C000026856

The only Official Guide to QUALITY

SELF-CATERING HOLIDAY HOMES

Beacon Hill Farm Holidays, Longhorsley

Welcome to this new and fully up-dated edition of Where to Stay

VisitBritain

VisitBritain is a new organisation created on 1 April 2003 to market Britain to the rest of the world and England to the British. Formed by the merger of the British Tourist Authority and the English Tourism Council, its mission is to build the value of tourism by creating world class destination brands and marketing campaigns. It will also build partnerships with – and provide insights to – other organisations which have a stake in British and English tourism.

1

The **only** official guide to quality accommodation in England

- This guide contains the widest choice of quality assured accommodation to suit all budgets and tastes.
- It includes an EXCLUSIVE listing of ALL Self-Catering Accommodation in VisitBritain's quality assurance standard.

Looking for accommodation in a particular area?

- The guide's divided into the English Regional Tourist Board areas and accommodation is listed alphabetically by place name.
- Use the regional maps which show every place with accommodation in the regional sections.
- Look in the town index at the back of the guide. It also includes tourism areas such as the New Forest or Cotswolds.
- A handy reference to counties is also at the back.

More information as well as places to stay

Each regional section is packed with information:

Visitor Attractions

A selection of places to visit highlighting those receiving our quality assurance marque.

Tourist Information Centres

Phone numbers are shown in the blue bands next to place names in accommodation entries.

Guides and maps

As well as contact details, we list tourist board free and saleable tourism publications.

Travel details

Directions for travel by road and rail to each region.

Town descriptions

At the end of each section is a brief description of the main places where accommodation is listed.

PICTURES
1. Bosinver Farm Cottage, St Austell
2. Olde Rectory, Whitbourne

KEY TO SYMBOLS:
A key to symbols can be found on the inside back cover. Keep it open for easy reference.

Contents

Accommodation, Places to Visit and Information:

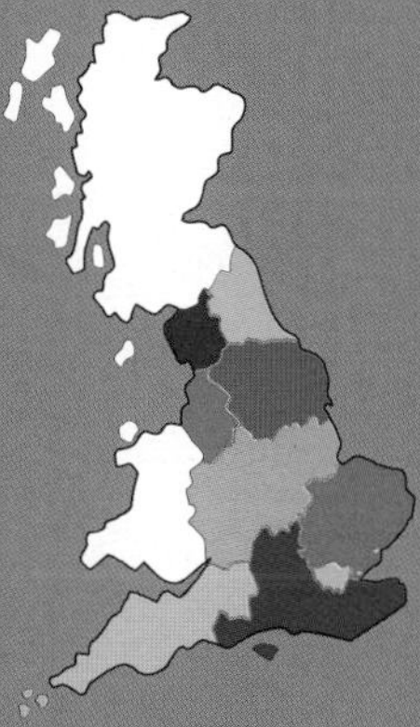

Everything you need to know for a great **English break**

1

Whether you're looking for country style, seaside splendour or city chic, you'll find nearly 9,000 places to stay here, all Star rated and with a range of prices for all pockets. Detailed entries and pictures help you make the right choice.

There's also advice on making a booking and an explanation of accommodation ratings and awards, handy location maps plus ideas on what to do and see in each region.

All **star rated** and with a range of prices for all **pockets**

2

3

4

5

6

You'll find nearly **9,000** places to stay, all **quality** assessed

PICTURES
1. The Homestead Barn, Brome
2. White House Farm, Knapton
3. Patterdale Hall Estate, Ullswater
4. Middletown Farm Cottages, Newent
5. Sea Tree House, Lyme Regis
6. View from Postern Close 43, York
7. The Olde Rectory, Whitbourne

7

Ratings and awards – your reliable guide to **quality**

Reliable, rigorous, easy to use – VisitBritain's ratings and awards system will help you choose with confidence.

All the accommodation in this guide has been inspected and rated for quality by VisitBritain, so you can be sure that the accommodation you choose will meet your expectations. Visitor attractions can also receive a special quality marque. These are the ratings and awards to look for:

Star ratings

Establishment's are awarded a rating of One to Five Stars for quality. VisitBritain has over 50 trained assessors who visit properties every year, generally on a day visit arranged in advance with the owner. They award ratings based on the overall level of quality and ensure that all requirements are met. There are strict guidelines to ensure every property is assessed to the same criteria. High standards of cleanliness are a major requirement; heating, lighting, comfort and convenience are also part of the assessment. There are strict guidelines to ensure every property is assessed to the same criteria.

National Accessible Scheme

Establishments with a National Accessible rating provide access and facilities for guests with visual, hearing and mobility impairment.

Excellence in England Awards

The 'Oscars' of the tourist industry, these awards are run by VisitBritain in association with England's 9 regional tourist boards. There are 12 categories including Self-Catering Holiday of the Year, and winners will be announced in Spring 2004.

Visitor Attraction Quality Assurance

To receive this award, attractions must achieve high standards in all aspects of the visitor experience, from initial telephone enquiries to departure, customer services to catering, as well as all facilities and activities. All participating attractions are visited every year by trained assessors.

Welcome to Excellence

VisitBritain's special 'Welcome to Excellence' plaque is awarded to accommodation and other tourism organisations that show a commitment to improving customer service through staff training.

PICTURES
1. Deer Park, Okehampton
2. Culver Cottage, Amberley
3. Orion Holidays, South Cerney

★★★
SELF CATERING

When you're looking for a place to stay, you need a rating system you can trust. VisitBritain's ratings give a clear guide to what to expect, in an easy-to-understand form. Properties are visited annually by trained, impartial assessors, so you can have the confidence that your accommodation has been thoroughly checked and rated for quality before you make your booking.

Star ratings

The Star ratings reflect the quality that you're looking for when booking accommodation. All properties have to meet an extensive list of minimum requirements to take part in the scheme. From there, increased levels of quality apply. For instance, you'll find acceptable quality at One Star, good to very good quality at Three Star and exceptional quality at Five Star establishments.

Quite simply, the more Stars, the higher the overall level of quality you can expect. Establishments at higher rating levels also have to meet additional requirements for facilities.

Minimum requirements include the following:

- High standard of cleanliness throughout
- Pricing and conditions of booking made clear
- Local information to help you make the best of your stay
- Comfortable accommodation with a range of furniture to meet your needs
- Colour television (where signal available) at no extra charge
- Kitchen equipped to meet all essential requirements

The brief explanation of the Star ratings for self-catering accommodation outlined below shows what is included at each rating level (note that each rating also includes what is provided at a lower Star rating).

★	An acceptable overall level of quality with adequate furniture furnishings and fittings.
★★	A good overall level of quality. All units are self-contained.
★★★	A good to very good overall level of quality with good standards of maintenance and decoration. Ample space and good quality furniture. All double beds have access from both sides. Microwave.
★★★★	An excellent overall level of quality with very good care and attention to detail throughout. Access to a washing machine and drier if it is not provided in the unit, or a 24 hour laundry service.
★★★★★	An exceptional overall level of quality with high levels of decor, fixtures and fittings, with personal touches. Excellent standards of management efficiency and guest services.

Many self-catering establishments have a range of accommodation units in the building or on the site, and in some cases the individual units may have different Star ratings. In such cases, the entry shows the range available. Further information about the scheme can be found at the back of this guide.

National Accessible **Scheme**

VisitBritain's National Accessible Scheme for accommodation includes standards for hearing and visually impaired guests in addition to standards for guests with mobility impairment.

Accommodation taking part in the National Accessible Scheme, and which appear in this guide are listed in the index at the back of this guide.

VisitBritian has a variety of accessible accommodation in its scheme, and the different accessible ratings will help you choose the one that best suits your needs.

When you see one of the symbols, you can be sure that the accommodation has been thoroughly assessed against demanding criteria.

If you have additional needs or special requirements we strongly recommend that you make sure these can be met by your chosen establishment before you confirm your booking. The criteria VisitBritain and National and Regional Tourist Boards have adopted do not necessarily conform to British Standards or to Building Regulations. They reflect what the Boards understand to be acceptable to meet the practical needs of guests with mobility or sensory impairment.

National Accessible Scheme ratings are also shown on the full list of VisitBritain-assessed establishments in the listings at the back of this guide.

Acccommodation is **assessed** against **demanding criteria**

PICTURES
1. Pimlico Farm Country Cottages, Bicester
2. Hidelow House Cottages, Malvern
3. Spixworth Hall Cottages, Norwich
4. Church Farm Country Cottages, Bath

The National Accessible Scheme forms part of the Tourism for All Campaign that is being promoted by VisitBritain and National and Regional Tourist Boards. Additional help and guidance on finding suitable holiday accommodation for those with special needs can be obtained from:

Holiday Care/Tourism for All Holidays Ltd
7th Floor - Sunley House,
4 Bedford Park
CROYDON CR0 2AP

Telephone: Admin/consultancy 0845 124 9974
Information helpline 0845 124 9971
(9-5 Mon, Tues and 9-1pm Wed-Fri)
Reservation/Friends 0845 124 9973
Fax: 0845 124 9972
Minicom: 0845 124 9976

Email: info@holidaycare.org
Web: www.holidaycare.org

HOLIDAY CARE

Access Symbols

Mobility

LEVEL 1 – Typically suitable for a person with sufficient mobility to climb a flight of steps but who would benefit from points of fixtures and fittings to aid balance.

LEVEL 2 – Typically suitable for a person with restricted walking ability and for those that may need to use a wheelchair some of the time.

LEVEL 3 – Typically suitable for a person who depends on the use of a wheelchair and transfers unaided to and from the wheelchair in a seated position.

LEVEL 4 – Typically suitable for a person who depends on the use of a wheelchair in a seated position. They can require personal/mechanical assistance to aid transfer (eg carer, hoist).

Hearing Impairment

1

LEVEL 1 – Minimum entry requirements to meet the National Accessible Standards for guests with hearing impairment, from mild hearing loss to profoundly deaf.

2

LEVEL 2 – Recommended (Best Practice) additional requirements to meet the National Accessible Standards for guests with hearing impairment, from mild hearing loss to profoundly deaf.

Visual Impairment

1

LEVEL 1 – Minimum entry requirements to meet the National Accessible Standards for visually impaired guests.

2

LEVEL 2 – Recommended (Best Practice) additional requirements to meet the National Accessible Standards for visually impaired guests.

2

3

4

South Coast
and New Forest

CHOICE
OF FOREST
OR COASTAL
LOCATIONS

With two high quality destinations to choose from, Shorefield Holidays offers you the best of both worlds in self-catering locations.

Both our parks are set in peaceful, unspoilt parkland in the beautiful New Forest or South Coast area. There are comprehensive facilities including entertainment and Free Leisure Club membership. For full details ask for our brochure or browse on-line.

For further details telephone:

01590 648331

SHOREFIELD
HOLIDAYS LIMITED

Oakdene Forest Park
St. Leonards, Ringwood, Hants BH24 2RZ

Shorefield Country Park
Shorefield Road, Milford on Sea,
Hants SO41 0LH

e-mail: holidays@shorefield.co.uk www.shorefield.co.uk Ref. WTS

The Excellence in England awards 2004

The Excellence in England Awards are all about blowing English tourism's trumpet and telling the world what a fantastic place England is to visit, whether it's for a day trip, a weekend break or a fortnight's holiday.

The Awards, now in their 15th year, are run by VisitBritain in association with England's regional tourist boards. This year there are 12 categories including B&B of the Year, Hotel of the Year and Visitor Attraction of the Year and an award for the best tourism website.

Winners of the 2004 awards will receive their trophies at an event to be held on Thursday 22nd April 2004 followed by a media event to be held on St George's Day (23 April) in London. The day will celebrate excellence in tourism in England.

The winners of the 2003 Excellence in England Self-Catering Holiday of the Year Award are:

Gold winner over 50 bedrooms:
Park Hall Country Cottages, St Osyth, Nr Clacton-on-Sea, Essex
Silver winners:
Barnacre Cottages, Barnacre, Garstang, Preston, Lancashire
Bruern Stable Cottages, Chipping Norton, Oxfordshire

For more information about the Excellence in England Awards visit
www.visitengland.com

EXCELLENCE IN ENGLAND
Awards for Tourism

Marketing English Tourism
VISIT BRITAIN

How do we arrive at a **Star Rating**

VisitBritain has more than 50 trained assessors throughout England who visit properties annually, generally on a day visit arranged in advance with the owner.

They award ratings based on the overall level of quality and ensure that all requirements are met. There are strict guidelines to ensure every property is assessed to the same criteria.

High standards of cleanliness are a major requirement; heating, lighting, comfort and convenience are also part of the assessment.

The assessor's role

An assessor takes into account everything a guest will experience.

This includes:

- how the initial enquiry is dealt with
- the brochure or information supplied
- the arrival procedure
- help and contact for guests during their stay
- the quality of the accommodation and facilities.

In fact all aspects which contribute to the overall comfort and convenience for guests who may hire the property for a holiday or short break.

During their visit the assessor will take into consideration the quality and condition of all the fixtures and fittings. Most importantly excellent standards of cleanliness are noted.

Personal touches which give a homely and welcoming feeling are encouraged. Spaciousness and convenience of use is also part of the assessment, taking into account the number of people who can be accommodated. The quality of information provided about places to visit, where to eat and how to operate equipment is all taken into account. To attract the highest Star rating everything must be of an exceptional standard, both inside and outside the property.

At the end of the visit the assessor will advise the owner of the Star rating they have awarded, discussing the reasons why, as well as suggesting areas for improvement. So you can see it's a very thorough process to ensure that when you book accommodation with a particular Star rating you can be confident it will meet your expectations. After all, meeting customer expectations is what makes happy guests.

50 **trained assessors** visit properties annually

PICTURES
1. Field Cottage, Lyonshall
2 & 3. Mill House, Somerton
4. Stanton Court, Stanton

Accommodation
entries explained

Each accommodation entry contains detailed information to help you decide if it is right for you.

This information has been provided by the proprietors themselves, and our aim has been to ensure that it is as objective and factual as possible. To the left of the establishment name you will find the Star rating.

At-a-glance symbols at the end of each entry give you additional information on services and facilities - a key can be found on the back cover flap. Keep this open to refer to as you read.

1 ROSS-ON-WYE Map ref 2A1 *Tourist Information Centre Tel: (01423) 537300*

2 ★★★★

3 1 Unit Sleeps 5

4

5 

THE COACH HOUSE 8

Ross-on-Wye
Contact: Mrs C Dower, Pine Combe,
24 Waylands Avenue, Weybridge, Surrey KT13 1RY
T: (01989) 000121 F: (01989) 000123
E: info@coachhouse.co.uk
I: www.coachhouse.ross.co.uk

6 *Converted from an old coach house, this beautiful character cottage has a delightful thatched roof. Spacious yet cosy and warm in winter with wood-burning stove. Two large bedrooms, recently fitted kitchen. Overlooking apple orchards with views of beautiful Herefordshire countryside. Town centre easily accessible, many fine amenities close by.*

OPEN All year
CC: Access, Visa
Switch/Delta 10

3 night stays available
Oct–Jan (excl Xmas
and New Year) 11

Low season per wk 9
£150.00–£170.00
High season per wk
£170.00–£210.00

7 P

1. Listing under town or village with map reference
2. VisitBritain Star rating
3. Number of units and how many they sleep
4. Accessible rating where applicable
5. Colour picture for enhanced entries
6. Description
7. At-a-glance facility symbols
8. Establishment name, contact address, telephone and fax numbers, e-mail and web site address
9. Prices per unit per week for low season and high season
10. Shows establishment is open all year and credit cards accepted
11. Special promotions (enhanced entries only)

Inspiring ideas for a **Short Break**

Live the dream for a few days, staying in a picturesque country cottage, traditional farmhouse, working farm or modern penthouse apartment. Whatever you're looking for, you'll find a wide range of accommodation in this guide, suitable for all kinds of holidays, from romantic, indulgent weekends to active, outdoor breaks and residential courses in everything from hedge laying to willow weaving.

Many places offer short breaks at reduced rates. Here's a selection of ideas - for more, look out for the special offers and promotions, highlighted in red in the guide.

1

Great for groups

Self-catering accommodation is the perfect choice for groups of all kinds and sizes: family gatherings, celebrations, and walking and cycling groups. At **Scoles Manor, Corfe Castle**, up to 20 people can stay in three cottages in 30 acres (12 ha) of grounds with panoramic views of the castle. Holders of the Devon Cycle Mark for cyclist-friendly accommodation, **Kerslake Cottage, Meldon** in the Dartmoor National Park, has a lockable cycle store in a barn and is an ideal base for small groups wanting to explore Devon by bike. And for groups of 2 to 12 golfers, **Colmworth Golf Club Holidays, Colmworth**, has luxury cottages overlooking the lakes of the 18-hole golf course.

Learning for fun

Refresh and de-stress with a residential course in a favourite hobby, or try something new for a complete change. At **Brentwood Farm Cottages, Burton-in-Lonsdale**, on a family-run dairy farm in the tranquil Yorkshire Dales, you can learn the traditional skills of hedge laying and walling, while professional tennis coaching can be arranged on the new court at **Romsey Oak Cottages, Wingfield**. Creative types will enjoy courses on floral portraits, willow weaving and clay sculpture in a converted barn at **Shatton Hall Farm, Bamford** in the heart of the Peak District.

2

Relax and unwind. Go on! You owe it to **yourself**

3

PICTURES
1 & 2. Shatton Hall Farm, Bamford
3. Blaize Barn, Lavenham
4. Brentwood Farm Cottages, Burton-in-Lonsdale
5. Hidelow House Cottages, Malvern

A glorious selection of **gourmet** breaks to suit all **tastes**

4

Country pursuits

Get a flavour of the country life with a Farm Trail weekend at **Cruck Cottage, Hartington** – the trail takes you from the farmyard through the spectacular and unspoilt countryside of the Derbyshire Dales. Fish for wild brown trout at **Dove Cottage, Alstonefield**, a Victorian fishing lodge on the River Dove, try clay-pigeon shooting, horse-riding and archery, staying in 17th century cottages at **Butcombe Farm, Butcombe**, or walking, fishing and riding at **Dolphin Lodge, East Harling**.

Break out the bubbly

Choose somewhere very special for a short romantic break. At **Hidelow House Cottages, Malvern**, spoil yourselves with four poster beds, log fires, champagne and roses, and an outdoor hot tub.

Blaize Barn, in the medieval village of **Lavenham**, will welcome you with soft music, champagne, chocolate and flowers, and can even prepare a special supper for you.

Offpeak pleasures

Beat the crowds with a break in autumn or winter. Christmas shopping can be a pleasure – **Widmouth Farm Cottages, Combe Martin**, come complete with festive decorations, and there's great shopping nearby at Atlantic Village factory outlet centre, the Dartington Glass factory shop and many individual specialists. Enjoy guided tours of historic York and North Yorkshire while staying at the chic and contemporary loft-style **Penthouse** in **York**.

5

Freedom...

Why not enjoy a perfect cottage holiday in Britain

Whatever you're looking for, Blakes have the holiday for you...

★★★★★ SELF-CATERING

The widest choice of self-catering accommodation throughout Britain, handpicked for quality and value. From couples seeking a romantic weekend retreat in heather-clad Scotland, to families looking for a fun-packed week on a beach in Cornwall. With almost every inch of fertile woodland, rolling moor and golden beach covered in our brochure, you're sure to find the perfect holiday.

Call now for your free 2004 brochure - quoting code BM080

08700 70 80 99

or look and book online @

www.blakes-cottages.co.uk

or visit your local travel agent

Blakes Country Cottages

Country Holidays

BRITAIN'S FAVOURITE COTTAGE HOLIDAYS

★★★★★ SELF-CATERING

live your dreams

Enjoy the perfect British cottage holiday

Would you like to get away from the hustle and bustle of everyday life and unwind and relax on a peaceful break in the country or on the coast? Then why not call Country Holidays and enjoy the perfect British cottage holiday.

- *Over 3000 cottages to choose from throughout Britain*
- *Cottages for couples to parties of ten or more*
- *All cottages quality graded annually to ETC standards*
- *Pets welcome at many cottages*
- *Short Breaks offer - 4 midweek nights for the same price as 3 weekend nights*
- *Save £25 on a fortnight's holiday*

***Call 08700 725 725** please quote CMO80*
for your FREE 2004 brochure or look and book at:
www.country-holidays.co.uk

www.visitengland.com

What makes the perfect break? Big city buzz or peaceful country panoramas? Take a fresh look at England and you may be surprised that everything is here on your very own doorstep. Where will you go? Make up your own mind and enjoy England in all its diversity.

Experience*....remember paddling on sandy beaches, playing Poohsticks in the forest, picnics at open-air concerts, tea-rooms offering home-made cakes........*

Discover*....make your own journey of discovery through England's cultural delights: surprising contrasts between old and new, traditional and trend-setting, time-honoured and contemporary........*

Explore*....while you're reading this someone is drinking in lungfuls of fresh air on a hill-side with heart-stopping views or wandering through the maze that can be the garden of a stately home or tugging on the sails of a boat skimming across a lake....*

Relax*....no rush to do anything or be anywhere, time to immerse yourself in your favourite book by a roaring log fire or glide from a soothing massage to a refreshing facial, ease away the tension......*

To enjoy England, visitengland.com

QUALITY ASSURED
VISITOR
ATTRACTION

Visitor Attraction Quality Assurance

VisitBritain operates a Visitor Attraction Quality Assurance Standard. Participating attractions are visited annually by trained, impartial assessors who look at all aspects of the visit, from initial telephone enquiries to departure, customer services to catering, as well as facilities and activities. Only those attractions which have been assessed by VisitBritain and meet the standard receive the quality marque, your sign of a 'Quality Assured Visitor Attraction'.

Look out for the quality marque and visit with confidence.

Location Maps

Every place name featured in the regional accommodation sections of this Where to Stay guide has a map reference to help you locate it on the maps which follow. For example, to find Colchester, Essex, which has 'Map ref 3B2', turn to Map 3 and refer to grid square B2.

All place names appearing in the regional sections are shown in black type on the maps. This enables you to find other places in your chosen area which may have suitable accommodation - the Town Index (at the back of this guide) gives page numbers.

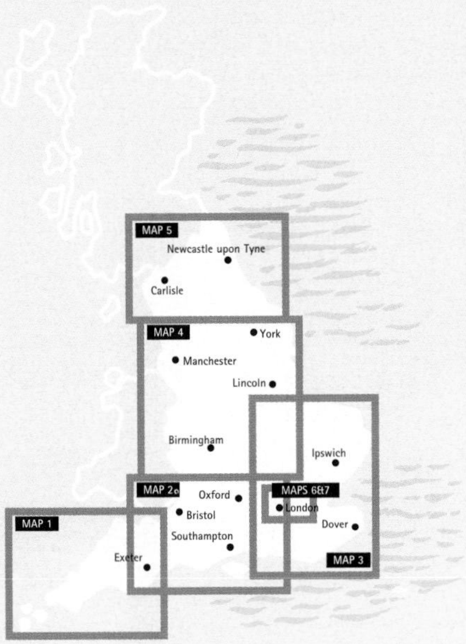

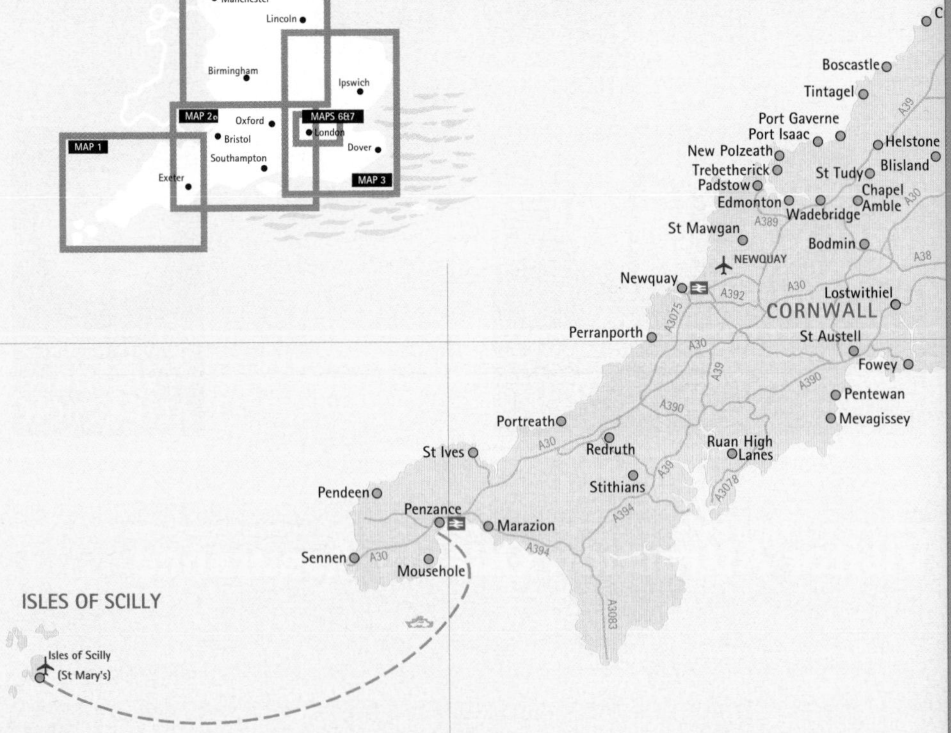

Key to regions: South West

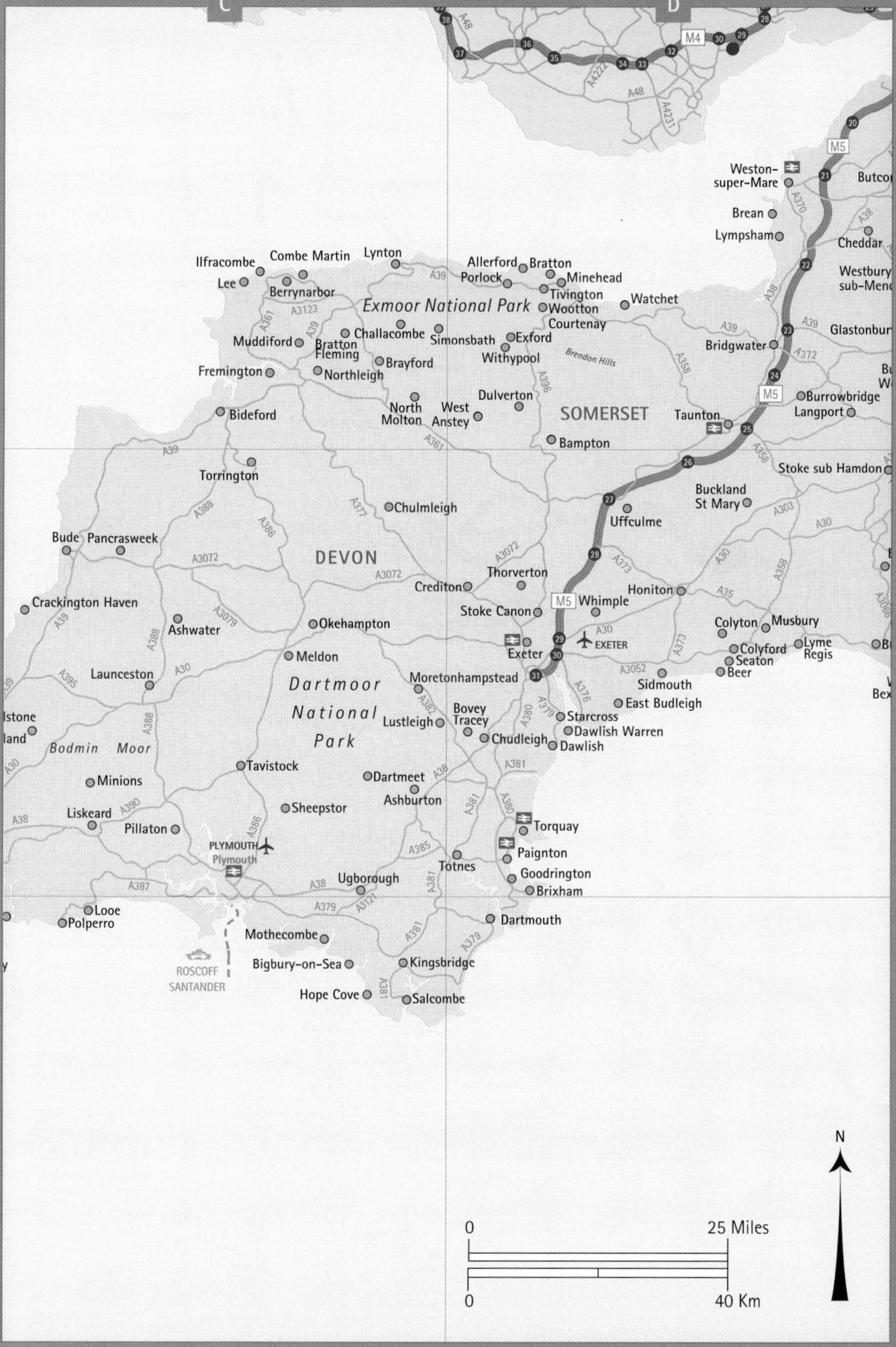

All place names in black offer accommodation in this guide.

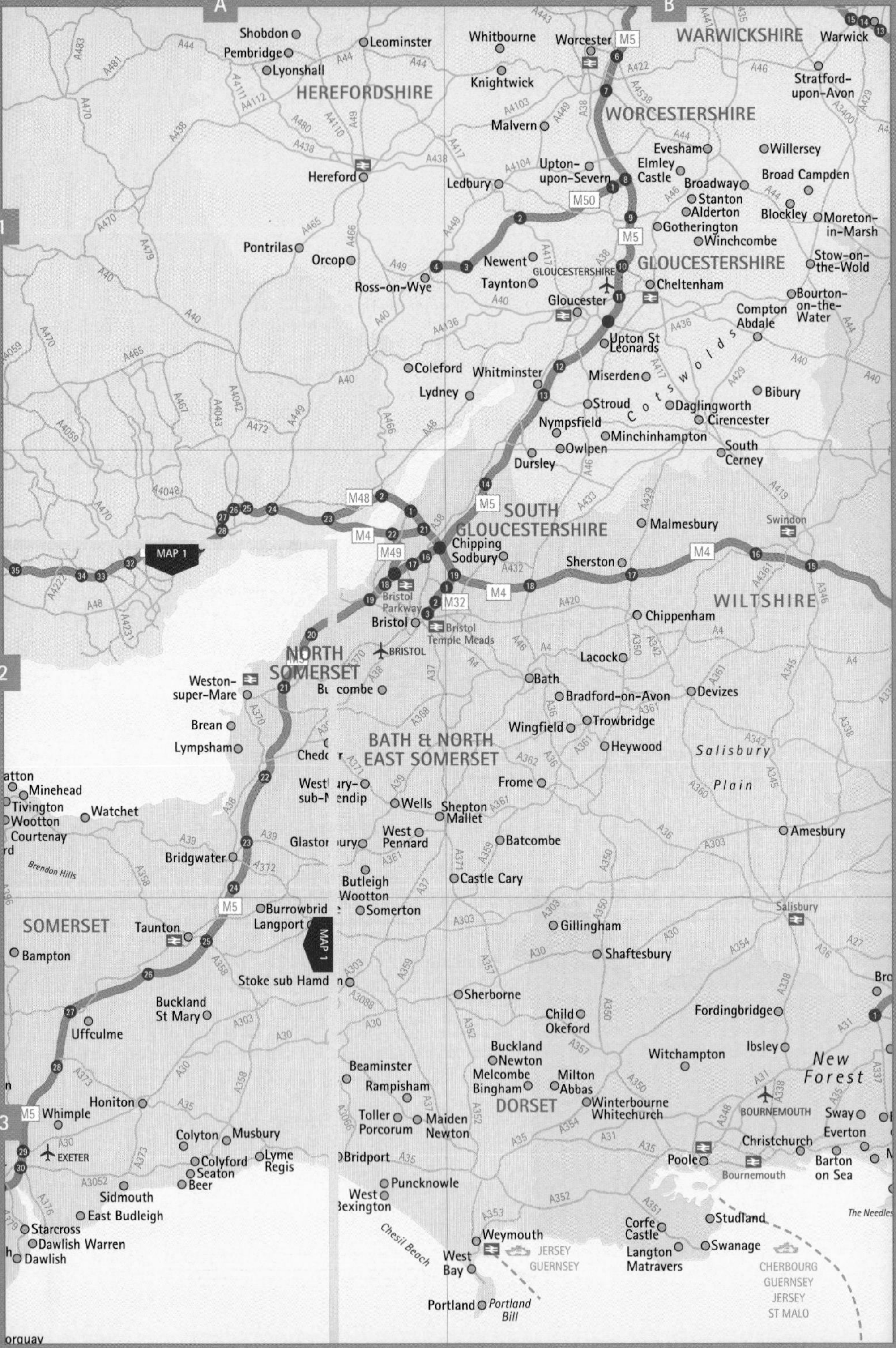

Key to regions: South West South of England Heart of England

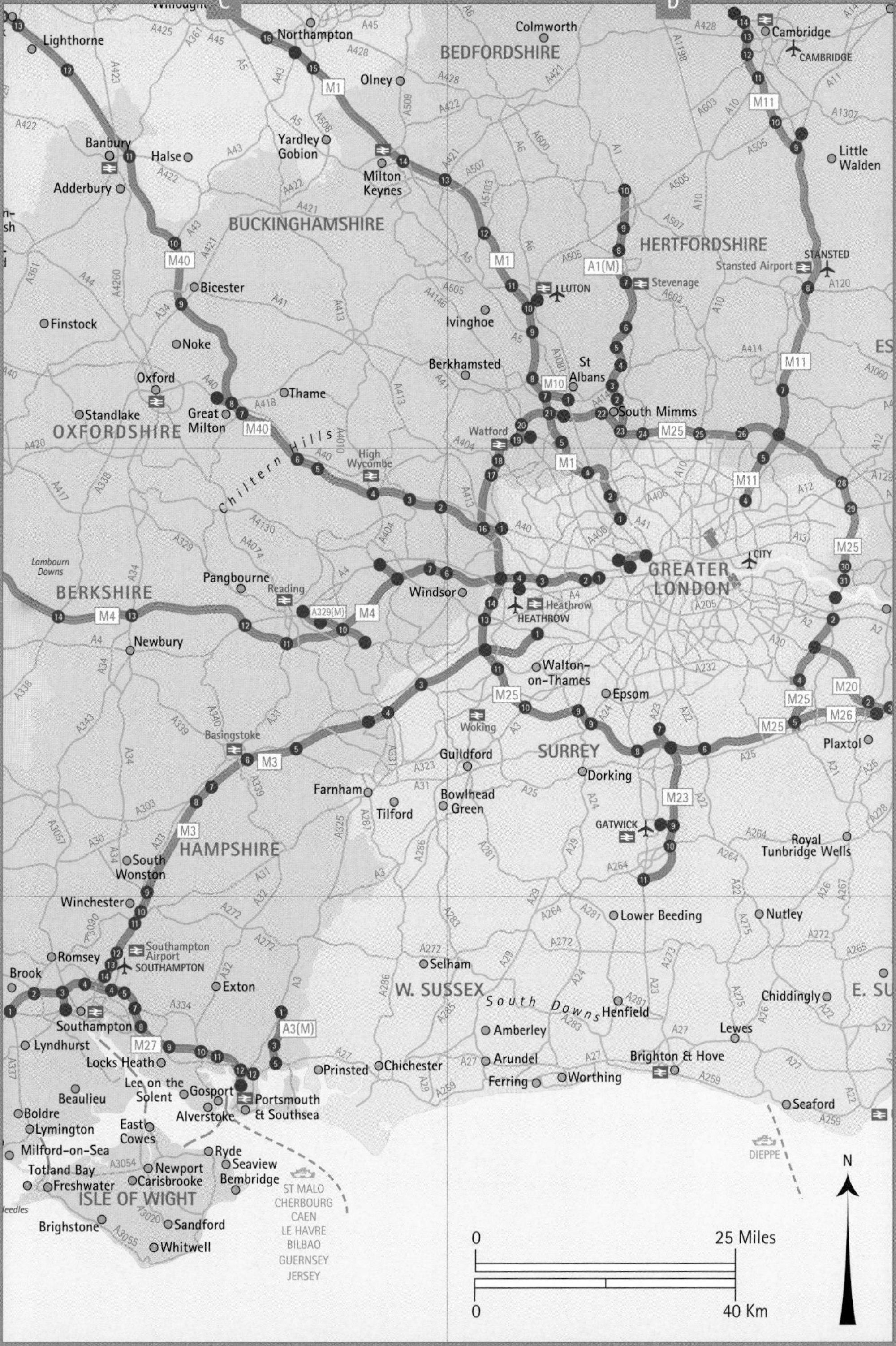

South East England East of England *All place names in black offer accommodation in this guide.*

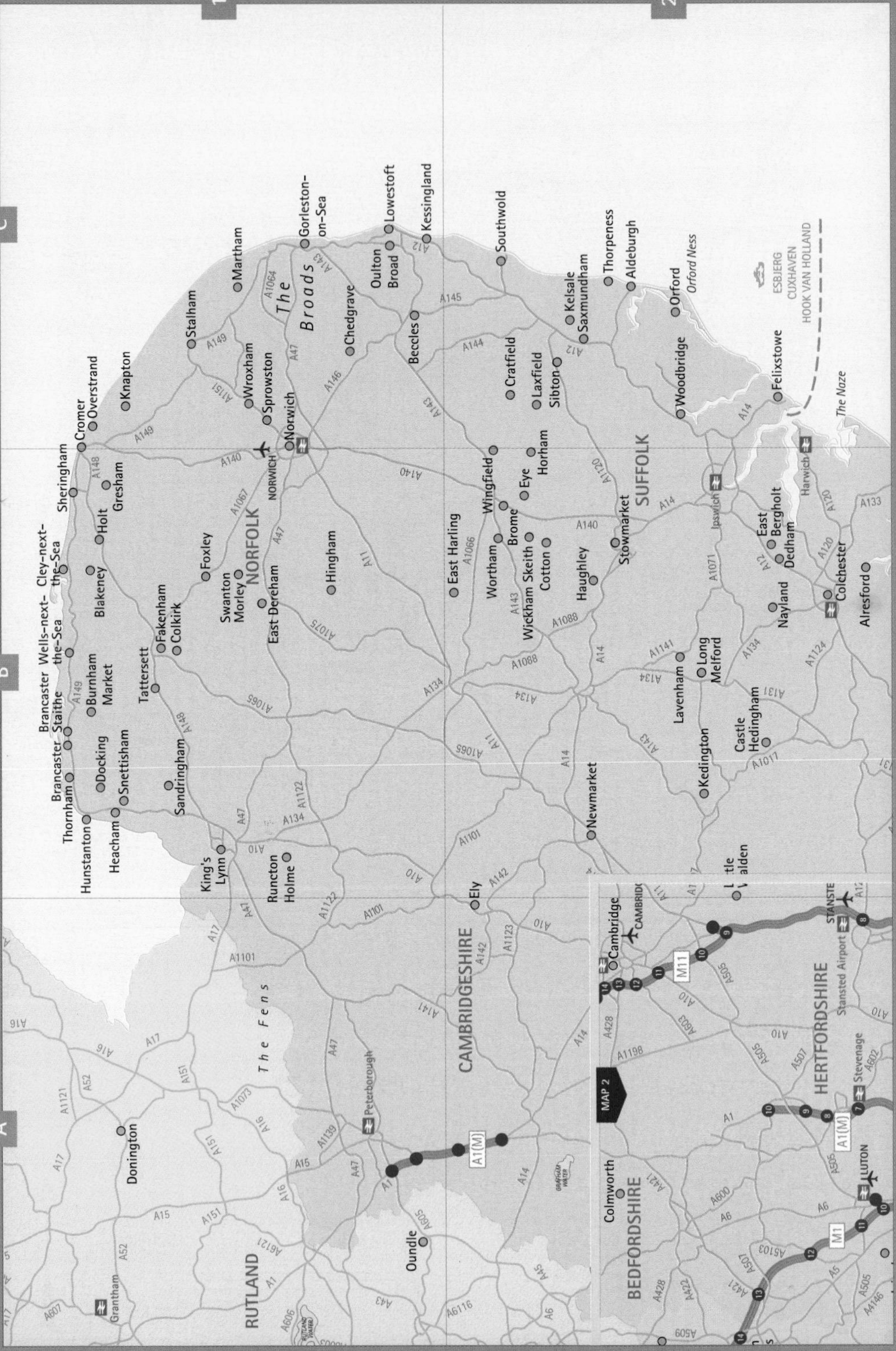

Key to regions: London East of England Heart of England South East England

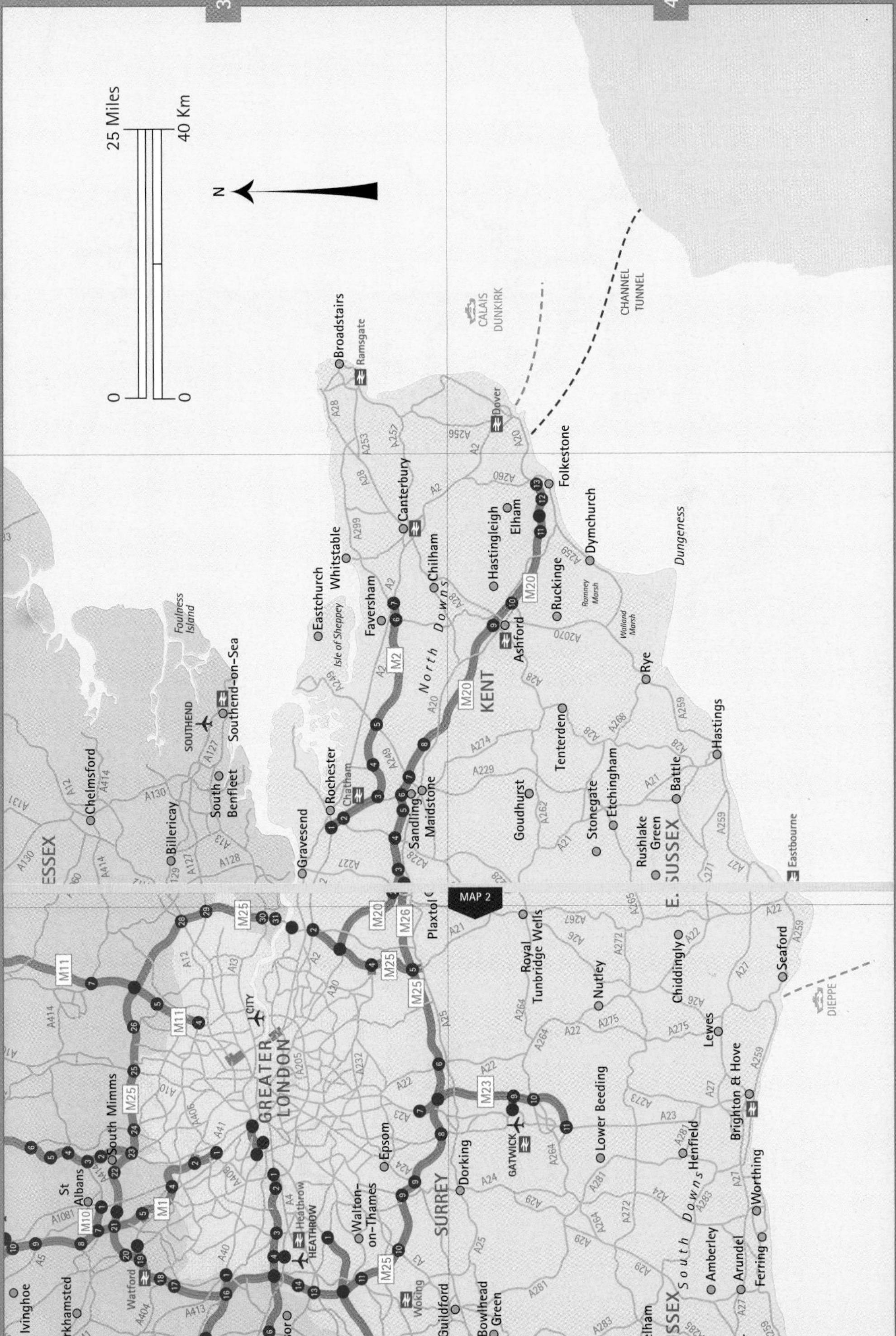

All place names in black offer accommodation in this guide.

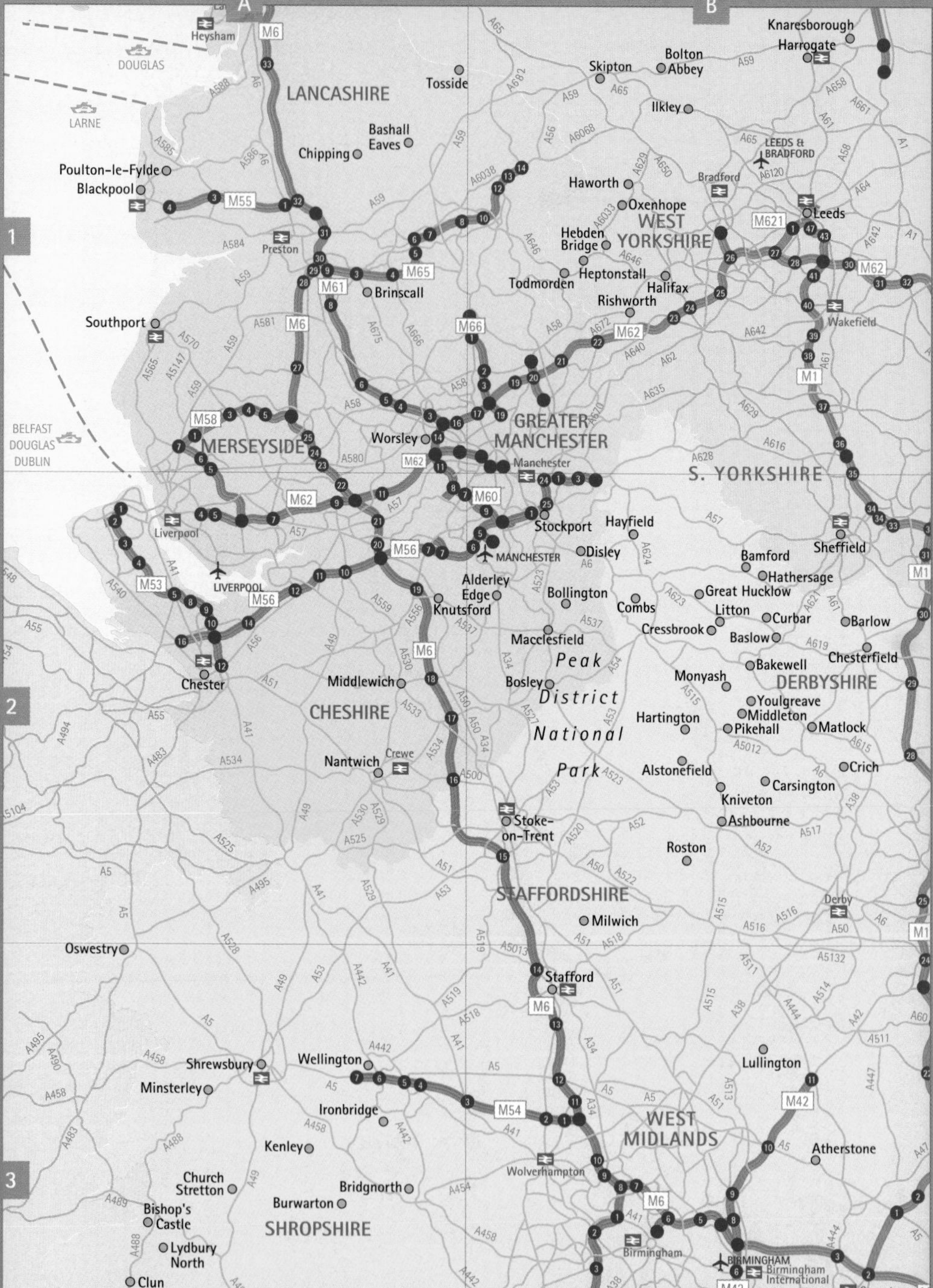

Key to regions: North West | Yorkshire | Heart of England | East of England

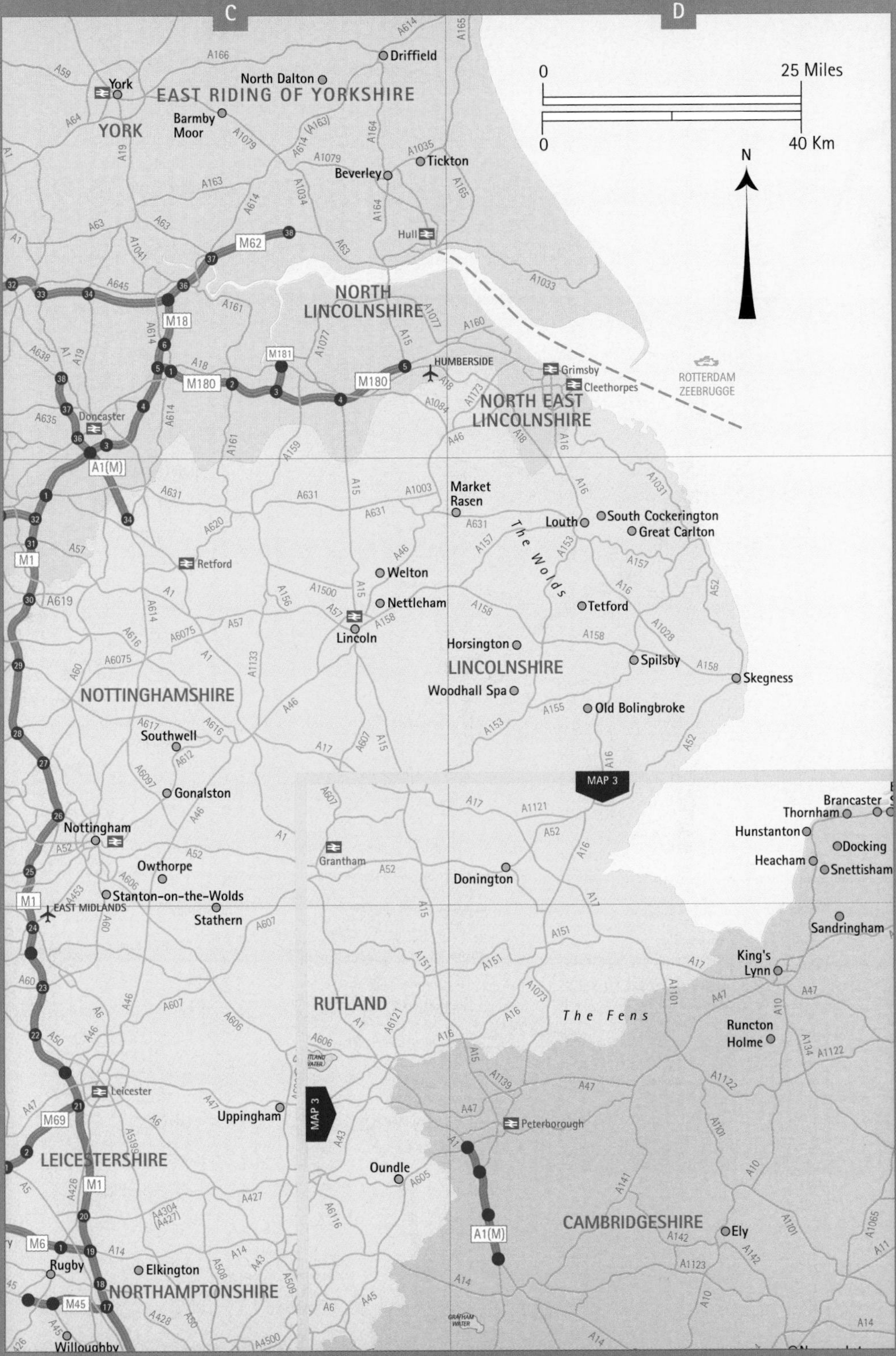

All place names in black offer accommodation in this guide.

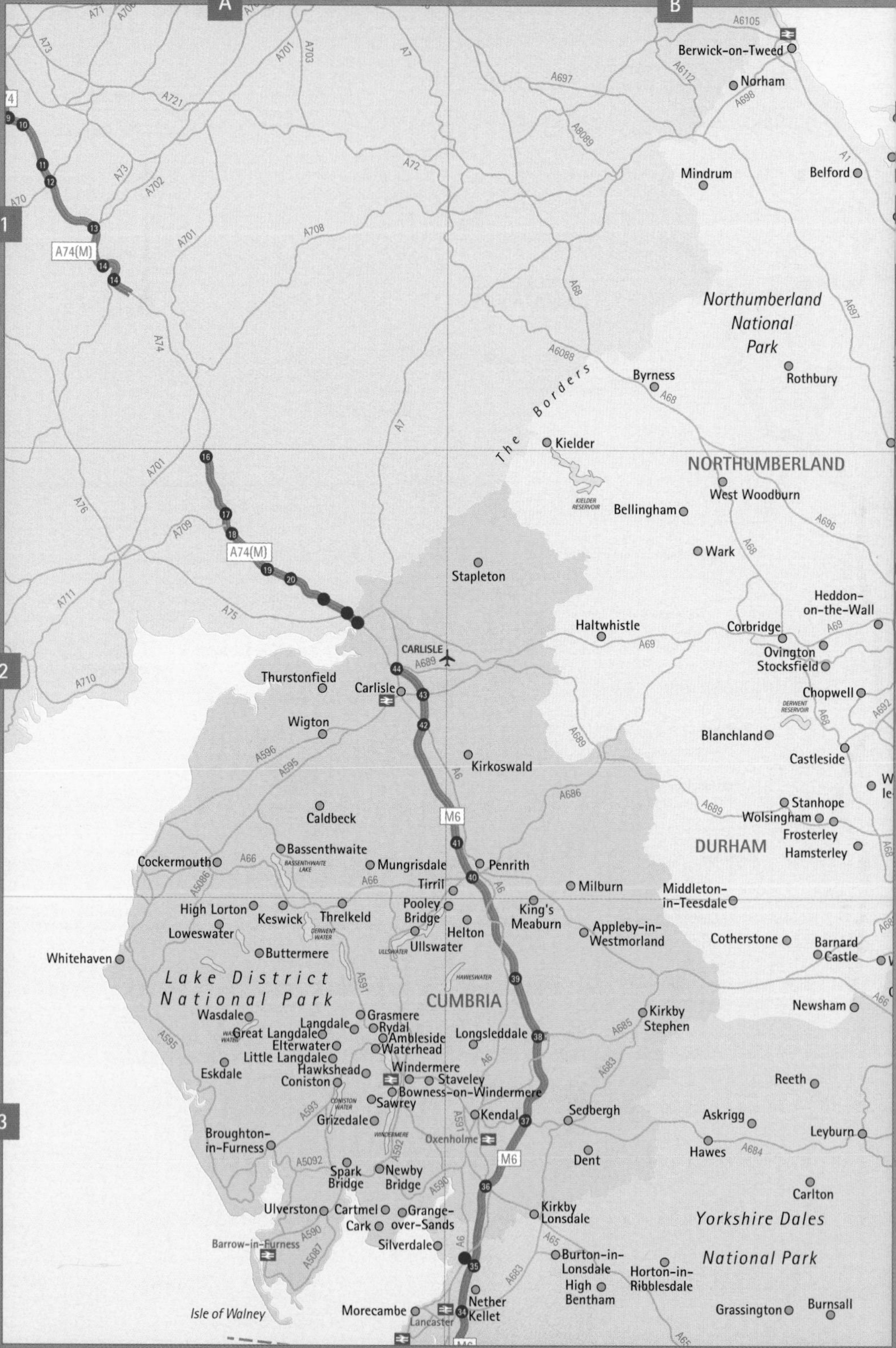

Key to regions: Cumbria Yorkshire Northumbria

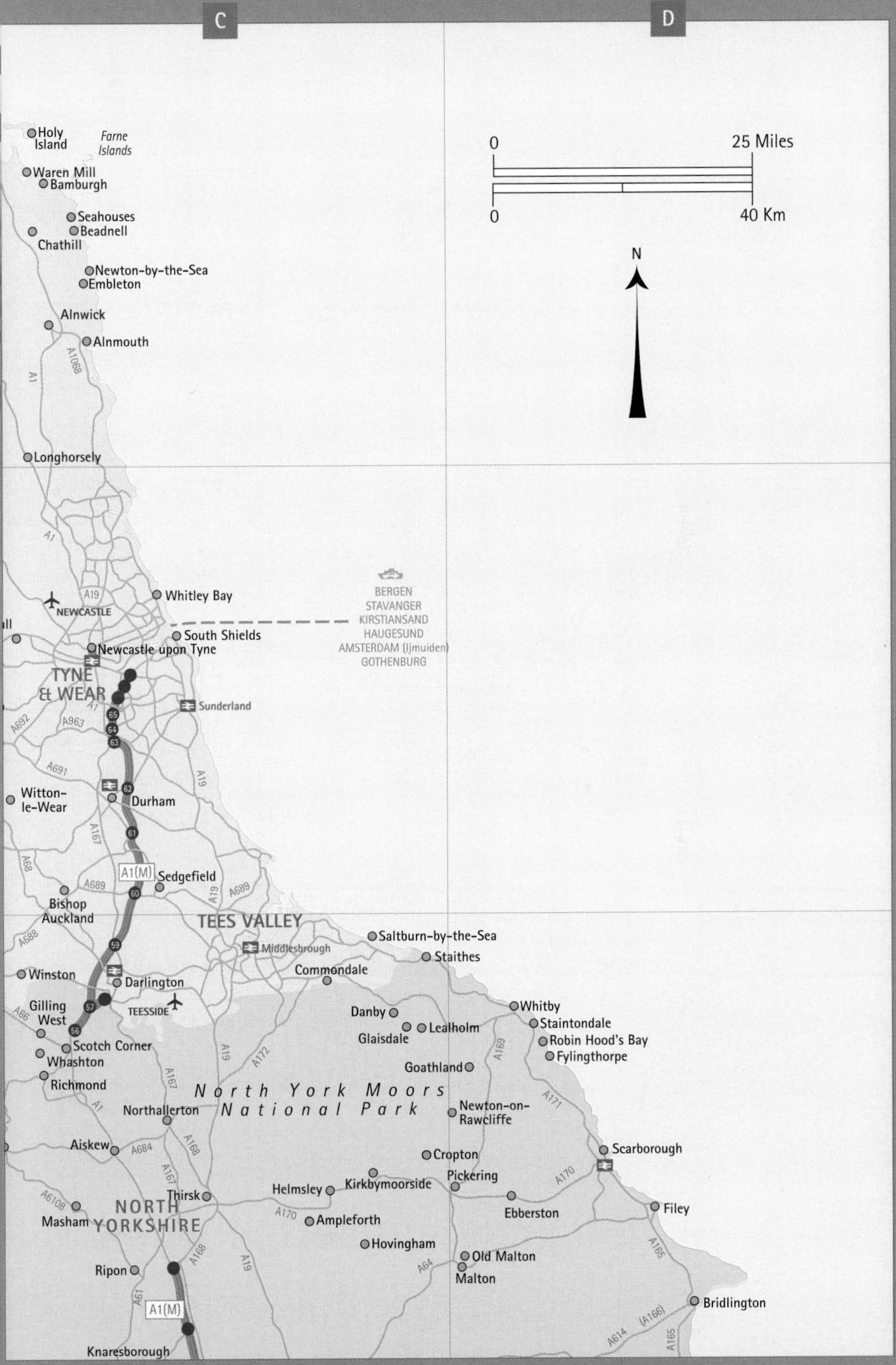

All place names in black offer accommodation in this guide.

BARNET
HARINGEY
HARROW
BRENT
ISLINGTON
CAMDEN
See map 7
WESTMINSTER
HILLINGDON
EALING
HAMMERSMITH & FULHAM
KENSINGTON & CHELSEA
LAMBETH
London Heathrow Airport
HOUNSLOW
WANDSWORTH
RICHMOND UPON THAMES
MERTON
SUTTON
KINGSTON UPON THAMES
NORTH CIRCULAR
M25
M1
M40
M4
M3
A1(M)
A40(M)

ENFIELD
WALTHAM FOREST
REDBRIDGE
HAVERING
HACKNEY
NEWHAM
TOWER HAMLETS
CITY
BARKING & DAGENHAM
SOUTHWARK
GREENWICH
BEXLEY
LEWISHAM
SOUTH CIRCULAR
BROMLEY
CROYDON
M25
M11
M20
M26
M2
A102(M)
A414
A113
A12
A218
A129
A127
A124
A118
A13
A1306
A206
A2226
A2
A20
A21
A25
A225
A227
A228
A22
A10
A406
A112
A104
A11
A2016
A207
A210
A222
A224
A232
© Arka Cartographics Ltd. 1999

Central London

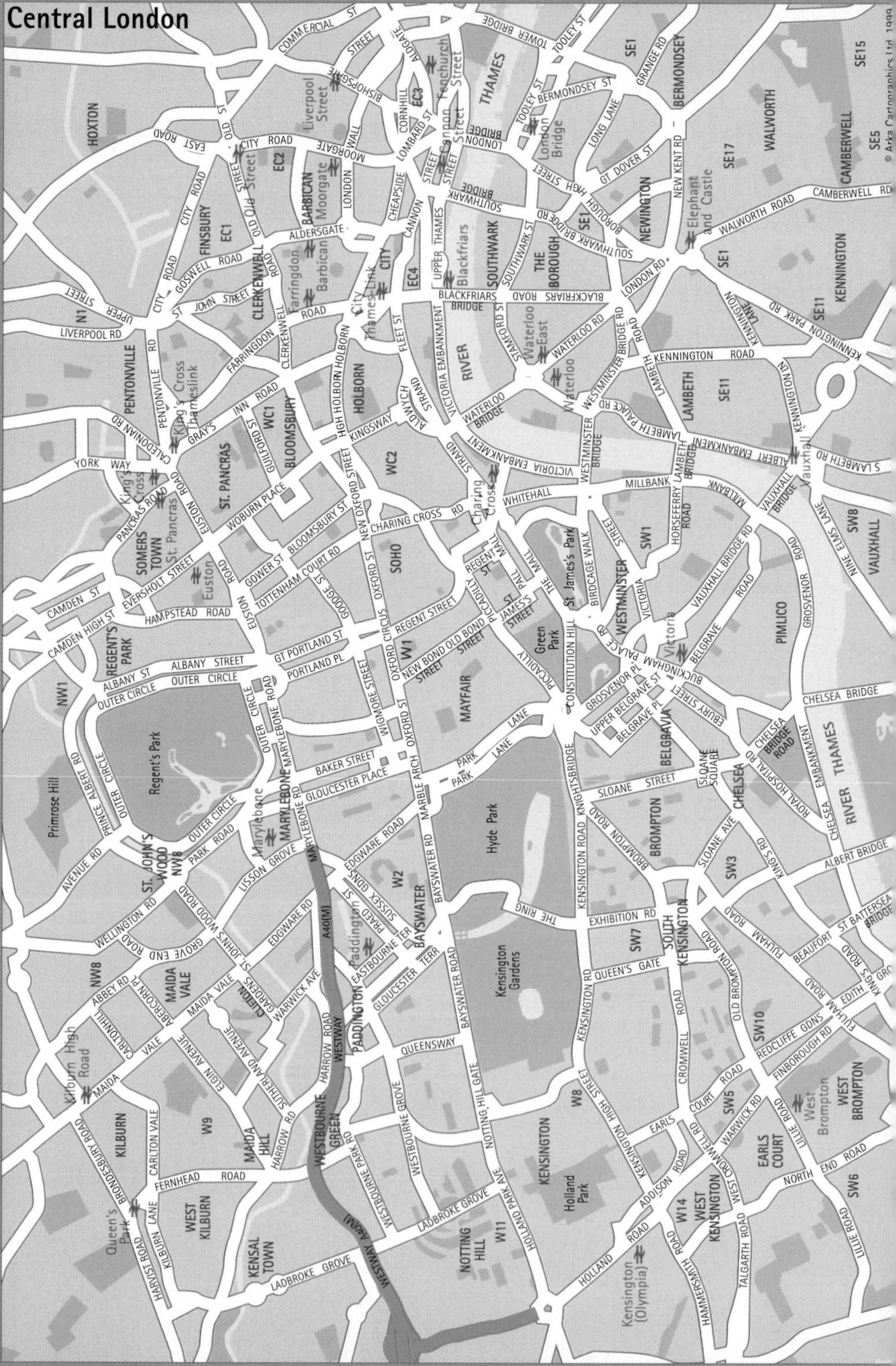

London

A dynamic mix of history and heritage, cool and contemporary. Great museums, stunning art collections, royal palaces, hip nightlife and stylish shopping, from ritzy Bond Street to cutting-edge Hoxton.

Classic sights
St Paul's Cathedral – Wren's famous church
Tower of London – 900 years of British history
London Eye – spectacular views from the world's highest 'big wheel'

Arts for all
National Gallery – Botticelli, Rembrandt, Turner and more
Tate Modern – 20thC art in a former power station
Victoria & Albert Museum – decorative arts

City lights
Theatre: Musicals – West End;
drama – Royal Court and National Theatre;
Music: Classical – Wigmore Hall and Royal Festival Hall;
jazz – Ronnie Scott's;
Ballet & Opera – Royal Opera House

Insider London
Dennis Severs's House, E1 – candlelit tours of this authentically 18thC house

Greater London, comprising the 32 London Boroughs

For more information contact:
Visit London
1 Warwick Row,
London SW1E 5ER

www.visitlondon.com

Telephone enquiries -
see London Line on page 36

1. Piccadilly Circus
2. Millennium Bridge across River Thames and St Paul's

1

Places to Visit

You will find hundreds of interesting places to visit during your stay, just some of which are listed in these pages. Contact any Tourist Information Centre in and around London for more ideas on days out.

Awarded VisitBritain's 'Quality Assured Visitor Attraction' marque.

British Airways London Eye
Jubilee Gardens, South Bank, SE1 7PB
Tel: 0870 5000600 www.ba-londoneye.com
The British Airways London eye is the world's largest observation wheel. Take in over 55 of London's most famous landmarks in just 30 minutes!

British Museum
Great Russell Street, WC1B 3DG
Tel: (020) 7323 8000
www.thebritishmuseum.ac.uk
One of the great museums of the world, showing the works of man from prehistoric to modern times with collections drawn from the whole world.

Cabinet War Rooms
Clive Steps, King Charles Street, SW1A 2AQ
Tel: (020) 7930 6961 www.iwm.org.uk
The underground headquarters used by Winston Churchill and the British Government during World War II. Includes Cabinet Room, Transatlantic Telephone Room and Map Room.

Chessington World of Adventures
Leatherhead Road, Chessington, KT9 2NE
Tel: (01372) 729560 www.chessington.com
Fun family adventures include the 'fang-tastic' New Vampire ride, Tomb Blaster, an action packed adventure ride, and a mischievous new attraction in Beanoland.

Design Museum
28 Shad Thames, SE1 2YD
Tel: (020) 7403 6933 www.designmuseum.org
The world's leading museum of industrial design, fashion and architecture. Its exhibition programme captures the excitement and ingenuity of design's evolution.

Hampton Court Palace
Hampton Court, East Molesey, KT8 9AU
Tel: (020) 8781 9500 www.hrp.org.uk
The oldest Tudor palace in England with many attractions including the Tudor kitchens, tennis courts, maze and State Apartments and King's Apartments.

HMS Belfast
Morgan's Lane, Tooley Street, SE1 2JH
Tel: (020) 7940 6300 www.iwm.org.uk
World War II cruiser weighing 11,500 tonnes, now a floating naval museum, with 9 decks to explore, from the Captain's Bridge to the Boiler and Engine rooms.

Imperial War Museum
Lambeth Road, SE1 6HZ
Tel: (020) 7416 5320 www.iwm.org.uk
Museum tells the story of 20thC war from Flanders to Bosnia. Special features include the Blitz Experience, the Trench Experience and the world of Espionage.

Kensington Palace State Apartments
Kensington Gardens, W8 4PX
Tel: 0870 7515180 www.hrp.org.uk
Furniture and ceiling paintings from Stuart-Hanoverian periods, rooms from Victorian era and works of art from the Royal Collection. Also Royal Ceremonial Dress Collection.

Kew Gardens (Royal Botanic Gardens)
Richmond, TW9 3AB
Tel: (020) 8332 5655 www.kew.org
300 acres (120ha) containing living collections of over 40,000 varieties of plants. Seven spectacular glasshouses, 2 art galleries, Japanese and rock garden.

London Aquarium
County Hall, Riverside Building, SE1 7PB
Tel: (020) 7967 8000
www.londonaquarium.co.uk
Dive down deep beneath the Thames and submerge yourself in one of Europe's largest displays of aquatic life from sharks and piranhas to seahorses and starfish.

London Planetarium
Marylebone Road, NW1 5LR
Tel: 0870 4003000
www.london-planetarium.com
Visitors can experience a virtual reality trip through space and find out about Black Holes and extra terrestrials in the interactive Space Zones before the show.

London Transport Museum
Covent Garden Piazza, WC2E 7BB
Tel: (020) 7379 6344 www.ltmuseum.co.uk
The history of transport for everyone, from spectacular vehicles, special exhibitions, actors and guided tours to film shows, gallery talks and children's craft workshops.

London Zoo
Regent's Park, NW1 4RY
Tel: (020) 7722 3333 www.londonzoo.co.uk
Escape the stress of city life and visit the amazing animals at the world famous London Zoo. See Asian lions, Sloth bears and the incredible 'Animals in Action'.

Museum of London
150 London Wall, EC2Y 5HN
Tel: (020) 7600 3699
www.museumoflondon.org.uk
Discover over 2000 years of the capital's history, from prehistoric to modern times. Regular temporary exhibitions and lunchtime lecture programmes.

National Gallery
Trafalgar Square, WC2N 5DN
Tel: (020) 7747 2885
www.nationalgallery.org.uk
Gallery displaying Western European painting from about 1250-1900. Includes work by Botticelli, Leonardo da Vinci, Rembrandt, Gainsborough, Turner, Renoir, Cezanne.

National Maritime Museum
Romney Road, SE10 9NF
Tel: (020) 8858 4422 www.nmm.ac.uk
This national museum explains Britain's worldwide influence through its explorers, traders, migrants and naval power. Features on ship models, costume, and ecology of the sea.

National Portrait Gallery
St Martin's Place, WC2H 0HE
Tel: (020) 7306 0055 www.npg.org.uk
Permanent collection of portraits of famous men and women from the Middle Ages to the present day. Free, but charge for some exhibitions.

Natural History Museum
Cromwell Road, SW7 5BD
Tel: (020) 7942 5000 www.nhm.ac.uk
Home of the wonders of the natural world with hundreds of exciting, interactive exhibits. Don't miss 'Dinosaurs', 'Creepy-Crawlies' and the new Darwin Centre.

Royal Mews
Buckingham Palace, SW1A 1AA
Tel: (020) 7321 2233 www.royal.gov.uk
One of the finest working stables in existence, the Royal Mews is responsible for all road travel arrangements for the Queen and Royal Family.

2

3

1. The London Eye
2. Buckingham Palace
3. Notting Hill Carnival

Royal Observatory Greenwich
Greenwich Park, SE10 9NF
Tel: (020) 8858 4422 www.nmm.ac.uk
Museum of time and space and site of the Greenwich Meridian. Working telescopes and planetarium, timeball, Wren's Octagon Room and intricate clocks and computer simulations.

St Paul's Cathedral
St Paul's Churchyard, EC4M 8AD
Tel: (020) 7236 4128 www.stpauls.co.uk
Wren's famous cathedral church of the diocese of London incorporating the Crypt, Ambulatory and Whispering Gallery.

Science Museum
Exhibition Road, SW7 2DD
Tel: 0870 8704868
www.sciencemuseum.org.uk
See, touch and experience the major scientific advances of the last 300 years at the largest Museum of its kind in the world.

Shakespeare's Globe Exhibition and Tour
Bankside, SE1 9DT
Tel: (020) 7902 1500
www.shakespeares-globe.org
Against the historical background of Elizabethan Bankside, the City of London's playground in Shakespeare's time, the exhibition focuses on actors, architecture and audiences.

Tate Britain
Millbank, SW1P 4RG
Tel: (020) 7887 8008 www.tate.org.uk
The world's greatest collection of British art including work by Constable, Gainsborough, Hockney, Rossetti and Turner, presented in a dynamic series of new displays and exhibitions.

Tate Modern
Bankside, SE1 9TG
Tel: (020) 7887 8008 www.tate.org.uk
Houses the Tate Collection of international modern art from 1900 to the present day, including major works by Matisse and Picasso plus contemporary work by Sarah Lucas and Rachel Whiteread.

Theatre Museum
Russell Street, WC2E 7PA
Tel: (020) 7943 4700 www.theatremuseum.org
Exhibitions, events based on the world's most exciting performing arts collections, and galleries brought to life by tour guides, all celebrate performance in Britain.

Tower Bridge Experience
Tower Bridge, SE1 2UP
Tel: (020) 7403 3761
www.towerbridge.org.uk
Exhibition explaining the history of the bridge and how it operates. Enjoy the panoramic views from the Walkway 150ft (45m) above the Thames and visit the original Engines.

Tower of London
Tower Hill, EC3N 4AB
Tel: 0870 7567070
www.hrp.org.uk
Home of the 'Beefeaters' and ravens, the building spans 900 years of British history. On display are the nation's Crown Jewels, regalia and armoury robes.

Victoria and Albert Museum
Cromwell Road, SW7 2RL
Tel: (020) 7942 2000 www.vam.ac.uk
Large and varied collections of decorative arts from 3000BC to the present day. The new British Galleries explore British art and design from Tudor times to the Victorian era.

Vinopolis - London's Wine Tasting Visitor Attraction
1 Bank End, SE1 9BU
Tel: 0870 2414040 www.vinopolis.co.uk
Vinopolis is London's Wine Tasting Visitor Attraction. For anyone who enjoys a glass of wine it is one of the few attractions where guests grow merrier as they walk through!

Westminster Abbey
Parliament Square, SW1P 3PA
Tel: (020) 7222 5152
www.westminster-abbey.org
One of Britain's finest Gothic buildings. Scene of the coronation, marriage and burial of British monarchs. Nave and cloisters, Royal Chapels and Undercroft Museum.

Visit London

1 Warwick Row, London SW1E 5ER
www.visitlondon.com

1. Tower Bridge
2. Houses of Paliament
3. Queens Guard

3

Tourist Information Centres

INNER LONDON

- **Britain and London Visitor Centre,** 1 Regent Street, Piccadilly Circus, SW1Y 4XT. Open: Mon 0930-1830,Tue-Fri 0900-1830, Sat & Sun 1000-1600; Jun-Oct, Sat 0900-1700.

- **Greenwich TIC,** Pepys House, 2 Cutty Sark Gardens, Greenwich SE10 9LW. Tel: 0870 608 2000; Fax: 020 8853 4607. Open: Daily 1000-1700.

- **Lewisham TIC,** Lewisham Library, 199-201 Lewisham High Street, SE13 6LG. Tel: 020 8297 8317; Fax: 020 8297 9241. Open: Mon 1000-1700, Tue-Fri 0900-1700, Sat 1000-1600.

- **London Visitors Centre,** Arrivals Hall, Waterloo International Terminal, SE1 7LT. Open: Daily 0830-2230.

OUTER LONDON

- **Bexley Hall Place TIC,** Bourne Road, Bexley, Kent, DA5 1PQ. Tel: 01322 558676; Fax 01322 522921. Open: Mon-Sat 1000-1630, Sun 1400-1730.

- **Croydon TIC, Katharine Street,** Croydon, CR9 1ET. Tel: 020 8253 1009; Fax: 020 8253 1008. Open: Mon-Wed & Fri 0900-1800, Thu 0930-1800, Sat 0900-1700, Sun 1400-1700.

- **Harrow TIC,** Civic Centre, Station Road, Harrow, HA1 2XF. Tel: 020 8424 1103; Fax: 020 8424 1134. Open: Mon-Fri 0900-1700.

- **Hillingdon TIC,** Central Library, 14-15 High Street, Uxbridge, UB8 1HD. Tel: 01895 250706; Fax: 01895 239794. Open: Mon, Tue & Thu 0930-2000, Wed 0930-1730, Fri 1000-1730, Sat 0930-1600.

- **Hounslow TIC,** The Treaty Centre, High Street, Hounslow, TW3 1ES. Tel: 0845 4562929; Fax: 0845 4562904 Open: Mon, Tues & Thurs 0930-2000; Wed, Fri & Sat 0930-1730; Sun 1130-1600.

- **Kingston TIC,** Market House, Market Place, Kingston upon Thames, KT1 1JS. Tel: 020 8547 5592; Fax: 020 8547 5594. Open: Mon-Sat 1000-1700.

- **Richmond TIC,** Old Town Hall, Whittaker Avenue; Richmond, TW9 1TP. Tel: 020 8940 6899; Fax: 020 8940 6899. Open: Mon-Sat 1000-1700; May-Sep, Sun 1030-1330.

- **Swanley TIC,** London Road, BR8 7AE. Tel: 01322 614660; Fax: 01322 666154. Open: Mon-Thu 0930-1730, Fri 0930-1800, Sat 0900-1600.

- **Twickenham TIC,** The Atrium, Civic Centre, York Street, Twickenham, Middlesex, TW1 3BZ. Tel: 020 8891 7272; Fax: 020 8891 7738. Open: Mon-Thu 0900-1715, Fri 0900-1700.

INFORMATION PACK
For a London information pack call 0870 240 4326. Calls are charged at national rate.

LONDON LINE
Visit London's recorded telephone information service provides information on museums, galleries, attractions, riverboat trips, sightseeing tours, accommodation, theatre, what's on, changing the Guard, children's London, shopping, eating out and gay and lesbian London.

Available 24 hours a day. Calls cost 60p per minute as at July 2003. Call 09068 663344.

ARTSLINE
London's information and advice service for disabled people on arts and entertainment. Call (020) 7388 2227.

HOTEL ACCOMMODATION SERVICE
Accommodation reservations can be made throughout London. Call Visit London's Telephone Accommodation Service on (020) 7932 2020 with your requirements and MasterCard/Visa/Switch details or email your request on book@visitlondon.com

WHICH PART OF LONDON
The majority of tourist accommodation is situated in the central parts of London and is therefore very convenient for most of the city's attractions and nightlife.

However, there are many hotels in outer London which provide other advantages, such as easier parking. In the 'Where to Stay' pages which follow, you will find accommodation listed under INNER LONDON (covering the E1 to W14 London Postal Area) and OUTER LONDON (covering the remainder of Greater London). Colour maps 6 and 7 at the front of the guide show place names and London Postal Area codes and will help you to locate accommodation in your chosen area of London.

1

Getting to London

BY ROAD: Major trunk roads into London include: A1, M1, A5, A10, A11, M11, A13, A2, M2, A23, A3, M3, A4, M4, A40, M40, A41, M25 (London orbital). London Transport is responsible for running London's bus services and the underground rail network. (020) 7222 1234 (24 hour telephone service; calls answered in rotation).

BY RAIL: Main rail termini: Victoria/Waterloo/Charing Cross - serving the South/South East; King's Cross - serving the North East; Euston - serving the North West/Midlands; Liverpool Street - serving the East; Paddington - serving the Thames Valley/West.

1. London Underground Station
2. The Mall

2

Where to stay in

London

Entries in this region are listed under Inner London (postcode areas E1 to W14) and Outer London (the remainder of Greater London).

All place names in the blue bands under which accommodation is listed, are shown on the maps at the front of this guide.

Symbols give useful information about services and facilities. Inside the back cover flap there's a key to these symbols which you can keep open for easy reference.

A complete listing of all the VisitBritain assessed accommodation covered by this guide appears at the back of this guide.

INNER LONDON
LONDON E14

★★★★

1 Unit
Sleeping 6

RIVER THAMES APARTMENT

London E14
Contact: Greta Paull
T: (020) 8530 2336
F: (020) 85302336
E: gretapaull@aol.com
I: www.riverthamesapartment.co.uk

All rooms and balcony overlooking river. First floor apartment (lift). Two bedrooms, two bathrooms, lounge/dining room, kitchen. Docklands Light Railway (South Quay) five-minute walk. Trains to City and West End 20 minutes or Greenwich five minutes.

OPEN All Year

Low season per wk
£500.00–£600.00
High season per wk
£600.00–£750.00

LONDON N7

★★-★★★

2 Units

CARENA HOLIDAY ACCOMMODATION

London N7
Contact: Mr M Chouthi, 98 St George's Avenue, Tufnell Park, London N7 0AH
T: (020) 7607 7453
F: (020) 7607 7453
E: c.chouthi@btopenworld.com

OPEN All Year

Low season per wk
£300.00–£500.00
High season per wk
£350.00–£550.00

In quiet road with free street parking. Comfortable apartments with a range of quality facilities and services. Perfectly positioned for easy access to London.

LONDON SE10

★★★★

1 Unit
Sleeping 4

HARBOUR MASTER'S HOUSE BASEMENT FLAT

London SE10
Contact: Professor French, The Harbour Master's House, 20 Ballast Quay, London SE10 9PD
T: (020) 8293 9597
F: (020) 8293 9597
E: harbourmaster@lineone.net
I: website.lineone.net/~harbourmaster/

OPEN All Year

Low season per wk
£540.00–£700.00
High season per wk
£540.00–£700.00

Superb self-contained flat, part of the historic Harbour Master's house (Grade II Listed). Situated on attractive riverside enclave on the Thames in maritime Greenwich.

LONDON SW7

★★-★★★

13 Units

SNOW WHITE PROPERTIES LTD

London SW7
Contact: Miss M White, Snow White Properties Ltd, 55 Ennismore Gardens, Knightsbridge, London SW7 1AJ
T: (020) 7584 3307
F: (020) 7581 4686
E: snow.white@virgin.net
I: www.snowwhitelondon.com

OPEN All Year
CC: Mastercard, Visa

Low season per wk
£630.00–£1,000.00
High season per wk
£700.00–£1,050.00

Elegant 19thC house situated in beautiful, quiet garden square close to Harrods, Hyde Park, museums and public transport. Your home away from home – a gem.

LONDON SW18

★★★★

2 Units
Sleeping 3–6

BEAUMONT APARTMENTS

London SW18
Contact: Mr & Mrs A Afriat, Beaumont Apartments, 24 Combemartin Road, Southfields, London SW18 5PR
T: (020) 8789 2663
F: (020) 8265 5499
E: alan@beaumont-london-apartments.co.uk
I: www.beaumont-london-apartments.co.uk

OPEN All Year
CC: Amex, Delta, JCB, Mastercard, Solo, Switch, Visa

Low season per wk
£490.00–£650.00
High season per wk
£520.00–£780.00

Well-appointed flats in leafiest suburb within 25 minutes of West End. Close to zone 3 underground, Wimbledon tennis and convenient for A3, M4, M41, M25, Heathrow, Gatwick.

LONDON SW20

★★★

2 Units

THALIA & HEBE HOLIDAY HOMES

London SW20
Contact: Mr & Mrs Briscoe-Smith, 150 Westway, Raynes Park, West Wimbledon, London SW20 9LS
T: (020) 8542 0505
F: (020) 8287 0637
E: peter@briscoe-smith.org.uk
I: www.briscoe-smith.org.uk/thalia/

OPEN All Year

Low season per wk
£550.00–£650.00
High season per wk
£550.00–£650.00

Thalia and Hebe are both three-bedroomed houses in the residential suburban area of West Wimbledon. Home from home, with easy access to central London.

LONDON W1

★★-★★★

10 Units

TUSTIN HOLIDAY FLATS

London W1
Contact: Reservations Office, Tustin Holiday Flats, 94 York Street, London W1H 1QX
T: (020) 7723 9611
F: (020) 7724 0224
E: pctustinuk@btconnect.com
I: www.pctustin.com

OPEN All Year
CC: Mastercard, Visa

Low season per wk
£360.00–£660.00
High season per wk
£365.00–£670.00

Fully furnished self-contained flats in central London, offering easy access to Oxford Street, places of interest and public transport.

RATING **All accommodation in this guide has been rated, or is awaiting a rating, by a trained VisitBritain assessor.**

LONDON W5

★★★★

3 Units

Ealing is a vibrant university suburb with great shops, restaurants and pavement cafes. Select from a garden apartment in a Victorian house, a brand new Art Deco-style two-bedroom, two-bathroom flat, or a two-bedroom apartment in a conservation area. Easy access to all types of transport. Free parking.

CLARENDON HOUSE APARTMENTS

London W5

Contact: Mrs A Pedley, 48 Ranelagh Road, Ealing, London W5 5RJ

T: (020) 8567 0314

F: (020) 8566 3241

E: clarendon.house@LineOne.net

I: www.clarendonhouseapartments.co.uk

OPEN All Year
CC: Mastercard, Solo, Switch, Visa

Low season per wk
£425.00–£725.00
High season per wk
£425.00–£725.00

LONDON W13

★★★

5 Units
Sleeping 3

APARTMENTS WEST LONDON

London W13
Contact: Bill Smith, Apartments West London, 94 Gordon Road, London W13 8PT
T: (020) 8566 8187
F: (020) 8566 7670
E: info@apartmentswestlondon.com
I: www.apartmentswestlondon.com

OPEN All Year
CC: Delta, JCB, Mastercard, Solo, Switch, Visa

Low season per wk
£352.00–£442.00
High season per wk
£352.00–£442.00

Attractive studio apartments for business or holiday. Short walk to Ealing Broadway underground station and shopping centre with lively bars, pubs and restaurants.

OUTER LONDON BECKENHAM

★-★★★

8 Units

OAKFIELD APARTMENTS

Beckenham

Contact: Mr J E Deane

T: (020) 8658 4441

F: (020) 8658 9198

E: hols@oakfield.co.uk

I: www.oakfield.co.uk

Victorian mansion with a large garden in a semi-rural setting, three minutes' walk to Eden Park rail station, 25 minutes by rail or 14 kilometres by road to central London. Mr and Mrs Deane live on the premises and welcome children but not pets.

OPEN All Year
CC: Mastercard, Solo, Switch, Visa

Low season per wk
£250.00–£625.00
High season per wk
£250.00–£625.00

CROYDON *Tourist Information Centre Tel: (020) 8253 1009*

★★★-★★★★

6 Units

Family-run business. Centrally situated, good train services to London. Apartments furnished to high standard. TV, telephone, kitchen fully equipped with microwave, fridge/freezer, washing machine, quality utensils and crockery. Mob: 07710 466870.

S N D APARTMENTS

Croydon

Contact: Mrs P Pereira, S N D Apartments, 1 Mulgrave Road, Croydon CR0 1BL

T: (020) 8686 7023

F: (020) 8686 7835

E: reservations@www.sndapartments.co.uk

I: www.sndapartments.co.uk

OPEN All Year
CC: Mastercard

Low season per wk
£350.00–£650.00
High season per wk
£350.00–£650.00

PINNER

★★★★

1 Unit
Sleeping 5

MOSS COTTAGE

Pinner
Contact: Ms B Le Quesne
T: (020) 8868 5507
F: (020) 8868 5507
E: info@moss-lane-cottages.com
I: www.moss-lane-cottages.com

This self-contained wing of a 17thC building has been renovated to provide quality accommodation in a traditional setting just 12 miles from central London. Conveniently located for shops, restaurants, underground, rail and bus services, Heathrow airport and M25. Spacious bedrooms, bathroom with shower, kitchen with laundry facilities, central heating, private patio.

OPEN All Year
CC: Mastercard, Switch, Visa

Short breaks available during low season.

Low season per wk
£600.00–£700.00
High season per wk
£700.00–£770.00

QUALITY ASSURANCE SCHEME

For an explanation of the quality and facilities represented by the Stars please refer to the front of this guide. A more detailed explanation can be found in the information pages at the back.

Cumbria

Cumbria's dynamic and breathtaking landscapes, from the famous Lakes to the rugged mountains and fells, have inspired poets and artists for hundreds of years.

The County of Cumbria

Classic sights
Hadrian's Wall – a reminder of Roman occupation
Lake Windermere – largest lake in England

Coast & country
Scafell Pike – England's highest mountain
Whitehaven – historic port

Literary links
William Wordsworth – the poet's homes: Wordsworth House, Dove Cottage and Rydal Mount
Beatrix Potter – her home, Hill Top; The Beatrix Potter Gallery; The World of Beatrix Potter attraction.

Distinctively different
The Gondola – sail Coniston Water aboard the opulent 1859 steam yacht Gondola
Cars of the Stars Museum – cars from TV and Film, including Chitty Chitty Bang Bang and the Batmobile

For more information contact:
Cumbria Tourist Board
Ashleigh, Holly Road,
Windermere, Cumbria
LA23 2AQ

E: info@golakes.co.uk
www.golakes.co.uk
www.lakedistrictoutdoors.co.uk
www.lastminutelakedistrict.co.uk

Telephone enquiries -
T: (015394) 44444
F: (015394) 44041

1. Jetty on Derwent Water
2. Snowboarder, near Alston
3. Bluebells at Brantwood

Places to Visit

You will find hundreds of interesting places to visit during your stay, just some of which are listed in these pages. Contact any Tourist Information Centre in the region for more ideas on days out.

QUALITY ASSURED VISITOR ATTRACTION

Awarded VisitBritain's 'Quality Assured Visitor Attraction' marque.

The Beacon
West Strand, Whitehaven
Tel: (01946) 592302
www.copelandbc.gov.uk
Award-winning attraction and museum superbly situated overlooking the Georgian harbour of Whitehaven, one of England's 'gem towns'.

Brantwood, Home of John Ruskin
Standish Street, Coniston
Tel: (015394) 41396 www.brantwood.org.uk
The most beautifully situated house in the Lake District, home of John Ruskin from 1872 until 1900. Discover the wealth of things to do at Brantwood.

Cars of the Stars Motor Museum
Keswick
Tel: (017687) 73757 www.carsofthestars.com
Features TV and film vehicles including the Batmobile, Chitty Chitty Bang Bang, the James Bond Aston Martin, Herbie, FAB 1 plus many other famous cars and motorcycles.

The Dock Museum
North Road, Barrow-in-Furness
Tel: (01229) 894444 www.dockmuseum.org.uk
Spectacular modern museum built over an original Victorian graving dock. Galleries include multi-media interactives, and impressive ship models.

Dove Cottage and Wordsworth Museum
Town End, Grasmere, Ambleside
Tel: (015394) 35544 www.wordsworth.org.uk
Wordsworth's home 1799-1808. Museum with manuscripts, farmhouse reconstruction, paintings and drawings. Special events throughout the year.

Furness Abbey (English Heritage)
Barrow-in-Furness
Tel: (01229) 823420
www.english heritage.org.uk
Ruins of 12thC Cistercian abbey, the 2nd wealthiest in England. Extensive remains include transepts, choir and west tower of church, canopied seats, arches, church.

Gleaston Water Mill
Gleaston, Ulverston
Tel: (01229) 869244 www.watermill.co.uk
A truly rural experience abounding with all things country - a water cornmill, artefacts, traditions, folklore and cooking and of course the acclaimed Pig's Whisper Store.

Heron Glass Ltd
The Lakes Glass Centre, Ulverston
Tel: (01229) 581121
www.herongiftware.com
Heron Glass Ltd and Cumbria Crystal, displays of making handblown glass giftware and lead crystal. Lighthouse cafe and restaurant.
A Gateway to Furness Exhibition.

Hill Top (National Trust)
Near Sawrey, Ambleside
Tel: (015394) 36269 www.nationaltrust.org.uk
Beatrix Potter wrote many of her popular Peter Rabbit stories and other books in this charming little house which still contains her own china and furniture.

Holker Hall and Gardens
Cark in Cartmel, Grange-over-Sands
Tel: (015395) 58328
www.holker-hall.co.uk
Including Victorian new wing, formal and woodland garden, deer park, motor museum, adventure playground, cafe and gift shop.

Jennings Brothers plc
The Castle Brewery, Cockermouth
Tel: 0845 1297185
www.jenningsbrewery.co.uk
Guided tours of Jennings traditional brewery and sampling of the ales in the Old Cooperage Bar.

K Village Outlet Centre
Lound Road, Kendal,
Tel: (01539) 732363 www.kvillage.co.uk
Famous named brands such as K-shoes, Van Heusen, Denby, National Trust Shop, Tog24 and Ponden Mill all at discounts. Open 7 days per week with full disabled access.

The Lake District Coast Aquarium Maryport
South Quay, Maryport,
Tel: (01900) 817760
www.lakedistrict-coastaquarium.co.uk
Purpose-built independent aquarium with over 35 displays. Largest collection of native marine species in Cumbria. Cafe and gift shop.

The Lake District Visitor Centre Brockhole
Windermere
Tel: (015394) 46601
www.lake-district.gov.uk
Brockhole is an Edwardian house on the shores of Windermere with extensive landscaped gardens, superb views, lake cruises, adventure playground, walks, events & activities.

Lakeland Sheep and Wool Centre
Egremont Road, Cockermouth
Tel: (01900) 822673
www.sheep-woolcentre.co.uk
Live farm show including cows, sheep, dogs and ducks, all displaying their working qualities. Large gift shop and licensed cafe/restaurant. All weather attraction.

Levens Hall
Levens, Kendal
Tel: (015395) 60321
www.levenshall.co.uk
Elizabethan home of the Bagot family incorporating 13thC pele tower, world-famous topiary gardens, Bellingham Buttery, Potting Shed gift shop, plant centre and play area.

Muncaster Castle, Gardens, Owl Centre and Meadow Vole Maze
Ravenglass
Tel: (01229) 717614 www.muncaster.co.uk
Muncaster Castle with the most beautifully situated Owl Centre in the world. See the birds fly, picnic in the gardens, visit the Pennington family home.

Ravenglass and Eskdale Railway
Ravenglass
Tel: (01229) 717171
www.ravenglass-railway.co.uk
England's oldest narrow-gauge railway runs for 7 miles (12km) through glorious scenery to the foot of England's highest hills. Most trains are steam hauled.

Rheged - The Village in the Hill
Redhills, Penrith
Tel: (01768) 868000 www.rheged.com
Award-winning Rheged is home to giant cinema screen showing 3 movies daily, the National Mountaineering Exhibition, speciality shops, indoor play area and restaurant.

The Rum Story
27 Lowther Street, Whitehaven
Tel: (01946) 592933 www.rumstory.co.uk
'The Rum Story' - the world's first exhibition depicting the unique story of the UK rum trade in the original Jefferson's wine merchant premises.

2

3

1. Lake Windermere
2. Esk River, Eskdale
3. Thirlmere Valley

Rydal Mount and Gardens
Rydal, Ambleside
Tel: (015394) 33002
www.wordsworthlakes.co.uk
Nestling between the majestic fells, Lake Windermere and Rydal Water, lies the 'most beloved' home of William Wordsworth from 1813-1850.

Senhouse Roman Museum
The Battery, Sea Brows, Maryport
Tel: (01900) 816168
www.senhousemuseum.co.uk
Once the headquarters of Hadrian's Coastal Defence system. UK's largest group of Roman altar stones and inscriptions on one site.

Sizergh Castle (National Trust)
Kendal
Tel: (015395) 60070 www.nationaltrust.org.uk
Strickland family home for 750 years, now National Trust owned, with 14thC pele tower, 15thC great hall, 16thC wings and Stuart connections. Rock garden, rose garden, daffodils.

South Lakes Wild Animal Park Ltd
Crossgates, Dalton-in-Furness
Tel: (01229) 466086
www.wildanimalpark.co.uk
Wild zoo park in over 17 acres (7ha) of grounds. Giraffe, rhino, tiger, lions, toilets, car/coach park. Miniature railway. Over 120 species of animals from all around the world.

South Tynedale Railway
Railway Station, Alston
Tel: (01434) 381696 www.strps.org.uk
Narrow gauge railway along part of the route of the former Alston to Haltwhistle branch line through South Tynedale with preserved steam and diesel engines.

Steam Yacht Gondola (National Trust)
Pier Cottage, Coniston
Tel: (015394) 41288
www.nationaltrust.org.uk/gondola
Victorian steam-powered vessel now National Trust owned and completely renovated with an opulently-upholstered saloon. Superb way to appreciate the beauty of Coniston Water.

Theatre by the Lake
Lakeside, Keswick
Tel: (017687) 74411
www.theatrebythelake.com
Offering a summer season of plays, a Christmas show and an Easter production. The theatre also hosts visiting drams, music, dance, talks and comedy.

Tullie House Museum and Art Gallery
Castle Street, Carlisle
Tel: (01228) 534781
www.tulliehouse.co.uk
Visit our Georgian Mansion housing our magnificent pre-Raphaelite collection, Victorian childhood gallery, 1689 fireplace and Jacobean oak staircase.

Ullswater 'Steamers'
The Pier House, Glenridding
Tel: (017684) 82229
www.ullswater-steamers.co.uk
Relax and enjoy a beautiful Ullswater cruise with walks and picnic areas. Boat services operating all year round.

Windermere Lake Cruises
Ambleside, Bowness-on-Windermere
Tel: (015395) 31188
www.windermere-lakecruises.co.uk
Steamers and launches sail daily throughout the year between Ambleside, Lakeside and Bowness. Seasonal sailings to Brockhole, L&H Steam Railway and Aquarium of the Lakes.

Windermere Steamboats & Museum
Rayrigg Road, Bowness-on-Windermere
Tel: (015394) 45565
www.steamboat.co.uk
A wealth of interest and information about life on bygone Windermere. Regular steam launch trips, vintage vessels and classic motorboats. Model boat pond, lakeside picnic area.

The World Famous Old Blacksmith's Shop Centre
Gretna Green
Tel: (01461) 338441 www.gretnagreen.com
The original Blacksmith's Shop museum and a shopping centre selling, cashmere and woollen knitwear, crystal and china. Taste local produce in the Old Smithy Restaurant.

Cumbria Tourist Board

Ashleigh, Holly Road, Windermere,
Cumbria L23 2AQ
T: (015394) 44444 F: (015394) 44041
E: info@golakes.co.uk
www.golakes.co.uk
www.lakedistrictoutdoors.co.uk
www.lastminutelakedistrict.co.uk

THE FOLLOWING PUBLICATIONS ARE AVAILABLE FROM THE CUMBRIA TOURIST BOARD

Cumbria – the Lake District Holidays & Breaks Guide (free) T: 08705 133059

The Flora and Fauna of Cumbria - the Lake District (free)

The Caravan and Camping Guide of Cumbria – the Lake District (free)

The Taste District (free) Food & drink guide
Events Listing (free)

Getting to Cumbria

BY ROAD: The M1/M6/M25/M40 provide a link with London and the South East and the M5/M6 provide access from the South West. The M6 links the Midlands and North West and the M62/M6 links the East of England and Yorkshire. Approximate journey time from London is 5 hours, from Manchester 1 hour 30 minutes.

BY RAIL: From London (Euston) to Oxenholme (Kendal) takes approximately 3 hours 30 minutes. From Oxenholme (connecting station for all main line trains) to Windermere takes approximately 20 minutes. From Carlisle to Barrow-in-Furness via the coastal route, with stops at many of the towns in between, takes approximately 2 hours. Trains from Edinburgh to Carlisle take approximately 2 hours 15 minutes. The historic Settle-Carlisle line also runs through the county bringing passengers from Yorkshire via the Eden Valley.

www.golakes.co.uk/transport.html

1. The village of Kikoswald, Eden Valley
2. Wordsworth House, Cockermouth

Heart of the Lakes & Cottage Life

Fisherbeck Mill, Old Lake Road, Ambleside, LA22 0DH

280 properties sleeping 2 - 12
Weekly Prices range from £200 - £1900

★★ - ★★★★★

Lakeland's Premier Holiday Letting Agency

For the best selection of self-catering homes in the very heart of England's beautiful Lake District.

Prime locations include Ambleside, Grasmere, Langdale, Keswick, Ullswater etc.

All properties include free leisure club membership. Call us now or visit our informative website.

Tel: 015394 32321 or Fax: 015394 33251

www.heartofthelakes.co.uk

e-mail: info@heartofthelakes.co.uk

Open all year round

Credit Cards: Visa, Access, Switch, Delta

Excellence in England 2002 Gold Winner Self Catering Holiday of the Year

INVESTOR IN PEOPLE

THE LAKELAND COTTAGE COMPANY

virtually yours
BECOME A VIRTUAL TOURIST AND DISCOVER OUR LAKE DISTRICT

Visit us at www.lakelandcottageco.com our 'Cumbria for Excellence 2003' award winning website and take the virtual tours around our unique selection of fabulous quality cottages.

What better way to see if a cottage is right for you than to pay a visit, get a feel for the layout, choose which bedroom will be yours, all from the comfort of your own home.

You can then see what else the Lake District has to offer and dip into our Lakeland Guide,visit our Towns & Villages or even take a spin around a calm Lakeshore or breathtaking Fell top.

Alternatively, give us a call for our colour brochure pack, crammed with reviews and full of fabulous pictures of our cottages and favourite Lakeland Locations.

TELEPHONE 015395 30024 FAX 015395 31932
WEBSITE www.lakelandcottageco.com E - MAIL john@lakelandcottageco.com
WATERSIDE HOUSE, NEWBY BRIDGE, CUMBRIA LA12 8AN

Where to stay in

Cumbria

All place names in the blue bands under which accommodation is listed, are shown on the maps at the front of this guide.

Symbols give useful information about services and facilities. Inside the back cover flap there's a key to these symbols which you can keep open for easy reference.

A complete listing of all the VisitBritain assessed accommodation covered by this guide appears at the back of this guide.

AMBLESIDE, Cumbria Map ref 5A3 *Tourist Information Centre Tel: (015394) 32582*

★★★

1 Unit
Sleeping 4

BIRCH COTTAGE
Ambleside
Contact: Dr L Nash, 47 Goring Road, Bounds Green, London N11 2BT
T: (020) 88881252
F: (020) 88881252
E: birchcottage@vithani.freeserve.co.uk

OPEN All Year

Low season per wk
Min £200.00
High season per wk
Max £390.00

Delightful 200-year-old traditional stone cottage in a quiet hamlet with mountain views. Five minutes' walk to village centre. Comfortably furnished, well equipped. No smokers.

The LAKE DISTRICT and CUMBRIA

Dales Holiday Cottages

Superb, personally inspected, self catering holiday properties in beautiful rural and coastal locations from Beatrix Potter and Wordsworth country to the Borders. Cosy cottages to country houses, many welcome pets and most are open all year.
Phone for free brochure.

01756 799821 & 790919
www.dalesholcot.com

English Tourism Council
Committed to ETC Quality Assurance

AMBLESIDE continued

★★★★

3 Units
Sleeping 4–6

CHESTNUTS, BEECHES & THE GRANARY

High Wray, Ambleside
Contact: Mr J R Benson, High Sett, Sun Hill Lane, Troutbeck Bridge, Windermere LA23 1HJ
T: (015394) 42731
F: (015394) 42731
E: sbenson@talk21.com
I: www.accommodationlakedistrict.com

Charming cottages and a bungalow converted from a former coach house and tack room, furnished to a high standard. Set in idyllic surroundings overlooking Lake Windermere with panoramic views of the Lakeland mountains. High Wray is a quiet hamlet between Ambleside and Hawkshead, an ideal base for walking/touring.

OPEN All Year

3-night stays available low season.

Low season per wk
£250.00–£500.00
High season per wk
£250.00–£500.00

★★★

1 Unit
Sleeping 5

DOWER HOUSE COTTAGE
Ambleside
Contact: Mrs M Rigg
T: (015394) 33211
F: (015394) 33211

OPEN All Year

Low season per wk
£256.00–£339.00
High season per wk
£387.00–£492.00

Self-catering cottage with two bedrooms, large kitchen, dining room, large sitting room, bathroom. French windows opening onto terrace and gardens.

★★★

1 Unit
Sleeping 8

SARUM
Ambleside
Contact: Ms J Hughes, 95 Lark Hill Lane, Formby, Liverpool L37 1LU
T: (01704) 831558
F: (01704) 874866
E: formbyphysio@bigfoot.com
I: sarum.co.uk

OPEN All Year except Christmas

Low season per wk
Min £400.00
High season per wk
Max £550.00

Comfortable Victorian stone-built house in centre of village. Three bathrooms and private parking. Convenient for all amenities. Well placed for walking and touring.

Rating Applied For

1 Unit
Sleeping 7

SCANDALE BRIDGE COTTAGE

Thirlmere, Keswick
Contact: Central Reservations, Kings Head Hotel, Thirlspot CA12 4TN
T: (017687) 72393
F: (017687) 72309
E: stay@lakedistrictinns.co.uk
I: www.lakedistrictinns.co.uk

A period Lakeland-stone house on the edge of Ambleside, fully-equipped to be your country home from home in the Lake District. Mature private gardens with river frontage, beautifully furnished, ample parking. This is a wonderful base for touring the Lake District.

OPEN All Year

Low season per wk
£250.00–£400.00
High season per wk
£400.00–£750.00

NB

IMPORTANT NOTE Information on accommodation listed in this guide has been supplied by the proprietors. As changes may occur you are advised to check details at the time of booking.

APPLEBY-IN-WESTMORLAND, Cumbria Map ref 5B3 *Tourist Information Centre Tel: (017683) 51177*

★★★★

1 Unit
Sleeping 9

DUNKIRK

Reagill, Penrith
Contact: Mr P Crosbie, 30 Eagle Wharf Court, Lafone Street, London SE1 2LZ
T: (020) 7403 7346
E: paulcrosbie147@msn.com
I: www.dunkirk.20m.com

OPEN All Year

Low season per wk
Min £350.00
High season per wk
Max £475.00

Well-equipped cottage/barn conversion, oil central heating, woodburning stove. In quiet location, spacious grounds. Ideal for northern lakes and Eden Valley.

BASSENTHWAITE, Cumbria Map ref 5A2

★★★★

5 Units
Sleeping 2–6

IRTON HOUSE FARM

Isel, Cockermouth
Contact: Mr & Mrs R W Almond, Irton House Farm, Isel, Cockermouth CA13 9ST
T: (017687) 76380
E: almond@farmersweekly.net
I: www.almondirtonhousefarm.com

OPEN All Year
CC: Mastercard, Visa

Low season per wk
£275.00–£295.00
High season per wk
£320.00–£360.00

Immaculate, spacious properties, all furnished to a high specification. Shopping at Keswick and Cockermouth. Superb views, walks and places of interest. Prices are for two people.

BOWNESS-ON-WINDERMERE, Cumbria Map ref 5A3

★★★★

3 Units
Sleeping 2–8

This traditional, Lakeland-stone house has been converted into three-bedroom suites and studio apartment to a very high, luxury standard. The suites have unsurpassed views of the lake, surrounding hills and mountains.

WATERS EDGE VILLA

Bowness-on-Windermere, Windermere
Contact: Michelle Weir & Anna Jex, Waters Edge Villa, Ferry Nab, Bowness-on-Windermere LA23 3JH
T: (015394) 43415
F: (015394) 88721
E: email@lakewindermere.net
I: www.lakewindermere.net

OPEN All Year
CC: Delta, Mastercard, Solo, Switch, Visa

Short breaks all year round. Weekends and mid-week breaks. Free entry into local leisure club. Special winter rates available.

Low season per wk
£235.00–£550.00
High season per wk
£375.00–£949.00

BROUGHTON-IN-FURNESS, Cumbria Map ref 5A3

★★★-★★★★

5 Units
Sleeping 2–6

Cottages set in the beautiful and unspoilt 'Woodland Valley' provide an excellent base for outdoor activities or relaxing short breaks. All cottages are centrally heated and fully-equipped, including bedding and towels. Electricity, gas and fuel for log fires are also included in the price you pay.

RING HOUSE COTTAGES

Broughton-in-Furness
Contact: Mr & Mrs S Harrison, Ring House Cottages, Woodland, Broughton-in-Furness LA20 6DG
T: (01229) 716578
F: (01229) 716850
E: info@ringhouse.co.uk
I: www.ringhouse.co.uk

OPEN All Year
CC: Delta, Mastercard, Switch, Visa

Weekend and mid-week breaks available all year round.

Low season per wk
£200.00–£385.00
High season per wk
£300.00–£475.00

BUTTERMERE, Cumbria Map ref 5A3

★★★★
6 Units
Sleeping 4–6

BRIDGE HOTEL SELF CATERING APARTMENTS

Buttermere, Cockermouth
Contact: Bridge Hotel, Buttermere, Cockermouth CA13 9UZ
T: (017687) 70252
F: (017687) 70215
E: enquiries@bridge-hotel.com
I: www.bridge-hotel.com

OPEN All Year
CC: Delta, Mastercard, Switch, Visa

High season per wk
£335.00–£620.00

Superbly situated, surrounded by fells in Area of Outstanding Natural Beauty. Each apartment is furnished to a high standard. All modern facilities. Dogs welcome.

★★★★
1 Unit
Sleeping 4

LANTHWAITE GREEN FARM COTTAGE

Buttermere, Cockermouth
Contact: Mrs P McGuire, Bridge Hotel, Buttermere, Cockermouth CA13 9UZ
T: (017687) 70252
F: (017687) 70215
E: enquiries@bridge-hotel.com
I: www.bridge-hotel.com

OPEN All Year
CC: Mastercard, Switch, Visa

High season per wk
£265.00–£495.00

Situated at the foot of Melbreak on a working farm. Looking towards Crummock Water, luxury, cosy, 16thC cottage. Boasts all modern facilities.

CALDBECK, Cumbria Map ref 5A2

★★★★
1 Unit
Sleeping 3

THE BARN, MANOR COTTAGE

Caldbeck, Wigton
Contact: Mrs A Wade, Manor Cottage, Fellside, Caldbeck, Wigton CA7 8HA
T: (016974) 78214
E: walterwade@tiscali.co.uk

OPEN All Year except Christmas

Low season per wk
£160.00–£250.00
High season per wk
£260.00–£300.00

Converted barn with pine beams, nestling in the Caldbeck Fells in unspoilt Northern Lakeland. Comfortable, well equipped. Panoramic views with garden and patio opening onto fells.

CARK IN CARTMEL, Cumbria Map ref 5A3

★★★
1 Unit
Sleeping 4

THE MILL APARTMENT

Cark in Cartmel, Grange-over-Sands
Contact: Mrs T Watson, 12 Millstream Court, Cark in Cartmel, Grange-over-Sands LA11 7NW
T: (015395) 58519
E: neiwatson@lineone.net
I: www.millholidayapartment.co.uk

OPEN All Year

Low season per wk
£195.00–£245.00
High season per wk
£295.00–£350.00

This very spacious yet cosy apartment is the ground floor of a converted corn mill. Short breaks available (excluding peak season).

CARLISLE, Cumbria Map ref 5A2 *Tourist Information Centre Tel: (01228) 625600*

★★★★
1 Unit
Sleeping 6

WEST COTTAGE

Cumwhinton, Carlisle
Contact: Mrs A Stamper, Cringles Farm, Cumwhinton, Carlisle CA4 8DL
T: (01228) 561600

A spacious, tastefully furnished and well-equipped cottage adjoining a Georgian Listed house in a village location three miles from historic Carlisle city. Village amenities include a shop, post office and pub serving good food. Relax on the patio or visit the beautiful Lake District, Hadrian's Wall and the Scottish Borders.

OPEN All Year

Short breaks available (excl Christmas and New Year when high season weekly rates apply).

Low season per wk
£200.00–£245.00
High season per wk
£280.00–£375.00

CONFIRM YOUR BOOKING
You are advised to confirm your booking in writing.

CARTMEL, Cumbria Map ref 5A3

★★★★

2 Units
Sleeping 6

Grange End, originally a Georgian barn, now holiday homes just oozing character and charm, complemented by solid tree-trunks supporting the ancient roof beams, exposed stone-work, wood-panelled window seats, 4-poster and, of course, a log fire. Step back in time, but luxuriate in the comforts of a modern, well-equipped home.

GRANGE END COTTAGES

Cark in Cartmel, Near Cartmel
Contact: Mr B T Colling, 7 Rushside Road, Cheadle Hulme, Stockport SK8 6NW
T: (0161) 4857015
F: (0161) 3556346
E: ibex32@aol.com
I: www.holidaycottagescumbria.com

OPEN All Year

Short breaks available, except in school holidays.

Low season per wk
£240.00–£320.00
High season per wk
£420.00–£560.00

COCKERMOUTH, Cumbria Map ref 5A2 *Tourist Information Centre Tel: (01900) 822634*

★★★

1 Unit
Sleeping 6

37 KIRKGATE

Cockermouth
Contact: Mr & Mrs N Chicken, 39 Kirkgate, Cockermouth CA13 9PJ
T: (01900) 823236
F: (01900) 825983
E: valandnelson@btopenworld.com
I: www.37kirkgate.com

OPEN All Year

Low season per wk
£200.00–£300.00
High season per wk
£275.00–£300.00

An ideal base for touring Cumbria, this spacious and comfortable three-bedroomed Georgian house overlooks tree-lined, cobbled area of Kirkgate.

CONISTON, Cumbria Map ref 5A3

★★★★

2 Units
Sleeping 6

1 & 2 ASH GILL COTTAGES

Torver, Coniston
Contact: Mrs D Cowburn, Lyndene, Pope Lane, Whitestake, Preston PR4 4JR
T: (01772) 612832

OPEN All Year

Low season per wk
Min £300.00
High season per wk
Max £450.00

Two houses equipped to the highest standard. Ample parking, gardens and patios. Excellent base for walking, touring, watersports and pony trekking.

3

★★★-★★★★★

12 Units
Sleeping 2–6

A range of quality cottages in superb surroundings in and around Coniston. Each well-equipped cottage is individually and tastefully furnished and has its own off-road parking and private patio or garden. Complimentary leisure club membership. Local activities include walking, horse-riding, mountain biking, canoeing and sailing.

CONISTON COUNTRY COTTAGES

Little Arrow, Coniston
Contact: Mr S & Mrs L Abbott
T: (015394) 41114
F: (015394) 41114
E: enquiry@conistoncottages.co.uk
I: www.conistoncottages.co.uk

OPEN All Year
CC: Delta, Mastercard, Switch, Visa

Short breaks available Nov-Mar (excl Christmas and New Year).

Low season per wk
£200.00–£350.00
High season per wk
£295.00–£595.00

QUALITY ASSURANCE SCHEME

Star ratings were correct at the time of going to press but are subject to change. Please check at the time of booking.

CONISTON continued

★★★

1 Unit
Sleeping 5

1 FAR END COTTAGES

Coniston
Contact: Mrs A H Batho, High Hollin Bank, Coniston
LA21 8AG
T: (015394) 41680
E: a.batho@virgin.net
I: www.cottagescumbria.com

This charming, Grade II Listed cottage is in a lovely, peaceful location at the foot of the fell, close to the village and the lake. It is furnished and equipped to a high standard. There is an open fire in the cosy sitting room and delighful views from the front rooms.

OPEN All Year

Low season per wk
£162.00–£270.00
High season per wk
£282.00–£399.00

★★★

1 Unit
Sleeping 8

5 HOLME GROUND COTTAGES

Coniston
Contact: Mrs K Bradshaw
T: (01434) 682526
E: rookery1@tiscali.co.uk

Tranquilly located, traditionally built (1860s), former quarryman's cottage in (usually unoccupied) terrace of eight. Cosy and comfortable with double-glazing and open fire. Rates include coal and electricity throughout the year. Well-equipped home from home surrounded by woodland and fell with attractive views. Enjoy great family fun and walking straight from the doorstep.

OPEN All Year

Free linen/towels supplied (up to 4 people) low season Oct-Feb.

Low season per wk
£225.00–£290.00
High season per wk
£350.00–£455.00

★★★

1 Unit
Sleeping 5

SHELT GILL

Coniston
Contact: Mrs R Dean, 9 The Fairway, Sheffield SI0 4LX
T: (0114) 2308077
F: (0114) 2308077
E: holiday@sheltgill.co.uk
I: www.sheltgill.co.uk

OPEN All Year

Low season per wk
Min £190.00
High season per wk
Max £400.00

Medieval cottage with a view of Lake Coniston from the timbered living room, a stream in the garden and easy access to hill walks.

★★-★★★★

7 Units
Sleeping 2–6

THURSTON HOUSE & THURSTON VIEW

Coniston
Contact: Mr & Mrs A Jefferson, 21 Chale Green, Harwood, Bolton BL2 3NJ
T: (01204) 419261
E: alan@jefferson99.freeserve.co.uk
I: www.jefferson99.freeserve.co.uk

Thurston View: lovely stone cottage with superb views. Sorry, no pets/smoking in cottage. Short walk to village centre. Parking for one car. Thurston House: large Victorian house converted into individual apartments. Quiet location close to village centre. Private parking at rear of property.

OPEN All Year

Short breaks may be available – please phone for details.

Low season per wk
£205.00–£295.00
High season per wk
£295.00–£375.00

DENT, Cumbria Map ref 5B3

★★

1 Unit
Sleeping 4

FERN LEA

Dent, Sedbergh
Contact: Mrs B Harlow, 32 Main Street, Woodborough, Nottingham NE14 6EA
T: (0115) 965 2795
F: (0115) 965 2795

Comfortable stone cottage in attractive cobbled village. Good local pubs, cafes and shops in village and at Sedbergh (five miles). Convenient for walking or touring West Yorkshire Dales. Within easy drive of southern end of Lake District – Cartmel, Levens, Kendal, Ambleside etc.

OPEN All Year

Low season per wk
£175.00–£210.00
High season per wk
£210.00–£295.00

★★★

2 Units
Sleeping 4

MIDDLETON'S COTTAGE & FOUNTAIN COTTAGE

Dent, Sedbergh
Contact: Mr & Mrs P M Ayers, The Old Rectory, Litlington, Polegate BN26 5RB
T: (01323) 870032
F: (01323) 870032
E: candpayers@mistral.co.uk
I: www.dentcottages.co.uk

Modernised mid-17thC cottages in centre of small, quaint village, comfortably furnished and decorated to high standards. Quiet, unspoilt Dentdale offers a good base for walking, touring and exploring the Yorkshire Dales or the Lake District, with Kendal and Hawes nearby. Brochure available. Open all year.

OPEN All Year

Short breaks from Oct-Mar, weekend or mid-week. Any combination, subject to availability.

Low season per wk
£175.00–£270.00
High season per wk
£225.00–£300.00

ELTERWATER, Cumbria Map ref 5A3

★★★

2 Units
Sleeping 4

LANE ENDS COTTAGES

Elterwater, Ambleside
Contact: Mrs M E Rice, Fellside,
3 and 4 Lane Ends Cottages, Elterwater, Ambleside
LA22 9HN
T: (015394) 37678

OPEN All Year

Low season per wk
£200.00–£350.00
High season per wk
£380.00–£440.00

Family-run stone-built cottages with open fireplaces. In a peaceful setting in Great Langdale on the edge of the common, with views of the surrounding fells.

★★★

2 Units
Sleeping 3–4

WISTARIA COTTAGE & 3 MAIN STREET

Elterwater, Ambleside
Contact: Mr G & Mrs D Beardmore, 2 Beech Drive,
Kidsgrove, Stoke-on-Trent ST7 1BA
T: (01782) 783170
F: (01782) 783170
E: geoff.doreen.beardmore@ntlworld.com

OPEN All Year

Low season per wk
£298.00–£320.00
High season per wk
£346.00–£398.00

Traditional 18thC cottages near village centre. Tastefully renovated, well equipped. Serviced and maintained by owners. Warm and comfortable, off-peak heating, open fires. Fell and valley walking.

10

CREDIT CARD BOOKINGS **If you book by telephone and are asked for your credit card number it is advisable to check the proprietor's policy should you cancel your reservation.**

ESKDALE, Cumbria Map ref 5A3

★★★

4 Units
Sleeping 6

FISHERGROUND FARM

Eskdale, Holmrook
Contact: Fisherground Farm Holidays, Fisherground, Eskdale, Holmrook CA19 1TF
T: (01946) 723319
E: holidays@fisherground.co.uk
I: www.fisherground.co.uk

Fisherground is a lovely traditional hill farm, offering accommodation in cottages and pine lodges. Ideal for walkers, nature lovers, dogs and children. We have a games room, an adventure playground, raft ponds and even our own station on the miniature Ravenglass and Eskdale Railway!

OPEN All Year

Short breaks available Nov-Mar.

Low season per wk
£225.00–£350.00
High season per wk
£390.00–£540.00

★★★★

1 Unit
Sleeping 6

OLD BRANTRAKE

Eskdale, Holmrook
Contact: Mr J B Tyson, Brant Rake, Eskdale, Holmrook CA19 1TT
T: (019467) 23340
F: (019467) 23340
E: tyson@eskdale1.demon.co.uk

OPEN All Year

Low season per wk
£240.00–£365.00
High season per wk
£335.00–£460.00

Recently restored, 17thC, Listed farmhouse in rural setting, ideal for central fells or touring. Three bedrooms, two wcs, bath, shower, wood fire, modern kitchen.

GRANGE-OVER-SANDS, Cumbria Map ref 5A3 *Tourist Information Centre Tel: (015395) 34026*

★★★

1 Unit
Sleeping 4

CORNERWAYS BUNGALOW

Grange-over-Sands
Contact: Mrs E Rigg, Prospect House, Barber Green, Grange-over-Sands LA11 6HU
T: (015395) 36329

Low season per wk
£250.00–£300.00
High season per wk
£300.00–£350.00

Pleasant bungalow in quiet situation, with double and twin bedroom. All-round views, private garden with parking. Ideal base for touring Lake District. Personal supervision.

4

★★★

1 Unit
Sleeping 6

DYER DENE

Witherslack, Grange-over-Sands
Contact: Mrs S Andrews, 121 Dorchester Road, Garstang, Preston PR3 1FE
T: (01995) 602769
E: dyerdene@fish.co.uk
I: www.dyerdene.com

Comfortable cottage in tranquil valley. Beautiful views and excellent local walking. Garage-cum-games room and garden. Ideal for children. Radiators in all bedrooms. On arrival, the peace is immediate. Unload, put the kettle on and relax with a log fire in winter or in the secluded garden in summer.

OPEN All Year except Christmas

Open all year round. 3-night stays available Nov-mid-Mar also 7 days over New year.

Low season per wk
£140.00–£260.00
High season per wk
£320.00–£390.00

WEB

www.visitengland.com

Log on for information and inspiration. The latest information on places to visit, events and quality assessed accommodation.

GRASMERE, Cumbria Map ref 5A3 *Tourist Information Centre Tel: (015394) 35245*

★★★-★★★★★

3 Units
Sleeping 2–4

With dramatic mountains, gentle rolling fells, glorious lakes and peaceful valleys, Broadrayne Farm is at the very heart of the Lake District, superbly located for wonderful views. The atmospheric traditional farm properties have been lovingly renovated with today's creature comforts, including open coal fires, central heating and off-street parking.

BROADRAYNE FARM COTTAGES

Grasmere, Ambleside
Contact: Mrs J Dennison Drake, Broadrayne Farm, Grasmere, Ambleside LA22 9RU
T: (015394) 35055
F: (015394) 35733
E: jo@grasmere-accommodation.co.uk
I: www.grasmere-accommodation.co.uk

OPEN All Year except Christmas
CC: Mastercard, Solo, Switch, Visa

A week booked in the year allows 10% off a second week booked in March.

Low season per wk
£222.00–£260.00
High season per wk
£375.00–£537.00

★★★

1 Unit
Sleeping 5

A personal welcome awaits you at this attractive Lakeland house furnished to a high standard. Ideal situation on village outskirts, within minutes of local amenities. Three bedrooms, large, modern kitchen, dining room, comfortable lounge with magnificent views of fells. Spacious, yet cosy and warm in winter (coal fire optional). Attractive garden.

SILVERGARTH

Grasmere, Ambleside
Contact: Mrs S Coward, Silvergarth, 1 Low Riddings, Grasmere, Ambleside LA22 9QY
T: (015394) 35828
F: (015394) 35828
E: cowards.silvergarth@btinternet.com
I: www.cowards.silvergarth.btinternet.co.uk

OPEN All Year

Low season per wk
£165.00–£285.00
High season per wk
£340.00–£410.00

GREAT LANGDALE, Cumbria Map ref 5A3

★★★★★

6 Units
Sleeping 4–6

ELTERWATER HALL

Great Langdale, Ambleside
Contact: Mrs P Leyland, The Langdale Estate, Great Langdale, Ambleside LA22 9JD
T: (015394) 37302
F: (015394) 37394
E: itsgreat@langdale.co.uk
I: www.langdale.co.uk

OPEN All Year
CC: Amex, Delta, JCB, Mastercard, Solo, Switch, Visa

Low season per wk
£585.00–£790.00
High season per wk
£1,080.00–£1,435.00

Elterwater Hall is situated in its own grounds and forms part of the award-winning Langdale Estate, with its hotel and country club a short walk away.

★★★★

10 Units
Sleeping 4–8

LANGDALE ESTATE CHAPEL STILE APARTMENTS

Great Langdale, Ambleside
Contact: Mrs P Leyland, The Langdale Estate, Great Langdale, Ambleside LA22 9JD
T: (015394) 37302
F: (015394) 37394
E: itsgreat@langdale.co.uk
I: www.langdale.co.uk

OPEN All Year
CC: Amex, Delta, Mastercard, Solo, Switch, Visa

Low season per wk
£465.00–£665.00
High season per wk
£810.00–£1,110.00

Chapel Stile is situated next to Wainwrights Inn and forms part of the award-winning Langdale Estate, with its hotel and country club a short walk away.

GREAT LANGDALE continued

★★★★★

82 Units
Sleeping 4–8

LANGDALE ESTATE LODGES

Great Langdale, Ambleside
Contact: Mrs P Leyland, The Langdale Estate,
Great Langdale, Ambleside LA22 9JD
T: (015394) 37302
F: (015394) 37394
E: itsgreat@langdale.co.uk
I: www.langdale.co.uk

OPEN All Year
CC: Amex, Delta, Mastercard, Solo, Switch, Visa

Low season per wk
£530.00–£825.00
High season per wk
£945.00–£1,585.00

Formerly an old gunpowder mill for the Elterwater Gunpowder Company and now a hotel and lodge complex, with a leisure centre and all facilities attached.

GRIZEDALE, Cumbria Map ref 5A3

★★★

2 Units
Sleeping 2–6

HIGH DALE PARK BARN

Satterthwaite, Ulverston
Contact: Mr P Brown, High Dale Park Farm,
High Dale Park, Satterthwaite, Ulverston LA12 8LJ
T: (01229) 860226
E: peter@lakesweddingmusic.com
I: www.lakesweddingmusic.com/Accomm

Delightfully situated, south-facing, 17thC converted barn attached to owner's farmhouse. Wonderful views down quiet, secluded valley, surrounded by beautiful, broadleaf woodland, rich in wildlife. Oak beams, log fire, central heating, patio. Hawkshead and Beatrix Potter's house three miles.

OPEN All Year

Low season per wk
Min £195.00
High season per wk
Max £670.00

HAWKSHEAD, Cumbria Map ref 5A3

★★★-★★★★

8 Units
Sleeping 2–6

BROOMRIGGS

Hawkshead, Ambleside
Contact: Mrs F Taylforth, Broomriggs, Hawkshead,
Ambleside LA22 0JX
T: (015394) 36280
E: broomriggs@zoom.co.uk
I: www.broomriggs.co.uk/location.htm

Large country house converted into comfortable apartments, set in 100 acres of gardens, woodlands and lake frontage with rowing boats. All apartments have views of Esthwaite Water and surrounding fells. Located one mile from Hawkshead on the B5286 to Windermere ferry. Within easy access of all areas of the Lake District.

OPEN All Year

3-night stays available.

Low season per wk
£220.00–£370.00
High season per wk
£315.00–£480.00

★★★

8 Units
Sleeping 6

THE CROFT HOLIDAY FLATS

Hawkshead, Ambleside
Contact: Mrs R E Barr, The Croft Holiday Flats,
North Lonsdale Road, Hawkshead, Ambleside LA22 0NX
T: (015394) 36374
F: (015394) 36544
E: enquiries@hawkshead-croft.com
I: www.hawkshead-croft.com

OPEN All Year
CC: Delta, Mastercard, Solo, Switch, Visa

Low season per wk
£185.00–£295.00
High season per wk
£320.00–£420.00

Large house with garden, converted into holiday flats. In village of Hawkshead on B5286 from Ambleside.

ACCESSIBILITY

Look for the symbols which indicate National Accessible Scheme standards for hearing and visually impaired guests in addition to standards for guests with mobility impairment. Additional participants are shown in the listings at the back.

HAWKSHEAD continued

★★

1 Unit
Sleeping 4

MEADOW VIEW
Hawkshead, Ambleside
Contact: Blakes Cottages, Spring Mill, Earby, Barnoldswick BB94 0AA
T: 08700 708090
F: 08705 851150
I: www.blakes.cottages.co.uk

OPEN All Year
CC: Amex, Delta, Mastercard, Switch, Visa

Low season per wk
£200.00–£250.00
High season per wk
£260.00–£430.00

Three-hundred-year-old cottage in the centre of Hawkshead. Entrance hall, bathroom, twin bedroom, double bedroom with wash basin and separate wc, kitchen and living accommodation. Central heating.

11

★★★★

2 Units
Sleeping 2–5

THE OLD BARN & BARN END COTTAGE

Outgate, Ambleside
Contact: Mrs A Gallagher, Hideaways, The Minstrels Gallery, The Square, Hawkshead, Ambleside LA22 0NZ
T: (015394) 42435
F: (015394) 36178
E: bookings@lakeland-hideaways.co.uk
I: www.lakeland-hideaways.co.uk

A superb barn conversion set amid stunning countryside. A quiet location within easy reach of Hawkshead village. Cosy, comfortable interior, furnished to a very high standard – all home comforts. Log fires. An excellent base for walking, cycling and sightseeing. Delightful private garden. Off-road parking. Lovely views.

OPEN All Year

Short breaks available autumn, winter and early spring.

Low season per wk
£220.00–£330.00
High season per wk
£310.00–£450.00

HELTON, Cumbria Map ref 5B3

★★★★

1 Unit
Sleeping 2

TALBOT STUDIO

Helton, Penrith
Contact: Mr M Cowell, Church Villa, Gamblesby, Penrith CA10 1HR
T: (01768) 881682
F: (01768) 889055
E: markcowell@amserve.com
I: www.gogamblesby.co.uk

Originally a Westmorland slate barn, this beautiful cottage has panoramic views over the Lowther Valley near Ullswater in the north-eastern corner of the Lake District National Park. Upstairs: large open living room and double bed in spacious alcove beyond. Down the spiral staircase: kitchen/diner, bathroom and utility. Shared garden. Own off-road parking.

OPEN All Year

3-night short breaks available Nov-Apr (excl Christmas, New Year and Easter).

Low season per wk
£185.00–£205.00
High season per wk
£219.00–£329.00

USE YOUR *i*s

There are more than 550 Tourist Information Centres throughout England offering friendly help with accommodation and holiday ideas as well as suggestions of places to visit and things to do. You'll find TIC addresses in the local Phone Book.

HIGH LORTON, Cumbria Map ref 5A3

★★★★

1 Unit
Sleeping 2

HOLEMIRE HOUSE BARN

High Lorton, Cockermouth
Contact: Mrs A Fearfield, Holemire House Barn, Holemire House, High Lorton, Cockermouth CA13 9TX
T: (01900) 85225
I: www.lakelandbarn.co.uk

Traditional Lakeland barn with exposed beams, converted to quality accommodation. In beautiful Lorton Vale, overlooking local fells. Close to Keswick and northern Lakes. Warm in winter, light and sunny in summer. Situated in the midst of superb walking country. All prices include electricity, central heating and linen.

OPEN All Year

Low season per wk
£210.00–£255.00
High season per wk
£295.00–£375.00

★★★★

2 Units
Sleeping 4

MIDTOWN COTTAGES

High Lorton, Cockermouth
Contact: Mr M Burrell, 20 Hillside, Abbotts Ann, Andover SP11 7DF
T: (01264) 710165
E: info@midtown-cottages.co.uk
I: www.midtowncottages.com

Delightful cottages set by a paved courtyard with small lawned garden. Situated in a picturesque corner of the Lake District National Park close to Crummock Water and Buttermere, an ideal base for walking, cycling or just relaxing! The cottages are warm, comfortably furnished, with nearby pub and hotel serving excellent meals.

OPEN All Year

Short breaks available. See website for details.

Low season per wk
£240.00
High season per wk
£420.00

KENDAL, Cumbria Map ref 5B3 *Tourist Information Centre Tel: (01539) 725758*

★★★-★★★★

9 Units
Sleeping 6–9

FIELD END BARNS & SHAW END MANSION

Patton, Kendal
Contact: Mr & Mrs E D Robinson, Field End Barns and Shaw End Mansion, Patton, Kendal LA8 9DU
T: (01539) 824220
F: (01539) 824464
E: robinson@fieldendholidays.co.uk
I: www.fieldendholidays.co.uk

Field End Barns and Shaw End Mansion are set on a 200-acre estate in a beautiful location. The Barns provide award-winning cottages of character with own private gardens, exposed oak beams and open fireplaces. Shaw End Mansion contains four spacious and elegant apartments in a restored Georgian mansion.

OPEN All Year
CC: Amex, Mastercard, Switch, Visa

Short breaks from 2 nights available most of the year, prices from £95.

Low season per wk
£175.00–£220.00
High season per wk
£230.00–£450.00

SB

SPECIAL BREAKS

Many establishments offer special promotions and themed breaks. These are highlighted in red. (All such offers are subject to availability.)

KESWICK, Cumbria Map ref 5A3 *Tourist Information Centre Tel: (017687) 72645*

★★★★-★★★★★

3 Units
Sleeping 5–6

ACORN APARTMENTS & ACORN VIEW

Keswick
Contact: Mr J Miller, South Barn, Fort Putnam, Greystoke, Penrith CA11 0UP
T: (017684) 80310
E: info@acornselfcatering.co.uk
I: www.acornselfcatering.co.uk

Ideally situated close to town centre and lake. Spacious two- and three-bedroom accommodation. Owner maintained to the highest standards. All bed linen and electricity included in price. No smoking or pets permitted. Private parking. Open all year. Special breaks available. Mob: 07816 867162.

OPEN All Year
CC: Solo

Short breaks available between Nov-Easter. 3-night weekend breaks or 4-night mid-week breaks.

Low season per wk
£180.00–£350.00
High season per wk
£350.00–£650.00

★★★★

1 Unit
Sleeping 6

BANNERDALE

Keswick
Contact: Ms H Hutton, Bannerdale, 39 Millfield Gardens, Keswick CA12 4PD
T: 07816 824253
F: (017687) 72546
E: hazel@bannerdale.info
I: www.bannerdale.info

Set at the foot of Walla Crag and only 10 minutes' walk from Keswick, Bannerdale offers all modern comforts: corner bath, separate shower, well-equipped kitchen with dishwasher, washer, fridge/freezer and tumble dryer. Elevated patio, with seating and lighting, overlooks fields and has magnificent fell views.

OPEN All Year

Short breaks available Nov-Mar.

Low season per wk
£290.00–£420.00
High season per wk
£560.00–£810.00

★★★-★★★★★

3 Units

BELLE VUE

Keswick
Contact: Mrs L G Ryder, Hillside, Portinscale, Keswick CA12 5RS
T: (017687) 71065
E: lexieryder@hotmail.com

Close to the heart of Keswick, this lovely Lakeland-stone residence has been superbly converted, providing very spacious,comfortable, well-appointed suites. Fell-top views from lounges of Catbells and Newlands Valley. Carefully owner maintained. Ideally located with Derwentwater and the famous Theatre by the Lake a short walk away.

OPEN All Year

Short breaks available Nov-Mar, minimum 3 nights. Reductions given for 2 people.

Low season per wk
£120.00–£210.00
High season per wk
£210.00–£360.00

★★★

1 Unit
Sleeping 5

3 CATHERINE COTTAGES

Keswick
Contact: Mr & Mrs P Hewitson, 17 Cedar Lane, Cockermouth CA13 9HN
T: (01900) 828039
E: peter.hewitson1@btinternet.com

Cottage in a quiet area near Fitz Park, 5 minutes' walk from the shops. Owner maintained. Car park. Phone or email for brochure.

OPEN All Year

Low season per wk
£130.00–£200.00
High season per wk
£200.00–£275.00

KESWICK continued

★★★

1 Unit
Sleeping 4

THE COTTAGE
Newlands, Keswick
Contact: Mrs M Beaty, The Cottage, Birkrigg, Newlands, Keswick CA12 5TS
T: (017687) 78278

OPEN All Year

Low season per wk
£170.00
High season per wk
£300.00–£320.00

100-acre farm. Clean, comfortable, beamed farm cottage with wonderful outlook. Five miles from Keswick between Braithwaite and Buttermere, in the peaceful Newlands Valley.

★★★★★

2 Units
Sleeping 2–4

CROFTLANDS COTTAGES

Thornthwaite, Keswick
Contact: Mrs S McGarvie, Croftlands, Thornthwaite, Keswick CA12 5SA
T: (017687) 78300
F: (017687) 78300
E: bobmcgarvie@lineone.net
I: www.croftlands-cottages.co.uk

Converted from the old stables, this cosy cottage enjoys a peaceful village setting with magnificent fell views all around. Spacious and warm with logburning stove, stone fireplace, oak beams and antiques. Two bedrooms, both with luxuriously appointed, en suite facilities. Keswick easily accessible. Pub food nearby. Walks from the doorstep.

OPEN All Year

Short breaks available Nov-Feb (excl Christmas and New Year). 3 nights weekend, 4 nights mid-week. Open all year.

Low season per wk
Max £270.00
High season per wk
Max £470.00

★★★

4 Units
Sleeping 6

DERWENT HOUSE & BRANDELHOWE

Portinscale, Keswick
Contact: Mr & Mrs O W Bull, Derwent House Holidays, Stone Heath, Hilderstone ST15 8SH
T: (01889) 505678
F: (01889) 505679
E: thebulls@globalnet.co.uk
I: www.dholidays-lakes.com

Traditional stone and slate Lakeland building of character in village on north shore of Derwentwater one mile from Keswick. Comfortable, well-equipped holiday suites, one retaining old cottage grate and range and another open beams. Various views over lake and to Skiddaw. Ideal centre for walking and resting.

OPEN All Year

Short breaks available Nov-Mar. Minimum 2 nights.

Low season per wk
£110.00–£275.00
High season per wk
£235.00–£350.00

6

★★★★

19 Units
Sleeping 2–4

DERWENT MANOR

Portinscale, Keswick
Contact: Mrs C Denwood
T: (017687) 72538
F: (017687) 71002
E: info@derwent-manor.com
I: www.derwent-manor.com

Enjoy village life at this former gentleman's residence. Refurbished to provide some of the most comfortable and well-equipped apartments available, or one-bedroomed cottage within grounds. Many extras including Sunday lunch, entry to local leisure club. Pets welcome. Lake on your doorstep, with 16 acres of conservation grounds.

OPEN All Year
CC: Amex, Delta, Diners, JCB, Mastercard, Solo, Switch, Visa

Short breaks subject to availability.

Low season per wk
£225.00–£435.00
High season per wk
£390.00–£630.00

KESWICK continued

★★★★

1 Unit
Sleeping 7

FOUNTAIN COTTAGE
Keswick
Contact: Dr and Mrs W E Preston, Bannest Hill House, Haltcliffe, Hesket Newmarket, Wigton CA7 8JT
T: (01768) 484394
F: (01768) 484394
E: preston@talk-101.com

OPEN All Year

Low season per wk
£199.00–£259.00
High season per wk
£325.00–£450.00

Owner-maintained, cosy, well-equipped cottage, on the edge of town with fell views. Three bedrooms, central heating, private parking. Pets accepted.

★★★

3 Units
Sleeping 8–12

ORCHARD BARN

Applethwaite, Keswick
Contact: Mr & Mrs I C Hall, Fisherground Farm, Eskdale CA19 1TF
T: (01946) 723319
E: holidays@fisherground.co.uk
I: www.orchardhouseholidays.co.uk

Superb family house with fabulous views. Aga, central heating, laundry, freezer, video etc. Huge lounge, fully-equipped kitchen, two bathrooms. Large garden. Pets welcome. Ideal for family or walking groups. Brochure on request, or see our website.

OPEN All Year

Short breaks available Oct-May, minimum 3 nights.

Low season per wk
£420.00–£590.00
High season per wk
£650.00–£990.00

KING'S MEABURN, Cumbria Map ref 5B3

★★★-★★★★★

4 Units
Sleeping 3–6

LYVENNET COTTAGES & HILL TOP BARN

King's Meaburn, Penrith
Contact: Mrs D M Addison, Keld, King's Meaburn, Penrith CA10 3BS
T: (01931) 714226
F: (01931) 714598
E: info@lyvennetcottages.co.uk
I: www.lyvennetcottages.co.uk

Attractive, well-furnished cottages in quiet village, overlooking the beautiful Lyvennet Valley and Lakeland hills. Some log fires in winter. Fishing, fuel and linen inclusive. Children and pets welcome. Good pub. Own woodland walks and bird-watching. Bring your own horse – excellent livery or grass. Ideal centre for Lakes, Dales, Hadrian's Wall and Scottish Borders.

OPEN All Year

Short breaks available Oct-Mar (excl Christmas and New Year). Minimum 3 nights.

Low season per wk
£180.00–£270.00
High season per wk
£280.00–£440.00

KIRKBY LONSDALE, Cumbria Map ref 5B3 *Tourist Information Centre Tel: (015242) 71437*

★★★

1 Unit
Sleeping 4

BARKINBECK COTTAGE
Gatebeck, Kendal
Contact: Mrs A Hamilton, Barkin House, Gatebeck, Kendal LA8 0HX
T: (015395) 67122
E: ann@barkin.fsnet.co.uk
I: www.barkinbeck.co.uk

OPEN All Year

Low season per wk
£200.00–£250.00
High season per wk
£250.00–£300.00

Converted barn in beautiful, peaceful countryside between Lakes and Dales, an ideal base for touring and walking. Log fire, owner maintained, spotlessly clean. Adapted for disabled.

12

CHECK THE MAPS

**The colour maps at the front of this guide show all the cities, towns and villages for which you will find accommodation entries.
Refer to the town index to find the page on which they are listed.**

KIRKBY LONSDALE continued

★★★★
3 Units
Sleeping 5–7

SELLET HALL COTTAGES

Kirkby Lonsdale, Carnforth
Contact: Mrs M Hall, Sellet Hall, Kirkby Lonsdale, Carnforth LA6 2QF
T: (01524) 271865
E: sellethall@hotmail.com
I: www.sellethall.com

Unique cottages converted from 17thC barn set in the grounds of Sellet Hall, surrounded by open countryside and complemented by far-distance views over the Lune Valley, Trough of Bowland and Yorkshire Dales. All have log fires, fitted kitchens, dishwasher, microwave etc. Own gardens, patio and parking.

OPEN All Year

Short breaks, subject to availability, (excl Christmas and New Year). Pets welcome.

Low season per wk
£250.00–£350.00
High season per wk
£350.00–£460.00

KIRKBY STEPHEN, Cumbria Map ref 5B3 *Tourist Information Centre Tel: (017683) 71199*

★★★★
5 Units
Sleeping 2–6

PENNISTONE GREEN

North Stainmore, Kirkby Stephen
Contact: Mr T F Jackson, Ashmere, Rakes Road, Monyash, Bakewell DE45 1JL
T: (01629) 815683
E: jackson@ashmere.fsnet.co.uk
I: www.uk-holiday-cottages.info

Delightful farmhouse/barn conversions equipped to a very high standard for your every comfort. Suitable for groups. Enjoy the splendid landscape surrounding you. Ideally situated for Lakes, Dales, Pennine Way. Abundance of footpaths and bridleways. Market town of Kirkby Stephen five miles, Appleby eight miles.

OPEN All Year

Low season per wk
£180.00–£225.00
High season per wk
£250.00–£325.00

KIRKOSWALD, Cumbria Map ref 5B2

★★★★
5 Units
Sleeping 3–4

HOWSCALES

Kirkoswald, Penrith
Contact: Mrs S E Webster
T: (01768) 898666
F: (01768) 898710
E: liz@howscales.fsbusiness.co.uk
I: www.eden-in-cumbria.co.uk/howscales

OPEN All Year
CC: Mastercard, Visa

Low season per wk
£200.00–£300.00
High season per wk
£280.00–£440.00

Cosy, well-equipped, converted, 17thC farm cottages set in open, tranquil countryside with superb views. Touring base for Eden Valley, lakes, Pennines. Brochure. Short breaks.

12

LANGDALE, Cumbria Map ref 5A3

★★★
2 Units
Sleeping 4

2 & 7 LINGMOOR VIEW

Langdale, Ambleside
Contact: Mr J Batho, High Hollin Bank, Coniston LA21 8AG
T: (015394) 41680
E: charlie.batho@wernethlow.fsnet.co.uk
I: www.cottagescumbria.com

Traditional, stone-built, Lakeland cottages situated in peaceful, unspoilt valley. Ideal position for fell and valley walking, 0.5 miles from village shop and pub. Cosy country interior with open fire and original features. Modern fitted kitchen, sitting room, bathroom and two bedrooms. Sunny aspect with magnificent views across hills.

OPEN All Year

Special long-weekend-break prices available during low season.

Low season per wk
£160.00–£255.00
High season per wk
£270.00–£350.00

LANGDALE continued

★★★-★★★★★

2 Units
Sleeping 2–10

In the centre of the unspoilt village of Elterwater, Meadow Bank has fine views towards the beck and fells. It is an exceptional property, completely renovated and beautifully furnished throughout. The house has four bedrooms and three bathrooms. There is also the Garden Chalet. Leisure Club facilities are included.

MEADOW BANK

Elterwater, Ambleside
Contact: Ms P Locke, Elterwater Investments Ltd, 17 Shay Lane, Hale Barns, Altrincham WA15 8NZ
T: (0161) 9049445
F: (0161) 9049877
E: lockemeadowbank@aol.com
I: www.langdalecottages.co.uk

OPEN All Year

4-night mid-week breaks for the price of 2 (Chalet £100, House £250-300).

Low season per wk
£210.00–£630.00
High season per wk
£290.00–£1,450.00

★★-★★★★★

63 Units
Sleeping 2–11

Welcome to Wheelwrights – an established family business featuring the very best in self-catering property in the heart of the English Lake District, with numerous quality properties. You are guaranteed a holiday to remember. For more information visit our website or telephone.

WHEELWRIGHTS HOLIDAY COTTAGES

Elterwater, Ambleside
Contact: Mr I Price, Wheelwrights Holiday Cottages, Elterwater, Ambleside LA22 9HS
T: (015394) 37635
F: (015394) 37618
E: enquiries@wheelwrights.com
I: www.wheelwrights.com

OPEN All Year
CC: Delta, Mastercard, Switch, Visa

Low season per wk
£268.00–£1,300.00
High season per wk
£368.00–£2,300.00

LITTLE LANGDALE, Cumbria Map ref 5A3

★★★

1 Unit
Sleeping 5

HIGHFOLD COTTAGE

Little Langdale, Ambleside
Contact: Mrs C E Blair, 8 The Glebe, Chapel Stile, Ambleside LA22 9JT
T: (015394) 37686

OPEN All Year

Low season per wk
£200.00–£260.00
High season per wk
£280.00–£340.00

Comfortable, well-equipped cottage, set in magnificent scenery. Ideally situated for walking and touring. Open fires, central heating. Pets and children welcome. Personally maintained.

LONGSLEDDALE, Cumbria Map ref 5B3

★★★

1 Unit
Sleeping 4

THE COACH HOUSE

Longsleddale, Kendal
Contact: Mrs Farmer, The Coach House, Capplebarrow House, Longsleddale, Kendal LA8 9BB
T: (01539) 823686
F: (01539) 823092
E: jenyfarmer@aol.com
I: www.capplebarrowcoachhouse.co.uk

OPEN All Year

Low season per wk
£150.00–£200.00
High season per wk
£200.00–£220.00

Stone-built, converted coach house with ground floor shower room and bedroom and open staircase to first floor kitchen and lounge. Excellent views.

TOWN INDEX

This can be found at the back of this guide. If you know where you want to stay, the index will give you the page number listing accommodation in your chosen town, city or village.

LOWESWATER, Cumbria Map ref 5A3

★★★★

1 Unit
Sleeping 8

HIGH MOSSER GATE

Mosser, Cockermouth
Contact: Mrs A Evens, Russetts, Highfield Road, Wigginton, Tring HP23 6EB
T: (01442) 825855
F: (01442) 828227
E: alison@highmossergate.co.uk
I: www.highmossergate.co.uk

Traditional farmhouse with superb views of nearby fell-side and Scotland. Spacious, comfortable, family accommodation: five bedrooms; large kitchen with range; two lounges, one with piano; lockable bike shed; two bathrooms; three wcs. Excellent for walkers and cyclists with fine, local routes. All facilities within 10 minutes' drive at Cockermouth.

OPEN All Year

Short breaks available. See website or call for details.

Low season per wk
Min £350.00
High season per wk
Max £790.00

★★★★-★★★★★

6 Units

LOWESWATER HOLIDAY COTTAGES

Loweswater, Cockermouth
Contact: Mr M E Thompson, Loweswater Holiday Cottages, Scale Hill, Loweswater, Cockermouth CA13 9UX
T: (01900) 85232
F: (01900) 85232
E: mike@loweswaterholidaycottages.co.uk
I: www.loweswaterholidaycottages.co.uk

Nestling among the magnificent Loweswater/Buttermere fells and lakes, our luxury cottages have open fires, en suite bathrooms, 4-poster, modern kitchens, gardens. Country inn with good food 0.5 miles. Crummock Water only 10 minutes' walk through NT woods. Children and pets welcome. Family run. Abandon the car – walks are from the doorstep.

OPEN All Year

Low season per wk
£150.00–£390.00
High season per wk
£310.00–£785.00

MILBURN, Cumbria Map ref 5B2

★★★★

1 Unit
Sleeping 4

BRAMLEY COTTAGE

Milburn, Penrith
Contact: Mr & Mrs G Heelis, Orchard Cottage, Milburn, Penrith CA10 1TN
T: (01768) 361074
F: (01768) 895528
E: Guyheelis@aol.com
I: www.uk-holiday-cottages.co.uk/bramley

OPEN All Year
CC: Delta, Mastercard, Solo, Switch, Visa

Low season per wk
£190.00–£230.00
High season per wk
£280.00–£390.00

Charming two-bedroomed cottage overlooking the large picturesque village green. Exposed beams, open fire, fully-equipped fitted kitchen, furnished and decorated to a high standard.

AT-A-GLANCE SYMBOLS

Symbols at the end of each accommodation entry give useful information about services and facilities. A key to symbols can be found inside the back cover flap. Keep this open for easy reference.

MUNGRISDALE, Cumbria Map ref 5A2

★★★★
2 Units
Sleeping 4–7

Cottages converted from old Cumbria barns, with views over fells. Use of large garden and well-stocked bar. Dinner available. Easy access to Lakes.

GRISEDALE VIEW, HOWE TOP

Mungrisdale, Penrith
Contact: Mrs C A Weightman, Grisedale View, Howe Top, Near Howe, Mungrisdale, Penrith CA11 0SH
T: (017687) 79678
F: (017687) 79462
E: nearhowe@btopenworld.com
I: www.nearhowe.co.uk

OPEN All Year

Low season per wk
£200.00–£280.00
High season per wk
£280.00–£500.00

NEWBY BRIDGE, Cumbria Map ref 5A3

★★★★
1 Unit
Sleeping 6

FELLCROFT COTTAGE

Backbarrow, Ulverston
Contact: Ms C Hale, 1 Low Row, Backbarrow, Ulverston LA12 8QH
T: (015395) 30316
E: cath@fellcroft.fsnet.co.uk

18thC terraced cottage, beautifully decorated and equipped to a high standard throughout. Located only 1.5 miles from Lake Windermere, giving easy access to all areas of the Lake District, Fellcroft Cottage provides an ideal base for a touring, cycling or walking holiday. Private parking.

OPEN All Year

Short breaks available – Ring or email for details.

Low season per wk
£205.00–£245.00
High season per wk
£360.00–£419.00

★★★★
1 Unit
Sleeping 4

WOODLAND COTTAGE

Newby Bridge
Contact: Mr P G Newton
T: (015395) 31030
F: (015395) 30105
E: info@cumbriancaravans.co.uk
I: www.cumbriancaravans.co.uk

CC: Delta, Mastercard, Switch, Visa

Low season per wk
£240.00–£365.00
High season per wk
£365.00–£490.00

Detached cottage with two en suite bedrooms, in own private gardens within the award-winning Newby Bridge Caravan Park. All on one level.

PENRITH, Cumbria Map ref 5B2 *Tourist Information Centre Tel: (01768) 867466*

★★★★
5 Units
Sleeping 3–8

Charming, well-equipped sandstone cottage clustered amongst attractive gardens with large grassed area. Situated in Eden Valley on the edge of a quiet country village with pub. Easy access to the amenities of the Lake District, northern England and southern Scotland. Walking, cycling, golf, swimming and fishing nearby. Prices fully inclusive.

WETHERAL COTTAGES

Great Salkeld, Penrith
Contact: Mr J Lowrey, Wetheral Cottages, Great Salkeld, Penrith CA11 9NA
T: (01768) 898779
F: (01768) 898943
E: wetheralcottages@btopenworld.com
I: www.wetheralcottages.co.uk

OPEN All Year
CC: Delta, Mastercard, Switch, Visa

Short breaks available between Nov 2003 and Easter 2004. 3-night weekend breaks or 4-night mid-week breaks.

Low season per wk
£190.00–£320.00
High season per wk
£370.00–£650.00

POOLEY BRIDGE, Cumbria Map ref 5A3

★★★★

3 Units
Sleeping 4–8

HIGH WINDER COTTAGES

Tirril, Penrith
Contact: Mr R A Moss, High Winder House, Celleron, Tirril, Penrith CA10 2LS
T: (017684) 86997
F: (017684) 86997
E: mossr@highwinder.freeserve.co.uk
I: www.highwindercottages.co.uk

OPEN All Year

Low season per wk
£175.00–£280.00
High season per wk
£310.00–£600.00

Cottages converted from a building in the grounds of the owner's secluded, 17thC farmhouse high in the fells and enjoying outstanding views.

RYDAL, Cumbria Map ref 5A3

★★

1 Unit
Sleeping 6

HALL BANK COTTAGE

Rydal, Ambleside
Contact: Mr Lambton, Rydal Estate Carter Jonas, 52 Kirkland, Kendal LA9 5AP
T: (01539) 722592
F: (01539) 729587
E: marilyn.staunton@carterjonas.co.uk

OPEN All Year

Low season per wk
£220.00–£450.00
High season per wk
£475.00–£575.00

Cottage at Rydal in the heart of the Lake District, providing comfortable accommodation with easy access to main attractions of the area. Central heating, open fire. Large garden.

SAWREY, Cumbria Map ref 5A3

★★★

1 Unit
Sleeping 4

DERWENTWATER COTTAGE

Near Sawrey, Ambleside
Contact: Mrs A Gallagher, Hideaways, The Minstrels Gallery, The Square, Hawkshead, Ambleside LA22 0NZ
T: (015394) 42435
F: (015394) 36178
E: bookings@lakeland-hideaways.co.uk
I: www.lakeland-hideaways.co.uk

Family-run self-catering accommodation consisting of traditional farm buildings converted into attractive apartments and cottages in beautiful rural setting. Sunny terraces overlooking private paddock. Access to private lakeshore. Free coarse and trout fishing. Log fires, cosy and comfortable, excellent base for walking, cycling and sightseeing.

OPEN All Year

Short breaks available autumn, winter and early spring.

Low season per wk
£220.00–£330.00
High season per wk
£330.00–£420.00

★★★★★

1 Unit
Sleeping 7

SAWREY STABLES

Far Sawrey, Ambleside
Contact: Mrs A Gallagher, Hideaways, The Minstrels Gallery, The Square, Hawkshead, Ambleside LA22 0NZ
T: (015394) 42435
F: (015394) 36178
E: bookings@lakeland-hideaways.co.uk
I: www.sawreystables.co.uk

OPEN All Year

Low season per wk
£480.00–£600.00
High season per wk
£600.00–£880.00

Superb, luxury, 5-star cottage above Lake Windermere. Complete with Aga, jacuzzi bath, open fire. Peaceful, yet with excellent local amenities.

MAP REFERENCES The map references refer to the colour maps at the front of this guide. The first figure is the map number; the letter and figure which follow indicate the grid reference on the map.

SEDBERGH, Cumbria Map ref 5B3

★★★★

2 Units
Sleeping 6–8

FELL HOUSE

Sedbergh
Contact: Mr S Wickham, 14 Home Meadows, Billericay CM12 9HQ
T: (01277) 652746
E: steve@higround.co.uk
I: www.higround.co.uk

OPEN All Year

Low season per wk £150.00–£800.00
High season per wk £230.00–£1,060.00

Luxurious character warehouse conversion with linked, self-contained flat. Spacious living areas tastefully furnished. Quiet, but very close to pubs, shops, restaurant. Weekend bookings taken.

★★★★

1 Unit
Sleeping 5

THWAITE COTTAGE

Sedbergh
Contact: Mrs D Parker, Thwaite Farm, Howgill, Sedbergh LA10 5JD
T: (015396) 20493
F: (015396) 20493
E: thwaitecottage@yahoo.co.uk

OPEN All Year

Low season per wk Min £180.00
High season per wk Min £320.00

Peaceful location with excellent views of the Howgill fells. Salmon and trout fishing, good walking. Central for touring Lakes and Dales. Lots of wildlife.

SPARK BRIDGE, Cumbria Map ref 5A3

★★

1 Unit
Sleeping 4

THURSTONVILLE HIGH LODGE

Lowick, Ulverston
Contact: Mr R N Lord, Thurstonville, Lowick, Ulverston LA12 7SX
T: (01229) 861271
F: (01229) 861271

Thurstonville High Lodge is the gatehouse to a privately owned country house, four miles south of Coniston Water. Convenient for central Lakes and quieter Furness peninsula. Nearest shops 1.5 miles, Ulverston four miles. Rural outlook, private garden, two bedrooms, bathroom (bath/shower), kitchen/diner, living room (open fire).

Low season per wk £170.00–£220.00
High season per wk £230.00–£270.00

STAPLETON, Cumbria Map ref 5B2

★★★

1 Unit
Sleeping 6

DROVE COTTAGE

Stapleton
Contact: Mr & Mrs K Hope
T: (01697) 748202
F: (01697) 748054
E: droveinn@hotmail.com

Our first floor cottage adjoins our busy 'Country Inn' which is family run with an excellent reputation for food – established 29 years! The cottage has a lounge/fitted kitchen, three twin rooms – one with extra futon – and one double room. Bathroom, shower room and one en suite room. Beautiful countryside location.

OPEN All Year
CC: Amex, Delta, JCB, Mastercard, Solo, Switch, Visa

Low season per wk £260.00–£300.00
High season per wk £380.00–£400.00

NB

IMPORTANT NOTE Information on accommodation listed in this guide has been supplied by the proprietors. As changes may occur you are advised to check details at the time of booking.

STAVELEY, Cumbria Map ref 5A3

★★★

4 Units
Sleeping 2–5

BRUNT KNOTT FARM HOLIDAY COTTAGES

Staveley, Kendal
Contact: Mr & Mrs W Beck, Brunt Knott Farm Holiday Cottages, Brunt Knott Farm, Staveley, Kendal LA8 9QX
T: (01539) 821030
F: (01539) 821221
E: margaret@bruntknott.demon.co.uk
I: www.bruntknott.demon.co.uk

Cosy cottages on small, secluded 17thC hill farm. Peaceful, elevated fellside location with superb panoramic views over Lakeland fells. Five miles from Windermere/Kendal. Cycling/lovely walks from your doorstep. Central heating. Three cottages with woodburner/open fire. Parking. Laundry facilities. Winter short breaks available. Brochure.

OPEN All Year

Low season per wk
£185.00–£215.00
High season per wk
£285.00–£400.00

THRELKELD, Cumbria Map ref 5A3

★★★

3 Units
Sleeping 4–6

BLENCATHRA CENTRE–LATRIGG VIEW, DERWENT VIEW, BORROWDALE VIEW
Threlkeld, Keswick
Contact: Mr A Simms, Blencathra Centre, Threlkeld, Keswick CA12 4SG
T: (017687) 79601
F: (017687) 79264
E: enquiries.bl@field-studies-council.org

OPEN All Year
CC: Delta, Mastercard, Switch, Visa

Low season per wk
£165.00–£280.00
High season per wk
£235.00–£375.00

Cottages high on the slopes of Blencathra, in grounds of award-winning Eco-Centre. Walking from the door. Brochure available, dogs welcome.

THURSTONFIELD, Cumbria Map ref 5A2

★★★★-★★★★★

7 Units
Sleeping 4–6

THE TRANQUIL OTTER LODGES

Thurstonfield, Carlisle
Contact: Richard & Wendy Wise
T: (01228) 576661
F: (01228) 576662
E: info@tranquilotter@aol.com
I: www.thetranquilotter.co.uk

Idyllic lodges right on the lakeshore. Peaceful beauty spot. Well-equipped lodges with picture-book views set in private nature reserve. Luxury lodges with logburner, jacuzzi bath / sauna or hot tub. Wonderful nature (including otters). Private lakeside walks. Own rowing boat. Fly fishing. Outstanding wheelchair access and wheely boat.

OPEN All Year
CC: Delta, Mastercard, Visa

Low season per wk
£281.00–£463.00
High season per wk
£495.00–£842.00

TIRRIL, Cumbria Map ref 5B2

★★★★

5 Units
Sleeping 2–9

TIRRIL FARM COTTAGES
Tirril, Penrith
Contact: Mr D Owens, Tirril View, Tirril, Penrith CA10 2JE
T: (01768) 864767
F: (01768) 864767
E: enquiries@tirrilfarmcottages.co.uk
I: www.tirrilfarmcottages.co.uk

OPEN All Year

Low season per wk
£120.00–£440.00
High season per wk
£210.00–£886.00

Situated in the village of Tirril, two miles from Ullswater, these tasteful barn conversions enjoy a quiet courtyard setting with outstanding views over the fells.

VISITBRITAIN'S WHERE TO STAY
Please mention this guide when making your booking.

ULLSWATER, Cumbria Map ref 5A3

★★★★

1 Unit
Sleeping 6

CHERRY HOLM BUNGALOW

Yanwath, Penrith
Contact: Mrs S Sheard
T: (01943) 830766

Luxury, spacious modern bungalow in peaceful country surroundings between Penrith and Ullswater. Ideal for exploring Lake District, Scottish Borders and North Pennines. Warm in winter. Open fire or electric. Exceptionally well equipped. Good food available locally. Riding, golf, boating and fishing nearby. Lockable bike shed. Three bedrooms, two bathrooms.

OPEN All Year

Short breaks available Nov-Mar, minimum 3 nights.

Low season per wk
£170.00–£335.00
High season per wk
£335.00–£420.00

★★★

4 Units
Sleeping 3–5

LAND ENDS

Watermillock, Penrith
Contact: Ms B Holmes
T: (017684) 86438
F: (017684) 86959
E: infolandends@btinternet.com
I: www.landends.co.uk

For those seeking total relaxation, Land Ends is ideal. Only one mile from Ullswater, our detached log cabins have a peaceful, fellside location in 25-acre grounds with two pretty lakes, red squirrels, ducks and wonderful birdlife. Inside, exposed logs and quality furnishings give a cosy, rustic appeal. Dogs welcome.

OPEN All Year

Short breaks available Oct-Mar.

Low season per wk
£234.00–£420.00
High season per wk
£290.00–£475.00

★★-★★★

17 Units
Sleeping 2–6

PATTERDALE HALL ESTATE

Glenridding, Penrith
Contact: Ms S Kay, Estate Office Patterdale Hall Estate, Glenridding, Penrith CA11 0PJ
T: (017684) 82308
F: (017684) 82308
E: welcome@patterdalehallestate.com
I: www.patterdalehallestate.com

Between Helvellyn and Ullswater, the private 300-acre estate with private foreshore, woodland and gardens offers a range of comfortable, centrally heated, self-catering properties all in an idyllic and relaxing setting. Perfect for leisurely holidays, ideally situated for outdoor activities, an excellent base from which to explore the Lake District.

OPEN All Year
CC: Delta, JCB, Mastercard, Solo, Switch, Visa

Short breaks available Nov-Mar or any time if booked within a fortnight of arrival date (subject to availability).

Low season per wk
£140.00–£230.00
High season per wk
£273.00–£452.00

QUALITY ASSURANCE SCHEME

Star ratings were correct at the time of going to press but are subject to change. Please check at the time of booking.

ULLSWATER continued

★★★-★★★★★

5 Units
Sleeping 8–14

SWARTHBECK FARM HOLIDAY COTTAGES

Howtown, Penrith
Contact: Mr & Mrs W H Parkin, Swarthbeck Farm, Howtown, Penrith CA10 2ND
T: (017684) 86432
E: whparkin@ukonline.co.uk
I: www.cumbria.com/horsehols

160-acre hill livestock farm. Properties overlook Ullswater and have colour TV, freezer, central heating, dishwasher and clothes washing and drying facilities. Private access to lake, visitors may bring own boats (motor boats, sailing dinghies, canoes, mountain bikes for hire). Horses available for riding.

OPEN All Year

Low season per wk
£195.00–£615.00
High season per wk
£240.00–£1,387.00

ULVERSTON, Cumbria Map ref 5A3 *Tourist Information Centre Tel: (01229) 587120*

★★★★

5 Units
Sleeping 4–12

ASHLACK COTTAGES

Grizebeck, Kirkby-in-Furness
Contact: Mrs A Keegan, Ashlack Hall, Grizebeck, Kirkby-in-Furness LA17 7XN
T: (01229) 889108
F: (01229) 889111
E: ashlackcottages@hotmail.com
I: ashlackcottages.co.uk

OPEN All Year
CC: Amex, Delta, Diners, Mastercard, Switch, Visa

Low season per wk
£245.00–£499.00
High season per wk
£450.00–£1,450.00

Luxury holiday cottages, surrounded by farmland, overlooking the Duddon estuary, providing excellent accommodation.

★★-★★★

6 Units
Sleeping 2–6

THE FALLS

Ulverston
Contact: Mrs Cheetham and Mrs Unger, The Falls, Mansriggs, Ulverston LA12 7PX
T: (01229) 583781
I: www.thefalls.co.uk

OPEN All Year

Low season per wk
£170.00–£390.00
High season per wk
£250.00–£520.00

17thC farmstead in beautiful surroundings, converted into holiday homes in traditional Lakeland style. Resident proprietors. Children and dogs welcome.

★★★★

1 Unit
Sleeping 2

LILE COTTAGE AT GLEASTON WATER MILL

Gleaston, Ulverston
Contact: Mrs V Brereton, Lile Cottage at Gleaston Water Mill, Gleaston Water Mill, Gleaston, Ulverston LA12 0QH
T: (01229) 869244
F: (01229) 869764
E: pigsty@watermill.co.uk
I: www.watermill.co.uk

Stay in a delightfully converted pigsty, set amidst rolling Furness farmland – ideal for couples seeking unspoilt peace and tranquillity. If you find it difficult to relax by the mill stream, try your hand at bee-keeping or make use of the computer with internet connections at no extra cost.

OPEN All Year
CC: Delta, Mastercard, Solo, Switch, Visa

3-night, mid-week or weekend breaks available in low season.

Low season per wk
£195.00–£250.00
High season per wk
£265.00–£315.00

VISITOR ATTRACTIONS **For ideas on places to visit refer to the introduction at the beginning of this section. Look out too for the ETC's Quality Assured Visitor Attraction signs.**

WASDALE, Cumbria Map ref 5A3

★★★

2 Units
Sleeping 4

WOODHOW FARM COTTAGES
Wasdale, Seascale
Contact: Mr D J Kaminski
T: (0161) 4289116
E: woodhow_farm@kaminsk.fsnet.co.uk
I: kaminski.fsnet.co.uk

OPEN All Year

Low season per wk
£300.00–£450.00
High season per wk
£450.00–£550.00

Grade II Listed, four-bedroomed, beamed farmhouse and converted byres in 210 acres of beautiful countryside including tarn. Lovely setting.

WATERHEAD, Cumbria Map ref 5A3

★★★

1 Unit
Sleeping 5

FLAT 2
Waterhead, Coniston
Contact: Mr S Elson, Waterhead Country Guest House, Coniston LA21 8AJ
T: (015394) 41442
F: (015394) 41476
E: waterheadsteve@aol.com
I: www.waterheadguesthouse.co.uk

OPEN All Year
CC: Delta, Mastercard, Switch, Visa

Low season per wk
£150.00–£250.00
High season per wk
£180.00–£300.00

First floor flat with one large bedroom. Excellent views of Coniston fells. Also kitchen, bathroom and lounge/dining area. Ample parking availabe.

WHITEHAVEN, Cumbria Map ref 5A3 *Tourist Information Centre Tel: (01946) 852939*

★★★★

2 Units
Sleeping 4–6

Cottages adjacent to Moresby Hall, a historical, 16thC Grade I Listed building. Semi-rural, private parking. Near Whitehaven, a Georgian harbour town. Managed by owners with care and attention. Superbly equipped. Delightful decor and furnishings. Welcome grocery pack, self-cater or dine in Moresby Hall. Lakes, fells, golf, cultural and tourist locations close by.

ROSMERTA & BRIGHIDA COTTAGES
Whitehaven
Contact: Mrs J Saxon, Rosmerta & Brighida Cottages, Moresby Hall, Moresby, Whitehaven CA28 6PJ
T: (01946) 696317
F: (01946) 694385
E: etc@moresbyhall.co.uk
I: www.moresbyhall.co.uk

OPEN All Year
CC: Amex, Delta, Diners, JCB, Mastercard, Switch, Visa

Short breaks (3 nights for the price of 2) available Nov-Mar (excl Christmas and New Year).

Low season per wk
£220.00–£330.00
High season per wk
£330.00–£520.00

WIGTON, Cumbria Map ref 5A2

★★★★

1 Unit
Sleeping 8

FOXGLOVES
Westward, Wigton
Contact: Mr & Mrs E Kerr, Greenrigg Farm, Westward, Wigton CA7 8AH
T: (016973) 42676
E: kerr_greenrigg@hotmail.com

Spacious, well-equipped, comfortable cottage on a working farm. Superlative setting and views, large kitchen/dining room, Aga, lounge, open fire, storage heaters, TV/video, dishwasher, three bedrooms, bathroom, shower room. Linen, towels, electricity, logs and coal inclusive. Children and pets very welcome. Extensive garden. Horse grazing and stabling available.

OPEN All Year

Short breaks and mid-week breaks.

Low season per wk
£180.00–£280.00
High season per wk
£305.00–£384.00

WINDERMERE, Cumbria Map ref 5A3 *Tourist Information Centre Tel: (015394) 46499*

★★★

2 Units
Sleeping 4–6

THE ABBEY COACH HOUSE

Windermere
Contact: Mrs P Bell, The Abbey Coach House,
St Mary's Park, Windermere LA23 1AZ
T: (015394) 44027
F: (015394) 44027
E: abbeycoach@aol.com
I: www.oas.co.uk/ukcottages

OPEN All Year

Low season per wk
£150.00–£295.00
High season per wk
£195.00–£425.00

Excellent location of ground floor apartment and bungalow in quiet, private area. Ample parking, extensive gardens. Ideal for families or retired.

★★★

9 Units
Sleeping 2–6

BIRTHWAITE EDGE

Windermere
Contact: Mr B Dodsworth, Birthwaite Edge,
Birthwaite Road, Windermere LA23 1BS
T: (015394) 42861
E: etc@lakedge.com
I: www.lakedge.com

Birthwaite Edge is the perfect holiday base from which to explore the north of England. Public transport and bus tours nearby. Set in an exclusive area 10 minutes' stroll from Windermere village and lake. Central for restaurants, cafes and inns. Resident proprietors guarantee comfortable, clean apartments. No smoking or pets.

OPEN All Year except Christmas
CC: Delta, Mastercard, Switch, Visa

Low season per wk
£180.00–£260.00
High season per wk
£300.00–£530.00

PRICES

Please check prices and other details at the time of booking.

LAKELOVERS

For the ultimate in Lakeland holidays, Lakelovers have it all, from traditional farmhouses sleeping up to 14 steeped in character, to luxury modern apartments sleeping 2, complete with private tennis facilities. Over 140 retreats to choose from. We pride ourselves on hand picking individual properties equipped to the highest standard to suit every taste and pocket. We include FREE leisure club membership with every holiday. Short breaks also available.

Belmont House, Lake Road, Bowness-on-Windermere, Cumbria LA23 3BJ
t: 015394 88855 f: 015394 88857 e: bookings@lakelovers.co.uk www.lakelovers.co.uk

WINDERMERE continued

★★-★★★ 5 Units Sleeping 2-7	**CANTERBURY FLATS** Bowness-on-Windermere, Windermere Contact: Mr M & Mrs I Zuniga, Bowness Holidays, 131 Radcliffe New Road, Whitefield, Manchester M45 7RP T: (0161) 7963896 F: (0161) 2721841 E: info@bownesslakelandholidays.co.uk I: www.bownesslakelandholidays.co.uk OPEN All Year *Wonderful location. Apartments in the centre of the village, close to all amenities. Full membership of private leisure club, indoor swimming complex. Short breaks available.*	Low season per wk £150.00–£175.00 High season per wk £200.00–£270.00
★★★★ 1 Unit Sleeping 4	**GAVEL COTTAGE** Bowness-on-Windermere Contact: Mr Screeton, Screetons, 25 Bridgegate, Howden, Goole DN14 7AA T: (01430) 431201 F: (01430) 432114 E: howden@screetons.co.uk I: screetons.co.uk OPEN All Year *Secluded period cottage close to marina. Tastefully furnished and well equipped. Two bedrooms, all modern facilities. Large garden with summer house. Member Burnside Leisure Complex.*	Low season per wk £225.00–£295.00 High season per wk £385.00–£460.00
★★★ 4 Units Sleeping 2-6	**LANGDALE VIEW HOLIDAY APARTMENTS** Bowness-on-Windermere, Windermere Contact: Mrs J Fletcher, Langdale View Holiday Apartments, 112 Craig Walk, Bowness-on-Windermere, Windermere LA23 3AX T: (015394) 46655 F: (015394) 46728 E: enquiries@langdale-view.co.uk I: www.langdale-view.co.uk OPEN All Year CC: Delta, JCB, Mastercard, Solo, Switch, Visa *Attractive, comfortable holiday apartments with car parking. Quiet, elevated position very close to village centre, lake, steamers, shops and restaurants.*	Low season per wk £165.00–£260.00 High season per wk £270.00–£420.00
Rating Applied For 1 Unit Sleeping 2	**THE OLD PICTURE HOUSE** Windermere Contact: Mr N Thompson, No 3, 511 Barlow Moor Road, Chorlton, Manchester M21 8AQ T: (0161) 861 7574 E: ndjthompson@hotmail.com OPEN All Year *Unwind and relax in this self-contained holiday home in the centre of Windermere village. Fully equipped and furnished to a high standard. Mob: 07957 661 362.*	Low season per wk £220.00–£270.00 High season per wk £270.00–£375.00

★★★
4 Units
Sleeping 2

Old spinnery tastefully converted into pleasant apartments, situated above Bowness village, close to Lake Windermere and fells. Ideal base from which to explore the Lake District at the end of the Dales Way. Quiet surroundings, private on-site car parking, leisure club facilities nearby, bargain breaks during the winter months.

SPINNERY COTTAGE HOLIDAY APARTMENTS

Bowness-on-Windermere, Windermere
Contact: Mr & Mrs Hood, Sylvan Wood, Underbarrow Road, Kendal, Cumbria LA8 8AH
T: (01539) 725153
F: (01539) 725153
E: Ray&barb@spinnerycottage.co.uk
I: www.spinnerycottage.co.uk

OPEN All Year
CC: Delta, Mastercard, Switch, Visa

Special breaks available Nov-Mar, minimum 2 nights.

Low season per wk
£225.00–£270.00
High season per wk
£300.00–£350.00

WINDERMERE continued

★★★★

3 Units
Sleeping 8

WINDERMERE MARINA VILLAGE
Bowness-on-Windermere, Windermere
Contact: Mrs C Burns, Windermere Marina Village,
Bowness-on-Windermere, Windermere LA23 3JQ
T: 0800 262902
F: (015394) 43233
E: info@wmv.co.uk
I: www.wmv.co.uk

OPEN All Year
CC: Amex, Delta, Mastercard, Switch, Visa

Low season per wk
£395.00–£665.00
High season per wk
£655.00–£1,075.00

Superbly appointed lakeside cottages with private leisure club and moorings. Short breaks and weekly bookings. Swimming pool, sauna, spas, bistro, playground.

★★★

3 Units
Sleeping 2

WINSTER HOUSE
Windermere
Contact: Mrs S Jump, Winster House, Sunnybank Road,
Windermere LA23 2EN
T: (015394) 44723
E: enquiries@winsterhouse.co.uk
I: www.winsterhouse.co.uk

Low season per wk
Min £165.00
High season per wk
Max £240.00

Private parking and use of secluded garden. Five minutes' walk to shops and restaurants, 10 minutes' walk to Lake Windermere. Brochure available.

TOWN INDEX

This can be found at the back of the guide. If you know where you want to stay, the index will give you the page number listing accommodation in your chosen town, city or village.

A brief guide to the main Towns and Villages offering accommodation in **Cumbria**

A AMBLESIDE, CUMBRIA - Market town situated at the head of Lake Windermere and surrounded by fells. The historic town centre is now a conservation area and the country around Ambleside is rich in historic and literary associations. Good centre for touring, walking and climbing.

APPLEBY-IN-WESTMORLAND, CUMBRIA - Former county town of Westmorland, at the foot of the Pennines in the Eden Valley. The castle was rebuilt in the 17th C, except for its Norman keep, ditches and ramparts. It now houses a Rare Breeds Survival Trust Centre. Good centre for exploring the Eden Valley.

B BOWNESS-ON-WINDERMERE, CUMBRIA - Bowness is the older of the 2 towns of Bowness and Windermere and dates from the 11th C. It is a busy tourist resort set on the shores of Lake Windermere, England's largest lake. Good location for touring, walking, boating and fishing.

BROUGHTON-IN-FURNESS, CUMBRIA - Old market village whose historic charter to hold fairs is still proclaimed every year on the first day of August in the market square. Good centre for touring the pretty Duddon Valley.

C CALDBECK, CUMBRIA - Quaint limestone village lying on the northern fringe of the Lake District National Park. John Peel, the famous huntsman who is immortalised in song, is buried in the churchyard. The fells surrounding Caldbeck were once heavily mined, being rich in lead, copper and barytes.

CARLISLE, CUMBRIA - Cumbria's only city is rich in history. Attractions include the small red sandstone cathedral and 900-year-old castle with magnificent view from the keep. The award-winning Tullie House Museum and Art Gallery brings 2,000 years of Border history dramatically to life. Excellent centre for shopping.

CARTMEL, CUMBRIA - Picturesque conserved village based on a 12th C priory with a well-preserved church and gatehouse. Just half a mile outside the Lake District National Park, this is a peaceful base for walking and touring, with historic houses and beautiful scenery.

COCKERMOUTH, CUMBRIA - Ancient market town at confluence of rivers Cocker and Derwent. Birthplace of William Wordsworth in 1770. The house where he was born is at the end of the town's broad, tree-lined main street and is now owned by the National Trust. Good touring base for the Lakes.

CONISTON, CUMBRIA - The 803m fell Coniston Old Man dominates the skyline to the east of this village at the northern end of Coniston Water. Arthur Ransome set his "Swallows and Amazons" stories here. Coniston's most famous resident was John Ruskin, whose home, Brantwood, is open to the public. Good centre for walking.

D DENT, CUMBRIA - Very picturesque village with narrow cobbled streets, lying within the boundaries of the Yorkshire Dales National Park.

E ELTERWATER, CUMBRIA - Attractive village at the foot of Great Langdale with a small village green as its focal point. Elterwater, one of the smallest lakes in the Lake District, was named by the Norsemen as "Swan Lake", and swans still frequent the lake.

ESKDALE, CUMBRIA - Several minor roads lead to the west end of this beautiful valley, or it can be approached via the east over the Hardknott Pass, the Lake District's steepest pass. Scafell Pike and Bow Fell lie to the north, and a miniature railway links the Eskdale Valley with Ravenglass on the coast.

G GRANGE-OVER-SANDS, CUMBRIA - Set on the beautiful Cartmel Peninsula, this tranquil resort, known as Lakeland's Riviera, overlooks Morecambe Bay. Pleasant seafront walks and beautiful gardens. The bay attracts many species of wading birds.

GRASMERE, CUMBRIA - Described by William Wordsworth as "the loveliest spot that man hath ever found", this village, famous for its gingerbread, is in a beautiful setting overlooked by Helm Crag. Wordsworth lived at Dove Cottage. The cottage and museum are open to the public.

GREAT LANGDALE, CUMBRIA - Picturesque valley at the foot of the Langdale Pikes, popular with walkers and climbers of every ability, with some of the Lake District's loveliest waterfalls.

H HAWKSHEAD, CUMBRIA - Lying near Esthwaite Water, this village has great charm and character. Its small squares are linked by flagged or cobbled alleys, and the main square is dominated by the market house, or Shambles, where the butchers had their stalls in days gone by.

HIGH LORTON, CUMBRIA - On the B5292 between Keswick and Cockermouth. Spectacular views from nearby Whinlatter Pass down this predominantly farming valley.

K KENDAL, CUMBRIA - The "Auld Grey Town" lies in the valley of the River Kent with a backdrop of limestone fells. Situated just outside the Lake District National Park, it is a good centre for touring the Lakes and surrounding country. Ruined castle, reputed birthplace of Catherine Parr.

KESWICK, CUMBRIA - Beautifully positioned town beside Derwentwater and below the mountains of Skiddaw and Blencathra. Excellent base for walking, climbing, watersports and touring. Motor-launches operate on Derwentwater, and motor boats, rowing boats and canoes can be hired.

KING'S MEABURN, CUMBRIA - Unspoilt Eden Valley village on the River Lyvennet.

KIRKBY LONSDALE, CUMBRIA - Charming old town of narrow streets and Georgian buildings, set in the superb scenery of the Lune Valley. The Devil's Bridge over the River Lune is probably 13th C.

KIRKBY STEPHEN, CUMBRIA - Old market town close to the River Eden, with many fine Georgian buildings and an attractive market square. St Stephen's Church is known as the "Cathedral of the Dales". Good base for exploring the Eden Valley and the Dales.

KIRKOSWALD, CUMBRIA - Village of red sandstone houses in the fertile Eden Valley, with the ruins of a 12th C castle. The village derives its name from the church of St Oswald.

L LANGDALE, CUMBRIA - The 2 Langdale valleys (Great Langdale and Little Langdale) lie in the heart of beautiful mountain scenery. The craggy Langdale Pikes are almost 2,500 ft high. An ideal walking and climbing area and base for touring.

LITTLE LANGDALE, CUMBRIA - See Langdale.

LONGSLEDDALE, CUMBRIA - Quiet valley in the south-eastern fells, stretching 6 miles and lying 5 miles north of Kendal. Narrow roads, bordered by rolling hillsides, woodlands and craggy valley head.

LOWESWATER, CUMBRIA - Scattered village lying between Loweswater, one of the smaller lakes, and Crummock Water. Mountains surround this quiet valley of three lakes, giving some marvellous views.

M MUNGRISDALE, CUMBRIA - Set in an unspoilt valley, this hamlet has a simple, white church with a 3-decker pulpit and box pews.

N NEWBY BRIDGE, CUMBRIA - At the southern end of Windermere on the River Leven, this village has an unusual stone bridge with arches of unequal size. The Lakeside and Haverthwaite Railway has a stop here, and steamer cruises on Lake Windermere leave from nearby Lakeside.

P PENRITH, CUMBRIA - Ancient and historic market town, the northern gateway to the Lake District. Penrith Castle was built as a defence against the Scots. Its ruins, open to the public, stand in the public park. High above the town is the Penrith Beacon, made famous by William Wordsworth.

POOLEY BRIDGE, CUMBRIA - The bridge is on the northern tip of Lake Ullswater and spans the River Eamont where it emerges from the lake. Good centre for exploring, walking and sailing.

S SAWREY, CUMBRIA - Far Sawrey and Near Sawrey lie near Esthwaite Water. Both villages are small, but Near Sawrey is famous for Hill Top Farm, home of Beatrix Potter, now owned by the National Trust and open to the public.

SEDBERGH, CUMBRIA - This busy market town, set below the Howgill Fells, is an excellent centre for walking and touring the Dales and Howgills. The noted boys' school was founded in 1525.

SPARK BRIDGE, CUMBRIA - Small, attractive village beside the River Crake, south of Coniston Water. Cumbria's last bobbin mill recently closed here.

STAVELEY, CUMBRIA - Large village built in slate, set between Kendal and Windermere at the entrance to the lovely Kentmere Valley.

T THRELKELD, CUMBRIA - This village is a centre for climbing the Saddleback range of mountains, which tower high above it.

U ULLSWATER, CUMBRIA - This beautiful lake, which is over 7 miles long, runs from Glenridding to Pooley Bridge. Lofty peaks ranging around the lake make an impressive background. A steamer service operates along the lake between Pooley Bridge, Howtown and Glenridding in the summer.

ULVERSTON, CUMBRIA - Market town lying between green fells and the sea. There is a replica of the Eddystone lighthouse on the Hoad which is a monument to Sir John Barrow, founder of the Royal Geographical Society. Birthplace of Stan Laurel, of Laurel and Hardy.

W WASDALE, CUMBRIA - A very dramatic valley with England's deepest lake, Wastwater, highest mountain, Scafell Pike, and smallest church. The eastern shore of Wastwater is dominated by the 1,500-ft screes dropping steeply into the lake. A good centre for walking and climbing.

WHITEHAVEN, CUMBRIA - Historic Georgian port on the west coast. The town was developed in the 17th C and many fine buildings have been preserved. The Beacon Heritage Centre includes a Meteorological Office Weather Gallery. Start or finishing point of Coast to Coast, Whitehaven to Sunderland cycleway.

WIGTON, CUMBRIA - Built on the site of a Roman fort, Wigton has a centuries-old market as well as cattle, sheep and horse auctions.

WINDERMERE, CUMBRIA - Once a tiny hamlet before the introduction of the railway in 1847, it now adjoins Bowness which is on the lakeside. Centre for sailing and boating. A good way to see the lake is a trip on a passenger steamer. Steamboat Museum has a fine collection of old boats.

QUALITY ASSURANCE SCHEME

Star ratings were correct at the time of going to press but are subject to change. Please check at the time of booking.

Northumbria

Romans, sailors and industrial pioneers have all left their mark here. Northunbria's exciting cities, castle-studded countyside and white-sanded coastline make it an undiscovered gem.

Classic sights
Lindisfarne Castle – on Holy Island
Housesteads Roman Fort – the most impressive Roman fort on Hadrian's Wall
Durham Cathedral & Hadrian's Wall – 2 World Heritage Sites

Coast & country
Kielder Water and Forest Park – perfect for walking, cycling and watersports
Saltburn – beach of broad sands
Seahouses – picturesque fishing village

Maritime history
HMS Trincomalee – magnificent 1817 British warship
Captain Cook – birthplace museum and replica of his ship, *Endeavour*
Grace Darling – museum commemorating her rescue of shipwreck survivors in 1838

Arts for all
Angel of the North – awe-inspiring sculpture by Antony Gormley
BALTIC – The Centre for Contemporary Art in Gateshead

Distinctively different
St Mary's Lighthouse – great views from the top

The Counties of Durham, Northumberland, Tees Valley and Tyne & Wear

For more information contact:
Northumbria Tourist Board
Aykley Heads,
Durham DH1 5UX

www.visitnorthumbria.com

Telephone enquiries -
T: (0191) 375 3049
F: (0191) 386 0899

1. The Angel of the North, Gateshead
2. Town Crier, Alnwick Fair
3. Walkers on the Northumbrian Coast

Places to **Visit**

You will find hundreds of interesting places to visit during your stay, just some of which are listed in these pages. Contact any Tourist Information Centre in the region for more ideas on days out.

QUALITY ASSURED VISITOR ATTRACTION

Awarded VisitBritain's 'Quality Assured Visitor Attraction' marque.

Alnwick Castle
Alnwick
Tel: (01665) 510777 www.alnwickcastle.com
Home of the Percy's, Dukes of Northumberland, since 1309, this imposing medieval fortress has magnificent 19thC interiors in the Italian Renaissance style.

Alnwick Garden
Alnwick
Tel: (01665) 511350 www.alnwickgarden.com
New 12-acre (5ha) garden with fabulous water feature, rose garden, ornamental garden, woodland walk and viewpoint.

BALTIC The Centre for Contemporary Art
Quayside, Gateshead
Tel: (0191) 478 1810 www.balticmill.com
A major international centre for contemporary art in a converted warehouse, with a constantly changing programme of exhibitions and events.

Bamburgh Castle
Bamburgh
Tel: (01668) 214515
www.bamburghcastle.com
Magnificent coastal castle completely restored in 1900. Collections of china, porcelain, furniture, paintings, arms and armour.

Beamish The North of England Open Air Museum
Beamish
Tel: (0191) 370 4000
www.beamish.org.uk
Visit the town, colliery village, working farm, Pockerley Manor and 1825 railway, recreating life in the North East in the early 1800s and 1900s.

Bede's World
Church Bank, Jarrow
Tel: (0191) 489 2106
www.bedesworld.co.uk
Discover the exciting world of the Venerable Bede, early medieval Europe's greatest scholar. Church, monastic site, museum with exhibitions and recreated Anglo-Saxon farm.

Belsay Hall, Castle and Gardens (English Heritage)
Belsay, Newcastle upon Tyne
Tel: (01661) 881636
www.english-heritage.org.uk
Home of the Middleton family for 600 years. 14thC castle, ruined 17thC manor house and neo-classical hall, set in 30 acres (12ha) of landscaped gardens and winter garden.

Blue Reef Aquarium
Grand Parade, Tynemouth
Tel: (0191) 258 1031
www.bluereefaquarium.co.uk
More than 30 living displays exploring the drama of the North Sea and the dazzling beauty of a spectacular coral reef with its own underwater tunnel.

Bowes Museum
Barnard Castle
Tel: (01833) 690606
www.bowesmuseum.org.uk
French-style chateau, housing art collections of national importance and archaeology of south west Durham.

Captain Cook Birthplace Museum
Stewart Park, Middlesborough
Tel: (01642) 311211
Early life and voyages of Captain Cook and the countries he visited. Temporary exhibitions. One person free with every group of 10 visiting.

Centre For Life
Times Square, Newcastle upon Tyne
Tel: (0191) 243 8210 www.centre-for-life.co.uk
Meet your 4 billion year old family, explore what makes us all different, test your brain power and enjoy the thrill of the crazy motion ride.

Cherryburn: Thomas Bewick Birthplace Museum (National Trust)
Station Bank, Stocksfield
Tel: (01661) 843276 www.nationaltrust.org.uk
Birthplace cottage (1700) and farmyard. Printing house using original printing blocks. Introductory exhibition of the life, work and countryside.

Chesters Roman Fort (Cilurnum), Hadrian's Wall
Chollerford, Humshaugh, Hexham
Tel: (01434) 681379
Fort built for 500 cavalrymen. Remains include 5 gateways, barrack blocks, commandant's house and headquarters. Finest military bath house in Britain.

Chillingham Castle
Chillingham, Wooler
Tel: (01668) 215359
www.chillingham-castle.com
Medieval fortress with Tudor additions, torture chamber, shop, dungeon, tearoom, woodland walks, furnished rooms and topiary garden.

Cragside House, Gardens and Estate (National Trust)
Rothbury, Morpeth
Tel: (01669) 620333 www.nationaltrust.org.uk
Built in 1864-84 for Tyneside industrialist Lord Armstrong, Cragside was the first house to be lit by electricity generated by water power.

Discovery Museum
Blandford Square, Newcastle upon Tyne
Tel: (0191) 232 6789 www.twmuseums.org.uk
Discovery Museum offers a wide variety of experiences for all the family to enjoy. Explore the Newcastle Story, Live Wires, Science Maze and Fashion Works.

Dunstanburgh Castle (English Heritage)
Craster, Alnwick
Tel: (01665) 576231
www.english-heritage.org.uk
Romantic ruins of extensive 14thC castle in dramatic coastal situation on 100ft (30.5km) cliffs. Built by Thomas, Earl of Lancaster. Remains include gatehouse and curtain wall.

Durham Castle
Palace Green, Durham
Tel: (0191) 374 3863 www.durhamcastle.com
Castle founded in 1072, Norman chapel dating from 1080. Kitchens and great hall dated 1499 and 1284 respectively. Fine example of motte-and-bailey castle.

Durham Cathedral
The College, Durham
Tel: (0191) 386 4266
www.durhamcathedral.co.uk
Durham Cathedral is thought by many to be the finest example of Norman church architecture in England. Contains the tombs of St Cuthbert and The Venerable Bede.

2

3

1. Lindisfarne Castle, Holy Island
2. Hadrian's Wall
3. Bridges over the Tyne, Newcastle

Hall Hill Farm
Lanchester, Durham
Tel: (01388) 730300 www.hallhillfarm.co.uk
Family fun set in attractive countryside with an opportunity to see and touch the animals at close quarters. Farm trailer ride, riverside walk, teashop and play area.

Hartlepool Historic Quay
Maritime Avenue, Hartlepool
Tel: (01429) 860006
www.destinationhartlepool.com
Hartlepool Historic Quay is an exciting reconstruction of a seaport of the 1800s with buildings and lively quayside, authentically reconstructed.

Housesteads Roman Fort (Vercovicium), Hadrian's Wall (National Trust)
Haydon Bridge, Hexham
Tel: (01434) 344363 www.nationaltrust.org.uk
Best preserved and most impressive of the Roman forts. Vercovicium was a 5-acre (2ha) fort for an extensive 800 civil settlement. Only example of a Roman hospital.

Killhope, The North of England Lead Mining Museum
Cowshill, Bishop Auckland
Tel: (01388) 537505
www.durham.gov.uk/killhope
Most complete lead mining site in Great Britain. Mine tours available, 34-ft- (10m-) diameter waterwheel, reconstruction of Victorian machinery, miners lodging and woodland walks.

Lindisfarne Castle (National Trust)
Holy Island, Berwick-upon-Tweed
Tel: (01289) 389244 www.nationaltrust.org.uk
The castle was built in 1550 and restored and converted into a private home for Edward Hudson by the architect Sir Edwin Lutyens in 1903.

National Glass Centre
Liberty Way, Sunderland
Tel: (0191) 515 5555
www.nationalglasscentre.com
A unique visitor attraction presenting the best in contemporary glass. Master craftspeople will demonstrate glass-making techniques. Classes and workshops available.

Nature's World at the Botanic Centre
Ladgate Lane, Middlesborough
Tel: (01642) 594895 www.naturesworld.org.uk
Demonstration gardens, wildlife pond, white garden, environmental exhibition hall, shop, tearoom and River Tees model. Hydroponicum and Eco centre now open.

Otter Trust's North Pennines Reserve
Bowes, Barnard Castle
Tel: (01833) 628339
A branch of the famous Otter Trust. Visitors can see Asian and British otters, red and fallow deer and several rare breeds of farm animals in this 230-acre (93ha) wildlife reserve.

Raby Castle
Staindrop, Darlington
Tel: (01833) 660202 www.rabycastle.com
The medieval castle, home of Lord Barnard's family since 1626, includes a 200-acre (80ha) deer park, walled gardens, carriage collection, adventure playground, shop and tearoom.

St Nicholas Cathedral
St Nicholas Street, Newcastle upon Tyne
Tel: (0191) 232 1939
www.newcastle-ang-cathedralstnicholas.org.uk
13thC and 14thC church, added to in 18thC-20thC. Famous lantern tower, pre-reformation font and font cover, 15thC stained glass roundel in the side chapel.

Wallington House, Walled Garden and Grounds (National Trust)
Wallington, Morpeth
Tel: (01670) 773600 www.nationaltrust.org.uk
Escape to the beautiful walled garden and its conservatory or enjoy a walk in the woods or along by the river. Bring the family to one of the many events at Wallington.

Washington Old Hall (National Trust)
The Avenue, Washington
Tel: (0191) 416 6879 www.nationaltrust.org.uk
From 1183 to 1399 the home of George Washington's direct ancestors, remaining in the family until 1613. The manor, from which the family took its name, was restored in 1936.

Wildfowl and Wetlands Trust Washington
District 15, Washington
Tel: (0191) 416 5454 www.wwt.org.uk
Collection of 1,000 wildfowl of 85 varieties. Viewing gallery, picnic areas, hides and winter wild bird-feeding station, flamingos and wild grey heron. Waterside cafe.

Northumbria Tourist Board

Aykley Heads, Durham DH1 5UX.
Tel: (0191) 375 3049 Fax: (0191) 386 0899
www.visitnorthumbria.com

THE FOLLOWING PUBLICATIONS ARE AVAILABLE FROM NORTHUMBRIA TOURIST BOARD UNLESS OTHERWISE STATED:

Northumbria 2004 –
information on the region, including hotels, bed and breakfast and self-catering accommodation, caravan and camping parks, attractions, shopping, eating and drinking

Group Travel & Education Directory –
guide contains information on group accommodation providers, places to visit, suggested itineraries, coaching information and events. Also provides information to help plan educational visits within the region. Uncover a wide variety of places to visit with unique learning opportunities

Discover Northumbria on two wheels –
information on cycling in the region including an order form allowing the reader to order maps/leaflets from a central ordering point

Discover Northumbria on two feet –
information on walking in the region including an order form allowing the reader to order maps/leaflets from a central ordering point

Getting to Northumbria

BY ROAD: The north/south routes on the A1 and A19 thread the region as does the A68. East/west routes like the A66 and A69 easily link with the western side of the country. Within Northumbria you will find fast, modern interconnecting roads between all the main centres, a vast network of scenic, traffic-free country roads to make motoring a pleasure and frequent local bus services operating to all towns and villages.

BY RAIL: London to Edinburgh InterCity service stops at Darlington, Durham, Newcastle and Berwick upon Tweed. 26 trains daily make the journey between London and Newcastle in just under 3 hours. The London to Middlesbrough journey (changing at Darlington) takes 3 hours. Birmingham to Darlington 3 hours 15 minutes. Bristol to Durham 5 hours and Sheffield to Newcastle just over 2 hours. Direct services operate to Newcastle from Liverpool, Manchester, Glasgow, Stranraer and Carlisle. Regional services to areas of scenic beauty operate frequently, allowing the traveller easy access. The Tyne & Wear Metro makes it possible to travel to many destinations within the Tyneside area, such as Gateshead, South Shields, Whitley Bay and Newcastle International Airport, in minutes.

1. Dunstanburgh Castle

Where to stay in

Northumbria

All place names in the blue bands under which accommodation is listed, are shown on the maps at the front of this guide.

Symbols give useful information about services and facilities. Inside the back cover flap there's a key to these symbols which you can keep open for easy reference.

A complete listing of all the VisitBritain assessed accommodation covered by this guide appears at the back of this guide.

ALNMOUTH, Northumberland Map ref 5C1

★★★★

1 Unit
Sleeping 7

SUNNYSIDE COTTAGE
Alnmouth, Near Alnwick
Contact: Mrs M Hollins, 2 The Grove, Whickham, Newcastle upon Tyne NE16 4QY
T: (0191) 4883939
F: (0191) 4883939
E: sunnysidecott@lineone.net

OPEN All Year

Low season per wk
Min £275.00
High season per wk
Min £610.00

Newly renovated cottage, yards from estuary and beach. Enclosed garden. Outside parking. Ideal for bird-watching, cycling, walking and Duchess' gardens.

NORTHUMBRIA, the BORDERS & COAST

Dales Holiday Cottages

Superb, personally inspected, self catering holiday properties in beautiful rural and coastal locations including the Northern Dales, the Land of the Prince Bishops and Hadrian's Wall country. Cosy cottages to country houses, many welcome pets and most are open all year.
Phone for free brochure.

01756 799821 & 790919
www.dalesholcot.com

English Tourism Council
Committed to ETC Quality Assurance

ALNMOUTH continued

★★-★★★
3 Units
Sleeping 4

WOODEN FARM HOLIDAY COTTAGES
Alnmouth, Alnwick
Contact: Mr W G Farr
T: (01665) 830342

OPEN All Year

Low season per wk £190.00–£200.00
High season per wk £190.00–£250.00

Stone-built cottages in a quiet farm setting, overlooking the coast and the picturesque village of Alnmouth. Only four miles from Alnwick Castle/garden.

ALNWICK, Northumberland Map ref 5C1 *Tourist Information Centre Tel: (01665) 510665*

★★★
1 Unit
Sleeping 2

GREEN BATT STUDIO
Alnwick
Contact: Clare Mills, 1 Percy Street, Alnwick NE66 1AE
T: (01665) 602742
E: paul@mills84.freeserve.co.uk

OPEN All Year

Low season per wk £160.00–£180.00
High season per wk £180.00–£220.00

Second floor studio apartment in a quiet conservation area, yet only 100 metres from town centre. Friendly hosts live on ground floor. Well-equipped accommodation, welcome pack provided.

★★★-★★★★★
13 Units
Sleeping 3–7

17thC farmhouse, cottages and beautifully appointed chalets complemented by excellent facilities – indoor heated swimming pool, health club, steam room, sauna, sunshower, beauty therapist, games room, tennis, riding, fishing and adventure playground. Situated between Alnwick and Heritage Coast. A warm, personal welcome.

VILLAGE FARM
Shilbottle, Alnwick
Contact: Mrs C M Stoker, Town Foot Farm, Shilbottle, Alnwick NE66 2HG
T: (01665) 575591
F: (01665) 575591
E: crissy@villagefarmcottages.co.uk
I: www.villagefarmcottages.co.uk

OPEN All Year

2/3-night stays available Nov-Easter (excl Christmas, New Year and half-terms).

Low season per wk £130.00–£385.00
High season per wk £240.00–£975.00

BAMBURGH, Northumberland Map ref 5C1

★★★★
1 Unit
Sleeping 6

BARN END
Bamburgh
Contact: Mr G E Bruce, The Steading, Westburn, Crawcrook, Ryton NE40 4EU
T: (0191) 4132353
E: george.e.bruce@talk21.com

Low season per wk Max £250.00
High season per wk £400.00–£450.00

Cottage with one twin, two double rooms, bathroom/wc, en suite shower/wc. Fully carpeted and equipped. Two hundred yards to village and beach. Sorry, no pets.

★★★
1 Unit
Sleeping 3

Cosy bungalow set in the heart of this charming village. Delightful views with fields to the front and Bamburgh Castle to the rear. Situated at the end of a cul-de-sac, only a few minutes' walk to village amenities, beach and castle. Attractively furnished to a high standard. Small garden.

CASTLE VIEW BUNGALOW
Bamburgh
Contact: Mr & Mrs I Nicol, Springwood, South Lane, Seahouses NE68 7UL
T: (01665) 720320
F: (01665) 720146
E: ian@slatehall.freeserve.co.uk
I: www.slatehallridingcentre.com

OPEN All Year

Low season per wk £225.00–£250.00
High season per wk £425.00–£475.00

BAMBURGH continued

★★★
1 Unit
Sleeping 4

THE COTTAGE
Bamburgh
Contact: Mrs S Turnbull, 1 Friars Court, Bamburgh NE69 7AE
T: (01668) 214494

OPEN All Year

Charming, quality accommodation minutes from the beautiful sandy beach, with wonderful views of the magnificent Bamburgh Castle. Large private gardens and parking.

Low season per wk
£225.00–£350.00
High season per wk
£350.00–£475.00

★★★★
5 Units
Sleeping 4–8

DUKESFIELD FARM HOLIDAY COTTAGES
Bamburgh
Contact: Mrs M Robinson, The Glebe, 16 Radcliffe Road, Bamburgh NE69 7AE
T: (01668) 214456
F: (01668) 214354
E: eric_j_robinson@compuserve.com
I: www.secretkingdom.com/dukes/field.htm

Situated just outside Bamburgh village, this attractive farmsteading offers easy access to coast, castle, beach and golf course. Spacious yet cosy cottages with first-class kitchens and bathrooms. Own paddocks. Children and pets welcome. Ample parking. An ideal base for walking and exploring Northumberland's Heritage Coast.

Special 2-person weekly prices and short breaks available.

Low season per wk
£200.00–£445.00
High season per wk
£375.00–£745.00

★★★
1 Unit
Sleeping 8

THE FAIRWAY
Bamburgh
Contact: Mrs Diana Middleton, High Close House, Wylam NE41 8BL
T: (01661) 852125
E: rsmiddleton@talk21.com

Beautifully situated cottage overlooking sea, one minute from beaches and golf course. Four bedrooms, open fire and central heating. Garden front and rear.

Low season per wk
£450.00–£480.00
High season per wk
£550.00–£600.00

★★★★★
2 Units
Sleeping 4–8

GLEBE HOUSE & GLEBE COTTAGE
Bamburgh
Contact: Mrs M Robinson, The Glebe, 16 Radcliffe Road, Bamburgh NE69 7AE
T: (01668) 214456
F: (01668) 214354
E: eric_j_robinson@compuserve.com
I: www.secretkingdom.com/glebe/house.htm

In Bamburgh village, this lovely 18thC vicarage has stunning views of church, castle and sea. Glebe House is spacious and well furnished with full central heating included. First-class kitchen. Children and pets welcome. Large, peaceful, private gardens. Separate cottage also available with ground floor bedrooms and private patio.

OPEN All Year

Special 2-person prices and short breaks available.

Low season per wk
£295.00–£475.00
High season per wk
£575.00–£995.00

CREDIT CARD BOOKINGS If you book by telephone and are asked for your credit card number it is advisable to check the proprietor's policy should you cancel your reservation.

BAMBURGH continued

★★★★

1 Unit
Sleeping 6

INGLENOOK COTTAGE

Bamburgh
Contact: Mrs A D Moore, Beckstones, Carperby, Leyburn DL8 4DA
T: (01969) 663363

Well-appointed, three-bedroomed, Listed 17thC cottage beside the grove (village green), only 550 yards from Bamburgh Castle and the beach. Large enclosed rear garden. The cottage is spacious with two bathrooms, fully fitted kitchen, dining room and sitting room with log/coalburning fires. Fully centrally heated.

OPEN All Year

Short breaks available Oct-Mar (excl Christmas and New Year), minimum 3 nights.

Low season per wk
£195.00–£285.00
High season per wk
£354.00–£597.00

★★★-★★★★

16 Units
Sleeping 4–6

OUTCHESTER & ROSS FARM COTTAGES

Belford
Contact: Mrs S McKie, 1 Cragview Road, Belford NE70 7NT
T: (01668) 213336
F: (01668) 219385
E: enquiry@rosscottages.co.uk
I: www.rosscottages.co.uk

Ross is in a superb location near the sea between Bamburgh and Holy Island – really 'away from it all'. Outchester Manor Cottages won the Northumbria Tourist Board 'Pride of Northumbria Award' for self-catering cottages in 2001. Please phone/fax for our colour brochure, or visit our website.

OPEN All Year

Low season per wk
£195.00–£350.00
High season per wk
£275.00–£590.00

★★★

5 Units
Sleeping 2–5

POINT COTTAGES

Bamburgh
Contact: Mrs E Sanderson
T: (0191) 2662800
F: (0191) 2151630
E: info@bamburgh-cottages.co.uk
I: www.bamburgh-cottages.co.uk

OPEN All Year

Low season per wk
£190.00–£250.00
High season per wk
£400.00–£450.00

Cluster of cottages, with fine sea views, located next to golf course. Furnished to a high standard with log fires and large garden.

★★

2 Units
Sleeping 7–10

SAINT OSWALD'S/SAINT AIDAN'S

Bamburgh
Contact: Anthony Smith, 10 Aldbourne Road, London W12 0LN
T: (020) 8248 9589
F: (020) 8248 9587
E: quintin.smith@btinternet.com

Large Victorian family house, three floors, divided into two independent holiday homes. Superbly placed at foot of Bamburgh's charming village and nearest castle, green, beach, dunes. Spacious rooms, conservatories, congenial atmosphere, ample parking, open fire places, garden. Owned by same family since 1892.

OPEN All Year

Low season per wk
£230.00–£320.00
High season per wk
£500.00–£590.00

BAMBURGH continued

★★★

1 Unit
Sleeping 4

WHINSTONE COTTAGE
Bamburgh
Contact: Mrs P J Tait
T: (0191) 2851363

OPEN All Year

Low season per wk
£225.00–£295.00
High season per wk
£295.00–£420.00

Victorian, stone, terraced cottage in Bamburgh. One double, one twin. Bathroom with bath/electric shower. Modern kitchen. Small, sunny garden. Sandy beaches within walking distance.

BARNARD CASTLE, Durham Map ref 5B3 *Tourist Information Centre Tel: (01833) 690909*

★★★★

2 Units
Sleeping 2–6

HAUXWELL COTTAGES (BUMPKIN BYRE AND PUDDLES END)
Barnard Castle
Contact: Mrs P A Clark, Hauxwell Grange, Marwood, Barnard Castle DL12 8QU
T: (01833) 695022
F: (01833) 695022
E: jdclark@mail.sci-net.co.uk

OPEN All Year

Low season per wk
£170.00–£195.00
High season per wk
£240.00–£330.00

Converted farm buildings.Cottage 1: two bedrooms, bathroom, sitting room, dining/kitchen, cloakroom. Cottage 2: bedroom, shower room, large sitting room/dining/kitchen. Separate garden terraces.

★★★★

2 Units
Sleeping 2–5

STAINDROP HOUSE MEWS & ARCHES

Staindrop, Darlington
Contact: Mrs D J Walton, Staindrop House, 14 Front Street, Staindrop, Darlington DL2 3NH
T: (01833) 660951
E: shmholidays@teesdaleonline.co.uk

Converted stable units comprising one/two reception rooms, bathroom, shower room, fitted kitchen and small balcony. The unit with two reception rooms also has a beamed ceiling. Pretty countryside village, A1 (M) 12 miles. Use of large, landscaped garden with children's play area. All linen provided.

OPEN All Year

Coal fire (first bucket of coal free). Bottle of wine in fridge.

Low season per wk
Min £180.00
High season per wk
Max £400.00

★★★★

1 Unit
Sleeping 3

VILLAGE GREEN COTTAGE

Ovington, Richmond
Contact: Mrs M J Green, The Cottage, Village Green, Ovington, Richmond DL11 7BW
T: (01833) 627331
I: www.teesdaleholidays.co.uk/villagegreencottage.htm

Enjoy a taste of luxury in this cosy 18thC cottage overlooking village green, with oak-beamed ceilings, wood-panelled hallway, timber flooring and pretty bedrooms enhanced by lace, porcelain and dried flowers. A walk leads from patio through delightful garden to heated summerhouse with fantastic views, field and pond.

OPEN All Year

Fresh fruit, flowers, wine and milk on arrival. 3-night stays available Oct-Mar (excl Christmas and New Year) – £120.

Low season per wk
£200.00
High season per wk
£262.00–£310.00

★★★

1 Unit
Sleeping 5

WACKFORD SQUEERS COTTAGE
Cotherstone, Barnard Castle
Contact: Mr John Braithwaite, Wackford Squeers Cottage, Wodencroft, Cotherstone, Barnard Castle DL12 9UQ
T: (01833) 650032
F: (01833) 650909
E: wodencroft@freenet.co.uk

OPEN All Year

Low season per wk
£160.00–£200.00
High season per wk
£240.00–£340.00

Open-beamed cottage on quiet Teesdale farm in unspoilt countryside. Easy access long-distance paths. Easy drive to Lakes and Yorkshire Dales.

BEADNELL, Northumberland Map ref 5C1

★★★

1 Unit
Sleeping 8

BEECHLEY
Beadnell, Chathill
Contact: Mrs D Baker, 22 Upper Green Way, Tingley, Wakefield WF3 1TA
T: (0113) 2189176
F: (0113) 2189176
E: deb_n_ade@hotmail.com

OPEN All Year except Christmas

Low season per wk
£300.00–£400.00
High season per wk
£450.00–£560.00

A four-bedroomed, centrally heated house on the seafront. Modern fitted kitchen, enclosed rear garden, sea view from all bedrooms. Fuel and linen included.

★★★-★★★★★

7 Units
Sleeping 2–5

TOWN FARM COTTAGES

Beadnell, Seahouses
Contact: Mr & Mrs P Thompson & Mrs License, Heritage Coast Holidays, 6G Greensfield Court, Alnwick NE66 2DE
T: (01655) 606022
F: (01670) 787336
E: paulthompson@alncom.net
I: www.northumberland-holidays.com

17thC stable block converted to cottages and apartments. Close to the sea and beaches, ideal for exploring lovely Northumbria. Easy walk to beach. Short distance to beautiful Bamburgh Castle and Holy Isle. Seahouses and Farne Isle three miles. Alnwick Gardens and Castle easily accessible, plus Heritage Coast and National Park.

OPEN All Year
CC: Amex, Delta, Mastercard, Switch, Visa

Short breaks available in low season.

Low season per wk
£145.00–£250.00
High season per wk
£225.00–£420.00

BELFORD, Northumberland Map ref 5B1

★★★

3 Units
Sleeping 4–6

3, 4 & 5 SWINHOE COTTAGES
Belford
Contact: Mrs V Nixon, Swinhoe Farm House, Belford NE70 7LJ
T: (01668) 213370
E: valerie@swinhoecottages.co.uk
I: www.swinhoecottages.co.uk

OPEN All Year

Low season per wk
Min £150.00
High season per wk
Max £380.00

Well-equipped cottages on working farm. Many walks including St Cuthbert's Cave. Approximately 10 minutes' drive from Bamburgh, with its sandy beaches, and Holy Island.

BELLINGHAM, Northumberland Map ref 5B2 *Tourist Information Centre Tel: (01434) 220616*

★★★★

1 Unit
Sleeping 5

CONHEATH COTTAGE
Bellingham, Hexham
Contact: Mrs Z Riddle, Blakelaw Farm, Bellingham, Hexham NE48 2EF
T: (01434) 220250
F: (01434) 220250
E: stay@conheath.co.uk
I: www.conheath.co.uk

OPEN All Year

Low season per wk
Min £200.00
High season per wk
Max £375.00

Quiet, semi-detached cottage. Stunning views. Very well equipped and comfortable. Centrally heated with open fire. Garden with accessories. Beautiful indoor heated swimming pool. Ideal location.

BERWICK-UPON-TWEED, Northumberland Map ref 5B1

★★★

1 Unit
Sleeping 5

BROADSTONE COTTAGE
Norham, Berwick-upon-Tweed
Contact: Mr E D Chantler, Broadstone Farm, Grafty Green, Maidstone ME17 2AT
T: (01622) 850207
F: (01622) 851750

OPEN All Year

Low season per wk
£130.00–£180.00
High season per wk
£200.00–£320.00

Village cottage. Ideal centre for touring, walking, fishing holidays. Twenty minutes beach. Shops, pubs nearby. Full central heating. Bathroom with shower.

BISHOP AUCKLAND, Durham Map ref 5C2 *Tourist Information Centre Tel: (01388) 604922*

★★★★

1 Unit
Sleeping 5

Victorian miner's cottage with country views, at edge of village, opposite the owners' guesthouse. Well-equipped, with facilities for five guests to sleep in two bedrooms. Lawn, gardens and parking to the front and side. Ideal centre for Durham City and World Heritage Site, Beamish, North Yorkshire and Northumbria. Dogs welcome.

FIVE GABLES COTTAGE

Binchester, Bishop Auckland
Contact: Mr P & Mrs J Weston, Five Gables Guest House, Binchester, Bishop Auckland DL14 8AT
T: (01388) 608204
F: (01388) 663092
E: cottage@fivegables.co.uk
I: www.fivegables.co.uk

OPEN All Year
CC: Delta, JCB, Mastercard, Solo, Switch, Visa

3-night breaks available in low season (excl Christmas and New Year). Special offers advertised on our website.

Low season per wk
£230.00–£260.00
High season per wk
£260.00–£330.00

★★★★

1 Unit
Sleeping 4

WEST COTTAGE
Rushyford, Ferryhill
Contact: Mrs E Wilkinson, Carrsides Farm, Rushyford, Ferryhill DL17 0NJ
T: (01388) 720252
F: (01388) 720252
E: carrsides@farming.co.uk

OPEN All Year
CC: Visa

Low season per wk
£200.00–£250.00
High season per wk
£250.00–£300.00

Delightful old cart shed converted into attractive 2-bedroomed cottage. Ideally situated for touring holiday.

BLANCHLAND, Northumberland Map ref 5B2

★★★

1 Unit
Sleeping 4

Set in beautiful moorland, this is our family retreat. Two-bedroomed stone cottage with log stove, historic features and comfortable pine furnishings. Main bedroom recently refurbished. Central heating, telephone, VCR, garden with barbecue and stunning views. Sailing, fishing and golf nearby, 40 minutes to Beamish, Hadrian's Wall and Durham. Favourite honeymoon destination!

BOLTSLAW COTTAGE

Blanchland, Consett
Contact: Mrs N Smith, 6 Selborne Avenue, Gateshead NE9 6ET
T: (0191) 4879456
F: (01670) 510300
E: asmith6000@aol.com
I: www.uk-holiday-cottages.co.uk/boltslaw

OPEN All Year
CC: Mastercard

Mid-week breaks outside school holidays £25 per night.

Low season per wk
£175.00–£195.00
High season per wk
£195.00–£260.00

CHECK THE MAPS

The colour maps at the front of this guide show all the cities, towns and villages for which you will find accommodation entries. Refer to the town index to find the page on which they are listed.

BYRNESS, Northumberland Map ref 5B1

★★★★

1 Unit
Sleeping 4

THE OLD SCHOOL HOUSE

Byrness, Rochester, Newcastle upon Tyne
Contact: Dales Holiday Cottages, Carleton Business Park, Carleton New Road, Skipton BD23 2DG
T: (01756) 799821
F: (01756) 797012

On Pennine Way with views over Kielder Forest Park. Northumbrian single-storey, stone cottage under slate. Exterior restored in vernacular style. Interior remodelled in pine with attic bedrooms and modern facilities. Spacious and cosy with oil-fired Rayburn for central heating and cooking. Excellent for touring Borders and Cheviot Hills.

OPEN All Year

Low season per wk
Min £214.00
High season per wk
Min £367.00

CASTLESIDE, Durham Map ref 5B2

★★-★★★

3 Units
Sleeping 4–5

GARDEN COTTAGE, DAIRY COTTAGE & THE FORGE

Castleside, Consett
Contact: Mr & Mrs Elliot, Derwent Grange Farm, Castleside, Consett DH8 9BN
T: (01207) 508358
E: ekelliot@aol.com

Charming cottages converted from farm buildings, set on a working sheep farm, provide a serene, relaxing holiday. Access to all the wonderful countryside, tourist attractions and the cities of Newcastle and Durham is easy. Local supermarkets are plentiful. Local pubs and hotels provide good food.

Low season per wk
£200.00–£225.00
High season per wk
£200.00–£250.00

CHATHILL, Northumberland Map ref 5C1

★★

2 Units
Sleeping 5

NEWSTEAD COTTAGE
Chathill
Contact: Mrs M Riddell
T: (01665) 589263

A mixed farm, four miles from unspoilt beaches. Ideal for touring. Numerous castles, golf courses and the famous Fenwick Gardens within a 10-mile radius.

Low season per wk
£160.00–£200.00
High season per wk
£300.00–£350.00

CHOPWELL, Tyne and Wear Map ref 5B2

★★★★

1 Unit
Sleeping 4

HIGH PASTURE COTTAGE

Chopwell, Newcastle upon Tyne
Contact: Mr A Low, Bowser Hill Farm, Chopwell, Newcastle upon Tyne NE17 7AY
T: (01207) 560881
E: alow@btinternet.com

Converted 17thC barn perched high above Derwent Valley with superb long-distance views. Furnished to a very high standard with beams and logburning stove. Conveniently situated 15 minutes from MetroCentre, 12 miles from Hexham market town and within easy reach of Hadrian's Wall, Durham City and the coast.

OPEN All Year

Low season per wk
£180.00–£220.00
High season per wk
£240.00–£340.00

VISITOR ATTRACTIONS **For ideas on places to visit refer to the introduction at the beginning of this section. Look out too for the ETC's Quality Assured Visitor Attraction signs.**

CORBRIDGE, Northumberland Map ref 5B2

★★★★

1 Unit
Sleeping 6

OSWALD COTTAGE

Corbridge
Contact: Mrs H K Harriman, Swarden House,
Kyloe House Farm, Eachwick, Newcastle upon Tyne
NE18 0BB
T: (01661) 852909
F: (01661) 854106
E: pwh@littonproperties.co.uk

Exceptional 18thC double-fronted large stone cottage. Carved external Latin inscription 'To the good all things are good' reflects interior ambience, beams and open fire. In heart of historic village but quiet. Stone's throw from river and superb local shops. Lovely patio garden. Perfect, winter or summer.

OPEN All Year

Low season per wk
£250.00–£350.00
High season per wk
£350.00–£500.00

★★★★

1 Unit
Sleeping 4

WALLHOUSES SOUTH FARM COTTAGE

Corbridge
Contact: Mrs E Lymburn, South Farm, Military Road,
Corbridge NE45 5PU
T: (01434) 672388
E: loraip@aol.com

OPEN All Year
CC: Visa

Low season per wk
£280.00–£340.00
High season per wk
£340.00–£390.00

Traditional two-bedroomed stone cottage in countryside location, on route of Roman Wall between Corbridge and Matfen. Pleasant garden, original features, fully refurbished.

COTHERSTONE, Durham Map ref 5B3

★★★

1 Unit
Sleeping 6

FARTHINGS

Cotherstone, Barnard Castle
Contact: Mr C J Bainbridge, Glen Leigh, Cotherstone,
Barnard Castle DL12 9QW
T: (01833) 650331

Comfortable stone-built bungalow overlooking village green. Two bedrooms (double and twin), gas central heating, living room fire. Well equipped and decorated.

OPEN All Year

Low season per wk
£100.00–£190.00
High season per wk
£190.00–£270.00

DARLINGTON, Tees Valley Map ref 5C3 *Tourist Information Centre Tel: (01325) 388666*

★★★

1 Unit
Sleeping 4

PEGASUS COTTAGE

Darlington
Contact: Mr & Mrs S Chapman, 4 Tees View,
Hurworth Place, Darlington DL2 2DH
T: (01325) 722542
F: (01325) 722542
E: stuart1948@msn.com
I: www.pegasuscottage.co.uk

OPEN All Year
CC: Delta, Mastercard,
Solo, Switch, Visa

Low season per wk
£220.00–£270.00
High season per wk
£270.00–£320.00

Converted stable block of a Grade II Listed building, c1850. Local mayor's Design Award winner 1995. Set in small village three miles from Darlington.

WEB

www.visitengland.com

Log on for information and inspiration. The latest information on places to visit, events and quality assessed accommodation.

DURHAM, Durham Map ref 5C2 *Tourist Information Centre Tel: (0191) 384 3720*

★★★★

1 Unit
Sleeping 4

THE OLD POWER HOUSE

Plawsworth, Chester-le-Street
Contact: Mrs A Hall, Garden Cottage, Southill Hall, Plawsworth, Chester-le-Street DH3 4EQ
T: (0191) 3873001
F: (0191) 3893569
E: g.s.hall@talk21.com

Recently redeveloped former power house set in walled garden of old hall, providing compact two-bedroomed country cottage set in three acres of landscaped gardens. Idyllic location midway between Durham City (three miles) and Chester-le-Street (three miles). Newcastle, Sunderland and MetroCentre (Gateshead) within 25 minutes' drive.

OPEN All Year except Christmas

Low season per wk
£220.00–£260.00
High season per wk
£250.00–£325.00

EMBLETON, Northumberland Map ref 5C1

★★★

4 Units
Sleeping 2–4

DUNSTANBURGH CASTLE COURTYARD COTTAGES

Embleton, Alnwick
Contact: Mr & Mrs P Thompson & Mrs License, Heritage Coast Holidays, 6G Greensfield Court, Alnwick NE66 2DE
T: (01665) 606022
F: (01670) 787336
E: paulthompson@alncom.net
I: www.northumberland-holidays.com

17thC coach house converted to cottages in the quiet village of Embleton. An easy walk to the superb Embleton Beach and Dunstanburgh Castle. Ideal for exploring lovely Northumbria, the Heritage Coastline, Holy Island, Alnwick Castle and gardens and the National Park.

OPEN All Year

Short breaks available in low season.

Low season per wk
£145.00–£250.00
High season per wk
£225.00–£420.00

★★★★

3 Units
Sleeping 3–6

NORTHUMBRIAN HOLIDAY COTTAGES

Embleton, Alnwick
Contact: Mr & Mrs C J Seal, 1 Westfield, Gosforth, Newcastle upon Tyne NE3 4YE
T: (0191) 2856930
F: (0191) 2856930
E: seal@northumbrian-holiday-cottages.co.uk
I: www.northumbrian-holiday-cottages.co.uk

Quality properties in Embleton village offering the ultimate in tranquillity, luxury and character. Secluded, south-facing gardens and great emphasis on the provision of comfort and peace of mind. Ideal location for exploring Northumbrian coast, hills and castles. Enjoy a warm welcome and personal attention. This is a family-run business.

OPEN All Year

Low season per wk
£210.00–£230.00
High season per wk
£490.00–£525.00

ACCESSIBILITY

Look for the symbols which indicate National Accessible Scheme standards for hearing and visually impaired guests in addition to standards for guests with mobility impairment. Additional participants are shown in the listings at the back.

FROSTERLEY, Durham Map ref 5B2

★★★★
1 Unit
Sleeping 9

THE OLD SUNDAY SCHOOL
Frosterley
Contact: Mrs P Blayney, The Old Sunday School, Bridge End, Frosterley DL13 2SN
T: (01388) 528913
F: (01388) 528913
E: pat@theoss.freeserve.co.uk

OPEN All Year

Low season per wk
£450.00–£545.00
High season per wk
£650.00–£760.00

Wing of an attractively converted school, in a peaceful designated Area of Outstanding Natural Beauty, convenient for all Northumbria and Cumbria.

HALTWHISTLE, Northumberland Map ref 5B2 *Tourist Information Centre Tel: (01434) 322002*

★★★★
5 Units
Sleeping 2–7

SCOTCHCOULTHARD
Haltwhistle
Contact: Mrs S Saunders, Scotchcoulthard, Haltwhistle NE49 9NH
T: (01434) 344470
F: (01434) 344020
E: cottages@scotchcoulthard.co.uk
I: www.scotchcoulthard.co.uk

OPEN All Year
CC: Amex, Mastercard, Switch, Visa

Low season per wk
£180.00–£350.00
High season per wk
£370.00–£740.00

Stone cottages set in 178 acres, north of Hadrian's Wall. Open fires, original beams, indoor pool and large games room. Spectacular views and wildlife.

HAMSTERLEY, Durham Map ref 5B2

★★★
2 Units
Sleeping 4

EDGE KNOLL FARM COTTAGES
Hamsterley, Bishop Auckland
Contact: Mr M G Edmonds, Edge Knoll Farm, Hamsterley, Bishop Auckland DL13 3PF
T: (01388) 488537
E: vacationfarm@hotmail.com

Converted from 17thC farm buildings, set around a peaceful cobbled courtyard amid beautiful countryside, the cottages are ideally placed for walking, sightseeing, wildlife and bird-watching. Within easy walking distance of the region's best attractions as well as the major shopping towns. Horse riding, shooting and fishing are all available locally.

OPEN All Year

Low season per wk
£300.00–£325.00
High season per wk
£325.00–£350.00

★★
2 Units
Sleeping 4

WEST HOPPYLAND CABINS
Hamsterley, Bishop Auckland
Contact: Mrs C J Atkinson, West Hoppyland Cabins, Hamsterley, Bishop Auckland DL13 3NP
T: (01388) 488196
E: westhoppyland@hotmail.com
I: www.geocities.com/westhoppyland

Cosy lodges set in peaceful birch wood with lovely views over Hamsterley Forest. Designated an Area of Outstanding Natural Beauty in the northern Dales. An ideal base for touring the Dales or for outdoor activities. Pony trekking and cycle hire on site. Owners at hand to help.

10% reduction on treks for people staying in lodges.

Low season per wk
£175.00–£200.00
High season per wk
£210.00–£280.00

HAMSTERLEY FOREST

See under Barnard Castle, Bishop Auckland, Frosterley, Stanhope, Wolsingham

SB

SPECIAL BREAKS
Many establishments offer special promotions and themed breaks. These are highlighted in red. (All such offers are subject to availability.)

HEDDON-ON-THE-WALL, Northumberland Map ref 5B2

★★★

1 Unit
Sleeping 7

2 EAST TOWN HOUSE
Heddon-on-the-Wall, Newcastle upon Tyne
Contact: Mr C & Mrs B Amos
T: (01661) 852277
F: (01661) 853063

OPEN All Year

Low season per wk
£230.00–£280.00
High season per wk
£340.00–£390.00

Stone-built, well-equipped house furnished to a high standard, in historic village on Hadrian's Wall. Only six miles to Newcastle, 20 minutes from Hexham.

HOLY ISLAND, Northumberland Map ref 5C1

★★★

2 Units
Sleeping 4

FARNE COURT COTTAGE, FARNE VIEW COTTAGE
Holy Island, Berwick-upon-Tweed
Contact: Mrs A J Batty, Orchard Gap, Aydon Road,
Corbridge NE45 5EJ
T: (01434) 632691
F: (01434) 634170
E: angelabatty@ukonline.co.uk

Low season per wk
£220.00–£250.00
High season per wk
£425.00–£495.00

18thC cottages in private courtyard setting. Stone built, one with private garden.

KIELDER, Northumberland Map ref 5B1

★★★★-★★★★★

33 Units
Sleeping 4–6

KIELDER LODGES
Kielder Water & Forest Park
Contact: Hoseasons Holidays Limited, Sunway House,
Lowestoft NR32 3LT
T: 0870 333 2000
F: (01502) 584962
E: kielder.water@nwl.co.uk
I: www.kielder.org

Luxury, Scandanavian-style forest lodges, quiet surroundings of Kielder Water and Forest Park. Excellent base for watersports, mountain biking and walking. Other facilities include swimming pool and sauna, lakeside restaurant and bar. Crazy golf, ferry trips and birds of prey centre.

CC: Mastercard, Switch, Visa

Short breaks available Feb-Dec (some exclusions apply at peak times).

Low season per wk
£230.00–£375.00
High season per wk
£375.00–£690.00

KIELDER WATER & FOREST PARK

See under Bellingham, Kielder, Wark, West Woodburn

LONGHORSLEY, Northumberland Map ref 5C1

★★★

1 Unit
Sleeping 2

CARTWHEEL COTTAGE
Longhorsley, Morpeth
Contact: Mr & Mrs J Chisholm, Westerheugh Farm,
Longhorsley, Morpeth NE65 8RH
T: (01665) 570661
E: sarah@cartwheelcottage.com

Cottage set on working farm. Central for coast and towns of Alnwick, Rothbury and Morpeth. Close to NT properties, Cragside and Wallington. Sleeps two upstairs, double or twin. Ground floor consists of sitting/dining room with sofa bed, large kitchen, and bathroom with a shower over bath. Brochure available.

OPEN All Year except Christmas

3 nights £120, Oct-Mar.

Low season per wk
£160.00–£200.00
High season per wk
£240.00–£260.00

CHECK THE MAPS

The colour maps at the front of this guide show all the cities, towns and villages for which you will find accommodation entries.
Refer to the town index to find the page on which they are listed.

MIDDLETON-IN-TEESDALE, Durham Map ref 5B3 *Tourist Information Centre Tel: (01833) 641001*

★★★
1 Unit
Sleeping 6

COUNTRY COTTAGE
Middleton-in-Teesdale
Contact: Mr R B Burman, Fairlawn, 1 Thorn Road, Bramhall, Stockport SK7 1HG
T: (0161) 8607123
E: robinburman@robinburman.com

OPEN All Year

Low season per wk
Min £150.00
High season per wk
Max £310.00

200-year-old cottage in quiet, peaceful location with superb views, surrounded by farmland. Excellent walking countryside.

★★★
1 Unit
Sleeping 2

FIRETHORN COTTAGE
Middleton-in-Teesdale, Barnard Castle
Contact: Mrs J Thompson, Cutbush Farmhouse, Hardingham Road, Hingham, Norwich NR9 4LY
T: (01953) 850364

OPEN All Year

Low season per wk
£120.00–£130.00
High season per wk
£130.00–£160.00

Stone-built lead miner's cottage, 1 up/1 down, flagstone floors, traditional rag rugs, beamed ceilings. Superb walking, fishing, pubs and restaurants.

MINDRUM, Northumberland Map ref 5B1

★★
1 Unit
Sleeping 4

BOWMONT COTTAGE
Mindrum
Contact: Mr & Mrs S Orpwood, Bowmont Hill, Mindrum TD12 4QW
T: (01890) 850266
F: (01890) 850245
E: s.orpwood@farmline.com
I: www.cottageguide.co.uk/bowmonthill

OPEN All Year

Low season per wk
£130.00–£175.00
High season per wk
£175.00–£275.00

Two-bedroomed cottage on arable and livestock farm with bathroom and separate shower. Log fire, kitchen/dining room with oil-fired Raeburn. Cot, high chair. Dogs by arrangement. Fishing.

NEWCASTLE UPON TYNE, Tyne and Wear Map ref 5C2 *Tourist Information Centre Tel: (0191) 277 8000*

★★★
1 Unit
Sleeping 6

135 AUDLEY ROAD
South Gosforth, Newcastle upon Tyne
Contact: Miss L K Wright, 137 Audley Road, South Gosforth, Newcastle upon Tyne NE3 1QH
T: (0191) 2856374
E: lkw@audleyender.fsnet.co.uk
I: www.audleyender.fsnet.co.uk

OPEN All Year

Low season per wk
£250.00–£300.00
High season per wk
£250.00–£300.00

Self-contained flat, close to shops and Metro and with easy access to city centre. All amenities.

NEWTON-BY-THE-SEA, Northumberland Map ref 5C1

★★★★
3 Units
Sleeping 5–6

NEWTON HALL COTTAGES
Newton-by-the-Sea, Alnwick
Contact: Mrs S A Patterson
T: (01665) 576239
F: (01665) 576900
E: patterson@newtonholidays.co.uk
I: www.recommended-cottages.co.uk

OPEN All Year
CC: Delta, JCB, Mastercard, Switch, Visa

Low season per wk
£215.00–£270.00
High season per wk
£240.00–£525.00

Quality, spacious, Georgian accommodation with two acres of gardens. Ideal base to enjoy magnificent coastline and panoramic countryside.

TOWN INDEX

This can be found at the back of this guide. If you know where you want to stay, the index will give you the page number listing accommodation in your chosen town, city or village.

NORHAM, Northumberland Map ref 5B1

★★★
1 Unit
Sleeping 10

THE BOATHOUSE
Norham, Berwick-upon-Tweed
Contact: Mr G J Crabtree & Mrs Chantler,
Great Humphries Farm, Grafty Green, Maidstone
ME17 2AX
T: (01622) 859672
F: (01622) 859672
E: chantler@humphreys46.fsnet.com
I: www.recommended-cottages.co.uk

OPEN All Year

Low season per wk
£400.00–£475.00
High season per wk
£500.00–£850.00

Period cottage with frontage to River Tweed and spectacular views. Spacious, well-equipped accommodation. Fishing can be arranged, subject to availability.

OVINGTON, Northumberland Map ref 5B2

★★★★
1 Unit
Sleeping 4

WESTGARTH COTTAGE
Ovington
Contact: Mrs C Graham, Stonecroft, Ovington
NE42 6EB
T: (01661) 832202

OPEN All Year

Low season per wk
£260.00–£300.00
High season per wk
£300.00–£400.00

Attractive stone-built cottage in a small, peaceful village surrounded by beautiful countryside, near the historic towns of Hexham and Corbridge.

ROTHBURY, Northumberland Map ref 5B1 *Tourist Information Centre Tel: (01669) 620887*

★★★★
1 Unit
Sleeping 4

THE OLD TELEPHONE EXCHANGE
Rothbury, Morpeth
Contact: Ms S Doncaster
T: (01669) 621858
E: tery.foreman@virgin.net

OPEN All Year

Low season per wk
£175.00–£180.00
High season per wk
£255.00–£290.00

A cleverly converted cottage in the village centre, yet quietly tucked away. Close to the hills, and the coast only a 20-mile drive away.

★★★★★
1 Unit
Sleeping 4

THE PELE TOWER
Rothbury
Contact: Mr D Malia, The Pele Tower, Whitton,
Rothbury NE65 7RL
T: (01669) 620410
F: (01669) 621006
E: davidmalia@aol.com
I: www.thepeletower.com

OPEN All Year
CC: Mastercard, Visa

Low season per wk
£240.00–£400.00
High season per wk
£400.00–£600.00

19thC wing of Northumbrian pele tower, origins 1380. Includes whirlpool bath, dishwasher, satellite TV and video. Mountain bikes. Sorry, no smoking and no pets.

SALTBURN-BY-THE-SEA, Tees Valley Map ref 5C3 *Tourist Information Centre Tel: (01287) 622422*

★★★
1 Unit
Sleeping 4

THE ZETLAND
Saltburn-by-the-Sea
Contact: Mrs J Carter, 1 Hawthorn Grove, Yarm
TS15 9EZ
T: (01642) 782507
E: graham@howard95.freeserve.co.uk
I: www.carter-steel.co.uk

OPEN All Year

Low season per wk
£180.00–£250.00
High season per wk
£250.00–£300.00

Most famous building in Saltburn, the old Zetland Hotel, an imposing Victorian building. Second floor, two-bedroom apartment with spectacular views of the sea, cliffs and surrounding countryside.

MAP REFERENCES The map references refer to the colour maps at the front of this guide. The first figure is the map number; the letter and figure which follow indicate the grid reference on the map.

SEAHOUSES, Northumberland Map ref 5C1

★★★

4 Units
Sleeping 3

Cottages in their own courtyard, close to the harbour. Within yards of the village and the country's most beautiful beaches and castles. An ideal base for walking, cycling, golfing etc. All cottages: one bedroom, lounge/kitchen/diner, shower room. Communal laundry room. Private parking. Linen and electricity included.

CLIFF HOUSE COTTAGES

Seahouses
Contact: Mrs J Forsyth, Westfield Farmhouse, North Sunderland, Seahouses NE68 7UR
T: (01665) 720161
F: (01665) 720713
E: enquiries@cliffhousecottages.co.uk
I: www.cliffhousecottages.co.uk

OPEN All Year
CC: Amex, Delta, Mastercard, Switch, Visa

Low season per wk
£200.00–£330.00
High season per wk
£250.00–£350.00

★★★★

1 Unit
Sleeping 4

KIPPER COTTAGE

Seahouses
Contact: Country Holidays Ref:80171, Country Holidays, Spring Mill, Earby, Barnoldswick BB94 0AA
T: 08700 781200
I: www.country-holidays.co.uk

OPEN All Year
CC: Amex, Delta, Mastercard, Visa

Low season per wk
£250.00–£350.00
High season per wk
£275.00–£500.00

Originally a former smoke house. Set in a quiet square close to all local amenities and harbour. Private parking.

12

SEDGEFIELD, Durham Map ref 5C2

★★

1 Unit
Sleeping 9

SPRUCELY FARM COTTAGE

Sedgefield, Stockton-on-Tees
Contact: Mr S R Harris, Sprucely Farm, Sedgefield, Stockton-on-Tees TS21 2BD
T: (01740) 620378
E: barbara@sprucely.fsnet.co.uk
I: sprucely.fsnet.co.uk

OPEN All Year

Low season per wk
£200.00–£400.00
High season per wk
£200.00–£400.00

A working farm surrounded by beautiful open countryside. Ideally situated as a touring holiday base, with easy access to the A1. Visit Northumberland or Yorkshire.

SOUTH SHIELDS, Tyne and Wear Map ref 5C2 *Tourist Information Centre Tel: (0191) 454 6612*

★★★

2 Units
Sleeping 4

36 & 38 ECCLESTON ROAD

South Shields
Contact: Mrs K Cole, 9 Sea Way, South Shields NE33 2NQ
T: (0191) 4561802

OPEN All Year

Low season per wk
Max £210.00
High season per wk
Max £210.00

Ground floor flat with two bedrooms. Living room, kitchen, bathroom and shower, TV/video, washing machine. Children welcome, linen provided. Near parks and seafront.

COUNTRY CODE Always follow the Country Code · Enjoy the countryside and respect its life and work · Guard against all risk of fire · Fasten all gates · Keep your dogs under close control · Keep to public paths across farmland · Use gates and stiles to cross fences, hedges and walls · Leave livestock, crops and machinery alone · Take your litter home · Help to keep all water clean · Protect wildlife, plants and trees · Take special care on country roads · Make no unnecessary noise

STANHOPE, Durham Map ref 5B2 *Tourist Information Centre Tel: (01388) 527650*

★★

1 Unit
Sleeping 6

PRIMROSE COTTAGE

Stanhope, Bishop Auckland
Contact: Mrs D P Dickson
T: (01228) 573337
F: (01228) 573338
E: enquiries@northumbria-byways.com
I: www.northumbria-byways.com

Large, stone-built, three-bedroomed cottage in England's last great wilderness, yet with all modern conveniences and within walking distance of shops, tourist information centre, banks etc. The cottage is in a high position with superb views of Weardale. Two separate central heating systems and double glazing throughout ensure comfort.

OPEN All Year
CC: Delta, JCB, Mastercard, Solo, Switch, Visa

Short breaks available (special conditions apply).

Low season per wk
£210.00–£260.00
High season per wk
£246.00–£349.00

STOCKSFIELD, Northumberland Map ref 5B2

★★★

1 Unit
Sleeping 4

MOUNT FLAGGON

Stocksfield
Contact: Mrs B Smith, North View House, Hedley on the Hill, Stocksfield NE43 7SW
T: (01661) 843867
F: (01661) 844097
E: gsmith@compuserve.com

OPEN All Year

Low season per wk
£220.00–£250.00
High season per wk
£310.00–£380.00

Semi-detached cottage with garden and patio in small picturesque village with wonderful views and superb pub food a stroll away. Close to Durham, Newcastle, Hexham.

WAREN MILL, Northumberland Map ref 5C1

★★★★

1 Unit
Sleeping 5

EIDER COTTAGE

Waren Mill, Belford
Contact: Mrs S Turnbull, 1 Friars Court, Bamburgh NE69 7AE
T: (01668) 214494
E: theturnbulls2k@btinternet.com

OPEN All Year

Low season per wk
£200.00–£350.00
High season per wk
£300.00–£450.00

This charming, stone-built, former miller's cottage is situated yards from Budle Bay, a renowned bird-watching area near Bamburgh. Ideal base for exploring Northumberland.

WARK, Northumberland Map ref 5B2

★★★★

1 Unit
Sleeping 6

THE HEMMEL

Wark, Hexham
Contact: Mrs A Nichol, Hetherington, Wark, Hexham NE48 3DR
T: (01434) 230260
F: (01434) 230260
E: alan_nichol@hotmail.com
I: www.hetheringtonfarm.co.uk

Low season per wk
£200.00–£250.00
High season per wk
£285.00–£387.00

Excellent converted farm building, all mod cons. Lovely rural setting close to Hadrian's Wall. Ideal walking, touring or relaxing holiday. Well recommended.

★★★

1 Unit
Sleeping 4

ROSES BOWER

Wark, Hexham
Contact: Mr L & Mrs S Watson, Roses Bower, Wark, Hexham NE48 3DX
T: (01434) 230779
F: (01434) 230779
E: sandlwatson@rosesbower.fsworld.co.uk
I: http://roses-bower.co.uk

OPEN All Year

Low season per wk
£157.00–£184.00
High season per wk
£190.00–£295.00

A cosy cottage in the grounds of Roses Bower, a working sheep farm in a magnificent location on The Warksburn, within the Northumbrian National Park.

WEST WOODBURN, Northumberland Map ref 5B2

★★★

1 Unit
Sleeping 4

THE HOLLOW

West Woodburn, Hexham
Contact: Mrs M S Robson, Nunnykirk East Lodge, Netherwitton, Morpeth NE61 4PB
T: (01670) 772580

Comfortable, 19thC, two-bedroomed cottage in peaceful, unspoilt wooded valley on edge of National Park. Fifteen miles north Corbridge, 0.25 miles A68, one mile south-west West Woodburn village. Within easy reach of golf courses, Hadrian's Wall, Kielder Reservoir, castles, houses, gardens and many other attractions of this beautiful border county of Northumberland.

OPEN All Year

3-night stays available autumn and spring. All year – reduced price for only 2 people staying.

Low season per wk
£195.00–£280.00
High season per wk
£280.00–£330.00

WHITLEY BAY, Tyne and Wear Map ref 5C2 *Tourist Information Centre Tel: (0191) 200 8535*

★★★

6 Units
Sleeping 2–6

SEAFRONT APARTMENTS

Cullercoats, By Whitley Bay
Contact: Mr A & Mrs R Webb, Seafront Apartments, 46 Beverley Terrace, Cullercoats, Tyne and Wear NE30 4NU
T: 07977 203379
E: stay@seafront.info
I: www.seafront.info

Smart, warm apartments in Victorian terrace with unrivalled views over picturesque Cullercoats Bay. Suitable for business/leisure. Whitley Bay, Cullercoats, Tynemouth beaches have cleanliness awards. Doorstep buses. Newcastle Metro, food shops and varied restaurants within five minutes' walk. Ideal base for Newcastle's culture, Hadrian's Wall, Northumbria's castles and Durham. Shoppers' paradise.

OPEN All Year

Low season per wk
£160.00–£290.00
High season per wk
£200.00–£360.00

WINSTON, Durham Map ref 5B3

★★★★

3 Units
Sleeping 5–6

HIGHCLIFFE WATERS

Winston, Darlington
Contact: Mr & Mrs Hodson
T: (01325) 730427
F: (01325) 730740
E: mrshodson@aol.com
I: www.countryholidays.co.uk

Beautiful, fully-equipped Danish pine lodges in the heart of Teesdale. Set on the banks of the River Tees and surrounded by woodland. Private salmon and trout fishing included, excellent walking as the Teesdale Way passes through the site. An ideal base for touring the northern counties and Lake District.

OPEN All Year

Low season per wk
£155.00–£185.00
High season per wk
£320.00–£450.00

NB

IMPORTANT NOTE **Information on accommodation listed in this guide has been supplied by the proprietors. As changes may occur you are advised to check details at the time of booking.**

WITTON-LE-WEAR, Durham Map ref 5C2

★★★★

1 Unit
Sleeping 8

CARRS TERRACE

Witton-le-Wear, Bishop Auckland
Contact: Miss M Law, 93-99 Upper Richmond Road, London SW15 2TG
T: (020) 8780 1084
F: (020) 8789 9199
E: merlynlaw@aol.com

Very comfortable stone-built Victorian cottage in the charming and picturesque village of Witton-le-Wear. Four bedrooms, two bathrooms. On the village green with open panoramic views of the Wear Valley from the south-facing patio/garden. Convenient location for both Durham City and its lovely Dales.

OPEN All Year

Low season per wk
£250.00–£350.00
High season per wk
£350.00–£550.00

WOLSINGHAM, Durham Map ref 5B2

★★★

2 Units
Sleeping 4

ARDINE & ELVET COTTAGES

Wolsingham, Bishop Auckland
Contact: Mrs M Gardiner, 3 Melbourne Place, Wolsingham, Bishop Auckland DL13 3EQ
T: (01388) 527538

OPEN All Year

Low season per wk
Min £130.00
High season per wk
Max £233.00

Cosy, two-bedroomed terraced cottages overlooking small village green in old part of Wolsingham. Excellent walking and touring centre.

★★★

1 Unit
Sleeping 7

WHITFIELD HOUSE COTTAGE

Wolsingham, Bishop Auckland
Contact: Mrs M E Shepheard, 25 Front Street, Wolsingham, Bishop Auckland DL13 3DF
T: (01388) 527466
E: enquiries@whitfieldhouse.clara.net
I: www.whitfieldhouse.clara.net

OPEN All Year

Low season per wk
£180.00–£250.00
High season per wk
£250.00–£400.00

Spacious accommodation in part of an attractive Queen Anne house. Near the centre of this small town, in a designated Area of Outstanding Natural Beauty.

QUALITY ASSURANCE SCHEME

For an explanation of the quality and facilities represented by the Stars please refer to the front of this guide. A more detailed explanation can be found in the information pages at the back.

A brief guide to the main Towns and Villages offering accommodation in **Northumbria**

A **ALNMOUTH, NORTHUMBERLAND** - Quiet village with pleasant old buildings, at the mouth of the River Aln where extensive dunes and sands stretch along Alnmouth Bay. 18th C granaries, some converted to dwellings, still stand.

ALNWICK, NORTHUMBERLAND - Ancient and historic market town, entered through the Hotspur Tower, an original gate in the town walls. The medieval castle, the second biggest in England and still the seat of the Dukes of Northumberland, was restored from ruin in the 18th C.

B **BAMBURGH, NORTHUMBERLAND** - Village with a spectacular red sandstone castle standing 150 ft above the sea. On the village green the magnificent Norman church stands opposite a museum containing mementoes of the heroine Grace Darling.

BARNARD CASTLE, DURHAM - High over the Tees, a thriving market town with a busy market square. Bernard Baliol's 12th C castle (now ruins) stands nearby. The Bowes Museum, housed in a grand 19th C French chateau, holds fine paintings and furniture. Nearby are some magnificent buildings.

BEADNELL, NORTHUMBERLAND - Charming fishing village on Beadnell Bay. Seashore lime kilns (National Trust), dating from the 18th C, recall busier days as a coal and lime port and a pub is built on to a medieval pele tower which survives from days of the border wars.

BELFORD, NORTHUMBERLAND - Small market town on the old coaching road, close to the coast, the Scottish border and the north-east flank of the Cheviots. Built mostly in stone and very peaceful now that the A1 has by-passed the town, Belford makes an ideal centre for excursions to the moors and coast.

BELLINGHAM, NORTHUMBERLAND - Set in the beautiful valley of the North Tyne close to the Kielder Forest, Kielder Water and lonely moorland below the Cheviots. The church has an ancient stone wagon roof fortified in the 18th C with buttresses.

BISHOP AUCKLAND, DURHAM - Busy market town on the bank of the River Wear. The Bishop's Palace, a castellated Norman manor house altered in the 18th C, stands in beautiful gardens. Entered from the market square by a handsome 18th C gatehouse, the park is a peaceful retreat of trees and streams.

BLANCHLAND, NORTHUMBERLAND - Beautiful medieval village rebuilt in the 18th C with stone from its ruined abbey, for lead miners working on the surrounding wild moors. The village is approached over a stone bridge across the Derwent or, from the north, through the ancient gatehouse.

BYRNESS, NORTHUMBERLAND - Forestry village in Redesdale Forest on the A68. Catcleugh Reservoir is nearby, the Pennine Way runs through the village, and there is a forest toll road to Kielder Water.

C **CASTLESIDE, DURHAM** - Village on the edge of the North Pennines on the A68, one of the main routes from England to Scotland.

CHATHILL, NORTHUMBERLAND - Rural hamlet with mainline station. Preston Tower, a border pele tower, is nearby.

CHOPWELL, TYNE AND WEAR - Small village, 3 miles south-east of Prudhoe. Ruined Prudhoe Castle stands on a wooded hillside overlooking the River Tyne.

CORBRIDGE, NORTHUMBERLAND - Small town on the River Tyne. Close by are extensive remains of the Roman military town Corstopitum, with a museum housing important discoveries from excavations. The town itself is attractive with shady trees, a 17th C bridge and interesting old buildings, notably a 14th C vicarage.

COTHERSTONE, DURHAM - Village with remains of Norman castle, 3 miles north-west of Barnard Castle. Home of Cotherstone cheese.

D **DARLINGTON, DURHAM** - Largest town in County Durham, standing on the River Skerne and home of the earliest passenger railway which first ran to Stockton in 1825, now the home of a railway museum. Originally a prosperous market town occupying the site of an Anglo-Saxon settlement, it still holds an open market.

DURHAM, DURHAM - Ancient city with its Norman castle and cathedral, now a World Heritage site, set on a bluff high over the Wear. A market and university town and regional centre, spreading beyond the market-place on both banks of the river.

F **FROSTERLEY, DURHAM** - Old quarrying village on the limestone slopes of Weardale. The rich Frosterley marble, black when polished, graces the fonts and columns of many local churches, including Durham Cathedral.

VISITOR ATTRACTIONS For ideas on places to visit refer to the introduction at the beginning of this section. Look out too for the ETC's Quality Assured Visitor Attraction signs.

HALTWHISTLE, NORTHUMBERLAND - Small market town with interesting 12th C church, old inns and blacksmith's smithy. North of the town are several important sites and interpretation centres of Hadrian's Wall. Ideal centre for archaeology, outdoor activities or touring holidays.

HAMSTERLEY, DURHAM - Small village near Bedburn Beck, at the edge of the North Pennines. Just westward lies moorland country of Hamsterley Common and the beautiful Hamsterley Forest with picnic areas and nature trails.

HEDDON-ON-THE-WALL, NORTHUMBERLAND - Village overlooking Hadrian's Wall near its eastern limit, at the edge of an industrial area spreading into Tyneside. The church, first rebuilt by the Normans, was originally constructed of stone from the Wall.

HOLY ISLAND, NORTHUMBERLAND - Still an idyllic retreat, a tiny island and fishing village and cradle of northern Christianity. It is approached from the mainland at low water by a causeway. The clifftop castle (National Trust) was restored by Sir Edwin Lutyens.

MIDDLETON-IN-TEESDALE, DURHAM - Small stone town of hillside terraces overlooking the river, developed by the London Lead Company in the 18th C. Five miles up-river is the spectacular 70-ft waterfall, High Force.

MINDRUM, NORTHUMBERLAND - Hamlet 4 miles south of Cornhill on Tweed by banks of Bowmont Water.

NEWCASTLE UPON TYNE, TYNE AND WEAR - Commercial and cultural centre of the North East, with a large indoor shopping centre, Quayside market, museums and theatres which offer an annual 6-week season by the Royal Shakespeare Company. Norman castle keep, medieval alleys, old Guildhall.

NEWTON-BY-THE-SEA, NORTHUMBERLAND - Attractive hamlet at the south end of Beadnell Bay with a sandy beach and splendid view of Dunstanburgh Castle. In a designated Area of Outstanding Natural Beauty, Low Newton, part of the village, is now owned by the National Trust.

OVINGTON, NORTHUMBERLAND - Quiet village on the north bank of the River Tyne, linked to the village of Ovingham which has a 17th C packhorse bridge and was the birthplace of the famous artist and engraver Thomas Bewick.

ROTHBURY, NORTHUMBERLAND - Old market town on the River Coquet near the Simonside Hills. It makes an ideal centre for walking and fishing or for exploring this beautiful area from the coast to the Cheviots. Cragside House and Gardens (National Trust) are open to the public.

SALTBURN-BY-THE-SEA, CLEVELAND - Set on fine cliffs just north of the Cleveland Hills, a gracious Victorian resort with later developments and wide, firm sands. A handsome Jacobean mansion at Marske can be reached along the sands.

SEAHOUSES, NORTHUMBERLAND - Small, modern resort developed around a 19th C herring port. Just offshore, and reached by boat from here, are the rocky Farne Islands (National Trust) where there is an important bird reserve. The bird observatory occupies a medieval pele tower.

SEDGEFIELD, DURHAM - Ancient market town, a centre for hunting and steeplechasing, with a racecourse nearby. Handsome 18th C buildings include the town council's former Georgian mansion and the rectory. The church, with its magnificent spire, has 17th C wood-carvings by a local craftsman.

SOUTH SHIELDS, TYNE AND WEAR - At the mouth of the Tyne, a shipbuilding and industrial centre developed around a 19th C coalport and occupying the site of an important Roman fort and granary port. The town's museum has mementoes of the earliest self-righting lifeboat, built here in 1789.

STANHOPE, DURHAM - Old market town, "Capital of Weardale", set amid moorland hills and former lead-mining country of the North Pennines. In the market square opposite the church is a mock medieval castle. Close to the town is a cave where important Bronze Age finds were made.

STOCKSFIELD, NORTHUMBERLAND - Pretty rural village in the Tyne Valley in an area of good agricultural land. Bywell Hall, the home of Lord Allendale, is nearby, as well as Cherryburn, the birthplace of Thomas Bewick, where a musuem dedicated to the life and works of this famous local engraver can be found.

WAREN MILL, NORTHUMBERLAND - On Budle Bay just north of Bamburgh, in a designated Area of Outstanding Natural Beauty. This area is a favourite place for bird-watchers.

WEST WOODBURN, NORTHUMBERLAND - Small hamlet on the River Rede in rolling moorland country.

WHITLEY BAY, TYNE AND WEAR - Traditional seaside resort with long beaches of sand and rock and many pools to explore. St Mary's lighthouse is open to the public.

WINSTON, DURHAM - Attractive village overlooking the valley of the River Tees. Interesting early English church and a manor house which once belonged to the powerful Neville family.

WITTON-LE-WEAR, DURHAM - Hillside village rising from the river to its Norman church and triangular green. From here can be seen across the river the 15th C castle. Set in woodland by a stream it makes a romantic sight and its grounds provide secluded spots for campers and caravanners.

WOLSINGHAM, DURHAM - Gateway to the moors of Upper Weardale, a small town set at the confluence of the Wear and Waskerley Beck. The moors abound in old lead-workings and quarries; on Waskerley Beck, Tunstall Reservoir is the haunt of bird-watchers. Well placed for exploring the fells and dales.

QUALITY ASSURANCE SCHEME

Star ratings are explained at the back of this guide.

2004 Where to Stay

The official and best selling guides, offering the reassurance of quality assured accommodation

Hotels, Townhouses and Travel Accommodation in England 2004

£10.99

Guesthouses, Bed & Breakfast, Farmhouses, Inns and Campus Accommodation in England 2004

£11.99

Self-Catering Holiday Homes in England 2004

£10.99

Camping & Caravan Parks, Hostels, Holiday Villages and Boat Accommodation in Britain 2004

£6.99

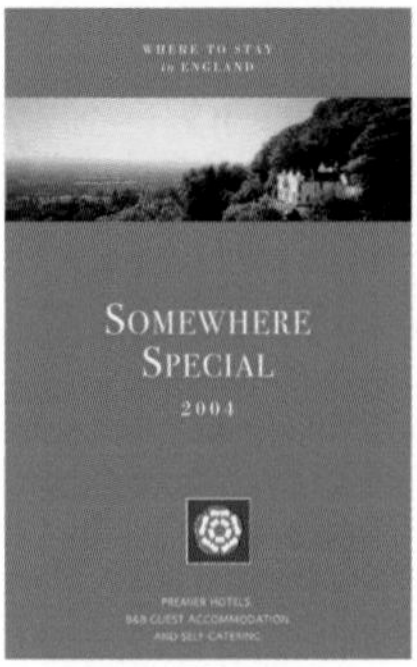

Somewhere Special in England 2004

£8.99

Look out also for:
SOMEWHERE SPECIAL IN ENGLAND 2004

Accommodation achieving the highest standards in facilities and quality of service - the perfect guide for the discerning traveller.

NOW ALSO FEATURING SELF-CATERING ACCOMMODATION

The guides include

• Accommodation entries packed with information • Full colour maps • Places to visit • Tourist Information Centres

INFORMATIVE • EASY TO USE • GREAT VALUE FOR MONEY

From all good bookshops or by mail order from the:
VisitBritain Fulfilment Centre,
C/o Westex Ltd, 7 St Andrews Way, Devons Road, Bromley-by-Bow, London E3 3PA
Tel: 0870 606 7204 Fax: 020 8563 3289 Email: fulfilment@visitbritain.org

North West

Home of pop stars, world-famous football teams, Blackpool Tower and Coronation Street, the great North West has vibrant cities, idyllic countryside and world-class art collections too.

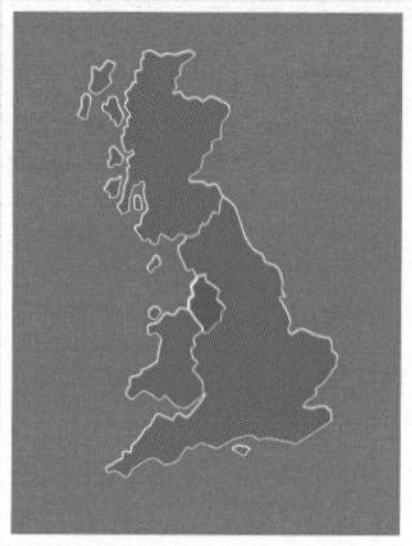

The Counties of Chesire, Greater Manchester, Lancashire, Merseyside and the High Peak District of Derbyshire

Classic sights
Blackpool Tower & Pleasure Beach – unashamed razzamatazz
Football – museums and tours at Manchester United and Liverpool football clubs
The Beatles – The Beatles Story, Magical Mystery Tour Bus and Macca's former home

Coast & country
The Ribble Valley – unchanged rolling landscapes
Formby – a glorious beach of sand dunes and pine woods
Wildfowl & Wetlands Trust, near Ormskirk – 120 types of birds including flamingos

Arts for all
The Tate Liverpool – modern art
The Lowry – the world's largest collection of LS Lowry paintings

For more information contact:
North West Tourist Board
Swan House,
Swan Meadow Road,
Wigan Pier, Wigan WN3 5BB

www.visitnorthwest.com

Telephone enquiries -
T: (01942) 821222
F: (01942) 820002

1. Blackpool Tower
2. Walkers on Kinder Scout, Derbyshire

Places to Visit

You will find hundreds of interesting places to visit during your stay, just some of which are listed in these pages. Contact any Tourist Information Centre in the region for more ideas on days out.

QUALITY ASSURED VISITOR ATTRACTION — Awarded VisitBritain's 'Quality Assured Visitor Attraction' marque.

Arley Hall and Gardens
Arley, Northwich
Tel: (01565) 777353
www.arleyestate.zuunet.co.uk
Early Victorian building set in 12 acres (5ha) of magnificent gardens, with a 15thC tithe barn. Plant nursery, gift shop and restaurant. A plantsman's paradise!

Astley Hall Museum and Art Gallery
Astley Park, Chorley
Tel: (01257) 515555 www.astleyhall.co.uk
Astley Hall dates from 1580 with subsequent additions. Unique collections of furniture including a fine Elizabethan bed and the famous Shovel Board Table.

The Beatles Story
Albert Dock, Liverpool
Tel: (0151) 709 1963 www.beatlesstory.com
Liverpool's award-winning visitor attraction with a replica of the original Cavern Club. Available for private parties.

Blackpool Pleasure Beach
Ocean Boulevard, Blackpool
Tel: 0870 4445566
www.blackpoolpleasurebeach.co.uk
Europe's greatest show and amusement park. Blackpool Pleasure Beach offers over 145 rides and attractions, plus spectacular shows.

Blackpool Tower and Circus
The Promenade, Blackpool
Tel: (01253) 292029
www.theblackpooltower.co.uk
Inside Blackpool Tower you will find the UK's best circus, world famous Tower Ballroom, children's entertainment plus Jungle Jim's Playground, Tower Top Ride and Undersea World.

Boat Museum
South Pier Road, Ellesmere Port
Tel: (0151) 355 5017
www.boatmuseum.org.uk
Home to the UK's largest collection of inland waterway craft. Working forge, Power Hall, Pump House, 7 exhibitions of industrial heritage. Gift shop and cafeteria.

Botany Bay Villages and Puddletown Pirates
Canal Mill, Chorley
Tel: (01257) 261220 www.botanybay.co.uk
A shopping, leisure and heritage experience including Puddletown Pirates, the North West's largest indoor adventure play centre.

Bridgemere Garden World
Bridgemere, Nantwich
Tel: (01270) 520381 www.bridgemere.co.uk
Bridgemere Garden World, 25 fascinating acres (10ha) of plants, gardens, greenhouses and shop. Coffee shop, restaurant and over 20 different display gardens in the Garden Kingdom.

Camelot Theme Park
Charnock Richard, Chorley
Tel: (01257) 453044
www.camelotthemepark.co.uk
The Magical Kingdom of Camelot voted Lancashire's Family Attraction of the Year 2002 is a world of thrilling rides, fantastic entertainment and family fun.

CATALYST: Science Discovery Centre
Mersey Road, Widnes
Tel: (0151) 420 1121 www.catalyst.org.uk
Catalyst is the award-winning family day out where science and technology fuse with fun.

Chester Zoo
Upton-by-Chester, Chester
Tel: (01244) 380280
www.chesterzoo.org.uk
Chester Zoo is one of Europe's leading conservation zoos, with over 7,000 animals in spacious and natural enclosures. Now featuring the 'Tsavo' African Black Rhino Experience.

Croxteth Hall and Country Park
Croxteth Hall Lane, Liverpool
Tel: (0151) 228 5311
www.croxteth.co.uk
An Edwardian stately home set in 500 acres (200ha) of countryside (woodlands and pasture), featuring a Victorian walled garden and animal collection.

Dunham Massey Hall Park and Garden (National Trust)
Altrincham
Tel: (0161) 941 1025
www.thenationaltrust.org.uk
An 18thC mansion in a 250-acre (100-ha) wooded deer park with furniture, paintings and silver. A 25-acre (10-ha) informal garden with mature trees and waterside plantings.

East Lancashire Railway
Bolton Street, Bury
Tel: (0161) 764 7790
www.east-lancs-rly.co.uk
Eight miles of preserved railway, operated principally by steam. Traction Transport Museum close by.

Jodrell Bank Science Centre, Planetarium and Arboretum
Lower Withington, Macclesfield
Tel: (01477) 571339 www.jb.man.ac.uk/scicen
Exhibition and interactive exhibits on astronomy, space, energy and the environment. Planetarium, 3D theatre and the world-famous Lovell telescope, plus a 35-acre (14-ha) arboretum.

Knowsley Safari Park
Prescot
Tel: (0151) 430 9009
www.knowsley.com
A 5-mile safari through 500 acres (200ha) of rolling countryside and the world's wildest animals roaming free - that's the wonderful world of freedom you'll find at the park.

Lady Lever Art Gallery
Port Sunlight Village, Wirral
Tel: (0151) 478 4136
www.ladyleverartgallery.org.uk
The 1st Lord Leverhulme's magnificent collection of British paintings dated 1750-1900, British furniture, Wedgewood pottery and oriental porcelain.

Lancaster Castle
Castle Parade, Lancaster
Tel: (01524) 64998 www.lancastercastle.com
Shire Hall has a collection of coats of arms, a crown court, a grand jury room, a 'drop room' and dungeons. Also external tour of castle.

Lyme Park (National Trust)
Disley, Stockport
Tel: (01663) 762023 www.nationaltrust.org.uk
Lyme Park is a National Trust country estate set in 1,377 acres (557ha) of moorland, woodland and park. This magnificent house has 17 acres (7ha) of historic gardens.

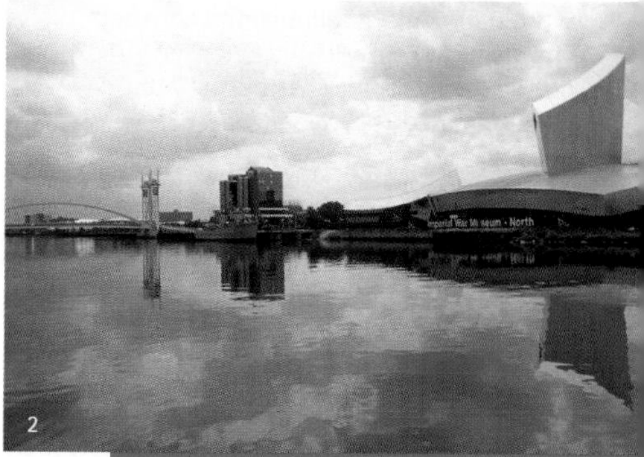

2

1. Rochdale Canal
2. Imperial War Museum North, Salford Quays, Manchester
3. Blackpool Pleasure Beach

Macclesfield Silk Museum
Roe Street, Macclesfield
Tel: (01625) 613210 www.silk-macclesfield.org
A silk museum is situated in the Heritage Centre, a Grade II Listed former Sunday school.

Merseyside Maritime Museum
Albert Dock, Liverpool
Tel: (0151) 478 4499
www.merseysidemaritimemuseum.org.uk
Liverpool's seafaring heritage brought to life in the historic Albert Dock.

The Museum of Science & Industry in Manchester
Castlefield, Manchester
Tel: (0161) 832 2244 www.msim.org.uk
Based in the world's oldest passenger railway station, this museum has galleries that amaze, amuse and entertain, full of working exhibits including industrial machines and historic planes.

The National Football Museum
Deepdale Stadium, Preston
Tel: (01772) 908442
www.nationalfootballmuseum.com
The National Football Museum exists to explain how and why football has become the people's game.

Norton Priory Museum and Gardens
Manor Park, Runcorn
Tel: (01928) 569895
www.nortonpriory.org
Medieval priory remains, purpose-built museum, St Christopher's statue, sculpture trail and award-winning walled garden, all set in 38 acres (15ha) of beautiful gardens.

Pleasureland Theme Park
Marine Drive, Southport
Tel: 0870 2200204 www.pleasureland.uk.com
Over 100 rides and attractions, including the TRAUMAtizer and the Lucozade Space Shot.

Rufford Old Hall (National Trust)
Rufford, Ormskirk
Tel: (01704) 821254 www.nationaltrust.org.uk
One of the finest 16thC buildings in Lancashire, with a magnificent hall, particularly noted for its immense moveable screen.

Sandcastle Tropical Waterworld
South Promenade, Blackpool
Tel: (01253) 343602
www.blackpool-sandcastle.co.uk
Wave pool, fun pools, giant water flumes, sauna, white-knuckle water slides, kiddies safe harbour, play area, catering, bar shops and amusements.

Southport Zoo and Conservation Trust
Princes Park, Southport
Tel: (01704) 538102 www.southportzoo.co.uk
Zoological gardens and conservation trust. Southport Zoo has been run by the Petrie family since 1964. Talks on natural history are held in the schoolroom.

Tate Liverpool
Albert Dock, Liverpool
Tel: (0151) 702 7400
www.tate.org.uk/liverpool/
The Tate Liverpool in historic Albert Dock has 4 floors of art and houses the National Collection of Modern Art.

Tatton Park (National Trust)
Knutsford
Tel: (01625) 534400
www.tattonpark.org.uk
Historic mansion with a 50-acre (20-ha) garden, traditional working farm, Tudor manor-house and a 1,000-acre (400-ha) deer park and children's adventure playground.

Wigan Pier
Trencherfield Mill, Wigan
Tel: (01942) 323666
www.wiganmbc.gov.uk
Wigan Pier combines interaction with displays and reconstructions and the Wigan Pier Theatre Company. Facilities include shops and a cafe.

Wildfowl and Wetland Trust Martin Mere
Burscough, Ormskirk
Tel: (01704) 895181 www.wwt.org.uk
Martin Mere Wildfowl and Wetland Centre is home to over 1,600 ducks, geese and swans.

North West Tourist Board

Swan House, Swan Meadow Road,
Wigan Pier, Wigan WN3 5BB
T: (01942) 821222 F: (01942) 820002
www.visitnorthwest.com

THE FOLLOWING PUBLICATIONS ARE AVAILABLE FROM NORTH WEST TOURIST BOARD:

Discover England's North West –
a guide to information on the region

Great Days Out in England's North West –
a non-accommodation guide, A1 (folded to A4) map including list of visitor attractions, what to see and where to go

Freedom –
forming part of a family of publications about camping and caravan parks in the north of England

Stay on a Farm –
a guide to farm accommodation in the north of England

Group Travel Planner –
a guide to choosing the right accommodation, attraction or venue for group organisers

1

Getting to the North West

BY ROAD: Motorways intersect within the region which has the best road network in the country. Travelling north or south use the M6, and east or west the M62.

BY RAIL: Most North West coastal resorts are connected to InterCity routes with trains from many parts of the country, and there are through trains to major cities and towns.

1. The Lowry, Salford Quays, Manchester
2. Chester Clock

2

Where to stay in the

North West

All place names in the blue bands under which accommodation is listed, are shown on the maps at the front of this guide.

Symbols give useful information about services and facilities. Inside the back cover flap there's a key to these symbols which you can keep open for easy reference.

A complete listing of all the VisitBritain assessed accommodation covered by this guide appears at the back of this guide.

ALDERLEY EDGE, Cheshire Map ref 4B2

★★★★

1 Unit
Sleeping 2

Set in a 0.75-acre garden surrounded by beautiful countryside and 'The Edge' (NT), yet close to the village, The Hayloft is a cosy and peaceful haven. Knutsford (Tatton RHS show), Macclesfield, Manchester, Chester and the Peak District are within easy reach, as are the airport and motorway network.

THE HAYLOFT

Alderley Edge
Contact: Mrs J Dawson, Interludes, Croft Cottage, Hough Lane, Alderley Edge SK9 7JE
T: (01625) 599802
F: (01625) 599802
E: info@interludes-uk.com
I: www.interludes-uk.com

OPEN All Year except Christmas
CC: Amex, Delta, Diners, Mastercard, Switch, Visa

Reduced rental for multiple weeks booked.

Low season per wk
Min £350.00
High season per wk
Max £500.00

BASHALL EAVES, Lancashire Map ref 4A1 *Tourist Information Centre Tel: (01200) 425566*

★★★★

1 Unit
Sleeping 4

THE COACH HOUSE

Bashall Eaves, Clitheroe
Contact: Country Holidays, Property Ref: 17177
T: 08700 781 200
E: ch.enquiry@holidaycottagesgroup.com

OPEN All Year
CC: Delta, JCB, Mastercard, Solo, Switch, Visa

Low season per wk
Min £230.00
High season per wk
Max £475.00

An organic farm set in idyllic surroundings. Historic buildings. Well maintained in superb grounds which are conservation focused.

BLACKPOOL, Lancashire Map ref 4A1 *Tourist Information Centre Tel: (01253) 478222*

Rating Applied For
8 Units
Sleeping 2–8

STRATFORD APARTMENTS

North Shore, Blackpool
Contact: Mr C Taylor
T: (01253) 500150
F: (01253) 591004
E: tonorthdene@hotmail.com
I: www.blackpoolbreaks.net/stratfordapartments

OPEN All Year
CC: Delta, Mastercard, Solo, Switch, Visa

Low season per wk £100.00–£290.00
High season per wk £145.00–£400.00

Situated close to Queens Promenade in Blackpool's select North Shore district with good local transport links to all attractions in central and South Shore areas.

BOLLINGTON, Cheshire Map ref 4B2 *Tourist Information Centre Tel: (01625) 504114*

★★★★★
1 Unit
Sleeping 8

HIGHER INGERSLEY BARN

Bollington, Macclesfield
Contact: Mr B Peacock
T: (01625) 572245
F: (01625) 574231
E: bw.peacock@ntlworld.com
I: www.higheringersleyfarm.co.uk

Low season per wk £380.00–£500.00
High season per wk £480.00–£800.00

Beautiful converted barn on edge of Peak District. Spectacular views. Oak beamed, elegant and comfortable. Sofa bed for two extra. Garden. Superb walking and sightseeing.

BOSLEY, Cheshire Map ref 4B2 *Tourist Information Centre Tel: (01625) 504114*

★★★
1 Unit
Sleeping 8

THE OLD BYRE

Bosley, Macclesfield
Contact: Mrs D Gilman, Woodcroft, Bosley, Macclesfield SK11 0PB
T: (01260) 223293
F: (01260) 273650

OPEN All Year except Christmas

Low season per wk £250.00–£350.00
High season per wk £400.00–£500.00

110-acre mixed farm. Old beamed shippon in beautiful walking area, edge of Peak District and moorlands, 15 miles from Alton Towers. Heating and linen included. Mob: 07762 095389

BRINSCALL, Lancashire Map ref 4A1

★★★
1 Unit
Sleeping 7

MOORS VIEW COTTAGE

Brinscall, Chorley
Contact: Mrs S Smith, Four Seasons Guest House, 9 Cambridge Road, Cleveleys, Blackpool FY5 1EP
T: (01253) 853537
F: (01624) 662190

Situated amid lovely countryside adjacent to canal, motorways, market towns and coast, this fully equipped cottage comprises two bedrooms and excellent bedsettee, luxury bathroom, separate shower and toilet, large through lounge and dining area, oak kitchen, off-road parking, large rear garden and sun room. Fuel, power and linen included. Mob: 07747 808406.

OPEN All Year

Low season per wk £250.00–£300.00
High season per wk £315.00–£375.00

CHESTER, Cheshire Map ref 4A2 *Tourist Information Centre Tel: (01244) 402111*

★★★
1 Unit
Sleeping 6

CAMBELL'S COTTAGE

3 The Mount, Chester
Contact: Mrs Henderson, 4 Lancaster Drive, Chester CH3 5JW
T: (01244) 326890
E: jeannetunnard@aol.com

OPEN All Year except Christmas

Low season per wk £230.00–£340.00
High season per wk £275.00–£405.00

Part Victorian, Grade II Listed property with a black and white exterior. Beautiful views onto the River Dee. Only one mile from the city centre.

CHESTER continued

★★★

2 Units
Sleeping 2–6

CITY WALLS APARTMENTS

Chester
Contact: Mr R Cox, Thompson Cox Partnership, 1 City Walls, Chester CH1 2JG
T: (01244) 313400
F: (01244) 400414
E: rc@thompsoncox.co.uk

Modern, second floor apartments, both with courtyard and garden views, parking, near everything. Large studio (one double bed) and two-bedroom (two doubles) in award-winning courtyard, half built 1990, half 1750, nestling on the city walls, housing craft shops, book shops, restaurants and Alexander's Jazz Bar. Everything included.

Short breaks if late availability (3 weeks ahead) only. Ring for prices.

Studio: £250.00 all year except Christmas
2 bed: £350.00 all year except Christmas

★★★

1 Unit
Sleeping 4

KINGSWOOD COACH HOUSE

Saughall, Chester
Contact: Mrs C Perry, Kingswood Coach House, Kingswood, Parkgate Road, Saughall, Chester CH1 6JS
T: (01244) 851204
F: (01244) 851244
E: caroline.mcvey@psmconsulting.co.uk

OPEN All Year except Christmas

Low season per wk £170.00–£200.00
High season per wk £200.00–£250.00

Ideal for couples. Large bedroom, fitted kitchen, living room, toilet and shower. Garden and patio, off-road parking. Close to bus route. Near Wales and Wirral.

★★

1 Unit
Sleeping 6

LITTLE MAYFIELD

Hoole Village, Chester
Contact: Mr M J Cullen, Little Mayfield, Mayfield House, Warrington Road, Hoole Village, Chester CH2 4EX
T: (01244) 300231
F: (01244) 300231

OPEN All Year except Christmas

Low season per wk £180.00
High season per wk £260.00

Self-contained wing of William IV house set in three acres of garden with hard tennis court. Spacious rooms. Seven minutes from Chester city centre.

CHIPPING, Lancashire Map ref 4A1 *Tourist Information Centre Tel: (01200) 425566*

★★★-★★★★

4 Units
Sleeping 4

RAKEFOOT BARN

Chaigley, Clitheroe
Contact: Mrs P M Gifford
T: (01995) 61332
F: (01995) 61296
E: info@rakefootfarm.co.uk
I: www.rakefootfarm.co.uk

OPEN All Year

Low season per wk Min £85.00
High season per wk Max £533.00

Traditional stone barn, original features, woodburners, en suites. Family farm. Forest of Bowland between Chipping/Clitheroe. NWTB Silver Award winner. Also bed and breakfast.

DISLEY, Cheshire Map ref 4B2 *Tourist Information Centre Tel: (0161) 474 4444*

★★★★

1 Unit
Sleeping 6

PLATTWOOD FARM COTTAGE

Lyme Park, Disley, Stockport
Contact: Mrs J Emmott
T: (01625) 872738
F: (01625) 872738
E: plattwoodfarm@talk21.com
I: www.plattwoodfarm.com

Low season per wk £350.00–£395.00
High season per wk £395.00–£595.00

Comfortable cottage tucked away from crowds and traffic. Enjoy cosy log fires, a master en suite bedroom with 4-poster bed. Ideal location for Peak District/ Manchester.

QUALITY ASSURANCE SCHEME

Star ratings are explained at the back of this guide.

KNUTSFORD, Cheshire Map ref 4A2 *Tourist Information Centre Tel: (01565) 632611*

★★★★
2 Units
Sleeping 4

6 THE SYCAMORES & 7 THE CEDARS

Mobberley, Knutsford
Contact: Mrs J Dawson, Interludes, Croft Cottage, Hough Lane, Alderley Edge SK9 7JE
T: (01625) 599802
F: (01625) 599802
E: info@interludes-uk.com
I: www.interludes-uk.com

Peaceful and relaxing with fluffy robes, Molton Brown toiletries and inclusive membership of the on-site leisure club, these special new apartments are surrounded by beautiful countryside. Manchester Airport and the motorway network are within easy reach, as are Knutsford (Tatton RHS show) Manchester, Chester, Macclesfield and the Peak District

OPEN All Year
CC: Amex, Delta, Diners, Mastercard, Switch, Visa

Reduced rental for multiple weeks booked.

Low season per wk
Min £400.00
High season per wk
Max £600.00

MACCLESFIELD, Cheshire Map ref 4B2 *Tourist Information Centre Tel: (01625) 504114*

★★★
1 Unit
Sleeping 6

MILL HOUSE FARM COTTAGE

Bosley, Macclesfield
Contact: Mrs L Whittaker, Mill House Farm, Bosley, Macclesfield SK11 0NZ
T: (01260) 226265
E: lynne-whittaker@yahoo.co.uk
I: www.geocities.com/farm_cottage/

OPEN All Year except Christmas

Low season per wk
£155.00–£175.00
High season per wk
£175.00–£250.00

Comfortable, spacious cottage on 130-acre dairy farm bordering the Peak District. Beautiful surrounding countryside and convenient for Alton Towers, Potteries, Chester, Manchester Airport.

MANCHESTER AIRPORT

See under Alderley Edge, Knutsford, Stockport

MIDDLEWICH, Cheshire Map ref 4A2

★★★-★★★★
3 Units
Sleeping 4–5

FORGE MILL FARM COTTAGES

Warmingham, Middlewich
Contact: Mrs S Moss, Forge Mill Farm, Forge Mill Lane, Warmingham, Middlewich CW10 0HQ
T: (01270) 526204
F: (01270) 526204
E: forgemill2@msn.com

Barn, newly converted to a high standard to create beautiful cottages. Located in a peaceful situation, ideal for a long-weekend break, peaceful holiday or business trip. Forge Masters is the larger cottage and is suitable for the partially disabled. Millers is smaller but has its own special charm. Equipped with all modern conveniences.

OPEN All Year

3-night stays available all year.

Low season per wk
£250.00–£350.00
High season per wk
£320.00–£450.00

MORECAMBE, Lancashire Map ref 5A3 *Tourist Information Centre Tel: (01524) 582808*

★
2 Units

RYDAL MOUNT

Morecambe
Contact: Mrs S Holmes
T: (01524) 411858

OPEN All Year except Christmas

Low season per wk
£150.00–£245.00
High season per wk
£180.00–£255.00

Situated on Morecambe promenade overlooking bay and Lakeland hills. Well-appointed, self-contained holiday apartments. Ideal base for Lake District. Car park, stair lift.

NANTWICH, Cheshire Map ref 4A2 *Tourist Information Centre Tel: (01270) 610983*

★★★
5 Units
Sleeping 1–6

BANK FARM COTTAGES
Hough, Crewe
Contact: Mrs A Vaughan
T: (01270) 841809
F: (01270) 841809

OPEN All Year

Low season per wk
£250.00
High season per wk
£300.00

Charming holiday cottages created from Victorian farm buildings, furnished to a high standard. Full gas central heating, washing machines, microwaves. Ample parking. Excellent base for North Wales potteries.

NETHER KELLET, Lancashire Map ref 5B3

★★★
1 Unit
Sleeping 4

THE APARTMENT
Nether Kellet, Carnforth
Contact: Mr S Richardson
T: (01524) 734969

OPEN All Year

Low season per wk
£140.00
High season per wk
£225.00

One-bedroomed, self-contained flat with extensive, private gardens in peaceful, rural village. Secluded cul-de-sac location. Also phone (01524) 736331.

★★★★
1 Unit
Sleeping 4

THE LOFT

Nether Kellet, Carnforth
Contact: Mr S Hinde
T: (01524) 734135
F: (01524) 734135
E: stevehinde@onetel.net.uk

A beautifully converted barn with oak beams which overlooks the village green. Large lounge with elevated diner/kitchen, two double bedrooms, patio area. Close to the historic city of Lancaster and Morecambe Bay. The Lake District and Yorkshire Dales are a short drive away. All amenities in village.

OPEN All Year

Short breaks all year. 2/3/4-night breaks available (excl Christmas and New Year).

Low season per wk
£170.00–£280.00
High season per wk
£280.00–£420.00

POULTON-LE-FYLDE, Lancashire Map ref 4A1

★★★★
6 Units
Sleeping 4

SWANS REST HOLIDAY COTTAGES
Singleton, Poulton-le-Fylde
Contact: Mrs I O'Connor, Swans Rest,
Garstang Road East, Singleton, Poulton-le-Fylde
FY6 8LX
T: (01253) 886617
F: (01253) 892563
E: swansrest@btconnect.com
I: www.swansrest.co.uk

OPEN All Year

Low season per wk
£151.00–£239.00
High season per wk
£245.00–£435.00

Luxury cottages set in eight acres, including two new log cabins overlooking pond area with swans and ducks. Within six miles of Blackpool.

RIBBLE VALLEY

See under Chipping

USE YOUR *i*s

There are more than 550 Tourist Information Centres throughout England offering friendly help with accommodation and holiday ideas as well as suggestions of places to visit and things to do. You'll find TIC addresses in the local Phone Book.

SILVERDALE, Lancashire Map ref 5A3

★★★★

1 Unit
Sleeping 3

THE STABLES

Silverdale, Carnforth
Contact: Mrs C M Ranford, The Stables, Lindeth House, Lindeth Road, Silverdale, Carnforth LA5 0TT
T: (01524) 702121
F: (01524) 702226
E: conquerors.maryk@virgin.net

The Stables are of 18thC construction and have been completely converted to a luxury standard. Large bedroom, en suite shower room. Additional shower room. Facilities for disabled. Wheelchair access to all rooms. Situated in peaceful surroundings. Area of Outstanding Natural Beauty. Village and coast 0.25 miles. RSPB and golf course one mile.

3-night stays available Oct-Feb (excl Christmas and New Year).

Low season per wk
£245.00–£275.00
High season per wk
£275.00–£325.00

SOUTHPORT, Merseyside Map ref 4A1 *Tourist Information Centre Tel: (01704) 533333*

★★★★

2 Units
Sleeping 4–6

MARTIN LANE FARMHOUSE HOLIDAY COTTAGES

Burscough, Ormskirk
Contact: Mrs Stubbs, Martin Lane Farmhouse Holiday Cottages, Martin Lane Farmhouse, Burscough, Ormskirk L40 8JH
T: (01704) 893527
F: (01704) 893527
E: mlfhc@btinternet.com
I: www.martinlanefarmhouse.btinternet.co.uk

Beautiful, award-winning country cottages, nestling in the rich arable farmland of West Lancashire and just four miles from Southport and the seaside. Our cottages have a friendly, relaxed, family atmosphere. The ideal base for visiting all the North West's major attractions.

OPEN All Year

Low season per wk
£150.00–£325.00
High season per wk
£225.00–£395.00

★★★

5 Units
Sleeping 2–6

SANDY BROOK FARM

Southport
Contact: Mr W Core, Sandy Brook Farm,
52 Wyke Cop Road, Scarisbrick, Southport PR8 5LR
T: (01704) 880337
F: (01704) 880337
E: sandybrookfarm@lycos.co.uk

OPEN All Year

Low season per wk
£100.00–£130.00
High season per wk
£250.00–£280.00

27-acre arable farm. Converted barn apartments furnished in traditional style. 3.5 miles from Southport in rural area of Scarisbrick. One apartment adapted for disabled.

STOCKPORT, Greater Manchester Map ref 4B2 *Tourist Information Centre Tel: (0161) 474 4444*

★★★

1 Unit
Sleeping 6

LAKE VIEW

Marple Bridge, Stockport
Contact: Mrs M Sidebottom, Shire Cottage,
Benches Lane, Marple Bridge, Stockport SK6 5RY
T: (01457) 866536
F: (01457) 866536

Well-equipped bungalow with magnificent views, in peaceful setting overlooking Etherow Country Park near Peak District. Cot available. Restaurant five minutes away. All rooms on ground floor level. Coal fire.

Low season per wk
£300.00–£350.00
High season per wk
£350.00–£450.00

COLOUR MAPS **Colour maps at the front of this guide pinpoint all places under which you will find accommodation listed.**

TOSSIDE, Lancashire Map ref 4A1

★★★★

5 Units

PRIMROSE COTTAGE, JENNY WREN, WAGTAIL, SWALLOWS, LOWER GILL FARMHOUSE

Tosside, Skipton

OPEN All Year

Contact: Holiday Cottages (Yorkshire), Water Street, Skipton BD23 1PB
T: (01756) 700510
E: brochure@holidaycotts.co.uk
I: www.holidaycotts.co.uk

Superb cottages with heated indoor pool, games room, tennis court and play area. Surrounded by open countryside.

Low season per wk
£235.00–£395.00
High season per wk
£416.00–£836.00

WORSLEY, Greater Manchester Map ref 4A1 *Tourist Information Centre Tel: (0161) 234 3157*

★★★

1 Unit
Sleeping 4

THE COTTAGE – WORSLEY

Worsley, Manchester
Contact: Mr & Mrs G R Atherton, 60 Worsley Road, Worsley, Manchester M28 2SH
T: (0161) 793 4157
F: (0161) 793 4157

Cosy, single-storey cottage six miles west of Manchester in picturesque conservation area. Close motorway access to Lake District, Scotland, Midlands, Merseyside and Wales.

Low season per wk
Min £300.00
High season per wk
Max £450.00

AT-A-GLANCE SYMBOLS

Symbols at the end of each accommodation entry give useful information about services and facilities. A key to symbols can be found inside the back cover flap. Keep this open for easy reference.

A brief guide to the main Towns and Villages offering accommodation in the **North West**

B **BLACKPOOL, LANCASHIRE -** Britain's largest fun resort, with Blackpool Pleasure Beach, 3 piers and the famous Tower. Host to the spectacular autumn illuminations.

C **CHESTER, CHESHIRE -** Roman and medieval walled city rich in treasures. Black and white buildings are a hallmark, including 'The Rows' - two-tier shopping galleries. 900-year-old cathedral and the famous Chester Zoo.

CHIPPING, LANCASHIRE - Charming, well-preserved 17th C village, on the edge of the Forest of Bowland on the Pendle Witches' Trail. Ancient church, pub, craft shops. A superb base for walking and touring the area. Best Kept Village award.

K **KNUTSFORD, CHESHIRE -** Delightful town with many buildings of architectural and historic interest. The setting of Elizabeth Gaskell's "Cranford". Annual May Day celebration and decorative "sanding" of the pavements are unique to the town. Popular Heritage Centre.

M **MACCLESFIELD, CHESHIRE -** Cobbled streets and quaint old buildings stand side by side with modern shops and 3 markets. Centuries of association with the silk industry; museums feature working exhibits and social history. Stunning views of the Peak District National Park.

N **NANTWICH, CHESHIRE -** Old market town on the River Weaver made prosperous in Roman times by salt springs. Fire destroyed the town in 1583 and many buildings were rebuilt in Elizabethan style. Churche's Mansion (open to the public) survived the fire.

P **POULTON-LE-FYLDE, LANCASHIRE -** Old market town, listed in the Domesday Book, whose most notable feature is the church of St Chad which has an early 17th C Perpendicular tower, Romanesque chancel, Georgian interior and wall monuments to the Fleetwoods and Hesketh's.

S **SILVERDALE, LANCASHIRE -** On the shores of Morecambe Bay, this picturesque village is in the centre of a designated Area of Outstanding Natural Beauty.

SOUTHPORT, MERSEYSIDE - Delightful Victorian resort noted for gardens, sandy beaches and 6 golf courses, particularly Royal Birkdale. Attractions include the Atkinson Art Gallery, Southport Railway Centre, Pleasureland and the annual Southport Flower Show. Excellent shopping, particularly in Lord Street's elegant boulevard.

STOCKPORT, GREATER MANCHESTER - Once an important cotton-spinning and manufacturing centre, Stockport has an impressive railway viaduct, a shopping precinct built over the River Mersey and a new leisure complex. Lyme Hall and Vernon Park Museum nearby.

T **TOSSIDE, LANCASHIRE -** Small hillside hamlet with village school, church, public house and early 18th C Congregational Chapel. In beautiful countryside on the edge of the Forest of Bowland, close to the Stocks Reservoir.

COUNTRY CODE Always follow the Country Code ✤ Enjoy the countryside and respect its life and work ✤ Guard against all risk of fire ✤ Fasten all gates ✤ Keep your dogs under close control ✤ Keep to public paths across farmland ✤ Use gates and stiles to cross fences, hedges and walls ✤ Leave livestock, crops and machinery alone ✤ Take your litter home ✤ Help to keep all water clean ✤ Protect wildlife, plants and trees ✤ Take special care on country roads ✤ Make no unnecessary noise

Their house is **your home**

Owners and agencies offering holiday homes in this guide want you to enjoy your holiday so please make yourself at home – but do also remember that it is someone else's property.

Here are a few tips to ensure a smooth-running, problem-free holiday:

Allow plenty of time for your journey but please do not arrive at the property before the stated time – and please leave by the stated time. This enables the owner to make sure everything is ready for you and for whoever follows you.

If you've booked for, say, six people please don't turn up with more.

Do respect the owner's rules on pets – if, for example, one small pet is allowed please don't take a Great Dane.

Do report any damages or breakages immediately (and offer the cost of repair), so that the owner can ensure everything is in order for the next letting.

Do leave the place clean and tidy – no dirty dishes in the sink, please – and all the furniture back where it was when you arrived.

Despite the best endeavours of the owners and agents, problems can occur from time to time. If you are dissatisfied in any way with your holiday home, please give the owner or agent a chance to put matters right by letting them know immediately.

Yorkshire

Yorkshire combines wild and brooding moors with historic cities, elegant spa towns and a varied coastline of traditional resorts and working fishing ports.

The Counties of North, South, East and West Yorkshire, and Northern Lincolnshire

Classic sights
Fountains Abbey & Studley Royal – 12thC Cistercian abbey and Georgian water garden
Nostell Priory – 18thC house with outstanding art collection
York Minster – largest medieval Gothic cathedral north of the Alps

Coast & country
The Pennines – dramatic moors and rocks
Whitby – unspoilt fishing port, famous for jet (black stone)

Literary links
Bronte parsonage, Haworth – home of the Bronte sisters; inspiration for 'Wuthering Heights' and 'Jane Eyre'

Arts for all
National Museum of Photography, Film and Television, Bradford – hi-tech and hands-on

Distinctively different
The Original Ghost Walk of York – spooky tours every night

For more information contact:
Yorkshire Tourist Board
312 Tadcaster Road,
York YO24 1GS

E: info@ytb.org.uk
www.yorkshirevisitor.com

Telephone enquiries -
T: (01904) 707070
(24-hr Brochure Line)
F: (01904) 701414

1. Yorkshire Dales
2. Castle Howard, North Yorkshire
3. Flamborough, East Riding of Yorkshire

You will find hundreds of interesting places to visit during your stay, just some of which are listed in these pages. Contact any Tourist Information Centre in the region for more ideas on days out.

QUALITY ASSURED VISITOR ATTRACTION

Awarded VisitBritain's 'Quality Assured Visitor Attraction' marque.

Beningbrough Hall & Gardens (National Trust)
Beningborough, York
Tel: (01904) 470666 www.nationaltrust.org.uk
Handsome Baroque house, built in 1716. With 100 pictures from the National Portrait Gallery, Victorian laundry, potting shed and restored walled garden.

Bolton Abbey Estate
Skipton
Tel: (01756) 718009 www.boltonabbey.com
Ruins of 12thC priory in a parkland setting by the River Wharfe. Tearooms, catering, nature trails, fishing, fell-walking and picturesque countryside.

Cusworth Hall Museum of South Yorkshire Life
Cusworth Lane, Doncaster
Tel: (01302) 782342
www.museum@doncaster.gov.uk
Georgian mansion in landscaped park containing Museum of South Yorkshire Life, with displays of costumes, childhood and transport. Special educational facilities.

The Deep
Hull
Tel: (01482) 381000 www.thedeep.co.uk
Find out all about the world's oceans in entertaining and informative displays. The Deep also has a learning centre and research facility.

Eden Camp Modern History Theme Museum
Malton
Tel: (01653) 697777 www.edencamp.co.uk
This museum transports you back to wartime Britain in a series of expertly-recreated scenes covering all aspects of World War II.

Eureka! The Museum for Children
Discovery Road, Halifax
Tel: (01422) 330069 www.eureka.org.uk
Eureka! is the first museum of its kind designed especially for children up to the age of 12 with over 400 hands-on exhibits.

Fountains Abbey and Studley Royal (National Trust)
Studley Park, Ripon
Tel: (01765) 608888
www.fountainsabbey.org.uk
Largest monastic ruin in Britain, founded by Cistercian monks in 1132. Landscaped garden laid between 1720-40 with lake, formal water garden, temples and deer park.

Freeport Hornsea Outlet Village
Rolston Road, Hornsea
Tel: (01964) 534211 www.freeportplc.com
Set in 25 acres (10ha) of landscaped gardens with over 40 quality high-street names all selling stock with discounts of up to 50%, licensed restaurant. Leisure attractions.

Helmsley Castle (English Heritage)
Helmsley, York
Tel: (01439) 770442
www.english-heritage.org.uk
Great ruined keep dominates the town. Other remains include a 16thC domestic range with original panelling and plasterwork. Spectacular earthwork defences.

JORVIK – The Viking City
Coppergate, York
Tel: (01904) 543403
www.vikingjorvik.com
Journey back to York in AD975 and experience the sights, sounds and even smells of the Viking Age. Special exhibitions complete the experience.

Last of the Summer Wine Exhibition (Compo's House)
30 Huddersfield Road, Holmfirth
Tel: (01484) 681408
Collection of photographs and memorabilia connected with the television series 'Last of the Summer Wine'.

Leeds City Art Gallery
The Headrow, Leeds
Tel: (0113) 247 8248
www.leeds.gov.uk/tourinfo/attract/museums/artgall.html
Interesting collections of British paintings, sculptures, prints and drawings of the 19th/20thC. Henry Moore gallery with permanent collection of 20thC sculpture.

Lightwater Valley Theme Park and Country Shopping Village
North Stainley, Ripon
Tel: 0870 4580060 www.lightwatervalley.net
Set in 175 acres (70ha) of parkland, Lightwater Valley features a number of white-knuckle rides and attractions for all the family, shopping, a restaurant and picnic areas.

Magna
Sheffield Road, Rotherham
Tel: (01709) 720002
www.magnatrust.org.uk
Magna is the UK's 1st Science Adventure Centre set in the vast Templeborough steelworks in Rotherham. Fun is unavoidable here with giant interactive displays.

National Centre for Early Music
St Margarets Church, York
Tel: (01904) 645738 www.yorkearlymusic.org
The National Centre for Early Music is a unique combination of music, heritage and new technology and offers a perfect venue for musicmaking, drama, recordings and conferences.

National Fishing Heritage Centre
Alexandra Dock, Grimsby
Tel: (01472) 323345
www.welcome.to/NFHCentre/
A journey of discovery, experience the reality of life on a deep-sea trawler. Interactive games and displays. Children's area.

National Museum of Photography, Film & Television
Bradford
Tel: (01274) 202030 www.nmpft.org.uk
Experience the past, present and future of photography, film and television with amazing interactive displays and spectacular 3D IMAX cinema. Museum admission is free.

National Railway Museum
Leeman Road, York
Tel: (01904) 621261 www.nrm.org.uk
Discover the story of the train in a great day out for all the family. The National Railway Museum mixes fascination and education with hours of fun. And best of all, it's free.

Newby Hall & Gardens
Ripon
Tel: (01423) 322583
www.newbyhall.com
Late 17thC house with additions, interior by Robert Adam, classical sculpture, Gobelins tapestries, 25 acres (10ha) of gardens, miniature railway, children's adventure garden.

2

3

1. Worsbrough Mill Museum, South Yorkshire
2. Staithes, North Yorkshire
3. North Yorkshire Moors, Railway Steam Train

North Yorkshire Moors Railway
Pickering Station, Pickering
Tel: (01751) 472508
www.nymr.demon.co.uk
Britain's most popular heritage railway travelling through the beautiful North York Moors National Park.

Nunnington Hall (National Trust)
Nunnington, York
Tel: (01439) 748283 www.nationaltrust.org.uk
Large 17thC manor-house situated on banks of River Rye. With hall, bedrooms, nursery, maid's room (haunted), Carlisle collection of miniature rooms. National Trust shop.

Pleasure Island Family Theme Park
Kings Road, Cleethorpes
Tel: (01472) 211511 www.pleasure-island.co.uk
The East Coast's biggest fun day out, with over 50 rides and attractions. Whatever the weather, fun is guaranteed with lots of undercover attractions. Shows from around the world.

Ripley Castle
Ripley, Harrogate
Tel: (01423) 770152
www.ripleycastle.co.uk
Ripley Castle, home to the Ingilby family for over 26 generations is set in the heart of a delightful estate with Victorian walled gardens, deer park and pleasure grounds.

Royal Armouries Museum
Armouries Drive, Leeds
Tel: (0113) 220 1916 www.armouries.org.uk
Experience more than 3,000 years of history covered by over 8,000 spectacular exhibits and stunning surroundings. Arms and armour.

Ryedale Folk Museum
Hutton-le-Hole, York
Tel: (01751) 417367
www.ryedalefolkmuseum.co.uk
Reconstructed local buildings including cruck-framed long-houses Elizabethan manor-house, furnished cottages, craftsmen's tools, household/agricultural implements.

Sea Life and Marine Sanctuary
Scalby Mills, Scarborough
Tel: (01723) 376125 www.sealife.co.uk
At the Sea Life Centre you have the opportunity to meet creatures that live in and around the oceans of the British Isles, ranging from starfish and crabs to rays and seals.

Sheffield Botanical Gardens
Clarkehouse Road, Sheffield
Tel: (0114) 267 6496 www.sbg.org.uk
Extensive gardens with over 5,500 species of plants, Grade II Listed garden pavilion (now closed).

Skipton Castle
Skipton
Tel: (01756) 792442
www.skiptoncastle.co.uk
Fully-roofed Skipton Castle is in excellent condition. One of the most complete and well-preserved medieval castles in England.

Wensleydale Cheese Visitor Centre
Gayle Lane, Hawes
Tel: (01969) 667664 www.wensleydale.co.uk
Viewing gallery, see real Wensleydale cheese being made by hand. Interpretation area, including rolling video, display and photographic boards. Museum, shop and cafe.

Wigfield Farm
Worsbrough Bridge, Barnsley
Tel: (01226) 733702
http://sites.barnsley.ac.uk/wigfield
Open working farm with rare and commercial breeds of farm animals including pigs, cattle, sheep, goats, donkeys, ponies and small pet animals.

York Castle Museum
The Eye of York, York
Tel: (01904) 653611 www.york.gov.uk
England's most popular museum of everyday life including reconstructed streets and period rooms.

York Minster
Deangate, York
Tel: (01904) 557200 www.yorkminster.org
York Minster is the largest medieval Gothic cathedral north of the alps. Museum of Roman/Norman remains. Chapter house.

Yorkshire Tourist Board

312 Tadcaster Road, York YO24 1GS.
T: (01904) 707070 (24-hour brochure line)
F: (01904) 701414
E: info@ytb.org.uk
www.yorkshirevisitor.com

THE FOLLOWING PUBLICATIONS ARE AVAILABLE FROM YORKSHIRE TOURIST BOARD:

Yorkshire Visitor Guide 2004 –
information on Yorkshire and Northern Lincolnshire, including hotels, self-catering, camping and caravan parks. Also attractions, shops, restaurants and major events

Walk Yorkshire –
a walking pack tailored to meet the individual's needs according to the area they are interested in

Hidden Yorkshire –
a guide to Yorkshire's less well known haunts

Yorkshire on Screen –
a guide to Yorkshire's TV, Movie, and Literary heritage

Eating out Guide –
information on eateries in Yorkshire

Getting to Yorkshire

BY ROAD: Motorways: M1, M62, M606, M621, M18, M180, M181, A1(M). Trunk roads: A1, A19, A57, A58, A59, A61, A62, A63, A64, A65, A66.

BY RAIL: InterCity services to Bradford, Doncaster, Harrogate, Kingston upon Hull, Leeds, Sheffield, Wakefield and York. Frequent regional railway services city centre to city centre including Manchester Airport service to Scarborough, York and Leeds.

1. The Humber Bridge
2. Whitby, North Yorkshire

Where to stay in

Yorkshire

All place names in the blue bands under which accommodation is listed, are shown on the maps at the front of this guide.

Symbols give useful information about services and facilities. Inside the back cover flap there's a key to these symbols which you can keep open for easy reference.

A complete listing of all the VisitBritain assessed accommodation covered by this guide appears at the back of this guide.

AISKEW, North Yorkshire Map ref 5C3

★★★★

4 Units
Sleeping 4–6

THE COURTYARD

Aiskew, Bedale
Contact: Mr & Mrs J Cartman
T: (01677) 423689
F: (01677) 425762
E: jill@courtyard.ndirect.co.uk
I: www.courtyard.ndirect.co.uk

Completely rebuilt with rustic brick and cobble, these delightful cottages, with their beamed ceilings, combine local country craftsmanship with all modern facilities. Cleverly designed and furnished, they provide superb holiday homes conveniently situated on the edge of the old market town of Bedale, James Herriot's "Gateway to the Dales".

OPEN All Year
CC: Mastercard, Switch, Visa

Off-peak short breaks by arrangement.

Low season per wk
£179.00–£221.00
High season per wk
£216.00–£360.00

QUALITY ASSURANCE SCHEME

Star ratings were correct at the time of going to press but are subject to change. Please check at the time of booking.

AMPLEFORTH, North Yorkshire Map ref 5C3

★★★★

1 Unit
Sleeping 4

Attractive stone cottage on the edge of National Park, enjoying splendid views. Immaculate decorative order throughout. Price fully inclusive. Close to village amenities. Superb eating hostelries locally. Ideally situated for walking, moors, coast. Twenty miles York, 10 miles Castle Howard. Non-smoking establishment. Personal attention by resident owners.

HILLSIDE COTTAGE

Ampleforth, York
Contact: Mrs P Noble, Hillside, West End, Ampleforth, York YO62 4DY
T: (01439) 788303
F: (01439) 788303
E: hillsidecottage@westend-ampleforth.co.uk
I: www.cottageguide.co.uk/hillsidecottage

OPEN All Year

Low season per wk
Min £185.00
High season per wk
Max £300.00

ASKRIGG, North Yorkshire Map ref 5B3

★★★-★★★★

9 Units
Sleeping 7

ASKRIGG COTTAGES

Askrigg, Leyburn
Contact: Mrs K M Empsall, Whitfield, Helm, Askrigg, Leyburn DL8 3JF
T: (01969) 650565
F: (01969) 650565
E: empsall@askrigg-cottages.co.uk
I: www.askrigg-cottages.co.uk

OPEN All Year
CC: Mastercard, Visa

Low season per wk
£170.00–£350.00
High season per wk
£240.00–£490.00

Traditional Dales cottages and farmhouses in peaceful locations near rivers and meadows in the heart of the Yorkshire Dales National Park. Pets welcome.

TOWN INDEX

This can be found at the back of the guide. If you know where you want to stay, the index will give you the page number listing accommodation in your chosen town, city or village.

YORKSHIRE'S DALES, MOORS & COAST

Dales Holiday Cottages

Superb, personally inspected, self catering holiday properties in beautiful rural and coastal locations including Heartbeat, Herriot and Brontë country. Cosy cottages to country houses, many welcome pets and most are open all year.
Phone for free brochure.

01756 799821 & 790919

www.dalesholcot.com

English Tourism Council
Committed to ETC Quality Assurance

BARMBY MOOR, East Riding of Yorkshire Map ref 4C1

★★★★

1 Unit
Sleeping 6

NORTHWOOD COACH HOUSE

Barmby Moor, York
Contact: Mrs A Gregory
T: (01759) 302305
E: annjgregory@hotmail.com

This pretty, three-bedroomed, converted Victorian coach house overlooks open countryside. Warm and cosy in winter, it is ideally situated in a picturesque village on the edge of the Wolds, only 12 miles from York and convenient for the coast and moors. Pubs, shops and restaurants nearby.

OPEN All Year

Short breaks (3 days) £250, bookable 28 days in advance.

Low season per wk
£350.00–£400.00
High season per wk
£400.00–£520.00

BEVERLEY, East Riding of Yorkshire Map ref 4C1 *Tourist Information Centre Tel: (01482) 867430*

★★★★

8 Units
Sleeping 2–6

RUDSTONE WALK COUNTRY ACCOMMODATION

South Cave, Brough
Contact: Mrs L Greenwood,
Rudstone Walk Country Cottages, South Cave, Brough, Nr Beverly HU15 2AH
T: (01430) 422230
F: (01430) 424552
E: admin@rudstone-walk.co.uk
I: www.rudstone-walk.co.uk

Superb sunsets and views across the Yorkshire Wolds surround our extremely comfortable, cottage-style apartments. Fully licensed, the 400-year-old farmhouse serves meals in your cottage or 'en-famille' in the beautiful beamed dining room, if required. B&B also available. Ideal location for Beverley, York, the Heritage Coastline or the Moors. Telephone for colour brochure.

OPEN All Year
CC: Amex, Delta, Diners, JCB, Mastercard, Solo, Switch, Visa

3-day, self-catering breaks available all year, including Christmas and New Year, for family gatherings.

Low season per wk
Min £225.00
High season per wk
Min £340.00

BOLTON ABBEY, North Yorkshire Map ref 4B1

Rating Applied For

1 Unit
Sleeping 6

THE BEAMSLEY PROJECT
Beamsley, Skipton
Contact: Margaret and John Tomlinson, The Beamsley Project, Beamsley, Skipton BD23 6JA
T: (01756) 710255
F: (01756) 710255
E: beamsley.project@virgin.net
I: www.beamsleyproject.org.uk

OPEN All Year

Low season per wk
£210.00–£350.00
High season per wk
£280.00–£420.00

Comfortable, three-twin-bedded cottage, fully equipped for people with disabilities; wheelchair lift, hoist, walk-in shower. Near Bolton Abbey with easy accessible footpaths for disabled.

CREDIT CARD BOOKINGS If you book by telephone and are asked for your credit card number it is advisable to check the proprietor's policy should you cancel your reservation.

BRIDLINGTON, East Riding of Yorkshire Map ref 5D3 *Tourist Information Centre Tel: (01262) 673474*

★-★★★

4 Units
Sleeping 2–5

HIGHCLIFFE HOLIDAY APARTMENTS

Bridlington
Contact: Mrs P Willcocks, Highcliffe Holiday Apartments, 19 Albion Terrace, Bridlington YO15 2PJ
T: (01262) 674127

On the seafront, south facing, only 50 metres from sandy beach and promenade. All apartments have uninterrupted views along the beach to the harbour. Ideal position for main shopping centre, restaurants and Leisure World complex. Fully equipped, with high standard of furnishing, each with own private bathroom facilities.

OPEN All Year

Low season per wk
£70.00–£200.00
High season per wk
£150.00–£350.00

BURNSALL, North Yorkshire Map ref 5B3

★★★★

1 Unit
Sleeping 6

THE SYCAMORES

Burnsall, Skipton
Contact: Mrs S Carr, DSC Holiday Lettings Ltd, Moor Green Farm, Threshfield, Skipton BD23 5NR
T: (01756) 752435
F: (01756) 752435
E: carr@totalise.co.uk

A large, spacious, well-equipped cottage overlooking the village green and river. Open fire in lounge. Patio with furniture and barbecue. Ideal for any time of year. Excellently situated for walking/touring the Dales.

OPEN All Year

Weekends and short breaks available Oct–Mar.

Low season per wk
£200.00–£250.00
High season per wk
£300.00–£475.00

BURTON-IN-LONSDALE, North Yorkshire Map ref 5B3

★★★★

2 Units
Sleeping 5

BRENTWOOD FARM COTTAGES

Burton-in-Lonsdale, Carnforth
Contact: Mrs A Taylor, Brentwood Farm Cottages, Barnoldswick Lane, Burton-in-Lonsdale, Carnforth LA6 3LZ
T: (015242) 62155
F: (015242) 62155
E: info@brentwoodfarmcottages.co.uk
I: www.brentwoodfarmcottages.co.uk

Relax in a spacious, yet cosy, new barn conversion located in a tranquil setting on a working dairy farm. Centrally situated for the Lake District, Yorkshire Dales, Lune Valley and Forest of Bowland. Ingleton waterfalls walk, three peaks and show caves nearby. Private walking and fishing available on site.

OPEN All Year
CC: Delta, JCB, Mastercard, Solo, Switch, Visa

Winter short breaks available. Seasonal hedge laying and walling and computer tuition available on request.

Low season per wk
Min £220.00
High season per wk
£440.00–£460.00

WEB
www.visitengland.com
Log on for information and inspiration. The latest information on places to visit, events and quality assessed accommodation.

COMMONDALE, North Yorkshire Map ref 5C3

★★★

3 Units
Sleeping 2–6

FOWL GREEN FARM

Commondale, Whitby
Contact: Mrs S Muir, Fowl Green Farm, Commondale, Whitby YO21 2HN
T: (01287) 660742
E: susan.muir@ukonline.co.uk
I: www.fowlgreenfarm.com

Three 18thC rough-stone pigsties and barn, converted to combine original features with 21stC comfort, set on a traditional hill sheep farm with footpaths and picnic sites across the farmland. The cottages are accesible to all having ground floor bedroom, adapted bath/shower facilities and outside patio, barbecues and garden areas.

OPEN All Year

Short breaks available – minimum 2 nights.

Low season per wk
£160.00–£380.00
High season per wk
£180.00–£460.00

CROPTON, North Yorkshire Map ref 5C3

★★★★

7 Units
Sleeping 2–12

BECKHOUSE COTTAGES

Cropton, Pickering
Contact: Mrs P Smith, Beckhouse Cottages, Beckhouse Farm, Cropton, Pickering YO18 8ER
T: (01751) 417235
F: (01751) 417218
E: beckhousecottages@hotmail.com
I: www.beckhousecottages.co.uk

OPEN All Year

Low season per wk
£170.00–£230.00
High season per wk
£260.00–£430.00

Working farm, keeping mostly horses for carriage driving and breeding. Private gardens. Beautiful walking countryside. Handy for forest, moors and sea. Winter breaks available.

DANBY, North Yorkshire Map ref 5C3

★★★

1 Unit
Sleeping 6

BLACKMIRES FARM

Danby, Whitby
Contact: Mrs G M Rhys
T: (01287) 660352
E: gl.rhys@freenet.co.uk

OPEN All Year except Christmas

Low season per wk
£275.00–£325.00
High season per wk
£325.00–£400.00

Stone cottage adjoining farmhouse. Two bedrooms and bathroom on ground floor, twin bedroom upstairs. Three miles from Danby village in North Yorkshire National Park.

★★

1 Unit
Sleeping 6

CLITHERBECKS FARM

Danby, Whitby
Contact: Mr N Harland, Clitherbecks Farm, Danby, Whitby YO21 2NT
T: (01287) 660321
E: nharland@clitherbecks.freeserve.co.uk
I: www.clitherbecks.freeserve.co.uk

OPEN All Year

Low season per wk
£160.00–£260.00
High season per wk
£190.00–£300.00

Get away from it all in this 18thC farmhouse at the head of its own valley in the North York Moors National Park.

DRIFFIELD, East Riding of Yorkshire Map ref 4C1

★★★

2 Units
Sleeping 5

MANOR FARM COTTAGES

Driffield
Contact: Mr & Mrs A Byass
T: (01377) 217324
F: (01377) 217840
E: lanpulses@aol.com

OPEN All Year

Low season per wk
£175.00–£250.00
High season per wk
£250.00–£375.00

Fully modernised Georgian cottages in pretty village. Ideal for exploring York, Beverley and east coast. Moors and many stately homes within easy driving distance.

RATING **All accommodation in this guide has been rated, or is awaiting a rating, by a trained VisitBritain assessor.**

EBBERSTON, North Yorkshire Map ref 5D3

★★★-★★★★

8 Units
Sleeping 2–6

CLIFF HOUSE
Ebberston, Scarborough
Contact: Mr S J Morris, Cliff House, Ebberston, Scarborough YO13 9PA
T: (01723) 859440
F: (01723) 850005
E: cliffhouseebberston@btinternet.com
I: www.cliffhouse-cottageholidays.co.uk

OPEN All Year

Low season per wk
£200.00–£325.00
High season per wk
£375.00–£850.00

Comfortable cottages in the grounds of a historic former manor house. Heated indoor pool, jacuzzi, hard tennis court, games room. Colour brochure available on request.

FILEY, North Yorkshire Map ref 5D3

★★-★★★

11 Units
Sleeping 2–7

BEACH HOLIDAY FLATS
Filey
Contact: Mr D Tindall, Beach Holiday Flats, 9-10 The Beach, Filey YO14 9LA
T: (01723) 513178
E: anntindall@aol.com
I: www.thebeach-holidayflats.co.uk

Probably the best position on the east coast, 25 yards from the seafront, fabulous views over Filey Brigg, Bempton Rocks and Flamborough Head. We pride ourselves on the quality of our decor, fixtures and fittings, cleanliness and hospitality. The perfect location for your east coast holiday. Filey – gem of the Yorkshire coast.

OPEN All Year

Low season per wk
£115.00–£185.00
High season per wk
£185.00–£455.00

★★★

5 Units
Sleeping 5

THE COTTAGES
Filey
Contact: Mr & Mrs D Teet, The Cottages, Muston Grange, Muston Road, Filey YO14 0HU
T: (01723) 516620
F: (01723) 516620
I: www.mustongrangefiley.co.uk

OPEN All Year
CC: Delta, JCB, Mastercard, Solo, Switch, Visa

Low season per wk
£250.00–£310.00
High season per wk
£380.00–£470.00

Situated between Muston and Filey, the cottages are a range of converted traditional ex-farm buildings providing quality accommodation in a private courtyard setting.

FYLINGTHORPE, North Yorkshire Map ref 5D3

★★★-★★★★

5 Units
Sleeping 2–10

SOUTH HOUSE FARMHOUSE & COTTAGES
Fylingthorpe, Whitby
Contact: Mrs N Pattinson, South House Farmhouse & Cottages, Millbeck, Fylingthorpe, Whitby YO22 4UQ
T: (01947) 880243
F: (01947) 880243
E: kmp@bogglehole.fsnet.co.uk
I: www.southhousefarm.co.uk

OPEN All Year

Low season per wk
£120.00–£700.00
High season per wk
£220.00–£1,000.00

Situated in 180 acres of farmland near Robin Hood's Bay. Wonderful walks in National Park. Beach 0.5 miles. Super refurbished farmhouse, and luxury cottages. Large garden. Parking.

CHECK THE MAPS

The colour maps at the front of this guide show all the cities, towns and villages for which you will find accommodation entries. Refer to the town index to find the page on which they are listed.

GILLING WEST, North Yorkshire Map ref 5C3

★★★★

3 Units
Sleeping 2–10

Magnificent properties converted from traditional stone barns situated in idyllic courtyard setting, overlooking delightful open countryside. An ideal base from which to explore Swaledale and surrounding area.

GILLING OLD MILL COTTAGES

Gilling West, Richmond
Contact: Mr & Mrs H Bird, Gilling Old Mill Waters Lane, Gilling West, Richmond DL10 5JD
T: (01748) 822771
F: (01748) 821734
E: admin@yorkshiredales-cottages.com
I: www.yorkshiredales-cottages.com

OPEN All Year

Low season per wk
£165.00–£335.00
High season per wk
£220.00–£695.00

GLAISDALE, North Yorkshire Map ref 5C3

★★

1 Unit
Sleeping 2

LANES COTTAGE
Glaisdale, Whitby
Contact: Mr & Mrs J Dale
T: (01947) 897316

OPEN All Year

Lanes Cottage is an old, stone-built cottage with beamed ceilings, adjoining owners' old farmhouse, close to moorland walks and Heartbeat country. Eight miles from Whitby.

Low season per wk
£160.00–£225.00
High season per wk
£225.00–£270.00

GOATHLAND, North Yorkshire Map ref 5D3

★★★★

1 Unit
Sleeping 8

ESKHOLME
Goathland, Whitby
Contact: Mrs J M Hodgson
T: (01924) 498154
E: ffsjan@aol.com

OPEN All Year

Four-bedroomed house tucked away in delightful moorland village in heart of National Park. Good walking country, regular steam trains to Pickering. Eight miles from Whitby.

Low season per wk
£225.00–£285.00
High season per wk
£375.00–£480.00

★★★★★

1 Unit
Sleeping 6

Located at the edge of the village on a private roadway, this charming cottage has been completely refurbished to the highest standards. Every luxury is included, and the property is ideally suited to families or a couple seeking a rather special retreat in the National Park. Open all year. Send for brochure.

ORCHARD COTTAGE

Goathland, Whitby
Contact: Mrs C Carr, Orchard Farm, Goathland, Whitby YO22 5JX
T: (01947) 896391
F: (01947) 896001
E: enquiries@theorchardcottages.co.uk
I: www.theorchardcottages.co.uk

OPEN All Year
CC: Delta, Mastercard, Solo, Switch, Visa

Low season per wk
£350.00–£390.00
High season per wk
£630.00–£700.00

GRASSINGTON, North Yorkshire Map ref 5B3 *Tourist Information Centre Tel: (01756) 752774*

★★★★

1 Unit
Sleeping 4

THE BARN
Grassington, Skipton
Contact: Mrs P G Evans
T: (01274) 561546
E: grassington@ukonline.co.uk
I: www.dalestay.co.uk/thebarn

OPEN All Year

Ground floor of a tastefully converted Yorkshire Dales barn. In quiet, private fold off the main square. Secluded, south-facing garden. Garage, plus parking facilities.

10

Low season per wk
£240.00–£265.00
High season per wk
£450.00–£475.00

GRASSINGTON continued

★★★★

1 Unit
Sleeping 4

An 18thC former lead miner's cottage which has been recently refurbished to show many of the original features. This cosy and comfortable cottage is ideally situated for exploring the Dales either on foot or by car. Relax in the evening by strolling down the main street to the pub.

MANNA COTTAGE

Grassington, Skipton
Contact: Mrs S Carr, Moor Green Farm, Tarns Lane, Threshfield, Skipton BD23 5NR
T: (01756) 752435
F: (01756) 752435
E: carr@totalise.co.uk
I: www.yorkshirenet.co.uk/stayat/mannacottage/

OPEN All Year

Weekend breaks available Oct-Mar.

Low season per wk
£180.00–£210.00
High season per wk
£270.00–£375.00

★★★

1 Unit
Sleeping 6

SUNNYSIDE COTTAGE

Grassington, Skipton
Contact: Mrs C Butt, Garris Lodge, Rylstone, Skipton BD23 6LJ
T: (01756) 730391
E: c.butt@daelnet.co.uk
I: www.cosycottages.com

OPEN All Year

Low season per wk
Min £180.00
High season per wk
Max £460.00

Beautiful 300-year-old barn conversion. Ideally situated overlooking open fields, yet only 150 metres from the quaint old cobbled village square. Mob: 07720 294391.

HALIFAX, West Yorkshire Map ref 4B1 *Tourist Information Centre Tel: (01422) 368725*

★★★★

2 Units
Sleeping 4

Warm, comfortable, stone-built cottages set in two acres of natural woodland/heather garden with superb Pennine views and direct access to open countryside and footpaths. Close to a quiet Calderdale village with good pubs and restaurants nearby. Ideal location for exploring Bronte country and Pennine Yorkshire.

CHERRY TREE COTTAGES

Barkisland, Halifax
Contact: Mr S & Mrs E Shaw, Cherry Tree Cottages, Wall Nook, Barkisland, Halifax HX4 0BL
T: (01422) 372662
F: (01422) 372662
E: cherry.tree@zen.co.uk
I: www.yorkshire-cottages.co.uk

OPEN All Year
CC: Delta, Mastercard, Visa

Short breaks available, minimum 3 nights. Check our website for late availability.

Low season per wk
£240.00–£250.00
High season per wk
£330.00–£395.00

COUNTRY CODE Always follow the Country Code · Enjoy the countryside and respect its life and work · Guard against all risk of fire · Fasten all gates · Keep your dogs under close control · Keep to public paths across farmland · Use gates and stiles to cross fences, hedges and walls · Leave livestock, crops and machinery alone · Take your litter home · Help to keep all water clean · Protect wildlife, plants and trees · Take special care on country roads · Make no unnecessary noise

HARROGATE, North Yorkshire Map ref 4B1 *Tourist Information Centre Tel: (01423) 537300*

★★★★

23 Units
Sleeping 3

ASHNESS APARTMENTS

Harrogate
Contact: Mr J Spinlove & Miss H Spinlove,
15 St Mary's Avenue, Harrogate HG2 0LP
T: (01423) 526894
F: (01423) 700038
E: office@ashness.com
I: www.ashness.com

High-quality apartments, superbly situated in a nice, quiet road of fine Victorian townhouses very near the town centre of Harrogate. Excellent shops, restaurants and cafes are a short walk away through Montpellier Gardens with the Stray and Valley Gardens just around the corner.

OPEN All Year
CC: Amex, Delta, JCB, Mastercard, Solo, Switch, Visa

Short breaks available from £60pn, minimum 2 nights.

Low season per wk
£270.00–£345.00
High season per wk
£330.00–£465.00

★★★-★★★★★

10 Units
Sleeping 2–8

BRIMHAM ROCKS COTTAGES

Fellbeck, Harrogate
Contact: Mrs J M Martin, Brimham Rocks Cottages, High North Farm, Fellbeck, Harrogate HG3 5EY
T: (01765) 620284
F: (01765) 620477
E: brimham@nascr.net
I: www.brimham.co.uk

Overlooking Brimham Rocks and with views of up to 60 miles, these individual cottages are ideally situated to explore both Dales and Moors, York, Ripon, Harrogate, Leeds and the east coast. Converted from old farm buildings, the cottages are warm, cosy, comfortable and decorated with flair and imagination. A warm welcome guaranteed.

OPEN All Year

Short breaks at 66% of weekly rate.

Low season per wk
£235.00–£335.00
High season per wk
£415.00–£595.00

★★★★

3 Units
Sleeping 3–5

DINMORE COTTAGES

Burnt Yates, Harrogate
Contact: Mrs Susan Chapman
T: (01423) 770860
F: (01423) 770860
E: aib@dinmore-cottages.freeserve.co.uk
I: www.dinmore-cottages.co.uk

Award-winning Dales cottages converted from 17thC farmstead. Peaceful situation, breathtaking views over Nidderdale, a protected Area of Outstanding Natural Beauty. Only seven miles to spa town of Harrogate, close to York and Herriot country. Ideal for walkers and bird-watchers and for touring and sightseeing in the Yorkshire Dales.

OPEN All Year

Low season per wk
£240.00–£325.00
High season per wk
£395.00–£580.00

ACCESSIBILITY

Look for the symbols which indicate National Accessible Scheme standards for hearing and visually impaired guests in addition to standards for guests with mobility impairment. Additional participants are shown in the listings at the back.

HARROGATE continued

★★★

3 Units
Sleeping 4–5

HOLLY HOUSE FARM COTTAGES

Darley, Harrogate
Contact: Miss M Owen, Holly House Farm Cottages, Holly House Farm, Moorcock Lane, Darley, Harrogate HG3 2QL
T: (01423) 780266
F: (01423) 780299
E: hollyhousecottages@supanet.com
I: www.hollyhousecottages.co.uk

OPEN All Year
CC: Delta, Mastercard, Visa

Low season per wk
£250.00–£275.00
High season per wk
£375.00–£400.00

Outstanding views in Nidderdale. Fully centrally heated character cottages in converted milking parlour outside Darley. One suitable mildly disabled. Pets welcome.

★★★★

1 Unit
Sleeping 4

KENT ROAD COTTAGE

Harrogate
Contact: Mrs E McCullough
T: (01423) 560223
E: Innuk@hotmail.com

OPEN All Year
CC: Delta, Mastercard, Switch, Visa

Low season per wk
£250.00–£300.00
High season per wk
£250.00–£375.00

Immaculate two-bedroomed, detached cottage in lovely neighbourhood. Walking distance to Harrogate centre. Recently renovated with lovely furnishings. Gift basket upon arrival.

★★★

1 Unit
Sleeping 3

MOOR VIEW COTTAGE

Harrogate
Contact: Mrs H L Sweeting, 45 Kingsley Drive, Harrogate HG1 4TH
T: (01423) 885498
E: hlsweeting@easicom.com
I: www.mvcottage.netfirms.com

OPEN All Year

Low season per wk
£175.00–£210.00
High season per wk
£210.00–£245.00

Moor View Cottage is a delightful, fully furnished, two-bedroomed cottage, 10 minutes' walk from Harrogate Conference Centre and town shops. Shorter stays available.

★★★★

3 Units
Sleeping 3–6

MOUNT PLEASANT FARM HOLIDAY COTTAGE

Killinghall, Harrogate
Contact: Mrs L Prest, Mount Pleasant Farm, Skipton Road, Killinghall, Harrogate HG3 2BU
T: (01423) 504694

Converted farm buildings which retain character, set in the countryside. Family pub nearby. Two miles from Harrogate spa town and ideal for exploring Yorkshire Dales. Briar Cottage is a detached cottage standing in its own priavte area.

OPEN All Year

Low season per wk
£195.00–£250.00
High season per wk
£290.00–£410.00

QUALITY ASSURANCE SCHEME

For an explanation of the quality and facilities represented by the Stars please refer to the front of this guide. A more detailed explanation can be found in the information pages at the back.

HARROGATE continued

★★★

10 Units
Sleeping 2–6

Choose from our traditional, stone-built houses in the beautiful grounds of Rudding Park or our timber lodges set in delightful woodland clearings, many overlooking a small lake. Three miles south of Harrogate, Deer House family pub, shop, swimming pool, children's playground, games room, 18-hole golf course and driving range.

RUDDING HOLIDAY PARK

Follifoot, Harrogate
Contact: Mr M Hutchinson, Rudding Holiday Park, Rudding Park, Follifoot, Harrogate HG3 1JH
T: (01423) 870439
F: (01423) 870859
E: holiday-park@ruddingpark.com
I: www.ruddingpark.com

OPEN All Year
CC: Delta, Diners, Mastercard, Solo, Switch, Visa

Receive £20 off your booking if you mention this advert when making your reservation.

Low season per wk
£250.00–£835.00

HAWES, North Yorkshire Map ref 5B3 *Tourist Information Centre Tel: (01969) 667450*

★★★★

4 Units
Sleeping 4–6

MILE HOUSE FARM COUNTRY COTTAGES

Hawes
Contact: Mrs A Fawcett, Mile House Farm Country Cottages, Mile House Farm, Hawes DL8 3PT
T: (01969) 667481
F: (01969) 667425
E: milehousefarm@hotmail.com
I: www.wensleydale.uk.com

OPEN All Year

Low season per wk
£175.00–£325.00
High season per wk
£375.00–£600.00

Traditional old Dales stone cottages with beamed ceilings and open fires. Peaceful locations with spectacular views. Well equipped, warm and comfortable. Free trout fishing on farm.

HAWORTH, West Yorkshire Map ref 4B1 *Tourist Information Centre Tel: (01535) 642329*

★★★-★★★★

5 Units
Sleeping 2–6

A fine range of historic cottages in the heart of Bronte country. Modern, spacious amenities, yet old world charm. Watch steam trains from your warm, cosy cottage or collect your own fresh eggs on a working farm! An ideal location for exploring all of Yorkshire and even the Lake District. Groups of 19 welcome.

BRONTE COUNTRY COTTAGES

Haworth, Keighley
Contact: Ms C Pickles
T: (01535) 644568
F: (01535) 646686
E: clare@brontecountrycottages.co.uk
I: www.brontecountrycottages.co.uk

OPEN All Year
CC: Delta, Mastercard, Switch, Visa

Short breaks available (minimum 3 nights). Discounts on second week of 2-week booking.

Low season per wk
£150.00–£320.00
High season per wk
£270.00–£520.00

★★★★

1 Unit
Sleeping 4

HERON COTTAGE

Haworth, Keighley
Contact: Mr & Mrs R Walker, Vale Barn, Mytholmes Lane, Haworth, Keighley BD22 0EE
T: (01535) 648537
E: jan_w@tinyworld.co.uk

OPEN All Year

Low season per wk
Max £230.00
High season per wk
Max £365.00

Comfortable cottage in peaceful location beside River Worth. Set in paddocks and woodland with abundant walks. Haworth village and steam trains nearby. Also Yorkshire Dales.

HAWORTH continued

★★★★

2 Units
Sleeping 4

HEWENDEN MILL COTTAGES

Cullingworth, Bradford
Contact: Mrs Janet Emanuel
T: (01535) 271834
F: (01535) 273943
E: info@hewendenmillcottages.co.uk
I: www.hewendenmillcottages.co.uk

Ideally located in idyllic Bronte country, our cottages provide a perfect base for exploring northern England. Set in 10 acres of ancient woodland, they form part of an old water-mill complex and have been recently renovated to provide luxury, self-catering accommodation. Ideal for lovers of walking, wildlife and Wuthering Heights!

OPEN All Year
CC: Mastercard, Solo, Switch, Visa

Short breaks our speciality: 3-night weekend and 4-night mid-week (excl Bank Holidays).

Low season per wk
£200.00–£300.00
High season per wk
£310.00–£450.00

HEBDEN BRIDGE, West Yorkshire Map ref 4B1 *Tourist Information Centre Tel: (01422) 843831*

★★★

1 Unit
Sleeping 4

3 BIRKS HALL COTTAGE

Cragg Vale, Hebden Bridge
Contact: Mrs H Wilkinson, 1 Birks Hall Cottage, Cragg Vale, Hebden Bridge HX7 5SB
T: (01422) 882064

OPEN All Year

Low season per wk
£100.00–£130.00
High season per wk
£130.00–£180.00

Country cottage with two bedrooms, bathroom, kitchen and lounge with Georgian windows. In a small, picturesque village near the Pennine centre of Hebden Bridge.

★★★

1 Unit
Sleeping 4

15 OLDGATE

Hebden Bridge
Contact: Mrs J Barker, Cobweb Cottage, Banks Farm, Mytholmroyd, Hebden Bridge HX7 5RF
T: (01422) 845929
F: (01422) 846354
E: janatcobweb@aol.com

OPEN All Year

Low season per wk
£250.00
High season per wk
£300.00

Riverside cottage, well furnished. Linen supplied. Centrally heated and very cosy. Ideal for walkers and ramblers. Situated at foot of Pennines.

HELMSLEY, North Yorkshire Map ref 5C3

★★★★

1 Unit
Sleeping 4

TOWNEND COTTAGE

Beadlam, Nawton, York
Contact: Mrs M Begg, Townend Farmhouse, High Lane, Beadlam, Nawton, York YO62 7SY
T: (01439) 770103
E: margaret.begg@ukgateway.net
I: www.visityorkshire.com

Originally part of an 18thC farmhouse, this is a very warm, comfortable, two-bedroomed stone cottage with oak beams. Situated off the main road in village three miles from charming market town of Helmsley. Ideal for walking or touring moors, coast and York. Central heating and log fire included in price.

OPEN All Year

Low season per wk
Min £175.00
High season per wk
£265.00–£330.00

HEPTONSTALL, West Yorkshire Map ref 4B1

★★

1 Unit
Sleeping 5

5 DRAPER CORNER

Heptonstall, Hebden Bridge
Contact: Mrs S A Taylor
T: (01422) 844323

OPEN All Year

Low season per wk
£180.00–£230.00
High season per wk
£230.00–£330.00

Delightful 18thC cottage overlooking spectacular moorland/National Park views. Easy access to cities and Dales. Author's home when in England, furnished with personal antiques, books, pictures.

HIGH BENTHAM, North Yorkshire Map ref 5B3

★★★★

1 Unit
Sleeping 4

HOLMES FARM COTTAGE

Low Bentham, Lancaster
Contact: Mrs L J Story, Holmes Farm Cottage, Holmes Farm, Low Bentham, Lancaster LA2 7DE
T: (015242) 61198
E: lucy@clucy.demon.co.uk

OPEN All Year

Low season per wk
Min £180.00
High season per wk
Max £255.00

Tastefully converted stone cottage with large landscaped garden, surrounded by 127 acres of beautiful pastureland. Ideal base for visiting Lake District, Dales and coast.

HOLMFIRTH, West Yorkshire Map ref 4B1

★★★★

3 Units
Sleeping 2–10

UPPERGATE FARM

Hepworth, Holmfirth, Huddersfield
Contact: Mrs A Booth
T: (01484) 681369
F: (01484) 687343
E: stevenal.booth@virgin.net
I: www.uppergatefarm.co.uk

Farm cottages set in beautiful countryside on the edge of Hepworth, a lovely Pennine village. The cottages form part of a small hamlet in a conservation area. Flagstone floors and exposed beams abound. Peaceful location with extensive gardens and woodland walks. One- and three-bedroom cottages available.

OPEN All Year
CC: Amex, Mastercard, Switch, Visa

Short breaks available throughout the year. Farm activities for children. Safe play areas. Excellent pub/restaurant within five minutes' walk.

Low season per wk
£120.00–£250.00
High season per wk
£200.00–£500.00

HORTON-IN-RIBBLESDALE, North Yorkshire Map ref 5B3 *Tourist Information Centre Tel: (01729) 860333*

★★★

1 Unit
Sleeping 5

BLIND BECK HOLIDAY COTTAGE

Horton-in-Ribblesdale, Settle
Contact: Mrs M Huddleston, Blind Beck, Horton-in-Ribblesdale, Settle BD24 0HT
T: (01729) 860396
E: h.huddleston@daelnet.co.uk
I: www.blindbeck.co.uk

OPEN All Year

Low season per wk
£175.00–£200.00
High season per wk
£200.00–£300.00

This 17thC cottage is full of character, in the centre of the Three Peaks area and near the Settle-Carlisle railway.

★★★-★★★★

2 Units
Sleeping 4–6

SELSIDE FARM HOLIDAY COTTAGES

Selside, Settle
Contact: Mrs S E Lambert, Selside Farm, Selside, Settle BD24 0HZ
T: (01729) 860367
E: shirley@lam67.freeserve.co.uk

OPEN All Year

Low season per wk
£130.00–£250.00
High season per wk
£250.00–£385.00

Converted barn and adjoining cottage – three and two bedrooms. In centre Three Peaks walking country, waterfalls and caves. Weekends and short breaks available. One pet allowed.

HOVINGHAM, North Yorkshire Map ref 5C3

★★★

1 Unit
Sleeping 4

WESTWOOD

Hovingham, York
Contact: Mrs S A Weston
T: (0191) 372 1785

OPEN All Year

Low season per wk
£180.00–£200.00
High season per wk
£260.00–£320.00

Comfortable, well-appointed, first floor cottage in one of North Yorkshire's prettiest villages, midway between Malton and Helmsley. Superb countryside walks nearby.

CONFIRM YOUR BOOKING
You are advised to confirm your booking in writing.

ILKLEY, West Yorkshire Map ref 4B1

★★★★-★★★★★

10 Units
Sleeping 2–6

FAWEATHER GRANGE

Ilkley
Contact: Mrs D Skinn
T: (01943) 878777
F: (01943) 878777
E: skinn@attglobal.net
I: www.faweathergrange.com

One of the most romantic hideaways in Britain, these luxury log houses feature 4-poster beds, outdoor hot tubs, saunas and the very latest fixtures and fittings. Membership of an exclusive health club completes your luxury break. Nominated as a finalist in the 2003 YHTB Self-Catering Holiday of the Year awards.

OPEN All Year
CC: Mastercard, Switch, Visa

Low season per wk
£400.00–£550.00
High season per wk
£500.00–£750.00

KIRKBYMOORSIDE, North Yorkshire Map ref 5C3

★★★★

1 Unit
Sleeping 6

CHERRY VIEW COTTAGE

Kirkbymoorside, York
Contact: Mrs SMP Drinkel, High Hagg Farm, Kirkbymoorside, York YO62 7JF
T: (01751) 431714

Cottage set at edge of farm, breathtaking views across Vale of Pickering. Spacious and self-contained, three-bedroomed accommodation, furnished to a high standard. Lawned garden, ample parking.

OPEN All Year

Low season per wk
£280.00–£350.00
High season per wk
£385.00–£425.00

★★★★

2 Units
Sleeping 3

THE CORNMILL

Kirkbymoorside, York
Contact: Mr & Mrs C Tinkler, The Cornmill, Kirby Mills, Kirkbymoorside, York YO62 6NP
T: (01751) 432000
F: (01751) 432300
E: cornmill@kirbymills.demon.co.uk
I: www.kirbymills.demon.co.uk

Converted stable mews cottages. Part of converted complex comprising 18thC watermill and Victorian farmhouse bed and breakfast. One cottage has the option of twin beds or king-size double.

OPEN All Year
CC: Delta, Mastercard, Switch, Visa

Low season per wk
£225.00–£300.00
High season per wk
£250.00–£300.00

USE YOUR *i*s

There are more than 550 Tourist Information Centres throughout England offering friendly help with accommodation and holiday ideas as well as suggestions of places to visit and things to do. You'll find TIC addresses in the local Phone Book.

KIRKBYMOORSIDE continued

★★★

2 Units
Sleeping 3

KELDHOLME COTTAGES

Kirkbymoorside, York
Contact: Mr B Hughes, Keldholme Cottages, Keldholme, Kirkbymoorside, York YO62 6NA
T: (01751) 431933

Restored, recently refurbished stone cottages set in approximately one acre of beautiful gardens in peaceful hamlet near small market town with excellent services and good local restaurants. Well-equipped modern kitchen. We take pride in our high standards of quality furnishings and cleanliness. Easy access to Moors, coast, Dales and York.

Early and late short breaks available on request. Minimum stay 3 nights.

Low season per wk
Min £140.00
High season per wk
Min £200.00

★★★★

2 Units
Sleeping 4

SURPRISE VIEW COTTAGE & FIELD BARN COTTAGE

Kirkbymoorside, York
Contact: Mrs R Wass, Sinnington Lodge, Sinnington, York YO62 6RB
T: (01751) 431345
F: (01751) 433418
E: info@surpriseviewcottages.co.uk
I: www.surpriseviewcottages.co.uk

OPEN All Year

Low season per wk
£195.00–£275.00
High season per wk
£280.00–£360.00

Historic barn conversions on farmstead (originally an old mill and tannery) giving good views over moorland edge and easy access to walks. Roomy and comfortable accommodation.

KNARESBOROUGH, North Yorkshire Map ref 4B1

★★★★

1 Unit
Sleeping 3

THE GRANARY

Farnham, Knaresborough
Contact: Mr & Mrs I Thornton, The Granary, Gibbet House Farm, Farnham Lane, Farnham, Knaresborough HG5 9JP
T: (01423) 862325
F: (01423) 862271

Traditional, converted granary adjacent to principal limestone-built farmhouse. Situated in 30 acres of parkland in an elevated position with stunning views of the Nidderdale Valley. Refurbished to a high standard. Five miles Harrogate, two miles Knaresborough. Central for Dales, Yorkshire Coast, 'Herriot' and 'Heartbeat' country. Mob: 07970 000068.

Short breaks available. 3-night stays Oct-Mar.

Low season per wk
£195.00–£210.00
High season per wk
£200.00–£250.00

AT-A-GLANCE SYMBOLS

Symbols at the end of each accommodation entry give useful information about services and facilities. A key to symbols can be found inside the back cover flap. Keep this open for easy reference.

KNARESBOROUGH continued

★★★-★★★★★

6 Units
Sleeping 2–8

Quality apartments in a spectacular setting. Tastefully appointed with many personal touches. Extensive grounds with woodland walks to River Nidd, Knaresborough and the Nidd Gorge, an Area of Outstanding Natural Beauty. Ideal holiday base with many nearby attractions. Convenient for Harrogate, York and Yorkshire Dales. Bed and breakfast also available.

WATERGATE LODGE HOLIDAY APARTMENTS

Knaresborough, Harrogate
Contact: Mr & Mrs P Guest, Watergate Lodge Holiday Apartments, Watergate Haven, Ripley Road, Knaresborough, Harrogate HG5 9BU
T: (01423) 864627
F: (01423) 861087
E: info@watergatehaven.com
I: www.watergatehaven.com

OPEN All Year
CC: Delta, Mastercard, Visa

Short breaks and mid-week bookings may be available. Discounts for advance payment.

Low season per wk
£219.00–£339.00
High season per wk
£329.00–£649.00

LEALHOLM, North Yorkshire Map ref 5C3

★★★

3 Units
Sleeping 3–6

Stone and pantile cottages converted from traditional farm buildings, providing well-equipped, comfortable, centrally heated accommodation. The lounges have solid fuel stoves and colour TVs. The kitchens are all equipped with electric cooker, microwave, washing machine and pleasant dining area. In beautiful moorland hamlet within North York Moors National Park, nine miles Whitby.

GREENHOUSES FARM COTTAGES

Lealholm, Whitby
Contact: Mr & Mrs N Eddleston, Greenhouses Farm Cottages, Greenhouses Farm, Lealholm, Whitby YO21 2AD
T: (01947) 897486
F: (01947) 897486
E: n_eddleston@yahoo.com
I: www.greenhouses-farm-cottages.co.uk

OPEN All Year

Low season per wk
£193.00–£237.00
High season per wk
£342.00–£520.00

LEEDS, West Yorkshire Map ref 4B1 *Tourist Information Centre Tel: (0113) 242 5242*

★★★★

2 Units
Sleeping 2–4

HARMAN SUITES

Leeds
Contact: Mr K Singh, Miss S P Kaur, Harman Suites, 48 St Martins Avenue, Leeds LS7 3LG
T: (0113) 295 5886
F: (0113) 295 5886
E: info@harmansuite.co.uk
I: www.harmansuite.co.uk

OPEN All Year
CC: Amex, Diners, Mastercard, Switch, Visa

Low season per wk
£210.00–£300.00
High season per wk
£225.00–£350.00

High-quality, ground floor apartments. Suite 1: king-size bed, en suite, double sofa bed. Suite 2: studio flat, en suite, double bed, single sofa bed. Private patio, car parking.

LEEDS/BRADFORD AIRPORT

See under Leeds

VISITBRITAIN'S WHERE TO STAY
Please mention this guide when making your booking.

LEYBURN, North Yorkshire Map ref 5B3 *Tourist Information Centre Tel: (01969) 623069*

★★★

5 Units
Sleeping 4–6

Stone-built period cottages and self-contained apartments form a secluded courtyard only 80 metres form Leyburn market place. Ample private parking, ideal touring and walking centre.

DALES VIEW HOLIDAY HOMES

Leyburn
Contact: Messrs J&M Chilton, Dales View Holiday Homes, Jenkins Garth, Leyburn DL8 5SP
T: (01969) 623707
F: (01969) 623707
E: daleshols@aol.com
I: www.daleshols.com

OPEN All Year

Short breaks available Oct-Apr.

Low season per wk
£140.00–£230.00
High season per wk
£230.00–£295.00

★★★★

1 Unit
Sleeping 2

Comfortable beamed stone cottage, thoughtfully converted, in a quiet cul-de-sac. Cosy in winter, with central heating and a coal/gas fire, with good walking from the doorstep. Leyburn is an excellent centre for touring, with good shops, pubs and eating places. Non-smokers only.

THE OLD FIRE STATION

Leyburn
Contact: Miss C Wallace-Lowell, 4 Shawl Terrace, Leyburn DL8 5DA
T: (01969) 623993

OPEN All Year

Short breaks available Oct, Nov, Dec, Mar. Minimum 3-night stay.

Low season per wk
£200.00–£245.00
High season per wk
£245.00–£300.00

MALTON, North Yorkshire Map ref 5D3 *Tourist Information Centre Tel: (01653) 600048*

★★★★

1 Unit
Sleeping 3

A cosy, two-bedroomed, fully equipped old farm cottage, caringly modernised to a very high standard, situated in the heart of rural Ryedale. Ideally located, being central to the North York Moors, Yorkshire Wolds, east coast seaside and the old City of York. Price includes logs and coal for multi-fuel stove.

SWANS NEST COTTAGE

Ryton, Malton
Contact: Mrs Y Dickinson, Abbots Farm House, Ryton, Malton YO17 6SA
T: (01653) 694970
E: swansnestcottage@hotmail.com
I: www.uk-holiday-cottages.co.uk/swans-nest

OPEN All Year
CC: Delta, Mastercard, Solo, Switch, Visa

Mid-week and weekend breaks generally available.

Low season per wk
£195.00–£265.00
High season per wk
£295.00–£345.00

TOWN INDEX

This can be found at the back of the guide. If you know where you want to stay, the index will give you the page number listing accommodation in your chosen town, city or village.

MASHAM, North Yorkshire Map ref 5C3

★★★★

1 Unit
Sleeping 4

THE MEWS

Masham, Ripon
Contact: Mrs J Jameson, Sutton Grange, Masham, Ripon HG4 4PB
T: (01765) 689068
E: jameson1@ukf.net
I: www.themews-masham.com

The Mews. 1.5 miles from Masham with panoramic views from the luxury, first floor accommodation. Set in over 1.5 acres of walled gardens with orchard, home to lambs and goslings, croquet lawn, table tennis, barbecue, picnic area, hammock, woodland walk with wildlife pond. Convenient for Moors, Dales and market towns.

OPEN All Year

Low season per wk
£200.00–£260.00
High season per wk
£260.00–£350.00

★★★

1 Unit
Sleeping 4

MEWS COTTAGE

Masham, Ripon
Contact: Mrs C Hallsworth, 5 Bridge Close, Harleston IP20 9HW
T: (01379) 853020
E: mashamcottage@hotmail.com

Charming mews cottage, built in traditional stone, quietly tucked away near the centre of delightful Dales market town. Spacious, yet cosy, with a choice of three double bedrooms (one twin). Ideally situated, being close to all Masham's amenities. Perfect base for exploring the surrounding area and beautiful Yorkshire Dales.

OPEN All Year except Christmas

Weekend and 3-day breaks available during low season. Peak season: available if booked within 10 days.

Low season per wk
£225.00–£250.00
High season per wk
£300.00–£325.00

NEWSHAM, North Yorkshire Map ref 5B3

★★★★

1 Unit
Sleeping 6

DYSON HOUSE BARN

Newsham, Richmond
Contact: Mr & Mrs R Clarkson, Dyson House, Newsham, Richmond DL11 7QP
T: (01833) 627365
E: dysonbarn@tinyworld.co.uk
I: www.cottageguide.co.uk/dysonhousebarn

Between Richmond and Barnard Castle this spacious, well-equipped, converted farm barn makes an ideal base for touring Teesdale, Swaledale, North Yorkshire, Durham and Cumbria. Retaining many original features there are three large bedrooms, one ground floor with shower room. Patio with barbecue. Two public house/restaurants, 10 minutes' walk. Brochure available.

OPEN All Year

Short stays available 6 Oct–31 Mar (excl school holidays), minimum 2 nights.

Low season per wk
£210.00–£430.00
High season per wk
£210.00–£430.00

NEWTON-ON-RAWCLIFFE, North Yorkshire Map ref 5D3

★★★★

3 Units
Sleeping 4–6

LET'S HOLIDAY

Newton-on-Rawcliffe, Pickering
Contact: Mr J Wicks, Let's Holiday, Mel House, Newton-on-Rawcliffe, Pickering YO18 8QA
T: (01751) 475396
E: holiday@letsholiday.com
I: www.letsholiday.com

OPEN All Year
CC: Delta, Mastercard, Switch, Visa

Low season per wk
£245.00–£305.00
High season per wk
£540.00–£695.00

Well equipped and comfortable with guests' indoor pool/jacuzzi/sauna in quiet village with pub next door. Ideal for steam railway, Moors, coast and York.

NORTH DALTON, East Riding of Yorkshire Map ref 4C1

★★★

1 Unit
Sleeping 4

OLD COBBLERS COTTAGE

North Dalton, Driffield
Contact: Miss C Wade & Mr Nigel Morton
T: (01377) 217523
F: (01377) 217754
E: chris@adastey.demon.co.uk

OPEN All Year

Low season per wk
Min £150.00
High season per wk
Min £300.00

19thC, beamed, mid-terraced cottage overlooking picturesque pond in a peaceful farming village between York and Yorkshire's Heritage Coast. Good for walking, sightseeing and relaxing.

NORTHALLERTON, North Yorkshire Map ref 5C3 *Tourist Information Centre Tel: (01609) 776864*

★★★

1 Unit
Sleeping 5

2 SUMMERFIELD COTTAGE

Welbury, Northallerton
Contact: Mrs S H Holmes, Summerfield House Farm, Welbury, Northallerton DL6 2SL
T: (01609) 882393
F: (01609) 882393
E: sallyhholmes@aol.com

OPEN All Year

Low season per wk
£120.00–£170.00
High season per wk
£170.00–£250.00

Enjoy the peaceful surroundings of this well-appointed, three-bedroomed farm cottage. Superb views over open countryside. Central for Yorkshire Dales, Moors, Herriot country and York.

OLD MALTON, North Yorkshire Map ref 5D3

Rating
Applied For

1 Unit
Sleeping 8

CORONATION FARM COTTAGE

Old Malton
Contact: Mr Beeley
T: (01653) 698251
E: enquiries@coronationfarmcottage.co.uk
I: www.coronationfarmcottage.co.uk

Superb, newly renovated cottage in lovely village of Old Malton on River Derwent. Four bedrooms and two bathrooms. Highly equipped, well-appointed, cosy and comfortable. Your gateway to the North Yorkshire Moors, Scarborough and York – the ideal holiday base. Private garden and parking. Pets very welcome. No smoking.

OPEN All Year

Low season short breaks from £125.

Low season per wk
£195.00
High season per wk
£195.00–£595.00

OXENHOPE, West Yorkshire Map ref 4B1

★★★

1 Unit
Sleeping 3

YATE COTTAGE

Oxenhope, Keighley
Contact: Mrs J Dunn, Yate House, Yate Lane, Oxenhope, Keighley BD22 9HL
T: (01535) 643638
E: jeanandhugh@dunnyate.freeserve.co.uk
I: www.uk-holiday-cottages.co.uk/yatecottage

OPEN All Year except Christmas
CC: Amex, Mastercard, Visa

Low season per wk
£100.00–£120.00
High season per wk
£160.00–£180.00

18thC cottage adjoining Yate House, a 'yeoman' house of striking architectural appearance. South-facing view over beautiful garden to hills. No short breaks.

CHECK THE MAPS

The colour maps at the front of this guide show all the cities, towns and villages for which you will find accommodation entries. Refer to the town index to find the page on which they are listed.

PICKERING, North Yorkshire Map ref 5D3 *Tourist Information Centre Tel: (01751) 473791*

★★★★-★★★★★

8 Units
Sleeping 2–10

BEECH FARM COTTAGES

Wrelton, Nr Pickering
Contact: Mr & Mrs P Massara, Beech Farm Cottages, Wrelton, Pickering YO18 8PG
T: (01751) 476612
F: (01751) 475032
E: holiday@beechfarm.com
I: www.beechfarm.com

Award-winning, luxury, stone cottages – Yorkshire's best. Heated indoor pool, sauna, children's play area, paddock. Delightful location in quiet village on edge of Moors National Park. Also convenient for coast and York. Cottages in courtyard setting backing onto fileds. Brochure available.

OPEN All Year
CC: Amex, Delta, Mastercard, Switch, Visa

Winner of Yorkshire Tourist Board's 'Self-Catering Holiday of the Year' Award 2001 and 2002.

Low season per wk
£255.00–£730.00
High season per wk
£345.00–£1,600.00

★★★

1 Unit
Sleeping 6

JOINERS COTTAGE

Pickering
Contact: Mr P & Mrs C Fisher, Farndale House, 103 Eastgate, Pickering YO18 7DW
T: (01751) 475158

Converted barn set in 0.75-acre lawned garden, situated in close proximity to the town centre, yet overlooking open fields. Personally supervised by the owners who live on site. The cottage provides spacious, 'upside down' accommodation with ground floor bedrooms (one fully en suite). Linen, towels, log fire and heating all included.

OPEN All Year

Open all year. 3-night stays available Nov-Mar (excl Christmas and New Year).

Low season per wk
£250.00–£375.00
High season per wk
£375.00–£500.00

REETH, North Yorkshire Map ref 5B3

★★★

1 Unit
Sleeping 6

ST ANDREWS CHAPEL

Marrick, Richmond
Contact: Mr D Bown, The Old Wesleyan Chapel, Marrick, Richmond DL11 7LQ
T: (01748) 884792
E: sarah@twochapels.free-online.co.uk
I: www.twochapels.free-online.co.uk

Self-catering accommodation in Swaledale, North Yorkshire, close to the popular village of Reeth and all its amenties. This extremely comfortable and beautifully converted chapel is the perfect rural retreat. Logburning stove and private gardens with stunning views. An ideal walking base, highly popular with couples and young families.

OPEN All Year

Low season per wk
£220.00–£250.00
High season per wk
£320.00–£350.00

SB

SPECIAL BREAKS

Many establishments offer special promotions and themed breaks. These are highlighted in red. (All such offers are subject to availability.)

RICHMOND, North Yorkshire Map ref 5C3 *Tourist Information Centre Tel: (01748) 850252*

★★★★
1 Unit
Sleeping 5

ROSE COTTAGE
Skeeby, Richmond
Contact: Mr D Hunt, 11 Richmond Road, Skeeby, Richmond DL10 5DR
T: (01748) 823080
E: huntsholidays@hotmail.com
I: www.huntsholidays.co.uk

OPEN All Year
CC: Amex, Delta, JCB, Mastercard, Switch, Visa

Low season per wk
£200.00–£295.00
High season per wk
£300.00–£420.00

Recently built, beautifully furnished (en suite bedrooms) cottage in small picturesque village (pub/meals) close to historic Richmond, Dales, A1. Ideal for touring, walking or relaxing.

RIPON, North Yorkshire Map ref 5C3

★★★★
1 Unit
Sleeping 8

INTAKE
Kirkby Malzeard, Ripon
Contact: Mrs K F McConnell, 3 Hippingstones Lane, Corbridge NE45 5JP
T: (01434) 632812
F: (01434) 633825
E: kfiona@tiscali.co.uk

OPEN All Year

Low season per wk
Min £300.00
High season per wk
Max £600.00

Traditional stone farmhouse, newly renovated. Furnished to high standard. Log fire, Stanley cooker. Lovely view over fields – listen to curlews. Many diverse attractions within easy reach.

RISHWORTH, West Yorkshire Map ref 4B1

★★★★
1 Unit
Sleeping 8

KIT HILL COTTAGE AT PIKE END FARM
Rishworth, Sowerby Bridge
Contact: Mrs C Ryder
T: (01422) 823949
F: (01422) 824626
E: carolineryder@pikeendfarm.net
I: www.pikeendfarm.net

Traditional Pennine hill cottage set high above beautiful Ryburn Valley. Furnished in the true cottage style with all mod cons. Four lovely bedrooms, master bedroom en suite. Wonderfully peaceful, yet close to amenities. Close to the Pennine Way. An ideal base for exploring the southern Pennines, on foot, bicycle or horseback.

OPEN All Year

Horse livery service available during summer months.

Low season per wk
£175.00–£325.00
High season per wk
£300.00–£450.00

10

ROBIN HOOD'S BAY, North Yorkshire Map ref 5D3

★★★
1 Unit
Sleeping 4

LINGERS HILL
Robin Hood's Bay, Whitby
Contact: Mrs F Harland, Lingers Hill Farm, Thorpe Lane, Robin Hood's Bay, Whitby YO22 4TQ
T: (01947) 880608

OPEN All Year

Low season per wk
£170.00–£220.00
High season per wk
£240.00–£310.00

Cosy character cottage situated on the edge of the village at Robin Hood's Bay. Close to amenities, ideal walking and cycling area. Lovely views.

SCARBOROUGH, North Yorkshire Map ref 5D3 *Tourist Information Centre Tel: (01723) 373333*

★★★
1 Unit
Sleeping 4

LENDAL HOUSE
Scarborough
Contact: Mrs P Scott
T: (01723) 372178
E: info@lendalhouse.co.uk
I: www.lendalhouse.co.uk

Low season per wk
£200.00–£250.00
High season per wk
£300.00–£350.00

Luxury, self-contained ground floor flat with 4-poster bed. Near cricket ground, five minutes' walk to North Bay Beach, town centre, also great for walks on North Yorkshire moors.

SCARBOROUGH continued

★★★
2 Units
Sleeping 4–6

SPIKERS HILL COUNTRY COTTAGES
West Ayton, Scarborough
Contact: Mrs J Hutchinson, Spikers Hill Country Cottages, Spikers Hill Farm, West Ayton, Scarborough YO13 9LB
T: (01723) 862537
F: (01723) 865511
E: janet@spikershill.ndo.co.uk
I: www.spikershill.ndo.co.uk

Low season per wk
£170.00–£225.00
High season per wk
£225.00–£450.00

Delightful cottages with beautiful view on a private 600-acre farm in North York Moors National Park. Ideal for countryside and coast (Scarborough five miles).

★★★★
9 Units
Sleeping 2–9

National winners of ETC 'England for Excellence' award for Best Self-Catering Holiday of the Year. Superb indoor heated swimming pool, jacuzzi and sauna. Stunning panoramic sea views and beautiful countryside on edge of National Park. Lovely, award-winning gardens. Parking. Furnished Teddy Bear's cottage and picnic park. York one hour, Whitby 30 minutes.

WREA HEAD COTTAGE HOLIDAYS

Scalby, Scarborough
Contact: Mr & Mrs C J Wood, Wrea Head Cottage Holidays, Wrea Head House, Barmoor Lane, Scalby, Scarborough YO13 0PG
T: (01723) 375844
F: (01723) 500274
E: ytb@wreahead.co.uk
I: www.wreahead.co.uk

OPEN All Year
CC: Delta, Mastercard, Switch, Visa

Excellent-value breaks, 4 nights for price of 3, 1 Nov 2003 to 20 Mar 2004. Christmas and New Year holidays for all.

Low season per wk
£245.00–£525.00
High season per wk
£486.00–£1,295.00

SCOTCH CORNER, North Yorkshire Map ref 5C3

★★★
1 Unit
Sleeping 4

5 CEDAR GROVE
Barton, Richmond
Contact: Mr & Mrs J P Lawson, The Close, Mill Lane, Cloughton, Scarborough YO13 0AB
T: (01723) 870455
E: jim@lawson5270fsnet.co.uk

OPEN All Year

Low season per wk
£200.00
High season per wk
£250.00

Semi-detached family home, near village green. Five miles south of Darlington, central for touring the Yorkshire Dales, Moors, Northumberland, Durham and Lake District. Enquiries: 01723 870017.

SHEFFIELD, South Yorkshire Map ref 4B2 *Tourist Information Centre Tel: (0114) 221 1900*

★★★★
1 Unit
Sleeping 6

HANGRAM LANE FARMHOUSE
Sheffield
Contact: Mrs J Clark, Hangram Lane Farmhouse, Hangram Lane Grange, Hangram Lane, Ringinglow, Sheffield S11 7TQ
T: (0114) 230 3570
F: (0114) 230 6573

OPEN All Year

Low season per wk
£258.50–£282.00
High season per wk
£293.75–£340.75

Comfortable, modernised farmhouse comprising large kitchen, dining room, lounge, one double bedroom, two twin-bedded rooms, bathroom and toilet. Two minutes' drive from the Peak District, shops and eating places.

CHECK THE MAPS

The colour maps at the front of this guide show all the cities, towns and villages for which you will find accommodation entries. Refer to the town index to find the page on which they are listed.

SKIPTON, North Yorkshire Map ref 4B1 *Tourist Information Centre Tel: (01756) 792809*

★★★-★★★★★

6 Units
Sleeping 2–4

Peaceful, tastefully converted farm cottages in open countryside, one mile from castle and historic market town of Skipton. Suitable for disabled.

CAWDER HALL COTTAGES

Skipton
Contact: Mr G Pearson, Cawder Hall Cottages, Cawder Lane, Skipton BD23 2TD
T: (01756) 791579
F: (01756) 797036
E: info@cawderhallcottages.co.uk
I: www.cawderhallcottages.co.uk

OPEN All Year
CC: Amex, Delta, Mastercard, Solo, Switch, Visa

Low season per wk
£160.00–£275.00
High season per wk
£210.00–£380.00

★★★★

1 Unit
Sleeping 5

THE LODGE
Horton, Skipton
Contact: Mrs E Thwaite
T: (01200) 445300
E: edithwaite@hotmail.com
I: www.thelodgehorton.co.uk

OPEN All Year

Low season per wk
£190.00–£230.00
High season per wk
£230.00–£290.00

Recently built in ancient stone, with verandah. One double, one twin room and sofa bed. Quiet location by a stream. With ramped access, wheelchair friendly.

★★★

1 Unit
Sleeping 6

Detached, Victorian, stone-built house in quiet location on edge of Yorkshire Dales National Park. Three bedrooms, separate dining room. Spacious and comfortably furnished. Rent includes heating, linen and electricity. Village amenities include shop, post office, playground, two pubs. Ideal base for walking or touring. Pets and families welcome.

7 PASTURE ROAD

Embsay, Skipton
Contact: JS&C Lunnon, 17 Cherry Tree Way, Helmshore, Rossendale BB4 4JZ
T: (01706) 230653
E: j.lunnon@blackburn.ac.uk
I: www.cjlunnon.co.uk

OPEN All Year

Low season per wk
Min £170.00
High season per wk
Max £395.00

STAINTONDALE, North Yorkshire Map ref 5D3

★★★

4 Units
Sleeping 2–6

Peace and tranquillity found on 170-acre sheep farm with stunning coastal and rural views. Ten minutes' walk from the Cleveland Way. Plenty of walks from the door amid cliffs, woodland and streams. 'Home from home', highly equipped, welcoming cottages. Ample parking. Pets made welcome.

WHITE HALL FARM HOLIDAY COTTAGES

Staintondale, Scarborough
Contact: Mr J & Mrs C White, White Hall Farm Holiday Cottages, White Hall Farm, Staintondale, Scarborough YO13 0EY
T: (01723) 870234
E: celia@white66fs.business.co.uk
I: www.whitehallcottages.co.uk

OPEN All Year

Low season per wk
£165.00–£280.00
High season per wk
£240.00–£450.00

STAITHES, North Yorkshire Map ref 5C3

★★ 1 Unit Sleeping 4

GLENCOE
Staithes, Saltburn-by-the-Sea
Contact: Rev D Purdy
T: (01751) 431452

OPEN All Year

Low season per wk £200.00–£240.00
High season per wk £240.00–£300.00

Cosy, harbourside, mid-terrace former fisherman's cottage in a picturesque fishing village steeped in history. Open fire. Two bedrooms. Close beach, shops, pubs, restaurants.

THIRSK, North Yorkshire Map ref 5C3 *Tourist Information Centre Tel: (01845) 522755*

★★★ 1 Unit Sleeping 5

THE OLD SCHOOL HOUSE
Catton, Thirsk
Contact: Mrs G Readman, School House, Catton, Thirsk YO7 4SG
T: (01845) 567308

OPEN All Year
CC: Visa

Low season per wk £130.00–£160.00
High season per wk £210.00

Formerly the village school, attached to the owner's residence at the School House. Two bedrooms, one double with a single bed and one twin-bedded room, all ground floor.

★★★★ 5 Units Sleeping 3–4

Pretty cottages in a large garden. Village shop and pub nearby. Friendly welcome. Owners' attention throughout your stay. Cottages comfortable and well equipped with dishwashers. We hope you will feel at home here and enjoy all this lovely part of Yorkshire has to offer – Moors, Dales, York and much more.

POPLARS HOLIDAY COTTAGES

Carlton Miniott, Thirsk
Contact: Mrs C M Chilton, Poplars Holiday Cottages, The Poplars, Carlton Miniott, Thirsk YO7 4LX
T: (01845) 522712
F: (01845) 522712
E: the_poplars_cottages@btopenworld.com
I: www.yorkshirebandb.co.uk

OPEN All Year

Low season per wk £150.00–£170.00
High season per wk £210.00–£295.00

TICKTON, East Riding of Yorkshire Map ref 4C1

★★★ 1 Unit Sleeping 6

BRIDGE HOUSE COTTAGE
Tickton, Beverley
Contact: Mr P White & Ms Adele Wilkinson, Bridge House Cottage, Hull Bridge House, Weel Road, Tickton, Beverley HU17 9RY
T: (01964) 542355
E: alw@amj.co.uk

OPEN All Year

Low season per wk £225.00–£275.00
High season per wk £275.00–£350.00

Secluded, refurbished cottage with excellent facilities. A warm welcome is assured.

TODMORDEN, West Yorkshire Map ref 4B1 *Tourist Information Centre Tel: (01706) 818181*

★★★ 1 Unit Sleeping 4

THE COTTAGE
Todmorden
Contact: Mr & Mrs A Bentham, The Cottage, Causeway East Farmhouse, Lee Bottom Road, Todmorden OL14 6HH
T: (01706) 815265
E: andrew@bentham5.freeserve.co.uk

OPEN All Year

Low season per wk £135.00–£165.00
High season per wk £165.00–£195.00

Part of a 17thC farmhouse beneath the Pennine Way. Ideal for walking and touring.

TOWN INDEX

This can be found at the back of this guide. If you know where you want to stay, the index will give you the page number listing accommodation in your chosen town, city or village.

TODMORDEN continued

★★★★
1 Unit
Sleeping 4

STANNALLY FARM COTTAGE
Todmorden
Contact: Mrs D Brunt
T: (01706) 813998
F: (01706) 813998
E: Bruntdennis@aol.com

OPEN All Year

Low season per wk
£170.00–£260.00
High season per wk
£260.00–£355.00

Luxurious 17thC stone cottage on Calderdale Way. South-facing access, rural Pennine foothills. Convenient for town, ideal centre for walking and touring.

WHASHTON, North Yorkshire Map ref 5C3

★★★
2 Units
Sleeping 4

MOUNT PLEASANT FARM

Whashton, Richmond
Contact: Mrs A Pittaway, Mount Pleasant Farm, Whashton, Richmond DL11 7JP
T: (01748) 822784
F: (01748) 822784
E: info@mountpleasantfarmhouse.co.uk
I: www.mountpleasantfarmhouse.co.uk

Enjoy a break in one of our beautifully converted, cosy cottages with wonderful views over open countryside. Peaceful, rural location with easy access to Richmond and Dales. Each cottage has a double and twin bedroom, fully equipped kitchen, comfy lounge, dining area, patio, lawn and car parking to front.

OPEN All Year

Low season per wk
£210.00
High season per wk
£320.00

WHITBY, North Yorkshire Map ref 5D3 *Tourist Information Centre Tel: (01947) 602674*

★★★★
9 Units
Sleeping 2–4

DISCOVERY ACCOMMODATION

Whitby
Contact: Mrs P Gilmore
T: (01947) 821598
F: (01947) 600406
E: pam@discoveryaccommodation.com
I: www.discoveryaccommodation.com

Spacious, modern apartments in historical 18thC building situated around peaceful courtyard convenient for seafront harbour, beach and amenities. Free private off-street parking. Our commitment is to provide superior quality accommodation for your holiday.

OPEN All Year
CC: Delta, Mastercard, Switch, Visa

Low season per wk
£250.00–£350.00
High season per wk
£300.00–£450.00

★★★
7 Units
Sleeping 4–7

EAST CLIFF COTTAGES, HARDWICK COTTAGE
Whitby
Contact: Dr S M Thornton, Brookhouse, Dam Lane, Leavening, Malton YO17 9SF
T: (01653) 658249
E: enquiries@seasideholiday.co.uk
I: www.seasideholiday.co.uk

OPEN All Year

Low season per wk
£180.00–£480.00

Listed fisherman's cottage. Old Whitby at foot of 199 steps. Great views from all windows. Private, sunny yard. Parking available. Has washing machine and dishwasher.

MAP REFERENCES The map references refer to the colour maps at the front of this guide. The first figure is the map number; the letter and figure which follow indicate the grid reference on the map.

WHITBY continued

★-★★★★★
3 Units
Sleeping 3–4

Refurbished flats in Victorian terrace. Ideal location for beach, shops and restaurants. Personally supervised by the owners who are committed to very high-quality standards. Linen and electricity included. Pets welcome. Unrestricted on-street parking outside the property on a 'first-come' basis. Phone for colour brochure.

ELIZABETH HOUSE HOLIDAY FLATS

Whitby
Contact: Mrs R A Cooper, Park View, 14 Chubb Hill Road, Whitby YO21 1JU
T: (01947) 604213
E: jakanann@btopenworld.com
I: www.elizabeth-house.biz

OPEN All Year

Bargain breaks from £70 per flat Nov-Mar (excl Christmas and New Year).

Low season per wk
£120.00–£200.00
High season per wk
£200.00–£360.00

★★★★
1 Unit
Sleeping 14

GRANGE FARM HOLIDAY COTTAGES

High Hawsker, Whitby
Contact: Miss D Hooning
T: (01947) 881080
F: (01947) 881080
E: info@grangefarm.net
I: www.grangefarm.net

OPEN All Year

Low season per wk
£650.00–£1,100.00
High season per wk
£1,100.00–£2,000.00

Comfortable, modernised, well-equipped farmhouse, perfect for friends/family wanting to holiday together. Excellent base to explore coast and Moors.

★★★
1 Unit
Sleeping 4

LOBSTER POT COTTAGE

Whitby
Contact: Mrs A Forbes, Whitby Fishermens Amateur Rowing Club, 10 Castle Road, Whitby YO21 3NJ
T: (01947) 605846
E: anne.forbes2@btopenworld.com

Lobster Pot Cottage is a delightful holiday home located in an old fishermans yard dating back to the 17thC close to the harbour and nearby beaches. The accommodation offered is clean, comfortable and cosy. It is an ideal base for touring or a holiday by the seaside.

OPEN All Year

Short breaks available.

Low season per wk
Min £170.00
High season per wk
Max £300.00

★★★★
1 Unit
Sleeping 7

1 PRINCESS PLACE

Whitby
Contact: Mr J Whitton
T: (01287) 660118

OPEN All Year

Low season per wk
£220.00–£480.00
High season per wk
£220.00–£500.00

A Grade II Listed Georgian terraced cottage offering high-quality accommodation over three floors. Quiet location but only one minute's walk from the harbour.

★★
4 Units
Sleeping 2–5

SWALLOW HOLIDAY COTTAGES

Stainsacre, Whitby
Contact: Mr & Mrs McNeil, Swallow Holiday Cottages, Long Lease Farm, Hawsker, Whitby YO22 4LA
T: (01947) 603790
F: (01947) 603790
I: www.swallowcottages.co.uk

OPEN All Year

Low season per wk
£120.00–£250.00
High season per wk
£160.00–£450.00

Mews of converted farm cottages in a private courtyard, in a small village close to the Moors and the sea. Ideal for couples or family groups. Part weeks available low season.

WHITBY continued

★★★-★★★★★

14 Units
Sleeping 1–6

WHITE ROSE HOLIDAY COTTAGES

Sleights, Whitby

Contact: Mrs J E Roberts, Greenacres, 5 Brook Park, Sleights, Whitby YO21 1RT
T: (01947) 810763
E: enquiries@whiterosecottages.co.uk
I: www.whiterosecottages.co.uk

New habourside apartments in Whitby and village properties in Sleights. Tastefully decorated and furnished for your pleasure and comfort. Centrally heated. Available all year. Ideal for coast country. We aim to please with our quality accommodation and friendly customer service.

OPEN All Year

Reduced rates for autumn/winter breaks. Cosy, festively decorated properties for Christmas/New Year.

Low season per wk
£180.00–£395.00
High season per wk
£200.00–£700.00

YORK, North Yorkshire Map ref 4C1 *Tourist Information Centre Tel: (01904) 621756*

★★★★★

1 Unit
Sleeping 8

ABBEYGATE HOUSE

York

Contact: Mr & Mrs C Halliday, 1 Grange Drive, Horsforth, Leeds LS18 5EQ
T: (0113) 258 9833

Luxurious Georgian-style townhouse overlooking the medieval city walls on prestigious Bishops Wharfe riverside development five minutes from city centre. Recently refurbished to a superior standard, it has every facility including large lounge with four co-ordinated leather sofas and south-facing balcony, jacuzzi, bath. Private parking for two to three.

OPEN All Year
CC: Mastercard, Visa

Short breaks available. Discounts for smaller groups.

Low season per wk
Min £295.00

6

★★★

1 Unit
Sleeping 6

ACER BUNGALOW

York

Contact: Mrs S Wreglesworth
T: (01904) 653839
F: (01904) 677017
E: info@acerhotel.co.uk
I: www.acerbungalow.co.uk

Delightful bungalow situated one mile from city centre and attractions. Comfort and good housekeeping are guaranteed. Power, heating, bed linen and towels are provided free. The bungalow is furnished to a high standard and is well equipped. Lovely gardens, and patio with seating and lighting.

OPEN All Year

Short breaks available low season. Special discounts during less-busy periods. Please telephone for details of our special offers.

Low season per wk
£250.00–£300.00
High season per wk
£350.00–£400.00

★★★

1 Unit
Sleeping 4

BARBICAN MEWS

York

Contact: Mrs H Jones, Homefinders Holidays, 11 Walmgate, York YO1 9TX
T: (01904) 632660
F: (01904) 615388
E: helen@letters-of-york.co.uk
I: www.letters-of-york.co.uk

OPEN All Year

Low season per wk
£230.00–£320.00
High season per wk
£340.00–£380.00

Two-bedroomed apartment, fully equipped to a high standard and with semi patio, ideally situated adjacent to city walls and leisure centre with pool.

YORK continued

★★★ 1 Unit Sleeping 6	**1 CLOISTERS WALK** York — OPEN All Year Contact: Mrs H Jones, Homefinders Holidays, 11 Walmgate, York YO1 9TX T: (01904) 632660 F: (01904) 651388 E: helen@letters-of-york.co.uk I: www.letters-of-york.co.uk *Comfortable, modern house, beautifully placed 500 yards from York Minster. Excellent views, tranquil and spacious garden. Your 'corner shop' is Sainsbury's (200 yards).*	Low season per wk £240.00–£330.00 High season per wk £350.00–£385.00
★★★★ 2 Units Sleeping 2–4	**9 CLOISTERS WALK** York — OPEN All Year Contact: Mr & Mrs G Jones, 2 Chalfonts, Off Tadcaster Road, York YO24 1EX T: (01904) 702043 F: (01904) 702043 E: hilary@yorkcloisters.com *Monkgate, near to the Minster and city centre, first floor apartment with two bedrooms. Well equipped and immaculate. Garden for residents.*	Low season per wk £300.00–£350.00 High season per wk £425.00–£450.00
★★ 6 Units Sleeping 2–4	**KNOWLE HOUSE APARTMENTS** York — OPEN All Year CC: Mastercard, Visa Contact: Mr G Harrand T: (01904) 637404 F: (01904) 639774 E: greg@hedleyhouse.com I: www.harrands.com *City-centre apartments next door to owner's hotel. Off-street parking. See website for more information.*	Low season per wk £150.00–£300.00 High season per wk £280.00–£450.00
★★★ 8 Unit Sleeping 2–8	**MERRICOTE COTTAGES** Stockton-on-the-Forest, York — OPEN All Year CC: Amex, Delta, Mastercard, Switch, Visa Contact: Mr A Williamson, Merricote Cottages, Malton Road, Stockton-on-the-Forest, York YO32 9TL T: (01904) 400256 F: (01904) 400846 E: merricote@hotmail.com I: www.merricote-holiday-cottages.co.uk *Beautiful spot from which to explore the historic city of York (three miles), moors and coast. The cottages and bungalows are well appointed. Many amenities nearby.*	Low season per wk £200.00–£300.00 High season per wk £360.00–£610.00
★★★★ 1 Unit Sleeping 3	**145 MOUNT VALE** York — OPEN All Year Contact: Mrs H Jones, Homefinders Holidays, 11 Walmgate, York YO1 9TJ T: (01904) 632660 F: (01904) 651388 E: helen@letters-of-york.co.uk I: www.letters-of-york.co.uk *Beautiful houses attached to owner's home. Patio at back, very private. About 15 minutes' walk to centre. Very quiet location.*	Low season per wk £240.00–£330.00 High season per wk £350.00–£385.00

NB

IMPORTANT NOTE Information on accommodation listed in this guide has been supplied by the proprietors. As changes may occur you are advised to check details at the time of booking.

YORK continued

★★★★★

1 Unit
Sleeping 2

Stunning riverside penthouse apartment with superb views of city including York Minster, Clifford's Tower etc. Contemporary décor. Five minutes' walk to city centre. No smoking/pets.

THE PENTHOUSE

York
Contact: Mrs K Hodgson, 1 Postern House, Bishop's Wharf, York YO23 1PH
T: (01904) 610351
F: (01904) 613687
E: hodgsonschoice@hotmail.com
I: www.hodgsons-choice.co.uk

OPEN All Year

Guided tours of York/North Yorkshire; York races package; short breaks available, minimum 2 nights.

Low season per wk
Min £350.00
High season per wk
Max £500.00

★★★★★

1 Unit
Sleeping 2

Stylish first floor apartment with lift, near to the city centre. The sitting room and balcony overlook the River Ouse. The corner site creates larger accommodation than many properties in the development, having a beautifully equipped separate dining kitchen with river views and a spacious bedroom with dressing area.

43 POSTERN CLOSE

York
Contact: Mr & Mrs G Jones, 2 Chalfonts, Off Tadcaster Road, York YO24 1EX
T: (01904) 702043
F: (01904) 702043
E: hilary@yorkcloisters.com
I: www.yorkcloisters.com

OPEN All Year

3-night breaks £200. During Jan and Feb 4 nights £200.

Low season per wk
£300.00–£350.00
High season per wk
£425.00–£450.00

★★★

1 Unit
Sleeping 6

29 RICHARDSON STREET

York
Contact: Mrs H Jones, Homefinders Holidays, 11 Walmgate, York YO1 9TX
T: (01904) 632660
F: (01904) 651388
E: helen@letters-of-york.co.uk
I: www.letters-of-york.co.uk

OPEN All Year

Low season per wk
£240.00–£330.00
High season per wk
£350.00–£385.00

Comfortable and spacious house, short walk along riverside to the city centre. Three bedrooms, well furnished.

★★★★

1 Unit
Sleeping 3

RIVERSIDE HOLIDAY FLAT

York
Contact: Mr P A Jackson, 17 Great Close, Cawood, Selby YO8 3UG
T: (01757) 268207
E: pajack@lineone.net
I: www.yorkriversideholidayflat.co.uk

OPEN All Year

Low season per wk
£270.00–£330.00
High season per wk
£340.00–£450.00

City-centre, double-bedroomed, first floor apartment with patio balcony. Overlooking the river and with fine views of the city. Own parking space.

8

QUALITY ASSURANCE SCHEME

Star ratings were correct at the time of going to press but are subject to change. Please check at the time of booking.

YORK continued

★★★★

3 Units
Sleeping 2

SHAMBLES HOLIDAY APARTMENTS

York
Contact: Mr & Mrs Fletcher, Shambles Holiday Apartments, The Art Shop, 27-27a Shambles, York YO1 7LX
T: (01904) 623898
F: (01904) 671283
E: shambleshoIiday-york@tinyworld.co.uk

OPEN All Year
CC: JCB, Mastercard, Solo, Switch, Visa

Low season per wk
Min £195.00
High season per wk
Max £395.00

Grade II Listed Georgian building in York's most famous medieval street, The Shambles. Adjacent open-air market and all city-centre facilities. No car parking.

★★★

1 Unit
Sleeping 4

WITHIN THE WALLS COTTAGE

York
Contact: Mr B Giles
T: (0115) 931 2070

OPEN All Year

Low season per wk
£250.00–£295.00
High season per wk
£300.00–£370.00

Completely modernised, fully equipped, very attractive accommodation in prime residential spot with parking. Just two minutes' walk to river and city attractions.

11

★★★★

1 Unit
Sleeping 2

24 WOODSMILL QUAY

York
Contact: Mrs H Jones, Homefinders Holidays, 11 Walmgate, York YO1 9TX
T: (01904) 632660
F: (01904) 651388
E: helen@letters-of-york.co.uk
I: www.letters-of-york.co.uk

OPEN All Year

Low season per wk
£235.00–£325.00
High season per wk
£345.00–£385.00

Beautiful flat on riverside with beams and brick wall in lounge. Situated in city centre. Private parking.

★★★★-★★★★★

16 Units
Sleeping 2

YORK LAKESIDE LODGES

York
Contact: Mr N Manasir, York Lakeside Lodges Ltd, Moor Lane, York YO24 2QU
T: (01904) 702346
F: (01904) 701631
E: neil@yorklakesidelodges.co.uk
I: www.yorklakesidelodges.co.uk

OPEN All Year

Low season per wk
£230.00–£385.00
High season per wk
£445.00–£735.00

Self-catering lodges and cottages in mature parkland around large fishing lake. Superstore across the road, coach to York centre every 10 minutes.

COUNTRY CODE Always follow the Country Code Enjoy the countryside and respect its life and work Guard against all risk of fire Fasten all gates Keep your dogs under close control Keep to public paths across farmland Use gates and stiles to cross fences, hedges and walls Leave livestock, crops and machinery alone Take your litter home Help to keep all water clean Protect wildlife, plants and trees Take special care on country roads Make no unnecessary noise

A brief guide to the main Towns and Villages offering accommodation in **Yorkshire**

A AMPLEFORTH, NORTH YORKSHIRE - Stone-built village in Hambleton Hills. Famous for its abbey and college, a Benedictine public school, founded in 1802, of which Cardinal Hume was once abbot. Romanesque-style church by Sir Giles Scott, completed in 1961 just after his death.

ASKRIGG, NORTH YORKSHIRE - The name of this Dales village means "ash tree ridge". It is centred on a steep main street of high, narrow, 3-storey houses and thrived on cotton and later wool in the 18th C. Once famous for its clock making.

B BEVERLEY, NORTH HUMBERSIDE - Beverley's most famous landmark is its beautiful medieval minster dating from 1220, with the Percy family tomb. Many attractive squares and streets, notably Wednesday and Saturday Market and North Bar Gateway. Famous racecourse. The market cross dates from 1714.

BRIDLINGTON, EAST RIDING OF YORKSHIRE - Lively seaside resort with long sandy beaches, Leisure World and busy harbour with fishing trips in cobles. Priory church of St Mary whose Bayle Gate is now a museum. Mementoes of flying pioneer, Amy Johnson, in Sewerby Hall. Harbour Museum and Aquarium.

BURNSALL, NORTH YORKSHIRE - Attractive village of grey-stone buildings with massive 5-arched bridge over the River Wharfe, popular for fishing, boating and walking excursions. Annual feast day games, notably the fell race held around maypole on the village green in August.

BURTON-IN-LONSDALE, NORTH YORKSHIRE - On a hillside above the River Greta, this town was once the centre for 7 potteries, the last of which closed in 1930.

C CARLTON, NORTH YORKSHIRE - At the edge of the Yorkshire Dales, Carlton is a good base for exploring Coverdale and visiting the National Park Centre.

CROPTON, NORTH YORKSHIRE - Moorland village at the top of a high ridge with stone houses, some of cruck construction, a Victorian church and the remains of a 12th C moated castle. Cropton Forest and Cropton Brewery are nearby.

D DANBY, NORTH YORKSHIRE - Eskdale village 12 miles west of Whitby. Visit the Moors Centre at Danby Lodge, a former shooting lodge in 13 acres of grounds including woodland and riverside meadow. Remains of medieval Danby Castle.

E EBBERSTON, NORTH YORKSHIRE - Picturesque village with a Norman church and hall, overlooking the Vale of Pickering.

F FILEY, NORTH YORKSHIRE - Resort with elegant Regency buildings along the front and 6 miles of sandy beaches bounded by natural breakwater, Filey Brigg. Starting point of the Cleveland Way. St Oswald's church, overlooking a ravine, belonged to Augustinian canons until the Dissolution.

FYLINGTHORPE, NORTH YORKSHIRE - Within a stone's throw of Robin Hood's Bay and the north- east coast.

G GLAISDALE, NORTH YORKSHIRE - Set in a wooded valley with the 350-year-old shingle stone arch "Beggars Bridge" spanning the River Esk. Often described as the "Queen of the Dales". Central for the North York Moors National Park and close to Whitby. Numerous lovely walks and bridle paths.

GOATHLAND, NORTH YORKSHIRE - Spacious village with several large greens grazed by sheep, an ideal centre for walking the North York Moors. Nearby are several waterfalls, among them Mallyan Spout. Plough Monday celebrations are held in January. Location for filming of TV's "Heartbeat" series.

GRASSINGTON, NORTH YORKSHIRE - Tourists visit this former lead-mining village to see its "smiddy", antique and craft shops and Upper Wharfedale Museum of country trades. Popular with fishermen and walkers. Cobbled market square, numerous prehistoric sites. Grassington Feast in October. National Park Centre.

H HALIFAX, WEST YORKSHIRE - Founded on the cloth trade, and famous for its building society, textiles, carpets and toffee. The most notable landmark is Piece Hall where wool merchants traded, now restored to house shops, museums and art gallery. Home also to Eureka! The Museum for Children.

HARROGATE, NORTH YORKSHIRE - Major conference, exhibition and shopping centre, renowned for its spa heritage and award-winning floral displays, spacious parks and gardens. Famous for antiques, toffee, fine shopping and excellent tea shops; also its Royal Pump Rooms and Baths. Annual Great Yorkshire Show in July.

HAWES, NORTH YORKSHIRE - The capital of Upper Wensleydale on the famous Pennine Way, Yorkshire's highest market town, renowned for great cheeses. Popular with walkers. Dales National Park Information Centre and Folk Museum. Nearby is spectacular Hardraw Force waterfall.

HAWORTH, WEST YORKSHIRE - Famous since 1820 as home of the Bronte family. The Parsonage is now a Bronte Museum where furniture and possessions of the family are displayed. The Moors and Bronte waterfalls are nearby and steam trains on the Keighley and Worth Valley Railway pass through.

HEBDEN BRIDGE, WEST YORKSHIRE - Originally a small town on a packhorse route, Hebden Bridge grew into a booming mill town in the 18th C with rows of "up-and-down" houses of several storeys built against hillsides. Ancient "pace-egg play" custom held on Good Friday.

HELMSLEY, NORTH YORKSHIRE - Delightful small market town with red roofs, warm stone buildings and cobbled market square, on the River Rye at the entrance to Ryedale and the North York Moors. Remains of 12th C castle, several inns and All Saints' Church.

HEPTONSTALL, WEST YORKSHIRE - Quaint village above Hebden Bridge with an assortment of narrow streets, weavers' cottages, weather-worn houses and the ruins of a 12th C church. The 17th C grammar school is situated in a churchyard.

HIGH BENTHAM, NORTH YORKSHIRE - Bentham is said to mean "Home on the Common". A weekly market has been held here since the 14th C. Good walking country.

I ILKLEY, WEST YORKSHIRE - Former spa with an elegant shopping centre and famous for its ballad. The 16th C manor house, now a museum, displays local prehistoric and Roman relics. Popular walk leads up Heber's Ghyll to Ilkley Moor, with the mysterious Swastika Stone and White Wells, 18th C plunge baths.

K KIRKBYMOORSIDE, NORTH YORKSHIRE - Attractive market town with remains of Norman castle. Good centre for exploring moors. Nearby are the wild daffodils of Farndale.

KNARESBOROUGH, NORTH YORKSHIRE - Picturesque market town on the River Nidd. The 14th C keep is the best-preserved part of John of Gaunt's castle, and the manor house, with its chequerboard walls, was presented by James I to his son Charles as a fishing lodge. Prophetess Mother Shipton's cave. Boating on river.

L LEALHOLM, NORTH YORKSHIRE - Pretty moorland village on the River Esk below Leaholm Moor.

LEEDS, WEST YORKSHIRE - Large city with excellent modern shopping centre and splendid Victorian architecture. Museums and galleries including Temple Newsam House (the Hampton Court of the North), Tetley's Brewery Wharf and the Royal Armouries Museum; also home of Opera North.

LEYBURN, NORTH YORKSHIRE - Attractive Dales market town where Mary Queen of Scots was reputedly captured after her escape from Bolton Castle. Fine views over Wensleydale from nearby.

M MALTON, NORTH YORKSHIRE - Thriving farming town on the River Derwent with large livestock market. Famous for racehorse training. The local museum has Roman remains, and the Eden Camp Modern History Theme Museum transports visitors back to wartime Britain. Castle Howard is within easy reach.

N NEWTON-ON-RAWCLIFFE, NORTH YORKSHIRE - Pretty village on the edge of the North York Moors National Park.

NORTHALLERTON, NORTH YORKSHIRE - Formerly a staging post on coaching route to the North and later a railway town. Today it is a lively market town and the administrative capital of North Yorkshire. The parish church of All Saints dates from 1200. Dickens stayed at The Fleece.

P PICKERING, NORTH YORKSHIRE - Market town and tourist centre on edge of North York Moors. The parish church has a complete set of 15th C wall paintings depicting the lives of saints. Part of the 12th C castle still stands. Beck Isle Museum. The North York Moors Railway begins here.

R REETH, NORTH YORKSHIRE - Once a market town and lead-mining centre, Reeth today serves holiday-makers in Swaledale with its folk museum and 18th C shops and inns lining the green at High Row.

RICHMOND, NORTH YORKSHIRE - Market town on the edge of Swaledale with 11th C castle and Georgian and Victorian buildings surrounding the cobbled market-place. Green Howards' Museum is in the former Holy Trinity Church. Attractions include the Georgian Theatre, restored Theatre Royal, Richmondshire Museum, and Easby Abbey.

RIPON, NORTH YORKSHIRE - Ancient city with impressive cathedral containing a Saxon crypt which houses church treasures from all over Yorkshire. Charter granted in 886 by Alfred the Great. "Setting the Watch" tradition kept nightly by horn-blower in Market Square. Fountains Abbey is nearby.

ROBIN HOOD'S BAY, NORTH YORKSHIRE - Picturesque village of red-roofed cottages with main street running from cliff top down ravine to seashore, a magnet for artists. Scene of much smuggling and shipwrecks in the 18th C. Robin Hood is reputed to have escaped to the continent by boat from here.

S SCARBOROUGH, NORTH YORKSHIRE - Large, popular East Coast seaside resort, formerly a spa town. Beautiful gardens and 2 splendid sandy beaches. Castle ruins date from 1100; fine Georgian and Victorian houses. Scarborough Millennium depicts 1,000 years of the town's history. Sea Life Centre.

CHECK THE MAPS

The colour maps at the front of this guide show all the cities, towns and villages for which you will find accommodation entries. Refer to the town index to find the page on which they are listed.

SCOTCH CORNER, NORTH YORKSHIRE - Famous milestone at the junction of the A1 and A66 near Richmond.

SHEFFIELD, SOUTH YORKSHIRE - Local iron ore and coal gave Sheffield its prosperous steel and cutlery industries. The modern city centre has many interesting buildings - cathedral, Cutlers' Hall, Crucible Theatre, Graves and Mappin Art Galleries. Meadowhall Shopping Centre is nearby.

SKIPTON, NORTH YORKSHIRE - Pleasant market town at gateway to Dales, with farming community atmosphere, a Palladian Town Hall, parish church and fully roofed castle at the top of the High Street. The Clifford family motto, "Desoramis", is sculpted in huge letters on the parapet over the castle gateway.

STAINTONDALE, NORTH YORKSHIRE - Moors village north-west of Scarborough with shire-horse farm and visitor centre.

STAITHES, NORTH YORKSHIRE - A busy fishing village until the growth of Whitby, Staithes is a maze of steep, cobbled streets packed with tall houses of red brick and bright paintwork. Smuggling was rife in the 18th C. Cotton bonnets worn by fisherwomen can still be seen. Strong associations with Captain Cook.

T THIRSK, NORTH YORKSHIRE - Thriving market town with cobbled square surrounded by old shops and inns. St Mary's Church is probably the best example of Perpendicular work in Yorkshire. House of Thomas Lord - founder of Lord's Cricket Ground - is now a folk museum.

TODMORDEN, WEST YORKSHIRE - In beautiful scenery on the edge of the Pennines at junction of 3 sweeping valleys. Until 1888 the county boundary between Yorkshire and Lancashire cut this old cotton town in half, running through the middle of the Town Hall.

W WHITBY, NORTH YORKSHIRE - Holiday town with narrow streets and steep alleys at the mouth of the River Esk. Captain James Cook, the famous navigator, lived in Grape Lane. 199 steps lead to St Mary's Church and St Hilda's Abbey overlooking harbour. Dracula connections. Gothic weekend every April.

Y YORK, NORTH YORKSHIRE - Ancient walled city nearly 2,000 years old, containing many well-preserved medieval buildings. Its minster has over 100 stained glass windows and is the largest Gothic cathedral in England. Attractions include Castle Museum, National Railway Museum, Jorvik Viking Centre and York Dungeon.

COUNTRY CODE

Always follow the Country Code · Enjoy the countryside and respect its life and work · Guard against all risk of fire · Fasten all gates · Keep your dogs under close control · Keep to public paths across farmland · Use gates and stiles to cross fences, hedges and walls · Leave livestock, crops and machinery alone · Take your litter home · Help to keep all water clean · Protect wildlife, plants and trees · Take special care on country roads · Make no unnecessary noise

Heart of England

A multi-cultural region with a diverse mix of vibrant cities, picturesque villages and dramatic countryside, the Heart of England has much to enjoy, from its industrial heritage to the famous 'balti' curry.

The Counties of Derbyshire, Gloucestershire, Herefordshire, Leicestershire, Lincolnshire, Northamptonshire, Nottinghamshire, Rutland, Shropshire, Staffordshire, Warrickshire, Worcestershire and West Midlands.

Classic sights
Chatsworth House – one of the great treasure houses of England
Ironbridge – birthplace of the industrial revolution
Pottery and porcelain – world-famous Royal Crown Derby, Wedgewood and Spode potteries

Coast and country
Herefordshire – peaceful countryside with black and white timber-framed villages
Skegness – seaside fun
Peak District – stunning landscapes in England's first National Park

City lights
Birmingham – world class visual and performing arts, designer labels, jewellery and the famous Balti Quarter
Nottingham, Leicester, Derby – lively, contemporary cities with bags of culture and style

Distinctively different
Ludlow – acclaimed Michelin-starred restaurants
National Space Centre – look into the future
Alton Towers – thrills, spills and white-knuckle rides galore

For more information contact:
Visit Heart of England –
The Regional Tourist Board
Larkhill Road, Worcester
WR5 2EZ

www.visitheartofengland.com

Telephone enquiries -
T: (01905) 761100
F: (01905) 763450

1. Chipping Campden
2. Burghley House, Lincolnshire
3. Rutland Water

Places to Visit

You will find hundreds of interesting places to visit during your stay, just some of which are listed in these pages. Contact any Tourist Information Centre in the region for more ideas on days out.

QUALITY ASSURED VISITOR ATTRACTION

Awarded VisitBritain's 'Quality Assured Visitor Attraction' marque.

Acton Scott Historic Working Farm
Wenlock Lodge, Church Stretton
Tel: (01694) 781306
www.actonscotmuseum.co.uk
This historic working farm demonstrates farming and rural life in south Shropshire at the close of the 19th century.

Alton Towers Theme Park
Alton, Stoke-on-Trent
Tel: 0870 5204060 www.altontowers.com
Theme park with over 125 rides and attractions such as Air, Oblivion, Nemesis, Congo River Rapids, Log Flume and many children's attractions including 'Blobmaster' live show.

The American Adventure
Ilkeston
Tel: 0845 3302929
www.americanadventure.co.uk
Action and entertainment for all ages, with The Missile white-knuckle rollercoaster, Europe's tallest skycoaster and the world's wettest log flume.

Belton House, Park and Gardens (National Trust)
Belton, Grantham
Tel: (01476) 566116
www.nationaltrust.org.uk
The crowning achievement of restoration country house architecture, built in 1685-88 for Sir John Brownlow with alterations by James Wyatt in 1777.

Belvoir Castle
Belvoir, Grantham
Tel: (01476) 871002 www.belvoircastle.com
The present castle is the 4th to be built on this site and dates from 1816. Art treasures include works by Poussin, Rubens, Holbein and Reynolds. Queens Royal Lancers display.

Birmingham Botanical Gardens and Glasshouses
Westbourne Road, Edgbaston
Tel: (0121) 454 1860
www.birminghambotanicalgardens.org.uk
15 acres (6ha) of ornamental gardens and glasshouses. Widest range of plants in the Midlands from tropical rainforest to arid desert. Aviaries with exotic birds, child's play area.

Black Country Living Museum
Tipton Road, Dudley
Tel: (0121) 557 9643 www.bclm.co.uk
A warm welcome awaits you at Britain's friendliest open-air museum. Wander around original shops and houses, or ride on fair attractions and take a look down the mine.

Museum of British Road Transport
Hales Street, Coventry
Tel: (024) 7683 2425 www.mbrt.co.uk
Two hundred cars and commercial vehicles from 1896 to date, 200 cycles from 1818 to date, 90 motorcycles from 1920 to date and 'Thrust 2' and 'Thrust SSC' land speed record cars.

Butlins
Roman Bank, Skegness
Tel: (01754) 762311
www.butlinsonline.co.uk
Butlins has a Skyline Pavilion, Toyland, Sub Tropical Waterworld, tenpin bowling and entertainment centre with live shows.

Cadbury World
Bournville, Birmingham
Tel: (0121) 451 4180 www.cadburyworld.co.uk
The story of Cadbury's chocolate includes chocolate-making demonstration and attractions for all ages, with free samples, free parking, shop and restaurant.

Chatsworth House, Garden, Farmyard & Adventure Playground
Chatsworth, Bakewell
Tel: (01246) 582204 www.chatsworth.org
Visitors to Chatsworth see more than 30 richly decorated rooms; the garden with fountains, a cascade and maze and the Farmyard and Adventure Playground.

Cotswold Farm Park
Guiting Power, Cheltenham
Tel: (01451) 850307
www.cotswoldfarmpark.co.uk
Collection of rare breeds of British farm animals. Pet's corner, adventure playground, Tractor School, picnic area, gift shop and cafe and seasonal farming displays.

Crich Tramway Village
Crich, Matlock
Tel: (01773) 852565 www.tramway.co.uk
A collection of over 70 trams from Britain and overseas from 1873-1969 with tram rides on a 1-mile (1.5-km) route, a period street scene, depots, a power station, workshops and exhibitions.

Drayton Manor Family Theme Park
Tamworth
Tel: (01827) 287979 www.draytonmanor.co.uk
A major theme park with over 100 rides and attractions, plus children's rides, Zoo, farm, museums and the new live 'Popeye Show'.

The Elgar Birthplace Museum
Lower Broadheath, Worcester
Tel: (01905) 333224 www.elgar.org
Country cottage birthplace of Sir Edward Elgar and the new Elgar Centre, giving a fascinating insight into his life, music, family, friends and inspirations.

The Galleries of Justice
Shire Hall, Nottingham
Tel: (0115) 952 0555
www.galleriesofjustice.org.uk
An atmospheric experience of justice over the ages located in and around an original 19thC courthouse and county gaol, brought to life by live actors.

The Heights of Abraham Cable Cars, Caverns and Hilltop Park
Matlock Bath, Matlock
Tel: (01629) 582365
www.heights-of-abraham.co.uk
A spectacular cable car ride takes you to the summit where, within the grounds, there are a wide variety of attractions for young and old alike. Gift shop and coffee shop.

Ikon Gallery
1 Oozells Square, Birmingham
Tel: (0121) 248 0708 www.ikon-gallery.co.uk
One of Europe's foremost galleries, presenting the work of national and international artists within an innovative educational framework.

Ironbridge Gorge Museum
Coalbrookdale, Telford
Tel: (01952) 433522
www.ironbridge.org.uk
World's first cast-iron bridge, Museum of the Gorge, Tar Tunnel, Jackfield Tile Museum, Coalport China Museum, Rosehill House, Blists Hill and Iron and Enginuity Museum.

Lincoln Castle
Castle Hill, Lincoln
Tel: (01522) 511068
www.lincolnshire.gov.uk/lccconnect/culturalservices/heritage/LincolnCastle
A medieval castle including towers and ramparts with a Magna Carta exhibition, a prison chapel experience, reconstructed Westgate and popular events throughout the summer.

2

3

1. Quayside Wharf, Birmingham
2. Rolling Hills and rural landscapes in the Heart of England
3. Robin Hood Statue, Nottingham

Midland Railway Centre
Butterley Station, Derby
Tel: (01773) 747674
www.midlandrailwaycentre.co.uk
Over 50 locomotives and over 100 items of historic rolling stock of Midland and LMS origin with a steam-hauled passenger service, a museum site, country and farm park.

National Sea Life Centre
The Water's Edge, Birmingham
Tel: (0121) 633 4700 www.sealife.co.uk
Over 55 fascinating displays. The opportunity to come face-to-face with literally 100's of fascinating sea creatures from sharks to shrimps. Now also includes otters.

Nottingham Industrial Museum
Courtyard Buildings, Nottingham
Tel: (0115) 915 3910
www.nottinghamcity.gov.uk
An 18thC stables presenting the history of Nottingham's industries: printing, pharmacy, hosiery and lace. There is also a Victorian beam engine, a horse gin and transport.

Peak District Mining Museum
The Pavilion, Matlock Bath
Tel: (01629) 583834 www.peakmines.co.uk
A large exhibition on 3500 years of lead mining with displays on geology, mines and miners, tools and engines. The climbing shafts make it suitable for children as well.

Rockingham Castle
Rockingham, Market Harborough
Tel: (01536) 770240
www.rockinghamcastle.com
An Elizabethan house within the walls of a Norman castle with fine pictures, extensive views and gardens with roses and an ancient yew hedge.

Rugby School Museum
10 Little Church Street, Rugby
Tel: (01788) 556109
www.rugbyschool.net/bt/museum_intro.htm
Rugby School Museum tells the story of the school, scene of 'Tom Brown's Schoolday's', and contains the earlier memorabilia of the game invented on the school close.

Severn Valley Railway
The Railway Station, Bewdley
Tel: (01299) 403816 www.svr.co.uk
Preserved standard gauge steam railway running 16 miles (27km) between Kidderminster, Bewdley and Bridgnorth. Collection of locomotives and passenger coaches.

Shakespeare's Birthplace
Henley Street, Stratford-upon-Avon
Tel: (01789) 201822 www.shakespeare.org.uk
The world famous house where William Shakespeare was born in 1564 and where he grew up. See the highly acclaimed Shakespeare Exhibition.

Shugborough Estate (National Trust)
Milford, Stafford
Tel: (01889) 881388
www.staffordshire.gov.uk/shugborough
18thC mansion house with fine collection of furniture. Gardens and park contain beautiful neo-classical monuments.

Skegness Natureland Seal Sanctuary
The Promenade, Skegness
Tel: (01754) 764345
www.skegnessnatureland.co.uk
Collection of performing seals, baby seals, penguins, aquarium, crocodiles, snakes, terrapins, scorpions, tropical birds, butterflies (April-October) and pets.

Snibston Discovery Park
Coalville, Leicester
Tel: (01530) 278444
www.leics.gov.uk/museums
Award-winning science and industrial heritage museum. Over 90 indoor and outdoor hands-on displays, plus exhibits from Leicestershire's industrial past.

Spode Visitor Centre
Church Street, Stoke-on-Trent
Tel: (01782) 744011 www.spode.co.uk
Visitors are shown the various processes in the making of bone china. Visitors can 'have a go' themselves in the craft demonstration area.

The Tales of Robin Hood
30-38 Maid Marian Way, Nottingham
Tel: (0115) 948 3284 www.robinhood.uk.com
Join the world's greatest medieval adventure. Ride through the magical green wood and play the Silver Arrow game, in the search for Robin Hood.

Twycross Zoo
Twycross, Atherstone
Tel: (01827) 880250
www.twycrosszoo.com
A zoo with gorillas, orang-utans, chimpanzees, a modern gibbon complex, elephants, lions, giraffes, a reptile house, pets' corner and rides.

Walsall Arboretum
Lichfield Street, Walsall
Tel: (01922) 653148
www.walsallarboretum.co.uk
Picturesque Victorian park with over 170 acres (70ha) of gardens, lakes and parkland. Home to the famous Walsall Illuminations each Autumn.

Warwick Castle
Warwick
Tel: 0870 4422000 www.warwick-castle.co.uk
Set in 60 acres (24ha) of grounds with state rooms, armoury, dungeon, torture chamber, 'A Royal Weekend Party 1898', 'Kingmaker' and the new Mill and Engine House attraction.

The Wedgwood Story Visitor Centre
Barlaston, Stoke-on-Trent
Tel: (01782) 204218
www.thewedgwoodstory.com
This £4.5 million visitor centre exhibits centuries of craftmanship on a plate. Audio-guided tour includes exhibition and demonstration areas. Shop and restaurants.

The Wildfowl and Wetlands Trust Slimbridge
Slimbridge, Gloucester
Tel: (01453) 890333 www.wwt.org.uk
Tropical house, hides, heated observatory, exhibits, shop, restaurant and children's playground, pond zone.

Worcester Cathedral
10A College Green, Worcester
Tel: (01905) 611002 www.cofe-worcester.org.uk
Worcester Cathedral is England's loveliest cathedral. We welcome families, groups and individuals with refreshments, gift shop and disabled access to all facilities and gardens.

1. Food and drink in the Heart of England
2. Stratford

Visit Heart of England – The Regional Tourist Board

Larkhill Road, Worcester WR5 2EZ.
T: (01905) 761100
F: (01905) 763450
www.visitheartofengland.com

THE FOLLOWING PUBLICATIONS ARE AVAILABLE FROM VISIT HEART OF ENGLAND:

Bed & Breakfast Touring Map including Camping and Caravan Parks 2004

Escape to the Heart 2004/5

Great Places to Visit in the Heart of England 2004

Getting to the Heart of England

BY ROAD: Britain's main motorways (M1/M6/M5) meet in the Heart of England; the M40 links with the M42 south of Birmingham while the M4 provides fast access from London to the south of the region. These road links ensure that the Heart of England is more accessible by road than any other region in the UK.

BY RAIL: The Heart of England lies at the centre of the country's rail network.
There are direct trains from London and other major cities to many towns and cities within the region.

1. Shrewsbury Castle
2. Stokesay Castle, Shropshire

Where to stay in the

Heart of England

Accommodation entries in this region are listed in alphabetical order of place name, and then in alphabetical order of establishment. As West Oxfordshire and Cherwell are promoted in both Heart of England and The South East, places in these areas with accommodation are listed in this section. See The South East for full West Oxfordshire and Cherwell entries.

All place names in the blue bands under which accommodation is listed, are shown on the maps at the front of this guide.

Symbols give useful information about services and facilities. Inside the back cover flap there's a key to these symbols which you can keep open for easy reference.

A complete listing of all the VisitBritain assessed accommodation covered by this guide appears at the back of this guide.

ABBERLEY, Worcestershire Map ref 4A3

★★★

4 Units
Sleeping 2–4

OLD YATES COTTAGES
Abberley, Worcester
Contact: Mr & Mrs R M Goodman, Old Yates Farm, Abberley, Worcester WR6 6AT
T: (01299) 896500
F: (01299) 896065
E: oldyates@aol.com
I: www.oldyatescottages.co.uk

OPEN All Year
CC: Delta, Mastercard, Switch, Visa

Low season per wk
£150.00–£200.00
High season per wk
£270.00–£370.00

Cosy cottages in tranquil surroundings amidst beautiful countryside. A personal welcome awaits you. Convenient for exploring the Midlands and Welsh Borders. Contact us for colour brochure.

QUALITY ASSURANCE SCHEME

For an explanation of the quality and facilities represented by the Stars please refer to the front of this guide. A more detailed explanation can be found in the information pages at the back.

BRUERN COTTAGES

National Winners of VisitBritain's Excellence in England Gold and Silver Award for Self-Catering Holiday of the Year 1998 and 2003, Bruern Cottages are the finest self-catering properties, not just in the Cotswolds but in the whole of Great Britain.

"For a taste of the upper crust Britain head for Bruern Cottages, twelve Merchant Ivoryesque cottages. Each antiques filled cottage offers one to five bedrooms, up-to-the-minute kitchens, and access to a secret garden of lavender and wisteria. Children will gallop straight for the playhouse, complete with Lilliputian tea set and canopied bed." *Condé Nast Traveller*

TOP 5 STAR GRADING

These twelve award winning cottages, in the heart of the Cotswolds, were converted from the Victorian stable yard and outbuildings of Bruern Abbey. They are stylish, luxurious and unusually well equipped, country houses in miniature, with open fires and four poster beds as well as state-of-the-art bathrooms and kitchens. They sleep two to ten. Each has a private enclosed terrace and many have their own secluded gardens.

In the beautifully landscaped communal gardens and grounds there is tennis, croquet and swimming. Children have their own special play area with a two storey playhouse, a climbing frame and an indoor playroom. There are wonderful wildlife walks in the neighbouring Nature Reserve at Foxholes and along the Oxfordshire Way, which runs through Bruern. Fly-fishing and riding are available near at hand and Bruern adjoins a challenging golf course.

London is only an hour and a half by train or by car, and Oxford just forty minutes.

SMALLEST COTTAGE

(sleeps 2 plus cot)

LOW SEASON	£526 p.w.
HIGH SEASON	£983 p.w.

LARGEST COTTAGE

(sleeps 10 plus cots)

LOW SEASON	£1,848 p.w.
HIGH SEASON	£3,921 p.w.

www.bruern-holiday-cottages.co.uk Tel: 01993 830415 Email: enquiries@bruern.co.uk

ALDERTON, Gloucestershire Map ref 2B1

★★★★

4 Units
Sleeping 6–10

Pretty cottages with their own gardens in Cotswold village with shop and pub. Barn conversion with walled garden; part-thatched 16thC cottage with large garden overlooking fields; black-and-white barn conversion with paved garden and lawn; stone house with own garden.

RECTORY FARM COTTAGES

Alderton, Tewkesbury
Contact: Mr & Mrs M A Burton, Rectory Farm Cottages, Alderton, Tewkesbury GL20 8NW
T: (01242) 620455
F: (01242) 620455
E: peterannabel@hotmail.com
I: www.rectoryfarmcottages.co.uk

OPEN All Year
CC: Switch

Low season per wk
£350.00–£600.00
High season per wk
£750.00–£1,000.00

ALSTONEFIELD, Staffordshire Map ref 4B2

★★★★-★★★★★

2 Units
Sleeping 4–6

Idyllic country cottage, cosy and warm, nestling in a truly peaceful setting. Also our Ancestral Barn with luxurious canopy beds (two king-size), all en suite bathrooms, full of old world charm, character and medieval ambience, with polished floors, rich colours and antiques. Rambles from door to Dales. Organic farm near Dovedale.

ANCESTRAL BARN & CHURCH FARM COTTAGE

Stanshope (Nr Dovedale), Ashbourne
Contact: Mrs S Fowler, Church Farm, Stanshope, Ashbourne DE6 2AD
T: (01335) 310243
F: (01335) 310243
E: sue@dovedalecottages.fsnet.co.uk
I: www.dovedalecottages.co.uk

OPEN All Year

Low season per wk
£320.00–£425.00
High season per wk
£425.00–£600.00

★★★★★

1 Unit
Sleeping 5–6

Situated in a beautiful and idyllic part of Wolfscote Dale, enjoying stunning views along the River Dove. Recently refurbished throughout, you will relax in a comfortable and highly maintained family home. Fires laid daily, welcome grocery basket and even hand cream! Large gardens (one enclosed), toys, videos and ride-ons.

DOVE COTTAGE FISHING LODGE

Alstonefield, Ashbourne
Contact: Ms M Hignett, Foxlease Court, Preston, Cirencester GL7 5PS
T: (01285) 655875
F: (01285) 655885
E: info@dovecottages.co.uk
I: www.dovecottages.co.uk

OPEN All Year except Christmas

2-rods fishing on River Dove (Apr-Oct). Short breaks available Oct-Apr (excl Christmas and New Year).

Low season per wk
£275.00–£480.00
High season per wk
£760.00–£990.00

CREDIT CARD BOOKINGS **If you book by telephone and are asked for your credit card number it is advisable to check the proprietor's policy should you cancel your reservation.**

ASHBOURNE, Derbyshire Map ref 4B2 *Tourist Information Centre Tel: (01335) 343666*

★★★★★

1 Unit
Sleeping 8

Part of 18thC coach house, many original features, converted into a spacious and cosy retreat. Elevated and tranquil with superb views. Good walking from the door, cycling on the trails. Bordering Dovedale and Peak Park. Alton Towers three miles. Woodburning stove, super-king beds, farmhouse kitchen. Dogs welcome.

THE GROOMS' QUARTERS

Ashbourne
Contact: Ray & Ann Thompson, The Grooms' Quarters, The Old Coach House, Hall Lane, Wootton, Ashbourne DE6 2GW
T: (01335) 324549
E: thompson.wootton@virgin.net
I: www.groomsquarters.co.uk

OPEN All Year

Short breaks available.

Low season per wk
£350.00–£460.00
High season per wk
£460.00–£750.00

★★★★

1 Unit
Sleeping 5

THE NOOK
Kniveton, Ashbourne
Contact: Mrs S E Osborn, Barracca, Ivydene Close, Earl Shilton, Leicester LE9 7NR
T: (01455) 842609
E: susan.osborn@virgin.net
I: www.come.to/thenook

OPEN All Year

Low season per wk
£185.00–£250.00
High season per wk
£250.00–£385.00

A stone cottage in a conservation area in the village centre of Kniveton. Two miles Carsington Water, close to village pub. Visit website for full details.

★★★-★★★★

30 Units
Sleeping 2–6

Set in the former grounds of Sandybrook Hall, an elegant 19thC manor house with woodland walks and wonderful views. Luxurious, fully equipped pine lodges furnished to the highest standards. Heated indoor swimming pool, indoor and outdoor play areas, restaurant and bar.

SANDYBROOK COUNTRY PARK

Ashbourne
Contact: Reservations, Pinelodge Holidays, Darley Moor, Two Dales, Matlock DE4 5LN
T: (01629) 732428
F: (01629) 735015
E: admin@pinelodgeholidays.co.uk
I: www.pinelodgeholidays.co.uk

OPEN All Year
CC: Delta, Mastercard, Solo, Switch, Visa

Mid-week and weekend breaks available all year round (excl Christmas and New Year). More offers upon application.

Low season per wk
£250.00–£380.00
High season per wk
£480.00–£795.00

USE YOUR *i*s

There are more than 550 Tourist Information Centres throughout England offering friendly help with accommodation and holiday ideas as well as suggestions of places to visit and things to do. You'll find TIC addresses in the local Phone Book.

ATHERSTONE, Warwickshire Map ref 4B3

★★★★

6 Units
Sleeping 2–7

Superb cottages carefully converted from old farm barns, each individually furnished to highest standards. Full central heating and all linen and towels included, fully equipped laundry. Enjoy the putting green, barbecue, lovely farm walks. Within easy reach of theatres, castles, cathedrals and museums of Stratford, Warwick, Lichfield and Birmingham.

HIPSLEY FARM COTTAGES

Hurley, Atherstone
Contact: Mrs A Prosser, Waste Farm, Hurley, Atherstone CV9 2LR
T: (01827) 872437
F: (01827) 872437
E: ann@hipsley.co.uk
I: www.hipsley.co.uk

OPEN All Year

Low season per wk
£260.00–£440.00
High season per wk
£285.00–£550.00

BAKEWELL, Derbyshire Map ref 4B2 *Tourist Information Centre Tel: (01629) 813227*

★★★★

1 Unit
Sleeping 6

EDGE VIEW

Bakewell
Contact: Mrs G P Rogers, Penylan, Monyash Road, Bakewell DE45 1FG
T: (01629) 813336
F: (01629) 813336

OPEN All Year

Low season per wk
£260.00–£300.00
High season per wk
£300.00–£395.00

Three-bedroomed bungalow, with two bedrooms and bathroom/toilet on ground floor. Extensive views. Lawn, garden, ample off-road parking. Lock-up garage. Owner maintained.

3

★★★

2 Units
Sleeping 4–6

SPOUT FARM

Bakewell
Contact: Mrs E M Patterson, The Bungalow, Elton, Matlock DE4 2BY
T: (01629) 650358

Barn conversion with original stonework, beams and logburning stove, standing in spacious grounds with ponds, pool and abundant wildlife. Magnificent views over unspoilt scenery. Convenient for many attractions including Haddon and Chatsworth. Surrounded by pretty villages and superb walking country. Total peace and seclusion.

OPEN All Year except Christmas

Short breaks available Oct-Mar, 3 nights minimum (excl Christmas and New Year).

Low season per wk
£190.00–£235.00
High season per wk
£260.00–£380.00

AT-A-GLANCE SYMBOLS

Symbols at the end of each accommodation entry give useful information about services and facilities. A key to symbols can be found inside the back cover flap. Keep this open for easy reference.

BAMFORD, Derbyshire Map ref 4B2

★★★★

3 Units

Comfortable barn-converted cottages, each with own garden or terrace, on this 'out of the way', beautifully situated farmstead, with good access. Waymarked woodland walks, trout lake, tennis court and gardens of interest, open National Garden Scheme. Each cottage has double and twin-bedded rooms and good size living areas with open fires.

SHATTON HALL FARM

Bamford, Hope Valley
Contact: Mrs A H Kellie, Shatton Hall Farm, Bamford, Hope Valley S33 0BG
T: (01433) 620635
F: (01433) 620689
E: ahk@peakfarmholidays.co.uk
I: www.peakfarmholidays.co.uk

OPEN All Year

Recently converted barn suitable for art, craft and special-interest groups.

Low season per wk
£250.00–£325.00
High season per wk
£350.00–£425.00

BARLOW, Derbyshire Map ref 4B2

★★★

5 Units
Sleeping 2–5

MILL FARM HOLIDAY COTTAGES

Barlow, Dronfield
Contact: Mr & Mrs R Ward
T: (0114) 2890543
F: (0114) 2891473
E: cottages@barfish.fsnet.co.uk
I: www.barlowlakes.co.uk

OPEN All Year

Low season per wk
£121.00–£187.00
High season per wk
£197.00–£248.00

Holiday cottages, some with 4-poster beds. Trout/coarse fishing included. On 50 acres of conservation land. Shop and pub 150 yards, bus at gate.

BASLOW, Derbyshire Map ref 4B2

★★★★

1 Unit
Sleeping 5

HALL COTTAGE

Baslow, Bakewell
Contact: Mr & Mrs R W Griffiths, Beechcroft, School Lane, Baslow, Bakewell DE45 1RZ
T: (01246) 582900
F: (01246) 583675
E: hallcottage@btinternet.com

OPEN All Year

Low season per wk
£250.00–£280.00
High season per wk
£280.00–£330.00

Small stone barn, tastefully restored. Beamed ceilings, fireplace. Quiet location in oldest part of village. Walking distance to shops, pubs, restaurants, Chatsworth and open countryside.

BEWDLEY, Worcestershire Map ref 4A3 *Tourist Information Centre Tel: (01299) 404740*

★★★

1 Unit
Sleeping 8

RIVERVIEW COTTAGE

Bewdley
Contact: Mr & Mrs J Giles
T: (01299) 403481
E: jgilesm81@aol.com
I: www.riverview-bdy.co.uk

OPEN All Year

Low season per wk
£210.00–£250.00
High season per wk
£400.00–£460.00

A 14thC, Grade II Listed cottage on the riverside. Three bedrooms, fully equipped and comfortably furnished. Five minutes' walk from the town centre.

TOWN INDEX

This can be found at the back of the guide. If you know where you want to stay, the index will give you the page number listing accommodation in your chosen town, city or village.

BIBURY, Gloucestershire Map ref 2B1

★★★★
2 Units
Sleeping 4

COTTESWOLD HOUSE COTTAGES

Bibury, Cirencester
Contact: Mrs J Underwood, Cotteswold House, Arlington, Bibury, Cirencester GL7 5ND
T: (01285) 740609
F: (01285) 740609
E: cotteswold.house@btconnect.com
I: home.btconnect.com/cotteswold.house

Situated in this picturesque village, these delightful cottages offer tastefully furnished, spacious accommodation. Equipped to a high standard to include all the comforts of home. Heating, linen and electricity included. Private parking. No smoking/pets. An ideal centre for touring Cotswolds and surrounding areas.

OPEN All Year
CC: Mastercard, Visa

Low season per wk
Min £240.00
High season per wk
Max £375.00

BISHOP'S CASTLE, Shropshire Map ref 4A3

★★★★
1 Unit
Sleeping 4

MOUNT COTTAGE
Bishop's Castle
Contact: Mrs H Willis, Mount Cottage, Bull Lane, Bishop's Castle SY9 5DA
T: (01588) 638288
F: (01588) 638288
E: adamheather@btopenworld.com
I: www.mountcottage.co.uk

OPEN All Year

Low season per wk
£175.00–£250.00
High season per wk
£250.00–£320.00

Converted 17thC barn. Very short walk to town. Well-equipped, modern fitted kitchen. Bathroom/wc with over-bath shower and second wc. Beams throughout.

BLOCKLEY, Gloucestershire Map ref 2B1

★★★★
9 Units
Sleeping 2–6

LOWER FARM COTTAGES

Blockley, Moreton-in-Marsh
Contact: Mrs K Batchelor, Lower Farm Cottages, Lower Farmhouse, Blockley, Moreton-in-Marsh GL56 9DP
T: (01386) 700237
F: (01386) 700237
E: lowerfarm@hotmail.com
I: www.lower-farm.co.uk

Converted barns and typical Cotswold cottages in an idyllic setting on the edge of this pretty village, ideally situated to explore the numerous attractions of the Cotswolds, including Stratford, castles, gardens and wildlife parks. Cottages tastefully furnished with a blend of antique and new furnishings, together with modern facilities.

OPEN All Year

Winter breaks. Short breaks in season at short notice, subject to availability.

Low season per wk
£253.00–£384.00
High season per wk
£368.00–£644.00

BOURTON-ON-THE-WATER, Gloucestershire Map ref 2B1 *Tourist Information Centre Tel: (01451) 820211*

★★★
1 Unit
Sleeping 3

BOBBLE COTTAGE
Bourton-on-the-Water
Contact: Country Holidays reference: 15430, Spring Mill, Barnoldswick BB94 0AS
T: 08700 723723

OPEN All Year

Low season per wk
£125.00–£175.00
High season per wk
£245.00–£345.00

A delightful Cotswold-stone cottage set within a secluded farmyard in the very heart of the Cotswold Hills.

5

VISITOR ATTRACTIONS For ideas on places to visit refer to the introduction at the beginning of this section. Look out too for the ETC's Quality Assured Visitor Attraction signs.

BOURTON-ON-THE-WATER continued

★★★★
4 Units
Sleeping 3–6

All of our luxuriously appointed 19thC cottages are spacious and centrally located, each having its own enclosed garden and parking and situated in a quiet backwater of Bourton-on-the-Water. They are a short walk to the many attractions of this lovely historic town. Children and pets welcome.

HATTIE'S, LUCY'S, CHAPEL & JACK'S

Bourton-on-the-Water
Contact: Pippa Arnott, Cotswolds Cottage Company, Wells Head, Temple Guiting, Cheltenham GL54 5RR
T: (01451) 850560
F: (0870) 128 0033
E: cotscotco@msn.com
I: www.cotswoldcottage.co.uk

OPEN All Year except Christmas
CC: Amex, Delta, Mastercard, Switch, Visa

Short breaks available out of season – minimum 3-night stay.

Low season per wk
£325.00–£460.00
High season per wk
£460.00–£575.00

★★★★
1 Unit
Sleeping 4

MAGNOLIA COTTAGE APARTMENT

Bourton-on-the-Water, Cheltenham
Contact: Mr & Mrs M Cotterill
T: (01451) 821841
F: (01451) 821841
E: cotterillmj@hotmail.com
I: www.cottageguide.co.uk/magnolia

OPEN All Year
CC: Delta, Mastercard, Visa

Low season per wk
£250.00–£325.00
High season per wk
£300.00–£360.00

First-floor apartment, tastefully furnished and fully carpeted. Two twin-bedded rooms. Easy walk to all village amenities. Not suitable for children under 10 and, sorry, no pets. Short breaks in low season.

10

★★★★
2 Units
Sleeping 6

OXLEIGH COTTAGES

Bourton-on-the-Water, Cheltenham
Contact: Mrs B Smith, Dairy House Farm, Croxton Lane, Middlewich CW10 9LA
T: (01606) 833245
F: (01606) 837139
E: bsmith@lazymeadow.fsnet.co.uk

OPEN All Year

Low season per wk
£298.00–£498.00
High season per wk
£528.00–£780.00

Three-bedroomed cottages, semi-detached. 4-poster beds. Log fires, central heating. TV/radio/stereo. Fully equipped kitchen. Lawned garden, private patio. Off-road parking.

BREDON, Gloucestershire

See display ad on opposite page

BRIDGNORTH, Shropshire Map ref 4A3 *Tourist Information Centre Tel: (01746) 763257*

★★★
5 Units

Superbly furnished cottage with stone feature walls. Fully equipped, centrally heated. Quiet location near owner's 17thC inn. Ideally situated for visiting the many places of interest nearby. Choice of other cottages/apartments (three on ground floor). Short breaks available.

BULLS HEAD COTTAGES

Chelmarsh, Bridgnorth
Contact: Mr D Baxter, The Bulls Head, Chelmarsh, Bridgnorth WV16 6BA
T: (01746) 861469
F: (01746) 862646
E: dave@bullshead.fsnet.co.uk
I: www.virtual-shropshire.co.uk/bulls-head-inn

OPEN All Year
CC: Delta, Mastercard, Solo, Switch, Visa

Low season per wk
£210.00–£280.00
High season per wk
£280.00–£575.00

BRIDGNORTH continued

★★★★

3 Units
Sleeping 4–5

Victorian cottages on a 330-acre dairy, arable and free-range poultry farm three miles south-west of Bridgnorth. Situated in beautiful countryside, the cottages are very comfortably furnished and well equipped with their own attractive gardens. Peaceful location, an ideal centre for exploring Shropshire and visiting Bridgnorth, Ironbridge, Ludlow and Shrewsbury.

EUDON BURNELL COTTAGES

Glazeley, Bridgnorth
Contact: Mrs M A Crawford Clarke, Eudon Burnell, Glazeley, Near Bridgnorth WV16 6UD
T: (01746) 789235
F: (01746) 789550
E: eudonburnell@virtual-shropshire.co.uk
I: www.eudon.co.uk

OPEN All Year

Winter/autumn short breaks, 2 nights minimum. £45-£65 per day. Log fire in 2 cottages.

Low season per wk
£240.00–£360.00
High season per wk
£260.00–£360.00

★★★

1 Unit
Sleeping 4

THE GRANARY

Bridgnorth
Contact: Mrs S Allen, The Granary, The Old Vicarage, Ditton Priors, Bridgnorth WV16 6SQ
T: (01746) 712272
F: (01746) 712288
E: allen@oldvicditton.freeserve.co.uk

OPEN All Year

Low season per wk
£130.00
High season per wk
£180.00

Farm granary in unspoilt South Shropshire countryside. Bridgnorth within easy reach, Ludlow 16 miles. Studio sitting room, bedroom, kitchen, bathroom. Excellent walking.

PRICES
Please check prices and other details at the time of booking.

The Moretons Vacation Houses
Nine self-catering houses, accommodating between 2 and 10. Each house is completely furnished down to a needle and thread. Indoor heated swimming pool with spa, 5 acres of gardens and children's play house. Flexible arrival and departure dates and short breaks. 10 miles from Cheltenham, 50 miles from Oxford. 2004 is our 31st year of operation.
Full brochure and price list available - contact us or visit our web site.
★★★★★ SELF CATERING
The Moretons Vacation Houses, Bredon, Tewkesbury, Gloucestershire, GL20 7EN
T: (01684) 772294
F: (01684) 772262
E: soutar@moretonsbredon.co.uk
www.moretons-soutar.co.uk

BROAD CAMPDEN, Gloucestershire Map ref 2B1

★★★
1 Unit
Sleeping 5

LION COTTAGE

Broad Campden, Chipping Campden
Contact: Mrs B L Rawcliffe, Lion Cottage,
Broad Campden, Chipping Campden GL55 6UR
T: (01386) 840077

OPEN All Year

Low season per wk
£225.00–£245.00
High season per wk
£260.00–£350.00

Cotswold-stone cottage with beamed ceilings and open fireplace. Open-plan living room with sitting, dining and kitchen areas; one double, one twin, one single bedroom.

BROADWAY, Worcestershire Map ref 2B1

★★★
1 Unit
Sleeping 2

HESTERS HOUSE

Broadway
Contact: Mrs L Dungate, Inglenook, Brokengate Lane,
Denham, Uxbridge UB9 4LA
T: (01895) 834357
F: (01895) 832904
E: pdungate@aol.com

OPEN All Year except Christmas

Low season per wk
£175.00
High season per wk
£225.00

Charming, oak-beamed end of terrace cottage with small courtyard, fronting Broadway High Street. A delightful cosy home from which to tour Cotswolds. Prices include gas, electricity.

5

Rating Applied For
1 Unit
Sleeping 6

ORCHARD COTTAGE

Saintbury, Broadway
Contact: Sheila Rolland, Campden Cottages, Paxford,
Chipping Campden GL55 6XG
T: (01386) 593315
F: (01386) 593057
E: info@campdencottages.co.uk
I: www.campdencottages.co.uk

16thC Cotswold stone cottage overlooking beautiful, peaceful countryside. Chipping Campden or Broadway three miles. Many original features including exposed elm beams, flagstone floor downstairs/ wood floors upstairs, inglenook fireplace in sitting room (with logs supplied), separate dining room, three double bedrooms, two bathrooms. Garden, barbecue. Parking.

OPEN All Year
CC: Delta, Mastercard, Switch, Visa

Short breaks – minimum 3 nights. Other cottages available (Chipping Campden area) sleeping 2-8.

Low season per wk
Min £360.00
High season per wk
Max £595.00

BROMSGROVE, Worcestershire Map ref 4B3 *Tourist Information Centre Tel: (01527) 831809*

★★★
1 Unit
Sleeping 4

EAST VIEW APARTMENT

Bromsgrove
Contact: Mrs A Westwood, Little Shortwood,
Brockhill Lane, Tardebigge, Bromsgrove B60 1LU
T: (01527) 63180
F: (01527) 63180
E: westwoodja@hotmail.com

OPEN All Year except Christmas

Low season per wk
Min £130.00
High season per wk
Max £180.00

Comfortable apartment in 17thC cottage in beautiful countryside. 10 minutes M5/ M42. Convenient for many local places of interest. Birmingham 30 minutes. Ideal for holidays/business.

10

WEB
www.visitengland.com
Log on for information and inspiration. The latest information on places to visit, events and quality assessed accommodation.

BURWARTON, Shropshire Map ref 4A3

★★★

1 Unit
Sleeping 8

THE WICKET

Burwarton, Bridgnorth
Contact: Mrs J M Millard, Brown Clee Holidays, Estate Office, Burwarton, Bridgnorth WV16 6QQ
T: (01746) 787207
F: (01746) 787422
E: millard@burwarton-estates.co.uk

Total peace and seclusion. Spacious, fully-fitted cottage on slopes of Brown Clee Hill on beautiful private estate. Paradise for nature lovers with beautiful walks. Dogs/horses welcome, fly fishing in small lake.

Low season per wk
£350.00–£400.00
High season per wk
£500.00–£550.00

CARSINGTON, Derbyshire Map ref 4B2

★★★-★★★★★

17 Units
Sleeping 3–11

KNOCKERDOWN HOLIDAY COTTAGES
Knockerdown, Ashbourne
Contact: Ms C Lambert
T: (01629) 540525
F: (01629) 540525
E: cathy@knockerdown-cottages.co.uk
I: www.derbyshireholidaycottages.co.uk

OPEN All Year
CC: Delta, Mastercard, Switch, Visa

Low season per wk
£412.00–£692.00
High season per wk
£701.00–£1,549.00

Adjacent to village inn. Indoor pool, sauna, gym, outdoor play area. Central for both Derbyshire and Staffordshire's many attractions. Five minutes to beautiful Carsington Reservoir.

CHELTENHAM, Gloucestershire Map ref 2B1 *Tourist Information Centre Tel: (01242) 522878*

★★★★

3 Units
Sleeping 2–4

HOLMER COTTAGES

Cheltenham
Contact: Mrs J Collins, Holmer Cottages, Haines Orchard, Woolstone, Cheltenham GL52 9RG
T: (01242) 672848
F: (01242) 672848
E: holmercottages@talk21.com
I: http://www.cottageguide.co.uk/holmercottages

Late-19thC, semi-detached brick cottages, each with own separate sun terrace and private garden, overlooking old apple orchard. Situated in a small rural hamlet convenient for Cotswolds, Malverns, Severn Valley and racing at Cheltenham.

OPEN All Year

1 Nov–1 May: 3-night stay £135.

Low season per wk
£190.00–£250.00
High season per wk
£290.00–£360.00

★★★

1 Unit
Sleeping 4

PRIORY COTTAGE

Southam, Cheltenham
Contact: Mr I S Mant, Church Gate, Southam Lane, Southam, Cheltenham GL52 3NY
T: (01242) 584693
F: (01242) 584693
E: iansmant@hotmail.com

Old Cotswold-stone cottage in own garden overlooking apple orchard. Cosy and warm in winter with woodburning stove. Two bedrooms: one double, one twin; sitting room, dining room, modern fitted kitchen. Ideal touring base for Gloucestershire and surrounds. By Area of Outstanding Natural Beauty. Nearby footpaths include Cotswold Way.

OPEN All Year

Short breaks available Oct–Mar. Minimum 3 nights.

Low season per wk
£250.00–£300.00
High season per wk
£300.00–£350.00

CHERWELL

See South East region for entries

CHESTERFIELD, Derbyshire Map ref 4B2 *Tourist Information Centre Tel: (01246) 345777*

★★★★

1 Unit
Sleeping 5

PLOUGHMANS COTTAGE

Chesterfield
Contact: Mr & Mrs W G Fry, Ploughmans Cottage, Low Farm, Main Road, Marsh Lane, Chesterfield S21 5RH
T: (01246) 435328
E: ploughmans.cottage@virgin.net

Fresh eggs from our hens, kisses from our llamas, skylarks and woodland walks. This delightful cottage is carefully and attractively maintained. It has a fenced garden with orchard, lawns, flower beds, patio and sandpit. Lovely open views and many places of interest within easy reach.

OPEN All Year

Short breaks available Oct-Mar (excl Christmas).

Low season per wk
£200.00–£240.00
High season per wk
£200.00–£240.00

CHURCH STRETTON, Shropshire Map ref 4A3

★★★

1 Unit
Sleeping 2

THE GARDEN FLAT

Church Stretton
Contact: Mrs C Hembrow, The Garden Flat, Ashfield House, Windle Hill, Church Stretton SY6 7AF
T: (01694) 723715
E: cj.hembrow@ukonline.co.uk

OPEN All Year

Low season per wk
£170.00–£185.00
High season per wk
£185.00–£200.00

Set amongst beautiful Shropshire hills, cosy, private, self-contained, ground floor flat within walking distance of Long Mynd and historic town. Near Ludlow, Shrewsbury, Ironbridge.

★★★★

2 Units
Sleeping 4–5

GRANARY COTTAGE & THE LONG BARN

Church Stretton
Contact: Mr & Mrs J Kirkwood
T: (01694) 771521
E: jim@lowerdayhouse.freeserve.co.uk
I: www.lowerdayhouse.freeserve.co.uk

Part of an 18thC farm courtyard, sited next to an oak-framed threshing barn. The cottage is tastefully furnished, retaining many original beams and features. With magnificent views of Wenlock Edge, Granary Cottage is ideally suited for those seeking the real 'heart of the country'. Sorry, no smoking or pets.

OPEN All Year

Short breaks available from end Oct-Easter.

Low season per wk
£195.00–£245.00
High season per wk
£250.00–£350.00

★★★★

1 Unit
Sleeping 3

LEASOWES COTTAGE

Longnor, Church Stretton
Contact: Mrs M Harris, Leasowes, Watling Street, Longnor, Shrewsbury SY5 7QG
T: (01694) 751351
E: paul-harris@c-stretton.fsnet.co.uk

A pretty barn conversion in beautiful, quiet countryside. Views to the nearby Stretton Hills offering excellent walking and touring opportunities. Large, comfortable furnished living room and well equipped kitchen. Exposed beams in the spacious, galleried, double bedroom. Easy access to Ludlow and Shrewsbury, with good restaurants in Church Stretton.

3-night stays available Apr-Sep.

Low season per wk
£185.00–£235.00
High season per wk
£240.00–£280.00

CHURCH STRETTON continued

★★★

7 Units
Sleeping 3–4

LONGMYND HOTEL
Church Stretton
Contact: Mr M Chapman, Longmynd Hotel, Cunnery Road, Church Stretton SY6 6AG
T: (01694) 722244
F: (01694) 722718
E: reservations@longmynd.co.uk
I: www.longmynd.co.uk

OPEN All Year
CC: Amex, Delta, Diners, Mastercard, Switch, Visa

Low season per wk
£145.00–£245.00
High season per wk
£275.00–£375.00

The hotel offers restaurant meals, afternoon tea, bar snacks and use of swimming pool, sauna, pitch 'n' putt and croquet lawn.

CIRENCESTER, Gloucestershire Map ref 2B1 *Tourist Information Centre Tel: (01285) 654180*

★★★★★

1 Unit
Sleeping 12

Beautifully appointed farmhouse in four acres of stunning, secluded countryside. Six bedrooms, all en suite. Large dining room, kitchen, hall, spacious drawing room with woodburning stove. Lawn, sheltered terrace and rough-games field. Gourmet catering if required. Five miles from Cirencester. Good walking.

THE TALLET COTTAGE
Cirencester
Contact: Mrs V J Arbuthnott, The Tallet, Calmsden, Cirencester GL7 5ET
T: (01285) 831437
F: (01285) 831437
E: vanessa@thetallet.demon.co.uk
I: www.thetallet.co.uk

OPEN All Year
CC: Delta, Mastercard, Switch, Visa

Low season per wk
£675.00–£890.00
High season per wk
£750.00–£995.00

CLUN, Shropshire Map ref 4A3

★★★

2 Units

LAKE HOUSE COTTAGES
Clun, Craven Arms
Contact: Mr & Mrs G Berry
T: (01588) 640148
F: (01588) 640152
E: graham.berry5@btopenworld.com

OPEN All Year

Low season per wk
£180.00–£275.00
High season per wk
£300.00–£425.00

Converted from a 17thC barn, incorporating clearview stoves, power showers, fitted kitchens and beautiful views over Shropshire countryside.

COLEFORD, Gloucestershire Map ref 2A1 *Tourist Information Centre Tel: (01594) 812388*

★★★

1 Unit
Sleeping 4

FIRTREES HOLIDAY BUNGALOW
Coalway, Coleford
Contact: Mrs C A Brain, Asgard House, 84 Park Road, Christchurch, Coleford GL16 7AZ
T: (01594) 832576
E: douglas.brain@genie.co.uk
I: www.firtreesatfod.co.uk

OPEN All Year

Low season per wk
£135.00–£170.00
High season per wk
£170.00–£250.00

Modern, detached, easily accessible, two-bedroomed bungalow. Large lounge with sloping, beamed ceiling. Small, private garden, integral garage. Near woodland, quiet and relaxing.

ACCESSIBILITY

Look for the symbols which indicate National Accessible Scheme standards for hearing and visually impaired guests in addition to standards for guests with mobility impairment. Additional participants are shown in the listings at the back.

COMBS, Derbyshire Map ref 4B2

★★★★★

1 Unit
Sleeping 4

Situated within the Peak District National Park and enjoying spectacular views, this cottage is finished and furnished to a very high standard whilst retaining original oak beams and many other interesting features. Ideal location for walking, golfing, the theatre (Buxton) or simply as an idyllic hideaway.

PYEGREAVE COTTAGE

Combs, High Peak
Contact: Mr N C Pollard, Pyegreave Farm, Combs, High Peak SK23 9UX
T: (01298) 813444
F: (01298) 815381
E: n.pollard@allenpollard.co.uk
I: www.holidayapartments.org

OPEN All Year except Christmas

Low season per wk
£230.00–£260.00
High season per wk
£290.00–£360.00

COMPTON ABDALE, Gloucestershire Map ref 2B1

★★★

2 Units
Sleeping 3–4

Charming cottages situated in countryside close to the village of Compton Abdale. These properties, with their magnificent views and rural surroundings, are ideal for those seeking complete relaxation and peace. Also within easy reach are Bath, Oxford and Stratford-upon-Avon. The Cotswold Way is readily accessible for walking.

SPRING HILL STABLE COTTAGES

Compton Abdale, Cheltenham
Contact: Mrs M L Smail, Spring Hill Stable Cottages, Spring Hill, Compton Abdale, Cheltenham GL54 4DU
T: (01242) 890263
F: (01242) 890266
E: springhillcottages@yahoo.co.uk

OPEN All Year

3-night stays available Oct-Feb (excl Christmas and New Year).

Low season per wk
£115.00–£170.00
High season per wk
£215.00–£335.00

COTSWOLDS

See under Alderton, Bibury, Blockley, Bourton-on-the-Water, Broad Campden, Broadway, Cheltenham, Cirencester, Compton Abdale, Daglingworth, Dursley, Gloucester, Minchinhampton, Miserden, Moreton-in-Marsh, Nympsfield, Owlpen, South Cerney, Stanton, Stow-on-the-Wold, Stroud, Upton St Leonards, Winchcombe

See also Cotswolds in South East region

CRESSBROOK, Derbyshire Map ref 4B2

★★★

3 Units

CRESSBROOK HALL COTTAGES

Cressbrook, Buxton
Contact: Mrs B H Bailey, Cressbrook Hall Cottages Ltd, Cressbrook Hall, Cressbrook, Buxton SK17 8SY
T: (01298) 871289
F: (01298) 871845
E: stay@cressbrookhall.co.uk
I: www.cressbrookhall.co.uk

OPEN All Year
CC: Delta, Mastercard, Solo, Switch, Visa

Low season per wk
£155.00–£375.00
High season per wk
£360.00–£895.00

Accommodation with a difference! Self-catering or B&B in magnificent surroundings. Special catering services and leisure facilities ensure a carefree holiday. Colour brochure.

SPECIAL BREAKS

Many establishments offer special promotions and themed breaks. These are highlighted in red. (All such offers are subject to availability.)

CURBAR, Derbyshire Map ref 4B2

★★★★

1 Unit
Sleeping 3

JACK'S COTTAGE

Curbar, Calver, Hope Valley
Contact: Mrs M North, Green Farm, Curbar, Calver, Hope Valley S32 3YH
T: (01433) 630120
F: (01433) 631829
E: Marsha.North1@btopenworld.com
I: www.peak-district-romantic-holidaycottages.co.uk

Romantic, luxury, detached 17thC stone cottage. Very pretty, private, traditional cottage garden with barbecue area. Beautifully furnished to offer an authentic country-cottage experience with the best 21stC comforts. Aga-style cooker and real fire. Centre of peaceful village. Excellent walking. Good local pubs.

OPEN All Year

Short breaks available throughout the year, minimum 2 nights.

Low season per wk
£340.00–£450.00
High season per wk
£470.00–£500.00

DAGLINGWORTH, Gloucestershire Map ref 2B1

★★★★

1 Unit
Sleeping 2

CORNER COTTAGE

Cirencester
Contact: Mrs V M Bartlett, Brook Cottage, 23 Farm Court, Daglingworth, Cirencester GL7 7AF
T: (01285) 653478
F: (01285) 653478

OPEN All Year

Tastefully furnished, well-equipped, traditional Cotswold cottage in small village in tranquil valley. Cosy base for walking or touring. Non-smokers only, please.

Low season per wk
£210.00
High season per wk
£210.00

DONINGTON, Lincolnshire Map ref 3A1

★★★

1 Unit
Sleeping 8

THE BARN

Donington, Spalding
Contact: Mrs M A Smith
T: (01775) 821242

OPEN All Year

This attractive converted and refurbished barn is situated on owner's large water-fowl gardens. One mile from village which offers excellent restaurants and pubs.

Low season per wk
£200.00–£250.00
High season per wk
£250.00

DURSLEY, Gloucestershire Map ref 2B2

★★★

1 Unit
Sleeping 4

TWO SPRINGBANK

Dursley
Contact: Mrs F A Jones, 32 Everlands, Cam, Dursley GL11 5NL
T: (01453) 543047

OPEN All Year

Renovated Victorian mid-terrace cottage, in pleasant rural location near 14thC church. Multi-fuel stove and night storage heaters. Close to Cotswold Way and an ideal touring centre.

Low season per wk
£138.00–£210.00
High season per wk
£186.00–£219.00

ELKINGTON, Northamptonshire Map ref 4C3

★★★★

2 Units

MANOR FARM

Elkington, Northampton
Contact: Mr & Mrs M Higgott
T: (01858) 575245
F: (01858) 575213

OPEN All Year

A Listed barn conversion in a historic hamlet. Easy access to the M1, M6, A14 and places of importance in the Midlands.

Low season per wk
£250.00–£380.00
High season per wk
£250.00–£380.00

CHECK THE MAPS

**The colour maps at the front of this guide show all the cities, towns and villages for which you will find accommodation entries.
Refer to the town index to find the page on which they are listed.**

ELMLEY CASTLE, Worcestershire Map ref 2B1

★★
1 Unit
Sleeping 2

THE COTTAGE, MANOR FARM HOUSE
Elmley Castle, Pershore
Contact: Mr & Mrs B D Lovett, Manor Farm House, Main Street, Elmley Castle, Pershore WR10 3HS
T: (01386) 710286
F: (01386) 710112

OPEN All Year

Low season per wk
£100.00–£130.00
High season per wk
£140.00–£160.00

Small cottage attached to original village farmhouse and beautiful garden, at the foot of Bredon Hill. Excellent for trekking and touring the Cotswolds and Malverns.

EVESHAM, Worcestershire Map ref 2B1 *Tourist Information Centre Tel: (01386) 446944*

★★★★
1 Unit
Sleeping 6

THATCHERS END

Evesham
Contact: Mr & Mrs Wilson, 60 Pershore Road, Evesham WR11 6PQ
T: (01386) 446269
F: (01386) 446269
E: trad.accom@virgin.net
I: http://freespace.virgin.net/trad.accom

Delightful Grade II Listed thatched black and white cottage with many traditional and original period features. Spacious, tastefully furnished, all modern facilities. Large enclosed garden, patio area, garden furniture. Private and peacefully situated. Ample parking. Ideal touring base. Family supervised. No pets. Brochures available.

OPEN All Year
CC: Amex, Delta, Diners, JCB, Mastercard, Solo, Switch, Visa

Low season per wk
£335.00–£430.00
High season per wk
£430.00–£500.00

FOREST OF DEAN

See under Coleford, Lydney, Newent

GLOUCESTER, Gloucestershire Map ref 2B1

★★★
1 Unit
Sleeping 6

THE VINEARY
Huntley, Gloucester
Contact: Mrs A Snow, Vinetree Cottage, Solomons Tump, Huntley, Gloucester GL19 3EB
T: (01452) 830006
E: anniesnow@btinternet.com

Low season per wk
£155.00–£195.00
High season per wk
£200.00–£250.00

Annexe to owner's cottage in country lane. Open views. Local post office, golf course, country inns. Garden play area – great for children. Peaceful, central setting.

GONALSTON, Nottinghamshire Map ref 4C2

★★★★
1 Unit
Sleeping 2

THE STUDIO COTTAGE

Gonalston, Nottingham
Contact: Mr & Mrs M G Carradice, Hill House, Gonalston, Nottingham NG14 7JA
T: (0115) 9664551
F: (0115) 9665097
E: carradice@btinternet.com
I: www.carradice@btinternet.co.uk

A charming, beautifully appointed, centrally heated cottage, facing the croquet lawn of a country house, which overlooks the Trent and Dover Beck valleys. Ideal for exploring Robin Hood country, the Dukeries, the Vale of Belvoir and Nottingham, Lincoln, Newark and the nearby minster town of Southwell.

OPEN All Year

3/4-night stays available throughout the year: £90–£190 depending on dates.

Low season per wk
£160.00–£190.00
High season per wk
£190.00–£220.00

SYMBOLS The symbols in each entry give information about services and facilities. A key to these symbols appears at the back of this guide.

GOTHERINGTON, Gloucestershire Map ref 2B1

★★★

1 Unit
Sleeping 4

BAKERY COTTAGE
Gotherington, Cheltenham
Contact: Mrs Weller
T: (01242) 236765

OPEN All Year

High season per wk
£200.00–£350.00

A two-bedroomed, Cotswold-stone cottage, recently renovated to provide up-to-date kitchen facilities with lounge/diner and modern facilities. Ample parking space.

GREAT CARLTON, Lincolnshire Map ref 4D2

★★★

1 Unit
Sleeping 5

WILLOW FARM
Great Carlton, Louth
Contact: Mr J Clark, Willow Farm, Great Carlton, Louth LN11 8JT
T: (01507) 338540

OPEN All Year

Low season per wk
£150.00–£180.00
High season per wk
£200.00–£250.00

Comprising two double and one single bedrooms. Fly and coarse fishing available on site. Touring caravans welcome by arrangement.

GREAT HUCKLOW, Derbyshire Map ref 4B2

★★★★

1 Unit
Sleeping 4

SOUTH VIEW COTTAGE
Great Hucklow, Buxton
Contact: Mrs M Waterhouse, Holme Cottage, Windmill, Great Hucklow, Buxton SK17 8RE
T: (01298) 871440
E: mo@mmwaterhouse.demon.co.uk
I: www.cottageguide.co.uk/southviewcottage

OPEN All Year

Low season per wk
Max £250.00
High season per wk
£250.00–£310.00

Modernised country cottage in the hamlet of Windmill in the middle of the Peak District. Owner maintained. Furnished and decorated to a high standard. No smoking. Lock-up garage.

HALSE, Northamptonshire Map ref 2C1

★★★★

6 Units
Sleeping 3

HILL FARM
Halse, Brackley
Contact: Mrs J Robinson, Hill Farm, Halse, Brackley NN13 6DY
T: (01280) 703300
F: (01280) 704999
E: jg.robinson@farmline.com

OPEN All Year except Christmas

Low season per wk
£120.00–£200.00
High season per wk
£150.00–£250.00

Hill Farm is set in 400 acres of rolling farmland. An ideal location to visit Silverstone, Oxford, Blenheim Palace, Stowe. One hour to Cotswolds.

HARTINGTON, Derbyshire Map ref 4B2

★★★

1 Unit
Sleeping 5

CHURCH VIEW
Hartington, Buxton
Contact: Miss K Bassett, Digmer, Hartington, Buxton SK17 0AQ
T: (01298) 84660

Stone-built cottage with lawns to the front and side. Storage heaters. Spacious, comfortable interior. Lounge, dining room, utility room, recently fitted kitchen. Three bedrooms, upstairs bathroom consisting of bath, toilet, wash basin and new walk-in shower. Open fire optional. Close to amenities. Owner maintained. Established 21 years.

OPEN All Year

Low season per wk
£170.00–£195.00
High season per wk
£195.00–£250.00

TOWN INDEX

This can be found at the back of this guide. If you know where you want to stay, the index will give you the page number listing accommodation in your chosen town, city or village.

HARTINGTON continued

★★★★

5 Units
Sleeping 4

CRUCK COTTAGE, WOLFSCOTE STABLE, GRACES COTTAGE, SWALLOWS & SWALLOWS RETURN

Hartington, Buxton
Contact: Mrs J Gibbs, Wolfscote Grange Farm, Hartington, Buxton SK17 0AX
T: (01298) 84342
E: wolfscote@btinternet.com
I: www.wolfscotegrangecottages.co.uk

The unique setting overlooking Dove Valley/Dale with miles of rolling countryside and picture views sells Wolfcote cottages as the perfect place to stay. Cruck Cottage – a hideaway. 'No neighbours, only sheep'. Beautifully oak beamed. Swallows Cottage – en suites, spa bathroom. Both highly recommended, offering comfort and character. Farm trail with freedom to roam.

OPEN All Year

Private farm trail weekend and short breaks available (especially Oct-Easter).

Low season per wk
£180.00–£200.00
High season per wk
£450.00–£550.00

★★★★

2 Units
Sleeping 5–6

1 STALEY COTTAGE & VICTORIA HOUSE

Hartington, Buxton
Contact: Mr & Mrs J Oliver, Carr Head Farm, Penistone, Sheffield S36 7GA
T: (01226) 762387

Spacious cottage with three bedrooms, dining room, lounge, ground floor bathroom, upstairs shower room/WC and garden. In a pretty village near amenities, shops and restaurants. Also second property.

OPEN All Year

Low season per wk
£300.00–£350.00
High season per wk
£350.00–£500.00

HATHERSAGE, Derbyshire Map ref 4B2

★★★

1 Unit
Sleeping 6

PAT'S COTTAGE

Dore, Sheffield
Contact: Mr J M Drakeford
T: (0114) 236 6014
F: (0114) 236 6014
E: johnmdrakeford@hotmail.com
I: www.patscottage.co.uk

OPEN All Year

Low season per wk
£220.00–£330.00
High season per wk
£240.00–£330.00

An attractive 18thC stone cottage, sympathetically refurbished, retaining original features including black beams. On the edge of the Peak District, close to Hathersage and the city of Sheffield.

★★★

1 Unit
Sleeping 4

ST MICHAEL'S COTTAGE

Hathersage, Hope Valley
Contact: Miss H Turton, St Michael's Environmental Education Centre, Main Road, Hathersage, Hope Valley S32 1BB
T: (01433) 650309
F: (01433) 650089
E: stmichaels@education.nottscc.gov.uk
I: www.eess.org.uk

OPEN All Year

Low season per wk
£170.00–£200.00
High season per wk
£240.00–£320.00

Cosy character cottage with one double and one twin bedroom. Dramatic scenery, walks from the door, close to all amenities.

3

VISITOR ATTRACTIONS **For ideas on places to visit refer to the introduction at the beginning of this section. Look out too for the ETC's Quality Assured Visitor Attraction signs.**

HAYFIELD, Derbyshire Map ref 4B2

★★★★
1 Unit
Sleeping 4

BOWDEN BRIDGE COTTAGE
Hayfield, High Peak
OPEN All Year
Contact: Mrs M Easter, Bowden Bridge Cottage, Kinder, Hayfield, High Peak SK22 2LH
T: (01663) 743975
F: (01663) 743812
E: j_easter@talk21.com

Low season per wk £140.00–£220.00
High season per wk £240.00–£270.00

Cottage flat attached to main house, with double bedroom, lounge, kitchen, bathroom. Additional twin bedroom with washbasin available if required. Full central heating.

HEREFORD, Herefordshire Map ref 2A1 *Tourist Information Centre Tel: (01432) 268430*

Rating Applied For
1 Unit
Sleeping 4

BARTON WEST
Hereford
OPEN All Year
Contact: Mrs Teresa Godbert, 24 Broomy Hill, Hereford HR4 0LH
T: 07966 100230
E: teresagodbert@hereford-hopes.co.uk
I: www.hereford-hopes.co.uk

Low season per wk £350.00–£500.00
High season per wk £500.00–£850.00

Everything this historic cathedral city has to offer the visitor is within easy walking distance of our beautiful luxury apartment. Gardens, balcony, garage and views. English, French and Spanish spoken.

★★★
6 Units

BREINTON COURT
Hereford
OPEN All Year
CC: Amex, Mastercard
Contact: Mrs G Hands
T: (01432) 268156
F: (01432) 265134
E: hentapeparkhotel@talk21.com

Low season per wk £195.00–£250.00
High season per wk £200.00–£450.00

Splendid homes with all modern facilities set in 11 acres of wooded grounds which include 9-hole mini golf and outdoor pool. Within 200 yards of River Wye but only two miles from Hereford.

★★★★
1 Unit
Sleeping 6

CASTLE CLIFFE EAST
Hereford
Contact: Mr M Hubbard and Mr P Wilson, Castle Cliffe West, 14 Quay Street, Hereford HR1 2NH
T: (01432) 272096
E: mail@castlecliffe.net
I: www.castlecliffe.net

Formerly the medieval watergate of Hereford Castle, Castle Cliffe provides luxury riverside accommodation. Period furnishings throughout, open fires and private, south-facing garden with beautiful views. Recently fitted kitchen and wonderful atmospheric bathroom. Set in historic parkland with town centre, cathedral and local amenities four minutes' walk.

OPEN All Year

Short breaks available all year. Claim a 10% discount by mentioning 'Where to Stay' or VisitBritain.

Low season per wk £350.00–£550.00
High season per wk £650.00–£850.00

CHECK THE MAPS

The colour maps at the front of this guide show all the cities, towns and villages for which you will find accommodation entries. Refer to the town index to find the page on which they are listed.

HEREFORD continued

★★★★

1 Unit
Sleeping 3

RUSHFORD

Holmer, Hereford
Contact: Mrs M W Roberts, Rushford,
7 Belle Bank Avenue, Holmer, Hereford HR4 9RL
T: (01432) 273380
F: (01432) 273380

Much-praised wing of owner's detached house in pleasant surroundings and pretty garden with ancient cider mill. Situated on city fringe with rural views, close to church, pub, shop and bus service, it is 30 minutes' walk into the city centre. Comfortable and peaceful, for non-smokers only.

OPEN All Year except Christmas

Low season per wk
£120.00–£150.00
High season per wk
£180.00–£200.00

HORSINGTON, Lincolnshire Map ref 4D2

★★★

1 Unit
Sleeping 4

WAYSIDE COTTAGE

Horsington, Woodhall Spa
Contact: Mr & Mrs I G Williamson, 72 Mill Lane,
Woodhall Spa LN10 6QZ
T: (01526) 353101
E: will@williamsoni.freeserve.co.uk
I: www.skegness.net/woodhallspa.htm

OPEN All Year

Low season per wk
£170.00–£200.00
High season per wk
£175.00–£200.00

Cottage bungalow in rural setting in sleepy Horsington, central to the county for exploring. Many walks.

IRONBRIDGE, Shropshire Map ref 4A3 *Tourist Information Centre Tel: (01952) 432166*

★★★

1 Unit
Sleeping 4

LANGDALE COTTAGE

Ironbridge, Telford
Contact: Mr A K Blight
T: 07768 830500
E: keithblight@aol.com

The comfortable, two-bedroomed restored 19thC cottage is situated in the beautiful Ironbridge Gorge just 0.5 miles from the famous Iron Bridge. It is an ideal base for exploring the town and the World Heritage museum sites as well as the ancient towns and hills of surrounding Shropshire.

OPEN All Year

Low season per wk
£130.00–£190.00
High season per wk
£230.00–£290.00

KENILWORTH, Warwickshire Map ref 4B3

★★★★

2 Units
Sleeping 4

JACKDAW COTTAGE & WREN'S NEST

Kenilworth
Contact: Mrs L Grierson, The White Bungalow,
6 Canterbury Close, Kenilworth CV8 2PU
T: (01926) 855616
F: (01926) 513189
E: kgrierson@ukonline.co.uk

OPEN All Year

Low season per wk
£250.00–£310.00
High season per wk
£340.00–£380.00

Cosy, well-furnished old world cottages in conservation area, on edge of historic town. Picturesque setting near castle. Convenient for Stratford, Warwick, Cotswolds, NEC and NAC.

MAP REFERENCES The map references refer to the colour maps at the front of this guide. The first figure is the map number; the letter and figure which follow indicate the grid reference on the map.

KENLEY, Shropshire Map ref 4A3

★★★★
2 Units
Sleeping 2–4

NO 1 & 2 COURTYARD COTTAGES
Kenley, Shrewsbury
Contact: Mrs A Gill
T: (01952) 510841
F: (01952) 510841
E: a-gill@lineone.net
I: www.courtyardcottages.com

OPEN All Year

Low season per wk
£200.00–£375.00
High season per wk
£225.00–£400.00

Immaculate, recently converted cottages with exposed oak beams. Large garden and stocked trout pools in lovely, peaceful valley with panoramic views of Wenlock Edge.

10

KNIGHTWICK, Worcestershire Map ref 2B1

★★★
2 Units

HARLEYS BARN & DAISY BARN
Knightwick, Worcester
Contact: Mr & Mrs D H Bentley
T: (01886) 821056
F: (01886) 821056

OPEN All Year

Low season per wk
Min £170.00
High season per wk
Min £210.00

Compact, two-bedroomed, self-contained wooden barn. Non-smoking. Near Malvern, Worcester, Bromyard. Ideal walking in beautiful countryside.

KNIVETON, Derbyshire Map ref 4B2

★★★★
1 Unit
Sleeping 4

WILLOW BANK
Kniveton, Ashbourne
Contact: Mrs M E Vaughan, Willow Bank, Kniveton, Ashbourne DE6 1JJ
T: (01335) 343308
E: willowbank@kniveton.net
I: www.kniveton.net

OPEN All Year

Low season per wk
£275.00–£300.00
High season per wk
£250.00–£350.00

Luxurious, recently fitted ground floor flat, one double bedroom, one twin, an acre of garden with stream. Peak District village, Ashbourne 15 minutes.

5

LEAMINGTON SPA, Warwickshire Map ref 4B3 *Tourist Information Centre Tel: (01926) 742762*

★★★★
1 Unit
Sleeping 2

Superbly appointed luxury cottage in delightful rural setting close to Warwick, Stratford and the Cotswolds. Tastefully decorated living/dining room, modern, well-equipped fitted kitchen and attractive twin-bedded room. Delightful, landscaped cottage garden with patio. Open views and nearby public right of way.

BARN OWL COTTAGE

Leamington Spa
Contact: Mrs B Norman, Fosseway Barns, Fosse Way, Offchurch, Leamington Spa CV33 9BQ
T: (01926) 614647
F: (01926) 614647
E: bnorman@fossebarn.prestel.co.uk
I: barnowlcottage.co.uk

OPEN All Year

Short breaks available. 10% discount if booking 2 weeks.

Low season per wk
£200.00–£270.00
High season per wk
£270.00–£335.00

★
2 Units
Sleeping 3–5

BLACKDOWN FARM COTTAGES
Blackdown, Leamington Spa
Contact: Mr & Mrs R Solt, Blackdown Farm, Sandy Lane, Leamington Spa CV32 6QS
T: (01926) 422522
F: (01926) 450996
E: bobby@solt.demon.co.uk

OPEN All Year

Low season per wk
Min £150.00
High season per wk
Max £350.00

Cottages converted from farm buildings, in the countryside between Leamington Spa and Kenilworth. Convenient for Shakespeare country, Warwick, Coventry and the Cotswolds.

QUALITY ASSURANCE SCHEME
Star ratings are explained at the back of this guide.

LEAMINGTON SPA continued

★★★
3 Units
Sleeping 4–7

FURZEN HILL FARM

Leamington Spa
Contact: Mrs C M Whitfield, Furzen Hill Farm, Cubbington Heath, Leamington Spa CV32 7UJ
T: (01926) 424791
F: (01926) 424791

OPEN All Year

Low season per wk
Min £180.00
High season per wk
Max £360.00

Cottages at Cubbington, ideally situated for Warwick, Stratford-upon-Avon and NEC. Large garden. Use of hard tennis court.

LEDBURY, Herefordshire Map ref 2B1 *Tourist Information Centre Tel: (01531) 636147*

★★★
1 Unit
Sleeping 4

COACH HOUSE APARTMENT

Ledbury
Contact: Mrs J Williams, Leadon House Hotel, Ross Road, Ledbury HR8 2LP
T: (01531) 631199
F: (01531) 631476
E: leadon.house@amserve.net

OPEN All Year
CC: Amex, Delta, Mastercard, Solo, Switch, Visa

Low season per wk
£175.00–£225.00
High season per wk
£245.00–£280.00

Former coach house in the attractive themed grounds of Leadon House Hotel. High-quality 2001 conversion provides comfortable and spacious ground floor accommodation.

★★★★
1 Unit
Sleeping 6

HONEYSUCKLE COTTAGE

Bromsberrow Heath, Ledbury
Contact: Mrs W S Hooper, Greenlands, Bromsberrow Heath, Ledbury HR8 1PG
T: (01531) 650360
E: ws.hooper@btopenworld.com

Three-bedroomed detached cottage in own private gardens. Beautifully furnished and well equipped accommodation. Village location in delightful Herefordshire countryside providing easy access to Malvern Hills, Forest of Dean, Gloucester, Hereford and Worcester. Ideal for touring or just relaxing in comfort.

OPEN All Year except Christmas

Short breaks available Oct-Mar (excl Christmas and New Year).

Low season per wk
Max £345.00
High season per wk
Max £655.00

★★★-★★★★★
5 Units

WHITE HOUSE COTTAGES

Ledbury
Contact: Mrs Marianne Hills, The White House, Aylton, Ledbury HR8 2RQ
T: (01531) 670349
F: (01531) 670057
E: hills1477@aol.com
I: www.whitehousecottages.co.uk

Aylton, a conservation area, is four miles from Ledbury. The cottages, former farm buildings, are set within the mature grounds of owner's 17thC property. An excellent centre for exploring the Wye Valley, the Malverns, Forest of Dean, the Welsh Borders and the cathedral cities of Hereford, Gloucester and Worcester.

OPEN All Year

3-night short breaks available all year, subject to certain booking restrictions. Please ring for details.

Low season per wk
£175.00–£265.00
High season per wk
£304.00–£491.00

NB

IMPORTANT NOTE Information on accommodation listed in this guide has been supplied by the proprietors. As changes may occur you are advised to check details at the time of booking.

LEINTWARDINE, Herefordshire Map ref 4A3

★★★

1 Unit
Sleeping 4

OAK COTTAGE
Leintwardine, Craven Arms
Contact: Mrs Faulkner, 24 Watling Street, Leintwardine, Craven Arms SY7 0LW
T: (01547) 540629
F: (01547) 540181
E: fmjones@skg.co.uk

OPEN All Year

16thC, Grade II Listed, timber-framed cottage, carefully restored and equipped, in borderland village on River Teme. Glorious walking, fishing, good food. You can even coracle.

Low season per wk
£180.00–£200.00
High season per wk
£250.00–£300.00

★★

2 Units

OAKLANDS FARM
Leintwardine, Craven Arms
Contact: Mrs S Swift
T: (01547) 540635
E: mrpaswift@aol.co.uk

OPEN All Year

Lovely conversion of a traditional barn offering excellent cottages in a perfect walking location, enjoying superb views over the River Teme. Ideal for those seeking a peaceful escape.

Low season per wk
£180.00–£200.00
High season per wk
£280.00–£393.00

LEOMINSTER, Herefordshire Map ref 2A1 *Tourist Information Centre Tel: (01568) 616460*

★★★

2 Units
Sleeping 5–8

ASHTON COURT FARM
Leominster
Contact: Mrs P Edwards
T: (01584) 711245

Our spacious farmhouse apartment and semi-detached cottage, converted from an old granary, are situated in a large garden with swings, play equipment and garden games. Table tennis and pool tables in the barn. Situated between Leominster and Ludlow, the location is central for touring the Welsh Borders, Shropshire and Worcestershire.

OPEN All Year

Low season per wk
£95.00–£120.00
High season per wk
£95.00–£275.00

★★★

1 Unit
Sleeping 4

MILL HOUSE FLAT
Leysters, Leominster
Contact: Mrs E M Thomas, Woonton Court Farm, Leysters, Leominster HR6 0HL
T: (01568) 750232
F: (01568) 750232
E: thomas.woontoncourt@farmersweekly.net
I: www.woontoncourt.co.uk

OPEN All Year

Comfortable converted cider house providing self-contained first floor flat. Excellent centre for Marches Gardens, NT properties, woodland walks, wildlife. Regret no smoking or pets.

Low season per wk
£140.00–£200.00
High season per wk
£200.00–£280.00

COUNTRY CODE Always follow the Country Code · Enjoy the countryside and respect its life and work · Guard against all risk of fire · Fasten all gates · Keep your dogs under close control · Keep to public paths across farmland · Use gates and stiles to cross fences, hedges and walls · Leave livestock, crops and machinery alone · Take your litter home · Help to keep all water clean · Protect wildlife, plants and trees · Take special care on country roads · Make no unnecessary noise

LIGHTHORNE, Warwickshire Map ref 2C1

★★★★

1 Unit
Sleeping 4

2 CHURCH COTTAGES

Lighthorne, Warwick
Contact: Mrs B Norman, Fosseway Barns, Fosse Way, Offchurch, Leamington Spa CV33 9BQ
T: (01926) 614647
F: (01926) 614647
E: bnorman@fossebarn.prestel.co.uk
I: twochurchcottages.co.uk

Attractive, Listed, stone period cottage in delightful Lighthorne village, close to Warwick, Stratford and the Cotswolds. Charming sitting/dining room with exposed timbers and handsome fireplace fitted with woodburning stove. Recently fitted modern kitchen, two bedrooms. Landscaped garden to the front and secluded patio to the rear.

OPEN All Year

Short breaks available. 10% discount if booking 2 weeks.

Low season per wk
£225.00–£300.00
High season per wk
£300.00–£370.00

LINCOLN, Lincolnshire Map ref 4C2

★★★

1 Unit
Sleeping 6

THE COBBLES

Lincoln
Contact: Mr J M Scott, Sunnyside, Lincoln Road, Brattleby, Lincoln LN1 2SQ
T: (01522) 730561
F: (01522) 513995
E: jmsco@lineone.net
I: www.lincolncottages.co.uk

Edwardian cottage on a quiet, cobbled lane in the historic quarter of the city. Ideal, central location for exploring and within walking distance of the cathedral and castle uphill and the shopping areas downhill. Enclosed, south-facing garden. Numerous pubs, restaurants, cafes and specialist shops nearby.

OPEN All Year

4 nights for the price of 3 in the low season.

Low season per wk
£220.00–£245.00
High season per wk
£245.00–£350.00

★★★★

1 Unit
Sleeping 5

19A LINDUM HILL

Lincoln
Contact: Mr S Richardson, 3 Marine Approach, Burton Waters, Lincoln LN1 2WW
T: (01522) 533119
F: (01522) 533119
E: stuart@disaster-care.co.uk
I: www.lindum-hill.co.uk

Sympathetically and tastefully restored, graceful, Georgian residence retaining many period features with well-proportioned, comprehensively equipped kitchen/dining room and a cosy and relaxing living room. Overlooked by the cathedral and castle, and the cultural quarter known as the Bailgate, home to the city's premier pubs and restaurants. Mob: 07957 622583.

OPEN All Year
CC: Amex, Mastercard, Switch, Visa

Welcome hamper that includes tea, coffee, sugar, milk, champagne and chocolates.

Low season per wk
£200.00–£275.00
High season per wk
£300.00–£350.00

PRICES
Please check prices and other details at the time of booking.

LINCOLN continued

★★★

1 Unit
Sleeping 2

MARTINGALE COTTAGE

Nettleham, Lincoln
Contact: Mrs P A Pate, 19 East Street, Nettleham, Lincoln LN2 2SL
T: (01522) 751795
E: patsy.pate@ntlworld.com

An 18thC stone cottage near the centre of the attractive village of Nettleham, 2.5 miles from Lincoln. Very comfortable, well-equipped accommodation with private parking. Use of owner's spacious, secluded garden. Good local shops and pubs, post office and library. Picturesque beckside and bus service to Lincoln. A warm welcome awaits.

OPEN All Year

Low season per wk
Min £120.00
High season per wk
Max £180.00

★★★★

1 Unit
Sleeping 3

OLD VICARAGE COTTAGE

Nettleham, Lincoln
Contact: Mrs S Downs, The Old Vicarage, East Street, Nettleham, Lincoln LN2 2SL
T: (01522) 750819
F: (01522) 750819
E: susan@oldvic.net

An 18thC, stone-built property, one of the oldest in the village. Spacious, well-equipped accommodation. Original exposed beams in the living room. Own south-facing garden, off-road parking. Quiet position, close to the centre of this very attractive village with its shops, pubs, village green and picturesque beckside.

OPEN All Year

Low season per wk
£135.00
High season per wk
£190.00

QUALITY ASSURANCE SCHEME

For an explanation of the quality and facilities represented by the Stars please refer to the front of this guide. A more detailed explanation can be found in the information pages at the back.

Poachers Hideaway
HOLIDAY COTTAGES

6 Luxury Cottages
Lincoln (40 mins)
Superb Views (area of outstanding natural beauty)
In isolated hidden valley
Hot tub/Jacuzzi
Private walks (5 miles)
Sauna (8 person)

Conference Facilities
Boot/drying room
Function/Meeting room
East Coast (40 mins)
Heart of Tennyson country
Fishing (Trout, Coarse & Carp)
On the Viking Way
Working farm

Welcome pack of Lincolnshire Produce
Cadwell Park (10 mins)
Resident owners
Explore our 170 acres of ancient woodland, wildflower pastures, natural hedgerows and water meadows

Flintwood Farm ❖ Belchford
Horncastle ❖ Lincolnshire ❖ LN9 6QN
Contact Sally & Andrew Tuxworth
Telephone 01507 533 555
Fax 01507 534 264
Mobile 07836 746865
www.poachershideaway.com

LINCOLN continued

★★★

1 Unit
Sleeping 4

PINGLES COTTAGE

Broxholme, Lincoln
Contact: Mrs P A Sutcliffe, Pingles Cottage, Grange Farm, Broxholme, Lincoln LN1 2NG
T: (01522) 702441

Well-equipped, secluded, cosy cottage with private garden and ample parking, only six miles from historic Lincoln and within easy reach of trunk roads (A57, A1500). Free-range hens' eggs and lamb are produced on the 100-acre organic farm. A good variety of wildlife regularly visits the garden. Coarse fishing in season at no extra cost.

OPEN All Year

Winter breaks; Nov-Easter, 3 nights £155.

Low season per wk
Min £240.00
High season per wk
Max £280.00

★★★

3 Units
Sleeping 2

SAINT CLEMENTS

Lincoln
Contact: Mrs G Marshall, Saint Clements, Langworth Gate, Lincoln LN2 4AD
T: (01522) 538087
F: (01522) 560642
E: jroywood@aol.com

Well-equipped, centrally heated apartments in comfortable Victorian rectory: one is twin-bedded, two are doubles. Situated down quiet drive lined with mature trees. Cathedral views and only five minutes' walk from historic up-hill area. Plenty of car parking. A peaceful retreat in the heart of the city. Short breaks when available.

OPEN All Year

Low season per wk
Min £110.00
High season per wk
Max £170.00

★★★★

1 Unit
Sleeping 4

THE STABLES

Brattleby, Lincoln
Contact: Mr J Scott, Sunnyside, Lincoln Road, Brattleby, Lincoln LN1 2SQ
T: (01522) 730561
E: jmsco@lineone.net
I: www.lincolncottages.co.uk

300-year-old cottage of character converted from a former stone and pantile stable. Peace and tranquillity in a conservation village yet only six miles from the historic cathedral city of Lincoln. Tastefully furnished and decorated. Own enclosed garden and views over open fields.

OPEN All Year

4 nights for the price of 3 in low season.

Low season per wk
£185.00–£240.00
High season per wk
£240.00–£350.00

USE YOUR *i*s

There are more than 550 Tourist Information Centres throughout England offering friendly help with accommodation and holiday ideas as well as suggestions of places to visit and things to do. You'll find TIC addresses in the local Phone Book.

LITTON, Derbyshire Map ref 4B2

★★★
1 Unit
Sleeping 6

2 CROSS VIEW, THE GREEN

Litton, Buxton
Contact: Mrs C Rowan-Olive, 44 Burnham Road, St Albans AL1 4QW
T: (01727) 844169
E: litton.cottage@ntworld.com
I: www.cross-view.co.uk

18thC stone cottage with traditional coal fire and modern comforts, including central heating and a fully equipped kitchen. It faces the green in Litton, a small, peaceful village with excellent pub and community shop. Fine views and beautiful walking country. Accessible for Tideswell, Chatsworth, Haddon Hall, Bakewell and Buxton.

OPEN All Year except Christmas

Short breaks available Oct–May (excl school half-terms, school holidays and Bank Holiday weekends).

Low season per wk
£210.00–£240.00
High season per wk
£270.00–£295.00

★★★★
1 Unit
Sleeping 7

FARM HANDS COTTAGE

Litton, Buxton
Contact: Mrs A Scott, Hall Farm House, Litton, Buxton SK17 8QP
T: (01298) 872172
E: jfscott@waitrose.com
I: www.users.waitrose.com/~jfscott

OPEN All Year

Low season per wk
£250.00–£350.00
High season per wk
£350.00–£450.00

Charming converted cottage. Superbly equipped, including woodburning stove. Spacious yet cosy. Easy parking. Situated in quiet village close to many attractions.

LLANFAIR WATERDINE, Shropshire Map ref 4A3

★★★★
1 Unit
Sleeping 6

LLANDINSHIP

Llanfair Waterdine, Knighton
Contact: Mr & Mrs A Beavan
T: (01547) 528909
F: (01547) 528909
E: andrew.beaven@telco4u.net
I: www.blackhallfarm.com

OPEN All Year

Low season per wk
£200.00–£250.00
High season per wk
£350.00–£450.00

Secluded position with private drive in beautiful countryside, ideal for a relaxing retreat. Exposed beams, woodburning stove, linen, towels, electricity and welcome pack included. Mob: 07974 416550.

LOUTH, Lincolnshire Map ref 4D2 *Tourist Information Centre Tel: (01507) 609289*

★★★
1 Unit
Sleeping 4

MILL LODGE

Donington on Bain, Louth
Contact: Mrs P Cade, Mill Lodge, Benniworth House Farm, Donington on Bain, Louth LN11 9RD
T: (01507) 343265
E: pamela@milllodge995fsnet.co.uk

Ezra and Pamela Cade welcome you to a comfortable, warm, detached cottage, with conservatory, garden and garage, on lovely farm/nature reserve. Fitted kitchen, open log fire. Free first snack with home-produced honey. Good footpaths join the Viking Way, open access to countryside stewardship area. Children welcome.

OPEN All Year

Special rates for just two visitors. Discounted honey available.

Low season per wk
£200.00–£300.00
High season per wk
£200.00–£350.00

3

CREDIT CARD BOOKINGS If you book by telephone and are asked for your credit card number it is advisable to check the proprietor's policy should you cancel your reservation.

LUDLOW, Shropshire Map ref 4A3 *Tourist Information Centre Tel: (01584) 875053*

★★★★

1 Unit
Sleeping 6

THE AVENUE FLAT
Ludlow
OPEN All Year
Contact: Mr R E Meredith, The Avenue Flat, The Avenue, Ashford Carbonell, Ludlow SY8 4DA
T: (01584) 831616
E: ronmeredithavenue@talk21.com

Second floor of large, attractive, peaceful country residence set in six acres. Completely independent access with fine views and very comfortable, well-equipped accommodation.

Low season per wk
£130.00–£170.00
High season per wk
£160.00–£290.00

★★★

1 Unit
Sleeping 6

BRIBERY COTTAGE
Ludlow
OPEN All Year
Contact: Mr & Mrs R Caithness, 2 Dinham, Ludlow SY8 1EJ
T: (01584) 872828
F: (01584) 872828
E: richard.caithness@virgin.net
I: www.virtual-shropshire.co.uk/bribery-cottage

Three-storey terraced house, c1830 and a Grade II Listed building, set in historic surroundings near market square and castle. Rear conservatory leads into attractive walled garden.

Low season per wk
£135.00–£175.00
High season per wk
£250.00–£320.00

★★

1 Unit
Sleeping 5

CHURCH BANK
Burrington, Ludlow
Contact: Mrs K R Laurie, Church Bank, Burrington, Ludlow SY8 2HT
T: (01568) 770426
E: laurie2502@lineone.net

This stone cottage lies in a beautiful, peaceful valley near River Teme. There are excellent walks on the hills and forest trails. Wildlife abounds. Historic Ludlow is five winding miles away. Large, comfortable sitting room with woodburner and many books. Dinner can be provided by arrangement. Available March to October.

Low season per wk
£160.00–£190.00
High season per wk
£200.00–£220.00

★★★-★★★★

2 Units
Sleeping 5

ELM LODGE APARTMENT & THE COACH HOUSE APARTMENT
Ludlow
Contact: Mrs B Weaver, Elm Lodge, Fishmore, Ludlow SY8 3DP
T: (01584) 877394
F: (01584) 877397
E: apartments@sjweaver.fsnet.co.uk
I: www.ludlow.org.uk/elmlodge

OPEN All Year
CC: Mastercard, Switch, Visa

Magnificent Georgian house and buildings on outskirts of town. Own golf course. Views to Ludlow and Welsh Borders. Short breaks available. B&B rooms also available.

Low season per wk
£250.00–£300.00
High season per wk
£320.00–£400.00

AT-A-GLANCE SYMBOLS

Symbols at the end of each accommodation entry give useful information about services and facilities. A key to symbols can be found inside the back cover flap. Keep this open for easy reference.

LUDLOW continued

★★★★

3 Units
Sleeping 4–6

GOOSEFOOT BARN COTTAGES

Diddlebury, Craven Arms
Contact: Mrs Loft, Goosefoot Barn Cottages, Pinstones, Diddlebury, Craven Arms SY7 9LB
T: (01584) 861326
E: sally@goosefoot.freeserve.co.uk

Converted in 2000 from stone and timbered barns, the cottages are individually decorated and equipped to the highest standards. Each cottage has en suite facilities and private garden or seating area. Situated in a secluded valley with walks from the doorstep through beautiful Corvedale. Ideally located for exploring South Shropshire.

OPEN All Year

Short breaks available, minimum 2 nights. Winter special offers.

Low season per wk
£190.00–£330.00
High season per wk
£320.00–£425.00

★★★

1 Unit
Sleeping 3

THE GRANARY

Clee St Margaret, Craven Arms
Contact: Mr & Mrs R Mercer, Tana Leas Farm, Clee St Margaret, Craven Arms SY7 9DZ
T: (01584) 823272
F: (01584) 823272
E: r.mercer@tinyworld.co.uk
I: www.southshropshire.org.uk/granary

OPEN All Year

Low season per wk
£175.00–£185.00
High season per wk
£185.00–£225.00

Recently refurbished converted granary in Area of Outstanding Natural Beauty. Ideal for quiet holiday. Ludlow six miles. Second property in Ludlow's historic Broad Street. Open all year.

★★★★

1 Unit
Sleeping 4

HAZEL COTTAGE

Onibury, Craven Arms
Contact: Mrs R E Sanders
T: (01584) 856342
F: (01584) 856696

Unspoilt period cottage, retaining its original features, with antiques. It comprises a living room with Victorian range (working perfectly), dining room, kitchen, hall, Victorian bathroom, two bedrooms with washbasins. Set in its own peaceful and private cottage garden with beautiful, panoramic views of the surrounding countryside. Five miles north of historic Ludlow. Open all year.

OPEN All Year

Short breaks available.

Low season per wk
Min £195.00
High season per wk
Max £410.00

★★★★

1 Unit
Sleeping 3

24 MILL STREET

Ludlow
Contact: Mrs D Brodie, Old Rectory Cottage, Wistanstow, Craven Arms SY7 8DQ
T: (01588) 672074
F: (01588) 672074

A delightful mix of 16thC and Georgian architecture. A Grade II Listed, three-storey townhouse situated in the heart of Ludlow old town only a few minutes walk from the castle, shops and award-winning restaurants. The home has a small but attractive courtyard area. Free parking just outside the door.

OPEN All Year

Low season per wk
£195.00–£275.00
High season per wk
£300.00–£375.00

LUDLOW continued

★★

1 Unit
Sleeping 4

POST HORN COTTAGE
Ludlow
Contact: Ms H Davis, 32 Leamington Drive, Chilwell, Beeston, Nottingham NG9 5JL
T: (0115) 9222383

OPEN All Year

Low season per wk £140.00–£175.00
High season per wk £180.00–£250.00

Charming two-storey cottage in historic town-centre building with exposed beams and small, private patio. In quiet courtyard off Broad Street.

★★★★

6 Units

SUTTON COURT FARM COTTAGES
Stanton Lacy, Ludlow
Contact: Mrs S J Cronin
T: (01584) 861305
F: (01584) 861441
E: suttoncourtfarm@hotmail.com
I: www.go2.co.uk/suttoncourtfarm

Comfortable cottages set around a peaceful courtyard in the beautiful Corvedale, just five miles from historic Ludlow. World Heritage Ironbridge Gorge, Shrewsbury, Hereford and the Welsh borders all within easy reach. Short breaks available all year. Cream teas and evening meals can be ordered in advance.

OPEN All Year

Short breaks from Oct–Mar (excl holidays). 3 nights for 2, 4 nights for 3.

Low season per wk £199.00–£350.00
High season per wk £290.00–£495.00

LULLINGTON, Derbyshire Map ref 4B3

★★★★

1 Unit
Sleeping 5

AUBRIETIA COTTAGE
Swadlincote
Contact: Mrs R Cooper, The Grange, Lullington, Swadlincote DE12 8ED
T: (01827) 373219
F: (01283) 515885
E: r.cooper@care4free.net

OPEN All Year

Low season per wk £160.00–£210.00
High season per wk £210.00–£280.00

Tastefully furnished cottage in Lullington, several-times winner of the Best Kept Village award. Pleasant outlook with many places of interest only a short drive away.

LYDBURY NORTH, Shropshire Map ref 4A3

★★★–★★★★

3 Units

WALCOT HALL HOLIDAY APARTMENTS
Lydbury North, Bishop's Castle
Contact: Miss Maria Higgs
T: (01588) 680570
F: (01588) 680361
E: maria@walcotthall.com
I: www.walcothall.com

OPEN All Year

Low season per wk £200.00–£390.00
High season per wk £300.00–£550.00

Spacious apartments with character in stately home once owned by Clive of India. Idyllic country setting with lakes, gardens and arboretum to explore.

LYDNEY, Gloucestershire Map ref 2B1

★★★

3 Units
Sleeping 2–5

HIGHBURY COACH HOUSE
Lydney
Contact: Mr A R Midgley, Highbury Coach House, Bream Road, Lydney GL15 5JH
T: (01594) 842339
F: (01594) 844948
E: midgleya1@aol.com

OPEN All Year

Low season per wk £140.00–£180.00
High season per wk £220.00–£290.00

Apartments in a Listed coach house close to Lydney, with panoramic views over the Forest of Dean and Severn Valley. Gardens, snooker and games rooms.

COLOUR MAPS Colour maps at the front of this guide pinpoint all places under which you will find accommodation listed.

LYONSHALL, Herefordshire Map ref 2A1

★★★★-★★★★★

3 Units
Sleeping 4–14

FIELD COTTAGE, THE SHERRIFFS & GARDENERS COTTAGE

Lyonshall, Kington
Contact: Mrs J Hilditch, Field Cottage, The Sherriffs & Gardeners Cottage, The Whittern Farms Ltd, Lyonshall, Kington HR5 3JA
T: (01544) 340241
F: (01544) 340253
E: info@whiteheronproperties.com
I: www.whiteheronproperties.com

Charming properties set in remote Herefordshire countryside, all recently refurbished in opulent style with open fires or logburners. Field Cottage is in panoramic orchard setting. Gardeners Cottage is in the old estate walled garden. The Sherriffs, a listed Queen Anne House, is spacious and comfortable with large, mature gardens.

OPEN All Year

Low season per wk
Min £350.00
High season per wk
Max £2,500.00

MALVERN, Worcestershire Map ref 2B1 *Tourist Information Centre Tel: (01684) 892289*

★★★

1 Unit
Sleeping 4

THE COACH HOUSE

Malvern
Contact: Mrs J Jones, 58 North Malvern Road, Malvern WR14 4LX
T: (01684) 569562
E: jjmalvern@onetel.net.uk

OPEN All Year

Low season per wk
£210.00–£250.00
High season per wk
£275.00–£350.00

Detached, turn-of-the-century coach house conversion in the heart of Great Malvern. Set in a secluded garden.

★★★

1 Unit
Sleeping 4

GREENBANK HOUSE GARDEN FLAT

Malvern
Contact: Mr D G Matthews, Greenbank House Garden Flat, 236 West Malvern Road, West Malvern, Malvern WR14 4BG
T: (01684) 567328
E: matthews.greenbank@virgin.net

OPEN All Year

Low season per wk
£140.00
High season per wk
£205.00

On the Malvern Hills, close to shop and on a bus route. Excellent walking and touring centre. Fine outlook. Conservatory and garden.

★★★★-★★★★★

6 Units
Sleeping 2–10

HIDELOW HOUSE COTTAGES

Malvern, Worcester
Contact: Mrs P Diplock, Hidelow House, Acton Green, Acton Beauchamp, Worcester WR6 5AH
T: (01886) 884547
F: (01886) 884658
E: stay@hidelow.co.uk
I: www.hidelow.co.uk

Relax and unwind in luxury for a short break or longer. A peaceful, rural retreat with exceptional views, on the edge of an Area of Outstanding Natural Beauty, yet only 2.5 hours from London and Manchester. Former hop-kilns and a tithe barn, now with 4-poster beds, log fires, private gardens and barbecues.

OPEN All Year
CC: Delta, JCB, Mastercard, Solo, Switch, Visa

Honeymoons and romantic breaks a speciality. Champagne and roses. Outdoor hot tub to hire. Home-cooked freezer meals, using local ingredients. Personal transport service.

Low season per wk
£229.00–£469.00
High season per wk
£479.00–£1,779.00

MARKET RASEN, Lincolnshire Map ref 4D2

★★★★
1 Unit
Sleeping 4

MEADOW FARM HOUSE

Bleasby Moor, Market Rasen
Contact: Mr N Grimshaw, Meadow Farm House, Bleasby Moor, Market Rasen LN8 3QL
T: (01673) 885909
F: (01673) 885909
E: nickgrimshaw@btconnect.com
I: www.meadowfarmhouse.co.uk

OPEN All Year

Low season per wk
£213.00–£260.00
High season per wk
£300.00–£406.00

Spacious country accommodation with high standard of comfort in a warm, relaxing environment. Ideal for walkers, cyclists, birdwatchers, antique hunters or a peaceful, relaxing break.

★★★-★★★★★
6 Units
Sleeping 2–6

PAPERMILL COTTAGES

Tealby, Market Rasen
Contact: Mr & Mrs P Rhodes, Vale Farm, Caistor Lane, Tealby, Market Rasen LN8 3XN
T: (01673) 838010
F: (01673) 838127
E: peter.rhodes1@btinternet.com

30-acre livestock farm in a conservation Area of Outstanding Natural Beauty. Very old stone buildings lovingly restored and furnished and equipped to a very high standard. Near Viking Way. Hard tennis court.

OPEN All Year
CC: Mastercard, Switch, Visa

Short breaks – minimum 2 nights.

Low season per wk
£145.00–£190.00
High season per wk
£285.00–£365.00

MATLOCK, Derbyshire Map ref 4B2 *Tourist Information Centre Tel: (01629) 583388*

★★★★
10 Units
Sleeping 4–8

DARWIN LAKE

Darley Moor, Matlock
Contact: Miss N Manning, Peak Village Ltd, Darwin Lake, Jaggers Lane, Darley Moor, Matlock DE4 5LH
T: (01629) 735859
F: (01629) 735859
E: enquiries@darwinlake.co.uk
I: www.darwinlake.co.uk

Set in 10 acres of private, wooded grounds surrounding Darwin Lake, these superb, luxury, stone-built cottages provide a perfect setting for a tranquil, relaxing holiday, or for exploring the Peaks and Dales. Bustling market towns, stately homes, quaint villages and many family attractions. Village shop and pub two miles. Pets welcome in selected cottages.

OPEN All Year
CC: Delta, JCB, Mastercard, Switch, Visa

3-and 4-night breaks available. Larger detatched cottages also available.

Low season per wk
£255.00–£436.00
High season per wk
£476.00–£984.00

★★★★
1 Unit
Sleeping 5

EAGLE COTTAGE

Birchover, Matlock
Contact: Mrs M E Prince, Haresfield House, Birchover, Matlock DE4 2BL
T: (01629) 650634
E: maryprince@msn.com
I: www.cressbrook.co.uk/youlgve/eagle/

A quiet end cottage in the centre of a small Peak District village having two pubs and a shop. The village is surrounded by a network of public footpaths and stunning scenery in an Area of Outstanding Natural Beauty. Many attractions, including stately Chatsworth House and Haddon Hall, are nearby.

OPEN All Year

Low season per wk
£190.00–£230.00
High season per wk
£220.00–£240.00

MATLOCK continued

★★

1 Unit
Sleeping 6

HADFIELD HOUSE

Matlock
Contact: Mrs M Evans, Christ Church Vicarage, Doncaster Road, Ardsley, Barnsley S71 5EF
T: (01226) 203784
E: rgrevans@compuserve.com

Century-old, double glazed, centrally heated stone cottage of character, well-equipped kitchen/diner, comfortable large lounge with VCR, two bedrooms and bathroom with shower. In a quiet area near Matlock town centre, an excellent base for walking, touring or just relaxing.

OPEN All Year

Short breaks (weekend or mid-week) available out of season – contact us for details.

Low season per wk
£150.00–£250.00
High season per wk
£250.00–£300.00

★★★★

2 Units

HONEYSUCKLE & CLEMATIS COTTAGES

Matlock
Contact: Mr J Lomas, Middle Hills Farm, Grangemill, Derby DE4 4HY
T: (01629) 650368
F: (01629) 650368
E: l.lomas@btinernet.com
I: www.peakdistrictfarmhols.co.uk

OPEN All Year

Low season per wk
£250.00–£350.00
High season per wk
£350.00–£450.00

Comfortable cottages with magnificent views. Two with patios, parquet floors, beams, rose arches. Clematis Cottage designed for wheelchair users and less able.

★★★

1 Unit
Sleeping 4

IVY COTTAGE

Matlock
Contact: Mrs P M Potter
T: (01629) 823018
E: ivy.cottage@ukgateway.net

OPEN All Year

Low season per wk
£200.00–£250.00
High season per wk
£250.00–£375.00

Delightful, well-equipped, 300-year-old country cottage with original beamed ceilings and woodburner. Beautiful gardens with views overlooking surrounding countryside. Pets welcome.

★★★★-★★★★★

3 Units
Sleeping 4–10

MOOREDGE BARNS

Tansley, Matlock
Contact: A M & P Barratt, Moor Edge Farm, Tansley, Matlock DE4 5FS
T: (01629) 583701
E: tonybar1921@aol.com
I: http://mooredgefarmcottages.co.uk

These barns are set in a very rural location down a quiet country lane, having splendid panoramic views from the grounds of the whole surrounding area with Riber Castle sitting on the horizon overlooking Matlock. Choice of cottages. Heated indoor pool.

OPEN All Year
CC: Solo

Enjoy swimming in our heated indoor pool all year round, free to cottage guests.

Low season per wk
£368.00–£523.00
High season per wk
£460.00–£800.00

MIDDLETON-BY-YOULGREAVE, Derbyshire Map ref 4B2

★★★★

1 Unit
Sleeping 6

HOLLY HOMESTEAD COTTAGE

Middleton-by-Youlgreave, Bakewell
Contact: Mr & Mrs D W Edge, Ridgeway House, Hillcliff Lane, Turnditch, Belper DE56 2EA
T: (01773) 550754
E: daveedge@turnditch82.freeserve.co.uk
I: www.holly-homestead.co.uk

OPEN All Year

Low season per wk
£240.00–£260.00
High season per wk
£285.00–£420.00

Cosy Peak District Grade II Listed cottage, 250 years old. Character accommodation in peaceful village. Excellent base for walking, cycling, sailing, golf and exploring National Park.

MILWICH, Staffordshire Map ref 4B2

★★★★

2 Units
Sleeping 5

SUMMERHILL FARM

Milwich, Stafford
Contact: Mrs P A Milward, Summerhill Farm, Milwich, Stafford ST18 0EL
T: (01889) 505546
F: (01889) 505692
E: p.milward@btinternet.com

OPEN All Year

Low season per wk
£120.00–£135.00
High season per wk
£135.00–£280.00

Fully-equipped apartments, close to Alton Towers, Peak District, Shugborough Hall and Wedgwood. Indoor heated swimming pool at owner's discretion.

MINCHINHAMPTON, Gloucestershire Map ref 2B1

★★★★

1 Unit
Sleeping 2

THE WOOLSACK

Minchinhampton, Stroud
Contact: Mrs E Hayward, The Woolsack, Hyde Wood House, Cirencester Road, Minchinhampton, Stroud GL6 8PE
T: (01453) 885504
F: (01453) 885504
E: info@hydewoodhhouse.co.uk
I: www.hydewoodhouse.co.uk

OPEN All Year

Low season per wk
£125.00–£155.00
High season per wk
£155.00–£275.00

First floor coach house, all rooms with exposed beamed ceilings creating cosy cottage atmosphere. Large, comfortable lounge with views over open countryside. Central for touring Cotswolds.

MINSTERLEY, Shropshire Map ref 4A3

★★★

1 Unit
Sleeping 4

OVENPIPE COTTAGE

Minsterley, Shrewsbury
Contact: Mr A B & Mrs P Thornton, Tankerville Lodge, Stiperstones, Minsterley, Shrewsbury SY5 0NB
T: (01743) 791401
F: (01743) 792305
E: tankervillelodge@supanet.com
I: www.ovenpipecottage.com

OPEN All Year

Low season per wk
£100.00–£160.00
High season per wk
£160.00–£190.00

Attractively restored barn in peaceful countryside setting, close to Stiperstones nature reserve and Long Mynd in dramatic Shropshire hills. Superb walking, touring. Shop, inn, post office nearby.

MISERDEN, Gloucestershire Map ref 2B1

★★★

3 Units

Attractive Cotswold-stone cottages overlooking fields in a peaceful hamlet on a no-through road. Footpaths lead through valleys, woods and pasture to picturesque villages while Cirencester, Stroud, Cheltenham and Gloucester are easily reached by car. You will find Sudgrove a place to relax and unwind.

SUDGROVE COTTAGES

Miserden, Stroud
Contact: Mr M G Ractliffe, Sudgrove Cottages, Miserden, Stroud GL6 7JD
T: (01285) 821322
F: (01285) 821322
E: enquiries@sudgrovecottages.co.uk
I: www.sudgrovecottages.co.uk

OPEN All Year

Short breaks available Oct-Apr. Minimum 2 nights.

Low season per wk
£200.00–£300.00
High season per wk
£250.00–£415.00

WEB
www.visitengland.com
Log on for information and inspiration. The latest information on places to visit, events and quality assessed accommodation.

MONYASH, Derbyshire Map ref 4B2

★★★★

2 Units
Sleeping 5

SHELDON COTTAGES
Monyash, Bakewell
Contact: Mrs L Fanshawe, Sheldon House,
Chapel Street, Monyash, Bakewell DE45 1JJ
T: (01629) 813067
F: (01629) 815768
E: steveandlou.fanshawe@vigin.net
I: www.sheldoncottages.co.uk

OPEN All Year

Low season per wk
£211.00–£234.00
High season per wk
£377.00–£413.00

Detached, self-catering cottage and flat in the heart of the Peak District; ideal for touring and walking. Dogs welcome by prior arrangement only.

MORETON-IN-MARSH, Gloucestershire Map ref 2B1

★★★

1 Unit
Sleeping 3

THE LAURELS
Moreton-in-Marsh
Contact: Mrs S I Billinger, Blue Cedar House,
Stow Road, Moreton-in-Marsh GL56 0DW
T: (01608) 650299

OPEN All Year

Low season per wk
Min £220.00
High season per wk
Max £371.00

Modern, centrally heated bungalow, tastefully decorated and furnished and with private garden. Set in an attractive location close to the village centre. Ideal touring centre.

NETTLEHAM, Lincolnshire Map ref 4C2

★★★★

1 Unit
Sleeping 4

CORNER COTTAGE
Nettleham, Lincoln
Contact: Mrs S Downs, The Old Vicarage, East Street,
Nettleham, Lincoln LN2 2SL
T: (01522) 750819
F: (01522) 750819
E: susan@oldvic.net

A detached, old stone cottage with its own front garden and garage, equipped with everything you need. Close to all amenities in this best-kept village.

OPEN All Year

Low season per wk
£195.00
High season per wk
£295.00

NEWENT, Gloucestershire Map ref 2B1 *Tourist Information Centre Tel: (01531) 822468*

★★★★

2 Units
Sleeping 2–3

MIDDLETOWN FARM COTTAGES
Upleadon, Newent
Contact: Mrs J A Elkins, Middletown Farm,
Middletown Lane, Upleadon, Newent GL18 1EQ
T: (01531) 828237
F: (01531) 822850
E: cottages@middletownfarm.co.uk
I: www.middletownfarm.co.uk

Cosy cottage in quiet countryside. Within grounds of 16thC timbered farmhouse, this delightful barn conversion is fully furnished to a high standard with lots of character and beams and has a private garden. Easy access to Cotswolds, Forest of Dean, Cheltenham, Gloucester, Stratford and Bath.

OPEN All Year

Low season per wk
£160.00–£220.00
High season per wk
£220.00–£295.00

ACCESSIBILITY

Look for the symbols which indicate National Accessible Scheme standards for hearing and visually impaired guests in addition to standards for guests with mobility impairment. Additional participants are shown in the listings at the back.

NORTHAMPTON, Northamptonshire Map ref 2C1 *Tourist Information Centre Tel: (01604) 622677*

★★★

1 Unit
Sleeping 9

MILL BARN COTTAGE

Earls Barton, Northampton
Contact: Mr R Wolens, Mill Barn Cottage, The Mill House, Mill Lane, Earls Barton, Northampton NN6 0NR
T: (01604) 810507
F: (01604) 810507
I: www.themillbarn.free-online.co.uk

A centuries-old riverside barn converted into a fully-equipped cottage, retaining all the original stone and oak-beam features. Unlimited access to gardens, river, barbecue etc. Private and secluded but offering easy access to major tourist attractions. Well equipped including microwave, dishwasher, washer/dryer, TV, video. Babysitting available. Six miles Northampton.

OPEN All Year

Special short-break and weekend rates from £50pn.

Low season per wk
£150.00–£200.00
High season per wk
£250.00–£450.00

NOTTINGHAM, Nottinghamshire Map ref 4C2 *Tourist Information Centre Tel: (0115) 915 5330*

★★★

48 Units
Sleeping 2–6

DAYS SERVICED APARTMENTS

Nottingham
Contact: Mr P Smith
T: (0115) 9241900
F: (0115) 9471500
E: psmith@premgroup.com
I: www.premgroup.com

Fully furnished, serviced apartments with one and two bedrooms, bathroom, kitchen and lounge. Located in the heart of the city with restaurants, bars and shopping five minutes' walk away.

OPEN All Year
CC: Amex, Delta, Diners, Mastercard, Switch, Visa

Available for 1 night, 1 week or 1 month – the ideal alternative to hotel accommodation.

Low season per wk
£420.00–£560.00
High season per wk
£420.00–£560.00

NYMPSFIELD, Gloucestershire Map ref 2B1

★★★

1 Unit
Sleeping 4

CROSSWAYS

Nympsfield, Stonehouse
Contact: Mr & Mrs F J Bowen
T: (01453) 860309

OPEN All Year except Christmas

Annexe to village house. Fully self-contained, own garden, patio, entrance. Fully fitted kitchen, large living room. Twin-bedded room, bathroom. Extra beds if necessary.

Low season per wk
£130.00
High season per wk
£150.00

OLD BOLINGBROKE, Lincolnshire Map ref 4D2

★★★★

1 Unit
Sleeping 3

1 HOPE COTTAGE

Old Bolingbroke, Spilsby
Contact: Mr & Mrs S Taylor, Clowery Cottage, Craypool Lane, Scothern, Lincoln LN2 2UU
T: (01673) 861412
F: (01673) 863336
E: no1hopecottage@aol.com
I: www.no1hopecottage.co.uk

Enjoy visiting this well-appointed country cottage, located in a quiet, royal village complete with castle ruins. Explore rolling Lincolnshire Wolds, nearby seaside or historic Lincoln and a host of market towns. Walking, cycling, fishing, nature reserves nearby – or just enjoy the peace and quiet!

OPEN All Year

Short breaks available.

Low season per wk
£185.00–£226.00
High season per wk
£247.00–£309.00

ORCOP, Herefordshire Map ref 2A1

★★★★

3 Units
Sleeping 2–5

THE BURNETT FARMHOUSE

Orcop, Hereford
Contact: Mr & Mrs M A Gooch, The Burnett Farmhouse, Orcop, Hereford HR2 8SF
T: (01981) 540999
F: (01981) 540999
E: burnett.farmhouse@talk21.com
I: www.burnettfarmhouse.co.uk

Set in magnificent rolling countryside, these beautifully renovated farm buildings adjoin The Burnett Farmhouse, with oak beams and old world charm. Far-reaching views across Orcop Valley to Garway Hill. Excellent base to discover the Wye Valley, Forest of Dean, Brecon Beacons, Malvern Hills, Welsh borders. Ideal walking/painting/wildlife. Payment by credit card welcomed.

OPEN All Year
CC: Amex, Mastercard, Visa

Short breaks available all year round.

Low season per wk
£215.00–£270.00
High season per wk
£325.00–£425.00

OSWESTRY, Shropshire Map ref 4A3 *Tourist Information Centre Tel: (01691) 662488 (Mile End)*

★★★

1 Unit
Sleeping 3

THE CROSS KEYS

Oswestry
Contact: Mr & Mrs P J Rothera
T: (01691) 650247

OPEN All Year

Converted shop and granary attached to pub, regularly featured in the 'Good Beer Guide'. In beautiful walking country. Easy access to Oswestry, Shrewsbury and Chester.

Low season per wk
£175.00
High season per wk
£175.00

OUNDLE, Northamptonshire Map ref 3A1 *Tourist Information Centre Tel: (01832) 274333*

★★★★

1 Unit
Sleeping 3

THE BOLT HOLE

Oundle, Peterborough
Contact: Mrs Spurrell, Rose Cottage, 70 Glapthorne Road, Oundle, Peterborough PE8 4PT
T: (01832) 273521
F: (01832) 275409

OPEN All Year

Comfortable, modern bungalow. Lounge/diner, fitted kitchen. Garden room/single bedroom, double bedroom, large en suite shower. Separate cloaks/utility room. Gas heating. Private garden and parking.

Low season per wk
£270.00
High season per wk
£270.00

OWLPEN, Gloucestershire Map ref 2B1

★★★★

9 Units
Sleeping 2–8

OWLPEN MANOR

Dursley
Contact: Ms J Webb, Owlpen Manor, Owlpen, Uley, Dursley GL11 5BZ
T: (01453) 860261
F: (01453) 860819
E: sales@owlpen.com
I: www.owlpen.com

OPEN All Year
CC: Amex, Delta, Mastercard, Solo, Switch, Visa

Period cottages in romantic Cotswold setting, on historic manorial estate in private wooded valley. Fully serviced, licensed restaurant, log fires, 4-poster beds, antiques.

Low season per wk
£250.00–£840.00
High season per wk
£395.00–£1,135.00

SB

SPECIAL BREAKS

Many establishments offer special promotions and themed breaks. These are highlighted in red. (All such offers are subject to availability.)

OWTHORPE, Nottinghamshire Map ref 4C2

★★★★

2 Units

WOODVIEW COTTAGES

Owthorpe, Nottingham
Contact: Mrs J Morley, Woodview Cottages, Newfields Farm, Owthorpe, Nottingham NG12 3GF
T: (01949) 81279
F: (01949) 81279
E: enquiries@woodviewcottages.co.uk
I: www.woodviewcottages.co.uk

Idyllic cottages set in picturesque gardens with wood view surrounded by open countryside. Recently converted and tastefully furnished to complement the exposed beams/stonework. Well-equipped kitchen/comfortable living area/two bedrooms/bath/shower. Ideal touring/walking base for nature lovers/wildlife enthusiasts. Located 20 minutes from Nottingham/Leicester on the edge of the Vale of Belvoir.

OPEN All Year

Short breaks available, minimum 3 nights.

Low season per wk
£325.00–£400.00
High season per wk
£350.00–£550.00

PEAK DISTRICT

See under Alstonefield, Ashbourne, Bakewell, Bamford, Barlow, Baslow, Cressbrook, Great Hucklow, Hartington, Hathersage, Hayfield, Litton, Middleton-by-Youlgreave, Monyash, Youlgreave

PEMBRIDGE, Herefordshire Map ref 2A1

★★★

2 Units
Sleeping 4

THE GRANARY & THE DAIRY

Pembridge, Leominster
Contact: Mrs N Owens, The Granary and The Dairy, The Grove, Pembridge, Leominster HR6 9HP
T: (01544) 388268
F: (01544) 388154
E: nancy@grovedesign.co.uk

OPEN All Year except Christmas

Low season per wk
Min £200.00
High season per wk
Max £300.00

Attractive barn conversions in 200-acre farm in secluded valley near black and white villages, Offa's Dyke and Mortimer Trail. Friendly farm atmosphere. Children and pets welcome.

★★

1 Unit
Sleeping 5

ROWENA COTTAGE

Pembridge, Leominster
Contact: Mrs D Malone, The Cottage, Holme, Newark NG23 7RZ
T: (01636) 672914
E: dianamalone56@hotmail.com

Charming black and white 16thC cottage with open fire and storage heaters in the picturesque village of Pembridge on the River Arrow. An ideal touring centre for the countless attractions of the Border country, Welsh Marches, Herefordshire, Shropshire and Offa's Dyke. Local shops and pubs. Fishing, riding and gliding nearby.

OPEN All Year except Christmas

Short breaks available out of school holidays. Minimum of 2 nights for £90.

Low season per wk
Min £220.00
High season per wk
Max £350.00

CHECK THE MAPS

The colour maps at the front of this guide show all the cities, towns and villages for which you will find accommodation entries.
Refer to the town index to find the page on which they are listed.

PIKEHALL, Derbyshire Map ref 4B2

★★★★

2 Units

THE OLD FARMHOUSE & THE GRANGE

Pikehall, Matlock
Contact: Mr & Mrs S Mavin
T: (01335) 390382

In a beautiful, secluded valley, both 18thC cottages are full of character and original features including woodburners. The Grange has four bedrooms, three bathrooms, spacious lounge. The Old Farmhouse has two bedrooms, one with 4-poster, and Aga in kitchen. Great for walking, cycling and touring. Located on The Roystone Grange Archaeological Trail.

OPEN All Year

3-night breaks. Packed lunches and home-cooked meals ready to cook. Available separately or as 1 unit.

Low season per wk
£300.00–£450.00
High season per wk
£500.00–£750.00

PONTRILAS, Herefordshire Map ref 2A1

★★

1 Unit
Sleeping 5

STATION HOUSE

Pontrilas, Hereford
Contact: Ms J Russell, Station House, Pontrilas, Hereford HR2 0EH
T: (01981) 240564
F: (01981) 240564
E: john.pring@tesco.net
I: www.golden-valley.co.uk/stationhouse

OPEN All Year

Low season per wk
£270.00
High season per wk
£270.00

Former Great Western Railway station retaining its unique character, in the beautiful Welsh Marches, midway between Hereford and Abergavenny. Watch the passing trains from the old station platform.

ROSS-ON-WYE, Herefordshire Map ref 2A1 *Tourist Information Centre Tel: (01989) 562768*

★★★

1 Unit
Sleeping 5

FAIRVIEW

Ross-on-Wye
Contact: Mrs M E Jones, Stoneleigh, Fourth Avenue, Greytrees, Ross-on-Wye HR9 7HR
T: (01989) 566301

OPEN All Year except Christmas

Low season per wk
£175.00
High season per wk
£230.00–£300.00

Completely refurbished to a high standard. A real home from home, with panoramic views towards the distant Welsh hills.

★★-★★★

2 Units
Sleeping 2–4

THE GAME LARDERS & THE OLD BAKEHOUSE

Walford, Ross-on-Wye
Contact: Mr M McIntyre,
The Game Larders & Old Bakehouse, Wythall, Walford, Ross-on-Wye HR9 5SD
T: (01989) 562688
F: (01989) 763225
E: wythall@globalnet.co.uk
I: www.wythallestate.co.uk

Self-contained cottages in the wing of a 16thC manor house in a secluded setting with garden, duck pond and wooded grounds. You will enjoy peace and quiet here and see an abundance of wildlife. Well equipped and furnished in period style, the cottages are warm and comfortable.

OPEN All Year

Short breaks available Oct-Mar. 3-night stay.

Low season per wk
£210.00–£290.00
High season per wk
£320.00–£450.00

RATING **All accommodation in this guide has been rated, or is awaiting a rating, by a trained VisitBritain assessor.**

ROSS-ON-WYE continued

★★★★
1 Unit
Sleeping 2

OLD CIDER HOUSE
Glewstone, Ross-on-Wye
Contact: Mrs H A Jackson, Lowcop, Glewstone, Ross-on-Wye HR9 6AN
T: (01989) 562827
F: (01989) 563877
E: man.of.ross.ltd@farming.co.uk

OPEN All Year

Low season per wk
Min £190.00
High season per wk
Max £260.00

Old cider house on fruit farm in Wye Valley, converted to character cottage with beams and antique furniture. Overlooking apple orchards. Warm in winter.

★★★
1 Unit
Sleeping 6

THE OLDE HOUSE
Ross-on-Wye
Contact: P J & J Fray, Keepers Cottage, Upton Bishop, Ross-on-Wye HR9 7UE
T: (01989) 780383
F: (01989) 780383
E: peter@pjfray.co.uk
I: www.oldehouse.com

OPEN All Year

Low season per wk
Min £195.00
High season per wk
Max £350.00

Cosy beamed cottage with open fire and full central heating. Large garden and panoramic views.

ROSTON, Derbyshire Map ref 4B2

★★★★
3 Units
Sleeping 4

DERBYSHIRE DALES HOLIDAYS
Roston, Ashbourne
Contact: Mrs B Wheeler, Town End Farm, Roston, Ashbourne DE6 2EH
T: (01335) 324062
F: (01335) 324062
E: wheelertef@supanet.com

OPEN All Year

Low season per wk
£160.00–£220.00
High season per wk
£220.00–£400.00

The terraced cottages have been tastefully decorated and furnished to a high standard to provide comfortable, centrally heated accommodation.

RUGBY, Warwickshire Map ref 4C3 *Tourist Information Centre Tel: (01788) 534970*

★★★★
3 Units
Sleeping 4–6

Attractive converted barns set within a farmyard. Fully equipped to ensure you are cosy and comfortable. Short breaks by arrangement. Fishing available. Located three miles from Rugby on Lawford Heath Lane. Midway between A428 and A45.

LAWFORD HILL FARM
Rugby
Contact: Mr & Mrs S Moses, Lawford Hill Farm, Lawford Heath Lane, Rugby CV23 9HG
T: (01788) 542001
F: (01788) 537880
E: lawford.hill@talk21.com
I: www.lawfordhill.co.uk

OPEN All Year
CC: Delta, JCB, Mastercard, Solo, Switch, Visa

Low season per wk
£350.00–£500.00
High season per wk
£400.00–£550.00

SHERWOOD FOREST

See under Gonalston, Southwell

SHOBDON, Herefordshire Map ref 2A1

★★★★
1 Unit
Sleeping 2

TYN-Y-COED
Shobdon, Leominster
Contact: Mr & Mrs J Andrews
T: (01568) 708277
F: (01568) 708277
E: jandrews@shobdondesign.kc3.co.uk

Low season per wk
£280.00
High season per wk
£280.00

Country house in beautiful North Herefordshire between Leominster and Presteigne. Good walking country, close to the Mortimer Trail. Historic sites and lovely gardens to explore nearby.

SHREWSBURY, Shropshire Map ref 4A3 *Tourist Information Centre Tel: (01743) 281200*

★★

1 Unit
Sleeping 4

INGLENOOK
Shrewsbury
Contact: Mrs J M Mullineux, Fach-Hir, Brooks, Welshpool SY21 8QP
T: (01686) 650361

OPEN All Year

Low season per wk
£80.00–£110.00
High season per wk
£175.00–£200.00

Bungalow in peaceful surroundings, three miles from the centre of historic Shrewsbury town. Ample parking alongside. Gardens and lawn.

SKEGNESS, Lincolnshire Map ref 4D2 *Tourist Information Centre Tel: (01754) 764821/(01754) 899887*

★★★★

4 Units
Sleeping 6–8

INGOLDALE PARK
Skegness
Contact: Ms C Whitehead, Ingoldale Park, Roman Bank, Ingoldmells, Skegness PE25 1LL
T: (01754) 872335
F: (01754) 873887
E: info@ingoldmells.net
I: www.ingoldmells.net

OPEN All Year

Low season per wk
£280.00–£400.00
High season per wk
£490.00–£580.00

Accessible apartments, level throughout, in heart of busy and popular resort.

SOUTH CERNEY, Gloucestershire Map ref 2B2

★★★★

18 Units

Luxury lakeside lodges offering quality accommodation within the Cotswold Water Park. Individually furnished, beautifully fitted, offering comfort and style. Two styles of lodges are available: New England and Turret. Superb country retreat for sightseeing, shopping, activity breaks and relaxing.

ORION HOLIDAYS

South Cerney, Cirencester
Contact: Mr M Thomas, Orion Holidays Orion House, Unit W, The Old Brickyard Works, North End, Ashton Keynes, Swindon SN6 6QR
T: (01285) 861839
F: (01285) 869188
E: bookings@orionholidays.com
I: www.orionholidays.com

OPEN All Year
CC: Delta, Mastercard, Switch, Visa

Short breaks available throughout the year. 20% 2-person discount offered during off-peak times.

Low season per wk
£475.00–£685.00
High season per wk
£595.00–£1,045.00

SOUTH COCKERINGTON, Lincolnshire Map ref 4D2

★★★

3 Units

WEST VIEW COTTAGES

South Cockerington, Louth
Contact: Mr R Nicholson & Mrs J Hand
T: (01507) 327209
E: richard@nicholson55.freeserve.co.uk

Beautifully converted, single-storey farm buildings tastefully decorated to a high standard. Ideally located in a quiet village with the market town of Louth four miles away. There are numerous quiet beaches along the coast (six miles). Suitable walking and cycling routes are close by. Come and relax in pleasant surroundings.

OPEN All Year

Low season per wk
£170.00–£190.00
High season per wk
£200.00–£270.00

CONFIRM YOUR BOOKING

You are advised to confirm your booking in writing.

SOUTHWELL, Nottinghamshire Map ref 4C2

★★★

2 Units
Sleeping 2–4

THE HAYLOFT & LITTLE TITHE

Fiskerton, Southwell
Contact: Mrs V M Wilson, Lodge Farm, Morton, Fiskerton, Southwell NG25 0XH
T: (01636) 830497
E: info@lodgebarns.co.uk
I: www.lodgebarns.co.uk

Situated on working farm in country village of Morton, these 18thC barn conversions offer you a high standard of self-contained facilities. Twin-bedded rooms, each with shower room, fully fitted kitchen, lounge. Set in an orchard courtyard and farmland. Within walking distance of village shop, local pubs and River Trent.

OPEN All Year

Low season per wk
£175.00–£300.00
High season per wk
£175.00–£300.00

SPILSBY, Lincolnshire Map ref 4D2

★★★

1 Unit
Sleeping 4

CORNER FARM COTTAGE

Spilsby
Contact: Mr M Fitzpatrick
T: (01790) 753476
F: (01790) 752810
E: smrfitzp@ukonline.co.uk

OPEN All Year except Christmas

Low season per wk
Min £200.00
High season per wk
Max £250.00

Pristine two-bedroomed cottage. Part of private 12 acre horse stud with stabling available. Close to sea, Wolds and historic Lincoln.

STAFFORD, Staffordshire Map ref 4B3 *Tourist Information Centre Tel: (01785) 619619*

★★★★

1 Unit
Sleeping 2

NO 4 THE ROW

Salt, Stafford
Contact: Miss S Moore, Downtop Farm, Sandon Bank, Stafford ST18 9TB
T: (01889) 508300

Exceptionally well-equipped 19thC terraced cottage in a peaceful, picturesque village in the heart of Staffordshire close to Shugborough, Cannock Chase and Wedgwood. Makes a good touring and walking base, as well as an ideal place to relax and unwind. Open all year.

OPEN All Year
CC: Mastercard, Switch, Visa

Short breaks available 3 or 4 nights.

Low season per wk
£200.00–£250.00
High season per wk
£250.00–£300.00

STANTON, Gloucestershire Map ref 2B1

★★★

1 Unit
Sleeping 6

CHARITY COTTAGE

Stanton, Broadway
Contact: Mrs V Ryland, Charity Farm, Stanton, Broadway WR12 7NE
T: (01386) 584339
F: (01386) 584270
E: kennethryland@ukonline.co.uk
I: www.myrtle-cottge.co.uk/ryland.htm

Charming Cotswold-stone cottage in picturesque village. Three bedrooms, two bathrooms, spacious accommodation. The pretty garden offers al fresco dining. Village pub five minutes' walk from cottage, and Broadway (two miles) has a selection of pubs and restaurants. Enjoy walking the Cotswold hills, or visit National Trust houses and gardens.

OPEN All Year
CC: Mastercard, Visa

Short breaks available.

Low season per wk
£280.00–£350.00
High season per wk
£350.00–£500.00

STANTON-ON-THE-WOLDS, Nottinghamshire Map ref 4C2

★★★★
1 Unit
Sleeping 6

FOXCOTE COTTAGE
Stanton-on-the-Wolds, Keyworth
Contact: Mrs J Hinchley
T: (0115) 9374337
F: (0115) 9374337

OPEN All Year

Low season per wk
£450.00
High season per wk
£450.00

Situated on the edge of the Vale of Belvoir, the cottage overlooks open countryside, with views of a lake, and is set in a private, well-maintained garden.

STATHERN, Leicestershire Map ref 4C2

★★★★
1 Unit
Sleeping 4

BRAMBLES BARN
Stathern, Melton Mowbray
Contact: Mrs J Newton
T: (01949) 860071
E: richard@bramblesbarn.co.uk
I: www.bramblesbarn.co.uk

Set in its own paddock, Brambles Barn offers an ideal base for walking, cycling, or bring your own horse and ride in the lovely countryside of Leicestershire. Only 18 miles from Nottingham, so you could shop 'til you drop or simply roam Sherwood Forest looking for Robin Hood! Available all year.

OPEN All Year
CC: Delta, Mastercard, Switch, Visa

Low season per wk
£200.00–£425.00
High season per wk
£375.00–£425.00

STOKE-ON-TRENT, Staffordshire Map ref 4B2 *Tourist Information Centre Tel: (01782) 236000*

★★★
2 Units
Sleeping 6

BANK END FARM COTTAGES
Stoke-on-Trent
Contact: Mr K & Mrs E Meredith
T: (01782) 502160
E: pete502@btopenworld.com
I: www.alton-village.com

OPEN All Year

Low season per wk
£199.00–£225.00
High season per wk
£225.00–£285.00

Set in pleasant countryside, with village amenities five minutes' walk away. Beautiful views. Ideal for visiting Potteries and Peak District. Children welcome. Ample parking.

★★★★
1 Unit
Sleeping 12

FIELD HEAD FARM HOUSE HOLIDAYS
Stoke-on-Trent
Contact: Mrs J Hudson, Stoney Rock Farm, Waterhouses, Stoke-on-Trent ST10 3LH
T: (01538) 308352
E: info@field-head.co.uk
I: www.field-head.co.uk

Grade II Listed farmhouse situated within the southern Peak District and the Staffordshire moorlands. Set in beautiful, secluded surroundings close to Dovedale and the Manifold Valley. Ideal country for the walker, horse-rider or cyclist. Well equipped, Sky TV. Alton Towers 15-minute drive. All pets and horses welcome.

OPEN All Year

Short breaks, late-booking discount.

Low season per wk
£540.00–£1,190.00

★★★
1 Unit
Sleeping 4

JAY'S BARN
Stoke-on-Trent
Contact: Mrs C Babb
T: (01889) 507444

OPEN All Year

Low season per wk
£230.00
High season per wk
£300.00

Self-catering unit specifically designed for disabled people, situated in own grounds.

VISITBRITAIN'S WHERE TO STAY
Please mention this guide when making your booking.

STOKE-ON-TRENT continued

★★★★

3 Units
Sleeping 6

MOORCOURT COTTAGES, MOORCOURT HOUSE

Stoke-on-Trent
Contact: Mrs V Bradshaw
T: (01538) 723008
F: (01538) 723008
E: vbradshaw@moorcourtcottages.co.uk
I: www.moorcourtcottages.co.uk

Converted cottages set in 17thC farmhouse courtyard. Three bedrooms. Fully equipped accommodation. New, modern appliances, central heating. Garden with patio at rear. Countryside location in small village, five minutes' drive to local high street. Central for all Staffordshire's attractions.

OPEN All Year

Weekend and mid-week breaks (3 nights) available.

High season per wk
£335.00–£365.00

STOW-ON-THE-WOLD, Gloucestershire Map ref 2B1 *Tourist Information Centre Tel: (01451) 831082*

★★★★★

4 Units
Sleeping 4

BROAD OAK COTTAGES

Stow-on-the-Wold, Cheltenham
Contact: Mrs M Wilson, The Counting House, Stow-on-the-Wold, Cheltenham GL54 1AL
T: (01451) 830794
F: (01451) 830794
E: mary@broadoakcottages.fsnet.co.uk
I: www.broadoakcottages.fsnet.co.uk

Delightful five-star cottages, all with character and all beautifully furnished and equipped. Each has twin and double bedrooms, kitchen complete with modern appliances, patio and garden. Three have parking, one is all on one level. Prices are unusually inclusive!

OPEN All Year

Short breaks available (except in high season).

Low season per wk
Min £275.00
High season per wk
Max £510.00

Rating
Applied For
1 Unit
Sleeping 10

ICOMB LODGE

Stow-on-the-Wold, Cheltenham
Contact: Mrs Taylor
T: (01423) 502355

Delightful 18thC Listed farmhouse with extensive private gardens, situated in Icomb, a very pretty, unspoilt village between Burford and Stow-on-the-Wold. Fully modernised and furnished to a high standard but retaining many original features including open fireplaces, flagstone floors and exposed beams.

OPEN All Year except Christmas

Special mid-week rates throughout the year.

High season per wk
£950.00–£1,750.00

TOWN INDEX

This can be found at the back of this guide. If you know where you want to stay, the index will give you the page number listing accommodation in your chosen town, city or village.

STOW-ON-THE-WOLD continued

★★★

1 Unit
Sleeping 5

JOHNSTON COTTAGE

Stow-on-the-Wold, Cheltenham
Contact: Mrs Y V Johnston, Poplars Barn, Evenlode, Moreton-in-Marsh GL56 0NN
T: (01608) 650816

Quiet location in a pretty terrace, five minutes from the town centre. Inglenook fireplace, exposed stonework and beams and a well fitted kitchen. South-facing patio with colourful flower tubs, hanging baskets and garden furniture. Ideal for visiting the many attractions which the Cotswolds have to offer. Parking close by.

OPEN All Year

Low season per wk
£200.00–£350.00
High season per wk
£350.00

★★★

3 Units

LUCKLEY HOLIDAYS

Longborough, Moreton-in-Marsh
Contact: Mr R Wharton
T: (01451) 870885
F: (01451) 831481
E: info@luckley-holidays.co.uk
I: www.luckley-holidays.co.uk

OPEN All Year

Low season per wk
£300.00–£420.00
High season per wk
£300.00–£820.00

In open countryside, pool, tennis court, games room, banquet hall. Ideal for weekend parties and families (up to 38 people). Also self-catering rooms for the night.

★★★★

4 Units
Sleeping 2–6

PARK FARM HOLIDAY COTTAGES

Stow-on-the-Wold, Cheltenham
Contact: Mrs J C Ricketts, Park Farm, Maugersbury, Cheltenham GL54 1HP
T: (01451) 830227
F: (01451) 870568
E: parkfarm.cottages@virgin.net

Situated on owners' mixed farm in small hamlet less than 10 minutes' walk from Stow-on-the-Wold where there are excellent pubs and restaurants. South-facing, single-storey, detached cottages with wonderful views. Romantic 4-poster beds in double rooms. Logburning stoves, plenty of parking and use of hard tennis court. Prices all inclusive.

OPEN All Year

Short breaks available Nov-Mar.

Low season per wk
£200.00–£250.00
High season per wk
£380.00–£560.00

★★★★

1 Unit
Sleeping 2

ROSE'S COTTAGE

Broadwell, Moreton-in-Marsh
Contact: Mr & Mrs R Drinkwater, Rose's Cottage, The Green, Broadwell, Moreton-in-Marsh GL56 0UF
T: (01451) 830007

OPEN All Year

Low season per wk
£220.00–£250.00
High season per wk
£250.00–£300.00

Delightful cottage overlooking the green of charming Cotswold village, in an Area of Outstanding Natural Beauty, 1.5 miles from Stow-on-the-Wold. Ideal for touring.

MAP REFERENCES The map references refer to the colour maps at the front of this guide. The first figure is the map number; the letter and figure which follow indicate the grid reference on the map.

STOW-ON-THE-WOLD continued

★★★★★

1 Unit
Sleeping 2

Quietly situated in lovely surroundings, Springbank is a Cotswold-stone coach house, furnished to the highest standards. Set in 11 acres of the Windrush valley which features a 0.5-acre pond with private coarse fishing. Soft colour schemes, oak floors with rugs, quality furnishings and fabrics feature in this superb conversion. Sorry no pets, no smoking preferred.

SPRINGBANK

Temple Guiting, Cheltenham
Contact: Mr Mather, Landgate House, Colman, Temple Guiting, Cheltenham GL54 5RT
T: (01451) 850571
F: (01451) 850614
E: landgatemathers@tesco.net
I: www.landgatetg.co.uk

OPEN All Year

Short breaks available Oct-Mar (excl Christmas and New Year): 3 nights £160 inclusive of power and linen.

Low season per wk
Max £275.00
High season per wk
Max £375.00

★★★★

1 Unit
Sleeping 4

A delightful Victorian Cotswold-stone semi-detached cottage in a quiet street just five minutes from the Market Square. A sympathetic, recent renovation has retained much of the character and original features. A conservatory situated at the rear of the cottage overlooks the pretty, enclosed garden.

2 UNION STREET

Stow-on-the-Wold, Cheltenham
Contact: Ms K Spiers, Cottage in the Country and Cottage Holidays, Forest Gate, Frog Lane, Milton-under-Wychwood, Oxford OX7 6JZ
T: (01993) 831495
F: (01993) 831095
E: enquiries@cottageinthecountry.co.uk
I: www.cottageinthecountry.co.uk

OPEN All Year
CC: Delta, Mastercard, Solo, Switch, Visa

Low season per wk
£270.00
High season per wk
£435.00–£475.00

STRATFORD-UPON-AVON, Warwickshire Map ref 2B1 *Tourist Information Centre Tel: (01789) 293127*

★★★

1 Unit
Sleeping 3

AS YOU LIKE IT
Stratford-upon-Avon
Contact: Mrs J Reid
T: (01789) 450266
F: (01789) 450266
I: www.alderminster99.freeserve.co.uk

OPEN All Year

Low season per wk
£260.00–£295.00
High season per wk
£295.00–£365.00

Quietly situated character cottage in 'Old Town', within easy walking distance of theatres, shops and riverside parks. Owner supervised.

★★★★

2 Units
Sleeping 4

First floor apartments, centrally heated, in a quiet lane within two minutes' walk of town centre, river and theatre. Number 20 has a balcony with wonderful views of the river bridge onto Holy Trinity spire. Apartments have off-road parking and are fully equipped.

20–21 BANCROFT PLACE

Stratford-upon-Avon
Contact: Mrs Carter, Park View Guest House, 57 Rother Street, Stratford-upon-Avon CV37 6LT
T: (01789) 266839
F: (01789) 266839

OPEN All Year

Low season per wk
£275.00–£375.00
High season per wk
£450.00–£475.00

STRATFORD-UPON-AVON continued

★★★

1 Unit
Sleeping 3

CHESTNUT COTTAGE

Pathlow, Stratford-upon-Avon
Contact: Mrs J Rush, Gospel Oak House, Pathlow, Stratford-upon-Avon CV37 0JA
T: (01789) 292764

OPEN All Year except Christmas

Low season per wk
£170.00
High season per wk
£200.00–£230.00

Set in splendid, secluded grounds by woodland, with far-reaching views. Well appointed, attractively furnished, ample parking. 2.5 miles from Stratford-upon-Avon.

★★★

2 Units
Sleeping 2–4

The Davy and Paradise Cottages are newly converted to a very high standard. The Davy has two bedrooms and Paradise has one bedroom, all ensuite. Surrounded by open countryside with stunning views over the Downs. Three local pubs nearby serving good food. Stratford-upon-Avon is five miles and Warwick 10 miles.

CRIMSCOTE DOWNS FARM HOLIDAY COTTAGES

Crimscote, Stratford-upon-Avon
Contact: Mrs J James, The Old Coach House, Whitchurch Farm, Wimpstone, Stratford-upon-Avon CV37 8NS
T: (01789) 450275
F: (01789) 450275
I: www.stratford-upon-avon.co.uk/crimscote.htm

OPEN All Year

3-night stays available Nov-Feb (excl Christmas and New Year).

Low season per wk
£190.00–£325.00
High season per wk
£350.00–£430.00

STROUD, Gloucestershire Map ref 2B1

★★–★★★

8 Units

WHITMINSTER HOUSE COTTAGES

Whitminster, Wheatenhurst
Contact: Mrs A R Teesdale, Whitminster House, Wheatenhurst, Whitminster GL2 7PN
T: (01452) 740204
F: (01452) 740204
E: whitminster@btconnect.com
I: www.whitminsterhousecottages..co.uk

OPEN All Year

Low season per wk
£225.00–£295.00
High season per wk
£625.00–£735.00

Picturesque, rural location ideally situated to explore Heart of England and Cotswolds. Range of different-sized cottages can be combined for larger parties. One wheelchair access.

TAYNTON, Gloucestershire Map ref 2B1

★★★★

1 Unit
Sleeping 2

OWLS BARN

Huntley, Gloucester
Contact: Mrs B Goodwin, Coldcroft Farm, Glasshouse Lane, Taynton, Huntley, Gloucester GL19 3HJ
T: (01452) 831290
F: (01452) 831544
E: goodies@coldcroft.freeserve.co.uk
I: www.coldcroft.freeserve.co.uk

OPEN All Year

Low season per wk
£195.00–£215.00
High season per wk
£265.00–£295.00

In the heart of glorious Gloucestershire, Owls Barn, which was beautifully renovated in 2002, has fantastic views, secure parking and a wealth of local attractions.

TETFORD, Lincolnshire Map ref 4D2

★★★

3 Units
Sleeping 3–4

GRANGE FARM COTTAGES

Salmonby, Horncastle
Contact: Mr & Mrs Downes
T: (01507) 534101
F: (01507) 534101

OPEN All Year

Low season per wk
Min £180.00
High season per wk
Max £383.00

Well-furnished, two-bedroomed cottages in old barn conversion. Children's play area, large gardens and fishing lakes. Lovely Wolds countryside. Pub/meals 250 yards. Idyllic retreat.

UPPINGHAM, Rutland Map ref 4C3

★★★

1 Unit
Sleeping 3

4 STOCKERSTON ROAD

Uppingham, Oakham
Contact: Mr & Mrs Lloyd, 4 Stockerston Road, Uppingham, Oakham LE15 9UD
T: (01572) 823478
F: (01572) 823955

OPEN All Year except Christmas

Low season per wk £160.00
High season per wk £170.00

Comfortably appointed flat with its own private walled garden. Designed for a couple, but can accommodate a third person. Enjoys a three Star rating with the ETC.

UPTON ST LEONARDS, Gloucestershire Map ref 2B1

★★

2 Units
Sleeping 5

HILL FARM COTTAGES

Upton St Leonards, Gloucester
Contact: Mrs M McLellan, Hill Farm Cottages, Hill Farm, Upton Hill, Upton St Leonards, Gloucester GL4 8DA
T: (01452) 614081

OPEN All Year

Low season per wk £180.00
High season per wk £250.00–£260.00

Located two miles from Gloucester, with panoramic views of the Cotswolds. Close to dry-ski slopes and golfing facilities. Ideal for walking. Country pub nearby providing food.

UPTON-UPON-SEVERN, Worcestershire Map ref 2B1 *Tourist Information Centre Tel: (01684) 594200*

★★★★

1 Unit
Sleeping 3

CAPTAINS' RETREAT

Upton-upon-Severn, Worcester
Contact: Mr M Cranton
T: (01684) 592023
F: (01684) 592023
E: michael@cranton.freeserve.co.uk

Converted from a 17thC inn, this fully renovated and spacious first floor apartment offers the perfect base for exploring and relaxing in this beautiful part of the country. 200 yards from open countryside, just off the centre of Upton, this beautiful timber-framed accommodation offers the perfect retreat.

OPEN All Year

Short 3-day breaks available, from £120.

Low season per wk £200.00–£250.00
High season per wk £250.00–£350.00

WARWICK, Warwickshire Map ref 2B1 *Tourist Information Centre Tel: (01926) 492212*

★★★

1 Unit
Sleeping 3

COPES FLAT

Warwick
Contact: Mrs E Draisey, Forth House, 44 High Street, Warwick CV34 4AX
T: (01926) 401512
F: (01926) 490809
E: info@forthhouseuk.co.uk
I: www.forthhouseuk.co.uk

OPEN All Year
CC: Delta, JCB, Mastercard, Solo, Switch, Visa

Low season per wk Min £220.00
High season per wk Max £320.00

Secluded, town centre, self-contained coach-house flat. Sitting room/dining room, bedroom, bathroom, kitchen, telephone. Adjacent to castle, close to restaurants. Large roof garden. Non-smokers only, please.

WELLINGTON, Shropshire Map ref 4A3

★★★★

1 Unit
Sleeping 4

THE COACH HOUSE

Wellington, Telford
Contact: Mrs M M Fellows, Old Vicarage, Wrockwardine, Wellington, Telford TF6 5DG
T: (01952) 244859
F: (01952) 255066
E: mue@mfellows@.freeserve.co.uk

OPEN All Year

Low season per wk £300.00–£350.00
High season per wk £400.00–£450.00

Detached private house providing centrally heated, two-bedroomed accommodation. Pleasant location, surrounded by farms yet close to Ironbridge, Shrewsbury and the Welsh Marches.

WELTON, Lincolnshire Map ref 4C2

★★★★

1 Unit
Sleeping 4

MILL COTTAGE

Welton, Lincoln
Contact: Mrs G E Gladwin
T: (01673) 860082
F: (01673) 863424
E: gill@millhousecottage.freeserve.co.uk

A Victorian steam mill newly converted to a high standard, situated in beautiful cottage gardens surrounded by open farmland. The location is quiet and peaceful. Seasonal salads, vegetables and eggs are available from the owners. An 18-hole golf course, with a public bar and restaurant, is within easy walking distance.

OPEN All Year

3-day breaks £100, by arrangement.

Low season per wk
£175.00–£200.00
High season per wk
£200.00–£250.00

WEST OXFORDSHIRE

See South East region for entries

WHITBOURNE, Herefordshire Map ref 2B1

★★★

1 Unit
Sleeping 11

CRUMPLEBURY FARMHOUSE

Whitbourne, Worcester
Contact: Mrs A Evans, Dial House, Whitbourne, Worcester WR6 5SG
T: (01886) 821534
F: (01886) 821534
E: a.evans@candaevans.fsnet.co.uk

OPEN All Year

Low season per wk
£310.00–£790.00
High season per wk
£360.00–£570.00

Owner-maintained, comfortable and cosy five-bedroomed farmhouse on family farm. Ideal reunions, family gatherings, walking. Enclosed garden. Quiet. Wheelchair access. Coarse fishing available.

WHITMINSTER, Gloucestershire Map ref 2B1

★★★

1 Unit
Sleeping 4

THE STABLE

Whitminster, Gloucester
Contact: Mr & Mrs A Beeby
T: (01452) 740969
E: beebyac@onet.co.uk
I: homepage.ntlworld.com/beebyac

OPEN All Year

Low season per wk
£244.00–£350.00
High season per wk
£350.00–£464.00

Two-hundred-year-old, recently converted stable with elm beams; cosy, comfortable and well equipped; rural setting yet easy access to wide area with many attractions.

WILLERSEY, Gloucestershire Map ref 2B1

★★

1 Unit
Sleeping 3

3 CHELTENHAM COTTAGES

Willersey, Broadway
Contact: Mrs G Malin, 28 Bibsworth Avenue, Broadway WR12 7BQ
T: (01386) 853248
F: (01386) 853181
E: g.malin@virgin.net

OPEN All Year

Low season per wk
£185.00–£200.00
High season per wk
£235.00–£295.00

Listed Cotswold-stone cottage with countryside views. Attractive garden. Award-winning village, excellent shop and pubs. Ideal centre for exploring the Cotswolds and Shakespeare country.

5

NB

IMPORTANT NOTE Information on accommodation listed in this guide has been supplied by the proprietors. As changes may occur you are advised to check details at the time of booking.

WILLOUGHBY, Warwickshire Map ref 4C3

★★★★★

1 Unit
Sleeping 6

THE SADDLERY

Willoughby, Rugby
Contact: Mrs E Heckford, Manor Farm, Brooks Close, Willoughby, Rugby CV23 8BY
T: (01788) 890256
E: office@thesaddlery.org.uk
I: thesaddlery.org.uk

A converted saddlery of the highest standard with luxurious accommodation. Tastefully furnished and centrally heated throughout. Situated in a quiet village on working farm in courtyard. Private parking and patio. Ideal location on Warwicks/Northants border. Close to Warwick, Stratford-upon-Avon, Leamington Spa, Silverstone and Althorpe.

OPEN All Year

Low season per wk
£320.00–£370.00
High season per wk
£430.00–£500.00

WINCHCOMBE, Gloucestershire Map ref 2B1

★★★★-★★★★★

5 Units
Sleeping 2–5

TRADITIONAL ACCOMMODATION

Winchcombe, Cheltenham
Contact: Mr & Mrs Wilson, 60 Pershore Road, Evesham WR11 2PQ
T: (01386) 446269
F: (01386) 446269
E: trad.accom@virgin.net
I: http://freespace.virgin.net/trad.accom

Traditional old barns of individual style and character finely restored to provide spacious, high-quality properties. Original period features. Quality furnishings and all modern facilities. Gardens/patios, private parking and countryside views to each property. Also detached stone cottage nearby. All family supervised. Ideal touring base. No pets. Brochures available.

OPEN All Year
CC: Amex, Delta, Diners, JCB, Mastercard, Solo, Switch, Visa

Low season per wk
£220.00–£430.00
High season per wk
£430.00–£500.00

WOODHALL SPA, Lincolnshire Map ref 4D2

★★

1 Unit
Sleeping 4

MILL LANE COTTAGE

Woodhall Spa
Contact: Mr & Mrs I G Williamson, 72 Mill Lane, Woodhall Spa LN10 6QZ
T: (01526) 353101
E: will@williamsoni.freeserve.co.uk
I: www.skegness.net/woodhallspa.htm

OPEN All Year

Low season per wk
£155.00–£185.00
High season per wk
£160.00–£190.00

Renovated cottage down quiet residential lane. Walks to river and pub. Cottage has all amenities, sports can be catered for.

WORCESTER, Worcestershire Map ref 2B1 *Tourist Information Centre Tel: (01905) 726311*

★★★

1 Unit
Sleeping 5

LITTLE LIGHTWOOD FARM

Cotheridge, Worcester
Contact: Mrs V A Rogers
T: (01905) 333236
F: (01905) 333236
E: lightwood.holidays@virgin.net

OPEN All Year
CC: Delta, Mastercard, Visa

Low season per wk
£140.00–£220.00
High season per wk
£260.00–£280.00

Working farm with delightful views of Malvern Hills. Just off the A44 Worcester to Leominster road, 3.5 miles from Worcester.

WYE VALLEY

See under Hereford, Ross-on-Wye

WYTHALL, Worcestershire Map ref 4B3

★★★-★★★★★

7 Units

INKFORD COURT COTTAGES

Wythall, Birmingham

Contact: Mr J S Bedford, Inkford Court Cottages, Alcester Road, Wythall, Birmingham B47 6DL

T: (01564) 822304

F: (01564) 829618

OPEN All Year

Low season per wk £195.00–£325.00

High season per wk £200.00–£365.00

Cottages, part of a restoration and conversion of 18thC period farm buildings, set in 6.5 acres. Ideally located for Heart of England.

YARDLEY GOBION, Northamptonshire Map ref 2C1

★★

1 Unit

Sleeping 4

THE STABLE

Yardley Gobion, Towcester

Contact: Mr A Paine, The Stable, Old Wharf Farm, The Wharf, Yardley Gobion, Towcester NN12 7UE

T: (01908) 542293

F: (01908) 542293

OPEN All Year

Low season per wk £250.00

High season per wk £325.00

Self-contained stable cottage in rural, canal-side location, built about 1850 by former French prisoners of war. Accommodation on ground and first floors.

YOULGREAVE, Derbyshire Map ref 4B2

★★★

1 Unit

Sleeping 2

SUNNYSIDE

Youlgreave, Bakewell

Contact: Ms J Steed

T: (01629) 636195

Sunnyside is a homely, self-contained, very private apartment. From its patio, which is well-stocked with hanging-baskets, various old farm implements and stone troughs, there are lovely views to the hills. Close to local amenities (including good pubs!), long/short walks from the door and tourist attractions (Chatsworth, Bakewell etc). Off-street parking.

OPEN All Year

3-night breaks available Nov-Apr.

Low season per wk £180.00–£210.00

High season per wk £245.00–£290.00

TOWN INDEX

This can be found at the back of the guide. If you know where you want to stay, the index will give you the page number listing accommodation in your chosen town, city or village.

A brief guide to the main Towns and Villages offering accommodation in the **Heart of England**

A **ABBERLEY, WORCESTERSHIRE -** Village with some interesting buildings including a pre-Reformation rectory and a Gothic clock tower with 20 bells. At Great Witley, nearby, is a magnificent 18th C church with rich plasterwork, paintings and carving and the gardens and ruins of Witley Court.

ALDERTON, GLOUCESTERSHIRE - Hillside village with wide views of Evesham Vale. The restored church has a 15th C tower, a broken Saxon font and some medieval glass. Some stone from the previous Norman church has been incorporated into its structure.

ALSTONEFIELD, STAFFORDSHIRE - Peaceful village, well situated for exploring the pleasant countryside of Dovedale, much of which is owned by the National Trust.

ASHBOURNE, DERBYSHIRE - Market town on the edge of the Peak District National Park and an excellent centre for walking. Its impressive church, with 212-ft spire, stands in an unspoilt old street. Ashbourne is well known for gingerbread and its Shrovetide football match.

ATHERSTONE, WARWICKSHIRE - Pleasant market town with some 18th C houses and interesting old inns. Every Shrove Tuesday a game of football is played in the streets, a tradition which dates from the 13th C. Twycross Zoo is nearby with an extensive collection of reptiles and butterflies.

B **BAKEWELL, DERBYSHIRE -** Pleasant market town, famous for its pudding. It is set in beautiful countryside on the River Wye and is an excellent centre for exploring the Derbyshire Dales, the Peak District National Park, Chatsworth and Haddon Hall.

BAMFORD, DERBYSHIRE - Village in the Peak District near the Upper Derwent Reservoirs of Ladybower, Derwent and Howden. An excellent centre for walking.

BARLOW, DERBYSHIRE - Lying 4 miles north-west of Chesterfield, its recorded history dates back to William the Conqueror. The major event is annual well-dressing week.

BASLOW, DERBYSHIRE - Small village on the River Derwent with a stone-built toll-house and a packhorse bridge. Chatsworth, home of the Duke of Devonshire, is nearby.

BEWDLEY, WORCESTERSHIRE - Attractive town on the River Severn, approached by a bridge designed by Telford. The town has many elegant buildings and an interesting craft and folk museum. On the Severn Valley Steam Railway.

BIBURY, GLOUCESTERSHIRE - Village on the River Coln with stone houses and the famous 17th C Arlington Row, former weavers' cottages. Arlington Mill is now a folk museum. Trout farm and Barnsley House Gardens, nearby, are open to the public.

BISHOP'S CASTLE, SHROPSHIRE - A 12th C Planned Town with a castle site at the top of the hill and a church at the bottom of the main street. There are many interesting buildings with original timber frames hidden behind present-day houses. On the Welsh border close to the Clun Forest in quiet, unspoilt countryside.

BLOCKLEY, GLOUCESTERSHIRE - This village's prosperity was founded in silk mills and other factories but now it is a quiet, unspoilt place. An excellent centre for exploring pretty Cotswold villages, especially Chipping Campden and Broadway.

BOURTON-ON-THE-WATER, GLOUCESTERSHIRE - The River Windrush flows through this famous Cotswold village which has a green and cottages and houses of Cotswold stone. Its many attractions include a model village, Birdland, a Motor Museum and the Cotswold Perfumery.

BRIDGNORTH, SHROPSHIRE - Red sandstone riverside town in 2 parts - High and Low - linked by a cliff railway. Much of interest including a ruined Norman keep, half-timbered 16th C houses, Midland Motor Museum and Severn Valley Railway.

BROAD CAMPDEN, GLOUCESTERSHIRE - Attractive village, with interesting church by Prichard of Llandaff, a mile outside the picturesque Cotswold town of Chipping Campden.

BROADWAY, WORCESTERSHIRE - Beautiful Cotswold village, called the "Show village of England", with 16th C stone houses and cottages. Near the village is Broadway Tower with magnificent views over 12 counties and a country park with nature trails and adventure playground.

BROMSGROVE, WORCESTERSHIRE - This market town near the Lickey Hills has an interesting museum and craft centre and 14th C church with fine tombs and a Carillon tower. The Avoncroft Museum of Buildings is nearby where many old buildings have been re-assembled, having been saved from destruction.

BURWARTON, SHROPSHIRE - Stately village between Ludlow and Bridgnorth, with the magnificent park of Burwarton Hall, an attractive Georgian inn and the ruin of an old Norman church.

C **CARSINGTON, DERBYSHIRE -** The visitor centre at Britain's newest reservoir, Carsington Water, allows visitors to learn about the surrounding countryside and wildlife. Around the reservoir many activities are available including cycling, sailing and horse-riding.

CHELTENHAM, GLOUCESTERSHIRE - Cheltenham was developed as a spa town in the 18th C and has some beautiful Regency architecture, in particular the Pittville Pump Room. It holds international music and literature festivals and is also famous for its race meetings and cricket.

CHESTERFIELD, DERBYSHIRE - Famous for the twisted spire of its parish church, Chesterfield has some fine modern buildings and excellent shopping facilities, including a large, traditional open-air market. Hardwick Hall and Bolsover Castle are nearby.

CHURCH STRETTON, SHROPSHIRE - Church Stretton lies under the eastern slope of the Longmynd surrounded by hills. It is ideal for walkers, with marvellous views, golf and gliding. Wenlock Edge is not far away.

CIRENCESTER, GLOUCESTERSHIRE - "Capital of the Cotswolds", Cirencester was Britain's second most important Roman town with many finds housed in the Corinium Museum. It has a very fine Perpendicular church and old houses around the market place.

CLUN, SHROPSHIRE - Small, ancient town on the Welsh border with flint and stone tools in its museum and Iron Age forts nearby. The impressive ruins of a Norman castle lie beside the River Clun, and there are some interesting 17th C houses.

COLEFORD, GLOUCESTERSHIRE - Small town in the Forest of Dean with the ancient iron mines at Clearwell Caves nearby, where mining equipment and geological samples are displayed. There are several forest trails in the area.

COMPTON ABDALE, GLOUCESTERSHIRE - High on the hills, this Cotswold village is quietly located 4 miles outside Northleach, off the main A40 towards Cheltenham, and is ideally located to tour the area and visit the main attractions.

CRESSBROOK, DERBYSHIRE - Delightful dale with stone hall and pleasant houses, steep wooded slopes and superb views.

D **DAGLINGWORTH, GLOUCESTERSHIRE -** Delightful village in the valley of the River Dunt near Cirencester, with a church which has remnants of Saxon work as well as 3 well-preserved sculptures. There is a medieval dovecote at the manor house.

DURSLEY, GLOUCESTERSHIRE - Market town with some Georgian houses and an 18th C arched market hall with a statue of Queen Anne. Nearby is the weaving village of Uley with 17th C houses.

E **EVESHAM, WORCESTERSHIRE -** Market town in the centre of a fruit-growing area. There are pleasant walks along the River Avon and many old houses and inns. A fine 16th C bell tower stands between 2 churches near the medieval Almonry Museum.

G **GLOUCESTER, GLOUCESTERSHIRE -** A Roman city and inland port, its cathedral is one of the most beautiful in Britain. Gloucester's many attractions include museums and the restored warehouses in the Victorian docks containing the National Waterways Museum, Robert Opie Packaging Collection and other attractions.

GOTHERINGTON, GLOUCESTERSHIRE - A small village 5 miles north of Cheltenham, at the edge of the Cotswolds, looking towards Langley Hill and Prescott Hill. Famous for the special classic car climbs. Close to Tewkesbury and Sudeley Castle.

GREAT HUCKLOW, DERBYSHIRE - Small village in the Peak District. Headquarters of the Derbyshire and Lancashire Gliding Club.

H **HARTINGTON, DERBYSHIRE -** Village with a large market-place set in fine surroundings near the River Dove, well known for its fishing and Izaak Walton, author of "The Compleat Angler".

HATHERSAGE, DERBYSHIRE - Hillside village in the Peak District, dominated by the church with many good brasses and monuments to the Eyre family which provide a link with Charlotte Bronte. Little John, friend of Robin Hood, is said to be buried here.

HAYFIELD, DERBYSHIRE - Village set in spectacular scenery at the highest point of the Peak District with the best approach to the Kinder Scout plateau via the Kinder Downfall. An excellent centre for walking. Three reservoirs close by.

HEREFORD, HEREFORDSHIRE - Agricultural county town, its cathedral containing much Norman work, a large chained library and the world-famous Mappa Mundi exhibition. Among the city's varied attractions are several museums, including the Cider Museum and the Old House.

I **IRONBRIDGE, SHROPSHIRE -** Small town on the Severn where the Industrial Revolution began. It has the world's first iron bridge, built in 1779. The Ironbridge Gorge Museum, of exceptional interest, comprises a rebuilt, turn-of-the-century town and sites spread over 6 square miles.

K **KENILWORTH, WARWICKSHIRE -** The main feature of the town is the ruined 12th C castle. It has many royal associations but was damaged by Cromwell. A good base for visiting Coventry, Leamington Spa and Warwick.

L **LEAMINGTON SPA, WARWICKSHIRE -** 18th C spa town with many fine Georgian and Regency houses and the refurbished 19th C Pump Rooms with Heritage Centre. The attractive Jephson Gardens are laid out alongside the river.

LEDBURY, HEREFORDSHIRE - Town with cobbled streets and many black and white timbered houses, including the 17th C market house and old inns. In attractive countryside nearby is Eastnor Castle, a venue for many events, with an interesting collection of tapestries and armour.

LEINTWARDINE, HEREFORDSHIRE - Attractive border village where the rivers Teme and Clun meet. It has some black and white cottages, old inns and an impressive church. It is near Hopton Castle and the beautiful scenery around Clun.

LEOMINSTER, HEREFORDSHIRE - The town owed its prosperity to wool, and has many interesting buildings, notably the timber-framed Grange Court, a former town hall. The impressive Norman priory church has 3 naves and a ducking stool. Berrington Hall (National Trust) is nearby.

LINCOLN, LINCOLNSHIRE - Ancient city dominated by the magnificent 11th C cathedral with its triple towers. A Roman gateway is still used and there are medieval houses lining narrow, cobbled streets. Other attractions include the Norman castle, several museums and the Usher Gallery.

LOUTH, LINCOLNSHIRE - Attractive old market town set on the eastern edge of the Lincolnshire Wolds. St James's Church has an impressive tower and spire and there are the remains of a Cistercian abbey. The museum contains an interesting collection of local material.

LUDLOW, SHROPSHIRE - Outstandingly interesting border town with a magnificent castle high above the River Teme, 2 half-timbered old inns and an impressive 15th C church. The Reader's House, with its 3-storey Jacobean porch, should also be seen.

LULLINGTON, DERBYSHIRE - In the extreme south of Derbyshire, near the Staffordshire border. Beautiful flowers and plants fill the village green, churchyard and gardens of the Great House.

LYDNEY, GLOUCESTERSHIRE - Small town in the Forest of Dean close to the River Severn, where Roman remains have been found. It has a steam centre with engines, coaches and wagons.

M **MALVERN, WORCESTERSHIRE -** A spa town in Victorian times, its water is today bottled and sold worldwide. Six resorts, set on the slopes of the Hills, form part of Malvern. Great Malvern Priory has splendid 15th C windows. It is an excellent walking centre.

MARKET RASEN, LINCOLNSHIRE - Market town on the edge of the Lincolnshire Wolds. The racecourse and the picnic site and forest walks at Willingham Woods are to the east of the town.

MATLOCK, DERBYSHIRE - The town lies beside the narrow valley of the River Derwent surrounded by steep, wooded hills. Good centre for exploring Derbyshire's best scenery.

MIDDLETON-BY-YOULGREAVE, DERBYSHIRE - Small hamlet nestling on the River Bradford, a mile from Youlgreave.

MILWICH, STAFFORDSHIRE - Village midway between Stone and Uttoxeter. The oldest-dated bell in Staffordshire, purported to have rung for Agincourt, is here.

MINSTERLEY, SHROPSHIRE - Village with a curious little church of 1692 and a fine old black and white hall. The lofty ridge, known as the Stiperstones, is 4 miles to the south.

MISERDEN, GLOUCESTERSHIRE - Village in wooded valley country with a church of late Saxon origin. The Camp is a hamlet with an interesting group of old houses, and Miserden Park Gardens can be visited between April and September.

MORETON-IN-MARSH, GLOUCESTERSHIRE - Attractive town of Cotswold stone with 17th C houses, an ideal base for touring the Cotswolds. Some of the local attractions include Batsford Park Arboretum, the Jacobean Chastleton House and Sezincote Garden.

N **NEWENT, GLOUCESTERSHIRE -** Small town with the largest collection of birds of prey in Europe at the Falconry Centre. Flying demonstrations daily. Glass workshop where visitors can watch glass being blown. There is a "seconds" shop. North of the village are the Three Choirs Vineyards.

NORTHAMPTON, NORTHAMPTONSHIRE - A bustling town and a shoe-manufacturing centre, with excellent shopping facilities, several museums and parks, a theatre and a concert hall. Several old churches include 1 of only 4 round churches in Britain.

NOTTINGHAM, NOTTINGHAMSHIRE - Attractive modern city with a rich history. Outside its castle, now a museum, is Robin Hood's statue. Attractions include "The Tales of Robin Hood"; the Lace Hall; Wollaton Hall; museums and excellent facilities for shopping, sports and entertainment.

O **OSWESTRY, SHROPSHIRE -** Town close to the Welsh border, the scene of many battles. To the north are the remains of a large Iron Age hill fort. An excellent centre for exploring Shropshire and Offa's Dyke.

OUNDLE, NORTHAMPTONSHIRE - Historic town situated on the River Nene with narrow alleys and courtyards and many stone buildings, including a fine church and historic inns.

OWLPEN, GLOUCESTERSHIRE - Near the Severn Estuary, the 15th C Owlpen Manor (open to visitors April-September), together with its outbuildings and church, forms a delightful group of Cotswold-stone buildings. The weaving village of Uley, with its 17th C houses, is close by.

P **PEMBRIDGE, HEREFORDSHIRE -** Delightful village close to the Welsh border with many black and white half-timbered cottages, some dating from the 14th C. There is a market hall supported by 8 wooden pillars in the market place, also old inns and a 14th C church with interesting separate bell tower.

R **ROSS-ON-WYE, HEREFORDSHIRE -** Attractive market town with a 17th C market hall, set above the River Wye. There are lovely views over the surrounding countryside from the Prospect, and the town is close to Goodrich Castle and the Welsh border.

RUGBY, WARWICKSHIRE - Town famous for its public school which gave its name to Rugby Union football and which featured in "Tom Brown's Schooldays".

S **SHREWSBURY, SHROPSHIRE -** Beautiful historic town on the River Severn retaining many fine old timber-framed houses. Its attractions include Rowley's Museum with Roman finds, remains of a castle, Clive House Museum, St Chad's 18th C round church, rowing on the river and the Shrewsbury Flower Show in August.

SKEGNESS, LINCOLNSHIRE - Famous seaside resort with 6 miles of sandy beaches and bracing air. Attractions include swimming pools, bowling greens, gardens, Natureland Marine Zoo, golf courses and a wide range of entertainment at the Embassy Centre. Nearby is Gibraltar Point Nature Reserve.

SOUTH CERNEY, GLOUCESTERSHIRE - The 15,000 acres of lakes and ponds and several Country Parks are being developed at South Cerney as the Cotswold Water Park, for sailing, fishing, bird-watching and other recreational activities.

SOUTHWELL, NOTTINGHAMSHIRE - Town dominated by the Norman minster which has some beautiful 13th C stone carvings in the Chapter House. Charles I spent his last night of freedom in one of the inns. The original Bramley apple tree can still be seen.

SPILSBY, LINCOLNSHIRE - Market town in attractive countryside on the edge of the Lincolnshire Wolds and the Fens. Birthplace of explorer Sir John Franklin, and it has associations with the poet Tennyson, born in nearby Somersby. There is a medieval market cross.

STAFFORD, STAFFORDSHIRE - The town has a long history, and some half-timbered buildings still remain, notably the 16th C High House. There are several museums in the town, and Shugborough Hall and the famous angler Izaak Walton's cottage, now a museum, are nearby.

STANTON, GLOUCESTERSHIRE - Unspoilt Cotswold village with picturesque stone houses built around 1600. The church dates from Norman times but has 20th C furnishings and glass. Nearby is Stanway House, a Jacobean manor, open to summer visitors, and ruins of Hailes Abbey (English Heritage).

STANTON-ON-THE-WOLDS, NOTTINGHAMSHIRE - Quiet village with golf course, just off the main route between Nottingham and Melton Mowbray, giving easy access to nearby attractions.

STOKE-ON-TRENT, STAFFORDSHIRE - Famous for its pottery. Factories of several famous makers, including Josiah Wedgwood, can be visited. The City Museum has one of the finest pottery and porcelain collections in the world.

STOW-ON-THE-WOLD, GLOUCESTERSHIRE - Attractive Cotswold wool town with a large market-place and some fine houses, especially the old grammar school. There is an interesting church dating from Norman times. Stow-on-the-Wold is surrounded by lovely countryside and Cotswold villages.

STRATFORD-UPON-AVON, WARWICKSHIRE - Famous as Shakespeare's home town, Stratford's many attractions include his birthplace, New Place where he died, the Royal Shakespeare Theatre and Gallery and Hall's Croft (his daughter's house).

STROUD, GLOUCESTERSHIRE - This old town, surrounded by attractive hilly country, has been producing broadcloth for centuries; the local museum has an interesting display on the subject. Many of the mills have been converted into centres for craft and other uses.

U **UPPINGHAM, RUTLAND -** Quiet market town dominated by its famous public school which was founded in 1584. It has many stone houses and is surrounded by attractive countryside.

UPTON ST LEONARDS, GLOUCESTERSHIRE - Village in a lovely setting below hills, with many old houses and a part-Norman church.

UPTON-UPON-SEVERN, WORCESTERSHIRE - Attractive country town on the banks of the Severn and a good river-cruising centre. It has many pleasant old houses and inns, and the pepperpot landmark is now the Heritage Centre.

W **WARWICK, WARWICKSHIRE -** Castle rising above the River Avon, 15th C Beauchamp Chapel attached to St Mary's Church, medieval Lord Leycester's Hospital almshouses and several museums. Nearby is Ashorne Hall and the National Heritage Museum at Gaydon.

WELLINGTON, SHROPSHIRE - On the west side of Telford district, under the Wrekin and with easy access to Shrewsbury and Ironbridge.

WHITBOURNE, HEREFORDSHIRE - Large parish on both sides of the Worcester to Bromyard road, the location of a medieval moated building, once the palace of the Bishops of Hereford. In the delightfully peaceful village are some houses of cruck construction and some unusual 16th C brick chimneys.

WINCHCOMBE, GLOUCESTERSHIRE - Ancient town with a folk museum and railway museum. To the south lies Sudeley Castle with its fine collection of paintings and toys and an Elizabethan garden.

WOODHALL SPA, LINCOLNSHIRE - Attractive town which was formerly a spa. It has excellent sporting facilities, with a championship golf course, and is surrounded by pine woods.

WORCESTER, WORCESTERSHIRE - Lovely riverside city dominated by its Norman and early English cathedral, King John's burial place. There are many old buildings, including the 15th C Commandery and the 18th C Guildhall. There are several museums and the Royal Worcester porcelain factory.

WYTHALL, WORCESTERSHIRE - On the southern outskirts of Birmingham heading towards Evesham.

Y **YARDLEY GOBION, NORTHAMPTONSHIRE -** Picturesque village in the southern tip of the county near the Grand Union Canal. Some expansion since the 1950s.

YOULGREAVE, DERBYSHIRE - Small town in the Peak District with an impressive church, much of which dates from Norman times. There are some interesting monuments in the church and stained glass by William Morris. The stone circle of Arbor Low is nearby.

RATING **All accommodation in this guide has been rated, or is awaiting a rating, by a trained VisitBritain assessor.**

Finding
accommodation
is as easy as **1 2 3**

Where to Stay makes it quick and easy to find a place to stay. There are several ways to use this guide.

1

TOWN INDEX

The town index at the back, lists all the places with accommodation featured in the regional sections. The index gives a page number where you can find full accommodation and contact details.

2

COLOUR MAPS

All the place names in black on the colour maps at the front have an entry in the regional sections. Refer to the town index for the page number where you will find one or more establishments offering accommodation in your chosen town or village.

3

ACCOMMODATION LISTING

Contact details for **all** VisitBritain assessed accommodation throughout England, together with their national Star rating are given in the listing section of this guide. Establishments with a full entry in the regional sections are shown in blue. Look in the town index for the page number on which their full entry appears.

East of England

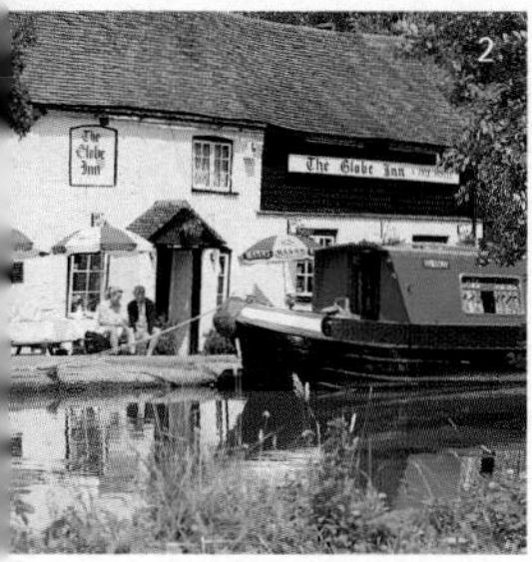

Discover England as you always thought it should be. Gently rolling countryside and unspoilt coastline, excellent for cycling, walking and bird-watching. Explore charming villages, historic market towns, traditional seaside resorts and bustling cities; awesome gothic cathedrals, magnificent stately homes and famous gardens.

Classic sights
Hatfield House – childhood home of Queen Elizabeth I
Blickling Hall – one of England's greatest Jacobean houses
Sutton Hoo – important burial site of Anglo-Saxon kings

Coast and country
The Chilterns – beautiful chalk life flora and fauna at the regions highest point
The Norfolk Broads – miles of reed-fringed waterways, man-made broads and nature reserves
The Fens – unique panorama of rivers and dykes, wide open skies and unforgettable sunsets

Glorious gardens
Anglesey Abbey – outstanding all year round gardens
The Gardens of the Rose – wander amongst 30,000 rose species
RHS Garden: Hyde Hall – rose, water and woodland gardens

Arts for all
Aldeburgh festival – internationally acclaimed festival of music and the arts
Luton Carnival – Britain's biggest one-day carnival

Delightfully different
Stilton – where each May they roll wooden cheeses down the High Street
St. Peters-on-the Wall – oldest Saxon church in England

The Counties of Bedfordshire, Cambridgeshire, Essex, Hertfordshire, Norfolk and Suffolk

For more information contact:
East of England Tourist Board
Toppesfield Hall, Hadleigh,
Suffolk IP7 5DN

E: jbowers@eetb.org.uk
www.eastofenglandtouristboard.com

Telephone enquiries -
T: 0870 225 4800
F: 0870 225 4890

1. Punting on the River Cam, Cambridge
2. Globe Inn, Linslade, Bedfordshire

Places to Visit

You will find hundreds of interesting places to visit during your stay, just some of which are listed in these pages. Contact any Tourist Information Centre in the region for more ideas on days out.

QUALITY ASSURED VISITOR ATTRACTION — Awarded VisitBritain's 'Quality Assured Visitor Attraction' marque.

Audley End House and Park (English Heritage)
Audley End, Saffron Walden
Tel: (01799) 522399
www.english-heritage.org.uk
A palatial Jacobean house remodelled in the 18th-19thC with a magnificent great hall with 17thC plaster ceilings. Rooms and furniture by Robert Adam and park by 'Capability' Brown.

Banham Zoo
Banham, Norwich
Tel: (01953) 887771
www.banhamzoo.co.uk
Wildlife spectacular which will take you on a journey to experience tigers, leopards and zebra and some of the world's most exotic, rare and endangered animals.

Barleylands Farm
Barleylands Road, Billericay
Tel: (01268) 290229
www.barleylandsfarm.co.uk
Visitor centre with a rural museum, animal centre, craft studios, blacksmith's shop, glass-blowing studio with a viewing gallery, miniature steam railway and a restaurant.

Blickling Hall (National Trust)
Blickling, Norwich
Tel: (01263) 738030 www.nationaltrust.org.uk
A Jacobean redbrick mansion with garden, orangery, parkland and lake. There is also a display of fine tapestries and furniture.

Bressingham Steam Experience and Gardens
Bressingham, Diss
Tel: (01379) 686900 www.bressingham.co.uk
Steam rides through 4 miles (6.5km) of woodland. Six acres (2.5ha) of the Island Beds plant centre. Main line locomotives, the Victorian Gallopers and over 50 steam engines.

Bure Valley Railway
Aylsham Station, Norwich
Tel: (01263) 733858 www.bvrw.co.uk
A 15-inch narrow-gauge steam railway covering 9 miles (14.5km) of track from Wroxham in the heart of the Norfolk Broads to the bustling market town of Aylsham.

Colchester Castle
Castle Park, Colchester
Tel: (01206) 282939
www.colchestermuseums.org.uk
A Norman keep on the foundations of a Roman temple. The archaeological material includes much on Roman Colchester (Camulodunum).

Colchester Zoo
Stanway, Colchester
Tel: (01206) 331292
www.colchester-zoo.co.uk
Zoo with 200 species and some of the best cat and primate collections in the UK, 60 acres (24ha) of gardens and lakes, award-winning animal enclosures and picnic areas.

Ely Cathedral
The College, Ely
Tel: (01353) 667735
www.cathedral.ely.anglican.org.uk
One of England's finest cathedrals with guided tours and tours of the Octagon and West Tower, monastic precincts and also a brass rubbing centre and Stained Glass Museum.

Fritton Lake Country World
Fritton, Great Yarmouth
Tel: (01493) 488208
www.frittonlake.co.uk
A 250-acre (100-ha) centre with a children's assault course, putting, an adventure playground, golf, fishing, boating, wildfowl, heavy horses, cart rides, falconry and flying displays.

The Gardens of the Rose
Chiswell Green, St Albans
Tel: (01727) 850461 www.roses.co.uk
The Royal National Rose Society's Garden with 27 acres (11ha) of garden and trial grounds for new varieties of rose. 30,000 roses of all types and 1,700 different varieties are on display .

Hatfield House, Park and Gardens
Hatfield
Tel: (01707) 287010
www.hatfield-house.co.uk
Magnificent Jacobean house, home of the Marquess of Salisbury. Exquisite gardens, model soldiers and park trails. Childhood home of Queen Elizabeth I.

Hedingham Castle
Castle Hedingham, Halstead
Tel: (01787) 460261
www.hedinghamcastle.co.uk
The finest Norman keep in England, built in 1140 by the deVeres, Earls of Oxford. Visited by Kings Henry VII and VIII and Queen Elizabeth I and besieged by King John.

Holkham Hall
Wells-next-the-Sea
Tel: (01328) 710806
www.holkham.co.uk
A classic 18thC Palladian-style mansion. Part of a great agricultural estate and a living treasure house of artistic and architectural history along with a bygones collection.

Ickworth House, Park and Gardens (National Trust)
Horringer, Bury St Edmunds
Tel: (01284) 735270 www.nationaltrust.org.uk
An extraordinary oval house with flanking wings, begun in 1795. Fine paintings, a beautiful collection of Georgian silver, an Italian garden and stunning parkland.

Imperial War Museum Duxford
Duxford, Cambridge
Tel: (01223) 835000 www.iwm.org.uk
Almost 200 aircraft on display with tanks, vehicles and guns, an adventure playground, shops and a restaurant.

Kentwell Hall
Long Melford, Sudbury
Tel: (01787) 310207 www.kentwell.co.uk
Tudor manor house, still a lived-in family home. Winner of the '2001 Heritage Building of the Year' in the Good Britain Guide.

Knebworth House, Gardens and Park
Knebworth, Stevenage
Tel: (01438) 812661
www.knebworthhouse.com
Tudor manor house, re-fashioned in the 19thC, housing a collection of manuscripts, portraits and Jacobean banquet hall. Formal gardens, parkland and adventure playground.

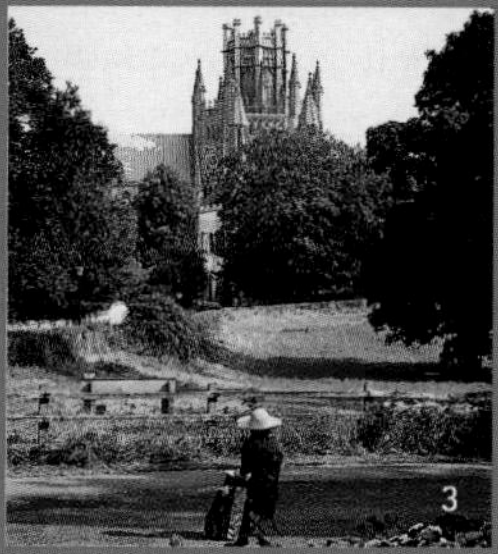

1. River Wensum, Norfolk
2. Cambridge
3. Ely Cathedral

Leighton Buzzard Railway
Page's Park Station, Leighton Buzzard
Tel: (01525) 373888 www.buzzrail.co.uk
An authentic narrow-gauge light railway, built in 1919, offering a 65 minute return journey into the Bedfordshire countryside.

Marsh Farm Country Park
South Woodham Ferrers, Chelmsford
Tel: (01245) 321552
www.marshfarmcountrypark.co.uk
A farm centre with sheep, a pig unit, free-range chickens, milking demonstrations, an indoor and outdoor adventure play areas, nature reserve, walks, picnic area and pet's corner.

Melford Hall (National Trust)
Long Melford, Sudbury
Tel: (01787) 880286
www.nationaltrust.org.uk/eastanglia
Turreted brick Tudor mansion with 18thC and Regency interiors. Collection of Chinese porcelain, gardens and a walk in the grounds. Dogs on leads, where permitted.

National Horseracing Museum and Tours
99 High Street, Newmarket
Tel: (01638) 667333 www.nhrm.co.uk
Award-winning display of the people and horses involved in racing's amazing history. Minibus tours to gallops, stables and equine pool. Hands-on gallery with horse simulator.

National Stud
Newmarket
Tel: (01638) 663464 x203
www.nationalstud.co.uk
A conducted tour which includes top thoroughbred stallions, mares and foals, and gives an insight into the day to day running of a modern stud farm.

New Pleasurewood Hills Leisure Park
Corton, Lowestoft
Tel: (01502) 586000
www.pleasurewoodhills.co.uk
Tidal wave watercoaster, log flume, chairlift, 2 railways, pirate ship, parrot/sealion shows, go-karts and rattlesnake coaster. Mega-Drop Tower and new circus theatre shows.

Norfolk Lavender Limited
Heacham, King's Lynn
Tel: (01485) 570384
www.norfolk-lavender.co.uk
Find out how lavender is distilled from the flowers and the oil made into a wide range of gifts. There is a slide show when the distillery is not working.

Norwich Cathedral
62 The Close, Norwich
Tel: (01603) 218321 www.cathedral.org.uk
A Norman cathedral from 1096 with 14thC roof bosses depicting bible scenes from Adam and Eve to the Day of Judgement, cloisters, cathedral close, shop and restaurant.

Oliver Cromwell's House
29 St Marys Street, Ely
Tel: (01353) 662062
www.elyeastcambs.co.uk
The family home of Oliver Cromwell with a 17thC kitchen, parlour, a haunted bedroom, a Tourist Information Centre, souvenirs and gift shop.

Peter Beales Roses
London Road, Attleborough
Tel: (01953) 454707 www.classicroses.co.uk
2.5-acre (1-ha) rose garden displaying most of the company's collection of 1200 varieties of roses, plus the national collection of Rosa species.

Pleasure Beach
South Beach Parade, Great Yarmouth
Tel: (01493) 844585 www.pleasure-beach.co.uk
Rollercoaster, Terminator, log flume, Twister, monorail, galloping horses, caterpillar, ghost train and fun house. Height restrictions are in force on some rides.

The Royal Air Force Air Defence Radar Museum
RAF Neatishead, Norwich
Tel: (01692) 633309
www.neatishead.raf.mod.uk
History of the development and use of radar in the UK and overseas from 1935 to date. Winner of the Regional Visitor Attraction (under 100,000 visitors). National Silver Award.

RSPB Minsmere Nature Reserve
Westleton, Saxmundham
Tel: (01728) 648281 www.rspb.org.uk
RSPB reserve on Suffolk coast with bird-watching hides and trails, year-round events and guided walk and visitor centre with large shop and welcoming tearoom.

Sainsbury Centre for Visual Arts
University of East Anglia, Norwich
Tel: (01603) 593199 www.uea.ac.uk/scva
Housing the Sainsbury Collection of works by artists such as Picasso, Bacon and Henry Moore alongside many objects of pottery and art from across time and cultures.

Sandringham
Sandringham, King's Lynn
Tel: (01553) 612908
www.sandringhamestate.co.uk
The country retreat of HM The Queen. A delightful house and 60 acres (24ha) of grounds and lakes. There is also a museum of royal vehicles and royal memorabilia.

Shuttleworth Collection
Old Warden Aerodrome, Biggleswade
Tel: (01767) 627288 www.shuttleworth.org
A unique historical collection of aircraft from a 1909 Bleriot to a 1942 Spitfire in flying condition and cars dating from an 1898 Panhard in running order.

Somerleyton Hall and Gardens
Somerleyton, Lowestoft
Tel: (01502) 730224
www.somerleyton.co.uk
Early Victorian stately mansion in Anglo-Italian style, with lavish features and fine state rooms. Beautiful 12-acre (5-ha) gardens, with historic Yew hedge maze, gift shop.

Stondon Museum
Henlow
Tel: (01462) 850339
www.transportmuseum.co.uk
A museum with transport exhibits from the early 1900s to the 1980s. The largest private collection in England of bygone vehicles from the beginning of the century.

Thursford Collection
Thursford, Fakenham
Tel: (01328) 878477
A live musical show with 9 mechanical organs and a Wurlitzer show starring Robert Wolfe.

Wimpole Hall and Home Farm (National Trust)
Arrington, Royston
Tel: (01223) 207257 www.wimpole.org
An 18thC house in a landscaped park with a folly, Chinese bridge, plunge bath and yellow drawing room in the house, the work of John Soane. Home Farm has a rare breeds centre.

Woburn Abbey
Woburn, Milton Keynes
Tel: (01525) 290666 www.woburnabbey.co.uk
An 18thC Palladian mansion, altered by Henry Holland, the Prince Regent's architect, containing a collection of English silver, French and English furniture and art.

Woburn Safari Park
Woburn, Milton Keynes
Tel: (01525) 290407
www.woburnsafari.co.uk
Drive through the safari park with 30 species of animals in natural groups just a windscreen's width away plus the action-packed Wild World Leisure Area.

1. Theme Park, Essex

East of England Tourist Board

Toppesfield Hall, Hadleigh, Suffolk IP7 5DN

T: 0870 225 4800 F: 0870 225 4890

E: jbowers@eetb.org.uk

www.eastofenglandtouristboard.com

THE FOLLOWING PUBLICATIONS ARE AVAILABLE FROM THE EAST OF ENGLAND TOURIST BOARD:

Great days out in the East of England 2004 – an information-packed A5 guide featuring all you need to know about places to visit and things to see and do in the East of England. From historic houses to garden centres, from animal collections to craft centres - this guide has it all, including film and TV locations, city, town and village information, events, shopping, car tours plus lots more! (£4.50 excl p&p)

England's Cycling Country – the East of England offers perfect cycling country - from quiet country lanes to ancient trackways. This free publication promotes the many Cycling Discovery Maps that are available to buy (£1.50 excl p&p), as well as providing useful information for anyone planning a cycling tour of the region

Getting to the East of England

BY ROAD: The region is easily accessible. From London and the south via the A1(M), M11, M25, A10, M1, A46 and A12. From the north via the A1(M), A15, A5, M1 and A6. From the west via the A14, A47, A421, A428, A418, A41, A422, A17 and A427.

BY RAIL: Regular fast trains run to all major cities and towns in the region. London stations which serve the region are Liverpool Street, Kings Cross, Fenchurch Street, St Pancras, London Marylebone and London Euston. Bedford, Luton and St Albans are on the Thameslink line which runs to Kings Cross and on to London Gatwick Airport. There is also a direct link between London Stansted Airport and Liverpool Street. Through the Channel Tunnel, there are trains direct from Paris and Brussels to Waterloo Station, London. A short journey on the Underground will bring passengers to those stations operating services into the East of England. Further information on rail journeys in the East of England can be obtained on 08457 484 950.

1

1. Windmill, Norfolk

Where to stay in the

East of England

All place names in the blue bands under which accommodation is listed, are shown on the maps at the front of this guide.

Symbols give useful information about services and facilities. Inside the back cover flap there's a key to these symbols which you can keep open for easy reference.

A complete listing of all the VisitBritain assessed accommodation covered by this guide appears at the back of this guide.

ALDEBURGH, Suffolk Map ref 3C2 *Tourist Information Centre Tel: (01728) 453637*

★★★

1 Unit
Sleeping 4

AMBER COTTAGE

Aldeburgh
Contact: Mr R Williams
T: (01359) 270444
F: (01359) 271226
E: roger.williams43@virgin.net
I: www.cottageguide.co.uk/ambercottage

Superb new property overlooking the Moor Green, foreshore and sea. One double bedroom with large balcony. Feature bathroom has Whirlpool spa. Double sofa bed in large lounge/diner. Power shower in ground floor bathroom. Fully equipped, luxury kitchen with breakfast bar. More pictures on website. No children, no pets, no smoking.

OPEN All Year

Short breaks available Oct-Feb (excl Christmas and New Year).

Low season per wk
£250.00–£350.00
High season per wk
£350.00–£450.00

QUALITY ASSURANCE SCHEME

Star ratings were correct at the time of going to press but are subject to change. Please check at the time of booking.

ALDEBURGH continued

★★★★

1 Unit
Sleeping 3

CRAGSIDE

Aldeburgh, Ipswich
Contact: Mrs L Valentine, Rookery Farm, Cratfield, Halesworth IP19 0QE
T: (01986) 798609
F: (01986) 798609
E: j.r.valentine@btinternet.com

Deceptively spacious accommodation in large house on Crag Path, recently completely refurbished. Twenty yards sea. Well equipped for a really comfortable holiday with two TVs, microwave, dishwasher, washer/dryer, telephone/answerphone. Inglenook fireplaces. Cosy for winter with central heating, down duvets, electric blankets. No pets and no children, please.

OPEN All Year

Short breaks available Oct-Mar. Minimum 3-night stay.

Low season per wk
£200.00–£280.00
High season per wk
£280.00–£370.00

★★★

1 Unit
Sleeping 4

THE DUTCH HOUSE FLAT

Aldeburgh
Contact: Mr C Bacon, Dodnash Priory Farm, Bentley, Ipswich IP9 2DF
T: (01473) 310682
F: (01473) 311131
E: cbacon@freeuk.com

Recently created, centrally heated ground floor flat in high street position near sea and shops. Two bedrooms, one double and one twin. Galley kitchen fully fitted with microwave, dishwasher and washing machine. Tastefully furnished accommodation. Lounge/dining room with stereo TV/VCR.

OPEN All Year

Weekend breaks available in low season.

Low season per wk
£300.00–£310.00
High season per wk
£320.00–£360.00

★★★

1 Unit
Sleeping 13

ORLANDO

Aldeburgh
Contact: Mr P Hatcher, Martlesham Hall, Church Lane, Martlesham, Woodbridge IP12 4PQ
T: (01394) 382126
F: (01394) 278600
E: orlando@hatcher.co.uk
I: www.hatcher/co.uk/orlando

Orlando is a spacious, six-bedroomed house adjacent to the beach with magnificent, panoramic views of the sea. The house is well equipped with all modern facilities. There is an open-plan kitchen with Aga and dining area for sociable meals. Two living rooms on two floors – ideal for grown-ups and kids alike.

OPEN All Year

Low season per wk
£600.00–£1,300.00
High season per wk
£1,300.00–£1,700.00

CREDIT CARD BOOKINGS **If you book by telephone and are asked for your credit card number it is advisable to check the proprietor's policy should you cancel your reservation.**

ALDEBURGH continued

★★★★★

1 Unit
Sleeping 2

Parklands is a ground floor apartment in a newly restored, imposing country house set in three acres, close to Thorpness, Minsmere and Snape Maltings. Twin-bedded accommodation offers five-star luxury in a very peaceful setting. Brochure available.

PARKLANDS

Aldringham, Nr Aldeburgh
Contact: Mr & Mrs R Allen, Garden Suite,
6 Aldringham House, Leiston Road, Aldringham, Leiston
IP16 4PT
T: (01728) 830139
F: (01728) 831034
E: aldringham@supanet.com
I: www.aldringham@supanet.com

OPEN All Year

Short breaks available
Oct–Jun.

Low season per wk
£200.00–£245.00
High season per wk
£245.00–£275.00

ALRESFORD, Essex Map ref 3B2

★★★

1 Unit
Sleeping 2

CREEK LODGE

Alresford, Colchester
Contact: Mrs P J Mountney, Creek Lodge, Ford Lane,
Alresford, Colchester CO7 8BE
T: (01206) 825411

OPEN All Year

Tranquil riverside cottage set in extensive landscaped gardens, perfectly situated for sailing, walking and bird-watching. Only five miles from historic Colchester.

Low season per wk
£150.00
High season per wk
£230.00

BECCLES, Suffolk Map ref 3C1

★★★

1 Unit
Sleeping 6

9 THE MALTINGS

Beccles
Contact: Mrs B Lanchester & Mr Birch
T: (01502) 717362
F: (01502) 711888
E: bircharch@aol.com

OPEN All Year except
Christmas

Riverside, converted maltings. Large, galleried living room. Two twin-bedded rooms (plus double sofa bed in living room). Kitchen and bathroom (ground floor). Adjacent moorings.

Low season per wk
£175.00–£320.00
High season per wk
£320.00–£450.00

BERKHAMSTED, Hertfordshire Map ref 2D1

★★★

2 Units
Sleeping 5

HOLLY TREE & JACK'S COTTAGE

Berkhamsted
Contact: Mrs D Barrington, 20 & 21 Ringshall,
Little Gaddesden, Berkhamsted HP4 1ND
T: (01442) 843464
F: (01442) 842051
E: rbbarrington@aol.com

OPEN All Year

Restored, period cottages with all modern amenities, large garden, parking. Set in NT village. London 28 miles. Excellent road and rail connections.

Low season per wk
Min £275.00
High season per wk
Max £350.00

CHECK THE MAPS

The colour maps at the front of this guide show all the cities, towns and villages for which you will find accommodation entries. Refer to the town index to find the page on which they are listed.

BILLERICAY, Essex Map ref 3B3

★★★★★

1 Unit
Sleeping 6

The apartment is on two floors and luxuriously furnished, with air conditioning. The accommodation comprises two living rooms, fully fitted kitchen/diner and the option of one, two or three bedrooms with one, two or three bath/shower rooms. Guests have use of heated outdoor pool (May-September), hot tub, gazebo and gardens. Personal supervision.

THE PUMP HOUSE APARTMENT

Billericay
Contact: Mrs E R Bayliss, Pump House, Church Street, Great Burstead, Billericay CM11 2TR
T: (01277) 656579
F: (01277) 631160
E: john.bayliss@willmottdixon.co.uk
I: www.thepumphouseapartment.co.uk

OPEN All Year
CC: Amex, Mastercard, Visa

5% discount for stays of 4 weeks. 10% discount for stays of 8 weeks against 2/3-bedroom options.

Low season per wk
£425.00–£850.00
High season per wk
£550.00–£950.00

BLAKENEY, Norfolk Map ref 3B1

★★★

3 Units
Sleeping 4–8

THE TANNING HOUSE
Blakeney, Holt
Contact: Mrs B Pope, The Lodge, Back Lane, Blakeney, Holt NR25 7NR
T: (01263) 740477
F: (01263) 741356

OPEN All Year

Low season per wk
£455.00–£555.00
High season per wk
£555.00–£730.00

Barn conversion in quiet cul-de-sac facing the harbour. Open log fires, ample parking. Local amenities. Ideal for golf, bird-watching, sailing, riding, walking.

BRANCASTER, Norfolk Map ref 3B1

★★★

5 Units
Sleeping 7–10

Beautifully restored, fully fitted, traditional-flint farm cottages. Stunning location, remote yet accessible to local amenities. Unspoilt rolling farmland, woodland, long empty beaches, cosy pubs, RSPB nature reserves, log fires, barbecues, gardens, tennis court, high chairs, cots, stairgates, wooden playhouse, linen supplied, laundry, microwave ovens, TVs, videos, radios, dishwashers.

THOMPSON BRANCASTER FARMS

Brancaster, King's Lynn
Contact: Mrs S Lane, 4 Stiffkey Road, Warham, Wells-next-the-Sea NR23 1NP
T: 07885 269538
F: (01328) 710144
E: info@tbfholidayhomes.co.uk
I: www.tbfholidayhomes.co.uk

OPEN All Year
CC: Delta, Mastercard, Solo, Switch, Visa

Open all year – short breaks available (excl peak times).

Low season per wk
£360.00–£430.00
High season per wk
£800.00–£953.00

COUNTRY CODE Always follow the Country Code · Enjoy the countryside and respect its life and work · Guard against all risk of fire · Fasten all gates · Keep your dogs under close control · Keep to public paths across farmland · Use gates and stiles to cross fences, hedges and walls · Leave livestock, crops and machinery alone · Take your litter home · Help to keep all water clean · Protect wildlife, plants and trees · Take special care on country roads · Make no unnecessary noise

BRANCASTER STAITHE, Norfolk Map ref 3B1 *Tourist Information Centre Tel: (01485) 210256*

★★★

2 Units
Sleeping 2–6

VISTA & CARPENTERS COTTAGES

Brancaster Staithe, King's Lynn
Contact: Mrs G J Smith, Dale View, Main Road, Brancaster Staithe, King's Lynn PE31 8BY
T: (01485) 210497
F: (01485) 210497

These lovely cottages enjoy one of the best views along the Norfolk coast (see picture). Walking down the cottage gardens you meet the saltmarsh and the Norfolk coastal path. The cottages have exposed beams and open fires as well as central heating throughout. Close to amenities. Pets welcome.

OPEN All Year

Short breaks (weekend and mid-week) available during low season or at short notice; minimum 3 nights.

Low season per wk
£210.00–£360.00
High season per wk
£300.00–£750.00

BROME, Suffolk Map ref 3B2

★★★★

1 Unit
Sleeping 4

THE HOMESTEAD BARN

Brome, Eye
Contact: Mr & Mrs D Downes, The Homestead Barn, Brome, Eye IP23 8AE
T: (01379) 870489
E: dianadownes@hotmail.com

Delightful Grade II Listed converted barn with exposed beams. Situated on smallholding, in small village within easy reach of coast. Central to Norwich, Bury St Edmonds, Ipswich. Large fenced garden/patio. Secure parking. Two bedrooms. Fully equipped kitchen. Comfortable sitting room. Available all year round.

OPEN All Year

Short breaks available Oct-Mar. Minimum 3 nights. £100.

Low season per wk
£200.00–£250.00
High season per wk
£250.00–£300.00

BURNHAM MARKET, Norfolk Map ref 3B1

★★★

1 Unit
Sleeping 6

BARLEY COTTAGE

Burnham Market, King's Lynn
Contact: Mr & Mrs A J Watley, 26 Mount Crescent, Brentwood CM14 5DB
T: (01277) 218116
E: a.s.watley@btinternet.com

OPEN All Year

Low season per wk
£200.00–£325.00
High season per wk
£325.00–£480.00

Brick and flint wood-beamed cottage, full of charm and character. Super village shops, sandy beaches, Titchwell Reserve. Visitors' book speaks for itself.

CAMBRIDGE, Cambridgeshire Map ref 2D1 *Tourist Information Centre Tel: 0906 586 2526 (premium rate number)*

★★★

1 Unit
Sleeping 4

GLEBE COTTAGE

Hardwick, Cambridge
Contact: Mrs F M Key
T: (01954) 212895
E: info@camcottage.co.uk
I: www.camcottage.co.uk

OPEN All Year except Christmas

Low season per wk
£190.00–£250.00
High season per wk
£250.00–£350.00

Ideally situated next to village church and pub, but only 10 minutes' drive from Cambridge! Lovely views from front with secluded garden at back. Single parking space.

WEB

www.visitengland.com
Log on for information and inspiration. The latest information on places to visit, events and quality assessed accommodation.

CAMBRIDGE continued

★★★-★★★★★

5 Units
Sleeping 2–5

HOME FROM HOME APARTMENTS

Cambridge
Contact: Mrs E Fasano, Bungalow rear of 78 Milton Road, Cambridge CB4 1LA
T: (01223) 323555
F: (01223) 236078
E: homefromhome@tesco.net
I: www.homefromhomecambridge.co.uk

OPEN All Year
CC: Amex, Delta, JCB, Mastercard, Solo, Switch, Visa

Low season per wk
£325.00–£420.00
High season per wk
£350.00–£560.00

Victorian house centrally located to river and colleges. Apartments are fully equipped and furnished to a high standard. Smoking is not permitted.

★★★★

1 Unit
Sleeping 8

THE SCHOOL HOUSE

Horningsea, Cambridge
Contact: Mr & Mrs T F Mann, The School House, High Street, Horningsea, Cambridge CB5 9JG
T: (01223) 440077
F: (01223) 441414
E: schoolhse1@aol.com

A wonderful Victorian headmaster's house situated in an unspoilt village four miles from Cambridge city centre. Three/four bedrooms, two bathrooms, garden room, patio garden. Beautiful interior, very well equipped. Local riverside walks and traditional pubs. A full brochure on request.

OPEN All Year except Christmas
CC: Delta, JCB, Mastercard, Solo, Switch, Visa

Low season per wk
£400.00–£750.00
High season per wk
£400.00–£750.00

Rating Applied For

1 Unit
Sleeping 9

79A VICTORIA ROAD

Cambridge
Contact: Mrs A Thoday, 40 High Street, Aldreth, Ely CB6 3PG
T: (01353) 740022
F: (01353) 740022
E: trojan.david@virgin.net

OPEN All Year
CC: Switch, Visa

Low season per wk
£400.00–£500.00
High season per wk
£550.00–£900.00

Well-appointed Victorian house within walking distance of Cambridge city centre. Refurbished spring 2003 to a very high standard. Garden with barbecue and furniture.

CASTLE HEDINGHAM, Essex Map ref 3B2

★★★★

2 Units
Sleeping 4–5

ROSEMARY FARM

Castle Hedingham, Halstead
Contact: Mr G I Henderson, Rosemary Farm, Rosemary Lane, Castle Hedingham, Halstead CO9 3AJ
T: (01787) 461653

Rosemary Farm is situated in a quiet country lane within view of Hedingham Castle, former home of the De Veres, Earls of Oxford, and is a convenient base for visiting the many nearby attractions. Cottages in barn conversion offering lounge, kitchen, one and two bedrooms, shower/toilet, tiled flooring throughout, patio area, parking.

OPEN All Year

Low season per wk
£200.00–£327.00
High season per wk
£200.00–£327.00

ACCESSIBILITY

Look for the symbols which indicate National Accessible Scheme standards for hearing and visually impaired guests in addition to standards for guests with mobility impairment. Additional participants are shown in the listings at the back.

CHEDGRAVE, Norfolk Map ref 3C1

★★★

3 Units
Sleeping 6

18thC barn converted into oak-beamed cottages. Set in grounds of country house. Fifteen minutes' walk to village, pubs and boat hire. Use of indoor heated swimming pool.

BARN OWL HOLIDAYS

Chedgrave, Norwich
Contact: Mrs R Beattie, Barn Owl Holidays, Bryons Green, Big Back Lane, Chedgrave, Norwich NR14 6HB
T: (01508) 528786
F: (01508) 528698
E: barnowls@bt.clara.co.uk
I: www.barnowlholidays.co.uk

OPEN All Year

Low season per wk
£180.00–£310.00
High season per wk
£320.00–£540.00

CHELMSFORD, Essex Map ref 3B3 *Tourist Information Centre Tel: (01245) 283400*

★★★★

1 Unit
Sleeping 4

BURY BARN COTTAGE

Chelmsford
Contact: Mr R Morris, Bury Barn Cottage, Bury Road, Pleshey, Chelmsford CM3 1HB
T: (01245) 237384
F: (01245) 237327
I: www.burybarncottage.co.uk

Bungalow cottage located within the boundaries of a Listed historic site, near to the historic village of Pleshey. Fully equipped with kitchen and washing machine, our cottage offers you a completely self-contained home. Beautifully furnished to exacting standards, you are within easy reach of London and Eastern England. Single- or multiple-night stay.

OPEN All Year

Single-night stays available with reduced rates for extra nights.

Low season per wk
£280.00–£455.00
High season per wk
£280.00–£455.00

CLEY NEXT THE SEA, Norfolk Map ref 3B1

★★★

1 Unit
Sleeping 7

ARCHWAY COTTAGE

Cley next the Sea, Holt
Contact: Mrs V Jackson, 3A Brickendon Lane, Brickendon, Hertford SG13 8NU
T: (01992) 511303
F: (01992) 511303

Pretty 18thC flint cottage, well furnished and comfortable, with four bedrooms, two bathrooms and garage. Near village centre, bird sanctuaries and the sea. Also, another similar cottage in Wells-next-the-Sea. Illustrated brochures available for both cottages.

OPEN All Year

Low season per wk
£200.00–£290.00
High season per wk
£350.00–£490.00

COLCHESTER, Essex Map ref 3B2 *Tourist Information Centre Tel: (01206) 282920*

★★★

1 Unit
Sleeping 5

50 ROSEBERY AVENUE

Colchester
Contact: Mrs K Webb, 51 Rosebery Avenue, Colchester CO1 2UP
T: (01206) 866888
E: rosebery.avenue@ntlworld.com

Modernised house in quiet town-centre location. Castle, park, shops, museums and sports centre within walking distance. Ideal for east coast. Bus/trains close by.

OPEN All Year

Low season per wk
£180.00–£200.00
High season per wk
£220.00–£250.00

VISITOR ATTRACTIONS For ideas on places to visit refer to the introduction at the beginning of this section. Look out too for the ETC's Quality Assured Visitor Attraction signs.

COLCHESTER continued

★★★★

1 Unit
Sleeping 4

THE TEA HOUSE

Colchester
Contact: Mr N Charrington
T: (01206) 330784
F: (01206) 330884
E: info@layermarneytower.co.uk
I: layermarneytower.co.uk

OPEN All Year except Christmas
CC: Mastercard, Visa

Low season per wk
£305.00–£385.00
High season per wk
£420.00–£585.00

Beautiful Edwardian folly in grounds of Tudor palace. Tastefully restored and fully equipped to highest standards. Peaceful, rural setting with spectacular views of Layer Marney Tower and surrounding countryside.

COLKIRK, Norfolk Map ref 3B1

★★★

2 Units
Sleeping 7

SADDLERY & HILLSIDE COTTAGE

Colkirk, Fakenham
Contact: Mrs C Joice
T: (01328) 862261
F: (01328) 856464
E: catherine.joice@btinternet.com

OPEN All Year

Low season per wk
£170.00–£325.00
High season per wk
£375.00–£480.00

Attractive, well-equipped cottages overlooking farmland. Large, fenced gardens and ample parking. Saddlery Cottage has a downstairs bathroom and bedroom. Winter lets available.

COLMWORTH, Bedfordshire Map ref 2D1

★★★

2 Units
Sleeping 5–6

Being located only minutes from major roads (A1, M1, A14), yet in a rural setting, makes Colmworth an attractive, get-away venue. The well-equipped, luxury, self-catering cottages are set in tranquil surroundings overlooking the lakes of the 12th green.

COLMWORTH GOLF COURSE HOLIDAY COTTAGES

Colmworth, Bedford
Contact: Mrs J Vesely
T: (01234) 378181
F: (01234) 376678
E: julie@colmworthgc.fsnet.co.uk
I: www.colmsworthgolfclub.co.uk

OPEN All Year
CC: JCB, Mastercard, Solo, Switch, Visa

Golf- and swimming-tuition breaks. Reduced green-fee rates for residents.

High season per wk
£325.00–£425.00

COTTON, Suffolk Map ref 3B2

★★★★

3 Units
Sleeping 2

A 17thC barn with original features has been converted into cottages set around a shared courtyard surrounded by the owner's farmland in mid-Suffolk. Each cottage has exposed beams, wooden floors and open brickwork as well as all the modern accessories needed for a very comfortable stay.

CODA COTTAGES

Cotton, Stowmarket
Contact: Mrs K Sida-Nicholls, Coda Cottages, Poplar Farm, Dandy Corner, Cotton, Stowmarket IP14 4QX
T: (01449) 780076
F: (01449) 780280
E: codacottages@dandycorner.co.uk
I: www.codacottages.co.uk

OPEN All Year

Short breaks available Oct–Jan.

Low season per wk
£150.00–£215.00
High season per wk
£215.00–£360.00

PRICES
Please check prices and other details at the time of booking.

CRATFIELD, Suffolk Map ref 3C2

★★★

1 Unit
Sleeping 6

CHERRY TREES

Cratfield, Halesworth
Contact: Mrs C Knox
T: (01379) 586709
F: (01379) 588033
E: J.L.Knox@farming.co.uk

A chalet/bungalow situated in Suffolk with an enclosed garden set well back from the road and in the grounds of a working farm. Facilities for children. Pets welcome.

OPEN All Year

Short breaks available (excl summer holidays).

Low season per wk
£198.00–£291.00
High season per wk
£312.00–£417.00

★★★★

4 Units
Sleeping 2–4

SCHOOL FARM COTTAGES

Cratfield, Halesworth
Contact: Mrs C Sillett
T: (01986) 798844
F: (01986) 798394
E: schoolfarmcotts@aol.com
I: www.schoolfarmcottages.com

OPEN All Year

Low season per wk
£150.00–£300.00
High season per wk
£350.00–£450.00

High-quality, well-equipped cottages converted from traditional farm buildings. Attractive setting on working farm in beautiful Suffolk countryside. Near Heritage Coast.

CROMER, Norfolk Map ref 3C1 *Tourist Information Centre Tel: (01263) 512497*

★

3 Units
Sleeping 4–6

CHALETS 28, 151, 152

Cromer
Contact: Russells Self Catering Holidays
T: (01263) 513139
F: (01263) 513139

Low season per wk
£100.00–£200.00
High season per wk
£220.00–£280.00

Chalets overlook spacious, grassed areas with trees. Owners carefully clean and prepare chalets. Nearby are picturesque cliff walks, woods and steps leading to the beach.

★★★

3 Units
Sleeping 2–4

THORPEWOOD COTTAGES

Thorpe Market, Norwich
Contact: Mr D Howarth
T: (01263) 834493
E: davidhowarth@thorpegate.fsnet.co.uk
I: www.thorpewoodcottages.co.uk

OPEN All Year

Low season per wk
£181.00–£391.00
High season per wk
£325.00–£420.00

Charming cottages enjoying a prime location close to the beaches of North Norfolk. Situated in the 8-acre grounds of the owner's grade II Listed farmhouse.

QUALITY ASSURANCE SCHEME

For an explanation of the quality and facilities represented by the Stars please refer to the front of this guide. A more detailed explanation can be found in the information pages at the back.

DEDHAM, Essex Map ref 3B2

★★★★

2 Units
Sleeping 10

In quiet, picturesque courtyard in heart of village, these spacious period houses have antique furnishings and well-equipped, walled, furnished gardens. Dedham, famous for Constable's 18thC English landscapes, is an Area of Outstanding Natural Beauty. Minutes to riverside walks, village green, historic pubs and gourmet restaurants.

THE TALLOW FACTORY & BRANNAM COTTAGE

Dedham, Colchester
Contact: Ms C Thompson, 14 School Lane, Lawford, Manningtree CO11 2HZ
T: (01206) 393711
I: www.tallowfactory.com

OPEN All Year

Low season per wk
£360.00–£625.00
High season per wk
£900.00–£1,250.00

DOCKING, Norfolk Map ref 3B1

★★★★★

2 Units
Sleeping 4–5

Victorian townhouse and character cottage. Luxurious accommodation fully equipped with every comfort. Individually and tastefully designed rooms in period or traditional Norfolk style with numerous curios, artworks and homely touches. Bedrooms en suite or with hand basins. A warm welcome, log fires, fresh flowers, music room with keyboard. Quality assurance.

NORFOLK HOUSE & COURTYARD COTTAGE

Docking
Contact: Tim & Liz Witley, Cherry Tree Cottage, 17 Peddars Way South, Ringstead, Hunstanton PE36 5LF
T: (01485) 525341
F: (01485) 532715
E: timwitley@norfolkholidays.demon.co.uk

OPEN All Year

Last-minute holidays at reduced rate. Winter breaks Nov-Mar from £165. Phone for tariff.

Low season per wk
Min £275.00
High season per wk
Min £395.00

EAST BERGHOLT, Suffolk Map ref 3B2

★★★

1 Unit
Sleeping 4

WOODSTOCK WING WOODSTOCK

East Bergholt, Colchester
Contact: Mr & Mrs K Alcoe, Woodstock Wing Woodstock, Gaston Street, East Bergholt, Colchester CO7 6SD
T: (01206) 298724
F: (01206) 298128
E: janetandkeith@familyalcoe.fsnet.co.uk

OPEN All Year

Low season per wk
£250.00
High season per wk
£260.00

Close to centre of picturesque village, John Constable's birthplace. Ideal location to explore Suffolk and beyond. Comfortably furnished, all facilities, parking. Brochure available on request.

SPECIAL BREAKS

Many establishments offer special promotions and themed breaks. These are highlighted in red. (All such offers are subject to availability.)

EAST DEREHAM, Norfolk Map ref 3B1

★★★★

2 Units
Sleeping 2–9

Handsomely appointed 18thC country house and detached bungalow. Both self-contained and very private, patios/garden, tennis/croquet. Quiet, rural retreat in pretty countryside, excellent centre for exploring East Anglia. Tastefully furnished accommodation. House has beautiful conservatory, wash basins in all four bedrooms, lounge with beams, inglenook and woodburner.

CLINTON COTTAGE & CLINTON HOUSE

Yaxham, Dereham
Contact: Mrs M R Searle, Clinton Willows, Cutthroat Lane, Yaxham, East Dereham NR19 1RZ
T: (01362) 692079
F: (01362) 692079
E: clintonholidays@tesco.net
I: www.norfolkcountrycottage.co.uk

OPEN All Year

Low season per wk
£155.00–£315.00
High season per wk
£430.00–£925.00

EAST HARLING, Norfolk Map ref 3B2

★★★★

2 Units
Sleeping 5

900-acre arable farm. Escape to the Norfolk countryside. Our cosy cottages, with beams and woodburners, are ideal for a relaxing break or a busy sightseeing holiday. Why not book both cottages and bring family and friends? Set in large garden by Thetford Forest, the cottages are fully equipped and carefully prepared for you.

DOLPHIN LODGE

East Harling, Norwich
Contact: Mrs E Jolly, Dolphin Lodge, Roudham Farm, East Harling, Norwich NR16 2RJ
T: (01953) 717126
F: (01953) 718593
E: jolly@roudhamfarm.co.uk
I: www.roudhamfarm.co.uk

OPEN All Year

Short breaks available autumn/spring. Themed breaks – cookery/riding/walking/trail cycling.

Low season per wk
£275.00–£320.00
High season per wk
£360.00–£450.00

★★★

1 Unit
Sleeping 2

Comfortable studio conversion, open-beamed interior, fully centrally heated, ideally situated for cycling or touring Norfolk and North Suffolk's historic sites, NT properties, coast, Thetford Forest, Snetterton racetrack. Norwich and Bury St Edmunds are a 30-minute drive. Village setting. Pubs, shops, fish & chips all easy walking distance.

TAPESTRY COTTAGE

East Harling, Norwich
Contact: Mr M Dolling
T: (01263) 741115
F: (01953) 717443
E: ok_to.mark_it@virgin.net

Low season per wk
£160.00–£200.00
High season per wk
£200.00–£240.00

CHECK THE MAPS

**The colour maps at the front of this guide show all the cities, towns and villages for which you will find accommodation entries.
Refer to the town index to find the page on which they are listed.**

ELY, Cambridgeshire Map ref 3A2 *Tourist Information Centre Tel: (01353) 662062*

★★★
1 Unit
Sleeping 5

19 CHIEFS STREET
Ely
Contact: Mrs P Coates
T: (01223) 290842
F: (01223) 290529
E: cheviotbob@aol.com

OPEN All Year

Low season per wk
£250.00–£300.00
High season per wk
£350.00–£450.00

House in quiet city street, walking distance from cathedral, museums, restaurants, shops, Cromwell's house and station. Frequent cultural events, fast trains for Cambridge and London.

EYE, Suffolk Map ref 3B2

★★★-★★★★★
4 Units
Sleeping 2–4

MANOR HOUSE COTTAGES
Yaxley, Eye
Contact: Mr D Mason
T: (01379) 788181
F: (01379) 788422
E: david@dmenterprises.demon.co.uk
I: www.manorhousecottages.co.uk

OPEN All Year

Low season per wk
£165.00–£213.00
High season per wk
£220.00–£330.00

Yaxley Manor House was built in 1520. In the rear courtyard, the cottages and barns are set in six acres of gardens and grazing.

FAKENHAM, Norfolk Map ref 3B1

★★★★
1 Unit
Sleeping 8

POLLYWIGGLE COTTAGE
West Raynham, Fakenham
Contact: Mrs M Farnham-Smith
T: (01603) 471990
F: (01603) 612221
E: marilyn@pollywigglecottage.co.uk
I: www.pollywigglecottage.co.uk

Brimming with character, this pretty, well-equipped home wraps you in its cosy, comfortable interior. Nestled in a secluded, rambling flower garden, Pollywiggle Cottage lies on the fringe of a tranquil village 15 miles from long, sandy beaches. A wealth of attractions and amenities are within an easy drive.

OPEN All Year

Small-party reductions and short breaks available – minimum 3 nights.

Low season per wk
£340.00–£500.00
High season per wk
£460.00–£700.00

FELIXSTOWE, Suffolk Map ref 3C2 *Tourist Information Centre Tel: (01394) 276770*

★★★
1 Unit
Sleeping 4

FLAT 2
Felixstowe
Contact: Mrs G Lynch
T: (01473) 328729

Low season per wk
£130.00–£160.00
High season per wk
£160.00–£200.00

Two-bedroomed, first floor flat with balcony overlooking the sea. In quiet area and within walking distance of the town centre, with own parking space.

★★
3 Units
Sleeping 2–7

KIMBERLEY HOLIDAY FLATS
Felixstowe
Contact: Mrs V Reed
T: (01394) 672157

OPEN All Year

Low season per wk
Min £175.00
High season per wk
Max £420.00

All flats are self-contained with balconies, and overlook the sea. The town centre is nearby. Off-road parking at rear. Telephone for brochure.

TOWN INDEX
This can be found at the back of this guide. If you know where you want to stay, the index will give you the page number listing accommodation in your chosen town, city or village.

FOXLEY, Norfolk Map ref 3B1

★★-★★★

12 Units
Sleeping 4–7

MOOR FARM STABLE COTTAGES

Foxley, Dereham
Contact: Mr P Davis
T: (01362) 688523
F: (01362) 688523
E: moorfarm@aol.com
I: www.moorfarmstablecottages.co.uk

Located on working farm, a courtyard of two- and three-bedroomed self-catering chalets, all fully equipped and centrally heated, two specially adapted for disabled. Ideally situated for coast, Broads, Norwich, Sandringham. 365 acres of mature woodland adjoining owners' farm to walk. Fishing available close by. Pets welcome.

OPEN All Year

Low season per wk
£170.00–£370.00
High season per wk
£310.00–£420.00

GORLESTON-ON-SEA, Norfolk Map ref 3C1

★★★

1 Unit
Sleeping 4

MANOR COTTAGE

Gorleston-on-Sea, Great Yarmouth
Contact: Mrs M Ward, North Manor House, 12 Pier Plain, Gorleston-on-Sea, Great Yarmouth NR31 6PE
T: (01493) 669845
F: (01493) 669845
E: manorcottage@wardm4.fsnet.co.uk
I: www.wardm4.fsnet.co.uk

OPEN All Year except Christmas

Low season per wk
£100.00–£160.00
High season per wk
£220.00–£320.00

Edwardian two-bedroomed cottage attached to manor house. Quiet location between high street, beach and harbour. Secure parking. Near Yarmouth, Lowestoft, Broads and nature reserves.

GRESHAM, Norfolk Map ref 3B1

★★

2 Units
Sleeping 3–4

ASTALOT & AVALON COTTAGES

Lower Gresham
Contact: Mrs J J Murray
T: (01263) 740404
F: (01263) 740404

OPEN All Year

Low season per wk
£130.00–£230.00
High season per wk
£230.00–£310.00

Attractive, adjoining flint/brick cottages over 160 years old. Completely renovated. Warm and very comfortable, with small enclosed gardens. Dogs welcome. Sea two miles. Electricity included.

HAUGHLEY, Suffolk Map ref 3B2

★★★

1 Unit
Sleeping 2

THE COTTAGE

Haughley, Stowmarket
Contact: Mrs M Noy, Red House Farm, Station Road, Haughley, Stowmarket IP14 3QP
T: (01449) 673323
F: (01449) 675413
E: mary@noy1.fsnet.co.uk
I: farmstayanglia.co.uk

OPEN All Year

Low season per wk
£200.00
High season per wk
£250.00

Delightful, well-equipped cottage adjoining farmhouse on small grassland farm. Ideal for exploring the many attractions in Suffolk, Norfolk and Essex.

HEACHAM, Norfolk Map ref 3B1

★★-★★★

7 Units
Sleeping 4–6

CEDAR SPRINGS

Heacham, King's Lynn
Contact: Mrs A Howe, Owl Lodge, Jubilee Road, Heacham, King's Lynn PE31 7AR
T: (01485) 570609
E: antoniahowe@aol.com

Low season per wk
£110.00–£160.00
High season per wk
£240.00–£320.00

Fully equipped two/three-bedroomed chalets on quiet garden site, 300 yards from beach, three miles from Hunstanton. Adjacent car parking. Sorry, no pets.

HEACHAM continued

★★★

1 Unit
Sleeping 7

STANEVE
Docking, King's Lynn
Contact: Mr & Mrs J Smith, 2B Church Road, Flitwick, Bedford MK45 1AE
T: (01525) 634935
E: amandalsmith@ntlworld.com
I: www.staneve.biz

OPEN All Year

Low season per wk
£175.00–£275.00
High season per wk
£275.00–£375.00

Delightful brick and flint, three-bedroom cottage. Modernised and cosy with woodburning stove. Located in coastal village with amenities. Beach five miles. Pub walking distance.

HINGHAM, Norfolk Map ref 3B1

★★★★

1 Unit
Sleeping 6

THE GRANARY

Hingham, Norwich
Contact: Mrs C Dunnett, College Farm, Hingham, Norwich NR9 4PP
T: (01953) 850596
F: (01953) 851364
E: christine.dunnett@lineone.net

Tastefully converted and furnished 18thC granary. Peaceful location on small thoroughbred stud farm with pets galore. Very attractive, well-equipped accommodation with original oak beams throughout. Warm and cosy in winter with woodburning stove. Children's play area with outdoor above-ground pool. Perfect location to explore Norfolk.

OPEN All Year

3-night low season breaks available for only £100.

Low season per wk
£170.00–£275.00
High season per wk
£275.00–£325.00

HOLT, Norfolk Map ref 3B1

★

1 Unit
Sleeping 4

ALBERT STREET
Holt
Contact: Mrs H North, Eldon House, Eldon Lane, Braishfield, Romsey SO51 0PT
T: (01794) 368864

OPEN All Year

Low season per wk
£140.00–£175.00
High season per wk
£250.00–£255.00

Warm and comfortable Victorian terraced cottage with small garden. Close to shops. On National Express coach route from London.

HORHAM, Suffolk Map ref 3B2

★★★

2 Units
Sleeping 4–5

ALPHA COTTAGES
Horham, Eye
Contact: Mr & Mrs B Cooper, Lodge Farm, The Street, Horham, Eye IP21 5DX
T: (01379) 384424
F: (01379) 384424

Low season per wk
£211.00–£300.00
High season per wk
£464.00–£508.00

Beautifully converted, well-equipped cottages in the heart of rural East Anglia. Fenced garden, patio with meadow and play equipment. Leisure facilities and good inns two miles.

HUNSTANTON, Norfolk Map ref 3B1 *Tourist Information Centre Tel: (01485) 532610*

★★

1 Unit
Sleeping 4

CHALET 4
Hunstanton
Contact: Mr & Mrs M Chestney, 35 West Raynham, Fakenham NR21 7EY
T: (01328) 838341
F: (01328) 838341

Low season per wk
£110.00–£145.00
High season per wk
£145.00–£190.00

A two-bedroomed chalet, 100 yards fom Beacy. Six miles from Sandringham. Bathroom/toilet, lounge/diner. Picnic table and bench outside.

SYMBOLS The symbols in each entry give information about services and facilities. A key to these symbols appears at the back of this guide.

HUNSTANTON continued

★★★

1 Unit
Sleeping 5

MINNA COTTAGE

Hunstanton
Contact: Mr T Cassie, 21 The Green, Hunstanton PE36 5AH
T: (01485) 532448
E: tonycassie@btconnect.com
I: www.minnacottage.com

This fully modernised coachman's cottage provides comfortable and private accommodation for five adults and one baby. Situated by the town green it has delightful and unobstructed views of the 'Wash' and is conveniently placed for the local shops, directly opposite the sea and about 200 yards from the beach.

OPEN All Year
CC: Delta, Mastercard, Switch, Visa

Low season per wk
£300.00–£365.00
High season per wk
£365.00–£435.00

KEDINGTON, Suffolk Map ref 3B2

★★★

1 Unit
Sleeping 2

THE COTTAGE AT ROWANS

Kedington, Haverhill
Contact: Mrs C Owen, Rowans House, Calford Green, Kedington, Haverhill CB9 7UN
T: (01440) 702408
F: (01440) 702408
E: cheryl@owen41.supanet.com
I: www.cottagesdirect.com/nfa.123

OPEN All Year

Low season per wk
£150.00–£230.00
High season per wk
£260.00–£330.00

Spacious, bright, well-appointed, one-bedroom cottage with double-sprung sofa bed. Cosy in winter. Stour Valley walks, golf and antique hunting nearby. Garden and patio.

USE YOUR *i*s

There are more than 550 Tourist Information Centres throughout England offering friendly help with accommodation and holiday ideas as well as suggestions of places to visit and things to do. You'll find TIC addresses in the local Phone Book.

Norfolk Holiday Homes

Visit this lovely area in one of our self-catering coastal or country holiday homes. Over 50 to choose from and all tourist board graded.

Pets, Children, Disabled, all welcome.

62 Westgate, Hunstanton, PE36 5EL
T: 01485 534267 24 Hours F: 01485 535230
E: shohol@birdsnorfolkholidayhomes.co.uk
FREE BROCHURE
www.norfolkholidayhomes-birds.co.uk

Norfolk Holiday Homes

KELSALE, Suffolk Map ref 3C2

★★★★

4 Units
Sleeping 6

EAST GREEN FARM COTTAGES

Kelsale, Saxmundham
Contact: Mr & Mrs R Gawthrop, East Green Maintenance Services, East Green Farm, Kelsale, Saxmundham IP17 2PH
T: (01728) 602316
F: (01728) 604408
E: claire@eastgreenproperty.co.uk
I: www.eastgreencottages.co.uk

Between Southwold and Aldeburgh and only two miles from the beautiful Heritage Coast. The Granary, The Old Stables, The Hayloft and The Dairy are charming, spacious, fully equipped, converted barns set in the grounds of a 500-year-old farmhouse. 13 acres of paddocks, horses, tennis court and outdoor swimming pool. Tennis coaching available.

OPEN All Year

Short breaks available Oct-Mar, minimum 3 nights.

Low season per wk
Min £240.00
High season per wk
Max £570.00

KESSINGLAND, Suffolk Map ref 3C1

★★★

1 Unit
Sleeping 4

CHURCH ROAD

Kessingland, Lowestoft
Contact: Mr J M Rayment, 28 Woollards Lane, Great Shelford, Cambridge CB2 5LZ
T: (01223) 843048

OPEN All Year

Low season per wk
£155.00–£200.00
High season per wk
£200.00–£260.00

Traditional, terraced, modernised cottage. Fully fitted kitchen including microwave oven, large lounge/diner with colour TV, and porch. One double and one twin room, bathroom/toilet.

3

★★★

1 Unit
Sleeping 5

KEW COTTAGE

Kessingland, Lowestoft
Contact: Mrs J Gill, 46 St Georges Avenue, Northampton NN2 6JA
T: (01604) 717301
F: (01604) 791424
E: b.s.g.@btopenworld.com

Modernised, two-bedroomed semi-detached cottage in the middle of village, 10 minutes' walk from the sea. Large back garden with patio area. Norfolk Broads three miles, Lowestoft three miles, Southwold five miles.

Low season per wk
£165.00–£190.00
High season per wk
£185.00–£240.00

KING'S LYNN, Norfolk Map ref 3B1 *Tourist Information Centre Tel: (01553) 763044*

★★★

1 Unit
Sleeping 4

THE STABLES TOO

King's Lynn
Contact: Ms S O'Brien, The Stables, 35a Goodwins Road, King's Lynn PE30 5QX
T: (01553) 774638
E: mikeandsueobrien@hotmail.com
I: www.cottageguide.co.uk/thestablestoo

Attractive converted Victorian stable with courtyard sitting area. Surprisingly secluded position, yet only a short walk into town. Convenient for Sandringham, coast, Broads, Cambridge and Norwich.

OPEN All Year

Low season per wk
£165.00–£275.00
High season per wk
£165.00–£275.00

MAP REFERENCES

Map references apply to the colour maps at the front of this guide.

KNAPTON, Norfolk Map ref 3C1

★★★★

2 Units
Sleeping 6

WHITE HOUSE FARM – THE GRANARY & WALLAGES COTTAGE

Knapton, North Walsham
Contact: Mr & Mrs C Goodhead, White House Farm, Knapton, North Walsham NR28 0RX
T: (01263) 721344
E: info@whitehousefarmnorfolk.co.uk
I: www.whitehousefarmnorfolk.co.uk

Converted from an original hay-loft, these cottages are set in the gardens of an 18thC farmhouse close to Broads, coast and Norwich. Many character features (including log fires) combined with modern comforts and recently fitted kitchens. Freshly prepared, farm-cooked meals available.

OPEN All Year
CC: Delta, JCB, Mastercard, Solo, Switch, Visa

3-night stays available Sep-May; also special Christmas and New Year breaks.

Low season per wk
£240.00–£325.00
High season per wk
£325.00–£475.00

LAVENHAM, Suffolk Map ref 3B2

★★★★★

1 Unit
Sleeping 4

BLAIZE BARN

Lavenham, Sudbury
Contact: Mr & Mrs J Keohane, Blaize House, Churst Street, Lavenham, Sudbury CO10 9QT
T: (01787) 247402
F: (01787) 247402
E: j.and.c.keohane@virgin.net

A Grade II Listed barn renovated to the highest standards in 2002 and located within a stunning, medieval village. Vaulted, oak-beam ceiling, log fire, large beds, well-equipped oak/granite kitchen, sky/DVD with cinema sound, large bath. Private parking and private gardens. Excellent restaurants and pubs within walking distance.

OPEN All Year
CC: Delta, Mastercard, Switch, Visa

3-day weekend breaks or 4-day mid-week breaks at 60% of weekly charge. Romantic breaks are a speciality.

Low season per wk
£400.00–£450.00
High season per wk
£500.00–£780.00

14

★★★★

5 Units
Sleeping 2–5

THE GROVE

Lavenham, Sudbury
Contact: Mark Scott
T: (01787) 211115
E: mark@grove-cottages.co.uk
I: www.grove-cottages.co.uk

Enjoy the romance of your own 300-year-old farm cottage – oak beams, open log fires, period furniture, ducks, roses and a touch of luxury. Our cottages are close to the lovely medieval Suffolk village of Lavenham – just two hours from London. Bikes free and canoes available.

OPEN All Year
CC: Delta, Diners, JCB, Mastercard, Solo, Switch, Visa

Our cosy cottages make up The Grove Farm, bookable for 2-15 guests, from 2-night short breaks upwards. Pets welcome.

Low season per wk
£177.00–£316.00
High season per wk
£427.00–£780.00

QUALITY ASSURANCE SCHEME
Star ratings are explained at the back of this guide.

LAVENHAM continued

★★★
1 Unit
Sleeping 6

OLD WETHERDEN HALL

Ipswich
Contact: Mrs J Elsden, Old Wetherden Hall, Hitcham, Ipswich IP7 7PZ
T: (01449) 740574
F: (01449) 740574
E: farm@wetheradenhall.force9.co.uk
I: www.oldwetherdenhall.co.uk

OPEN All Year

Low season per wk
Min £200.00
High season per wk
Max £375.00

15thC oak-beamed house, enclosed moated site on arable farm. Beautiful secluded setting, large garden, abundance of wildlife. Inglenook fireplace.

★★★★
4 Units
Sleeping 4–6

QUAKERS YARD

Lavenham, Sudbury
Contact: Mr D Aldous, Two A's Hoggards Green, Stanningfield, Bury St Edmunds IP29 4RG
T: (01284) 827271
E: val@quakersyard.com
I: www.quakersyard.com

OPEN All Year
CC: Delta, Mastercard, Switch, Visa

Low season per wk
£200.00–£250.00
High season per wk
£250.00–£400.00

Bungalows and cottage-style units in Lavenham, set in landscaped gardens and with off-road parking. Open all year. Short breaks available.

★★★
1 Unit
Sleeping 2

THE RECTOR'S RETREAT

Kettlebaston, Ipswich
Contact: Mr & Mrs P Gutteridge, The Rector's Retreat, The Old Convent, The Street, Kettlebaston, Ipswich IP7 7QA
T: (01449) 741557
E: holidays@kettlebaston.fsnet.co.uk
I: www.kettlebaston.fsnet.co.uk

Timber building within the curtilage of a Grade II thatched cottage. Recently completely refurbished and renovated to provide wheelchair access. Complimentary basic provisions (milk/beverages). The Retreat comprises a double bedroom with en suite shower, lounge/diner, kitchen, electric storage heaters. Electricity and linen included. Brochure available. Minimum three nights' stay.

OPEN All Year

Jun & Sep: 7 nights for £210.

Low season per wk
£200.00–£250.00
High season per wk
£250.00–£300.00

LAXFIELD, Suffolk Map ref 3C2

★★★
2 Units
Sleeping 4

THE LOOSE BOX & THE OLD STABLES

Laxfield, Woodbridge
Contact: Mr & Mrs J Reeve, Laxfield Leisure Ltd, High Street, Laxfield, Woodbridge IP13 8DU
T: (01986) 798019
F: (01986) 798155
E: laxfieldleisure@talk21.com
I: www.villastables.co.uk

OPEN All Year

Low season per wk
£175.00–£310.00
High season per wk
£275.00–£415.00

The Loose Box and Old Stables are Listed properties in the village centre. Superb modern conversions retaining all their character.

MAP REFERENCES The map references refer to the colour maps at the front of this guide. The first figure is the map number; the letter and figure which follow indicate the grid reference on the map.

LAXFIELD continued

★★★★

1 Unit
Sleeping 5

Pretty Victorian cottage offering spacious accommodation in the centre of Laxfield. Ideal base for exploring Suffolk's Heritage Coast or the heart of Suffolk. Extremely well appointed, the cottage is cosy and comfortable in the summer or winter and overlooks peaceful meadowland. Two pubs/restaurants within 100 yards.

MEADOW COTTAGE

Laxfield, Woodbridge
Contact: Mr & Mrs W Ayers, Meadow Cottage Leisure, Quinton House, Gorhams Mill lane, Laxfield, Woodbridge IP13 8DN
T: (01986) 798345
F: (01986) 798345
E: will.ayers@btinternet.com

OPEN All Year

Free first basket of logs for woodburner from 1/10/03 to 1/4/04; further logs available from owner.

Low season per wk
£210.00–£290.00
High season per wk
£290.00–£480.00

LITTLE WALDEN, Essex Map ref 2D1

★★★

4 Units
Sleeping 3–4

ORCHARD VIEW NUMBERS 1-4
Little Walden, Saffron Walden
Contact: Mrs M Chapman-Barker, Little Bowsers Farm, Bowsers Lane, Little Walden, Saffron Walden CB10 1XQ
T: (01799) 527315
F: (01799) 527315
E: sales@farmerkit.co.uk
I: www.farmerkit.co.uk

OPEN All Year

Low season per wk
£200.00–£250.00
High season per wk
£200.00–£250.00

Little Bowsers Farm is a 30-acre organic holding. The farm produces free range, organic eggs. There are apple, plum, pear and cherry orchards, planted over the past five years.

LONG MELFORD, Suffolk Map ref 3B2

★★★★

1 Unit
Sleeping 4

Delightful Grade II Listed flint cottage in the heart of this historic and picturesque village. Recently renovated, retaining many traditional features. Attractively furnished to high levels of comfort. Secluded garden backing onto meadowlands. All amenities in the village are close by, including restaurants and shops. Mob: 07970 808701.

HOPE COTTAGE

Long Melford, Sudbury
Contact: Ms S Jamil, Hill Farm Cottage, Glemsford, Sudbury CO10 7PP
T: (01787) 282338
F: (01787) 282338
E: sns.jam@tesco.net
I: www.hope-cottage-suffolk.co.uk

OPEN All Year

Short breaks available all year (subject to availability in high season).

Low season per wk
Min £230.00
High season per wk
Max £355.00

LOWESTOFT, Suffolk Map ref 3C1 *Tourist Information Centre Tel: (01502) 533600*

★★★

1 Unit
Sleeping 4

SUFFOLK SEASIDE & BROADLANDS
Lowestoft
Contact: Ms Collecott, 282 Gorleston Road, Oulton, Lowestoft NR32 3AJ
T: (01502) 564396

OPEN All Year

Low season per wk
£185.00–£215.00
High season per wk
£260.00–£375.00

Beautifully furnished, well-equipped bungalow with conservatory, garden and garage. Two bedrooms, two bathrooms, sitting room, dining room and large, fully fitted kitchen.

MARTHAM, Norfolk Map ref 3C1

★★★

1 Unit
Sleeping 5

GREENSIDE COTTAGE

Martham, Great Yarmouth
Contact: Mrs B I Dyball, Greenside, 30 The Green, Martham, Great Yarmouth NR29 4PA
T: (01493) 740375

OPEN All Year

Low season per wk
£160.00–£220.00
High season per wk
£220.00–£390.00

Part-thatched cottage overlooking village green. Fitted kitchen, shower with hand basin and toilet, double bedroom (3 beds), single bedroom, lounge and lounge/diner. No pets.

NAYLAND, Suffolk Map ref 3B2

★★★★-★★★★★

9 Units
Sleeping 2–9

GLADWINS FARM

Nayland
Contact: Mrs P Dossor, Gladwins Farm, Harpers Hill, Nayland, Colchester CO6 4NU
T: (01206) 262261
F: (01206) 263001
E: gladwinsfarm@aol.com
I: www.gladwinsfarm.co.uk

22 acres of wooded grounds in Suffolk's rolling Constable country with marvellous views make our lovely cottages a wonderful location. Charming villages and gardens to explore - only 30 minutes from the sea. Heated indoor swimming pool, sauna, tennis court, fishing, animals and playground. Pets welcome.

OPEN All Year
CC: Delta, JCB, Mastercard, Solo, Switch, Visa

Short breaks Oct-Easter. 3-night weekends or 4-night mid-week breaks @ 65% full-week rate.

Low season per wk
£220.00–£650.00
High season per wk
£450.00–£1,400.00

NEWMARKET, Suffolk Map ref 3B2 *Tourist Information Centre Tel: (01638) 667200*

★★★★

1 Unit
Sleeping 2

SWALLOWS REST

Woodditton, Newmarket
Contact: Mrs G Woodward, Swallows Rest, 6 Ditton Green, Woodditton, Newmarket CB8 9SQ
T: (01638) 730823
F: (01638) 731767
E: gillian@swallowsrest.f9.co.uk

Low season per wk
£170.00–£200.00
High season per wk
£200.00–£240.00

Comfortable annexe off owners' secluded property in quiet rural village three miles from Newmarket. Own entrance and garden. Pub with food 400 yards. Country walks. Cambridge 20 minutes.

NORFOLK BROADS

See under Beccles, Gorleston-on-Sea, Lowestoft, Norwich, Oulton Broad, Sprowston, Stalham, Wroxham

NORWICH, Norfolk Map ref 3C1 *Tourist Information Centre Tel: (01603) 727927*

★★★★

1 Unit
Sleeping 7

MILL HOUSE

Norwich
Contact: Ms F Godin, 3 Mill Cottages, Hellesdon Mill Lane, Norwich NR6 5AZ
T: (01603) 415061
E: villa.cott@virgin.net

This attractive, timber-clad house lies adjacent to the site of Hellesdon Mill and overlooks a tranquil part of the River Wensum. The building dates back to the 18thC, but has been remodelled over the years. The riverside garden is the perfect setting to see the local wildlife.

OPEN All Year

Low season per wk
£370.00–£500.00
High season per wk
£520.00–£775.00

NORWICH continued

★★★-★★★★★

8 Units
Sleeping 4–9

SPIXWORTH HALL COTTAGES

Spixworth, Norwich
Contact: Mrs S Cook, Grange Farm, Buxton Road, Spixworth, Norwich NR10 3PR
T: (01603) 898190
F: (01603) 897176
E: hallcottages@btinternet.com
I: www.hallcottages.co.uk

These delightful cottages, situated in seclusion on our farm, are ideal for exploring Norwich, the Broads and coast. They have quality furnishings and equipment, log fires and attractive gardens. We offer a warm welcome, farm and woodland walks, swimming, tennis, fishing, a games barn and space to relax and unwind.

OPEN All Year
CC: Delta, JCB, Mastercard, Solo, Switch, Visa

3-night breaks Oct-Mar from £150. 4 nights for the price of 3, Mon-Thu. Snowdrop and Bluebell walks.

Low season per wk
£225.00–£400.00
High season per wk
£330.00–£640.00

ORFORD, Suffolk Map ref 3C2

★★★★

1 Unit
Sleeping 5

70 BROOM COTTAGES

Sudbourne, Woodbridge
Contact: Mrs S Pool, High House Fruit Farm, 69 Broom Cottages, High House Farm Road, Sudbourne, Woodbridge IP12 2BL
T: (01394) 450378
F: (01394) 450124
E: cottage@high-house.co.uk

Situated in an Area of Outstanding Natural Beauty on Suffolk's Heritage Coast two miles from Orford, with its excellent restaurants, and four miles from Snape, home of the Aldeburgh Festival. Spacious, yet cosy and warm in winter with a log fire. Overlooking apple orchards and woodlands. Gardens at front and rear.

OPEN All Year

Short breaks available Oct-Mar, minimum 3 nights.

Low season per wk
£290.00–£350.00
High season per wk
£360.00–£440.00

★★★

1 Unit
Sleeping 5

47 DAPHNE ROAD

Orford, Woodbridge
Contact: Mrs S Hitchcock, Church Farm Cottage, Sudbourne, Woodbridge IP12 2BP
T: (01394) 450714
F: (01394) 450714
E: barryhitchcock@tesco.com

OPEN All Year

Low season per wk
£180.00–£225.00
High season per wk
£250.00–£380.00

Delightful three-bedroomed Edwardian cottage in centre of village. Quiet road with unrestricted parking. Electric heating and open fire. Near Woodbridge, Aldeburgh and Minsmere.

★★★

1 Unit
Sleeping 4

VESTA COTTAGE

Orford, Woodbridge
Contact: Mrs P Kay, 74 Broad Street, Orford, Woodbridge IP12 2NQ
T: (01394) 450652
F: (01394) 450097
E: kaycottages@pobox.com
I: www.vestacottage.co.uk

OPEN All Year
CC: Mastercard, Switch, Visa

Low season per wk
£290.00–£325.00
High season per wk
£360.00–£396.00

Attractive two-bedroom (double and double-bunk) cottage with garden. Next to medieval friary, near Orford Castle and Quay. Suit sailors, bird-watchers, walkers, etc.

OULTON BROAD, Suffolk Map ref 3C1

★★★

2 Units
Sleeping 2–6

MALTINGS HOLIDAY ACCOMMODATION

Oulton Broad, Lowestoft
Contact: Ivy House Farm Hotel
T: (01502) 501353
F: (01502) 501539
E: reception@ivyhousefarm.co.uk
I: www.ivyhousefarm.co.uk

A spacious, yet cosy, one-bedroom, second floor apartment in converted Maltings. Also a well-appointed mews house with south-facing patio garden overlooking Oulton Broad. Quiet location and private parking. Enjoy 10% discount at the Crooked Barn, a 2-Rosette restaurant, when staying in either property.

OPEN All Year except Christmas
CC: Amex, Delta, Diners, JCB, Mastercard, Solo, Switch, Visa

Short breaks available throughout the year.

Low season per wk
£199.00–£399.00
High season per wk
£209.00–£525.00

OVERSTRAND, Norfolk Map ref 3C1

★★★

1 Unit
Sleeping 7

31 HARBORD ROAD

Overstrand, Cromer
Contact: Mrs J Langley, 28 Esher Place Avenue, Esher KT10 8PY
T: (01372) 463063
F: (01372) 463063
E: jane@harbordholidays.co.uk
I: www.harbordholidays.co.uk

A beautifully refurbished, extended Edwardian house in poppy land. Quiet village off coast road. Two hundred yards from cliff-top, leading to sandy beach. Downstairs bedroom and bathroom, two further bedrooms and second bathroom. Large playroom in garden. Carpeted throughout. Short walk to village shop, post office, cafes, pubs, hotels.

OPEN All Year

3/4 night-stays available Nov-Mar (excl Christmas and New Year). Reductions for under-occupancy during same period.

Low season per wk
£300.00–£400.00
High season per wk
£480.00–£600.00

RUNCTON HOLME, Norfolk Map ref 3B1

★★★★

2 Units
Sleeping 4–5

THORPLAND MANOR BARNS

Runcton Holme, King's Lynn
Contact: Mrs M Caley
T: (01553) 810409
F: (01553) 811831
E: w.p.caley@tesco.net

A 17thC barn, skilfully converted into cottages retaining traditional features, beams and interesting memorablilia. Offering a high quality of comfort, rural views, fishing, farm walks, heated outdoor swimming pool (May to end October). Price all inclusive. Easily accessible from A10. Shop, post office and pubs within two miles.

OPEN All Year

Short breaks available (3-night stay) Nov-Apr.

Low season per wk
Min £231.00
High season per wk
Max £564.00

NB

IMPORTANT NOTE Information on accommodation listed in this guide has been supplied by the proprietors. As changes may occur you are advised to check details at the time of booking.

ST ALBANS, Hertfordshire Map ref 2D1 *Tourist Information Centre Tel: (01727) 864511*

★★★★

1 Unit
Sleeping 2

THE HOLLIES

Sandridge, St Albans
Contact: Mrs A Newbury, The Hollies, 11 Spencer Place, Sandridge, St Albans AL4 9DW
T: (01727) 859845
E: martin.newbury@ntlworld.co.uk

Delightful, self-contained, ground floor annexe attached to owner's home. Pretty double bedroom, shower room/wc and sunny kitchen/diner. The lounge has French doors onto patio leading to large, peaceful garden which guests are welcome to enjoy. Close to countryside yet only 2.5 miles from historic St Albans.

OPEN All Year

Low season per wk
Min £280.00
High season per wk
Min £280.00

SANDRINGHAM, Norfolk Map ref 3B1

★★★★

1 Unit
Sleeping 7

FOLK ON THE HILL

Dersingham, King's Lynn
Contact: Mrs L Skerritt, Mill Cottage, Mill Road, Dersingham, King's Lynn PE31 6HY
T: (01485) 544411
E: lili@skerritt-euwe.freeserve.co.uk

Delightfully converted 18thC coach house, set in large gardens, close to the North Norfolk coast with local facilities only 0.5 miles. A luxurious holiday barn for all seasons with four bedrooms, three bathrooms, games room, woodburner, barbecue. Ideal for children, and pets welcome. Popular beach hut at Old Hunstanton.

OPEN All Year except Christmas

Special 3-day breaks – prices negotiable.

Low season per wk
£440.00–£570.00
High season per wk
£535.00–£780.00

SAXMUNDHAM, Suffolk Map ref 3C2

★★★

4 Units
Sleeping 2–6

SNAPE MALTINGS

Snape, Saxmundham
Contact: Ms D Hannan, Snape Maltings, Snape, Saxmundham IP17 1SR
T: (01708) 688303
F: (01708) 688930
E: accom@snapemaltings.co.uk
I: www.snapemaltings.co.uk

Snape Maltings is a unique collection of Victorian granaries and malthouses set on the River Alde – now housing a variety of shops, galleries and restaurants, and famous as home to the Aldeburgh Festival. The cottages and flat have been tastefully converted to make an ideal base for touring the Suffolk coast.

OPEN All Year
CC: Amex, Delta, Mastercard, Switch, Visa

Low season per wk
£275.00–£515.00
High season per wk
£340.00–£595.00

SHERINGHAM, Norfolk Map ref 3B1

Rating Applied For

2 Units
Sleeping 4

CLIFFTOP COTTAGES

Sheringham
Contact: Mrs L Fenn, Clifftops, 19 Vincent Road, Sheringham NR26 8BP
T: (01263) 825409

New cottages. Superb position and sea views. Access beach/cliff walks. Ground floor bedroom, shower room. Upstairs bedroom, bathroom. Garden, parking. Walking distance town centre.

OPEN All Year

Low season per wk
£200.00–£250.00
High season per wk
£280.00–£400.00

SHERINGHAM continued

★★★★

2 Units
Sleeping 4

VICTORIA COURT

Sheringham
Contact: Mr G R Simmons, Camberley, 62 Cliff Road,
Sheringham NR26 8BJ
T: (01263) 823101
F: (01263) 821433
E: graham@camberleyguesthouse.co.uk
I: www.camberleyguesthouse.co.uk

OPEN All Year

Low season per wk
£185.00–£330.00
High season per wk
£360.00–£445.00

Immaculate, fully equipped apartments enjoying excellent coastal and sea views. Direct access to beach. Safe parking in own grounds.

SIBTON, Suffolk Map ref 3C2

★★★★

1 Unit
Sleeping 5

CARDINAL COTTAGE

Sibton, Saxmundham
Contact: Mr & Mrs Belton, Cardinal Cottage, Pouy Street,
Sibton, Saxmundham IP17 2JH
T: (01728) 660111
E: jan.belton@btopenworld.com
I: www.cardinalcottagehoidays.co.uk

Delightful period timber-framed cottage with spectactular beams. Three bedrooms, fully equipped to high standard. Close to Heritage Coast, Minsmere, Aldeburgh and Southwold. Ideal base for walkers and bird-watchers, family history researchers or those after a quiet country retreat.

OPEN All Year

Low season per wk
Max £350.00
High season per wk
Max £425.00

SNETTISHAM, Norfolk Map ref 3B1

★★★★

1 Unit
Sleeping 4

CURSONS COTTAGE

Snettisham, King's Lynn
Contact: Mrs A Campbell, Craven House, Lynn Road,
Snettisham, King's Lynn PE31 7LW
T: (01485) 541179
F: (01485) 543259
E: ian.averilcampbell@btinternet.com
I: www.cottageguide.co.uk/cursonscottage

OPEN All Year

Low season per wk
£200.00–£300.00
High season per wk
£300.00–£375.00

Attractive and comfortable stone cottages in centre of by-passed village. Near Sandringham and north-west Norfolk Heritage Coastline. Sensitively modernised to retain character.

SOUTH BENFLEET, Essex Map ref 3B3

★★★

1 Unit
Sleeping 4

ALICE'S PLACE

South Benfleet
Contact: Mr & Mrs S Millward, 43 Danesfield,
South Benfleet SS7 5EE
T: (01268) 756283
F: (01268) 756283
E: info@alices-place.co.uk
I: www.alices-place.co.uk

OPEN All Year

Low season per wk
£300.00–£350.00
High season per wk
£350.00–£450.00

Spacious two-bedroom bungalow within walking distance of shops, railway station and country park. Easy access to seafront, London and all attractions.

SOUTH MIMMS, Hertfordshire Map ref 2D1

★★-★★★

2 Units
Sleeping 3–6

THE BLACK SWAN

South Mimms, Potters Bar
Contact: Mr W A Marsterson, The Black Swan,
62-64 Blanche Lane, South Mimms, Potters Bar
EN6 3PD
T: (01707) 644180
F: (01707) 642344

OPEN All Year

Low season per wk
£185.00–£220.00
High season per wk
£245.00–£295.00

Cottage and self-contained flats, 16thC Listed building. Rail connections at Potters Bar and London Underground at Barnet allow travel to London within 45 minutes.

SOUTHEND-ON-SEA, Essex Map ref 3B3 *Tourist Information Centre Tel: (01702) 215120*

★★
1 Unit
Sleeping 6

EVERHOME APARTMENTS
Southend-on-Sea
Contact: Mr M Taylor, 26 Drake Road, Westcliff-on-Sea SS0 8LP
T: (01702) 343030
E: malcolmt@zoom.co.uk

OPEN All Year
CC: Amex, Diners, Mastercard, Solo, Switch, Visa

Low season per wk
£300.00–£350.00
High season per wk
£350.00–£450.00

Large two-bedroom apartment in conservation area, five minutes' walk to seafront, 10 minutes' walk to high street, pubs, restaurants and station.

SOUTHWOLD, Suffolk Map ref 3C2 *Tourist Information Centre Tel: (01502) 724729*

★★★
1 Unit
Sleeping 4

GARDEN COTTAGE
Southwold
Contact: A T Bent Properties Ltd, Home Lodge, Beccles NR34 9AS
T: (01502) 712259
F: (01502) 712086
E: wbent@atbentproperties.fsbusiness.co.uk

A very appealing, tastefully furnished, two-bedroom, ground floor cottage, set in pretty herb and rose patio garden. One double and one twin room offering comfortable, orthopaedic mattresses. Garden Cottage is 50 yards from the seafront, and Southwold's pier, shops and amenities are within easy walking distance.

OPEN All Year except Christmas

Low season per wk
£325.00–£400.00
High season per wk
£435.00–£510.00

5

★★★
1 Unit
Sleeping 6

HORSESHOE COTTAGE
Southwold
Contact: Ms D Frost & Ms J Tallon, Acanthus Property Letting Services, 9 Trinity Street, Southwold IP18 6JH
T: (01502) 724033
F: (01502) 725168
E: sales@southwold-holidays.co.uk
I: www.southwold-holidays.co.uk

OPEN All Year
CC: Amex, Mastercard, Visa

Low season per wk
£270.00–£345.00
High season per wk
£340.00–£560.00

A comfortable family house with views over South Green. Near to sea, shops and common. Small rear yard. Open fire. New kitchen and bathroom 2002.

★★
1 Unit
Sleeping 4

THE LITTLE BLUE HOUSE
Southwold
Contact: Mrs D Wright, The Kiln, The Folley, Layer-de-la-Haye, Colchester CO2 0HZ
T: (01206) 738003

OPEN All Year

Low season per wk
£230.00–£270.00
High season per wk
£270.00–£380.00

Small, cosy cottage close to shops and seafront with an attractive enclosed paved garden at the rear.

★★★
1 Unit
Sleeping 2

THE NEST
Southwold
Contact: Mrs D Hall
T: (01502) 723292
E: haadnams_lets@ic24.net
I: www.thenest-southwold.info

OPEN All Year

Low season per wk
£210.00–£273.00
High season per wk
£299.00–£394.00

Centrally located on one of Southwold's prettiest greens, near the lighthouse and beach, a peaceful, cosy hideaway with sea views. Well equipped and double-glazed throughout.

QUALITY ASSURANCE SCHEME
Star ratings were correct at the time of going to press but are subject to change. Please check at the time of booking.

SPROWSTON, Norfolk Map ref 3C1

★★ 1 Unit Sleeping 4

HOLME
Sprowston, Norwich
Contact: Mrs P Guyton, 2 Recreation Ground Road, Sprowston, Norwich NR7 8EN
T: (01603) 465703

OPEN All Year

Low season per wk £145.00–£170.00
High season per wk £180.00–£230.00

Traditional, detached bungalow two miles north of Norwich. Non-smoking accommodation consists of two twin bedrooms, lounge, kitchen/diner, bathroom. Enclosed garden with patio furniture.

STALHAM, Norfolk Map ref 3C1

★★ 1 Unit Sleeping 4

144 BROADSIDE CHALET PARK
Stalham, Norwich
Contact: Mr J J Crawford, 5 Collingwood Avenue, Surbiton KT5 9PT
T: (020) 833 74487
F: (020) 833 74487
E: crawfcall@aol.com
I: www.norfolkholiday.co.uk

OPEN All Year

Low season per wk £85.00–£150.00
High season per wk £155.00–£259.00

South-facing, detached chalet in landscaped park, with pleasant lawns for quiet relaxation or where children may play safely. Swimming pool, licensed club, shop. Four miles to Blue Flag beach.

STOWMARKET, Suffolk Map ref 3B2 *Tourist Information Centre Tel: (01449) 676800*

★★★★ 5 Units Sleeping 2

BARN COTTAGES
Stonham Aspal, Stowmarket
Contact: Mrs M Tydeman, Goldings, East End Lane, Stonham Aspal, Stowmarket IP14 6AS
T: (01449) 711229
E: maria@barncottages.co.uk
I: www.barncottages.co.uk

Immaculate, spacious cottages for two people amidst four acres of peaceful and tranquil surroundings in the heart of the Suffolk countryside. Cottages fully equipped and owner maintained. Ideally situated for exploring Constable country, Lavenham, Southwold and the Heritage Coast.

OPEN All Year

Low season per wk £160.00–£280.00
High season per wk £280.00–£310.00

SWANTON MORLEY, Norfolk Map ref 3B1

★★★ 3 Units Sleeping 4–5

TEAL, HERON & GREBE COTTAGES
Swanton Morley, East Dereham
Contact: Mrs S Marsham, Waterfall Farm, Worthing Road, Swanton Morley, East Dereham NR20 4QD
T: (01362) 637300
F: (01362) 637300
E: waterfallfarm@tesco.net

Situated in a peaceful area of mid-Norfolk, the cottages have been converted from old farm buildings into beautiful holiday homes and are an ideal base for exploring Norfolk. Spacious, well-equipped accommodation with underfloor central heating. With a play area and small animals to see, it is ideal for children. No smoking. Open all year.

OPEN All Year

Nightly stays available. Fishing locally – permits provided. New cottage awaiting inspection (Glebe Cottage).

Low season per wk Min £185.00
High season per wk Max £280.00

CREDIT CARD BOOKINGS If you book by telephone and are asked for your credit card number it is advisable to check the proprietor's policy should you cancel your reservation.

TATTERSETT, Norfolk Map ref 3B1

★★★-★★★★★

5 Units
Sleeping 4–6

These luxury barn conversions offer accommodation to the highest standards, whilst retaining many original features. A large games barn with facilities for all ages is an added bonus for this tranquil setting. Tatt Valley Cottages are situated on a working farm in beautiful North Norfolk near to Burnham Market and the Norfolk coast.

TATT VALLEY HOLIDAY COTTAGES

Tattersett, Fakenham
Contact: Mr T W Hurn, Tatt Valley Holiday Cottages, Lower Farm, Tattersett, King's Lynn PE31 8RT
T: (01485) 528506
E: enquiries@norfolkholidayhomes.co.uk
I: www.norfolkholidayhomes.co.uk

OPEN All Year

3-night stays available Oct-Mar (excl holiday periods).

Low season per wk
£195.00–£265.00
High season per wk
£375.00–£490.00

THORNHAM, Norfolk Map ref 3B1

★★

1 Unit
Sleeping 4

1 MALTHOUSE COTTAGES

Thornham, Hunstanton
Contact: Mrs L K Rigby, Brindle cottage, 6 Church Hill, Castor, Peterborough PE5 7AU
T: (01733) 380399
F: (01733) 380399
E: leslierigby@castor.freeserve.co.uk

OPEN All Year

Low season per wk
£175.00–£230.00
High season per wk
£320.00–£400.00

Charming traditional Norfolk cottage in lovely coastal village with bakery, post office and two pubs. Area renowned for sailing/walking/bird-watching and golfing.

THORPENESS, Suffolk Map ref 3C2

★★★★

11 Units
Sleeping 4–7

Two- and three-bedroomed family apartments and houses with sea views. Fully fitted kitchens with dishwasher and washing machine. TV in lounge. Linen, towels, electricity included. Pets and smoking allowed in some apartments. Discounted tennis and golf facilities. Beach, cycling and wonderful walks make up this perfect holiday.

THE COUNTRY CLUB APARTMENTS

Thorpeness, Leiston
Contact: Thorpeness Golf Club and Hotel Limited, Lakeside Avenue, Thorpeness, Leiston IP16 4NH
T: (01728) 452176
F: (01728) 453868
E: info@thorpeness.co.uk
I: www.thorpeness.co.uk

OPEN All Year
CC: Delta, Mastercard, Solo, Switch, Visa

Short breaks available, maximum 4 days, from Nov-Feb.

Low season per wk
£231.00–£263.00
High season per wk
£693.00–£835.00

AT-A-GLANCE SYMBOLS

Symbols at the end of each accommodation entry give useful information about services and facilities. A key to symbols can be found inside the back cover flap. Keep this open for easy reference.

THORPENESS continued

★★★

1 Unit
Sleeping 12

THE HOUSE IN THE CLOUDS

Thorpeness, Leiston
Contact: Mrs S Le Comber, The House in The Clouds, 4 Hinde House, 14 Hinde Street, London W1U 3BG
T: (020) 7224 3615
F: (020) 7224 3615
E: houseintheclouds@btopenworld.com

A true family holiday in this wonderfully eccentric 'fantasy unmatched in England'. The House in the Clouds has five bedrooms, three bathrooms and unrivalled views from the 'Room at the Top'. Play billiards, snooker, table tennis, tennis and boules. Overlooking sea, golf course and Meare. Bird-watching on RSPB reserves.

OPEN All Year

Low season per wk
£1,500.00–£1,820.00
High season per wk
£1,820.00–£2,200.00

WELLS-NEXT-THE-SEA, Norfolk Map ref 3B1

★★★

1 Unit
Sleeping 4

HONEYPOT COTTAGE

Wells-next-the-Sea
Contact: Mrs J Price, Shingles, Southgate Close, Wells-next-the-Sea NR23 1HG
T: (01328) 711982
F: (01328) 711982
E: walker.al@talk21.com
I: www.wells-honeypot.co.uk

OPEN All Year

Low season per wk
£200.00–£300.00
High season per wk
£300.00–£400.00

Offering comfortable accommodation on the picturesque North Norfolk coast with quaint shopping streets and harbour within easy walking distance. Ideally situated for bird-watching, walking, sightseeing etc.

★★★

1 Unit
Sleeping 4

SEASHELL COTTAGE

Wells-next-the-Sea
Contact: Mrs C Fox, Middle Cottage, Church Street, Brisley, East Dereham NR20 5AA
T: (01362) 668534
F: (01362) 668534
I: www.seashellcottage.co.uk

Pretty Victorian terraced cottage. Extremely well equipped and very well maintained with country-pine-furnished interior. Private patio-style garden to sit out in. Free parking behind patio with rear gate access. Wine, flowers, open fire. Central heating inclusive. Non-smoking. No dogs. Warm welcome.

OPEN All Year

Winter weekend breaks (4 nights), £120, Nov-beginning Mar (excl Christmas and New Year).

Low season per wk
£165.00–£210.00
High season per wk
£263.00–£360.00

WICKHAM SKEITH, Suffolk Map ref 3B2

★★★

1 Unit
Sleeping 4

THE NETUS BARN

Wickham Skeith, Eye
Contact: Mrs J Homan
T: (01449) 766275
E: joygeoffhoman@amserve.net

OPEN All Year

Low season per wk
£175.00–£210.00
High season per wk
£225.00–£260.00

Single-storey period barn, well-equipped kitchen-cum-living room, bathroom with shower, two twin bedrooms, disabled friendly, parking and patio garden. Rural views.

WEB

www.visitengland.com

Log on for information and inspiration. The latest information on places to visit, events and quality assessed accommodation.

WINGFIELD, Suffolk Map ref 3B2

★★★★
1 Unit
Sleeping 4

BEECH FARM MALTINGS
Wingfield, Diss
Contact: Mrs R Gosling, Beech Farm, Wingfield, Eye IP21 5RG
T: (01379) 586630
F: (01379) 586630
E: maltings.beechfarm@virgin.net
I: http://freespace.virgin.net/maltings.beechfarm

OPEN All Year except Christmas

Low season per wk
£215.00–£343.00
High season per wk
£350.00–£424.00

Charming, spacious, converted Maltings, Norfolk/Suffolk border. Fully equipped, rural, parking, garden. Base for Heritage Coast (Aldeburgh, Southwold, Sutton Hoo), North Norfolk coast/broads.

10

WOODBRIDGE, Suffolk Map ref 3C2 *Tourist Information Centre Tel: (01394) 382240*

★★★★
2 Units
Sleeping 6–10

Beautiful and cosy cottages located at Easton Farm Park, a well-established open farm. Set in 35 acres of attractive countryside beside the River Deben, Easton Farm Park is ideal for a relaxing, rural family holiday down on the farm. Fifteen miles from the Suffolk Heritage Coast.

EASTON FARM PARK
Woodbridge
Contact: Fiona Kerr, Easton Farm Park, Easton, Woodbridge IP13 0EQ
T: (01728) 746475
F: (01728) 747861
E: easton@eastonfarmpark.co.uk
I: www.eastonfarmpark.co.uk

OPEN All Year
CC: Delta, Mastercard, Switch, Visa

Short breaks available in low season. Minimum 3 nights. Visit our website for details of events and promotions.

Low season per wk
£385.00–£900.00
High season per wk
£700.00–£1,250.00

★★★★
4 Units
Sleeping 4–6

Authentic round-log cabins set around a private fishing lake in the heart of the countryside. Enjoy a swim in our indoor heated pool or relax in your own secluded, outdoor hot tub.

WINDMILL LODGES
Saxtead, Woodbridge
Contact: Mrs B Coe, Windmill Lodges Ltd, Red House Farm, Saxtead, Woodbridge IP13 9RD
T: (01728) 685338
F: (01728) 685338
E: holidays@windmilllodges.co.uk
I: www.windmilllodges.co.uk

OPEN All Year
CC: Mastercard, Switch, Visa

Short breaks available.

Low season per wk
£185.00–£345.00
High season per wk
£400.00–£670.00

★★★
1 Unit
Sleeping 4

THE WING
Burgh, Woodbridge
Contact: Mrs G M Gurden, Burgh House, Woodbridge IP13 6PU
T: (01473) 735273

OPEN All Year

Low season per wk
£180.00
High season per wk
£200.00

Well-appointed wing of country house with lagre garden near Woodbridge and Snape. Lovely location.

ACCESSIBILITY

Look for the symbols which indicate National Accessible Scheme standards for hearing and visually impaired guests in addition to standards for guests with mobility impairment. Additional participants are shown in the listings at the back.

WORTHAM, Suffolk Map ref 3B2

★★★★

5 Units
Sleeping 4–10

IVY HOUSE FARM

Wortham, Diss
Contact: Mr & Mrs P Bradley
T: (01379) 898395
E: prjsbrad@aol.com
I: www.ivyhousefarmcottages.co.uk

This peaceful complex, set in spacious grounds surrounded by common-land in the heart of East Anglia, consists of a 17thC farmhouse and purpose-built cottages, one of which has facilities for the disabled. Other facilities include heated indoor swimming pool and cosy barn with table-tennis, pool, piano, snooker table and library.

OPEN All Year

Low season per wk
£237.00–£571.00
High season per wk
£508.00–£1,283.00

WROXHAM, Norfolk Map ref 3C1

★★★★

9 Units
Sleeping 8

DAISY BROAD LODGES
Wroxham, Norwich
Contact: Mr D Thwaites, Barnes Brinkcraft, Riverside Road, Wroxham, Norwich NR12 8UD
T: (01603) 782625
F: (01603) 784072
E: daniel@barnesbrinkcraft.co.uk
I: www.barnesbrinkcraft.co.uk

OPEN All Year
CC: Delta, JCB, Mastercard, Solo, Switch, Visa

Low season per wk
£514.00–£622.00
High season per wk
£794.00–£1,193.00

New in 1998/2000, river frontage. First floor living area and balcony allows for superb views. Two minutes' walk from Wroxham village. Daylaunch FOC (not Jul/Aug).

★★★★

1 Unit
Sleeping 6

KINGFISHER LODGE

Wroxham, Norwich
Contact: Mrs D Campling, Kingfisher Lodge, Fineway Cruisers, Riverside Road, Wroxham, Norwich NR12 8UD
T: (01603) 782309
E: steve@fineway.freeserve.co.uk
I: www.finewayleisure.co.uk

Built in 1999, the lodge has spacious accommodation with full gas central heating. Three large bedrooms (two doubles, one twin). Two toilets, one with shower and one with bath. Large communal room with kitchen/diner. Lawn to river frontage with own dinghy. Quietly situated but within walking distance of village.

OPEN All Year
CC: Delta, Mastercard, Solo, Switch, Visa

Low season per wk
Min £320.00
High season per wk
Max £760.00

TOWN INDEX

This can be found at the back of the guide. If you know where you want to stay, the index will give you the page number listing accommodation in your chosen town, city or village.

WROXHAM continued

★★★★

2 Units
Sleeping 2–6

NUTMEG & PLUM TREE COTTAGES

Wroxham, Norwich
Contact: Mrs J Pond, East View Farm, Stone Lane, Ashmanhaugh, Norwich NR12 8YW
T: (01603) 782225
F: (01603) 782225
E: john.pond@tinyworld.co.uk
I: www.eastviewfarm.co.uk

Stunning barn conversion in a tranquil, rural setting, close to all facilities. Furnished to a high standard, spacious and cosy with woodburners and 4-poster bed. Wroxham/Broads two miles. Norwich/beaches 10 miles. Good pubs and restaurants nearby. Open all year.

OPEN All Year

3-night stays available Oct-Apr (excl Christmas and New Year).

Low season per wk
£196.00–£422.00
High season per wk
£218.00–£642.00

★★★

1 Unit
Sleeping 2

WHITEGATES APARTMENT

Wroxham, Norwich
Contact: Mrs C M Youd, Whitegates Apartment, 181 Norwich Road, Wroxham, Norwich NR12 8RZ
T: (01603) 781037

Whitegates Apartment is a fully equipped self-catering ground floor apartment with en suite facilities, secure parking, swimming pool, sauna, games room and barbecue. Ten minutes' walk from Wroxham with boat hire and restaurants, eight miles from Norwich and within easy reach of Great Yarmouth and the North Norfolk coast.

OPEN All Year

3-night stays available Oct-Mar (incl Christmas and New Year).

Low season per wk
£200.00–£225.00
High season per wk
£250.00–£280.00

CHECK THE MAPS

The colour maps at the front of this guide show all the cities, towns and villages for which you will find accommodation entries. Refer to the town index to find the page on which they are listed.

A brief guide to the main Towns and Villages offering accommodation in the **East of England**

A **ALDEBURGH, SUFFOLK** - A prosperous port in the 16th C, now famous for the Aldeburgh Music Festival held annually in June. The 16th C Moot Hall, now a museum, is a timber-framed building once used as an open market.

ALRESFORD, ESSEX - Village easily accessible from the Essex Sunshine Coast and Colchester.

B **BECCLES, SUFFOLK** - Fire destroyed the town in the 16th C and it was rebuilt in Georgian red brick. The River Waveney, on which the town stands, is popular with boating enthusiasts and has an annual regatta. Home of Beccles and District Museum.

BERKHAMSTED, HERTFORDSHIRE - Hilltop town on Grand Union Canal surrounded by pleasant countryside and a 1200-acre common. It has remains of an important castle with earthworks and moat. Birthplace of William Cowper, the poet.

BILLERICAY, ESSEX - Site of both Roman and Saxon settlements and a popular overnight stop for Canterbury pilgrims. Historic links with famous Mayflower voyage. Now a flourishing town with a wide variety of sports, leisure and cultural activities and some fine examples of Georgian architecture.

BLAKENEY, NORFOLK - Picturesque village on the north coast of Norfolk and a former port and fishing village. 15th C Guildhall. Marshy creeks extend towards Blakeney Point (National Trust) and are a paradise for naturalists, with trips to the reserve and to see the seals from Blakeney Quay.

BRANCASTER, NORFOLK - On the North Norfolk coast. One mile from the pebble beach. Close to Holkham Hall and Sandringham. Many nature reserves nearby.

BRANCASTER STAITHE, NORFOLK - Small harbour with a boat service to Scolt Head Island, a bird sanctuary and nature-study area.

C **CAMBRIDGE, CAMBRIDGESHIRE** - A most important and beautiful city on the River Cam with 31 colleges forming one of the oldest universities in the world. Numerous museums, good shopping centre, restaurants, theatres, cinema and fine bookshops.

CASTLE HEDINGHAM, ESSEX - Here is a splendid Norman keep, built by the famous deVeres, Earls of Oxford, with the finest Norman arch in England, all beside a medieval village with a fine Norman church.

CHELMSFORD, ESSEX - The county town of Essex, originally a Roman settlement, Caesaromagus, thought to have been destroyed by Boudicca. Growth of the town's industry can be traced in the excellent museum in Oaklands Park. The 15th C parish church has been Chelmsford Cathedral since 1914.

CLEY NEXT THE SEA, NORFOLK - Due to land reclamation, the village has not been 'next the sea' since the 17th C. Behind the old quay the main street winds between flint-built houses. The marshes between Cley and Salthouse are bird reserves. Cley Windmill is a 160-year-old tower mill converted into a guesthouse.

COLCHESTER, ESSEX - Britain's oldest-recorded town standing on the River Colne and famous for its oysters. Numerous historic buildings, ancient remains and museums. Plenty of parks and gardens, extensive shopping centre, theatre and zoo.

CROMER, NORFOLK - Once a small fishing village and now famous for its fishing boats that still work off the beach and offer freshly caught crabs. Excellent bathing on sandy beaches fringed by cliffs. The town boasts a fine pier, theatre, museum and a lifeboat station.

D **DEDHAM, ESSEX** - A former wool town. Dedham Vale is an Area of Outstanding Natural Beauty, and there is a countryside centre in the village. This is John Constable country, and Sir Alfred Munnings lived at Castle House which is open to the public.

DOCKING, NORFOLK - Conservation village still retaining village stocks, lock-up, blacksmith's forge and ponds. Well situated for the North Norfolk coast 5 miles away.

E **EAST BERGHOLT, SUFFOLK** - John Constable, the famous East Anglian artist, was born here in 1776 and at the church of St Mary are reminders of his family's associations with the area. One mile south of the village are Flatford Mill and Willy Lott's cottage, both made famous by Constable in his paintings.

EAST HARLING, NORFOLK - In the heart of Norfolk countryside, near Thetford forest.

ELY, CAMBRIDGESHIRE - Until the 17th C, when the Fens were drained, Ely was an island. The cathedral, completed in 1189, dominates the surrounding area. One particular feature is the central octagonal tower with a fan-vaulted timber roof and wooden lantern.

EYE, SUFFOLK - "Eye" means island, and this town was once surrounded by marsh. The fine church of SS Peter and Paul has a tower over 100 ft high. A carving of the Archangel Gabriel can be seen on the 16th C Guildhall.

F FAKENHAM, NORFOLK - Attractive, small market town which dates from Saxon times and was a Royal Manor until the 17th C. Its market place has 2 old coaching inns, both showing traces of earlier work behind Georgian facades, and the parish church has a commanding 15th C tower.

FELIXSTOWE, SUFFOLK - Seaside resort that developed at the end of the 19th C, lying in a gently curving bay with a 2-mile-long beach and backed by a wide promenade of lawns and floral gardens.

FOXLEY, NORFOLK - Small, quiet, rural village close to Fakenham and East Dereham.

G GRESHAM, NORFOLK - A rural village with a round-towered church which has a fine Seven Sacraments font.

H HAUGHLEY, SUFFOLK - In the heart of Suffolk, very well placed for touring.

HEACHAM, NORFOLK - The portrait of a Red Indian princess who married John Rolfe of Heacham Hall in 1614 appears on the village sign. Caley Mill is the centre of lavender growing.

HINGHAM, NORFOLK - Small market town with a 14th C church, 15 miles from Norwich.

HUNSTANTON, NORFOLK - Seaside resort which faces the Wash. The shingle and sand beach is backed by striped cliffs, and many unusual fossils can be found here. The town is predominantly Victorian. The Oasis family leisure centre has indoor and outdoor pools.

K KESSINGLAND, SUFFOLK - Seaside village whose church tower has served as a landmark to sailors for generations. Nearby is the Suffolk Wildlife and Country Park.

KING'S LYNN, NORFOLK - A busy town with many outstanding buildings. The Guildhall and Town Hall are both built of flint in a striking chequer design. Behind the Guildhall in the Old Gaol House the sounds and smells of prison life 2 centuries ago are recreated.

KNAPTON, NORFOLK - The church is visited for the beauty of its roof and font. The former, dated 1504, is 30 ft wide and adorned with a host of angels. The latter is 13th C, built of Purbeck marble, and has an interesting Decorative cover.

L LAVENHAM, SUFFOLK - A former prosperous wool town of timber-framed buildings with the cathedral-like church and its tall tower. The market-place is 13th C and the Guildhall now houses a museum.

LONG MELFORD, SUFFOLK - One of Suffolk's loveliest villages, remarkable for the length of its main street. Holy Trinity Church is considered to be the finest village church in England. The National Trust own the Eizabethan Melford Hall, and nearby Kentwell Hall is also open to the public.

LOWESTOFT, SUFFOLK - Seaside town with wide sandy beaches. Important fishing port with picturesque fishing quarter. Home of the famous Lowestoft porcelain and birthplace of Benjamin Britten. East Point Pavilion's exhibition describes the Lowestoft story.

N NEWMARKET, SUFFOLK - Centre of the English horse-racing world and the headquarters of the Jockey Club and National Stud. Racecourse and horse sales. The National Horse Racing Museum traces the history and development of the Sport of Kings.

NORWICH, NORFOLK - Beautiful cathedral city and county town on the River Wensum with many fine museums and medieval churches. Norman castle, Guildhall and interesting medieval streets. Good shopping centre and market.

O ORFORD, SUFFOLK - Once a thriving port, now a quiet village of brick and timber buildings, famous for its castle. Orford comes to life during the summer when boats tie up at the quay.

OVERSTRAND, NORFOLK - Village with extensive sandy beach. The church of St Martin, built in 14th C but much rebuilt since, has a round tower and ancient oven for baking the sacrament.

S ST ALBANS, HERTFORDSHIRE - As Verulamium this was one of the largest towns in Roman Britain, and its remains can be seen in the museum. The Norman cathedral was built from Roman materials to commemorate Alban, the first British Christian martyr.

SANDRINGHAM, NORFOLK - Famous as the country retreat of Her Majesty the Queen. The house and grounds are open to the public at certain times.

SAXMUNDHAM, SUFFOLK - The church of St John the Baptist has a hammer-beam roof and contains a number of good monuments.

SHERINGHAM, NORFOLK - Holiday resort with Victorian and Edwardian hotels and a sand and shingle beach where the fishing boats are hauled up. The North Norfolk Railway operates from Sheringham station during the summer. Other attractions include museums, theatre and Splash Fun Pool.

SNETTISHAM, NORFOLK - Village with a superb Decorated church. The 17th C Old Hall is a distinguished-looking house with Dutch gables over the 2 bays. Snettisham Pits is a reserve of the Royal Society for the Protection of Birds. Red deer herd and other animals, farm trails and nature walks at Park Farm.

SOUTH MIMMS, HERTFORDSHIRE - Best known today for its location at the junction of the M25 and the A1M.

SOUTHEND-ON-SEA, ESSEX - On the Thames Estuary and the nearest seaside resort to London. Famous for its pier and unique pier trains. Other attractions include Peter Pan's Playground, indoor swimming pools, indoor rollerskating and ten pin bowling.

SOUTHWOLD, SUFFOLK - Pleasant and attractive seaside town with a triangular market square and spacious greens around which stand flint, brick and colour-washed cottages. The parish church of St Edmund is one of the greatest churches in Suffolk.

SPROWSTON, NORFOLK - 2 miles north of Norwich, 6 miles from the Broads.

STALHAM, NORFOLK - Lies on the edge of the Broads.

STOWMARKET, SUFFOLK - Small market town where routes converge. There is an open-air museum of rural life at the Museum of East Anglian Life.

SWANTON MORLEY, NORFOLK - All Saints Church, built around 1400, has an eye-catching west tower with large bell-openings at the top. The remains of a cottage belonging to the ancestors of Abraham Lincoln can also be seen.

THORPENESS, SUFFOLK - A planned mock-Tudor seaside resort, built in the early 20th C, with a 65-acre artificial lake. The House in the Clouds was built to disguise a water-tower. The windmill contains an exhibition on Suffolk's Heritage Coast.

WELLS-NEXT-THE-SEA, NORFOLK - Seaside resort and small port on the north coast. The Buttlands is a large, tree-lined green surrounded by Georgian houses, and from here narrow streets lead to the quay.

WOODBRIDGE, SUFFOLK - Once a busy seaport, the town is now a sailing centre on the River Deben. There are many buildings of architectural merit including the Bell and Angel Inns. The 18th C Tide Mill is now restored and open to the public.

WROXHAM, NORFOLK - Yachting centre on the River Bure which houses the headquarters of the Norfolk Broads Yacht Club. The church of St Mary has a famous doorway, and the manor house nearby dates back to 1623.

USE YOUR *i*s

There are more than 550 Tourist Information Centres throughout England offering friendly help with accommodation and holiday ideas as well as suggestions of places to visit and things to do. There may well be a centre in your home town which can help you before you set out. You'll find addresses in the local Phone Book.

South West

A land of myths and legends – and beautiful beaches. The region has cathedral cities, Georgian Bath and maritme Bristol, mysterios castles, evocative country houses and sub tropical gardens to discover, too.

Classic sights
Eden Project – plant life from around the world
English Riviera – family-friendly beaches
Dartmoor & Exmoor – wild open moorland, rocky tors and woodland

Coast & country
Jurassic Coast – World Heritage Coastline
Runnymede – riverside meadows and woodland
Pegwell Bay & Goodwin Sands – a haven for birds and seals

Glorious gardens
Stourhead – 18thC landscaped garden
Westonbirt Arboretum – Over 3,700 different varieties of tree

Art for all
Tate Gallery St Ives – modern art and the St Ives School
Arnolfini Gallery, Bristol – contemporary arts

Distinctively different
Daphne du Maurier – Cornwall inspired many of her novels
Agatha Christie – follow the trail in Torquay

The Counties of Bath & Bristol, Cornwall & Isles of Scilly, Devon, Dorset (Western), Gloucestershire South, Somerset and Wiltshire

For more information contact:
South West Tourism
Admail 3186,
Exeter EX2 7WH

E: info@westcountryholidays.com
www.visitsouthwest.co.uk

Telephone enquiries -
T: (0870) 442 0880

1. Roman Bath, Bath

Places to Visit

You will find hundreds of interesting places to visit during your stay, just some of which are listed in these pages. Contact any Tourist Information Centre in the region for more ideas on days out.

QUALITY ASSURED VISITOR ATTRACTION — Awarded VisitBritain's 'Quality Assured Visitor Attraction' marque.

At Bristol
Harbourside, Bristol
Tel: 08453 451235 www.at-bristol.org.uk
3 exciting new attractions which will take you on the interactive adventure of a lifetime – Explore, Wildwalk and the IMAX Theatre.

Atwell-Wilson Motor Museum Trust
Stockley Lane, Calne
Tel: (01249) 813119 www.atwell-wilson.org
Motor museum with vintage, post-vintage and classic cars, including American models. Classic motorbikes. A 17thC water meadow walk. Car clubs welcome for rallies. Play area.

Babbacombe Model Village
Babbacombe, Torquay
Tel: (01803) 315315
www.babbacombemodelvillage.co.uk
Over 400 models many with sound and animation with 4 acres (1.6ha) of award-winning gardens. See modern towns, villages and rural areas. Stunning illuminations and Aquaviva.

Bristol City Museum & Art Gallery
Queen's Road, Bristol
Tel: (0117) 922 3571
www.bristol-city.gov.uk/museums
Outstanding collections of applied, oriental and fine art, archaeology, geology, natural history, ethnography and Egyptology.

Bristol Zoo Gardens
QUALITY ASSURED VISITOR ATTRACTION
Clifton, Bristol
Tel: (0117) 974 7300
www.bristolzoo.org.uk
Enjoy an exciting real life experience and see over 300 species of wildlife in beautiful gardens. Favourites include Gorilla Island, Bug World and Sea and Penguin Coasts with underwater viewing.

Buckland Abbey (National Trust)
Yelverton
Tel: (01822) 853607 www.nationaltrust.org.uk
Originally Cistercian monastery, then home of Sir Francis Drake. Ancient buildings, exhibitions, herb garden, craft workshops and estate walks. Elizabethan garden.

Cheddar Caves and Gorge
Cheddar
Tel: (01934) 742343 www.cheddarcaves.co.uk
Beautiful caves located in Cheddar Gorge. Gough's Cave with its cathedral-like caverns and Cox's Cave with stalagmites and stalactites. Also 'The Crystal Quest' fantasy adventure.

Combe Martin Wildlife and Dinosaur Park
Combe Martin, Ilfracombe
Tel: (01271) 882486 www.dinosaur-uk.com
The land that time forgot. A subtropical paradise with hundreds of birds and animals, and animatronics dinosaurs, so real they're alive!

Crealy Park
Clyst St Mary, Exeter
Tel: (01395) 233200 www.crealy.co.uk
One of Devon's largest animal farms. Milk a cow, feed a lamb and pick up a piglet. Adventure playgrounds. Dragonfly Lake and farm trails.

Dairyland Farm World
QUALITY ASSURED VISITOR ATTRACTION
Summercourt, Newquay
Tel: (01872) 510246
www.dairylandfarmworld.com
120 cows milked in Clarabelle's 'Spage-age' orbiter, adventure playground, country life museum, nature trail, farm park, pets and daily events.

Eden Project
Bodelva, St Austell
Tel: (01726) 811911 www.edenproject.com
An unforgettable experience in a breathtaking epic location. Eden is a gateway into the fascinating world of plants and people.

Exmoor Falconry & Animal Farm
West Lynch Farm, Minehead
Tel: (01643) 862816
www.exmoorfalconry.co.uk
Historic 15thC farm with hand-tame, rare breed farm animals, pets' corner, birds of prey and owls. Flying displays daily. Short activity breaks.

Flambards Village
Culdrose Manor, Helston
Tel: (01326) 573404 www.flambards.co.uk
Life-size Victorian village with fully stocked shops, carriages and fashions. 'Britain in the Blitz' life-size wartime street, historic aircraft. Science centre and rides.

Heale Garden & Plant Centre
Middle Woodford, Salisbury
Tel: (01722) 782504
Mature traditional garden with shrubs, musk and other roses, and kitchen garden. Authentic Japanese teahouse in water garden. Magnolias. Snowdrops and aconites in winter.

International Animal Rescue
Animal Tracks, South Molton
Tel: (01769) 550277 www.iar.org.uk
A 60-acre (24-ha) animal sanctuary with a wide range of rescued animals from monkeys to chinchillas and from shire horses and ponies to donkeys, goats and pigs. Also rare plant nursery.

Jamaica Inn Museums (Potters Museum of Curiosity)
Bolventor, Launceston
Tel: (01566) 86838
www.pottersjamaicainn.com
Museums contain lifetime work of Walter Potter, a Victorian taxidermist. Exhibits include 'Kittens' Wedding' and 'Death of Cock Robin' and 'The Story of Smuggling'.

Longleat
Longleat, Warminster
Tel: (01985) 844400 www.longleat.co.uk
Elizabethan stately home, safari park plus a wonderland of 10 family attractions. 'World's Longest Hedge Maze', Safari Boats, Pets Corner, Longleat railway and Adventure Castle.

The Lost Gardens of Heligan
Heligan, St Austell
Tel: (01726) 845100 www.heligan.com
Gardeners' World 'The Nation's Favourite Garden' 2002. The world famous, award winning garden restoration is now complemented by a pioneering wildlife conservation project.

Lyme Regis Philpot Museum
Bridge Street, Lyme Regis
Tel: (01297) 443370
www.lymeregismuseum.co.uk
Fossils, geology, local history, literary connections – The story of Lyme in its landscape.

2

3

1. Stourhead Gardens, Wiltshire
2. Clifton Suspension Bridge, Bristol
3. Water sports in Torquay

National Marine Aquarium
Rope Walk, Plymouth
Tel: (01752) 600301
www.national-aquarium.co.uk
The United Kingdom's only world-class aquarium, located in the heart of Plymouth. Visitor experiences include a mountain stream and Caribbean reef complete with sharks.

Newquay Zoo
Trenance Park, Newquay
Tel: (01637) 873342
www.newquayzoo.co.uk
A modern award-winning zoo, where you can have fun and learn at the same time. A varied collection of animals, from Antelope to Zebra.

Paignton Zoo Environmental Park
Totnes Road, Paignton
Tel: (01803) 697500
www.paigntonzoo.org.uk
One of England's largest zoos with over 1,200 animals in the beautiful setting of 75 acres (30ha) of botanical gardens. The zoo is one of Devon's most popular family days out.

Plant World
St Marychurch Road, Newton Abbot
Tel: (01803) 872939
Four acres of gardens including the unique 'map of the world' gardens. Cottage garden. Panoramic views. Comprehensive nursery of rare and more unusual plants.

Powderham Castle
Kenton, Exeter
Tel: (01626) 890243 www.powderham.co.uk
Built c1390, restored in 18thC, Georgian interiors, china, furnishings and paintings. Family home of the Courtenays for over 600 years. Fine views across deer park and River Exe.

Railway Village Museum
34 Faringdon Road, Swindon
Tel: (01793) 466553
www.steam-museum.org.uk
Foreman's house in original Great Western Railway village. Furnished to re-create a Victorian working-class home.

Roman Baths
Pump Room, Bath
Tel: (01225) 477785
www.romanbaths.co.uk
2000 years ago, around Britain's hot springs, the Romans built this great temple and spa that still flows with natural hot water.

St Michael's Mount
Marazion, Penzance
Tel: (01736) 710507
www.stmichaelsmount.co.uk
Originally the site of a Benedictine chapel, castle on its rock dates from 12thC. Fine views towards Land's End and the Lizard. Reached by foot, or ferry at high tide in summer.

Smugglers Barn
Abbotsbury, Weymouth
Tel: (01305) 871817
www.abbotsbury-tourism.co.uk
Soft play undercover with a smuggling theme for children under 11 years. Other activities include rabbit and guinea pig cuddling. Pony rides (extra charge).

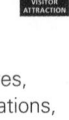

Steam – Museum of the Great Western Railway
Kemble Drive, Swindon
Tel: (01793) 466646
www.steam-museum.org.uk
Historic Great Western Railway locomotives, wide range of nameplates, models, illustrations, posters and tickets.

Stonehenge
Amesbury, Salisbury
Tel: (01980) 624715
www.stonehengemasterplan.org
World-famous prehistoric monument built as a ceremonial centre. Started 5000 years ago and remodelled several times in next 1500 years.

Stourhead House and Garden (National Trust)
Stourton, Warminster
Tel: (01747) 841152 www.nationaltrust.org.uk
Landscaped garden laid out c1741-80, with lakes, temples, rare trees and plants. House begun in c1721 by Colen Campbell, contains fine paintings and Chippendale furniture.

Tate Gallery St Ives
Porthmeor Beach, St Ives
Tel: (01736) 796226 www.tate.org.uk
Opened in 1993 and offering a unique introduction to modern art. Changing displays focus on the modern movement St Ives is famous for. Major contemporary exhibitions.

Teignmouth Museum
29 French Street, Teignmouth
Tel: (01626) 777041
www.lineone.net/-teignmuseum
Exhibits include 16thC cannon and artefacts from Armada wreck and local history, 1920s pier machines and c1877 cannon.

Tintagel Castle (English Heritage)
Tintagel
Tel: (01840) 770328
www.english-heritage.org.uk
Medieval ruined castle on wild, wind-swept coast. Famous for associations with Arthurian legend. Built largely in 13thC by Richard, Earl of Cornwall.

Totnes Costume Museum – Devonshire Collection of Period Costume
Bogan House, Totnes
Tel: (01803) 863821
New exhibition of costumes and accessories each season, displayed in one of the historic merchant's houses of Totnes, Bogan House, restored by Mitchell Trust.

Woodlands Leisure Park
Blackawton, Totnes
Tel: (01803) 712598
www.woodlandspark.com
All weather fun guaranteed; unique combination indoor and outdoor attractions, 3 water coasters, toboggan run, indoor venture centre with rides. Falconry and animals.

Wookey Hole Caves and Papermill
Wookey Hole, Wells
Tel: (01749) 672243 www.wookey.co.uk
Spectacular caves and legendary home of the Witch of Wookey. Working Victorian paper mill including Old Penny Arcade, Magical Mirror Maze and Cave Diving Museum.

1

1. Land's End, Cornwall

SOUTH WEST

South West Tourism
Admail 3186,
Exeter EX2 7WH
T: (0870) 442 0880
E: info@westcountryholidays.com
www.visitsouthwest.co.uk

THE FOLLOWING OFFICIAL GUIDES ARE AVAILABLE FREE FROM SOUTH WEST TOURISM:

Quality Bed & Breakfast

Holiday Homes, Cottages & Apartments

Hotels and Guesthouses

Holiday Parks, Camping and Caravan

Attractions and Days Out

Trencherman's Restaurant Guide

South West Walks

Sailing and Watersports

Getting to the South West

BY ROAD: The region is easily accessible from London, the South East, the North and Midlands by the M6/M5 which extends just beyond Exeter, where it links in with the dual carriageways of the A38 to Plymouth, A380 to Torbay and the A30 into Cornwall. The North Devon Link Road A361 joins Junction 37 with the coast of North Devon and the A39, which then becomes the Atlantic Highway into Cornwall.

BY RAIL: The main towns in the South West are served throughout the year by fast, direct and frequent rail services from all over the country. Trains operate from London (Paddington) to Chippenham, Swindon, Bath, Bristol, Weston-super-Mare, Taunton, Exeter, Plymouth and Penzance, and also from Scotland, the North East and the Midlands to the South West. A service runs from London (Waterloo) to Exeter, via Salisbury, Yeovil and Crewkerne. Sleeper services operate between Devon and Cornwall and London as well as between Bristol and Glasgow and Edinburgh. Motorail services operate from strategic points to key South West locations.

1. Salisbury Cathedral, Wiltshire
2. Selworthy, Somerset

Where to stay in the
South West

All place names in the blue bands under which accommodation is listed, are shown on the maps at the front of this guide.

Symbols give useful information about services and facilities. Inside the back cover flap there's a key to these symbols which you can keep open for easy reference.

A complete listing of all the VisitBritain assessed accommodation covered by this guide appears at the back of this guide.

ALLERFORD, Somerset Map ref 1D1

★★★★

7 Units
Sleeping 2–8

Delightful country house in woodland setting, overlooking moors and sea, tastefully converted to comfortable apartments. 7-acre, informal gardens. Lynch is an ideal base for those on a walking holiday. There are many well-made paths leading to combes, moors and wooded hillsides.

LYNCH COUNTRY HOUSE HOLIDAY APARTMENTS

Allerford, (Exmoor National Park)
Contact: Mr & Mrs B Tacchi, Lynch Country House Holiday Apartments, Allerford, Minehead TA24 8HJ
T: (01643) 862800
F: (01643) 862800
E: anntacchi@beeb.net
I: www.lynchcountryhouse.co.uk

OPEN All Year

Low season per wk
£235.00–£390.00
High season per wk
£280.00–£580.00

SPECIAL BREAKS
Many establishments offer special promotions and themed breaks. These are highlighted in red. (All such offers are subject to availability.)

Three Superb Properties, One Superb Holiday!

Kirk House

PierInn House

PierInn Studio

Located in the picturesque, ancient fishing village of Polperro are three unique ETC Five Star rated self-catering holiday homes. Kirk House is a converted 1838 Chapel with secluded courtyard, balcony with harbour views and superb accommodation for ten. Historic PierInn House at the head of the harbour, provides luxury accommodation for six and boasts superb views of the harbour and sea beyond. PierInn Studio, with it's harbourside balcony, is a superbly appointed, romantic apartment for two and can be combined with PierInn House to provide accommodation for eight guests.

Contact: Sarah Sullivan, Holiday Cottages Polperro,
Talland Street, Polperro, Cornwall. PL13 2RE
Tel: 01503 272320 Fax: 01503 272560
Email: wts@holidaycottagespolperro.co.uk www.holidaycottagespolperro.co.uk

Your first visit
won't be your last
adventure.

MARSDENS
COTTAGE HOLIDAYS

The quality and variety of our 200 hand picked, inspected and graded North Devon cottages will ensure that your first Marsdens Cottage Holiday won't be your last.

www.marsdens.co.uk
for information and 24 hour on line booking

For a free brochure, contact holidays@marsdens.co.uk, phone 01271 813777 or write 2 The Square, Braunton EX33 2JB

ALLERFORD continued

★★★

1 Unit
Sleeping 4

ORCHARD COTTAGE

Allerford, Minehead
Contact: Mrs D M Williams, Brandish Street Farm, Allerford, Minehead TA24 8HR
T: (01643) 862383

Delightful character National Trust cottage on a traditional working farm, surrounded by beautiful scenery. Old beams, log fire, cosy, clean and comfortable. Situated near Allerford, Minehead, and central for exploring the Exmoor coast and countryside. Many attractions nearby. Village shops, pubs and restaurants five minutes' drive away. Colour brochure available.

OPEN All Year

Low season per wk
£250.00–£290.00
High season per wk
£310.00–£340.00

★★★

5 Units
Sleeping 3–6

THE PACK HORSE

Allerford, Minehead
Contact: Mr & Mrs Garner, The Pack Horse, Allerford, Minehead TA24 8HW
T: (01643) 862475
F: (01643) 862475
E: holidays@thepackhorse.net
I: www.thepackhorse.net

Idyllic location in the NT village of Allerford alongside the shallow River Aller, overlooking the ancient pack-horse bridge. Paths and bridleways give immediate access to beautiful countryside on the edge of Exmoor. Self-contained accommodation, outstanding views; private car parking and stabling available. Open all year round.

OPEN All Year

2- and 3-night breaks available Oct–Jun from £105.

Low season per wk
£210.00–£295.00
High season per wk
£310.00–£450.00

AMESBURY, Wiltshire Map ref 2B2 *Tourist Information Centre Tel: (01980) 622833*

★★★★

1 Unit
Sleeping 5

THE STABLES

Netheravon, Salisbury
Contact: Mrs A Thatcher, Ivy Cottage, Netheravon, Salisbury SP4 9QW
T: (01980) 670557
F: (01980) 670557
E: athatcher@bigfoot.com
I: www.uk-holiday-cottages.co.uk/thestables

OPEN All Year
CC: Delta, Mastercard, Switch, Visa

Low season per wk
Min £220.00
High season per wk
Max £420.00

Charming cottage, in village five miles north of Stonehenge, in Avon valley. Self-catering or half board. Short breaks available.

DREAM COTTAGES LTD

5 Hope Square, Weymouth, DT4 8TR
Tel: (01305) 789000 Fax: (01305) 761347

Self-catering accommodation located throughout glorious Dorset and on the picturesque borders of Devon and Wiltshire in coastal and country locations. A good selection of properties are suitable for Christmas and New Year. Accommodation is offered at very competitive rates.

Email: admin@dream-cottages.co.uk
www.dream-cottages.co.uk

ASHBURTON, Devon Map ref 1C2

★★★

7 Units
Sleeping 4–12

Cottages nestled in picturesque valley in Dartmoor National Park. Peaceful location, beautiful views of woodland, moors and granite tors. Tour Devon, explore Dartmoor, the coast, NT properties and attractions. Clean and very well equipped. Gardens. Off-road parking. Good food at two local inns 0.5 and 0.75 miles. Colour brochure.

WOODER MANOR HOLIDAY HOMES

Widecombe-in-the-Moor, Newton Abbot
Contact: Mrs A M Bell, Wooder Manor Holiday Homes, Widecombe-in-the-Moor, Newton Abbot TQ13 7TR
T: (01364) 621391
F: (01364) 621391
E: angela@woodermanor.com
I: www.woodermanor.com

OPEN All Year
CC: Amex, Delta, Mastercard, Solo, Switch, Visa

Short breaks available.

Low season per wk
Min £160.00
High season per wk
Max £950.00

★★★★

2 Units
Sleeping 2–4

WREN & ROBIN COTTAGES
Ashburton, Newton Abbot
Contact: Mrs Phipps, Wren & Robin Cottages, New Cott Farm, Poundsgate, Ashburton, Newton Abbot TQ13 7PD
T: (01364) 631421
F: (01364) 631421
E: enquiries@newcott-farm.co.uk
I: www.newcott-farm.co.uk

CC: JCB, Mastercard, Solo, Visa

Low season per wk
£185.00–£210.00
High season per wk
£230.00–£450.00

Cottages situated in a beautiful, peaceful location. Fully equipped, beautifully furnished, user friendly for less-able guests. Eden project 90 minutes away. Dartmoor National Park for walking.

ASHWATER, Devon Map ref 1C2

★★★

6 Units
Sleeping 6–8

BRADDON COTTAGES
Ashwater, Beaworthy
Contact: Mr G & Mrs A Ridge, Braddon Cottages, Ashwater, Beaworthy EX21 5EP
T: (01409) 211350
F: (01409) 211350
E: holidays@braddoncottages.co.uk
I: www.braddoncottages.co.uk

OPEN All Year
CC: Delta, Diners, Mastercard, Solo, Switch, Visa

Low season per wk
£90.00–£240.00
High season per wk
£250.00–£1,100.00

For country lovers, cottages in secluded location. Games field, adults' snooker and children's games rooms. Wood fires, licensed shop. Colour brochure, extensive website.

BAMPTON, Devon Map ref 1D1

★★★★

5 Units
Sleeping 2–6

Relax in one of our excellent converted barns, in the beautiful Devonshire countryside. Spend hours in our superb indoor heated pool, sauna or fitness room. Play in the grounds, with play tower and games rooms. The perfect place to unwind and explore the beaches, river valleys and attractions of Devon.

THREE GATES FARM

Huntsham, Tiverton
Contact: Mrs A Spencer, Three Gates Farm, Huntsham, Tiverton EX16 7QH
T: (01398) 331280
E: threegatesfarm@hotmail.com
I: www.threegatesfarm.co.uk

OPEN All Year

Short breaks available Oct–Mar (excl Christmas and New Year), also short break B&B.

Low season per wk
£125.00–£275.00
High season per wk
£315.00–£855.00

COLOUR MAPS Colour maps at the front of this guide pinpoint all places under which you will find accommodation listed.

BAMPTON continued

★★★
4 Units
Sleeping 4–8

VELTHAM COTTAGES

Morebath, Tiverton
Contact: Mrs P Krombas
T: (01398) 331465
F: (01392) 425529

In a quiet village on edge of Exmoor, eight miles from Wimbleball Lake. Beautiful walking, fishing, riding area. Sauna and fitness room available.

Low season per wk
£185.00–£300.00
High season per wk
£265.00–£430.00

★★★
1 Unit
Sleeping 6

WONHAM BARTON

Bampton, Tiverton
Contact: Mrs A McLean Williams
T: (01398) 331312
F: (01398) 331312
E: wonham.barton@virgin.net
I: www.wonham-country-holidays.co.uk

From friendly accommodation overlooking Exe Valley, conveniently explore secretive, historic Devon, rolling moorlands and dramatic coastlines; enjoy country pursuits and leisurely cream teas. Savour 300 tranquil acres, glimpsing Exmoor red deer, soaring buzzards and traditional shepherding; share romantic scenes from TV drama and 'Landgirls' filmed here. Tell us when you're coming!

OPEN All Year
CC: Delta, Mastercard, Solo, Switch, Visa

Short breaks available Oct-Mar. Min 2 nights. Prices on request. Dogs accepted by arrangement.

Low season per wk
£165.00–£305.00
High season per wk
£305.00–£375.00

BATCOMBE, Somerset Map ref 2B2

★★★★
1 Unit
Sleeping 4

THE COACH HOUSE AT BOORDS FARM

Batcombe, Shepton Mallet
Contact: Mr & Mrs M Page, The Coach House at Boords Farm, Batcombe, Shepton Mallet BA4 6HD
T: (01749) 850372
F: (01749) 850372
E: boordsfarm@michaelp.demon.co.uk

Recently converted coach house in grounds of 16thC thatched farmhouse equipped to high standard for comfort. Rural setting on edge of beautiful village. Twin and double bedrooms, each with own bathroom. Woodburning stove, central heating. Local walks, good touring location Stourhead, Longleat, Bath, Wells. Short walk to excellent pub.

OPEN All Year

Short breaks available. Flexible changeover days on all lengths of bookings.

Low season per wk
£375.00–£400.00
High season per wk
£410.00–£425.00

COUNTRY CODE Always follow the Country Code ✤ Enjoy the countryside and respect its life and work ✤ Guard against all risk of fire ✤ Fasten all gates ✤ Keep your dogs under close control ✤ Keep to public paths across farmland ✤ Use gates and stiles to cross fences, hedges and walls ✤ Leave livestock, crops and machinery alone ✤ Take your litter home ✤ Help to keep all water clean ✤ Protect wildlife, plants and trees ✤ Take special care on country roads ✤ Make no unnecessary noise

BATH, Bath and North East Somerset Map ref 2B2 *Tourist Information Centre Tel: 0906 711 2000 (premium rate number)*

★★★★

7 Units
Sleeping 2–5

Tastefully converted, well-equipped single-storey cottages, formerly old cow byres. Working farm in Area of Outstanding Natural Beauty. Heated indoor swimming pool (12 metres x 5 metres) and games room. Pub/shop 500 metres. Bath five miles. Longleat and NT properties nearby. Kennet and Avon Canal 0.75 miles for boating/cycling/walking. Regular buses. Welcome cream tea.

CHURCH FARM COUNTRY COTTAGES

Winsley, Bradford-on-Avon
Contact: Mrs T Bowles
T: (01225) 722246
F: (01225) 722246
E: stay@churchfarmcottages.com
I: www.churchfarmcottages.com

OPEN All Year
CC: Delta, Mastercard, Switch, Visa

A mid-week break (Mon-Thu) or weekend break (Fri-Sun) can be booked 14 days before commencement of intended stay.

Low season per wk
£195.00–£270.00
High season per wk
£325.00–£575.00

★★★

1 Unit
Sleeping 3

2 DEVONSHIRE VILLAS

Bath
Contact: Mr & Mrs D Wall, 2 Devonshire Villas, Wellsway, Bath BA2 4SX
T: (01225) 331539
E: Daniel@wallsbath.freeserve.co.uk

OPEN All Year

Low season per wk
£240.00–£310.00
High season per wk
£270.00–£340.00

Spacious ground floor flat. Double bedroom, single bed in anteroom. Free parking. City 15 minutes' walk. Local shops/take-aways/pubs five minute's walk. Public transport within yards.

★★★★-★★★★★

5 Units
Sleeping 4

GREYFIELD FARM COTTAGES

High Littleton, Bristol
Contact: Mrs J Merry, Greyfield Farm Cottages, Greyfield Road, High Littleton, Bristol BS39 6YQ
T: (01761) 471132
F: (01761) 471132
E: june@greyfieldfarm.com
I: www.greyfieldfarm.com

OPEN All Year

Low season per wk
£190.00–£285.00
High season per wk
£295.00–£395.00

Quality cottages set in peaceful, private location with panoramic views of Mendips. Use of sauna, hot tub, fitness centre and video library included. Brochure available.

★★

1 Unit
Sleeping 5

RIVERSIDE COTTAGE

Wick, Bristol
Contact: Mr B Trezise
T: (0117) 9372304
F: (0117) 9372304
E: b.trezise@btopenworld.com

OPEN All Year

Low season per wk
Min £220.00
High season per wk
Max £425.00

Riverside cottage in popular village five miles from Bath and Bristol. Riverside garden, easy parking. Ideal touring base for many attractions. Local pubs and restaurants.

BEAMINSTER, Dorset Map ref 2A3

★★★

3 Units
Sleeping 4

GREENS CROSS FARM

Beaminster
Contact: Mr D G Baker, Greens Cross Farm, Stoke Road, Beaminster DT8 3JL
T: (01308) 862661
F: (01308) 863800

OPEN All Year

Low season per wk
£100.00–£190.00
High season per wk
£200.00–£300.00

Well-equipped holiday units within walking distance of Beaminster in heart of Dorset and close to coast. Short winter breaks. Field for horse.

BEAMINSTER continued

★★★★
1 Unit
Sleeping 3

STABLE COTTAGE
Beaminster
Contact: Mrs D M Clarke
T: (01308) 862305
F: (01308) 863972
E: meerhay@aol.com
I: www.meerhay.co.uk

OPEN All Year except Christmas

Low season per wk
Min £150.00
High season per wk
Max £375.00

New ground floor conversion of old barn in grounds of old manor. Wheelchair accessible. Forty acres farmland, plantsman's garden, tennis court, stabling. Seven miles coast, idyllic setting.

BEER, Devon Map ref 1D2

★★★★
2 Units
Sleeping 4

BEER VIEW & NEW NOOKIES
Beer, Seaton
Contact: Mrs J Forbes-Harriss, Beer View and New Nookies, Berry House, Berry Lane, Beer, Seaton EX12 3JS
T: (01297) 20096
F: (01297) 20096
E: forbesh@globalnet.co.uk

Lovely, peaceful location in the gardens of period house. Comfortable, no-smoking flat and newly built, no-smoking cottage. Superb seaviews over a delightful, picturesque, Devon fishing village. Short walk to village shops. Restaurants, pubs and beach. Sorry, no pets or children under 12 years old.

Low season per wk
£200.00–£230.00
High season per wk
£250.00–£450.00

12

BERRYNARBOR, Devon Map ref 1C1

★★★-★★★★
4 Units
Sleeping 4

SMYTHEN FARM COASTAL HOLIDAY COTTAGES
Berrynarbor, Ilfracombe
Contact: Mr & Ms Thompson & Elstone, Smythen Farm Coastal Holiday Cottages, Smythen, Sterridge Valley, Berrynarbor, Ilfracombe EX34 9TB
T: (01271) 882875
F: (01271) 882875
E: jayne@smythenfarmholidaycottages.co.uk
I: www.smythenfarmholidaycottages.co.uk

Near golden sands with sea and coastal views. Heated, covered swimming pool in a suntrap enclosure, gardens and games room with pool table, table tennis, football machine. Tree-house on two levels. Free pony rides, ball pond and bouncy castle, 14-acre recreation field and dog walk. For colour brochure phone Jayne.

Low season per wk
£95.00–£267.00
High season per wk
£267.00–£699.00

BIDEFORD, Devon Map ref 1C1 *Tourist Information Centre Tel: (01237) 477676*

★★★
1 Unit
Sleeping 2

COACHMANS COTTAGE
Monkleigh, Bideford
Contact: Mr & Mrs T M Downie, Staddon House, Monkleigh, Bideford EX39 5JR
T: (01805) 623670
E: tom.downie@ukonline.co.uk
I: www.creamteacottages.co.uk

OPEN All Year

Low season per wk
£130.00–£165.00
High season per wk
£165.00–£215.00

Charming character cottage in courtyard setting, within easy reach of national parks and beaches. Price includes cream tea on arrival, linen and fuel for woodburner.

RATING **All accommodation in this guide has been rated, or is awaiting a rating, by a trained VisitBritain assessor.**

BIDEFORD continued

★★★★
1 Unit
Sleeping 4

Converted from the wing of an old house, this beautiful mews-type cottage in a peaceful, semi-rural location has been renovated to a very high standard. Airy and spacious, but warm in winter. Two large bedrooms, lounge, farmhouse kitchen, utility room and garden. Beaches, shops and local amenities nearby.

LITTLE MELVILLE HOLIDAY COTTAGE

Northam, Bideford
Contact: Mr & Mrs Moore, Melville Cottage, Heywood Road, Northam, Bideford EX39 3QB
T: (01237) 471140
F: (01237) 471140
E: anb@melvillecot.freeserve.co.uk
I: www.litmel.freeserve.co.uk

OPEN All Year

Low season per wk
£230.00–£280.00
High season per wk
£320.00–£375.00

BIGBURY-ON-SEA, Devon Map ref 1C3

★★★★★
1 Unit
Sleeping 4

Luxury modern ground floor apartment set into cliff with panoramic southerly views from large patio. Facilities include pool, gym, sauna, cafe/bar, grassy cliff-top grounds and direct access to beautiful large sandy beach and coastal path. Popular for surfing and near golf course and village shop/post office.

APARTMENT 5, BURGH ISLAND CAUSEWAY

Bigbury-on-Sea, Kingsbridge
Contact: Helpful Holidays, Mill Street, Chagford, Newton Abbot TQ13 8AW
T: (01647) 433593
F: (01647) 433694
E: help@helpfulholidays.com
I: www.helpfulholidays.com

OPEN All Year
CC: Delta, Mastercard, Switch, Visa

Bargain weekend and short-stay breaks available in autumn and winter months.

Low season per wk
£392.00–£814.00
High season per wk
£878.00–£1,228.00

★★★★
1 Unit
Sleeping 6

FERRYCOMBE
Bigbury-on-Sea, Kingsbridge
Contact: Mrs J Fooks, 15 Mouchotte Close, Biggin Hill, Kent TN16 3ES
T: 07050 030231

OPEN All Year

Unique, old Devon-stone barn in small courtyard with private gardens. Spectacular sea views overlook the sweep of Bigbury Bay with its glorious sandy beaches and famous Burgh Island. Ideal for the family with children.

Low season per wk
£250.00–£400.00
High season per wk
£300.00–£750.00

QUALITY ASSURANCE SCHEME

For an explanation of the quality and facilities represented by the Stars please refer to the front of this guide. A more detailed explanation can be found in the information pages at the back.

BLISLAND, Cornwall Map ref 1B2

★★★★

2 Units
Sleeping 4

TORR HOUSE COTTAGES

Blisland, Bodmin
Contact: Mr & Mrs M Wilson
T: (01208) 851601
F: (01208) 851601
E: wilson@millbanks.fsworld.co.uk
I: www.torrhouseholidays.co.uk

Delightful, comfortable barn conversions set in peaceful, secluded grounds with outstanding views of the picturesque village of Blisland and the surrounding countryside. 20 minutes from Eden, 10 miles from North and South coast beaches, and one mile from the Camel Trail. Walking distance to CAMRA pub serving food.

OPEN All Year

Weekend and mid-week breaks available all year except Jul, Aug, Christmas and New Year.

Low season per wk
£275.00–£400.00
High season per wk
£400.00–£750.00

BODMIN, Cornwall Map ref 1B2 *Tourist Information Centre Tel: (01208) 76616*

★★★★

1 Unit
Sleeping 8

LANJEW PARK

Withiel, Bodmin
Contact: Mrs E Biddick, Lanjew Park, Lanjew Farm, Withiel, Bodmin PL30 5PB
T: (01726) 890214
F: (01726) 890214
E: biddick@lanjew.co.uk
I: www.lanjew.co.uk

Tastefully furnished house on working farm. Well-equipped kitchen, dining area, separate lounge with open fire. Central heating included. Idyllic, peaceful setting. Large gardens, swings, sandpit, barbecue. Within easy reach Eden Project, Camel Trail, Newquay. Perfect secluded location for a delightful, relaxing, get-away-from-it all holiday. Personal attention from owner.

OPEN All Year

3-night breaks available Nov-Mar. (Christmas/New Year: minimum 5 nights).

Low season per wk
Min £245.00
High season per wk
Max £660.00

BOSCASTLE, Cornwall Map ref 1B2

★★★★

9 Units
Sleeping 4–6

CARGURRA FARM

St Juliot, Boscastle
Contact: Mrs Gillian Elson, Hennett, St Juliot, Boscastle PL35 0BT
T: (01840) 261206
F: (01840) 261206
E: gillian@cargurra.co.uk
I: www.cargurra.co.uk

Secluded farm setting within the beautiful Valency Valley where Thomas Hardy met his love. A well-appointed, traditional cottage with log fire and central heating. Spacious gardens with barbecue, games room with pool and table tennis. Private road, ample parking. Country and coastal walks. Also, cottages converted from Victorian barn.

OPEN All Year
CC: Delta, JCB, Mastercard, Solo, Switch, Visa

Low season per wk
£140.00–£250.00
High season per wk
£250.00–£520.00

CHECK THE MAPS

The colour maps at the front of this guide show all the cities, towns and villages for which you will find accommodation entries.
Refer to the town index to find the page on which they are listed.

BOSCASTLE continued

★★★
1 Unit
Sleeping 5

PARADISE FARM COTTAGE
Boscastle
Contact: Mrs D M Hancock
T: (01840) 250528

OPEN All Year

Low season per wk £170.00–£225.00
High season per wk £290.00–£430.00

Peaceful, bygone surroundings, magical harbour village. Pets, ponies, ducks. Suntrap garden, fields, views. Log fire. Super pub meals, shop, cliff and country walks from the doorstep.

★★★
1 Unit
Sleeping 5

SHEPHERD'S COTTAGE

Boscastle
Contact: Mr H Jenkins, Endellion House, Parc Road, Llangybi, Usk NP15 1NL
T: (01633) 450417
E: jenkins@choicecornishcottages.com
I: www.choicecornishcottages.com

Situated above the picturesque village of Boscastle, fairytale charm exudes from this traditional 17thC detached cottage. Original features add to the romance, while every modern convenience ensures a totally relaxing retreat. A large, sunny garden commands breathtaking views of the NT countryside and coastline. Beautiful beaches and attractions nearby.

OPEN All Year

Short breaks available. Reduced rates for couples at off-season weekends.

Low season per wk £250.00–£400.00
High season per wk £450.00–£600.00

BOVEY TRACEY, Devon Map ref 1D2

★★★★
1 Unit
Sleeping 12

WARMHILL FARM
Hennock, Bovey Tracey, Newton Abbot
Contact: Mr & Mrs B Marnham, Warmhill Farm, Bovey Tracey, Newton Abbot TQ13 9QH
T: (01626) 833229
E: marnham@agriplus.net

OPEN All Year

Low season per wk £350.00–£650.00
High season per wk £850.00–£1,200.00

100-acre working farm. Superb thatched farmhouse in Dartmoor National Park. Ideal for moor and sea. Spacious and comfortable, with many old features preserved.

BRADFORD-ON-AVON, Wiltshire Map ref 2B2 *Tourist Information Centre Tel: (01225) 865797*

★★★
1 Unit
Sleeping 4

GREYSTONE COTTAGE
Bradford-on-Avon
Contact: Mrs G M Patel, 19 Church Street, Bradford-on-Avon BA15 1LN
T: (01225) 868179
F: (01225) 867084
E: vivandgill@yahoo.co.uk
I: www.greystoneboa.co.uk

OPEN All Year

Low season per wk £220.00–£280.00
High season per wk £280.00–£340.00

Comfortable, 18thC, Grade II Listed terraced cottage, overlooking medieval town bridge. Ample public parking nearby. Close to all amenities. Garden with patio and views. Welcome tray.

5

USE YOUR *i*s

There are more than 550 Tourist Information Centres throughout England offering friendly help with accommodation and holiday ideas as well as suggestions of places to visit and things to do. You'll find TIC addresses in the local Phone Book.

BRATTON, Somerset Map ref 1D1

★★★★
8 Units
Sleeping 2–12

Timber lodges and stone cottages in a tranquil, rural setting on the edge of Exmoor National Park. Standing in a beautiful, 2.5-acre garden with wonderful views towards the wooded slopes of Exmoor. Minehead's seafront, harbour, shops etc 1.5 miles. Close to Dunster, Selworthy, Porlock and many local beauty spots. Mob: 07860 667325.

WOODCOMBE LODGES

Minehead
Contact: Mrs N Hanson, Woodcombe Lodges, Bratton Lane, Minehead TA24 8SQ
T: (01643) 702789
F: (01643) 702789
E: nicola@woodcombelodge.co.uk
I: www.woodcombelodge.co.uk

OPEN All Year
CC: Delta, Mastercard, Visa

Short breaks available Nov-Easter, minimum 3 nights.

Low season per wk
£130.00–£500.00
High season per wk
£250.00–£1,100.00

BRATTON FLEMING, Devon Map ref 1C1

★★★★
1 Unit
Sleeping 2

BRACKEN ROOST

Bratton Fleming, Barnstaple
Contact: Mr L Scott, Bracken House, Bratton Fleming, Barnstaple EX31 4TG
T: (01598) 710320
E: lawrie@brackenhousehotel.com
I: www.brackenhousehotel.com

OPEN All Year
CC: Delta, Mastercard, Solo, Switch, Visa

Low season per wk
£140.00–£200.00
High season per wk
£220.00–£320.00

Two-person cottage adjacent to Bracken House, a small, award-winning hotel. All set in eight peaceful acres of garden, woodland, pond and paddocks.

BRAYFORD, Devon Map ref 1C1

★★
1 Unit
Sleeping 6

MUXWORTHY COTTAGE

Brayford, Barnstaple
Contact: Mrs G M Bament, Muxworthy Farm, Brayford, Barnstaple EX32 7QP
T: (01598) 710342

OPEN All Year

Low season per wk
£145.00–£190.00
High season per wk
£260.00–£290.00

Secluded old world cottage with oak beams in the heart of Exmoor. Warm and cosy in winter with woodburning stove. Ideal for a peaceful and relaxing holiday.

BREAN, Somerset Map ref 1D1

★★
1 Unit
Sleeping 8

GADARA BUNGALOW

Brean, Burnham-on-Sea
Contact: Mr T M Hicks, Gadara Bungalow, Diamond Farm, Weston Road, Brean, Burnham-on-Sea TA8 2RL
T: (01278) 751263
E: trevor@diamondfarm42.freeserve.co.uk
I: www.diamondfarm.co.uk

OPEN All Year

Low season per wk
£150.00–£200.00
High season per wk
£200.00–£380.00

A spacious, three-bedroomed bungalow in its own grounds with direct access to beach. Accommodation includes lounge, kitchen. Central heating is provided for main rooms.

BRIDGWATER, Somerset Map ref 1D1

★★★★
2 Units
Sleeping 4

ASH-WEMBDON FARM COTTAGES

Wembdon, Bridgwater
Contact: Mr C Rowe, Ash-Wembdon Farm Cottages, Ash-Wembdon Farm, Hollow Lane, Wembdon, Bridgwater TA5 2BD
T: (01278) 453097
F: (01278) 445856
E: c.a.rowe@btinternet.com
I: www.farmaccommodation.co.uk

OPEN All Year
CC: Delta, JCB, Mastercard, Solo, Switch, Visa

High season per wk
£200.00–£430.00

Escape and spoil yourselves at our luxury farm cottages, fully equipped to a very high standard. Disabled facilities. Non-smokers preferred. No pets.

BRIDPORT, Dorset Map ref 2A3 *Tourist Information Centre Tel: (01308) 424901*

★★★

4 Units
Sleeping 6

CONISTON HOLIDAY APARTMENTS
Bridport
Contact: Mrs J Murphy, Coniston Holiday Apartments, Coniston House, Victoria Grove, Bridport DT6 3AE
T: (01308) 424049
F: (01308) 424049

OPEN All Year

Low season per wk
Min £100.00
High season per wk
Max £455.00

Spacious, self-contained, fully equipped apartments with summer swimming pool. Play area, gardens and garage parking. Overlooking the Dorset hills, yet only two minutes' walk to market town.

★★★

3 Units
Sleeping 4–6

HIGHLANDS END HOLIDAY PARK
Eype, Bridport
Contact: Mr M Cox, Highlands End Holiday Park, Eype, Bridport DT6 6AR
T: (01308) 422139
F: (01308) 425672
E: holidays@wdlh.co.uk
I: www.wdlh.co.uk

CC: Mastercard, Switch, Visa

Low season per wk
£220.00–£290.00
High season per wk
£275.00–£500.00

Flats in secluded grounds, 150 metres from entrance to select holiday park on West Dorset Heritage coastline. Indoor swimming pool.

BRISTOL Map ref 2A2 *Tourist Information Centre Tel: 0906 586 2313 (premium rate number)*

★★★

1 Unit
Sleeping 4

AVONSIDE
Sea Mills, Bristol
Contact: Mrs D M Ridout, Avonside, 19 St Edyth's Road, Sea Mills, Bristol BS9 2EP
T: (0117) 968 1967

OPEN All Year

Low season per wk
Min £250.00
High season per wk
Max £275.00

Comfortable first floor flat, well furnished, equipped and maintained to a high standard. Convenient, pleasant residential area three miles from city centre. Motorway nearby.

BRIXHAM, Devon Map ref 1D2 *Tourist Information Centre Tel: 0906 680 1268 (Premium rate number)*

★★★★★

10 Units
Sleeping 6

Luxury waterfront apartments with panoramic sea views and private balcony. Own parking. Close to beach and town.

BLUE CHIP VACATIONS – MOORINGS REACH

Brixham
Contact: Mrs S Cutting
T: (01803) 855282
F: (01803) 851825
E: bluechip@eclipse.co.uk
I: www.bluechipvacations.com

OPEN All Year
CC: Amex, Delta, Diners, JCB, Mastercard, Switch, Visa

Low season per wk
£295.00–£450.00
High season per wk
£450.00–£695.00

AT-A-GLANCE SYMBOLS

Symbols at the end of each accommodation entry give useful information about services and facilities. A key to symbols can be found inside the back cover flap. Keep this open for easy reference.

BRIXHAM continued

★★★★

1 Unit
Sleeping 7

Grade II Listed character stone cottage, beautifully refurbished, features beams and logburning stove, sea views from top floor. Centrally heated. Beach, marina, harbour, shops and restaurants all within short walk. A relaxing and comfortable holiday retreat with modern facilities.

CRABBERS COTTAGE

Brixham
Contact: Ms T Cornish, 8 The Queensway, Austenwood Common, Gerrards Cross SL9 8NF
T: (01753) 882482
F: (01753) 882546
E: info@cornish-cottage.com
I: www.cornish-cottage.com

OPEN All Year

Short breaks available – please phone for info/prices.

Low season per wk
£390.00–£430.00
High season per wk
£450.00–£700.00

★★

6 Units
Sleeping 5

Panoramic sea views from your balcony and lounge over Torbay, Brixham harbour and marina. The beach is opposite, only 50 metres. Each flat is fully self-contained, with colour TV, full cooker, fully carpeted. Private gardens. Car park. Children, pets and credit cards welcome. For colour brochure telephone 01803 853748 or 07050 338889.

DEVONCOURT HOLIDAY FLATS

Brixham
Contact: Mr R Hooker, Devoncourt Holiday Flats, Berry Head Road, Brixham TQ5 9AB
T: (01803) 853748
F: (01803) 855775
E: robinhooker@devoncourt.net
I: www.devoncourt.net

OPEN All Year
CC: Delta, Mastercard, Switch, Visa

10% discount for Senior Citizens.

Low season per wk
£199.00–£249.00
High season per wk
£249.00–£499.00

★★★

2 Units
Sleeping 4–7

Excellently furnished and equipped house occupying an enviable position with magnificent views over busy fishing harbour, marina and Torbay. House is divided into flat and maisonette which are let seperately or jointly. Two minutes from harbour, town and coastal walks. Open all year. Phone for colour brochure.

HARBOUR REACH

Brixham
Contact: Mrs J Pocock, Totley Hall Farm, Totley Hall Lane, Totley, Sheffield S17 4AA
T: (0114) 236 4761
F: (0114) 236 4761

OPEN All Year except Christmas

Low season short breaks available.

Low season per wk
£130.00–£240.00
High season per wk
£175.00–£430.00

TOWN INDEX

This can be found at the back of this guide. If you know where you want to stay, the index will give you the page number listing accommodation in your chosen town, city or village.

BUCKLAND NEWTON, Dorset Map ref 2B3

★★★★

3 Units
Sleeping 4

Delightful, Victorian, two-bedroomed cottages, comfortably furnished and equipped and maintained to highest standards. Surrounded by beautiful gardens with patios. Heated summer swimming pool. Peaceful location on village edge in heart of Hardy's Dorset. Well situated for touring Wessex, walking and country pursuits. Regret no pets. Children 5+ and babies welcome.

DOMINEYS COTTAGES

Buckland Newton, Dorchester
Contact: Mrs J D Gueterbock, Domineys Cottages, Domineys Yard, Buckland Newton, Dorchester DT2 7BS
T: (01300) 345295
F: (01300) 345596
E: cottages@domineys.com
I: www.domineys.com

OPEN All Year

Low season per wk
£190.00–£300.00
High season per wk
£360.00–£460.00

BUCKLAND ST MARY, Somerset Map ref 1D2

★★★★

1 Unit
Sleeping 4

HILLSIDE END APARTMENT

Buckland St Mary, Chard
Contact: Mr R Harkness, Hillside, Buckland St Mary, Chard TA20 3TQ
T: (01460) 234599
F: (01460) 234599
E: royandmarge@hillsidebsm.freeserve.co.uk
I: www.theaa.com/hotels/103591.html

OPEN All Year

Low season per wk
£135.00–£175.00
High season per wk
£180.00–£240.00

Tastefully extended Victorian cottage on the edge of Blackdown Hills (off A303), bordering South Somerset and North Devon. Comfortable and quiet. Ideal for Lyme, Exmoor, Dartmoor, Quantocks.

BUDE, Cornwall Map ref 1C2 *Tourist Information Centre Tel: (01288) 354240*

★★★

3 Units
Sleeping 4

DOWNLANDS

Bude
Contact: Mr C Bloy, Downlands, Maer Lane, Bude EX23 9EE
T: (01288) 356920
E: sonia@downlands.net
I: www.downlands.net

OPEN All Year
CC: Amex, Delta, JCB, Mastercard, Switch, Visa

Low season per wk
£160.00–£348.00
High season per wk
£260.00–£540.00

Garden apartments nestled behind spectacular coastline minutes from coastal path and beaches. Patio overlooking tennis court. Riding and golf nearby. Off-peak discount for couples.

★★★★

7 Units
Sleeping 4–6

Beautiful period cottages with exposed beams, some 4-poster beds, en suite facilities and double spa baths. Set in five acres of tranquil countryside on Grade II Listed Georgian estate but only 10 minutes' drive to Bude and sandy beaches. Cellar bar and restaurant serving superb, home-cooked food. Baby-listening monitors.

GLEBE HOUSE COTTAGES

Bridgerule, Holsworthy
Contact: Mr & Mrs J Varley, Glebe House Cottages Limited, Bridgerule, Holsworthy EX22 7EW
T: (01288) 381272
E: etc@glebehousecottages.co.uk
I: www.glebehousecottages.co.uk

OPEN All Year
CC: Delta, JCB, Mastercard, Solo, Switch, Visa

Short breaks available most of the year (excl school summer holidays).

Low season per wk
£240.00–£525.00
High season per wk
£395.00–£825.00

BUDE continued

★★★★★

19 Units
Sleeping 2–10

KENNACOTT COURT

Widemouth Bay, Bude
Contact: Mr & Mrs R H Davis, Kennacott Court, Widemouth Bay, Bude EX23 0ND
T: (01288) 362000
F: (01288) 361434
E: maureen@kennacottcourt.co.uk
I: www.kennacottcourt.co.uk

An outstanding collection of cottages which are beautifully furnished, very comfortable and comprehensively equipped. Kennacott Court has a wide range of activities: indoor swimming pool, games room, badminton, snooker and children's room, together with tennis courts and our own golf course. All set in 75 acres overlooking the sea at Widemouth Bay.

OPEN All Year
CC: Delta, JCB, Mastercard, Solo, Switch, Visa

Open all year with attractive out-of-season short breaks.

Low season per wk
£240.00–£700.00
High season per wk
£520.00–£2,100.00

★★★

7 Units
Sleeping 2–6

LANGFIELD MANOR

Bude
Contact: Mr K Freestone, Langfield Manor, Broadclose, Bude EX23 8DP
T: (01288) 352415
E: info@langfieldmanor.co.uk
I: www.langfieldmanor.co.uk

Quality apartments within fine Edwardian house. Games room with full-sized snooker table, pool and table-tennis tables. Three minutes' walk to the shops and 10 to beautiful sandy beaches, yet peacefully situated in delightful, sheltered, south-facing gardens with heated outdoor swimming pool. Golf course adjacent.

OPEN All Year except Christmas
CC: Mastercard, Solo, Switch, Visa

Low season per wk
£165.00–£300.00
High season per wk
£300.00–£730.00

★★★

2 Units
Sleeping 6–8

PENHALT FARM

Widemouth Bay, Bude
Contact: Mr & Mrs D Marks
T: (01288) 361210
F: (01288) 361210
E: denandjennie@penhaltfarm.fsnet.co.uk
I: www.holidaybank.co.uk/penhaltfarm

Spectacular sea and country views. The farmhouse has comfortable accommodation with enclosed garden. Ample parking. Close to coastal footpath. Ideal for walking, surfing and touring the North Cornwall coast and countryside. Outside children's play area.

OPEN All Year except Christmas
CC: Mastercard, Switch, Visa

Reduced rates for smaller parties Sep-Easter.

Low season per wk
Min £150.00
High season per wk
Max £650.00

★★★

2 Units
Sleeping 2–5

SOUTH LYNSTONE BARNS

Bude
Contact: Mrs J Armstrong, East Lodge, Back Lane, Paddockhurst Road, Turners Hill, Crawley RH10 4SF
T: (01342) 716355
E: armstrongsydney@aol.co.uk

OPEN All Year

Low season per wk
£125.00–£225.00
High season per wk
£200.00–£600.00

Delightful barn conversions with all facilities situated midway between Bude and Widemouth Bay and within easy reach of Summerleaze Beach.

BURROWBRIDGE, Somerset Map ref 1D1

★★★

1 Unit
Sleeping 2

HILLVIEW

Burrowbridge, Bridgwater
Contact: Mrs R Griffiths, Hillview, Stanmoor Road, Burrowbridge, Bridgwater TA7 0RX
T: (01823) 698308
F: (01823) 698308

OPEN All Year

Low season per wk
Min £140.00
High season per wk
Min £175.00

Compact bungalow, fully equipped and centrally heated, in its own grounds. Conservatory. Short breaks available in low season.

BUTCOMBE, North Somerset Map ref 2A2

★★★

8 Units
Sleeping 2–6

BUTCOMBE FARM

Butcombe
Contact: Ms S Moss, Butcombe Farm, Aldwick Lane, Butcombe, Bristol BS40 7UW
T: (01761) 462380
F: (01761) 462300
E: info@butcombe-farm.demon.co.uk
I: www.butcombe-farm.demon.co.uk

Originally a 14thC medieval hall, Butcombe Farm is now a beautiful manor house with en suite bed and breakfast and self-catering accommodation. Set in several acres amid peaceful countryside with heated outdoor pool. Close to Bath, Bristol, Cheddar, Wells. For more information please contact Sandra and Brian Moss.

OPEN All Year
CC: Mastercard, Solo, Switch, Visa

Breaks available with clay pigeon shoots, horse-riding, archery, aromatherapy massage, wine tasting and more.

Low season per wk
£290.00–£560.00
High season per wk
£350.00–£590.00

BUTLEIGH WOOTTON, Somerset Map ref 2A2

★★

1 Unit
Sleeping 5

LITTLE BROADWAY

Butleigh Wootton, Glastonbury
Contact: Mrs M Butt, Proprietor, Broadway Farm, Butleigh Wootton, Glastonbury BA6 8TX
T: (01458) 442824
F: (01458) 442824

OPEN All Year

Low season per wk
£250.00–£325.00
High season per wk
£275.00–£325.00

Part of a 17thC farmhouse owned by the Acland Hood estate. Comfortable and spacious. Quiet area. Ideal for touring Somerset.

TOWN INDEX

This can be found at the back of the guide. If you know where you want to stay, the index will give you the page number listing accommodation in your chosen town, city or village.

CASTLE CARY, Somerset Map ref 2B2

★★★★

3 Units
Sleeping 2–7

Really special, Grade II Listed buildings. Old beams and other original features are combined with full central heating and every top-quality comfort. Set either in lovely countryside, by a small working farm, or in nearby Castle Cary. All are ideally placed for touring this fascinating county.

THE ANCIENT BARN, THE OLD STABLES & THE WEAVER'S COTTAGE

Castle Cary
Contact: Ms A Peppin, The Ancient Barn, The Old Stables, and The Weaver's Cottage, Lower Cockhill Farm, Castle Cary BA7 7NZ
T: (01963) 351288
F: (01963) 351288
E: bookings@medievalbarn.co.uk
I: www.medievalbarn.co.uk

OPEN All Year
CC: Delta, JCB, Mastercard, Solo, Switch, Visa

Off-peak short breaks often possible, minimum 3 nights. Contact us to discuss your needs.

Low season per wk
£225.00–£250.00
High season per wk
£250.00–£550.00

CHALLACOMBE, Devon Map ref 1C1

★★★

7 Units
Sleeping 2–6

HOME PLACE FARM COTTAGES

Challacombe, Barnstaple
Contact: Mr M Ravenscroft, Home Place Farm Cottages, Challacombe, Barnstaple EX31 4TS
T: (01598) 763283
F: (01598) 763283
E: mark@holidayexmoor.co.uk
I: www.holidayexmoor.co.uk

OPEN All Year
CC: Mastercard, Visa

Low season per wk
£145.00–£500.00
High season per wk
£145.00–£500.00

Comfortable cottages in the tranquil River Bray valley Exmoor National Park. Excellent walking from the door. Spa facilities and treatments available to guests.

6

CHAPEL AMBLE, Cornwall Map ref 1B2

★★★★

4 Units
Sleeping 2–6

CARCLAZE COTTAGES

Chapel Amble, Wadebridge
Contact: Mrs J Nicholls
T: (01208) 813886
E: enquire@carclaze.dabsol.co.uk
I: www.carclaze.co.uk

Peaceful setting in the heart of the countryside with superb views, yet only 10 minutes from the spectacular coast. An ideal location to explore North Cornwall with its sailing, surfing, sandy beaches, golf and cliff walks. Quality cottages furnished to high standards, suitable for those who seek something special.

OPEN All Year

Open all year. Short breaks available.

Low season per wk
£330.00–£430.00
High season per wk
£510.00–£1,140.00

★★★★

3 Units
Sleeping 4–6

HOMELEIGH FARM

Chapel Amble, Wadebridge
Contact: Mrs A J Rees
T: (01208) 812411
F: (01208) 815025
E: homeleigh@eclipse.co.uk
I: www.eclipse.co.uk/homeleigh

OPEN All Year

Low season per wk
£200.00–£350.00
High season per wk
£300.00–£750.00

Two- and three-bedroomed converted farm cottages in traditional Cornish stone, on edge of village, 1.5 miles off A39.

CHEDDAR, Somerset Map ref 1D1

Rating Applied For
6 Units
Sleeping 2–4

Characterful, beamed, converted farm buildings, providing an ideal place to relax and an excellent base for Cheddar, Bath, Wells, Bristol and Weston-super-Mare. Many lovely walks in the area and comfortable, well-equipped cottages to return to. Set in two acres adjacent to farmhouse.

HOME FARM COTTAGES

Barton, Winscombe, Cheddar
Contact: Mr C Sanders, Home Farm Cottages, Home Farm, Barton, Winscombe, Cheddar BS25 1DX
T: (01934) 842078
F: (01934) 842500
E: mail@homefarmcottages.com
I: www.homefarmcottages.com

OPEN All Year
CC: Delta, JCB, Mastercard, Solo, Switch, Visa

Short breaks available.

Low season per wk
£220.00–£350.00
High season per wk
£420.00–£580.00

★★★★
3 Units
Sleeping 2

Charming one-bedroom cottages in converted barn in two acres of gardens/grounds between the Mendip Hills and Somerset Levels. The famous Cheddar Gorge and caves are within walking distance. Ideally situated for touring the West Country. Nearby opportunities for most sports/interests. No smoking. Ample off-road parking. Dogs welcome.

SPRING COTTAGES

Cheddar
Contact: Mrs J Buckland, Spring Cottage, Venns Gate, Cheddar BS27 3LW
T: (01934) 742493
F: (01934) 742493
E: buckland@springcottages.co.uk
I: www.springcottages.co.uk

OPEN All Year
CC: JCB, Mastercard, Solo, Switch, Visa

Mon-Wed break for 2 people: £99 with Thu free. Jan-May, subject to availability. Basic heating included.

Low season per wk
£205.00–£217.00
High season per wk
£245.00–£290.00

★★★
4 Units
Sleeping 3–4

SUNGATE HOLIDAY APARTMENTS
Cheddar
Contact: Mrs M M Fieldhouse, Pyrenmount, Parsons Way, Winscombe BS25 1BU
T: (01934) 842273
F: (01934) 844994
I: sunholapartment@aol.com

OPEN All Year

Low season per wk
£112.00–£140.00
High season per wk
£140.00–£168.00

Delightful apartments in beautiful Listed Georgian house. Well furnished and equipped. In the centre of Cheddar village. Well-behaved children and pets welcome.

CHECK THE MAPS

The colour maps at the front of this guide show all the cities, towns and villages for which you will find accommodation entries. Refer to the town index to find the page on which they are listed.

CHIPPENHAM, Wiltshire Map ref 2B2 *Tourist Information Centre Tel: (01249) 706333*

★★★★

2 Units
Sleeping 2–4

Character cottages converted from traditional farm barns with many original features. Set on a small farm in peaceful Wiltshire countryside with easy access to Bath, Cotswolds and many local attractions. Each cottage has its own garden or patio, is fully equipped and very comfortable.

ROWARD FARM

Draycot Cerne, Chippenham
Contact: Mr D Humphrey, Roward Farm, Draycot Cerne, Chippenham SN15 4SG
T: (01249) 758147
F: (01249) 758149
E: d.humphrey@roward.demon.co.uk
I: www.roward.demon.co.uk

OPEN All Year
CC: JCB, Solo

Low season per wk
£245.00–£285.00
High season per wk
£295.00–£395.00

★★★★

1 Unit
Sleeping 6

Imagine a delightful, comfortable, well-equipped cottage on a working dairy farm, converted to offer the luxuries of modern living but retaining its traditional features. Bed settee available for extra guests. Perfectly positioned for days out in Wiltshire, Bath and the Cotswolds. Convenient M4. Brochure available.

SWALLOW COTTAGE

Dauntsey, Chippenham
Contact: Mrs S Candy, Olivemead Farm, Olivemead Lane, Dauntsey, Chippenham SN15 4JQ
T: (01666) 510205
F: (01666) 510205
E: olivemead@farmholidays@tesco.net
I: www.olivemead.farmholidays.com

OPEN All Year

New, 2-bedroom cottage available.

Low season per wk
£200.00–£300.00
High season per wk
£300.00–£450.00

CHIPPING SODBURY, South Gloucestershire Map ref 2B2

★★★

1 Unit
Sleeping 8

TAN HOUSE FARM COTTAGE

Yate, Bristol
Contact: Mrs C E James, Tan House Farm Cottage, Tan House Farm, Yate, Bristol BS37 7QL
T: (01454) 228280
F: (01454) 228777

OPEN All Year

Low season per wk
Max £250.00
High season per wk
Max £270.00

Cottage situated on the edge of the Cotswolds. Full oil-fired central heating with open fireplace if required. Parking. Rear view overlooks own fishing lake. Children and dogs welcome.

CHUDLEIGH, Devon Map ref 1D2

★★★

3 Units
Sleeping 6

COOMBESHEAD FARM

Chudleigh, Newton Abbot
Contact: Mr & Mrs R Smith, Coombeshead Farm, Coombeshead Cross, Chudleigh, Newton Abbot TQ13 0NQ
T: (01626) 853334
E: anne-coombeshead@supanet.com

Low season per wk
£180.00–£300.00
High season per wk
£320.00–£400.00

Comfortable holiday cottages converted from stone farm buildings. Quiet but not isolated, between Dartmoor and sea. Owners in residence.

ACCESSIBILITY

Look for the symbols which indicate National Accessible Scheme standards for hearing and visually impaired guests in addition to standards for guests with mobility impairment. Additional participants are shown in the listings at the back.

CHUDLEIGH continued

★★★

1 Unit
Sleeping 4

SILVER COTTAGE

Chudleigh, Newton Abbot
Contact: Mr E J Gardner, 75 Old Exeter Street, Chudleigh, Newton Abbot TQ13 0JX
T: (01626) 854571
F: (01626) 854571
E: ejgardner@care4free.net

Delightful character cottage ideally situated for shops, country walks and surrounding attractions of Dartmoor, Teignmouth, Torbay, Plymouth (Maritime Museum), Paignton (Zoo) and the seaside towns of Dawlish and Torquay, and of special interest The Eden Project with restaurants, cafes and picnic areas – whatever the weather – within easy distance via A38.

OPEN All Year

Low season short breaks from £78. Discounts for Senior Citizens. Brochure and details upon request. Book early for Silver Cottage.

Low season per wk
£130.00–£235.00
High season per wk
£260.00–£290.00

CHULMLEIGH, Devon Map ref 1C2

★★★★

10 Units
Sleeping 2–8

BEALY COURT HOLIDAY COTTAGES

Chulmleigh
Contact: Mr R & Mrs J Lea
T: (01769) 580312
F: (01769) 508986
E: bealycourt@msn.com
I: www.bealycourt.co.uk

Set in 24 acres of undulating Devonshire countryside, Bealy Court offers delightful properties with an extensive range of leisure facilities to suit all ages, perfect for family holidays. An ideal base for exploring the wolds of Exmoor and Dartmoor and the golden beaches of the North Devon coast.

OPEN All Year

Short breaks available (3 nights) Oct-Apr (excl Christmas and New Year).

Low season per wk
£191.00–£543.00
High season per wk
£420.00–£1,222.00

★★★★

1 Unit
Sleeping 2

DEER COTT

Chulmleigh
Contact: Mr & Mrs Simpson, Deer Cott, Middle Garland, Chulmleigh EX18 7DU
T: (01769) 581318
F: (01769) 580461
E: enquiries@deercott.co.uk
I: www.deercott.co.uk

Discover the peace and beauty of the Devonshire countryside and relax in comfortable accommodation offering every convenience for two at any time of the year. In a park-like setting of 20 acres within the Devon heartland, handy for the moors and shores. Amenities at South Molton/ Barnstaple a short drive away.

OPEN All Year

Low season per wk
£210.00
High season per wk
£225.00–£375.00

COLYFORD, Devon Map ref 1D2

★★★★★

4 Units
Sleeping 2–10

WHITWELL FARM COTTAGES

Colyford, Colyton
Contact: Mr M Williams, Whitwell Farm Cottages, Colyford, Colyton EX24 6HS
T: 0800 090 2419
F: (01297) 552911
E: 100755.66@compuserve.com
I: www.a5star.co.uk

OPEN All Year
CC: Delta, Mastercard, Switch, Visa

Low season per wk
£190.00–£500.00
High season per wk
£300.00–£1,290.00

Award-winning cottages with en suite bathrooms, 4-posters, jacuzzis, wooden beams, log fires, stunning views, farm animals and ostriches! Renowned for our comfort, location and decor.

COLYTON, Devon Map ref 1D2

★★★★

5 Units
Sleeping 2–8

SMALLICOMBE FARM

Northleigh, Colyton
Contact: Mrs M A Todd
T: (01404) 831310
F: (01404) 831431
E: maggie_todd@yahoo.com
I: www.smallicombe.com

Relax in award-winning converted barns, with superb rural views yet close to the World Heritage Coastline. Roam over 70 acres of pasture and ancient woodland abounding with wildlife and enjoy the sights and sounds of the countryside. Visit our Ruby Devon cattle, Dorset Down sheep or prize-winning rare breed pigs.

OPEN All Year
CC: Switch, Visa

Low season per wk
£125.00–£295.00
High season per wk
£325.00–£725.00

COMBE MARTIN, Devon Map ref 1C1

★★★★

6 Units
Sleeping 3–6

YETLAND FARM COTTAGES

Berry Down, Combe Martin, Ilfracombe
Contact: Mrs A Balcombe
T: (01271) 883655
F: (01271) 883655
E: enquiries@yetlandcottages.co.uk
I: www.yetlandcottages.co.uk

OPEN All Year
CC: Delta, Mastercard, Switch, Visa

Low season per wk
£180.00–£480.00
High season per wk
£351.00–£650.00

Luxury, well-equipped barn conversions set around a courtyard on the edge of Exmoor in a quiet, rural location. Towels, linen and electricity included.

CRACKINGTON HAVEN, Cornwall Map ref 1C2

★★★★

1 Unit
Sleeping 4

THE OLD CIDER PRESS

Crackington Haven, Bude
Contact: Mr S Bennett, 64 Park Drive, London W3 8NA
T: (020) 8993 2628
F: (08709) 223 563
E: booking@theoldcidерpress.co.uk
I: www.theoldciderpress.co.uk

Luxury, self-catering accommodation. This stunning, two-bedroom barn conversion has been furnished to the highest standards. Superbly appointed kitchen and bathroom. Computer with free internet access. Views towards Cornwall's rugged coastline which is just two miles away. Ideal for relaxing breaks, any time of year.

OPEN All Year
CC: Amex, Delta, Mastercard, Switch, Visa

Short breaks of 3 or more nights available Sep- mid-June.

Low season per wk
£320.00–£520.00
High season per wk
£520.00–£655.00

★★★

5 Units
Sleeping 4–6

TRENANNICK COTTAGES

Warbstow, Launceston
Contact: Ms L Harrison, Trenannick Cottages, Trenannick Farm, Warbstow, Launceston PL15 8RP
T: (01566) 781443
F: (01566) 781443
E: lorraine.trenannick@j12.com
I: www.trenannickcottages.co.uk

Delightful cottages standing in three acres of lawn and woodland at the end of a private, tree-lined drive in peaceful, rural setting. Five miles from beach at Crackington Haven. Excellent touring base for North Cornish coast. Pets welcome. Open all year, with log fires for those colder evenings.

OPEN All Year

Short breaks and special reduced rates for small parties available Oct-Mar (excl school holidays).

Low season per wk
£130.00–£200.00
High season per wk
£185.00–£495.00

CREDITON, Devon Map ref 1D2 *Tourist Information Centre Tel: (01363) 772006*

★★★★

2 Units
Sleeping 5–7

Beautiful beamed barn and comfortable cottage on 177-acre livestock farm situated in lovely Devonshire countryside. A perfect base for touring and exploring Dartmoor, Exmoor, north and south coasts, or why not just unwind in your own enclosed lawned garden. Swimming, fishing, riding, cycling and golf available nearby.

RUDGE REW COTTAGE & COLTS HILL BARN

Crediton
Contact: Mrs Bailey, Rudge Rew Cottage & Colts Hill Barn, Rudge Rew Farm, Morchard Bishop, Crediton EX17 6NG
T: (01363) 877309
F: (01363) 877309
E: rudgerew@talk21.com
I: www.rudgerewfarm.btinternet.co.uk

OPEN All Year

5% discount for 2-week booking. Short breaks available Oct-Apr (excl Christmas, New Year and Easter).

Low season per wk
£180.00–£195.00
High season per wk
£345.00–£420.00

DARTMEET, Devon Map ref 1C2

★★★★

1 Unit
Sleeping 4

In the heart of Dartmoor National Park, this granite cottage, recently converted from an old coach house, enjoys a breathtaking view of the Dart Valley and surrounding tors. Fully equipped kitchen/dining room. Spacious bedrooms can be arranged as double or twin. Immediate access to riverbank, woodland and open moorland.

COACHMAN'S COTTAGE

Princetown, Yelverton
Contact: Mrs T Evans, Coachman's Cottage, Hunter's Lodge, Dartmeet, Princetown, Yelverton PL20 6SG
T: (01364) 631173
E: mail@dartmeet.com
I: www.dartmeet.com

OPEN All Year
CC: Amex, JCB, Mastercard, Solo, Switch, Visa

Mid-week (Mon-Fri) and weekend (Fri-Mon) breaks available.

Low season per wk
£180.00–£250.00
High season per wk
£275.00–£320.00

DARTMOOR

See under Ashburton, Bovey Tracey, Dartmeet, Lustleigh, Moretonhampstead, Okehampton, Tavistock

DARTMOUTH, Devon Map ref 1D3 *Tourist Information Centre Tel: (01803) 834224*

★★★

5 Units
Sleeping 2–6

THE OLD BAKEHOUSE
Dartmouth
Contact: Mrs S R Ridalls, The Old Bakehouse, 7 Broadstone, Dartmouth TQ6 9NR
T: (01803) 834585
F: (01803) 834585
E: pioneerparker@aol.com
I: www.oldbakehousedartmouth.co.uk

OPEN All Year

Low season per wk
£200.00–£360.00
High season per wk
£360.00–£630.00

Character cottages, some with beams and old stone fireplaces. In a conservation area, two minutes from historic town centre and river. Free parking. Beach 15 minutes' drive.

NB

IMPORTANT NOTE **Information on accommodation listed in this guide has been supplied by the proprietors. As changes may occur you are advised to check details at the time of booking.**

DAWLISH, Devon Map ref 1D2

★★★★

5 Units
Sleeping 4–6

On the edge of privately owned Cofton Country Holiday Park, converted 100-year-old farm buildings overlooked by ancient Cofton church. Coarse-fishing lakes. Woodland walks. Within a short drive to the Exe estuary and Dawlish Warren. All amenities of the park available during season, including swimming pool and pub.

COFTON COUNTRY COTTAGE HOLIDAYS

Exeter
Contact: Cofton Country Cottage Holidays, Starcross, Nr Dawlish, Exeter EX6 8RP
T: (01626) 890111
F: (01626) 891572
E: info@croftonholidays.co.uk
I: www.coftonholidays.co.uk

OPEN All Year
CC: Delta, Mastercard, Solo, Switch, Visa

Short breaks early and late season. 3- or 4-night breaks at most times. Free coarse fishing Nov-Mar.

Low season per wk £235.00–£399.00
High season per wk £355.00–£649.00

DAWLISH WARREN, Devon Map ref 1D2

★★★★

9 Units
Sleeping 4–6

Magnificent 18thC house converted into luxury apartments. Woodside Cottages – estate workers' cottage conversions. Exe estuary views, surrounded by fields and 50 acres of unspoilt woodlands. Quiet and restful holidays in a perfect setting. Amenities at Cofton during season.

EASTDON ESTATE

Dawlish
Contact: Cofton Country Holidays, Dawlish EX6 8RP
T: (01626) 890111
F: (01626) 891572
E: info@coftonholidays.co.uk
I: www.coftonholidays.co.uk

OPEN All Year
CC: Delta, Mastercard, Switch, Visa

Short breaks early and late season. 3- or 4-night breaks at most times. Free coarse fishing Nov-Mar.

Low season per wk £245.00–£435.00
High season per wk £375.00–£679.00

★★★

1 Unit
Sleeping 4

SHUTTERTON FARM

Dawlish Warren, Dawlish
Contact: Ms K Mitchell, Shutterton Farm, Shutterton Lane, Dawlish Warren, Dawlish EX7 0PD
T: (01626) 863766
F: (01626) 863766
E: shuttertonfarm@aol.com
I: shuttertonfarm.co.uk

OPEN All Year

Low season per wk £275.00–£300.00
High season per wk £350.00–£400.00

16thC Listed thatched cottage, accommodation in former dairy, set in 1.5 acres surrounded by farmland. 1.5 miles from beach and nature reserve.

DEVIZES, Wiltshire Map ref 2B2 *Tourist Information Centre Tel: (01380) 729408*

★★★★

3 Units
Sleeping 4

THE OLD STABLES

Devizes
Contact: Mr & Mrs J Nash, The Old Stables, Tichbornes Farm, Etchilhampton, Devizes SN10 3JL
T: (01380) 862971
F: (01380) 862971
E: info@tichbornes.co.uk
I: www.tichbornes.co.uk

OPEN All Year
CC: Amex, Delta, Diners, JCB, Mastercard, Switch, Visa

Low season per wk Max £200.00
High season per wk Max £415.00

Single-storey cottages, converted from former stables within a courtyard setting in an Area of Outstanding Natural Beauty on the edge of Pewsey Vale.

DEVIZES continued

★★★★

1 Unit
Sleeping 5

OWLS COTTAGE
Easterton, Devizes
Contact: Mrs G C Whittome, Owls Cottage,
48 White Street, Easterton, Devizes SN10 4PA
T: (01380) 818804
F: (01380) 818804
E: gill_whittome@yahoo.co.uk
I: www.owlscottage.homestead.com

OPEN All Year

Low season per wk
£195.00–£290.00
High season per wk
£420.00

Superior quality cottage in peaceful, rural location, outstanding downland views. Excellent walking, White Horse way, Wiltshire cycle way, bird-watching. Ideal for Stonehenge and Bath. Brochure.

DULVERTON, Somerset Map ref 1D1

★★★★

2 Units
Sleeping 4–22

NORTHMOOR HOUSE & LODGE
Dulverton
Contact: Mr T Tarling, Northmoor, Dulverton TA22 9QF
T: (01398) 323720
F: (01398) 324537
E: timtarling@northmoor.fsnet.co.uk
I: www.northmoorhouse.co.uk

Victorian country house set in four acres of lovely garden and surrounded by woodland of the Barle River Valley. Perfect for family and other gatherings in the peace and beauty of Exmoor.

OPEN All Year
CC: Delta, JCB, Mastercard, Solo, Switch, Visa

3-night breaks out of high season.

Low season per wk
Min £276.00
High season per wk
Max £2,700.00

★★★

1 Unit
Sleeping 4

PADDONS
Dulverton
Contact: Mrs McMichael, Paddons, Northmoor Road, Dulverton TA22 9PW
T: (01398) 323514
F: (01398) 324283
E: marymm@paddons.fsnet.co.uk

OPEN All Year

Low season per wk
£215.00–£270.00
High season per wk
£280.00–£455.00

Comfortable, attractive, self-contained flat overlooking River Barle. Beautiful setting. 0.25-mile private fishing. 12 acres private woodland. Large, sunny garden. Ten minutes from Dulverton shops.

★★★★

1 Unit
Sleeping 5

VENFORD COTTAGE
Dulverton
Contact: Mr H Stratton
T: (01398) 341308
E: harleyhstratton@aol.com
I: www.venfordcottage.co.uk

Venford Cottage is a traditional, secluded, three bedroom stone cottage on a smallholding in Exmoor National Park, surrounded by farmland and moorland. The cottage has a downstairs shower room, fully equipped kitchen, dining room, sitting room with woodburner. Upstairs are three bedrooms and a bathroom.

OPEN All Year

Short breaks available most of the year, minimum 3 nights.

Low season per wk
£285.00
High season per wk
£325.00–£425.00

4

QUALITY ASSURANCE SCHEME
Star ratings were correct at the time of going to press but are subject to change. Please check at the time of booking.

EAST BUDLEIGH, Devon Map ref 1D2

★★★★
1 Unit
Sleeping 8

BROOK COTTAGE
East Budleigh, Budleigh Salterton
Contact: Mrs J Simons
T: (01242) 574031
E: josimons@tesco.net
I: http://homepage.ntlworld.com/jim.simons

OPEN All Year

Low season per wk
£230.00–£365.00
High season per wk
£485.00–£650.00

Comfortable, well-equipped, thatched cottage in quiet village, two miles from sea. Plenty to do for the whole family. Also walking, golf and bird-watching.

EDMONTON, Cornwall Map ref 1B2

★★★
2 Units
Sleeping 4

QUARRYMAN'S COTTAGES NO 20 & NO 1
Edmonton, Wadebridge
Contact: Mr H Jenkins, Endellion House, Parc Road, Llangybi, Usk NP15 1NL
T: (01633) 450417
E: jenkins@choicecornishcottages.com
I: www.choicecornishcottages.com

OPEN All Year

Low season per wk
£200.00–£350.00
High season per wk
£400.00–£550.00

Cottages situated in a courtyard of converted 19thC slate workers' terraced dwellings, above the Camel Estuary.

EXETER, Devon Map ref 1D2 *Tourist Information Centre Tel: (01392) 265700*

★★★★★
1 Unit
Sleeping 4

COACH HOUSE FARM
Exeter
Contact: Mr J Bale, Coach House Farm, Moor Lane, Broadclyst, Exeter EX5 3JH
T: (01392) 461254
F: (01392) 460931
E: selfcatering@mpprops.co.uk

OPEN All Year
CC: Mastercard, Switch, Visa

Low season per wk
£185.00–£380.00
High season per wk
£400.00–£500.00

Surrounded by the National Trust Killerton estate, the converted stables provide ground floor accommodation with private entrance and garden. Spectacular East Devon coastline. Good access from M5/A30.

★★★★
2 Units
Sleeping 2–6

REGENT HOUSE
Starcross, Exeter
Contact: Mrs J Goss
T: (01626) 891947
F: (01626) 899126
E: regenthouse@eclipse.co.uk
I: www.cottageguide.co.uk/regenthouse

OPEN All Year
CC: Amex, Delta, Diners, JCB, Mastercard, Solo, Switch, Visa

Low season per wk
£180.00–£500.00
High season per wk
£200.00–£580.00

Self-catering holiday flats. Boating, walking, wildlife. Linen, towels, TV and parking all inclusive. Open all year. Long and short lets. Sea view. See our website.

EXFORD, Somerset Map ref 1D1

★★★
1 Unit
Sleeping 6

2 AUCTION FIELD COTTAGES
Exford, Minehead
Contact: Mr & Mrs Batchelor, Bulbarrow Farm, Bulbarrow, Blandford Forum DT11 0HQ
T: (01258) 817801
F: (01258) 817004

OPEN All Year

Low season per wk
£210.00–£250.00
High season per wk
Max £350.00

Available all year. Short walk from village. Superb woodland and moorland walking. Very well equipped, comfortable and relaxing. An ideal base for exploring Exmoor.

CREDIT CARD BOOKINGS **If you book by telephone and are asked for your credit card number it is advisable to check the proprietor's policy should you cancel your reservation.**

EXFORD continued

★★★-★★★★

6 Units
Sleeping 4–8

WESTERMILL FARM

Exford, Minehead
Contact: Mr & Mrs Oliver & Jill Edwards
T: (01643) 831238
F: (01643) 831216
E: holidays@westermill-exmoor.co.uk
I: www.exmoorfarmholidays.co.uk

Escape to the tranquillity of Westermill, holder of David Bellamy Gold Conservation Award. Cottages on lawns, warm and cosy with log fires. A beautiful valley in the heart of Exmoor. Watch birds in trees, explore working farm on waymarked walks, paddle or fish in our two miles of shallow River Exe.

OPEN All Year

Low season per wk
£150.00–£300.00
High season per wk
£330.00–£480.00

EXMOOR

See under Allerford, Bratton, Brayford, Challacombe, Combe Martin, Dulverton, Exford, Lynton, Minehead, North Molton, Porlock, Simonsbath, West Anstey, Withypool, Wootton Courtenay

FALMOUTH, Cornwall

See display ad below

WEB

www.visitengland.com
Log on for information and inspiration. The latest information on places to visit, events and quality assessed accommodation.

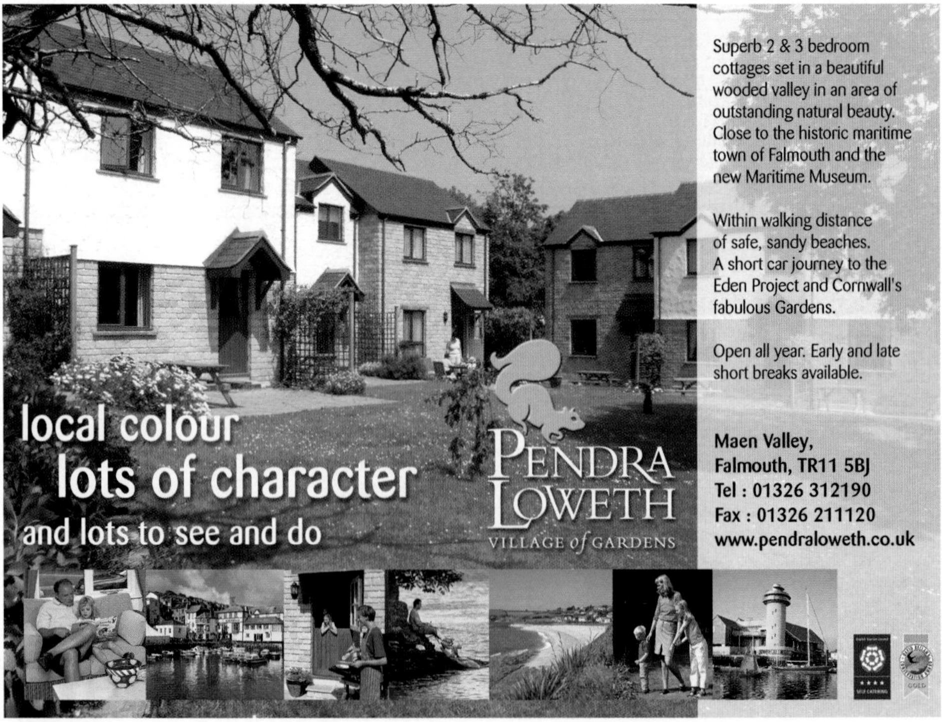

local colour
lots of character
and lots to see and do
PENDRA LOWETH
VILLAGE of GARDENS
Superb 2 & 3 bedroom cottages set in a beautiful wooded valley in an area of outstanding natural beauty. Close to the historic maritime town of Falmouth and the new Maritime Museum.
Within walking distance of safe, sandy beaches. A short car journey to the Eden Project and Cornwall's fabulous Gardens.
Open all year. Early and late short breaks available.
Maen Valley,
Falmouth, TR11 5BJ
Tel : 01326 312190
Fax : 01326 211120
www.pendraloweth.co.uk

FOWEY, Cornwall Map ref 1B3 *Tourist Information Centre Tel: (01726) 833616*

★★★

1 Unit
Sleeping 6

HARBOUR COTTAGE

Fowey
Contact: Fowey Harbour Cottages (W J B Hill & Son), 3 Fore Street, Fowey PL23 1AH
T: (01726) 832211
F: (01726) 832901
E: hillandson@talk21.com

A pleasant cottage situated overlooking the harbour with direct steps to the water and a mooring for a small dinghy. Patio garden. Linen included. Town-centre location close to shops and restaurants. Ideal sailing and walking base.

OPEN All Year

Low season per wk
£275.00–£550.00
High season per wk
£500.00–£900.00

★★★★

4 Units
Sleeping 4–7

THE SQUARE RIG
Fowey
Contact: Mrs H Astley-Morton, Square Rig Holidays, Ladybird House, 26 The Avenue, Rubery, Birmingham B45 9AL
T: (0121) 457 6664
F: (0121) 457 6685
E: info@sqrighol.co.uk
I: www.sqrighol.co.uk

OPEN All Year

Low season per wk
£263.00–£509.00
High season per wk
£425.00–£981.00

Waterside flats on the beautiful Fowey estuary. All flats have balconies with river views. We offer boating facilities, games room and in-house launderette.

FREMINGTON, Devon Map ref 1C1

★★★

1 Unit
Sleeping 6

LOWER YELLAND FARM

Fremington, Barnstaple
Contact: Mr P Day
T: (01271) 860101
F: (01271) 860101
E: pday@loweryellandfarm.co.uk
I: www.loweryellandfarm.co.uk

Built in 1658, modernised in 1990. Adjacent to RSPB Bird Sanctuary and Tarka Trail (footpath and cycle path). Borders River Taw. Ideal centre for touring North Devon. Good access to motorway. Sandy beach at Instow one mile. Winner of Golden Achievement Award of Excellence for Devon Retreat of the Year.

OPEN All Year

Low season per wk
Max £199.00
High season per wk
Max £575.00

FROME, Somerset Map ref 2B2 *Tourist Information Centre Tel: (01373) 467271*

★★★★-★★★★★

17 Units
Sleeping 2–14

EXECUTIVE HOLIDAYS
Oldford, Frome
Contact: Mr R A Gregory, Executive Holidays, Whitemill Farm, Iron Mills Lane, Oldford, Frome BA11 2NR
T: (01373) 452907
F: (01373) 453253
E: info@executiveholidays.co.uk
I: www.executiveholidays.co.uk

OPEN All Year
CC: Mastercard, Visa

Low season per wk
£220.00–£1,540.00
High season per wk
£380.00–£3,360.00

16thC mill and cottage, courtyard cottages and 16thC farmhouse. Country setting in own grounds with private trout stream. Twelve miles from Bath. Free brochure on request.

ACCESSIBILITY

Look for the symbols which indicate National Accessible Scheme standards for hearing and visually impaired guests in addition to standards for guests with mobility impairment. Additional participants are shown in the listings at the back.

GLASTONBURY, Somerset Map ref 2A2 *Tourist Information Centre Tel: (01458) 832954*

★★★★

8 Units
Sleeping 2–6

Delightful cottages converted from a Listed farmhouse and barns. Set in eight acres of garden, apple orchards and meadows. The cottages have old world charm and country-style decor. There is also an indoor heated swimming pool. Beautiful views of the Somerset Levels and Mendip hills. Central for many places of interest.

MIDDLEWICK HOLIDAY COTTAGES

Glastonbury
Contact: Mr & Mrs M Kavanagh, Middlewick Holiday Cottages, Middlewick, Wick Lane, Glastonbury BA6 8JW
T: (01458) 832351
F: (01458) 832351
E: info@middlewickholidaycottages.co.uk
I: www.middlewickcottages.co.uk

OPEN All Year
CC: Mastercard, Visa

Short breaks Oct-Mar.

Low season per wk
£180.00–£290.00
High season per wk
£290.00–£380.00

GOODRINGTON, Devon Map ref 1D2

★★★

5 Units
Sleeping 2–4

Detached property comprising self-contained apartments. Private parking. Goodrington Sands 150 yards. Close to zoo and water park.

ASHDENE HOLIDAY APARTMENTS

Goodrington, Paignton
Contact: Mrs & Mr J & D Beckett, Ashdene Holiday Apartments, Cliff Park Road, Goodrington, Paignton TQ4 6NB
T: (01803) 558397
E: ashdene.apts@goodrington.fsbusiness.co.uk
I: www.ashdeneapartments.co.uk

OPEN All Year

Low season per wk
£145.00–£220.00
High season per wk
£175.00–£450.00

HELSTONE, Cornwall Map ref 1B2

★★★-★★★★

5 Units
Sleeping 4–6

Off quiet country lane, Cornish-stone farm cottages set in 18 acres of fields with views overlooking picturesque Allen Valley. Cosy whitewashed interiors, some logburners. Linen and towels provided. Heated outdoor pool, friendly farm animals for the children.

MAYROSE FARM

Helstone, Camelford
Contact: Mrs J Maunder, Mayrose Farm, Helstone, Camelford PL32 9RN
T: (01840) 213509
F: (01840) 213509
E: info@mayrosefarmcottages.co.uk
I: www.mayrosefarmcottages.co.uk

OPEN All Year
CC: Amex, Mastercard, Visa

Low season per wk
£200.00–£400.00
High season per wk
£500.00–£670.00

SB

SPECIAL BREAKS

Many establishments offer special promotions and themed breaks. These are highlighted in red. (All such offers are subject to availability.)

HEYWOOD, Wiltshire Map ref 2B2

★★★★★

2 Units
Sleeping 15

HEYWOOD HOLIDAY COTTAGES

Heywood, Westbury
Contact: Mr J Boyce
T: (01225) 868393
F: (01225) 868393
E: enquiries@ashecottage-holidaylets.co.uk
I: www.ashecottage-holidaylets.co.uk

Delightful old cottage with annexe. Oak beams and low ceilings add to the charm. Large dining room. Private gardens onto open countryside. Barbecue terrace. Log fire in winter, swimming pool in summer! Private parking. Village pub with great food. Local farm shop. A superb secluded country hideaway.

OPEN All Year
CC: Delta, Mastercard, Switch, Visa

3-night stays available Sep-Jun and some high season dates (excl Christmas and New Year).

Low season per wk
£1,295.00–£1,450.00
High season per wk
£1,650.00–£1,975.00

★★★★★

1 Unit
Sleeping 14

THE WILDERNESS

Heywood, Westbury
Contact: Mrs J Boyce
T: (01225) 868393
F: (01225) 868393
E: contact@uk-holiday-cottages.org
I: www.uk-holiday-cottages.org

Gorgeous 17thC house with attached annexe, featuring oak beams, low ceilings and inglenook fireplace. Two kitchens, range cooker, large dining room. Absolutely bursting with character! Extensive private gardens onto open countryside, barbecue patio, private parking. Village pub with great food. Local farm shop.

OPEN All Year
CC: Delta, Mastercard, Switch, Visa

3-night stays available Sep-Jun and some high season dates (excl Christmas and New Year).

Low season per wk
£1,295.00–£1,450.00
High season per wk
£1,650.00–£1,975.00

HONITON, Devon Map ref 1D2 *Tourist Information Centre Tel: (01404) 43716*

★★★★★

6 Units
Sleeping 3–6

RED DOORS FARM

Beacon, Honiton
Contact: Mr C Shrubb
T: (01404) 890067
F: (01404) 890067
E: info@reddoors.co.uk
I: www.reddoors.co.uk

Grade II Listed Red Doors Farm forms an enchanting, private hamlet nestling in the Blackdown Hills yet only three miles from the market town of Honiton. Our cottages are perfect for both family holidays and couples looking for a relaxing break, each having been refurbished to an extremely high standard.

OPEN All Year

3- or 4-night breaks available Oct-Mar.

Low season per wk
£395.00–£550.00
High season per wk
£550.00–£850.00

CHECK THE MAPS

The colour maps at the front of this guide show all the cities, towns and villages for which you will find accommodation entries. Refer to the town index to find the page on which they are listed.

HOPE COVE, Devon Map ref 1C3

★★★

10 Units
Sleeping 2–4

Large flat, mews cottages and split-level bungalow in pretty, south-facing garden, 400 yards from the beach. Superb cliff walks, swimming and sailing. Kingsbridge and Salcombe 10 minutes' drive. Windsurfing and riding nearby. Wide range of good restaurants and pubs in the locality.

THORNLEA MEWS HOLIDAY COTTAGES

Hope Cove, Salcombe
Contact: Mr J & Mrs A Wilton, Thornlea Mews Holiday Cottages, Hope Cove, Salcombe TQ7 3HB
T: (01548) 561319
F: (01548) 561319
E: thornleamews@ukonline.co.uk
I: www.thornleamews-holidaycottages.co.uk

Short breaks available in the low season.

Low season per wk
£95.00–£475.00
High season per wk
£148.00–£600.00

ILFRACOMBE, Devon Map ref 1C1

★★★

10 Units
Sleeping 2–6

Delightful cottages, some early 1800s (including a unique round barn conversion), set in 35 acres of National Heritage coastland with private beach. The coastal footpath borders our land and the views are stunning. Easily accessible. Activities for all ages. Grocery and meal-delivery services. Pets welcome.

WIDMOUTH FARM COTTAGES

Watermouth, Ilfracombe
Contact: Mrs E Sansom
T: (01271) 863743
F: (01271) 866479
E: holidays@widmouthfarmcottages.co.uk
I: www.widmouthfarmcottages.co.uk

OPEN All Year
CC: Amex, Delta, JCB, Mastercard, Solo, Switch, Visa

Short stays accepted. Christmas shopping offers. Christmas drinks party and decorations in cottages.

Low season per wk
£185.00–£315.00
High season per wk
£360.00–£730.00

KINGSBRIDGE, Devon Map ref 1C3 *Tourist Information Centre Tel: (01548) 853195*

★★★

2 Units
Sleeping 2–6

READS FARM

Loddiswell, Kingsbridge
Contact: Mrs A Pethybridge, Reads Farm, Loddiswell, Kingsbridge TQ7 4RT
T: (01548) 550317
F: (01548) 550317

Flats are part of farmhouse in an Area of Outstanding Natural Beauty. Farmland adjoins River Avon. Fishing. Heated swimming pool. No through traffic.

Low season per wk
£100.00–£200.00
High season per wk
£200.00–£390.00

COUNTRY CODE Always follow the Country Code ♣ Enjoy the countryside and respect its life and work ♣ Guard against all risk of fire ♣ Fasten all gates ♣ Keep your dogs under close control ♣ Keep to public paths across farmland ♣ Use gates and stiles to cross fences, hedges and walls ♣ Leave livestock, crops and machinery alone ♣ Take your litter home ♣ Help to keep all water clean ♣ Protect wildlife, plants and trees ♣ Take special care on country roads ♣ Make no unnecessary noise

KINGSBRIDGE continued

★★★★
8 Units
Sleeping 2–10

WEST CHARLETON GRANGE

West Charleton, Kingsbridge
Contact: Mrs A Lubrani, West Charleton Grange, West Charleton, Kingsbridge TQ7 2AD
T: (01548) 531779
F: (01548) 531100
E: admin@westcharletongrange.com
I: www.westcharletongrange.com

One of Devon's best locations for individual and family holidays. A private hamlet of comfortable cottages in a peaceful, hidden, 15-acre valley just five minutes from Kingsbridge. Superb indoor pool, outdoor play area, tennis court, wildlife lake, coarse fishing. Easy access to Salcombe, Dartmouth, Dartmoor and the best of South Devon's beaches.

OPEN All Year except Christmas
CC: Amex, Delta, JCB, Mastercard, Solo, Switch, Visa

Short breaks and couples breaks available. Colour brochure and details on request.

Low season per wk
£199.00–£1,400.00
High season per wk
£400.00–£2,400.00

LACOCK, Wiltshire Map ref 2B2

★★★★
2 Units
Sleeping 4–5

CYDER HOUSE & CHEESE HOUSE AT WICK FARM

Lacock, Chippenham
Contact: Mr & Mrs P H King, Cyder House and Cheese House, Wick Farm, Wick Lane, Lacock, Chippenham SN15 2LU
T: (01249) 730244
F: (01249) 730072
E: kingsilverlands2@btinternet.com
I: www.cheeseandcyderhouses.co.uk

Tastefully converted, beamed farm building with many original features, 1.5 miles from National Trust village. Cheese House has an extra seating area on the second floor with portable TV. Stepped fireplace with woodburning stove. Private garden with furniture and barbecue. Bath 11 miles.

OPEN All Year
CC: Amex, Mastercard, Visa

'Silver Lands' coarse-fishing lake. 3-night stays Oct-Apr (excl holiday times).

Low season per wk
£220.00–£335.00
High season per wk
£390.00–£470.00

LANGPORT, Somerset Map ref 1D1

★★★-★★★★
2 Units
Sleeping 4–5

MUCHELNEY HAM FARM

Muchelney, Langport
Contact: Mr J Woodborne
T: (01458) 250737
F: (01458) 250737

OPEN All Year

Cider house, extension built in c1979 to main farmhouse. Two bedrooms, one double, one double and single, two bathrooms-one shower en suite. Large sitting, dining, kitchen. Ample parking.

Low season per wk
£160.00–£250.00
High season per wk
£250.00–£410.00

TOWN INDEX

This can be found at the back of this guide. If you know where you want to stay, the index will give you the page number listing accommodation in your chosen town, city or village.

LAUNCESTON, Cornwall Map ref 1C2 *Tourist Information Centre Tel: (01566) 772321*

★★★-★★★★

8 Units
Sleeping 4–8

BAMHAM FARM COTTAGES

Launceston
Contact: Mrs J A Chapman, Bamham Farm Cottages, Higher Bamham Farm, Launceston PL15 9LD
T: (01566) 772141
F: (01566) 775266
E: jackie@bamhamfarm.co.uk
I: www.bamhamfarm.co.uk

Individually designed cottages, ideally situated in beautiful countryside one mile from Launceston, the ancient capital of Cornwall, dominated by its Norman castle. The north and south coasts are easily accessible as are both Dartmoor and Bodmin Moor. Facilities include a heated indoor swimming pool, sauna, solarium, video recorders and trout fishing.

OPEN All Year
CC: Delta, Mastercard, Solo, Switch, Visa

For special offers see our website.

Low season per wk
£210.00–£330.00
High season per wk
£490.00–£1,060.00

★★★-★★★★

4 Units
Sleeping 2–4

LANGDON FARM HOLIDAY COTTAGES
Boyton, Launceston
Contact: Mrs F Rawlinson, Langdon Farm, Boyton, Launceston PL15 8NW
T: (01566) 785389
E: g.f.rawlinson@btinternet.com
I: www.langdonholidays.com

OPEN All Year

Low season per wk
£120.00–£200.00
High season per wk
£210.00–£350.00

One- and two-bedroom, well-equipped cottages, 4-poster beds, countryside setting, near pub, 10 miles from sea. Easy drive to Eden Project. Short breaks available.

★★★

1 Unit
Sleeping 6

SWALLOWS
Launceston
Contact: Mrs K Broad, Lower Dutson Farm, Launceston PL15 9SP
T: (01566) 776456
F: (01566) 776456
E: francis.broad@btclick.com
I: www.farm-cottage.co.uk

OPEN All Year

Low season per wk
£140.00–£280.00
High season per wk
£300.00–£480.00

Pretty walks on traditional family farm, central for visiting NT properties, moors, coasts and beaches. Well-equipped cottage with two bathrooms. River and lake fishing.

LEE, Devon Map ref 1C1

★★★-★★★★

7 Units
Sleeping 4–8

LOWER CAMPSCOTT FARM

Lee, Ilfracombe
Contact: Mrs M Cowell, Lower Campscott Farm, Lee, Ilfracombe EX34 8LS
T: (01271) 863479
F: (01271) 867639
E: holidays@lowercampscott.co.uk
I: www.lowercampscott.co.uk

Charming, tastefully furnished character cottages converted from our farm buildings. Everything supplied to make your stay special. Also holiday homes and lodge home. Peaceful farm setting with views across the Bristol Channel. Lee and Woolacombe beaches are easily accessible.

OPEN All Year
CC: Delta, Switch, Visa

Short breaks available out of school holidays.

Low season per wk
Min £299.00
High season per wk
Max £620.00

CONFIRM YOUR BOOKING
You are advised to confirm your booking in writing.

LISKEARD, Cornwall Map ref 1C2

★★★★

3 Units
Sleeping 4–6

LOWER TRENGALE FARM

Liskeard
Contact: Brian & Terri Shears, Lower Trengale Farm, Liskeard PL14 6HF
T: (01579) 321019
F: (01579) 321432
E: lowertrengale@aol.com
I: www.trengaleholidaycottages.co.uk

OPEN All Year

Low season per wk
£150.00–£260.00
High season per wk
£380.00–£650.00

Quality cottages situated in beautiful countryside 20 miles from Eden. Set in six acres. Expect warmth, comfort, peace and tranquillity. Good dogs welcome.

LOOE, Cornwall Map ref 1C3

★★★★

3 Units
Sleeping 4

BOCADDON HOLIDAY COTTAGES

Looe
Contact: Mrs A Maiklem, Bocaddon, Lanreath, Looe PL13 2PG
T: (01503) 220192
F: (01503) 220192
E: bocaddon@aol.com

Warm, welcoming and peaceful, this tastefully converted barn on a working farm nestles deep in beautiful Cornish countryside, yet is near the famous beaches and fishing harbours of Looe, Polperro and Fowey. Walking, fishing, wonderful houses and gardens are easily available, or just relax in comfort. Very wheelchair friendly.

OPEN All Year

Short breaks available Oct-Mar.

Low season per wk
£160.00–£270.00
High season per wk
£280.00–£480.00

★★★★-★★★★★

5 Units
Sleeping 4–8

BUCKLAWREN FARM

Looe
Contact: Mrs J Henly, Bucklawren Farm, St Martins, Looe PL13 1NZ
T: (01503) 240738
F: (01503) 240481
E: bucklawren@btopenworld.com
I: www.bucklawren.com

Set deep in unspoilt countryside, with a large garden and exceptional sea views, these delightful stone cottages on an award-winning farm are just one mile from the beach and three miles from the fishing port of Looe. The Granary Restaurant is close by.

OPEN All Year
CC: Mastercard, Visa

Short breaks from Nov-Apr (excl Christmas and New Year).

Low season per wk
£150.00–£250.00
High season per wk
£250.00–£850.00

★★★★

35 Units
Sleeping 4

CRYLLA VALLEY COTTAGES

Notter Bridge, Saltash
Contact: Mr M Walsh
T: (01752) 851133
F: (01752) 851666
E: sales@cryllacottages.co.uk
I: www.cryllacottages.co.uk

Award-winning cottages and bungalows in beautiful riverside setting between Looe and Plymouth. 18 acres of grounds and attractive flower gardens. Play area. Ideal for fishing, golf, walking, riding, sailing, town and coast, visiting historic houses and gardens and touring Cornwall and Devon. Country inn close by for good food.

OPEN All Year
CC: Delta, Mastercard, Switch, Visa

Free leisure membership to nearby Golf and Country Club: 3 pools, gym, sauna, jacuzzi, racquets and reduced golf rates.

Low season per wk
£160.00–£277.00
High season per wk
£267.00–£738.00

LOOE continued

★★★★

10 Units
Sleeping 4–8

Situated in a commanding position right on the seafront in Looe, these apartments provide high-quality accommodation with a very high level of facilities. The views from each apartment are stunning, and the location is an ideal base for exploring the rest of Cornwall and South Devon.

ROCK TOWERS APARTMENTS

West Looe, Looe
Contact: Mr C J Dixon, Cornish Collection,
73 Bodrigan Road, Barbican, East Looe, Looe PL13 1EH
T: (01503) 262736
F: (01503) 262736
E: cornishcol@aol.com
I: www.cornishcollection.co.uk

OPEN All Year
CC: Delta, Mastercard, Switch, Visa

5% discount Nov-Mar (excluding Christmas and New Year) if you quote this advertisement.

Low season per wk
£185.00–£325.00
High season per wk
£485.00–£855.00

★★★★

5 Units
Sleeping 1–4

Tastefully converted and very comfortable stone holiday cottages set around 17thC non-working farmstead. Set in unspoilt, peaceful countryside with breathtaking coastal walks/beaches nearby. Close to Eden Project, Lost Gardens of Heligan and many NT properties. An ideal base for exploring the many varied delights of Cornwall.

TALEHAY

Pelynt, Looe
Contact: Mr P R Brumpton, Talehay, Tremaine, Pelynt, Looe PL13 2LT
T: (01503) 220252
F: (01503) 220252
E: paul@talehay.co.uk
I: www.talehay.co.uk

OPEN All Year
CC: Amex, Delta, Diners, JCB, Mastercard, Solo, Switch, Visa

Short breaks available Oct-Mar (excl Christmas and New Year), minimum 2 nights.

Low season per wk
£145.00–£320.00
High season per wk
£250.00–£650.00

LOSTWITHIEL, Cornwall Map ref 1B2

Rating
Applied For
3 Units
Sleeping 2–4

CHARK COUNTRY HOLIDAYS

Redmoor, Bodmin
Contact: Ms J Littleton, Chark Country Holidays, Chark, Redmoor, Bodmin PL30 5AR
T: (01208) 871118
F: (01208) 871118
E: charkcountryholidays@farmersweekly.net
I: www.charkcountryholidays.co.uk

OPEN All Year

Delightful barn conversions in beautiful rural location, yet near Eden Project and many other attractions and beaches. Ideal base for touring, walking, cycling and riding.

Low season per wk
£180.00–£250.00
High season per wk
£250.00–£450.00

QUALITY ASSURANCE SCHEME

For an explanation of the quality and facilities represented by the Stars please refer to the front of this guide. A more detailed explanation can be found in the information pages at the back.

LOSTWITHIEL continued

★★★-★★★★

7 Units
Sleeping 2–6

LANWITHAN MANOR, FARM & WATERSIDE COTTAGES

Lostwithiel
Contact: Mr H F Edward-Collins
T: (01208) 872444
F: (01208) 872444
E: info@lanwithancottages.co.uk
I: www.lanwithancottages.co.uk

Charming selection of Georgian estate cottages nestling in the Fowey Valley with two delightful waterside properties. Cottages with leaded-light windows, crackling log fires, 4-poster bed and glass-topped well. Parkland, river frontage and boat. Woodland and riverside walks from your cottage door. So much more than just a cottage!

OPEN All Year

Short breaks out of season. Last minute reduced green fees. Pets accepted in some cottages.

Low season per wk
£195.00–£370.00
High season per wk
£200.00–£790.00

★★★★

9 Units
Sleeping 2–6

TREDETHICK FARM COTTAGES

Lostwithiel
Contact: Mr & Mrs Reed, Tredethick Farm Cottages, Lostwithiel PL22 OLE
T: (01208) 873618
F: (01208) 873618
E: holidays@tredethick.co.uk
I: www.tredethick.co.uk

Winners of six awards in five years, including 'Best Self-Catering Holiday of the Year' for the whole of England. With all the ingredients for a perfect holiday you are bound to want to come back. Equally suitable for couples or families. Visit our website or phone for a brochure.

OPEN All Year
CC: Amex, Delta, Diners, JCB, Mastercard, Solo, Switch, Visa

Short breaks from Nov-Apr (excl Christmas and New Year).

Low season per wk
£200.00–£300.00
High season per wk
£300.00–£1,150.00

LUSTLEIGH, Devon Map ref 1C2

★★★-★★★★

2 Units
Sleeping 2–4

LUSTLEIGH MILLS
Lustleigh, Newton Abbot
Contact: Mrs J A Rowe
T: (01647) 277357
E: lustleighmills@ukgateway.net
I: www.lustleighmills.btinternet.co.uk

OPEN All Year

Idyllic riverside situation on edge of picturesque Dartmoor village, historic millhouse and bakery with many character features including old beams, bake-ovens, antique furniture, delightful gardens.

Low season per wk
£180.00–£300.00
High season per wk
£350.00

USE YOUR *i*s

There are more than 550 Tourist Information Centres throughout England offering friendly help with accommodation and holiday ideas as well as suggestions of places to visit and things to do. You'll find TIC addresses in the local Phone Book.

LYME REGIS, Dorset Map ref 1D2 *Tourist Information Centre Tel: (01297) 442138*

★★★

2 Units
Sleeping 5–6

NORTHAY FARM

Hawkchurch, Axminster
Contact: Mrs D Olof, Northay Farm, Hawkchurch, Axminster EX13 5UU
T: (01297) 678591
F: (01297) 678591
E: deeolof@hotmail.com
I: www.northay.com

Relax in our cosy 16thC cottages, surrounded by the 200-acre, picturesque, working family farm. Enjoy the outdoor heated swimming pool, barbecue and children's adventure playground, ponies and shire horses. Log fires, central heating, video, dishwasher, microwave and old world charm all await you. Lyme Regis coast nearby.

OPEN All Year
CC: Delta, Switch, Visa

Weekend or mid-week breaks at £40 per night.

Low season per wk
£210.00–£280.00
High season per wk
£380.00–£550.00

★★★★

2 Units
Sleeping 4

SEA TREE HOUSE

Lyme Regis
Contact: Mr D Parker, Sea Tree House, 18 Broad Street, Lyme Regis DT7 3QE
T: (01297) 442244
F: (01297) 442244
E: seatree.house@ukonline.co.uk
I: www.lymeregis.com/seatreehouse

Romantic, elegant apartments overlooking the sea, three minutes from the beach. Spacious living room with dining area overlooking the sea. Central position giving easy access to restaurants, pubs and walks in Area of Outstanding Natural Beauty. Warm, friendly welcome from owners.

OPEN All Year

Short breaks available in the low season.

Low season per wk
£215.00–£365.00
High season per wk
£415.00–£595.00

LYMPSHAM, Somerset Map ref 1D1

★★

4 Units
Sleeping 4

DULHORN FARM CARAVAN PARK

Lympsham, Weston-super-Mare
Contact: Mr & Mrs J E Bowden, Dulhorn Farm Caravan Park, Weston Road, Lympsham, Weston-super-Mare BS24 0JQ
T: (01934) 750298
F: (01934) 750913

On working farm. Ideal touring and fishing, country surroundings. Beaches approximately four miles. Easy access to motorway. Pets welcome.

Low season per wk
£115.00–£180.00
High season per wk
£180.00–£299.00

LYNTON, Devon Map ref 1C1 *Tourist Information Centre Tel: 0845 660 3232*

★★★-★★★★

8 Units
Sleeping 2–8

COASTAL EXMOOR HIDEAWAYS

Parracombe, Barnstaple
Contact: Mr P Hitchen, Coastal Exmoor Hideaways, Heddon Valley Hill, Parracombe, Barnstaple EX31 4PU
T: 08717 170772
F: 08717 170773
E: info@coastalexmoorhideaways.co.uk
I: www.coastalexmoorhideaways.co.uk

OPEN All Year
CC: Delta, Mastercard, Switch, Visa

Coastal Devon cottages on Exmoor in private 50-acre valley with heated indoor pool and jacuzzi. 4-posters, log fires, dogs welcome. Short breaks also available.

Low season per wk
£248.00–£398.00
High season per wk
£598.00–£948.00

VISITBRITAIN'S WHERE TO STAY
Please mention this guide when making your booking.

LYNTON continued

★★★★

1 Unit
Sleeping 2

ROYAL CASTLE LODGE

Lynton
Contact: Mr M Wolverson, Royal Castle Lodge, c/o Stag Cottage, Holdstone Down, Combe Martin EX34 0PF
T: (01271) 882449

Something special! High-quality, 16thC, detached, thatched stone cottage with rustic balcony, stable door, real fire, garden. Idyllic coastal setting in England's 'Little Switzerland'. Exmoor National Park, wooded outlook with harbour, pubs, restaurants, shops within walking distance. Spectacular walks. Spotless, warm and cosy. Off-season short breaks. Perfect honeymoon/anniversaries.

OPEN All Year

De-stressing breaks Nov-Mar. All welcome who appreciate quality, privacy and no petty restrictions.

Low season per wk
Min £235.00
High season per wk
Max £545.00

MAIDEN NEWTON, Dorset Map ref 2A3

★★★★

6 Units
Sleeping 2–5

LANCOMBE COUNTRY COTTAGES

Maiden Newton, Dorchester
Contact: Mr M & Mrs J Provis & Schofield
T: (01300) 320562
F: (01300) 320562
E: info@lancombe.co.uk
I: www.lancombe.co.uk

Lovingly converted from original farm buildings, the cottages offer comfort and warmth, some having 4-poster beds. There is a super indoor heated pool and sauna, a games room and large garden to enhance any summer holiday or cosy winter break. There are magnificent views over the lovely surrounding countryside.

OPEN All Year

Low season per wk
£226.00–£322.00
High season per wk
£250.00–£640.00

MALMESBURY, Wiltshire Map ref 2B2 *Tourist Information Centre Tel: (01666) 823748*

★★★

2 Units
Sleeping 3

COW BYRE & BULL PEN

Charlton, Malmesbury
Contact: Mrs E Edwards, Cow Byre & Bull Pen, Stonehill Farm, Charlton, Malmesbury SN16 9DY
T: (01666) 823310
F: (01666) 823310
E: johnedna@stonehillfarm.fsnet.co.uk
I: www.smoothhound.co.uk/hotels/stonehill.html

Superbly located on the Wiltshire/ Gloucestershire border on the edge of the Cotswolds in lush, rolling countryside. Explore quiet villages, stately homes, market towns, walk in the beautiful countryside, visit fantastic gardens, or just stay at the farm and watch the cows come home. The perfect place for a holiday.

OPEN All Year

Low season per wk
Min £195.00
High season per wk
Max £250.00

MAP REFERENCES The map references refer to the colour maps at the front of this guide. The first figure is the map number; the letter and figure which follow indicate the grid reference on the map.

MARAZION, Cornwall Map ref 1B3

★★★

1 Unit
Sleeping 8

Spacious, seafront, early 19thC character cottage, wonderful views, retaining its old world charm and relaxed atmosphere. Situated in a superb coastal location, two minutes' walk from the centre of Marazion, St Michael's Mount and the beach. Surrounded by seascapes, countryside, walks, close to surfing, gardens, art galleries, pubs and restaurants.

TREVARA

Marazion
Contact: Mrs S Laird, Pheasant Copse, Bere Court Road, Pangbourne, Reading RG8 8JU
T: (0118) 984 5500
F: (0118) 984 3966
E: sallylaird@talk21.com
I: www.thebestcottageincornwall.co.uk

OPEN All Year

Short breaks, 4 nights or less, with 20% reduction on weekly price. Peak-season breaks, late availability only.

Low season per wk
£300.00–£475.00
High season per wk
£540.00–£750.00

MELCOMBE BINGHAM, Dorset Map ref 2B3

★★★★

1 Unit
Sleeping 7

Rural peace in spacious, well-equipped stone cottage with delightful views. Hardy country, on edge of friendly village with well-known pub. Four bedrooms, one on ground floor. Log fire. Wendy house in garden. In an Area of Outstanding Natural Beauty, just off Wessex Ridgeway walkers' path. Coast, abbeys, castles, gardens, many attractions within 0.5-hour drive.

GREYGLES

Melcombe Bingham, Dorchester
Contact: Mr P Sommerfeld, 22 Tiverton Road, Willesden, London NW10 3HL
T: (020) 8969 4830
F: (020) 8960 0069
E: enquiry@greygles.co.uk
I: www.greygles.co.uk

OPEN All Year
CC: JCB, Solo

Short breaks available outside summer peak, Christmas and Easter. Minimum 3-night stay. All linen, towels, heating included.

Low season per wk
£375.00–£425.00
High season per wk
£525.00–£775.00

MELDON, Devon Map ref 1C2

★★★★

1 Unit
Sleeping 7

Old Dartmoor country cottage, tastefully restored with exposed beams and woodburner. Well equipped. En suite shower/wc, plus bathroom. Private, enclosed garden. Ideal centre for family holidays, golf, fishing etc. Very close to moorland, Cycleway 27, woods and streams. North and South coasts, numerous attractions (eg. Eden Project) within easy reach.

KERSLAKE COTTAGE

Meldon, Okehampton
Contact: Ms L St George, Kerslake Farm, Meldon, Okehampton EX20 4LU
T: (01837) 54892
F: (01837) 54892
E: booking@kerslakemeldon.co.uk
I: www.kerslakemeldon.co.uk

OPEN All Year

Holders of Devon Cycle Mark for cyclist-friendly accommodation. Short breaks available in autumn, winter and spring.

Low season per wk
£200.00–£350.00
High season per wk
£300.00–£600.00

VISITOR ATTRACTIONS **For ideas on places to visit refer to the introduction at the beginning of this section. Look out too for the ETC's Quality Assured Visitor Attraction signs.**

MEVAGISSEY, Cornwall Map ref 1B3

★★★
13 Units
Sleeping 2–6

TRELOEN HOLIDAY APARTMENTS
Mevagissey, St Austell
Contact: Mrs P Seamark, Treloen Holiday Apartments, Dept E, Polkirt Hill, Mevagissey, St Austell PL26 6UX
T: (01726) 842406
F: (01726) 842406
E: holidays@treloen.co.uk
I: www.treloen.co.uk

OPEN All Year
CC: Delta, JCB, Mastercard, Solo, Switch, Visa

Low season per wk
£175.00–£230.00
High season per wk
£320.00–£580.00

Quality apartments in secluded clifftop setting, all with spectacular sea views and private balconies/patios. 450 metres picturesque harbour, shops, beach. Ten miles Eden Project.

MINEHEAD, Somerset Map ref 1D1 *Tourist Information Centre Tel: (01643) 702624*

★★★★
1 Unit
Sleeping 4

ANCHOR COTTAGE
Minehead
Contact: Dr J C Malin
T: (01643) 707529
F: (01643) 708712
E: jmalin@btinternet.com

Low season per wk
£260.00–£305.00
High season per wk
£310.00–£425.00

Delightful 17thC fisherman's cottage facing Bristol Channel, with rear patio giving superb views. Two double bedrooms, attic bedroom, bathroom/wc, fully-equipped kitchen, lounge and downstairs wc.

7

★★★★
3 Units
Sleeping 4

HUNTINGBALL LODGE
Blue Anchor, Minehead
Contact: Mr B & Mrs K Hall, Huntingball Lodge, Blue Anchor, Minehead TA24 6JP
T: (01984) 640076
F: (01984) 640076
I: www.huntingball-lodge.co.uk

Elegant country house with magnificent, far-reaching views across the West Somerset coast and surrounding Exmoor countryside from all of its luxurious and spacious apartments. Park-like grounds. Pubs/restaurants plus shop and tea rooms within easy walking distance. Open all year. A guaranteed warm welcome from the resident owners.

OPEN All Year

Short breaks available Oct-Mar (excl Christmas and New Year).

Low season per wk
£200.00–£225.00
High season per wk
£260.00–£450.00

★★★★
1 Unit
Sleeping 6

LA MER
Minehead
Contact: Mrs A Bowden
T: (01643) 704405
F: (01643) 704405

Low season per wk
Min £210.00
High season per wk
Max £550.00

Three-bedroomed mews-type house on the harbour. Large studio with balcony. Wonderful sea views. Private parking. Quiet, interesting location.

7

AT-A-GLANCE SYMBOLS
Symbols at the end of each accommodation entry give useful information about services and facilities. A key to symbols can be found inside the back cover flap. Keep this open for easy reference.

MINIONS, Cornwall Map ref 1C2

★★★★

3 Units
Sleeping 3–4

TREWALLA FARM

Minions, Liskeard
Contact: F Cotter
T: (01579) 342385
F: (01579) 342385
E: cotter.trewalla@virgin.net
I: http://cotter.trewalla@virgin.net

Cottages equipped and furnished to a high standard on a small farm in an Area of Outstanding Natural Beauty overlooking Siblyback Lake. The location offers perfect peace and an ideal base for walking; conveniently located for both coastlines and visiting the Eden Project – if you can tear yourself away!

Weekend breaks available in low season.

Low season per wk
£220.00–£260.00
High season per wk
£395.00–£425.00

MORETONHAMPSTEAD, Devon Map ref 1C2

★★-★★★★

7 Units
Sleeping 2–4

BUDLEIGH FARM

Moretonhampstead, Newton Abbot
Contact: Mrs J Harvey, Budleigh Farm, Moretonhampstead, Newton Abbot TQ13 8SB
T: (01647) 440835
F: (01647) 440436
E: swharvey@budleighfarm.co.uk
I: www.budleighfarm.co.uk

Properties created with flair from granite barns, on a farm at the end of a stunning valley – rural but not remote. Easy to find. Superb gardens, pubs of character, beaches and castles are all accessible. Superb walking country. In Dartmoor National Park.

OPEN All Year
CC: Mastercard, Visa

Low season per wk
£135.00–£280.00
High season per wk
£260.00–£430.00

MOTHECOMBE, Devon Map ref 1C3

★★★★-★★★★★

10 Units
Sleeping 4–12

THE FLETE ESTATE HOLIDAY COTTAGES

Holbeton, Plymouth
Contact: Miss J Webb, The Flete Estate Holiday Cottages, Pamflete, Holbeton, Plymouth PL8 1JR
T: (01752) 830234
F: (01752) 830500
E: cottages@flete.co.uk
I: www.flete.co.uk

The Flete Estate is undoubtedly the Jewel in the Crown of the beautiful South Hams. This private 5000-acre estate is designated an Area of Outstanding Natural Beauty, encompassing large, broadleaf woodlands, rolling pastures, cliff paths and sandy beaches, secluded cottages, little hamlets and a tantalising lacework of private drives and pathways.

OPEN All Year

Winter breaks Nov-Mar (excl Christmas and New Year) from £117pn, minimum 3 nights.

Low season per wk
£411.00–£800.00
High season per wk
£640.00–£1,670.00

NB

IMPORTANT NOTE Information on accommodation listed in this guide has been supplied by the proprietors. As changes may occur you are advised to check details at the time of booking.

MOUSEHOLE, Cornwall Map ref 1A3

★★★

1 Unit
Sleeping 8

Listed 16thC granite cottage located only a few metres from the water's edge at the heart of the picturesque former fishing village of Mousehole (pronounced Mowzel). Very well equipped and very comfortable. Equally suitable for family holiday or quiet break. Village has sandy beaches, harbour, shops, galleries, post office, pubs and restaurants.

2 THE OLD STANDARD

Mousehole, Penzance
Contact: Mr & Mrs J Underhill, The Old Vicarage, Collingbourne Kingston, Marlborough SN8 3SE
T: (01264) 850234
F: (01264) 850703
E: j.underhill@oldstandard.co.uk
I: www.oldstandard.co.uk

OPEN All Year

Short breaks available in low season – minimum 3 nights (excl Christmas and New Year).

Low season per wk
£250.00–£460.00
High season per wk
£465.00–£700.00

MUDDIFORD, Devon Map ref 1C1

★★★★

1 Unit
Sleeping 8

Restored to a high standard in 2002 this country cottage, with south-facing views over the Devon countryside, has retained its character and charm. Lounge/diner featuring inglenook fireplace and woodburning stove. Fully equipped kitchen and utility room. Four bedrooms, family bathroom/shower. Large gardens. Off-road parking.

ROSE COTTAGE

Muddiford, Barnstaple
Contact: Ms H Knight, Score Farm Developments, Score Farm, Chapel Street, Braunton EX33 1EL
T: (01271) 814815
F: (01271) 817973
E: sunshinenel@btinternet.com
I: www.scorefarmholidays.co.uk

OPEN All Year

Walking Festival in May: discounts available. North Devon Festival in June: 2 weeks of entertainment, arts, heritage, horticulture and Oceanfest.

Low season per wk
£260.00–£335.00
High season per wk
£390.00–£635.00

MUSBURY, Devon Map ref 1D2

★★★★★

1 Unit
Sleeping 6

This spacious, detached, stone cottage, with its own fully enclosed garden, has a woodburning stove in the sitting room and a well-equipped, modern fitted kitchen/dining room. Set in an Area of Outstanding Natural Beauty, it's an ideal base for exploring Devon and neighbouring Dorset and Somerset.

MAIDENHAYNE FARM COTTAGE

Musbury, Axminster
Contact: Mrs T Colley, Maidenhayne Farmhouse, Maidenhayne Lane, Musbury, Axminster EX13 8AG
T: (01297) 552469
F: (01297) 551109
E: graham@maidenhayne-farm-cottage.co.uk
I: www.Maidenhayne-farm-cottage.co.uk

OPEN All Year

3- or 4-night stays available Oct-Mar.

Low season per wk
£350.00–£460.00
High season per wk
£360.00–£600.00

QUALITY ASSURANCE SCHEME

Star ratings were correct at the time of going to press but are subject to change. Please check at the time of booking.

NEW POLZEATH, Cornwall Map ref 1B2

★★★-★★★★★

2 Units
Sleeping 5–14

ATLANTIC VIEW & ATLANTIC VIEW COACH HOUSE
New Polzeath, Wadebridge
Contact: Dr S Garthwaite
T: (01892) 722264
F: (01892) 724022
E: enquiries@atlanticview.net
I: www.atlanticview.net

OPEN All Year

Low season per wk
£400.00–£1,070.00
High season per wk
£790.00–£2,500.00

Luxury, refurbished properties overlooking one of the finest beaches on the North Cornwall coast. Enjoy surfing, walking, golf, sailing, gardens, health club and much more.

★★★

1 Unit
Sleeping 6

TREHEATHER
New Polzeath, Wadebridge
Contact: Dr E Mayall, Osmond House, Stoke Canon, Exeter EX5 4AA
T: (01392) 841219

Low season per wk
Min £350.00
High season per wk
Max £650.00

Spacious, modern bungalow. About 200 yards from sandy surfing beach with rock pools. Garden, coastal walks.

NEWQUAY, Cornwall Map ref 1B2 *Tourist Information Centre Tel: (01637) 854020*

★★

9 Units
Sleeping 2–6

CROFTLEA HOLIDAY FLATS

Newquay
Contact: Croftlea Holiday Flats, Wildflower Lane, Newquay TR7 2QB
T: (01637) 852505
F: (01637) 877183
E: info@croftlea.co.uk
I: www.croftlea.co.uk

Croftlea flats are fully self-contained and are ideally situated close to beaches, shops, station, leisure and sports facilities. Croftlea overlooks Trenance Leisure Park with zoo, tennis courts, bowls, boating, crazy golf and skateboarding. Croftlea stands in its own grounds with swimming pool, barbecue area, gardens and ample car parking.

OPEN All Year

Low season per wk
£150.00–£250.00
High season per wk
£300.00–£700.00

NORTH MOLTON, Devon Map ref 1C1

★★-★★★

3 Units
Sleeping 2–8

WEST MILLBROOK FARM

Twitchen, South Molton
Contact: Mrs R J Courtney
T: (01598) 740382
E: wmbselfcatering@aol.com
I: www.north.molton.co.uk

Farm bordering Exmoor surrounded by pleasant gardens and beautiful, peaceful countryside. Situated a mile from North Molton village with easy access from North Devon link road. Ideal for touring Exmoor and North Devon/Somerset coast and beaches. Games room, play area. Out-of-season short breaks. Colour brochure available.

OPEN All Year

Low season per wk
Min £70.00
High season per wk
Max £375.00

CREDIT CARD BOOKINGS If you book by telephone and are asked for your credit card number it is advisable to check the proprietor's policy should you cancel your reservation.

NORTHLEIGH, Devon Map ref 1D2

★★★★
3 Units
Sleeping 4–6

NORTHLEIGH FARM

Northleigh, Colyton
Contact: Mr & Mrs S Potter
T: (01404) 871217
F: (01404) 871217
E: simon-potter@msn.com
I: www.northleighfarm.co.uk

OPEN All Year

Low season per wk
£250.00–£350.00
High season per wk
£350.00–£575.00

Fully equipped barn conversions in peaceful farm courtyard. Beautiful views over Coly Valley. Coast six miles.

OKEHAMPTON, Devon Map ref 1C2

★★★★
4 Units
Sleeping 4–6

BEER FARM

Okehampton
Contact: Mr R & Mrs S Annear, Beer Farm, Okehampton EX20 1SG
T: (01837) 840265
F: (01837) 840245
E: beerfarm.oke@which.net
I: www.beerfarm.co.uk

Enjoy a peaceful holiday on our small farm situated on the northern edge of Dartmoor in mid-Devon. Comfortable and well-equipped two- and three-bedroomed cottages with VCRs and CD-players. One offers accessibility for the less mobile. Games room, some covered parking. Dogs/horses by arrangement. Good walking, cycling and touring base.

OPEN All Year

5% discount on second (lower price) cottage if booked together. Short breaks available (excl school holidays), minimum 3 nights.

Low season per wk
£170.00–£340.00
High season per wk
£350.00–£595.00

★★★★★
1 Unit
Sleeping 6

DEER PARK

Petrockstow, Okehampton
Contact: Mrs J Buckland, Deer Park, Berry Farm, Petrockstow, Okehampton EX20 3ET
T: (01837) 811187
F: (01837) 810037
E: judy@berryfarm.co.uk
I: www.deerparkcottage.co.uk

As you drive down the track through the dappled tunnel of trees you are lost in unspoilt countryside with abundant wildlife and birdsong. A lovely cottage with two inglenooks. Five-star standard and breathtaking views. Bedrooms furnished with soft colours, exuding comfort and warmth. Time to pause, gaze, stand and wonder.

OPEN All Year

Low season per wk
£300.00–£350.00
High season per wk
£450.00–£600.00

★★★★
2 Units
Sleeping 6

MELDON COTTAGES

Okehampton
Contact: Mr Plant & Mrs Roberts, Meldon Cottages, Meldon, Okehampton EX20 4LU
T: (01837) 54363
E: enquiries@meldoncottages.co.uk
I: www.meldoncottages.co.uk

OPEN All Year

Low season per wk
Min £100.00
High season per wk
Max £550.00

Well-equipped cottage situated within Dartmoor National Park. Many attractions within easy reach.

PRICES

Please check prices and other details at the time of booking.

OKEHAMPTON continued

★★★★

4 Units
Sleeping 4–8

Delightful barn conversions on working sheep farm, furnished to high standards. Lounge, well-equipped fitted kitchens/dining areas, outdoor heated swimming pool, gardens and patio, barbecue areas. Dartmoor just a walk away. Pony trekking, walking, cycling, fishing or just simply relax. Home from home, cream tea. Three new coarse-fishing lakes.

WEEK FARM COUNTRY HOLIDAYS

Bridestowe, Okehampton
Contact: Mrs M K Hockridge, Week Farm Country Holidays, Week Farm, Bridestowe, Okehampton EX20 4HZ
T: (01837) 861221
F: (01837) 861221
E: accom@weekfarmonline.com
I: www.weekfarmonline.com

OPEN All Year
CC: Amex, Mastercard, Visa

Fishing weekends based on 3 well-stocked coarse-fishing lakes.

Low season per wk
£250.00–£520.00
High season per wk
£540.00–£840.00

PADSTOW, Cornwall Map ref 1B2 *Tourist Information Centre Tel: (01841) 533449*

★★★-★★★★

4 Units
Sleeping 3–8

Situated in an Area of Outstanding Natural Beauty near Padstow, these stone and slate cottages have been refurbished to provide a high standard of accommodation. An excellent location for touring, walking, cycling or just relaxing. Children and pets welcome. Daily rates for winter bookings available. Ample parking.

THE LAURELS HOLIDAY PARK

Whitecross, Wadebridge
Contact: Mr A D Nicholson, The Laurels Holiday Park, Padstow Road, Whitecross, Wadebridge PL27 7JQ
T: (01208) 813341
F: (01208) 816590
E: anicholson@thelaurelsholidaypark.co.uk
I: www.thelaurelsholidaypark.co.uk

OPEN All Year

Daily rates available Oct-Mar (excl Christmas and New Year): from £25 per night. Ideal for weekend break.

Low season per wk
£150.00–£250.00
High season per wk
£370.00–£650.00

★★★★

3 Units
Sleeping 8

THE OLD BAKERY

Padstow
Contact: Mr T Tippett, T W Properties, 6 Cross Street, Padstow PL28 8AT
T: (01841) 532885
E: tony.twproperties@aol.com
I: www.TWPROPERTIES.co.uk

OPEN All Year

Low season per wk
£220.00–£600.00
High season per wk
£350.00–£825.00

Adjoining cottages set in the heart of Padstow. Three minutes' walk from harbour, shops, restaurants and inns. Comfortable accommodation at any time of year.

★★★

3 Units
Sleeping 4–6

PADSTOW HOLIDAY COTTAGES

Padstow
Contact: Mrs P Walker, 1 Sarah's Gate, Little Petherick, Wadebridge PL27 7QT
T: (01841) 541180
E: info@padstow-holiday-cottages.co.uk
I: www.padstow-holiday-cottages.co.uk

OPEN All Year
CC: Mastercard, Visa

Low season per wk
£170.00–£270.00
High season per wk
£360.00–£590.00

Padstow properties in quiet locations a short walk from the harbour. Providing comfortable, quality accommodation. Private parking. Patio gardens. Gas/electricity and linen included. Owner-supervised.

SYMBOLS The symbols in each entry give information about services and facilities. A key to these symbols appears at the back of this guide.

PADSTOW continued

★★★

7 Units
Sleeping 5–6

Delightfully situated, well-equipped apartments set in large gardens with panoramic sea views. Just a short walk through fields to a natural swimming pool and Trevone beach. Swimming, surfing, sailing, rambling and golfing nearby. Ample parking, laundry room, table tennis, children's play area and Wendy house. Pets welcome.

POLS PIECE HOLIDAYS

Trevone, Padstow
Contact: Mrs J E Olivey, Pols Piece Holidays, Dobbin Lane, Trevone, Padstow PL28 8QP
T: (01841) 520372
F: (01841) 520372
E: polspiece@virgin.net
I: www.polspieceholidays.co.uk

OPEN All Year

Short breaks available Nov-Mar.

Low season per wk
£200.00–£345.00
High season per wk
£385.00–£695.00

★★★

1 Unit
Sleeping 4

34 SARAH'S VIEW

Padstow
Contact: Mrs M A Thomas
T: (01841) 532243

OPEN All Year except Christmas

Modern, well-equipped cottage on edge of town (Tesco nearby). Open all year. Owner supervised. Close to Camel Trail, lovely coastal walks.

Low season per wk
£195.00–£275.00
High season per wk
£300.00–£425.00

★★★★

1 Unit
Sleeping 8

The Spinney House is a newly renovated property now offering luxury four-bedroom accommodation. Spacious, yet cosy and warm in winter with full central heating and double glazing. Fully fitted kitchen, separate utility room, lounge/diner plus cloakroom. One en suite bedroom, three others plus full bathroom. Close to Padstow, beaches and Eden Project.

THE SPINNEY HOUSE

St Ervan
Contact: Mr Clarke, The Old Rectory, St Ervan, Wadebridge PL27 7TA
T: (01841) 540255
F: (01841) 540255
E: mail@stervanmanor.freeserve.co.uk
I: www.stervanmanor.co.uk

OPEN All Year
CC: Delta, Mastercard, Switch, Visa

Open all year. Short breaks available – please ring for details.

Low season per wk
£600.00–£800.00
High season per wk
£900.00–£1,500.00

★★★★-★★★★★

2 Units
Sleeping 2–4

Beautifully restored, tastefully furnished cottages in old part of Padstow. Ideal location for those who appreciate comfort and quality. Lovers of good food are catered for by fine restaurants including three Rick Stein establishments. Three minutes' walk to the delightful harbour. Beautiful unspoilt coastline and beaches all around.

SUNDAY & SUNRISE COTTAGE

Padstow
Contact: Mrs D E Hoe, 14 The Green, Snitterfield, Stratford-upon-Avon CV37 0JG
T: (01789) 730223
F: (01789) 730199
E: mail@sundaycottage.co.uk
I: www.sundaycottage.co.uk

OPEN All Year

Low season per wk
£210.00–£290.00
High season per wk
£360.00–£610.00

PAIGNTON, Devon Map ref 1D2 *Tourist Information Centre Tel: 0906 680 1268 (Premium rate number)*

★★★
4 Units
Sleeping 4–6

Quality apartments and a celebration suite with 4-poster, ideally situated on level ground close to beach, shops and all amenities. Our apartments all have lounge with TV and VCR, separate kitchens and full-size, fully tiled bathrooms containing bath and shower. Cleanliness is assured. We are a non-smoking and no pets establishment.

ALL SEASONS HOLIDAY APARTMENTS

Paignton
Contact: Mr M Dessi
T: (01803) 552187
F: (01803) 552187
E: mikedessi@allseasonsholiday.freeserve.co.uk
I: www.allseasonsholidayapartments.co.uk

OPEN All Year

Short breaks available from Oct-Apr and last minute at all other times, subject to availability.

Low season per wk
£140.00–£245.00
High season per wk
£210.00–£440.00

★★★★
3 Units
Sleeping 2–6

"Best of Both Worlds" – enjoy the freedom that self-catering can offer, with facilities of a 2-star hotel. We offer beautifully appointed holiday apartments, some with sea views and balconies, all with every home comfort. Idyllic location, fronting onto open parkland and safe, sandy beaches.

HARWIN HOTEL APARTMENTS

Paignton
Contact: Mr & Mrs S Gorman, Harwin Hotel & Apartments, Alta Vista Road, Goodrington Sands, Paignton TQ4 6DA
T: (01803) 558771
F: 0870 831 3998
E: harwin@blueyonder.co.uk
I: www.harwinapartments.co.uk

OPEN All Year
CC: Delta, Mastercard, Solo, Switch, Visa

Short breaks available Sep-Apr, minimum 3 nights.

Low season per wk
£195.00–£440.00
High season per wk
£250.00–£700.00

★★★
8 Units

JULIE COURT HOLIDAY APARTMENTS
Paignton
Contact: Owner/Proprietor
T: (01803) 551012
E: info@juliecourt.co.uk
I: www.juliecourt.co.uk

Quoted by our guests as 'best in Paignton' and 'great for location'. Quality self-contained apartments, minutes from award-winning beach. Secured private car park. Mob: 0776 481 2875.

Low season per wk
£115.00–£200.00
High season per wk
£210.00–£475.00

PANCRASWEEK, Devon Map ref 1C2

★★
1 Unit
Sleeping 7

TAMARSTONE FARM
Pancrasweek, Holsworthy
Contact: Mrs M Daglish, Tamarstone Farm, Bude Road, Pancrasweek, Holsworthy EX22 7JT
T: (01288) 381734
E: cottage@tamarstone.co.uk
I: www.tamarstone.co.uk

OPEN All Year

Three-bedroomed, centrally heated cottage peacefully situated on the Devon/Cornwall borders, ideal for touring both counties.

Low season per wk
£220.00–£340.00
High season per wk
£315.00–£495.00

MAP REFERENCES
Map references apply to the colour maps at the front of this guide.

PENDEEN, Cornwall Map ref 1A3

★★★-★★★★

5 Units
Sleeping 2–5

TREWELLARD MANOR FARM

Pendeen, Penzance
Contact: Mrs M Bailey, Trewellard Manor Farm, Pendeen, Penzance TR19 7SU
T: (01736) 788526
F: (01736) 788526
E: marionbbailey@hotmail.com
I: www.trewellardmanor.co.uk

A warm, all-year-round welcome awaits you in our tastefully converted stables and granary. Spectacular moorland scenery and rugged cliffs. Ideal walking area. Stoves for cooler days. Heated swimming pool May to September. Play area and barbecue.

OPEN All Year
CC: Delta, Mastercard, Switch, Visa

Low season per wk
Min £180.00
High season per wk
Max £630.00

PENTEWAN, Cornwall Map ref 1B3

★★★

1 Unit
Sleeping 4

CROFTERS END

Pentewan, St Austell
Contact: Mr & Mrs Radmore
T: (01872) 501269

Pretty, well-equipped cottage. Pecaeful, yet close to village amenities. Minutes from the long sandy beach. The coastal footpath and cycle trail lead from the village. Ideally positioned for a quiet break or for visiting many of Cornwall's attractions: Lost Gardens of Heligan, Eden Project, Mevagissey, Charlestown etc.

OPEN All Year

Short breaks available Oct–Mar.

Low season per wk
£120.00–£300.00
High season per wk
£300.00–£450.00

PENZANCE, Cornwall Map ref 1A3 *Tourist Information Centre Tel: (01736) 362207*

★★★

2 Units
Sleeping 3–8

ROSPANNEL FARM

Penzance
Contact: Mr G B Hocking, Rospannel Farm, Crows-an-Wra, Penzance TR19 6HS
T: (01736) 810262
E: gbernard@thefreeinternet.co.uk
I: www.rospannel.com

OPEN All Year

Low season per wk
£200.00–£300.00
High season per wk
£300.00–£400.00

Old-fashioned, very quiet and peaceful farm. Own pool and hide for bird-watchers. Moth light for insect enthusiasts. Badgers, foxes and lots of wildlife.

★★★-★★★★

6 Units
Sleeping 4

SAINT PIRANS COTTAGES

Perranuthnoe, Penzance
Contact: Mrs C Gresswell
T: (01962) 774379
E: perranhols@aol.com

The cottages provide well-equipped, comfortable accommodation with a pretty, communal garden, in the centre of Perranuthoe, a traditional, coastal, Cornish village. The village enjoys a lovely pub, a large, sandy beach 400 metres from the cottages and superb coastal walks. Golf, riding, sailing close by. Regret no pets.

OPEN All Year

Low season per wk
£140.00–£150.00
High season per wk
£430.00–£450.00

PERRANPORTH, Cornwall Map ref 1B2

★★★★

1 Unit
Sleeping 6

4 EUREKA VALE

Perranporth
Contact: Mr & Mrs J A Cuthill, Claremont, St Georges Hill, Perranporth TR6 0JS
T: (01872) 573624

OPEN All Year

Low season per wk
£190.00–£345.00
High season per wk
£360.00–£495.00

Early Victorian cottage in a quiet, private location with a sheltered garden, 150 metres from a sandy surfing beach. Close to all amenities.

PILLATON, Cornwall Map ref 1C2

★★★★

2 Units
Sleeping 2

UPALONG & DOWNALONG

Pillaton, Saltash
Contact: Mr G M Barnicoat, Trefenten, Pillaton, Saltash PL12 6QX
T: (01579) 350141
F: (01579) 351520
E: trefenten@beeb.net
I: www.trefenten.co.uk

Character barn conversion. Own parking within four acres of grounds. Close St Mellion Golf and Leisure Centre. We provide many extra items you will not find elsewhere included in reasonable rates. No hidden extras. Local fishing, horse-riding. Short drive several NT properties, Moors, seaside and Plymouth. Eden Project 27 miles.

CC: Delta, JCB, Mastercard, Solo, Switch, Visa

High season per wk
£200.00–£299.00

POLPERRO, Cornwall Map ref 1C3

★★★★-★★★★★

17 Units
Sleeping 2–16

CLASSY COTTAGES

Polperro, Looe
Contact: Mrs & Mr F & M Nicolle, Blanches Windsor, Polperro, Looe PL13 2PT
T: (01720) 423000
E: nicolle@classycottages.co.uk
I: www.classycottages.co.uk

Romantic fishermen's cottages sitting on Polperro's harbour wall, plus isolated houses situated in three acres of gardens with sea views, short walk down valley to deserted cove and rock pools. Log fires. Use of private indoor swimming pool, sauna, spa, solarium at our farm cottages. Cornish cream tea to complete our welcome.

OPEN All Year
CC: Delta, JCB, Mastercard, Solo, Switch, Visa

Weekend breaks – out of season, mid-week breaks.

Low season per wk
£95.00–£890.00
High season per wk
£350.00–£3,200.00

★★★-★★★★

7 Units
Sleeping 2–5

CRUMPLEHORN COTTAGES

Polperro, Looe
Contact: Mr M Collings, Crumplehorn Cottages, The Anchorage, Portuan Road, Hannafore, Looe PL13 2DN
T: (01503) 262523
F: (01503) 262523
E: gloria@crumplehorncottages.co.uk
I: www.crumplehorncottage.co.uk

Traditional Cornish cottages, close to harbour, safe sandy beaches. Resident local owner. Not part of a holiday complex – individually sited within the village. Cottage at Looe also available.

OPEN All Year

3-day breaks Nov-Mar: £120 for 2 people (excl Christmas and New Year).

Low season per wk
£175.00–£300.00
High season per wk
£310.00–£540.00

POLPERRO continued

★★★★★

1 Unit
Sleeping 10

KIRK HOUSE

Polperro, Looe
Contact: Ms K Boniface
T: (01789) 205522
F: (01789) 298899
E: wts@kirkhouseholidays.co.uk
I: www.kirkhouseholidays.co.uk

Nestling in the heart of Polperro, Kirk House is a lovingly converted 19thC chapel offering spacious and stylish holiday accommodation. Kirk House has five bedrooms (two doubles, two twins and one bunk bed) and every facility needed to provide a perfect holiday home.

OPEN All Year
CC: Amex, Delta, Diners, JCB, Mastercard, Solo, Switch, Visa

Long weekend and short breaks available Oct-Feb (excl Christmas and New Year). Corporate conferences catered for.

Low season per wk
£800.00–£1,000.00
High season per wk
£1,300.00–£2,000.00

★★★★-★★★★★

2 Units
Sleeping 2–6

PIER INN HOUSE & STUDIO

Polperro, Looe
Contact: Ms K Boniface
T: (01789) 205522
F: (01789) 298899
E: wts@pierinnholidays.co.uk
I: www.pierinnholidays.co.uk

Pier Inn is situated at the head of Polperro harbour, commanding panoramic sea and harbour views. Pier Inn House offers one double and two twins, and Pier Inn Studio, with its harbourside balcony, is a romantic self-contained apartment. Both are furnished and equipped to the highest standard.

OPEN All Year
CC: Amex, Delta, Diners, JCB, Mastercard, Switch, Visa

Off-season short breaks available plus discounts for taking combined facility for 8 people.

Low season per wk
£240.00–£460.00
High season per wk
£500.00–£1,320.00

PORLOCK, Somerset Map ref 1D1

★★★★

1 Unit
Sleeping 4

GREEN CHANTRY

Porlock, Minehead
Contact: Mrs M Payton, Home Farm, Burrowbridge, Bridgwater TA7 0RF
T: (01823) 698330
F: (01823) 698169
E: maggie_payton@hotmail.com

Pretty Victorian cottage in a tranquil setting, close to the high street of this charming village with its range of shops and restaurants. Pretty fabrics, wooden floors downstairs, brightly coloured rugs and co-ordinating bedlinen make this a perfect place to unwind. Sun-trap garden. Garage nearby.

OPEN All Year

Short breaks Nov-Easter, minimum 2 nights. Special offers for Christmas and New Year.

Low season per wk
Min £190.00
High season per wk
Max £400.00

WEB
www.visitengland.com
Log on for information and inspiration. The latest information on places to visit, events and quality assessed accommodation.

PORT GAVERNE, Cornwall Map ref 1B2

★★★-★★★★★

10 Units
Sleeping 2–8

Comfortable, restored 18thC cottages with enclosed, sheltered courtyard, and prestigious apartments with panoramic sea views. Picturesque, tranquil cove, 0.5 miles from ancient fishing village of Port Isaac, on Cornish coast path. Traditional pub opposite. Polzeath surfing beach and Camel Trail 15 minutes. Dogs welcome. Short breaks.

GREEN DOOR COTTAGES

Port Gaverne, Port Isaac
Contact: Mrs M Ross, Green Door Cottages, Port Gaverne, Port Isaac PL29 3SQ
T: (01208) 880293
F: (01208) 880151
E: enquiries@greendoorcottages.co.uk
I: www.greendoorcottages.co.uk

OPEN All Year
CC: Amex, Delta, Diners, JCB, Mastercard, Switch, Visa

Low season per wk
£279.00–£456.00
High season per wk
£456.00–£955.00

PORT ISAAC, Cornwall Map ref 1B2

★★★-★★★★★

10 Units
Sleeping 2–12

TREVATHAN FARM
St Endellion, Port Isaac
Contact: Mrs J Symons, Trevathan Farm, St Endellion, Port Isaac PL29 3TT
T: (01208) 880248
F: (01208) 880248
E: symons@trevathanfarm.com
I: www.trevathanfarm.com

OPEN All Year

Low season per wk
£100.00–£400.00
High season per wk
£460.00–£1,300.00

Beautiful cottages with countryside views, games room, fishing lake, tennis court, set on working farm. Beaches, golf, riding within three miles. Also large period house available.

PORTLAND, Dorset Map ref 2B3

★★★

1 Unit
Sleeping 4

LILAC COTTAGE
Portland
Contact: Ms S Hepple
T: (01977) 619453
E: hepple@lilaccott171.fs.co.uk
I: www.portlandholiday.co.uk

OPEN All Year

Low season per wk
Min £125.00
High season per wk
Max £350.00

A delightful Victorian terraced cottage with modern amenities but which retains many of its original features. Located in a highly scenic area five minutes from Church Ope Cove.

PORTREATH, Cornwall Map ref 1B3

★★★

7 Units
Sleeping 2–6

TRENGOVE FARM COTTAGES

Illogan, Redruth
Contact: Mrs L Richards, Trengove Farm, Cot Road, Illogan, Redruth TR16 4PU
T: (01209) 843008
F: (01209) 843682
E: richards@farming.co.uk

Traditional, well-equipped cottages and farmhouse on a 140-acre arable farm. Close to beautiful beaches, cliffs and countryside park, yet within easy reach of the main towns. Centrally heated, some with woodburners – ideal for inexpensive winter breaks. A superb location for walking, swimming, touring or just switching off.

OPEN All Year
CC: JCB, Mastercard, Solo, Switch, Visa

Short breaks available from £90 during low season.

Low season per wk
£150.00–£320.00
High season per wk
£250.00–£650.00

PUNCKNOWLE, Dorset Map ref 2A3

★★★★

2 Units
Sleeping 6–13

DAISY DOWN COTTAGE & PUNCKNOWLE MANOR FARMHOUSE

Puncknowle, Dorchester
Contact: Mrs L Hopkins, Hazel Lane Farmhouse, Puncknowle, Dorchester DT2 9BU
T: (01308) 898107
F: (01308) 898107
E: cottages@pknlest.com

Pretty farm cottage and newly converted farmhouse in idyllic position overlooking the peaceful Bride Valley. Just two minutes' drive from the Jurassic Coast. The farmhouse is bright and adaptable for large family holidays. Set in the heart of rural Dorset on a working farm.

OPEN All Year

Short breaks available during Oct-Mar.

Low season per wk
£200.00–£1,000.00
High season per wk
£400.00–£1,400.00

RAMPISHAM, Dorset Map ref 2A3

★★★★

1 Unit
Sleeping 2

STABLE COTTAGE

Rampisham, Dorchester
Contact: Mr J & Mrs D Read, School House, Rampisham, Dorchester DT2 0PR
T: (01935) 83555

OPEN All Year

Charming stone cottage surrounded by fields and woodland. Birds and wildlife abound. Fully heated and carpeted. Within easy reach of World Heritage Coast and many towns.

Low season per wk
£130.00–£150.00
High season per wk
£250.00–£270.00

REDRUTH, Cornwall Map ref 1B3

★★-★★★

2 Units
Sleeping 4–5

MORTHANA FARM HOLIDAYS

Scorrier, Redruth
Contact: Mrs S Pearce, Morthana Farm Holidays, Morthana Farm, Wheal Rose, Scorrier, Redruth TR16 5DF
T: (01209) 890938
F: (01209) 890938

Modern, semi-detached cottages. Equipped to a high standard. Suntrap patios and rural views. Friendly animals. Central for all attractions. Beaches nearby. Couples and children welcome.

Low season per wk
£135.00–£300.00
High season per wk
£330.00–£410.00

RUAN HIGH LANES, Cornwall Map ref 1B3

★★★★

1 Unit
Sleeping 8

CHY TYAK

Ruan High Lanes, Truro
Contact: Mrs P Carbis
T: (01872) 501339
F: (01872) 501339
E: pam@trenonafarmholidays.co.uk
I: www.trenonafarmholidays.co.uk

This former farmhouse, which has been completely refurbished, is set in the heart of a 250-acre, mixed, working farm in a peaceful location on the beautiful Roseland Peninsula. All modern furnishings and equipped to a high standard including en suite master bedroom. Private garden and patio. Eden Project nearby.

OPEN All Year

Short breaks available Oct-Mar.

Low season per wk
£220.00–£350.00
High season per wk
£350.00–£640.00

ACCESSIBILITY

Look for the symbols which indicate National Accessible Scheme standards for hearing and visually impaired guests in addition to standards for guests with mobility impairment. Additional participants are shown in the listings at the back.

ST AUSTELL, Cornwall Map ref 1B3 *Tourist Information Centre Tel: (01726) 879500*

★★-★★★★★

18 Units
Sleeping 3–8

BOSINVER FARM COTTAGES

Trelowth, St Austell
Contact: Mrs P A Smith
T: (01726) 72128
F: (01726) 72128
E: bosinver@holidays2000.freeserve.co.uk
I: www.bosinver.co.uk

Nestling in a hidden valley near the sea, Heligan Gardens and the Eden Project, our small farm has friendly animals and ponies. 16thC thatched farmhouse or cottages, privately set in their own mature gardens, surrounded by wildflower meadows. Fishing, tennis, swimming pool. A short walk to the village pub.

OPEN All Year
CC: Delta, Mastercard, Switch, Visa

Short breaks Sep-May, £45 per night for 2 persons (minimum 3 nights).

Low season per wk
£130.00–£500.00
High season per wk
£250.00–£1,500.00

ST IVES, Cornwall Map ref 1B3 *Tourist Information Centre Tel: (01736) 796297*

★★★

7 Units
Sleeping 2–4

CHY MOR & PREMIER APARTMENTS

St Ives
Contact: Mr M Gill
T: (01736) 798798
F: (01736) 796831
E: mgill@stivesharbour.com
I: www.stivesharbour.com

OPEN All Year
CC: Mastercard, Switch, Visa

Low season per wk
£150.00–£170.00
High season per wk
£445.00–£600.00

Situated on St Ives harbour front with uninterrupted views of the harbour and bay. Visit our website, www.stivesharbour.com.

ST MARY'S, Isles of Scilly Map ref 1A3 *Tourist Information Centre Tel: (01720) 422536*

★★★★

1 Unit
Sleeping 2

CARNWETHERS COUNTRY HOUSE

St Mary's
Contact: Mr R Graham, Carnwethers Country House, Pelistry Bay, St Mary's TR21 0NX
T: (01720) 422415
F: (01720) 422415

Low season per wk
£350.00–£375.00
High season per wk
£450.00–£475.00

Situated in peaceful Area of Outstanding Natural Beauty, 2.5 miles from Hughtown. Solar-heated pool, prize-winning gardens with croquet lawn. Games room and sauna.

12

SPECIAL BREAKS

Many establishments offer special promotions and themed breaks. These are highlighted in red. (All such offers are subject to availability.)

tregenna
CASTLE
St. Ives - Cornwall

Luxury Cottages and Apartments set in a private estate overlooking the fishing harbour of St Ives. Fabulous leisure facilities including indoor/outdoor pools, steam room, sauna, jacuzzi, badminton, squash, tennis and 18 hole golf course.

Phone 01736 795588 or visit www.tregenna-castle.co.uk

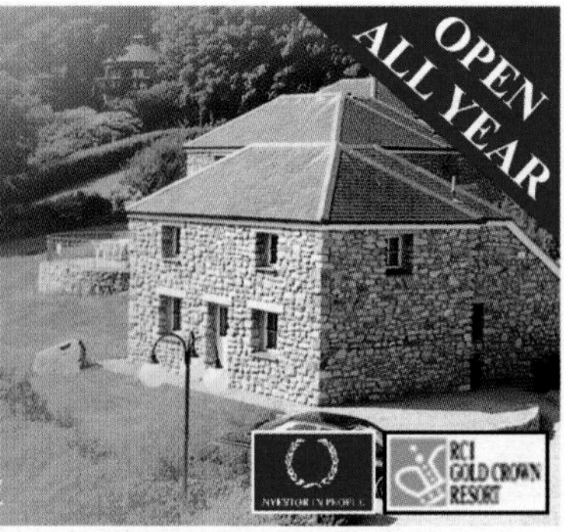

ST MAWGAN, Cornwall Map ref 1B2

★★

1 Unit
Sleeping 4

POLGREEN MANOR
St Mawgan, Newquay
Contact: Mrs J A Wake, NDD, Polgreen Manor,
St Mawgan, Newquay TR8 4AG
T: (01637) 860700
F: (01637) 875165

Cottage adjoining former Cornish farmhouse, home of artist Judith Wake and ornithologist Robin Wake. Very attractive country setting, near beaches, NT cliffs/ gardens, Eden, etc.

High season per wk
£450.00–£495.00

ST MAWES, Cornwall

See display ad below

ST TUDY, Cornwall Map ref 1B2

★★★★

1 Unit
Sleeping 6

POTTERS
St Tudy, Bodmin
Contact: Susan Enderby, 48 Little Heath, London SE7 8BH
T: (020) 8855 8532
F: (020) 8855 8532
E: susanenderby@aol.com
I: www.westcountrynow.com

Well-equipped, furnished and maintained, 4-bedroomed country cottage with secluded garden in attractive, friendly village. Easy access to panoramic beaches and coastal paths on both coasts, the Camel Trail and Eden Project. Ideal base for beaches, watersports, cycling, walking, riding, golf, houses, gardens, pubs and restaurants. Detailed brochure available. Wadebridge five miles.

2 nights, 2 people, Oct-Apr £99. Christmas, New Year, Easter, negotiable.

Low season per wk
£199.00–£299.00
High season per wk
£399.00–£499.00

TOWN INDEX

This can be found at the back of the guide. If you know where you want to stay, the index will give you the page number listing accommodation in your chosen town, city or village.

specialplaces

ETC 2-5 STARS ALL PROPERTIES INSPECTED

www.specialplacescornwall.co.uk

Self-catering at its best. A small selection of very Special Places at beautiful waterside and countryside locations, including St. Mawes, Falmouth, Flushing, Feock, Perranwell and Truro. Well placed for Eden, Heligan and Western Cornwall. Comfortable, well equipped and carefully maintained. Sleeping from 2 to 8 people. A warm welcome awaits you at any time of year. Also member of Cornwall Tourist Board.

SPECIAL PLACES IN CORNWALL TELEPHONE 01872 864400

SALCOMBE, Devon Map ref 1C3 *Tourist Information Centre Tel: (01548) 843927*

★★★

1 Unit
Sleeping 6

Delightfully appointed period residence, with magnificent views over harbour and estuary and lying close to shops, pubs, restaurants and ferry to beaches, in this superb sailing resort. Hall, cloaks/shower room, lounge, kitchen/breakfast room, laundry, three bedrooms, bathroom, patio, central heating. Free use of indoor swimming pool.

COXSWAIN'S WATCH

Salcombe
Contact: Mr A Oulsnam, Robert Oulsnam & Co, 79 Hewell Road, Barnt Green, Birmingham B45 8NL
T: (0121) 445 3311
F: (0121) 445 6026
E: barntgreen@oulsnam-online.com
I: www.oulsnam-online.com

OPEN All Year
CC: Amex, Delta, Mastercard, Switch, Visa

Low season per wk
Min £500.00
High season per wk
Max £1,500.00

SALISBURY PLAIN

See under Amesbury

SEATON, Devon Map ref 1D2 *Tourist Information Centre Tel: (01297) 21660*

★★★

1 Unit
Sleeping 5

Comfortably furnished bungalow on elevated ground in 1.5 acres of lawns and gardens. Beautiful, panoramic views of Axe Estuary and sea. Close by are Beer and Branscombe. Lyme Regis seven miles, Sidmouth 10 miles. An excellent centre for touring, walking, sailing, fishing, golf. Full gas central heating, double glazing throughout.

WEST RIDGE BUNGALOW

Seaton
Contact: Mrs H Fox, West Ridge Bungalow, Harepath Hill, Seaton EX12 2TA
T: (01297) 22398
F: (01297) 22398
E: foxfamily@westridge.fsbusiness.co.uk
I: www.cottageguide.co.uk/westridge

10% reduction for 2 persons only, throughout booking period.

Low season per wk
£195.00–£295.00
High season per wk
£325.00–£425.00

SENNEN, Cornwall Map ref 1A3

★★★

2 Units

Two granite farm buildings, now single-storey cosy cottages with open fires. At end of lane in peaceful valley with countryside/sea views. Equidistant Sennen and St Just (2.5 miles). Wonderful walks/beaches. Attractions include Minack Theatre, art galleries (Tate, St Ives), archaeological sites, golf, fishing, wildlife havens, theme parks and more.

3 & 4 WESLEY COTTAGES

St Just-in-Penwith
Contact: Mrs J J Davey, Rosteague, Raginnis Farm, Mousehole, Penzance TR19 6NJ
T: (01736) 731933
F: (01736) 732344
E: wesley@raginnis.demon.co.uk
I: www.wesleyatnanquidno.co.uk

OPEN All Year

Low season per wk
Min £120.00
High season per wk
Max £380.00

SHALDON, Devon

See display ad on opposite page

SHEEPSTOR, Devon Map ref 1C2

★★★-★★★★★

3 Units
Sleeping 4–8

BURRATOR HOUSE
Yelverton
Contact: Ms S Bridger
T: (01822) 855669
E: sarah.bridger@btopenworld.com
I: www.burratorhouse.com

OPEN All Year

Low season per wk
£200.00–£450.00
High season per wk
£350.00–£750.00

Set in beautiful, secluded surroundings amidst the glorious Dartmoor National Park, these cottages offer the very best in country holidays, together with every modern comfort.

SHEPTON MALLET, Somerset Map ref 2A2 *Tourist Information Centre Tel: (01749) 345258*

★★★

4 Units
Sleeping 2–6

KNOWLE FARM COTTAGES
West Compton, Shepton Mallet
Contact: Ms H Trotman
T: (01749) 890482
F: (01749) 890405
E: info@knowle-farm-cottages.co.uk
I: www.knowle-farm-cottages.co.uk

OPEN All Year

Low season per wk
£150.00–£360.00
High season per wk
£285.00–£450.00

Cottages converted from traditional farm buildings, set in a pleasant garden in quiet, unspoilt countryside. Ideal for touring. Separate play area for children.

SHERBORNE, Dorset Map ref 2B3 *Tourist Information Centre Tel: (01935) 815341*

★★★

1 Unit
Sleeping 4

BLACKBERRY COTTAGE
Sherborne
Contact: Mr J M Farr, 17 Marsh Lane, Yeovil BA21 3BX
T: (01935) 423148

OPEN All Year

Low season per wk
£160.00–£190.00
High season per wk
£230.00–£330.00

An ideal base for discovering the delights of Dorset. This 19thC stone cottage is close to the centre of the historic town of Sherborne.

SHERSTON, Wiltshire Map ref 2B2

★★★★

1 Unit
Sleeping 3

MAY COTTAGE
Sherston, Malmesbury
Contact: Mrs S M Bristow, Mill Cottage, Thompsons Hill, Sherston, Malmesbury SN16 0PZ
T: (01666) 840655

Cotswold-stone cottage rebuilt in 1991 from original stable and hayloft. Situated in quiet valley in Area of Outstanding Natural Beauty on edge of village designated a conservation area. Secluded gardens with river running through. Parking adjacent to cottage. No pets and no smoking, please.

OPEN All Year except Christmas

Low season per wk
Min £220.00
High season per wk
Max £275.00

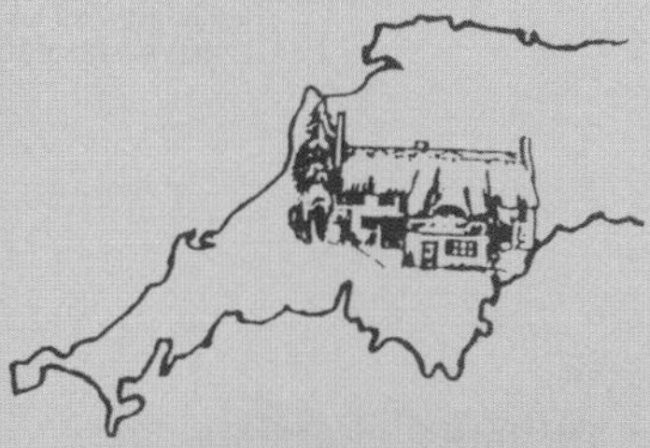

www.cottagesw.vir.co.uk

COTTAGES SOUTH WEST

A wide selection of self-catering cottages and apartments in picturesque Shaldon & Teignmouth.

Phone for a free colour brochure

01626 872314 (24hrs)

16C Fore Street, Shaldon DEVON TQ14 0DE
email: lets@cottagessw.vir.co.uk

SIDMOUTH, Devon Map ref 1D2 *Tourist Information Centre Tel: (01395) 516441*

★★★★

7 Units
Sleeping 4–6

BOSWELL FARM COTTAGES

Sidford, Sidmouth
Contact: Mr & Mrs B P Dillon
T: (01395) 514162
F: (01395) 514162
E: dillon@boswell-farm.co.uk
I: www.boswell-farm.co.uk

Two miles from the World Heritage Coastline and beaches, cradled in 45 acres of idyllic, peaceful valley. Listed, 17thC farmhouse with period cottages, lovingly converted from original farm buildings, each with own delightful, enclosed garden. Studio facilities in restored Victorian kennels. Tennis court, trout pond. 14thC inn and amenities within walking distance.

OPEN All Year
CC: Delta, Mastercard, Switch, Visa

25% reduction – 2 people (or 2 people and baby) Nov-Mar (for full week only, excl Bank Holidays).

Low season per wk
£185.00–£339.00
High season per wk
£385.00–£852.00

★★★★

4 Units
Sleeping 4

LEIGH FARM

Weston, Sidmouth
Contact: Mr G & Mrs G Davis, Leigh Farm, Weston, Sidmouth EX10 0PH
T: (01395) 516065
F: (01395) 579582
E: leigh.farm@virgin.net
I: www.streets-ahead.com/leighfarm

We are 150 yards from a National Trust valley which leads to the coastal path and Weston beach. Excellent walking and touring area. Our bungalows face south onto a lawn and each has a patio table and chairs for your use. Perfect location for an interesting and relaxing holiday.

OPEN All Year
CC: Delta, JCB, Mastercard, Solo, Switch, Visa

Low season per wk
£152.00–£186.00
High season per wk
£214.00–£487.00

SIMONSBATH, Somerset Map ref 1C1

★★★★

5 Units
Sleeping 2–6

WINTERSHEAD FARM

Simonsbath, Minehead
Contact: Mrs J Styles, Wintershead Farm, Simonsbath, Minehead TA24 7LF
T: (01643) 831222
I: www.wintershead.co.uk

Off the beaten track, hidden away in the hills of Exmoor, where time stands still. Converted stone cottages, perfectly situated for you to explore the moor any time of the year. A place where a lot of the traffic has four legs and the only street lighting comes from the stars above. Colour brochure.

Low season per wk
£195.00–£395.00
High season per wk
£355.00–£385.00

WEB

www.visitengland.com
Log on for information and inspiration. The latest information on places to visit, events and quality assessed accommodation.

SOMERTON, Somerset Map ref 2A3

★★★★

3 Units
Sleeping 2–3

SLEEPY HOLLOW

Barton St. David, Somerton
Contact: Mr & Mrs P Raine
T: (01458) 850584
F: (01458) 850584
E: paul&rhian@sleepyhollowcottages.com
I: www.sleepyhollowcottages.com

OPEN All Year
CC: Delta, JCB, Mastercard, Solo, Switch, Visa

Low season per wk
£165.00–£230.00
High season per wk
£220.00–£340.00

Stables converted to charming, single-storey cottages. Peaceful setting on edge of small village. Ideal for touring, cycling, walking. Mountain-bike hire.

STITHIANS, Cornwall Map ref 1B3

★★★★

1 Unit
Sleeping 4

CHARIS COTTAGE

Stithians, Truro
Contact: Mr A Drees & Ms T Schneider, Treweege, Trewithen Moor, Stithians, Truro TR3 7DU
T: (01209) 861003
E: astondrees@hotmail.com
I: www.chariscottage.co.uk

Enjoy peace and tranquillity in this secluded, semi-detached, 250-year-old, spacious cottage. Midway between the Eden Project and Land's End. Excellent for West Cornwall and both the south and north coasts. Walking distance from a good lakeside country pub/restaurant. A beautiful character building with modern luxuries.

OPEN All Year

Short breaks available Oct-pre-Easter (excl Christmas and New Year). Up to 5 nights at 75% of weekly rental.

Low season per wk
£200.00–£300.00
High season per wk
£330.00–£500.00

STOKE CANON, Devon Map ref 1D2

★★★★

7 Units
Sleeping 6–7

BUSSELLS FARM COTTAGES

Huxham, Exeter
Contact: Mr A Hines, Bussells Farm, Huxham, Exeter EX5 4EN
T: (01392) 841238
F: (01392) 841345
E: hinesandrew@netscape.net
I: www.bussellsfarm.co.uk

High-quality barn-conversion cottages, heated swimming pool, adventure playground, well-equipped games room and excellent coarse fishing in the private lakes. We offer a wonderful base from which to explore the beautiful Exe valley, Dartmoor, the south Devon beaches and the ancient city of Exeter.

OPEN All Year
CC: Delta, Mastercard, Switch, Visa

3-night stays available. Home-cooked meals/hampers on request.

Low season per wk
£330.00–£600.00
High season per wk
£560.00–£785.00

CHECK THE MAPS

The colour maps at the front of this guide show all the cities, towns and villages for which you will find accommodation entries. Refer to the town index to find the page on which they are listed.

STOKE SUB HAMDON, Somerset Map ref 1D2

★★★★

1 Unit
Sleeping 4

Golden hamstone cottage in quiet, picturesque village. Lovely countryside with wonderful walks. Many NT properties and gardens nearby. Ideal touring area. Two bedrooms and bathroom with shower, well-equipped kitchen overlooking pretty cottage garden, comfortable sitting room with open log fire, colour TV and video. Linen provided. Brochure available.

ONE FAIR PLACE

Stoke sub Hamdon
Contact: Mrs A A Wright, Holly Lodge, 39 The Avenue, Crowthorne RG45 6PB
T: (01344) 772461
F: (01344) 778389
E: aawright@btopenworld.com
I: www.somersetcottageholidays.co.uk

OPEN All Year

Short breaks available Oct-Mar, minimum 2 nights.

Low season per wk
£190.00–£230.00
High season per wk
£270.00–£350.00

★★★

1 Unit
Sleeping 2

TOP O HILL

Stoke sub Hamdon
Contact: Mrs M Gane
T: (01935) 822089

OPEN All Year except Christmas

Low season per wk
£90.00–£100.00
High season per wk
£100.00–£200.00

Annexe of 150-year-old house in private road, close to A303. Excellent touring base for many places of interest.

TAUNTON, Somerset Map ref 1D1 *Tourist Information Centre Tel: (01823) 336344*

★★★-★★★★

4 Units
Sleeping 2–8

Comfortable holiday cottages with character set in idyllic countryside – either converted barns or adjoin the historic 17thC Listed farmhouse. Spacious and equipped to a high standard, surrounded by the beautiful countryside of our working dairy farm. Horse riding can be arranged nearby. Ideal for exploring the West Country. Outdoor swimming pool. Taunton, jct 25 M5,4 miles. Mob: 07980 601670.

MEARE COURT HOLIDAY COTTAGES

Wrantage, Taunton
Contact: Mrs E J Bray, Meare Court Holiday Cottages, Meare Court, Wrantage, Taunton TA3 6DA
T: (01823) 480570
F: 0870 167 3067
E: mearecourt@farming.co.uk
I: www.mearecourt.co.uk

OPEN All Year
CC: Amex, Delta, Diners, JCB, Mastercard, Solo, Switch, Visa

Short breaks/weekends available (excl Aug), minimum 2 nights. Linen, towels etc. provided.

Low season per wk
£150.00–£375.00
High season per wk
£360.00–£1,050.00

TAVISTOCK, Devon Map ref 1C2 *Tourist Information Centre Tel: (01822) 612938*

★★★

1 Unit
Sleeping 4

HIGHER CHADDLEHANGER FARM

Tavistock
Contact: Mrs R Cole, Higher Chaddlehanger Farm, Tavistock PL19 0LG
T: (01822) 810268
F: (01822) 810268

OPEN All Year

Low season per wk
Min £140.00
High season per wk
Max £140.00

Holiday flatlet in farmhouse on beef and sheep farm, close to moors. Own entrance, private garden.

QUALITY ASSURANCE SCHEME
Star ratings are explained at the back of this guide.

TAVISTOCK continued

★★★

2 Units
Sleeping 4–6

OLD SOWTONTOWN

Peter Tavy, Tavistock
Contact: Mr C Boswell, Old Sowtontown, Peter Tavy, Tavistock PL19 9JR
T: (01822) 810687
F: (01822) 810687
E: chrisboswe@aol.com
I: www.dartmoorholidays.co.uk

OPEN All Year

Low season per wk
£155.00–£255.00
High season per wk
£285.00–£430.00

On Dartmoor, cosy and well-equipped barn conversions with magnificent views. Friendly welcome. Ideal place to get away from it all any time of year.

THORVERTON, Devon Map ref 1D2

★★★

1 Unit
Sleeping 6

RATCLIFFE FARM

Thorverton, Exeter
Contact: Mr M & Mrs T Ayre, Ratcliffe Farm, Thorverton, Exeter EX5 5PN
T: (01392) 860434
E: ayre.ratcliffe@virgin.net

OPEN All Year except Christmas
CC: Visa

Low season per wk
Min £280.00
High season per wk
Max £480.00

Thatched farmhouse, spacious and comfortable, full of original features. One mile from pretty cobbled village in Exe Valley. Central for West Country coasts and moors.

TINTAGEL, Cornwall Map ref 1B2

★★★

1 Unit
Sleeping 4

TREGEATH COTTAGE

Tintagel
Contact: Mrs E M Broad, Davina, Trevillett, Tintagel PL34 0HL
T: (01840) 770217
F: (01840) 770217

OPEN All Year

Low season per wk
Min £100.00
High season per wk
Max £400.00

Old modernised detached cottage, built of stone and slate. Coal grate, six night-storage heaters, TV/video, payphone, microwave. One dog, no cats. Parking space. Washing machine. Separate tumble dryer.

TIVINGTON, Somerset Map ref 1D1

★★★★

1 Unit
Sleeping 5

TETHINSTONE COTTAGE

Tivington, Minehead
Contact: Mr N G Challis, Tethinstone Cottage, Tivington, Minehead TA24 8SX
T: (01643) 706757
F: (01643) 706757

Very comfortable thatched cottage, secluded but not isolated, in idyllic position between Minehead and Porlock. Charges include all electricity, hot water and heating.

OPEN All Year

Low season per wk
£250.00–£350.00
High season per wk
£350.00–£450.00

TOLLER PORCORUM, Dorset Map ref 2A3

★★★

1 Unit
Sleeping 6

11 HIGH STREET

Toller Porcorum, Dorchester
Contact: Mrs D Thornton
T: (01962) 732700
E: dot.thornton@virgin.net

18thC cottage in quiet village amidst beautiful countryside. Sea and coastal path seven miles. Weekend and mid-week breaks available during winter – £150 inclusive of nightstore heating and logs for two woodburning stoves. Off-street parking for two cars.

OPEN All Year

Low season per wk
Max £300.00
High season per wk
Max £450.00

TORQUAY, Devon Map ref 1D2 *Tourist Information Centre Tel: 0906 680 1268 (Premium rate number)*

★★

5 Units
Sleeping 2–4

ATHERTON HOLIDAY FLATS

Torquay
Contact: Mrs B K Kaye, Atherton Holiday Flats,
41 Morgan Avenue, Torquay TQ2 5RR
T: (01803) 296884

OPEN All Year

Low season per wk
£75.00–£150.00
High season per wk
£145.00–£250.00

Centrally located, our clean, modern, fully equipped flats offer excellent value for money.

★★★

4 Units
Sleeping 2–6

ATLANTIS HOLIDAY APARTMENTS

Torquay
Contact: Mrs P Roberts, Atlantis Holiday Apartments,
Solsbro Road, Chelston, Torquay TQ2 6PF
T: (01803) 607929
F: (01803) 391313
E: enquiry@atlantistorquay.co.uk
I: www.atlantistorquay.co.uk

OPEN All Year
CC: Amex, Delta, JCB, Mastercard, Solo, Switch, Visa

Low season per wk
£150.00–£210.00
High season per wk
£240.00–£490.00

Non-smoking, fully-equipped apartments. Close to Torquay seafront, station and shops. Car park. Garden. Dishwasher and washer/dryer in all apartments.

★★-★★★

5 Units

BEDFORD HOUSE

Torquay
Contact: Mrs E J MacDonald-Smith
T: (01803) 296995
F: (01803) 296995
E: bedfordhotorquay@btconnect.com
I: www.bedfordhousetorquay.co.uk

An elegant, Tudor-style house built in 1888 and set in a sunny, pleasant garden. Well situated in a conservation area, only 500 metres from harbour, shops and entertainment. Comfortable, self-contained and well-equipped apartments. Colour TV and microwaves. Bath or shower room. Bed linen. Guest laundry. Central heating. Private car park.

OPEN All Year
CC: Amex, Mastercard, Visa

Short breaks available Oct-Apr, minimum 3 nights.

Low season per wk
£120.00–£200.00
High season per wk
£150.00–£410.00

★★★

14 Units
Sleeping 6

BURLEY COURT APARTMENTS

Torquay
Contact: Mrs B Palmer
T: (01803) 607879
F: (01803) 605516
E: burley.court@virgin.net
I: www.burleycourt.co.uk

OPEN All Year
CC: Mastercard, Switch, Visa

Low season per wk
£105.00–£285.00
High season per wk
£245.00–£560.00

Architecturally designed apartments furnished to a high standard, many with sea views and private sun terrace. Situated in south-facing, secluded gardens, 200 yards beach.

COUNTRY CODE Always follow the Country Code · Enjoy the countryside and respect its life and work · Guard against all risk of fire · Fasten all gates · Keep your dogs under close control · Keep to public paths across farmland · Use gates and stiles to cross fences, hedges and walls · Leave livestock, crops and machinery alone · Take your litter home · Help to keep all water clean · Protect wildlife, plants and trees · Take special care on country roads · Make no unnecessary noise

TORQUAY continued

★★★

24 Units
Sleeping 2–4

Well-appointed, self-contained apartments providing superior accommodation. Close to shops and seafront and an ideal base for touring. Superb leisure facilities including indoor/outdoor pools, spa, sauna and gymnasium. Beauty salon, solarium, games room, licensed bar and restaurant also available.

MAXTON LODGE HOLIDAY APARTMENTS

Chelston, Torquay
Contact: Mr R Hassell, Maxton Lodge Holiday Apartments, Rousdown Road, Chelston, Torquay TQ2 6PB
T: (01803) 607811
F: (01803) 605357
E: stay@redhouse-hotel.co.uk
I: www.redhouse-hotel.co.uk

OPEN All Year
CC: Delta, Mastercard, Solo, Switch, Visa

Fully serviced apartments available with a choice of meals built into an inclusive tariff.

Low season per wk
£170.00–£270.00
High season per wk
£300.00–£700.00

★★★

6 Units
Sleeping 2–6

Beautifully appointed, spacious, Victorian, self-contained apartments in level woodland setting in exclusive, peaceful conservation area. Walks through woods to beaches, close to excellent shops. One mile from harbour. Regular bus service. Gardens, off-road parking. All accommodation is well equipped, tastefully decorated and immaculately maintained. Pets and children welcome.

MOORCOT SELF CONTAINED HOLIDAY APARTMENTS

Torquay
Contact: Mrs M C Neilson, Moorcot Self Contained Holiday Apartments, Kents Road, Wellswood, Torquay TQ1 2NN
T: (01803) 293710
E: holidayflats@moorcot.com
I: www.moorcot.com

OPEN All Year

Short breaks Oct-Apr, 4 nights for the price of 3.

Low season per wk
£120.00–£200.00
High season per wk
£200.00–£390.00

★★★

18 Units
Sleeping 1–5

Specifically designed holiday apartments offering a high degree of comfort and cleanliness. Spacious and tastefully decorated with fitted kitchens. Apartments with bath or shower. No meters. Towels available upon request. Ground and first floor only. Seafront location. Beach 100 yards. Main bus route. Families and couples only.

SOUTH SANDS APARTMENTS

Torquay
Contact: Mr P W Moorhouse, South Sands Apartments, Torbay Road, Torquay TQ2 6RG
T: (01803) 293521
F: (01803) 293502
E: southsands.torquay@virgin.net
I: www.southsands.co.uk

OPEN All Year
CC: Amex, Delta, Mastercard, Switch, Visa

Short breaks and mid-week bookings in low season. Holiday cancellation insurance included. Discount available 2 weeks or more.

Low season per wk
£115.00–£195.00
High season per wk
£230.00–£425.00

TORQUAY continued

★★★

18 Units
Sleeping 2–4

SUNNINGDALE APARTMENTS

Torquay
Contact: Mr A Carr, Sunningdale Apartments,
11 Babbacombe Downe Road, Torquay TQ1 3LF
T: (01803) 325786
F: (01803) 329611
E: allancarr@yahoo.com
I: www.sunningdaleapartments.co.uk

Spacious apartments, many with stunning sea views. Self-contained with bathroom and shower, fitted kitchen and lounge with dining area. Large car park, laundry room, gardens. All double glazed with sun patio and central heating. Level walk to shops, restaurants, bar and theatre. Excellent touring centre.

OPEN All Year except Christmas

Low season per wk
£180.00–£295.00
High season per wk
£350.00–£615.00

★★★

8 Units
Sleeping 2–6

WOODFIELD HOLIDAY APARTMENTS

Torquay
Contact: Mr & Mrs T W Gaylard, Woodfield Holiday Apartments, Lower Woodfield Road, Torquay TQ1 2JY
T: (01803) 295974

Grade II Listed neo-Gothic villa built in 1841, of architectural and historic interest. Clean, homely apartments, most with views over Torquay harbour. Convenient for all amenities. Six hundred yards to harbour and town. Free car parking, central heating for early/late-season visitors. Family-run business, resident proprietors. Telephone or write for free colour brochure.

OPEN All Year

Low season per wk
£105.00–£200.00
High season per wk
£255.00–£470.00

TORRINGTON, Devon Map ref 1C2 *Tourist Information Centre Tel: (01805) 626140*

★★★

6 Units
Sleeping 4–6

STOWFORD LODGE & SOUTH HILL COTTAGES

Torrington
Contact: Mrs S Milsom, Stowford Lodge, Langtree, Torrington EX38 8NU
T: (01805) 601540
F: (01805) 601487
E: stowford@dial.pipex.com
I: www.stowford.dial.pipex.com

OPEN All Year
CC: Delta, JCB, Mastercard, Solo, Switch, Visa

Low season per wk
£200.00–£290.00
High season per wk
£250.00–£520.00

Delightful cottages converted from Victorian stone farm buildings. Heated indoor pool. Also, pair of period cottages on edge of farm. Pets welcome.

TOTNES, Devon Map ref 1D2 *Tourist Information Centre Tel: (01803) 863168*

★★★★

1 Unit
Sleeping 8

CASTLE FOOT

Totnes
Contact: Mr D G R Hales
T: (01803) 865282
E: davidg.r.hales@sagainternet.co.uk

OPEN All Year

Low season per wk
£195.00–£285.00
High season per wk
£395.00–£470.00

Four-bedroomed house right in the centre of this Elizabethan town, set in rolling South Hams countryside. Near castle. Dartmoor and many beaches within short drive.

TOWN INDEX

This can be found at the back of this guide. If you know where you want to stay, the index will give you the page number listing accommodation in your chosen town, city or village.

TREBETHERICK, Cornwall Map ref 1B2

Rating Applied For
1 Unit
Sleeping 6

HILLCROFT BUNGALOW
Trebetherick, Wadebridge
Contact: Mr & Mrs P Beach, Longwood, West Street, Odiham, Hook RG29 1NX
T: (01256) 702650

Comfortable, well-equipped bungalow with lovely views across farmland towards Roserrow golf course. 0.5 miles from Polzeath and Daymer beaches. Two bathrooms.

Low season per wk
£235.00–£700.00

TROWBRIDGE, Wiltshire Map ref 2B2 *Tourist Information Centre Tel: (01225) 777054*

★★★★
1 Unit
Sleeping 4

One-hundred-year-old snug, rural, detached cottage, recently restored and equipped to high standard. Beautiful views to Salisbury Plain. 4-poster bed, log fire, oil central heating, private cottage garden with barbecue, play space for children, bikes available on request. Private parking for two cars. Excellent eating pub within walking distance.

HINTON LODGE
Devizes
Contact: Mrs C Gompels, Hinton House, Great Hinton, Trowbridge BA14 6BS
T: (01380) 871067
F: 0870 870 7026
E: sam@gompels.co.uk
I: www.hintonlodge.co.uk

OPEN All Year

Complimentary starter hamper with wine. Linen and towels provided. Short stays usually available.

Low season per wk
£290.00–£395.00
High season per wk
£420.00–£550.00

UFFCULME, Devon Map ref 1D2

★★★★
13 Units
Sleeping 6

Clustered around the thatched pumphouse, each of our spacious, individually styled cottages offers home from home comfort. Our extensive grounds have a safe children's play area, a restored, walled fruit garden, and with the whole of Devon awaiting your discovery, where better?

OLD BRIDWELL HOLIDAY COTTAGES
Uffculme, Cullompton
Contact: Ms J Kind, Old Bridwell Holiday Cottages, Uffculme, Cullompton EX15 3BU
T: (01884) 841464
E: bridwellholidays@aol.com
I: www.oldbridwell.co.uk

OPEN All Year

Discounts for reduced occupancy.

Low season per wk
Min £245.00
High season per wk
Max £1,090.00

UGBOROUGH, Devon Map ref 1C2

★★★★
1 Unit
Sleeping 4

DONKEY COTTAGE
Ugborough, Ivybridge
Contact: Mrs G Barker, 5 Meade King Grove, Woodmancote, Cheltenham GL52 9UD
T: (01242) 678568
E: gill@donkeycottage.co.uk
I: www.donkeycottage.co.uk

OPEN All Year
CC: Delta, Mastercard, Switch, Visa

Cosy, 16thC cottage with oak beams and open fire in pretty South Hams village, a few miles from coast and close to Dartmoor.

Low season per wk
£250.00–£350.00
High season per wk
£390.00–£490.00

MAP REFERENCES The map references refer to the colour maps at the front of this guide. The first figure is the map number; the letter and figure which follow indicate the grid reference on the map.

WADEBRIDGE, Cornwall Map ref 1B2 *Tourist Information Centre Tel: (01208) 813725*

★★★★

2 Units
Sleeping 7

COLESENT COTTAGES

St Tudy, Wadebridge
Contact: Mrs S Zamaria
T: (01208) 850112
F: (01208) 850112
E: holiday@colesent.co.uk
I: www.colesent.co.uk

Converted barn, luxury self-catering cottages near Wadebridge. Found along a leafy drive, with wonderful views beside the lazy, twisting Camel River with its 'Trail' for walking and cycling. Cornwall Tourism Awards 2002: Self-catering Establishment of the Year – Highly Commended.

OPEN All Year

Special offers – 20% reduction for 2 people; 10% for 4 people. Short breaks available (excl high season and Bank Holidays).

Low season per wk
£375.00–£395.00
High season per wk
£890.00–£945.00

★★

2 Units
Sleeping 6

15 & 16 MICHAELSTOW MANOR HOLIDAY PARK

St Tudy, Bodmin
Contact: Mr & Mrs J Hartill, 17 St Leonards, Bodmin PL31 1LA
T: (01208) 73676
F: (01208) 73676
E: pamhartill@ukonline.co.uk

Low season per wk
Min £80.00
High season per wk
Min £360.00

Privately owned chalets within holiday park. Full use of all facilities. Situated on edge of Bodmin Moor, yet only a short drive from the coast.

WATCHET, Somerset Map ref 1D1

★★★★

6 Units
Sleeping 4–8

THE CROFT HOLIDAY COTTAGES

Watchet
Contact: Mr & Mrs A M Musgrave, The Croft Holiday Cottages, The Croft, Anchor Street, Watchet TA23 0BY
T: (01984) 631121
F: (01984) 631134
E: croftcottages@talk21.com
I: www.cottageguide.co.uk/croft-cottages

OPEN All Year

Low season per wk
£115.00–£230.00
High season per wk
£335.00–£530.00

Cottages and bungalows in quiet backwater location. Lawned children's play area. Heated indoor pool. Individual barbecues. Easy level walking to shops and harbour/marina etc.

WELLS, Somerset Map ref 2A2 *Tourist Information Centre Tel: (01749) 672552*

★★★

1 Unit
Sleeping 2

HART COTTAGE

Wells
Contact: Mr A Williams, 21 St John Street, Wells BA5 1SW
T: (01749) 674897
E: nandi@clara.co.uk

OPEN All Year

Low season per wk
£195.00–£265.00
High season per wk
£265.00–£320.00

Charming period cottage, ideally located for exploring Wells and surrounding countryside. Comfortably furnished with woodburning stove. Near Glastonbury, Cheddar Gorge, Bath and many beautiful gardens.

★★★

2 Units
Sleeping 2–3

MODEL FARM COTTAGES

Milton, Wells
Contact: Mrs G Creed, Model Farm Cottages, Model Farm, Milton, Wells BA5 3AE
T: (01749) 673363
F: (01749) 671566
E: gill_creed@talk21.com

OPEN All Year except Christmas

Low season per wk
£195.00–£235.00
High season per wk
£220.00–£300.00

These well-equipped cottages are situated in peaceful countryside away from traffic. Both have private patios leading on to open fields with wonderful views.

COLOUR MAPS **Colour maps at the front of this guide pinpoint all places under which you will find accommodation listed.**

WELLS continued

★★★

1 Unit
Sleeping 6

VICARS' CLOSE HOLIDAY HOUSE
Wells
Contact: Mrs D Jones
T: (01749) 674483
F: (01749) 832210
E: visits@wellscathedral.uk.net

OPEN All Year
CC: Amex, Delta, Mastercard, Switch, Visa

Low season per wk
£500.00–£625.00
High season per wk
£625.00–£750.00

Beautiful 14thC house in the oldest-inhabited street in Europe. In the shadow of Wells Cathedral and a short walk from the city centre.

WEST ANSTEY, Devon Map ref 1D1

★★★★

1 Unit
Sleeping 9

BRIMBLECOMBE
West Anstey, South Molton
Contact: Mrs C Hutsby
T: (01789) 840261
F: (01789) 842270
E: charhutsby@talk21.com
I: www.brimblecombe-exmoor.co.uk

Nestling in a secluded valley on the edge of Exmoor National Park, this Devon longhouse offers accommodation of the highest standard, comprising four double rooms en suite, large well-equipped farmhouse kitchen, extremely comfortable sitting room with inglenook fireplace. Stabling for five horses, eight acres, trout ponds.

OPEN All Year

Low season per wk
£500.00–£800.00
High season per wk
£500.00–£1,000.00

WEST BAY, Dorset Map ref 2B3

★★★-★★★★★

7 Units
Sleeping 2–4

WESTPOINT APARTMENTS
West Bay, Bridport
Contact: Mr D & Mrs B Slade, Westpoint Apartments, The Esplanade, West Bay, Bridport DT6 4HE
T: (01308) 423636
F: (01308) 458871
E: bed@westpoint-apartments.co.uk
I: www.westpointapartments.co.uk

OPEN All Year
CC: JCB, Mastercard, Solo, Switch, Visa

Low season per wk
£160.00–£285.00
High season per wk
£320.00–£520.00

Quality self-catering apartments on seafront overlooking sea and harbour. Fishing, 18-hole golf course, beautiful cliff walks, Thomas Hardy country. Three- and four-day breaks available.

5

WEST BEXINGTON, Dorset Map ref 2A3

★★★-★★★★★

5 Units
Sleeping 4–6

TAMARISK FARM COTTAGES
West Bexington, Dorchester
Contact: Mrs J Pearse, Tamarisk Farm Cottages, West Bexington, Dorchester DT2 9DF
T: (01308) 897784
F: (01308) 897784
E: tamarisk@eurolink.ltd.net
I: www.tamariskfarm.co.uk

On organic farm sloping to Chesil Beach. All cottages in own gardens, glorious sea views. Excellent walking country, dogs allowed on Chesil Beach all year. Abbotsbury Swannery and gardens nearby. Variety of beaches and fossil-hunting possibilities, abundant bird life. Hardy's Wessex, prehistoric sites, tourist attractions. Quiet at home!

OPEN All Year
CC: Mastercard, Visa

Low season per wk
£195.00–£225.00
High season per wk
£490.00–£650.00

RATING **All accommodation in this guide has been rated, or is awaiting a rating, by a trained VisitBritain assessor.**

WESTBURY-SUB-MENDIP, Somerset Map ref 2A2

★★★

1 Unit
Sleeping 3

THE DAIRY

Westbury-sub-Mendip, Wells
OPEN All Year
Contact: Mrs C Hancock, The Dairy, Cottage Farm, The Hollow, Westbury-sub-Mendip, Wells BA5 1HH
T: (01749) 870351
I: www.westbury-sub-mendip.org

Low season per wk
£150.00–£200.00
High season per wk
£200.00–£280.00

Peaceful 17thC cottage annexe with beams, spiral stairs and romantic, canopied bed. In beautiful Mendip village, overlooking Somerset levels. Wonderful walking/cycling. Four miles Wells/Cheddar.

WESTON-SUPER-MARE, Somerset Map ref 1D1 *Tourist Information Centre Tel: (01934) 888800*

★★

1 Unit
Sleeping 8

BATCH FARM COTTAGE

Lympsham, Weston-super-Mare
Contact: Mrs I D Wall
T: (01934) 750287
F: (01934) 750287

Low season per wk
Min £150.00
High season per wk
Max £420.00

Self-contained holiday cottage adjoining a working dairy and livestock farm in the picturesque village of Lympsham. Four bedrooms, one on ground floor. Children welcome.

★★★★

4 Units
Sleeping 4

HOPE FARM COTTAGES

Lympsham, Weston-super-Mare
OPEN All Year
Contact: Mrs L Stirk, Hope Farm Cottages, Brean Road, Lympsham, Weston-super-Mare BS24 0HA
T: (01934) 750506
F: (01934) 750506
E: stirkhopefarm@aol.com
I: www.hopefarmcottages.co.uk

Low season per wk
£190.00–£320.00
High season per wk
£365.00–£590.00

Tranquil ground floor cottages, each with two en suites. Overlooking level, landscaped courtyard. Wheelchair and other aids available. Play areas, games room, laundry. Dogs welcomed.

WEYMOUTH, Dorset Map ref 2B3 *Tourist Information Centre Tel: (01305) 785747*

★★★★★

2 Units
Sleeping 6

Seafront homes with garage or private parking, 18thC cottages with garage and seafront parking, all newly refurbished. Bedrooms with king-size beds, the majority with en suite bathrooms, some with jacuzzi. Beamed ceilings, open fires, designer kitchens with every modern convenience.

BAY LODGE SELF-CATERING ACCOMMODATION

Weymouth
Contact: Mr & Mrs G Dubben, Bay Lodge, 27 Greenhill, Weymouth DT4 7SW
T: (01305) 782419
F: (01305) 782828
E: barbara@baylodge.co.uk
I: www.baylodge.co.uk

OPEN All Year
CC: Amex, Delta, Diners, JCB, Mastercard, Solo, Switch, Visa

Winter breaks available: Fri-Mon or Mon-Fri, from £8.34pppn for maximum occupancy of cottage.

Low season per wk
Min £300.00
High season per wk
Max £875.00

★★★

1 Unit
Sleeping 6

TREZISE HOLIDAY HOME

Weymouth
OPEN All Year
Contact: Mr B Trezise
T: (0117) 937 2304
E: b.trezise@btopenworld.com

Low season per wk
Min £150.00
High season per wk
Max £460.00

Holiday house near harbour, town and sandy beaches. Quiet position. Easy parking outside on road. Sun-trap garden. TV and amenities.

WHIMPLE, Devon Map ref 1D2

★★★

2 Units
Sleeping 4–6

LSF HOLIDAY COTTAGES

Whimple, Exeter
Contact: Mrs S Lang
T: (01404) 822989
F: (01404) 822989
E: lowersouthbrookfarm@btinternet.com

Lovely, comfortable, well-equipped cottages in beautiful countryside. Set in peaceful location, yet convenient for the cathedral city of Exeter, beaches and other popular tourist attractions. Heated swimming pool and large playing area for children. Fully centrally heated for early/late holidays. Brochure available.

OPEN All Year

Short breaks available throughout year. Please ring for availability.

Low season per wk
£165.00–£240.00
High season per wk
£300.00–£396.00

WINGFIELD, Wiltshire Map ref 2B2

★★

5 Units
Sleeping 2–5

ROMSEY OAK COTTAGES

Wingfield, Trowbridge
Contact: Mr A R Briars, Romsey Oak Cottages, Romsey Oak Farmhouse, Bradford Road, Wingfield, Trowbridge BA14 9LS
T: (01225) 753950
F: (01225) 753950
E: enquiries@romseyoakcottages.co.uk
I: www.romseyoakcottages.co.uk

Converted farm building around courtyard of main house in open countryside. Bath 10 miles, Bradford on Avon three miles. Fully equipped kitchen, TV, heating, pay phone, laundry. Bed linen provided. Dogs accepted. Residents' garden and tennis court (professional coaching can be provided). Numerous good eating places and public houses nearby. Brochure available.

OPEN All Year
CC: Amex, Delta, Mastercard, Switch, Visa

Special deals for tennis weeks to include professional coaching. Short breaks available – call for prices.

Low season per wk
£150.00–£235.00
High season per wk
£220.00–£275.00

1

WITHYPOOL, Somerset Map ref 1D1

★★★

1 Unit
Sleeping 3

LANDACRE BUNGALOW

Withypool, Minehead
Contact: Mrs P G Hudson, Landacre Cottage, Landacre Farm, Withypool, Minehead TA24 7SD
T: (01643) 831223

OPEN All Year

Warm, clean, quiet, comfortable and well-equipped bungalow, in an area of outstanding beauty. Situated on farm overlooking moors and river.

Low season per wk
£110.00–£160.00
High season per wk
£160.00–£210.00

WOOTTON COURTENAY, Somerset Map ref 1D1

★★

1 Unit
Sleeping 6

BRIDGE COTTAGE

Wootton Courtenay, Minehead
Contact: Mrs M Hawksford, Bridge Cottage, Crockford House, Wootton Courtenay, Minehead TA24 8RE
T: (01643) 841286

OPEN All Year

Charming 16thC thatched cottage with enclosed garden on Exmoor. Pretty village with shop and church. Idyllic situation for walking, riding, seaside, steam train. Minehead five miles.

Low season per wk
£250.00–£300.00
High season per wk
£300.00–£350.00

NB

IMPORTANT NOTE **Information on accommodation listed in this guide has been supplied by the proprietors. As changes may occur you are advised to check details at the time of booking.**

A brief guide to the main Towns and Villages offering accommodation in the **South West**

A **ALLERFORD, SOMERSET** - Village with picturesque stone and thatch cottages and a packhorse bridge, set in the beautiful Vale of Porlock.

AMESBURY, WILTSHIRE - Standing on the banks of the River Avon, this is the nearest town to Stonehenge on Salisbury Plain. The area is rich in prehistoric sites.

ASHBURTON, DEVON - Formerly a thriving wool centre and important as one of Dartmoor's 4 stannary towns. Today's busy market town has many period buildings. Ancient tradition is maintained in the annual ale-tasting and bread-weighing ceremony. Good centre for exploring Dartmoor or the South Devon coast.

ASHWATER, DEVON - Village 6 miles south-east of Holsworthy, with a pleasant village green dominated by its church.

B **BAMPTON, DEVON** - Riverside market town, famous for its fair each October.

BATCOMBE, SOMERSET - Village tucked into a fold of the hills, close to the uppermost reaches of the River Alham, giving superb views of the countryside. The church has a splendid 15th C tower.

BATH, BATH AND NORTH EAST SOMERSET - Georgian spa city beside the River Avon. Important Roman site with impressive reconstructed baths, uncovered in 19th C. Bath Abbey was built on the site of the monastery where the first king of England was crowned (AD 973). Fine architecture in mellow local stone. Pump Room and museums.

BEAMINSTER, DORSET - Old country town of mellow local stone set amid hills and rural vales. Mainly Georgian buildings; attractive almshouses dating from 1603. The 17th C church, with its ornate, pinnacled tower, was restored inside by the Victorians. Parnham, a Tudor manor house, lies 1 mile south.

BERRYNARBOR, DEVON - Picturesque, old-world village, winner of best-kept village awards, adjoining the lovely, wooded Sterridge Valley. On scenic route between Ilfracombe and Combe Martin.

BIDEFORD, DEVON - The home port of Sir Richard Grenville, the town, with its 17th C merchants' houses, flourished as a shipbuilding and cloth town. The bridge of 24 arches was built in about 1460. Charles Kingsley stayed here while writing Westward Ho!

BIGBURY-ON-SEA, DEVON - Small resort on Bigbury Bay at the mouth of the River Avon. Wide sands, rugged cliffs. Burgh Island can be reached on foot at low tide.

BODMIN, CORNWALL - County town south-west of Bodmin Moor with a ruined priory and church dedicated to St Petroc. Nearby are Lanhydrock House and Pencarrow House.

BOSCASTLE, CORNWALL - Small, unspoilt village in Valency Valley. Active as a port until the onset of the railway era, its natural harbour affords rare shelter on this wild coast. Attractions include spectacular blow-hole, Celtic field strips, part-Norman church. Nearby St Juliot Church was restored by Thomas Hardy.

BOVEY TRACEY, DEVON - Standing by the river just east of Dartmoor National Park, this old town has good moorland views. Its church, with a 14th C tower, holds one of Devon's finest medieval rood screens.

BRADFORD-ON-AVON, WILTSHIRE - Huddled beside the river, the buildings of this former cloth-weaving town reflect continuing prosperity from the Middle Ages. There is a tiny Anglo-Saxon church, part of a monastery. The part-14th C bridge carries a medieval chapel, later used as a gaol.

BRATTON, SOMERSET - Hamlet on the edge of the Exmoor National Park, close to the resort of Minehead.

BRAYFORD, DEVON - Village which lies 6 miles north-west of South Molton and marks the crossing of the River Bray by one of the main roads from Exmoor to the sea.

BREAN, SOMERSET - Caravans and holiday bungalows are situated by sand dunes on the flat shoreline south of Brean Down. This rocky promontory has exhilarating cliff walks, bird-watching and an Iron Age fort.

BRIDGWATER, SOMERSET - Former medieval port on the River Parrett, now a small industrial town with mostly 19th C or modern architecture. Georgian Castle Street leads to West Quay and the site of a 13th C castle razed to the ground by Cromwell. The birthplace of Cromwellian Admiral Robert Blake is now a museum. Arts centre.

BRIDPORT, DORSET - Market town and chief producer of nets and ropes just inland of dramatic Dorset coast. Old, broad streets built for drying and twisting and long gardens for rope-walks. Grand arcaded Town Hall and Georgian buildings. The local-history museum has Roman relics.

BRISTOL - Famous for maritime links, historic harbour, Georgian terraces and Brunel's Clifton suspension bridge. Many attractions including SS Great Britain, Bristol Zoo, museums and art galleries and top-name entertainments. Events include Balloon Fiesta and Regatta.

BRIXHAM, DEVON - Famous for its trawling fleet in the 19th C, a steeply built fishing port overlooking the harbour and fish market. A statue of William of Orange recalls his landing here before deposing James II. There is an aquarium and museum. Good cliff views and walks.

BUCKLAND NEWTON, DORSET - Village in an Area of Outstanding Natural Beauty, on the edge of the Dorset Downs midway between Dorchester and Sherborne.

BUDE, CORNWALL - Resort on dramatic Atlantic coast. High cliffs give spectacular sea and inland views. Golf course, cricket pitch, folly, surfing, coarse-fishing and boating. Mother-town Stratton was base of Royalist Sir Bevil Grenville.

C **CASTLE CARY, SOMERSET -** One of south Somerset's most attractive market towns with a picturesque, winding high street of golden stone and thatch, market-house and famous round 18th C lock-up.

CHALLACOMBE, DEVON - Small, attractive village surrounded by the stunning countryside of the Exmoor National Park. Close to the North Devon coast, a number of National Trust properties and family attractions.

CHAPEL AMBLE, CORNWALL - Village 2 miles north of Wadebridge and within easy reach of the Camel Estuary and the North Cornwall coast.

CHEDDAR, SOMERSET - Large village at foot of Mendips just south of the spectacular Cheddar Gorge. Close by are Roman and Saxon sites and famous show caves. Traditional Cheddar cheese is still made here.

CHIPPENHAM, WILTSHIRE - Ancient market town with modern industry. Notable early buildings include the medieval Town Hall and the gabled 15th C Yelde Hall, now a local history museum. On the outskirts, Hardenhuish has a charming hilltop church designed by the Georgian architect John Wood of Bath.

CHIPPING SODBURY, SOUTH GLOUCESTERSHIRE - Old market town, its buildings a mixture of Cotswold stone and mellowed brickwork. The 15th C church and the market cross are of interest. Horton Court (National Trust) stands 4 miles north-east and preserves a very rare Norman hall.

CHUDLEIGH, DEVON - Small market town close to main Exeter to Plymouth road. To the south is Chudleigh Rock, a dramatic limestone outcrop containing prehistoric caves.

CHULMLEIGH, DEVON - Small, hilly town above the Little Dart River, long since by-passed by the main road. The large 15th C church is noted for its splendid rood screen and 38 carved wooden angels on the roof.

COLYTON, DEVON - Surrounded by fertile farmland, this small riverside town was an early Saxon settlement. Medieval prosperity from the wool trade built the grand church tower, with its octagonal lantern, and the church's fine west window.

COMBE MARTIN, DEVON - On the edge of the Exmoor National Park, this seaside village is set in a long, narrow valley with its natural harbour lying between towering cliffs. The main beach is a mixture of sand, rocks and pebbles and the lack of strong currents ensures safe bathing.

CRACKINGTON HAVEN, CORNWALL - Tiny village on the North Cornwall coast, with a small sandy beach and surf bathing. The highest cliffs in Cornwall lie to the south.

CREDITON, DEVON - Ancient town in fertile valley, once prosperous from wool, now active in cider-making. Said to be the birthplace of St Boniface. The 13th C Chapter House, the church governors' meeting place, holds a collection of armour from the Civil War.

D **DARTMOUTH, DEVON -** Ancient port at mouth of Dart. Has fine period buildings, notably town houses near Quay and Butterwalk of 1635. Harbour castle ruin. In the 12th C Crusader fleets assembled here. Royal Naval College dominates from hill. Carnival, June; Regatta, August.

DAWLISH, DEVON - Small resort, developed in Regency and Victorian periods beside Dawlish Water. The town centre has ornamental riverside gardens with black swans. One of England's most scenic stretches of railway was built by Brunel alongside jagged red cliffs between the sands and the town.

DAWLISH WARREN, DEVON - Popular with campers and caravanners, a sandy spit of land at the mouth of the River Exe. The sand dunes, with their golf links, are rich in plant and bird life. Brunel's atmospheric railway once ran along the dramatic line between jagged red cliffs and sandy shore.

DEVIZES, WILTSHIRE - Old market town standing on the Kennet and Avon Canal. Rebuilt Norman castle, good 18th C buildings. St John's church has 12th C work and a Norman tower. Museum of Wiltshire's archaeology and natural history reflects a wealth of prehistoric sites in the county.

DULVERTON, SOMERSET - Set among woods and hills of south-west Exmoor, a busy riverside town with a 13th C church. The rivers Barle and Exe are rich in salmon and trout. The information centre at the Exmoor National Park Headquarters at Dulverton is open throughout the year.

E **EXETER, DEVON -** University city rebuilt after the 1940s around its cathedral. Attractions include 13th C cathedral with fine west front; notable waterfront buildings; Guildhall; Royal Albert Memorial Museum; underground passages; Northcott Theatre.

F **FOWEY, CORNWALL -** Set on steep slopes at the mouth of the Fowey River, an important clayport and fishing town. Ruined forts guarding the shore recall the days of "Fowey Gallants" who ruled the local seas. The lofty church rises above the town. Ferries to Polruan and Bodinnick; August Regatta.

FROME, SOMERSET - Old market town with modern light industry, its medieval centre watered by the River Frome. Above Cheap Street, with its flagstones and watercourse, is the church, showing work of varying periods. Interesting buildings include 18th C wool merchants' houses.

G **GLASTONBURY, SOMERSET -** Market town associated with Joseph of Arimathea and the birth of English Christianity. Built around its 7th C abbey, said to be the site of King Arthur's burial. Glastonbury Tor, with its ancient tower, gives panoramic views over flat country and the Mendip Hills.

H **HONITON, DEVON -** Old coaching town in undulating farmland. Formerly famous for lace-making, it is now an antiques-trade centre and market town. Small museum.

HOPE COVE, DEVON - Sheltered by the 400-ft headland of Bolt Tail, Hope Cove lies close to a small resort with thatched cottages, Inner Hope. Between Bolt Tail and Bolt Head lie 6 miles of beautiful National Trust cliffs.

K **KINGSBRIDGE, DEVON -** Formerly important as a port, now a market town overlooking head of beautiful, wooded estuary winding deep into rural countryside. Summer art exhibitions; Cookworthy Museum.

L **LACOCK, WILTSHIRE -** Village of great charm. Medieval buildings of stone, brick or timber-frame have jutting storeys, gables and oriel windows. The magnificent church has Perpendicular fan-vaulted chapel with grand tomb to benefactor who, after Dissolution, bought Augustinian nunnery, Lacock Abbey.

LANGPORT, SOMERSET - Small market town with Anglo-Saxon origins, sloping to River Parrett. Well known for glove making and, formerly, for eels. Interesting old buildings include some fine local churches.

LAUNCESTON, CORNWALL - Medieval "Gateway to Cornwall", county town until 1838, founded by the Normans under their hilltop castle near the original monastic settlement. This market town, overlooked by its castle ruin, has a square with Georgian houses and an elaborately carved granite church.

LEE, DEVON - Village 2 miles west of Ilfracombe, nestling in a coombe leading down to Lee Bay and sometimes called Fuchsia Valley.

LISKEARD, CORNWALL - Former stannary town with a livestock market and light industry, at the head of a valley running to the coast. Handsome Georgian and Victorian residences and a Victorian Guildhall reflect the prosperity of the mining boom. The large church has an early 20th C tower and a Norman font.

LOOE, CORNWALL - Small resort developed around former fishing and smuggling ports occupying the deep estuary of the East and West Looe rivers. Narrow, winding streets, with old inns; the museum and art gallery are housed in interesting old buildings. Shark-fishing centre, boat trips; busy harbour.

LOSTWITHIEL, CORNWALL - Cornwall's ancient capital which gained its Royal Charter in 1189. Tin from the mines around the town was smelted and coined in the Duchy Palace. Norman Restormel Castle, with its circular keep and deep moat, overlooks the town.

LYNTON, DEVON - Hilltop resort on Exmoor coast linked to its seaside twin, Lynmouth, by a water-operated cliff railway which descends from the town hall. Spectacular surroundings of moorland cliffs with steep chasms of conifer and rocks through which rivers cascade.

M **MALMESBURY, WILTSHIRE -** Overlooking the River Avon, an old town dominated by its great church, once a Benedictine abbey. The surviving Norman nave and porch are noted for fine sculptures, 12th C arches and musicians' gallery.

MARAZION, CORNWALL - Old town sloping to Mount's Bay with views of St Michael's Mount and a causeway to the island revealed at low tide. In medieval times it catered for pilgrims. The Mount is crowned by a 15th C castle built around the former Benedictine monastery of 1044.

MEVAGISSEY, CORNWALL - Small fishing town, a favourite with holidaymakers. Earlier prosperity came from pilchard fisheries, boat-building and smuggling. By the harbour are fish cellars, some converted, and a local history museum is housed in an old boat-building shed. Handsome Methodist chapel; shark fishing, sailing.

MINEHEAD, SOMERSET - Victorian resort with spreading sands developed around old fishing port on the coast below Exmoor. Former fishermen's cottages stand beside the 17th C harbour; cobbled streets climb the hill in steps to the church. Boat trips, steam railway. Hobby Horse festival 1 May.

MINIONS, CORNWALL - Village on the southern edge of Bodmin Moor with many prehistoric sites nearby. Paths lead to the Cheesewring, a stone formation where thick, oval slabs balance precariously.

MORETONHAMPSTEAD, DEVON - Small market town, with a row of 17th C almshouses, standing on the Exeter road. Surrounding moorland is scattered with ancient farmhouses and prehistoric sites.

MOTHECOMBE, DEVON - Situated on the western side of the Erme Estuary and close to the coast of Bigbury Bay. Within easy reach of Plymouth and Kingsbridge.

MOUSEHOLE, CORNWALL - Old fishing port completely rebuilt after its destruction in the 16th C by Spanish raiders. Twisting lanes and granite cottages with luxuriant gardens rise steeply from the harbour; just south is a private bird sanctuary.

N **NEWQUAY, CORNWALL -** Popular resort spread over dramatic cliffs around its old fishing port. Many beaches with abundant sands, caves and rock pools; excellent surf. Pilots' gigs are still raced from the harbour, and on the headland stands the stone Huer's House from the pilchard-fishing days.

NORTH MOLTON, DEVON - Village on the southern slopes of Exmoor, a centre for local copper mines in the 19th C. A 17th C monument in the church shows the effigies of a mining landlord and his family.

OKEHAMPTON, DEVON - Busy market town near the high tors of northern Dartmoor. The Victorian church, with William Morris windows and a 15th C tower, stands on the site of a Saxon church. A Norman castle ruin overlooks the river to the west of the town. Museum of Dartmoor Life in a restored mill.

PADSTOW, CORNWALL - Old town encircling its harbour on the Camel Estuary. The 15th C church has notable bench-ends. There are fine houses on North Quay and Raleigh's Court House on South Quay. Tall cliffs and golden sands along the coast, and ferry to Rock. Famous 'Obby 'Oss Festival on 1 May.

PAIGNTON, DEVON - Lively seaside resort with a pretty harbour. Bronze Age and Saxon sites are occupied by the 15th C church, which has a Norman door and font. The beautiful Chantry Chapel was built by local landowners, the Kirkhams.

PENZANCE, CORNWALL - Resort and fishing port on Mount's Bay with mainly Victorian promenade and some fine Regency terraces. Former prosperity came from tin trade and pilchard fishing. Grand Georgian-style church by harbour. Georgian Egyptian building at head of Chapel Street and Morrab Gardens.

PERRANPORTH, CORNWALL - Small seaside resort developed around a former mining village. Today's attractions include exciting surf, rocks, caves and extensive sand dunes.

PILLATON, CORNWALL - Peaceful village on the slopes of the River Lynher in steeply wooded country near the Devon border. Within easy reach of the coast and rugged walking country on Bodmin Moor.

POLPERRO, CORNWALL - Picturesque fishing village clinging to steep valley slopes about its harbour. A river splashes past cottages, and narrow lanes twist between. The harbour mouth, guarded by jagged rocks, is closed by heavy timbers during storms.

PORLOCK, SOMERSET - Village set between steep Exmoor hills and the sea at the head of beautiful Porlock Vale. The narrow street shows a medley of building styles. South-westward is Porlock Weir, with its old houses and tiny harbour, and further along the shore at Culbone is England's smallest church.

PORT ISAAC, CORNWALL - Old fishing port of whitewashed cottages, twisting stairways and narrow alleys. A stream splashes down through the centre to the harbour. Nearby stands a 19th C folly, Doyden Castle, with a magnificent view of the coast.

PORTREATH, CORNWALL - Formerly developed as a mining port, now a small resort with some handsome 19th C buildings. Cliffs, sands and good surf.

RUAN HIGH LANES, CORNWALL - Village at the northern end of the Roseland Peninsula.

ST AUSTELL, CORNWALL - Leading market town, the meeting point of old and new Cornwall. One mile from St Austell Bay with its sandy beaches, old fishing villages and attractive countryside. Ancient narrow streets, pedestrian shopping precincts. Fine church of Pentewan stone and Italianate Town Hall.

ST IVES, CORNWALL - Old fishing port, artists' colony and holiday town with good surfing beach. Fishermen's cottages, granite fish cellars, a sandy harbour and magnificent headlands typify a charm that has survived since the 19th C pilchard boom. Tate Gallery opened in 1993.

ST MAWGAN, CORNWALL - Pretty village of great historic interest, on wooded slopes in the Vale of Lanherne. At its centre, an old stone bridge over the River Menahyl is overlooked by the church with its lofty, buttressed tower. Among ancient stone crosses in the churchyard is a 15th C lantern cross with carved figures.

SALCOMBE, DEVON - Sheltered yachting resort of whitewashed houses and narrow streets in a balmy setting on the Salcombe Estuary. Palm, myrtle and other Mediterranean plants flourish. There are sandy bays and creeks for boating.

SEATON, DEVON - Small resort lying near the mouth of the River Axe. A mile-long beach extends to the dramatic cliffs of Beer Head. Annual art exhibition in July.

SHEPTON MALLET, SOMERSET - Historic town in the Mendip foothills, important in Roman times and site of many significant archaeological finds. The cloth industry reached its peak in the 17th C, and many fine examples of cloth merchants' houses remain. Beautiful parish church, market cross, local history museum, Collett Park.

SHERSTON, WILTSHIRE - Village situated 5 miles south-west of Malmesbury, with 16th C to 18th C houses in the High Street. Site of a battle against the Danes in 1016.

SIDMOUTH, DEVON - Charming resort set amid lofty red cliffs where the River Sid meets the sea. The wealth of ornate Regency and Victorian villas recalls the time when this was one of the south coast's most exclusive resorts. Museum; August International Festival of Folk Arts.

SOMERTON, SOMERSET - Old market town, important in Saxon times, situated at a gap in the hills south-east of Sedgemoor. Attractive red-roofed stone houses surround the 17th C octagonal market cross, and among other handsome buildings are the Town Hall and almshouses of about the same period.

VISITOR ATTRACTIONS For ideas on places to visit refer to the introduction at the beginning of this section. Look out too for the ETC's Quality Assured Visitor Attraction signs.

TAUNTON, SOMERSET - County town, well known for its public schools, sheltered by gentle hill-ranges on the River Tone. Medieval prosperity from wool has continued in marketing and manufacturing, and the town retains many fine period buildings. Museum.

TAVISTOCK, DEVON - Old market town beside the River Tavy on the western edge of Dartmoor. Developed around its 10th C abbey, of which some fragments remain, it became a stannary town in 1305 when tin-streaming thrived on the moors. Tavistock Goose Fair, October.

TINTAGEL, CORNWALL - Coastal village near the legendary home of King Arthur. There is a lofty headland with the ruin of a Norman castle, and traces of a Celtic monastery are still visible in the turf.

TORQUAY, DEVON - Devon's grandest resort, developed from a fishing village. Smart apartments and terraces rise from the seafront, and Marine Drive along the headland gives views of beaches and colourful cliffs.

TORRINGTON, DEVON - Perched high above the River Torridge, with a charming market square, Georgian Town Hall and a museum. The famous Dartington Crystal Factory, Rosemoor Gardens and Plough Arts Centre are all located in the town.

TOTNES, DEVON - Old market town steeply built near the head of the Dart Estuary. The remains of a motte and bailey castle, medieval gateways, a noble church, 16th C Guildhall and medley of period houses recall former wealth from cloth and shipping, continued in rural and water industries.

TROWBRIDGE, WILTSHIRE - Wiltshire's administrative centre, a handsome market and manufacturing town with a wealth of merchants' houses and other Georgian buildings.

WADEBRIDGE, CORNWALL - Old market town with Cornwall's finest medieval bridge, spanning the Camel at its highest navigable point. Twice widened, the bridge is said to have been built on woolpacks sunk in the unstable sands of the river bed.

WATCHET, SOMERSET - Small port on Bridgwater Bay, sheltered by the Quantocks and the Brendon Hills. A thriving paper industry keeps the harbour busy; in the 19th C it handled iron from the Brendon Hills. Cleeve Abbey, a ruined Cistercian monastery, is 3 miles to the south-west.

WELLS, SOMERSET - Small city set beneath the southern slopes of the Mendips. Built between 1180 and 1424, the magnificent cathedral is preserved in much of its original glory and, with its ancient precincts, forms one of our loveliest and most unified groups of medieval buildings.

WEST BAY, DORSET - Picturesque resort with a busy harbour, the perfect base for exploring this spectacular stretch of coastline.

WEST BEXINGTON, DORSET - Village on the stretch of Dorset coast known as Chesil Beach. Close to the famous Abbotsbury Subtropical Gardens and Swannery.

WESTON-SUPER-MARE, NORTH SOMERSET - Large, friendly resort developed in the 19th C. Traditional seaside attractions include theatres and a dance hall. The museum has a Victorian seaside gallery and Iron Age finds from a hill fort on Worlebury Hill in Weston Woods.

WEYMOUTH, DORSET - Ancient port and one of the south's earliest resorts. Curving beside a long, sandy beach, the elegant Georgian esplanade is graced with a statue of George III and a cheerful Victorian Jubilee clock tower. Museum, Sea Life Centre.

WITHYPOOL, SOMERSET - Pretty village high on Exmoor near the beautiful River Barle. On Winsford Hill (National Trust) are Bronze Age barrows known as the Wambarrows.

TOWN INDEX

This can be found at the back of the guide. If you know where you want to stay, the index will give you the page number listing accommodation in your chosen town, city or village.

South East

From Kent, the 'Garden of England', to the breathtaking Dorset Coast and from the magical Isle of Wight to the mellow Oxfordshire Cotswolds, the South East provides the perfect holiday mix – quaint villages, rolling countryside, dramatic coastline, seaside chic and cool heritage cities.

Classic sights
Stonehenge – ancient and mysterious standing stones
Battle Abbey – the site that marked the end of the Battle of Hastings in 1066
Blenheim Palace – birthplace of Sir Winston Churchill

Coast and country
Runnymede Meadow – the Magna Carta was signed here by King John in 1215
Chiltern Hills – tranquil country walks
The Needles – chalk pillars extending out into the Solent
New Forest – 900 year old historic wood and heathland

Glorious gardens
Leonardslee Lakes and Gardens – rhododendrons and azaleas ablaze with colour in May
Mottisfont Abbey – the perfect English rose garden designed by Graham Stuart Thomas
Savill Garden – woodland garden with royal connections
Sheffield Park Gardens – great 18thC, Capability Brown-designed landscaped gardens

Literary links
Jane Austen – her home in Chawton is now a museum and she is buried in Winchester Cathedral
Charles Dickens – Rochester; his home, Gad's Hill Place

The Counties of Berkshire, Buckinghamshire, Dorset (Eastern), East Sussex, Hampshire, Isle of Wight, Kent, Oxfordshire, Surrey, and West Sussex.

For more information contact:
Tourism South East
The Old Brew House
Warwick Park, Tunbridge Wells,
Kent TN2 5TU

Telephone enquiries -
T: (01892) 540766
F: (01892) 511008

Tourism South East
40 Chamberlayne Road
Eastleigh,
Hampshire SO50 5JH

Telephone enquiries -
T: (023) 8062 5505
F: (023) 8062 0010

E: enquiries@tourismse.com
www.gosouth.co.uk

1. Stonehenge, Wiltshire
2. Oast House, Kent

Places to Visit

You will find hundreds of interesting places to visit during your stay, just some of which are listed in these pages. Contact any Tourist Information Centre in the region for more ideas on days out.

Awarded VisitBritain's 'Quality Assured Visitor Attraction' marque.

A Day at the Wells
The Pantiles, Royal Tunbridge Wells
Tel: (01892) 546545
www.heritageattractions.co.uk
With commentary on personal stereos visitors experience the sights and sounds of 18thC Tunbridge Wells in its heyday as a spa town, escorted by Beau Nash, renowned dandy and MC.

Amberley Working Museum
Amberley, Arundel
Tel: (01798) 831370
www.amberleymuseum.co.uk
Open-air industrial history centre in chalk quarry. Working craftsmen, narrow-gauge railway, early buses, working machines and other exhibits. Nature trail and visitor centre.

Arundel Castle
Arundel
Tel: (01903) 883136 www.arundelcastle.org
An impressive Norman stronghold in extensive grounds, much restored 18/19thC, 11thC keep, 13thC barbican. Barons' hall, armoury, chapel. Van Dyck and Gainsborough paintings.

Battle Abbey and Battlefield
High Street, Battle
Tel: (01424) 773792
www.english-heritage.org.uk
Abbey founded by William the Conqueror on the site of the Battle of Hastings. The church altar is on the spot where King Harold was killed. Battlefield views and exhibition.

Bekonscot Model Village
Warwick Road, Beaconsfield
Tel: (01494) 672919 www.bekonscot.org.uk
The oldest model village in the world, Bekonscot depicts rural England in the 1930s, where time has stood still for 70 years. Narrow gauge ride-on railway.

Bentley Wildfowl and Motor Museum
Halland, Lewes
Tel: (01825) 840573 www.bentley.org.uk
Over 1,000 wildfowl in parkland with lakes. Motor museum with vintage cars, house, children's play facilities and woodland walk.

Blenheim Palace
Woodstock
Tel: (01993) 811325 www.blenheimpalace.com
Home of the 11th Duke of Marlborough. Birthplace of Sir Winston Churchill. Designed by Vanbrugh in the English baroque style. Landscaped by `Capability' Brown.

Breamore House
Breamore, Fordingbridge
Tel: (01725) 512233
Elizabethan manor house of 1583, with fine collection of works of art. Furniture, tapestries, needlework, paintings mainly Dutch School 17th and 18thC.

Brooklands Museum
Brooklands Road, Weybridge
Tel: (01932) 857381
www.brooklandsmuseum.com
Original 1907 motor racing circuit. Features the most historic and steepest section of the old banked track and 1-in-4 test hill. Motoring village and Grand Prix exhibition.

The Canterbury Tales
St Margaret's Street, Canterbury
Tel: (01227) 479227
www.canterburytales.org.uk
An audiovisual recreation of life in medieval England. Join Chaucer's pilgrims on their journey from the Tabard Inn in London to St. Thomas Becket's shrine at Canterbury.

Chatley Heath Semaphore Tower
Pointers Road, Cobham
Tel: (01372) 458822
A restored historic semaphore tower displaying the history of overland naval communications in early 19thC set in woodland. Working semaphore mast and models.

Compton Acres
Canford Cliffs, Poole
Tel: (01202) 700778 www.comptonacres.co.uk
11 distinct gardens of the world. The gardens include Italian, Japanese, Spanish water garden. Deer sanctuary with treetop lookout. Restaurant and a craft centre.

Dapdune Wharf (National Trust)
Wharf Road, Guildford
Tel: (01483) 561389
www.nationaltrust.org.uk/southern
Dapdune Wharf is the home of 'Reliance', a restored Wey barge, as well as an interactive exhibition which tells the story of the waterway and those who lived and worked on it.

Didcot Railway Centre
Great Western Society, Didcot
Tel: (01235) 817200
www.didcotrailwaycentre.org.uk
Living museum recreating the golden age of the Great Western Railway. Steam locomotives and trains, engine shed and small relics museum.

Dover Castle and Secret Wartime Tunnels (English Heritage)
Dover
Tel: (01304) 211067
www.english-heritage.org.uk
One of the most powerful medieval fortresses in Western Europe. St Mary-in-Castro Saxon church. Roman lighthouse, secret wartime tunnels, Henry II Great Keep.

Eagle Heights
Hulberry Farm, Eynsford, Dartford
Tel: (01322) 866466 www.eagleheights.co.uk
Bird of prey centre housed undercover where visitors can see eagles, hawks, falcons, owls and vultures from all over the world. Reptile centre, play area and sandpit.

Gilbert White's House and The Oates Museum
Selbourne, Alton
Tel: (01420) 511275
Historic house and garden, home of Gilbert White, author of 'The Natural History of Selborne'. Exhibition on Frank Oates, explorer and Captain Lawrence Oates of Antarctic fame.

Hastings Castle and 1066 Story
West Hill, Hastings
Tel: (01424) 781112
www.smugglersadventure.co.uk
Fragmentary remains of Norman Castle built on West Hill after William the Conqueror's victory at the Battle of Hastings. 1066 Story interpretation centre in siege tent.

2

3

1. The Stade, Hastings
2. The Needles, Isle of Wight
3. Shefield Park Gardens, East Sussex

The Hawk Conservancy and Country Park
Andover
Tel: (01264) 772252
www.hawk-conservancy.org
Unique to Great Britain – 'Valley of the Eagles' held here daily at 1400, plus 250 birds of prey and 22 acres (9ha) of woodland gardens.

High Beeches Gardens
Handcross, Haywards Heath
Tel: (01444) 400589
www.highbeeches.com
25 acres (10ha) of peaceful, landscaped woodland and water gardens with many rare plants, wildflower meadow, spring bulbs and glorious autumn colour.

QUALITY ASSURED VISITOR ATTRACTION

Kent & East Sussex Railway
Tenterden Town Station, Tenterden
Tel: (01580) 765155 www.kesr.org.uk
Full-size steam railway with restored Edwardian stations at Tenterden and Northiam, 14 steam engines, Victorian coaches and Pullman carriages. Museum and children's play area.

QUALITY ASSURED VISITOR ATTRACTION

Kingston Lacy (National Trust)
Wimborne Minster
Tel: (01202) 883402
www.kingstonlacy@ntrust.org.uk
A 17thC house designed for Sir Ralph Bankes by Sir Roger Pratt altered by Sir Charles Barry in 19thC. Collection of paintings, 250-acre (101-ha) wooded park, herd of Devon cattle.

QUALITY ASSURED VISITOR ATTRACTION

LEGOLAND Windsor
Winkfield Road, Windsor
Tel: 0870 5040404 www.legoland.co.uk
A family park with hands-on activities, rides, themed playscapes and more LEGO bricks than you ever dreamed possible.

The Living Rainforest
Thatcham, Newbury
Tel: (01635) 202444 www.livingrainforest.org
Two tropical rainforests, all under cover, approximately 20,000 sq ft (1,858sq m). Collection of rare and exotic tropical plants together with small representation of wildlife in rainforest.

Manor Farm (Farm and Museum)
Botley, Southampton
Tel: (01489) 787055
www.hants.gov.uk/countryside/manorfarm
Traditional Hampshire farmstead with a range of buildings, farm animals, machinery and equipment. Pre-1950's farmhouse and 13thC church set for 1900 living history site.

National Motor Museum
Beaulieu, Brockenhurst
Tel: (01590) 612345 www.beaulieu.co.uk
Motor museum with over 250 exhibits showing history of motoring from 1896. Also Palace House, Wheels Experience, Beaulieu Abbey ruins and a display of monastic life.

Newport Roman Villa
Cypress Road, Newport
Tel: (01983) 529720
Underfloor heated bath system; tesselated floors displayed in reconstructed rooms; corn-drying kiln, small site museum of objects recovered.

Oceanarium
West Beach, Bournemouth
Tel: (01202) 311993 www.oceanarium.co.uk
Situated in the heart of Bournemouth, next to the pier, the Oceanarium will take you on a fascinating voyage on the undersea world from elegant seahorses to sinister sharks.

Osborne House (English Heritage)
Yorke Avenue, East Cowes
Tel: (01983) 200022
www.english-heritage.org.uk
Queen Victoria and Prince Albert's seaside holiday home. Swiss Cottage where royal children learnt cooking and gardening. Victorian carriage rides.

The Oxford Story
6 Broad Street, Oxford
Tel: (01865) 728822 www.oxfordstory.co.uk
Take your seat on our amazing 'dark' ride and journey through scenes from 900 years of university's history, complete with sights, sounds and smells!

Port Lympne Wild Animal Park, Mansion and Gardens
Lympe, Hythe
Tel: (01303) 264647 www.howletts.net
Set in 400 acres (160 ha) with historic mansion and gardens, black rhino, tigers, elephants, small cats, monkeys, Barbary lions, red pandas, tapirs and 'Palace of the Apes'.

Portsmouth Historic Dockyard
1/7 College Road, HM Naval Base, Portsmouth
Tel: (023) 9286 1533
www.historicdockyard.co.uk
A fascinating day out – Action Stations, Mary Rose, HMS Victory, HMS Warrior 1860, Royal Naval Museum, 'Warships by water' harbour tours, Dockyard Apprentice exhibition.

St Mary's House and Gardens
Bramber, Steyning
Tel: (01903) 816205
A medieval timber-framed Grade I house with rare 16thC wall-leather, fine panelled rooms and a unique painted room. Topiary gardens.

The Sir Harold Hillier Gardens and Arboretum
Ampfield, Romsey
Tel: (01794) 368787 www.hillier.hants.gov.uk/
Established in 1953, The Sir Harold Hillier Gardens and Arboretum comprises the greatest collection of wild and cultivated woody plants in the world.

South of England Rare Breeds Centre
Highlands Farm, Woodchurch
Tel: (01233) 861493 www.rarebreeds.org.uk
Large collection of rare farm breeds on a working farm with children's play activities. Home to the 'Tamworth Two'. Woodland walks.

Swanage Railway
Station House, Swanage
Tel: (01929) 425800
www.swanagerailway.co.uk
Enjoy a nostalgic steam-train ride on the Purbeck line. Steam trains run every weekend throughout the year with daily running April to October.

The Tank Museum
Bovington, Wareham
Tel: (01929) 405096 www.tankmuseum.co.uk
The world's finest display of armoured fighting vehicles. Experimental vehicles, interactive displays, disabled access and facilities.

The Vyne (National Trust)
Sherborne St John, Basingstoke
Tel: (01256) 881337
www.nationaltrust.org.uk/places/thevyne
Original house dating back to Henry VIII's time. Extensively altered in mid 17thC. Tudor chapel, beautiful gardens and lake.

Waterperry Gardens Limited
Waterperry, Oxford
Tel: (01844) 339254
www.waterperrygardens.co.uk
Ornamental gardens covering 6 acres (2.4ha) of the 83-acre (33.5-ha) 18thC Waterperry House estate. A Saxon village church, garden shop teashop, art and craft gallery are found within the grounds.

Weald and Downland Open Air Museum
Singleton, Chichester
Tel: (01243) 811348 www.wealddown.co.uk
Over 40 rescued historic buildings from South East England, reconstructed on a downland country park site. Homes and workplaces of the past include a medieval farmstead.

West Dean Gardens
West Dean, Chichester
Tel: (01243) 818210
www.westdean.org.uk
Extensive downland garden with specimen trees, 300-ft (91-m) pergola, rustic summerhouses and restored walled kitchen garden. Walk in parkland and 45-acre (18-ha) arboretum.

Whitchurch Silk Mill
28 Winchester Street, Whitchurch
Tel: (01256) 892065
www.whitchurchsilkmill.org.uk
Unique Georgian silk-weaving watermill, now a working museum producing fine silk fabrics on Victorian machinery. Riverside garden, tearoom for light meals, silk gift shop.

Wilderness Wood
Hadlow Down, Uckfield
Tel: (01825) 830509
www.wildernesswood.co.uk
A family-run working woodland of 60 acres (24ha), beautiful in all seasons. There are trails, a bluebell walk, a play area, workshop and a timber barn with exhibition.

Winchester Cathedral
The Close, Winchester
Tel: (01962) 857225
www.winchester-cathedral.org.uk
Magnificent medieval cathedral, soaring gothic nave converted from original Norman. 12thC illuminated Winchester Bible, Jane Austen's tomb, library, gallery, crypt, chapels.

Winkworth Arboretum (National Trust)
Hascombe, Godalming
Tel: (01483) 208477
www.nationaltrust.org.uk/winkworthar boretum
100 acres (40ha) of hillside planted with rare trees and shrubs. Good views, lakes, newly-restored boathouse, azaleas, bluebells, wild spring flowers and autumn colours.

Tourism South East

The Old Brew House,
Warwick Park, Tunbridge Wells,
Kent TN2 5TU
T: (01892) 540766
F: (01892) 511008

40 Chamberlayne Road,
Eastleigh,
Hampshire, SO50 5JH
T: (023) 8062 5505
F: (023) 8062 0010

E: enquiries@tourismse.com
www.gosouth.co.uk

1

THE FOLLOWING PUBLICATIONS ARE AVAILABLE FROM TOURISM SOUTH EAST:

South East Breaks
Southern England
Days Out in Southern England
Days Out in Thames & Chilterns Country
Favourite Gardens & Garden Stays in South East England
Glorious Gardens & Historic Houses in Southern England
Walk South East England
Escape into the Countryside

Getting to the South East

BY ROAD: From the north east – M1 & M25; the north west – M6, M40 & M25; the west and Wales – M4 & M25; the east – M25; the south west – M5, M4 & M25; London – M25, M2, M20, M23, M3, M4 or M40.

BY RAIL: Regular services from London's Charing Cross, Victoria, Waterloo and Waterloo East stations to all parts of the South East. Further information on rail journeys in the South East can be obtained on 08457 484950.

1. Savill Garden
2. Dreaming Spires, Oxford

2

Where to stay in the

South East

All place names in the blue bands under which accommodation is listed, are shown on the maps at the front of this guide.

Symbols give useful information about services and facilities. Inside the back cover flap there's a key to these symbols which you can keep open for easy reference.

A complete listing of all the VisitBritain assessed accommodation covered by this guide appears at the back of this guide.

ADDERBURY, Oxfordshire Map ref 2C1

★★★★
1 Unit
Sleeping 2

HANNAH'S COTTAGE AT FLETCHER'S
Adderbury, Banbury
Contact: Mrs C A Holmes
T: (01295) 810308
E: charlotteaholmes@hotmail.com
I: www.holiday-rentals.com

OPEN All Year

Low season per wk
£250.00–£300.00
High season per wk
£300.00–£350.00

Hannah's, a recently restored Victorian garden cottage which incorporates a former hayloft as first floor lounge, is cosy and quiet although in the centre of this lovely village.

ALVERSTOKE, Hampshire Map ref 2C3

★★
1 Unit
Sleeping 6

28 THE AVENUE
Alverstoke, Gosport
Contact: Mr M Lawson
T: (01923) 244042
F: (01923) 244042

OPEN All Year

Low season per wk
£300.00–£350.00
High season per wk
£350.00–£370.00

Three-bedroomed house with pleasant garden, 10 minutes from Stokes Bay. Opportunities for fishing, sailing and windsurfing. Close to Portsmouth, Southampton and New Forest.

NB

IMPORTANT NOTE Information on accommodation listed in this guide has been supplied by the proprietors. As changes may occur you are advised to check details at the time of booking.

BRUERN COTTAGES

National Winners of VisitBritain's Excellence in England Gold and Silver Award for Self-Catering Holiday of the Year 1998 and 2003, Bruern Cottages are the finest self-catering properties, not just in the Cotswolds but in the whole of Great Britain.

"For a taste of the upper crust Britain head for Bruern Cottages, twelve Merchant Ivoryesque cottages. Each antiques filled cottage offers one to five bedrooms, up-to-the-minute kitchens, and access to a secret garden of lavender and wisteria. Children will gallop straight for the playhouse, complete with Lilliputian tea set and canopied bed." *Condé Nast Traveller*

TOP 5 STAR GRADING

These twelve award winning cottages, in the heart of the Cotswolds, were converted from the Victorian stable yard and outbuildings of Bruern Abbey. They are stylish, luxurious and unusually well equipped, country houses in miniature, with open fires and four poster beds as well as state-of-the-art bathrooms and kitchens. They sleep two to ten. Each has a private enclosed terrace and many have their own secluded gardens.

In the beautifully landscaped communal gardens and grounds there is tennis, croquet and swimming. Children have their own special play area with a two storey playhouse, a climbing frame and an indoor playroom. There are wonderful wildlife walks in the neighbouring Nature Reserve at Foxholes and along the Oxfordshire Way, which runs through Bruern. Fly-fishing and riding are available near at hand and Bruern adjoins a challenging golf course.

London is only an hour and a half by train or by car, and Oxford just forty minutes.

SMALLEST COTTAGE
(sleeps 2 plus cot)

LOW SEASON	£526 p.w.
HIGH SEASON	£983 p.w.

LARGEST COTTAGE
(sleeps 10 plus cots)

LOW SEASON	£1,848 p.w.
HIGH SEASON	£3,921 p.w.

www.bruern-holiday-cottages.co.uk Tel: 01993 830415 Email: enquiries@bruern.co.uk

AMBERLEY, West Sussex Map ref 2D3

★★

1 Unit
Sleeping 4

CULVER COTTAGE

Amberley, Arundel
Contact: Mrs B Cruttenden
T: (01903) 746610
F: (01903) 743332

One of a pair of secluded cottages in the heart of Amberley. Hidden up a twitten winding through neighbours' gardens. Beautiful South Downs views. Thatched houses, flowering stone walls, Norman church, castle and the Wildbrooks ancient water meadows add to the charm of this walking paradise. Pubs and restaurants within walking distance.

OPEN All Year

Short stays by arrangement.

Low season per wk
£400.00–£500.00
High season per wk
£500.00–£600.00

ARUNDEL, West Sussex Map ref 2D3 *Tourist Information Centre Tel: (01903) 882268*

★★★

2 Units
Sleeping 4

THE COACHMAN'S FLAT AND THE COTTAGE

Slindon, Arundel
Contact: Mrs J Fuente, Mill Lane House, Slindon, Arundel BN18 0RP
T: (01243) 814440
F: (01243) 814436
E: jan.fuente@btopenworld.com
I: mill-lane-house.co.uk

OPEN All Year

Low season per wk
£165.00–£250.00
High season per wk
£250.00–£375.00

Flat and cottage in 17thC property. Spectacular views to coast. In National Trust village on South Downs. Use of large gardens. Animals by arrangement.

ASHDOWN FOREST

See under Nutley

ASHFORD, Kent Map ref 3B4 *Tourist Information Centre Tel: (01233) 629165*

★★★

6 Units
Sleeping 4

EVERSLEIGH WOODLAND LODGES

Shadoxhurst, Ashford
Contact: Mrs C J Drury, Eversleigh Woodland Lodges, Eversleigh House, Hornash Lane, Shadoxhurst, Ashford TN26 1HX
T: (01233) 733248
F: (01233) 733248
E: cjdrury@freeuk.com
I: www.eversleighlodges.co.uk

CC: Mastercard, Visa

Low season per wk
£235.00–£380.00
High season per wk
£425.00–£570.00

Spacious detached lodges in woodland setting. Heated indoor swimming pool, games room, gymnasium, solarium, gardens. Easy access South Coast, London, Canterbury, Channel ports and tunnel.

BANBURY, Oxfordshire Map ref 2C1 *Tourist Information Centre Tel: (01295) 259855*

★★★★

1 Unit
Sleeping 6

LITTLE GOOD LODGE

Little Bourton, Banbury
Contact: Ms L Aries, Little Good Farm, Little Bourton, Banbury OX17 1QZ
T: (01295) 750069
F: (01295) 750069
E: littlegoodfarm@btopenworld.com
I: http://littlegoodfarm.users.btopenworld.com

OPEN All Year

Low season per wk
£200.00–£239.00
High season per wk
£330.00–£400.00

Single-storey barn conversion on its own in beautiful countryside, ideal for unwinding or as a base for seeing Oxford, Stratford, Cotswolds (M40 jct 11 four miles).

QUALITY ASSURANCE SCHEME

Star ratings were correct at the time of going to press but are subject to change. Please check at the time of booking.

FOR SELF CATERING HOLIDAYS IN THE SOUTH EAST OF ENGLAND, SEASCA MEMBERS OFFER THE WIDEST CHOICE PLUS FRIENDLY HELP AND EXPERT LOCAL KNOWLEDGE

Best of Brighton & Sussex Cottages

Tel: 01273 308779 Fax: 01273 390211
Email:enquiries@bestofbrighton.co.uk
www.bestofbrighton.co.uk

FAIRHAVEN HOLIDAY COTTAGES

Tel: 08452 304334 Fax: 01634 570157
Email: enquiries@fairhaven-holidays.co.uk
www.fairhaven-holidays.co.uk

Garden of England Cottages

Tel: 01732 369168 Fax: 01732 358817
Email: holidays@gardenofenglandcottages.co.uk
www.gardenofenglandcottages.co.uk

All SEASCA (South East Association of Self Catering Agencies) agencies are members of Tourism South East and participate in the VisitBritain Star Grading Scheme

Freedom Holiday Homes

We offer the largest choice of quality self-catering accommodation in cottages, barn conversions, granaries, Oast houses and apartments throughout the beautiful counties of Kent & East Sussex.

Our friendly, professional staff who have extensive local knowledge will be pleased to assist you with your requirements. Ideal locations for visiting the many castles, gardens, historic houses, National Trust and English Heritage properties in the area, or alternatively take a visit to London, the coast or a day trip to Europe. All the accommodations are ETC graded and inspected.

Pets welcome at many properties. Mini-breaks and longer lets available all year (subject to availability). Rentals from £125pw - £1000pw.

15 High Street, Cranbrook, Kent, TN17 3EB Tel: 01580 720770 Fax: 01580 720771
Email: mail@freedomholidayhomes.co.uk www.freedomholidayhomes.co.uk

BANBURY continued

★★★★

1 Unit
Sleeping 2–4

MILL WHEEL COTTAGE

Banbury
Contact: Mrs S A Nichols, Mill House Farm, King's Sutton, Banbury OX17 3QP
T: (01295) 811637
F: (01295) 811637
I: www.holiday-rentals.com

Idyllic, private and very comfortable, well-equipped cottage on River Cherwell, converted to a high standard with original beams. Full of character, surrounded by water-meadows with abundant wildlife, the unltimate in tranquillity and relaxation. Canal close by. Ideal for exploring Cotswolds, Stratford and Oxford. Enjoy a warm welcome and personal attention.

OPEN All Year

Low season per wk
£260.00–£310.00
High season per wk
£360.00–£450.00

BARTON ON SEA, Hampshire Map ref 2B3

★★★★★

1 Unit
Sleeping 4

SOLENT HEIGHTS

Barton on Sea, New Milton
Contact: Mrs D Philpott
T: (01425) 616066
F: (01425) 616066

OPEN All Year

Low season per wk
£265.00–£525.00
High season per wk
£525.00–£630.00

New luxury apartment with balcony, adjacent golf course. Two double bedrooms, two bathrooms, lounge/diner, fully equipped kitchen. Full central heating. Peaceful seafront location overlooking Needles, IOW to Purbeck Hills.

BATTLE, East Sussex Map ref 3B4 *Tourist Information Centre Tel: (01424) 773721*

★★★

1 Unit

HENLEY BRIDGE STUD

Ashburnham, Battle
Contact: Mr & Mrs M White
T: (01424) 892076
F: (01424) 893990
E: martan@hbstud.fsnet.co.uk

OPEN All Year

Low season per wk
£250.00–£300.00
High season per wk
£350.00–£500.00

This converted byre with oak beams and inglenook fireplace offers comfort and privacy with peace and tranquillity in the heart of the beautiful Sussex countryside.

BEAULIEU, Hampshire Map ref 2C3

★★★

1 Unit
Sleeping 7

IVY COTTAGE

East Boldre, Brockenhurst
Contact: Mr & Mrs B R Gibb, 28 Church Street, Littlehampton BN17 5PX
T: (01903) 715595
F: (01903) 719176
E: gibb28@breathemail.net

Low season per wk
Min £390.00
High season per wk
Max £575.00

Comfortable, well-equipped, four-bedroomed holiday cottage between Beaulieu and Lymington, with direct access to open forest. Village shop and pub nearby. Open March-October.

BEMBRIDGE, Isle of Wight Map ref 2C3

★★★

1 Unit
Sleeping 10

NINE

Bembridge
Contact: Mrs B C Cripps
T: (01444) 454474

OPEN All Year

Low season per wk
£210.00–£280.00
High season per wk
£310.00–£800.00

Ideal holiday home 400 yards from sea. Five double bedrooms, sun parlour, good garden. TV, video, washing machine/dryer, dishwasher, fridge/freezer. Parking. Dogs welcome.

RATING **All accommodation in this guide has been rated, or is awaiting a rating, by a trained VisitBritain assessor.**

BICESTER, Oxfordshire Map ref 2C1 *Tourist Information Centre Tel: (01869) 369055*

★★★★

5 Units
Sleeping 4–6

Top-quality cottages, in Cotswold-stone barn conversions situated in the Oxfordshire Cotswolds on a 500-acre working farm. Free, on-farm fishing. Close to Oxford, Stratford-upon-Avon, Warwick, with easy day trips to London, Legoland, Bath. Wealth of historic houses nearby. Resident owners will make guests welcome.

PIMLICO FARM COUNTRY COTTAGES

Tusmore, Bicester
Contact: Mr & Mrs J Harper, Pimlico Farm Country Cottages, Pimlico Farm, Tusmore, Bicester OX27 7SL
T: (01869) 810306
F: (01869) 810309
E: enquiries@pimlicofarm.co.uk
I: www.pimlicofarm.co.uk

OPEN All Year
CC: Mastercard, Switch, Visa

Low season per wk
£245.00–£375.00
High season per wk
£329.00–£515.00

BOLDRE, Hampshire Map ref 2C3

★★★

1 Unit
Sleeping 2

CLOSE COTTAGE

Boldre, Lymington
Contact: Mr & Mrs C J White, Close Cottage, Brockenhurst Road, Battramsley, Boldre, Lymington SO41 8PT
T: (01590) 675343

Cosy annexe of period cottage with beamed ceilings and antique decor. French doors to garden with rural views. Totally self-contained, with double bed. Ample parking. Nearest neighbour is country pub serving meals. Ideal for forest walks, two miles to Lymington and coast, two miles to Brockenhurst shops/eating.

OPEN All Year

Short breaks available.

Low season per wk
£140.00–£180.00
High season per wk
£200.00–£250.00

BOWLHEAD GREEN, Surrey Map ref 2C2

★★

1 Unit
Sleeping 2

THE BARN FLAT

Thursley, Godalming
Contact: Mrs G P Ranson, Bowlhead Green Farm, Bowlhead Green, Thursley, Godalming GU8 6NW
T: (01428) 682687

Attractive, small, self-contained flat overlooking garden of old farmhouse. Double sofa bed, kitchenette, shower and wc. No pets.

OPEN All Year except Christmas

Low season per wk
£120.00
High season per wk
£140.00

BRIGHSTONE, Isle of Wight Map ref 2C3

★★★

13 Units

Attractive stone cottages in courtyard setting on our 700-acre working farm. Large garden with barbecue and two tennis courts. In beautiful countryside. Five minutes' walk to sea. Car park and laundry room. A very warm welcome assured.

CHILTON FARM COTTAGES

Brighstone
Contact: Mrs S Fisk, Chilton Farm Cottages, Chilton Farm, Chilton Lane, Brighstone PO30 4DS
T: (01983) 740338
F: (01983) 741370
E: info@chiltonfarm.co.uk
I: www.chiltonfarm.co.uk

3-night stays available Oct-Jan, Mar-May (excl New Year and Christmas).

Low season per wk
£150.00–£250.00
High season per wk
£350.00–£650.00

BRIGHSTONE continued

★★★
4 Units
Sleeping 6–10

GRANGE FARM – BRIGHSTONE BAY

Brighstone, Newport
Contact: Mr D J Dunjay
T: (01983) 740296
F: (01983) 741233
E: grangefarm@brighstonebay.fsnet.co.uk
I: www.brighstonebay.fsnet.co.uk

CC: Amex, Delta, JCB, Mastercard, Solo, Switch, Visa

Low season per wk
£275.00–£415.00
High season per wk
£575.00–£665.00

3- or 4-bedroom self-catering barn conversions on small working farm on south-west coast with beach and chine. Safe swimming, walkers' paradise.

BRIGHTON & HOVE, East Sussex Map ref 2D3

★-★★
41 Units
Sleeping 2

THE ABBEY SELF-CATERING FLATLETS

Brighton
Contact: Mr R A Smith
T: (01273) 778771
F: (01273) 729147
E: theabbey@brighton.co.uk
I: www.brighton.co.uk/hotels/theabbey

OPEN All Year
CC: Delta, JCB, Mastercard, Solo, Switch, Visa

Low season per wk
£138.00–£215.00
High season per wk
£156.00–£259.00

Specialising in self-catering. Lift, licensed bar. Everything provided. Prices to suit everyone. Easy parking. Children welcome. Open all year. All major credit cards.

★★★★
3 Units

BRIGHTON MARINA HOLIDAY APARTMENTS

Brighton
Contact: Mrs A M Wills
T: (020) 8940 6945
F: (020) 8940 8907
E: info@brightonmarinaholidayapartments.co.uk
I: www.brightonmarinaholidayapartments.co.uk

Luxury two-bedroom apartments overlooking the inner harbour with private balconies or terrace. Each individually furnished apartment has a separate living room, modern kitchen, bathroom, en suite shower room and private parking. Situated a mile east of Brighton, the Marina boasts an extensive range of leisure, shopping and dining facilities. Enquiries 01273 693569.

OPEN All Year

Low season per wk
£350.00–£450.00
High season per wk
£450.00–£600.00

★★★
3 Units
Sleeping 5

DALE COURT FAMILY HOLIDAY FLATS

Brighton
Contact: Ms B Goodman, Dale Court Family Holiday Flats, 9 Florence Road, Brighton BN1 6DL
T: (01273) 326963

OPEN All Year

High season per wk
£200.00–£350.00

Victorian house divided into self-contained flats of two and three bedrooms. Centrally located, comfortably furnished and very well equipped. Ample free street parking. Open all year.

QUALITY ASSURANCE SCHEME

For an explanation of the quality and facilities represented by the Stars please refer to the front of this guide. A more detailed explanation can be found in the information pages at the back.

BRIGHTON & HOVE continued

★★★★★
1 Unit
Sleeping 5

KILCOLGAN BUNGALOW

Rottingdean, Brighton
Contact: Mr J St George
T: (020) 7250 3678
F: (020) 7250 1955
E: jc.stgeorge@virgin.net

Welcome to excellence in self-catering accommodation. Exceptional, detached, three-bedroomed bungalow comprehensively equipped, with emphasis on comfort. Secluded, landscaped garden overlooking farmland. Garage and parking for two vehicles. Rottingdean is a delightful seaside village with seafront and promenade. Ideal, quiet retreat. Brighton four miles.

OPEN All Year

Minimum 3-night stays available Nov-Mar, £420-£450.

Low season per wk
£550.00–£600.00
High season per wk
£650.00–£750.00

★★★★★
1 Unit

19A METROPOLE COURT

Brighton
Contact: Mr R T Harris, Best of Brighton & Sussex Cottages Ltd, Windmill Lodge, Vicarage Lane, Rottingdean, Brighton BN2 7HD
T: (01273) 308779
F: (01273) 390211
E: enquiries@bestofbrighton.co.uk
I: www.bestofbrighton.co.uk

This luxury three-bedroomed, two-bathroomed balcony penthouse apartment is set right on top of the famous Hilton Metropole hotel on the seafront. Close to shops, theatres and Conference Centre. Outstanding views. One free car space. Daily access available, on a payment basis, to the luxury gym and indoor heated swimming pool.

OPEN All Year
CC: Delta, Mastercard, Switch, Visa

Reduced prices for 2 and 4 people. 3-day short breaks available out of season at 75% of weekly rate; 4 days at 85%.

Low season per wk
£800.00–£900.00
High season per wk
£900.00–£1,000.00

★★
1 Unit
Sleeping 4

UPPER MARKET STREET
Hove, Brighton
Contact: Ms M Stanton
T: (020) 8979 1792
F: (020) 8399 6639

Lovely, fully equipped studio apartments with entrance patio. Central location, close to seafront, shopping, entertainment and public transport facilities.

OPEN All Year

Low season per wk
£225.00–£250.00
High season per wk
£225.00–£250.00

BROADSTAIRS, Kent Map ref 3C3 *Tourist Information Centre Tel: (01843) 583333/583334*

BRAY HOLIDAY HOMES

BROADSTAIRS — Tel: 0208 660 1925

Our holiday home is situated within just a few minutes walk from the centre of Broadstairs and a large selection of restaurants and the cinema. The delightful, sandy and picturesque Viking Bay beach is also just as close.

The end of terrace town house is on three floors with some sea views and a balcony that catches the evening sun. There is one twin bedroom and two double bedrooms plus a cot.

Prices: Low season per week £200.00 to £390.00
High season per week £450.00 to £550.00

Contact: Mr D J Bray • 34 Smitham Downs Road • Purley • Surrey • CR8 4ND

BROADSTAIRS continued

★★★

1 Unit
Sleeping 4

SECRET COTTAGE

Broadstairs
Contact: Mr J Ferris, Blue Sky, 15 St Peters Park Road, Broadstairs CT10 2BG
T: (01843) 602656
F: (01843) 602656
E: info@bluesky-apart.com
I: www.bluesky-apart.com

OPEN All Year

Low season per wk
£199.00–£349.00
High season per wk
£349.00–£399.00

Charming, detatched, Victorian two-bedroomed cottage with walled garden. Ten minutes from Viking Bay. Great for kids. Pets welcome.

BROOK, Hampshire Map ref 2C3

★★★

1 Unit
Sleeping 8

WITTENSFORD LODGE

Brook, Lyndhurst
Contact: Ms C Smith
T: (01277) 623997
F: (01277) 634976
E: mbmcarol@dircon.co.uk
I: www.wittensfordlodge.freeservers.com

OPEN All Year

Low season per wk
£300.00–£400.00
High season per wk
£500.00–£600.00

Detached cottage set in woodland with 0.33-acre garden. Superb base for touring this lovely area.

CREDIT CARD BOOKINGS If you book by telephone and are asked for your credit card number it is advisable to check the proprietor's policy should you cancel your reservation.

WOODLANDS LEISURE

SACKETTS HILL FARM, SACKETTS HILL, BROADSTAIRS CT10 2QS
T:(01843) 603133 F:(01843) 601996

Set in acres of mature woodlands, with abundance of wildlife including owls.

Accommodation available ranging from tastefully decorated log cabins to a beautifully furnished 16thC farmhouse renovated to its original grandeur with special features including beams and inglenook fireplace.

If you prefer to stay closer to the nearby coastal town rent the Fisherman's Cottage.

All accommodation fully equipped for your every need.

Short breaks available October to March (excluding Christmas and New Year).

E:phil@ukholidayz.co.uk www.ukholidayz.co.uk

CANTERBURY, Kent Map ref 3B3 *Tourist Information Centre Tel: (01227) 766567*

★★★★
3 Units
Sleeping 4–6

THE CANTERBURY HOTEL & APARTMENTS

Canterbury
Contact: Mrs J Wigginton, The Canterbury Hotel and Apartments, 71 New Dover Road, Canterbury CT1 3DZ
T: (01227) 450551
F: (01227) 780145
E: canterbury.hotel@btinternet.com
I: www.canterbury-hotel-apartments.co.uk

OPEN All Year
CC: Amex, Delta, Diners, Mastercard, Solo, Switch, Visa

Low season per wk
£290.00–£440.00
High season per wk
£320.00–£480.00

Superior apartments in hotel grounds, close to city centre. Colour TV, direct-dial telephone, fully equipped. Out of season, long-stay discounts.

★★★
1 Unit
Sleeping 3

HENRY'S OF ASH

Ash, Canterbury
Contact: Mr P H Robinson, Henry's of Ash, Darrington, Durlock Road, Ash, Canterbury CT3 2HU
T: (01304) 812563

OPEN All Year

Low season per wk
£120.00–£160.00
High season per wk
£170.00–£185.00

Comfortable self-contained maisonette, over central village antiques shop. Double glazing. Handy for touring East Kent and for Channel trips.

★★★★
3 Units
Sleeping 1–3

ORIEL LODGE

Canterbury
Contact: Mr Keith Rishworth, Oriel Lodge, 3 Queens Avenue, Canterbury CT2 8AY
T: (01227) 462845
F: (01227) 462845
E: info@oriel-lodge.co.uk
I: www.oriel-lodge.co.uk

High-quality apartments in a lovely Edwardian house, set in a tree-lined residential area five minutes' walk from shops, restaurants and city centre. Self-contained, peaceful and very comfortable accommodation with clean, up-to-date facilities. Heating, bed linen and towels included. No smoking; no pets; children welcome from age six. Private car park.

OPEN All Year
CC: Delta, Mastercard, Solo, Switch, Visa

Weekend and weekday short breaks available all year.

Low season per wk
£200.00–£270.00
High season per wk
£260.00–£380.00

6

★★★
2 Units
Sleeping 2–4

WAGONERS & SHEPHERDS COTTAGES

Blean, Canterbury
Contact: Ms H Long, Wagoners & Shepherds Cottages, Denstroude Farm, Blean, Canterbury CT2 9JZ
T: (01227) 471513

OPEN All Year

Low season per wk
£170.00–£195.00
High season per wk
£200.00–£240.00

Two small, comfortable cottages on working farm. Close to Canterbury and within easy reach of Dover and many places of interest. Ideal for walking and bird-watching.

CARISBROOKE, Isle of Wight Map ref 2C3

★★★★
1 Unit
Sleeping 6

DAIRY COTTAGE

Carisbrooke, Newport
Contact: Mrs E R Yapp, Luckington Farm, Bowcombe Road, Carisbrooke, Newport PO30 3HT
T: (01983) 822951

OPEN All Year

Low season per wk
Min £350.00
High season per wk
Max £550.00

Detached stone cottage in rural position. Castle close by, excellent walking and beaches nearby. Separate garden, barbecue.

CHERWELL

See under Adderbury, Banbury, Bicester, Noke

CONFIRM YOUR BOOKING
You are advised to confirm your booking in writing.

CHICHESTER, West Sussex Map ref 2C3 *Tourist Information Centre Tel: (01243) 775888*

★★★★
1 Unit
Sleeping 4

APPLE TREE COTTAGE

Chichester
Contact: Mrs D Vickers
T: (01243) 839770
F: (01243) 839771
E: vickersdaphne@aol.com

Beautiful detached flint cottage with secluded walled garden, five minutes' walk from city centre and Festival Theatre. Furnished and equipped to highest standard. Three bedrooms: one double, one small (4ft) double, one single. Gas central heating, electricity, linen and weekly cleaning included. Colour brochure with tariff and availability. Open all year.

OPEN All Year

Low season per wk
£250.00–£320.00
High season per wk
£310.00–£550.00

★★★★
1 Unit
Sleeping 6

5 CALEDONIAN ROAD

Chichester
Contact: Miss V A Chubb, 33 Hillier Road, London SW11 6AX
T: (020) 7924 5446
E: victoriachubb@hotmail.com
I: www.visitsussex.org

Recently restored old townhouse with high-quality, contemporary interior in quiet road. Modern kitchen, real fire, books and games. Patio garden. City centre three minutes' walk. Ideal for beach or exploring the South Downs, Goodwood and evenings at theatre, cinema, restaurants. Wonderful location, summer or winter.

OPEN All Year

Low season per wk
£275.00–£350.00
High season per wk
£300.00–£425.00

★★★★
1 Unit
Sleeping 6

CORNERSTONES

Runcton, Chichester
Contact: Mrs V J Higgins, Greenacre, Goodwood Gardens, Runcton, Chichester PO20 1SP
T: (01243) 839096
F: (01243) 779658
E: vjrmhiggins@hotmail.com
I: www.visitbritain.com

Built in local style. Two bedrooms upstairs, one downstairs. Quiet village south of Chichester. Easy walking distance to pub/restaurant, church and post office/shop. Recently renovated, central heating. Equipped/furnished to a high standard. Garaging for two cars. Enclosed gardens with patio, tables and chairs. No smoking. Brochure available.

OPEN All Year
CC: Mastercard, Visa

Low season per wk
£375.00–£540.00
High season per wk
£540.00–£625.00

WEB
www.visitengland.com
Log on for information and inspiration. The latest information on places to visit, events and quality assessed accommodation.

CHICHESTER continued

★★★★

1 Unit
Sleeping 2

Distinctive, modernised, one-bedroomed cottage. Quiet village south of Chichester. Within easy walking distance of pub/restaurant, church, village post office/shop. Equipped and furnished to a high standard. Gas central heating. Off-road parking. Sun-trap patio with table and chairs. No smoking. Brochure available.

CYGNET COTTAGE

Runcton, Chichester

Contact: Mrs V J Higgins, Greenacre, Goodwood Gardens, Runcton, Chichester PO20 1SP
T: (01243) 839096
F: (01243) 779658
E: vjrmhiggins@hotmail.com
I: www.visitbritain.com

OPEN All Year
CC: Mastercard, Visa

Low season per wk
£215.00–£285.00
High season per wk
£285.00–£330.00

Rating
Applied For
2 Units

Beautiful one-bedroom flats on the first and second floor of this wing of a Victorian country house. Overlooking extensive garden, fields and downland just one mile from the city centre, Norman cathedral and Festival Theatre. Chichester Harbour five miles. Motor-racing circuit and horse-racing at Goodwood three miles.

FLATS 1 & 5 WEST BROYLE HOUSE

Chichester

Contact: Mrs P Gurland, Flat 6, 21 De Vere Gardens, London W8 5AN
T: (020) 7937 6337
F: (0207) 9382199

OPEN All Year

Low season per wk
£140.00–£220.00
High season per wk
£180.00–£450.00

★★★-★★★★

5 Units
Sleeping 2–5

18thC windmill and adjoining buildings converted into comfortable holiday homes, set in nearly an acre of attractive gardens with croquet, putting and barbecue. Situated in the country between the historic city of Chichester and the sea, with views over farmland, golf course and to the Downs.

HUNSTON MILL

Hunston, Chichester

Contact: Mr & Mrs R Beeny, Hunston Mill, Selsey Road, Hunston, Chichester PO20 1AU
T: (01243) 783375
F: (01243) 785179
E: rbeeny@freenetname.co.uk
I: www.hunstonmill.co.uk

OPEN All Year
CC: Mastercard, Visa

Low season per wk
£185.00–£245.00
High season per wk
£250.00–£400.00

ACCESSIBILITY

Look for the symbols which indicate National Accessible Scheme standards for hearing and visually impaired guests in addition to standards for guests with mobility impairment. Additional participants are shown in the listings at the back.

CHIDDINGLY, East Sussex Map ref 2D3

★★★-★★★★

6 Units
Sleeping 8–11

Spacious oast house, cottages and wing of Tudor manor in extensive grounds. Hard tennis court, indoor heated pool, sauna, jacuzzi, solarium. Children and pets welcome. Off-peak and short breaks available. Prices shown are for the cottages. Oast house is £1200-£1500.

PEKES

Chiddingly, Lewes
Contact: Ms E Morris, 124 Elm Park Mansions, Park Walk, London SW10 0AR
T: (020) 7352 8088
F: (020) 7352 8125
E: pekes.afa@virgin.net
I: www.pekesmanor.com

OPEN All Year
CC: Switch

Low season per wk
Min £385.00
High season per wk
Max £945.00

CHILD OKEFORD, Dorset Map ref 2B3

★★★

1 Unit
Sleeping 4

HILLCREST

Child Okeford, Blandford Forum
Contact: Mrs S Salisbury, Orchard Cottage, Duck Street, Child Okeford, Blandford Forum DT11 8ET
T: (01258) 861476
E: mikesal66@yahoo.co.uk
I: www.heartofdorset.easynet.co.uk

OPEN All Year

Low season per wk
£200.00–£300.00
High season per wk
£285.00–£375.00

Two-bedroomed character cottage in quiet village location. Flagstone floors, inglenook with woodburning stove. Well equipped throughout. Excellent walking, cycling, within easy reach of coast.

CHILHAM, Kent Map ref 3B3

★★★

2 Units
Sleeping 3

Charming, peaceful cottages in 15thC manor set in three acres. Picturesque setting on North Downs Way alongside Chilham Castle's parkland. Perfect for walking, exploring ancient woodland, chalk downs, Tudor village, castles. Canterbury six miles. Own large gardens, oak beams, inglenook fire/ woodburning stove. Immaculate, well equipped. New bathrooms/ kitchen installed 2002. Detailed brochure.

MONCKTON COTTAGES

Chilham, Canterbury
Contact: Mrs Helen Kirwan, Monckton Cottages, Heron Manor, Mountain Street, Chilham, Canterbury CT4 8DG
T: (01227) 730256
F: (01227) 732423
E: monckton@rw-kirwan.demon.co.uk

OPEN All Year

Low season per wk
£170.00–£320.00
High season per wk
£310.00–£340.00

USE YOUR *i*s

There are more than 550 Tourist Information Centres throughout England offering friendly help with accommodation and holiday ideas as well as suggestions of places to visit and things to do. You'll find TIC addresses in the local Phone Book.

CHRISTCHURCH, Dorset Map ref 2B3 *Tourist Information Centre Tel: (01202) 471780*

★★★

4 Units

The Black House, formerly a boat builder's house, dating back some two centuries, is set in a stunning maritime location on the sand spit at Mudeford which guards the entrance to Christchurch Harbour. With water on three sides it affords stunning, panoramic views in every direction. Self-contained apartments. No pets/smoking.

THE BLACK HOUSE

Bournemouth

Contact: The Black House, 51 Carbery Avenue, Southbourne, Bournemouth BH6 3LN
T: 07855 280191
F: (01202) 483555
E: theblackhouse@hotmail.com
I: www.theblackhouse.co.uk

OPEN All Year

Low season per wk
£295.00–£495.00
High season per wk
£655.00–£895.00

★★★★

1 Unit
Sleeping 10

Luxurious, south-facing, three-storey property with river frontage, outdoor jacuzzi and private mooring. Ten minutes' walk from Christchurch town centre. Quiet location. Parking for four cars.

RIVERBANK HOUSE

Christchurch

Contact: Ms S Burrows, Oakdene Orchard, Ringwood Road, Three Legged Cross, Wimborne Minster BH21 6RB
T: (01202) 828487
F: (01202) 828487
E: handbleisure@amserve.net
I: riverbankholidays.co.uk

OPEN All Year

Short breaks available.

Low season per wk
£550.00–£780.00
High season per wk
£820.00–£1,300.00

CORFE CASTLE, Dorset Map ref 2B3

★★★★

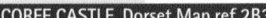

6 Units
Sleeping 5–6

Scoles Manor Barns are next to historic Scoles Manor (Listed Grade II) and have been converted into beautifully appointed units. They are in a superb rural setting with 30 acres of meadows and woodlands and spectacular views over Corfe Castle and the Purbeck countryside.

SCOLES MANOR

Kingston, Corfe Castle

Contact: Mr & Mrs P B Bell, Scoles Manor, Kingston, Corfe Castle BH20 5LG
T: (01929) 480312
F: (01929) 481237
E: peter@scoles.co.uk
I: www.scoles.co.uk

OPEN All Year

Winter breaks – perfect for groups up to 20.

Low season per wk
£225.00–£375.00
High season per wk
£550.00–£1,025.00

COTSWOLDS

See under Standlake

See also Cotswolds in Heart of England region

SB

SPECIAL BREAKS

Many establishments offer special promotions and themed breaks. These are highlighted in red. (All such offers are subject to availability.)

DORKING, Surrey Map ref 2D2

★★★
2 Units
Sleeping 2–4

BULMER FARM

Holmbury St Mary, Dorking
Contact: Mrs G M Hill, Bulmer Farm, Holmbury St Mary, Dorking RH5 6LG
T: (01306) 730210

OPEN All Year

Low season per wk £220.00–£300.00
High season per wk £290.00–£380.00

30-acre beef farm. Two single-storey units converted from 17thC farm building. Two-person unit suitable for disabled and four-person unit together form a courtyard to the farmhouse.

DYMCHURCH, Kent Map ref 3B4

★★★★
1 Unit
Sleeping 7

DYMCHURCH HOUSE

Dymchurch, Romney Marsh
Contact: 53 Crescent Road, Sidcup DA15 7HW
T: (020) 8300 2100
E: dymchurchhouse@btopenworld.com

OPEN All Year

Low season per wk £280.00–£330.00
High season per wk £390.00–£550.00

Spacious, well-equipped, detached property in a prime position. Ideal for its superb sandy beach accessed direct via footpath. Excellent location for visiting tourist attractions.

EAST COWES, Hampshire Map ref 2C3

★★★★
1 Unit
Sleeping 5

BUTTERCUP COTTAGE

Whippingham, East Cowes
Contact: Mr G Newnham, Alberts Dairy, Heathfield Farm, Whippingham, Isle of Wight PO32 6NQ
T: (01983) 884553
E: post@newnhams.freeserve.co.uk

Beautifully converted dairy in rural location situated midway between Ryde and Newport, with easy access to all island attractions. Two bedrooms, sitting room, fully fitted kitchen and dining area. French doors opening onto patio and enclosed garden. Views across farmland to the River Medina.

OPEN All Year

Short breaks available Oct–Mar.

Low season per wk £350.00–£400.00
High season per wk £450.00–£550.00

EASTCHURCH, Kent Map ref 3B3

★★★-★★★★
5 Units
Sleeping 4–6

CONNETTS FARM HOLIDAY COTTAGES

Eastchurch, Sheerness
Contact: Mrs M A Phipps, Connetts Farm Holiday Cottages, Plough Road, Eastchurch, Sheerness ME12 4JL
T: (01795) 880358
F: (01795) 880358
E: connetts@btconnect.com
I: www.connettsfarm.co.uk

Tastefully converted barns on 130-acre working farm. South Barn (two bedrooms) overlooks lawns, ponds and open farmland and North Barn (three bedrooms, one with en suite shower and basin) overlooks the farm and the sea. Sheerness beach, naturist beach and RSPB reserve. London 50 miles, Canterbury 30 miles.

OPEN All Year

Low season per wk £140.00–£420.00
High season per wk £260.00–£495.00

CHECK THE MAPS

**The colour maps at the front of this guide show all the cities, towns and villages for which you will find accommodation entries.
Refer to the town index to find the page on which they are listed.**

ELHAM, Kent Map ref 3B4

★★★★

1 Unit
Sleeping 4

LOWER COURT COTTAGE

Ottinge, Canterbury
Contact: Mr & Mrs J G Caunce, Lower Court, Shuttlesfield Lane, Ottinge, Canterbury CT4 6XJ
T: (01303) 862124
F: (01303) 864231
E: caunce@ottinge.fsnet.co.uk

Refurbished, light and airy country cottage near the beautiful village of Elham. Easy access to Canterbury, Hythe and the Channel Tunnel. Peaceful courtyard setting off delightful country lane. Two bathrooms, one en suite, sitting and dining rooms, modern kitchen, garden, tennis court and secluded patio.

OPEN All Year

Enquire about short breaks. Minimum price £225.

Low season per wk
£265.00–£320.00
High season per wk
£300.00–£520.00

EPSOM, Surrey Map ref 2D2

★★★

1 Unit
Sleeping 5

7 GREAT TATTENHAMS

Epsom
Contact: Mrs M K Willis, 7 Great Tattenhams, Epsom KT18 5RF
T: (01737) 354112

OPEN All Year

Low season per wk
£150.00–£175.00
High season per wk
£200.00–£225.00

Modern, spacious, comfortably furnished first floor flat. A good touring centre for London and the South East. Superstore nearby.

ETCHINGHAM, East Sussex Map ref 3B4

★★★★

1 Unit
Sleeping 5

MOON COTTAGE

Etchingham, Wadhurst
Contact: Mrs J L Harrison
T: (01580) 879328
F: (01580) 879729
E: enquiries@harrison-holidays.co.uk
I: www.harrison-holidays.co.uk

Beautifully refurbished/equipped cottage. Country walks in Area of Outstanding Natural Beauty. Convenient for many places of interest, NT properties and coastal resorts. Station two miles, with trains to London (one hour) and south coast. Conservatory, large garden and patio with furniture and barbecue. Log burner and central heating. Off-road parking. Pets welcome.

OPEN All Year

Short breaks available Nov-May, minimum 3 days.

Low season per wk
£250.00–£300.00
High season per wk
£365.00–£475.00

AT-A-GLANCE SYMBOLS

Symbols at the end of each accommodation entry give useful information about services and facilities. A key to symbols can be found inside the back cover flap. Keep this open for easy reference.

EVERTON, Hampshire Map ref 2B3

★★★★

1 Unit
Sleeping 8

2 UPLAY COTTAGES

Everton, Lymington
Contact: Ms J Taylor, Three Corners, Centre Lane, Everton, Lymington SO41 0JP
T: (01590) 645217
F: (01590) 673633
E: tommy.tiddles@virgin.net
I: www.halcyonholidays.com

A beautifully refurbished, comfortable Edwardian cottage set in the heart of the village with shops, pub, coast and forest nearby. Larger cottages/two-person studio in Lymington and Brockenhurst with direct forest access, large gardens, open fires, antique furniture. Weekly or weekend/mid-week breaks. Detailed information and pictures on website.

OPEN All Year
CC: Amex, Delta, Mastercard, Solo, Switch, Visa

Mid-week/weekend bookings. 70% off-peak discount for 1-2 persons. Available all year round.

Low season per wk
£238.00–£460.00
High season per wk
£367.00–£790.00

EXTON, Hampshire Map ref 2C3

★★★★

4 Units
Sleeping 5

BEACON HILL FARM COTTAGES
Exton, Southampton
Contact: Mrs J Smith
T: (01730) 829724
F: (01730) 829833
E: chris@martin4031.freeserve.co.uk
I: www.beaconhillcottages.co.uk

OPEN All Year

Low season per wk
Max £300.00
High season per wk
Max £450.00

Cottages in a converted barn, formerly part of a working farm. Idyllic setting, stunning views of Meon Valley farmland.

FARNHAM, Surrey Map ref 2C2 *Tourist Information Centre Tel: (01252) 715109*

★★

3 Units
Sleeping 2–5

HIGH WRAY
Farnham
Contact: Mrs A G N Crawford, High Wray, 73 Lodge Hill Road, Farnham GU10 3RB
T: (01252) 715589
F: (01252) 715746
E: crawford@highwray73.co.uk

OPEN All Year

Low season per wk
£175.00–£350.00
High season per wk
£200.00–£450.00

Open-plan studio in private corner of the garden plus garden flats purpose built for disabled people. Bed and breakfast also available.

★★★★

13 Units
Sleeping 2–6

TILFORD WOODS

Tilford, Farnham
Contact: The Booking Manager
T: (01252) 792199
F: (01252) 781027
E: admin@tilfordwoods.co.uk
I: www.tilfordwoods.co.uk

Tilford Woods comprises one- to three-bedroom, fully fitted and equipped, luxury timber lodges. The one-bedroom 'Cobbett' lodges have a 4-poster bed, en suite bathroom with sauna, spa and outside hot tub. Tilford Woods is the ideal base for exploring the wonderful surrounding countryside and the many local attractions.

OPEN All Year
CC: Delta, Mastercard, Solo, Switch, Visa

Short breaks available.

Low season per wk
£371.00–£413.00
High season per wk
£595.00–£700.00

VISITBRITAIN'S WHERE TO STAY
Please mention this guide when making your booking.

FAVERSHAM, Kent Map ref 3B3 *Tourist Information Centre Tel: (01795) 534542*

★★★★

1 Unit
Sleeping 4

MONKS COTTAGE

Leaveland, Faversham
Contact: Mr & Mrs G A Darby, Monks Cottage, Leaveland, Faversham ME13 0NP
T: (01233) 740419
F: (01233) 740419

Modern cottage of brick construction in grounds of period thatched family home. Set in four acres in quiet, picturesque valley. Ideal for country walks. Situated within four miles M2/M20. Easy access to coastal resorts and Channel ports.

High season per wk
£300.00–£400.00

FERRING, West Sussex Map ref 2D3

★★★

1 Unit
Sleeping 4

5 LAMORNA GARDENS

Ferring, Worthing
Contact: Mrs Elsden & Mary Fitzgerald
T: (01903) 238582
F: (01903) 230266

OPEN All Year

Spacious, detached bungalow situated on the seafront, just three miles from Worthing. Supermarket and tearooms six minutes' walk. Non-smokers only. Mob: 07860 699268.

Low season per wk
£300.00
High season per wk
£380.00–£500.00

FINSTOCK, Oxfordshire Map ref 2C1

★★

1 Unit
Sleeping 5

WYCHWOOD

Finstock, Chipping Norton
Contact: Mrs B Grain, 40 School Road, Finstock, Oxford OX7 3DJ
T: (01993) 868249
E: bgrain@wychwoodcottage.co.uk
I: www.wychwoodcottage.co.uk

17thC cottage situated on the edge of the Cotswolds in peaceful Oxfordshire village. Many attractions include scenic countryside, walking and easy access to Oxford and Stratford.

OPEN All Year

Low season per wk
£200.00–£250.00
High season per wk
£250.00–£350.00

FOLKESTONE, Kent Map ref 3B4 *Tourist Information Centre Tel: (01303) 258594*

★★-★★★

12 Units

THE GRAND

Folkestone
Contact: Mr M Stainer
T: (01303) 220440
F: (01303) 220220
E: enquiries@grand-uk.com
I: www.grand-uk.com

The Grand is a fine listed building situated on The Leas, the world famous grassy clifftop promenade running from the town centre along the southern side of the spacious and gracious west end of Folkestone. It enjoys uninterrupted views across the ever changing seascape to France.

OPEN All Year
CC: Delta, JCB, Mastercard, Solo, Switch, Visa

Short breaks, Mon-Fri or Fri-Mon: low season – min £60, max £140; high season – min £125, max £255.

Low season per wk
£90.00–£210.00
High season per wk
£190.00–£380.00

VISITOR ATTRACTIONS **For ideas on places to visit refer to the introduction at the beginning of this section. Look out too for the ETC's Quality Assured Visitor Attraction signs.**

FORDINGBRIDGE, Hampshire Map ref 2B3

★★★★
8 Units
Sleeping 4–18

BURGATE MANOR FARM HOLIDAYS

Fordingbridge
Contact: Mrs B D Stallard, Burgate Manor Farm Holidays, Burgate Manor Farm, Fordingbridge SP6 1LX
T: (01425) 653908
F: (01425) 653908
E: info@newforestcottages.com
I: www.newforestcottages.com

OPEN All Year

Low season per wk
£248.00–£1,000.00
High season per wk
£358.00–£2,600.00

New Forest/Avon Valley. Farm cottages and large, newly converted, galleried, beamed barn. Short walk pub/restaurant. Games barn. Fishing. Grazing. Beach 15 miles.

★★★★
1 Unit
Sleeping 5

FIR TREE FARM COTTAGE

Stuckton, Fordingbridge
Contact: Mr & Mrs C Proctor, Fir Tree Farm, Frogham Hill, Stuckton, Fordingbridge SP6 2HH
T: (01425) 654001
E: cjproctor@onetel.net.uk
I: www.firtreefarmcottage.co.uk

Spacious, comfortable, three-bedroomed cottage situated on owners' farm in small hamlet within New Forest boundary. Fully fitted kitchen, large secluded garden with patio. Short walk to open forest, farm shop, two excellent pubs and restaurant. Ideally situated for south coast beaches, country walks, horse-riding, golf and fishing. Brochure available.

OPEN All Year

Short breaks available Oct-Mar.

Low season per wk
Min £250.00
High season per wk
£350.00–£485.00

★★★
1 Unit
Sleeping 4

GLENCAIRN

Damerham, Fordingbridge
Contact: Mrs C Tiller, 2 Fernlea, Sandleheath, Fordingbridge SP6 1PN
T: (01425) 652506

Low season per wk
£200.00–£260.00
High season per wk
£260.00–£390.00

Detached cottage in pleasant, friendly village close to New Forest. Comfortably furnished and well maintained. Three bedrooms, well-equipped kitchen, large, quiet garden. Brochure available.

3

FRESHWATER, Isle of Wight Map ref 2C3

★★★
29 Units
Sleeping 4

FARRINGFORD HOTEL

Freshwater Bay
Contact: Miss L Hollyhead, Farringford Hotel, Bedbury Lane, Freshwater PO40 9PE
T: (01983) 752500
F: (01983) 756515
E: enquiries@farringford.co.uk
I: www.farringford.co.uk

Once the home of Alfred Lord Tennyson, now a country-style house with self-catering units of three different styles to suit individual needs. Set within 35 acres of mature pastureland incorporating a 9-hole par 3 golf course, tennis, outdoor heated pool, Bistro Bar and bowls.

OPEN All Year
CC: Amex, Delta, Mastercard, Switch, Visa

Fully inclusive Christmas packages available. Ferry-inclusive deals available. Subsidised child and pet rates available.

Low season per wk
Min £315.00
High season per wk
Min £749.00

PRICES
Please check prices and other details at the time of booking.

FRESHWATER continued

★★★

1 Unit
Sleeping 4

LITTLE RABBITS

Freshwater
Contact: Mrs H Long, Windrush, Wellow, Yarmouth PO41 0TA
T: (01983) 761506
E: hugh7@bushinternet.com

Delightful modern holiday bungalow in an exclusive, quiet development overlooking open wildlife landscape to front and The Needles and Solent to side and rear. Wooded walks to nearby Yarmouth and beyond, with Blue Flag bathing beach a few minutes' walk away. Ideal base to explore this lovely island. Owner managed.

3- or 4-night stays welcome according to availability – phone for prices and ferry offers out of season.

Low season per wk
Min £150.00
High season per wk
Max £290.00

GILLINGHAM, Dorset Map ref 2B3

★★★★

1 Unit
Sleeping 6

MEADS FARM

Gillingham
Contact: Mrs J A Wallis, Meads Farm, Stour Provost, Gillingham SP8 5RX
T: (01747) 838265
F: (01258) 821123

Superb detached bungalow with spacious, very well-equipped accommodation. Two double, one twin bedroom. 0.5 acres of lawns. Coarse fishing 150 yards, also lake fishing 0.5 miles. Outstanding views over the Blackmore Vale. Many places of interest just a short car ride away.

OPEN All Year

Low season per wk
£240.00–£350.00
High season per wk
£385.00–£430.00

★★★★

1 Unit
Sleeping 2

WOOLFIELDS BARN

Gillingham
Contact: Mr & Mrs B Thomas, Woolfields Barn, Woolfields Farm, Milton on Stour, Gillingham SP8 5PX
T: (01747) 824729
F: (01747) 824986
E: OThomas453@aol.com

OPEN All Year

Low season per wk
Min £150.00
High season per wk
Max £250.00

Superb, very comfortable barn conversion equipped to a high standard. Games room, centrally heated, linen provided. Near Stourhead.

GOSPORT, Hampshire Map ref 2C3 *Tourist Information Centre Tel: (023) 9252 2944*

★★★

1 Unit
Sleeping 10

CAPTAINS FOLLY

Gosport
Contact: Mr J M White, 8 Cambridge Road, Lee on the Solent PO13 9DH
T: (023) 9255 0883
I: www.brook.white1.btinternet.co.uk/index.html

OPEN All Year

Low season per wk
£375.00–£450.00
High season per wk
£450.00–£500.00

Character house with four bedrooms and three bathrooms. Large garden leading to shore. Adjacent Priddy's Hard waterbus to Portsmouth. Ideal for New Forest, Winchester and Salisbury. Parking.

GOUDHURST, Kent Map ref 3B4

★★★★

3 Units

THREE CHIMNEYS FARM

Goudhurst, Cranbrook
Contact: Mrs M Fuller
T: (01580) 212175
F: (01580) 212175
E: marionfuller@threechimneysfarm.co.uk
I: www.threechimneysfarm.co.uk

OPEN All Year
CC: Delta, JCB, Mastercard, Solo, Switch, Visa

Low season per wk
£200.00–£400.00
High season per wk
£300.00–£700.00

80-acre mixed farm. Spacious cottages in a beautiful location, very quiet but not isolated.

GRAVESEND, Kent Map ref 3B3 *Tourist Information Centre Tel: (01474) 337600*

★★★★

1 Unit
Sleeping 4

A two-bedroom, en suite, first floor flat overlooking the frequently trafficked River Thames, fitted and furnished to a high standard. On-site parking, but close to all town centre amenities and railway station. Convenient for London sightseeing, and a good base for touring Kent, Sussex and Essex.

RUSSELL QUAY

Gravesend
Contact: Mr T M Dickety, 1 Brimstone Hill, Meopham, Gravesend DA13 0BN
T: (01474) 573045
F: (01474) 573049
E: mikedickety@beeb.net
I: www.halcyon-gifts.co.uk/holidaylet.html

OPEN All Year
CC: Mastercard, Visa

Short breaks (mid-week and weekend) available all year. Must be booked within 4 weeks of start date.

Low season per wk
£190.00–£300.00
High season per wk
£300.00–£420.00

GREAT MILTON, Oxfordshire Map ref 2C1

★★★★

6 Units
Sleeping 4

VIEWS FARM BARNS

Great Milton, Oxford
Contact: Mr & Mrs C O Peers, Views Farm Barns, Views Farm, Great Milton, Oxford OX44 7NW
T: (01844) 279352
F: (01844) 279362
E: info@viewsfarmbarns.co.uk
I: www.viewsfarmbarns.co.uk

OPEN All Year
CC: JCB, Mastercard, Solo, Switch, Visa

Low season per wk
£220.00–£265.00
High season per wk
£370.00–£435.00

400-acre arable and mixed farm. Converted stable block forming well-appointed holiday flats. Close to Oxford and the M40. Superb views of Thame Valley.

GUILDFORD, Surrey Map ref 2D2 *Tourist Information Centre Tel: (01483) 444333*

★★★

1 Unit
Sleeping 6

LAVENDER

Guildford
Contact: Mr & Mrs E Liew, Mandarin, Pewley Point, Pewley Hill, Guildford GU1 4LF
T: (01483) 506819
F: (01483) 506819
E: shirleyliew9@hotmail.com

OPEN All Year

Low season per wk
£450.00–£550.00
High season per wk
£450.00–£550.00

Well-presented, fully furnished, comfortable house, conveniently situated in town centre, close to high street shops, river, theatre, leisure facilities and railway station. Airports 40 minutes.

★★

36 Units
Sleeping 4–6

UNIVERSITY OF SURREY

Guildford
Contact: Conference Office, University of Surrey, Guildford GU2 7XH
T: (01483) 689157
F: (01483) 579266
E: k.stacey@surrey.ac.uk
I: www.surrey.ac.uk/conferences

CC: Delta, Mastercard, Switch, Visa

Low season per wk
£310.00–£370.00
High season per wk
£310.00–£370.00

Modern, self-contained accommodation for self-catering holidays on attractive campus. One mile from Guildford centre. Ideal base to enjoy London and South East England.

TOWN INDEX

This can be found at the back of this guide. If you know where you want to stay, the index will give you the page number listing accommodation in your chosen town, city or village.

HASTINGLEIGH, Kent Map ref 3B4

★★★★

1 Unit
Sleeping 2

STAPLE FARM

Hastingleigh, Ashford
Contact: Mr & Mrs C H Martindale, Staple Farm, Hastingleigh, Ashford TN25 5HF
T: (01233) 750248
F: (01233) 750249

Stable conversion displaying beams and original features, yet offering all modern amenities. Situated in Area of Outstanding Natural Beauty with excellent walks from front door, including the North Downs Way. Within easy reach of Canterbury, Eurostar terminals, Channel ports of Dover and Folkestone, plus many places of historic interest.

Low season per wk
£250.00
High season per wk
£250.00–£350.00

HASTINGS, East Sussex Map ref 3B4 *Tourist Information Centre Tel: (01424) 781111*

★★★

1 Unit
Sleeping 4

ROSE HOUSE
Hastings
Contact: Mrs S E Hill
T: (01424) 754812
F: (01424) 754812
E: hillbusybee@aol.com

OPEN All Year
CC: JCB, Mastercard, Solo, Switch, Visa

Low season per wk
Max £195.00
High season per wk
Max £285.00

Home from home, fully furnished flat, short walking distance to all attractions.

HAYLING ISLAND, Hampshire

See display ad below

HENFIELD, West Sussex Map ref 2D3

★★★

2 Units
Sleeping 4–5

NEW HALL COTTAGE & NEW HALL HOLIDAY FLAT

Small Dole, Henfield
Contact: Mrs M W Carreck, New Hall, Small Dole, Henfield BN5 9YJ
T: (01273) 492546

Self-contained flat and 17thC cottage attached to manor house. Set in 3.5 acres of mature gardens and surrounded by farmland. Within easy reach of famous Sussex gardens, Nymans, High Beeches, Wakehurst Place, Leonardslee, and less than an hour from Wisley. Or visit the towns of Brighton, Arundel, Lewes and Chichester, the South Downs and the coast.

OPEN All Year

Short breaks available. Nov-Mar: £90 for 2 nights, each extra night £35. Apr-Oct: £130 for 2 nights, each extra night £40.

Low season per wk
£175.00–£250.00
High season per wk
£270.00–£335.00

Millers

SELF-CATERING HOLIDAY ACCOMMODATION

HAYLING ISLAND, HAMPSHIRE

Self-Catering houses, bungalow's and flats near the seafront. Free colour brochure.

19 Mengham Road, Hayling Island, Hampshire PO11 9BG
T: 023 9246 5951
E: millers@haylingproperty.co.uk W: www.haylingproperty.co.uk

HOVE

See under Brighton & Hove

IBSLEY, Hampshire Map ref 2B3

★★★★

1 Unit
Sleeping 6

CHOCOLATE BOX COTTAGE
Ibsley, Ringwood
Contact: Mrs F A Higham
T: (01268) 741036
F: (01268) 741990
E: enquiries@chocolateboxcottage.co.uk
I: www.chocolateboxcottage.co.uk

OPEN All Year

Low season per wk
£485.00
High season per wk
£600.00–£685.00

Beautiful 'chocolate box' cottage set in 0.5-acre grounds, on the edge of the New Forest. High-standard accommodation. Pets welcome. Smoking permitted.

ISLE OF WIGHT

See under Bembridge, Brighstone, Carisbrooke, Freshwater, Newport, Ryde, Seaview, Totland Bay, Whitwell

IVINGHOE, Buckinghamshire Map ref 2D1

★★★

7 Units
Sleeping 6

TOWN FARM HOLIDAY COTTAGES
Ivinghoe, Leighton Buzzard
Contact: Mrs A Leach, Town Farm Holiday Cottages, Town Farm, Ivinghoe, Leighton Buzzard LU7 9EL
T: (01296) 660279
F: (01296) 668455
E: angie@unlimitedlets.com
I: www.unlimitedlets.com

OPEN All Year
CC: Delta, Mastercard, Switch, Visa

Low season per wk
£325.00–£350.00
High season per wk
£350.00–£450.00

600-acre mixed farm. Some of the cottages have views over Ivinghoe Beacon and are situated on the B489 outside Ivinghoe.

LANGTON MATRAVERS, Dorset Map ref 2B3

★★★

1 Unit
Sleeping 5

FLAT 5 GARFIELD HOUSE
Langton Matravers, Swanage
Contact: Miss S A Inge, Flat A, 147 Holland Road, London W14 8AS
T: (020) 7602 4945
E: sueinge@hotmail.com
I: www.langton-matravers.co.uk

OPEN All Year

Low season per wk
£210.00–£280.00
High season per wk
£280.00–£350.00

Spacious and homely, well-equipped apartment in old Purbeck-stone house in friendly village. Lovely views over sea and hills. Ten minutes' walk to cliff top.

5

MAP REFERENCES The map references refer to the colour maps at the front of this guide. The first figure is the map number; the letter and figure which follow indicate the grid reference on the map.

Island Cottage Holidays
ISLE OF WIGHT

ETC ★★★ - ★★★★★
Low season (October-May)
£135-£595

High season (June-September)
£198-£1,225

T:(01929) 480080
F:(01929) 481070
E:enq@islandcottageholidays.com
I:www.islandcottageholidays.com

Short breaks also available.

Charming cottages in delightful rural surroundings and close to the sea. Beautiful views - attractive gardens - some with swimming pools. Situated throughout the Isle of Wight. Properties sleeping 1-14.

LEE ON THE SOLENT, Hampshire Map ref 2C3

★★★

1 Unit
Sleeping 6

THE CHART HOUSE

Lee on the Solent
Contact: Ms M Kinnear-White, 6 Cambridge Road, Lee on the Solent PO13 9DH
T: (023) 9255 4145
E: marion_kinnear-white@talk21.com
I: www.brook.white1.btinternet.co.uk

OPEN All Year

Low season per wk £250.00–£300.00
High season per wk £350.00–£390.00

Comfortable, detached, three-bedroomed family home, close to seafront. Enclosed patio/garden. Off-road parking. Heated indoor pool available for private hire next door.

LEWES, East Sussex Map ref 2D3 *Tourist Information Centre Tel: (01273) 483448*

★★★

1 Unit
Sleeping 4

5 BUCKHURST CLOSE

Lewes
Contact: Mrs S Foulds, 66 Houndean Rise, Lewes BN7 1EJ
T: (01273) 474755
F: (01273) 474755

OPEN All Year

Low season per wk Min £210.00
High season per wk Max £230.00

Modern terraced house, fully equipped. Small garden, parking space. Easy walking distance to town. Five minutes' drive to station or Glyndebourne.

LOCKS HEATH, Hampshire Map ref 2C3

★★★★

1 Unit
Sleeping 2

STEPPING STONES

Locks Heath, Southampton
Contact: Mrs B A Habens
T: (01489) 572604
E: jimhabens@aol.com
I: http://members.lycos.co.uk/selfcateringannexe/

OPEN All Year except Christmas

Low season per wk £250.00
High season per wk £250.00

One-bedroom annexe adjoining owners' bungalow. Very high-standard accommodation in a delightful, secluded garden. Easy reach of historic Portsmouth and Winchester, New Forest, Bournemouth etc.

LOWER BEEDING, West Sussex Map ref 2D3

★★★-★★★★★

3 Units
Sleeping 4–6

BLACK COTTAGE, THE LITTLE BARN & THE OLD DAIRY

Lower Beeding, Horsham
Contact: Mrs V Storey, Newells Farm, Newells Farmhouse, Newells Lane, Lower Beeding, Horsham RH13 6LN
T: (01403) 891326
F: (01403) 891530
E: vicky.storey@btinternet.com

OPEN All Year

Low season per wk £220.00–£280.00
High season per wk £270.00–£495.00

Secluded 19thC cottage with lovely views. Also newly converted cottages in farmyard. All with gardens. 650-acre arable and woodland farm.

LYMINGTON, Hampshire Map ref 2C3

★★★★

1 Unit
Sleeping 6

BOURNE HOUSE

Lymington
Contact: Mr & Mrs P J Mare, Maybury Wood Cottage, The Ridge, Woking GU22 7EG
T: (01483) 772086
F: (01483) 772086
E: jppmare@aol.com

OPEN All Year

Low season per wk £350.00–£595.00
High season per wk £650.00

Beautifully furnished detached house near marina. Pretty garden/patio. Spacious living/dining room, ground floor double bedroom, bathroom, two double bedrooms, upstairs bathroom, balcony, garage.

★★★

1 Unit
Sleeping 5

FIR TREE COTTAGE

Lymington
Contact: Mrs B Saword, 1 Merlewood Court, Lyon Avenue, New Milton BH25 6AP
T: (01425) 617219

OPEN All Year except Christmas

Low season per wk £200.00–£205.00
High season per wk £270.00–£420.00

Period cottage 1.5 miles from open forest. Enclosed garden, good for pets and children. Traditional furnishings, books, fitted carpets, double glazing, toys.

LYMINGTON continued

★★★★ 1 Unit Sleeping 5	**17 SOUTHAMPTON ROAD** Lymington Contact: J Stevens & Andrew Baxendine, Elm Cottage, Pilley Bailey, Pilley, Lymington SO41 5QT T: (01590) 676445 E: juleestevens@aol.com *Beautifully presented three-bedroom Georgian townhouse. Close proximity to shops, restaurants and pretty town quay. Unwind with fresh flowers and welcome pack on arrival.*	OPEN All Year except Christmas	Low season per wk £300.00–£400.00 High season per wk £500.00–£600.00

LYNDHURST, Hampshire Map ref 2C3

★★★★ 1 Unit Sleeping 4	**HOLLY COTTAGE** Lyndhurst Contact: Mr & Mrs F S Turner, Greensward, The Crescent, Woodlands Road, Ashurst, Southampton SO40 7AQ T: (023) 8029 2374 F: (023) 8029 2374 E: sam@turner402.fsnet.co.uk I: http://mysite.freeserve.com/hollycottnewforest *Cosy, comfortably furnished 19thC cottage 50 yards from forest. Personally renovated and maintained by local owner. Children welcome. No short breaks.*	OPEN All Year	Low season per wk £275.00–£375.00 High season per wk £375.00–£475.00
★★★★ 1 Unit Sleeping 4	**YORKE COTTAGE** Lyndhurst Contact: Mr J Drew, Burwood Lodge, 27 Romsey Road, Lyndhurst SO43 7AA T: (023) 8028 2445 F: (023) 8028 4104 E: burwood.1@ukonline.co.uk I: www.burwoodlodge.co.uk *Pretty Victorian cottage in peaceful location, minutes from open forest and village high street. Superbly and tastefully appointed. Linen, gas, electricity included. Private parking.*	OPEN All Year	Low season per wk £195.00–£390.00 High season per wk £390.00–£500.00

MAIDSTONE, Kent Map ref 3B3 *Tourist Information Centre Tel: (01622) 602169*

★★ 1 Unit Sleeping 3	**LAVENDER COTTAGE** Maidstone Contact: Mr & Mrs L R Hulm, Lavender Cottage, Headcorn Road, Grafty Green, Maidstone ME17 2AN T: (01622) 850287 F: (01622) 850287 E: lavender@nascr.net I: www.oas.co.uk/ukcottages/lavender *17thC, oak-beamed, 2-bedroomed cottage. Log fire, fully equipped. In pretty village, close to Leeds Castle, with easy access to M20, Channel Tunnel and ports and London.* 5	OPEN All Year	Low season per wk £150.00–£180.00 High season per wk £180.00–£250.00

MILFORD-ON-SEA, Hampshire Map ref 2C3

★★★★ 1 Unit Sleeping 5	**BETHANY** Milford-on-Sea, Lymington Contact: Mrs J A Green, The Vicarage, Station Road, Sway, Lymington SO41 6BA T: (01590) 683389 F: (01590) 683389 E: jackiegreen@onetel.net.uk I: www.bethany-milford.com *Spacious, well-appointed bungalow. Quiet setting. Close to village centre, beach. South-facing, secluded walled garden/patio. Discount for couples. Ideal for exploring forest, coast, IOW.* 8		Low season per wk £250.00–£350.00 High season per wk £420.00–£580.00

SYMBOLS The symbols in each entry give information about services and facilities. A key to these symbols appears at the back of this guide.

MILFORD-ON-SEA continued

★★★

1 Unit
Sleeping 5

WINDMILL COTTAGE
Milford-on-Sea, Lymington
Contact: Mrs S M Perham
T: (01590) 643516
F: (01590) 641255

OPEN All Year

Low season per wk
£215.00–£235.00
High season per wk
£265.00–£515.00

Three-bedroomed, Georgian-style house in select residential area close to village, sea and the New Forest.

MILTON ABBAS, Dorset Map ref 2B3

★★★★★

1 Unit
Sleeping 4

LITTLE HEWISH BARN

Milton Abbas, Blandford Forum
Contact: Mr T M Dunn, 2 Little Hewish Cottages, Milton Abbas, Blandford Forum DT11 0DP
T: (01258) 881235
F: (01258) 881393
E: terry@littlehewish.co.uk
I: www.littlehewish.co.uk

Converted 150-year-old brick and flint barn in lovely rural setting. Spacious, open-plan living/dining area, woodburning stove, small private garden. Children welcome, well-behaved pets by arrangement. Pre-arrival shopping/baby-sitting available at cost. Flexible, family-run business. Fully inclusive prices, no hidden extras!

OPEN All Year

'Per person per night' pricing (excl peak periods).

Low season per wk
Min £210.00
High season per wk
Max £550.00

★★-★★★★★

2 Units
Sleeping 5–10

PARK FARM

Milton Abbas, Blandford Forum
Contact: Mrs A Burch
T: (01258) 880828
E: burch@parkfarmcottages.co.uk
I: www.parkfarmcottages.co.uk

Beautiful architect-designed conversion of Grade II Listed thatched barn with very spacious accommodation. Underfloor heating, inglenook fireplaces with woodburners. Set 0.5 miles from the village with stunning views to Poole harbour and the Purbeck hills. A peaceful and relaxing site with superb woodland walking, cycling and horse-riding.

OPEN All Year

2- or 3-night stays are offered in off-peak periods.

Low season per wk
£250.00–£625.00
High season per wk
£385.00–£780.00

★★★★

1 Unit
Sleeping 6

PRIMROSE COTTAGE

Milton Abbas, Blandford Forum
Contact: Mrs G D Garvey, Brook Cottage, 1 Long Street, Cerne Abbas, Dorchester DT2 7JF
T: (01300) 341352
F: (01300) 341352
E: tgarvey@ragtime99.freeserve.co.uk
I: www.miltonabbas-primrosecottage.co.uk

Grade II Listed, 18thC thatched cob cottage set in The Street in the unique village of Milton Abbas, created by Lord Milton and landscaped by 'Capability' Brown. This cosy and comfortable cottage has everything you would expect, from low doors to inglenook fireplace. In the centre of Hardy country, an ideal base for walkers and romantics.

OPEN All Year

Low season per wk
£195.00–£345.00
High season per wk
£345.00–£445.00

MILTON KEYNES, Buckinghamshire Map ref 2C1

★★★
2 Units
Sleeping 2

33 & 35 BROOKSIDE CLOSE
Old Stratford, Milton Keynes
Contact: Mrs A Hepher, The Old Bakery, 5 Main Street, Cosgrove, Milton Keynes MK19 7JL
T: (01908) 562253
F: (01908) 562228
E: mksh@hepher.demon.co.uk
I: www.mksh.co.uk

OPEN All Year
CC: Amex, Delta, Diners, JCB, Mastercard, Solo, Switch, Visa

Low season per wk
Min £275.00

One of several high-quality, self-catering apartments, available by the week. Fully serviced, furnished to a high standard. Quiet residential area. Personal service.

NEW FOREST

See under Barton on Sea, Beaulieu, Boldre, Brook, Fordingbridge, Lymington, Lyndhurst, Milford-on-Sea, Sway

NEWBURY, Berkshire Map ref 2C2 *Tourist Information Centre Tel: (01635) 30267*

★★★★★
1 Unit
Sleeping 5

PEREGRINE COTTAGE
Enborne, Newbury
Contact: Mrs E A Knight, Peregrine House, Enborne Street, Enborne, Newbury RG14 6RP
T: (01635) 42585
F: (01635) 528775
E: lizknight@amserve.net

South of historic Newbury in open countryside. Five minutes from M4 jct 13. Town centre 10 minutes, London one hour, Heathrow 45 minutes. Beautifully furnished and cared for with private terrace by old orchard. Use of swimming pool, tennis court and barbecue. Extra cleaning if required. Given highest rating. Sorry, no smoking.

OPEN All Year
CC: Delta, Mastercard, Switch, Visa

Low season per wk
£420.00–£575.00
High season per wk
£420.00–£575.00

6

★★★-★★★★★
2 Units
Sleeping 3–6

YAFFLES
Hermitage, Thatcham
Contact: Mr & Mrs A Bradford, Yaffles, Red Shute Hill, Hermitage, Thatcham RG18 9QH
T: (01635) 201100
F: (01635) 201100
E: yaffles@ukonline.co.uk
I: www.cottagesdirect.com/yaffles

OPEN All Year

Low season per wk
Min £245.00
High season per wk
Min £245.00

Comfortable, secluded, self-contained garden flat and studio set in spacious, peaceful grounds just north of Newbury yet near jct 13 of M4 motorway. Prices are for two people.

NEWPORT, Isle of Wight Map ref 2C3 *Tourist Information Centre Tel: (01983) 813818*

Rating Applied For
2 Units
Sleeping 6–8

WEST STANDEN FARM
Newport
Contact: Mr & Mrs E Burt
T: (01983) 522099
I: www.weststandenfarm.co.uk

OPEN All Year

Low season per wk
£300.00–£450.00
High season per wk
£400.00–£1,000.00

Tastefully converted Victorian barns, set on a working farm, surrounded by rural views and an abundance of wildlife. Ideal, central location. Year-round appeal.

NOKE, Oxfordshire Map ref 2C1

★★★★
1 Unit
Sleeping 4

MANOR BARN
Noke, Oxford
Contact: Ms E Righton
T: (01865) 373766
F: (01865) 371911
E: er@oxfordshortlets.co.uk
I: isisnokelets.co.uk

OPEN All Year
CC: Delta, Mastercard, Solo, Switch, Visa

Low season per wk
£300.00–£425.00
High season per wk
£375.00–£500.00

Stylish, well-equipped, two-bedroom Cotswold-stone cottage in quiet village, ideally sited for access to Oxford and to A34/A40/M40.

NUTLEY, East Sussex Map ref 2D3

★★-★★★

10 Units

Former smallholding overlooking open countryside and Ashdown Forest. Shower room, kitchen/diner/lounge. Fully equipped. Wheelchair, pet and smoker-friendly cottages available. Spare campbeds. Ideally situated for London, castles, gardens and coast. Both Friday and Saturday turnaround.

WHITEHOUSE FARM HOLIDAY COTTAGES

Nutley, Uckfield
Contact: Mr K Wilson, Whitehouse Farm Holiday Cottages, Whitehouse Farm, Horney Common, Nutley, Uckfield TN22 3EE
T: (01825) 712377
F: (01825) 712377
E: keith.g.r.wilson@btinternet.com
I: www.streets-ahead.com/whitehousefarm

OPEN All Year
CC: Delta, Mastercard, Visa

Low season per wk
£220.00–£409.00
High season per wk
£306.00–£409.00

OLNEY, Buckinghamshire Map ref 2C1

★★★★

2 Units

HYDE FARM COTTAGES

Olney
Contact: Mrs P J Reynolds
T: (01234) 711223
F: (01234) 714305
E: accomm@thehyde.fsbusiness.co.uk

Beautifully situated at the end of a long drive with lovely views over open farmland, these cottages are comfortable and homely with their own garden, patio and parking. Ideal central location for many tourist attractions, with easy access to Milton Keynes, Northampton and Bedford. Olney market town just 1.5 miles.

OPEN All Year

Low season per wk
Max £300.00
High season per wk
£375.00

OXFORD, Oxfordshire Map ref 2C1 *Tourist Information Centre Tel: (01865) 726871*

★★★★

2 Units
Sleeping 2–4

MANOR HOUSE COTTAGES
Wheatley
Contact: Mr & Mrs E Hess, Manor House Cottages, The Manor House, Wheatley OX33 1XX
T: (01865) 875022
F: (01865) 875023
E: chess@harcourtchambers.law.co.uk

OPEN All Year
CC: Amex, Mastercard, Visa

Low season per wk
£325.00–£400.00
High season per wk
£375.00–£450.00

Family-run, period cottages, charmingly refurbished, in the grounds of an attractive and historic Tudor manor house enjoying rural aspect in village close to Oxford.

TOWN INDEX

This can be found at the back of the guide. If you know where you want to stay, the index will give you the page number listing accommodation in your chosen town, city or village.

PANGBOURNE, Berkshire Map ref 2C2

★★★

1 Unit
Sleeping 5

BRAMBLY THATCH

Nr Pangbourne, Reading
Contact: Mr & Mrs J N Hatt, Merricroft Farming, Goring Heath, Reading RG8 7TA
T: (0118) 9843121
F: (0118) 9844662
I: www.easisites.co.uk/bramblycottages

Picturebook, brick and flint thatched cottage on 300-acre beef and arable farm. Ideal base for visiting London, Oxford, Stonehenge and Stratford, and for sightseeing in the Thames Valley, Chilterns, Cotswolds and beyond. A warm and friendly home from home or a holiday to remember.

OPEN All Year
CC: Delta, JCB, Mastercard, Solo, Switch, Visa

Pay by credit card free of charge if you mention this advert. Also special monthly rates in winter.

Low season per wk
£345.00–£395.00
High season per wk
£395.00–£425.00

PLAXTOL, Kent Map ref 2D2

★★★

1 Unit
Sleeping 5

GOLDING HOP FARM COTTAGE

Plaxtol, Sevenoaks
Contact: Mrs J Vincent, Golding Hop Farm, Bewley Lane, Plaxtol, Sevenoaks TN15 0PS
T: (01732) 885432
F: (01732) 885432
E: adrian@mvvincent.freeserve.co.uk
I: www.mvvincent.freeserve.co.uk

OPEN All Year

Low season per wk
£200.00–£280.00
High season per wk
£240.00–£380.00

12-acre cobnut farm. South-facing cottage with garden and all modern conveniences. Quiet position but not isolated.

POOLE, Dorset Map ref 2B3 *Tourist Information Centre Tel: (01202) 253253*

★★-★★★

2 Units
Sleeping 6–7

FLATS 5 & 6 SANDACRES

Poole
Contact: Mrs R C Bond
T: (01202) 631631
F: (01202) 625749
I: www.beaconhilltouringpark.co.uk

OPEN All Year except Christmas

Low season per wk
Min £185.00
High season per wk
Min £380.00

First floor flats, a stone's throw from beach. Free parking, TV/video, washing machine, microwave and linen. Sorry, no pets or smokers.

PORTSMOUTH & SOUTHSEA, Hampshire Map ref 2C3

★★★

6 Units
Sleeping 1–6

ATLANTIC APARTMENTS

Southsea
Contact: Mr F Hamdani, Atlantic Apartments, 61A Festing Road, Southsea PO4 0NQ
T: (023) 9282 3606
F: (023) 9229 7046
E: atlantic@portsmouth-apartments.co.uk
I: www.portsmouth-apartments.co.uk

OPEN All Year

Low season per wk
£150.00–£300.00
High season per wk
£200.00–£320.00

Situated in one of the most attractive areas of Southsea, only a few yards from the canoe lake and seafront. All apartments are fully self-contained. Large car park.

2

★★★

10 Units

LAKESIDE HOLIDAY & BUSINESS APARTMENTS

Southsea, Portsmouth
Contact: Mrs V Hamza, Lakeside Holiday & Business Apartments, 5 Helena Road, Southsea, Portsmouth PO4 9RH
T: 07810 436981
I: www.lakesidesouthsea.com

OPEN All Year
CC: Amex, Diners, Mastercard, Switch, Visa

Low season per wk
£150.00–£200.00
High season per wk
£180.00–£220.00

Self-catering apartments in lovely detached house, two minutes' walk to sea, rose gardens, bowling greens and lake. Top 3-Star award. Open all year, parking available, rear garden.

3

PORTSMOUTH & SOUTHSEA continued

★★★
6 Units
Sleeping 4

OCEAN APARTMENTS

Southsea, Portsmouth
Contact: Mr F Hamdani, Ocean Hotel & Apartments, 8-10 St Helens Parade, Southsea PO4 0RW
T: (023) 9273 4233
F: (023) 9229 7046
I: www.portsmouth-apartments.co.uk

OPEN All Year
CC: Mastercard, Visa

Low season per wk
£140.00–£400.00
High season per wk
£250.00–£600.00

Imposing seafront building with magnificent views. Recently refurbished. Very spacious one- to four-bedroomed self-contained apartments, lift, private car parking. Executive suites available.

★★★
6 Units
Sleeping 6

SALISBURY APARTMENTS

Southsea
Contact: Mr F Hamdani, Atlantic Apartments, 61A Festing Road, Southsea PO4 0NQ
T: (023) 9282 3606
F: (023) 9229 7046
E: salisbury@portsmouth-apartments.co.uk
I: www.portsmouth-apartments.co.uk

OPEN All Year
CC: Mastercard, Visa

Low season per wk
£120.00–£300.00
High season per wk
£250.00–£450.00

Situated two minutes' walk from the sea, next door to the Atlantic Apartments. Recently refurbished, self-contained apartments. Large, private car park.

PRINSTED, West Sussex Map ref 2C3

★★
1 Unit
Sleeping 4

4 THE SQUARE

Prinsted, Emsworth
Contact: Mrs A P Brooks
T: (01243) 377489
E: brooksems@btclick.com
I: www.fourthesquare.co.uk

Charming 18thC thatched cottage, comfortably furnished and in the centre of a quiet Sussex village. Sunny walled garden. 250 yards from the sea with good walking, both coastal and in the South Downs. Historic cities of Chichester and Portsmouth nearby with plenty to see and do. Unrestricted local parking. Leaflet available.

OPEN All Year

Weekend or mid-week short breaks available – minimum stay 3 nights.

Low season per wk
£250.00–£280.00
High season per wk
£300.00–£400.00

ROCHESTER, Kent Map ref 3B3 *Tourist Information Centre Tel: (01634) 843666*

★★★★
4 Units
Sleeping 4

STABLE COTTAGES

St Mary's Hoo, Rochester
Contact: Mr & Mrs J Symonds, Stable Cottages, Fenn Croft, Newlands Farm Road, St Mary's Hoo, Rochester ME3 8QS
T: (01634) 272439
F: (01634) 272205
E: stablecottages@btinternet.com
I: www.stable-cottages.com

These luxury, oak-beamed cottages are set in 20 acres of secluded farmland close to RSPB reserve with panoramic views of the Thames. Access to motorways and ports. London/Canterbury 45 minutes. Perfect base for walking, bird-watching, sightseeing or just getting away from it all. Two bedrooms. Warm welcome. Family run.

Short breaks and split weeks available.

Low season per wk
£250.00
High season per wk
£400.00

MAP REFERENCES

Map references apply to the colour maps at the front of this guide.

ROMSEY, Hampshire Map ref 2C3 *Tourist Information Centre Tel: (01794) 512987*

★★★

1 Unit
Sleeping 4

THE OLD SMITHY COTTAGE

Romsey
Contact: Mr P K Reeves, The Old Smithy Cottage, Awbridge Hill, Romsey SO51 0HF
T: (01794) 511778
E: paul@smithycottage.co.uk
I: www.smithycottage.co.uk

Grade II Listed building, once a blacksmith's shop, dating back to early 1700. Recently completely renovated, it comprises a spacious, open-plan room with a cathedral ceiling, exposed oak beams and a galleried mezzanine floor. It stands in almost an acre of garden with exceptional views across the Test Valley.

OPEN All Year except Christmas

High season per wk
£250.00–£350.00

ROYAL TUNBRIDGE WELLS, Kent Map ref 2D2 *Tourist Information Centre Tel: (01892) 515675*

★★★

2 Units
Sleeping 4

FORD COTTAGE

Royal Tunbridge Wells
Contact: Mrs W A Cusdin
T: (01892) 531419
E: FordCottage@tinyworld.co.uk
I: www.fordcottage.co.uk

Ford Cottage is a picturesque Victorian cottage three minutes' walk from the Pantiles. Self-contained studio flats with own front doors, fully fitted kitchens, en suites and showers. Off-street parking. Ideal for visiting many local gardens, castles and historic houses.

1

OPEN All Year except Christmas

Short breaks available – terms on request.

Low season per wk
£220.00–£280.00
High season per wk
£275.00–£325.00

★★★★

6 Units
Sleeping 4

ITARIS PROPERTIES LIMITED

Royal Tunbridge Wells
Contact: Mrs A May, Itaris Properties Ltd, 12 Mount Ephraim, Royal Tunbridge Wells TN4 8AS
T: (01892) 511065
F: (01892) 540171
E: itaris_properties@yahoo.co.uk
I: www.itaris.co.uk

Royal Tunbridge Wells is surrounded by beautiful and unspoilt countryside and is the ideal location for a short break or relaxing holiday. Our self-contained and fully equipped holiday apartments are situated in the very heart of Tunbridge Wells within walking distance of its many amenities.

OPEN All Year

Low season per wk
£225.00–£275.00
High season per wk
£275.00–£370.00

★★★★

1 Unit
Sleeping 4

KENNETT
Southborough, Royal Tunbridge Wells
Contact: Mrs L Clements, Kennett, London Road, Southborough, Royal Tunbridge Wells TN4 0UJ
T: (01892) 533363
E: gravels@onetel.net.uk

OPEN All Year except Christmas

Low season per wk
£250.00
High season per wk
£300.00–£450.00

Refurbished duplex apartment. One-two double bedrooms, view over countryside. Open-plan lounge, kitchen and dining area with doors to private patio. Convenient for local amenities.

RUCKINGE, Kent Map ref 3B4

★★

1 Unit
Sleeping 7

THE OLD POST OFFICE

Ruckinge, Ashford
Contact: Mr C Cook
T: (020) 8655 4466
F: (020) 8656 7755
E: c.cook@btinternet.com
I: www.ruckinge.info

A comprehensively equipped large house, very suitable for two families holidaying together – two bathrooms, two kitchens, a huge garden from which public footpaths lead off, canal walks 100 yards. Digital TV and many books if it rains! Owner's website at www.ruckinge.info has pictures of all the rooms.

OPEN All Year except Christmas
CC: Delta, Mastercard, Solo, Switch, Visa

Short breaks Oct-Mar.

Low season per wk
£285.00–£325.00
High season per wk
£365.00–£495.00

RUSHLAKE GREEN, East Sussex Map ref 3B4

★★★★

1 Unit
Sleeping 2

THE COACH HOUSE

Beech Hill Farm, Rushlake Green, Heathfield
Contact: Mrs J B Desch, Beech Hill Farm, Cowbeech Road, Rushlake Green, Heathfield TN21 9QB
T: (01435) 830203
F: (01435) 830203
E: desch@lineone.net
I: www.sussexcountryretreat.co.uk

Historical, 18thC coach house, artistically converted, on small, organically run smallholding with panoramic views, in Area of Outstanding Natural Beauty. Ideal location for peaceful retreat. Own entrance, parking and garden area. Bike storage. Bird/music/garden lovers' haven. First-class pubs, walks, historic castles and coast within easy distance. Easy access Glyndebourne.

OPEN All Year
CC: Amex, Delta, Diners, Mastercard, Switch, Visa

Short breaks, minimum 3 nights, any season.

Low season per wk
£200.00–£275.00
High season per wk
£275.00–£350.00

12

RYDE, Isle of Wight Map ref 2C3 *Tourist Information Centre Tel: (01983) 813818*

★★★

1 Unit
Sleeping 4

CLAVERTON HOUSE

Ryde
Contact: Dr H Metz
T: (01983) 613015
F: (01983) 613015
E: clavertonhouse@aol.com

OPEN All Year

Low season per wk
£150.00–£200.00
High season per wk
£250.00–£300.00

Beautiful holiday residence at Ryde's seafront, overlooking the Solent. Ten minutes' walk to town centre, bus station and passenger ferries.

RYE, East Sussex Map ref 3B4 *Tourist Information Centre Tel: (01797) 226696*

★★

1 Unit
Sleeping 2

ELLIS BROS (IRONMONGERS) LTD

Rye
Contact: Miss H K Gill, Ellis Bros (Ironmongers) Ltd, 1 High Street, Rye TN31 7JE
T: (01797) 222110

OPEN All Year
CC: Delta, JCB, Mastercard, Solo, Switch, Visa

Low season per wk
£160.00
High season per wk
£160.00

Open-plan studio flat suitable for two, overlooking private courtyard. Situated close to shops, restaurants, parking. Bookings taken from 0930 to 1700 Monday-Friday.

NB

IMPORTANT NOTE **Information on accommodation listed in this guide has been supplied by the proprietors. As changes may occur you are advised to check details at the time of booking.**

SANDFORD, Isle of Wight Map ref 2C3

★★★

1 Unit
Sleeping 9

Delightful Grade II 16thC thatched cottage. Set in large, enclosed gardens, gated access. Spacious, comfortbale accommodation. Three bedrooms, three bathrooms. Large open plan lounge/dining room, original oak beams, two inglenook fireplaces (non-functioning). Well-equipped kitchen with breakfast table. Utilities included. Godshill and coastal resort of Shanklin five minutes' drive.

THE COTTAGE

Sandford, Ventnor
Contact: Ms S Dyer, S D Residential, 6 Velsheda Close, Totland Bay PO39 0AJ
T: (01983) 759861
F: (01983) 759861
E: sue.dyer2@virgin.net
I: www.iowcottage.com

OPEN All Year

3-night stays available Oct-Mar (excl Christmas and New Year).

Low season per wk
£325.00–£450.00
High season per wk
£550.00–£850.00

SANDLING, Kent Map ref 3B3

★★★★

2 Units
Sleeping 8

Tastefully, fully furnished and equipped cottages converted from former stables and coach house annexed to a historical country manor house made famous in Charles Dickens' 'The Pickwick Papers'. Conveniently located in Kent, only 50 minutes by rail/car to London, and in a beautiful country setting.

DINGLEY COTTAGE & DELL COTTAGE

Sandling, Maidstone
Contact: Mr R J Lawty, Cobtree Manor House, Forstal Road, Sandling, Maidstone ME14 3AX
T: (01622) 671160
F: (01622) 750378
E: mail@cobtree.com
I: www.cobtree.com

OPEN All Year
CC: Delta, Mastercard, Switch, Visa

Low season per wk
£350.00–£450.00
High season per wk
£500.00–£650.00

SEAFORD, East Sussex Map ref 2D3 *Tourist Information Centre Tel: (01323) 897426*

★★★★

1 Unit
Sleeping 5

2 KINGSWAY COURT

Seaford
Contact: Mrs P Gower, 6 Sunningdale Close, Southdown Road, Seaford BN25 4PF
T: (01323) 895233
E: sific@bgower.f9.co.uk

Fully equipped, spacious, semi-detached house. Gardens, balcony, parking. Five minutes from sea, open country, station and town centre. One single and two double bedrooms.

OPEN All Year

Low season per wk
£250.00–£300.00
High season per wk
£300.00–£400.00

CHECK THE MAPS

The colour maps at the front of this guide show all the cities, towns and villages for which you will find accommodation entries. Refer to the town index to find the page on which they are listed.

SEAVIEW, Isle of Wight Map ref 2C3

★★★

1 Unit
Sleeping 6

1 POND LANE

Seaview
Contact: Mrs S M Capon, 11 Circular Road, Ryde PO33 1AL
T: (01983) 564267
F: (01983) 564267
E: smcapon@aol.com

Detatched property set in a large garden with off-road parking. Situated on the outskirts of the tranquil village of Seaview, the beach is only a two-minute stroll with local shops, boutiques and restaurants within easy walking distance. A well-equipped cottage, open all year round, offering comfortable, homely accommodation.

OPEN All Year

Low season per wk
£173.00–£288.00
High season per wk
£288.00–£520.00

SELHAM, West Sussex Map ref 2C3

★★★

1 Unit
Sleeping 2

THE ANNEX

Selham, Petworth
Contact: Mrs B Hurst, Great Ham Mead, Selham, Petworth GU28 0PJ
T: (01798) 861450

Self-contained ground floor accommodation overlooking farmland. One double bedroom, en suite bathroom, kitchenette and spacious, comfortable living room.

High season per wk
£200.00–£250.00

SHAFTESBURY, Dorset Map ref 2B3 *Tourist Information Centre Tel: (01747) 853514*

★★

1 Unit
Sleeping 4

DAIRY COTTAGE

Sutton Waldron, Blandford Forum
Contact: Mrs Pope, Broadlea Farm, Sutton Waldron, Blandford Forum DT11 8NS
T: (01747) 811330
F: (01747) 811330
E: maryp2@tinyworld.co.uk

OPEN All Year

Fully equipped cottage amidst lovely countryside, south of Shaftesbury. Two bedrooms, spacious lounge/dining room, separate kitchen and bathroom. Good base for visiting tourist attractions.

Low season per wk
£210.00
High season per wk
£240.00

★★★-★★★★★

3 Units

STABLE COTTAGE, SHIRE COTTAGE & GRANARY COTTAGE

Fifehead Magdalen, Gillingham
Contact: Mrs Trevor, Middle Farm, Fifehead Magdalen, Gillingham SP8 5RR
T: (01258) 820220
F: (01258) 820220

OPEN All Year

Charming detached cottages situated in courtyard of working farm. Picturesque walks along the river, riding, cycling, golf and fishing are available. Coast within an hour.

Low season per wk
£175.00–£300.00
High season per wk
£350.00–£600.00

★★★★

2 Units
Sleeping 4

VALE FARM HOLIDAY COTTAGES

Sutton Waldron, Blandford Forum
Contact: Mrs S A Drake, Vale Farm, Sutton Waldron, Blandford Forum DT11 8PG
T: (01747) 811286
F: (01747) 811286
E: jandsdrake@ukonline.co.uk
I: www.valeholidays.co.uk

OPEN All Year

Luxury barn conversion, beautifully furnished, in outstanding area. Short drive to coast and many tourist attractions. Arrive as a guest, leave as a friend.

Low season per wk
£145.00–£250.00
High season per wk
£275.00–£520.00

QUALITY ASSURANCE SCHEME

Star ratings were correct at the time of going to press but are subject to change. Please check at the time of booking.

SOUTH WONSTON, Hampshire Map ref 2C3

★★★★

1 Unit
Sleeping 4

'BURWOOD'
South Wonston, Winchester
Contact: Mrs A Lowery
T: (01962) 881690
E: lowery@euphony.net

OPEN All Year

Low season per wk
Max £250.00
High season per wk
Max £350.00

'Burwood' is a tastefully furnished, self-contained bungalow annexe in the village of South Wonston, five miles north of Winchester. A warm welcome guaranteed.

SOUTHAMPTON, Hampshire Map ref 2C3

★★★

2 Units
Sleeping 2

PINEWOOD LODGE APARTMENTS
Southampton
Contact: Dr or Mrs S W Bradberry, Pinewood Lodge Apartments, Pinewood Lodge, Kanes Hill, Southampton SO19 6AJ
T: (023) 8040 2925
E: stan.bradberry@tesco.net

OPEN All Year

Low season per wk
£148.00–£155.00
High season per wk
£182.00

Double or twin-bedded, fully-equipped, self-contained apartments, in pleasant wooded area, each with separate kitchen, bathroom and lounge. Private verandah or patio.

SOUTHSEA

See under Portsmouth & Southsea

STANDLAKE, Oxfordshire Map ref 2C1

★★★★

1 Unit
Sleeping 2

WHEELWRIGHTS COTTAGE

Standlake, Witney
Contact: Mrs N Hunt
T: (01865) 300536
E: bobnora@huntb1.fsnet.co.uk
I: www.oxtowns.co.uk/wheelwrights

Converted Cotswold-stone barn in pretty vilage of Standlake. Cosy, yet spacious, with exposed stone and oak beams, plus high-standard fittings providing a homely atmosphere. Own patio/garden and use of owners' garden edging River Windrush. Situated in Thames Valley on the egde of Cotswolds with Oxford easily accessible.

OPEN All Year

Short breaks available at short notice, Oct-Mar; also in summer if cottage not pre-booked.

Low season per wk
£215.00–£290.00
High season per wk
£325.00

STONEGATE, East Sussex Map ref 3B4

★★★★★

1 Unit
Sleeping 4

COOPERS COTTAGE

Stonegate, Wadhurst
Contact: Ms J Howard, Coopers Farm, Stonegate, Wadhurst TN5 7EH
T: (01580) 200386
E: jane@coopersfarmstonegate.co.uk
I: www.coopersfarmstonegate.co.uk

Coopers Cottage combines the charm of an ancient building – huge inglenook fireplace and a wealth of beams – with the supreme comfort of 21st-century living. Enjoy the peace and seclusion of this traditional working farm situated in the High Weald Area of Outstanding Natural Beauty. Horses also welcome.

OPEN All Year

From Nov-Mar: £200 for the weekend or a 4-night, mid-week break.

Low season per wk
£350.00–£450.00
High season per wk
£520.00–£650.00

CREDIT CARD BOOKINGS If you book by telephone and are asked for your credit card number it is advisable to check the proprietor's policy should you cancel your reservation.

STUDLAND, Dorset Map ref 2B3

★★
1 Unit
Sleeping 9

CORNER COTTAGE
Studland, Swanage
OPEN All Year
Contact: Mrs A D Ives, Faun's Cottage, Swanage Road, Studland, Swanage BH19 3AE
T: (01929) 450309
E: antnives@aol.com
I: www.members.aol.com/antnives

Low season per wk
£215.00–£525.00
High season per wk
£525.00–£820.00

Five-bedroom, cottage-style residence with one en suite. In centre of village with rural and sea views, close to safe, sandy beaches.

SWANAGE, Dorset Map ref 2B3 *Tourist Information Centre Tel: (01929) 422885*

★★★★
1 Unit

COASTGUARDS RETURN
Swanage
Contact: Mrs A L Morrison, 6 Sunnydale Villas, Durlston Road, Swanage BH19 2HY
T: (01929) 424630
F: (01929) 424630
E: jamesrmorrison@aol.com

Low season per wk
£250.00–£350.00
High season per wk
£370.00–£495.00

Renovated and refurbished to a high standard, offering very attractive, comfortable and well-equipped accommodation. Beautiful World Heritage-site location.

★★★
1 Unit
Sleeping 3

FLAT 3 SUNNYBANK COURT
Swanage
OPEN All Year
Contact: Mrs P M Oliver, 27 Prospect Crescent, Swanage BH19 1BD
T: (01929) 425984
E: rob@oliverr80.fsnet.co.uk

Low season per wk
£200.00–£240.00
High season per wk
£250.00–£360.00

Comfortably furnished, first floor flat in Victorian house. Large double bedroom and pleasant outlook from south-facing lounge. Two minutes' walk to buses/shops/beach.

5

★★-★★★
3 Units
Sleeping 6–8

THE ISLES APARTMENTS
Swanage
OPEN All Year
Contact: Ms P McGrath
T: (0118) 973 3116
F: (0118) 973 3116

Low season per wk
£110.00–£330.00
High season per wk
£275.00–£600.00

Spacious seafront apartments enjoying unspoilt view over Swanage Bay and close to the heart of the town.

★★★★
1 Unit

NO 3 EXETER ROAD
Swanage
Contact: Mrs A L Morrison, 6 Sunnydale Villas, Durlston Road, Swanage BH19 2HY
T: (01929) 424630
F: (01929) 424630
E: jamesrmorrison@aol.com

Low season per wk
£375.00–£525.00
High season per wk
£560.00–£825.00

Completely modernised and refurbished period house offering very comfortable, well-equipped, attractive accommodation. Conveniently located for beach, town and countryside.

SWAY, Hampshire Map ref 2C3

★★★
1 Unit
Sleeping 6

HACKNEY PARK
Sway, Lymington
OPEN All Year
Contact: Mrs H Beale, Hackney Park, Mount Pleasant Lane, Sway, Lymington SO41 8LS
T: (01590) 682049

Low season per wk
£190.00–£280.00
High season per wk
£280.00–£370.00

Modern, spacious and comfortable, self-contained apartment (more bedrooms available if required) in tranquil setting with delightful forest views. Excellent touring, walking and horse-riding area.

QUALITY ASSURANCE SCHEME
Star ratings are explained at the back of this guide.

TENTERDEN, Kent Map ref 3B4

★★★★

1 Unit
Sleeping 5

QUINCE COTTAGE

Tenterden
Contact: Mrs H E Crease, Laurelhurst, 38 Ashford Road, Tenterden TN30 6LL
T: (01580) 765636
F: (01580) 765922
E: quincott@zetnet.co.uk
I: quincecottage.co.uk

Listed, beamed cottage on residential side of tree-lined high street. Comfortable home from home, one single, two double bedrooms, cot available. Rear secluded courtyard. Close to all amenities, including steam railway and leisure centre. Children welcome. Sorry no pets, no smoking. Good centre for exploring Kent and East Sussex. Brochure available.

OPEN All Year

5% discount on bookings for 2 or more consecutive weeks. Short breaks (minimum 3 nights) possible during low season.

Low season per wk
£220.00–£320.00
High season per wk
£360.00–£410.00

THAME, Oxfordshire Map ref 2C1 *Tourist Information Centre Tel: (01844) 212834*

★★★★

1 Unit
Sleeping 6

THE HOLLIES

Thame
Contact: Ms J Tanner, Little Acre, 4 High Street, Tetsworth, Thame OX9 7AT
T: (01844) 281423
E: info@theholliesthame.co.uk
I: www.theholliesthame.co.uk

OPEN All Year

Beautifully appointed, luxury cottage-style bungalow with peaceful gardens, situated in a secluded backwater near the oldest part of Thame, five minutes' walk from the centre of our historic market town.

Low season per wk
£350.00–£400.00
High season per wk
£400.00–£500.00

TOTLAND BAY, Isle of Wight Map ref 2C3

★★★

1 Unit
Sleeping 6

STONEWIND FARM

Totland Bay
Contact: Mrs P Hayles, Barn Cottage, Middleton, Freshwater PO40 9RW
T: (01983) 752912
F: (01983) 752912

OPEN All Year

Charming two-bedroomed farmhouse, in peaceful area with fine views. Central heating, fully equipped kitchen. Electricity, linen, towels provided. Secluded gardens with barbecue.

Low season per wk
£150.00–£200.00
High season per wk
£200.00–£450.00

TUNBRIDGE WELLS

See under Royal Tunbridge Wells

WALTON-ON-THAMES, Surrey Map ref 2D2

★★★★

1 Unit
Sleeping 4

GUEST WING

Walton-on-Thames
Contact: Mr A R Dominy
T: (01932) 241223

OPEN All Year

Attractive, two-bedroomed, self-contained wing of neo-Georgian house in residential cul-de-sac, adjacent to Walton station. Ideal for London, Hampton Court, Windsor and motorway network.

Low season per wk
£240.00–£300.00
High season per wk
£300.00–£335.00

WEST OXFORDSHIRE

See under Finstock, Standlake

WEB

www.visitengland.com

Log on for information and inspiration. The latest information on places to visit, events and quality assessed accommodation.

WHITSTABLE, Kent Map ref 3B3 *Tourist Information Centre Tel: (01227) 275482*

★★★
1 Unit
Sleeping 6

TRAPPERS END
Whitstable
Contact: Mrs J M Reed, 11 Woodlands Avenue, New Malden KT3 3UL
T: (020) 8942 0342
F: (020) 8942 0344
E: janette.reed07@btopenworld.com
I: www.kenttourism.co.uk/trappers

CC: Amex, Delta, Mastercard, Visa

Low season per wk
£400.00–£500.00
High season per wk
£500.00–£600.00

Detached house overlooking Whitstable. Fresh linen and towels provided, central heating, dishwasher, video/TV, garage and parking for two cars.

WHITWELL, Isle of Wight Map ref 2C3

★★★
1 Unit

PYRMONT COTTAGE
Whitwell, Ventnor
Contact: Hose Rhodes Dickson, Residential and Holiday Letting Agents, 177 High Street, Ryde PO33 2HW
T: (01983) 616644
F: (01983) 568822
E: rental_office@hose-rhodes-dickson.co.uk
I: island-holiday-homes.net

Low season per wk
£375.00–£425.00
High season per wk
£485.00–£575.00

A varied selection of properties throughout the Isle of Wight. Visit unspoilt villages, safe, sandy beaches and places of historical interest. A perfect place to relax.

WINCHESTER, Hampshire Map ref 2C3 *Tourist Information Centre Tel: (01962) 840500*

★★★★★
1 Unit
Sleeping 4

GYLEEN
Winchester
Contact: Mr & Mrs P Tipple, 9 Mount View Road, Olivers Battery, Winchester SO22 4JJ
T: (01962) 861918
F: 08700 542801
E: pauliz@tipple.demon.co.uk
I: www.cottageguide.co.uk/gyleen

OPEN All Year
CC: Delta, JCB, Mastercard, Switch, Visa

Low season per wk
£278.00–£370.00
High season per wk
£381.00–£410.00

Detached, centrally heated, two-bedroomed bungalow with large, mature garden in quiet cul-de-sac overlooking golf course, two miles west of Winchester city centre.

WINDSOR, Berkshire Map ref 2D2 *Tourist Information Centre Tel: (01753) 743900*

★★★
1 Unit

FLAT 6 THE COURTYARD
Windsor
Contact: Mr G M Gordon, 5 Temple Mill Island, Marlow SL7 1SG
T: (01628) 824267
F: (01628) 828949
E: gavingordon@totalise.co.uk

OPEN All Year

Low season per wk
£450.00
High season per wk
£450.00

An elegant, well-equipped, first floor (lift) apartment centrally situated in a quiet courtyard almost opposite Windsor Castle. One double and one twin bedroom. Parking.

Rating Applied For
2 Units
Sleeping 5

WISTERIA & GARDENERS BOTHY
Windsor
Contact: Mr P Smith & Sarah Everitt, The Old Place, Lock Path, Dorney, Windsor SL4 6QQ
T: (01753) 827037
F: (01753) 855022
E: sarah@pjsmith.co.uk
I: www.pjsmith.co.uk

OPEN All Year

Low season per wk
£455.00–£665.00
High season per wk
£455.00–£665.00

Suitable for families. Secure, rural setting yet only 10 minutes from London train connections. Easy reach of Legoland etc. Flexible booking arrangements. Rowers welcome.

COLOUR MAPS Colour maps at the front of this guide pinpoint all places under which you will find accommodation listed.

WINTERBORNE WHITECHURCH, Dorset Map ref 2B3

★★★

1 Unit
Sleeping 4

3 ROSE COTTAGES

Winterborne Whitechurch, Blandford Forum
Contact: Mrs A Macfarlane, Barn Court, West Street, Winterborne Kingston, Blandford Forum DT11 9AX
T: (01929) 471612
F: (01929) 472293
E: rosecottages5137@aol.com
I: www.cottageguide.co.uk/rose.cottage

A pretty 17thC thatched cottage, overlooking the unspoilt Dorset countryside. Perfectly situated for exploring the beautiful Thomas Hardy country and the dramatic coastline from Lulworth Cove to Chesil beach. Dorchester 12 miles, Blandford Forum five miles. Weymouth, Poole and Bournemouth all within easy reach.

OPEN All Year

Short breaks (3 or 4 days) available as well as weekend breaks – minimum 2 nights.

Low season per wk
Min £180.00
High season per wk
Max £400.00

WITCHAMPTON, Dorset Map ref 2B3

★★★★

1 Unit
Sleeping 2

THE OLD EXCHANGE

Witchampton, Wimborne Minster
Contact: Mr & Mrs M R Smith, The Old Exchange, c/o High Lea Cottage, Witchampton Lane, Witchampton, Wimborne Minster BH21 5AF
T: (01258) 840809
E: msmithhighlea@aol.com
I: www.heartofdorset.easynet.co.uk

Converted in 2002/3, from probably the oldest telephone exchange in the south into a delightful holiday cottage for two people, The Old Exchange affords modern fixtures and fittings to a very high standard. One double bedroom (super en suite bathroom), separate wc, fully fitted kitchen, triple-aspect lounge, wonderful countryside views.

OPEN All Year

3/4-night stays sometimes available Oct-Mar (excl Christmas and New Year).

Low season per wk
£180.00–£220.00
High season per wk
£310.00–£340.00

WORTHING, West Sussex Map ref 2D3 *Tourist Information Centre Tel: (01903) 210022*

★★

1 Unit
Sleeping 4

6 HEENE TERRACE

Worthing
Contact: Mr R G Brew, Promenade Holiday Homes, 165 Dominion Road, Worthing BN14 8LD
T: (01903) 201426
F: (01903) 201426
E: robert@promhols.fsbusiness.co.uk
I: www.promenadeholidayhomes.co.uk

OPEN All Year

Low season per wk
£230.00–£260.00
High season per wk
£340.00–£370.00

Spacious seafront ground floor flat in historic Regency terrace. Glorious sea views over award-winning, formal gardens. Other flats, bungalows, houses (2-4 star rating) available.

COUNTRY CODE Always follow the Country Code · Enjoy the countryside and respect its life and work · Guard against all risk of fire · Fasten all gates · Keep your dogs under close control · Keep to public paths across farmland · Use gates and stiles to cross fences, hedges and walls · Leave livestock, crops and machinery alone · Take your litter home · Help to keep all water clean · Protect wildlife, plants and trees · Take special care on country roads · Make no unnecessary noise

WORTHING continued

★★

3 Units

TORRINGTON HOLIDAY FLATS

Worthing
Contact: Mrs Elsden & Mary Fitzgerald
T: (01903) 238582
F: (01903) 230266

Handsome Edwardian house in quiet conservation area, close to sea and shops. Spacious, well-furnished flats in excellent condition. Mobile number: 07860 699268.

OPEN All Year

Low season per wk
£160.00–£250.00
High season per wk
£160.00–£350.00

QUALITY ASSURANCE SCHEME

For an explanation of the quality and facilities represented by the Stars please refer to the front of this guide. A more detailed explanation can be found in the information pages at the back.

A brief guide to the main Towns and Villages offering accommodation in the **South East**

A ALVERSTOKE, HAMPSHIRE - Village located at the head the Haslar Creek. Within easy reach of Gosport.

ARUNDEL, WEST SUSSEX - Picturesque, historic town on the River Arun, dominated by Arundel Castle, home of the Dukes of Norfolk. There are many 18th C houses, the Wildfowl and Wetlands Centre and Museum and Heritage Centre.

ASHFORD, KENT - Once a market centre, the town has a number of Tudor and Georgian houses and a museum. Eurostar trains stop at Ashford International station.

B BANBURY, OXFORDSHIRE - Famous for its cattle market, cakes, nursery rhyme and Cross. Founded in Saxon times, it has some fine houses and interesting old inns. A good centre for touring Warwickshire and the Cotswolds.

BARTON ON SEA, HAMPSHIRE - Seaside village with views of the Isle of Wight. Within easy driving distance of the New Forest.

BATTLE, EAST SUSSEX - The Abbey at Battle was built on the site of the Battle of Hastings, when William defeated Harold II and so became the Conqueror in 1066. The museum has a fine collection relating to the Sussex iron industry, and there is a social history museum - Buckleys Yesterday's World.

BEAULIEU, HAMPSHIRE - Beautifully situated among woods and hills on the Beaulieu river, the village is both charming and unspoilt. The 13th C ruined Cistercian abbey and 14th C Palace House stand close to the National Motor Museum. There is a maritime museum at Bucklers Hard.

BEMBRIDGE, ISLE OF WIGHT - Village with harbour and bay below Bembridge Down - the most easterly village on the island. Bembridge Sailing Club is one of the most important in southern England.

BICESTER, OXFORDSHIRE - Market town with a large army depot and well-known hunting centre with hunt established in the late 18th C. The ancient parish church displays work of many periods. Nearby is the Jacobean mansion of Rousham House with gardens landscaped by William Kent.

BOLDRE, HAMPSHIRE - An attractive village with pretty views of the village from the bridge. The white plastered church sits on top of a hill.

BRIGHSTONE, ISLE OF WIGHT - Excellent centre for visitors who want somewhere quiet. Calbourne, nearby, is ideal for picnics, and the sea at Chilton Chie has safe bathing at high tide.

BRIGHTON & HOVE, EAST SUSSEX - Brighton's attractions include the Royal Pavilion, Volks Electric Railway, Sea Life Centre, Marina Village, Conference Centre, The Lanes and several theatres.

BROADSTAIRS, KENT - Popular seaside resort with numerous sandy bays. Charles Dickens spent his summers at Bleak House where he wrote parts of "David Copperfield". The Dickens Festival is held in June, when many people wear Dickensian costume.

C CANTERBURY, KENT - Place of pilgrimage, since the martyrdom of Becket in 1170, and the site of Canterbury Cathedral. Visit St Augustine's Abbey, St Martin's (the oldest church in England), Royal Museum and Art Gallery and the Canterbury Tales. Nearby is Howletts Wild Animal Park. Good shopping centre.

CARISBROOKE, ISLE OF WIGHT - Situated at the heart of the Isle of Wight and an ideal base for touring. Boasts a Norman church, formerly a monastic church, and a castle built on the site of a Roman fortress.

CHICHESTER, WEST SUSSEX - The county town of West Sussex with a beautiful Norman cathedral. Noted for its Georgian architecture but also has modern buildings like the Festival Theatre. Surrounded by places of interest, including Fishbourne Roman Palace, Weald and Downland Open-Air Museum and West Dean Gardens.

CHILHAM, KENT - Extremely pretty village of mostly Tudor and Jacobean houses. The village rises to the spacious square with the castle and the 15th C church.

CHRISTCHURCH, DORSET - Tranquil town lying between the Avon and Stour just before they converge and flow into Christchurch Harbour. A fine 11th C church and the remains of a Norman castle and house can be seen.

CORFE CASTLE, DORSET - One of the most spectacular ruined castles in Britain. Norman in origin, the castle was a Royalist stronghold during the Civil War and held out until 1645. The village had a considerable marble-carving industry in the Middle Ages.

D DORKING, SURREY - Ancient market town and a good centre for walking, delightfully set between Box Hill and the Downs. Denbies Wine Estate - England's largest vineyard - is situated here.

DYMCHURCH, KENT - For centuries the headquarters of the Lords of the Level, the local government of this area. Probably best known today because of the fame of its fictional parson, the notorious Dr Syn, who has inspired a regular festival.

E EPSOM, SURREY - Horse races have been held on the slopes of Epsom Downs for centuries. The racecourse is the home of the world-famous Derby. Many famous old homes are here, among them the 17th C Waterloo House.

F FARNHAM, SURREY - Town noted for its Georgian houses. Willmer House (now a museum) has a facade of cut and moulded brick with fine carving and panelling in the interior. The 12th C castle has been occupied by Bishops of both Winchester and Guildford.

FAVERSHAM, KENT - Historic town, once a port, dating back to prehistoric times. Abbey Street has more than 50 listed buildings. Roman and Anglo-Saxon finds and other exhibits can be seen in a museum in the Maison Dieu at Ospringe. Fleur de Lys Heritage Centre.

FINSTOCK, OXFORDSHIRE - This charming village on the edge of the Wychwood Forest was the home of John Wesley.

FOLKESTONE, KENT - Popular resort. The town has a fine promenade, the Leas, from where orchestral concerts and other entertainments are presented. Horse-racing at Westenhanger Racecourse nearby.

FORDINGBRIDGE, HAMPSHIRE - On the north-west edge of the New Forest. A medieval bridge crosses the Avon at this point and gave the town its name. A good centre for walking, exploring and fishing.

FRESHWATER, ISLE OF WIGHT - This part of the island is associated with Tennyson, who lived in the village for 30 years. A monument on Tennyson's Down commemorates the poet.

G GILLINGHAM, DORSET - A good shopping centre for tourists in the dairy vale of Dorset on the River Stour. Acclaimed as a beauty spot by the painter John Constable.

GOSPORT, HAMPSHIRE - From a tiny fishing hamlet, Gosport has grown into an important centre with many naval establishments, including HMS Dolphin, the submarine base, with the Naval Submarine Museum which preserves HMS Alliance and Holland I.

GOUDHURST, KENT - Village on a hill surmounted by a square-towered church with fine views of orchards and hop fields. Achieved prosperity through weaving in the Middle Ages. Finchcocks houses a living museum of historic, early keyboard instruments.

GREAT MILTON, OXFORDSHIRE - One of Oxfordshire's most famous villages situated in the Chiltern foothills. Thought to once be the home of John Milton who it is suggested wrote Paradise Lost while living here.

GUILDFORD, SURREY - Bustling town with Lewis Carroll connections and many historic monuments, one of which is the Guildhall clock jutting out over the old High Street. The modern cathedral occupies a commanding position on Stag Hill.

H HASTINGS, EAST SUSSEX - Ancient town which became famous as the base from which William the Conqueror set out to fight the Battle of Hastings. The later became one of the Cinque Ports, and is now a leading resort. Castle, Hastings Embroidery, inspired by the Bayeux Tapestry, and Sea Life Centre.

HENFIELD, WEST SUSSEX - Ancient village with many old houses and good shopping facilities, on a ridge of high ground overlooking the Adur Valley. Views to the South Downs.

L LANGTON MATRAVERS, DORSET - 18th C Purbeck-stone village surrounded by National Trust downland, about a mile from the sea and 350 ft above sea level. Excellent walking.

LEE ON THE SOLENT, HAMPSHIRE - Resort and residential area with fine views across the Solent to Cowes and Calshot.

LEWES, EAST SUSSEX - Historic county town with Norman castle. The steep High Street has mainly Georgian buildings. There is a folk museum at Anne of Cleves House, and the archaeological museum is in Barbican House.

LOWER BEEDING, WEST SUSSEX - Close to St Leonard's Forest, once a royal hunting ground. The area is also well known for its hammer ponds, used when the iron was smelted here. Leonardslee Gardens are especially beautiful in spring and autumn.

LYME REGIS, DORSET - Pretty, historic fishing town and resort set against the fossil-rich cliffs of Lyme Bay. In medieval times it was an important port and cloth centre. The Cobb, a massive stone breakwater, shelters the ancient harbour which is still lively with boats.

LYMINGTON, HAMPSHIRE - Small, pleasant town with bright cottages and attractive Georgian houses, lying on the edge of the New Forest with a ferry service to the Isle of Wight. A sheltered harbour makes it a busy yachting centre.

LYNDHURST, HAMPSHIRE - The "capital" of the New Forest, surrounded by attractive woodland scenery and delightful villages. The town is dominated by the Victorian Gothic-style church where the original Alice in Wonderland is buried.

M MAIDSTONE, KENT - Busy county town of Kent on the River Medway which has many interesting features and is an excellent centre for excursions. Museum of Carriages, Museum and Art Gallery, Mote Park.

MILFORD-ON-SEA, HAMPSHIRE - Victorian seaside resort with shingle beach and good bathing, set in pleasant countryside and looking out over the Isle of Wight. Nearby is Hurst Castle, built by Henry VIII.

MILTON ABBAS, DORSET - Sloping village street of thatched houses. A boys' school lies in Capability Brown's landscaped gardens amid hills and woods where the town once stood. The school chapel, former abbey church, can be visited.

MILTON KEYNES, BUCKINGHAMSHIRE - Designated a New Town in 1967, Milton Keynes offers a wide range of housing, and is abundantly planted with trees. It has excellent shopping facilities and 3 centres for leisure and sporting activities. The Open University is based here.

N NEWBURY, BERKSHIRE - Ancient town surrounded by the Downs, on the Kennet and Avon Canal. It has many buildings of interest, including the 17th C Cloth Hall, which is now a museum. The famous racecourse is nearby.

NUTLEY, EAST SUSSEX - Richard II had a hunting lodge at Nutley, which he used when hunting in the Ashdown Forest. To the north of the village is Nutley Mill, built in 1690.

O OXFORD, OXFORDSHIRE - Beautiful university town with many ancient colleges, some dating from the 13th C, and numerous buildings of historic and architectural interest. The Ashmolean Museum has outstanding collections. Lovely gardens and meadows with punting on the Cherwell.

P PANGBOURNE, BERKSHIRE - A pretty stretch of river where the Pang joins the Thames with views of the lock, weir and toll bridge. Once the home of Kenneth Grahame, author of "Wind in the Willows".

PLAXTOL, KENT - Village standing high above the Kent Weald, with a 17th C church in the centre and a rare medieval domestic house.

POOLE, DORSET - A tremendous natural harbour makes Poole a superb boating centre. The harbour area is crowded with historic buildings including the 15th C Town Cellars housing a maritime museum.

PORTLAND, DORSET - Joined by a narrow isthmus to the coast, a stony promontory sloping from the lofty landward side to a lighthouse on Portland Bill at its southern tip. Villages are built of the white limestone for which the "isle" is famous.

PORTSMOUTH & SOUTHSEA, HAMPSHIRE - There have been connections with the Navy since early times, and the first dock was built in 1194. HMS Victory, Nelson's flagship, is here and Charles Dickens' former home is open to the public. Neighbouring Southsea has a promenade with magnificent views of Spithead.

R ROCHESTER, KENT - Ancient cathedral city on the River Medway which has many places of interest connected with Charles Dickens (who lived nearby) including the fascinating Dickens Centre. There is also a massive castle overlooking the river and Guildhall Museum.

ROMSEY, HAMPSHIRE - Town which grew up around the important abbey and which lies on the banks of the River Test, famous for trout and salmon. Broadlands House, home of the late Lord Mountbatten, is open to the public.

ROYAL TUNBRIDGE WELLS, KENT - This "Royal" town became famous as a spa in the 17th C and much of its charm is retained, as in the Pantiles, a shaded walk lined with elegant shops. Heritage attraction "A Day at the Wells". Excellent shopping centre.

RYDE, ISLE OF WIGHT - The island's chief entry port, connected to Portsmouth by ferries and hovercraft. Seven miles of sandy beaches with a half-mile pier, esplanade and gardens.

RYE, EAST SUSSEX - Cobbled, hilly streets and fine old buildings make Rye, once a Cinque Port, a most picturesque town. Noted for its church with ancient clock, potteries and antique shops. Town Model Sound and Light Show gives a good introduction to the town.

S SEAFORD, EAST SUSSEX - The town was a bustling port until 1579 when the course of the River Ouse was diverted. The downlands around the town make good walking country, with fine views of the Seven Sisters cliffs.

SHAFTESBURY, DORSET - Hilltop town with a long history. The ancient and cobbled Gold Hill is one of the most attractive in Dorset. There is an excellent small museum containing a collection of buttons, for which the town is famous.

SHERBORNE, DORSET - Dorset's "Cathedral City" of medieval streets, golden hamstone buildings and great abbey church, resting place of Saxon kings. Formidable 12th C castle ruins and Sir Walter Raleigh's splendid Tudor mansion and deer park. Street markets, leisure centre, many cultural activities.

SOUTHAMPTON, HAMPSHIRE - One of Britain's leading seaports with a long history, now a major container port. In the 18th C it became a fashionable resort with the assembly rooms and theatre. The old Guildhall and the Wool House are now museums. Sections of the medieval wall can still be seen.

STANDLAKE, OXFORDSHIRE - 13th C church with an octagonal tower and spire standing beside the Windrush. The interior of the church is rich in woodwork.

STUDLAND, DORSET - On a beautiful stretch of coast and good for walking, with a National Nature Reserve to the north. The Norman church is the finest in the country, with superb rounded arches and vaulting. Brownsea Island, where the first scout camp was held, lies in Poole Harbour.

SWANAGE, DORSET - Began life as an Anglo-Saxon port, then a quarrying centre of Purbeck marble. The safe, sandy beach is set in a sweeping bay flanked by downs, making it an ideal resort and good walking country.

SWAY, HAMPSHIRE - Small village on the south-western edge of the New Forest. It is noted for its 220-ft tower, Peterson's Folly, built in the 1870s by a retired Indian judge to demonstrate the value of concrete as a building material.

T TENTERDEN, KENT - Most attractive market town with a broad main street full of 16th C houses and shops. The tower of the 15th C parish church is the finest in Kent. Fine antiques centre.

THAME, OXFORDSHIRE - Historic market town on the River Thames. The wide, unspoilt High Street has many styles of architecture with medieval timber-framed cottages, Georgian houses and some famous inns.

TOTLAND BAY, ISLE OF WIGHT - On the Freshwater Peninsula. It is possible to walk from here around to Alum Bay.

WALTON-ON-THAMES, SURREY - Busy town beside the Thames, retaining a distinctive atmosphere despite being only 12 miles from central London. Close to Hampton Court Palace, Sandown Park racecourse and Claremont Landscape Garden (National Trust), Esher.

WHITSTABLE, KENT - Seaside resort and yachting centre on Kent's north shore. The beach is shingle, and there are the usual seaside amenities and entertainments and also a museum.

WHITWELL, ISLE OF WIGHT - West of Ventnor, with interesting church, thatched inn and youth hostel. Good walking area.

WINCHESTER, HAMPSHIRE - King Alfred the Great made Winchester the capital of Saxon England. A magnificent Norman cathedral, with one of the longest naves in Europe, dominates the city. Home of Winchester College, founded in 1382.

WINDSOR, BERKSHIRE - Town dominated by the spectacular castle, home of the Royal Family for over 900 years. Parts are open to the public. There are many attractions including the Great Park, Eton and trips on the river.

WORTHING, WEST SUSSEX - Town in the West Sussex countryside and by the south coast, with excellent shopping and many pavement cafes and restaurants. Attractions include the award-winning Museum and Art Gallery, beautiful gardens, pier, elegant town houses, Cissbury Ring hill fort and the South Downs.

AT-A-GLANCE SYMBOLS

Symbols at the end of each accommodation entry give useful information about services and facilities. A key to symbols can be found inside the back cover flap. Keep this open for easy reference.

Self-Catering Agencies

This section of the guide lists agencies which have a selection of holiday homes to let in various parts of the country. Some agencies specialise in a particular area or region while others have properties in all parts of England.

The agencies listed here are grouped first into those who have had all properties assessed by VisitBritain, secondly into those who have had at least 75% of their properties assessed and thirdly those who have had at least 50% of their properties assessed.

To obtain further information on individual properties please contact the agency or agencies direct, indicating the time of year when the accommodation is required, the number of people to be accommodated and any preferred locations.

* The agencies listed in green have an advertisement in this guide.

Totally Quality Assessed

These agencies promote only properties which have been assessed under VisitBritain's National Quality Assurance Standard

Appledore Holiday Letting Agency
T: (01237) 476191
F: (01237) 479621
E: enquiries@appledore-letting.co.uk
I: www.appledore-letting.co.uk

Bath Centre-Stay Holidays
T: (01225) 313205
F: (01225) 313205
E: holidays@bathcentrestay.freeserve.co.uk
I: www.bcsh.co.uk

Bath Holiday Homes
T: (01225) 332221
E: bhh@virgin.net
I: www.bathholidayhomes.co.uk

Bembridge Holiday Homes
T: (01983) 873163
F: (01983) 873163
E: mail@bembridge-holiday-homes.co.uk
I: www.bembridge-holiday-homes.co.uk

The Coppermines & Coniston Lanes Cottages
T: (015394) 41765
F: (015394) 41944
E: info@coppermines.co.uk
I: www.coppermines.co.uk

Cornish Holiday Cottages
T: (01326) 250339
F: (01326) 250339
E: postmaster@cornishholidaycottages.net
I: www.cornishholidaycottages.net

Cottages South West
T: (01626) 872314
F: (01626) 872314
E: lets@cottagessw.vir.co.uk
I: cottagessw.vir.co.uk

Country Hideaways
T: (01969) 663559
F: (01969) 663559
E: ubr@countryhidaways.co.uk
I: www.countryhideaways.co.uk

Cumbrian Cottages Ltd
T: (01228) 599950
F: (01228) 599970
E: enquiries@cumbrian-cottages.co.uk
I: www.cumbrian-cottages.co.uk

Dartmouth Cottages
T: (01803) 839499
E: holidays@dartmouthcottages.com
I: www.dartmouthcottages.com

Diana Bullivant Holidays
T: (01208) 831336
F: (01208) 831336
E: diana@bullivant.fsnet.co.uk
I: www.cornwall-online.co.uk/diana-bullivant

Dream Cottages
T: (01305) 761347
F: (01305) 789000
E: admin@dream-cottages.co.uk
I: www.dream-cottages.co.uk

Freedom Holiday Homes
T: (01580) 720770
F: (01580) 720771
E: mail@freedomholidayhomes.co.uk
I: www.freedomholidayhomes.co.uk

Garden of England Cottages Limited
T: (01732) 369168
F: (01732) 358817
E: holidays@gardenofenglandcottages.co.uk
I: www.gardenofenglandcottages.co.uk

Harbour Holidays, Padstow

Heart of the Lakes and Cottage Life
T: (015394) 32321
F: (015394) 33251
E: info@heartofthelakes.co.uk
I: www.heartofthelakes.co.uk

Holiday Home Services (Seaview)
T: (01983) 811418
F: (01983) 616900
E: mail@seaviewholidayhomes.co.uk
I: www.seaview-holiday-homes.co.uk

Holiday Homes and Cottages SW
T: (01803) 663650
F: (01803) 664037
E: holcotts@aol.com
I: www.swcottages.co.uk

Holiday Homes Owners Services (West Wight)
T: (01983) 753423

Home from Home Holidays
T: (01983) 854340
F: (01983) 855524
E: admin@hfromh.co.uk
I: www.hfromh.co.uk

In the English Manner (London Apartments)
T: (01559) 371600
F: (01559) 371601
E: london@english-manner.com
I: www.english-manner.com

Island Cottage Holidays
T: (01929) 480080
F: (01929) 481070
E: enq@islandcottageholidays.com
I: www.islandcottageholidays.com

Island Properties
T: (01720) 422211
F: (01720) 422211
E: enquiries@islesofscillyholidays.com
I: www.islesofscillyholidays.com

Jean Bartlett Cottage Holidays Ltd
T: (01297) 23221
F: (01297) 23303
E: holidays@jeanbartlett.com
I: www.jeanbartlett.com

Lakeland Cottage Company
T: (015395) 30024
F: (015395) 31932
E: john@lakelandcottages.com
I: www.lakelandcottageco.com

Lakeland Cottage Holidays
T: (017687) 76065
F: (017687) 76869
E: info@lakelandcottages.co.uk
I: www.lakelandcottages.co.uk

Lakelovers Holiday Homes
T: (015394) 88855
F: (015394) 88857
E: bookings@lakelovers.co.uk
I: www.lakelovers.co.uk

Linstone Chine Holiday Services Ltd
T: (01983) 755933
F: (01983) 755933
E: enquiries@linstone-chine.co.uk
I: www.linstone-chine.co.uk

Mackay's Agency
T: (0131) 225 3539
F: (0131) 226 5284
E: patricia@mackays-scotland.co.uk
I: www.mackays-scotland.co.uk

Marsdens Cottage Holidays
T: (01271) 813777
F: (01271) 813664
E: holidays@marsdens.co.uk
I: www.marsdens.co.uk

Milkbere Cottage Holidays
T: (01297) 20729
F: (01297) 22925
E: info@milkberehols.com
I: www.milkberehols.com

Millers
T: (023) 9246 5951
F: (023) 9246 1321
E: millers@haylingproperty.co.uk
I: www.millers@haylingproperty.co.uk

Miraleisure Ltd
T: (01424) 730298
F: (01424) 212500

Red Rose Cottages
T: (01200) 420101
F: (01200) 420103
E: info@redrosecottages.co.uk
I: www.redrosecottages.co.uk

Special Places
T: (01872) 864400
E: office@specialplacescornwall.co.uk
I: www.specialplacescornwall.co.uk

Suffolk Secrets
T: (01379) 651297
F: (01379) 650116
E: holidays@suffolk-secrets.co.uk
I: www.suffolk-secrets.co.uk

Sutherland Estate
T: (01408) 633268
F: (01408) 633800
E: estateoffice@sutherlandestate.com
I: www.sutherlandestates.com

Wheelwrights
T: (015394) 37635
F: (015394) 37618
E: enquiries@wheelwrights.com
I: www.wheelwrights.com

Whitby Holiday Cottages
T: (01947) 603010
F: (01947) 821133
E: enquiries@whitby-cottages.co.uk
I: www.whitby-cottages.co.uk

Yealm Holidays
T: (0870) 747 2987
F: (01752) 873173
E: info@yealm-holidays.co.uk
I: www.yealm-holidays.co.uk

York Holiday Homes
T: (01904) 641997
F: (01904) 613453
I: www.yorkshirenet.co.uk/accgde/yorkholidayhomes

Commited to VisitBritain Quality Assurance with at least 75% assessed

At least 75% of the properties promoted by each of these agencies has been assessed under VisitBritain's National Quality Assurance Standard

Best of Brighton and Sussex Cottages Ltd
T: (01273) 308779
F: (01273) 390211
E: enquiries@bestofbrighton.co.uk
I: www.bestofbrighton.co.uk

Norfolk Holiday Homes
T: (01485) 534267
F: (01485) 535230
E: shohol@birdsnorfolkholidayhomes.co.uk
I: www.norfolkholidayhomes-birds.co.uk

Rumsey Holiday Homes
T: (08456) 444 852
F: (01202) 701955
E: info@rhh.org
I: www.rhh.org

Homefinders Holidays
T: (01904) 632660
F: (01904) 651388
E: c.thomas-letters.of.york@btinternet.com
I: www.letters-of-york.co.uk

Rock Holidays
T: (01208) 863399
F: (01208) 862218
E: rockhols@aol.com
I: www.rockholidays.co.uk

Shoreline Cottages Ltd
T: (0113) 244 8410
F: (0113) 244 9826
E: reservations@shoreline-cottages.com
I: www.shoreline-cottages.com

Committed to VisitBritain Quality Assurance with at least 50% assessed

At least 50% of the properties promoted by each of these agencies has been assessed under VisitBritain's National Quality Assurance Standard

Albion Rose Properties
T: (01763) 249999
F: (01763) 247793
E: albioncottages@aol.com
I: www.albionrose.co.uk

Cottage in the Country & Cottage Holidays
T: (01993) 831495
F: (01993) 831095
E: info@cottageinthecountry.co.uk
I: www.cottageinthecountry.co.uk

Dales Holiday Cottages
T: (01756) 799821
F: (01756) 797012
E: Enq@dales-holiday-cottages.com
I: www.dales-holiday-cottages.com

Fowey Harbour Cottages (W J B Hill & Son)
T: (01726) 832211
F: (01726) 832901
E: hillandson@talk21.com

Island Holiday Homes
T: (01983) 616644
F: (01983) 616640
E: enquiries@island-holiday-homes.net
I: www.island-holiday.homes.net

Lambert & Russell
T: (01263) 513139
F: (01263) 513139
E: property@lamberttw.fslife.co.uk

Manor Cottages
T: (01993) 824252
F: (01993) 824443
E: mancott@netcomuk.co.uk
I: www.manorcottages.co.uk

Mullion Cottages
T: (01326) 240315
F: (01326) 241090
E: enquiries@mullioncottages.com
I: www.mullioncottages.com

Peak Cottages
T: (0114) 262 0777
F: (0114) 262 0777
E: enquiries@peakcott
I: www.peakcottages.com

Tourist INFORMATION Centres

When it comes to your next England break, the first stage of your journey could be closer than you think. You've probably got a tourist information centre nearby which is there to serve the local community - as well as visitors. Knowledgeable staff will be happy to help you, wherever you're heading.

Many tourist information centres can provide you with maps and guides, and often it's possible to book accommodation and travel tickets too.

Across the country, there are more than 550 TICs. You'll find the address of your nearest centre in your local phone book.

QUALITY ASSURED
VISITOR
ATTRACTION

Visitor Attraction Quality Assurance

VisitBritain operates a Visitor Attraction Quality Assurance Standard. Participating attractions are visited annually by trained, impartial assessors who look at all aspects of the visit, from initial telephone enquiries to departure, customer services to catering, as well as facilities and activities. Only those attractions which have been assessed by VisitBritain and meet the standard receive the quality marque, your sign of a 'Quality Assured Visitor Attraction'.

Look out for the quality marque and visit with confidence.

VisitBritain's
assessed accommodation

On the following pages you will find an exclusive listing of every self-catering establishment in England that has been assessed for quality by VisitBritain.

The information includes brief contact details for each place to stay, together with its Star rating. The listing also shows if an establishment has a National Accessible rating (see the front of the guide for further information).

More detailed information on all the places shown in blue can be found in the regional sections (where establishments have paid to have their details included). To find these entries please refer to the appropriate regional section, or look in the town index at the back of this guide.

The list which follows was compiled slightly later than the regional sections. For this reason you may find that, in a few instances, a Star rating may differ between the two sections. This list contains the most up-to-date information and was correct at the time of going to press.

LONDON

E1

Hamlet UK Ltd ★★-★★★
Contact: Miss R Naufal, Hamlet UK Ltd, 74 Onslow Gardens, Muswell Hill, London N10 3JX
T: (020) 8883 0024
F: (020) 8444 1118
E: hamlet_uk@globalnet.co.uk
I: www.users.globalnet.co.uk/~hamlet_uk/

E11

S.T.A.Y! ★★★
Contact: Mrs Teresa Farnham, 17 Greenstone Mews, Wanstead, London E11 2RS
T: (020) 8530 6729
F: (020) 8530 6729
E: stayfarnham@aol.com

E14

Bridge House-London Docklands ★★★★
Contact: Mr J K Graham, 31 Falcon Way, London E14 9UP
T: (020) 7538 8980
F: (020) 7538 8980
E: johnkgraham@hotmail.com
I: www.johnkgraham.com

River Thames Apartment ★★★★
Contact: Mrs Greta Paull, 35 Cheyne Avenue, South Woodford, London E18 2DP
T: (020) 8530 2336
F: (020) 8530 2336
E: gretapaull@aol.com
I: www.riverthamesapartment.co.uk

Riverside ★★★★
Contact: Ms Christine James, Riverside, 35 Fairfield Drive, Codsall, Wolverhampton WV8 2AE
T: (01902) 843545
F: (01902) 843545
E: christine@capstansq.fsnet.co.uk
I: www.capstansq.fsnet.co.uk

E16

Sheerness Apartments ★★★★
Serviced Apartments
Contact: Mr Colin Stares, Spectrum Property, 8 Fordwich Hill, Hertford SG14 2BQ
T: (01992) 422100
F: (01992) 301351
E: cjstares@aol.com

N7

Carena Holiday Accommodation ★★-★★★
Contact: Mr M Chouthi, 98 St George's Avenue, Tufnell Park, London N7 0AH
T: (020) 7607 7453
F: (020) 7607 7453
E: c.chouthi@btopenworld.com

N21

Firs Apartments ★★★★
Contact: Mrs A M Turanli, 30 Firs Lane, London N21 3ES
T: (020) 8360 3890
F: (020) 8364 2232
E: information@firsapartments.com
I: www.firsapartments.com

SE1

London Riverside Apartments ★★★★
Contact: Mr John Dillon, London Riverside Apartments, 566 Manhattan Building, Bow Quarter, London E3 2UL
T: (020) 8983 1260
I: www.londonriverside.co.uk

SE3

Sunfields ★★
Contact: Mrs J Poole, Sunfields, 135 Shooters Hill Road, Basement Flat, London SE3 8UQ
T: (020) 8858 1420
E: jacquipoole@sunfieldsfsnet.co.uk

SE6

Glenthurston Holiday Apartments ★★★-★★★★
Contact: Miss Sue Halliday & Mrs C E Halliday, Glenthurston Holiday Apartments, 27-29 Canadian Avenue, London SE6 3AU
T: (020) 8690 3992
F: (020) 8265 5872
E: via website
I: www.glenthurston.co.uk

SE10

Harbour Master's House Basement Flat★★★★
Contact: Professor Chris French, The Harbour Master's House, 20 Ballast Quay, London SE10 9PD
T: (020) 8293 9597
F: (020) 8293 9597
E: harbourmaster@lineone.net
I: website.lineone.net/~harbourmaster/

SE13

Studio Cottage ★★★
Contact: Ms Pamela Burke, Welcome Homes & Hotels, 21 Kellerton Road, London SE13 5RB
T: (020) 8265 1212
F: (020) 8852 3243
E: info@welcomehomes.co.uk
I: www.welcomehomes.co.uk

SW1

The Apartments Knightsbridge ★★★★-★★★★★
Contact: Ms Maureen Boyle, Panorama Property Services Ltd, The Garage, 22 Queensgate Place Mews, London SW7 5BQ
T: (020) 7589 3271
F: (020) 7589 3274
E: maureen@theapartments.co.uk

Club Suites ★★★★
Contact: Ms Anne-Marie Webster, 52 Lower Sloane Street, London SW1W 8BS
T: (020) 7730 9131
F: (020) 7730 6146
E: reservations@sloaneclub.co.uk
I: www.sloaneclub.co.uk

SW3

The Apartments ★★★★
Contact: Ms Maureen Boyle, Panorama Property Services Ltd The Garage, 22 Queensgate Place Mews, London SW7 5BQ
T: (020) 7589 3271
F: (020) 7589 3274
E: maureen@theapartments.co.uk
I: www.cheapartments.co.uk

Beaufort House ★★★★★
Serviced Apartments
Contact: Mr J Garcia, Beaufort House, 45-47 Beaufort Gardens, London SW3 1PN
T: (020) 7584 2600
F: (020) 7584 6532
E: info@beauforthouse.co.uk
I: www.beauforthouse.co.uk

SW5

Emperors Gate Short Stay Apartments ★★★
Contact: Mr R G Arnold, Emperors Gate Short Stay Apartments, 8 Knaresborough Place, Kensington, London SW5 0TG
T: (020) 7244 8409
F: (020) 7373 6455
E: info@apartment-hotels.com
I: www.apartment-hotels.com

SW7

Queensberry Mews ★★★
Contact: Mrs P Owen, 37 Norham Road, Oxford OX2 6SQ
T: (01865) 511835
F: (01865) 463340
E: paulejeanne@yahoo.co.uk
I: www.queensberrymews.co.uk

Snow White Properties Ltd ★★-★★★
Contact: Miss M White, Snow White Properties Ltd, 55 Ennismore Gardens, Knightsbridge, London SW7 1AJ
T: (020) 7584 3307
F: (020) 7581 4686
E: snow.white@virgin.net
I: www.snowwhitelondon.com

SW14

East Sheen Studio Flat Flat 1 ★★★
Contact: Mrs Angela Butt, 179 Mortlake Road, Kew, Richmond TW9 4AW
T: (020) 8876 0584
F: (020) 8876 0584

SW18

Beaumont Apartments ★★★★
Contact: Mr & Mrs A Afriat, Beaumont Apartments, 24 Combemartin Road, Southfields, London SW18 5PR
T: (020) 8789 2663
F: (020) 8265 5499
E: alan@beaumont-london-apartments.co.uk
I: www.beaumont-london-apartments.co.uk

SW19

Honey Cottage ★★★
Contact: Mrs Jenny Humphries, 5 Homefield Road, Wimbledon, London SW19 4QE
T: (020) 8947 9636
F: (020) 8395 7353
E: mikejenny@compuserve.com
I: www.honeycottage.com

SW20

Thalia & Hebe Holiday Homes ★★★
Contact: Mr & Mrs Briscoe-Smith, 150 Westway, Raynes Park, West Wimbledon, London SW20 9LS
T: (020) 8542 0505
F: (020) 8287 0637
E: peter@briscoe-smith.org.uk
I: www.briscoe-smith.org.uk/thalia/

TW9

Flat 4 Friston House ★★★
Contact: Mr Arthur Shipp, 19 Larkfield Road, Richmond TW9 2PG
T: (020) 8948 6620
E: shipplets@ukgateway.net
I: www.shipplets.com

W1

The Ascott Mayfair ★★★★-★★★★★
Serviced Apartments
Contact: Mr Martin King, Ascott International, 16 Charles Street, London W1J 5DS
T: (020) 7499 6868
F: (020) 7499 0705
E: enquiry.london@the-ascott.com
I: www.the-ascott.com

23 Greengarden House ★★★★
Serviced Apartments
Contact: Miss Nikki Pybus, 23 Greengarden House, St Christopher's Place, London W1U 1NL
T: (020) 7935 9191
F: (020) 7935 8858
E: info@greengardenhouse.com
I: www.greengardenhouse.com

Marylebone Apartment Rating Applied For
Contact: Mr Richard Sutherland, Marylebone Apartment, 9 Molyneux Street, London W1H 5HP
T: (020) 7262 9843
E: rsutherland@ayli.com

Tustin Holiday Flats ★★-★★★
Contact: Reservations Office, Tustin Holiday Flats, 94 York Street, London W1H 1QX
T: (020) 7723 9611
F: (020) 7724 0224
E: pctustinuk@btconnect.com
I: www.pctustin.com

W2

Royal Court Apartments ★★
Contact: Ms Tesse, Royal Court Apartments, 51-53 Gloucester Terrace, London W2 3DQ
T: (020) 7402 5077
F: (020) 7724 0286
E: info@royalcourtapartments.co.uk
I: www.royalcourtapartments.co.uk

W5

Clarendon House Apartments ★★★★
Contact: Mrs Anne Pedley, 48 Ranelagh Road, Ealing, London W5 5RJ
T: (020) 8567 0314
F: (020) 8566 3241
E: clarendon.house@LineOne.net
I: www.clarendonhouse apartments.co.uk

W8

51 Kensington Court ★★★★
Contact: 51 Kensington Court, London W8 5DB
T: (020) 7937 2030
F: (020) 7938 5312
E: bookings@kensingtoncourt.co.uk
I: www.kensingtoncourt.co.uk

W13

Apartments West London ★★★
Contact: Bill Smith, Apartments West London, 94 Gordon Road, London W13 8PT
T: (020) 8566 8187
F: (020) 8566 7670
E: info@apartmentswestlondon.com
I: www.apartmentswestlondon.com

BECKENHAM

Oakfield Apartments ★-★★★
Contact: Mr J E Deane
T: (020) 8658 4441
F: (020) 8658 9198
E: hols@oakfield.co.uk
I: www.oakfield.co.uk

CROYDON

Ballards Farm Cottage ★★★
Contact: Mr & Mrs M McDermott, Ballards Farm Cottage, 2 Ballards Farm Road, Croydon CR0 5RL
T: (020) 8657 1080
I: www.website.lineone.net/~michaelmed

London Country Apartments Ltd ★★★★-★★★★★
Contact: Ms Rochelle Anselm, London Country Apartments Ltd, 121 Cherry Orchard Road, Croydon CR0 6BE
T: (020) 8686 8068
F: (020) 8686 0678
E: enquiries@londoncountryapartments.co.uk
I: www.londoncountryapartments.co.uk

S N D Apartments ★★★-★★★★★
Contact: Mrs Pamela Pereira, S N D Apartments, 1 Mulgrave Road, Croydon CR0 1BL
T: (020) 8686 7023
F: (020) 8686 7835
E: reservations@www.sndapartments.co.uk
I: www.sndapartments.co.uk

HAMPTON WICK

Wick Cottage & The Barn Rating Applied For
Contact: Ms Pippa Stevens, Chase Lodge Hotel, 10 Park Road, Hampton Wick, Kingston upon Thames KT1 4AS
T: (020) 8943 1862
F: (020) 8943 9363
E: info@chaselodgehotel.com
I: www.chaselodgehotel.com

KINGSTON UPON THAMES

Sunny House ★
Contact: Mrs Denise Haworth, Chase Lodge Hotel, 10 Park Road, Hampton Wick, Kingston upon Thames KT1 4AS
T: (020) 8943 1862
F: (020) 8943 9363
E: info@chaselodgehotel.com

PETTS WOOD

3 Maple Close ★★
Contact: Mrs Debra Sutch, 3 Maple Close, Petts Wood, Orpington BR5 1LP
T: (01689) 603037

PINNER

Moss Cottage ★★★★
Contact: Ms Barbara Le Quesne
T: (020) 8868 5507
F: (020) 8868 5507
E: info@moss-lane-cottages.com
I: www.moss-lane-cottages.com

TWICKENHAM

Houseboat Sunray ★★
Contact: Ms Lynn Gould, 17 The Grove, Isleworth TW7 4JS
T: (020) 8560 5630
E: sunray@dial.pipex.com
I: www.sunray.dial.pipex.com

CUMBRIA

AINSTABLE Cumbria

The Old Dairy Cottage ★★★★
Contact: Mrs Jackie Moffat, Rowfoot, Ainstable, Broadwath, Heads Hook, Carlisle CA4 9PZ
T: (01768) 896409
F: (01768) 896409
E: jackie@rowfoot.fsnet.co.uk

ALLITHWAITE Cumbria

Shamrock Cottage ★★★
Contact: Mr Peter Durbin, Cumbrian Cottages, 2 Lonsdale Street, Carlisle CA1 1DB
T: (01228) 599960
F: (01228) 599970
E: enquiries@cumbrian-cottages.co.uk
I: www.cumbrian-cottages.co.uk

ALLONBY Cumbria

Crookhurst ★★★★
Contact: Mrs Brenda Wilson, Allonby, Maryport CA15 6RB
T: (01900) 881228
F: (01900) 881228
E: brendawilson@zoom.co.uk
I: www.crookhurst.co.uk

Spring Lea ★★★★
Contact: Mr Williamson, Spring Lea Caravan Park, Main Road, Allonby, Maryport, Maryport CA15 6QF
T: (01900) 881331
F: (01900) 881209
E: mail@springlea.co.uk
I: www.springlea.co.uk

ALSTON Cumbria

Connelly ★★★
Contact: Mr D A Timms, 51 Silver Street, Ely CB7 4JB
T: (01353) 662171

Ghyll Burn Cottage ★★★
Contact: Mrs Susan Huntley, Hartside Nursery Garden, Alston CA9 3BL
T: (01434) 381372
F: (01434) 381372
E: ghyllburn@macunlimited.net
I: www.cumbria1st.com/towns

Stone Barn Cottage ★★★★★
Contact: Mrs Dee Ellis, Stone Barn Cottage, Low Galligill Farm, Nentsberry, Alston CA9 3LW
T: (01434) 381672
E: tim@hillfarmer.com
I: www.btinternet.com/~stonebarncottage

AMBLESIDE Cumbria

1,2,3,4 & 5 Riverside Cottages ★★★
Contact: Mr Paul Liddell, Lakelovers, Belmont House, Lake Road, Bowness-on-Windermere, Windermere LA23 3BJ
T: (015394) 88855
F: (015394) 88857
E: bookings@lakelovers.co.uk
I: www.lakelovers.co.uk

Above Stock ★★★★
Contact: Mr Paul Liddell, Lakelovers, Belmont House, Lake Road, Bowness-on-Windermere, Windermere LA23 3BJ
T: (015394) 88855
F: (015394) 88857
E: bookings@lakelovers.co.uk
I: www.lakelovers.co.uk

Acorns ★★★★
Contact: Mrs Susan Jackson, Heart of the Lakes, Fisherbeck Mill, Old Lake Road, Ambleside LA22 0DH
T: (015394) 32321
F: (015394) 33251
E: info@heartofthelakes.co.uk
I: www.heartofthelakes.co.uk

Altar End ★★★★
Contact: Mrs Susan Jackson, Heart of the Lakes, Fisherbeck Mill, Old Lake Road, Ambleside LA22 0DH
T: (015394) 32321
F: (015394) 33251
E: info@heartofthelakes.co.uk
I: www.heartofthelakes.co.uk

Amblers Rest ★★★★
Contact: Mr Peter Durbin, Cumbrian Cottages, 2 Lonsdale Street, Carlisle CA1 1DB
T: (01228) 599960
F: (01228) 599970
E: enquiries@cumbrian-cottages.co.uk
I: www.cumbrian-cottages.co.uk

20 and 21 The Falls ★★★
Contact: Mr Paul Liddell, Lakelovers, Belmont House, Lake Road, Bowness-on-Windermere, Windermere LA23 3BJ
T: (015394) 88855
F: (015394) 88857
E: bookings@lakelovers.co.uk
I: www.lakelovers.co.uk

Appletree Cottage ★★★★
Contact: Mrs Susan Jackson, Heart of the Lakes, Fisherbeck Mill, Old Lake Road, Ambleside LA22 0DH
T: (015394) 32321
F: (015394) 33251
E: info@heartofthelakes.co.uk
I: www.heartofthelakes.co.uk

Ashburne Cottage ★★★
Contact: Mrs Susan Jackson, Heart of the Lakes, Fisherbeck Mill, Old Lake Road, Ambleside LA22 0DH
T: (015394) 32321
F: (015394) 33251
E: info@heartofthelakes.co.uk
I: www.heartofthelakes.co.uk

Ashness ★★★★
Contact: Mrs Susan Jackson, Heart of the Lakes, Fisherbeck Mill, Old Lake Road, Ambleside LA22 0DH
T: (015394) 32321
F: (015394) 33251
E: info@heartofthelakes.co.uk
I: www.heartofthelakes.co.uk

Babbling Brook ★★★★
Contact: Mrs Susan Jackson, Heart of the Lakes, Fisherbeck Mill, Old Lake Road, Ambleside LA22 0DH
T: (015394) 32321
F: (015394) 33251
E: info@heartofthelakes.co.uk
I: www.heartofthelakes.co.uk

7 Badgers Rake (The Garden Flat) ★★★
Contact: Mr Peter Durbin, Cumbrian Cottages, 2 Lonsdale Street, Carlisle CA1 1DB
T: (01228) 599960
F: (01228) 599970
E: enquiries@cumbrian-cottages.co.uk
I: www.cumbrian-cottages.co.uk

9 Badgers Rake ★★★
Contact: Mr Peter Durbin, Cumbrian Cottages, 2 Lonsdale Street, Carlisle CA1 1DB
T: (01228) 599960
F: (01228) 599970
E: enquiries@cumbrian-cottages.co.uk
I: www.cumbrian-cottages.co.uk

10 Badgers Rake ★★★★
Contact: Mr Peter Durbin, Cumbrian Cottages, 2 Lonsdale Street, Carlisle CA1 1DB
T: (01228) 599960
F: (01228) 599970
E: enquiries@cumbrian-cottages.co.uk
I: www.cumbrian-cottages.co.uk

Bakestones Cottage ★★★★
Contact: Mrs Susan Jackson, Heart of the Lakes, Fisherbeck Mill, Old Lake Road, Ambleside LA22 0DH
T: (015394) 32321
F: (015394) 33251
E: info@heartofthelakes.co.uk
I: www.heartofthelakes.co.uk

Barn Waterhead ★★★★
Contact: Mrs Susan Jackson, Heart of the Lakes, Fisherbeck Mill, Old Lake Road, Ambleside LA22 0DH
T: (015394) 32321
F: (015394) 33251
E: info@heartofthelakes.co.uk
I: www.heartofthelakes.co.uk

Birch Cottage ★★★
Contact: Dr L Nash, 47 Goring Road, Bounds Green, London N11 2BT
T: (020) 8888 1252
F: (020) 8888 1252
E: birchcottage@vithani.freeserve.co.uk

Birch Knoll ★★★★
Contact: Mr Paul Liddell, Lakelovers, Belmont House, Lake Road, Bowness-on-Windermere, Windermere LA23 3BJ
T: (015394) 88855
F: (015394) 88857
E: bookings@lakelovers.co.uk

Birchcroft ★★★★
Contact: Mrs Susan Jackson, Heart of the Lakes, Fisherbeck Mill, Old Lake Road, Ambleside LA22 0DH
T: (015394) 32321
F: (015394) 33251
E: info@heartofthelakes.co.uk
I: www.heartofthelakes.co.uk

Blelham Tarn at Neaum Crag ★★★★
Contact: Mr Andy Witts, P O Box 73, Newport TF10 8WG
T: 07740 486947
F: (01952) 810102
E: sales@logcabin.bz
I: www.pad-lok.com

Blue Hill Cottage ★★★
Contact: Mr Peter Durbin, Cumbrian Cottages, 2 Lonsdale Street, Carlisle CA1 1DB
T: (01228) 599960
F: (01228) 599970
E: enquiries@cumbrian-cottages.co.uk
I: www.cumbrian-cottages.co.uk

Bobbin Cottage ★★★
Contact: Mr Paul Liddell, Lakelovers, Belmont House, Lake Road, Bowness-on-Windermere, Windermere LA23 3BJ
T: (015394) 88855
F: (015394) 88857
E: bookings@lakelovers.co.uk
I: www.lakelovers.co.uk

Borrans View Cottage ★★★
Contact: Mr Peter Durbin, Cumbrian Cottages, 2 Lonsdale Street, Carlisle CA1 1DB
T: (01228) 599960
F: (01228) 599970
E: enquiries@cumbrian-cottages.co.uk
I: www.cumbrian-cottages.co.uk

Bowfell ★★★
Contact: Mrs Susan Jackson, Heart of the Lakes, Fisherbeck Mill, Old Lake Road, Ambleside LA22 0DH
T: (015394) 32321
F: (015394) 33251
E: info@heartofthelakes.co.uk
I: www.heartofthelakes.co.uk

Brackenrigg ★★★
Contact: Mr Paul Liddell, Lakelovers, Belmont House, Lake Road, Bowness-on-Windermere, Windermere LA23 3BJ
T: (015394) 88855
F: (015394) 88857
E: bookings@lakelovers.co.uk
I: www.lakelovers.co.uk

Brae Cottage ★★★
Contact: Mr Paul Liddell, Lakelovers, Belmont House, Lake Road, Bowness-on-Windermere, Windermere LA23 3BJ
T: (015394) 88855
F: (015394) 88857
E: bookings@lakelovers.co.uk
I: www.lakelovers.co.uk

Braebeck ★★★★
Contact: Mr Paul Liddell, Lakelovers, Belmont House Lake Road, Bowness-on-Windermere, Windermere LA23 3BJ
T: (015394) 88855
F: (015394) 88857
E: bookings@lakelovers.co.uk
I: www.lakelovers.co.uk

15 Brathay ★★★★
Contact: Mrs Susan Jackson, Heart of the Lakes, Fisherbeck Mill, Old Lake Road, Ambleside LA22 0DH
T: (015394) 32321
F: (015394) 33251
E: info@heartofthelakes.co.uk
I: www.heartofthelakes.co.uk

Briar Nook ★★★★
Contact: Mr Peter Durbin, Cumbrian Cottages, 2 Lonsdale Street, Carlisle CA1 1DB
T: (01228) 599960
F: (01228) 599970
E: enquiries@cumbrian-cottages.co.uk
I: www.cumbrian-cottages.co.uk

Briardale Cottage ★★★
Contact: Mrs Susan Jackson, Heart of the Lakes, Fisherbeck Mill, Old Lake Road, Ambleside LA22 0DH
T: (015394) 32321
F: (015394) 33251
E: info@heartofthelakes.co.uk
I: www.heartofthelakes.co.uk

Broad Oak ★★★
Contact: Mrs Susan Jackson, Heart of the Lakes, Fisherbeck Mill, Old Lake Road, Ambleside LA22 0DH
T: (015394) 32321
F: (015394) 33251
E: info@heartofthelakes.co.uk
I: www.heartofthelakes.co.uk

Brunt How ★★★
Contact: Mrs Susan Jackson, Heart of the Lakes, Fisherbeck Mill, Old Lake Road, Ambleside LA22 0DH
T: (015394) 32321
F: (015394) 33251
E: info@heartofthelakes.co.uk
I: www.heartofthelakes.co.uk

Buttermere ★★★
Contact: Mr Paul Liddell, Lakelovers, Belmont House, Lake Road, Bowness-on-Windermere, Windermere LA23 3BJ
T: (015394) 88855
F: (015394) 88857
E: bookings@lakelovers.co.uk
I: www.lakelovers.co.uk

Byways ★★
Contact: Mrs Susan Jackson, Heart of the Lakes, Fisherbeck Mill, Old Lake Road, Ambleside LA22 0DH
T: (015394) 32321
F: (015394) 33251
E: info@heartofthelakes.co.uk
I: www.heartofthelakes.co.uk

Cedar House ★★★★
Contact: Mrs Susan Jackson, Heart of the Lakes, Fisherbeck Mill, Old Lake Road, Ambleside LA22 0DH
E: info@heartofthelakes.co.uk
I: www.heartofthelakes.co.uk

Chestnuts, Beeches & The Granary ★★★★
Contact: Mr J R Benson, High Sett, Sun Hill Lane, Troutbeck Bridge, Windermere LA23 1HJ
T: (015394) 42731
F: (015394) 42731
E: sbenson@talk21.com
I: www.accommodationlakedistrict.com

Church View ★★★
Contact: Mr Peter Durbin, Cumbrian Cottages, 2 Lonsdale Street, Carlisle CA1 1DB
T: (01228) 599960
F: (01228) 599970
E: enquiries@cumbrian-cottages.co.uk
I: www.cumbrian-cottages.co.uk

Clover Cottage ★★★
Contact: Mrs Susan Jackson, Heart of the Lakes, Fisherbeck Mill, Old Lake Road, Ambleside LA22 0DH
T: (015394) 32321
F: (015394) 33251
E: info@heartofthelakes.co.uk
I: www.heartofthelakes.co.uk

The Coach House ★★★
Contact: Mrs Susan Jackson, Heart of the Lakes, Fisherbeck Mill, Old Lake Road, Ambleside LA22 0DH
T: (015394) 32321
F: (015394) 33251
E: info@heartofthelakes.co.uk
I: www.heartofthelakes.co.uk

Cobblestone House ★★★★
Contact: Mr Peter Durbin, Cumbrian Cottages, 2 Lonsdale Street, Carlisle CA1 1DB
T: (01228) 599960
F: (01228) 599970
E: enquiries@cumbrian-cottages.co.uk
I: www.cumbrian-cottages.co.uk

Cobblestones ★★★★
Contact: Mr Peter Durbin, Cumbrian Cottages, 2 Lonsdale Street, Carlisle CA1 1DB
T: (01228) 599960
F: (01228) 599970
E: enquiries@cumbrian-cottages.co.uk
I: www.cumbrian-cottages.co.uk

Conifers ★★★
Contact: Mrs Susan Jackson, Heart of the Lakes, Fisherbeck Mill, Old Lake Road, Ambleside LA22 0DH
T: (015394) 32321
F: (015394) 33251
E: info@heartofthelakes.co.uk
I: www.heartofthelakes.co.uk

Cooksons Garth ★★★★
Contact: Mrs Susan Jackson, Heart of the Lakes, Fisherbeck Mill, Old Lake Road, Ambleside LA22 0DH
T: (015394) 32321
F: (015394) 33251
E: info@heartofthelakes.co.uk
I: www.heartofthelakes.co.uk

Crag View ★★★
Contact: Mrs Davies, 21 Dowhills Road, Blundellsands, Liverpool L23 8SH
T: (0151) 924 6995
F: (0151) 285 9107
E: pfdavies@blueyonder.co.uk

Cranford Cottage ★★
Contact: Ref: 301 Sykes Cottages, Sykes Cottages, York House, York Street, Chester CH1 3LR
T: (01244) 345700
F: (01244) 321442
E: info@sykescottages.co.uk
I: www.sykescottages.co.uk

Cringol Cottage ★★★
Contact: Mrs Susan Jackson, Heart of the Lakes, Fisherbeck Mill, Old Lake Road, Ambleside LA22 0DH
T: (015394) 32321
F: (015394) 33251
E: info@heartofthelakes.co.uk
I: www.heartofthelakes.co.uk

Crinkle Crags ★★★
Contact: Mrs Susan Jackson, Heart of the Lakes, Fisherbeck Mill, Old Lake Road, Ambleside LA22 0DH
T: (015394) 32321
F: (015394) 33251
E: info@heartofthelakes.co.uk
I: www.heartofthelakes.co.uk

Derby Cottage ★★★
Contact: Mr Peter Durbin, Cumbrian Cottages, 2 Lonsdale Street, Carlisle CA1 1DB
T: (01228) 599960
F: (01228) 599970
E: enquiries@cumbrian-cottages.co.uk
I: www.cumbrian-cottages.co.uk

Dower House Cottage ★★★
Contact: Mrs Margaret Rigg, The Dower House, Wray Castle, Ambleside LA22 0JA
T: (015394) 33211
F: (015394) 33211

Dwarf Studio ★★★
Contact: Mr Peter Durbin, Cumbrian Cottages, 2 Lonsdale Street, Carlisle CA1 1DB
T: (01228) 599960
F: (01228) 599970
E: enquiries@cumbrian-cottages.co.uk
I: www.cumbrian-cottages.co.uk

Ecclerigg Cottage ★★★
Contact: Mrs Susan Jackson, Heart of the Lakes, Fisherbeck Mill, Old Lake Road, Ambleside LA22 0DH
T: (015394) 32321
F: (015394) 33251
E: info@heartofthelakes.co.uk
I: www.heartofthelakes.co.uk

Ecclerigg Old farm ★★★
Contact: Mrs Susan Jackson, Heart of the Lakes, Fisherbeck Mill, Old Lake Road, Ambleside LA22 0DH
T: (015394) 32321
F: (015394) 33251
E: info@heartofthelakes.co.uk
I: www.heartofthelakes.co.uk

Edelweiss ★★★★
Contact: Mrs Susan Jackson, Heart of the Lakes, Fisherbeck Mill, Old Lake Road, Ambleside LA22 0DH
T: (015394) 32321
F: (015394) 33251
E: info@heartofthelakes.co.uk
I: www.heartofthelakes.co.uk

Ellerview ★★★
Contact: Mr Paul Liddell, Lakelovers, Belmont House, Lake Road, Bowness-on-Windermere, Windermere LA23 3BJ
T: (015394) 88855
F: (015394) 88857
E: bookings@lakelovers.co.uk
I: www.lakelovers.co.uk

Eskdale ★★★★
Contact: Mr Peter Durbin, Cumbrian Cottages, 2 Lonsdale Street, Carlisle CA1 1DB
T: (01228) 599960
F: (01228) 599970
E: enquiries@cumbrian-cottages.co.uk
I: www.cumbrian-cottages.co.uk

Evening Primrose Cottage ★★★
Contact: Mr Peter Durbin, Cumbrian Cottages, 2 Lonsdale Street, Carlisle CA1 1DB
T: (01228) 599960
F: (01228) 599970
E: enquiries@cumbrian-cottages.co.uk
I: www.cumbrian-cottages.co.uk

Fairview
Rating Applied For
Contact: Mrs Susan Jackson, Fisherbeck Mill, Old Lake Road, Ambleside LA22 0DH
T: (015394) 33110
F: (015394) 33251
E: info@heartofthelakes.co.uk

Falls View Cottage ★★★
Contact: Mrs Susan Jackson, Heart of the Lakes, Fisherbeck Mill, Old Lake Road, Ambleside LA22 0DH
T: (015394) 32321
F: (015394) 33251
E: info@heartofthelakes.co.uk
I: www.heartofthelakes.co.uk

Fellcroft ★★★★
Contact: Mrs Susan Jackson, Heart of the Lakes, Fisherbeck Mill, Old Lake Road, Ambleside LA22 0DH
T: (015394) 32321
F: (015394) 33251
E: info@heartofthelakes.co.uk
I: www.heartofthelakes.co.uk

Fellmere
Rating Applied For
Contact: Mr & Mrs Philip & Jane Butcher, Fellmere, Kirkstone Road, Ambleside LA22 9ET
T: (015394) 31569
E: fellmere@bestofthelakes.com

Fellside ★★★
Contact: Mr Paul Liddell, Lakelovers, Belmont House, Lake Road, Bowness-on-Windermere, Windermere LA23 3BJ
T: (015394) 88855
F: (015394) 88857
E: bookings@lakelovers.co.uk
I: www.lakelovers.co.uk

Fern Ghyll ★★★★
Contact: Mrs Susan Jackson, Heart of the Lakes, Fisherbeck Mill, Old Lake Road, Ambleside LA22 0DH
T: (015394) 32321
F: (015394) 33251
E: info@heartofthelakes.co.uk
I: www.heartofthelakes.co.uk

Field Cottage ★★★
Contact: Mrs Susan Jackson, Heart of the Lakes, Fisherbeck Mill, Old Lake Road, Ambleside LA22 0DH
T: (015394) 32321
F: (015394) 33251
E: info@heartofthelakes.co.uk
I: www.heartofthelakes.co.uk

The Flat ★★★
Contact: Mrs Susan Jackson, Heart of the Lakes, Fisherbeck Mill, Old Lake Road, Ambleside LA22 0DH
T: (015394) 32321
F: (015394) 33251
E: info@heartofthelakes.co.uk
I: www.heartofthelakes.co.uk

Forge Side ★★★
Contact: Mrs Susan Jackson, Heart of the Lakes, Fisherbeck Mill, Old Lake Road, Ambleside LA22 0DH
T: (015394) 32321
F: (015394) 33251
E: info@heartofthelakes.co.uk
I: www.heartofthelakes.co.uk

Four Seasons Cottage ★★★
Contact: Mrs Susan Jackson, Heart of the Lakes, Fisherbeck Mill, Old Lake Road, Ambleside LA22 0DH
T: (015394) 32321
F: (015394) 33251
E: info@heartofthelakes.co.uk
I: www.heartofthelakes.co.uk

Gable End ★★★★
Contact: Mr Peter Durbin, Cumbrian Cottages, 2 Lonsdale Street, Carlisle CA1 1DB
T: (01228) 599960
F: (01228) 599970
E: enquiries@cumbrian-cottages.co.uk
I: www.cumbrian-cottages.co.uk

Gale House Cottage ★★★★
Contact: Mrs Susan Jackson, Heart of the Lakes, Fisherbeck Mill, Old Lake Road, Ambleside LA22 0DH
T: (015394) 32321
F: (015394) 33251
E: info@heartofthelakes.co.uk
I: www.heartofthelakes.co.uk

Gale Howe Barn ★★★★
Contact: Mrs Susan Jackson, Heart of the Lakes, Fisherbeck Mill, Old Lake Road, Ambleside LA22 0DH
T: (015394) 32321
F: (015394) 33251
E: info@heartofthelakes.co.uk
I: www.heartofthelakes.co.uk

Gale Mews ★★★★
Contact: Mrs Susan Jackson, Heart of the Lakes, Fisherbeck Mill, Old Lake Road, Ambleside LA22 0DH
T: (015394) 32321
F: (015394) 33251
E: info@heartofthelakes.co.uk
I: www.heartofthelakes.co.uk

The Garden Flat ★★★
Contact: Mr & Mrs Alan Wardle, Bateman Fold Barn, Crook, Kendal LA8 8LN
T: (015395) 68074
I: www.lakedistrictholidays.net

The Gate ★★★★
Contact: Mrs Susan Jackson, Heart of the Lakes, Fisherbeck Mill, Old Lake Road, Ambleside LA22 0DH
T: (015394) 32321
F: (015394) 33251
E: info@heartofthelakes.co.uk
I: www.heartofthelakes.co.uk

Ghyll Bank ★★★★
Contact: Mrs Susan Jackson, Heart of the Lakes, Fisherbeck Mill, Old Lake Road, Ambleside LA22 0DH
T: (015394) 32321
F: (015394) 33251
E: info@heartofthelakes.co.uk
I: www.heartofthelakes.co.uk

Ghyll Heights ★★★
Contact: Mr Peter Durbin, Cumbrian Cottages, 2 Lonsdale Street, Carlisle CA1 1DB
T: (01228) 599960
F: (01228) 599970
E: enquiries@cumbrian-cottages.co.uk
I: www.cumbrian-cottages.co.uk

Ghyll View ★★★
Contact: Mrs Susan Jackson, Heart of the Lakes, Fisherbeck Mill, Old Lake Road, Ambleside LA22 0DH
T: (015394) 32321
F: (015394) 33251
E: info@heartofthelakes.co.uk
I: www.heartofthelakes.co.uk

3 Ghyllside ★★
Contact: Mr Paul Liddell, Lakelovers, Belmont House, Lake Road, Bowness-on-Windermere, Windermere LA23 3BJ
T: (015394) 88855
F: (015394) 88857
E: bookings@lakelovers.co.uk
I: www.lakelovers.co.uk

Gillybeck, The Falls ★★★★
Contact: Mrs Susan Jackson, Heart of the Lakes, Fisherbeck Mill, Old Lake Road, Ambleside LA22 0DH
T: (015394) 32321
F: (015394) 33251
E: info@heartofthelakes.co.uk
I: www.heartofthelakes.co.uk

Glenmore Cottage ★★★
Contact: Mr Peter Durbin, Cumbrian Cottages, 2 Lonsdale Street, Carlisle CA1 1DB
T: (01228) 599960
F: (01228) 599970
E: enquiries@cumbrian-cottages.co.uk
I: www.cumbrian-cottages.co.uk

The Granny Flat ★★★
Contact: Mrs Susan Jackson, Heart of the Lakes, Fisherbeck Mill, Old Lake Road, Ambleside LA22 0DH
T: (015394) 32321
F: (015394) 33251
E: info@heartofthelakes.co.uk
I: www.heartofthelakes.co.uk

Green Moss ★★★★
Contact: Mrs Susan Jackson, Heart of the Lakes, Fisherbeck Mill, Old Lake Road, Ambleside LA22 0DH
T: (015394) 32321
F: (015394) 33251
E: info@heartofthelakes.co.uk
I: www.heartofthelakes.co.uk

Greenways ★★★★
Contact: Mr Paul Liddell, Lakelovers, Belmont House, Lake Road, Bowness-on-Windermere, Windermere LA23 3BJ
T: (015394) 88855
F: (015394) 88857
E: bookings@lakelovers.co.uk
I: www.lakelovers.co.uk

The Grove Cottages
★★★★-★★★★★
Contact: Mrs Zorika Thompson, The Grove Cottages, Stockghyll Lane, Ambleside LA22 9LG
T: (015394) 33074
F: (015394) 31881
E: grovecottages@clara.co.uk
I: www.grovecottages.com

Hayrake ★★★
Contact: Mrs Susan Jackson, Heart of the Lakes, Fisherbeck Mill, Old Lake Road, Ambleside LA22 0DH
T: (015394) 32321
F: (015394) 33251
E: info@heartofthelakes.co.uk
I: www.heartofthelakes.co.uk

Hazelhurst ★★★★
Contact: Mr Peter Durbin, Cumbrian Cottages, 2 Lonsdale Street, Carlisle CA1 1DB
T: (01228) 599960
F: (01228) 599970
E: enquiries@cumbrian-cottages.co.uk
I: www.cumbrian-cottages.co.uk

Heather Cottage ★★★
Contact: Mr Paul Liddell, Lakelovers, Belmont House, Lake Road, Bowness-on-Windermere, Windermere LA23 3BJ
T: (015394) 88855
F: (015394) 88857
E: bookings@lakelovers.co.uk
I: www.lakelovers.co.uk

Herald Cottage ★★★★
Contact: Mr Peter Durbin, Cumbrian Cottages, 2 Lonsdale Street, Carlisle CA1 1DB
T: (01228) 599960
F: (01228) 599970
E: enquiries@cumbrian-cottages.co.uk
I: www.cumbrian-cottages.co.uk

High Bank ★★★
Contact: Mrs Susan Jackson, Heart of the Lakes, Fisherbeck Mill, Old Lake Road, Ambleside LA22 0DH
T: (015394) 32321
F: (015394) 33251
E: info@heartofthelakes.co.uk
I: www.heartofthelakes.co.uk

High Bank Cottage ★★★★
Contact: Mrs Susan Jackson, Heart of the Lakes, Fisherbeck Mill, Old Lake Road, Ambleside LA22 0DH
T: (015394) 32321
F: (015394) 33251
E: info@heartofthelakes.co.uk
I: www.heartofthelakes.co.uk

High Nook ★★★
Contact: Mrs Susan Jackson, Heart of the Lakes, Fisherbeck Mill, Old Lake Road, Ambleside LA22 0DH
T: (015394) 32321
F: (015394) 33251
E: info@heartofthelakes.co.uk
I: www.heartofthelakes.co.uk

High Pike Cottage ★★★
Contact: Mrs Susan Jackson, Heart of the Lakes, Fisherbeck Mill, Old Lake Road, Ambleside LA22 0DH
T: (015394) 32321
F: (015394) 33251
E: info@heartofthelakes.co.uk
I: www.heartofthelakes.co.uk

Hilber Cottage
Rating Applied For
Contact: Mrs Susan Jackson, Fisherbeck Mill, Old Lake Road, Ambleside LA22 0DH
T: (015394) 33110
F: (015394) 33251
E: info@heartofthelakes.co.uk

Hillandale ★★★
Contact: Mr Paul Liddell, Lakelovers, Belmont House, Lake Road, Bowness-on-Windermere, Windermere LA23 3BJ
T: (015394) 88855
F: (015394) 88857
E: bookings@lakelovers.co.uk
I: www.lakelovers.co.uk

Hillside Cottage ★★★
Contact: Mrs Susan Jackson, Heart of the Lakes, Fisherbeck Mill, Old Lake Road, Ambleside LA22 0DH
T: (015394) 32321
F: (015394) 33251
E: info@heartofthelakes.co.uk
I: www.heartofthelakes.co.uk

Hilltop (Loughrigg Suite)
★★★★★
Contact: Mrs Susan Jackson, Heart of the Lakes, Fisherbeck Mill, Old Lake Road, Ambleside LA22 0DH
T: (015394) 32321
F: (015394) 33251
E: info@heartofthelakes.co.uk
I: www.heartofthelakes.co.uk

Holbeck ★★★★★
Contact: Mrs Susan Jackson, Heart of the Lakes, Fisherbeck Mill, Old Lake Road, Ambleside LA22 0DH
T: (015394) 32321
F: (015394) 33251
E: info@heartofthelakes.co.uk
I: www.heartofthelakes.co.uk

Hole House ★★★
Contact: Mrs Clare Irvine, Tock How Farm, High Wray, Ambleside LA22 0JF
T: (015394) 36106
F: (015394) 36294
E: info@tock-how-farm.com
I: www.tock-how-farm.com

The Hollies ★★★
Contact: Mr Peter Durbin, Cumbrian Cottages, 2 Lonsdale Street, Carlisle CA1 1DB
T: (01228) 599960
F: (01228) 599970
E: enquiries@cumbrian-cottages.co.uk
I: www.cumbrian-cottages.co.uk

Holly Cottage ★★★
Contact: Mrs Susan Jackson, Heart of the Lakes, Fisherbeck Mill, Old Lake Road, Ambleside LA22 0DH
T: (015394) 32321
F: (015394) 33251
E: info@heartofthelakes.co.uk
I: www.heartofthelakes.co.uk

Hollybrook ★★★★
Contact: Mr Peter Durbin, Cumbrian Cottages, 2 Lonsdale Street, Carlisle CA1 1DB
T: (01228) 599960
F: (01228) 599970
E: enquiries@cumbrian-cottages.co.uk
I: www.cumbrian-cottages.co.uk

Honeypot Cottage ★★★★
Contact: Mrs Susan Jackson, Heart of the Lakes, Fisherbeck Mill, Old Lake Road, Ambleside LA22 0DH
T: (015394) 32321
F: (015394) 33251
E: info@heartofthelakes.co.uk
I: www.heartofthelakes.co.uk

Horseshoe Cottage ★★★
Contact: Mrs Susan Jackson, Heart of the Lakes, Fisherbeck Mill, Old Lake Road, Ambleside LA22 0DH
T: (015394) 32321
F: (015394) 33251
E: info@heartofthelakes.co.uk
I: www.heartofthelakes.co.uk

2 How Head ★★★
Contact: Mrs Susan Jackson, Heart of the Lakes, Fisherbeck Mill, Old Lake Road, Ambleside LA22 0DH
T: (015394) 32321
F: (015394) 33251
E: info@heartofthelakes.co.uk
I: www.heartofthelakes.co.uk

4 How Head ★★★
Contact: Mr D Holland, How Head Cottage, East of Lake, Coniston LA21 8AA
T: (015394) 41594
E: howhead@lineone.net
I: www.howheadcottages.co.uk

How Head Barn ★★★
Contact: Mrs Susan Jackson, Heart of the Lakes, Fisherbeck Mill, Old Lake Road, Ambleside LA22 0DH
T: (015394) 32321
F: (015394) 33251
E: info@heartofthelakes.co.uk
I: www.heartofthelakes.co.uk

Iona ★★★
Contact: Mrs Susan Jackson, Heart of the Lakes, Fisherbeck Mill, Old Lake Road, Ambleside LA22 0DH
T: (015394) 32321
F: (015394) 33251
E: info@heartofthelakes.co.uk
I: www.heartofthelakes.co.uk

Juniper Cottage ★★★
Contact: Mr Paul Liddell, Lakelovers, Belmont House, Lake Road, Bowness-on-Windermere, Windermere LA23 3BJ
T: (015394) 88855
F: (015394) 88857
E: bookings@lakelovers.co.uk
I: www.lakelovers.co.uk

Kiln Cottage ★★★★
Contact: Mr Paul Liddell, Lakelovers, Belmont House, Lake Road, Bowness-on-Windermere, Windermere LA23 3BJ
T: (015394) 88855
F: (015394) 88857
E: bookings@lakelovers.co.uk
I: www.lakelovers.co.uk

Kirkstone Cottage ★★★
Contact: Mr Peter Durbin, Cumbrian Cottages, 2 Lonsdale Street, Carlisle CA1 1DB
T: (01228) 599960
F: (01228) 599970
E: enquiries@cumbrian-cottages.co.uk
I: www.cumbrian-cottages.co.uk

Kirkstone Foot Cottages and Apartments
★★★★-★★★★★
Contact: Mr Norfolk, Kirkstone Foot Cottages and Apartments, Kirkstone Pass Road, Ambleside LA22 9EH
T: (015394) 32232
F: (015394) 32805
E: kirkstone@breathemail.net
I: www.kirkstonefoot.co.uk

Lakeland Cottage ★★★★
Contact: Mr Paul Liddell, Lakelovers, Belmont House, Lake Road, Bowness-on-Windermere, Windermere LA23 3BJ
T: (015394) 88855
F: (015394) 88857
E: bookings@lakelovers.co.uk
I: www.lakelovers.co.uk

The Lakelands ★★★★
Contact: Mrs Catrina Fletcher, The Lakelands, Lower Gale, Ambleside LA22 0BD
T: (015394) 33777
F: (015394) 31301
E: lakeland@globalnet.co.uk
I: www.the-lakelands.com

19 The Lakelands ★★★★
Contact: Mr Paul Liddell, Lakelovers, Belmont House, Lake Road, Bowness-on-Windermere, Windermere LA23 3BJ
T: (015394) 88855
F: (015394) 88857
E: bookings@lakelovers.co.uk
I: www.lakelovers.co.uk

The Larches ★★★
Contact: Mrs Susan Jackson, Heart of the Lakes, Fisherbeck Mill, Old Lake Road, Ambleside LA22 0DH
T: (015394) 32321
F: (015394) 33251
E: info@heartofthelakes.co.uk
I: www.heartofthelakes.co.uk

Leafy Nook ★★★★
Contact: Mrs Susan Jackson, Heart of the Lakes, Fisherbeck Mill, Old Lake Road, Ambleside LA22 0DH
T: (015394) 32321
F: (015394) 33251
E: info@heartofthelakes.co.uk
I: www.heartofthelakes.co.uk

Lingmell Gale Lodge ★★★★
Contact: Mrs Susan Jackson, Fisherbeck Mill, Old Lake Road, Ambleside LA22 0DH
T: (015394) 32321
F: (015394) 33251
E: info@heartofthelakes.co.uk
I: www.heartofthelakes.co.uk

Little Robin Cottage ★★
Contact: Mr Peter Durbin, Cumbrian Cottages, 2 Lonsdale Street, Carlisle CA1 1DB
T: (01228) 599960
F: (01228) 599970
E: enquiries@cumbrian-cottages.co.uk
I: www.cumbrian-cottages.co.uk

Long Mynd ★★★
Contact: Mr Peter Durbin, Cumbrian Cottages, 2 Lonsdale Street, Carlisle CA1 1DB
T: (01228) 599960
F: (01228) 599970
E: enquiries@cumbrian-cottages.co.uk
I: www.cumbrian-cottages.co.uk

Longmeadow ★★★★
Contact: Mr Peter Durbin, Cumbrian Cottages, 2 Lonsdale Street, Carlisle CA1 1DB
T: (01228) 599960
F: (01228) 599970
E: enquiries@cumbrian-cottages.co.uk
I: www.cumbrian-cottages.co.uk

The Lookout ★★★★★
Contact: Mrs Susan Jackson, Heart of the Lakes, Fisherbeck Mill, Old Lake Road, Ambleside LA22 0DH
T: (015394) 32321
F: (015394) 33251
E: info@heartofthelakes.co.uk
I: www.heartofthelakes.co.uk

Loughrigg ★★★★
Contact: Mr Peter Durbin, Cumbrian Cottages, 2 Lonsdale Street, Carlisle CA1 1DB
T: (01228) 599960
F: (01228) 599970
E: enquiries@cumbrian-cottages.co.uk
I: www.cumbrian-cottages.co.uk

Loughrigg ★★★★
Contact: Mrs Susan Jackson, Heart of the Lakes, Fisherbeck Mill, Old Lake Road, Ambleside LA22 0DH
T: (015394) 32321
F: (015394) 33251
E: info@heartofthelakes.co.uk
I: www.heartofthelakes.co.uk

5 Loughrigg Park ★★★
Contact: Mr Paul Liddell, Lakelovers, Belmont House, Lake Road, Bowness-on-Windermere, Windermere LA23 3BJ
T: (015394) 88855
F: (015394) 88857
E: bookings@lakelovers.co.uk
I: www.lakelovers.co.uk

Loughrigg Suite ★★★★★
Contact: Mrs Susan Jackson, Heart of the Lakes, Fisherbeck Mill, Old Lake Road, Ambleside LA22 0DH
T: (015394) 32321
F: (015394) 33251
E: info@heartofthelakes.co.uk
I: www.heartofthelakes.co.uk

Loughrigg View ★★★
Contact: Mrs Susan Jackson, Heart of the Lakes, Fisherbeck Mill, Old Lake Road, Ambleside LA22 0DH
T: (015394) 32321
F: (015394) 33251
E: info@heartofthelakes.co.uk
I: www.heartofthelakes.co.uk

Low Brow Barn ★★★★
Contact: Mrs Susan Jackson, Heart of the Lakes, Fisherbeck Mill, Old Lake Road, Ambleside LA22 0DH
T: (015394) 32321
F: (015394) 33251
E: info@heartofthelakes.co.uk
I: www.heartofthelakes.co.uk

Low Grove Cottage ★★★★
Contact: Mrs Susan Jackson, Heart of the Lakes, Fisherbeck Mill, Old Lake Road, Ambleside LA22 0DH
T: (015394) 32321
F: (015394) 33251
E: info@heartofthelakes.co.uk
I: www.heartofthelakes.co.uk

Low White Stones ★★★★
Contact: Mrs Susan Jackson, Heart of the Lakes, Fisherbeck Mill, Old Lake Road, Ambleside LA22 0DH
T: (015394) 32321
F: (015394) 33251
E: info@heartofthelakes.co.uk
I: www.heartofthelakes.co.uk

Lyndhurst
Rating Applied For
Contact: Mrs Susan Jackson, Heart of the Lakes, Fisherbeck Mill, Old Lake Road, Ambleside LA22 0DH
T: (015394) 33110
F: (015394) 33251
E: info@heartofthelakes.co.uk

Martins Nest ★★★★
Contact: Mrs Susan Jackson, Heart of the Lakes, Fisherbeck Mill, Old Lake Road, Ambleside LA22 0DH
T: (015394) 32321
F: (015394) 33251
E: info@heartofthelakes.co.uk
I: www.heartofthelakes.co.uk

Melverley ★★★
Contact: Mrs Susan Jackson, Heart of the Lakes, Fisherbeck Mill, Old Lake Road, Ambleside LA22 0DH
T: (015394) 32321
F: (015394) 33251
E: info@heartofthelakes.co.uk
I: www.heartofthelakes.co.uk

Milestones ★★★★
Contact: Mr Paul Liddell, Lakelovers, Belmont House, Lake Road, Bowness-on-Windermere, Windermere LA23 3BJ
T: (015394) 88855
F: (015394) 88857
E: bookings@lakelovers.co.uk
I: www.lakelovers.co.uk

Mill Brow Farm Cottage ★★★★
Contact: Mrs Pat Long, Mill Brow Farm, Skelwith Bridge, Loughrigg, Ambleside LA22 9NH
T: (015394) 33253

Millerbeck ★★★★
Contact: Mrs Susan Jackson, Heart of the Lakes, Fisherbeck Mill, Old Lake Road, Ambleside LA22 0DH
T: (015394) 32321
F: (015394) 33251
E: info@heartofthelakes.co.uk
I: www.heartofthelakes.co.uk

Mountain View ★★★
Contact: Mr Peter Durbin, Cumbrian Cottages, 2 Lonsdale Street, Carlisle CA1 1DB
T: (01228) 599960
F: (01228) 599970
E: enquiries@cumbrian-cottages.co.uk
I: www.cumbrian-cottages.co.uk

Nook End Annexe ★★★
Contact: Mr John Serginson, Waterside House, Newby Bridge, Ulverston LA12 8AN
T: (015395) 30024
F: (015395) 31932
E: john@lakelandcottageco.com
I: www.lakeland-cottage-company.co.uk

Nook End Farm ★★★★
Contact: Mr John Serginson, Waterside House, Newby Bridge, Ulverston LA12 8AN
T: (015395) 30024
F: (015395) 31932
E: john@lakelandcottageco.com
I: www.lakeland-cottage-company.co.uk

Nook End Studio ★★★
Contact: Mr John Serginson, Waterside House, Newby Bridge, Ulverston LA12 8AN
T: (015395) 30024
F: (015395) 31932
E: john@lakelandcottageco.com
I: www.lakelandcottageco.com

North Cottage ★★★
Contact: Mrs Susan Jackson, Heart of the Lakes, Fisherbeck Mill, Old Lake Road, Ambleside LA22 0DH
T: (015394) 32321
F: (015394) 33251
E: info@heartofthelakes.co.uk
I: www.heartofthelakes.co.uk

Oak Cottage ★★★
Contact: Mrs Susan Jackson, Heart of the Lakes, Fisherbeck Mill, Old Lake Road, Ambleside LA22 0DH
T: (015394) 32321
F: (015394) 33251
E: info@heartofthelakes.co.uk
I: www.heartofthelakes.co.uk

Oaklands ★★★
Contact: Mr Peter Durbin, Cumbrian Cottages, 2 Lonsdale Street, Carlisle CA1 1DB
T: (01228) 599960
F: (01228) 599970
E: enquiries@cumbrian-cottages.co.uk
I: www.cumbrian-cottages.co.uk

The Old Bakehouse ★★★
Contact: Mr Peter Durbin, Cumbrian Cottages, 2 Lonsdale Street, Carlisle CA1 1DB
T: (01228) 599960
F: (01228) 599970
E: enquiries@cumbrian-cottages.co.uk
I: www.cumbrian-cottages.co.uk

Old Coach House, Riverside and Garden Cottages★★★★
Contact: Mr V R Vyner-Brooks, Old Coach House, Riverside and Garden Cottages, Middle Barrows Green, Kendal LA8 0JG
T: (0151) 526 5451/9321
F: (0151) 526 1331
E: vyner-brooks@btconnect.com
I: www.primecottages.co.uk

Old Coachman's Cottage ★★★★
Contact: Mr Paul Liddell, Belmont House, Lake Road, Bowness-on-Windermere, Windermere LA23 3BJ
T: (015394) 88855
F: (015394) 88857
E: bookings@lakelovers.co.uk

Old Gale Farmhouse ★★★
Contact: Mr Peter Durbin, Cumbrian Cottages, 2 Lonsdale Street, Carlisle CA1 1DB
T: (01228) 599960
F: (01228) 599970
E: enquiries@cumbrian-cottages.co.uk
I: www.cumbrian-cottages.co.uk

Old Mill Cottage ★★★
Contact: Mrs Susan Jackson, Heart of the Lakes, Fisherbeck Mill, Old Lake Road, Ambleside LA22 0DH
T: (015394) 32321
F: (015394) 33251
E: info@heartofthelakes.co.uk
I: www.heartofthelakes.co.uk

Orchard House
Rating Applied For
Contact: Mrs Susan Jackson, Fisherbeck Mill, Old Lake Road, Ambleside LA22 0DH
T: (015394) 33110
F: (015394) 33251
E: info@heartoflakes.co.uk

Otters Holt ★★★★
Contact: Mrs Susan Jackson, Heart of the Lakes, Fisherbeck Mill, Old Lake Road, Ambleside LA22 0DH
T: (015394) 32321
F: (015394) 33251
E: info@heartofthelakes.co.uk
I: www.heartofthelakes.co.uk

Overbeck Cottage ★★★★
Contact: Mr & Mrs Alan Rhone, Riverside Lodge, Rothay Bridge, Ambleside LA22 0EH
T: (015394) 34208
E: alanrhone@riversidelodge.co.uk
I: www.riversidelodge.co.uk

Overghyll ★★★★
Contact: Mrs Susan Jackson, Heart of the Lakes, Fisherbeck Mill, Old Lake Road, Ambleside LA22 0DH
T: (015394) 32321
F: (015394) 33251
E: info@heartofthelakes.co.uk
I: www.heartofthelakes.co.uk

Parkwood ★★★★
Contact: Mrs Susan Jackson, Heart of the Lakes, Fisherbeck Mill, Old Lake Road, Ambleside LA22 0DH
T: (015394) 32321
F: (015394) 33251
E: info@heartofthelakes.co.uk
I: www.heartofthelakes.co.uk

Printers Cottage ★★★
Contact: Mrs Susan Jackson, Heart of the Lakes, Fisherbeck Mill, Old Lake Road, Ambleside LA22 0DH
T: (015394) 32321
F: (015394) 33251
E: info@heartofthelakes.co.uk
I: www.heartofthelakes.co.uk

Pudding Cottage ★★★★★
Contact: Mr Paul Liddell, Lakelovers, Belmont House, Lake Road, Bowness-on-Windermere, Windermere LA23 3BJ
T: (015394) 88855
F: (015394) 88857
E: bookings@lakelovers.co.uk
I: www.lakelovers.co.uk

Raaesbeck ★★★★
Contact: Mr Paul Liddell, Belmont House, Lake Road, Bowness-on-Windermere, Windermere LA23 3BJ
T: (015394) 88855
F: (015394) 88857
E: bookings@lakelovers.co.uk

Ramsteads ★-★★
Contact: Mr G Evans, Ramsteads, Outgate, Ambleside LA22 0NH
T: (015394) 36583

Redwoods ★★★
Contact: Mrs Susan Jackson, Heart of the Lakes, Fisherbeck Mill, Old Lake Road, Ambleside LA22 0DH
T: (015394) 32321
F: (015394) 33251
E: info@heartofthelakes.co.uk
I: www.heartofthelakes.co.uk

The Retreat ★★★★
Contact: Mrs Susan Jackson, Heart of the Lakes, Fisherbeck Mill, Old Lake Road, Ambleside LA22 0DH
T: (015394) 32321
F: (015394) 33251
E: info@heartofthelakes.co.uk
I: www.heartofthelakes.co.uk

River Falls View ★★★★
Contact: Mr Paul Liddell, Lakelovers, Belmont House, Lake Road, Bowness-on-Windermere, Windermere LA23 3BJ
T: (015394) 88855
F: (015394) 88857
E: bookings@lakelovers.co.uk
I: www.lakelovers.co.uk

The Rock Shop Flat ★★★★
Contact: Ms Louise Burhouse, Quarmby Mills, Tanyard Road, Oakes, Huddersfield HD3 4YD
T: (01484) 485104
F: (01484) 460036
E: rockshopflat@burhouse.com

Rose Cottage ★★★
Contact: Mrs Susan Jackson, Heart of the Lakes, Fisherbeck Mill, Old Lake Road, Ambleside LA22 0DH
T: (015394) 32321
F: (015394) 33251
E: info@heartofthelakes.co.uk
I: www.heartofthelakes.co.uk

Roselea ★★★★
Contact: Mr Paul Liddell, Lakelovers, Belmont House, Lake Road, Bowness-on-Windermere, Windermere LA23 3BJ
T: (015394) 88855
F: (015394) 88857
E: bookings@lakelovers.co.uk

Rushbrook Cottage ★★★★
Contact: Mrs Susan Jackson, Heart of the Lakes, Fisherbeck Mill, Old Lake Road, Ambleside LA22 0DH
T: (015394) 32321
F: (015394) 33251
E: info@heartofthelakes.co.uk
I: www.heartofthelakes.co.uk

Rydal ★★★
Contact: Mrs Susan Jackson, Heart of the Lakes, Fisherbeck Mill, Old Lake Road, Ambleside LA22 0DH
T: (015394) 32321
F: (015394) 33251
E: info@heartofthelakes.co.uk
I: www.heartofthelakes.co.uk

Sarum ★★★
Contact: Ms J Hughes, 95 Lark Hill Lane, Formby, Liverpool L37 1LU
T: (01704) 831558
F: (01704) 874866
E: formbyphysio@bigfoot.com
I: sarum.co.uk

Scafell Gale Lodge ★★★★
Contact: Mrs Susan Jackson, Heart of the Lakes, Fisherbeck Mill, Old Lake Road, Ambleside LA22 0DH
T: (015394) 32321
F: (015394) 33251
E: info@heartofthelakes.co.uk
I: www.heartofthelakes.co.uk

Scandale Bridge Cottage Rating Applied For
Contact: Central Reservations, Kings Head Hotel, Thirlspot CA12 4TN
T: (017687) 72393
F: (017687) 72309
E: stay@lakedistrictinns.co.uk
I: www.lakedistrictinns.co.uk

Sheenfell ★★★
Contact: Mrs Susan Jackson, Heart of the Lakes, Fisherbeck Mill, Old Lake Road, Ambleside LA22 0DH
T: (015394) 32321
F: (015394) 33251
E: info@heartofthelakes.co.uk
I: www.heartofthelakes.co.uk

Shepherds Fold ★★★★
Contact: Mrs Susan Jackson, Heart of the Lakes, Fisherbeck Mill, Old Lake Road, Ambleside LA22 0DH
T: (015394) 32321
F: (015394) 33251
E: info@heartofthelakes.co.uk
I: www.heartofthelakes.co.uk

Spring Cottage ★★★
Contact: Mr Paul Liddell, Lakelovers, Belmont House, Lake Road, Bowness-on-Windermere, Windermere LA23 3BJ
T: (015394) 88855
F: (015394) 88857
E: bookings@lakelovers.co.uk
I: www.lakelovers.co.uk

Spring Cottage ★★★★
Contact: Mrs Susan Jackson, Heart of the Lakes, Fisherbeck Mill, Old Lake Road, Ambleside LA22 0DH
T: (015394) 32321
F: (015394) 33251
E: info@heartofthelakes.co.uk
I: www.heartofthelakes.co.uk

Squirrel Bank ★★★
Contact: Mr D Hogarth, Cumbrian Cottages, 7 The Crescent, Carlisle CA1 1QW
T: (01228) 599960
F: (01228) 599970
E: enquiries@cumbrian-cottages.co.uk
I: www.cumbrian-cottages.co.uk

Squirrel's Nest ★★★★
Contact: Mr Peter Durbin, Cumbrian Cottages, 2 Lonsdale Street, Carlisle CA1 1DB
T: (01228) 599960
F: (01228) 599970
E: enquiries@cumbrian-cottages.co.uk
I: www.cumbrian-cottages.co.uk

The Stables ★★★★★
Contact: Mrs Susan Jackson, Heart of the Lakes, Fisherbeck Mill, Old Lake Road, Ambleside LA22 0DH
T: (015394) 32321
F: (015394) 33251
E: info@heartofthelakes.co.uk
I: www.heartofthelakes.co.uk

Steeple View ★★★
Contact: Mrs Susan Jackson, Heart of the Lakes, Fisherbeck Mill, Old Lake Road, Ambleside LA22 0DH
T: (015394) 32321
F: (015394) 33251
E: info@heartofthelakes.co.uk
I: www.heartofthelakes.co.uk

Stepping Stones ★★★★
Contact: Mrs Susan Jackson, Heart of the Lakes, Fisherbeck Mill, Old Lake Road, Ambleside LA22 0DH
T: (015394) 32321
F: (015394) 33251
E: info@heartofthelakes.co.uk
I: www.heartofthelakes.co.uk

Stockghyll Court ★★★
Contact: Mr Peter Durbin, Cumbrian Cottages, 2 Lonsdale Street, Carlisle CA1 1DB
T: (01228) 599960
F: (01228) 599970
E: enquiries@cumbrian-cottages.co.uk
I: www.cumbrian-cottages.co.uk

Striding Home ★★★★
Contact: Mrs Susan Jackson, Heart of the Lakes, Fisherbeck Mill, Old Lake Road, Ambleside LA22 0DH
T: (015394) 32321
F: (015394) 33251
E: info@heartofthelakes.co.uk
I: www.heartofthelakes.co.uk

Studio Cottage ★★★★
Contact: Mrs Susan Jackson, Heart of the Lakes, Fisherbeck Mill, Old Lake Road, Ambleside LA22 0DH
T: (015394) 32321
F: (015394) 33251
E: info@heartofthelakes.co.uk
I: www.heartofthelakes.co.uk

2 Sunny Bank Cottages ★★★
Contact: Mrs Susan Jackson, Heart of the Lakes, Fisherbeck Mill, Old Lake Road, Ambleside LA22 0DH
T: (015394) 32321
F: (015394) 33251
E: info@heartofthelakes.co.uk
I: www.heartofthelakes.co.uk

Sunset Cottage ★★★★
Contact: Mrs Susan Jackson, Heart of the Lakes, Fisherbeck Mill, Old Lake Road, Ambleside LA22 0DH
T: (015394) 32321
F: (015394) 33251
E: info@heartofthelakes.co.uk
I: www.heartofthelakes.co.uk

Swallowdale ★★★★
Contact: Mrs Susan Jackson, Heart of the Lakes, Fisherbeck Mill, Old Lake Road, Ambleside LA22 0DH
T: (015394) 32321
F: (015394) 33251
E: info@heartofthelakes.co.uk
I: www.heartofthelakes.co.uk

Sweden Bank ★★★
Contact: Mrs Susan Jackson, Heart of the Lakes, Fisherbeck Mill, Old Lake Road, Ambleside LA22 0DH
T: (015394) 32321
F: (015394) 33251
E: info@heartofthelakes.co.uk
I: www.heartofthelakes.co.uk

Thomas Fold Cottage ★★★★
Contact: Mrs Susan Jackson, Heart of the Lakes, Fisherbeck Mill, Old Lake Road, Ambleside LA22 0DH
T: (015394) 32321
F: (015394) 33251
E: info@heartofthelakes.co.uk
I: www.heartofthelakes.co.uk

1 Tom Fold ★★★
Contact: Mr Paul Liddell, Lakelovers, Belmont House, Lake Road, Bowness-on-Windermere, Windermere LA23 3BJ
T: (015394) 88855
F: (015394) 88857
E: bookings@lakelovers.co.uk
I: www.lakelovers.co.uk

Top O' The Stairs ★★★
Contact: Mrs Susan Jackson, Heart of the Lakes, Fisherbeck Mill, Old Lake Road, Ambleside LA22 0DH
T: (015394) 32321
F: (015394) 33251
E: info@heartofthelakes.co.uk
I: www.heartofthelakes.co.uk

Tottle Bank ★★★
Contact: Mr Paul Liddell, Lakelovers, Belmont House Lake Road, Bowness-on-Windermere, Windermere LA23 3BJ
T: (015394) 88855
F: (015394) 88857
E: bookings@lakelovers.co.uk
I: www.lakelovers.co.uk

Tree Tops ★★★★
Contact: Mr D Hogarth, Cumbrian Cottages, 7 The Crescent, Carlisle CA1 1QW
T: (01228) 599960
F: (01228) 599970
E: enquiries@cumbrian-cottages.co.uk
I: www.cumbrian-cottages.co.uk

Troutbeck ★★★★
Contact: Mrs Susan Jackson, Heart of the Lakes, Fisherbeck Mill, Old Lake Road, Ambleside LA22 0DH
T: (015394) 32321
F: (015394) 33251
E: info@heartofthelakes.co.uk
I: www.heartofthelakes.co.uk

Walkers Cottage ★★★
Contact: Mr D Hogarth, Cumbrian Cottages, 7 The Crescent, Carlisle CA1 1QW
T: (01228) 599960
F: (01228) 599970
E: enquiries@cumbrian-cottages.co.uk
I: www.cumbrian-cottages.co.uk

Wansfell ★★★★★
Contact: Mrs Susan Jackson, Heart of the Lakes, Fisherbeck Mill, Old Lake Road, Ambleside LA22 0DH
T: (015394) 32321
F: (015394) 33251
E: info@heartofthelakes.co.uk
I: www.heartofthelakes.co.uk

Waterfalls ★★★★
Contact: Mrs Susan Jackson, Heart of the Lakes, Fisherbeck Mill, Old Lake Road, Ambleside LA22 0DH
T: (015394) 32321
F: (015394) 33251
E: info@heartofthelakes.co.uk
I: www.heartofthelakes.co.uk

Wayside Cottage ★★★★
Contact: Dr Dennis Leech, 22 Styvechale Avenue, Coventry CV5 6DX
T: (02476) 677549
E: waysidecottage@lineone.net
I: website.lineone.net/~waysidecottage

Wetherlam ★★★★
Contact: Mr Paul Liddell, Belmont House, Lake Road, Bowness-on-Windermere, Windermere LA23 3BJ
T: (015394) 88855
F: (015394) 88857
E: bookings@lakelovers.co.uk

Wilmar Cottage ★★
Contact: Mrs Susan Jackson, Heart of the Lakes, Fisherbeck Mill, Old Lake Road, Ambleside LA22 0DH
T: (015394) 32321
F: (015394) 33251
E: info@heartofthelakes.co.uk
I: www.heartofthelakes.co.uk

Winander ★★★★★
Contact: Mrs Susan Jackson, Heart of the Lakes, Fisherbeck Mill, Old Lake Road, Ambleside LA22 0DH
T: (015394) 32321
F: (015394) 33251
E: info@heartofthelakes.co.uk
I: www.heartofthelakes.co.uk

Windermere Suite ★★★★★
Contact: Mrs Susan Jackson, Heart of the Lakes, Fisherbeck Mill, Old Lake Road, Ambleside LA22 0DH
T: (015394) 32321
F: (015394) 33251
E: info@heartofthelakes.co.uk
I: www.heartofthelakes.co.uk

Woolly End ★★★★
Contact: Mr Paul Liddell, Lakelovers, Belmont House, Lake Road, Bowness-on-Windermere, Windermere LA23 3BJ
T: (015394) 88855
F: (015394) 88857
E: bookings@lakelovers.co.uk
I: www.lakelovers.co.uk

Wren Cottage ★★★
Contact: Mrs Susan Jackson, Heart of the Lakes, Fisherbeck Mill, Old Lake Road, Ambleside LA22 0DH
T: (015394) 32321
F: (015394) 33251
E: info@heartofthelakes.co.uk
I: www.heartofthelakes.co.uk

Wykefield Cottages ★★★-★★★★★
Contact: Mrs Susan Jackson, Heart of the Lakes, Fisherbeck Mill, Old Lake Road, Ambleside LA22 0DH
T: (015394) 32321
F: (015394) 33251
E: info@heartofthelakes.co.uk
I: www.heartofthelakes.co.uk

Yew Tree Cottage ★★★
Contact: Mrs Susan Jackson, Heart of the Lakes, Fisherbeck Mill, Old Lake Road, Ambleside LA22 0DH
T: (015394) 32321
F: (015394) 33251
E: info@heartofthelakes.co.uk
I: www.heartofthelakes.co.uk

APPLEBY-IN-WESTMORLAND
Cumbria

Black Bull ★★★
Contact: Mr Peter Durbin, Cumbrian Cottages, 2 Lonsdale Street, Carlisle CA1 1DB
T: (01228) 599960
F: (01228) 599970
E: enquiries@cumbrian-cottages.co.uk
I: www.cumbrian-cottages.co.uk

Dunkirk ★★★★
Contact: Mr Paul Crosbie, 30 Eagle Wharf Court, Lafone Street, London SE1 2LZ
T: (020) 7403 7346
E: paulcrosbie147@msn.com
I: www.dunkirk.20m.com

Holly Lodge ★★★
Contact: Mr Nigel Hodgkinson, Holly Lodge, Roman Road, Kirkby Stephen, Kirkby Stephen CA16 6JH
T: (017683) 51850

Ivy Cottage ★★★
Contact: Mrs H Grisdale, Penerin, Long Marton, Appleby-in-Westmorland CA16 6BN
T: (017683) 61233

The Little House ★★★★
Contact: Mr & Mrs Roger & Lesley Hiscox, Bradshaw Gate Main Street, Hackthorn, Welton, Lincoln LN2 3PF
T: (01673) 860047
F: (01673) 861380
E: rogerhiscox@beeb.net
I: www.thelittlehouse.20m.com

Milburn Grange Holidays ★★★
Contact: Mr & Mrs Peter Baker, Milburn Grange Holidays, Milburn Grange, Knock, Appleby-in-Westmorland CA16 6DR
T: (017683) 61867
F: (01768) 362337
E: holidays@milburngrange.co.uk
I: www.milburngrange.co.uk/cottages-fr.htm

The Old Smithy
Rating Applied For
Contact: Mrs Kay Smith, The Old Smithy, Far Uose, Knock, Appleby-in-Westmorland CA16 6DN
T: (017683) 61333
E: smithies.com@talk21.com

Owl Cottage ★★
Contact: The Manager Dales Hol Cot Ref:2923, Carleton Business Park, Carleton New Road, Skipton BD23 2AA
T: (01756) 799821
F: (01756) 797012
E: info@dalesholcot.com
I: www.dalesholcot.com

APPLETHWAITE
Cumbria

Applewick Cottage ★★★
Contact: Mr Peter Durbin, Cumbrian Cottages, 2 Lonsdale Street, Carlisle CA1 1DB
T: (01228) 599960
F: (01228) 599970
E: enquiries@cumbrian-cottages.co.uk
I: www.cumbrian-cottages.co.uk

Emily's Escape ★★★★
Contact: Mr David Miller, 24 Elm Court, Whickham, Newcastle upon Tyne NE16 4PS
T: (0191) 488 0549
F: (0191) 422 3303
E: mtekk@ic24.net

The Manesty ★★★★
Contact: Mr Peter Durbin, Cumbrian Cottages, 2 Lonsdale Street, Carlisle CA1 1DB
T: (01228) 599960
F: (01228) 599970
E: enquiries@cumbrian-cottages.co.uk
I: www.cumbrian-cottages.co.uk

No 1 - No 5 Gale Cottages ★★★★
Contact: Mr Thomas Ryan, Gale Cottage, Applethwaite, Keswick CA12 4PL
T: (017687) 72413
F: (017687) 75706
E: ryan@applethwaite.com
I: www.galecottages.com

Sarah's Secret ★★★★
Contact: Mr David Miller, 24 Elm Court, Whickham, Newcastle upon Tyne NE16 4PS
T: (0191) 488 0549
F: (0191) 422 3303
E: mtekk@ic24.net

Whiteside ★★★
Contact: Mr David Burton, Melbecks, Bassenthwaite, Keswick CA12 4QX
T: (017687) 76065
F: (017687) 76869
E: info@lakelandcottages.co.uk
I: www.lakelandcottages.co.uk

ARMATHWAITE
Cumbria

Coombs Cottage ★★★★
Contact: Mr Peter Durbin, Cumbrian Cottages, 2 Lonsdale Street, Carlisle CA1 1DB
T: (01228) 599960
F: (01228) 599970
E: enquiries@cumbrian-cottages.co.uk
I: www.cumbrian-cottages.co.uk

Longdales Cottage ★★★
Contact: Mr Peter Durbin, Cumbrian Cottages, 2 Lonsdale Street, Carlisle CA1 1DB
T: (01228) 599960
F: (01228) 599970
E: enquiries@cumbrian-cottages.co.uk
I: www.cumbrian-cottages.co.uk

ASKHAM
Cumbria

Park View ★★★
Contact: Mrs Lyn Page, Lowther Estate Office, Hackthorpe, Penrith CA10 2HG
T: (01931) 712577
F: (01931) 712679
E: lyn.page@lowther.co.uk
I: lowther-estatecottages.co.uk

ASPATRIA
Cumbria

Halls Bank Farm ★★★★★
Contact: Messrs G H Wilkinson, Arkleby House, Arkleby, Aspatria, Carlisle CA5 2BP
T: (016973) 20374

AYSIDE
Cumbria

Brookfield Cotttage ★★★★
Contact: The Manager Dales Hol Cot Ref:2649, Carleton Business Park, Carleton New Road, Skipton BD23 2AA
T: (01756) 799821
F: (01756) 797012
E: info@dalesholcot.com
I: www.dalesholcot.com

BACKBARROW
Cumbria

Cark Cottage ★★★
Contact: Mr Peter Durbin, Cumbrian Cottages, 2 Lonsdale Street, Carlisle CA1 1DB
T: (01228) 599960
F: (01228) 599970
E: enquiries@cumbrian-cottages.co.uk
I: www.cumbrian-cottages.co.uk

Kate's Cottage ★★★
Contact: Irene Zuniga, Bowness Lakeland Holidays, 131 Radcliffe New Road, Whitefield, Manchester M25 7RP

BAILEY
Cumbria

Bailey Mill ★★
Contact: Mrs Pamela Copeland, Bailey Mill, Bailey, Roadhead, Carlisle TD9 0TR
T: (016977) 48617
F: (016977) 48074
E: pam@baileymill.fsnet.co.uk
I: www.holidaycottagescumbria.co.uk

Cuddy's Hall Holiday Cottage ★★★
Contact: Mrs Joanna Furness, No 2 Cuddy's Hall, Bailey, Newcastleton TD9 0TP
T: (016977) 48160
F: (016977) 48160

Saughs Farm Cottages ★★★★
Contact: Mrs Jane Gray, Saughs Farm Cottages, Saughs Farm, Bailey, Newcastleton TD9 0TT
T: (016977) 48346
F: (016977) 48180
E: skylark@onholiday.co.uk
I: www.skylarkcottages.co.uk

BAMPTON
Cumbria

Tethera ★★★★
Contact: Mr Martin Wardle, Lakes and Valleys, Bateman Fold Barn, Crook, Kendal LA8 8LN
T: (015394) 68103
F: (015394) 68104
E: lakesandvalleys@aol.com
I: www.lakesandvalleys.co.uk

BASSENTHWAITE
Cumbria

Apple Tree Cottage ★★★★
Contact: Mrs Jill Pointon, The Lodge, Low Lorton, Lorton, Cockermouth CA13 9UP
T: (01900) 85011
I: www.cottageappletree.co.uk

Brook Cottage ★★★★
Contact: Mr Peter Durbin, Cumbrian Cottages, 2 Lonsdale Street, Carlisle CA1 1DB
T: (01228) 599960
F: (01228) 599970
E: enquiries@cumbrian-cottages.co.uk
I: www.cumbrian-cottages.co.uk

Brookfield ★★★★
Contact: Mr Peter Durbin, Cumbrian Cottages, 2 Lonsdale Street, Carlisle CA1 1DB
T: (01228) 599960
F: (01228) 599970
E: enquiries@cumbrian-cottages.co.uk
I: www.cumbrian-cottages.co.uk

Castle Hill Cottage ★★★★
Contact: Mr Peter Durbin, Cumbrian Cottages, 2 Lonsdale Street, Carlisle CA1 1DB
T: (01228) 599960
F: (01228) 599970
E: enquiries@cumbrian-cottages.co.uk
I: www.cumbrian-cottages.co.uk

Garries Cottage ★★★
Contact: Mr D Hogarth, Cumbrian Cottages, 7 The Crescent, Carlisle CA1 1QW
T: (01228) 599960
F: (01228) 599970
E: enquiries@cumbrian-cottages.co.uk
I: www.cumbrian-cottages.co.uk

Glencrest ★★★
Contact: Mr Peter Durbin, Cumbrian Cottages, 2 Lonsdale Street, Carlisle CA1 1DB
T: (01228) 599960
F: (01228) 599970
E: enquiries@cumbrian-cottages.co.uk
I: www.cumbrian-cottages.co.uk

High Spy ★★★
Contact: Mr Peter Durbin, Cumbrian Cottages, 2 Lonsdale Street, Carlisle CA1 1DB
T: (01228) 599960
F: (01228) 599970
E: enquiries@cumbrian-cottages.co.uk
I: www.cumbrian-cottages.co.uk

Irton House Farm ★★★★
Contact: Mr & Mrs R W Almond, Irton House Farm, Isel, Cockermouth CA13 9ST
T: (017687) 76380
E: almond@farmersweekly.net
I: www.almondirtonhousefarm.com

6 Low Kiln Court ★★★
Contact: Mr Peter Durbin, Cumbrian Cottages, 2 Lonsdale Street, Carlisle CA1 1DB
T: (01228) 599960
F: (01228) 599970
E: enquiries@cumbrian-cottages.co.uk
I: www.cumbrian-cottages.co.uk

Melbecks Holidays Homes: Skiddaw, Dodd, Dash, Randel ★★★-★★★★★
Contact: Mr Burton, Lakeland Cottage Holidays, Melbecks, Bassenthwaite, Keswick CA12 4QX
T: (017687) 76065
F: (017687) 76869
E: info@lakelandcottages.co.uk
I: www.lakelandcottages.co.uk

Peter House Farm Cottage ★★★★
Contact: Mrs Trafford, Peter House Farm Cottage, Peter House Farm, Bassenthwaite, Keswick CA12 4QX
T: (017687) 76278
I: www.peterhousefarm.co.uk

Random Stones ★★★★
Contact: Mrs Susan Jackson, Heart of the Lakes, Fisherbeck Mill, Old Lake Road, Ambleside LA22 0DH
T: (015394) 32321
F: (015394) 33251
E: info@heartofthelakes.co.uk
I: www.heartofthelakes.co.uk

Riggs Cottage ★★★★
Contact: Mr Peter Durbin, Cumbrian Cottages, 2 Lonsdale Street, Carlisle CA1 1DB
T: (01228) 599960
F: (01228) 599970
E: enquiries@cumbrian-cottages.co.uk
I: www.cumbrian-cottages.co.uk

The Ruddings ★★
Contact: Mr Peter Durbin, Cumbrian Cottages, 2 Lonsdale Street, Carlisle CA1 1DB
T: (01228) 599960
F: (01228) 599970
E: enquiries@cumbrian-cottages.co.uk
I: www.cumbrian-cottages.co.uk

Uldale ★★★★
Contact: Mr David Burton, Melbecks, Bassenthwaite, Keswick CA12 4QX
T: (017687) 76065
F: (017687) 76869
E: info@lakelandcottages.co.uk
I: www.lakelandcottages.co.uk

BASSENTHWAITE LAKE
Cumbria

Underwood ★★★
Contact: Mr Peter Durbin, Cumbrian Cottages, 2 Lonsdale Street, Carlisle CA1 1DB
T: (01228) 599960
F: (01228) 599970
E: enquiries@cumbrian-cottages.co.uk
I: www.cumbrian-cottages.co.uk

BECKFOOT
Cumbria

Seaview Farmhouse ★★★★★
Contact: Mr & Mrs Graham & Betty Walton, Annandale, Blitterlees Silloth, Wigton CA7 4JN
T: (016973) 31030
I: www.english-country-cottages.co.uk

BERRIER
Cumbria

Bells Farm ★★★
Contact: Mr Peter Durbin, Cumbrian Cottages, 2 Lonsdale Street, Carlisle CA1 1DB
T: (01228) 599960
F: (01228) 599970
E: enquiries@cumbrian-cottages.co.uk
I: www.cumbrian-cottages.co.uk

BEWCASTLE
Cumbria

Arch View ★★★-★★★★
Contact: Mrs James, Arch View, Midtodhills Farm, Roadhead, Carlisle CA6 6PF
T: (016977) 48213
F: (016977) 48213
E: jjames@v21mail.co.uk
I: www.holidaycottagescarlisle.co.uk

Bank End Farm Cottages (Old Farm Cottage and Barn Cottage) ★★★
Contact: Mrs Jean Liddle, Bank End Farm, Bewcastle, Roadhead, Carlisle CA6 6NU
T: (016977) 48644
F: (016977) 48644
E: bankendfarm@tiscali.co.uk

BLAWITH
Cumbria

Birchbank Cottage ★★★★
Contact: Mrs Linda Nicholson, Birchbank, Blawith, Ulverston LA12 8EW
T: (01229) 885277
E: birchbank@btinternet.com
I: www.lakedistrictfarmhouseholidays.co.uk/birchbankcottage

Blea Brows Cottage ★★★
Contact: Mr Philip Johnston, The Coppermines & Lakes Cottages, The Estate Office, The Bridge, Coniston LA21 8HJ
T: (015394) 41765
F: (015394) 41944
E: info@@coppermines.co.uk
I: www.coppermines.co.uk

Brown Howe Cottage ★★★★
Contact: Mr Philip Johnston, The Coppermines & Lakes Cottages, The Estate Office, The Bridge, Coniston LA21 8HJ
T: (015394) 41765
F: (015394) 41944
E: info@@coppermines.co.uk
I: www.coppermines.co.uk

BLEATARN
Cumbria

Sawbridge Hall ★★★★
Contact: Mrs R I Paul, Sawbridge Hall, Bleatarn, Appleby-in-Westmorland CA16 6PY

BOLTON
Cumbria

Glebe Hayloft and Glebe Stable ★★★★
Contact: Mr Martin Wardle, Goosemire Cottages, North Lodge, Longtail Hill, Bowness-on-Windermere, Windermere LA23
T: (015394) 47477
F: (015394) 48988
E: goosemirecottage@aol.com
I: www.goosemirecottages.co.uk

BORROWDALE
Cumbria

Barrowgate ★★★
Contact: Mr David Burton, Melbecks, Bassenthwaite, Keswick CA12 4QX
T: (017687) 76065
F: (017687) 76869
E: info@lakelandcottages.co.uk
I: www.lakelandcottages.co.uk

Derwent Farmhouse ★★★
Contact: Mr David Burton, Melbecks, Bassenthwaite, Keswick CA12 4QX
T: (017687) 76065
F: (017687) 76869
E: info@lakelandcottages.co.uk
I: www.lakelandcottages.co.uk

Grange Cottage ★★★
Contact: Mr Peter Durbin, Cumbrian Cottages, 2 Lonsdale Street, Carlisle CA1 1DB
T: (01228) 599960
F: (01228) 599970
E: enquiries@cumbrian-cottages.co.uk
I: www.cumbrian-cottages.co.uk

Hazel Bank Cottage ★★★★
Contact: Mr & Mrs Glen & Brenda Davies, Hazel Bank Country House, Rosthwaite, Borrowdale, Keswick CA12 5XB
T: (017687) 77248
F: (017687) 77373
E: enquiries@hazelbankhotel.co.uk
I: www.hazelbankhotel.co.uk

The Hollies ★★★★
Contact: Mr David Burton, Melbecks, Bassenthwaite, Keswick CA12 4QX
T: (017687) 76065
F: (017687) 76869
E: info@lakelandcottages.co.uk

Rockery Cottage & Maiden Moor Cottage★★★
Contact: Mrs Wood, Greenbank Countryhouse Hotel, Borrowdale, Keswick CA12 5UY
T: (017687) 77215

Rose Cottage Holiday Apartments ★★★
Contact: Mr Steve Cooke, Rose Cottage Holiday Flats, Rosthwaite, Borrowdale, Keswick CA12 5XB
T: (017687) 77678
E: stevecooke@rosthwaite.freeserve.co.uk
I: borrowdalecottages.co.uk

Scale Force ★★★
Contact: Mr David Burton, Melbecks, Bassenthwaite, Keswick CA12 4QX
T: (017687) 76065
F: (017687) 76869
E: info@lakelandcottages.co.uk
I: www.lakelandcottages.co.uk

BOTHEL
Cumbria

The Lodge ★★★★
Contact: Mrs Diane Shankland, Quarry House, Bothel, Carlisle CA7 2HH
T: (016973) 21674
E: lodge.bothel@virgin.net
I: www.lodge-bothel.co.uk

Meadow View ★★★
Contact: Mr David Burton, Melbecks, Bassenthwaite, Keswick CA12 4QX
T: (017687) 76065
F: (017687) 76869
E: info@lakelandcottages.co.uk
I: www.lakelandcottages.co.uk

BOUTH
Cumbria

Crag House Cottage ★★★★
Contact: Mr John Serginson, Waterside House, Newby Bridge, Ulverston LA12 8AN
T: (015395) 30024
F: (015395) 31932
E: john@lakelandcottageco.com
I: www.lakeland-cottage-company.co.uk

No 1 Rose Cottage ★★★★
Contact: Mr John Serginson, Waterside House, Newby Bridge, Ulverston LA12 8AN
T: (015395) 30024
F: (015395) 31932
E: john@lakelandcottageco.com
I: www.lakelandcottageco.com

BOWMANSTEAD
Cumbria

Number 1 Lake View Cottages ★★★★
Contact: Mr Philip Johnston, The Coppermines Coniston Cottages, The Estate Office, The Bridge, Coniston LA21 8HJ
T: (015394) 41765
E: bookings@coppermines.co.uk
I: www.coppermines.co.uk

BOWNESS-ON-WINDERMERE
Cumbria

Waters Edge Villa ★★★★
Contact: Michelle Weir & Anna Jex, WLHA, Waters Edge Villa, Ferry Nab, Bowness-on-Windermere LA23 3JH
T: (015394) 43415
F: (015394) 88721
E: email@lakewindermere.net
I: www.lakewindermere.net

BOWSTON
Cumbria

Winstanley Cottage ★★★
Contact: Mr Peter Durbin, Cumbrian Cottages, 2 Lonsdale Street, Carlisle CA1 1DB
T: (01228) 599960
F: (01228) 599970
E: enquiries@cumbrian-cottages.co.uk
I: www.cumbrian-cottages.co.uk

BRAITHWAITE
Cumbria

Barrow View Cottage and Cedar Cottage★★★★
Contact: Mr Horton, 5 St John's Street, Keswick CA12 5AP
T: (01768) 774627
E: c.c.horton@talk21.com

Coledale House ★★★★
Contact: Mr Peter Durbin, Cumbrian Cottages, 2 Lonsdale Street, Carlisle CA1 1DB
T: (01228) 599960
F: (01228) 599970
E: enquiries@cumbrian-cottages.co.uk
I: www.cumbrian-cottages.co.uk

Cosy Cottage ★★★
Contact: Mr David Burton, Melbecks, Bassenthwaite, Keswick CA12 4QX
T: (017687) 76065
F: (017687) 76869
E: info@lakelandcottages.co.uk
I: www.lakelandcottages.co.uk

Eastern Cottage ★★
Contact: Mr Peter Durbin, Cumbrian Cottages, 2 Lonsdale Street, Carlisle CA1 1DB
T: (01228) 599960
F: (01228) 599970
E: enquiries@cumbrian-cottages.co.uk
I: www.cumbrian-cottages.co.uk

Glen Cottage ★★★★
Contact: Mrs J Pilling, The Shiel, Applethwaite, Keswick CA12 4PL
T: (017687) 72171
F: (017687) 72171
E: lel@btinternet.com
I: www.cottagel.freeserve.co.uk

Highbridge Cottage ★★★★
Contact: Mr Peter Rigg, High Bridge, Braithwaite, Thornthwaite, Keswick CA12 5SX
T: (017687) 78161
E: peter.rigg@ntlworld.com
I: www.braithwaite-cottage.co.uk

Olives Cottage ★★★★
Contact: Mr Peter Durbin, Cumbrian Cottages, 2 Lonsdale Street, Carlisle CA1 1DB
T: (01228) 599960
F: (01228) 599970
E: enquiries@cumbrian-cottages.co.uk
I: www.cumbrian-cottages.co.uk

The Shieling ★★★
Contact: Mr David Burton, Melbecks, Bassenthwaite, Keswick CA12 4QX
T: (017687) 76065
F: (017687) 76869
E: info@lakelandcottages.co.uk
I: www.lakelandcottages.co.uk

Windrush ★★★★
Contact: Mr David Burton, Melbecks, Bassenthwaite, Keswick CA12 4QX
T: (017687) 76065
F: (017687) 76869
E: info@lakelandcottages.co.uk
I: www.lakelandcottages.co.uk

Wychwood ★★★
Contact: Mr David Burton, Melbecks, Bassenthwaite, Keswick CA12 4QX
T: (017687) 76065
F: (017687) 76869
E: info@lakelandcottages.co.uk
I: www.lakelandcottages.co.uk

BRAMPTON
Cumbria

Chapel House ★★★
Contact: Mrs Potts, Chapel House, Talkin, Brampton CA8 1LP
T: (01228) 670535
F: (01228) 670535
E: potts@chapelhouse10.fsnet.co.uk
I: www.chapelhouse10.fsnet.co.uk

Long Byres at Talkin Head ★★-★★★
Contact: Mrs Harriet Sykes, Talkin Head, Brampton CA8 1LT
T: (016977) 3435
F: (016977) 2228
E: harriet@talkinhead.co.uk
I: www.talkinhead.demon.co.uk

South View Cottage ★★★★
Contact: Marie Hodgson, 141 Nell Lane, West Didsbury, Manchester M20 2LG
T: (0161) 374 0110
E: mariehodgson@southviewbanks.f9.co.uk
I: www.southviewbanks.f9.co.uk/cottage/index.htm

Warren Bank Cottage ★★★★★
Contact: Mrs Margaret Douglas, c/o The Coach House, Halliwell Dene, Hexham NE46 1HW
T: (01434) 607544
E: margie@warrenbankcottage.com
I: www.warrenbankcottage.com

BRIDEKIRK
Cumbria

Ellwood ★★★★★
Contact: Mr Peter Durbin, Cumbrian Cottages, 2 Lonsdale Street, Carlisle CA1 1DB
T: (01228) 599960
F: (01228) 599970
E: enquiries@cumbrian-cottages.co.uk
I: www.cumbrian-cottages.co.uk

BRIGHAM
Cumbria

Garron Lodge ★★★
Contact: Sykes Ref 879, Sykes Cottages, York House, York Street, Chester CH1 3LR
T: (01244) 345700
F: (01244) 321442
E: info@sykescottages.co.uk
I: www.sykescottages.co.uk

BRIGSTEER
Cumbria

Garden Cottage ★★★★
Contact: Mr Peter Durbin, Cumbrian Cottages, 2 Lonsdale Street, Carlisle CA1 1DB
T: (01228) 599960
F: (01228) 599970
E: enquiries@cumbrian-cottages.co.uk
I: www.cumbrian-cottages.co.uk

Moss Rigg ★★★
Contact: Mr Peter Durbin, Cumbrian Cottages, 2 Lonsdale Street, Carlisle CA1 1DB
T: (01228) 599960
F: (01228) 599970
E: enquiries@cumbrian-cottages.co.uk
I: www.cumbrian-cottages.co.uk

The Old Barn
Rating Applied For
Contact: Mr Paul Liddell, Belmont House, Lake Road, Bowness-on-Windermere, Windermere LA23 3BJ
T: (015394) 88855
F: (015394) 88857
E: bookings@lakelovers.co.uk

BROADWATH
Cumbria

Stonerigg Barn ★★★★
Contact: Mr Peter Durbin, Cumbrian Cottages, 2 Lonsdale Street, Carlisle CA1 1DB
T: (01228) 599960
F: (01228) 599970
E: enquiries@cumbrian-cottages.co.uk
I: www.cumbrian-cottages.co.uk

BROUGHTON-IN-FURNESS
Cumbria

Holebeck Farm Cottages ★★★-★★★★
Contact: Mr Philip Johnston, The Coppermines Coniston Cottages, Coppermines Valley, Coniston LA21 8HX
T: (015394) 41765
F: (015394) 41765
E: bookings@coppermines.co.uk
I: www.coppermines.co.uk

Ring House Cottages ★★★-★★★★
Contact: Mr & Mrs Stuart & Lynda Harrison, Ring House Cottages, Woodland, Broughton-in-Furness LA20 6DG
T: (01229) 716578
F: (01229) 716850
E: info@ringhouse.co.uk
I: www.ringhouse.co.uk

Rose Cottage & Honeysuckle Cottage ★★★★
Contact: Mrs M Harrison, Lane End Farm, Broughton Mills, Broughton-in-Furness LA20 6AX
T: (01229) 716332
I: www.lakesbreaks.co.uk

Thornthwaite Farm ★★★
Contact: Mrs J Jackson, Thornthwaite Farm, Woodland Hall, Woodland, Broughton-in-Furness LA20 6DF
T: (01229) 716340
F: (01229) 716340
I: www.lakedistrictcottages.co.uk

BROUGHTON MILLS
Cumbria

Hobkin Cottage ★★★
Contact: Mr Philip Johnston, The Coppermines Coniston Cottages, The Estate Office, The Bridge, Coniston LA21 8HJ
T: (015394) 41765
E: bookings@coppermines.co.uk
I: www.coppermines.co.uk

BURNESIDE
Cumbria

Carling Barn ★★★
Contact: Mr Peter Durbin, Cumbrian Cottages, 2 Lonsdale Street, Carlisle CA1 1DB
T: (01228) 599960
F: (01228) 599970
E: enquiries@cumbrian-cottages.co.uk
I: www.cumbrian-cottages.co.uk

St Oswald's View ★★★
Contact: Mr Peter Durbin, Cumbrian Cottages, 2 Lonsdale Street, Carlisle CA1 1DB
T: (01228) 599960
F: (01228) 599970
E: enquiries@cumbrian-cottages.co.uk
I: www.cumbrian-cottages.co.uk

BURTON-IN-KENDAL
Cumbria

Cornmillers Cottage ★★★★
Contact: Mrs Kathleen Duckett, Coat Green Farm, Burton, Burton-in-Kendal, Kendal LA6 1JG
T: (01524) 781535
F: (01524) 781535
E: cornmiller@supanet.com

East Wing ★★★★
Contact: Mr Peter Durbin, Cumbrian Cottages, 2 Lonsdale Street, Carlisle CA1 1DB
T: (01228) 599960
F: (01228) 599970
E: enquiries@cumbrian-cottages.co.uk
I: www.cumbrian-cottages.co.uk

BUTTERMERE
Cumbria

Beck House ★★★★
Contact: Mrs Shelagh Hughes, 13 St Leonards Close, Watlington, Oxford OX49 5PQ
T: (01491) 612841
F: (01491) 614668
E: shelagh@beckhouseholidays.co.uk
I: www.beckhouseholidays.co.uk

Bridge Hotel Self Catering Apartments★★★★
Contact: Bridge Hotel, Buttermere, Cockermouth CA13 9UZ
T: (017687) 70252
F: (017687) 70215
E: enquiries@bridge-hotel.com
I: www.bridge-hotel.com

Lanthwaite Green Farm Cottage ★★★★
Contact: Mrs Pippa McGuire, Bridge Hotel, Buttermere, Cockermouth CA13 9UZ
T: (017687) 70252
F: (017687) 70215
E: enquiries@bridge-hotel.com
I: www.bridge-hotel.com

Rannerdale Close & Rannerdale Croft★★★★
Contact: Mrs Elaine Beard, Rannerdale Close & Rannderdale Croft, Rannerdale Farm Cottages, Buttermere, Cockermouth CA13 9UY
T: (017687) 70232

CALDBECK
Cumbria

The Barn, Manor Cottage ★★★★
Contact: Mrs Ann Wade, Manor Cottage, Fellside, Caldbeck, Wigton CA7 8HA
T: (016974) 78214
E: walterwade@tiscali.co.uk

Ellwood House ★★★★
Contact: Mr D Hogarth, Cumbrian Cottages, 7 The Crescent, Carlisle CA1 1QW
T: (01228) 599960
F: (01228) 599970
E: enquiries@cumbrian-cottages.co.uk
I: www.cumbrian-cottages.co.uk

Greenside ★★★
Contact: Mr Peter Durbin, Cumbrian Cottages, 2 Lonsdale Street, Carlisle CA1 1DB
T: (01228) 599960
F: (01228) 599970
E: enquiries@cumbrian-cottages.co.uk
I: www.cumbrian-cottages.co.uk

High Greenrigg House Country Cottages★★★★
Contact: Mrs Sonia Hill, High Greenrigg House, Caldbeck, Wigton CA7 8HD
T: (016974) 78430
F: (016974) 78430
E: info@highgreenrigghouse.co.uk

Monkhouse Hill ★★★★-★★★★★
Contact: Mrs Jennifer Collard, Monkhouse Hill, Sebergham, Nr Caldbeck, Welton, Carlisle CA5 7HW
T: (016974) 76254
F: (016974) 76254
E: cottages@monkhousehill.co.uk
I: www.monkhousehill.co.uk

1 Riverside Cottage ★★★★
Contact: Mr Peter Durbin, Cumbrian Cottages, 2 Lonsdale Street, Carlisle CA1 1DB
T: (01228) 599960
F: (01228) 599970
I: www.cumbrian-cottages.co.uk

CARK IN CARTMEL
Cumbria

Batters Cottage ★★★
Contact: Mr John Serginson, Waterside House, Newby Bridge, Ulverston LA12 8AN
T: (015395) 30024
F: (015395) 31932
E: john@lakelandcottageco.com
I: www.lakelandcotco.com

The Mill Apartment ★★★
Contact: Mrs Teresa Watson, 12 Millstream Court, Cark in Cartmel, Grange-over-Sands LA11 7NW
T: (015395) 58519
E: neiwatson@lineone.net
I: www.millholidayapartment.co.uk

Salesbrook ★★★★
Contact: Mr John Serginson, Waterside House, Newby Bridge, Ulverston LA12 8AN
T: (015395) 30024
F: (015395) 31932
E: john@lakelandcottageco.com
I: www.lakeland-cottage-company.co.uk

CARLETON
Cumbria

Newbiggin Hall ★★★★
Contact: Mr & Mrs David & June Bates, Newbiggin Hall, Carleton, Carlisle CA4 0AJ
T: (01228) 527549
E: all.bates@virgin.net

CARLISLE
Cumbria

Bessiestown Farm Country Cottages ★★★★
Contact: Mr John Sisson, Bessiestown Farm Country Cottages, Catlowdy, Longtown, Carlisle CA6 5QP
T: (01228) 577219
F: (01228) 577219
E: info@bessiestown.co.uk
I: www.bessiestown.co.uk

Meadow View, Burn Cottage & Ald Pallyards★★★★
Contact: Mrs G Elwen, Meadow View, Burn Cottage & Ald Pallyards, New Pallyards, Hethersgill, Carlisle CA6 6HZ
T: (01228) 577308
F: (01228) 577308
E: info@newpallyards.freeserve.co.uk
I: www.newpallyards.freeserve.co.uk

University of Northumbria (Carlisle Campus)★★★
Contact: Mrs Dee Carruthers, University of Northumbria (Carlisle Campus), Old Brewery Residences, Bridge Lane, Caldewgate, Carlisle CA2 5SR
T: (01228) 597352
F: (01228) 597352
E: dee.carruthers@unn.ac.uk

West Cottage ★★★★
Contact: Mrs Allison Stamper, Cringles Farm, Cumwhinton, Carlisle CA4 8DL
T: (01228) 561600

CARTMEL
Cumbria

Grange End Cottages ★★★★
Contact: Mr Brian Colling, 7 Rushside Road, Cheadle Hulme, Stockport SK8 6NW
T: (0161) 485 7015
F: (0161) 355 6346
E: ibex32@aol.com
I: www.holidaycottagescumbria.com

Longlands at Cartmel ★★★★
Contact: Mr Martin Ainscough, Longlands at Cartmel, Cartmel, Grange-over-Sands LA11 6HG
T: (015395) 36475
F: (015395) 36172
E: longlands@cartmel.com
I: www.cartmel.com

Longlands Farm Cottage ★★★
Contact: Mrs Valerie Dixon, Longlands Farm Cottage, Aynsome Road, Cartmel, Grange-over-Sands LA11 6HJ
T: (015395) 36406
E: longlandsfarm@freeuk.com
I: longlands.golakes.co.uk

The Old Vicarage ★★★★
Contact: Mrs Veronica Sharphouse, The Old Vicarage, Field Broughton, Grange-over-Sands LA11 6HW
T: (015395) 36540
E: theflat@sharphouse.co.uk
I: www.sharphouse.co.uk/theflat

Springfield Lodge ★★★
Contact: Mr & Mrs Jack & Maureen Craig, Plane Tree Cottage, Leasgill, Milnthorpe LA7 7EX
T: (015395) 64787
E: Craigplanetree@aol.com
I: www.springfield-lodge.com

Wharton Barn ★★★★
Contact: Mr John Serginson, Waterside House, Newby Bridge, Ulverston LA12 8AN
T: (015395) 30024
F: (015395) 31932
E: john@lakelandcottageco.com
I: www.lakeland-cottage-company.co.uk

Wharton Cottage ★★★★
Contact: Mr John Serginson, Waterside House, Newby Bridge, Ulverston LA12 8AN
T: (015395) 30024
F: (015395) 31932
E: john@lakelandcottageco.com
I: www.lakeland-cottage-company.co.uk

Wharton House ★★★★
Contact: Mr John Serginson, Waterside House, Newby Bridge, Ulverston LA12 8AN
T: (015395) 30024
F: (015395) 31932
E: john@lakelandcottageco.com
I: www.lakelandcottageco.com

CARTMEL FELL
Cumbria

The Byre ★★★★
Contact: Mr John Serginson, Waterside House, Newby Bridge, Ulverston LA12 8AN
T: (015395) 30024
F: (015395) 31932
E: john@lakelandcottageco.com
I: www.lakelandcottageco.com

CASTLE CARROCK
Cumbria

Tottergill Farm ★★★★-★★★★★
Contact: Mrs Alison Bridges, Tottergill Farm, Castle Carrock, Carlisle CA8 9DP
T: (01228) 670615
F: (01228) 670727
E: alison@tottergill.demon.co.uk
I: www.tottergill.demon.co.uk

CHAPEL STILE
Cumbria

Bank View ★★★
Contact: Mr Peter Durbin, Cumbrian Cottages, 2 Lonsdale Street, Carlisle CA1 1DB
T: (01228) 599960
F: (01228) 599970
E: enquiries@cumbrian-cottages.co.uk
I: www.cumbrian-cottages.co.uk

Dulcanter ★★★
Contact: Mr Peter Durbin, Cumbrian Cottages, 2 Lonsdale Street, Carlisle CA1 1DB
T: (01228) 599960
F: (01228) 599970
E: enquiries@cumbrian-cottages.co.uk
I: www.cumbrian-cottages.co.uk

Fir Garth ★★★
Contact: Mr Peter Durbin, Cumbrian Cottages, 2 Lonsdale Street, Carlisle CA1 1DB
T: (01228) 599960
F: (01228) 599970
E: enquiries@cumbrian-cottages.co.uk
I: www.cumbrian-cottages.co.uk

1 Lingmoor View ★★★
Contact: Mrs Pauline Robinson, 3 Whinfield Road, Ulverston LA12 7HG
T: (01229) 583889
E: paulinerobinson@lakelandcottage.com
I: www.lakelandcottage.com

3 Lingmoor View ★★★
Contact: Mr & Mrs Geoffrey & Sheila Smith, 21 Cross Bank, Oughtershaw, Skipton BD23 6AH
T: (01756) 791779
E: g.s.smith@btinternet.com

8 Lingmoor View ★★
Contact: Mr Paul Liddell, Lakelovers, Belmont House, Lake Road, Bowness-on-Windermere, Windermere LA23 3BJ
T: (015394) 88855
F: (015394) 88857
E: bookings@lakelovers.co.uk
I: www.lakelovers.co.uk

CLAPPERSGATE
Cumbria

Blackcombe, Whitecrags ★★★★
Contact: Mrs Susan Jackson, Heart of the Lakes, Fisherbeck Mill, Old Lake Road, Ambleside LA22 0DH
T: (015394) 32321
F: (015394) 33251
E: info@heartofthelakes.co.uk
I: www.heartofthelakes.co.uk

The Clock ★★★★
Contact: Mr Paul Liddell, Lakelovers, Belmont House, Lake Road, Bowness-on-Windermere, Windermere LA23 3BJ
T: (015394) 88855
F: (015394) 88857
E: bookings@lakelovers.co.uk
I: www.lakelovers.co.uk

Fell View ★★★
Contact: Mrs Susan Jackson, Heart of the Lakes, Fisherbeck Mill, Old Lake Road, Ambleside LA22 0DH
T: (015394) 32321
F: (015394) 33251
E: info@heartofthelakes.co.uk
I: www.heartofthelakes.co.uk

The Hayloft ★★★
Contact: Mrs Susan Jackson, Heart of the Lakes, Fisherbeck Mill, Old Lake Road, Ambleside LA22 0DH
T: (015394) 32321
F: (015394) 33251
E: info@heartofthelakes.co.uk
I: www.heartofthelakes.co.uk

Rock Cottage ★★★
Contact: Mrs Susan Jackson, Heart of the Lakes, Fisherbeck Mill, Old Lake Road, Ambleside LA22 0DH
T: (015394) 32321
F: (015394) 33251
E: info@heartofthelakes.co.uk
I: www.heartofthelakes.co.uk

Scafell Pike, White Crags ★★★★
Contact: Mrs Susan Jackson, Heart of the Lakes, Fisherbeck Mill, Old Lake Road, Ambleside LA22 0DH
T: (015394) 32321
F: (015394) 33251
E: info@heartofthelakes.co.uk
I: www.heartofthelakes.co.uk

Skiddaw, Whitecrags ★★★★
Contact: Mrs Susan Jackson, Heart of the Lakes, Fisherbeck Mill, Old Lake Road, Ambleside LA22 0DH
T: (015394) 32321
F: (015394) 33251
E: info@heartofthelakes.co.uk
I: www.heartofthelakes.co.uk

COCKERMOUTH
Cumbria

Corner Cottage ★★★
Contact: Mrs Sue Hannah, Grand Theatre, Station Road, Cockermouth CA13 9PZ
T: (01900) 822480
F: (01900) 823105
E: suehannah@limelighting.demon.co.uk
I: www.cottageguide.co.uk/greatbroughton

Fellside ★★★
Contact: Mr Peter Durbin, Cumbrian Cottages, 2 Lonsdale Street, Carlisle CA1 1DB
T: (01228) 599960
F: (01228) 599970
E: enquiries@cumbrian-cottages.co.uk
I: www.cumbrian-cottages.co.uk

Garden Cottage ★★★
Contact: Mr Colin Wornham, Dower Cottage, Pardshaw Hall, Cockermouth CA13 0SP
T: (01900) 823531
F: (01900) 823531
E: wornham2@aol.com
I: www.lakesnw.co.uk/gardencottage

Ghyll Yeat ★★★★
Contact: Mrs Haworth, 1 Park Villas, Keswick CA12 5LQ
T: (017687) 80321
E: peter_anneghyllyeat@lineone.net
I: www.ghyllyeat.co.uk

Highside Cottage ★★★★
Contact: Mr Peter Durbin, Cumbrian Cottages, 2 Lonsdale Street, Carlisle CA1 1DB
T: (01228) 599960
F: (01228) 599970
E: enquiries@cumbrian-cottages.co.uk
I: www.cumbrian-cottages.co.uk

Jenkin Cottage ★★★★
Contact: Mrs Margaret Teasdale, Jenkin Cottage, Embleton, Cockermouth CA13 9TN
T: (017687) 76387

Kirkbrae Cottage ★★★
Contact: Dr P Spencer Davis, 15 Lochend Road, Bearsden, Glasgow G61 1DX
T: (0141) 576 0234
E: psd@dmgovan.com
I: www.kirkbraecottage.fsnet.co.uk

37 Kirkgate ★★★
Contact: Mr & Mrs Nelson Chicken, 39 Kirkgate, Cockermouth CA13 9PJ
T: (01900) 823236
F: (01900) 825983
E: valandnelson@btopenworld.com
I: www.37kirkgate.com

46 Kirkgate ★★★★
Contact: Mrs Livesey, Fawcett House, High Brigham, Cockermouth CA13 0TG
T: (01900) 825442
F: (01900) 825442
E: tricia.livesey@euphony.net

Lanefoot Barn ★★★★
Contact: Mr & Mrs Tony & Betty Fielden, Pardshaw Hall, Brow Howe, Cockermouth CA13 0SP
T: (01900) 827780
E: Brow.howe@virgin.net

Moorside ★★★
Contact: Mr Peter Durbin, Cumbrian Cottages, 2 Lonsdale Street, Carlisle CA1 1DB
T: (01228) 599960
F: (01228) 599970
E: enquiries@cumbrian-cottages.co.uk
I: www.cumbrian-cottages.co.uk

Southwaite Mill Holiday Cottages ★★★★
Contact: Mr David Warner, Greysouthern House, The Went Greysouthen, Greysouthen, Cockermouth CA13 0UQ
T: (01900) 827270
F: (01900) 821168

Wood Hall ★★★
Contact: Mrs Dorothy Jackson, Wood Hall, Apartment 1, Cockermouth CA13 0NX
T: (01900) 823585
E: wood.hall@ukonline.co.uk
I: www.wood-hall.co.uk

COLTHOUSE
Cumbria

Croft Foot Barn ★★★
Contact: Mrs Susan Jackson, Heart of the Lakes, Fisherbeck Mill, Old Lake Road, Ambleside LA22 0DH
T: (015394) 32321
F: (015394) 33251
E: info@heartofthelakes.co.uk
I: www.heartofthelakes.co.uk

Croft Head Cottage ★★★★
Contact: Mr Peter Durbin, Cumbrian Cottages, 2 Lonsdale Street, Carlisle CA1 1DB
T: (01228) 599960
F: (01228) 599970
E: enquiries@cumbrian-cottages.co.uk
I: www.cumbrian-cottages.co.uk

CONISTON
Cumbria

Acorn Cottage ★★★
Contact: Mr Peter Briggs, 52 Kendal Green, Kendal LA9 5PT
T: (01539) 735802
E: pb@haytonwinkleykendal.co.uk

Acorn Cottage ★★★
Contact: Mrs Susan Jackson, Heart of the Lakes, Fisherbeck Mill, Old Lake Road, Ambleside LA22 0DH
T: (015394) 32321
F: (015394) 33251
E: info@heartofthelakes.co.uk
I: www.heartofthelakes.co.uk

1 & 2 Ash Gill Cottages ★★★★
Contact: Mrs Dorothy Cowburn, Lyndene, Pope Lane, Whitestake, Preston PR4 4JR
T: (01772) 612832

Atkinson Ground Cottage ★★★
Contact: Mr John Serginson, Waterside House, Newby Bridge, Ulverston LA12 8AN
T: (015395) 30024
F: (015395) 31932
E: john@lakelandcottageco.com
I: www.lakelandcottageco.com

Bank Ground Farm Cottages ★★-★★★★
Contact: Mrs Lucy Batty, The Barn, Bank Ground, Coniston LA21 8AA
T: (015394) 41264
F: (015394) 41900
E: info@bankground.co.uk
I: www.bankground.com

Banks Ghyll Cottage ★★★★
Contact: Mr Philip Johnston, The Coppermines Coniston Cottages, The Estate Office, The Bridge, Coniston LA21 8HJ
T: (015394) 41765
E: bookings@coppermines.co.uk
I: www.coppermines.co.uk

Beck Yeat Cottage ★★★
Contact: Mr Philip Johnston, The Coppermines Coniston Cottages, The Estate Office, The Bridge, Coniston LA21 8HJ
T: (015394) 41765
F: (015394) 41944
E: info@coppermines.co.uk
I: www.coppermines.co.uk

Beech Grove ★★★★
Contact: Mrs Jean Johnson, Orchard Cottage, Yewdale Road, Hawkshead, Ambleside LA21 8DU
T: (015394) 41319
E: jean.orchardcottage@virgin.net
I: www.conistonholidays.co.uk

Bramble Cottage ★★★★
Contact: Mr R Newport, Bannisdale Head, Selside, Kendal LA8 9JZ
T: (01539) 823450
F: (01539) 441092
E: gill@lakesabout.co.uk
I: www.lakesabout.co.uk

The Bridge Cottages ★★★★
Contact: Mr Philip Johnston, The Coppermines Coniston, Coppermines Valley, Coniston LA21 8HX
T: (015394) 41765
F: (015394) 41944
E: bookings@coppermines.co.uk
I: www.coppermines.co.uk

Carries Gate ★★★
Contact: Mrs Susan Jackson, Heart of the Lakes, Fisherbeck Mill, Old Lake Road, Ambleside LA22 0DH
T: (015394) 32321
F: (015394) 33251
E: info@heartofthelakes.co.uk
I: www.heartofthelakes.co.uk

Cherry Tree Cottage ★★★
Contact: Mr Philip Johnston, The Coppermines Coniston Cottages, The Estate Office, The Bridge, Coniston LA21 8HJ
T: (015394) 41765
F: (015394) 41944
E: info@coppermines.co.uk
I: www.coppermines.co.uk

The Coach House ★★★★
Contact: Mrs Gillian Newport, Bannisdale Head, Selside, Longsleddale, Kendal LA8 9JZ
T: (01539) 823450
E: info@lakesabout.co.uk
I: www.lakesabout.co.uk

Coniston Country Cottages ★★★-★★★★
Contact: Mr S & Mrs L Abbott
T: (015394) 41114
F: (015394) 41114
E: enquiry@conistoncottages.co.uk
I: www.conistoncottages.co.uk

Coniston View Cottage ★★★
Contact: Mrs Susan Jackson, Heart of the Lakes, Fisherbeck Mill, Old Lake Road, Ambleside LA22 0DH
T: (015394) 32321
F: (015394) 33251
E: info@heartofthelakes.co.uk
I: www.heartofthelakes.co.uk

The Coppermines Coniston Cottages ★★-★★★★
Contact: Mr Philip Johnston, The Coppermines Coniston Cottages, Coniston LA21 8HJ
T: (015394) 41765
F: (015394) 41944
E: bookings@coppermines.co.uk
I: www.coppermines.co.uk

4 Coppermines Cottages ★★★
Contact: Mr Philip Johnston, The Coppermines Coniston Cottages, Coppermines Valley, Coniston LA21 8HX
T: (015394) 41765
E: bookings@coppermines.co.uk
I: www.coppermines.co.uk

Curdle Dub ★★★
Contact: Mr Paul Liddell, Lakelovers, Belmont House, Lake Road, Bowness-on-Windermere, Windermere LA23 3BJ
T: (015394) 88855
F: (015394) 88857
E: bookings@lakelovers.co.uk
I: www.lakelovers.co.uk

Damson Cottage ★★★★
Contact: Mr Peter Durbin, Cumbrian Cottages, 2 Lonsdale Street, Carlisle CA1 1DB
T: (01228) 599960
F: (01228) 599970
E: enquiries@cumbrian-cottages.co.uk
I: www.cumbria-cottages.co.uk

25 Days Bank ★★★
Contact: Mrs Thornton, 43 Dovedale Gardens, Pendas Fields, Cross Gates, Leeds LS15 8UP
T: (0113) 260 2455

Dixon Ground ★★★
Contact: Mr Philip Johnston, The Coppermines Coniston Cottages, The Estate Office, The Bridge, Coniston LA21 8HJ
T: (015394) 41765
E: bookings@coppermines.co.uk
I: www.coppermines.co.uk

Fair Snape Cottage ★★★★
Contact: Mr Philip Johnston, The Coppermines Coniston Cottages, The Estate Office, The Bridge, Coniston LA21 8HJ
T: (015394) 41765
E: bookings@coppermines.co.uk
I: www.coppermines.co.uk

1 Far End Cottages ★★★
Contact: Mrs Andrea Batho, High Hollin Bank, Coniston LA21 8AG
T: (015394) 41680
E: a.batho@virgin.net
I: www.cottagescumbria.com

The Firemans Cottage ★★★
Contact: Mr Philip Johnston, The Coppermines Coniston Cottages, The Estate Office, The Bridge, Coniston LA21 8HJ
T: (015394) 41765
E: bookings@coppermines.co.uk
I: www.coppermines.co.uk

Fisherbeck Fold ★★★★
Contact: Mr Paul Liddell, Belmont House, Lake Road, Bowness-on-Windermere, Windermere LA23 3BJ
T: (015394) 88855
F: (015394) 88857
E: bookings@lakelovers.co.uk

Fisherbeck Nest ★★★
Contact: Mr Paul Liddell, Belmont House, Lake Road, Bowness-on-Windermere, Windermere LA23 3BJ
T: (015394) 88855
F: (015394) 88857
E: bookings@lakelovers.co.uk

Forest Cottage ★★★★
Contact: Mr John Serginson, Waterside House, Newby Bridge, Ulverston LA12 8AN
T: (015395) 30024
F: (015395) 31932
E: john@lakelandcottageco.com
I: www.lakelandcottageco.com

Gable Cottage ★★★
Contact: Mr Philip Johnston, The Coppermines Coniston Cottages, The Estate Office, The Bridge, Coniston LA21 8HJ
T: (015394) 41765
E: bookings@coppermines.co.uk
I: www.coppermines.co.uk

Gable End ★★★
Contact: Mr John Serginson, Waterside House, Newby Bridge, Ulverston LA12 8AN
T: (015395) 30024
F: (015395) 31932
E: john@lakelandcottageco.com
I: www.lakelandcottageco.com

10 Green Cottages ★★★★
Contact: The Bridge, Lowick Bridge, Ulverston LA21 8HS
T: (015394) 41765

Heathwaite Farm Cottages Heathwaite Farm House, The Old Cottage★★★-★★★★
Contact: Mr Philip Johnston, The Coppermines Coniston Cottages, The Estate Office, The Bridge, Coniston LA21 8HJ
T: (015394) 41765
E: bookings@coppermines.co.u
I: www.coppermines.co.uk

High Arnside ★★★
Contact: Mrs Meredith, High Arnside, High Arnside Farm, Coniston LA21 8DW
T: (015394) 32261
E: JanMeredith@bigwig.net
I: www.higharnsidefarm.co.uk

High Dixon Barn ★★★
Contact: Mrs Susan Jackson, Heart of the Lakes, Fisherbeck Mill, Old Lake Road, Ambleside LA22 0DH
T: (015394) 32321
F: (015394) 33251
E: info@heartofthelakes.co.uk
I: www.heartofthelakes.co.uk

High Dixon Ground ★★★
Contact: Mrs Susan Jackson, Heart of the Lakes, Fisherbeck Mill, Old Lake Road, Ambleside LA22 0DH
T: (015394) 32321
F: (015394) 33251
E: info@heartofthelakes.co.uk
I: www.heartofthelakes.co.uk

Hollin & Richmond House Apartments ★★★
Contact: Mrs Jean Johnson, Orchard Cottage, Yewdale Road, Hawkshead, Ambleside LA21 8DU
T: (015394) 41319
E: jean.orchardcottage@virgin.net
I: www.conistonholidays.co.uk

Hollygarth ★★★★
Contact: Mrs Susan Jackson, Heart of the Lakes, Fisherbeck Mill, Old Lake Road, Ambleside LA22 0DH
T: (015394) 32321
F: (015394) 33251
E: info@heartofthelakes.co.uk
I: www.heartofthelakes.co.uk

5 Holme Ground Cottages ★★★
Contact: Mrs Kate Bradshaw, The Rookery, Oaklands, Riding Mill NE44 6AR
T: (01434) 682526
E: rookery1@tiscali.co.uk

How Head Cottages ★★★
Contact: Mr D Holland, How Head Cottages, East of Lake, Coniston LA21 8AA
T: (015394) 41594
E: howhead@lineone.net
I: www.howheadcottages.co.uk

Howhead ★★★★
Contact: Mr John Serginson, Waterside House, Newby Bridge, Ulverston LA12 8AN
T: (015395) 30024
F: (015395) 31932
E: john@lakelandcottageco.com
I: www.lakeland-cottage-company.co.uk

Lake View Cottage ★★★
Contact: Mrs Susan Jackson, Heart of the Lakes, Fisherbeck Mill, Old Lake Road, Ambleside LA22 0DH
T: (015394) 32321
F: (015394) 33251
E: info@heartofthelakes.co.uk
I: www.heartofthelakes.co.uk

Low Brow ★★★
Contact: Mrs Susan Jackson, Heart of the Lakes, Fisherbeck Mill, Old Lake Road, Ambleside LA22 0DH
T: (015394) 32321
F: (015394) 33251
E: info@heartofthelakes.co.uk
I: www.heartofthelakes.co.uk

Lower Barn ★★★
Contact: Mr John Serginson, The Lakeland Cottage Company, Waterside House, Newby Bridge, Ulverston LA12 8AN
T: (015395) 30024
F: (015395) 31932
E: john@lakelandcottageco.com
I: www.lakelandcottageco.com

Mountain Ash Cottage ★★★
Contact: Mr Philip Johnston, The Coppermines Coniston Cottages, The Estate Office, The Bridge, Coniston LA21 8HJ
T: (015394) 41765
E: bookings@coppermines.co.uk
I: www.coppermines.co.uk

Red Dell Cottage ★★★★
Contact: Mr Philip Johnston, The Coppermines & Lakes Cottages, The Estate Office, The Bridge, Coniston LA21 8HJ
T: (015394) 41765
F: (015394) 41944
E: info@coppermines.co.uk
I: www.coppermines.co.uk

Rockleigh ★★★★
Contact: Mr Paul Liddell, Lakelovers, Belmont House, Lake Road, Bowness-on-Windermere, Windermere LA23 3BJ
T: (015394) 88855
F: (015394) 88857
E: bookings@lakelovers.co.uk
I: www.lakelovers.co.uk

Rose Cottage ★★★★
Contact: Mr John Serginson, The Lakeland Cottage Company, Waterside House, Newby Bridge, Ulverston LA12 8AN
T: (015395) 30024
F: (015395) 31932
E: john@lakelandcottageco.com
I: www.lakelandcottageco.com

Shelt Gill ★★★
Contact: Mrs R Dean, 9 The Fairway, Sheffield SI0 4LX
T: (0114) 230 8077
F: (0114) 230 8077
E: holiday@sheltgill.co.uk
I: www.sheltgill.co.uk

The Shieling ★★★
Contact: Mr Paul Liddell, Lakelovers, Belmont House, Lake Road, Bowness-on-Windermere, Windermere LA23 3BJ
T: (015394) 88855
F: (015394) 88857
E: bookings@lakelovers.co.uk
I: www.lakelovers.co.uk

Sunbeam Cottage ★★★
Contact: Mr Paul Liddell, Lakelovers, Belmont House, Lake Road, Bowness-on-Windermere, Windermere LA23 3BJ
T: (015394) 88855
F: (015394) 88857
E: bookings@lakelovers.co.uk
I: www.lakelovers.co.uk

Sunny Bank Farm ★★★★
Contact: Mrs Daphne Libby, St James Vicarage, Goschen Road, Carlisle CA2 5PF
T: (01228) 515639
F: (01228) 524569
E: sunnybankfarm@btinternet.com
I: www.bbbweb.com/sunnybank

Three Springs ★★★
Contact: Mr John Serginson, Waterside House, Newby Bridge, Ulverston LA12 8AN
T: (015395) 30024
F: (015395) 31932
E: john@lakelandcottageco.com
I: www.lakeland-cottage-company.co.uk

Thurston House & Thurston View ★★-★★★★
Contact: Mr & Mrs A Jefferson, 21 Chale Green, Harwood, Bolton BL2 3NJ
T: (01204) 419261
E: alan@jefferson99.freeserve.co.uk
I: www.jefferson99.freeserve.co.uk

Tilberthwaite Farm Cottage ★★★
Contact: Mrs Dorothy Wilkinson, Tilberthwaite Farm Cottage, Tilberthwaite Farm, Coniston LA21 8DG
T: (015394) 37281
E: tilberthwaite.farm@lineone.net
I: tilberthwaitefarmcottage.com

Tinkler Beck Farm ★★★★★
Contact: Mr John Serginson, Waterside House, Newby Bridge, Ulverston LA12 8AN
T: (015395) 30024
F: (015395) 31932
E: john@lakelandcottageco.com
I: www.lakeland-cottage-company.co.uk

Townson Ground ★★★
Contact: Mrs B E Nelson, Townson Ground, East of Lake, Coniston LA21 8AA
T: (015394) 41272
F: (015394) 41110
E: barbara@townsonground.freeserve.co.uk
I: www.townsonground.co.uk

COUPLAND BECK
Cumbria

Westmorland Cottages ★★★★
Contact: Mrs Clare Patterson, Westmorland Cottages, Coupland Beck Farm, Coupland Beck, Appleby-in-Westmorland CA16 6LN
T: (017683) 51449
E: westmorlandcott@btconnect.com
I: www.couplandbeckfarm.demon.co.uk

COWAN HEAD
Cumbria

River View ★★★
Contact: Mr Peter Durbin, Cumbrian Cottages, 2 Lonsdale Street, Carlisle CA1 1DB
T: (01228) 599960
F: (01228) 599970
E: enquiries@cumbrian-cottages.co.uk
I: www.cumbrian-cottages.co.uk

COWGILL
Cumbria

Hill Farmhouse ★★★
Contact: Mr & Mrs Ron and Yvonne Metcalfe, Hill Farmhouse, Cowgill, Sedbergh LA10 5RF
T: (015396) 25144

CROOK
Cumbria

Brackenrigg ★★★
Contact: Mr Peter Durbin, Cumbrian Cottages, 2 Lonsdale Street, Carlisle CA1 1DB
T: (01228) 599960
F: (01228) 599970
E: enquiries@cumbrian-cottages.co.uk
I: www.cumbrian-cottages.co.uk

Lyth View Cottage ★★★
Contact: Mr Peter Durbin, Cumbrian Cottages, 2 Lonsdale Street, Carlisle CA1 1DB
T: (01228) 599960
F: (01228) 599970
E: enquiries@cumbrian-cottages.co.uk
I: www.cumbrian-cottages.co.uk

Mitchelland Farm Bungalow ★★★★
Contact: Mr Stuart Higham & Ms Farrer, Mitchelland Farm, Off Crook Road, Bowness-on-Windermere, Crook, Kendal LA8 8LL
T: (015394) 47421

Old Mill Cottage ★★★
Contact: Mr Peter Durbin, Cumbrian Cottages, 2 Lonsdale Street, Carlisle CA1 1DB
T: (01228) 599960
F: (01228) 599970
E: enquiries@cumbrian-cottages.co.uk
I: www.cumbrian-cottages.co.uk

Tan Smithy Cottage ★★★★
Contact: Mr Peter Durbin, Cumbrian Cottages, 2 Lonsdale Street, Carlisle CA1 1DB
T: (01228) 599960
F: (01228) 599970
E: enquiries@cumbrian-cottages.co.uk
I: www.cumbrian-cottages.co.uk

CROOKLANDS
Cumbria

Hillview Cottage ★★★★
Contact: Mrs Simpson, Craig Mount, 10 Kentrigg, Kendal LA9 6EE
T: (015395) 67467
F: (01539) 728528
E: bouncershire6746@aol.com

CROSBY GARRETT
Cumbria

The Old Wash House Cottage ★★★
Contact: Mrs Shirley Thompson, Clark Scott-Harden, 1 Little Dockray, Penrith CA11 2HL
T: (01768) 864541
F: (01768) 865578
E: Shirley.Thompson@csh.co.uk
I: www.csh.co.uk

CROSBY-ON-EDEN
Cumbria

Crosby House Cottages ★★★★
Contact: Mrs Dickson, Crosby House Cottages, Crosby House, Crosby-on-Eden, Carlisle CA6 4QZ
T: (01228) 573239
F: (01228) 573338
E: info@norbyways.demon.co.uk
I: www.northumbria-byways.com/crosby

CROSBY RAVENSWORTH
Cumbria

The Stable ★★★★
Contact: Mrs Christine Jackson, Wickerslack Farm, Crosby Ravensworth, Pooley Bridge, Penrith CA10 2LN
T: (01931) 715236

CROSTHWAITE
Cumbria

Acorn Lodge ★★★★
Contact: Mr Peter Durbin, Cumbrian Cottages, 2 Lonsdale Street, Carlisle CA1 1DB
T: (01228) 599960
F: (01228) 599970
E: enquiries@cumbrian-cottages.co.uk
I: www.cumbrian-cottages.co.uk

Barf Lodge ★★★★
Contact: Mr Peter Durbin, Cumbrian Cottages, 2 Lonsdale Street, Carlisle CA1 1DB
T: (01228) 599960
F: (01228) 599970
E: enquiries@cumbrian-cottages.co.uk
I: www.cumbrian-cottages.co.uk

Bega ★★★★
Contact: Mr Peter Durbin, Cumbrian Cottages, 2 Lonsdale Street, Carlisle CA1 1DB
T: (01228) 599960
F: (01228) 599970
E: enquiries@cumbrian-cottages.co.uk
I: www.cumbrian-cottages.co.uk

Corner Cottage ★★★
Contact: Mary Smith, 51 Rennie Court, 11 Upper Ground, London SE1 9LP
T: (01744) 894196
E: mary@sgcornercottage.co.uk

Crosthwaite Cottages ★★★
Contact: Mr John Serginson, Waterside House, Newby Bridge, Ulverston LA12 8AN
T: (015395) 30024
F: (015395) 31932
E: john@lakelandcottageco.com
I: www.lakeland-cottage-company.co.uk

Crosthwaite Spring Cottage ★★★
Contact: Mr Paul Liddell, Lakelovers, Belmont House, Lake Road, Bowness-on-Windermere, Windermere LA23 3BJ
T: (015394) 88855
F: (015394) 88857
E: bookings@lakelovers.co.uk
I: www.lakelovers.co.uk

Ennerdale ★★★★
Contact: Mr Peter Durbin, Cumbrian Cottages, 2 Lonsdale Street, Carlisle CA1 1DB
T: (01228) 599960
F: (01228) 599970
E: enquiries@cumbrian-cottages.co.uk
I: www.cumbrian-cottages.co.uk

Ghyllbank ★★★★
Contact: Mr Paul Liddell, Lakelovers, Belmont House, Lake Road, Bowness-on-Windermere, Windermere LA23 3BJ
T: (015394) 88855
F: (015394) 88857
E: bookings@lakelovers.co.uk
I: www.lakelovers.co.uk

Gilpin View ★★★
Contact: Mr Paul Liddell, Lakelovers, Belmont House, Lake Road, Bowness-on-Windermere, Windermere LA23 3BJ
T: (015394) 88855
F: (015394) 88857
E: bookings@lakelovers.co.uk
I: www.lakelovers.co.uk

Greenbank ★★★★
Contact: Jackie Gaskell, Greenbank, Crosthwaite, Kendal LA8 8JD
T: (015395) 68598
E: greenbank@nascr.net
I: www.greenbank-cumbria.co.uk

High Beck Cottage ★★★★
Contact: Mr Paul Liddell, Lakelovers, Belmont House, Lake Road, Bowness-on-Windermere, Windermere LA23 3BJ
T: (015394) 88855
F: (015394) 88857
E: bookings@lakelovers.co.uk
I: www.lakelovers.co.uk

CUNSEY
Cumbria

Deer Holm ★★★★
Contact: Mr John Serginson, Waterside House, Newby Bridge, Ulverston LA12 8AN
T: (015395) 30024
F: (015395) 31932
E: john@lakelandcottageco.com
I: www.lakelandcottageco.com

DEEPDALE
Cumbria

Willans ★★
Contact: Ms Kathleen Bentham, Willans, Deepdale, Dent, Sedbergh LA10 5QZ
T: (015396) 25285
E: kathbentham@hotmail.com
I: www.cottageguide.co.uk/willans

DENT
Cumbria

Brooks Barn ★★★★
Contact: The Manager Dales Hol Cot Ref 3306, Dales Holiday Cottages, Carleton Business Centre, Carleton New Road, Skipton BD23 2AA
T: (01756) 799821
F: (01756) 797012
E: info@dalesholcot.com
I: www.dalesholcot.com

Buzzard's Cottage ★★★★
Contact: The Manager Dales Hol Cot Ref:2865, Carleton Business Park, Carleton New Road, Skipton BD23 2AA
T: (01756) 799821
F: (01756) 797012
E: info@dalesholcot.com
I: www.dalesholcot.com

Fern Lea ★★
Contact: Mrs B Harlow, 32 Main Street, Woodborough, Nottingham NE14 6EA
T: (0115) 965 2795
F: (0115) 965 2795

Gibbs Hall Barn ★★★★
Contact: The Manager Dales Hol Cot Ref:3488, Carleton Business Park, Carleton New Road, Skipton, BD23 2AA
T: (01756) 790919
F: (01756) 797012
E: fiona@dales-holiday-cottages.com
I: www.dales-holiday-cottages.com

High Chapel Cottage ★★★★
Contact: The Manager Dales Hol Cot Ref:2074, Carleton Business Park, Carleton New Road, Skipton BD23 2AA
T: (01756) 799821
F: (01756) 797012
E: info@dalesholcot.com
I: www.dalesholcot.com

Lea Yeat Cottage ★★★★
Contact: Mrs Jo Chapman, Wray Rigg, Dent, Sedbergh LA10 5RF
T: (015396) 25091
E: billyjo@tesco.net
I: www.cottageguide.co.uk/leayeat

Middleton's Cottage & Fountain Cottage★★★
Contact: Mr & Mrs P M Ayers, The Old Rectory, Litlington, Polegate BN26 5RB
T: (01323) 870032
F: (01323) 870032
E: candpayers@mistral.co.uk
I: www.dentcottages.co.uk

Mire Garth ★★★
Contact: Mrs Jean Middleton, Deepdale Head, Dent, Sedbergh LA10 5RA
T: (015396) 25235

Old Parsonage ★★★
Contact: The Manager Dales Hol Cot Ref:2595, Carleton Business Park, Carleton New Road, Skipton BD23 2AA
T: (01756) 799821
F: (01756) 797012
E: info@dalesholcot.com
I: www.dalesholcot.com

Stonecroft ★★★
Contact: Country Holidays Ref:5555, Spring Mill, Earby, Barnoldswick BB94 0AA
T: 0870 723723
F: (01282) 844288
E: sales@holidaycottagesgroup.com
I: www.country-holidays.co.uk

Wilsey House ★★★
Contact: Mrs Joan Saunders, 21 Church Street, Somersham, Huntingdon PE28 3EG
T: (01487) 841556
E: enquiries@wilsey.co.uk

DOCKRAY
Cumbria

Lookin How ★★★★★
Contact: Mr Peter Durbin, Cumbrian Cottages, 2 Lonsdale Street, Carlisle CA1 1DB
T: (01228) 599960
F: (01228) 599970
E: enquiries@cumbrian-cottages.co.uk
I: www.cumbrian-cottages.co.uk

DRUMBURGH
Cumbria

Grange Cottages ★★★-★★★★
Contact: Mrs Sarah Hodgson, The Grange, Wigton, Drumburgh, Carlisle CA7 5DW
T: (01228) 576551
E: messrs.hodgson@tesco.net

EDDERSIDE
Cumbria

Centre Farm ★★★
Contact: Mr Peter Durbin, Cumbrian Cottages, 2 Lonsdale Street, Carlisle CA1 1DB
T: (01228) 599960
F: (01228) 599970
E: enquiries@cumbrian-cottages.co.uk
I: www.cumbrian-cottages.co.uk

ELTERWATER
Cumbria

Bridge End Cottage ★★★★
Contact: Mr Paul Liddell, Lakelovers, Belmont House, Lake Road, Bowness-on-Windermere, Windermere LA23 3BJ
T: (015394) 88855
F: (015394) 88857
E: bookings@lakelovers.co.uk
I: www.lakelovers.co.uk

Bridge Syke Cottage ★★★★
Contact: Mr Paul Liddell, Lakelovers, Belmont House, Lake Road, Bowness-on-Windermere, Windermere LA23 3BJ
T: (015394) 88855
F: (015394) 88857
E: bookings@lakelovers.co.uk
I: www.lakelovers.co.uk

Eltermere Old Barn ★★★★
Contact: Mrs Susan Jackson, Heart of the Lakes, Fisherbeck Mill, Old Lake Road, Ambleside LA22 0DH
T: (015394) 32321
F: (015394) 33251
E: info@heartofthelakes.co.uk
I: www.heartofthelakes.co.uk

Gunpowder Cottage ★★★★
Contact: Mr Paul Liddell, Lakelovers, Belmont House, Lake Road, Bowness-on-Windermere, Windermere LA23 3BJ
T: (015394) 88855
F: (015394) 88857
E: bookings@lakelovers.co.uk
I: www.lakelovers.co.uk

Lane Ends Cottages ★★★
Contact: Mrs M E Rice, Fellside, 3 and 4 Lane Ends Cottages, Elterwater, Ambleside LA22 9HN
T: (015394) 37678

Maple Tree Corner Rating Applied For
Contact: Mrs Susan Jackson, Heart of the Lakes, Fisherbeck Mill, Old Lake Road, Ambleside LA22 0DH
T: (015394) 33110
F: (015394) 33251
E: info@heartofthelakes.co.uk

Mill Race Cottage Rating Applied For
Contact: Mrs Susan Jackson, Fisherbeck Mill, Old Lake Road, Ambleside LA22 0DH
T: (015394) 33110
F: (015394) 33251
E: info@heartofthelakes.co.uk

Oakbank ★★★★
Contact: Mrs Susan Jackson, Heart of the Lakes, Fisherbeck Mill, Old Lake Road, Ambleside LA22 0DH
T: (015394) 32321
F: (015394) 33251
E: info@heartofthelakes.co.uk
I: www.heartofthelakes.co.uk

St Giles ★★★
Contact: Mrs Susan Jackson, Heart of the Lakes, Fisherbeck Mill, Old Lake Road, Ambleside LA22 0DH
T: (015394) 32321
F: (015394) 33251
E: info@heartofthelakes.co.uk
I: www.heartofthelakes.co.uk

Wistaria Cottage and 3 Main Street ★★★
Contact: Mr G & Mrs D Beardmore, 2 Beech Drive, Kidsgrove, Stoke-on-Trent ST7 1BA
T: (01782) 783170
F: (01782) 783170
E: geoff.doreen.beardmore@ntlworld.com

EMBLETON
Cumbria

Sunny Bank Cottage ★★★
Contact: Mrs Margaret Bell, 2 Rakefoot Cottages, Embleton, Cockermouth CA13 9XU
T: (017687) 76273

ENDMOOR
Cumbria

West View Flat ★★★
Contact: Mrs M Bainbridge, West View Flat, West View Farm, Endmoor, Kendal LA8 0HY
T: (015395) 67278

ESKDALE
Cumbria

Bridge End Farm Cottages ★★★★-★★★★★
Contact: Mr Greg Poole, Bridge End Farm Cottages, Boot, Holmrook CA19 1TG
T: 08700 735328
F: 08700 735328
E: greg@selectcottages.com
I: www.selectcottages.com

Fisherground Farm ★★★
Contact: Fisherground Farm Holidays, Fisherground, Eskdale, Holmrook CA19 1TF
T: (01946) 723319
E: holidays@fisherground.co.uk
I: www.fisherground.co.uk

Longrigg Green ★★★★★
Contact: Mrs Christine Carter, Forest How, Eskdale, Holmrook CA19 1TR
T: (019467) 23201
F: (019467) 23190
E: fcarter@easynet.co.uk
I: www.longrigg.green.btinternet.co.uk

Old Brantrake ★★★★
Contact: Mr J B Tyson, Brant Rake, Eskdale, Holmrook CA19 1TT
T: (019467) 23340
F: (019467) 23340
E: tyson@eskdale1.demon.co.uk

Whin Rigg ★★★★
Contact: Mrs Jennifer Prestwood, The Ferns, Eskdale, Holmrook CA19 1UA
T: (019467) 23217
F: (019467) 23217
E: info@eskdalebreaks.com
I: www.eskdalebreaks.com

FAR SAWREY
Cumbria

1 & 2 Church Cottage ★★★★
Contact: Mrs Susan Jackson, Heart of the Lakes, Fisherbeck Mill, Old Lake Road, Ambleside LA22 0DH
T: (015394) 32321
F: (015394) 33251
E: info@heartofthelakes.co.uk
I: www.heartofthelakes.co.uk

Claife Cottage ★★★
Contact: Mr Peter Durbin, Cumbrian Cottages, 2 Lonsdale Street, Carlisle CA1 1DB
T: (01228) 599960
F: (01228) 599970
E: enquiries@cumbrian-cottages.co.uk
I: www.cumbrian-cottages.co.uk

Rowan Cottage ★★★★
Contact: Mrs Susan Jackson, Heart of the Lakes, Fisherbeck Mill, Old Lake Road, Ambleside LA22 0DH
T: (015394) 32321
F: (015394) 33251
E: info@heartofthelakes.co.uk
I: www.heartofthelakes.co.uk

Sawrey Knotts ★★★★-★★★★★
Contact: Mr Kevin McCarten, Sawrey Knotts, Far Sawrey, Sawrey, Ambleside LA22 0LG
T: (01539) 488625
E: sawreyknotts@aol.com
I: www.sawreyknotts.co.uk

Tower Cottage ★★★★
Contact: Mr Philip Johnston, The Coppermines Coniston Cottages, The Estate Office, The Bridge, Coniston LA21 8HJ
T: (01539) 441265
F: (01539) 441944
E: bookings@coppermines.co.uk
I: www.coppermines.co.uk

FARLAM
Cumbria

Calf Close Cottage ★★★★★
Contact: Mr Peter Durbin, Cumbrian Cottages, 2 Lonsdale Street, Carlisle CA1 1DB
T: (01228) 599960
F: (01228) 599970
E: enquiries@cumbrian-cottages.co.uk
I: www.cumbrian-cottages.co.uk

FINSTHWAITE
Cumbria

The Barn ★★★★★
Contact: Mr John Serginson, Waterside House, Newby Bridge, Ulverston LA12 8AN
T: (015395) 30024
F: (015395) 31932
E: john@lakelandcottageco.com
I: www.lakelandcottagecompany.co.uk

Sheiling Barn ★★★★
Contact: Mr Paul Liddell, Lakelovers, Belmont House, Lake Road, Bowness-on-Windermere, Windermere LA23 3BJ
T: (015394) 88855
F: (015394) 88857
E: bookings@lakelovers.co.uk
I: www.lakelovers.co.uk

GARNETT BRIDGE
Cumbria

Cocks Close ★★★
Contact: Mrs Denny, Lindens, Ashley Park Road, Walton-on-Thames KT12 1JU
T: (01932) 246432
F: (01932) 253174
E: mikericky@aol.com

GARRIGILL
Cumbria

Brook Cottage ★★★★
Contact: Mrs Fiona Gifford, Moordale, Garrigill, Alston CA9 3EB
T: (01434) 381688
F: (01434) 381688
E: mcgarrigill@aol.com
I: members.aol.com/brookcot

GARSDALE
Cumbria

Cloughside Cottage ★★★★
Contact: The Manager Dales Hol Cot Ref:2599, Carleton Business Park, Carleton New Road, Skipton BD23 2AA
T: (01756) 799821
F: (01756) 797012
E: info@dalesholcot.com
I: www.dalesholcot.com

GARSDALE HEAD
Cumbria

Dandry Cottage ★★★
Contact: Dales Hol Cot Ref:1637, Carleton Business Park, Carleton New Road, Skipton BD23 2AA
T: (01756) 799821
F: (01756) 797012
E: info@dalesholcot.com
I: www.dalesholcot.com

GILCRUX
Cumbria

Ellen Hall ★★-★★★★
Contact: Mrs Alison Dunlop, Wigton, Gilcrux, Carlisle CA7 2QB
T: (016973) 21439
F: (016973) 22675
E: data.dunlop@virgin.net
I: www.cottagesmadefortwo.co.uk

GILSLAND
Cumbria

Working Dales Pony Centre ★★★
Contact: Mr C & G Parker, Clarks Hill, Gilsland, Brampton CA8 7DF
T: (016977) 47208

GLASSONBY
Cumbria

Chapel House ★★★★
Contact: Mr Duncan Lowis, Drovers Ghyll, Glassonby, Penrith CA10 1DU
T: (01768) 898747
E: duncanlowis@hotmail.com

GLENRIDDING
Cumbria

Beech House Apartments 1 & 2 ★★★
Contact: Mr Paul Liddell, Lakelovers, Belmont House, Lake Road, Bowness-on-Windermere, Windermere LA23 3BJ
T: (015394) 88855
F: (015394) 88857
E: bookings@lakelovers.co.uk
I: www.lakelovers.co.uk

Birkside Cottage ★★★
Contact: Mr Peter Durbin, Cumbrian Cottages, 2 Lonsdale Street, Carlisle CA1 1DB
T: (01228) 599960
F: (01228) 599970
E: enquiries@cumbrian-cottages.co.uk
I: www.cumbrian-cottages.co.uk

Chapel Cottage ★★★★
Contact: Mrs Susan Jackson, Heart of the Lakes, Fisherbeck Mill, Old Lake Road, Ambleside LA22 0DH
T: (015394) 32321
F: (015394) 33251
E: info@heartofthelakes.co.uk
I: www.heartofthelakes.co.uk

Chapel House ★★★★
Contact: Mrs Susan Jackson, Heart of the Lakes, Fisherbeck Mill, Old Lake Road, Ambleside LA22 0DH
T: (015394) 32321
F: (015394) 33251
E: info@heartofthelakes.co.uk
I: www.heartofthelakes.co.uk

Crag Close ★★★★★
Contact: Mr Paul Liddell, Lakelovers, Belmont House, Lake Road, Bowness-on-Windermere, Windermere LA23 3BJ
T: (015394) 88855
F: (015394) 88857
E: bookings@lakelovers.co.uk
I: www.lakelovers.co.uk

Fell View Holidays ★★★★
Contact: Mr & Mrs Burnett, Fell View Holidays, Fell View, Grisedale Bridge, Patterdale, Penrith CA11 0PJ
T: (017684) 82342
F: (017684) 82342
E: enquiries@fellviewholidays.com

Grassthwaite How ★★★★
Contact: Mrs Susan Jackson, Heart of the Lakes, Fisherbeck Mill, Old Lake Road, Ambleside LA22 0DH
T: (015394) 32321
F: (015394) 33251
E: info@heartofthelakes.co.uk
I: www.heartofthelakes.co.uk

Grisedale Cottage ★★★
Contact: Mrs Susan Jackson, Heart of the Lakes, Fisherbeck Mill, Old Lake Road, Ambleside LA22 0DH
T: (015394) 32321
F: (015394) 33251
E: info@heartofthelakes.co.uk
I: www.heartofthelakes.co.uk

Halton Cottage ★★★
Contact: Mr Peter Durbin, Cumbrian Cottages, 2 Lonsdale Street, Carlisle CA1 1DB
T: (01228) 599960
F: (01228) 599970
E: enquiries@cumbrian-cottages.co.uk
I: www.cumbrian-cottages.co.uk

Mistal Cottage ★★★★
Contact: Mrs Susan Jackson, Heart of the Lakes, Fisherbeck Mill, Old Lake Road, Ambleside LA22 0DH
T: (015394) 32321
F: (015394) 33251
E: info@heartofthelakes.co.uk
I: www.heartofthelakes.co.uk

Rathmore ★★★
Contact: Mrs Susan Jackson, Heart of the Lakes, Fisherbeck Mill, Old Lake Road, Ambleside LA22 0DH
T: (015394) 32321
F: (015394) 33251
E: info@heartofthelakes.co.uk
I: www.heartofthelakes.co.uk

Stybarrow Cottage ★★★
Contact: Mr Peter Durbin, Cumbrian Cottages, 2 Lonsdale Street, Carlisle CA1 1DB
T: (01228) 599960
F: (01228) 599970
E: enquiries@cumbrian-cottages.co.uk
I: www.cumbrian-cottages.co.uk

Ullswater House Maisonette ★★
Contact: The Manager Dales Hol Cot Ref: 1978, Carleton Business Park, Carleton New Road, Skipton BD23 2AA
T: (01756) 799821
F: (01756) 797012
E: info@dalesholcot.com
I: www.dalesholcot.com

GOSFORTH
Cumbria

Kell Bank Cottage ★★★
Contact: Mr Peter Durbin, Cumbrian Cottages, 2 Lonsdale Street, Carlisle CA1 1DB
T: (01228) 599960
F: (01228) 599970
E: enquiries@cumbrian-cottages.co.uk
I: www.cumbrian-cottages.co.uk

Potters Barn ★★★★
Contact: Mrs Barbara Wright, Potters Barn, Gosforth Pottery, Gosforth, Seascale CA20 1AH
T: (019467) 25296
E: mail@potters-barn.co.uk
I: www.potters-barn.co.uk

GRANGE-OVER-SANDS
Cumbria

The Chalet Studio ★★★
Contact: Mrs Margaret Wilson, Highfield Road, Allithwaite, Grange-over-Sands LA11 7JA
T: (015395) 34695

Cornerways Bungalow ★★★
Contact: Mrs Eunice Rigg, Prospect House, Barber Green, Grange-over-Sands LA11 6HU
T: (015395) 36329

Dyer Dene ★★★
Contact: Mrs S Andrews, 121 Dorchester Road, Garstang, Preston PR3 1FE
T: (01995) 602769
E: dyerdene@fish.co.uk
I: www.dyerdene.com

Hazelwood Court Country House Self-Catering ★★★★
Contact: Mr M Stilling, Hazelwood Court Country House Self-Catering, Lindale Road, Grange-over-Sands LA11 6SP
T: (015395) 34196
F: (01539) 534196
E: markstilling.hazelcourt@virgin.net
I: hazelwoodcourt.co.uk

The Nook ★★★
Contact: Mr John Serginson, Waterside House, Newby Bridge, Ulverston LA12 8AN
T: (015395) 30024
F: (015395) 31932
E: john@lakelandcottageco.com
I: www.lakeland-cottage-company.co.uk

Spring Bank Cottage ★★★★
Contact: Mrs Janet Brocklebank, Spring Bank Farm, Spring Bank Road, Grange-over-Sands, Grange-over-Sands LA11 6HA
T: (015395) 32606

Swimmers Farm ★★★★★
Contact: Mr Peter Durbin, 2 Lonsdale Street, Carlisle CA1 1DB
T: (01228) 599960
F: (01228) 599970
E: enquiries@cumbrian-cottages.co.uk
I: www.cumbrian-cottages.co.uk

Wycombe Holiday Flats ★★★
Contact: Mr W G Benson, Wycombe Holiday Flats, Wycombe, The Esplanade, Grange-over-Sands LA11 7HH
T: (015395) 32297
F: (015395) 32295
E: mail@whf.info
I: www.wycombeholidayflats.co.uk

GRASMERE
Cumbria

Above Beck ★★★
Contact: Mr Paul Liddell, Lakelovers, Belmont House, Lake Road, Bowness-on-Windermere, Windermere LA23 3BJ
T: (015394) 88855
F: (015394) 88857
E: bookings@lakelovers.co.uk

Acorn Cottage ★★★★
Contact: Mr Paul Liddell, Lakelovers, Belmont House, Lake Road, Bowness-on-Windermere, Windermere LA23 3BJ
T: (015394) 88855
F: (015394) 88857
E: bookings@lakelovers.co.uk
I: www.lakelovers.co.uk

April Cottage ★★★★
Contact: Mrs Susan Jackson, Heart of the Lakes, Fisherbeck Mill, Old Lake Road, Ambleside LA22 0DH
E: info@heartofthelakes.co.uk
I: www.heartofthelakes.co.uk

Beck Allans ★★★-★★★★
Contact: Mrs Taylor, Beck Allans, College Street, Grasmere, Ambleside LA22 9SZ
T: (015394) 35563
F: (015394) 35563
E: mail@beckallans.com
I: www.beckallans.com

Becksteps ★★★★
Contact: Becksteps, Grasmere, Ambleside LA22 9SY
T: (015394) 32321
F: (015394) 33251
E: info@leisuretime.co.uk
I: www.leisuretime.co.uk

Beechghyll ★★★★
Contact: Mrs Susan Jackson, Heart of the Lakes, Fisherbeck Mill, Old Lake Road, Ambleside LA22 0DH
T: (015394) 32321
F: (015394) 33251
E: info@heartofthelakes.co.uk
I: www.heartofthelakes.co.uk

Bellfoot ★★★★
Contact: Mrs Susan Jackson, Heart of the Lakes, Fisherbeck Mill, Old Lake Road, Ambleside LA22 0DH
T: (015394) 32321
F: (015394) 33251
E: info@heartofthelakes.co.uk
I: www.heartofthelakes.co.uk

Blind Tarn ★★★
Contact: Mrs Susan Jackson, Heart of the Lakes, Fisherbeck Mill, Old Lake Road, Ambleside LA22 0DH
T: (015394) 32321
F: (015394) 33251
E: info@heartofthelakes.co.uk
I: www.heartofthelakes.co.uk

Bramrigg ★★★★
Contact: Mrs Susan Jackson, Heart of the Lakes, Fisherbeck Mill, Old Lake Road, Ambleside LA22 0DH
T: (015394) 32321
F: (015394) 33251
E: info@heartofthelakes.co.uk
I: www.heartofthelakes.co.uk

Broad Oak ★★★★
Contact: Mrs Susan Jackson, Heart of the Lakes, Fisherbeck Mill, Old Lake Road, Ambleside LA22 0DH
T: (015394) 32321
F: (015394) 33251
E: info@heartofthelakes.co.uk
I: www.heartofthelakes.co.uk

Broadrayne Farm Cottages ★★★-★★★★★
Contact: Mrs Jo Dennison Drake, Broadrayne Farm, Grasmere, Ambleside LA22 9RU
T: (015394) 35055
F: (015394) 35733
E: jo@grasmere-accommodation.co.uk
I: www.grasmere-accommodation.co.uk

Coachmans Cottage ★★★★
Contact: Mrs Susan Jackson, Heart of the Lakes, Fisherbeck Mill, Old Lake Road, Ambleside LA22 0DH
T: (015394) 32321
F: (015394) 33251
E: info@heartofthelakes.co.uk
I: www.heartofthelakes.co.uk

The Cottage ★★
Contact: Mr Peter Durbin, Cumbrian Cottages, 2 Lonsdale Street, Carlisle CA1 1DB
T: (01228) 599960
F: (01228) 599970
E: enquiries@cumbrian-cottages.co.uk
I: www.cumbrian-cottages.co.uk

Crag Cottage ★★★
Contact: Mrs Susan Jackson, Heart of the Lakes, Fisherbeck Mill, Old Lake Road, Ambleside LA22 0DH
T: (015394) 32321
F: (015394) 33251
E: info@heartofthelakes.co.uk
I: www.heartofthelakes.co.uk

3 Dale End ★★★
Contact: Mrs Anne Truelove, 98 Antrobus Road, Sutton Coldfield B73 5EL
T: (0121) 354 7915
E: p.f.truelove@aston.ac.uk
I: my.genie.co.uk/p.f.truelove

Dale Head Cottage ★★★
Contact: Mrs Susan Jackson, Heart of the Lakes, Fisherbeck Mill, Old Lake Road, Ambleside LA22 0DH
T: (015394) 32321
F: (015394) 33251
E: info@heartofthelakes.co.uk
I: www.heartofthelakes.co.uk

Dippers Bank ★★★★
Contact: Mrs Susan Jackson, Heart of the Lakes, Fisherbeck Mill, Old Lake Road, Ambleside LA22 0DH
T: (015394) 32321
F: (015394) 33251
E: info@heartofthelakes.co.uk
I: www.heartofthelakes.co.uk

Dove Holme ★★★★
Contact: Mr Peter Durbin, Cumbrian Cottages, 2 Lonsdale Street, Carlisle CA1 1DB
T: (01228) 599960
F: (01228) 599970
E: enquiries@cumbrian-cottages.co.uk
I: www.cumbrian-cottages.co.uk

Dunnabeck ★★★★
Contact: Mrs Susan Jackson, Heart of the Lakes, Fisherbeck Mill, Old Lake Road, Ambleside LA22 0DH
T: (015394) 32321
F: (015394) 33251
E: info@heartofthelakes.co.uk
I: www.heartofthelakes.co.uk

Easedale ★★★
Contact: Mrs Susan Jackson, Heart of the Lakes, Fisherbeck Mill, Old Lake Road, Ambleside LA22 0DH
T: (015394) 32321
F: (015394) 33251
E: info@heartofthelakes.co.uk
I: www.heartofthelakes.co.uk

Fairfield, Wood Close ★★★★
Contact: Mrs Susan Jackson, Heart of the Lakes, Fisherbeck Mill, Old Lake Road, Ambleside LA22 0DH
T: (015394) 32321
F: (015394) 33251
E: info@heartofthelakes.co.uk
I: www.heartofthelakes.co.uk

Fairfield Cottage ★★★★
Contact: Mrs Susan Jackson, Heart of the Lakes, Fisherbeck Mill, Old Lake Road, Ambleside LA22 0DH
T: (015394) 32321
F: (015394) 33251
E: info@heartofthelakes.co.uk
I: www.heartofthelakes.co.uk

Fellside Cottage ★★★★
Contact: Mrs Susan Jackson, Heart of the Lakes, Fisherbeck Mill, Old Lake Road, Ambleside LA22 0DH
T: (015394) 32321
F: (015394) 33251
E: info@heartofthelakes.co.uk
I: www.heartofthelakes.co.uk

1 Field Foot ★★★
Contact: Mrs Jean Morrison, 11 Park Crescent, Wigan WN1 1RZ
T: (01942) 236350

Glendene ★★★★
Contact: Mrs Susan Jackson, Heart of the Lakes, Fisherbeck Mill, Old Lake Road, Ambleside LA22 0DH
T: (015394) 32321
F: (015394) 33251
E: info@heartofthelakes.co.uk
I: www.heartofthelakes.co.uk

Glenview Cottage ★★★★
Contact: Mrs Susan Jackson, Heart of the Lakes, Fisherbeck Mill, Old Lake Road, Ambleside LA22 0DH
E: info@heartofthelakes.co.uk
I: www.heartofthelakes.co.uk

Goody Bridge Barn ★★★★
Contact: Mrs Susan Jackson, Heart of the Lakes, Fisherbeck Mill, Old Lake Road, Ambleside LA22 0DH
T: (015394) 32321
F: (015394) 33251
E: info@heartofthelakes.co.uk
I: www.heartofthelakes.co.uk

Goody Bridge Cottage ★★★★
Contact: Mrs Susan Jackson, Heart of the Lakes, Fisherbeck Mill, Old Lake Road, Ambleside LA22 0DH
T: (015394) 32321
F: (015394) 33251
E: info@heartofthelakes.co.uk
I: www.heartofthelakes.co.uk

Grasmere Cottages ★★★★
Contact: Mr Martin Wood, Grasmere Cottages, Moss Grove Hotel, Hawkshead, Ambleside LA22 9SW
T: (015394) 35395
F: (015394) 35691
E: martinw@globalnet.co.uk
I: www.grasmerecottage accommodation.co.uk

Grasmere Lodge ★★
Contact: Mr B Watt, Forest Side Hotel, Grasmere, Ambleside LA22 9RN
T: (015394) 35250
F: (015394) 35947
E: hotel@forestsidehotel.com
I: www.forestsidehotel.com

Grasmere View ★★★
Contact: Mr Peter Durbin, Cumbrian Cottages, 2 Lonsdale Street, Carlisle CA1 1DB
T: (01228) 599960
F: (01228) 599970
E: enquiries@cumbrian-cottages.co.uk
I: www.cumbrian-cottages.co.uk

Grey Crag Barn ★★★★★
Contact: Mr Paul Liddell, Lakelovers, Belmont House Lake Road, Bowness-on-Windermere, Windermere LA23 3BJ
T: (015394) 88855
F: (015394) 88857
E: bookings@lakelovers.co.uk
I: www.lakelovers.co.uk

Helm Cottage ★★★★
Contact: Mr Paul Liddell, Lakelovers, Belmont House, Lake Road, Bowness-on-Windermere, Windermere LA23 3BJ
T: (015394) 88855
F: (015394) 88857
E: bookings@lakelovers.co.uk

Helm Crag ★★★
Contact: Mr & Mrs Alan Wardle, Bateman Fold Barn, Crook, Kendal LA8 8LN
T: (015395) 68074
I: www.lakedistrictholidays.net

Heron View Cottage ★★★★
Contact: Mr Peter Durbin, Cumbrian Cottages, 2 Lonsdale Street, Carlisle CA1 1DB
T: (01228) 599960
F: (01228) 599970
E: enquiries@cumbrian-cottages.co.uk
I: www.cumbrian-cottages.co.uk

Heronsyde ★★★★
Contact: Mrs Susan Jackson, Heart of the Lakes, Fisherbeck Mill, Old Lake Road, Ambleside LA22 0DH
T: (015394) 32321
F: (015394) 33251
E: info@heartofthelakes.co.uk
I: www.heartofthelakes.co.uk

Holly Cottage ★★★★
Contact: Mr Peter Durbin, Cumbrian Cottages, 2 Lonsdale Street, Carlisle CA1 1DB
T: (01228) 599960
F: (01228) 599970
E: enquiries@cumbrian-cottages.co.uk
I: www.cumbrian-cottages.co.uk

Huntingstile South ★★★★
Contact: Mrs Susan Jackson, Heart of the Lakes, Fisherbeck Mill, Old Lake Road, Ambleside LA22 0DH
T: (015394) 32321
F: (015394) 33251
E: info@heartofthelakes.co.uk
I: www.heartofthelakes.co.uk

Juniper Cottage ★★★★
Contact: Mrs Susan Jackson, Heart of the Lakes, Fisherbeck Mill, Old Lake Road, Ambleside LA22 0DH
T: (015394) 32321
F: (015394) 33251
E: info@heartofthelakes.co.uk
I: www.heartofthelakes.co.uk

Lake View Holiday Apartments ★★★
Contact: Mr & Mrs Stephen & Michelle King, Lake View Holiday Apartments, Lake View Drive, Grasmere LA22 9TD
T: (015394) 35167
E: michelleking@buryend.freeserve.co.uk
I: www.lakeview-grasmere.com

Le Tholonet ★★★★
Contact: Mrs Susan Jackson, Heart of the Lakes, Fisherbeck Mill, Old Lake Road, Ambleside LA22 0DH
T: (015394) 32321
F: (015394) 33251
E: info@heartofthelakes.co.uk
I: www.heartofthelakes.co.uk

Little Beeches ★★★
Contact: Mrs Susan Jackson, Heart of the Lakes, Fisherbeck Mill, Old Lake Road, Ambleside LA22 0DH
T: (015394) 32321
F: (015394) 33251
E: info@heartofthelakes.co.uk
I: www.heartofthelakes.co.uk

Low Croft, Croft End & Tongue Ghyll ★★★★
Contact: Mrs Ann Dixon, Low Croft, Croft End & Tongue Ghyll, 1 Tongue Ghyll, Grasmere, Ambleside LA22 9QS
T: (015394) 35571
F: 08707 063180
E: ann@grasmere-holidays.co.uk
I: www.grasmere-holidays.co.uk

Mews Cottage ★★★★
Contact: Mrs Susan Jackson, Heart of the Lakes, Fisherbeck Mill, Old Lake Road, Ambleside LA22 0DH
T: (015394) 32321
F: (015394) 33251
E: info@heartofthelakes.co.uk
I: www.heartofthelakes.co.uk

North Lodge ★★★
Contact: Mrs Susan Jackson, Heart of the Lakes, Fisherbeck Mill, Old Lake Road, Ambleside LA22 0DH
T: (015394) 32321
F: (015394) 33251
E: info@heartofthelakes.co.uk
I: www.heartofthelakes.co.uk

Oak Bank Apartment ★★★
Contact: Mr Peter Durbin, Cumbrian Cottages, 2 Lonsdale Street, Carlisle CA1 1DB
T: (01228) 599960
F: (01228) 599970
E: enquiries@cumbrian-cottages.co.uk
I: www.cumbrian-cottages.co.uk

Old Bakers Cottage & Bakers Rest ★★★★
Contact: Mr Peter Durbin, Cumbrian Cottages, 2 Lonsdale Street, Carlisle CA1 1DB
T: (01228) 599960
F: (01228) 599970
E: enquiries@cumbrian-cottages.co.uk
I: www.cumbrian-cottages.co.uk

The Old Police House Rating Applied For
Contact: Mrs Susan Jackson, Heart of the Lakes, Fisherbeck Mill, Old Lake Road, Ambleside LA22 0DH
T: (015394) 32321
F: (015394) 33251
E: info@heartofthelakes.co.uk

Overmere ★★★★
Contact: Mrs Susan Jackson, Heart of the Lakes, Fisherbeck Mill, Old Lake Road, Ambleside LA22 0DH
T: (015394) 32321
F: (015394) 33251
E: info@heartofthelakes.co.uk
I: www.heartofthelakes.co.uk

Poets View Cottage ★★★★
Contact: Mr Peter Durbin, Cumbrian Cottages, 2 Lonsdale Street, Carlisle CA1 1DB
T: (01228) 599960
F: (01228) 599970
E: enquiries@cumbrian-cottages.co.uk
I: www.cumbrian-cottages.co.uk

Ramblers Roost ★★★
Contact: Mr Howard King, The Old West Quay Travel Inn, Maritime Avenue, Hartlepool TS24 0XZ
F: (01964) 590106
E: hk.developments@virgin.net

Rothay Lodge Garden Apartment ★★★★
Contact: Mrs Jean Allan, Rothay Lodge Garden Apartment, White Bridge, Grasmere, Ambleside LA22 9RH
T: (015394) 35341
F: (015394) 39545
E: jean@rothay-lodge.co.uk
I: www.rothay-lodge.co.uk

Rowan Cottage ★★★★
Contact: Mr Peter Durbin, Cumbrian Cottages, 2 Lonsdale Street, Carlisle CA1 1DB
T: (01228) 599960
F: (01228) 599970
E: enquiries@cumbrian-cottages.co.uk
I: www.cumbrian-cottages.co.uk

Silvergarth ★★★
Contact: Mrs Susan Coward, Silvergarth, 1 Low Riddings, Grasmere, Ambleside LA22 9QY
T: (015394) 35828
F: (015394) 35828
E: cowards.silvergarth@btinternet.com
I: www.cowards.silvergarth.btinternet.co.uk

Spinners ★★★★
Contact: Mrs Susan Jackson, Heart of the Lakes, Fisherbeck Mill, Old Lake Road, Ambleside LA22 0DH
T: (015394) 32321
F: (015394) 33251
E: info@heartofthelakes.co.uk
I: www.heartofthelakes.co.uk

Stonebeck ★★★★
Contact: Mrs Susan Jackson, Heart of the Lakes, Fisherbeck Mill, Old Lake Road, Ambleside LA22 0DH
T: (015394) 32321
F: (015394) 33251
E: info@heartofthelakes.co.uk
I: www.leisuretime.co.uk

Swallows Cottage ★★★★
Contact: Mr Paul Liddell, Lakelovers, Belmont House, Lake Road, Bowness-on-Windermere, Windermere LA23 3BJ
T: (015394) 88855
F: (015394) 88857
E: bookings@lakelovers.co.uk
I: www.lakelovers.co.uk

3 Tarn Cottages ★★★
Contact: Mrs Isobel Yates, Brookside, Underbarrow, Kendal LA8 8HH
T: (015395) 68843
E: iayates@btopenworld.com
I: www.tarncottage.co.uk

Thirlmere Cottage ★★★
Contact: Mrs Susan Jackson, Heart of the Lakes, Fisherbeck Mill, Old Lake Road, Ambleside LA22 0DH
T: (015394) 32321
F: (015394) 33251
E: info@heartofthelakes.co.uk
I: www.heartofthelakes.co.uk

Tilly's Cottage ★★★★
Contact: Mr Paul Liddell, Lakelovers, Belmont House, Lake Road, Bowness-on-Windermere, Windermere LA23 3BJ
T: (015394) 88855
F: (015394) 88857
E: bookings@lakelovers.co.uk
I: www.lakelovers.co.uk

2 Townhead Cottages ★★★
Contact: Mr Paul Liddell, Lakelovers, Belmont House, Lake Road, Bowness-on-Windermere, Windermere LA23 3BJ
T: (015394) 88855
F: (015394) 88857
E: bookings@lakelovers.co.uk
I: www.lakelovers.co.uk

Underheron ★★★★
Contact: Mrs Susan Jackson, Heart of the Lakes, Fisherbeck Mill, Old Lake Road, Ambleside LA22 0DH
T: (015394) 32321
F: (015394) 33251
E: info@heartofthelakes.co.uk
I: www.heartofthelakes.co.uk

Weavers ★★★
Contact: Mr Paul Liddell, Lakelovers, Belmont House, Lake Road, Bowness-on-Windermere, Windermere LA23 3BJ
T: (015394) 88855
F: (015394) 88857
E: bookings@lakelovers.co.uk

The West House ★★★
Contact: Mrs Susan Jackson, Heart of the Lakes, Fisherbeck Mill, Old Lake Road, Ambleside LA22 0DH
T: (015394) 32321
F: (015394) 33251
E: info@heartofthelakes.co.uk
I: www.heartofthelakes.co.uk

Willowbank ★★★
Contact: Mrs Susan Jackson, Heart of the Lakes, Fisherbeck Mill, Old Lake Road, Ambleside LA22 0DH
T: (015394) 32321
F: (015394) 33251
E: info@heartofthelakes.co.uk
I: www.heartofthelakes.co.uk

Woodland Crag Cottage ★★★★
Contact: Mrs Susan Jackson, Heart of the Lakes, Fisherbeck Mill, Old Lake Road, Ambleside LA22 0DH
T: (015394) 32321
F: (015394) 33251
E: info@heartofthelakes.co.uk
I: www.heartofthelakes.co.uk

GRAYRIGG
Cumbria

Punchbowl House ★★★
Contact: Mrs D Johnson, Punchbowl House, Grayrigg, Kendal LA8 9BU
T: (01539) 824345
F: (01539) 824345
E: enquiries@punchbowlhouse.co.uk
I: www.punchbowlhouse.co.uk

GREAT ASBY
Cumbria

Town Head Farm Cottages ★★★★
Contact: Ms Debbie Lucas, Town Head Farm Cottages, Town Head Farm, Great Asby, Appleby-in-Westmorland CA16 6EX
T: (017683) 51499
E: info@townheadfarm.co.uk
I: www.townheadfarm.co.uk

Wray Cottage ★★★
Contact: Mrs Pamela Cowey, Wray Cottage, The Hunting House, Great Asby, Appleby-in-Westmorland CA16 6HD
T: (017683) 52485

GREAT BROUGHTON
Cumbria

Fern Cottage ★★★★
Contact: Mr M Winks, 179 Eccleshall Road, Stafford ST16 1PD
T: (01785) 661365

GREAT LANGDALE
Cumbria

Elterwater Hall ★★★★★
Contact: Mrs Paula Leyland, The Langdale Estate, Great Langdale, Ambleside LA22 9JD
T: (015394) 37302
F: (015394) 37394
E: itsgreat@langdale.co.uk
I: www.langdale.co.uk

Harry Place Farm Cottage ★★★★
Contact: Mrs Susan Jackson, Heart of the Lakes, Fisherbeck Mill, Old Lake Road, Ambleside LA22 0DH
T: (015394) 32321
F: (015394) 33251
E: info@heartofthelakes.co.uk
I: www.heartofthelakes.co.uk

Langdale Estate Chapel Stile Apartments★★★★
Contact: Mrs Paula Leyland, The Langdale Estate, Great Langdale, Ambleside LA22 9JD
T: (015394) 37302
F: (015394) 37394
E: itsgreat@langdale.co.uk
I: www.langdale.co.uk

Langdale Estate Lodges ★★★★★
Contact: Mrs Paula Leyland, The Langdale Estate, Great Langdale, Ambleside LA22 9JD
T: (015394) 37302
F: (015394) 37394
E: itsgreat@langdale.co.uk
I: www.langdale.co.uk

Middlefell Farm Cottage ★★★
Contact: Mrs Susan Jackson, Heart of the Lakes, Fisherbeck Mill, Old Lake Road, Ambleside LA22 0DH
T: (015394) 32321
F: (015394) 33251
E: info@heartofthelakes.co.uk
I: www.heartofthelakes.co.uk

Rawfell ★★★★
Contact: Mrs Susan Jackson, Heart of the Lakes, Fisherbeck Mill, Old Lake Road, Ambleside LA22 0DH
T: (015394) 32321
F: (015394) 33251
E: info@heartofthelakes.co.uk
I: www.heartofthelakes.co.uk

GREAT MUSGRAVE
Cumbria

Blandswath Cottage ★★★
Contact: The Manager Dales Hol Cot Ref:1914, Carleton Business Park, Carleton New Road, Skipton BD23 2AA
T: (01756) 799821
F: (01756) 797012
E: info@dalesholcot.com
I: www.dalesholcot.com

GREYSOUTHEN
Cumbria

Swallow Barn Cottage ★★★★
Contact: Mr & Mrs Roger James, 6 Evening Hill View, Brigham Road, Thornthwaite, Keswick CA13 0BB
T: (01900) 823016
F: (01900) 821446
E: enquiry@swallowbarn.co.uk
I: www.swallowbarn.co.uk

GREYSTOKE
Cumbria

Duck Down Cottage ★★★★
Contact: Mr Kevin Duckenfield, 10 Leconfield Garth, Follifoot, Harrogate HG3 1NF
T: (01423) 870490
F: (01423) 816216
E: sales@duckdowncottage.co.uk
I: www.duckdowncottage.co.uk

Thanetwell Lodge ★★★★
Contact: Ms Judith Robson, The Office, Mardale Road, Penrith CA11 9EH
T: (01768) 868555
F: (01768) 868777
I: www.thanetwell-lodge.co.uk

Whakatane ★★★★
Contact: The Manager Dales Hol Cot Ref:2955, Carleton Business Park, Carleton New Road, Skipton BD23 2AA
T: (01756) 799821
F: (01756) 797012
E: info@dalesholcot.com
I: www.dalesholcot.com

GRIZEBECK
Cumbria

The Cart House ★★★★
Contact: Mr John Serginson, Waterside House, Newby Bridge, Ulverston LA12 8AN
T: (015395) 30024
F: (015395) 31932
E: john@lakelandcottageco.com
I: www.lakeland-cottage-company.co.uk

GRIZEDALE
Cumbria

High Dale Park Barn ★★★
Contact: Mr P Brown, High Dale Park Farm, High Dale Park, Satterthwaite, Ulverston LA12 8LJ
T: (01229) 860226
E: peter@lakesweddingmusic.com
I: www.lakesweddingmusic.com/Accomm

HARTLEY
Cumbria

The Barn ★★★
Contact: The Manager Dales Hol Cot Ref:2852, Carleton Business Park, Carleton New Road, Skipton BD23 2AA
T: (01756) 799821
F: (01756) 797012
E: info@dalesholcot.com
I: www.dalesholcot.com

Hartley Castle Barn ★★★★
Contact: Mrs Sally Dixon, Hartley Castle Barn, Hartley, Nateby, Kirkby Stephen CA17 4JJ
T: (017683) 71331
E: djs@hartleycastle.freeserve.co.uk

HARTSOP
Cumbria

Caudale Beck ★★★
Contact: Mrs Susan Jackson, Heart of the Lakes, Fisherbeck Mill, Old Lake Road, Ambleside LA22 0DH
T: (015394) 32321
F: (015394) 33251
E: info@heartofthelakes.co.uk
I: www.heartofthelakes.co.uk

Dovedale ★★
Contact: Mrs Susan Jackson, Heart of the Lakes, Fisherbeck Mill, Old Lake Road, Ambleside LA22 0DH
T: (015394) 32321
F: (015394) 33251
E: info@heartofthelakes.co.uk
I: www.heartofthelakes.co.uk

Greenbank ★★★★
Contact: Mrs Susan Jackson, Heart of the Lakes, Fisherbeck Mill, Old Lake Road, Ambleside LA22 0DH
T: (015394) 32321
F: (015394) 33251
E: info@heartofthelakes.co.uk
I: www.heartofthelakes.co.uk

High Beckside ★★★
Contact: Mrs Susan Jackson, Heart of the Lakes, Fisherbeck Mill, Old Lake Road, Ambleside LA22 0DH
T: (015394) 32321
F: (015394) 33251
E: info@heartofthelakes.co.uk
I: www.leisuretime.co.uk

Weavers Cottage ★★★
Contact: Mrs Susan Jackson, Heart of the Lakes, Fisherbeck Mill, Old Lake Road, Ambleside LA22 0DH
E: info@heartofthelakes.co.uk
I: www.heartofthelakes.co.uk

HAVERIGG
Cumbria

Haverings ★★★
Contact: Country Hols Ref:4902, Holiday Cottages Group Owner Services Dept, Spring Mill, Earby, Barnoldswick BB94 0AA
T: 08700 723723
F: (01282) 844288
E: sales@holidaycottagesgroup.com
I: www.country-holidays.co.uk

Lazey Cottage ★★★★★
Contact: Mrs Gloria Parsons and Mrs P Jenkinson, Orchard House, The Hill, Millom LA18 5HE
T: (01229) 772515

The Quiet Cottage ★★★
Contact: Mr Haston, 2 Poolside, Haverigg, Millom LA18 4HW
T: (01229) 772974
E: quietcottage@tiscali.co.uk
I: quietcottage.golakes.co.uk

HAVERTHWAITE
Cumbria

Close Cottage ★★★★
Contact: Mr John Serginson, Waterside House, Newby Bridge, Ulverston LA12 8AN
T: (015395) 30024
F: (015395) 31932
E: john@lakelandcottageco.com
I: www.lakeland-cottage-company.co.uk

Woodcroft House ★★★★
Contact: Mr John Serginson, Waterside House, Newby Bridge, Ulverston LA12 8AN
T: (015395) 30024
F: (015395) 31932
E: john@lakelandcottageco.com
I: www.lakeland-cottage-company.co.uk

HAWKSHEAD
Cumbria

Barn Syke ★★★★
Contact: Mr Paul Liddell, Lakelovers, Belmont House, Lake Road, Bowness-on-Windermere, Windermere LA23 3BJ
T: (015394) 88855
F: (015394) 88857
E: bookings@lakelovers.co.uk
I: www.lakelovers.co.uk

Ben Fold ★★★★
Contact: Mrs Susan Jackson, Heart of the Lakes, Fisherbeck Mill, Old Lake Road, Ambleside LA22 0DH
E: info@heartofthelakes.co.uk
I: www.heartofthelakes.co.uk

Birkwray Farmhouse ★★★★
Contact: Mr Paul Liddell, Lakelovers, Belmont House, Lake Road, Bowness-on-Windermere, Windermere LA23 3BJ
T: (015394) 88855
F: (015394) 88857
E: bookings@lakelovers.co.uk
I: www.lakelovers.co.uk

Bridge View ★★★
Contact: Mrs S Dewhurst, Bridge View, 2 Bridge View, Hawkshead, Ambleside LA22 0PL
T: (015394) 36340

Broomriggs ★★★-★★★★
Contact: Mrs F Taylforth, Broomriggs, Hawkshead, Ambleside LA22 0JX
T: (015394) 36280
E: broomriggs@zoom.co.uk
I: www.broomriggs.co.uk/location.htm

Cherry Tree Lodge & Apple Tree Lodge
Rating Applied For
Contact: Mr Paul Liddell, Lakelover, Belmont House, Lake Road, Bowness-on-Windermere, Windermere LA23 3BJ
T: (015394) 88855
F: (015394) 88857
E: bookings@lakelovers.co.uk

Coachman's Loft ★★★★
Contact: Mrs Susan Jackson, Heart of the Lakes, Fisherbeck Mill, Old Lake Road, Ambleside LA22 0DH
E: info@heartofthelakes.co.uk
I: www.heartofthelakes.co.uk

Columbine Cottage ★★★
Contact: Mr Paul Liddell, Lakelovers, Belmont House, Lake Road, Bowness-on-Windermere, Windermere LA23 3BJ
T: (015394) 88855
F: (015394) 88857
E: bookings@lakelovers.co.uk
I: www.lakelovers.co.uk

The Croft Holiday Flats ★★★
Contact: Mrs R E Barr, The Croft Holiday Flats, North Lonsdale Road, Hawkshead, Ambleside LA22 0NX
T: (015394) 36374
F: (015394) 36544
E: enquiries@hawkshead-croft.com
I: www.hawkshead-croft.com

Fair Cop ★★★★
Contact: Mrs Susan Jackson, Heart of the Lakes, Fisherbeck Mill, Old Lake Road, Ambleside LA22 0DH
T: (015394) 32321
F: (015394) 33251
E: info@heartofthelakes.co.uk
I: www.heartofthelakes.co.uk

Gilpin Cottage ★★★
Contact: Mrs Susan Jackson, Heart of the Lakes, Fisherbeck Mill, Old Lake Road, Ambleside LA22 0DH
T: (015394) 32321
F: (015394) 33251
E: info@heartofthelakes.co.uk
I: www.heartofthelakes.co.uk

Goosifoot ★★★
Contact: Mrs Susan Jackson, Heart of the Lakes, Fisherbeck Mill, Old Lake Road, Ambleside LA22 0DH
T: (015394) 32321
F: (015394) 33251
E: info@heartofthelakes.co.uk
I: www.heartofthelakes.co.uk

Greenbank House ★★★
Contact: Mrs Susan Jackson, Heart of the Lakes, Fisherbeck Mill, Old Lake Road, Ambleside LA22 0DH
T: (015394) 32321
F: (015394) 33251
E: info@heartofthelakes.co.uk
I: www.heartofthelakes.co.uk

Hatters Cottage ★★★
Contact: Mr & Mrs Gunner, Hawkshead Hill Farm, Hawkshead Hill, Ambleside LA22 0PW
T: (015394) 36203
E: mail9@hatterscottage.freeserve.co.uk
I: www.hatters-cottage.freeserve.co.uk

Heron Cottage ★★★
Contact: Mr Paul Liddell, Lakelovers, Belmont House, Lake Road, Bowness-on-Windermere, Windermere LA23 3BJ
T: (015394) 88855
F: (015394) 88857
E: bookings@lakelovers.co.uk
I: www.lakelovers.co.uk

High Orchard ★★★★
Contact: Mrs Susan Jackson, Heart of the Lakes, Fisherbeck Mill, Old Lake Road, Ambleside LA22 0DH
E: info@heartofthelakes.co.uk
I: www.heartofthelakes.co.uk

Hillcrest ★★★★★
Contact: Mrs Susan Jackson, Heart of the Lakes, Fisherbeck Mill, Old Lake Road, Ambleside LA22 0DH
T: (015394) 32321
F: (015394) 33251
E: info@heartofthelakes.co.uk
I: www.heartofthelakes.co.uk

Keen Ground Cottage ★★★
Contact: Mr John Serginson, The Lakeland Cottage Company, Waterside House, Newby Bridge, Ulverston LA12 8AN
T: (015395) 30024
F: (015395) 31932
E: john@lakelandcottageco.com
I: www.lakeland-cottage-company.co.uk

Kings Yard Cottage ★★★
Contact: Mr Peter Durbin, Cumbrian Cottages, 2 Lonsdale Street, Carlisle CA1 1DB
T: (01228) 599960
F: (01228) 599970
E: enquiries@cumbrian-cottages.co.uk
I: www.cumbrian-cottages.co.uk

Lantern Cottage ★★★
Contact: Mr Peter Durbin, Cumbrian Cottages, 2 Lonsdale Street, Carlisle CA1 1DB
T: (01228) 599960
F: (01228) 599970
E: enquiries@cumbrian-cottages.co.uk
I: www.cumbrian-cottages.co.uk

Larch Cottage ★★★
Contact: Mrs Susan Jackson, Heart of the Lakes, Fisherbeck Mill, Old Lake Road, Ambleside LA22 0DH
T: (015394) 32321
F: (015394) 33251
E: info@heartofthelakes.co.uk
I: www.heartofthelakes.co.uk

Meadow View ★★
Contact: Blakes Cottages, Spring Mill, Earby, Barnoldswick BB94 0AA
T: 08700 708090
F: 08705 851150
I: www.blakes.cottages.co.uk

Oak Apple Barn ★★★★
Contact: Mrs Nancy Penrice, Oak Apple Cottage, Violet Bank, Hawkshead, Outgate, Ambleside LA22 0PL
T: (015394) 36222
E: Nancy@vboa.fsnet.co.uk
I: www.oak-apple.co.uk

The Old Barn & Barn End Cottage ★★★★
Contact: Mrs Anne Gallagher, Hideaways, The Minstrels Gallery, The Square, Hawkshead, Ambleside LA22 0NZ
T: (015394) 42435
F: (015394) 36178
E: bookings@lakeland-hideaways.co.uk
I: www.lakeland-hideaways.co.uk

Old Farm ★★★★
Contact: Mr John Serginson, The Lakeland Cottage Company, Waterside House, Newby Bridge, Ulverston LA12 8AN
T: (015395) 30024
F: (015395) 31932
E: john@lakelandcottageco.com
I: www.lakeland-cottage-company.co.uk

Rigges Wood Cottage ★★★★
Contact: Mr Paul Liddell, Lakelovers, Belmont House, Lake Road, Bowness-on-Windermere, Windermere LA23 3BJ
T: (015394) 88855
F: (015394) 88857
E: bookings@lakelovers.co.uk
I: www.lakelovers.co.uk

The Rockery Suite ★★★★
Contact: Mrs Susan Jackson, Heart of the Lakes, Fisherbeck Mill, Old Lake Road, Ambleside LA22 0DH
T: (015394) 32321
F: (015394) 33251
E: info@heartofthelakes.co.uk
I: www.heartofthelakes.co.uk

Rose Cottage ★★★★★
Contact: Mrs Shirley Whiteside, Sawrey House Country Hotel & Restaurant, Near Sawrey, Sawrey, Ambleside LA22 0LF
T: (015394) 36956
F: (015394) 36010
E: email@sawrey-house.com
I: www.hawksheadcottages.co.uk

Rose Howe ★★★★
Contact: Mrs Susan Jackson, Heart of the Lakes, Fisherbeck Mill, Old Lake Road, Ambleside LA22 0DH
T: (015394) 32321
F: (015394) 33251
E: info@heartofthelakes.co.uk
I: www.heartofthelakes.co.uk

Sand Ground Barn ★★★
Contact: Mrs Susan Jackson, Heart of the Lakes, Fisherbeck Mill, Old Lake Road, Ambleside LA22 0DH
T: (015394) 32321
F: (015394) 33251
E: info@heartofthelakes.co.uk

Sandy Wyke ★★★
Contact: Mrs Susan Jackson, Heart of the Lakes, Fisherbeck Mill, Old Lake Road, Ambleside LA22 0DH
T: (015394) 32321
F: (015394) 33251
E: info@heartofthelakes.co.uk
I: www.heartofthelakes.co.uk

Sergeant Man ★★★★
Contact: Mrs Susan Jackson, Heart of the Lakes, Fisherbeck Mill, Old Lake Road, Ambleside LA22 0DH
T: (015394) 32321
F: (015394) 33251
E: info@heartofthelakes.co.uk
I: www.heartofthelakes.co.uk

Shepherd's Cottage ★★★★
Contact: Hideaways, The Minstrels Gallery, The Square, Hawkshead, Ambleside LA22 0NZ
T: (015394) 42435
F: (015394) 36178
E: bookings@lakeland-holidays.co.uk
I: www.lakeland-hideaways.co.uk

Swallow's Nest ★★★★
Contact: Mrs Susan Jackson, Heart of the Lakes, Fisherbeck Mill, Old Lake Road, Ambleside LA22 0DH
T: (015394) 32321
F: (015394) 33251
E: info@heartofthelakes.co.uk
I: www.heartofthelakes.co.uk

Swallows Nest Cottage ★★★
Contact: Mr Philip Johnston, The Coppermines Coniston Cottages, The Estate Office, The Bridge, Coniston LA21 8HJ
T: (015394) 41765
F: (015394) 41944
E: info@coppermines.co.uk
I: www.coppermines.co.uk

Syke Cottage ★★★★
Contact: Mrs Susan Jackson, Heart of the Lakes, Fisherbeck Mill, Old Lake Road, Ambleside LA22 0DH
T: (015394) 32321
F: (015394) 33251
E: info@heartofthelakes.co.uk
I: www.heartofthelakes.co.uk

Tarn Hows ★★★★
Contact: Mrs Susan Jackson, Heart of the Lakes, Fisherbeck Mill, Old Lake Road, Ambleside LA22 0DH
T: (015394) 32321
F: (015394) 33251
E: info@heartofthelakes.co.uk
I: www.heartofthelakes.co.uk

Walker Ground Barn ★★★★
Contact: Mrs Susan Jackson, Heart of the Lakes, Fisherbeck Mill, Old Lake Road, Ambleside LA22 0DH
T: (015394) 32321
F: (015394) 33251
E: info@heartofthelakes.co.uk
I: www.heartofthelakes.co.uk

Woodlands, Roger Ground ★★★★
Contact: Mrs Susan Jackson, Heart of the Lakes, Fisherbeck Mill, Old Lake Road, Ambleside LA22 0DH
T: (015394) 32321
F: (015394) 33251
E: info@heartofthelakes.co.uk
I: www.heartofthelakes.co.uk

Yew Trees ★★★
Contact: Mrs Susan Jackson, Heart of the Lakes, Fisherbeck Mill, Old Lake Road, Ambleside LA22 0DH
T: (015394) 32321
F: (015394) 33251
E: info@heartofthelakes.co.uk
I: www.heartofthelakes.co.uk

HAWKSHEAD HILL
Cumbria

Summerhill Country House ★★★
Contact: Mr Philip Johnston, The Coppermines Coniston Cottages, The Estate Office, The Bridge, Coniston LA21 8HJ
T: (015394) 41765
F: (015394) 41944
E: info@coppermines.co.uk
I: www.coppermines.co.uk

HELTON
Cumbria

Talbot Studio ★★★★
Contact: Mr Martin Cowell, Church Villa, Gamblesby, Penrith CA10 1HR
T: (01768) 881682
F: (01768) 889055
E: markcowell@amserve.com
I: www.gogamblesby.co.uk

HESKET NEWMARKET
Cumbria

Beech Cottage ★★★
Contact: Mr Peter Durbin, Cumbrian Cottages, 2 Lonsdale Street, Carlisle CA1 1DB
T: (01228) 599960
F: (01228) 599970
E: enquiries@cumbrian-cottages.co.uk
I: www.cumbrian-cottages.co.uk

Syke House ★★★
Contact: Sykes Cottages Ref: 692, Sykes Cottages, York House, York Street, Chester CH1 3LR
T: (01244) 345700
F: (01244) 321442
E: info@sykescottages.co.uk
I: www.sykescottages.co.uk

HETHERSGILL
Cumbria

Newlands ★★★★
Contact: Mr Peter Durbin, Cumbrian Cottages, 2 Lonsdale Street, Carlisle CA1 1DB
T: (01228) 599960
F: (01228) 599970
E: enquiries@cumbrian-cottages.co.uk
I: www.cumbrian-cottages.co.uk

HIGH LORTON
Cumbria

Brewery House ★★★★★
Contact: Mr Peter Durbin, Cumbrian Cottages, 2 Lonsdale Street, Carlisle CA1 1DB
T: (01228) 599960
F: (01228) 599970
E: enquiries@cumbrian-cottages.co.uk
I: www.cumbrian-cottages.co.uk

Dale House
Rating Applied For
Contact: Mr Peter Durbin, Cumbrian Cottages, 2 Lonsdale Street, Carlisle CA1 1DB
T: (01228) 599960
F: (01228) 599970
E: enquiries@cumbrian-cottages.co.uk
I: www.cumbrian-cottages.co.uk

Holemire House Barn ★★★★
Contact: Mrs A Fearfield, Holemire House Barn, Holemire House, High Lorton, Cockermouth CA13 9TX
T: (01900) 85225
I: www.lakelandbarn.co.uk

Midtown Cottages ★★★★
Contact: Mr M Burrell, 20 Hillside, Abbotts Ann, Andover SP11 7DF
T: (01264) 710165
E: info@midtown-cottages.co.uk
I: www.midtowncottages.com

Wayside Cottage ★★★
Contact: The Manager Dales Hol Cot Ref:2376, Carleton Business Park, Carleton New Road, Skipton BD23 2AA
T: (01756) 799821
F: (01756) 797012
E: info@dalesholcot.com
I: www.dalesholcot.com

HOLMROOK
Cumbria

Randle How
Rating Applied For
Contact: Mrs Susan Wedley, Long Yocking How, Eskdale, Holmrook CA19 1UA
T: (01946) 723126
F: (01946) 723490
E: js.wedley@btopenworld.com

Yattus ★★★★★
Contact: Mr Peter Durbin, Cumbrian Cottages, 2 Lonsdale Street, Carlisle CA1 1DB
T: (01228) 599960
F: (01228) 599970
E: enquiries@cumbrian-cottages.co.uk
I: www.cumbrian-cottages.co.uk

HOWGILL
Cumbria

Blandsgill Cottage ★★★
Contact: Mr Peter Durbin, Cumbrian Cottages, 2 Lonsdale Street, Carlisle CA1 1DB
T: (01228) 599960
F: (01228) 599970
E: enquiries@cumbrian-cottages.co.uk
I: www.cumbrian-cottages.co.uk

HUTTON ROOF
Cumbria

Barn Cottage ★★★
Contact: Dr Joyce Newton, Hegglehead, Hutton Roof, Mungrisdale, Penrith CA11 0XS
T: (017684) 84566
F: (017684) 84460
E: hegglehead@aol.com
I: www.hegglehead.co.uk

Carrock Cottages ★★★★
Contact: Mr & Mrs Malcolm & Gillian Iredale, Carrock Cottages, Carrock House, Howhill, Hutton Roof, Penrith CA11 0XY
T: (017684) 84111
F: (017684) 88850
I: www.carrockcottages.co.uk

INGS
Cumbria

Topiary Cottage ★★★★
Contact: Mr Paul Liddell, Lakelovers, Belmont House, Lake Road, Bowness-on-Windermere, Windermere LA23 3BJ
T: (015394) 88855
F: (015394) 88857
E: bookings@lakelovers.co.uk
I: www.lakelovers.co.uk

IREBY
Cumbria

Daleside Farm ★★★★
Contact: Mrs Isabel Teasdale, Daleside Farm, Allonby, Maryport CA5 1EW
T: (016973) 71268
E: info@dalesidefarm.co.uk
I: www.dalesidefarm.co.uk

Fell Cottage ★★★★★
Contact: Mr Peter Durbin, 2 Lonsdale Street, Carlisle CA1 1DB
T: (01228) 599960
F: (01228) 599970
E: enquiries@cumbrian-cottages.co.uk
I: www.cumbrian-cottages.co.uk

KENDAL
Cumbria

Dora's Cottage ★★★
Contact: Mrs Val Sunter, Oxenholme Lane, Natland, Kendal LA9 7QH
T: (015395) 61177
F: (015395) 61520

Field End Barns & Shaw End Mansion ★★★-★★★★
Contact: Mr & Mrs E D Robinson, Field End Barns and Shaw End Mansion, Patton, Kendal LA8 9DU
T: (01539) 824220
F: (01539) 824464
E: robinson@fieldendholidays.co.uk
I: www.fieldendholidays.co.uk

Great Gable ★★★★★
Contact: Mr Peter Durbin, Cumbrian Cottages, 2 Lonsdale Street, Carlisle CA1 1DB
T: (01228) 599960
F: (01228) 599970
E: enquiries@cumbrian-cottages.co.uk
I: www.cumbrian-cottages.co.uk

High Swinklebank Farm ★★★
Contact: Mrs Olive Simpson, High Swinklebank Farm, Longsleddale, Kendal LA8 9BD
T: (01539) 823682

Hylands ★★★★
Contact: Mr S Lambeth, 5 Stable Close, Finmere, Buckingham MK18 4AD
T: (01280) 848779
F: (01280) 847519
E: simonlambeth@aol.com
I: www.hylands-lakedistrict.co.uk

Middle Swinklebank ★★★
Contact: Mrs Helen Todd, Saddler Croft, Longsleddale, Kendal LA8 9BD
T: (01539) 823275

Moresdale Bank Cottage ★★★★
Contact: Mrs Helen Parkins, Moresdale Bank Cottage, Lambrigg, Kendal LA8 0DH
T: (01539) 824227
E: mclamb@ukonline.co.uk
I: www.diva-web.co.uk/moresdale

The Old Vicarage ★★★★
Contact: Mr Peter Durbin, Cumbrian Cottages, 2 Lonsdale Street, Carlisle CA1 1DB
T: (01228) 599960
F: (01228) 599970
E: enquiries@cumbrian-cottages.co.uk
I: www.cumbrian-cottages.co.uk

Todd Meadow ★★★
Contact: Mr D Hogarth, Cumbrian Cottages, 7 The Crescent, Carlisle CA1 1QW
T: (01228) 599960
F: (01228) 599970
E: enquiries@cumbrian-cottages.co.uk
I: www.cumbrian-cottages.co.uk

KENTMERE
Cumbria

Fell View ★★★
Contact: The Manager Dales Hol Cot Ref:2035, Carleton Business Park, Carleton New Road, Skipton BD23 2AA
T: (01756) 799821
F: (01756) 797012
E: info@dalesholcot.com
I: www.dalesholcot.com

High Fold ★★★★
Contact: Mr Peter Durbin, Cumbrian Cottages, 2 Lonsdale Street, Carlisle CA1 1DB
T: (01228) 599960
F: (01228) 599970
E: enquiries@cumbrian-cottages.co.uk
I: www.cumbrian-cottages.co.uk

Nook Cottage - Kentmere Valley ★★★
Contact: Mr John Serginson, Waterside House, Newby Bridge, Ulverston LA12 8AN
T: (015395) 30024
F: (015395) 31932
E: john@lakelandcottageco.com
I: www.lakeland-cottage-company.co.uk

Rawe Cottage ★★★★
Contact: Mr John Serginson, Waterside House, Newby Bridge, Ulverston LA12 8AN
T: (015395) 30024
F: (015395) 31932
E: john@lakelandcottageco.com
I: www.lakelandcottageco.com

KESWICK
Cumbria

Acorn Apartments & Acorn View ★★★★-★★★★★
Contact: Mr J Miller, South Barn, Fort Putnam, Greystoke, Penrith CA11 0UP
T: (017684) 80310
E: info@acornselfcatering.co.uk
I: www.acornselfcatering.co.uk

Alice's Nook ★★★★
Contact: Mr Peter Durbin, Cumbrian Cottages, 2 Lonsdale Street, Carlisle CA1 1DB
T: (01228) 599960
F: (01228) 599970
E: enquiries@cumbrian-cottages.co.uk
I: www.cumbrian-cottages.co.uk

Alison's Cottage and Alison's View and Laal Yan ★★★-★★★★★
Contact: Mrs Alison Milner, 9 Fearon Close, Gunthorpe, Nottingham NG14 7FA
T: (0115) 966 4049
E: MILNER@fearon9.fsnet.co.uk
I: www.alisonscottages.co.uk

Amba ★★★★
Contact: Mr Peter Durbin, Cumbrian Cottages, 2 Lonsdale Street, Carlisle CA1 1DB
T: (01228) 599960
F: (01228) 599970
E: enquiries@cumbrian-cottages.co.uk
I: www.cumbrian-cottages.co.uk

Applemere ★★★★
Contact: Mr Peter Durbin, Cumbrian Cottages, 2 Lonsdale Street, Carlisle CA1 1DB
T: (01228) 599960
F: (01228) 599970
E: enquiries@cumbrian-cottages.co.uk
I: www.cumbrian-cottages.co.uk

Appletree ★★★★
Contact: Mr Peter Durbin, Cumbrian Cottages, 2 Lonsdale Street, Carlisle CA1 1DB
T: (01228) 599960
F: (01228) 599970
E: enquiries@cumbrian-cottages.co.uk
I: www.cumbrian-cottages.co.uk

Armathwaite Hall ★★★★-★★★★★
Contact: Ms Laura Sharpe, Armathwaite Hall, Bassenthwaite, Keswick CA12 4RE
T: (017687) 76551
F: (017687) 76220
E: reservations@armathwaite-hall.com
I: www.armathwaite-hall.com

Ashbrooke ★★★★
Contact: Mr Peter Durbin, Cumbrian Cottages, 2 Lonsdale Street, Carlisle CA1 1DB
T: (01228) 599960
F: (01228) 599970
E: enquiries@cumbrian-cottages.co.uk
I: www.cumbrian-cottages.co.uk

Ashness ★★★★
Contact: Mr Peter Durbin, Cumbrian Cottages, 2 Lonsdale Street, Carlisle CA1 1DB
T: (01228) 599960
F: (01228) 599970
E: enquiries@cumbrian-cottages.co.uk
I: www.cumbrian-cottages.co.uk

Aysgarth ★★★
Contact: Mr Peter Durbin, Cumbrian Cottages, 2 Lonsdale Street, Carlisle CA1 1DB
T: (01228) 599960
F: (01228) 599970
E: enquiries@cumbrian-cottages.co.uk
I: www.cumbrian-cottages.co.uk

3 Balmoral House ★★★
Contact: Mr Peter Durbin, Cumbrian Cottages, 2 Lonsdale Street, Carlisle CA1 1DB
T: (01228) 599960
F: (01228) 599970
E: enquiries@cumbrian-cottages.co.uk
I: www.cumbrian-cottages.co.uk

6 Balmoral House (Mountain View) ★★★
Contact: Mr Peter Durbin, Cumbrian Cottages, 2 Lonsdale Street, Carlisle CA1 1DB
T: (01228) 599960
F: (01228) 599970
E: enquiries@cumbrian-cottages.co.uk
I: www.cumbrian-cottages.co.uk

Bannerdale ★★★★
Contact: Ms Hazel Hutton, Bannerdale, 39 Millfield Gardens, Keswick CA12 4PD
T: 07816 824253
F: (017687) 72546
E: hazel@bannerdale.info
I: www.bannerdale.info

3 Beech ★★★
Contact: Mrs S Johnstone, 6 Nethertown Close, Whalley, Clitheroe BB7 9SF
T: (01254) 822733

Beech Nut ★★★
Contact: Mr Peter Durbin, Cumbrian Cottages, 2 Lonsdale Street, Carlisle CA1 1DB
T: (01228) 599960
F: (01228) 599970
E: enquiries@cumbrian-cottages.co.uk
I: www.cumbrian-cottages.co.uk

Belle Vue ★★★-★★★★
Contact: Mrs L G Ryder, Hillside, Portinscale, Keswick CA12 5RS
T: (017687) 71065
E: lexieryder@hotmail.com

Bleach Green Cottages ★★★
Contact: Mr Peter Durbin, Cumbrian Cottages, 2 Lonsdale Street, Carlisle CA1 1DB
T: (01228) 599960
F: (01228) 599970
E: enquiries@cumbrian-cottages.co.uk
I: www.cumbrian-cottages.co.uk

The Blencathra ★★★
Contact: Mr Peter Durbin, Cumbrian Cottages, 2 Lonsdale Street, Carlisle CA1 1DB
T: (01228) 599960
F: (01228) 599970
E: enquiries@cumbrian-cottages.co.uk
I: www.cumbrian-cottages.co.uk

Blencathra House ★★★★
Contact: Mr Peter Durbin, Cumbrian Cottages, 2 Lonsdale Street, Carlisle CA1 1DB
T: (01228) 599960
F: (01228) 599970
E: enquiries@cumbrian-cottages.co.uk
I: www.cumbrian-cottages.co.uk

Bobbin Cottage ★★★★
Contact: Mr D Hogarth, Cumbrian Cottages, 7 The Crescent, Carlisle CA1 1QW
T: (01228) 599960
F: (01228) 599970
E: enquiries@cumbrian-cottages.co.uk
I: www.cumbrian-cottages.co.uk

Bracken Lodge ★★★★
Contact: Mr Peter Durbin, Cumbrian Cottages, 2 Lonsdale Street, Carlisle CA1 1DB
T: (01228) 599960
F: (01228) 599970
E: enquiries@cumbrian-cottages.co.uk
I: www.cumbrian-cottages.co.uk

Brandelhow ★★★★
Contact: Mrs Susan Jackson, Heart of the Lakes, Fisherbeck Mill, Old Lake Road, Ambleside LA22 0DH
T: (015394) 32321
F: (015394) 33251
E: info@heartofthelakes.co.uk
I: www.heartofthelakes.co.uk

Brigham Farm ★★★★
Contact: Mr Norman Green, Fornside House, St Johns-in-the-Vale, Keswick CA12 4TS
T: (017687) 79666
E: selfcatering@keswickholidays.co.uk
I: www.keswickholidays.co.uk

Brundholme Keswick ★★★★
Contact: Mr Peter Durbin, Cumbrian Cottages, 2 Lonsdale Street, Carlisle CA1 1DB
T: (01228) 599960
F: (01228) 599970
E: enquiries@cumbrian-cottages.co.uk
I: www.cumbrian-cottages.co.uk

Bunbury Cottage ★★★★
Contact: Mr Peter Durbin, Cumbrian Cottages, 2 Lonsdale Street, Carlisle CA1 1DB
T: (01228) 599960
F: (01228) 599970
E: enquiries@cumbria-cottages.co.uk
I: www.cumbria-cottages.co.uk

11 Burnside Park ★★★★
Contact: Mr Peter Durbin, Cumbrian Cottages, 2 Lonsdale Street, Carlisle CA1 1DB
T: (01228) 599960
F: (01228) 599970
E: enquiries@cumbrian-cottages.co.uk
I: www.cumbrian-cottages.co.uk

Cairnway ★★★★
Contact: Mr Peter Durbin, Cumbrian Cottages, 2 Lonsdale Street, Carlisle CA1 1DB
T: (01228) 599960
F: (01228) 599970
E: enquiries@cumbrian-cottages.co.uk
I: www.cumbrian-cottages.co.uk

Carlton Cottage ★★★★
Contact: Mr Peter Durbin, Cumbrian Cottages, 2 Lonsdale Street, Carlisle CA1 1DB
T: (01228) 599960
F: (01228) 599970
E: enquiries@cumbrian-cottages.co.uk
I: www.cumbrian-cottages.co.uk

Carolyn's Cottage ★★★★
Contact: Mr D Hogarth, Cumbrian Cottages, 7 The Crescent, Carlisle CA1 1QW
T: (01228) 599960
F: (01228) 599970
E: enquiries@cumbrian-cottages.co.uk
I: www.cumbrian-cottages.co.uk

Castlerigg Manor Lodge ★★★★
Contact: Mr D Hogarth, Cumbrian Cottages, 7 The Crescent, Carlisle CA1 1QW
T: (01228) 599960
F: (01228) 599970
E: enquiries@cumbrian-cottages.co.uk
I: www.cumbrian-cottages.co.uk

3 Catherine Cottages ★★★
Contact: Mr & Mrs Peter & Margaret Hewitson, 17 Cedar Lane, Cockermouth CA13 9HN
T: (01900) 828039
E: peter.hewitson1@btinternet.com

Cosy Nook ★★★
Contact: Mr Peter Durbin, Cumbrian Cottages, 2 Lonsdale Street, Carlisle CA1 1DB
T: (01228) 599960
F: (01228) 599970
E: enquiries@cumbrian-cottages.co.uk
I: www.cumbrian-cottages.co.uk

The Cottage ★★★
Contact: Mrs M Beaty, The Cottage, Birkrigg, Newlands, Keswick CA12 5TS
T: (017687) 78278

The Cottage ★★★★
Contact: Mrs Susan Jackson, Heart of the Lakes, Fisherbeck Mill, Old Lake Road, Ambleside LA22 0DH
T: (015394) 32321
F: (015394) 33251
E: info@heartofthelakes.co.uk
I: www.heartofthelakes.co.uk

Crag Lea ★★★
Contact: Mr Peter Durbin, Cumbrian Cottages, 2 Lonsdale Street, Carlisle CA1 1DB
T: (01228) 599960
F: (01228) 599970
E: enquiries@cumbrian-cottages.co.uk
I: www.cumbrian-cottages.co.uk

The Croft ★★★
Contact: Mr Peter Durbin, Cumbrian Cottages, 2 Lonsdale Street, Carlisle CA1 1DB
T: (01228) 599960
F: (01228) 599970
E: enquiries@cumbrian-cottages.co.uk
I: www.cumbrian-cottages.co.uk

Croft House Holidays ★★★★
Contact: Mrs Jan Boniface, Croft House, Applethwaite, Keswick CA12 4PN
T: (017687) 73693
E: holidays@crofthouselakes.co.uk
I: www.crofthouselakes.co.uk

Croftlands Cottages ★★★★★
Contact: Mrs S McGarvie, Croftlands, Thornthwaite, Keswick CA12 5SA
T: (017687) 78300
F: (017687) 78300
E: bobmcgarvie@lineone.net
I: www.croftlands-cottages.co.uk

Dale Head Hall Lakeside Hotel ★★★★-★★★★★
Contact: Mr Hans Bonkenburg, Dale Head Hall Lakeside Hotel, Thirlmere, Keswick CA12 4TN
T: (017687) 72478
F: (017687) 71070
E: selfcater@dale-head-hall.co.uk
I: www.dale-head-hall.co.uk

Dalrymple ★★★
Contact: Mr David Burton, Melbecks, Bassenthwaite, Keswick CA12 4QX
T: (017687) 76065
F: (017687) 76869
E: info@lakelandcottages.co.uk
I: www.lakelandcottages.co.uk

Denholm ★★★
Contact: Mr Peter Durbin, Cumbrian Cottages, 2 Lonsdale Street, Carlisle CA1 1DB
T: (01228) 599960
F: (01228) 599970
E: enquiries@cumbrian-cottages.co.uk
I: www.cumbrian-cottages.co.uk

Derwent Cottage ★★★
Contact: Mr Peter Durbin, Cumbrian Cottages, 2 Lonsdale Street, Carlisle CA1 1DB
T: (01228) 599960
F: (01228) 599970
E: enquiries@cumbrian-cottages.co.uk
I: www.cumbrian-cottages.co.uk

Derwent Cottage Mews ★★★★★
Contact: Mrs Susan Newman, Derwent Cottage, Portinscale, Applethwaite, Keswick CA12 5RF
T: (017687) 74838
E: enquiries@dercott.demon.co.uk
I: www.dercott.demon.co.uk

Derwent House & Brandelhowe ★★★
Contact: Mr & Mrs Oliver Bull, Derwent House Holidays, Stone Heath, Hilderstone ST15 8SH
T: (01889) 505678
F: (01889) 505679
E: thebulls@globalnet.co.uk
I: www.dholidays-lakes.com

Derwent Manor ★★★★
Contact: Mrs C Denwood
T: (017687) 72538
F: (017687) 71002
E: info@derwent-manor.com
I: www.derwent-manor.com

Dove House ★★★
Contact: Mrs Susan Jackson, Heart of the Lakes, Fisherbeck Mill, Old Lake Road, Ambleside LA22 0DH
T: (015394) 32321
F: (015394) 33251
E: info@heartofthelakes.co.uk
I: www.heartofthelakes.co.uk

Dowthwaite ★★★★
Contact: Mrs Susan Jackson, Heart of the Lakes, Fisherbeck Mill, Old Lake Road, Ambleside LA22 0DH
T: (015394) 32321
F: (015394) 33251
E: info@heartofthelakes.co.uk
I: www.heartofthelakes.co.uk

Duck Pool ★★★
Contact: Mr David Burton, Melbecks, Bassenthwaite, Keswick CA12 4QX
T: (017687) 76065
F: (017687) 76869
E: info@lakelandcottages.co.uk
I: www.lakelandcottages.co.uk

Dunmallet ★★★
Contact: Mr Peter Durbin, Cumbrian Cottages, 2 Lonsdale Street, Carlisle CA1 1DB
T: (01228) 599960
F: (01228) 599970
E: enquiries@cumbrian-cottages.co.uk
I: www.cumbrian-cottages.co.uk

14 Elm Court ★★★
Contact: Mr Peter Durbin, Cumbrian Cottages, 2 Lonsdale Street, Carlisle CA1 1DB
T: (01228) 599960
F: (01228) 599970
E: enquiries@cumbrian-cottages.co.uk
I: www.cumbrian-cottages.co.uk

15 Elm Court ★★★★
Contact: Mr Peter Durbin, Cumbrian Cottages, 2 Lonsdale Street, Carlisle CA1 1DB
T: (01228) 599960
F: (01228) 599970
E: enquiries@cumbrian-cottages.co.uk
I: www.cumbrian-cottages.co.uk

Fell View ★★★
Contact: Mr Peter Durbin, Cumbrian Cottages, 2 Lonsdale Street, Carlisle CA1 1DB
T: (01228) 599960
F: (01228) 599970
E: enquiries@cumbrian-cottages.co.uk
I: www.cumbrian-cottages.co.uk

Fell View Lodge ★★★★
Contact: Mr Peter Durbin, Cumbrian Cottages, 2 Lonsdale Street, Carlisle CA1 1DB
T: (01228) 599960
F: (01228) 599970
E: enquiries@cumbrian-cottages.co.uk
I: www.cumbrian-cottages.co.uk

The Fells ★★★★
Contact: Mr Peter Durbin, Cumbrian Cottages, 2 Lonsdale Street, Carlisle CA1 1DB
T: (01228) 599960
F: (01228) 599970
E: enquiries@cumbrian-cottages.co.uk
I: www.cumbrian-cottages.co.uk

Fernbank House ★★★★★
Contact: Mr Stephen Mason, Stonegarth Guest House, 2 Eskin Street, Keswick CA12 4DH
T: (017687) 74457
E: info@fernbankhouse.com
I: www.fernbankhouse.com

Ferndale ★★★
Contact: Mr David Burton, Melbecks, Bassenthwaite, Keswick CA12 4QX
T: (017687) 76065
F: (017687) 76869
E: info@lakelandcottages.co.uk
I: www.lakelandcottages.co.uk

Fieldside Grange ★★★-★★★★★
Contact: Mr David Mitchell, Fieldside, Keswick CA12 4RN
T: (017687) 74444
F: (017687) 75088
E: fsg@lakebreaks.co.uk
I: www.lakebreaks.co.uk

Fieldside Lodge ★★★★
Contact: Mr Peter Durbin, Cumbrian Cottages, 2 Lonsdale Street, Carlisle CA1 1DB
T: (01228) 599960
F: (01228) 599970
E: enquiries@cumbrian-cottages.co.uk
I: www.cumbrian-cottages.co.uk

Fornside Farm Cottages ★★★★
Contact: Mr & Mrs Hall, St Johns-in-the-Vale, Thirlmere, Keswick CA12 4TS
T: (017687) 79173
F: (017687) 79174
E: cottages@fornside.co.uk
I: www.fornside.co.uk

Fountain Cottage ★★★★
Contact: Dr and Mrs W E Preston, Bannest Hill House, Haltcliffe, Hesket Newmarket, Wigton CA7 8JT
T: (01768) 484394
F: (01768) 484394
E: preston@talk-101.com

Friars Cottage ★★★★
Contact: Mr Peter Durbin, Cumbrian Cottages, 2 Lonsdale Street, Carlisle CA1 1DB
T: (01228) 599960
F: (01228) 599970
E: enquiries@cumbrian-cottages.co.uk
I: www.cumbrian-cottages.co.uk

Gable Cottage ★★★
Contact: Mr Peter Durbin, Cumbrian Cottages, 2 Lonsdale Street, Carlisle CA1 1DB
T: (01228) 599960
F: (01228) 599970
E: enquiries@cumbrian-cottages.co.uk
I: www.cumbrian-cottages.co.uk

Gabriel's Cottage ★★★★
Contact: Mr Peter Durbin, Cumbrian Cottages, 2 Lonsdale Street, Carlisle CA1 1DB
T: (01228) 599960
F: (01228) 599970
E: enquiries@cumbrian-cottages.co.uk
I: www.cumbrian-cottages.co.uk

Gallery Mews Cottages ★★★
Contact: Mr Graham, Mockerkin, Cockermouth CA13 0ST
T: (01946) 861018
E: enquiries@thornthwaite.net
I: www.thornthwaite.net

Glaramara ★★★★
Contact: Mr D Hogarth, Cumbrian Cottages, 7 The Crescent, Carlisle CA1 1QW
T: (01228) 599960
F: (01228) 599970
E: enquiries@cumbrian-cottages.co.uk
I: www.cumbrian-cottages.co.uk

Glendera ★★★
Contact: Mr David Burton, Melbecks, Bassenthwaite, Keswick CA12 4QX
T: (017687) 76065
F: (017687) 76869
E: info@lakelandcottages.co.uk
I: www.lakelandcottages.co.uk

Glenmore ★★★
Contact: Mr Peter Durbin, Cumbrian Cottages, 2 Lonsdale Street, Carlisle CA1 1DB
T: (01228) 599960
F: (01228) 599970
E: enquiries@cumbrian-cottages.co.uk
I: www.cumbrian-cottages.co.uk

Greenbank ★★★
Contact: Mr Peter Durbin, Cumbrian Cottages, 2 Lonsdale Street, Carlisle CA1 1DB
T: (01228) 599960
F: (01228) 599970
E: enquiries@cumbrian-cottages.co.uk
I: www.cumbrian-cottages.co.uk

2 Greta Grove House ★★★★
Contact: Mr Peter Durbin, Cumbrian Cottages, 2 Lonsdale Street, Carlisle CA1 1DB
T: (01228) 599960
F: (01228) 599970
E: enquiries@cumbrian-cottages.co.uk
I: www.cumbrian-cottages.co.uk

Greta Side Court ★★★
Contact: Mrs Laura Atkinson, 3 Felsted, Bolton BL1 5EY
T: (01204) 493138
E: johnlaura3@btopenworld.com

1 Greta Side Court ★★★
Contact: Mr Peter Durbin, Cumbrian Cottages, 2 Lonsdale Street, Carlisle CA1 1DB
T: (01228) 599960
F: (01228) 599970
E: enquiries@cumbrian-cottages.co.uk
I: www.cumbrian-cottages.co.uk

2 Greta Side Court ★★★
Contact: Mr Peter Durbin, Cumbrian Cottages, 2 Lonsdale Street, Carlisle CA1 1DB
T: (01228) 599960
F: (01228) 599970
E: enquiries@cumbrian-cottages.co.uk
I: www.cumbrian-cottages.co.uk

4 Greta Side Court ★★★
Contact: Mr Peter Durbin, Cumbrian Cottages, 2 Lonsdale Street, Carlisle CA1 1DB
T: (01228) 599960
F: (01228) 599970
E: enquiries@cumbrian-cottages.co.uk
I: www.cumbrian-cottages.co.uk

Gretaside ★★★
Contact: Mr Cowman, 10 The Forge, High Hill, Applethwaite, Keswick CA12 5NX
T: (017687) 72650
E: ajcowman@hotmail.com

Haystacks ★★★
Contact: Mr Peter Durbin, Cumbrian Cottages, 2 Lonsdale Street, Carlisle CA1 1DB
T: (01228) 599960
F: (01228) 599970
E: enquiries@cumbrian-cottages.co.uk
I: www.cumbrian-cottages.co.uk

Herries ★★★
Contact: Mr David Burton, Melbecks, Bassenthwaite, Keswick CA12 4QX
T: (017687) 76065
F: (017687) 76869
E: info@lakelandcottages.co.uk
I: www.lakelandcottages.co.uk

High Rigg ★★★★
Contact: Mr T C Sayer, High Rigg, Fasnakyle, Oldhill Wood, Studham, Dunstable LU6 2NF
T: (01582) 872574

Highbank ★★★★
Contact: Mr Peter Durbin, Cumbrian Cottages, 2 Lonsdale Street, Carlisle CA1 1DB
T: (01228) 599960
F: (01228) 599970
E: enquiries@cumbrian-cottages.co.uk
I: www.cumbrian-cottages.co.uk

Holly Cottage ★★★★
Contact: Mr Richard Wilson, 92 Banner Cross Road, Ecclesall, Sheffield S11 9HR
T: (0114) 296 0491
F: (0114) 296 0491
E: r.e.t.wilson@btinternet.com
I: www.hollycottage.info

11 Howrah's Court ★★★★
Contact: Mr Peter Durbin, Cumbrian Cottages, 2 Lonsdale Street, Carlisle CA1 1DB
T: (01228) 599960
F: (01228) 599970
E: enquiries@cumbrian-cottages.co.uk
I: www.cumbrian-cottages.co.uk

Keswick Timeshare Limited ★★★★
Contact: Mr David Etherden, Keswick Timeshare Limited, Keswick Bridge, Brundholme Road, Keswick CA12 4NL
T: (017687) 73591
F: (017687) 75811
E: enquiries@keswickb.com
I: www.keswickb.com

Kingsfell & Kingstarn ★★★★
Contact: Mr Nicholas Gillham, 3 Salisbury House, Abbey Mills, Abbey Mill Lane, St Albans AL3 4HG
T: (01727) 853531
E: nick@lakebreaks.co.uk
I: www.lakebreaks.co.uk

Kintail ★★★★★
Contact: Mr Peter Durbin, Cumbrian Cottages, 2 Lonsdale Street, Carlisle CA1 1DB
T: (01228) 599960
F: (01228) 599970
E: enquiries@cumbrian-cottages.co.uk
I: www.cumbrian-cottages.co.uk

Kylesku ★★★
Contact: Mr Peter Durbin, Cumbrian Cottages, 2 Lonsdale Street, Carlisle CA1 1DB
T: (01228) 599960
F: (01228) 599970
E: enquiries@cumbrian-cottages.co.uk
I: www.cumbrian-cottages.co.uk

Latrigg View ★★★★
Contact: Mr Peter Durbin, Cumbrian Cottages, 2 Lonsdale Street, Carlisle CA1 1DB
T: (01228) 599960
F: (01228) 599970
E: enquiries@cumbrian-cottages.co.uk
I: www.cumbrian-cottages.co.uk

Leander ★★★★
Contact: Mr Peter Durbin, Cumbrian Cottages, 2 Lonsdale Street, Carlisle CA1 1DB
T: (01228) 599960
F: (01228) 599970
E: enquiries@cumbrian-cottages.co.uk
I: www.cumbrian-cottages.co.uk

Little Chestnut Hill ★★★
Contact: Mr David Burton, Melbecks, Bassenthwaite, Keswick CA12 4QX
T: (017687) 76065
F: (017687) 76869
E: info@lakelandcottages.co.uk
I: www.lakelandcottages.co.uk

1 Lonsdale House ★★★★
Contact: Mr D Hogarth, Cumbrian Cottages, 7 The Crescent, Carlisle CA1 1QW
T: (01228) 599960
F: (01228) 599970
E: enquiries@cumbrian-cottages.co.uk
I: www.cumbrian-cottages.co.uk

5 Lonsdale House ★★★★
Contact: Mr Peter Durbin, Cumbrian Cottages, 2 Lonsdale Street, Carlisle CA1 1DB
T: (01228) 599960
F: (01228) 599970
E: enquiries@cumbrian-cottages.co.uk
I: www.cumbrian-cottages.co.uk

Low Briery Cottages ★★★★
Contact: Mr Michael Atkinson, Low Briery Holiday Village, Penrith Road, Keswick CA12 4RN
F: (017687) 72044
E: info@lowbriery.fsnet.co.uk
I: www.keswick.uk.com

Luxurious Lakeland ★★-★★★
Contact: Mr John Mitchell, Luxurious Lakeland, 35 Main Street, Keswick CA12 5BL
T: (017687) 72790
F: (017687) 75750

8 Lydia's Cottages ★★★★
Contact: Mrs Jean Hutchinson, 6 Mountain View, Borrowdale, Keswick CA12 5XH
T: (017687) 77631
E: jean@jhutch.demon.co.uk
I: www.jhutch.demon.co.uk/jean/lydias.htm

Meadow Cottage ★★★
Contact: Mr David Burton, Melbecks, Bassenthwaite, Keswick CA12 4QX
T: (017687) 76065
F: (017687) 76869
E: info@lakelandcottages.co.uk
I: www.lakelandcottages.co.uk

Mill House ★★★★
Contact: Mr Peter Durbin, Cumbrian Cottages, 2 Lonsdale Street, Carlisle CA1 1DB
T: (01228) 599960
F: (01228) 599970
E: enquiries@cumbrian-cottages.co.uk
I: www.cumbrian-cottages.co.uk

Millbeck Cottages ★★★★
Contact: Mr Peter Durbin, Cumbrian Cottages, 2 Lonsdale Street, Carlisle CA1 1DB
T: (01228) 599960
F: (01228) 599970
E: enquiries@cumbrian-cottages.co.uk
I: www.cumbrian-cottages.co.uk

Newlands View ★★★★
Contact: Mr David Burton, Melbecks, Bassenthwaite, Keswick CA12 4QX
T: (017687) 76065
F: (017687) 76869
E: info@lakelandcottages.co.uk
I: www.lakelandcottages.co.uk

Olivet ★★★
Contact: Mr Peter Durbin, Cumbrian Cottages, 2 Lonsdale Street, Carlisle CA1 1DB
T: (01228) 599960
F: (01228) 599970
E: enquiries@cumbrian-cottages.co.uk
I: www.cumbrian-cottages.co.uk

Orchard Barn ★★★
Contact: Mr & Mrs I C Hall, Fisherground Farm, Eskdale CA19 1TF
T: (01946) 723319
E: holidays@fisherground.co.uk
I: www.orchardhouseholidays.co.uk

Peak View ★★★★
Contact: Mr Peter Durbin, Cumbrian Cottages, 2 Lonsdale Street, Carlisle CA1 1DB
T: (01228) 599960
F: (01228) 599970
E: enquiries@cumbrian-cottages.co.uk
I: www.cumbrian-cottages.co.uk

Poet's Corner ★★★★
Contact: Mr Peter Durbin, Cumbrian Cottages, 2 Lonsdale Street, Carlisle CA1 1DB
T: (01228) 599960
F: (01228) 599970
E: enquiries@cumbrian-cottages.co.uk
I: www.cumbrian-cottages.co.uk

Poplar Cottage ★★★
Contact: Mr Peter Durbin, Cumbrian Cottages, 2 Lonsdale Street, Carlisle CA1 1DB
T: (01228) 599960
F: (01228) 599970
E: enquiries@cumbrian-cottages.co.uk
I: www.cumbrian-cottages.co.uk

Primrose Cottage ★★★★
Contact: Mr & Mrs Geoff & Julia Holloway, Bramble Cottage, Helmingham Road, Otley, Ipswich IP6 9NS
T: (01473) 890035
E: primrose.cott@btinternet.com
I: www.primrose.cott.btinternet.co.uk

Ptarmigan House ★★★★
Contact: Mr Peter Durbin, Cumbrian Cottages, 2 Lonsdale Street, Carlisle CA1 1DB
T: (01228) 599960
F: (01228) 599970
E: enquiries@cumbrian-cottages.co.uk
I: www.cumbrian-cottages.co.uk

Quintok ★★★★
Contact: Mr David Burton, Melbecks, Bassenthwaite, Keswick CA12 4QX
T: (017687) 76065
F: (017687) 76869
E: info@lakelandcottages.co.uk
I: www.lakelandcottages.co.uk

24 Ratcliffe Place ★★★
Contact: Mrs Wendy Plant, The Rectory, Church Lane, Garforth, Leeds LS25 1NR
T: (0113) 286 3737
E: wendy@plant.go-legend.net

The Retreat ★★★
Contact: Mr Peter Durbin, Cumbrian Cottages, 2 Lonsdale Street, Carlisle CA1 1DB
T: (01228) 599960
F: (01228) 599970
E: enquiries@cumbrian-cottages.co.uk
I: www.cumbrian-cottages.co.uk

Rheda Cottage ★★★★
Contact: Mr Peter Durbin, Cumbrian Cottages, 2 Lonsdale Street, Carlisle CA1 1DB
T: (01228) 599960
F: (01228) 599970
E: enquiries@cumbrian-cottages.co.uk
I: www.cumbrian-cottages.co.uk

Rivendell ★★★
Contact: Mr David Burton, Melbecks, Bassenthwaite, Keswick CA12 4QX
T: (017687) 76065
F: (017687) 76869
E: info@lakelandcottages.co.uk
I: www.lakelandcottages.co.uk

Riverside Cottage ★★★★
Contact: Mrs Daphne Barron, Fell View, Bassenthwaite, Keswick CA12 4QP
T: (017687) 76007
E: info@riversideholidays.com
I: www.riversideholidays.com

Riverside Cottage ★★★
Contact: Mrs Susan Jackson, Heart of the Lakes, Fisherbeck Mill, Old Lake Road, Ambleside LA22 0DH
T: (015394) 32321
F: (015394) 33251
E: info@heartofthelakes.co.uk
I: www.heartofthelakes.co.uk

Robin's Nest ★★★★
Contact: Mr Peter Durbin, Cumbrian Cottages, 2 Lonsdale Street, Carlisle CA1 1DB
T: (01228) 599960
F: (01228) 599970
E: enquiries@cumbrian-cottages.co.uk
I: www.cumbrian-cottages.co.uk

Rock House ★★★★
Contact: Mrs Susan Jackson, Heart of the Lakes, Fisherbeck Mill, Old Lake Road, Ambleside LA22 0DH
T: (015394) 32321
F: (015394) 33251
E: info@heartofthelakes.co.uk
I: www.heartofthelakes.co.uk

The Rowans ★★★
Contact: Mr Peter Durbin, Cumbrian Cottages, 2 Lonsdale Street, Carlisle CA1 1DB
T: (01228) 599960
F: (01228) 599970
E: enquiries@cumbrian-cottages.co.uk
I: www.cumbrian-cottages.co.uk

Rowanwood & Beechwood ★★★
Contact: Mr & Mrs Davison, Northfield House, Northfield Drive, Mansfield NG18 3DD
T: (01623) 627370

Saddleback Cottage ★★★
Contact: Mr Peter Durbin, Cumbrian Cottages, 2 Lonsdale Street, Carlisle CA1 1DB
T: (01228) 599960
F: (01228) 599970
E: enquiries@cumbrian-cottages.co.uk
I: www.cumbrian-cottages.co.uk

19 Saint John's Street ★★
Contact: Mr Peter Gee, 19 Saint John's Street, Keswick CA12 5AE
T: (017687) 73571

Sandburne Cottage ★★★★
Contact: Mrs Susan Jackson, Heart of the Lakes, Fisherbeck Mill, Old Lake Road, Ambleside LA22 0DH
T: (015394) 32321
F: (015394) 33251
E: info@heartofthelakes.co.uk
I: www.heartofthelakes.co.uk

Shelter Stone ★★★
Contact: Mr David Burton, Melbecks, Bassenthwaite, Keswick CA12 4QX
T: (017687) 76065
F: (017687) 76869
E: info@lakelandcottages.co.uk
I: www.lakelandcottags.co.uk

The Shieling ★★★★
Contact: Mr Peter Durbin, Cumbrian Cottages, 2 Lonsdale Street, Carlisle CA1 1DB
T: (01228) 599960
F: (01228) 599970
E: enquiries@cumbrian-cottages.co.uk
I: www.cumbrian-cottages.co.uk

Skiddaw View ★★★
Contact: Mr Peter Durbin, Cumbrian Cottages, 2 Lonsdale Street, Carlisle CA1 1DB
T: (01228) 599960
F: (01228) 599970
E: enquiries@cumbrian-cottages.co.uk
I: www.cumbrian-cottages.co.uk

Skiddaw View ★★★
Contact: Mrs Winifred Cartmell, Skiddaw View, 1 Heads Road, Applethwaite, Keswick CA12 5HA
T: (017687) 73574

Slate Cottage ★★★★
Contact: Mr Peter Durbin, Cumbrian Cottages, 2 Lonsdale Street, Carlisle CA1 1DB
T: (01228) 599960
F: (01228) 599970
E: enquiries@cumbrian-cottages.co.uk
I: www.cumbrian-cottages.co.uk

South View ★★★★★
Contact: Mrs Susan Jackson, Heart of the Lakes, Fisherbeck Mill, Old Lake Road, Ambleside LA22 0DH
T: (015394) 32321
F: (015394) 33251
E: info@heartofthelakes.co.uk
I: www.heartofthelakes.co.uk

Sprys View Cottage ★★★
Contact: Mr Peter Durbin, Cumbrian Cottages, 2 Lonsdale Street, Carlisle CA1 1DB
T: (01228) 599960
F: (01228) 599970
E: enquiries@cumbrian-cottages.co.uk
I: www.cumbrian-cottages.co.uk

Squirrel Cottage ★★★
Contact: Mr David Burton, Melbecks, Bassenthwaite, Keswick CA12 4QX
T: (017687) 76065
F: (017687) 76869
E: info@lakelandcottages.co.uk

The Steps ★★★★
Contact: Mr Peter Durbin, Cumbrian Cottages, 2 Lonsdale Street, Carlisle CA1 1DB
T: (01228) 599960
F: (01228) 599970
E: enquiries@cumbrian-cottages.co.uk
I: www.cumbrian-cottages.co.uk

Stone Ledges ★★★
Contact: Mr Peter Durbin, Cumbrian Cottages, 2 Lonsdale Street, Carlisle CA1 1DB
T: (01228) 599960
F: (01228) 599970
E: enquiries@cumbrian-cottages.co.uk
I: www.cumbrian-cottages.co.uk

Stone Steps ★★★
Contact: Mr Peter Durbin, Cumbrian Cottages, 2 Lonsdale Street, Carlisle CA1 1DB
T: (01228) 599960
F: (01228) 599970
E: enquiries@cumbrian-cottages.co.uk
I: www.cumbrian-cottages.co.uk

Threeways ★★★★
Contact: Mr Peter Durbin, Cumbrian Cottages, 2 Lonsdale Street, Carlisle CA1 1DB
T: (01228) 599960
F: (01228) 599970
E: enquiries@cumbrian-cottages.co.uk
I: www.cumbrian-cottages.co.uk

Topsey Turvey ★★★
Contact: Mr Peter Durbin, Cumbrian Cottages, 2 Lonsdale Street, Carlisle CA1 1DB
T: (01228) 599960
F: (01228) 599970
E: enquiries@cumbrian-cottages.co.uk
I: www.cumbrian-cottages.co.uk

Twentymans Court ★★★
Contact: Mr Peter Durbin, Cumbrian Cottages, 2 Lonsdale Street, Carlisle CA1 1DB
T: (01228) 599960
F: (01228) 599970
E: enquiries@cumbrian-cottages.co.uk
I: www.cumbrian-cottages.co.uk

Underne ★★★
Contact: Mr David Burton, Melbecks, Bassenthwaite, Keswick CA12 4QX
T: (017687) 76065
F: (017687) 76869
E: info@lakelandcottages.co.uk
I: www.lakelandcottages.co.uk

Underscar ★★★★★
Contact: Mrs Susan Jackson, Heart of the Lakes, Fisherbeck Mill, Old Lake Road, Ambleside LA22 0DH
T: (015394) 32321
F: (015394) 33251
E: info@heartofthelakes.co.uk
I: www.heartofthelakes.co.uk

Upton Glen ★★★
Contact: Mr Peter Durbin, Cumbrian Cottages, 2 Lonsdale Street, Carlisle CA1 1DB
T: (01228) 599960
F: (01228) 599970
E: enquiries@cumbrian-cottages.co.uk
I: www.cumbrian-cottages.co.uk

Wendover ★★★
Contact: Mr Peter Durbin, Cumbrian Cottages, 2 Lonsdale Street, Carlisle CA1 1DB
T: (01228) 599960
F: (01228) 599970
E: enquiries@cumbrian-cottages.co.uk
I: www.cumbrian-cottages.co.uk

White Wicket ★★★
Contact: Mr Peter Durbin, Cumbrian Cottages, 2 Lonsdale Street, Carlisle CA1 1DB
T: (01228) 599960
F: (01228) 599970
E: enquiries@cumbrian-cottages.co.uk
I: www.cumbrian-cottages.co.uk

Woodleigh ★★★★
Contact: Mr Peter Durbin, Cumbrian Cottages, 2 Lonsdale Street, Carlisle CA1 1DB
T: (01228) 599960
F: (01228) 599970
E: enquiries@cumbrian-cottages.co.uk
I: www.cumbrian-cottages.co.uk

KILLINGTON
Cumbria

Ghyll Stile Mill Cottage ★★★
Contact: Mrs Janet Chetwood, Ghyll Stile Mill Cottage, Killington, Sedbergh LA10 5EH
T: (015396) 21715
E: janetghyll@aol.com

Valley View & The Granary ★★★
Contact: Mr & Mrs Isabel & Peter Sugden, Greenholme, Killington, Sedbergh LA10 5EP
T: (015396) 21153
E: peter@greenholme.fsnet.co.uk
I: www.greenholme.fsnet.co.uk

KING'S MEABURN
Cumbria

Lyvennet Cottages ★★★-★★★★
Contact: Mrs D M Addison, Keld, King's Meaburn, Penrith CA10 3BS
T: (01931) 714226
F: (01931) 714598
E: info@lyvennetcottages.co.uk
I: www.lyvennetcottages.co.uk

KIRKBY LONSDALE
Cumbria

Barkinbeck Cottage ★★★
Contact: Mrs A Hamilton, Barkin House, Gatebeck, Kendal LA8 0HX
T: (015395) 67122
E: ann@barkin.fsnet.co.uk
I: www.barkinbeck.co.uk

The Old Stables ★★★★
Contact: Mr Peter Durbin, Cumbrian Cottages, 2 Lonsdale Street, Carlisle CA1 1DB
T: (01228) 599960
F: (01228) 599970
E: enquiries@cumbrian-cottages.co.uk
I: www.cumbrian-cottages.co.uk

Sellet Hall Cottages ★★★★
Contact: Mrs M Hall, Sellet Hall, Kirkby Lonsdale, Carnforth LA6 2QF
T: (01524) 271865
E: sellethall@hotmail.com
I: www.sellethall.com

Wisteria Cottage ★★★★
Contact: Mr Peter Durbin, Cumbrian Cottages, 2 Lonsdale Street, Carlisle CA1 1DB
T: (01228) 599960
F: (01228) 599970
E: enquiries@cumbrian-cottages.co.uk
I: www.cumbrian-cottages.co.uk

KIRKBY STEPHEN
Cumbria

Hatygill Cottage ★★★
Contact: The Manager Dales Hol Cott Ref: 1459, Carleton Business Park, Carleton New Road, Skipton BD23 2AA
T: (01756) 790919
F: (01756) 797012
E: info@dalesholcot.com
I: www.dalesholcot.com

Pennistone Green ★★★★
Contact: Mr T F Jackson, Ashmere, Rakes Road, Monyash, Bakewell DE45 1JL
T: (01629) 815683
E: jackson@ashmere.fsnet.co.uk
I: www.uk-holiday-cottages.info

Swallows Barn ★★★★
Contact: Mrs J Atkinson, Swallows Barn, Augill House Farm, Brough, Kirkby Stephen CA17 4DX
T: (017683) 41272
I: www.ukworld.net/swallowsbarn

KIRKBY THORE
Cumbria

Holme Lea ★★★
Contact: Mr Alan Price, 27 Church Close, Buxton, Norwich NR10 5ER
T: (01603) 279713
E: jprice@albatross.co.uk

KIRKLAND
Cumbria

Kirkland Hall Cottages ★★★★
Contact: Mr & Mrs Ian Howes, Kirkland Hall Cottages, Kirkland Hall, Kirkland, Penrith CA10 1RN
T: (01768) 88295
F: (01768) 88295
E: kirklandhallcottages@hotmail.com
I: www.kirkland-hall-cottages.co.uk

KIRKLINTON
Cumbria

Dovecote ★★★★
Contact: Mrs Sherann Chandley, Cleughside Farm, Kirklinton, Carlisle CA6 6BE
T: (01228) 675650
F: (01228) 675870
E: slc@cleughside.co.uk
I: www.cleughside.co.uk

Keepers Cottage ★★★★
Contact: Mrs Pat Armstrong, Slealands, Longtown, Carlisle CA6 5RQ
T: (01228) 791378
E: info@keepers-cottage.co.uk
I: www.keepers-cottage.co.uk

KIRKOSWALD
Cumbria

Crossfield Cottages ★★★
Contact: Mrs Susan Bottom, Crossfield Cottages, Staffield, Kirkoswald, Penrith CA10 1EU
T: (01768) 898711
F: (01768) 898711
E: info@crossfieldcottages.co.uk

Howscales ★★★★
Contact: Mrs S E Webster, Howscales, Kirkoswald, Penrith CA10 1JG
T: (01768) 898666
F: (01768) 898710
E: liz@howscales.fsbusiness.co.uk
I: www.eden-in-cumbria.co.uk/howscales

LAKESIDE
Cumbria

Flat 2 Stock Park Mansion ★★★
Contact: Mrs Diane Watson, 17 Argarmeols Road, Formby, Liverpool L37 7BX
T: (01704) 871144
E: rogerwatson@ic24.net

Nutwood ★★★★
Contact: Mr Paul Liddell, Lakelovers, Belmont House, Lake Road, Bowness-on-Windermere, Windermere LA23 3BJ
T: (015394) 88855
F: (015394) 88857
E: bookings@lakelovers.co.uk
I: www.lakelovers.co.uk

LAMONBY
Cumbria

Half Crown Cottage ★★★★
Contact: Mr Paul Durbin, Cumbrian Cottages, 2 Lonsdale Street, Carlisle CA1 1DB
T: (01228) 599960
F: (01228) 599970

LAMPLUGH
Cumbria

2 Folly ★★★★
Contact: Mrs Alison Wilson, Dockray Nook, Lamplugh, Workington CA14 4SH
T: (01946) 861151
E: dockraynook@talk21.com
I: www.felldykecottageholidays.co.uk

LANGDALE
Cumbria

2 & 7 Lingmoor View ★★★
Contact: Mr J Batho, High Hollin Bank, Coniston LA21 8AG
T: (015394) 41680
E: charlie.batho@wernethlow.fsnet.co.uk
I: www.cottagescumbria.com

Long House Cottages ★★★
Contact: Mr Ian Grayston, Long House Cottages, Great Langdale, Grasmere, Ambleside LA22 9JS
T: (015394) 37222
E: enquiries@longhousecottages.co.uk
I: www.longhousecottages.co.uk

The Maple Loft
Rating Applied For
Contact: Mrs Susan Jackson, Fisherbeck Mill, Old Lake Road, Ambleside LA22 0DH
T: (015394) 33110
F: (015394) 33251
E: info@heartofthelakes.co.uk

Maple Tree Holiday Cottages ★★★-★★★★
Contact: Mrs Judith Fry, Contrast, Great Langdale, Ambleside LA22 9HW
T: (015394) 37210
F: (015394) 37311
E: info@britinn.co.uk
I: www.britinn.co.uk

Meadow Bank ★★★-★★★★★
Contact: Ms Patricia Locke, Elterwater Investments Ltd, 17 Shay Lane, Hale Barns, Altrincham WA15 8NZ
T: (0161) 904 9445
F: (0161) 904 9877
E: lockemeadowbank@aol.com
I: www.langdalecottages.co.uk

Weir Cottage
Rating Applied For
Contact: Mrs Susan Jackson, Fisherbeck Mill, Old Lake Road, Ambleside LA22 0DH
T: (015394) 33110
F: (015394) 33251
E: info@heartofthelakes.co.uk

Wheelwrights Holiday Cottages ★★-★★★★★
Contact: Mr I Price, Wheelwrights Holiday Cottages, Elterwater, Ambleside LA22 9HS
T: (015394) 37635
F: (015394) 37618
E: enquiries@wheelwrights.com
I: www.wheelwrights.com

LANGWATHBY
Cumbria

Byre Cottage ★★★★
Contact: Mrs Frances Flower, 2 Eden Garth, Langwathby, Penrith CA10 1NT
T: (01768) 881923
E: francesflower@tiscali.co.uk
I: www.byrecottage.co.uk

LAZONBY
Cumbria

Bracken Bank Lodge & Bracken Bank Cottage
Rating Applied For
Contact: Mrs Hilary Burton, Bracken Bank Lodge & Bracken Bank Cottage, Lazonby, Penrith CA10 1AX
T: (01768) 898241
F: (01768) 898221

LEASGILL
Cumbria

The Cottage ★★★
Contact: Mrs Beverly Keatings, The Cottage, 1 Eversley Gardens, Leasgill, Milnthorpe LA7 7EY
T: (015395) 63008
F: (015395) 62920
E: eversleycottage@going-away.co.uk

LEVENS
Cumbria

Gilpin Farmhouse Cottage
Rating Applied For
Contact: Mr & Mrs William & Judy Park, Gilpin Farmhouse, Levens, Kendal LA8 8EW
T: (015395) 52450

Underhill ★★★★
Contact: Mrs Phillips, Underhill, Levens, Kendal LA8 8PH
T: (015395) 60298
E: underhillcottage@aol.com

LINDALE
Cumbria

Bank House ★★★★
Contact: Mr John Serginson, The Lakeland Cottage Company, Waterside House, Newby Bridge, Ulverston LA12 8AN
T: (015395) 30024
F: (015395) 31932
E: john@lakeland-cottage-company.co.uk
I: www.lakeland-cottage-company.co.uk

Horseshoe Cottage ★★★★
Contact: Mr Peter Durbin, Cumbrian Cottages, 2 Lonsdale Street, Carlisle CA1 1DB
T: (01228) 599960
F: (01228) 599970
E: enquiries@cumbrian-cottages.co.uk
I: www.cumbrian-cottages.co.uk

7 New Cottages ★★★
Contact: Country Holidays Ref: 3625, Holiday Cottages Group Owner Services Dept, Spring Mill, Earby, Barnoldswick BB94 0AA
T: 08700 723723
F: (01282) 844288
E: sales@holidaycottagesgroup.com
I: www.country-holidays.co.uk

LITTLE ARROW
Cumbria

Penny Rigg, Nether Fell & Spring Bank★★★-★★★★
Contact: Mr & Mrs Roger and Joan Lupton, Penny Rigg, Nether Fell & Spring Bank, Little Arrow, Coniston LA21 8AU
T: (015394) 41114
F: (015394) 41114
E: rlupton@conistoncottages.co.uk
I: www.conistoncottages.co.uk

LITTLE LANGDALE
Cumbria

The Bield ★★★★
Contact: Mrs Susan Jackson, Heart of the Lakes, Fisherbeck Mill, Old Lake Road, Ambleside LA22 0DH
T: (015394) 32321
F: (015394) 33251
E: info@heartofthelakes.co.uk
I: www.heartofthelakes.co.uk

Birch House ★★★★
Contact: Mr Paul Liddell, Lakelovers, Belmont House, Lake Road, Bowness-on-Windermere, Windermere LA23 3BJ
T: (015394) 88855
F: (015394) 88857
E: bookings@lakelovers.co.uk
I: www.lakelovers.co.uk

Farragrain ★★★★
Contact: Mrs Susan Jackson, Heart of the Lakes, Fisherbeck Mill, Old Lake Road, Ambleside LA22 0DH
T: (015394) 32321
F: (015394) 33251
E: info@heartofthelakes.co.uk
I: www.heartofthelakes.co.uk

Hacket Forge ★★★
Contact: Mrs Judith Amos, Hacket Forge, Little Langdale, Elterwater, Ambleside LA22 9NU
T: (015394) 37630

Highfold Cottage ★★★
Contact: Mrs C E Blair, 8 The Glebe, Chapel Stile, Ambleside LA22 9JT
T: (015394) 37686

Lang Parrock ★★★
Contact: Mrs Susan Jackson, Heart of the Lakes, Fisherbeck Mill, Old Lake Road, Ambleside LA22 0DH
T: (015394) 32321
F: (015394) 33251
E: info@heartofthelakes.co.uk
I: www.heartofthelakes.co.uk

LITTLE STRICKLAND
Cumbria

Spring Bank ★★★★
Contact: Mrs Joan Ostle, Meadowfield, Little Strickland, Penrith CA10 3EG
T: (01931) 716246
E: springbank17@hotmail.com

LONGSLEDDALE
Cumbria

The Coach House ★★★
Contact: Mrs Farmer, The Coach House, Capplebarrow House, Longsleddale, Kendal LA8 9BB
T: (01539) 823686
E: jenyfarmer@aol.com
I: www.capplebarrowcoachhouse.co.uk

Mill Cottage
Rating Applied For
Contact: Mrs Jeanie Thom, Garnett Bridge, Longsleddale, Kendal LA8 9AZ
T: (01539) 823030
F: (01539) 823030
E: jeanie@corn-mill.fsnet.co.uk
I: www.country-holidays.co.uk

LORTON
Cumbria

Swaledale Cottage ★★★
Contact: Miss Christine England, Hope Farm, Lorton, Cockermouth CA13 9UD
T: (01900) 85226
F: (01900) 85226

LOUGHRIGG
Cumbria

Lane Head ★★★★
Contact: Mrs Susan Jackson, Fisherbeck Mill, Old Lake Road, Ambleside LA22 0DH
T: (015394) 32321
F: (015394) 33251
E: info@heartofthelakes.co.uk

The Poppies
Rating Applied For
Contact: Mrs Susan Jackson, Heart of the Lakes, Fisherbeck Mill, Old Lake Road, Ambleside LA22 0DH
T: (015394) 33110
F: (015394) 33251
E: info@heartofthelakes.co.uk

LOW COTEHILL
Cumbria

Oakville Cottage ★★★★
Contact: Mr Peter Durbin, Cumbrian Cottages, 2 Lonsdale Street, Carlisle CA1 1DB
T: (01228) 599960
F: (01228) 599970
E: enquiries@cumbrian-cottages.co.uk
I: www.cumbrian-cottages.co.uk

Oakville Garden Cottage ★★★★
Contact: Mr Peter Durbin, Cumbrian Cottages, 2 Lonsdale Street, Carlisle CA1 1DB
T: (01228) 599960
F: (01228) 599970
E: enquiries@cumbrian-cottages.co.uk
I: www.cumbrian-cottages.co.uk

LOWESWATER
Cumbria

The Coach House ★★★★★
Contact: Mrs Naomi Kerr, Looking Stead, Loweswater, Cockermouth CA13 0RS
T: (01900) 85660
E: naomi.kerr@which.net
I: www.country-holidays.co.uk

Crummock Water Holiday Cottages and Foulsyke House ★★★★★
Contact: Mrs Carol Thompson, Foulsyke, Loweswater, Cockermouth CA13 0RS
T: (01900) 85637
E: cjt@crummockcottages.co.uk
I: www.crummockcottages.co.uk

High Mosser Gate ★★★★
Contact: Mrs A Evens, Russetts, Highfield Road, Wigginton, Tring HP23 6EB
T: (01442) 825855
F: (01442) 828227
E: alison@highmossergate.co.uk
I: www.highmossergate.co.uk

The Howe ★★★★
Contact: Mrs M Townson, The Howe, Mosser, Cockermouth CA13 0RA
T: (01900) 823660
E: millie@mosserhowe.freeserve.co.uk
I: www.mosserhowe.co.uk

Low Park Cottage ★★★
Contact: Mr Robert Watkins, Low Park Cottage, Loweswater, Cockermouth CA13 0RU
T: (01900) 85242

Loweswater Holiday Cottages ★★★★-★★★★★
Contact: Mr M E Thompson, Loweswater Holiday Cottages, Scale Hill, Loweswater, Cockermouth CA13 9UX
T: (01900) 85232
F: (01900) 85232
E: mike@loweswaterholidaycottages.co.uk
I: www.loweswaterholidaycottages.co.uk

LOWICK
Cumbria

Allt Maen ★★★
Contact: Mr John Serginson, Waterside House, Newby Bridge, Ulverston LA12 8AN
T: (015395) 30024
F: (015395) 31932
E: john@lakelandcottageco.com
I: www.lakeland-cottage-company.co.uk

Bark Cottage ★★★
Contact: Miss Jenny Tancock & Mr Joe Fairclough, Tannery Barn, The Meadows, Lowick Green, Ulverston LA12 8DX
T: (01229) 885416
E: barkcottage@tannerybarn.freeserve.co.uk
I: www.tannerybarn.freeserve.co.uk

Tsukudu ★★★★
Contact: Mr Martin Wardle, Lakes and Valleys, Bateman Fold Barn, Crook, Kendal LA8 8LN
T: (015394) 68103
F: (015394) 68104
E: lakesandvalleys@aol.com
I: www.lakesandvalleys.co.uk

LOWICK BRIDGE
Cumbria

Coniston Retreat ★★★★
Contact: Mr Paul Liddell, Belmont House, Lake Road, Bowness-on-Windermere, Windermere LA23 3BJ
T: (015394) 88855
F: (015394) 88857
E: bookings@lakelovers.co.uk

Langholme Cottage ★★★
Contact: Mr Philip Johnston, The Coppermines Coniston Cottages, The Estate Office, The Bridge, Coniston LA21 8HJ
T: (015394) 41765
F: (015394) 41944
E: info@coppermines.co.uk
I: www.coppermines.co.uk

LOWICK GREEN
Cumbria

The Hidden Cottage ★★★
Contact: Mr Philip Johnston, The Coppermines Coniston Cottages, The Estate Office, The Bridge, Coniston LA21 8HJ
T: (015394) 41765
E: bookings@coppermines.co.uk
I: www.coppermines.co.uk

LYTH
Cumbria

Fellside Farm ★★★
Contact: Bowness Lakeland Holidays, 131 Radcliffe New Road, Whitefield, Manchester M45 7RP
T: (0161) 796 3896

MALLERSTANG
Cumbria

Old Faw Cottage ★★★
Contact: Mr Wales, Water Street, Oughtershaw, Skipton BD23 1PB
T: (01756) 700510
E: brochure@holidaycotts.co.uk

MANESTY
Cumbria

The Coppice ★★
Contact: Mr David Burton, Melbecks, Bassenthwaite, Keswick CA12 4QX
T: (017687) 76065
F: (017687) 76869
E: info@lakelandcottages.co.uk
I: www.lakelandcottages.co.uk

High Ground ★★★
Contact: Mr David Burton, Melbecks, Bassenthwaite, Keswick CA12 4QX
T: (017687) 76065
F: (017687) 76869
E: info@lakelandcottages.co.uk
I: www.lakelandcottages.co.uk

Manesty Holiday Cottages ★★★-★★★★
Contact: Mr & Mrs Leyland, Manesty Holiday Cottages, Youdale Knot, Manesty, Keswick CA12 5UG
T: (017687) 77216
F: (017687) 77384
E: cottages@manesty.co.uk
I: www.manesty.co.uk

MARTINDALE
Cumbria

Beckside Cottage ★★★★
Contact: Mrs Caroline Ivinson, Beckside Farm, Sandwick, Ullswater, Penrith CA10 2NF
T: (017684) 86239
F: (017684) 86239
E: ivinson_becksidefarm@hotmail.com

Townhead Cottage ★★★
Contact: Mr John Serginson, Waterside House, Newby Bridge, Ulverston LA12 8AN
T: (015395) 30024
F: (015395) 31932
E: john@lakelandcottageco.com
I: www.lakelandcottageco.com

MAULDS MEABURN
Cumbria

Harrys Barn ★★★★
Contact: Mrs Julie Hatton, Coat Flatt Mill, Orton, Penrith CA10 3RE
T: (01539) 624664
F: (01539) 624527
E: hattonjulie@hotmail.com
I: www.harrysbarn.co.uk

MEALSGATE
Cumbria

West Court and East Court ★★★
Contact: The Manager Dales Hol Cot Ref:2315/2075, Carleton Business Park, Carleton New Road, Skipton BD23 2AA
T: (01756) 799821
F: (01756) 797012
E: info@dalesholcot.com
I: www.dalesholcot.com

MILBURN
Cumbria

Bramley Cottage ★★★★
Contact: Mr & Mrs G Heelis, Orchard Cottage, Milburn, Penrith CA10 1TN
T: (01768) 361074
F: (01768) 895528
E: Guyheelis@aol.com
I: www.uk-holiday-cottages.co.uk/bramley

Gullom Cottage ★★★
Contact: Mr Peter Durbin, Cumbrian Cottages, 2 Lonsdale Street, Carlisle CA1 1DB
T: (01228) 599960
F: (01228) 599970
E: enquiries@cumbrian-cottages.co.uk
I: www.cumbrian-cottages.co.uk

High Slakes ★★★★
Contact: Mr Wales, Water Street, Oughtershaw, Skipton BD23 1PB
T: (01756) 700510
E: brochure@holidaycotts.co.uk

MILLBECK
Cumbria

Millbeck Cottages ★★★★
Contact: Mr Richard Watson, 20 Hebing End, Benington, Stevenage SG2 7DD
T: (01438) 359311
F: (01438) 740127
E: r.watson@bbwlaw.biz

MORLAND
Cumbria

Lowergate House East ★★★★
Contact: The Manager Dales Hol Cot Ref:3148, Carleton Business Park, Carleton New Road, Skipton BD23 2AA
T: (01756) 799821
F: (01756) 797012
E: info@dalesholcot.com
I: www.dalesholcot.com

Shorrocks House, Torbock House & The Coach House ★★★★★
Contact: Mrs G Crossley, Morland Hall, Morland, Penrith CA10 3BB
T: (01931) 714029
F: (01931) 714714

MOTHERBY
Cumbria

Nettle How Cottage ★★★
Contact: The Manager Dales Hol Cot Ref: 3362, Carleton Business Park, Carleton New Road, Skipton BD23 2AA
T: (01756) 790919
F: (01756) 799821
E: fiona@dales-holiday-cottages.com
I: www.dales-holiday-cottages.com

MUNGRISDALE
Cumbria

The Garth & Elind ★★★★
Contact: Mrs Susan Jackson, Dales Holiday Cottages, Carleton Business Park, Carleton New Road, Skipton BD23 2AA
T: (015394) 32321
F: (015394) 33251
E: info@heartofthelakes.co.uk
I: www.dalesholcot.com

Grisedale View, Howe Top ★★★★
Contact: Mrs C A Weightman, Grisedale View, Howe Top, Near Howe, Mungrisdale, Penrith CA11 0SH
T: (017687) 79678
F: (017687) 79462
E: nearhowe@btopenworld.com
I: www.nearhowe.co.uk

NADDLE
Cumbria

The Bungalow ★★★
Contact: Mrs Jane Nicholson, St Johns-in-the-Vale, Keswick CA12 4TF
T: (017687) 72290
E: jackie@causewayfoot.co.uk
I: www.causewayfoot.co.uk

NATLAND
Cumbria

Stonegable ★★★
Contact: Mr Peter Durbin, Cumbrian Cottages, 2 Lonsdale Street, Carlisle CA1 1DB
T: (01228) 599960
F: (01228) 599970
E: enquiries@cumbrian-cottages.co.uk
I: www.cumbrian-cottages.co.uk

NEAR SAWREY
Cumbria

Smithy Cottage ★★★
Contact: Mr Paul Liddell, Lakelovers, Belmont House, Lake Road, Bowness-on-Windermere, Windermere LA23 3BJ
T: (015394) 88855
F: (015394) 88857
E: bookings@lakelovers.co.uk
I: www.lakelovers.co.uk

NENTHEAD
Cumbria

Rock House Estate ★★★★
Contact: Mr & Mrs Paul & Carol Huish, Valley View, Rock House Estate, Nenthead, Alston CA9 3NA
T: (01434) 382684
F: (01434) 382685
E: Paul@RockHouseEstate.co.uk
I: www.rockhouseestate.co.uk

NEWBIGGIN
Cumbria

The Old Post Office ★★★★
Contact: The Manager Dales Hol Cot Ref:2799, Carleton Business Park, Carleton New Road, Skipton BD23 2AA
T: (01756) 799821
F: (01756) 797012
E: info@dalesholcot.com
I: www.dalesholcot.com

NEWBIGGIN-ON-LUNE
Cumbria

Ashley Cottage ★★★
Contact: Mr & Mrs Hickman, Ashley Cottage, Ashley Bank, Newbiggin-on-Lune, Kirkby Stephen CA17 4LZ
T: (015396) 23214
F: (015396) 23214
E: ashleybnk@aol.com
I: www.eden-in-cumbria.co.uk/ashleybank

Green Bell View ★★★
Contact: The Manager Dales Hol Cot Ref: 2076, Carleton Business Park, Carleton New Road, Skipton BD23 2AA
T: (01756) 790919
F: (01756) 797012
E: info@dalesholcot.com
I: www.dalesholcot.com

Pleasant View
Rating Applied For
Contact: The Manager Dales Hol Cot Ref: 2392, Carleton Business Park, Carleton New Road, Skipton BD23 2AA
T: (01756) 790919
F: (01756) 797012
E: info@dalesholcot.com
I: www.dalesholcot.com

NEWBY
Cumbria

Midtown Cottage & Dairy Cottage ★★★★-★★★★★
Contact: Wardle Family, Bateman Fold Barn, Crook, Kendal LA8 8LN
T: (015395) 68102
F: (015395) 68104
E: goosemirecottage@aol.com
I: www.holidaycottage.org.uk

NEWBY BRIDGE
Cumbria

Cherry Tree House ★★★★
Contact: Mrs Susan Jackson, Heart of the Lakes, Fisherbeck Mill, Old Lake Road, Ambleside LA22 0DH
E: info@heartofthelakes.co.uk
I: www.heartofthelakes.co.uk

Fellcroft Cottage ★★★★
Contact: Ms Cath Hale, 1 Low Row, Backbarrow, Ulverston LA12 8QH
T: (015395) 30316
E: cath@fellcroft.fsnet.co.uk

Woodland Cottage ★★★★
Contact: Mr Peter Newton, Fellside Lodge, Newby Bridge Caravan Park, Canny Hill, Newby Bridge LA12 8NF
T: (015395) 31030
F: (015395) 30105
E: info@cumbriancaravans.co.uk
I: www.cumbriancaravans.co.uk

NEWLAND
Cumbria

Curlew Rise and Heron Beck ★★★★
Contact: Mr John Serginson, Waterside House, Newby Bridge, Ulverston LA12 8AN
T: (015395) 30024
F: (015395) 31932
E: john@lakelandcottageco.com
I: www.lakeland-cottage-company.co.uk

NEWLANDS
Cumbria

Fell Cottage ★★★
Contact: Mr David Burton, Melbecks, Bassenthwaite, Keswick CA12 4QX
T: (017687) 76065
F: (017687) 76869
E: info@lakelandcottages.co.uk
I: www.lakelandcottages.co.uk

NIBTHWAITE
Cumbria

Fell View ★★★
Contact: Mrs Susan Jackson, Heart of the Lakes, Fisherbeck Mill, Old Lake Road, Ambleside LA22 0DH
T: (015394) 32321
F: (015394) 33251
E: info@heartofthelakes.co.uk
I: www.heartofthelakes.co.uk

The Hovel ★★★★
Contact: Mr John Serginson, Waterside House, Newby Bridge, Ulverston LA12 8AN
T: (015395) 30024
F: (015395) 31932
E: john@lakelandcottageco.uk
I: www.lakelandcottagecompany.co.uk

ORTON
Cumbria

Chapel Beck Cottage ★★★★
Contact: Mrs Leonne Hodgson, Coat Flatt Hall, Tebay, Orton, Penrith CA10 3SZ
T: (015396) 24379
F: (015396) 24379
E: leonne@coatflatt.force9.co.uk

OUSBY
Cumbria

Hole Bank ★★★★
Contact: Mrs Lesley McVey, 10 Helvellyn Court, Penrith CA11 8PZ
T: (01768) 892247
F: (01768) 892247

OUTGATE
Cumbria

Borwick Fold Cottages ★★★★
Contact: Mr & Mrs J Johnson, Borwick Fold, Hawkshead, Ambleside LA22 0PU
T: (015394) 36742
F: (015394) 36094
E: borwickfold.cottages@btopenworld.com
I: www.borwickfold.com

Honey Pot Cottage (Currier) ★★★★
Contact: Mr Philip Johnston, The Coppermines & Lakes Cottages, The Estate Office, The Bridge, Coniston LA21 8HJ
T: (015394) 41765
F: (015394) 41944
E: info@coppermines.co.uk
I: www.coppermines.co.uk

Pepper Cottage ★★★★
Contact: Mr Paul Liddell, Lakelovers, Belmont House, Lake Road, Bowness-on-Windermere, Windermere LA23 3BJ
T: (015394) 88855
F: (015394) 88857
E: bookings@lakelovers.co.uk
I: www.lakelovers.co.uk

OUTHGILL
Cumbria

Ing Hill Barn Apartments ★★★★
Contact: Country Holidays Ref:14815, 21a Roydon Road, Stanstead Abbotts, Ware SG12 8HQ
T: (01282) 445096
F: (01282) 844288

PAPCASTLE
Cumbria

Sunny Brae ★★★
Contact: Mr Peter Durbin, Cumbrian Cottages, 2 Lonsdale Street, Carlisle CA1 1DB
T: (01228) 599960
F: (01228) 599970
E: enquiries@cumbrian-cottages.co.uk
I: www.cumbrian-cottages.co.uk

PARDSHAW
Cumbria

Stoneygate Cottage ★★★★
Contact: Country Hols Ref: 12243, Holiday Cottages Group Owner Services Dept, Spring Mill, Earby, Barnoldswick BB94 0AA
T: 08700 723723
F: (01282) 844288
E: sales@holidaycottagesgroup.com
I: www.country-holidays.co.uk

PATTERDALE
Cumbria

Bleaze End ★★★★
Contact: Mrs Susan Jackson, Heart of the Lakes, Fisherbeck Mill, Old Lake Road, Ambleside LA22 0DH
T: (015394) 32321
F: (015394) 33251
E: info@heartofthelakes.co.uk
I: www.heartofthelakes.co.uk

Broad How ★★★★
Contact: Country Holidays Ref: 8478, Holiday Cottages Group Owner Servic, Spring Mill, Earby, Barnoldswick BB18 6RN
T: 0870 723723
F: (01282) 844288
E: sales@holidaycottagegroup.com
I: www.country-holidays.co.uk

Deepdale Hall Cottage ★★★
Contact: Mr Chris Brown, Patterdale, Penrith CA11 0NR
T: (017684) 82369
F: (017684) 82608
E: brown@deepdalehall.freeserve.co.uk
I: www.deepdalehall.co.uk

Elm How, Cruck Barn & Eagle Cottage ★★★-★★★★
Contact: Mrs Marsden, Estate Office, Matson Ground, Windermere LA23 2NH
T: (015394) 45756
F: (015394) 47892
I: www.matsonground.co.uk

Fellside ★★★
Contact: Mrs Susan Jackson, Heart of the Lakes, Fisherbeck Mill, Old Lake Road, Ambleside LA22 0DH
T: (015394) 32321
F: (015394) 33251
E: info@heartofthelakes.co.uk

Grove Cottage ★★★
Contact: Miss Helen Griffiths, Hartsop, Near Patterdale, Ullswater, Penrith CA11 0NZ
T: (017684) 82647
E: helen@lakes-hartsop.co.uk

Hartsop Fold ★★★
Contact: Mrs Lesley Hennedy, Merlin Crag, Marthwaite, Sedbergh LA10 5HU
T: (015396) 22069
F: (015396) 20899
E: lesleyhennedy@hartsop-fold.co.uk
I: www.hartsop-fold.co.uk

Lower Grisedale Lodge ★★★★
Contact: Mrs Susan Jackson, Heart of the Lakes, Fisherbeck Mill, Old Lake Road, Ambleside LA22 0DH
T: (015394) 32321
F: (015394) 33251
E: info@heartofthelakes.co.uk
I: www.heartofthelakes.co.uk

Old Police House Apartment ★★★★
Contact: Mrs Joan Carver, Old Police House Apartment, The Old Police House, Patterdale, Penrith CA11 0PJ
T: (017684) 82760
E: carver@oldpolicehse.fsnet.co.uk
I: www.oldpolicehouseapartment.co.uk

PENRITH
Cumbria

Bankside ★★★★
Contact: Mr Peter Durbin, Cumbrian Cottages, 2 Lonsdale Street, Carlisle CA1 1DB
T: (01228) 599960
F: (01228) 599970
E: enquiries@cumbrian-cottages.co.uk
I: www.cumbrian-cottages.co.uk

Barn Croft and Barn End ★★★★
Contact: Mrs Brenda Walton, Carthanet, Soulby, Pooley Bridge, Penrith CA11 0JF
T: (017684) 86376
E: brenda@waltoncottages.fsnet.co.uk

Croft House ★★
Contact: The Manager Dales Hol Cot Ref:3007, Carleton Business Park, Carleton New Road, Skipton BD23 2AA
T: (01756) 799821
F: (01756) 797012
E: info@dalesholcot.com
I: www.dalesholcot.com

Daisy Cottage ★★★★
Contact: Mr David Burton, Melbecks, Bassenthwaite, Keswick CA12 4QX
T: (017687) 76065
F: (017687) 76869
E: info@lakelandcottages.co.uk

Lavender Cottage ★★★★
Contact: Mr David Burton, Melbecks, Bassenthwaite, Keswick CA12 4QX
T: (017687) 76065
F: (017687) 76869
E: info@lakelandcottages.co.uk

Oak View Cottage ★★★★
Contact: Mr & Mrs David & Jackie Dearling, Bampton, Penrith CA10 2RQ
T: (01931) 713121
F: (01931) 713121
E: david.dearling@tesco.net

Skirwith Hall Cottage & Smithy Cottage ★★★-★★★★
Contact: Mrs Wilson, Skirwith Hall Cottage & Smithy Cottage, Skirwick Hall, Skirwith, Penrith CA10 1RH
T: (01768) 88241
F: (01768) 88241
E: idawilson@aol.com
I: www.eden-in-cumbria.co.uk/skirwith

Stonefold Cottages ★★★★
Contact: Mrs Gill Harrington, Stonefold Cottages, Stonefold, Newbiggin, Penrith CA11 0HP
T: (01768) 866383
E: gill@stonefold.co.uk
I: www.stonefold.co.uk

West View Cottages ★★★★
Contact: Mr & Mrs A J Grave, West View Farm, Winskill, Penrith CA10 1PD
T: (01768) 881356
F: (01768) 881356
E: westviewcottages@btinternet.com
I: www.eden-in-cumbria.co.uk/westview

Wetheral Cottages ★★★★
Contact: Mr John Lowrey, Wetheral Cottages, Great Salkeld, Penrith CA11 9NA
T: (01768) 898779
F: (01768) 898943
E: wetheralcottages@btopenworld.com
I: www.wetheralcottages.co.uk

PENRUDDOCK
Cumbria

Beckses Cottage ★★★★
Contact: Mr Peter Durbin, Cumbrian Cottages, 2 Lonsdale Street, Carlisle CA1 1DB
T: (01228) 599960
F: (01228) 599970
E: enquiries@cumbrian-cottages.co.uk
I: www.cumbrian-cottages.co.uk

Beckside Cottage ★★★
Contact: The Manager Dales Hol Cot Ref:2591, Carleton Business Park, Carleton New Road, Skipton BD23 2AA
T: (01756) 799821
F: (01756) 797012
E: info@dalesholcot.com
I: www.dalesholcot.com

Low Garth Cottage ★★★★
Contact: The Manager Dales Hol Cott Ref: 3317, Carleton Business Park, Carleton New Road, Skipton BD23 2AA
T: (01756) 790919
F: (01756) 797012
E: info@dalesholcot.com
I: www.dalesholcot.com

POOLEY BRIDGE
Cumbria

Barton Hall Farm Holiday Cottages ★★★★
Contact: Mrs Amanda Strong, Barton Hall Farm Holiday Cottages, Pooley Bridge, Penrith CA10 2NG
T: (017684) 86034
E: amanda@bartonhallfarmfsnet.co.uk

Beauthorn Coach House ★★★
Contact: Mr Martin Wardle, Lakes and Valleys, Bateman Fold Barn, Crook, Kendal LA8 8LN
T: (015394) 68103
F: (015394) 68104
E: lakesandvalleys@aol.com

Blacksmith's Cottages ★★★★
Contact: Mr Peter Durbin, Cumbrian Cottages, 2 Lonsdale Street, Carlisle CA1 1DB
T: (01228) 599960
F: (01228) 599970
E: enquiries@cumbrian-cottages.co.uk
I: www.cumbrian-cottages.co.uk

High Winder Cottages ★★★★
Contact: Mr R A Moss, High Winder House, Celleron, Tirril, Penrith CA10 2LS
T: (017684) 86997
F: (017684) 86997
E: mossr@highwinder.freeserve.co.uk
I: www.highwindercottages.co.uk

Winn's Cottage ★★★★
Contact: Mrs Jean Young, Winn's Cottage, Bowerbank, Pooley Bridge, Penrith CA10 2NG
T: (017684) 86642

PORTINSCALE
Cumbria

The Cottage and Cosey Cottage, Twentyman Court ★★★★
Contact: Mr David Brown, Portinscale, Applethwaite, Keswick CA12 5RF
T: (017687) 74324
E: information@keswickholidaycottages.co.uk
I: www.keswickcumbria.freeserve.co.uk

Grizedale View ★★★
Contact: Mr Peter Durbin, Cumbrian Cottages, 2 Lonsdale Street, Carlisle CA1 1DB
T: (01228) 599960
F: (01228) 599970
E: enquiries@cumbrian-cottages.co.uk
I: www.cumbrian-cottages.co.uk

High Portinscale Rating Applied For
Contact: Mr Peter Durbin, Cumbrian Cottages, 2 Lonsdale Street, Carlisle CA1 1DB
T: (01228) 599960
F: (01228) 599970
E: enquiries@cumbrian-cottages.co.uk
I: www.cumbrian-cottages.co.uk

Jasmine Cottage ★★★
Contact: Mr Peter Durbin, Cumbrian Cottages, 2 Lonsdale Street, Carlisle CA1 1DB
T: (01228) 599960
F: (01228) 599970
E: enquiries@cumbrian-cottages.co.uk
I: www.cumbrian-cottages.co.uk

Middle Howe ★★★★
Contact: Mr Peter Durbin, Cumbrian Cottages, 2 Lonsdale Street, Carlisle CA1 1DB
T: (01228) 599960
F: (01228) 599970
E: enquiries@cumbrian-cottages.co.uk
I: www.cumbrian-cottages.co.uk

Smithy Cottage ★★★
Contact: Mr Peter Durbin, Cumbrian Cottages, 2 Lonsdale Street, Carlisle CA1 1DB
T: (01228) 599960
F: (01228) 599970
E: enquiries@cumbrian-cottages.co.uk
I: www.cumbrian-cottages.co.uk

Stable Cottage ★★★
Contact: Mrs Margaret Pope, Thirnbeck, Portinscale, Applethwaite, Keswick CA12 5RD
T: (017687) 75161

Watendlath ★★★★
Contact: Mr Peter Durbin, Cumbrian Cottages, 2 Lonsdale Street, Carlisle CA1 1DB
T: (01228) 599960
F: (01228) 599970
E: enquiries@cumbrian-cottages.co.uk
I: www.cumbrian-cottages.co.uk

RAVENSTONEDALE
Cumbria

Moss Cottages ★★★
Contact: Mrs Shallcross, Moss Cottages, Newbiggin-on-Lune, Kirkby Stephen CA17 4NB
T: (015396) 23316
F: (015396) 23491
E: shallmoss@aol.com

REDMAIN
Cumbria

Huddlestone Cottage and The Hayloft ★★★★
Contact: Mrs Christine Neale, Huddlestone Cottage and The Hayloft, Pooley House, Redmain, Cockermouth CA13 0PZ
T: (01900) 825695
F: (01900) 829228
E: hudcot@lakesnw.co.uk
I: www.lakesnw.co.uk/hudcot

ROSTHWAITE
Cumbria

Borrowdale Self-Catering Holidays ★★★
Contact: Mr & Mrs Peter Davis-Merry, Borrowdale Self-Catering Holidays, Kiln How, Borrowdale, Keswick CA12 5XB
T: (017687) 77356
F: (017687) 77727
E: info@kilnhow.com
I: www.kilnhow.com

Castle How ★★★
Contact: Mr Peter Durbin, Cumbrian Cottages, 2 Lonsdale Street, Carlisle CA1 1DB
T: (01228) 599960
F: (01228) 599970
E: enquiries@cumbrian-cottages.co.uk
I: www.cumbrian-cottages.co.uk

Clare's Cottage ★★
Contact: Ms Janice Diamond, 20 James Street, Horwich, Bolton BL6 7QS
T: (01204) 668681
E: janctb@clarescottage.com
I: www.clarescottage.com

High Knott ★★★★
Contact: Mr Peter Durbin, Cumbrian Cottages, 2 Lonsdale Street, Carlisle CA1 1DB
T: (01228) 599960
F: (01228) 599970
E: enquiries@cumbrian-cottages.co.uk
I: www.cumbrian-cottages.co.uk

Larch Cottage ★★★
Contact: Mr David Burton, Melbecks, Bassenthwaite, Keswick CA12 4QX
T: (017687) 76065
F: (017687) 76869
E: info@lakelandcottages.co.uk
I: www.lakelandcottages.co.uk

Nokka and Lobstone Cottages ★★★
Contact: Mr Peter Durbin, Cumbrian Cottages, 2 Lonsdale Street, Carlisle CA1 1DB
T: (01228) 599960
F: (01228) 599970
E: enquiries@cumbrian-cottages.co.uk
I: www.cumbrian-cottages.co.uk

Thwaite How ★★★
Contact: Mr & Mrs Brewerton, 3 Sycamore Way, Market Bosworth, Nuneaton CV13 0LU
T: (01455) 290168

RUCKCROFT
Cumbria

Ruckcroft Cottage ★★★
Contact: Mr Peter Durbin, Cumbrian Cottages, 2 Lonsdale Street, Carlisle CA1 1DB
T: (01228) 599960
F: (01228) 599970
E: enquiries@cumbrian-cottages.co.uk
I: www.cumbrian-cottages.co.uk

RYDAL
Cumbria

Daffodils ★★★
Contact: Mrs Susan Jackson, Heart of the Lakes, Fisherbeck Mill, Old Lake Road, Ambleside LA22 0DH
T: (015394) 32321
F: (015394) 33251
E: info@heartofthelakes.co.uk
I: www.heartofthelakes.co.uk

Fox Cottage ★★★★
Contact: Mrs Susan Jackson, Heart of the Lakes, Fisherbeck Mill, Old Lake Road, Ambleside LA22 0DH
T: (015394) 32321
F: (015394) 33251
E: info@heartofthelakes.co.uk
I: www.heartofthelakes.co.uk

Hall Bank Cottage ★★
Contact: Mr Lambton, Rydal Estate Carter Jonas, 52 Kirkland, Kendal LA9 5AP
T: (01539) 722592
F: (01539) 729587
E: marilyn.staunton@carterjonas.co.uk

Hart Head Barn ★★★★
Contact: Mrs Susan Jackson, Heart of the Lakes, Fisherbeck Mill, Old Lake Road, Ambleside LA22 0DH
T: (015394) 32321
F: (015394) 33251
E: info@heartofthelakes.co.uk
I: www.heartofthelakes.co.uk

Rydal Mount Cottage ★★★★
Contact: Mrs Susan Jackson, Heart of the Lakes, Fisherbeck Mill, Old Lake Road, Ambleside LA22 0DH
T: (015394) 32321
F: (015394) 33251
E: info@heartofthelakes.co.uk
I: www.heartofthelakes.co.uk

ST JOHNS-IN-THE-VALE
Cumbria

Lowthwaite Cottage ★★★★
Contact: Mr Peter Durbin, Cumbrian Cottages, 2 Lonsdale Street, Carlisle CA1 1DB
T: (01228) 599960
F: (01228) 599970
E: enquiries@cumbrian-cottages.co.uk
I: www.cumbrian-cottages.co.uk

Pine Cottage ★★★
Contact: Mr David Burton, Melbecks, Bassenthwaite, Keswick CA12 4QX
T: (017687) 76065
F: (017687) 76869
E: info@lalelandcottages.co.uk

The Studio ★★★★
Contact: Mrs Jill Green, The Studio, Fornside House, St Johns-in-the-Vale, Keswick CA12 4TS
T: (017687) 79666
E: selfcatering@keswickholidays.co.uk
I: www.keswickholidays.co.uk

SATTERTHWAITE
Cumbria

Church Cottage ★★★
Contact: Mrs Susan Jackson, Heart of the Lakes, Fisherbeck Mill, Old Lake Road, Ambleside LA22 0DH
T: (015394) 32321
F: (015394) 33251
E: info@heartofthelakes.co.uk
I: www.heartofthelakes.co.uk

Hawkrigg House ★★★★
Contact: Mrs Susan Jackson, Heart of the Lakes, Fisherbeck Mill, Old Lake Road, Ambleside LA22 0DH
T: (015394) 32321
F: (015394) 33251
E: info@heartofthelakes.co.uk
I: www.heartofthelakes.co.uk

Tanwood Barn ★★★★
Contact: Mrs Susan Jackson, Heart of the Lakes, Fisherbeck Mill, Old Lake Road, Ambleside LA22 0DH
T: (015394) 32321
F: (015394) 33251
E: info@heartofthelakes.co.uk
I: www.heartofthelakes.co.uk

SAWREY
Cumbria

Anvil Cottage ★★★★
Contact: Mr Peter Durbin, Cumbrian Cottages, 2 Lonsdale Street, Carlisle CA1 1DB
T: (01228) 599960
F: (01228) 599970
E: enquiries@cumbrian-cottages.co.uk
I: www.cumbrian-cottages.co.uk

Apple Tree Cottage ★★★
Contact: Mr Paul Liddell, Belmont House, Lake Road, Bowness-on-Windermere, Windermere LA23 3BJ
T: (015394) 88855
F: (015394) 88857
E: bokkings@lakelovers.co.uk

2 Cunsey House ★★★
Contact: Country Holidays Ref: 11039, Holiday Cottages Group Owner Services Dept, Spring Mill, Earby, Barnoldswick BB94 0AA
T: 08700 723723
F: (01282) 844288
E: sales@holidaycottagesgroup.com
I: www.country-holidays.co.uk

Derwentwater Cottage ★★★
Contact: Mrs Anne Gallagher, Hideaways, The Minstrels Gallery, The Square, Hawkshead, Ambleside LA22 0NZ
T: (015394) 42435
F: (015394) 36178
E: bookings@lakeland-hideaways.co.uk
I: www.lakeland-hideaways.co.uk

The Forge ★★★
Contact: Mr Paul Liddell, Lakelovers, Belmont House, Lake Road, Bowness-on-Windermere, Windermere LA23 3BJ
T: (015394) 88855
F: (015394) 88857
E: bookings@lakelovers.co.uk
I: www.lakelovers.co.uk

Fountain Cottage ★★★
Contact: Mr Paul Liddell, Belmont House, Lake Road, Bowness-on-Windermere, Windermere LA23 3BJ
T: (015394) 88855
F: (015394) 88857
E: bookings@lakelovers.co.uk

Lakefield ★★★-★★★★
Contact: Mr & Mrs John and Ann Taylor, Lakefield, Near Sawrey, Sawrey, Ambleside LA22 0JZ
T: (015394) 36635
F: (015394) 36635
E: lakefieldacom@aol.com
I: lakefield.golakes.co.uk

Meadowside ★★★★
Contact: Mr Paul Liddell, Lakelovers, Belmont House, Lake Road, Bowness-on-Windermere, Windermere LA23 3BJ
T: (015394) 88855
F: (015394) 88857
E: bookings@lakelovers.co.uk
I: www.lakelovers.co.uk

Sawrey Stables ★★★★★
Contact: Mrs Anne Gallagher, Hideaways, The Minstrels Gallery, The Square, Hawkshead, Ambleside LA22 0NZ
T: (015394) 42435
F: (015394) 36178
E: bookings@lakeland-hideaways.co.uk
I: www.sawreystables.co.uk

Sunnyside Cottage ★★★★
Contact: Mr John Serginson, Waterside House, Newby Bridge, Ulverston LA12 8AN
T: (015395) 30024
F: (015395) 31932
E: john@lakelandcottageco.com
I: www.lakeland-cottge-company.co.uk

Top Garden Suite ★★★★
Contact: Mrs Susan Jackson, Fisherbeck Mill, Old Lake Road, Ambleside LA22 0DH
T: (015394) 32321
F: (015394) 33251
E: info@heartoflakes.co.uk

Town End Cottage
Rating Applied For
Contact: Mr Paul Liddell, Belmont House, Lake Road, Bowness-on-Windermere, Windermere LA23 3BJ
T: (015394) 88855
F: (015394) 88857
E: bokkings@lakelovers.co.uk

West Vale Cottage ★★★
Contact: Mrs Dee Pennington, West Vale Cottage, West Vale, Far Sawrey, Sawrey, Ambleside LA22 0LQ
T: (015394) 42817
F: (015394) 45302
E: enquiries@westvalecountryhouse.co.uk
I: www.westvalecountryhouse.co.uk

SEATHWAITE
Cumbria

Rose Cottage ★★★★
Contact: Mr John Serginson, Waterside House, Newby Bridge, Ulverston LA12 8AN
T: (015395) 30024
F: (015395) 31932
E: john@lakelandcottageco.com
I: www.lakelandcottageco.com

SEATOLLER
Cumbria

The Barn ★★★★
Contact: Mr Peter Durbin, Cumbrian Cottages, 2 Lonsdale Street, Carlisle CA1 1DB
T: (01228) 599960
F: (01228) 599970
E: enquiries@cumbrian-cottages.co.uk
I: www.cumbrian-cottages.co.uk

Bell Crags ★★★
Contact: Mr David Burton, Melbecks, Bassenthwaite, Keswick CA12 4QX
T: (017687) 76065
F: (017687) 76869
E: info@lakelandcottages.co.uk
I: www.lakelandcottages.co.uk

Brasscam ★★★★
Contact: Mr Peter Durbin, Cumbrian Cottages, 2 Lonsdale Street, Carlisle CA1 1DB
T: (01228) 599960
F: (01228) 599970
E: enquiries@cumbrian-cottages.co.uk
I: www.cumbrian-cottages.co.uk

Ghyllside ★★★
Contact: Mr Peter Durbin, Cumbrian Cottages, 2 Lonsdale Street, Carlisle CA1 1DB
T: (01228) 599960
F: (01228) 599970
E: enquiries@cumbrian-cottages.co.uk
I: www.cumbrian-cottages.co.uk

Hause Gill ★★★
Contact: Mr David Burton, Melbecks, Bassenthwaite, Keswick CA12 4QX
T: (017687) 76065
F: (017687) 76869
E: info@lakelandcottages.co.uk
I: www.lakelandcottages.co.uk

High Stile ★★★
Contact: Mr David Burton, Melbecks, Bassenthwaite, Keswick CA12 4QX
T: (017687) 76065
F: (017687) 76869
E: info@lakelandcottages.co.uk
I: www.lakelandcottages.co.uk

Honister ★★★
Contact: Mr Peter Durbin, Cumbrian Cottages, 2 Lonsdale Street, Carlisle CA1 1DB
T: (017687) 71071
F: (017687) 75036
E: info@lakelandcottages.co.uk
I: www.cumbrian-cottages.co.uk

SEDBERGH
Cumbria

The Bungalow & The Cottage ★★★
Contact: The Manager Dales Hol Cot Ref:3302/3303, Carleton Business Park, Carleton New Road, Skipton BD23 2AA
T: (01756) 799821
F: (01756) 797012
E: info@dalesholcot.com
I: www.dalesholcot.com

Carriers Cottage ★★★
Contact: Mr T & Mrs K Ellis, Sun Ridge, Joss Lane, Sedbergh LA10 5AS
T: (015396) 20566

Fell House ★★★★
Contact: Mr Stephen Wickham, 14 Home Meadows, Billericay CM12 9HQ
T: (01277) 652746
E: steve@higround.co.uk
I: www.higround.co.uk

Ingmire Hall ★★★★
Contact: Mr & Mrs S Gardner, Ingmire Hall, Sedbergh LA10 5HR
T: (015396) 21012
F: (015396) 21116

Merlin Cottage ★★★★
Contact: Mrs Christine Linley, 31 Greenside, Underbarrow, Kendal LA9 5DU
T: (01539) 738677
F: (01539) 740615
E: christine@merlincottage.com
I: www.merlincottage.com

The Mount ★★★★
Contact: Mrs Suzan Sedgwick, Howgill Lane, Sedbergh LA10 5HE
T: (015396) 20252
E: lockbank@uk4free.net
I: www.themountatlockbank.com

4 Railway Cottages ★★★
Contact: Mrs Mills, 131 Glendale Gardens, Leigh-on-Sea SS9 2BE
T: (01702) 478846
F: (01702) 482088
E: trewen@clara.co.uk
I: www.dalescottages.com

Randall Hill Cottage ★★★
Contact: The Manager Dales Hol Cot Ref:2177, Carleton Business Park, Carleton New Road, Skipton BD23 2AA
T: (01756) 799821
F: (01756) 797012
E: info@dalesholcot.com
I: www.dalesholcot.com

Thwaite Cottage ★★★★
Contact: Mrs Dorothy Parker, Thwaite Farm, Howgill, Sedbergh LA10 5JD
T: (015396) 20493
F: (015396) 20493
E: thwaitecottage@yahoo.co.uk

SEDGWICK
Cumbria

High House Barn ★★★★★
Contact: Mr Peter Durbin, Cumbrian Cottages, 2 Lonsdale Street, Carlisle CA1 1DB
T: (01228) 599960
F: (01228) 599970
E: enquiries@cumbrian-cottages.co.uk
I: www.cumbrian-cottages.co.uk

Woodside Cottage ★★★★
Contact: Mr Peter Durbin, Cumbrian Cottages, 2 Lonsdale Street, Carlisle CA1 1DB
T: (01228) 599960
F: (01228) 599970
E: enquiries@cumbrian-cottages.co.uk
I: www.cumbrian-cottages.co.uk

SETMURTHY
Cumbria

Derwent View ★★★
Contact: Mr Peter Durbin, Cumbrian Cottages, 2 Lonsdale Street, Carlisle CA1 1DB
T: (01228) 599960
F: (01228) 599970
E: enquiries@cumbrian-cottages.co.uk
I: www.cumbrian-cottages.co.uk

SILECROFT
Cumbria

Lowsha Cottage ★★★
Contact: The Manager Dales Hol Cot Ref:3126, Carleton Business Park, Carleton New Road, Skipton BD23 2AA
T: (01756) 799821
F: (01756) 797012
E: info@dalesholcot.com
I: www.dalesholcot.com

SKELWITH BRIDGE
Cumbria

Brathay View ★★★
Contact: Mrs Susan Jackson, Heart of the Lakes, Fisherbeck Mill, Old Lake Road, Ambleside LA22 0DH
T: (015394) 32321
F: (015394) 33251
E: info@heartofthelakes.co.uk
I: www.heartofthelakes.co.uk

Brow Foot ★★★★
Contact: Mrs Susan Jackson, Heart of the Lakes, Fisherbeck Mill, Old Lake Road, Ambleside LA22 0DH
T: (015394) 32321
F: (015394) 33251
E: info@heartofthelakes.co.uk
I: www.heartofthelakes.co.uk

The Coach House ★★★★
Contact: Mr Paul Liddell, Lakelovers, Belmont House, Lake Road, Bowness-on-Windermere, Windermere LA23 3BJ
T: (015394) 88855
F: (015394) 88857
E: bookings@lakelovers.co.uk
I: www.lakelovers.co.uk

The Courtyard ★★★
Contact: Mrs Susan Jackson, Heart of the Lakes, Fisherbeck Mill, Old Lake Road, Ambleside LA22 0DH
T: (015394) 32321
F: (015394) 33251
E: info@heartofthelakes.co.uk
I: www.heartofthelakes.co.uk

Ghyll Pool Lodge ★★★
Contact: Mr Peter Durbin, Cumbrian Cottages, 2 Lonsdale Street, Carlisle CA1 1DB
T: (01228) 599960
F: (01228) 599970
E: enquiries@cumbrian-cottages.co.uk
I: www.cumbrian-cottages.co.uk

Greenbank ★★★★
Contact: Mrs Lilian Green, Little Greenbank & Low Greenbank, Skelwith Bridge, Clappersgate, Ambleside LA22 9NW
T: (015394) 33236
E: info@visitgreenbank.co.uk
I: www.visitgreenbank.co.uk

Ivy Cottage ★★★★
Contact: Mr Peter Durbin, Cumbrian Cottages, 2 Lonsdale Street, Carlisle CA1 1DB
T: (01228) 599960
F: (01228) 599970
E: enquiries@cumbrian-cottages.co.uk
I: www.cumbrian-cottages.co.uk

Merlin's ★★★★
Contact: Mrs Susan Jackson, Heart of the Lakes, Fisherbeck Mill, Old Lake Road, Ambleside LA22 0DH
T: (015394) 32321
F: (015394) 33251
E: info@heartofthelakes.co.uk
I: www.heartofthelakes.co.uk

2 Neaum Crag Court ★★★
Contact: Mr Peter Durbin, Cumbrian Cottages, 2 Lonsdale Street, Carlisle CA1 1DB
T: (01228) 599960
F: (01228) 599970
E: enquiries@cumbrian-cottages.co.uk
I: www.cumbrian-cottages.co.uk

Oakdene ★★★★
Contact: Mrs Susan Jackson, Heart of the Lakes, Fisherbeck Mill, Old Lake Road, Ambleside LA22 0DH
T: (015394) 32321
F: (015394) 33251
E: info@heartofthelakes.co.uk
I: www.heartofthelakes.co.uk

Ramblers Rest ★★★★
Contact: Mr Paul Liddell, Lakelovers, Belmont House, Lake Road, Bowness-on-Windermere, Windermere LA23 3BJ
T: (015394) 88855
F: (015394) 88857
E: bookings@lakelovers.co.uk
I: www.lakelovers.co.uk

Tarn Hows ★★
Contact: Mr Paul Liddell, Lakelovers, Belmont House, Lake Road, Bowness-on-Windermere, Windermere LA23 3BJ
T: (015394) 88855
F: (015394) 88857
E: bookings@lakelovers.co.uk
I: www.lakelovers.co.uk

Tarn Moss ★★★
Contact: Mr Peter Durbin, Cumbrian Cottages, 2 Lonsdale Street, Carlisle CA1 1DB
T: (01228) 599960
F: (01228) 599970
E: enquiries@cumbrian-cottages.co.uk
I: www.cumbrian-cottages.co.uk

Wordsworth, Neaum Crag ★★★
Contact: Mrs Susan Jackson, Heart of the Lakes, Fisherbeck Mill, Old Lake Road, Ambleside LA22 0DH
T: (015394) 32321
F: (015394) 33251
E: info@heartofthelakes.co.uk
I: www.heartofthelakes.co.uk

SKELWITH FOLD
Cumbria

Hillcrest ★★★★
Contact: Mr Paul Liddell, Lakelovers, Belmont House, Lake Road, Bowness-on-Windermere, Windermere LA23 3BJ
T: (015394) 88855
F: (015394) 88857
E: bookings@lakelovers.co.uk
I: www.lakelovers.co.uk

The Hobbit ★★★
Contact: Mr Peter Durbin, Cumbrian Cottages, 2 Lonsdale Street, Carlisle CA1 1DB
T: (01228) 599960
F: (01228) 599970
E: enquiries@cumbrian-cottages.co.uk
I: www.cumbrian-cottages.co.uk

Rivendell Cottage ★★★
Contact: Mrs Susan Jackson, Heart of the Lakes, Fisherbeck Mill, Old Lake Road, Ambleside LA22 0DH
T: (015394) 32321
F: (015394) 33251
E: info@heartofthelakes.co.uk
I: www.heartofthelakes.co.uk

SKINBURNESS
Cumbria

Lucknow ★★★★
Contact: Mrs Joy Ross, 10 Brittons Close, Sharnbrook, Bedford MK44 1PN
T: 07774 888480
F: 07860 275142
E: lucknowcottage@btinternet.com
I: www.btinternet.com/~lucknowcottage

SMARDALE
Cumbria

Leases ★★★
Contact: Mrs Christina Galloway, Leases, Swardale, Soulby, Kirkby Stephen CA17 4HQ
T: (017683) 71198
E: leasesgal@aol.com

SOCKBRIDGE
Cumbria

Eastwards Cottage ★★★★
Contact: Mr Martin Wardle, Lakes and Valleys, Bateman Fold Barn, Crook, Kendal LA8 8LN
T: (015394) 68103
F: (015394) 68104
E: lakesandvalleys@aol.com
I: www.lakesandvalleys.co.uk

SOUTHWAITE
Cumbria

Serendipity Cottage ★★★
Contact: The Manager Dales Hol Cot Ref:2814, Carleton Business Park, Carleton New Road, Skipton BD23 2AA
T: (01756) 799821
F: (01756) 797012
E: info@dalesholcot.com
I: www.dalesholcot.com

SPARK BRIDGE
Cumbria

Dicky Cragg ★★★
Contact: Mrs D Lever, 27 East Beach, Lytham, Lytham St Annes FY8 5EX
T: (01253) 736438
F: (01253) 731555
E: lettings@jgl.co.uk
I: www.jgl.co.uk/dickycragg

Riversdale ★★★
Contact: Mr John Serginson, Waterside House, Newby Bridge, Ulverston LA12 8AN
T: (015395) 30024
F: (015395) 31932
E: john@lakelandcottageco.com
I: www.lakeland-cottage-company.co.uk

Summer Hill Holidays ★★★-★★★★
Contact: Mrs Rosemary Campbell, Summer Hill Holidays, Summer Hill, Spark Bridge, Ulverston LA12 7SS
T: (01229) 861510
F: (01229) 861090
E: rosemary@summerhill.co.uk
I: www.summerhill.co.uk

Thurstonville High Lodge ★★
Contact: Mr R N Lord, Thurstonville, Lowick, Ulverston LA12 7SX
T: (01229) 861271
F: (01229) 861271

The Turners Cottage ★★★
Contact: Mr Philip Johnston, The Coppermines Coniston Cottages, The Estate Office, The Bridge, Coniston LA21 8HJ
T: (015394) 41765
E: bookings@coppermines.co.uk
I: www.coppermines.co.uk

STAINTON
Cumbria

The Cottage at Andrew House ★★★
Contact: The Manager Dales Hol Cot Ref:2098, Carleton Business Park, Carleton New Road, Skipton BD23 2AA
T: (01756) 799821
F: (01756) 797012
E: info@dalesholcot.com
I: www.dalesholcot.com

Mill Race View ★★★
Contact: The Manager Dales Hol Cot Ref:2264, Carleton Business Park, Carleton New Road, Skipton BD23 2AA
T: (01756) 799821
F: (01756) 797012
E: info@dalesholcot.com
I: www.dalesholcot.com

STAIR
Cumbria

Clairgarth ★★★
Contact: Mr Peter Durbin, Cumbrian Cottages, 2 Lonsdale Street, Carlisle CA1 1DB
T: (01228) 599960
F: (01228) 599970
E: enquiries@cumbrian-cottages.co.uk
I: www.cumbrian-cottages.co.uk

Grizedale Cottage ★★★
Contact: Mr David Burton, Melbecks, Bassenthwaite, Keswick CA12 4QX
T: (017687) 76065
F: (017687) 76869
E: info@lakelandcottages.co.uk
I: www.lakelandcottages.co.uk

Stair Mill ★★★
Contact: Mrs Jacqueline Williams, Stair, Keswick CA12 5UF
T: (017687) 78333

STAPLETON
Cumbria

Drove Cottage ★★★
Contact: Mr & Mrs K Hope
T: (01697) 748202
F: (01697) 748054
E: droveinn@hotmail.com

STAVELEY Cumbria

Ashleigh ★★★★
Contact: Mr John Serginson, Waterside House, Newby Bridge, Ulverston LA12 8AN
T: (015395) 30024
F: (015395) 31932
E: john@lakelandcottageco.com
I: www.lakeland-cottage-company.co.uk

Avondale ★★★
Contact: Miss Helen Whalley, 2 Lynstead, Thornbarrow Road, Windermere LA23 2DG
T: (015394) 45713
E: enquiries@avondale.uk.net
I: www.avondale.uk.net

Bobbin Cottage ★★★
Contact: The Manager Dales Hol Cot Ref:2284, Carleton Business Park, Carleton New Road, Skipton BD23 2AA
T: (01756) 799821
F: (01756) 797012
E: info@dalesholcot.com
I: www.dalesholcot.com

Brunt Knott Farm Holiday Cottages ★★★
Contact: Mr & Mrs William and Margaret Beck, Brunt Knott Farm Holiday Cottages, Brunt Knott Farm, Staveley, Kendal LA8 9QX
T: (01539) 821030
F: (01539) 821221
E: margaret@bruntknott.demon.co.uk
I: www.bruntknott.demon.co.uk

The Chapel ★★★
Contact: Mr Peter Durbin, Cumbrian Cottages, 2 Lonsdale Street, Carlisle CA1 1DB
T: (01228) 599960
F: (01228) 599970
E: enquiries@cumbrian-cottages.co.uk
I: www.cumbrian-cottages.co.uk

Ghyll Bank House ★★★
Contact: Mrs Sylvia Beaty, Garnett House Farm, Burnesdie, Underbarrow, Kendal LA8 5SF
T: (01539) 724542
F: (01539) 724542
E: info@garnetthousefarm.co.uk
I: www.garnetthousefarm.co.uk

Marsden ★★★
Contact: Mr Peter Durbin, Cumbrian Cottages, 2 Lonsdale Street, Carlisle CA1 1DB
T: (01228) 599960
F: (01228) 599970
E: enquiries@cumbrian-cottages.co.uk
I: www.cumbrian-cottages.co.uk

Mill House ★★★
Contact: Mr Peter Durbin, Cumbrian Cottages, 2 Lonsdale Street, Carlisle CA1 1DB
T: (01228) 599960
F: (01228) 599970
E: enquiries@cumbrian-cottages.co.uk
I: www.cumbrian-cottages.co.uk

Nook House ★★★
Contact: Mr John Serginson, Waterside House, Newby Bridge, Ulverston LA12 8AN
T: (015395) 30024
F: (015395) 31932
E: john@lakelandcottageco.com
I: www.lakeland.cottage-company.co.uk

STAVELEY-IN-CARTMEL Cumbria

April Cottage ★★★
Contact: Mr Peter Durbin, Cumbrian Cottages, 2 Lonsdale Street, Carlisle CA1 1DB
T: (01228) 599960
F: (01228) 599970
E: enquiries@cumbrian-cottages.co.uk
I: www.cumbrian-cottages.co.uk

Croft Cottage ★★★
Contact: Mr Paul Liddell, Lakelovers, Belmont House, Lake Road, Bowness-on-Windermere, Windermere LA23 3BJ
T: (015394) 88855
F: (015394) 88857
E: bookings@lakelovers.co.uk
I: www.lakelovers.co.uk

Staveley House Cottage ★★★★
Contact: Mr John Serginson, Waterside House, Newby Bridge, Ulverston LA12 8AN
T: (015395) 30024
F: (015395) 31932
E: john@lakelandcottageco.com
I: www.lakeland-cottage-company.co.uk

THORNTHWAITE Cumbria

Barf Cottage ★★★
Contact: Mrs Susan Jackson, Heart of the Lakes, Fisherbeck Mill, Old Lake Road, Ambleside LA22 0DH
T: (015394) 32321
F: (015394) 33251
E: info@heartofthelakes.co.uk
I: www.heartofthelakes.co.uk

Hallgarth ★★★★
Contact: Mr Peter Durbin, Cumbrian Cottages, 2 Lonsdale Street, Carlisle CA1 1DB
T: (01228) 599960
F: (01228) 599970
E: enquiries@cumbrian-cottages.co.uk
I: www.cumbrian-cottages.co.uk

Harriets Hideaway ★★★★
Contact: Mrs Jane Miller, 24 Elm Court, Whickham, Newcastle upon Tyne NE16 4PS
T: (0191) 488 0549
F: (0191) 422 3303
E: mtekk@ic24.net

Holly Bank Cottage ★★★★
Contact: Ms Kate Danchin, Thornthwaite, Keswick CA12 5SA
T: (017687) 78192
E: enquiries@hollybankcottage.co.uk
I: www.hollybankcottage.co.uk

The Larches ★★★
Contact: Mr David Burton, Melbecks, Bassenthwaite, Keswick CA12 4QX
T: (017687) 76065
F: (017687) 76869
E: info@lakelandcottages.co.uk
I: www.lakelandcottages.co.uk

Old School House ★★★
Contact: Mr Peter Durbin, Cumbrian Cottages, 2 Lonsdale Street, Carlisle CA1 1DB
T: (01228) 599960
F: (01228) 599970
E: enquiries@cumbrian-cottages.co.uk
I: www.cumbrian-cottages.co.uk

Seat Howe ★★★
Contact: Mrs Dorothy Bell, Seat Howe, Thornthwaite, Keswick CA12 5SQ
T: (017687) 78371

Talcomb ★★★
Contact: Mr Howard King, 14 Brooklands, Ponteland, Newcastle upon Tyne NE20 9LZ
E: hk.developments@virgin.net

Thornthwaite Grange ★★★
Contact: Mrs Joan Berwick, Thornthwaite Grange, Thornthwaite, Keswick CA12 5SA
T: (017687) 78205
E: joan_berwick@hotmail.com
I: www.thornthwaite-grange.co.uk

Thwaite Hill Cottage ★★
Contact: Mr David Burton, Melbecks, Bassenthwaite, Keswick CA12 4QX
T: (017687) 76065
F: (017687) 76869
E: info@lakelandcottages.co.uk
I: www.lakelandcottages.co.uk

THRELKELD Cumbria

1 The Barns ★★★
Contact: Mrs Joan Browne, Merritts Hill, Illogan, Redruth TR16 4DF
T: (01209) 215553
E: tom.joan@lineone.net

Blease Cottage ★★★★
Contact: Mr Peter Durbin, Cumbrian Cottages, 2 Lonsdale Street, Carlisle CA1 1DB
T: (01228) 599960
F: (01228) 599970
E: enquiries@cumbrian-cottages.co.uk
I: www.cumbrian-cottages.co.uk

Blencathra Centre – Latrigg View, Derwent View, Borrowdale View★★★
Contact: Mr A Simms, Blencathra Centre, Threlkeld, Keswick CA12 4SG
T: (017687) 79601
F: (017687) 79264
E: enquiries.bl@field-studies-council.org

Heather View ★★★
Contact: Mr Peter Durbin, Cumbrian Cottages, 2 Lonsdale Street, Carlisle CA1 1DB
T: (01228) 599960
F: (01228) 599970
E: enquiries@cumbrian-cottages.co.uk
I: www.cumbrian-cottages.co.uk

Katellen Cottage ★★★
Contact: Mr Peter Durbin, Cumbrian Cottages, 2 Lonsdale Street, Carlisle CA1 1DB
T: (01228) 599960
F: (01228) 599970
E: enquiries@cumbrian-cottages.co.uk
I: www.cumbrian-cottages.co.uk

Latcrag ★★★★
Contact: Mrs Dorothy Benson, High Row Farm, Threlkeld, Keswick CA12 4SF
T: (017687) 79256

Lingclose Cottage ★★★★
Contact: The Manager Dales Hol Cot Ref:2469, Carleton Business Park, Carleton New Road, Skipton BD23 2AA
T: (01756) 799821
F: (01756) 797012
E: info@dalesholcot.com
I: www.dalesholcot.com

Old Manse Barn ★★★
Contact: Mrs Deadman, Old Manse Barn, Threlkeld, Keswick CA12 4SQ
T: (017687) 79270
E: jon@deadman.freeserve.co.uk
I: www.deadman.freeserve.co.uk

The Old School House ★★★★
Contact: Ms Lucy Swarbrick, 12 Bonville Chase, Altrincham WA14 4QA
T: (0161) 928 6290
E: info@cottageinthethrelkeld.co.uk

Townhead Barn ★★★
Contact: Mr David Burton, Melbecks, Bassenthwaite, Keswick CA12 4QX
T: (017687) 76065
F: (017687) 76869
E: info@lakelandcottages.co.uk
I: www.lakelandcottages.co.uk

Townhead Byre ★★★
Contact: Mr David Burton, Melbecks, Bassenthwaite, Keswick CA12 4QX
T: (017687) 76065
F: (017687) 76869
E: info@lakelandcottages.co.uk
I: www.lakelandcottages.co.uk

White Pike ★★★★
Contact: Mr Peter Durbin, Cumbrian Cottages, 2 Lonsdale Street, Carlisle CA1 1DB
T: (01228) 599960
F: (01228) 599970
E: enquiries@cumbrian-cottages.co.uk
I: www.cumbrian-cottages.co.uk

THURSTONFIELD Cumbria

The Tranquil Otter Lodges ★★★★-★★★★★
Contact: Richard & Wendy Wise
T: (01228) 576661
F: (01228) 576662
E: info@tranquilotter@aol.com
I: www.thetranquilotter.co.uk

TIRRIL
Cumbria

Tirril Farm Cottages ★★★★
Contact: Mr David Owens, Tirril View, Tirril, Penrith CA10 2JE
T: (01768) 864767
F: (01768) 864767
E: enquiries@tirrilfarmcottages.co.uk
I: www.tirrilfarmcottages.co.uk

TORVER
Cumbria

Brocklebank Ground Cottages Old Pottery, Old Stable, Old Dairy★★★
Contact: Mr Philip Johnston, The Coppermines Coniston Cottages, The Estate Office, The Bridge, Coniston LA21 8HJ
T: (015394) 41765
E: bookings@coppermines.co.uk
I: www.coppermines.co.uk

Ellice Howe ★★★★
Contact: Mr Paul Liddell, Lakelovers, Belmont House, Lake Road, Bowness-on-Windermere, Windermere LA23 3BJ
T: (015394) 88855
F: (015394) 88857
E: bookings@lakelovers.co.uk
I: www.lakelovers.co.uk

Scarr Head Cottage ★★★★
Contact: Mr Peter Durbin, Cumbrian Cottages, 2 Lonsdale Street, Carlisle CA1 1DB
T: (01228) 599960
F: (01228) 599970
E: enquiries@cumbrian-cottages.co.uk
I: www.cumbrian-cottages.co.uk

Station House & Station Cottage★★★
Contact: Mr Philip Johnston, The Coppermines Coniston Cottages, The Estate Office, The Bridge, Coniston LA21 8HJ
T: (015394) 41765
F: (015394) 41944
E: info@coppermines.co.uk
I: www.coppermines.co.uk

Sunny Bank Mill ★★★
Contact: Mr Paul Liddell, Lakelovers, Belmont House, Lake Road, Bowness-on-Windermere, Windermere LA23 3BJ
T: (015394) 88855
F: (015394) 88857
E: bookings@lakelovers.co.uk
I: www.lakelovers.co.uk

TROUTBECK
Cumbria

1 & 2 Butt Hill Cottage ★★★-★★★★
Contact: Mr Paul Liddell, Lakelovers, Belmont House, Lake Road, Bowness-on-Windermere, Windermere LA23 3BJ
T: (015394) 88855
F: (015394) 88857
E: bookings@lakelovers.co.uk
I: www.lakelovers.co.uk

Barn Cottage ★★★
Contact: Mr Paul Liddell, Lakelovers, Belmont House, Lake Road, Bowness-on-Windermere, Windermere LA23 3BJ
T: (015394) 88855
F: (015394) 88857
E: bookings@lakelovers.co.uk
I: www.lakelovers.co.uk

Betty's Cottage ★★★★
Contact: Mrs Susan Jackson, Heart of the Lakes, Fisherbeck Mill, Old Lake Road, Ambleside LA22 0DH
T: (015394) 32321
F: (015394) 33251
E: info@heartofthelakes.co.uk
I: www.heartofthelakes.co.uk

Fell Cottage ★★★★
Contact: Mr Paul Liddell, Lakelovers, Belmont House, Lake Road, Bowness-on-Windermere, Windermere LA23 3BJ
T: (015394) 88855
F: (015394) 88857
E: bookings@lakelovers.co.uk
I: www.lakelovers.co.uk

Field Cottage ★★★★
Contact: Mrs Susan Jackson, Fisherbeck Mill, Old Lake Road, Ambleside LA22 0DH
T: (015394) 32321
F: (015394) 33251
E: info@heartofthelakes.co.uk

Glenside ★★★
Contact: Mrs Susan Jackson, Heart of the Lakes, Fisherbeck Mill, Old Lake Road, Ambleside LA22 0DH
T: (015394) 32321
F: (015394) 33251
E: info@heartofthelakes.co.uk
I: www.heartofthelakes.co.uk

Granary Cottage ★★★
Contact: Mr Peter Durbin, Cumbrian Cottages, 2 Lonsdale Street, Carlisle CA1 1DB
T: (01228) 599960
F: (01228) 599970
E: enquiries@cumbrian-cottages.co.uk
I: www.cumbrian-cottages.co.uk

Holbeck Ghyll Lodge ★★★★
Contact: Mrs Maggie Kaye, Holmdene, Stoney Bank Road, Thongsbridge, Holmfirth, Huddersfield HD9 7SL
T: (01484) 684605
F: (01484) 689051
E: maggiekaye@hotmail.com

Ivy Cottage ★★★
Contact: Mr Paul Liddell, Lakelovers, Belmont House, Lake Road, Bowness-on-Windermere, Windermere LA23 3BJ
T: (015394) 88855
F: (015394) 88857
E: bookings@lakelovers.co.uk
I: www.lakelovers.co.uk

Knotts Farm Cottage ★★★
Contact: Mrs Susan Jackson, Heart of the Lakes, Fisherbeck Mill, Old Lake Road, Ambleside LA22 0DH
T: (015394) 32321
F: (015394) 33251
E: info@heartofthelakes.co.uk
I: www.heartofthelakes.co.uk

Knotts Farmhouse ★★★★
Contact: Mrs Susan Jackson, Heart of the Lakes, Fisherbeck Mill, Old Lake Road, Ambleside LA22 0DH
T: (015394) 32321
F: (015394) 33251
E: info@heartofthelakes.co.uk
I: www.heartofthelakes.co.uk

Long Mire Yeat ★★★
Contact: Mrs Susan Jackson, Heart of the Lakes, Fisherbeck Mill, Old Lake Road, Ambleside LA22 0DH
T: (015394) 32321
F: (015394) 33251
E: info@heartofthelakes.co.uk
I: www.heartofthelakes.co.uk

Low House ★★★★
Contact: Mrs Eileen Dale, Moorend, Troutbeck, Penrith CA11 0SX
T: (017687) 79388

Myley Ghyll ★★★★★
Contact: Mr Paul Liddell, Lakelovers, Belmont House, Lake Road, Bowness-on-Windermere, Windermere LA23 3BJ
T: (015394) 88855
F: (015394) 88857
E: bookings@lakelovers.co.uk
I: www.lakelovers.co.uk

Orchard Cottage ★★★★
Contact: Mr Paul Liddell, Lakelovers, Belmont House, Lake Road, Bowness-on-Windermere, Windermere LA23 3BJ
T: (015394) 88855
F: (015394) 88857
E: bookings@lakelovers.co.uk
I: www.lakelovers.co.uk

South View ★★★
Contact: Mr Peter Durbin, Cumbrian Cottages, 2 Lonsdale Street, Carlisle CA1 1DB
T: (01228) 599960
F: (01228) 599970
E: enquiries@cumbrian-cottages.co.uk
I: www.cumbrian-cottages.co.uk

Stamp Howe ★★★★
Contact: Mrs Susan Jackson, Heart of the Lakes, Fisherbeck Mill, Old Lake Road, Ambleside LA22 0DH
T: (015394) 32321
F: (015394) 33251
E: info@heartofthelakes.co.uk
I: www.heartofthelakes.co.uk

Storeythwaite ★★★★
Contact: Mrs Susan Jackson, Heart of the Lakes, Fisherbeck Mill, Old Lake Road, Ambleside LA22 0DH
T: (015394) 32321
F: (015394) 33251
E: info@heartofthelakes.co.uk
I: www.heartofthelakes.co.uk

Syke Villa ★★★
Contact: Mr Paul Liddell, Lakelovers, Belmont House, Lake Road, Bowness-on-Windermere, Windermere LA23 3BJ
T: (015394) 88855
F: (015394) 88857
E: bookings@lakelovers.co.uk
I: www.lakelovers.co.uk

Troutbeck Mews ★★★★
Contact: Mr & Mrs T J Bowers, Troutbeck Mews, Troutbeck Inn, Troutbeck, Penrith CA11 0SJ
T: (017684) 83635
F: (017684) 83928
E: enquiries@troutbeck-inn.com
I: www.troutbeck-inn.com

Wetherlam ★★★
Contact: Mrs Susan Jackson, Heart of the Lakes, Fisherbeck Mill, Old Lake Road, Ambleside LA22 0DH
T: (015394) 32321
F: (015394) 33251
E: info@heartofthelakes.co.uk
I: www.heartofthelakes.co.uk

TROUTBECK BRIDGE
Cumbria

Briery Lodge ★★★
Contact: Mrs Susan Jackson, Heart of the Lakes, Fisherbeck Mill, Old Lake Road, Ambleside LA22 0DH
T: (015394) 32321
F: (015394) 33251
E: info@heartofthelakes.co.uk
I: www.heartofthelakes.co.uk

Grooms Cottage ★★★★
Contact: Mr Peter Durbin, Cumbrian Cottages, 2 Lonsdale Street, Carlisle CA1 1DB
T: (01228) 599960
F: (01228) 599970
E: enquiries@cumbrian-cottages.co.uk
I: www.cumbrian-cottages.co.uk

Howarth Cottage ★★★
Contact: Mr Peter Durbin, Cumbrian Cottages, 2 Lonsdale Street, Carlisle CA1 1DB
T: (01228) 599960
F: (01228) 599970
E: enquiries@cumbrian-cottages.co.uk
I: www.cumbrian-cottages.co.uk

Lowther Cottage ★★★
Contact: Mrs Susan Jackson, Heart of the Lakes, Fisherbeck Mill, Old Lake Road, Ambleside LA22 0DH
T: (015394) 32321
F: (015394) 33251
E: info@heartofthelakes.co.uk
I: www.heartofthelakes.co.uk

Quarry Garth Lodge ★★★★
Contact: Mr Richard Bee, Lakeland Estates, Quarry Garth, Windermere LA23 1LF
T: (015394) 45111
F: (015394) 45333

School Cottage ★★★
Contact: Mrs Susan Jackson, Heart of the Lakes, Fisherbeck Mill, Old Lake Road, Ambleside LA22 0DH
T: (015394) 32321
F: (015394) 33251
E: info@heartofthelakes.co.uk
I: www.heartofthelakes.co.uk

ULDALE
Cumbria

Coach House and Groom Cottage ★★★
Contact: Mr D Hogarth, Cumbrian Cottages, 7 The Crescent, Carlisle CA1 1QW
T: (01228) 599960
F: (01228) 599970
E: enquiries@cumbrian-cottages.co.uk
I: www.cumbrian-cottages.co.uk

Knaifan Cottage ★★★★
Contact: Mr Peter Durbin, Cumbrian Cottages, 2 Lonsdale Street, Carlisle CA1 1DB
T: (01228) 599960
F: (01228) 599970
E: enquiries@cumbrian-cottages.co.uk
I: www.cumbrian-cottages.co.uk

Trusmadoor ★★★★
Contact: Mr Peter Durbin, Cumbrian Cottages, 2 Lonsdale Street, Carlisle CA1 1DB
T: (01228) 599960
F: (01228) 599970
E: enquiries@cumbrian-cottages.co.uk
I: www.cumbrian-cottages.co.uk

ULLOCK
Cumbria

Tree Tops ★★★★
Contact: The Manager Dales Hol Cot Ref:2884, Carleton Business Park, Carleton New Road, Skipton BD23 2AA
T: (01756) 799821
F: (01756) 797012
E: info@dalesholcot.com
I: www.dalesholcot.com

ULLSWATER
Cumbria

Cherry Holm Bungalow ★★★★
Contact: Mrs Susanne Sheard, 7 Bark Lane, Addingham, Ilkley LS29 0RA
T: (01943) 830766

Ghyll Cottage ★★★★
Contact: Mrs Elizabeth Darbyshire, Crossgates Farm, Hartsop, Patterdale, Ullswater, Penrith CA11 0NZ
T: (017684) 82566
F: (017684) 82566
E: erdarbyshire@aol.com
I: www.lakesinfo.com/ghyllcottage

Knottsbank and Halsteads Garden Cottage★★★★
Contact: Mr C Riley & Miss M George, Woodbank, The Knotts, Watermillock, Penrith CA11 0JP
T: (017684) 86355

Lakefield ★★★★
Contact: Mrs Susan Jackson, Heart of the Lakes, Fisherbeck Mill, Old Lake Road, Ambleside LA22 0DH
T: (015394) 32321
F: (015394) 33251
E: info@heartofthelakes.co.uk
I: www.heartofthelakes.co.uk

Land Ends ★★★
Contact: Ms Barbara Holmes
T: (017684) 86438
F: (017684) 86959
E: infolandends@btinternet.com
I: www.landends.co.uk

Low Wood View ★★★
Contact: Mrs Jennifer Wear, Green Lane, Hartsop, Ullswater, Penrith CA11 0NZ
T: (017684) 82396

Patterdale Hall Estate ★★-★★★
Contact: Ms Sue Kay, Estate Office Patterdale Hall Estate, Glenridding, Penrith CA11 0PJ
T: (017684) 82308
F: (017684) 82308
E: welcome@patterdalehallestate.com
I: www.patterdalehallestate.com

Swarthbeck Farm Holiday Cottages ★★★-★★★★
Contact: Mr & Mrs W H Parkin, Swarthbeck Farm, Howtown, Penrith CA10 2ND
T: (017684) 86432
E: whparkin@ukonline.co.uk
I: www.cumbria.com/horsehols

ULPHA
Cumbria

Brigg House Cottage ★★★★
Contact: Mr Philip Johnston, The Coppermines Coniston Cottages, The Estate Office, The Bridge, Coniston LA21 8HJ
T: (015394) 41765
E: bookings@coppermines.co.uk
I: www.coppermines.co.uk

Fishermans Cottage (Church House) ★★★★
Contact: Mr Philip Johnston, The Coppermines & Lakes Cottages, The Estate Office, The Bridge, Coniston LA21 8HJ
T: (015394) 41765
F: (015394) 41944
E: info@coppermines.co.uk
I: www.coppermines.co.uk

Low Birks ★★★★
Contact: Mr John Serginson, Waterside House, Newby Bridge, Ulverston LA12 8AN
T: (015395) 30024
F: (015395) 31932
E: john@lakelandcottageco.com
I: www.lakelandcottages.com

ULVERSTON
Cumbria

Ashlack Cottages ★★★★
Contact: Mrs Amanda Keegan, Ashlack Hall, Grizebeck, Kirkby-in-Furness LA17 7XN
T: (01229) 889108
F: (01229) 889111
E: ashlackcottages@hotmail.com
I: ashlackcottages.co.uk

The Falls ★★-★★★
Contact: Mrs Cheetham and Mrs Unger, The Falls, Mansriggs, Ulverston LA12 7PX
T: (01229) 583781
I: www.thefalls.co.uk

Lile Cottage at Gleaston Water Mill ★★★★
Contact: Mrs V Brereton, Lile Cottage at Gleaston Water Mill, Gleaston, Ulverston LA12 0QH
T: (01229) 869244
F: (01229) 869764
E: pigsty@watermill.co.uk
I: www.watermill.co.uk

Orchard Cottage ★★★
Contact: Mrs Martin, Mascalles Bungalow, Ulverston LA12 0TQ
T: (01229) 463591

3 Rosside Cottages ★★★
Contact: Sykes Cottages Ref:608, Sykes Cottages, York House, York Street, Chester CH1 3LR
T: (01244) 345700
F: (01244) 321442
E: info@sykescottages.co.uk
I: www.sykescottages.co.uk

Staveley Chapel Cottage Rating Applied For
Contact: Mr Peter Durbin, Cumbrian Cottages, 2 Lonsdale Street, Carlisle CA1 1DB
T: (01228) 599960
F: (01228) 599970
E: enquiries@cumbriancottages.co.uk

Swarthmoor Hall ★★★-★★★★
Contact: Mr Steven Deeming, Swarthmoor Hall, Swarthmoor, Ulverston LA12 0JQ
T: (01229) 583204
F: (01229) 583283
E: swarthmrhall@gn.apc.org
I: www.swarthmoorhall.co.uk

Waters Yeat Mill ★★★
Contact: Mr Peter Durbin, Cumbrian Cottages, 2 Lonsdale Street, Carlisle CA1 1DB
T: (01228) 599960
F: (01228) 599970
E: enquiries@cumbrian-cottages.co.uk
I: www.cumbrian-cottages.co.uk

Wood View & Stable End ★★★★
Contact: Mr John Serginson, Waterside House, Newby Bridge, Ulverston LA12 8AN
T: (015395) 30024
F: (015395) 31932
E: john@lakelandcottageco.com
I: www.lakeland-cottage-company.co.uk

UNDERBARROW
Cumbria

Honey Pot ★★★★★
Contact: Mr Peter Durbin, 2 Lonsdale Street, Carlisle CA1 1DB
T: (01228) 599960
F: (01228) 599970
E: enquiries@cumbrian-cottages.co.uk
I: www.cumbrian-cottages.co.uk

Nanny Goat ★★★★★
Contact: Mr Peter Durbin, 2 Lonsdale Street, Carlisle CA1 1DB
T: (01228) 599960
F: (01228) 599970
E: enquiries@cumbrian-cottages.co.uk
I: www.cumbrian-cottages.co.uk

UNDERSKIDDAW
Cumbria

Apartment 1, Oakfield House ★★★★
Contact: Mr Hogarth, Cumbrian Cottages, 2 Lonsdale Street, Carlisle CA1 1DB
T: (01228) 599960
F: (01228) 599970
E: enquiries@cumbrian-cottages.co.uk
I: www.cumbrian-cottages.co.uk

Garth Cottage ★★★★
Contact: Mr Peter Durbin, Cumbrian Cottages, 2 Lonsdale Street, Carlisle CA1 1DB
T: (01228) 599960
F: (01228) 599970
E: enquiries@cumbrian-cottages.co.uk
I: www.cumbrian-cottages.co.uk

White Stones Cottage ★★★
Contact: Mr & Mrs John Houldershaw, White Stones Cottage, Underskiddaw, Thornthwaite, Keswick CA12 4QD
T: (017687) 72762

WASDALE
Cumbria

Greendale Holiday Apartments ★★★
Contact: Mr & Mrs M D Burnett, Greendale Holiday Apartments, Greendale, Wasdale CA20 1EU
T: (019467) 26243

Sundial Cottage ★★★
Contact: Mr & Mrs Michael & Christine McKinley, Galesyke, Wasdale, Seascale CA20 1ET
T: (01946) 726267

Woodhow Farm Cottages Rating Applied For
Contact: Mr D J Kaminski, The Squirrels, 55 Broadway, Cheadle SK8 1LB
T: (0161) 428 9116
E: woodhow_farm@kaminsk.fsnet.co.uk
I: kaminski.fsnet.co.uk

Yewtree Farm ★★★-★★★★
Contact: Mrs Pauline Corley, Yewtree Farm, Wasdale Head, Wasdale, Seascale CA20 1EU
T: (019467) 26285
E: pauline@corleyp.freeserve.co.uk
I: www.yewtreeholidays.co.uk

WATER YEAT
Cumbria

Bee Bole House/The Farmstead/The Garden Cottage/Horseshoe Cottage ★★★-★★★★
Contact: Mr Philip Johnston, The Coppermines Coniston Cottages, The Estate Office, The Bridge, Coniston LA21 8HJ
T: (015394) 41765
F: (015394) 41944
E: info@coppermines.co.uk
I: www.coppermines.co.uk

Lake Bank Cottage ★★
Contact: Mr Philip Johnston, The Coppermines Coniston Cottages, The Estate Office, The Bridge, Coniston LA21 8HJ
T: (01539) 441765
E: bookings@coppermines.co.uk
I: www.coppermines.co.uk

WATERHEAD
Cumbria

Betamere ★★★★
Contact: Mrs Susan Jackson, Heart of the Lakes, Fisherbeck Mill, Old Lake Road, Ambleside LA22 0DH
T: (015394) 32321
F: (015394) 33251
E: info@heartofthelakes.co.uk
I: www.heartofthelakes.co.uk

Flat 2 ★★★
Contact: Mr Steve Elson, Waterhead Country Guest House, Coniston LA21 8AJ
T: (015394) 41442
F: (015394) 41476
E: waterheadsteve@aol.com
I: www.waterheadguesthouse.co.uk

High Borrans ★★★★
Contact: Mrs Susan Jackson, Heart of the Lakes, Fisherbeck Mill, Old Lake Road, Ambleside LA22 0DH
T: (015394) 32321
F: (015394) 33251
E: info@heartofthelakes.co.uk
I: www.heartofthelakes.co.uk

Jenkins Crag ★★★★★
Contact: Mrs Susan Jackson, Heart of the Lakes, Fisherbeck Mill, Old Lake Road, Ambleside LA22 0DH
T: (015394) 32321
F: (015394) 33251
E: info@heartofthelakes.co.uk
I: www.heartofthelakes.co.uk

Latterbarrow ★★★★★
Contact: Mrs Susan Jackson, Heart of the Lakes, Fisherbeck Mill, Old Lake Road, Ambleside LA22 0DH
T: (015394) 32321
F: (015394) 33251
E: info@heartofthelakes.co.uk
I: www.heartofthelakes.co.uk

Romney Grange ★★★★★
Contact: Mrs Susan Jackson, Heart of the Lakes, Fisherbeck Mill, Old Lake Road, Ambleside LA22 0DH
T: (015394) 32321
F: (015394) 33251
E: info@heartofthelakes.co.uk
I: www.heartofthelakes.co.uk

Skelghyll ★★★★
Contact: Mrs Susan Jackson, Heart of the Lakes, Fisherbeck Mill, Old Lake Road, Ambleside LA22 0DH
T: (015394) 32321
F: (015394) 33251
E: info@heartofthelakes.co.uk
I: www.heartofthelakes.co.uk

WATERMILLOCK
Cumbria

Beauthorn Cottage ★★★
Contact: Mr Martin Wardle, Lakes and Valleys, Bateman Fold Barn, Crook, Kendal LA8 8LN
T: (015394) 68103
F: (015394) 68104
E: lakesandvalleys@aol.com
I: www.lakesandvalleys.co.uk

Fair Place Cottage ★★★
Contact: CH Ref: 11224, 13649, Holiday Cottages Group Owner Services Dept, Spring Mill, Earby, Barnoldswick BB94 0AA
T: 08700 723723
F: (01282) 844288
E: sales@holidaycottagesgroup.com
I: www.country-holidays.co.uk

Gatesgarth Cottage ★★★
Contact: The Manager Dales Hol Cot Ref:2297, Carleton Business Park, Carleton New Road, Skipton BD23 2AA
T: (01756) 790919
F: (01756) 797012
E: info@dalesholcot.com
I: www.dalesholcot.com

Low House ★★★★★
Contact: Mrs Susan Jackson, Heart of the Lakes, Fisherbeck Mill, Old Lake Road, Ambleside LA22 0DH
T: (015394) 32321
F: (015394) 33251
E: info@heartofthelakes.co.uk
I: www.heartofthelakes.co.uk

Middlegate ★★★
Contact: Mrs Susan Jackson, Heart of the Lakes, Fisherbeck Mill, Old Lake Road, Ambleside LA22 0DH
T: (015394) 32321
F: (015394) 33251
E: info@heartofthelakes.co.uk
I: www.heartofthelakes.co.uk

WESTNEWTON
Cumbria

Home Farm Cottage ★★★★
Contact: Mr Martin King, Home Farmhouse, Westnewton, Carlisle CA7 3NX
T: (016973) 22480
E: martin@homefarmhouse.freeserve.co.uk
I: www.homefarmhouse.freeserve.co.uk

WESTWARD
Cumbria

High Hall Cottage ★★★★
Contact: Mrs Jane Thompson, High Hall, Westward, Wigton CA7 8NQ
T: (016973) 42584

WETHERAL
Cumbria

Geltsdale ★★★★★
Contact: Mr Peter Durbin, Cumbrian Cottages, 2 Lonsdale Street, Carlisle CA1 1DB
T: (01228) 599960
F: (01228) 599970
E: enquiries@cumbrian-cottages.co.uk
I: www.cumbrian-cottages.co.uk

Sarah's Cottage ★★★★★
Contact: Mr Peter Durbin, 2 Lonsdale Street, Carlisle CA1 1DB
T: (01228) 599960
F: (01228) 599970
E: enquiries@cumbrian-cottages.co.uk
I: www.cumbrian-cottages.co.uk

WHALE
Cumbria

Whale Farm Cottage ★★★★★
Contact: Mrs Lyn Page, Estate Office, Lowther, Hackthorpe, Penrith CA10 2HG
T: (01931) 712577
F: (01931) 712679
E: lyn.page@lowther.co.uk
I: www.lowther-estatecottages.co.uk

WHARTON
Cumbria

Lammerside Cottage ★★★★
Contact: The Manager Dales Hol Cottage Ref:3461, Carleton Business Park, Carleton New Road, Skipton BD23 2AA
T: (01756) 790919
F: (01756) 797012
E: info@dalesholcot.com
I: www.dalesholcot.com

WHITE MOSS
Cumbria

Ladywood Lodge ★★
Contact: Mrs Susan Jackson, Heart of the Lakes, Fisherbeck Mill, Old Lake Road, Ambleside LA22 0DH
T: (015394) 32321
F: (015394) 33251
E: info@heartofthelakes.co.uk
I: www.heartofthelakes.co.uk

WHITEHAVEN
Cumbria

Rosmerta & Brighida Cottages ★★★★
Contact: Mrs Jane Saxon, Rosmerta & Brighida Cottages, Moresby Hall, Moresby, Whitehaven CA28 6PJ
T: (01946) 696317
F: (01946) 694385
E: etc@moresbyhall.co.uk
I: www.moresbyhall.co.uk

Swallows Return and Owls Retreat ★★★★
Contact: Mr & Mrs James & Joyce Moore, Swallows Return and Owls Retreat, Moresby Hall Cottage, Moresby, Low Moresby, Whitehaven CA28 6PJ
T: (01946) 64078
E: mhc.moresby@virgin.net
I: www.cottageguide.co.uk/moresby

WIGTON
Cumbria

Foxgloves ★★★★
Contact: Mr & Mrs E Kerr, Greenrigg Farm, Westward, Wigton CA7 8AH
T: (016973) 42676
E: kerr_greenrigg@hotmail.com

Lane Head Apartment Rating Applied For
Contact: David & Marion Colborn & Ms Fitzgerald, Lane Head Apartment, Lane Head Farmhouse, Bolton Low Houses, Wigton CA7 8PA
T: (016973) 43888
F: (016973) 656134
E: info@laneheadapartment.co.uk

Leegate House Cottage ★★★
Contact: The Manager Dales Hol Cot Ref:2658, Carleton Business Park, Carleton New Road, Skipton BD23 2AA
T: (01756) 799821
F: (01756) 797012
E: info@dalesholcot.com
I: www.dalesholcot.com

WINDERMERE
Cumbria

The Abbey Coach House ★★★
Contact: Mrs P Bell, The Abbey Coach House, St Mary's Park, Windermere LA23 1AZ
T: (015394) 44027
F: (015394) 44027
E: abbeycoach@aol.com
I: www.oas.co.uk/ukcottages

Above Cot ★★★
Contact: Mr Peter Durbin, Cumbrian Cottages, 2 Lonsdale Street, Carlisle CA1 1DB
T: (01228) 599960
F: (01228) 599970
E: enquiries@cumbrian-cottages.co.uk
I: www.cumbrian-cottages.co.uk

Annisgarth ★★★
Contact: Mr Paul Liddell, Lakelovers, Belmont House, Lake Road, Bowness-on-Windermere, Windermere LA23 3BJ
T: (015394) 88855
F: (015394) 88857
E: bookings@lakelovers.co.uk
I: www.lakelovers.co.uk

April Cottage ★★★★
Contact: Mr Sam Lindley, G E Lindley & Son, Pontey Farm, Meltham Road, Honley, Huddersfield HD7
T: (01484) 661723
F: (01484) 663839
E: lindleys@ponteyfarm.fsnet.co.uk
I: www.lakeholidays.com

Bank Cottage ★★★★
Contact: Captain and Mrs Beighton, The Gables, 180 Singlewell Road, Gravesend DA11 7RB
T: (01474) 533028

Bears Den ★★★★
Contact: Mr Peter Durbin, Cumbrian Cottages, 2 Lonsdale Street, Carlisle CA1 1DB
T: (01228) 599960
F: (01228) 599970
E: enquiries@cumbrian-cottages.co.uk
I: www.cumbrian-cottages.co.uk

Beau Penny ★★★
Contact: Mr Paul Liddell, Lakelovers, Belmont House, Lake Road, Bowness-on-Windermere, Windermere LA23 3BJ
T: (015394) 88855
F: (015394) 88857
E: bookings@lakelovers.co.uk
I: www.lakelovers.co.uk

Beaumont ★★★
Contact: Mr & Mrs Bob Theobald, Beaumont, Thornbarrow Road, Windermere LA23 2DG
T: (015394) 45521
F: (015394) 46267
E: etc@beaumont-holidays.co.uk
I: beaumont-holidays.co.uk

Bedes Cottage ★★★
Contact: Mr Peter Durbin, Cumbrian Cottages, 2 Lonsdale Street, Carlisle CA1 1DB
T: (01228) 599960
F: (01228) 599970
E: enquiries@cumbrian-cottages.co.uk
I: www.cumbrian-cottages.co.uk

Beech How Cottage ★★★
Contact: Mr Paul Liddell, Lakelovers, Belmont House, Lake Road, Bowness-on-Windermere, Windermere LA23 3BJ
T: (015394) 88855
F: (015394) 88857
E: bookings@lakelovers.co.uk
I: www.lakelovers.co.uk

Beechmount
Rating Applied For
Contact: Mrs Susan Jackson, Heart of the Lakes, Fisherbeck Mill, Old Lake Road, Ambleside LA22 0DH
T: (015394) 33110
F: (015394) 33251
E: info@heartofthelakes.co.uk

Birch Cottage ★★★
Contact: Mr Roland Brown, 32 Tavistock Park, Leeds LS12 4DD
T: (0113) 263 4260
F: (0113) 263 4260
E: roland.brown@virgin.net
I: www.birchcottagewindermere.freeserve.co.uk

1 Birchmill Cottages ★★★
Contact: Mr Paul Liddell, Lakelovers, Belmont House, Lake Road, Bowness-on-Windermere, Windermere LA23 3BJ
T: (015394) 88855
F: (015394) 88857
E: bookings@lakelovers.co.uk
I: www.lakelovers.co.uk

The Birds Nest ★★★
Contact: Mrs Susan Jackson, Heart of the Lakes, Fisherbeck Mill, Old Lake Road, Ambleside LA22 0DH
T: (015394) 32321
F: (015394) 33251
E: info@heartofthelakes.co.uk
I: www.heartofthelakes.co.uk

Birthwaite Edge ★★★
Contact: Mr Bruce Dodsworth, Birthwaite Edge, Birthwaite Road, Windermere LA23 1BS
T: (015394) 42861
E: etc@lakedge.com
I: www.lakedge.com

Biskey Rise ★★★★
Contact: Mrs Susan Jackson, Heart of the Lakes, Fisherbeck Mill, Old Lake Road, Ambleside LA22 0DH
T: (015394) 32321
F: (015394) 33251
E: info@heartofthelakes.co.uk
I: www.heartofthelakes.co.uk

Black Beck Cottage ★★★★★
Contact: Mr Peter Durbin, Cumbrian Cottages, 2 Lonsdale Street, Carlisle CA1 1DB
T: (01228) 599960
F: (01228) 599970
E: enquiries@cumbrian-cottages.co.uk
I: www.cumbrian-cottages.co.uk

The Bothy ★★★
Contact: Mr Peter Durbin, Cumbrian Cottages, 2 Lonsdale Street, Carlisle CA1 1DB
T: (01228) 599960
F: (01228) 599970
E: enquiries@cumbrian-cottages.co.uk
I: www.cumbrian-cottages.co.uk

Bowmere ★★★★
Contact: Mr Peter Durbin, Cumbrian Cottages, 2 Lonsdale Street, Carlisle CA1 1DB
T: (01228) 599960
F: (01228) 599970
E: enquiries@cumbrian-cottages.co.uk
I: www.cumbrian.cottages.co.uk

Brackenrigg Lodge ★★★★★
Contact: Mrs Susan Jackson, Heart of the Lakes, Fisherbeck Mill, Old Lake Road, Ambleside LA22 0DH
T: (015394) 32321
F: (015394) 33251
E: info@heartofthelakes.co.uk
I: www.heartofthelakes.co.uk

4 Brantfell Cottages ★★★
Contact: Mr Peter Durbin, Cumbrian Cottages, 2 Lonsdale Street, Carlisle CA1 1DB
T: (01228) 599960
F: (01228) 599970
E: enquiries@cumbrian-cottages.co.uk
I: www.cumbrian-cottages.co.uk

Brantfield Cottage ★★★
Contact: Mr Paul Liddell, Lakelovers, Belmont House, Lake Road, Bowness-on-Windermere, Windermere LA23 3BJ
T: (015394) 88855
F: (015394) 88857
E: bookings@lakelovers.co.uk
I: www.lakelovers.co.uk

Brantmere ★★★
Contact: Mr & Mrs Norman & Christine McVeigh, 24 Oak Street, Windermere LA23 1EN
T: (015394) 43404
E: cmcveigh@gocumbria.org

Brent Cottage ★★★★
Contact: Mr Paul Liddell, Lakelovers, Belmont House, Lake Road, Bowness-on-Windermere, Windermere LA23 3BJ
T: (015394) 88855
F: (015394) 88857
E: bookings@lakelovers.co.uk
I: www.lakelovers.co.uk

Briarwood ★★★
Contact: Mr Peter Durbin, Cumbrian Cottages, 2 Lonsdale Street, Carlisle CA1 1DB
T: (01228) 599960
F: (01228) 599970
E: enquiries@cumbrian-cottages.co.uk
I: www.cumbrian-cottages.co.uk

Briscoe Lodge ★★★
Contact: Mrs Margaret Cook, Briscoe Lodge, Ellerthwaite Road, Windermere LA23 2AH
T: (015394) 42928

1 Brookside Cottages ★★
Contact: Mr Paul Liddell, Lakelovers, Belmont House, Lake Road, Bowness-on-Windermere, Windermere LA23 3BJ
T: (015394) 88855
F: (015394) 88857
E: bookings@lakelovers.co.uk
I: www.lakelovers.co.uk

Brow Edge ★★★
Contact: Mr Peter Durbin, Cumbrian Cottages, 2 Lonsdale Street, Carlisle CA1 1DB
T: (01228) 599960
F: (01228) 599970
E: enquiries@cumbrian-cottages.co.uk
I: www.cumbrian-cottages.co.uk

Burkesfield Cottage ★★★★
Contact: Mr Paul Liddell, Lakelovers, Belmont House, Lake Road, Bowness-on-Windermere, Windermere LA23 3BJ
T: (015394) 88855
F: (015394) 88857
E: bookings@lakelovers.co.uk
I: www.lakelovers.co.uk

Burnside Park ★★★★
Contact: Mrs Candy Philip, Burnside Park, The Lodge, Windermere LA23 3EW
T: (015394) 46624
F: (015394) 47754
E: cottages@burnsidehotel.com
I: www.burnsidehotel.com

Calgarth ★★★
Contact: Mr D Hogarth, Cumbrian Cottages, 7 The Crescent, Carlisle CA1 1QW
T: (01228) 599960
F: (01228) 599970
E: enquiries@cumbrian-cottages.co.uk
I: www.cumbrian-cottages.co.uk

Canons Craig ★★★★
Contact: Bowness Lakeland Holidays, 131 Radcliffe New Road, Whitefield, Manchester M45 7RP
T: (0161) 796 3896
E: dougie@freeneasy.net
I: www.freeyellow.com/pdfedrkd/

Canterbury Flats ★★-★★★
Contact: Mr M & Mrs I Zuniga, Bowness Holidays, 131 Radcliffe New Road, Whitefield, Manchester M45 7RP
T: (0161) 796 3896
F: (0161) 272 1841
E: info@bownesslakelandholidays.co.uk
I: www.bownesslakelandholidays.co.uk

The Carriage House ★★★★★
Contact: Mrs Susan Jackson, Heart of the Lakes, Fisherbeck Mill, Old Lake Road, Ambleside LA22 0DH
T: (015394) 32321
F: (015394) 33251
E: info@heartofthelakes.co.uk
I: www.heartofthelakes.co.uk

Chapel House ★★★★
Contact: Mr Paul Liddell, Lakelovers, Belmont House, Lake Road, Bowness-on-Windermere, Windermere LA23 3BJ
T: (015394) 88855
F: (015394) 88857
E: bookings@lakelovers.co.uk
I: www.lakelovers.co.uk

Cherry Tree Cottage ★★★★
Contact: Mr Peter Durbin, Cumbrian Cottages, 2 Lonsdale Street, Carlisle CA1 1DB
T: (01228) 599960
F: (01228) 599970
E: enquiries@cumbrian-cottages.co.uk
I: www.cumbrian-cottages.co.uk

Cherry Vale ★★★★
Contact: Mr Peter Durbin, Cumbrian Cottages, 2 Lonsdale Street, Carlisle CA1 1DB
T: (01228) 599960
F: (01228) 599970
E: enquiries@cumbrian-cottages.co.uk
I: www.cumbrian-cottages.co.uk

Cinnamon Cottage
Rating Applied For
Contact: Mrs Susan Jackson, Heart of the Lakes, Fisherbeck Mill, Old Lake Road, Ambleside LA22 0DH
T: (015394) 32321
F: (015394) 33251
E: info@heartofthelakes.co.uk
I: www.heartofthelakes.co.uk

Cinnamon Cottage
Rating Applied For
Contact: Mrs Susan Jackson, Heart of the Lakes, Fisherbeck Mill, Old Lake Road, Ambleside LA22 0DH
T: (015394) 33110
F: (015394) 33251
E: info@heartofthelakes.co.uk

Claife View ★★★
Contact: Mr Peter Durbin, Cumbrian Cottages, 2 Lonsdale Street, Carlisle CA1 1DB
T: (01228) 599960
F: (01228) 599970
E: enquiries@cumbrian-cottages.co.uk
I: www.cumbrian-cottages.co.uk

Clara's Cottage ★★★
Contact: Mr Peter Durbin, Cumbrian Cottages, 2 Lonsdale Street, Carlisle CA1 1DB
T: (01228) 599960
F: (01228) 599970
E: enquiries@cumbrian-cottages.co.uk
I: www.cumbrian-cottages.co.uk

Claremont ★★★
Contact: Mrs Susan Jackson, Heart of the Lakes, Fisherbeck Mill, Old Lake Road, Ambleside LA22 0DH
T: (015394) 32321
F: (015394) 33251
E: info@heartofthelakes.co.uk
I: www.heartofthelakes.co.uk

Coach House ★★★
Contact: Mr Nigel Hamblett, 16 Turpins Chase, Welwyn AL6 0RA
T: (01438) 717077
F: (01438) 717287
E: fiona99@ukonline.co.uk
I: www.windermere-accommodation.co.uk

Cobblestones ★★★
Contact: Mr Paul Liddell, Lakelovers, Belmont House, Lake Road, Bowness-on-Windermere, Windermere LA23 3BJ
T: (015394) 88855
F: (015394) 88857
E: bookings@lakelovers.co.uk
I: www.lakelovers.co.uk

Cockshott Wood ★★★★
Contact: Mrs Susan Jackson, Heart of the Lakes, Fisherbeck Mill, Old Lake Road, Ambleside LA22 0DH
T: (015394) 32321
F: (015394) 33251
E: info@heartofthelakes.co.uk
I: www.heartofthelakes.co.uk

3 College Court ★★★
Contact: Mr Paul Liddell, Lakelovers, Belmont House, Lake Road, Bowness-on-Windermere, Windermere LA23 3BJ
T: (015394) 88855
F: (015394) 88857
E: bookings@lakelovers.co.uk
I: www.lakelovers.co.uk

4 College Court ★★★
Contact: Mr Paul Liddell, Lakelovers, Belmont House, Lake Road, Bowness-on-Windermere, Windermere LA23 3BJ
T: (015394) 88855
F: (015394) 88857
E: bookings@lakelovers.co.uk
I: www.lakelovers.co.uk

8 College Court ★★★
Contact: Mr Paul Liddell, Lakelovers, Belmont House, Lake Road, Bowness-on-Windermere, Windermere LA23 3BJ
T: (015394) 88855
F: (015394) 88857
E: bookings@lakelovers.co.uk
I: www.lakelovers.co.uk

Coppice Corner ★★★★★
Contact: Mr Paul Liddell, Lakelovers, Belmont House, Lake Road, Bowness-on-Windermere, Windermere LA23 3BJ
T: (015394) 88855
F: (015394) 88857
E: bookings@lakelovers.co.uk
I: www.lakelovers.co.uk

Coppice View ★★★★
Contact: Mr Peter Durbin, 2 Lonsdale Street, Carlisle CA1 1DB
T: (01228) 599960
F: (01228) 599970
E: enquiries@cumbrian-cottages.co.uk
I: www.cumbrian-cottages.co.uk

Corner Cottage ★★★
Contact: Mr Peter Durbin, Cumbrian Cottages, 2 Lonsdale Street, Carlisle CA1 1DB
T: (01228) 599960
F: (01228) 599970
E: enquiries@cumbrian-cottages.co.uk
I: www.cumbrian-cottages.co.uk

Craglands ★★★★
Contact: Mr Peter Durbin, Cumbrian Cottages, 2 Lonsdale Street, Carlisle CA1 1DB
T: (01228) 599960
F: (01228) 599970
E: enquiries@cumbrian-cottages.co.uk
I: www.cumbrian-cottages.co.uk

Craigside ★★★★
Contact: Mr Paul Liddell, Lakelovers, Belmont House, Lake Road, Bowness-on-Windermere, Windermere LA23 3BJ
T: (015394) 88855
F: (015394) 88857
E: bookings@lakelovers.co.uk
I: www.lakelovers.co.uk

Cross Cottage ★★★
Contact: Mr D Hogarth, Cumbrian Cottages, 7 The Crescent, Carlisle CA1 1QW
T: (01228) 599960
F: (01228) 599970
E: enquiries@cumbrian-cottages.co.uk
I: www.cumbrian-cottages.co.uk

Crowmire Wood
Rating Applied For
Contact: Mrs Susan Jackson, Heart of the Lakes, Fisherbeck Mill, Old Lake Road, Ambleside LA22 0DH
T: (015394) 33110
F: (015394) 33251
E: info@heartofthelakes.co.uk

Cumbria View ★★★
Contact: Mr Peter Durbin, Cumbrian Cottages, 2 Lonsdale Street, Carlisle CA1 1DB
T: (01228) 599960
F: (01228) 599970
E: enquiries@cumbrian-cottages.co.uk
I: www.cumbrian-cottages.co.uk

Daisy Bank Cottage ★★★
Contact: Mr Peter Durbin, Cumbrian Cottages, 2 Lonsdale Street, Carlisle CA1 1DB
T: (01228) 599960
F: (01228) 599970
E: enquiries@cumbrian-cottages.co.uk
I: www.cumbrian-cottages.co.uk

Deloraine ★★★
Contact: Mr G H and Mrs Pauline Fanstone, Deloraine, Helm Road, Bowness-on-Windermere, Windermere LA23 2HS
T: (015394) 45557
F: (015394) 43221
E: gordon@deloraine.demon.co.uk
I: www.deloraine.demon.co.uk

The Den ★★★
Contact: Mr Paul Liddell, Lakelovers, Belmont House, Lake Road, Bowness-on-Windermere, Windermere LA23 3BJ
T: (015394) 88855
F: (015394) 88857
E: bookings@lakelovers.co.uk
I: www.lakelovers.co.uk

Elim Cottage ★★★
Contact: Mr Peter Durbin, Cumbrian Cottages, 2 Lonsdale Street, Carlisle CA1 1DB
T: (01228) 599960
F: (01228) 599970
E: enquiries@cumbrian-cottages.co.uk
I: www.cumbrian-cottages.co.uk

Fair View ★★★★
Contact: Mrs Susan Jackson, Heart of the Lakes, Fisherbeck Mill, Old Lake Road, Ambleside LA22 0DH
T: (015394) 32321
F: (015394) 33251
E: info@heartofthelakes.co.uk
I: www.heartofthelakes.co.uk

6 Fairfield ★★★★
Contact: Mrs Killip, 6 Fairfield, Off Brantfell Road, Bowness-on-Windermere, Windermere LA23 3AL
T: (015394) 45305

9 Fairfield ★★★★
Contact: Mr Peter Durbin, Cumbrian Cottages, 2 Lonsdale Street, Carlisle CA1 1DB
T: (01228) 599960
F: (01228) 599970
E: enquiries@cumbrian-cottages.co.uk
I: www.cumbrian-cottages.co.uk

Fairhaven ★★★★
Contact: Mr Peter Durbin, Cumbrian Cottages, 2 Lonsdale Street, Carlisle CA1 1DB
T: (01228) 599960
F: (01228) 599970
E: enquiries@cumbrian-cottages.co.uk
I: www.cumbria-cottages.co.uk

Fir Cones ★★★★
Contact: Mr Peter Durbin, Cumbrian Cottages, 2 Lonsdale Street, Carlisle CA1 1DB
T: (01228) 599960
F: (01228) 599970
E: enquiries@cumbrian-cottages.co.uk
I: www.cumbrian-cottages.co.uk

Firbank ★★★
Contact: Mr Peter Durbin, Cumbrian Cottages, 2 Lonsdale Street, Carlisle CA1 1DB
T: (01228) 599960
F: (01228) 599970
E: enquiries@cumbrian-cottages.co.uk
I: www.cumbrian-cottages.co.uk

Four Winds ★★★★
Contact: Mrs Monks, Four Winds, Victoria Road, Windermere LA23 2DP
T: (015394) 43612
E: brigid@fourwind.demon.co.uk

Gable Dene ★★★★
Contact: Mr Paul Liddell, Lakelovers, Belmont House, Lake Road, Bowness-on-Windermere, Windermere LA23 3BJ
T: (015394) 88855
F: (015394) 88857
E: bookings@lakelovers.co.uk
I: www.lakelovers.co.uk

The Gallery ★★★★★
Contact: Mrs Susan Jackson, Heart of the Lakes, Fisherbeck Mill, Old Lake Road, Ambleside LA22 0DH
T: (015394) 32321
F: (015394) 33251
E: info@heartofthelakes.co.uk
I: www.heartofthelakes.co.uk

Gardens View ★★★
Contact: Mr Paul Liddell, Lakelovers, Belmont House, Lake Road, Bowness-on-Windermere, Windermere LA23 3BJ
T: (015394) 88855
F: (015394) 88857
E: bookings@lakelovers.co.uk
I: www.lakelovers.co.uk

Gavel Cottage ★★★★
Contact: Mr Screeton, Screetons, 25 Bridgegate, Howden, Goole DN14 7AA
T: (01430) 431201
F: (01430) 432114
E: howden@screetons.co.uk
I: screetons.co.uk

Gildabrook Cottage ★★★
Contact: Mrs Susan Jackson, Heart of the Lakes, Fisherbeck Mill, Old Lake Road, Ambleside LA22 0DH
T: (015394) 32321
F: (015394) 33251
E: info@heartofthelakes.co.uk
I: www.heartofthelakes.co.uk

Glebe Holme ★★★★
Contact: Mr Peter Durbin, Cumbrian Cottages, 2 Lonsdale Street, Carlisle CA1 1DB
T: (01228) 599960
F: (01228) 599970
E: enquiries@cumbrian-cottages.co.uk
I: www.cumbrian-cottages.co.uk

Grace Cottage ★★★★
Contact: Mr Paul Liddell, Lakelovers, Belmont House, Lake Road, Bowness-on-Windermere, Windermere LA23 3BJ
T: (015394) 88855
F: (015394) 88857
E: bookings@lakelovers.co.uk
I: www.lakelovers.co.uk

Greenrigg ★★★★
Contact: Mr Peter Durbin, Cumbrian Cottages, 2 Lonsdale Street, Carlisle CA1 1DB
T: (01228) 599960
F: (01228) 599970
E: enquiries@cumbrian-cottages.co.uk
I: www.cumbrian-cottages.co.uk

Greystones ★★★
Contact: Mr Peter Durbin, Cumbrian Cottages, 2 Lonsdale Street, Carlisle CA1 1DB
T: (01228) 599960
F: (01228) 599970
E: enquiries@cumbrian-cottages.co.uk
I: www.cumbrian-cottages.co.uk

The Hayloft ★★★
Contact: Mr Peter Durbin, Cumbrian Cottages, 2 Lonsdale Street, Carlisle CA1 1DB
T: (01228) 599960
F: (01228) 599970
E: enquiries@cumbrian-cottages.co.uk
I: www.cumbrian-cottages.co.uk

The Heaning ★★★
Contact: Mrs Hazel Moulding, The Heaning, Heaning Lane, Windermere LA23 1JW
T: (015394) 43453
F: (015394) 43453
E: info@theheaning.co.uk
I: www.theheaning.co.uk

Heatherbank ★★★
Contact: Mr Peter Durbin, Cumbrian Cottages, 2 Lonsdale Street, Carlisle CA1 1DB
T: (01228) 599960
F: (01228) 599970
E: enquiries@cumbrian-cottages.co.uk
I: www.cumbrian-cottages.co.uk

Helm Farm ★★★
Contact: Miss Madeleine Scott, Estate Office, Matson Ground, Windermere LA23 2NH
T: (015394) 45756
F: (015394) 47892
E: info@matsonground.co.uk
I: www.matsonground.co.uk

5 Helm Rigg ★★★
Contact: Mr Paul Liddell, Lakelovers, Belmont House, Lake Road, Bowness-on-Windermere, Windermere LA23 3BJ
T: (015394) 88855
F: (015394) 88857
E: bookings@lakelovers.co.uk
I: www.lakelovers.co.uk

Hermitage Cottage ★★★
Contact: Mr Paul Liddell, Lakelovers, Belmont House, Lake Road, Bowness-on-Windermere, Windermere LA23 3BJ
T: (015394) 88855
F: (015394) 88857
E: bookings@lakelovers.co.uk
I: www.lakelovers.co.uk

High Croft ★★★★
Contact: Mrs Susan Jackson, Heart of the Lakes, Fisherbeck Mill, Old Lake Road, Ambleside LA22 0DH
T: (015394) 32321
F: (015394) 33251
E: info@heartofthelakes.co.uk
I: www.heartofthelakes.co.uk

High Langrigge ★★★★★
Contact: Mr Paul Liddell, Lakelovers, Belmont House, Lake Road, Bowness-on-Windermere, Windermere LA23 3BJ
T: (015394) 88855
F: (015394) 88857
E: bookings@lakelovers.co.uk
I: www.lakelovers.co.uk

2 Hodge How ★★★
Contact: Mr John Serginson, Waterside House, Newby Bridge, Ulverston LA12 8AN
T: (015395) 30024
F: (015395) 31932
E: john@lakelandcottageco.com
I: www.lakelandcottageco.com

Hodge Howe ★★★★★
Contact: Mrs Susan Jackson, Heart of the Lakes, Fisherbeck Mill, Old Lake Road, Ambleside LA22 0DH
T: (015394) 32321
F: (015394) 33251
E: info@heartofthelakes.co.uk
I: www.heartofthelakes.co.uk

Hollinfield ★★★★
Contact: Mrs Susan Jackson, Heart of the Lakes, Fisherbeck Mill, Old Lake Road, Ambleside LA22 0DH
T: (015394) 32321
F: (015394) 33251
E: info@heartofthelakes.co.uk
I: www.heartofthelakes.co.uk

Honeysuckle Cottage ★★★
Contact: Mr Peter Durbin, Cumbrian Cottages, 2 Lonsdale Street, Carlisle CA1 1DB
T: (01228) 599960
F: (01228) 599970
E: enquiries@cumbrian-cottages.co.uk
I: www.cumbrian-cottages.co.uk

Honeysuckle Cottage ★★★
Contact: Mr Paul Liddell, Lakelovers, Belmont House, Lake Road, Bowness-on-Windermere, Windermere LA23 3BJ
T: (015394) 88855
F: (015394) 88857
E: bookings@lakelovers.co.uk
I: www.lakelovers.co.uk

Howe Cottage ★★★
Contact: Mr Peter Durbin, Cumbrian Cottages, 2 Lonsdale Street, Carlisle CA1 1DB
T: (01228) 599960
F: (01228) 599970
E: enquiries@cumbrian-cottages.co.uk
I: www.cumbrian-cottages.co.uk

Howe Top ★★★
Contact: Mr Paul Liddell, Lakelovers, Belmont House, Lake Road, Bowness-on-Windermere, Windermere LA23 3BJ
T: (015394) 88855
F: (015394) 88857
E: bookings@lakelovers.co.uk
I: www.lakelovers.co.uk

Hunters Moon ★★★★
Contact: Mr Paul Liddell, Lakelovers, Belmont House, Lake Road, Bowness-on-Windermere, Windermere LA23 3BJ
T: (015394) 88855
F: (015394) 88857
E: bookings@lakelovers.co.uk
I: www.lakelovers.co.uk

Hydaway ★★★
Contact: Mr Peter Durbin, Cumbrian Cottages, 2 Lonsdale Street, Carlisle CA1 1DB
T: (01228) 599960
F: (01228) 599970
E: enquiries@cumbrian-cottages.co.uk
I: www.cumbrian-cottages.co.uk

Karis Cottage ★★★
Contact: Mr Peter Durbin, Cumbrian Cottages, 2 Lonsdale Street, Carlisle CA1 1DB
T: (01228) 599960
F: (01228) 599970
E: enquiries@cumbrian-cottages.co.uk
I: www.cumbrian-cottages.co.uk

Kent Cottage ★★★
Contact: Mr Paul Liddell, Lakelovers, Belmont House, Lake Road, Bowness-on-Windermere, Windermere LA23 3BJ
T: (015394) 88855
F: (015394) 88857
E: bookings@lakelovers.co.uk
I: www.lakelovers.co.uk

Knotts View ★★★★
Contact: Mr Paul Liddell, Lakelovers, Belmont House, Lake Road, Bowness-on-Windermere, Windermere LA23 3BJ
T: (015394) 88855
F: (015394) 88857
E: bookings@lakelovers.co.uk
I: www.lakelovers.co.uk

Lake Lodge ★★★★
Contact: Mr Paul Liddell, Lakelovers, Belmont House, Lake Road, Bowness-on-Windermere, Windermere LA23 3BJ
T: (015394) 88855
F: (015394) 88857
E: bookings@lakelovers.co.uk
I: www.lakelovers.co.uk

Lake View ★★★★
Contact: Mr Paul Liddell, Lakelovers, Belmont House, Lake Road, Bowness-on-Windermere, Windermere LA23 3BJ
T: (015394) 88855
F: (015394) 88857
E: bookings@lakelovers.co.uk
I: www.lakelovers.co.uk

Lakeside View ★★★★
Contact: Mr Paul Liddell, Lakelovers, Belmont House, Lake Road, Bowness-on-Windermere, Windermere LA23 3BJ
T: (015394) 88855
F: (015394) 88857
E: bookings@lakelovers.co.uk
I: www.lakelovers.co.uk

Lakeview ★★★
Contact: Mr Peter Durbin, Cumbrian Cottages, 2 Lonsdale Street, Carlisle CA1 1DB
T: (01228) 599960
F: (01228) 599970
E: enquiries@cumbrian-cottages.co.uk
I: www.cumbrian-cottages.co.uk

Langdale View Holiday Apartments ★★★
Contact: Mrs Janice Fletcher, Langdale View Holiday Apartments, 112 Craig Walk, Bowness-on-Windermere, Windermere LA23 3AX
T: (015394) 46655
F: (015394) 46728
E: enquiries@langdale-view.co.uk
I: www.langdale-view.co.uk

Langrigge Cottage ★★★★★
Contact: Mr Paul Liddell, Lakelovers, Belmont House, Lake Road, Bowness-on-Windermere, Windermere LA23 3BJ
T: (015394) 88855
F: (015394) 88857
E: bookings@lakelovers.co.uk
I: www.lakelovers.co.uk

Larch House ★★★★
Contact: Mr Paul Liddell, Lakelovers, Belmont House, Lake Road, Bowness-on-Windermere, Windermere LA23 3BJ
T: (015394) 88855
F: (015394) 88857
E: bookings@lakelovers.co.uk
I: www.lakelovers.co.uk

Ling Howe ★★★★★
Contact: Mr Peter Durbin, Cumbrian Cottages, 2 Lonsdale Street, Carlisle CA1 1DB
T: (01228) 599960
F: (01228) 599970
E: enquiries@cumbrian-cottages.co.uk
I: www.cumbrian-cottages.co.uk

Little Ghyll ★★★★
Contact: Mr Peter Durbin, Cumbrian Cottages, 2 Lonsdale Street, Carlisle CA1 1DB
T: (01228) 599960
F: (01228) 599970
E: enquiries@cumbrian-cottages.co.uk
I: www.cumbrian-cottages.co.uk

Low Fell Cottage ★★★
Contact: Mr Peter Durbin, Cumbrian Cottages, 2 Lonsdale Street, Carlisle CA1 1DB
T: (01228) 599960
F: (01228) 599970
E: enquiries@cumbrian-cottages.co.uk
I: www.cumbrian-cottages.co.uk

Low How ★★★★
Contact: Mrs Susan Jackson, Heart of the Lakes, Fisherbeck Mill, Old Lake Road, Ambleside LA22 0DH
T: (015394) 32321
F: (015394) 33251
E: info@heartofthelakes.co.uk
I: www.heartofthelakes.co.uk

Marybank ★★★
Contact: Mr Peter Durbin, Cumbrian Cottages, 2 Lonsdale Street, Carlisle CA1 1DB
T: (01228) 599960
F: (01228) 599970
E: enquiries@cumbrian-cottages.co.uk
I: www.cumbrian-cottages.co.uk

1 Meadowcroft ★★★★
Contact: Mr Peter Durbin, Cumbrian Cottages, 2 Lonsdale Street, Carlisle CA1 1DB
T: (01228) 599960
F: (01228) 599970
E: enquiries@cumbrian-cottages.co.uk
I: www.cumbrian-cottages.co.uk

3 Meadowcroft ★★★★
Contact: Mr Peter Durbin, 2 Lonsdale Street, Carlisle CA1 1DB
T: (01228) 599960
F: (01228) 599970
E: enquiries@cumbrian-cottages.co.uk
I: www.cumbrian-cottages.co.uk

6 Meadowcroft ★★★★
Contact: Mr Paul Liddell, Lakelovers, Belmont House, Lake Road, Bowness-on-Windermere, Windermere LA23 3BJ
T: (015394) 88855
F: (015394) 88857
E: bookings@lakelovers.co.uk
I: www.lakelovers.co.uk

7 Meadowcroft ★★★★
Contact: Mr Peter Durbin, 2 Lonsdale Street, Carlisle CA1 1DB
T: (01228) 599960
F: (01228) 599970
E: enquiries@cumbrian-cottages.co.uk
I: www.cumbrian-cottages.co.uk

8 Meadowcroft ★★★★
Contact: Mr Peter Durbin, Cumbrian Cottages, 2 Lonsdale Street, Carlisle CA1 1DB
T: (01228) 599960
F: (01228) 599970
E: enquiries@cumbrian-cottages.co.uk
I: www.cumbrian-cottages.co.uk

12 Meadowcroft ★★★★
Contact: Mr Peter Durbin, 2 Lonsdale Street, Carlisle CA1 1DB
T: (01228) 599960
F: (01228) 599970
E: enquiries@cumbrian-cottages.co.uk
I: www.cumbrian-cottages.co.uk

14 Meadowcroft ★★★★
Contact: Mr Paul Liddell, Belmont House, Lake Road, Bowness-on-Windermere, Windermere LA23 3BJ
T: (015394) 88855
F: (015394) 88857
E: bookings@lakelovers.co.uk

Meadows End ★★★
Contact: Mr Peter Durbin, Cumbrian Cottages, 2 Lonsdale Street, Carlisle CA1 1DB
T: (01228) 599960
F: (01228) 599970
E: enquiries@cumbrian-cottages.co.uk
I: www.cumbrian-cottages.co.uk

Mere View ★★★★
Contact: Mr Paul Liddell, Lakelovers, Belmont House, Lake Road, Bowness-on-Windermere, Windermere LA23 3BJ
T: (015394) 88855
F: (015394) 88857
E: bookings@lakelovers.co.uk
I: www.lakelovers.co.uk

Meregarth ★★★
Contact: Mr Paul Liddell, Lakelovers, Belmont House, Lake Road, Bowness-on-Windermere, Windermere LA23 3BJ
T: (015394) 88855
F: (015394) 88857
E: bookings@lakelovers.co.uk
I: www.lakelovers.co.uk

Merewood Stables ★★★★★
Contact: Mrs Susan Jackson, Heart of the Lakes, Fisherbeck Mill, Old Lake Road, Ambleside LA22 0DH
T: (015394) 32321
F: (015394) 33251
E: info@heartofthelakes.co.uk
I: www.heartofthelakes.co.uk

Middlerigg ★★★★
Contact: Mrs Susan Jackson, Heart of the Lakes, Fisherbeck Mill, Old Lake Road, Ambleside LA22 0DH
T: (015394) 32321
F: (015394) 33251
E: info@heartofthelakes.co.uk
I: www.heartofthelakes.co.uk

Moss Bank Cottage ★★★★
Contact: Mr Peter Durbin, Cumbrian Cottages, 2 Lonsdale Street, Carlisle CA1 1DB
T: (01228) 599960
F: (01228) 599970
E: enquiries@cumbrian-cottages.co.uk
I: www.cumbrian-cottages.co.uk

North Lodge & North Cottage ★★★★
Contact: Mr Alan Wardle, Bateman Fold Farm, Crook, Kendal LA8 8LN
T: (015395) 68074
F: (015395) 68104
E: lakedistricthols@aol.com

Oakdene ★★★★
Contact: Country Holidays Ref:12088, Spring Mill, Earby, Barnoldswick BB94 0AA
T: 08700 723723
F: (01282) 844288
E: sales@ttgihg.co.uk
I: www.country-holidays.co.uk

The Oaks ★★★★
Contact: Mr Peter Durbin, Cumbrian Cottages, 2 Lonsdale Street, Carlisle CA1 1DB
T: (01228) 599960
F: (01228) 599970
E: enquiries@cumbrian-cottages.co.uk
I: www.cumbrian-cottages.co.uk

Oakwood Cottages ★★★
Contact: Mrs J Moore, Pavey Ark, Brantfell Road, Bowness-on-Windermere, Windermere LA23 3AE
T: (015394) 88685
F: (015394) 88685
E: mooredsr@freeserve.co.uk
I: www.oakwoodcottages.co.uk

Octavia Cottage ★★★
Contact: Mr Peter Durbin, Cumbrian Cottages, 2 Lonsdale Street, Carlisle CA1 1DB
T: (01228) 599960
F: (01228) 599970
E: enquiries@cumbrian-cottages.co.uk
I: www.cumbrian-cottages.co.uk

Old Oak Cottage ★★★
Contact: Mr Peter Durbin, Cumbrian Cottages, 2 Lonsdale Street, Carlisle CA1 1DB
T: (01228) 599960
F: (01228) 599970
E: enquiries@cumbrian-cottages.co.uk
I: www.cumbrian-cottages.co.uk

The Old Picture House Rating Applied For
Contact: Mr N Thompson, No 3, 511 Barlow Moor Road, Chorlton, Manchester M21 8AQ
T: (0161) 861 7574
E: ndjthompson@hotmail.com

Olde Coach House and Stables ★★★
Contact: Mr & Mrs Alan & Margaret Wardle, Bateman Fold Barn, Crook, Kendal LA8 8LN
T: (015395) 68074
E: lakedistricthols@aol.com
I: www.lakedistrictholidays.net

Orchard Fold ★★★
Contact: Mr Peter Durbin, Cumbrian Cottages, 2 Lonsdale Street, Carlisle CA1 1DB
T: (01228) 599960
F: (01228) 599970
E: enquiries@cumbrian-cottages.co.uk
I: www.cumbrian-cottages.co.uk

Orchard House ★★★★
Contact: Mr Paul Liddell, Lakelovers, Belmont House, Lake Road, Bowness-on-Windermere, Windermere LA23 3BJ
T: (015394) 88855
F: (015394) 88857
E: bookings@lakelovers.co.uk
I: www.lakelovers.co.uk

Pear Tree Cottage ★★★
Contact: Mr Peter Durbin, Cumbrian Cottages, 2 Lonsdale Street, Carlisle CA1 1DB
T: (01228) 599960
F: (01228) 599970
E: enquiries@cumbrian-cottages.co.uk
I: www.cumbrian-cottages.co.uk

Penny Place ★★★★
Contact: Mr Paul Liddell, Lakelovers, Belmont House, Lake Road, Bowness-on-Windermere, Windermere LA23 3BJ
T: (015394) 88855
F: (015394) 88857
E: bookings@lakelovers.co.uk
I: www.lakelovers.co.uk

Penny's Nest ★★★★
Contact: Mr Paul Liddell, Lakelovers, Belmont House, Lake Road, Bowness-on-Windermere, Windermere LA23 3BJ
T: (015394) 88855
F: (015394) 88857
E: bookings@lakelovers.co.uk
I: www.lakelovers.co.uk

Pilgrim's Rest ★★★
Contact: Mr & Mrs John & Anne Ruck, 121 Bournbrook Road, Selly Park, Birmingham B29 7BY
T: (0121) 415 4036
E: JohnAnne@Ruckja.freeserve.co.uk

Pine Lodge ★★★★
Contact: Mr Paul Liddell, Lakelovers, Belmont House, Lake Road, Bowness-on-Windermere, Windermere LA23 3BJ
T: (015394) 88855
F: (015394) 88857
E: bookings@lakelovers.co.uk
I: www.lakelovers.co.uk

Pine Rigg ★★★
Contact: Mr Peter Durbin, Cumbrian Cottages, 2 Lonsdale Street, Carlisle CA1 1DB
T: (01228) 599960
F: (01228) 599970
E: enquiries@cumbrian-cottages.co.uk
I: www.cumbrian-cottages.co.uk

Pine View ★★★
Contact: Mr Peter Durbin, Cumbrian Cottages, 2 Lonsdale Street, Carlisle CA1 1DB
T: (01228) 599960
F: (01228) 599970
E: enquiries@cumbrian-cottages.co.uk
I: www.cumbrian-cottages.co.uk

Pinethwaite Holiday Cottages ★★★
Contact: Mr Paul Legge, Pinethwaite Holiday Cottages, Old Laundry Cottage, Pinethwaite, Windermere LA23 2NQ
T: (015394) 44558
E: p.legge@talk21.com
I: www.pinecottages.co.uk

Pipers Howe ★★★★
Contact: Mr Paul Liddell, Lakelovers, Belmont House, Lake Road, Bowness-on-Windermere, Windermere LA23 3BJ
T: (015394) 88855
F: (015394) 88857
E: bookings@lakelovers.co.uk
I: www.lakelovers.co.uk

Post Masters House ★★★★
Contact: Mr Peter Durbin, Cumbrian Cottages, 2 Lonsdale Street, Carlisle CA1 1DB
T: (01228) 599960
F: (01228) 599970
E: enquiries@cumbrian-cottages.co.uk
I: www.cumbrian-cottages.co.uk

Primrose Cottage ★★★
Contact: Mr Peter Durbin, Cumbrian Cottages, 2 Lonsdale Street, Carlisle CA1 1DB
T: (01228) 599960
F: (01228) 599970
E: enquiries@cumbrian-cottages.co.uk
I: www.cumbrian-cottages.co.uk

Priory Coach House ★★★★
Contact: Mr Paul Liddell, Lakelovers, Belmont House, Lake Road, Bowness-on-Windermere, Windermere LA23 3BJ
T: (015394) 88855
F: (015394) 88857
E: bookings@lakelovers.co.uk
I: www.lakelovers.co.uk

Priory Lodge ★★★★
Contact: Mr Paul Liddell, Lakelovers, Belmont House, Lake Road, Bowness-on-Windermere, Windermere LA23 3BJ
T: (015394) 88855
F: (015394) 88857
E: bookings@lakelovers.co.uk
I: www.lakelovers.co.uk

2 Priory Manor ★★★★
Contact: Mr Paul Liddell, Lakelovers, Belmont House, Lake Road, Bowness-on-Windermere, Windermere LA23 3BJ
T: (015394) 88855
F: (015394) 88857
E: bookings@lakelovers.co.uk
I: www.lakelovers.co.uk

48A Quarry Rigg ★★★
Contact: Mr Paul Liddell, Lakelovers, Belmont House, Lake Road, Bowness-on-Windermere, Windermere LA23 3BJ
T: (015394) 88855
F: (015394) 88857
E: bookings@lakelovers.co.uk
I: www.lakelovers.co.uk

35A Quarry Rigg-Lookout Post ★★★
Contact: Mr Peter Durbin, Cumbrian Cottages, 2 Lonsdale Street, Carlisle CA1 1DB
T: (01228) 599960
F: (01228) 599970
E: enquiries@cumbrian-cottages.co.uk
I: www.cumbrian-cottages.co.uk

Rainbows End ★★★
Contact: The Manager Dales Hol Cot Ref: 3338, Carleton Business Park, Carleton New Road, Skipton BD23 2AA
T: (01756) 799821
F: (01756) 797012
E: info@dalesholcot.com
I: www.dalesholcot.com

Rattle Beck ★★★★
Contact: Mr Peter Durbin, Cumbrian Cottages, 2 Lonsdale Street, Carlisle CA1 1DB
T: (01228) 599960
F: (01228) 599970
E: enquiries@cumbrian-cottages.co.uk
I: www.cumbrian-cottages.co.uk

Ravenclaw Cottage ★★★
Contact: Mr D Hogarth, Cumbrian Cottages, 7 The Crescent, Carlisle CA1 1QW
T: (01228) 599960
F: (01228) 599970
E: enquiries@cumbrian-cottages.co.uk
I: www.cumbrian-cottages.co.uk

Rayrigg Roost ★★★
Contact: Mr Peter Durbin, Cumbrian Cottages, 2 Lonsdale Street, Carlisle CA1 1DB
T: (01228) 599960
F: (01228) 599970
E: enquiries@cumbrian-cottages.co.uk
I: www.cumbrian-cottages.co.uk

Rivendell ★★★
Contact: Mr Peter Durbin, Cumbrian Cottages, 2 Lonsdale Street, Carlisle CA1 1DB
T: (01228) 599960
F: (01228) 599970
E: enquiries@cumbrian-cottages.co.uk
I: www.cumbrian-cottages.co.uk

Robin Cottage ★★★★
Contact: Mr Paul Liddell, Lakelovers, Belmont House, Lake Road, Bowness-on-Windermere, Windermere LA23 3BJ
T: (015394) 88855
F: (015394) 88857
E: bookings@lakelovers.co.uk
I: www.lakelovers.co.uk

Rogerground ★★★★
Contact: Mr Paul Liddell, Lakelovers, Belmont House, Lake Road, Bowness-on-Windermere, Windermere LA23 3BJ
T: (015394) 88855
F: (015394) 88857
E: bookings@lakelovers.co.uk
I: www.lakelovers.co.uk

Rose Cottage ★★★
Contact: Mr & Mrs Alan Wardle, Bateman Fold Barn, Crook, Kendal LA8 8LN
T: (015395) 68074
I: www.lakedistrictholidays.net

Rose Cottage ★★★★
Contact: Mr Peter Durbin, Cumbrian Cottages, 2 Lonsdale Street, Carlisle CA1 1DB
T: (01228) 599960
F: (01228) 599970
E: enquiries@cumbrian-cottages.co.uk
I: www.cumbrian-cottages.co.uk

Saw Mill Cottage ★★★
Contact: Mrs Susan Jackson, Heart of the Lakes, Fisherbeck Mill, Old Lake Road, Ambleside LA22 0DH
T: (015394) 32321
F: (015394) 33251
E: info@heartofthelakes.co.uk
I: www.heartofthelakes.co.uk

Skylark ★★★★
Contact: Mr Peter Durbin, Cumbrian Cottages, 2 Lonsdale Street, Carlisle CA1 1DB
T: (01228) 599960
F: (01228) 599970
E: enquiries@cumbrian-cottages.co.uk
I: www.cumbrian-cottages.co.uk

Solstice Cottage ★★★
Contact: Mr Paul Liddell, Lakelovers, Belmont House, Lake Road, Bowness-on-Windermere, Windermere LA23 3BJ
T: (015394) 88855
F: (015394) 88857
E: bookings@lakelovers.co.uk
I: www.lakelovers.co.uk

Southside Cottage ★★★
Contact: Mr Paul Liddell, Lakelovers, Belmont House, Lake Road, Bowness-on-Windermere, Windermere LA23 3BJ
T: (015394) 88855
F: (015394) 88857
E: bookings@lakelovers.co.uk
I: www.lakelovers.co.uk

Spinnery Cottage Holiday Apartments ★★★
Contact: Mr & Mrs Ray Hood, Sylvan Wood, Underbarrow Road, Kendal, Cumbria LA8 8AH
T: (01539) 725153
F: (01539) 725153
E: Ray&barb@spinnerycottage.co.uk
I: www.spinnerycottage.co.uk

Stable Cottage ★★★★★
Contact: Mrs Susan Jackson, Heart of the Lakes, Fisherbeck Mill, Old Lake Road, Ambleside LA22 0DH
T: (015394) 32321
F: (015394) 33251
E: info@heartofthelakes.co.uk
I: www.heartofthelakes.co.uk

Storrs Hall ★★★
Contact: Mr Peter Durbin, Cumbrian Cottages, 2 Lonsdale Street, Carlisle CA1 1DB
T: (01228) 599960
F: (01228) 599970
E: enquiries@cumbrian-cottages.co.uk
I: www.cumbrian-cottages.co.uk

Sunny Brook Cottage ★★★
Contact: Mr Peter Durbin, Cumbrian Cottages, 2 Lonsdale Street, Carlisle CA1 1DB
T: (01228) 599960
F: (01228) 599970
E: enquiries@cumbrian-cottages.co.uk
I: www.cumbrian-cottages.co.uk

Swallow's Rest ★★★
Contact: Mr Paul Liddell, Lakelovers, Belmont House, Lake Road, Bowness-on-Windermere, Windermere LA23 3BJ
T: (015394) 88855
F: (015394) 88857
E: bookings@lakelovers.co.uk
I: www.lakelovers.co.uk

Thwaites Cottage ★★★
Contact: Mr Peter Durbin, Cumbrian Cottages, 2 Lonsdale Street, Carlisle CA1 1DB
T: (01228) 599960
F: (01228) 599970
E: enquiries@cumbrian-cottages.co.uk
I: www.cumbrian-cottages.co.uk

Tree Tops ★★★
Contact: Mr Paul Liddell, Lakelovers, Belmont House, Lake Road, Bowness-on-Windermere, Windermere LA23 3BJ
T: (015394) 88855
F: (015394) 88857
E: bookings@lakelovers.co.uk
I: www.lakelovers.co.uk

Treetops ★★★★
Contact: Mr & Mrs Alcock, 6 Ghyllside, Ambleside LA22 0QU
T: (015394) 32819
E: pat.john@lakedistrictcumbria.co.uk
I: www.lakedistrictcumbria.co.uk

Troutbeck Barn ★★★
Contact: Mr Paul Liddell, Lakelovers, Belmont House, Lake Road, Bowness-on-Windermere, Windermere LA23 3BJ
T: (015394) 88855
F: (015394) 88857
E: bookings@lakelovers.co.uk
I: www.lakelovers.co.uk

24 Victoria Terrace ★★
Contact: Mrs Eileen Lishman, 22 Victoria Terrace, Windermere LA23 1AB
T: (015394) 42982

Waterfall Cottage ★★★
Contact: Mr D Hogarth, Cumbrian Cottages, 7 The Crescent, Carlisle CA1 1QW
T: (01228) 599960
F: (01228) 599970
E: enquiries@cumbrian-cottages.co.uk
I: www.cumbrian-cottages.co.uk

Welkom Cottage ★★★★
Contact: Mr Paul Liddell, Lakelovers, Belmont House, Lake Road, Bowness-on-Windermere, Windermere LA23 3BJ
T: (015394) 88855
F: (015394) 88857
E: bookings@lakelovers.co.uk
I: www.lakelovers.co.uk

The Wendy House ★★★
Contact: Mr Paul Liddell, Lakelovers, Belmont House, Lake Road, Bowness-on-Windermere, Windermere LA23 3BJ
T: (015394) 88855
F: (015394) 88857
E: bookings@lakelovers.co.uk
I: www.lakelovers.co.uk

Westwood ★★★★★
Contact: Mr Paul Liddell, Lakelovers, Belmont House, Lake Road, Bowness-on-Windermere, Windermere LA23 3BJ
T: (015394) 88855
F: (015394) 88857
E: bookings@lakelovers.co.uk
I: www.lakelovers.co.uk

White Moss ★★★★
Contact: Mrs Susan Jackson, Heart of the Lakes, Fisherbeck Mill, Old Lake Road, Ambleside LA22 0DH
T: (015394) 32321
F: (015394) 33251
E: info@heartofthelakes.co.uk
I: www.heartofthelakes.co.uk

Wind Force ★★★★
Contact: Mr Paul Liddell, Lakelovers, Belmont House, Lake Road, Bowness-on-Windermere, Windermere LA23 3BJ
T: (015394) 88855
F: (015394) 88857
E: bookings@lakelovers.co.uk
I: www.lakelovers.co.uk

Windermere Marina Village ★★★★
Contact: Mrs C Burns, Windermere Marina Village, Bowness-on-Windermere, Windermere LA23 3JQ
T: 0800 262902
F: (015394) 43233
E: info@wmv.co.uk
I: www.wmv.co.uk

Winster Fields
Rating Applied For
Contact: Mrs Susan Jackson, Heart of the Lakes, Fisherbeck Mill, Old Lake Road, Ambleside LA22 0DH
T: (015394) 33110
F: (015394) 33251
E: info@heartofthelakes.co.uk
I: www.heartofthelakes.co.uk

Winster House ★★★
Contact: Mrs S Jump, Winster House, Sunnybank Road, Windermere LA23 2EN
T: (015394) 44723
E: enquiries@winsterhouse.co.uk
I: www.winsterhouse.co.uk

3 Woodland Grove ★★★
Contact: Mr Paul Liddell, Lakelovers, Belmont House, Lake Road, Bowness-on-Windermere, Windermere LA23 3BJ
T: (015394) 88855
F: (015394) 88857
E: bookings@lakelovers.co.uk
I: www.lakelovers.co.uk

Woodland View ★★★
Contact: Mr D Hogarth, Cumbrian Cottages, 7 The Crescent, Carlisle CA1 1QW
T: (01228) 599960
F: (01228) 599970
E: enquiries@cumbrian-cottages.co.uk
I: www.cumbrian-cottages.co.uk

Woodside ★★★★
Contact: Mrs Susan Jackson, Heart of the Lakes, Fisherbeck Mill, Old Lake Road, Ambleside LA22 0DH
T: (015394) 32321
F: (015394) 33251
E: info@heartofthelakes.co.uk
I: www.heartofthelakes.co.uk

WINTON
Cumbria

Manor House ★★★
Contact: Mr Peter Durbin, Cumbrian Cottages, 2 Lonsdale Street, Carlisle CA1 1DB
T: (01228) 599960
F: (01228) 599970
E: enquiries@cumbrian-cottages.co.uk
I: www.cumbrian-cottages.co.uk

WITHERSLACK
Cumbria

Fern Lea Rose Mount Mole End Ingle Nook Primrose Cottage Delph Cottage★★-★★★
Contact: CH Ref:11182-11184,4970,4971, Holiday Cottages Group Owner Services Dept, Spring Mill, Earby, Barnoldswick BB94 0AA
T: (01282) 445096
F: (01282) 844288
E: sales@holidaycottagesgroup.com
I: www.country-holidays.co.uk

The Old Coachouse ★★★★
Contact: Mr John Serginson, Waterside House, Newby Bridge, Ulverston LA12 8AN
T: (015395) 30024
F: (015395) 31932
E: john@lakelandcottageco.com
I: www.lakeland-cottage-company.co.uk

Spa Inn House ★★★★
Contact: Mr Peter Durbin, Cumbrian Cottages, 2 Lonsdale Street, Carlisle CA1 1DB
T: (01228) 599960
F: (01228) 599970
E: enquiries@cumbrian-cottages.co.uk
I: www.cumbrian-cottages.co.uk

Thornbarrow Hill Cottage ★★★
Contact: Mr John Serginson, Waterside House, Newby Bridge, Ulverston LA12 8AN
T: (015395) 30024
F: (015395) 31932
E: john@lakelandcottageco.com
I: www.lakeland-cottage-company.co.uk

WYTHOP
Cumbria

Sty Cottage ★★★
Contact: Mr Peter Durbin, Cumbrian Cottages, 2 Lonsdale Street, Carlisle CA1 1DB
T: (01228) 599960
F: (01228) 599970
E: enquiries@cumbrian-cottages.co.uk
I: www.cumbrian-cottages.co.uk

YANWATH
Cumbria

Copper Beech Cottage ★★★★
Contact: S M Beattie, 2 Barnside, Glendowlin Park, Yanwath, Penrith CA10 2LA
T: (01768) 892855

YEARNGILL
Cumbria

Hill House ★★★
Contact: Mrs Mary Kinsella, Hill House, Yearngill, Aspatria, Wigton CA7 3JX
T: (016973) 22399
E: mary@mkinsella.fsbusiness.co.uk
I: www.mkinsella.fsbusiness.co.uk

NORTHUMBRIA

ACKLINGTON
Northumberland

Low Park Cottage ★★★
Contact: Mrs Louise Howie, Acklington Park Farm, Acklington, Morpeth NE65 9AA
T: (01670) 760360
F: (01670) 761261

Morwick Farm Cottage ★★
Contact: Sykes Cottages Ref:6 Sykes Cottages Ref:642, Sykes Cottages, York House, York Street, Chester CH1 3LR
T: (01244) 345700
F: (01244) 321442
E: info@sykescottages.co.uk
I: www.sykescottages.co.uk

The Railway Inn
Rating Applied For
Contact: Mrs Linda Osborne, The Railway Inn, Acklington, Morpeth NE65 9BP
T: (01670) 760320
E: linda.osborne1@btopenworld.com
I: www.wishingwellcottages.co.uk

ALLENDALE
Northumberland

Allen Mill Cottages ★★★★
Contact: Mrs Kerry Crellin, Ashy Bank, Shilburn, Allendale, Hexham NE47 9LQ
T: (01434) 683358
E: crellin@ukgateway.net

Station House Caravan Park ★★
Contact: Mrs A G Dodsworth, Station House Caravan Park, Catton, Hexham NE47 9QF
T: (01434) 683362

ALLENHEADS
Northumberland

Englewood ★★★
Contact: Sykes Cottages Ref:2 Sykes Cottages Ref:291, Sykes Cottages, York House, York Street, Chester CH1 3LR
T: (01244) 345700
F: (01244) 321442
E: info@sykescottages.co.uk
I: www.sykescottages.co.uk

ALNMOUTH
Northumberland

Bilton Barns ★★★-★★★★
Contact: Mrs Dorothy Jackson, Bilton Barns, 8 North Street, Seahouses NE68 7SB
T: (01665) 830427
F: (01665) 833909
E: dorothy@biltonbarns.com

Curlew's Calling
Rating Applied For
Contact: Alan and Sheila Worsley, Curlew's Calling, rear of 10 Riverside Road, Alnmouth, Alnwick NE66 2SD
T: (01665) 830888
F: (01665) 830888

Garden Cottage
Rating Applied For
Contact: Mr Robin Winder, Garden Cottage, 4 Garden Terrace, Alnmouth, Alnwick NE66 2SF
T: (0191) 440 8586
E: robin75up@hotmail.com

Grange Cottages – Old Watch Tower & The Coach House ★★★★
Contact: Ms Nicola Brierley, 20 Northumberland Street, Alnmouth, Foxton, Alnwick NE66 2RJ
T: (01665) 830783
F: (01665) 830783
E: enquiries@thegrange-alnmouth.com

Old Hall Cottage, High Buston Hall ★★★★★
Contact: Mrs Therese Atherton, High Buston Hall, High Buston, Alnmouth, Alnwick NE66 3QH
T: (01665) 830606
F: (01665) 830707
E: highbuston@aol.com
I: www.highbuston.com

The Old Stables, High Buston Hall ★★★★
Contact: Mr Edwards, The Stables, High Buston Hall, High Buston, Alnmouth, Alnwick NE66 3QH
T: (01665) 830341
F: (01665) 830005
E: info@holiday-cottages-northumberland.com
I: www.holiday-cottages-northumberland.com

Prospect House ★★★
Contact: Mrs Yeadon, 2 Prospect Place, Alnmouth, Alnwick NE66 2RL
T: (01665) 830649
E: prospect.holidays@talk21.com
I: www.cottageguide.co.uk/alnmouth

Quality Self Catering ★★★★
Contact: Mrs Vicki Taylor, Letton Lodge, Alnmouth, Alnwick NE66 2RJ
T: (01665) 830633
F: (01665) 830122
E: NTB@QSCmail.co.uk
I: www.alnmouth.co.uk

Shepherds House ★★★
Contact: Mrs Lyn Frater, High Buston Farm, Alnmouth, Alnwick NE66 3QH
T: (01665) 830361
F: (01665) 830361
E: lynpfrater@aol.com

Sunnyside Cottage ★★★★
Contact: Mrs Mary Hollins, 2 The Grove, Whickham, Newcastle upon Tyne NE16 4QY
T: (0191) 488 3939
F: (0191) 488 3939
E: sunnysidecott@lineone.net

Wooden Farm Holiday Cottages ★★-★★★
Contact: Mr W G Farr, Wooden Farm Holiday Cottages, Wooden Farm, Lesbury, Alnwick NE66 2TW
T: (01665) 830342

ALNWICK
Northumberland

Barbican View ★★★★
Contact: Mrs Hazel Wintrip, 22 Lesbury Road, Alnwick NE66 3NB
T: (01665) 830148
E: halwintrip@hotmail.com

Bog Mill Farm Holiday Cottages ★★★★
Contact: Mrs Ann Mason, Bog Mill Farm Holiday Cottages, Bog Mill Farm, Alnwick NE66 3PA
T: (01665) 604529
F: (01665) 606972
E: stay@bogmill.co.uk
I: www.bogmill.co.uk

The Buie ★★★
Contact: Ms Diana Norris, Cosaig, Glenelg, Kyle of Lochalsh IV40 8LB
T: (01599) 522365
F: (01599) 522365
E: diana_norris@hotmail.com

Cheviot View and Dipper Cottage ★★★-★★★★
Contact: CH Ref: 13062, N625, Holiday Cottages Group Owner Services Dept, Spring Mill, Earby, Barnoldswick BB94 0AA
T: 08700 723723
F: (01282) 844288
E: sales@holidaycottagesgroup.com
I: www.country-holidays.co.uk

Dene View Cottage and Moor Croft Cottage★★★★
Contact: Mrs Margaret McGregor, Dene View Cottage and Moor Croft Cottage, Broome Hill Farm, Alnwick NE66 2BA
T: (01665) 574460
F: (01665) 574460
E: margaret@broomehillfarm.co.uk
I: www.visitnorthumbria.com

Farm Cottage ★★★
Contact: Mrs Renner, Farmhouse, Shipley Hill, Eglingham, Alnwick NE66 2LX
T: (01665) 579266

Garden Cottages ★★★★
Contact: Mr & Mrs Harrison, Garden Cottages, Lemmington Hall, Alnwick NE66 2BH
T: (01665) 574129
F: (01665) 574129
E: gardencottage@lemmington.fsbusiness.co.uk

Green Batt Cottages ★★★
Contact: Dr Emma Wady, Green Batt House, The Pinfold, Denwick, Alnwick NE66 1TY
T: (01665) 602429
F: (01665) 602429
E: wadyone@aol.com
I: www.cottageguide.co.uk/greenbatt

Green Batt Studio ★★★
Contact: Mrs Clare Mills, 1 Percy Street, Alnwick NE66 1AE
T: (01665) 602742
E: paul@mills84.freeserve.co.uk

Henhill and Birchwood Hall Cottages ★★★★
Contact: Mrs Jane Mallen, Northumberland Estates, Alnwick Castle, Denwick, Alnwick NE66 1NQ
T: (01665) 602094
F: (01665) 608126
E: northumberland.est.hols@farmline.com
I: www.alnwickcastle.com/holidaycottages/

1 Howick Street ★★★
Contact: Mr Thomas Payton, Austrey House, 3 Grosvenor Terrace, Alnwick NE66 1LG
T: (01665) 510484
E: tompayton@whsmithnet.co.uk
I: www.howickhols.fsnet.co.uk

Limpet Cottage ★★★★
Contact: Mrs Jane Mallen, Northumberland Estates, Alnwick Castle, Denwick, Alnwick NE66 1NQ
T: (01665) 602094
F: (01665) 608126
E: nehc@farmline.com
I: www.alnwickcastle.com/holidaycottages/

Reiver Cottage - Ref 3607 ★★★
Contact: Ms Hannah Cook, Carleton Business Park, Carleton New Road, Skipton BD23 2AA
T: (01756) 799821
E: info@dales-holiday-cottages.com

Sawmill Cottage ★★★
Contact: Ms Alison Wrangham, Harehope Hall, Eglingham, Alnwick NE66 2DP
T: (01668) 217329
F: (01668) 217346
E: ali.wrangham@bt.connect.com

Stamford & Embleton Mill Farm Cottages★★★★
Contact: Mrs Grahamslaw, The Farmhouse, Gallowmoor, Embleton, Alnwick NE66 3SB
T: (01665) 579425
F: (01665) 579425

Thorn Rigg ★★★★
Contact: Country Hols Ref: 12730, Holiday Cottages Group Owner Services Dept, Spring Mill, Earby, Barnoldswick BB94 0AA
T: 08700 723723
F: (01282) 844288
E: sales@holidaycottagesgroup.com
I: www.country-holidays.co.uk

Village Farm ★★★-★★★★★
Contact: Mrs C M Stoker, Town Foot Farm, Shilbottle, Alnwick NE66 2HG
T: (01665) 575591
F: (01665) 575591
E: crissy@villagefarmcottages.co.uk
I: www.villagefarmcottages.co.uk

2 White House Folly Cottages ★★★
Contact: Mrs Joan Gilroy, White House Folly Farm, Alnwick NE66 2LW
T: (01665) 579265

ALWINTON
Northumberland

Stonecrop Cottage ★★★
Contact: Mrs Mason, Flat 1, 2 Percy Gardens, Tynemouth, North Shields NE30 4HG
T: (0191) 257 0892

AMBLE
Northumberland

Sea Swallows ★★★
Contact: Mr Colin Storey, 31 Bourne Avenue, Fenham, Newcastle upon Tyne NE4 9XL
T: (0191) 274 5203
E: seaswallows@yahoo.co.uk
I: www.seaswallows-self-catering.co.uk

Seashells ★★★
Contact: Mr & Mrs Rochester, 22 Hauxley Way, Amble, Morpeth NE65 0AL
T: (01665) 713448
F: (01665) 713448
E: ian@roch11.freeserve.co.uk

AMBLE-BY-THE-SEA
Northumberland

Braid View ★★★
Contact: Mrs Joyce Crass, 11 Morwick Road, Warkworth, Morpeth NE65 0TG
T: (01665) 711623
E: northumbriabreaks@hotmail.com

Brent Cottage ★★★
Contact: Mr Clarke, 18 The Green, Thrussington, Leicester LE7 4UH
T: (01664) 424480

Coastguard Cottage ★★★★
Contact: Mr & Mrs N Aitchison, Lords Moor Lane, Strensall, York YO32 5XF
T: (01904) 490408
E: neville@aitchison.co.uk
I: coastguardcottage.co.uk

Collingwood ★★★
Contact: Mrs Gwen Young, 69 Castle View, Amble by the Sea, Morpeth NE65 0NN
T: (01665) 710303
E: info@collingwoodamble.co.uk

Kew Cottage ★★★★
Contact: Mrs Linda Kewin, 3 Promontory Terrace, Whitley Bay NE26 2PF
T: (0191) 253 4404

Marina Cottage ★★★★
Contact: Mr Dennis Black, Marina Villa, The Wynd, Amble, Morpeth NE65 0HH
T: (01665) 711019
F: (01665) 711019
E: mangotree@supanet.com

BALDERSDALE
Durham

Clove Lodge Cottage ★★★
Contact: Mrs Ann Heys, Clove Lodge Farm, Baldersdale, Barnard Castle DL12 9UP
T: (01833) 650030
E: ann@heys70.freeserve.co.uk
I: www.thepennineway.co.uk

Lartington Hall Rating Applied For
Contact: Mr Robin Rackham, Lartington Lettings, Lartington Hall, Lartington, Baldersdale, Barnard Castle DL12 9BW
T: (01833) 650495
F: (01833) 650419
E: robin.rackham@btconnect.com

The Old Chapel and Bluebell Barn ★★★★-★★★★★
Contact: Mrs J Moore, Briscoe Farm, Baldersdale, Barnard Castle DL12 9UL
T: (01833) 650822

BAMBURGH
Northumberland

Barn End ★★★★
Contact: Mr George Bruce, The Steading, Westburn, Crawcrook, Ryton NE40 4EU
T: (0191) 413 2353
E: george.e.bruce@talk21.com

Bradford Country Cottages Rating Applied For
Contact: Mr L W Robson, Bradford Country Cottages, Bradford House, Bamburgh NE70 7JT
T: (01668) 213432
F: (01668) 213891
E: lwrob@tiscali.co.uk

Bridge End ★★★★
Contact: Mr & Mrs Roger and Linda Topping, 98 Dowanhill Street, Glasgow G12 9EG
T: (0141) 334 4833

The Bungalow ★★★
Contact: Miss Eve Humphreys, Burton Hall, East Burton, Bamburgh NE69 7AR
T: (01668) 214213
F: (01668) 214538
E: evehumphreys@aol.com
I: www.burtonhall.co.uk

Castle View Bungalow ★★★
Contact: Mr & Mrs I Nicol, Springwood, South Lane, Seahouses NE68 7UL
T: (01665) 720320
F: (01665) 720146
E: ian@slatehall.freeserve.co.uk
I: www.slatehallridingcentre.com

The Cottage ★★★
Contact: Mrs S Turnbull, 1 Friars Court, Bamburgh NE69 7AE
T: (01668) 214494

Dukesfield Farm Holiday Cottages ★★★★
Contact: Mrs Maria Eliana Robinson, The Glebe, 16 Radcliffe Road, Bamburgh NE69 7AE
T: (01668) 214456
F: (01668) 214354
E: eric_j_robinson@compuserve.com
I: www.secretkingdom.com/dukes/field.htm

The Fairway ★★★
Contact: Mrs Diana Middleton, High Close House, Wylam NE41 8BL
T: (01661) 852125
E: rsmiddleton@talk21.com

Glebe House and Glebe Cottage ★★★★★
Contact: Mrs Maria Eliana Robinson, The Glebe, 16 Radcliffe Road, Bamburgh NE69 7AE
T: (01668) 214456
F: (01668) 214354
E: eric_j_robinson@compuserve.com
I: www.secretkingdom.com/glebe/house.htm

The Granary ★★★
Contact: Mrs Patricia Cowen, Thornleigh, Wetheral, Carlisle CA4 8ES
T: (01228) 560245
E: cowen-home@hotmail.com

Harelaw House ★★★★
Contact: Ms Zana Juppenlatz, Kimbolton Road, Hail Weston, St Neots, Huntingdon PE19 5LA
T: (01480) 475667
F: (01480) 404783
E: zjuppenlatz@aol.com

The Haven ★★★★
Contact: Miss Lynn Gregory, Earsdon Hill Farm, Earsdon, Morpeth NE61 3ES
T: (01670) 787392
F: (01670) 787392
E: pg@africaselect.com
I: www.cottageguide.co.uk/thehaven/

High Tutlaw House ★★★★★
Contact: Mrs Jane Mallen, Park Farm House, Hulne Park, Alnwick NE66 3HZ
T: (01665) 602094
F: (01665) 608126
E: tutlaw@farming.co.uk

Hillside ★★★★
Contact: Ms Michelle Mattinson, Hillside Bed & Breakfast, 25 Lucker Road, Bamburgh NE69 7BS
T: (01668) 214674
F: (01668) 214674
E: enquiries@hillside-bamburgh.com
I: www.hillside-bamburgh.com

Hoppen Hall Farm Cottages ★★★★
Contact: Mrs Jane Mallen, Northumberland Estates Holiday Cottages, Alnwick Castle, Denwick, Alnwick NE66 1NQ
T: (01665) 602094
F: (01665) 608126
E: nehc@farmline.com
I: www.alnwickcastle.com/holidaycottages/

Inglenook Cottage ★★★★
Contact: Mrs A D Moore, Beckstones, Carperby, Leyburn DL8 4DA
T: (01969) 663363

Millhouse Cottage ★★★★
Contact: Mrs Sarah Nelson, Low Bleakhope, Powburn, Alnwick NE66 4NZ
T: (01665) 578361
E: sarah.nelson@ukonline.co.uk

Nineteen ★★★★
Contact: Mr John McDougal, Whitestacks, 24 Ingram Road, Bamburgh NE69 7BT
T: (01668) 214395
F: (01668) 214100
E: clem500@btinternet.com

The Old Coach House ★★★★
Contact: Country Holidays Ref:12179, Spring Mill, Earby, Barnoldswick BB94 0AA
T: 08700 723723
F: (01282) 844288
E: sales@holidaycottagesgroup.com
I: www.country-holidays.co.uk

Outchester & Ross Farm Cottages ★★★-★★★★
Contact: Mrs Shirley McKie, 1 Cragview Road, Belford NE70 7NT
T: (01668) 213336
F: (01668) 219385
E: enquiry@rosscottages.co.uk
I: www.rosscottages.co.uk

Point Cottages ★★★
Contact: Mrs E Sanderson
T: (0191) 266 2800
F: (0191) 215 1630
E: info@bamburgh-cottages.co.uk
I: www.bamburgh-cottages.co.uk

Saint Oswald's/Saint Aidan's ★★
Contact: Mr Anthony Smith, 10 Aldbourne Road, London W12 0LN
T: (020) 8248 9589
F: (020) 8248 9587
E: quintin.smith@btinternet.com

Smugglers Court ★★★★
Contact: Mr Gordon Begg, Smugglers Court, Waren Mill, Belford NE70 7EE
T: (01668) 214047
F: (01668) 214047
E: gordon@budle-bay.com
I: www.budle-bay.com

Springhill Farm Cottages ★★★★
Contact: Mrs Julie Gregory, Springhill Farm Holiday Cottages, Springhill Farmhouses, Springhill Farm, Seahouses NE68 7UR
T: (01665) 721820
F: (01665) 721820
E: enquiries@springhill-farm.co.uk
I: www.springhill-farm.co.uk

Struan ★★★
Contact: Mr Charles Wilkie-Smith, 27 Ridley Place, Jesmond, Newcastle upon Tyne NE1 8LE
T: (0191) 232 8058
F: (0191) 222 1391
E: kerry@daviesbellreed.co.uk

Swallows Nest
Rating Applied For
Contact: Ms Jo Tattersall, 19 Belle Vue Avenue, Gosforth, Newcastle upon Tyne NE3 1AH
T: (0191) 285 3334
F: (0191) 285 3334

Whinstone Cottage ★★★
Contact: Mrs P J Tait, Lyndale, 15 Kenton Road, Gosforth, Newcastle upon Tyne NE3 4NE
T: (0191) 285 1363

Wynding Down ★★★★★
Contact: Mrs Stanger, 6 Cottingwood Lane, Morpeth NE61 1EA
T: (01670) 511162
E: distanger@hotmail.com

BARDON MILL
Northumberland

The Hott ★★★
Contact: Mrs Harding, West End Town Farm, Thorngrafton, Bardon Mill, Hexham NE47 7JJ
T: (01434) 344258

BARNARD CASTLE
Durham

Boot and Shoe Cottage ★★★★
Contact: Mrs Rachel Peat, Waterside Cottage, Wycliffe, Barnard Castle DL12 9TR
T: (01833) 627200
F: (01833) 627200
E: info@bootandshoecottage.co.uk
I: www.bootandshoecottage.co.uk

East Briscoe Farm Cottages ★★★★
Contact: Mr Chris Tarpey, East Cottage, East Briscoe Farm, Baldersdale, Romaldkirk, Barnard Castle DL12 9UL
T: (01833) 650087
F: (01833) 650027
E: peter@eastbriscoe.co.uk
I: www.eastbriscoe.co.uk

Hauxwell Cottages (Bumpkin Byre and Puddles End) ★★★★
Contact: Mrs Penny Clark, Hauxwell Grange, Marwood, Barnard Castle DL12 8QU
T: (01833) 695022
F: (01833) 695022
E: jdclark@mail.sci-net.co.uk

Lanquitts Cottage ★
Contact: Mrs Brenda Kidd, Strathmore Arms Farm, Baldersdale, Barnard Castle DL12 9UR
T: (01833) 650345

5A Market Place ★★★
Contact: Mr & Mrs C Armstrong, 77 Galgate, Barnard Castle DL12 8ES
T: (01833) 690726
E: cajamara@aol.com

Staindrop House Mews & Arches ★★★★
Contact: Mrs D J Walton, Staindrop House, 14 Front Street, Staindrop, Darlington DL2 3NH
T: (01833) 660951
E: shmholidays@teesdaleonline.co.uk

Thorngate Coach House ★★★★
Contact: Mrs Clare Terry, Thorngate Coach House, Thorngate House, Thorngate, Barnard Castle DL12 8PY
T: (01833) 637791
F: (01833) 637791
E: markterry101@hotmail.com

Village Green Cottage ★★★★
Contact: Mrs M J Green, The Cottage, Village Green, Ovington, Richmond DL11 7BW
T: (01833) 627331
I: www.teesdaleholidays.co.uk/villagegreencottage.htm

Wackford Squeers Cottage ★★★
Contact: Mr John Braithwaite, Wackford Squeers Cottage, Wodencroft, Cotherstone, Barnard Castle DL12 9UQ
T: (01833) 650032
F: (01833) 650909
E: wodencroft@freenet.co.uk

Woodland House Cottage ★★★
Contact: Mr Harding, Woodland House, Woodland, Barnard Castle DL13 5RH
T: (01388) 718659
E: cottage@woodland-house.freeserve.co.uk
I: www.cottageguide.co.uk/woodlandhouse

BARNINGHAM
Durham

The Cottage ★★★★
Contact: Mrs Helen Lowes, The Cottage, Wilson House, Barningham, Richmond DL11 7EB
T: (01833) 621218
F: (01833) 621110

Dove Cottage ★★★
Contact: Miss Sheila Catton, Heath House, Barningham, Richmond DL11 7DU
T: (01833) 621374
E: dove@smithj90.fsnet.co.uk
I: www.cottageguide.co.uk/dove-cottage

Silver Hill Farm ★★★
Contact: Mrs Daphne Metcalf, Park House farm, Barningham, Richmond DL11 7DX
T: (01833) 621277
F: (01833) 621277
E: metcalf@parkhouse.flife.co.uk

BARRASFORD
Northumberland

Barrasford Arms Cottage ★★
Contact: Mr Milburn, Barrasford Arms, Barrasford, Chollerton, Hexham NE48 4AA
T: (01434) 681237
F: (01434) 681237

BEADNELL
Northumberland

Annstead Farm ★★★★
Contact: Mrs Susan Mellor, Annstead Farm, Beadnell, Chathill NE67 5BT
T: (01665) 720387
F: (01665) 721494
E: susan@annstead.co.uk
I: www.annstead.co.uk

Beadnell House Cottage ★★★
Contact: Mrs Val Litherland, Beadnell House, Chathill NE67 5AT
T: (01665) 721380
F: (01665) 720217
E: enquiries@beadnellhouse.co.uk
I: www.beadnellhouse.co.uk

Beechley ★★★
Contact: Mrs Deborah Baker, 22 Upper Green Way, Tingley, Wakefield WF3 1TA
T: (0113) 218 9176
F: (0113) 218 9176
E: deb_n_ade@hotmail.com

Benthall ★★★★
Contact: Mr & Mrs E Davidson, 6 Benthall, Beadnell, Chathill NE67 5BQ
T: (01665) 720269

The Bothy ★★★★
Contact: Mrs Beryl Seaward-Birchall, The Bothy, Shepherds Cottage, Beadnell, Chathill NE67 5AD
T: (01665) 720497
F: (01665) 720497
I: www.shepherdscottage.ntb.org.uk

The Dells ★★★
Contact: Mr & Mrs Iain and Andrea Slater, 25 Northumberland Gardens, Jesmond, Newcastle upon Tyne NE2 1HA
T: (0191) 239 9934
E: andreaslater@beadnell.fsnet.co.uk

Low Dover Beadnell Bay ★★★★
Contact: Mrs Kath Thompson, Low Dover Beadnell Bay, Harbour Road, Beadnell, Chathill NE67 5BJ
T: (01665) 720291
F: (01665) 720291
E: kathandbob@lowdover.co.uk
I: www.lowdover.co.uk

Nook End Cottage ★★★★★
Contact: Ms Fiona McKeith, 174 Warkworth Woods, Newcastle Great Park, Gosforth, Newcastle upon Tyne NE3 5RD
T: (0191) 236 5971
E: info@coastalretreats.co.uk
I: www.coastalretreats.co.uk

The Rowans ★★★
Contact: Mr Trotter, South Cottage, Pasture Hill, Seahouses NE68 7UU
T: (01665) 720891
E: thomasjtrotter@tiscali.co.uk

Torwoodlee & Shorestone ★★★
Contact: Dales Hol Cot Ref:1892,1893, Dales Holiday Cottages, Carleton Business Park, Carleton New Road, Skipton BD23 2AA
T: (01756) 799821
F: (01756) 797012
E: info@dalesholcot.com
I: www.dalesholcot.com

Town Farm Cottages ★★★-★★★★
Contact: Mr & Mrs P Thompson & Mrs License, Heritage Coast Holidays, 6G Greensfield Court, Alnwick NE66 2DE
T: (01655) 606022
F: (01670) 787336
E: paulthompson@alncom.net
I: www.northumberland-holidays.com

BEAL
Northumberland

Bee Hill Properties ★★★★-★★★★★
Contact: Mr David Nesbitt, Bee Hill Properties, Beal, Berwick-upon-Tweed TD15 2PB
T: (01289) 381102
F: (01289) 381418
E: info@beehill.co.uk
I: www.beehill.co.uk

BEAMISH
Durham

Chapel House Studio Apartments ★★★
Contact: Mr MacLennan, Chapel House, Causey Row, Marley Hill, Beamish, Stanley NE16 5EJ
T: (01207) 290992

BELFORD
Northumberland

3, 4 and 5 Swinhoe Cottages ★★★
Contact: Mrs V Nixon, Swinhoe Farm House, Belford NE70 7LJ
T: (01668) 213370
E: valerie@swinhoecottages.co.uk
I: www.swinhoecottages.co.uk

Belford Court ★★★★
Contact: Louise Nixon, Market Place, Belford NE70 7NE
T: (01668) 213543
F: (01668) 213787
E: bluebel@globalnet.co.uk
I: www.belfordcourt.com

Church View ★★★
Contact: Mrs Susan Oates, 27 Whitfield Place, Wolsingham, Bishop Auckland DL13 3DF
T: (01388) 527127
F: (01377) 526547
E: johnoates@pro-streamlimited.co.uk

Elwick Farm Cottages ★★★-★★★★
Contact: Mrs Roslyn Reay, Elwick Farm Cottages, Elwick Farm, Belford NE70 7EL
T: (01668) 213242
F: (01668) 213783
E: w.r.reay@talk21.com
I: www.elwickcottages.co.uk

Grange Cottage ★★★★
Contact: Mrs Susan Mellor, Annstead Farm, Beadnell NE67 5BT
T: (01665) 720387
F: (01665) 721494
E: susan@annstead.co.uk
I: www.annstead.co.uk

Hollyhock House ★★★★
Contact: Miss Alison Turnbull, 95 St Matthew's Road, London SW2 1NE
T: (0207) 733 4904
E: ali_turnbull@hotmail.com
I: www.highstreetbelford.freeserve.co.uk

Owls Rest ★★★★
Contact: Ms Christine Brown, The Old Manse, New Road, Chatton, Alnwick NE66 5PU
T: (01668) 215343
F: (01668) 215343
E: chattonbb@aol.com
I: www.owlsrestbelford.co.uk

Shepherds Cottage ★★★★
Contact: Mrs Iris Oates, Easington Farm, Belford NE70 7EG
T: (01668) 213298

Teal Cottage ★★★★
Contact: Mrs Burn, Fenham-le-Moor, Belford NE70 7PN
T: (01668) 213247
F: (01668) 213247
E: katie@fenhamlemoor.com

BELLINGHAM
Northumberland

Boat Farm Cottages (Heron Cottage and Otter Cottage) ★★★★
Contact: Mrs Young, Boat Farm Cottages (Heron Cottage and Otter Cottag, Boat Farm, Bellingham, Wark, Hexham NE48 2AR
T: (01434) 220989
E: barbaraattheboat@hotmail.com

Buteland Bothy ★★
Contact: Mrs Alison Williams, Buteland Bothy, Buteland House, Bellingham, Wark, Hexham NE48 2EX
T: (01434) 220389
F: (01434) 220389
E: buteland@aol.com

Castle Hill View ★★★
Contact: Mr & Mrs Len & Joan Batey, Front Street, Bellingham, Hexham NE48 2AA
T: (01434) 220263

Conheath Cottage ★★★★
Contact: Mrs Zaina Riddle, Blakelaw Farm, Bellingham, Hexham NE48 2EF
T: (01434) 220250
F: (01434) 220250
E: stay@conheath.co.uk
I: www.conheath.co.uk

Riverdale Court ★★★★
Contact: Mr John and Iben Cocker, Riverdale Court, Bellingham, Hexham NE48 2JT
T: (01434) 220254
F: (01434) 220457
E: iben@riverdalehall.demon.co.uk
I: www.riverdalehall.demon.co.uk

BERWICK-UPON-TWEED
Northumberland

Broadstone Cottage ★★★
Contact: Mr E D Chantler, Broadstone Farm, Grafty Green, Maidstone ME17 2AT
T: (01622) 850207
F: (01622) 851750

2, The Courtyard
Rating Applied For
Contact: Mrs Joan Morton, 2, The Courtyard, Church Street, Berwick-upon-Tweed TD15 1EE
T: (01289) 308737
E: jim@patmosphere.uklinux.net

Courtyard Cottage
Rating Applied For
Contact: Mr Peter Howard, 30 Great Lime Road, Newcastle upon Tyne NE12 7AH
T: (0191) 268 0788
E: susanhoward@cwcom.net

Gainslawhill Farm Cottage ★★★
Contact: Mrs Susan Wight, Gainslawhill Farm, Berwick-upon-Tweed TD15 1SZ
T: (01289) 386210
I: www.gainslawhill.co.uk

Honeysuckle Cottage and Bluebell Cottage ★★★★
Contact: Mr Robert Whitten, West Longridge Farm, Berwick-upon-Tweed TD15 2JX
T: (01289) 331112
F: (01289) 304591
E: robert@westlongridge.co.uk
I: www.westlongridge.co.uk

Kingsway Cottage ★★★★
Contact: Mrs Judith King, East Ord Farmhouse, East Ord, Tweedmouth, Berwick-upon-Tweed TD15 2NS
T: (01289) 306228
E: jking4kingsway@aol.com
I: www.kingswaycottage.co.uk

Lark Rise ★★★★
Contact: Mrs Deirdre Dickson, Crosby House, Crosby-on-Eden, Carlisle CA6 4QZ
T: (01228) 573239
F: (01228) 573338
E: enquires@norbyways.demon.co.uk
I: www.northumbria-byways.com/larkrise

Mill Lane Apartments ★★★★
Contact: Mr John Haswell, Mill Lane Apartments, 2A Palace Street East, Berwick-upon-Tweed TD15 1HT
T: (01289) 304492
F: (01289) 304848
E: john@millane.fsnet.co.uk
I: www.millane.co.uk

The Old Barn ★★★★
Contact: Mr & Mrs Richard & Susan Persse, High Letham Farmhouse, High Letham, Berwick-upon-Tweed TD15 1UX
T: (01289) 306585
F: (01289) 304194
E: hlfb@fantasyprints.co.uk
I: www.ntb.org.uk

1 The Old Smokehouse ★★★
Contact: Mrs Jackie Sell, 46 Queenhythe Road, Jacobs Well, Guildford GU4 7NX
T: (01483) 533757

6 Palace Green
Rating Applied For
Contact: Mr Louis Heward-Mills, 73 Bengeo Street, Hertford SG14 3ET
T: (01992) 534828
F: (01992) 534858
E: louis@cctr-london.demon.co.uk

18 Parade ★★★
Contact: Mrs Brenda Crowcroft, The Sycamores, Cardingmill Valley, Church Stretton SY6 6JF
T: (01694) 722219
E: b.crowcroft@talk21.com

The Retreat ★★★★
Contact: Mrs Muckle, 40 Ravensdowne, Berwick-upon-Tweed TD15 1DQ
T: (01289) 306992
F: (01289) 331606
E: petedot@dmuckle.freeserve.co.uk

South Ord Farm Bungalow ★★★★
Contact: Dales Hol Cot Ref:2203, Dales Holiday Cottages, Carleton Business Park, Carleton New Road, Skipton BD23 2AA
T: (01756) 799821
F: (01756) 797012
E: info@dalesholcot.com
I: www.dalesholcot.com

Tigh Na Rudh Rating Applied For
Contact: Sykes Ref 891, Sykes Cottages, York House, York Street, Chester CH1 3LR
T: (01244) 345700
F: (01244) 321442
E: info@sykescottages.co.uk
I: www.sykescottages.co.uk

Trevone ★★★★
Contact: Mr Peter Herdman, Devonia, 13 Bankhill, Berwick-upon-Tweed TD15 1BE
T: (01289) 307524

West Kyloe Cottages ★★★
Contact: Mrs Teresa Smalley, Garden Cottage, 1 West Kyloe, Fenwick, Berwick-upon-Tweed TD15 2PG
T: (01289) 381279
F: (01289) 381279
E: teresasmalley@westkyloe.demon.co.uk
I: www.westkyloe.co.uk

West Ord Holiday Cottages ★★★★
Contact: Mrs Carol Lang, West Ord Cottages, West Ord Farm, Berwick-upon-Tweed TD15 2XQ
T: (01289) 386631
F: (01289) 386800
E: stay@westord.co.uk
I: www.westord.co.uk

Whitecroft ★★★
Contact: Mrs Moira Kay, Tweed Cottage, Berwick-upon-Tweed TD15 2XW
T: (01289) 386066
F: (01289) 386066
E: enquiries@whitecroftcottage.co.uk
I: www.whitecroftcottage.co.uk

BISHOP AUCKLAND
Durham

Five Gables Cottage ★★★★
Contact: Mr P & Mrs J Weston, Five Gables Guest House, Binchester, Bishop Auckland DL14 8AT
T: (01388) 608204
F: (01388) 663092
E: cottage@fivegables.co.uk
I: www.fivegables.co.uk

Gill Bank Farm Cottage ★★★
Contact: Mrs Anne Marley, Butterknowle, Bishop Auckland DL13 5QF
T: (01388) 718614

Meadow View ★★★
Contact: Dales Hol Cot Ref:14 Dales Hol Cot Ref:1462, Dales Holiday Cottages, Carleton Business Park, Carleton New Road, Skipton BD23 2AA
T: (01756) 799821
F: (01756) 797012
E: info@dalesholcot.com
I: www.dalesholcot.com

West Cottage ★★★★
Contact: Mrs E Wilkinson, Carrsides Farm, Rushyford, Ferryhill DL17 0NJ
T: (01388) 720252
F: (01388) 720252
E: carrsides@farming.co.uk

BLANCHLAND
Northumberland

Bail Hill ★★★
Contact: Mrs Graham, Allenshields, Blanchland, Consett DH8 9PP
T: (01434) 675274

Boltsburn Holiday Cottages ★★
Contact: Mr Cecil Ernest Davison, Bolts Brae, 10 Watergate Road, Castleside, Consett DH8 9QS
T: (01207) 583076

Boltslaw Cottage ★★★
Contact: Mrs N Smith, 6 Selborne Avenue, Gateshead NE9 6ET
T: (0191) 487 9456
F: (01670) 510300
E: asmith6000@aol.com
I: www.uk-holiday-cottages.co.uk/boltslaw

BOULMER
Northumberland

North Cottage Rating Applied For
Contact: Mrs Madeleine Frater, North Cottage, Boulmer, Alnwick NE66 3BX
T: (01665) 577308
E: madeleinefrater@hotmail.com

BOWSDEN
Northumberland

The Cottage ★★★
Contact: Mr & Mrs John Dunn, Lickar Lea Bungalow, Bowsden, Berwick-upon-Tweed TD15 2TP
T: (01289) 388500
F: (01289) 388507
E: janet.dunn@lickarlea.co.uk
I: www.lickarlea.co.uk

BRANTON
Northumberland

Breamish Valley Cottages ★★★★-★★★★★
Contact: Mrs Michele Moralee, Breamish Valley Cottages, Branton West Side, Branton, Alnwick NE66 4LW
T: (01665) 578263
F: (01665) 578263
E: peter@breamishvalley.co.uk
I: www.breamishvalley.co.uk

BUTTERKNOWLE
Durham

Folly Cottage ★★★
Contact: Dales Hol Cot Ref:2112, Carleton Business Park, Carleton New Road, Skipton BD23 2AA
T: (01756) 799821
F: (01756) 797012
E: info@dalesholcot.com
I: www.dalesholcot.com

BYRNESS
Northumberland

Catcleugh Farm ★★★
Contact: Mr Walter Nieuwkoop, Catcleugh, Byrness, Otterburn, Newcastle upon Tyne NE19 1TX
T: (01670) 772607
F: (01670) 772607
E: catcleugh@hotmail.com
I: www.catcleugh.com

The Old School House ★★★★
Contact: Dales Holiiday Cottages, Carleton Business Park, Carleton New Road, Skipton BD23 2DG
T: (01756) 799821
F: (01756) 797012

CALLALY
Northumberland

Dene Cottage ★★★★
Contact: Mrs Maureen Winn, Dene Cottage, Dene House, Callaly, Alnwick NE66 4TA
T: (01665) 574513

CARLTON IN CLEVELAND
Tees Valley

The Coachman's Cottage ★★★
Contact: Dales Hol Cot Ref:10 Dales Hol Cot Ref:1075, Dales Holiday Cottages, Carleton Business Park, Carleton New Road, Skipton BD23 2AA
T: (01756) 799821
F: (01756) 797012
E: info@dalesholcot.com
I: www.dalesholcot.com

Stables Cottage ★★★
Contact: Dales Hol Cot Ref:2697, Dales Holiday Cottages, Carleton Business Park, Carleton New Road, Skipton BD23 2AA
T: (01756) 799821
F: (01756) 797012
E: info@dalesholcot.com
I: www.dalesholcot.com

CARRVILLE
Durham

62 Wantage Road ★★
Contact: Mr & Mrs Norman and Anne Walker, 62 Wantage Road, Carrville, Durham DH1 1LR
T: (0191) 386 2290
I: www.cottageguide.co.uk/carrville

CASTLESIDE
Durham

Garden Cottage, Dairy Cottage & The Forge ★★-★★★
Contact: Mr & Mrs Elliot, Derwent Grange Farm, Castleside, Consett DH8 9BN
T: (01207) 508358
E: ekelliot@aol.com

Manor Park Cottage (Manor Park Ltd) ★★
Contact: Mr Brian Elstrop, Manor Park Ltd, Broadmeadows, Rippon Burn, Tow Law, Bishop Auckland DH8 9HD
T: (01207) 501000
F: (01207) 509271

Pondfield Villa Farm Cottages ★★★
Contact: Mrs Margaret Steel, Pondfield Villa Farm, Millershill Lane, Rowley, Consett DH8 9HF
T: (01207) 582703
E: k.a.steel@btinternet.co.uk

Willerby Grange ★★★
Contact: Mr & Mrs Gavin & Patricia Jopling, Willerby Grange, Pemberton Road, Allensford, Consett DH8 9BA
T: (01207) 508752
F: (01207) 508752
E: stay@willerbygrange.co.uk

CAWBURN
Northumberland

Rowan Cottage ★★★★
Contact: Mrs Margaret Swallow, Rowan Cottage, High Edges Green, Cawburn, Haltwhistle NE49 9PP
T: (01434) 320352
F: (01434) 320352
E: swallow@rowan78.freeserve.co.uk
I: www.rowan78.freeserve.co.uk

CHATHILL
Northumberland

Charlton Hall Holiday Cottages Rating Applied For
Contact: Mr Robert Thorp, Charlton Hall Holiday Cottages, Charlton Hall, Chathill NE67 5DZ
T: (01665) 579378

The Lodge and Head Gardener's House ★★★★
Contact: Mrs J. Shirley Burnie, The Lodge and Head Gardener's House, Doxford Hall, Ellingham, Chathill NE67 5DN
T: (01665) 589499
F: (01665) 589499
E: doxfordhall@aol.com

Newstead Cottage ★★
Contact: Mrs M Riddell, Newstead Farm, Chathill NE67 5LH
T: (01665) 589263

Tower Cottage ★★
Contact: Mrs Cresswell, Preston Tower, Ellingham, Chathill NE67 5DH
T: (01665) 589227

CHATTON
Northumberland

Mill Cottage ★★★★
Contact: Ms Kim Stewart, Ros View, 14 Mill Hill, Chatton, Alnwick NE66 5PR
T: (01668) 215289
E: spearfish@btinternet.com

Sunny and Primrose Cottages ★★★★
Contact: Mr Ian Fenwick, Castle Street, Warkworth, Morpeth NE65 0UW
T: (01665) 711136
F: (01727) 844901
E: stay@millcottages.co.uk

CHESTER-LE-STREET
Durham

The Old Stables ★★★★
Contact: Mr & Mrs Cutter, The Old Stables, Hollycroft, 11 The Parade, Chester-le-Street DH3 3LR
T: (0191) 388 7088
E: cutter@hollycroft11.freeserve.co.uk

Plawsworth Hall Farm ★★★★
Contact: Mr Harry Johnson, Plawsworth, Chester-le-Street DH2 3LD
T: (0191) 371 0251
F: (0191) 371 2101
E: hmj2109@aol.com

CHILLINGHAM
Northumberland

Chillingham Castle ★★★
Contact: Chillingham Castle, Chillingham, Alnwick NE66 5NJ
T: (01668) 215359
F: (01668) 215463
E: enquiries@chillingham-castle.com
I: www.chillingham-castle.com

CHOLLERTON
Northumberland

The Old Church ★★★★
Contact: Mrs Marilyn Framrose, Old Church Cottage, Chollerton, Hexham NE46 4TF
T: (01434) 681930
E: oldchurch@supanet.com
I: www.urscene.net

CHOPWELL
Tyne and Wear

High Pasture Cottage ★★★★
Contact: Mr Allan Low, Bowser Hill Farm, Chopwell, Newcastle upon Tyne NE17 7AY
T: (01207) 560881
E: alow@btinternet.com

COANWOOD
Northumberland

Mill Hill Farmhouse ★★★
Contact: Mrs Wigham, Hargill House, Haltwhistle NE49 0PQ
T: (01434) 320256
E: millhill@fsmail.net
I: www.cottageguide.co.uk/millhill

COCKFIELD
Durham

New Cottage ★★★
Contact: Mrs Margaret Partridge, New Cottage, Law One, Hollymoor Farm, Cockfield, Bishop Auckland DL13 5HF
T: (01388) 718567
F: (01388) 718567

Rose Cottage ★★★
Contact: Mrs M E Elstob, Rose Cottage, Highlands, Cockfield, Bishop Auckland DL13 5BG
T: (01388) 718941

Stonecroft and Swallows Nest ★★★★
Contact: Mrs Alison Tallentire, Low Lands Farm, Cockfield, Bishop Auckland DL13 5AW
T: (01388) 718251
F: (01388) 718251
E: info@farmholidaysuk.com
I: www.farmholidaysuk.com

COLWELL
Northumberland

Lance-Surtees Cottage ★★★
Contact: Mrs Dorothea Nelson, Chapel Cottages, Prescott, Uffculme, Cullompton EX15 3BA
T: (01884) 841320

CORBRIDGE
Northumberland

April Cottage ★★★
Contact: Mrs Kate Dean, 21 Woodland Close, Chelford, Macclesfield SK11 9BZ
T: (01625) 861718
E: peterandkatedean@btopenworld

The Hayes ★★
Contact: Mrs Monica Matthews, The Hayes, Newcastle Road, Corbridge NE45 5LP
T: (01434) 632010
F: (01434) 633069
E: mjct@mmatthews.fsbusiness.co.uk
I: www.hayes-corbridge.co.uk

Nosbor Cottage ★★★
Contact: Mrs Veronica Robson, 7 Runnymede Road, Darras Hall, Ponteland, Newcastle upon Tyne NE20 9HE
T: (01661) 871135
F: (01661) 871135
E: nosboruk@yahoo.co.uk

Oswald Cottage ★★★★
Contact: Mrs H K Harriman, Swarden House, Kyloe House Farm, Eachwick, Newcastle upon Tyne NE18 0BB
T: (01661) 852909
F: (01661) 854106
E: pwh@littonproperties.co.uk

14 Princes Street ★★★★
Contact: Mrs Hendry, The Old Post Office, Kiln Pit Hill, Consett DH8 9RW
T: (01207) 255283
E: olwen.hendry@btopenworld.com

Wallhouses South Farm Cottage ★★★★
Contact: Mrs E Lymburn, South Farm, Military Road, Corbridge NE45 5PU
T: (01434) 672388
E: loraip@aol.com

West Fell Cottage ★★★
Contact: Smith, West Fell House, Corbridge NE45 5RZ
T: (01434) 632044

CORNHILL-ON-TWEED
Northumberland

East Moneylaws Farm Cottage Rating Applied For
Contact: Mr Robin Lathangle, East Moneylaws Farm Cottage, No 4 Cottage, East Moneylaws, Cornhill-on-Tweed TD12 4QD
T: (01890) 850328

Herds Hoose, Cherry Cottage ★★★
Contact: Mrs Diana Tweedie, Tithe Hill, Cornhill-on-Tweed TD12 4QD
T: (01890) 850286
E: info@tithehill.co.uk
I: www.tithehill.co.uk

Jasmine Cottage ★★★
Contact: Dales Hol Cot Ref:22 Dales Hol Cot Ref:2257, Dales Holiday Cottages, Carleton Business Park, Carleton New Road, Skipton BD23 2AA
T: (01756) 799821
F: (01756) 797012
E: info@dalesholcot.com
I: www.dalesholcot.com

Melkington Lodge ★★★★★
Contact: Mrs Veronica Barber, Melkington Lodge, Cornhill-on-Tweed TD12 4UP
T: (01890) 882313
F: (01890) 882300
E: barber@melkington.demon.co.uk
I: www.melkington.co.uk

Orchard Cottage ★★★★
Contact: Mrs Lucy Carroll, Old Egypt, Tiptoe, Cornhill-on-Tweed TD12 4XD
T: (01890) 882177
F: (01890) 883060
E: fish@till-fishing.co.uk
I: www.till-fishing.co.uk

The Stables ★★★★
Contact: Mrs Margaret Buckle, Tor Cottage, Cornhill-on-Tweed TD12 4QA
T: (01890) 882390
F: (01890) 883778
E: david.buckle@btinternet.com
I: www.thestables.cornhill.btinternet.co.uk/

Tillmouth Cottage ★★★★
Contact: Mrs Binnie, Tillmouth Farm, Cornhill-on-Tweed TD12 4XA
T: (01289) 382482
F: (01289) 342482

COTHERSTONE
Durham

Farthings ★★★
Contact: Mr C J Bainbridge, Glen Leigh, Cotherstone, Barnard Castle DL12 9QW
T: (01833) 650331

Thwaite Hall ★★★
Contact: Mrs Audrey Wickham, Hillcrest, 6 Front Street, Whitburn, Sunderland SR6 7JD
T: (0191) 529 3793
F: (0191) 529 2362

COWSHILL
Durham

Dales Farm Cottage ★★★
Contact: Dales Hol Cot Ref:1322, Dales Holiday Cottages, Carleton Business Park, Carleton New Road, Skipton BD23 2AA
T: (01756) 799821
F: (01756) 797012
E: info@dalesholcot.com
I: www.dalesholcot.com

CRAMLINGTON
Northumberland

Burradon Farm Cottages Rating Applied For
Contact: Mrs Judith Younger, Burradon Farm Cottages, Burradon Farm, Burradon, Cramlington NE23 7ND
T: (0191) 268 3203
E: judy_younger@burradonfarm.co.uk

CRASTER
Northumberland

Craster Pine Lodges ★★★★
Contact: Mr & Mrs Robson, Craster Pine Lodges, 9 West End, Craster, Dunstan, Alnwick NE66 3TS
T: (01665) 576286
F: (01665) 576983
E: pinelodges@barkpots.co.uk
I: www.barkpots.co.uk

Ebor ★★★
Contact: Mr Mawhinney, Gosforth, Newcastle upon Tyne NE3 1UL
T: (0191) 284 6294
E: whbmawhinney@supanet.com

Proctor's Stead Cottages ★★★
Contact: Mr Ruth Anne Davidson, Proctor's Stead, Dunstan, Alnwick NE66 3TF
T: (01665) 576613
F: (01665) 576311
I: www.proctorsstead.ntb.org.uk

Rock Ville ★★★★
Contact: Mr & Mrs Robson, 9 West End, Craster, Dunstan, Alnwick NE66 3TS
T: (01665) 576286
F: (01665) 576286
E: rockville@barkpots.co.uk
I: www.rockvillecraster.co.uk

Seahaven ★★★
Contact: Mrs Imrie, 90 Allerburn Lea, Denwick, Alnwick NE66 2NQ
T: (01665) 602275

CROOKHAM
Northumberland

Askew Cottage ★★★★
Contact: Mrs Heather Pentland, 32 Crookham Village, Cornhill-on-Tweed TD12 4SY
T: (01890) 820201
F: (01890) 820201
E: hjpentland@waitrose.com

DARLINGTON
Tees Valley

63 Cumberland Street Rating Applied For
Contact: Mrs Kathleen Reeve, 63 Cumberland Street, Darlington DL3 0LY
T: (01933) 387945
F: (01933) 350203
E: barry.reeve1@ntlworld.com

High House Farm Cottages ★★★-★★★★
Contact: Mr & Mrs Harry and Peggy Wood, High House Farm Cottages, High House Farm, Houghton-le-Side, Darlington DL2 2UU
T: (01388) 834879
F: (01388) 834879
E: wood@houghtonleside.fsnet.co.uk
I: www.farmstaynorth.co.uk

Pegasus Cottage ★★★
Contact: Mr & Mrs Stuart and Denise Chapman, 4 Tees View, Hurworth Place, Darlington DL2 2DH
T: (01325) 722542
F: (01325) 722542
E: stuart1948@msn.com
I: www.pegasuscottage.co.uk

DENWICK
Northumberland

Riverside Cottage Rating Applied For
Contact: Ms Alison Wrangham, Harehope Hall, Eglingham, Alnwick NE66 2DP
T: (01668) 217329
F: (01668) 217346
E: ali.wrangham@farming.co.uk

Waterside Cottage ★★★
Contact: Mrs Deborah Philipson, Waterside House, Denwick, Alnwick NE66 3RA
T: (01665) 603082
F: (01665) 603082
E: debbiephilipson@hopeandanchorholidays.fsnet.co.uk

DETCHANT
Northumberland

Peace Cottage
Rating Applied For
Contact: Mr William Quinn, Peace Cottage, 1 Kettleburn Farm Cottages, Detchant, Belford NE70 7PQ
T: (01668) 219459
E: victorquinn@l12.com

DIPTON
Durham

Westlea ★★★★
Contact: Mrs A C Watson, Evergreen, Hilltop Road, Dipton, Stanley DH9 9JY
T: (01207) 570072
F: (01207) 570072
E: westlea@unitynet.co.uk
I: www.country.holidays.co.uk

DURHAM
Durham

26a and 26b Hallgarth Street ★★
Contact: Ms Sue Pitts, 27 Hallgarth Street, Durham DH1 3AT
T: (0191) 384 1611

Arbour House Bungalow and Cottage ★★★
Contact: Mrs Rena Hunter, Arbour House Bungalow and Cottage, Arbour House Farm, Crossgate Moor, Durham DH1 4TQ
T: (0191) 384 2418
F: (0191) 386 0738
E: enquiries@arbourhouse.co.uk
I: www.arbourhouse.ntb.org.uk

Baxter Wood Cottages ★★★★
Contact: Mr & Mrs Trevor and Tricia Jones, Baxter Wood Cottages, Baxter Wood Farm, Crossgate Moor, Nevilles Cross, Durham DH1 4TG
T: (0191) 386 5820
F: (0191) 386 5820

Dove Cottage ★★★★
Contact: Mrs Eileen Woods, 25 Orchard Drive, Gilesgate, Durham DH1 1LA
T: (0191) 386 4176
E: durhamcottages@aol.com
I: www.durhamcottages.com

Jubilee House ★★
Contact: Mrs C Reay, Jubilee House, 9 Sidegate, Durham DH1 5SY
T: (0191) 384 4894

The Old Power House ★★★★
Contact: Mrs Anne Hall, Garden Cottage, Southill Hall, Plawsworth, Chester-le-Street DH3 4EQ
T: (0191) 387 3001
F: (0191) 389 3569
E: g.s.hall@talk21.com

Sands Cottage ★★★
Contact: Mrs Greta Hodgson, Sands House, The Sands, Gilesgate, Durham DH1 1JY
T: (0191) 384 4731
F: (0191) 384 4731
E: greta@sandshouse.fsnet.co.uk

Stowhouse Farm Cottages
Rating Applied For
Contact: Mr Peter Swinburne, Stowhouse Farm Cottages, Stowhouse Farm, Old Cornsay, Lanchester, Durham DH7 9EN
T: (0191) 373 9990

EAGLESCLIFFE
Tees Valley

Aislaby Grange Farm Cottages ★★★
Contact: Mr Hutchinson, Aislaby Grange Farm Cottages, Aislaby Grange, Aislaby, Eaglescliffe, Stockton-on-Tees TS16 0QP
T: (01642) 782170
F: (01642) 782170

EASINGTON
Tees Valley

Swan Cottage
Rating Applied For
Contact: Mr Thistlethwaite, 23 Fir Trees Crescent, Lostock Hill, Preston PR5 5SL
T: (01772) 312818
F: (01772) 312818

EASTFIELD
Northumberland

Little Dormer Cottage ★★★★
Contact: Mr Clive Sykes, Sykes Cottages, York House, York Street, Chester CH1 3LR
T: (01244) 345700
F: (01244) 321442
E: info@sykescottages.co.uk
I: www.sykescottages.co.uk

EDLINGHAM
Northumberland

Briar, Rose And Clematis Cottage ★★★★
Contact: Mrs Helen Wyld, Briar, Rose And Clematis Cottage, New Moor House, Edlingham, Alnwick NE66 2BT
T: (01665) 574638
E: stay@newmoorhouse.co.uk
I: www.newmoorhouse.co.uk

Hazelnuthouse ★★★★
Contact: Ms Hazel Bennett, 61 Portsmouth Road, Guildford GU2 4BS
T: (01483) 569346
F: (01483) 569346
E: hazelnuthouse@dial.pipex.com
I: www.bigfoot.com/~hazelnuthouse

Lumbylaw & Garden Cottages ★★★★
Contact: Mrs Lee, Edlingham, Alnwick NE66 2BW
T: (01665) 574277
F: (01665) 574277
E: holidays@lumbylaw.co.uk
I: www.lumbylaw.co.uk

EGGLESTON
Durham

The Granary ★★★
Contact: Mrs Gray, The Cottage, Eggleston Hall, Eggleston, Barnard Castle DL12 0AG
T: (01833) 650403
F: (01833) 650378

The Stobbs ★★★
Contact: Mrs D Bainbridge, East Carnigill, Baldersdale, Barnard Castle DL12 9UX
T: (01833) 650472
E: madbain@ukonline.co.uk
I: www.thestobbs@ntb.org.uk

Swinkly Cottage ★★★
Contact: Mrs Mary Robinson (FROM 2004 SEASON), Dales Holiday Cottages, 3 Dene Hall Drive, Bishop Auckland DL14 6UF
T: (01388) 605620
I: www.dalesholcot.com

ELSDON
Northumberland

Dunns Farm & Bilsmoorfoot ★★★-★★★★★
Contact: Mrs Carruthers, Dunns Farm, Elsdon, Newcastle upon Tyne NE19 1AL
T: (01669) 640219
I: www.dunnsfarm.ntb.org.uk

EMBLETON
Northumberland

Cra-na-ge ★★★
Contact: Sykes Cottages Ref: 694, Sykes Cottages, York House, York Street, Chester CH1 3LR
T: (01244) 345700
F: (01244) 321442
E: info@sykescottages.co.uk
I: www.sykescottages.co.uk

Doxford Farm Cottages ★★-★★★★★
Contact: Mrs Sarah Shell, Doxford Farm Cottages, Doxford Farm, Doxford, Chathill NE67 5DY
T: (01665) 579348
F: (01665) 579331
E: doxfordfarm@hotmail.com
I: www.doxfordfarmcottages.com

Dunstanburgh Castle Courtyard Cottages★★★
Contact: Mr & Mrs P Thompson & Mrs License, Heritage Coast Holidays, 6G Greensfield Court, Alnwick NE66 2DE
T: (01665) 606022
F: (01670) 787336
E: paulthompson@alncom.net
I: www.northumberland-holidays.com

Dunstanburgh View ★★★★
Contact: Mrs B R Astbury, 9 Sunnybrae Cottages, Embleton, Alnwick NE66 3UU
T: (01665) 576509
F: (01665) 576509
E: dunstanburgh_view@hotmail.com
I: www.dunstanburghview.ntb.org.uk

Eider ★★★★
Contact: Mrs Jan Straughan, Riverside, Lesbury, Alnwick NE66 3SG
T: (01665) 830032

Embleton Cottage & The Nook ★★★
Contact: Mrs Ella Unwin, Lynecroft, Seahouses NE66 3XN
T: (01665) 576639

Glebe Cottage ★★★
Contact: Mrs Sybil Goldthorpe, Glebe Farmhouse, Embleton, Alnwick NE66 3UX
T: (01665) 576465

The Haberderdashers 2A Front Street ★★★
Contact: Mrs Mary Axelby, 86 Crimicar Lane, Sheffield S10 4FB
T: (0114) 230 5090
F: (01141) 230 5090
E: graham.axelby@btinternet.com

Mansard Cottage ★★★★
Contact: Mr & Mrs Nic & Pauline Grant, 11 Holeyn Hall Road, Wylam NE41 8BB
T: (01661) 853513
F: (01661) 852152
E: pauline.grant@btinternet.com
I: www.mansard.cottage.btinternet.co.uk

Northumbrian Holiday Cottages ★★★★
Contact: Mr & Mrs Chris Seal, 1 Westfield, Gosforth, Newcastle upon Tyne NE3 4YE
T: (0191) 285 6930
F: (0191) 285 6930
E: seal@northumbrian-holiday-cottages.co.uk
I: www.northumbrian-holiday-cottages.co.uk

ESCOMB
Durham

Muskoka ★★★★
Contact: Dales Hol Cot Ref:3372, Dales Holiday Cottages, Carleton Business Park, Carleton New Road, Skipton BD23 2AA
T: (01756) 790919
F: (01756) 797012
E: info@dalesholcot.com
I: www.dalesholcot.com

FALSTONE
Northumberland

Station Cottage
Rating Applied For
Contact: Mrs June Banks, Station House, Falstone, Hexham NE48 1AB
T: (01434) 240311

FELTON
Northumberland

Eshottheugh Farm Cottage ★★★
Contact: Ms Fay Shead, Eshotteugh Farm, Felton, Morpeth NE65 9QH
T: (01670) 787817
F: (01670) 787817

FERRYHILL
Durham

Farnless Farm Cottage ★★
Contact: Mrs Daphne Anderson, Farnless Farm Cottage, Bishop Middleham, Ferryhill DL17 9EB
T: (0191) 377 1428
E: farnless@btopenworld.co.uk

FOREST-IN-TEESDALE
Durham

Laneside ★★★★
Contact: Mrs N J Liddle, Raby Estate Office, Middleton-in-Teesdale, Barnard Castle DL12 0QH
T: (01833) 640209
F: (01833) 640963
E: teesdaleestate@rabycastle.com
I: www.rabycastle.com

FOXTON
Northumberland

Greybarns ★★★★
Contact: Ms Jane Mallen, Northumberland Estates Holiday Cottages, Alnwick Castle, Denwick, Alnwick NE66 1NQ
T: (01665) 602094
F: (01665) 608126
E: nehc@farmline.com
I: www.alnwickcastle.com/holidaycottages

Out of Bounds ★★★★
Contact: Mrs Hazel Tate, 19 Lawhead Road West, Berwick-upon-Tweed KY16 9NE
T: (01334) 470200
E: golftate@aol.com

FROSTERLEY
Durham

The Old Sunday School ★★★★
Contact: Mrs Pat Blayney, The Old Sunday School, Bridge End, Frosterley DL13 2SN
T: (01388) 528913
F: (01388) 528913
E: pat@theoss.freeserve.co.uk

Roseli Court ★★★
Contact: Mrs Vivian Rayne, 68 Front Street, Wolsingham, Bishop Auckland DL13 2QS
T: (01388) 526488
F: (01388) 526488

GAINFORD
Durham

Corner Cottage & Barn House Mews ★★-★★★
Contact: Dales Hol Cot Ref:1283/1285, Dales Holiday Cottages, Carleton Business Park, Carleton New Road, Skipton BD23 2AA
T: (01756) 799821
F: (01756) 797012
E: info@dalesholcot.com
I: www.daleshocot.com

East Greystone Farm Cottages ★★★★
Contact: Mrs Sue Hodgson, East Greystone Farm Cottages, East Greystone Farm, Main Road, Gainford, Darlington DL2 3BL
T: (01325) 730236
F: (01325) 730236
E: sue@holidayfarmcottages.co.uk

The Mansion House ★★★
Contact: Mr & Mrs Christopher Wain, High Row, Gainford, Darlington DL2 3DN
E: chris.wain@ukonline.co.uk
I: www.themansionhousegainford.co.uk

GILESGATE
Durham

Fern Cottage and Rose Cottage ★★★★
Contact: Mrs Eileen Woods, 25 Orchard Drive, Gilesgate, Durham DH1 1LA
T: (0191) 386 4176
E: durhamcottages@aol.com

GLANTON
Northumberland

Coniston Cottage ★★★
Contact: Mrs Helen Jean Mossman, Coniston House, Whittingham Road, Glanton, Alnwick NE66 4AS
T: (01665) 578305

Holly Cottage ★★★
Contact: Mr Robert Johnston, Crag View Cottage, Glanton, Alnwick NE66 4AU
T: (01665) 578200
F: (01665) 578336
E: glantonvillagestore@yahoo
I: www.hollycottage-glanton.com

GREENHAUGH
Northumberland

Bought-Hill Mill ★★★★
Contact: Mrs Cowan, Bimmer-Hill, Greenhaugh, Hexham NE48 1PG
T: (01434) 240373

GREENHEAD
Northumberland

Holmhead Farm Cottage ★★★
Contact: Mrs Pauline Staff, Holmhead Farm Cottage, Thirlwall Castle Farm, Hadrian's Wall, Greenhead, Brampton CA8 7HY
T: (016977) 47402
F: (016977) 47402
E: Holmhead@hadrianswall.freeserve.co.uk
I: www.bandbhadrianswall.com

Stanegate Cottage ★★★★
Contact: Mrs Shelagh Potts, Stanegate Cottage, Braeside, Bank Top, Greenhead, Brampton CA8 7HA
T: (01697) 747443
E: smpotts@talk21.com
I: www.braeside-banktop.co.uk

GUYZANCE
Northumberland

Garden Cottage ★★★
Contact: Lady Milburn, Guyzance Hall, Guyzance, Morpeth NE65 9AG
T: (01665) 513047
F: (01665) 513042

HALTON LEA GATE
Northumberland

The Old Chapel ★★★★★
Contact: Mr Stephen Jackson, 18 Grange Road, Fenham, Newcastle upon Tyne NE4 9LD
T: (0191) 274 6125
E: info@theoldcountrychapel.fsnet.co.uk

HALTWHISTLE
Northumberland

Ald White Craig Farm Cottages ★★★-★★★★
Contact: Mrs Cherine Zard, Near Hadrian's Wall, Haltwhistle NE49 9NW
T: (01434) 320565
F: (01434) 322004
E: info@hadrianswallholidays.com
I: www.hadrianswallholidays.com

Gibbs Hill Farm Cottages ★★★★
Contact: Mrs Valerie Gibson, Gibbs Hill Farm Cottages, Gibbs Hill, Once Brewed, Cawburn, Haltwhistle NE47 7AP
T: (01434) 344030
F: (01434) 344030
E: val@gibbshillfarm.co.uk
I: www.gibbshillfarm.co.uk

Kellah Farm Cottages ★★★-★★★★
Contact: Mrs Lesley Teasdale, Kellah Cottages, Kellah Farm, Kellah, Featherstone, Haltwhistle NE49 0JL
T: (01434) 320816
E: teasdale@ukonline.co.uk
I: www.kellah.co.uk

St Wilfrid's House ★★★★
Contact: Mrs Hilary Cloughley, The Old Presbytery, Castle Hill, Haltwhistle NE49 0DW
T: (01434) 321697
E: clogs55@aol.com
I: clogs55@aol.com

Scotchcoulthard ★★★★
Contact: Mrs Susan Saunders, Scotchcoulthard, Haltwhistle NE49 9NH
T: (01434) 344470
F: (01434) 344020
E: cottages@scotchcoulthard.co.uk
I: www.scotchcoulthard.co.uk

HAMSTERLEY
Durham

Edge Knoll Farm Cottages ★★★
Contact: Mr M G Edmonds, Edge Knoll Farm, Hamsterley, Bishop Auckland DL13 3PF
T: (01388) 488537
E: vacationfarm@hotmail.com

Hoppyland House ★★★
Contact: Mr & Mrs Bainbridge, Hoppyland House, West Hoppyland Farm, Hamsterley, Bishop Auckland DL13 3NP

Jasmine Cottage ★★★
Contact: Mrs A Roberts, Jessamine House, Hamsterley, Bishop Auckland DL13 3QF
T: (01388) 488630

1 South View Cottage ★★★
Contact: Dales Hol Cot Ref:2893, Dales Holiday Cottages, Carleton Business Park, Carleton New Road, Skipton BD23 2AA
T: (01756) 799821
F: (01756) 797012
E: info@dalesholcot.com
I: www.dalesholcot.com

West Hoppyland Cabins ★★
Contact: Mrs C J Atkinson, West Hoppyland Cabins, Hamsterley, Bishop Auckland DL13 3NP
T: (01388) 488196
E: westhoppyland@hotmail.com
I: www.geocities.com/westhoppyland

HARBOTTLE
Northumberland

Hillview and Woodbine Cottage ★★★-★★★★
Contact: Mrs Deirdre Dickson, Crosby House, Crosby-on-Eden, Carlisle CA6 4QZ
T: (01228) 573239
F: (01228) 573338
E: stay@northumbrian-cottages.co.uk
I: www.northumbrian-cottages.co.uk

Honeysuckle Cottage ★★
Contact: Mrs Bickmore, Wayside, Harbottle, Morpeth NE65 7DQ
T: (01669) 650348
I: www.honeysuckleharbottle.ntb.org.uk

Woodhall Farm Holiday Cottage ★★★
Contact: Mrs J D Blakey, Woodhall Farm Holiday Cottage, Harbottle, Sharperton, Morpeth NE65 7AD
T: (01669) 650245
F: (01669) 650245
E: blakey@woodhall65.freeserve.co.uk
I: www.woodhallcottage.co.uk

HARPERLEY
Durham

Bushblades Farm Cottage ★★★
Contact: Mrs Gibson, Bushblades Farm, Harperley, Stanley DH9 9UA
T: (01207) 232722

HARWOOD
Durham

Frog Hall Cottage ★★★
Contact: Ms Kath Toward, Herdship Farm, Harwood, Barnard Castle DL12 0YB
T: (01833) 622215
F: (01833) 622215
E: kath@hership.freeserve.co.uk

Honey Pot Cottage ★★
Contact: Mrs Liddle, Upper Teesdale Estate (Raby Estates), Raby Estate Office, Middleton-in-Teesdale, Barnard Castle DL12 0QH
T: (01833) 640209
F: (01833) 640963
E: teesdaleestate@rabycastle.com
I: www.rabycastle.com

HAYDON BRIDGE
Northumberland

Airlea Bungalow ★★★
Contact: Dales Hol Cot Ref:32 Dales Hol Cot Ref:3230, Dales Holiday Cottages, Carleton Business Park, Carleton New Road, Skipton BD23 2AA
T: (01756) 799821
F: (01756) 797012
E: info@dalesholcot.com
I: www.dalesholcot.com

Hadrian's Wall Country Cottages ★★★
Contact: Mrs Lyn Murray, Hadrian's Wall Country Cottages, Hindshield Moss, North Road, Haydon Bridge, Hexham NE47 6NF
T: (01434) 688688
F: (01434) 688688
E: cottages@hadrianswall.co.uk
I: www.hadrianswall.co.uk

Holiday Cottage ★★★★
Contact: Mrs Cynthia Bradley, Edenholme, John Martin Street, Haydon Bridge, Hexham NE47 6AA
T: (01434) 684622
E: edenholme@btinternet.com
I: www.edenholme.btinternet.co.uk

Scotch Corner ★★★★
Contact: Mrs Pauline Wallis, Scotch Arms, Langley-on-Tyne, Hexham NE47 6BJ
T: (01434) 684061
E: wallis@scotcharms.fsnet.co.uk
I: www.scotcharms.com

HEBBURN
Tyne and Wear

26 Hazelmoor ★★★★
Contact: Mr Goodall, 18 Coleridge Square, Hebburn NE31 1QD
T: 07941 611551

HEDDON-ON-THE-WALL
Northumberland

2 East Town House ★★★
Contact: Mr C & Mrs B Amos, 1 East Town House, Heddon-on-the-Wall, Newcastle upon Tyne NE15 0DR
T: (01661) 852277
F: (01661) 853063

HEPPLE
Northumberland

The Barn ★★★★
Contact: Country Holidays Ref: 4166, Holiday Cottages Group Owner Services Dept, Spring Mill, Earby, Barnoldswick BB94 0AA
T: 08700 723723
F: (01282) 844288
E: sales@holidaycottagesgroup.com
I: www.country-holidays.co.uk

HEXHAM
Northumberland

Brokenheugh Lodge ★★★★
Contact: Mrs Renee Jamieson, Brokenheugh Lodge, Brokenheugh Hall, Haydon Bridge, Hexham NE47 6JT
T: (01434) 684206
F: (01434) 684557
E: stay@brokenheugh.co.uk
I: www.brokenheugh.co.uk

Holy Island House ★★★★★
Contact: Mrs Judith Youens, Holy Island House, Gilesgate, Holy Island, Hexham NE46 3QL
T: (01434) 609386
E: stay@holyislandhouse.co.uk

Moorgair Cottage ★★★★
Contact: Mrs Vicki Ridley, Moorgair Cottage, Slaley, Hexham NE47 0AN
T: (01434) 673473
E: g_ridley@lineone.net
I: www.moorgair.co.uk

Rosebank Cottage ★★★
Contact: Ms Colette Gullery, Rosebank Cottage Rental, 9A Elsinore Road, London SE23 2SH
T: 07816 909737
F: (0208) 699 5825
E: info@rosebankcottage.co.uk
I: www.rosebankcottage.co.uk

Rye Hill Farm The Old Byre ★★★★
Contact: Mrs Elizabeth Courage, Rye Hill Farm The Old Byre, Rye Hill Farm, Slaley, Hexham NE47 0AH
T: (01434) 673259
F: (01434) 673259
E: info@ryehillfarm.co.uk
I: www.ryehillfarm.co.uk

Sammy's Place ★★★★★
Contact: Mr Roger McKechnie, Dilston House, Corbridge NE45 5RH
T: (01434) 633653
F: (01434) 634640
E: relax@sammyshideaways.com
I: www.sammyshideaways.com

HOLY ISLAND
Northumberland

Britannia House and The Cottage ★★★★
Contact: Mrs Katherine Tiernan, St Andrews House, College Place, Berwick-upon-Tweed TD15 1DA
T: (01289) 309826
E: ktiernan@onetel.net.uk

Farne Court Cottage, Farne View Cottage★★★
Contact: Mrs A J Batty, Orchard Gap, Aydon Road, Corbridge NE45 5EJ
T: (01434) 632691
F: (01434) 634170
E: angelabatty@ukonline.co.uk

The Haven ★★★
Contact: Mr C Souter, 30 Brandling Place South, Jesmond, Newcastle upon Tyne NE2 4RU
T: (0191) 281 7421
F: (0191) 212 0600

Ivy Cottage ★★★
Contact: Mr Keith Mitcheson, 18 Meckridge Gardens, Benton, Newcastle upon Tyne NE7 7GQ
T: (0191) 266 4661
E: go.mitch@ic24.net

Memnon Cottage ★★★★
Contact: Ms Shirley Douglas, 71 Mayors Road, Knutsford WA15 9RW
T: (0161) 941 1963
E: shirleyandouglas@aol.com

HOWICK
Northumberland

South Cottage ★★
Contact: Sykes Cottages Ref:625, Sykes Cottages, York House, York Street, Chester CH1 3LR
T: (01244) 345700
F: (01244) 321442
E: info@sykescottages.co.uk
I: www.sykescottages.co.uk

HUMSHAUGH
Northumberland

East Farm Cottage ★★★
Contact: Mrs Gwen Dodds, East Farm House, Wall, Hexham NE46 4AT
T: (01434) 689150
E: charles.dodds@btopenworld.com

ILDERTON
Northumberland

Coach House & Coach House Cottage ★★★
Contact: Mrs Margaret Sale, Ilderton Glebe, Ilderton, Alnwick NE66 4YD
T: (01668) 217293
E: margaretsale@amserve.com

INGRAM
Northumberland

Cheviot Holiday Cottages ★★★★★
Contact: Mrs Trysha Stephenson, The Old Rectory, Ingram, Powburn, Alnwick NE66 4LT
T: (01665) 578236
E: trysha@cheviotholidaycottages.co.uk
I: www.cheviotholidaycottages.co.uk

IRESHOPEBURN
Durham

High Barnes Holiday Cottage ★★★★
Contact: Mr & Mrs John and Frederique Wilson, High Barnes Holiday Cottage, Ireshopeburn, Wearhead, St John's Chapel, Bishop Auckland DL13 1PY
T: (01388) 537556
E: jwilsonis@yahoo.co.uk

Hillview Cottage ★★★
Contact: Miss Rachel O'Halleron, 1 Collindale Road, South Ferring, Worthing BN12 3JF
T: (01903) 245345
E: racmarglen@hotmail.com

KIELDER
Northumberland

Kielder Lodges ★★★★-★★★★★
Contact: Hoseasons Holidays Limited, Sunway House, Lowestoft NR32 3LT
T: 0870 333 2000
F: (01502) 584962
E: kielder.water@nwl.co.uk
I: www.kielder.org

KIELDER WATER
Northumberland

Calvert Trust Kielder ★★★★
Contact: Calvert Trust Kielder, Falstone, Kielder Water, Hexham NE48 1BS
T: (01434) 250232
F: (01434) 250015
E: enquiries@calvert-kielder.com
I: www.calvert-trust.org.uk

KIRKNEWTON
Northumberland

Hillview Cottage ★★★★
Contact: Dales Hol Cot Ref:2043, Dales Holiday Cottages, Carleton Business Park, Carleton New Road, Skipton BD23 2AA
T: (01756) 799821
F: (01756) 797012
E: info@dalesholcot.com
I: www.dalesholcot.com

KIRKWHELPINGTON
Northumberland

Herdsman Cottage ★★★★
Contact: Mrs Lorna Thornton, Cornhills, Kirkwhelpington, Newcastle upon Tyne NE19 2RE
T: (01830) 540232
F: (01830) 540388
E: cornhills@farming.co.uk
I: www.northumberlandfarmhouse.co.uk

LANCHESTER
Durham

Browney Cottage & Browney Close ★★★
Contact: Mrs Ann Darlington, Hall Hill Farm, Lanchester, Durham DH7 0TA
T: (01207) 521476
F: (01388) 730300
E: hhf@freenetname.co.uk
I: www.hallhillfarm.co.uk

Stable Cottage ★★★★
Contact: Dales Hol Cot Ref: 3358, Dales Holiday Cottages, Carleton Business Park, Carleton New Road, Skipton BD23 2AA
T: (01756) 799821
F: (01756) 797012
E: info@dalesholcot.com
I: www.dalesholcot.com

LANGLEY-ON-TYNE
Northumberland

West Deanraw Bungalow ★★★
Contact: Mr John Drydon, West Deanraw Farm, Langley-on-Tyne, Hexham NE47 5LY
T: (01434) 684228
F: (01434) 684228

LESBURY
Northumberland

Lesbury Glebe Cottage ★★★★★
Contact: Mrs D. Gillian Brunton, Lesbury Glebe Cottage, Glebe Garden Cottage, Lesbury, Alnwick NE66 3AU
T: (01665) 830732
E: gillieray@tiscali.co.uk

LOFTUS
Tees Valley

Liverton Lodge ★★
Contact: Dales Hol Cot Ref:17
Dales Hol Cot Ref:1778, Dales Holiday Cottages, Carleton Business Park, Carleton New Road, Skipton BD23 2AA
T: (01756) 799821
F: (01756) 797012
E: info@dalesholcot.com
I: www.dalesholcot.com

LONGFRAMLINGTON
Northumberland

Dene House Farm Cottages Poppy, Bluebell, Primrose, Buttercup★★★
Contact: Mrs Wilson, Dene House Farm Cottages Poppy, Bluebell, Primrose, B, Dene House, Longframlington, Morpeth NE65 8EE
T: (01665) 570549
F: (01665) 570549

Picklewood Cottage ★★★★★
Contact: Mrs Di Jevons, Picklewood Cottage, Felton Road, Longframlington, Morpeth NE65 8BD
T: (01665) 570221
F: (01665) 570221
E: di@picklewood.info
I: www.picklewood.info

LONGHORSLEY
Northumberland

Beacon Hill Farm Holidays ★★★★-★★★★★
Contact: Mr Moore, Beacon Hill House, Longhorsley, Morpeth NE65 8QW
T: (01670) 780900
F: (01670) 780901
E: alun@beaconhill.co.uk
I: www.beaconhill.co.uk

Cartwheel Cottage ★★★
Contact: Mr & Mrs James & Sarah Chisholm, Westerheugh Farm, Longhorsley, Morpeth NE65 8RH
T: (01665) 570661
E: sarah@cartwheelcottage.com

Garrett Lee Cottage ★★★★
Contact: Ms Linda Wilson, Garrett Lee Cottage, Garrett Lee Farm, Longhorsley, Morpeth NE65 8RJ
T: (01670) 788474
F: (01670) 788976
E: info@garrettleefarm.com
I: www.garrettleefarm.com

Green Yard Cottage ★★★
Contact: Mr & Mrs George and Susan Lowes, Green Yard Cottage, Todburn West Farm, Longhorsley, Morpeth NE65 8QZ
T: (01670) 788416

LONGHOUGHTON
Northumberland

Harlaw Hill Farm Cottages ★★-★★★
Contact: Mrs Joan Pringle, Harlaw Hill Farm Cottages, Harlaw Hill, Longhoughton, Alnwick NE66 3AA
T: (01665) 577215

Rose Cottage & Croft Cottage ★★★
Contact: Mrs Margaret Forsyth, Low Steads, Longhoughton, Howick, Alnwick NE66 3AL
T: (01665) 577227
I: www.lowsteads.co.uk

LOWICK
Northumberland

Barmoor Ridge Cottage ★★★★
Contact: Mrs Patricia Adrienne Reavley, Barmoor Ridge Cottage, Barmoor Ridge, Lowick, Berwick-upon-Tweed TD15 2QD
T: (01289) 388226
F: (01289) 388688
E: jimpyreavley@aol.com

Barmoor South Moor ★★★
Contact: Mrs Ann Gold, Barmoor South Moor, Lowick, Berwick-upon-Tweed TD15 2QF
T: (01289) 388205
F: (01289) 388205
E: barryandanngold@aol.com

Black Bull Cottage ★★★
Contact: Mr & Mrs Nigel and Margaret Lambert, Black Bull Hotel, Main Street, Lowick, Berwick-upon-Tweed TD15 2UA
T: (01289) 388228
E: tom@blackbullowick.freeserve.co.uk
I: www.secretkingdom.com/black/bull.htm

South View Cottage ★★★★
Contact: Mrs Carol Waugh, 8 South Road, Lowick, Berwick-upon-Tweed TD15 2TX
T: (01289) 388640

LUCKER
Northumberland

Lucker Hall Steading ★★★★-★★★★★
Contact: Mrs Jane Mallen, Northumberland Estates Holiday, Cottages, Alnwick Castle, Denwick, Alnwick NE66 1NQ
T: (01665) 602094
F: (01665) 608126
E: nehc@farmline.com
I: www.alnwickcastle.com/holidaycottages

Lucker Mill ★★★★★
Contact: Mrs Jane Mallen, Northumberland Estates Holiday Cottages, Alnwick Castle, Denwick, Alnwick NE66 1NQ
T: (01665) 602094
F: (01665) 608126
E: nehc@farmline.com
I: www.alnwickcastle.com/holidaycottages/

MARSKE-BY-THE-SEA
Tees Valley

4 Church Street ★★★
Contact: Mrs Barbara Mosey, 27 The Avenue, Billericay CM12 9HG
T: (01277) 652778
E: brmosey@yahoo.co.uk

White Rose Cottage ★★★
Contact: Mr & Mrs Philip Phillips, 21 Church Howle Crescent, Marske-by-the-Sea TS11 7EJ
T: (01642) 481064
F: (01642) 481064
E: phillipspcp@aol.com

MELKRIDGE
Northumberland

Common House Farm ★★★
Contact: Mr & Mrs Richard and Gloria Goodchild, Common House Farm, Melkridge, Haltwhistle NE49 9PF
T: (01434) 321680
E: stay@commonhousefarm.com
I: www.commonhousefarm.com

MICKLETON
Durham

Blackthorn Cottage ★★★
Contact: Mrs Diane Garrett, 3 Mariam Gardens, Upminster RM12 6QA
T: (01708) 447260
E: coldigar@btinternet.com
I: www.teesdalecottages.co.uk

Kirkcarrion Cottage Rating Applied For
Contact: Mrs Gail Foster, 1 Syke Cottage, Mickleton, Barnard Castle DL12 0LH
T: (01833) 640132
E: gailfoster.sykecott@virgin.net

West Tofts ★★★★
Contact: Mrs Stoddart, Wemmergill Hall Farm, Lunedale, Middleton-in-Teesdale, Barnard Castle DL12 0PA
T: (01833) 640379
E: wemmergill@freenet.co.uk
I: www.wemmergill-farm.co.uk

MIDDLETON-IN-TEESDALE
Durham

The Barn ★★★
Contact: Mrs Ann Whitfield, Garden House, Low Side, Mickleton, Barnard Castle DL12 0JR
T: (01833) 640759

Brock Scar Cottage ★★★★
Contact: Mrs Winfred Gargate, Brock Scar Farm, West Pasture, Middleton-in-Teesdale, Barnard Castle DL12 0PW
T: (01833) 640495
F: (01833) 640495
E: wyngargate@btopenworld.com
I: www.brockscar.co.uk

Castle Cottage ★★★
Contact: Mrs Lynch, Pikestone House, Holwick, Middleton-in-Teesdale, Barnard Castle DL12 0NR
T: (01833) 640474

The Coach House ★★★★
Contact: Mrs Finn, Belvedere House, 54 Market Place, Middleton-in-Teesdale, Barnard Castle DL12 0QH
T: (01833) 640884
F: (01883) 640884
E: info@thecoachhouse.net
I: www.thecoachhouse.net

Country Cottage ★★★
Contact: Mr R B Burman, Fairlawn, 1 Thorn Road, Bramhall, Stockport SK7 1HG
T: (0161) 860 7123
E: robinburman@robinburman.com

Firethorn Cottage ★★★
Contact: Mrs J Thompson, Cutbush Farmhouse, Hardingham Road, Hingham, Norwich NR9 4LY
T: (01953) 850364

Green Acres, Meadow's Edge, Shepherds Cottage★★★
Contact: Mrs Glennis Scott, Low Way Farm, Holwick, Middleton-in-Teesdale, Barnard Castle DL12 0NJ
T: (01833) 640506

Grooms Cottage and The Stables ★★★★
Contact: Mr Nicholas Hamer, 25 Village Way, Kirkby Fleetham, Northallerton DL7 0TW
T: (01609) 748938
F: (01609) 748938
E: clocktower@supanet.com

Hush Cottage ★★
Contact: Mrs Mulholland, Knapp Cottage, Corton, Warminster BA12 0SZ
T: (01985) 850450
E: mul.cort@btinternet.com

Hyland View and The Hideaway ★★★
Contact: Mrs Kathryn Guy, Granary Cottage, Whashton, Richmond DL11 7JL
T: (01748) 825640

North Wythes Hill ★★★
Contact: Mrs June Dent, Laneside, Middleton in Teesdale, Middleton-in-Teesdale, Barnard Castle DL12 0RY
T: (01833) 640573
E: wytheshill@teesdaleonline.co.uk

Rosedale ★★★
Contact: Mrs Mary Wilkinson, Ladnek, School Road, Kirkby-in-Furness LA17 7TF
T: (01229) 889420
F: (01229) 889766

Snaisgill Farm Cottage ★★★
Contact: Mrs Susan Parmley, Snaisgill Farm Cottage, Snaisgill Road, Middleton-in-Teesdale, Barnard Castle DL12 0RP
T: (01833) 640343

Summerville Cottage ★★★
Contact: Mr Fletcher, Friar House Farm, Newbiggin-in-Teesdale, Middleton-in-Teesdale, Barnard Castle DL12 0XG
T: (01833) 622202
I: www.summervillecottage.co.uk

Town View Cottage ★★★
Contact: Mrs Marshall, The Bungalow, The Green, Gainford, Darlington DL2 3HA
T: (01325) 730989
F: (01325) 730989

Westfield Cottage ★★★★
Contact: Mrs Doreen Scott, Westfield House, Laithkirk, Middleton-in-Teesdale, Barnard Castle DL12 0PN
T: (01833) 640942
F: (01833) 640942

Willow Cottage ★★
Contact: Mrs Diane Garrett, 3 Mariam Gardens, Upminster RM12 6QA
T: (01708) 447260
E: coldigar@btinternet.com

MIDDLETON-ON-LEVEN
North Yorkshire

Harvest Cottage ★★★★
Contact: Mrs Caroline Bainbridge, Middleton Grove Farm, Middleton-on-Leven, Yarm TS15 0JU
T: (01642) 599669

MIDDLETON ST GEORGE
Durham

The Barn ★★★★
Contact: Mr Ian Atkinson, The Barn, Oak Tree Farm, Yarm Road, Middleton St George, Darlington DL2 1HN
T: (01325) 333322
F: (01325) 333555
E: ian@ingenius.co.uk
I: www.ingenius.co.uk/inservice/thebarn.html

MILFIELD
Northumberland

Barley Hill Cottage ★★★
Contact: Mr David Bell, 20 Balmoral Terrace, Gosforth, Newcastle upon Tyne NE3 1YH
T: (0191) 285 2526
E: rosemary.bell@newcastle.gov.uk

Milfield Hill Cottage ★★★★
Contact: Mrs Judith Craig, Milfield Hill House, Wooler NE71 6JE
T: (01668) 216338
F: (01668) 216095
E: craig@milfield1.freeserve.co.uk
I: www.milfield1.freeserve.co.uk

Mill Barn ★★★★
Contact: Mr & Mrs Denise & David Elgie, 8 Millfield Gardens, Tynemouth, North Shields NE30 2PX
T: (0191) 259 2078
F: (0191) 259 2111
E: daveelgie@hotmail.com

MINDRUM
Northumberland

Bowmont Cottage ★★
Contact: Mr & Mrs S Orpwood, Bowmont Hill, Mindrum TD12 4QW
T: (01890) 850266
F: (01890) 850245
E: s.orpwood@farmline.com
I: www.cottageguide.co.uk/bowmonthill

MITFORD
Northumberland

The Old Blacksmiths Cottage ★★★★
Contact: Mrs Glass, The Old Blacksmiths Cottage, Mitford, Morpeth NE61 3PR
T: (01670) 512074
E: emma@emglass.freeserve.co.uk

MORPETH
Northumberland

Barnacre ★★★★
Contact: Mrs Linda Rudd, Warren Cottage, Longhirst Village, Morpeth NE61 3LX
T: (01670) 790116
E: linda@mrudd.fslife.co.uk

The Carriage House Rating Applied For
Contact: Mr Joseph Evans, The Old Vicarage, Ulgham Village, Morpeth NE61 3AR
T: (01670) 790225
E: joe@ulgham.demon.co.uk

5 Copper Chare ★★★
Contact: Mr G.M. Gagie, Hillside Cottage, Wood Lane, Uttoxeter ST14 8JR
T: (01889) 562838

High Barn Cottage ★★★
Contact: Mr Martin Downing, Waterside Cottage, Felton, Morpeth NE65 9EG
T: (01670) 783398
F: (01670) 783398
E: downing@mdaconsultancy.co.uk

Meldon Park Holiday Apartment ★★★
Contact: Mrs Janet Wilson, Flat 1, Meldon Park, Morpeth NE61 3SW
T: (01670) 772622
F: (01670) 772341
E: mrscookson@compuserve.com

Morpeth Court ★★★★
Contact: Mrs Carol Edmundson, Morpeth Court, Castle Bank, Morpeth NE61 1YJ
T: (01670) 517217
F: (01670) 517217
E: carol_edmundson@hotmail.com

Netherwitton Hall Cottages ★★★
Contact: Mrs Anne-Marie Trevelyan, Netherwitton Hall Cottages, Netherwitton Hall, Netherwitton, Morpeth NE61 4NW
T: (01670) 772249
F: (01670) 772510
E: anne-marie@netherwitton.com

Old Barn Cottages ★★★
Contact: Mrs Jo Mancey, Benridge Hagg, Morpeth NE61 3SB
T: (01670) 518507
I: benridge_cottages_uk.tripod.com

Peigh Hills Farm Cottages ★★★★
Contact: Mr A Tench, Peighs Hills Farm, Morpeth NE61 3EU
T: (01670) 790332
F: (01670) 791390

NEWCASTLE UPON TYNE
Tyne and Wear

135 Audley Road ★★★
Contact: Miss Linda Wright, 137 Audley Road, South Gosforth, Newcastle upon Tyne NE3 1QH
T: (0191) 285 6374
E: lkw@audleyender.fsnet.co.uk
I: www.audleyender.fsnet.co.uk

Bavington Hall, Stable Court ★★★
Contact: Mr Patrick, Bavington Hall, Stable Court, Little Bavington, Newcastle upon Tyne NE19 2BA
T: (01830) 530394
F: (01830) 530394
E: enquiries@bavingtonhall.co.uk
I: www.bavingtonhall.co.uk

Walbottle Farm House ★★★★★
Contact: Mr & Mrs Dominic Aston, Walbottle Farmhouse, Walbottle, Newcastle upon Tyne NE15 8JD
T: (0191) 267 1368
E: aston@walbottle.fsnet.co.uk

Walbottle House ★★★★★
Contact: Mrs Sharon Kent, Walbottle House, Walbottle, Newcastle upon Tyne NE15 8JD
T: (0191) 264 1108

NEWTON
Northumberland

The Piggery Cottage ★★★★
Contact: Mrs Barbara Hill, Middle Barns, Newton, Stocksfield NE43 7UL
T: (01661) 844550
E: bhhill@talk21.com

NEWTON-BY-THE-SEA
Northumberland

3A & 3B Coastguard Cottages ★★★
Contact: Mr & Mrs M Cottam, 13 St Georges Crescent, Monkseaton, Whitley Bay NE25 8BJ
T: (0191) 251 2506
F: (0191) 222 1017
E: mbc@bradleyhall.co.uk
I: www.geocities.com/coastguardcottages.

Link House Farm ★★★★
Contact: Mrs Jayne Hellmann, The Granary, Link House Farm, Newton-by-the-Sea, Alnwick NE66 3DF
T: (01665) 576820
F: (01665) 576820
E: jayne.hellman@virgin.net

Newton Hall Cottages ★★★★
Contact: Mrs S A Patterson, Newton Hall, Newton-by-the-Sea, Alnwick NE66 3DZ
T: (01665) 576239
F: (01665) 576900
E: patterson@newtonholidays.co.uk
I: www.newtonholidays.co.uk

Seawinds ★★★★
Contact: Miss Jo Park, Low Buston Hall, Warkworth, Eastfield, Morpeth NE65 0XY
T: (01665) 714805
F: (01665) 711345
E: jopark@farming.co.uk
I: www.seawinds.ntb.org.uk

NORHAM
Northumberland

The Boathouse ★★★
Contact: Mr G J Crabtree & Mrs Chantler, Great Humphries Farm, Grafty Green, Maidstone ME17 2AX
T: (01622) 859672
F: (01622) 859672
E: chantler@humphreys46.fsnet.com
I: www.recommended-cottages.co.uk

Boathouse Cottage ★★★★
Contact: Mrs Susan Dalgety, The Columns, Norham, Berwick-upon-Tweed TD15 2JZ
T: (01289) 382300
F: (01289) 382334
E: susan@boathousecottage.co.uk
I: www.boathousecottage.co.uk

Falcon's Gate 5 Grievestead Farm Cottages★★★★
Contact: Mrs Margaret Wright, 19 Houghton Avenue, Whitley Bay NE30 3NQ
T: (0191) 252 0627
F: (0191) 297 1984
E: ron.wright2@virgin.net

Rosemary Cottage Rating Applied For
Contact: Mrs Barbara Piercy, Rosemary Cottage, 14 West Street, Norham, Berwick-upon-Tweed TD15 2LB
T: (01289) 382247

NORTH TOGSTON
Northumberland

Orchard Cottage ★★★★
Contact: Mr & Mrs Matthew & Joy Pettifer, Orchard Cottage, Togston House, North Togston, Morpeth NE65 0HR
T: (01665) 710145
F: (01665) 714428
E: matthew.pettifer@btinternet.com

OAKENSHAW
Durham

Stockley Fell Farm Cottages ★★★★
Contact: Mrs Carter, Stockley Fell Farm Cottages, Stockley Fell Farm, Oakenshaw, Crook DL15 0TN
T: (01388) 745938
F: (01388) 745938

OTTERBURN
Northumberland

Woodhill ★★★★★
Contact: Mrs Corrinne Knight, Woodhill, Otterburn, Newcastle upon Tyne NE19 1JX
T: (01830) 520657
E: christopher@knightc41.fsbusiness.co.uk

OUSTON
Durham

Katie's Cottage ★★★★
Contact: Mrs Hilary Johnson, Katie's Cottage, Low Urpeth Farm, Ouston, Chester-le-Street DH2 1BD
T: (0191) 410 2901
F: (0191) 410 0088
E: stay@lowurpeth
I: www.lowurpeth.co.uk

OVINGTON
Northumberland

Appletree Cottage ★★★★
Contact: Mrs Lesley Rowell, Appletree Cottage, Ovington Hall Farm, Ovington, Prudhoe NE42 6ED
T: (01661) 832355

High Fewster Gill Cottage ★★★
Contact: Dales Hol Cot Ref:32 Dales Hol Cot Ref:3228, Dales Holiday Cottages, Carleton Business Park, Carleton New Road, Skipton BD23 2AA
T: (01756) 799821
F: (01756) 797012
E: info@dalesholcot.com
I: www.dalesholcot.com

Porch Cottage ★★★
Contact: Dales Hol Cot Ref: 3351, Carleton Business Park, Carleton New Road, Skipton BD23 2AA
T: (01756) 790919
F: (01756) 797012
E: fiona@dalesholcot.com
I: www.dales-holiday-cottages.com

Westgarth Cottage ★★★★
Contact: Mrs C Graham, Stonecroft, Ovington NE42 6EB
T: (01661) 832202

PIERCEBRIDGE
Durham

The Bungalow ★★★
Contact: Mrs Jean Lowe, The Bungalow, Bolam Grange, Piercebridge, Darlington DL2 3UL
T: (01388) 832779

POWBURN
Northumberland

The Cottage ★★★
Contact: Mrs Helen Arnott, 21 Cottonwood, Biddick Woods, Houghton-le-Spring DH4 7TA
T: (0191) 385 7167
E: harnott@talk21.com

Shepherd's Cottage ★★★
Contact: Mrs Sarah Wilson, Ingram Farm, Powburn, Alnwick NE66 4LT
T: (01665) 578243
F: (01665) 578243
E: swingram@ukonline.co.uk

REDCAR
Tees Valley

Dove House ★★★
Contact: Mrs McGovern, Redcar TS10 1NS
T: (01642) 479311

ROMALDKIRK
Durham

Jesmond Cottage ★★★★
Contact: Mrs Dorothy West, Yew Trees, Lartington, Baldersdale, Barnard Castle DL12 9BP
T: (01833) 650454
F: (01833) 650454
E: john@westcotts.demon.co.uk
I: www.westcotts.co.uk

Romaldkirk Self Catering Cottages ★★-★★★★★
Contact: Mrs Gwen Wall, Kleine Cottage, Romaldkirk, Barnard Castle DL12 9ED
T: (01833) 650794
I: www.cottageguide.co.uk/romaldkirk

Sycamore Cottage ★★★★
Contact: Dales Hol Cot Ref:69 Dales Hol Cot Ref:698, Dales Holiday Cottages, Carleton Business Park, Carleton New Road, Skipton BD23 2AA
T: (01756) 799821
F: (01756) 797012
E: info@dalesholcot.com
I: www.dalesholcot.com

ROOKHOPE
Durham

Brandon Cottage ★★★★
Contact: Mr & Mrs Anthony Newbon, Brandon Cottage, High Brandon, Rookhope-in-Weardale, Rookhope, Bishop Auckland DL13 2AF
T: (01388) 517673
E: highbrandonbb@aol.com
I: members.aol.com/highbrandonbb

ROTHBURY
Northumberland

The Cottage ★★★
Contact: Mrs Isabelle Anthea Wilbie-Chalk, The Cottage, Well Close, Townfoot, Rothbury, Morpeth NE65 7NZ
T: (01669) 620430
E: visitors@wellclose.com
I: www.rothbury.co.uk

Featherwood House ★★★
Contact: Mrs S M Piper, Apperley House, Hillside Road East, Rothbury, Morpeth NE65 7PT
T: (01669) 620565

Garden Cottage At Silverton Lodge ★★★★★
Contact: Mr & Mrs Bruce & Jeannette Hewison, Silverton Lane, Rothbury, Morpeth NE65 7RJ
T: (01669) 620144
E: info@silvertonlodge.co.uk
I: www.silvertonlodge.co.uk

The Granary ★★★★★
Contact: Ms Mandy Lance and Mr George Snaith, The Granary, Charity Hall Farm, Sharperton, Morpeth NE65 7AG
T: (01669) 650219
F: (01669) 650219
E: mandy@charityhallfarm.com
I: www.charityhallfarm.com

Low Alwinton Holiday Cottages ★★★★
Contact: Mrs Jackie Stothard, Mountain View, Haugh Head Road, Wooler NE71 6QJ
T: (01668) 283572
E: jackie@lowalwinton.co.uk
I: www.lowalwinton.co.uk

The Old Telephone Exchange ★★★★
Contact: Ms Susan Doncaster, 34 Ashburnham Road, Abington, Northampton NN1 4QY
T: (01669) 621858
E: tery.foreman@virgin.net

The Pele Tower ★★★★★
Contact: Mr & Mrs J D Malia, The Pele Tower, Whitton, Rothbury NE65 7RL
T: (01669) 620410
F: (01669) 621006
E: davidmalia@aol.com
I: www.thepeletower.com

Riverside Lodge ★★★★
Contact: Mr Eric Jensen, Edgecombe, Hillside Road, Rothbury, Morpeth NE65 7PT
T: (01669) 620464
F: (01669) 621031
E: info@theriversidelodge.com
I: www.theriversidelodge.com

Tosson Tower Farm ★★★-★★★★★
Contact: Mrs Ann Foggin, Tosson Tower Farm, Rothbury, Great Tosson, Morpeth NE65 7NW
T: (01669) 620228
F: (01669) 620228
E: stay@tossontowerfarm.com
I: www.tossontowerfarm.com

Whitton Lodge ★★★★
Contact: Mrs Monaghan, Whitton Grange, Rothbury, Morpeth NE65 7RL
T: (01669) 620929
F: (01669) 620471
E: john.monaghan@ukonline.co.uk
I: www.visit-rothbury.co.uk/members

ROWLANDS GILL
Tyne and Wear

The Stables ★★★★
Contact: Mrs Jenny Dicks, Barton, Low Thornley, Rowlands Gill NE39 1BE
T: (01207) 544486

ST JOHN'S CHAPEL
Durham

Burnbrae ★★★★
Contact: Mrs Ann Robson, 37 Park Drive, Deuchar Park, Morpeth NE61 2SX
T: (01670) 518129
E: william@robson637.freeserve.co.uk

SALTBURN-BY-THE-SEA
Tees Valley

Coastguard Cottages ★★★
Contact: Mrs Cecilia Daly, 1 Coastguard Cottage, Huntcliffe, Saltburn-by-the-Sea TS12 1HG
T: (01287) 625235

Seagal Holiday Bungalow ★★★★
Contact: Ms Chris Priestman, 47 Severn Drive, Guisborough TS14 8AT
T: (01287) 633754
E: chrissiepriestman@hotmail.com

The Zetland ★★★
Contact: Mrs Joan Carter, 1 Hawthorn Grove, Yarm TS15 9EZ
T: (01642) 782507
E: graham@howard95.freeserve.co.uk
I: www.carter-steel.co.uk

SEAHOUSES
Northumberland

Cliff House Cottages ★★★
Contact: Mrs Jackie Forsyth, Westfield Farmhouse, North Sunderland, Seahouses NE68 7UR
T: (01665) 720161
F: (01665) 720713
E: enquiries@cliffhousecottages.co.uk
I: www.cliffhousecottages.co.uk

Crabhouse Cottage ★★★★
Contact: Mrs Jackie Forsyth, Westfield Farmhouse, North Sunderland, Seahouses NE68 7UR
T: (01665) 720161
F: (01665) 727713
E: info@crabhouse.co.uk

Crewe Cottage ★★★
Contact: Mrs Sarah Steed, 3 Grants Crescent, Paisley PA2 6BD
T: (0141) 884 1064
F: (0141) 884 1064
E: msdfsteed@aol.com

Driftwood Cottage ★★★★
Contact: Mr Ian Longstaff, 3 Lamb Court, Tweedmouth, Berwick-upon-Tweed TD15 2YR
T: (01289) 303034

Fahren House ★★★★
Contact: Ms Caroline Shiel, The Bield, 37 St Aidans, Seahouses NE68 7SS
T: (01665) 721375
F: (01665) 721375
E: carolinebryan@ukonline.co.uk
I: www.farne-islands.com

Fisherlasses Flat ★★★
Contact: Mrs Karen Wilkin, Fisherlasses Flat, Swallow Fish Ltd., 2 South Street, Seahouses NE68 7RB
T: (01665) 720470
F: (01665) 721177
E: wilkin@swallowfish.co.uk
I: www.swallowfish.co.uk

Fishermans Mid Cottage ★★★
Contact: Mrs Dorothy Jackson, Fishermans Mid Cottage, 8 North Street, Seahouses NE68 7SB
T: (01665) 830427
F: (01665) 833909
E: dorothy@biltonbarns.com
I: www.biltonbarns.co.uk

Fisherman's Retreat Rating Applied For
Contact: Ms Fiona McKeith, Northumberland Coastal Retreats, 174 Warkworth Woods, Newcastle Great Park, Newcastle upon Tyne NE3 5RD
T: (0191) 236 5971
F: (0191) 236 4586
E: info@coastalretreats.co.uk

Kipper Cottage ★★★★
Contact: Country Holidays Ref:80171, Country Holidays, Spring Mill, Earby, Barnoldswick BB94 0AA
T: 08700 781200
I: www.country-holidays.co.uk

Lynbank and Dalfaber ★★★
Contact: Mrs Louise Donaldson, 4 Broad Road, Seahouses NE68 7UP
T: (01665) 721066
F: (01665) 721066
I: www.dalfaber-lynbank.ntb.org.uk

Peregrine ★★★
Contact: Miss Ursula Wanglin, Bolton Mill, Alnwick NE66 2EH
T: (01665) 574304
F: (01665) 574304

Quarry Cottage ★★★
Contact: Mrs Mary Alston, Woodlea, 36 St Aidans, Seahouses NE68 7SS
T: (01665) 720235
F: (01665) 720235
E: george.alston@ic24.net

Rose Cottages
Rating Applied For
Contact: Mr Michael Townsend, Rose Cottages, c/o Dunstanburgh Castle Hotel, Embleton, Seahouses NE66 3UN
T: (01665) 576111
F: (01665) 576203
E: stay@dunstanburghcastlehotel.co.uk

Sparrowhawk
Rating Applied For
Contact: Miss Ursula Wanglin, Bolton Mill, Alnwick NE66 2EH
T: (01665) 574304
F: (01665) 574304

SEDGEFIELD
Durham

The Granary ★★★
Contact: Mr & Mrs Edgoose, The Granary, Todds House Farm, Sedgefield, Stockton-on-Tees TS21 3EL
T: (01740) 620244
F: (01740) 620244
E: edgoosej@aol.com
I: www.toddshousefarm.co.uk

Sprucely Farm Cottage ★★
Contact: Mr S R Harris, Sprucely Farm, Sedgefield, Stockton-on-Tees TS21 2BD
T: (01740) 620378
E: barbara@sprucely.fsnet.co.uk
I: sprucely.fsnet.co.uk

SHADFORTH
Durham

Bourne Cottages ★★★★
Contact: Mrs Judith Heron, Bourne House Farm, Church Villas Shadforth, Shadforth, Durham DH6 1LQ
T: (0191) 372 0730
F: (0191) 372 0730
E: judithheron@aol.com

SHARPERTON
Northumberland

North Sharperton Farm Cottage ★★★★
Contact: Ms Carolyn Banks, North Sharperton Farm Cottage, Rothbury, Sharperton, Morpeth NE65 7AE
T: (01669) 650321
F: (01669) 650321
E: ormnthsharperton@bushinternet.com

Ryecroft Cottage ★★★
Contact: Mrs Rosalind Kerven, Swindonburn Cottage West, Sharperton, Morpeth NE65 7AP
T: (01669) 640291
E: roskerven@hotmail.com

SHILBOTTLE
Northumberland

Sycamore and Honeysuckle Cottages ★★★
Contact: Mrs Janet Brewis, Sycamore and Honeysuckle Cottages, Woodhouse, Shilbottle, Alnwick NE66 2HR
T: (01665) 575222
I: www.woodhousefarmholidays.co.uk

SHOTLEY BRIDGE
Durham

River's Edge Cottage
Rating Applied For
Contact: Mrs Jean Johnson, 7 Shotley Grove Road, Shotley Bridge, Consett DH8 8SF
T: (01207) 501194

SKELTON
Tees Valley

Barn Cottage and Newbrook ★★★★
Contact: English Country Cottages, Barn Cottage and Newbrook, Trout Hall Lane, Skelton Green, Saltburn-by-the-Sea TS12 2DE
T: 08700 781100

SLALEY
Northumberland

Clairmont Cottage ★★★★
Contact: Mrs Evelyn Allsop, Clairmont Cottage, Slaley, Hexham NE47 0AD
T: (01434) 673686
F: (01434) 673921
E: david.allsop4@which.net
I: www.clairmontslaley.freeserve.co.uk

Combhills Farm ★★★
Contact: Mrs Ogle, Combhills Farm, Slaley, Hexham NE47 0AQ
T: (01434) 673475
F: (01434) 673778
E: m.ogle@lineone.net

SOUTH SHIELDS
Tyne and Wear

36 & 38 Eccleston Road ★★★
Contact: Mrs K Cole, 9 Sea Way, South Shields NE33 2NQ
T: (0191) 456 1802

22 Hartington Terrace ★★★
Contact: Mrs Patricia Capps, Cheer-me-up Barn, 2 Cundall Road, Asenby, Thirsk YO7 3QR
T: (01845) 578657
E: m.capps@aol.com

Sandhaven Beach Chalets ★★★
Contact: Mrs Christine Rowell, Sandhaven Beach Chalets, South Promenade, Sea Road, South Shields NE33 2LD
T: (0191) 455 8319
F: (0191) 455 8319
E: crowell@btconnect.com
I: www.sandhavenchalets.co.uk

SPARTY LEA
Northumberland

Isaac's and Hannah's Cottages ★★★
Contact: Mrs Heather Robson, Allenheads Farm, Allenheads, Hexham NE47 9HJ
T: (01434) 685312

SPENNYMOOR
Durham

The Green Tree ★★★
Contact: Mrs Yvonne Parker, The Green Tree, 41 Tudhoe Village, Spennymoor DL16 6LE
T: (01388) 818557
F: (01388) 813243

Highview Country House -Apartment ★★★
Contact: Mr J Thompson, Highview Country House, Kirkmerrington, Spennymoor DL16 7JT
T: (01388) 811006

SPITTAL
Northumberland

21 Billendean Terrace ★★★
Contact: Mrs Ingham, 8 Burnaby Crescent, Chiswick, London W4 3LH
T: (020) 8747 0425
E: inghamfive@hotmail.com

Silvester Properties ★★★
Contact: Mrs Fiona Silvester, Silvester Properties, 51 Church Street, Berwick-upon-Tweed TD15 1EE
T: (01289) 306666
E: silprops@aol.com

STAINTON
Durham

The Old Granary ★★★★
Contact: Dales Hol Cot Ref:1691, Dales Holiday Cottages, Carleton Business Park, Carleton New Road, Skipton BD23 2AA
T: (01756) 790919
F: (01756) 797012
E: info@dalesholcot.com
I: www.dalesholcot.com

STANHOPE
Durham

Primrose Cottage ★★
Contact: Mrs D P Dickson
T: (01228) 573337
F: (01228) 573338
E: enquiries@northumbria-byways.com
I: www.northumbria-byways.com

STOCKSFIELD
Northumberland

The Granary and Stable Cottage ★★★
Contact: Mrs Susan Astbury, The Granary and Stable Cottage, Old Ridley Farm, New Ridley, Stocksfield NE43 7RU
T: (01661) 842043
F: (01661) 842043

Mount Flaggon ★★★
Contact: Mrs Bridget Smith, North View House, Hedley on the Hill, Stocksfield NE43 7SW
T: (01661) 843867
F: (01661) 844097
E: gsmith@compuserve.com

The Old Bakery Cottages ★★★★
Contact: Mr & Mrs Bolton, Greencroft, 56 New Ridley Road, Stocksfield NE43 7EE
T: (01661) 843217
F: 07974 910970

Old Ridley Hall ★★★
Contact: Mrs Aldridge, Old Ridley Hall, New Ridley, Stocksfield NE43 7RU
T: (01661) 842816
E: oldridleyhall@talk21.com

Tithe Cottage & Wash House Cottage ★★★
Contact: Mrs Harrison, Eltringham Farm, Mickley, Ovington, Prudhoe NE43 7DF
T: (01661) 842833

SUNDERLAND
Tyne and Wear

15 Ashdale Court ★★★★
Contact: Mrs Christine Whincop, Nicholas Avenue, Whitburn, Sunderland SR6 7DB
T: (0191) 529 3578

Mill View – 45 Poplar Drive ★★
Contact: Mrs Bethan Farrar, 50 Beechhill Road, Eltham, London SE9 1HH
T: (020) 8850 4863
E: cass.farrar@virgin.net

22 Topcliff ★★★
Contact: Mr & Mrs M B Farrar, 50 Beechhill Road, Eltham, London SE9 1HH
T: (020) 8850 4863
E: cass.farrar@virgin.net

SWARLAND
Northumberland

Swarland Hall Golf Club ★★★
Contact: Mrs Denise Bell, Swarland Hall Golf Club, Coast View, Swarland, Morpeth NE65 9JG
T: (01670) 787940
F: (01670) 787214
I: wwww.swarlandgolf.co.uk

TARSET
Northumberland

Highfield Farm Cottage ★★
Contact: Mrs Miriam Elizabeth Tweddle, Highfield Farm Cottage, Highfield, Tarset, Hexham NE48 1RT
T: (01434) 240219

THROPTON
Northumberland

Black Chirnells, The Cottage ★★★★
Contact: Mrs Liz Juppenlatz, PO Box 97, Leimuiden, Netherlands
T: 00311 7250 6020
E: 100663.1174@compuserve.com

Mordue's Cottage & Grandma's Cottage ★★★
Contact: Mrs Helen Farr, Mordue's Cottage & Grandma's Cottage, Lorbottle West Steads, Thropton, Morpeth NE65 7JT
T: (01665) 574672
F: (01665) 574672
E: Helen.Farr@farming.co.uk
I: www.cottageguide.co.uk/lorbottle.html

North Croft
Rating Applied For
Contact: Mrs Marilyn Chalk, The Old School, Wingates, Morpeth NE65 8RW
T: (01670) 788655
E: northcroftMC@aol.com

Physic Cottage ★★★★
Contact: Mr & Mrs Andrew and Helen Duffield, Riverview, Physic Lane, Thropton, Morpeth NE65 7HU
T: (01669) 620450
E: physiccottage@aol.com

Westfield Cottage ★★★★
Contact: Mr & Mrs Alastair & Catherine Hardie, Westfield House Farm, Thropton, Morpeth NE65 7LB
T: (01669) 640263
E: alicat@btinternet.com

TOW LAW
Durham

Greenwell Farm Cottages ★★★
Contact: Mrs Linda Vickers, Greenwell Farm Cottages, Greenwell Farm, nr Wolsingham, Wolsingham, Bishop Auckland DL13 4PH
T: (01388) 527248
E: greenwell@farming.co.uk
I: www.greenwellfarm.co.uk

Pennine View ★★★★
Contact: Mrs Margo Farrow, Thornley, Tow Law, Wolsingham, Bishop Auckland DL13 4PQ
T: (01388) 731329
E: enquiries@bracken-hill.com
I: www.bracken-hill.com

TWEEDMOUTH
Northumberland

Rowandene ★★★★
Contact: Lorna Chappell, 1 Ravensdowne, Berwick-upon-Tweed TD15 1HX
T: (01289) 331300
E: lornachappell127@hotmail.com

WAREN MILL
Northumberland

Eider Cottage ★★★★
Contact: Mrs S Turnbull, 1 Friars Court, Bamburgh NE69 7AE
T: (01668) 214494
E: theturnbulls2k@btinternet.com

Waren Lea Hall ★★★★★
Contact: . Country Holidays Ref:14111, Holiday Cottages Group Owner Services Department, Spring Mill, Earby, Barnoldswick BB94 0AA
T: 0870 444 6603
F: (01282) 841539
E: ownerservices@holidaycottagesgroup.com
I: www.country-holidays.co.uk

WARENFORD
Northumberland

Etive Cottage ★★★★
Contact: Mr & Mrs David and Jan Thompson, The Cott, Warenford, Belford NE70 7HZ
T: (01668) 213233

WARK
Northumberland

Coachmans and Stable Cottages ★★★
Contact: Mr & Mrs Bruce and Sally Napier, Coachmans and Stable Cottages, The Old Rectory, Wark, Hexham NE48 3PP
T: (01434) 230223
E: bruce_napier@talk21.com

The Green ★★★
Contact: Sykes Cottages Ref:683, Sykes Cottages, York House, York Street, Chester CH1 3LR
T: (01244) 345700
F: (01244) 321442
E: info@sykescottages.co.uk
I: www.sykescottages.co.uk

The Hemmel ★★★★
Contact: Mrs A Nichol, Hetherington, Wark, Hexham NE48 3DR
T: (01434) 230260
F: (01434) 230260
E: alan_nichol@hotmail.com
I: www.hetheringtonfarm.co.uk

Rainbow Cottage ★★★
Contact: Mr & Mrs Sydney and Susan Thorkildsen, Tweedbank Cottage, Wark, Cornhill-on-Tweed TD12 4RH
T: (01890) 882218
F: (01890) 882218
E: winston44@ntlworld.com

Riverside Cottage ★★★
Contact: Mrs Stella Jackson, 16 Moss Side, Wrekenton, Gateshead NE9 7UU
T: (0191) 487 6531
E: jands@wrekenton.freeserve.co.uk

Roses Bower ★★★
Contact: Mr L & Mrs S Watson, Roses Bower, Wark, Hexham NE48 3DX
T: (01434) 230779
F: (01434) 230779
E: sandlwatson@rosesbower.fsworld.co.uk
I: http://roses-bower.co.uk

WARKWORTH
Northumberland

Birling Vale ★★★
Contact: Mrs Janet Brewis, Woodhouse, Shilbottle, Alnwick NE66 2HR
T: (01665) 575222
I: www.woodhousefarmholidays.co.uk

Buston Farm Holiday Cottages ★★★★
Contact: Miss Jo Park, Low Buston Hall, Warkworth, Eastfield, Morpeth NE65 0XY
T: (01665) 714805
F: (01665) 711345
E: stay@buston.co.uk
I: www.buston.co.uk

Coquet Cottage ★★★★
Contact: Mrs Barbara Jean Purvis, Fynder, 3 Dovecote Steadings, Morpeth NE61 6DN
T: (01670) 789516
F: (01670) 789520
I: www.castle-cottages.co.uk

Old Barns Farmhouse Holiday Cottage ★★★★
Contact: Mrs Wilkes, Old Barns Farmhouse Holiday Cottage, Morwick Road, Warkworth, Morpeth NE65 0TH
T: (01665) 713427
E: scott.wilkes@virgin.net
I: www.oldbarnsholidaycottage.co.uk

Riverview Cottage ★★★★
Contact: Mr & Mrs Paul & Helen Skuse, 20 Bristol Road, Winterbourne, Bristol BS36 1RG
T: (01454) 775441
E: pmskuse@hotmail.com
I: www.riverview-warkworth.co.uk

Southmede Cottage ★★★★
Contact: Mr & Mrs Mike and Carol Smith, Southmede, Beal Bank, Warkworth, Morpeth NE65 0TB
T: (01665) 711360
E: info@southmede.co.uk
I: www.southmede.co.uk

WEARHEAD
Durham

Far End Cottage ★★★
Contact: Mrs S Kebell, Deneholme, Deneholme Terrace, Holmside, Edmondsley, Durham DH7 6ER
T: (0191) 371 8369
E: richkebell@aol.com

WEST WOODBURN
Northumberland

The Hollow ★★★
Contact: Mrs Marlene Robson, Nunnykirk East Lodge, Netherwitton, Morpeth NE61 4PB
T: (01670) 772580

WESTGATE-IN-WEARDALE
Durham

The Old Barn ★★★★
Contact: Mrs Angela Hackett, The Old Barn, High Kitty Crag, Westgate, Westgate-in-Weardale, Bishop Auckland DL13 1LF
T: (01388) 517562
F: (01388) 526122
E: matthackett@talk21.com

Rowan Cottage ★★★
Contact: Dales Hol Cottage Ref: 2007, Carleton Business Park, Carleton New Road, Skipton BD23 2AA
T: (01756) 790919
F: (01756) 797012
E: info@dalesholcot.com
I: www.dalesholcot.com

WHITBURN
Tyne and Wear

Seawynds ★★★
Contact: Mrs Christine Whincop, Seawynds, 12A Nicholas Avenue, Whitburn, Sunderland SR6 7DB
T: (0191) 529 3578

WHITLEY BAY
Tyne and Wear

Seafront Apartments ★★★
Contact: Mr A & Mrs R Webb, Seafront Apartments, 46 Beverley Terrace, Cullercoats, Tyne and Wear NE30 4NU
T: 07977 203379
E: stay@seafront.info
I: www.seafront.info

WHITTINGHAM
Northumberland

The Lodge ★★★
Contact: Mrs Jenny Sordy, Alnham House, Alnham, Whittingham, Alnwick NE66 4TJ
T: (01669) 630210
F: (01669) 630310
E: jennysordy@hotmail.com
I: www.country-holidays.co.uk

WIDDRINGTON
Northumberland

Seaspray Cottage ★★★
Contact: Mrs Carole Wood, Tudor House, Parkway, Wilmslow SK9 1LS
T: (01625) 525857
E: carole@woodc43.fsnet.co.uk

WINSTON
Durham

Highcliffe Waters ★★★★
Contact: Mr & Mrs Hodson
T: (01325) 730427
F: (01325) 730740
E: mrshodson@aol.com
I: www.countryholidays.co.uk

Strathmore Barns ★★★★
Contact: Mrs Marion Boyes, Strathmore House, Cleatlam, Winston, Darlington DL2 3QS
T: (01833) 660302
F: 0709 228 5603
E: johnboyes@boyesj.freeserve.co.uk

WITTON-LE-WEAR
Durham

Carrs Terrace ★★★★
Contact: Miss Merlyn Law, 93-99 Upper Richmond Road, London SW15 2TG
T: (020) 8780 1084
F: (020) 8789 9199
E: merlynlaw@aol.com

Old Joiner's Shop ★★★★
Contact: Dales Hol Cot Ref:2630, Dales Holiday Cottages, Carleton Business Park, Carleton New Road, Skipton BD23 2AA
T: (01756) 799821
F: (01756) 797012
E: info@dalesholcot.com
I: www.dalesholcot.com

WOLSINGHAM
Durham

Ardine and Elvet Cottages ★★★
Contact: Mrs M Gardiner, 3 Melbourne Place, Wolsingham, Bishop Auckland DL13 3EQ
T: (01388) 527538

Bradley Burn Holiday Cottages ★★★
Contact: Mrs Judith Stephenson, Bradley Burn Holiday Cottages, Bradley Burn Farm, Wolsingham, Bishop Auckland DL13 3JH
T: (01388) 527285
F: (01388) 527285
I: www.bradleyburn.co.uk

High Doctor Pasture ★★★★
Contact: Mr & Mrs Painter, High Doctor Pasture, Wolsingham, Bishop Auckland DL13 3LR
T: (01388) 526354
F: (01388) 526583

Sandycarr Farm Cottage ★★★★
Contact: Mrs Marjorie Love, Holywell Farm, Wolsingham, Bishop Auckland DL13 3HB
T: (01388) 527249
F: (01388) 527249

Whitfield House Cottage ★★★
Contact: Mrs M E Shepheard, 25 Front Street, Wolsingham, Bishop Auckland DL13 3DF
T: (01388) 527466
E: enquiries@whitfieldhouse.clara.net
I: www.whitfieldhouse.clara.net

WOODLAND
Durham

Mayland Farm Cottage ★★★
Contact: Mrs Mortimer, Mayland Farm, Woodland, Barnard Castle DL13 5NH
T: (01388) 718237

WOOLER
Northumberland

Bushyfield Cottage and Airidh Bhan ★★★★
Contact: Mrs Liz Turnbull, 4 Wood Terrace, South Shields NE33 4UU
T: (0191) 427 6203
F: (0191) 420 6987
E: turnbullliz@aol.com

Byram House ★★★
Contact: Mrs Catherine Easton, Byram House, High Humbleton, Wooler NE71 6SU
T: (01668) 281647

Castle Hill Cottage ★★★
Contact: Mr James Nall-Cain, Rarick Ltd, Waterend Lane, Wheathampstead, St Albans AL4 8EP
T: (01582) 831083
F: (01582) 831081
E: manussj@aol.com

The Castle Tower ★★★★
Contact: Dales Hol Cot Ref:16 Dales Hol Cot Ref:1636, Dales Holiday Cottages, Carleton Business Park, Carleton New Road, Skipton BD23 2AA
T: (01756) 799821
F: (01756) 797012
E: info@dalesholcot.com
I: www.dalesholcot.com

Coldgate Mill ★★★★
Contact: Mr & Mrs Diana Stone, Coldgate Mill, North Middleton, Wooler NE71 6QZ
T: (01668) 217259
E: diana_coldgatemill@hotmail.com
I: www.coldgatemill.co.uk

The Croft ★★★
Contact: Mrs Joan Renner, Lilburn Grange, West Lilburn, Alnwick NE66 4PP
T: (01668) 217274

Fenton Hill Farm Cottages ★★★★
Contact: Mrs Margaret Logan, Fenton Hill, Wooler NE71 6JJ
T: (01668) 216228
F: (01668) 216169
E: stay@fentonhillfarm.co.uk
I: www.fentonhillfarm.co.uk

Firwood Bungalow & Humphrey House ★★★-★★★★★
Contact: Mrs Sylvia Elizabeth Armstrong, North Charlton Farm, Chathill NE67 5HP
T: (01665) 579443
F: (01665) 579407
E: ncharlton1@agricplus.net
I: www.cottageguide.co.uk/firwood

Harehope Hall ★★★★
Contact: Ms Alison Wrangham, Harehope Hall, Creswell Wing, Eglingham, Alnwick NE66 2DP
T: (01668) 217329
F: (01688) 217346
E: ali.wrangham@btconnect.com

Hayloft & Yearle Tower ★★★★
Contact: CH Ref:N377,N376, Alnham, Whittingham, Alnwick NE66 4TJ
T: 08700 723723
F: (01282) 844288
E: sales@holidaycottagesgroup.com
I: www.country-holidays.co.uk

Kimmerston Riding Centre ★★★
Contact: Mr Jeffreys, Kimmerston Riding Centre, Kimmerston Farm, Wooler NE71 6JH
T: (01668) 216283
E: jane@kimmerston.com
I: www.kimmerston.com

28 Oliver Road ★★
Contact: Davidson/Pearson, 21 Roselands Avenue, Sale M33 4BH
T: (0161) 973 0894
F: (0161) 973 0894
E: aitken777@hotmail.com

Rose Cottage ★★★
Contact: Mrs Christine Andrews, 1 Littleworth Lane, Esher KT10 9PF
T: (01372) 464284
F: (01372) 467715
E: andrews@playfactors.demon.co.uk

Westnewton Estate ★★★
Contact: Mrs Jean Davidson, Westnewton Estate, Westnewton, Kirknewton, Wooler NE71 6XL
T: (01668) 216077
E: jd@westnewtonestate.co.uk
I: www.westnewtonestate.co.uk

YARM
Tees Valley

Yarm Holiday Homes ★★★★
Contact: Mr Geoff Rowley, Yarm Holiday Homes, Far End Farm, Worsall Road, Yarm TS15 9PE
T: (01642) 787017
E: enquiries@yarmholidayhomes.co.uk
I: www.yarmholidayhomes.co.uk

NORTH WEST

ABBEYSTEAD
Lancashire

Higher Lee ★★★★
Contact: Hoseasons Cottages, Lowestoft NR32 2LW

Whitemoor Cottage ★★★★
Contact: Mr Martin McShane, Red Rose Cottages, 6 King Street, Clitheroe BB7 2EP
T: (01200) 420101
F: (01200) 420103
I: www.redrosecottages.co.uk

ACCRINGTON
Lancashire

Low Moorside Farm Cottage ★★★
Contact: Mr & Mrs C & E Hallworth, Burnley Road, Clayton-le-Moors, Altham, Accrington BB5 5UG
T: (01254) 237053

ADLINGTON
Cheshire

Carr Cottage ★★★★
Contact: Mrs Isobel Worthington, Holiday Cottages Group Owner Services Dept, Carr House Farm, Mill Lane, Macclesfield SK10 4LG
T: (01625) 828337
F: (01625) 828337
I: www.country-holidays.co.uk

ALDERLEY EDGE
Cheshire

The Hayloft ★★★★
Contact: Mrs Jenny Dawson, Interludes, Croft Cottage, Hough Lane, Alderley Edge SK9 7JE
T: (01625) 599802
F: (01625) 599802
E: info@interludes-uk.com
I: www.interludes-uk.com

Interludes Rating Applied For
Contact: Mrs Jenny Dawson, Royles Square, Alderley Edge Sk9 7GN
T: (01625) 599802
F: (01625) 599802
E: info@interludes-uk.com

ARKHOLME
Lancashire

Redwell Fisheries ★★★
Contact: Mrs D Campbell-Barker & Mr Hall, Redwell Fisheries, Mere House, Kirkby Lonsdale Road, Arkholme, Carnforth LA6 1BQ
T: (015242) 21979
E: kenanddiane@redwellfisheries.co.uk
I: www.redwellfisheries.co.uk

BACUP
Lancashire

Oakenclough Farm ★★★
Contact: Mr Martin Mcshane, Red Rose Cottages, 6 King Street, Clitheroe BB7 2EP
T: (01200) 420101
F: (01200) 420103
E: info@redrosecottages.co.uk
I: www.redrosecottages.co.uk

BARROWFORD
Lancashire

Alondra ★★★★
Contact: Mr Martin McShane, Red Rose Cottages, 6 King Street, Clitheroe BB7 2EP
T: (01200) 420101
F: (01200) 420103

Toll House ★★★
Contact: Country Holidays Ref:13226, Holiday Cottages Group Owner Services Department, Spring Mill, Earby, Barnoldswick BB94 0AA
T: 08700 723723
F: (01282) 844288
E: sales@holidaycottagesgroup.com
I: www.country-holidays.co.uk

BASHALL EAVES
Lancashire

The Coach House ★★★★
Contact: Country Holidays, Property Ref: 17177
T: 08700 781200
E: ch.enquiry@holidaycottagesgroup.com

BEESTON
Cheshire

The Lodge ★★★★
Contact: Mrs Pauline & Alexandra Davies, Whitegate Farm, Peckforton Hall Lane, Spurstow, Tarporley CW6 9TG
T: (01829) 781457
F: (01829) 781457

BILLINGTON
Lancashire

Croft View ★★★★
Contact: Mr Martin McShane, Red Rose Cottages, 6 King Street, Clitheroe BB7 2EP
T: (01200) 420101
F: (01200) 420103
I: www.redrosecottages.co.uk

Riverview ★★★★
Contact: Mr Martin Mcshane, Red Rose Cottages, 6 King Street, Clitheroe BB7 2EP
T: (01200) 420101
F: (01200) 420103
E: info@redrosecottages.co.uk
I: www.redrosecottages.co.uk

Weavers Cottage
Rating Applied For
Contact: Mr Martin McShane, Red Rose Cottages, 6 King Street, Clitheroe BB7 2EP
T: (01200) 420101
F: (01200) 420103
E: info@redrosecottages

BISPHAM
Lancashire

Burbage Holiday Lodge
★★★-★★★★
Contact: Mrs Sheila Chick, 200 Queens Promenade, Bispham, Ormskirk FY2 9JS
T: (01253) 356657
E: enquiries@burbageholidaylodge.co.uk
I: www.burbageholidaylodge.co.uk

Queens Mansions Holiday Apartments ★★★
Contact: Mr & Mrs Conrad, Queens Mansions Holiday Apartments, 224 Queens Promenade, Bispham, Ormskirk FY2 9HP
T: (01253) 355689

BLACKPOOL
Lancashire

Abingdon Holiday Flats ★★
Contact: Mr & Mrs Douglas Nelson, Abingdon Holiday Apartments, 33 Holmfield Road, Blackpool FY2 9TB
T: (01253) 356181
I: www.accommodation-blackpool.co.uk

Beachcliffe Holiday Flats
★★★
Contact: Mrs Alison Salisbury, Beachcliffe Holiday Flats, 3 King Edward Avenue, Blackpool FY2 9TD
T: (01253) 357147
I: www.holidayflatsblackpool.com

Bridle Lodge Apartments
★★★
Contact: Ms Valerie Taylor, Bridle Lodge Apartments, 91 Withnell Road, South Shore, Blackpool FY4 1HE
T: (01253) 404117
E: bridlelodge@hotmail.com

Crystal Lodge Holiday Flats
★★
Contact: Mr & Mrs T and C Cray, Crystal Lodge, 10-12 Crystal Road, Blackpool FY1 6BS
I: http://blackpool1.com/crystallodge

Donange ★★-★★★
Contact: Mrs Myra Hasson, Donange, 29 Holmfield Road, Blackpool FY2 9TB
T: (01253) 355051
I: www.de-zineuk.co.uk/donange

Grand Hotel Holiday Flats
★★-★★★
Contact: Mr Smith, The Grand Hotel Holiday Flats, Station Road, Blackpool FY4 1EU
T: (01253) 343741
F: (01253) 408228
I: www.grandholidayflats.co.uk

The Holiday Lodge ★★
Contact: Mr & Mrs R Threadgold, The Holiday Lodge, 115 Homefield Road, Blackpool FY2 9RF
T: (01253) 352934
I: www.holidaylodge.co.uk

San Remo Holiday Flats ★★
Contact: Mrs Morgan, San Remo Holiday Flats, Apartments and Bungalows, 7 Empress Drive North, Blackpool FY2 9SE
T: (01253) 353487

Sea Cote Holiday Flats ★★★
Contact: Mrs Anne Cunningham, Sea Cote Holiday Flats, 172 Queens Promenade, Bispham, Ormskirk FY2 9JN
T: (01253) 354435

Stratford Apartments
Rating Applied For
Contact: Mr C Taylor, 36-38 Empress Drive, Blackpool FY2 9SD
T: (01253) 500150
F: (01253) 591004
I: www.blackpoolbreaks.net/stratfordapartments

Thorncliffe Holiday Flats
★★-★★★
Contact: Mr Al Badani, Thorncliffe Holiday Flats, 1 Holmfield Road, Gynn Square, Blackpool FY2 9SL
T: (01253) 357561
F: (01253) 508770

BOLLINGTON
Cheshire

Higher Ingersley Barn
★★★★★
Contact: Mr Brian Peacock, Higher Ingersley Farm, Oakenbank Lane, Bollington, Macclesfield SK10 5RP
T: (01625) 572245
F: (01625) 574231
E: bw.peacock@ntlworld.com
I: www.higheringersleyfarm.co.uk

BOLTON-BY-BOWLAND
Lancashire

Springhead Farm Holiday Cottages ★★★★
Contact: Mr Martin Mcshane, Red Rose Cottages, 6 King Street, Clitheroe BB7 2EP
T: (01200) 420101
F: (01200) 420103
E: info@redrosecottages.co.uk
I: www.redrosecottages.co.uk

BOLTON-LE-SANDS
Lancashire

Fairhaven Holiday Home ★★★
Contact: Mr & Mrs A Smith, 2 Whin Avenue, Bolton-le-Sands, Carnforth LA5 8DA
T: (01524) 733996
F: (01524) 733996
E: andycaroline.smith@btopenworld.com
I: www.fairhavenholidayhomebythebay.users.btopenworld.com

Salt-Pie Cottage ★★★★
Contact: Mrs Allison Wardle, Cobblers Cottage, 12 The Nook, Carnforth LA5 8LG
T: (01524) 824692

BOSLEY
Cheshire

Old Byre, The ★★★
Contact: Mrs D Gilman, Woodcroft, Bosley, Macclesfield SK11 0PB
T: (01260) 223293
F: (01260) 273650

Strawberry Duck Holidays
Rating Applied For
Contact: Mr Bruce Carter & Emma Cowley, Strawberry Duck Holidays, Bryher Cottage, Bullgate Lane, Bosley, Macclesfield SK11 0PP
T: (01260) 223591
F: (01260) 223591

BRIERCLIFFE
Lancashire

Delph Cottage ★★★
Contact: Mr Martin McShane, Red Rose Cottages, 6 King Street, Clitheroe BB7 2EP
T: (01200) 420101
F: (01200) 420103
I: www.redrosecottages.co.uk

BRINSCALL
Lancashire

Moors View Cottage ★★★
Contact: Mrs Sheila Smith, Four Seasons Guest House, 9 Cambridge Road, Cleveleys, Blackpool FY5 1EP
T: (01253) 853537
F: (01624) 662190

BROXTON
Cheshire

Summerfield House ★★★
Contact: Mrs Morris, Nantwich Road, Broxton, Chester CH3 9JH
T: (01829) 782293

BURROW
Lancashire

River Bank Cottage ★★★★
Contact: Dales Holiday Cottages, Dales Holiday Cottages, Carelton Business Park, Skipton BD23 2AA
T: (01756) 799821
F: (01756) 797012
E: info@dalesholcot.com
I: www.dalesholcot.com

BURTON
Cheshire

Honeysuckle Cottage ★★★★
Contact: Mrs C E Nevett, Honeysuckle Cottage and Primrose Cottage, Warren House Farm, Burton Road, Burton, Tarporley CW6 0ES
T: (01829) 781178

CARNFORTH
Lancashire

Deroy Cottage ★★★
Contact: Mr & Mrs Cross, Deroy, The Heights, Carnforth LA5 9LA
T: (01524) 733196
E: colin@colincross.co.uk
I: www.colincross.co.uk

Mansergh Farm House Cottages ★★★★
Contact: Mr & Mrs A D Morphy, Mansergh Farm House Cottages, Borwick, Carnforth LA6 1JS
T: (01524) 732586
E: linda@manserghcottages.co.uk
I: www.manserghcottages.co.uk

Pine Lake Lodges ★★★★
Contact: Mr Tony Commons, Cumbrian Cottages, 2 Lonsdale Street, Carlisle CA1 1DB
T: (01228) 599960
F: (01228) 599970
I: www.cumbrian-cottages.co.uk

CATON
Lancashire

Marybank Barn ★★★
Contact: Mrs Julie Fisher, Marybank Barn, Caton Green, Lancaster LA2 9JG
T: (01524) 770339

CHESTER
Cheshire

The Bijou ★★★
Contact: Mrs Sue Byrne, Walnut Cottage, Rake Lane, Chester CH2 4DB
T: (01244) 379824
E: sueandkevin@chestergems.freeserve.co.uk

Cambell's Cottage ★★★
Contact: Mrs Henderson, 4 Lancaster Drive, Chester CH3 5JW
T: (01244) 326890
E: jeannetunnard@aol.com

Cheshire Country Cottages
★★★★
Contact: Mr Robert Menzies, Sandy Lane, Tarvin Sands, Chester CH3 8JQ
I: www.cheshirecottages.com

The City Apartments ★★★★
Contact: Moira Martland, Upton Lodge, Wealstone Lane, Chester CH2 1HD
T: (01244) 372091
F: (01244) 374779
I: www.chesterholidays.co.uk

City Walls Apartments ★★★
Contact: Mr Rod Cox, Thompson Cox Partnership, 1 City Walls, Chester CH1 2JG
T: (01244) 313400
F: (01244) 400414
E: rc@thompsoncox.co.uk

Domini Mews & Romana Court ★★★
Contact: Mr & Mrs Massey, 46 York Road, Connahs Quay, Connah's Quay, Deeside CH5 4YE
T: (01244) 815664
F: (01244) 815664

Duchess Apartment ★★★★★
Contact: Mrs W J Appleton, Blakemere Lane, Norley, Warrington WA6 6NW
T: (01928) 788355
F: (01928) 788507
E: ches@williamj99.freeserve.co.uk
I: www.wickentreefarm.co.uk

Fir Tree Cottage ★★★
Contact: Mrs Ursula Owen, 71 Heath Road, Upton, Chester CH2 1HT
T: (01244) 382681

Handbridge Village ★★★
Contact: Mr Owen, 18 Eaton Road, Handbridge, Chester CH4 7EN
T: (01244) 676159
F: (01244) 676159

Ivy Cottage ★★★
Contact: Mr & Mrs Joseph & Sonia Barry, Woodsorrel, 18 Dee Fords Avenue, Chester CH3 5UP
T: (01244) 403630
F: (01244) 403699
E: rmd.heritage@btconnect.com
I: rmd-heritage.co.uk

Jasmine Cottage ★★★★★
Contact: Mrs Karen Buchan, Auchmacoy House, Llanfair Road, Abergele LL22 8DH
T: (01745) 825880
F: (01745) 825880
E: k.buchan@btinternet.com
I: www.chesterholidaycottages.com

Jocsam Cottage ★★
Contact: J M Hughes, Chester Road, Sandycroft, Deeside CH5 2QN
T: (01244) 530312

Kingswood Coach House ★★★
Contact: Mrs Caroline Perry, Kingswood Coach House, Kingswood, Parkgate Road, Saughall, Chester CH1 6JS
T: (01244) 851204
F: (01244) 851244
E: caroline.mcvey@psmconsulting.co.uk

Little Mayfield ★★
Contact: Mr M J Cullen, Little Mayfield, Mayfield House, Warrington Road, Hoole Village, Chester CH2 4EX
T: (01244) 300231
F: (01244) 300231

Russia House ★★
Contact: Ian Bennion, 32 Oldfield Crescent, Chester CH4 7PE
T: (01244) 629177

Stapleford Hall Cottage ★★★
Contact: Mrs M J Winward, Stapleford Hall Cottage, Stapleford Hall, Tarvin, Chester CH3 8HH
T: (01829) 740202
F: (01829) 740202
E: margaretwinward@hotmail.com
I: www.staplefordhallcottage.com

Tattersall Gate ★★★
Contact: Mrs R A Randle, PO Box 247, Chester CH1 2WA
T: (01244) 401591
F: (01244) 401591
E: rosrandle@cs.com
I: www.woodbank.co.uk/thatch

2 Towergate ★★★
Contact: Peter Davies, Tan-y-Bryn Lodge, Ffordd-y-Berth, Abergele LL22 9AU
T: (01745) 822113
F: (01745) 833770
E: peterdavies800@hotmail.com

York House ★★★★
Contact: Mrs Pauline & Alexandra Davies, Whitegate Farm, Peckforton Hall Lane, Spurstow, Tarporley CW6 9TG
T: (01829) 261601
F: (01829) 261602

CHIPPING
Lancashire

Fell View ★★★★
Contact: Mr Martin McShane, Red Rose Cottages, 6 King Street, Clitheroe BB7 2EP
T: (01200) 420101
F: (01200) 420103
I: www.redrosecottages.co.uk

Hall Trees Barn West ★★★★
Contact: Mr & Mrs Lesley Lloyd, Turnleys Farm, Off Four Acre Lane, Thornley, Preston PR3 2TD
T: 07801 496610
F: (01772) 783294
E: lesleylloyd@btconnect.com

Pale Farm Cottages ★★★★
Contact: Mrs Lynn Ollerton, 113 Halfpenny Lane, Longridge, Preston PR3 2EA
T: (01772) 783082

Rakefoot Barn ★★★-★★★★
Contact: Mrs P M Gifford, Rakefoot Barn, Thornley Road, Rakefoot Farm, Chaigley, Clitheroe BB7 3LY
T: (01995) 61332
F: (01995) 61296
E: info@rakefootfarm.co.uk
I: www.rakefootfarm.co.uk

The Waterwheel ★★★★
Contact: Mr Martin Mcshane, Red Rose Cottages, 6 King Street, Clitheroe BB7 2EP
T: (01200) 420101
F: (01200) 420103
E: info@redrosecottages.co.uk
I: www.redrosecottages.co.uk

Wolfen Mill Country Retreats ★★★★
Contact: Mr Martin McShane, Red Rose Cottages, 6 King Street, Clitheroe BB7 2EP
T: (01995) 61574
I: www.wolfenmill.co.uk

CLAYTON LE DALE
Lancashire

Whiteholme Studio ★★★★
Contact: Mr Graham Gardner-Boyes, Whiteholme, Ribchester Road, Clayton Le Dale, Blackburn BB1 9EY
T: (01254) 245893
E: gardnerboyes@hotmail.com

CLITHEROE
Lancashire

Brownhills Cottage Rating Applied For
Contact: Mr Martin McShane, Red Rose Cottages, 6 King Street, Clitheroe BB7 2EP
T: (01200) 420101
F: (01200) 420103
E: info@redrosecottages

Chestnut Cottage ★★★★
Contact: Mr Martin McShane, Red Rose Cottages, 6 King Street, Clitheroe BB7 2EP
T: (01200) 420101
F: (01200) 420103
I: www.redrosecottages.co.uk

Five Fells Cottage ★★★
Contact: Mr & Mrs R Hailwood, Albion House, Kirkmoor Road, Clitheroe BB7 2DU
T: (01200) 424240
E: roland.hailwood@talk21.com

Greenbank Cottages ★★★★
Contact: Mr Gordon Greenwood, Greenbank Cottages, Greenbank Farm, Whalley Road, Sabden, Clitheroe BB7 9DT
T: (01254) 823064
F: (01254) 822314
E: gordon.greenwood@ntlworld.com

Hawk Cottage ★★★★
Contact: Mr Martin Mcshane, Red Rose Cottages, 6 King Street, Clitheroe BB7 2EP
T: (01200) 420101
F: (01200) 420103
E: info@redrosecottages.co.uk
I: www.redrosecottages.co.uk

Higher Gills Farm ★★★★
Contact: Mrs Freda Pilkington, Higher Gills Farm, Rimington, Clitheroe BB7 4DA
T: (01200) 445370
I: www.highergills.co.uk

Hydes Farm Holiday Cottages ★★★
Contact: Mrs Jean Howard, Hydes Farm, Newton-in-Bowland, Clitheroe BB7 3DY
T: (01200) 446353

Number 10 ★★★
Contact: Mrs Newhouse, Clitheroe BB7 3ER
T: (01200) 446620
F: (01200) 446620

Painters Cottage ★★★★
Contact: Mr Martin Mcshane, Red Rose Cottages, 6 King Street, Clitheroe BB7 2EP
T: (01200) 420101
F: (01200) 420103
E: info@redrosecottages.co.uk
I: www.redrosecottages.co.uk

Ribble Cottage ★★★
Contact: Mr Martin Mcshane, Red Rose Cottages, 6 King Street, Clitheroe BB7 2EP
T: (01200) 420101
F: (01200) 420103
E: info@redrosecottages.co.uk
I: www.redrosecottages.co.uk

Saetr Cottage ★★★
Contact: Mrs Victoria Wood, Harrod Fold, Bolton-by-Bowland, Clitheroe BB7 4PJ
T: (01200) 447600

COCKERHAM
Lancashire

Near Moss Farm Holidays ★★★
Contact: Mr Sutcliffe, Near Moss Farm Holidays, Gulf Lane, Cockerham, Lancaster LA2 0ER
T: (01253) 790504
F: (01253) 790043
I: www.nearmossfarmholidays.com

CONGLETON
Cheshire

Acorn Cottages ★★★
Contact: Mr & Mrs Mark Bullock, Oaklands, North Rode, Congleton CW12 2PH
I: www.acorncottages-england.co.uk

CROSTON
Lancashire

Cockfight Barn ★★★★
Contact: Mr Martin Mcshane, Red Rose Cottages, 6 King Street, Clitheroe BB7 2EP
T: (01200) 420101
F: (01200) 420103
E: info@redrosecottages.co.uk
I: www.redrosecottages.co.uk

DELAMERE
Cheshire

Wickentree Farm 1 & 2 Stable Cottage★★★
Contact: Mrs Libby Appleton, Wicken Tree Farm, Blakemere Lane, Norley, Warrington WA6 6NW
I: www.wickentreefarm.co.uk

DINCKLEY

Aspinall Cottage ★★★★
Contact: Mr Martin McShane, Red Rose Cottages, 6 King Street, Clitheroe BB7 2EP
T: (01200) 420101
F: (01200) 420103
E: info@redrosecottages

DISLEY
Cheshire

Plattwood Farm Cottage ★★★★
Contact: Mrs Jill Emmott, Plattwood Farm, Lyme Park, Disley, Stockport SK12 2NT
T: (01625) 872738
F: (01625) 872738
E: plattwoodfarm@talk21.com
I: www.plattwoodfarm.com

DOWNHAM
Lancashire

Stables Lodge Cottage ★★★
Contact: Mr Taylor, Stables Lodge Cottage, The Post Office, Downham, Clitheroe BB7 4BJ
T: (01200) 441242

EATON
Cheshire

The Old Shippon ★★★★
Contact: Mr & Mrs L Syson, Church House, Eaton, Congleton CW12 2NH
T: (01260) 274331
E: les.syson@ukonline.co.uk

ECCLESTON
Cheshire

Riverside Cottage ★★★★
Contact: Suzanne Butterfield, Church Road, Eccleston, Chester CH4 9HT
T: (01244) 675705

EGERTON
Cheshire

Manor Farm Holiday Cottages Rating Applied For
Contact: Mr Tim Dilworth, Manor Farm Holiday Cottages, Chomondley, Egerton, Malpas SY14 8AW
T: (01829) 720261

FADDILEY
Cheshire

Old Cart House Rating Applied For
Contact: Mrs Ruth Robinson, Wood Hey Hall, Wood Hey Hall Lane, Faddiley, Nantwich CW5 8JH
T: (01270) 524215
F: (01270) 524677
I: www.cheshireaccommodation.com

FARNDON
Cheshire

Woodpecker Cottage ★★★★
Contact: Sue Heyworth, Woodpecker Cottage, Caldecott Green, Farndon, Chester CH3 6PE
T: (01829) 270927

GALGATE
Lancashire

Lakewood Cottages ★★★★
Contact: Mr Martin McShane, Red Rose Cottages, 6 King Street, Clitheroe BB7 2EP
T: (01200) 420101
F: (01200) 420103
I: www.redrosecottages.co.uk

GARSTANG
Lancashire

Barnacre Cottages ★★★★★
Contact: Mr Sharples, Barnacre Cottages, Arkwright Farm, Eidsforth Lane, Barnacre, Preston PR3 1GN
T: (01995) 600918
F: (01995) 600918
E: sue@barnacre-cottages.co.uk
I: www.barnacre-cottages.co.uk

GREAT BARROW
Cheshire

Hawthorn Cottage ★★★
Contact: Eileen M. Pratt, Woodleigh, 44 Guilden Sutton Lane, Guilden Sutton, Chester CH3 7EY
T: (01244) 317287

Milton Brook Farm Cottages ★★★★
Contact: Mrs Charlotte Allwood, Milton Brook Cottage, Barrow Lane, Chester CH3 7HW

GREENFIELD
Greater Manchester

Clifton Cottage ★★★
Contact: Mrs J Wood, 113 Chew Valley Road, Greenfield, Oldham OL3 7JJ
T: (01457) 872098
F: (01457) 870760
E: ced117@aol.com
I: members.aol.com/ajb1912/ajbutterworthltd.html

GRESSINGHAM
Lancashire

Garden Cottage ★★★
Contact: Mrs Margaret Burrow, Garden Cottage, High Snab, Gressingham, Carnforth LA2 8LS
T: (01254) 221347
F: (01254) 221347
I: www.highsnab.freeserve.co.uk

HARROP FOLD
Lancashire

Harrop Fold Cottages ★★★
Contact: Mr Frank Robinson, Dales Holiday Cottages, Harrop Fold, Bolton-by-Bowland, Clitheroe BB7 4PJ
T: (01200) 447665
I: www.dalesholcot.com

HOOLE
Cheshire

St James Apartments ★★★★
Contact: Mrs June Smith, 65 Hoole Road, Hoole, Chester CH2 3NJ
I: www.chesterholidayrentals.co.uk

HOYLAKE
Merseyside

AAA North Villa Apartments ★★★-★★★★
Contact: Ms Sandra Verkade, AAA North Villa Apartments, 33 Cable Road, Hoylake, Wirral CH47 2AU
T: 632 3982
F: 632 3982
E: sandraverkade@aol.com
I: www.northvilla.com

HURST GREEN
Lancashire

Hunters Rest ★★★★
Contact: Mr Martin McShane, Red Rose Cottages, 6 King Street, Clitheroe BB7 2EP
T: (01200) 420101
F: (01200) 420103
I: www.redrosecottages.co.uk

KNUTSFORD
Cheshire

Danebury Apartments Rating Applied For
Contact: Mr & Mrs Stephen and Pauline West, Danebury Apartments, 8 Tabley Road, Knutsford WA16 0NB
T: (01565) 755219
E: enquiries@daneburyapartments.co.uk
I: www.danebury.uk.com

Mile End Apartment Rating Applied For
Contact: Ms Diane Graziano, Mile End, 9 Tabley Road, Knutsford WA16 0NB
T: (01565) 632079
F: (01606) 44417
E: david.graziano@ntlworld.com

6 The Sycamores & 7 The Cedars ★★★★
Contact: Mrs Jenny Dawson, Interludes, Croft Cottage, Hough Lane, Alderley Edge SK9 7JE
T: (01625) 599802
F: (01625) 599802
E: info@interludes-uk.com
I: www.interludes-uk.com

LANCASTER
Lancashire

Mulberry Cottage ★★★
Contact: Mrs Catherine Fatkin, Mulberry Cottage, 8 Castle Park, Cartmel, Grange-over-Sands LA1 1YQ
T: (01524) 64755
I: www.mulberrycottages.uk.com

Rose Cottage ★★★
Contact: Mr Martin Mcshane, Red Rose Cottages, 6 King Street, Clitheroe BB7 2EP
T: (01200) 420101
F: (01200) 420103
E: info@redrosecottages.co.uk
I: www.redrosecottages.co.uk

The Stables ★★★
Contact: Mr & Mrs Quinn, The Stables, Conder Green Cottage, Conder Green, Lancaster LA2 0BG
T: (01524) 751568
F: (01524) 751568

LANESHAW BRIDGE
Lancashire

Spaw Cottage ★★★★
Contact: Mr Martin McShane, Red Rose Cottages, 6 King Street, Clitheroe BB7 2EP

LIVERPOOL
Merseyside

Days Serviced Appartments (Howard Johnson)★★★★
Contact: Mr Richard Howard, Premier Apartments, L3 Complex, 15 Hatton Garden, Liverpool L3 2HB
T: 07951 539040
F: (0151) 227 9468
E: sales@liverpool.premgroup.com
I: www.liverpool-apartments.com

Mersey Waterfront Apartments Rating Applied For
Contact: Mr & Mrs Ian and Janet Shields, Mersey Waterfront Apartments, 135 Royal Quay, Kings Dock, Liverpool L3 4EX
T: (0151) 7440
E: merseywaterfrontapartments@aol.com

Quay Flat ★★★
Contact: Mr & Mrs FA & J Majeed & Saleh, Apartment 45, 2 Royal Quay, Liverpool l3 4et
T: (0151) 625 7298
F: (0151) 625 1749

Trafalgar Warehouse ★★★★
Contact: Mr Ray Gibson, 25 Rosedale Road, Wavertree, Liverpool L18 5JD
T: (0151) 734 4924
F: (0151) 734 4924

Waterfront Penthouse ★★★★
Contact: Mrs Muriel Simpson, Waterfront Penthouse, 424 South Ferry Quay, Clippers Quay, Liverpool L2 4EZ
E: rod+muir@stayinginliverpool.com
I: www.stayinginliverpool.com

LYTHAM ST ANNES
Lancashire

The Chymes Holiday Flats ★★★
Contact: Mrs L Winstanley, The Chymes Holiday Flats, 21 Fairhaven Road, Lytham St Annes FY8 1NN
T: (01253) 726942
F: (01253) 726942

MACCLESFIELD
Cheshire

Mellow Brook Cottage ★★★★
Contact: Susan Stevenson, Harrop Fold Farm, Macclesfield Road, Macclesfield SK10 5UU
T: (01625) 560085
E: susan@harropstudio.fsnet.co.uk

Mill House Farm Cottage ★★★
Contact: Mrs L Whittaker, Mill House Farm, Bosley, Macclesfield SK11 0NZ
T: (01260) 226265
E: lynne-whittaker@yahoo.co.uk
I: www.geocities.com/farm_cottage/

The Teachers Cottage ★★★
Contact: Peak Cottages, School House, Macclesfield Forest, Macclesfield SK11 0AR
I: www.peakcottages.com

MANCHESTER
Greater Manchester

Days Serviced Apartments ★★★
Contact: Mrs Valerie Smith, Days Serviced Apartments, 3, Dale Street, Manchester M1 1JA
T: 236 8963
F: 238 8762
E: vsmith@premgroup.com
I: www.manchester-apartments.com

La Suisse Service Apartments (Bury Old Road)★★★
Contact: Mr Michael Phillips, La Suisse Service Apartments (Bury Old Road), 444, Bury Old Road, Prestwich, Manchester M25 1PQ
T: 796 0545
F: 796 0545
E: reservations@lasuisse.co.uk
I: www.lasuisse.co.uk

The Place Apartment Hotel ★★★★
Contact: Ms Clare Johnson, The Place Apartment Hotel, Ducie Street, Piccadilly, Manchester M1 2TP
T: (0161) 778 7500
F: (0161) 778 7507
I: www.theplaceforliving.com

Establishments printed in blue have a detailed entry in this guide

MARPLE
Greater Manchester

Top Lock Bungalow ★★★
Contact: Country Holidays Ref: 10561, Holiday Cottages Group Owner Services Dept, Spring Mill, Earby, Barnoldswick BB94 0AA
T: 08700 723723
F: (01282) 844288
E: ownerservices@holidaycottagesgroup.com
I: www.country-holidays.co.uk

MIDDLEWICH
Cheshire

Forge Mill Farm Cottages ★★★-★★★★
Contact: Mrs S Moss, Forge Mill Farm, Forge Mill Lane, Warmingham, Middlewich CW10 0HQ
T: (01270) 526204
F: (01270) 526204
E: forgemill2@msn.com

MORECAMBE
Lancashire

Eden Vale Luxury Holiday Flats ★★★
Contact: Mr Jason Coombs, Eden Vale Luxury Holiday Flats, 338 Marine Road, Morecambe LA4 5AB
T: (01524) 415544

Mountfield Holiday Flats ★★
Contact: Mrs Janet Mayers, Mountfield Holiday Flats, 67 Balmoral Road, Morecambe LA4 4JS
T: (01524) 423518

Northumberland House ★★
Contact: Mr Neil Briggs, Northumberland House, 42 Northumberland Street, Morecambe LA4 4BA
T: (01524) 412039
E: j.s.shaw@tesco.net

Rydal Mount ★
Contact: Mrs S Holmes, Rydal Mount, 361 Marine Road East, Morecambe LA4 5AQ
T: (01524) 411858

Sandown Holiday Flats ★★
Contact: Mr & Mrs Colin Matthews, 367 Marine Road East, Morecambe LA4 5AQ
T: (01524) 410933

NANTWICH
Cheshire

Bank Farm Cottages ★★★
Contact: Mrs Ann Vaughan, Bank Farm Cottages, Hough, Crewe CW2 5JG
T: (01270) 841809
F: (01270) 841809

Fields Farm ★★
Contact: Mr David Heys, Fields Farm, Off Queens Drive, Edleston, Nantwich CW5 5JL
T: (01270) 625769
F: (01270) 625769

Stoke Grange Mews ★★★★
Contact: Mrs Georgina West, Stoke Grange Mews, Stoke Grange Farm, Chester Road, Nantwich CW5 6BT
T: (01270) 625525
F: (01270) 625525
I: www.topfarms.co.uk/stokegrangefarm.htm

NESTON
Cheshire

The Field House ★★★★
Contact: Mrs Anna Wild, The Field House, Upper Raby Road, Neston, South Wirral CH64 7TZ
T: 336 1728

NETHER KELLET
Lancashire

The Apartment ★★★
Contact: Mr S Richardson
T: (01524) 734969

The Loft ★★★★
Contact: Mr Stephen Hinde
T: (01524) 734135
F: (01524) 734135
E: stevehinde@onetel.net.uk

ORMSKIRK
Lancashire

Tristrams Farm Holiday Cottages ★★★
Contact: Mr David Swift, Sunset Cottage, Narrow Lane, Halsall, Ormskirk L39 8RL

OSCROFT
Cheshire

Ash Farm Cottage ★★★
Contact: Administration Manager, Spring Mill, Earby, Barnoldswick BB94 0AA
T: (01282) 445096
F: (01282) 844288
I: www.country-holidays.co.uk

OVER KELLET
Lancashire

Lime Tree Cottage ★★
Contact: Mrs Greaves, Lime Tree Cottage, The Green, Over Kellet, Carnforth LA6 1DA
T: (01524) 732165

POULTON
Cheshire

Half Mile Cottage Rating Applied For
Contact: Mrs Margaret Walker, 6 Straight Mile, Poulton, Chester CH4 9EQ
T: (01244) 570435
F: (01244) 570435
E: wallpoul@bytecraft.net

POULTON-LE-FYLDE
Lancashire

Hardhorn Breaks ★★★★
Contact: Mr Martin McShane, Red Rose Cottages, 6 King Street, Clitheroe BB7 2EP
T: (01200) 420101
F: (01200) 420103
I: www.redrosecottages.co.uk

Swans Rest Holiday Cottages ★★★★
Contact: Mrs Irene O'Connor, Swans Rest, Garstang Road East, Singleton, Poulton-le-Fylde FY6 8LX
T: (01253) 886617
F: (01253) 892563
E: swansrest@btconnect.com
I: www.swansrest.co.uk

PRESTON
Lancashire

Cloggers Cottage ★★★★
Contact: Mr Martin McShane, Red Rose Cottages, 6 King Street, Clitheroe BB7 2EP
T: (01200) 420101
F: (01200) 420103
E: info@redrosecottages.co.uk
I: www.redrosecottages.co.uk

University of Central Lancashire ★★
Contact: Miss Maria Dominguez, University of Central Lancashire, Hospitality Services, Marsh Building, Preston PR1 2HE
T: (01772) 892650
F: (01772) 892977
E: hospitalityservices@uclan.ac.uk
I: www.uclan.ac.uk

QUERNMORE
Lancashire

Daisy Bank Cottage ★★★
Contact: Mrs Janette Callon, Daisy Bank Cottage, The Bungalow, Daisy Bank, Scotforth, Lancaster LA1 3JN
T: (01524) 35493

Lodge View Cottages ★★★
Contact: Mr David Gardner, Far Lodge, Quernmore, Lancaster LA2 9EF
T: (01524) 63109
E: djkagardner@ukgateway.net

RIMINGTON
Lancashire

Raikes Barn ★★★★
Contact: Mrs Robinson, Beckside Farm, Cross Hill Lane, Rimington, Clitheroe BB7 4EE
T: (01200) 445287
F: (01200) 445287
I: www.btclickforbusiness.com

Tewit and Badger Cottages ★★★★
Contact: Mrs Anne Smith, No. 1 Howcroft Cottages, Stopper Lane, Rimington, Clitheroe BB7 4EJ
T: (01200) 445598
F: (01200) 444188

ROCHDALE
Greater Manchester

31 Butterworth Hall ★★★★
Contact: Mrs Judith Hirst, 31 Butterworth Hall, Milnrow, Rochdale OL16 3PE
E: gatehouse@faxvia.net

SADDLEWORTH
Greater Manchester

Friar Lodge ★★★
Contact: Mrs Burke, Friar Lodge, Lodge Lane, Delph, Oldham OL3 5HG
T: (01457) 872718

SAWLEY
Lancashire

Riverside Cottage ★★★★
Contact: Mr Martin Mcshane, Red Rose Cottages, 6 King Street, Clitheroe BB7 2EP
T: (01200) 420101
F: (01200) 420103
E: info@redrosecottages.co.uk
I: www.redrosecottages.co.uk

SILVERDALE
Lancashire

Old Waterslack Farmhouse Caravan Cottages★★★
Contact: Mrs N Hevey, Old Waterslack Farmhouse Caravan Cottages, Old Waterslack Farmhouse, Silverdale, Carnforth LA5 0UH
T: (01524) 701108
F: (01524) 844280
E: n.hevey@oldwaterslackfarm.ukf.net
I: www.oldwaterslackfarm.ukf.net

Pheasant Field ★★★
Contact: Sykes Cottages Ref: 684, Sykes Cottages, York House, York Street, Chester CH1 3LR
T: (01244) 345700
F: (01244) 321442
E: info@sykescottages.co.uk
I: www.sykescottages.co.uk

The Stables ★★★★
Contact: Mrs C M Ranford, The Stables, Lindeth House, Lindeth Road, Silverdale, Carnforth LA5 0TT
T: (01524) 702121
F: (01524) 702226
E: conquerors.maryk@virgin.net

Virginia Cottage ★★★★
Contact: Mr David Hogarth, Cumbrian Cottages, 7 The Crescent, Carlisle CA1 1QW
T: (01228) 599960
F: (01228) 599970
E: enquiries@cumbrian-cottages.co.uk
I: www.cumbrian-cottages.co.uk

Wolf House Cottage ★★★-★★★★
Contact: Mrs Denise Dowbiggin, Wolf House Cottage, Gibraltar, Silverdale, Carnforth LA5 0TX
T: (01524) 701573
F: (01524) 701573
E: denise@wolfhouse-gallery.co.uk
I: www.wolfhouse-gallery.co.uk

SLAIDBURN
Lancashire

Burn Fell View ★★★
Contact: Red Rose Cottages Red Rose Cottages, Red Rose Cottages, 6 King Street, Clitheroe BB7 2EP
T: (01200) 420101
F: (01200) 420103
I: www.redrosecottages.co.uk

Laythams Farmhouse & Cottage ★★★
Contact: Mr Ian Roger Driver, 1 Laythams Farm, Back Lane, Slaidburn, Clitheroe BB7 3AJ
T: (01200) 446454
F: (01200) 446454
E: iandriver@talk21.com

The Olde Stables ★★★★
Contact: Mrs Margaret Robinson, The Olde Stables, Woodhouse Gate Farm, Slaidburn, Clitheroe BB7 3AQ
T: (01200) 446240
F: (01200) 446412

SOUTHPORT
Merseyside

Barford House Apartments ★★★
Contact: Mr Graham Watson, Barford House Apartments, 32 Avondale Road, Southport PR9 0ND
E: graham@barfordhouse.co.uk
I: www.barfordhouse.co.uk

Beaucliffe Holiday Flats ★★-★★★
Contact: Mrs Lewis, 9 Leicester St, Widnes PR9 0ER
T: 537 207

Castle Mews ★★★
Contact: Mr Graham Watson, 32 Avondale Road, Southport PR9 0ND
E: graham@barfordhouse.co.uk
I: barfordhouse.co.uk

Martin Lane Farmhouse Holiday Cottages ★★★★
Contact: Mrs Stubbs, Martin Lane Farmhouse Holiday Cottages, Martin Lane Farmhouse, Burscough, Ormskirk L40 8JH
T: (01704) 893527
F: (01704) 893527
E: mlfhc@btinternet.com
I: www.martinlanefarmhouse.btinternet.co.uk

Sandcroft Holidy Flats ★
Contact: Mr Best, Sandcroft Holiday Flats, 13 Albany Road, Southport PR9 0JF
T: 537 497

Sandy Brook Farm ★★★
Contact: Mr W Core, Sandy Brook Farm, 52 Wyke Cop Road, Scarisbrick, Southport PR8 5LR
T: (01704) 880337
F: (01704) 880337
E: sandybrookfarm@lycos.co.uk

STOCKPORT
Greater Manchester

Lake View ★★★
Contact: Mrs M Sidebottom, Shire Cottage, Benches Lane, Marple Bridge, Stockport SK6 5RY
T: (01457) 866536
F: (01457) 866536

STONYHURST
Lancashire

Alden Cottage ★★★★
Contact: Mrs B Carpenter, Alden Cottage, Kemple End, Birdy Brow, Bashall Eaves, Clitheroe BB7 9QY
T: (01254) 826468
F: (01254) 826468
E: carpenter@aldencottagef9.co.uk
I: http://fp.aldencottage.f9.co.uk

SUTTON
Cheshire

Lower Pethills Farm Cottage ★★★★
Contact: Mr & Mrs Greg Rowson, Lower Pethills Farm Cottages, Lower Pethills Farm, Sutton, Wincle, Macclesfield SK11 0NJ

TARVIN
Cheshire

Cheese Makers Cottage ★★★
Contact: Elaine Sherwin, Broomheath Lane, Stapleford, Tarvin, Chester CH3 8HE
T: (01829) 140439

THORNLEY
Lancashire

Thornley Hall ★★★
Contact: Mrs Airey, Thornley Hall, Thornley Hall Farm, Thornley, Preston PR3 2TN
T: (01995) 61243

TOSSIDE
Lancashire

Primrose Cottage, Jenny Wren, Wagtail, Swallows, Lower Gill Farmhouse ★★★★
Contact: Holiday Cottages (Yorkshire), Water Street, Skipton BD23 1PB
T: (01756) 700510
E: brochure@holidaycotts.co.uk
I: www.holidaycotts.co.uk

WENNINGTON
Lancashire

Easter Cottage ★★★★
Contact: Mrs Jenny Herd, Mill Farm, Wennington, Lancaster LA2 8NU
T: (015242) 21690
I: www.eastercottage.net

WESTHOUSE
Lancashire

Hillcrest ★★
Contact: Mr Brown, West House, Westhouse, Ingleton, Carnforth LA6 3PA
T: (015242) 41331

WHALLEY
Lancashire

Tabgha ★★★
Contact: Mr Martin McShane, Red Rose Cottages, 6 King Street, Clitheroe BB7 2EP

WIGAN
Greater Manchester

Oysterber Farm Cottage Holidays
Rating Applied For
Contact: Mrs Cathy Cartledge, Oysterber Farm Cottage Holidays, Oysterber Farm, Burton Road, Wigan LA2 7ET
T: (015242) 61567
F: (015242) 62885

WILDBOARCLOUGH
Cheshire

Lower House Cottage ★★
Contact: Mrs F Waller, Blaze Farm, Wildboarclough, Macclesfield SK11 0BL
T: (01260) 227229

WILLINGTON
Cheshire

Delamere Cottage ★★★★
Contact: Mr & Mrs Sidebotham, Delamere Cottage, Willington Road, Willington, Tarporley CW6 0ND
T: (01829) 751628
E: jhs@sebden.com

WINCLE
Cheshire

Clough Brook Cottage ★★★★
Contact: Mr John Henshall, Clough Brook Cottage, Almeadows Farm, Wincle, Macclesfield SK11 0QJ
T: (01260) 227209
F: (01260) 227209
E: henshalls@btinternet.com
I: www.allmeadows.co.uk

WISWELL
Lancashire

New Row Cottage ★★★
Contact: Mr Martin Mcshane, Red Rose Cottages, 6 King Street, Clitheroe BB7 2EP
T: (01200) 420101
F: (01200) 420103
E: info@redrosecottages.co.uk
I: www.redrosecottages.co.uk

WORSLEY
Greater Manchester

The Cottage - Worsley ★★★
Contact: Mr & Mrs G R Atherton, 60 Worsley Road, Worsley, Manchester M28 2SH
T: (0161) 793 4157
F: (0161) 793 4157

YEALAND REDMAYNE
Lancashire

Brackenthwaite Cottage ★★★
Contact: Mrs Susan Clarke, Brackenthwaite Farm, Yealand Redmayne, Carnforth LA5 9TE
T: (015395) 63276
F: (015395) 63276
I: www.brackenthwaitecottages.co.uk

YORKSHIRE

ACKLAM
North Yorkshire

Beck Side Cottage @ Trout Pond Barn ★★★★
Contact: Mrs Margaret Phillips, Trout Pond Barn, Acklam, Malton YO17 9RG
T: (01653) 658468
F: (01653) 698688
E: margaret@troutpondbarn.co.uk

ADDINGHAM
West Yorkshire

Number Nine ★★★★
Contact: Mr & Mrs Ian & Jean Francis, Old Lane, Addingham, Ilkley LS29 0SA
T: (01943) 831254

AIKE
East Riding of Yorkshire

The Old Chapel ★★★
Contact: Sykes Cottages Ref:323, Sykes Cottages, York House, York Street, Chester CH1 3LR
T: (01244) 345700
F: (01244) 321442
E: info@sykescottages.co.uk
I: www.sykescottages.co.uk

AIRTON
North Yorkshire

13 Riverside Walk
Rating Applied For
Contact: Agent, Embsay Mills, Embsay, Skipton BD23 6QR
T: (01756) 696868
F: (01756) 702235

Scosthrop Old School House ★★★★
Contact: Agent Dales Hol Cot Ref:1741, Carleton Business Park, Carleton New Road, Skipton BD23 2AA
T: (01756) 799821
F: (01756) 797012
E: info@dalesholcot.com
I: www.dalesholcot.com

AISKEW
North Yorkshire

The Courtyard ★★★★
Contact: Mr & Mrs J Cartman
T: (01677) 423689
F: (01677) 425762
E: jill@courtyard.ndirect.co.uk
I: www.courtyard.ndirect.co.uk

AISLABY
North Yorkshire

Aislaby Hall Cottage ★★★★
Contact: Mrs Janet Hartshorne, Aislaby Hall, Aislaby, Pickering YO18 8PE
T: (01751) 477777
F: (01751) 477766

Eskbridge Cottage ★★★★
Contact: Mrs Julie Tuby, 54 Carr Hill Lane, Briggswath, Sleights, Whitby YO21 1RS
T: (01947) 810388
F: (01947) 820466

Low Newbiggin House
★★★-★★★★★
Contact: Miss Charlotte Etherington, Low Newbiggin House, Aislaby, Whitby YO21 1TQ
T: (01947) 811811
F: (01947) 810348
E: enquires@lownewbiggin.co.uk
I: www.lownewbiggin.co.uk

Stable Cottage & Byre Cottage
Rating Applied For
Contact: Mrs Adele Thompson & Vanessa Hickings, Whitby Holiday Cottages, 47 Flowergate, Whitby YO21 3BB
T: (01947) 603010
F: (01947) 821133
E: enquiries@whitby-cottages.co.uk
I: www.whitby-cottages.co.uk

ALDBROUGH
North Yorkshire

Greencroft Cottage ★★★
Contact: Mrs Baxter, Aldbrough St John, Aldbrough, Richmond DL11 7TJ
T: (01325) 374550
E: ray.baxter@btinternet.com
I: www.greencroft.org.uk

Lilac Cottage ★★★★
Contact: Mrs Helen Stubbs, 19 Seaside Road, Aldbrough, Hull HU11 4RX
T: (01964) 527645
E: helen@seasideroad.freeserve.co.uk
I: www.aer96.dial.pipex.com/lilac-cottage

ALDFIELD
North Yorkshire

Trips Cottage ★★★
Contact: Mrs S V Leeming, Trips Cottage, Bay Tree Farm, Aldfield, Ripon HG3 4BE
T: (01765) 620394
I: www.yorkshirebandb.co.uk

ALKBOROUGH
North Lincolnshire

Corner Cottage ★★★★
Contact: Ms Annette Dexter, 169 Abbots Road, Abbots Langley, Watford WD5 0BN
T: (01923) 330022
F: (01923) 330022
E: annette.dexter@ntlworld.com

ALLERSTON
North Yorkshire

The Old Station ★★★★
Contact: Mr & Mrs Mark & Carol Benson, The Old Station, Main Street, Allerston, Pickering YO18 7PG
T: (01723) 859024
E: mcrbenson@aol.com
I: www.cottageguide.co.uk/theoldstation

Rains Farm ★★★★
Contact: Mrs L Allanson, Rains Farm, Allerston, Pickering YO18 7PQ
T: (01723) 859333
E: allan@rainsfarm.freeserve.co.uk
I: www.rains-farm-holidays.co.uk

ALLERTHORPE
East Riding of Yorkshire

The Old Gravel Pits ★★★★
Contact: Dr Edward Moll, Allerthorpe, York YO42 4RW
T: (01759) 302192

AMPLEFORTH
North Yorkshire

Beckside Cottage ★★★
Contact: Agent Dales Hol Cot Ref:2474, Carleton Business Park, Carleton New Road, Skipton BD23 2AA
T: (01756) 799821
F: (01756) 797012
E: info@dalesholcot.com
I: www.dalesholcot.com

Brook House ★★★★
Contact: Mrs Mary Sturges, Brook House Cottage, West End, Ampleforth, York YO62 4DY
T: (01439) 788563
F: (01439) 788563
E: mpsturge@aol.com

2 Carmel Cottage ★★★
Contact: Miss Jennings, West End, Ampleforth, York YO62 4DU
T: (01439) 788467
F: (01439) 788467
E: carmelcott@onetel.net.uk

Hillside Cottage ★★★★
Contact: Mrs P Noble, Hillside, West End, Ampleforth, York YO62 4DY
T: (01439) 788303
F: (01439) 788303
E: hillsidecottage@westend-ampleforth.co.uk
I: www.cottageguide.co.uk/hillsidecottage

APPERSETT
North Yorkshire

The Coach House ★★★
Contact: Mr W Head, The Coach House, Rigg House, High Abbotside, Appersett, Hawes DL8 3LR
T: (01969) 667375
F: (01969) 667375
E: walterhead@rigghouse.freeserve.co.uk

APPLETON-LE-MOORS
North Yorkshire

The Carthouse ★★★
Contact: Mrs Diane Peirson, Cockpit Farmhouse, Appleton-le-Moors, York YO62 6TF
T: (01751) 417363
F: (01751) 417636
E: bob.peirson@tiscali.co.uk

Darley Cottage ★★★★
Contact: Mr & Mrs James Brooke, The Pottery, Appleton-le-Moors, York YO62 6TE
T: (01751) 417514
E: jbrooke@pottery1.fsnet.co.uk

Hamley Hagg Cottage ★★★
Contact: Mrs Feaster, Hamley Hagg Cottage, Hamley Hagg Farm, Appleton-le-Moors, York YO62 6TG
T: (01751) 417413
F: (01751) 417413
I: www.appletonlemoors.fsnet.co.uk

Three Faces Cottage ★★★
Contact: Mrs Firth, 4 West End Lane, Horsforth, Leeds LS18 5JP
T: (0113) 258 8940
E: the3faces@hotmail.com

APPLETREEWICK
North Yorkshire

Fell Cottage
Rating Applied For
Contact: Mr & Mrs Nigel and Tracey Wain, Andras Farm, Appletreewick, Skipton BD23 6DA
T: (01756) 720286
F: (01756) 720286
E: fellcottage@appletreewick.net

Fell View
Rating Applied For
Contact: Sykes Ref 817, Sykes Cottages, York House, York Street, Chester CH1 3LR
T: (01244) 345700
F: (01244) 321442
E: info@sykescottages.co.uk
I: www.sykescottages.co.uk

Fellside ★★★
Contact: Mrs Murphy, 5 Barns Close, Kirby Muxloe, Leicester LE9 2BA
T: (0116) 239 5713
F: (0116) 239 5713
E: murphyjayne@hotmail.com

ARKENGARTHDALE
North Yorkshire

Low Lock Slack Cottage ★★★
Contact: Sykes Cottages Ref:62, Sykes Cottages, York House, York Street, Chester CH1 3LR
T: (01244) 345700
F: (01244) 321442
E: info@sykescottages.co.uk
I: www.sykescottages.co.uk

The Old School House ★★
Contact: Sykes Cottages Ref:279, Sykes Cottages, York House, York Street, Chester CH1 3LR
T: (01244) 345700
F: (01244) 321442
E: info@sykescottages.co.uk
I: www.sykescottages.co.uk

ARNCLIFFE
North Yorkshire

Green Farm Cottage ★★★
Contact: Agent Dales Hol Cot Ref:1523, Carleton Business Park, Carleton New Road, Skipton BD23 2AA
T: (01756) 799821
F: (01756) 797012
E: info@dalesholcot.com
I: www.dalesholcot.com

ASKRIGG
North Yorkshire

Askrigg Cottage Holidays
★★★★
Contact: Mr & Mrs Ken Williamson, Askrigg Cottage Holidays, Thwaite House, Moor Road, Askrigg, Leyburn DL8 3HH
T: (01969) 650022
E: stay@askrigg.com
I: www.askrigg.com

Askrigg Cottages
★★★-★★★★★
Contact: Mrs Kate Empsall, Whitfield, Helm, Askrigg, Leyburn DL8 3JF
T: (01969) 650565
F: (01969) 650565
E: empsall@askrigg-cottages.co.uk
I: www.askrigg-cottages.co.uk

Carr End Cottage ★★★
Contact: Agent Dales Hol Cot Ref:2467, Carleton Business Park, Carleton New Road, Skipton BD23 2AA
T: (01756) 790919
F: (01756) 797012
E: fiona@dales-holiday-cottages.com
I: www.dales-holiday-cottages.com

Cowlingholme Cottage
★★★★
Contact: Mrs Nadine H Bell, Country Hideaways, Margaret's Cottage, West Burton, Askrigg, Leyburn DL8 4JN
T: (01969) 663559
F: (01969) 663559
E: nadine@countryhideaways.co.uk
I: www.countryhideaways.co.uk

Elm Hill Holiday Cottages
★★★
Contact: Mr & Mrs Peter Haythornthwaite, Biggins Wood, High Biggins, Kirkby Lonsdale, Carnforth LA6 2NP
T: (015242) 71127
F: (015242) 71127
E: enquiries@elmhillholidaycottages.co.uk
I: www.browcottage-askrigg.co.uk

Faith Hill Cottage ★★★
Contact: Ms Jennifer Kirkbride, Town Head Farm, Moor Road, Askrigg, Leyburn DL8 3HH
T: (01969) 650325
E: allenkirkbride@hotmail.com

Greystones ★★★
Contact: Mrs Nadine Bell, Country Hideaways, Margaret's Cottage, West Burton, Askrigg, Leyburn DL8 4JN
T: (01969) 663559
F: (01969) 663559
E: nadine@countryhideaways.co.uk
I: www.countryhideaways.co.uk

Lavender Cottage ★★★★
Contact: Sykes Cottages Ref:729, Sykes Cottages, York House, York Street, Chester CH1 3LR
T: (01244) 345700
F: (01244) 321442
E: info@sykescottages.co.uk
I: www.sykescottages.co.uk

Lukes Barn ★★★
Contact: Agent Dales Hol Cot Ref:1675, Dales Holiday Cottages, Carleton Business Park, Carleton New Road, Skipton BD23 2AA
T: (01756) 799821
F: (01756) 797012
E: info@dalesholcot.com
I: www.dalesholcot.com

Old Mill II ★★★
Contact: Mrs Nadine Bell, Country Hideaways, Margaret's Cottage, West Burton, Askrigg, Leyburn DL8 4JN
T: (01969) 663559
F: (01969) 663559
E: nadine@countryhideaways.co.uk
I: www.countryhideaways.co.uk

School House ★★★
Contact: Mrs Nadine H Bell, Country Hideaways, Margaret's Cottage, West Burton, Askrigg, Leyburn DL8 4JN
T: (01969) 663559
F: (01969) 663559
E: nadine@countryhideaways.co.uk
I: www.countryhideaways.co.uk

Shaw Cote Cottage ★★★
Contact: Sykes Cottages Ref:218, Sykes Cottages, York House, York Street, Chester CH1 3LR
T: (01244) 345700
F: (01244) 321442
E: info@sykescottages.co.uk
I: www.sykescottages.co.uk

The Shippon ★★★
Contact: Mrs Nadine Bell, Country Hideaways, Margaret's Cottage, West Burton, Askrigg, Leyburn DL8 4JN
T: (01969) 663559
F: (01969) 663559
E: nadine@countryhideaways.co.uk
I: www.countryhideaways.co.uk

Thorndale House ★★★★
Contact: Mrs Kate Empsall, Whitfield/Askrigg Cottages, Askrigg, Leyburn DL8 3JF
T: (01969) 650565
F: (01969) 650565
E: empsall@askrigg-cottages.co.uk
I: www.askrigg.yorks.net

Yoredale Cottage ★★
Contact: Mrs Elizabeth Miller, The Orchard, West Burton, Askrigg, Leyburn DL8 4JN
T: (01969) 663359
E: bmiller@wensleydale.n-yorks.sch.uk

AUSTWICK
North Yorkshire

Rawlinshaw Farm ★★★★
Contact: Dales Hol Cottages Ref:3335, Dales Holiday Cottages, Carleton Business Park, Carleton New Road, Skipton BD23 2AA
T: (01756) 799821
F: (01756) 797012
E: info@dalesholcot.com
I: www.dalesholcot.com

Spoutscroft Cottage ★★★★
Contact: Mrs Christine Hartland, Leigh Cottage, Austwick, Lancaster LA2 8BN
T: (01524) 251052
E: mikehartland@onetel.net.uk

AYSGARTH
North Yorkshire

Yore Mews ★★
Contact: Mrs Nadine H Bell, Country Hideaways, Margarets Cottage, West Burton, Leyburn DL8 4JN
T: (01969) 663559
F: (01969) 663559
E: nadine@countryhideaways.co.uk
I: www.countryhideaways.co.uk

BALDERSBY
North Yorkshire

The Barn ★★★
Contact: Mrs Sylvia Thain, Baldersby, Thirsk YO7 4PE
T: (01765) 640561
F: (01765) 640561
E: sthain@zoom.co.uk

Elm Cottage ★★
Contact: Dales 2557,3135, Carleton Business Park, Carleton New Road, Skipton BD23 2AA
T: (01756) 799821
F: (01756) 797012
E: info@dalesholcot.com
I: www.dalesholcot.com

BARDEN
North Yorkshire

The Shippon ★★★
Contact: Dales Hol Cot Ref:2877, Carleton Business Park, Carleton New Road, Skipton BD23 2AA
T: (01756) 799821
F: (01756) 797012
E: info@dalesholcot.com
I: www.dalesholcot.com

BARMBY MOOR
East Riding of Yorkshire

Calley Barn ★★★★
Contact: Mrs Steel, Kimberley House, The Green, Barmby Moor, York YO42 4EY
T: (01759) 302514
F: (01759) 302514

Northwood Coach House ★★★★
Contact: Mrs A Gregory, Northwood House, St Helen's Square, Barmby Moor, York YO42 4HF
T: (01759) 302305
E: annjgregory@hotmail.com

BARNOLDBY-LE-BECK
Lincolnshire

Grange Farm Cottages & Riding School★★★★
Contact: Mrs Suzette & Miss Jenkins, Grange Farm Cottages & Riding School, Waltham Road, Barnoldby-le-Beck, Grimsby DN37 0AR
T: (01472) 622216
F: (01472) 311101
E: sueuk4000@netscape.net
I: grangefarmcottages.com

BARROW UPON HUMBER
North Lincolnshire

Papist Hall ★★★
Contact: Mrs Marion Dawson, 22 Lynwood Avenue, Anlaby, Hull HU10 7DP
T: (01482) 657930
F: (01482) 657553
E: info@papisthall.co.uk
I: www.papisthall.co.uk

BARTON-LE-WILLOWS
North Yorkshire

The Old Granary ★★★★
Contact: Mrs Hudson, The Old Granary, Green Farm, Barton le Willows, Whitwell-on-the-Hill, York YO60 7PD
T: (01653) 618387
F: (01653) 618387
E: bartonlewillows@netscapeonline.co.uk
I: www.oldgranary.com

BAYSDALE
North Yorkshire

Baysdale Abbey ★★★
Contact: Agent, Stoney Bank, Earby, Barnoldswick BB94 0AA
T: 0870 585 1155
F: (01282) 841539

BECKWITHSHAW
North Yorkshire

The Old Mistal Cottage ★★★★
Contact: Mrs Christine Williams, Bluecoat Farm, Howhill Road, Beckwithshaw, Harrogate HG3 1QJ
T: (01423) 561385
F: (01423) 561385
E: c.williams@mistal.fsnet.co.uk
I: www.mistal.fsnet.co.uk

BEDALE
North Yorkshire

High Grange Holiday Cottages ★★★★
Contact: Mr & Mrs Trevor and Janet Ripley, High Grange Holiday Cottages, High Grange, Exelby, Bedale DL8 2HQ
T: (01677) 422740
E: highgrange@yorks.net
I: www.highgrange.yorks.net

Stabann ★★★★
Contact: Mr Michael Hall, Georgian Bed and Breakfast, 16 North End, Bedale DL8 1AB
T: (01677) 424454
E: georgianbandb@aol.com
I: www.georgian@bedale-town.com

BELLERBY
North Yorkshire

Boar Cottage ★★★★
Contact: Mr & Mrs B Gray, The Boar Inn House, Bellerby, Leyburn DL8 5QP
T: (01969) 622220
F: (01969) 62220
E: graydales@aol.com
I: www.boarcottage.co.uk

Eastvale Cottage ★★★
Contact: Ms Trish Borrill, Stores Cottage, Moor Road, Bellerby, Leyburn DL8 5QT
T: (01969) 623152
E: trish@eastvalecottage.fslife.co.uk

Scott Cottage ★★★
Contact: Mrs Maughan, Scott Cottage, Bellerby, Leyburn DL8 5QP
T: (01969) 622498
F: (01969) 622498

BEMPTON
East Riding of Yorkshire

Primrose Cottage ★★★★
Contact: Agent Dales Hol Cot Ref:2122, Carleton Business Park, Carleton New Road, Skipton BD23 2AA
T: (01756) 799821
F: (01756) 797012
E: info@dalesholcot.com
I: www.dalesholcot.com

BEVERLEY
East Riding of Yorkshire

Apple Tree Cottages Rating Applied For
Contact: Mrs Linda Chamberlain, Apple Tree House, Norwood, Beverley HU17 9HN
T: (01482) 873615
F: (01482) 866666

Beckside Cottage ★★★
Contact: Mr King, Beckside Cottage, 66 Beckside, Beverley HU17 0PD
T: (01482) 872291
E: kings@three.karoo.co.uk

Beverley Holiday Cottages ★★-★★★
Contact: Mr Paul Eastburn, 32 Wood Lane, Beverley HU17 8BS
T: (01482) 882699
E: eastburn@eastburn1066.karoo.co.uk
I: www.eastburn1066.karoo.net

Chapel View ★★★
Contact: Mr Philip Hillman, 138 Norwood, Beverley HU17 9HL
T: (01482) 867465

The Coach House Rating Applied For
Contact: Mr D & Mrs H Wright, The Coach House, Newbegin House, 10 Newbegin, Beverley HU17 8EG

The Cottage ★★★★
Contact: Mr Kenneth Hearne, 25 All Hallows Road, Walkington, Beverley HU17 8SH
T: (01482) 868310
E: knhearne@talk21.com
I: www.akcottage.com

Foremans Cottage ★★★
Contact: Mrs Hayward, Lane House, Beverley Road, Bishop Burton, Beverley HU17 8QY
T: (01964) 550821
F: (01964) 550898
E: paulwhay@aol.com

Lempicka Cottage ★★★★
Contact: Mrs Linda Boyeson, 13 Wednesday Market, Beverley HU17 0DH
T: (01482) 863665
F: (01482) 866960

Old Walkergate & The Cabin ★★-★★★
Contact: Mrs Margaret Abbey, 5 Laughton Road, Beverley HU17 9JR
T: (01482) 860005
F: (01482) 860005
E: margaretabbey@beverleyselfcatering.freeserve.co.uk
I: www.beverleyselfcatering.freeserve.co.uk

Rudstone Walk Country Accommodation ★★★★
Contact: Mrs L Greenwood, Rudstone Walk Country Cottages, South Cave, Brough, Nr Beverly HU15 2AH
T: (01430) 422230
F: (01430) 424552
E: admin@rudstone-walk.co.uk
I: www.rudstone-walk.co.uk

BEWERLEY
North Yorkshire

Bewerley Hall Farm ★★★★
Contact: Mrs Smith, Bewerley Hall Farm, Bewerley, Harrogate HG3 5JA
T: (01423) 711636
E: chris@farmhouseholidays.freeserve.co.uk
I: www.bewerleyhallfarm.co.uk

4 The Green ★★★
Contact: Mr Wales, Water Street, Oughtershaw, Skipton BD23 1PB
T: (01756) 700510

BIRSTWITH
North Yorkshire

3 The Square ★★★★
Contact: Mr Wales, Water Street, Oughtershaw, Skipton BD23 1PB
T: (01756) 700510

BISHOP MONKTON
North Yorkshire

Granary Cottage ★★★
Contact: Ms Allison Hewson, Laurel Bank Farm, Hungate Lane, Bishop Monkton, Harrogate HG3 3QL
T: (01765) 677677

Hall Farm Cottage ★★★★
Contact: Mrs Jennifer Barker, Boroughbridge Road, Bishop Monkton, Harrogate HG3 3QN
T: (01765) 677200
E: barkerhallfarm@onetel.net.co.uk
I: www.yorkshirebandb.co.uk

BISHOP THORNTON
North Yorkshire

The Courtyard at 'Dukes Place' ★★★-★★★★
Contact: Mrs Jaki Moorhouse, The Courtyard at 'Dukes Place', Bishop Thornton, Harrogate HG3 3JY
T: (01765) 620229
F: (01765) 620454
E: jakimoorhouse@onetel.net.uk

BISHOP WILTON
East Riding of Yorkshire

Low Callis Granary ★★★★
Contact: J Stringer & Sons, Low Callis Granary, Low Callis Wold, Bishop Wilton, York YO42 1TD
T: (01759) 368831
E: thegranary@lowcallis.plus.com

BOLSTERSTONE
South Yorkshire

Nook Farm Holiday Cottage ★★★
Contact: Ms Wainwright, Nook Farm Holiay Cottage, Nook Farm, More Hall Lane, Bolsterstone, Sheffield S36 3ST
T: (0114) 288 3335

BOLTBY
North Yorkshire

The Coach House ★★★
Contact: Blakes Cottages, 21a Roydon Road, Stanstead Abbotts, Earby, Barnoldswick SG12 8HQ
T: 08704 446603
F: (01282) 841539
I: www.boltbytrekking.co.uk

BOLTON
East Riding of Yorkshire

Croft House ★★★★
Contact: Mrs Sampson, Bolton House, Bolton, Fangfoss, York YO41 5QX
T: (01759) 368210

BOLTON ABBEY
North Yorkshire

The Beamsley Project Rating Applied For
Contact: Margaret and John Tomlinson, The Beamsley Project, Beamsley, Skipton BD23 6JA
T: (01756) 710255
F: (01756) 710255
E: beamsley.project@virgin.net
I: www.beamsleyproject.org.uk

Low Laithe Barn ★★★★★
Contact: Mrs Susan Gray, Beech House Farm, Langbar, Ilkley LS29 0EP
T: (01943) 609819
F: (01943) 609337
E: info@beechhousebarns

BOLTON PERCY
North Yorkshire

Manor Cottages ★★★
Contact: Mrs Jane Houseman, Hornington Manor, Bolton Percy, York YO23 7AS
T: (01937) 833157
F: (01937) 833157

BORROWBY
North Yorkshire

Muttling Corner Cottage ★★★★
Contact: Mrs Jane McBretney, Danby Wiske, Northallerton DL7 0AL
T: (01325) 378297
E: muttlingcorner@dial.pipex.com
I: www.yorkshireescapes.com

BOUTHWAITE
North Yorkshire

Granary Cottage ★★★
Contact: Mr & Mrs John and Sheila Lofthouse, Ramsgill in Nidderdale, Bouthwaite, Harrogate HG3 5RW
T: (01423) 755306
F: (01423) 755306
E: sales@jandsenterprises.co.uk
I: www.jandsenterprises.co.uk

BRADFIELD
South Yorkshire

Foxholes Farm ★★★
Contact: Ms Jean & Rachel Hague, High Bradfield, Bradfield, Sheffield S6 6LJ
T: (0114) 285 1551
F: (0114) 285 1559

BRAMHAM
West Yorkshire

Chestnut Chase ★★★
Contact: Mrs P Machin, Chestnut Chase, 9 Prospect Bank, Bramham, Wetherby LS23 6RS
T: (01937) 842559

BRIDLINGTON
East Riding of Yorkshire

Acorn House ★★★
Contact: Mr & Mrs Morton, 9 Belgrave Road, Bridlington YO15 3JP
T: (01262) 672451
E: marieoak24@hotmail.com

Angie's Imp-press Holiday Apartments★★
Contact: Mrs Angela Boxer, Imp-press Holiday Flats, 17 Blackburn Avenue, Bridlington YO15 2ER
T: (01262) 608838

Arncliffe ★-★★★
Contact: Mrs Shirley Drew, Arncliffe, 39 Blackburn Avenue, Bridlington YO15 2ER
T: (01262) 677945

Ash Lee Holiday Apartments ★★-★★★
Contact: Mrs Greatorex, Ash Lee Holiday Apartments, 4 Vernon Road, Bridlington YO15 2HQ
T: (01262) 400485
I: www.bridlington-flats.co.uk

Ashton Holiday Flats ★
Contact: Mr & Mrs Samuel & Helen Levitt, Ashton Holiday Flats, 5 Belgrave Road, Bridlington YO15 3JP
T: (01262) 675132

Beach House ★★★
Contact: Doreen Hirst, 47 Bond Road, Barnsley S75 2TW
T: (01226) 206847

Beaconsfield House ★★★
Contact: Mrs Loraine Stuart, 5 Park Avenue, Bridlington YO15 2HL
T: (01262) 401482

Bluebell Holiday Apartment ★★★
Contact: Mrs Lorna Shaw, 8a Sands Lane, Bridlington YO15 2JE
T: (01262) 401445

Claran Holiday Flats ★
Contact: Mr Newham, Claran Holiday Flats, 27 Tennyson Avenue, Bridlington YO15 2EX
T: (01262) 675978

East Coast Holiday Cottages ★★-★★★
Contact: Mrs Cynthia Dean, East Coast Holiday Cottages, 77 Bempton Crescent, Sewerby, Bridlington YO16 7HH
T: (01262) 601543
I: www.bridlington.net/business.eastcoast

Ellwyn Holiday Flats ★★
Contact: Mr & Mrs James & Susan Thornton, Ellwyn Holiday Flats, 47 Wellington Road, Bridlington YO15 2AX
T: (01262) 606896
E: elliethodsq@supanet.com
I: www.bridlington.net/business.ellwyn

Fairholme Holiday Flats ★
Contact: Mr Nicholas Geraghty, Fairholme Holiday Flats, 12 Pembroke Terrace, Bridlington YO15 3BX
T: (01262) 676269
E: nicholasscott@geraghty2.fsnet.co.uk

Finley Cottages ★★★
Contact: Mrs Pauline Halstead, 33 Beverley Road, Wansford, Driffield YO25 6RZ
T: (01377) 253985
F: (01377) 253232
E: winston.halstead@virgin.net

Fir Lodge Holiday Apartments ★★-★★★
Contact: Mr & Mrs Chris & Les Day, Fir Lodge Holiday Apartments, 14 Sands Lane, Bridlington YO15 2JE
T: (01262) 671400
E: firlodge@bridlington.co.uk

Fountain House ★
Contact: Mr Shuttleworth, Fountain House, 4 Marlborough Terrace, Bridlington YO15 2PA
T: (01262) 604850

The Grosvenor Holiday Flats ★★★★
Contact: Mrs Elizabeth Otulakowski, 32 Effingham Road, Harden, Bingley BD16 1LQ
T: (01535) 272172
F: (01535) 272172
E: nicehols@aol.com

Hemsley Holiday Flats ★-★★
Contact: Mrs Christine Tranmer, Hemsley Holiday Flats, 5 Alexandra Drive, Bridlington, Bridlington YO15 2HZ
T: (01262) 672603

Highcliffe Holiday Apartments ★-★★★
Contact: Mrs Pat Willcocks, Highcliffe Holiday Apartments, 19 Albion Terrace, Bridlington YO15 2PJ
T: (01262) 674127

Lunbelle ★★
Contact: Mr Colin Ward, 19 Birch Close, Hull HU5 5YR
T: (01482) 572641
E: brid-accom@talk21.com

Marina Holiday Apartments ★★★
Contact: Mrs Shaw, 8a Sands Lane, Bridlington YO15 2JE
T: (01262) 401445

Marton Manor Cottages ★★★★
Contact: Mrs Jane Waind, Marton Manor Cottages, Marton Manor, Flamborough Road, Sewerby, Bridlington YO15 1DU
T: (01262) 672552
F: (01262) 672552
E: martonmanor@btopenworld.com
I: www.martonmanor.fsnet.co.uk

23 Mount Drive ★★★
Contact: Mrs Helen Gudggon, 6 Westfield Avenue, Leeds LS12 3SJ
T: (0113) 226 1298
F: (0113) 226 3735
E: rkgudgeon@hotmail.com

Mowbray Holiday Flats ★
Contact: Mr Carl Chambers, Mowbray Holiday Flats, 8 The Crescent, Bridlington YO15 2NX
T: (01262) 676218
E: mowbrayflats@amserve.com
I: mowbrayflats.co.uk

Oakwell Holiday Apartments ★★-★★★
Contact: Ms Kay Williams, Oakwell Holiday Apartments, 35-39 & 43 Horsforth Avenue, Bridlington YO15 3DG
T: (01262) 403666
F: (01262) 403666

Orchard Court Holiday Cottages ★★★
Contact: Mr C Dare, Orchard Court Holiday Cottages, 65 Jewison Lane, Sewerby, Bridlington YO15 1DX
T: (01262) 671829
F: (01262) 671829

Pembroke Holiday Flats ★★★
Contact: Mr & Mrs Eaton, Pembroke Holiday Flats, 18 Pembroke Terrace, Bridlington YO15 3BX
T: (01262) 677376
E: ampembroke@btopenworld.com

Rialto Holiday Flats ★-★★
Contact: Mrs Audrey Marshall, Rialto Holiday Flats, 63-65 Trinity Road, Bridlington YO15 2HF
T: (01262) 677653
E: enquiries@rialto-bridlington.co.uk
I: www.rialto-bridlington.co.uk

St Margarets Holiday Apartments ★★-★★★
Contact: Mr & Mrs John & Liz Stuart, St Margarets Holiday Apartments, 5 Marlborough Terrace, Bridlington YO15 2PA
T: (01262) 673698

San Remo ★★-★★★
Contact: Mrs Ann Jackson, 3 Kingston Road, Bridlington YO15 3NF
T: (01262) 676585

Sea View Holiday Flats ★-★★
Contact: Mr & Mrs Stanley & Margaret Benson, Seaview Holiday Flats, 8 Belgrave Road, Bridlington YO15 3JR
T: (01262) 676974

Sewerby Apartments ★★★
Contact: Mr Philip Richardson, Sewerby Apartments, 447C Sewerby Road, Bridlington YO15 1ER
T: (01262) 676819

Swalesmoor Holiday Flats ★★★
Contact: Mr Bernard Swales, Swalesmoor Holiday Flats, 11 Trinity Road, Bridlington YO15 2EZ
T: (01262) 675480
E: bernard.swales@btinternet.com

Victoria Holidays ★★★★
Contact: Mr & Mrs Barry & Anne Hatfield, c/o 25 Victoria Road, Bridlington YO15 2AT
T: (01262) 673871
F: (01262) 609431
E: victoria.hotel@virgin.net
I: www.victoriahotelbridlington.co.uk

Winston Court Holiday Apartments ★-★★
Contact: Mr Ian Reed & Catherine Cook, 7-8 Fort Terrace, Bridlington YO15 2PE
T: (01262) 677819
E: holiday-apartments@winston-court.fsbusiness.co.uk

York Holiday Flats ★★
Contact: Mrs Joan Cash, York Holiday Flats, York Road, Bridlington YO15 2PQ
T: (01262) 675956
F: (01262) 675956
I: www.yorksholidayflats.co.uk

BRIGSLEY
Lincolnshire

Prospect Farm Cottages ★★★★★
Contact: Mrs Janet Speight, Prospect Farm, Waltham Road, Brigsley, Grimsby DN37 0RQ
T: (01472) 826491
E: prospectfarm@btconnect.com

BROUGHTON
North Yorkshire

Summertree Granary & The Studio, Summertree Farm ★★★
Contact: Mr & Mrs B Eldridge, Summertree Farm, High Marishes, Thornton Dale, Pickering YO17 6UH
T: (01751) 474625
E: bridget.m.eldridge@talk21.com
I: www.summertree.sagenet.co.uk

BUCKDEN
North Yorkshire

Dalegarth and The Ghyll Cottages★★★★
Contact: Mr & Mrs D Lusted, 9 Dalegarth, Buckden, Skipton BD23 5JU
T: (01756) 760877
F: (01756) 760877
E: dalegarth@aol.com
I: www.dalegarth.co.uk

BURNSALL
North Yorkshire

Bland Place and Manor Cottage ★★★
Contact: Ms Diana Rosemary Lodge, Bland Place and Manor Cottage, Main Street, High Croft, Burnsall, Skipton BD23 6BP
T: (01756) 720668

Oatcroft Farm Barn Apartment ★★★
Contact: Mrs Jane Stockdale, Oatcroft Farm Apartment, Oatcroft Farm, Burnsall, Skipton BD23 6BN
T: (01756) 720268

Pipit Cottage ★★★
Contact: Agent Dales Hol Cot Ref:1430, Carleton Business Park, Carleton New Road, Skipton BD23 2AA
T: (01756) 799821
F: (01756) 797012
E: info@dalesholcot.com
I: www.dalesholcot.com

Riversyde Cottage ★★★
Contact: Sykes Cottages Ref:214, Sykes Cottages, York House, York Street, Chester CH1 3LR
T: (01244) 345700
F: (01244) 321442
E: info@sykescottages.co.uk
I: www.sykescottages.co.uk

The Sycamores ★★★★
Contact: Mrs Sheila Carr, DSC Holiday Lettings Ltd, Moor Green Farm, Threshfield, Skipton BD23 5NR
T: (01756) 752435
F: (01756) 752435
E: carr@totalise.co.uk

BURNT YATES
North Yorkshire

North Gate Cottage ★★★
Contact: Dales Hol Cot Ref:3045, Carleton Business Park, Carleton New Road, Skipton BD23 2AA
T: (01756) 799821
F: (01756) 797012
E: info@dalesholcot.com
I: www.dalesholcot.com

BURTERSETT
North Yorkshire

2 Middlegate ★★★
Contact: Mr V Punchard, Beckstones, Woodburn Yard, Main Street, Askrigg, Leyburn DL8 3HQ
T: (01969) 650607
E: tpunchard@aol.com

BURTON-IN-LONSDALE
North Yorkshire

Brentwood Farm Cottages ★★★★
Contact: Mrs Anita Taylor, Brentwood Farm Cottages, Barnoldswick Lane, Burton-in-Lonsdale, Carnforth LA6 3LZ
T: (015242) 62155
F: (015242) 62155
E: info@brentwoodfarmcottages.co.uk
I: www.brentwoodfarmcottages.co.uk

Greta Cottage ★★★★
Contact: Mrs Jane Burns, Bridge Cottage, Bridge End, Burton in Lonsdale, Burton-in-Lonsdale, Carnforth LA6 3LJ
T: (015242) 61081

Riverside Cottage ★★★★★
Contact: Ms Leverton, 1 Manor Fold, Cottingley, Bingley BD16 1TE
T: (01274) 560542
E: riversidecott@whsmith.net

BURTON LEONARD
North Yorkshire

Park House Holiday Cottages ★★★★
Contact: Mr Russell Hammond, Park House Holiday Cottages, Park House, Station Lane, Burton Leonard, Harrogate HG3 3RX
T: (01765) 677387
E: mail@parkhouseholidays.com
I: www.parkhouseholidays.com

BURYTHORPE
North Yorkshire

The Granary ★★★★
Contact: Mrs Margaret Raines, The Hermitage, Burythorpe, Malton YO17 9LF
T: (01653) 658201

CARLETON
North Yorkshire

Ivy Cottage ★★★
Contact: Dales Hol Cot Ref:2713, Carleton Business Park, Carleton New Road, Skipton BD23 2AA
T: (01756) 799821
F: (01756) 797012
E: info@dalesholcot.com
I: www.dalesholcot.com

Rombalds Cottage and Crookrise Cottage★★★
Contact: Dales Hol Cot Ref:786/787, Dales Holiday Cottages, Carleton Business Park, Carleton New Road, Skipton BD23 2AA
T: (01756) 799821
F: (01756) 797012
E: info@dalesholcot.com
I: www.dalesholcot.com

CARLTON
North Yorkshire

Coverdale Lodge Cottage ★★★★
Contact: Mrs Daphne Joy Beardsmore, Coverdale Lodge, Carlton, Leyburn DL8 4BA
T: (01969) 640602

Hillcrest ★★★
Contact: Mrs Sarah Scott, 9 Otley Old Road, Lawnswood, Leeds LS16 6HB
T: (0113) 261 4130
E: thescotts@totalise.co.uk

CARLTON MINIOTT
North Yorkshire

Avalon ★★★
Contact: Country Hols Ref: 816, Holiday Cottages Group Owner Services Dept, Spring Mill, Earby, Barnoldswick BB94 0AA
T: 08700 723723
F: (01282) 844288
E: sales@holidaycottagesgroup.com
I: www.country-holidays.co.uk

Holly Barn ★★★★
Contact: Mr William Edward Lawson, Holly House, Carlton Miniott, Thirsk YO7 4NJ
T: (01845) 522099

CARPERBY
North Yorkshire

Barnbrook ★★★
Contact: Sykes Cottages Ref:567, Sykes Cottages, York House, York Street, Chester CH1 3LR
T: (01244) 345700
F: (01244) 321442
E: info@sykescottages.co.uk
I: www.sykescottages.co.uk

The Granary ★★★★
Contact: Agent Dales Hol Cot Ref:1159, Carleton Business Park, Carleton New Road, Skipton BD23 2AA
T: (01756) 799821
F: (01756) 797012
E: info@dalesholcot.com
I: www.dalesholcot.com

Pencroft Cottage ★★★
Contact: Mr D Nichol, 49 Ashfield Park, Whickham, Newcastle upon Tyne NE16 4SQ
T: (0191) 488 1519
F: (0191) 488 1519

Sunnybank Cottage ★★★
Contact: Mrs Dolphin, Sunnybank Cottage, Sunnybank Farm, Carperby, Leyburn DL8 4DR
T: (01969) 663131
F: (01969) 663131
E: mdcmadol@supanet.com

Woodsomme Cottage ★★★★
Contact: Dales Hol Cot Ref:3305, Carleton Business Park, Carleton New Road, Skipton BD23 2AA
T: (01756) 799821
F: (01756) 797012
E: info@dalesholcot.com
I: www.dalesholcot.com

CASTLETON
North Yorkshire

Primrose Cottage ★★★★
Contact: Mrs June Graham, Craigower, 34 West Lane, Danby, Sandsend, Whitby YO21 2LY
T: (01287) 660248
E: june@grahamdanby.com

CATTERICK
North Yorkshire

Gallery Cottage ★★★
Contact: Dales Hol Cot Ref:1993, Carleton Business Park, Carleton New Road, Skipton BD23 2AA
T: (01756) 799821
F: (01756) 797012
E: info@dalesholcot.com
I: www.dalesholcot.com

CAWOOD
North Yorkshire

Cawood Holiday Park ★★★★
Contact: Mr Archer, Cawood Holiday Park, Ryther Road, Cawood, Selby YO8 3TT
T: (01757) 268450
F: (01757) 268537
E: william.archer13@btopenworld.com
I: www.ukparks.co.uk/cawood

CAWTHORNE
South Yorkshire

The Cottage ★★★
Contact: Mr C & Mrs M Rowlands, Hilltop Cottage, North Lane, Cawthorne, Barnsley S75 4AG
T: (01226) 791984
F: (01226) 792383
E: RowlandsCM@aol.com

CAYTON
North Yorkshire

Killerby Old Hall ★★★★
Contact: Mrs Margery Middleton, Killerby Old Hall, Killerby, Cayton, Scarborough YO11 3TW
T: (01723) 583799

CHAPEL LE DALE
North Yorkshire

Netherscar ★★
Contact: Sykes Cottages Ref:281, Sykes Cottages, York House, York Street, Chester CH1 3LR
T: (01244) 345700
F: (01244) 321442
E: info@sykescottages.co.uk
I: www.sykescottages.co.uk

4 Salt Lake Cottages ★★★
Contact: Mrs Lees, Barnstead, New Houses, Horton-in-Ribblesdale, Selside, Settle BD24 0JE
T: (01729) 860485

CHOP GATE
North Yorkshire

Broadfields Cottage ★★★★
Contact: Mrs Judith Staples, Broadfields Cottage, Broadfields, Chop Gate, Stokesley, Middlesbrough TS9 7JB
T: (01642) 778384
I: www.diamond.org/broadfields

Lavrock Hall Farmhouse Cottage ★★★
Contact: Mrs Jane Brack, Lavrock Hall, Chop Gate, Stokesley, Middlesbrough TS9 7LQ
T: (01439) 798275
F: (01439) 798337
E: info@lavrockhall.co.uk
I: www.lavrockhall.co.uk

Low Ellermire Farm Cottage ★★★
Contact: Dales Hol Cot Ref:3027, Dales Holiday Cottages, Carleton Business Park, Carleton New Road, Skipton BD23 2AA
T: (01756) 799821
F: (01756) 797012
E: info@dalesholcot.com
I: www.dalesholcot.com

CLAPHAM
North Yorkshire

Coppy House Stable ★★★★
Contact: Sykes Cottages Ref:763, Sykes Cottages, York House, York Street, Chester CH1 3LR
T: (01244) 345700
F: (01244) 321442
E: info@sykescottages.co.uk
I: www.sykescottages.co.uk

CLAYTON
West Yorkshire

Brow Top Farm ★★★
Contact: Mrs Margaret Priestley, Brow Top Farm, Brow Top, Bandwin Lane, Clayton, Bradford BD14 6PS
T: (01274) 882178
F: (01274) 882178
E: ruthpriestley@farmersweekly.net
I: www.browtopfarm.co.uk

CLOUGHTON
North Yorkshire

Gowland Farm Holiday Cottages ★★★★
Contact: Mr J A Donnelly, Gowland Farm Holiday Cottages, Gowland Lane, Cloughton, Scarborough YO13 0DU
T: (01723) 870924
F: (01723) 870524
E: jeff@gfarm.fsworld.co.uk
I: www.gowlandfarm.co.uk

COMMONDALE
North Yorkshire

Fowl Green Farm ★★★
Contact: Mrs Susan Muir, Fowl Green Farm, Commondale, Whitby YO21 2HN
T: (01287) 660742
E: susan.muir@ukonline.co.uk
I: www.fowlgreenfarm.com

CONISBROUGH
South Yorkshire

Cosy Terrace Cottage ★★
Contact: Mr John Perrin, 8 Denaby Lane, Old Denaby, Doncaster DN12 4LA
T: (01709) 580612
E: john@cosyterrace.fsnet.co.uk

CONONLEY
North Yorkshire

The Cottage ★★★
Contact: Dales Hol Cot Ref:521, Carleton Business Park, Carleton New Road, Skipton BD23 2AA
T: (01756) 799821
F: (01756) 797012
E: info@dalesholcot.com

CONSTABLE BURTON
North Yorkshire

Park Gate Cottage ★★★★
Contact: Agent Dales Hol Cot Ref: 1785, Carleton Business Park, Carleton New Road, Skipton BD23 2AA
T: (01756) 799821
F: (01756) 797012
E: info@dalesholcot.com
I: www.dalesholcot.com

COUNTERSETT
North Yorkshire

Bee-Bole Cottage ★★★
Contact: Sykes Cottages Ref:353, Sykes Cottages, York House, York Street, Chester CH1 3LR
T: (01244) 345700
F: (01244) 321442
E: info@sykescottages.co.uk
I: www.sykescottages.co.uk

COWLING
North Yorkshire

Starmire Cottage ★★★★
Contact: Mrs Fiona Moody, Dales Holiday Cottages, Carleton Business Park, Carleton New Road, Skipton BD23 2AA
T: (01756) 790919
F: (01756) 797012
E: info@dalesholcot.com
I: www.dalesholcot.com

Swallow Cottage ★★★★
Contact: Dales Hol Cot Ref:2643, Carleton Business Park, Carleton New Road, Skipton BD23 2AA
T: (01756) 799821
F: (01756) 797012
E: info@dalesholcot.com
I: www.dalesholcot.com

CRAGG VALE
West Yorkshire

Rudd Clough Holiday Cottages ★★★★★
Contact: Mr & Mrs James and Juliet Barker, Cragg Vale, Hebden Bridge HX7 5TB
T: (01422) 882755
F: (01422) 886044
E: james.barker@hemscott.net

CRAKEHALL
North Yorkshire

St Edmund's Country Cottages ★★-★★★
Contact: Ms Sue Cooper, St Edmund's Country Cottages, St Edmund's, The Green, Crakehall, Bedale DL8 1HP
T: (01677) 423584
F: (01677) 427397
E: stedmundscountrycottages@hotmail.com
I: www.crakehall.org.uk

CROCKEY HILL
North Yorkshire

Wigman Hall Cottage ★★★
Contact: Mrs Gillian Duncan, Wigman Hall, Crockey Hill, York YO19 4SQ
T: (01904) 448221
F: (01904) 449288
E: gillduncan@aol.com

CROPTON
North Yorkshire

Allerdale ★★★
Contact: Mrs Feaster, Fernwood, Cropton, Pickering YO18 8HL
T: (01751) 417692

Beckhouse Cottages ★★★★
Contact: Mrs P Smith, Beckhouse Cottages, Beckhouse Farm, Cropton, Pickering YO18 8ER
T: (01751) 417235
F: (01751) 417218
E: beckhousecottages@hotmail.com
I: www.beckhousecottages.co.uk

2 Corner Cottage ★★
Contact: Mrs Rowlands, 1 Corner Cottage, Cropton, Pickering YO18 8HH
T: (01751) 417562

High Farm Holiday Cottages ★★★★
Contact: Mrs Ruth Feaster, High Farm Holiday Cottages, High Farm, Cropton, Pickering YO18 8HL
T: (01751) 417461
E: highfarmcropton@aol.com
I: www.hhml.com/cottages/highfarmcropton.htm

DALTON
North Yorkshire

Badgerway Stoop Cottage ★★★
Contact: Dales Hol Cot Ref:3119, Dales Holiday Cottages, Carleton Business Park, Carleton New Road, Skipton BD23 2AA
T: (01756) 799821
F: (01756) 797012
E: info@dalesholcot.com
I: www.dalesholcot.com

Hilltop Cottage ★★★★
Contact: Mr Farr, Dalton, Ravensworth, Richmond DL11 7HU
T: (01833) 621234
F: (01833) 621092
E: hilltopcottage@rfarr.freeserve.co.uk
I: www.hilltop-dales-cottage.co.uk

DANBY
North Yorkshire

Ainthorpe Farm Cottage ★★★★
Contact: Mrs Sheila Hide, Ainthorpe Farm House, Easton Lane, Ainthorpe, Danby, Whitby YO21 2JW
T: (01287) 660358

Beckwith House ★★★
Contact: Mrs Heather Mather, Ainthorpe Lane, Ainthorpe, Danby, Whitby YO21 2NG
T: (01287) 669104
E: colinheather@ainthorpemather.freeserve.co.uk

Blackmires Farm ★★★
Contact: Mrs G M Rhys, Blackmires Farm, Danby Head, Danby, Whitby YO21 2NN
T: (01287) 660352
E: gl.rhys@freenet.co.uk

Clitherbecks Farm ★★
Contact: Mr Neil Harland, Clitherbecks Farm, Danby, Whitby YO21 2NT
T: (01287) 660321
E: nharland@clitherbecks.freeserve.co.uk
I: www.clitherbecks.freeserve.co.uk

Margold Cottage ★★★
Contact: Dales Hol Cot Ref:2505, Carleton Business Park, Carleton New Road, Skipton BD23 2AA
T: (01756) 799821
F: (01756) 797012
E: info@dalesholcot.com
I: www.dalesholcot.com

DARLEY
North Yorkshire

days2go.com ★★★
Contact: Mrs Kish, days2go.com, Sheepcote Lane, Darley, Harrogate HG3 2RW
T: (01423) 780661
F: (01423) 780661

Meadow Cottages ★★★★
Contact: Mr & Mrs Anthony & Rachael Harris, Meadow Cottages, Stumps Farm, Stumps Lane, Darley, Harrogate HG3 2RR
T: (01423) 781336

DENHOLME
West Yorkshire

Blacksmith's Cottages ★★
Contact: Mrs Janet Nella Ackroyd, Blacksmith's Cottages, Forge End, 2 Edge Bottom, Denholme, Bradford BD13 4JW
T: (01274) 832850
F: (01274) 832850

DONCASTER
South Yorkshire

The Green Gable ★★★★
Contact: Mr Smeaton, 161 Carr House Road, Doncaster DN4 5DP
T: (01302) 327782
F: (01302) 327774
E: qjs@freeuk.com

DOWNHOLME
North Yorkshire

Coldstorms Farm ★★★
Contact: Mrs Diana Greenwood, Walburn Hall, Downholme, Richmond DL11 6AF
T: (01748) 822152
F: (01748) 822152

DRIFFIELD
East Riding of Yorkshire

Manor Farm Cottages ★★★
Contact: Mr & Mrs A Byass, R F Byass & Co, North Dalton Manor, Driffield YO25 9UX
T: (01377) 217324
F: (01377) 217840
E: lanpulses@aol.com

DUGGLEBY
North Yorkshire

Highbury Farm Cottage ★★★★
Contact: Mr & Mrs Sawdon, Highbury Farm, Duggleby, Malton YO17 8BN
T: (01944) 738664
E: highburyfarmcott@aol.com
I: www.highbury-farm-holiday-cottage.co.uk

DUNNINGTON
North Yorkshire

Dunnington Lodge & Dunnington Lodge Cottage ★★★
Contact: Dales Hol Cot Ref:2938/3234, Dales Holiday Cottages, Carleton Business Park, Carleton New Road, Skipton BD23 2AA
T: (01756) 799821
F: (01756) 797012
E: info@dalesholcot.com
I: www.dalesholcot.com

DUNSLEY
North Yorkshire

The Shippon & The Stable ★★★
Contact: Dales Hol Cot Ref:1988/1989, Dales Holiday Cottages, Carleton Business Park, Carleton New Road, Skipton BD23 2AA
T: (01756) 799821
F: (01756) 797012
E: info@dalesholcot.com
I: www.dalesholcot.com

EASINGWOLD
North Yorkshire

Mooracres Bungalow ★★★
Contact: Dales Hol Cot Ref:753, Carleton Business Park, Carleton New Road, Skipton BD23 2AA
T: (01756) 799821
F: (01756) 797012
E: info@dalesholcot.com
I: www.dalesholcot.com

Oak Mews ★★★
Contact: Agent Dales Hol Cot Ref:1795, Carleton Business Park, Carleton New Road, Skipton BD23 2AA
T: (01756) 799821
F: (01756) 797012
E: info@dalesholcot.com
I: www.dalesholcot.com

EAST HALTON
Lincolnshire

The Cottage ★★★★
Contact: Mrs Florence Sampson, Woodland View, Swinster Lane, East Halton, Immingham DN40 3NR
T: (01469) 540523

EAST MORTON
West Yorkshire

8 The Butts ★★★
Contact: Mrs Irene Holdsworth, Moor Cottage, The Butts, East Morton, Keighley BD20 5RU
T: (01274) 563985

EAST WITTON
North Yorkshire

Wayland Cottage ★★★
Contact: Agent Dales Hol Cot Ref:2379, Carleton Business Park, Carleton New Road, Skipton BD23 2AA
T: (01756) 799821
F: (01756) 797012
E: info@dalesholcot.com
I: www.dalesholcot.com

EBBERSTON
North Yorkshire

Cliff House ★★★-★★★★
Contact: Mr Simon Morris, Cliff House, Ebberston, Scarborough YO13 9PA
T: (01723) 859440
F: (01723) 850005
E: cliffhouseebberston@btinternet.com
I: www.cliffhouse-cottageholidays.co.uk

Cow Pasture Cottage ★★★
Contact: Mrs B Green, Studley House, 67 Main Street, Ebberston, Scarborough YO13 9NR
T: (01723) 859285
F: (01723) 859285
E: ernie@jhodgson.fsnet.co.uk
I: www.studley-house.co.uk

Nesfield Cottage ★★★★
Contact: Mrs Janet Wood, Ingleside, Burton Road, Annswell, Ashby-de-la-Zouch LE65 2TF
T: (01530) 416094
E: chris.wood4@virgin.net

EGTON
North Yorkshire

Barn Cottages ★★★★
Contact: Mrs Barbara Howard, Deepdale House, Wintringham, Thorpe Bassett, Malton YO17 8HX
T: (01944) 758910
F: (01944) 758910
E: enquiries@barncottages.com
I: www.barncottages.com

The Hayloft & Pine Cottage ★★★
Contact: Mrs Hilary Walker, The Nurseries, Egton, Whitby YO21 1TT
T: (01947) 895640
E: hilary_phenix@hotamil.com

Westonby Cottage ★★
Contact: Mrs Joan Flintoft, Egton, Glaisdale, Whitby YO21 1UH
T: (01947) 895296

EGTON BRIDGE
North Yorkshire

Broom Cottage ★★★★
Contact: Mrs Maria White, Egton Bridge, Whitby YO21 1XD
T: (01947) 895279
F: (01947) 895657
E: mw@broom-house.co.uk

EMBSAY
North Yorkshire

Crag View Cottage ★★★★
Contact: Dales Holiday Cot Ref:0869, Carleton Business Park, Carleton New Road, Skipton BD23 2AA
T: (01756) 799821
F: (01756) 797012
E: info@dalesholcot.com
I: www.dalesholcot.com

Elm Garth Cottage ★★★
Contact: Mrs Margaret Mewies, The Craggs, Kirk Lane, Eastby, Skipton BD23 6SH
T: (01756) 799188
E: m.mewies@talk21.com
I: www.elmgarth.co.uk

FADMOOR
North Yorkshire

North Farm Cottages ★★★★
Contact: Mr & Mrs David and Gill Broadbent, North Farm, Main Street, Fadmoor, Gillamoor, York YO62 7HY
T: (01751) 431934
F: (01751) 431934

FARNDALE
North Yorkshire

The Old Post Office and The Chapel ★★★★
Contact: Sykes Cottages Ref:657,760, Sykes Cottages, York House, York Street, Chester CH1 3LR
T: (01244) 345700
F: (01244) 321442
E: info@sykescottages.co.uk
I: www.sykescottages.co.uk

FEIZOR
North Yorkshire

Scar Close Barn ★★★★
Contact: Dales Hol Cot Ref:2953, Carleton Business Park, Carleton New Road, Skipton BD23 2AA
T: (01756) 799821
F: (01756) 797012
E: info@dalesholcot.com
I: www.dalesholcot.com

Stockdale Barn ★★★★
Contact: Sykes Cottages Ref:312, Sykes Cottages, York House, York Street, Chester CH1 3LR
T: (01244) 345700
F: (01244) 321442
E: info@sykescottages.co.uk
I: www.sykescottages.co.uk

FELLBECK
North Yorkshire

1 and 2 North Oaks Farm Cottages ★★★
Contact: Mrs Sue Loveless, 1 and 2 North Oaks Farm Cottages, North Oaks Farm, Fellbeck, Pateley Bridge, Harrogate HG3 5EP
T: (01423) 712446
F: (01423) 712457
E: cottages@loveless.co.uk
I: www.loveless.co.uk

South Oaks ★★★
Contact: Mrs Land, South Oaks, Fellbeck, Pateley Bridge, Harrogate HG3 5EP
T: (01423) 711379
F: (01423) 711919
E: pam@landp.fsbusiness.co.uk

Troutbeck Cottage ★★★★
Contact: Mrs C E Nelson, Nidderdale Lodge Farm, Fellbeck, Harrogate HG3 5EU
T: (01423) 711677

FILEY
North Yorkshire

Beach Holiday Flats ★★-★★★
Contact: Mr David Tindall, Beach Holiday Flats, 9-10 The Beach, Filey YO14 9LA
T: (01723) 513178
E: anntindall@aol.com
I: www.thebeach-holidayflats.co.uk

The Cottages ★★★
Contact: Mr & Mrs David Teet, The Cottages, Muston Grange, Muston Road, Filey YO14 0HU
T: (01723) 516620
F: (01723) 516620
I: www.mustongrangefiley.co.uk

Ennerdale Holiday Flats ★-★★
Contact: Mr Thompson, Ennerdale Holiday Flats, 31-33 Station Avenue, Filey YO14 9AE
T: (01723) 513798

Holiday House ★★★
Contact: Mrs Anne Cooper, 41 Northstead Manor Drive, Scarborough YO12 6AF
T: (01723) 365263

Nostell Holiday Flats ★-★★★
Contact: Mr Rowland Winn, Nostell Holiday Flats, 30/36 Rutland Street, Filey YO14 9JB
T: (01723) 515437

84 Queen Street ★★★★
Contact: Ms Suzan Brown, 26 Church Close, Wingerworth, Chesterfield S42 6QA
T: (01246) 200780

FITLING
East Riding of Yorkshire

Stables Cottage ★★★★
Contact: Mrs Patricia Cockshutt, Fitling Garth, Humbleton Road, Fitling, Hull HU12 9AJ
I: www.scope.karoo.net/fitling

FLAXTON
North Yorkshire

Griffon Forest Holiday Lodges ★★★★
Contact: Mr Julian Darnley, Griffon Forest Ltd, Scotchman Lane, Flaxton, York YO60 7RG
T: (01904) 468787
F: (01904) 468791
E: juliandarnley@btconnect.com
I: www.griffonforest.co.uk

FOLLIFOOT
North Yorkshire

Marlin Cottage ★★★★
Contact: Mrs Evelyn Clayton, April Cottage, Crimple Lane, Follifoot, Harrogate HG3 1DF
T: (01423) 883696
E: clayton.clayton@virgin.net

FRAISTHORPE
East Riding of Yorkshire

North Kingsfield Holiday Cottages ★★★★
Contact: Mr & Mrs Milner, North Kingsfield Farm, Fraisthorpe, Bridlington YO15 3QP
T: (01262) 673743
E: helen@northkingsfield.co.uk

FYLINGDALES
North Yorkshire

Browdale Cottage ★★★
Contact: Mr M & Mrs S Earnshaw, Browdale Cottage, Thorney Brow Farm, Fylingdales, Whitby YO22 4UL
T: (01947) 880052

Swallows Cottage & The Granary ★★★
Contact: Mrs Adele Thompson, Whitby Holiday Cottages, 47 Flowergate, Whitby YO21 3BB
T: (01947) 603010
F: (01947) 821133
E: enquiries@whitby-cottages.co.uk
I: www.whitby-cottages.co.uk

FYLINGTHORPE
North Yorkshire

Croft Farm Cottage ★★★
Contact: Mrs Joanne Braithwaite, Croft Farm, Church Lane, Fylingthorpe, Robin Hood's Bay, Whitby YO22 4PW
T: (01947) 880231
F: (01947) 880231
E: croftfarmbb@aol.com

The Peat House ★★★★
Contact: Mrs Adele Thompson & Vanessa Hickings, Whitby Holiday Cottages, 47 Flowergate, Whitby YO21 3BB
T: (01947) 603010
F: (01947) 821133
E: enquiries@whitby-cottages.co.uk
I: www.whitby-cottages.co.uk

South House Farmhouse & Cottages ★★★-★★★★
Contact: Mrs N Pattinson, South House Farmhouse & Cottages, Millbeck, Fylingthorpe, Whitby YO22 4UQ
T: (01947) 880243
F: (01947) 880243
E: kmp@bogglehole.fsnet.co.uk
I: www.southhousefarm.co.uk

GARGRAVE
North Yorkshire

Bobbin ★★★
Contact: Mr Sykes Cottages Ref:696, Sykes Cottages, York House, York Street, Chester CH1 3LR
T: (01244) 345700
F: (01244) 321442
E: info@sykescottages.co.uk
I: www.sykescottages.co.uk

GARTON-ON-THE-WOLDS
East Riding of Yorkshire

Foldyard Cottage & The Granary ★★
Contact: Mr & Mrs Brian & Mavis Walsh, Church Farm, Pump Lane, Garton-on-the-Wolds, Driffield YO25 3ES
T: (01377) 253988

Rolella ★★★
Contact: Mr Garvey, 10 Main Street, Garton-on-the-Wolds, Driffield YO25 3ET
T: (01377) 253656
F: (01377) 241408

GAYLE
North Yorkshire

Aysgill Cottage ★★★
Contact: Mrs Deborah Allen, Scaur Head Farm, Gayle, Hawes DL8 3SF
T: (01969) 667477

Foss Cottage ★★★
Contact: Mrs Brenda Watering, Force Head Farm, Gayle, Burtersett, Hawes DL8 3RZ
T: (01969) 667518
F: (01969) 667518

Gayle Farmhouse ★★
Contact: Dales Hol Cot Ref:636, Carleton Business Park, Carleton New Road, Skipton BD23 2AA
T: (01756) 799821
F: (01756) 797012
E: info@dalesholcot.com
I: www.dalesholcot.com

GIGGLESWICK
North Yorkshire

Bookend Cottage ★★★
Contact: Sykes Cottages Ref:713, Sykes Cottages, York House, York Street, Chester CH1 3LR
T: (01244) 345700
F: (01244) 321442
E: info@sykescottages.co.uk
I: www.sykescottages.co.uk

Close House Cottage Holidays ★★★★
Contact: Mr & Mrs Richard & Sue Hargreaves, Close House Cottage Holidays, Close House, Giggleswick, Settle BD24 0EA
T: (01729) 822778
F: (01729) 822778
E: chcottages@aol.com
I: www.close-house.co.uk

Foxholes Lodge ★★★
Contact: Mrs Lynn Scruton, Station Road, Giggleswick, Settle BD24 0AB
T: (01729) 823505
F: (01729) 824088

2 Gildersleets ★★★★
Contact: Griffiths, 9 Polefield Road, Blackley, Manchester M9 6FN
T: (0161) 795 9713
F: (0161) 653 6570
E: doctor.g@gconnect.com

Ivy Cottage ★★★★
Contact: Dales Hol Cot Ref:629, Carleton Business Park, Carleton New Road, Skipton BD23 2AA
T: (01756) 799821
F: (01756) 797012
E: info@dalesholcot.com
I: www.dalesholcot.com

Rowan House, Willow Cottage ★★★★
Contact: Sykes Cottages Ref:398,652, Sykes Cottages, York House, York Street, Chester CH1 3LR
T: (01244) 345700
F: (01244) 321442
E: info@sykescottages.co.uk
I: www.sykescottages.co.uk

Stanton Cottage ★★★
Contact: Mrs Alison Boswell, 3 Bankwell Close, Giggleswick, Settle BD24 0BX
T: (01729) 822400
F: (01729) 822400
E: pboswell@ukonline.co.uk

Sutcliffe Cottage ★★
Contact: Sykes Cottages Ref:31, Sykes Cottages, York House, York Street, Chester CH1 3LR
T: (01244) 345700
F: (01244) 321442
E: info@sykescottages.co.uk
I: www.sykescottages.co.uk

GILLAMOOR
North Yorkshire

Gales House Farm ★★★★
Contact: Mrs Kathy Ward, Gales House Farm, Kirkby Lane, Gillamoor, York YO62 7HT
T: (01751) 431258
F: 07050 650741
E: cottages@gillamoor.com
I: www.gillamoor.com

Hen House ★★★★★
Contact: Mr & Mrs Stephen & Georgina Hackett, Church View, Main Street, Gillamoor, York YO62 7HX
T: (01751) 430135

GILLING EAST
North Yorkshire

Sunset Cottages ★★★-★★★★
Contact: Mr & Mrs Kelsey, Sunset Cottages, Grimston Manor Farm, Gilling East, York YO62 4HR
T: (01347) 888654
F: (01347) 888347
E: info@sunsetcottages.co.uk
I: www.sunsetcottages.co.uk

GILLING WEST
North Yorkshire

Gilling Old Mill Cottages ★★★★
Contact: Mr & Mrs H Bird, Gilling Old Mill Waters Lane, Gilling West, Richmond DL10 5JD
T: (01748) 822771
F: (01748) 821734
E: admin@yorkshiredales-cottages.com
I: www.yorkshiredales-cottages.com

GILSTEAD
West Yorkshire

Thimble, Bobbin & Shuttle ★★★-★★★★★
Contact: Mrs L Jean Warin, March Cote Farm, Lee Lane, Cottingley, Bingley BD16 1UB
T: (01274) 487433
F: (01274) 561074
E: jean.warin@nevisuk.net
I: www.yorkshirenet.co.uk/accgde/marchcote

GLAISDALE
North Yorkshire

Lanes Cottage ★★
Contact: Mr & Mrs J Dale
T: (01947) 897316

London Lodge ★★★
Contact: Mrs Mary Danaher, Dales Holiday Cottages, London House Farm, Glaisdale, Whitby YO21 2PZ
T: (01947) 897166
F: (01947) 897166
E: gdanaherg@aol.com
I: www.londonhousefarm.com

The Studio Flat ★★★★
Contact: Mr & Mrs John & Mary Thompson, Postgate Farm, Glaisdale, Whitby YO21 2PZ
T: (01947) 897353
F: (01947) 897353
E: j-m.thompson.bandb@talk21.com
I: www.eskvalley.com/postgate/postgate.html

Tailors Cottage ★★★
Contact: Mr Clive Sykes, Sykes Cottages, York House, York Street, Chester CH1 3LR
T: (01244) 345700
F: (01244) 321442
E: info@sykescottages.co.uk
I: www.sykescottages.co.uk

GOATHLAND
North Yorkshire

Eskholme ★★★★
Contact: Mrs J M Hodgson, Woodlands, 31 Shillbank View, Mirfield WF14 0QG
T: (01924) 498154
E: ffsjan@aol.com

14 Oakfield Avenue ★★★
Contact: Mrs Adele Thompson & Vanessa Hickings, Whitby Holiday Cottages, 47 Flowergate, Whitby YO21 3BB
T: (01947) 603010
F: (01947) 821133
E: enquiries@whitby-cottages.co.uk
I: www.whitby-cottages.co.uk

Orchard Cottage ★★★★★
Contact: Mrs Clare Carr, Orchard Farm, Goathland, Whitby YO22 5JX
T: (01947) 896391
F: (01947) 896001
E: enquiries@theorchardcottages.co.uk
I: www.theorchardcottages.co.uk

Rosedean ★★
Contact: Mrs Eileen Cox, Abbot's House Farm, Goathland, Robin Hood's Bay, Whitby YO22 5NH
T: (01947) 896270
F: (01947) 896270
E: goathland@enterprise.net
I: www.homepages.enterprise.net/goathland/index

The Stone Cottage ★★★
Contact: Dales Holiday Cottages, Carleton Business Park, Sandylands Business Centre, Carleton N, Skipton BD23 2DG
T: (01756) 799821
F: (01756) 799821

Woodpecker Cottage ★★★★
Contact: Dales Hol Cot Ref:3125, Carleton Business Park, Carleton New Road, Skipton BD23 2AA
T: (01756) 799821
F: (01756) 797012
E: info@dalesholcot.com
I: www.dalesholcot.com

GRASSINGTON
North Yorkshire

The Barn ★★★★
Contact: Mrs P G Evans, 3 Delph Wood Close, Gilstead, Bingley BD16 3LQ
T: (01274) 561546
E: grassington@ukonline.co.uk
I: www.dalestay.co.uk/thebarn

The Coach House ★★★
Contact: Dales Hol Cot Ref:3176, Carleton Business Park, Carleton New Road, Skipton BD23 2AA
T: (01756) 799821
F: (01756) 797012
E: info@dalesholcot.com
I: www.dalesholcot.com

Garrs House Apartment ★★★
Contact: Mr & Mrs Ann & Malcolm Wadsworth, 25 Watson Road, Blackpool FY4 1EG
T: (01253) 404726

3 Garrs Lane ★★★★
Contact: Country Hols Ref: 582, Holiday Cottages Group Owner Services Dept, Spring Mill, Earby, Barnoldswick BB94 0AA
T: 08700 723723
F: (01282) 844288
E: sales@holidaycottagesgroup.com
I: www.country-holidays.co.uk

6a Garrs Lane ★★★
Contact: Mr Borrill, Garrs Lane, Grassington, Thorpe, Skipton BD23 5AT
T: (01756) 752436
F: (01756) 753260
E: paborrill@supanet.com

Manna Cottage ★★★★
Contact: Mrs Sheila Carr, Moor Green Farm, Tarns Lane, Threshfield, Skipton BD23 5NR
T: (01756) 752435
F: (01756) 752435
E: carr@totalise.co.uk
I: www.yorkshirenet.co.uk/stayat/mannacottage/

Riverside ★★★
Contact: Mrs Marilyn Brown, 12 Bridge End, Grassington, Threshfield, Skipton BD23 5NH
T: (01756) 753886
I: www.dales.accommodation.com

Scala Glen Barn ★★★★
Contact: Mr & Mrs Hugh & Caroline Roundhill, 43 Main Street, Grassington, Skipton BD23 5AA
T: (01756) 752011
E: scalaglen@aol.com
I: www.oas.co.uk/ukcottages.scalaglen

Sunnyside Cottage ★★★
Contact: Mrs Carolyn Butt, Garris Lodge, Rylstone, Skipton BD23 6LJ
T: (01756) 730391
E: c.butt@daelnet.co.uk
I: www.cosycottages.com

Theatre Cottage ★★★
Contact: Agent Dales Hol Cot Ref:2214, Carleton Business Park, Carleton New Road, Skipton BD23 2AA
T: (01756) 799821
F: (01756) 797012
E: info@dalesholcot.com
I: www.dalesholcot.com

Wellhead Cottage & Hilltop Fold Cottage ★★★★
Contact: Mr & Mrs Halliday, P O Box 177, Horsforth, Leeds LS18 5WZ
T: (0113) 258 4212
F: (0113) 281 9455
E: lesley.halliday@virgin.net

GREAT AYTON
North Yorkshire

Flat 2 ★★
Contact: Mrs Metcalfe, 89 Newton Road, Great Ayton, Middlesbrough TS9 6DY
T: (01642) 722935

The Old Stables ★★★★
Contact: Mrs Catherine Hawman, Park House, Great Ayton, Easby, Middlesbrough TS9 6JQ
T: (01642) 722560
F: (01642) 722560
E: theoldstables@btopenworld.com

The Stable Cottage ★★★
Contact: Mrs Anne Gregory, 1 Overbrook, Great Ayton, Middlesbrough TS9 6NX
T: (01642) 724226
E: iang@overbrookone.fsnet.co.uk

GREAT EDSTONE
North Yorkshire

Cowldyke Farm ★★★-★★★★
Contact: Mrs Janet Benton, Salton Road, Great Edstone, Salton, York YO62 6PE
T: (01751) 431242
E: info@cowldyke-farm.co.uk
I: www.cowldyke-farm.co.uk

GREAT LANGTON
North Yorkshire

Stanhow Bungalow ★★★★
Contact: Mrs Mary Furness, Stanhow Farm, Great Langton, Northallerton DL7 0TJ
T: (01609) 748614
F: (01609) 748614
E: mary.stanhow@freenet.co.uk

GREEN HAMMERTON
North Yorkshire

Wasp's Nest Holiday Cottages ★★★-★★★★
Contact: Mrs M Nixon, The Wasp's Nest, Green Hammerton, York YO26 8AE
T: (01423) 330153
F: (01423) 331204
E: waspsnest@phnixon.demon.co.uk
I: www.phnixon.demon.co.uk

GREETLAND
West Yorkshire

The Barn, Lower High Trees Farm ★★★
Contact: Mrs Kate Griffiths, Lower High Trees Farm, High Trees Lane, Greetland, Halifax HX4 8PP
T: (01422) 375205
F: (01422) 375205
E: griffs@freeuk.com
I: www.greetland.org.uk

GREWELTHORPE
North Yorkshire

Crown Cottage ★★★
Contact: Dales Hol Cot Ref:718, Carleton Business Park, Carleton New Road, Skipton BD23 2AA
T: (01756) 799821
F: (01756) 797012
E: info@dalesholcot.com
I: www.dalesholcot.com

Sunnyside Cottage ★★★★
Contact: Mrs Jane Shuttleworth, 224 Bradway Road, Bradway, Sheffield S17 4PE
T: (0114) 235 2783

GRISTHORPE
North Yorkshire

Dove Cottage ★★★★
Contact: Dales Hol Cot Ref:3035, Carleton Business Park, Carleton New Road, Skipton BD23 2AA
T: (01756) 799821
F: (01756) 797012
E: info@dalesholcot.com
I: www.dalesholcot.com

GRISTHORPE BAY
North Yorkshire

58 Clarence Drive ★★★
Contact: Mrs Mary Graves, 99 Muston Road, Filey YO14 0AJ
T: (01723) 512791
E: graves19@freeserve.co.uk

St Kitts ★★★★
Contact: Mrs K Rook, North Cliffe, York YO43 4XE
T: (01430) 827661

GROSMONT
North Yorkshire

East Farm Cottage ★★★
Contact: Mrs Adele Thompson & Vanessa Hickings, Whitby Holiday Cottages, 47 Flowergate, Whitby YO21 3BB
T: (01947) 603010
F: (01947) 821133
E: enquiries@whitby-cottages.co.uk
I: www.whitby-cottages.co.uk

Engineman's Lodge ★★
Contact: Mrs Adele Thompson & Vanessa Hickings, 47 Flowergate, Whitby YO21 3BB
T: (01947) 603010
F: (01947) 821133
E: enquiries@whitby-cottages.co.uk
I: www.whitby-cottages.co.uk

Porter's Lodge ★★
Contact: Mrs Adele Thompson & Vanessa Hickings, 47 Flowergate, Whitby YO21 3BB
T: (01947) 603010
F: (01947) 821133
E: enquiries@whitby-cottages.co.uk
I: www.whitby-cottages.co.uk

Signalman's Lodge ★★
Contact: Mrs Adele Thompson & Vanessa Hickings, Whitby Holiday Cottages, 47 Flowergate, Whitby YO21 3BB
T: (01947) 603010
F: (01947) 821133
E: enquiries@whitby-cottages.co.uk
I: www.whitby-cottages.co.uk

GUNNERSIDE
North Yorkshire

Appletons ★★★★
Contact: Mr John Burnham, Great Becketts, Duddenhoe End Road, Arkesden, Duddenhoe End, Saffron Walden CB11 4HG
T: (01799) 550661

Brooklyn ★★★
Contact: Mrs Emmott, 6 Nether Way, Darley Dale, Matlock DE4 2TS
T: (01629) 734270

Croft Cottage ★★
Contact: Mrs Margaret Batty, Croft House, Low Row, Gunnerside, Richmond DL11 6ND
T: (01748) 886460

Dene Holme ★★★★
Contact: Mrs Annie Porter, Gunnerside, Richmond DL11 6JJ
T: (01748) 886253
F: (01748) 886253

Dufton House ★★★★
Contact: Mrs Annie Porter, Gunnerside, Richmond DL11 6JJ
T: (01748) 886253
F: (01748) 886253

High Oxnop ★★★★
Contact: Mrs Annie Porter, Oxnop Hall, Gunnerside, Richmond DL11 6JJ
T: (01748) 886253
F: (01748) 886253

Manfield Cottage ★★★
Contact: Dales Hol Cot Ref:3110, Carleton Business Park, Carleton New Road, Skipton BD23 2AA
T: (01756) 799821
F: (01756) 797012
E: info@dalesholcot.com
I: www.dalesholcot.com

Roof House Cottage ★★★
Contact: Agent Dales Hol Cot Ref:1761, Carleton Business Park, Carleton New Road, Skipton BD23 2AA
T: (01756) 799821
F: (01756) 797012
E: info@dalesholcot.com
I: www.dalesholcot.com

Sundale ★★
Contact: Mr Wales, Water Street, Oughtershaw, Skipton BD23 1PB
T: (01756) 700510

HACKNESS
North Yorkshire

Poachers ★★★★
Contact: Mr & Mrs Howarth, Hunters Cottage, Wrench Green, Hackness, Scarborough YO13 9AB
T: (01723) 882266
E: robert.elaine@lineone.net

HALIFAX
West Yorkshire

Cherry Tree Cottages ★★★★
Contact: Mr & Mrs Stan & Elaine Shaw, Cherry Tree Cottages, Wall Nook, Barkisland, Halifax HX4 0BL
T: (01422) 372662
F: (01422) 372662
E: cherry.tree@zen.co.uk
I: www.yorkshire-cottages.co.uk

The Fall ★★★★
Contact: Mrs Knight, 4 Lane Ends, Shibden, Halifax HX3 7UW
T: (01422) 363346

Nina's Cottage ★★★
Contact: Mr Kevin Hellowell, The Barn Moorside, Old Lindley, Holywell Green, Halifax HX4 9DF

HAMBLETON
North Yorkshire

Casten Cottage ★★★
Contact: Sykes Cottages Ref:549, Sykes Cottages, York House, York Street, Chester CH1 3LR
T: (01244) 345700
F: (01244) 321442
E: info@sykescottages.co.uk
I: www.sykescottages.co.uk

HARMBY
North Yorkshire

1,2,3 and 4 Harmby Grange Cottages ★★★★
Contact: Dales Holiday Cottages, Carleton Business Park, New Road, Skipton BD23 2AA
T: (01756) 799821
F: (01756) 790919

Hillfoot House ★★
Contact: Mrs Jones, Hillfoot House, Hillfoot, Harmby, Leyburn DL8 5PH
T: (01969) 623632

HARROGATE
North Yorkshire

Ashness Apartments ★★★★
Contact: Mr J Spinlove & Miss H Spinlove, 15 St Mary's Avenue, Harrogate HG2 0LP
T: (01423) 526894
F: (01423) 700038
E: office@ashness.com
I: www.ashness.com

Brimham Rocks Cottages ★★★-★★★★★
Contact: Mrs J M Martin, Brimham Rocks Cottages, High North Farm, Fellbeck, Harrogate HG3 5EY
T: (01765) 620284
F: (01765) 620477
E: brimham@nascr.net
I: www.brimham.co.uk

Cheltenham Apartments ★★★
Contact: Mr Andrew Moss, 20 Hollins Lane, Hampsthwaite, Birstwith, Harrogate HG3 2EJ
T: (01423) 770864
F: (01423) 770864
E: andrew_moss@ic24.net

6B Cornwall Road ★★★
Contact: Mrs Patricia Anne Sugden, Waterlane Cottage, Middle Street, Rudston, Driffield YO25 4UF
T: (01262) 420796
F: (01262) 602066
E: john@sugden278.freeserve.co.uk

Dinmore Cottages ★★★★
Contact: Mrs Susan Mabel Chapman
T: (01423) 770860
F: (01423) 770860
E: aib@dinmore-cottages.freeserve.co.uk
I: www.dinmore-cottages.co.uk

Flat 1 ★★★★
Contact: Mrs Pamela Wright, Applegarth House, Sleingford Grange, North Stainley, Ripon HG4 3HX
T: (01765) 635367

Holly House Farm Cottages ★★★
Contact: Miss Mary Owen, Holly House Farm Cottages, Holly House Farm, Moorcock Lane, Darley, Harrogate HG3 2QL
T: (01423) 780266
F: (01423) 780299
E: hollyhousecottages@supanet.com
I: www.hollyhousecottages.co.uk

Kent Road Cottage ★★★★
Contact: Mrs E McCullough
T: (01423) 560223
E: lnnuk@hotmail.com

1 Mayfield Terrace Rating Applied For
Contact: Harrogate Holiday Cottages, Crimple Head House, Beckwithshaw, Harrogate HG3 1QU

Moor View Cottage ★★★
Contact: Mrs H L Sweeting, 45 Kingsley Drive, Harrogate HG1 4TH
T: (01423) 885498
E: hlsweeting@easicom.com
I: www.mvcottage.netfirms.com

Mount Pleasant Farm Holiday Cottage ★★★★
Contact: Mrs Linda Prest, Mount Pleasant Farm, Skipton Road, Killinghall, Harrogate HG3 2BU
T: (01423) 504694

Regent Cottage ★★★★
Contact: Mr Robert Blake, 1A Moorfield Road, Woodbridge IP12 4JN
T: (01394) 382565
E: deben@btclick.com

Rudding Holiday Park ★★★
Contact: Mr Martin Hutchinson, Rudding Holiday Park, Rudding Park, Follifoot, Harrogate HG3 1JH
T: (01423) 870439
F: (01423) 870859
E: holiday-park@ruddingpark.com
I: www.ruddingpark.com

HARTON
North Yorkshire

W Todd & Sons ★★★
Contact: Mr & Mrs Todd, W Todd & Sons, Harton, York YO60 7NP
T: (01904) 468487
F: (01904) 468487
E: colin.todd@ukgateway.com
I: www.visityorkshire.com

HARTWITH
North Yorkshire

Brimham Lodge Cottage ★★★
Contact: Mrs Sue Clarke, Brimham Rocks Road, Hartwith, Burnt Yates, Harrogate HG3 3HE
T: (01423) 771770
F: (01423) 770370
E: neil.clarke@virgin.net

Cow Close Barn ★★★★
Contact: Mrs Diana Kitzing, Cow Close Barn, Stripe Lane, Hartwith, Burnt Yates, Harrogate HG3 3EY
T: (01423) 770850
F: (01423) 770993
E: rainerkitzing@aol.com

HATFIELD WOODHOUSE
South Yorkshire

Cosy Executive Accommodation ★★★
Contact: Mr John Perrin, 8 Denaby Lane, Old Denaby, Doncaster DN12 4LA
T: (01709) 580612
F: (01709) 585149
E: john@cosyterrace.fsnet.co.uk

HAWES
North Yorkshire

Chapel House ★★★
Contact: Agent Dales Hol Cot Ref:2320, Carleton Business Park, Carleton New Road, Skipton BD23 2AA
T: (01756) 799821
F: (01756) 797012
E: info@dalesholcot.com
I: www.dalesholcot.com

Cherry Tree Cottage ★★★
Contact: Mrs Nadine Bell, Country Hideaways, Margaret's Cottage, West Burton, Askrigg, Leyburn DL8 4JN
T: (01969) 663559
F: (01969) 663559
E: nadine@countryhideaways.co.uk
I: www.countryhideaways.co.uk

Gaudy House Farm ★★★
Contact: Mrs Jane Allison, Gayle, Hawes DL8 3NA
T: (01969) 667231

Jane Ann Cottage ★★
Contact: Mrs E Irene Sunter, Simonstone, Hawes DL8 3LY
T: (01969) 667186
E: irene.sunter@tiscali.co.uk
I: www.cloud-nine.org.uk/dales

Low Shaw Barn ★★★
Contact: Agent Dales Hol Cot Ref:2367, Carleton Business Park, Carleton New Road, Skipton BD23 2AA
T: (01756) 799821
F: (01756) 797012
E: info@dalesholcot.com
I: www.dalesholcot.com

Mile House Farm Country Cottages ★★★★
Contact: Mrs Anne Fawcett, Mile House Farm Country Cottages, Mile House Farm, Hawes DL8 3PT
T: (01969) 667481
F: (01969) 667425
E: milehousefarm@hotmail.com
I: www.wensleydale.uk.com

Sandy Sike ★★★
Contact: Mrs Margaret Hill, Widdale Foot, Hawes DL8 3LX
T: (01969) 667383
F: (01969) 667417
E: widdalefoot@talk21.com
I: www.wensleydale.org

Yore View ★★★
Contact: Mrs Elizabeth Pedley, Yore House, Lunds, Sedbergh LA10 5PX
T: (01969) 667358
E: yoreviewcottage@talk21.com

Yorkshire Dales Country Cottages ★★★-★★★★
Contact: Mrs Brenda Stott, Yorkshire Dales Country Cottages, Shaw Ghyll, High Shaw, Simonstone, Hawes DL8 3LY
T: (01969) 667359
F: (01969) 667894
E: rogerstott@aol.com
I: www.yorkshirenet.co.uk/accgde/ydcotts.htm

HAWKSWICK
North Yorkshire

Redmire Farm ★★★★★
Contact: Mr Neil Tomlinson, c/o MC (Keighley) Ltd, Unit 2, Newbridge Industrial Estate, Pitt Street, Keighley BD21 4PQ
T: (01535) 610491
F: (01535) 610469
E: neil@mckeighley.co.uk
I: www.redmirefarm.com

HAWORTH
West Yorkshire

Balcony Farm ★★★★
Contact: Mrs Raine, Balcony Farm, Balcony, Haworth, Stanbury, Keighley BD22 8QR
T: (01535) 643627

Bottoms Farm Cottages ★★★★
Contact: Mrs Littler, Bottoms Farm Cottages, Bottoms Farm, Grey Stones Lane, Laycock, Cowling, Keighley BD22 0QD
T: (01535) 607720
F: (01535) 607720

Bronte Country Cottages ★★★-★★★★★
Contact: Ms Clare Pickles, Bronte Country Cottages, Westfield Farm, Tim Lane, Haworth, Keighley BD22 7SA
T: (01535) 644568
F: (01535) 646686
E: clare@brontecountrycottages.co.uk
I: www.brontecountrycottages.co.uk

Heathcliffe Cottage ★★★★
Contact: Mrs Vicky Walker, 35 Norr Lane, Wilsden, Bradford BD15 0DL
T: 07989 557201
F: 07989 557201

Heather, Bilberry Cottage and Grandad's Loft★★★★
Contact: Mrs Janet Milner, Heather & Bilberry Cottages, Hole Farm, Hole, Haworth, Oxenhope, Keighley BD22 8QT
T: (01535) 644755
F: (01535) 644755
E: janet@bronteholidays.co.uk
I: www.bronteholidays.co.uk

Heron Cottage ★★★★
Contact: Mr & Mrs Richard and Jan Walker, Vale Barn, Mytholmes Lane, Haworth, Keighley BD22 0EE
T: (01535) 648537
E: jan_w@tinyworld.co.uk

Hewenden Mill Cottages ★★★★
Contact: Mrs Janet & Susan Emanuel, Hewenden Mill Cottages, Hewenden Mill, Cullingworth, Bradford BD13 5BP
T: (01535) 271834
F: (01535) 273943
E: info@hewendenmillcottages.co.uk
I: www.hewendenmillcottages.co.uk

Little Nook ★★★
Contact: Mr & Mrs Anton and Sheila Murray, 50 West Lane, Haworth, Stanbury, Keighley BD22 8DU
T: (01535) 607013
F: (01535) 690110
E: info@littlenook.co.uk
I: www.littlenook.co.uk

Penny Cottage ★★★
Contact: Ms Lynn Majakas & Mrs Sara Packham, 5 Charles Court, Station Road, Oxenhope, Keighley BD22 9HG
T: (01535) 647796
E: pennycottage@haworth-cottage.co.uk

September Cottage ★★★★
Contact: Mrs Joy Page, Heathcliff, Providence Lane, Oakworth, Keighley BD22 7QR
T: (01535) 644091
E: robjoypagecromer@supanet.com

Spring Cottage ★★★
Contact: Agent Dales Hol Cot Ref:2389, Carleton Business Park, Carleton New Road, Skipton BD23 2AA
T: (01756) 790919
F: (01756) 797012
E: info@dalesholcot.com
I: www.dalesholcot.com

Tanera ★★★
Contact: Agent Dales Hol Cot Ref:0751, Carleton Business Park, Carleton New Road, Skipton BD23 2AA
T: (01756) 790919
F: (01756) 797012
E: info@dalesholcot.com
I: www.dalesholcot.com

Weavers Cottage & Weavers Loft ★★★
Contact: Gaye Bond, 47 North Street, Haworth, Stanbury, Keighley BD22 8EP
T: (01535) 647402
E: g.j.bond@blueyonder.co.uk

Woolcombers Cottage ★★★
Contact: Ms Barbara Clayton, 30 Sun Street, Haworth, Stanbury, Keighley BD22 8BP
T: (01535) 646778
E: woolcombers@clara.co.uk
I: www.bronte-country.com/accomm/woolcombers

HAWSKER
North Yorkshire

Ling Hill Farm ★★
Contact: Mr B Tordoff and Miss A Trotter, Ling Hill Farm, Whitby Laithes, Hawsker, Whitby YO22 4JY
T: (01947) 603914

West End Farm Cottage ★★★★
Contact: Agent Dales Hol Cot Ref:1228, Carleton Business Park, Carleton New Road, Skipton BD23 2AA
T: (01756) 799821
F: (01756) 797012
E: info@dalesholcot.com
I: www.dalesholcot.com

HEALAUGH
North Yorkshire

Lockheather ★★★
Contact: Mrs K Donbavand, 4 Lulworth Road, Birkdale, Southport PR8 2AT
T: (01704) 566317
E: lockheather@amserve.com

HEALEY
North Yorkshire

Grange End
Rating Applied For
Contact: Ms Ruth Henderson, Dales Holiday Cottages, Carleton Business Park, Carleton New Road, Skipton BD23 2AA
T: (01756) 799821
F: (01756) 790919

HEATON
West Yorkshire

Honeysuckle Cottage ★★★
Contact: Mrs Pamela Stobart, 29 Haworth Road, Heaton, Bradford BD9 5PB
T: (01274) 541181
F: (01274) 496169

HEBDEN
North Yorkshire

High Dene House
Rating Applied For
Contact: Dales Hol Cot Ref: 3503, Carleton Business Park, Carleton New Road, Skipton BD23 2AA
T: (01756) 790919
F: (01756) 797012
E: fiona@dalesholcot.com
I: www.dales-holiday-cottages.com

Reservoir Cottage ★★★
Contact: Sykes Cottages Ref:209, Sykes Cottages, York House, York Street, Chester CH1 3LR
T: (01244) 345700
F: (01244) 321442
E: info@sykescottages.co.uk
I: www.sykescottages.co.uk

HEBDEN BRIDGE
West Yorkshire

3 Birks Hall Cottage ★★★
Contact: Mrs H Wilkinson, 1 Birks Hall Cottage, Cragg Vale, Hebden Bridge HX7 5SB
T: (01422) 882064

Lumb Cottage ★★★
Contact: Mrs Maureen Audsley, 14 Myrtle Grove, Hebden Bridge HX7 8HL
T: (01422) 846078
E: myrtlegrove@btinternet.com

15 Oldgate ★★★
Contact: Mr J Barker, Cobweb Cottage, Banks Farm, Mytholmroyd, Hebden Bridge HX7 5RF
T: (01422) 845929
F: (01422) 846354
E: janatcobweb@aol.com

HELMSLEY
North Yorkshire

Beadlam Farm Cottage ★★★
Contact: Mrs Jenny Rooke, Beadlam Grange, Pockley, York YO62 7TD
T: (01439) 770303
E: mark.rooke@farming.co.uk
I: www.stayfarmnorth.co.uk

Bell Cottage ★★★
Contact: Mrs Liz Hudson-Forster, Slingsby Walk, Harrogate HG2 7RZ
T: (01423) 884774

Church View ★★★★
Contact: Mrs Sally Ann Foster, Chestnut Tree Farm, Doncaster Road, Thrybergh, Rotherham S65 4NS
T: (01709) 852929
E: sally.f@ntlworld.com
I: www.fosterl.force9.co.uk

Fleur-de-lys ★★★★
Contact: Mrs Pat Anderson, Mrs Anderson's Country Cottages, Boonhill Cottage, Newton-on-Rawcliffe, Stape, Pickering YO18 8QF
T: (01751) 472172
E: fleurdelys@boonhill69.freeserve.co.uk
I: www.swiftlink.pnc-uk.net/sc/1236a.htm

Honeysuckle Cottage ★★★
Contact: Mrs Margaret Stringer, Cornfield House, Bransdale, Fadmoor, Kirkbymoorside, York YO62 7JW
T: (01751) 431983
E: stringercornfield@talk21.com

Osbourne & Orchard Cottage ★★★
Contact: Miss Wilcox & Mrs J Beckwith, Nice Things Cafe, 10 Market Place, Helmsley, York YO62 5BL
T: (01439) 770632
F: (01439) 770632

Plum Tree Cottage ★★★★
Contact: Mrs T Dzierzek, 46 High Street, Farningham, Dartford DA4 0DB
T: (01322) 863168
F: (01322) 863168
E: dzierzek@btinternet.com
I: www.farninghampine.co.uk

Rose Beck ★★★★
Contact: Ms Steph Woolhouse, 9 Main Street, Ravenfield, Rotherham S65 4NA
T: (01709) 852483
E: steph.woolhouse@hotmail.com

Townend Cottage ★★★★
Contact: Mrs M Begg, Townend Farmhouse, High Lane, Beadlam, Nawton, York YO62 7SY
T: (01439) 770103
E: margaret.begg@ukgateway.net
I: www.visityorkshire.com

Wardy's ★★★
Contact: Miss Joanne Ward, 1 Storey Close, Helmsley, Sproxton, York YO62 5DP
T: (01439) 770124

HELPERTHORPE
North Yorkshire

The Old Dairy & The Granary ★★★★
Contact: Dales Hol Cot Ref:3194/3195, Dales Holiday Cottages, Carleton Business Park, Carleton New Road, Skipton BD23 2AA
T: (01756) 799821
F: (01756) 797012
E: info@dalesholcot.com
I: www.dalesholcot.com

HEPTONSTALL
West Yorkshire

5 Draper Corner ★★
Contact: Mrs S A Taylor, 4 Northfield Terrace, Hebden Bridge HX7 7NG
T: (01422) 844323

The Hayloft Flat ★★★
Contact: Mrs H M Harrison, Fields Farm, Heptonstall, Hebden Bridge HX7 7PD
T: (01422) 843145

HEPWORTH
West Yorkshire

The Old Barn ★★★★
Contact: Mrs Alison Golden, Law Farm, Penistone Road, Hepworth, Holmfirth, Huddersfield HD9 2TR
T: (01226) 762926
F: (01484) 697973

HIGH BENTHAM
North Yorkshire

Batty Farm ★★★
Contact: Agent Dales Hol Cot Ref:1362, Carleton Business Park, Carleton New Road, Skipton BD23 2AA
T: (01756) 799821
F: (01756) 797012
E: info@dalesholcot.com
I: www.dalesholcot.com

Holmes Farm Cottage ★★★★
Contact: Mrs L J Story, Holmes Farm Cottage, Holmes Farm, Low Bentham, Lancaster LA2 7DE
T: (015242) 61198
E: lucy@clucy.demon.co.uk

Low Ben Cottage ★★★
Contact: Dales Hol Cot Ref:587, Dales Holiday Cottages, Carleton Business Park, Carleton New Road, Skipton BD23 2AA
T: (01756) 799821
F: (01756) 797012
E: info@dalesholcot.com
I: www.dalesholcot.com

Parkside & Woodside ★★★★
Contact: Mr & Mrs Thomas and Jane Marshall, Knowe Top, Low Bentham Road, Bentham, Low Bentham, Lancaster LA2 7BN
T: (015242) 62163
F: (015242) 62163
E: info@riversidecaravanpark.co.uk
I: www.riversidecaravanpark.co.uk

HIGH NORMANBY
North Yorkshire

Abbey View Farm Cottage ★★
Contact: Agent Dales Hol Cot Ref:2148, Carleton Business Park, Carleton New Road, Skipton BD23 2AA
T: (01756) 799821
F: (01756) 797012
E: info@dalesholcot.com
I: www.dalesholcot.com

HINDERWELL
North Yorkshire

Jasmine Cottage ★★★★
Contact: Mrs Adele Thompson, Whitby Holiday Cottages, 47 Flowergate, Whitby YO21 3BB
T: (01947) 603010
F: (01947) 821133
E: enquiries@whitby-cottages.co.uk
I: www.whitby-cottages.co.uk

Rhuss Cottage ★★★
Contact: Mrs Louise Robson, Broom House Farm, Ugthorpe, Whitby YO21 2BJ
T: (01947) 840454
F: (01947) 840454
E: john@broomhse.fsnet.co.uk

HOLMBRIDGE
West Yorkshire

Ivy Cottage ★★★
Contact: Mr & Mrs Ian and Joyce Bangham and Carter, Ivy Cottage, Woodhead Road, Holmbridge, Holmfirth, Huddersfield HD9 2NQ
T: (01484) 682561
E: bangham77@hotmail.com

Weavers Cottage ★★★★
Contact: Mr Gillian Blewett, 96 Woodhead Road, Holmbridge, Holmfirth, Huddersfield HD9 2NL
T: (01484) 666319
F: (01484) 665715
E: martinblewett@aol.com

HOLMFIRTH
West Yorkshire

Dal-a-fr-sa ★★★★
Contact: Mr & Mrs David Babbings, 52 Meltham Road, Honley, Huddersfield HD9 6HL
T: (01484) 666545
F: (01484) 323990
E: davidbabbings@ntlworld.com

Fern Mount Cottage ★★★
Contact: Mr & Mrs Roger and Sally Carrier, 36 Back Lane, Holmfirth, Huddersfield HD9 1HG
T: (01484) 688755
F: (01484) 689378

Old Yew Barn ★★★
Contact: Mrs Doris Thorpe, Royd Lane, Holmfirth, Huddersfield HD9 2JA
T: (028) 928 2334

The Studio & Victoria Flats ★★★-★★★★★
Contact: Mrs Newby, Foxhill Keepers Cottage, Skipton Road, Hampsthwaite, Pateley Bridge, Harrogate HG3 2LZ
T: (01423) 771730
F: (01484) 771730

Summerwine Cottages ★★★
Contact: Mrs Susan Meakin, Summerwine Cottages, West Royd Farm, Marsh Lane, Shepley, Huddersfield HD8 8AY
T: (01484) 602147
F: (01484) 609427
E: summerwinecottages@lineone.net
I: www.summerwinecottages.co.uk

Uppergate Farm ★★★★
Contact: Mrs Alison Booth
T: (01484) 681369
F: (01484) 687343
E: stevenal.booth@virgin.net
I: www.uppergatefarm.co.uk

HOLTBY
North Yorkshire

Garden Cottage ★★★★
Contact: Agent Dales Hol Cot Ref:1472, Carleton Business Park, Carleton New Road, Skipton BD23 2AA
T: (01756) 799821
F: (01756) 797012
E: info@dalesholcot.com
I: www.dalesholcot.com

HORNSEA
East Riding of Yorkshire

Cobble Cottage ★★★
Contact: Mrs Mary Everington, Risingfield, Strawberry Gardens, Hornsea HU18 1US
T: (01964) 536159

Horseshoe Cottage ★★
Contact: Mr & Mrs Barron, Horseshoe Cottage, Suffolk House, Suffolk Road, Hornsea HU18 1RT
T: (01964) 532088
E: a.barron1@talk21.com

Westgate Mews ★★
Contact: Mrs Walker, 27 Westgate, Hornsea HU18 1BP
T: (01964) 533430
E: lettings@walkerhornsea.plus.com
I: www.eastyorkshire.co.uk

HORSEHOUSE
North Yorkshire

East Close ★★★
Contact: Ms L Townsley, 70 Parish Ghyll Drive, Ilkley LS29 9PR
T: (01943) 609012
E: lindseytownsley@cs.com
I: www.dalescharactercottages.co.uk

HORTON-IN-RIBBLESDALE
North Yorkshire

Blind Beck Holiday Cottage ★★★
Contact: Mrs M Huddleston, Blind Beck, Horton-in-Ribblesdale, Settle BD24 0HT
T: (01729) 860396
E: h.huddleston@daelnet.co.uk
I: www.blindbeck.co.uk

Churchgate ★★★
Contact: Dales Hol Cot Ref:3115, Dales Holiday Cottages, Carleton Business Park, Carleton New Road, Skipton BD23 2AA
T: (01756) 799821
F: (01756) 797012
E: info@dalesholcot.com
I: www.dalesholcot.com

Douk Ghyll Cottage ★★★★
Contact: Mr & Mrs Teal and Mr & Mrs Traher, Valley Hotel, 93-95 Valley Drive, Harrogate HG2 0JP
T: (01423) 504868
F: (01423) 531940
E: valley@harrogate.com
I: www.valleyhotel.co.uk

The Flat ★★★
Contact: Mrs Sheila Fleming, South View, New Houses, Horton-in-Ribblesdale, Selside, Settle BD24 0JE
T: (01729) 860394
F: (01729) 860394
E: info@south-view.org.uk

Fourways Cottage ★★★
Contact: Mr & Mrs Dermot & Deborah Griffin, 2 Openview, London SW18 3PF
T: (0208) 870 6784
F: (0208) 870 7668
E: enquiries@escapetothedales.co.uk
I: www.escapetothedales.co.uk

Hollybush Cottage
Rating Applied For
Contact: Sykes Ref 827, Sykes Cottages, York House, York Street, Chester CH1 3LR
T: (01244) 345700
F: (01244) 321442
E: info@sykescottages.co.uk
I: www.sykescottages.co.uk

Selside Farm Holiday Cottages
★★★-★★★★
Contact: Mrs S E Lambert, Selside Farm, Selside, Settle BD24 0HZ
T: (01729) 860367
E: shirley@lam67.freeserve.co.uk

HOVINGHAM
North Yorkshire

Westwood ★★★
Contact: Mrs S A Weston, Elemore Grange Farm, Littletown, Durham DH6 1QE
T: (0191) 372 1785

HUDDERSFIELD
West Yorkshire

Ashes Farm Cottages
★★★-★★★★
Contact: Mrs Barbara Lockwood, Ashes Farm Cottages, Ashes Common Farm, Ashes Lane, Newsome, Huddersfield HD4 6TE
T: (01484) 426507
F: (01484) 426507
E: enquiries@ashescommonfarm.co.uk
I: www.ashesfarm.demon.co.uk

Castle House Farm Cottages
★★★★
Contact: Mr & Mrs Philip Coates, Castle House Farm Cottages, Castle House Farm, Berry Brow, Huddersfield, Huddersfield HD4 6TS
T: (01484) 663808
F: (01484) 661464
E: philip@castlehousefarm.co.uk
I: www.castlehousefarm.co.uk

Elam & Coates ★★★
Contact: Mrs Anne Mullany, 49 Lowerhouses Lane, Lowerhouses, Huddersfield HD5 8JP
T: (01484) 431432
E: mullany@tesco.net

Swallow Cottage ★★★★
Contact: Mrs Margaret Kucharczyk, Rockley House, High Flatts, Huddersfield HD8 8XU
T: (01484) 607072
F: (01484) 607072
E: swallow@care4free.net

HUGGATE
East Riding of Yorkshire

Manor House Farm ★★★
Contact: Mrs S Frumin, Manor House Farm, The Green, Huggate, York YO42 1YZ
T: (01377) 288368
F: (01377) 288127
E: manorhouse-huggate@ukonline.co.uk

HULL
East Riding of Yorkshire

Walton House ★★
Contact: Mr David Bradley, 9 Minnies Grove, Walton Street, Hull HU3 6JP
T: (01482) 352733

Waters Edge Executive Apartments ★★★★
Contact: Mrs J L Langton, 719 Beverley Road, Hull HU6 7JN
T: (01482) 853248
F: (01482) 853148

HUNMANBY
North Yorkshire

Honeysuckle Cottage ★★★
Contact: Dales Hol Cot Ref:1984, Carleton Business Park, Carleton New Road, Skipton BD23 2AA
T: (01756) 799821
F: (01756) 797012
E: info@dalesholcot.com
I: www.dalesholcot.com

HUNTON
North Yorkshire

Emberton
Rating Applied For
Contact: Mr & Mrs Trevor & Wendy Mills, 131 Glendale Gardens, Leigh-on-Sea SS9 2BE
T: (01702) 478846
F: (01702) 482088
E: info@dalescottages.com
I: www.dalescottages.com

HURST
North Yorkshire

Shiney Row Cottage ★★★
Contact: Dales Hol Cot Ref:2786, Carleton Business Park, Carleton New Road, Skipton BD23 2AA
T: (01756) 799821
F: (01756) 797012
E: info@dalesholcot.com
I: www.dalesholcot.com

HUSTHWAITE
North Yorkshire

Greg's Cottage ★★★
Contact: Mr Greg Harrand, 3 Bootham Terrace, York YO30 7DH
T: (01904) 637404
F: (01904) 639774
E: greg@harrands.com

Kate's Cottage ★★
Contact: Mrs Anne Cox, The Nookin, Husthwaite, York YO61 4PY
T: (01845) 526550
E: c.anne.cox@virgin.net

HUTTON-LE-HOLE
North Yorkshire

Moorlands Cottage ★★★
Contact: Ms Kate Seekings and Mr B Jenkinson, Moorlands of Hutton-le-Hole, Hutton-le-Hole, York YO62 6UA
T: (01751) 417548
F: (01751) 417760
E: stay@moorlandshouse.com
I: www.moorlandshouse.com

Waterswallow Cottage ★★★
Contact: Mrs Barbara Grabowski, Halfway House, Hutton-le-Hole, York YO62 6UQ
T: (01751) 431596
F: (01751) 431596

HUTTON SESSAY
North Yorkshire

White Rose Holiday Cottages
★★★
Contact: Ms Natalie Jessop, White Rose Holiday Cottages, Rowan Cottage, Hutton Sessay, Thirsk YO7 3BA
T: (01845) 501180
F: (01845) 501180

ILKLEY
West Yorkshire

Faweather Grange
★★★★-★★★★★
Contact: Mrs D Skinn
T: (01943) 878777
F: (01943) 878777
E: skinn@attglobal.net
I: www.faweathergrange.com

Westwood Lodge, Ilkley Moor
★★★★-★★★★★
Contact: Mr & Mrs Tim & Paula Edwards, Wells Road, Ilkley LS29 9JF
T: (01943) 433430
F: (01943) 433431
E: welcome@westwoodlodge.co.uk
I: www.westwoodlodge.co.uk

INGLEBY CROSS
North Yorkshire

Hill House ★★★★
Contact: Mr & Mrs Richard & Vee Kitteridge, Ingleby Cross, Northallerton DL6 3NH
T: (01609) 882109
E: kitteridge@ukgateway.net

INGLEBY GREENHOW
North Yorkshire

Ingleby Manor ★★★★
Contact: Mrs Christine Bianco, Ingleby Manor, Ingleby Greenhow, Great Ayton, Middlesbrough TS9 6RB
T: (01642) 722170
F: (01642) 722170
E: christine@inglebymanor.co.uk
I: www.inglebymanor.co.uk

INGLETON
North Yorkshire

Bank Hall ★★★
Contact: Mr Philip Angus, Brooklyn, Ingleton, Carnforth LA6 3DE
T: (015242) 41127
E: philip.angus@ukgateway.net
I: www.bankhall-ingleton.co.uk

Kingsdale Head Cottage ★★★
Contact: Mrs Stephanie Faraday, Westhouse, Ingleton, Carnforth LA6 3PH
T: (015242) 41393
F: (015242) 41393

Little Storrs ★★★★
Contact: Mrs Kuhlmann, Storrs Dale, Ingleton, Carnforth LA6 3AN
T: (015242) 41843
F: (015242) 41690
E: debbykuhlmann@aol.com

Primrose Cottage ★★★
Contact: Mr & Mrs John and Celia Jones, Spring View, Ingleton, Carnforth LA6 3HE
T: (015242) 41407
F: (015242) 41407
E: topclub.john@virgin.net

KEARBY WITH NETHERBY
North Yorkshire

Nethercroft Cottage ★★★★
Contact: Mrs Webb, The Riddings, Spring Lane, Kearby, Kearby With Netherby, Wetherby LS22 4DA
T: (0113) 288 6234
F: (0113) 288 6234
E: info@maustin.co.uk
I: www.maustin.co.uk

KEIGHLEY
West Yorkshire

Opal Apartment ★★
Contact: Mr David Mortimer, 5 Opal Street, Ingrow, Keighley BD22 7BP
T: (01535) 604175
F: (01535) 604175
E: david@brackenbankstores.co.uk
I: www.nosurrender.freeserve.co.uk

KELD
North Yorkshire

Hillcrest Holiday Cottage
★★★
Contact: Mrs Barbara Rukin, Park Lodge, Keld, Richmond DL11 6LJ
T: (01748) 886274
E: babrarukin@ukonline.co.uk

Keld Cottages ★★★
Contact: Mr Stuart Brier, The Smithy, Keld, Richmond DL11 6LJ
T: (01748) 886436

KETTLENESS
North Yorkshire

Eastwater Cottage ★★★
Contact: Agent Dales Hol Cot Ref:1537, Carleton Business Park, Carleton New Road, Skipton BD23 2AA
T: (01756) 799821
F: (01756) 797012
E: info@dalesholcot.com
I: www.dalesholcot.com

KETTLEWELL
North Yorkshire

Cam Cottage ★★★★
Contact: Dales Hol Cot Ref:3015, Dales Holiday Cottages, Carleton Business Park, Carleton New Road, Skipton BD23 2AA
T: (01756) 799821
F: (01756) 797012
E: info@dalesholcot.com
I: www.dalesholcot.com

Fold Farm Cottages ★★★★
Contact: Mrs Barbara Lambert, Fold Farm Cottages, Fold Farm, Kettlewell, Starbotton, Skipton BD23 5RH
T: (01756) 760886
F: (01756) 760464
E: info@foldfarm.co.uk
I: www.foldfarm.co.uk

Heathlands ★★★
Contact: Dales Hol Cot Ref:931, Carleton Business Park, Carleton New Road, Skipton BD23 2AA
T: (01756) 799821
F: (01756) 797012
E: info@dalesholcot.com
I: www.dales-holiday-cottages.com

Primrose Cottage ★★★★
Contact: Dales Hol Cot Ref:2504, Carleton Business Park, Carleton New Road, Skipton BD23 2AA
T: (01756) 799821
F: (01756) 797012
E: info@dalesholcot.com
I: www.dalesholcot.com

Townsley Dales Cottages ★★★
Contact: Ms L Townsley, 70 Parish Ghyll Drive, Ilkley LS29 9PR
T: (01943) 609012
E: charactercottages@hotmail.com
I: www.dalescharactercottages.co.uk

Wayside Cottage ★★★
Contact: Mrs Georgina Drew, 5 The Coombe, Dartmouth TQ6 9PG
T: (01803) 839295
E: craig.drew@tesco.net

KILDALE
North Yorkshire

Bernard's Barn ★★★★
Contact: Agent Dales Hol Cot Ref:1566, Carleton Business Park, Carleton New Road, Skipton BD23 2AA
T: (01756) 799821
F: (01756) 797012
E: info@dalesholcot.com
I: www.dales-holiday-cottages.com

KILHAM
East Riding of Yorkshire

Raven Hill Holiday Farmhouse ★★★
Contact: Mr & Mrs Savile, Raven Hill Farm, Kilham, Langtoft, Driffield YO25 4EG
T: (01377) 267217
F: (01377) 267217

KIPLIN
North Yorkshire

Maryland Cottage & Baltimore Cottage ★★
Contact: Ms Elaine Bird, Maryland Cottage & Baltimore Cottage, Kiplin Hall, Kiplin, Scorton, Richmond DL10 6AT
T: (01748) 812863
F: (01748) 818178
E: info@kiplinhall.co.uk
I: www.kiplinhall.co.uk

KIRBY HILL
North Yorkshire

Manor Cottage ★★★
Contact: Mrs Diana Whitby, Manor House, Kirby Hill, Whashton, Richmond DL11 7JH
T: (01748) 825634
E: dianawhitby@hotmail.com

KIRBY MISPERTON
North Yorkshire

2 Rose Cottages ★★★
Contact: Mrs Kathryn Greenwood, Main Street, Kirby Misperton, Malton YO17 6XL
T: (01422) 364880
E: kathryn@sillaford.com
I: www.cottageguide.co.uk/kirbymisperton

KIRKBY MALZEARD
North Yorkshire

Alma Cottage ★★★★
Contact: Mrs Janet Barclay, 12 St Stephens Road, Cold Norton, Purleigh, Chelmsford CM3 6JE
T: (01621) 828576
F: (01621) 828539
E: janet@lbarclay.demon.co.uk
I: www.almacottage.co.uk

The Cottage ★★★
Contact: Dales Hol Cot Ref:3146, Carleton Business Park, Carleton New Road, Skipton BD23 2AA
T: (01756) 799821
F: (01756) 797012
E: info@dalesholcot.com
I: www.dalesholcot.com

The Woodpeckers ★★★
Contact: Mrs Elizabeth Drewery, The Woodpeckers, Main Street, Kirkby Malzeard, Laverton, Ripon HG4 3SE
T: (01765) 658206

KIRKBYMOORSIDE
North Yorkshire

Burton House ★★★
Contact: Country Hols Ref:13729, Country Holidays Group Owner Services Dept, Spring Mill, Earby, Barnoldswick BB94 0AA
T: 08700 723723
F: (01282) 844288
E: sales@holidaycottagesgroup.com
I: www.country-holidays.co.uk

Catterbridge Farm Cottage ★★★★
Contact: Mrs Jayne Peace, Catterbridge Farm, Kirkbymoorside, York YO62 6NF
T: (01751) 433271

Cherry View Cottage ★★★★
Contact: Mrs SMP Drinkel, High Hagg Farm, Kirkbymoorside, York YO62 7JF
T: (01751) 431714

The Cornmill ★★★★
Contact: Mr & Mrs Chris & Karen Tinkler, The Cornmill, Kirby Mills, Kirkbymoorside, York YO62 6NP
T: (01751) 432000
F: (01751) 432300
E: cornmill@kirbymills.demon.co.uk
I: www.kirbymills.demon.co.uk

Ellerslie ★★★
Contact: Mrs Elizabeth Davison, 26 Castlegate, Kirkbymoorside, York YO62 6BJ
T: (01751) 431112
E: mail@lizdavison.co.uk

Horseshoe Cottage ★★★
Contact: Mr & Mrs David and Susan Snowden, Hollyhock, Brawby, Malton YO17 6PY
T: (01653) 668470
E: rd.snowden@btopenworld.com

Keldholme Cottages ★★★
Contact: Mr B Hughes, Keldholme Cottages, Keldholme, Kirkbymoorside, York YO62 6NA
T: (01751) 431933

Oak Lodge ★★★
Contact: Mrs Andrea Turnbull, Oak Lodge, Whitethorn Farm, Rook Barugh, Kirkbymoorside, York YO62 6PF
T: (01751) 431298

The Retreat ★★★★
Contact: Mrs A J Schulze, The Grange, Sinnington, York YO62 6RB
T: (01751) 430806
F: (01751) 430369
E: tish.mill@virgin.net

Sinnington Common Farm ★★★-★★★★
Contact: Mrs Felicity Wiles, Sinnington Common Farm, Cartoft, Kirkbymoorside, Sinnington, York YO62 6NX
T: (01751) 431719
F: (01751) 431719
E: felicity@scfarm.demon.co.uk
I: www.scfarm.demon.co.uk

Sleightholmedale Cottages ★★★★
Contact: Mrs James, Sleightholmedale Cottages, Sleightholmedale, Kirkbymoorside, York YO62 7JG
T: (01751) 431942
F: (01751) 430106
E: wshoot@aol.com

Surprise View Cottage & Field Barn Cottage ★★★★
Contact: Mrs Ruth Wass, Sinnington Lodge, Sinnington, York YO62 6RB
T: (01751) 431345
F: (01751) 433418
E: info@surpriseviewcottages.co.uk
I: www.surpriseviewcottages.co.uk

KIRKSTALL
West Yorkshire

The Tops ★★
Contact: Mr Merton Miles, 21 Wadlands Drive, Farsley, Pudsey LS28 5JS
T: (0113) 257 2197
F: (0113) 257 2197

KNARESBOROUGH
North Yorkshire

Acorn Cottage ★★★★
Contact: Mrs & Mrs C&S Webster, Oakwood Farm, Hay-A-Park, Knaresborough HG5 0RX
T: (01423) 863144
F: (01423) 865375
I: www.acorn-cottage.com

Badger Hill Properties ★★★-★★★★
Contact: Mr McGrath, Dropping Well Village Ltd, Badger Hill Properties, Harrogate Road, Knaresborough HG5 8DP
T: (01423) 862352
F: (01423) 868021
E: manager@badgerhill.co.uk
I: www.badgerhill.co.uk

6 Cheapside ★★
Contact: Mrs Doreen Cook, 21 Manor Road, Knaresborough HG5 0BN
T: (01423) 862641

Garden Apartment ★★★
Contact: Mrs Rowinski, Garden Apartment, 3 Aspin Way, Knaresborough HG5 8HL
T: (01423) 860463

The Granary ★★★★
Contact: Mr & Mrs I Thornton, The Granary, Gibbet House Farm, Farnham Lane, Farnham, Knaresborough HG5 9JP
T: (01423) 862325
F: (01423) 862271

Knaresborough Holiday Apartments ★★★
Contact: Mr & Mrs C A Cheney, 2A Aspin Lane, Knaresborough HG5 8ED
T: (01423) 862629
F: (01423) 862629

Uncle Tom's Holiday Cabins ★★★
Contact: Mrs Pat Ridsdale, Uncle Tom's Holiday Cabins, 22 Waterside, Knaresborough, Knaresborough HG5 8DF
T: (01423) 867045
F: (01423) 867045

Watergate Lodge Holiday Apartments ★★★-★★★★
Contact: Mr & Mrs Peter & Lesley Guest, Watergate Lodge Holiday Apartments, Watergate Haven, Ripley Road, Knaresborough, Harrogate HG5 9BU
T: (01423) 864627
F: (01423) 861087
E: info@watergatehaven.com
I: www.watergatehaven.com

LANGTHWAITE
North Yorkshire

Arklehurst ★★★
Contact: Mrs Julie Bissicks, Langthwaite, Arkengarthdale, Richmond DL11 6RE
T: (01748) 884912
I: www.arkengarthdalecottage.co.uk

LASTINGHAM
North Yorkshire

Lastingham Holiday Cottage - Brook Cottage ★★★-★★★★
Contact: Mrs Cattle, Lastingham Holiday Cottages, Littlegarth, Low Street, Lastingham, York YO62 6TJ
E: lastinghamhols@aol.com
I: www.members.aol.com/lastinghamhols

LAVERTON
North Yorkshire

Laverton Holiday Cottages ★★★
Contact: Mrs Brassington, Laverton Holiday Cottages, Laverton Grange, Laverton, Ripon HG4 3SX
T: (01765) 658262
E: ron@brasso95.freeserve.co.uk
I: www.cottageguide.co.uk/lavertoncottages

LEALHOLM
North Yorkshire

Greenhouses Farm Cottages ★★★
Contact: Mr & Mrs Nick Eddleston, Greenhouses Farm Cottages, Greenhouses Farm, Lealholm, Whitby YO21 2AD
T: (01947) 897486
F: (01947) 897486
E: n_eddleston@yahoo.com
I: www.greenhouses-farm-cottages.co.uk

Poets Cottage Holiday Flat ★★
Contact: Mrs Blanche Rees, 25 Roseberry Road, Billingham TS20 1JZ
T: (01642) 532413
E: rees@btinternet.com

West Banks Farmhouse ★★★
Contact: Agent Dales Hol Cot Ref:1671, Carleton Business Park, Carleton New Road, Skipton BD23 2AA
T: (01756) 799821
F: (01756) 797012
E: info@dalesholcot.com
I: www.dalesholcot.com

LEAVENING
North Yorkshire

Sunset Cottage at the Jolly Farmers Inn★★★★
Contact: Mr & Mrs John Parkinson, Sunset Cottage, Main Street, Leavening, Malton YO17 9SA
T: (01653) 658276
I: www.yorkshireholidays.com

LEEDS
West Yorkshire

Harman Suites ★★★★
Contact: Mr K Singh & Miss Simerpreet Kaur, Harman Suites, 48 St Martins Avenue, Leeds LS7 3LG
T: (0113) 295 5886
F: (0113) 295 5886
E: info@harmansuite.co.uk
I: www.harmansuite.co.uk

LEVEN
East Riding Of Yorkshire

Leven Park Lake ★★★★
Contact: Mr & Mrs Graham & Lisa Skinner, South Street, Leven, Beverley HU17 5NY
T: (01964) 544510

LEVISHAM
North Yorkshire

The Hopper, The Granary & The Cottage★★-★★★★
Contact: Mr Dales Hol Cot:2317/1813/3171, Carleton Business Park, Carleton New Road, Skipton BD23 2AA
T: (01756) 799821
F: (01756) 797012
E: info@dalesholcot.com
I: www.dalesholcot.com

Lilac Farm ★★★
Contact: Mrs Heather Eddon, Lilac Farm Cottage & End House Farm, Main Street, Levisham, Lockton, Pickering YO18 7NL
T: (01751) 460281
E: heather@lilacfarm.f9.co.uk
I: www.lilacfarm.f9.co.uk

Moorlands Cottage ★★★★★
Contact: Mr & Mrs Ron and Gill Leonard, Main Street, Levisham, Lockton, Pickering YO18 7NL
T: (01751) 460229
F: (01751) 460470
E: ronaldoleonardo@aol.com
I: www.moorlandslevisham.co.uk

LEYBURN
North Yorkshire

Calverts of Leyburn ★★★
Contact: Mrs Ann Calvert, Smithy Lane, Leyburn DL8 5DZ
T: (01969) 623051
F: (01969) 624345
E: cottages@calverts.co.uk
I: www.calverts.co.uk

2 Crown Court Cottage ★★★
Contact: Mr & Mrs Roland & Diane Terry, Old Farm, Barden, Leyburn DL8 5JS
T: (01969) 624448
F: (01969) 624448
E: dalescottages@sniffout.com
I: www.yorkshiredalesholidaycottages.co.uk

Dales View Holiday Homes ★★★
Contact: Messrs J&M Chilton, Dales View Holiday Homes, Jenkins Garth, Leyburn DL8 5SP
T: (01969) 623707
F: (01969) 623707
E: daleshols@aol.com
I: www.daleshols.com

Eastburn Cottage ★★★★
Contact: Mrs Nadine H Bell, Country Hideaways, Margaret's Cottage, West Burton, Askrigg, Leyburn DL8 4JN
T: (01969) 663559
E: nadine@countryhideaways.co.uk
I: www.countryhideaways.co.uk

Foal Barn ★★★
Contact: Mrs Canham, Foal Barn, Spennithorne, Leyburn DL8 5PR
T: (01969) 622580

Low Riseborough ★★
Contact: Mr John Rowntree, 95 Chiswick Village, London W4 3BZ
T: (020) 8994 9837
F: (020) 8995 4674

The Old Fire Station ★★★★
Contact: Miss C Wallace-Lowell, 4 Shawl Terrace, Leyburn DL8 5DA
T: (01969) 623993

Penn Hill View
Rating Applied For
Contact: Mr David Smith, 10 Strickland Close, Leeds LS17 8JY
T: (0113) 273 7452
E: david.smith@persimmonhomes.com

Thorney Cottages ★★★
Contact: Mrs Nadine Bell, Country Hideaways, Margaret's Cottage, West Burton, Askrigg, Leyburn DL8 4JN
T: (01969) 663559
F: (01969) 663559
E: nadine@countryhideaways.co.uk
I: www.countryhideaways.co.uk

Throstlenest Holiday Cottages ★★★
Contact: Mrs Tricia Smith, Throstlenest Holiday Cottages, Walk Mill Lane, Leyburn DL8 5HF
T: (01969) 623694
F: (01969) 624755
E: info@throstlenestcottages.co.uk
I: www.throstlenestcottages.co.uk

LINTON
North Yorkshire

Wharfedene ★★★
Contact: Miss Liquorish, 6 Hope Street, Beeston, Nottingham NG9 1DR
T: (0115) 922 3239
E: eliquorish@learnall.net

LINTON-ON-OUSE
North Yorkshire

Nursery View & Fuchsia Cottage ★★★
Contact: Dales Hol Cot Ref:1463/1464, Dales Holiday Cottages, Carleton Business Park, Carleton New Road, Skipton BD23 2AA
T: (01756) 799821
F: (01756) 797012
E: info@dalesholcot.com
I: www.dalesholcot.com

LITTLE OUSEBURN
North Yorkshire

Hawtree Cottage ★★★★
Contact: Mrs Anne Llewellyn, Hawtree House, Main Street, Little Ouseburn, York YO26 9TD
T: (01423) 331526
E: annellewellyn@yahoo.com

LITTLE THIRKLEBY
North Yorkshire

Old Oak Cottages ★★★★
Contact: Mrs Tattersall, High House Farm, Little Thirkleby, Thirsk YO7 2BB
T: (01845) 501258
F: (01845) 501258

LITTLEBECK
North Yorkshire

Kelp House ★★★★
Contact: Mr Ray Flute, Ingrid Flute, 1 Hillcrest Avenue, Scarborough YO12 6RQ
T: (01723) 376777
F: (01723) 376777
E: info@ingridflute.co.uk

LITTON
North Yorkshire

Stonelands ★★★★
Contact: Mrs Cowan, Arncliffe, Skipton BD23 5QE
T: (01756) 770293

LOCKTON
North Yorkshire

Ashfield Cottage ★★★
Contact: Mrs Carol Fisk, Ashfield Cottage, Lockton, Pickering YO18 7PZ
T: (01751) 460397
E: ashfieldcottage@beeb.net

Barn Cottage ★★★
Contact: Mrs Gill Grant, Buslingthorpe, Lincoln LN3 5AQ
T: (01673) 842283
E: emmalouise.grant@btopenworld.co.uk

Bell Cottage Ref 3466
Rating Applied For
Contact: Miss Ruth Henderson, Dales Holiday Cottages, Carleton Business Park, Carleton New Road, Skipton BD23 2AA
T: (01756) 79982
F: (01756) 797012

Old Barn Cottage ★★★★
Contact: Dales Hol Cot Ref:3237, Carleton Business Park, Carleton New Road, Skipton BD23 2AA
T: (01756) 799821
F: (01756) 797012
E: info@dalesholcot.com
I: www.dalesholcot.com

West View Farm ★★★
Contact: Mrs J Welburn, Lockton, Pickering YO18 7QB
T: (01751) 460286
F: (01751) 460286

LOFTHOUSE
North Yorkshire

Acorn Quality Cottages ★★★★
Contact: Mrs Kerr, 82 Trafalgar Road, Birkdale, Southport PR8 2NJ
T: (01704) 568941
E: acornqualitycottages@supanet.com
I: www.acornqualitycottages.co.uk

Blayshaw Farmhouse ★★★★
Contact: Mr Ian Walker, Studfold Farm, Lofthouse, Harrogate HG3 5SG
T: (01423) 755399

Thrope Farm Cottage ★★★
Contact: Mr Stephen Harker, Thrope Farm, Lofthouse, Harrogate HG3 5SN
T: (01423) 755607

LONG MARSTON
North Yorkshire

The Cottage ★★★
Contact: Mrs Gilmour, The Cottage, Old Lane, Long Marston, York YO26 7LF
T: (01904) 738535
F: (01904) 738535
E: bob.gilmour@btopenworld.com
I: www.bob.gilmour.btinternet.co.uk

LOTHERSDALE
North Yorkshire

Great Gib Cottage ★★★
Contact: Agent Dales Hol Cot Ref:1859, Carleton Business Park, Carleton New Road, Skipton BD23 2AA
T: (01756) 799821
F: (01756) 797012
E: info@dalesholcot.com
I: www.dalesholcot.com

Street Head Farm ★★★★★
Contact: Mrs J Gooch, Tow Top Farm, Cononley, Skipton BD20 8HY
T: (01535) 632535
F: (01535) 632535
E: streethead@towtop.fsnet.co.uk
I: www.towtop.co.uk

LOW BENTHAM
North Yorkshire

Borrans Cottage ★★★
Contact: Mrs Fiona Moody, Carleton Business Park, Carleton New Road, Skipton BD23 2AA
T: (01756) 799821
E: info@dalesholcot.com
I: www.dalesholcot.com

The Old Dairy Ref 3327
Rating Applied For
Contact: Ms Ruth Henderson, Dales Holiday Cottages, Carleton Business Park, Carleton New Road, Skipton BD23 2AA
T: (01756) 799821
F: (01756) 797012

LOW CATTON
East Riding of Yorkshire

2 Appletree Cottages ★★★★
Contact: Hoseasons Country Cottages Ltd, Raglan Road, Lowestoft NR32 2LW
T: (01502) 500505
F: (01502) 514298

LOW LAITHE
North Yorkshire

Springside ★★★★
Contact: Mrs Cathie Murrell, Old Coach Road, Low Laithe, Harrogate HG3 4DE
T: (01423) 781383
F: (01423) 781383

LOW ROW
North Yorkshire

High Smarber ★★★
Contact: Mrs Kathleen Hird, Smarber Hall, Richmond DL11 6PX
T: (01748) 886738
E: rentals@swaledalecottage.com
I: www.swaledalecottage.com

Intake Cottage ★★★
Contact: Dales Hol Cot Ref: 3346, Dales Holiday Cottages, Carleton Business Park, Carleton New Road, Skipton BD23 2AA
T: (01756) 790919
F: (01756) 797012
E: info@dalesholcot.com
I: www.dalesholcot.com

MALHAM
North Yorkshire

The Old School ★★★★
Contact: Ms Victoria Spence, King House, Malham, Skipton BD23 4DD
T: (01729) 830445
E: spences@whsmithnet.co.uk

Waterside Cottage ★★★★
Contact: Sykes Cottages Ref:641, Sykes Cottages, York House, York Street, Chester CH1 3LR
T: (01244) 345700
F: (01244) 321442
E: info@sykescottages.co.uk
I: www.sykescottages.co.uk

MALTON
North Yorkshire

Rowgate Cottage ★★★★
Contact: Mrs Janet Clarkson, Thorpe Bassett, Malton YO17 8LU
T: (01944) 758277
F: (01944) 758277

Swans Nest Cottage ★★★★
Contact: Mrs Yvonne Dickinson, Abbots Farm House, Ryton, Malton YO17 6SA
T: (01653) 694970
E: swansnestcottage@hotmail.com
I: www.uk-holiday-cottages.co.uk/swans-nest

4 Wellgarth ★★
Contact: Mrs Waudby, 5 Wellgarth, Swinton, Amotherby, Malton YO17 6SS
T: (01653) 697548
E: diannewaudby@onetel.net.uk

MARISHES
North Yorkshire

Bellafax Holiday Cottage ★★★★
Contact: Dales Hol Cot Ref:2798, Carleton Business Park, Carleton New Road, Skipton BD23 2AA
T: (01756) 799821
F: (01756) 797012
E: info@dalesholcot.com
I: www.dalesholcot.com

MARSKE
North Yorkshire

Home Farm ★★★★
Contact: Mrs V Simpson, Home Farm, Marske, Richmond DL11 7LT
T: (01748) 824770
F: (01748) 826357

MARTON
North Yorkshire

Orchard House ★★★★
Contact: Mr & Mrs Paul Richardson, Orchard House, Marton, Sinnington, York YO62 6RD
T: (01751) 432904
F: (01751) 430733
E: orchardhouse@tinyworld.co.uk
I: www.orchardhouse.biz

Wildsmith Court ★★★★
Contact: Mr & Mrs David & Joan Milner, Wildsmith Court, The Granary, Marton, Sinnington, York YO62 6RD
T: (01751) 431358
E: milner@wildsmithcourt.freeserve.co.uk

MARTON CUM SEWERBY
East Riding of Yorkshire

Grange Farm Cottages ★★★★
Contact: Mr Richard Dibb, Ryal, Flamborough Road, Sewerby, Bridlington YO15 1DU
T: (01262) 671137
E: richard.dibb@btclick.com
I: www.grangefarmcottages.net

MASHAM
North Yorkshire

Barn Owl Cottage ★★★
Contact: Agent Dales Hol Cot Ref:1178, Carleton Business Park, Carleton New Road, Skipton BD23 2AA
T: (01756) 799821
F: (01756) 797012
E: info@dalesholcot.com
I: www.dalesholcot.com

Masham Cottages ★★★
Contact: Mr John Airton, Masham Cottages, 27 Red Lane, Masham, Ripon HG4 4HH
T: (01765) 689327
E: airton@bronco.co.uk
I: www.mashamcottages.co.uk

The Mews ★★★★
Contact: Mrs J Jameson, Sutton Grange, Masham, Ripon HG4 4PB
T: (01765) 689068
E: jameson1@ukf.net
I: www.themews-masham.com

Mews Cottage ★★★
Contact: Mrs C Hallsworth, 5 Bridge Close, Harleston IP20 9HW
T: (01379) 853020
E: mashamcottage@hotmail.com

Yoredale ★★★★
Contact: Simon, 42 Market Place, Masham, Ripon HG4 4EF
T: (01756) 688707

MELMERBY
North Yorkshire

Field Cottage ★★★
Contact: Mrs Nadine Bell, Country Hideaways, Margaret's Cottage, West Burton, Askrigg, Leyburn DL8 4JN
T: (01969) 663559
F: (01969) 663559
E: nadine@countryhideaways.co.uk
I: www.countryhideaways.co.uk

West Close Cottage ★★★
Contact: Mrs Nadine H Bell, Country Hideaways, Margaret's Cottage, West Burton, Askrigg, Leyburn DL8 4JN
T: (01969) 663559
F: (01969) 663559
E: nadine@countryhideaways.co.uk
I: www.countryhideaways.co.uk

MELTHAM
West Yorkshire

Constance Cottage ★★★★
Contact: Mr Esposito & Ms J B Jackman, 148 Huddersfield Road, Meltham, Huddersfield HD9 4AL
T: (01484) 851811

Cuish Cottages ★★★★
Contact: Mrs Mairi Binns, 5 Cliff Hill Court, Holmfirth, Huddersfield HD9 1JF
T: (01484) 681532
E: martin@crepes.freeserve.co.uk

MENWITH HILL
North Yorkshire

Delves Ridge Cottages ★★★
Contact: Mrs Karen MacLaverty, Delves Ridge Cottages, Menwith Hill, Harrogate HG3 2RA
T: (01943) 880346

MIDDLEHAM
North Yorkshire

Castle Hill Cottage ★★★
Contact: Agent Dales Hol Cot Ref:1506, Dales Holiday Cottages, Carleton Business Park, Carleton New Road, Skipton BD23 2AA
T: (01756) 799821
F: (01756) 797012
E: info@dalesholcot.com
I: www.dalesholcot.com

The Cottage ★★★
Contact: Mrs Jacqueline Welch, 67 Saughton Road North, Kingskerswell, Newton Abbot EH12 7JB
T: (0131) 334 3118

The Garth ★★★
Contact: Mrs Nadine Bell, Country Hideaways, Margaret's Cottage, West Burton, Askrigg, Leyburn DL8 4JN
T: (01969) 663559
F: (01969) 663559
E: nadine@countryhideaways.co.uk
I: www.countryhideaways.co.uk

Honeykiln Cottage ★★★
Contact: Dales Hol Cot Ref:3197, Dales Holiday Cottages, Carleton Business Park, Carleton New Road, Skipton BD23 2AA
T: (01756) 799821
F: (01756) 797012
E: info@dalesholcot.com
I: www.dalesholcot.com

Jade Cottage ★★★★
Contact: Mrs Joanne E Long, Jade Cottage, Market Place, Middleham, Leyburn DL8 4NU
T: (01969) 622858
E: enquiries@jasminehouse.net

Stonecroft ★★★★
Contact: Mrs Best, Chapel Farmhouse, Whaw, Arkengarthdale, Richmond DL11 6RT
T: (01748) 884062
E: chapelfarmbb@aol.com
I: www.middlehamcottage.co.uk

Sunnyside Cottage ★★★
Contact: Dales Hol Cot Ref:2531, Dales Holiday Cottages, Carleton Business Park, Carleton New Road, Skipton BD23 2AA
T: (01756) 799821
F: (01756) 797012
E: info@dalesholcot.com
I: www.dalesholcot.com

Teal Cottage ★★★★
Contact: Country Holidays Ref: 15566, Holiday Cottages Group Owner Services Dept, Spring Mill, Earby, Barnoldswick BB94 0AA
T: 08700 723723
F: (01282) 844288
E: sales@holidaycottagesgroup.com
I: www.country-holidays.co.uk

West Hill ★★★★
Contact: Mrs Nadine Bell, Country Hideaways, Margaret's Cottage, West Burton, Askrigg, Leyburn DL8 4JN
T: (01969) 663559
F: (01969) 663559
E: nadine@countryhideaways.co.uk
I: www.countryhideaways.co.uk

MIDDLESMOOR
North Yorkshire

Abbey Holiday Cottages ★★★★
Contact: Mrs Katrina Holmes, 12 Panorama Close, Pateley Bridge, Bewerley, Harrogate HG3 5NY
T: (01423) 712062
F: (01423) 712776
E: abbeyholiday.cottages@virgin.net

MUKER
North Yorkshire

Corner Cottage ★★★
Contact: Dales Hol Cot Ref:914, Carleton Business Park, Carleton New Road, Skipton BD23 2AA
T: (01756) 799821
F: (01756) 797012
E: info@dalesholcot.com
I: www.dalesholcot.com

Stoneleigh ★★★
Contact: Mr Michael Peacock, Stoneleigh, Stoneleigh Cottage, Muker, Richmond DL11 6QQ
T: (01748) 886375
F: (01748) 886375

MURTON
North Yorkshire

Windy Ridge ★★★★
Contact: Dales Hol Cot Ref:3175, Carleton Business Park, Carleton New Road, Skipton BD23 2AA
T: (01756) 799821
F: (01756) 797012
E: info@dalesholcot.com
I: www.dalesholcot.com

MYTON-ON-SWALE
North Yorkshire

Plump House Farm Cottages ★★★
Contact: Mrs Maxine Walker, York Road, Myton on Swale, York YO61 2RA
T: (01423) 360650
F: (01347) 823184
E: plumphousefarm@aol.com
I: www.plumphousefarm.co.uk

NAFFERTON
East Riding of Yorkshire

Heapfield Cottage ★★★
Contact: Agent Dales Hol Cot Ref:2047, Carleton Business Park, Carleton New Road, Skipton BD23 2AA
T: (01756) 799821
F: (01756) 797012
E: info@dalesholcot.com
I: www.dalesholcot.com

NAWTON
North Yorkshire

Valley View Lodges
Rating Applied For
Contact: Mrs Linda Johnson, Valley View Lodges, Station Road, Nawton, York YO62 7RG
T: (01439) 770555
E: info@valleyviewlodges.co.uk

NEWBIGGIN
North Yorkshire

The Rowans ★★★
Contact: Agent Dales Hol Cot Ref:210, Carleton Business Park, Carleton New Road, Skipton BD23 2AA
T: (01756) 799821
F: (01756) 797012
E: info@dalesholcot.com
I: www.dalesholcot.com

NEWSHAM
North Yorkshire

Dyson House Barn ★★★★
Contact: Mr & Mrs R Clarkson, Dyson House, Newsham, Richmond DL11 7QP
T: (01833) 627365
E: dysonbarn@tinyworld.co.uk
I: www.cottageguide.co.uk/dysonhousebarn

High Dalton Hall Cottage ★★★★
Contact: Mrs Elizabeth Jopling, High Dalton Hall, Newsham, Barningham, Richmond DL11 7RG
T: (01833) 621450
F: (01833) 621450

The Mill Cottage ★★★
Contact: Dales Hol Cot Ref:323, Carleton Business Park, Carleton New Road, Skipton BD23 2AA
T: (01756) 799821
F: (01756) 797012
E: info@dalesholcot.com
I: www.dalesholcot.com

NEWTON-LE-WILLOWS
North Yorkshire

The Shippon ★★★
Contact: Mrs Valerie Nelson, Woodbine House, Newton le Willows, Bedale DL8 1TG
T: (01677) 450227
E: andrew.nelson3@virgin.net
I: www.theshippon.co.uk

NEWTON-ON-OUSE
North Yorkshire

Village Farm Holidays ★★★★
Contact: Mr Wales, Water Street, Oughtershaw, Skipton BD23 1PB
T: (01756) 700510

NEWTON-ON-RAWCLIFFE
North Yorkshire

Hill Rise Cottage ★★★★
Contact: Agent Dales Hol Cot Ref:1617, Carleton Business Park, Carleton New Road, Skipton BD23 2AA
T: (01756) 799821
F: (01756) 797012
E: info@dalesholcot.com
I: www.dalesholcot.com

Hillcrest Cottage ★★★★
Contact: Mrs Orgill, November Cottage, Brinton Road, Stody, Hunworth, Melton Constable NR24 2ED
T: (01263) 862917

Let's Holiday ★★★★
Contact: Mr John Wicks, Let's Holiday, Mel House, Newton-on-Rawcliffe, Pickering YO18 8QA
T: (01751) 475396
E: holiday@letsholiday.com
I: www.letsholiday.com

Manor Farm Cottages ★★★★
Contact: Lady Kirk, Manor Farm Cottages, Manor Farm, Newton-on-Rawcliffe, Pickering YO18 8QA
T: (01751) 472601
F: (01751) 472601
E: emkirkmanorfarm@aol.com
I: www.members.aol.com/ManorfarmNewton

Stable Cottage ★★★
Contact: Mr & Mrs Gardner, The Old Vicarage, Toftly View, Newton-on-Rawcliffe, Pickering YO18 8QD
T: (01751) 476126
E: sueashburn2007@aol.com

Sunset Cottage ★★★★
Contact: Mrs Pat Anderson, Mrs Anderson's Country Cottages, Boonhill Cottage, Newton-on-Rawcliffe, Stape, Pickering YO18 8QF
T: (01751) 472172
E: bookings@boonhill69.freeserve.co.uk
I: www.swiftlink.pnc-uk.net/sc/1236.htm

NORTH COWTON
North Yorkshire

Millstone ★★★
Contact: Sykes Cottages Ref:613, Sykes Cottages, York House, York Street, Chester CH1 3LR
T: (01244) 345700
F: (01244) 321442
E: info@sykescottages.co.uk
I: www.sykescottages.co.uk

NORTH DALTON
East Riding of Yorkshire

Old Cobblers Cottage ★★★
Contact: Miss Chris Wade & Mr Nigel Morton
T: (01377) 217523
F: (01377) 217754
E: chris@adastey.demon.co.uk

NORTHALLERTON
North Yorkshire

The Byre ★★★★
Contact: Mrs M Crowe, The Byre, Hill View Farm, Bullamoor, Northallerton DL6 3QW
T: (01609) 776072

Hill House Farm Cottages ★★★★
Contact: Mr Griffith, Little Langton, Northallerton DL7 0PZ
T: (01609) 770643
F: (01609) 760438
E: info@hillhousefarmcottages.com

2 Summerfield Cottage ★★★
Contact: Mrs S H Holmes, Summerfield House Farm, Welbury, Northallerton DL6 2SL
T: (01609) 882393
F: (01609) 882393
E: sallyhholmes@aol.com

NORTON
North Yorkshire

Anson House
Rating Applied For
Contact: Mrs Susan Camacho, Star Cottage, Welham Road, Norton, Malton YO17 9DU
T: (01653) 694916
F: (01653) 694901

The Cottage ★★★
Contact: Mrs Barber, 69 Welham Road, Norton, Malton YO17 9DS
T: (01653) 693409
E: Patricia.barber@Btinternet.com

NUNNINGTON
North Yorkshire

The Cottage ★★★
Contact: Agent Dales Hol Cot Ref:200, Carleton Business Park, Carleton New Road, Skipton BD23 2AA
T: (01756) 799821
F: (01756) 797012
E: info@dalesholcot.com
I: www.dalesholcot.com

Orchard Cottage ★★
Contact: Mr & Mrs Foxton, Ness Farm, Ness, Nunnington, York YO62 5XE
T: (01439) 748226

Strawberry Cottage ★★★★
Contact: Mrs Angela Ward, Strawberry Cottage, c/o Rosedene, Church Street, Nunnington, York YO62 5US
T: (01439) 748399

OAKWORTH
West Yorkshire

Moorcock Cottage ★★★★
Contact: Dales Hol Cot Ref:2896, Dales Holiday Cottages, Carleton Business Park, Carleton New Road, Skipton BD23 2AA
T: (01756) 799821
F: (01756) 797012
E: info@dalesholcot.com
I: www.dalesholcot.com

OLD BYLAND
North Yorkshire

Tylas Lodge ★★★
Contact: Mrs Jane Holmes, Tylas Farm, Old Byland, York YO62 5LH
T: (01439) 798308
F: (01439) 798461
E: holmesivan@btinternet.com

Valley View Farm ★★★★
Contact: Mrs C S Robinson, Valley View Farm, Old Byland, York YO62 5LG
T: (01439) 798221
E: sally@valleyviewfarm.com
I: www.valleyviewfarm.com

OLD MALTON
North Yorkshire

Coronation Farm Cottage
Rating Applied For
Contact: Mr David Beeley
T: (01653) 698251
E: enquiries@coronationfarmcottage.co.uk
I: www.coronationfarmcottage.co.uk

OSGODBY
North Yorkshire

Sea Views and Sea Views Too ★★★★-★★★★★
Contact: Mr & Mrs O'Connor, 15 Halifax Road, Brighouse HD62AA
T: (01484) 401757
E: pat@oconn100.freeserve.co.uk
I: www.sea-views-scarborough.co.uk

OSMOTHERLEY
North Yorkshire

Monk's Walk ★★★★
Contact: Agent Dales Hol Cot Ref:2041, Carleton Business Park, Carleton New Road, Skipton BD23 2AA
T: (01756) 799821
F: (01756) 797012
E: info@dalesholcot.com
I: www.dalesholcot.com

Weavers Cottage ★★★
Contact: Miss Margaret Cook, Ash View, Battersby, Whitby TS9 6LU
T: (01642) 724123

OSWALDKIRK
North Yorkshire

Angel Cottage ★★★★
Contact: Mrs Jane Sweeney, Wheatfield, Newton Grange, Oswaldkirk, York YO62 5YG
T: (01439) 788493
E: jane.sweeney@lineone.net
I: www.pb-design.com/swiftlink/sc/1325.htm

OXENHOPE
West Yorkshire

Hawksbridge Cottage ★★★
Contact: Mrs Hazel Holmes, 2 Hawksbridge Lane, Oxenhope, Keighley BD22 9QU
T: (01535) 642203

Lynden Barn Cottage ★★★★
Contact: Mrs I Spencer, Lynden Barn, Sawood Lane, Oxenhope, Keighley BD22 9SP
T: (01535) 645074
E: lyndenbarn@ukonline.co.uk
I: members.netscapeonline.co.uk/lyndenbarn/index.html

2 Mouldgreave Cottages
★★★★
Contact: Mrs Mackrell, Mouldgreave House, Mouldgreave, Oxenhope, Keighley BD22 9RT
T: (01535) 642325
F: (01535) 640370
E: mackrells@lineone.net

Yate Cottage ★★★
Contact: Mrs Jean M M Dunn, Yate House, Yate Lane, Oxenhope, Keighley BD22 9HL
T: (01535) 643638
E: jeanandhugh@dunnyate.freeserve.co.uk
I: www.uk-holiday-cottages.co.uk/yatecottage

PATELEY BRIDGE
North Yorkshire

Ashfield House ★★★
Contact: Mr & Mrs Myers, Ashfield House, Ashfield, Pateley Bridge, Bewerley, Harrogate HG3 5HJ
T: (01423) 711491
F: (01423) 711491
E: john.myers@virgin.net
I: www.freespace.virgin.net/john.myers

Blue Plain Cottage ★★★
Contact: Mrs Jane Ninness, 125 Hinckley Road, Stoke Golding, Dadlington, Nuneaton CV13 6ED
T: (01455) 213086
E: ninness@ninness.screaming.net

Grassfield Country Cottage
★★★★
Contact: Country Hols Ref: 9177, Holiday Cottages Group Owner Services Dept, Spring Mill, Earby, Barnoldswick BB94 0AA
T: 08700 723723
F: (01282) 844288
E: sales@holidaycottagesgroup.com
I: www.country-holidays.co.uk

Helme Pasture, Old Spring Wood ★★★★
Contact: Mrs Helme, Old Spring Wood Lodges and Cottages, Hartwith Bank, Summerbridge, Summer Bridge, Harrogate HG3 4DR
T: (01423) 780279
F: (01423) 780994
E: info@helmepasture.co.uk
I: www.oldspringwoodlodges.co.uk

Kirklea Cottage ★★★★
Contact: Mrs Elizabeth Anne Challis, Cobblestone Top, Studfold Farm, Lofthouse, Harrogate HG3 5SG
T: (01423) 755228

Rainbows End ★★★
Contact: Sykes Cottages Ref:61, Sykes Cottages, York House, York Street, Chester CH1 3LR
T: (01244) 345700
F: (01244) 321442
E: info@sykescottages.co.uk
I: www.sykescottages.co.uk

Rolling Mill Stable ★★★
Contact: Sykes Cottages Ref:244, Sykes Cottages, York House, York Street, Chester CH1 3LR
T: (01244) 345700
F: (01244) 321442
E: info@sykescottages.co.uk
I: www.sykescottages.co.uk

PICKERING
North Yorkshire

Barker Stakes Farm ★★★
Contact: Mrs Susannah Hardy, Barker Stakes Farm, Lendales Lane, Pickering YO18 8EE
T: (01751) 476759
F: (01751) 476759
E: barkerstakes@virgin.net

Beech Farm Cottages
★★★★-★★★★★
Contact: Mr & Mrs Pat Massara, Beech Farm Cottages, Wrelton, Pickering YO18 8PG
T: (01751) 476612
F: (01751) 475032
E: holiday@beechfarm.com
I: www.beechfarm.com

Bramwood Cottages ★★★★
Contact: Mr John Butler, 19 Hall Garth, Pickering YO18 7AW
T: (01751) 474066
F: (01751) 475849
E: bramwood19@aol.com
I: www.bramwoodguesthouse.co.uk

Dandelion Cottage
Rating Applied For
Contact: Mr & Mrs Mark & Sandra Ward, 22 Eastgate, Pickering YO18 7DU
T: (01751) 473349

East Kingthorpe House
★★★★
Contact: Mr & Mrs Geoff & Flo Abbott, Buckthorn House, Malton Road, Pickering YO18 8EA
T: (01751) 473848
E: geoffabbott@supanet.com
I: kingthorpe.freeservers.com/

Eastgate Cottages ★★★★
Contact: Mr & Mrs Kevin & Elaine Bedford, Eastgate Cottages, 117 Eastgate, Pickering YO18 7DW
T: (01751) 476653
F: (01751) 471310
E: info@northyorkshirecottages.co.uk
I: www.northyorkshirecottages.co.uk

Easthill Farm House and Gardens ★★★★
Contact: Mrs Diane Stenton, Easthill Farm House and Gardens, Wilton Road, Thornton Dale, Pickering YO18 7QP
T: (01751) 474561
E: info@easthill-farm-holidays.co.uk
I: www.easthill-farm-holidays.co.uk

Eastside Cottage ★★★
Contact: Mrs E Evans, Eastside Farm, Newton upon Rawcliffe, Pickering YO18 8QA
T: (01751) 477204

The Hayloft ★★★
Contact: Ms Karen Auker, Newton-on-Rawcliffe, Stape, Pickering YO18 8QA
T: (01851) 477075
E: granaryhayloft@hotmail.com

27A Hungate ★★★★
Contact: Mrs Diana Ellis, 29 Hartington Close, Dorridge, Solihull B93 8SU
T: (01564) 779573
E: diana@ems-knowle.demon.co.uk

Joiners Cottage ★★★
Contact: Mr P & Mrs C Fisher, Farndale House, 103 Eastgate, Pickering YO18 7DW
T: (01751) 475158

Keld Head Farm Cottages
★★★★
Contact: Mr & Mrs Julian & Penny Fearn, Keld Head Farm Holiday Cottages, Keld Head, Middleton, Pickering YO18 8LL
T: (01751) 473974
E: julian@keldheadcottages.com
I: www.keldheadcottages.com

Lilac Cottage ★★★
Contact: Mr R & Mrs D Munn, Lilac Cottage, 23 Westgate, Pickering YO18 8BA
T: (01751) 472193

Low Costa Mill Cottages
★★★★
Contact: Mrs Eileen Thomas, Costa Lane, Pickering YO18 8LP
T: (01751) 472050
E: thomas@lowcostamill.freeserve.co.uk

Lynton Cottage ★★★
Contact: Dales Hol Cot Ref:2800, Carleton Business Park, Carleton New Road, Skipton BD23 2AA
T: (01756) 799821
F: (01756) 797012
E: info@dalesholcot.com
I: www.dalesholcot.com

New Meadows ★★★
Contact: Mrs K J Hill, New Meadows, 66 Ruffa Lane, Pickering YO18 7HT
T: (01751) 473258

Newton Cottage ★★★
Contact: Mr Tony Danks, Rosamund Avenue, Lockton, Pickering YO18 7HF
T: (01751) 477913
E: mal.danks@btinternet.com

One Oak Lodge ★★★
Contact: Mr Baker, Kirkham Lane, Pickering YO18 7AS
T: (01751) 472200

11 Potter Hill
Rating Applied For
Contact: Mr Michael Jones, 26 Royal Hill, London SE10 8RT
T: (020) 8305 0401
F: (020) 8305 0401
E: michael@cheese-board.co.uk

Rawcliffe House Farm ★★★★
Contact: Mr & Mrs Duncan & Jan Allsopp, Rawcliffe House Farm, Stape, Pickering YO18 8JA
T: (01751) 473292
F: (01751) 473766
E: office@yorkshireaccommodation.com
I: www.yorkshireaccommodation.com

The Sidings ★★★
Contact: Mr & Mrs Lloyd & Liz Varley, 21 Redwood, Compton Acres, West Bridgford, Nottingham NG2 7UL
T: (0115) 945 5543
F: (0115) 945 5543
E: varleyfm@supanet.com

Skelton Cottage & Rowntree Cottages ★★★★
Contact: Mr & Mrs Kevin & Elaine Bedford, 117 Eastgate, Pickering YO18 7DW
T: (01751) 476653
F: (01751) 471310
E: info@northyorkshirecottages.co.uk
I: www.northyorkshirecottages.co.uk

South View Cottages
★★★-★★★★
Contact: Mr Simpson, 107 Church Street, Whitby YO22 4DE
T: (01937) 832192
E: info@southviewcottage.co.uk

1 Tannery Cottages ★★★
Contact: Mr & Mrs Robert and Diana Ellis, 29 Hartington Close, Dorridge, Solihull B93 8SU
T: (015464) 779573
F: 0870 052 5303
E: bob@ems-knowle.demon.co.uk

Town End Farm Cottage ★★★
Contact: Mr Peter Holmes, Town End Farm Cottage, Eastfield Road, Pickering YO18 7HU
T: (01751) 472713

Upper Carr Chalet and Touring Park ★★★
Contact: Mr M Harker, Upper Carr Chalet and Touring Park, Upper Carr Lane, Malton Road, Pickering YO18 7JP
T: (01751) 473115
F: (01751) 473115
E: harker@uppercarr.demon.co.uk
I: www.upercarr.demon.co.uk

1 Westgate
Rating Applied For
Contact: Miss S Toothill, 2 Summerfields Drive, Blaxton, Doncaster DN9 3BG
T: (01302) 770601

White Lodge Cottage ★★★
Contact: Mrs Briggs, White Lodge Cottage, 54 Eastgate, Pickering YO18 7DU
T: (01751) 473897

PORT MULGRAVE
North Yorkshire

Haefen Cottage ★★★
Contact: Dales Hol Cot Ref:2522, Carleton Business Park, Carleton New Road, Skipton BD23 2AA
T: (01756) 799821
F: (01756) 797012
E: info@dalesholcot.com
I: www.dalesholcot.com

PRESTON-UNDER-SCAR
North Yorkshire

Anna's Cottage at Rocky View ★★★
Contact: Mrs Nadine H Bell, Country Hideaways, Margaret's Cottage, West Burton, Askrigg, Leyburn DL8 4JN
T: (01969) 663559
F: (01969) 663559
E: nadine@countryhideaways.co.uk
I: www.countryhideaways.co.uk

Croxford Cottage Rating Applied For
Contact: Ms Hannah Cook, Carleton Business Park, Carleton New Road, Skipton BD23 2AA
T: (01756) 799821
F: (01756) 797012
E: info@dalesholcot.com
I: www.dalesholcot.com

Mallyan Wynd ★★
Contact: Mrs Nadine H Bell, Country Hideaways, Margaret's Cottage, West Burton, Askrigg, Leyburn DL8 4JN
T: (01969) 663559
F: (01969) 663559
E: nadine@countryhideaways.co.uk
I: www.countryhideaways.co.uk

PRIMROSE VALLEY
North Yorkshire

Calm Waters Bungalow ★★★
Contact: Dales Hol Cot Ref:2478, Carleton Business Park, Carleton New Road, Skipton BD23 2AA
T: (01756) 799821
F: (01756) 797012
E: info@dalesholcot.com
I: www.dalesholcot.com

RATHMELL
North Yorkshire

Layhead Farm Cottages ★★★★
Contact: Mrs H R Hyslop, Field House, Rathmell, Settle BD24 0LD
T: (01729) 840234
F: (01729) 840775
E: rosehyslop@layhead.co.uk
I: www.layhead.co.uk

RAVENSCAR
North Yorkshire

Raven Lea ★★★★
Contact: Mrs Turner, Raven Lea, Station Road, Ravenscar, Scarborough YO13 0LX
T: (01723) 870949
E: ravenlea@ic24.net

Smugglers Rock Country House ★★★-★★★★
Contact: Mrs Sharon Gregson, Smugglers Rock Country House, Staintondale Road, Ravenscar, Scarborough YO13 0ER
T: (01723) 870044
E: info@smugglersrock.co.uk
I: www.smugglersrock.co.uk

RAVENSWORTH
North Yorkshire

Beckside Barn ★★★
Contact: Sykes Ref 893, Sykes Cottages, York House, York Street, Chester CH1 3LR
T: (01244) 345700
F: (01244) 321442
E: info@sykescottages.co.uk
I: www.sykescottages.co.uk

REETH
North Yorkshire

Barn End Cottage Ref 3639 Rating Applied For
Contact: Miss Ruth Henderson, Dales Holiday Cottages, Carleton Business Park, Carleton New Road, Skipton BD23 2AA
T: (01756) 799821
F: (01756) 797012

Burton House, Greystones, Turbine House and Charlies Stable★★★★
Contact: Mrs Procter, Hill Cottage, Reeth, Richmond DL11 6SQ
T: (01748) 884273
E: cprocter@aol.com
I: www.uk-cottages.com

The Cobbles Cottage ★★
Contact: Mrs Kate Empsall, Whitfield/Askrigg Cottages, Askrigg, Leyburn DL8 3JF
T: (01969) 650565
F: (01969) 650565
E: empsall@askrigg-cottages.co.uk
I: www.askrigg.yorks.net

St Andrews Chapel ★★★
Contact: Mr David & Sarah Don Bown, The Old Wesleyan Chapel, Marrick, Richmond DL11 7LQ
T: (01748) 884792
E: sarah@twochapels.free-online.co.uk
I: www.twochapels.free-online.co.uk

Swaledale Cottages ★★★★
Contact: Mrs Janet Hughes, Swaledale Cottages, Thiernswood Hall, Healaugh, Richmond DL11 6UJ
T: (01748) 884526
F: (01748) 884834

Winmaur Cottage ★★★★
Contact: Dales Hol Cot Ref:2995, Carleton Business Park, Carleton New Road, Skipton BD23 2AA
T: (01756) 799821
F: (01756) 797012
E: info@dalesholcot.com
I: www.dalesholcot.com

Wraycroft Holiday Cottages ★★★★
Contact: Mrs F Hodgson, Wraycroft Holiday Cottages, Wraycroft, Reeth, Richmond DL11 6SU
T: (01748) 884497
F: (01748) 884497

REIGHTON
North Yorkshire

St Helen's Cottage ★★★★★
Contact: Mrs Janice T Carter, Hilla Green Farm, Hackness, Scarborough YO13 0BS
T: (01723) 882274
F: (01723) 882274

RICHMOND
North Yorkshire

Barn Owl Cottage and Kingfisher Cottage★★★★
Contact: Mr & Mrs George Fothergill, Barn Owl Cottage and Kingfisher Cottage, Red House Farm, Easby, Brompton-on-Swale, Richmond DL10 7EU
T: (01748) 822038

The Bungalow ★★★
Contact: Mr CH Ref: 5527, Holiday Cottages Group Owner Services Dept, Spring Mill, Earby, Barnoldswick BB94 0AA
T: 08700 723723
F: (01282) 841539
E: sales@holidaycottagesgroup.com
I: www.country-holidays.co.uk

Castle View ★★★★
Contact: English Country Cottages, Stoney Bank, Earby, Barnoldswick BB94 0AA
T: 0870 585 1155
F: 0870 585 1150
I: www.english-country-cottages.co.uk

Chestnut Cottage ★★★
Contact: Mr & Mrs P Donaldson, Cowstand Farm, Catterick, Richmond DL10 7PP
T: (01748) 811911
E: pdonal5069@aol.com
I: www.cottageguide.co.uk/chestnutcottage

Coach House ★★★★
Contact: Mrs M F Turnbull, Coach House, Whashton Springs Farm, Whashton, Richmond DL11 7JS
T: (01748) 822884
F: (01748) 826285
E: whashton@turnbullg.freeserve.co.uk
I: www.whashtonsprings.co.uk

Croft Cottage ★★
Contact: Mrs Wakeling-Stretton, 5 Vermont Grove, Richmond CV31 1SE
T: (01926) 428784
E: stretton7@aol.com

Fox Cottage ★★★
Contact: Mr & Mrs D J Fryer, 17 High Green, Catterick, Richmond DL10 7LN
T: (01748) 811772

Fryers Cottage ★★★
Contact: Mr & Mrs Oliver & Valerie Blease, 26 Newbiggin, Richmond DL10 4DT
T: (01748) 823344
F: (01748) 821319

Nuns Cottage Yard ★★★
Contact: Mrs Susan Parks, 5 Hurgill Road, Richmond DL10 4AR
T: (01748) 822809
F: (01429) 864320
E: nunscottage@richmond.org.uk
I: richmond.org.uk/business/nunscottage

Rose Cottage ★★★★
Contact: Mr David Hunt, 11 Richmond Road, Skeeby, Richmond DL10 5DR
T: (01748) 823080
E: huntsholidays@hotmail.com
I: www.huntsholidays.co.uk

Thornlea Cottage ★★★
Contact: Mr Sykes, Sykes Cottages, York House, York Street, Chester CH1 3LR
T: (01244) 345700
F: (01244) 321442
E: info@sykescottages.co.uk
I: www.sykescottages.co.uk

RILLINGTON
North Yorkshire

Thorpe-Rise ★★★
Contact: Mrs Marilyn Legard, Thorpe-Rise, 10 High Street, Rillington, Malton YO17 8LA
T: (01944) 758446

RIPLEY
North Yorkshire

The Old Smithy ★★★★★
Contact: Mrs Lesley Halliday, PO Box 177, Horsforth, Leeds LS18 5WZ
T: (0113) 258 4212
F: (0113) 281 9455

RIPON
North Yorkshire

Bondgate Green ★★★
Contact: Mrs Norris, Downe, Baldersby, Thirsk YO7 4PP
T: (01765) 640283
E: BondgateGreen@aol.com

22 Doublegates Court ★★★
Contact: Mrs Peggy Wilding, 9 Stephenson Close, Knaresborough HG5 8EG
T: (01423) 797068
E: peggywilding@yahoo.co.uk

Intake ★★★★
Contact: Mrs K F McConnell, 3 Hippingstones Lane, Corbridge NE45 5JP
T: (01434) 632812
F: (01434) 633825
E: kfiona@tiscali.co.uk

Mallorie Bungalow ★★★
Contact: Agent Dales Hol Cot Ref:2176, Carleton Business Park, Carleton New Road, Skipton BD23 2AA
T: (01756) 799821
F: (01756) 797012
E: info@dalesholcot.com
I: www.dalesholcot.com

Waterfront House ★★★★★
Contact: Mrs Lesley Halliday, PO Box 177, Horsforth, Leeds LS18 5WZ
T: (0113) 258 4212
F: (0113) 281 9455

RISHWORTH
West Yorkshire

Kit Hill Cottage at Pike End Farm ★★★★
Contact: Mrs Caroline Ryder
T: (01422) 823949
F: (01422) 824626
E: carolineryder@pikeendfarm.net
I: www.pikeendfarm.net

The Old Post Office Rating Applied For
Contact: Mr Steven Edwards, Calder House, 264 Oldham Road, Rishworth, Sowerby Bridge HX6 4QB
T: (01422) 823840

ROBIN HOOD'S BAY
North Yorkshire

1 and 2 Wragby Barn ★★★★
Contact: Mrs Fenby, Whin Sill, Station Road, Robin Hoods Bay, Whitby YO22 4RA
T: (01947) 880719
F: (01947) 880719
E: marilyn@fenby.fsbusiness.co.uk

Farsyde House Farm Cottages ★★★-★★★★★
Contact: Mrs A Green, Farsyde House Farm Cottages, Robin Hood's Bay, Whitby YO22 4UG
T: (01947) 880249
F: (01947) 880877
E: farsydestud@talk21.com

Inglenook ★★★★
Contact: Mrs Lesley Abbott, 7 Goodwood Grove, York YO24 1ER
T: (01904) 622059
F: (01904) 622059
I: www.inglenook-cottage.co.uk

Lingers Hill ★★★
Contact: Mrs F Harland, Lingers Hill Farm, Thorpe Lane, Robin Hood's Bay, Whitby YO22 4TQ
T: (01947) 880608

4 Martin's Row ★★★
Contact: Mrs Adele Thompson & Vanessa Hickings, Whitby Holiday Cottages, 47 Flowergate, Whitby YO21 3BB
T: (01947) 603010
F: (01947) 821133
E: enquiries@whitby-cottages.co.uk
I: www.whitby-cottages.co.uk

Meadowcroft
Rating Applied For
Contact: Mrs Adele Thompson & Vanessa Hickings, Whitby Holiday Cottages, 47 Flowergate, Whitby YO21 3BB
T: (01947) 603010
F: (01947) 821133
E: enquiries@whitby-cottages.co.uk
I: www.whitby-cottages.co.uk

The Moorings ★★
Contact: Mrs Adele Thompson, Whitby Holiday Cottages, 47 Flowergate, Whitby YO21 3BB
T: (01947) 603010
F: (01947) 821133
E: enquiries@whitby-cottages.co.uk
I: www.whitby-cottages.co.uk

The White Owl Holiday Apartments ★★★
Contact: Mr David Higgins, The White Owl Holiday Apartments, Station Road, Robin Hood's Bay, Robin Hood's Bay, Whitby YO22 4RL
T: (01947) 880879
E: higgins@whiteowlrhb.freeserve.co.uk

ROSEDALE ABBEY
North Yorkshire

Coach House ★★★★
Contact: Mrs L Sugars, Coach House, Sevenford House, Rosedale Abbey, Pickering YO18 8SE
T: (01751) 417283
F: (01751) 417505
E: sevenford@aol.com
I: www.sevenford.com

Craven Garth Holiday Cottages ★★★
Contact: Mrs Ena Dent, Craven Garth Holiday Cottages, Craven Garth Farm, Rosedale Abbey, Pickering YO18 8RH
T: (01751) 417506
F: (01751) 417506
E: ena@cravengarth.com
I: www.cravengarth.com

Rowan Cottage ★★★
Contact: Dales Hol Cot Ref:2566, Carleton Business Park, Carleton New Road, Skipton BD23 2AA
T: (01756) 799821
F: (01756) 797012
E: info@dalesholcot.com
I: www.dalesholcot.com

Stable Cottage ★★★
Contact: Mrs Christine Ewington, Stable Cottage, Medds Farmhouse, Thorgill, Rosedale Abbey, Pickering YO18 8SQ
T: (01751) 417583
E: holidays@medds.co.uk
I: www.medds.co.uk

White Horse Farm ★★★
Contact: Mrs Penny Biglin, White Horse Farm Hotel, Gill Lane, Rosedale Abbey, Pickering YO18 8SE
T: (01751) 417239
E: sales@whitehorsefarmhotel.co.uk

Woodlea ★★★★
Contact: Mr Mark Belt, 2 Low Green, Askham Bryan, York YO23 3SB
T: (01904) 705549
F: (01904) 709420
E: m.belt@daviscoleman.com

ROSEDALE EAST
North Yorkshire

East Coast Holiday Bungalows Briar Cottage & Florence Terrace★★★
Contact: Mrs Lorraine Johnson, 8 Florence Terrace, Rosedale East, Pickering YO18 8RJ
T: (01751) 417785

1 Hill Houses ★★★
Contact: Mrs Harrison, 28 George Street, Driffield YO25 6RA
T: (01377) 253042
E: mary.harrison@btinternet.com

RUSWARP
North Yorkshire

Croft Farm Holiday Cottages ★★★★
Contact: Ms Emma Carpenter, 1 Croft Farm, The Avenue, Whitby YO21 1NY
E: ejc@dircon.co.uk

Egton Cottage ★★★
Contact: Sykes Cottages Ref:734, Sykes Cottages, York House, York Street, Chester CH1 3LR
T: (01244) 345700
F: (01244) 321442
E: info@sykescottages.co.uk
I: www.sykescottages.co.uk

Esk Moor Cottage ★★★
Contact: Mrs Marion Corner & Pauline Walker, 15 Mulgrave Road, Whitby YO21 3JS
T: (01947) 605836

Esk View Cottage ★★★
Contact: Dales Hol Cot Ref:1912, Carleton Business Park, Carleton New Road, Skipton BD23 2AA
T: (01756) 799821
F: (01756) 797012
E: info@dalesholcot.com
I: www.dalesholcot.com

Maybeck Cottage ★★★
Contact: Agent Dales Hol Cot Ref:1674, Carleton Business Park, Carleton New Road, Skipton BD23 2AA
T: (01756) 799821
F: (01756) 797012
E: info@dalesholcot.com
I: www.dalesholcot.com

Skipper Lodge ★★★
Contact: Mrs Adele Thompson & Vanessa Hickings, Whitby Holiday Cottages, 47 Flowergate, Whitby YO21 3BB
T: (01947) 603010
F: (01947) 821133
E: enquiries@whitby-cottages.co.uk
I: www.whitby-cottages.co.uk

Turnerdale Cottage ★★★★★
Contact: Mr David Haycox & Mrs Sue Brooks, Shoreline Cottages, PO Box 135, Thorner, Leeds LS14 3XJ
T: (0113) 244 8410
F: (0113) 244 9826
E: reservations@shoreline-cottages.com
I: www.shoreline-cottages.com

SALTAIRE
West Yorkshire

Overlookers Cottage ★★★★
Contact: Mrs Anne Heald, 2 Victoria Road, Saltaire, Shipley BD18 3LA
T: (01274) 774993
F: (01274) 774464
I: www.saltaire.yorks.com/touristinfo/overlookers.html

SALTON
North Yorkshire

Dove Court ★★★★
Contact: Mrs Helen Earnshaw, Dove Court, Sparrow Hall, Salton, York YO62 6RW
T: (01751) 431697
E: helen@dovecourt.com
I: www.dovecourt.com

SALTWICK BAY
North Yorkshire

Brook House Barn ★★★
Contact: Agent Dales Hol Cot Ref:1340, Carleton Business Park, Carleton New Road, Skipton BD23 2AA
T: (01756) 799821
F: (01756) 797012
E: info@dalesholcot.com
I: www.dalesholcot.com

SANDSEND
North Yorkshire

Caedmon House
Rating Applied For
Contact: Mrs Sue Brooks, Shoreline Cottages, PO Box 135, Thorner, Leeds LS14 3XJ
T: (0113) 244 8410
F: (0113) 244 9826
E: reservations@shoreline-cottages.com

Harlow Cottage ★★★★
Contact: Mrs Brooks, Shoreline Cottages, PO Box 135, Thorner, Leeds LS14 3XJ
T: (0113) 244 8410
F: (0113) 244 9826
E: reservations@shoreline-cottages.com
I: www.shoreline-cottages.com

Howdale Cottage ★★★★
Contact: Mrs Adele Thompson & Vanessa Hickings, Whitby Holiday Cottages, 47 Flowergate, Whitby YO21 3BB
T: (01947) 603010
F: (01947) 821133
E: enquiries@whitby-cottages.co.uk
I: www.whitby-cottages.co.uk

Melrose ★★★
Contact: Mrs Adele Thompson & Vanessa Hickings, Whitby Holiday Cottages, 47 Flowergate, Whitby YO21 3BB
T: (01947) 603010
F: (01947) 821133
E: enquiries@whitby-cottages.co.uk
I: www.whitby-cottages.co.uk

Pebble Cottage Ref 3502
Rating Applied For
Contact: Miss Ruth Henderson, Dales Holiday Cottages, Carleton Business Park, Carleton New Road, Skipton BD23 2AA
T: (01756) 799821
F: (01756) 797021

Plovers Nest ★★★★
Contact: Dales Hol Cot Ref:2785, Dales Holiday Cottages, Carleton Business Park, Carleton New Road, Skipton BD23 2AA
T: (01756) 799821
F: (01756) 797012
E: info@dalesholcot.com
I: www.dalesholcot.com

Prospect House, Flat 1 ★★★★
Contact: Mrs Adele Thompson & Vanessa Hickings, 47 Flowergate, Whitby YO21 3BB
T: (01947) 603010
F: (01947) 821133
E: enquiries@whitby-cottages.co.uk
I: www.whitby-cottages.co.uk

Prospect House Flat 3 ★★★★
Contact: Mrs Adele Thompson & Vanessa Hickings, Whitby Holiday Cottages, 47 Flowergate, Whitby YO21 3BB
T: (01947) 603010
F: (01947) 821133
E: enquiries@whitby-cottages.co.uk
I: www.whitby-cottages.co.uk

Puzzle Corner ★★★
Contact: Agent Dales Hol Cot Ref:1679, Carleton Business Park, Carleton New Road, Skipton BD23 2AA
T: (01756) 799821
F: (01756) 797012
E: info@dalesholcot.com
I: www.dalesholcot.com

2 Sunnyside ★★★
Contact: Mrs Adele Thompson & Vanessa Hickings, Whitby Holiday Cottages, 47 Flowergate, Whitby YO21 3BB
T: (01947) 603010
F: (01947) 821133
E: enquiries@whitby-cottages.co.uk
I: www.whitby-cottages.co.uk

Toll Bar ★★★★
Contact: Agent Dales Hol Cot Ref:2243, Carleton Business Park, Carleton New Road, Skipton BD23 2AA
T: (01756) 799821
F: (01756) 797012
E: info@dalesholcot.com
I: www.dalesholcot.com

Woodbine Cottage ★★★
Contact: Mrs Adele Thompson & Vanessa Hickings, Whitby Holiday Cottages, 47 Flowergate, Whitby YO21 3BB
T: (01947) 603010
F: (01947) 821133
E: enquiries@whitby-cottages.co.uk
I: www.whitby-cottages.co.uk

SAWLEY
North Yorkshire

Lacon Hall Cottages ★★
Contact: Mr & Mrs A C Cook, Lacon Hall Cottages, Lacon Hall, Sawley, Ripon HG4 3EE
T: (01765) 620658

Sawley Arms Cottages ★★★★
Contact: Mrs June Hawes, Sawley Arms, Sawley, Ripon HG4 3EQ
T: (01765) 620642
F: (01765) 620642

SCALBY
North Yorkshire

Away From The Madding Crowd ★★★★
Contact: Mr & Mrs Peter Ward, Spring Farm, Scalby Nabs, Scalby, Scarborough YO13 0SL
T: (01723) 360502

Barmoor Farmhouse Holiday Cottages ★★★★
Contact: Mr D A Sharp, 16 Throxenby Lane, Newby, Scarborough YO12 5HW
T: (01723) 363256

SCARBOROUGH
North Yorkshire

Abbey Holiday Flats ★★
Contact: Mrs Catherine Cook, 7-8 Fort Terrace, Bridlington YO15 2PE
T: (01262) 677819
E: holiday-flats@abbey-flats.fsnet.co.uk

Atlantis Holiday Flats ★★
Contact: Mrs Ros Dyson, Atlantis Holiday Flats, 73 Queen's Parade, Scarborough YO12 7HT
T: (01723) 375087
F: (01723) 375087

Avenwood Apartments ★★
Contact: Mr D I Atkinson, Avenwood Apartments, 129 Castle Road, Scarborough YO11 1HX
T: (01723) 374640
E: dave@avenwood.freeserve.co.uk

Avondale Holiday Flats ★★-★★★
Contact: Mrs Norma Dalgleish, Avondale, 75 Queens Parade, Scarborough YO12 7HY
T: (01723) 364836

Bay View Cottage ★★★★
Contact: Ms Sally Jubb, 43 North Street, Scalby, Scarborough YO13 0RP
T: (01723) 378711

Blenheim Holiday Flats ★★-★★★
Contact: Mr & Mrs Denis Middleton, Blenheim Holiday Flats, 7 Blenheim Terrace, Scarborough YO12 7HF
T: (01723) 363643
F: (01723) 363767

Brialene Holiday Apartments ★★-★★★
Contact: Mrs Marlene Witty, Brialene Holiday Apartments, 35-37 Valley Road, Scarborough, Scarborough YO11 2LX
T: (01723) 367158
I: www.scarborough-brialene.co.uk

Broadcliffe Holiday Flats ★
Contact: Mrs Gillian Ryan, Flat 3, Greyfriars, 19 Granville Road, Scarborough YO11 2RA
T: (01723) 374912
F: (01723) 374912
E: broadcliffeflat@amserve.net
I: www.yorkshirecoast.co.uk/broadcliffe

Brompton Holiday Flats ★★★
Contact: Mr Kenneth Broadbent, Selomar Hotel, 23 Blenheim Terrace, Scarborough YO12 7HD
T: (01723) 364964
F: (01723) 364964
E: info@bromptonholidayflats.co.uk

Cherry Trees Holiday Flats ★-★★
Contact: Mrs Helen Sanderson, Cherry Trees Holiday Flats, 72 North Marine Road, Scarborough YO12 7PE
T: (01723) 501433
E: info@cherrytrees.vholiday.co.uk

Chomley Self-contained Holiday Apartments ★★★
Contact: Mrs Witty, Chomley Self-contained Holiday Apartments, 68 Columbus Ravine, Scarborough YO12 7QU
T: (01723) 367292
E: chomley@yahoo.co.uk

Cresta House Flats ★★★★
Contact: Ms L S Dobie, 4 Riversvale Drive, Nether Poppleton, York YO26 6JY
T: (01904) 799703
E: crestahouse@hotmail.com

Cromwell Court ★★★
Contact: Mrs Walker, 9 The Garlands, Scarborough YO11 2SU
T: (01723) 376008
I: www.yorkshirecoast.co.uk/cromwell

Crown Holiday Apartments ★★★★
Contact: Miss Melinda Dowson, 13 Crown Terrace, Scarborough YO11 2BL
T: (01723) 341786

East Farm Country Cottages ★★★★
Contact: Ms Janice Hutchinson, 6 Jameson Crescent, Scarborough YO12 5BZ
T: (01723) 506406
I: www.eastfarmcottages.co.uk

Elizabethan Court ★★★
Contact: Mrs Paula Randall, 43 Church Avenue, Harrogate HG1 4HG
T: (01423) 549436

Executive Apartments ★★★
Contact: Mrs H C Alderwick, 3 Oriel Bank, Scarborough YO11 2SZ
T: (01723) 369043
I: www.s-h-a.dircon.co.uk

Forge Valley Cottages ★★★★
Contact: Mr David Beeley, Main Street, East Ayton, Scarborough YO13 9HL
T: (01653) 698251
F: (01653) 691962
E: enquiries@forgevalleycottages.co.uk
I: www.forgevalleycottages.co.uk

Glaisdale Holiday Flats and Cottage ★★★
Contact: Mr Michael Holliday FHCIMA, Glaisdale Holiday Flats and Cottage, 49 West Street, Scarborough YO11 2QR
T: (01723) 372728
F: (01723) 372728
E: michael.holliday@tesco.net
I: www.s-h-a.dircon.co.uk

Green Gables Hotel Holiday Flats ★★-★★★
Contact: Mrs J McGovern, Green Gables Hotel Holiday Flats, West Bank, Scarborough YO12 4DX
T: (01723) 361005
E: ggables@netcomuk.co.uk

Harbour View Holiday Flats ★★
Contact: Mr David Gordon Jenkinson, Harbour View Holiday Flats, 37/37A Sandside, Scarborough YO11 1PG
T: (01723) 361162

The Hayloft ★★★★
Contact: Mr & Mrs Ray & Lucette Flute, Ingrid Flute Holiday Accommodation, 1 Hillcrest Avenue, Scarborough YO12 6RQ
T: (01723) 376777
F: (01723) 376777
E: info@ingridflute.co.uk
I: www.ingridflute.co.uk

Hydeaway Haven ★
Contact: Mr & Mrs John Hyde, 18 Roslyn Close, Broxbourne EN10 7DA
T: (01992) 465509
F: (020) 8270 6451
E: hydehaven@ntlworld.com

Kimberley Holiday Flats ★★-★★★
Contact: Mr S Costello & Mr G Quilter, Q C Associates, The Gatehouse, Barker Lane, Snainton, Scarborough YO13 9BG
T: (01723) 850552
F: (01723) 859362
E: stagedoorsteve@yahoo.co.uk

Lawnswood ★-★★★
Contact: Mr & Mrs Kevin & Carys Makepeace, 2 Sea View Grove, Scarborough YO11 3JA
T: (01723) 363653
F: (01723) 353521
E: flats@scarborough.co.uk
I: www.scarborough-flats.co.uk

Lendal House ★★★
Contact: Mrs Petra Scott
T: (01723) 372178
E: info@lendalhouse.co.uk
I: www.lendalhouse.co.uk

Marlborough Flats ★★
Contact: Mrs Julie Ellard, Marlborough Flats, 22 Blenheim Terrace, Scarborough YO12 7HD
T: (01723) 373116
E: julieellard@hotmail.com

Meenagoland Holiday Flats ★★-★★★
Contact: Mr & Mrs Joseph McGrath, 5 Weldon Court, Weaponness Park, Scarborough YO11 2UA
T: (01723) 350991

Neville House Apartments ★★★
Contact: Mr & Mrs Smailes, The Rise, 27 Seamer Road, Scarborough YO12 4DU
T: (01723) 366123

Parade Holiday Flats ★★
Contact: Mrs Sue Sayers, 31 Cornelian Avenue, Scarborough YO11 3AN
T: (01723) 374307

Penny Apartments ★-★★★
Contact: Jimmy Corrigan Enterprises, 17-18 Sandside, Scarborough YO11 1PE
T: (01723) 378058

Rambling Rose Holiday Flats ★★★
Contact: Mrs Helen Benson, Rambling Rose Holiday Flats, 3 Marlborough Street, Scarborough YO12 7HG
T: (01723) 351171
E: htbenson007@hotmail.com

Rosewood Holiday Flat ★★★
Contact: Mrs Lynne Redley, 1 Scholes Park Road, Scarborough YO12 6RE
T: (01723) 367696
E: lynne.redley@talk21.com

St Olives Holiday Flats ★★★
Contact: Mr & Mrs John & Elza Fail, 28 New Queen Street, Scarborough YO12 7HJ
T: (01723) 360441
E: enquiries@scarborough-holidayflats.co.uk
I: www.scarborough-holidayflats.co.uk

Sea Vista Holiday Bungalow ★★★★
Contact: Mr & Mrs Alan Roper, Bradford Road, Bingley BD16 1TT
T: (01274) 564741
F: (01274) 548525
E: info@sea-vista.com
I: www.sea-vista.com

Seacliffe Holiday Flats ★-★★
Contact: Mrs Lumley, Manor Farm, East Heslerton, Malton YO17 8RN
T: (01944) 728277
F: (01944) 728277
E: dclumley@scarborough.co.uk
I: www.seacliffeholidays.co.uk

Spikers Hill Country Cottages ★★★
Contact: Mrs J Hutchinson, Spikers Hill Country Cottages, Spikers Hill Farm, West Ayton, Scarborough YO13 9LB
T: (01723) 862537
F: (01723) 865511
E: janet@spikershill.ndo.co.uk
I: www.spikershill.ndo.co.uk

Town Farm Cottages ★★★★
Contact: Mr & Mrs Joe Green, Town Farm, High Street, Cloughton, Burniston, Scarborough YO13 0AE
T: (01723) 870278
E: mail@greenfarming.co.uk
I: www.greenfarming.co.uk

Valley View Holiday Flats ★★
Contact: Mr Wilkinson, Valley View Holiday Flats, 13 Grosvenor Road, Scarborough YO11 2LZ
T: (01723) 364709
F: (01723) 364709
E: valleyview@btconnect.com
I: www.valleyview.org.uk

Victoria House Select Self-contained Holiday Apartments ★★★
Contact: Miss Ann Mason, Coverdale House, 1 Granville Road, South Cliff, Scarborough YO11 2RA
T: (01723) 368854

Vincent Holiday Complex ★★★
Contact: Mr & Mrs Alan & Sandra Hopkins, Vincent Holiday Complex, 42-43 Sandside, Scarborough YO11 1PG
T: (01723) 500997
E: vincents.scarborough@btinternet.com
I: www.s-h-a.dircon.co.uk

Wayside Farm Holiday Cottages ★★-★★★
Contact: Mr & Mrs Peter Halder, Wayside Farm Holiday Cottages, Whitby Road, Cloughton, Scarborough YO13 0DX
T: (01723) 870519

Wheatlands Holiday Flats ★★★
Contact: Mr & Mrs John and Josie Perry, Perry's Court, 1 & 2 Rutland Terrace, Queens Parade, Scarborough YO12 7JB
T: (01723) 373768
F: (01723) 353274
E: john@perryscourthotel.fsnet.co.uk
I: www.perryscourthotel.com

White Acre ★★★
Contact: Mr Squire, 54 Falsgrave Road, Scarborough YO12 5AX
T: (01723) 374220
F: (01723) 366693
E: squiresc@clara.co.uk

White Gable ★★★★
Contact: Mr Squire, 54 Falsgrave Road, Scarborough YO12 5AX
T: (01723) 374220
F: (01723) 366693
E: squiresc@clara.co.uk

Windsor Holiday Flats ★
Contact: Mr Andrew Eadie, 6 Newlands Drive, Manchester M20 5NW
T: (01723) 375986
E: andrew@windsorholidayflats.com

Wrea Head Cottage Holidays ★★★★
Contact: Mr & Mrs Chris & Andrea Wood, Wrea Head Cottage Holidays, Wrea Head House, Barmoor Lane, Scalby, Scarborough YO13 0PG
T: (01723) 375844
F: (01723) 500274
E: ytb@wreahead.co.uk
I: www.wreahead.co.uk

Yorkshire Rose Seaview Holiday Flat ★★★
Contact: Mr & Mrs Benson, Yorkshire Rose Seaview Holiday Flat, 28 Blenheim Terrace, Scarborough YO12 7HD
T: (01723) 351171
E: htbenson@hotmail.com

SCAWTON
North Yorkshire

Forresters Cottage ★★★★
Contact: Mrs Charlotte de Klee, Lockiehead Farm, Berwick-upon-Tweed KY14 7EH
T: (01337) 828217
F: (01337) 828686
E: charlotte@lcokiehead.freeserve.co.uk

SCHOLES
West Yorkshire

1 Cross Barn ★★★★
Contact: Mr & Mrs John & Janet Armitage, Cross Farm, Dunford Road, Scholes, Holmfirth, Huddersfield HD9 2RR
T: (01484) 683664

SCOTCH CORNER
North Yorkshire

5 Cedar Grove ★★★
Contact: Mr & Mrs J P Lawson, The Close, Mill Lane, Cloughton, Scarborough YO13 0AB
T: (01723) 870455
E: jim@lawson5270fsnet.co.uk

SEDBUSK
North Yorkshire

The Coach House ★★★
Contact: Agent Dales Hol Cot Ref:2016, Carleton Business Park, Carleton New Road, Skipton BD23 2AA
T: (01756) 799821
F: (01756) 797012
E: info@dalesholcot.com
I: www.dalesholcot.com

Wagtail Cottage ★★★★
Contact: Mrs Shirley Smith, C/O Mrs A Riley, The Old Goat House, Thornton Rust, Leyburn DL8 3AAN
T: (01969) 650297
E: roger@oldcamms.fsnet.uk
I: www.cottageguide.co.uk/wagtail/

West Cottage ★★★
Contact: Mrs Nadine H Bell, Country Hideaways, Margaret's Cottage, West Burton, Askrigg, Leyburn DL8 4JN
T: (01969) 663559
F: (01969) 663559
E: nadine@countryhideaways.co.uk
I: www.countryhideaways.co.uk

SELBY
North Yorkshire

Lund Farm Cottages ★★★-★★★★
Contact: Mr & Mrs Chris and Helen Middleton, Lund Farm Cottages, Lund Farm, Gateforth, Selby YO8 9LE
T: (01757) 228775
F: (01757) 228775
E: chris.middleton@farmline.com
I: www.lundfarm.co.uk

Rusholme Cottage ★★★
Contact: Mrs Anne Roberts, Rusholme Grange, Drax, Selby YO8 8PW
T: (01757) 618257
F: (01757) 618257
E: anne@rusholmegrange.co.uk
I: www.rusholmegrange.co.uk

SETTLE
North Yorkshire

Cragdale Cottage Rating Applied For
Contact: Mr Paul Whitehead, 75 New North Road, Reigate RH2 8LZ
T: (020) 8288 0505
F: (020) 8288 0505

Devonshire Flat ★★★
Contact: Mr Aspden, Devonshire House, 27 Duke Street, Settle BD24 9DJ
T: (01729) 825781

Hazel Cottage ★★★
Contact: Mrs Jennie Crawford, Moorside Services, Malt Kiln Lane, Thornton, Bradford BD13 3SX
T: (01274) 832368
I: www.country-holidays.co.uk

Ingleborough Cottage ★★★★
Contact: Mr & Mrs Jean Needham, 14 St Leonards Avenue, Lostock, Hawkshaw, Bury BL6 4JE
T: (01204) 696786
E: info@goldielands.co.uk
I: www.goldielands.co.uk

Lock Cottage Rating Applied For
Contact: Sykes Ref 816, Sykes Cottages, York House, York Street, Chester CH1 3LR
T: (01244) 345700
F: (01244) 321442
E: info@sykescottages.co.uk
I: www.sykescottages.co.uk

Old Brew House, Brewhouse Cottage & Robin Hill★★★★
Contact: Mrs Carr, 17 Midland Terrace, Hellifield, Long Preston, Skipton BD23 4HJ
T: (01729) 850319
E: jmcarr@tesco.net
I: www.settle-selfcatering.co.uk

The Old Brewhouse,The Old Brewhouse & Robin Hill ★★★★
Contact: Mrs J M Carr, 17 Midland Terrace, Hellifield, Skipton BD23 4HJ
T: (01729) 850319
E: jmcarr@tesco.net
I: www.settle-selfcatering.co.uk

4 St John's Row ★★★
Contact: Mrs Sowerby, 15 Netherfield Road, Guiseley, Leeds LS20 9DN
T: (01943) 875552
F: (01924) 267341
E: marysowerby@yahoo.com

SEWERBY
East Riding of Yorkshire

Field House Farm Cottages ★★★★
Contact: Mrs Angela Foster, Field House, Jewison Lane, Sewerby, Bridlington YO16 6YG
T: (01262) 674932
F: (01262) 608688
E: john.foster@farmline.com
I: www.field-house-farm-cottages.co.uk

Park Cottage ★★★
Contact: Mrs Sue Ashby, The Old Manse, East Hardwick, Pontefract WF8 3EB
T: (01977) 620359

Peach Tree Cottage ★★★
Contact: Mrs Adams, 15 Redwing Drive, Wansford, Driffield YO25 5HJ
T: (01377) 240650
F: (01377) 272220

Sunnyside Cottages Rating Applied For
Contact: Mr & Mrs Andrew & Caroline Pond, Manor Farm, Newsham Hill Lane, Bempton, Bridlington YO15 1HL
T: (01262) 850680
F: (01262) 850680
E: allponds@btopenworld.com

SHAW MILLS
North Yorkshire

Fern Bank ★★★★
Contact: Mr Wales, Water Street, Oughtershaw, Skipton BD23 1PB
T: (01756) 700510

SHEFFIELD
South Yorkshire

Apartment Nine ★★★★
Contact: Mr Walker-Kane, The Parsonage House, Manchester Road, Thurlstone, Sheffield S36 8QS
T: (01226) 761408

The Clough ★★★★
Contact: Mrs King & Mr N Ritchie, The Clough, Mayfield House, Mayfield Road, Sheffield S10 4PR
T: (0114) 230 1949
F: (0114) 230 2014
E: breking@hotmail.com

The Flat ★★★
Contact: Mrs M J Cox, The Flat, 152 Whirlowdale Road, Sheffield S7 2NL
T: (0114) 221 5553

Hangram Lane Farmhouse ★★★★
Contact: Mrs J Clark, Hangram Lane Farmhouse, Hangram Lane Grange, Hangram Lane, Ringinglow, Sheffield S11 7TQ
T: (0114) 230 3570
F: (0114) 230 6573

Mill Lane Farm Cottage and Orchard Cottage★★★★★
Contact: Miss Jayne Middleton, Mill Lane Farm Cottage and Orchard Cottage, Mayfield Road, Sheffield S10 4PR
T: (0114) 263 0188
F: (0114) 230 6647
E: milllanefarmcottages@hotmail.com
I: milllanefarmcottages.tripod.com

Moor Royd House ★★★-★★★★
Contact: Mrs Janet Hird, Moor Royd House, Manchester Road, Millhouse Green, Penistone, Sheffield S36 9FG
T: (01226) 763353
F: (01226) 763353
E: janet@moorroydhouse.freeserve.uk
I: www.moorroydhouse.com

Sale Hill Lodge ★★★★
Contact: Mrs Geraldine Williams, 40 Stainton Road, Sheffield S11 7AX
T: (0114) 267 8630
F: (0114) 268 6953
E: stayinsheff@hotmail.com
I: www.stayinsheffield.com

SHERBURN
North Yorkshire

Westfield Granary ★★★-★★★★
Contact: Mr Wales, Holiday Cottages (Yorkshire) Ltd, Water Street, Oughtershaw, Skipton BD23 1PB
T: (01756) 700510

SHERIFF HUTTON
North Yorkshire

Grooms Cottage
Rating Applied For
Contact: Mrs Lynne Fawcett, Castle Farm House, Sheriff Hutton, York YO60 6ST
T: (01347) 878311
E: lfawcett@personneltraining.freeserve.co.uk

SILSDEN
West Yorkshire

Croft Cottage ★★★★
Contact: Agent Dales Hol Cot Ref:1622, Carleton Business Park, Carleton New Road, Skipton BD23 2AA
T: (01756) 790919
F: (01756) 797012
E: info@dalesholcot.com
I: www.dalesholcot.com

Ford Cottage ★★★
Contact: Dales Hol Cot Ref:89, Carleton Business Park, Carleton New Road, Skipton BD23 2AA
T: (01756) 799821
F: (01756) 797012
E: info@dalesholcot.com
I: www.dalesholcot.com

SINNINGTON
North Yorkshire

Bridle Cottage ★★★
Contact: Agent Dales Hol Cot Ref:1720, Carleton Business Park, Carleton New Road, Skipton BD23 2AA
T: (01756) 799821
F: (01756) 797012
E: info@dalesholcot.com
I: www.dalesholcot.com

Goose End of Seven House ★★★
Contact: Agent Dales Hol Cot Ref:1779, Carleton Business Park, Carleton New Road, Skipton BD23 2AA
T: (01756) 799821
F: (01756) 797012
E: info@dalesholcot.com
I: www.dalesholcot.com

Pear Tree Barn ★★★★
Contact: Ms Hannah Cook, Carleton Business Park, Carleton New Road, Skipton BD23 2AA
T: (01756) 799821
F: (01756) 797012

Sevenside Holiday Bungalow ★★★
Contact: Mrs Elizabeth Allan, Station House, Sinnington, York YO62 6RA
T: (01751) 431812
E: jdallan@care4free.net

SKIPSEA
East Riding of Yorkshire

Sea Holme Cottage ★★★
Contact: Mrs Susan Allen, Chapel House, Beeford Road, Skipsea, Driffield YO25 8TG
T: (01262) 468663
E: sumic@seaholme.fsnet.co.uk

SKIPTON
North Yorkshire

Airedale House
Rating Applied For
Contact: Mr & Mrs Barrie & Carole Thomas, Airedale House, 20 Gargrave Road, Oughtershaw, Skipton BD23 1PJ
T: (01756) 709581

Cawder Hall Cottages ★★★-★★★★★
Contact: Mr Graham Pearson, Cawder Hall Cottages, Cawder Lane, Skipton BD23 2TD
T: (01756) 791579
F: (01756) 797036
E: info@cawderhallcottages.co.uk
I: www.cawderhallcottages.co.uk

Dales Flat ★★
Contact: Mrs Margaret Little, Skipton Road, Steeton, Keighley BD20 6PD
T: (01756) 791688
F: (01535) 653637

Dalestone ★★★
Contact: Mr & Mrs Ann & Malcolm Wadsworth, 25 Watson Road, Blackpool FY4 1EG
T: (01253) 404726

7 Elliot Street
Rating Applied For
Contact: Mr Wales, Water Street, Oughtershaw, Skipton BD23 1PB
T: (01756) 700510
E: brochure@holidaycotts.co.uk
I: www.holidaycotts.co.uk

Garden Cottage ★★★
Contact: Mrs Barbara Anne Ross, 56 Otley Street, Oughtershaw, Skipton BD23 1ET
T: (01756) 799867

Ginnel Mews ★★★
Contact: Sykes Cottages Ref:46, Sykes Cottages, York House, York Street, Chester CH1 3LR
T: (01244) 345700
F: (01244) 321442
E: info@sykescottages.co.uk
I: www.sykescottages.co.uk

Hallams Yard ★★★
Contact: Dales Hol Cot Ref:255, Carleton Business Park, Carleton New Road, Skipton BD23 2AA
T: (01756) 799821
F: (01756) 797012
E: info@dalesholcot.com
I: www.dalesholcot.com

The Hide ★★★
Contact: Sykes Cottages Ref:617, Sykes Cottages, York House, York Street, Chester CH1 3LR
T: (01244) 345700
F: (01244) 321442
E: info@sykescottages.co.uk
I: www.sykescottages.co.uk

High Malsis Farmhouse ★★★
Contact: Mrs Sheila Fort, High Malsis Farmhouse, High Malsis, Sutton-in-Craven, Keighley BD20 8DU
T: (01535) 633309
I: www.jfort.co.uk/holiday/

The Lodge ★★★★
Contact: Mrs Edith Ann Thwaite
T: (01200) 445300
E: editththwaite@hotmail.com
I: www.thelodgehorton.co.uk

Low Skibeden Farm Cottage ★★★
Contact: Mrs Heather Simpson, Low Skibeden Farmhouse, Harrogate Road, Skipton BD23 6AB
T: (01756) 793849
F: (01756) 793804
E: skibhols.yorksdales@talk21.com
I: www.yorkshirenet.co.uk/accgde.lowskibeden

Maypole Cottage ★★★★
Contact: Mrs Elizabeth Gamble, Blackburn House, Thorpe, Skipton BD23 6BJ
T: (01756) 720609
E: gamble@daelnet.co.uk

None-go-Bye Farm Cottage ★★★
Contact: Mrs Lawn, Grassington Road, Stirton, Skipton BD23 3LB
T: (01756) 793165
F: (01756) 793203
E: cottage@nonegobye.co.uk
I: www.yorkshiredales.net/stayat/nonegobyefarm/index.htm

7 Pasture Road ★★★
Contact: JS&C Lunnon, 17 Cherry Tree Way, Helmshore, Rossendale BB4 4JZ
T: (01706) 230653
E: j.lunnon@blackburn.ac.uk
I: www.cjlunnon.co.uk

SLEDMERE
North Humberside

Life Hill Farm ★★★★
Contact: Mr & Mrs Andrew & Fay Grace, Life Hill Farm, Wetwang, Sledmere, Driffield YO25 3EY
T: (01377) 236224
F: (01377) 236685
E: info@lifehillfarm.co.uk
I: www.lifehillfarm.co.uk

SLEIGHTS
North Yorkshire

April Cottage
Rating Applied For
Contact: Ms Vanessa Hicking, 47 Flowergate, Whitby YO21 3BB
T: (01947) 603010

Bracken Edge ★★★
Contact: Sykes Ref 887, Sykes Cottages, York House, York Street, Chester CH1 3LR
T: (01244) 345700
F: (01244) 321442
E: info@sykescottages.co.uk
I: www.sykescottages.co.uk

Groves Dyke ★★★
Contact: Mr Niall Carson, Woodlands, Sleights, Whitby YO21 1RY
T: (01947) 811404
F: (01947) 810220
E: relax@grovesdyke.co.uk
I: www.grovesdyke.co.uk

The Stable ★★★★
Contact: Dales Hol Cot Ref:2892, Carleton Business Park, Carleton New Road, Skipton BD23 2AA
T: (01756) 799821
F: (01756) 797012
E: info@dalesholcot.com
I: www.dalesholcot.com

SLINGSBY
North Yorkshire

Church Cottage
Rating Applied For
Contact: Ms Ann Beaufoy, 5 Church Street, Kirkbymoorside, York YO62 6AZ
T: (01751) 433121
F: (01751) 433121

Dawson Cottage ★★★
Contact: Mrs Julia Snowball, Harlsey House, Railway Street, Slingsby, York YO62 4AL
T: (01653) 628136
F: (01653) 628413
E: julia.snowball@talk21.com

Home Farm Holiday Cottages ★★★★
Contact: Mr & Mrs Prest, Castle Farm, High Street, Slingsby, York YO62 4AE
T: (01653) 628277
F: (01653) 628277
E: sgprest@farming.co.uk
I: www.yorkshire-holiday-cottage.co.uk

Keepers Cottage Holidays ★★★
Contact: Mrs Joanna Pavey, Railway Street, Slingsby, York YO62 4AN
T: (01653) 628656

SNAINTON
North Yorkshire

Foxglove Cottage ★★★★★
Contact: Mrs Sandra Simpson, The Old Post Office, Thorpe Bassett, Malton YO17 8LU
T: (01944) 758047
F: (01944) 758047
E: ssimpsoncottages@aol.com

SNAPE
North Yorkshire

Jasmine Cottage ★★★
Contact: Mr & Mrs Colette Leyshon, 131 Shackleton Close, Old Hall, Bewsey, Warrington WA5 9QG
T: (01925) 413907
E: jasminecottage@ntlworld.com

SNEATON
North Yorkshire

Rose Cottage ★★★
Contact: Mrs Adele Thompson & Vanessa Hickings, Whitby Holiday Cottages, 47 Flowergate, Whitby YO21 3BB
T: (01947) 603010
F: (01947) 821133
E: enquiries@whitby-cottages.co.uk
I: www.whitby-cottages.co.uk

SNEATON THORPE
North Yorkshire

Rose Cottage Apartment ★★★
Contact: Mrs Eirene Toshach, Rose Cottage Apartment, Rose Cottage, Sneaton Thorpe, Whitby YO22 5JG
T: (01947) 881192
E: info@rosecottageapartment.co.uk

Sorrel Cottage
Rating Applied For
Contact: Mrs Sue Brooks, Shoreline Cottages, PO Box 135, Thorner, Leeds LS14 3XJ
T: (0113) 244 8410
F: (0113) 244 9826
E: reservations@shoreline-cottages.com

SOUTH KILVINGTON
North Yorkshire

Mowbray Stable Cottages ★★★
Contact: Mrs Margaret Backhouse, Mowbray, Stockton Road, South Kilvington, Thirsk YO7 2LY
T: (01845) 522605

SOWERBY
North Yorkshire

Long Acre Lodge ★★★
Contact: Mrs R Dawson, The Lodge, 86A Topcliffe Road, Sowerby, Thirsk YO7 1RY
T: (01845) 522360

The Old Granary ★★★
Contact: Country Hols Ref: 23, Holiday Cottages Group Owner Services Dept, Spring Mill, Earby, Barnoldswick BB94 0AA
T: (01282) 445096
F: (01282) 844288
E: sales@holidaycottagesgroup.com
I: www.country-holidays.co.uk

St Claire House ★★★★
Contact: Mrs Judy Periam, St Claire House, Front Street, Sowerby, Thirsk YO7 1JJ
T: (01845) 526085

SOWERBY BRIDGE
West Yorkshire

Shield Hall Holiday Cottage ★★★
Contact: Mr John R Broadbent, Shield Hall, Shield Hall Lane, Sowerby Bridge HX6 1NJ
T: (01422) 832165

SPEETON
North Yorkshire

Woodbine Farm Holiday Cottages ★★★★
Contact: Mrs Karen Dyson, Speeton, Filey YO14 9TG
T: (01723) 890783

SPROXTON
North Yorkshire

Lavender Cottage
Rating Applied For
Contact: Mr & Mrs Robin & Sue Houlston, 3 Roseacres, Hook, Goole DN14 5PP
T: (01405) 764598
E: robin.houlston@ntlworld.com

Sproxton Hall Cottages ★★★
Contact: Mr Chris Pearson, Ingrid Flute Holiday Accommodation Agency, Bondgate, Helmsley, York YO62 5EZ
T: (01439) 770980
E: info@helmslep.biz

STACKHOUSE
North Yorkshire

Langcliffe Locks
Rating Applied For
Contact: Mr Colin Hibbert, 8 Undercliffe Rise, Ilkley LS29 8RF
T: (01943) 601729
E: catherine.hibbert@blueyonder.co.uk

Woodend ★★★
Contact: Country Hols Ref: 1827, Holiday Cottages Group Owner Services Dept, Spring Mill, Earby, Barnoldswick BB94 0AA
T: 08700 723723
F: (01282) 844288
E: sales@holidaycottagesgroup.com
I: www.country-holidays.co.uk

STAINTONDALE
North Yorkshire

White Hall Farm Holiday Cottages ★★★
Contact: Mr & Mrs James and Celia White, White Hall Farm Holiday Cottages, White Hall Farm, Staintondale, Scarborough YO13 0EY
T: (01723) 870234
E: celia@white66fs.business.co.uk
I: www.whitehallcottages.co.uk

STAITHES
North Yorkshire

The Cottage ★★★
Contact: Mrs Adele Thompson & Vanessa Hickings, Whitby Holiday Cottages, 47 Flowergate, Whitby YO21 3BB
T: (01947) 603010
F: (01947) 821133
E: enquiries@whitby-cottages.co.uk
I: www.whitby-cottages.co.uk

The Cottage ★★
Contact: Mrs Adele Thompson & Vanessa Hickings, Whitby Holiday Cottages, 47 Flowergate, Whitby YO21 3BB
T: (01947) 603010
F: (01947) 821133
E: enquiries@whitby-cottages.co.uk
I: www.whitby-cottages.co.uk

11 Cowbar Cottage ★★★
Contact: Country Holidays, Spring Mill, Earby, Barnoldswick BB94 0AS
T: 08700 723723
E: sales@ttgigh.co.uk
I: www.country-holidays.co.uk

Glencoe ★★
Contact: Rev David Purdy, The Vicarage, Church Street, Kirkbymoorside, York YO62 6AZ
T: (01751) 431452

Roxby Cottage ★★★
Contact: Mrs Adele Thompson & Vanessa Hickings, Whitby Holiday Cottages, 47 Flowergate, Whitby YO21 3BB
T: (01947) 603010
F: (01947) 821133
E: enquiries@whitby-cottages.co.uk
I: www.whitby-cottages.co.uk

Springfields ★★★
Contact: Mrs J Watson, Springfields, 42 Staithes Lane, Staithes, Saltburn-by-the-Sea TS13 5AD
T: (01947) 841465

STAMFORD BRIDGE
East Riding of Yorkshire

The Cottage ★★★★
Contact: Mrs Foster, The Cottage, High Catton Grange, High Catton, Stamford Bridge, York YO41 1EP
T: (01759) 371374
F: (01759) 371374

Sparrow Hall Holiday Cottages ★★★
Contact: Mr & Mrs Nick & Pam Gaunt, 7 Ox Close, Stamford Bridge, York YO41 1JW
T: (01759) 607999

STANBURY
West Yorkshire

High Scholes Cottage
Rating Applied For
Contact: Mrs Catherine O'Leary, Higher Scholes, Oakworth, Stanbury, Keighley BD22 0RP
T: (01535) 646793
E: olly@mopsy66552.freeserve.co.uk

Sarah's Cottage ★★★★
Contact: Mr Brian Fuller, 101 Stanbury, Haworth, Keighley BD22 0HA
T: (01535) 643015
E: brian.fuller2@btinternet.com

Upper Heights Farm ★★★★
Contact: Mr & Mrs Baxter, Upper Heights Farm, Stanbury, Keighley BD22 0HH
T: (01535) 644592
I: brontemoor-breaks.co.uk

STANNINGTON
South Yorkshire

Wesley Cottage ★★★
Contact: Colin MacQueen, Strawberry Lee Lane, Totley Rise, Sheffield S17 3BA
T: (0114) 262 0777
F: (0114) 262 0666
E: enquiries@peakcottages.com
I: www.peakcottages.com

STARBOTTON
North Yorkshire

Horseshoe Cottage
Rating Applied For
Contact: Mrs Lynn May, 7 The Street, Leighterton, Tetbury GL8 8UN
T: (01666) 890336
E: kevin@may1561.fsnet.co.uk

Ivy Cottage (Ref. 3390) ★★★★
Contact: Agent, Carleton Business Park, Carleton New Road, Skipton BD23 2AA
T: (01756) 799821
F: (01756) 797012
E: info@dalesholcot.com
I: www.dales-holiday-cottages.com

STIRTON
North Yorkshire

Cockpit Corner ★★★
Contact: Agent Dales Hol Cot Ref:1699, Carleton Business Park, Carleton New Road, Skipton BD23 2AA
T: (01756) 799821
F: (01756) 797012
E: info@dalesholcot.com
I: www.dalesholcot.com

STOKESLEY
North Yorkshire

Levenside ★★★★
Contact: Agent Dales Hol Cot Ref:2156, Carleton Business Park, Carleton New Road, Skipton BD23 2AA
T: (01756) 799821
F: (01756) 797012
E: info@dalesholcot.com
I: www.dalesholcot.com

STORWOOD

Paradise Leisure
Rating Applied For
Contact: Mrs Valerie Cranmer-Gordon, Paradise Leisure, Ballhall Lane, Storwood, York YO42 4TD
T: (01759) 318452
F: (01759) 318368
E: info@paradiseleisure.com

SUTTON-ON-THE-FOREST
North Yorkshire

K M Knowlson Holiday Cottages ★★★
Contact: Mrs Heather Knowlson, K M Knowlson Holiday Cottages, Thrush House, Well Lane, Sutton-on-the-Forest, York YO61 1ED
T: (01347) 810225
F: (01347) 810225
E: kmkholcottyksuk@aol.com

TERRINGTON
North Yorkshire

The Barn ★★★
Contact: Mrs Jo Gibson, The Barn, Birkdale Farm, Mowthorpe, Terrington, York YO60 6QE
T: (01653) 648301

Terrington Holiday Cottages ★★★-★★★★
Contact: Mrs Sally Goodrick, Terrington Holiday Cottages, 3 Springfield Court, Terrington, York YO60 6PY
T: (01653) 648370
E: goodrick@terrington10.freeserve.co.uk
I: www.terrington10.freeserve.co.uk

THIRSK
North Yorkshire

The Granary ★★★★
Contact: Mrs Mary Harrison, East Farm, Thirlby, Thirsk YO7 2DJ
T: (01845) 597554
E: mary@thegranary36.fsnet.co.uk
I: www.thegranary.20m.com

The Old School House ★★★
Contact: Mrs G Readman, School House, Catton, Thirsk YO7 4SG
T: (01845) 567308

Pasture Field House ★★
Contact: Mrs Emma Hunter, Pasture Field House, Newsham, Borrowby, Thirsk YO7 4DE
T: (01845) 587230
F: (01845) 587230

Poplars Holiday Cottages ★★★★
Contact: Mrs C M Chilton, Poplars Holiday Cottages, The Poplars, Carlton Miniott, Thirsk YO7 4LX
T: (01845) 522712
F: (01845) 522712
E: the_poplars_cottages@btopenworld.com
I: www.yorkshirebandb.co.uk

Shires Court ★★★
Contact: Mrs Judy Rennie, Shires Court, Moor Road, Knayton, Thirsk YO7 4BS
T: (01845) 537494

80 St James Green ★★★
Contact: Mrs Joanna Todd, 79 St James Green, Thirsk YO7 1AJ
T: (01845) 523522

THONGSBRIDGE
West Yorkshire

Mytholmbridge Studio Cottage ★★★★
Contact: Mrs Clay, Mytholmbridge Farm, Luke Lane, Thongsbridge, Holmfirth, Huddersfield HD9 7TB
T: (01484) 686642
E: cottages@mytholmbridge.co.uk

THORALBY
North Yorkshire

High Green Cottage ★★★
Contact: Mr Clive Sykes, Sykes Holiday Cottages, York House, York Street, Chester CH1 3LR
T: (01244) 345700
F: (01244) 321442
E: info@sykescottages.co.uk
I: www.sykescottages.co.uk

Low Green House ★★★★
Contact: Mrs Nadine H Bell, Country Hideaways, Margarets Cottage, West Burton, Leyburn DL8 4JN
T: (01969) 663559
F: (01969) 663559
E: nadine@countryhideaways.co.uk
I: www.countryhideaways.co.uk

Meadowcroft ★★★
Contact: Mr M C Mason, 43 Llythrid Avenue, Uplands, Swansea SA2 0JJ
T: (01792) 280068
F: (01792) 280068
E: mcmason@globalnet.co.uk

The Old Barn ★★★
Contact: Mrs Nadine Bell, Country Hideaways, Margaret's Cottage, West Burton, Askrigg, Leyburn DL8 4JN
T: (01969) 663559
E: nadine@countryhideaways.co.uk
I: www.countryhideaways.co.uk

The Old Corn Mill ★★★
Contact: Mrs Nadine Bell, Country Hideaways, Margaret's Cottage, West Burton, Askrigg, Leyburn DL8 4JN
T: (01969) 663559
F: (01969) 663559
E: nadine@countryhideaways.co.uk
I: www.countryhideaways.co.uk

Woodpecker Cottage ★★★★
Contact: Mrs Nadine H Bell, Country Hideaways, Margaret's Cottage, West Burton, Askrigg, Leyburn DL8 4JN
T: (01969) 663559
F: (01969) 663559
E: nadine@countryhideaways.co.uk
I: www.countryhideaways.co.uk

THORGILL
North Yorkshire

Appledore Cottage ★★★★
Contact: Mrs Emma Glover, St Margaret's Rectory, South Street, Durham DH1 4QP
T: (0191) 384 3623
E: emmag@fish.co.uk

THORNTON DALE
North Yorkshire

Brookwood ★★★★
Contact: Mrs Balderson & Claire Lealman, Brookwood, Welcome Cafe, Thornton Dale, Pickering YO18 7RW
T: (01751) 474272
F: (01751) 472372
E: baldersons@hotmail.com

Hillcroft ★★★
Contact: Country Hols Ref: 1004, Holiday Cottages Group Owner Services Dept, Spring Mill, Earby, Barnoldswick BB94 0AA
T: 08700 723723
F: (01282) 841539
E: sales@holidaycottagesgroup.com
I: www.country-holidays.co.uk

Orchard House ★★★
Contact: Dales Hol Cot Ref:3118, Dales Holiday Cottages, Carleton Business Park, Carleton New Road, Skipton BD23 2AA
T: (01756) 799821
F: (01756) 797012
E: info@dalesholcot.com
I: www.dalesholcot.com

THORNTON IN CRAVEN
North Yorkshire

The Cottage ★★★
Contact: Agent Dales Hol Cot Ref:2166, Carleton Business Park, Carleton New Road, Skipton BD23 2AA
T: (01756) 799821
F: (01756) 797012
E: info@dalesholcot.com
I: www.dalesholcot.com

THORNTON RUST
North Yorkshire

The Old Goat House ★★★★
Contact: Mrs Annette Riley, South View, Thornton Rust, Aysgarth, Leyburn DL8 3AN
T: (01969) 663716
E: riley@oldgoathouse.freeserve.co.uk
I: www.wensleydale.org/accommodation/theoldgoathouse

Outgang Cottage ★★★
Contact: Agent Dales Hol Cot Ref:1468, Carleton Business Park, Carleton New Road, Skipton BD23 2AA
T: (01756) 799821
F: (01756) 797012
E: info@dalesholcot.com
I: www.dales-holiday-cottages.com

THORPE BASSETT
North Yorkshire

The Old Post Office ★★★★
Contact: Mrs Sandra Simpson, The Old Post Office, Thorpe Bassett, Malton YO17 8LU
T: (01944) 758047
F: (01944) 758047
E: ssimpsoncottages@aol.com

THRESHFIELD
North Yorkshire

Brazengate ★★★
Contact: Sykes Cottages Ref:55, Sykes Cottages, York House, York Street, Chester CH1 3LR
T: (01244) 345700
F: (01244) 321442
E: info@sykescottages.co.uk
I: www.sykescottages.co.uk

Dalesgate ★★
Contact: Agent Dales Hol Cot Ref:1006, Carleton Business Park, Carleton New Road, Skipton BD23 2AA
T: (01756) 799821
F: (01756) 797012
E: info@dalesholcot.com
I: www.dalesholcot.com

THURLSTONE
South Yorkshire

The Parsonage House ★★★★
Contact: Mr Walker-Kane, The Parsonage House, Manchester Road, Thurlstone, Sheffield S36 9QS
T: (01226) 761408
F: (01226) 761044

THWAITE
North Yorkshire

The Cottage ★★★
Contact: Mrs Nadine Bell, Country Hideaways, Margaret's Cottage, West Burton, Askrigg, Leyburn DL8 4JN
T: (01969) 663559
F: (01969) 663559
E: nadine@countryhideaways.co.uk
I: www.countryhideaways.co.uk

Greystones ★★★
Contact: Mr Ken Williamson, Askrigg Cottage Holidays, Thwaite House, Moor Road, Askrigg, Leyburn DL8 3HH
T: (01969) 650022
E: stay@askrigg.com
I: www.upperswaledale.co.uk

Thwaite Farm Cottages ★★★-★★★★
Contact: Mrs Gillian Whitehead, Thwaite Farm, Thwaite, Richmond DL11 6DR
T: (01748) 886444
F: (01748) 886444
E: info@thwaitefarmcottages.co.uk
I: www.thwaitefarmcottages.co.uk

Thwaitedale Cottages ★★★★
Contact: Miss Valerie Hunter, 52 Moira Road, Donisthorpe, Burton upon Trent DE12 7QE
T: (01530) 272794
F: (01530) 272794
E: valerie@theturret.freeserve.co.uk
I: www.thwaitecottages.co.uk

Turfy Gill Hall ★★★★
Contact: Mr & Mrs Keith & Ivy Moseley, Turfy Gill Hall, Angram, Richmond DL11 6DT
T: (01748) 886369
F: (01748) 886593
E: info@turfygill.com
I: www.turfygill.com

TICKTON
East Riding of Yorkshire

Bridge House Cottage ★★★
Contact: Mr Peter White & Ms Adele Wilkinson, Bridge House Cottage, Hull Bridge House, Weel Road, Tickton, Beverley HU17 9RY
T: (01964) 542355
E: alw@amj.co.uk

TIMBLE
North Yorkshire

The Old Dairy ★★★★
Contact: Mrs Dawn Meeks, Southcroft, Timble, Otley LS21 2NN
T: (01943) 880363
E: meeksdawn@hotmail.com
I: www.theolddairy.info

TODMORDEN
West Yorkshire

Butterworth Cottage ★★★
Contact: Mr & Mrs Neil and Patricia Butterworth, Butterworth Cottage, Cinder Hill Farm, Cinderhill Road, Todmorden OL14 8AA
T: (01706) 813067
F: 08700 884807
E: bookings@cottage-holiday.co.uk
I: www.cottage-holiday.co.uk

The Cottage ★★★
Contact: Mr & Mrs A Bentham, The Cottage, Causeway East Farmhouse, Lee Bottom Road, Todmorden OL14 6HH
T: (01706) 815265
E: andrew@bentham5.freeserve.co.uk

Stannally Farm Cottage ★★★★
Contact: Mrs Dineen Ann Brunt, Stannally Farm, Stoney Royd Lane, Todmorden OL14 8EP
T: (01706) 813998
F: (01706) 813998
E: Bruntdennis@aol.com

Staups Barn Holiday Cottage ★★★
Contact: Mr & Mrs D Crabtree, Staups Cottage, Staups Lane, Higher Eastwood, Todmorden OL14 8RU
T: (01706) 812730
F: (01706) 812730
I: www.staups1@supanet.com

TOLLERTON
North Yorkshire

Gill Cottage ★★★★
Contact: Dales Hol Cot Ref:1977, Carleton Business Park, Carleton New Road, Skipton BD23 2AA
T: (01756) 799821
F: (01756) 797012
E: info@dalesholcot.com
I: www.dalesholcot.com

UGGLEBARNBY
North Yorkshire

Howlet Hall Farm Cottage ★★★
Contact: Agent Dales Hol Cot Ref:1556, Carleton Business Park, Carleton New Road, Skipton BD23 2AA
T: (01756) 799821
F: (01756) 797012
E: info@dalesholcot.com
I: www.dalesholcot.com

WALSDEN
West Yorkshire

Henshaw Farm Cottage ★★
Contact: Mr Paul Hunt, 9 Outgaits Lane, Hunmanby, Filey YO14 0PX
T: (01723) 891826
E: paulhunt@ukonline.co.uk
I: www.cottagesdirect.com/henshawfarm

WANSFORD
East Riding of Yorkshire

Watersedge Cottage ★★★★
Contact: Dales Hol Cot Ref:3301, Dales Holiday Cottages, Carleton Business Park, Carleton New Road, Skipton BD23 2AA
T: (01756) 799821
F: (01756) 797012
E: info@dalesholcot.com
I: www.dalesholcot.com

WARLEY
West Yorkshire

Greystones Farm Cottage ★★★★
Contact: Mrs Alison Phillips, Greystones Road, Luddendenfoot, Warley, Halifax HX2 6BY
T: (01422) 882445

WASS
North Yorkshire

High Woods Farm Holiday Cottages ★★★★
Contact: Mr & Mrs Jonathan & Susan Evans, High Woods Farm Holiday Cottages, High Woods Farm, Wass, York YO61 4AY
T: (01347) 868188
E: jon&sue@highwoodsfarm.co.uk
I: www.highwoodsfarm.demon.co.uk

WELBURN
North Yorkshire

Castle View ★★★
Contact: Mr & Mrs Michael Cockerill, West End, Welburn, York YO60 7DX
T: (01653) 618344

Oak Tree Cottage Rating Applied For
Contact: Mr Mark Rees, Oak Tree Cottage, Welburn, York YO60 7DX
E: mark.rees@northyorkshire.pnn.police.uk

WEST BRETTON
West Yorkshire

Parkside Cottage ★★★★
Contact: Mr & Mrs Philip & Joyce Platts, Parkside Cottage, 31 Park Lane, Bretton, West Bretton, Wakefield WF4 4JT
T: (01924) 830215
F: (01924) 830215
E: jmplatts@hotmail.com
I: www.parksidecottage.co.uk

WEST BURTON
North Yorkshire

Cherry Tree Cottage ★★★
Contact: Mrs Nadine H Bell, Country Hideaways, Margaret's Cottage, West Burton, Askrigg, Leyburn DL8 4JN
T: (01969) 663559
F: (01969) 663559
E: nadine@countryhideaways.co.uk
I: www.countryhideaways.co.uk

First Floor Apartment, The Mill ★★★
Contact: Mrs Nadine Bell, Country Hideaways, Margaret's Cottage, West Burton, Askrigg, Leyburn DL8 4JN
T: (01969) 663559
F: (01969) 663559
E: nadine@countryhideaways.co.uk
I: www.countryhideaways.co.uk

The Garden Level Apartment, The Mill★★★
Contact: Mrs Nadine H Bell, Country Hideaways, Margaret's Cottage, West Burton, Askrigg, Leyburn DL8 4JN
T: (01969) 663559
F: (01969) 663559
E: nadine@countryhideaways.co.uk
I: www.countryhideaways.co.uk

Grange House ★★★★
Contact: Mrs Zoe Mort, Walden, West Burton, Leyburn DL8 4LF
T: (01969) 663641

Green Bank ★★★
Contact: Mrs Nadine Bell, Country Hideaways, Margaret's Cottage, West Burton, Askrigg, Leyburn DL8 4JN
T: (01969) 663559
F: (01969) 663559
E: nadine@countryhideaways.co.uk
I: www.countryhideaways.co.uk

The Ground Floor Apartment, The Mill★★★
Contact: Mrs Nadine H Bell, Country Hideaways, Margaret's Cottage, West Burton, Askrigg, Leyburn DL8 4JN
T: (01969) 663559
F: (01969) 663559
E: nadine@countryhideaways.co.uk
I: www.countryhideaways.co.uk

Ivy Cottage ★★★
Contact: Mr Wales, Water Street, Oughtershaw, Skipton BD23 1PB
T: (01756) 700510

Jesmond Cottage ★★★
Contact: Mrs Nadine Bell, Country Hideaways, Margaret's Cottage, West Burton, Askrigg, Leyburn DL8 4JN
T: (01969) 663559
F: (01969) 663559
E: nadine@countryhideaways.co.uk
I: www.countryhideaways.co.uk

Penny Farthings ★★★
Contact: Mrs Nadine H Bell, Country Hideaways, Margaret's Cottage, West Burton, Askrigg, Leyburn DL8 4JN
T: (01969) 663559
F: (01969) 663559
E: nadine@countryhideaways.co.uk
I: www.countryhideaways.co.uk

Post Office Barn ★★★★
Contact: Mrs Nadine H Bell, Country Hideaways, Margarets Cottage, West Burton, Leyburn DL8 4JN
T: (01969) 663559
F: (01969) 663559
E: nadine@countryhideaways.co.uk
I: www.countryhideaways.co.uk

Studio Apartment, The Mill ★★
Contact: Mrs Nadine H Bell, Country Hideaways, Margaret's Cottage, West Burton, Askrigg, Leyburn DL8 4JN
T: (01969) 663559
F: (01969) 663559
E: nadine@countryhideaways.co.uk
I: www.countryhideaways.co.uk

WEST HESLERTON
North Yorkshire

Whin Moor Cottage ★★★
Contact: Agent Dales Hol Cot Ref:1575, Carleton Business Park, Carleton New Road, Skipton BD23 2AA
T: (01756) 799821
F: (01756) 797012
E: info@dalesholcot.com
I: www.dalesholcot.com

WEST WITTON
North Yorkshire

1 Chestnut Garth ★★★
Contact: Sykes Cottages Ref:779, Sykes Cottages, York House, York Street, Chester CH1 3LR
T: (01244) 345700
F: (01244) 321442
E: info@sykescottages.co.uk
I: www.sykescottages.co.uk

Dairy Cottage ★★★
Contact: Mrs Nadine H Bell, Country Hideaways, Margaret's Cottage, West Burton, Askrigg, Leyburn DL8 4JN
T: (01969) 663559
F: (01969) 663559
E: nadine@countryhideaways.co.uk
I: www.countryhideaways.co.uk

The Granary ★★★
Contact: Dales Hol Cot Ref:398, Dales Holiday Cottages, Carleton Business Park, Carleton New Road, Skipton BD23 2AA
T: (01756) 799821
F: (01756) 797012
E: info@dalesholcot.com
I: www.dalesholcot.com

Ivy Dene Cottage ★★★
Contact: Mr Bob Dickinson, Ivy Dene Guesthouse, Main Street, West Witton, Leyburn DL8 4LP
T: (01969) 622785
F: (01969) 622785
E: info@ivydeneguesthouse.co.uk
I: www.ivydeneguesthouse.co.uk

Wrang View and Garth End ★★
Contact: Dales Hol Cot Ref:1117/1118, Carleton Business Park, Carleton New Road, Skipton BD23 2AA
T: (01756) 799821
F: (01756) 797012
E: info@dalesholcot.com
I: www.dalesholcot.com

WHASHTON
North Yorkshire

Mount Pleasant Farm ★★★
Contact: Mrs A Pittaway, Mount Pleasant Farm, Whashton, Richmond DL11 7JP
T: (01748) 822784
F: (01748) 822784
E: info@mountpleasantfarmhouse.co.uk
I: www.mountpleasantfarmhouse.co.uk

WHITBY
North Yorkshire

Abbey Holiday Apartments ★-★★★
Contact: Mr & Mrs Ted & Sandra Smith, 17 Esk Terrace, Whitby YO21 1PA
T: (01947) 820025
E: smiths@tedsandra.co.uk

Abbey View ★★★
Contact: Mrs Adele Thompson & Vanessa Hickings, 47 Flowergate, Whitby YO21 3BB
T: (01947) 603010
F: (01947) 821133
E: enquiries@whitby-cottages.co.uk
I: www.whitby-cottages.co.uk

Abbey View ★★★★
Contact: Mr Peter Simpson, 107 Church Street, Whitby YO22 4DE
T: (01947) 604406

Abbey View Cottage ★★★★
Contact: Mr David Haycox & Mrs Sue Brooks, Shoreline Cottages, PO Box 135, Thorner, Leeds LS14 3XJ
T: (0113) 244 8410
F: (0113) 244 9826
E: reservations@shoreline-cottages.com
I: www.shoreline-cottages.com

Albany Flat ★★★
Contact: Mrs Adele Thompson & Vanessa Hickings, Whitby Holiday Cottages, 47 Flowergate, Whitby YO21 3BB
T: (01947) 603010
F: (01947) 821133
E: enquiries@whitby-cottages.co.uk
I: www.whitby-cottages.co.uk

Albany House ★★★★
Contact: Mrs Adele Thompson & Vanessa Hickings, 47 Flowergate, Whitby YO21 3BB
T: (01947) 603010
F: (01947) 821133
E: enquiries@whitby-cottages.co.uk
I: www.whitby-cottages.co.uk

Ammonite Cottage ★★★
Contact: Dales Hol Cot Ref:3038, Carleton Business Park, Carleton New Road, Skipton BD23 2AA
T: (01756) 799821
F: (01756) 797012
E: info@dalesholcot.com
I: www.dalesholcot.com

The Anchorage ★★
Contact: Sykes Cottages Ref:360, Sykes Cottages, York House, York Street, Chester CH1 3LR
T: (01244) 345700
F: (01244) 321442
E: info@sykescottages.co.uk
I: www.sykescottages.co.uk

Bakehouse Cottage ★★★★
Contact: Mr David Haycox & Mrs Sue Brooks, Shoreline Cottages, PO Box 135, Thorner, Leeds LS14 3XJ
T: (0113) 244 8410
F: (0113) 244 9826
E: reservations@shoreline-cottages.com
I: www.shoreline-cottages.com

Bennison House Farm ★★★★
Contact: Mr & Mrs R G & H E Thompson, Beacon Way, Sneaton, Whitby YO22 5HS
T: (01947) 820292

1 Bensons Yard ★★★
Contact: Mrs Lonsdale, 1 Bensons Yard, Meadowcroft, Oakley Walls, Lealholm, Whitby YO21 2AU
T: (01947) 897472

Breckon Cottage ★★★
Contact: Mrs Adele Thompson & Vanessa Hickings, Whitby Holiday Cottages, 47 Flowergate, Whitby YO21 3BB
T: (01947) 603010
F: (01947) 821133
E: enquiries@whitby-cottages.co.uk
I: www.whitby-cottages.co.uk

Bridle Cottage ★★★
Contact: Mr J J Stanway, Lamberhurst, St Hilda's Terrace, Whitby YO21 3AG
T: (01947) 602725

Brook House Farm Holiday Cottages ★★★★
Contact: Mrs Sallie White, Brook House Farm Holiday Cottages, Brook House Farm, Houlsyke, Whitby YO21 2LH
T: (01287) 660064

Broom Cottage ★★
Contact: Mrs Adele Thompson & Vanessa Hickings, Whitby Holiday Cottages, 47 Flowergate, Whitby YO21 3BB
T: (01947) 603010
F: (01947) 821133
E: enquiries@whitby-cottages.co.uk
I: www.whitby-cottages.co.uk

12A Brunswick Street ★★★
Contact: Mrs Adele Thompson & Vanessa Hickings, Whitby Holiday Cottages, 47 Flowergate, Whitby YO21 3BB
T: (01947) 603010
F: (01947) 821133
E: enquiries@whitby-cottages.co.uk
I: www.whitby-cottages.co.uk

Bumblebee Cottage ★★★
Contact: Mrs Julie Asher, Bumblebee Cottage, 4 Princess Place, Whitby YO21 1DZ
T: (01947) 821803
E: jash@dracula68.fsnet.co.uk

5 Burns Yard ★★★★
Contact: Mrs Adele Thompson & Vanessa Hickings, Whitby Holiday Cottages, 47 Flowergate, Whitby YO21 3BB
T: (01947) 603010
F: (01947) 821133
E: enquiries@whitby-cottages.co.uk
I: www.whitby-cottages.co.uk

Captain Cook's Haven ★★★-★★★★
Contact: Mrs Anne Barrowman, Upton Hall, Lythe, Whitby YO21 3RU
T: (01947) 893573
F: (01947) 893573
I: www.hoseasons.co.uk

Captain's Quarters ★★★★★
Contact: Mrs Brooks, Shoreline Cottages, P O Box 135, Thorner, Leeds LS14 3XJ
T: (0113) 244 8410
F: (0113) 244 9826
E: reservations@shoreline-cottages.com
I: www.shoreline-cottages.com

Carlton House Holiday Accommodation★-★★
Contact: Mrs Susan Brookes, Carlton House Holiday Accommodation, 5 Royal Crescent, West Cliff, Whitby YO21 3EJ
T: (01947) 602868
F: (01947) 602868

Cherry Trees ★★★
Contact: Mr P Dowson, Aislaby, Whitby YO21 1SX
T: (01947) 810324
F: (01747) 810324

Church Cottage ★★★
Contact: Mrs Adele Thompson & Vanessa Hickings, 47 Flowergate, Whitby YO21 3BB
T: (01947) 603010
F: (01947) 821133
E: enquiries@whitby-cottages.co.uk
I: www.whitby-cottages.co.uk

Cliff House ★★
Contact: Mrs Beale, Ryedale House, Coach Road, Sleights, High Normanby, Whitby YO22 5EQ
T: (01947) 810534
F: (01947) 810534

5A Cliff Street ★★★
Contact: Mrs Adele Thompson, Whitby Holiday Cottages, 47 Flowergate, Whitby YO21 3BB
T: (01947) 603010
F: (01947) 821133
E: enquiries@whitby-cottages.co.uk
I: www.whitby-cottages.co.uk

Cobble Cottage ★★★
Contact: Agent Dales Hol Cot Ref:1808, Carleton Business Park, Carleton New Road, Skipton BD23 2AA
T: (01756) 799821
F: (01756) 797012
E: info@dalesholcot.com
I: www.dalesholcot.com

Coble Cottage ★★★
Contact: Mrs Adele Thompson & Vanessa Hickings, 47 Flowergate, Whitby YO21 3BB
T: (01947) 603010
F: (01947) 821133
E: enquiries@whitby-cottages.co.uk
I: www.whitby-cottages.co.uk

Copper Beeches ★-★★
Contact: Mrs Hilary Walker, The Nurseries, Egton, Egton Bridge, Whitby YO21 1TT
T: (01947) 895640
F: (01947) 895641
E: hilary_phenix@hotmail.com

Corner Cottage ★★★★
Contact: Mrs Adele Thompson & Vanessa Hickings, 47 Flowergate, Whitby YO21 3BB
T: (01947) 603010
F: (01947) 821133
E: enquiries@whitby-cottages.co.uk
I: www.whitby-cottages.co.uk

The Cottage ★★★
Contact: Mrs Adele Thompson & Vanessa Hickings, Whitby Holiday Cottages, 47 Flowergate, Whitby YO21 3BB
T: (01947) 603010
F: (01947) 821133
E: enquiries@whitby-cottages.co.uk
I: www.whitby-cottages.co.uk

1 The Croft ★★★★
Contact: Mrs Adele Thompson & Vanessa Hickings, Whitby Holiday Cottages, 47 Flowergate, Whitby YO21 3BB
T: (01947) 603010
F: (01947) 821133
E: enquiries@whitby-cottages.co.uk
I: www.whitby-cottages.co.uk

The Crows Nest ★★★
Contact: Mrs A Thompson, 47 Flowergate, Whitby YO21 3BB
T: (01947) 603010
F: (01947) 821133
E: enquiries@whitby-cottages.co.uk
I: www.whitby-cottages.co.uk

Cuddy Cottage ★★★★
Contact: Mr David Haycox & Mrs Sue Brooks, Shoreline Cottages, PO Box 135, Thorner, Leeds LS14 3XJ
T: (0113) 244 8410
F: (0113) 244 9826
E: reservations@shoreline-cottages.com
I: www.shoreline-cottages.com

Discovery Accommodation ★★★★
Contact: Mrs Pam Gilmore, Milward Properties Ltd, Viking Lodge, Mulgrave Road, Whitby YO21 3JS
T: (01947) 821598
F: (01947) 600406
E: pam@discoveryaccommodation.com
I: www.discoveryaccommodation.com

East Cliff Cottages, Hardwick Cottage★★★
Contact: Dr S M Thornton, Brookhouse, Dam Lane, Leavening, Malton YO17 9SF
T: (01653) 658249
E: enquiries@seasideholiday.co.uk
I: www.seasideholiday.co.uk

Elizabeth House Holiday Flats ★-★★★★
Contact: Mrs Rosaline Cooper, Park View, 14 Chubb Hill Road, Whitby YO21 1JU
T: (01947) 604213
E: jakanann@btopenworld.com
I: www.elizabeth-house.biz

24 Endeavour Court ★★★
Contact: Mrs Adele Thompson & Vanessa Hickings, Whitby Holiday Cottages, 47 Flowergate, Whitby YO21 3BB
T: (01947) 603010
F: (01947) 821133
E: enquiries@whitby-cottages.co.uk
I: www.whitby-cottages.co.uk

7 Esk Terrace ★★★
Contact: Mrs Adele Thompson & Vanessa Hickings, Whitby Holiday Cottages, 47 Flowergate, Whitby YO21 3BB
T: (01947) 603010
F: (01947) 821133
E: enquiries@whitby-cottages.co.uk
I: www.whitby-cottages.co.uk

Fayvan Holiday Apartments ★★★★
Contact: Mr & Mrs Ian & Pauline Moore, Fayvan Holiday Apartments, 43 Crescent Avenue, Whitby YO21 3EQ
T: (01947) 604813
F: (01947) 604813
E: info@fayvan.co.uk
I: www.fayvan.co.uk

Flat 12 ★★★
Contact: Mrs Mohammed, 1 Marine Parade, Whitby YO21 3PR
T: (01947) 604727

Forget-Me-Not ★★★
Contact: Whitby Holiday Cottages, 47 Flowergate, Whitby YO21 3BB
T: (01947) 603010
F: (01947) 821133
E: enquiries@whitby-cottages.co.uk
I: www.whitby-cottages.co.uk

Glencoe - Garden Flat ★★★★
Contact: Mrs Julie Charlton, Glencoe Holiday Flats, 18 Linden Close, Briggs Wath, Whitby YO21 1TA
T: (01947) 811531
F: (01947) 602474

Glencoe Holiday Flats ★-★★★
Contact: Mrs Julie Charlton, 18 Linden Close, Briggswath, Sleights, Whitby YO21 1TA
T: (01947) 811531

Grange Farm Holiday Cottages ★★★★
Contact: Miss D Hooning
T: (01947) 881080
F: (01947) 881080
E: info@grangefarm.net
I: www.grangefarm.net

Greencroft ★★
Contact: Mrs Susan Welford, Greencroft, 9 Esplanade, Whitby YO21 3HH
T: (01947) 603019

Harbour Lights ★★★★
Contact: Mrs Adele Thompson & Vanessa Hickings, 47 Flowergate, Whitby YO21 3BB
T: (01947) 603010
F: (01947) 821133
E: enquiries@whitby-cottages.co.uk
I: www.whitby-cottages.co.uk

Harbourside Apartments ★★★-★★★★
Contact: Mr & Mrs Ian & June Roberts, 51 Church Street, Whitby YO22 4AS
T: (01947) 810763
E: marketing@whiterosecottages.co.uk

Harbourside Cottage ★★★
Contact: Mrs Adele Thompson & Vanessa Hickings, Whitby Holiday Cottages, 47 Flowergate, Whitby YO21 3BB
T: (01947) 603010
F: (01947) 821133
E: enquiries@whitby-cottages.co.uk
I: www.whitby-cottages.co.uk

Henrietta Cottage ★★★★
Contact: Mr David Haycox & Mrs Sue Brooks, Shoreline Cottages, PO Box 135, Thorner, Leeds LS14 3XJ
T: (0113) 244 8410
F: (0113) 244 9826
E: reservations@shoreline-cottages.com
I: www.shoreline-cottages.com

7 Henrietta Street ★★★
Contact: Mr Usher, 2 Southlands Avenue, Whitby YO21 3DY
T: (01947) 605868

Hightrees Garden Apartment ★★★
Contact: Miss Sarah Elizabeth Clancy, 34A Bagdale, Whitby YO21 1QL
T: (01947) 601926

8 Horse Road ★★★
Contact: Whitby Holiday Cottages, 47 Flowergate, Whitby YO21 3BB
T: (01947) 603010
F: (01947) 821133
E: enquiries@whitby-cottages.co.uk
I: www.whitby-cottages.co.uk

5 Hydings Yard ★★★
Contact: Mrs Adele Thompson & Vanessa Hickings, Whitby Holiday Cottages, 47 Flowergate, Whitby YO21 3BB
T: (01947) 603010
F: (01947) 821133
E: enquiries@whitby-cottages.co.uk
I: www.whitby-cottages.co.uk

Jet Cottage ★★★
Contact: Mrs Adele Thompson & Vanessa Hickings, 47 Flowergate, Whitby YO21 3BB
T: (01947) 603010
F: (01947) 821133
E: enquiries@whitby-cottages.co.uk
I: www.whitby-cottages.co.uk

Kiln Cottage ★★★★
Contact: Mr David Haycox & Mrs Sue Brooks, Shoreline Cottages, PO Box 135, Thorner, Leeds LS14 3XJ
T: (0113) 244 8410
F: (0113) 244 9826
E: reservations@shoreline-cottages.com
I: www.shoreline-cottages.com

Kingfisher Cottage ★★★
Contact: Dales Hol Cot Ref:2588, Carleton Business Park, Carleton New Road, Skipton BD23 2AA
T: (01756) 799821
F: (01756) 797012
E: info@dalesholcot.com
I: www.dalesholcot.com

Kipper Cottage ★★★★
Contact: Mrs Adele Thompson & Vanessa Hickings, Whitby Holiday Cottages, 47 Flowergate, Whitby YO21 3BB
T: (01947) 603010
F: (01947) 821133
E: enquiries@whitby-cottages.co.uk
I: www.whitby-cottages.co.uk

The Lamp House ★★★★
Contact: Mrs Adele Thompson & Vanessa Hickings, Whitby Holiday Cottages, 47 Flowergate, Whitby YO21 3BB
T: (01947) 603010
F: (01947) 821133
E: enquiries@whitby-cottages.co.uk
I: www.whitby-cottages.co.uk

Little Venice ★★★
Contact: Dales Hol Cot Ref:2642, Carlton Business Park, Carleton New Road, Skipton BD23 2AA
T: (01756) 799821
F: (01756) 797012
E: info@dalesholcot.com
I: www.dalesholcot.com

Lobster Pot Cottage ★★★
Contact: Mrs Anne Forbes, Whitby Fishermens Amateur Rowing Club, 10 Castle Road, Whitby YO21 3NJ
T: (01947) 605846
E: anne.forbes2@btopenworld.com

Loen Cottage ★★★
Contact: Ms Hannah Cook, Carleton Business Centre, Carleton New Road, Skipton BD23 2AA
T: (01756) 799821
F: (01756) 797012

The Lookout ★★
Contact: Mrs Adele Thompson & Vanessa Hickings, Whitby Holiday Cottages, 47 Flowergate, Whitby YO21 3BB
T: (01947) 603010
F: (01947) 821133
E: enquiries@whitby-cottages.co.uk
I: www.whitby-cottages.co.uk

Magenta House Rating Applied For
Contact: Mr Jeffrey Roy Fox, Magenta House, 7 Esplanade, Whitby YO21 3HH
T: (01947) 820915

Mallard ★★★★
Contact: Mr & Mrs Granger, Gunpowder House, Wades Lane, East Barnby, Whitby YO21 3SB
T: (01947) 893444
F: (01947) 893777
E: mgranger@eastbarnby.freeserve.co.uk
I: www.mallardwhitby.co.uk

Manor Cottage ★★★★
Contact: Agent Dales Hol Cot Ref:2448, Carleton Business Park, Carleton New Road, Skipton BD23 2AA
T: (01756) 799821
F: (01756) 797012
E: info@dalesholcot.com
I: www.dalesholcot.com

Margherita Cottage ★★★★
Contact: Mrs Adele Thompson & Vanessa Hickings, Whitby Holiday Cottages, 47 Flowergate, Whitby YO21 3BB
T: (01947) 603010
F: (01947) 821133
E: enquiries@whitby-cottages.co.uk
I: www.whitby-cottages.co.uk

Marina View & Riverside ★★★-★★★★
Contact: Dales Hol Cot Ref:3321&3322, Dales Holiday Cottages, Carleton Business Park, Carleton New Road, Skipton BD23 2AA
T: (01756) 799821
F: (01756) 797012
E: info@dalesholcot.com
I: www.dalesholcot.com

Mariners Cottage ★★★
Contact: Mrs Adele Thompson & Vanessa Hickings, Whitby Holiday Cottages, 47 Flowergate, Whitby YO21 3BB
T: (01947) 603010
F: (01947) 821133
E: enquiries@whitby-cottages.co.uk
I: www.whitby-cottages.co.uk

Mariner's Cottage ★★★★
Contact: Mr David Haycox & Mrs Sue Brooks, Shoreline Cottages, PO Box 135, Thorner, Leeds LS14 3XJ
T: (0113) 244 8410
F: (0113) 244 9826
E: reservations@shoreline-cottages.com
I: www.shoreline-cottages.com

Midships
Rating Applied For
Contact: Mrs Vanessa Hicking, 12 The Cragg, Whitby YO21 3QA
T: (01947) 603010
F: (01947) 821133

New Hills ★★★
Contact: Dales Hol Cot Ref:2586, Carleton Business Park, Carleton New Road, Skipton BD23 2AA
T: (01756) 799821
F: (01756) 797012
E: info@dalesholcot.com
I: www.dalesholcot.com

Old Boatman's Shelter ★★★★
Contact: Mrs Alison Halidu, 50 Carr Hill Lane, Briggswath, Sleights, Whitby YO21 1RS
T: (01947) 811089
E: oldboatshelter@aol.com

6 Old Coastguard Cottages ★★★★
Contact: Ms J M Noble, Howdale House, Browside, Fylingdales, Whitby YO22
T: (01947) 881064

Olive Tree Cottage ★★★★
Contact: Mrs Adele Thompson & Vanessa Hickings, 47 Flowergate, Whitby YO21 3BB
T: (01947) 603010
F: (01947) 821133
E: enquiries@whitby-cottages.co.uk
I: www.whitby-cottages.co.uk

Pantiles
Rating Applied For
Contact: Mr & Mrs Peter & Alison Lawson, 51 Greenbank Crescent, Kingskerswell, Newton Abbot EH10 5TD
T: (0131) 446 0225
E: holidays@mountsquarewhitby.fsnet.co.uk

2 Pear Tree Cottages ★★★★
Contact: Mrs Adele Thompson & Vanessa Hickings, Whitby Holiday Cottages, 47 Flowergate, Whitby YO21 3BB
T: (01947) 603010
F: (01947) 821133
E: enquiries@whitby-cottages.co.uk
I: www.whitby-cottages.co.uk

Penny Hedge House ★★★★
Contact: Agent Dales Hol Cot Ref:2994, Carleton Business Park, Carleton New Road, Skipton BD23 2AA
T: (01756) 799821
F: (01756) 797012
E: info@dalesholcot.com
I: www.dalesholcot.com

Perkins Cottage ★★★★
Contact: Mrs Adele Thompson & Vanessa Hickings, Whitby Holiday Cottages, 47 Flowergate, Whitby YO21 3BB
T: (01947) 603010
F: (01947) 821133
E: enquiries@whitby-cottages.co.uk
I: www.whitby-cottages.co.uk

Primrose & Bluebell Cottages ★★★-★★★★
Contact: Mr & Mrs Robin & Barbara Hopps, Primrose & Bluebell Cottages, Low Newbiggin North Farm, Aislaby, Sleights, Whitby YO21 1TQ
T: (01947) 810948
F: (01947) 810948
E: barbara@bhopps.freeserve.co.uk
I: www.stilwell.co.uk

Prince of Wales Cottage ★★★★
Contact: Mr David Haycox & Mrs Sue Brooks, Shoreline Cottages, PO Box 135, Thorner, Leeds LS14 3XJ
T: (0113) 244 8410
F: (0113) 244 9826
E: reservations@shoreline-cottages.com
I: www.shoreline-cottages.com

1 Princess Place ★★★★
Contact: Mr John Whitton, Brook House, Brook Lane, Ainthorpe, Whitby YO21 2JR
T: (01287) 660118

8 Prospect Place ★★★
Contact: Mrs Adele Thompson & Vanessa Hickings, Whitby Holiday Cottages, 47 Flowergate, Whitby YO21 3BB
T: (01947) 603010
F: (01947) 821133
E: enquiries@whitby-cottages.co.uk
I: www.whitby-cottages.co.uk

Quayside Cottage ★★★★
Contact: Mr & Mrs Paul & Di Wicks, Orchard Cottage, High Street, Cloughton, Scarborough YO13 0AE
T: (01723) 871028
F: (01723) 871379
E: di@whitbycottages.com

Quayside Cottage ★★★★
Contact: Mr David Haycox & Mrs Sue Brooks, Shoreline Cottages, PO Box 135, Thorner, Leeds LS14 3XJ
T: (0113) 244 8410
F: (0113) 244 9826
E: reservations@shoreline-cottages.com
I: www.shoreline-cottages.com

Sailing By ★★★
Contact: Mrs Adele Thompson & Vanessa Hickings, 47 Flowergate, Whitby YO21 3BB
T: (01947) 603010
F: (01947) 821133
E: enquiries@whitby-cottages.co.uk
I: www.whitby-cottages.co.uk

St Joseph's Cottage ★★★★★
Contact: Mr David Haycox & Mrs Sue Brooks, Shoreline Cottages, PO Box 135, Thorner, Leeds LS14 3XJ
T: (0113) 244 8410
F: (0113) 244 9826
E: reservations@shoreline-cottages.com
I: www.shoreline-cottages.com

Sandglass Cottage ★★★★
Contact: Mr David Haycox & Mrs Sue Brooks, Shoreline Cottages, PO Box 135, Thorner, Leeds LS14 3XJ
T: (0113) 244 8410
F: (0113) 244 9826
E: reservations@shoreline-cottages.com
I: www.shoreline-cottages.com

Seacrest ★★★★
Contact: Mrs Adele Thompson & Vanessa Hickings, Whitby Holiday Cottages, 47 Flowergate, Whitby YO21 3BB
T: (01947) 603010
F: (01947) 821133
E: enquiries@whitby-cottages.co.uk
I: www.whitby-cottages.co.uk

Seagull Cottage ★★★
Contact: Mrs Adele Thompson & Vanessa Hickings, Whitby Holiday Cottages, 47 Flowergate, Whitby YO21 3BB
T: (01947) 603010
F: (01947) 821133
E: enquiries@whitby-cottages.co.uk
I: www.whitby-cottages.co.uk

Seagull Cottage ★★★★
Contact: Mr David Haycox & Mrs Sue Brooks, Shoreline Cottages, PO Box 135, Thorner, Leeds LS14 3XJ
T: (0113) 244 8410
F: (0113) 244 9826
E: reservations@shoreline-cottages.com
I: www.shoreline-cottages.com

23 Silver Street ★★★
Contact: Mrs Adele Thompson & Vanessa Hickings, Whitby Holiday Cottages, 47 Flowergate, Whitby YO21 3BB
T: (01947) 603010
F: (01947) 821133
E: enquiries@whitby-cottages.co.uk
I: www.whitby-cottages.co.uk

Southern Cross ★★★
Contact: Mrs Adele Thompson & Vanessa Hickings, Whitby Holiday Cottages, 47 Flowergate, Whitby YO21 3BB
T: (01947) 603010
F: (01947) 821133
E: enquiries@whitby-cottages.co.uk
I: www.whitby-cottages.co.uk

Spindletop ★★★
Contact: Mrs Adele Thompson & Vanessa Hickings, Whitby Holiday Cottages, 47 Flowergate, Whitby YO21 3BB
T: (01947) 603010
F: (01947) 821133
E: enquiries@whitby-cottages.co.uk
I: www.whitby-cottages.co.uk

Spring Cottage ★★★★
Contact: Ms Hannah Cook, Carleton Business Park, Carleton New Road, Skipton BD23 2AA
T: (01756) 790919
F: (01756) 797012

Spring Vale ★★★★
Contact: Mr David Haycox & Mrs Sue Brooks, Shoreline Cottages, PO Box 135, Thorner, Leeds LS14 3XJ
T: (0113) 244 8410
F: (0113) 244 9826
E: reservations@shoreline-cottages.com
I: www.shoreline-cottages.com

Stable Cottage ★★★★
Contact: Mr & Mrs Martin & Chrissie Warner, Sandfield House Farm, Sandsend Road, Whitby YO21 3SR
T: (01947) 602660
E: info@sandfieldhousefarm.co.uk

Steps Cottage ★★★
Contact: Mrs Adele Thompson & Vanessa Hickings, Whitby Holiday Cottages, 47 Flowergate, Whitby YO21 3BB
T: (01947) 603010
F: (01947) 821133
E: enquiries@whitby-cottages.co.uk
I: www.whitby-cottages.co.uk

Stoneleigh ★★★★★
Contact: Mrs Adele Thompson & Vanessa Hickings, Whitby Holiday Cottages, 47 Flowergate, Whitby YO21 3BB
T: (01947) 603010
F: (01947) 821133
E: enquiries@whitby-cottages.co.uk
I: www.whitby-cottages.co.uk

Storm Cottage ★★
Contact: Mrs Adele Thompson & Vanessa Hickings, Whitby Holiday Cottages, 47 Flowergate, Whitby YO21 3BB
T: (01947) 603010
F: (01947) 821133
E: enquiries@whitby-cottages.co.uk
I: www.whitby-cottages.co.uk

Studio Flat 6 ★★★
Contact: Mrs Adele Thompson & Vanessa Hickings, 47 Flowergate, Whitby YO21 3BB
T: (01947) 603010
F: (01947) 821133
E: enquiries@whitby-cottages.co.uk
I: www.whitby-cottages.co.uk

Swallow Cottage ★★★★
Contact: Mrs Adele Thompson & Vanessa Hickings, Whitby Holiday Cottages, 47 Flowergate, Whitby YO21 3BB
T: (01947) 603010
F: (01947) 821133
E: enquiries@whitby-cottages.co.uk
I: www.whitby-cottages.co.uk

Swallow Holiday Cottages ★★
Contact: Mr & Mrs McNeil, Swallow Holiday Cottages, Long Lease Farm, Hawsker, Whitby YO22 4LA
T: (01947) 603790
F: (01947) 603790
I: www.swallowcottages.co.uk

Swallows Nest & Wheelhouse Cottages ★★★★
Contact: Mr Peter Hamilton, Greystones Farm, Newholm, Whitby YO21 3QR
T: (01947) 605886

Swan Cottage ★★★
Contact: Mrs M A Smith, Swan Farm, High Hawsker, Whitby YO22 4LH
T: (01947) 880682

Thimble Cottage, 15 Loggerhead Yard ★★
Contact: Mr & Mrs Paul & Janet Breeze, The Barn, Gun End, Heaton, Rushton Spencer, Macclesfield SK11 0SJ
T: (01260) 227391
E: pbreeze@tiscali.co.uk

108 Upgang Lane ★★★
Contact: Mrs Adele Thompson & Vanessa Hickings, Whitby Holiday Cottages, 47 Flowergate, Whitby YO21 3BB
T: (01947) 603010
F: (01947) 821133
E: enquiries@whitby-cottages.co.uk
I: www.whitby-cottages.co.uk

Waverley ★★★
Contact: Mrs Adele Thompson & Vanessa Hickings, Whitby Holiday Cottages, 47 Flowergate, Whitby YO21 3BB
T: (01947) 603010
F: (01947) 821133
E: enquiries@whitby-cottages.co.uk
I: www.whitby-cottages.co.uk

Welsby Cottage ★★★
Contact: Mrs Adele Thompson & Vanessa Hickings, Whitby Holiday Cottages, 47 Flowergate, Whitby YO21 3BB
T: (01947) 603010
F: (01947) 821133
E: enquiries@whitby-cottages.co.uk
I: www.whitby-cottages.co.uk

West End Cottage ★★★★
Contact: Mr David Haycox & Mrs Sue Brooks, Shoreline Cottages, PO Box 135, Thorner, Leeds LS14 3XJ
T: (0113) 244 8410
F: (0113) 244 9826
E: reservations@shoreline-cottages.com
I: www.shoreline-cottages.com

White Horse Cottage ★★★
Contact: Mr George & Steven Walker, The Shakespeare Inn, 120 Eldon Road, Rotherham S65 1RD
T: (01709) 367031

6 White Horse Yard ★★★
Contact: Mrs Adele Thompson & Vanessa Hickings, Whitby Holiday Cottages, 47 Flowergate, Whitby YO21 3BB
T: (01947) 603010
F: (01947) 821133
E: enquiries@whitby-cottages.co.uk
I: www.whitby-cottages.co.uk

White Rose Holiday Cottages ★★★-★★★★
Contact: Mrs J E Roberts, Greenacres, 5 Brook Park, Sleights, Whitby YO21 1RT
T: (01947) 810763
E: enquiries@whiterosecottages.co.uk
I: www.whiterosecottages.co.uk

Windrush Cottage ★★★
Contact: Mrs Adele Thompson & Vanessa Hickings, Whitby Holiday Cottages, 47 Flowergate, Whitby YO21 3BB
T: (01947) 603010
F: (01947) 821133
E: enquiries@whitby-cottages.co.uk
I: www.whitby-cottages.co.uk

WHITWELL-ON-THE-HILL
North Yorkshire

The Hay Loft ★★★
Contact: Mrs Anne Polley, El Paso, Barton Hill, Whitwell-on-the-Hill, York YO60 7JX
T: (01653) 618324
E: anne.polley1@btopenworld.com

WILTON
North Yorkshire

The Old Forge Cottages ★★★
Contact: Mrs Bernice Graham, The Old Forge Cottages, The Old Forge, Wilton, Pickering YO18 7JY
T: (01751) 477399
F: (01751) 473122
E: theoldforge@themutual.net
I: www.forgecottages.themutual.net/fc.html

Sands Farm Country Cottages ★★★★
Contact: Miss Tomlinson, Sands Farm Country Cottages, Wilton, Allerston, Pickering YO18 7JY
T: (01751) 474405
F: (01751) 476866
E: sandsfarm@faxvia.net

WINKSLEY
North Yorkshire

Meadow View Cottage ★★★
Contact: Mr Les Broadbent, 9 Roydscliffe Road, Heaton, Bradford BD9 5PT
T: (01274) 541622

WOLD NEWTON
East Riding of Yorkshire

Owl Cottage Ref 2325
Rating Applied For
Contact: Miss Ruth Henderson, Dales Holiday Cottages, Carleton Business Park, Carleton New Road, Skipton BD23 2AA
T: (01756) 799821
F: (01756) 797012

WOMBLETON
North Yorkshire

Rosebud Cottage ★★★★
Contact: Ms L Smith & Mr D Barnacle, 48 Piercy End, Kirkbymoorside, York YO62 6DF
T: (01751) 433452
F: (01751) 430778

WORSBROUGH
South Yorkshire

Delf Cottage ★★★★
Contact: Mrs Julie Elmhirst, Delf House, Houndhill Lane, Worsbrough, Barnsley S70 6TX
T: (01226) 282430
F: (01226) 282430
E: t.elmhirst@btinternet.com
I: www.delfcottage.co.uk

WORTLEY
South Yorkshire

Pennine Equine
Rating Applied For
Contact: Mrs Lynn Berry, Bromley Farm, Bromley, Wortley, Sheffield S35 7DE
T: (0114) 284 7140
F: (0114) 284 7644
E: alex@tuefarming.freeserve.co.uk

WORTON
North Yorkshire

Stoney End Holidays ★★★-★★★★
Contact: Mrs Pamela Hague, Stoney End, Worton, Leyburn DL8 3ET
T: (01969) 650652
F: (01969) 650077
E: pmh@stoneyend.co.uk
I: www.stoneyend.co.uk

WRELTON
North Yorkshire

Croft Head Cottage ★★★★
Contact: Mr & Mrs Sue & Chris Halstead, Croft Head, Wrelton, Aislaby, Pickering YO18 8PF
T: (01751) 477918
F: (01751) 477918
E: suehalstead@richardburbridge.co.uk

Hallgarth ★★★★
Contact: Mrs Carol Marsh, Orchard House, Main Street, Wrelton, Pickering YO18 8PG
T: (01751) 476081

Vale Cottage ★★★★
Contact: Mr & Mrs Scaling, Cliff Farm, Sinnington, York YO62 6SS
T: (01751) 473792
F: (01751) 473792
E: jeanscaling@btinternet.com

WROOT
North Lincolnshire

Rye House Granary ★★★
Contact: Mr Robin Aconley, Rye House, High Street, Wroot, Doncaster DN9 2BT
T: (01302) 770196
E: janeaconley@tinyworld.co.uk

YAPHAM
East Riding of Yorkshire

Wolds View Holiday Cottages ★★★★
Contact: Mrs Woodliffe, Wolds View Holiday Cottages, Mill Farm, Yapham, York YO42 1PH
T: (01759) 302172

YEADON
West Yorkshire

Gillcroft Cottage ★★★★
Contact: Mrs Croft, 41 Gill Lane, Yeadon, Leeds LS19 7DE
T: (0113) 250 4198

YORK
North Yorkshire

9 Cloisters Walk ★★★★
Contact: Mr & Mrs Gordon & Hilary Jones, 2 Chalfonts, Off Tadcaster Road, York YO24 1EX
T: (01904) 702043
F: (01904) 702043
E: hilary@yorkcloisters.com

Abbeygate House ★★★★★
Contact: Mr & Mrs C Halliday, 1 Grange Drive, Horsforth, Leeds LS18 5EQ
T: (0113) 258 9833

Acer Bungalow ★★★
Contact: Mrs Sandra Wreglesworth
T: (01904) 653839
F: (01904) 677017
E: info@acerhotel.co.uk
I: www.acerbungalow.co.uk

Aisling House
Rating Applied For
Contact: Mr Ian Addyman, 5 Cherry Hill House, Bishopgate Street, York YO23 1LY
T: (01904) 636921
F: (01904) 636921
E: info@yorkselfcatering.fsnet.co.uk

Apple Cottage ★★★
Contact: Mrs Jean Corrigan, Highfields, Beckdale Road, Helmsley, York YO62 5AS
T: (01439) 770705
F: (01439) 770705

Baile Hill Cottage ★★★
Contact: Mr & Mrs Paul Hodgson, Avalon, North Lane, Wheldrake, York YO19 6AY
T: (01904) 448670
F: (01904) 448908
E: enquiries@holiday-cottage.org.uk
I: www.holiday-cottage.org.uk

Barbican Mews ★★★
Contact: Mrs Helen Jones, Homefinders Holidays, 11 Walmgate, York YO1 9TX
T: (01904) 632660
F: (01904) 615388
E: helen@letters-of-york.co.uk
I: www.letters-of-york.co.uk

Bishopgate Pavilion–Bishops Wharf ★★★★★
Contact: Mr John Graham, 31 Falcon Way, Clippers Quay, London E14 9UP
T: (020) 7538 8980
F: (020) 7538 8980
E: johnkgraham@hotmail.com
I: www.johnkgraham.com

Bishops Hotel Apartment ★★★★
Contact: Mr & Mrs Magson, Bishops Hotel, 135 Holgate Road, Acomb, York YO24 4DF
T: (01904) 628000
F: (01904) 628181
E: bishops@ukonline.co.uk
I: www.bishopshotel.co.uk

Centre York Cottages ★★-★★★
Contact: Mr William Richardson, Catton Park, Wilberfoss, York YO41 5QA
T: (01759) 388280
F: (01759) 388280
E: william@centre-yorkcottages.fsnet.co.uk
I: www.centre.yorkcottages.fsnet.co.uk

Chestnut Farm Holiday Cottages ★★★★
Contact: Mrs Alison Smith, Chestnut Farm Holiday Park, Acaster Malbis, York YO23 2UQ
T: (01904) 704676
F: (01904) 704676
E: enquiries@yorkholidaycottages.co.uk
I: www.yorkholidaycottages.co.uk

Classique Select Holiday Accommodation ★★-★★★
Contact: Mr Rodney Inns, 21 Larchfield, Stockton Lane, York YO31 1JS
T: (01904) 421339
F: (01904) 421339
E: rodela_2194_inns@hotmail.com
I: www.classique-york.co.uk

1 Cloisters Walk ★★★
Contact: Mrs Helen Jones, Homefinders Holidays, 11 Walmgate, York YO1 9TX
T: (01904) 632660
F: (01904) 651388
E: helen@letters-of-york.co.uk
I: www.letters-of-york.co.uk

Cloisters Walk Holiday Accommodation ★★★
Contact: Mrs Susan Burrows, 15 Knapton Close, Strensall, York YO32 5ZF
T: (01904) 490729

Colonia Holidays ★★★
Contact: Mrs Margaret Booth, Hutton Street, Hutton Wandesley, York YO26 7ND
T: (01904) 738579

17 Escrick Street ★★★
Contact: Mrs Helen Jones, 11 Walmgate, York YO1 9TX
T: (01904) 632660
F: (01904) 651388
E: helen@letters-of-york.co.uk

Five Pennies ★★★★
Contact: Mrs Wilson, Five Pennies, Broad Lane, Appleton Roebuck, York YO23 7DS
T: (01904) 744562
E: nosliw90@hotmail.com

Flat 24 Middleton House ★★★★
Contact: Mrs Carole Bowes, Melrose House Farm, Sutton, Thirsk YO7 2ES
T: (01845) 597334
E: rce.bowes@lineone.net
I: www.yorkcityflat.co.uk

The Garden Cottage ★★★★
Contact: Mr & Mrs Ann Hart, Meadowville, Grimstone Bar, Heslington, York YO19 5LA
T: (01904) 413353
F: (01904) 431559
E: ann@yorkgardencottage.co.uk

Garden Cottage ★★★
Contact: Mrs Katy Harvey, Moat View House, 28 Lord Mayors Walk, York YO31 7HA
T: (01904) 623329
E: katy.harvey1@ntlworld.com

Hilary's Holiday Homes ★★★★
Contact: Mrs Hilary Kernohan, Duncanne House, Roecliffe Lane, Roecliffe, York YO51 9LN
T: (01423) 325417
E: hilarysholidayhomes@btconnect.com
I: www.hilarysholidayhomes.co.uk

Knowle House Apartments ★★
Contact: Mr Graham Harrand
T: (01904) 637404
F: (01904) 639774
E: greg@hedleyhouse.com
I: www.harrands.com

Merricote Cottages ★★★
Contact: Mr Andrew Williamson, Merricote Cottages, Malton Road, Stockton-on-the-Forest, York YO32 9TL
T: (01904) 400256
F: (01904) 400846
E: merricote@hotmail.com
I: www.merricote-holiday-cottages.co.uk

Minster View ★★★★
Contact: Mrs Helen Jones, 11 Walmgate, York YO1 9TX
T: (01904) 632660
F: (01904) 651388
E: helen@letter-of-york.co.uk

12 Monkbridge Court ★★★★
Contact: Mrs Angela Bush, Burtonfields Hall, Bridlington Road, Stamford Bridge, York YO41 1SA
T: (01759) 371308
F: (01759) 371308
E: angelabush@monkbridge.co.uk

145 Mount Vale ★★★★
Contact: Mrs Helen Jones, Homefinders Holidays, 11 Walmgate, York YO1 9TJ
T: (01904) 632660
F: (01904) 651388
E: helen@letters-of-york.co.uk
I: www.letters-of-york.co.uk

Owl Cottage ★★
Contact: Mrs Rosemary Fletcher, Owl Cottage, Long Acres, The Village, Osbaldwick, York YO10 3NP
T: (01904) 410438
F: (01904) 414404
E: rjf@cfga.co.uk

The Penthouse ★★★★★
Contact: Mr Ian Berg, 1 Kenwood Avenue, Bramhall, Stockport SK7 1BP
T: (0161) 439 8964
E: rtib@currantbun.com

The Penthouse ★★★★★
Contact: Mrs Kim Hodgson, 1 Postern House, Bishop's Wharf, York YO23 1PH
T: (01904) 610351
F: (01904) 613687
E: hodgsonschoice@hotmail.com
I: www.hodgsons-choice.co.uk

43 Postern Close ★★★★★
Contact: Mr & Mrs Gordon & Hilary Jones, 2 Chalfonts, Off Tadcaster Road, York YO24 1EX
T: (01904) 702043
F: (01904) 702043
E: hilary@yorkcloisters.com
I: www.yorkcloisters.com

44 Postern Close ★★★★
Contact: Mrs Christine Turner, Meadowcroft, Millfield, Willingham, Cambridge CB4 5HD
T: (01954) 201218
E: cmt22@hermes.cam.ac.uk
I: www.yorkholidayflat.co.uk

29 Richardson Street ★★★
Contact: Mrs Helen Jones, Homefinders Holidays, 11 Walmgate, York YO1 9TX
T: (01904) 632660
F: (01904) 651388
E: helen@letters-of-york.co.uk
I: www.letters-of-york.co.uk

Riverside Holiday Flat ★★★★
Contact: Mr P A Jackson, 17 Great Close, Cawood, Selby YO8 3UG
T: (01757) 268207
E: pajack@lineone.net
I: www.yorkriversideholidayflat.co.uk

Roman Retreat ★★★
Contact: Mr S O Hedderick, 4 Crummock, York YO24 2SU
T: (01904) 331803
E: hedderick@ntlworld.com

Shambles Holiday Apartments ★★★★
Contact: Mr & Mrs Fletcher, Shambles Holiday Apartments, The Art Shop, 27-27a Shambles, York YO1 7LX
T: (01904) 623898
F: (01904) 671283
E: shamblesholiday-york@tinyworld.co.uk

Stakesby Holiday Flats ★★
Contact: Mr Anthony Bryce, Stakesby Holiday Flats, 4 St Georges Place, York YO24 1DR
T: (01904) 634835
E: ant@stakesby.co.uk

Swallow Hall ★★★
Contact: Mrs Christine Scutt, Swallow Hall, Wheldrake Lane, Crockey Hill, York YO19 4SG
T: (01904) 448219
E: jtscores@hotmail.com

Thornfield House ★★★
Contact: Ms Regina Longjaloux, 14 Thirlmere Drive, Heworth, York YO31 0LZ
T: (01904) 415478
E: r.d@longjaloux.freeserve.co.uk

Westgate ★★★★
Contact: Mrs Helen Jones, 11 Walmgate, York YO1 9TX
T: (01904) 632660
F: (01904) 651388
E: helen@letters-of-york.co.uk

Westgate Apartments ★★★★★
Contact: Mr Kenneth Irving, 142 Bonnyton Drive, Eaglesham, Glasgow G76 0LU
T: (01355) 302508

Within the Walls Cottage ★★★
Contact: Mr Barry Giles
T: (0115) 931 2070

24 Woodsmill Quay ★★★★
Contact: Mrs Helen Jones, Homefinders Holidays, 11 Walmgate, York YO1 9TX
T: (01904) 632660
F: (01904) 651388
E: helen@letters-of-york.co.uk
I: www.letters-of-york.co.uk

York Holiday Apartments ★★★★
Contact: Mr Malcolm Bradley, Old Quarry Lane, Lumby, South Milford, Leeds LS25 5JA
T: (01977) 683499
F: (01977) 680110
E: malcolmrbradley@farmersweekly.net
I: www.yorkholidayapartments.co.uk

York Holiday Homes ★★★-★★★★
Contact: Mrs Dorothy Preece & Mrs D Widdicombe, York Holiday Homes, 53 Goodramgate, York YO1 7LS
T: (01094) 641997
F: (01904) 613453

York Holiday Homes ★★★
Contact: Mrs Dorothy Preece, York Holiday Homes, 53 Goodramgate, York YO1 7LS
T: (01904) 641997
F: (01904) 613453

York Lakeside Lodges ★★★★-★★★★★
Contact: Mr N Manasir, York Lakeside Lodges Ltd, Moor Lane, York YO24 2QU
T: (01904) 702346
F: (01904) 701631
E: neil@yorklakesidelodges.co.uk
I: www.yorklakesidelodges.co.uk

HEART OF ENGLAND

ABBERLEY
Worcestershire

Hill Farm ★★★
Contact: Mr & Mrs Reece, Hill Farm, Wynniatts Way, Worcester WR6 6BZ
T: (01299) 896415

Old Yates Cottages ★★★
Contact: Mr & Mrs R M Goodman, Old Yates Farm, Abberley, Worcester WR6 6AT
T: (01299) 896500
F: (01299) 896065
E: oldyates@aol.com
I: www.oldyatescottages.co.uk

ACTON BURNELL
Shropshire

Rosehay ★★★★
Contact: Mr Clive Sykes, Sykes Cottages, York House, York Street, Chester CH1 3LR
T: (01244) 345700
F: (01244) 321442
E: info@sykescottages.co.uk

ADMASTON
Staffordshire

Blithfield Lakeside Barns
Rating Applied For
Contact: Ms Lisa Brown, St Stephens Hill Farm, Steenwood Lane, Admaston, Rugeley WS15 3NQ
T: (01889) 500458
F: (01889) 500288

ALCESTER
Warwickshire

The Croft Cottage ★★★★
Contact: Mrs Catherine Harris, Bidford Road, Broom, Alcester B50 4HH
T: (01789) 490543
E: cathy@thecroftcottage.co.uk
I: www.thecroftcottage.co.uk

Dorset House Cottage and Dorset House★★★★
Contact: Mrs Plummer, Dorset House, Church Street, Alcester B49 5AJ
T: (01789) 762856
F: (01789) 766165
E: dorsethac@aol.com

HeronView ★★★★
Contact: Mr & Mrs Mike and Heather Bosworth, HeronView, Cross Guns Cottage, Mill Lane, Oversley Green, Arrow, Alcester B49 6LF
T: (01789) 766506
F: (01789) 400851
E: heather@heronview.freeserve.co.uk
I: www.heronview.freeserve.co.uk

ALDERLEY
Gloucestershire

La Vacherie and The Gunroom ★★★★
Contact: Mr & Mrs A Shearer, Awssome Partnership, The Old Farmhouse, Alderley, Wotton-under-Edge GL12 7QT
T: 07930 367621
E: awssomeuk@aol.com
I: www.awssome.com

ALDERTON
Gloucestershire

Rectory Farm Cottages ★★★★
Contact: Mr & Mrs M A Burton, Rectory Farm Cottages, Alderton, Tewkesbury GL20 8NW
T: (01242) 620455
F: (01242) 620455
E: peterannabel@hotmail.com
I: www.rectoryfarmcottages.co.uk

ALDERWASLEY
Derbyshire

Church View ★★★
Contact: Mr S Mihulka, Knob Cottage, Alderwasley, Belper DE56 2RA
T: (01629) 823728
F: (01629) 823728

ALDSWORTH
Gloucestershire

Aldsworth Place ★★★
Contact: Mr & Mrs Munson-Kingham, Aldsworth Place, Aldsworth, Cirencester GL54 3RE
T: (01451) 844461
F: (01451) 844871

ALDWARK
Derbyshire

The Old Coach House ★★★★
Contact: Mr Nigel John Smith, 94 Northwood Lane, Darley Dale, Matlock DE4 2HR
T: (01629) 733114

ALFORD
Lincolnshire

Woodthorpe Hall Country Cottage ★★★★
Contact: Mrs Stubbs, Woodthorpe Hall Country Cottage, Woodthorpe, Alford LN13 0DD
T: (01507) 450294
F: (01507) 450885
E: enquiries@woodthorpehall.com
I: www.woodthorpehall.co.uk

ALFRETON
Derbyshire

The Coach House ★★★★
Contact: Mr & Mrs D M Whitaker, The Old Vicarage, 136 Derby Road, Swanwick, Alfreton DE55 1AD
T: (01773) 605116
F: (01773) 528703
E: pwhitaker@dial.pipex.com

ALKMONTON
Derbyshire

The Looseboxes Dairy House Farm ★★★★
Contact: Mr Andy Harris, The Looseboxes Dairy House Farm, Alkmonton, Ashbourne DE6 3DG
T: (01335) 330359
F: (01335) 330359
E: b&b@dairyhousefarm.org.uk
I: www.dairyhousefarm.org.uk/

ALL STRETTON
Shropshire

The Pottery
Rating Applied For
Contact: Mr Chris Cotter, Overbatch House, Castle Hill, All Stretton, Church Stretton SY6 6JX
T: (01694) 723511
E: chrisjcotter@yahoo.co.uk

ALSOP-EN-LE-DALE
Derbyshire

Church Farm Cottages ★★★★
Contact: Mrs Christine Duffell, Church Farm, Alsop-en-le-Dale, Ashbourne DE6 1QP
T: (01335) 390216
F: (01335) 390216
E: churchfarmcottages.alsop@virgin.net
I: www.cressbrook.co.uk/ashborn/churchfarm

ALSTONEFIELD
Staffordshire

Ancestral Barn & Church Farm Cottage★★★★-★★★★★
Contact: Mrs S Fowler, Church Farm, Stanshope, Ashbourne DE6 2AD
T: (01335) 310243
F: (01335) 310243
E: sue@dovedalecottages.fsnet.co.uk
I: www.dovedalecottages.co.uk

Dove Cottage Fishing Lodge ★★★★★
Contact: Ms M Hignett, Foxleaze Court, Preston, Cirencester GL7 5PS
T: (01285) 655875
F: (01285) 655885
E: info@dovecottages.co.uk
I: www.dovecottages.co.uk

The Gables
Rating Applied For
Contact: Mr McKee, Timewell Estates Plc, PO Box 15, West Kirby, Wirral CH48 1QQ
T: (0151) 625 3264
E: timewell@rtconnect.com
I: www.dovedale.org.uk

Gateham Grange Cottage & The Coach House ★★★-★★★★★
Contact: Mrs Teresa Flower, Gateham Grange Cottage & The Coach House, Gateham Grange, Alstonefield, Hartington, Buxton DE6 2FT
T: (01335) 310349
E: gateham.grange@btinternet.com
I: gateham.grange@btinternet.com

The Haybarn ★★★
Contact: Mrs Coralie Smith, The Haybarn, Hope Green Farm, Alstonfield, Alstonefield, Ashbourne DE6 2GE
T: (01335) 310328
I: www.peakcottages.com

Hope Farm House Barn ★★★★
Contact: Ms Su Hanson, 4 Stone Row, Osmaston, Ashbourne DE6 1LW
T: (01335) 347757
F: (01335) 342717
E: su.hanson@virgin.net

Hope Marsh Cottage ★★★
Contact: Peak Cottages, Strawberry Lee Lane, Totley Bents, Sheffield S17 3BA
T: (0114) 262 0777
F: (0114) 262 0666
E: enquries@peakcottages.com
I: www.peakcottages.com

ALTON
Staffordshire

Dale Farm Cottage ★★★
Contact: Mrs Moult, Dale Farm, The Dale, Alton, Stoke-on-Trent ST10 4BG
T: (01538) 702022
F: (01538) 702022
E: njmoult@aol.com

Fox House Cottages ★★★★
Contact: Mr & Mrs Aston, Fox House, Tithe Barn, Alton, Stoke-on-Trent ST10 4AZ
T: (01538) 702367

Foxglove Cottage ★★★★
Contact: Country Holidays Ref 11949, Spring Mill, Earby, Barnoldswick BB18
T: 08700 723723
E: sales@ttgihg.co.uk
I: www.country-holidays.co.uk

The Homesteads ★★★
Contact: Mrs A Smith, 24 Dove Lane, Rocester, Uttoxeter ST14 5LA
T: (01889) 590062

The Raddle Inn ★★
Contact: Mr Wilkinson, The Raddle Inn, Quarry Bank, Tean, Stoke-on-Trent ST10 4HQ
T: (01889) 507278
F: (01889) 507520
E: peter@logcabin.co.uk
I: www.logcabin.co.uk

ALVESTON
Warwickshire

Elm Cottage ★★★★
Contact: Mr & Mrs Baker, Penny Well Cottage, 4 Lower End, Alveston, Stratford-upon-Avon CV37 7QH
T: (01789) 299101
F: (01789) 262998
E: petro_baker@compuserve.com

Tods Earth ★★★★
Contact: Mr & Mrs V Selby, 88 Old Town Mews, Stratford-upon-Avon CV37 6GR
T: (01789) 414626

AMBERLEY
Gloucestershire

The Squirrels ★★★
Contact: Mrs Valerie Bowen, The Squirrels, Theescombe, Amberley, Stroud GL5 5AU
T: (01453) 836940
E: valeriebowen@thesquirrels.fsbusiness.co.uk

ARNOLD
Nottinghamshire

The Grannary ★★★
Contact: Mrs P A Lamin, The Grannary, Top House Farm, Mansfield Road, Arnold, Nottingham NG5 8PH
T: (0115) 926 8330

ASFORDBY
Leicestershire

Amberley Gardens Self-catering ★★★★
Contact: Mr Bruce Brotherhood, Amberley Gardens Self-catering, 4 Church Lane, Asfordby, Melton Mowbray LE14 3RU
T: (01664) 812314
F: (01664) 813740
E: doris@amberleygardens.net
I: www.amberleygardens.net

Stable Cottage ★★★★
Contact: The Old Rectory, Church Lane, Asfordby, Melton Mowbray LE14 3RU
T: (01664) 813679
F: (0115) 924 2450

ASHBOURNE
Derbyshire

Ashfield And Dove Cottages ★★★
Contact: Mr Tatlow, Ashfield Farm, Ashbourne DE6 2EB
T: (01335) 324279

Borrowdale Cottage ★★★
Contact: Mrs W Parratt, 24 Weydon Lane, Farnham GU9
T: (01252) 712562

Callow Top Cottages 1 and 2 ★★★
Contact: Mrs Sue Deane, Callow Top Cottages 1 and 2, Callow Top Holiday Park, Buxton Road, Ashbourne DE6 2AQ
T: (01335) 344020
F: (01335) 343726
E: enquiries@callowtop.freeserve.co.uk
I: www.callotop.co.uk

Daisy Bank Cottage ★★★★
Contact: Mr & Mrs John & Liz Hanford, Kelmscott, Congree Lane, Mayfield, Ashbourne DE6 2HW
T: (01335) 343253
E: liz.john@hanford.freeserve.co.uk

Dove Farm ★★★★
Contact: Mrs Jane Stretton, Dove Farm, Ellastone, Ashbourne DE6 2GY
T: (01335) 324357
E: jane@dovefarm.co.uk
I: www.dovefarm.co.uk

The Grooms' Quarters ★★★★★
Contact: Ray & Ann Thompson, The Grooms' Quarters, The Old Coach House, Hall Lane, Wootton, Ashbourne DE6 2GW
T: (01335) 324549
E: thompson.wootton@virgin.net
I: www.groomsquarters.co.uk

Haifa ★★★
Contact: Mr David Dudley, 8 Esher Court, The Arbours, Little Billing, Northampton NN3 3RN
T: (01604) 403625
F: (01604) 403646

Hillside Croft ★★★★★
Contact: Mrs Pat Walker, Offcote Grange, Offcote, Kniveton, Ashbourne DE6 1JQ
T: (01335) 344795
F: (01335) 348358
E: cottages@hillsidecroft.co.uk
I: www.hillsidecroft.co.uk

Home Farm Cottages ★★★★-★★★★★
Contact: Mrs P Longley, Home Farm Cottages, Hall Lane, Wootton, Ashbourne DE6 2GW
T: (01335) 324433

Moore's Cottage Farm ★★★-★★★★
Contact: David Restrick and Janet Watson, Moore's Cottage Farm, Slack Lane, Upper Mayfield, Thorpe, Ashbourne DE6 2JX
T: (01335) 346121
F: (01335) 300668
E: janetwatson@waitrose.com
I: www.cressbrook.co.uk/ashborn/moorescottage

The Nook ★★★★
Contact: Mrs S E Osborn, Barracca, Ivydene Close, Earl Shilton, Leicester LE9 7NR
T: (01455) 842609
E: susan.osborn@virgin.net
I: www.come.to/thenook

The Old Laundry
Rating Applied For
Contact: Mr Colin MacQueen, Strawberry Lee Lane, Totley Bents, Sheffield S17 3BA
T: (0114) 262 0777
F: (0114) 262 0666
E: enquiries@peakcottages.com

Old Miller's Cottage ★★★
Contact: Mrs Hewitt, 45 Portway Drive, Tutbury, Burton upon Trent DE13 9HU
T: (01283) 815895

The Orchards ★★★★
Contact: Mrs Vanessa Holland, Rushley Farm, Ilam, Ashbourne DE6 2BA
T: (01538) 308205
E: rushley.farm@talk21.com
I: www.peakdistrict-tourism.gov.uk/peakdistrict/accomm/theorchards/

Sandybrook Country Park ★★★-★★★★
Contact: Reservations, Pinelodge Holidays, Darley Moor, Two Dales, Matlock DE4 5LN
T: (01629) 732428
F: (01629) 735015
E: admin@pinelodgeholidays.co.uk
I: www.pinelodgeholidays.co.uk/sandybrook.ihtml

Slade House Farm ★★★★-★★★★★
Contact: Mr & Mrs Alan and Pat Philp, Ilam, Ashbourne DE6 2BB
T: (01538) 308123
F: (01538) 308777
E: alanphilp@sladehousefarm.co.uk
I: www.sladehousefarm.co.uk

Strawberry Cottage ★★★
Contact: Mrs Wendy Boddy, Cliff Bank Cottage, Calwich, Ashbourne DE6 2EB
T: (01335) 324210
E: wendyboddy@handbag.com

Thorpe Cloud View ★★★★★
Contact: Mr Ray Neilson, Thorpe Cloud View, Thorpe House, Thorpe, Ashbourne DE6 2AW
T: (01335) 350215
E: rayneilson@aol.com

Yeldersley Hall ★★★★-★★★★★
Contact: Mr Andrew Bailey, Yeldersley Hall, Ashbourne DE6 1LS
T: (01335) 343432

ASHBY-DE-LA-ZOUCH
Leicestershire

Sylvan ★★★
Contact: Mrs Doreen Gasson, 13 Babelake Street, Packington, Ashby-de-la-Zouch LE65 1WD
T: (01530) 412012
E: egg-deg@packington.freeserve.co.uk

Upper Rectory Farm Cottages ★★★★★
Contact: Mrs Jean Corbett, Cottage Farm, Norton-Juxta-Twycross, Atherstone CV9 3QH
T: (01827) 880448
E: info@upperrectoryfarmcottages.co.uk
I: www.upperrectoryfarmcottages.co.uk

ASHFORD IN THE WATER
Derbyshire

Ashford Barns ★★★★
Contact: Mr C MacQueen, Peak Cottages, Strawberry Lee Lane, Totley Bents, Sheffield S17 3BA
T: (0114) 262 0777
F: (0114) 262 0666
E: enquiries@peakcottages.com
I: www.peakcottages.com

Churchdale Holidays ★★★★★
Contact: Mrs Sarah Winkworth-Smith, Churchdale Holidays, Churchdale Farm, Ashford-in-the-Water, Bakewell DE45 1NX
T: (01629) 640269
F: (01629) 640608
E: info@churchdaleholidays.co.uk
I: www.churchdaleholidays.co.uk

Clematis Cottage ★★★
Contact: Mr & Mrs Bernard & Kate Armstrong, Holmedene, Ashford Road, Bakewell DE45 1GL
T: (01629) 813448
E: bernard-armstrong@lineone.net

Corner Cottage ★★★★★
Contact: Mrs Staley, Bolehill Farm, Monyash Road, Over Haddon, Bakewell DE45 1QW
T: (01629) 815699
F: (01629) 812359
E: tonystaley@hotmail.com
I: www.bolehillfarmcottages.co.uk

End Cottage ★★★★
Contact: Mrs Wright, Stancil House, Barn Furlong, Great Longstone, Little Longstone, Bakewell DE45 1TR
T: (01629) 640136

Foxglove Cottage ★★★★
Contact: Mr C MacQueen, Peak Cottages, Strawberry Lee Lane, Totley Bents, Sheffield S17 3BA
T: (0114) 262 0777
F: (0114) 262 0666

Green Gates ★★★
Contact: Mr MacQueen, Peak Cottages, Strawberry Lee Lane, Totley Bents, Totley Rise, Sheffield S17 3BA
T: (0114) 262 0777
F: (0114) 262 0666
E: enquiries@peakcottages.com
I: www.peakcottages.com

Orchard House ★★★
Contact: Mr C MacQueen, Peak Cottages, Strawberry Lee Lane, Totley Bents, Sheffield S17 3BA
T: (0114) 262 0777
F: (0114) 262 0666
E: enquiries@peakcottages.com
I: www.peakcottages.com

The Smithy ★★★★
Contact: Ms Susan Akeroyd, The Smithy, Devonshire Weir, Watts Green, Bakewell DE45 1QE
T: (01629) 812693
E: akeroydsusie@aol.com

Thorpe Cottage ★★★★
Contact: Mrs Sheila Newman, 14 Pool Drive, Bessacarr, Doncaster DN4 6UX
T: (01302) 536763
F: (01302) 536763
E: msnewman@care4free.co.uk
I: www.thorpecottage.co.uk

Thyme Cottage
Rating Applied For
Contact: Mrs H Bell, Nether Croft, Eaton Place, Baslow, Bakewell DE45 1RW
T: (01246) 583564
E: nethercroftbandb@aol.com

Underwood ★★★★
Contact: Mrs P E Hollingworth, Brushfield House, Church Street, Ashford in the Water, Bakewell DE45 1QB
T: (01629) 812128

ASHLEWORTH
Gloucestershire

Little Manor ★★★★
Contact: Mrs Sylvia Mary Barnes, Little Manor, Ashleworth Manor, Ashleworth, Gloucester GL19 4LA
T: (01452) 700350
F: (01452) 700350
E: rjb@ashleworthmanor.fsnet.co.uk

ASHLEY
Gloucestershire

Wisteria Cottage ★★★
Contact: Mrs Alison Smith, 4 Manor Farm Cottages, Ashley, Tetbury GL8 8ST
T: (01666) 577540

ASHOVER
Derbyshire

Holestone Moor Barns ★★★★-★★★★★
Contact: Mr & Mrs Steve & Vicki Clemerson, Holestone Moor Barns, Holestone Moor Farm, Holestone Moor, Ashover, Chesterfield S45 0JS
T: (01246) 591263
F: (01246) 591263
E: hmbarns@aol.com
I: www.hmbarns.co.uk

ASHTON
Northamptonshire

Vale Farm House ★★★★
Contact: Mrs Zanotto, Vale Farm House, Stoke Road, Roade, Northampton NN7 2JN
T: (01604) 863697
F: (01604) 862859

ASLACKBY
Lincolnshire

Workshop Cottage ★★★★
Contact: Mr & Mrs A Cole, Martins, Temple Road, Aslackby, Sleaford NG34 0HJ
T: (01778) 440113
F: (01778) 440920

ASTON CANTLOW
Warwickshire

Cantlow Cottage ★★★
Contact: Mr & Mrs John & Jane Nickless, The Corner House, Henley Road, Great Alne, Alcester B49 6HX
T: (01789) 488513

ASTON-ON-CLUN
Shropshire

The Granary ★★★★
Contact: Mrs L Morgan, Rowton Grange, Aston-on-Clun, Craven Arms SY7 0PA
T: (01588) 660227
F: (01588) 660227
E: all@rowtongrange.freeserve.co.uk

ATHERSTONE
Warwickshire

Hipsley Farm Cottages ★★★★
Contact: Mrs A Prosser, Waste Farm, Hurley, Atherstone CV9 2LR
T: (01827) 872437
F: (01827) 872437
E: ann@hipsley.co.uk
I: www.hipsley.co.uk

AVENING
Gloucestershire

The Shoeing Forge ★★★★★
Contact: Miss Sharon Connolly, The Shoeing Forge, 31 Tetbury Hill, Avening, Tetbury GL6 8LF
T: (01295) 730212
E: lamadonett@aol.co.uk

AVERHAM
Nottinghamshire

Wynberg ★★★
Contact: Mrs Maureen Justice, Wynberg, Staythorpe Road, Averham, Kelham, Newark NG23 5RA
T: (01636) 702874
F: (01636) 702874

AYLBURTON
Gloucestershire

The Old Pumphouse Rating Applied For
Contact: Mr Nicholas Pash, Hideaways, Chapel House, Luke Street, Berwick St John, Shaftesbury SP7 0HQ
T: (01747) 828170
I: www.hideaways.co.uk

AYMESTREY
Herefordshire

The Bungalow ★★★
Contact: Mr & Mrs Price, The Bungalow, Sussex Acres, Lower Lye, Aymestrey, Leominster HR6 9TA
T: (01568) 770582
E: price2k@fsmail.net

BAGNALL
Staffordshire

Cordwainer Cottage ★★★
Contact: Mrs Muriel Buckle, Cordwainer Cottage, Stoney Villa Farm, Salters Wells, Bagnall, Stoke-on-Trent ST9 9JY
T: (01782) 302575

BAKEWELL
Derbyshire

Anne Cottage and Barn Cottage ★★★★★
Contact: Mrs Adrienne Howarth, Bakewell Holidays, Long Meadow House, Coombs Road, Bakewell DE45 1AQ
T: (01629) 812500
E: amshowarth@aol.com

Bakewell Holiday Cottage (Coach Cottage) ★★★★
Contact: Mr & Mrs J Gough, The Gatehouse, Riverside Court, Calver, Curbar, Hope Valley S32 3YW
T: (01433) 639582
E: john@gough57.fsnet.co.uk
I: www.bakewellcottages.co.uk

Ball Cross Farm Cottages ★★★★
Contact: Mrs J Edwards, Ball Cross Farm Cottages, Chatsworth Estate, Bakewell DE45 1PE
T: (01629) 815215
E: info@ballcrossfarm.com
I: www.ballcrossfarm.com

The Barn ★★★★
Contact: Mr G J Raymont, 44 Newland Lane, Ash Green, Coventry CV7 9BA
T: (024) 7664 4173

Bay Tree Cottage ★★★★
Contact: Mr Philip Ryder, Bay Tree Cottage, 8 Old Lumford Cottages, Bakewell DE45 1GG
T: (01663) 762724
F: (01663) 762724
E: baytree@smartone.co.uk

Bolehill Farm Holiday Cottages ★★-★★★
Contact: Mr Staley, Bolehill Farm Holiday Cottages, Bolehill Farm, Monyash Road, Over Haddon, Bakewell DE45 1QW
T: (01629) 812359
F: (01629) 812359
E: tonystaley@hotmail.com
I: www.bolehillfarmcottages.co.uk

Butts Cottage ★★★
Contact: Mr C MacQueen, Peak Cottages, Strawberry Lee Lane, Totley Bents, Sheffield S17 3BA
T: (0114) 262 0777
F: (0114) 262 0666
E: enquiries@peakcottages.com
I: www.peakcottages.com

Carter's Mill Cottage ★★★★
Contact: Mr & Mrs Marsden, Mill Farm, Haddon Grove, Over Haddon, Bakewell DE45 1JF
T: (01629) 812013
F: (01629) 814734
E: MARSDEN.MILLFARM@BTINTERNET.COM

Cosy Cottage ★★★★
Contact: Peak Cottages, Strawberry Lee Lane, Totley Bents, Sheffield S17 3BA
T: (0114) 262 0777
F: (0114) 262 0666
E: enquiries@peakcottages.com
I: www.peakcottages.com

The Cottage ★★★★
Contact: Mrs L Wright, Stancil House, Barn Furlong, Great Longstone, Bakewell DE45 1TR
T: (01629) 640136

Dale End Farm ★★★
Contact: Mrs Elizabeth Hague, Dale End Farm, Gratton Dale, Youlgreave, Bakewell DE45 1LN
T: (01629) 650453
E: john.elizabeth.hague@talk21.com

Dale View Farm Rating Applied For
Contact: Mrs Janet Frost, Dale View Farm, Gratton, Bakewell DE45 1LN
T: (01629) 650670

East View ★★★★
Contact: Mr & Mrs F Dickinson, Meadow View, Coombes Road, Bakewell DE45 1AQ
T: (01629) 812961

Edge View ★★★★
Contact: Mrs G P Rogers, Penylan, Monyash Road, Bakewell DE45 1FG
T: (01629) 813336
F: (01629) 813336

Four Winds ★★★
Contact: Mr Sykes, Sykes Cottages, York House, York Street, Chester CH1 3LR
T: (01244) 345700
F: (01244) 321442
E: info@sykescottages.co.uk
I: www.sykescottages.co.uk

Gingerbread Cottage ★★★★
Contact: Mrs Jane Bond, The Shooting Lodge, Derwent, Bamford, Hope Valley S33 0AQ
T: (01433) 659767
F: (01433) 659767

Haddon Grove Farm Cottages ★★★
Contact: Mr & Mrs John & Barbara Boxall, Haddon Grove Farm Cottages, Haddon Grove Farm, Monyash Road, Over Haddon, Bakewell DE45 1JF
T: (01629) 813551
F: (01629) 815684

Limestone Cottage ★★★
Contact: Mrs V Hartley, 1 Church Street, Ashford in the Water, Bakewell DE45 1QB
T: (01629) 813230
E: b&b@hartleycons.co.uk

Meadows ★★★★
Contact: Peak Cottages, Strawberry Lee Lane, Totley Bents, Totley Rise, Sheffield S17 3BA
T: (0114) 262 0777
F: (0114) 262 0666
E: enquiries@peakcottages.com
I: www.peakcottages.com

36 North Church Street ★★★
Contact: Mr Phillip Dobbin, Bryants Bottom Road, Great Missenden HP16 0JU
T: (01494) 488463
E: phillip.dobbin@pipemedia.co.uk

Rozel ★★★★
Contact: Mr Colin MacQueen, Peak Cottages, Strawberry Lee Lane, Totley Bents, Sheffield S17 3BA
T: (0114) 262 0777
F: (0114) 262 0666
E: enquiries@peakcottages.com
I: www.peakcottages.com

Shutts Farm ★★★★
Contact: Mr & Mrs Corbridge, Orchard Close, The Shutts, Bakewell DE45 1JA
T: (01629) 813639

Spout Farm ★★★
Contact: Mrs Ena Patterson, The Bungalow, Elton, Matlock DE4 2BY
T: (01629) 650358

Yuletide Cottage ★★★
Contact: Mr & Mrs Figg, Yuletide Cottage, Church Street, Youlgrave, Bakewell DE45 1UR
T: (01629) 636234

BALLIDON
Derbyshire

Ballidon Moor Farmhouse ★★★★
Contact: Mrs Vicki Lambert, Ballidon Moor Farmhouse, Brassington, Ballidon, Ashbourne DE4 4HP
T: (01629) 540327
F: (01629) 540661

Rachels Croft ★★★★
Contact: Mrs Alison Edge, Oldfield House, Ballidon, Ashbourne DE6 1QX
T: (01335) 390587

BAMFORD
Derbyshire

Derwent View ★★★★
Contact: Mrs Joyce Mannion, 12 Ashopton Drive, Bamford, Hope Valley S33 0BU
T: (01433) 651637
E: jamcottage@talk21.com

Shatton Hall Farm ★★★★
Contact: Mrs A H Kellie, Shatton Hall Farm, Bamford, Hope Valley S33 0BG
T: (01433) 620635
F: (01433) 620689
E: ahk@peakfarmholidays.co.uk
I: www.peakfarmholidays.co.uk

Thornhill View ★★★
Contact: Mrs Joyce Fairbairn, Thornhill View, Hope Road, Bamford, Hope Valley S33 0AL
T: (01433) 651823

Thornseat Cottage ★★★
Contact: Mr Colin MacQueen, Peak Cottages, Strawberry Lee Lane, Totley Bents, Sheffield S17 3BA
T: (0114) 262 0777
F: (0114) 262 0666
E: enquiries@peakcottages.com
I: www.peakcottages.com

BARLASTON
Staffordshire

Wedgwood Memorial College ★★
Contact: Ms Elaine Heather, Wedgwood Memorial College, Station Road, Barlaston, Stoke-on-Trent ST12 9DG
T: (01782) 372105
F: (01782) 372393
E: wedgwood.college@staffordshire.gov.uk
I: www.aredu.org.uk/wedgwoodcollege

BARLOW
Derbyshire

Mill Farm Holiday Cottages ★★★
Contact: Mr & Mrs R Ward, Mill Farm Holiday Cottages, Mill Farm, Barlow, Dronfield S18 7TJ
T: (0114) 289 0543
F: (0114) 289 1473
E: cottages@barfish.fsnet.co.uk
I: www.barlowlakes.co.uk

PCB Holiday Cottages ★★★-★★★★★
Contact: Mr & Mrs Moffatt, PCB Holiday Cottages, Oxton Rakes Hall Farm, Dronfield S18 7SE
T: (0114) 289 9290
F: (0114) 289 9260
E: bookings@heron-lodge.hypermart.net
I: heron-lodge.hypermart.net

BARROW UPON SOAR
Leicestershire

Kingfisher Cottage ★★★★
Contact: Mr J Matthews, 114 Main Street, Woodhouse Eaves, Loughborough LE12 8RZ
T: (01509) 890244
E: nikkidavid@aol.com
I: www.englishcottage.com

BARTESTREE
Herefordshire

St James's House ★★★★
Contact: Mr Giles Mason, Perkins Rail, Peatree Green, Brockhampton, Hereford HR1 4SA
T: (01989) 740669
F: (01989) 740354
E: hugo@perkinsrail.co.uk

BASLOW
Derbyshire

Goose Green Apartment ★★★★
Contact: Mr D W Bailey, Goose Green Apartment, c/o Goose Green Tearooms, Nether End, Baslow, Bakewell DE45 1SR
T: (01246) 583000

Goose Green Cottage ★★★★★
Contact: Mr & Mrs Smith, Long Meadow House, Coombs Road, Bakewell DE45 1AQ
T: (01246) 582140

Hall Cottage ★★★★
Contact: Mr & Mrs R W Griffiths, Beechcroft, School Lane, Baslow, Bakewell DE45 1RZ
T: (01246) 582900
F: (01246) 583675
E: hallcottage@btinternet.com

Stable Cottage ★★★★
Contact: Ms Anne O'Connor, Woodside Cottage, Nether End, Baslow, Bakewell DE45 1SR
T: (01246) 582285
F: (01246) 583007
E: ourstablecottage@aol.com

Tom's Cottage ★★★
Contact: Ms Hazel Bell, Nether Croft, Eaton Place, Baslow, Bakewell DE45 1RW
T: (01246) 583564
E: nethercroftBandB@aol.com

Wrose Cottage ★★★
Contact: Mrs J Cartledge, Bramley Court, Waterside, Calver Road, Baslow, Bakewell DE45 1RR
T: (01246) 583131
F: (01246) 583131

BAUMBER
Lincolnshire

Gathman's Cottage ★★★
Contact: Mrs Wendy Harrison, Hemingby, Baumber, Horncastle LN9 5QF
T: (01507) 578352
F: (01507) 578417
E: gathmans@freenetname.co.uk
I: www.gathmanscottage.co.uk

BAYTON
Worcestershire

The Mill House ★★★
Contact: Mrs Jane Chance, The Mill House, Bayton, Clows Top, Kidderminster DY14 9LP
T: (01299) 832608
F: (01299) 832137
I: www.themillhouse-bayton.co.uk

BECKFORD
Worcestershire

The Old Stable Block Rating Applied For
Contact: Mr & Mrs Geoff Stringer, Beckford Stores, Main Street, Beckford, Tewkesbury GL20 7AD
T: (01386) 881248
E: info@beckford-stores.co.uk

BELMESTHORPE
Rutland

Elder Flower Cottage ★★★
Contact: Mr & Mrs Wilkinson, Meadow View, Shepherds Walk, Belmesthorpe, Stamford PE9 4JG
T: (01780) 757188
F: (01780) 757188

BELPER
Derbyshire

Chevin Green Farm ★★★
Contact: Mr C A Postles, Chevin Green Farm, Chevin Road, Belper, Derby DE56 2UN
T: (01773) 822328
F: (01773) 822328
E: spostles@globalnet.co.uk
I: chevingreenfarm.co.uk

Chevin House Farm Cottages ★★★
Contact: Mr & Mrs Jordan, Chevin House Farm Cottages Chevin House Farm, Chevin Road, Belper DE56 2UN
T: (01773) 823144
F: (01773) 823144

The Sheiling ★★★
Contact: Country Holidays Ref: 12853 Sales, Holidays Cottages Group Limited, Spring Mill, Earby, Barnoldswick BB94 0AA
T: 08700 723723
F: (01282) 844288
E: sales@ttgihg.co.uk
I: www.country-holidays.co.uk

Wiggonlea Stable ★★★★
Contact: Mrs Spendlove, Wiggonlea Stable, Wiggonlea Farm, Alderwasley, Belper DE56 2RE
T: (01773) 852344

BEOLEY
Worcestershire

The Granary ★★★★
Contact: Mrs Lang, The Granary, Dagnell End Farm, Dagnell End Road, Redditch B98 9BE
T: (01527) 596406
E: donnalang@aol.com

BEWDLEY
Worcestershire

The Brant ★★★★
Contact: Mrs Helen Robson, The Brant, Heightington, Bewdley DY12 2XY
T: (01299) 825603
F: (01299) 825603
E: paulandhelen@hotmail.com

Manor Holding ★★★
Contact: Mr & Mrs Nigel & Penny Dobson-Smyth, 32 Church Street, Hagley, Clent, Stourbridge DY9 0NA
T: 07970 260010
E: nds@landscapeconsultancy.freeserve.co.uk

Painsmore Cottage ★★
Contact: Mrs Drummy, Dowles House, Bewdley DY12 3AA
T: (01299) 403137
E: painsmore@hotmail.com

Peacock Coach House ★★★★
Contact: Mrs P Hall, Peacock House, Lower Park, Bewdley DY12 2DP
T: (01299) 400149
E: priscahall@hotmail.com

Riverview Cottage ★★★
Contact: Mr & Mrs J Giles, The Lodge, Station Road, Bewdley DY12 1BT
T: (01299) 403481
E: jgilesm81@aol.com
I: www.riverview-bdy.co.uk

The White Cottage Garden Flat ★★★★
Contact: Mrs S A Tallents, The White Cottage, Kinlet, Bewdley DY12 3BD
T: (01299) 841238
F: (01299) 841482

BIBURY
Gloucestershire

Bibury Holiday Cottages ★★★-★★★★★
Contact: Mr & Mrs R Hedgeland Cotswold Heritage Ltd, Coln Court, Arlington, Cirencester GL7 5NL
T: (01285) 740314
F: (01285) 740314
E: rogerhedgeland@btopenworld.com

Cotteswold House Cottages ★★★★
Contact: Mrs Judith Underwood, Cotteswold House, Arlington, Bibury, Cirencester GL7 5ND
T: (01285) 740609
F: (01285) 740609
E: cotteswold.house@btconnect.com
I: home.btconnect.com/cotteswold.house

Hartwell Farm Cottages ★★★★
Contact: Mrs Caroline Mann, Hartwell Farm, Ready Token, Cirencester GL7 5SY
T: (01285) 740210
F: (01285) 740210
E: caroline@hartwell89.freeserve.co.uk
I: www.selfcateringcotswolds.co.uk

BIDFORD-ON-AVON
Warwickshire

Corner Cottage ★★★★
Contact: Mr & Mrs W A Lucas, Tanglewood, Park Close, Wilmcote, Stratford-upon-Avon CV37 9XE
T: (01789) 293932
F: (01789) 261855
E: lucasstratford@aol.com

BIGGIN-BY-HARTINGTON
Derbyshire

Cheese Press Cottage, The Old Farrowings & Courtyard Creamery★★★★
Contact: Mr C MacQueen, Peak Cottages, Strawberry Lee Lane, Totley Bents, Sheffield S17 3BA
T: (0114) 262 0777
F: (0114) 262 0666
E: enquiries@peakcottages.com
I: www.peakcottages.com

BIRCH VALE
Derbyshire

Hallishaw Cote ★★★★
Contact: Mrs Jennifer Hallam, Cold Harbour Farm, New Mills, High Peak SK22 4QJ
T: (01663) 746155
E: jenny@coldharbour.fslife.co.uk
I: www.hallishawcote.co.uk

BIRCHOVER
Derbyshire

Birchover Cottages ★★★
Contact: Mr C MacQueen, Peak Cottages, Strawberry Lee Lane, Totley Bents, Sheffield S17 3BA
T: (0114) 262 0777
F: (0114) 262 0666

Uppertown Hayloft ★★★
Contact: Mr Colin MacQueen, Peak Cottages, Strawberry Lee Lane, Totley Bents, Sheffield S17 3BA
T: (0114) 262 0777
F: (0114) 262 0666
E: enquiries@peakcottages.com
I: www.peakcottages.com

BIRTLEY
Shropshire

Hinds Cottage ★★★★
Contact: Mrs Newby, White House Farm, Deerfold, Lingen, Bucknell SY7 0EF
T: (01568) 770242
E: geof.newby@lycos.com
I: www.hindscottage.co.uk

BISHOP'S CASTLE
Shropshire

Claremont ★★★
Contact: Mrs Price, Claremont, Claremont Holiday Cottages, Bull Lane, Bishop's Castle SY9 5BW
T: (01588) 638170
F: (01588) 638170
E: price@claremontcottages.freeserve.co.uk
I: www.priceclaremont.co.uk

The Firs ★★★
Contact: Mr Sykes, Sykes Cottage, York House, York Street, Chester CH1 3LR
T: (01244) 345700
F: (01244) 321442
E: info@sykescottages.co.uk
I: www.sykescottages.co.uk

Mount Cottage ★★★★
Contact: Mrs H Willis, Mount Cottage, Bull Lane, Bishop's Castle SY9 5DA
T: (01588) 638288
F: (01588) 638288
E: adamheather@btopenworld.com
I: www.mountcottage.co.uk

Walkmill Cottage ★★★
Contact: Mr Barry Preston, Walkmill Cottage, Wentnor, Bishop's Castle SY9 5DZ
T: (01588) 650671

BISHOPS FROME
Herefordshire

Five Bridges Inn ★★★★
Contact: Mr & Mrs Chatterton, Five Bridges Inn, Bishops Frome, Worcester WR6 5BX
T: (01531) 640340
E: mark@5bridges.freeserve.co.uk

BISLEY
Gloucestershire

Coopers Cottage ★★★
Contact: Mr & Mrs Flint, Wells Cottage, Bisley, Stroud GL6 7AG
T: (01452) 770289

BITTERLEY
Shropshire

Angel House ★★★
Contact: Mr & Mrs Henry & Doreen Mears, Angel House, Angel Bank, Near Bitterley, Ludlow SY8 3HT
T: (01584) 890755
F: (01584) 890755

BLACKBROOK
Staffordshire

Nags Head Farm Cottages ★★★
Contact: Mr David William Leathem, Nags Head Farm Cottages, Nags Head Farm, Nantwich Road, Blackbrook, Newcastle-under-Lyme ST5 5EH
T: (01782) 680334
F: (01782) 680334
E: nagsheadfarm.@aol.com

BLAKENEY
Gloucestershire

Orchard Cottage & Granny's Apple Lodge★★★-★★★★
Contact: Mrs S Thomas, Orchard Cottage & Granny's Apple Lodge, c/o Gable Cottage, Furnace Valley, Blakeney GL15 4DH
T: (01594) 510537
F: (01594) 516336

BLANKNEY
Lincolnshire

Blankney Golf Club ★★★
Contact: Mr D Priest, Blankney Golf Club, Blankney, Lincoln LN4 3AZ
T: (01526) 320263
F: (01526) 322521
I: www.blankneygolf.co.uk

BLOCKLEY
Gloucestershire

Angel Cottage ★★
Contact: Mr & Mrs Peter & Sue Knights, 104 Little Sutton Lane, Sutton Coldfield B75 6PG
T: (0121) 308 0519
E: sue_knights@hotmail.com

Julianas Court ★★★★
Contact: Mr T R Lomas, The Cedars, 92 Prestbury Road, Macclesfield SK10 3BN
T: (01625) 613701
E: erl@xaniels.uk.com

Lower Farm Cottages ★★★★
Contact: Mrs K Batchelor, Lower Farm Cottages, Lower Farmhouse, Blockley, Moreton-in-Marsh GL56 9DP
T: (01386) 700237
F: (01386) 700237
E: lowerfarm@hotmail.com
I: www.lower-farm.co.uk

BOCKLETON
Worcestershire

1 Grafton Cottage ★★★
Contact: Mrs Sue Thomas, Grafton Farm, Bockleton, Tenbury Wells WR15 8PT
T: (01568) 750602
F: (01568) 750602
E: grafton.farm@btinternet.com

BODENHAM
Herefordshire

Bodenham Forge ★★★★
Contact: Mrs Mary Nickols, Bodenham Forge, The Forge, Bodenham, Hereford HR1 3JZ
T: (01568) 797144
E: sgnickols@yahoo.co.uk
I: www.bodenhamforge.co.uk

BONSALL
Derbyshire

Croft Cottage ★★★★
Contact: Mr Colin MacQueen, Peak Cottages Ltd, Strawberry Lee Lane, Totley Bents, Totley Rise, Sheffield S17 3BA
T: (0114) 262 0777
F: (0114) 262 0666
E: enquiries@peakcottages.com
I: www.peakcottages.com

Hollies Cottage ★★★
Contact: Mrs Mountney, 38 High Street, Bonsall, Matlock DE4 2AR
T: (01629) 823162

BOSTON
Lincolnshire

The Annexe ★★★
Contact: Mrs Lindsey McBarrow, Walnuts Farmhouse, Frampton Bank, Boston PE20 1SW
T: (01205) 290067
E: mcbcastle@aol.com

The Lodge at Pinewood ★★★
Contact: Ms Sylvia Kilshaw, Pinewood, Ralphs Lane, Frampton West, Boston PE20 1QZ
T: (01205) 723739
F: (01205) 723739

BOURTON-ON-THE-WATER
Gloucestershire

Acorn Cottage ★★★★
Contact: Mrs Ann Oakes, White Rails Farm, Atch Lench, Church Lench, Evesham WR11 4SZ
T: (01386) 870727
F: (01386) 870727
E: oakescottages@bigfoot.com

Annes Cottage ★★★★
Contact: Mrs Ann Oakes, White Rails Farm, Atch Lench, Church Lench, Evesham WR11 4SZ
T: (01386) 870727
F: (01386) 870727
E: oakescottages@bigfoot.com

Bobble Cottage ★★★
Contact: Country Holidays Ref: 15430, Spring Mill, Barnoldswick BB94 0AS
T: 08700 723723

The Chesters ★★★★★
Contact: Miss Wendy Ratcliffe, Avalon, Rissington Road, Little Rissington, Cheltenham GL54 2DX
T: (01451) 821014

The Coach House of the Dower House ★★
Contact: Mrs Philomena Adams, The Dower House, Bourton-on-the-Water, Cheltenham GL54 2AP
T: (01451) 820629

Farncombe Apartment ★★★★
Contact: Mrs Julia Wright, Farncombe Apartment, Clapton, Bourton-on-the-Water, Cheltenham GL54 2LG
T: (01451) 820120
F: (01451) 820120
E: jwrightbb@aol.com
I: www.SmoothHound.co.uk/hotels/farncombe.html

Florries Cottage ★★★
Contact: Country Holidays - 1362 Sales, Holiday Cottages Group Limited, Spring Mill, Earby, Barnoldswick BB94 0AA
T: 08700 723723
F: (01282) 844288
E: sales@ttgihg.co.uk
I: www.country-holidays.co.uk

Greenleighs ★★★★
Contact: Mrs Tombs, The Old Forge, Tytherington, Wotton-under-Edge GL12 8UH
T: (01454) 419760

Hattie's, Lucy's, Chapel and Jack's ★★★★
Contact: Pippa Arnott, Cotswolds Cottage Company, Wells Head, Temple Guiting, Cheltenham GL54 5RR
T: (01451) 850560
F: (0870) 128 0033
E: cotscotco@msn.com
I: www.cotswoldcottage.co.uk

Inglenook Cottage ★★★
Contact: Mrs Vicki Garland, Mythe Farm, Pinwall Lane, Atherstone CV9 3PF
T: (01827) 712367
F: (01827) 715738

Magnolia Cottage Apartment ★★★★
Contact: Mr & Mrs M Cotterill, Magnolia Cottage, Lansdowne, Bourton-on-the-Water, Cheltenham GL54 2AR
T: (01451) 821841
F: (01451) 821841
E: cotterillmj@hotmail.com
I: www.cottageguide.co.uk/magnolia

Oxleigh Cottages ★★★★
Contact: Mrs B Smith, Dairy House Farm, Croxton Lane, Middlewich CW10 9LA
T: (01606) 833245
F: (01606) 837139
E: bsmith@lazymeadow.fsnet.co.uk

Pheasant Walk ★★★★
Contact: Mrs Penny Avery, Pheasant Walk, Grove Farm, Cold Aston, Cheltenham GL54 3BJ
T: (01451) 810942
F: (01451) 810942
E: grovefarm@coldaston.fsnet.co.uk

Southview, Courtyard & Tallet Cottage ★★★★-★★★★★
Contact: Mr & Mrs Nando & Joyce Fracasso, Southview and Courtyard Cottages, c/o Home Farm House, Little Rissington, Cheltenham GL54 2NA
T: (01451) 820691

Tagmoor Hollow Apartment ★★★★
Contact: Mrs G Bennett, Tagmoor Hollow, Marshmouth Lane, Bourton-on-the-Water, Cheltenham GL54 2EE
T: (01451) 821307

Well Cottage ★★★★
Contact: Mr & Mrs J Roberts, Wayside Cottage, Letch Lane, Bourton-on-the-Water, Cheltenham GL54 2DG
T: (01451) 824059

Wrights Cottage ★★★★
Contact: Mr & Mrs Marsh, Applegarth, Hilcote Drive, Little Rissington, Cheltenham GL54 2DU
T: (01451) 820568

BRACKENFIELD
Derbyshire

Ruardean ★★★
Contact: Mr Clive Sykes, Sykes Cottages, York House, York Street, Chester CH1 3LR
T: (01244) 345700
F: (01244) 321442
E: info@sykescottages.co.uk

BRACKLEY
Northamptonshire

Iletts Courtyard ★★★★
Contact: Mrs Sally Bellingham, Iletts Courtyard, Iletts Farm, Whitfield, Brackley NN13 7TY
T: (01280) 703244
F: (01280) 703244
E: iletts@clara.co.uk
I: home.clara.net/iletts

BRADLEY
Derbyshire

Briar, Primrose and Bluebell Cottages★★★-★★★★
Contact: Mrs Janet Hinds, Briar, Primrose and Bluebell Cottages, Yeldersley Old Hall Farm, Yeldersley Lane, Bradley, Ashbourne DE6 1PH
T: (01335) 344504
F: (01335) 344504
E: janethindsfarm@yahoo.co.uk
I: www.ashbourne-accommodation.co.uk/detail/briar.htm

Shepherds Folly ★★★★
Contact: Mrs Kathy Cowley, Shepherds Folly, Bradley, Ashbourne DE6 1LL
T: (01335) 343315

BRADNOP
Staffordshire

Millstones ★★★
Contact: Mrs J Edwards, Millstones, Ashbourne Road, Bottomhouse, Bradnop, Leek ST13 7NZ
T: (01538) 304548
F: (01538) 304101
E: stephan@swepme.fsnet.co.uk

School House ★★★★★
Contact: Mr Sykes, Sykes Cottages, York House, York Street, Chester CH1 3LR
T: (01244) 345700
F: (01244) 321442
E: info@sykescottages.co.uk
I: www.sykescottages.co.uk

BRADWELL
Derbyshire

Bridge End Barn ★★★★
Contact: Mrs Gill Gascoyne, Bridge End Barn, Brough, Hope, Hope Valley S33 9HG
T: (01433) 621258

The Croft and Edge View ★★★-★★★★
Contact: Mr Sykes, Sykes Cottage, York House, York Street, Chester CH1 3LR
T: (01244) 345700
F: (01244) 321442
E: info@sykescottage.co.uk
I: www.sykescottge.co.uk

Derwent Cottage ★★★
Contact: Mr Mark Gilbertson, 124 Cranbrook Road, Chiswick, London W4 2LJ
T: (020) 8747 9450
E: markanddoona@hotmail.com

Smalldale ★★★★
Contact: Mr Sykes, Sykes Cottages, York House, York Street, Chester CH1 3LR
T: (01244) 345700
F: (01244) 321442
E: info@sykescottages.co.uk
I: www.sykescottages.co.uk

BRAILES
Warwickshire

Mill Holm Cottage and Mill Flat ★★★
Contact: Mr Rod Case, Mill Holm Cottage and Mill Flat, Whichford Mill, Cherington, Banbury CV36 5JB
T: (01608) 686537
E: RODCASE29@HOTMAIL.COM

BRAILSFORD
Derbyshire

The Cottage ★★★★
Contact: Mrs C Phillips, The Cottage, Culland Mount Farm, Brailsford, Ashbourne DE6 3BW
T: (01335) 360313

BRAMPTON BRYAN
Herefordshire

Hicks Farm Holidays-Rose Cottage ★★★★
Contact: Mrs Susan Bywater, Hicks Farm, Boresford, Brampton Bryan, Bucknell LD8 2NB
T: (01544) 260237
E: holidays@hicksfarm.fsbusiness.co.uk

BRASSINGTON
Derbyshire

Hillocks Barn ★★★★
Contact: Mr MacQueen, Peak Cottages, Strawberry Lee Lane, Totley Bents, Totley Rise, Sheffield S17 3BA
T: (0114) 262 0777
F: (0114) 262 0666
E: enquiries@peakcottages.com
I: www.peakcottages.com

Jack's Cottage ★★★★
Contact: Mrs E Rodrigues, 48 Grove Avenue, Chilwell, Nottingham NG9 4DZ
T: (0115) 925 1441
E: jacks.cottage@tinyworld.co.uk

Maddock Lake House ★★★★
Contact: Ms Diane Moore, 48a Nottingham Road, Eastwood, Nottingham NG16 3NQ
T: (01773) 532110

BREDON
Worcestershire

The Moretons Vacation Houses ★★★★★
Contact: Mr & Mrs Soutar, The Moretons, Bredon, Tewkesbury GL20 7EN
T: (01684) 772294
F: (01684) 772262
E: soutar@moretonsbredon.co.uk
I: www.worcs.com/moretonswww.moretonsbredon.co.uk

BRIDGNORTH
Shropshire

Bulls Head Cottages ★★★
Contact: Mr D Baxter, The Bulls Head, Chelmarsh, Bridgnorth WV16 6BA
T: (01746) 861469
F: (01746) 862646
E: dave@bullshead.fsnet.co.uk
I: www.virtual-shropshire.co.uk/bulls-head-inn

Eudon Burnell Cottages ★★★★
Contact: Mrs M A Crawford Clarke, Eudon Burnell, Glazeley, Near Bridgnorth WV16 6UD
T: (01746) 789235
F: (01746) 789550
E: eudonburnell@virtual-shropshire.co.uk
I: www.eudon.co.uk

The Gatehouse ★★★★
Contact: Mrs B Cash, Upton Cressett Hall, Bridgnorth WV16 6UH
T: (01746) 714307
F: (01746) 714506

The Granary ★★★
Contact: Mrs Sarah Allen, The Granary, The Old Vicarage, Ditton Priors, Bridgnorth WV16 6SQ
T: (01746) 712272
F: (01746) 712288
E: allen@oldvicditton.freeserve.co.uk

Jacob's Cottage ★★★★
Contact: Mrs Gilly Wooldridge, 2 Allscott, Nr Worfield, Worfield, Bridgnorth WV15 5JX
T: (01746) 716687
F: (01746) 716687
E: peterwulf@lineone.net

Lobby Stables ★★★★
Contact: Mrs Helen Danks, Lobby Stables, Lobby Farm, Oldfield, Chelmarsh, Bridgnorth WV16 6AQ
T: (01746) 789218
E: lobby_farm@lineone.net
I: cottageguide.co.uk/lobbyfarmwww.shropshire-cottage.co.uk

The Loosebox and The Hayloft Ellerdine★★★-★★★★
Contact: Mr & Mrs G J Higgins, Ellerdine, Occupation Lane, Chelmarsh, Bridgnorth WV16 6BE
T: (01746) 861397
F: (01746) 861397
E: ghig158852@aol.com

Severn Rest ★★★
Contact: Miss Cartwright, 8 Riverside, Bridgnorth WV16 4BH
T: (01746) 768242
E: jacky.cartwright@virgin.net

Tudor Cottage ★★
Contact: Mrs Henshaw, 17 High Street, Claverley, Bridgnorth WV5 7DR
T: (01746) 710262

BRIERLEY
Herefordshire

Walnut Tree Cottage ★★★★
Contact: Ms Elaine Johnson, Walnut Tree Cottage, Brierley, Leominster HR6 0NU
T: (01568) 620033
F: (01568) 620011
E: elaine@walnuttreecottage.net

BRIGSTOCK
Northamptonshire

The Gable End ★★★
Contact: Mrs Clarke, The Gables, 2 Benefield Road, Brigstock, Kettering NN14 3ES
T: (01536) 373674
F: (01536) 373674
E: marcus@clark1999.freeserve.co.uk

BRIMPSFIELD
Gloucestershire

Brimpsfield Farmhouse (West Wing) ★★★
Contact: Mrs Valerie Partridge, Brimpsfield Farmhouse (West Wing), Brimpsfield Farm, Brimpsfield, Gloucester GL4 8LD
T: (01452) 863568

BROAD CAMPDEN
Gloucestershire

Lion Cottage ★★★
Contact: Mrs B L Rawcliffe, Lion Cottage, Broad Campden, Chipping Campden GL55 6UR
T: (01386) 840077

BROADWAY
Worcestershire

Hesters House ★★★
Contact: Mrs L Dungate, Inglenook, Brokengate Lane, Denham, Uxbridge UB9 4LA
T: (01895) 834357
F: (01895) 832904
E: pdungate@aol.com

Orchard Cottage
Rating Applied For
Contact: Sheila Rolland, Campden Cottages, Paxford, Chipping Campden GL55 6XG
T: (01386) 593315
F: (01386) 593057
E: info@campdencottages.co.uk
I: www.campdencottages.co.uk

BROADWELL
Warwickshire

Little Biggin ★★★
Contact: Mr & Mrs Adrian & Linda Denham, Little Biggin, Broadwell House Farm, Broadwell, Rugby CV23 8HF
T: (01926) 812347
F: (01926) 812347
E: broadwellhouse@ntlworld.com

BROBURY
Herefordshire

Brobury House Cottages ★★-★★★
Contact: Mrs P Cartwright, Brobury House, Brobury, Hereford HR3 6BS
T: (01981) 500229
F: (01981) 500229
I: www.broburyhouse.co.uk

BROCKTON
Shropshire

Old Quarry Cottage Apartment ★★★
Contact: Mrs Thorpe, Old Quarry Cottage, Brockton, Much Wenlock TF13 6JR
T: (01746) 785596
E: rod@brockton.fsbusiness.co.uk

BROMSBERROW
Gloucestershire

Perrins Court Holiday Cottages Rating Applied For
Contact: Mr & Mrs A Stow, Stow House, Chase End Street, Bromesberrow, Ledbury HR8 1SD
T: (01531) 650670
E: stow@perrinscourt.org

BROMSGROVE
Worcestershire

East View Apartment ★★★
Contact: Mrs A Westwood, Little Shortwood, Brockhill Lane, Tardebigge, Bromsgrove B60 1LU
T: (01527) 63180
F: (01527) 63180
E: westwoodja@hotmail.com

BROMYARD
Herefordshire

Mintridge ★★★★
Contact: Mr & Mrs Richard and Sally Barrett, Hodgebatch Manor, Bromyard HR7 4QQ
T: (01885) 483262
F: (01885) 483262
E: hodgebatch@aol.com

BROSELEY
Shropshire

Aynsley Cottages ★★★
Contact: Mr & Mrs Keith & Elsie Elcock, Shalimar, 4 Fox Lane, Broseley TF12 5LR
T: (01952) 882695
E: aynsleycottages@hotmail.com

BROWN EDGE
Staffordshire

Ladymoor View Cottage ★★★
Contact: Mrs M E Adams, Ladymoor View, Hill Top, Brown Edge, Stoke-on-Trent ST6 8UB
T: (01782) 504668

BROXWOOD
Herefordshire

The Coach House ★★★★★
Contact: Mr & Mrs Mike & Anne Allen, Broxwood Court, Broxwood, Leominster HR6 9JJ
T: (01544) 340245
F: (01544) 340573
E: mikeanne@broxwood.kc3.co.uk

BUCKLAND
Gloucestershire

Hillside Cottage and The Bothy ★★★★
Contact: Mr C Edmondson, Burhill, Buckland, Broadway WR12 7LY
T: (01386) 858842
F: (01386) 853900

BURGHILL
Herefordshire

Manor Barn ★★★★
Contact: Mr Christie, Manor Barn, Burghill Manor, Burghill, Hereford HR4 7RX
T: (01432) 761447
F: (01432) 761447
I: www.herefordshire-cottages.com

BURLEY GATE
Herefordshire

Holly Lodge ★★★
Contact: Mr Barry Lawrence, Holly Tree Cottage, Burley Gate, Hereford HR1 3QS
T: (01432) 820493
E: lawrence3@supanet.com
I: www.cottageguide.co.uk/hollylodge.html

BURTON
Lincolnshire

10 Bridge Walk Cottage ★★★★★
Contact: Mrs Elliott, Ednaston House, Ednaston, Brailsford, Ashbourne DE6 3AE
T: (01335) 360664
F: (01335) 361466

The Conifers Guest Annexe ★★★★
Contact: Mr Martin Gray, The Conifers Guest Annexe, The Conifers, Occupation Lane, Burton, Lincoln LN1 2NB
T: (01522) 703196
E: mjgtheconifers@supanet.com

Waterside Cottage ★★★★★
Contact: Ms A M Moore, 18 Monkton Way, Dunholme, Lincoln LN2 3WQ
T: (01673) 863008

BURWARTON
Shropshire

The Wicket ★★★
Contact: Mrs J M Millard, Brown Clee Holidays, Estate Office, Burwarton, Bridgnorth WV16 6QQ
T: (01746) 787207
F: (01746) 787422
E: millard@burwarton-estates.co.uk

BUTTERTON
Staffordshire

Croft Head Farm ★★★
Contact: Mr M Clark, Croft Head Farm, Butterton, Leek ST13 7TD
T: (01538) 304347
F: (01538) 304347
E: manon@lineone.net
I: www.farmholidays.co.uk

Swainsley Farm ★★★★★
Contact: Mr & Mrs C J Snook, Swainsley Farm, Butterton, Leek ST13 7SS
T: (01298) 84530

BUXTON
Derbyshire

Cavendish Apartment ★★★★
Contact: Mr John Limer, Cavendish Apartment, Apartment 1, 3 Cavendish Villas, Buxton SK17 6JE
T: (01298) 78827
E: jblimer@compuserve.com

Glen Apartment ★★★
Contact: Peak Cottages, Strawberry Lee Lane, Totley Bents, Sheffield S17 3BA
T: (0114) 262 0777
F: (0114) 262 0666
E: enquries@peakcottages.com
I: www.peakcottages.com

Harefield Garden Flat ★★★★
Contact: Mr & Mrs Hardie, Harefield Garden Flat, 15 Marlborough Road, Fairfield, Buxton SK17 6RD
T: (01298) 24029
F: (01298) 24029
E: hardie@harefieldl.freeserve.co.uk
I: www.harefield1.freeserve.co.uk

Hargate Hall ★★★
Contact: Mr J Jackson, Hargate Hall, Wormhill, Buxton SK17 8TA
T: (01298) 872591
I: www.hargate-hall.co.uk

High Needham Cottage ★★★★
Contact: Mrs Paula Bradbury, High Needham Cottage, High Needham Farm, Earl Sterndale, Buxton SK17 0OD
T: (01298) 83242

Hill Side House ★★★★
Contact: Mrs M Swain, 1 Spencer Road, Fairfield, Buxton SK17 9DX
T: (01298) 25451

Lake View ★★★
Contact: Mr C MacQueen, Peak Cottages, Strawberry Lee Lane, Totley Bents, Sheffield S17 3BA
T: (0114) 262 0777
F: (0114) 262 0666

Meadow Barn Cottage ★★★★
Contact: Peak Cottages, Strawberry Lee Lane, Totley Bents, Totley Rise, Sheffield S17 3BA
T: (0114) 262 0777
F: (0114) 262 0666
E: enqurries@peakcottages.com
I: www.peakcottages.com

The Old Stables ★★★
Contact: Mrs J Cowlishaw, 136 Green Lane, Buxton SK17 9DQ
T: (01298) 71086
F: (01298) 77678
E: j.cowlishaw@endeavour.co.uk

Outlow ★★★
Contact: Mr Colin MacQueen, Peak Cottages, Strawberry Lee Lane, Totley Bents, Totley Rise, Sheffield S17 3BA
T: (0114) 262 0777
F: (0114) 262 0666
E: enquiries@peakcottages.com
I: www.peakcottages.com

Priory Lea Holiday Flats ★-★★★
Contact: Mrs Gillian Taylor, Priory Lea Holiday Flats, 50 White Knowle Road, Fairfield, Buxton SK17 9NH
T: (01298) 23737

9 Silverlands Close ★★★
Contact: Mrs N Oldfield, Twelve Trees Guesthouse, 13 Burlington Road, Buxton SK17 9AH
T: (01298) 24371
E: info@buxtonlet.com
I: www.buxtonlet.com

Sittinglow Farm Cottage ★★★
Contact: Mrs Ann S Buckley, Sittinglow Farm Cottage, Cottage Meadow Lane, Dove Holes, Chapel-en-le-Frith, High Peak SK17 8DA
T: (01298) 812271
E: louise@sittinglow.freeserve.co.uk

Thorn Heyes House & Holiday cottage ★★
Contact: Ms Sylvia Hicken & Mr Melvyn Hadfield, Thorn Heyes House & Holiday Cottage, 137 London Road, Buxton SK17 9NW
T: (01298) 23539
F: (01298) 22638
E: syl.mel@hartingtonhotel.co.uk
I: www.hartingtonhotel.co.uk

CALDECOTT
Northamptonshire

Rose Cottage ★★★★
Contact: Mrs Jill Bartlett, The Dog House, 7 The Green, Caldecott, Market Harborough LE16 8RR
T: (01536) 770149
E: mcldoghouse@aol.com
I: www.northamptonshire.co.uk/hotels/rosecottage.htm

CALLOW
Herefordshire

The Loft at Cold Nose ★★★★
Contact: Mr John Evans, Cottage Life, Cold Nose Cottage, Callow, Hereford HR2 8DE
T: (01432) 340954
E: john@cottagelife.freeserve.co.uk

CALVER
Derbyshire

Barn Cottage ★★★★
Contact: Mr B P Finney, The Barn, Lowside, Calver, Hope Valley S32 3XQ
T: (01433) 631672
E: enquiries@barncottage.com

Knouchley Cottage ★★★★
Contact: Peak Cottages, Strawberry Lee Lane, Totley Bents, Sheffield S17 3BA
T: (0114) 262 0777
F: (0114) 262 0666

Sunnyside ★★★
Contact: Peak Cottages, Strawberry Lee Lane, Totley Bents, Totley Rise, Sheffield S17 3BA
T: (0114) 262 0777
F: (0114) 262 0666
E: enquiries@peakcottages.com
I: www.peakcottages.com

CALVERTON
Nottinghamshire

Beryls Cottage ★★★
Contact: Mrs Sandra Pepper, 1 Doveys Orchard, Calverton, Nottingham NG14 6PT
T: (0115) 965 4660
F: (0115) 965 4275
E: pep@doveysorchard.freeserve.co.uk

CAREBY
Lincolnshire

Linnet Cottage ★★★
Contact: Mrs Barbara Cooper, Linnet Cottage, Main Street, Careby, Stamford PE9 4EA
T: (01780) 410580
F: (01780) 410580

CAREY
Herefordshire

Carey Dene and Rock House ★★★
Contact: Mrs Slater, Ruxton Farm, Kings Caple, Hereford HR1 4TX
T: (01432) 840493
F: (01432) 840493
E: milly@ruxton.co.uk

The Stable ★★★★
Contact: Mrs Janette McDonnell, Mews Cottage, Carey, Hereford HR2 6NF
T: (01432) 840463
E: Jan@Mcdonellfamily.com

CARSINGTON
Derbyshire

Breach Farm ★★★★
Contact: Mrs Michelle Wilson, Breach Farm, Carsington, Matlock DE4 4DD
T: (01629) 540265

Knockerdown Holiday Cottages ★★★-★★★★
Contact: Ms Cathy Lambert, Gainsborough Leisure Limited, T/A Knockerdown Farm, Knockerdown, Ashbourne DE6 1NQ
T: (01629) 540525
F: (01629) 540525
E: cathy@knockerdown-cottages.co.uk
I: www.derbyshireholidaycottages.co.uk

Owslow ★★★
Contact: Mr Peter Oldfield, Owslow, Owslow Farm, Carsington, Matlock DE4 4DD
T: (01629) 540510
F: (01629) 540445
E: peter.oldfield@ukonline.co.uk

CASTLETON
Derbyshire

Cave End Cottage ★★★★
Contact: Mr Colin MacQueen, Peak Cottages, Strawberry Lee Lane, Totley Bents, Totley Rise, Sheffield S17 3BA
T: (0114) 262 0777
F: (0114) 262 0666
E: enquiries@peakcottages.com
I: www.peakcottages.com

Eastry Cottage ★★★★
Contact: Mrs Webster, Hillside House, Pindale Road, Castleton, Hope Valley S33 8WU
T: (01433) 620312
F: (01433) 620312

High View Cottage ★★★
Contact: Mr C MacQueen, Peak Cottages, Strawberry Lee Lane, Totley Bents, Sheffield S17 3BA
T: (0114) 262 0777
F: (0114) 262 0666
E: enquiries@peakcottages.com
I: www.peakcottages.com

Millbridge Cottage ★★★★
Contact: Mrs Cutts, Millbridge House, Millbridge, Castleton, Hope Valley S33 8WR
T: (01433) 621556
E: cuttssue@aol.com

Oatcake Cottage ★★★★
Contact: Mrs Sue Baxter, 305 Ecclesall Road South, Ecclesall, Sheffield S11 9PW
T: (0114) 236 4590
F: (0114) 236 3966
E: suebax@btopenworld.com
I: www.cressbrook.co.uk/hopev/oatcake

Trickett Gate Barn ★★★★
Contact: Mrs L Woollacott, Trickett Gate Barn, Castleton, Hope Valley S33 8WR
T: (01433) 620007

CHAPEL-EN-LE-FRITH
Derbyshire

Hawthorn Cottage ★★★
Contact: Mrs Olive Fraser, Rose Cottage, Hawthorn Cottage, Bagshaw, Chapel-en-le-Frith, High Peak SK23 0QU
T: (01298) 813294

Herb View at Newlyn ★★★
Contact: Mr & Mrs Mike & Helen Cullen, Newlyn, Crossings Road, Chapel-en-le-Frith, High Peak SK23 9RY
T: (01298) 814775
E: culherbs@ukonline.co.uk

Keepers Cottage ★★★
Contact: Mrs Mary Hayward, Keepers Cottage, Castleton Road, Chapel-en-le-Frith, High Peak SK23 0QS
T: (01298) 812845
F: (01298) 812845

Sweetpiece Cottage ★★★★
Contact: Mr Colin MacQueen, Peak Cottages, Strawberry Lee Lane, Totley Bents, Totley Rise, Sheffield S17 3BA
T: (0114) 262 0777
F: (0114) 262 0666
E: enquiries@peakcottages.com
I: www.peakcottages.com

CHARLTON KINGS
Gloucestershire

Coxhorne Farm ★★★
Contact: Mr & Mrs Close, Coxhorne Farm, London Road, Cheltenham GL52 6UY
T: (01242) 236599

CHEADLE
Staffordshire

Marmadukes Folly ★★★★
Contact: English Country Cottages, Stoney Bank, Earby, Barnoldswick BB94 0AA
T: 0870 5 851155

CHEDDLETON
Staffordshire

Cheddleton Grange Farm ★★★★
Contact: Mr & Mrs J Goodwin, Cheddleton Grange Farm, Cheddleton, Leek ST13 7HN
T: (01538) 360344

CHEDWORTH
Gloucestershire

Tiddley Dyke ★★★★
Contact: Mrs Jenny Bull, Buffers, School Lane, Chedworth, Winchcombe, Cheltenham GL54 4AJ
T: (01285) 720673

CHELMARSH
Shropshire

Duck, Drake & Cart Cottages ★★★
Contact: Mrs M Roberts, Dinney Farm, Chelmarsh, Bridgnorth WV16 6AU
T: (01746) 861070
F: (01746) 861002
I: www.smoothhound.co.uk/hotels/dinney.html

CHELMORTON
Derbyshire

The Hall ★★★
Contact: Mrs Lucilla Marsden, The Hall, Town End Farm, Chelmorton, Buxton SK17 9SH
T: (01298) 85249
E: charles.marsden@nottingham.ac.uk

Lilac Cottage Rating Applied For
Contact: Ms S Goodall, 1 Bride Hall Cottages, Bride Hall Lane, Ayot St Lawrence, Welwyn AL6 9DB
T: (01582) 834763
F: (01582) 834763
E: lilaccottage@mail.com

Swallow Barn ★★★★
Contact: Mrs Gill Chapman, The Green, Chelmorton, Buxton SK17 9SL
T: (01298) 85355
E: gechapman@btinternet.com

CHELTENHAM
Gloucestershire

The Annexe ★★★
Contact: Mrs Corbett, The Annexe, 11 Oldfield Crescent, St Marks, Cheltenham GL51 7BB
T: (01242) 524608

Balcarras Farm Holiday Cottages ★★★
Contact: Mr & Mrs David & Judith Ballinger, Balcarras Farm, London Road, Cheltenham GL52 6UT
T: (01242) 584837
E: cottage@balcarras-farm.co.uk
I: www.balcarras-farm.co.uk

Beechgarden Apartments ★★★
Contact: Miss Denise Holman, Beechcroft B&B, 295 Gloucester Road, Cheltenham GL5017AD
T: (01242) 519564
F: (01242) 519564
E: beechcroft.chelenham@dial.pipex .com
I: www.geocities.com/beechcroftuk.

The Courtyard ★★★★
Contact: Mrs Jane Reynolds, Austwick, Lancaster LA2 8BY
T: (015242) 51224
F: (015242) 51796
E: jane@22montpellier.co.uk
I: www.22montpellier.co.uk

Flat 2 ★★★★
Contact: Serviced Let, Cheltenham GL50
T: 0800 093 5383
E: reservations@servicedlet.com
I: www.cheltenhamlet.com

The Garden Flat ★★★★
Contact: Ms Jenny Wardle, Change Forum Ltd, 20 Lansdown Parade, Cheltenham GL50 2LH
T: (01242) 577450
E: jennyw@changeforum.co.uk

The Garden Studio ★★★★
Contact: Mrs I Ellams, The Garden Studio, 53 Gratton Road, Cheltenham GL50 2BZ
T: (01242) 575572

Holmer Cottages ★★★★
Contact: Mrs Jill Collins, Holmer Cottages, Haines Orchard, Woolstone, Cheltenham GL52 9RG
T: (01242) 672848
F: (01242) 672848
E: holmercottages@talk21.com
I: http://www.cottageguide.co.uk/holmercottages

Oakfield Rise ★★★★
Contact: Mr Tony Russell, Oakfield Rise, Ashley Road, Battledown, Cheltenham GL52 6NU
T: (01242) 222220
E: oakfieldrise@hotmail.com
I: www.oakfieldrise.com

Priory Cottage ★★★
Contact: Mr I S Mant, Church Gate, Southam Lane, Southam, Cheltenham GL52 3NY
T: (01242) 584693
F: (01242) 584693
E: iansmant@hotmail.com

Regency Maisonette ★★★★
Contact: Mrs Jane Reynolds, 16 Montpellier Spa Road, Cheltenham GL50 1UL
T: (015242) 51224
F: (015242) 51796
E: jane@22montpellier.co.uk
I: www.22montpellier.co.uk

7 Royal Parade ★★★★
Contact: Serviced Let, Cheltenham GL50
T: 0800 093 5383
E: reservations@servicedlet.com
I: www.cheltenhamlet.com

Top Flat
Rating Applied For
Contact: Mr & Mrs S Morris, Huntley Farm, Patch Elm Lane, Rangeworthy, Bristol BS37 7LU
T: (01454) 227322
F: (01454) 227323
E: cotswold.cottage@btopenworld.com

Ullenwood Court Cottages ★★★★
Contact: Mrs Shand, 90 Redgrove Park, Hatherley Lane, Cheltenham GL51 6YZ
T: (01242) 239751

The Vergus ★★★
Contact: Mrs R M Preen, Ashley, Staverton Village, Cheltenham GL51 0TW
T: (01242) 680511
E: ritapreen@aol.com
I: ritapreen@aol.com

Vine Court
Rating Applied For
Contact: Mrs Linda Hennessy, Vine Court, 59 Leckhampton Road, Cheltenham GL53 0BS
T: (01242) 222403
E: lindyhennessy@hotmail.com

Willoughby House Hotel and Apartments★★★-★★★★
Contact: Mr & Mrs F P Eckermann, Willoughby House Hotel, 1 Suffolk Square, Cheltenham GL50 2DR
T: (01242) 522798
E: bookings@willoughbyhouse.com
I: www.willoughbyhouse.com

CHERINGTON
Warwickshire

Steele's Cottage ★★★★
Contact: Mrs C Russell, Home Farm House, Cherington, Shipston-on-Stour CV36 5HL
T: (01608) 686540
F: (01608) 686333

CHESTERFIELD
Derbyshire

Chryslinash ★★★
Contact: Mrs Tina Cave, Chryslinash, Lower Pilsley, North Wingfield, Chesterfield S45 8DG
T: (01246) 853467
E: chryslinash@aol.com

Heatherlea ★★★
Contact: Mrs J Pearson, Oakwood, George Street, Old Whittington, Chesterfield S41 9DR
T: (01246) 261579
F: (01246) 455001

Pear Tree Cottage ★★★
Contact: Mrs Beckett, 46 Hardstoft Road, Pilsley, Chesterfield S45 8BL
T: (01773) 872767

Ploughmans Cottage ★★★★
Contact: Mr & Mrs W G Fry, Ploughmans Cottage, Low Farm, Main Road, Marsh Lane, Chesterfield S21 5RH
T: (01246) 435328
E: ploughmans.cottage@virgin.net

CHINLEY
Derbyshire

Fernbank ★★★
Contact: Mrs J Storer, 34 Beresford Road, Chapel-en-le-Frith, High Peak SK23 0NY
T: (01298) 813458

Monks Meadow Cottage ★★★★
Contact: Mrs Pauline Gill, Monks Meadow Cottage, Hayfield Road, Chinley Head, Chinley, High Peak SK23 6AL
T: (01663) 750329
E: monksmeadow@yahoo.com
I: www.monksmeadow.co.uk

CHIPPING CAMPDEN
Gloucestershire

Bank Cottage ★★★★
Contact: Mr Robert Hutsby, Middle Hill Farm, Charlecote, Warwick CV35 9EH
T: (01789) 841525
F: (01789) 841523
E: robert.hutsby@btinternet.com
I: www.broadway-cotswolds.co.uk/bank.html

Barnstones ★★★★★
Contact: Mr & Mrs Jones, Barnstones, Aston Road, Chipping Campden GL55 6HR
T: (01386) 840975
F: (01386) 840975
E: jonesbarnstones@aol.com

Box Tree Cottage ★★★
Contact: Mr Robert Hutsby, Middle Hill Farm, Charlecote, Warwick CV35 9EH
T: (01789) 841525
F: (01789) 841523
E: robert.hutsby@btinternet.com
I: www.broadway-cotswolds.co.uk/boxtree.html

Chapter Cottage ★★★★
Contact: Mr Revers, The Tyning, Blind Lane, Chipping Campden GL55 6ED
T: (01386) 841450
E: admin@perpetuare.com
I: www.perpetuare.com

Cotswold Charm ★★★★
Contact: Mr & Miss Michael & Margaret Haines, Cotswold Charm, Top Farm, Blind Lane, Chipping Campden GL55 6ED
T: (01386) 840164
F: (01386) 841883
I: www.cotswoldcharm.co.uk

Cowfair ★★★★
Contact: Mrs Whitehouse, Weston Park Farm, Dovers Hill, Chipping Campden GL55 6UW
T: (01386) 840835
E: jane_whitehouse@hotmail.com

Dragon House ★★★★
Contact: Country Holidays Ref: 8386 Sales, Holiday Cottages Group Limited, Spring Mill, Earby, Barnoldswick BB94 0AA
T: 08700 723723
F: (01282) 844288
E: sales@ttgihg.co.uk
I: www.country-holidays.co.uk

Fox Cottage ★★★★
Contact: Miss Sheila Rolland, Campden Cottages, Folly Cottage, Paxford, Chipping Campden GL55 6XG
T: (01386) 593315
F: (01386) 593057
E: info@campdencottages.co.uk
I: www.campdencottages.co.uk

Grafton Mews ★★★★
Contact: Ms Sheila Rolland, Campden Cottages, Folly Cottage, Paxford, Chipping Campden GL55 6XG
T: (01386) 593315
F: (01386) 593057
E: info@campdencottages.co.uk
I: www.campdencottages.co.uk

Little Thatch ★★★★
Contact: Mrs D Gadsby, 'Hillsdown', Aston Road, Chipping Campden GL55 6PL
T: (01386) 840234

Lychgate Cottage ★★★★
Contact: Mr Robert Hutsby, Middle Hill Farm, Charlecote, Warwick CV35 9EH
T: (01789) 841525
F: (01789) 841523
E: robert.hutsby@btinternet.com
I: www.broadway-cotswolds.co.uk/lychgate.html

Merlin Cottage ★★★★
Contact: Miss Sheila Rolland, Campden Cottages, Folly Cottage, Paxford, Chipping Campden GL55 6XG
T: (01386) 593315
F: (01386) 593057
E: info@campdencottages.co.uk
I: www.campdencottages.co.uk

Millers Cottage ★★★★
Contact: Mrs Susan Jessup, Old Palace Cottage, Hatfield Park, Hatfield AL9 5NE
T: (01707) 287042
F: (01707) 287033
E: info@millerscottage.co.uk
I: www.millerscottage.co.uk

Shepherd's Cottage ★★★★
Contact: Miss Sheila Rolland, Campden Cottages, Folly Cottage, Paxford, Chipping Campden GL55 6XG
T: (01386) 593315
F: (01386) 593057
E: info@campdencottages.co.uk
I: www.campdencottages.co.uk

Walkers Retreat ★★★
Contact: Mrs Whitehouse, Weston Park Farm, Dovers Hill, Chipping Campden GL55 6UW
T: (01386) 840835

Whistlers Corner Cottage ★★★★
Contact: Mr Robert Hutsby, Middle Hill Farm, Charlecote, Warwick CV35 9EH
T: (01789) 841525
F: (01789) 841523
E: robert.hutsby@btinternet.com
I: www.broadway-cotswolds.co.uk/whistlers.html

CHRISTCHURCH
Gloucestershire

Glenwood ★★★
Contact: Mr & Mrs Keith & Joan Harvey, Glenwood, Coleford GL16 7NR
T: (01594) 833128
F: (01594) 833128

CHURCH STRETTON
Shropshire

The Barn, Daisy's Place and Goose Yard★★★★
Contact: Mr Sykes, Sykes Cottage, York House, York Street, Chester CH1 3LR
T: (01244) 345700
F: (01244) 321442
E: info@sykescottage.co.uk
I: www.sykescottge.co.uk

Berry's Coffee House ★★★★
Contact: Mr John Gott, Berry's Coffee House, 17 High Street, Church Stretton, Church Stretton SY6 6BU
T: (01694) 724452
E: all@berryscoffeehouse.co.uk
I: www.berryscoffehouse.co.uk

Botvyle Farm ★★★-★★★★
Contact: Mrs Gill Bebbington, Botvyle Farm, All Stretton, Church Stretton SY6 7JN
T: (01694) 722869
F: (01694) 722869
E: tlmgill@bebbington28.fsnet.co.uk

Broome Farm Cottages ★★★★★
Contact: Mr & Mrs Cavendish, Broome Farm Cottages, Broome Farm, Chatwall, Church Stretton SY6 7LD
T: 0796 805 1873
F: (01694) 771784
E: mark@broome-farm.co.uk
I: broome-farm.co.uk

Caradoc Cottage ★★★★
Contact: Mrs Wendy Lewis, Caradoc House, Comley, Church Stretton SY6 7JS
T: (01694) 751488
F: (01694) 751488
E: w-lewis@lineone.net

Elizas Cottage ★★★★
Contact: Mrs Wendy Lewis, Caradoc House, Comley Leebotwood, Church Stretton SY67JS
T: (01694) 751488
F: (01694) 751488

The Garden Flat ★★★
Contact: Mrs Carol Hembrow, The Garden Flat, Ashfield House, Windle Hill, Church Stretton SY6 7AF
T: (01694) 723715
E: cj.hembrow@ukonline.co.uk

Granary Cottage and The Long Barn ★★★★
Contact: Mr & Mrs J Kirkwood, Lower Day House, Church Preen, Church Stretton SY6 7LH
T: (01694) 771521
E: jim@lowerdayhouse.freeserve.co.uk
I: www.lowerdayhouse.freeserve.co.uk

Hodghurst Cottage ★★★
Contact: Mrs Forsyth, Hodghurst Farm, Lower Wood, Church Stretton SY6 6LF
T: (01694) 751403

Jasleigh Cottage ★★★-★★★★
Contact: Mrs Wendy Lewis, Caradoc House, Comley, Church Stretton SY67JS
T: (01694) 751488
F: (01694) 751488

Leasowes Cottage ★★★★
Contact: Mrs M Harris, Leasowes, Watling Street, Longnor, Shrewsbury SY5 7QG
T: (01694) 751351
E: paul-harris@c-stretton.fsnet.co.uk

The Links ★★
Contact: Mrs Onions, The Links, Trevor Hill, Church Stretton SY6 6JH
T: (01694) 724669

Longmynd Hotel ★★★
Contact: Mr M Chapman, Longmynd Hotel, Cunnery Road, Church Stretton SY6 6AG
T: (01694) 722244
F: (01694) 722718
E: reservations@longmynd.co.uk
I: www.longmynd.co.uk

Parkgate Cottages ★★★
Contact: Mrs Audrey Hill, Parkgate Cottages, Parkgate Farmhouse, Pulverbatch, Shrewsbury SY5 8DH
T: (01694) 751303
E: park-gate@lineone.net
I: www.shropshiretourism.com

The Retreat ★★★
Contact: Mr & Mrs Bennett, The Retreat, 72 Watling Street South, Church Stretton SY6 7BH
T: (01694) 723370

The Sapling at Oakwood Cottage ★★★
Contact: Mrs Jan Oram, Oakwood Cottage, Marshbrook, Church Stretton SY6 6RG
T: (01694) 781347
E: oakwoodcottage01@aol.com

Woodview ★★★
Contact: Mrs J Brereton, Woolston Farm, Church Stretton SY6 6QD
T: (01694) 781201
F: (01694) 781201

Ye Olde Stables at Jinlye ★★★★
Contact: Miss Kate Tory, Ye Olde Stables at Jinlye, Castle Hill, All Stretton, Church Stretton SY6 6JP
T: (01694) 723243
F: (01694) 723243
E: info@jinlye.co.uk
I: www.jinlye.co.uk

CIRENCESTER
Gloucestershire

Glebe Farm Holiday Lets ★★★★
Contact: Mrs Handover, Glebe Farm Holiday Lets, Glebe Farm, Barnsley Road, Cirencester GL7 5DY
T: (01285) 659226
F: (01285) 642622

The Malthouse Granary ★★★★
Contact: Mrs B O'Leary, The Malthouse, Poulton, Cirencester GL7 5HN
T: (01285) 850006
F: (01285) 850437
E: bernie.oleary@btinternet.com

Old Mill Cottages ★★★★
Contact: Mrs Catherine Hazell, Ermin House Farm, Syde, Cheltenham GL53 9PN
T: (01285) 821255
F: (01285) 821531
E: catherine@oldmillcottages.fsnet.co.uk
I: www.oldmillcottages.co.uk

The Tallet Cottage ★★★★★
Contact: Mrs V J Arbuthnott, The Tallet, Calmsden, Cirencester GL7 5ET
T: (01285) 831437
F: (01285) 831437
E: vanessa@thetallet.demon.co.uk
I: www.thetallet.co.uk

Warrens Gorse Cottages ★★
Contact: Mrs Nanette Randall, Warrens Gorse Cottages, Home Farm, Warrens Gorse, Cirencester GL7 7JD
T: (01285) 831261

Westley Farm ★★★
Contact: Mr Usborne, Westley Farm, Charlford, Stroud GL6 8HP
T: (01285) 760262
F: (01285) 760262
I: www.westleyfarm.co.uk

CLAXBY
Lincolnshire

The Coach House ★★★
Contact: Mrs Elizabeth Wilson, Claxby Manor, Claxby, Alford LN13 0HJ
T: (01507) 466374
F: (01507) 466374
E: liffa@claxby.fsnet.co.uk

CLAYWORTH
Nottinghamshire

The Shambles ★★★★
Contact: Mrs Roberts, 143 Bawtry Road, Bessacarr, Doncaster DN4 7AH
T: (01302) 537110

CLEE ST MARGARET
Shropshire

Titchbourne Cottage ★★★★
Contact: Country Holidays Ref: 9882 Sales, Holiday Cottages Group Limited, Spring Mill, Earby, Barnoldswick BB94 0AA
T: 08700 723723
F: (01282) 844288
E: sales@ttgihg.co.uk
I: www.country-holidays.co.uk

CLEEVE HILL
Gloucestershire

The Old Dairy ★★★★
Contact: Mr & Mrs Rickie & Jenny Gauld, Slades Farm, Bushcombe Lane, Woodmancote, Cheltenham GL52 3PN
T: (01242) 676003
F: (01242) 676003
E: rickieg@btinternet.com
I: www.cotswoldscottages.btinternet.co.uk

CLEEVE PRIOR
Worcestershire

Top Farm Cottage ★★★
Contact: Country Holidays Ref 11842, Spring Mill, Earby, Barnoldswick BB18
T: 08700 723723
E: sales@ttgihg.co.uk
I: www.country-holidays.co.uk

CLEOBURY MORTIMER
Shropshire

Hop Barn ★★★★
Contact: Mrs Birgit Jones, Neen Court, Neen Sollars, Cleobury Mortimer, Kidderminster DY14 0AH
T: (01299) 271204
F: (01299) 271916
E: birgitanne@aol.com
I: www.virtual-shropshire.co.uk/hopbarn

Prescott Mill ★★★
Contact: Mrs W Etchells, Prescott Mill, Stottesdon, Cleobury Mortimer DY14 8RR
T: (01746) 718721
F: (01746) 718718
E: mail@prescott-mill-cottage.co.uk
I: www.prescott-mill-cottage.co.uk

CLUN
Shropshire

Dick Turpin Cottage at Cockford Hall ★★★★★
Contact: Mr Roger Wren, Dick Turpin Cottage at Cockford Hall, Cockford Bank, Clun, Craven Arms SY7 8LR
T: (01588) 640327
F: (01588) 640881
E: cockford.hall@virgin.net
I: www.dickturpincottage.com

Lake House Cottages ★★★
Contact: Mr & Mrs G Berry, Lake House Cottages, Lake House, Guilden Down Road, Clun, Craven Arms SY7 8NY
T: (01588) 640148
F: (01588) 640152
E: graham.berry5@btopenworld.com

The Miller's House and Mill Stream Cottage ★★★★
Contact: Ms Gill Della Casa, Birches Mill, Clun, Craven Arms SY7 8NL
T: (01588) 640409
F: (01588) 640409
E: gill@birchesmill.fsnet.co.uk
I: www.virtual-shropshire.co.uk/mullerhouse

Wagtail Cottage ★★★★
Contact: Mrs Williams, Wagtail Cottage, Hurst Mill Farm, Clun, Clunton, Craven Arms SY7 0JA
T: (01588) 640224
F: (01588) 640224
E: hurstmillholidays@tinyworld.co.uk

Woolbury Barn ★★★★
Contact: Mrs F Morris, Woolbury Barn, Hollybush Farm, Woodside, Clun, Craven Arms SY7 0JB
T: (01588) 640481

CLUNBURY
Shropshire

Brookside Rating Applied For
Contact: Mr & Mrs S Seabury, Clunbury, Craven Arms SY7 0HG
T: (01588) 660494

CLUNTON
Shropshire

Kingfisher Apartment ★★★
Contact: Mrs Pittam, Kingfisher Apartment, Tawny Cottage, Clunton, Craven Arms SY7 0HP
T: (01588) 660327
F: (01588) 660327

COALBROOKDALE
Shropshire

Coalbrookdale, Tea Kettle Row Cottages ★★★-★★★★
Contact: Mrs Mary Jones, 34 Darby Road, Coalbrookdale, Telford TF8 7EW
T: (01952) 433202
E: mary@teakettlecottages.co.uk
I: www.teakettlecottages.co.uk

COLEFORD
Gloucestershire

Firtrees Holiday Bungalow ★★★
Contact: Mrs C A Brain, Asgard House, 84 Park Road, Christchurch, Coleford GL16 7AZ
T: (01594) 832576
E: douglas.brain@genie.co.uk
I: www.firtreesatfod.co.uk

Little Millend Rating Applied For
Contact: Mr Nicholas Pash, Hideaways, Chapel House, Luke Street, Berwick St John, Shaftesbury SP70 0HQ
T: (01747) 828170
E: enq@hideaways.co.uk

32 Tudor Walk ★★★
Contact: Mrs Beale, 82 Park Road, Christchurch, Coleford GL16 7AZ
T: (01594) 832061

Woodside Cottage ★★★
Contact: Mrs Helen Evans, Peaked Rocks Cottage, The Rocks, Joys Green, Lydbrook GL17 9RF
T: (01594) 861119
F: (01594) 823408
E: evens@evansholidays.freeserve.co.uk

COLWALL
Herefordshire

Threshing Barn ★★★★
Contact: Mr R Coates, Lower House Farm, Evendine Lane, Colwall, Malvern WR13 6DT
T: (01684) 540284

COMBS
Derbyshire

Pyegreave Cottage ★★★★★
Contact: Mr N C Pollard, Pyegreave Farm, Combs, High Peak SK23 9UX
T: (01298) 813444
F: (01298) 815381
E: n.pollard@allenpollard.co.uk
I: www.holidayapartments.org

COMPTON ABDALE
Gloucestershire

Spring Hill Stable Cottages ★★★
Contact: Mrs M L Smail, Spring Hill Stable Cottages, Spring Hill, Compton Abdale, Cheltenham GL54 4DU
T: (01242) 890263
F: (01242) 890266
E: springhillcottages@yahoo.co.uk

CORLEY
West Midlands

St Ives Lodge ★★★★
Contact: Mr Ruffett, St Ives Cottage, Church Lane, Corley, Coventry CV7 8BA
T: (01676) 542994
F: (01676) 549088
E: tim@ruffett.co.uk

CORSE LAWN
Gloucestershire

The Lodge ★★★★★
Contact: Mrs E Gardner, Little Manor, Corse Lawn, Gloucester GL19 4LU
T: (01452) 780363
F: (01452) 780363
E: carnbargus@aol.com
I: www.holidaybank.co.uk

COSTOCK
Nottinghamshire

Costock Manor Luxury Cottages ★★★★★
Contact: Mr & Mrs Simblet, Costock Manor Luxury Cottages, The Manor, Church Lane, Costock, Loughborough LE12 6UZ
T: (01509) 852250
F: (01509) 853337
E: simblet@costock-manor.co.uk
I: www.costock-manor.co.uk

COTTESMORE
Rutland

Thompson's Barn ★★★
Contact: Mrs M E Cheetham, Thompson's Barn, 12 The Leas, Cottesmore, Oakham LE15 7DG
T: (01572) 812231

COUND
Shropshire

The Cottage ★★★
Contact: Mr & Mrs Willetts, The Cottage, Severnside, Cound, Shrewsbury SY5 6AF
T: (01952) 510352

CRASWALL
Herefordshire

Rose Cottage ★★★
Contact: Mrs Myra Howard, The Three Horse Shoes, Crawell, Craswall, Hereford HR2 0PL
T: (01981) 510631

CRAVEN ARMS
Shropshire

Gwynfa ★★★
Contact: Mrs Delysia Wall, The Balkans, Longmeadow End, Craven Arms SY7 8ED
T: (01588) 673375

Halford Holiday Homes ★★★-★★★★★
Contact: Mr & Mrs E James, Halford Holiday Homes, Halford Farm, Craven Arms SY7 9JG
T: (01588) 672382
I: www.go2.co.uk/halford

Malt House ★★★★★
Contact: Mrs Margaret Mellings, Long Meads, Lower Barns Road, Ludford, Ludlow SY8 4DS
T: (01584) 873315
E: jean@mellings.freeserve.co.uk
I: www.mellings.freeserve.co.uk

Orchard Cottage ★★★★
Contact: Mr & Mrs Lewis, Orchard Cottage, Strefford House, Strefford, Craven Arms SY7 8DE
T: (01588) 673340
F: (01588) 673340
E: webb.streffordhouse@virgin.net

Swallows Nest and Robin's Nest ★★★★
Contact: Mrs Caroline Morgan, Strefford Hall, Craven Arms SY7 8DE
T: (01588) 672383
I: www.streffordhall.co.uk

Upper Onibury Cottages ★★★★
Contact: Mrs Hickman, Upper Onibury Cottages, Upper Onibury, Craven Arms SY7 9AW
T: (01584) 856206
F: (01584) 856236
E: info@shropshirecottages.com
I: www.information-britain.co.uk

CRESSAGE
Shropshire

Jasmine Lodge ★★
Contact: Ms Kate Hogwood, Jasmine Lodge, Wood Lane, Cressage, Shrewsbury SY5 6DY
T: (01952) 510375
F: (01952) 510350
E: shrop.mus@lineone.net
I: www.accomodata.co.uk/270699.htm

CRESSBROOK
Derbyshire

8 Bobbin Mill ★★★★
Contact: Mrs Wendy Hicks, Chert Cottage, Main Road, Little Longstone, Bakewell DE45 1TG
T: (01629) 640410

Cressbrook Hall Cottages ★★★
Contact: Mrs B H Bailey, Cressbrook Hall Cottages Ltd, Cressbrook Hall, Cressbrook, Buxton SK17 8SY
T: (01298) 871289
F: (01298) 871845
E: stay@cressbrookhall.co.uk
I: www.cressbrookhall.co.uk

Monsal View ★★★
Contact: Mr C MacQueen, Peak Cottages, Strawberry Lee Lane, Totley Bents, Sheffield S17 3BA
T: (0114) 262 0777
F: (0114) 262 0666
E: enquiries@peakcottages.com
I: www.peakcottages.com

CRICH
Derbyshire

Avista Property Partnership ★★★★
Contact: Mr Keith William Bendon, Avista Property Partnership, Penrose, Sandy Lane, Tansley, Matlock DE4 5DE
T: (01773) 852625
E: keith@avista.freeserve.co.uk
I: www.s-h-systems.co.uk/hotels/avista.html

Clover Stable ★★★★
Contact: Mr David Worthy, Clover Stable, Crich Pottery, Market Place, Tansley, Matlock DE4 5DD
T: (01773) 853171
F: (01773) 857325
E: davidworthy@hotmail.com
I: www.peakcottages.com

Primrose Cottage ★★★★
Contact: Mrs P Dwyer, 101 Ripley Road, Heage, Belper DE56 2HU
T: (01773) 857964

CROMFORD
Derbyshire

1 High Peak Cottages ★★★
Contact: Mr & Mrs David & Lorraine Wolsey, 5 High Peak Cottages, High Peak Junction, Cromford, Matlock DE4 5HN
T: (01629) 823402
E: stay@highpeakcottage.co.uk
I: www.highpeakcottage.co.uk

The Lock Up ★★★
Contact: Mrs Angela Ash, The Old Printing Works, Scarthin, Cromford, Matlock DE4 3QF
T: (01629) 822541

CROPWELL BISHOP
Nottinghamshire

Corner Cottage ★★★★
Contact: Ms Hilary Hawkins, 1 Kinoulton Road, Cropwell Bishop, Nottingham NG12 3BH
T: (0115) 989 9889
F: (0115) 989 9880
E: hilary@weekendco.com
I: weekendco.com

CURBAR
Derbyshire

Jack's Cottage ★★★★
Contact: Mrs M North, Green Farm, Curbar, Calver, Hope Valley S32 3YH
T: (01433) 630120
F: (01433) 631829
E: Marsha.North1@btopenworld.com
I: www.peak-district-romantic-holidaycottages.co.uk

The Old Vicarage ★★★★
Contact: Mr MacQueen, Peak Cottages, Strawberry Lee Lane, Totley Bents, Totley Rise, Sheffield S17 3BA
T: (0114) 262 0777
F: (0114) 262 0666
E: enquiries@peakcottages.com
I: www.peakcottages.com

Upper Barn and Lower Barn ★★★
Contact: Mr & Mrs Pierce, Upper Barn and Lower Barn, Orchard House, Curbar, Calver, Hope Valley S32 3YJ
T: (01433) 631885
F: (0114) 290 3309
E: mjfp@bvickers.co.uk
I: www.bvickers.co.uk

CUTTHORPE
Derbyshire

Cow Close Farm Cottages ★★★
Contact: Mr & Mrs S E Gaskin, Cow Close Farm, Overgreen, Cutthorpe, Chesterfield S42 7BA
T: (01246) 232055
E: cowclosefarm.cottages@virgin.net

DAGLINGWORTH
Gloucestershire

Corner Cottage ★★★★
Contact: Mrs V M Bartlett, Brook Cottage, 23 Farm Court, Daglingworth, Cirencester GL7 7AF
T: (01285) 653478
F: (01285) 653478

DARLEY DALE
Derbyshire

Housekeepers Cottage ★★★★★
Contact: Mrs Rudkin, The Winnatts, Long Hill, Darley Dale, Matlock DE4 2HE
T: (01629) 733270
F: (01629) 733270
E: enquiries@housekeeperscottage.co.uk
I: www.housekeeperscottage.co.uk

Meadow Cottage ★★★
Contact: Mrs Cynthia Davies, The Spinney, Lincombe Drive, Torquay TQ1 2HH
T: (01803) 294218
E: davies@spinney382.freeserve.co.uk

Nether End c/o Nether Hall ★★★★
Contact: Mrs Lynne Wilson, Nether End c/o Nether Hall, Hallmoor Road, Daley Dale, Hackney, Matlock DE4 2HF
T: (01629) 732131
F: (01629) 735716
E: lynne.netherhall@dial.pippex.com
I: www.cottageguide.co.uk/netherend

DENSTONE
Staffordshire

Keepers Cottage ★★★★
Contact: Mr Christopher Ball, Keepers Cottage, Manor House Farm, Denstone, Prestwood, Uttoxeter ST14 5DD
T: (01889) 590415
F: (01335) 342198
E: cm_ball@yahoo.co.uk
I: 4posteraccom.com

DERBY
Derbyshire

Bank Cottage ★★★
Contact: Mrs Pym, Mickleover, Derby DE3 0DG
T: (01332) 515607

DILHORNE
Staffordshire

Birchenfields Farm ★★★
Contact: Mr & Mrs Peter Edge, Birchenfields Farm, Dilhorne, Stoke-on-Trent ST10 2PX
T: (01538) 753972

DOCKLOW
Herefordshire

Docklow Manor Holiday Cottages ★★★
Contact: Mrs Jane Viner, Docklow Manor Holiday Cottages, Docklow Manor, Docklow, Leominster HR6 0RX
T: (01568) 760668
F: (01568) 760572
E: jane@docklowmanor.freeserve.co.uk
I: www.docklow-manor.co.uk

DONINGTON
Lincolnshire

The Barn ★★★
Contact: Mrs Margaret A Smith, The Barn, 110 Quadring Road, Donington, Spalding PE11 4SJ
T: (01775) 821242

DORSINGTON
Warwickshire

Windmill Grange Cottage ★★★★
Contact: Mrs Lorna Hollis, Windmill Grange, Dorsington, Stratford-upon-Avon CV37 8BQ
T: (01789) 720866
F: (01789) 721872
E: lorna@windmillgrange.co.uk
I: www.windmillgrange.co.uk

DRAYCOTT-IN-THE-CLAY
Staffordshire

Granary Court Holiday Cottages ★★★★
Contact: Mrs Lynne Statham, Granary Court Holiday Cottages, Stubby Lane, Draycott-in-the-Clay, Ashbourne DE6 5BU
T: (01283) 820917

DUNNINGTON
Warwickshire

Shakespeare Cottage ★★★★
Contact: Mrs Jill Morton, Old Mudwalls Cottage, Dunnington, Alcester B49 5PA
T: (01386) 870152
E: jill@shakespearecottage.com
I: www.shakespearecottage.com

DUNTISBOURNE ABBOTS
Gloucestershire

The Old Cottage ★★★★
Contact: Mrs Simpson, Church Barn, Hawling, Cheltenham GL54 5TA
T: (01451) 850118
F: (01451) 850118
E: simpson@glos68.fsnet.co.uk
I: www.cottageguide.co.uk/cotswold-cottages

DUNTISBOURNE ROUSE
Gloucestershire

Swallow Barns ★★★★★
Contact: Mr & Mrs Anthony & Jean Merrett, Swallow Barns, Duntisbourne Rouse, Cirencester GL7 7AP
T: (01285) 651031
I: www.cottageinthecountry.co.uk

DURSLEY
Gloucestershire

Badgers Mead Downhouse Farm ★★★
Contact: Mrs Maureen Marsh Downhouse Farm, Springhill, Upper Cam, Dursley GL11 5HQ
T: (01453) 546001

Two Springbank ★★★
Contact: Mrs F A Jones, 32 Everlands, Cam, Dursley GL11 5NL
T: (01453) 543047

EAGLE
Lincolnshire

Eagle & Thorpe Crossing Cottage ★★★
Contact: Mr Patrick Britton, 95 Lauriston Road, Victoria Park, London E9 7HJ
T: (020) 8986 5601
F: (020) 8986 5601
E: p.j.britton@amserve.net

EARDISLAND
Herefordshire

The Stables Rating Applied For
Contact: Mr Albert Priday, The Old Vicarage, Eardisland, Leominster HR6 9BP
T: (01544) 388570
F: (01544) 388570
E: pridays@aol.com

EARL STERNDALE
Derbyshire

Wheeldon Trees Farm Holiday Cottages★★★★
Contact: Mr Hollands, Wheeldon Trees Farm Holiday Cottages, Wheeldon Trees Farm, Earl Sterndale, Buxton SK17 0AA
T: (01298) 83219
F: (01298) 83219
E: hollands@earlsterndale.fsnet.co.uk
I: www.wheeldontreesfarm.co.uk

EAST HADDON
Northamptonshire

East Haddon Grange ★★★★
Contact: Mr & Mrs Pike, East Haddon Grange, East Haddon, Northampton NN6 8DR
T: (01604) 770368
F: (01604) 770368
E: ged.pike@u.genie.co.uk

Mulberry Cottage ★★★★★
Contact: Mr & Mrs M Smerin, Lane Cottage, St Andrews Road, East Haddon, Northampton NN6 8DE
T: (01604) 770244
F: (01327) 844822
E: liz@smerin.freeserve.co.uk

Rye Hill Country Cottages ★★★★
Contact: Mrs Margaret Widdowson, Clematis Cottage, 33 Chelford Road, Brig o' Turk, Callander WA16 8NN
T: (01565) 654343
F: (01604) 770237
E: info@ryehillcottages.evesham.net
I: www.ryehillcottages.co.uk

EAST MARKHAM
Nottinghamshire

Stables Cottage ★★★★
Contact: Mrs Juliet Hagger, York House, York Street, East Markham, Newark NG22 0QW
T: (01777) 870683

EASTMOOR
Derbyshire

Bilberry Lodge ★★★
Contact: Mr Richard Gill, Nether Rod Knowle Farm, Eastmoor, Chesterfield S42 7DB
T: (01246) 566151
E: enquiries@peakcottages.com
I: www.peakcottages.com

EASTON ON THE HILL
Northamptonshire

The Old Bakery ★★★
Contact: Mrs Yogasundram, The Old Bakery, 25 West Street, Easton on the Hill, Stamford PE9 3LS
T: (01780) 753898
E: yogiandmel@theoldbakery25.freeserve.co.uk

EATON-UNDER-HEYWOOD
Shropshire

Eaton Manor Rural Escapes ★★★★
Contact: Miss Nichola Madeley, Eaton Manor Rural Escapes, Eaton Manor, Eaton-under-Heywood, Church Stretton SY6 7DH
T: (01694) 724814
F: (01694) 722048
E: ruralescapes@eatonmanor.co.uk
I: eatonmanor.co.uk

EBRINGTON
Gloucestershire

Pump Cottage ★★★
Contact: Mr Robert Hutsby, Middle Hill Farm, Charlecote, Warwick CV35 9EH
T: (01789) 841525
F: (01789) 841523
E: robert.hutsby@btinternet.com
I: www.broadway-cotswolds.co.uk/pump.html

ECCLESHALL
Staffordshire

Cadbury Cottage Rating Applied For
Contact: Mrs Margaret Housiaux, Cadbury Cottage, The Old Creamery, Pershall, Eccleshall, Stafford ST21 6NE
T: (01785) 851402

EDALE
Derbyshire

Grindslow House ★★★
Contact: Mrs Crook, c/o Meller Braggins, The Estate Office, Rostherne, Knutsford WA16 6SW
T: (01565) 830395
F: (01565) 830241

Hathaway & Heath Cottages ★★★
Contact: Mrs S Gee, Cotefield Farm, Ollerbrook, Edale, Hope Valley S33 2ZG
T: (01433) 670273
F: (01433) 670273

Ollerbrook Cottages ★★★★
Contact: Mrs Paula Greenlees, Ollerbrook Cottages, Middle Ollerbrook House, Ollerbrook, Edale, Hope Valley S33 7LG
T: (01433) 670083
I: www.ollerbrook-cottages.co.uk

Taylor's Croft ★★★★★
Contact: Mrs Susan Favell, Taylor's Croft, Skinners Hall, Edale, Hope Valley S33 7ZE
T: (01433) 670281
F: (01433) 670481
E: sue@skinnershall.freeserve.co.uk
I: www.skinnershall.freeserve.co.uk

EDLASTON
Derbyshire

Church Farm Cottages ★★★
Contact: Mrs Lois Blake, Wyaston, Ashbourne DE6 2DQ
T: (01335) 348776

ELKINGTON
Northamptonshire

Manor Farm ★★★★
Contact: Mr & Mrs Michael & Hilary Higgott, Manor Farm, Elkington, Northampton NN6 6NH
T: (01858) 575245
F: (01858) 575213

ELKSTONE
Gloucestershire

The Dolls House ★★★
Contact: Mrs Cooch, Enfield Farm, Elkstone, Cheltenham GL53 9PB
T: (01242) 870244

Stable Cottage ★★★
Contact: Mrs Veronica Lawrenson, Grove House, Elkstones, Buxton SK17 0LU
T: (01538) 300487
E: elkstone@talk21.com

ELMLEY CASTLE
Worcestershire

The Cottage, Manor Farm House ★★
Contact: Mr & Mrs B D Lovett, Manor Farm House, Main Street, Elmley Castle, Pershore WR10 3HS
T: (01386) 710286
F: (01386) 710112

ELTON
Derbyshire

Barn Croft Cottage ★★★
Contact: Mr Clive Sykes, Sykes Cottages, York House, York Street, Chester CH1 3LR
T: (01244) 345700
F: (01244) 321442
E: info@sykescottages.co.uk

The Stable ★★★★
Contact: Mrs Jean Carson, The Stable, Homestead Farm, Main Street, Elton, Matlock DE4 2BW
T: (01629) 650359

ENGLISH BICKNOR
Gloucestershire

Upper Tump Farm ★★★
Contact: Mrs M Merrett, Upper Tump Farm, Tump Lane, Eastbach, English Bicknor, Coleford GL16 7EU
T: (01594) 860072

EPPERSTONE
Nottinghamshire

The Loft House ★★★★
Contact: Mrs Jenny Esam, The Loft House, Criftin Farm, Woodborough, Nottingham NG14 6AT
T: (0115) 965 2039
F: (0115) 965 2039
E: jenny@criftinfarm.com
I: www.nottsfarmtourism.co.uk

The Mews ★★★
Contact: Mrs Susan Santos, Eastwood Farm, Hagg Lane, Epperstone, Nottingham NG14 6AX
T: (0115) 966 3018
E: santosthemews@hotmail.com
I: www.nottsfarmtourism.co.uk

The Mistal ★★★★
Contact: Mr & Mrs Peake, Ricketwood Farm, Chapel Lane, Epperstone, Nottingham NG14 6AR
T: (0115) 965 2086
E: edipper@aol.com

EVENLODE
Gloucestershire

Swallow Cottage ★★★
Contact: Ms Cheryl Lamb, 1B, Block 2 Pacific View, 38 Taitam Road, Hong Kong
T: 852 2813 7504
F: 852 2813 7504
E: chlamb@netvigator.com

EVESHAM
Worcestershire

Nubarn Cottage ★★★★
Contact: Mrs Pauline Taylor, Anvil House, 9a Badsey Road, Dumbleton, Evesham WR11 5DS
T: (01386) 442787

Thatchers End ★★★★
Contact: Mr & Mrs Wilson, 60 Pershore Road, Evesham WR11 6PQ
T: (01386) 446269
F: (01386) 446269
E: trad.accom@virgin.net
I: http://freespace.virgin.net/trad.accom

EYAM
Derbyshire

Alice Cottage ★★★★
Contact: Mrs Judy Downes, Cliffe Cottage, Jaggers Lane, Hathersage, Hope Valley S32 1AZ
T: (01433) 650364
E: judy@alice-cottage.co.uk

Dalehead Court Cottages ★★★★-★★★★★
Contact: Mrs D M Neary, Laneside Farm, Hope, Hope Valley S33 6RR
T: (01433) 620214
F: (01433) 620214
E: laneside@lineone.net
I: www.laneside.fsbusiness.co.uk

Fern & Brosterfield Cottage Brosterfield Hall★★★★
Contact: Mrs Jenny Vickers, Fern & Brosterfield Cottage Brosterfield Hall, Bakewell Road, Foolow S32 5QB
T: (01433) 631254
F: (01433) 639180
E: rcv@bvickers.co.uk
I: www.peak-cottages.com

Lark Cottage ★★★★★
Contact: Mr & Mrs R T Bell, Peak District Holidays, Nether Croft, Eaton Place, Baslow, Bakewell DE45 1RW
T: (01246) 583564

1 Lydgate Cottages ★★★★
Contact: Mrs Harrop, Townfield House, Townfield Lane, Warburton, Lymm WA13 9SR
T: (01925) 752118
E: lydgatecottage@townfieldhouse.freeserve.co.uk
I: lydgatecottage@townfieldhouse.freeserve.co.uk

Steeple Barn ★★★★
Contact: Mrs Yvonne Pursglove, The Well House, Highcliff, Eyam, Hope Valley, Eyam, Hope Valley S32 5QW
T: (01433) 639030
E: info@onetorent.com
I: www.onetorent.com

The Trap House ★★★★
Contact: Peak Cottages, Strawberry Lee Lane, Totley Bents, Sheffield S17 3BA
T: (0114) 262 0777
F: (0114) 262 0666
E: enquiries@peakcottages.com
I: www.peakcottages.com

Watchmakers Cottage ★★★★
Contact: Mrs N J Carmichael, Croft View Cottage, Foolow, Eyam, Hope Valley S32 5QA
T: (01433) 630711
E: carmichael@msn.com

EYDON
Northamptonshire

Crockwell Farm ★★★★
Contact: Mrs Lucy Pellerin, Crockwell Farm, Eydon, Daventry NN11 3QA
T: (01327) 361358
F: (01327) 361573
E: info@crockwellfarm.co.uk
I: www.crockwellfarm.co.uk

FAIRFORD
Gloucestershire

The Cottage, East End House ★★★★★
Contact: Mrs D Ewart, East End House, Fairford GL7 4AP
T: (01285) 713715
F: (01285) 713505
E: eastendho@cs.com
I: www.eastendhouse.co.uk

FENNY BENTLEY
Derbyshire

Swallows Cottage Rating Applied For
Contact: Mrs Angela Hughes, Woodleaves, Fenny Bentley, Ashbourne DE6 1LF
T: (01335) 350238
E: hughes.priory@virgin.net
I: www.country-holidays.co.uk

FLAGG
Derbyshire

Box Tree Cottage ★★★
Contact: Mr C MacQueen, Peak Cottages, Strawberry Lee Lane, Totley Bents, Sheffield S17 3BA
T: (0114) 262 0777
F: (0114) 262 0666
E: enquiries@peakcottages.com
I: www.peakcottages.com

Sonny Cottage ★★★★
Contact: Mr MacQueen, Peak Cottages, Strawberry Lee Lane, Totley Bents, Totley Rise, Sheffield S17 3BA
T: (0114) 262 0777
F: (0114) 262 0666
E: enquiries@peakcottages.com
I: www.peakcottages.com

FLASH
Staffordshire

Northfield Farm ★★-★★★
Contact: Mrs E Andrews, Northfield Farm, Flash, Quarnford, Buxton SK17 0SW
T: (01298) 22543
F: (01298) 27849
E: northfield@btinternet.com

FLORE
Northamptonshire

Brewer's Cottage ★★★★
Contact: Mrs Loasby, Brewer's Cottage, Old Baker's Arms (No 16), Kings Lane, Flore, Northampton NN7 4LQ
T: (01327) 349737
F: (01327) 349747
E: mloasby@btinternet.com

FOOLOW
Derbyshire

Sycamore Cottage ★★★
Contact: Mrs Maueen Norton, The Rest, Foolow S32 5QR
T: (01433) 630186
E: mnortonfoolow@aol.com

FORD
Shropshire

Longmore Cottage ★★★★
Contact: Mrs Mary Powell, Home Farm, Rowton, Halfway House, Ford, Shrewsbury SY5 9EN
T: (01743) 884201

FOWNHOPE
Herefordshire

Birds Farm Cottage ★★★
Contact: Mrs Margaret Edwards, White House, How Caple, Foy, Ross-on-Wye HR1 4SR
T: (01989) 740644
F: (01989) 740388
E: birdscottage@yahoo.com
I: www.holidaybank.co.uk/uk/heuk/h0529.htm

FRAMPTON MANSELL
Gloucestershire

Twissells Mill ★★
Contact: Mr & Mrs Daphne & Martin Neville, Bakers Mill, Frampton Mansell, Stroud GL6 8JH
T: (01285) 760234

FRAMPTON-ON-SEVERN
Gloucestershire

Clair Cottage ★★★★
Contact: Mrs Cullen, Church Court Cottage, Church End, Frampton-on-Severn, Gloucester GL2 7EH
T: (01452) 740289
E: claircottage@waitrose.com

Old Priest Cottage & Old Stable Cottage ★★★★-★★★★★
Contact: Mr & Mrs Mike & Caroline Williams, Tan House Farm, Frampton-on-Severn, Gloucester GL2 7EH
T: (01452) 741072
F: (01452) 741072
E: tanhouse.farm@lineone.net

FROCESTER
Gloucestershire

Kestrel Cottage ★★★★
Contact: Mr F J Holpin, F J Holpin & Sons Ltd, 1 Leaze Close, Berkeley GL13 9BZ
T: (01453) 810486

FRODESLEY
Shropshire

The Haven ★★★
Contact: Mr & Mrs Richard & Jennifer Pickard, The Haven, Frodesley, Shrewsbury SY5 7EY
T: (01694) 731672
E: the-haven@frodesley-fsnet.co.uk
I: www.cottageguide.co.uk/the-haven

FROGHALL
Staffordshire

Foxtwood Cottages ★★★★
Contact: Mr & Mrs Clive & Alison Worrall, Foxtwood Cottages, Foxt Road, Froghall, Stoke-on-Trent ST10 2HJ
T: (01538) 266160
E: info@foxtwood.co.uk

FULLETBY
Lincolnshire

High Beacon Cottage ★★★★
Contact: Mr & Mrs Andrew & Susan Walker, High Beacon Cottage, High Beacon Farm, Fulletby, Horncastle LN9 6LB
T: (01507) 534009
F: (01507) 534009
E: beacon.cottage@virgin.net
I: www.highbeaconcottage.co.uk

GATCOMBE
Gloucestershire

Oatfield Country Cottages ★★★★-★★★★★
Contact: Mr & Mrs Julian & Pennie Berrisford, Oatfield Country Cottages, Oatfield House Farm, Etloe, Blakeney GL15 4AY
T: (01594) 510372
F: (01594) 510372

GAYDON
Warwickshire

The Wagon House ★★★★
Contact: Miss G A Malsbury, Manor Farm, Gaydon, Warwick CV35 0HB
T: (01926) 640232
F: (01926) 640232

GLOSSOP
Derbyshire

Tingley Dell ★★★★
Contact: Mr C MacQueen, Peak Cottages, Strawberry Lee Lane, Totley Bents, Sheffield S17 3BA
T: (0114) 262 0777
F: (0114) 262 0666
E: enquiries@peakcottages.com
I: www.peakcottages.com

GLOUCESTER
Gloucestershire

Norfolk House ★★★
Contact: Mrs P J Jackson, 3 Wood Street, Higham Ferrers, Wellingborough NN9 8DL
T: (01452) 300997
E: nor39@fsmail.net

Number Ten ★★★
Contact: Mr M A Lampkin, Number Ten, 10 Albion Street, Gloucester GL1 1UE
T: (01452) 304402
E: lampkinternet.com@bushinternet.com

The Vineary ★★★
Contact: Mrs A Snow, Vinetree Cottage, Solomons Tump, Huntley, Gloucester GL19 3EB
T: (01452) 830006
E: anniesnow@btinternet.com

GONALSTON
Nottinghamshire

The Studio Cottage ★★★★
Contact: Mr & Mrs M G Carradice, Hill House, Gonalston, Nottingham NG14 7JA
T: (0115) 966 4551
F: (0115) 966 5097
E: carradice@btinternet.com
I: www.carradice@btinternet.co.uk

GOTHERINGTON
Gloucestershire

Bakery Cottage ★★★
Contact: Mrs Weller, Wortheal House, Southam Lane, Southam, Cheltenham GL52 3NY
T: (01242) 236765

Barn Cottages ★★★★
Contact: Mr Paul Tilley, Barn Cottages, Moat Farm, 34 Malleson Road, Cheltenham GL52 9ET
T: (01242) 672055
F: 07050 665639
E: jo@moatfarm.free-online.co.uk
I: www.moatfarm.free-online.co.uk

GRANTHAM
Lincolnshire

Belvior Cottage
Rating Applied For
Contact: Mrs Ursula Soar, Belvior Cottage, Old Millhouse, Branston Road, Eaton, Grantham NG32 1SF
T: (01476) 870797
E: belvoircottage@aol.com

Granary Cottage ★★★★
Contact: Miss Pepper, Granary Cottage, The Farmhouse, Little Humby, Grantham NG33 4HW
T: (01476) 585311

GREAT CARLTON
Lincolnshire

Willow Farm ★★★
Contact: Mr J Clark, Willow Farm, Great Carlton, Louth LN11 8JT
T: (01507) 338540

GREAT COMBERTON
Worcestershire

The Granary ★★★★
Contact: Mr & Mrs Newbury, Tibbitts Farm, Great Comberton, Pershore WR10 3DT
T: (01386) 710210
F: (01386) 710210

GREAT HALE
Lincolnshire

The Old Stable ★★★★
Contact: Mr & Mrs Redmond, The Old Stable, The Old Vicarage, 9 Church Street, Great Hale, Sleaford NG34 9LF
T: (01529) 460307
E: c.redmond@virgin.net

GREAT HUCKLOW
Derbyshire

Burrs Cottage ★★★
Contact: Mr Sykes, Sykes Cottages, York House, York Street, Chester CH1 3LR
T: (01244) 345700
F: (01244) 321442
E: info@sykescottages.co.uk
I: www.sykescottages.co.uk

The Hayloft ★★★★
Contact: Mrs Margot Darley, Stanley House Farm, Great Hucklow, Buxton SK17 8RL
T: (01298) 871044
E: margot.darley@btinternet.com
I: peakdistrictfarmhols.co.uk

South View Cottage ★★★★
Contact: Mrs M Waterhouse, Holme Cottage, Windmill, Great Hucklow, Buxton SK17 8RE
T: (01298) 871440
E: mo@mmwaterhouse.demon.co.uk
I: www.cottageguide.co.uk/southviewcottage

GREAT LONGSTONE
Derbyshire

Ivy Cottage
Rating Applied For
Contact: Mrs H Bell, Nether Croft, Eaton Place, Baslow, Bakewell DE45 1RW
T: (01246) 583564
E: nethercroftbandb@aol.com

Netherdale ★★
Contact: Country Hols Ref: 8134, Country Holidays Group Owner Services Dept, Spring Mill, Earby, Barnoldswick BB94 0AA
T: 08700 723723
F: (01282) 844288
E: sales@ttgihg.co.uk
I: www.countryhoildays.co.uk

Two Bears Cottage ★★★★
Contact: Mrs Valerie Squire, 185 Crimicar Lane, Sheffield S10 4EH
T: (0114) 230 3274
E: roger.squire@virgin.net

GREAT RISSINGTON
Gloucestershire

The Dairy Barn ★★★★
Contact: Manor Cottages, Manor Cottages, 33A Priory Mews, Burford, Oxford OX18 4SG
T: (01993) 824252
E: mancott@netcomuk.co.uk

GRIMBLETHORPE
Lincolnshire

Shepherds Cottage ★★★★★
Contact: Mrs E A Codling, Grimblethorpe Hall Country Cottages, Grimblethorpe, Louth LN11 0RB
T: (01507) 313671
F: (01507) 313854

GRIMLEY
Worcestershire

The Whitehouse Annex ★★★
Contact: Mrs O'Neill, The Whitehouse, Monkwood Green, Grimley, Worcester WR2 6NX
T: (01886) 888743

GRINDLEFORD
Derbyshire

Middle Cottage ★★★
Contact: Peak Cottages, Paddock Cottage, Strawberry Lee Lane, Totley Bents, Sheffield S17 3BA
T: (0114) 262 0777
F: (0114) 262 0666
E: enquiries@peakcottages.com
I: www.peakcottages.com

GRINDON
Staffordshire

Manifold Retreat ★★★★
Contact: Mr Robert Magnier, Manifold Retreat, Cawbrook Cottage, Grindon, Leek ST13 7TP
T: (01538) 304535
E: bwmag@freeuk.com

GRINSHILL
Shropshire

Barleycorn Barns ★★★★
Contact: Mr Neil Lewis & Ms Kerry Taylor, Barleycorn Cottage, Grinshill, Shrewsbury SY4 3BH
T: (01939) 220333
F: (01952) 608275
E: booking@barleycornbarns.com

Chestnut Croft Self-Catering Cottage ★★★
Contact: Mr R J Good, 61 The Hill, Grinshill, Shrewsbury SY4 3BU
T: (01939) 220573
F: (01939) 220573
E: roger@goodrj.fsnet.co.uk
I: www.chestnutcroft.com

HALLINGTON
Lincolnshire

The Paddy House & Blacksmiths Shop ★★★★
Contact: Mrs Canter, The Paddy House & Blacksmiths Shop, Home Farm, Hallington, Louth LN11 9QX
T: (01507) 605864
F: (01472) 250365
E: canter.hallington@virgin.net
I: freespace.virginnet.co.uk/canter.hallington/index.htm

HALLOW
Worcestershire

The New Cottage ★★★★
Contact: Mr & Mrs Michael & Doreen Jeeves, The New Cottage, Bridles End House, Greenhill Lane, Worcester WR2 6LG
T: (01905) 640953
E: jeeves@thenewcottage.co.uk
I: www.thenewcottage.co.uk

HALSE
Northamptonshire

Hill Farm ★★★★
Contact: Mrs J Robinson, Hill Farm, Halse, Brackley NN13 6DY
T: (01280) 703300
F: (01280) 704999
E: jg.robinson@farmline.com

HANDLEY
Derbyshire

Ridgewell Farm ★★★★
Contact: Mrs Ann Kerry, Ridgewell Farm, Handley Lane, Handley, Clay Cross, Chesterfield S45 9AT
T: (01246) 590698
F: (01246) 590698

HANLEY CASTLE
Worcestershire

Orchard Cottage
Rating Applied For
Contact: Mrs Nicola Whittaker, Whitehall Farm, Brotheridge Green, Hanley Castle, Worcester WR8 0BB
T: (01684) 310376
F: (01684) 310376
E: nicki@aol.com

HANLEY SWAN
Worcestershire

Little Merebrook ★★★★
Contact: Mr Bishop, Little Merebrook, Hanley Swan, Worcester WR8 0EH
T: (01684) 310899
F: (01684) 310899
I: www.hanleyholidays@yahoo.co.uk

HARBY
Leicestershire

New Farm Cottage ★★★
Contact: Mrs Jean Stanley, New Farm Cottage, Waltham Road, Stathern, Melton Mowbray LE14 4DB
T: (01949) 860640
F: (01949) 861165

HARLEY
Shropshire

Old Mill Cottages ★★★★
Contact: Mr W J Cooper, Old Mill Cottages, The Old Mill, Harley, Shrewsbury SY5 6LP
T: (01952) 510726

HARTINGTON
Derbyshire

Beech Cottage ★★★
Contact: Mrs Lesley Birch, Dale House, Hartington, Buxton SK17 0AS
T: (01298) 84532
E: lesley@beechcottage99.freeserve.co.uk
I: www.beechcottage99.freeserve.co.uk

Church View ★★★
Contact: Miss K Bassett, Digmer, Hartington, Buxton SK17 0AQ
T: (01298) 84660

Cotterill Farm Cottages ★★★★
Contact: Mrs Frances Skemp, Cotterill Farm Cottages, Cotterill Farm, Biggin-by-Hartington, Hartington, Buxton SK17 0DJ
T: (01298) 84447
F: (01298) 84664
E: enquire@cotterillfarm.co.uk
I: www.skemp.u-net.com

Cruck Cottage, Wolfscote Stable, Graces Cottage, Swallows & Swallows Return ★★★★
Contact: Mrs Jane Gibbs, Wolfscote Grange Farm, Hartington, Buxton SK17 0AX
T: (01298) 84342
E: wolfscote@btinternet.com
I: www.wolfscotegrangecottages.co.uk

Dairy Cottage, Piggery Place, Shire's Rest ★★★-★★★★
Contact: Mrs S Flower, Dairy Cottage, Piggery Place, Shire's Rest, Newhaven, Hartington, Buxton SK17 0DY
T: (01629) 636268
F: (01629) 636268
E: s.flower1@virgin.net
I: freespace.virgin.net/s.flower1

Dalescroft Cottage and Apartment ★★★★-★★★★★
Contact: Mr B J Leese, 19 Lansdowne Road, Buxton SK17 6RR
T: (01298) 24263
E: mail@dalescroft.co.uk
I: www.dalescroft.co.uk

Dove Valley Centre ★★★
Contact: Mr & Mrs Walker, Dove Valley Centre, Under Whitle, Sheen, Hartington, Buxton SK17 0PR
T: (01298) 83282
E: walker@dovevalleycentre.co.uk
I: www.dovevalleycentre.co.uk

Hartington Cottages ★★★★-★★★★★
Contact: Mr & Mrs Patrick & Frances Skemp, Cotterill Farm, Biggin by Hartington, Hartington, Buxton SK17 0DJ
F: (01298) 84447
E: enquiries@hartingtoncottages.co.uk
I: www.haartingtoncottages.co.uk

Raikes Barn ★★★★
Contact: Mr C MacQueen, Peak Cottages, Strawberry Lee Lane, Totley Bents, Sheffield S17 3BA
T: (0114) 262 0777
F: (0114) 262 0666
E: enquiries@peakcottages.com
I: www.peakcottages.com

1 Staley Cottage & Victoria House ★★★★
Contact: Mr & Mrs J Oliver, Carr Head Farm, Penistone, Sheffield S36 7GA
T: (01226) 762387

HATHERSAGE
Derbyshire

Oaks Farm ★★★
Contact: Mrs P M Bardwell, Oaks Farm, Highlow, Hathersage, Hope Valley S32 1AX
T: (01433) 650494
E: oaksfarm@fsdial.co.uk
I: ukonline.co.uk/oaksfarm/index.html

Pat's Cottage ★★★
Contact: Mr John Drakeford, 110 Townhead Road, Dore, Sheffield S17 3GB
T: (0114) 236 6014
F: (0114) 236 6014
E: johnmdrakeford@hotmail.com
I: www.patscottage.co.uk

St Michael's Cottage ★★★
Contact: Miss H Turton, St Michael's Environmental Education Centre, Main Road, Hathersage, Hope Valley S32 1BB
T: (01433) 650309
F: (01433) 650089
E: stmichaels@education.nottscc.gov.uk
I: www.eess.org.uk

HATTON
Lincolnshire

The Gables ★★★★★
Contact: Mrs Merivale, The Gables, Hatton Hall Farm, Wragby, Market Rasen LN8 5QG
T: (01673) 858862
I: www.thegables-hatton.co.uk

The Stable ★★★
Contact: Mr & Mrs Hall, White House, Affcot, Church Stretton SY6 6RL
T: (01694) 781202

HAWLING
Gloucestershire

The Bothy ★★★★
Contact: Mrs S Watters, Brocklehurst, Hawling, Cheltenham GL54 5TA
T: (01451) 850772
E: hawling@aol.com

Middle Farm Cottages ★★★★
Contact: Mr & Mrs Woollacott, Middle Farm Cottages, Middle Farm, Hawling, Cheltenham GL54 5SZ
T: (01451) 850744

HAYFIELD
Derbyshire

Bowden Bridge Cottage ★★★★
Contact: Mrs Margrith Easter, Bowden Bridge Cottage, Kinder, Hayfield, High Peak SK22 2LH
T: (01663) 743975
F: (01663) 743812
E: j_easter@talk21.com

HAZELWOOD
Derbyshire

Duck Pond View
Rating Applied For
Contact: Ms Liz Chisman, Knowle Farm, Nether Lane, Hazelwood, Belper DE56 4AP
T: (01773) 550686
F: (01773) 550686
E: liz@chisman.co.uk

HENLEY-IN-ARDEN
Warwickshire

Irelands Farm ★★★★
Contact: Mr & Mrs Stephanie Williams, Irelands Farm, Irelands Lane, Henley-in-Arden, Solihull B95 5SA
T: (01564) 792476
F: (01564) 792476
E: stephanie.williams1@btinternet.com
I: www.irelandsfarmcottages.com

HENNOR
Herefordshire

Hennor House ★★-★★★
Contact: Mrs Sally Hall, Hennor Holidays, Hennor House, Hennor, Leominster HR6 0QR
T: (01568) 760665
F: (01568) 760665
E: salihall@aol.com

HEREFORD
Herefordshire

Anvil Cottage ★★★★
Contact: Mrs Jennie Layton, Grafton Villa Farm House, Grafton, Hereford HR2 8ED
T: (01432) 268689
F: (01432) 268689
E: jennielayton@ereal.net
I: www.s-h-system@uk/hotels/graftonv.html

Barton West
Rating Applied For
Contact: Mrs Teresa Godbert, 24 Broomy Hill, Hereford HR4 0LH
T: 07966 100230
E: teresagodbert@hereford-hopes.co.uk
I: www.hereford-hopes.co.uk

Breinton Court ★★★
Contact: Mrs G Hands, Breinton Court, Lower Breinton, Hereford HR4 7PG
T: (01432) 268156
F: (01432) 265134
E: hentapeparkhotel@talk21.com

Castle Cliffe East ★★★★
Contact: Mr M Hubbard & Mr P Wilson, Castle Cliffe West, 14 Quay Street, Hereford HR1 2NH
T: (01432) 272096
E: mail@castlecliffe.net
I: www.castlecliffe.net

Cross In Hand Farm Cottage ★★★★
Contact: Dr Thornton, Cross In Hand Farm Cottage, Cross In Hand Farm, Callow, Hereford HR2 8EF
T: (01981) 540957
E: julia@crossinhand.com

Home From Home Holidays ★★
Contact: Mr & Mrs Bill & Maggie Matthews, 16 St Martins Avenue, Hereford HR2 7RQ
T: (01432) 272259
E: bandm@prospectpl.fsnet.co.uk
I: bandm@prospectpl.fsnet.co.uk

Longwood Cottage ★★★
Contact: Mrs Veronica Harris, S L C (Services) Limited, Ashfield House, Sollers Hope, Fownhope, Hereford HR1 4RL
T: (01989) 740248
F: (01989) 740214
E: kenverharris@aol.com

Rushford ★★★★
Contact: Mrs M W Roberts, Rushford, 7 Belle Bank Avenue, Holmer, Hereford HR4 9RL
T: (01432) 273380
F: (01432) 273380

Treago Castle Cottages ★★★
Contact: Lady Mynors, Treago Castle Cottages, St Weonards, Hereford HR2 8QB
T: (01981) 580208
E: fiona.mynors@cmail.co.uk

HIMBLETON
Worcestershire

Phepson Farm Cottages ★★★
Contact: Mr & Mrs David & Trica Havard, Phepson Farm Cottages, Phepson Farm, Himbleton, Droitwich WR9 7JZ
T: (01905) 391205
F: (01905) 391338
E: havard@globalnet.co.uk
I: www.phepsonfarm.co.uk

HINCKLEY
Leicestershire

Crossways Country Holidays ★★★★
Contact: Mrs Carol Mac, Crossways Country Holidays, Crossways Farm, Lutterworth Road, Burbage, Hinckley LE10 3AH
T: (01455) 239261
F: (01445) 221121
E: user@burbage60.fsnet.co.uk
I: www.crossways-holidays.co.uk

HOARWITHY
Herefordshire

Old Mill Cottage ★★★
Contact: Mrs Carol Probert, Old Mill, Hoarwithy, Hereford HR2 6QH
T: (01432) 840602
F: (01432) 840602

HODTHORPE
Derbyshire

Southview ★★★
Contact: Mrs J Hogg, 11 Queens Road, Hodthorpe, Worksop S80 4UN
T: (01909) 720410

HOGNASTON
Derbyshire

The Flintstones – Barney's Cottage & Fred's Place Rating Applied For
Contact: Mrs Gillian Pearson, 4 Bank House Court, Hognaston, Ashbourne DE6 1PR
T: (01335) 372189
F: (01335) 370231
E: gillian.pearson@virgin.net

HOLBEACH
Lincolnshire

Poachers Den ★★★
Contact: Mr Flynn, 34 Fen Road, Holbeach, Spalding PE12 8QA
T: (01406) 423625
F: (01406) 423625
E: MFlynn8748@aol.com
I: www.Smoothhound.co.uk/hotels/poachers.html

HOLLINGTON
Staffordshire

Rowan Cottage ★★★
Contact: Mrs Campbell, Great Gate Road, Winnoth Dale, Tean, Stoke-on-Trent ST10 4HB
T: (01538) 722031

HOLYMOORSIDE
Derbyshire

Millclose Cottage ★★★★
Contact: Mr & Mrs Stockton, Millclose Cottage, Millclose Farm, Nether Loads, Holymoorside, Chesterfield S42 7HW
T: (01246) 567624
F: (01246) 567624
E: allan.stockton@btinternet.com

HOPE
Derbyshire

Aston Cottages ★★★★
Contact: Mrs Rachel Morley, Aston Cottages, The Dimings, Aston Lane, Hope Valley S33 6RA
T: (01433) 621619
E: rmorley@dimings.freeserve.co.uk
I: www.sallydog.co.uk/astoncottages/

Farfield Farm Cottages ★★★★
Contact: Mrs Elliott, Farfield Farm Cottages, Farfield Farm, Hope Valley S33 6RA
T: (01433) 620640
F: (01433) 620640
I: www.farfield.gemsoft.co.uk

Keepers Lodge ★★★★★
Contact: Mrs Christine Bell, Keeper's lodge, Spring House Farm, Castleton, Hope Valley S33 8WB
T: (01433) 620962
E: thebells@btinternet.com
I: www.peak-district-holiday-cottages.co.uk

Laneside Farm Cottages ★★★★
Contact: Mrs D M Neary, Laneside Farm, Hope Valley S33 6RR
T: (01433) 620214
F: (01433) 620214
E: laneside@lineone.net
I: www.laneside.fsbusiness.co.uk

Oaker Farm Holiday Cottages ★★★★
Contact: Mrs Julie Ann Hadfield, Oaker Farm Holiday Cottages, Off Edale Road, Hope Valley S33 6RF
T: (01433) 621955
E: julieannhadfield@hotmail.com
I: www.oakerfarm.fsnet.co.uk

The Old Bell & Ebenezer Barn ★★★
Contact: Mr M Davis, Bennet Grange, Jefferys Green, Sheffield S10 4PA
T: (0114) 230 3463
F: (0114) 230 8808

Tiggy's Cottage ★★★★
Contact: Mr C MacQueen, Peak Cottages, Strawberry Lee Lane, Totley Bents, Sheffield S17 3BA
T: (0114) 262 0777
F: (0114) 262 0666
E: enquiries@peakcottages.com
I: www.peakcottages.com

Twitchill Farm Cottages ★★★-★★★★
Contact: Mrs S Atkin, Twitchill Farm Cottages, Edale Road, Hope Valley S33 6RF
T: (01433) 621426
I: members.aol.com/sarahatkin

HOPESAY
Shropshire

Hesterworth Holidays ★★-★★★
Contact: Mr Roger Davies, Hesterworth Holidays, Hopesay, Craven Arms SY7 8EX
T: (01588) 660487
F: (01588) 660153
I: www.hesterworth.co.uk

HOPTON
Derbyshire

Peakside ★★★
Contact: Mr C MacQueen, Peak Cottages, Strawberry Lee Lane, Totley Bents, Sheffield S17 3BA
T: (0114) 262 0777
F: (0114) 262 0666
E: enquiries@peakcottages.com
I: www.peakcottages.com

HORNCASTLE
Lincolnshire

Coach House ★★★
Contact: Country Holidays Ref 11456 Holiday Cottages Group, Spring Mill, Earby, Barnoldswick BB94 0AA
T: 08700 723723
E: sales@ttgihg.co.uk
I: www.country-holidays.co.uk

Southolme Cottage ★★★
Contact: Mr David Gresham, Glebe Cottage, Valenders Lane, Ilmington, Shipston-on-Stour CV36 4LB
T: (0121) 449 5666
E: david@gartongresham.co.uk

HORSINGTON
Lincolnshire

Wayside Cottage ★★★
Contact: Mr & Mrs I G Williamson, 72 Mill Lane, Woodhall Spa LN10 6QZ
T: (01526) 353101
E: will@williamsoni.freeserve.co.uk
I: www.skegness.net/woodhallspa.htm

HORSLEY
Gloucestershire

The Coach House c/o The Old Vicarage★★★
Contact: Mrs Stella Knight, The Old Vicarage, Rockness, Horsley, Nailsworth, Stroud GL6 0PJ
T: (01453) 832265
F: (01453) 832865
E: andrew.knight@ukgateway.net

HULLAND WARD
Derbyshire

Valley View ★★★
Contact: Mrs Audrey Gray, Biggin by Hulland, Ashbourne DE6 3FJ
T: (01335) 370204
F: (01333) 70204
E: hayes.farm@lineone.net

HULME END
Staffordshire

East & West Cawlow Barn ★★★★
Contact: Mr Clive Sykes, Sykes Cottages, York House, York Street, Chester CH1 3LR
T: (01244) 345700
F: (01244) 321442
E: info@sykescottages.co.uk
I: www.sykescottages.co.uk

The Old Dairy ★★★
Contact: Mrs Marianne Grayson, The Old Dairy, Endon House Farm, Hulme End, Buxton SK17 0HG
T: (01298) 84515
F: (01298) 84476
E: mariannechalcraft@endonhouse.fsnet.co.uk
I: www.cressbrook.co.uk

HUNTLEY
Gloucestershire

The Olde Brew House Rating Applied For
Contact: Mr Maurice Estop, The Farmers Arms, Ledbury Road, Huntley, Gloucester GL19 3DR
T: (01452) 780307

IBSTOCK
Leicestershire

Lavender Cottage ★★★★
Contact: Mrs Lorraine Rajput, The Cottage, 155 High Street, Ibstock, Leicester LE67 6JQ
T: (01530) 450451

ILAM
Staffordshire

Beechenhill Cottage & The Cottage by the Pond★★★★
Contact: Mrs Sue Prince, Beechenhill Cottage & The Cottage by the Pond, Beechenhill Farm, Ilam, Ashbourne DE6 2BD
T: (01335) 310274
F: (01335) 310467
I: www.beechenhill.co.uk

Throwley Hall Farm ★★★-★★★★
Contact: Mrs M A Richardson, Throwley Hall Farm, Ilam, Ashbourne DE6 2BB
T: (01538) 308202
F: (01538) 308243
E: throwleyhall@talk21.com
I: throwleyhallfarm.co.uk

ILMINGTON
Warwickshire

Cotswold Retreat at Folly Farm Cottage★★★-★★★★
Contact: Mrs Sheila Lowe, Folly Farm Cottage, Back Street, Ilmington, Shipston-on-Stour CV36 4LJ
T: (01608) 682425
F: (01608) 682425

Featherbed Cottage ★★★★
Contact: Mr David Price, Featherbed Cottage, Featherbed Lane, 8 Nellands Close, Ilmington, Shipston-on-Stour CV36 4NF
T: (01608) 682215
E: featherbedcottage@hotmail.com

INGHAM
Lincolnshire

3 Anyans Row ★★★
Contact: Mr & Mrs T Taylor, Ivy Cottage, Stow Road, Sturton by Stow, Sturton-by-Stow, Lincoln LN1 2BZ
T: (01427) 788023

IPSTONES
Staffordshire

Coach House Stables ★★★
Contact: Mrs Susan Wyncoll, Coach House Stables, The Noggin, Ipstones, Stoke-on-Trent ST10 2LQ
T: (01538) 266579
E: susan@the-noggin.freeserve.co.uk

Meadow Place ★★★★
Contact: Mr Sykes, Sykes Cottages, York House, York Street, Chester CH1 3LR
T: (01244) 345700
F: (01244) 321442
E: info@sykescottages.co.uk
I: www.sykescottages.co.uk

Old Hall Farm Cottages ★★
Contact: Mr & Mrs D R Glover, Old Hall Farm Cottages, Old Hall Farm, Church Lane, Ipstones, Stoke-on-Trent ST10 2LF
T: (01538) 266465

The Stables & The Cart Shed ★★★
Contact: Mr & Mrs Michael & Hilary Hall, Shay Lane, Ipstones, Stoke-on-Trent ST10 2LZ
T: (01538) 266259

IRONBRIDGE
Shropshire

Bottom End Cottage ★★★★
Contact: Mr P A Ottley, 8 Ladywood, Ironbridge, Telford TF8 7JR
T: (01952) 883770
F: (01952) 884647
E: ironbridge@theironbridge.co.uk
I: www.theironbridge.co.uk

Bryher Cottage ★★★
Contact: Mr Ian Roberts, 25 St Philips Avenue, Wolverhampton WV3 7DU
T: (01902) 655419

Eleys of Ironbridge ★★★-★★★★★
Contact: Ms Jayne Mountford, Eleys of Ironbridge, 13 Tontine Hill, Ironbridge, Telford TF8 7AL
T: (01952) 684249
F: (01952) 432030
I: www.eleys-ironbridge.co.uk

Langdale Cottage ★★★
Contact: Mr A K Blight
T: 07768 830500
E: keithblight@aol.com

Martha's Cottage ★★★
Contact: Mr Brian Richards, Thorpe House, High Street, Coalport, Telford TF8 7HP
T: (01952) 586789
F: (01952) 586789
E: thorpehouse@tiscali.co.uk

Murton Cottage Rating Applied For
Contact: Mrs Shan Murton, Mickleden, Sutherland Avenue, Wellington, Telford TF1 3BL
T: (01952) 415019
E: shanmurton@aol.com

Paradise House ★★-★★★
Contact: Mrs M Gilbride, Paradise House, 3 Paradise, Coalbrookdale, Telford TF8 7NR
T: (01952) 433379
E: marjorie@gilbride.co.uk

The Uplands Flat ★★★
Contact: Mrs B M Eccleston, The Uplands, Buildwas Road, Ironbridge, Telford TF8 7BJ
T: (01952) 433408

KENILWORTH
Warwickshire

Castle Cottages ★★★★
Contact: Mrs Sheila Tomalin, 7 Castle Green, Kenilworth CV8 1NE
T: (01926) 852204
E: sheilatomalin@tinyonline.co.uk

Jackdaw Cottage & Wren's Nest ★★★★
Contact: Mrs L Grierson, The White Bungalow, 6 Canterbury Close, Kenilworth CV8 2PU
T: (01926) 855616
F: (01926) 513189
E: kgrierson@ukonline.co.uk

The Little Barn ★★★
Contact: Mrs Oliver, Crewe Farm Barns, Crewe Lane, Kenilworth CV8 2LA
T: (01926) 850692

Wren's Nest ★★★★
Contact: Mrs Lynn Grierson, The White Bungalow, 6 Canterbury Close, Kenilworth CV8 2PU
T: (01926) 855616
F: (01926) 513189
E: kgrierson@ukonline.co.uk

KENLEY
Shropshire

No 1 & 2 Courtyard Cottages ★★★★
Contact: Mrs A Gill, No 1 & 2 Courtyard Cottages, Lower Springs Farm, Kenley, Shrewsbury SY5 6PA
T: (01952) 510841
F: (01952) 510841
E: a-gill@lineone.net
I: www.courtyardcottages.com

KERSALL
Nottinghamshire

Rose & Sweetbriar Cottages ★★★
Contact: Mrs Brenda Wood, Rose & Sweetbriar Cottages, Hill Farm, Kersall, Newark NG22 0BJ
T: (01636) 636274
I: www.roseandsweetbriar.fsbusiness.co.uk

KETTERING
Northamptonshire

The Villiers Suite, Cranford Hall ★★★
Contact: Mr & Mrs John Robinson, The Villiers Suite, Cranford Hall, Cranford, Kettering NN14 4AL
T: (01536) 330248
F: (01536) 330203
E: cranford@farmline.com
I: cranfordhall.co.uk

KETTON
Rutland

Dove Cottage ★★★
Contact: Mr & Mrs Don & Margaret Bradley, 27 High Street, Ketton, Stamford PE9 3TA
T: (01780) 720248

Randolph Cottage ★★★★
Contact: Mrs M Forster, Randolph Cottage, 11 Church Road, Ketton, Stamford PE9 3RD
T: (01780) 720802
E: forster.ketton@virgin.net

KIMBOLTON
Herefordshire

Rowley Farm ★★★
Contact: Mrs & Mrs Jean & Sue Pugh, Rowley Farm, Kimbolton, Leominster HR6 0EX
T: (01568) 616123
F: (01568) 611101
E: rowley@farmersweekley.net
I: www.rowleyholidaypark.co.uk

KING'S STANLEY
Gloucestershire

Rectory Cottage ★★★★
Contact: Country Holidays Ref: 9131 Sales, Holiday Cottages Group Limited, Spring Mill, Earby, Barnoldswick BB94 0AA
T: 08700 723723
F: (01282) 844288
E: sales@holidaycottagesgroup.com
I: www.country-holidays.co.uk

KINGS CAPLE
Herefordshire

Ruxton Mill ★★★★
Contact: Mrs M Slater, Ruxton Farm, Kings Caple, Hereford HR1 4TX
T: (01432) 840493
F: (01432) 840493
E: milly@ruxton.co.uk
I: www.wyevalleycottages.com

KINGTON
Herefordshire

Cider Press Cottage Rating Applied For
Contact: Mrs Lorraine Wright, Bredward Farm, Kington HR5 3HP
T: (01544) 231462

KINWARTON
Warwickshire

The Granary ★★★
Contact: Mrs Kinnersley, The Granary, Glebe Farm, Kinwarton, Alcester B49 6HB
T: (01789) 762554
F: (01789) 762554
E: johnandsusan@kinnersley.fsworld.co.uk

KIRK IRETON
Derbyshire

Bluebell, Buttercup & Clover Barn ★★★★
Contact: Mr & Mrs Pollard, Bluebell, Buttercup & Clover Barn, Alton Nether Farm, Tinkerley Lane, Kirk Ireton, Derby DE6 3LF
T: (01335) 370270
F: (01335) 370270
E: ben@redpepperpictures.freeserve.co.uk

Grange Holidays ★★★★
Contact: Mr Malcolm Race, Grange Holidays, Tinkerley Lane, Kirk Ireton, Derby DE6 3LF
T: (01335) 370880
E: malcolm@malcolmrace.fsnet.co.uk
I: www.ashbourne-accommodation.co.uk

Ivy Cottage ★★★
Contact: Peak Cottages Ltd, Strawberry Lee Lane, Totley Bents, Totley Rise, Sheffield S17 3BA
T: (0114) 262 0777
F: (0114) 262 0666

KIRK LANGLEY
Derbyshire

The Cart Hovel and The Stables ★★★★
Contact: Mrs Sue Gibbs, Brun Farm View, Brun Lane, Kirk Langley, Ashbourne DE6 4LU
T: (01332) 824214

KNIGHTCOTE
Warwickshire

Knightcote Farm Cottages ★★★★★
Contact: Mrs Fiona Walker, Knightcote Farm Cottages, The Bake House, Knightcote, Southam CV47 2EF
T: (01295) 770637
F: (01295) 770135
E: fionawalker@farmcottages.com
I: www.farmcottages.com

KNIGHTWICK
Worcestershire

Harleys Barn & Daisy Barn ★★★
Contact: Mr & Mrs D H Bentley, The Courtyard, Highfields Farm, Worcester WR6 5QG
T: (01886) 821056
F: (01886) 821056

KNIVETON
Derbyshire

Meadow Cottages ★★★
Contact: Peak Cottages, Strawberry Lee Lane, Totley Bents, Sheffield S17 3BA
T: (0114) 262 0777
F: (0114) 262 0666
E: enquiries@peakcottages.com
I: www.peakcottages.com

Willow Bank ★★★★
Contact: Mrs M E Vaughan, Willow Bank, Kniveton, Ashbourne DE6 1JJ
T: (01335) 343308
E: willowbank@kniveton.net
I: www.kniveton.net

KNOCKIN
Shropshire

The Coach House Rating Applied For
Contact: Mrs P Calvert, The Oak Barn, The Old Estate Yard, Knockin, Oswestry SY10 8HQ
T: (01691) 682154
E: trishcalvert@talk21.com

LAMBLEY
Nottinghamshire

Dickman's Cottage ★★★
Contact: Mr William Marshall Marshall Smith, Springsyde, Birdcage Walk, Otley LS21 3HB
T: (01943) 462719
F: (01943) 850925
E: marshallsmithuk@hotmail.com
I: marshallsmithuk@hotmail.com

LEA
Derbyshire

Coach House ★★★
Contact: Mr & Mrs Hobson, Coach House, Main Road, Lea, Matlock DE4 5GJ
T: (01629) 534346
E: alanandbarbara@coachhouselea.co.uk
I: www.coachhouselea.co.uk

Moorlands ★★★
Contact: Mrs White, Moors Farm, Lea, Ross-on-Wye HR9 7JY
T: (01989) 750230

The Old Stable ★★★
Contact: Mr Philip Waterfall, The Old Stable, 5 Main Road, Lea, Matlock DE4 5GJ
T: (01629) 534546

LEAMINGTON SPA
Warwickshire

Barn Owl Cottage ★★★★
Contact: Mrs B Norman, Fosseway Barns, Fosse Way, Offchurch, Leamington Spa CV33 9BQ
T: (01926) 614647
F: (01926) 614647
E: bnorman@fossebarn.prestel.co.uk
I: barnowlcottage.co.uk

Blackdown Farm Cottages ★
Contact: Mr & Mrs R Solt, Blackdown Farm, Sandy Lane, Leamington Spa CV32 6QS
T: (01926) 422522
F: (01926) 450996
E: bobby@solt.demon.co.uk

Furzen Hill Farm ★★★
Contact: Mrs C M Whitfield, Furzen Hill Farm, Cubbington Heath, Leamington Spa CV32 7UJ
T: (01926) 424791
F: (01926) 424791

Riplingham ★★★★
Contact: Ms Shevlin, 1 The Old Courtyard, Alderman Way, Weston under Wetherley, Leamington Spa CV33 9GF
T: (01926) 633790
E: riplingham@hotmail.com

LEATON
Shropshire

Vicarage Cottage ★★★★★
Contact: Mrs Joan Mansell-Jones, Vicarage Cottage, The Old Vicarage, Shrewsbury SY4 3AP
T: (01939) 290989
F: (01939) 290989
E: m-j@oldvicleaton.com
I: www.oldvicleaton.com

LEDBURY
Herefordshire

Coach House Apartment ★★★
Contact: Mrs J Williams, Leadon House Hotel, Ross Road, Ledbury HR8 2LP
T: (01531) 631199
F: (01531) 631476
E: leadon.house@amserve.net

Homend Bank Cottage ★★★
Contact: Mrs E F Hughes, R H & R W Clutton, The Estate Office, Leighton Court, Ledbury HR8 2UN
T: (01531) 640262
F: (01531) 640719

Honeysuckle Cottage ★★★★
Contact: Mrs W S Hooper, Greenlands, Bromsberrow Heath, Ledbury HR8 1PG
T: (01531) 650360
E: ws.hooper@btopenworld.com

The Old Kennels Farm ★★★-★★★★
Contact: Mrs Wilce, The Old Kennels Farm, Bromyard Road, Ledbury HR8 1LG
T: (01531) 635024
F: (01531) 635241
E: wilceoldkennelsfarm@btinternet.com
I: www.visitorlinks.com

The Studio ★★★
Contact: Mr & Mrs David Riley, The Studio, Kynaston Place, Kynaston, Ledbury HR8 2PD
T: (01531) 670321
E: david@criley56.freeserve.co.uk

White House Cottages ★★★-★★★★
Contact: Mrs Marianne Hills, The White House, Aylton, Ledbury HR8 2RQ
T: (01531) 670349
F: (01531) 670057
E: hills1477@aol.com
I: www.whitehousecottages.co.uk

LEEK
Staffordshire

Blackshaw Grange ★★★-★★★★
Contact: Mr & Mrs K Williams, Blackshaw Grange, Blackshaw Moor, Leek ST13 8TL
T: (01538) 300165
E: kevwilliams@btinternet.com
I: website.lineone.net/~blackshawgrange

Broomyshaw Country Cottages Lower Broomyshaw Farm Rating Applied For
Contact: Mr & Mrs G T Saul, Broomyshaw Country Cottages Lower Broomyshaw Farm, Winkhill, Leek ST13 7QZ
T: (01538) 308298

Candy Cottage ★★★★
Contact: Mrs Sylvia Plant, Candy Cottage, Upper Cadlow Farm, Winkhill, Leek ST13 7QX
T: (01538) 266243
E: splantuppercadlow@hotmail.com
I: www.cottageguide.co.uk/candycottage/

Larks Rise ★★★
Contact: Mrs Laura Melland, Larks Rise, New House Farm, Bottom House, Leek ST13 7PA
T: (01538) 304350
E: newhousefarm@btinternet.com

Overton Bank Cottage Rating Applied For
Contact: Mr Sykes, Sykes Cottages, York House, York Street, Chester CH1 3LR
T: (01244) 345700
F: (01244) 321442
E: info@sykescottages.co.uk
I: www.sykescottages.co.uk

Rosewood ★★★
Contact: Mr & Mrs T & E Mycock, Rosewood, Lower Berkhamsytch Farm, Bottom House, Leek ST13 7QP
T: (01538) 308213
F: (01538) 308213

Wren Cottage ★★★★
Contact: Mr & Mrs Robert & Elizabeth Lowe, Fairboroughs Farm, Rudyard, Leek ST13 8PR
T: (01260) 226341
F: (01260) 226341

LEICESTER
Leicestershire

Romany ★★
Contact: Mrs E Harris, 86 Station Lane, Scraptoft, Leicester LE7 9UF
T: (0116) 292 7161
E: romany1@talk21.com
I: homepage.ntworld.com/monopoly1

LEINTWARDINE
Herefordshire

Badgers Bluff Holiday Cottages ★★★★
Contact: Mr Norton, The Todding Farmhouse, Leintwardine, Craven Arms SY7 0LX
T: (01547) 540648
F: (01547) 540648
E: reg@badgersbluff.co.uk
I: www.badgersbluff.co.uk

Dower Cottage ★★★★
Contact: Ms Anne & Susan Douthwaite, Dower Cottage, Dower House, Leintwardine, Craven Arms SY7 0LS
T: (01547) 540446
E: info@dower-cottage.co.uk
I: www.dower-cottage.co.uk

Oak Cottage ★★★
Contact: Mrs Vivienne Faulkner, 24 Watling Street, Leintwardine, Craven Arms SY7 0LW
T: (01547) 540629
F: (01547) 540181
E: fmjones@skg.co.uk

Oaklands Farm ★★
Contact: Mrs Sally Ann Swift
T: (01547) 540635
E: mrpaswift@aol.co.uk

LEOMINSTER
Herefordshire

Ashton Court Farm ★★★
Contact: Mrs P Edwards
T: (01584) 711245

The Buzzards ★★★★
Contact: Ms E Povey, The Buzzards, Kingsland, Leominster HR6 9QE
T: (01568) 708941
E: holiday@thebuzzards.co.uk

Eaton Farm Cottage ★★★
Contact: Mrs Audrey Pritchard, Eaton Farm Cottage, Eaton Court Farm, Stoke Prior Road, Leominster HR6 0NA
T: (01568) 612095

Ford Abbey ★★★★★
Contact: Mr Michael Wildmore, Ford Abbey, Pudleston, Leominster HR6 0RZ
T: (01568) 760700
F: (01568) 760264
E: info@fordabbey.co.uk
I: www.fordabbey.co.uk

Ledicot Granary Rating Applied For
Contact: Mr & Mrs Crawford and Vanessa Gibbons, Ledicot Farm, Shobdon, Leominster, Leominster HR6 9NX
T: (01568) 709245

Mill House Flat ★★★
Contact: Mrs E M Thomas, Woonton Court Farm, Leysters, Leominster HR6 0HL
T: (01568) 750232
F: (01568) 750232
E: thomas.woontoncourt@farmersweekly.net
I: www.woontoncourt.co.uk

LIGHTHORNE
Warwickshire

2 Church Cottages ★★★★
Contact: Mrs Beatrice Norman, Fosseway Barns, Fosse Way, Offchurch, Leamington Spa CV33 9BQ
T: (01926) 614647
F: (01926) 614647
E: bnorman@fossebarn.prestel.co.uk
I: twochurchcottages.co.uk

LINCOLN
Lincolnshire

Bight House ★★★★
Contact: Mrs Mavis Sharpe, Bight House, 17 East Bight, Lincoln LN2 1QH
T: (01522) 534477

Burton Cottage ★★★
Contact: Mrs Sharen Clark, 30 Burton Road, Lincoln LN1 3LB
T: (01522) 524990
F: (01522) 560845

The Cobbles ★★★
Contact: Mr J M Scott, Sunnyside, Lincoln Road, Brattleby, Lincoln LN1 2SQ
T: (01522) 730561
F: (01522) 513995
E: jmsco@lineone.net
I: www.lincolncottages.co.uk

9 Dorron Court ★★★
Contact: Mr Barry Dean, Thackers Lane, Lincoln LN4 1LT
T: (01522) 791442
F: (01522) 523067

The Flat ★★★
Contact: Mrs E A Slingsby, The Flat, 3 Greestone Place, Lincoln LN2 1PP
T: (01522) 560880
F: (01522) 535600
E: auction@thosmawer.co.uk
I: www.greestoneplacelincoln.co.uk

Kenton ★★★
Contact: Mr Michael Taylor, 2 Ventnor Place, Danesgate, Lincoln LN2 1LZ
T: (01522) 532136
E: mikefs@compuserve.com

Lilac Cottage ★★★
Contact: Mrs Veronica Verner, Lincoln LN2 1LP
T: (01522) 533347

19a Lindum Hill ★★★★
Contact: Mr S Richardson, 3 Marine Approach, Burton Waters, Lincoln LN1 2WW
T: (01522) 533119
F: (01522) 533119
E: stuart@disaster-care.co.uk
I: www.lindum-hill.co.uk

Martingale Cottage ★★★
Contact: Mrs P A Pate, 19 East Street, Nettleham, Lincoln LN2 2SL
T: (01522) 751795
E: patsy.pate@ntlworld.com

The Needleworkers ★★★★
Contact: Mr & Mrs Rochester, 5 Industrial Cottages, Long Leys Road, Lincoln LN1 1DZ
T: (01522) 522113
E: john@jrochester.fsnet.co.uk

Old Vicarage Cottage ★★★★
Contact: Mrs S Downs, The Old Vicarage, East Street, Nettleham, Lincoln LN2 2SL
T: (01522) 750819
F: (01522) 750819
E: susan@oldvic.net

Pingles Cottage ★★★
Contact: Mrs P A Sutcliffe, Pingles Cottage, Grange Farm, Broxholme, Lincoln LN1 2NG
T: (01522) 702441

Saint Clements ★★★
Contact: Mrs G Marshall, Saint Clements, Langworth Gate, Lincoln LN2 4AD
T: (01522) 538087
F: (01522) 560642
E: jroywood@aol.com

The Stables ★★★★
Contact: Mr J Scott, Sunnyside, Lincoln Road, Brattleby, Lincoln LN1 2SQ
T: (01522) 730561
E: jmsco@lineone.net
I: www.lincolncottages.co.uk

Tennyson Court ★★
Contact: Mr Andrew Carnell, Tennyson Court, Tennyson House, 3 Tennyson Street, Lincoln LN1 1LZ
T: (01522) 569892
F: (01522) 887997
E: andrew@tennyson-court.co.uk
I: www.tennyson-court.co.uk

Witham View ★★★★
Contact: Miss S Reynolds, 43 Mons Road, Lincoln LN1 3UF
T: (01522) 851631

LITTLE DEWCHURCH
Herefordshire

The Granary ★★★★
Contact: Mrs K Tibbetts, The Granary, Henclose Farm, Little Dewchurch, Hereford HR2 6PP
T: (01432) 840826
F: (01432) 840826

LITTLE EVERDON
Northamptonshire

Home Farm Barn ★★★★
Contact: Mrs Howell-Williams, Home Farm Barn, Little Everdon, Daventry NN11 3BG
T: (01327) 361233
F: (01327) 361543
E: howellwilliams@lineone.net

LITTLE HUCKLOW
Derbyshire

Glider View Cottage ★★★★
Contact: Mrs C Sherman, Two Barns, Main Street, Elton, Matlock DE4 2BW
T: (01629) 650196

The Parlour & The Dairy ★★★★
Contact: Mrs Wendy Mycock, The Parlour & The Dairy, Forest Lane Farm, Little Hucklow, Buxton SK17 8JE
T: (01298) 871226
F: (01298) 871226

LITTLE LONGSTONE
Derbyshire

The Lodge & Dove Cottage ★★★
Contact: Mrs A Davey, Chestnut House, Little Longstone, Bakewell DE45 1NN
T: (01629) 640542
F: (01629) 640450
E: annie@littlelongstone.freeserve.co.uk
I: www.clessbrook.co.uk/bakewell/lodgedove

Orrs Barn ★★★★
Contact: Peak Cottages, Strawberry Lee Lane, Totley Bents, Totley Rise, Sheffield S17 3BA
T: (0114) 262 0777
F: (0114) 262 0666
E: enquiries@peakcottages.com
I: www.peakcottages.com

LITTLE TARRINGTON
Herefordshire

Stock's Cottage ★★★★
Contact: Mrs Angela Stock, Stock's Cottage, Little Tarrington, Hereford HR1
T: (01432) 890243
F: (01432) 890243
E: stay@stockscottage.co.uk
I: www.stockscottage.co.uk

LITTON
Derbyshire

Ashleigh Cottage ★★★
Contact: Mrs S A Maxted, Ashleigh, Litton, Buxton SK17 8QU
T: (01298) 872505

2 Cross View, The Green ★★★
Contact: Mrs C Rowan-Olive, 44 Burnham Road, St Albans AL1 4QW
T: (01727) 844169
E: litton.cottage@ntworld.com
I: www.cross-view.co.uk

Farm Hands Cottage ★★★★
Contact: Mrs Annette Scott, Hall Farm House, Litton, Buxton SK17 8QP
T: (01298) 872172
E: jfscott@waitrose.com
I: www.users.waitrose.com/~jfscott

The Hillock ★★★★
Contact: Mrs L G Burrows, The Hillock, Litton, Buxton SK17 8QU
T: (01298) 871018

LLANFAIR WATERDINE
Shropshire

Llandinship ★★★★
Contact: Mr & Mrs A Beavan, Blackhall, Llanfair Waterdine, Knighton LD7 1TU
T: (01547) 528909
F: (01547) 528909
E: andrew.beaven@telco4u.net
I: www.blackhallfarm.com

LLANYBLODWEL
Shropshire

The Coach House ★★★★★
Contact: Mr & Mrs Malcolm & Sylvia Perks, The Coach House, Huntsmans Lodge, Llanyblodwel, Oswestry SY10 8NF
T: (01691) 828038
E: coach.house@micro-plus-web.net
I: www.thecoachhouse.micro-plus-web.net

LOBTHORPE
Lincolnshire

Old Moat Barn ★★★
Contact: Mrs S Grindal, Hall Farm, Lobthorpe, Grantham NG33 5LS
T: (01476) 860350
F: (01476) 861724
E: grindal@freeuk.com

LONG BUCKBY
Northamptonshire

Meadowview Cottages ★★★★
Contact: Mrs Judith Jelley, Meadowview Cottages, Perkins Lodge Farm, Brington Road, Long Buckby, Northampton NN6 7NT
T: (01327) 842205
F: (01327) 842205
E: meadowview.cottages@farming.co.uk
I: meadowview.cottages@farming.co.uk

LONGBOROUGH
Gloucestershire

Cottage Barn ★★★★
Contact: Mr & Mrs Williams-Ellis, Cottage Barn, Sunnybank, Chapel Lane, Longborough, Moreton-in-Marsh GL56 0QR
T: (01451) 830695
F: (01451) 830695
E: rupert.williams-ellis@talk21.com

Hope Cottage ★★★★
Contact: Miss E.M Langton, Hope Cottage, School Square, Longborough, Moreton-in-Marsh GL56 0QD
T: (01451) 830343
F: (01451) 832043
E: e.langton@200m.co.uk

Stonecroft ★★★
Contact: Mr & Mrs Williams, Sitch Estates, Bell House, Salford, Chipping Norton OX7 5FE
T: (01608) 645397
F: (01608) 645397
E: sitchestate@aol.com

Studio Cottage ★★★
Contact: Mrs C H Green, Ganborough House, Longborough, Moreton-in-Marsh GL56 0QZ
T: (01451) 830466

LONGHOPE
Gloucestershire

The Old Farm ★★★★★
Contact: Ms Lucy Rodger, The Old Farm, Barrel Lane, Longhope GL17 0LR
T: (01452) 830252
F: (01452) 830255
E: lucy@the-old-farm.co.uk

LONGNOR
Staffordshire

Vincent Cottage ★★★★
Contact: Mr Colin MacQueen, Peak Cottages, Strawberry Lee Lane, Totley Bents, Totley Rise, Sheffield S17 3BA
T: (0114) 262 0777
F: (0114) 262 0666
E: enquiries@peakcottages.com
I: www.peakcottages.com

LOUGHBOROUGH
Leicestershire

The Woodlands ★★★
Contact: Mr & Mrs Grudgings, 14 Beacon Drive, Loughborough LE11 2BD
T: (01509) 214596
E: thewoodlands@bushinternet.com

LOUTH
Lincolnshire

Ashwater House ★★★-★★★★
Contact: Mrs Holly Mapletoft, Ashpot Cottage, Willow Drive, Louth LN11 0AH
T: (01507) 609295
F: (01507) 354624
E: robnholly@tesco.net
I: www.ashwaterhouse.co.uk

Canal Farm Cottages ★★★★
Contact: Mr & Mrs Richard Drinkel, Canal Farm Cottages, Canal Farm, Austen Fen, Grainthorpe, Louth LN11 0NX
T: (01472) 388825
F: (01472) 388825
E: canalfarm@ukhome.net
I: www.oas.co.uk/ukcottages/canalfarm

Mill Lodge ★★★
Contact: Mrs P Cade, Mill Lodge, Benniworth House Farm, Donington on Bain, Louth LN11 9RD
T: (01507) 343265
E: pamela@milllodge995fsnet.co.uk

LOWER APPERLEY
Gloucestershire

Rofield Barn ★★★★★
Contact: Mrs Hazel Lewis, Lower Apperley, Gloucester GL19 4DR
T: (01452) 780555
F: (01452) 780777
E: jeremy@tewkbury.freeserve.co.uk

LOWER BENEFIELD Northamptonshire

Granary Cottage ★★★
Contact: Mrs Judith Singlehurst, Granary Cottage, Brook Farm, Lower Benefield, Peterborough PE8 5AE
T: (01832) 205215

LOWER SLAUGHTER Gloucestershire

The Burrows & Sloe Trees ★★★-★★★★
Contact: CH Ref: 10192,10193, Country Holidays Group Owner Services Deptartment, Spring Mill, Earby, Barnoldswick BB94 0AA
T: 08700 723723
F: (01282) 844288
E: sales@ttgihg.co.uk

Malt House Cottage ★★★★
Contact: Mrs C E Hutsby, Little Hill Farm, Wellesbourne, Warwick CV35 9EB
T: (01789) 840261
F: (01789) 842270
I: www.accomodata.co.uk/06099.htm

LOWER SOUDLEY Gloucestershire

Beechwood Bungalow ★★★
Contact: Mrs Judith Anderton, Brookside Cottage, Lower Soudley, Cinderford GL14 2UB
T: (01594) 825864
E: raanderton@ntlworld.com

LUDLOW Shropshire

The Avenue Flat ★★★★
Contact: Mr R E Meredith, The Avenue Flat, The Avenue, Ashford Carbonell, Ludlow SY8 4DA
T: (01584) 831616
E: ronmeredithavenue@talk21.com

The Bakery Apartment ★★★
Contact: Mrs Deborah Cook, 6 Vashon Close, Ludlow SY8 1XG
T: (01584) 877051

9 Brand Lane Rating Applied For
Contact: Mrs Angela Wells, High Street, Leintwardine, Craven Arms SY7 0LB
T: (01547) 540383

Bribery Cottage ★★★
Contact: Mr & Mrs R Caithness, 2 Dinham, Ludlow SY8 1EJ
T: (01584) 872828
F: (01584) 872828
E: richard.caithness@virgin.net
I: www.virtual-shropshire.co.uk/bribery-cottage

Broadgate Cottage ★★★★
Contact: Mrs Jane Chance, Broad Meadows Farmhouse, Bayton, Kidderminster DY14 9LP
T: (01299) 832608
F: (01299) 832137
E: janechnc@aol.com
I: www.characterholidaycottages.co.uk

Cariad Holiday Cottages ★★★
Contact: Mrs Fitzmaurice, 16 Morden Road, Newport NP19 7EU
T: (01633) 666732
F: (01633) 666732
E: carol.fitzmaurice@ntlworld.com
I: www.southshropshire.org.uk/cariad

Casa Dona Marcella ★★★★
Contact: Mrs Mills-Pereira, Middlewood Stables, Lowerwood Road, Ludlow SY8 2JG
T: (01584) 856401
F: (01584) 856512
E: casadonamarcella@msn.com
I: www.casadonamarcella.co.uk

Church Bank ★★
Contact: Mrs K R Laurie, Church Bank, Burrington, Ludlow SY8 2HT
T: (01568) 770426
E: laurie2502@lineone.net

Criterion Cottage ★★★
Contact: Mrs Christine Hodgson, Criterion House, Clee Hill, Ludlow SY8 3NZ
T: (01584) 890344

Elm Lodge Apartment & The Coach House Apartment ★★★-★★★★
Contact: Mrs B Weaver, Elm Lodge, Fishmore, Ludlow SY8 3DP
T: (01584) 877394
F: (01584) 877397
E: apartments@sjweaver.fsnet.co.uk
I: www.ludlow.org.uk/elmlodge

Garden Apartment ★★★
Contact: Ms Sue Walsh, Holloway Farm, Hungerford, Craven Arms SY7 9HG
T: (01584) 841225
F: (01584) 841225
E: suewalsh@tesco.net
I: www.virtual-shropshire.co.uk/greenwich

Garden Cottage ★★★★
Contact: Mr Pash, Chapel House, Luke Street, Berwick St John, Shaftesbury SP7 0HQ
T: (01747) 828170
F: (01747) 829090
E: enq@hideways.co.uk
I: www.hideaways.co.uk/property2.cfm?ref=H182

Goosefoot Barn Cottages ★★★★
Contact: Mrs Sally Loft, Goosefoot Barn Cottages, Pinstones, Diddlebury, Craven Arms SY7 9LB
T: (01584) 861326
E: sally@goosefoot.freeserve.co.uk

The Granary ★★★
Contact: Mr & Mrs R Mercer, Tana Leas Farm, Clee St Margaret, Craven Arms SY7 9DZ
T: (01584) 823272
F: (01584) 823272
E: r.mercer@tinyworld.co.uk
I: www.southshropshire.org.uk/granary

Grazers Cottage, Calvers Cottage, Threshers Cottage, Little Huntington ★★★★
Contact: Mr & Mrs Norman Tudge, Grazers Cottage, Calvers Cottage, Threshers Cottage, Ashford Farm, Ashford Carbonell, Ludlow SY8 4DB
T: (01584) 831243
F: (01584) 831243
E: ashfordfarms@aol.com
I: www.ashfordfarms.co.uk

Hazel Cottage ★★★★
Contact: Mrs R E Sanders, Duxmoor Farm, Onibury, Craven Arms SY7 9BQ
T: (01584) 856342
F: (01584) 856696

Horseshoe Cottage ★★★★
Contact: Mr & Mrs T R Gill, 3 Fosse Close, Sharnford, Hinckley LE10 3PQ
T: (01455) 272874
F: (01455) 272874
E: trgill@btinternet.com

Lilac Cottage ★★★★
Contact: Mrs Elizabeth Grant, Wheelers Hope Cottage Farm, Easthope, Much Wenlock TF13 6DN
T: (01746) 785564
E: cottagefarm@farmersweekly.co.uk

Ludford View ★★★
Contact: Mr & Mrs Christopher & Laura Birkett & Rutty, Ludlowlife, 22A Temeside, Ludlow SY81PB
T: (01584) 873249
F: (01584) 873249
E: ludlowlet@aol.com
I: www.ludlowlife.co.uk

Maryvale Lodge ★★★★
Contact: Mrs Alison Cundall, Maryvale, Mill Street, Ludlow SY8 1GH
T: (01584) 873272
F: (01584) 878347
E: mail@maryvalecottages.co.uk

24 Mill Street ★★★★
Contact: Mrs D Brodie, Old Rectory Cottage, Wistanstow, Craven Arms SY7 8DQ
T: (01588) 672074
F: (01588) 672074

Mocktree Barns Holiday Cottages ★★★
Contact: Mr & Mrs Clive & Cynthia Prior, Mocktree Barns Holiday Cottages, Mocktree Barns, Leintwardine, Craven Arms SY7 0LY
T: (01547) 540441

Post Horn Cottage ★★
Contact: Ms H Davis, 32 Leamington Drive, Chilwell, Beeston, Nottingham NG9 5JL
T: (0115) 922 2383

Ravenscourt Manor ★★★★
Contact: Mrs Elizabeth Purnell, Ravenscourt Manor, Woofferton, Stanford Bishop, Worcester SY8 4AL
T: (01584) 711905
E: ravenscourtmanor@amsgrve.com
I: www.virtual-shropshire.co.uk/ravencourt-manor

The Studio, The Rhyse Farm Rating Applied For
Contact: Mr & Mrs Barnard, The Rhyse Farm, Ashford Bowdler, Ludlow SY8 4AE
T: (01584) 831128
E: cbarn1937@aol.com

Sutton Court Farm Cottages ★★★★
Contact: Mrs S J Cronin
T: (01584) 861305
F: (01584) 861441
E: suttoncourtfarm@hotmail.com
I: www.go2.co.uk/suttoncourtfarm

Toad Hall ★★★
Contact: Mrs Jean Taylor, Lindisfarne, 12 Toll Gate Road, Ludlow SY8 1TQ
T: (01584) 874161
F: (01584) 874161

The Town Flat ★★★
Contact: Mr G Kidd, 12 Corve Street, Ludlow SY8 1DA
T: (01584) 877946
F: (01584) 878256
E: gk@nka.co.uk

Wandering William Barn Rating Applied For
Contact: Mr Richard Maddicott, Foldgate Farm, Foldgate Lane, Ludlow SY8 4BN
T: (01584) 877899
F: (01584) 878480
E: richard@maddicott.com

1 Whitcliffe Cottages ★★★★
Contact: Ms H Murphy, Period Properties (Ludlow) Ltd, 9 Lower Broad Street, Ludlow SY8 1PQ
T: (01584) 876931
F: (01584) 879548
E: bookings@periodpropertiesludlow.co.uk
I: www.periodpropertiesludlow.co.uk

The Wool Shop ★★
Contact: Mr & Mrs Mercer, Tana Leas Farm, Clee St Margaret, Craven Arms SY7 9DZ
T: (01584) 823272
F: (01584) 823272
E: r.mercer@tinyworld.co.uk

LULLINGTON Derbyshire

Aubrietia Cottage ★★★★
Contact: Mrs R Cooper, The Grange, Lullington, Swadlincote DE12 8ED
T: (01827) 373219
F: (01283) 515885
E: r.cooper@care4free.net

LYDBURY NORTH Shropshire

Walcot Hall Holiday Apartments ★★★-★★★★
Contact: Miss Maria Higgs
T: (01588) 680570
F: (01588) 680361
E: maria@walcotthall.com
I: www.walcothall.com

LYDNEY Gloucestershire

Arlin Cottage ★★★★
Contact: Mrs Sharon Freeman, Arlin Cottage, Lower Road, Yorkley, Lydney GL15 4TH
T: (01594) 562187
F: (01594) 562187

Bream Cross Farm ★★★
Contact: Mr & Mrs Jock & Margaret Reeks, Bream Cross Farm, Coleford GL16 6EU
T: (01594) 562208
F: (01594) 564399

Highbury Coach House ★★★
Contact: Mr A R Midgley, Highbury Coach House, Bream Road, Lydney GL15 5JH
T: (01594) 842339
F: (01594) 844948
E: midgleya1@aol.com

Nagshead Cottage ★★★★
Contact: Mr & Mrs A McCrindle, Thistle Cottage, Viney Woodside, Lydney GL15 4LX
T: (01594) 510695
E: info@forest-cottages.co.uk
I: www.forest-cottages.co.uk

Squirrel Cottage ★★★
Contact: Mr & Mrs A McCrindle, Forest Cottages, Thistle Cottage, Viney Woodside, Blakeney GL15 4LX
T: (01594) 510695
E: info@forest-cottages.co.uk

Wisteria Cottage ★★★★
Contact: Mrs E Rye, Rose Cottage, Church Walk, Viney Hill, Lydney GL15 4NY
T: (01594) 510435
E: ericarye@onetel.net.uk

LYONSHALL
Herefordshire

Field Cottage, The Sherriffs & Gardeners Cottage
★★★★-★★★★★
Contact: Mrs Joanna Hilditch, Field Cottage, The Sherriffs & Gardeners Cottage, The Whittern Farms Ltd, Lyonshall, Kington HR5 3JA
T: (01544) 340241
F: (01544) 340253
E: info@whiteheronproperties.com
I: www.whiteheronproperties.com

MADELEY
Shropshire

Fletcher House
★★★★-★★★★★
Contact: Mrs Moira Shean, Fletcher House, The Old Vicarage, Church Street, Madeley, Telford TF7 5BN
T: (01952) 525522
E: houseoffletcher@aol.com
I: www.fletcherhouse.co.uk

MADLEY
Herefordshire

Canon Bridge House ★★★★
Contact: Mrs Anscomb, Canon Bridge House, Canon Bridge, Madley, Hereford HR2 9JF
T: (01981) 251104
F: (01981) 251412
E: timothy.anscomb4@virgin.net
I: www.oas.co.uk/ukcottages

MALTBY LE MARSH
Lincolnshire

Yew Tree Cottage & The Granary ★★★★
Contact: Mrs Ann Graves, Grange Farm, Maltby-Le-Marsh, Maltby le Marsh, Alford LN13 0JP
T: (01507) 450267
F: (01507) 450180
E: grangefarm@beeb.net
I: www.grange-farmhouse.co.uk

MALVERN
Worcestershire

Annexe to Blue Cedars ★★★
Contact: Mrs P M Longmire Blue Cedars, Peachfield Close, Malvern Wells, Malvern WR14 4AN
T: (01684) 566689

April Cottage ★★★
Contact: Mrs P M Longmire, 2 Peachfield Close, Malvern WR14 4AN
T: (01684) 566689
E: pml@peachfield.freeserve.co.uk

The Coach House
Rating Applied For
Contact: Mrs J Bury, David E J Prosser, 71 Church Street, Malvern WR14 2AE
T: (01684) 561411
F: (01684) 564748
E: dprosser@supanet.com

The Coach House ★★★
Contact: Mrs J Jones, 58 North Malvern Road, Malvern WR14 4LX
T: (01684) 569562
E: jjmalvern@onetel.net.uk

The Cottages at Westwood House ★★★★
Contact: Mrs J Wright & Mrs J Staddon, The Cottages at Westwood House, Park Road, West Malvern, Malvern WR14 4DS
T: (01684) 892308
F: (01684) 892882
E: davidwright2@compuserve.com
I: www.oas.co.uk/ukcottages/westwood

Farmhouse Cottage ★★★
Contact: Mrs Stringer, Farmhouse Cottage, Cowleigh Park Farm, Cowleigh Road, Malvern WR13 5HJ
T: (01684) 566750
F: (01684) 566750
E: cowleighpark@ukonline.co.uk
I: www.SmoothHound.co.uk/a13380.html

Four Seasons ★★★
Contact: Mr M E James, Four Seasons, 7 Newtown Road, Malvern WR14 1PD
T: (01684) 575045
E: james@markeric.freeserve.co.uk

Greenbank House Garden Flat ★★★
Contact: Mr D G Matthews, Greenbank House Garden Flat, 236 West Malvern Road, West Malvern, Malvern WR14 4BG
T: (01684) 567328
E: matthews.greenbank@virgin.net

Hidelow House Cottages
★★★★-★★★★★
Contact: Mrs P Diplock, Hidelow House, Acton Green, Acton Beauchamp, Worcester WR6 5AH
T: (01886) 884547
F: (01886) 884658
E: stay@hidelow.co.uk
I: www.hidelow.co.uk

Maynard Lodge ★★★★★
Contact: Mr Michael & Elaine Roberts, Maynard Lodge, Croft Bank, Malvern WR1 4DU
T: (01684) 564568
F: (01684) 563201

The Old Bakery ★★★
Contact: Mrs Aldridge, West End House, Lower Dingle, West Malvern, Malvern WR14 4BQ
T: (01684) 566044
F: (01684) 566044
E: westendhouse@btopenworld.com
I: www.oldbakerymelvern.co.uk

25 Queens Drive ★★★
Contact: Mrs A Jeffs, 25 Queens Drive, Malvern WR14 4RE
T: (01684) 561337
F: (01684) 562526

The Studio ★★★
Contact: Mrs Gwyneth Sloan, The Studio, Rosehill Cottage, Holywell Road, Malvern WR14 4LF
T: (01684) 561074
F: (01684) 561074
E: sloaniain@hotmail.com

Whitewells Farm Cottages ★★★★
Contact: Mr & Ms Denis & Kate Kavanagh, Whitewells Farm Cottages, Whitewells Farm, Ridgeway Cross, Malvern WR13 5JR
T: (01886) 880607
F: (01886) 880360
E: info@whitewellsfarm.co.uk
I: www.whitewellsfarm.com

MANSFIELD
Nottinghamshire

Blue Barn Cottage ★★★
Contact: Mrs June Ibbotson, Blue Barn Cottage, Langwith, Nether Langwith, Mansfield NG20 9JD
T: (01623) 742248
F: (01623) 742248
E: bluebarnfarm@supanet.com

MARKET DRAYTON
Shropshire

The Old Smithy Holiday Cottages ★★★★
Contact: Mrs Carmel Simpson, The Old Smithy Holiday Cottages, The Lightwoods, Market Drayton TF9 2LR
T: (01630) 661661

MARKET HARBOROUGH
Leicestershire

Newbold Farm Holiday Cottages ★★★★
Contact: Mr & Mrs Gilbert, Newbold Farm Holiday Cottages, Newbold Farm, Dicks Hill, Clipston, Market Harborough LE16 9TT
T: (01858) 525272
F: (01858) 525565
E: enquiries@nbfhc.co.uk
I: www.nbfhc.co.uk

Short Lodge ★★★
Contact: Ms Durham, Short Lodge, Arthingworth, Market Harborough LE16 8LB
T: (01858) 525323

MARKET RASEN
Lincolnshire

Meadow Farm House ★★★★
Contact: Mr N Grimshaw, Meadow Farm House, Bleasby Moor, Market Rasen LN8 3QL
T: (01673) 885909
F: (01673) 885909
E: nickgrimshaw@btconnect.com
I: www.meadowfarmhouse.co.uk

Papermill Cottages
★★★-★★★★★
Contact: Mr & Mrs Peter & Joyce Rhodes, Vale Farm, Caistor Lane, Tealby, Market Rasen LN8 3XN
T: (01673) 838010
F: (01673) 838127
E: peter.rhodes1@btinternet.com

Pelham Arms Farm ★★★★
Contact: Mrs Margaret Henderson, Pelham Arms Farm, Claxby Moor, Market Rasen LN8 3YP
T: (01673) 828261
E: pelhamarmsfarm@btinternet.com

MARSH LANE
Derbyshire

Fold Farm ★★★
Contact: Mr & Mrs Ryan, 10 Hawkshead Avenue, Dronfield Woodhouse, Dronfield S18 8NB
T: (01246) 415143
E: foldfarm@fwryan.freeserve.co.uk
I: www.fwryan.freeserve.co.uk

MARSHCHAPEL
Lincolnshire

Dove Cottage
Rating Applied For
Contact: Mrs J Houghton, Dove Cottage, c/o Sedgebeck, West End Lane, Marshchapel, Grimsby DN36 5TN
T: (01472) 388520
E: june.houghton@tesco.net

MARTON
Shropshire

Highgate Cottage ★★★
Contact: Mr Sykes, Sykes Cottage, York House, York Street, Chester CH1 3LR
T: (01244) 345700
F: (01244) 321442
E: info@sykescottages.co.uk
I: www.sykescottages.co.uk

MATLOCK
Derbyshire

Carsington Cottages ★★★
Contact: Mrs Valerie Riach, Carsington Cottages, Swiers Farm, Carsington, Wirksworth, Derby DE4 4DE
T: (01629) 540513
F: (01629) 540513
E: riachclan@btinternet.com

Croft Edge ★★★★
Contact: Dr Miller, 21 Plover Wharf, Castle Marina, Sandyway, South Molton NG7 1TL
T: (0115) 958 2766
E: info@croftedge.co.uk
I: www.croftedge.co.uk

Darwin Lake ★★★★
Contact: Miss N Manning, Peak Village Ltd, Darwin Lake, Jaggers Lane, Darley Moor, Matlock DE4 5HL
T: (01629) 735859
F: (01629) 735859
E: enquiries@darwinlake.co.uk
I: www.darwinlake.co.uk

Dene Cottage ★★★★
Contact: Ms A Latham, 11 The Charters, Lichfield WS13 7LX
T: (01543) 319440
F: (01543) 319441
E: amanda@threespires.net
I: www.peakdistrictcottage.co.uk

Eagle Cottage ★★★★
Contact: Mrs M E Prince, Haresfield House, Birchover, Matlock DE4 2BL
T: (01629) 650634
E: maryprince@msn.com
I: www.cressbrook.co.uk/youlgve/eagle/

Florence Nightingale Chapel ★★★★
Contact: Mrs Susan Metcalf, 14 Chapel Lane, Holloway, Whatstandwell, Matlock DE4 5AU
T: (01629) 534652
F: (01629) 534977
E: paulmetcalf@tiscali.co.uk

The Fold ★★★
Contact: Mrs Audrey Hinman, The Fold, 31 Main Road, Darley Dale, Matlock DE4 2JY
T: (01629) 734333

Hadfield House ★★
Contact: Mrs M Evans, Christ Church Vicarage, Doncaster Road, Ardsley, Barnsley S71 5EF
T: (01226) 203784
E: rgrevans@compuserve.com

Honeysuckle & Clematis Cottages ★★★★
Contact: Mr J Lomas, Middle Hills Farm, Grangemill, Derby DE4 4HY
T: (01629) 650368
F: (01629) 650368
E: l.lomas@btinernet.com
I: www.peakdistrictfarmhols.co.uk

Ivonbrook Grange Farm Cottage ★★★
Contact: Ms Christine Heathcote, Ivonbrook Grange Farm Cottage, Ivanbrook Grange Farm, Grangemill, Derby DE4 4HU
T: (01629) 650221
F: (01629) 650221

Ivy Cottage ★★★
Contact: Mrs P M Potter, Highfields, Pounder Lane, Bonsall, Matlock DE4 2AT
T: (01629) 823018
E: ivy.cottage@ukgateway.net

Little Hallmoor Castle Rating Applied For
Contact: The Manager, 90 Cavendish Road, Matlock DE4 3HD
T: (01629) 583545
F: (01629) 583545
E: enquiries@derbyshirecountrycottages.co.uk

Masson Leys Farm ★★★★
Contact: Mrs Brenda Dawes, Masson Leys Farm, Salters Lane, Matlock DE4 2PA
T: (01629) 582944

Mooredge Barns ★★★★-★★★★★
Contact: A M & P Barratt, Moor Edge Farm, Tansley, Matlock DE4 5FS
T: (01629) 583701
E: tonybar1921@aol.com
I: http://mooredgefarmcottages.co.uk

The Studio ★★
Contact: Mrs Reuss, 247 Starkholmes Road, Matlock DE4 5JE
T: (01629) 584622

Swallow Cottage ★★★
Contact: Mrs Lois Clark, 19 Melvin Way, Histon, Cambridge CB4 9HY
T: (01223) 235596
E: lois.j.clark@btinternet.com
I: www.btinternet.com/~lois.j.clark

Thimble Cottage Rating Applied For
Contact: Mr & Mrs B Armstrong, Holmedene, Ashford Road, Bakewell DE45 1GL
T: (01629) 813448
E: bernard-armstrong@lineone.net

Tinkersley Barn ★★★★
Contact: Mrs H Bradford, Tinkersley Barn, Tinkersley, Rowsley, Matlock DE4 2NJ
T: (01629) 735451

Wayside Farm Holidays ★★★
Contact: Mrs Janet Hole, Wayside Farm Holidays, Wayside Farm, Matlock Moor, Tansley, Matlock DE4 5LZ
T: (01629) 582967
I: www.waysidefarm-holidays.co.uk

MATLOCK BATH
Derbyshire

Derwent View ★★★
Contact: Mr Tim Heathcote, 3 Wellington House, Waterloo Road, Matlock Bath, Matlock DE4 3PH
T: (01629) 57473
F: (01629) 57473

Nonsuch Apartment ★★★★
Contact: Mr Dennis Smith, Wilson Lane Farm House, Main Street, Heath Village, Chesterfield S44 5SA
T: (01246) 851421

Rambler Cottage ★★★
Contact: Mrs Singer, Peak Cottages, Strawberry Lee Lane, Totley Bents, Totley Rise, Sheffield S17 3BA
T: (0114) 262 0777
F: (0114) 262 0666
E: enquiries@peakcottages.com
I: www.peakcottages.com

Weavers Cottage Rating Applied For
Contact: Mr Colin MacQueen, Peak Cottages, Strawberry Lee Lane, Totley Bents, Totley Rise, Sheffield S17 3BA
T: (0114) 262 0777
F: (0114) 262 0666
E: enquiries@peakcottages.com

MAVESYN RIDWARE
Staffordshire

Stable Cottage ★★★★
Contact: Mrs Susan Clift, Manor Farm Cottage, Church Lane, Rugeley WS15
T: (01543) 491579
F: (01543) 491579
E: dmsaclift@farming.co.uk

MELBOURNE
Derbyshire

Orchard Barn ★★★★
Contact: Mrs Hendley, 7 Holm Avenue, Little Eaton, Derby DE21 5DX
T: (01332) 833584
E: hendleysfour@aol.uk

MELTON MOWBRAY
Leicestershire

28 Melton Road ★★★★
Contact: Mrs Watchorn, Chester House, 26 Melton Road, Waltham on the Wolds, Melton Mowbray LE14 4AJ
T: (01664) 464255
E: awatchorn1314@yahoo.com

MEOLE BRACE
Shropshire

Stable Cottage ★★
Contact: Mrs U Baugh, Glebe House, Vicarage Road, Meole Brace, Shrewsbury SY3 9EZ
T: (01743) 236914
E: s.baugh@virgin.net

MIDDLE DUNTISBOURNE
Gloucestershire

Flowers Barn ★★★★
Contact: Mrs Tina Barton, Flowers Barn, Manor Farm, Duntisbourne Rouse, Cirencester GL7 7AR
T: (01285) 658145
F: (01285) 641504
E: duntisbourne@aol.com
I: www.SmoothHound.co.uk/hotels/manorfar.html

MIDDLETON
Derbyshire

The Barn ★★★
Contact: Mr Peter John Smith, The Barn, 14 Main Street, Middleton by Wirksworth, Middleton, Matlock DE4 4LQ
T: (01629) 824519

MIDDLETON-BY-YOULGREAVE
Derbyshire

The Coach House Rating Applied For
Contact: Mr Colin MacQueen, Peak Cottages, Strawberry Lee Lane, Totley Bents, Totley Rise, Sheffield S17 3BA
T: (0114) 262 0777
F: (0114) 262 0666
E: enquiries@peakcottages.com

Curlew Cottage, Abbot's Flight & Monks Rest★★★★
Contact: Mrs Carole Brister, Lowfield Farm, Middleton-by-Youlgrave, Bakewell DE45 1LR
T: (01629) 636180
F: (01629) 636513
E: brister@quista.net

Holly Homestead Cottage ★★★★
Contact: Mr & Mrs D W Edge, Ridgeway House, Hillcliff Lane, Turnditch, Belper DE56 2EA
T: (01773) 550754
E: daveedge@turnditch82.freeserve.co.uk
I: www.holly-homestead.co.uk

MIDDLETON SCRIVEN
Shropshire

Harry's House ★★★★
Contact: Mrs Patrica Round, Coates Farm, Middleton Scriven, Bridgnorth WV16 6AG
T: (01746) 789224

MILLER'S DALE
Derbyshire

Miller's Dale Cottages & Monks Retreat★★★-★★★★
Contact: Mrs Pamela Wilkson, Monks Dale Farm, Miller's Dale, Buxton SK17 8SN
T: (01298) 871306
F: (01298) 871306
E: pamwilkson@hotmail.com
I: www.cressbrook.co.uk/tidza/monksdale

MILLTHORPE
Derbyshire

Millthorpe Cottage ★★★★
Contact: Mr & Mrs Nich & Liz Barrett, Sleaford Property Services Ltd, Sleaford House, Cordwell Lane, Millthorpe, Holmesfield, Dronfield S18 7WH
T: (0114) 289 1071
F: (0114) 289 1071
E: cottage.holidays@btopenworld.com
I: www.cottage-vacations.co.uk

MILLTOWN
Derbyshire

Greenfield Barn ★★★★
Contact: Mr & Mrs T Page, Greenfield House, Oakstedge Lane, Milltown, Ashover S45 0HA
T: (01246) 590119

Hay Ho Cottage ★★★★
Contact: Mrs Susan Howe, Hay House, The Hay, Milltown, Ashover, Chesterfield S45 0HB
T: (01246) 590538
F: (01246) 590538

MILWICH
Staffordshire

Summerhill Farm ★★★★
Contact: Mrs P A Milward, Summerhill Farm, Milwich, Stafford ST18 0EL
T: (01889) 505546
F: (01889) 505692
E: p.milward@btinternet.com

MINCHINHAMPTON
Gloucestershire

Vine House Flat ★★★★
Contact: Mrs Veronica Finn, Vine House, Friday Street, Minchinhampton, Stroud GL6 9JL
T: (01453) 884437
E: finnatminch@aol.com

The Woolsack ★★★★
Contact: Mrs E Hayward, The Woolsack, Hyde Wood House, Cirencester Road, Minchinhampton, Stroud GL6 8PE
T: (01453) 885504
F: (01453) 885504
E: info@hydewoodhhouse.co.uk
I: www.hydewoodhouse.co.uk

MINSTERLEY
Shropshire

Brookland ★★★
Contact: Mrs Davies, New House Farm, Minsterley, Shrewsbury SY5 0HR
T: (01743) 791217

Ovenpipe Cottage ★★★
Contact: Mr A B & Mrs P Thornton, Tankerville Lodge, Stiperstones, Minsterley, Shrewsbury SY5 0NB
T: (01743) 791401
F: (01743) 792305
E: tankervillelodge@supanet.com
I: www.ovenpipecottage.com

Upper House Farm Cottage ★★★★
Contact: Mrs K Stanhope, Upper House Farm, Minsterley, Shrewsbury SY5 0AA
T: (01743) 792831
F: (01743) 792831
E: k.stanhope@ukonline.co.uk

MISERDEN
Gloucestershire

Sudgrove Cottages ★★★
Contact: Mr M G Ractliffe, Sudgrove Cottages, Miserden, Stroud GL6 7JD
T: (01285) 821322
F: (01285) 821322
E: enquiries@sudgrovecottages.co.uk
I: www.sudgrovecottages.co.uk

MITCHELDEAN
Gloucestershire

Church Farm Holidays Church Farm ★★★
Contact: Mr John Verity, Church Farm Holidays Church Farm, Church Lane, Abenhall, Mitcheldean GL17 0DX
T: (01594) 541211
F: (01594) 541212
I: www.churchfarm.uk.net

MONSAL DALE
Derbyshire

Heron Cottage Upperdale Farm ★★★
Contact: Mr & Mrs Clarke, Heron Cottage Upperdale Farm, Upperdale, Monsal Dale, Buxton SK17 8SZ
T: (01629) 640536

Riversdale Farm Holiday Cottages ★★★★
Contact: Mrs Jackson, Riversdale Farm Holiday Cottages, Riversdale, Little Longstone, Bakewell SK17 8SZ
T: (01629) 640500
I: www.riversdalefarm.co.uk

MONTFORD BRIDGE
Shropshire

Mytton Mill Flat ★★★
Contact: Mrs Patrica Minshall, Mytton Mill House, Forton Heath, Montford Bridge, Shrewsbury SY4 1HA
T: (01743) 850497

MONYASH
Derbyshire

The Barn ★★★★
Contact: Mr Staley, Bolehill Farm, Monyash Road, Over Haddon, Bakewell DE45 1QW
T: (01629) 815699
F: (01629) 812359
E: tonystaley@hotmail.com
I: www.bolehillfarmcottages.co.uk

Rose Cottage ★★★
Contact: Brian & Heather Read, 20 Church Street, Monyash, Bakewell DE45 1JH
T: (01629) 813629

Sheldon Cottages ★★★★
Contact: Mrs L Fanshawe, Sheldon House, Chapel Street, Monyash, Bakewell DE45 1JJ
T: (01629) 813067
F: (01629) 815768
E: steveandlou.fanshawe@virgin.net
I: www.sheldoncottages.co.uk

MORETON-IN-MARSH
Gloucestershire

The Flat ★★★★
Contact: Ms Sheila Rolland, Campden Cottages, Folly Cottage, Paxford, Chipping Campden GL55 6XG
T: (01386) 593315
F: (01386) 593057
E: info@campdencottages.co.uk
I: www.campdencottages.co.uk

Hayloft ★★★
Contact: Mrs Jan Wright, Hayloft, Twostones, Evenlope, Moreton-in-Marsh GL56 0NY
T: (01608) 651104

The Laurels ★★★
Contact: Mrs S I Billinger, Blue Cedar House, Stow Road, Moreton-in-Marsh GL56 0DW
T: (01608) 650299

Little Milton ★★★★
Contact: Mrs Heather Bates, Milton House, High Street, Moreton-in-Marsh GL56 9ET
T: (01386) 701163
F: (01386) 701163
E: heb@henmarsh.freeserve.co.uk

Little Pinners ★★★
Contact: Mrs Mariam Gilbert, Country House Interiors, High Street, Moreton-in-Marsh GL56 0AT
T: (01608) 650007
F: (01608) 650007

Michaelmas Cottage ★★★★
Contact: Mr M J Gaffney, Mulberry, Shrubbs Hill Lane, Sunningdale, Ascot SL5 0LD
T: (01344) 624833
F: (01344) 624693
E: michael@spoonerco.com
I: www.country-cottages.org.uk

Michaelmas Daisy Cottage ★★★
Contact: Mrs R K Alexander, The Folly, Fifield, Chipping Norton OX7 6HW
T: (01993) 830484
F: (01993) 832022
E: rosemaryalex@onetel.net.uk

2 Rose Terrace ★★★
Contact: Ms Richards, Manor Cottages, Priory Mews, 33A Priory Lane, Burford, Oxford OX18 4SG
T: (01993) 824252
F: (01993) 824443
E: mancott@netcomuk.co.uk
I: manorcottage.co.uk

Sarum ★★★★
Contact: Mrs Brooks, Ashlar, Todenham Road, Lower Lemington, Moreton-in-Marsh GL56 9NJ
T: (01608) 650821
E: jobrooks41@btinternet.com

Toms Cottage ★★★★
Contact: Mrs Hall, Chanonry, St Leonards Hill, Windsor SL4 4AT
T: (01753) 855086

The Trees ★★★
Contact: Mrs Ward, 15 Gisborough Way, Bailey's Meadow, Loughborough LE11 4FU
T: (01509) 646135
E: rosemaryanne.ward@virgin.net

Woodkeepers ★★★★★
Contact: Mrs Wendy Hicks, Woodkeepers, Barton-on-the-Heath, Moreton-in-Marsh GL56 0PL
T: (01608) 674236
E: wendy@woodkeepers.co.uk
I: www.woodkeepers.co.uk

MORTON
Lincolnshire

Gills Cottage ★★★★
Contact: Mrs E Berry, 7 Saddler Drive, Morton, Bourne PE10 0XS
T: (01778) 571217
E: keith.berry@amserve.net

MORTON BAGOT
Warwickshire

Manor Farm Cottages, Royland Farms Ltd★★★★
Contact: Mrs Green, Manor Farm, Morton Bagot, Studley B80 7ED
T: (01527) 852219
F: (01527) 852219
E: roylands@farmersweekly.net
I: www.manorfarmcottages.co.uk

MORVILLE
Shropshire

Hurst Farm Cottages ★★★★
Contact: Mr & Mrs D Brick, Hurst Farm, Morville, Bridgnorth WV16 4TF
T: (01746) 714375
F: (01746) 714375
E: hurstfarm@talk21.com

MOUNTSORREL
Leicestershire

The Bungalow ★★★
Contact: Mr & Mrs Tony & Lyn Bartle, The Lindens, 22 Halstead Road, Mountsorrel, Loughborough LE12 7HF
T: (0166) 230 2163

Stonehurst Lodge ★★
Contact: Mrs Marilyn Duffin, Stonehurst Lodge, Stonehurst Farm, 141 Loughborough Road, Mountsorrel, Loughborough LE12 7AR
T: (01509) 413216
I: www.farm18.fsnet.co.uk/index.html

MUCH COWARNE
Herefordshire

Old Bridgend Cottage ★★★
Contact: Mrs Angela Morgan, 32 Chestnut Grove, New Malden KT3 3JN
T: (020) 8942 0702
F: (020) 8949 4950

MUCH MARCLE
Herefordshire

Shepherds Rest Rating Applied For
Contact: Mrs Fiona Wilcox, Shepherds Rest, Hill Farm, Much Marcle, Ledbury HR8 2PH
T: (01531) 660285
E: fjwilcox@waitrose.com

Wolton Brook ★★★★
Contact: Mrs A Putley, Lower Wolton Farm, Much Marcle, Ledbury HR8 2NY
T: (01531) 660429
F: (01531) 660429

MUCH WENLOCK
Shropshire

The Priory ★★★
Contact: Mrs A Croft, The Priory, Bull Ring, Much Wenlock TF13 6HS
T: (01952) 728280
E: ahcl@supanet.com

Priory Cottage ★★★
Contact: Mrs J Cumberland, Priory Cottage, Bull Ring, Much Wenlock TF13 6HS
T: (01952) 727386

3 Queen Street ★★★
Contact: Mrs Elizabeth Ann Williams, 68 Church Hill, Penn, Wolverhampton WV4 5JD
T: (01902) 341399
E: williams_letting@hotmail.com

18 Sheinton Street ★★★★
Contact: Country Holidays Ref: 8371 Sales, Holiday Cottages Group Limited, Spring Mill, Earby, Barnoldswick BB94 0AA
T: 08700 723723
F: (01282) 844288
E: sales@ttgihg.co.uk
I: www.country-holidays.co.uk

2 St Marys Lane ★★★★★
Contact: Mr & Mrs Gray, Penkridge Cottage, Sheinton Road, Much Wenlock TF13 6NS
T: (01952) 728169
F: (01952) 728415
E: dgray@dgray96.fsnet.co.uk

Stokes Cottage ★★★
Contact: Mrs Suzanne Hill, Stokes Cottage, Newtown House Farm, Much Wenlock TF13 6DB
T: (01952) 727293
F: (01952) 728130
E: stokesbarn@hotmail.com

MUNSLOW
Shropshire

Green Gates Apartment ★★★
Contact: Ms S Walsh, Holloway Farm, Munslow, Craven Arms SY7 9HG
T: (01584) 841225
E: suewalsh@tesco.net
I: www.virtual.shropshire.co.uk/greengates

NAUNTON
Gloucestershire

Mill Barn Cottage ★★
Contact: Mrs Madeleine Hindley, Mill Barn Cottage, Mill Barn, Naunton, Winchcombe, Cheltenham GL54 3AF
T: (01451) 850417
F: (01451) 850196

Yew Tree House ★★★★
Contact: Mrs Patrica Smith, White Gables, Woodcote Park Road, Epsom KT18 7EX
T: (01372) 723166
F: (01372) 723166
E: patriciasmith43@hotmail.com
I: www.yewtreehouse.com

NEEN SOLLARS
Shropshire

Live and Let Live ★★★
Contact: Mr C & Mrs I Ferguson, Live and Let Live, Neen Sollars, Kidderminster DY14 9AB
T: (01299) 832391

NETHERSEAL
Staffordshire

Grangefields ★★★★
Contact: Mrs Rita Hill & Mrs Alison Hill, Grangefields, Clifton Lane, Netherseal, Burton upon Trent DE12 8BT
T: (01827) 373253

NETTLEHAM
Lincolnshire

Corner Cottage ★★★★
Contact: Mrs Susan Downs, The Old Vicarage, East Street, Nettleham, Lincoln LN2 2SL
T: (01522) 750819
F: (01522) 750819
E: susan@oldvic.net

NEW MILLS
Derbyshire

Shaw Farm ★★★
Contact: Mrs Nicky Burgess, Shaw Farm, Shaw Marsh, New Mills, High Peak SK22 4QE
T: (0161) 427 1841
E: nicky.burgess@talk21.com
I: www.shawfarmholidays.co.uk

NEWENT
Gloucestershire

Middletown Farm Cottages ★★★★
Contact: Mrs J A Elkins, Middletown Farm, Middletown Lane, Upleadon, Newent GL18 1EQ
T: (01531) 828237
F: (01531) 822850
E: cottages@middletownfarm.co.uk
I: www.middletownfarm.co.uk

NEWLAND
Gloucestershire

Birchamp Coach House ★★★★
Contact: Mrs Karen Davies, Birchamp Coach House, Birchamp House, Newland, Coleford GL16 8NP
T: (01594) 833143
F: (01594) 836775
E: karen@wyedeancottages.co.uk
I: www.wyedeancottages.co.uk

NEWTON GRANGE
Derbyshire

New Hanson Bungalow ★★★★
Contact: Mrs Linda Bonsall, New Hanson Grange Farm, Newton Grange, Ashbourne DE6 1NN
T: (01335) 310258
F: (01335) 310258
E: NHGFarmHoliday@tiscali.co.uk
I: www.ashbourne-town.com/accom/new-hanson

NORBURY
Staffordshire

Oulton House Farm Garden Cottages ★★★★
Contact: Mrs Judy Palmer, Oulton House Farm, Norbury, Stafford ST20 0PG
T: (01785) 284264
F: (01785) 284264
E: judy@oultonhousefarm.co.uk
I: www.oultonhousefarm.co.uk

NORTH CARLTON
Lincolnshire

Cliff Farm Cottage ★★★★
Contact: Mrs Rae Marris, Cliff Farm, North Carlton, Lincoln LN1 2RP
T: (01522) 730475
E: rae.marris@farming.co.uk

NORTH LUFFENHAM
Rutland

Old School Cottage ★★★★
Contact: Mrs Elaine Handley, Wytchley House, Empingham Road, Ketton, Stamford PE9 3UP
T: (01780) 721768
F: (01780) 720214
E: emhand@hotmail.com

NORTHAMPTON
Northamptonshire

The Long Barn ★★★★★
Contact: Mrs L Carter, Broombank, Upper Harlestone, Northampton NN7 4EL
T: (01604) 583237
F: (01604) 751865
E: longbarn@carter2861.fsnet.co.uk

Mill Barn Cottage ★★★
Contact: Mr Roger Wolens, Mill Barn Cottage, The Mill House, Mill Lane, Earls Barton, Northampton NN6 0NR
T: (01604) 810507
F: (01604) 810507
I: www.themillbarn.free-online.co.uk

NORTHLEACH
Gloucestershire

1 College Row ★★★
Contact: Mr & Mrs S Morris, Huntley Farm, Patch Elm Lane, Rangeworthy, Bristol BS37 7LU
T: (01454) 227322
F: (01454) 227323
E: cotswold.cottage@btopenworld.com

NOTTINGHAM
Nottinghamshire

Days Serviced Apartments ★★★
Contact: Mr Paul Smith
T: (0115) 924 1900
F: (0115) 947 1500
E: psmith@premgroup.com
I: www.premgroup.com

46 Riverview ★★★
Contact: Mrs Margaret Hallam, 364 Loughborough Road, West Bridgford, Nottingham NG2 7FD
T: (0115) 923 3372

Tree Tops
Rating Applied For
Contact: Mrs Ann Turner, Tree Tops, 103 Castle Boulevard, Nottingham NG7 1FE
T: (0115) 117580
F: (0115) 947 2819
E: ann.turnel@ntlworld.com

NYMPSFIELD
Gloucestershire

Crossways ★★★
Contact: Mr & Mrs F J Bowen, Crossways, Tinkley Lane, Nympsfield, Stonehouse GL10 3TU
T: (01453) 860309

ODDINGTON
Gloucestershire

Lower Court Cottages ★★★-★★★★
Contact: Mrs Juliet Pauling, Lower Court Farm, Chadlington, Oxford OX7 3NQ
T: (01608) 676422
F: (01608) 676422
E: jpauling@lineone.net

OLD BOLINGBROKE
Lincolnshire

1 Hope Cottage ★★★★
Contact: Mr & Mrs S Taylor, Clowery Cottage, Craypool Lane, Scothern, Lincoln LN2 2UU
T: (01673) 861412
F: (01673) 863336
E: no1hopecottage@aol.com
I: www.no1hopecottage.co.uk

OLD BRAMPTON
Derbyshire

Chestnut Cottage & Willow Cottage ★★★★
Contact: Mr & Mrs Jeffery & Patrica Green, Chestnut Cottage & Willow Cottage, Priestfield Grange, Hollins, Old Brampton, Chesterfield S42 7JH
T: (01246) 566159

OLDCROFT
Gloucestershire

Cider Press Cottage ★★★★
Contact: Mr & Mrs Hinton, Cider Press Cottage, 1 Westleigh Villa, St Swithens Road, Oldcroft, Lydney GL15 4NF
T: (01594) 510285
F: (01594) 510285

ORCOP
Herefordshire

Barn Cottage ★★★
Contact: Mrs Jan Brown, Barn Cottage, Star Acre Farm, Orcop, Hereford HR2 8HD
T: (01981) 240363

The Burnett Farmhouse ★★★★
Contact: Mr & Mrs M A Gooch, The Burnett Farmhouse, Orcop, Hereford HR2 8SF
T: (01981) 540999
F: (01981) 540999
E: burnett.farmhouse@talk21.com
I: www.burnettfarmhouse.co.uk

Bury Farm ★★
Contact: Mrs G Goodwin, Old Kitchen Farm, Garway Hill, Hereford HR2 0DE
T: (01981) 240383
F: (01981) 241475

OSWESTRY
Shropshire

The Cross Keys ★★★
Contact: Mr & Mrs P J Rothera, The Cross Keys, Selattyn, Oswestry SY10 7DH
T: (01691) 650247

The Old Rectory Cottage ★★
Contact: Mrs Maggie Barnes, The Old Rectory Cottage, The Old Rectory, Glyn Road, Selattyn, Oswestry SY10 7DH
T: (01691) 659708
F: (01691) 661366

Underhill House ★★★★
Contact: Mr G Hughes, Underhill House, Racecourse Road, Oswestry SY10 7PN
T: (01691) 661660
F: (01691) 656893
E: info@underhillhouse.co.uk
I: www.underhillhouse.co.uk

OUNDLE
Northamptonshire

The Bolt Hole ★★★★
Contact: Mrs Anita Spurrell, Rose Cottage, 70 Glapthorne Road, Oundle, Peterborough PE8 4PT
T: (01832) 273521
T: (01832) 275409

The Coffee Tavern ★★★
Contact: Mr & Mrs Groom, The Coffee Tavern, 34 Market Place, Peterborough PE8 4BE
T: (01832) 272524
F: (01832) 270156
E: pat@coffeetavernoundle.freeserve.co.uk
I: www.northamptonshire.co.uk

13 Cotterstock Road ★★★
Contact: Mr & Mrs J S Czwortek, 13 Cotterstock Road, Oundle, Peterborough PE8 4PN
T: (01832) 273371

Oundle Cottage Breaks ★★★-★★★★★
Contact: Mr & Mrs Simmonds, Oundle Cottage Breaks, 30 Market Place, Oundle, Peterborough PE8 4BE
T: (01832) 273531
F: (01832) 274938
E: ricard@Simmondsatoundle.co.uk
I: www.oundlecottagebreaks.co.uk

OVER HADDON
Derbyshire

Burton Manor Barns ★★★★
Contact: Mr C MacQueen, Peak Cottages, Strawberry Lee Lane, Totley Bents, Sheffield S17 3BA
T: (0114) 262 0777
F: (0114) 262 0666

May Cottage
Rating Applied For
Contact: Mrs Margaret Corbridge, Shutts Farm, Shutts Lane, Over Haddon, Bakewell DE45 1JA
T: (01629) 813639

Mount Pleasant ★★★
Contact: Mr C MacQueen, Peak Cottages, Strawberry Lee Lane, Totley Bents, Sheffield S17 3BA
T: (0114) 262 0777
F: (0114) 262 0666
E: enquiries@peakcottages.com
I: www.peakcottages.com

OWLPEN
Gloucestershire

Owlpen Manor ★★★★
Contact: Ms Julia Webb, Owlpen Manor, Owlpen, Uley, Dursley GL11 5BZ
T: (01453) 860261
F: (01453) 860819
E: sales@owlpen.com
I: www.owlpen.com

OWTHORPE
Nottinghamshire

Woodview Cottages ★★★★
Contact: Mrs Judith Morley, Woodview Cottages, Newfields Farm, Owthorpe, Nottingham NG12 3GF
T: (01949) 81279
F: (01949) 81279
E: enquiries@woodviewcottages.co.uk
I: www.woodviewcottages.co.uk

OXTON
Nottinghamshire

Wesley Farm Cottage ★★★★
Contact: Mr & Mrs Des & Heather Palmer, Windmill Farm, Forest Road, Oxton, Southwell NG25 0SZ
T: (0115) 965 2043
I: wesleycottage.com

PAINSWICK
Gloucestershire

1 Hambutts Cottages ★★★★
Contact: Mr G A Hawkins, Bath Place, Birdlip, Gloucester GL4 8JH
T: (01452) 863140
E: godfrey.hawkins@btinternet.com

Verlands Retreats ★★★★★
Contact: Mrs & Mr M Young, Verlands, Vicarage Street, Painswick, Stroud GL6 6XP
T: (01452) 812099
F: (01452) 814215
E: accommodation@painswick.com
I: www.painswick.com

PANTON
Lincolnshire

Ex St Andrew's Church
Rating Applied For
Contact: Mrs J K Haller, The Old Rectory, Panton, Market Rasen LN8 5LQ
T: (01673) 857302

PARKEND
Gloucestershire

The Coach House ★★★★
Contact: Mrs C Yeatman, Deanfield, Royal Forest of Dean, Parkend, Lydney GL15
T: (01594) 562256

PARWICH
Derbyshire

Brook Lodge ★★★
Contact: Peak Cottages, Strawberry Lee Lane, Totley Bents, Totley Rise, Sheffield S17 3BA
T: (0114) 262 0777
F: (0114) 262 0666
E: enquiries@peakcottages.com
I: www.peakcottages.com

Church Gates Cottage ★★★
Contact: Mr MacQueen, Peak Cottages, Strawberry Lee Lane, Totley Bents, Totley Rise, Sheffield S17 3BA
T: (0114) 262 0777
F: (0114) 262 0666
E: enquiries@peakcottages.com
I: www.peakcottages.com

Croft Cottage ★★★★
Contact: Mrs Saskia Tallis, Croft Cottage, Creamery Lane, Parwich, Ashbourne DE6 1QB
T: (01335) 390440
F: (01335) 390440
E: enquiries@croftcottage.co.uk
I: www.croftcottage.co.uk

Curlew, Wheatear & Redstart Cottages★★★
Contact: Mr Colin McQueen, Peak Cottages, Paddock Cottage, Strawberry Lane, Totley Bents, Sheffield S17 3BA
T: (0114) 262 0777
F: (0114) 262 0666

Tom's Barn ★★★★★
Contact: Mr & Mrs J Fuller-Sessions, Orchard Farm, Parwich, Ashbourne DE6 1QB
T: (01335) 390519
E: tom@orchardfarm.demon.co.uk

PEMBRIDGE
Herefordshire

The Cottage ★★★
Contact: Mr & Mrs Jones, The Cottage, Clearbrook, Pembridge, Leominster HR6 9HL
T: (01544) 388569
E: jonescottage@aol.com
I: www.cottageguide.co.uk/clearbrook

The Granary & The Dairy ★★★
Contact: Mrs N Owens, The Granary & The Dairy, The Grove, Pembridge, Leominster HR6 9HP
T: (01544) 388268
F: (01544) 388154
E: nancy@grovedesign.co.uk

Luntley Court Farm ★★★★
Contact: Mrs Sandra Owens, Luntley Court Farm, Pembridge, Leominster HR6 9EH
T: (01544) 388422
F: (01544) 388422
E: luntley.court.farm@faarming.co.uk

Orchard Lodge & Tippet's Lodge Tibhall Lodges ★★★-★★★★
Contact: Mr & Mrs Gwatkin, Tibhall Lodge, Tibhall, Pembridge, Leominster HR6 9JR
T: (01544) 388428

Pilgrims Cottage ★★★
Contact: Mrs Anna Pollock, Yew Tree Cottage, Bearwood, Leominster HR6 9EE
T: (01544) 388953
F: (01544) 388953
E: anna.pollock@btinternet.com
I: www.pilgrimscottage.com

Rowena Cottage ★★
Contact: Mrs D Malone, The Cottage, Holme, Newark NG23 7RZ
T: (01636) 672914
E: dianamalone56@hotmail.com

PENKRIDGE
Staffordshire

Dalraddy Cottage
Rating Applied For
Contact: Mrs Sonia Young, Pottal Pool House, Pottal Pool, Teddesley Hay, Penkridge, Stafford ST19 5RR
T: (01785) 715700
F: (01785) 712216
E: sonia@adamsyoung.fsnet.co.uk

PERSHORE
Worcestershire

Court Close Farm ★★★
Contact: Mrs Fincher, Court Close Farm, Manor Road, Eckington, Pershore WR10 3BH
T: (01386) 750297
F: (01386) 750297
E: fincher@ukonline.co.uk

Treaford ★★★
Contact: Mrs Lila Bailey, Treaford, The Grange, Little Comberton, Pershore WR10 3EH
T: (01386) 710331
I: www.cottageguide.co.uk/treaford

PICKLESCOTT
Shropshire

Bank Farm Cottage ★★★★
Contact: Mrs Alison Lucas, Bank Farm Cottage, Bank Farm, Picklescott, Church Stretton SY6 6NT
T: (01694) 751219
E: a-lucas@lineone.net

PIKEHALL
Derbyshire

The Old Farmhouse & The Grange ★★★★
Contact: Mr & Mrs S Mavin, Roystone Grange, Roystone Lane, Pikehall, Matlock DE4 2PQ
T: (01335) 390382

PILLERTON HERSEY
Warwickshire

Roman Acres Cottage ★★★
Contact: Mrs Williams, Roman Acres Cottage, Roman Acres, Oxhill Bridle Road, Pillerton Hersey, Warwick CV35 0QB
T: (01789) 740360

PLUNGAR
Leicestershire

The Cottage ★★★
Contact: Ms Anne Chatterton, Merrivale Farm, Plungar, Nottingham NG13 0JE
T: (01949) 860267
F: (01949) 861316
E: mikechatt@lineone.net

The Old Wharf ★★★★★
Contact: Mrs Elaine Pell, Grange Farm, Granby Lane, Plungar, Nottingham NG13 0JJ
T: (01949) 860630
E: pellelaine@hotmail.com

PONTRILAS
Herefordshire

Station House ★★
Contact: Ms J Russell, Station House, Pontrilas, Hereford HR2 0EH
T: (01981) 240564
F: (01981) 240564
E: john.pring@tesco.net
I: www.golden-valley.co.uk/stationhouse

PONTSHILL
Herefordshire

The Coach House ★★★
Contact: Mr V & Mrs B Hoare, Croome Hall, Pontshill, Ross-on-Wye HR9 5TB
T: (01989) 750335
E: brendan@croomehall.freeserve.co.uk

POTTERHANWORTH
Lincolnshire

Skelghyll Cottage ★★★★
Contact: Mrs Hawes, Skelghyll Cottage, Moor Lane, Potterhanworth, Lincoln LN4 2DZ
T: (01522) 790043

PRESTBURY
Gloucestershire

Home Farm ★★★★
Contact: Mr Charles Banwell, Home Farm, Mill Street, Prestbury, Cheltenham GL52 3BG
T: (01242) 583161
F: (01242) 583161

PRESTON
Gloucestershire

The Tallet ★★★
Contact: Mrs Susan Spivey, The Tallet, The Old Farmhouse, Preston, Cirencester GL7 5PR
T: (01285) 653405
F: (01285) 651152

PRESTON GUBBALS
Shropshire

Gubbals House Cottage Rating Applied For
Contact: Mrs Valerie Nunn, Gubbals House Cottage, Preston Gubbals, Shrewsbury SY4 3AN
T: (01939) 290644
F: (01939) 290644
E: mikenunn@onetel.net.uk

PRESTON WYNNE
Herefordshire

Wisteria Cottage ★★★
Contact: Mrs Jenni Maund, Lower Town, Preston Wynne, Hereford HR1 3PB
T: (01432) 820608
F: (01432) 820608
E: lowertown@onetel.net.uk

PRESTWOOD
Staffordshire

Swallows Loft ★★★★
Contact: Mrs Joyce Beeson, Swallows Loft, Brook Cottage, Quixhill Lane, Prestwood, Uttoxeter ST14 5DD
T: (01889) 590464
F: (01335) 300093
E: bookings@swallows-loft.fsnet.co.uk
I: www.swallows-loft.fsnet.co.uk

PRINCETHORPE
Warwickshire

Stretton Lodge Barns ★★★
Contact: Mrs Best, Stretton Lodge, Oxford Road, Princethorpe, Rugby CV23 9QD
T: (01926) 632351
F: (01926) 456209
E: c.best@btinternet.com

PRIORS HARDWICK
Warwickshire

Pepperpot Lodge ★★★
Contact: Mrs A Prophet, School Cottage, London End, Priors Hardwick, Southam CV47 7SL
T: (01327) 262015
F: (01327) 264663

PULVERBATCH
Shropshire

2 Holly Grove Cottages ★★★★
Contact: Mrs Sue Morris, Holly Grove Farm, Pulverbatch, Shrewsbury SY5 8DD
T: (01743) 718300
E: pulverbatch@farmersweekly.net
I: www.virtual-shropshire.co.uk/holly

Wilderley Cottage ★★★
Contact: Mrs Gill Swain, Wilderley Lane Farm, Pulverbatch, Shrewsbury SY5 8DF
T: (01743) 718152
E: gill@crosswaysstud.com
I: www.crosswaysstud.com

QUARNFORD
Derbyshire

Black Clough Farmhouse ★★-★★★
Contact: Mrs A Brocklesby, 4 St Georges Square, London SW1V 2HP
T: (01327) 860991
F: (01327) 860994
E: edwina@globalnet.co.uk

Colshaw Cottage ★★★
Contact: Country Holidays Ref: 5291 Sales, Holiday Cottages Group Limited, Spring Mill, Earby, Barnoldswick BB94 0AA
T: 08700 723723
F: (01282) 844288
E: sales@ttgihg.co.uk
I: www.country-holidays.co.uk

Greens Farm ★★★
Contact: Mrs Audrey Gould, Flash Head, Quarnford, Buxton SK17 0TE
T: (01298) 25172

New Colshaw Farm ★★★
Contact: Mr John Belfield, New Colshaw Farm, Hollinsclough, Quarnford, Buxton SK17 0SL
T: (01298) 73266

RANBY
Nottinghamshire

Spruce Cottage ★★★
Contact: Ms Penny Mason, 58 Newbattle Terrace, Edinburgh EH10 4RX
T: (0131) 447 6886
E: bpmason@blueyonder.co.uk

REDMARLEY
Gloucestershire

Playley Green Cottages ★★★★
Contact: Mr A McKechnie, Playley Green Cottages, Playley Green Farm, Redmarley, Gloucester GL19 3NB
T: (01531) 650309
F: (01531) 650375
E: playley-cottages@lineone.net
I: play-cottages@lineone.net

RICHARDS CASTLE
Shropshire

The Barn ★★★★
Contact: Mr & Mrs Peter & Sue Plant, The Barn, Richards Castle, Ludlow SY8 4EU
T: (01584) 831224
F: (01584) 831224
E: ryecroftbarn@hotmail.com
I: www.ludlow.org.uk/ryecroft

ROCK
Worcestershire

The Barn ★★★
Contact: Mr M S Deall, Chinook, Bliss Gate, Rock, Kidderminster DY14 9YE
T: (01299) 266047

ROSS-ON-WYE
Herefordshire

The Ashe ★★★
Contact: Mrs M.R Ball, The Ashe, Ashe Holiday Cottages, Bridstow, Ross-on-Wye HR9 6QA
T: (01989) 563336
I: www.burnett24.freeserve.co.uk

Barn House & Oaklands ★★★
Contact: Mrs Angela Farr, Farr Cottages, Southwell Court, Broad Oak, Hereford HR2 8RA
T: (01600) 750333
E: farrcottages@yahoo.com
I: www.farrcottages.co.uk

Browns Cottage ★★★★
Contact: Country Holidays Ref: 67504 Sales, Country Holidays, Spring Mill, Earby, Barnoldswick BB94 0AA
T: 08700 723723
F: (01282) 844288
E: sales@ttgihg.co.uk
I: www.country-holidays.co.uk

Columbine Cottage ★★★
Contact: Mrs Sue Wall, Radcliffe House, Wye Street, Ross-on-Wye HR9 7BS
T: (01989) 563895
E: radcliffegh@bt.internet.com

Fairview ★★★
Contact: Mrs M E Jones, Stoneleigh, Fourth Avenue, Greytrees, Ross-on-Wye HR9 7HR
T: (01989) 566301

The Game Larders & The Old Bakehouse★★-★★★
Contact: Mr Mr McIntyre, The Game Larders & Old Bakehouse, Wythall, Walford, Ross-on-Wye HR9 5SD
T: (01989) 562688
F: (01989) 763225
E: wythall@globalnet.co.uk
I: www.wythallestate.co.uk

Highview ★★
Contact: Mr J Perry, Westfield House, Wye Street, Ross-on-Wye HR9 7BT
T: (01989) 564149
F: (01989) 566884

Little Trereece Holiday Cottages ★★★
Contact: Mr & Mrs Cinderey, Little Trereece Holiday Cottages, Little Trereece Farmhouse, Llangarron, Ross-on-Wye HR9 6NH
T: (01989) 770145
E: trereece@nasuwt.net
E: http://homepages.nasuwt.net/trereece

Mainoaks Farm Cottages ★★★-★★★★★
Contact: Mrs Unwin, Hill House, Chase End, Bromsberrow, Ledbury HR8 1SE
T: (01531) 650448
E: mainoaks@lineone.net

Man of Ross House ★★
Contact: Mr David Campkin, 8 Maitland Road, Reading RG1 6NL
T: (0118) 957 2561
F: (0118) 959 4867

Mill Cottage ★★★★
Contact: Mrs H J Gammond, Rudhall Farm, Ross-on-Wye HR9 7TL
T: (01989) 780240

Old Cider House ★★★★
Contact: Mrs H A Jackson, Lowcop, Glewstone, Ross-on-Wye HR9 6AN
T: (01989) 562827
F: (01989) 563877
E: man.of.ross.ltd@farming.co.uk

Old Forge Cottage ★★★
Contact: Mrs J S Jennings, The Tower House, Priory Road, Dodford, Bromsgrove B61 9DF
T: (01527) 833880
F: (01527) 833880

The Old Hall ★★★
Contact: Mrs Heather Lovett, The Old Hall, 7 Hom Green, Ross-on-Wye HR9 7TG
T: (01989) 567864
F: (01989) 567869
E: grather.lovett@btoprnnolld.com

The Olde House ★★★
Contact: P J & J Fray, Keepers Cottage, Upton Bishop, Ross-on-Wye HR9 7UE
T: (01989) 780383
F: (01989) 780383
E: peter@pjfray.co.uk
I: www.oldehouse.com

Orchard View ★★★
Contact: Mr & Mrs G Powell, Underhill Farm, Foy, Ross-on-Wye HR9 6RD
T: (01989) 567950

Paddocks Farm ★★★★★
Contact: Ms Catherine Gaskell, Paddocks Farm, Deep Dean, Ross-on-Wye HR9 5SQ
T: (01989) 768699
F: (01989) 768699
E: info@pakkocksfarm.co.uk
I: www.paddocksfarm.co.uk

Perrystone Cottage ★★★
Contact: Mrs Sanders, Woodlands Farm, Little Dewchurch, Hereford HR2 6QD
T: (01432) 840488
F: (01432) 840700
E: upperhouse@hotmail.com

River View ★★
Contact: Country Holidays Ref: 8216 Sales, Holiday Cottages Group Limited, Spring Mill, Earby, Barnoldswick BB94 0AA
T: 08700 723723
F: (01282) 844288
E: sales@ttgihg.co.uk
I: www.country-holidays.co.uk

Riverview Apartment ★★★
Contact: Ms Jane Roberts, Riverview Apartment, Edde Cross House, Edde Cross Street, Ross-on-Wye HR9 7BZ
T: (01989) 563299
E: info-tb@riverviewapartment.com
I: www.riverviewapartment.com

Watchmaker's Cottage ★★★★
Contact: Mrs Jennifer Clark, Watchmaker's Cottage, Daffaluke House, Glewstone, Ross-on-Wye HR9 6BB
T: (01989) 770369
F: (01989) 770369
E: watchmakerscottage@madasafish.com
I: watchmakerscottage@madasafish.com

Wharton Lodge Cottages ★★★★★
Contact: Mrs Cross, Wharton Lodge Cottages, Weston under Penyard, Ross-on-Wye HR9 7JX
T: (01989) 750140
F: (01989) 750140
E: ncross@whartonlodge.co.uk
I: www.whartonlodge.co.uk

Willows ★★★★
Contact: Ms Jenny Taylor, Cavendish Cottage, Buckcastle Hill, Bridstow, Ross-on-Wye HR9 6QF
T: (01989) 562619
F: (01989) 563304

Y Crwys ★★★
Contact: Mr & Mrs Colin and Angie Fuller, 3 The Square, Goodrich, Ross-on-Wye HR9
T: (01600) 890799
E: colinfuller@hotmail.com
I: www.pimlico@demon.co.uk

ROSTON
Derbyshire

Derbyshire Dales Holidays ★★★★
Contact: Mrs Beryl Wheeler, Town End Farm, Roston, Ashbourne DE6 2EH
T: (01335) 324062
F: (01335) 324062
E: wheelertef@supanet.com

ROWSLEY
Derbyshire

Bluebell Cottage ★★★★
Contact: Mr & Mrs M Henderson, 67 Dalewood Avenue, Beauchief, Sheffield S8 0EG
T: (0114) 281 7217
F: (0114) 281 7217
E: jane77@blueyonder.co.uk
I: www.bluebellcountrycottage.co.uk

New Fallinge Cottage ★★★★
Contact: Mrs Mona Haylock, New Fallinge Cottage, New Fallinge Farm, Rowsley, Matlock DE4 2NN
T: (01629) 734936
E: mona@newfallinge.fsworld.co.uk

RUARDEAN
Gloucestershire

Anne's Cottage ★★★★
Contact: Mrs Anne Seager, South View, Crooked End, Ruardean GL17 9XF
T: (01594) 543217
F: (01594) 543217
E: anneseager@aol.com

The Old Post Office Annexe ★★★
Contact: Mr & Mrs C Harrison, Hope Cottage, High Street, The Pludds, Ruardean GL17 9TU
T: (01594) 860229

RUGBY
Warwickshire

Lawford Hill Farm ★★★★
Contact: Mr & Mrs Susan Moses, Lawford Hill Farm, Lawford Heath Lane, Rugby CV23 9HG
T: (01788) 542001
F: (01788) 537880
E: lawford.hill@talk21.com
I: www.lawfordhill.co.uk

RUSHBURY
Shropshire

Lilywood Cottage ★★★★
Contact: Mrs Lole, Lilywood Cottage, Lilywood Barn, Lilywood Lane, Rushbury, Church Stretton SY6 7EA
T: (01694) 771286
E: ruth.lole@ukonline.co.uk

RUSHTON SPENCER
Staffordshire

Cosy Nook ★★★★★
Contact: Mrs Jackie Matravers, Ivydene, Rushton Spencer, Macclesfield SK11 0QU
T: (01260) 226570
F: (01260) 226570
E: 106366.3376@compuserve.com
I: www.cottageguide.co.uk/cosynook

RUTLAND WATER
Rutland

Barn Owl House ★★★★★
Contact: Mr & Mrs Roger Page, 33 Coniston Road, Edith Weston, Oakham LE15 8HP
T: (01780) 720413
F: (01780) 720413

Barns at Wing & Garden View Apartment
Rating Applied For
Contact: Mr Curley, Barns at Wing & Garden View Apartment, Wing Hall, Rutland Water, Oakham LE15 8RY
T: (01572) 737283
F: (01572) 737709
E: winghall@postmark.net
I: www.rutnet.co.uk

RYTON
Shropshire

Fairfield Bungalow ★★★
Contact: Country Holidays Ref 10994, Holiday Cottages Group, Spring Mill, Earby, Barnoldswick BB94 0AA
T: 08700 723723
F: (01282) 841539
E: sales@ttgihg.co.uk
I: www.country-holidays.co.uk

SELSTON
Nottinghamshire

Cottages in the Square ★★★-★★★★
Contact: Mr Keith Hill, Cottages in the Square, 62 Nottingham Road, Selston, Nottingham NG16 6DE
T: (01773) 812029
F: (01623) 559849
E: cottages2000@yahoo.com
I: www.cottages2000.com

Kinnaird ★★★
Contact: Mrs Karen Barton, 10 Searwood Avenue, Kirby-In-Ashfield, Kirkby-in-Ashfield, Nottingham NG17 8HL
T: (01623) 441278
F: (01623) 441278

SEVERN STOKE
Worcestershire

Roseland Annexe ★★★★
Contact: Mr & Mrs Guy & Mary Laurent, Roseland Annexe, Roseland, Clifton, Severn Stoke, Worcester WR8 9JF
T: (01905) 371463
F: (01905) 371463
E: guy@guy-laurent.demon.co.uk
I: www.roselandworcs.demon.co.uk

SHARDLOW
Derbyshire

The Old Workshop ★★★★
Contact: Mrs Hansen, 24 Mill Green, The Wharf, Shardlow, Derby DE72 2WE
T: (01332) 799820
E: hansendorothy@hotmail.com
I: www.workshop-shardlow.fsnet.co.uk

SHEEN
Staffordshire

Bank Top Lodge ★★★★
Contact: Mrs N Birch, Bank Top Farm, Sheen, Buxton SK17 0HN
T: (01298) 84768

Ferny Knowle ★★★★★
Contact: Mr & Mrs George & Pauline Grindon, Ferny Knowle, Sheen, Hartington, Buxton SK17 0ER
T: (01298) 83264

SHEEPSCOMBE
Gloucestershire

Longridge Meend ★★★
Contact: Mr R Cound, Longridge Meend, Bulls Cross, Sheepscombe, Stroud GL7 7HU
T: (01452) 813225
F: (01452) 812006
E: richardcound@beeb.net

SHELDON
Derbyshire

Townend Cottage ★★★
Contact: Mrs Ethel Plumtree, Townend Cottage, Sheldon, Bakewell DE45 1QS
T: (01629) 813322

SHIFNAL
Shropshire

The Old Stable ★★★
Contact: Mr & Mrs R Wild, The Old Stable, 4 Church Street, Shifnal TF11 9AA
T: (01952) 461136
E: wildthings@raphaelsrestaurant.co.uk

Silvermere Mews ★★★
Contact: Mrs Sylvia Blake, Hawkshutt Farm, Stretton, Stafford ST19 9QU
T: (01785) 840808
I: www.silvermere.co.uk

SHIPSTON-ON-STOUR
Warwickshire

Little Barn ★★★★
Contact: Mrs Karen Lawrence, Little Barn, Ascott, Whichford, Shipston-on-Stour CV36 5PP
T: (01608) 684240
E: johnandkaren.lawrence@ic24.net
I: www.littlebarn.members.easyspace.com.index.htm

SHIPTON OLIFFE
Gloucestershire

Paddock Barn ★★★★★
Contact: Mrs E Doyle, Southwold Farm, Compton Abdale, Cheltenham GL54 4DS
T: (01242) 890147
E: emma@paddockbarn.co.uk
I: www.paddockbarn.co.uk

SHIRLEY
Derbyshire

Shirley Hall Farm ★★★
Contact: Mrs Sylvia Foster, Shirley Hall Farm, Ashbourne, Shirley, Ashbourne DE6 3AS
T: (01335) 360346
F: (01335) 360346
E: sylviafoster@shirleyhallfarm.com
I: shirleyhallfarm.com

Yew Tree Cottage ★★★★★
Contact: Mrs Tracey Griffin, Yew Tree Cottage, Mill Lane, Shirley, Ashbourne DE6 3AR
T: (01332) 720870
F: (01332) 720870
E: yewtree.cottage@ntlworld.com
I: www.yewtreecountrycottage.co.uk

SHOBDON
Herefordshire

Tyn-y-Coed ★★★★
Contact: Mr & Mrs J Andrews, Tyn-y-Coed, Shobdon, Leominster HR6 9NY
T: (01568) 708277
F: (01568) 708277
E: jandrews@shobdondesign.kc3.co.uk

SHREWSBURY
Shropshire

8 Cross Hill ★★★
Contact: Mrs Elizabeth Ann Williams, 68 Church Hill, Penn, Wolverhampton WV4 5JD
T: (01902) 341399
E: williams_letting@hotmail.com

Inglenook ★★
Contact: Mrs J M Mullineux, Fach-Hir, Brooks, Welshpool SY21 8QP
T: (01686) 650361

Mill House Farm ★★★
Contact: Mrs Christine Burton, Mill House Farm, Cruckmeole, Shrewsbury SY5 8JN
T: (01743) 860325
E: christine@millhousefarmholidays.fsnet.co.uk

Newton Meadows Holiday Cottages ★★★★
Contact: Mr & Mrs Simcox, Wem Road, Harmer Hill, Shrewsbury SY2 3DZ
T: (01939) 290346
F: (01939) 290346
E: e.simcox@btopenworld.com
I: www.virtual-shropshire.co.uk/newton

Yews Barn ★★★★
Contact: Ms Hiorns, 5 Humbers Way, Telford TF2 8LH
T: (01952) 605915

SIBBERTOFT
Northamptonshire

Brook Meadow Holiday Chalets ★★★-★★★★
Contact: Mrs Mary Hart, Brook Meadow Holiday Chalets, The Wrongs, Welford Road, Sibbertoft, Market Harborough LE16 9UJ
T: (01858) 880886
F: (01858) 880485
I: www.brookmeadow.co.uk

SIBSEY
Lincolnshire

Sweetbriar ★★★
Contact: Mrs Alison Twiddy, Sweetbriar, Main Road, Sibsey, Boston PE22 0TT
T: (01205) 750837

SKEGNESS
Lincolnshire

Ingoldale Park ★★★★
Contact: Ms Cathryn Whitehead, Ingoldale Park, Roman Bank, Ingoldmells, Skegness PE25 1LL
T: (01754) 872335
F: (01754) 873887
E: info@ingoldmells.net
I: www.ingoldmells.net

Lyndene Holiday Apartments ★-★★★
Contact: Mr Bailey, 11A St Margarets Avenue, Skegness PE25 2LX
T: (01754) 766108
E: info@lyndene-uk.com
I: www.lyndene-uk.com

Springfield & Island Holiday Apartments★-★★★
Contact: Mr & Mrs John & Carol Haines, Springfield & Island Holiday Apartments, 30-32 Scarborough Avenue, Skegness PE25 2TA
T: (01754) 762660
E: carol@springfield-island.fsnet.co.uk
I: www.skegness-resort.co.uk/springfield

SLAD
Gloucestershire

Little Vatch
Rating Applied For
Contact: Mr Hoy, Upper Vatch Mill, The Vatch, Slad, Stroud GL6 7JY
T: (01453) 764270
F: (01453) 755233
E: i.hodgkins@dial.pipex.com

SNAILBEACH
Shropshire

The Blessing ★★★
Contact: Mr & Mrs M J Dennis, 3 Farm Cottages, Snailbeach, Shrewsbury SY5 0LP
T: (01743) 791489

SNELSTON
Derbyshire

Owls Roost ★★★★
Contact: Mrs M Kay, Brook Farm, Snelston, Ashbourne DE6 2GP
T: (01335) 324602

SOUDLEY
Gloucestershire

The Cottage ★★★
Contact: Mrs Helen Evans, Peaked Rocks Cottage, The Rocks, Joys Green, Lydbrook GL17 9RF
T: (01594) 861119
F: (01594) 823408
E: evans@evansholidays.freeserve.co.uk

SOUTH CERNEY
Gloucestershire

Beau Lodge ★★★★
Contact: Ms G Parfitt, Flat 1, 156/8 Wandsworth Bridge Road, Fulham, London SW6 2UH
T: 07976 610157
F: 07970 701378
E: gloria@parfittdirect.com

Orion Holidays ★★★★
Contact: Mr M Thomas, Orion Holidays Orion House, Unit W, The Old Brickyard Works, North End, Ashton Keynes, Swindon SN6 6QR
T: (01285) 861839
F: (01285) 869188
E: bookings@orionholidays.com
I: www.orionholidays.com

The Watermark Club ★★★-★★★★★
Contact: Ms Miles, The Watermark Club, Isis Lake, South Cerney, Cirencester GL7 5TL
T: (01285) 869181
F: (01285) 862488
E: enquiries@watermarkclub.co.uk
I: www.watermarkclub.co.uk

SOUTH COCKERINGTON
Lincolnshire

West View Cottages ★★★
Contact: Mr Richard Nicholson & Mrs J Hand, West View, South View Lane, South Cockerington, Louth LN11 7ED
T: (01507) 327209
E: richard@nicholson55.freeserve.co.uk

SOUTH LUFFENHAM
Rutland

Country View Holiday Home ★★★★
Contact: Mr Terry Langley, Birch House, The Row, Sutton, Ely CB6 2PD
T: (01353) 777762
F: (01353) 777762

SOUTH WILLINGHAM
Lincolnshire

The Cottage ★★★★
Contact: Mrs Donocik, The Cottage, Church Farm, Station Road, South Willingham, Market Rasen LN8 6NJ
T: (01507) 313737

SOUTHWELL
Nottinghamshire

The Hayloft & Little Tithe ★★★
Contact: Mrs V M Wilson, Lodge Farm, Morton, Fiskerton, Southwell NG25 0XH
T: (01636) 830497
E: info@lodgebarns.co.uk
I: www.lodgebarns.co.uk

The Nest ★★★★
Contact: Mrs Diana Dawes, The Nest, Cooks Lane, Morton-Cum-Fiskerton, Bleasby, Nottingham NG25 0XQ
T: (01636) 830140
E: rlgdawes@hotmail.com

SPARROWPIT
Derbyshire

Daisy Bank Cottage & Hope Cottage ★★★
Contact: Mrs Hilary Batterbee, Daisy Bank, Sparrowpit, Buxton SK17 8ET
T: (01298) 813027
F: (01298) 816012
E: batterbees@btopenworld.com

Whitelee Cottage ★★★★
Contact: Mr Colin MacQueen, Peak Cottages, Strawberry Lee Lane, Totley Bents, Totley Rise, Sheffield S17 3BA
T: (0114) 262 0777
F: (0114) 262 0666
E: enquiries@peakcottages.com
I: www.peakcottages.com

SPILSBY
Lincolnshire

Corner Farm Cottage ★★★
Contact: Mr M Fitzpatrick
T: (01790) 753476
F: (01790) 752810
E: smrfitzp@ukonline.co.uk

Northfields Farm Cottages ★★★
Contact: Mrs C A Miller, Northfields Farm Cottages, Northfields Farm, Mavis Enderby, Spilsby PE23 4EW
T: (01507) 588251
F: (01507) 588251
E: chrismiller@tiacali.co.uk
I: www.lineone.net/~holidaycottages/

SPROXTON
Leicestershire

Appletree Cottage ★★★
Contact: Mrs C Slack, Appletree Cottage, The Green, Sproxton, Melton Mowbray LE14 4QS
T: (01476) 860435
F: (01476) 860435

STAFFORD
Staffordshire

No 4 The Row ★★★★
Contact: Miss S Moore, Downtop Farm, Sandon Bank, Stafford ST18 9TB
T: (01889) 508300

Soapsuds Cottage ★★★★
Contact: Mrs Bristow, Chebsey, Stafford ST21 6JU
T: (01785) 760208
F: (01785) 760731
E: bristow@rvb1.fsnet.co.uk

STAMFORD
Lincolnshire

Palm Cottage ★★★
Contact: Mrs Webster, Palm House, The Green, Ketton, Stamford PE9 3RA
T: (01780) 721499

STANFORD BRIDGE
Worcestershire

The Riseling ★★★★
Contact: Mrs Margaret Lane, The Rise, Stanford Bridge, Worcester WR6 6SP
T: (01886) 853438

STANLEY
Derbyshire

Yew Tree Farm ★★★★★
Contact: Mrs Gail Newman, Yew Tree Farm, Morley Lane, Stanley Village, Ilkeston DE7 6EZ
T: (0115) 932 9803
E: gailnewman@yewtreefarm94.freeserve.co.uk

STANSHOPE
Staffordshire

Lower Damgate Barns,Reuben's Roost, Bremen's Barn, Hope's Hideaway★★★★
Contact: Mr R & Mrs C Wilderspin, Lower Damgate Farm, Stanshope, Ashbourne DE6 2AD
T: (01335) 310367
F: (01335) 310001
E: DAMGATE@HOTMAIL.COM
I: www.damgate.com

STANTON
Gloucestershire

Charity Cottage ★★★
Contact: Mrs V Ryland, Charity Farm, Stanton, Broadway WR12 7NE
T: (01386) 584339
F: (01386) 584270
E: kennethryland@ukonline.co.uk
I: www.myrtle-cottge.co.uk/ryland.htm

Stanton Court Cottages ★★★★
Contact: Mrs Sheila Campbell, Stanton Court Cottages, Stanton Court, Toddington, Cheltenham WR12 7NE
T: (01386) 584527
F: (01386) 584682
I: www.stantoncourt.co.uk

STANTON IN PEAK
Derbyshire

Lathkill Cottage ★★★
Contact: Country Holidays Ref 4504, Spring Mill, Earby, Barnoldswick BB18
T: 08700 723723
E: sales@ttgihg.co.uk
I: www.country-holidays.co.uk

STANTON-ON-THE-WOLDS
Nottinghamshire

Foxcote Cottage ★★★★
Contact: Mrs Joan Hinchley, Foxcote Cottage, Hill Farm (Foxcote), Melton Road, Stanton-on-the-Wolds, Keyworth NG12 5PJ
T: (0115) 937 4337
F: (0115) 937 4337

STARKHOLMES
Derbyshire

Hazel Cottage ★★★★
Contact: Mr Colin MacQueen, Peak Cottages, Strawberry Lee Lane, Totley Bents, Totley Rise, Sheffield S17 3BA
T: (0114) 262 0777
F: (0114) 262 0666
E: enquiries@peakcottages.com
I: www.peakcottages.com

STATHERN
Leicestershire

Brambles Barn ★★★★
Contact: Mrs J Newton
T: (01949) 860071
E: richard@bramblesbarn.co.uk
I: www.bramblesbarn.co.uk

Sycamore Farm ★★★★
Contact: Mrs Jean Stanley, Waltham Road, Harby, Stathern, Melton Mowbray LE14 4DB
T: (01949) 860640
F: (01949) 861165

STIPERSTONES
Shropshire

The Resting Hill ★★★
Contact: Mrs Rowson, Resting Hill, 46 Snailbeach, Shrewsbury SY5 0LT
T: (01743) 791219

STOKE BRUERNE
Northamptonshire

3 Canalside ★★★
Contact: Mr Trevor Morley, 29 Main Road, Shutlanger, Towcester NN12 7RU
T: (01604) 862107
F: (01604) 864098
I: www.stokebruerneboats.co.uk

STOKE-ON-TRENT
Staffordshire

Bank End Farm Cottages ★★★
Contact: Mr K & Mrs E Meredith
T: (01782) 502160
E: pete502@btopenworld.com
I: www.alton-village.com

Coach House ★★★
Contact: Mrs Janet Lowery, 2 Moss Cottage, Mossfields, Stoke-on-Trent ST7 1EL
T: (01782) 786821

Field Head Farm House Holidays ★★★★
Contact: Mrs Janet Hudson, Stoney Rock Farm, Waterhouses, Stoke-on-Trent ST10 3LH
T: (01538) 308352
E: info@field-head.co.uk
I: www.field-head.co.uk

Jay's Barn ★★★
Contact: Mrs C Babb, Rest Cottage, Bradley in the Moor, Stoke-on-Trent ST10 4DF
T: (01889) 507444

Lockwood Hall Farm ★★★★
Contact: Mrs Rebecca Sherratt, Lockwood Hall Farm, Lockwood Road, Kingsley Holt, Stoke-on-Trent ST10 2DH
T: (01538) 752270
F: (01538) 752270
E: sherratt@lockwoodhall.freeserve.co.uk
I: www.peakdistrictfarmhols.co.uk

Low Roofs ★★★
Contact: Mrs Malkin, 62 Albert Terrace, Wolstanton, Newcastle-under-Lyme ST5 8AY
T: (01782) 627087
F: (01782) 627087

Moorcourt Cottages, Moorcourt House★★★★
Contact: Mrs V Bradshaw, Moor Court House, Leigh Lane, Upper Leigh, Stoke-on-Trent ST10 4NU
T: (01538) 723008
F: (01538) 723008
E: vbradshaw@moorcourtcottages.co.uk
I: www.moorcourtcottages.co.uk

STOULTON
Worcestershire

Stables Flat ★★★★
Contact: Mrs Marchant, The Hay Loft, The Old Vicarage, Stoulton, Worcester WR7 4RE
T: (01905) 841554
F: (01905) 841553
E: smarchant@wyenet.co.uk

STOURBRIDGE
West Midlands

41 Hagley Road ★★★
Contact: Mrs M Lee, 59 Warwick Avenue, Bromsgrove B60 2AP
T: (01527) 876973

STOURPORT-ON-SEVERN
Worcestershire

Winnall House Cottage and Caravan Park★★★★
Contact: Mrs Sheila Wilson, Winnall House Cottage and Caravan Park, Winnall House, Lincomb, Stourport-on-Severn DY13 9RG
T: (01299) 250389

STOW-ON-THE-WOLD
Gloucestershire

Broad Oak Cottages ★★★★★
Contact: Mrs M Wilson, The Counting House, Stow-on-the-Wold, Cheltenham GL54 1AL
T: (01451) 830794
F: (01451) 830794
E: mary@broadoakcottages.fsnet.co.uk
I: www.broadoakcottages.fsnet.co.uk

Charlie's Cottage ★★★★
Contact: Mrs Veronica Woodford, 21 Wyck Rissington, Stow-on-the-Wold, Cheltenham GL54 2PN
T: (01451) 821496
E: iwoodford@wyckriss.freeserve.co.uk

Charlton Cottage ★★★★
Contact: Mr Les Gardner, T F Travel, 44 Kingsway, Stoke-on-Trent ST4 1JH
T: (01782) 411141
F: (01782) 747061
E: tftravel@aol.com

Cotswold Cottages ★★★
Contact: Mr Spiers, Forest Gate, Frog Lane, Shipton-under-Wychwood, Oxford OX7 6JZ
T: (01993) 831495
F: (01993) 831095
E: info@cottageinthecountry.co.uk
I: www.cottageinthecountry.co.uk

Foden Lodge ★★★
Contact: Mr & Mrs Beryl Gypps, 77 Park Lane, Waltham Cross EN8 8AD
T: (01992) 301800
E: thefodenlodge@hotmail.com
I: www.come.to/fodenlodge

Horseshoe Cottage ★★★★
Contact: Mr & Mrs McHale, Horseshoe Cottage, Forge House, Lower Oddington, Stow-on-the-Wold, Cheltenham GL56 0UP
T: (01451) 831556

Icomb Lodge
Rating Applied For
Contact: Mrs Dawn Taylor
T: (01423) 502355

Johnston Cottage ★★★
Contact: Mrs Yvonne Johnston, Poplars Barn, Evenlode, Moreton-in-Marsh GL56 0NN
T: (01608) 650816

Luckley Holidays ★★★
Contact: Mr Robert Wharton
T: (01451) 870885
F: (01451) 831481
E: info@luckley-holidays.co.uk
I: www.luckley-holidays.co.uk

Maugersbury Manor ★★★
Contact: Mr C S Martin, Maugersbury Manor, Stow-on-the-Wold, Cheltenham GL54 1HP
T: (01451) 830581
F: (01451) 870902
I: www.manorholidays.co.uk

Old Corner Cottage ★★★★
Contact: Mrs Cathy Terry, St Helens Vicarage, St Helens Gardens, London W10 6LP
T: (0208) 960 5067
F: (0208) 965782
E: cathy.terry@cornercottage23.fsbusiness.co.uk

The Old School House ★★★★
Contact: Mrs Anita McKinney, Beresford, Cliveden Mead, Maidenhead SL6 8HE
T: (01628) 638190
E: information@heartofthecotswolds.com

3 The Old Shop ★★★★
Contact: Mrs Norma Marfell, Hillside Cottage, Broadwell, Moreton-in-Marsh GL56 0UA
T: (01451) 830617
F: (01451) 830617

Park Farm Holiday Cottages ★★★★
Contact: Mrs J C Ricketts, Park Farm, Maugersbury, Cheltenham GL54 1HP
T: (01451) 830227
F: (01451) 870568
E: parkfarm.cottages@virgin.net

Park House Cottage ★★★
Contact: Mr & Mrs Sutton, Park House, 8 Park Street, Stow-on-the-Wold, Cheltenham GL54 1AQ
T: (01451) 830159
F: (01451) 870809
E: info@parkhousecottage.co.uk
I: www.parkhousecottage.co.uk

Rose's Cottage ★★★★
Contact: Mr & Mrs R Drinkwater, Rose's Cottage, The Green, Broadwell, Moreton-in-Marsh GL56 0UF
T: (01451) 830007

Springbank ★★★★★
Contact: Mr Mather, Landgate House, Colman, Temple Guiting, Cheltenham GL54 5RT
T: (01451) 850571
F: (01451) 850614
E: landgatemathers@tesco.net
I: www.landgatetg.co.uk

Sycamore Cottage ★★★★
Contact: Mrs S Jones, 111 Bicester Road, Long Crendon, Aylesbury HP18 9EF
T: (01844) 208615
E: suejones16@hotmail.com

Twinkle Toes Cottage ★★★★
Contact: Mrs Christine Gowing, Barley Cottage, Churchill, Kingham, Oxford OX7 6NW
T: (01608) 658579
E: kcgowing@talk21.com

2 Union Street ★★★★
Contact: Ms K Spiers, Cottage in the Country and Cottage Holidays, Forest Gate, Frog Lane, Milton-under-Wychwood, Oxford OX7 6JZ
T: (01993) 831495
F: (01993) 831095
E: enquiries@cottageinthecountry.co.uk
I: www.cottageinthecountry.co.uk

Valley View ★★★
Contact: Mr & Mrs P J Craddock, 25 Avenue Road, Dorridge, Solihull B93 8LD
T: (01564) 770143

Weavers Cottage ★★
Contact: Country Holidays Ref: 9400 Sales, Country Holidays, Spring Mill, Earby, Barnoldswick BB94 0AA
T: 08700 723723
F: (01282) 844288
E: sales@ttgihg.co.uk
I: www.country-holidays.co.uk

STRATFORD-UPON-AVON
Warwickshire

Anne's House ★★★★
Contact: Mrs Cauvin, 34 Evesham Place, Stratford-upon-Avon CV37 6HT
T: (01789) 550197
F: (01789) 295322
E: karenc@anneshouse.com
I: www.anneshouse.com

As You Like It ★★★
Contact: Mrs J Reid, Inwood House, New Road, Alderminster, Stratford-upon-Avon CV37 8PE
T: (01789) 450266
F: (01789) 450266
I: www.alderminster99.freeserve.co.uk

20-21 Bancroft Place ★★★★
Contact: Mrs Stella Carter, Park View Guest House, 57 Rother Street, Stratford-upon-Avon CV37 6LT
T: (01789) 266839
F: (01789) 266839

Bard Cottage ★★★★
Contact: Mrs Hicks, 2 Beech Court, Stratford-upon-Avon CV37 7UQ
T: (01789) 205039
F: (01789) 261386
E: Maureen.Hicks@btinternet.com
I: www.stratford-upon-avon.co.uk/bardcott.htm

66 Bull Street ★★★
Contact: Sir W Lawrence, The Knoll, Walcote, Alcester B49 6LZ
T: 07836 636932
F: 07971 434810
I: www.stratforduponavonselfcatering.co.uk

Charlecote Cottage 2 Willicote Pastures★★★★
Contact: Mr John Lea, 6 Oak Wharf Mews, Birchdale Road, Appleton, Warrington WA4 5AS
T: (01925) 604106
F: (0151) 424 6785
E: jplea@aol.com
I: jplea@aol.com

Chestnut Cottage ★★★
Contact: Mrs J Rush, Gospel Oak House, Pathlow, Stratford-upon-Avon CV37 0JA
T: (01789) 292764

1 College Mews ★★★★
Contact: Mr I R Reid, Inwood House, New Road, Alderminster, Stratford-upon-Avon CV37 8PE
T: (01789) 450266
F: (01789) 450266
I: www.alderminster99.freeserve.co.uk

Crimscote Downs Farm Holiday Cottages★★★
Contact: Mrs J James, The Old Coach House, Whitchurch Farm, Wimpstone, Stratford-upon-Avon CV37 8NS
T: (01789) 450275
F: (01789) 450275
I: www.stratford-upon-avon.co.uk/crimscote.htm

Elmhurst ★★★★
Contact: Mrs Davenport, Lygon Arms Hotel, High Street, Chipping Campden GL55 6HB
T: (01386) 840318
F: (01386) 841088
E: sandra@elmhurstcottage.co.uk
I: www.elmhurstcottage.co.uk

Ely Street ★★★
Contact: Mr Pash, Chapel House, Luke Street, Berwick St John, Shaftesbury SP7 0HQ
T: (01747) 828170
F: (01747) 829090
E: enq@hideaways.co.uk
I: www.hideaways.co.uk

Flower Court ★★★★
Contact: Mrs Rachel Liddell, Settlestones, Hidcote Boyce, Chipping Campden GL55 6LT
T: (01386) 438833
F: (01386) 438833
E: liddellrachel@aol.com
I: www.flowercourt.freeservers.com

Fosbroke Cottage ★★★
Contact: Mrs Susan Swift, Fosbroke Cottage, 4 High Street, Bidford-on-Avon, Alcester B50 4BU
T: (01789) 772327
E: mark@swiftrilla.fsnet.co.uk

Guild Court ★★★-★★★★
Serviced Apartments
Contact: Miss Tanya Moss, Guild Court, 3 Guild Street, Stratford-upon-Avon CV37 6QZ
T: (01789) 293007
F: (01789) 296301
E: info@guildcourt.co.uk
I: www.guildcourt.co.uk

Kingzett ★★★★
Contact: Country Holidays Ref: 10858 Sales, Holiday Cottages Group Limited, Spring Mill, Earby, Barnoldswick BB94 0AA
T: 08700 723723
F: (01282) 844288
E: sales@ttgihg.co.uk
I: www.country-holidays.co.uk

Loaf Cottage ★★★
Contact: Sir William Lawrence, The Knoll, Walcote, Alcester B49 6LZ
T: 07836 636932
F: 07971 434810
I: www.stratforduponavonselfcatering.co.uk

The Mill House ★★★-★★★★
Contact: Mrs Sheila Greenwood, The Mill House, Mill Lane, Stratford-upon-Avon CV37 8EW
T: (01789) 750267
F: (01789) 750267
I: www.stratford-upon-avon.co.uk/millhouse.htm

No 7 Bull Street ★★★
Contact: Mrs Salmon, 80 Fentham Road, Hampton in Arden, Solihull B92 0AY
T: (01675) 443613
F: (01675) 443613
E: sallyannsalmon@talk21.com

3 Queens Court ★★★
Contact: Sir William Lawrence, The Knoll, Walcote, Alcester B49 6LZ
T: 07836 636932
F: 07971 434810
I: www.stratforduponavonselfcatering.co.uk

42 Shakespeare Street ★★★
Contact: Mr Field, Avon House, Mulberry Street, Stratford-upon-Avon CV37 6RS
T: (01789) 298141
F: (01789) 262272

Woodcote ★★★★★
Contact: Mr & Mrs Lucas, Tanglewood, Park Close, Wilmcote, Stratford-upon-Avon CV37 9XE
T: (01789) 293932
F: (01789) 261855
E: lucasstratford@aolco.uk
I: www.lucasstratford.co.uk

STRETTON
Staffordshire

Anvil Cottage ★★★★
Contact: Mrs Blake, Anvil Cottage, Hawkshutt Farm, Stretton, Stafford ST19 9QU
T: (01785) 840808

STRETTON ON FOSSE
Warwickshire

Woodfield Cottage ★★★
Contact: Mrs Best, 4 Bear Close, Henley-in-Arden, Solihull B95 5HS
T: (01564) 793354

STROUD
Gloucestershire

Lypiatt Hill House ★★-★★★
Contact: Mr Pyke, Lypiatt Hill House, Bisley Road, Stroud, Stroud GL6 7LQ
T: (01453) 764785
F: (01453) 751782
E: john.pyke@virgin.net

Whitminster House Cottages ★★-★★★
Contact: Mrs A R Teesdale, Whitminster House, Wheatenhurst, Whitminster GL2 7PN
T: (01452) 740204
F: (01452) 740204
E: whitminster@btconnect.com
I: www.whitminsterhousecottages.co.uk

The Yew Tree ★★★★
Contact: Mrs Elizabeth Peters, The Yew Tree, Walls Quarry, Brimscombe, Stroud GL5 2PA
T: (01453) 887594
F: (01453) 883428
E: elizabeth.peters@tesco.net
I: www.holidaycottages-uk.com/gloucestershire

SUCKLEY
Worcestershire

Tundridge Mill ★★★★
Contact: Mrs Penny Beard, Tundridge Mill, Suckley, Worcester WR6 5DP
T: (01886) 884478
F: (01886) 884478

SUTTERTON
Lincolnshire

Somercotes ★★★
Contact: Dr J V Sharp, Irish Fail, Orchard Close, East Hendred, Wantage OX12 8JJ
T: (01235) 833367
F: (01235) 833367
E: j.v.sharp@btinternet.com
I: www.j.v.sharp.btinternet.co.uk/somercotes.htm

SUTTON ON THE HILL
Derbyshire

The Chop House and The Hay Loft ★★★★
Contact: Mr & Mrs Keith & Joan Lennard, Windle Hill Farm, Sutton on the Hill, Ashbourne DE6 5JH
T: (01283) 732377
F: (01283) 732377
E: windlehill@btinternet.com
I: www.windlehill.btinternet.co.uk

SUTTON ST JAMES
Lincolnshire

Foremans Bridge Caravan Park ★★★★
Contact: Mrs Alison Negus, Foremans Bridge Caravan Park, Sutton Road, Sutton St James, Spalding PE12 0HU
T: (01945) 440346
F: (01945) 440346
I: www.foremans.bridge.co.uk

SWADLINCOTE
Derbyshire

Barne Cottage
Rating Applied For
Contact: Mrs M Fallon, Ivy Cottage, 96 Woodville Road, Hartshorne, Swadlincote DE11 7EX
T: (01283) 221511
F: 0870 133 2707
E: mim@mim-properties.co.uk

Manor Farm Cottages Manor Farm ★★★
Contact: Mr John Busby, Manor Farm, Church Lane, Chilcote, Swadlincote DE12 8DL
T: (01827) 373282
F: (01827) 373561
E: cottages@jwbusby.co.uk

SWAYFIELD
Lincolnshire

Greystones Lodge ★★★★
Contact: Mrs C Stanley, Greystones, Overgate Road, Swayfield, Grantham NG33 4LG
T: (01476) 550909
F: (01476) 550989
E: jslog@mcmail.com

SYMONDS YAT
Herefordshire

Old Court Farm ★★★★
Contact: Mrs Edwina Gee, Old Court Farm, Symonds Yat, Ross-on-Wye HR9 6DA
T: (01600) 890316
F: (01600) 890316
E: teddy.gee@breathemail.net
I: www.holidaybank.com/oldcourtfarm/

SYMONDS YAT WEST
Herefordshire

Up Beyond ★★★
Contact: Mrs K Harvey, 149 Marlborough Road, Stoke, Coventry CV2 4ES
T: (02476) 443466
F: (02476) 445007

TADDINGTON
Derbyshire

Ash Barn ★★★
Contact: Ms Judith Hawley, Ash Barn, Main Road, Taddington, Priestcliffe, Buxton SK17 9UB
T: (01298) 85453
E: jah@ashtreebarn.fsnet.co.uk

Lodley View Farm ★★★★
Contact: Mr & Mrs Nicholas, Adagio Ltd, Hollybank, Lumb Lane, Darley Dale, Matlock DE4 2HP
T: (01629) 732151
F: (01629) 735002
I: www.peakcottages.co.uk

Middle Farm Holiday Cottages
Rating Applied For
Contact: Mr & Mrs B Mullan, Middle Farm Holiday Cottages, Middle Farm, Brushfield, Taddington, Buxton SK17 9UQ
T: (01298) 85787
E: bmullan1@aol.com
I: www.cressbrook.co.uk/tidza/brushfield

Town End House ★★★★
Contact: Mr C MacQueen, Peak Cottages, Strawberry Lee Lane, Totley Bents, Sheffield S17 3BA
T: (0114) 262 0777
F: (0114) 262 0666
E: enquiries@peakcottages.com

TANSLEY
Derbyshire

Blakelow Cottages ★★★★
Contact: Mr Colin MacQueen, Peak Cottages, Strawberry Lee Lane, Totley Bents, Sheffield S17 3BA
T: (0114) 262 0777
F: (0114) 262 0666
E: enquiries@peakcottages.com
I: www.peakcottages.com

Lair Barn
Rating Applied For
Contact: Mrs Anne McLean, Roystone Lodge, Chesterfield Road, Matlock Moor, Tansley, Matlock DE4 5LZ
T: (01629) 580456
F: (01629) 580327
E: anne@pwltd.net

TAYNTON
Gloucestershire

Owls Barn ★★★★
Contact: Mrs Barbara Goodwin, Coldcroft Farm, Glasshouse Lane, Taynton, Huntley, Gloucester GL19 3HJ
T: (01452) 831290
F: (01452) 831544
E: goodies@coldcroft.freeserve.co.uk
I: www.coldcroft.freeserve.co.uk

TEAN
Staffordshire

Old School Cottage ★★★
Contact: County Holidays Ref 11351, Spring Mill, Earby, Barnoldswick BB18
T: 08700 723723
I: www.country-holidays.co.uk

The Old Smithy
Rating Applied For
Contact: Mrs Judy Dronzek, Quarry Bank, Hollington, Tean, Stoke-on-Trent ST10 4HQ
T: (01889) 507249

The Rockery ★★★★
Contact: Mrs Rushton, The Rockery, Abbey View Cottage, Quarry Road, Tean, Stoke-on-Trent ST10 4HP
T: (01889) 507434

TELFORD
Shropshire

Church Farm Cottages ★★★
Contact: Mrs Virginia Evans, Church Farm Cottages, Rowton, Wellington, Telford TF6 6QY
T: (01952) 770381
F: (01952) 770381
E: church.farm@bigfoot.com
I: www.virtual-shropshire.co.uk/churchfarm

Old Stables Cottage ★★★
Contact: Mrs Ferriday, 4 Laburnum Drive, Madeley, Telford TF7 5SE
T: (01952) 684238
E: ferriday@madeley6.freeserve.co.uk

7 Pool View ★★★
Contact: Country Holidays Ref 4385, Spring Mill, Earby, Barnoldswick BB18
T: 08700 723723
E: sales@ttgihg.co.uk
I: www.country-holidays.co.uk

Witchwell Cottage ★★★★
Contact: Mrs Carter, Wenboro Cottage, Church Lane, Little Wenlock, Telford TF6 5BB
T: (01952) 505573
E: rcarter@wenboro.freeserve.co.uk
I: www.witchwellcottage.co.uk

TEMPLE GUITING
Gloucestershire

The Furrow ★★★★
Contact: Mrs Valerie Hughes, The Furrow, The Ploughmans Cottage, Temple Guiting, Cheltenham GL54 5RW
T: (01451) 850733
F: (01451) 850733

TEMPLE NORMANTON
Derbyshire

Rocklea Private House ★★★
Contact: Mr & Mrs Roger & Tricia Stirling, 8 Ranworth Road, Bramley, Rotherham S66 2SN
T: (01709) 543108

TENBURY WELLS
Worcestershire

Colleybatch Pine Lodges
★★★★
Contact: Mr R & Mrs E Tebbett, Colleybatch Pine Lodges, Colleybatch, Boraston Bank, Tenbury Wells WR15 8LQ
T: (01584) 810153
F: (01299) 827011

TETBURY
Gloucestershire

Folly Farm Cottages ★★★
Contact: Mr Julian Benton, Folly Farm, Tetbury GL8 8XA
T: (01666) 502475
F: (01666) 502358
E: info@gtb.co.uk
I: www.gtb.co.uk

TETFORD
Lincolnshire

Cornerways & The Garth
★★★★-★★★★★
Contact: Country Holidays Holiday Cottages Group Ltd, Spring Mill, Earby, Barnoldswick BB94 0AA
T: 08700 723723
F: (01282) 841539
E: sales@ttgihg.co.uk
I: www.country-holidays.co.uk

Grange Farm Cottages ★★★
Contact: Mr & Mrs Downes
T: (01507) 534101
F: (01507) 534101

Poachers Hideaway ★★★★
Contact: Mr Andrew Tuxworth, Flintwood Farm, Belchford, Tetford, Horncastle LN9 6QN
T: (01507) 533555
F: (01507) 534264

TETNEY
Lincolnshire

Beech Farm Cottages ★★★★
Contact: Mr & Mrs N L Smith, Beech Farm Cottages, Beech Farm, Station Road, Tetney, Grimsby DN36 5HX
T: (01472) 815935
E: norman@beechfarm.fsworld.co.uk
I: www.beechfarmcottages.co.uk

TEWKESBURY
Gloucestershire

Courtyard Cottages
★★★★-★★★★★
Contact: Mr H W Herford, Upper Court, Kemerton, Tewkesbury GL20 7HY
T: (01386) 725351
F: (01386) 725472
E: diana@uppercourt.co.uk
I: www.uppercourt.co.uk

9 Millbank ★★
Contact: Mr Hunt, 139 Perryfields Road, Bromsgrove B61 8TH
T: (01527) 875384
F: (01527) 875384
E: billhunt139@ic24.net

The Stable Rose Hill Farm
★★★
Contact: Mrs Elizabeth Collinson, The Stable Rose Hill Farm, Stokes Lane, Bushley, Tewkesbury GL20 6HS
T: (01684) 293598

THORPE
Derbyshire

Hawthorn Studio ★★★
Contact: Mrs Suzanne Walton, Hawthorn Cottage, Church Lane, Thorpe, Ashbourne DE6 2AW
T: (01335) 350494

Paxtons Studio ★★★
Contact: Mrs Wilford, Paxtons Studio, Paxtons, Thorpe, Ashbourne DE6 2AW
T: (01335) 350302
F: (01335) 350302
I: www.derbyshire-online.co.uk

THORPE WATERVILLE
Northamptonshire

The Loft ★★★★
Contact: Mrs Sue Goodall, Thorpe Castle House, Thorpe Waterville, Kettering NN14 3ED
T: (01832) 720549
F: (01832) 720549
E: sugoodall@aol.com

TIDESWELL
Derbyshire

Geil Torrs ★★
Contact: Ms Buttle, Geil Torrs, Buxton Road, Tideswell, Buxton SK17 8QJ
T: (01298) 871302

Goldstraws ★★★
Contact: Mr & Mrs D J Sutherland, 2 Curzon Terrace, Litton Mill, Buxton SK17 8SR
T: (01298) 871100
F: (01298) 871641
E: eng@goldstrawshouse.co.uk
I: www.goldstrawshouse.co.uk

Lane End Cottage ★★★★
Contact: Mr John Snowden, 6 Winterbank Close, Sutton in Ashfield NG17 1LS
T: (01623) 557279

Markeygate Cottage & Barn
★★★★
Contact: Mrs Greening-James, Markeygate Cottage & Barn, Markeygate House, Bank Square, Tideswell, Buxton SK17 8NT
T: (01298) 871260
E: markeygatehouse@hotmail.com
I: www.lineone.net/~markeygate.co.uk

The Nook ★★★★
Contact: Peak Cottages, Strawberry Lee Lane, Totley Bents, Sheffield S17 3BA
T: (0114) 262 0777
F: (0114) 262 0666
E: enquiries@peakcottages.com
I: www.peakcottage.com

Stanley Barn ★★★
Contact: Ms Jean Hopkin, Stanley Barn, Stanley House, Sherwood Road, Tideswell, Buxton SK17 8HJ
T: (01298) 872327
E: jeanhopkin@aol.com

TODENHAM
Gloucestershire

Applegate ★★★★
Contact: Mrs Crump, Applegate, The Retreat, Springbank, Moreton-in-Marsh GL56 9PA
T: (01608) 651307

TREFONEN
Shropshire

Little Barn ★★★★
Contact: Mrs Sue Batley, Wulfruna Cottage, Old Post Office Lane, Trefonen, Oswestry SY10 9DL
T: (01691) 653387
E: info@little-barn.co.uk
I: www.little-barn.co.uk

TRUMPET
Herefordshire

The Trumpet Inn ★★★
Contact: Mr Riga, The Trumpet Inn, Trumpet, Ledbury HR8 2RA
T: (01531) 670277
F: (01531) 670277
I: www.trumpetinn.com

TUFFLEY
Gloucestershire

The Bungalow ★★
Contact: Mr & Mrs Witham, 42 Holmwood Drive, Tuffley, Gloucester GL4 0PP
T: (01452) 500826
F: (01452) 500826
E: kenwitham@msn.com

TWO DALES
Derbyshire

Darwin Forest Country Park ★★★-★★★★
Contact: Mr Ian Grant, Pinelodge Holidays Ltd, Riverside Works, Bakewell DE45 1GS
T: (01629) 814481
F: (01629) 814634
E: igrant@pinelog.co.uk

Piggery ★★★
Contact: Mr Colin MacQueen, Peak Cottages, Strawberry Lee Lane, Totley Bents, Sheffield S17 3BA
T: (0114) 262 0777
F: (0114) 262 0666
E: enquiries@peakcottages.com
I: www.peakcottages.com

UFTON
Warwickshire

Wood Farm ★★★★
Contact: Mr Derek Hiatt, Wood Farm, Ufton, Leamington Spa CV33 9PH
T: (01926) 612270

ULEY
Gloucestershire

Blacknest Cottage ★★★★
Contact: Mr Grindley, Blacknest Cottage, Owlpen, Uley, Dursley GL11 5BZ
T: (01453) 860034
F: (01453) 860034
I: www.blacknestcottage.co.uk

Coopers Cottage ★★★★
Contact: Mrs Griffiths, 48 Orchard Leaze, Cam, Dursley GL11 6HX
T: (01453) 542861

Hydehill ★★★
Contact: Sales Country Holidays Ref 14663 Sping Mill, Stoney Bank Road, Earby, Barnoldswick BB18
T: 08700 723723
E: sales@ttgihg.co.uk
I: www.country-holidays.co.uk

UPPER HULME
Staffordshire

Hurdlow Cottage ★★★★
Contact: Mrs Belfield, Hurdlow Cottage, Hurdlow Farm, Upper Hulme, Leek ST13 8TX
T: (01538) 300406
F: (01538) 300406
E: robertruth@hurdlowfarm.fsnet.co.uk
I: www.peakcottages.com

Little Ramshaw
Rating Applied For
Contact: Peak Cottages, Strawberry Lee Lane, Totley Bents, Totley Rise, Sheffield S17 3BA
T: (0114) 262 0777
F: (0114) 262 0666
E: enquiries@peakcottages.com
I: www.peakcottages.com

The Old Chapel
Rating Applied For
Contact: Mr Paul Hancock, The Old Schoolhouse, Schoolgreen, Ipstones, Stoke-on-Trent ST10 2LX
T: (01538) 266977
E: paul.cathie@virgin.net

Paddock Farm Holiday Cottages ★★★★
Contact: Mr & Mrs M Barlow, Paddock Farm, Upper Hulme, Leek ST13 8TY
T: (01538) 300345

UPPER QUINTON
Warwickshire

Gable Cottage ★★★★
Contact: Ms Angela Richards, Manor Cottages, 33 Priory Lane, Burford, Oxford OX18 4SG
T: (01993) 824252
F: (01993) 824443
E: mancott@netcomuk.co.uk

1 Meon View ★★★★
Contact: Mrs A Rimell, 1 Meon View, Taylors Lane, Upper Quinton, Stratford-upon-Avon CV37 8LG
T: (01789) 720080

Winton House Cottage ★★★★
Contact: Mrs Lyon, Winton House Cottage, The Green, Upper Quinton, Stratford-upon-Avon CV37 8SX
T: (01789) 720500
E: gail@wintonhouse.com
I: www.wintonhouse.com

UPPER SLAUGHTER
Gloucestershire

Home Farm Stable ★★★★★
Contact: Mrs Bayetto, Home Farm Stable, Home Farmhouse, Upper Slaughter, Cheltenham GL54 2JF
T: (01451) 820487
F: (01451) 820487
E: maureen.bayetto@virgin.net
I: www.home-farm-stable.co.uk

UPPINGHAM
Rutland

4 Stockerston Road ★★★
Contact: Mr & Mrs Lloyd, 4 Stockerston Road, Uppingham, Oakham LE15 9UD
T: (01572) 823478
F: (01572) 823955

UPTON ST LEONARDS
Gloucestershire

Hill Farm Cottages ★★
Contact: Mrs M McLellan, Hill Farm Cottages, Hill Farm, Upton Hill, Upton St Leonards, Gloucester GL4 8DA
T: (01452) 614081

UPTON-UPON-SEVERN
Worcestershire

Captain's Retreat ★★★★
Contact: Mr M Cranton, White Cottage, Church End, Hanley Castle, Worcester WR8 0BL
T: (01684) 592023
F: (01684) 592023
E: michael@cranton.freeserve.co.uk

UPTON WARREN
Worcestershire

The Durrance ★★★★
Contact: Mrs Helen Hirons, The Durrance, Berry Lane, Upton Warren, Bromsgrove B61 9EL
T: (01562) 777533
F: (01562) 777533
E: helenhirons@thedurrance.fsnet.co.uk
I: www.hedurrance.co.uk

UTTOXETER
Staffordshire

Chestnut Cottage ★★★
Contact: Mrs Susan Tania Sketchley, Chestnut Cottage, Marston Bank, Marston Montgomery, Uttoxeter ST14 5BT
T: (01889) 590736
F: (01889) 590736

VINEY HILL
Gloucestershire

Lower Viney Farm Cottage ★★★★
Contact: Ms Carole Youngs, North Lodge, Church Road, Clearwell, Coleford GL16 8LG
T: (01594) 564600
F: (01594) 564656
E: carole@synapse-ar.co.uk

VOWCHURCH
Herefordshire

The Dingle
Rating Applied For
Contact: Mrs Ruth Watkins, Upper Gilvach Farm, St Margarets, Vowchurch, Hereford HR2 0QY
T: (01981) 510618
E: ruth@uppergilvach.freeserve.co.uk

The Front Dore ★★★
Contact: Mrs M Layton, The Front Dore, Ponty Pinna Farm, Vowchurch, Hereford HR2 0QE
T: (01981) 550266

WADDINGWORTH
Lincolnshire

Redhouse Cottage ★★★★
Contact: Mr & Mrs A Pritchard, Redhouse Farm, Waddingworth, Woodhall Spa LN10 5EE
T: (01507) 578285
F: (01507) 578285

WARMINGTON
Northamptonshire

Papley Farm Cottages ★★★★
Contact: Mrs Joyce Lane, Slade House, Papley Farm, Warmington, Peterborough PE8 6UU
T: (01832) 272583
F: (01832) 272583

WARSLOW
Staffordshire

Shay Side Barn and Cottage ★★★★
Contact: Mr Sykes, Sykes Cottage, York House, York Street, Chester CH1 3LR
T: (01244) 345700
F: (01244) 321442
E: info@sykescottages.co.uk
I: www.sykescottages.co.uk

WARWICK
Warwickshire

Copes Flat ★★★
Contact: Mrs E Draisey, Forth House, 44 High Street, Warwick CV34 4AX
T: (01926) 401512
F: (01926) 490809
E: info@forthhouseuk.co.uk
I: www.forthhouseuk.co.uk

Whitley Elm Cottages ★★★★
Contact: Mr & Mrs Clive & Pat Bevins, Whitley Elm Cottages, Case Lane, Mousley End, Rowington, Warwick CV35 7JE
T: (01926) 484577
F: (01926) 484577
E: clive.bevins@btclick.com
I: www.cottagesdirect.com/whitleyelm/

WATERHOUSES
Staffordshire

Broadhurst Farm ★★★★
Contact: Mr R Clowes, Broadhurst Farm, Waterhouses, Stoke-on-Trent ST10 3LQ
T: (01538) 308261
E: enquiries@broadhurstfarm.com
I: www.broadhurstfarm.com

Greenside and Greenside Cottage ★★★-★★★★
Contact: Mr Sykes, Sykes Cottage, York House, York Street, Chester CH1 3LR
T: (01244) 345700
F: (01244) 321442
E: info@sykescottages.co.uk
I: www.sykescottages.co.uk

Limestone View Cottage ★★★
Contact: Mrs Wendy Webster, Limestone View Farm, Stoney Lane, Cauldon, Waterhouses, Stoke-on-Trent ST10 3EP
T: (01538) 308288
E: wendywebster@limestoneviewfarm.freeserve.co.uk
I: www.peakdistrictfarmhols.co.uk

WELFORD-ON-AVON
Warwickshire

The Granary ★★★★
Contact: Mr & Mrs Spink, The Granary, Rumer Hall Cottage, Welford-on-Avon, Stratford-upon-Avon CV37 8AF
T: (01789) 750752
F: (01789) 750752
E: bruce_spink@btopenworld.com

Peacock Thatch ★★★★
Contact: Mr Peter Holden, The Little Cottage, 3 Siddals Lane, Allestree, Derby DE22 2DY
T: (01332) 551155
F: (01332) 551155
E: peterpeacockthatch@dmserve.com

WELLAND
Worcestershire

Mutlows Farm Cottages ★★★★
Contact: Mrs Price, Mutlows Farm Cottages, Drake Street, Welland, Malvern WR13 6LP
T: (01684) 310552
E: mavepice@hotmail.com

WELLESBOURNE
Warwickshire

Walton Hall ★★★
Contact: Mrs Jane Gulliver, Walton Hall, Walton, Wellesbourne, Warwick CV35 9HU
T: (01789) 842424
F: (01789) 470418
E: reservations@waltonhall.com
I: www.waltonhall.co.uk/waltonhall

WELLINGTON
Shropshire

The Coach House ★★★★
Contact: Mrs M M Fellows, Old Vicarage, Wrockwardine, Wellington, Telford TF6 5DG
T: (01952) 244859
F: (01952) 255066
E: mue@mfellows@freeserve.co.uk

WELLOW
Nottinghamshire

Foliat Cottages ★★★
Contact: Mr & Mrs Carr, Jordan Castle Farm, Wellow, Newark NG22 0EL
T: (01623) 861088
F: (01623) 861088
E: janet.carr@farmline.com
I: www.sherwoodforestholidaycottages.com

The White House and Studio ★★★
Contact: Mrs Angela Holding, Rose Cottage, Maypole Green, Wellow, Newark NG22 0FE
T: (01623) 835798
E: alan.holding@btinternet.com
I: www.whitehouse@wellow.co.uk

WELTON
Lincolnshire

Mill Cottage ★★★★
Contact: Mrs G E Gladwin, Mill House, Mill Lane, Welton, Lincoln LN2 3PB
T: (01673) 860082
F: (01673) 863424
E: gill@millhousecottage.freeserve.co.uk

WEM
Shropshire

Soulton Hall Cottages ★★★
Contact: Mrs A P Ashton, Soulton Hall Cottages, Soulton Hall, Wem, Shrewsbury SY4 5RS
T: (01939) 232786
F: (01939) 234097
E: jiashton@soultonhall.fsbusiness.co.uk

WENSLEY
Derbyshire

Ivy Cottage ★★★
Contact: Mr Sykes, Sykes Cottage, York House, York Street, Chester CH1 3LR
T: (01244) 345700
F: (01244) 321442
E: info@sykescottages.co.uk
I: www.sykescottages.co.uk

Yew Tree Cottage ★★★
Contact: Mr C MacQueen, Peak Cottages, Strawberry Lee Lane, Totley Bents, Sheffield S17 3BA
T: (0114) 262 0777
F: (0114) 262 0666
E: enquiries@peakcottages.com
I: www.peakcottages.com

WESSINGTON
Derbyshire

Dell Farm ★★★
Contact: Mr & Mrs T Anthony, Dell Farm, Wessington, Alfreton DE55 6DU
T: (01773) 832889
F: (01773) 832889

WEST FELTON
Shropshire

The Stables ★★★★
Contact: Mr & Mrs Edward & Kirsten Nicholas, The Stables, Sutton Farm, West Felton, Oswestry SY11 4HX
T: (01691) 610230
E: edwardnicholas@freeuk.com

WESTBURY
Shropshire

Garden Cottage ★★★
Contact: Mrs Halliday, Garden Cottage, Whitton Hall, Westbury, Shrewsbury SY5 9RD
T: (01743) 884270
F: (01743) 884158
E: whittonhall@farmersweekly.net
I: www.shropshiretourism.com

WESTBURY-ON-SEVERN
Gloucestershire

Gatwick Cottage ★★
Contact: Mrs Andrews, Rock Farm, Rock Lane, Westbury-on-Severn GL14 1QJ
T: (01452) 760210

WESTON-ON-AVON
Warwickshire

March Font, Hurnberry, Brickall & The Arbales★★★★
Contact: Mr & Mrs Richard Bluck, Weston Farm, Weston-on-Avon, Stratford-upon-Avon CV37 8JY
T: (01789) 750688
E: r.bluckwestonfarm@amserve.net

WESTON RHYN
Shropshire

Mill Cottage ★★★
Contact: Mr & Mrs H Brannick, Mill Cottage, Mill House, The Wern, Weston Rhyn, Oswestry SY10 7ER
T: (01691) 659738

WESTON SUBEDGE
Gloucestershire

Buff's Cottage ★★★★
Contact: Mrs Nelson, The Old Baptist Manse, Sheep Street, Stow-on-the-Wold, Cheltenham GL54 1AA
T: (01451) 870813
E: caroline.nelson@virgin.net

WESTON UNDERWOOD
Derbyshire

Brook Cottage & Honeysuckle Cottage★★★-★★★★
Contact: Mrs Linda Adams, Parkview Farm, Weston Underwood, Ashbourne DE6 4PA
T: (01335) 360352
F: (01335) 360352
E: enquiries@parkviewfarm.co.uk
I: parkviewfarm.co.uk

WETTON
Staffordshire

Manor Barn ★★★
Contact: Mr & Mrs Higton, Manor Barn, Manor House Farm, Wetton, Ashbourne DE6 2AF
T: (01335) 310223
I: www.peakcottages.com

Old Sunday School ★★★★
Contact: Peak Cottages, Strawberry Lee Lane, Totley Bents, Sheffield S17 3BA
T: (0114) 262 0777
F: (0114) 262 0666
E: enquiries@peakcottages.com
I: www.peakcottages.com

Stable Barn ★★★
Contact: Mrs Higton, The Old Post Office, Thorpe, Ashbourne DE6 2AP
T: (01335) 310312

Wetton Barns ★★★★-★★★★★
Contact: Mrs F Reason, Wetton Barns Holiday Cottages, Wensley, Matlock DE451PJ
T: (01246) 565379
F: (01246) 583464
E: wettonbarns@chatsworth.org

WHALEY BRIDGE
Derbyshire

Cloud Cottage and Nimbus House ★★★★
Contact: Country Holidays - 9405 Sales, Country Holidays, Spring Mill, Earby, Barnoldswick BB94 0AA
T: 08700 723723
F: (01282) 844288
E: sales@ttgihg.co.uk
I: www.country-holidays.co.uk

Cote Bank Cottages ★★★★
Contact: Mrs Pamela Broadhurst, Cote Bank Cottages, Buxworth, Whaley Bridge, High Peak SK23 7NP
T: (01663) 750566
F: (01663) 750566
E: cotebank@btinternet.com
I: www.peakdistrictfamhols.co.uk

WHATELEY
Staffordshire

33 Rosemary Cottage ★★★
Contact: Mrs Voilet Coles, 31 Old Forge Cottage, Whateley, Tamworth B78 2ET
T: (01827) 280826

WHATSTANDWELL
Derbyshire

Smithy Forge Cottages ★★★
Contact: Mr Chris Buxton, End Cottage, 32 Station Road, Denby, Ripley DE5 8ND
T: (01332) 881758
F: (01332) 780232
E: chris@smithyforgecottages.co.uk
I: www.smithyforgecottage.co.uk

WHICHFORD
Warwickshire

Hillside Cottage ★★★★
Contact: Mrs Janet Haines, Ascott House Farm, Whichford, Shipston-on-Stour CV36 5PP
T: (01608) 684655
F: (01608) 684539
E: djhaines@ascott6.fsnet.co.uk
I: www.smoothhound.co.uk/hotels/ascottho.html

The Hops & The Vines ★★★★
Contact: Mrs C Garner, The Hops & The Vines, The Norman Knight, Whichford, Shipston-on-Stour CV36 5PE
T: (01608) 684621
F: (01608) 684621
E: carole@thenormanknight.co.uk
I: www.thenormanknight.co.uk

Horseshoe Cottage ★★★
Contact: Mrs S Gore, Holly Cottage, The Green, Whichford, Shipston-on-Stour CV36 5PE
T: (01608) 684310
F: (01608) 684310
E: suevaudin@community.co.uk

WHITBOURNE
Herefordshire

Crumplebury Farmhouse ★★★
Contact: Mrs A Evans, Dial House, Whitbourne, Worcester WR6 5SG
T: (01886) 821534
F: (01886) 821534
E: a.evans@candaevans.fsnet.co.uk

Establishments printed in blue have a detailed entry in this guide

Elcocks Cottage ★★★
Contact: Mr Mike Hogg, 61 Pereira Road, Harborne, Birmingham B17 9JB
T: (0121) 427 1395
E: mikehogguk@aol.com

The Olde Rectory ★★★★-★★★★★
Contact: Mr & Mrs Cliff and Gilly Poultney, The Olde Rectory, Boat Lane, Whitbourne, Worcester WR6 5RS
T: (01886) 822000
F: (01886) 822100
E: stay@olde-rectory.co.uk
I: www.olde-rectory.co.uk

Stone House ★★★★★
Contact: Mr Patrick Priest, High Lea, Whitbourne, Worcester WR6 5SP
T: (01886) 821648

WHITCHURCH
Shropshire

Combermere Abbey Cottages ★★★★★
Contact: Mrs Fiona Grundy, Combermere Abbey Cottages, Whitchurch SY13 4AJ
T: (01948) 662876
F: (01948) 660920
E: cottages@combermereabbey.co.uk
I: www.combermereabbey.co.uk

The Granary ★★★
Contact: Mrs Maggie White, The Granary, The Old Rectory, Calverhall, Whitchurch SY13 4PE
T: (01948) 890696

Holiday Cottage ★★★★
Contact: Mr & Mrs Wright, Holiday Cottage, The Park, Tilstock, Whitchurch SY13 3NL
T: (01948) 880669
F: (01948) 880669

WHITECROFT
Gloucestershire

The Sidings ★★★
Contact: Mrs V Long, Fiddlers Green, Mitchel Troy Common, Monmouth NP25 4JQ
T: (01600) 714464
F: (01600) 714464
E: glong4464@aol.com

WHITMINSTER
Gloucestershire

The Stable ★★★
Contact: Mr & Mrs A Beeby
T: (01452) 740969
E: beebyac@onet.co.uk
I: homepage.ntlworld.com/beebyac

WHITTINGTON MOOR
Derbyshire

20 Sanforth Street ★★★
Contact: Mr & Mrs B Armstrong, Holmedene, Ashford Road, Bakewell DE45 1GL
T: (01629) 813448
E: bernard-armstrong@lineone.net

WHITTLEBURY
Northamptonshire

Dolly's Cottage ★★
Contact: Mrs Clapp, 6 High Street, Whittlebury, Towcester NN12 8XJ
T: (01327) 857896
F: (01327) 857896
E: patcandalan@tesco.net

WILLERSEY
Gloucestershire

3 Cheltenham Cottages ★★
Contact: Mrs G Malin, 28 Bibsworth Avenue, Broadway WR12 7BQ
T: (01386) 853248
F: (01386) 853181
E: g.malin@virgin.net

Rex Cottage ★★
Contact: Mrs Baldwin, Rex House, Willersey, Broadway WR12 7PJ
T: (01386) 852365

WILLOUGHBY
Warwickshire

The Saddlery ★★★★★
Contact: Mrs E Heckford, Manor Farm, Brooks Close, Willoughby, Rugby CV23 8BY
T: (01788) 890256
E: office@thesaddlery.org.uk
I: thesaddlery.org.uk

WILMCOTE
Warwickshire

Apple Loft ★★★★
Contact: Mrs Margaret Mander, Peartree Cottage, 5 Church Road, Wilmote, Pathlow, Stratford-upon-Avon CV37 9UX
T: (01789) 205889
F: (01789) 262862
E: peartree3@hotmail.com

WILTON
Herefordshire

Benhall Farm ★★★
Contact: Mrs Carol Brewer, Benhall Farm, Wilton, Ross-on-Wye HR9 6AG
T: (01989) 563900
I: carol_m_brewer@hotmail.com

WINCHCOMBE
Gloucestershire

Briar Cottage ★★★★
Contact: Mrs Parker, The Olde Bakehouse, Castle Street, Winchcombe, Cheltenham GL54 5JA
T: (01242) 602441
F: (01242) 602441
E: deniseparker@onetel-net.uk

Cockbury Court Cottages ★★★★
Contact: Mr & Mrs J Charlton, Cotswold Cottages Limited, Rowan Lodge, Neata Farm, Greet, Cheltenham GL54 5BL
T: (01242) 604806
F: (01242) 604806
E: john@rowan-lodge.demon.co.uk
I: www.cotswoldcottagesltd.co.uk/bookings

Dunbar Cottage ★★★
Contact: Ms Linda Andrews, 73 Gloucester Street, Winchcombe, Cheltenham GL54 5LX
T: (01242) 604946

Muir Cottage ★★★★
Contact: Mr Mark Grassick, Postlip Estate Co, Muir Cottage, Postlip, Winchcombe, Cheltenham GL54 5AQ
T: (01242) 603124
F: (01242) 603602
E: enquiries@thecotswoldretreat.co.uk

The Old Stables ★★★
Contact: Miss Jane Eayrs, The Old Stables, Hill View, Farmcote, Winchcombe, Cheltenham GL54 5AU
T: (01242) 603860
F: (01242) 603860

Orchard Cottage ★★★
Contact: Mrs S M Rolt, Orchard Cottage, Stanley Pontlarge, Winchcombe, Cheltenham GL54 5HD
T: (01242) 602594
E: cottages@rolt99.freeserve.co.uk
I: www.cottageguide.co.uk/orchard-cottage

Styche Cottage ★★★★
Contact: Mrs Anne Bayston, 276A Myton Road, Warwick CV34 6PT
T: (01926) 831508
E: stychecottage@bayston.f9.co.uk
I: styche-cottage.co.uk

Sudeley Castle Country Cottages ★★★
Contact: Mrs Olive Byng, Sudeley Castle Country Cottages, Castle Street, Winchcombe, Cheltenham GL54 5JA
T: (01242) 604181
F: (01242) 604181
E: olive.byng@sudeley.org.uk

Traditional Accommodation ★★★★-★★★★★
Contact: Mr & Mrs Wilson, 60 Pershore Road, Evesham WR11 2PQ
T: (01386) 446269
F: (01386) 446269
E: trad.accom@virgin.net
I: http://freespace.virgin.net/trad.accom

WINDLEY
Derbyshire

The Old Cheese Factory ★★★★★
Contact: Mrs Sally Wallwork, Windley Hall, Windley, Belper DE56 2LP
T: (01773) 550947
F: (01773) 550944
E: sawallwork@aol.com

WINKHILL
Staffordshire

Alma Cottage ★★★★
Contact: Mrs Diana Cope, Alma Cottage, Little Paradise Farm, Blackbrook, Winkhill, Leek ST13 7QR
T: (01538) 308909
F: (01538) 308910

WINSTER
Derbyshire

Blakelow Farm Holiday Cottages Rating Applied For
Contact: Mr Stephen Ogan, Blakelow Farm Holiday Cottages, Blakelow Farm, Bonsall Lane, Winster, Matlock DE4 2PD
T: (01629) 650814
F: (01629) 650814
E: blakelowfarm@breathe.com

Briar Cottage ★★★★
Contact: Mrs Anne Walters, Briar Cottage, Heathcote House, Main Street, Winster, Matlock DE4 2DJ
T: (01629) 650342

Gingerbread Cottage ★★★★
Contact: Mrs Jill Wild, Gingerbread Cottage, September Cottage, East Bank, Winster, Matlock DE4 2DT
T: (01629) 650071
E: wildgray@hotmail.com
I: www.wildgray.fsnet.co.uk

The Headlands Fold ★★★
Contact: Mrs Janet Shiers, The Headlands Fold, The Headlands, East Bank, Winster, Matlock DE4 2DS
T: (01629) 650523
E: cottage@familyshier.org.uk
I: www.familyshier.org.uk

Jasmine Cottage ★★★★
Contact: Ms Ann Banister, Clough Vista, West Bank, Winster, Matlock DE4 2DQ
T: (01629) 650096
I: www.winster-cottages.co.uk

WIRKSWORTH
Derbyshire

Hillside Cottage ★★★
Contact: Mrs A Simons, 4 Tippendell Lane, Chiswell Green, St Albans AL2 3HL
T: (01727) 852684

Hog Cottage ★★★★
Contact: Ms Anna Fern, Blue Lagoon, 46 London Road, Alderley Edge SK9 7DZ
T: (01625) 583107
F: (01625) 890001
E: hogcottage@bluelagoon.co.uk
I: www.bluelagoon.co.uk

Hopton Estates ★★★★-★★★★★
Contact: Mr & Mrs Bill & Eddy Brogden, Hopton Estates, Hopton Hall, Hopton, Wirksworth, Derby DE4 4DF
T: (01629) 540458
F: (01629) 540712
E: h.e@saqnet.co.uk
I: www.hoptonhall.co.uk

Snuffless Dip ★★★
Contact: Mrs Margaret Doxey, Chandlers, West End, Wirksworth, Derby DE4 4EG
T: (01629) 824466

Weathericks & Bradstone ★★★★
Contact: Mr MacQueen, Peak Cottages, Strawberry Lee Lane, Totley Bents, Totley Rise, Sheffield S17 3BA
T: (0114) 262 0777
F: (0114) 262 0666
E: enquiries@peakcottages.com
I: www.peakcottages.com

WITCOMBE
Gloucestershire

Witcombe Park Holiday Cottages ★★★
Contact: Mrs Hicks-Beach, Great Witcombe, Gloucester GL3 4TR
T: (01452) 863591
F: (01452) 863591

WITHERN
Lincolnshire

Park Farm Holidays
Rating Applied For
Contact: Mrs E H Burkitt, Aby Road, Withern, Alford LN13 0DF
T: (01507) 450331
F: (01507) 450331
E: alan@park-farm25.fsnet.co.uk

WITHINGTON
Gloucestershire

Ballingers Farmhouse Cottages ★★★★
Contact: Mrs Judith Pollard, Ballingers Farmhouse, Withington, Cheltenham GL54 4BB
T: (01242) 890335
E: pollardfam@compuserve.com
I: www.smoothhound.co.uk/hotels/ball.html

WOODHALL SPA
Lincolnshire

Cuckoo Land ★★★
Contact: Mr & Mrs Coates, 16 The Broadway, Woodhall Spa LN10 6ST
T: (01526) 353336
E: cuckoo.land@ic24.net

Merrimoles ★★★
Contact: Mrs Margot Mills, The Vale, 50 Tor-o-Moor Road, Woodhall Spa LN10 6SB
T: (01526) 353022
E: thevale@amserve.net

Mill Lane Cottage ★★
Contact: Mr & Mrs I G Williamson, 72 Mill Lane, Woodhall Spa LN10 6QZ
T: (01526) 353101
E: will@williamsoni.freeserve.co.uk
I: www.skegness.net/woodhallspa.htm

Old Forge Cottage ★★★★
Contact: Mr David Mawer, 47 Witham Road, Woodhall Spa LN10 6RG
T: (01526) 353813
F: (01526) 353996
E: tanyamawer@hotmail.com

WOODMANCOTE
Gloucestershire

25 Chapel Lane Lanes End ★★★★
Contact: Mrs Deirdre Taylor, 23 Chapel Lane, Woodmancote, Cheltenham GL52 9HT
T: (01242) 676685
E: taylor@danskin80.fsnet.co.uk
I: www.danskin80.fsnet.co.uk

WORCESTER
Worcestershire

College Street Apartments ★★★★
Contact: Mr & Mrs A Manning, Malvern View, Broad Green, Worcester WR6 5NW
T: (01886) 822114
E: info@primaproperties.co.uk
I: www.primaproperties.co.uk

Honeysuckle Cottages ★★★
Contact: Mr R J Gilchrist, 32 Barbourne Road, Knights Rest, Worcester WR1 1HU
T: (01905) 24257
F: (01905) 26202

Little Lightwood Farm ★★★
Contact: Mrs V A Rogers, Little Lightwood Farm, Lightwood Lane, Cotheridge, Worcester WR6 5LT
T: (01905) 333236
F: (01905) 333236
E: lightwood.holidays@virgin.net

Maybury & Malvern View ★★★
Contact: Mr & Mrs Houghton, Upper Lightwood Farm, Lower Broadheath, Cotheridge, Worcester WR2 6RL
T: (01905) 333202
E: jph6@hotmail.com

Mill Cottage ★★★★
Contact: Mrs Valerie Baylis, Mill Cottage, Mildenham Mill, Egg Lane, Claines, Worcester WR3 7SA
T: (01905) 451554

Peter Jackson Apartments ★★★★
Contact: Mr & Mrs Peter & Marilyn Jackson, 1 Birchwood, Peachley Lane, Worcester WR2 6QR
T: (01905) 25822
I: www.peterjacksonapartments.com

Stildon Manor Cottage ★★★★
Contact: Mr & Mrs Wilding-Davies, Stildon Manor, Menith Wood, Worcester WR6 6UL
T: (01299) 832720
F: (01299) 832720

WORMELOW
Herefordshire

Old Forge Cottage ★★★
Contact: Mrs Shirley Wheeler, Forge Cottage, Lyston Smithy, Wormelow, Hereford HR2 8EL
T: (01981) 540625

WOTTON-UNDER-EDGE
Gloucestershire

The Burrow ★★★
Contact: Blakes Ref B5831 Spring Mill, Earby, Barnoldswick BB18
T: 08700 708090
E: sales@ttgihg.co.uk
I: www.blakes-cottages.co.uk

Hill Mill Cottage ★★★★
Contact: Mrs Nash, Hill Mill Cottage, Hill Mill House, Ozleworth, Wotton-under-Edge GL12 7QR
T: (01453) 842401
F: (01453) 842401
E: pnash@hillmillcottage.co.uk
I: www.hillmillcottage.co.uk

WYRE PIDDLE
Worcestershire

Peaceavon ★★★★
Contact: Mr & Mrs Price, 15 The Paddock, Newbold Verdon, Leicester LE9 9NW
T: (01455) 821723
E: pricenr@aol.com

WYTHALL
Worcestershire

Inkford Court Cottages ★★★-★★★★
Contact: Mr J S Bedford, Inkford Court Cottages, Alcester Road, Wythall, Birmingham B47 6DL
T: (01564) 822304
F: (01564) 829618

YARDLEY GOBION
Northamptonshire

The Stable ★★
Contact: Mr Alan Paine, The Stable, Old Wharf Farm, The Wharf, Yardley Gobion, Towcester NN12 7UE
T: (01908) 542293
F: (01908) 542293

YOULGREAVE
Derbyshire

Appletree Cottage ★★★
Contact: Mr C MacQueen, Peak Cottages, Strawberry Lee Lane, Totley Bents, Sheffield S17 3BA
T: (0114) 262 0777
F: (0114) 262 0666

April Cottage ★★★
Contact: Mrs Avril Naybour, April Cottage, Church Street, Youlgreave, Bakewell DE45 1WL
T: (01629) 636151
F: (01629) 636151
E: anaybour@talk21.com
I: www.cottageguide.co.uk/aprilcottage

The Cottage ★★★
Contact: Mr & Mrs John & Carol Sutcliffe, The Old School Hall House, Main Street, Youlgrave, Youlgreave, Bakewell DE45 1UW
T: (01629) 636570
E: carolandjohn@coalmoor.fsnet.co.uk

Easter Cottage ★★★
Contact: Country Holidays - 13178 Sales, Holiday Cottages Group Limited, Spring Mill, Earby, Barnoldswick BB94 0AA
T: 08700 723723
F: (01282) 844288
E: sales@ttgihg.co.uk
I: www.country-holidays.co.uk

Hope Cottage ★★★
Contact: Mrs Rachel McQueen, 1 Broad Meadows, Alport, Youlgreave, Bakewell DE45 1LH
T: (01629) 636812
F: (01629) 815783
E: info@peakparkcottages.com
I: www.peakparkcottages.com

The Old Dairy & Buttermilk Cottage ★★★
Contact: Mrs P Twose, Manor Cottage, Healaugh Manor Farm, Wighill Lane, Tadcaster LS24 8HG
T: 07798 830467
I: www.peakcottages.com

Rose Cottages ★★★★
Contact: Mr & Mrs John & Carol Upton, Rose Cottages, Copper Pot, Conksbury Lane, Youlgreave, Bakewell DE45 1WR
T: (01629) 636487
E: enquiries@rosecottages.co.uk
I: www.rosecottages.co.uk

Sunnyside ★★★
Contact: Ms J Steed, Falkland House, 10 New Road, Youlgreave, Bakewell DE45 1WP
T: (01629) 636195

Tempus Cottage ★★★
Contact: Mr & Mrs A Thornelow, Tempus Cottage, 67 Ingle Road, Chatham ME4 5SD
T: (01634) 401479

Thimble Cottage ★★★
Contact: Mr Colin MacQueen, Peak Cottages, Strawberry Lee Lane, Totley Bents, Sheffield S17 3BA
T: (0114) 262 0777
F: (0114) 262 0666
E: enquiries@peakcottages.com
I: www.peakcottages.com

Thyme Cottage ★★★★
Contact: Mrs MacDonald, Hardanger, Main Street, Youlgreave, Bakewell DE45 1UW
T: (01629) 636472
F: (01629) 636472
E: lm@maccolour.co.uk

EAST OF ENGLAND

ACLE
Norfolk

Station Cottage ★★★★
Contact: Mr David Harris, Station Cottage, Station Road, Acle, Norwich NR13 3BZ
T: (01493) 751136
F: (01493) 752930
E: broadsman@lineone.net
I: www.oas.co.uk/ukcottages/station

ALDBOROUGH
Norfolk

Waverley ★★★
Contact: Mrs Margery Skipper, Doctor's Corner, Aldborough, Norwich NR11 7NR
T: (01263) 761512

ALDBURY
Hertfordshire

Aldbury Cottage
Rating Applied For
Contact: Mrs Pamela Dickens, Toms Hill Road, Aldbury, Tring HP23 5SA
T: (01442) 851277
F: (01442) 851125
E: pam@dickens1.com

ALDEBURGH
Suffolk

Aldeburgh Court House & Aldeburgh Court Studio
★★★-★★★★
Contact: Mrs Susie Hayward, Poplar Farm Barn, Sweffling, Saxmundham IP17 2BW
T: (01728) 664014

29 Aldeburgh Lodge ★★★
Contact: Ms Francoise Cresson, Eastridge Nr Leiston, Eastbridge, Leiston IP16 4SG
T: (01728) 830499

Amber Cottage ★★★
Contact: Mr Roger Williams
T: (01359) 270444
F: (01359) 271226
E: roger.williams43@virgin.net
I: www.cottageguide.co.uk/ambercottage

Avon Cottage
Rating Applied For
Contact: Suffolk Secrets, 7 Frenze Road, Diss IP22 4PA
T: (01379) 651297
F: (01379) 641555
E: holidays@suffolk-secrets.co.uk

Braid House ★★★
Contact: Miss Ying Tan, Sweffling, Rendham, Saxmundham IP17 2BU
T: (01728) 663432
F: (01728) 663532
E: tanying4488@aol.com

Bramcote ★★★
Contact: Mrs Diana Biddlecombe, 1 Barley Lands, Aldeburgh IP15 5LW
T: 07817 724643

8 Coastguard Court ★★★
Contact: Mr & Mrs John Mauger, Redisham, Beccles NR34 8LU
T: (01502) 575896
F: (01502) 575896
E: john.mauger@blythweb.net
I: www.blythweb.co.uk/coastguard-court

Cosy Corner ★★★
Contact: Mrs Fryer, Cosy Corner, 41 Mariners Way, Aldeburgh IP15 5QH
T: (01728) 453121

The Cottage ★★★
Contact: Mrs Alexander, Old Church Road, Ufford, Woodbridge IP13 6DH
T: (01394) 383822

21 Crag Path ★★★
Contact: Ms Lisabeth Hoad, Aldeburgh IP15 5BY
T: (01728) 453933

Cragside ★★★★
Contact: Mrs L Valentine, Rookery Farm, Cratfield, Halesworth IP19 0QE
T: (01986) 798609
F: (01986) 798609
E: j.r.valentine@btinternet.com

Dial Flat ★
Contact: Mrs Pam Harrison, 5 Dial Lane, Aldeburgh IP15 5AG
T: (01728) 453212
E: pam@harpd.freeserve.co.uk

The Dutch House Flat ★★★
Contact: Mr Christopher Bacon, Dodnash Priory Farm, Bentley, Ipswich IP9 2DF
T: (01473) 310682
F: (01473) 311131
E: cbacon@freeuk.com

Fig Tree ★★★
Contact: Mr & Mrs Martin Jinks, 94 Leiston Road, Aldeburgh IP15 5PX
T: (01728) 453037
E: martin@jinsky.fsnet.co.uk

Hall Cottage ★★★★
Contact: Ms Buchanan, Debach, Woodbridge IP13 6JW
T: (01473) 735456
F: (01473) 738887
E: miriam@greenlabel.co.uk

290 High Street ★★★
Contact: Mr & Mrs Martin Jinks, 94 Leiston Road, Aldeburgh IP15 5PX
T: (01728) 453037
E: martin@jinksy.fsnet.co.uk

65 High Street ★★★★
Contact: Mr Richard Pither, 7 Frenze Road, Diss IP22 4PA
T: (01379) 651297

Kingfisher & Swallow Cottages ★★★★
Contact: Mr & Mrs Robert Barr, James Barr & Sons (Farmers) Ltd, Manor Farm, Grove Road, Friston, Saxmundham IP17 1TL
T: (01728) 603196
F: (01728) 603196
E: manorfarmcottages@hotmail.com

38 Lee Road ★★★★
Contact: Mrs Elizabeth Wagener, Cox Hill, Boxford, Sudbury CO10 5JG
T: (01787) 210223
E: lizwagener@aol.com

Magenta ★★★
Contact: Mr & Mrs Martin Jinks, 94 Leiston Road, Aldeburgh IP15 5PX
T: (01728) 453037
E: martin@jinksy.fsnet.co.uk

May Lodge ★★★★
Contact: 7 Frenze Road, Diss IP22 3PA
T: (01379) 651297
F: (01379) 641555
E: holidays@suffolk-secrets.co.uk
I: www.suffolk-secrets.co.uk

Melody Cottage
Rating Applied For
Contact: Miss Sarah Bayley, The Dower House, Lower Street, Ufford, Woodbridge IP13 6DW
T: (01394) 461235
E: melodycottage@yahoo.co.uk

Mermaid Cottage ★★★★
Contact: Mrs Jacqueline Collier, Clopton Hall, Grundisburgh, Woodbridge IP13 6QB
T: (01473) 735004

Orlando ★★★
Contact: Mr Peter Hatcher, Martlesham Hall, Church Lane, Martlesham, Woodbridge IP12 4PQ
T: (01394) 382126
F: (01394) 278600
E: orlando@hatcher.co.uk
I: www.hatcher/co.uk/orlando

Parklands ★★★★★
Contact: Mr & Mrs Roy Allen, Garden Suite, 6 Aldringham House, Leiston Road, Aldringham, Leiston IP16 4PT
T: (01728) 830139
F: (01728) 831034
E: aldringham@supanet.com
I: www.aldringham@supanet.com

Telegraph Cottage and Barn ★★★
Contact: Mr Richard John Balls, Gorse Hill, Leiston Road, Aldeburgh IP15 5QD
T: (01728) 452162
F: (01728) 452162
E: info@aldeburghproperties.co.uk
I: www.aldeburghproperties.co.uk

ALRESFORD
Essex

Creek Lodge ★★★
Contact: Mrs Patricia Mountney, Creek Lodge, Ford Lane, Alresford, Colchester CO7 8BE
T: (01206) 825411

ASHDON
Essex

Whitensmere Farm Cottages ★★★★-★★★★★
Contact: Mrs Susan Ford, Ashdon, Saffron Walden CB10 2JQ
T: (01799) 584244
F: (01799) 584244
E: gford@lineone.net
I: www.holidaycottagescambridge.co.uk

AYLMERTON
Norfolk

Moorland Park ★★★
Contact: Mrs Elaine Field, Moorland Park, Holt Road, Aylmerton, Norwich NR11 8QA
T: (01263) 837508
F: (01263) 837508

Rodavia ★★★
Contact: Mr & Mrs David and Rosemary Wilson, Northbank, Church Road, Aylmerton, Norwich NR11 8PZ
T: (01263) 837338
E: rodavia@hotmail.com

Thyme Untied ★★★
Contact: Mr Tony Mackay, Sheringham NR26 8RT
T: (01263) 824955
F: (01263) 824955
E: tonyandpat@pinecones.fsnet.co.uk

AYLSHAM
Norfolk

Bay Cottage ★★★★
Contact: Mr Stuart Clarke, Bay Cottage, Colby Corner, Colby, Aylsham, Norwich NR11 7EB
T: (01263) 734574
F: (01263) 734574
E: jsclarke@colbycorner.fsnet.co.uk
I: www.cottagesdirect.com

Holly Cottage ★★★
Contact: Mr & Mrs Burr, Burgh House, Burgh Road, Aylsham, Norwich NR11 6AT
T: (01263) 733567

The Old Windmill ★★★★★
Contact: Mr & Mrs Tim Bower, Old Mill House, Cawston Road, Aylsham, Norwich NR11 6NB
T: (01263) 732118
E: timatmill@aol.com

BACTON
Norfolk

Swiss Cottage ★★★★
Contact: Mrs Linda Weinberg, Buehl Str 6, 8113 Boppelsen, Switzerland
T: 00411 844 2222
F: 00411 840 0222
E: info@swissonthebeach.com
I: www.swissonthebeach.com

BADINGHAM
Suffolk

The Nest ★★★
Contact: Mrs Susan Long, Wood Farm, Bruisyard, Saxmundham IP17 2EZ
T: (01728) 660360
F: (01728) 660131

BALE
Norfolk

Chapel Field Cottage ★★★
Contact: Mrs Judith Everitt, Field Dalling Road, Bale, Fakenham NR21 0QS
T: (01328) 878419

BANHAM
Norfolk

Olde Farm Cottage ★★★
Contact: Mrs Girling, New Buckenham Road, Banham, Norwich NR16 2DA
T: (01953) 860023
F: (01953) 860023
E: kathygirling@aol.com
I: www.greystokegraphics.co.uk.

BANNINGHAM
Norfolk

Bridge Bungalow ★★★★
Contact: Miss D Kingsley, Norfolk Country Cottages, Carlton House, Market Place, Reepham, Norwich NR10 4JJ
T: (01603) 871872
F: (01603) 870304
E: info@norfolkcottages.co.uk
I: www.norfolkcottages.co.uk

BARNEY
Norfolk

The Stables ★★★
Contact: Mrs Christine Blackman, The Street, Fakenham NR21 0AD
T: (01328) 878204

BARTON TURF
Norfolk

Gunns Cottage ★★★
Contact: Miss D Kingsley, Norfolk Country Cottages, Carlton House, Market Place, Reepham, Norwich NR10 4JJ
T: (01603) 871872
F: (01603) 870304
E: info@norfolkcottages.co.uk
I: www.norfolkcottages.co.uk

BAWDESWELL
Norfolk

Jotts Cottage ★★★★
Contact: Mr & Mrs John Clarke, Dereham Road, Bawdeswell, East Dereham NR20 4AA
T: (01362) 688444
F: (01362) 688172
E: clarkes.jasmine@virgin.net

BAWDSEY
Suffolk

Bawdsey Manor ★★★-★★★★★
Contact: Mr Niels Toettcher, Bawdsey, Woodbridge IP12 3AZ
T: (01394) 411633
F: (01394) 410417
E: info@bawdseymanor.co.uk

BAYLHAM
Suffolk

Baylham House Annexe & Baylham House Flat★★★
Contact: Mrs Ann Storer, Mill Lane, Baylham, Ipswich IP6 8LG
T: (01473) 830264
F: (01473) 830264
E: ann@baylham-house-farm.co.uk
I: www.baylham-house-farm.co.uk

BEACHAMWELL
Norfolk

Carole Wilson's Rectory Holidays ★★★
Contact: Mrs Carole Wilson, Carole Wilson's Rectory Holidays, The Old Rectory, Old Hall Lane, Beachamwell, Swaffham PE37 8Ba
T: (01366) 328628
E: wilson@rectoryholidays.com
I: www.rectoryholidays.com

BECCLES
Suffolk

9 The Maltings ★★★
Contact: Mrs Brenda Lanchester & Mr Birch, Brick Kiln Barn, Kings Lane, Weston, Beccles NR34 8TG
T: (01502) 717362
F: (01502) 711888
E: bircharch@aol.com

Redisham Hall ★★★★
Contact: Agent, Country Holidays, Spring Mill, Earby, Barnoldswick BB94 0AA
T: 08700 723723
I: www.country-holidays.co.uk

BEDFORD
Bedfordshire

The Dovecote ★★★★
Contact: Mrs Rosalind Northern, The Dovecote, Priory Farm, High Street, Bedford MK43 7EE
T: (01234) 720293
F: (01234) 720292

BEESTON
Norfolk

Holmdene Farm ★★★
Contact: Mrs Davidson, Holmdene Farm, Syers Lane, Beeston, King's Lynn PE32 2NJ
T: (01328) 701284
F: (01328) 701284
E: holmdenefarm@farmersweekly.net
I: www.northnorfolk.co.uk/holmdenefarm

BELCHAMP ST PAUL
Essex

Colefair Cottage ★★★★
Contact: Mr Kirk Forrest, Suffolk & Norfolk Country Cottages, Hillside Orchard, Rectory Farm Lane, Orwell, Royston SG8 5RB
T: (01223) 207946
F: (01223) 208893
E: admin@suffolkandnorfolkcottages.co.uk
I: www.suffolkandnorfolkcottages.co.uk

BERKHAMSTED
Hertfordshire

Holly Tree & Jack's Cottage ★★★
Contact: Mrs D Barrington, 20 & 21 Ringshall, Little Gaddesden, Berkhamsted HP4 1ND
T: (01442) 843464
F: (01442) 842051
E: rbbarrington@aol.com

Walnut Cottage ★★★★
Contact: Mrs Knowles, Berkhamsted HP4 2RR
T: (01442) 866541
F: (01442) 866541
E: aknowles@broadway.nildram.co.uk

BEYTON
Suffolk

The Coach House ★★
Contact: Mrs Barbara Jeffery, The Green, Hessett, Bury St Edmunds IP30 9AD
T: (01359) 270219

Manorflat ★★★★
Contact: Mr & Mrs Kay & Mark Dewsbury, The Green, Hessett, Bury St Edmunds IP30 9AF
T: (01359) 270960
E: manorhouse@beyton.com
I: www.beyton.com

BILDESTON
Suffolk

Christmas Hall & The Coach House ★★★★
Contact: Mrs Christina Hawkins, Christmas Hall, Market Place, Bildeston, Ipswich IP7 7EN
T: (01449) 741428
F: (01449) 744161
E: christmashall@macmail.com

Friar's Cottage ★★★★★
Contact: Mrs Sewell, 21 High Street, Bildeston, Ipswich IP7 7EX
T: (01449) 741108
F: (01449) 741108
E: patricia@pmsewell.fsnet.co.uk
I: www.friarscottage.co.uk

Minto Cottage ★★★★
Contact: Mr & Mrs Cox, 74 High Street, Bildeston, Ipswich IP7 7EA
T: (01449) 744988
F: (01449) 740086
E: andycox@eidosnet.co.uk
I: www.mintoholidays.co.uk

BILLERICAY
Essex

The Pump House Apartment ★★★★★
Contact: Mrs E R Bayliss, Pump House, Church Street, Great Burstead, Billericay CM11 2TR
T: (01277) 656579
F: (01277) 631160
E: john.bayliss@willmottdixon.co.uk
I: www.thepumphouseapartment.co.uk

BILLINGTON
Bedfordshire

Brewery Cottage ★★★
Contact: Mrs Angie Leach & Mrs J Franlin, Lets Unlimited, Town Farm, Ivinghoe, Leighton Buzzard LU7 9EZ
T: (01296) 668455
F: (01296) 668455
E: w.h.leach.and.sons@farmline.com
I: members.farmline.com/angie

BINHAM
Norfolk

The Barn
Rating Applied For
Contact: Miss Dawn Kinsley, Norfolk Country Cottages, Carlton House, Market Place, Reepham, Norwich NR10 4JJ
T: (01603) 871872
F: (01603) 870304
E: info@norfolkcottages.co.uk

Betty's Cottage & Bob's Cottage ★★★★
Contact: Ms Fiona Thompson, Betty's Cottage & Bob's Cottage, Field House, Walsingham Road, Binham, Fakenham NR21 0BU
T: (01328) 830639

Fairfield Cottage ★★★
Contact: Mrs Sheila Thornton, Apple Acre, Bleasby Road, Thurgarton, Norwich NG14 7FW
T: (01636) 830395
F: (0115) 987 8011

BISHOP'S STORTFORD
Hertfordshire

Cedar Court ★★
Contact: Mrs Paula Sewell, Spellbrook Farm, London Road, Spellbrook, Bishop's Stortford CM23 4AX
T: (01279) 600191
F: (01279) 722758

13 Priory Court ★★★
Contact: Mrs Oakes, 102 Havers Lane, Bishop's Stortford CM23 3PD
T: (01279) 507304

BLAKENEY
Norfolk

The Friary ★★★
Contact: Mrs Cooke, 31 Bracondale, Norwich NR1 2AT
T: (01603) 624827
E: cookehd@paston.co.uk

51 High Street ★★
Contact: Miss Dawn Kinsley, Norfolk Country Cottages Ref. 674, Market Place, Reepham, Norwich NR10 4JJ
T: (01603) 871872
F: (01603) 870304
E: info@norfolkcottages.co.uk
I: www.swallow-tail.com

Pimpernel Cottage ★★
Contact: Mrs D. Kinsley, Market Place, Reepham, Norwich NR10 4JJ
T: (01603) 871872
F: (01603) 870304
E: info@norfolkcottages.co.uk
I: www.swallow-tail.com

Quayside Cottages ★★-★★★★★
Contact: Mrs Alvarez, New Wellbury Farmhouse, Wellbury Park, Hitchin SG5 3BP
T: (01462) 768627
F: (01462) 768320
E: veronicaAlvarez@compuserve.com
I: www.blakeneycottages.co.uk

Roslyn ★★
Contact: Mrs Brenda Eke, 169 Fakenham Road, Melton Constable NR24 2DN
T: (01263) 860111

The Stable Court and Apartments ★★★
Contact: Mr & Mrs Peter Darling, Langham, Holt NR25 7BX
T: (01328) 830375
F: (01328) 830775
E: peter.darling1@btinternet.com
I: www.ukcoastalholidays.com/go/langhamhall

The Tanning House ★★★
Contact: Mrs B Pope, The Lodge, Back Lane, Blakeney, Holt NR25 7NR
T: (01263) 740477
F: (01263) 741356

Wren Cottage
Rating Applied For
Contact: Mr & Mrs Ian Mashiter, 11 Branksome Close, Norwich NR4 6SP
T: (01603) 457560
E: cleycottage@aol.com

BLAXHALL
Suffolk

Willows ★★
Contact: Mrs Elizabeth Simmonds, Bedford MK40 2NA
T: (01234) 214686
E: liz@simmonds1941.freeserve.co.uk

BLYTHBURGH
Suffolk

Whitehouse Barns ★★★★
Contact: Mrs Penelope Roskell-Griffiths, London N16 7AR
T: (020) 8806 5969
E: peneloperoskell@yahoo.co.uk

BRADWELL
Norfolk

Aardvark House ★★★
Contact: Mr Brown, 2 Avington, Milton Keynes MK8 9DQ
T: (01908) 569628
I: www.alex.brown.hemscott.net

BRADWELL-ON-SEA
Essex

Mill House ★★
Contact: Mr & Mrs Steve & Sylvia Cruse, Mill House, Mill End, Bradwell-on-Sea, Southminster CM0 7HL
T: (01621) 776525

BRAINTREE
Essex

1 Red Lion Cottages ★★
Contact: Mrs Moran McKellar Ratcliffe, 2 Red Lion Cottages, Lanham Green Road, Cressing, Braintree CM77 8DR
T: (01376) 584043
F: (01376) 584043
E: moran.ratcliffe@btconnect.com
I: www.stilwell.co.uk

BRAMFIELD
Suffolk

Japonica House ★★★
Contact: 7 Frenze Road, Diss IP22 4PA
T: (01379) 651297
F: (01379) 641555
E: holidays@suffolk-secrets.co.uk
I: www.suffolk-secrets.co.uk

BRANCASTER
Norfolk

11 Anchorage View ★★★
Contact: Mrs Sandra Hohol, 62 Westgate, Hunstanton PE36 5EL
T: (01485) 534267
F: (01485) 535230
E: shohol@birdsnorfolkholidayhomes.co.uk
I: www.norfolkholidayhomes-birds.co.uk

Dunlin ★★
Contact: Mrs Sandra Hohol, 62 Westgate, Hunstanton PE36 5EL
T: (01485) 534267
F: (01485) 535230
E: shohol@birdsnorfolkholidayhomes.co.uk
I: www.norfolkholidayhomes-birds.co.uk

The Old Stores ★★★
Contact: Miss D Kingsley, Norfolk Country Cottages, Carlton House, Market Place, Reepham, Norwich NR10 4JJ
T: (01603) 871872
F: (01603) 870304
E: info@norfolkcottages.co.uk
I: www.swallow-tail.com

Russett Lodge ★★★
Contact: Mrs Sandra Hohol, 62 Westgate, Hunstanton PE36 5EL
T: (01485) 534267
F: (01485) 535230
E: shohol@birdsnorfolkholidayhomes.co.uk
I: www.norfolkholidayhomes-birds.co.uk

The Stalls ★★★
Contact: Mrs Judith Rippon, The Annex, The Old Stables, Broad Lane, Brancaster, King's Lynn PE31 8AU
T: (01485) 210774
F: (01485) 210774
E: judyrippon@theoldstables123.fslife.co.uk

Stubton Cottage ★★★★
Contact: Mrs Sandra Hohol, 62 Westgate, Hunstanton PE36 5EL
T: (01485) 534267
F: (01485) 535230
E: shohol@birdsnorfolkholidayhomes.co.uk
I: www.norfolkholidayhomes-birds.co.uk

Thompson Brancaster Farms ★★★
Contact: Mrs Sue Lane, 4 Stiffkey Road, Warham, Wells-next-the-Sea NR23 1NP
T: 07885 269538
F: (01328) 710144
E: info@tbfholidayhomes.co.uk
I: www.tbfholidayhomes.co.uk

BRANCASTER STAITHE
Norfolk

21 Dale End ★★★★
Contact: Mrs Debbie Clark, 19 Main Street, Seaton, Oakham LE15 9HU
T: (01572) 747389
F: (01572) 747693
E: debbieclark@btopenworld.com
I: www.hemingwayclark.com/norfolk

Island Cottage ★
Contact: Mrs Sandra Hohol, 62 Westgate, Ringstead, Hunstanton PE36 5BU
T: (01485) 534267
F: (01485) 535230
E: shohol@birdsnorfolkholidayhomes.co.uk
I: www.norfolkholidayhomes-birds.co.uk

Vista & Carpenters Cottages ★★★
Contact: Mrs G J Smith, Dale View, Main Road, Brancaster Staithe, King's Lynn PE31 8BY
T: (01485) 210497
F: (01485) 210497

Westbourne ★★★
Contact: Mrs Sandra Hohol, 62 Westgate, Hunstanton PE36 5EL
T: (01485) 534267
F: (01485) 535230
E: shohol@birdsnorfolkholidayhomes.co.uk
I: www.norfolkholidayhomes-birds.co.uk

BRANDON
Suffolk

Deacons Cottage ★★
Contact: Mrs Deacon, South Street, Hockwold, Thetford IP26 4JG
T: (01842) 828023

Poplar Hall ★★★★
Contact: Mrs Anna Garwood, Poplar Hall, Frostenden Corner, Frostenden, Wangford, Beccles NR34 7JA
T: (01502) 578549
I: www.southwold.co.uk/poplar-hall

BRANTHAM
Suffolk

Brantham Hall
Rating Applied For
Contact: Ms Caroline Williams, J R Keeble & Son Ltd, Brantham Lodge, Brantham, Manningtree CO11 1PT
T: (01473) 327090
F: (01473) 327090
E: hwilliams@branmann.freeserve.co.uk

BRAUGHING
Hertfordshire

Edwinstree Chapel ★★★★
Contact: Mrs Pamela Bradley, Edwinstree Chapel, Edwinstree, Dassels, Braughing, Ware SG11 2RR
T: (01763) 289509
E: edwinstree@tesco.net
I: www.Edwinstree.com

BRININGHAM
Norfolk

Moriah Cottage ★★★★
Contact: Miss Dawn Kinsley, Norfolk Country Cottages Ref. 139, Market Place, Reepham, Norwich NR10 4JJ
T: (01603) 871872
F: (01603) 870304
E: info@norfolkcottages.co.uk
I: www.norfolk-cottages.co.uk

BRISLEY
Norfolk

Church Farm Cottages & Pond Farm Studio★★★
Contact: Mrs G.V Howes, Church Farm Cottages & Pond Farm Studio, The Green, Brisley, East Dereham NR20 5LL
T: (01362) 668332
F: (01362) 668332

Mill Farm Barn ★★★★
Contact: Norfolk Country Cottages, Carlton House, Market Place, Reepham, Norwich NR10 4JJ
T: (01603) 871872
F: (01603) 870304
E: info@norfolkcottages.co.uk
I: www.norfolkcottages.co.uk

The Old Stable Annexe ★★
Contact: Mrs Jean Gaymer, The Old Stable Annexe, School Road, Brisley, East Dereham NR20 5LH
T: (01362) 668793

BRISTON
Norfolk

45 Chequers Close ★★★
Contact: Miss D Kingsley, Carlton House, Market Place, Reepham, Norwich NR10 4JJ
T: (01603) 871872
F: (01603) 870304
E: info@norfolkcottages.co.uk
I: www.swallow-tail.com

Koukounaries ★★★
Contact: Mrs Burgin, 9 Ashwell Road, Bygrave, Baldock SG7 5DT
T: (01462) 894930

BROME
Suffolk

The Homestead Barn ★★★★
Contact: Mr & Mrs David & Diana Downes, The Homestead Barn, Brome, Eye IP23 8AE
T: (01379) 870489
E: dianadownes@hotmail.com

BRUISYARD
Suffolk

Bruisyard Hall ★★★★
Contact: Mr Robert Rous, The Country House, Dennington, Woodbridge IP13 8AU
T: (01728) 638712
F: (01728) 638712
E: dennington@farmline.com
I: www.bruisyardhall.co.uk

Shelley Lodge ★★★
Contact: Mrs Kathleen Bowman, Shelley Lodge, Bruisyard, Saxmundham IP17 2HB
T: (01728) 660312

BRUNDISH
Suffolk

Potash Barns ★★★★
Contact: Mr Rob Spendlove, Potash Barns, Potash Farm, The Street, Brundish, Woodbridge IP13 8BL
T: (01379) 384819
F: (01379) 388697
E: enquiries@potashbarns.co.uk

BUNGAY
Suffolk

Garden Cottage & Courtyard Cottage ★★★★
Contact: Mr & Mrs Slater, St Margarets Road, Bungay NR35 1PQ
T: (01986) 896895
F: (01986) 896840

BURNHAM MARKET
Norfolk

Barley Cottage ★★★
Contact: Mr & Mrs A J Watley, 26 Mount Crescent, Brentwood CM14 5DB
T: (01277) 218116
E: a.s.watley@btinternet.com

Chapel Cottage ★★★
Contact: Miss D Kingsley, Norfolk Country Cottages, Carlton House, Market Place, Reepham, Norwich NR10 4JJ
T: (01603) 871872
F: (01603) 870304
E: info@norfolkcottages.co.uk
I: www.norfolk-cottages.co.uk

Clippers Cottage ★★★
Contact: Mrs Kinsley, Swallow Tail Holiday Homes, Carlton House, Market Place, Reepham, Norwich NR10 4JJ
T: (01603) 871872
F: (01603) 870304
E: holidays@swallow-tail.com
I: www.swallow-tail.com

Easterly ★★
Contact: Mrs D. Kinsley, Market Place, Reepham, Norwich NR10 4JJ
T: (01603) 871872
F: (01603) 870304
E: info@norfolkcottages.co.uk
I: www.swallow-tail.com

Foundry Barn ★★★★
Contact: Mr & Mrs Mike Benson, Badgers Croft, Nottwood Lane, Stoke Row, Henley-on-Thames RG9 5PU
T: (01491) 681644
F: (01491) 681644
E: mikebenson@btopenworld

Fuchsia Cottage ★★★
Contact: Mr Tinsley, 6 The Green, Stanhoe, King's Lynn PE31 8QE
T: (01485) 518896
E: tinsley.co@virgin.net

Granary Cottage ★★★
Contact: Ms Julie Levitt, Castle Cottage, Polopit, Titchmarsh, Kettering NN14 3DL
T: (01832) 735150
F: (01832) 735150
E: levitt.smarter@virgin.net

Rose Cottage ★★★
Contact: Mrs Anne Manning, Sussex Farm, Claythorpe, Alford PE31 8JY
T: (01328) 730775
F: (01328) 738470

The Shielings & Ebenezer Cottage ★★★-★★★★
Contact: Mrs Dawn Kinsley, Market Place, Reepham, Norwich NR10 4JJ
T: (01603) 871872
F: (01603) 870304
E: info@norfolkcottages.co.uk
I: www.swallow-tail.com

Stable Cottage ★★★★
Contact: Mrs Anne Cringle, Market Place, Burnham Market, Burnham Overy Town, King's Lynn PE31 8HD
T: (01328) 738456
E: pmcringle@aol.com

BURNHAM-ON-CROUCH
Essex

38 Petticrow Quays
Rating Applied For
Contact: Mr Paul Ayling, The Lodge, 23 Orsett Avenue, Leigh-on-Sea SS9 4TT
T: (01702) 522857

BURNHAM OVERY TOWN
Norfolk

Mill House Annexe ★★★
Contact: Mrs Anthea Moore Ede, The Mill House, Burnham Overy Town, King's Lynn PE31 8DX
T: (0207) 584 8826
F: (0207) 581 8694
E: antheamooreede@zoom.co.uk

BURNHAM THORPE
Norfolk

12 The Pightle ★★
Contact: Mr Pocock, Swallow Tail Holiday Homes, Carlton House, Market Place, Reepham, Norwich NR10 4JJ
T: (01603) 308108
F: (01603) 870304
E: holidays@swallow-tail.com
I: www.swallow-tail.com

BURY ST EDMUNDS
Suffolk

Brook Villa ★★★
Contact: Mr David Manning, Brook Villa, Rushbrooke Lane, Bury St Edmunds IP33 2RR
T: (01284) 764387
E: suffolksaddlery@supanet.com

The Court & The Granary Suites ★★-★★★★
Contact: Mrs Roberta Truin, The Court & The Granary Suites, Melford Road, Lawshall, Bury St Edmunds IP29 4PX
T: (01284) 830385
F: (01284) 830674
E: info@brighthousefarm.fsnet.co.uk
I: www.brighthousefarm.fsnet.co.uk

Garden Corner ★★★★
Contact: Mr Stemp, 91a Kings Road, Bury St Edmunds IP33 3DT
T: (01284) 702848

The Granary & The Cartlodge ★★★★
Contact: Mrs Sarah Worboys, Worboys Farms Ltd, Francis Farm, Upper Somerton, Bury St Edmunds IP29 4NE
T: (01284) 789241
F: (01284) 789241
E: francisfarmcottages@farmline.com

Kitchen Flat ★★★
Contact: Mrs Eileen Storey, Bury St Edmunds IP33 1HP
T: (01284) 755744
F: (01284) 755744
E: eileen@queequeg.demon.co.uk

Pump Lane House ★★★
Contact: Mr & Mrs Neil & Lucy Taylor, Pump Lane House, Pump Lane, Bury St Edmunds IP33 1HN
T: (01284) 755248

Theatre Royal, Bury St Edmunds ★
Contact: Theatre Royal, Westgate Street, Bury St Edmunds IP33 1QR
T: (01284) 755127
E: admin@theatreroyal.org
I: www.theatreroyal.org

1 Vinefields Cottage
Rating Applied For
Contact: Mr Paul Jacobs, Withams Cottage, Ousden, Newmarket CB8 8TS
T: (01284) 850179

BYLAUGH
Norfolk

Meadowview ★★★
Contact: Mrs Jenny Lake, Meadowview, Park Farm, Bylaugh, East Dereham NR20 4QE
T: (01362) 688584

CALIFORNIA
Norfolk

Bella Vista T/A Beachside Holidays ★★★★
Contact: Mrs S J Sampson, Wakefield Court, Rottenstone Lane, Scratby, Great Yarmouth NR29 3QT
T: (01493) 730279
E: holidays@theseaside.org
I: www.beachside-holidays.co.uk

CAMBRIDGE
Cambridgeshire

Brookacre Self Catering Accommodation
Rating Applied For
Contact: Mr & Mrs Colin Blackburn, Brookacre Self Catering Accommodation, 60 Birdwood Road, Cambridge CB1 3SU
T: (01223) 708967
F: (01223) 708967
E: paragon.holdings@ntlworld.com

Brooklands Court ★★★★
Contact: Mr & Mrs Oliver Digney, Stapleford, Cambridge CB2 5JE
T: (01223) 841294
F: (01223) 841294
E: sdigney@clarencehouse.fsnet.co.uk
I: www.clarencehouse.org.uk

Canonbury House & 53 Richmond Road
Rating Applied For
Contact: Mr A C Kiddy, Radwinter Park, Radwinter End, Saffron Walden CB10 2UE
T: (01799) 599272
F: (01799) 599172
E: ajkiddy@cambridge-vacation-homes.com
I: www.cambridge-vacation-homes.com

Clarence House ★★★★
Contact: Mr & Mrs Oliver Digney, Stapleford, Cambridge CB2 5JE
T: (01223) 841294
F: (01223) 841294
E: sdigney@clarencehouse.fsnet.co.uk
I: www.clarencehouse.org.uk

First Floor Apartment ★★★
Contact: Mr Desmond Hirsch, 31 Grantchester Street, Newnham, Cambridge CB3 9HY
T: (01223) 360200
F: (01223) 741543
E: cambridge.accommodation@virgin.net

Glebe Cottage ★★★
Contact: Mrs F M Key
T: (01954) 212895
E: info@camcottage.co.uk
I: www.camcottage.co.uk

28 Hanover Court ★★
Contact: Mr Young, 53 Devonshire Road, Cambridge CB1 2BL
T: (01223) 529653
E: riyo50@yahoo.com

Home From Home Apartments ★★★-★★★★
Contact: Mrs E Fasano, Bungalow rear of 78 Milton Road, Cambridge CB4 1LA
T: (01223) 323555
F: (01223) 236078
E: homefromhome@tesco.net
I: www.homefromhomecambridge.co.uk

The School House ★★★★
Contact: Mr & Mrs T F Mann, The School House, High Street, Horningsea, Cambridge CB5 9JG
T: (01223) 440077
F: (01223) 441414
E: schoolhse1@aol.com

79a Victoria Road
Rating Applied For
Contact: Mrs Anita Thoday, 40 High Street, Aldreth, Ely CB6 3PG
T: (01353) 740022
F: (01353) 740022
E: trojan.david@virgin.net

Warkworth Villa ★★★
Contact: Ms Wendy Whistler, Rose Lodge, 9 Boxworth End, Swavesey, Cambridge CB4 5RA
T: (01954) 231850
F: (01954) 204100
E: selective.studios@dial.pipex.com

CASTLE ACRE
Norfolk

Cherry Tree Cottage ★★★★
Contact: Mr & Mrs Boswell, Back Lane, Castle Acre, King's Lynn PE32 2AR
T: (01760) 755000
F: (01760) 755000
E: boswell@paston.co.uk

The Cottage ★★★★
Contact: Mrs Jane Famous, 45 Hawthorn Avenue, Palmers Green, London N13 4JS
T: (020) 8886 0800
E: jane-famous@virgin.net

Friars Croft ★★★
Contact: Mrs McGrath, Mill Road, Shipdham, Thetford IP25 7LU
T: (01362) 820408

Peddars Cottage ★★
Contact: Mrs Angela Swindell, St Saviour's Rectory, St Saviour, Jersey JE2 7NP
T: (01534) 727480
F: (01534) 727480
E: jsyedu71@localdial.com

1 Sandles Court ★★
Contact: Mrs Jane Wood, Swaffham PE37 7RY
T: (01760) 722455
E: j.wood1@tinyonline.co.uk

CASTLE HEDINGHAM
Essex

Keepers Cottage ★★★★
Contact: Mr David Brown, Keepers Cottage, Rosemary Lane, Castle Hedingham, Halstead CO9 3AH
T: (01787) 462685
F: (01787) 462685
E: davidmbrown@btinternet.com
I: www.keeperscottage.20m.com

Rosemary Farm ★★★★
Contact: Mr Garry Ian Henderson, Rosemary Farm, Rosemary Lane, Castle Hedingham, Halstead CO9 3AJ
T: (01787) 461653

CASTOR
Cambridgeshire

The Wrens Nest ★★★
Contact: Mrs Huckle, Cobnut Cottage, 45 Peterborough Road, Castor, Peterborough PE5 7AX
T: (01733) 380745
F: (01733) 380745
E: huckle.cobnut@talk21.com

CHEDGRAVE
Norfolk

Barn Owl Holidays ★★★
Contact: Mrs R Beattie, Barn Owl Holidays, Bryons Green, Big Back Lane, Chedgrave, Norwich NR14 6HB
T: (01508) 528786
F: (01508) 528698
E: barnowls@bt.clara.co.uk
I: www.barnowlholidays.co.uk

CHELMSFORD
Essex

Bury Barn Cottage ★★★★
Contact: Mr Richard Morris, Bury Barn Cottage, Bury Road, Pleshey, Chelmsford CM3 1HB
T: (01245) 237384
F: (01245) 237327
I: www.burybarncottage.co.uk

CLACTON-ON-SEA
Essex

Brunton House ★★
Contact: Mr & Mrs Kirk, Brunton House, 15 Carnarvon Road, Clacton-on-Sea CO15 6PH
T: (01255) 420431

Taylors Self-Contained Flats ★★
Contact: Mr Terence Taylor, 41 Thoroughgood Road, Clacton-on-Sea CO15 6DD
T: (01255) 431646

CLEY NEXT THE SEA
Norfolk

Archway Cottage ★★★
Contact: Mrs V Jackson, 3A Brickendon Lane, Brickendon, Hertford SG13 8NU
T: (01992) 511303
F: (01992) 511303

Dolphin Cottage ★★★★
Contact: Mr & Mrs Ian Mashiter, 11 Branksome Close, Norwich NR4 6SP
T: (01603) 457560
E: cleycottage@aol.com

Little Cottage ★★★
Contact: Miss D Kingsley, Carlton House, Market Place, Reepham, Norwich NR10 4JJ
T: (01603) 871872
F: (01603) 870304
E: info@norfolkcottages.co.uk

Orchard Cottage ★★★★
Contact: Mrs Sarah Godfrey, Town House, Easthorpe, Southwell NG25 0HY
T: (01636) 816398
F: (01636) 816398
E: sarah@spaces.demon.co.uk

South Knoll ★★★
Contact: Mrs Trench, 186 New North Road, London N1 7BJ
T: (020) 7359 6093
E: jo-trench@lineone.net

Thurn Cottage ★★★★
Contact: Mr & Mrs Chris & Carol Smith, Runwell, Wickford SS11 7DR
T: (01268) 769801
E: cjcksmith@btinternet.com

Tickers and Skylarks ★★★★
Contact: Mrs Nicola Arrowsmith-Brown, The Street, South Walsham, Norwich NR13 6DQ
T: (01603) 270457
F: (01603) 270142
E: arrows270@aol.com
I: www.cottageguide.co.uk/ticketswww.cottageguide.co.uk/skylarks

Woodbine Cottage & Captiva Cottage ★★★
Contact: Mr & Mrs Fraser & Louise Wibberley, Old Town Hall House, Coast Road, Cley, Cley next the Sea, Holt NR25 7RZ
T: (01263) 740284
I: www.woodbinecottagecley.co.uk

CLIPPESBY
Norfolk

Clippesby Hall ★★★
Contact: Mrs Jean Lindsay, Clippesby Hall, Hall Road, Clippesby, Great Yarmouth NR29 3BL
T: (01493) 367800
E: holidays@clippesby.com
I: www.clippesby.com

COLCHESTER
Essex

Castle Road Cottages ★★★★-★★★★★
Contact: Mrs Patsie Ford, 19 High Street, Nayland, Colchester CO6 4JG
T: (01206) 262210
F: (01206) 262210

Glinska House ★★★★
Contact: Mrs Angela Hawkins, 2 Queens Road, Colchester CO3 3NP
T: (01206) 540881
F: (01206) 503406
E: rhawki@msn.com
I: www.glinskahouse.co.uk

The Laurels ★★★★
Contact: Mrs Morgan, 5 St Johns Close, Colchester CO4 0HP
T: (01206) 842646
F: (01206) 842646
E: morgan.landywood@tesco.net

50 Rosebery Avenue ★★★
Contact: Mrs K Webb, 51 Rosebery Avenue, Colchester CO1 2UP
T: (01206) 866888
E: rosebery.avenue@ntlworld.com

The Tea House ★★★★
Contact: Mr Nicholas Charrington, Layer Marney Tower, Colchester CO5 9US
T: (01206) 330784
F: (01206) 330884
E: info@layermarneytower.co.uk
I: layermarneytower.co.uk

COLKIRK
Norfolk

Saddlery & Hillside Cottage ★★★
Contact: Mrs Catherine Joice
T: (01328) 862261
F: (01328) 856464
E: catherine.joice@btinternet.com

COLMWORTH
Bedfordshire

Colmworth Golf Course Holiday Cottages★★★
Contact: Mrs Julie Vesely
T: (01234) 378181
F: (01234) 376678
E: julie@colmworthgc.fsnet.co.uk
I: www.colmsworthgolfclub.co.uk

COLTISHALL
Norfolk

Broadgates ★★★★
Contact: Mrs Dack, Broadgates, 1 Wroxham Road, Coltishall, Norwich NR12 7DU
T: (01603) 737598
E: 2.richard@4broads.fsnet.co.uk
I: www.norfolkbroads.com/broadgates

COPDOCK
Suffolk

The Briars & Mansard Cottage ★★★★
Contact: Mrs Steward, Back Lane, Washbrook, Copdock, Ipswich IP8 3JA
T: (01473) 730494
E: rosanna.steward@virgin.net

CORPUSTY
Norfolk

Daisy Cottage ★★★
Contact: Miss D Kingsley, Norfolk Country Cottages, Carlton House, Market Place, Reepham, Norwich NR10 4JJ
T: (01603) 871872
F: (01603) 870304
E: info@norfolkcottages.co.uk
I: www.norfolk-cottages.co.uk

COTTON
Suffolk

Coda Cottages ★★★★
Contact: Mrs Kate Sida-Nicholls, Coda Cottages, Poplar Farm, Dandy Corner, Cotton, Stowmarket IP14 4QX
T: (01449) 780076
F: (01449) 780280
E: codacottages@dandycorner.co.uk
I: www.codacottages.co.uk

CRANMER
Norfolk

Home Farm ★★★★
Contact: Mrs Lynne & John Johnson, Home Farm, Cranmer, Sculthorpe, Fakenham NR21 9HY
T: (01328) 823135
F: (01328) 823136
E: booking@homefarmcranmer.co.uk
I: www.homefarmcranmer.co.uk

CRATFIELD
Suffolk

Cherry Trees ★★★
Contact: Mrs Chris Knox, Cherry Trees, Cratfield Hall, Cratfield, Halesworth IP19 0DR
T: (01379) 586709
F: (01379) 588033
E: J.L.Knox@farming.co.uk

The Old Granary ★★★★
Contact: Mr & Mrs O'Brien, Town Farm, Cratfield, Halesworth IP19 0QL
T: (01986) 785315
E: jukeservicesltd@aol.com

School Farm Cottages ★★★★
Contact: Mrs Claire Sillett
T: (01986) 798844
F: (01986) 798394
E: schoolfarmcotts@aol.com
I: www.schoolfarmcottages.com

CROMER
Norfolk

Albion House ★★★
Contact: Mrs Angela Forsyth, 8 Pearwood Close, Tarporley CW6 0UF
T: (01829) 733467
F: (01829) 733467
E: forsythleisure@aol.com

Allseasons ★-★★
Contact: Mr & Mrs Teagle, Sustead Road, Lower Gresham, Norwich NR11 8RE
T: (01263) 577205
E: sue@allseasons-cromer-co.uk

Avenue Holiday Flats ★★★
Contact: Mr John Bradley, Flat 1, 24 Cliff Avenue, Cromer NR27 0AN
T: (01263) 513611
F: (01263) 515009

Beverley House Holiday Apartments ★-★★★
Contact: Mr & Mrs Peter & Gill Day, Beverley House Holiday Apartments, 17 Alfred Road, Cromer NR27 9AN
T: (01263) 512787
F: (01263) 512787
I: www.broadland.com/beverleyhouse

Broadgates Cottages ★★-★★★
Contact: Mrs Gill Sargent, Northrepps Holiday Properties, Forest Park Caravan Site, Northrepps, Overstrand, Cromer NR27 0JR
T: (01263) 513969
F: (01263) 511992
E: gill@broadgates.co.uk

Chalet No 130 ★★
Contact: Mrs Lotta Fox, Russells Self Catering Holidays, 15 West Street, Cromer NR27 9HZ
T: (01263) 513139
F: (01263) 513139
E: property@lambertw.fslife.co.uk

Chalets 28, 151, 152 ★
Contact: Russells Self Catering Holidays, 15 West Street, Cromer NR27 9HZ
T: (01263) 513139
F: (01263) 513139

Cliff Hollow ★★
Contact: Miss L Willins, 35 Overstrand Road, Cromer NR27 0AL
T: (01263) 512447
F: (01263) 512447

15 Clifton Park ★★★★
Contact: Norfolk Country Cottages, Carlton House, Market Place, Reepham, Norwich NR10 4JJ
T: (01603) 871872
F: (01603) 870304

Coach House Cottage ★★★
Contact: Mrs Dorothy Casburn, 81 Station Road, Great Massingham, King's Lynn PE32 2JQ
T: (01485) 520569
F: (01485) 520569
E: ccasburn@britishsugar.co.uk

9a Cornerstreet ★★★
Contact: Mrs Lotta Fox, 15 West Street, Cromer NR27 9HZ
T: (01263) 511028
F: (01263) 513139
E: property@lambertw.fslife.co.uk

Drift Barn Cottage ★★★
Contact: Mr Payne, Felbrigg, Norwich NR11 8PL
T: (01263) 513765

Flat 2 ★★
Contact: Miss Denise Lewis, 15 West Street, Cromer NR27 9HZ
T: (01263) 513139
F: (01263) 513139
E: property@lambertw.fslife.co.uk

Flat 2 Bernard House ★★★
Contact: 15 West Street, Cromer NR27 9HZ
T: (01263) 513139
F: (01263) 513139
I: www.seaglimpse.demon.co.uk

Foxglade Lodge ★★★
Contact: Russells Self Catering Holidays, Russell & Company, 15 West Street, Cromer NR27 9HZ
T: (01263) 511028
F: (01263) 513139

2 The Gangway ★★
Contact: Mrs B L Price, Misterton, Kendal Avenue, Epping CM16 4PN
T: (01992) 572672

Greenwood Holiday Cottage ★★★
Contact: Mrs Hemming, The Lookout, 11 Cliff Drive, Overstrand, Cromer NR27 0AW
T: (01263) 514139

The Grove ★★★
Contact: Mrs Graveling, The Grove, 95 Overstrand Road, Overstrand, Cromer NR27 0DJ
T: (01263) 512412
F: (01263) 513416
E: thegrovecromer@btopenworld.com
I: www.thegrovecromer.co.uk

Kings Chalet Park ★★
Contact: Mrs Bateman, Stenson, 32 Overstrand Road, Overstrand, Cromer NR27 0AJ
T: (01263) 511308

Kings Chalet Park ★★
Contact: Mr Arthur Pritchard, East Beckham, Gresham, Norwich NR11 8RP
T: (01263) 824693
F: (01263) 824736
E: arthur@afjpritchard.fsnet.co.uk

103 Kings Chalet Park ★★
Contact: Mrs Lotta Fox, Russells Self Catering Holidays, 15 West Street, Cromer NR27 9HZ
T: (01263) 511028
F: (01263) 513139
E: property@lambertw.fslife.co.uk

110 King's Chalet Park ★★
Contact: Mrs Scotlock, Shangri-La, Little Cambridge, Duton Hill, Great Dunmow CM6 3QU
T: (01371) 870482

119 Kings Chalet Park ★★
Contact: Russells Self Catering Holidays, 15 West Street, Cromer NR27 9HZ
T: (01263) 513139
F: (01263) 513139

150 Kings Chalet Park ★★
Contact: Mr & Mrs P & M Cole, 201 Roughton Road, Overstrand, Cromer NR27 9LN
T: (01263) 513932

2 King's Chalet Park ★★
Contact: Russells Self Catering Holidays, 15 West Street, Cromer NR27 9HZ
T: (01263) 511028
F: (01263) 513139

22 Kings Chalet Park ★★
Contact: Russells Self Catering Holidays, 15 West Street, Cromer NR27 9HZ
T: (01263) 513139
F: (01263) 513139

Maynard House ★★★
Contact: Lambert & Russell, 15 West Street, Cranmer, Sculthorpe, Fakenham NR21 9HZ
T: (01263) 513139
F: (01263) 513139

The Old Forge ★★
Contact: Lambert & Russell Self Catering Holidays, 15 West Street, Cromer NR27 9HZ
T: (01263) 513139

Suncourt Holiday Flats ★★
Contact: Mr & Mrs A. R. Hams, Walcott Road, Bacton, Walcott, Norwich NR12 0HB
T: (01692) 650022
E: suncourtflats@mail.com
I: www.suncourt.freeservers.com

Thorpewood Cottages ★★★
Contact: Mr David Howarth, Nursery Farm, Cromer Road, Thorpe Market, Norwich NR11 8TU
T: (01263) 834493
E: davidhowarth@thorpegate.fsnet.co.uk
I: www.thorpewoodcottages.co.uk

CROXTON
Cambridgeshire

Croxton Old Rectory Rating Applied For
Contact: Mrs Margaret Williams, Croxton Old Rectory, Cambridge Road, Croxton, St Neots, Huntingdon PE19 6SU
T: (01480) 880344
F: (01480) 880344

CULFORD
Suffolk

Culford Farm Cottages Rating Applied For
Contact: Mrs Rosemary Flack, Culford Farm Cottages, Home Farm, Culford, Bury St Edmunds IP28 6DS
T: (01284) 728334
F: (01284) 728334
E: stephen@flack1712.freeserve.co.uk

DALLINGHOO
Suffolk

Robins Nest ★★★★
Contact: Mr Robert Blake, Woodbridge IP12 4JN
T: (01394) 382565
E: deben@btclick.com

DARSHAM
Suffolk

The Granary ★★★
Contact: Mrs S. Bloomfield, Priory Farm, Darsham, Saxmundham IP17 3QD
T: (01728) 668459

Rolletts Marsh ★★★
Contact: 7 Frenze Road, Diss IP22 4PA
T: (01379) 651297
F: (01379) 641555
E: holidays@suffolk-secrets.co.uk
I: www.suffolk-secrets.co.uk

DEBDEN
Essex

The Old Granary ★★★★
Contact: Ms Jessica Sperryn, Deynes House, Deynes Road, Debden, Saffron Walden CB11 3LG
T: (01799) 540232
E: sperryn@nascr.net

DEDHAM
Essex

The Tallow Factory & Brannam Cottage★★★★
Contact: Ms Christine Thompson, 14 School Lane, Lawford, Manningtree CO11 2HZ
T: (01206) 393711
I: www.tallowfactory.com

DENVER
Norfolk

West Hall Farm Holidays and Lakeside Fisheries★★★
Contact: Mrs Riches, West Hall Lodge, Sandy Lane, Denver, Downham Market PE38 0EB
T: (01366) 383291
F: (01366) 387074
I: www.west-hall-farm-holidays.co.uk

DERSINGHAM
Norfolk

Magnolia Cottage ★★★
Contact: Mrs Sandra Hohol, 62 Westgate, Hunstanton PE36 5EL
T: (01485) 534267
F: (01485) 535230
E: shohol@birdsnorfolkholidayhomes.co.uk

The Oaks Cottage ★★★★
Contact: Mr & Mrs Ben Mullarkey, Dersingham, King's Lynn PE31 6PN
T: (01485) 540761
E: jb.mullarkey@eidosnet.co.uk
I: www.oakscottage.co.uk

The Old Forge ★★★★
Contact: Peter & Kate Webb & Ms Oakes, 4 Manor Road, Dersingham, King's Lynn PE31 6LD
T: (01485) 544410
F: (01485) 544410
E: catherine.oakes1@btopenworld.com

Quince Cottage ★★★★
Contact: Mrs Karen Kennedy-Hill, 9 Wheatfields, Hillington, King's Lynn PE31 6BH
T: (01485) 600850
E: karen.kennedyhill@btopenworld.com

DILHAM
Norfolk

Dairy Farm Cottages ★★★★
Contact: Mr James Paterson, Manor Farm, Smallburgh, Norwich NR28 9PZ
T: (01692) 535178
F: (01692) 536723
E: japdilman@farmline.com

DISS
Norfolk

Honey Bee Cottage ★★★
Contact: Mrs Rachel Davy, Honey End, Upper Street, Billingford, Diss IP21 4HR
T: (01379) 741449
F: (01379) 741449
E: chrisjdavy@freenetname.co.uk
I: www.honeybeecott.co.uk

Norfolk Cottages Malthouse Farm ★★★★
Contact: Mrs Sue Austin, Anglo Euro Properties Ltd, Malthouse Lane, Gissing, Diss IP22 5UT
T: (01379) 677512
F: (01379) 677510
E: bookings@norfolkcottages.net
I: www.norfolkcottages.net

Old Mill Farm ★★★
Contact: Mrs Pauline Ward, Old Mill Farm, Hopton Road, Garboldisham, Hopton, Diss IP22 2RJ
T: (01953) 681350
F: (01953) 681752
I: www.oldmillfarm.co.uk

Walcot Green Farm Cottage ★★★★
Contact: Mrs Nannette Catchpole, Walcot Green Farm, Walcot Green, Diss IP22 5SU
T: (01379) 652806
F: (01379) 652806
E: n.catchpole.wgf@virgin.net
I: website.lineone.net/~walcotgreenfarm

DOCKING
Norfolk

Courtyard Stable ★★★★
Contact: Mr & Mrs Roger Roberts, North Farmhouse, Station Road, King's Lynn PE31 8LS
T: (01485) 518493
F: (01485) 518493
E: northfarmhouse@aol.com

Hollywell ★★★
Contact: Mrs Claire Lanham, Bank House, Sampford Road, Radwinter, Saffron Walden CB10 2TL
T: (01799) 599571
F: (01799) 599182
E: claire@hollywell.org.uk

Honeysuckle Cottage ★★★★
Contact: Miss Amanda Cox, 49 Chertsey Road, Byfleet, West Byfleet KT14 7AP
T: 07901 822621

Norfolk House & Courtyard Cottage ★★★★★
Contact: Tim & Liz Witley, Cherry Tree Cottage, 17 Peddars Way South, Ringstead, Hunstanton PE36 5LF
T: (01485) 525341
F: (01485) 532715
E: timwitley@norfolkholidays.demon.co.uk

White Cottage ★★★
Contact: Mrs Sandra Hohol, 62 Westgate, Hunstanton PE36 5EL
T: (01485) 534267
F: (01485) 535230
E: shohol@birdsnorfolkholidayhomes.co.uk

Woodbine Cottage ★★★★
Contact: Mrs Karen Kennedy-Hill, 9 Wheatfields, Hillington, King's Lynn PE31 6BH
T: (01485) 600850
E: kkh@tinyonline.co.uk

DOWNHAM MARKET
Norfolk

Bridge Cottage
Rating Applied For
Contact: Mrs Sandra Hohol, 62 Westgate, Hunstanton PE36 5EL
T: (01485) 534267
F: (01485) 535230
E: shohol@birdsnorfolkholidayshomes.co.uk
I: www.norfolkholidayhomes-birds.co.uk

DUDDENHOE END
Essex

Cosh Cottage ★★★★
Contact: Mrs Perks, The Cosh, Duddenhoe End, Saffron Walden CB11 4UX
T: (01763) 838880
E: susan.perks@virgin.net

DUNWICH
Suffolk

Cliff House Holiday Park ★★★
Contact: Mr Hay & Mr S Johnson, Cliff House, Minsmere Road, Dunwich, Saxmundham IP17 3DQ
T: (01728) 648282
F: (01728) 648996
E: info@cliffhouseholidays.co.uk
I: www.cliffhouseholidays.co.uk

Lodge Cottage ★★★
Contact: Mr Pither, Suffolk Secrets, 7 Frenze Road, Diss IP22 4PA
T: (01379) 651297
F: (01379) 641555
E: holidays@suffolk-secrets.co.uk

Tinkers Cottage ★★
Contact: 7 Frenze Road, Diss IP22 4PA
T: (01379) 651297
F: (01379) 641555
E: holidays@suffolk-secrets.co.uk
I: www.suffolk-secrets.co.uk

EARSHAM
Norfolk

Dukes Cottage ★★★
Contact: Miss D Kingsley, Norfolk Country Cottages, Carlton House, Market Place, Reepham, Norwich NR10 4JJ
T: (01603) 871872
F: (01603) 870304
E: info@norfolkcottages.co.uk
I: www.norfolk-cottages.co.uk

EAST BERGHOLT
Suffolk

Woodstock Wing Woodstock ★★★
Contact: Mr & Mrs Keith & Janet Alcoe, Woodstock Wing Woodstock, Gaston Street, East Bergholt, Colchester CO7 6SD
T: (01206) 298724
F: (01206) 298128
E: janetandkeith@familyalcoe.fsnet.co.uk

EAST DEREHAM
Norfolk

Clinton Cottage & Clinton House ★★★★
Contact: Mrs M R Searle, Clinton Willows, Cutthroat Lane, Yaxham, East Dereham NR19 1RZ
T: (01362) 692079
F: (01362) 692079
E: clintonholidays@tesco.net
I: www.norfolkcountrycottage.co.uk

EAST HARLING
Norfolk

Berwick Cottage ★★★
Contact: Mr Tickner, 25 Webbscroft Road, Dagenham RM10 7NL
T: (020) 8595 7056

Dolphin Lodge ★★★★
Contact: Mrs E Jolly, Dolphin Lodge, Roudham Farm, East Harling, Norwich NR16 2RJ
T: (01953) 717126
F: (01953) 718593
E: jolly@roudhamfarm.co.uk
I: www.roudhamfarm.co.uk

Tapestry Cottage ★★★
Contact: Mr Michael Dolling, Tapestry Cottage, 44 White Hart Street, East Harling, Norwich NR16 2NE
T: (01263) 741115
F: (01953) 717443
E: ok_to.mark_it@virgin.net

EAST RUDHAM
Norfolk

Bumble Barn ★★
Contact: Mr David Kernon, Bumble Barn, Broomsthorpe Road, East Rudham, King's Lynn PE31 8RG
T: (01485) 528717

Rose Cottage Annex ★★
Contact: Mrs E. Maureen Mawby, Bagthorpe Road, East Rudham, King's Lynn PE31 8RA
T: (01485) 528274

EAST RUNTON
Norfolk

Mallards Rest ★★★
Contact: Mrs Nicola Thompson, Mallards Rest, Ravenna, Lower Common, East Runton, Cromer NR27 9PG
T: (01263) 512496

Poplars Caravan and Chalet Park ★★-★★★
Contact: Mr & Mrs Kevin and Dena Parfitt, Poplars Caravan and Chalet Park, Brick Lane, West Runton, Cromer NR27 9PL
T: (01263) 512892

Woodhill House ★★★
Contact: Mr & Mrs Patricia & John Neal, Woodhill House, High Street, East Runton, Cromer NR27 9PB
T: 001281 3200254
E: jpneal@sbcglobal.net

EAST RUSTON
Norfolk

Swallowtail Cottage ★★★
Contact: Mrs Brenda Taylor, 21a Roydon Road, Stanstead Abbotts, Ware SG12 8HQ
T: (01920) 870079
E: swallowcottage@hotmail.com

ELMSTEAD MARKET
Essex

Birds Farm ★★★-★★★★
Contact: Mrs Joanna Burke, School Road, Elmstead, Elmstead Market, Colchester CO7 7EY
T: (01206) 823838
E: birdsfarm@btinternet.com

ELMSWELL
Suffolk

Kiln Farm ★★★
Contact: Mrs Jacqueline Macaree, Kiln Farm, Kiln Lane, Elmswell, Bury St Edmunds IP30 9QR
T: (01359) 240442
E: paul_jacky@kilnfarm.fsnet.co.uk

Oak Farm ★★★★★
Contact: Mr & Mrs Dyball, Ashfield Road, Elmswell, Bury St Edmunds IP30 9HG
T: (01359) 240263
F: (01359) 240263

ELSWORTH
Cambridgeshire

Meadow Farm Cottage ★★★★
Contact: Mr & Mrs Anthony & Sue Taylor, Meadow Farm, Broad End, Elsworth, Cambridge CB3 8JD
T: (01954) 268042
F: (01954) 268044

ELY
Cambridgeshire

19 Chiefs Street
Rating Applied For
Contact: Mrs P Coates
T: (01223) 290842
F: (01223) 290529
E: cheviotbob@aol.com

Hill House Farm Cottage & The Old Granary ★★★★★
Contact: Mrs Hilary Nix, Hill House Farm Cottage & The Old Granary, Hill House Farm, 9 Main Street, Coveney, Ely CB6 2DJ
T: (01353) 778369
F: (01353) 778369
E: hillhouse@madasafish.com

9 Lisle Lane ★★★
Contact: Mr Ken Davis, Hurdle Drove, West Row, Bury St Edmunds IP28 8RG
T: (01353) 675249
E: fortyfarm@aol.com

47a Waterside ★★★
Contact: Mrs Florence Nolan, 47a Waterside, Ely CB7 4AU
T: (01353) 664377

ERISWELL
Suffolk

Church Cottage ★★★★★
Contact: Ms Yolande Goode, Estate Office, London Road, Elveden, Thetford IP24 3TQ
T: 08704 441155
F: 08704 441150
E: elveden@farmline.com

Cranhouse ★★★★★
Contact: Ms Yolande Goode, Estate Office, London Road, Elveden, Thetford IP24 3TQ
T: (01638) 533318
F: (01842) 890070
E: elveden@farmline.com

ERPINGHAM
Norfolk

Grange Farm ★★★
Contact: Mrs Jane Bell, Erpingham, Norwich NR11 7QX
T: (01263) 761241
F: (01263) 761241
E: jez.bell@internet.com
I: www.grangefarmholidays.co.uk

Keepers Cottage ★★★
Contact: Mrs Daniels, Woodbine Cottage, Blacksmith Lane, Erpingham, Norwich NR11 7QF
T: (01263) 761724

EYE
Suffolk

Manor House Cottages ★★★-★★★★
Contact: Mr David Mason, Manor House Cottages, Yaxley Manor House, Mellis Road, Yaxley, Eye IP23 8DG
T: (01379) 788181
F: (01379) 788422
E: david@dmenterprises.demon.co.uk
I: www.manorhousecottages.co.uk

FAKENHAM
Norfolk

The Cottage ★★★
Contact: Miss Dawn Kinsley, Norfolk Country Cottages Ref. 672, Market Place, Reepham, Norwich NR10 4JJ
T: (01603) 871872
F: (01603) 870304
E: info@norfolkcottages.co.uk
I: www.swallow-tail.com

Idyllic Cottages at Vere Lodge ★★★-★★★★★
Contact: Mrs Jane Bowlby, Holiday Complex, South Raynham, Fakenham NR21 7HE
T: (01328) 838261
F: (01328) 838300
E: major@verelodge.co.uk

Manor Farm ★★★★
Contact: Mr Abram, Manor Farm, Oxwick, Fakenham NR21 7HZ
T: (01328) 700300
F: (01328) 700755

The Paddocks ★★★★
Contact: Mr Keith Hatfield, Little Barney Lane, Barney, Fakenham NR21 0NL
T: (01328) 878305
F: (01328) 878948
E: oldbrickkilns@aol.com
I: www.old-brick-kilns-co.uk

Pollywiggle Cottage ★★★★
Contact: Mrs Marilyn Farnham-Smith, 79 Earlham Road, Norwich NR2 3RE
T: (01603) 471990
F: (01603) 612221
E: marilyn@pollywigglecottage.co.uk
I: www.pollywigglecottage.co.uk

Stables Cottage & Oxford Barn ★★★
Contact: Mr & Mrs John & Jill Matthews, West Raynham, Fakenham NR21 7EZ
T: (01328) 838509
E: oldalehousecottages@hotmail.com

FELBRIGG
Norfolk

Boundary Farm Cottage Rating Applied For
Contact: Mrs Wendy Congreve, Smiths Farm, Gedney, Spalding PE12 0AZ
T: (01406) 363618

FELIXSTOWE
Suffolk

Fairlight Detached Bungalow ★★★
Contact: Mrs Daphne Knights, 127 High Road East, Felixstowe IP11 9PS
T: (01394) 277730

Flat 2 ★★★
Contact: Mrs Gwen Lynch
T: (01473) 328729

Honeypot Cottage ★★★
Contact: Mrs Theresa Adams, Falkenham, Ipswich IP10 0RA
T: (01394) 448564
F: (01394) 448564
E: adams99@btinternet.com

Kimberley Holiday Flats ★★
Contact: Mrs Valerie Reed, Kimberley Holiday Flats, 105-107 Undercliff Road, Felixstowe IP11 2AF
T: (01394) 672157

Sea View Holiday Flat ★★★★
Contact: Mrs Sue Brady, 50 St Georges Road, Felixstowe IP11 9PN
T: (01394) 274231
E: suembrady@talk21.com

FIELD DALLING
Norfolk

The Annexe ★★★
Contact: Mrs Betty Ringer, 2 Binham Road, Field Dalling, Wells-next-the-Sea NR25 7LJ
T: (01328) 830206

Oak Barn ★★★★
Contact: Mrs Angela Harcourt, Little Marsh Lane, Field Dalling, Holt NR25 7LL
T: (01328) 830655
F: (01328) 830257
E: harcog@farming.co.uk

FILBY
Norfolk

Wychwood ★★★★
Contact: Miss D Kingsley, Norfolk Country Cottages, Carlton House, Market Place, Reepham, Norwich NR10 4JJ
T: (01603) 871872
F: (01603) 870304
E: info@norfolkcottages.co.uk
I: www.norfolkcottages.co.uk

FORNHAM ALL SAINTS
Suffolk

Fornham Hall Cottage ★★★
Contact: Mrs Helene Sjolin, Fornham All Saints, Bury St Edmunds IP28 6JJ
T: (01284) 703424
E: cottage@sjolin.demon.co.uk

FOXLEY
Norfolk

Moor Farm Stable Cottages ★★-★★★★
Contact: Mr P Davis
T: (01362) 688523
F: (01362) 688523
E: moorfarm@aol.com
I: www.moorfarmstablecottages.co.uk

FRAMLINGHAM
Suffolk

Boundary Farm ★★★-★★★★★
Contact: Mrs Susan Seabrook, Boundary Farm, Saxtead Road, Framlingham, Woodbridge IP13 9PZ
T: (01728) 621026
F: (01728) 621026

Wood Lodge ★★★
Contact: Mr Tim Kindred, High House Farm, Cransford, Woodbridge IP13 9PD
T: (01728) 663461
F: (01728) 663409
E: woodlodge@highhousefarm.co.uk
I: www.highhousefarm.co.uk

FRING
Norfolk

Owl Barn ★★★★
Contact: Mrs Heather Habbin, West Winch, King's Lynn PE33 0PR
T: (01553) 840655
E: owlbarnfring@aol.com

FRINTON-ON-SEA
Essex

Quartette ★★★
Contact: Mr Robert Bucke, Boydens, 73 Connaught Avenue, Frinton-on-Sea CO13 9PP
T: 07010 716013
F: 08707 653746
E: ipsw2@btinternet.com
I: www.ipsw.btinternet.co.uk/quartette.htm

GARBOLDISHAM
Norfolk

Burnside ★★★★
Contact: Mrs Connie Atkins, Burnside, Alderwood, Hopton Road, Garboldisham, Hopton, Diss IP22 2RQ
T: (01953) 688376
F: (01953) 681743
E: douconatkins@waitrose.com

GAYTON
Norfolk

Chalk Barn ★★★★
Contact: Mrs S Thompson, Chalk Barn Cottage, Winch Road, Gayton, King's Lynn PE32 1QP
T: (01553) 636353

Field View ★★★
Contact: Mr & Mrs Watkinson, Lynn Road, Gayton, King's Lynn PE32 1QJ
T: (01553) 636629
F: (01553) 636629
E: fieldviewcottage@hotmail.com

Willow Cottage ★★★
Contact: Mr Michael Pooley, West Hall Farm, Winch Road, Gayton, King's Lynn PE32 1QP
T: (01553) 636519
F: (01553) 636519
E: mike@westhallfarm.co.uk
I: www.westhallfarm.co.uk

GEDGRAVE
Suffolk

The Gedgrave Broom ★★★★
Contact: Mrs Alison Watson, Newton Farm, Orford, Woodbridge IP12 2AG
T: (01394) 450488

GORLESTON-ON-SEA
Norfolk

Manor Cottage ★★★
Contact: Mrs Margaret Ward, North Manor House, 12 Pier Plain, Gorleston-on-Sea, Great Yarmouth NR31 6PE
T: (01493) 669845
F: (01493) 669845
E: manorcottage@wardm4.fsnet.co.uk
I: www.wardm4.fsnet.co.uk

GOSFIELD
Essex

Casita Rating Applied For
Contact: Mrs Christine Jones, Church Cottage, Church Road, Gosfield, Halstead CO9 1UD
T: (01787) 474863
F: (01787) 473449
E: christine.jones7@btinternet.com

GREAT ABINGTON
Cambridgeshire

Appletree Cottage Rating Applied For
Contact: Pamela & Brian Parris, Appletree Cottage, 36 South Road, Abington, Great Abington, Cambridge CB1 6AU
T: (01223) 892026

GREAT BIRCHAM
Norfolk

The Guest Flat ★★★
Contact: Mrs Sandra Hohol, 62 Westgate, Ringstead, Hunstanton PE36 5EL
T: (01485) 534267
F: (01485) 535230
E: shohol@birdsnorfolkholidayhomes.co.uk
I: www.norfolkholidayhomes-birds.co.uk

Humphrey Cottage ★★★
Contact: Mrs Elly Chalmers, Great Bircham, King's Lynn PE31 6SJ
T: (01485) 578393
E: info@birchamwindmill.co.uk
I: www.birchamwindmill.co.uk

GREAT DUNMOW
Essex

The Granary ★★★★
Contact: Mr & Mrs Philip & Cathy Burton, The Granary, Moor End Farm, Broxted, Great Dunmow CM6 2EL
T: (01371) 870821
F: (01371) 870821
E: cathy@moorendfarm.com
I: www.moorendfarm.com

Old Piggeries ★★★
Contact: Mr Kirby, Grange Farm, Great Dunmow CM6 3HY
T: (01371) 820205
F: (01377) 820205

GREAT HOCKHAM
Norfolk

Old School Cottage ★★★★
Contact: Mr & Mrs Colin & Karin Titley, Wretham Road, Great Hockham, Thetford IP24 1NY
T: (01953) 498277
E: oscott@clara.net
I: www.4starcottage.co.uk

GREAT MASSINGHAM
Norfolk

Eves Cottage ★★★
Contact: Mrs Kinsley, Carlton House, Market Place, Reepham, Norwich NR10 4JJ
T: (01603) 871872
F: (01603) 870304
E: info@norfolkcottages.co.uk
I: www.swallow-tail.com

Old Swan Cottage & The Stables at the Old Swan ★★★★
Contact: Mrs Sara Barns, The Old Swan, School Road, Great Massingham, King's Lynn PE32 2JA
T: (01485) 520151
E: ssbarns@hotmail.com

Primrose Cottage ★★★
Contact: Mrs Christine Riches, 21 Weasenham Road, Great Massingham, King's Lynn PE32 2EY
T: (01485) 520216
E: christine-riches@supanet.com
I: www.christine-riches.supanet.com

GREAT PLUMSTEAD
Norfolk

Windfalls ★★★
Contact: Mrs Jane Jones, Middle Road, Norwich NR13 5EF
T: (01603) 720235
F: (01603) 722008
E: hall.farm@btinternet.com

GREAT SNORING
Norfolk

Home Cottage ★★★
Contact: Mr Tony Rivett, Holt Road, Wood Norton, Swanton Novers, Melton Constable NR20 5BN
T: (01263) 860462

Rose Cottage ★★★★
Contact: Mrs Gilly Paramor, Pedlars Lane, Fulmodestone, Fakenham NR21 0NH
T: (01328) 878867
F: (01328) 878867
E: gilly@gparamor.freeserve.co.uk
I: www.clevencycottages.freeserve.co.uk

3 The Terrace ★★★
Contact: Miss Dawn Kinsley, Market Place, Reepham, Norwich NR10 4JJ
T: (01603) 871872
F: (01603) 870304
E: info@norfolkcottages.co.uk
I: www.swallow-tail.com

GREAT WALSINGHAM
Norfolk

The Tailor's House ★★★
Contact: Mr Andrew Howlett, Estate Office, Walsingham NR22 6BP
T: (01328) 820259
F: (01328) 820098
E: walsingham.estate@farmline.com

GREAT WIGBOROUGH
Essex

Honeysuckle Cottage ★★★★
Contact: Mr Kevin Benner, Honeysuckle Cottage, Mistletoe Cottage, Maldon Road, Great Wigborough, Colchester CO5 7RH
T: (01206) 735282
E: kevinbenner@btopenworld.com
I: www.honeysucklecot.co.uk

GREAT YARMOUTH
Norfolk

Arrandale Apartments ★★★
Contact: Mr Peter Meah, Arrandale Apartments, 39 Wellesley Road, Great Yarmouth NR30 1EU
T: (01493) 855046
F: (01493) 300434
I: www.arrandaleapartments.co.uk

Cambridge Court Holiday Apartments ★★★-★★★★
Contact: Ms Linda Dyble, Cambridge Court Holiday Apartments, 10 North Denes Road, Great Yarmouth NR30 4LW
T: (01493) 304913
F: (01493) 304913

Kenwood Holiday Flats ★★
Contact: Mrs V Forbes, 82 North Denes Road, Great Yarmouth NR30 4LW
T: (01493) 852740
E: kev@forbeseys.fsnet.co.uk

GRESHAM
Norfolk

Astalot & Avalon Cottages ★★
Contact: Mrs J J Murray
T: (01263) 740404
F: (01263) 740404

The Little Place ★★
Contact: Mr & Mrs Paul Hill, Loke End Cottage, The Loke, Gresham, Norwich NR11 8RJ
T: (01263) 577344
I: www.broadland.com/littleplace

GRUNDISBURGH
Suffolk

The Stable ★★★
Contact: Mrs Louisa Davies, The Green, Grundisburgh, Woodbridge IP13 6TA
T: (01473) 738827

GUNTHORPE
Norfolk

Chimney Cottage ★★★
Contact: Mr Preston, Langham, Holt NR25 7AE
T: (01328) 830411
F: (01328) 830411

The Stables Courtyard ★★★★
Contact: Mrs Irene Vallance, 10 Ashburnham Road, Bedford MK40 2RH
T: (01525) 404898

HADLEIGH
Suffolk

Stable Cottages ★★★★
Contact: Mrs Margaret Langton, Stable Cottages, The Granary, Chattisham Place, Chattisham, Ipswich IP8 3QD
T: (01473) 652210
F: (01473) 652210
E: margaret.langton@talk21.com
I: www.farmstayanglia.co.uk/chattisham

HAINFORD
Norfolk

Four Sticks ★★★
Contact: Norfolk Country Cottages, Carlton House, Market Place, Reepham, Norwich NR10 4JJ
T: (01603) 871872
F: (01603) 870304
E: info@norfolkcottages.co.uk
I: www.norfolkcottages.co.uk

HALESWORTH
Suffolk

Bucks Farm ★★★★
Contact: Mrs Bradshaw, Bucks Farm, Walpole, Halesworth IP19 0LX
T: (01986) 784216
F: (01986) 784216
I: www.bucksfarm-holidays.co.uk

HALSTEAD
Essex

Froyz Hall Barn ★★★★
Contact: Mrs Judi Butler, Froyz Hall Farm, Halstead CO9 1RS
T: (01787) 476684
F: (01787) 474647
E: mjudibutler6@aol.com

Gainsford Hall ★★★★
Contact: Mr Chris Barnard & Ms Archer, Houghtons Farm, Gainsford End, Toppesfield, Halstead CO9 4EH
T: (01787) 237334

HAPPISBURGH
Norfolk

Heather Cottage ★★★★
Contact: Miss D Kingsley, Carlton House, Market Place, Reepham, Norwich NR10 4JJ
T: (01603) 871872
F: (01603) 870304
E: info@norfolkcottages.co.uk
I: www.norfolkcottages.co.uk

Lanthorn Cottage ★★★★
Contact: Mr Brown, Church Lane House, Vicarage Lane, Bovingdon, Hemel Hempstead HP3 0LT
T: (01442) 832263
I: www.country-holidays.co.uk

HARPLEY
Norfolk

Rosedene ★★★★
Contact: Mr Roger Osborne, 22 Westgate Green, Hevingham, Norwich NR10 5RF
T: (01603) 754349
F: 0870 138 3280
E: rogero@pobox.com
I: www.pobox.com/~rogero

HARROLD
Bedfordshire

Ouse View ★★★
Contact: Mrs R Northern, The Priory, Priory Farm, High Street, Harrold, Bedford MK43 7EE
T: (01234) 720293
F: (01234) 720292
E: ros.northern@farmline.com
I: www.prioryfarmholidays.co.uk

Priory Farm Chalet ★★
Contact: Mrs R Northern, The Priory, Priory Farm, High Street, Harrold, Bedford MK43 7EE
T: (01234) 720293
F: (01234) 720292
E: ros.northern@farmline.com
I: www.prioryfarmholidays.co.uk

HARTEST
Suffolk

Crown Cottage ★★★
Contact: Holiday Cottages Ref: 10981, Holiday Cottages Group, Spring Mill, Earby, Barnoldswick BB94 0AA
T: 08700 723723
F: (01282) 844288
E: sales@holidaycottagesgroup.com
I: www.country-holidays.co.uk

HAUGHLEY
Suffolk

The Cottage ★★★
Contact: Mrs Mary Noy, Red House Farm, Station Road, Haughley, Stowmarket IP14 3QP
T: (01449) 673323
F: (01449) 675413
E: mary@noy1.fsnet.co.uk
I: farmstayanglia.co.uk

HEACHAM
Norfolk

1 Canon Pott Close ★★★★
Contact: Mrs Sandra Hohol, Birds Norfolk Holiday Homes, 62 Westgate, Hunstanton PE36 5EL
T: (01485) 534267
F: (01485) 535230
E: shohol@birdsnorfolkholidayhomes.co.uk
I: www.norfolkholidayhomes-birds.co.uk

Cedar Springs ★★-★★★
Contact: Mrs A Howe, Owl Lodge, Jubilee Road, Heacham, King's Lynn PE31 7AR
T: (01485) 570609
E: antoniahowe@aol.com

Cedar Springs Chalets ★★
Contact: Mr & Mrs Michael & Ann Chestney, 35 West Raynham, 35 The Street, West Raynham, Fakenham NR21 7EY
T: (01328) 838341
F: (01328) 838341

Cheney Hollow Cottages ★★★★
Contact: Mrs Thelma Holland, Cheney Hollow, 3-5 Cheney Hill, Heacham, King's Lynn PE31 7BX
T: (01485) 572625
F: (01485) 572625
E: thelma@cheneyhollow.co.uk
I: www.cheneyhollow.co.uk

Dora's Cottage
Rating Applied For
Contact: Mrs Sandra Hohol, Birds Norfolk Holiday Homes, 62 Westgate, Hunstanton PE36 5EL
T: (01485) 534267
F: (01485) 535230
E: shohol@birdsnorfolkholidayhomes.co.uk
I: www.norfolkholidayhomes-birds.co.uk

11 The Drift ★★★★
Contact: Holiday Cottages Ref: 17149, Holiday Cottages Group, Spring Mill, Earby, Barnoldswick BB94 0AA
T: 08700 723723
F: (01282) 844288
E: sales@holidaycottagesgroup.com

The Hayloft ★★★★
Contact: Mrs O'Callaghan, The Hermitage, Wilton Road, Heacham, King's Lynn PE31 7AD
T: (01485) 571838
F: (01485) 571838
E: sunnymeadholpark@aol.com

Holly Cottage ★★★
Contact: Mrs O'Callaghan, The Hermitage, Wilton Road, Heacham, King's Lynn PE31 7AD
T: (01485) 571838
F: (01485) 571838
E: sunnymeadholpark@aol.com
I: www.heacham1.fsnet.co.uk

Little Allington ★★★
Contact: Mrs Jane Shulver, Norfolk Country Cottages, Carlton House, Market Place, Reepham, Norwich NR10 4JJ
T: (01603) 871872
I: www.norfolk-cottages.co.uk

The Lookout ★★
Contact: Mrs Sandra Hohol, Birds Norfolk Holiday Homes, 62 Westgate, Hunstanton PE36 5EL
T: (01485) 534267
F: (01485) 535230
E: shohol@birdsnorfolkholidayhomes.co.uk
I: www.norfolkholidayhomes-birds.co.uk

Manor Farm Cottage ★★★
Contact: Mrs C. M. Wallace, Hunstanton Road, Heacham, King's Lynn PE31 7JX
T: (01485) 570567
F: (01485) 570567
E: carolewallace@talk21.com

The Old Station Waiting Rooms ★★★
Contact: Mr & Mrs Clay, Station Road, Heacham, King's Lynn PE31 7AW
T: (01485) 570712
I: www.cottageguide.co.uk/waitingrooms

Painters Corner ★★★★
Contact: Mrs N. J. O'Callaghan, The Hermitage, 2 Wilton Road, Heacham, King's Lynn PE31 7AD
T: (01485) 571838
F: (01485) 571838
E: hideawaya1@aol.com
I: www.sunnymead-holidays.co.uk

4 Pretoria Cottages ★★★
Contact: Mrs Barnes, 58 High Drive, New Malden KT3 3UB
T: (020) 8255 8834

2 Retreat Cottage ★★★
Contact: Mrs Rooth, 32 Church Green, Hunstanton Road, Heacham, King's Lynn PE31 7HH
T: (01485) 572072
E: sl.rooth@virgin.net

Robin Hill ★★
Contact: Mrs Gidney, Robin Hill, Hunstanton Road, Heacham, King's Lynn PE31 7JX
T: (01485) 570309

Roseleigh Villa ★★★
Contact: Mrs Sandra Hohol, Birds Norfolk Holiday Homes, 62 Westgate, Hunstanton PE36 5EL
T: (01485) 534267
F: (01485) 535230
E: shohol@birdsnorfolkholidayshomes.co.uk
I: www.norfolkholidayhomes-birds.co.uk

Staneve ★★★
Contact: Mr & Mrs J Smith, 2B Church Road, Flitwick, Bedford MK45 1AE
T: (01525) 634935
E: amandalsmith@ntlworld.com
I: www.staneve.biz

1 Sunnyside Cottages ★★★
Contact: Miss D Kingsley, Norfolk Country Cottages, Carlton House, Market Place, Reepham, Norwich NR10 4JJ
T: (01603) 871872
F: (01603) 870304
E: info@norfolkcottages.co.uk
I: www.norfolk-cottages.co.uk

Tawny Cottage ★★★★
Contact: Miss D Kingsley, Norfolk Country Cottages, Carlton House, Market Place, Reepham, Norwich NR10 4JJ
T: (01603) 871872
F: (01603) 870304
E: info@norfolkcottages.co.uk

Victoria House ★★★
Contact: Mrs Penny Rumble, Causeway End Farmhouse CB5 9PW
T: (01223) 861831
E: penny@therumbles.freeserve.co.uk

HERTFORD
Hertfordshire

Dalmonds Barns ★★★★
Contact: Mrs Ann Reay, Jepps Farm, Mangrove Lane, Hertford SG13 8QJ
T: (01992) 479151
F: (01992) 479151
E: ann.reay@virgin.net
I: www.dalmondsbarns.comwww.dalmondsbarns.co.uk

HESSETT
Suffolk

Wilwyn & Chapel Cottages ★★★
Contact: Mr & Mrs Chris & Nicky Glass, The Street, Hessett, Bury St Edmunds IP30 9AZ
T: (01359) 270736
F: (01359) 270736
E: chris.glass@free4all.co.uk
I: www.cottageguide.co.uk/hessett

HICKLING
Norfolk

The Conifers ★★★★
Contact: Miss D Kingsley, Carlton House, Market Place, Reepham, Norwich NR10 4JJ
T: (01603) 871872
F: (01603) 870304
E: info@norfolkcottages.co.uk
I: www.norfolk-cottages.co.uk

The Cottage ★★★
Contact: Miss D Kingsley, Norfolk Country Cottages, Carlton House, Market Place, Reepham, Norwich NR10 4JJ
T: (01603) 871872
F: (01603) 870304
E: info@norfolkcottages.co.uk
I: www.norfolk-cottages.co.uk

HIGH KELLING
Norfolk

Lynton Loft ★★★
Contact: Miss D Kingsley, Norfolk Country Cottages, Carlton House, Market Place, Reepham, Norwich NR10 4JJ
T: (01603) 871872
F: (01603) 870304
E: info@norfolkcottages.co.uk
I: www.norfolk-cottages.co.uk

HILLINGTON
Norfolk

The Old Rectory
Rating Applied For
Contact: Mrs Sarah Thompsett, The Old Rectory, Station Road, Hillington, King's Lynn PE31 6DE
T: (01485) 600177

HINDOLVESTON
Norfolk

Lavender Cottage ★★★★
Contact: Ms Jacqui Rose & Mr Phillip Archer, Thatches, Nedging Road, Nedging Tye, Ipswich IP7 7HL
T: (01449) 741396
E: philarcher_uk@yahoo.co.uk

Pine Cottage ★★★
Contact: Mr & Mrs Scammell, Potters Bar EN6 1QW
T: (01707) 651734

HINDRINGHAM
Norfolk

Cockle Cottage ★★★
Contact: Mrs Susan Heath, Packwood, Hillesden, Buckingham MK18 4DE
T: (01280) 820742

HINGHAM
Norfolk

The Granary ★★★★
Contact: Mrs C Dunnett, College Farm, Hingham, Norwich NR9 4PP
T: (01953) 850596
F: (01953) 851364
E: christine.dunnett@lineone.net

HITCHAM
Suffolk

Mill House Holiday Cottages ★★-★★★
Contact: Ms Melanie Rieger, Mill Acres Limited t/a Mill House, c/o Mill House, Water Run, Hitcham, Ipswich IP7 7LN
T: (01449) 740315
F: (01449) 740315
E: hitcham@aol.com
I: millhouse-hitcham.co.uk

HOCKWOLD
Norfolk

Lilac Barns ★★★★
Contact: Agent, Hoseasons Country Cottages, Sunway House, Raglan Road, Lowestoft NR32 2LW
T: (01502) 501515
I: www.hoseasons.co.uk

HOLBROOK
Suffolk

The Flat
Rating Applied For
Contact: Mrs Hilary Goodwin, Hyams Lane, Holbrook, Ipswich IP9 2QF
T: (01473) 327668
F: (01473) 328335

HOLME NEXT THE SEA
Norfolk

Beach Cottage ★★★★
Contact: Mrs Stephanie Jones, Beach Road, Hunstanton PE36 6LG
T: (01485) 525201
E: robertjones@samphire1.demon.co.uk

Brook Bungalow ★★★
Contact: Mrs Whitsed, Ailsworth, Peterborough PE5 7AQ
T: (01733) 380028
F: (01733) 380028
E: john@jwhitsed.freeserve.co.uk

Eastgate Barn ★★★
Contact: Mrs Shirley' Simeone, Eastgate Barn, Eastgate Road, Holme next the sea, Hunstanton PE36 6LL
T: (01485) 525218

Rose Cottage ★★★★
Contact: Mrs Stephanie Hedge, Cottenham, Cambridge CB4 8UL
T: (01954) 250470
F: (01954) 250470

Sunnymead Corner ★★★★
Contact: Mrs Nicola O'Callaghan, The Hermitage, Wilton Road, Heacham, King's Lynn PE31 7AD
T: (01485) 571838
E: sunnymeadholpark@aol.com

Swift Cottage ★★★
Contact: Mr Richard Simmonds, Market Place, Oundle, Peterborough PE8 4BE
T: (01832) 273531
F: (01832) 274938
E: richard@simmondsatoundle.co.uk
I: www.oundlecottagebreaks.co.uk

Tudor Lodge Cottage ★★★★
Contact: Mrs Sandra Hohol, 62 Westgate, Ringstead, Hunstanton PE36 5BU
T: (01485) 534267
F: (01485) 535230
E: shohol@birdsnorfolkholidayhomes.co.uk
I: www.norfolkholidayhomes-birds.co.uk

HOLT
Norfolk

Albert Street ★
Contact: Mrs Helen North, Eldon House, Eldon Lane, Braishfield, Romsey SO51 0PT
T: (01794) 368864

Arcadia ★★★
Contact: Mrs Elizabeth McGill, 8 Sunmead Road, Sunbury-on-Thames TW16 6PE
T: (01932) 770207
E: elizabethmcgill@dialstart.net

Blickling Bungalow ★★★
Contact: Miss Dawn Kinsley, Norfolk Country Cottages Ref. 123, Market Place, Reepham, Norwich NR10 4JJ
T: (01603) 871872
F: (01603) 870304
E: info@norfolkcottages.co.uk
I: www.swallow-tail.com

6 Carpenters Cottage ★★★
Contact: Mrs Beament, Moorlake Cross, Crediton EX17 5EL
T: (01363) 773789
E: sallybeament@hotmail.com

5 Carpenters Cottages ★★★
Contact: Mr Christopher Knights, The Hollies Farmhouse, Rushmere, Lowestoft NR33 8EP
T: (01493) 842289
F: (01502) 742022

Cherry Tree Cottage ★★★
Contact: Mr & Mrs Bailey, 9 Branksome Close, Norwich NR4 6SP
T: (01603) 501341
E: glyn.bailey@tesco.net

1 Crowlands Cottage & 4 Carpenters Cottage ★★★
Contact: Mrs Julie Pell, Spalding PE11 2HL
T: (01775) 725126
F: (01775) 725126
E: julie.pell@talk21.com

Halcyon House ★★★★
Contact: Mrs Judith Everitt, Field Dalling Road, Bale, Fakenham NR21 0QS
T: (01328) 878419

Hidden Talents ★★★★
Contact: Mr & Mrs Barker, 19 Quay Street, Woodbridge IP12 1BX
T: (01394) 382649
F: (01394) 610212

Honeysuckle Cottage ★★★
Contact: Miss Allison, Withers Close, Holt NR25 6NH
T: (01263) 712457

Sunnyside Cottage ★★★
Contact: Mr Michael Drake, Station New Road, Brundall, Norwich NR13 5PQ
T: (01603) 712524
F: (01603) 712524
E: michael.drake@ukgateway.net

Wood Farm Cottages ★★★-★★★★
Contact: Mrs Diana Elsby, Plumstead Road, Edgefield, Melton Constable NR24 2AQ
T: (01263) 587347
F: (01263) 587347
E: info@wood-farm.com
I: www.wood-farm.com

HOLTON ST MARY
Suffolk

The Coach House ★★★★
Contact: Mrs Anne Selleck, Holton St Mary, Colchester CO7 6NT
T: (01206) 298246
F: (01206) 298246
E: fjs.stratho@brutus.go-plus.net

HOLYWELL
Cambridgeshire

Reed Cottage
Rating Applied For
Contact: Mrs Jane Powell, 76 Boxworth End, Swavesey, Cambridge CB4 5RA
T: (01954) 232831
F: (01954) 202425

HORHAM
Suffolk

Alpha Cottages ★★★
Contact: Mr & Mrs Brian Cooper, Lodge Farm, The Street, Horham, Eye IP21 5DX
T: (01379) 384424
F: (01379) 384424

Athelington Hall
Rating Applied For
Contact: Hamilton Smith Management & Letting, 6b Church Street, Woodbridge IP12 1DS
T: (01394) 386688
E: woodbridge@hamilton-smith.com

HORNING
Norfolk

Boy's Own Cottage Riverside ★★★★
Contact: Ms Alison Atkins, Great Heath Farm, Chelmsford Road, Hatfield Heath, Bishop's Stortford CM22 7BQ
T: (01279) 739443
F: (01279) 739443
E: alirick@daynet.co.uk
I: www.boysowncottage.co.uk

Bure House ★★★★
Contact: Mrs Bryan, Scalford, Melton Mowbray LE14 4SS
T: (01664) 444206
E: ebryan@rutland.gov.uk
I: www.norfolkcottages.co.uk

Ferry Marina ★★★
Contact: Ferry Road, Horning, Norwich NR12 8PS
T: (01692) 630392
I: www.ferry-marina.co.uk

Hall Farm Cottages ★★★★
Contact: Mr & Mrs Hudson, Hall Farm Cottages, Hall Farm, Ludham, Great Yarmouth NR12 8NJ
T: (01692) 630385
I: www.hallfarm.com

Horning Lodges 1,2,3, Kates & Lady Lodge & Eagle Cottage ★★★-★★★★★
Contact: Mr Robert King, 4 Pinewood Drive, Horning, Norwich NR12 8LZ
T: (01692) 630297
F: (01692) 630297
E: kingline@norfolk-broads.co.uk
I: www.norfolk-broads.co.uk

Little River View ★★★
Contact: Mrs Free, Newlands Spring, Chelmsford CM1 4YE
T: (01245) 441981
E: victoria@littleriverview.co.uk
I: www.littlerivervew.co.uk

The Windmill ★★★
Contact: Ms Sandra Hohol, Norfolk Holiday Homes, 62 Westgate, Hunstanton PE36 5EL
T: (01485) 534267
F: (01485) 535230
E: shohol@birdsnorfolkholidayhomes.co.uk

HORNINGTOFT
Norfolk

The Old Stables ★★★
Contact: Mr Ivan Baker, The Old Stables, Church Farm, Oxwich Road, Horningtoft, East Dereham NR20 5DX
T: (01328) 700262

HUNSTANTON
Norfolk

19,33 South Beach Road ★★
Contact: Mrs Sandra Hohol, 62 Westgate, Hunstanton PE36 5EL
T: (01485) 534267
F: (01485) 535230
E: shohol@birdsnorfolkholidayhomes.co.uk
I: www.norfolkholidayhomes-birds.co.uk

Altera ★★★
Contact: Mrs J. H. Larman, 64 Hillview Road, Hatch End, Pinner HA5 4PE
T: (020) 8421 3815
E: jeanlarman@tinyworld.co.uk

Ashdale House ★★★★
Contact: Mrs Sandra Hohol, 62 Westgate, Hunstanton PE36 5EL
T: (01485) 534267
F: (01485) 535230
E: shohol@birdsnorfolkholidayhomes.co.uk
I: www.norfolkholidayhomes-birds.co.uk

Beat 'n' Retreat ★★
Contact: Mrs Sandra Hohol, 62 Westgate, Hunstanton PE36 5EL
T: (01485) 534267
F: (01485) 535230
E: shohol@birdsnorfolkholidayhomes.co.uk
I: www.norfolkholidayhomes-birds.co.uk

Beeches ★★★
Contact: Mr & Mrs Judd, Hunstanton Holidays, 64 Tudor Road, Godmanchester, Huntingdon PE29 2DW
T: (01480) 411509
F: (01480) 411509
E: hunstantonholidays@dsl.pipex.com
I: www.hunstantonholidays.co.uk

Belle Vue Apartment ★★★-★★★★★
Contact: Mrs Sandra Bowman, Belle Vue Apartments, 28 St Edmunds Avenue, Hunstanton PE36 6BW
T: (01485) 532826

Brincliffe ★★★★
Contact: Mrs Sandra Hohol, 62 Westgate, Hunstanton PE36 5EL
T: (01485) 534267
F: (01485) 535230
E: shohol@birdsnorfolkholidayhomes.co.uk
I: www.norfolkholidayhomes-birds.co.uk

The Bungalow ★★★
Contact: Mrs Harris, 3 Ratby Meadow Lane, St Johns Enderby, Leicester LE19 2BN
T: (0116) 286 2943

Chalet 4 ★★
Contact: Mr & Mrs Michael Chestney, 35 West Raynham, Fakenham NR21 7EY
T: (01328) 838341
F: (01328) 838341

Cleeks ★★★
Contact: Mrs Sandra Hohol, 62 Westgate, Hunstanton PE36 5EL
T: (01485) 534267
F: (01485) 535230
E: shohol@birdsnorfolkholidayhomes.co.uk
I: www.norfolkholidayhomes-birds.co.uk

70 Cliff Parade ★★
Contact: Mrs Sandra Hohol, 62 Westgate, Hunstanton PE36 5EL
T: (01485) 534267
F: (01485) 535230
E: shohol@birdsnorfolkholidayhomes.co.uk
I: www.norfolkholidayhomes-birds.co.uk

40 Collingwood Road ★★★
Contact: Mrs Sandra Hohol, 62 Westgate, Hunstanton PE36 5EL
T: (01485) 534267
F: (01485) 535230
E: shohol@birdsnorfolkholidayhomes.co.uk
I: www.norfolkholidayhomes-birds.co.uk

End of the Road ★★
Contact: Mrs Sandra Hohol, 62 Westgate, Hunstanton PE36 5EL
T: (01485) 534267
F: (01485) 535230
E: shohol@birdsnorfolkholidayhomes.co.uk
I: www.norfolkholidayhomes-birds.co.uk

Flat 11 ★★★
Contact: Mrs Sandra Hohol, 62 Westgate, Hunstanton PE36 5EL
T: (01485) 534267
F: (01485) 535230
E: shohol@birdsnorfolkholhomes.co.uk
I: www.norfolkholidayhomes-birds.co.uk

Ground Floor Flat ★★★
Contact: Mrs Sandra Hohol, 62 Westgate, Hunstanton PE36 5EL
T: (01485) 534267
F: (01485) 535230
E: shohol@birdsnorfolkholidayhomes.co.uk
I: www.norfolkholidayhomes-birds.co.uk

Hermits Lea ★★★
Contact: Mrs Cheri Crosley, Cromer Road, Hunstanton PE36 6HW
T: (01485) 533332
F: (01485) 533332
E: chericrosley@aol.com

4 Homefields Road ★★★
Contact: Ms Elizabeth Anderson, Prospect House, 92 North End, Bassingbourn, Royston SG8 5PD
T: (01763) 243067

Jaskville ★★★
Contact: Mr & Mrs John & Ann Smith, 11 Nene Road, Hunstanton PE36 5BZ
T: (01485) 533404

1 Lower Lincoln Street ★★★
Contact: Mr Emsden, 24 Northgate, Hunstanton PE36 6AP
T: (01485) 532552
E: mikeemsden@totalise.co.uk
I: www.hotelshunstanton.co.uk

Midway ★★★
Contact: Mrs Sandra Hohol, 62 Westgate, Hunstanton PE36 5EL
T: (01485) 534267
F: (01485) 535230
E: shohol@birdsnorfolkholidayhomes.co.uk
I: www.norfolkholidayhomes-birds.co.uk

Minna Cottage ★★★
Contact: Mr T Cassie, 21 The Green, Hunstanton PE36 5AH
T: (01485) 532448
E: tonycassie@btconnect.com
I: www.minnacottage.com

No 2, 39 South Beach Road ★★
Contact: Mrs Sandra Hohol, 62 Westgate, Hunstanton PE36 5EL
T: (01485) 534267
F: (01485) 535230
E: sholhol@birdsnorfolkholidayhomes.co.uk
I: www.norfolkholidayhomes-birds.co.uk

Number 14 ★★★
Contact: Mr King, North Wootton, King's Lynn PE30 3RU
T: (01553) 675696

Roundstones ★★★
Contact: Mrs Sandra Hohol, 62 Westgate, Denver, Downham Market PE38 5EL
T: (01485) 534267
F: (01485) 535230
E: shohol@birdsnorfolkholidayshomes.co.uk
I: www.norfolkholidayhomes-birds.co.uk

St Crispin ★★★
Contact: Mrs Lesley Poore, Saint Crispin, 3 Wodehouse Road, Old Hunstanton, Hunstanton PE36 6JD
T: (01485) 534036
E: st.crispins@btinternet.com

Sandpiper Cottage ★★★★
Contact: Mrs Sandra Hohol, 62 Westgate, Hunstanton PE36 5EL
T: (01485) 534267
F: (01485) 535230
E: shohol@birdsnorfolkholidayhomes.co.uk
I: www.norfolkholidayhomes-birds.co.uk

Sea Breeze ★★★
Contact: Mrs Sandra Hohol, 62 Westgate, Hunstanton PE36 5EL
T: (01485) 534267
F: (01485) 534267
E: shohol@birdsnorfolkholidayhomes.co.uk

1 Sea Lane ★★★
Contact: Mrs Kinsley, Swallow Tail Holiday Homes, Carlton House, Market Place, Reepham, Norwich NR10 4JJ
T: (01603) 308108
F: (01603) 870304
E: holidays@swallow-tail.com
I: www.swallow-tail.com

44 Sea Lane ★★
Contact: Mrs Sandra Hohol, 62 Westgate, Hunstanton PE36 5EL
T: (01485) 534267
F: (01485) 535230
E: shohol@birdsnorfolkholidayhomes.co.uk
I: www.norfolkholidayhomes-birds.co.uk

Sea View ★★
Contact: Mr Jeremy Roberts, Peterborough PE1 2TH
T: (01733) 342172

58 Seagate Road ★★
Contact: Mrs Sandra Hohol, 62 Westgate, Ringstead, Hunstanton PE36 5BU
T: (01485) 534267
F: (01485) 535230
E: shohol@birdsnorfolkholidayhomes.co.uk
I: www.norfolkholidayhomes-birds.co.uk

Spindrift ★★★★
Contact: Mrs Sandra Hohol, 62 Westgate, Hunstanton PE36 5EL
T: (01485) 534267
F: (01485) 535230
E: shohol@birdsnorfolkholidayhomes.co.uk
I: www.norfolkholidayhomes-birds.co.uk

1st & 2nd Floor Flat ★★★
Contact: Mrs Sandra Hohol, 62 Westgate, Hunstanton PE36 5EL
T: (01485) 534267
F: (01485) 535230
E: shohol@birdsnorfolkholidayhomes.co.uk
I: www.norfolkholidayhomes-birds.co.uk

Victory Cottage ★★★
Contact: Mrs Sandra Hohol, 62 Westgate, Hunstanton PE36 5EL
T: (01485) 534267
F: (01485) 535230
E: shohol@birdsnorfolkholidayhomes.co.uk
I: www.norfolkholidayhomes-birds.co.uk

West Lodge ★★★
Contact: Mrs Geraldine Tibbs, Cole Green, Sedgeford, Hunstanton PE36 5LS
T: (01485) 571770
F: (01485) 571770

Westacre ★★★
Contact: Mrs Sandra Hohol, 62 Westgate, Hunstanton PE36 5EL
T: (01485) 534267
F: (01485) 535230
E: shohol@birdsnorfolkholidayhomes.co.uk
I: www.norfolkholidayhomes-birds.co.uk

Westgate Flat ★★
Contact: Mrs Jean Chilleystone, Hunstanton PE36 6HQ
T: (01485) 533646

HUNTINGDON
Cambridgeshire

The Forge White Gates ★★★
Contact: Mr Robert Pickard, Grange Farm, Abbots Ripton, Huntingdon PE28 2PH
T: (01487) 773555
F: (01487) 773545
E: admin@arfco.co.uk

HUNWORTH
Norfolk

Green Farm Barn ★★★★
Contact: Mrs Patricia Hoskison, Green Farm Barn, The Green, Hunworth, Melton Constable NR24 2AA
T: (01263) 713177
F: (01263) 710083
E: alan@tagsy.freeserve.co.uk

Spink's Nest ★★
Contact: Mrs Angela Hampshire, Kings Street, Hunworth, Melton Constable NR24 2EH
T: (01263) 713891

IKEN
Suffolk

The Old Stable ★★★★
Contact: Mrs Gunilla Hailes, The Anchorage, Church Lane, Iken, Woodbridge IP12 2ES
T: (01728) 688263
F: (01728) 688262

River Cottage ★★★★
Contact: Mrs Kate Kilburn, The River House, Iken Cliff, Iken, Woodbridge IP12 2EN
T: (01728) 688267
F: (01728) 688267
E: dkilburn@cmpinformation.com

INGOLDISTHORPE
Norfolk

Fox Cottage ★★★
Contact: Ms Eileen Fox, 5 Handel Road, Canvey Island SS8 7HL
T: (01268) 680616

Foxes Croft ★★
Contact: Mrs Christine Riches, 21 Weasenham Road, Great Massingham, King's Lynn PE32 2EY
T: (01485) 520216
E: christine-riches@supanet.com
I: www.christine-riches.supanet.com

Pond View ★★★
Contact: Mrs Joy Kelly, 14 Robert Balding Road, Dersingham, King's Lynn PE31 6UP
T: (01485) 542751

Swan Cottage ★★★★
Contact: Mr Alex Swan, Ingoldisthorpe, King's Lynn PE31 6NZ
T: (01485) 543882
E: swans.norfolk@virgin.net

Timekeepers Cottage ★★★★
Contact: Mrs Lyn Storry Leathersich, 32 Manor Road, King's Lynn PE31 6LD
T: (01485) 540700
E: lynsl@supanet.com
I: www.lynsl.supanet.com

KEDINGTON
Suffolk

The Cottage at Rowans ★★★
Contact: Mrs Cheryl Owen, Rowans House, Calford Green, Kedington, Haverhill CB9 7UN
T: (01440) 702408
F: (01440) 702408
E: cheryl@owen41.supanet.com
I: www.cottagesdirect.com/nfa.123

KELLING
Norfolk

The Plough Wheel ★★★
Contact: Miss D Kingsley, Norfolk Country Cottages, Carlton House, Market Place, Reepham, Norwich NR10 4JJ
T: (01603) 871872
F: (01603) 870304
E: info@norfolkcottages.co.uk
I: www.norfolkcottages.co.uk

KELSALE
Suffolk

East Green Farm Cottages ★★★★
Contact: Mr & Mrs R Gawthrop, East Green Maintenance Services, East Green Farm, Kelsale, Saxmundham IP17 2PH
T: (01728) 602316
F: (01728) 604408
E: claire@eastgreenproperty.co.uk
I: www.eastgreencottages.co.uk

KESSINGLAND
Suffolk

32 Alandale Drive ★★★
Contact: Miss D Kingsley, Norfolk Country Cottages, Carlton House, Market Place, Reepham, Norwich NR10 4JJ
T: (01603) 871872
F: (01603) 870304
E: info@norfolkcottages.co.uk
I: www.swallow-tail.com

Church Road ★★★
Contact: Mr James Rayment, 28 Woollards Lane, Great Shelford, Cambridge CB2 5LZ
T: (01223) 843048

74 The Cliff ★★
Contact: Mrs Saunders, 159 The Street, Rockland St Mary, Hellington, Norwich NR14 7HL
T: (01508) 538340

Four Winds Retreat ★★★★
Contact: Mr & Mrs Peter & Jane Garner, Four Winds, Holly Grange Road, Kessingland, Lowestoft NR33 7RR
T: (01502) 740044
E: garner@four-winds-retreat.fsnet.co.uk

Geneva Cottage
Rating Applied For
Contact: Mr Timothy Nathan, Brambleside, Field Lane, Kessingland, Lowestoft NR33 7QB
T: (01502) 740308

11 Kessingland Cottages ★★
Contact: Mr John Ryan, 17 The Byway, Potters Bar EN6 2LN
T: (01707) 643511

Kew Cottage ★★★
Contact: Mrs J Gill, 46 St Georges Avenue, Northampton NN2 6JA
T: (01604) 717301
F: (01604) 791424
E: b.s.g.@btopenworld.com

Knights Holiday Homes ★-★★
Contact: Mr Michael Knights, 198 Church Road, Kessingland, Lowestoft NR33 7SF
T: (01502) 588533
E: khols@suffolk70.freeserve.co.uk

5 Seaview ★★★
Contact: Mrs Carol Head, Oulton Broad, Lowestoft NR33 9DG
T: (01502) 584880

KING'S LYNN
Norfolk

Granery ★★★
Contact: Mrs Ann Jones, Churchgate Way, Terrington St Clement, King's Lynn PE34 4LZ
T: (01553) 828700
E: interiormotiv@aol.com

10 North Hirne Court ★★★
Contact: Ms Alison Gifford, Mileham, King's Lynn PE30 1HT
T: (01553) 763983
E: alisongifford@hotmail.com

The Stables Too ★★★
Contact: Ms Sue O'Brien, The Stables, 35a Goodwins Road, King's Lynn PE30 5QX
T: (01553) 774638
E: mikeandsueobrien@hotmail.com
I: www.cottageguide.co.uk/thestablestoo

KNAPTON
Norfolk

Cornerstone Cottage ★★★★
Contact: Mr & Mrs Eves, Cornerstone House, The Street, Knapton, North Walsham NR28 0AD
T: (01263) 722884
I: www.broadland.com/cornerstone

High House Cottage ★★★
Contact: Mr Hall, High House, Hall Lane, Knapton, North Walsham NR28 0SG
T: (01263) 721827

White House Farm – The Granary & Wallages Cottage ★★★★
Contact: Mr & Mrs C Goodhead, White House Farm, Knapton, North Walsham NR28 0RX
T: (01263) 721344
E: info@whitehousefarmnorfolk.co.uk
I: www.whitehousefarmnorfolk.co.uk

KNODISHALL
Suffolk

Forget-Me-Not ★★★
Contact: 7 Frenze Road, Diss IP22 4PA
T: (01379) 651297
F: (01379) 641555
E: holiday@suffolk-secrets.co.uk
I: www.suffolk-secrets.co.uk

LANGHAM
Norfolk

Amersham House ★★★
Contact: Miss Dawn Kinsley, Norfolk Country Cottages Ref. 455, Market Place, Reepham, Norwich NR10 4JJ
T: (01603) 871872
F: (01603) 870304
E: info@norfolkcottages.co.uk
I: www.swallow-tail.com

Sunnyside Cottage ★★★★
Contact: Mr & Mrs Shephard, 11 Faire Road, Glenfield, Leicester LE3 8EE
T: (0116) 287 2739
E: jt@faireroad.freeserve.co.uk

LAVENHAM
Suffolk

Blaize Barn ★★★★★
Contact: Mr & Mrs Jim Keohane, Blaize House, Churst Street, Lavenham, Sudbury CO10 9QT
T: (01787) 247402
F: (01787) 247402
E: j.and.c.keohane@virgin.net

Glebe Cottage ★★★★
Contact: Mrs Klair Bauly, Malting Farm, Hessett, Bury St Edmunds IP30 9BJ
T: (01359) 271528
F: (01359) 271528
E: kbauly@waitrose.com

Granary Cottage ★★★★
Contact: Mrs Wendy Williams, Granary Cottage, Mill Farm, Lavenham Road, Cockfield, Bury St Edmunds IP30 0HX
T: (01284) 828458

The Grove ★★★★
Contact: Mark Scott
T: (01787) 211115
E: mark@grove-cottages.co.uk
I: www.grove-cottages.co.uk

Lavender Cottage ★★★★
Contact: Mrs Joyce Taylor, Bray Road, Maidenhead SL6 1UQ
T: (01628) 627741

Lavenham Cottages ★★★★★
Contact: Mrs Sheila Lane, Hartest, Bury St Edmunds IP29 4DW
T: (01284) 830771
F: (01284) 830771
E: sheila@lavenhamcottages.co.uk
I: www.lavenhamcottages.co.uk

Old Wetherden Hall ★★★
Contact: Mrs J Elsden, Old Wetherden Hall, Hitcham, Ipswich IP7 7PZ
T: (01449) 740574
F: (01449) 740574
E: farm@wetheradenhall.force9.co.uk
I: www.oldwetherdenhall.co.uk

Quakers Yard ★★★★
Contact: Mr David Aldous, Two A's Hoggards Green, Stanningfield, Bury St Edmunds IP29 4RG
T: (01284) 827271
E: val@quakersyard.com
I: www.quakersyard.com

The Rector's Retreat ★★★
Contact: Mr & Mrs Peter Gutteridge, The Rector's Retreat, The Old Convent, The Street, Kettlebaston, Ipswich IP7 7QA
T: (01449) 741557
E: holidays@kettlebaston.fsnet.co.uk
I: www.kettlebaston.fsnet.co.uk

12 Ropers Court ★★★
Contact: Mr Roger Arnold, Queen's House, Church Square, Bures CO8 5AB
T: (01787) 227760
F: (01787) 227082
E: rogerarnold2@aol.com
I: www.queenscottages.com

LAXFIELD
Suffolk

The Loose Box & The Old Stables ★★★
Contact: Mr & Mrs John & Jane Reeve, Laxfield Leisure Ltd, High Street, Laxfield, Woodbridge IP13 8DU
T: (01986) 798019
F: (01986) 798155
E: laxfieldleisure@talk21.com
I: www.villastables.co.uk

Meadow Cottage ★★★★
Contact: Mr & Mrs William Ayers, Meadow Cottage Leisure, Quinton House, Gorhams Mill Lane, Laxfield, Woodbridge IP13 8DN
T: (01986) 798345
F: (01986) 798345
E: will.ayers@btinternet.com

LEISTON
Suffolk

Abbey View Lodge ★★★-★★★★★
Contact: Mrs Sally Stobbart, Abbey View Lodge, 105 Abbey Road, Theberton, Leiston IP16 4TA
T: (01728) 831128
F: (01728) 832633
E: info@abbeyview.co.uk
I: www.abbeyview.co.uk

Micawbers ★★★★
Contact: Mrs Joan Hockley, Albury End, Ware SG11 2HS
T: (01279) 771281
F: (01279) 771517
E: j.hockley@whestates.com

Reckham Lodge ★★★
Contact: Mrs Helen Denny, Reckham Lodge, Sandy Lane, Sizewell, Leiston IP16 4UL
T: (01728) 832831
E: lovelybubblymum@aol.com

The Studio Cottage ★★★
Contact: 7 Frenze Road, Diss IP22 4PA
T: (01379) 651297
F: (01379) 641555

LITCHAM
Norfolk

4 Canaan Row ★★★
Contact: Mr David Court, Norfolk Country Cottages, Carlton House, Market Place, Reepham, Norwich NR10 4JJ
T: (01603) 871872
F: (01603) 870304
E: cottages@paston.co.uk
I: www.norfolkcottages.co.uk/litcham.htm

The Old Farmhouse ★★★
Contact: Mrs Judith Archer, Chalk Farm, Druids Lane, Litcham, King's Lynn PE32 2YA
T: (01328) 701331
F: (01328) 700719
E: judiarcher@aol.com

LITTLE ELLINGHAM
Norfolk

Horseshoes ★★★
Contact: Mrs Julie Abbs, Wood Lane, Little Ellingham, Attleborough NR17 1JZ
T: (01953) 454514
F: (01953) 454514
E: miriclemaker@hotmail.com

LITTLE FRANSHAM
Norfolk

Lyons Green & Little Flint ★★-★★★★★
Contact: Mrs Jenny Mallon, The Old Hall, Little Fransham, East Dereham NR19 2AD
T: (01362) 687649
F: (01362) 687419
E: office@franshamfarm.co.uk
I: www.franshamfarm.co.uk

LITTLE HENHAM
Essex

Stable Cottage ★★★★
Contact: Mrs Kate Muskett, Little Henham, Saffron Walden CB11 3XR
T: (01279) 850228
F: (01279) 850397
E: kgmletting@aol.com

LITTLE RYBURGH
Norfolk

Cherry Pip Cottage ★★★★
Contact: Norfolk Country Cottages, Carlton House, Market Place, Reepham, Norwich NR10
T: (01603) 871872
E: info@norfolkcottages.co.uk
I: www.norfolkcottages.co.uk

LITTLE SNORING
Norfolk

Sunset Cottage ★★★★
Contact: Mr & Mrs Fuller, Canards, The Street, Little Snoring, Fakenham NR21 0HU
T: (01328) 878836
F: (01328) 878836

The White House Cottage & Barn Lodge★★★
Contact: Mrs Lee, The White House, The Street, Little Snoring, Fakenham NR21 0AJ
T: (01328) 878789
E: celia.lee@freenet.co.uk

LITTLE WALDEN
Essex

Orchard View Numbers 1 - 4 ★★★
Contact: Mrs Maureen Chapman-Barker, Little Bowsers Farm, Bowsers Lane, Little Walden, Saffron Walden CB10 1XQ
T: (01799) 527315
F: (01799) 527315
E: sales@farmerkit.co.uk
I: www.farmerkit.co.uk

LITTLE WALSINGHAM
Norfolk

The Old Coach House ★★★★
Contact: Mr & Mrs Geoff & Julia Holloway, Helmingham Road, Otley, Ipswich IP6 9NS
T: (01473) 890035
E: theoldcoach.house@btinternet.com
I: www.theoldcoach.house.btinternet.co.uk

LITTLEPORT
Cambridgeshire

Caves Farm Barns ★★★
Contact: Mr Stephen Kerridge, Hale Fen, Littleport, Ely CB6 1EJ
T: (01353) 861423
F: (01353) 861423
E: cb6steve@aol.com
I: www.cavesfarmbarns.co.uk

LONG MELFORD
Suffolk

4 Church Walk ★★★
Contact: Mr Mark Thomas, 33 Patshull Road, Kentish Town, London NW5 2JX
T: (020) 7267 3653
F: (01932) 568933
E: markthomas@rmc-group.com

Hope Cottage ★★★★
Contact: Ms S Jamil, Hill Farm Cottage, Glemsford, Sudbury CO10 7PP
T: (01787) 282338
F: (01787) 282338
E: sns.jam@tesco.net
I: www.hope-cottage-suffolk.co.uk

LOWER GRESHAM
Norfolk

The Roost ★★★
Contact: Mr & Mrs Entwistle, Sustead Road, Lower Gresham, Norwich NR11 8RE
T: (01263) 577388
E: enthome@compuserve.com

LOWESTOFT
Suffolk

10 Banner Court ★★★
Contact: Mrs Aisha Khalaf, Lowestoft NR33 0DB
T: (01502) 511876
F: (01502) 580738
E: aishakhalaf100@hotmail.com

Lowestoft Holiday Flat ★★
Contact: Mrs Courtauld, 83 Aberfeldy House, Pyes Hall, London Road, Wrentham, Beccles NR34 7HL
T: (01502) 675209
E: mcourtauld@onetel.net.uk

Shaftsbury House ★★★★
Contact: Mrs C Wigg, Jacaranda House & Home Services, Lowestoft
T: (01502) 568580

Suffolk Seaside & Broadlands ★★★
Contact: Ms Collecott, 282 Gorleston Road, Oulton, Lowestoft NR32 3AJ
T: (01502) 564396

Tides Reach Holiday Flats ★★
Contact: Mrs Tallamy, Hulven Road, Hulver Road Ellough, Ellough, Beccles NR34 7TP
T: (01502) 476658

16 Wilson Road ★★★
Contact: Mr & Mrs Murray, Chelmsford CM1 2PA
T: (01245) 266018
F: (01245) 287000

LYNG
Norfolk

Holly Cottage ★★
Contact: Mr Thomas, Lyng, Norwich NR9 5LH
T: (01603) 880158
F: (01603) 881228

Utopia Paradise Rating Applied For
Contact: Mrs Susan Jarvis, Utopia Paradise, Stone House Farm, Farman Close, Lyng, Norwich NR9 5RD
T: (01603) 870812
E: utopia-paradise@talk21.com

MALDON
Essex

Little Wintersleet Farm ★★★
Contact: Mrs Merie Keeble, Little Wintersleet Farm, Little Wintersleet, London Road, Maldon CM9 6LJ
T: (01621) 856354

MARHOLM
Lincolnshire

Woodcroft Castle Coach House Rating Applied For
Contact: Mr Dan O'Donoghue, Woodcroft Castle, Marholm, Peterborough PE6 7HW
T: (01733) 252844
F: (01733) 252844
I: www.cottagenet.co.uk/woodcroftcastle

MARLESFORD
Suffolk

Hollyhock Cottage ★★★
Contact: John Hammond & Elizabeth Ardill, 34 Seckford Street, Woodbridge IP12 4LY
T: (01394) 384007
E: lizzie@suffolkcottageholidays.com

MARSWORTH
Hertfordshire

Field House ★★★
Contact: Mr Pash, Hideaways, Chapel House, Luke Street, Berwick St John, Shaftesbury SP7 0HQ
T: (01747) 828170
F: (01747) 829090
E: enq@hideaways.co.uk
I: www.hideaways.co.uk

MARTHAM
Norfolk

Greenside Cottage ★★★
Contact: Mrs B I Dyball, Greenside, 30 The Green, Martham, Great Yarmouth NR29 4PA
T: (01493) 740375

MENDHAM
Suffolk

Tom, Dick & Harry ★★★
Contact: Mrs Audrey Carless, Church Farm Barn, Withersdale Street, Mendham, Harleston IP20 0JR
T: (01379) 588091
F: (01379) 586009
E: enquiries@bacatchurchfarm.co.uk
I: www.bacatchurchfarm.co.uk

MIDDLETON
Suffolk

The Old Church Room ★★★★
Contact: 7 Frenze Road, Diss IP22 4PA
T: (01379) 651297
F: (01379) 641555
E: holidays@suffolk-secrets.co.uk
I: www.suffolk-secrets.co.uk

Rose Farm Barns ★★★★
Contact: Mrs Janet Maricic, Rose Farm, Mill Street, Middleton, Saxmundham IP17 3NG
T: (01728) 648456

MILDENHALL
Suffolk

The Coach House & Stables Rating Applied For
Contact: Mrs Anne Greenfield, Orchard House, 23 North Terrace, Mildenhall, Bury St Edmunds IP28 7AA
T: (01638) 711237
E: orchardhouse23@aol.com
I: www.mildenhallorchardhouse.com

MILEHAM
Norfolk

Mallards ★★★
Contact: Mrs Joscelin Colborne, Mallards, The Street, Mileham, King's Lynn PE32 2RA
T: (01328) 700602
F: (01328) 700061
E: joscelin.colborne@malards.co.uk

MUCH HADHAM
Hertfordshire

Blackcroft Farmhouse ★★★★
Contact: Mrs Gill Trundle, Blackcroft Farmhouse, Kettle Green, Much Hadham SG10 6AD
T: (01279) 843832

MUNDESLEY
Norfolk

The Anchorage ★★★
Contact: Miss D Kingsley, Norfolk Country Cottages, Market Place, Reepham, Norwich NR10 4JJ
T: (01603) 871872
F: (01603) 870304
E: info@norfolkcottages.co.uk
I: www.swallow-tail.com

Holiday Properties (Mundesley) Ltd ★-★★★
Contact: Mr & Mrs Mark & Nadine Gray, Holiday Properties (Mundesley) Ltd, 6A Paston Road, Mundesley, Norwich NR11 8BN
T: (01263) 720719
F: (01263) 720719
E: holidayproperties@tesco.net
I: www.holidayprops.freeuk.com

Paddock Bungalow ★★★
Contact: Mrs Christine Harding, Gimingham Road, Mundesley, Norwich NR11 8DG
T: (01263) 721060
F: (01263) 722998
E: christine.m.harding@btinternet.com

10 Royal Chalet Park ★★★
Contact: Miss D Kingsley, Norfolk Country Cottages, Carlton House, Market Place, Reepham, Norwich NR10 4JJ
T: (01603) 871872
F: (01603) 870304
E: info@norfolkcottages.co.uk
I: www.norfolk-cottages.co.uk

Schooner Cottage ★★★
Contact: Mr & Mrs Martin Webb, The Grange, Victoria Road, Mundesley, Norwich NR11 8JG
T: (01692) 582290

Sunshine Cottages ★★★★
Contact: Mr & Mrs Fiske, 28 High Street, Mundesley, Norwich NR11 8LH
T: (01263) 722342
F: (01263) 722342
E: bookings@fiskies.co.uk
I: www.fiskies.co.uk

Wild Rose Cottage ★★★
Contact: Mr Tuckett, 127 Writtle Road, Chelmsford CM1 3BP
T: (01245) 252397
F: (01245) 252397
E: ruffelsandtuckett@hotmail.com

MUNDON Essex

Wayside Annexe ★★★★
Contact: Mrs Vivien Clark, Wayside Annexe, Wayside, Main Road, Mundon, Maldon CM9 6NU
T: (01621) 740374
E: peter.clark@care4free.net

NAYLAND Suffolk

Gladwins Farm ★★★★-★★★★★
Contact: Mrs Pauline Dossor, Gladwins Farm, Harpers Hill, Nayland, Colchester CO6 4NU
T: (01206) 262261
F: (01206) 263001
E: gladwinsfarm@aol.com
I: www.gladwinsfarm.co.uk

NEWMARKET Suffolk

6 Belmont Court ★★
Contact: Mrs Jennie Collingridge, Chapel Street, Exning, Newmarket CB8 7HA
T: (01638) 577952
F: (01638) 577952
E: jennie@harratonstables.freeserve.co.uk

Gipsy Hall ★★★★
Contact: Mrs Francis Dow, Gipsy Hall, Dullingham Ley, Dullingham, Newmarket CB8 9XF
T: (01638) 508443
E: gipsyhall@onetel.com

Swallows Rest ★★★★
Contact: Mrs Gill Woodward, Swallows Rest, 6 Ditton Green, Woodditton, Newmarket CB8 9SQ
T: (01638) 730823
F: (01638) 731767
E: gillian@swallowsrest.f9.co.uk

NORTH WOOTTON Norfolk

Winsdail ★★★★
Contact: Mr Andrew Booth, Fern Hill, Dersingham, King's Lynn PE31 6HT
T: (01485) 543639
F: (01485) 543639
E: mail@winsdailcottage.com
I: www.winsdailcottage.com

NORTHREPPS Norfolk

Acorn Cottage ★★★
Contact: Mrs Louise Strong, Woodland House, Cromer Road, Overstrand, Cromer NR27 0JY
T: (01263) 579736

The Old Post Office Rating Applied For
Contact: Mr Andrew Banner, Odd Fellows Hall, Black Street, Martham, Great Yarmouth NR29 4PN
T: 08456 444018
E: info@theoldpostoffice-northrepps.co.uk
I: www.theoldpostoffice-northrepps.co.uk

Torridon & Yeomans Cottage ★★★★
Contact: Mrs Youngman, Shrublands Farm, Northrepps, Cromer NR27 0AA
T: (01263) 579297
F: (01263) 579297
E: youngman@farming.co.uk
I: www.broadland.com/torridon

NORWICH Norfolk

The Garden Flat ★★★
Contact: Mrs Eunice Edwards, 70 Earlham Road, Norwich NR2 3DF
T: (01603) 612579
F: (01603) 619367
E: bookings@gardenflat70.co.uk
I: www.gardenflat70.co.uk

The Hideaway & Pondside ★★★-★★★★★
Contact: Mrs Reilly, Heath Bungalow, Woodbastwick Road, Blofield Heath, Norwich NR13 4AB
T: (01603) 715052
E: pondside@talk21.com
I: www.norfolkbroads.com/thehideaway

30 Kingsley Road ★★★
Contact: Miss Sally Clarke, 3 Kingsley Road, Norwich NR1 3RB
T: (01603) 473547
F: (01603) 473547
E: kingsley@paston.co.uk
I: www.selfcateringnorwich.co.uk

Mabels Cottage ★★★
Contact: Mr & Mrs Randon, Sunnyside Cottage, Fritton Common, Norwich NR15 2QS
T: (01508) 499279
F: (01508) 499279
E: judy.randon@virgin.net
I: www.mabels-cottage.co.uk

Mill House ★★★★
Contact: Ms Fay Godin, 3 Mill Cottages, Hellesdon Mill Lane, Norwich NR6 5AZ
T: (01603) 415061
E: villa.cott@virgin.net

Parlours ★★★★
Contact: Mr & Mrs Derek Wright, Earlham Guesthouse, 147 Earlham Road, Norwich NR2 3RG
T: (01603) 454169
E: earlhamgh@hotmail.com

Poolside Lodges ★★★
Contact: Mrs Sally-Anne Hinkley, South Lodge, Woods End, Salhouse Road, Rackheath Park, Norwich NR13 6LD
T: (01603) 720000
F: (01603) 721483
E: sally.hinkley@btinternet.com

Sommersby ★★★
Contact: Miss Jackson, 31 Guy Cook Close, Great Cornard, Sudbury CO10 0JX
T: (01787) 372903
E: djackson@sommersby.freeserve.co.uk

Spixworth Hall Cottages ★★★-★★★★★
Contact: Mrs Sheelah Jane Cook, Grange Farm, Buxton Road, Spixworth, Norwich NR10 3PR
T: (01603) 898190
F: (01603) 897176
E: hallcottages@btinternet.com
I: www.hallcottages.co.uk

Thyme Cottage ★★★★
Contact: Mr David Lythell, Woodbastwick Road, Blofield Heath, Norwich NR13 4AB
T: (01603) 414443
F: (01603) 789472
E: dave@lythell.demon.co.uk

OLD BUCKENHAM Norfolk

Ox & Plough Cottages ★★★
Contact: Mrs Sally Bishop, Ox & Plough Cottages, The Ox & Plough Freehouse, Old Buckenham, Attleborough NR17 1RN
T: (01953) 860004
F: (01953) 860004
E: oxandplough.bishop@barbox.net
I: www.oxandploughcottages.co.uk

OLD HUNSTANTON Norfolk

Cameo Cottage Rating Applied For
Contact: Sandra Hohol, Norfolk Holiday Homes, 62 Westgate, Hunstanton PE36 5EL
T: (01485) 534267
F: (01485) 535230
E: shohol@birdsnorfolkholidayhomes.co.uk
I: www.norfolkholidayhomes-birds.co.uk

Fireman's Cottage Rating Applied For
Contact: Sandra Hohol, Norfolk Holiday Homes, 62 Westgate, Hunstanton PE36 5EL
T: (01485) 534267
F: (01485) 535230
E: shohol@birdsnorfolkholidayhomes.co.uk
I: www.norfolkholidayhomes-birds.co.uk

ORFORD Suffolk

70 Broom Cottages ★★★★
Contact: Mrs Suvi Pool, High House Fruit Farm, 69 Broom Cottages, High House Farm Road, Sudbourne, Woodbridge IP12 2BL
T: (01394) 450378
F: (01394) 450124
E: cottage@high-house.co.uk

47 Daphne Road ★★★
Contact: Mrs Sheila Hitchcock, Church Farm Cottage, Sudbourne, Woodbridge IP12 2BP
T: (01394) 450714
F: (01394) 450714
E: barryhitchcock@tesco.com

Vesta Cottage ★★★
Contact: Mrs Penny Kay, 74 Broad Street, Orford, Woodbridge IP12 2NQ
T: (01394) 450652
F: (01394) 450097
E: kaycottages@pobox.com
I: www.vestacottage.co.uk

ORWELL Cambridgeshire

The Retreat ★★★★
Contact: Mrs M Meikle, The Retreat, Malton Road, Orwell, Cambridge SG8 5QR
T: (01223) 208005

OULTON Norfolk

Willowbank Cottage ★★★
Contact: Mrs E. Poynder, 25 Champneys Walk, Newnham, Cambridge CB3 9AW
T: (01223) 462470

OULTON BROAD Suffolk

7 Holly Road ★★
Contact: Mrs Tonia Moore, 97A Normanston Drive, Oulton Broad, Lowestoft NR32 2PX
T: (01502) 563868
E: tonia@moore97a.fsnet.co.uk

Maltings Holiday Accommodation ★★★
Contact: Ivy House Farm Hotel
T: (01502) 501353
F: (01502) 501539
E: reception@ivyhousefarm.co.uk
I: www.ivyhousefarm.co.uk

White House Farm ★★★
Contact: Mr & Mrs Andrew Hughes, Burnt Hill Lane, Carlton Colville, Oulton Broad, Lowestoft NR33 8HU
T: (01502) 564049
E: mail@whitehousefarm.org.uk
I: www.whitehousefarm.org.uk

OVERSTRAND Norfolk

Beaches ★★★
Contact: Miss Denise Lewis, Holiday Cottages, Chalets & Flats, 15 West Street, Cromer NR27 9HZ
T: (01263) 511028
F: (01263) 513139
E: property@lambertw.fslife.co.uk
I: lambertandrussell.com

Buckthorns Rating Applied For
Contact: Mrs Mandy Reeve, 'Crackers', Wignals-Gate, Holbeach, Lincolnshire PE12 7HR
T: (01406) 422953
F: (01406) 425192
E: mail@ealing74.fsnet.co.uk

Cherry Burn ★★★★
Contact: Mr Bert Rose, Hill Farm House, Thorpe Market Road NR11 8TB
T: (01263) 834229
E: bertrocity@aol.com

4 Grange Gorman ★★★
Contact: Lambert & Russell, 15 West Street, Cromer NR27 9HZ
T: (01263) 511028
F: (01263) 513139
E: property@lambertw.fslife.co.uk

31 Harbord Road ★★★
Contact: Mrs Jane Langley, 28 Esher Place Avenue, Esher KT10 8PY
T: (01372) 463063
F: (01372) 463063
E: jane@harbordholidays.co.uk
I: www.harbordholidays.co.uk

Poppyland Holiday Cottages ★★★★
Contact: Mrs Riches, 21 Regent Street, Wickmere, Norwich NR11 7ND
T: (01263) 577473
F: (01265) 570087
E: poppyland@totalise.co.uk
I: www.broadland.com/poppyland

Summersville ★★★
Contact: Mr J C Laidlow, 19 High Street, Overstrand, Cromer NR27 0AB
T: (01263) 579368
E: john.laidlow@lineone.net

OXBOROUGH
Norfolk

Ferry Farm Cottage ★★★
Contact: Mrs Margaret Wilson, Ferry Road, Oxborough, King's Lynn PE33 9PT
T: (01366) 328287
E: margaretwil@btinternet.com

Hythe Cottage ★★★
Contact: Dr Barbara Sommerville, 23 Portugal Place, Cambridge CB5 8AF
T: (01366) 328946
E: bas@flora-garden-tours.co.uk
I: www.flora-garden-tours.co.uk/holidaycottage.htm

OXNEAD
Norfolk

Keepers Cottage ★★★
Contact: Norfolk Country Cottages, Carlton House, Market Place, Reepham, Norwich NR10 4JJ
T: (01603) 871872
F: (01603) 870304
E: cottages@paston.co.uk

PAKEFIELD
Suffolk

Cliff Cottage ★★★
Contact: Mrs Thelma Bruce, Fishermans Cottage, Pakefield Street, Oulton Broad, Lowestoft NR33 0JS
T: (01502) 501955

Holiday Cottage ★★★★
Contact: Mrs Victoria Mead, Coastguard Lane, Kessingland, Lowestoft NR33 9RE
T: (01502) 740304

PASTON
Norfolk

Garden Cottage ★★★
Contact: Mr Paul Parker, Paston, North Walsham NR28 0SQ
T: (01692) 407008

PELDON
Essex

Rose Barn Cottage ★★★★
Contact: Mrs Ariette Everett, Mersea Road/Colchester Road, Peldon, Colchester CO5 7QJ
T: (01206) 735317
F: (01206) 735311
E: everettaj@aol.com

PENTNEY
Norfolk

Bradmoor Cottage
Rating Applied For
Contact: Mrs Sandra Hohol, 62 Westgate, Hunstanton PE36 5EL
T: (01485) 534267
F: (01485) 535230
E: shohol@birdsnorfolkholidayhomes.co.uk

PIN MILL
Suffolk

Alma Cottage ★★★
Contact: Mr John Pugh, Amberley, Stroud GL5 5AG
T: (01453) 872551
F: (01453) 843225
E: john.pugh@talk21.com

POLSTEAD
Suffolk

The Stables ★★★
Contact: Mr & Mrs Richard English, Sprotts Farm, Holt Road, Polstead, Colchester CO6 5BT
T: (01787) 210368
E: R.J.English@btinternet.com

POTTER HEIGHAM
Norfolk

Herbert Woods ★★★-★★★★
Contact: Mr Andy Risborough, Herbert Woods, Broads Haven, Bridge Road, Potter Heigham, Great Yarmouth NR29 5JD
F: (01603) 784272
I: www.broads.co.uk

RADLETT
Hertfordshire

Constance
Rating Applied For
Contact: Mr & Mrs Clive Miles, Constance, 39 Homefield Road, Radlett WD7 8PX
T: (01923) 854444
E: cayd@homefield39.fsnet.co.uk

RADWINTER
Essex

Plough Hill Farm ★★★★
Contact: Mr Richard Martin, Plough Hill Farm, Hempstead Road, Radwinter, Saffron Walden CB10 2TQ
T: (01799) 599411
I: homepages.tesco.net/~richard.martin3/index.html

RATTLESDEN
Suffolk

The Dower House ★★★★
Contact: Mrs Voysey, Clopton Green, Rattlesden, Bury St Edmunds IP30 0RN
T: (01449) 736332
E: all@voysey.freeserve.co.uk

REDBOURN
Hertfordshire

The Beeches ★★★★
Contact: Mrs June Surridge, Hemel Hempstead Road, Redbourn, St Albans AL3 7AG
T: (01582) 792638
F: (01582) 792638

REEDHAM
Norfolk

Norton Marsh Mill ★★★
Contact: Mrs Kinsley, Swallow Tail Holiday Homes, Carlton House, Market Place, Reepham, Norwich NR10 4JJ
T: (01603) 308108
F: (01603) 870304
E: holidays@swallow-tail.com
I: www.swallow-tail.com

REEPHAM
Norfolk

Rookery Farm ★★★
Contact: Mrs Jan Ashford, Church Street, Reepham, Norwich NR10 4JW
T: (01603) 871847

RENDHAM
Suffolk

The Cottage ★★★
Contact: Mrs Elizabeth Spinney, Rendham, Saxmundham IP17 2AF
T: (01728) 663656
F: (01728) 663656
E: elizabethspinney@suffolkonline.net

REPPS WITH BASTWICK
Norfolk

Grove Farm Holidays
Rating Applied For
Contact: Mr & Mrs P W Pratt, Grove Farm Holidays, Repps With Bastwick, Great Yarmouth NR29 5JN
T: (01692) 670205
E: enquiries@grovefarmholidays.co.uk
I: www.grovefarmholidays.co.uk

REYDON
Suffolk

The Ark ★★★
Contact: 7 Frenze Road, Diss IP22 4PA
T: (01379) 651297
F: (01379) 641555
E: holidays@suffolk.secrets.co.uk
I: www.suffolk-secrets.co.uk

Church Cottage ★★★
Contact: 7 Frenze Road, Diss IP22 4PA
T: (01379) 651297
F: (01379) 641555
E: holidays@suffolk-secrets.co.uk
I: www.suffolk-secrets.co.uk

Furze Patch ★★★★
Contact: 7 Frenze Road, Diss IP22 4PA
T: (01379) 651297
F: (01379) 641555
E: holidays@suffolk-secrets.co.uk
I: www.suffolk-secrets.co.uk

Lily Cottage & Rose Cottage ★★★
Contact: Mr Dennis Reavell, Waystar Holdings Limited, Whitenhall Farm, Stoke Road, Hoo, Rochester ME3 9NP
T: (01634) 250251
F: (01634) 251112
E: reavell@waystarltd.freeserve.co.uk
I: www.selfkater.com

Quay House Chalet ★★
Contact: Mrs Claire Guppy, Woodleys Yard, High Street, Southwold IP18 6HP
T: (01502) 723323
F: (01502) 723323
E: baskerville@hotdoggy.demon.co.uk
I: www.southwold-quayhouse.co.uk

Richmond ★★★
Contact: 7 Frenze Road, Diss IP22 4PA
T: (01379) 651297
F: (01379) 641555
E: holidays@suffolk-secrets.co.uk
I: www.suffolk-secrets.co.uk

Whimbrel Cottage ★★★
Contact: 7 Frenze Road, Diss IP22 4PA
T: (01379) 651297
F: (01379) 641555
E: holidays@suffolk-secrets.co.uk
I: www.suffolk-secrets.co.uk

RINGSTEAD
Norfolk

April Cottage & Tamarisk Cottage ★★★★
Contact: Ms Laurice Jarman, Church Farm House, 33 Nursery Lane, North Wootton, King's Lynn PE30 3NG
T: (01553) 676060
F: (01553) 671211
E: bookings@jariard.fsnet.co.uk

Crossways ★
Contact: Mrs Sandra Hohol, 62 Westgate, Hunstanton PE36 5EL
T: (01485) 534267
F: (01485) 535230
E: shohol@birdsnorfolkholidayhomes.co.uk
I: www.norfolkholidayhomes-birds.co.uk

7 Langford Cottages ★★★★
Contact: Mr Douglas Hill, Shootersway Lane, Berkhamsted HP4 3NW
T: (01442) 864387
F: (01442) 871589
E: djbhill@waitrose.com

Lindsay Cottage ★★★
Contact: Miss Dawn Kinsley, Market Place, Reepham, Norwich NR10 4JJ
T: (01603) 871872
F: (01603) 870304
E: info@norfolkcottages.co.uk
I: www.norfolkcottages.co.uk

North Cottage ★★★★
Contact: Mrs Rachel Priest, 17 Chapel Lane, Ringstead, Hunstanton PE36 5JX
T: (01485) 525121

Orchard House ★★★
Contact: Mrs Sandra Hohol, 62 Westgate, Ringstead, Hunstanton PE36 5BU
T: (01485) 534267
F: (01485) 535230
E: shohol@birdsnorfolkholidayhomes.co.uk
I: www.norfolkholidayhomes-birds.co.uk

RISELEY
Bedfordshire

Coldham Cottages ★★★★
Contact: Ms Jean Felce, Risley Lodge Farm, Bowers Lane, Riseley, Bedford MK44 1DL
T: (01234) 708489
F: (01234) 708372
E: felce@talk21.com
I: www.coldhamcottages.co.uk

ROCKLAND ST MARY
Norfolk

Oxnead Holiday Cottages ★★★
Contact: Mrs Wendy Futter, Oxnead Holiday Cottages, 5 New Inn Hill, Hellington, Norwich NR14 7HP
T: (01508) 538295
F: (01603) 787496
E: oxnead@supanet.com

ROUGHTON
Norfolk

Jonas Farm Holiday Barns Ltd ★★★★
Contact: Ms Tracey Hampshire, Jonas Farm Holiday Barns Ltd, Cromer Road, Roughton, Felbrigg, Norwich NR11 8PF
T: (01263) 515438
F: (01263) 731866
E: info@jonasfarmholidaybarns.co.uk
I: www.jonasfarmholidaybarns.co.uk

Nora Blogg's Cottage ★★
Contact: Mr Varden, Chalden Cottage, Felbrigg Road, Roughton, Cromer NR11 8PA
T: (01263) 513353

Pond Farm Cottages ★★★★
Contact: Russells Self Catering Holidays, Spring Mill, Arby, Earby, Barnoldswick bb94 0aa
T: 08700 781300

Rogues & Rascals Barns ★★★★
Contact: Mrs Clare Wilson, Grove Farm, Back Lane, Roughton, Cromer NR11 8QR
T: (01263) 761594
F: (01263) 761605
E: grove-farm@homestay.co.uk

RUNCTON HOLME
Norfolk

Thorpland Manor Barns ★★★★
Contact: Mrs Mary Caley, Thorpland Manor Barns, Downham Road, Runcton Holme, King's Lynn PE33 0AD
T: (01553) 810409
F: (01553) 811831
E: w.p.caley@tesco.net

SAFFRON WALDEN
Essex

The Barn ★★★
Contact: Mrs Katy Bicknell, Pond Cottages, 6 Little Green, Cheveley, Saxon Street, Newmarket CB8 9RG
T: (01638) 730518

The Byre ★★★
Contact: Mrs Tineke Westerhuis, Rockells Farm, Duddenhoe End, Saffron Walden CB11 4UY
T: (01763) 838053
F: (01763) 837001

The Cottage ★★★★
Contact: Dr Rigby, 38 Gold Street, Saffron Walden CB10 1EJ
T: (01799) 501373
E: Mike@MCRigby.co.uk

Little Bulls Farmhouse ★★★★
Contact: Mr A C Kiddy, Radwinter Park, Radwinter End, Saffron Walden CB10 2UE
T: (01799) 599272
F: (01799) 599172
E: ajkiddy@cambridge-vacation-homes.com
I: www.cambridge-vacation-homes.com

Newhouse Farm ★★★★
Contact: Mrs Emma Redcliffe, Newhouse Farm, Walden Road, Radwinter, Saffron Walden CB10 2SP
T: (01799) 599211
F: (01799) 599967
E: emmaredcliffe@hotmail.com

ST ALBANS
Hertfordshire

69 Albert Street & 20 Keyfield Terrace ★★
Contact: Mrs Carol Nicol, 178 London Road, St Albans AL1 1PL
T: (01727) 846726
F: (01727) 831267

High Meadows ★★★★
Contact: Mrs Jenny Hale, High Meadows, 32 Lancaster Road, St Albans AL1 4ET
T: (01727) 865092
E: jenny.hale@ntlworld.com
I: www.akomodation.co.uk

The Hollies ★★★★
Contact: Mrs Anne Newbury, The Hollies, 11 Spencer Place, Sandridge, St Albans AL4 9DW
T: (01727) 859845
E: martin.newbury@ntlworld.co.uk

Holmes Court Apartment ★★★
Contact: Ms Margot Choo, 12 Wyton, Welwyn Garden City AL7 2PF
T: (01707) 327977
E: margot_monworth@hotmail.com

ST OSYTH
Essex

Park Hall Country Cottages ★★★★★
Contact: Mrs Trisha Ford, Park Hall Country Cottages, Park Farm, St Osyth, Colchester CO16 8HG
T: (01255) 820922
E: Trish@parkhall.fslife.co.uk
I: www.parkhall-countrycottages.com

SALLE
Norfolk

Lodge Cottage ★★★
Contact: Mr Douglas Whitelaw, Salle, Norwich NR10 4SB
T: (01603) 879046
F: (01603) 879047
E: douglaswhitelaw@sallemoorfm.u-net.co.uk

SALTHOUSE
Norfolk

Dun Cow Public House ★★★
Contact: Mrs Kay Groom, Public House, Coast Road, Salthouse, Wells-next-the-Sea NR25 7XG
T: (01263) 740467

SANDRINGHAM
Norfolk

Folk on the Hill ★★★★
Contact: Mrs L Skerritt, Mill Cottage, Mill Road, Dersingham, King's Lynn PE31 6HY
T: (01485) 544411
E: lili@skerritt-euwe.freeserve.co.uk

SANDY
Bedfordshire

Acorn Cottage ★★★★
Contact: Mrs Margaret Codd, Tempsford Road, Great North Road, Sandy SG19 2AQ
T: (01767) 682332
F: (01767) 692503
E: margaret@highfield-farm.co.uk

SAXMUNDHAM
Suffolk

Flora Cottage ★★★★
Contact: 7 Frenze Road, Diss IP22 4PA
T: (01379) 651297
F: (01379) 641555
I: www.suffolk-secrets.co.uk

Harvey's Mill ★★★★
Contact: Mrs Christine Baker, Harvey's Mill, Benstead, Main Road, Kelsale, Saxmundham IP17 2RD
T: (01728) 603212
F: (01728) 603637
E: mail@bensteadhouse.freeserve.co.uk
I: www.blythweb.co.uk/harveysmill

Quince Cottage ★★
Contact: Mr & Mrs John Andrew, Mutton Lane, Brandeston, Woodbridge IP13 7AR
T: (01728) 685953
E: tedischa@aol.com

Red Lodge Barn ★★★★
Contact: Mr & Mrs Michael & Lesley Bowler, Red Lodge Barn, Middleton Moor, Middleton, Saxmundham IP17 3LN
T: (01728) 668100

Riverside Cottage ★★★
Contact: 7 Frenze Road, Diss IP22 4PA
T: (01379) 651297
F: (01379) 641555
E: holidays@suffolk-secrets.co.uk
I: www.suffolk-secrets.co.uk

Snape Maltings ★★★
Contact: Ms Dawn Hannan, Snape Maltings, Snape, Saxmundham IP17 1SR
T: (01708) 688303
F: (01708) 688930
E: accom@snapemaltings.co.uk
I: www.snapemaltings.co.uk

SAXON STREET
Cambridgeshire

Rose Cottage
Rating Applied For
Contact: Mrs Lamb, 28 The Street, Saxon Street, Newmarket CB8 9RU
T: (01638) 730134

SCULTHORPE
Norfolk

Clarence's & Edna's Lodges ★★★
Contact: Mrs Beryl Engledow, Caxton House, Creake Road, Sculthorpe, Fakenham NR21 9NG
T: (01328) 864785

The Cottage ★★★
Contact: Mrs Chapman, 30 Lambert Cross, Saffron Walden CB10 2DP
T: (01799) 527287

Greenacre Bungalow ★★
Contact: Mrs Tuddenham, 1 The Street, Sculthorpe, Fakenham NR21 9QD
T: (01328) 862858

SEA PALLING
Norfolk

The Bolt Hole ★★★
Contact: Miss D Kingsley, Carlton House, Market Place, Reepham, Norwich NR10 4JJ
T: (01603) 871872
F: (01603) 870304
E: info@norfolkcottages.co.uk

Vila Voer ★★★
Contact: Mrs Jane Shulver, Point House, Ridlington, Walcott, Norwich NR28 9TY
T: (01692) 651126
F: (01692) 650180
E: pointhouse@hotmail.com
I: www.norfolkcottages.co.uk

SEDGEFORD
Norfolk

Highlands
Rating Applied For
Contact: Mrs Sandra Hohol, 62 Westgate, Hunstanton PE36 5EL
T: (01485) 534267
F: (01485) 535230
E: shohol@birdsnorfolkholidayhomes.co.uk
I: www.norfolkholidayhomes-birds.co.uk

Lavender Cottage ★★★★
Contact: Mrs Karen Kennedy-Hill, 9 Wheatfields, Hillington, King's Lynn PE31 6BH
T: (01485) 600850
E: mkh@tinyonline.co.uk
I: www.lavendercottage.co.uk

Victoria Cottage ★★★
Contact: Ms Charlotte Forbes-Robertson, Victoria House, Heacham Road, Sedgeford, Hunstanton PE36 5LU
T: (01485) 571082
E: charlotte@charard.com

SHARRINGTON
Norfolk

Daubeney Cottage ★★★
Contact: Ms Nina Ogier, Daubeney Hall Farm, Lower Hall Lane, Sharrington, Melton Constable NR24 2PQ
T: (01263) 861412
E: ninaogier@hotmail.com

Gable Cottage ★★
Contact: Miss M Lakey, Ashyard, Sharrington, Melton Constable NR24 2PH
T: (01263) 860393

Stone Cottage ★★★★
Contact: Miss D Kingsley, Market Place, Reepham, Norwich NR10 4JJ
T: (01603) 871872
F: (01603) 870304
E: info@norfolkcottages.co.uk
I: www.norfolk-cottages.co.uk

SHELLEY
Suffolk

Ivy Tree Cottage Annexe ★★★
Contact: Mrs Lock, Ivy Tree Cottage, Shelley, Ipswich IP7 5RE
T: (01473) 827632

SHERINGHAM
Norfolk

The Annexe ★★★
Contact: Mrs Kinsley, Swallow Tail Holiday Homes, Carlton House, Market Place, Reepham, Norwich NR10 4JJ
T: (01603) 308108
F: (01603) 870304
E: holidays@swallow-tail.com
I: www.swallow-tail.com

Augusta & Bennett ★★★
Contact: Mr Trevor Claydon, Owlet House, Laurel Drive, Holt NR25 6JR
T: (01263) 713998
E: trevor.claydon@which.net
I: www.broadland.com/augusta.html

Clifftop Cottages
Rating Applied For
Contact: Mrs L Fenn, Clifftops, 19 Vincent Road, Sheringham NR26 8BP
T: (01263) 825409

The Croft ★★★
Contact: Mr Dale McKean, 124 Eye Road, Peterborough PE1 4SG
E: DaleMcK@cyberware.co.uk

The Duncan ★★★
Contact: Mr & Mrs Wolsey, The Duncan, Burlington House, No 2 The Esplanade, Sheringham NR26 8LG
T: (01263) 821267

Fisherman's Cottage, Fisherman's Hyde Cottage and Fisherman's Rest★★-★★★
Contact: Mrs Bernadette Bennett, London SW6 2BD
T: (020) 7381 0771

Flat 2 ★★
Contact: Mrs Valerie Muggridge, 8 Warren Close, High Kelling, Holt NR25 6QX
T: (01263) 712688

Glendalough ★★★
Contact: Mrs Janet Teather, Sheringham NR26 8RR
T: (01263) 825032
E: janetandbrian@telinco.co.uk
I: www.broadland.com/glendalough

Hall Cottage ★★★
Contact: Mrs Dawn Kinsley, Market Place, Reepham, Norwich NR10 4JJ
T: (01603) 871872
F: (01603) 870304
E: info@norfolkcottages.co.uk
I: www.norfolkcottages.co.uk

The Haven
Rating Applied For
Contact: Mrs Irene Buck & Audrey Challoner, 19 Marriotts Way, Sheringham NR26 8RJ
T: (01263) 821281
E: irene@buck1065.fsnet.co.uk

The Haven ★★★
Contact: Mrs Pilkington, Newthorpe, Nottingham NG16 2FB
T: (01773) 763010

High Lee ★★
Contact: Mr & Mrs Nelson, Chelmsford CM2 8AA
T: (01245) 262436

Pinecones ★★★
Contact: Mrs Pat Harvey, Pinecones, 70 Cromer Road, Sheringham NR26 8RT
T: (01263) 824955
F: (01263) 824955
E: tonyandpat@pinecones.fsnet.co.uk

Poppy Cottage ★★★
Contact: Mr Peter Crook, Thorpe End, Norwich NR13 5DQ
T: (01603) 300324
F: (01603) 633638
E: peter.jacqui@virginnet.co.uk

4 Seaview ★★★★
Contact: Mrs Howes, Hampton Hargate, Sheringham PE7 8BB
T: (01733) 315321

8 Seaview ★★★
Contact: Mrs Joan Munday, 18 Station Road, Sheringham NR26 8RE
T: (01263) 823010
F: (01263) 821449
E: info@keys-holidays.co.uk
I: www.keys-holidays.co.uk

Victoria Court ★★★★
Contact: Mr Graham Simmons, Camberley, 62 Cliff Road, Sheringham NR26 8BJ
T: (01263) 823101
F: (01263) 821433
E: graham@camberleyguesthouse.co.uk
I: www.camberleyguesthouse.co.uk

16 Wyndham Street ★★★
Contact: Mrs Joan Munday, 18 Station Road, Sheringham NR26 8RE
T: (01263) 823010
F: (01263) 821449
E: info@keys-holidays.co.uk
I: www.keys-holidays.co.uk

SHOTLEY
Suffolk

The Apartment ★★★
Contact: Ms Deborah Baynes, Main Road, Shotley, Ipswich IP9 1PW
T: (01473) 788300
F: (01473) 787055

Box Iron Cottage ★★★
Contact: Mrs Broadway, The Street, Holbrook, Ipswich IP9 2PX
T: (01473) 327673
E: debroadway@macunlimited.net

SIBLE HEDINGHAM
Essex

Brickwall Farm ★★★★
Contact: Mrs Jean Fuller, Brickwall Farm, Queen Street, Sible Hedingham, Halstead CO9 3RH
T: (01787) 460329
F: (01787) 462584
E: brickwallfarm@btinternet.com

Pevors Farm Cottages ★★★★
Contact: Mr & Mrs Margaret & John Lewis, Pevors Farm Cottages, Southey Green, Sible Hedingham, Halstead CO9 3RN
T: (01787) 460830

SIBTON
Suffolk

Bluebell, Bonny, Buttercup & Bertie ★★★★
Contact: Mrs Margaret Gray, Park Farm, Sibton, Yoxford, Saxmundham IP17 2LZ
T: (01728) 668324
F: (01728) 668564
E: margaret.gray@btinternet.com
I: www.farmstayanglia.co.uk/parkfarm

Cardinal Cottage ★★★★
Contact: Mr & Mrs Belton, Cardinal Cottage, Pouy Street, Sibton, Saxmundham IP17 2JH
T: (01728) 660111
E: jan.belton@btopenworld.com
I: www.cardinalcottageholidays.co.uk

SLOLEY
Norfolk

Piggery Cottage & Hewitts Cottage ★★★★
Contact: Mrs Ann Jones, Piggery Cottage & Hewitts Cottage, Sloley Farm, Sloley, Norwich NR12 8HJ
T: (01692) 536281
F: (01692) 535162
E: sloley@farmhotel.u-net.com

SNAPE
Suffolk

The Granary & The Forge ★★★★
Contact: Mrs Sally Gillett, Snape, Saxmundham IP17 1QU
T: (01728) 688254
E: e.r.gillett@btinternet.com
I: www.croftfarmsnape.co.uk

Jubilee Cottage ★★★★
Contact: 7 Frenze Road, Diss IP22 4PA
T: (01379) 651297
F: (01379) 641555
E: holidays@suffolk-secrets.co.uk
I: www.suffolk-secrets.co.uk

Mulberry Cottage ★★★★
Contact: 7 Frenze Road, Diss IP22 4PA
T: (01379) 651297
F: (01379) 641555
E: holidays@suffolk-secrets.co.uk
I: www.suffolk-secrets.co.uk

Smithy Cottage ★★★★
Contact: 7 Frenze Road, Diss IP22 4PA
T: (01379) 651297
F: (01379) 641555
E: holidays@suffolk-secrets.co.uk
I: www.suffolk-secrets.co.uk

The Studio Flat ★★★
Contact: Ms Kathy Ball, Church Garage, Farnham Road, Snape, Saxmundham IP17 1QW
T: (01728) 688327
F: (01728) 688500

Valley Farm Barns ★★★★
Contact: Mr Nicholson, Valley Farm Barns, Aldeburgh Road, Snape, Saxmundham IP17 1QH
T: (01728) 689071

Whitewalls ★★
Contact: 7 Frenze Road, Diss IP22 4PA
T: (01379) 651297
F: (01379) 641555
E: holidays@suffolk-secrets.co.uk
I: www.suffolk-secrets.co.uk

SNETTISHAM
Norfolk

Alexandra Villas ★★★
Contact: Mrs Sandra Hohol, Birds Norfolk Holiday Homes, 62 Westgate, Hunstanton PE36 5EL
T: (01485) 534267
F: (01485) 535230
E: shohol@birdsnorfolkholidayhomes.co.uk
I: www.norfolkholidayhomes-birds.co.uk

21 Brent Avenue ★★
Contact: Mrs Sandra Hohol, Birds Norfolk Holiday Homes, 62 Westgate, Hunstanton PE36 5EL
T: (01485) 534267
F: (01485) 535230
E: shohol@birdsnorfolkholidayhomes.co.uk
I: www.norfolkholidayhomes-birds.co.uk

Carpenters Lodge ★★★
Contact: Mr Nigel Madgett, Carpenters Lodge, Norton Hill, Snettisham, King's Lynn PE31 7LZ
T: (01485) 541580
E: nmmadgett@hotmail.com

The Coach House ★★★
Contact: Mrs Marion Peters-Loader, The Coach House, Snettisham House, St Thomas's Lane, Snettisham, King's Lynn PE31 7RZ
T: (01485) 544902
E: clive.loader@freeserve.co.uk
I: www.clive.loader@virgin.net

Cobb Cottage ★★★
Contact: Ms Sarah Pink, The Workshop, Snettisham, King's Lynn PE31 7RZ
T: (01485) 544602
E: sarahpink@hotmail.co.uk

Cobbe Court ★★★
Contact: Mr & Mrs James Douglas, Cobbe Court, Snettisham House, St Thomas's Lane, Snettisham, King's Lynn PE31 7RZ
T: (01485) 543986

4 The Courtyard ★★★
Contact: Mrs Jennifer Overson, 9 Fakenham Chase, Holbeach, Spalding PE12 7QU
T: (01406) 422569
E: jennyoverson@norfolkholidaycottages.co.uk
I: www.cottageguide.co.uk/4.thecourtyard

Cursons Cottage ★★★★
Contact: Mrs A Campbell, Craven House, Lynn Road, Snettisham, King's Lynn PE31 7LW
T: (01485) 541179
F: (01485) 543259
E: ian.averilcampbell@btinternet.com
I: www.cottageguide.co.uk/cursonscottage

Hollies Cottage & Grooms Cottage ★★★★
Contact: Mrs Elaine Aldridge, The Hollies, 12 Lynn Road, Snettisham, King's Lynn PE31 7LS
T: (01485) 541294
F: (01485) 541294

The Old Barn ★★★★
Contact: Mrs Lynn Shannon, The Grove, 17 Collins Lane, Heacham, King's Lynn PE31 7DZ
T: (01485) 570513
E: tm.shannon@virgin.net
I: www.thegroveandoldbarn.fsnet.co.uk

The Old Farm House Cottage ★★★
Contact: Mrs Jacqueline Sandy, The Old Farm House Cottage, Bircham Road, Snettisham, King's Lynn PE31 7NG
T: (01485) 543106
E: jacqueline.sandy@tesco.net

Orangery Lodge ★★★★
Contact: Mrs Marion Goldsworthy, East Wing, Snettisham House, Snettisham, King's Lynn PE31 7RZ
T: (01485) 541187
E: picaroon2@aol.com

The Smithy ★★★
Contact: Mrs Sandra Hohol, Birds Norfolk Holiday Homes, 62 Westgate, Hunstanton PE36 5EL
T: (01485) 534267
F: (01485) 535230
E: shohol@birdsnorfolkholidayhomes.co.uk
I: www.norfolkholidayhomes-birds.co.uk

Wagtail Cottage ★★★★
Contact: Mrs Sandra Hohol, Birds Norfolk Holiday Homes, 62 Westgate, Hunstanton PE36 5EL
T: (01485) 534267
F: (01485) 535230
E: shohol@birdsnorfolkholidayhomes.co.uk

SOHAM
Cambridgeshire

Poppies ★★★★
Contact: Ms Roseann Allum, Poppies (The Styx), Eye Hill Drove, Soham, Ely CB7 5XF
T: (01353) 624541
F: (01353) 624541

SOUTH BENFLEET
Essex

Alice's Place ★★★
Contact: Mr & Mrs S Millward, 43 Danesfield, South Benfleet SS7 5EE
T: (01268) 756283
F: (01268) 756283
E: info@alices-place.co.uk
I: www.alices-place.co.uk

SOUTH CREAKE
Norfolk

Primrose Cottage ★★★
Contact: Mrs Jane Shulver, Norfolk Country Cottages, Carlton House, Market Place, Reepham, Norwich NR10 4JJ
T: (01603) 871872
I: www.norfolk-cottages.co.uk

Stoneycott Cottage ★★
Contact: Mrs M. Haw, Fir Tree Cottage, 1A Station Road, Brundall, Norwich NR13 5LA
T: (01603) 715588

SOUTH MIMMS
Hertfordshire

The Black Swan ★★-★★★
Contact: Mr W A Marsterson, The Black Swan, 62-64 Blanche Lane, South Mimms, Potters Bar EN6 3PD
T: (01707) 644180
F: (01707) 642344

SOUTH WALSHAM
Norfolk

Charity Barn ★★★★
Contact: Mr & Mrs Colin & Lynda Holmes, Charity Farm, 10 Wymers Lane, South Walsham, Norwich NR13 6EA
T: (01603) 270410

SOUTHEND-ON-SEA
Essex

Essex County Hotel Rating Applied For
Contact: Miss Clare Keane, Essex County Hotel, Aviation Way, Southend-on-Sea SS2 6UN
T: (01702) 279955
F: (01702) 541961
E: mail@essexcountyhotel.com
I: www.essexcountyhotel.com

Everhome Apartments ★★
Contact: Mr Malcom Taylor, 26 Drake Road, Westcliff-on-Sea SS0 8LP
T: (01702) 343030
E: malcolmt@zoom.co.uk

Family Bungalow ★★★
Contact: Mrs Kim Frederick, 199 Caufield Road, Shoeburyness, Southend-on-Sea SS3 9LU
T: (01702) 297328

Royal Apartments ★★★
Contact: Mrs Monk, 12 Royal Terrace, Southend-on-Sea SS1 1DY
T: (01702) 345323
F: (01702) 390415
E: pat@french-property.com

SOUTHMINSTER
Essex

Avonmore ★★★★
Contact: Mr & Mrs I Bull, Rose House, Poole Street, Cavendish, Sudbury CO10 8BD
T: (01787) 280063
F: (01787) 282617
E: mrd@teambull.co.uk

SOUTHREPPS
Norfolk

Clipped Hedge Cottages ★★★-★★★★
Contact: Mr Blyth, Sheringham NR26 8NH
T: (01263) 822817

SOUTHWOLD
Suffolk

Blackshore Corner ★★★★
Contact: 7 Frenze Road, Diss IP22 4PA
T: (01379) 651297
F: (01379) 641555
E: holidays@suffolk-secrets.co.uk
I: www.suffolk-secrets.co.uk

Blackshore Cottage ★★★
Contact: 7 Frenze Road, Diss IP22 4PA
T: (01379) 651297
F: (01379) 641555
E: holidays@suffolk-secrets.co.uk
I: www.suffolk-secrets.co.uk

The Bolt Hole ★★★
Contact: 7 Frenze Road, Diss IP22 4PA
T: (01379) 651297
F: (01379) 641555
E: holidays@suffolk-secrets.co.uk
I: www.suffolk-secrets.co.uk

Caterer House ★★★
Contact: 7 Frenze Road, Diss IP22 4PA
T: (01379) 651297
F: (01379) 641555
E: holidays@suffolk-secrets.co.uk
I: www.suffolk-secrets.co.uk

Cherry Trees ★★★★
Contact: 7 Frenze Road, Diss IP22 4PA
T: (01379) 651297
F: (01379) 641555
E: holidays@suffolk-secrets.co.uk
I: www.suffolk-secrets.co.uk

Corner Cottage ★★★
Contact: Mrs Daphne Hall, Adnams, 98 High Street, Southwold IP18 6DP
T: (01502) 723292
F: (01502) 724797

The Cottage ★★★★
Contact: Mr Thomas, Pier Avenue, Southwold IP18 6BL
T: (01502) 723561

Dolphin Cottage ★★★
Contact: 7 Frenze Road, Diss IP22 3PA
T: (01379) 651297
F: (01379) 641555
E: holidays@suffolk-secrets.co.uk
I: www.suffolk-secrets.co.uk

8 Dunwich Road ★★★
Contact: H A Adnams, 98 High Street, Southwold IP18
T: (01502) 723292
F: (01502) 724794
E: haadnams_lets6ic24.net

Fern Cottage ★★★
Contact: Mr Richard Pither, Suffolk Secrets, 7 Frenze Road, Diss IP22 3PA
T: (01379) 651297
F: (01379) 641555
E: holidays@suffolk-secrets.co.uk
I: www.suffolk-secrets.co.uk

Garden Cottage ★★★
Contact: A T Bent Properties Ltd, Home Lodge, Beccles, Suffolk NR34 9AS
T: (01502) 712259
F: (01502) 712086
E: wbent@atbentproperties.fsbusiness.co.uk

Harbour Cottage ★★★
Contact: 7 Frenze Road, Diss IP22 4PA
T: (01379) 651297
F: (01379) 641555
E: holidays@suffolk-secrets.co.uk
I: www.suffolk-secrets.co.uk

Harbour Cottage ★★★
Contact: Mrs Sylvia Harris, The Anchor Inn, Main Street, Walberswick, Southwold IP18 6UA
T: (01502) 722112
F: (01502) 724464

Horseshoe Cottage ★★★
Contact: Ms D Frost & Ms J Tallon, Acanthus Property Letting Services, 9 Trinity Street, Southwold IP18 6JH
T: (01502) 724033
F: (01502) 725168
E: sales@southwold-holidays.co.uk
I: www.southwold-holidays.co.uk

The Little Blue House ★★
Contact: Mrs Diana Wright, The Kiln, The Folley, Layer-de-la-Haye, Colchester CO2 0HZ
T: (01206) 738003

Little Garth ★★★
Contact: Joe Tynan, 30 Tovells Road, Ipswich IP4 4DY
T: 01473 434642
E: bill_tynan@hotmail.com

Mary's House ★★★
Contact: Ms Pip Fielder, Watford WD19 7PU
T: (020) 8428 6103
F: (020) 8420 1326
E: pipjoe74@aol.com
I: www.maryshousesouthwold.co.uk

Mill Way Cottage ★★★
Contact: Mr Martyn Elmy, 6 Hudson Close, Lidlington, Bedford MK43 0RE
F: (01525) 404332
E: info@blythburgh-southwold.co.uk

The Nest ★★★
Contact: Mrs Daphne Hall
T: (01502) 723292
E: haadnams_lets@ic24.net
I: www.thenest-southwold.info

No 70 Pebble Rock Cottage ★★★
Contact: Mrs Judi Butler, Froyz Hall Farm, Halstead CO9 1RS
T: (01787) 476684
F: (01787) 474647
E: mjudibutler6@aol.com

The Old Rope House ★★★★
Contact: Mrs Sian Mortlock, 16 Jermyns Road, Reydon, Southwold IP18 6QB
T: (01502) 724769
E: sian@theoldropehouse.co.uk

15 Pier Avenue ★★★
Contact: 7 Frenze Road, Diss IP22 4PA
T: (01379) 651297
F: (01379) 641555
E: holidays@suffolk-secrets.co.uk
I: www.suffolk-secrets.co.uk

Pippins ★★★
Contact: Mrs Daphne Hall, H A Adnams, 98 High Street, Southwold IP18 6DP
T: (01502) 723292
F: (01502) 724794

Red Roofs ★★
Contact: 7 Frenze Road, Diss IP22 4PA
T: (01379) 651297
F: (01379) 641555
E: holidays@suffolk-secrets.co.uk
I: www.suffolk-secrets.co.uk

The Reeds ★★★★
Contact: 7 Frenze Road, Diss IP22 3PA
T: (01379) 651297
F: (01379) 641555
E: holidays@suffolk-secrets.co.uk
I: www.suffolk-secrets.co.uk

Rosemary Cottage ★★★
Contact: 7 Frenze Road, Diss IP22 4PA
T: (01379) 651297
F: (01379) 641555
I: www.suffolk-secrets.co.uk

Saltings ★★★
Contact: 7 Frenze Road, Diss IP22 4PA
T: (01379) 651297
F: (01379) 641555
E: holidays@suffolk-secrets.co.uk
I: www.suffolk-secrets.co.uk

September Cottage ★★★
Contact: Mrs Sylvia Hayward, 19 Calverley Park, Royal Tunbridge Wells TN1 2SL
T: (01892) 520350
E: sylvia@septembercottage.info
I: www.septembercottage.info

The Shed ★★
Contact: 7 Frenze Road, Diss IP22 3PA
T: (01379) 651297
F: (01379) 641555
E: holidays@suffolk-secrets.co.uk
I: www.suffolk-secrets.co.uk

Shell House ★★★★
Contact: Mrs Elisabeth Fairs, Heveningham, Halesworth IP19 0EL
T: (01986) 798250
F: (01986) 798754

Shrimp Cottage ★★★
Contact: 7 Frenze Road, Diss IP22 3PA
T: (01379) 651297
F: (01379) 641555
E: holidays@suffolk-secrets.co.uk
I: www.suffolk-secrets.co.uk

Solely Southwold ★★★
Contact: Miss Kathy Oliver, Norfolk Road, Wangford, Beccles NR34 8RE
T: (01502) 578383
E: kathy@solely-southwold.co.uk
I: www.solely-southwold.co.uk

20 St James Green ★★
Contact: Mrs Doris Burley, Reydon, Southwold IP18 6RS
T: (01502) 724096

Suffolk House ★★★
Contact: Mrs Betty Freeman, Suffolk House, 18 Dunwich Road, Southwold IP18 6LJ
T: (01502) 723742

Suton Cottage ★★
Contact: 7 Frenze Road, Diss IP22 4PA
T: (01379) 651297
F: (01379) 641555
E: holidays@suffolk-secrets.co.uk
I: www.suffolk-secrets.co.uk

SPEXHALL
Suffolk

Rose Cottage ★★★
Contact: Mrs Hammond, South Lodge, Redisham Hall, Redisham, Beccles NR34 8LZ
T: (01502) 575894

SPROWSTON
Norfolk

Holme ★★
Contact: Mrs P Guyton, 2 Recreation Ground Road, Sprowston, Norwich NR7 8EN
T: (01603) 465703

STALHAM
Norfolk

144 Broadside Chalet Park ★★
Contact: Mr J J Crawford, 5 Collingwood Avenue, Surbiton KT5 9PT
T: (020) 8337 4487
F: (020) 8337 4487
E: crawfcall@aol.com
I: www.norfolkholiday.co.uk

Chapelfield Cottage Flat ★★★
Contact: Mr Gary Holmes, Chapel Field, Stalham, Norwich NR12 9EN
T: (01692) 582173
F: (01692) 583009
E: gary@cinqueportsmarine.freeserve.co.uk

STANBRIDGE
Bedfordshire

A G Bunker & Sons ★★
Contact: Mr George Bunker, A G Bunker & Sons, Stud Farm, Stanbridge, Leighton Buzzard LU7 9SF
T: (01525) 210984

STANHOE
Norfolk

Cherry Tree Cottage ★★★★
Contact: Miss D Kingsley, Norfolk Country Cottages, Carlton House, Market Place, Reepham, Norwich NR10 4JJ
T: (01603) 871872
F: (01603) 870304
E: info@norfolkcottages.co.uk

4 The Green ★★★
Contact: Mrs Priscilla Ash, Moat Road, Terrington St Clement, King's Lynn PE34 4PN
T: (01553) 827157
F: (01553) 827410
E: bramble@scillaash.fsnet.co.uk

Pilgrims ★★★
Contact: Miss D Kingsley, Carlton House, Market Place, Reepham, Norwich NR10 4JJ
T: (01603) 871872
F: (01603) 870304
E: info@norfolkcottages.co.uk

Sarahs Cottage ★★
Contact: Mrs Sandra Hohol, 62 Westgate, Hunstanton PE36 5EL
T: (01485) 534267
F: (01485) 535230
E: shohol@birdsnorfolkholidayhomes.co.uk

STANSTED
Essex

Cedar Court Apartment ★★★
Contact: Mrs Jean Windus, 16 Grailands, Bishop's Stortford CM23 2RG
T: (01279) 653614
E: jeanwindus@ntlworld.com
I: angleseyhouse.com

STANSTED MOUNTFITCHET
Essex

Walpole Farm House ★★★-★★★★
Contact: Mrs Jill Walton, Walpole Farm House, Cambridge Road, Stansted CM24 8TA
T: (01279) 812265
F: (01279) 812098

West Barn Cottage ★★★★
Contact: Ms Sarah Woodhouse, West Barn Cottage, Alsa Lodge, Ugley, Bishop's Stortford CM24 8SX
T: (01279) 813244
F: (01279) 812010

STAPLEFORD
Cambridgeshire

Inglenook Cottage
Rating Applied For
Contact: Mr & Mrs Vernon Spencer, PO Box 115, Toft, Cambridge CB3 7WU
T: (01954) 211147
E: cottage@dial.pipex.com

STIFFKEY
Norfolk

Apple Tree Cottage ★★★
Contact: Mr Brian Braid, 23a Sandown Road, Stoneygate, Leicester LE2 3TN
T: (0116) 271 6783

Grays Cottage ★★★
Contact: Miss D Kingsley, Norfolk Country Cottages, Carlton House, Market Place, Reepham, Norwich NR10 4JJ
T: (01603) 871872
F: (01603) 870304
E: info@norfolkcottages.co.uk
I: www.swallow-tail.com

Harbour House ★★★★
Contact: Mr Bindley, Hill House, 20 Hill House Road, Thorpe St Andrew, Norwich NR1 4BQ
T: (01603) 270637

Hawthorns ★★★
Contact: Mrs M. Hickey-Smith, 18 Poplar Road, Histon, Cambridge CB4 9LN
T: (01223) 572316
E: maddy@hawthorns.info

Manor Cottage ★★★
Contact: Mrs Cooke, Stiffkey, Wells-next-the-Sea NR23 1QP
T: (01328) 830439
E: chrisccooke@aol.com

Mount Tabor ★★★
Contact: Mrs Pat Norris, Royton, Oldham OL2 5HD
T: (0161) 633 6834
E: roger@stiffkeycottage.fsnet.co.uk

Primrose Cottage ★★★
Contact: Mrs Pearson, Wells Road, Stiffkey, Wells-next-the-Sea NR23 1AJ
T: (01328) 830303

2 Red Lion Cottages ★★★
Contact: Ms Jane Whitaker, The Avenue, Comberbach, Northwich CW9 6HT
T: (01606) 892368
E: jane.pathways@virgin.net

Shrimp Cottage ★★
Contact: Mrs D. Kinsley, Carlton House, Market Place, Reepham, Norwich NR10 4JJ
T: (01603) 871872
F: (01603) 870304
E: info@norfolkcottages.co.uk
I: www.swallow-tail.com

STILTON
Cambridgeshire

Orchard Cottage ★★★★
Contact: Mrs Jennifer Higgo, Manton, Rutland Water, Oakham LE15 8SY
T: (01572) 737420
E: jhiggo@freeuk.com
I: www.higgo.com/orchard

STISTED
Essex

Ballaglass ★★★★
Contact: Mrs Sally Dunn, Ballaglass Cottage, Coggeshall Road, Stisted, Braintree CM77 8AB
T: (01376) 331409
F: (01376) 331405
E: ballaglass@btopenworld.com

STOKE-BY-NAYLAND
Suffolk

Jums Cottage & Cobbs Cottage ★★
Contact: Mr H. Engleheart, The Priory, Stoke-by-Nayland, Colchester CO6 4RL
T: (01206) 262216
F: (01206) 262373

STOVEN
Suffolk

Stringers Woodlands, Wood Farm Stables & Dairy★★★★
Contact: Mrs Melody Kidner, North Green, Stoven, Beccles NR34 8DF
T: (01502) 575744

STOWMARKET
Suffolk

Barn Cottages ★★★★
Contact: Mrs M Tydeman, Goldings, East End Lane, Stonham Aspal, Stowmarket IP14 6AS
T: (01449) 711229
E: maria@barncottages.co.uk
I: www.barncottages.co.uk

Kimberley Cottage ★★★
Contact: Mr Brian Whiting, Moats Tye, Stowmarket IP14 2EZ
T: (01449) 677766
F: (01449) 677766
E: brianwhiting.kimberleyhall@virgin.net

STRADBROKE
Suffolk

Cornhouse Cottage ★★★★
Contact: Mrs Charmaine Cooper, Cornhouse Cottage, Hepwood Lodge, Wilby Road, Stradbroke, Eye IP21 5JN
T: (01379) 384256
F: (01379) 384256
I: www.hepwoodcottages.co.uk

STRATFORD ST ANDREW
Suffolk

Toad Hall Flat ★★★
Contact: Mr & Mrs P. J. Hunt, Stratford Lodge, Stratford St Andrew, Saxmundham IP17 1LJ
T: (01728) 603463
F: (01728) 604501
E: peregrine.hunt@btinternet.com

SUDBOURNE
Suffolk

The Cartlodge Studio Flat ★★★
Contact: Mrs Susan Crane, The White House, Ferry Road, Sudbourne, Woodbridge IP12 2BQ
T: (01394) 450033
F: (01394) 450033
E: sue@langtree192.freeserve.co.uk

Gamekeepers Cottage & Holly Cottage ★★★★★
Contact: Mel Glazer, Marshland House Farm, Captains Wood, Sudbourne, Woodbridge IP12 2HA
T: (01394) 450364
F: (01394) 450279
E: mel.alderney@virgin.net

SUDBURY
Suffolk

The Compasses ★★★
Contact: Mr & Mrs Mark Blows, The Compasses, High Street, Stansfield, Sudbury CO10 8LN
T: (01284) 789486
E: mark@thecompasses.com
I: www.thecompasses.com

Six Bells ★★★
Contact: Ms Janet Martin, Preston St Mary, Sudbury CO10 9NQ
T: 0700 278 2000
F: (01787) 248413
E: janet.martin@tesco.net

SUTTON
Norfolk

Sutton Staithe Boathouse Rating Applied For
Contact: Mrs Patricia Holloway, Sutton Staithe Boathouse, Sutton Staithe Boatyard Ltd, Sutton, Norwich NR12 9QS
T: (01692) 581653
F: (01692) 582938
E: ssboatyard@paston.co.uk

SWAFFHAM
Norfolk

Hall Barn ★★★
Contact: Ms Brenda Wilbourn, Hall Barn, Old Hall Lane, Beachamwell, Swaffham PE37 8BG
T: (01366) 328794
F: (01366) 328794
E: hallbarn@supanet.com

SWANTON ABBOT
Norfolk

Magnolia Cottage ★★
Contact: Mrs Christine Nockolds, Hill Farm House, Swanton Hill, Swanton Abbot, Norwich NT10 5EA
T: (01692) 538481

Walnut Tree Barn ★★★★
Contact: Mr & Mrs Mark & Sally Page, Walnut Tree Farm, Aylsham Road, Swanton Abbott, Swanton Abbot, Norwich NR10 5DL
T: (01692) 538888
F: (01692) 538100

Willow Tree Cottage ★★★★★
Contact: Mrs Nixon, Pheasant Cottage, Long Common Lane, Swanton Abbot, Norwich NR10 5BH
T: (01692) 538169
F: (01692) 538169

SWANTON MORLEY
Norfolk

Teal, Heron & Grebe Cottages ★★★
Contact: Mrs Sally Marsham, Waterfall Farm, Worthing Road, Swanton Morley, East Dereham NR20 4QD
T: (01362) 637300
F: (01362) 637300
E: waterfallfarm@tesco.net

SWANTON NOVERS
Norfolk

Daneway ★★★★
Contact: Mrs Eileen Summerlee, Thursford, Fakenham NR21 0BG
T: (01263) 712062
F: (01263) 712062
E: summerleecottage@aol.com

SYDERSTONE
Norfolk

Harrow Barn Rating Applied For
Contact: Miss Catherine Ringer, Buildings Farm, Creake Road, Syderstone, King's Lynn PE31 8SH
T: (01485) 578287
F: (01485) 576030
E: chringeris@hotmail.com

TATTERSETT
Norfolk

Tatt Valley Holiday Cottages ★★★-★★★★★
Contact: Mr T W Hurn, Tatt Valley Holiday Cottages, Lower Farm, Tattersett, King's Lynn PE31 8RT
T: (01485) 528506
E: enquiries@norfolkholidayhomes.co.uk
I: www.norfolkholidayhomes.co.uk

TERRINGTON ST CLEMENT
Norfolk

Northgate Lodge Flat ★★★
Contact: Mrs Howling, Northgate Way, Terrington St Clement, King's Lynn PE34 4LG
T: (01553) 828428
E: jbh@interads.co.uk

THAXTED
Essex

Thaxted Holiday Cottages ★★★★
Contact: Mrs Yolanda De Bono, Thaxted Holiday Cottages, Dunmow Road, Thaxted, Great Dunmow CM6 2LU
T: (01371) 830233
E: enquiries@thaxtedholidaycottages.co.uk
I: www.thaxtedholidaycottages.co.uk

THEBERTON
Suffolk

Woodpecker Cottage ★★★
Contact: 7 Frenze Road, Diss IP22 4PA
T: (01379) 651297
F: (01379) 641555
I: www.suffolk-secrets.co.uk

THETFORD
Norfolk

River Lodge ★★★★
Contact: Mrs Susan Burton, River House, River Lane, Thetford IP25 7TQ
T: (01362) 821570
F: (01362) 820639
E: andy@abaltd.demon.co.uk

THORNAGE
Norfolk

Daisy Lodge ★★
Contact: Mrs Melanie Hickling, Back Lane, Roughton, Cromer NR11 8QR
T: (01263) 761705

THORNHAM
Norfolk

Bay Tree Cottage ★★
Contact: Mrs Jean Wilson, Bay Tree Cottage, High Street, Thornham, Hunstanton PE36 6LY
T: (01485) 512204

Linzel Cottage ★★★★
Contact: Mrs Sandra Hohol, 62 Westgate, Ringstead, Hunstanton PE36 5BU
T: (01485) 534267
F: (01485) 535230
E: shohol@birdsnorfolkholidayhomes.co.uk
I: www.norfolkholidayhomes-birds.co.uk

1 Malthouse Cottages ★★
Contact: Mrs L K Rigby, Brindle Cottage, 6 Church Hill, Castor, Peterborough PE5 7AU
T: (01733) 380399
F: (01733) 380399
E: leslierigby@castor.freeserve.co.uk

4 Malthouse Court ★★★
Contact: Mrs Wendy Seaton, Manor Farm, Church Street, Thriplow, Royston SG8 7RE
T: (01763) 209154

8 Malthouse Court ★★★
Contact: Sue Sadler, 7 Malthouse Court, Thornham, Hunstanton PE36 6NW
T: (01485) 512085
F: (01485) 512085

Manor Cottage ★★
Contact: Mrs Sandra Hohol, 62 Westgate, Hunstanton PE36 5EL
T: (01485) 534267
F: (01485) 535230
E: shohol@birdsnorfolkholidayhomes.co.uk
I: www.norfolkholidayhomes-birds.co.uk

Manor Farm Cottages ★★★-★★★★
Contact: Mrs Margaret Goddard, Thornham, Hunstanton PE36 6NB
T: (01485) 512272
F: (01485) 512241

Oyster Cottage ★★★
Contact: Mrs Geraldine Tibbs, Sedgeford, Hunstanton PE36 5LS
T: (01485) 571770
F: (01485) 571770

Rosemary Cottage ★★★★
Contact: Mrs Jane Shulver, Norfolk Country Cottages, Carlton House, Market Place, Reepham, Norwich NR10 4JJ
T: (01603) 871872
I: www.norfolk-cottages.co.uk

Rushmeadow Studio ★★★
Contact: Mr Wyett, Main Road, Thornham, Hunstanton PE36 6LZ
T: (01485) 512372
F: (01485) 512372
E: rushmeadow@lineone.net
I: www.rushmeadow.com

21 Shepherds Pightle ★★★★
Contact: Mrs Sue Sadler, Green Lane, Thornham, Hunstanton PE36 6NW
T: (01485) 512085
F: (01485) 512085

1 West End Cottages ★★
Contact: Mr & Mrs Hardy, Barton, Cambridge CB3 7AZ
T: (01223) 263859

THORNHAM PARVA
Suffolk

Chandos Barn ★★★
Contact: Mr & Mrs Kevin & Judy O'Keefe, Chandos Barn, Chandos Farmhouse, Bull Road, Thornham Parva, Eye IP23 8ES
T: (01379) 783791

THORPE MORIEUX
Suffolk

Maltings Farm Holiday Cottages ★★★
Contact: Mrs Rachel Bell, Maltings Farm Holiday Cottages, Thorpe Morieux, Bury St Edmunds IP30 0NG
T: (01284) 828843
F: (01284) 827444
E: tim-bell@fsbdial.co.uk

THORPENESS
Suffolk

The Country Club Apartments ★★★★
Contact: Thorpeness Golf Club & Hotel Limited, Lakeside Avenue, Thorpeness, Leiston IP16 4NH
T: (01728) 452176
F: (01728) 453868
E: info@thorpeness.co.uk
I: www.thorpeness.co.uk

Hope Cove Cottage ★★★★
Contact: Mrs Irene Pearman, Albury End, Ware SG11 2HS
T: (01279) 771281
F: (01279) 771517
E: ipearman@whestates.com

The House in the Clouds ★★★
Contact: Mrs S Le Comber, The House in The Clouds, 4 Hinde House, 14 Hinde Street, London W1U 3BG
T: (020) 7224 3615
F: (020) 7224 3615
E: houseintheclouds@btopenworld.com

7 The Uplands ★★★
Contact: Mrs Diane Holmes, 2 Red House Cottage, Uplands Road, Thorpeness, Leiston IP16 4NG
T: (01728) 454648

THROCKING
Hertfordshire

Bluntswood Hall Cottages ★★★
Contact: Mrs Sally Smyth, Bluntswood Hall Cottages, Bluntswood Hall, Throcking, Buntingford SG9 9RN
T: (01763) 281204
F: (01763) 281204

THURLEIGH
Bedfordshire

Scald Farm ★
Contact: Mr Reg Towler, C V Towler & Sons, Scald Farm, Thurleigh, Bedford MK44 2DP
T: (01234) 771996
F: (01234) 771996
E: scaldendfarm@tesco.net

THURSFORD
Norfolk

Hayloft ★★★
Contact: Mrs Ann Green, Thursford, Fakenham NR21 0BD
T: (01328) 878273

Ransome Lodge The Meadows ★★★★
Contact: Miss D Kingsley, Norfolk Country Cottages, Carlton House, Market Place, Reepham, Norwich NR10 4JJ
T: (01603) 871872
F: (01603) 870304
E: info@norfolkcottages.co.uk
I: www.swallow-tail.com

Wallis Lodge ★★★★
Contact: Miss D Kingsley, Norfolk Country Cottages, Carlton House, Market Place, Reepham, Norwich NR10 4JJ
T: (01603) 871872
F: (01603) 870304
E: info@norfolkcottages.co.uk
I: www.swallow-tail.com

TOLLESBURY
Essex

Fernleigh ★★★
Contact: Mrs Gillian Willson, Fernleigh, 16 Woodrolfe Farm Lane, Tollesbury, Maldon CM9 8SX
T: (01621) 868245
F: (01621) 868245
E: Gill_Willson@lineone.net

TRIMINGHAM
Norfolk

Church Farm Cottage ★★
Contact: Mrs Turner, Church Lane, Gimingham, Norwich NR11 8AL
T: (01263) 833269

High Lawns ★★★
Contact: Mrs Gillian Kerr, 94 Overstrand Road, Overstrand, Cromer NR27 0DN
T: (01263) 512910
F: (01263) 519169
E: gill@gkerr37.freeserve.co.uk

TRIMLEY
Suffolk

Treacle Pot Cottage ★★★
Contact: Mr Richard Borley, Felixstowe IP11 0SA
T: (01394) 275367

TRIMLEY ST MARTIN
Suffolk

Gemini ★★★
Contact: Mr Stephen Olden, Gemini, 256 High Road, Trimley St Martin, Felixstowe IP11 0RG
T: (01394) 214093

TRUNCH
Norfolk

South Cottage & Briar Cottage ★★★
Contact: Mr & Mrs P Lomax, Malthouse Cottage, Mundesley Road, Trunch, North Walsham NR28 0QB
T: (01263) 721973
E: ronbet@fdn.co.uk

TUNSTALL
Suffolk

Knoll Cottage ★★★★
Contact: Mrs Jill Robinson, Timbertop Farm, Ashfield, Stowmarket IP14 6NA
T: (01728) 685084
F: (01728) 685084
E: jill@timbertop.co.uk

Walnut Tree Cottage ★★★★
Contact: 7 Frenze Road, Diss IP22 4PA
T: (01379) 651297
F: (01379) 641555
E: holidays@suffolk-secrets.co.uk
I: www.suffolk-secrets.co.uk

UPPER SHERINGHAM
Norfolk

Barn Owl Cottage ★★★
Contact: Mr & Mrs Russell, Lodge Hill, Upper Sheringham, Sheringham NR26 8TJ
T: (01263) 821445
E: stay@lodgecottage.co.uk
I: www.lodgecottage.co.uk

WALBERSWICK
Suffolk

1 Blackshore Rating Applied For
Contact: Suffolk Secrets, 7 Frenze Road, Diss IP22 4PA
T: (01379) 651297
F: (01379) 641555
E: holidays@suffolk-secrets.co.uk

The Shieling ★★★
Contact: Adnams, 98 High Street, Southwold IP18 6DP
T: (01502) 723292
F: (01502) 724794
E: h.a.adnams_lets@i.c.24.net

Shrublands ★★★★
Contact: 7 Frenze Road, Diss IP22 4PA
T: (01379) 651297
F: (01379) 641555
E: holidays@suffolk-secrets.co.uk
I: www.suffolk-secrets.co.uk

Stukie Ben Rating Applied For
Contact: Suffolk Secrets, 7 Frenze Road, Diss IP22 4PA
T: (01379) 651297
F: (01379) 641555
E: holidays@suffolk-secrets.co.uk

WALCOTT
Norfolk

Spindrift ★★
Contact: Miss D Kingsley, Norfolk Country Cottages, Carlton House, Market Place, Reepham, Norwich NR10 4JJ
T: (01603) 871872
F: (01603) 870304
E: info@norfolkcottages.co.uk
I: www.swallow-tail.com

Tamarisk ★★★★
Contact: Mrs Shulver, Norfolk Country Cottages, Carlton House, Market Place, Reepham, Norwich NR10 4JJ
T: (01692) 651126
F: (01692) 650180
E: info@norfolkcottages.co.uk

WALDRINGFIELD
Suffolk

Low Farm Estate Services ★★★
Contact: Mr Lee York, Low Farm Estate Services, Ipswich Road, Waldringfield, Woodbridge IP12 4QU
T: (01473) 736475
F: (01473) 736475

WALTON HIGHWAY
Cambridgeshire

Espalier Cottage ★★★
Contact: Mrs Catherine Harvey, St Pauls Road South, Walton Highway, Wisbech PE14 7DD
T: (01945) 476627
F: (01945) 463937
E: espalier@pdh.co.uk

WANGFORD
Suffolk

15 Elms Lane ★★★
Contact: Mr David Weight, Reydon, Southwold IP18 6RS
T: (01502) 724705
E: weight@onetel.net.uk

WASHBROOK
Suffolk

Stebbings Cottage ★★★
Contact: Mrs Caroline Fox, Back Lane, Washbrook, Copdock, Ipswich IP8 3JA
T: (01473) 730216
E: caroline@foxworld.fsnet.co.uk

WELLS-NEXT-THE-SEA
Norfolk

Annie's ★★★
Contact: Mrs Sarah Orford, Great Ashfield, Bury St Edmunds IP31 3HF
T: (01359) 240340

Barnacles ★★★★
Contact: Mr Andrew Wace, Eastgate Farm, Great Walsingham NR22 6AB
T: (01328) 820028
F: (01328) 821100
E: waceptnrs@farming.co.uk
I: wellstown@fsnet.co.uk

Briar Cottage ★★★
Contact: Mr & Mrs P Rainsford, The Old Custom House, East Quay, Wells-next-the-Sea NR23 1LD
T: (01328) 711463
F: (01328) 710277
E: briar@eastquay.co.uk
I: www.eastquay.co.uk

Canary Cottage ★★★
Contact: Ms Sally Maufe, Egmere, Walsingham NR23 1SB
T: (01328) 710246
F: (01328) 711524
E: branthill.farms@macunlimited.net

Chantry ★★★
Contact: Mrs Jackson, Brickendon, Hertford SG13 8NU
T: (01992) 511303
F: (01992) 511303

7 Chapel Yard ★★★★
Contact: Mrs Elizabeth Buxton, Barn House, Hempstead, Holt NR25 6TP
T: (01263) 714082
E: elizabethbuxton@tinyworld.co.uk

14 Church Street ★★
Contact: Mrs Rita Piesse, Convent House, 1 Longwater Lane, Costessey, Norwich NR8 5AH
T: (01603) 744233
E: rr.piesse@mailbox.tv

Fisherman's Cottage ★★★
Contact: Ms Lesley Whitby, 170 Leighton Road, London NW5 2RE
T: (020) 7679 9477
E: l.whitby@ucl.ac.uk

Gabriel Cottage ★★★★
Contact: Dr M. Strong, Saltings, 6 Ramms Court, Wells-next-the-Sea NR23 1JN
T: (01328) 710743

The Glebe ★★★
Contact: Miss Dawn Kinsley, Market Place, Reepham, Norwich NR10 4JJ
T: (01603) 871872
F: (01603) 870304
E: info@norfolkcottages.co.uk
I: www.swallow-tail.com

Hillside ★★★
Contact: Ms Carol Goulding, Hillside, Plummers Hill, Wells-next-the-Sea NR23 1ES
T: (01328) 710037

Holly Tree Cottage ★★★★
Contact: Mr Graham Wild, 26 Dogger Lane, Wells-next-the-Sea NR23 1BE
T: (01328) 711190

Honeypot Cottage ★★★
Contact: Mrs Joan Price, Shingles, Southgate Close, Wells-next-the-Sea NR23 1HG
T: (01328) 711982
F: (01328) 711982
E: walker.al@talk21.com
I: www.wells-honeypot.co.uk

4 Laylands Yard ★★★
Contact: Mrs Ann Heaton, 5 Laylands Yard, Freeman Street, Wells-next-the-Sea NR23 1DA
T: (01328) 711361

Luggers Cottage ★★★★
Contact: Miss D Kingsley, Norfolk Country Cottages, Market Place, Reepham, Norwich NR10 4JJ
T: (01603) 871872
F: (01603) 870304
E: info@norfolkcottages.co.uk
I: www.swallow-tail.com

No 5 Coastguard Cottages ★★★
Contact: Mrs Wace, Eastgate Farm, Scarborough Road, Walsingham NR22 6AB
T: (01328) 820028
F: (01328) 821100

Poppy Cottage ★★★
Contact: Mrs Christine Curtis, Ship Cottage, East Quay, Wells-next-the-Sea NR23 1LE
T: (01328) 710395

Ranters Cottage ★★★
Contact: Mrs Hilary Marsden, 22 Charles Street, Berkhamsted HP4 3DF
T: (01442) 872486
E: hilaryamarsden@aol.com

Seashell Cottage ★★★
Contact: Mrs Cecilia Fox, Middle Cottage, Church Street, Brisley, East Dereham NR20 5AA
T: (01362) 668534
F: (01362) 668534
I: www.seashellcottage.co.uk

Skylark Cottage ★★★
Contact: Mrs Bridget Jones, Bellaire, Wellingborough EX31 1QZ
T: (01271) 372225
E: bridget.jones@ukgateway.net
I: www.bridget.jones.ukgateway.net

Swamp Cottage ★★
Contact: Miss Dawn Kinsley, Norfolk Country Cottages Ref. 647, Market Place, Reepham, Norwich NR10 4JJ
T: (01603) 871872
F: (01603) 870304
E: info@norfolkcottages.co.uk
I: www.swallow-tail.com

13 Tunns Yard
Rating Applied For
Contact: Ms Jean Clitheroe, 14 Shop Lane, Wells-next-the-Sea NR23 1DF
T: (01328) 711362
E: jean@theoldexchange.fsnet.co.uk

Wagtails ★★★
Contact: Ms Frances Poulton, Wells-next-the-Sea NR23 1HT
T: (01328) 710014
E: wagtailswells@aol.com

Wherry Cottage ★★★
Contact: Miss D Kingsley, Carlton House, Market Place, Reepham, Norwich NR10 4JJ
T: (01603) 871872
F: (01603) 870304
E: info@norfolkcottages.co.uk
I: www.swallow-tail.com

WELWYN
Hertfordshire

Gamekeeper's Lodge & Shire Barn ★★★★
Contact: Mr & Mrs Marinus Buisman, Lockley Farm, Welwyn AL6 0BL
T: (01438) 718641
F: (01438) 714238
E: liz@lockleyfarm.co.uk
I: www.lockleyfarm.co.uk

WENDENS AMBO
Essex

The Chapel (Cottage) ★★
Contact: Mrs Rosemary Barratt, London NW3 1RR
T: (020) 7435 1126

WENHASTON
Suffolk

The Buntings ★★★
Contact: Mr L. E. Freeman, Blyford Lane, Wenhaston, Halesworth IP19 9BS
T: (01502) 478677
F: (01502) 478677

Holmview ★★★
Contact: Mr & Mrs Saunders, Foxdale, 159 The Street, Rockland St Mary, Hellington, Norwich NR14 7HL
T: (01508) 538340

Poplar Cottage ★★★★
Contact: 7 Frenze Road, Diss IP22 4PA
T: (01379) 651297
F: (01379) 641555
I: www.suffolk-secrets.co.uk

WEST BECKHAM
Norfolk

Flint Farm Cottages ★★-★★★★
Contact: Mrs Wilson, Flint Farm Cottages, Chestnut Farm, Church Road, West Beckham, Holt NR25 6NX
T: (01263) 822241
F: (01263) 822243

WEST RUDHAM
Norfolk

North, Bertie's Cottages ★★-★★★
Contact: Blakes Holidays, Blakes, Stoney Bank Road, Earby, Barnoldswick BB94 0AA
T: 08700 708090

WEST RUNTON
Norfolk

8 & 13 Travers Court ★★★
Contact: Mrs Oliver, Maple Cottage, Arkesden Road, Saffron Walden CB11 4QU
T: (01799) 550265
F: (01799) 550296
E: louise44@btinternet.com

Beacon Hill ★★
Contact: Mrs Justina Morris, Beacon Hill, Sandy Lane, West Runton, Cromer NR27 9NB
T: (01263) 838162

6 Cromer Road ★★★
Contact: Ms Lotta Fox, Lambert & Russell, 15 West Street, Cromer NR27 9HZ
T: (01263) 511028
E: property@lambertw.fslife.co.uk

Old Farm Cottage ★★★
Contact: Mrs Jackie Hack, Sheringham NR26 8HH
T: (01263) 824729
F: (01263) 825239

Roman Camp Brick Chalets ★★★
Contact: Mr Julian, West Runton, Cromer NR27 9ND
T: (01263) 837256

Roseacre Country House ★-★★
Contact: Mr & Mrs Lunken, Roseacre Country House, The Hurn, West Runton, Sheringham NR27 9QS
T: (01263) 837221

WESTCLIFF-ON-SEA
Essex

Thames Estuary Holiday Apartments ★★★
Contact: Mr Donald Watson, Leigh-on-Sea SS9 3SJ
T: (01702) 477255
F: (01702) 477255

Thames Estuary Holiday Apartments ★★★
Contact: Mr & Mrs Moxon, Leigh-on-Sea SS9 3RH
T: (01702) 555155
E: mandy@amoxon.freeserve.co.uk

WESTLETON
Suffolk

Apple Tree Cottage ★★★
Contact: 7 Frenze Road, Diss IP22 4PA
T: (01379) 651297
F: (01379) 641555
E: holidays@suffolk-secrets.co.uk

Easter Cottage ★★★★
Contact: 7 Frenze Road, Diss IP22 4PA
T: (01379) 651297
F: (01379) 641555
E: holidays@suffolk-secrets.co.uk
I: www.suffolk-secrets.co.uk

Ebenezer House, 1 & 3 & 5 Ebenezer Row ★★-★★★
Contact: 7 Frenze Road, Diss IP22 4PA
T: (01379) 651297
F: (01379) 641555
E: holidays@suffolk-secrets.co.uk
I: www.suffolk-secrets.co.uk

Mulleys Cottage ★★★★
Contact: Mr & Mrs Richard Pither, 7 Frenze Road, Diss IP22 4PA
T: (01379) 651297
F: (01379) 641553
E: holidays@suffolk-secrets.co.uk

Spring Cottage ★★★★
Contact: Dr Ruth Whittaker, 2 Clematis Close, Westleton, Saxmundham IP17 3BN
T: (01728) 648380
F: (01728) 648380

WEYBOURNE
Norfolk

Appletree Cottage ★★★★
Contact: Miss D Kingsley, Norfolk Country Cottages, Carlton House, Market Place, Reepham, Norwich NR10 4JJ
T: (01603) 871872
F: (01603) 870304
E: info@norfolkcottages.co.uk
I: www.norfolk-cottages.co.uk

Bolding Way Holiday Cottages ★★★★
Contact: Mr Charlie Harrison, Bolding Way Holiday Cottages, Bolding Way, Weybourne, Holt NR25 7SW
T: (01263) 588666
F: (01263) 588666
E: holidays@boldingway.co.uk
I: www.boldingway.co.uk

Home Farm Cottages ★★★
Contact: Mrs Sally Middleton, Home Farm Cottage, Home Farm, Holt Road, Weybourne, Holt NR25 7ST
T: (01263) 588334
E: sallymiddleton@virgin.com

Lower Byre ★★★
Contact: Ms Valerie James, Spalding PE11 2HL
T: (01775) 760938
F: (01775) 762856
E: valeriejames@waitrose.com

The Old Stables ★★★
Contact: Mr Maureen Hudson, Sheringham Road, Weybourne, Holt NR25 7EY
T: (01263) 588231
F: (01263) 588231
E: maureen.hudson@btinternet.com

The Treehouse ★★★
Contact: Mrs Sharon Moss, Priory Barn, Mendham, Harleston IP20 0JH
T: (01379) 854601
E: sharonmoss@pgen.net

Wayside Cottage ★★★
Contact: Countryside Cottages, 5 Old Stable Yard, High Street, Holt NR25 6BN
T: (01263) 713133

Weybourne Forest Lodges ★★
Contact: Mr & Mrs Chris & Sue Tansley, Weybourne Forest Lodges, Sandy Hill Lane, Weybourne, Holt NR25 7HW
T: (01263) 588440
F: (01263) 588588
E: chris_tansley@hotmail.com

Weybourne Holiday Homes ★★★
Contact: Mrs Lawson, Weybourne, Holt NR25 7EX
T: (01263) 588255
E: weyholhome@aol.com

WHEATACRE
Norfolk

Bluebell Cottage ★★★
Contact: Mrs Vera Thirtle, Playters Old Farm, Church Road, Ellough, Beccles NR34 7TN
T: (01502) 712325
F: (01502) 712325
E: thirtle.playters@virgin.net

WHEPSTEAD
Suffolk

Rowney Cottage ★★★
Contact: Mrs Kati Turner, Whepstead, Bury St Edmunds IP29 4TQ
T: (01284) 735842
E: nick.turner@farming.co.uk

WHISSONSETT
Norfolk

No 2 Sunnyside ★★★
Contact: Mrs Rand, Gormans Lane, Colkirk, Fakenham NR21 7NP
T: (01328) 855960
F: (01328) 864745
E: teresa.rand@virgin.net

WHITE RODING
Essex

Josselyns ★★★★
Contact: Mrs Dawn Becker, Josselyns, New Hall Farm, White Roding, Great Dunmow CM6 1RY
T: (01279) 876734
F: (01279) 876938
E: nb@artbecco.co.uk

WICKHAM SKEITH
Suffolk

The Netus Barn ★★★
Contact: Mrs Joy Homan, Street Farm, Wickham Skeith, Eye IP23 8LP
T: (01449) 766275
E: joygeoffhoman@amserve.net

WICKMERE
Norfolk

Swallow Cottages (Poppyland Holiday Cottages)★★★★
Contact: Mr & Mrs Riches, Wickmere, Norwich NR11 7ND
T: (01263) 577473
F: (01263) 570087
E: poppyland@totalise.co.uk
I: www.broadland.com/poppyland

WIGHTON
Norfolk

Malthouse ★★★
Contact: Mrs Linden Green, Copys Green, Wells-next-the-Sea NR23 1NY
T: (01328) 820204
F: (01328) 820175

Old Barn Cottage ★★★
Contact: Miss Dawn Kinsley, Norfolk Country Cottages Ref. 493, Market Place, Reepham, Norwich NR10 4JJ
T: (01603) 871872
F: (01603) 870304
E: info@norfolkcottages.co.uk
I: www.swallow-tail.com

WILBURTON
Cambridgeshire

Australia Farmhouse ★★★★
Contact: Mrs Rebecca Howard, Australia Farmhouse, Twentypence Road, Wilburton, Ely CB6 3PX
T: (01353) 740322
F: (01353) 740322
E: fenflat@hotmail.com
I: www.sakernet.com/jameshoward

WINGFIELD
Suffolk

Beech Farm Maltings ★★★★
Contact: Mrs Rosemary Gosling, Beech Farm, Wingfield, Eye IP21 5RG
T: (01379) 586630
F: (01379) 586630
E: maltings.beechfarm@virgin.net
I: http://freespace.virgin.net/maltings.beechfarm

Keeley's Farm ★★★
Contact: Mrs Gloria Elsden, Solomon Place, Syleham, Eye IP21 4LT
T: (01379) 668409
E: glori@solomonsplace.com

WINTERTON-ON-SEA
Norfolk

Transacre Ltd ★★★★
Contact: Mrs Rita Walker, Burnley Hall, East Somerton, Great Yarmouth NR29 4DZ
T: (01493) 393206
F: (01493) 393745
E: rita@burnleyhall.co.uk

WISBECH
Cambridgeshire

Common Right Barns ★★★★
Contact: Mrs Teresa Fowler, Plash Lane, Tholomas Drove, Wisbech St Mary, Wisbech PE13 4SP
T: (01945) 410424
F: (01945) 410424
E: teresa@commonrightbarns.co.uk
I: www.commonrightbarns.co.uk

WISBECH ST MARY
Cambridgeshire

Fenland Self Catering Holidays ★★★
Contact: Mr Michael Southern, Fenland Self Catering Holidays, Mandalay, Station Road, Wisbech St Mary, Wisbech PE13 4RY
T: (01945) 410680

WIVETON
Norfolk

Laneway Cottage ★★★★
Contact: Mrs Catherine Joice, Hall Lane, Colkirk, Fakenham NR21 7ND
T: (01328) 862261
F: (01328) 856464
E: catherine.joice@btinternet.com

WOOD NORTON
Norfolk

Acorn Cottages ★★★★
Contact: Ms Ann Pope, Foulsham Road, Wood Norton, East Dereham NR20 5BG
T: (01362) 683615
F: (01362) 683615
E: rjpope@lineone.net

Hall Farm Cottage ★★★★
Contact: Mr Barry Mark Griss, Hall Farm House, Church Road, Wood Norton, East Dereham NR20 5AR
T: (01362) 683341

The Small Barn Rating Applied For
Contact: Miss Jane Lister, The Small Barn, Severals Grange, Holt Road, Wood Norton, East Dereham NR20 5BL
T: (01362) 684206
E: hoecroft@acedial.co.uk

WOODBRIDGE
Suffolk

Colston Cottage ★★★★
Contact: Mr John Bellefontaine, Colston Hall Cottage, Colston Hall, Badingham, Woodbridge IP13 8LB
T: (01728) 638375
F: (01728) 638084
E: lizjohn@colstonhall.com

Easton Farm Park ★★★★
Contact: Fiona Kerr, Easton Farm Park, Easton, Woodbridge IP13 0EQ
T: (01728) 746475
F: (01728) 747861
E: easton@eastonfarmpark.co.uk
I: www.eastonfarmpark.co.uk

Mousehole Cottage ★★★★
Contact: Mr John Hammond, 34 Seckford Street, Woodbridge IP12 4LY
T: (01394) 384007
F: (01394) 384007
E: john@suffolkcottageholidays.com
I: www.cottageguide.co.uk/mousehole

The Old Forge Rating Applied For
Contact: Mr Robert Blake, The Old Forge, 6 Station Road, Melton, Woodbridge IP12 1PX
T: (01394) 382565

Quayside Cottage ★★★
Contact: Mr Richard Leigh, Quayside, The Quay, Waldringfield, Woodbridge IP12 4QZ
T: (01473) 736724
E: quayside@waldringfield.org.uk

Sampsons Mill ★★★
Contact: Mr Gordon J. Turner, Sampsons Mill, Mill Lane, Wickham Market, Woodbridge IP13 0SF
T: (01728) 746791
F: (01728) 746791
E: sampsons.mill@ntlworld.com

Sunbeams ★★★
Contact: Mrs Penny Moon, Little Bass, Ferry Quay, Woodbridge IP12 1BW
T: (01394) 382770
F: (01394) 382770
E: theoffice@mrsjanegoodltd.co.uk
I: www.mrsjanegoodltd.co.uk

Windmill Lodges ★★★★
Contact: Mrs Bobbie Coe, Windmill Lodges Ltd, Red House Farm, Saxtead, Woodbridge IP13 9RD
T: (01728) 685338
F: (01728) 685338
E: holidays@windmilllodges.co.uk
I: www.windmilllodges.co.uk

The Wing ★★★
Contact: Mrs G M Gurden, Burgh House, Woodbridge IP13 6PU
T: (01473) 735273

WOOLPIT
Suffolk

The Bothy ★★★★
Contact: Mrs Kathryn Parker, Woolpit Green, Woolpit, Bury St Edmunds IP30 9RG
T: (01359) 241143
F: (01359) 244296
E: grangefarm@btinternet.com
I: www.farmstayanglia.co.uk/grangefarm/

WOOTTON
Bedfordshire

The Stable Yard Rating Applied For
Contact: Mrs Rachael Thomas, Hunters Lodge, Wood Farm, Wootton Green, Wootton, Bedford MK43 9EF
T: (01234) 765351
F: (01234) 764278
E: thestableyard@tiscali.co.uk

EAST OF ENGLAND

WORSTEAD
Norfolk

Poppyfields Cottages ★★★
Contact: Mrs Jane Shulver, Carlton House, Market Place, Reepham, Norwich NR10 4JJ
T: (01603) 871872
F: (01603) 870304
E: info@norfolkcottages.co.uk
I: www.norfolk-cottages.co.uk

WORTHAM
Suffolk

Ivy House Farm ★★★★
Contact: Mr & Mrs Paul Bradley, Ivy House Farm, Long Green, Wortham, Diss IP22 1RD
T: (01379) 898395
E: prjsbrad@aol.com
I: www.ivyhousefarmcottages.co.uk

Olde Tea Shoppe Apartment ★★★★
Contact: Mrs Alison Dumbell, Wortham, Diss IP22 1PP
T: (01379) 783210
E: teashop@wortham.freeserve.co.uk

WROXHAM
Norfolk

Daisy Broad Lodges ★★★★
Contact: Mr Daniel Thwaites, Barnes Brinkcraft, Riverside Road, Wroxham, Norwich NR12 8UD
T: (01603) 782625
F: (01603) 784072
E: daniel@barnesbrinkcraft.co.uk
I: www.barnesbrinkcraft.co.uk

Helen's ★★★
Contact: Miss D Kingsley, Norfolk Country Cottages, Carlton House, Market Place, Reepham, Norwich NR10 4JJ
T: (01603) 871872
F: (01603) 870304
E: info@norfolkcottages.co.uk
I: www.swallow-tail.com

Kingfisher Lodge ★★★★
Contact: Mrs D Campling, Kingfisher Lodge, Fineway Cruisers, Riverside Road, Wroxham, Norwich NR12 8UD
T: (01603) 782309
E: steve@fineway.freeserve.co.uk
I: www.finewayleisure.co.uk

Nutmeg & Plum Tree Cottages ★★★★
Contact: Mrs J Pond, East View Farm, Stone Lane, Ashmanhaugh, Norwich NR12 8YW
T: (01603) 782225
F: (01603) 782225
E: john.pond@tinyworld.co.uk
I: www.eastviewfarm.co.uk

20 Trail Quay Cottages ★★★
Contact: Miss D Kingsley, Norfolk Country Cottages, Carlton House, Market Place, Reepham, Norwich NR10 4JJ
T: (01603) 871872
F: (01603) 870304
E: info@norfolkcottages.co.uk
I: www.swallow-tail.com

Whitegates Apartment ★★★
Contact: Mrs C M Youd, Whitegates Apartment, 181 Norwich Road, Wroxham, Norwich NR12 8RZ
T: (01603) 781037

YOXFORD
Suffolk

Wolsey Farm House ★★★★
Contact: Mrs Marion Anthony, Wrentham, Beccles NR34 7NH
T: (01502) 675674
F: (01502) 675674
E: marion.anthony1@virgin.net

SOUTH WEST

ABBOTSBURY
Dorset

The Cottage ★★★
Contact: Mrs Val Dredge, The Cottage, Grove Lane, Abbotsbury, Weymouth DT3 4JH
T: (01305) 871462
E: val@thecottage-abbotsbury.co.uk
I: www.thecottage-abbotsbury.co.uk

Elworth Farmhouse & Poppy's Cottage★★★★-★★★★★
Contact: Mrs Christine Wade, Elworth, Portesham, Weymouth DT3 4HF
T: (01305) 871693
E: elworthfarmhouse@aol.com
I: www.elworth.supanet.com

Gorwell Farm Cottages ★★★★-★★★★★
Contact: Mrs Mary Pengelly, Gorwell Farm Cottages, Gorwell, Abbotsbury, Weymouth DT3 4JX
T: (01305) 871401
F: (01305) 871441
E: mary@gorwellfarm.co.uk
I: www.gorwellfarm.co.uk

Lawrence's Cottage ★★★
Contact: Mr Zachary Stuart-Brown, Dream Cottages, 41 Maiden Street, Weymouth DT4 8AZ
T: (01305) 761347
E: admin@dream-cottages.co.uk
I: www.dream-cottages.co.uk

The Old Coastguards ★★★★
Contact: Mr & Mrs John & Cheryl Varley, The Old Coastguards, Abbotsbury, Weymouth DT3 4LB
T: (01305) 871335
F: (01305) 871766
E: enquiries@oldcoastguards.com
I: www.oldcoastguards.com

ABBOTSHAM
Devon

Bowood Farm Cottages ★★★★
Contact: Toad Hall Cottages, Elliot House, Church Street, Kingsbridge TQ7 1BY
T: (01548) 853089
F: (01548) 853086
E: thc@toadhallcottages.com
I: www.toadhallcottages.com

ADVENT
Cornwall

Aldermoor ★★★-★★★★
Contact: Mrs H Golding, Aldermoor, Advent, Camelford PL32 9QQ
T: (01840) 213366
F: (01840) 213366

Widewalls Farm Rating Applied For
Contact: Mrs Pauline Metters, Widewalls Farm, Advent, Camelford PL32 9PY

ALLERFORD
Somerset

Lynch Country House Holiday Apartments★★★★
Contact: Mr & Mrs B Tacchi, Lynch Country House Holiday Apartments, Allerford, Minehead TA24 8HJ
T: (01643) 862800
F: (01643) 862800
E: anntacchi@beeb.net
I: www.lynchcountryhouse.co.uk

Orchard Cottage ★★★
Contact: Mrs Diana Williams, Brandish Street Farm, Allerford, Minehead TA24 8HR
T: (01643) 862383

The Pack Horse ★★★
Contact: Mr & Mrs Garner, The Pack Horse, Allerford, Minehead TA24 8HW
T: (01643) 862475
F: (01643) 862475
E: holidays@thepackhorse.net
I: www.thepackhorse.net

ALTON PANCRAS
Dorset

Bookham Court ★★★★-★★★★★
Contact: Mr & Mrs Andrew Foot, Whiteways, Bookham, Buckland Newton, Dorchester DT2 7RP
T: (01300) 345511
F: (01300) 345511
E: andy.foot1@btopenworld.com
I: www.bookhamcourt.co.uk

AMESBURY
Wiltshire

The Stables ★★★★
Contact: Mrs A Thatcher, Ivy Cottage, Netheravon, Salisbury SP4 9QW
T: (01980) 670557
F: (01980) 670557
E: athatcher@bigfoot.com
I: www.uk/holidays-cottages.co.uk/thestables

Wilsford Cottage H108 Rating Applied For
Contact: Chapel House, Luke Street, Berwick St John, Shaftesbury SP7 0HQ
T: (01747) 828170
F: (01747) 829090
E: enq@hideaways.co.uk

APPLEDORE
Devon

Appledown ★★★
Contact: Farm & Cottage Holidays, Victoria House, 12 Fore Street, Northam, Bideford EX39 1AW
T: (01237) 479146
F: (01237) 421512
E: enquiries@farmcott.co.uk

Crab Apple Cottage ★★★
Contact: Mr & Mrs Peter & Janet Cornwell, Marsden's Cottage Holidays, 2 The Square, Braunton EX33 2JB
T: (01271) 813777
F: (01271) 813664
E: holidays@marsdens.co.uk
I: www.marsdens.co.uk

Meander, Bimbo's and Two Rivers ★★★
Contact: Farm & Cottage Holidays, Victoria House, 12 Fore Street, Northam, Bideford EX39 1AW
T: (01237) 479146
F: (01237) 421512
E: enquiries@farmcott.co.uk

Nanashaven ★★
Contact: Farm & Cottage Holidays, Victoria House, 12 Fore Street, Northam, Bideford EX39 1AW
T: (01237) 479146
F: (01237) 421512
E: bookings@farmcott.co.uk

Sailmakers ★★
Contact: Mrs Palmer, Marlheath, 179 Old Woking Road, Maybury, Woking GU22 8HP
T: (01483) 761982

Establishments printed in blue have a detailed entry in this guide

The Waterfront ★★★★
Contact: Farm & Cottage Holidays, Victoria House, 12 Fore Street, Northam, Bideford EX39 1AW
T: (01237) 479146
F: (01237) 421512
E: enquiries@farmcott.co.uk

Waters Reach ★★★
Contact: Mrs Foley, Mandevyll, The Ridgeway, Potters Bar EN6 5QS
T: (01707) 657644
E: viv@vfoley.freeserve.co.uk

APPLEY
Somerset

Stone Barn Cottages ★★★★
Contact: Mrs A Champion, Stawley, Appley, Wellington TA21 0HJ
T: (01823) 673263
F: (01823) 673287
E: goappleycourt@aol.com
I: www.goappleycourt@aol.com

ASHBRITTLE
Somerset

Court Place
Rating Applied For
Contact: Mrs Alex Simpson, Court Place, Ashbrittle, Wellington TA21 0LF
T: (01823) 673362
F: (01823) 673163
E: alexsimpson@courtplace.co.uk

ASHBURTON
Devon

Stares Nest Cottage ★★
Contact: Mrs Hemingway, 188 Sutton Court Road, London 020
T: (0208) 995 5676

Wooder Manor Holiday Homes ★★★
Contact: Mrs Angela Bell, Wooder Manor Holiday Homes, Widecombe-in-the-Moor, Newton Abbot TQ13 7TR
T: (01364) 621391
F: (01364) 621391
E: angela@woodermanor.com
I: www.woodermanor.com

Wren & Robin Cottages ★★★★
Contact: Mrs Margaret Phipps, Wren & Robin Cottages, New Cott Farm, Poundsgate, Ashburton, Newton Abbot TQ13 7PD
T: (01364) 631421
F: (01364) 631421
E: enquiries@newcott-farm.co.uk
I: www.newcott-farm.co.uk

ASHFORD
Devon

Ashford Holt Cottage ★★
Contact: Toad Hall Cottages, Elliot House, Church Street, Kingsbridge TQ7 1BY
T: (01548) 853089
F: (01548) 853086
E: thc@toadhallcottages.com
I: www.toadhallcottages.com

Garden Cottage ★★★
Contact: Marsden's Cottage Holidays, 2 The Square, Braunton EX33 2JB
T: (01271) 813777
F: (01271) 813664
E: holidays@marsdens.co.uk
I: www.marsdens.co.uk

Helliers Farm ★★★★
Contact: Mrs Lancaster, Helliers Farm, Ashford, Aveton Gifford, Kingsbridge TQ7 4NB
T: (01548) 550689
F: (01548) 550689
I: www.helliersfarm.co.uk

Incledon Barn ★★★
Contact: Mr P & Mrs J Cornwell, Marsden's Cottage Holidays, 2 The Square, Braunton EX33 2JB
I: www.marsdens.co.uk

ASHREIGNEY
Devon

Colehouse Farm ★★★★
Contact: Farm & Cottage Holidays, Victoria House, 12 Fore Street, Westward Ho!, Bideford EX39 1AW
T: (01237) 479146
F: (01237) 421512
E: enquiries@farmcott.co.uk

Northcott Barton Farm Holiday Cottage★★★★
Contact: Mrs S J Gay, Northcott Barton Farm Holiday Cottage, Northcott Barton, Ashreigney, Chulmleigh EX18 9PR
T: (01769) 520259
E: sandra@northcottbarton.co.uk
I: www.northcottbarton.co.uk

ASHTON
Cornwall

Chycarne Farm Cottages ★★★
Contact: Mrs P. J. Ross, Chycarne Farm Cottages, Balwest, Ashton, Helston TR13 9TE
T: (01736) 762473
F: (01736) 762473
E: a-g-ross@supanet.com
I: www.chycarne-farm-cottages.co.uk

ASHWATER
Devon

Blagdon Farm Country Holidays ★★★★-★★★★★
Contact: Mr & Mrs Tucker, Ashwater, Beaworthy EX21 5DF
T: (01409) 211509
F: (01409) 211510

Braddon Cottages ★★★
Contact: Mr & Mrs George & Anne Ridge, Braddon Cottages, Ashwater, Beaworthy EX21 5EP
T: (01409) 211350
F: (01409) 211350
E: holidays@braddoncottages.co.uk
I: www.braddoncottages.co.uk

ASKERSWELL
Dorset

Court Farm Cottages ★★★★-★★★★★
Contact: Mrs Rebecca Bryan, Court Farm Cottages, Askerswell, Dorchester DT2 9EJ
T: (01308) 485668
E: courtfarmcottages@eclipse.co.uk
I: www.eclipse.co.uk/courtfarmcottages/webpg2

Little Court ★★★★★
Contact: Mr Leonard Vickery, The Barn House, Moens Farm, Uploders, Bridport DT6 4PH
T: (01308) 421933
E: vicklen@tesco.net

Little Grey Cottage ★★★
Contact: Mrs Marcia Machin, Little Grey Cottage, Askerswell, Dorchester DT2 9EL
T: (01308) 485317
E: marciamachin@hotmail.com
I: www.littlegreycottage.co.uk/index

West Hembury Farm ★★★★
Contact: Dr & Mrs A Hunt, West Hembury Farm, Askerswell, Dorchester DT2 9EN
T: (01308) 485289
F: (01308) 485041
E: hunt@westhembury.com
I: www.westhembury.com

ATHELHAMPTON
Dorset

River Cottage
Rating Applied For
Contact: Miss Tracy Winder, River Cottage, Athelhampton, Dorchester DT2 7LG
T: (01305) 848363
F: (01305) 848135
E: enquiry@athelhampton.co.uk

AWLISCOMBE
Devon

Godford Farm ★★★
Contact: Mrs Sally Lawrence, Godford Farm, Otter Holt & Owl Hayes, Godford Farm, Awliscombe, Honiton EX14 3PW
T: (01404) 42825
F: (01404) 42825
E: lawrencesally@hotmail.com
I: www.devon-farm-holidays.co.uk

AXBRIDGE
Somerset

George's Cottage ★★★★
Contact: Ms Margaret Crawford, Midway Cottage, Church Lane, Axbridge BS26 2BW
T: (01934) 733351

AXMINSTER
Devon

Beckford Cottage ★★★★
Contact: Mrs Jill Bellamy, Beckford Cottage, Dalwood, Membury, Axminster EX13 7HQ
T: (01404) 881641
F: (01404) 881108
E: beckfordcottage@hotmail.com

Cider Room Cottage ★★★★
Contact: Mrs Steele, Cider Room Cottage, Hasland Farm, Tolcis, Membury, Axminster EX13 7JF
T: (01404) 881558
F: (01404) 881834

Furzeleigh House Country Cottages & Gardens★★★★
Contact: Mr & Mrs Rob & Shirley Blatchford, Furzeleigh House Country Cottages & Gardens, Lyme Road, Axminster EX13 5SW
T: (01297) 34448
E: shirley.blatchford@tesco.net

Symondsdown Cottages ★★★-★★★★
Contact: Mr & Mrs Stuart & Jenny Hynds, Symondsdown Cottages, Woodbury Lane, Woodbury Cross, Axminster EX13 5TL
T: (01297) 32385
I: www.symondsdownholidaycottages.co.uk

AXMOUTH
Devon

Coastguards ★★★★
Contact: Milkbere Holidays, 3 Fore Street, Seaton EX12 2LE
T: (01297) 20729
F: (01297) 22925
E: info@milkbere.com
I: www.milkbere.com

Combe Farm Cottages ★★-★★★
Contact: Ms Bows, Combe Farm Cottages, Combe Farm, Axmouth, Seaton EX12 4AU
T: (01297) 23822

3 Old Coastguards Cottages
Rating Applied For
Contact: Milkbere Holidays, 3 Fore Street, Seaton EX12 2LE
T: (01297) 20729
F: (01297) 22925
E: info@milkbere.com
I: www.milkbere.com

Stepps Barn ★★★★★
Contact: Jean Bartlett Cottage Holidays, Fore Street, Beer, Seaton EX12 3JB
T: (01297) 23221
F: (01297) 23303
E: holidays@jeanbartlett.com
I: www.netbreaks.com/jeanb

Stepps Cross Cottage ★★★★
Contact: Ms Kate Bartlett, Jean Bartlett Cottage Holidays, Fore Street, Seaton EX12 3JB
T: (01297) 23221
F: (01297) 23303
E: holidays@jeanbartlett.com
I: www.netbreaks.com/jeanb

Stepps Orchard ★★★★
Contact: Ms Kate Bartlett, Jean Bartlett Cottage Holidays, Fore Street, Seaton EX12 3JB
T: (01297) 23221
F: (01297) 23303
E: holidays@jeanbartlett.com
I: www.netbreaks.com/jeanb

AYLESBEARE
Devon

Alpine Park Cottages ★★★
Contact: Mrs Wendy Atkin, Alpine Park Cottages, Sidmouth Road, Aylesbeare, Exeter EX5 2JW
T: (01395) 233619
F: (01395) 239096
E: alpinians@eclipse.co.uk

BABBACOMBE
Devon

Rose Court Holiday Apartments ★★★
Contact: Mrs J Henshall, Rose Court Holiday Apartments, York Road, Babbacombe, St Marychurch, Torquay TQ1 3SG
T: (01803) 327203
E: holidays@rosecourtorquay.co.uk
I: www.rosecourtorquay.co.uk

Sunnybank ★★★
Contact: Holiday Homes & Cottages South West, 365A Torquay Road, Paignton TQ3 2BT
T: (01803) 663650
F: (01803) 664037
E: holcotts@aol.com
I: www.swcottages.co.uk

Willow Cottage ★★★
Contact: Holiday Homes & Cottages South West, 365A Torquay Road, Paignton TQ3 2BT
T: (01803) 663650
F: (01803) 664037
E: holcotts@aol.com
I: www.swcottages.co.uk

BACKWELL
North Somerset

The Coach House
Rating Applied For
Contact: Mrs Iola Solari, 73 West Town Road, Backwell, Bristol BS48 3BH
T: (01275) 464635
E: coachhousebackwell@hotmail.com

BAMPTON
Devon

Three Gates Farm ★★★★
Contact: Mrs Alison Spencer, Three Gates Farm, Huntsham, Tiverton EX16 7QH
T: (01398) 331280
E: threegatesfarm@hotmail.com
I: www.threegatesfarm.co.uk

Veltham Cottages ★★★
Contact: Mrs Pauline Krombas, Veltham Cottages, Veltham House, Morebath, Tiverton EX16 9AL
T: (01398) 331465
F: (01392) 425529

Westbrook House ★★★
Contact: Mrs Patricia Currie, Westbrook House, Bampton, Washfield, Tiverton EX16 9HU
T: (01398) 331418
F: (01398) 331418
E: brian@currie.co.uk
I: www.westbrookhouse.co.uk

Wonham Barton ★★★
Contact: Mrs A McLean Williams, Wonham Barton, Bampton, Tiverton EX16 9JZ
T: (01398) 331312
F: (01398) 331312
E: wonham.barton@virgin.net
I: www.wonham-country-holidays.co.uk

BARBICAN
Devon

Barbican Hideaway ★★★★★
Contact: Ms Julie Burdett, 58 Fulcher Avenue, Cromer, Cromer NR27 9SG
T: (01263) 515208
F: (01263) 519220
E: info@home-from-home-holidays.com

Greyfriars ★★★★
Contact: Mrs Summers, Yealm Holidays, 8 Whittingham Road, Yealmpton, Noss Mayo, Plymouth PL8 2NF
T: 0870 747 2987

The Harlequin ★★★★★
Contact: Ms Julie Burdett, 58 Fulcher Avenue, Cromer NR27 9SG
T: (01263) 515208
F: (01263) 519220
E: info@home-from-home-holidays.com

BARBROOK
Devon

New Mill Farm ★★★
Contact: Mr Bingham, Outovercott Riding Stables, Barbrook, Parracombe, Barnstaple EX35 6JR
T: (01598) 753341
E: susan@exmoor-outdoors.co.uk
I: www.newmillfarm.co.uk

West Lyn Farmhouse ★★★
Contact: Mrs Sally Barber, West Lyn Farmhouse, Barbrook, Lynton EX35 6LD
T: (01598) 753618
F: (01598) 753618
E: info@westlynfarm.co.uk
I: www.westlynfarm.co.uk

Woodside ★★★
Contact: Mrs Sally Gunn, Woodside, Barbrook, Lynton EX35 6PD
T: (01598) 753298
E: woodside@salian.fsnet.co.uk

BARKLA SHOP
Cornwall

The Owl House ★★★★★
Contact: Ms Lyn Hicks, Chy Ser Rosow, Barkla Shop, St Agnes TR5 0XN
T: (01872) 553644

BARNSTAPLE
Devon

Country Ways ★★★★
Contact: Mrs Kate Price, Country Ways, Little Knowle Farm, High Bickington, Umberleigh EX37 9BJ
T: (01769) 560503
F: (01769) 560503
E: country.ways@virgin.net
I: www.devon-holiday.co.uk

Humes Farm Cottages ★★★-★★★★
Contact: Marsden's Cottage Holidays, 2 The Square, Braunton EX33 2JB
T: (01271) 813777
F: (01271) 813664
E: holidays@marsdens.co.uk
I: www.marsdens.co.uk

Meadow Cottage ★★★
Contact: Mr & Mrs Peter & Janet Cornwell, Marsden's Cottage Holidays, 2 The Square, Braunton EX33 2JB
T: (01271) 813777
F: (01271) 813664
E: holidays@marsdens.co.uk
I: www.marsdens.co.uk

North Hill Cottages ★★★
Contact: Mrs Liz Duffield, North Hill Cottages, North Hill, Shirwell, Barnstaple EX31 4LG
T: (01271) 850611
F: (01271) 850693
E: enquiries@bestleisure.co.uk
I: www.bestleisure.co.uk

Willesleigh Farm ★★★★
Contact: Mr & Mrs Esmond-Cole, Willesleigh Farm, Goodleigh, Barnstaple EX32 7NA
T: (01271) 343763
F: (01271) 343763

BATCOMBE
Somerset

The Coach House at Boords Farm ★★★★
Contact: Mr & Mrs Michael & Anne Page, The Coach House at Boords Farm, Batcombe, Shepton Mallet BA4 6HD
T: (01749) 850372
F: (01749) 850372
E: boordsfarm@michaelp.demon.co.uk

BATH
Bath and North East Somerset

Bath Centre Stay Holidays ★★★
Contact: Mr Gerald Davey, 163 Newbridge Hill, Bath BA1 3PX
T: (01225) 313205
F: (01225) 313205
E: holidays@bathcentrestay.freeserve.co.uk

Beau Street Apartments 1 & 2 ★★★
Contact: Mr Brian Taylor, 49 Reynolds Road, Beaconsfield HP9 2NQ
T: (01494) 681212
F: (01494) 681231
E: bath.heritage@which.net
I: www.bath-selfcatering.co.uk

The Beeches Farmhouse - Pig Wig Cottages★★★★★
Contact: Mr & Mrs Kevin & Sharon Gover, The Beeches Farmhouse, Holt Road, Holt, Trowbridge BA15 1TS
T: (01225) 863475
F: (01225) 863996
E: beeches-farmhouse@netgates.co.uk
I: www.beeches-farmhouse.co.uk

Calverley Wing ★★★
Contact: Mrs Jenny John, Calverley Wing, South Stoke Hall, Southstoke, Bath BA2 7DL
T: (01225) 833387
F: (01225) 833387
E: tandjjohn@aol.com

Camden Garden Apartment ★★★
Contact: Mrs Ros Pritchard, Camden Garden Apartment, 5 Upper Camden Place, Camden Road, Bath BA1 5HX
T: (01225) 338730

Church Farm Country Cottages ★★★★
Contact: Mrs Trish Bowles, Church Farm, Winsley, Bradford-on-Avon BA15 2JH
T: (01225) 722246
F: (01225) 722246
E: stay@churchfarmcottages.com
I: www.churchfarmcottages.com

The Coach House (Bath) ★★★★
Contact: Mrs Marilyn Quiggin, The Coach House (Bath), Lansdown Road, Woolley, Bath BA1 5TJ
T: (01225) 331341
F: (01225) 482202
E: mq@bathselfcatering.fsnet.co.uk
I: www.bathselfcatering.demon.co.uk

Courtyard Apartment ★★★★★
Contact: Ms Karen Werrett, PO Box 3100, Bathwick, Bath BA2 6WA
T: 07817 306934
F: 0870 132 1656
E: enquiries@bathvacationrentals.com
I: www.bathvacationrentals.com

2 Devonshire Villas ★★★
Contact: Mr & Mrs D Wall, 2 Devonshire Villas, Wellsway, Bath BA2 4SX
T: (01225) 331539
E: Daniel@wallsbath.freeserve.co.uk

Flat 2 ★★
Contact: Miss Sophie Rosser-Rees, Glenhazel, 3 Warminster Road, Monkton Combe, Bath BA2 7HZ
T: (01225) 723545
E: srosserrees@hotmail.com

Georgian Apartment ★★★
Contact: Mrs Susanne Marie Cragg, Summerhaze, 2 Ludwells Orchard, Paulton, Bristol BS39 7XW
T: (01761) 415655
F: (01761) 419706
E: info@rentingplaces.com
I: www.rentingplaces.com

Georgian Apt ★★★★
Contact: Mrs C Besley, The Old Red House, 37 Newbridge Road, Bath BA1 3HE
T: (01225) 330464
F: (01225) 331661
E: georgianapt@amserve.net
I: www.georgianapt.co.uk

Greyfield Farm Cottages ★★★★-★★★★★
Contact: Mrs J Merry, Greyfield Farm Cottages, Greyfield Road, High Littleton, Bristol BS39 6YQ
T: (01761) 471132
F: (01761) 471132
E: june@greyfieldfarm.com
I: www.greyfieldfarm.com

Margaret's Building Apartment ★★★★
Contact: Mr Pash, Luke Street, Berwick St John, Shaftesbury SP7 0HQ
T: (01747) 828170
F: (01747) 829090
E: enq@hideaways.co.uk
I: www.hideaways.co.uk

Nailey Cottages ★★★★
Contact: Mrs Brett Gardner, Nailey Cottages, Nailey Farm, St Catherines Valley, Bath BA1 8HD
T: (01225) 852989
F: (01225) 852989
E: cottages@naileyfarm.co.uk
I: www.naileyfarm.co.uk

Riverside Apartment ★★★
Contact: Mr Graham Wilson, Riverside Apartment, 1 Norfolk Buildings, Bath BA1 2BP
T: (01225) 337968

Riverside Cottage ★★
Contact: Mr Barrie Trezise, Riverside Cottage, 1 High Street, Wick, Bristol BS30 5QJ
T: (0117) 937 2304
F: (0117) 937 2304
E: b.trezise@btopenworld.com

Russel Street Apartment ★★★★★
Contact: Mrs Clare Margaret Travers, 9 Prior Park Buildings, Widcombe, Bath BA2 4NP
T: (01225) 312011
E: traversa@aol.com
I: www.bathbreaks.co.uk

Second Floor Flat ★★★★
Contact: Mrs Lindsay Bishop, 15 Heatherdale Road, Camberley GU15 2LR
T: (01276) 29033
E: lindsay.bishop@btopenworld.com

Spring Farm Holiday Cottages ★★★-★★★★
Contact: Mrs Sue Brown, Spring Farm Holiday Cottages, Carlingcott, Peasedown St John, Bath BA2 8AP
T: (01761) 435524
F: (01761) 439461
E: suebrown@springfarmcottages.co.uk
I: www.springfarmcottages.co.uk

Time-2-Relax-Holidays ★★★★★
Contact: Ms Sue Thornton, Eastwood House, Stroudley Crescent, Preston, Weymouth DT3 6NT
T: (01305) 837474
F: (01305) 777515
E: sue@eastwoodquay.freeserve.co.uk

BATHEALTON
Somerset

Woodlands Farm ★★★
Contact: Mrs Joan Greenway, Woodlands Farm, Bathealton, Taunton TA4 2AH
T: (01984) 623271

BATHEASTON
Bath and North East Somerset

Avondale Riverside ★★★★-★★★★★
Contact: Mr & Mrs Pecchia, 104 Lower Northend, North End, Batheaston, Bath BA1 7HA
T: (01225) 852226
F: (01225) 852226
E: sheilapex@questmusic.co.uk

BATHWICK
Bath and North East Somerset

Flat 1, 17 Argyle Street Rating Applied For
Contact: Mr Tim Doyle, Flat 1, 17 Argyle Street, Bathwick, Bath BA2 4BQ
T: (01225) 329773
F: (01248) 644 5902
E: bathluxuryapt@aol.com

BEAMINSTER
Dorset

The Cottage Rating Applied For
Contact: Ms Trish Mitchell, North Buckham Farm, Beaminster DT8 3SH
T: (01308) 863054
F: (01308) 863054
E: trish@northbuckham.fsnet.co.uk

Greens Cross Farm ★★★
Contact: Mr D G Baker, Greens Cross Farm, Stoke Road, Beaminster DT8 3JL
T: (01308) 862661
F: (01308) 863800

Lewesdon Farm Holidays ★★★★
Contact: Mr & Mrs Michael & Linda Smith, Lewesdon Farm Holidays, Lewesdon Farm, Stoke Abbott, Beaminster DT8 3JZ
T: (01308) 868270
E: lewesdonfarmholiday@tinyonline.co.uk

Orchard End ★★★★
Contact: Mrs P M Wallbridge, Watermeadow House, Bridge Farm, Hooke, Beaminster DT8 3PD
T: (01308) 862619
F: (01308) 862619
E: enquiries@watermeadowhouse.co.uk
I: www.watermeadowhouse.co.uk

Stable Cottage ★★★★
Contact: Mrs Diana Clarke, Meerhay Manor, Beaminster DT8 3SB
T: (01308) 862305
F: (01308) 863972
E: meerhay@aol.com
I: www.meerhay.co.uk

Virginia Cottage ★★★
Contact: Mrs A Dunn, Chideock House Hotel, Main Street, Chideock, Bridport DT6 6JN
T: (01297) 489242
F: (01297) 489184
E: WDHG@chideockhousehotel.com
I: www.chideockhousehotel.com

BEAWORTHY
Devon

Tillislow Barn ★★★★
Contact: Farm & Cottage Holidays, Victoria House, 12 Fore Street, Westward Ho!, Bideford EX39 1AW
T: (01237) 479146
F: (01237) 421512
E: bookings@farmcott.co.uk

BEER
Devon

The Admirals View ★★★★
Contact: Jean Bartlett Cottage Holidays, Fore Street, Seaton EX12 3JB
T: (01297) 23221
F: (01297) 23303
E: holidays@jeanbartlett.com
I: www.netbreaks.com/jeanb

Bakery Cottage ★★★★
Contact: Jean Bartlett Cottage Holidays, Fore Street, Seaton EX12 3JB
T: (01297) 23221
F: (01297) 23303
E: holidays@jeanbartlett.com
I: www.netbreaks.com/jeanb

Beer View & New Nookies ★★★★
Contact: Mrs Jean Forbes-Harriss, Beer View & New Nookies, Berry House, Berry Lane, Beer, Seaton EX12 3JS
T: (01297) 20096
F: (01297) 20096
E: forbesh@globalnet.co.uk

Brooksyde ★★
Contact: Jean Bartlett Cottage Holidays, Fore Street, Beer, Seaton EX12 3JB
T: (01297) 23221
F: (01297) 23303
E: holidays@jeanbartlett.com
I: www.netbreaks.com/jeanb

Bung Ho ★★★★
Contact: Jean Bartlett Holidays, Beer, Seaton EX12
T: (01297) 23221

Captains Cabin ★★★★
Contact: Jean Bartlett Cottage Holidays, Fore Street, Seaton EX12 3JB
T: (01297) 23221
F: (01297) 23303
E: holidays@jeanbartlett.com
I: www.netbreaks.com/jeanb

Church View ★★★★
Contact: Milkbere Holidays, 3 Fore Street, Seaton EX12 2LE
T: (01297) 20729
F: (01297) 22925
E: info@milkberehols.com
I: www.milkbere.com

The Cottage ★★★★
Contact: Ms Kate Bartlett, Jean Bartlett Cottage Holidays, The Old Dairy, Fore Street, Beer, Seaton EX12 3JB
I: www.jeanbartlett.com

Craft Cottage ★★★★
Contact: Ms Kate Bartlett, Jean Bartlett Cottage Holidays, Fore Street, Seaton EX12 3JB
T: (01297) 23221
F: (01297) 23303
E: holidays@jeanbartlett.com
I: www.netbreaks.com/jeanb

Farnham House ★★★
Contact: Ms Kate Bartlett, Jean Bartlett Cottage Holidays, The Old Dairy, Fore Street, Seaton EX12 3JB
T: (01297) 23221
F: (01297) 23303
E: holidays@jeanbartlett.com
I: www.netbreaks.com/jeamb

Hardergraft ★★★
Contact: Jean Bartlett Cottage Holidays, Fore Street, Beer, Seaton EX12 3JB
T: (01297) 23221
F: (01297) 23303
E: holidays@jeanbartlett.com
I: www.netbreaks.com/jeanb

Hollyhocks ★★★★
Contact: Jean Bartlett Cottage Holidays, Fore Street, Beer, Seaton EX12 3JB
T: (01297) 23221
F: (01297) 23303
E: holidays@jeanbartlett
I: www.netbreaks.com/jeanb

Hooknell House ★★★★
Contact: Milkbere Holidays, 3 Fore Street, Seaton EX12 2LE
T: (01297) 20729
F: (01297) 22925
E: info@milkbere.com
I: www.milkbere.com

Hope Cottage and Creole Cottage ★★★★
Contact: Jean Bartlett Cottage Holidays, Fore Street, Beer, Seaton EX12 3JB
T: (01297) 23221
F: (01297) 23303
E: holidays@jeanbartlett.com
I: www.netbreaks.com/jeanb

Images ★★★
Contact: Ms Kate Bartlett, Jean Bartlett Cottage Holidays The Old Dairy, Fore Street, Seaton EX12 3JB
T: (01297) 23221
F: (01297) 23303
E: holidays@jeanbartlett.com
I: www.netbreaks.com/jeamb

The Lilacs ★★★
Contact: Ms Kate Bartlett, Jean Bartlett Cottage Holidays, Fore Street, Seaton EX12 3JB
T: (01297) 23221
F: (01297) 23303
E: holidays@jeanbartlett.com
I: www.netbreaks.com/jeanb

Little Jacks Corner ★★★
Contact: Jean Bartlett Holidays, Beer, Seaton EX12
T: (01297) 23221

Marine House Apartments & Twyford Cottage ★★★★
Contact: Jean Bartlett Cottage Holidays, Fore Street, Seaton EX12 3JB
T: (01297) 23221
F: (01297) 23303
E: holidays@jeanbartlett.com
I: www.netbreaks.com/jeanb

The Old Lace Shop ★★★
Contact: Jean Bartlett Cottage Holidays, Fore Street, Seaton EX12 3JB
T: (01297) 23221
F: (01297) 23303
E: holidays@jeanbartlett.com
I: www.netbreaks.com/jeanb

Otteys Cottage ★★★
Contact: Milkbere Holidays, 3 Fore Street, Seaton EX12 2LE
T: (01297) 20729
F: (01297) 22925
E: info@milkbere.com
I: www.milkbere.com

Pioneer 6 ★★★
Contact: Jean Bartlett Cottage Holidays, Fore Street, Seaton EX12 3JB
T: (01297) 23221

12 Pioneer Cottage ★★★
Contact: Ms Kate Bartlett, Jean Bartlett Cottage Holidays, The Old Dairy, Fore Street, Beer, Seaton EX12 3JB
I: www.jeanbartlett.com

3 Pioneer Cottage ★★★
Contact: Ms Kate Bartlett, Jean Bartlett Cottage Holidays, The Old Dairy, Fore Street, Beer, Seaton EX12 3JB
I: www.jeanbartlett.com

7 Pioneer Cottages ★★★
Contact: Ms Kate Bartlett, Jean Bartlett Cottage Holidays, The Old Dairy, Fore Street, Seaton EX12 3JB
T: (01297) 23221
F: (01297) 23303
E: holidays@jeanbartlett.com
I: www.jeanbartlett.com

Pugwash Cottage ★★
Contact: Ms Kate Bartlett, Jean Bartlett Cottage Holidays, The Old Dairy, Fore Street, Seaton EX12 3JB
T: (01297) 23221
F: (01297) 23303
E: holidays@jeanbartlett.com
I: www.netbreaks.com/jeamb

Purley ★★★
Contact: Jean Bartlett Cottage Holidays, Fore Street, Beer, Seaton EX12 3JB
T: (01297) 23221
F: (01297) 23303
E: holidays@jeanbartlett.com
I: www.netbreaks.com/jeanb

Ramblers ★★★
Contact: Jean Bartlett Cottage Holidays, Fore Street, Beer, Seaton EX12 3JB
T: (01297) 23221
F: (01297) 23303
E: holidays@jeanbartlett.com
I: www.netbreaks.com/jeanb

Rattenbury Cottage ★★★
Contact: Ms Kate Bartlett, Jean Bartlett Cottage Holidays, The Old Dairy, Fore Street, Seaton EX12 3JB
T: (01297) 23221
F: (01297) 23303
E: holidays@jeanbartlett.com
I: www.netbreaks.com/jeamb

Rock Cottage ★★★★
Contact: Ms Kate Bartlett, Jean Bartlett Cottage Holidays, Fore Street, Seaton EX12 3JB
T: (01297) 23221
F: (01297) 23303
E: holidays@jeanbartlett.com
I: www.netbreaks.com/jeanb

Rock Farm Cottage ★★★★
Contact: Ms Kate Bartlett, Jean Bartlett Cottage Holidays, The Old Dairy, Fore Street, Seaton EX12 3JB
T: (01297) 23221
F: (01297) 23303
E: holidays@jeanbartlett.com
I: www.netbreaks.com/jeamb

5 Rose Cottage ★★
Contact: Jean Bartlett Cottage Holidays, Fore Street, Seaton EX12 3JB
T: (01297) 23221

Sea Mist ★★★
Contact: Ms Kate Bartlett, Jean Bartlett Cottage Holidays, The Old Dairy, Fore Street, Seaton EX12 3JB
T: (01297) 23221
F: (01297) 23303
E: holidays@jeanbartlett.com
I: www.netbreaks.com/jeamb

Sea View ★★★
Contact: Jean Bartlett Cottage Holidays, Fore Street, Seaton EX12 3JB
T: (01297) 23221
F: (01297) 23303
E: holidays@jeanbartlett.com
I: www.netbreaks.com/jeanb

Shannon Cottage ★★★★
Contact: Jean Bartlett Cottage Holidays, Fore Street, Seaton EX12 3JB
T: (01297) 23221

Snowdrops ★★★
Contact: Jean Bartlett Cottage Holidays, Fore Street, Beer, Seaton EX12 3JB
T: (01297) 23221

Spring Garden ★★★
Contact: Ms Kate Bartlett, Jean Bartlett Cottage Holidays, The Old Dairy, Fore Street, Seaton EX12 3JB
T: (01297) 23221
F: (01297) 23303
E: holidays@jeanbartlett.com
I: www.netbreaks.com/jeamb

Starre Cottage ★★★★
Contact: Ms Kate Bartlett, Jean Bartlett Cottage Holidays, Fore Street, Seaton EX12 3JB
T: (01297) 23221
F: (01297) 23303
E: holidays@jeanbartlett.com
I: www.netbreaks.com/jeanb

Summerfold ★★★★
Contact: Milkbere Holidays, 3 Fore Street, Seaton EX12 2LE
T: (01297) 20729
F: (01297) 22925
E: info@milkberehols.com
I: www.milkbere.com

Tanglewood ★★★★
Contact: Ms Kate Bartlett, Jean Bartlett Cottage Holidays, The Old Dairy, Fore Street, Beer, Seaton EX12 3JB
T: (01297) 23221
F: (01297) 23303
E: holidays@jeanbartlett.com
I: www.netbreaks.com/jeamb

1 West View ★★
Contact: Jean Bartlett Cottage Holidays, Fore Street, Beer, Seaton EX12 3JB
T: (01297) 23221
F: (01297) 23303
E: holidays@jeanbartlett.com
I: www.netbreaks.com/jeanb

Westview Cottage ★★★★
Contact: Jean Bartlett Cottage Holidays, Fore Street, Seaton EX12 3JB
T: (01297) 23221
F: (01297) 23303
E: holidays@jeanbartlett.com
I: www.netbreaks.com/jeanb

BEESON
Devon

Andryl ★★★
Contact: Ms Beryl Wotton, Andryl, Lower Farm, Beeson, Beesands, Kingsbridge TQ7 2HW
T: (01548) 580527

BELOWDA
Cornwall

Treickle Barn ★★★★
Contact: Miss Alabaster, Three Chimneys, Lane End, Belowda, Roche, St Austell PL26 8NQ
T: (01726) 890566

BELSTONE
Devon

Brentor Cottage ★★
Contact: Mr Zachary Stuart-Brown, Dream Cottages, 41 Maiden Street, Weymouth DT4 8AZ
T: (01305) 761347
E: admin@dream-cottages.co.uk
I: www.dream-cottages.co.uk

BERRYNARBOR
Devon

Adventure Cottage ★★★★
Contact: Mr & Mrs Cornwell, Marsden's Cottage Holidays, 2 The Square, Braunton EX33 2JB
I: www.marsdens.co.uk

Forge Cottage ★★★★
Contact: Marsden's Cottage Holidays, 2 The Square, Braunton EX33 2JB
T: (01271) 813777
F: (01271) 813664
E: holidays@marsdens.co.uk
I: www.marsdens.co.uk

Glebe House & Coach House ★★★★
Contact: Marsden's Cottage Holidays, 2 The Square, Braunton EX33 2JB
T: (01271) 813777
F: (01271) 813664
E: holidays@marsdens.co.uk
I: www.marsdens.co.uk

Langleigh House ★★★-★★★★
Contact: Mr & Mrs Roy & Jackie Pierpoint, Langleigh House, The Village, Berrynarbor, Ilfracombe EX34 9SG
T: (01271) 883410
F: (01271) 882396
E: langleigh@hotmail.com

Lee Copse ★★★
Contact: Mr & Mrs Peter & Janet Cornwell, Marsden's Cottage Holidays, 2 The Square, Braunton EX33 2JB
T: (01271) 813777
F: (01271) 813664
E: holidays@marsdens.co.uk
I: www.marsdens.co.uk

Ropes End ★★★
Contact: Mrs B Y Davey, Ropes End, Newberry Hill, Berrynarbor, Ilfracombe EX34 9SS
T: (01271) 883476
E: yvonne@ropesend.eclipse.co.uk

Smythen Farm Coastal Holiday Cottages★★★-★★★★
Contact: Mr & Ms Thompson & Elstone, Smythen Farm Coastal Holiday Cottages, Smythen, Sterridge Valley, Berrynarbor, Ilfracombe EX34 9TB
T: (01271) 882875
F: (01271) 882875
E: jayne@smythenfarmholidaycottages.co.uk
I: www.smythenfarmholidaycottages.co.uk

Watermouth Cove Cottages ★★★
Contact: Mrs Janette Menday, Narracott Down, Honiton Road, South Molton EX36 4JA
T: 08702 413168
F: (01769) 573921
E: stay@watermouthcove.co.uk
I: www.watermouthcove.co.uk

BERWICK ST JAMES
Wiltshire

Rose Cottage ★★★
Contact: Mr & Mrs John & Mildred Read, 124 Greenwood Avenue, Laverstock, Salisbury SP1 1PE
T: (01722) 328934

BERWICK ST JOHN
Wiltshire

Easton Farm ★★★★
Contact: Mr Nicholas Pash, Chapel House, Luke Street, Berwick St John, Shaftesbury SP7 0HQ
T: (01747) 828170
F: (01747) 829090
E: enq@hideaways.co.uk
I: www.hideaways.co.uk

BETTISCOMBE
Dorset

Conway Bungalow ★★★
Contact: Mrs Margaret Smith, Conway Bungalow, Bettiscombe, Bridport DT6 5NT
T: (01308) 868313
F: (01308) 868313
E: info@conway-bungalow.co.uk
I: www.conway-bungalow.co.uk

BICKINGTON
Devon

East Burne Farm
Rating Applied For
Contact: Mike & Emma Pallett, East Burne Farm, Bickington, Newton Abbot TQ12 6PA
T: (01626) 821496
F: (01626) 821105
E: eastburnefarm@screaming.net
I: www.eastburnefarm.8k.com/

BIDDESTONE
Wiltshire

Barn End ★★★★
Contact: Mrs Davis, Barn End, The Barn, Manor Farm, Biddestone, Hartham, Corsham SN14 7DH
T: (01249) 712104
E: jennyandbob@biddestone.demon.co.uk

BIDEFORD
Devon

Britannia House ★★★
Contact: Farm & Cottage Holidays, Victoria House, 12 Fore Street, Northam, Bideford EX39 1AW
T: (01237) 479146
F: (01237) 421512
E: enquiries@farmcott.co.uk

Coachmans Cottage ★★★
Contact: Mr & Mrs T M Downie, Staddon House, Monkleigh, Bideford EX39 5JR
T: (01805) 623670
E: tom.downie@ukonline.co.uk
I: www.creamteacottages.co.uk

Copinger's Cottage ★★★★
Contact: Mr & Mrs Dennis and Sonia Heard, Copinger's Cottage, Galsham Farm, Hartland, Bideford EX39 6DN
T: (01237) 441262
E: jollyrogers@another.com
I: www.galsham.co.uk

Ford Farm Cottage ★★★
Contact: Mr & Mrs Peter & Janet Cornwell, Marsden's Cottage Holidays, 2 The Square, Braunton EX33 2JB
T: (01271) 813777
F: (01271) 813664
E: holidays@marsdens.co.uk
I: www.marsdens.co.uk

Little Melville Holiday Cottage ★★★★
Contact: Mr & Mrs Moore, Melville Cottage, Heywood Road, Northam, Bideford EX39 3QB
T: (01237) 471140
F: (01237) 471140
E: anb@melvillecot.freeserve.co.uk
I: www.litmel.freeserve.co.uk

Pillhead Farm ★★★-★★★★
Contact: Mr Richard Hill, Pillhead Farm, Old Barnstaple Road, Bideford EX39 4NF
T: (01237) 479337
F: (01237) 479337
E: hill@pillheadfarm.fsnet.co.uk

BIGBURY-ON-SEA
Devon

Apartment 2 ★★★★★
Contact: Helpful Holidays, Mill Street, Chagford, Newton Abbot TQ13 8AW
T: (01647) 433593
F: (01647) 433694
E: help@helpfulholidays.com
I: www.helpfulholidays.com

Apartment 29 ★★★★★
Contact: Helpful Holidays, Mill Street, Chagford, Newton Abbot TQ13 8AW
T: (01647) 433593
F: (01647) 433694
E: help@helpfulholidays.com
I: www.helpfulholidays.com

Apartment 5, Burgh Island Causeway ★★★★★
Contact: Helpful Holidays, Mill Street, Chagford, Newton Abbot TQ13 8AW
T: (01647) 433593
F: (01647) 433694
E: help@helpfulholidays.com
I: www.helpfulholidays.com

Ferrycombe ★★★★
Contact: Mrs Juliet Fooks, 15 Mouchotte Close, Biggin Hill, Kent TN16 3ES
T: 07050 030231

1 Sharpland Crest ★★★
Contact: Mrs Amanda Hough, 7 Oriole Drive, Pennsylvania, Exeter EX4 4SJ
T: (01392) 438234
E: amandahough@talk21.com

Thornbury ★★★★
Contact: Mrs Tagent, Challaborough Cottage, Ringmore, Kingsbridge TQ7 4HW
T: (01548) 810520
F: (01548) 810520
E: met@cix.co.uk
I: www.cottagesdirect.co.uk/thornbury

BINEGAR
Somerset

Spindle Cottage ★★★★
Contact: Ms Angela Bunting, Spindle Cottage, Binegar Green, Binegar, Shepton Mallet BA3 4UE
T: (01749) 840497
E: spindle.cottage@ukonline.co.uk

BISHOP'S CAUNDLE
Dorset

Ryalls Stud Cottage ★★★
Contact: Mr & Mrs Rawlins, Ryalls Stud Farmhouse, Bishops Caundle, Bishop's Caundle, Sherborne DT9 5NG
T: (01963) 23036
F: (01963) 23179

BISHOP'S NYMPTON
Devon

Crosse Farm ★★★
Contact: Mrs D A Verney, Crosse Farm, Wing of Farmhouse, Bishop's Nympton, South Molton EX36 4PB
T: (01769) 550288

BISHOP'S TAWTON
Devon

Horswell Farm Cottages ★★★★
Contact: Mr Roger Stanbury, Horswell Farm Cottages, Bishop's Tawton, Barnstaple EX32 0ED
T: (01271) 343505
F: (01271) 326393
E: horswellfarm@freeuk com
I: www.horswellcottages.co.uk

BISHOPS DOWN
Dorset

Monks Barn ★★★★
Contact: Mrs Caryll Perry, Glebe Farm House, Stakes Lane, Bishops Down, Sherborne DT9 5PN
T: (01963) 23259

BISHOPS HULL
Somerset

Leat Cottage ★★★★★
Contact: Mr William Beaumont, Leat Cottage, Longaller Mill, Bishops Hull, Taunton TA4 1AD
T: (01823) 326071
E: jo.beaumont@btopenworld.com

1 Old School Cottages ★★
Contact: Mrs Randle, Shute Cottage,Shutewater Hill, Bishops Hull, Taunton TA1 5EQ
T: (01823) 331189

BISHOPSTEIGNTON
Devon

Rose Cottage ★★
Contact: Holiday Homes & Cottages South West, 365A Torquay Road, Paignton TQ3 2BT
T: (01803) 663650
F: (01803) 664037
E: holcotts@aol.com
I: www.swcottages.co.uk

BISHOPSTROW
Wiltshire

Eastleigh Farm ★★★★
Contact: Mr Roz Walker, Eastleigh Farm, Bishopstrow, Warminster BA12 7BE
T: (01985) 212325

BITTON
Gloucestershire

The Gate House ★★
Contact: Mr Stone, The Gate House, Green Gables, Redfield Hill, Bitton, Bristol BS30 6NX
T: (0117) 932 5303
F: (0117) 932 5303
E: thegatehouse@houseofstone.co.uk
I: www.houseofstone.co.uk

BLACK TORRINGTON
Devon

Kingsley Mill ★★★★
Contact: Farm & Cottage Holidays, Victoria House, 12 Fore Street, Northam, Bideford EX39 1AW
T: (01237) 479146
F: (01237) 421512
E: enquiries@farmcott.co.uk

BLACKAWTON
Devon

Chuckle Too ★★★
Contact: Jill Hanlon, Chuckle Cottage, Main Street, Blackawton, Dartmouth TQ9 7BG
T: (01803) 712455
F: (01803) 712455
E: jillyhanlon@beeb.net

Lower Collaton Farmhouse ★★★★
Contact: Mr & Mrs James & Rosy Mussen, Lower Collaton Farmhouse, Blackawton, Totnes TQ9 7DW
T: (01803) 712260
E: Mussen@lower-collaton-farm.co.uk

BLACKBOROUGH
Devon

Bodmiscombe Farm ★★★
Contact: Mrs B M Northam, Bodmiscombe Farm, Blackborough, Cullompton EX15 2HR

South Farm Holiday Cottages & Fishery★★★
Contact: Mrs Susan Chapman, South Farm, Blackborough, Sheldon, Honiton EX15 2JE
T: (01823) 681078
F: (01823) 680483
E: chapman@southfarm.co.uk
I: www.sourthfarm.co.uk

BLATCHBRIDGE
Somerset

Mill Cottage ★★★★
Contact: Mrs Thelma Morris, Mill Cottage, Blatchbridge MIll, Frome BA11 5EJ
T: (01373) 464784

BLISLAND
Cornwall

Beech View
Rating Applied For
Contact: Mr Len Croney, Beech View, Higher Pengelly, Blisland, Bodmin PL30 4HR
T: (01208) 821116
E: len@pengellyconsult.com

Bridge Pool Cottage ★★★★
Contact: Mr & Mrs Trevor & Kathryn Sobey, Pengover, Merrymeet, Liskeard PL14 3NJ
T: (01579) 343382

Torr House Cottages ★★★★
Contact: Mr & Mrs Martin & Carolyn Wilson
T: (01208) 851601
F: (01208) 851601
E: wilson@millbanks.fsworld.co.uk
I: www.torrhouseholidays.co.uk

BODIEVE
Cornwall

Cornish Cottage ★★★
Contact: Mrs Holder, Roseley, Wadebridge PL27 6EG
T: (01208) 813024

BODMIN
Cornwall

Glynn Barton Cottages ★★★
Contact: Ms Lucy Orr, Glynn Barton Cottages, Glynn Barton, Glynn, Bodmin PL30 4AX
T: (01208) 821375
F: (01208) 821104
E: cottages@glynnbarton.fsnet.co.uk

Great Brightor Farm ★★★★★
Contact: Mr & Mrs Frank & Kay Chapman, St Kew Highway, Bodmin PL30 3DR
T: (01208) 850464
F: (01208) 850464

Lanjew Park ★★★★
Contact: Mrs E Biddick, Lanjew Park, Lanjew Farm, Withiel, Bodmin PL30 5PB
T: (01726) 890214
F: (01726) 890214
E: biddick@lanjew.co.uk
I: www.lanjew.co.uk

Little Talana ★★★
Contact: Mr & Mrs Peter & Cathy Osborne, Cornish Horizons, Higher Trehemborne, St Merryn, Padstow PL28 8JU
T: (01841) 520889

Mennabroom Farm ★★★★
Contact: Mrs Lucas, Mennabroom Farm, Warleggan, Mount, Bodmin PL30 4HE
T: (01208) 821272
F: (01208) 821555
E: lucas@mennabroom.co.uk
I: www.mennabroom.co.uk

Mount Pleasant Cottages ★★★
Contact: Mrs Capper, Mount Pleasant Cottages, Mount Pleasant Farm, Mount, Bodmin PL30 4EX
T: (01208) 821342
E: collette@capper61.fsnet.co.uk
I: www.peacefulholiday.co.uk

Outer Colvannick ★★★
Contact: Farm & Cottage Holidays, Victoria House, 12 Fore Street, Westward Ho!, Bideford EX39 1AW
T: (01237) 479146
F: (01237) 421512
E: enquiries@farmcott.co.uk

Penrose Burden Holiday Cottages ★★★-★★★★
Contact: Ms N Hall, Penrose Burden Holiday Cottages, St Breward, Bodmin PL30 4LZ
T: (01208) 850277
I: www.penroseburden.co.uk

The Stable ★★★
Contact: Mrs Elizabeth Tidy, Penbugle Farm, The Stable Penbugle, Bodmin PL31 2NT
T: (01208) 72844

Tor View ★★★-★★★★
Contact: Mr & Mrs Rob & Helen Watson, Tor View, Trebell Green, Lanivet, Bodmin PL30 5HR
T: (01208) 831472
F: (01208) 831472

Trethorne Cottage ★★★★★
Contact: Mr Stephen Chidgey, Cornwall Quality Cottages, The Old Barn, Tregonetha, St Columb TR9 6EL
T: (01637) 880630
E: oldbarncornwall@btinternet.com

BOSCASTLE
Cornwall

Anneth Lowen ★★★★
Contact: Mr K M Dougan, Kernow Holidays, 40A Oriental Road, Woking GU22 7AR
T: (01483) 765446
F: 0870 321 4658
E: info@annethlowen.co.uk
I: www.annethlowen.co.uk

Barn Park Gallery ★★★★
Contact: Mr J Holliday, Drewenna, Manor Close, Kingsdon, Somerton TA11 7LW
T: (01935) 842089
E: kingsdonman@aol.com

The Boathouse ★★★★
Contact: Mrs Webster, Seagulls, The Harbour, Boscastle PL35 0AG
T: (01840) 250413
I: www.buiness.thisiscornwall.co.uk/boathouse/

Boscastle Holidays ★★★
Contact: Mrs J Congdon, Boscastle Holidays, Tremorle, Boscastle PL35 0BU
T: (01840) 250233

Cargurra Farm ★★★★
Contact: Mrs Gillian Elson, Hennett, St Juliot, Boscastle PL35 0BT
T: (01840) 261206
F: (01840) 261206
E: gillian@cargurra.co.uk
I: www.cargurra.co.uk

Courtyard Farm & Cottages ★★★-★★★★★
Contact: Mr Jan Compton, Courtyard Farm & Cottages, Lesnewth, St Juliot, Boscastle PL35 0HR
T: (01840) 261256
F: (01840) 261794
E: courtyard.farm@virgin.net
I: www.cornwall-online.co.uk/courtyard-farm-cottages

The Garden Place ★★★★
Contact: Ms Celia Knox, Penagar, Boscastle PL35 0AB
T: (01840) 250817
E: celia.knox@btinternet.com

Gull Cottage ★★★
Contact: Mr & Mrs Chris & Ann Gooderham, Fir Cottage, 16 Church Close, Hose, Long Clawson, Melton Mowbray LE14 4JJ
T: (01949) 860564
F: (01949) 860084
E: cottages@gooderham44.freeserve.co.uk

Harbour Holidays ★★★-★★★★★
Contact: Mrs Christine Morgan, The Boscastle Hideaway, The Harbour Restaurant, Riverside Walk, Boscastle PL35 0HD
T: (01840) 250380
I: lanhydrock@btinternet.co.uk

Home Farm Cottage ★★★★
Contact: Mrs J Haddy, Home Farm Cottage, Boscastle PL35 0BN
T: (01840) 250195
F: (01840) 250195
E: jackie.haddy@btclick.com

Honeysuckle Cottage ★★★
Contact: Mr P & Mrs T Bunker, 89 Austin Road, Luton LU3 1TZ
T: (01582) 619314

1 Jordan Vale ★★★
Contact: Mrs Scott, 1 Jordan Vale, Old Road, Boscastle PL35 0AJ
T: (01840) 250463

Lewarne ★★★
Contact: Mr Purvis, 4 Alder Lane, Balsall Common, Coventry CV7 7DZ
T: (01676) 534648

Little Cobwebs ★★★★
Contact: Mr & Mrs Jeff & Judi Covelle, Cobwebs, Marshgate, Tresparrett, Camelford PL32 9YN
T: (01840) 261766
F: 07092 363351
E: jeff@jcovelle.freeserve.co.uk
I: www.jcovelle.freeserve.co.uk

No 4 Pennally Cottage ★★★
Contact: Mrs Janet Welch, 104 Rochester Drive, Bexley DA5 1QF
T: (01322) 522240
F: (01322) 522240

Paradise Farm Cottage ★★★
Contact: Mrs D M Hancock, Paradise Farm Cottage, Boscastle PL35 0BL
T: (01840) 250528

Shepherd's Cottage ★★★
Contact: Mr H Jenkins, Endellion House, Parc Road, Llangybi, Usk NP15 1NL
T: (01633) 450417
E: jenkins@choicecornishcottages.com
I: www.choicecornishcottages.com

Tregatherall Farm ★★★★
Contact: Mrs Seldon, Tregatherall Farm, Boscastle PL35 0EQ
T: (01840) 250277

Trehane House ★★
Contact: Mrs Cynthia Taylor, Gwel-an-Mor, Tintagel Road, Boscastle PL35 0DS
T: (01840) 250052

Trewannett Bungalow ★★★
Contact: Mr & Mrs James Sleep, Trewannett Bungalow, Boscastle PL35 0HJ
T: (01840) 250295

Welltown Farmhouse ★★★
Contact: Mrs Diane Kehoe, Welltown Farmhouse, Trevalga, Boscastle PL35 0DY
T: (01840) 250718
E: stella210@hotmail.com

Westerings ★★★
Contact: Mrs Shirley Wakelin, Westerings, Forrabury, Boscastle PL35 0DJ
T: (01840) 250314
E: shirley@westeringsholidays.co.uk
I: www.westeringsholidays.co.uk

BOVEY TRACEY
Devon

Lower Elsford Farm ★★★★
Contact: Helpful Holidays, Mill Street, Chagford, Newton Abbot TQ13 8AN
T: (01647) 433593

Stickwick Farm ★★★
Contact: Mrs L Harvey, Frost Farm, Bovey Tracey, Newton Abbot TQ13 9PP
T: (01626) 833266
E: linda@frostfarm.co.uk
I: www.frostfarm.co.uk

Tracey Cottage ★★★
Contact: Mr Ian Butterworth, Holiday Homes & Cottages South West, 365A Torquay Road, Paignton TQ3 2BT
T: (01803) 663650

Warmhill Farm ★★★★
Contact: Mr & Mrs B Marnham, Warmhill Farm, Bovey Tracey, Newton Abbot TQ13 9QH
T: (01626) 833229
E: marnham@agriplus.net

BOWERCHALKE
Wiltshire

Pennywort Cottage ★★★
Contact: Mr Nicholas Pash, Chapel House, Luke Street, Berwick St John, Shaftesbury SP7 0HQ
T: (01747) 828170
F: (01747) 829090
E: enq@hideaways.co.uk
I: www.hideaways.co.uk

BOX
Wiltshire

Henley Farmhouse ★★★
Contact: Mrs P Cordle, Henley Farmhouse, Box, Corsham SN13 8BX
T: (01225) 742447
E: penart@onetel.net.uk

BRADFORD-ON-AVON
Wiltshire

Greystone Cottage ★★★
Contact: Mrs Gillian Patel, 19 Church Street, Bradford-on-Avon BA15 1LN
T: (01225) 868179
F: (01225) 867084
E: vivandgill@yahoo.co.uk
I: www.greystoneboa.co.uk

The Loft ★★★★
Contact: Mrs Helen Rawlings, Great Ashley Farm, Ashley Lane, Bradford-on-Avon BA15 2PP
T: (01225) 864563
F: (01225) 309117
E: greatashleyfarm@farmersweekly.net
I: www.greatashleyfarm.co.uk

BRADNINCH
Devon

Highdown Organic Farm ★★★★
Contact: Mrs Vallis, Highdown Organic Farm, Cranishaies Lane, Bradninch, Exeter EX5 4LJ
T: (01392) 881028
F: (01392) 881272
E: svallis@highdownfarm.co.uk
I: www.highdownfarm.co.uk

BRADWORTHY
Devon

Lympscott Farm Holidays ★★★★
Contact: Mrs Caroline Furse, Lympscott Farm Holidays, Bradworthy, Holsworthy EX22 7TR
T: (01409) 241607
F: (01409) 241607
I: www.lympscott.co.uk

Teddies ★★★
Contact: Mr & Mrs Peter & Janet Cornwell, Marsden's Cottage Holidays, 2 The Square, Braunton EX33 2JB
T: (01271) 813777
F: (01271) 813664
E: holidays@marsdens.co.uk
I: www.marsdens.co.uk

BRANSCOMBE
Devon

Bank Cottage ★★★
Contact: Ms Kate Bartlett, Jean Bartlett Cottage Holidays, The Old Dairy, Fore Street, Seaton EX12 3JB
T: (01297) 23221
F: (01297) 23303
E: holidays@jeanbartlett.com
I: www.netbreaks.com/jeamb

The Chapel at Borcombe Farm ★★★
Contact: Ms Kate Bartlett, Jean Bartlett Cottage Holidays, The Old Dairy, Fore Street, Seaton EX12 3JB
T: (01297) 23221
F: (01297) 23303
E: holidays@jeanbartlett.com
I: www.netbreaks.com/jeamb

Chapel Row ★★★★
Contact: Ms Kate Bartlett, Jean Bartlett Cottage Holidays, The Old Dairy, Fore Street, Seaton EX12 3JB
T: (01297) 23221
F: (01297) 23303
E: holidays@jeanbartlett.com
I: www.netbreaks.com/jeamb

Cliffhayes ★★★
Contact: Ms Kate Bartlett, Jean Bartlett Cottage Holidays, The Old Dairy, Fore Street, Seaton EX12 3JB
T: (01297) 23221
F: (01297) 23303
E: holidays@jeanbartlett.com
I: www.jeanbartlett.com

Combe Way ★★★
Contact: Ms Kate Bartlett, Jean Bartlett Cottage Holidays, The Old Dairy, Fore Street, Seaton EX12 3JB
T: (01297) 23221
F: (01297) 23303
E: holidays@jeanbartlett.com
I: www.netbreaks.com/jeamb

Gill Cottage ★★★
Contact: Ms Kate Bartlett, Jean Bartlett Cottage Holidays, The Old Dairy, Fore Street, Seaton EX12 3JB
T: (01297) 23221
F: (01297) 23303
E: holidays@jeanbartlett.com
I: www.netbreaks.com/jeamb

Hole House ★★★★
Contact: Ms Kate Bartlett, Jean Bartlett Cottage Holidays, The Old Dairy, Fore Street, Seaton EX12 3JB
T: (01297) 23221
F: (01297) 23303
E: holidays@jeanbartlett.com
I: www.netbreaks.com/jeamb

Jasmine Cottage ★★
Contact: Ms Kate Bartlett, Jean Bartlett Cottage Holidays, The Old Dairy, Fore Street, Seaton EX12 3JB
T: (01297) 23221
F: (01297) 23303
E: holidays@jeanbartlett.com
I: www.netbreaks.com/jeamb

The Old Sunday School ★★★★
Contact: Jean Bartlett Cottage Holidays, Fore Street, Seaton EX12 3JB
T: (01297) 23221
F: (01297) 23303
E: holidays@jeanbartlett.com
I: www.netbreaks.com/jeanb

Pitt Farm Lodge ★★★
Contact: Ms Kate Bartlett, Jean Bartlett Cottage Holidays, The Old Dairy, Fore Street, Seaton EX12 3JB
T: (01297) 23221
F: (01297) 23303
E: holidays@jeanbartlett.com
I: www.netbreaks.com/jeamb

Roslyn Cottage ★★★
Contact: Jean Bartlett, Cottage Holidays, Seaton EX12 3JB
T: (01297) 23221
I: www.jeanbartlett.com

Sellerswood ★★
Contact: Jean Bartlett Cottage Holidays, Fore Street, Seaton EX12 3JB
T: (01297) 23221
F: (01297) 23303
E: holidays@jeanbartlett.com
I: www.netbreaks.com/jeanb

Terry Holt, Nook ★★★★
Contact: Ms Kate Bartlett, Jean Bartlett Cottage Holidays The Old Dairy, Fore Street, Seaton EX12 3JB
T: (01297) 23221
F: (01297) 23303
E: holidays@jeanbartlett.com
I: www.netbreaks.com/jeamb

BRATTON
Somerset

Woodcombe Lodges ★★★★
Contact: Mrs N Hanson, Woodcombe Lodges, Bratton Lane, Minehead TA24 8SQ
T: (01643) 702789
F: (01643) 702789
E: nicola@woodcombelodge.co.uk
I: www.woodcombelodge.co.uk

BRATTON CLOVELLY
Devon

Jersey Cottage ★★★★
Contact: Mr Bob Williamson, Jersey Cottage, Headson Farm, Bratton Clovelly, Okehampton EX20 4JP
T: (01837) 871417
F: (01837) 871417
E: bob@rjwillamson.fsnet.co.uk

Lavender Cottage ★★
Contact: Mrs Carol Blatchford, Laveddon Cottage, Blowinghouse Lane, Bodmin PL30 5JU
T: (01208) 74278

BRATTON FLEMING
Devon

Bracken Roost ★★★★
Contact: Mr Lawrie Scott, Bracken House, Bratton Fleming, Barnstaple EX31 4TG
T: (01598) 710320
E: lawrie@brackenhousehotel.com
I: www.brackenhousehotel.com

Capelands Farm ★★★
Contact: Toad Hall Cottages, Elliot House, Church Street, Kingsbridge TQ7 1BY
T: (01548) 521366
F: (01548) 853086
E: thc@toadhallcottages.com
I: www.toadhallcottages.com

The Tops ★★★
Contact: Mrs Hamner, Elliot House, Church Street, Kingsbridge TQ7 1BY
T: (01584) 853089

Wallover Barton Cottages ★★★
Contact: 2 The Square, Braunton EX33 2JB
T: (01271) 813777
F: (01271) 813664
E: holidays@marsdens.co.uk
I: www.marsdens.co.uk

BRAUNTON
Devon

Britton Lodge ★★★
Contact: Mr & Mrs Peter & Janet Cornwell, Marsden's Cottage Holidays, 2 The Square, Braunton EX33 2JB
T: (01271) 813777
F: (01271) 813664
E: holidays@marsdens.co.uk
I: www.marsdens.co.uk

Buckland Manor Cottage ★★★
Contact: Marsden's Cottage Holidays, 2 The Square, Braunton EX33 2JB
T: (01271) 813777
F: (01271) 813664
E: holidays@marsdens.co.uk
I: www.marsdens.co.uk

Buckland Mews ★★★
Contact: Marsden's Cottage Holidays, 2 The Square, Braunton EX33 2JB
T: (01271) 813777
F: (01271) 813664
E: holidays@marsdens.co.uk
I: www.marsdens.co.uk

Casquets ★★★★
Contact: 2 The Square, Braunton EX33 2JB
T: (01271) 813777
F: (01271) 813664
E: holidays@marsdens.co.uk
I: www.marsdens.co.uk

Courtyard, Cob & Coach House ★★★
Contact: Marsden's Cottage Holidays, 2 The Square, Braunton EX33 2JB
T: (01271) 813777
F: (01271) 813664
E: holidays@marsdens.co.uk
I: www.marsdens.co.uk

Farmhouse Cottage ★★★
Contact: 2 The Square, Braunton EX33 2JB
T: (01271) 813777
F: (01271) 813664
E: holidays@marsdens.co.uk
I: www.marsdens.co.uk

The Garden Flat ★★★
Contact: Marsden's Cottage Holidays, 2 The Square, Braunton EX33 2JB
T: (01271) 813777
F: (01271) 813664
E: holidays@marsdens.co.uk
I: www.marsdens.co.uk

Goadgates ★★★
Contact: Marsden's Cottage Holidays, 2 The Square, Braunton EX33 2JB
T: (01271) 813777
F: (01271) 813664
E: holidays@marsdens.co.uk
I: www.marsdens.co.uk

Higher Spreacombe Farm ★★★
Contact: Mrs Colleen McCammond, Higher Spreacombe Farm, Higher Spreacombe, Woolacombe EX33 1JA
T: (01271) 870443

Incledon Farmhouse ★★★
Contact: Marsden's Cottage Holidays, 2 The Square, Braunton EX33 2JB
T: (01271) 813777
F: (01271) 813664
E: holidays@marsdens.co.uk
I: www.marsdens.co.uk

Leacroft ★★★
Contact: 2 The Square, Braunton EX33 2JB
T: (01271) 813777
F: (01271) 813664
E: holidays@marsdens.co.uk
I: www.marsdens.co.uk

Lime Tree Nursery ★★★★
Contact: Marsden's Cottage Holidays, 2 The Square, Braunton EX33 2JB
T: (01271) 813777
F: (01271) 813664
E: holidays@marsdens.co.uk
I: www.marsdens.co.uk

Little Comfort Farm ★★★
Contact: Mrs Jackie Milsom, Little Comfort Farm, Braunton EX33 2NJ
T: (01271) 812414
F: (01271) 817975
E: jackie.milsom@btclick.com
I: www.littlecomfortfarm.co.uk

1 Millhouse Cottage ★★★
Contact: Marsden's Cottage Holidays, 2 The Square, Braunton EX33 2JB
T: (01271) 813777
F: (01271) 813664
E: holidays@marsdens.co.uk
I: www.marsdens.co.uk

2 Millhouse Cottage ★★★
Contact: 2 The Square, Braunton EX33 2JB
T: (01271) 813777
F: (01271) 813664
E: holidays@marsdens.co.uk
I: www.marsdens.co.uk

The Nook ★★★★
Contact: Marsden's Cottage Holidays, 2 The Square, Braunton EX33 2JB
T: (01271) 813777
F: (01271) 813664
E: holidays@marsdens.co.uk
I: www.marsdens.co.uk

The Old Byre ★★★★
Contact: Marsden's Cottage Holidays, 2 The Square, Braunton EX33 2JB
T: (01271) 813777
F: (01271) 813664
E: holidays@marsdens.co.uk
I: www.marsdens.co.uk

Orchard House ★★★
Contact: 2 The Square, Braunton EX33 2JB
T: (01271) 813777
F: (01271) 813664
E: holidays@marsdens.co.uk
I: www.marsdens.co.uk

Owl Cottage
Rating Applied For
Contact: Marsden's Cottage Holidays, 2 The Square, Braunton EX33 2JB
T: (01271) 813777
F: (01271) 813664
E: holidays@marsdens.co.uk
I: www.marsdens.co.uk

Ramblers Return ★★★
Contact: Marsden's Cottage Holidays, 2 The Square, Braunton EX33 2JB
T: (01271) 813777
F: (01271) 813664
E: holidays@marsdens.co.uk
I: www.marsdens.co.uk

Saunton Beach Villas ★★
Contact: Mr David Marshall, Broadfield Holidays, 1 Park Villas, Taw Vale, Barnstaple EX32 8NJ
T: (01271) 322033
F: (01271) 378558

Thorn Close Cottage ★★★★
Contact: Mr & Mrs Cornwell, Marsden's Cottage Holidays, 2 The Square, Braunton EX33 2JB
T: (01271) 813777

Waverley ★★★
Contact: Marsden's Cottage Holidays, 2 The Square, Braunton EX33 2JB
T: (01271) 813777
F: (01271) 813664
E: holidays@marsdens.co.uk
I: www.marsdens.co.uk

Well Cottage ★★★★
Contact: Mr & Mrs Peter & Janet Cornwell, Marsden's Cottage Holidays, 2 The Square, Braunton EX33 2JB
T: (01271) 815266
F: (01271) 813664
E: holidays@marsdens.co.uk
I: www.marsdens.co.uk

Willoways ★★★
Contact: Mr & Mrs P Cornwell, Marsden's Cottage Holidays, 2 The Square, Braunton EX33 2JB
T: (01271) 813777
F: (01271) 813664
E: holidays@marsdens.co.uk
I: www.marsdens.co.uk

Windspray ★★★
Contact: Marsden's Cottage Holidays, 2 The Square, Braunton EX33 2JB
T: (01271) 813777
F: (01271) 813664
E: holidays@marsdens.co.uk
I: www.marsdens.co.uk

BRAYFORD
Devon

Muxworthy Cottage ★★
Contact: Mrs G M Bament, Muxworthy Farm, Brayford, Barnstaple EX32 7QP
T: (01598) 710342

Rockley Farmhouse – The Stable Barn ★★★★
Contact: Mrs Renee Dover, Rockley Farmhouse, Brayford, Barnstaple EX32 7QR
T: (01598) 710429
F: (01598) 710429
E: info@rockley.co.uk
I: www.rockleyfarmhouse.co.uk

BREAGE
Cornwall

Pump House ★★★★
Contact: Cornish Cottage Holidays, Godolphin Road, Helston TR13 8AA
T: (01326) 573808
F: (01326) 564992
E: enquiry@cornishcottageholidays.co.uk
I: www.cornishcottageholidays.co.uk

BREAN
Somerset

Gadara Bungalow ★★
Contact: Mr T M Hicks, Gadara Bungalow, Diamond Farm, Weston Road, Brean, Burnham-on-Sea TA8 2RL
T: (01278) 751263
E: trevor@diamondfarm42.freeserve.co.uk
I: www.diamondfarm.co.uk

BRENT KNOLL
Somerset

West Croft Farm Dairy Cottage ★★★
Contact: Mrs Janet Harris, West Croft Farm Dairy Cottage, Brent Street, Brent Knoll, Highbridge TA9 4BE
T: (01278) 760259

BRENTOR
Devon

The Smithy ★★★
Contact: Mrs Wetherbee, Thorn Cottage, Burn Lane, Brentor, Tavistock PL19 0ND
T: (01822) 810285

BRIDESTOWE
Devon

Embleton Cottage ★★★
Contact: Country Holidays, Spring Mill, Earby, Barnoldswick BB94 0AA
T: 08700 781200

Knole Farm ★★★★
Contact: Farm & Cottage Holidays, Victoria House, 12 Fore Street, Northam, Bideford EX39 1AW
T: (01237) 479146
F: (01237) 421512
E: enquiries@farmcott.co.uk

BRIDGWATER
Somerset

Ash-Wembdon Farm Cottages ★★★★
Contact: Mr Clarence Rowe, Ash-Wembdon Farm Cottages, Ash-Wembdon Farm, Hollow Lane, Wembdon, Bridgwater TA5 2BD
T: (01278) 453097
F: (01278) 445856
E: c.a.rowe@btinternet.com
I: www.farmaccommodation.co.uk

Grange Barn ★★★★★
Contact: Mr Matthew Wheeler, Grange Barn, Cannington, Bridgwater TA5 2LD
T: (01278) 652216
F: (01278) 653611
E: grangehols@aol.com
I: www.grangehols.co.uk

BRIDPORT
Dorset

Chestnut Cottage ★★★
Contact: Mr Kenneth Savill, 25 Daneswood Close, Weybridge KT13 9AY
T: (01932) 821101
F: (01932) 821101
I: chideockcottages.com

Clearview Bungalow ★★★
Contact: Mr Zachary Stuart-Brown, Dream Cottages, 41 Maiden Street, Weymouth DT4 8AZ
T: (01305) 761347
E: admin@dream-cottages.co.uk
I: www.dream-cottages.co.uk

Coniston Holiday Apartments ★★★
Contact: Mrs Jackie Murphy, Coniston Holiday Apartments, Coniston House, Victoria Grove, Bridport DT6 3AE
T: (01308) 424049
F: (01308) 424049

1 Crockhaven Cottage ★★★
Contact: Mr D & Mrs B Slade, Westpoint Apartments, The Esplanade, West Bay, Bridport DT6 4HG
T: (01308) 423636
F: (01308) 458871
E: bea@westpoint-apartments.co.uk
I: www.westpoint-apartments.co.uk

Fern Down Farm ★★★
Contact: Mrs S Solly, Fern Down Farm, Shatcombe Lane, Wynford Eagle, Dorchester DT2 0EZ
T: (01300) 320810
E: pdnsolly@hotmail.com

Hayday ★★★★
Contact: Mrs Day, Hayday, 29 Howard Road, Bridport DT6 4SG
T: (01308) 424438
F: (01308) 424438

Highlands End Holiday Park ★★★
Contact: Mr Martin Cox, Highlands End Holiday Park, Eype, Bridport DT6 6AR
T: (01308) 422139
F: (01308) 425672
E: holidays@wdlh.co.uk
I: www.wdlh.co.uk

Highway Farm ★★★
Contact: Mrs Pauline Bale, Highway Farm, West Road, Bridport DT6 6AE
T: (01308) 424321
E: bale@highwayfarm.co.uk

Holiday Cottages Numbers 1 & 3 Stanley Place ★★
Contact: Mrs Barford, Bowood, Post Lane, Cotleigh, Upottery, Honiton EX14 9HZ
T: (01404) 861566

Lancombes House ★★★
Contact: Mr & Mrs Mansfield, Lancombes House, West Milton, Bridport DT6 3TN
T: (01308) 485375

Rope Cottage ★★★
Contact: Mrs Reichter, Rope Cottage, Rope Walks, West Bay, Bridport DT6 3RH
T: (01308) 425122
F: (01308) 425122
E: ropecott22@lycos.com

Rudge Farm ★★★★
Contact: Mrs Sue Diment, Rudge Farm, Chilcombe, Bridport DT6 4NF
T: (01308) 482630
E: sue@rudgefarm.co.uk
I: www.rudgefarm.co.uk

Strongate Cottage ★★★
Contact: Mrs Sandra Huxter, Strongate Farm, Salwayash, Bridport DT6 5JD
T: (01308) 488295
F: (01380) 488295

Sunset ★★★
Contact: Mr Dan Walker FHCIMA, c/o Eypeleaze, 117 West Bay Road, West Bay, Bridport DT6 4EQ
T: (01308) 423363
F: (01308) 420228
E: cdan@walker42.freeserve.co.uk

30 Victoria Grove ★★
Contact: Mr & Mrs Brook, 30 Victoria Grove, Victoria Grove, Bridport DT6 3AD
T: (01308) 424605

Wooth Manor Cottage ★★★
Contact: Mrs Gaby Martelli, St James Road, Netherbury, Waytown, Bridport DT6 5LW
T: (01308) 488348
E: amyasmartelli40@hotmail.com

BRISTOL

Avonside ★★★
Contact: Mrs D M Ridout, Avonside, 19 St Edyth's Road, Sea Mills, Bristol BS9 2EP
T: (0117) 968 1967

503 City Centre Apartment ★★★★★
Contact: Ms Grace Carleton, Carleton Estates, 1 Aspen Close, Green Park, Wootton Bassett, Swindon SN4 7HN
T: (01793) 850421
I: www.carletonestates.com

Days Serviced Apartments ★★★
Contact: Miss Emma Potter, Days Serviced Apartments, 30-38 St Thomas Street, Bristol BS1 6JZ
T: (01179) 544800
F: (01179) 544900
I: www.hojoservicedapartments.com

Harbourside Apartment ★★★★
Contact: Mrs Flick Selway, Savernake, 11 Hillside Road, Long Ashton, Bristol BS41 9LG
T: (01275) 541296
E: flickSelway@Pselway.freeserve.co.uk

Harbourside View ★★★★★
Contact: Mr & Mrs Kevin & Alison Davies, Abbotts Wootten Cottage, Wootton Fitzpaine, Bridport DT6 6NL
T: (01297) 560189
F: (01297) 560730
E: alisondavies21@hotmail.com

Redland Flat ★★★
Contact: Mr H I Jones, Flat 1, Elm Lodge, Elm Grove, London NW2 3AE
T: (020) 8450 6761
E: redlandflat.btc@onmail.co.uk

Waterside ★★★★★
Contact: Mr Pete Hodges, 37 Montague Court, Cotham, Bristol BS2 8HT
E: pete.hodges@virgin.net
I: www.watersidebristol.co.uk

BRIXHAM
Devon

Abri ★★★★
Contact: Holiday Homes & Cottages South West, 365A Torquay Road, Paignton TQ3 2BT
T: (01803) 663650
F: (01803) 664037
I: www.swcottages.co.uk

9 Albion Court
Rating Applied For
Contact: Mr Ian Butterworth, Holiday Homes & Cottages South West, 365A Torquay Road, Paignton TQ3 2BT
T: (01803) 663650

Arlington Holiday Flats ★★★
Contact: Ms Denise Buggins, 14 Station Road, Blackwell, Bromsgrove B60 1PZ
T: (0121) 447 7387
E: denise.bugins@btinternet.com

Beachcomber ★★★
Contact: Holiday Homes & Cottages South West, 365A Torquay Road, Paignton TQ3 2BT
T: (01803) 663650
F: (01803) 664037
E: holcotts@aol.co.uk
I: www.swcottages.co.uk

Berry Head ★★★
Contact: Holiday Homes & Cottages South West, 365a Torquay Road, Paignton TQ3 2BT
T: (01803) 663650
F: (01803) 664037
E: holcotts@aol.com
I: www.swcottages.co.uk

Blue Chip Vacations-Moorings Reach ★★★★★
Contact: Mrs S Cutting
T: (01803) 855282
F: (01803) 851825
E: bluechip@eclipse.co.uk
I: www.bluechipvacations.com

Captain's Quarters ★★★★★
Contact: Mrs Gretchen Tricker, The Hill House, 23 St Peter's Hill, Brixham TQ5 9TE
T: (01803) 857937
F: (01803) 857937
E: gtricker@aol.com
I: www.captainsquarters.co.uk

Caravella ★★★
Contact: Mr Ian Butterworth, Holiday Homes & Cottages South West, 365A Torquay Road, Paignton TQ3 2BT
T: (01803) 663650
F: (01803) 664037
E: holcotts@aol.com
I: www.swcottages.co.uk

Cobblers Cottage ★★★
Contact: Mr E & Mrs I Williamson, 71 Above Town, Dartmouth TQ6 9RH
T: (01803) 833591

Crabbers Cottage ★★★★
Contact: Ms Tegan Cornish, 8 The Queensway, Austenwood Common, Gerrards Cross SL9 8NF
T: (01753) 882482
F: (01753) 882546
E: info@cornish-cottage.com
I: www.cornish-cottage.com

Devoncourt Holiday Flats ★★
Contact: Mr Robin Hooker, Devoncourt Holiday Flats, Berry Head Road, Brixham TQ5 9AB
T: (01803) 853748
F: (01803) 855775
E: robinhooker@devoncourt.net
I: www.devoncourt.net

Harbour Lights Holiday Flats ★-★★
Contact: Mr Robert Walker, 69 Berry Head Road, Brixham TQ5 9AA
T: (01803) 854816
F: (01803) 854816
E: harbourlights@compuserve.com

Harbour Reach ★★★
Contact: Mrs J Pocock, Totley Hall Farm, Totley Hall Lane, Totley, Sheffield S17 4AA
T: (0114) 236 4761
F: (0114) 236 4761

Harbour View ★★★★
Contact: Holiday Homes & Cottages South West, 365A Torquay Road, Paignton TQ3 2BT
T: (01803) 663650
F: (01803) 664037
E: holcotts@aol.com
I: www.swcottages.co.uk

The Harbour's Edge ★★★
Contact: Mr & Mrs Booth, 24 The Close, Brixham TQ5 8RF
T: (01803) 859859

The Hatchway and the Porthole
Rating Applied For
Contact: Holiday Homes and Cottages SW, 365a Torquay Road, Paignton TQ3 2BT
T: (01803) 663650
F: (01803) 664037
E: holcotts@aol.com

Kings Barton Cottage ★★★
Contact: Holiday Homes & Cottages South West, 365A Torquay Road, Paignton TQ3 2BT
T: (01803) 663650
F: (01803) 664037
E: holcotts@eol.com
I: www.swcottages.co.uk

Lily Cottage ★★★
Contact: Holiday Homes & Cottages South West, 365A Torquay Road, Paignton TQ3 2BT
T: (01803) 663650
F: (01803) 664307
E: holcotts@aol.com

Linden Court Holiday Apartments ★★★
Contact: Mr & Mrs Brian & Carol McCandlish, Linden Court Holiday Apartments, South Furzeham Road, Brixham TQ5 8JA
T: (01803) 851491
F: (01803) 558761
E: linden_court@mail.com

Lytehouse Cottage ★★★
Contact: Mr Ian Butterworth, Holiday Homes & Cottages South West, 365A Torquay Road, Paignton TQ3 2BT
T: (01803) 663650
F: (01803) 664037
E: holcotts@aol.com
I: www.swcottages.co.uk

Mudberry House ★★★
Contact: Holiday Homes & Cottages South West, 365A Torquay Road, Paignton TQ3 2BT
T: (01803) 663650
F: (01803) 664037
E: holcotts@aol.com
I: www.swcottages.co.uk

Outlook ★★★
Contact: Holiday Homes & Cottages South West, 365A Torquay Road, Paignton TQ3 2BT
T: (01803) 663650
F: (01803) 664037
E: holcotts@aol.com
I: www.swcottages.co.uk

Sailor's Haunt ★★★★
Contact: Mr Richard Haycock, Beaumont House, 25 Siston Common, Warmley, Bristol BS15 4NY
T: (0117) 967 6659
F: (0117) 967 6659
I: www.beaumontcottages.co.uk

Seacat Cottage ★★★★
Contact: Holiday Homes & Cottages South West, 365A Torquay Road, Paignton TQ3 2BT
T: (01803) 663650
F: (01803) 664037
E: holcotts@aol.co.uk
I: www.swcottages.co.uk

Seashell Cottage ★★★
Contact: Mr Ian Butterworth, Holiday Homes & Cottages South West, 365A Torquay Road, Paignton TQ3 2BT
T: (01803) 663650
F: (01803) 664037
E: holcotts@aol.com
I: www.swcottages.co.uk

Torbay Holiday Chalets
Rating Applied For
Contact: Mr & Mrs Martyn & Jane Swift, Torbay Holiday Chalets, Fishcombe Road, Brixham TQ5 8RA
T: (01803) 853313

Trade Winds ★★★
Contact: Mr & Mrs Williamson, 71 Above Town, Dartmouth TQ6 9RH
T: (01803) 833591

Windjammer Apartment ★★★
Contact: Mr & Mrs Skeggs, Windjammer Apartment, Windjammer Lodge, Parkham Road, Brixham TQ5 9BU
T: (01803) 854279
E: windjammerapartments@yahoo.co.uk
I: www.geocities.com/windjammerapartments

BROADCLYST
Devon

Hue's Piece ★★★★
Contact: Mrs Anna Hamlyn, Hue's Piece, Paynes Farm, Broadclyst, Exeter EX5 3BJ
T: (01392) 466720
F: (01392) 468285
E: nchamlyn@fsbdial.co.uk
♿

Wares Cottage ★★★★
Contact: Farm & Cottage Holidays, Victoria House, 12 Fore Street, Westward Ho!, Bideford EX39 1AW
T: (01237) 479146
F: (01237) 421512
E: bookings@farmcott.co.uk

BROADMAYNE
Dorset

Holcombe Valley Cottages ★★★
Contact: Mr & Mrs Peter & Jane Davies, Holcombe Valley Cottages, Chalky Road, Broadmayne, Dorchester DT2 8PW
T: (01305) 852817
F: (01305) 854539
E: holvalcots@aol.com
I: www.holcombe-cottages.co.uk

BROADOAK
Dorset

Stoke Mill Farm ★★-★★★
Contact: Mrs Anthea Bay, Stoke Mill Farm, Broadoak, Bridport DT6 5NR
T: (01308) 868036
F: (01308) 868036
I: www.stokemillholidays.20m.com

BROADSANDS
Devon

Broadsands ★★★
Contact: Holiday Homes & Cottages South West, 365A Torquay Road, Paignton TQ3 2BT
T: (01803) 663650
F: (01803) 664037
E: holcotts@aol.com
I: www.swcottages.co.uk

BROMHAM
Wiltshire

The Byres ★★
Contact: Mr & Mrs G, B Myers, The Byres, 84 Westbrook, Bromham, Chippenham SN15 2EE
T: (01380) 850557

Farthings ★★★
Contact: Mrs Gloria Steed, Farthings, The Cottage, Westbrook, Bromham, Chippenham SN15 2EE
T: (01380) 850255
E: RJSteed@cottage16.freeserve.co.uk

BROMPTON RALPH
Somerset

Oddwell Cottage ★★★
Contact: CH Ref: 68023, Country Holidays Group Owner Services Dept, Spring Mill, Earby, Barnoldswick BB94 0AA
E: sales@holidaycottagesgroup.com
I: www.country-holidays.co.uk

BROMPTON REGIS
Somerset

Weatherham Farm Cottages ★★★★
Contact: Mrs Anne Caldwell, Weatherham Farm Cottages, Weather Farm, Brompton Regis, Dulverton TA22 9LG
T: (01398) 371303
F: (01398) 371104
E: enquiries@weatherhamfarm.co.uk

BROUGHTON GIFFORD
Wiltshire

Church Farm Holiday Cottages ★★★★
Contact: Mrs Sharon Hooper, J Hooper & Son, Church Farm, Broughton Gifford, Melksham SN12 8PR
T: (01225) 783413
F: (01225) 783467
E: shooper@churchfarmcottages.fsnet.co.uk
I: www.smoothhound.co.uk

BRUSHFORD
Somerset

Orchard Cottage ★★★
Contact: Mr & Mrs Peter & Janet Cornwell, Marsden's Cottage Holidays, 2 The Square, Braunton EX33 2JB
T: (01271) 813777
F: (01271) 813664
E: holidays@marsdens.co.uk
I: www.marsdens.co.uk

BRYHER
Cornwall

Atlanta Holiday Accommodation ★★★
Contact: Mrs Langdon, Atlanta Holiday Accommodation, Bryher TR23 0PR
T: (01720) 422823

Glenhope ★★★
Contact: Mr R E Langdon, Glenhope, Bryher TR23 0PR
T: (01720) 423136
F: (01720) 423166
E: glenhope@ukonline.co.uk

Hebe, Fernside & Shippen Cottage ★★★
Contact: Mrs K Taylor, Veronica Farm, Bryher TR23 0PR
T: (01720) 422862

Hillside Farm ★★★★
Contact: Mrs Ruth Jenkins, Bryher TR23 0PR
T: (01720) 423156
E: ruthbryher@aol.com
I: www.bryher-ios.co.uk/hfs

South Hill ★★★
Contact: Mrs M Bennett, Firmans, Bryher TR23
T: (01720) 422411
E: marianbennett@excite.co.uk

The White House Flat ★★★
Contact: Mr R F Bushell, The White House, Bryher TR23 0PR
T: (01720) 422010
F: (01720) 422010

BUCKLAND BREWER
Devon

Adipit ★★★★
Contact: High Street, Freystrop, Haverfordwest SA69 9EJ
T: (01834) 812791
F: (01834) 811731
E: info@powells.co.uk
I: www.powells.co.uk

Craneham Court ★★★★
Contact: North Devon Holiday Homes, 19 Cross Street, Barnstaple EX31 1BD
T: (01271) 376322

BUCKLAND IN THE MOOR
Devon

Pine Lodge ★★★
Contact: Holiday Homes & Cottages South West, 365A Torquay Road, Paignton TQ3 2BT
T: (01803) 663650
F: (01803) 664037
E: holcotts@aol.com
I: www.swcottages.co.uk

BUCKLAND NEWTON
Dorset

Church Farm Stables ★★★★
Contact: Mr & Mrs Neville Archer, Church Farm Stables, Buckland Newton, Dorchester DT2 7BX
T: (01300) 345315
F: (01300) 345320
E: enquiries@staydorset.co.uk
I: www.staydorset.co.uk

Domineys Cottages ★★★★
Contact: Mrs J D Gueterbock, Domineys Cottages, Domineys Yard, Buckland Newton, Dorchester DT2 7BS
T: (01300) 345295
F: (01300) 345596
E: cottages@domineys.com
I: www.domineys.com

BUCKLAND ST MARY
Somerset

Hillside End Apartment ★★★★
Contact: Mr Roy Harkness, Hillside, Buckland St Mary, Chard TA20 3TQ
T: (01460) 234599
F: (01460) 234599
E: royandmarge@hillsidebsm.freeserve.co.uk
I: www.theaa.com/hotels/103591.html

Leveret Cottage ★★★
Contact: Mrs Suzie Float, Leveret Cottage, Hare House, Blackwater, Buckland St Mary, Chard TA20 3LE
T: (01460) 234638
E: info@leveretcottage.co.uk

BUDE
Cornwall

Atlantic View Bungalows ★★★
Contact: Mr & Mrs Chris & Brenda Raven, Atlantic View Bungalows, Marine Drive, Widemouth Bay, Bude EX23 0AG
T: (01288) 361716
E: enquiries@atlanticview.co.uk
I: www.atlanticview.co.uk

Brannel Cottage ★★★
Contact: Mrs Christine Parker, The Crescent, Crapstone, Yelverton PL20 7PS
T: (01822) 855614
E: hannafordpc@Aol.com

Broomhill Manor Country Estate★★★★-★★★★★
Contact: Mr C B Mower, Broomhill Manor Country Estate, Bude EX23 9HA
T: (01288) 352940
F: (01288) 356526
E: chris@broomhill-manor.demon.co.uk
I: www.broomhillmanor.co.uk

Can Cleave ★★★
Contact: Mr & Mrs C Tippett, Millook House, Mineshop Holiday Cottages, Bude EX23 0NR
T: (01840) 230338
F: (01840) 230103
E: tippett.mineshop@btinternet.com

Conna-Mara ★★★
Contact: Ms Tina Collins, Maer Down, Bude EX23 8NG
T: (01288) 356354
F: (01288) 356354
E: t.collins@v.net

Downlands ★★★
Contact: Mr Clive Bloy, Downlands, Maer Lane, Bude EX23 9EE
T: (01288) 356920
E: sonia@downlands.net
I: www.downlands.net

The Falcon Hotel ★★★
Contact: Mr & Mrs T Browning, The Falcon Hotel, Breakwater Road, Bude EX23 8SD
T: (01288) 352005
F: (01288) 356359
E: reception@falconhotel.com
I: www.falconhotel.com

Flat 16 Kiming ★★★
Contact: Mrs Chris Ellis, 10 Parkfield Road, Topsham, Exeter EX3 0DR
T: (01392) 873666

Forda Lodges ★★★★-★★★★★
Contact: Mr & Mrs J Chibbett, Forda Lodges, Kilkhampton, Bude EX23 9RZ
T: (01288) 321413
F: (01288) 321413
E: forda.lodges@virgin.net
I: www.fordalodges.co.uk

Glebe House Cottages ★★★★
Contact: Mr & Mrs James Varley, Glebe House Cottages Limited, Bridgerule, Holsworthy EX22 7EW
T: (01288) 381272
E: etc@glebehousecottages.co.uk
I: www.glebehousecottages.co.uk

Hersham Carpentry Annexe ★★★
Contact: Mrs D Tillinghast, Hersham Carpentry Annexe, Hersham Carpentry, Launcells, Bude EX23 9LZ
T: (01288) 321369
F: (01288) 321369
E: tillinghast@ndirect.co.uk

Hilton Farm Holiday Cottages ★★★-★★★★
Contact: Mr & Mrs Ian & Fiona Goodman, Hilton Farm Holiday Cottages, Hilton Road, Marhamchurch, Bude EX23 0HE
T: (01288) 361521
F: (01288) 361521
E: ian@hiltonfarmhouse.freeserve.co.uk
I: www.hiltonfarmhouse.co.uk

Houndapitt Farm Cottages ★★★
Contact: Mr Heard, Houndapitt Farm Cottages, Sandymouth Bay, Stibb, Bude, Bude EX23 9HW
T: (01288) 355455
E: info@houndapitt.co.uk
I: www.houndapitt.co.uk

Ivyleaf Barton Cottages Rating Applied For
Contact: Mr Robert Barrett, Ivyleaf Barton Cottages, Ivyleaf Hill, Stratton, Bude EX23 9LD
T: (01288) 321237
F: (01288) 321937
E: ivyleafbarton@hotmail.com

Karibu ★★
Contact: Mrs Anna Rutlidge, Karibu, 3 Downs View, Bude EX23 8RF
T: (01288) 356519

Kennacott Court ★★★★★
Contact: Mr & Mrs R H Davis, Kennacott Court, Widemouth Bay, Bude EX23 0ND
T: (01288) 362000
F: (01288) 361434
E: maureen@kennacottcourt.co.uk
I: www.kennacottcourt.co.uk

Langfield Manor ★★★
Contact: Mr Keith Freestone, Langfield Manor, Broadclose, Bude EX23 8DP
T: (01288) 352415
E: info@langfieldmanor.co.uk
I: www.langfieldmanor.co.uk

Little Orchard ★★★
Contact: Mrs Gosney, Little Orchard, Old Orchard, Lynstone, Bude EX23 0LR
T: (01288) 355617

Lower Northcott Farmhouse ★★★
Contact: Mrs Mary Trewin, Court Farm, Marhamchurch, Bude EX23 0EN
T: (01288) 361494
F: (01288) 361494
E: mary@courtfarm-holidays.co.uk

Manby ★★★
Contact: Mrs L Hoole, 54 Western Road, Oxford OX1 4LG
T: (01865) 245268
E: hoole@patrol.1-way.co.uk

Millook House ★★★
Contact: Mr & Mrs C Tippett, Millook House, Mineshop Holiday Cottages, Bude EX23 0NR
T: (01840) 230338
F: (01840) 230103
E: tippett.mineshop@btinternet.com

Mornish Holiday Apartments ★★★★
Contact: Mr & Mrs John & Julia Hilder, Mornish Holiday Apartments, 20 Summerleaze Crescent, Bude EX23 8HJ
T: (01288) 352972
F: (01288) 352972
E: johnhilder@classicfm.net
I: www.bude.co.uk/mornish-apartments

Old Lifeboat House ★★-★★★
Contact: Ms Bader, Lifeboat Flats, c/o Brendon Arms, Falcon Terrace, Bude EX23 8SD
T: (01288) 354542
F: (01288) 354542
E: enquiries@brendonarms.co.uk
I: www.brendonarms.co.uk

Penhalt Farm ★★★
Contact: Mr & Mrs D Marks
T: (01288) 361210
F: (01288) 361210
E: denandjennie@penhaltfarm.fsnet.co.uk
I: www.holidaybank.co.uk/penhaltfarm

Penrhyn ★★★
Contact: Mr Brett, Penrhyn, 1 Flexbury Avenue, Bude EX23 8RE
T: (01288) 355039

Rosecare Farm Cottages ★★★★-★★★★★
Contact: Mr & Mrs John & Gillian Stone, Rosecare Farm Cottages, Rosecare, St Gennys, Bude EX23 0BE
T: (01840) 230375
E: gilljohn@rosecare.freeserve.co.uk
I: www.cottageguide.co.uk/rosecare

St Annes ★★
Contact: Mr & Mrs Butler, 97 Great Tattenhams, Epsom KT18 5RB
T: (01737) 362117

St Annes Bungalow ★★★
Contact: Mrs Britten, 6 Woodside Avenue N, Green Lane, Coventry CV3 6BB
T: (02476) 692410

South Lynstone Barns ★★★
Contact: Mrs J Armstrong, East Lodge, Back Lane, Paddockhurst Road, Turners Hill, Crawley RH10 4SF
T: (01342) 716355
E: armstrongsydney@aol.co.uk

Stable Cottages ★★★
Contact: Ms K Gregory, 10 Pathfields, Bude EX23 8DW
T: (01288) 354237

Trevalgas Manor ★★★★
Contact: Mr & Mrs Richard & Anita Smith, Trevalgas Manor, Pughill, Bude EX23 9EX
T: (01288) 359777
E: accounts@exsel5.freeserve.co.uk

29 Valley Road ★★★
Contact: Ms Tania Gibbs, 83 Victoria Road, Bude EX23 8RH
T: (01288) 352613

Wild Pigeon Holidays ★★
Contact: Mrs Anne Longley, Wild Pigeon Holidays, 8 Breakwater Road, Bude EX23 8LQ
T: (01288) 353839

Woolstone Manor Farm ★★★★
Contact: Farm & Cottage Holidays, Victoria House, 12 Fore Street, Northam, Bideford EX39 1AW
T: (01237) 479146
F: (01237) 421512
E: enquiries@farmcott.co.uk

BUDLEIGH SALTERTON
Devon

Christophers ★★★★★
Contact: Mrs Barlow, 56 Fore Street, Otterton, Budleigh Salterton EX9 7HB
T: (01395) 567676
F: (01395) 567440
E: info@thethatchedcottagecompany.com
I: www.thethatchedcottagecompany.com

Lufflands ★★★★
Contact: Mr & Mrs Goode, Lufflands, Yettington, East Budleigh, Budleigh Salterton EX9 7BP
T: (01395) 568422
F: (01395) 568810
E: cottages@lufflands.co.uk
I: www.lufflands.co.uk

Pebbles ★★
Contact: Jean Bartlett Cottage Holidays, Fore Street, Beer, Seaton EX12 3JB
T: (01297) 23221
F: (01297) 23303
E: holidays@jeanbartlett.com
I: www.netbreaaks.com/jeanb

BUGLE
Cornwall

Higher Menadew ★★★★
Contact: Mr & Mrs Andrew & Anita Higman, Higher Menadew, Bugle, St Austell PL26 8QW
T: (01726) 850310
F: (01726) 850310
E: mail@stayingincornwall.com
I: www.stayingincornwall.com

BURLAWN
Cornwall

**The Old Chapel
Rating Applied For**
Contact: Mrs Angela Byrne, The Old Chapel, Burlawn, Wadebridge PL27 7LA
T: (01208) 812075
F: (01208) 815421

Wren Cottage ★★★
Contact: Ms Rosina Shepherd, Harbour Holidays - Rock, Trebetherick House, Trebetherick, Wadebridge PL27 6SB
T: (01208) 863399
F: (01208) 862218

BURNHAM-ON-SEA
Somerset

Glenlora ★★
Contact: Mrs S Street, Glenlora, 44 Cross Street, Burnham-on-Sea TA8 1PF
T: (01278) 786877

Hurn Farm ★★★
Contact: Mrs Holdom, Hurn Farm, Hurn Lane, Berrow, Brean, Burnham-on-Sea TA8 2QT
T: (01278) 751418
E: hurnfarm@hurnfarmcottages.co.uk
I: www.hurnfarmcottages.co.uk

**Kingsway Road
Rating Applied For**
Contact: Miss Andrea Morris, 33 Kilmorie Road, London SE23 2SS
T: (020) 8699 1000
F: (020) 8699 1022

Prospect Farm ★★★-★★★★
Contact: Mrs Gillian Wall, Prospect Farm, Strowlands, East Brent, Highbridge TA9 4JH
T: (01278) 760507

Stable Cottage & Coach House ★★★-★★★★
Contact: Mr & Mrs Bigwood, Brean Farm, Brean Down, Burnham-on-Sea TA8 2RR
T: (01278) 751055
F: (01278) 751055

Stoddens Farm Holiday Cottages ★★★
Contact: Mrs Sandra Tipling, Stoddens Farm, Stoddens Road, Burnham-on-Sea TA8 2DE
T: (01278) 782505
F: (01278) 792221
E: stoddens-cottage@btconnect.com

BURROWBRIDGE
Somerset

Hillview ★★★
Contact: Mrs Rosalind Griffiths, Hillview, Stanmoor Road, Burrowbridge, Bridgwater TA7 0RX
T: (01823) 698308
F: (01823) 698308

BURSTOCK
Dorset

Whetham Farm, The Flat★★
Contact: Mrs Curtis, Whetham Farm The Flat, Burstock, Beaminster DT8 3LH
T: (01308) 868293

BURTON BRADSTOCK
Dorset

Apple Tree Cottage ★★★
Contact: Dream Cottages, 41 Maiden Street, Weymouth DT4 8AZ
T: (01305) 761347
F: (01305) 789000

Berwick House ★★★★
Contact: Mr Zachary Stuart-Brown, Dream Cottages, 41 Maiden Street, Weymouth DT4 8AZ
T: (01305) 761347
E: admin@dream-cottages.co.uk
I: www.dream-cottages.co.uk

Bramble Cottage ★★★
Contact: Mr Zachary Stuart-Brown, Dream Cottages, 41 Maiden Street, Weymouth DT4 8AZ
T: (01305) 761347
E: admin@dream-cottages.co.uk
I: www.dream-cottages.co.uk

Bryer Lea ★★★
Contact: Mr Zachary Stuart-Brown, Dream Cottages, 41 Maiden Street, Weymouth DT4 8AZ
T: (01305) 761347
E: admin@dream-cottages.co.uk
I: www.dream-cottages.co.uk

Cliff Farm ★★★
Contact: Mr Zachary Stuart-Brown, Dream Cottages, 41 Maiden Street, Weymouth DT4 8AZ
T: (01305) 761347
E: admin@dream-cottages.co.uk
I: www.dream-cottages.co.uk

The Doves ★★★
Contact: Mr Zachary Stuart-Brown, Dream Cottages, 41 Maiden Street, Weymouth DT4 8AZ
T: (01305) 761347
E: admin@dream-cottages.co.uk
I: www.dream-cottages.co.uk

Graston Farm Cottage ★★★
Contact: Mrs S J Bailey, Graston Farm Cottage, Annings Lane, Burton Bradstock, Bridport DT6 4NG
T: (01308) 897603
F: (01308) 897016
E: graston@ukgateway.net

Hillview Bungalow ★★★
Contact: Mr Zachary Stuart-Brown, Dream Cottages, 41 Maiden Street, Weymouth DT4 8AZ
T: (01305) 761347
E: admin@dream-cottages.co.uk
I: www.dream-cottages.co.uk

Jasmine Cottage ★★★
Contact: Mr Zachary Stuart-Brown, Dream Cottages, 41 Maiden Street, Weymouth DT4 8AZ
T: (01305) 761347
E: admin@dream-cottages.co.uk
I: www.dream-cottages.co.uk

Little Berwick ★★★
Contact: Mr Zachary Stuart-Brown, Dream Cottages, 41 Maiden Street, Weymouth DT4 8AZ
T: (01305) 761347
E: admin@dream-cottages.co.uk
I: www.dream-cottages.co.uk

Pebble Beach Lodge ★★★
Contact: Mrs Jan Hemingway, Pebble Beach Lodge, Burton Bradstock, Bridport DT6 4RJ
T: (01308) 897428
I: www.burtonbradstock.org.uk

Smugglers Cottage ★★★★
Contact: Dream Cottages, 41 Maiden Street, Weymouth DT4 8AZ
T: (01305) 761347
F: (01305) 789000

BUTCOMBE
North Somerset

Butcombe Farm ★★★
Contact: Ms Sandra Moss, Butcombe Farm, Aldwick Lane, Butcombe, Bristol BS40 7UW
T: (01761) 462380
F: (01761) 462300
E: info@butcombe-farm.demon.co.uk
I: www.butcombe-farm.demon.co.uk

BUTLEIGH WOOTTON
Somerset

Little Broadway ★★
Contact: Mrs Mary Butt, Proprietor, Broadway Farm, Butleigh Wootton, Glastonbury BA6 8TX
T: (01458) 442824
F: (01458) 442824

CADGWITH
Cornwall

Pennard ★★★
Contact: Mr Martin Raftery, Mullion Cottages, Churchtown, Mullion, Helston TR12 7HQ
T: (01326) 240315
F: (01326) 241090
E: martin@mullioncottages.com
I: www.mullioncottages.com

CALLINGTON
Cornwall

Cadson Manor Farm ★★★★
Contact: Mrs Brenda Crago, Cadson Manor Farm, Callington PL17 7HW
T: (01579) 383969
F: (01579) 383969
E: brenda.crago@btclick.com
I: www.chycor.co.uk/cottages/cadson-manor

CAMELFORD
Cornwall

Juliots Well Holiday Park Rating Applied For
Contact: Mrs Kim Boundy, Camelford PL32 9RF
T: (01840) 213302
F: (01840) 212700
E: juliotswell@holidaysincornwall.net

Lane End Farm Bungalow ★★★
Contact: Mr Keith Vasey, Victoria Road, Camelford PL32 9XB
T: (01840) 212452
F: (01840) 212452
E: keith@laneend47.fsnet.co.uk

Rose Cottage ★★
Contact: Ms Melanie Blake, 27 Anthony Road, Woodside, London SE25 5HA
T: (020) 8656 7842
F: (020) 8656 7842
E: mblake@mars-letts.com
I: www.cosycornwall.com

Vilnius ★★★
Contact: CH Ref: 66068, Holiday Cottages Group Owner Services Dept, Spring Mill, Earby, Barnoldswick BB18 6RN
T: 08700 723723
F: (01282) 844288
E: sales@holidaycottagesgroup.com
I: www.country-holidays.co.uk

CANNINGTON
Somerset

The Courtyard ★★★★
Contact: Mrs Dyer, Blackmore Lane, Cannington, Bridgwater TA5 2NE
T: (01278) 653442
F: (01278) 653427
E: dyerfarm@aol.com
I: www.dyerfarm.co.uk

CAPE CORNWALL
Cornwall

Nanpean Barn Holiday Flats ★★★
Contact: Mrs Turvil, Nanpean Barn Holiday Flats, Cape Cornwall, St Just, Penzance TR19 7NL
T: (01736) 788731
F: (01736) 788731
E: jt@cametech.freeserve.co.uk

CARBIS BAY
Cornwall

Laity Vean Cottage ★★★★
Contact: Ms Suzanne Belton, Long Barn, Yattendon Road, Hermitage, Newbury RG18 9RQ
T: (01635) 200316

Rotorua Apartments ★★★★
Contact: Mrs Linda Roach, Rotorua Apartments, Trencrom Lane, Carbis Bay, St Ives TR26 2TD
T: (01736) 795419
F: (01736) 795419
E: rotorua@btconnect.com
I: www.stivesapartments.com

Topaz & Azure ★★★★
Contact: Powells Cottage Holidays, Springmill, Earby, Freystrop, Haverfordwest BB94 0AA
T: 0870 514 3076
F: (01834) 811731
E: info@powells.co.uk
I: www.powells.co.uk

CARDINHAM
Cornwall

Muckle Byre Cottage ★★★
Contact: Mr & Mrs Steve & Viv Clemens, Muckle Byre Cottage, Muckle Byre, Welltown, Cardinham, Bodmin PL30 4EG
T: (01208) 821477
E: stevclem@aol.com

CARGREEN
Cornwall

Pilgrim Cottage ★★★★
Contact: Mr Paul Rippon, Pilgrim Cottage, Fore Street, Cargreen, Saltash PL12 6PA
T: (01752) 842727
E: pilgrim@cargreencornwall.co.uk

CARHARRACK
Cornwall

Old Alma Stores Bosuns Locker Holiday Flat★★★
Contact: Mr & Mrs M L Holmes, Old Alma Stores, Alma Terrace, Carharrack, Redruth TR16 5RT
T: (01209) 820417

CASTLE CARY
Somerset

The Ancient Barn, The Old Stables and The Weaver's Cottage★★★★
Contact: Ms Anthea Peppin, The Ancient Barn, The Old Stables, and The Weaver's Cottage, Lower Cockhill Farm, Castle Cary BA7 7NZ
T: (01963) 351288
F: (01963) 351288
E: bookings@medievalbarn.co.uk
I: www.medievalbarn.co.uk

Clanville Manor Tallet ★★★★
Contact: Mrs Snook, Clanville Manor Tallet, Clanville Manor, Clanville, Castle Cary BA7 7PJ
T: (01963) 350124
F: (01963) 350719
E: info@clanvillemanor.co.uk
I: www.clanvillemanor.co.uk

Orchard Farm Cottages ★★★
Contact: Mr & Mrs R D Boyer, Orchard Farm, Cockhill, Castle Cary BA7 7NY
T: (01963) 350418
F: (01963) 350418
E: boyer@talk21.com
I: www.leisurehuntcom

CATTISTOCK
Dorset

4 The Rocks ★★★★
Contact: Mrs Ann Stockwell, The Old Vicarage, Yarcombe, Honiton EX14 9BD
T: (01404) 861594
F: (01404) 861594
E: jonannstockwell@aol.com
I: www.members.aol.com/jonannstockwell/

Upshalls ★★★
Contact: Mr J G Walmsley, Castle Hill Cottage, Duck Street, Cattistock, Dorchester DT2 0JH
T: (01300) 320550
F: (01300) 320550

CAUNDLE MARSH
Dorset

Marsh Court Home Farm ★★
Contact: Ms Heidi Harris, 7 Roselyn Crescent, Alweston, Sherborne DT9 5HX
T: (01963) 23769

CERNE ABBAS
Dorset

Old Gaol Cottage ★★★★★
Contact: Ms Nicky Willis, 10 Dorchester Road, Dorchester DT2 9NU
T: (01300) 341659
F: (01300) 341699
E: nickywillis@tesco.net

CHAGFORD
Devon

Hunters Moon ★★★★
Contact: Dr & Mrs David Spear, Hunters Moon, Manor Road, Chagford, Newton Abbot TQ13 8AW
T: (01647) 433323
E: woof@mail.eclipse.co.uk

Springfield Cottage ★★★★
Contact: Helpful Holidays, Mill Street, Chagford, Newton Abbot TQ13 8AW
T: (01647) 433593
F: (01647) 433694
E: help@helpfulholidays.com

Yelfords ★★★★★
Contact: Mrs Ghislaine Caine, Helpful Holidays, Chagford, Newton Abbot TQ13 8ES
T: (01647) 432856

CHALLACOMBE
Devon

Home Place Farm Cottages ★★★
Contact: Mr Mark Ravenscroft, Home Place Farm Cottages, Challacombe, Barnstaple EX31 4TS
T: (01598) 763283
F: (01598) 763283
E: mark@holidayexmoor.co.uk
I: www.holidayexmoor.co.uk

Town Tenement ★★★
Contact: Mr & Mrs S M Yendell, Town Tenement, Challacombe, Barnstaple EX31 4TS
T: (01598) 763320
E: david@yendell0.fsnet.co.uk

Whitefield Barton ★★★
Contact: Mrs Rosemarie Kingdon, Whitefield Barton, Challacombe, Barnstaple EX31 4TU
T: (01598) 763271
I: www.exmoorholidays.co.uk

2 Yelland Cottages ★★★
Contact: Mrs M J Kingdon, West Whitefield, Challacombe, Barnstaple EX31 4TU
T: (01598) 763433

CHAPEL AMBLE
Cornwall

Ambledown Cottage ★★★★★
Contact: Bookings and Enquiries, English Country Cottages, Stoney Bank, Earby, Barnoldswick BB94 0AA
T: 0870 585 1155
F: 0870 585 1150

Carclaze Cottages ★★★★
Contact: Mrs J Nicholls, Carclaze Cottages, Chapel Amble, Wadebridge PL27 6EP
T: (01208) 813886
E: enquire@carclaze.dabsol.co.uk
I: www.carclaze.co.uk

Coombe Mill ★★★
Contact: Harbour Holidays - Rock, Trebetherick House, Polzeath, Wadebridge PL27 6SB
T: (01208) 863399
F: (01208) 862218

Down Below ★★★
Contact: Mrs V Davey, Carns Farm, Chapel Amble, Wadebridge PL27 6ER
T: (01208) 880398

Homeleigh Farm ★★★★
Contact: Mrs A J Rees, Homeleigh Farm, Chapel Amble, Wadebridge PL27 6EU
T: (01208) 812411
F: (01208) 815025
E: homeleigh@eclipse.co.uk
I: www.eclipse.co.uk/homeleigh

The Olde House ★★★
Contact: Mr & Mrs A Hawkey, The Olde House, Chapel Amble, Wadebridge PL27 6EN
T: (01208) 813219
F: (01208) 815689
E: info@theoldehouse.co.uk
I: www.theoldehouse.co.uk

Rooke Country Cottages ★★★★★
Contact: Mrs Gill Reskelly, Rooke Country Cottages, Rooke Farm, Chapel Amble, Wadebridge PL27 6ES
T: (01208) 880368
F: (01208) 880600
E: info@rookecottages.com
I: www.rookecottages.com

Rooke Mill ★★★★
Contact: Mrs Diana Bullivant, Diana Bullivant Holidays, Trebell Green, Lanivet, Bodmin PL30 5HR
T: (01208) 831336
F: (01208) 831336
E: diana@dbullivant.fsnet.co.uk
I: www.cornwall-online.co.uk/diana-bullivant

CHARD
Somerset

Yew Tree Cottage ★★★★
Contact: Mr & Mrs Phillip & Viv Hopkins, Yew Tree Cottage, Hornsbury Hill, Chard TA20 3DB
T: (01460) 64735
F: (01460) 68029
E: ytcottage@aol.com
I: www.yewtreecottage.org.uk

CHARDSTOCK
Devon

Barn Owls Cottage ★★★★
Contact: Mrs Jean Hafner, Barn Owls Cottage, Chardstock, Axminster EX13 7BY
T: (01460) 220475
F: (01460) 220475
E: Jean.hafnet@BTinternet.com

Cherryhazel
Rating Applied For
Contact: Milkbere Holidays, 3 Fore Street, Seaton EX12 2LE
T: (01297) 20729
E: info@milkberehols.com

CHARLTON MUSGROVE
Somerset

Pigsty, Cowstall & Bullpen Cottages ★★★
Contact: Mrs B C Chilcott, Pigsty, Cowstall & Bullpen Cottages, Barrow Lane Farm, Charlton Musgrove, Wincanton BA9 8HJ
T: (01963) 33217
F: (01963) 31449
E: chrischilcott@farmersweekly.net

CHARMOUTH
Dorset

Beachcomber ★★★★
Contact: Mr Zachary Stuart-Brown, Dream Cottages, 41 Maiden Street, Weymouth DT4 8AZ
T: (01305) 761347
E: admin@dream-cottages.co.uk
I: www.dream-cottages.co.uk

Befferlands Farm ★★★★★
Contact: Mr & Mrs Andrews, Befferlands Farm, Charmouth, Bridport DT6 6RD
T: (01297) 560203
E: befferlands@netscape.net

Charleston Holiday Cottages ★★★
Contact: Mrs Kim Wood, Grosvenor Cottage, The Street, Charmouth, Bridport DT6

The Coach House ★★★
Contact: Ms Kate Bartlett, Jean Bartlett Cottage Holidays, The Old Dairy, Fore Street, Seaton EX12 3JB
T: (01297) 23221
F: (01297) 23303
E: jeanb@netbreaks.com
I: www.netbreaks.com/jeamb

23 Fernhill Heights ★★★★
Contact: Mrs A Webb, Uplands Cottages, Shipham Lane, Winscombe BS25 1PX
T: (01934) 842257

Little Catherston Farm ★★-★★★
Contact: Mrs R J White, Little Catherston Farm, Charmouth, Wootton Fitzpaine, Bridport DT6 6LZ
T: (01297) 560550

Manor Farm Holiday Centre ★★
Contact: Mr Robin Loosmore, Manor Farm Holiday Centre, The Street, Charmouth, Bridport DT6 6QL
T: (01297) 560226
E: enq@manorfarmholidaycentre.co.uk
I: www.manorfarmholidaycentre.co.uk

Nookies ★★★★
Contact: Ms Kate Bartlett, Jean Bartlett Cottage Holidays, Fore Street, Seaton EX12 3JB
T: (01297) 23221
F: (01297) 23303
E: holidays@jeanbartlett.com
I: www.netbreaks.com/jeanb

The Poplars ★★★
Contact: Mrs Jane Pointing, Wood Farm Caravan and Camping Park, Axminster Road, Charmouth, Bridport DT6 6BT
T: (01297) 560697
F: (01297) 561243
E: holiday@woodfarm.co.uk
I: www.woodfarm.co.uk

Shadows ★★★
Contact: I Ward, Lower Sea Lane, Charmouth, Bridport DT6 6LW
T: (01297) 489609
F: (01297) 489609

CHEDDAR
Somerset

Applebee(formerly South)Barn Cottage★
Contact: Mrs Richardson, South Barn Cottage, The Hayes, Cheddar Gorge, Cheddar BS27 3AN
T: (01934) 743146
F: (01934) 743146

Cheddar Lodge ★★★
Contact: Mr Jon Rawlings, Cheddar Lodge, Draycott Road, Cheddar BS27 3RP
T: (01934) 743859
F: (01934) 741550
E: jon@1rawlings.freeserve.co.uk
I: www.cheddarlodge.pwp.blueyonder.co.uk

Home Farm Cottages
Rating Applied For
Contact: Mr C Sanders, Home Farm Cottages, Home Farm, Barton, Winscombe, Cheddar BS25 1DX
T: (01934) 842078
F: (01934) 842500
E: mail@homefarmcottages.com
I: www.homefarmcottages.com

Millyard Cottage ★★★★
Contact: Mr Stuart Fisher, Millhaven, Stoke Street, Rodney Stoke, Cheddar BS27 3UP
T: (01749) 870704
E: stuartfisher2@aol.com
I: www.stuarts-holidays.bc1.net

Orchard Court & Bungalow ★★★★
Contact: Mrs Carol Roberts, Orchard Lodge, Tweentown, Cheddar BS27 3HY
T: (01934) 742116

Spring Cottages ★★★★
Contact: Mrs Jennifer Buckland, Spring Cottages, Venns Gate, Cheddar BS27 3LW
T: (01934) 742493
F: (01934) 742493
E: buckland@springcottages.co.uk
I: www.springcottages.co.uk

Sungate Holiday Apartments ★★★
Contact: Mrs M M Fieldhouse, Pyrenmount, Parsons Way, Winscombe BS25 1BU
T: (01934) 842273
F: (01934) 844994
I: sunholapartment@aol.com

Uplands Cottages ★★★
Contact: Mrs A Webb, Uplands Cottages, Shipham Lane, Winscombe BS25 1PX
T: (01934) 842257

CHEDZOY
Somerset

Nelson Cottage ★★★★
Contact: Mr & Mrs Robbins, Nelson Lodge, Chedzoy Lane, Chedzoy, Bridgwater TA7 8QR
T: (01278) 453492
E: robbinsm@bridgwater.ac.uk

CHELSTON
Devon

Chelston Hall Holiday Apartments ★★★
Contact: Mr & Mrs Peter & Shirley Archer-Moy, Chelston Hall Holiday Apartments, Old Mill Road, Chelston, Torquay TQ2 6HW
T: (01803) 605520

CHEW MAGNA
Bath and North East Somerset

Chew Hill Farm ★★★
Contact: Mrs S Lyons, Chew Hill Farm, Chew Magna, Bristol BS40 8QP
T: (01275) 332496
F: (01275) 332496

Woodbarn Farm Cottages ★★★-★★★★
Contact: Mrs Judi Hasell, Woodbarn Farm, Denny Lane, Chew Magna, Bristol BS40 8SZ
T: (01275) 332599
F: (01275) 332599
E: woodbarnfarm@hotmail.com

CHICKERELL
Dorset

Pastures Green ★★★★
Contact: Mr Zachary Stuart-Brown, Dream Cottages, 41 Maiden Street, Weymouth DT4 8AZ
T: (01305) 761347
E: admin@dream-cottages.co.uk
I: www.dream-cottages.co.uk

Tidmoor Stables ★★★★
Contact: Mr & Mrs Townsend/ Wills, Tidmoor Stables, 431 Chickerell Road, Chickerell, Weymouth DT3 4DG
T: (01305) 787867
E: sarah@tidmoorstables.co.uk
I: www.tidmoorstables.co.uk

CHIDEOCK
Dorset

Chideock Coachhouse ★★★★
Contact: Mr Zachary Stuart-Brown, Dream Cottages, 41 Maiden Street, Weymouth DT4 8AZ
T: (01305) 761347
E: admin@dream-cottages.co.uk
I: www.dream-cottages.co.uk

Guard House Cottage ★★★★
Contact: Mrs Joyce Whittaker, Seatown House, Seatown, Chideock, Bridport DT6 6JU
T: (01297) 489417
F: (01297) 489151
E: info@guardhouse.co.uk
I: www.guardhouse.co.uk

CHILCOMBE
Dorset

Cherry Tree Cottage & Willow Tree Cottage★★★
Contact: Mr Zachary Stuart-Brown, Dream Cottages, 41 Maiden Street, Weymouth DT4 8AZ
T: (01305) 761347
E: admin@dream-cottages.co.uk
I: www.dream-cottages.co.uk

CHILLINGTON
Devon

Friends Cottage ★★★
Contact: Powell's Cottage Holidays, High Street, Freystrop, Haverfordwest SA69 9EJ
T: (01834) 812791
F: (01834) 811731
E: info@powells.co.uk
I: www.powells.co.uk

CHILTON TRINITY
Somerset

Chilton Farm ★★★★
Contact: Farm & Cottage Holidays, Victoria House, 12 Fore Street, Westward Ho!, Bideford EX39 1AW
T: (01237) 479146
F: (01237) 421512
E: enquiries@farmcott.co.uk

CHIPPENHAM
Wiltshire

Nut Tree Cottage ★★★
Contact: Mrs Margaret Payne, Nut Tree Cottage, Longdean, Yatton Keynell, Chippenham SN14 7EX
T: (01249) 782354

Roward Farm ★★★★
Contact: Mr David Humphrey, Roward Farm, Draycot Cerne, Chippenham SN15 4SG
T: (01249) 758147
F: (01249) 758149
E: d.humphrey@roward.demon.co.uk
I: www.roward.demon.co.uk

Swallow Cottage ★★★★
Contact: Mrs Suzanne Candy, Olivemead Farm, Olivemead Lane, Dauntsey, Chippenham SN15 4JQ
T: (01666) 510205
F: (01666) 510205
E: olivemead@farmholidays@tesco.net
I: www.olivemead.farmholidays.com

CHIPPING SODBURY
South Gloucestershire

Tan House Farm Cottage ★★★
Contact: Mrs C E James, Tan House Farm Cottage, Tan House Farm, Yate, Bristol BS37 7QL
T: (01454) 228280
F: (01454) 228777

CHITTLEHAMHOLT
Devon

Simmons Farm Cottage ★★★
Contact: Marsden's Cottage Holidays, 2 The Square, Braunton EX33 2JB
T: (01271) 813777
F: (01271) 813664
E: holidays@marsdens.co.uk
I: www.marsdens.co.uk

Treetops ★★★★
Contact: Marsden's Cottage Holidays, 2 The Square, Braunton EX33 2JB
T: (01271) 813777
F: (01271) 813664
E: holidays@marsdens.co.uk
I: www.marsdens.co.uk

CHUDLEIGH
Devon

Coombeshead Farm ★★★
Contact: Mr & Mrs R Smith, Coombeshead Farm, Coombeshead Cross, Chudleigh, Newton Abbot TQ13 0NQ
T: (01626) 853334
E: anne-coombeshead@supanet.com

Farmborough House ★★★★
Contact: Mrs Deirdre Aldridge, Farmborough House, Old Exeter Road, Chudleigh, Moretonhampstead, Newton Abbot TQ13 0DR
T: (01626) 853258
F: (01626) 853258
E: holidays@farmborough-house.com
I: www.farmborough-house.com

Silver Cottage ★★★
Contact: Mr E J Gardner, 75 Old Exeter Street, Chudleigh, Newton Abbot TQ13 0JX
T: (01626) 854571
F: (01626) 854571
E: ejgardner@care4free.net

CHULMLEIGH
Devon

Bealy Court Holiday Cottages ★★★★
Contact: Mr & Mrs Richard & Jane Lea
T: (01769) 580312
F: (01769) 508986
E: bealycourt@msn.com
I: www.bealycourt.co.uk

Bridleway Cottages ★★★
Contact: Mrs Fiona Lincoln-Gordon, Bridleway Cottages, Golland Farm, Golland Lane, Burrington, Umberleigh EX37 9JP
T: (01769) 520263
F: (01769) 520263
E: golland@btinternet.com
I: www.golland.btinternet.co.uk

Deer Cott ★★★★
Contact: Mr & Mrs George & Mary Simpson, Deer Cott, Middle Garland, Chulmleigh EX18 7DU
T: (01769) 581318
F: (01769) 580461
E: enquiries@deercott.co.uk
I: www.deercott.co.uk

Wembworthy Down ★★★
Contact: CH Ref:6188,11495,15181, Holiday Cottages Group Owner Services Dept, Spring Mill, Earby, Barnoldswick BB94 0AA
T: 08700 723723
F: (01282) 844288
E: sales@holidaycottagesgroup.com
I: www.country-holidays.co.uk

CHURCHINFORD
Somerset

Mow Barton ★★★★
Contact: Ms Louise Hayman, Milkbere Cottage Holidays, 3 Fore Street, Seaton EX12 2LE
T: (01297) 20729
F: (01297) 22925
E: info@milkberehols.com

Royston Cottage ★★★★
Contact: Farm & Cottage Holidays, Victoria House, 12 Fore Street, Northam, Bideford EX39 1AW
T: (01237) 479146
F: (01237) 421512
E: enquiries@farmcott.co.uk

South Cleeve Bungalow ★★★★
Contact: Mrs V D Manning, Holiday Cottages Group Owner Services Dept, Churchinford, Taunton TA3 7PR
T: (01823) 601378
I: www.country-holidays.co.uk

CLAWTON
Devon

The Coach House ★★★
Contact: Mrs Pix, The Old Vicarage Coach House, The Old Vicarage, Clawton, Holsworthy EX22 6PS
T: (01409) 271100
E: enquiries@oldvicarageclawton.co.uk
I: www.oldvicarageclawton.co.uk

CLIFTON
Bristol

Lansdown Serviced Apartments ★★★★
Contact: Ms Whife, Lansdown Serviced Apartments, 8 Lansdown Place, Clifton, Bristol BS8 3AE
T: (0117) 974 1414

COCKINGTON
Devon

Spyglass ★★★
Contact: Mr Ian Butterworth, Holiday Homes & Cottages South West, 365A Torquay Road, Paignton TQ3 2BT
T: (01803) 663650
F: (01803) 664037
E: holcotts@aol.com
I: www.swcottages.co.uk

COLERNE
Wiltshire

Thickwood House (Garden Cottages) ★★★
Contact: Mr Colin Agombar, Thickwood House, Thickwood Lane, Colerne, Chippenham SN14 8BN
T: (01225) 744377
F: (01225) 742329

COLYFORD
Devon

Chequers ★★★
Contact: Milkbere Holidays, 3 Fore Street, Seaton EX12 2LE
T: (01297) 20729
F: (01297) 22925
E: info@milkberehols.com
I: www.milkbere.com

Riverside ★★★★
Contact: Ms Louise Hayman, Milkbere Cottage Holidays Ltd, 3 Fore Street, Seaton EX12 2LE
T: (01297) 20729
F: (01297) 24831
E: info@milkberehols.com
I: www.milkbere.com

Whitwell Farm Cottages ★★★★★
Contact: Mr Mike Williams, Whitwell Farm Cottages, Colyford, Colyton EX24 6HS
T: 0800 090 2419
F: (01297) 552911
E: 100755.66@compuserve.com
I: www.a5star.co.uk

COLYTON
Devon

Berry House ★★★-★★★★
Contact: Ms Kate Bartlett, Jean Bartlett Cottage Holidays, The Old Dairy, Fore Street, Seaton EX12 3JB
T: (01297) 23221
F: (01297) 23303
E: holidays@jeanbartlett.com
I: www.netbreaks.com/jeamb

Bonehayne Farm Cottage ★★★
Contact: Sandra & Ruth Gould, Bonehayne Farm Cottage, Bonehayne Farm, Colyton EX24 6SG
T: (01404) 87396
E: gould@bonehayne.co.uk
I: www.members.netscapeonline.co.uk/thisfarm33

Coles House ★★★★
Contact: Jean Bartlett Cottage Holidays, Fore Street, Seaton EX12 3JB
T: (01297) 23221
F: (01297) 23303
E: holidays@jeanbartlett.com
I: www.netbreaks.com/jeanb

Colycroft ★★
Contact: Jean Bartlett Cottage Holidays, Fore Street, Seaton EX12 3JB
T: (01297) 23221
F: (01297) 23303
E: holidays@jeanbartlett.com
I: www.netbreaks.com/jeanb

65 Govers Meadow ★★★
Contact: Jean Bartlett Cottage Holidays, Fore Street, Seaton EX12 3JB
T: (01297) 23221
F: (01297) 23303
E: holidays@jeanbartlett.com
I: www.netbreaks.com/jeanb

Hill End Bungalow ★★★★
Contact: Fore Street, Seaton EX12 3JB
T: (01297) 23221

Lovehayne Farm Cottages ★★★★
Contact: Mrs Philippa Bignell, Lovehayne Farm, Southleigh, Colyton EX24 6JE
T: (01404) 871216
F: (01404) 871216
E: cottages@fairway.globalnet.co.uk
I: www.lovehayne.co.uk

Malt House ★★★
Contact: Milkbere Holidays, 3 Fore Street, Seaton EX12 2LE
T: (01297) 20729
F: (01297) 22925
E: info@milkberehols.com
I: www.milkbere.com

Millstream ★★★
Contact: Ms Kate Bartlett, Jean Bartlett Cottage Holidays, The Old Dairy, Fore Street, Seaton EX12 3JB
T: (01297) 23221
F: (01297) 23303
E: holidays@jeanbartlett.com
I: www.netbreaks.com/jeamb

Smallicombe Farm ★★★★
Contact: Mrs M A Todd
T: (01404) 831310
F: (01404) 831431
E: maggie_todd@yahoo.com
I: www.smallicombe.com
♿

Southcot ★★★★
Contact: Ms Kate Bartlett, Jean Bartlett Cottage Holidays, The Old Dairy, Fore Street, Seaton EX12 3JB
T: (01297) 23221
F: (01297) 23303
E: holidays@jeanbartlett.com
I: www.netbreaks.com/jeamb

Sunnyside ★★★★
Contact: Jean Bartlett Cottage Holidays, Fore Street, Seaton EX12 3JB
T: (01297) 23221
F: (01297) 23303
E: holidays@jeanbartlett.com
I: www.netbreaks.com/jeanb

Valley View ★★★
Contact: Jean Bartlett Cottage Holidays, Fore Street, Seaton EX12 3JB
T: (01297) 23221
F: (01297) 23303
E: holidays@jeanbartlett.com
I: www.netbreaks.com/jeanb

Waterloo Cottage ★★★
Contact: Ms Kate Bartlett, Jean Bartlett Cottage Holidays, The Old Dairy, Fore Street, Seaton EX12 3JB
T: (01297) 23221
F: (01297) 23303
E: holidays@jeanbartlett.com
I: www.netbreaks.com/jeamb

COMBE DOWN
Bath and North East Somerset

Kingham Cottage ★★★★
Contact: Mr & Mrs Peter & Christine Davis, Kingham Cottage, Summer Lane, Combe Down, Bath BA2 7EU
T: (01225) 837909
F: (01225) 837909
E: kinghamcottage@aol.com
I: www.kingham-cottage.co.uk

COMBE MARTIN
Devon

Beech & Ash Cottages ★★★★
Contact: Marsden's Cottage Holidays, 2 The Square, Braunton EX33 2JB
T: (01271) 813777
F: (01271) 813664
E: holidays@marsdens.co.uk
I: www.marsdens.co.uk

Bosun's Cottage ★★★
Contact: Mr & Mrs Martin and Margaret Wolverson, Primespot Character Cottages, c/o Stag Cottage, Holdstone Down, Combe Martin, Ilfracombe EX34 0PF
T: (01271) 882449

Callemonda ★★★★
Contact: 2 The Square, Braunton EX33 2JB
T: (01271) 813777
F: (01271) 813664
E: holidays@marsdens.co.uk
I: www.marsdens.co.uk

Coulscott ★★★★-★★★★★
Contact: Ms Trish Twigger, Coulscott, Nutcombe Hill, Combe Martin, Ilfracombe EX34 0PQ
T: (01271) 883339
E: stay@coulscott.co.uk
I: www.coulscott.co.uk

Ebrington Holiday Cottage ★★★
Contact: Mrs Irwin, Glen Lyn, Borough Road, Combe Martin, Ilfracombe EX34 0AN
T: (01271) 882292
F: (01271) 882391
E: mail@ebringtoncottage.co.uk

Jewells Holiday Villas ★★★★★
Contact: Ms Katie Jewell, 37 - 39 King Street, Mortimer Common, Mortimer West End, Reading RG7 3RS
T: (01189) 333935
F: (01189) 332737
E: katie-kewell@talk21.com

Pretoria ★★★★
Contact: Mrs Heather Trueman, 6 Crossmead, Lynton EX35 6DG
T: (01598) 753517
E: JanolHtrueman@aol.com

1 Stattens Cottages ★★★
Contact: Mrs Peggy Crees, 47 Kingcup Drive, Bisley, West End, Woking GU24 9HH
T: (01483) 488790
F: (01932) 562638
E: peggy.crees@virgin.net
I: www.romseyassoc.com/holidayhomes

Wheel Farm Country Cottages ★★★★
Contact: Mr & Mrs John Robertson, Wheel Farm Country Cottages, Berry Down, Combe Martin, Ilfracombe EX34 0NT
T: (01271) 882100
F: (01271) 883120
E: holidays@wheelfarmcottages.co.uk
I: wheelfarmcottages.co.uk

Wood Sorrell ★★★
Contact: Marsden's Cottage Holidays, 2 The Square, Braunton EX33 2JB
T: (01271) 813777
F: (01271) 813664
E: holidays@marsdens.co.uk
I: www.marsdens.co.uk

Yetland Farm Cottages ★★★★
Contact: Mrs C Gillio, Yetland Farm Cottages, Yetland Farm Holiday Cottages, Berry Down, Combe Martin, Ilfracombe EX34 0NT
T: (01271) 883655
F: (01271) 883655
E: enquiries@yetlandcottages.co.uk
I: www.yetlandcottages.co.uk

COMBEINTEIGNHEAD
Devon

The Old Bakery ★★
Contact: Holiday Homes & Cottages South West, 365A Torquay Road, Paignton TQ3 2BT
T: (01803) 663650
F: (01803) 664037
E: holcotts@aol.com
I: www.swcottages.co.uk

THORN COTTAGE ★★★
Contact: Mr Ian Butterworth, 365A Torquay Road, Paignton TQ3 2BT
T: (01803) 663650
F: (01803) 664037
E: holcotts@aol.com
I: www.swcottages.co.uk

COMPTON DUNDON
Somerset

Castlebrook Holiday Cottages ★★★
Contact: Mr & Mrs Smith, Castlebrook Holiday Cottages, Castlebrook, Compton Dundon, Somerton TA11 6PR
T: (01458) 841680
F: (01458) 441680

Wisteria Cottage ★★★★
Contact: Mrs Georgina Baston, The Old Farmhouse, Compton Street, Compton Dundon, Somerton TA11 6PS
T: (01458) 442848

CONSTANTINE
Cornwall

Anneth Lowen ★★★★
Contact: Cornish Cottage Holidays, Godolphin Road, Helston TR13 8AA
T: (01326) 573808
F: (01326) 564992
E: enquiry@cornishcottageholidays.co.uk
I: www.cornishcottageholidays.co.uk

Chynoweth ★★★
Contact: Mrs E. W. Combellack, Seworgan, Constantine, Falmouth TR11 5QN
T: (01326) 340196

The Fuchsias ★★★
Contact: Cornish Traditional Cottages, Blisland, Bodmin PL30 4HS
T: (01208) 821666
F: (01208) 821766

Jackdaw Cottage ★★★★
Contact: Mrs Castling, Rock Farm, Llandenny, St Briavels, Lydney NP15 1DL
T: (01291) 690069
E: jill.castling@tesco.net
I: www.cornwall-online.co.uk

Swallow Barn ★★★★
Contact: Cornish Cottage Holidays, Godolphin Road, Helston TR13 8AA
T: (01326) 573808
F: (01326) 564992
E: enquiry@cornishcottageholidays.co.uk
I: www.cornishcottageholidays.co.uk

CONSTANTINE BAY
Cornwall

1 & 2 Tremawr ★★★
Contact: Mr & Mrs Peter & Cathy Osborne, Cornish Horizons, Higher Trehemborne, St Merryn, Padstow PL28 8JU
T: (01841) 520889
F: (01841) 521523
E: cottages@cornishhorizons.co.uk
I: www.cornishhorizons.co.uk

Cowries ★★★
Contact: Mr & Mrs Peter & Cathy Osborne, Cornish Horizons, Higher Trehemborne, St Merryn, Padstow PL28 8JU
T: (01841) 520889
F: (01841) 521523
E: cottages@cornishhorizons.co.uk
I: www.cornishhorizons.co.uk

Flat 7 Sandhills ★★
Contact: Mrs J Vaughan, Chestnut Lodge, Oulton, Stone ST15 8UR
T: (01785) 813864
F: (01785) 813864
E: tim-and-jen@chestnut1.freeserve.co.uk

Flat 12 Sandhills ★★★
Contact: Mr & Mrs Keith & Marie Hull, 18 Caernarvon Gardens, Beacon Park, Plymouth PL22 2RY
T: (01752) 772519

The Garden Cottage Holiday Flats ★★★
Contact: Mrs Elizabeth Harris, The Garden Cottage, Padstow PL28 8JJ
T: (01841) 520262
F: (01741) 520262
E: gardencottage@cornwall-county.com

The Greens ★★★
Contact: Mr & Mrs Peter & Cathy Osborne, Cornish Horizons, Higher Trehemborne, St Merryn, Padstow PL28 8JU
T: (01841) 520889

Kalundu ★★★★
Contact: Mr & Mrs Peter & Cathy Osborne, Cornish Horizons, Higher Trehemborne, St Merryn, Padstow PL28 8JU
T: (01841) 520889
F: (01841) 521523
E: cottages@cornishhorizons.co.uk
I: www.cornishhorizons.co.uk

Kittiwake ★★★★
Contact: Mr & Mrs Peter & Cathy Osborne, Cornish Horizons, Higher Trehemborne, St Merryn, Padstow PL28 8JU
T: (01841) 520889
F: (01841) 521523
E: cottages@cornishhorizons.co.uk
I: www.cornishhorizons.co.uk

Lees Nook ★★-★★★
Contact: Mrs Stuttaford, Lees Nook, Constantine Bay, Padstow PL28 8JJ
T: (01841) 520344

Little Trevelyan ★★★
Contact: Ms Nicky Stanley, Harbour Holidays - Padstow, 1 North Quay, Padstow PL28 8AF
T: (01841) 532555
F: (01841) 533115
E: sales@jackie-stanley.co.uk
I: www.harbourholidays.co.uk

Pippins & Dinas View ★★
Contact: Mr & Mrs Peter & Cathy Osborne, Cornish Horizons, Higher Trehemborne, St Merryn, Padstow PL28 8JU
T: (01841) 520889
F: (01841) 521523
E: cottages@cornishhorizons.co.uk
I: www.cornishhorizons.co.uk

Porth Clyne ★★★
Contact: Mr & Mrs Peter & Cathy Osborne, Cornish Horizons, Higher Trehemborne, St Merryn, Padstow PL28 8JU
T: (01841) 520889
F: (01841) 521523
E: cottages@cornishhorizons.co.uk
I: www.cornishhorizons.co.uk

Portol ★★★
Contact: Mr A N Grayson, Alcester, Sunhill, Hook Heath Road, Woking GU22 0QL
T: (01483) 755539
E: alecjenny@aol.com

Quilletts ★★★★
Contact: Mr & Mrs Peter & Cathy Osborne, Cornish Horizons, Higher Trehemborne, St Merryn, Padstow PL28 8JU
T: (01841) 520889
F: (01841) 521523
E: cottages@cornishhorizons.co.uk
I: www.cornishhorizons.co.uk

Rose Campion ★★★
Contact: Mr & Mrs Peter & Cathy Osborne, Cornish Horizons, Higher Trehemborne, St Merryn, Padstow PL28 8JU
T: (01841) 520889
F: (01841) 521523
E: cottages@cornishhorizons.co.uk
I: www.cornishhorizons.co.uk

Stone's Throw ★★★
Contact: Mr & Mrs Temple, Fernleigh Road, Wadebridge PL27 7AZ
T: (01208) 812612
F: 08701 325817
E: iantemple@bigfoot.com
I: www.northcornwall.fsnet.co.uk

Trefebus ★★★★
Contact: Mr & Mrs Peter & Cathy Osborne, Cornish Horizons, Higher Trehemborne, St Merryn, Padstow PL28 8JU
T: (01841) 520889
F: (01841) 521523
E: cottages@cornishhorizons.co.uk
I: www.cornishhorizons.co.uk

Treglos ★★★
Contact: Mr Barlow, Treglos, Constantine Bay, Padstow PL28 8JH
T: (01841) 520727
E: enquiries@treglos-hotel.co.uk
I: www.treglos-hotel.co.uk

Treglyn ★★
Contact: Mr & Mrs Peter & Cathy Osborne, Cornish Horizons, Higher Trehemborne, St Merryn, Padstow PL28 8JU
T: (01841) 520889
F: (01841) 521523
E: cottages@cornishhorizons.co.uk
I: www.cornishhorizons.co.uk

Treless ★★★★
Contact: Mr & Mrs Peter & Cathy Osborne, Cornish Horizons, Higher Trehemborne, St Merryn, Padstow PL28 8JU
T: (01841) 520889
F: (01841) 521523
E: cottages@cornishhorizons.co.uk
I: www.cornishhorizons.co.uk

Trescore ★★★
Contact: Mr & Mrs Peter & Cathy Osborne, Cornish Horizons, Higher Trehemborne, St Merryn, Padstow PL28 8JU
T: (01841) 520889
F: (01841) 521523
E: cottages@cornishhorizons.co.uk
I: www.cornishhorizons.co.uk

Trevanion ★★★
Contact: Ms Nicky Stanley Harbour Holidays - Padstow, 1 North Quay, Padstow PL28 8AF
T: (01841) 532555
F: (01841) 533115
E: sales@jackie-stanley.co.uk
I: www.harbourholidays.co.uk

Turnstones ★★★
Contact: Mr & Mrs Peter & Cathy Osborne, Cornish Horizons, Higher Trehemborne, St Merryn, Padstow PL28 8JU
T: (01841) 520889

COOMBE BISSETT
Wiltshire

Cross Farm Cottage ★★★
Contact: Mrs S Kittermaster, Cross Farm Cottage, Cross Farm, Coombe Bissett, Salisbury SP5 4LY
T: (01722) 718293
F: (01722) 718665
E: s.j.kittermaster@talk21.com

CORSCOMBE
Dorset

Underhill Farm Holidays Bramble Down★★★★
Contact: Mrs Joanna Vassie, Underhill Farm Holidays Finch Rise, Corscombe, Dorchester DT2 0PA
T: (01935) 891245
F: (01935) 891245
E: vassie@fwi.co.uk
I: www.underhillfarm.co.uk

CORSHAM
Wiltshire

Linleys Farm Cottages ★★★★★
Contact: Ms Han Warr, Linleys Farm Cottages, Linleys Farm, Linleys, Corsham SN13 9PG
T: (01249) 715578
F: (01249) 715578
E: linleysfarm@aol.com

Wadswick Barns ★★★★★
Contact: Mr & Mrs Tim & Carolyn Barton, Wadswick Barns, Wadswick, Box, Corsham SN13 8JB
T: (01225) 810733
F: (01225) 810307
E: barns@wadswick.co.uk
I: www.wadswick.co.uk

COTLEIGH
Devon

Authers Cottage ★★★
Contact: Milkbere Holidays, 3 Fore Street, Seaton EX12 2LE
T: (01297) 20729
F: (01297) 22925
E: info@milkberehols.com
I: www.milkbere.com

COVERACK
Cornwall

Heath Farm Cottage ★★-★★★★
Contact: Mr Andy Goodman, Ponsongath, Coverack, Helston TR12 6SQ
T: (01326) 280521
F: (01326) 281272
E: info@heath-farm-holidays.co.uk
I: www.heath-farm-holidays.co.uk

CRACKINGTON HAVEN
Cornwall

Bremor Holiday Bungalows and Cottages★★★
Contact: Mr & Mrs Rogers, Bremor Holiday Bungalows and Cottages, Crackington Haven, Bude EX23 0JN
T: (01840) 230340

Cleave Farm Cottages ★★-★★★
Contact: Mrs Carole Zoeftig, Cleave Farm Cottages, St Gennys, Bude EX23 0NQ
T: (01840) 230426
E: carole@cleavefm.force9.co.uk

Longstones ★★★★
Contact: Mrs Pat Bird, Longstones, Middle Crackington Farm, Crackington Haven, Bude EX23 0JW
T: (01840) 230445
F: (01840) 230445
E: pat.bird@btinternet.com
I: www.cottagesonline.co.uk/cornwall/longstones.htm

9 Lundy Drive ★★★
Contact: Mrs Anderson, 1 Long-A-Row Close, Crackington Haven, Bude EX23 0PG
T: (01840) 230504
E: paul@panderson60.freeserve.co.uk

The Old Cider Press ★★★★
Contact: Mr Stephen Bennett, 64 Park Drive, London W3 8NA
T: (020) 8993 2628
F: (08709) 223 563
E: booking@theoldciderpress.co.uk
I: www.theoldciderpress.co.uk

Trenannick Cottages ★★★
Contact: Ms L Harrison, Trenannick Cottages, Trenannick Farm, Warbstow, Launceston PL15 8RP
T: (01566) 781443
F: (01566) 781443
E: lorraine.trenannick@j12.com
I: www.trenannickcottages.co.uk

Trevigue Cottages ★★★★
Contact: Ms Gayle Crocker, Trevigue Cottages, Trevigue Farm, Crackington Haven, Bude EX23 0LQ
T: (01840) 230418
E: trevigue@talk21.com
I: www.trevigue.co.uk

Trevigue Cottages ★★★-★★★★
Contact: Mr Francis Crocker, Barton Cottage, St Gennys, Bude EX23
T: (01840) 230492

CREDITON
Devon

Creedy Manor ★★★★
Contact: Ms Sandra Turner, Creedy Manor, Long Barn Farm, Crediton EX17 4AB
T: (01363) 772684
E: sandra@creedymanor.com
I: www.creedymanor.com

Eastacott Farm ★★★
Contact: Farm & Cottage Holidays, Victoria House, 12 Fore Street, Westward Ho!, Bideford EX39 1AW
T: (01237) 479146
F: (01237) 421512
E: enquiries@farmcott.co.uk

Rudge Rew Cottage & Colts Hill Barn ★★★★
Contact: Mrs Bailey, Rudge Rew Cottage & Colts Hill Barn, Rudge Rew Farm, Morchard Bishop, Crediton EX17 6NG
T: (01363) 877309
F: (01363) 877309
E: rudgerew@talk21.com
I: www.rudgerewfarm.btinternet.co.uk

White Witches and Stable Lodge ★★★-★★★★
Contact: Mrs Gillbard, Hele Barton, Black Dog, Oakford, Tiverton EX17 4QJ
T: (01884) 860278
F: (01884) 860278
E: gillbard@eclipse.co.uk
I: www.eclipse.co.uk/helebarton

CROCKERTON
Wiltshire

Glebe Lodge ★★★
Contact: Mrs Margaret Askew, Glebe Lodge, Foxholes, Crockerton, Warminster BA12 7DB
T: (01985) 219367
E: askew.easter@btinternet.com

CROWLAS
Cornwall

Cuckoo Cottage ★★★
Contact: Mrs Jackman, Mowshurst Farmhouse, Swan Lane, Edenbridge TN8 6AH
T: (01732) 862064

Millers Loft ★★★
Contact: Farm & Cottage Holidays, Victoria House, 12 Fore Street, Westward Ho!, Bideford EX39 1AW
T: (01237) 479146
F: (01237) 421512
E: bookings@farmcott.co.uk

CROYDE
Devon

Baggy Point Apartment ★★★
Contact: Marsden's Cottage Holidays, 2 The Square, Braunton EX33 2JB
T: (01271) 813777
F: (01271) 813664
E: holidays@marsdens.co.uk
I: www.marsdens.co.uk

Bramleys ★★★
Contact: Marsden's Cottage Holidays, 2 The Square, Braunton EX33 2JB
T: (01271) 813777
F: (01271) 813664
E: holidays@marsdens.co.uk
I: www.marsdens.co.uk

Bridge Cottage ★★★★
Contact: Mr & Mrs Peter & Janet Cornwell, Marsden's Cottage Holidays, 2 The Square, Braunton EX33 2JB
T: (01271) 813777
F: (01271) 813664
E: holidays@marsdens.co.uk
I: www.marsdens.co.uk

The Bungalow ★★★★
Contact: Marsden's Cottage Holidays, 2 The Square, Braunton EX33 2JB
T: (01271) 813777
F: (01271) 813664
E: holidays@marsdens.co.uk
I: www.marsdens.co.uk

Cock Rock Cottage ★★★★★
Contact: Marsden's Cottage Holidays, 2 The Square, Braunton EX33 2JB
T: (01271) 813777
F: (01271) 813664
E: holidays@marsdens.co.uk
I: www.marsdens.co.uk

Croyde Bay Lodge Apartments 1 & 2 ★★★★
Contact: Mrs Jenny Penny, Croyde, Croyde Bay, Braunton EX33 1PA
T: (01271) 890270

Cubbies Corner ★★★
Contact: Marsden's Cottage Holidays, 2 The Square, Braunton EX33 2JB
T: (01271) 813777
F: (01271) 813664
E: holidays@marsdens.co.uk
I: www.marsdens.co.uk

Denham House ★★★
Contact: Mr Hugh Bond, Denham House, North Buckland, Braunton EX33 1HY
T: (01271) 890297
F: (01271) 890297
I: www.denhamhouse.co.uk

Dunehaven ★★★★
Contact: Marsden's Cottage Holidays, 2 The Square, Braunton EX33 2JB
T: (01271) 813777
F: (01271) 813664
E: holidays@marsdens.co.uk
I: www.marsdens.co.uk

The Dunes ★★★★
Contact: Marsden's Cottage Holidays, 2 The Square, Braunton EX33 2JB
T: (01271) 813777
F: (01271) 813664
E: holidays@marsdens.co.uk
I: www.marsdens.co.uk

Embleton ★★★★
Contact: Marsden's Cottage Holidays, 2 The Square, Braunton EX33 2JB
T: (01271) 813777
F: (01271) 813664

Fujikawa ★★★
Contact: Mr & Mrs Peter & Janet Cornwell, Marsden's Cottage Holidays, 2 The Square, Braunton EX33 2JB
T: (01271) 813777
F: (01271) 813664
E: holidays@marsdens.co.uk
I: www.marsdens.co.uk

Hillview ★★★★
Contact: Marsden's Cottage Holidays, 2 The Square, Braunton EX33 2JB
T: (01271) 813777
F: (01271) 813664
E: holidays@marsdens.co.uk
I: www.marsdens.co.uk

Honeycott ★★★
Contact: Marsdens Cottage Holidays, 2 The square, Braunton EX33 2JB
T: (01271) 813777
E: holidays@marsdens.co.uk
I: www.marsdens.co.uk

Keats Lodge ★★★★
Contact: Marsden's Cottage Holidays, 2 The Square, Braunton EX33 2JB
T: (01271) 813777
F: (01271) 813664
E: holidays@marsdens.co.uk
I: www.marsdens.co.uk

Little Doone ★★★★
Contact: 2 The Square, Braunton EX33 2JB
T: (01271) 813777
F: (01271) 813664
E: holidays@marsdens.co.uk
I: www.marsdens.co.uk

Lundy Lodge ★★★★
Contact: Mr & Mrs Cornwell, Marsden's Cottage Holidays, 2 The Square, Braunton EX33 2JB
I: www.marsdens.co.uk

The Mallows ★★★
Contact: Marsden's Cottage Holidays, 2 The Square, Braunton EX33 2JB
T: (01271) 813777
F: (01271) 813664
E: holidays@marsdens.co.uk
I: www.marsdens.co.uk

Montana ★★★
Contact: Mr & Mrs Cornwell, Marsden's Cottage Holidays, 2 The Square, Braunton EX33 2JB
I: www.marsdens.co.uk

Mountain Ash ★★★
Contact: Mr & Mrs Peter & Janet Cornwell, Marsden's Cottage Holidays, 2 The Square, Braunton EX33 2JB
T: (01271) 813777
F: (01271) 813664
E: holidays@marsdens.co.uk
I: www.marsdens.co.uk

Myrtle Cottage ★★★★
Contact: Marsden's Cottage Holidays, 2 The Square, Braunton EX33 2JB
T: (01271) 813777
F: (01271) 813664
E: holidays@marsdens.co.uk
I: www.marsdens.co.uk

Nauwai ★★★★
Contact: Mr & Mrs Peter & Janet Cornwell, Marsden's Cottage Holidays, 2 The Square, Braunton EX33 2JB
T: (01271) 813777
F: (01271) 813664
E: holidays@marsdens.co.uk
I: www.marsdens.co.uk

Oceanus & Poseidon ★★★
Contact: Marsden's Cottage Holidays, 2 The Square, Braunton EX33 2JB
T: (01271) 813777
F: (01271) 813664
E: holidays@marsdens.co.uk
I: www.marsdens.co.uk

Oyster Falls ★★★★
Contact: Marsden's Cottage Holidays, 2 The Square, Braunton EX33 2JB
T: (01271) 813777
F: (01271) 813664
E: holidays@marsdens.co.uk
I: www.marsdens.co.uk

Rose Villa ★★★★
Contact: Marsden's Cottage Holidays, 2 The Square, Braunton EX33 2JB
T: (01271) 813777
F: (01271) 813664
E: holidays@marsdens.co.uk
I: www.marsdens.co.uk

Sands End ★★★★
Contact: Marsden's Cottage Holidays, 2 The Square, Braunton EX33 2JB
T: (01271) 813777
F: (01271) 813664
E: holidays@marsdens.co.uk
I: www.marsdens.co.uk

Seahaven ★★★★
Contact: Marsden's Cottage Holidays, 2 The Square, Braunton EX33 2JB
T: (01271) 813777
F: (01271) 813664
E: holidays@marsdens.co.uk
I: www.marsdens.co.uk

Sennen Cottage ★★★
Contact: Marsden's Cottage Holidays, 2 The Square, Braunton EX33 2JB
T: (01271) 813777
F: (01271) 813664
E: holidays@marsdens.co.uk
I: www.marsdens.co.uk

Sundowner ★★★★
Contact: Mr & Mrs Cornwell, Marsden's Cottage Holidays, 2 The Square, Braunton EX33 2JB
T: (01271) 813777

Sunny Skies ★★★★
Contact: Marsden's Cottage Holidays, 2 The Square, Braunton EX33 2JB
T: (01271) 813777
F: (01271) 813664
E: holidays@marsdens.co.uk
I: www.marsdens.co.uk

Sunnyside ★★★★
Contact: Marsden's Cottage Holidays, 2 The Square, Braunton EX33 2JB
T: (01271) 813777
F: (01271) 813664
E: holidays@marsdens.co.uk
I: www.marsdens.co.uk

Sunset View ★★★
Contact: Marsden's Cottage Holidays, 2 The Square, Braunton EX33 2JB
T: (01271) 813777
F: (01271) 813664
E: holidays@marsdens.co.uk
I: www.marsdens.co.uk

Suntana & Little Suntana ★★★
Contact: Marsden's Cottage Holidays, 2 The Square, Braunton EX33 2JB
T: (01271) 813777
F: (01271) 813664
E: holidays@marsdens.co.uk
I: www.marsdens.co.uk

Sweets Cottage ★★★★
Contact: Marsden's Cottage Holidays, 2 The Square, Braunton EX33 2JB
T: (01271) 813777
F: (01271) 813664
E: holidays@marsdens.co.uk
I: www.marsdens.co.uk

Wayside ★★★★
Contact: Mr & Mrs Cornwell, Marsden's Cottage Holidays, 2 The Square, Braunton EX33 2JB
I: www.marsdens.co.uk

Withyside ★★★★
Contact: Marsden's Cottage Holidays, 2 The Square, Braunton EX33 2JB
T: (01271) 813777
F: (01271) 813664
E: holidays@marsdens.co.uk
I: www.marsdens.co.uk

CROYDE BAY
Devon

Cotilla
Rating Applied For
Contact: Marsdens Cottage Holidays, 2 The Square, Braunton EX33 2JB
T: (01271) 813777
F: (01271) 813664
E: holidays@marsdens.co.uk

Sundowner ★★★★
Contact: Marsdens Cottage Holidays, 2 The Square, Braunton EX33 2JB
T: (01271) 813777
F: (01271) 813664
E: holidays@marsdens.co.uk

CRUGMEER
Cornwall

Old Lifeboat Station ★★★
Contact: Ms Nicky Stanley, Harbour Holidays - Padstow, 1 North Quay, Padstow PL28 8AF
T: (01841) 532555
F: (01841) 533115
E: sales@jackie-stanley.co.uk
I: www.harbourholidays.co.uk

Webbers ★★★
Contact: Ms Nicky Stanley, Harbour Holidays - Padstow, 1 North Quay, Padstow PL28 8AF
T: (01841) 532555
F: (01841) 533115
E: sales@jackie-stanley.co.uk
I: www.harbourholidays.co.uk

CUCKLINGTON
Somerset

Hale Farm ★★★
Contact: Mrs David, Hale Farm, Cucklington, Wincanton BA9 9PN
T: (01963) 33342

CURRY MALLET
Somerset

Buzzards View ★★★★
Contact: Holiday Cottages Group, Spring Mill, Earby, Barnoldswick BB94 0AA
T: 08700 723723

CURY
Cornwall

Nanplough Farm ★★★
Contact: Mr William Lepper, Nanplough Farm, Cury Cross Lanes, Mullion, Helston TR12 7BQ
T: (01326) 241088
E: william.lepper@btopenworld.com
I: www.nanplough.co.uk

Treloskan Farm ★★★
Contact: Mrs Lane, Treloskan Farm, Porthallow, St Keverne, Helston TR12 6PW
T: (01326) 240493

DALWOOD
Devon

Millwater 1 & 2 ★★★
Contact: Mr Zachary Stuart-Brown, Dream Cottages, 41 Maiden Street, Weymouth DT4 8AZ
T: (01305) 761347
E: admin@dream-cottages.co.uk
I: www.dream-cottages.co.uk

Old Symes Cottages ★★★★
Contact: Mr & Mrs John & Kathleen Brennan, The Green, Kilmington, Axminster EX13 7RG
T: (01297) 35982
F: (01297) 34982
E: brennans@oldsymes.fsnet.co.uk

DARTINGTON
Devon

Billany ★★★
Contact: Farm & Cottage Holidays, Victoria House, 12 Fore Street, Westward Ho!, Bideford EX39 1AW
T: (01237) 479146
F: (01237) 421512
E: enquiries@farmcott.co.uk

DARTMEET
Devon

Coachman's Cottage ★★★★
Contact: Mrs Toni Evans, Coachman's Cottage, Hunter's Lodge, Dartmeet, Princetown, Yelverton PL20 6SG
T: (01364) 631173
E: mail@dartmeet.com
I: www.dartmeet.com

DARTMOUTH
Devon

Barrington House ★★★★★
Contact: Mrs E Baldwin, Barrington House, Mount Boome, Dartmouth TQ6 9HZ
T: (01803) 835545
E: enq@barrington-house.com
I: www.barrington-house.com

Beauford House ★★★★
Contact: Dartmouth Cottages, 14 Mayors Avenue, Dartmouth TQ6 9NG
T: (01803) 839499

Cairn Cottage ★★★
Contact: Mr & Mrs D Cawley, Dartmouth Cottages, 14 Mayors Avenue, Dartmouth TQ6 9NG
T: (01803) 839499
E: holidays@dartmouthcottages.com
I: www.dartmouthcottages.com

Captains Cabin ★★
Contact: Mr & Mrs D Cawley, Dartmouth Cottages, 14 Mayors Avenue, Dartmouth TQ6 9NG
T: (01803) 839499
E: holidays@dartmouthcottages.com
I: www.dartmouthcottages.com

Chipton House ★★★
Contact: Mr & Mrs D Cawley, Dartmouth Cottages, 14 Mayors Avenue, Dartmouth TQ6 9NG
T: (01803) 839499
E: holidays@dartmouthcottages.com
I: www.dartmouthcottages.com

33 Clarence Hill ★★★★
Contact: Mrs Sally Pool, Lansdown, Magpie Lane, Coleshill, Amersham HP7 0LS
T: (01494) 727687
E: poolfamily@btinternet.com

Cornwood ★★★
Contact: Dartmouth Cottages, 14 Mayors Avenue, Dartmouth TQ6 9NG
T: (01803) 839499

Cotterbury ★★★
Contact: Dartmouth Cottages, 14 Mayors Avenue, Dartmouth TQ6 9NG
T: (01803) 839499

Cove Cottage ★★
Contact: Mr & Mrs D Cawley, Dartmouth Cottages, 14 Mayors Avenue, Dartmouth TQ6 9NG
T: (01803) 839499
E: holidays@dartmouthcottages.com
I: www.dartmouthcottages.com

Fairview ★★★★
Contact: Mr & Mrs D Cawley, Dartmouth Cottages, 14 Mayors Avenue, Dartmouth TQ6 9NG
T: (01803) 839499
E: holidays@dartmouthcottages.com
I: www.dartmouthcottages.com

Foss View ★★★
Contact: Dartmouth Cottages, 14 Mayors Avenue, Dartmouth TQ6 9NG
T: (01803) 839499

Freshford ★★★★
Contact: Dartmouth Cottages, 14 Mayors Avenue, Dartmouth TQ6 9NG
T: (01803) 839499

Full Deck ★★★
Contact: Mr & Mrs D Cawley, Dartmouth Cottages, 14 Mayors Avenue, Dartmouth TQ6 9NG
T: (01803) 839499
E: holidays@dartmouthcottages.com
I: www.dartmouthcottages.com

Fulmar Cottage ★★★
Contact: Mr & Mrs D Cawley, Dartmouth Cottages, 14 Mayors Avenue, Dartmouth TQ6 9NG
T: (01803) 839499
E: holidays@dartmouthcottages.com
I: www.dartmouthcottages.com

The Gallery ★★★★★
Contact: Mrs R James, 43 Faraday Drive, Shenley Lodge, Milton Keynes MK5 7DD
T: (01908) 604449

Green Meadows ★★★
Contact: Dartmouth Cottages, 14 Mayors Avenue, Dartmouth TQ6 9NG
T: (01803) 839499

Harbour Lights ★★★★
Contact: Mr & Mrs D Cawley, Dartmouth Cottages, 14 Mayors Avenue, Dartmouth TQ6 9NG
T: (01803) 839499
E: holidays@dartmouthcottages.com
I: www.dartmouthcottages.com

Harbour Views ★★★★
Contact: Mr & Mrs D Cawley, Dartmouth Cottages, 14 Mayors Avenue, Dartmouth TQ6 9NG
T: (01803) 839499
E: holidays@dartmouthcottages.com
I: www.dartmouthcottages.com

Harbourside ★★★★★
Contact: Mr & Mrs D Cawley, Dartmouth Cottages, 14 Mayors Avenue, Dartmouth TQ6 9NG
T: (01803) 839499
E: holidays@dartmouthcottages.com
I: www.dartmouthcottages.com

Herons ★★★
Contact: Mr & Mrs D Cawley, Dartmouth Cottages, 14 Mayors Avenue, Dartmouth TQ6 9NG
T: (01803) 839499
E: holidays@dartmouthcottages.com
I: www.dartmouthcottages.com

Higher Venice ★★★★
Contact: Mr Ian Butterworth, Holiday Homes & Cottages South West, 365A Torquay Road, Paignton TQ3 2BT
T: (01803) 663650
F: (01803) 664037
E: holcotts@aol.com
I: www.swcottages.co.uk

Huffin ★★★★★
Contact: Dartmouth Cottages, 14 Mayors Avenue, Dartmouth TQ6 9NG
T: (01803) 839499

Island Cottage ★★★
Contact: Mr & Mrs D Cawley, Dartmouth Cottages, 14 Mayors Avenue, Dartmouth TQ6 9NG
T: (01803) 839499
E: holidays@dartmouthcottages.com
I: www.dartmouthcottages.com

Lake Victoria Cottage ★★★
Contact: Dartmouth Cottages, 14 Mayors Avenue, Dartmouth TQ6 9NG
T: (01803) 839499

Lilliput House ★★★★
Contact: Mr & Mrs D Cawley, Dartmouth Cottages, 14 Mayors Avenue, Dartmouth TQ6 9NG
T: (01803) 839499
E: holidays@dartmouthcottages.com
I: www.dartmouthcottages.com

Lily Cottage ★★★
Contact: Dartmouth Cottages, 14 Mayors Avenue, Dartmouth TQ6 9NG
T: (01803) 839499

Little Coombe Cottage ★★★★★
Contact: Mr & Mrs Phil & Ann Unitt, Little Coombe Cottage, Dittisham, Dartmouth TQ6 0JB
T: (01803) 722599
F: (01803) 722599
I: www.dartvalleycottages.co.uk

The Little White House ★★★★
Contact: Mr & Mrs D Cawley, Dartmouth Cottages, 14 Mayors Avenue, Dartmouth TQ6 9NG
T: (01803) 839499
E: holidays@dartmouthcottages.com
I: www.dartmouthcottages.com

Lower Swannaton Farm ★★
Contact: Farm & Cottage Holidays, Victoria House, 12 Fore Street, Westward Ho!, Bideford EX39 1AW
T: (01237) 479146
F: (01237) 421512
E: enquiries@farmcott.co.uk

Mews Cottage ★★★
Contact: Mr & Mrs D Cawley, Dartmouth Cottages, 14 Mayors Avenue, Dartmouth TQ6 9NG
T: (01803) 839499
E: holidays@dartmouthcottages.com
I: www.dartmouthcottages.com

Middle Clifton ★★★★
Contact: Mr & Mrs D Cawley, Dartmouth Cottages, 14 Mayors Avenue, Dartmouth TQ6 9NG
T: (01803) 839499
E: holidays@dartmouthcottages.com
I: www.dartmouthcottages.com

Moonrakers ★★★★
Contact: Dartmouth Cottages, 14 Mayors Avenue, Dartmouth TQ6 9NG
T: (01803) 839499

The Old Bakehouse ★★★
Contact: Mrs S R Ridalls, The Old Bakehouse, 7 Broadstone, Dartmouth TQ6 9NR
T: (01803) 834585
F: (01803) 834585
E: pioneerparker@aol.com
I: www.oldbakehousedartmouth.co.uk

Old Globe House ★★★
Contact: Mr & Mrs D Cawley, Dartmouth Cottages, 14 Mayors Avenue, Dartmouth TQ6 9NG
T: (01803) 839499
E: holidays@dartmouthcottages.com
I: www.dartmouthcottages.com

Palladium Mews ★★★★
Contact: Dartmouth Cottages, 14 Mayors Avenue, Dartmouth TQ6 9NG
T: (01803) 839499

Puffin ★★★★★
Contact: Dartmouth Cottages, 14 Mayors Avenue, Dartmouth TQ6 9NG
T: (01803) 839499

The Quay ★★
Contact: Mr & Mrs D Cawley, Dartmouth Cottages, 14 Mayors Avenue, Dartmouth TQ6 9NG
T: (01803) 839499
E: holidays@dartmouthcottages.com
I: www.dartmouthcottages.com

Rose Cottage ★★★★
Contact: Mr Ian Butterworth, Holiday Homes & Cottages South West, 365A Torquay Road, Paignton TQ3 2BT
T: (01803) 663650

Rose Cottage ★★★
Contact: Mr & Mrs D Cawley, Dartmouth Cottages, 14 Mayors Avenue, Dartmouth TQ6 9NG
T: (01803) 839499
E: holidays@dartmouthcottages.com
I: www.dartmouthcottages.com

Serica ★★★★★
Contact: Dartmouth Cottages, 14 Mayors Avenue, Dartmouth TQ6 9NG
T: (01803) 839499

Slippery Causeway ★★★★
Contact: Mr & Mrs D Cawley, Dartmouth Cottages, 14 Mayors Avenue, Dartmouth TQ6 9NG
T: (01803) 839499
E: holidays@dartmouthcottages.com
I: www.slipperycauseway.co.uk

Speedwell ★★★
Contact: Dartmouth Cottages, 14 Mayors Avenue, Dartmouth TQ6 9NG
T: (01803) 839499

Sunny Bank ★★★★
Contact: Mr & Mrs D Cawley, Dartmouth Cottages, 14 Mayors Avenue, Dartmouth TQ6 9NG
T: (01803) 839499
E: holidays@dartmouthcottages.com
I: www.dartmouthcottages.com

Top View ★★★
Contact: Mr & Mrs D Cawley, Dartmouth Cottages, 14 Mayors Avenue, Dartmouth TQ6 9NG
T: (01803) 839499
E: holidays@dartmouthcottages.com
I: www.dartmouthcottages.com

Town View ★★★
Contact: Mr & Mrs D Cawley, Dartmouth Cottages, 14 Mayors Avenue, Dartmouth TQ6 9NG
T: (01803) 839499
E: holidays@dartmouthcottages.com
I: www.dartmouthcottages.com

Upper Tremorvah ★★
Contact: Toad Hall Cottages, Elliot House, Church Street, Kingsbridge TQ7 1BY
T: (01548) 853089
F: (01548) 853086
E: thc@toadhallcottages.com

DAWLISH
Devon

Brook Cottage ★★★★
Contact: Mr Ian Butterworth, Holiday Homes & Cottages South West, 365A Torquay Road, Paignton TQ3 2BT
T: (01803) 663650
F: (01803) 664037
E: holcotts@aol.com
I: www.swcottages.co.uk

Brookdale ★★★★
Contact: Mr Ian Butterworth, Holiday Homes & Cottages South West, 365A Torquay Road, Paignton TQ3 2BT
T: (01803) 663650
F: (01803) 664037
E: holcotts@aol.com
I: www.swcottages.co.uk

Cofton Country Cottage Holidays ★★★★
Contact: Cofton Country Cottage Holidays, Starcross, Nr Dawlish, Exeter EX6 8RP
T: (01626) 890111
F: (01626) 891572
E: info@coftonholidays.co.uk
I: www.coftonholidays.co.uk

Erminhurst ★★★★
Contact: Holiday Homes & Cottages South West, 365A Torquay Road, Paignton TQ3 2BT
T: (01803) 663650
F: (01803) 664037
E: holcotts@aol.com
I: www.swcottages.co.uk

Rockstone ★★★★
Contact: Holiday Homes & Cottages South West, 365a Torquay Road, Paignton TQ3 2BT
T: (01803) 663650
F: (01803) 664037
E: holcotts@aol.com
I: www.swcottages.co.uk

Shell Cove House ★★★★
Contact: Ms Jameson, Shell Cove House, Old Teignmouth Road, Dawlish EX7 0NJ
T: (01626) 862523
F: (01626) 862523

DAWLISH WARREN
Devon

Devondale ★★★
Contact: Holiday Homes & Cottages South West, 365a Torquay Road, Paignton TQ3 2BT
T: (01803) 663650
F: (01803) 664037
E: holcotts@aol.com
I: www.swcottages.co.uk

Eastdon Estate ★★★★
Contact: Cofton Country Holidays, Dawlish EX6 8RP
T: (01626) 890111
F: (01626) 891572
E: info@coftonholidays.co.uk
I: www.coftonholidays.co.uk

Shutterton Farm ★★★
Contact: Ms Karen Mitchell, Shutterton Farm, Shutterton Lane, Dawlish Warren, Dawlish EX7 0PD
T: (01626) 863766
F: (01626) 863766
E: shuttertonfarm@aol.com
I: shuttertonfarm.co.uk

DEVIZES
Wiltshire

The Derby ★★★
Contact: Mrs Janet Tyler, The Derby, Heddington, Calne SN11 0PL
T: (01380) 850523
F: (01380) 850523
E: W.S.Tyler@farmline.com

2 Eastfield Cottages ★★★
Contact: Mr & Mrs David & Nina Lamb, Eastfield House, London Road, Devizes SN10 2DW
T: (01380) 721562
F: (01380) 721562
E: david@devizes.force9.co.uk

The Gate House ★★★★
Contact: Mrs Laura Stratton, The Gate House, Wick Lane, Devizes SN10 5DW
T: (01380) 725283
F: (01380) 722382
E: info@visitdevizes.co.uk

The Old Stables ★★★★
Contact: Mr & Mrs J Nash, The Old Stables, Tichbornes Farm, Etchilhampton, Devizes SN10 3JL
T: (01380) 862971
F: (01380) 862971
E: info@tichbornes.co.uk
I: www.tichbornes.co.uk

Owls Cottage ★★★★
Contact: Mrs G C Whittome, Owls Cottage, 48 White Street, Easterton, Devizes SN10 4PA
T: (01380) 818804
F: (01380) 818804
E: gill_whittome@yahoo.co.uk
I: www.owlscottage.homestead.com

Rendells Farm Holiday Cottages ★★★★
Contact: Mr & Mrs Keith & Sue Baron, The Barn, All Cannings, Devizes SN10 3PA
T: (01380) 860243
F: (01895) 270708
E: sroper@waitrose.com
I: www.rendellsfarmcottages.com

DEVORAN
Cornwall

Anne's Cottage ★★★
Contact: Mrs Margie Lumby, Poachers Reach, Harcourt, Feock, Truro TR3 6SQ
T: (01872) 864400
E: office@specialplacescornwall.co.uk
I: www.specialplacescornwall.co.uk

Tinners ★★★
Contact: Mrs Margie Lumby, Poachers Reach, Harcourt, Feock, Truro TR3 6SQ
T: (01872) 864400
E: office@specialplacescornwall.co.uk
I: www.specialplacescornwall.co.uk

DEWLISH
Dorset

Ashbank ★★★
Contact: Messrs Bissell, Lower Dairy House, Crawthorne Farm, Crawthorne, Dorchester DT2 7NG
T: (01258) 837788

DIDWORTHY
Devon

Didworthy House ★★★★
Contact: Mr & Ms Reg & Jill Tavendale & Hamilton, Didworthy, South Brent TQ10 9EF
T: (01364) 72655
F: (01364) 73022
E: didworthhouse@aol.com
I: www.didworthyhouse.co.uk

DINTON
Wiltshire

The Cottage, Marshwood Farm Rating Applied For
Contact: Mrs Fiona Lockyer, The Cottage, Marshwood Farm, Dinton, Salisbury SP3 5ET
T: (01722) 716334
F: (01722) 716334

Fitz Farm Cottage ★★★
Contact: Mr Nicholas Pash, Chapel House, Luke Street, Berwick St John, Shaftesbury SP7 0HQ
T: (01747) 828170
F: (01747) 829090
E: enq@hideaways.co.uk
I: www.hideaways.co.uk

DIPTFORD
Devon

Ley Farm ★★★
Contact: Mrs Sophia Hendy, Ley Farm, Diptford, North Huish, South Brent TQ9 7NN
T: (01548) 821200

DITCHEAT
Somerset

Long Batch Cottage ★★★★
Contact: Mrs Christine Smallbone, Ditcheat, Shepton Mallet BA4 6RE
T: (01749) 860421
E: chrissmallbone@aol.com

DITTISHAM
Devon

Cobwebs ★★★★
Contact: Dart Valley Cottages, Parklands, Dartmouth Road, Stoke Fleming, Dartmouth TQ6 0QY
T: (01803) 771127
F: (01803) 771128
E: enquiries@dartvalleycottages.co.uk
I: www.dartvalleycottages.co.uk

Orchard House ★★★★
Contact: Toad Hall Cottages, Elliot House, Church Street, Kingsbridge TQ7 1BY
T: (01548) 853089
F: (01548) 853086
E: thc@toadhallcottages.com

Sarah Elliots ★★★★
Contact: Dart Valley Cottages, Parklands, Dartmouth Road, Stoke Fleming, Dartmouth TQ6 0QY
T: (01803) 722561
F: (01803) 722561
E: enquiries@dartvalleycottages.co.uk
I: www.dartvalleycottages.co.uk

DOBWALLS
Cornwall

An Penty ★★★★
Contact: Farm & Cottage Holidays, Victoria House, 12 Fore Street, Westward Ho!, Bideford EX39 1AW
T: (01237) 479146
F: (01237) 421512
E: enquiries@farmcott.co.uk

DODDISCOMBSLEIGH
Devon

Shippen Barton ★★★
Contact: Farm & Cottage Holidays, Victoria House, 12 Fore Street, Northam, Bideford EX39 1AW
T: (01237) 479146
F: (01237) 421512
E: enquiries@farmcott.co.uk

DOLTON
Devon

Ham Farm ★★★★-★★★★★
Contact: Mr & Mrs Cobbledick, Hebron, Calf Street, Torrington EX38 8EG
T: (01805) 624000
F: (01805) 623058

DONHEAD ST ANDREW
Wiltshire

Sparrow Cottage ★★★
Contact: Mr Nicholas Pash, Chapel House, Luke Street, Berwick St John, Shaftesbury SP7 0HQ
T: (01747) 828170
F: (01747) 829090
E: enq@hideaways.co.uk
I: www.hideaways.co.uk

DORCHESTER
Dorset

Bridle House ★★★★
Contact: Dream Cottages, 41 Maiden Street, Weymouth DT4 8AZ
T: (01305) 761347
F: (01305) 789000

Damers Cottage ★★★
Contact: Mrs Rosemary Hodder, Damers Cottage, East Chaldon, Dorchester DT2 8DN
T: (01305) 852829
F: (01305) 852025
E: RH@cottage-holidays-dorset.co.uk
I: www.cottage-holidays-dorset.co.uk

Greenwood Grange Farm Cottages ★★★★-★★★★★
Contact: Mrs Jayne O'Brien, Greenwood Grange Farm Cottages, Higher Bockhampton, Dorchester DT2 8QH
T: (01305) 268874
F: (01305) 267512
E: enquiries@greenwoodgrange.co.uk
I: www.greenwoodgrange.co.uk

Hardy Country Holidays ★★★★
Contact: Mrs Frances Carroll, Hardy Country Holidays, Rew Manor, Rew, Dorchester DT2 9HB
T: (01305) 889222

Hastings Farm Cottages ★★★★
Contact: Mr David Hills, Hastings Farm Cottages, Tincleton, Dorchester DT2 8QP
T: (01305) 848627
E: djh@hastingsfarm.freeserve.co.uk
I: www.hastingsfarm.freeserve.co.uk

Lower Wrackleford Farm ★★★
Contact: Mr & Mrs Steve & Caroline Foot, Lower Wrackleford Farm, Wrackleford, Dorchester DT2 9SN
T: (01305) 265390
E: footsteve@aol.com
I: www.wracklefordfarm.fsnet.co.uk

8 Maiden Castle Road ★★★★
Contact: Mr & Mrs Kolodynski, 8 Maiden Castle Road, Dorchester DT1 2ER
T: (01305) 257211
F: 08700 561547
E: tk@mailmatic.demon.co.uk

The Stables ★★★★
Contact: Mrs Elizabeth Peckover, The Barn, Pallington, Tincleton, Dorchester DT2 8QU
T: (01305) 849344
E: stables@epeckover.fsnet.co.uk

2 Trinity Cottages ★★★
Contact: Mrs J R Bunce 13 The Old Barns, Fordington Dairy, Athelstan Road, Dorchester DT1 1FD
T: (01305) 250456

Wolfeton Lodge ★★★
Contact: Mrs K Thimbleby, Wolfeton House, Dorchester DT2 9QN
T: (01305) 263500
F: (01305) 265090
E: kthimbley@wolfeton.freeserve.co.uk

Woodlands Cottage ★★★
Contact: Dream Cottages, 41 Maiden Street, Weymouth DT4 8AZ
T: (01305) 761347
F: (01305) 789000

DOULTING
Somerset

Brottens Lodge ★★★
Contact: Mrs Caroline Gent, Brottens Lodge, Doulting, Shepton Mallet BA4 4RB
T: (01749) 880601
F: (01749) 880601
E: brottens@ukgateway.net

DOWLISH FORD
Somerset

Number 3 New Buildings ★★★
Contact: Mrs Hillary Mead, Greenclose Cottage, Knowle St Giles, Chard TA20 4AX
T: (01460) 61996

DOWN THOMAS
Devon

Bayfield ★★★
Contact: CH Ref: 10143, Holiday Cottages Group, Spring Mill, Earby, Barnoldswick BB94 0AA
T: 08700 723723
F: (01282) 844288
E: sales@ttgihg.co.uk
I: www.country-holidays.co.uk

DRAYCOTT
Somerset

Martindale ★★★
Contact: CH Ref: 10687, Holiday Cottages Group Owner Services Dept, Spring Mill, Earby, Barnoldswick BB94 0AA
T: 08700 723723
F: (01282) 844288
I: www.country-holidays.co.uk

DREWSTEIGNTON
Devon

East Underdown ★★★★★
Contact: Mr Tim Clarke, Helpful Holidays, Drewsteignton, Exeter EX6 6PE
T: (01647) 231339
F: (01647) 231339

Michaelmas & Gardeners Cottages ★★★★★
Contact: Mr & Mrs Thomas, Netherton Vine, Drewsteignton, Exeter EX6 6RB
T: (01647) 281602

DULVERTON
Somerset

Anstey Mills Cottages ★★★★
Contact: Mrs Doris Braukmann-Pugsley, Anstey Mills Cottages, East Liscombe, Dulverton TA22 9RZ
T: (01398) 341329
E: ansteymills@yahoo.com
I: www.ansteymillscottagedevon.co.uk

Ashway Cottage ★★★
Contact: Mr George Vellacott, Ashway Cottage, Ashway Farm, Dulverton TA22 9QD
T: (01398) 323577
F: (01398) 323577

Liscombe Farm Holiday Cottages ★★★★
Contact: Mrs Sally Wade, Liscombe Farm Holiday Cottages, Tarr Steps, Dulverton TA22 9QA
T: (01643) 851551
E: info@liscombe.co.uk
I: www.liscombefarm.co.uk

Northmoor House & Lodge ★★★★
Contact: Mr Tim Tarling, Northmoor, Dulverton TA22 9QF
T: (01398) 323720
F: (01398) 324537
E: timtarling@northmoor.fsnet.co.uk
I: www.northmoorhouse.co.uk

Paddons ★★★
Contact: Mrs Mary McMichael, Paddons, Northmoor Road, Dulverton TA22 9PW
T: (01398) 323514
F: (01398) 324283
E: marymm@paddons.fsnet.co.uk

Venford Cottage ★★★★
Contact: Mr Harley Stratton
T: (01398) 341308
E: harleyhstratton@aol.com
I: www.venfordcottage.co.uk

Whitehall House ★★★
Contact: Mr Kevin Reeves, 22 Fitzwilliam Avenue, Hill Head PO14 3SD
T: (01329) 665792
E: kevin.reeves4@ntlworld.com

DUNSFORD
Devon

Poppy Cottage ★★★
Contact: Miss Hazel Cant, 23 Fox Brook, Wootton Bassett, Swindon SN4 8QD
T: (01793) 850555
E: hazel@hcart.freeserve.co.uk

DUNSTER
Somerset

5 Chapel Row ★★★
Contact: Ms E J Hall, 14 Rue De L'Equerre, 78290 Croissy-sur-Seine, France
T: 00331 3053 6730
E: familydavidmhall@compuserve.com

Duddings Country Holidays ★★★★
Contact: Mr Richard Tilke, Duddings Country Holidays, Timberscombe, Minehead TA24 7TB
T: (01643) 841123
F: (01643) 841165
E: richard@duddings.co.uk
I: www.duddings.co.uk

Grooms Cottage ★★★★
Contact: Ms Disney, Grooms Cottage, Knowle Lane, Dunster, Minehead TA24 6TX
T: (01643) 821497

Little Quarme Cottages ★★★★-★★★★★
Contact: Mrs Tammy Cody-Boutcher, Little Quarme Cottages, Wheddon Cross, Minehead TA24 7EA
T: (01643) 841249
F: (01643) 841249
E: info@littlequarme-cottages.co.uk
I: www.littlequarme-cottages.co.uk

Pound ★★★
Contact: Mrs Sherrin, The Bungalow, Orchard Road, Carhampton, Minehead TA24 6NW
T: (01643) 821366
F: (01643) 821366

The Studio & Courtyard Flats ★★★
Contact: Mrs G C Harwood, 1 Church Street, Dunster, Minehead TA24 6SH
T: (01643) 821485

EAST ALLINGTON
Devon

Flear Farm Cottages ★★★★-★★★★★
Contact: Mrs Julie Ford, Flear Farm Cottages, Flear Farm, East Allington, Kingsbridge TQ9 7RF
T: (01548) 521227
F: (01548) 521600
E: flearfarm@btinternet.com

Honeysuckle Barn ★★★★
Contact: Mrs Rita Jeanette Pickering, Hutcherleigh Barn, Blackawton, East Allington, Totnes TQ9 7AD
T: (01548) 521309
F: (01548) 521593
E: info@honeysucklebarn.com

Pitt Farm ★★★★
Contact: Mr & Mrs Christopher & Denise Bates, Pitt Farm, Green Lane, East Allington, Totnes TQ9 7QD
T: (01548) 521234
F: (01548) 521518
E: christopher.bates@ukonline.co.uk
I: www.pitt-farm.co.uk

EAST BRENT
Somerset

Knoll Farm ★★★
Contact: Mrs Jeanne Champion, Knoll Farm, Jarvis Lane, East Brent, Highbridge TA9 4HS
T: (01278) 760227

EAST BUDLEIGH
Devon

Brook Cottage ★★★★
Contact: Mrs Jo Simons, Foxcote, Noverton Lane, Prestbury, Cheltenham GL52 5BB
T: (01242) 574031
E: josimons@tesco.net
I: http://homepage.ntlworld.com/jim.simons

EAST CHINNOCK
Somerset

Weston House ★★★★
Contact: Mrs Susan Gliddon, Weston House, East Chinnock, Yeovil BA22 9EL
T: (01935) 863712
E: westonhouseuk@netscapeonline.co.uk

EAST COKER
Somerset

Little Prymleigh ★★★★
Contact: Mrs Williams, Prymleigh, Yeovil Road, East Coker, Yeovil BA22 9HW
T: (01935) 863313

EAST KNOYLE
Wiltshire

Spring Cottage ★★★★★
Contact: Mr Nicholas Pash, Chapel House, Luke Street, Berwick St John, Shaftesbury SP7 0HQ
T: (01747) 828170
F: (01747) 829090
E: enq@hideaways.co.uk
I: www.hideaways.co.uk

EAST LOOE
Cornwall

Admiralty Court Apartments ★★★★
Contact: Mrs Sheila Summers, Admiralty Court Apartments, Apartment 5, Church End, East Looe, Looe PL13 1BU
T: (01503) 264617

Endymion ★★★★★
Contact: Mr David Pearn, 2 Lower Street, Polperro, Looe PL13 1DA
T: (01503) 262244
F: (01503) 262244
E: endymion@exclusivevacations.co.uk

Holly House ★★
Contact: Powell's Cottage Holidays, High Street, Saundersfoot SA69 9EJ
T: (01834) 812791

EAST PORTLEMOUTH
Devon

Gara Rock Hotel ★★-★★★★
Contact: Ms Ann Carr, East Portlemouth, Salcombe TQ8 8PH
T: (01548) 842342
F: (01548) 843033
E: gara@gara.co.uk
I: www.gara.co.uk

Two West Waterhead ★★★★
Contact: Mr & Mrs Stokes, 12 Elmcroft Crescent, Horfield, Bristol BS7 9NF
T: (0117) 951 6333

EAST PRAWLE
Devon

Higher House Farm ★★★
Contact: Mrs Vicky Tucker, Higher House Farm, Higher House Farm, East Prawle, Kingsbridge TQ7 2BU
T: (01548) 511332
F: (01548) 511332
E: tuckersatprawle@btconnect.com

EASTERTON
Wiltshire

Stable End ★★★
Contact: CH Ref 64003, Country Holidays, Spring Mill, Earby, Barnoldswick BB18
E: sales@holidacottagesgroup.com
I: www.country-holidays.co.uk

EASTON
Somerset

Mill Lodge ★★★★
Contact: Ms Lesley Burt, Wookey Road, Burcott, Easton, Wells BA5 1NJ
T: (01749) 673118
F: (01749) 677376
E: theburts@burcottmill.com

EDINGTON
Wiltshire

Cheam House ★★★★
Contact: Val & Chris Harding & White, Cheam House, 17 Greatwoods, Greater Lane, Edington, Westbury BA13 4QA
T: (01380) 830631

Greengrove Cottage ★★★★
Contact: Ref: E2483, Raglan Road, Lowestoft NR32 2LW
T: 0870 534 2342
F: 0870 902 2090
I: www.hoseasons.co.uk/images/2002/ukcottages/cottages/aa98.html

Moor House Farm ★★★
Contact: Ms Angela Bastable, Moor House Farm, Edington, Bridgwater TA7 9LA
T: (01278) 722329
I: www.idass.com/moor_house/index.htm

EDMONTON
Cornwall

16 Quarrymans ★★★
Contact: Ms Nicky Stanley, Harbour Holidays - Padstow, 1 North Quay, Padstow PL28 8AF
T: (01841) 532555
F: (01841) 533115
E: sales@jackie-stanley.co.uk
I: www.harbourholidays.co.uk

Quarryman's Cottages No 20 & No 1 ★★★
Contact: Mr Hugh Jenkins, Endellion House, Parc Road, Llangybi, Usk NP15 1NL
T: (01633) 450417
E: jenkins@choicecornishcottages.com
I: www.choicecornishcottages.com

EGLOSHAYLE
Cornwall

Watermill Cottage ★★★
Contact: Mrs Ruth Varcoe, Lemail Quinnies, Egloshayle, Wadebridge PL27 6JQ
T: (01208) 895127
F: (01208) 895127
E: varcoeuk@aol.com

EGLOSKERRY
Cornwall

Treburtle Cottage ★★★★
Contact: Mrs W F Wyldbore-Smith, Bremhill Manor, Calne SN11 9LA
T: (01249) 814969

EVERSHOT
Dorset

Pippins Cottage ★★★
Contact: Mr Zachary Stuart-Brown, Dream Cottages, 41 Maiden Street, Weymouth DT4 8AZ
T: (01305) 761347
E: admin@dream-cottages.co.uk
I: www.dream-cottages.co.uk

EXETER
Devon

Augusta Court
Rating Applied For
Contact: Ms Juliet Ware, 9-10 Augusta Court, Smythen Street, Exeter EX1 1DL
T: (01392) 477727
F: (01392) 477727
E: enquiries@wareedwards.co.uk

Coach House Farm ★★★★★
Contact: Mr J Bale, Coach House Farm, Moor Lane, Broadclyst, Exeter EX5 3JH
T: (01392) 461254
F: (01392) 460931
E: selfcatering@mpprops.co.uk

Fairwinds Holiday Bungalow ★★★★
Contact: Mrs W Price, Fairwinds Hotel, Kennford, Exeter EX6 7UD
T: (01392) 832911
E: fairwindshotbun@aol.com

Regent House ★★★★
Contact: Mrs Jewel Goss, Regent House, Starcross, Exeter EX6 8PA
T: (01626) 891947
F: (01626) 899126
E: regenthouse@eclipse.co.uk
I: www.cottageguide.co.uk/regenthouse

EXFORD
Somerset

2 Auction Field Cottages ★★★
Contact: Mr & Mrs Batchelor, Bulbarrow Farm, Bulbarrow, Blandford Forum DT11 0HQ
T: (01258) 817801
F: (01258) 817004

Bailiffs Cottage ★★★
Contact: Mr Martin Burnett, Bailiffs Cottage, Muddicombe Lane, Exford, Minehead TA24 7NH
T: (01643) 831342
F: (01643) 831342
E: jycburnett@aol.com

Court Farm ★★★-★★★★
Contact: Mrs Beth Horstmann, Court Farm, Exford, Minehead TA24 7LY
T: (01643) 831207
F: (01643) 831207
E: beth@courtfarm.co.uk
I: www.courtfarm.co.uk

Riscombe Farm Holiday Cottages and Stabling ★★★★
Contact: Mr & Mrs Brian & Leone Martin, Riscombe Farm Holiday Cottages and Stabling, Exford, Minehead TA24 7NH
T: (01643) 831480
F: (01643) 831480
E: info@riscombe.co.uk
I: www.riscombe.co.uk

Rocks Bungalow ★★★★
Contact: Mrs Kathryn Tucker, Stetfold Rocks Farm, Exford, Minehead TA24 7NZ
T: (01643) 831213
F: (01643) 831426
E: tucker@exfordfsbusiness.co.uk

Stilemoor Bungalow ★★★★
Contact: Mrs Joan Atkins, 2 Edgcott Cottages, Exford, Minehead TA24 7QG
T: (01643) 831564
F: (01643) 831564
E: info@stilemoorexmoor.co.uk
I: www.stilemoorexmoor.co.uk

Westermill Farm ★★★-★★★★
Contact: Mr & Mrs Oliver & Jill Edwards
T: (01643) 831238
F: (01643) 831216
E: holidays@westermill-exmoor.co.uk
I: www.exmoorfarmholidays.co.uk

EXMOUTH
Devon

2 & 4 Channel View ★★★-★★★★
Contact: Mr & Mrs Lenn, St Andrews Holiday Homes, Channel View, The Esplanade, Exmouth EX8 2AZ
T: (01395) 222555
F: (01395) 270766
E: st-andrews@lineone.net

Apartment 2 ★★★★
Contact: Mr & Mrs Griffiths, 21 Phoenix Grove, Westbury Park, Bristol, Bristol BS6 7XX
T: (0117) 989 2658

Pilot Cottage ★★★★
Contact: Mr & Mrs Woods, 131 Victoria Road, Exmouth EX8 1DR
T: (01395) 222882
E: seahorse@exmouth.net
I: www.xmouth.co.uk

Saxonbury Annexe ★★★
Contact: Mrs Elliott, 43 Seymour Road, Exmouth EX8 3JG
T: (01395) 264323
E: jojohn@elliott.fsnet.co.uk

EXTON
Somerset

Oakley Lodge ★★★
Contact: Mrs Anne Pantall, Upper House, Staunton-on-Wye, Staunton on Wye, Hereford HR4 7LW
T: (01981) 500249
E: anne.pantall@amserve.net
I: www.oakley-lodge.co.uk

FALMOUTH
Cornwall

Captains Corner, Sunrise & The Brig ★★★-★★★★
Contact: Mrs Margie Lumby, Special Places in Cornwall, Poachers Reach, Harcourt, Feock, Truro TR3 6SQ
T: (01872) 864400
E: office@specialplacescornwall.co.uk
I: www.specialplacescornwall.co.uk

The Charthouse ★★★
Contact: The Proprietor, The Charthouse, 56 High Street, Falmouth TR11

Chy Nessa ★★★
Contact: Mrs Shirley Keene, Chy Nessa, 29 Church Street, Newlyn, Penzance TR18 5JY
T: (01736) 366697
E: chynessa@netscape.net

The Moorings ★★★★
Contact: Mrs Margie Lumby, Special Places In Cornwall, Poachers Reach, Harcourt, Feock, Truro TR3 6SQ
T: (01872) 864400
E: office@specialplacescornwall.co.uk

Pantiles ★★★
Contact: Mr Colin Kemp, Pantiles, Stracey Road, Newlyn, Penzance TR11 4DW
T: (01326) 211838
F: (01326) 211668
E: colinkemp@lineone.net

Parklands ★★★
Contact: Mrs Simmons, 215a Perry Street, Billericay CM12 0NZ
T: (01277) 654425
E: steve@simmo58.freeserve.co.uk

Pendra Loweth Holiday Cottages ★★★★
Contact: Ms Janet Dawes, Pendra Loweth Holiday Cottages, Maen Valley, Goldenbank, Maenporth, Falmouth TR11 5BJ
T: (01326) 312190
F: (01326) 211120
E: maenvalley@aol.com
I: www.maenvalley.co.uk

Seaworthy ★★★★
Contact: Mr & Mrs Hinton, Cornish Cottage Holidays, The Old Turnpike Dairy, Godolphin, Meneage Street, Helston TR13 8AA
T: (01326) 573808
F: (01326) 564992
E: enquiry@cornishcottageholidays.co.uk
I: www.cornishcottageholidays.co.uk

Stable Cottage ★★★★
Contact: Mrs Margie Lumby, Special Places, Poachers Reach, Feock, Truro TR3 6SQ
T: (01872) 864400
F: (01872) 864900
E: office@specialplacescornwall.co.uk
I: www.specialplacescornwall.co.uk

Tall Ships ★★★★★
Contact: Mr M Couldry, 8 Campbeltown Way, Port Pendennis, Falmouth TR11 3YE
T: (01326) 311440
F: (01326) 316781
E: mike.couldry@virgin.net
I: www.cornwall-online.co.uk/tallships

Toldeen Waterside Studio ★★★
Contact: Mrs Margie Lumby, Special Places in Cornwall, Poachers Reach, Harcourt, Feock, Truro TR3 6SQ
T: (01872) 864400
E: office@specialplacescornwall.co.uk
I: www.specialplacescornwall.co.uk

West Winds ★★★-★★★★
Contact: Mr Brian Watmore, West Winds, Stracey Road, Newlyn, Penzance TR11 4DW
T: (01326) 211707
F: (01326) 319158
I: www.cornwall-online.co.uk/west-winds

Wodehouse Place ★★★
Contact: Shelagh Spear, Wodehouse Place, Woodlane, Falmouth TR11 4RA
T: (01326) 314311

FAULKLAND
Somerset

The Green Farm ★★★★★
Contact: Mrs Gatley, The Green Farm House, The Green, Faulkland, Bath BA3 5UY
T: (01373) 834331
F: (01373) 834331
E: AnneGatley@greenfarmhouse.fsworld.co.uk

Lime Kiln Farm ★★★★★
Contact: Mrs Merinda Kendall, Lime Kiln Farm, Faulkland, Bath BA3 5XE
T: (01373) 834305
F: (01373) 834026
E: lime_kiln@hotmail.com

FENNY BRIDGES
Devon

Skinners Ash Farm ★★★★
Contact: Mrs Jill Godfrey, Skinners Ash Farm, Fenny Bridges, Alfington, Ottery St Mary EX14 3BH
T: (01404) 850231
F: (01404) 850231
I: www.cottageguide.co.uk/skinnersash/

FEOCK
Cornwall

Brambles ★★★
Contact: Cornish Cottage Holidays, The Old Turnpike Dairy, Godolphin, Meneage Street, Helston TR13 8AA
T: (01326) 573808
F: (01326) 564992
E: enquiry@cornishcottageholidays.co.uk
I: www.cornishcottageholidays.co.uk

Seaview Farm Cottage ★★
Contact: Mrs Margie Lumby, Poachers Reach, Harcourt, Feock, Truro TR3 6SQ
T: (01872) 864400
E: office@specialplacescornwall.co.uk
I: www.specialplacescornwall.co.uk

FIVE LANES
Cornwall

The Little Barn ★★★★
Contact: Ms Sheila Taylor, The Little Barn, Thorn Cottage, Five Lanes, Launceston PL15 7RX
T: (01566) 86689
F: (01566) 86936
E: sheilataylor@littlebarn.demon.co.uk
I: www.littlebarn.demon.co.uk

FLEET
Dorset

The Lugger Inn
Rating Applied For
Contact: Mr John Parker, 30 West Street, Chickerell, Fleet, Weymouth DT3 4DY
T: (01305) 766611
E: john@theluggerinn.co.uk

FLUSHING
Cornwall

Quay Cottage ★★★
Contact: Mrs Margie Lumby, Poachers Reach, Harcourt, Feock, Truro TR3 6SQ
T: (01872) 864400
E: office@specialplacescornwall.co.uk
I: www.specialplacescornwall.co.uk

Sea Pie Cottage ★★★★
Contact: Mrs Margie Lumby, Poachers Reach, Harcourt, Feock, Truro TR3 6SQ
T: (01872) 864400
E: office@specialplacescornwall.co.uk
I: www.specialplacescornwall.co.uk

Waterside House ★★★★
Contact: Mrs Margie Lumby, Poachers Reach, Harcourt, Feock, Truro TR3 6SQ
T: (01872) 864400
E: office@specialplacescornwall.co.uk
I: www.specialplacescornwall.co.uk

FOLKE
Dorset

Glebe House - Guests' Suite ★★★★
Contact: Mr S Friar, Glebe House - Guests' Suite, Folke, Sherborne DT9 5HP
T: (01963) 210337
F: (01963) 210337
E: friarwinter@btinternet.com

FONTHILL BISHOP
Wiltshire

Rose Cottage ★★★
Contact: Mr Nicholas Pash, Chapel House, Luke Street, Berwick St John, Shaftesbury SP7 0HQ
T: (01747) 828170
F: (01747) 829090
E: enq@hideaways.co.uk
I: www.hideaways.co.uk

FORSTON
Dorset

Watcombe House ★★★★
Contact: Mr Zachary Stuart-Brown, Dream Cottages, 41 Maiden Street, Weymouth DT4 8AZ
T: (01305) 761347
E: admin@dream-cottages.co.uk
I: www.dream-cottages.co.uk

FORTUNESWELL
Dorset

Cama Cottage ★★★★
Contact: Mr Zachary Stuart-Brown, Dream Cottages, 41 Maiden Street, Weymouth DT4 8AZ
T: (01305) 761347
E: admin@dream-cottages.co.uk
I: www.dream-cottages.co.uk

Ocean Views ★★★
Contact: Mr Charles Gollop, 93 Graham Road, London SW19 3SP
T: (020) 8408 9800
F: (020) 8408 9804
E: charles@oceanviews.uk.com

Parkers Cottage
Rating Applied For
Contact: Ms Lesley Gyte, Amhurst Lodge Cottages & Apartments, 4 Spring Gardens, Fortuneswell, Portland DT5 1JG
T: (01305) 860960
F: (01305) 860960

Quiet Nook ★★★
Contact: Dream Cottages, 41 Maiden Street, Weymouth DT4 8AZ
T: (01305) 761347
F: (01305) 789000

Sues Cottage ★★★
Contact: Mr Zachary Stuart-Brown, Dream Cottages, 41 Maiden Street, Weymouth DT4 8AZ
T: (01305) 761347
E: admin@dream-cottages.co.uk
I: www.dream-cottages.co.uk

FOWEY
Cornwall

1 & 2 Harbour Cottages ★★-★★★
Contact: Estuary Cottages, Estuary House, Fore Street, Fowey PL23 1AH
T: (01726) 832965
F: (01726) 832866
E: info@estuarycottages.co.uk
I: www.estuarycottages.co.uk

Chy Vounder & Rose Villa ★★
Contact: Fowey Harbour Cottages (W Hill & Son), 3 Fore Street, Polruan, Fowey PL23 1AH
T: (01726) 832211
F: (01726) 832901
E: hillandson@talk21.com

Crow's Nest & West Wing ★★★★
Contact: Estuary House, Fore Street, Polruan, Fowey PL23 1AH
T: (01726) 832965
F: (01726) 832866
E: info@estuarycottages.co.uk
I: www.estuarycottages.co.uk

Harbour Cottage ★★★
Contact: Fowey Harbour Cottages (W J B Hill & Son), 3 Fore Street, Fowey PL23 1AH
T: (01726) 832211
F: (01726) 832901
E: hillandson@talk21.com

Little Quoin ★★★★
Contact: Estuary Cottages, Estuary House, Fore Street, Fowey PL23 1AH
T: (01726) 832965
F: (01726) 832866
E: info@estuarycottages.co.uk
I: www.estuarycottages.co.uk

Palm Trees ★★
Contact: 3 Fore Street, Polruan, Fowey PL23 1AH
T: (01726) 832211
F: (01726) 832901
E: hillandson@talk21.com

The Penthouse ★★★
Contact: 3 Fore Street, Polruan, Fowey PL23 1AH
T: (01726) 832211
F: (01726) 832901
E: hillandson@talk21.com

River Watch ★★★★
Contact: Estuary Cottages, Estuary House, Fore Street, Fowey PL23 1AH
T: (01726) 832965
F: (01726) 832866
E: info@estuarycottages.co.uk
I: www.estuarycottages.co.uk

Sideways Cottage ★★★★
Contact: 3 Fore Street, Polruan, Fowey PL23 1AH
T: (01726) 832211
F: (01726) 832901
E: hillandson@talk21.com

The Square Rig ★★★★
Contact: Mrs H Astley-Morton, Square Rig Holidays, Ladybird House, 26 The Avenue, Rubery, Birmingham B45 9AL
T: (0121) 457 6664
F: (0121) 457 6685
E: info@sqrighol.co.uk
I: www.sqrighol.co.uk

17a St Fimbarrus Road ★★★
Contact: 3 Fore Street, Polruan, Fowey PL23 1AH
T: (01726) 832211
F: (01726) 832901
E: hillandson@talk21.com

Star Cottage ★★★★
Contact: Estuary Cottages, Estuary House, Fore Street, Fowey PL23 1AH
T: (01726) 832965
F: (01726) 832866
E: info@estuarycottages.co.uk
I: www.estuarycottages.co.uk

9 Troy Court ★★★★★
Contact: Mrs Sarah Wateridge, Estuary Cottages, Estuary House, Fowey PL23 1AH
T: (01726) 832965
F: (01726) 832866
I: www.estuarycottages.co.uk

Waterfront Apartment ★★★
Contact: Estuary House, Fore Street, Polruan, Fowey PL23 1AH
T: (01726) 832965
F: (01726) 832866
E: info@esturarycottages.co.uk
I: www.estuarycottages.co.uk

FRAMPTON
Dorset

Wingreen Manor Farm Cottages
Rating Applied For
Contact: Mr & Mrs Jon & Sandra Desborough, 354 Hatfield Road, St Albans AL4 0DU
T: (01727) 853853
E: afe24@dial.pipex.com

FREMINGTON
Devon

Lower Yelland Farm ★★★
Contact: Mr Peter Day
T: (01271) 860101
F: (01271) 860101
E: pday@loweryellandfarm.co.uk
I: www.loweryellandfarm.co.uk

FRESHFORD
Bath and North East Somerset

The Barton Cottage ★★★
Contact: Mrs C Foster, 57 Hillcrest Drive, Southdown, Bath BA2 1HD
T: (01225) 429756

Dolphin Cottage ★★★★★
Contact: Mrs Rowena Wood, Park Corner, Freshford, Limpley Stoke, Bath BA2 7UQ
T: (01225) 722100
F: (01225) 723741
E: rowena_wood@compuserve.com
I: www.dolphincottage.com

FRITHELSTOCK
Devon

Honeysuckle Cottage ★★★★
Contact: Farm & Cottage Holidays, Victoria House, 12 Fore Street, Northam, Bideford EX39 1AW
T: (01237) 479146
F: (01237) 421512
E: enquiries@farmcott.co.uk

FROME
Somerset

Bollow Hill Farm ★★★★
Contact: Mr & Mrs Mark & Emma Kaye, Bollow Hill Farm, Friggle Street, Frome BA11 5LJ
T: (01373) 463007
I: www.farmhousecottages.co.uk

Executive Holidays ★★★★-★★★★★
Contact: Mr R A Gregory, Executive Holidays, Whitemill Farm, Iron Mills Lane, Oldford, Frome BA11 2NR
T: (01373) 452907
F: (01373) 453253
E: info@executiveholidays.co.uk
I: www.executiveholidays.co.uk

Hill View ★★
Contact: Mrs Margaret House, Forest View, Gare Hill, Frome BA11 5EZ
T: (01985) 844276
E: wells@packsaddle11.freeserve.co.uk

St Katharine's Lodge ★★★★
Contact: Mrs Tania Maynard, St Katharine's Cottage, East Woodlands, Frome BA11 5LQ
T: (01373) 471434
F: (01373) 474499
E: rogermaynard@csi.com
I: www.stkaths.com

GALMPTON
Devon

Dart View ★★★
Contact: Mr Ian Butterworth, Holiday Homes & Cottages South West, 365A Torquay Road, Paignton TQ3 2BT
T: (01803) 663650
F: (01803) 664037
E: holcotts@aol.com
I: www.swcottages.co.uk

Georgia ★★★
Contact: Holiday Homes & Cottages South West, 365A Torquay Road, Paignton TQ3 2BT
T: (01803) 663650
F: (01803) 664037
E: holcotts@aol.com
I: www.swcottages.co.uk

GEORGE NYMPTON
Devon

East Trayne Cottage ★★★★
Contact: Marsden's Cottage Holidays, 2 The Square, Braunton EX33 2JB
T: (01271) 813777
F: (01271) 813664
E: holidays@marsdens.co.uk
I: www.marsdens.co.uk

GEORGEHAM
Devon

Appletree Cottage ★★★
Contact: Marsden's Cottage Holidays, 2 The Square, Braunton EX33 2JB
T: (01271) 813777
F: (01271) 813664
E: holidays@marsdens.co.uk
I: www.marsdens.co.uk

Bryher ★★★★
Contact: Marsden's Cottage Holidays, 2 The Square, Braunton EX33 2JB
T: (01271) 813777
F: (01271) 813664
E: holidays@marsdens.co.uk
I: www.marsdens.co.uk

Burver Cottage ★★★★
Contact: Marsden's Cottage Holidays, 2 The Square, Braunton EX33 2JB
T: (01271) 813777
F: (01271) 813664
E: holidays@marsdens.co.uk
I: www.marsdens.co.uk

Callum Cottage ★★★
Contact: Marsden's Cottage Holidays, 2 The Square, Braunton EX33 2JB
T: (01271) 813777
F: (01271) 813664
E: holidays@marsdens.co.uk
I: www.marsdens.co.uk

16 David's Hill ★★★
Contact: Marsden's Cottage Holidays, 2 The Square, Braunton EX33 2JB
T: (01271) 813777
F: (01271) 813664
E: holidays@marsdens.co.uk
I: www.marsdens.co.uk

Little Dene ★★★
Contact: Marsden's Cottage Holidays, 2 The Square, Braunton EX33 2JB
T: (01271) 813777
F: (01271) 813664
E: holidays@marsdens.co.uk

Pickwell Barton Cottages ★★-★★★
Contact: Mrs Sheila Cook, Pickwell Barton Cottages, Pickwell Barton, Georgeham, Braunton EX33 1LA
T: (01271) 890987
F: (01271) 890987
I: www.pickwellbarton.co.uk

Rock Cottage ★★
Contact: Marsden's Cottage Holidays, 2 The Square, Braunton EX33 2JB
T: (01271) 813777
F: (01271) 813664
E: holidays@marsdens.co.uk
I: www.marsdens.co.uk

Wester David ★★★★
Contact: 2 The Square, Braunton EX33 2JB
T: (01271) 813777
F: (01271) 813664
E: holidays@marsdens.co.uk
I: www.marsdens.co.uk

GERMOE
Cornwall

Bosverbas ★★★
Contact: Mr & Mrs Bearryman, Bosverbas, Praa Sands, Penzance TR20 9AA
T: (01736) 762277

GITTISHAM
Devon

Westgate Cottage ★★★★
Contact: Jean Bartlett Cottage Holidays, Fore Street, Seaton EX12 3JB
T: (01297) 23221
F: (01297) 23303
E: holidays@jeanbartlett.com
I: www.netbreaks.com/jeanb

GLASTONBURY
Somerset

60 Bove Town ★★★
Contact: Mrs Robertson, Well Lane, St Keverne, Helston TR12 6LZ
T: (01326) 280514
E: losowek.herbs@btinternet.com

The Lightship ★★★
Contact: Ms R Rose, The Lightship, 82 Bove Town, Glastonbury BA6 8JG
T: (01458) 833698
E: roselightship2001@yahoo.co.uk
I: www.lightship.ukf.net

Middlewick Holiday Cottages ★★★★
Contact: Mr & Mrs Martin & Shirley Kavanagh, Middlewick Holiday Cottages, Middlewick, Wick Lane, Glastonbury BA6 8JW
T: (01458) 832351
F: (01458) 832351
E: info@middlewickholidaycottages.co.uk
I: www.middlewickcottages.co.uk

St Edmunds Cottage ★★★★
Contact: Mrs Jeannette Heygate-Browne, St Edmunds Cottage, 26 Wells Road, Glastonbury BA6 9BS
T: (01458) 830461
E: rheygatebrowne@aol.com
I: www.members.aol.com/rheygatebrowne/stedmundscottage/homepage.html

GODNEY
Somerset

Swallow Barn ★★★★
Contact: Mrs Hilary Millard, Swallow Barn, Double Gate Farm, Godney, Wells BA5 1RX
T: (01458) 832217
F: (01458) 835612
E: doublegatefarm@aol.com
I: www.doublegatefarm.com

Tor View & Church Cottages ★★★
Contact: Mr & Mrs Michael & Jenny Churches, Godney Farm Holiday Cottages, Godney, Wells BA5 1RX
T: (01458) 831141
F: (01458) 831141
E: m.churches@farmersweekly.net.co.uk

GOLANT
Cornwall

Church Meadow ★★★★
Contact: Mrs Varco, Church Meadow, Penquite Farm, Golant, Fowey PL23 1LB
T: (01726) 833319
F: (01726) 833319
E: varco@farmersweekly.net
I: www.cornwall-online.co.uk/churchmeadow

Coaches Rest
Rating Applied For
Contact: Mrs Ruth Varco, Penquite, Golant, Fowey PL23 1LB
T: (01726) 833319
F: (01726) 833319
E: varco@farmersweekly.net

GOODLEIGH
Devon

Bampfield Cottages ★★★★
Contact: Mrs Lynda Thorne, Bampfield Cottages, Bampfield Farm, Goodleigh, Barnstaple EX32 7NR
T: (01271) 346566
I: www.bampfieldfarm.co.uk

GOODRINGTON
Devon

Ashdene Holiday Apartments ★★★
Contact: Mrs & Mr Jill & David Beckett, Ashdene Holiday Apartments, Cliff Park Road, Goodrington, Paignton TQ4 6NB
T: (01803) 558397
E: ashdene.apts@goodrington.fsbusiness.co.uk
I: www.ashdeneapartments.co.uk

GORRAN HAVEN
Cornwall

Haven Cottage & Seamew ★★★-★★★★
Contact: Miss P Teague, Clovelly, Rice Lane, Gorran Haven, St Austell PL26 6JD
T: (01726) 842977
I: www.gorranhavencottages.co.uk

Tregillan ★★★
Contact: Mr & Mrs Pike, Tregillan, Trewollock Lane, Gorran Haven, St Austell PL26 6NT
T: (01726) 842452

GREAT CHEVERELL
Wiltshire

Downswood ★
Contact: Mrs Ros Shepherd, Downswood, Great Cheverell, Devizes SN10 5TW
T: (01380) 813304

GRITTENHAM
Wiltshire

Orchard View ★★★★
Contact: Mr & Mrs P Cary, Orchard View, Grittenham, Chippenham SN15 4JX
T: (01666) 510747

GUNWALLOE
Cornwall

Hingey Farm ★★★★
Contact: Cornish Cottage Holidays, The Old Turnpike Dairy, Godolphin, Meneage Street, Helston TR13 8AA
T: (01326) 573808
F: (01326) 564992
E: enquiry@cornishcottageholidays.co.uk
I: www.cornishcottageholidays.co.uk

HALWILL
Devon

Anglers Paradise ★★★★
Contact: Mr Zyg Gregorek, Anglers Paradise, The Gables, Winsford, Halwill, Beaworthy EX21 5XT
T: (01409) 221559
F: (01409) 221559
I: www.anglers-paradise.co.uk

Westcroft Coach House & Wheelwright Cottage ★★★★
Contact: Mrs Barbara Dalton, Westcroft Coach House & Wheelwright Cottage, Westcroft Farm, Halwill, Beaworthy EX21 5UL
T: (01409) 221328
F: (01409) 221836
E: bdalton@waitrose.com

HARCOMBE
Devon

Chapel Cottage ★★★
Contact: Ms Kate Bartlett, Jean Bartlett Cottage Holidays, Fore Street, Beer, Seaton EX12 3JB
T: (01297) 23221
F: (01297) 23303
E: holidays@jeanbartlett.com
I: www.netbreaks.com/jeanb

HARDINGTON MANDEVILLE
Somerset

Stable Cottage ★★★
Contact: Farm & Cottage Holidays, Victoria House, 12 Fore Street, Northam, Bideford EX39 1AW
T: (01237) 479146
F: (01237) 421512
E: enquiries@farmcott.co.uk

HARLYN BAY
Cornwall

The Croft ★★
Contact: Ms Nicky Stanley, Harbour Holidays - Padstow, 1 North Quay, Padstow PL28 8AF
T: (01841) 532555
F: (01841) 533115
E: sales@jackie-stanley.co.uk
I: www.harbourholidays.co.uk

Harlyn Bay Cottages ★★★
Contact: Mrs Sally Albright, 10 Trewithan Parc, Lostwithiel PL22 0BD
T: (01208) 873856
E: trewithan@hotmail.com

Harlyn Farmhouse ★★★★
Contact: Mrs Hazel Perry, 35 Westbury Hill, Westbury on Trym, Bristol BS9 3AG
T: (0117) 962 4831
F: (0117) 962 4831
E: hazelperry@blueyonder.co.uk

4 Polmark Drive ★★★
Contact: Mr Neville Powell, 7 Pellew Close, Padstow PL28 8EY
T: (01841) 532156

Yellow Sands Holiday Apartments & House★★★
Contact: Mr Martin Dakin, Yellow Sands Holiday Apartments & House, Harlyn Bay, St Merryn, Padstow PL28 8SE
T: (01841) 520376

HARTLAND
Devon

Mettaford Farm Cottages ★★★-★★★★★
Contact: Mr & Mrs Peter & Janet Cornwell, Marsden's Cottage Holidays, 2 The Square, Braunton EX33 2JB
T: (01271) 813777
F: (01271) 813664
E: holidays@marsdens.co.uk
I: www.marsdens.co.uk

The Old Dairy & Polly's Cottage ★★★-★★★★★
Contact: Mrs S J Heywood, East Milford, Hartland, Bideford EX39 6EA
T: (01237) 441268
E: sue@gorvincottages.co.uk

HATHERLEIGH
Devon

Prudence Cottage ★★★
Contact: Ms H Stoner, Light Rock Systems Ltd, 67 Dorking Road, Epsom KT18 7JU
T: (01372) 741123
E: info@yourcountrycottages.co.uk
I: www.yourcountrycottage.co.uk

HAWKCHURCH
Devon

The Lodge Cottage ★★★
Contact: Mr & Mrs Ian & Valerie Spacie, The Lodge Cottage, 9 Tunnel Road, Hawkchurch, Axminster DT8 3BQ
T: (01308) 863468
F: (01308) 863468
E: ivspacie@hotmail.com

Sandford Cottage ★★★★
Contact: Mr & Mrs Golding, Sandford Cottage, Southmoor Farm, Hawkchurch, Axminster EX13 5UF
T: (01297) 678440
F: (01297) 678668
E: petergolding@ic24.net

HAWKRIDGE
Somerset

West Hollowcombe Cottages ★★★★
Contact: Farm & Cottage Holidays, Victoria House, 12 Fore Street, Northam, Bideford EX39 1AW
T: (01237) 479146
F: (01237) 421512
E: enquiries@farmcott.co.uk

HAYLE
Cornwall

Brunnion Barns H620 & H621 ★★★★
Contact: Chapel House, Luke Street, Berwick St John, Shaftesbury SP7 0HQ
T: (01747) 828170
F: (01747) 829090
E: enq@hideaways.co.uk

74 Gwithian Towans ★★★
Contact: Mr & Mrs Ray & Nicola Skinner, 7 The Gardens, Doddinghurst, Brentwood CM15 0LU
T: (01277) 822924

Manor House ★★★★
Contact: Powell's Cottage Holidays, High Street, Saundersfoot SA69 9EJ
T: (01834) 812791
F: (01834) 811731
E: info@powells.co.uk
I: www.powells.co.uk

Penellen Rating Applied For
Contact: Mr Peter Beare, Penellen, Penellen Hotel, Riviere Towans, Hayle TR27 5AF
T: (01736) 753777
E: pjbeare@aol.com

Truthwall Farm ★★★
Contact: Mrs Goldsworthy, Truthwall Farm, Leedstown, Hayle TR27 5EU
T: (01736) 850266

HEANTON
Devon

Grange House ★★★★
Contact: Marsden's Cottage Holidays, 2 The Square, Braunton EX33 2JB
T: (01271) 813777
F: (01271) 813664
E: holidays@marsdens.co.uk
I: www.marsdens.co.uk

HEATHFIELD
Somerset

Higher House Rating Applied For
Contact: Mrs Kirsten Horton, Higher House, Hillcommon, Heathfield, Taunton TA4 1DU
T: (01823) 400570
F: (01823) 400765
E: tedandkirsten@tiscali.co.uk

HEDDINGTON
Wiltshire

Harley Bungalow ★★
Contact: Mrs Mary Fox, Harley Bungalow, Harley Farm, Stockley Road, Heddington, Calne SN11 0PS
T: (01380) 850214
F: (01380) 850214
E: harley@luna.co.uk

HELE
Devon

Hele Payne Farm Cottages ★★★
Contact: Mrs Maynard, Hele Payne Farm, Hele, Exeter EX5 4PH
T: (01392) 881530
F: (01392) 881530

HELLANDBRIDGE
Cornwall

Silverstream Holidays ★★★
Contact: Mr Cameron, Silverstream Holidays, Hellandbridge, Bodmin PL30 4QR
T: (01208) 74408

HELSTON
Cornwall

Brick Cottage ★★
Contact: Mullion Cottages, Sea View Terrace, Churchtown, Mullion, Helston TR12 7HN
T: (01326) 240315
F: (01326) 241090
E: martin@mullioncottages.com

Chestnut Cottage ★★★
Contact: Mullion Cottages, Sea View Terrace, Churchtown, Mullion, Helston TR12 7HN
T: (01326) 240315
F: (01326) 241090
E: martin@mullioncottages.com

Church View ★★★★
Contact: Mullion Cottages, Sea View Terrace, Churchtown, Mullion, Helston TR12 7HN
T: (01326) 240315
F: (01326) 241090
E: martin@mullioncottage.com

Chy Barn ★★
Contact: Mullion Cottages, Sea View Terrace, Churchtown, Mullion, Helston TR12 7HN
T: (01326) 240315
F: (01326) 241090
E: martin@mullioncottages.com

Clies Farmhouse ★★
Contact: Mullion Cottages, Sea View Terrace, Churchtown, Mullion, Helston TR12 7HN
T: (01326) 240315
F: (01326) 241090
E: martin@mullioncottages.com

5 Coastguard Cottage ★★★
Contact: Mr Martin Raftery, Sea View Terrace, Churchtown, Mullion, Helston TR12 7HN
T: (01326) 240315
F: (01326) 241090
E: martin@mullioncottages.com

The Crag ★★★★
Contact: Mr Martin Raftery, Sea View Terrace, Churchtown, Mullion, Helston TR12 7HN
T: (01326) 240315
F: (01326) 241090
E: martin@mullioncottages.com

Driftwood ★★★
Contact: Mullion Cottages, Sea View Terrace, Churchtown, Mullion, Helston TR12 7HN
T: (01326) 240315
F: (01326) 241090
E: martin@mullioncottages.com

Flat 11a Rating Applied For
Contact: 22 Trevallion Park, Feock, Truro TR3 6RS
T: (01872) 863537

Ginentonic ★★★★
Contact: Mullion Cottages, Sea View Terrace, Churchtown, Mullion, Helston TR12 7HN
T: (01326) 240315
F: (01326) 241090
E: martin@mullioncottages.com

Goonhilly View ★★
Contact: Mullion Cottages, Sea View Terrace, Churchtown, Mullion, Helston TR12 7HN
T: (01326) 240315
F: (01326) 241090
E: martin@mullioncottages.com

The Linhay ★★
Contact: Mr Martin Raftery, Sea View Terrace, Churchtown, Mullion, Helston TR12 7HN
T: (01326) 240315
F: (01326) 241090
E: martin@mullioncottages.com

Little Criccieth ★★★
Contact: Mr Martin Raftery, Sea View Terrace, Churchtown, Mullion, Helston TR12 7HN
T: (01326) 240315
F: (01326) 241090
E: martin@mullioncottages.com

Lobster Pot ★★★
Contact: Mr & Mrs A Hinton, Cornish Cottage Holidays, The Old Turnpike Dairy, Godolphin Road, Helston TR13 8AA
T: (01326) 573808

The Longbarn ★★★
Contact: Mullion Cottages, Sea View Terrace, Churchtown, Mullion, Helston TR12 7HN
T: (01326) 240315
F: (01326) 241090
E: martin@mullioncottages.com

Midsummer Barn ★★★★
Contact: Mr Martin Raftery, Sea View Terrace, Churchtown, Mullion, Helston TR12 7HN
T: (01326) 240315
F: (01326) 241090
E: martin@mullioncottages.com

Neid Cottage ★★★
Contact: Mr Martin Raftery, Sea View Terrace, Churchtown, Mullion, Helston TR12 7HN
T: (01326) 240315
F: (01326) 241090
E: martin@mullioncottages.com

Newlyn Cottage ★★
Contact: Mr Martin Raftery, Sea View Terrace, Churchtown, Mullion, Helston TR12 7HN
T: (01326) 240315
F: (01326) 241090
E: martin@mullioncottages.com

The Nook ★★★
Contact: Mr Martin Raffery, Sea View Terrace, Churchtown, Mullion, Helston TR12 7HN
T: (01326) 240315
F: (01326) 241090
E: martin@mullioncottages.com

Pemboa Holiday Cottages Rating Applied For
Contact: Mrs Angela Crapp, Pemboa Holiday Cottages, Pemboa Farm, Helston TR13 0QF
T: (01326) 572380

Pras-Gwylas ★★★
Contact: Mr Martin Raftery, Sea View Terrace, Churchtown, Mullion, Helston TR12 7HN
T: (01326) 240315
F: (01326) 241090
E: martin@mullioncottages.com

Tregevis Farm ★★★★
Contact: Mrs Bray, Tregevis Farm, St Martin, Helston TR12 6DN
T: (01326) 231265
F: (01326) 231265

Trelawney House Self Catering Holidays★★★
Contact: Mr E J Cardnell, Trelawney House, Gunwalloe, Helston TR12 7QB
T: (01326) 240260
F: (01326) 240260
E: ejcardnell@aol.com

Westward House
Rating Applied For
Contact: Mr Martin Raftery, Sea View Terrace, Churchtown, Mullion, Helston TR12 7HN
T: (01326) 240315
F: (01326) 241090
E: martin@mullioncottages.com

Westward Mews
Rating Applied For
Contact: Mr Martin Raftery, Sea View Terrace, Churchtown, Mullion, Helston TR12 7HN
T: (01326) 240315
F: (01326) 241090
E: martin@mullioncottages.com

HELSTONE
Cornwall

Mayrose Farm ★★★-★★★★
Contact: Mrs Jane Maunder, Mayrose Farm, Helstone, Camelford PL32 9RN
T: (01840) 213509
F: (01840) 213509
E: info@mayrosefarmcottages.co.uk
I: www.mayrosefarmcottages.co.uk

HENWOOD
Cornwall

Clouds Hill Cottage
Rating Applied For
Contact: Mr Stephen Bennett, 64 Park Drive, London W3 8NA
T: (020) 8993 2628
F: 08709 223563
E: staphen@cloudshillcottage.co.uk

Henwood Barns
Rating Applied For
Contact: Mrs C Crossey, Henwood Barns, Henwood, Liskeard PL14 5BP
T: (01579) 363576
F: (01579) 363576
E: henwoodbarns@aol.com

HERODSFOOT
Cornwall

Coombe Farm Holiday Cottages ★★★★
Contact: Mrs Claire Trevelyan, Coombe Farm Holiday Cottages, Coombe Farm, Herodsfoot, Liskeard PL14 4RS
T: (01579) 320548
F: (01579) 321789
E: trevelyan@coombe-farm.co.uk
I: www.coombe-farm.co.uk

HEYWOOD
Wiltshire

Heywood Holiday Cottages ★★★★★
Contact: Mr John Boyce
T: (01225) 868393
F: (01225) 868393
E: enquiries@ashecottage-holidaylets.co.uk
I: www.ashecottage-holidaylets.co.uk

Pine Lodge ★
Contact: Mrs Mary Prince, Lea Cottage, 12 Church Road, Heywood, Westbury BA13 4LP
T: (01373) 822949
E: Pinelodgex@aol.com

The Wilderness ★★★★★
Contact: Mrs J Boyce
T: (01225) 868393
F: (01225) 868393
E: contact@uk-holiday-cottages.org
I: www.uk-holiday-cottages.org

HIGH BICKINGTON
Devon

Barn Owl Cottage ★★★★
Contact: 2 The Square, Braunton EX33 2JB
T: (01271) 813777
F: (01271) 813664
E: holidays@marsdens.co.uk
I: www.marsdens.co.uk

The Corn Mill ★★★★★
Contact: Mrs Glenda Tucker, The Corn Mill, Lee Barton, High Bickington, Umberleigh EX37 9BX
T: (01769) 560796
F: (01769) 560796
I: www.Lee-Barton.co.uk

Lee Meadow ★★★★★
Contact: Mrs Glenda Tucker, Lee Barton, High Bickington, Umberleigh EX37 9BX
T: (01769) 560796
E: tucker.leebarton@virgin.net

Millbrook ★★★★
Contact: Marsdens Cottage Holidays, 2 The Square, Braunton EX33 2JB
T: (01271) 813777
F: (01271) 813664
E: holidays@marsdens.co.uk

HIGHAMPTON
Devon

Orchard House
Rating Applied For
Contact: Mrs Sames, 28 Creslow Way, Stone, Aylesbury HP17 8YW
T: (01296) 747425
E: j.l.pearce@tesco.net

HIGHBRIDGE
Somerset

164 Burnham Road ★★
Contact: Mrs Carolyn Boley, 164 Burnham Road, Highbridge TA9 3EH
T: (01278) 788265

The Cottage ★★★★
Contact: Mrs Sarah Alderton, Grenacre Place, Bristol Road, Edithmead, Highbridge TA9 4HA
T: (01278) 785227
F: (01278) 785227
E: sm.alderton@btopenworld.com

HILFIELD
Dorset

Good Hope Studio Flat ★★★
Contact: Mrs Caroline Frew, The Good Hope, Hilfield, Dorchester DT2 7BD
T: (01963) 210551
E: caroline@thegoodhope.co.uk
I: www.thegoodhope.co.uk

HILPERTON
Wiltshire

Ashton Lodge Cottage ★★★
Contact: Mrs Daphne Richards, Ashton Lodge Cottage, Ashton Lodge, Ashton Road, Trowbridge BA14 7QY
T: (01225) 751420
E: daphne.richards@blueyonder.co.uk

HINTON ST GEORGE
Somerset

Summer Hill Cottage ★★★★
Contact: Mr & Mrs Leslie & Joan Farris, Summer Hill Cottage, Niddons House, Green Street, Hinton St George TA17 8SQ
T: (01460) 74475

HOLBETON
Devon

Devon Farm Cottages ★★★
Contact: Mrs Zoe Sayers, Devon Farm Cottages, Carswell, Holbeton, Plymouth PL8 1HH
T: (01752) 830492
F: (01752) 830565
E: carsfarm@farming.co.uk
I: www.devonfarmcottages.com

HOLCOMBE
Devon

Manor Farm
Rating Applied For
Contact: Mr Humphrey Clements, Manor Farm, Holcombe Village, Holcombe, Dawlish EX7 0JT
T: (01626) 863020
F: (01626) 863020
E: humphreyclem@aol.com

HOLCOMBE ROGUS
Devon

Whipcott Heights ★★★★
Contact: Mrs S M Gallagher, Whipcott Heights, Holcombe Rogus, Wellington TA21 0NA
T: (01823) 672339
F: (01823) 672339

HOLSWORTHY
Devon

Beech House ★★★★
Contact: Mrs M Heard, Thorne Park, Chilsworthy, Holsworthy EX22 7BL
T: (01409) 253339
F: (01409) 253339

Higher Sellick Farm Cottages ★★★★
Contact: Ms Denise Grafton, Higher Sellick Farm Cottages, Clawton, Holsworthy EX22 6PS
T: (01409) 271456
F: (01409) 271144
E: denisegrafton@devonholidays.org
I: www.devonholidays.org

Leworthy Cottage ★★★
Contact: Mrs Patricia Jennings, Leworthy Cottage, Pyworthy, Holsworthy EX22 6SJ
T: (01409) 259469

Thorne Manor Holiday Cottages ★★★-★★★★
Contact: Mr & Mrs Julian & Angela Plank, Thorne Manor Holiday Cottages, Thorne Manor, Holsworthy EX22 7JD
T: (01409) 253342
E: thornemanor@ex227jd.freeserve.co.uk
I: www.thorne-manor-holiday-cottages.co.uk

HOLWORTH
Dorset

Aura Holworth ★★★
Contact: Mr Zachary Stuart-Brown, Dream Cottages, 41 Maiden Street, Weymouth DT4 8AZ
T: (01305) 761347
E: admin@dream-cottages.co.uk
I: www.dream-cottages.co.uk

HOLYWELL BAY
Cornwall

Ocean Sands ★★★-★★★★
Contact: Mrs Penna, Ocean Sands, Holywell Bay, Newquay TR8 5PQ
T: (01637) 830447
F: (01637) 830447
E: www.sheilapenna@lineone.net

The Studio ★★★
Contact: Mr & Mrs Peter & Cathy Osborne, Cornish Horizons, Higher Trehemborne, St Merryn, Padstow PL28 8JU
T: (01841) 520889
F: (01841) 521523
E: cottages@cornishhorizons.co.uk
I: www.cornishhorizons.co.uk

HONITON
Devon

Devon Cottage Holidays ★★★★-★★★★★
Contact: Mr & Mrs Paul & Julia Hardy, Devon Cottage Holidays, Buckerell, Honiton EX14 3EP
T: (01404) 850292
F: (01404) 850292
E: info@devoncottage.com
I: www.devoncottage.com

March Cottage ★★★★
Contact: Ms Louise Hayman, Milkbere Cottage Holidays Ltd, 3 Fore Street, Seaton EX12 2LE
T: (01297) 20729
F: (01297) 24831
E: info@milkberehols.com
I: www.milkbere.com

Red Doors Farm ★★★★★
Contact: Mr Chris Shrubb
T: (01404) 890067
F: (01404) 890067
E: info@reddoors.co.uk
I: www.reddoors.co.uk

HOOKE
Dorset

Greenlands Bungalow ★★
Contact: Mr Zachary Stuart-Brown, Dream Cottages, 41 Maiden Street, Weymouth DT4 8AZ
T: (01305) 761347
E: admin@dream-cottages.co.uk
I: www.dream-cottages.co.uk

HOPE COVE
Devon

Blue Bay Apartments ★★★
Contact: Mrs J H Moon, Little Orchard, Kellaton, Kingsbridge TQ7 2ES
T: (01548) 511400
F: (01548) 511400
E: bbayapts@aol.co.uk

Seascape ★★★
Contact: Mrs Hazel Kolb, 57 The Whiteway, Cirencester GL7 2HQ
T: (01285) 654781
F: (01285) 654781
E: kolb@btinternet.com
I: www.englishholidayhouses.co.uk

Thornlea Mews Holiday Cottages ★★★
Contact: Mr & Mrs John & Ann Wilton, Thornlea Mews Holiday Cottages, Hope Cove, Salcombe TQ7 3HB
T: (01548) 561319
F: (01548) 561319
E: thornleamews@ukonline.co.uk
I: www.thornleamews-holidaycottages.co.uk

HORSINGTON
Somerset

Lois Country Cottages ★★★★
Contact: Mr & Mrs Paul & Penny Constant, Lois Barns, Lois Farm, Horsington, Templecombe BA8 0EW
T: (01963) 370496
F: (01963) 370496
E: info@loisfarm.com
I: www.somerset-farm-holiday.co.uk

HORTON
Gloucestershire

Bridle Path Cottage ★★★
Contact: Mr Clive Sykes, Sykes Cottage, York House, York Street, Chester CH1 3LR
T: (01244) 345700
E: info@sykescottages.co.uk

HUISH CHAMPFLOWER
Somerset

The Cottage ★★★
Contact: Mrs Mary Reynolds, Manor Farmhouse, Huish Champflower, Taunton TA4 2EY
T: (01984) 624915
F: (01984) 624915
E: reynolds@aol.com

ILFRACOMBE
Devon

The Admirals House ★★★★
Contact: Miss Marshall, Runnacleave Road, Ilfracombe EX34 8AR
T: (01271) 862446
F: (01271) 865379
I: www.theadmiralshouse.co.uk

Benricks ★★
Contact: Marsden's Cottage Holidays, 2 The Square, Braunton EX33 2JB
T: (01271) 813777
F: (01271) 813664
E: holidays@marsdens.co.uk
I: www.marsdens.co.uk

Brookdale Lodge ★★★
Contact: Marsden's Cottage Holidays, 2 The Square, Braunton EX33 2JB
T: (01271) 813777
F: (01271) 813664
E: holidays@marsdens.co.uk
I: www.marsdens.co.uk

Cheyne Flat ★★★
Contact: Marsden's Cottage Holidays, 2 The Square, Braunton EX33 2JB
T: (01271) 813777
F: (01271) 813664
E: holidays@marsdens.co.uk
I: www.marsdens.co.uk

Cornmill Cottage ★★★★
Contact: Marsden's Cottage Holidays, 2 The Square, Braunton EX33 2JB
T: (01271) 813777
F: (01271) 813664
E: holidays@marsdens.co.uk
I: www.marsdens.co.uk

Farthings Nest ★★★
Contact: Marsden's Cottage Holidays, 2 The Square, Braunton EX33 2JB
T: (01271) 813777
F: (01271) 813664
E: holidays@marsdens.co.uk
I: www.marsdens.co.uk

Gull Cottage ★★★
Contact: Marsden's Cottage Holidays, 2 The Square, Braunton EX33 2JB
T: (01271) 813777
F: (01271) 813664
E: holidays@marsdens.co.uk
I: www.marsdens.co.uk

Horne Cottage ★★★
Contact: 2 The Square, Braunton EX33 2JB
T: (01271) 813777
F: (01271) 813664
E: holidays@marsdens.co.uk
I: www.marsdens.co.uk

The Knapps
Rating Applied For
Contact: Marsdens Cottage Holidays, 2 The Square, Braunton EX33 2JB
T: (01271) 813777
F: (01271) 813664
E: holidays@marsdens.co.uk

The Lodge & Stables ★★★
Contact: Marsden's Cottage Holidays, 2 The Square, Braunton EX33 2JB
T: (01271) 813777
F: (01271) 813664
E: holidays@marsdens.co.uk
I: www.marsdens.co.uk

Middle Lee Farm
★★★-★★★★
Contact: Mr & Mrs Robin & Jenny Downer, Middle Lee Farm, Berrynarbor, Ilfracombe EX34 9SD
T: (01271) 882256
F: (01271) 882256
E: info@middleleefarm.co.uk
I: www.middleleefarm.co.uk

The Mill House ★★★★
Contact: Marsden's Cottage Holidays, 2 The Square, Braunton EX33 2JB
T: (01271) 813777
F: (01271) 813664
E: holidays@marsdens.co.uk
I: www.marsdens.co.uk

Mimosa Cottage ★★★
Contact: Marsden's Cottage Holidays, 2 The Square, Braunton EX33 2JB
T: (01271) 813777
F: (01271) 813664
E: holidays@marsdens.co.uk
I: www.marsdens.co.uk

Mostyn ★★★
Contact: Marsden's Cottage Holidays, 2 The Square, Braunton EX33 2JB
T: (01271) 813777
F: (01271) 813664
E: holidays@marsdens.co.uk
I: www.marsdens.co.uk

Norwood Holiday Flats ★★★
Contact: Mrs Betty Bulled, Norwood Holiday Flats, Highfield Road, Ilfracombe EX34 9LH
T: (01271) 862370

Rockcliffe ★★★★
Contact: Mr & Mrs Peter & Janet Cornwell, Marsden's Cottage Holidays, 2 The Square, Braunton EX33 2JB
T: (01271) 813777
F: (01271) 813664
E: holidays@marsdens.co.uk
I: www.marsdens.co.uk

The Round House ★★★★
Contact: Mr & Mrs P Cornwell, Marsden's Cottage Holidays, 2 The Square, Braunton EX33 2JB
T: (01271) 813777
I: www.marsdens.co.uk

White Pebbles ★★★
Contact: Mrs J M Foreshew, White Pebbles, The Torrs, Torrs Walk Avenue, Ilfracombe EX34 8AU
T: (01271) 864579

Widmouth Farm Cottages ★★★
Contact: Mrs Elizabeth Sansom, Widmouth Farm Cottages, Watermouth, Ilfracombe EX34 9RX
T: (01271) 863743
F: (01271) 866479
E: holidays@widmouthfarmcottages.co.uk
I: www.widmouthfarmcottages.co.uk

ILMINSTER
Somerset

Myrtle House ★★★★
Contact: Mr & Mrs Gordon & Marion Denman, 16 Challis Green, Barrington, Cambridge CB2 5RJ
T: (01223) 871294
E: denman@appleorchard.freeserve.co.uk
I: www.appleorchard.freeserve.co.uk

INSTOW
Devon

Bath House ★★★
Contact: Marsden's Cottage Holidays, 2 The Square, Braunton EX33 2JB
T: (01271) 813777
F: (01271) 813664
E: holidays@marsdens.co.uk

Chandlers Court ★★★
Contact: Farm & Cottage Holidays, Victoria House, 12 Fore Street, Northam, Bideford EX39 1AW
T: (01237) 479146
F: (01237) 421512
E: bookings@farmcott.co.uk

Driftwood ★★★★
Contact: 2 The Square, Braunton EX33 2JB
T: (01271) 813777
F: (01271) 813664
E: holidays@marsdens.co.uk
I: www.marsdens.co.uk

Garden House ★★★★
Contact: Marsden's Cottage Holidays, 2 The Square, Braunton EX33 2JB
T: (01271) 813777
F: (01271) 813664
E: holidays@marsdens.co.uk
I: www.marsdens.co.uk

Inglenook Cottage ★★★★
Contact: Marsden's Cottage Holidays, 2 The Square, Braunton EX33 2JB
T: (01271) 813777
F: (01271) 813664
E: holidays@marsdens.co.uk
I: www.marsdens.co.uk

Oak Tree Cottage ★★★
Contact: Mr & Mrs Peter & Janet Cornwell, Marsden's Cottage Holidays, 2 The Square, Braunton EX33 2JB
T: (01271) 813777
F: (01271) 813664
E: holidays@marsdens.co.uk
I: www.marsdens.co.uk

The Old Dairy ★★★★
Contact: Marsden's Cottage Holidays, 2 The Square, Braunton EX33 2JB
T: (01271) 813777
F: (01271) 813664
E: holidays@marsdens.co.uk
I: www.marsdens.co.uk

IPPLEPEN
Devon

Bulleigh Park ★★★
Contact: Mrs Angela Dallyn, Bulleigh Park, Bulleigh Park Farm, Ipplepen, Newton Abbot TQ12 5UA
T: (01803) 872254
F: (01803) 872254
E: bulleigh@lineone.net

Dainton Lodge ★★★
Contact: Mr Ian Butterworth, Holiday Homes & Cottages South West, 365A Torquay Road, Paignton TQ3 2BT
T: (01803) 663650
F: (01803) 664037
E: holcotts@aol.com
I: www.swcottages.co.uk

Roselands Holiday Chalets ★★
Contact: Mr & Mrs Simon & Eileen Whale, Roselands Holiday Chalets, Totnes Road, Ipplepen, Newton Abbot TQ12 5TD
T: (01803) 812701
E: enquiries@roselands.net
I: www.roselands.net

ISLE BREWERS
Somerset

Old School House
Rating Applied For
Contact: Mr Alan Coles, Stoke Hill Barton, Stoke St Mary, Henlade, Taunton TA3 5BT
T: (01823) 443759
F: (01823) 443759
E: ajcoles@supanet.com

ISLES OF SCILLY

3 & 4 Well Cross ★-★★
Contact: Mr A M Perry, Treboeth Guest House, St Mary's TR21 0HX
T: (01720) 422548

An Oberva ★★
Contact: Mrs J Berryman, Chy an Mor, 4 Fore Street, Porthleven, Helston TR13 9HQ
T: (01326) 574113

Boswartreth ★★★
Contact: Island Properties Holidays Lettings & Management, Porthmellon, St Mary's TR21 0JY
T: (01720) 422082
F: (01720) 422211
E: enquiries@islesofscillyholidays.com
I: www.islesofscillyholidays.com

Green Farm Cottage ★★★
Contact: Mr D Wright, Green Farm, St Mary's TR21 0NX
T: (01720) 422324
F: (01720) 423406
E: wright.d@btconnect.com
I: www.scillybulbs.co.uk

Harbour View ★★★-★★★★
Contact: Mr Chris Hopkins, Bryher TR23 0PR
T: (01720) 422222
I: www.bryher-ios.co.uk/hv

Holy Vale Holiday Houses ★★★
Contact: Mr J R & Mrs K Banfield, Holy Vale Holiday Houses, Holy Vale Farmhouse, St Mary's TR21 0NT
T: (01720) 422429
F: (01720) 422429
E: johnkayholyvale@lineone.net

Leumeah House ★★
Contact: Island Properties, Porthmellon, St Mary's
T: (01720) 422082
F: (01720) 422211
E: enquiries@islesofscillyholidays.com
I: www.islesofscillyholidays.com

Moonrakers Holiday Flats ★★★
Contact: Mr R J Gregory, Moonrakers Holiday Flats, St Mary's TR21 0JF
T: (01720) 422717
E: gregory@moonrakersholidayflats.fsnet.co.uk
I: www.moonrakersholidayflats.fsnet.co.uk

Mount Flagon ★★★★
Contact: Mr & Mrs Crawford, Mount Flagon, Porthloo, St Mary's TR21 0NE
T: (01720) 422598
F: (01720) 422529

Pednbrose ★★★
Contact: Miss Elizabeth Astbury, 23 Wonford Road, Exeter EX2 4LH
T: (01392) 250050

Puffin Burrow ★★★★
Contact: Mrs Carol Sargeant, Willow Tree House, Kingstone Winslow, Ashbury, Swindon SN6 8NG
T: (01793) 710062
F: (01793) 710387

Seaways Flower Farm ★★★-★★★★★
Contact: Mrs Juliet May, Seaways Flower Farm, St Mary's TR21 0NF
T: (01720) 422845
F: (01720) 423224

IVYBRIDGE
Devon

Beacon Cottage ★★★★
Contact: Mrs S Edwards, Moorhedge Farm, David's Lane, Ivybridge PL21 0DP
T: (01752) 894820

Ivybridge ★★★
Contact: Mr & Mrs John & Christine Crew, 40 Sheridan Way, Longwell Green, Bristol BS30 9UE
T: (01179) 328968

KELSTON
Bath and North East Somerset

Coombe Barn Holidays
Rating Applied For
Contact: Mr George Cullimore, Coombe Barn Holidays, Coombe Barn, Kelston, Bath BA1 9AJ
T: (01225) 448757

KENNFORD
Devon

Tapstone Barn ★★★★
Contact: Holiday Homes and Cottages SW, 365a Torquay Road, Paignton TQ3 2BT
T: (01803) 663650
F: (01803) 664037
E: holcotts@aol.com

KENTISBURY
Devon

Northcote Manor Farm Holiday Cottages★★★★
Contact: Mrs Peter & Pat Bunch, Northcote Manor Farm Cottages, Kentisbury, Kentisbury Ford, Barnstaple EX31 4NB
T: (01271) 882376
E: info@northcotemanorfarm.co.uk
I: www.northcotemanorfarm.co.uk

South Patchole Farm Cottage ★★★★
Contact: Mrs Heywood, South Patchole Farm Cottage, Kentisbury, Barnstaple
T: (01271) 883223

KENTISBURY FORD
Devon

Friars Cottages ★★★★
Contact: Mrs Helen Vine, Kentisbury, Kentisbury Ford, Barnstaple EX31 4ND
T: (01271) 882207
E: relax@friarscottages.co.uk

Old Stable Cottage ★★★★
Contact: Mrs Christine Hewitt, Old Stable Cottage, South Sandpark, Kentisbury Ford, Barnstaple EX31 4NG
T: (01271) 882305
E: christine@kentisburyford.fsnet.co.uk

KILKHAMPTON
Cornwall

Carefree Holidays ★★
Contact: Mr & Mrs Alan & Geraldine Glover, 180 Gloucester Road, Patchway, Bristol BS34 5BD
T: (0117) 969 3699
F: (0117) 969 3699
E: carefreeholsglover1@activemail.co.uk

East Thorne Cottages ★★★
Contact: Mrs Margaret Stears, East Thorne Cottages, Kilkhampton, Bude EX23 9RY
T: (01288) 321618

South Forda Holidays ★★★
Contact: Mr Rose, South Forda Holidays, South Forda, Kilkhampton, Bude EX23 9RZ
T: (01288) 321524
E: southforda@hotmail.com
I: www.southfordaholidays.co.uk

Spanish Villas 7&8 ★★
Contact: Mr & Mrs M D Sumner, 4 Park Court, Kilkhampton, Bude EX23 9PA
T: (01288) 321832

KILMERSDON
Somerset

The Creamery ★★★★
Contact: Mr & Mrs Knatchbull & Sons, The Creamery, Kilmersdon, Bath BA3 5SP
T: (01373) 812337
F: (01373) 813781

KILMINGTON
Devon

Orfield ★★★
Contact: Milkbere Holidays, 3 Fore Street, Seaton EX12 2LE
T: (01297) 20729
F: (01297) 22925
E: info@milkbere.com
I: www.milkbere.com

Stable Loft ★★
Contact: Mr Nicholas Pash, Chapel House, Luke Street, Berwick St John, Shaftesbury SP7 0HQ
T: (01747) 828170
F: (01747) 829090
E: enq@hideaways.co.uk
I: www.hideaways.co.uk

KING'S NYMPTON
Devon

Venn Farm Cottages ★★★
Contact: Mrs Pauline Caine, Venn Farm Holidays, Venn Farm, King's Nympton, Umberleigh EX37 9TR
T: (01769) 572448
E: twelvetwentyfive@msn.com
I: www.bmvenn.demon.co.uk

KINGSBRIDGE
Devon

Dairymans Corner & Shepherds Rest ★★★
Contact: Mrs Anne Rossiter, Burton Farmhouse & Garden Restaurant, Galmpton, Kingsbridge TQ7 3EY
T: (01548) 561210
F: (01548) 562257
E: anne@burtonfarm.co.uk

The Laurels, Coach House & Coachmans Lodge ★★★-★★★★
Contact: Mrs Barbara Baker, South Allington, Chivelstone, Kingsbridge TQ7 2NB
T: (01548) 511272
F: (01548) 511421
E: barbara@sthallingtonbnb.demon.co.uk
I: www.sthallingtonbnb.demon.co.uk

Malston Mill Farm Holiday Cottages ★★★★
Contact: Mr & Mrs Tony & Linda Gresham, Malston Mill Farm, Kingsbridge TQ7 2DR
T: (01548) 852518
F: (01548) 854084
E: gresham@malstonmill.fsnet.co.uk
I: www.malstonmill.co.uk

Reads Farm ★★★
Contact: Mrs A Pethybridge, Reads Farm, Loddiswell, Kingsbridge TQ7 4RT
T: (01548) 550317
F: (01548) 550317

Sloop Inn ★★★★
Contact: Mr Girling, Bantham, Kingsbridge TQ7 3AJ
T: (01548) 560489
F: (01548) 561940

Trouts Holiday Apartments ★★★-★★★★
Contact: Mrs Jill Norman, Prospect Cottage Trouts Holiday Apartments, South Hallsands, Kingsbridge TQ7 2EY
T: (01548) 511296
F: (01548) 511296
E: trouts.holiday@virgin.net
I: www.selfcateringdevon.com

West Charleton Grange
★★★★
Contact: Mrs Amanda Lubrani, West Charleton Grange, West Charleton, Kingsbridge TQ7 2AD
T: (01548) 531779
F: (01548) 531100
E: admin@westcharletongrange.com
I: www.westcharletongrange.com

KINGSDON
Somerset

The Lodge ★★★★
Contact: Mrs Jo Furneaux, The Lodge, Kingsdon, Somerton TA11 7LE
T: (01935) 841194

KINGSDOWN
Wiltshire

Sheylors Farm ★★★★★
Contact: Mrs S Sanders, Ashley, Box, Kingsdown, Corsham SN13 8AN
T: (01225) 743
F: (01225) 743998
E: sam@sheylorsfarm.co.uk

KINGSHEANTON
Devon

The Welkin ★★★★
Contact: Marsden's Cottage Holidays, 2 The Square, Braunton EX33 2JB
T: (01271) 813777
F: (01271) 813664
E: holidays@marsdens.co.uk
I: www.marsdens.co.uk

KINGSTEIGNTON
Devon

Plumb Corner ★★★★
Contact: Holiday Homes & Cottages South West, 365A Torquay Road, Paignton TQ3 2BT
T: (01803) 663650
F: (01803) 664037
E: holcotts@aol.com
I: www.swcottages.co.uk

KINGSTON SEYMOUR
North Somerset

Bullock Farm & Fishing Lakes
★★★
Contact: Mr & Mrs Philip & Jude Simmons, Bullock Farm & Fishing Lakes, Back Lane, Kingston Seymour, Clevedon BS21 6XA
T: (01934) 835020
F: (01934) 835927
E: bullockfarm@kingstonseymour1.freeserve.co.uk

LACOCK
Wiltshire

Cyder House & Cheese House at Wick Farm★★★★
Contact: Mr & Mrs Philip & Susan King, Cyder House & Cheese House, Wick Farm, Wick Lane, Lacock, Chippenham SN15 2LU
T: (01249) 730244
F: (01249) 730072
E: kingsilverlands2@btinternet.com
I: www.cheeseandcyderhouses.co.uk

The Paddocks Whitehall Garden Centre
Rating Applied For
Contact: CH Ref: 13672, Country Holidays, Spring Mill, Earby, Barnoldswick BB94 0AA
T: 08700 723723

LADOCK
Cornwall

Higher Hewas ★★★★
Contact: Mrs Pamela Blake, Lower Hewas, Ladock, Truro TR2 4QH
T: (01726) 882318

LAMORNA
Cornwall

Lamorna Vean ★★★★
Contact: Mr & Mrs M & S Searle, Lamorna, Penzance TR19 6NY
T: (01904) 481951
F: (01904) 489349
E: lamornavean@yorktrain.demon.co.uk

Round Chapel Barn ★★-★★★
Contact: Mr Ian Butterworth, Holiday Homes & Cottages South West, 365A Torquay Road, Paignton TQ3 2BT
T: (01803) 663650
F: (01803) 664037
E: holcotts@aol.com
I: www.swcottages.co.uk

LAMORNA COVE
Cornwall

Bal Red ★★
Contact: Miss Sarah Daniel, Sarah's Cottage, Lamorna, Penzance TR19 6XJ
T: (01736) 731227

LANDCROSS
Devon

Beaconside Cottages ★★★★
Contact: Mr Singer, Beaconside Cottages, Beaconside, Weare Giffard, Bideford EX39 5JL
T: (01237) 475118

LANDRAKE
Cornwall

The Coach House ★★★★
Contact: Mrs N Walker, The Coach House, Lantallack Farm, Landrake, Saltash PL12 5AE
T: (01752) 851281
F: (01752) 851281
E: Lantallack@ukgateway.net
I: www.lantallack.co.uk

Markwell Farm ★★★
Contact: Mrs Allison Brazington, Markwell Farm, Landrake, Saltash PL12 5EQ
T: (01752) 851185
F: (01752) 851185
E: markwellfarm@aol.com
I: www.markwellfarm.co.uk

LANGLEY BURRELL
Wiltshire

Cedarwood ★★★★
Contact: Mrs Helen Miflin Grove Farm, Sutton Lane, Langley Burrell, Chippenham SN15 4LW
T: (01249) 721500
F: (01249) 720413
E: miflin@btinternet.com

LANGLEY MARSH
Somerset

Vickery View Cottages ★★★
Contact: The Agent, Farm & Cottage Holidays, Victoria House, 12 Fore Street, Northam, Bideford EX39 1AW
T: (01237) 479146
F: (01237) 421512

LANGPORT
Somerset

2 Bow Cottage ★★
Contact: CH Ref: 10997, Holiday Cottages Group Owner Services Dept, Spring Mill, Earby, Barnoldswick BB94 0AA
T: 08700 723723
F: (01282) 844288
E: sales@ttgihg.co.uk
I: www.country-holidays.co.uk

Hay Loft & Stables ★★★
Contact: Mrs Pauline Pickard, Hay Loft & Stables, Dairy House Farm, Muchelney Ham, Langport TA10 0DJ
T: (01458) 253113

Laurel Wharf ★★★★
Contact: Mr John Neale, Laurel Wharf, c/o Laurel Cottage, West, Westport, Langport TA10 0BN
T: (01460) 281713

Muchelney Ham Farm
★★★-★★★★
Contact: Mr Jim Woodborne, Muchelney Ham Farm, Muchelney, Langport TA10 0DJ
T: (01458) 250737
F: (01458) 250737

LANGRIDGE
Bath and North East Somerset

Langridge Studio ★★★★
Contact: Mr Brian Shuttleworth, Langridge House, Langridge, Bath BA1 9BX
T: (01225) 338874
F: (01225) 338874
E: info@langridge-studio.co.uk
I: www.langridge-studio.co.uk

LANGTON HERRING
Dorset

Angel Cottage ★★★
Contact: Mr Zachary Stuart-Brown, Dream Cottages, 41 Maiden Street, Weymouth DT4 8AZ
T: (01305) 761347
E: admin@dream-cottages.co.uk
I: www.dream-cottages.co.uk

Hazel Copse & Orchard View
★★★
Contact: Mr Zachary Stuart-Brown, Dream Cottages, 41 Maiden Street, Weymouth DT4 8AZ
T: (01305) 761347
E: admin@dream-cottages.co.uk
I: www.dream-cottages.co.uk

3 Lower Farm, Chelsea Cottage, The Brambles, The Sycamores,★★★★
Contact: Mrs A E Mayo, Higher Farm, Rodden, Weymouth DT3 4JE
T: (01305) 871347
F: (01305) 871347
E: jane@mayo.fsbusiness.co.uk

LANGTREE
Devon

2 Moors View ★★★
Contact: Farm & Cottage Holidays, Victoria House, 12 Fore Street, Northam, Bideford EX39 1AW
T: (01237) 479146
F: (01237) 421512
E: enquiries@farmcott.co.uk

LANHYDROCK
Cornwall

Little Cutmadoc Farm
★★★★★
Contact: Ms Helen Cobb, 17 Waterside Tower, Imperial Wharf, London SW6 2SW
T: (020) 7348 7532
E: helen@luxurybreaks.co.uk

LANNER
Cornwall

Little Shalom ★★★★
Contact: Powell's Cottage Holidays, High Street, Freystrop, Haverfordwest SA69 9EJ
T: (01834) 812791
F: (01834) 811731
E: info@powells.co.uk
I: www.powells.co.uk

LANREATH-BY-LOOE
Cornwall

The Old Rectory ★★★
Contact: Mr & Mrs C Duncan, The Old Rectory, Lanreath-by-Looe, Looe PL13 2NU
T: (01503) 220247
F: (01503) 220108
E: ask@oldrectory-lanreath.co.uk
I: www.oldrectory-lanreath.co.uk

LANSALLOS
Cornwall

West Kellow Farmhouse
★★★★
Contact: Mrs Evelyn Julian, Tremadart Farm, Lansallos, Looe PL13 2QL
T: (01503) 272089
F: (01503) 272089
E: westkellow@aol.com

LANTEGLOS-BY-FOWEY
Cornwall

Trehaida Cottage ★★★★★
Contact: Ms Ann Hair, Trefawl, Lanreath, Looe PL13 2PB
T: (01503) 220229
F: (01503) 220229

LATCHLEY
Cornwall

The Apple Loft ★★★★
Contact: Mrs Margaret Blake, The Apple Loft, Old Solomons Farm, Latchley, Gunnislake PL18 9AX
T: (01822) 833242
F: (01822) 833242
E: info@oldsolomonsfarm.co.uk
I: www.oldsolomonsfarm.co.uk

LAUNCESTON
Cornwall

Bamham Farm Cottages ★★★-★★★★
Contact: Mrs J A Chapman, Bamham Farm Cottages, Higher Bamham Farm, Launceston PL15 9LD
T: (01566) 772141
F: (01566) 775266
E: jackie@bamhamfarm.co.uk
I: www.bamhamfarm.co.uk

Langdon Farm Holiday Cottages ★★★-★★★★
Contact: Mrs F Rawlinson, Langdon Farm, Boyton, Launceston PL15 8NW
T: (01566) 785389
E: g.f.rawlinson@btinternet.com
I: www.langdonholidays.com

Swallows ★★★
Contact: Mrs Kathryn Broad, Lower Dutson Farm, Launceston PL15 9SP
T: (01566) 776456
F: (01566) 776456
E: francis.broad@btclick.com
I: www.farm-cottage.co.uk

Ta Mill ★★★-★★★★
Contact: Mrs Helen Harvey, Ta Mill, St Clether, Launceston PL15 8PS
T: (01840) 261797
F: (01840) 261381
E: helen@tamill.co.uk
I: www.tamill.co.uk

Trefursdon Cottage ★★★
Contact: Mrs Fraser, Trefuge Cottage, Coads Green, Launceston PL15 7NB
T: (01566) 782484

Trevadlock Farm Cottages Platt and Trotters Cottages ★★★★
Contact: Mrs Barbara Sleep, Trevadlock Farm Cottages Platt and Trotters Cottages, Trevadlock Farm, Congdon's Shop, Launceston PL15 7PW
T: (01566) 782239
F: (01566) 782239
E: trevadlockfarm@compuserve.com
I: www.trevadlock.co.uk

West Barton – Cider Annexe ★★★
Contact: Mr & Mrs Brian & Fiona Perris, West Barton, North Petherwin, Launceston PL15 8LR
T: (01566) 785710
E: enquiries@westbarton.co.uk
I: www.westbarton.co.uk

Wheatley Cottage and Barn ★★★★
Contact: Mrs V Griffin, Wheatley Cottage and Barn, Wheatley Farm, Maxworthy, Launceston PL15 8LY
T: (01566) 781232
F: (01566) 781232
E: valerie@wheatleyfrm.com
I: www.chycor.co.uk/cottages/wheatley

LAVERSTOCK
Wiltshire

Church Cottage H090 ★★★★
Contact: Hideaways, Chapel House, Luke Street, Berwick St John, Shaftesbury SP7 0HQ
T: (01747) 828170
F: (01747) 829090
E: enq@hideaways.co.uk

LEA
Wiltshire

Oak Tree Loft ★★
Contact: Mr & Mrs Herbert, Oak Tree Loft, White Cottage, 5 Cresswell Lane, Lea, Little Somerford, Chippenham SN16 9PE
T: (01666) 822165
E: peter5whitecot@aol.com

LEE
Devon

Eliot House ★★★-★★★★
Contact: Marsden's Cottage Holidays, 2 The Square, Braunton EX33 2JB
T: (01271) 813777
F: (01271) 813664
E: holidays@marsdens.co.uk
I: www.marsdens.co.uk

Grange Apartment ★★★
Contact: Mr & Mrs Peter & Janet Cornwell, Marsden's Cottage Holidays, 2 The Square, Braunton EX33 2JB
T: (01271) 813777
F: (01271) 813664
E: holidays@marsdens.co.uk
I: www.marsdens.co.uk

Lincombe House ★★★
Contact: Mr & Mrs Ian & Cynthia Stuart, Lincombe House, Lincombe, Lee, Ilfracombe EX34 8LL
T: (01271) 864834
F: (01271) 864834
E: stuart.lincombehouse@btinternet.com
I: www.lincombehouse.co.uk

Lower Campscott Farm ★★★-★★★★
Contact: Mrs M Cowell, Lower Campscott Farm, Lee, Ilfracombe EX34 8LS
T: (01271) 863479
F: (01271) 867639
E: holidays@lowercampscott.co.uk
I: www.lowercampscott.co.uk

Smugglers Cottage ★★★★
Contact: Marsden's Cottage Holidays, 2 The Square, Braunton EX33 2JB
T: (01271) 813777
F: (01271) 813664
E: holidays@marsdens.co.uk
I: www.marsdens.co.uk

Vine Cottage ★★★★
Contact: Mr & Mrs Peter & Janet Cornwell, Marsden's Cottage Holidays, 2 The Square, Braunton EX33 2JB
T: (01271) 813777
F: (01271) 813664
E: holidays@marsdens.co.uk
I: www.marsdens.co.uk

LEIGH
Dorset

1 Church Farm Cottages ★★
Contact: CH Ref: 11740, Holiday Cottages Group Owner Services Dept, Spring Mill, Earby, Barnoldswick BB94 0AA
T: 08700 723723
F: (01282) 844288
E: sales@ttgihg.co.uk
I: www.country-holidays.co.uk

LELANT
Cornwall

Trevethoe Farm Cottages ★★★
Contact: Mrs Rogers, Trevethoe Farm Cottages, Trevethoe Farm, Trevethoe, Lelant, St Ives TR26 3HG
T: (01736) 753279
F: (01736) 753279
E: holidaycottages@trevethoe.co.uk

LERRYN
Cornwall

Puddleduck Cottage ★★★★
Contact: Estuary House, Fore Street, Polruan, Fowey PL23 1AH
T: (01726) 832965
F: (01726) 832866
E: info@estuarycottages.co.uk
I: www.estuarycottages.co.uk

LEWDOWN
Devon

The Honey House ★★★★
Contact: Mr Richard Baker, Bidlake Mill, Lewdown, Okehampton EX20 4ED
T: (01837) 861323
E: rrdb123@aol.com

LEZANT
Cornwall

East Penrest Barn ★★★★★
Contact: Mrs J Rider, East Penrest Barn, East Penrest, Lezant, Launceston PL15 9NR
T: (01579) 370186
F: (01579) 370477
E: jorider@eastpenrest.freeserve.co.uk
I: www.eastpenrest.freeserve.co.uk

LIDDINGTON
Wiltshire

Gables End ★★★
Contact: Mrs Rosemarie Watson, Gables End, Medbourne Lane, Liddington, Swindon SN4 0EY
T: (01793) 790927
F: (01793) 525588
E: rosemarie@carriagesatthree.co.uk

LISKEARD
Cornwall

Beechleigh Cottage ★★★★
Contact: Mrs Stephanie Rowe, Tregondale Farm, Menheniot, Liskeard PL14 3RG
T: (01579) 342407
F: (01579) 342407
E: tregondale@connectfree.co.uk
I: www.tregondalefarm.co.uk

Coach House Cottages ★★★★
Contact: Mr & Mrs Jeremy & Jane Hall, Coach House Cottages, Treworgey Manor, Liskeard PL14 6RN
T: (01579) 347755
F: (01579) 347755
E: cotttages@treworgay.co.uk

Lodge Barton ★★★
Contact: Mrs Hodin, Lodge Barton, Lamellion, Liskeard PL14 4JX
T: (01579) 344432
F: (01579) 344432
E: lodgebart@aol.com
I: www.selectideas.co.uk/lodgebarton

Lower Trengale Farm ★★★★
Contact: Brian & Terri Shears, Lower Trengale Farm, Liskeard PL14 6HF
T: (01579) 321019
F: (01579) 321432
E: lowertrengale@aol.com
I: www.trengaleholidaycottages.co.uk

Old Post Office
Rating Applied For
Contact: Farm & Cottage Holidays, Victoria House, 12 Fore Street, Westward Ho!, Bideford EX39 1AW
T: (01237) 479146
F: (01237) 421512
E: bookings@farmcott.co.uk

Treworgey Cottages ★★★★★
Contact: Mr & Mrs Bevis & Linda Wright, Treworgey Cottages, Duloe, Liskeard PL14 4PP
T: (01503) 262730
F: (01503) 263757
E: treworgey@enterprise.net

LITTLE PETHERICK
Cornwall

Quay House ★★★
Contact: Mrs Allison Hatcher, Quay House, Petherick Creek, Padstow PL27 7QT
T: (01841) 540431
F: (01841) 540431
I: www.Quay-House-Holidays.co.uk

Swallow Court Cottages ★★★★
Contact: Mr Geoffrey French, Molesworth Manor, Little Petherick, Padstow PL27 7QT
T: (01841) 540292
E: molesworthmanor@aol.com
I: www.molesworthmanor.co.uk

Tregonna Farm Barn and Cottage ★★★-★★★★
Contact: Mr & Mrs Peter & Cathy Osborne, Cornish Horizons, Higher Trehemborne, St Merryn, Padstow PL28 8JU
T: (01841) 520889
F: (01841) 521523
E: cottages@cornishhorizons.co.uk
I: www.cornishhorizons.co.uk

Tregwythen ★★★
Contact: Mr & Mrs Peter & Cathy Osborne, Cornish Horizons, Higher Trehemborne, St Merryn, Padstow PL28 8JU
T: (01841) 520889
F: (01841) 521523
E: cottages@cornishhorizons.co.uk
I: www.cornishhorizons.co.uk

Trenant ★★★★
Contact: Mr & Mrs Peter & Cathy Osborne, Cornish Horizons, Higher Trehemborne, St Merryn, Padstow PL28 8JU
T: (01841) 520889

Westcreek ★★★★
Contact: Cornish Cottage Holidays, The Old Turnpike Dairy, Godolphin, Meneage Street, Helston TR13 8AA
T: (01326) 573808
F: (01326) 564992
E: enquiry@cornishcottageholidays.co.uk
I: www.cornishcottageholidays.co.uk

LITTLE TORRINGTON
Devon

Torridge House Cottages ★★★
Contact: Mrs B Terry, Torridge House Cottages, Little Torrington, Torrington EX38 8PS
T: (01805) 622542
F: (01805) 622360
E: bookings@torridgehouse.co.uk
I: www.torrridgehouse.co.uk

LITTLEHAM
Devon

Robin Hill Farm Cottages ★★★★
Contact: Ref:FAD,FKH,FA,FKK, English Country Cottages, Holiday Cottages Group Owner Services Department, Spring Mill, Earby, Barnoldswick BB94 0AA
T: 08700 723723
F: (01282) 841539
E: sales@ttgihg.co.uk
I: www.english-country-cottages.co.uk

LITTON CHENEY
Dorset

Baglake Barn & Brewery Cottage ★★★★-★★★★★
Contact: Mrs Barbour, Baglake Barn & Brewery Cottage, Baglake Farm, Litton Cheney, Dorchester DT2 9AD
T: (01308) 482222
National Accessible Scheme Rating Applied For

Chimney Sweep ★★★★
Contact: Mr Zachary Stuart-Brown, Dream Cottages, 41 Maiden Street, Weymouth DT4 8AZ
T: (01305) 761347
E: admin@dream-cottages.co.uk
I: www.dream-cottages.co.uk

3 Manor Farm Close ★★★★
Contact: Mrs Jackson, Glebe Cottage, Oldbury Lane, Seal, Sevenoaks TN15 9DG
T: (01732) 884277
E: janet@kortoll.fsnet.co.uk

LIVERTON
Devon

Lookweep Farm Cottages ★★★
Contact: Mr & Mrs John & Helen Griffiths, Lookweep Farm Cottages, Liverton, Newton Abbot TQ12 6HT
T: (01626) 834412
F: (01626) 834412
E: holidays@lookweep.co.uk
I: www.lookweep.co.uk

Moor Copse Farm Cottages ★★★
Contact: Mr & Mrs Cross, Moor Copse Farm Cottages, Liverton, Newton Abbot TQ12 6HT
T: (01626) 833920
F: (01626) 833920
E: cross@moorcopse.fslife.co.uk

LOBB
Devon

South Lobb Cottage and House ★★★
Contact: Farm & Cottage Holidays, Victoria House, 12 Fore Street, Northam, Bideford EX39 1AW
T: (01237) 479146
F: (01237) 421512
E: enquiries@farmcott.co.uk

LONGBRIDGE DEVERILL
Wiltshire

Copperfield ★★★
Contact: Farm & Cottage Holidays, Victoria House, 12 Fore Street, Northam, Bideford EX39 1AW
T: (01237) 479146
F: (01237) 421512
E: enquiries@farmcott.co.uk

Sturgess Farmhouse ★★★★
Contact: Mr Ramsay, Sturgess Farmhouse, The Marsh, Longbridge Deverill, Warminster BA12 7EA
T: (01985) 840329
F: (01985) 841329
E: info@sturgessbarns.co.uk
I: www.sturgessbarns.co.uk

LOOE
Cornwall

Alices Cottage ★★★★
Contact: Cornish Cottage Holidays, Goldophin Road, Helston TR13 8AA
T: (01326) 573808
F: (01326) 564992
E: enquiry@cornishcottageholidays.co.uk
I: www.cornishcottageholidays.co.uk

Badham Farm Holiday Cottages ★★★
Contact: Mr & Mrs Brown, Badham Farm Holiday Cottages, St Keyne, Liskeard PL14 4RW
T: (01579) 343572
F: (01579) 343572

Barclay House Cottages ★★★★★
Contact: Mr Barclay, Barclay House, The Hotel, Restaurant & Luxury Cottages, St Martins Road, Looe PL13 1LP
T: (01503) 262929
F: (01503) 262632
E: info@barclayhouse.co.uk
I: www.barclayhouse.co.uk

Bocaddon Holiday Cottages ★★★★
Contact: Mrs Alison Maiklem, Bocaddon, Lanreath, Looe PL13 2PG
T: (01503) 220192
F: (01503) 220192
E: bocaddon@aol.com

Bucklawren Farm ★★★★-★★★★★
Contact: Mrs J Henly, Bucklawren Farm, St Martins, Looe PL13 1NZ
T: (01503) 240738
F: (01503) 240481
E: bucklawren@btopenworld.com
I: www.bucklawren.com

Crylla Valley Cottages ★★★★
Contact: Mr M Walsh
T: (01752) 851133
F: (01752) 851666
E: sales@cryllacottages.co.uk
I: www.cryllacottages.co.uk

Highwood ★★★★
Contact: Mrs Beatrix Windle, 118 Horsham Road, Ewhurst, Cranleigh GU6 8DY
T: (01483) 277894
E: beatrix@talk21.com

Lemain Garden Apartments ★★★-★★★★
Contact: Mr & Mrs Alan & Dee Palin, Lemain Garden Apartments, Portuan Road, Looe PL13 2DR
T: (01503) 262073
F: (01503) 265288
E: sales@lemain.com
I: www.lemain.com

Little Cottage ★★★
Contact: Mrs Annette Tolputt, Little Cottage, Lesquite Lansallos, Looe PL13 2QE
T: (01503) 220315

Penvith Cottages ★★★★
Contact: Mrs Beatrix Windle, 118 Horsham Road, Ewhurst, Cranleigh GU6 8DY
T: (01483) 277894
E: beatrix@talk21.com
I: www.cornwall-online.co.uk/penvith

Rock Towers Apartments ★★★★
Contact: Mr Clive Dixon, Cornish Collection, 73 Bodrigan Road, Barbican, East Looe, Looe PL13 1EH
T: (01503) 262736
F: (01503) 262736
E: cornishcol@aol.com
I: www.cornishcollection.co.uk

Summercourt Coastal Cottages ★★★★
Contact: Mr & Mrs Steve & Lisa Rawlins, Summercourt Coastal Cottages, Bodigga Cliff, St Martin, Looe PL13 1NZ
T: (01503) 263149
E: lisa.rawlins@virgin.net

Talehay ★★★★
Contact: Mr P R Brumpton, Talehay, Tremaine, Pelynt, Looe PL13 2LT
T: (01503) 220252
F: (01503) 220252
E: paul@talehay.co.uk
I: www.talehay.co.uk

LOOE
Cornwall

Well Meadow Cottage ★★★★
Contact: Mrs Kaye Chapman, Duloe, Liskeard PL14 4QF
T: (01503) 220251
E: kaye@coldrinnick.fsnet.co.uk
I: www.cornishcottage.net

LOSCOMBE
Dorset

Garden Cottage ★★★
Contact: Major J L Poe, Pear Tree Farm, Loscombe, Bridport DT6 3TL
T: (01308) 488223
E: poe@loscombe.freeserve.co.uk

LOSTWITHIEL
Cornwall

Chark Country Holidays Rating Applied For
Contact: Ms Jenny Littleton, Chark Country Holidays, Chark, Redmoor, Bodmin PL30 5AR
T: (01208) 871118
F: (01208) 871118
E: charkcountryholidays@farmersweekly.net
I: www.charkcountryholidays.co.uk

Hartswheal Barn ★★★
Contact: Mrs Wendy Jordan, Hartswheal Barn, Saint Winnow, Downend, Lostwithiel PL22 0RB
T: (01208) 873419
F: (01208) 873419
E: hartswheal@connexions.co.uk
I: www.connexions.co.uk/hartswheal/index.htm

Lanwithan Manor, Farm & Waterside Cottages ★★★-★★★★★
Contact: Mr H F Edward-Collins, Lanwithan Cottages, Lostwithiel PL22 0LA
T: (01208) 872444
F: (01208) 872444
E: info@lanwithancottages.co.uk
I: www.lanwithancottages.co.uk

Newham Farm Cottages ★★★★
Contact: Mrs Bolsover, Newham Farm Cottages, Newham Farm, Lostwithiel PL22 0LD
T: (01208) 872262
F: (01208) 872262

Tredethick Farm Cottages ★★★★
Contact: Mr & Mrs Reed, Tredethick Farm Cottages, Lostwithiel PL22 0LE
T: (01208) 873618
F: (01208) 873618
E: holidays@tredethick.co.uk
I: www.tredethick.co.uk

LOWER HENLADE
Somerset

The Stables ★★★★
Contact: Mrs Jane Harris, The Stables, Lower Henlade, Henlade, Taunton TA3 5NA
T: (01823) 444888
F: (01823) 444688
E: hilly.home@virgin.net
I: www.henladecottages.com

LOWER ODCOMBE
Somerset

The Cottage ★★★
Contact: Mrs N C Worledge, The Cottage, Old Dairy House, Lower Odcombe, Yeovil BA22 8TX
T: (01935) 862874
E: john.worledge@lineone.net
I: www.john.worledge@lineone.net

LUCCOMBE
Somerset

Wychanger ★★★-★★★★
Contact: Mr & Mrs David & Sue Dalton, Wychanger, Luccombe, Minehead TA24 8TA
T: (01643) 862526
E: holidays@wychanger.net
I: www.wychanger.net

LUSTLEIGH
Devon

Lustleigh Mills ★★★-★★★★
Contact: Mrs J A Rowe, Lustleigh Mills, Lustleigh, Newton Abbot TQ13 9SS
T: (01647) 277357
E: lustleighmills@ukgateway.net
I: www.lustleighmills.btinternet.co.uk

LUXBOROUGH
Somerset

The Old Granary ★★★★
Contact: Mr & Mrs Ivan & Anne Simpson, The Old Granary, Luxborough, Watchet TA23 0SJ
T: (01984) 640909
E: theoldgranaryexmoor@talk21.com

LYDEARD ST LAWRENCE
Somerset

Oaklea House ★★★★
Contact: Mrs Peta-Elaine Barker, Oaklea House, Tolland, Lawrence, Lydeard St Lawrence, Taunton TA4 3PW
T: (01984) 667373
F: (01984) 667373
E: Barker@Oakleahouse.fsnet.co.uk

LYME REGIS
Dorset

Appletrees ★★★★
Contact: Mr & Mrs Charles & Liz Teall, Salford Mill, Salford, Chipping Norton OX7 5YQ
T: (01608) 641304
F: (01608) 644442
E: teall@compuserve.com

Bay Cottage ★★
Contact: Ms Lynn Cable, Boat Close, Shire Lane, Uplyme, Lyme Regis DT7 3ET
T: (01297) 444593
F: (01297) 444693
E: thecables@btopenworld.com

Blacksmith Cottage ★★★★
Contact: Mrs Su Jolley, Westward, Loves Lane, Morcombelake, Bridport DT6 6DZ
T: (01297) 489778
F: (01297) 489778
E: su@westward.fsbusiness.co.uk

Cliff Cottage ★★★
Contact: Mrs Sue Rose, New Road, Whitehill, Bordon GU35 9AX
T: (01420) 472512

The Coach House - End House ★★
Contact: Mrs Lucy Watt, Ware Wood, Ware Lane, Lyme Regis DT7 3EL
T: (01297) 445100

Cobb House ★★
Contact: Ms Kate Bartlett, Jean Bartlett Cottage Holidays, Fore Street, Beer, Seaton EX12 3JB
T: (01297) 23221
F: (01297) 23303
E: holidays@jeanbartlett.com
I: www.netbreaks.com/jeanb

Coombe House Flat ★★★
Contact: Mrs Dympna Duncan, Coombe House Flat, 41 Coombe Street, Lyme Regis DT7 3PY
T: (01297) 443849
F: (01297) 443849
E: dymps@coombe-house.co.uk
I: www.coombe-house.co.uk

Coram Tower Holidays Ltd. ★★★
Contact: Mr & Mrs John & Margaret McLaren, Coram Tower Holidays, Coram Tower, Pound Road, Uplyme, Lyme Regis DT7 3HX
T: (01297) 442012
E: jmmclaren@coramtower.co.uk
I: www.coramtower.co.uk

Crystal ★★★
Contact: Miss Bridget Horner, Lyme Road, Yawl, Uplyme, Lyme Regis DT7 3UZ
T: (01297) 442231
E: bridget.horner@talk21.com
I: www.lymeregis.com/crystal

3 Dolphin Cottages ★★
Contact: Mrs D Lindfield, Sunnyside, Itchingfield, Southwater, Horsham RH13 0NX
T: (01403) 791258

Fairfield Cottage ★★★
Contact: Mr Davies, Fairfield Cottage, Charmouth Road, Lyme Regis DT7 3HH
T: (01297) 445362

Flat 1 Pyne House★★
Contact: Ms Sue Dare, 117 Leander Road, London SW2 2NB
T: (020) 8671 8587

Flat 1 Burton House ★★★
Contact: Mrs Elaine Windust, 5 Pound Street, Uplyme, Lyme Regis DT7 3HZ
T: (01297) 443548
E: lymeregisflat1@aol.com
I: lymeregisflat1@aol.com

The Gables Holiday Apartments ★★★
Contact: Mr & Mrs Alan & Christine Simpson, Church Street, Lyme Regis DT7 3BX
T: (01297) 442536

Greystones Flat ★★★★
Contact: Mrs Joan Gollop, Greystones, View Road, Lyme Regis DT7 3AA
T: (01297) 443678
E: greystones.flat@btopenworld.com
I: www.greystones-lymeregis.com

Harbour House Flats ★★★
Contact: Mrs Monica Cary, Briseham, Broadway Road, Kingsteignton, Newton Abbot TQ12 3EH
T: (01626) 364779

Haye Farm Bungalow, Stables, Hayloft & Dairy★★★-★★★★
Contact: Mr & Mrs Bob & Grace Anderson, Haye Farm, Haye Lane, Uplyme, Lyme Regis DT7 3UD
T: (01297) 442400
F: (01297) 442745

Hobbs Cottage ★★★
Contact: Mr Zachary Stuart-Brown, Dream Cottages, 41 Maiden Street, Weymouth DT4 8AZ
T: (01305) 761347
E: admin@dream-cottages.co.uk
I: www.dream-cottages.co.uk

Ilex House ★★★
Contact: Mr Royson Davies, Fairfield Cottage, Charmouth Road, Lyme Regis DT7 3HH
T: (01297) 445362

Jericho ★★★
Contact: Mrs K E Start, Monks Hall, Bowsers Lane, Little Walden, Saffron Walden CB10 1XQ
T: (01799) 522096

Kamloops & Nanaimo Apartments ★★★
Contact: Mr Sweet, Grove Cottage, Hollybush Lane, Sneyd Park, Bristol BS9 1BH
T: (0117) 968 1866
E: sw55t@msn.com

Kippis Cottage ★★★
Contact: Mr Royson Davies, Fairfield Cottage, Charmouth Road, Lyme Regis DT7 3HH
T: (01297) 445362

La Casa ★★★
Contact: Mr Royson Davies, Fairfield Cottage, Charmouth Road, Lyme Regis DT7 3HH
T: (01297) 445362

Little Cleve ★★★★
Contact: Mr Alister Mackenzie, Smithams Hill, East Harptree, Bristol BS40 6BZ
T: (01761) 221554

Lucerne Apartment ★★★
Contact: Bos House, 44 Church Street, Lyme Regis DT7 3DA
T: (01297) 444756
F: (01297) 445576
E: email@lymebayholidays.co.uk

Monmouth Cottage ★★★
Contact: Mrs W R Fisk, 28 Station Road, Crewkerne TA18 8AJ
T: (01460) 73878

Northay Farm ★★★
Contact: Mrs D Olof, Northay Farm, Hawkchurch, Axminster EX13 5UU
T: (01297) 678591
F: (01297) 678591
E: deeolof@hotmail.com
I: www.northay.com

Queen Ann's Lodge ★★★★
Contact: Mr Royson Davies, Fairfield Cottage, Charmouth Road, Lyme Regis DT7 3HH
T: (01297) 445362

Rose & Honeysuckle Cottages ★★★★
Contact: Mr Matthew Strong, Braden Chartered Surveyors, Laverstoke Grange, Whitchurch RG28 7PF
T: (01256) 896444
F: (01256) 896555
E: braden@andover.co.uk

St Andrews Holiday Flats ★★★
Contact: Mrs Cynthia Wendy McHardy, St Andrews Holiday Flats, Uplyme Road, Lyme Regis DT7 3LP
T: (01297) 445495
F: (01297) 445495

Sea Tree House ★★★★
Contact: Mr David Parker, Sea Tree House, 18 Broad Street, Lyme Regis DT7 3QE
T: (01297) 442244
F: (01297) 442244
E: seatree.house@ukonline.co.uk
I: www.lymeregis.com/seatreehouse

35 Sherborne Lane ★★★
Contact: Bos House, 44, Church Street, Lyme Regis DT7 3DA
T: (01297) 443363
E: email@lymebayholidays.co.uk

57a Silver Street ★★
Contact: Ms Rhoda Elwick, Thatch, Uplyme Road, Uplyme, Lyme Regis DT7 3LP
T: (01297) 442212
F: (01297) 443485
E: thethatch@lineone.net
I: www.holidaycottages-uk.com

Spring Cottage ★★★
Contact: Mr Zachary Stuart-Brown, Dream Cottages, 41 Maiden Street, Weymouth DT4 8AZ
T: (01305) 761347
E: admin@dream-cottages.co.uk
I: www.dream-cottages.co.uk

Stable Cottage ★★★★
Contact: Mrs Penny Jones, Stable Cottage, The Coach House, Haye Lane, Uplyme, Lyme Regis DT7 3NQ
T: (01297) 442656
F: (01297) 442656

Talbot Road – C4267 ★★★★
Contact: Boshouse, 44 Church Street, Lyme Regis DT7 3DA
T: (01297) 443363
F: (01297) 445576
E: email@lymebayholidays.co.uk

Water Cottage ★★★
Contact: Mrs Claire Laven-Morris, 67 Montholme Road, London SW11 6HX
T: (020) 7924 6194
F: (020) 7228 6779

1 Wellhayes ★★★
Contact: Mrs P Boyland, Barn Park Farm, Stockland Hill, Nr Cotleigh, Honiton EX14 9JA
T: (01404) 861297
F: (01404) 861297

2 Wellhayes Cottage ★★★
Contact: Ms Sandra Hailes, The Granary, Harbourneford, South Brent TQ10 9DT
T: (01364) 72515
E: shailes@freeuk.com
I: www.coinage.co.uk/wellhayes

Westfield
Rating Applied For
Contact: Mrs Stella Alford, Moonrakers, Claverton Down Road, Widcombe, Bath BA2 6DZ
T: (01225) 465430
F: (01225) 465430

Westover Farm Cottages ★★★
Contact: Mrs Debby Snook, Westover Farm Cottages, Westover Farm, Wootton Fitzpaine, Bridport DT6 6NE
T: (01297) 560451
E: wfcottages@aol.com
I: www.lymeregis.com/westover-farm-cottages

LYMPSHAM
Somerset

Dulhorn Farm Caravan Park ★★
Contact: Mr & Mrs J E Bowden, Dulhorn Farm Caravan Park, Weston Road, Lympsham, Weston-super-Mare BS24 0JQ
T: (01934) 750298
F: (01934) 750913

Lower Wick Farm ★★★
Contact: Mr & Ms Bishop & Coles, Lower Wick Farm, Wick Lane, Lympsham, Weston-super-Mare BS24 0HG
T: (01278) 751333

LYMPSTONE
Devon

Clays Cottage ★★★
Contact: Ms Kate Bartlett, Jean Bartlett Cottage Holidays, The Old Dairy, Fore Street, Beer, Seaton EX12 3JB
T: (01297) 23221
F: (01297) 23303
E: holidays@jeanbartlett.com
I: www.netbreaks.com/jeamb

LYNMOUTH
Devon

The Beacon ★★★★
Contact: Mr & Mrs Michael & Tracy Ann Burnside, The Beacon, Countisbury Hill, Lynmouth EX35 6ND
T: (01598) 753268
F: (01598) 752340
E: thebeacon@btinternet.com

Clooneavin Holidays ★★★
Contact: Mr & Mrs John & Gill Davidson, Clooneavin Holidays, Clooneavin Path, Lynmouth EX35 6EE
T: (01598) 753334
I: www.northdevon.co.uk/clooneavin.htm

Clovelly House ★★★★
Contact: Mrs Linda Dobie, 1 Ducks Meadow, Marlborough SN8 4DE
T: (01672) 513621
F: (01488) 684824
E: clovelly@hotmail.com
I: www.clovellyhouse.co.uk

Lynmouth Post Office Apartment ★★★
Contact: Mr & Mrs Peter & Janet Cornwell, Marsden's Cottage Holidays, 2 The Square, Braunton EX33 2JB
T: (01271) 813777
F: (01271) 813664
E: holidays@marsdens.co.uk
I: www.marsdens.co.uk

Riverview ★★★
Contact: Marsden's Cottage Holidays, 2 The Square, Braunton EX33 2JB
T: (01271) 813777
F: (01271) 813664

Water's Edge Cottage ★★★★
Contact: Mr M Wolverson, Primespot Character Cottages, c/o Stag Cottage, Holdstone Down, Combe Martin, Ilfracombe EX34 0PF
T: (01271) 882449

Wilrose ★★★
Contact: Marsden's Cottage Holidays, 2 The Square, Braunton EX33 2JB
T: (01271) 813777
F: (01271) 813664
E: holidays@marsdens.co.uk
I: www.marsdens.co.uk

LYNTON
Devon

Buttershaw Cottage ★★★★
Contact: Marsden's Cottage Holidays, 2 The Square, Braunton EX33 2JB
T: (01271) 813777
F: (01271) 813664
E: holidays@marsdens.co.uk
I: www.marsdens.co.uk

Coastal Exmoor Hideaways ★★★
Contact: Mr P Hitchen, Coastal Exmoor Hideaways, Heddon Valley Hill, Parracombe, Barnstaple EX31 4PU
T: 08717 170772
F: 08717 170773
E: info@coastalexmoorhideaways.co.uk
I: www.coastalexmoorhideaways.co.uk

Lyn Cottage ★★★
Contact: Mr & Mrs Peter & Janet Cornwell, Marsden's Cottage Holidays, 2 The Square, Braunton EX33 2JB
T: (01271) 813777
F: (01271) 813664
E: holidays@marsdens.co.uk
I: www.marsdens.co.uk

Nettlecombe Cottage ★★★
Contact: Marsden's Cottage Holidays, 2 The Square, Braunton EX33 2JB
T: (01271) 813777
F: (01271) 813664
E: holidayds@marsdens.co.uk
I: www.marsdens.co.uk

Royal Castle Lodge ★★★★
Contact: Mr M Wolverson, Royal Castle Lodge, c/o Stag Cottage, Holdstone Down, Combe Martin EX34 0PF
T: (01271) 882449

West Ilkerton Farm ★★★★
Contact: Mrs Eveleigh, West Ilkerton Farm, Parracombe, Barnstaple EX35 6QA
T: (01598) 752310
F: (01598) 752310
E: eveleigh@westilkerton.co.uk
I: www.westilkerton.co.uk

Wringcliffe, Sillery ★★★-★★★★★
Contact: Mr P Shimwell, Wringcliffe, Sillery, Burlington House, 11 Lee Road, Lynton EX35 6HW
T: (01598) 753352
F: (01598) 753352
E: art@gunnsgallery.co.uk

MAIDEN NEWTON
Dorset

Lancombe Country Cottages ★★★★
Contact: Mr & Mrs Myles & Janet Provis & Schofield
T: (01300) 320562
F: (01300) 320562
E: info@lancombe.co.uk
I: www.lancombe.co.uk

MAIDENCOMBE
Devon

Langley Manor ★★★
Contact: Holiday Homes & Cottages South West, 365A Torquay Road, Paignton TQ3 2BT
T: (01803) 663650
F: (01803) 664037
E: holcotts@aol.com
I: www.swcottages.co.uk

MALMESBURY
Wiltshire

Cow Byre & Bull Pen ★★★
Contact: Mrs Edna Edwards, Cow Byre & Bull Pen, Stonehill Farm, Charlton, Malmesbury SN16 9DY
T: (01666) 823310
F: (01666) 823310
E: johnedna@stonehillfarm.fsnet.co.uk
I: www.smoothhound.co.uk/hotels/stonehill.html

King's Cottage H139
Rating Applied For
Contact: Luke Street, Berwick St John, Shaftesbury SP7 0HQ
T: (01747) 828170
F: (01747) 829090
E: enq@hideaways.co.uk

MALPAS
Cornwall

Curlews ★★★★
Contact: Mrs Margie Lumby, Poachers Reach, Harcourt, Feock, Truro TR3 6SQ
T: (01872) 864400
E: office@specialplacescornwall.co.uk
I: www.specialplacescornwall.co.uk

The Quarterdeck ★★★★
Contact: Mrs Margie Lumby, Poachers Reach, Harcourt, Feock, Truro TR3 6SQ
T: (01872) 864400
E: office@specialplacescornwall.co.uk
I: www.specialplacescornwall.co.uk

Trelowthas ★★★★
Contact: Mr Chris Churm, 2 The Rookery, Tythby Road, Cropwell Butler, Nottingham NG12 3AA
T: (01159) 334707
F: (01159) 334707

MANACCAN
Cornwall

Discovery ★★★
Contact: Cornish Cottage Holidays, Godolphin Road, Helston TR13 8AA
T: (01326) 573808
F: (01326) 564992
E: enquiry@cornishcottageholidays.co.uk
I: www.cornishcottageholidays.co.uk

Hallowarren Cottage ★★★★
Contact: Cornish Cottage Holidays, The Old Turnpike Dairy, Godolphin Road, Helston TR13 8AA
T: (01326) 573808
F: (01326) 564992
E: enquiry@cornishcottageholidays.co.uk
I: www.cornishcottageholidays.co.uk

Hillside & Chy-Pyth ★★★-★★★★★
Contact: Cornish Cottage Holidays, The Old Turnpike Dairy, Godolphin, Meneage Street, Helston TR13 8AA
T: (01326) 573808
F: (01326) 564992
E: enquiry@cornishcottageholidays.co.uk
I: www.cornishcottageholidays.co.uk

Lestowder Farm ★★-★★★★
Contact: Mrs Janet Martin, Lestowder, Manaccan, Helston TR12 6ES
T: (01326) 231400
F: (01326) 231400
E: lestowderfarm@hotmail.com
I: www.lestowderfarmcottages.co.uk

MANATON
Devon

Homer Heales ★★
Contact: Mrs Moreton, Great Houndtor, Manaton, Newton Abbot TQ13 9UW
T: (01647) 221202

MANNINGFORD ABBOTS
Wiltshire

The Old Tulip Barn ★★★
Contact: Mrs Margot Andrews, The Old Tulip Barn, c/o Huntlys, Manningford Abbots, Manningford Bruce, Pewsey SN9 6HZ
T: (01672) 563663
F: (01672) 851249
E: meg@gimspike.fsnet.co.uk

MARAZION
Cornwall

The Captain's House ★★★★★
Contact: Mr & Mrs Pettit, Tregullas, Kea, Truro TR3 6AJ
T: (01872) 865403
E: treduma@tiscali.co.uk
I: www.cornwall-online.co.uk/accommodation-selfcatering.htm

The Engine House ★★★★
Contact: Mr & Mrs Rick & Jane Davy, The Engine House, Tregurtha Downs, Plain-an-Gwarry, Penzance TR17 0DR
T: (01736) 711604
F: (01736) 711604
E: rickandjane@mac.com
I: www.the-enginehouse.co.uk

Polgew ★★★★
Contact: Mrs Diane Hickman, Paddock Wood, Crenver Corner, Praze-an-Beeble, Camborne TR14 0PE
T: (01209) 831740
F: (01209) 832007
E: polgew1@ntlworld.com
I: www.westcornwallholidays.co.uk

St Aubyn Estates ★★★-★★★★★
Contact: Ms Clare Sandry, St Aubyn Estates, The Manor Office, West End, Marazion, Marazion TR17 0EF
T: (01736) 710507
F: (01736) 719930
E: godolphin@manor-office.co.uk

Tregew Holiday Bungalows ★★
Contact: Mr Rodney Pool, Rose Hill, Marazion TR17 0HB
T: (01736) 710247

Trevara ★★★
Contact: Mrs Sally Laird, Pheasant Copse, Bere Court Road, Pangbourne, Reading RG8 8JU
T: (0118) 984 5500
F: (0118) 984 3966
E: sallylaird@talk21.com
I: www.thebestcottageincornwall.co.uk

The White House, Courtyard Cottage & Whitehouse Mews Flat★★★
Contact: Ms Jo Sewell, Exmoor House, Porlock, Minehead TA24 8EY
T: (01643) 863155
F: (01643) 863371
E: info@cornwall-holiday-cottages.com

MARHAMCHURCH
Cornwall

Budds Barns ★★★
Contact: Mr & Mrs David & Carol Richardson, Budds Barns, Titson, Marhamchurch, Poundstock, Bude EX23 0HQ
T: (01288) 361339
F: (01288) 361339
E: relax@buddsbarns.co.uk
I: www.buddsbarns.co.uk

Corner Cottage ★★★
Contact: Mr & Mrs Colin & Suzanne Burke, Two Waters, Park Road, Toddington, Dunstable LU5 6AB
T: (01525) 878100
F: (01525) 878119
E: colin@gardnerburke.co.uk

Court Farm ★★★-★★★★
Contact: Mrs Mary Trewin, Court Farm Cottages, Marhamchurch, Bude EX23 0EN
T: (01288) 361494
F: (01288) 361494
E: mary@courtfarm-holidays.co.uk
I: www.courtfarm-holidays.co.uk

Knowle Farm Cottage ★★★
Contact: Mr & Mrs S Youldon, Marhamchurch, Bude EX23 0HG
T: (01288) 381215
F: (01288) 381215

The Old Bakery ★★
Contact: Mrs Sally Herman, The Old Bakery, Hobbacott Lane, Marhamchurch, Bude EX23 0HD
T: (01288) 361532
E: david@activ8.fsnet.co.uk

Sharlands Farm ★★★★
Contact: Farm & Cottage Holidays, Victoria House, 12 Fore Street, Westward Ho!, Bideford EX39 1AW
T: (01237) 479146
F: (01237) 421512
E: enquiries@farmcott.co.uk

Trelay Farmhouse ★★★★
Contact: Farm & Cottage Holidays, Victoria House, 12 Fore Street, Northam, Bideford EX39 1AW
T: (01237) 479146
F: (01237) 421512
E: enquiries@farmcott.co.uk

Wooldown Farm Cottages ★★★-★★★★
Contact: Mrs Susan Blewett, Wooldown Farm Cottages, Wooldown Farm, Marhamchurch, Bude EX23 0HP
T: (01288) 361216
F: (01288) 361216
E: rogersueblewett@aol.com
I: www.wooldown.co.uk

MARK
Somerset

Pear Tree Cottage ★★★
Contact: Mrs Susan Slocombe, Pear Tree Cottage, Northwick Road, Mark, Highbridge TA9 4PG
T: (01278) 641228
E: northwickfarm@breathemail.net

MARKET LAVINGTON
Wiltshire

Hazel Cottage ★★★★
Contact: Mrs Janette Hodgkinson, 7 Parsonage Lane, Market Lavington, West Lavington, Devizes SN10 4AA
T: (01380) 813516
F: (01380) 813516
E: okasan@waitrose.com

MARLDON
Devon

Millmans Cottages Rating Applied For
Contact: Mr & Mrs Edward & Tina Girard, Millmans Farm, Village Road, Marldon, Paignton TQ3 1SJ
T: (01803) 558213
F: (01803) 558213
E: tina@millmanfarm.co.uk

WILDWOODS ★★
Contact: Mr Ian Butterworth, Holiday Homes & Cottages South West, 365A Torquay Road, Paignton TQ3 2BT
T: (01803) 663650
F: (01803) 664037
E: holcotts@aol.com
I: www.swcottages.co.uk

MARSHFIELD

The Old Inn Rating Applied For
Contact: Mrs Judy Brason, The Old Inn, Market Place, Marshfield, Chippenham SN14 8NP
T: (01225) 891803
F: (01225) 891301
E: judy@theoldinnatmarshfield.co.uk

MARSTON
Wiltshire

Barn Cottage & Stable Cottage ★★★★
Contact: Mrs Joy Reardon, Barn Cottage & Stable Cottage, Home Farm, Close Lane, Marston, Devizes SN10 5SN
T: (01380) 725484
E: maupicereardon@lineone.net

MARTINHOE
Devon

Hollowbrook Lodge & Cottage ★★★★
Contact: Mr Christopher Richmond, Marsden's Cottage Holidays, Martinhoe, Parracombe, Barnstaple EX31 4QT
T: (01598) 763368
F: (01598) 763567
E: cottages@oldrectoryhotel.co.uk

Ivy Cottage ★★★★
Contact: Marsden's Cottage Holidays, 2 The Square, Braunton EX33 2JB
T: (01271) 813777
F: (01271) 813664
E: holidays@marsdens.co.uk
I: www.marsdens.co.uk

MARTINSTOWN
Dorset

Blackbird Cottage ★★★
Contact: Mr Zachary Stuart-Brown, Dream Cottages, 41 Maiden Street, Weymouth DT4 8AZ
T: (01305) 761347
E: admin@dream-cottages.co.uk
I: www.dream-cottages.co.uk

Greatstone Cottage ★★★
Contact: Dream Cottages, 41 Maiden Street, Weymouth DT4 8AZ
T: (01305) 761347
F: (01305) 789000

Hope Cottage ★★★
Contact: Dream Cottages, 41 Maiden Street, Weymouth DT4 8AZ
T: (01305) 761347
F: (01305) 789000

MARTOCK
Somerset

Anne's Place ★★★
Contact: Anne's Place, Spring Mill, Earby, Barnoldswick BB94 0AA
T: 08700 723723

MARWOOD
Devon

The Pump House ★★★★
Contact: Marsdens Cottage Holidays, 2 The Square, Braunton EX33 2JB
T: (01271) 813777
F: (01271) 813644
E: holidays@marsdens.co.uk

The Tallett ★★★
Contact: Marsden's Cottage Holidays, 2 The Square, Braunton EX33 2JB
T: (01271) 813777
F: (01271) 813664
E: holidays@marsdens.co.uk
I: www.marsdens.co.uk

MAWGAN
Cornwall

The Studio ★★★
Contact: Mr Martin Raftery, Churchtown, Mullion, Helston TR12 7HQ
T: (01326) 240315
F: (01326) 241090
E: martin@mullioncottages.com
I: www.mullioncottages.com

MAWGAN PORTH
Cornwall

Lanson ★★★
Contact: Mr/Ms Paynter/Phelps, 57 Dunheved Road, Launceston PL15 9JH
T: (01566) 773420
E: philip.paynter@talk21.com
I: holidaysatmawganporth.co.uk

Tredragon Lodges Rating Applied For
Contact: Mr James Mcluskie, Mawgan Porth, Newquay TR8 4BW
T: (01637) 881610
F: (01637) 860383
E: tredragonlodge@hotmail.com.uk

Trelawns ★★★★
Contact: Cornish Cottage Holidays, The Old Turnpike Dairy, Godolphin, Meneage Street, Helston TR13 8AA
T: (01326) 573808
F: (01326) 564992
E: enquiry@cornishcottageholidays.co.uk
I: www.cornishcottageholidays.co.uk

MELCOMBE BINGHAM
Dorset

Greygles ★★★★
Contact: Mr P Sommerfeld, 22 Tiverton Road, Willesden, London NW10 3HL
T: (020) 8969 4830
F: (020) 8960 0069
E: enquiry@greygles.co.uk
I: www.greygles.co.uk

MELDON
Devon

Kerslake Cottage ★★★★
Contact: Ms Lizzie St George, Kerslake Farm, Meldon, Okehampton EX20 4LU
T: (01837) 54892
F: (01837) 54892
E: booking@kerslakemeldon.co.uk
I: www.kerslakemeldon.co.uk

MELKSHAM
Wiltshire

Moorlands Self Catering Holiday Homes★★★★
Contact: Mrs Jackie Moore, Moorlands Self Catering Holiday Homes, The Coach House, Station Approach, Melksham SN12 8BN
T: (01225) 702155
F: (01225) 702155
E: moorlands@aol.com
I: www.moorlandsuk.co.uk

MELPLASH
Dorset

Binghams Farm ★★★
Contact: Mr & Mrs Roy & Barbara Philpott, Binghams Farm, Melplash, Bridport DT6 3TT
T: (01308) 488234
E: royphilpott@msn.com
I: www.binghamsfarm.co.uk

MEMBURY
Devon

Bowditch Farm ★★★★
Contact: Mr & Mrs Sarah & Michael Bell, Bowditch Farm, Membury, Stockland, Honiton EX13 7TY
T: 0845 456 0290
F: (01404) 881801

Bowditch Farm Lodge Rating Applied For
Contact: Milkbere Holidays, 3 Fore Street, Seaton EX12 2LE
T: (01297) 20729
E: info@milkbere.com

Oxenways Estate Cottages ★★★★-★★★★★
Contact: Mr Ken Beecham, Oxenways Estate Cottages, Oxenways, Chapelcroft Road, Membury, Axminster EX13 7JR
T: (01404) 881785
F: (01404) 881778
E: info@oxenways.com

MENHENIOT
Cornwall

Hayloft Courtyard Cottages ★★★-★★★★★
Contact: Mr & Mrs Hore, Hoseasons Country Cottages, Raglan Road, Lowestoft NR32 2LW
T: (01502) 501515
I: www.hoseasons.co.uk

Trewint Farm ★★★-★★★★
Contact: Mrs Elizabeth Rowe, Trewint Farm, Menheniot, Liskeard PL14 3RE
T: (01579) 347155
F: (01579) 347155
I: www.geocities.com/trewint_2000

MERE
Wiltshire

2 Chance Cottages ★★★★
Contact: Mr & Mrs White, Chance Cottage, Shaftesbury Road, Mere, Warminster BA12 6BW
T: (01747) 861401
F: (01747) 861401
E: mail@wiltshirecottageholidays.co.uk
I: www.wiltshirecottageholidays.co.uk

Lower Mere Park Farm ★★★★
Contact: Mrs Nicky Mitchell, Lower Mere Park Farm, Mere, Warminster BA12 6AD
T: (01747) 830771

Whistley Waters ★★★-★★★★★
Contact: Mrs Cleo Campbell, Whistley Waters, Milton-on-Stour, Silton, Gillingham SP8 5PT
T: (01747) 840666
F: (01747) 840666
E: campbell.whistley@virgin.net
I: whistlewaters.co.uk

MERTON
Devon

Pinkhill Farm ★★
Contact: Farm & Cottage Holidays, Victoria House, 12 Fore Street, Northam, Bideford EX39 1AW
T: (01237) 479146
F: (01237) 421512
E: enquiries@farmcott.co.uk

MEVAGISSEY
Cornwall

The Poppins Rating Applied For
Contact: Cornish Cottage Holidays, The Old Turnpike Dairy, Godolphin Road, Helston TR13 8AA
T: (01326) 573808

Treleaven Farm Cottages ★★★★
Contact: Mr Linda Hennah, Treleaven Farm, Valley Road, Mevagissey, St Austell PL26 6RZ
T: (01726) 843558
F: (01726) 843558
I: www.treleavenfarm.co.uk

Treloen Holiday Apartments ★★★
Contact: Mrs P Seamark, Treloen Holiday Apartments, Dept E, Polkirt Hill, Mevagissey, St Austell PL26 6UX
T: (01726) 842406
F: (01726) 842406
E: holidays@treloen.co.uk
I: www.treloen.co.uk

MIDDLE MARWOOD
Devon

Primrose House ★★★★
Contact: Marsden's Cottage Holidays, 2 The Square, Braunton EX33 2JB
T: (01271) 813777
F: (01271) 813664
E: holidays@marsdens.co.uk
I: www.marsdens.co.uk

MIDDLECOMBE
Somerset

Periton Park Court & Riding Stables ★★-★★★
Contact: Mr John Borland, Middlecombe, Minehead TA24 8SN
T: (01643) 705970
F: (01643) 705970
E: peritonparkcourt@btinternet.com

MIDDLEMARSH
Dorset

White Horse Farm ★★★★
Contact: Mr David Wilding, White Horse Farm, Middlemarsh, Sherborne DT9 5QN
T: (01963) 210222
F: (01963) 210222
E: enquiries@whitehorsefarm.co.uk
I: www.whitehorsefarm.co.uk

MILLBROOK
Cornwall

The Retreat/The Studio ★★★-★★★★★
Contact: Mrs Sarah Blake, Stone Farm, Millbrook, Torpoint PL10 1JJ
T: (01752) 822267

MILLPOOL
Cornwall

Nutkin Lodge ★★★★
Contact: Mr John Bass, Nutkin Lodge, Millpool Grange, Bodmin PL30 4HZ
T: (01208) 821596

MILTON COOMBE
Devon

Tower Cottage ★★★★
Contact: Mrs Sarah Stone, Tower Cottage, Buckland Abbey, Milton Coombe, Yelverton PL20 6EZ
T: (01822) 853285
E: sarah.stone@cider-house.co.uk

MINEHEAD
Somerset

Anchor Cottage ★★★★
Contact: Dr J C Malin, 3 The Courtyard, Bancks Street, Minehead TA24 5DJ
T: (01643) 707529
F: (01643) 708712
E: jmalin@btinternet.com

Combe Cottages ★★★★
Contact: Mrs B D Parks, Mead House, 104 Periton Lane, Minehead TA24 8DZ
T: (01643) 704939

Dome Flat ★★★★
Contact: Mr J Lowin, 176A Harefield Road, Uxbridge UB8 1PP
T: (01895) 236972

Dove Cottage ★★★
Contact: Mr B B Waterman, 38 Fernleigh Road, Winchmore Hill, London N21 3AL
T: (0208) 882 4920
F: (0208) 882 4920

The Freight Shed ★★★
Contact: Mr & Mrs Alison & Duncan Waller, Wheddon Cross, Minehead TA24 7BY
T: (01643) 851386
F: (01643) 851532
E: barlevalley@hotmail.com

Harbour Cottage ★★★
Contact: Ms E J Hall, 12 Rue Gabriel Faure, 78290 Croissy-Sur-Seine, France
T: 00331 3053 6730
E: family davidm.hall@compuserve.com

The Haven Holiday Flats ★★
Contact: Mr G P Thorpe, The Haven Holiday Flats, 41 Blenheim Road, Minehead TA24 5QA
T: (01643) 705167

Higher Rodhuish Farm ★★
Contact: Mrs J Thomas, Higher Rodhuish Farm, Minehead TA24 6QL
T: (01984) 640253
F: (01984) 640253

Hindon Organic Farm ★★★-★★★★★
Contact: Mrs Webber, Hindon Organic Farm, Minehead TA24 8SH
T: (01643) 705244
F: (01643) 705244
E: info@hindonfram.co.uk
I: www.hindonfarm.co.uk

Huntingball Lodge ★★★★
Contact: Mr & Mrs Brian & Kim Hall, Huntingball Lodge, Blue Anchor, Minehead TA24 6JP
T: (01984) 640076
F: (01984) 640076
I: www.huntingball-lodge.co.uk

La Mer ★★★★
Contact: Mrs A Bowden, 4 Tides Reach, The Harbour, Minehead TA24 5UL
T: (01643) 704405
F: (01643) 704405

Little Barn Cottage ★★★★
Contact: Mrs Marian Padgett, Little Barn Cottage, Selworthy, Minehead TA24 8TL
T: (01643) 862303

Little Stoke ★★★
Contact: Ms Lucy Hutchings, Little Stoke, Blenheim Road, Minehead TA24 5QB
T: (01643) 708585
E: lucy@littlestoke.evesham.net

Luxury Flat ★★
Contact: Mr & Mrs D J Coward, 28 Parks Lane, Minehead TA24 8BT
T:(01643) 705634

Old Black Boy Cottage ★★★
Contact: Mr & Mrs Harvey, 42 Bampton Street, Minehead TA24 5TT
T: (01643) 705016

The Old Kennels ★★★★
Contact: Mr Vivian Perkins, The Old Kennels, 4a Periton Lane, Minehead TA24 8AQ
T: (01643) 705754

Parkside ★★
Contact: Mrs Janet Bond, Parkside, 31 Blenheim Road, Minehead TA24 5PZ
T: (01643) 703720
I: www.travel.to/parkside

Peake Cottage ★★★
Contact: Mr H. J. Davies, Meadowcroft, Whitelane Road, Minehead TA24 8BB
T: (01643) 704634

Pella ★★★
Contact: Mrs Yendole, Western Lane, Minehead TA24 8BZ
T: (01643) 703277
E: hyendole@ukonline.co.uk

Rosanda House ★★★
Contact: Mr & Mrs Richard & Lorna Robbins, Rosanda House, 2 Northfield Road, Minehead TA24 5QQ
T: (01643) 704958
E: enquiries@rosanda.co.uk
I: www.rosanda.co.uk

Seagate Cottage ★★★★
Contact: Dr & Mr Eaton & Ball, Applegarth, West Chinnock, Crewkerne TA18 7PW
T: (01935) 881436
E: meganeaton@ukonline.co.uk

Wydon Farm Cottages ★★★
Contact: Farm & Cottage Holidays, Victoria House, 12 Fore Street, Northam, Bideford EX39 1AW
T: (01237) 479146
F: (01237) 421512
E: enquiries@farmcott.co.uk

MINIONS
Cornwall

Trewalla Farm ★★★★
Contact: Fiona Cotter
T: (01579) 342385
F: (01579) 342385
E: cotter.trewalla@virgin.net
I: http://cotter.trewalla@virgin.net

MODBURY
Devon

Garden Cottage ★★★★
Contact: Powell's Cottage Holidays, High Street, Saundersfoot SA69 9EJ
T: (01834) 812791

Oldaport Farm Cottages ★★★★
Contact: Miss C M Evans, Oldaport Farm Cottages, Modbury, Ivybridge PL21 0TG
T: (01548) 830842
F: (01548) 830998
E: cathy@oldaport.com
I: www.oldaport.dial.pipex.com

Pinewood Lodge ★★★★
Contact: Mrs Fiona Dukes, 188 Solihull Road, Shirley, Solihull B90 3LG
T: (0121) 744 1162
F: (0121) 744 1162
E: fdukes@globalnet.co.uk

The Popples ★★★★
Contact: Elliot House, Church Street, Kingsbridge TQ7 1BY
T: (01548) 853089
F: (01548) 853086
E: thc@toadhallcottages.com

MONTACUTE
Somerset

Abbey Farm ★★★
Contact: Mrs Jenkins, Abbey Farm, Montacute TA15 6UA
T: (01935) 823572
F: (01935) 823572
E: xxe70@dial.pipex.com
I: www.dial.pipex.com

MORCOMBELAKE
Dorset

Norchard Farmhouse ★★★
Contact: Mrs Mary Ollard, Norchard Farmhouse, Norchard Barn, Morcombelake, Bridport DT6 6EP
T: (01297) 489263
F: (01297) 489661

MORETONHAMPSTEAD
Devon

Budleigh Farm ★★-★★★★
Contact: Mrs J Harvey, Budleigh Farm, Moretonhampstead, Newton Abbot TQ13 8SB
T: (01647) 440835
F: (01647) 440436
E: swharvey@budleighfarm.co.uk
I: www.budleighfarm.co.uk

Great Doccombe Farm ★★★★
Contact: Mr & Mrs D G Oakey, Great Doccombe Farm, Doccombe, Moretonhampstead, Newton Abbot TQ13 8SS
T: (01647) 440694

Yarningale ★★★
Contact: Mrs Sarah (Sally) Radcliffe, Yarningale, Exeter Road, Moretonhampstead, Newton Abbot TQ13 8SW
T: (01647) 440560
F: (01647) 440560

MORTEHOE
Devon

Combesgate House ★★★
Contact: Mr & Mrs Keith & Virginia Sprason, Ferndale Leisure, Hagley Mews, Hagley Hall, Hall Drive, Hagley, Stourbridge DY9 9LQ
T: (01562) 883038
F: (01562) 886592
E: combesgate.house@virgin.net
I: www.combesgate.fsnet.co.uk

Crows Nest & The Lookout ★★★
Contact: Marsden's Cottage Holidays, 2 The Square, Braunton EX33 2JB
T: (01271) 813777
F: (01271) 813664
E: holidays@marsdens.co.uk
I: www.marsdens.co.uk

The Grange ★★★-★★★★
Contact: Mr & Mrs Peter & Jill Lawley, The Grange, North Morte Road, Mortehoe, Woolacombe EX34 7EG
T: (01271) 870580
E: the-grange-mortehoe@supanet.com

Mailscot & Wykeham ★★-★★★
Contact: Marsden's Cottage Holidays, 2 The Square, Braunton EX33 2JB
T: (01271) 813777
F: (01271) 813664
E: holidays@marsdens.co.uk
I: www.marsdens.co.uk

Seaview ★★★
Contact: Mr & Mrs Peter & Janet Cornwell, Marsden's Cottage Holidays, 2 The Square, Braunton EX33 2JB
T: (01271) 813777
F: (01271) 813664
E: holidays@marsdens.co.uk
I: www.marsdens.co.uk

MORVAL
Cornwall

Wringworthy Holiday Cottages ★★★★
Contact: Ms Francis & Cheryl Howard, Farm & Cottage Holidays, Wringworthy, Morval, Looe PL13 1PR
T: (01503) 240685
F: (01503) 240830
E: wrinholcot@aol.com
I: www.cornwallwringworthycottages.co.uk

MORWENSTOW
Cornwall

Gooseham Barton Cottages ★★★-★★★★
Contact: Miss D Hamilton, Gooseham Barton Cottages, Gooseham Barton, Morwenstow, Bude EX23 9PG
T: (01288) 331204
E: debbiehmltn@aol.com
I: www.gooseham-barton.com

West Woolley Barns ★★★-★★★★
Contact: Mr & Mrs Chris & Jan Everard, West Woolley Barns, West Woolley Farm, Woolley, Morwenstow, Bude EX23 9PP
T: (01288) 331202
E: info@westwoolleyfarm.co.uk

MOTHECOMBE
Devon

The Flete Estate Holiday Cottages ★★★★-★★★★★
Contact: Miss J Webb, The Flete Estate Holiday Cottages, Pamflete, Holbeton, Plymouth PL8 1JR
T: (01752) 830234
F: (01752) 830500
E: cottages@flete.co.uk
I: www.flete.co.uk

MOUNT HAWKE
Cornwall

Wayside ★★
Contact: Cornish Cottage Holidays, Godolphin Road, Helston TR13 8AA
T: (01326) 573808
F: (01326) 564992
E: enquiry@cornishcottageholidays.co.uk
I: www.cornishcottageholidays.co.uk

MOUSEHOLE
Cornwall

Fern Cottage ★★★
Contact: Mr & Mrs Phillip & Melanie Stephens, Fore Street, Mousehole, Penzance TR19 6TQ
T: (01736) 731363
E: stephens@churleys.freeserve.co.uk

Harbourside Cottage ★★★★
Contact: Mrs Sandra Hall, The Square, Marazion TR17 0AP
T: (01736) 710424
F: (01736) 710424
E: info@cornwall-holiday-cottages.com

2 The Old Standard ★★★
Contact: Mr & Mrs J Underhill, The Old Vicarage, Collingbourne Kingston, Marlborough SN8 3SE
T: (01264) 850234
F: (01264) 850703
E: j.underhill@oldstandard.co.uk
I: www.oldstandard.co.uk

Tide's Reach ★★★★
Contact: Mr & Mrs Peter & Sandra Hall, White House, The Square, Marazion TR17 0AP
T: (01736) 710424
F: (01736) 710424
E: info@cornwall-holiday-cottages.com

Wootton Gray ★★★
Contact: Mrs Jenifer Bower, 4 Coldharbour Close, Henley-on-Thames RG9 1QF
T: (01491) 575297
F: (01491) 575297

MUCHELNEY
Somerset

Gothic House (The Old Dairy) ★★★
Contact: Mrs Joy Thorne, Gothic House (The Old Dairy), Muchelney, Langport TA10 0DW
T: (01458) 250626
E: joy-thorne@totalserve.co.uk

MUDDIFORD
Devon

Ashtree Cottage ★★★★
Contact: Marsden's Cottage Holidays, 2 The Square, Braunton EX33 2JB
T: (01271) 813777
F: (01271) 813664
E: holidays@marsdens.co.uk
I: www.marsdens.co.uk

Rose Cottage ★★★★
Contact: Ms Helen Knight, Score Farm Developments, Score Farm, Chapel Street, Braunton EX33 1EL
T: (01271) 814815
F: (01271) 817973
E: sunshinenel@btinternet.com
I: www.scorefarmholidays.co.uk

MUDGLEY
Somerset

Hayloft Cottage ★★★
Contact: Mr Hugh Tucker, Hayloft Cottage, Court Farm, Mudgley, Wedmore BS28 4TY
T: (01934) 712367
E: htucker@courtfarmcottages.co.uk
I: www.courtfarmcottages.co.uk/

MULLION
Cornwall

Anchordown ★★★
Contact: Mr Martin Raftery, Mullion Cottages, Churchtown, Mullion, Helston TR12 7HQ
T: (01326) 240315
F: (01326) 241090
E: martin@mullioncottages.com
I: www.mullioncottages.com

Atlantic Suite ★★★
Contact: Mr Martin Raftery, Churchtown, Mullion, Helston TR12 7HQ
T: (01326) 240315
F: (01326) 241090
E: martin@mullioncottages.com
I: www.mullioncottages.com

The Cedars ★★★
Contact: Mr Martin Raftery, Churchtown, Mullion, Helston TR12 7HQ
T: (01326) 240315
F: (01326) 241090
E: martin@mullioncottages.com
I: www.mullioncottages.com

Chy-an-Mor ★★★
Contact: Mr Martin Raftery, Churchtown, Mullion, Helston TR12 7HQ
T: (01326) 240315
F: (01326) 241090
E: martin@mullioncottages.com
I: www.mullioncottages.com

2 Coastguard Cottage ★★★
Contact: Mr Martin Raftery, Churchtown, Mullion, Helston TR12 7HQ
T: (01326) 240315
F: (01326) 241090
E: martin@mullioncottages.com
I: www.mullioncottages.com

6 Coastguard Cottage ★★★
Contact: Mr Martin Raftery, Churchtown, Mullion, Helston TR12 7HQ
T: (01326) 240315
F: (01326) 241090
E: martin@mullioncottages.com
I: www.mullioncottages.com

Cornerways ★★★
Contact: Mr Martin Raftery, Churchtown, Mullion, Helston TR12 7HQ
T: (01326) 240315
F: (01326) 241090
E: martin@mullioncottages.com
I: www.mullioncottages.com

The Cottage ★★★
Contact: Mr Raftery, Mullion Cottages, Mullion, Helston TR12 7EU
T: (01326) 240315
F: (01326) 241090
E: martin@mullioncottages.com
I: www.mullioncottages.com

Creigan House ★★★
Contact: Mr Martin Raftery, Churchtown, Mullion, Helston TR12 7HQ
T: (01326) 240315
F: (01326) 241090
E: martin@mullioncottages.com
I: www.mullioncottages.com

Deu-Try ★★★
Contact: Mr Martin Raftery, Mullion Cottages, Churchtown, Mullion, Helston TR12 7HQ
T: (01326) 240315
F: (01326) 241090
E: martin@mullioncottages.com
I: www.mullioncottages.com

The Garden Suite ★★★★
Contact: Mr Martin Raftery, Churchtown, Mullion, Helston TR12 7HQ
T: (01326) 240315
F: (01326) 241090
E: martin@mullioncottages.com
I: www.mullioncottages.com

Green Cottage ★★★
Contact: Mr Martin Raftery, Mullion Cottages, Churchtown, Mullion, Helston TR12 7HQ
T: (01326) 240315
F: (01326) 241090
E: martin@mullioncottages.com
I: www.mullioncottages.com

Gulls ★★★
Contact: Mr Martin Raftery, Mullion Cottages, Churchtown, Mullion, Helston TR12 7HQ
T: (01326) 240315
F: (01326) 241090
E: martin@mullioncottages.com
I: www.mullioncottages.com

Higher Lampra ★★★
Contact: Mr Martin Raftery, Mullion Cottages, Churchtown, Mullion, Helston TR12 7HQ
T: (01326) 240315
F: (01326) 241090
E: martin@mullioncottages.com
I: www.mullioncottages.com

Lampra Mill ★★★★
Contact: Mr Raftery, Mullion Cottages, Sea View Terrace, Churchtown, Mullion, Helston TR12 7HN
T: (01326) 240512
F: (01326) 241090
E: martin@mullioncottages.com
I: www.mullioncottages.com

Mullion Mill Cottage ★★★
Contact: Mrs Lane, Treloskan Farm, Cury, Helston TR12
T: (01326) 240493

Nythfa ★★★
Contact: Cornish Cottage Holidays, The Old Turnpike Dairy, Godolphin Road, Helston TR13 8AA
T: (01326) 573808
F: (01326) 564992
E: enquiry@cornishcottageholidays.co.uk
I: www.cornishcottageholidays.co.uk

Ogo-Dour ★★★
Contact: Cornish Cottage Holidays, The Old Turnpike Dairy, Godolphin Road, Helston TR13 8AA
T: (01326) 573808
F: (01326) 564992
E: enquiry@cornishcottageholidays.co.uk
I: www.cornishcottageholidays.co.uk

Redannack Bungalow ★★★
Contact: Mr Martin Raftery, Churchtown, Mullion, Helston TR12 7HQ
T: (01326) 240315
F: (01326) 241090
E: martin@mullioncottages.com
I: www.mullioncottages.com

Sea Breezes ★★★★
Contact: Mr Martin Raftery, Churchtown, Mullion, Helston TR12 7HQ
T: (01326) 240315
F: (01326) 241090
E: martin@mullioncottages.com
I: www.mullioncottages.com

Stable Cottage ★★★
Contact: Mr Martin Raftery, Churchtown, Mullion, Helston TR12 7HQ
T: (01326) 240315
F: (01326) 241090
E: martin@mullioncottages.com
I: www.mullioncottages.com

Tregonning ★★★
Contact: Cornish Cottage Holidays, The Old Turnpike Dairy, Godolphin Road, Helston TR13 8AA
T: (01326) 573808
F: (01326) 564992
E: enquiry@cornishcottageholidays.co.uk
I: www.cornishcottageholidays.co.uk

Trenance Barton ★★★
Contact: Mr Martin Raftery, Churchtown, Mullion, Helston TR12 7HQ
T: (01326) 240315
F: (01326) 241090
E: martin@mullioncottages.com
I: www.mullioncottages.com

Trenance Farm Cottages ★★★
Contact: Mr & Mrs Richard & Jennifer Tyler Street, Trenance Farm Cottages, Trenance Farm, Mullion, Helston TR12 7HB
T: (01326) 240639
F: (01326) 240639
E: info@trenancefarmholidays.co.uk
I: www.trenancefarmholidays.co.uk

Trencrom ★★★★
Contact: Mr Martin Raftery, Churchtown, Mullion, Helston TR12 7HQ
T: (01326) 240315
F: (01326) 241090
E: martin@mullioncottages.com
I: www.mullioncottages.com

Trewenna & Scrumpy Cottage ★★★★
Contact: Farm & Cottage Holidays, Victoria House, 12 Fore Street, Westward Ho!, Bideford EX39 1AW
T: (01237) 479146
F: (01237) 421512
E: enquiries@farmcott.co.uk

The Vestry ★★
Contact: Mr Martin Raftery, Mullion Cottages, Churchtown, Mullion, Helston TR12 7HQ
T: (01326) 240315
F: (01326) 241090
E: martin@mullioncottages.com
I: www.mullioncottages.com

MUSBURY
Devon

Green Meadows ★★★★
Contact: Milkbere Holidays, 3 Fore Street, Seaton EX12 2LE
T: (01297) 20729
F: (01297) 22925
E: info@milkberehols.com
I: www.milkbere.com

Maidenhayne Farm Cottage ★★★★★
Contact: Mrs T Colley, Maidenhayne Farmhouse, Maidenhayne Lane, Musbury, Axminster EX13 8AG
T: (01297) 552469
F: (01297) 551109
E: graham@maidenhayne-farm-cottage.co.uk
I: www.Maidenhayne-farm-cottage.co.uk

Rosslyn ★★★
Contact: The Proprietor, Rosslyn, 4 Doatshayne Close, Musbury, Axminster EX13

Wood Cottage ★★★★
Contact: Ms Kate Bartlett, Jean Bartlett Cottage Holidays, The Old Dairy, Fore Street, Seaton EX12 3JB
T: (01297) 23221
F: (01297) 23303
E: holidays@jeanbartlett.com
I: www.netbreaks.com/jeamb

MYLOR
Cornwall

Albion House Cottages ★★★★
Contact: Mr & Mrs Patrick & Penelope Polglase, Albion House Cottages, Bells Hill, Mylor Bridge, Mylor, Falmouth TR11 5SQ
T: (01326) 373607
F: (01326) 377607

NANSTALLON
Cornwall

The Gate House ★★★★
Contact: Mr & Mrs Hamley, Nanscarne, Nanstallon, Bodmin PL30 5LG
T: (01208) 74291
E: mikekathhamley@clara.co.uk
I: www.trailcottage.co.uk

Stables Cottage ★★★★
Contact: Mr & Mrs Michael & Norma Hinde, Stables Cottage, Lower Mulberry Farm, Nanstallon, Bodmin PL30 5LJ
T: (01208) 831636
E: hind831636@aol.com
I: www.members.aol.com/hind831636

Tregarthen Cottages ★★★★★
Contact: Mrs Margaret Bealing, Tregarthen Cottages, Nanstallon, Bodmin PL30 5LB
T: (01208) 831570
F: (01208) 831570
E: enquiries@tregarthencottages.co.uk
I: www.tregarthencottages.co.uk

NETHER STOWEY
Somerset

The Old House ★★★-★★★★
Contact: Mr J Douglas Gee, The Old House, St Mary Street, Nether Stowey, Bridgwater TA5 1LJ
T: (01278) 732392
E: dgeetheoldhouse@ision.co.uk
I: www.theoldhouse.ision.co.uk

NETHERBURY
Dorset

Little Thatch ★★★
Contact: Mr Zachary Stuart-Brown, Dream Cottages, 41 Maiden Street, Weymouth DT4 8AZ
T: (01305) 761347
E: admin@dream-cottages.co.uk
I: www.dream-cottages.co.uk

NETTLECOMBE
Dorset

Wren Cottage ★★★★
Contact: Mrs Eirlys Johnson, 9 The Berkeleys, Fetcham, Leatherhead KT22 9DW
T: (01372) 378907
E: eirlys.johnson@tinyworld.co.uk

NEW POLZEATH
Cornwall

Atlantic View & Atlantic View Coachhouse★★★-★★★★★
Contact: Dr S Garthwaite, Atlantic View Holidays, Matfield Oast, Chestnut Lane, Matfield, Tonbridge TN12 7JJ
T: (01892) 722264
F: (01892) 724022
E: enquiries@atlanticview.net
I: www.atlanticview.net

Hilcote ★★★
Contact: Harbour Holidays - Rock, Trebetherick House, Polzeath, Wadebridge PL27 6SB
T: (01208) 863399
F: (01208) 862218

Treheather ★★★
Contact: Dr E Mayall, Osmond House, Stoke Canon, Exeter EX5 4AA
T: (01392) 841219

NEWBRIDGE
Cornwall

Bostrase Stables ★★★
Contact: CH Ref:13843, Holiday Cottages Group Owner Services Dept, Spring Mill, Earby, Barnoldswick BB94 0AA
T: 08700 723723
E: sales@holidaycottagesgroup.com
I: www.country-holidays.co.uk

NEWLYN
Cornwall

Chywoone Farm ★★★
Contact: CH Ref: 8803,8804, 8805, Holiday Cottages Group Owner Services Dept, Spring Mill, Earby, Barnoldswick BB94 0AA
T: 08700 723723
I: www.country-holidays.co.uk

Fuchsia Cottage Rating Applied For
Contact: Ms Victoria Howard, 3 The Bowjey Hill, Newlyn, Penzance TR18 5LP
T: (01736) 330672
E: bookings@victoriahoward.freeserve.co.uk

Shamaal ★★★★
Contact: Powell's Cottage Holidays, High Street, Freystrop, Haverfordwest SA69 9EJ
T: (01834) 813232
F: (01834) 811731

NEWQUAY
Cornwall

Croftlea Holiday Flats ★★
Contact: Croftlea Holiday Flats, Wildflower Lane, Newquay TR7 2QB
T: (01637) 852505
F: (01637) 877183
E: info@croftlea.co.uk
I: www.croftlea.co.uk

Gillyn ★★
Contact: Mrs Betty Barry, Gillyn, 21 Towan Blystra Road, Newquay TR7 2RP
T: (01637) 876104

Manuels Farm ★★★★
Contact: Mr & Mrs James & Tracy Wilson, Manuels Farm, Quintrell Downs, Newquay TR8 4NY
T: (01637) 878300
F: (01637) 878300
I: www.manuelsfarm.co.uk

Tregurrian Hotel Apartments ★★★★
Contact: Mr Paul Mills, Tregurrian Hotel Apartments, Watergate Bay, Newquay TR8 4AB
T: (01637) 860280
E: tregurrian@holidaysincornwall.net

Trendrean Farm Barns ★★★★
Contact: Mr & Mrs I Marshall, Trendrean Farm Barns, St Newlyn East, Newquay TR8 5LY
T: (01208) 813228
E: ivor.gill@btopenworld.com

NEWTON ABBOT
Devon

Chipley Mill ★★★★
Contact: Mr L Coleman, Chipley Mill, Bickington, Newton Abbot TQ12 6JW
T: (01626) 821681
E: laurence@colemanx.org.uk
I: www.chipleymill.co.uk

Lower Bramble Farm ★★★★
Contact: Mr Howard Lewis, Lower Bramble Farm, Chudleigh, Trusham, Newton Abbot TQ13 0DU
T: (01626) 852294
F: (01626) 852294

Oak Cottage ★★
Contact: Holiday Homes & Cottages South West, 365A Torquay Road, Paignton TQ3 2BT
T: (01803) 663650
F: (01803) 664037
E: holcotts@aol.com
I: www.swcottages.co.uk

2 Thorne Cottages Rating Applied For
Contact: Ms Debbie Sanders, Combeinteignhead, Newton Abbot TQ12 4RB
T: (01626) 872779
E: debbie@saunders17.freeserve.co.uk

NEWTON FERRERS
Devon

Anchor Cottage ★★★★
Contact: Mrs Vivienne Summers, Yealm Holidays, 8 Whittingham Road, Yealmpton, Plymouth PL8 2NF
T: 0870 7 472987
E: info@yealm-holidays.co.uk
I: www.yealm-holidays.co.uk

Crown Yealm Apartment ★★
Contact: Mrs Vivienne Summers, Yealm Holidays, 8 Whittingham Road, Yealmpton, Plymouth PL8 2NF
T: 0870 7 472987
E: info@yealm-holidays.co.uk
I: www.yealm-holidays.co.uk

Glen Cottage ★★★
Contact: Mrs Vivienne Summers, Yealm Holidays, 8 Whittingham Road, Yealmpton, Plymouth PL8 2NF
T: 0870 7 472987
E: info@yealm-holidays.co.uk
I: www.yealm-holidays.co.uk

Lezant Pine Lodge ★★★★
Contact: Mrs Vivienne Summers, Yealm Holidays, 8 Whittingham Road, Yealmpton, Plymouth PL8 2NF
T: 0870 7 472987
F: (01752) 873173
E: info@yealm-holidays.co.uk
I: www.yealm-holidays.co.uk

The Penthouse ★★★★
Contact: Mrs Vivienne Summers, Yealm Holidays, 8 Whittingham Road, Yealmpton, Plymouth PL8 2NF
T: 0870 7 472987
F: (01752) 873173
E: info@yealm-holidays.co.uk
I: www.yealm-holidays.co.uk

Upwood ★★★
Contact: Mrs Aline Stackhouse, Upwood, Court Road, Newton Ferrers, Plymouth PL8 1DA
T: (01752) 872286
E: aline@upwood64.freeserve.co.uk

NEWTON POPPLEFORD
Devon

21 Otter Reach ★★★
Contact: Holiday Homes & Cottages South West, 365A Torquay Road, Paignton TQ3 2BT
T: (01803) 663650
F: (01803) 664037
E: holcott@aol.com

Umbrella Cottage ★★★
Contact: Mrs M Woodley, Burrow, Newton Poppleford, Sidmouth EX10 0BP
T: (01395) 568687
F: (01395) 568883

NEWTON ST LOE
Bath and North East Somerset

Pennsylvania Farm ★★★-★★★★
Contact: Mr & Mrs Paul & Peggy Foster, Pennsylvania Farm, The Cheese House, The Stables, Newton St Loe, Bath BA2 9JD
T: (01225) 314912

NORTH CHIDEOCK
Dorset

Hell Barn Cottages, Hell Farmhouse ★★★
Contact: Mr & Mrs Shigeaki & Diana Takezoe, Hell Farmhouse, Hell Lane, Chideock, Wootton Fitzpaine, Bridport DT6 6LA
T: (01297) 489589
F: (01297) 489043
E: diana@hellbarn.co.uk
I: www.hellbarn.co.uk

NORTH HILL
Cornwall

The Granary at Eastgate Barn ★★★★
Contact: Ms Jill Goodman, Challs, Landreyne, North Hill, Launceston PL15 7LZ
T: (01566) 782573
E: jill@eastgatebarn.co.uk
I: www.eastgatebarn.co.uk

NORTH MOLTON
Devon

Bampfylde ★★★★★
Contact: Mr & Mrs P Cornwell, Marsden's Cottage Holidays, 2 The Square, Braunton EX33 2JB
T: (01271) 813777
F: (01271) 813664
E: holidays@marsdens.co.uk
I: www.marsdens.co.uk

Lambscombe Farm Cottages Rating Applied For
Contact: Mr & Mrs Farenden, Lambscombe Farm Cottages, Twitchen, South Molton EX36 3JT
T: (01598) 740558
I: www.lambscombefarm.co.uk

Pitt Farm ★★★★
Contact: Mrs Gladys Ayre, Pitt Farm, Stable Cottage, North Molton, Twitchen, South Molton EX36 3JR
T: (01598) 740285
E: royayre@tiscali.co.uk
I: www.devonfarms.co.uk

West Millbrook Farm ★★-★★★
Contact: Mrs R J Courtney, West Millbrook Farm, West Millbrook, Twitchen, South Molton EX36 3LP
T: (01598) 740382
E: wmbselfcatering@aol.com
I: www.north.molton.co.uk

NORTH PETHERWIN
Cornwall

Castle Milford Mill ★★★★
Contact: Farm & Cottage Holidays, Victoria House, 12 Fore Street, Westward Ho!, Bideford EX39 1AW
T: (01237) 479146
F: (01237) 421512
E: enquiries@farmcott.co.uk

Stenhill Farm
Rating Applied For
Contact: Mrs Phyllis Reddock, Stenhill Farm, North Petherwin, Launceston PL15 8NN
T: (01566) 785686
E: e.reddock@btinternet.com

Waterloo Farm ★★★★
Contact: Farm & Cottage Holidays, Victoria House, 12 Fore Street, Westward Ho!, Bideford EX39 1AW
T: (01237) 479146
F: (01237) 421512
E: enquiries@farmcott.co.uk

NORTH TAMERTON
Cornwall

Eastcott Farm & Lodges ★★-★★★
Contact: Mrs Candida Whitmill, Eastcott Farm & Lodges, Eastcott Farm, North Tamerton, Holsworthy EX22 6SB
T: (01409) 271172
F: (01409) 271308
E: eastcott@fsmail.net
I: www.eastcottcornwall.co.uk

Hill Cottage ★★★★
Contact: Mr & Mrs R & E Green, Beer Mill Farm, Clawton, Holsworthy EX22 6PF
T: (01409) 253093
F: (01409) 253024
E: lgsg@supanet.com

Tamar Valley Cottages ★★★★
Contact: Mr & Mrs Stephen & Jane Rhodes, Tamar Valley Cottages, North Tamerton House, North Tamerton, Holsworthy EX22 6SA
T: (01409) 271284
E: smrhodes@btinternet.com
I: www.tamarvalleycottages.co.uk

NORTH TAWTON
Devon

Cider Cottage ★★★★
Contact: Ms Daniel Kirst, Cider Cottage, Yeo Lane, North Tawton EX20 2DD
T: (01837) 89002
F: (01837) 89237

East Hill Bungalow Farm ★★★
Contact: Helpful Holidays, Mill Street, Chagford, Newton Abbot TQ13 8AW
T: (01647) 433593
F: (01647) 433694
E: help@helpfulholidays.com
I: www.pyle-farm-holidays.co.uk

Westacott Barton Farm ★★★★
Contact: Farm & Cottage Holidays, 12 Fore Street, Northam, Westward Ho!, Bideford EX39 1AW
T: (01237) 479146
E: enquiries@farmcott.co.uk

NORTH WHILBOROUGH
Devon

Long Barn Luxury Holiday Cottages ★★★★★
Contact: Mr Peter Tidman, Long Barn Luxury Holiday Cottages, Long Barn, Whilborough, Kingskerswell, Newton Abbot TQ12 5LP
T: (01803) 875044
F: (01803) 875705
E: tidman@lineone.net

NORTH WRAXALL
Wiltshire

Home Farm ★★★★
Contact: Mr & Mrs Drew, Home Farm, Upper North Wraxall, Chippenham SN14 7AG
T: (01225) 891238

NORTHAM
Devon

Bay View Maisonette ★★★
Contact: Farm & Cottage Holidays, Victoria House, 12 Fore Street, Northam, Bideford EX39 1AW
T: (01237) 479146
F: (01237) 421512
E: enquiries@farmcott.co.uk

The Cabin ★★★★
Contact: Marsden's Cottage Holidays, 2 The Square, Braunton EX33 2JB
T: (01271) 813777
F: (01271) 813664
E: holidays@marsdens.co.uk
I: www.marsdens.co.uk

Fordlands ★★★
Contact: Farm & Cottage Holidays, Victoria House, 12 Fore Street, Westward Ho!, Bideford EX39 1AW
T: (01237) 479146
F: (01237) 421512
E: enquiries@farmcott.co.uk

Lenwood ★★★
Contact: Farm & Cottage Holidays, Victoria House, 12 Fore Street, Westward Ho!, Bideford EX39 1AW
T: (01237) 479146
F: (01237) 421512
E: bookings@farmcott.co.uk

NORTHLEIGH
Devon

Chilcombe ★★★
Contact: Milkbere Holidays, 3 Fore Street, Seaton EX12 2LE
T: (01297) 20729
F: (01297) 22925
E: info@milkberehols.com
I: www.milkbere.com

4 The Malt House ★★★
Contact: Ms Louise Hayman, Milkbere Cottage Holidays Ltd, 3 Fore Street, Seaton EX12 2LE
T: (01297) 20729
F: (01297) 24831
E: info@milkberehols.com
I: www.milkbere.com

Northleigh Farm ★★★★
Contact: Mr & Mrs Simon & Sue Potter, Northleigh Farm, Northleigh, Colyton EX24 6BL
T: (01404) 871217
F: (01404) 871217
E: simon-potter@msn.com
I: www.northleighfarm.co.uk

NORTON SUB HAMDON
Somerset

Little Norton Mill ★★★★-★★★★★
Contact: Mrs Lynn Hart, Little Norton, Stoke sub Hamdon TA14 6TE
T: (01935) 881337
F: (01935) 881337
E: tom.hart@dial.pipex.com
I: www.littlenortonmill.co.uk

NOSS MAYO
Devon

The Galley & Post House ★★★★
Contact: Mrs Vivienne Summers, Yealm Holidays, 8 Whittingham Road, Yealmpton, Plymouth PL8 2NF
T: 0870 7 472987
F: (01752) 873173
E: info@yealm-holidays.co.uk
I: www.yealm-holidays.co.uk

Mallards ★★★
Contact: Mrs Vivienne Summers, Yealm Holidays, 8 Whittingham Road, Yealmpton, Plymouth PL8 2NF
T: 0870 7 472987
E: info@yealm-holidays.co.uk
I: www.yealm-holidays.co.uk

NOTTON
Dorset

Notton Hill Holiday Cottages ★★★-★★★★★
Contact: Mr & Mrs D Smith, Notton, Dorchester DT2 0BZ
T: (01300) 321299
F: (01300) 321299

NUNNEY
Somerset

Riverside Cottage ★★★★
Contact: Mrs Clare Hulley, 1 Hill House, 37 Innox Hill Gardens, Frome BA11 2LN
T: (01373) 464712

OAKHILL
Somerset

The Chapel ★★★
Contact: Mrs Jeanne Kirby, 166 West Street, Marlow SL7 2BU
T: (01628) 481239
E: kirbyjeanne@hotmail.com

OAKSEY
Wiltshire

Woodpecker Cottage ★★★
Contact: Mr & Mrs Martin & Ann Shewry-Fitzgerald, Manby's Farm, Oaksey, Malmesbury SN16 9SA
T: (01666) 577399
F: (01666) 577241
E: manbys@oaksey.junglelink.co.uk
I: www.manbysfarm.com

OGWELL
Devon

Rydon Ball ★★★★
Contact: Mr Ian Butterworth, Holiday Homes & Cottages South West, 365A Torquay Road, Paignton TQ3 2BT
T: (01803) 663650
F: (01803) 664037
E: holcotts@aol.com
I: www.swcottages.co.uk

OKEHAMPTON
Devon

Beer Farm ★★★★
Contact: Mr R & Mrs S Annear, Beer Farm, Okehampton EX20 1SG
T: (01837) 840265
F: (01837) 840245
E: beerfarm.oke@which.net
I: www.beerfarm.co.uk

Bowerland ★★★★
Contact: Mr Ray Quirke, East Bowerland Farm, Okehampton EX20 4LZ
T: (01837) 55979
E: bowerland@devonhols.com

Deer Park ★★★★★
Contact: Mrs Judy Buckland, Deer Park, Berry Farm, Petrockstow, Okehampton EX20 3ET
T: (01837) 811187
F: (01837) 810037
E: judy@berryfarm.co.uk
I: www.deerparkcottage.co.uk

East Hook Cottages ★★-★★★★
Contact: Mrs Ruth Maile, East Hook Cottages, West Hook, Okehampton EX20 1RL
T: (01837) 52305
E: marystevens@westhookfarm.fsnet.co.uk

Fourwinds Self-Catering Properties ★★★★
Contact: Miss Sue Collins, Fourwinds Self-Catering Properties, Tavistock Road, Meldon, Okehampton EX20 4LX
T: (01837) 55785
F: (01837) 55785
E: fourwinds@eclipse.co.uk
I: eclipse.co.uk/fourwinds

Fowley House ★★★
Contact: Farm & Cottage Holidays, Victoria House, 12 Fore Street, Northam, Bideford EX39 1AW
T: (01237) 479146
F: (01237) 421512
E: enquiries@farmcott.co.uk

Hayrish ★★★★-★★★★★
Contact: Mr David Judge, 1 Telegraph Street, London EC2R 7AR
T: (020) 7256 9013
F: (020) 7588 2051
E: hayrish@easynet.co.uk

Little Bidlake Barns ★★★★
Contact: Mrs Joanna Down, Little Bidlake Barns, Bridestowe, Okehampton EX20 4NS
T: (01837) 861233
F: (01837) 861233
E: bidlakefrm@aol.com
I: www.littlebidlakefarm.co.uk

Meldon Cottages ★★★★
Contact: Mr Plant & Mrs Roberts, Meldon Cottages, Meldon, Okehampton EX20 4LU
T: (01837) 54363
E: enquiries@meldoncottages.co.uk
I: www.meldoncottages.co.uk

Week Farm Country Holidays
★★★★
Contact: Mrs Margaret Hockridge, Week Farm Country Holidays, Week Farm, Bridestowe, Okehampton EX20 4HZ
T: (01837) 861221
F: (01837) 861221
E: accom@weekfarmonline.com
I: www.weekfarmonline.com

OSMINGTON
Dorset

Emmies Cottage ★★★★
Contact: Mr Zachary Stuart-Brown, Dream Cottages, 41 Maiden Street, Weymouth DT4 8AZ
T: (01305) 761347
E: admin@dream-cottages.co.uk
I: www.dream-cottages.co.uk

Gardeners Cottage ★★★
Contact: Mr Zachary Stuart-Brown, Dream Cottages, 41 Maiden Street, Weymouth DT4 8AZ
T: (01305) 761347
E: admin@dream-cottages.co.uk
I: www.dream-cottages.co.uk

Honeybun ★★★★
Contact: Mr Zachary Stuart-Brown, Dream Cottages, 41 Maiden Street, Weymouth DT4 8AZ
T: (01305) 761347
E: admin@dream-cottages.co.uk
I: www.dream-cottages.co.uk

Norden Cottage ★★★
Contact: Mr Zachary Stuart-Brown, Dream Cottages, 41 Maiden Street, Weymouth DT4 8AZ
T: (01305) 761347
E: admin@dream-cottages.co.uk
I: www.dream-cottages.co.uk

The Old Milking Parlour
★★★★★
Contact: Mrs Karenlee Knott, Halls Farm, Church Lane, Osmington, Weymouth DT3 6EW
T: (01305) 837068
F: (01305) 837068
E: halls.farm@lineone.net

OSMINGTON MILLS
Dorset

Vine Cottage
Rating Applied For
Contact: Dream Cottages, 41 Maiden Street, Weymouth DT4 8AZ
T: (01305) 761347
E: admin@dream-cottages.co.uk

OTHERY
Somerset

Middlefield Farm Cottage
★★★
Contact: Mrs Anita Winslade, Elmgrove Bungalow, Holloway Road, Othery, Bridgwater TA7 0QF
T: (01823) 698368
F: (01823) 698368

Willows Cottage
Rating Applied For
Contact: Mrs Christine Ellis, Bagenham Farm, Rye Lane, Othery, Bridgwater TA7 0PT
T: (01823) 698166

OTTERHAM
Cornwall

Old Newham Farm ★★★
Contact: Mrs Mary Purdue, Old Newham Farm, Otterham, Camelford PL32 9SR
T: (01840) 230470
F: (01840) 230303
E: cottages@old-newham.co.uk
I: www.old-newham.co.uk

Saint Tinney Farm Holidays
★★★-★★★★★
Contact: Mrs Windley, Saint Tinney Farm Holidays, Otterham, Camelford PL32 9TA
T: (01840) 261274
E: info@st-tinney.co.uk
I: www.st-tinney.co.uk

OTTERTON
Devon

Jodies ★★★
Contact: Jean Bartlett Cottage Holidays, Fore Street, Beer, Seaton EX12 3JB
T: (01297) 23221
F: (01297) 23303
E: holidays@jeanbartlett.com
I: www.netbreaks.com/jeanb

OTTERY ST MARY
Devon

Deblins Brook Farm Cottage
★★★★
Contact: Mr Graham Butler, Deblins Brook Farm Cottage, Sandgate Lane, Wiggaton, Ottery St Mary EX11 1PX
T: (01404) 811331
F: (01404) 811331

Over the Top ★★★
Contact: Milkbere Holidays, 3 Fore Street, Seaton EX12 2LE
T: (01297) 20729
F: (01297) 22925
E: info@milkberehols.com
I: www.milkbere.com

OVER COMPTON
Dorset

Uplands ★★★
Contact: Mr & Mrs Suellen Brake, Uplands, Over Compton, Sherborne DT9 4QS
T: (01935) 477043

OWERMOIGNE
Dorset

Jasmine Cottage ★★
Contact: Mrs Lawton, 9 Moreton Road, Owermoigne, Dorchester DT2 8HT
T: (01305) 854457
F: (01305) 854457

Vinney Cottage
Rating Applied For
Contact: Dream Cottages, 41 Maiden Street, Weymouth DT4 8AZ
T: (01305) 761347
E: admin@dream-cottages.co.uk

Wooden Tops ★★★
Contact: Mr Zachary Stuart-Brown, Dream Cottages, 41 Maiden Street, Weymouth DT4 8AZ
T: (01305) 761347
E: admin@dream-cottages.co.uk
I: www.dream-cottages.co.uk

PADSTOW
Cornwall

7/9 Grove Place ★★★
Contact: Ms Nicky Stanley, Harbour Holidays - Padstow, 1 North Quay, Padstow PL28 8AF
T: (01841) 532555
F: (01841) 533115
E: sales@jackie-stanley.co.uk
I: www.harbourholidays.co.uk

Alexandra House ★★★★
Contact: Mrs Moreen Williams, Alexandra House, 30 Dennis Road, Padstow PL28 8DE
T: (01841) 532503

The Backs and Rhetts ★★★
Contact: Ms Nicky Stanley, Harbour Holidays - Padstow, 1 North Quay, Padstow PL28 8AF
T: (01841) 532555
F: (01841) 533115
E: sales@jackie-stanley.co.uk
I: www.harbourholidays.co.uk

9 Barry's Lane ★★★
Contact: Ms Nicky Stanley, Harbour Holidays - Padstow, 1 North Quay, Padstow PL28 8AF
T: (01841) 532555
F: (01841) 533115
E: sales@jackie-stanley.co.uk
I: www.harbourholidays.co.uk

Beau Vista ★★★★
Contact: Mr Peter Haseldine, 34 Raleigh Close, Padstow PL28 8BQ
T: (01841) 533270
F: (01841) 533270
E: peter@beauvista.co.uk
I: www.padstow.uk.com/beauvista

Bellagio ★★★★
Contact: Mrs Annette Bassett, The Anchorage, Green Lane, Lelant, St Ives TR26 3JU
T: (01736) 752136
E: bassett@btinternet.com

Bloomfield ★★★
Contact: Mr Michael Bennett, 52 Church Street, Padstow PL28 8BG
T: (01841) 533890
E: mikeswave@onetel.net.uk

Bobbins ★★★
Contact: Ms Nicky Stanley Harbour Holidays - Padstow, 1 North Quay, Padstow PL28 8AF
T: (01841) 532555
F: (01841) 533115
E: sales@jackie-stanley.co.uk
I: www.harbourholidays.co.uk

Brambles ★★★
Contact: Mr & Mrs Peter & Cathy Osborne, Cornish Horizons, Higher Trehemborne, St Merryn, Padstow PL28 8JU
T: (01841) 520889
F: (01841) 521523
E: cottages@cornishhorizons.co.uk
I: www.cornishhorizons.co.uk

10 Broad Street, 2 Mill Road, 5 Mill Road★★-★★★
Contact: Mrs Susan Farr, Sheepcombe House, Washingpool Hill Road, Tockington, Bristol BS32 4NZ
T: (01454) 614861
F: (01454) 613252

Broomleaf Cottage ★★★
Contact: Mr & Mrs Peter & Cathy Osborne, Cornish Horizons, Higher Trehemborne, St Merryn, Padstow PL28 8JU
T: (01841) 520889
F: (01841) 521523
E: cottages@cornishhorizons.co.uk
I: www.cornishhorizons.co.uk

Camel Cottage ★★★
Contact: Mr & Mrs Peter & Cathy Osborne, Cornish Horizons, Higher Trehemborne, St Merryn, Padstow PL28 8JU
T: (01841) 520889
F: (01841) 521523
E: cottages@cornishhorizons.co.uk
I: www.cornishhorizons.co.uk

Catherine's ★★★
Contact: Mrs Olive Lovell, Catherine's, 13A Duke Street, Padstow PL28 8AB
T: (01841) 533859
E: bob@lovell281142.fsnet.co.uk

Catty Clew ★★★
Contact: Mr & Mrs Peter & Cathy Osborne, Cornish Horizons, Higher Trehemborne, St Merryn, Padstow PL28 8JU
T: (01841) 520889
F: (01841) 521523
E: cottages@cornishhorizons.co.uk
I: www.cornishhorizons.co.uk

10 Church Lane ★★★
Contact: Ms Nicky Stanley, Harbour Holidays - Padstow, 1 North Quay, Padstow PL28 8AF
T: (01841) 532555
F: (01841) 533115
E: sales@jackie-stanley.co.uk
I: www.harbourholidays.co.uk

20 Church Lane ★★★
Contact: Harbour Holidays - Padstow, 1 North Quay, Padstow PL28 8AF
T: (01841) 532555
F: (01841) 533115
E: sales@jackie-stanley.co.uk
I: www.harbourholidays.co.uk

23 Church Lane ★★★
Contact: Ms Nicky Stanley, Harbour Holidays - Padstow, 1 North Quay, Padstow PL28 8AF
T: (01841) 532555
F: (01841) 533115
E: sales@jackie-stanley.co.uk
I: www.harbourholidays.co.uk

Coachyard Mews ★★★
Contact: Mr Stephen Andrews, Raidean Ltd., 44 Blundells Road, Bradville, Heelands, Milton Keynes MK13 7HF
T: (01841) 521198
F: (01908) 225708
E: raideanltd@aol.com
I: www.holidayinpadstow.co.uk

Cobblers ★★★
Contact: Ms Nicky Stanley Harbour Holidays - Padstow, 1 North Quay, Padstow PL28 8AF
T: (01841) 532555
F: (01841) 533115
E: sales@jackie-stanley.co.uk
I: www.harbourholidays.co.uk

Crabcatchers ★★★
Contact: Mr & Mrs Peter & Cathy Osborne, Cornish Horizons, Higher Trehemborne, St Merryn, Padstow PL28 8JU
T: (01841) 520889

Crenella Barn ★★★
Contact: Ms Nicky Stanley, Harbour Holidays - Padstow, 1 North Quay, Padstow PL28 8AF
T: (01841) 532555
F: (01841) 533115
E: sales@jackie-stanley.co.uk
I: www.harbourholidays.co.uk

1 Cross Street ★★★
Contact: Mrs Hollest, Bath Road, Shaw, Melksham SN12 8EF
T: (01225) 707519
F: (01225) 709787
E: susanne.roger@virgin.net

14 Cross Street ★★★
Contact: Ms Nicky Stanley, Harbour Holidays - Padstow, 1 North Quay, Padstow PL28 8AF
T: (01841) 532555
F: (01841) 533115
E: sales@jackie-stanley.co.uk
I: www.harbourholidays.co.uk

Curlews ★★★
Contact: Ms Nicky Stanley, Harbour Holidays - Padstow, 1 North Quay, Padstow PL28 8AF
T: (01841) 532555
F: (01841) 533115
E: sales@jackie-stanley.co.uk
I: www.harbourholidays.co.uk

Dingly Dell ★★★
Contact: Ms Nicky Stanley Harbour Holidays - Padstow, 1 North Quay, Padstow PL28 8AF
T: (01841) 532555
F: (01841) 533115
E: sales@jackie-stanley.co.uk
I: www.harbourholidays.co.uk

Dodo's Cottage ★★
Contact: Harbour Holidays - Padstow, 1 North Quay, Padstow PL28 8AF
T: (01841) 532555
F: (01841) 533115
E: sales@jackie-stanley.co.uk
I: www.harbourholidays.co.uk

Dove Cottage ★★★
Contact: Harbour Holidays - Padstow, 1 North Quay, Padstow PL28 8AF
T: (01841) 532555

The Drang House ★★★
Contact: Ms Nicky Stanley Harbour Holidays - Padstow, 1 North Quay, Padstow PL28 8AF
T: (01841) 532555
F: (01841) 533115
E: sales@jackie-stanley.co.uk
I: www.harbourholidays.co.uk

15 Egerton Road ★★★
Contact: Harbour Holidays - Padstow, 1 North Quay, Padstow PL28 8AF
T: (01841) 532555
F: (01841) 533115
E: sales@jackie-stanley.co.uk
I: www.harbourholidays.co.uk

17 Egerton Road ★★
Contact: Ms Nicky Stanley Harbour Holidays - Padstow, 1 North Quay, Padstow PL28 8AF
T: (01841) 532555
F: (01841) 533115
E: sales@jackie-stanley.co.uk
I: www.harbourholidays.co.uk

22 Egerton Road ★★★
Contact: Ms Nicky Stanley, Harbour Holidays - Padstow, 1 North Quay, Padstow PL28 8AF
T: (01841) 532555
F: (01841) 533115
E: sales@jackie-stanley.co.uk
I: www.harbourholidays.co.uk

42 Egerton Road ★★★
Contact: Harbour Holidays - Padstow, 1 North Quay, Padstow PL28 8AF
T: (01841) 532555
F: (01841) 533115
E: sales@jackie-stanley.co.uk
I: www.harbourholidays.co.uk

Estuary View ★★★
Contact: Harbour Holidays - Padstow, 1 North Quay, Padstow PL28 8AF
T: (01841) 532555

Estuary View ★★★
Contact: Mrs Pamela Thomas, Tilmore House, Reservoir Lane, Petersfield GU32 2HX
T: (01730) 263135

Ferndale ★★★
Contact: Mr & Mrs Peter & Cathy Osborne, Cornish Horizons, Higher Trehemborne, St Merryn, Padstow PL28 8JU
T: (01841) 520889
F: (01841) 521523
E: cottages@cornishhorizons.co.uk
I: www.cornishhorizons.co.uk

Fisherman's Cottage ★★
Contact: Mr & Mrs Angelinetta, 18 Church Street, Banwell BS29 6EA
T: (01934) 822688
F: (01934) 822688

Fishermans Cottage ★★★★
Contact: Ms Nicky Stanley, Harbour Holidays - Padstow, 1 North Quay, Padstow PL28 8AF
T: (01841) 532555
F: (01841) 533115
E: sales@jackie-stanley.co.uk
I: www.harbourholidays.co.uk

Fuchsia Cottage ★★★
Contact: Mrs Lumley, Magnolia Cottage, 1 College Mews, Stokesley, Middlesbrough TS9 5DJ
T: (01642) 710732
E: lumley@magnolia1.fsnet.co.uk
I: www.fuchsiacottage.co.uk

The Furs ★★★
Contact: Mr & Mrs Peter & Cathy Osborne, Cornish Horizons, Higher Trehemborne, St Merryn, Padstow PL28 8JU
T: (01841) 520889
F: (01841) 521523
E: cottages@cornishhorizons.co.uk
I: www.cornishhorizons.co.uk

Garden Flat ★★★
Contact: Mr & Mrs Peter & Cathy Osborne, Cornish Horizons, Higher Trehemborne, St Merryn, Padstow PL28 8JU
T: (01841) 520889

Grove Cottage ★★★
Contact: Ms Claudia Dierks, 6 Rosse Wehe 3, 26160 Bad Zwischenahn, Germany, Germany
T: (01432) 275084
E: inquiries@padstowcottages.info
I: www.padstowcottages.info

Harbour View Holiday Flats ★★★
Contact: Mrs Oliver, Trewornan Manor, St Minver, Wadebridge PL27 6EX
T: (01208) 816422
E: beach.hols@dial.pipex.com

Harmony ★★★
Contact: Mr & Mrs Peter & Cathy Osborne, Cornish Horizons, Higher Tremborne, St Merryn, Padstow PL28 8JU
T: (01841) 520889
F: (01841) 521523
E: cottages@cornishhorizons.co.uk
I: www.cornishhorizons.co.uk

Hidden Cottage ★★★★★
Contact: Ms Nicky Stanley Harbour Holidays - Padstow, 1 North Quay, Padstow PL28 8AF
T: (01841) 532555
F: (01841) 533115
E: sales@jackie-stanley.co.uk
I: www.harbourholidays.co.uk

19 High Street ★★★
Contact: Ms Nicky Stanley, Harbour Holidays - Padstow, 1 North Quay, Padstow PL28 8AF
T: (01841) 532555
F: (01841) 533115
E: sales@jackie-stanley.co.uk
I: www.harbourholidays.co.uk

Hollyhocks ★★★★
Contact: Mrs Jo Robinson, 26 The Culvery, Trevanion Road, Wadebridge PL27 7DX
T: (01208) 815746
E: info@westcountry-life.co.uk

Honey Cottage ★★★
Contact: Mr & Mrs Peter & Cathy Osborne, Cornish Horizons, Higher Trehemborne, St Merryn, Padstow PL28 8JU
T: (01841) 520889
F: (01841) 521523
E: cottages@cornishhorizons.co.uk
I: www.cornishhorizons.co.uk

Honeysuckle Cottage ★★★
Contact: Harbour Holidays - Padstow, 1 North Quay, Padstow PL28 8AF
T: (01841) 532555
F: (01841) 533115

Honeysuckle Cottage ★★★
Contact: Mrs D Clarke, Manor Croft, Colebrooke, Crediton EX17 5DL
T: (01363) 84292
F: (01363) 84559
E: honeysucklecottage@cchaulage.com

Jasmine Cottage ★★★★
Contact: Ms Nicky Stanley Harbour Holidays - Padstow, 1 North Quay, Padstow PL28 8AF
T: (01841) 532555
F: (01841) 533115
E: sales@jackie-stanley.co.uk
I: www.harbourholidays.co.uk

Kessells Cottage ★★★
Contact: Mr & Mrs Peter & Cathy Osborne, Cornish Horizons, Higher Trehemborne, St Merryn, Padstow PL28 8JU
T: (01841) 520889
F: (01841) 521523
E: cottages@cornishhorizons.co.uk
I: www.cornishhorizons.co.uk

Kittiwake ★★★
Contact: Ms Nicky Stanley Harbour Holidays - Padstow, 1 North Quay, Padstow PL28 8AF
T: (01841) 532555
F: (01841) 533115
E: sales@jackie-stanley.co.uk
I: www.harbourholidays.co.uk

Lantern House ★★★
Contact: Mr Alistair Wright, Lantern House, 38/40 Duke Street, Padstow PL28 8AD
T: (01841) 532566

The Laurels Holiday Park ★★★-★★★★
Contact: Mr A D Nicholson, The Laurels Holiday Park, Padstow Road, Whitecross, Wadebridge PL27 7JQ
T: (01208) 813341
F: (01208) 816590
E: anicholson@thelaurelsholidaypark.co.uk
I: www.thelaurelsholidaypark.co.uk

Lawn Cottage ★★★★
Contact: Ms Heather Buckingham, Buckingham Properties, Coventry Road, Coleshill, Birmingham B46 3EX
T: 08704 423684
F: 08704 423685
E: heather@bprops.co.uk

Lelissick ★★★
Contact: Ms Nicky Stanley
Harbour Holidays - Padstow, 1 North Quay, Padstow PL28 8AF
T: (01841) 532555
F: (01841) 533115
E: sales@jackie-stanley.co.uk
I: www.harbourholidays.co.uk

Little Dolphins ★★★
Contact: Mr & Mrs Peter & Cathy Osborne, Cornish Horizons, Higher Trehemborne, St Merryn, Padstow PL28 8JU
T: (01841) 520889
F: (01841) 521523
E: cottages@cornishhorizons.co.uk
I: www.cornishhorizions.co.uk

Little Dukes ★★
Contact: Mr & Mrs Peter & Cathy Osborne, Cornish Horizons, Higher Trehemborne, St Merryn, Padstow PL28 8JU
T: (01841) 520889

The Lobster Pot ★★★
Contact: Ms Kay Wood, Trevilllador Farm, St Issey, Padstow PL27 7SD
T: (01841) 540226
E: kaywood@onetel.net.uk

Louand ★★★
Contact: Mr & Mrs Peter & Cathy Osborne, Cornish Horizons, Higher Trehemborne, St Merryn, Padstow PL28 8JU
T: (01841) 520889

Marine Villa – Harbour End ★★★
Contact: Harbour Holidays - Padstow, 1 North Quay, Padstow PL28 8AF
T: (01841) 532555
F: (01841) 533115
E: sales@jackie-stanley.co.uk
I: www.harbourholidays.co.uk

Market Square Holiday Apartments ★★★-★★★★
Contact: Mrs M Higgins, Tregolds, Whitecross, Wadebridge PL27 7JB
T: (01208) 813379
F: (01841) 533339
E: msh@padstow.com
I: www.padstow.com

Maypole Cottage ★★★
Contact: Harbour Holidays - Padstow, 1 North Quay, Padstow PL28 8AF
T: (01841) 532555
F: (01841) 533115
E: sales@jackie-stanley.co.uk
I: www.harbourholidays.co.uk

3 Meadow Court ★★★★
Contact: Harbour Holidays - Padstow, 1 North Quay, Padstow PL28 8AF
T: (01841) 532555

6 Meadow Court ★★★
Contact: Harbour Holidays - Padstow, 1 North Quay, Padstow PL28 8AF
T: (01841) 532555
E: contact@harbourholidays.co.uk

Mevagh ★★★
Contact: Ms Nicky Stanley, Harbour Holidays - Padstow, 1 North Quay, Padstow PL28 8AF
T: (01841) 532555
F: (01841) 533115
E: sales@jackie-stanley.co.uk
I: www.harbourholidays.co.uk

Middle Street Apartments ★★-★★★
Contact: Mrs Joan Hull, 24 Hawkins Road, Padstow PL28 3EU
T: (01841) 533545
F: (01841) 832630
E: jim@jwhull.fsnet.co.uk

14 Mill Road ★★★★
Contact: Mrs McCall, St Merryn Holiday Village, St Merryn, Padstow PL28 8QA
T: (01841) 520998

Moonfleet & Tarisk ★★★
Contact: Mrs Jenny O'Sullivan, 12 Champion Road, Upminster RM14 2SY
T: (01708) 229872

The Mowhay ★★
Contact: Harbour Holidays - Padstow, 1 North Quay, Padstow PL28 8AF
T: (01841) 532555
F: (01841) 533115
E: sales@jackie-stanley.co.uk
I: www.harbourholidays.co.uk

12 Netherton Road ★★★
Contact: Mr & Mrs Peter & Cathy Osborne, Cornish Horizons, Higher Trehemborne, St Merryn, Padstow PL28 8JU
T: (01841) 520889
F: (01841) 521523
E: cottages@cornishhorizons.co.uk
I: www.cornishhorizons.co.uk

10 New Street ★★
Contact: Ms Nicky Stanley, Harbour Holidays - Padstow, 1 North Quay, Padstow PL28 8AF
T: (01841) 532555
F: (01841) 533115
E: sales@jackie-stanley.co.uk
I: www.harbourholidays.co.uk

Nooks Cottage ★★★
Contact: Mr & Mrs Peter & Cathy Osborne, Cornish Horizons, Higher Trehemborne, St Merryn, Padstow PL28 8JU
T: (01841) 520889
F: (01841) 521523
E: cottages@cornishhorizons.co.uk
I: www.cornishhorizons.co.uk

The Old Bakery ★★★★
Contact: Mr Tony Tippett, T W Properties, 6 Cross Street, Padstow PL28 8AT
T: (01841) 532885
E: tony.twproperties@aol.com
I: www.TWPROPERTIES.co.uk

12 The Old Boatyard ★★★
Contact: Mrs McCall, Upper Deck, St Merryn Village, St Merryn, Padstow PL28 8QA
T: (01841) 520998

The Old Coach House ★★★
Contact: Ms Nicky Stanley, Harbour Holidays - Padstow, 1 North Quay, Padstow PL28 8AF
T: (01841) 532555
F: (01841) 533115
E: sales@jackie-stanley.co.uk
I: www.harbourholidays.co.uk

The Old Mill ★★★★
Contact: CH Ref: 12054, Holiday Cottages Group Owner Services Dept, Spring Mill, Earby, Barnoldswick BB94 0AA
T: 08700 723723
F: (01282) 844288
E: sales@ttgihg.co.uk
I: www.country-holidays.co.uk

18 Old School Court ★★★
Contact: Ms Nicky Stanley, Harbour Holidays - Padstow, 1 North Quay, Padstow PL28 8AF
T: (01841) 532555
F: (01841) 533115
E: sales@jackie-stanley.co.uk
I: www.harbourholidays.co.uk

25 Old School Court ★★★
Contact: Ms Nicky Stanley, Harbour Holidays - Padstow, 1 North Quay, Padstow PL28 8AF
T: (01841) 532555
F: (01841) 533115
E: sales@jackie-stanley.co.uk
I: www.harbourholidays.co.uk

Ossmill Cottage ★★★
Contact: Ms Nicky Stanley, Harbour Holidays - Padstow, 1 North Quay, Padstow PL28 8AF
T: (01841) 532555
F: (01841) 533115
E: sales@jackie-stanley.co.uk
I: www.harbourholidays.co.uk

Overcliff ★★★★
Contact: Mr & Mrs John & Gillian Hammond, The Mount Farm, Foxton, Market Harborough LE16 7RD
T: (0116) 251 7171
F: (01858) 545950
E: pjh@pjh.u-net.com

Padstow Holiday Cottages ★★★
Contact: Mrs Pat Walker, 1 Sarah's Gate, Little Petherick, Wadebridge PL27 7QT
T: (01841) 541180
E: info@padstow-holiday-cottages.co.uk
I: www.padstow-holiday-cottages.co.uk

Parnalls ★★★
Contact: Ms Nicky Stanley, Harbour Holidays - Padstow, 1 North Quay, Padstow PL28 8AF
T: (01841) 532555
F: (01841) 533115
E: sales@jackie-stanley.co.uk
I: www.harbourholidays.co.uk

Pebble Cottage ★★★
Contact: Ms Nicky Stanley Harbour Holidays - Padstow, 1 North Quay, Padstow PL28 8AF
T: (01841) 532555
F: (01841) 533115
E: sales@jackie-stanley.co.uk
I: www.harbourholidays.co.uk

Pensers ★★★★
Contact: Ms Nicky Stanley, Harbour Holidays - Padstow, 1 North Quay, Padstow PL28 8AF
T: (01841) 532555
F: (01841) 533115
E: sales@jackie-stanley.co.uk
I: www.harbourholidays.co.uk

Pentire Apartment ★★★★
Contact: Ms Nicky Stanley, Harbour Holidays - Padstow, 1 North Quay, Padstow PL28 8AF
T: (01841) 532555
F: (01841) 533115
E: sales@jackie-stanley.co.uk
I: www.harbourholidays.co.uk

Peponi ★★★
Contact: Ms Nicky Stanley, Harbour Holidays - Padstow, 1 North Quay, Padstow PL28 8AF
T: (01841) 532555
F: (01841) 533115
E: sales@jackie-stanley.co.uk
I: www.harbourholidays.co.uk

Pinmill Cottage ★★★
Contact: Ms Nicky Stanley, Harbour Holidays - Padstow, 1 North Quay, Padstow PL28 8AF
T: (01841) 532555
F: (01841) 533115
E: sales@jackie-stanley.co.uk
I: www.harbourholidays.co.uk

Pippits ★★★
Contact: Mr & Mrs Peter & Cathy Osborne, Cornish Horizons, Higher Trehemborne, St Merryn, Padstow PL28 8JU
T: (01841) 520889
F: (01841) 521523
E: cottages@cornishhorizons.co.uk
I: www.cornishhorizons.co.uk

Pols Piece Holidays ★★★
Contact: Mrs J E Olivey, Pols Piece Holidays, Dobbin Lane, Trevone, Padstow PL28 8QP
T: (01841) 520372
F: (01841) 520372
E: polspiece@virgin.net
I: www.polspieceholidays.co.uk

Poppies ★★★
Contact: Harbour Holidays - Padstow, 1 North Quay, Padstow PL28 8AF
T: (01841) 532555

Porthilly View ★★★
Contact: Harbour Holidays, 4 North Quay, Padstow PL28 8AF
T: (01841) 532555
F: (01741) 533115
E: contact@harbourholidays.co.uk

Portloe ★★
Contact: Harbour Holidays - Padstow, 1 North Quay, Padstow PL28 8AF
T: (01841) 532555

Primrose House ★★★★
Contact: Mr & Mrs Peter & Cathy Osborne, Cornish Horizons, Higher Trehemborne, St Merryn, Padstow PL28 8JU
T: (01841) 520889
F: (01841) 521523
E: cottages@cornishhorizons.co.uk
I: www.cornishhorizons.co.uk

Puffin Cottage ★★★
Contact: Ms Nicky Stanley
Harbour Holidays - Padstow, 1 North Quay, Padstow PL28 8AF
T: (01841) 532555
F: (01841) 533115
E: sales@jackie-stanley.co.uk
I: www.harbourholidays.co.uk

Quayside Cottage ★★★
Contact: Mrs Andrea Richards, Petrocstowe, 30 Treverbyn Road, Padstow PL28 8DW
T: (01841) 532429

The Quies
Rating Applied For
Contact: Harbour Holidays - Padstow, 1 North Quay, Padstow PL28 8AF
T: (01841) 532555

12 Rainyfields Close ★★★
Contact: Mrs D Bullingham, Treann, 24 Dennis Road, Padstow PL28 8DE
T: (01841) 533 855

3 Redbrick Building ★★★
Contact: Harbour Holidays - Padstow, 1 North Quay, Padstow PL28 8AF
T: (01841) 532555

Robins Nest ★★★
Contact: Mr & Mrs Peter & Cathy Osborne, Cornish Horizons, Higher Trehemborne, St Merryn, Padstow PL28 8JU
T: (01841) 520889
F: (01841) 521523
E: cottages@cornishhorizons.co.uk
I: www.cornishhorizons.co.uk

Rockview
Rating Applied For
Contact: Harbour Holidays, 1 North Quay, Padstow PL28 8AF
T: (01841) 532555
F: (01841) 533115
E: contact@harbourholidays.co.uk

Rose Cottage ★★★
Contact: Ms Nicky Stanley, Harbour Holidays - Padstow, 1 North Quay, Padstow PL28 8AF
T: (01841) 532555
F: (01841) 533115
E: sales@jackie-stanley.co.uk
I: www.harbourholidays.co.uk

Rosehill Holiday Accommodation ★★★
Contact: Mr Dave Kean, Rosehill Holiday Accommodation, Little Petherick, Padstow PL27 7QT
T: (01841) 541475

Rosehill House ★★★
Contact: Ms Nicky Stanley, Harbour Holidays - Padstow, 1 North Quay, Padstow PL28 8AF
T: (01841) 532555
F: (01841) 533115
E: sales@jackie-stanley.co.uk
I: www.harbourholidays.co.uk

Sable Cottage ★★★-★★★★
Contact: Ms Denise Daw, 16 Harbury Road, Henleaze, Bristol BS9 4PL
T: (0117) 907 9348
E: mddaw@harbury56.co.uk

Sail Loft ★★★
Contact: Ms Nicky Stanley, Harbour Holidays - Padstow, 1 North Quay, Padstow PL28 8AF
T: (01841) 532555
F: (01841) 533115
E: sales@jackie-stanley.co.uk
I: www.harbourholidays.co.uk

Saint Breock ★★★
Contact: Ms Nicky Stanley
Harbour Holidays - Padstow, 1 North Quay, Padstow PL28 8AF
T: (01841) 532555
F: (01841) 533115
E: sales@jackie-stanley.co.uk
I: www.harbourholidays.co.uk

Sanderlings ★★★★
Contact: Mrs Gill Vivian, Holiday Padstow, 4 St Saviours Lane, Padstow PL28 8BD
T: (01841) 533791
F: (01841) 533843
E: neil.vivian@btopenworld.com
I: www.holiday-padstow.co.uk

Sarahs View
Rating Applied For
Contact: Harbour Holidays, 4 North Quay, Padstow PL28 8AF
T: (01841) 532555
F: (01841) 533115
E: contact@harbourholidays.co.uk

28 Sarah's View ★★★
Contact: Mr R & Mrs S Clapp, 12 Grenville Road, Padstow PL28 8EX
T: (01841) 532294
E: obbyoss@hotmail.com

34 Sarah's View ★★★
Contact: Mrs M A Thomas, 31 Dennis Road, Padstow PL28 8DF
T: (01841) 532243

62 Sarah's View ★★★
Contact: Mrs Amey, 45 Southern Road, Southborne, Southbourne, Bournemouth BH6 3SS
T: (01202) 258769

The School House ★★★★
Contact: Mr & Mrs Martin & Jacqui Wilson, Egloshayle Road, Hildenborough, Tonbridge PL27 6AQ
T: (01732) 832085
F: (01732) 832228
E: Martin.Jacqui@virgin.net

Seal Cottage ★★★
Contact: Ms Nicky Stanley, Harbour Holidays - Padstow, 1 North Quay, Padstow PL28 8AF
T: (01841) 532555
F: (01841) 533115
E: sales@jackie-stanley.co.uk
I: www.harbourholidays.co.uk

Serendipity ★★★
Contact: Ms Nicky Stanley
Harbour Holidays - Padstow, 1 North Quay, Padstow PL28 8AF
T: (01841) 532555
F: (01841) 533115
E: sales@jackie-stanley.co.uk
I: www.harbourholidays.co.uk

Shore Lodge ★★★★★
Contact: Mrs Vivian, 4 St Saviours Lane, Padstow PL28 8BD
T: (01841) 533791
F: (01841) 533843
E: Neil.Vivian@btopenworld.com
I: www.holiday-padstow.co.uk

Skipper Cottage ★★★
Contact: Mrs MacRae, Skipper Cottage, 18 Riverside, Padstow PL28 8BY
T: (01841) 540237
E: m4crae@aol.com

The Slate House ★★★
Contact: Ms Nicky Stanley
Harbour Holidays - Padstow, 1 North Quay, Padstow PL28 8AF
T: (01841) 532555
F: (01841) 533115
E: sales@jackie-stanley.co.uk
I: www.harbourholidays.co.uk

The Spinney House ★★★★
Contact: Mr Clarke, The Old Rectory, St Ervan, Wadebridge PL27 7TA
T: (01841) 540255
F: (01841) 540255
E: mail@stervanmanor.freeserve.co.uk
I: www.stervanmanor.co.uk

Squirrels ★★★
Contact: Mr & Mrs Peter & Cathy Osborne, Cornish Horizons Holiday Cottages, Higher Trehemborne, St Merryn, Padstow PL28 8JU
T: (01841) 520889
F: (01841) 521523
E: cottages@cornishhorizons.co.uk
I: www.cornishhorizons.co.uk

10 St Petroc's Meadow ★★★
Contact: Mr Neville Powell, 7 Pellew Close, Padstow PL2 8EY
T: (01841) 532156

Stable Cottage, Bay Tree Cottage & Clover Cottage ★★★★
Contact: Mrs Jill Hagley, Stable Cottage, Bay Tree Cottage & Clover Cottage, Trevethan Farm, Sarah's Lane, Padstow PL28 8LE
T: (01841) 532874
F: (01841) 532874
I: www.padstowcottages.co.uk

Stone Cottage ★★
Contact: Dr Richardson, 45A Cassiobury Park Avenue, Watford WD18 7LD
T: (01923) 226218
F: (01923) 226218
E: jrichardson09@aol.com

Stonesthrow Cottage ★★★★
Contact: Mr & Mrs Peter & Cathy Osborne, Cornish Horizons, Higher Trehemborne, St Merryn, Padstow PL28 8JU
T: (01841) 520889
F: (01841) 521523
E: cottages@cornishhorizons.co.uk
I: www.cornishhorizons.co.uk

2 The Strand ★★★
Contact: Ms Nicky Stanley, Harbour Holidays - Padstow, 1 North Quay, Padstow PL28 8AF
T: (01841) 532555
F: (01841) 533115
E: sales@jackie-stanley.co.uk
I: www.harbourholidays.co.uk

Strand Flats ★★★
Contact: Mr Brown, Strand Flats, Treoell, Cardinham, Bodmin PL30 4BL
T: (01208) 821611
F: (01208) 821611
E: Jill.P.Brown@btinternet.com
I: www.strandflats.co.uk

Summer Court ★★★★
Contact: Mr & Mrs Whitehead, Great North Road, Micklefield, Leeds LS25 4AG
T: (0113) 286 0036

Sunbeam Cottage ★★★★
Contact: Ms Wendy Gidlow, Sunbeam Cottage, 39 Duke Street, Padstow PL28 8AD
T: (01841) 533634
F: (01841) 532271
E: wendy@wgidlow.fsnet.co.uk
I: www.sunbeam_cottage.co.uk

Sunday & Sunrise Cottage ★★★★-★★★★★
Contact: Mrs D E Hoe, 14 The Green, Snitterfield, Stratford-upon-Avon CV37 0JG
T: (01789) 730223
F: (01789) 730199
E: mail@sundaycottage.co.uk
I: www.sundaycottage.co.uk

Sunnyhill Cottage ★★★★
Contact: Ms Nicky Stanley, Harbour Holidays - Padstow, 1 North Quay, Padstow PL28 8AF
T: (01841) 532555
F: (01841) 533115
E: sales@jackie-stanley.co.uk
I: www.harbourholidays.co.uk

Teal ★★★
Contact: Ms Nicky Stanley
Harbour Holidays - Padstow, 1 North Quay, Padstow PL28 8AF
T: (01841) 532555
F: (01841) 533115
E: sales@jackie-stanley.co.uk
I: www.harbourholidays.co.uk

Teazers ★★★
Contact: Ms Nicky Stanley
Harbour Holidays - Padstow, 1 North Quay, Padstow PL28 8AF
T: (01841) 532555
F: (01841) 533115
E: sales@jackie-stanley.co.uk
I: www.harbourholidays.co.uk

Tregirls ★★★-★★★★
Contact: Mrs Watson Smyth, Tregirls, Padstow PL28 8RR
T: (01841) 532648

Trenoder ★★★
Contact: Mr & Mrs Peter & Cathy Osborne, Cornish Horizons, Higher Trehemborne, St Merryn, Padstow PL28 8JU
T: (01841) 520889
F: (01841) 521523
E: cottages@cornishhorizons.co.uk

Treverbyn Road
Rating Applied For
Contact: Harbour Holidays, 4 North Quay, Padstow PL28 8AF
T: (01841) 532555
F: (01841) 533115
E: contact@harbourholidays.co.uk

4 Treverbyn Road ★★★★
Contact: Mrs Vivian, Holiday - Padstow, 4 St Saviours Lane, Padstow PL28 8BD
T: (01841) 533791
F: (01841) 533843
E: Neil.Vivian@btopenworld.com
I: www.holiday-padstow.co.uk

Trevorrick Farm ★★★
Contact: Mr & Mrs M Topliss & Benwell, Trevorrick Farm, St Issey, Wadebridge PL27 7QH
T: (01841) 540574
F: (01841) 540574
E: info@trevorrick.co.uk
I: www.trevorrick.co.uk

Valerian ★★★
Contact: Mrs Vivian, Holiday - Padstow, 4 St Saviours Lane, Padstow PL28 8BD
T: (01841) 533791
F: (01481) 533843
E: Neil.Vivian@btopenworld.com
I: www.holiday-padstow.co.uk

The White Hart ★★★★
Contact: Ms Patricia Jacoby-Blake, The White Hart, New Street, Padstow PL28 8EA
T: (01841) 532350
E: whitehartpad@aol.com

Zefyros ★★★★
Contact: Mrs Harris, The Pheasantry, Easthope, Much Wenlock TF13 6DN
T: (01746) 785504

't Sandt ★★★
Contact: Mr & Mrs Peter & Cathy Osborne, Cornish Horizons, Higher Trehemborne, St Merryn, Padstow PL28 8JU
T: (01841) 520889
F: (01841) 521523
E: cottages@cornishhorizons.co.uk
I: www.cornishhorizons.co.uk

PAIGNTON
Devon

All Seasons Holiday Apartments ★★★
Contact: Mr Mike Dessi, All Seasons Holiday Apartments, 18 Garfield Road, Paignton TQ4 6AX
T: (01803) 552187
F: (01803) 552187
E: mikedessi@allseasonsholiday.freeserve.co.uk
I: www.allseasonsholidayapartments.co.uk

Alpenrose Holiday Apartments ★★★★
Contact: Mrs Margaret Taylor, Alpenrose Holiday Apartments, 20 Polsham Park, Paignton TQ3 2AD
T: (01803) 558430
F: (01803) 407959
E: alpenrose@blueyonder.co.uk
I: www.alpenrose.eurobell.co.uk

Beachway Holiday Flats ★★
Contact: Mr Edwin Toms, 11 Kernou Road, Paignton, Paignton TQ4 6BA
T: (01803) 555717

Bedford Holiday Flats and Flatlets ★-★★★
Contact: Mr & Mrs S Dunster, Bedford Holiday Flats and Flatlets, 10 Adelphi Road, Paignton TQ4 6AW
T: (01803) 557737
E: pat@bedfordflats.co.uk
I: www.bedfordflats.co.uk

Big Tree Holiday Flats ★★★
Contact: Mrs Pam Siddall, Big Tree Holiday Flats, 68 Fisher Street, Paignton TQ4 5ES
T: (01803) 559559
E: bigtree@eidosnet.co.uk
I: www.bigtreeholidayflats.co.uk

Bosuns Cottage ★★★★
Contact: Holiday Homes & Cottages South West, 365A Torquay Road, Paignton TQ3 2BT
T: (01803) 663650
F: (01803) 664037
E: holcotts@aol.co.uk
I: www.swcottages.co.uk

Broadshade Holiday Flats ★-★★★
Contact: Mr & Mrs John & Dot Barber, 9 St Andrews Road, Paignton TQ4 6HA
T: (01803) 559647
F: (01803) 529400
E: broadshade@hotmail.com

Brocklehurst Lodge
Rating Applied For
Contact: Holiday Homes & Cottages SW, 365a Torquay Road, Paignton TQ3 2BT
T: (01803) 663650
F: (01803) 664037
E: holcotts@aol.com

Casa Marina Holiday Apartments ★★★
Contact: Mr & Mrs Bob & Andrea Wooller, Casa Marina Holiday Apartments, 2 Keysfield Road, Paignton TQ4 6EP
T: (01803) 558334
I: enquiries@casamarina.co.uk

Compton Pool Farm ★★★-★★★★
Contact: Mr & Mrs Phipps, Compton Pool Farm, Compton, Marldon, Paignton TQ3 1TA
T: (01803) 872241
F: (01803) 874012
E: enquiries@comptonpool.co.uk
I: www.comptonpool.clara.co.uk

The Conifers ★★★
Contact: Holiday Homes & Cottages South West, 365A Torquay Road, Paignton TQ3 2BT
T: (01803) 663650
F: (01803) 664037
E: holcotts@aol.com
I: www.swcottages.co.uk

Cranmore Lodge ★★★
Contact: Mr Deryck Edwards, Cranmore Lodge, 45 Marine Drive, Paignton TQ3 2NS
T: (01803) 556278
F: (01803) 665797
E: cranlodge@btopenworld.com

Denby House Holiday Apartments ★★★
Contact: Mr & Mrs Ford, Denby House Holiday Apartments, Belle Vue Road, Paignton TQ4 6ES
T: (01803) 559121
E: lina@denbyhouse.co.uk
I: www.denbyhouse.co.uk

Fairsea Holiday Flats
Rating Applied For
Contact: Mr J Hallett, 12 St Andrews Road, Paignton TQ4 6HA
T: (01803) 556903
E: fairsea@amserve.net

Fortescue ★★★
Contact: Holiday Homes & Cottages South West, 365A Torquay Road, Paignton TQ3 2BT
T: (01803) 663650
F: (01803) 664037
E: holcotts@aol.com
I: www.swcottages.co.uk

Glencoe Holiday Flats ★★★
Contact: Mrs Patricia Jill Ayles, Glencoe Holiday Flats, Seafront, 7 Esplanade Road, Paignton TQ4 6EB
T: (01803) 557727
F: (01803) 666512
E: info@glencoeapartments.com

Grassington Court Holiday Apartments★★★
Contact: Mrs J M Crompton, 28 Sands Road, Paignton TQ4 6EJ
T: (01803) 557979

Harbour Reach Holiday Flats ★★-★★★
Contact: Ms Christine Grindrod, Holiday Flats, 36 Old Torquay Road, Paignton TQ3 2RA
T: (01803) 525857

Harbourside Holiday Apartments ★★★
Contact: Ms Kathleen Quaid, Roundham Road, Paignton TQ4 6DS
T: (01803) 550181
F: (01803) 550181

Harwin Hotel Apartments ★★★★
Contact: Mr & Mrs Steve Gorman, Harwin Hotel & Apartments, Alta Vista Road, Goodrington Sands, Paignton, Devon TQ4 6DA
T: (01803) 558771
F: 0870 831 3998
E: harwin@blueyonder.co.uk
I: www.harwinapartments.co.uk

Harwood Lodge ★★★★
Contact: Mr & Mrs Holgate, Harwood Lodge, 14 Roundham Road, Paignton TQ4 6DN
T: (01803) 391538
F: (01803) 401357
E: enq@harwoodlodge.co.uk
I: www.harwoodlodge.co.uk

Hennock ★★★★
Contact: Holiday Homes & Cottages South West, 365A Torquay Road, Paignton TQ3 2BT
T: (01803) 663650
F: (01803) 664037
E: holcotts@aol.com
I: www.swcottages.co.uk

Julie Court Holiday Apartments★★★
Contact: Abu & Wahida, Owner/Proprietor, Julie Court Holiday Apartments
T: (01803) 551012
E: info@juliecourt.co.uk
I: www.juliecourt.co.uk

Kimberley Holiday Flats ★★-★★★
Contact: Mr & Ms Nigel & Fran Boon & Moreby, Kimberley Holiday Flats, 39 Sands Road, Paignton TQ4 6EG
T: (01803) 551576
I: www.kimberleyholidayflats.co.uk

Laverna Palms
Rating Applied For
Contact: Mr Michael Craft, Laverna Palms, 5 Kernou Road, Paignton TQ4 6BA
T: (01803) 557620

The Lawn Holiday Apartments ★★★
Contact: Mrs Linda Harrison, The Lawn Holiday Apartments, St Andrews Road, Paignton TQ4 6HA
T: (01803) 528983
F: (01803) 528983
E: the.lawn@4mymail.co.uk
I: www.thelawn.info

7 Louville Close ★★★
Contact: Holiday Homes & Cottages South West, 365A Torquay Road, Paignton TQ3 2BT
T: (01803) 663650

24 Marine Parade
Rating Applied For
Contact: Holiday Homes & Cottages SW, 365a Torquay Road, Paignton TQ3 2BT
T: (01803) 663650
F: (01803) 664037
E: holcotts@aol.com

Montana ★-★★★
Contact: Mr Roger Seaward, Montana Holidays, 10 Belle Vue Road, Paignton TQ4 6ER
T: (01803) 559783

Preston Down ★★★
Contact: Holiday Homes & Cottages South West, 365A Torquay Road, Paignton TQ3 2BT
T: (01803) 663650
F: (01803) 664037
E: holcotts@aol.com
I: www.swcottages.co.uk

148 Preston Down Road ★★★★
Contact: Holiday Homes & Cottages South West, 365A Torquay Road, Paignton TQ3 2BT
T: (01803) 663650

Primley ★★★
Contact: Holiday Homes & Cottages South West, 365A Torquay Road, Paignton TQ3 2BT
T: (01803) 663650
F: (01803) 664037
E: holcotts@aol.com
I: www.swcottages.com

San Remo Holiday Apartments ★★-★★★
Contact: Mr C & Mrs E Hannant, San Remo Holiday Apartments, 15 Marine Drive, Paignton TQ3 2NJ
T: (01803) 550293

Sandmoor Holiday Apartments ★★★
Contact: Mr & Mrs Rita & Brian Ellis, St Andrews Road, Paignton TQ4 6HA
T: (01803) 525909
F: (01803) 525909

Stanley House ★★★
Contact: Mr & Mrs E & D Baldry, Stanley House Holiday Flats, Cliff Road, Paignton TQ4 6DG
T: (01803) 557173
E: stanley.house@btinternet.com

Suncrest ★★-★★★
Contact: Mr Neil Carr, Adelphi Lane, Paignton TQ4 6AS
T: (01803) 665571
E: neilcarr@fsmail.net

Sunnybeach Holiday Flats ★-★★★
Contact: Mr & Mrs Schaedl, 6 Esplanade Road, Paignton TQ4 6EB
T: (01803) 558729
F: (01803) 558729
E: jshadll@btconnect.com

Surfline Holiday Flats ★★
Contact: Stephanie & David Cox & Brophy, Surfline Holiday Flats, 15 Esplanade Road, Paignton TQ4 6EB
T: (01803) 555414
E: surfline@blueyonder.co.uk

Thatcher View ★★★
Contact: Mr David Morey, Thatcher View, 25A Cliff Road, Paignton TQ4 6DH
T: (01803) 555759
E: moreyfamily@tiscali.co.uk

Torbay Holiday Motel ★★
Contact: Mr G P Booth, Torbay Holiday Motel, Totnes Road, Paignton TQ4 7PP
T: (01803) 558226
F: (01803) 663375
E: enquries@thm.co.uk
I: www.thm.co.uk

Tregarth ★-★★
Contact: Mr Barry Haskins, Tregarth, 8 Adelphi Road, Paignton TQ4 6AW
T: (01803) 558458

PANBOROUGH
Somerset

Panborough Batch House ★★★
Contact: Mrs Sheila Booth, Panborough Batch House, Panborough, Wells BA5 1PN
T: (01934) 712769
E: sdb.antiques@ukgateway.co.uk

PANCRASWEEK
Devon

Tamarstone Farm ★★
Contact: Mrs Megan Daglish, Tamarstone Farm, Bude Road, Pancrasweek, Holsworthy EX22 7JT
T: (01288) 381734
E: cottage@tamarstone.co.uk
I: www.tamarstone.co.uk

PARRACOMBE
Devon

Martinhoe Cleave Cottages ★★★★
Contact: Mr & Mrs RM J Deville, Parracombe, Barnstaple EX31 4PT
T: (01598) 763313
E: info@hgate.co.uk

Voley Farm ★★★★
Contact: Ms Judith Killen, Voley Farm, Parracombe, Barnstaple EX31 4PG
T: (01598) 763315
E: voleyfarm@tesco.net
I: www.voleyfarm.com

Woodcote ★★★★
Contact: Marsden's Cottage Holidays, 2 The Square, Braunton EX33 2JB
T: (01271) 813777
F: (01271) 813664
E: holidays@marsdens.co.uk
I: www.marsdens.co.uk

PAUL
Cornwall

Susies Cottage ★★★
Contact: Mrs Susan Hales, 14 Long Row, Sheffield, Paul, Penzance TR19 6UN
T: (01736) 731703
F: (01736) 731703

PAULTON
Bath and North East Somerset

The Coach House ★★★-★★★★★
Contact: Mrs Jenny Ahlberg, The Coach House, Hanham Lane, Paulton, Bristol BS39 7PF
T: (01761) 413121
F: (01761) 413121
E: jennyahlberg@aol.com

PEDWELL
Somerset

Higher Nythe Farm ★★★
Contact: Farm & Cottage Holidays, Victoria House, 12 Fore Street, Westward Ho!, Bideford EX39 1AW
T: (01237) 479146
F: (01237) 421512
E: enquiries@farmcott.co.uk

Sunnyside ★★★★
Contact: Ms Sheila Caruso, Sunnyside, 34 Taunton Road, Pedwell, Bridgwater TA7 9BG
T: (01458) 210097
E: sunnyside@pedwell.freeuk.com

PELYNT
Cornwall

Penrose Cottage ★★★★
Contact: Mr Paul Brumpton, Talehay, 5 Summer Lane, Pelynt, Looe PL13 2LP
T: (01503) 220252
F: (01503) 220252
E: paul@talehay.co.uk
I: www.talehay.co.uk

Tremaine Green Country Cottages ★★-★★★
Contact: Mr Spreckley, Tremaine Green, Pelynt, Looe PL13 2LT
T: (01503) 220333
F: (01503) 220633
E: stay@tremainegreen.co.uk
I: www.tremainegreen.co.uk

PENDEEN
Cornwall

Kerenza ★★
Contact: Cornish Cottage Holidays, Godolphin Road, Helston TR13 8AA
T: (01326) 573808
F: (01326) 564992
E: enquiry@cornishcottageholidays.co.uk
I: www.cornishcottageholidays.co.uk

Porthmear Farm ★★★
Contact: Mrs Lee Berryman, Porthmear Farm, Pendeen, Penzance TR20 8YX
T: (01736) 796923
F: (01736) 796923
E: l.berryman@whsmith.co.uk

Trewellard Manor Farm ★★★-★★★★★
Contact: Mrs M Bailey, Trewellard Manor Farm, Pendeen, Penzance TR19 7SU
T: (01736) 788526
F: (01736) 788526
E: marionbbailey@hotmail.com
I: www.trewellardmanor.co.uk

PENDOGGETT
Cornwall

Mays Cottage ★★★★★
Contact: Mrs Diana Bullivant, South Winds, Trebell Green, Lanivet, Bodmin PL30 5HR
T: (01208) 831336
F: (01208) 831336
E: diana@dbullivant.fsnet.co.uk

PENHALLOW
Cornwall

Nutmeg & Peppercorn ★★★★
Contact: Cornish Cottage Holidays, The Old Turnpike Dairy, Godolphin, Meneage Street, Helston TR13 8AA
T: (01326) 573808
F: (01326) 564992
E: enquiry@cornishcottageholidays.co.uk
I: www.cornishcottageholidays.co.uk

PENSELWOOD
Somerset

Pen Mill Cottage ★★★★
Contact: Mrs Sarah Fitzgerald, Pen Mill Farm, Coombe Street, Pen Selwood, Penselwood, Wincanton BA9 8NF
T: (01747) 840895
F: (01747) 840429
E: fitzgeraldatpen@aol.com

PENSFORD
Bath and North East Somerset

Leigh Farm ★-★★
Contact: Mrs Smart, Leigh Farm, Old Road, Pensford BS39 4BA
T: (01761) 490281
F: (01761) 490281

PENTEWAN
Cornwall

Crofters End ★★★
Contact: Mr & Mrs Radmore
T: (01872) 501269

PENWITHICK
Cornwall

Penwithick
Rating Applied For
Contact: Holiday Homes & Cottages SW, 365a Torquay Road, Paignton TQ3 2BT
T: (01803) 663650
F: (01803) 664037
E: holcotts@aol.com

PENZANCE
Cornwall

Boskennal Farm ★★★★
Contact: Ms Beryl Richards, Boskennal Farm, Ludgvan, Penzance TR20 8AR
T: (01736) 740293
F: (01736) 740293
E: alan@boskennal.fsnet.co.uk

Chyandaunce and Chyancrowse ★★★
Contact: Mrs Sampson, Gulval Cottages, 55 Albemarle Gate, Cheltenham GL50 4PH
T: (01242) 232769
F: (01242) 232769
E: tjwsampson@aol.com
I: www.gulvalcottages.co.uk

Countryview
Rating Applied For
Contact: Mrs C P Wright, Countryview, 9 Old Court, Kenegie Manor, Penzance TR20 8YN
T: (01354) 638282
E: tony@wright113.freeserve.co.uk

The Old Farmhouse ★★★★★
Contact: Mrs Vivienne Hall, The Old Farmhouse, Chegwidden Farm, St Levan, Penzance TR19 6LP
T: (01736) 810516
F: (01736) 810516
E: halls@thegwidden.fsnet.co.uk
I: www.chegwidden.fsnet.co.uk

Rospannel Farm ★★★
Contact: Mr G B Hocking, Rospannel Farm, Crows-an-Wra, Penzance TR19 6HS
T: (01736) 810262
E: gbernard@v21.me.uk
I: www.rospannel.com

Saint Pirans Cottages ★★★-★★★★★
Contact: Mrs Caroline Gresswell
T: (01962) 774379
E: perranhols@aol.com

Seascape ★★★
Contact: Mr & Mrs A Hinton, Cornish Cottage Holidays, The Old Turnpike Dairy, Godolphin Road, Helston TR13 8AA

Summer Breeze ★★★
Contact: Mrs Roberts, The Barn, Trewarveneth Vean, Tredaude Lane, Penzance TR18 5DL
T: (01736) 351949

Trevenen ★★★★
Contact: Cornish Cottage Holidays, The Old Turnpike Dairy, Godolphin Road, Helston TR13 8AA
T: (01326) 573808
F: (01326) 564992
E: enquiry@cornishcottageholidays.co.uk
I: www.cornishcottageholidays.co.uk

The Wharf Apartments ★★★★
Contact: Mrs Penny O'Neill, The Wharf Apartments, The Wharfhouse, Wharf Road, Penzance TR18 2JY
T: (01736) 366888
F: (01736) 331129
E: info@wharfapartments.com
I: www.wharfapartments.com

PERRANPORTH
Cornwall

4 Eureka Vale ★★★
Contact: Mr & Mrs J A Cuthill, Claremont, St Georges Hill, Perranporth TR6 0JS
T: (01872) 573624

PERRANWELL STATION
Cornwall

The Barn ★★★★
Contact: Mrs Margie Lumby, Poachers Reach, Harcourt, Feock, Truro TR3 6SQ
T: (01872) 864400
E: office@specialplacescornwall.co.uk
I: www.specialplacescornwall.co.uk

Greenwith Cottage ★★★★
Contact: The Proprietor, Greenwith Cottage, Greenwith Hill, Perranwell Station, Truro TR3 7LS
T: (01872) 863338

Lymington Cottage ★★★★
Contact: The Proprietor, Lymington Cottage, Tarrandean Lane, Perranwell Station, Truro TR3 7NP

Lymington Snug ★★★★
Contact: Mrs Margie Lumby, Poachers Reach, Harcourt, Feock, Truro TR3 6SQ
T: (01872) 864400
E: office@specialplacescornwall.co.uk
I: www.specialplacescornwall.co.uk

Postbox Cottage ★★★★
Contact: Mrs Margie Lumby, Poachers Reach, Harcourt, Feock, Truro TR3 6SQ
T: (01872) 864400
E: office@specialplacescornwall.co.uk
I: www.specialplacescornwall.co.uk

Woodpeckers ★★★
Contact: Mrs Margie Lumby, Poachers Reach, Harcourt, Feock, Truro TR3 6SQ
T: (01872) 864400
E: office@specialplacescornwall.co.uk
I: www.specialplacescornwall.co.uk

PIDDLETRENTHIDE
Dorset

Coach House ★★★★
Contact: Mr & Mrs Drewe, Coach House, Lackington Farmhouse, Piddletrenthide, Dorchester DT2 7QU
T: (01300) 348253
F: (01300) 348222
E: info@lackingtonfarmhouse.co.uk

PILLATON
Cornwall

Upalong & Downalong ★★★★
Contact: Mr G M Barnicoat, Trefenten, Pillaton, Saltash PL12 6QX
T: (01579) 350141
F: (01579) 351520
E: trefenten@beeb.net
I: www.trefenten.co.uk

PLAYING PLACE
Cornwall

Kernewek ★★★
Contact: Cornish Cottage Holidays, The Old Turnpike Dairy, Godolphin, Meneage Street, Helston TR13 8AA
T: (01326) 573808
F: (01326) 564992
E: enquiry@cornishcottageholidays.co.uk
I: www.cornishcottageholidays.co.uk

PLYMOUTH
Devon

All Seasons Holiday Homes ★★★★
Contact: Mr & Mrs Budd, 20 Pearn Road, Plymouth PL3 5JF
T: (01752) 767730
F: (01752) 767048
E: abudd@talk21.com
I: www.allseasonsholidayhomes.com

Gatehouse Cottage ★★★★
Contact: Mr Ian Butterworth, Holiday Homes & Cottages South West, 365A Torquay Road, Paignton TQ3 2BT
T: (01803) 663650

Haddington House Apartments ★★★★
Contact: Mr Fairfax Luxmoore, Estate Yard Cottage, High Street, Beaulieu, Brockenhurst SO42 7YB
T: 07966 256984
I: www.abudd.co.uk

Hoeside Holiday Flats ★★★
Contact: Mrs Dianne Seymour, Old Rectory, 20 Penlee Way, Stoke, Plymouth PL3 4AW
T: (01752) 563504
F: (01752) 563504
E: hoeside.dsfs@virgin.net

POLBATHIC
Cornwall

Higher Tredis Farm ★★
Contact: Mrs Cindy Rice, Higher Tredis Farm, Sheviock, Polbathic, Torpoint PL11 3ER
T: (01503) 230184
E: cindyrice@btopenworld.com

POLPERRO
Cornwall

Brent House ★★
Contact: Mrs R Bristowe, Brent House, Talland Hill, Polperro, Looe PL13 2RY
T: (01503) 272495

Classy Cottages ★★★★-★★★★★
Contact: Mrs & Mr Fiona & Martin Nicolle, Blanches Windsor, Polperro, Looe PL13 2PT
T: (01720) 423000
E: nicolle@classycottages.co.uk
I: www.classycottages.co.uk

Crumplehorn Cottages ★★★-★★★★
Contact: Mr M Collings, Crumplehorn Cottages, The Anchorage, Portuan Road, Hannafore, Looe PL13 2DN
T: (01503) 262523
F: (01503) 262523
E: gloria@crumplehorncottages.co.uk
I: www.crumplehorncottage.co.uk

Kirk House ★★★★★
Contact: Ms Kay Boniface
T: (01789) 205522
F: (01789) 298899
E: wts@kirkhouseholidays.co.uk
I: www.kirkhouseholidays.co.uk

Little Laney and Polhaven ★★★★
Contact: Mrs Tegan Cornish, 8 The Queensway, Chalfont St Peter, Gerrards Cross SL9 8NF
T: (01753) 882482
F: (01753) 882546
E: tegan@cornish-cottage.com
I: www.cornish-cottage.com

Lucy's ★★★
Contact: Mrs Jackie Leftly, Talland Hill, Polperro, Looe PL13 2JL
T: (01503) 272271
F: (01503) 272271
E: info@leftly.com

Osprey Holidays ★★★
Contact: Mr Ian Ferguson, Osprey Holidays, Talland Hill, Polperro, Looe PL13 2RX
T: (01503) 272819

Pier Inn House and Studio ★★★★-★★★★★
Contact: Ms Kay Boniface
T: (01789) 205522
F: (01789) 298899
E: wts@pierinnholidays.co.uk
I: www.pierinnholidays.co.uk

POLRUAN
Cornwall

The Hideaway ★★
Contact: 3 Fore Street, Polruan, Fowey PL23 1AH
T: (01726) 832211
F: (01726) 832901
E: hillandson@talk21.com

POLRUAN-BY-FOWEY
Cornwall

Peppercorn Cottage ★★★
Contact: Mr David Hill, 3 Fore Street, Polruan, Fowey PL23 1AH
T: (01726) 832211
F: (01726) 832901
E: hillandson@talk21.com

Tremaine Cottage ★★★
Contact: Mr David Hill, 3 Fore Street, Polruan, Fowey PL23 1AH
T: (01726) 832211
F: (01726) 832901
E: hillandsun@talk21.com

POLYPHANT
Cornwall

Darkes Court Cottages ★★★
Contact: Mr Richard Sowerby, Darkes Court Cottages, Polyphant, Launceston PL15 7PS
T: (01566) 86598
F: (01566) 86795
E: sowerby@darkesfarm.fsnet.co.uk

Tregarth ★★★
Contact: Farm & Cottage Holidays, Victoria House, 12 Fore Street, Westward Ho!, Bideford EX39 1AW
T: (01237) 479146
F: (01237) 421512
E: enquiries@farmcott.co.uk

POLZEATH
Cornwall

Godolphin House ★★★★
Contact: Ms J Stanley, Harbour Holidays, Ferry Point, Rock PL27 6LD

Honeysuckle Hill
Rating Applied For
Contact: Mrs Carolyn Crutcher, The Homestead, Rusper Road, Newdigate, Dorking RH5 5BX
T: (01306) 631568
E: carrie@crutchersfarm.freeserve

The Lookout ★★★
Contact: Harbour Holidays - Rock, Trebetherick House, Polzeath, Wadebridge PL27 6SB
T: (01208) 863399
F: (01208) 862218

Marmarra ★★★
Contact: Harbour Holidays - Rock, Trebetherick House, Polzeath, Wadebridge PL27 6SB
T: (01208) 863399
F: (01208) 862218

Millbank ★★★
Contact: Harbour Holidays - Rock, Trebetherick House, Polzeath, Wadebridge PL27 6SB
T: (01208) 863399
F: (01208) 862218

Pentire View ★★★
Contact: Mrs Diana Bullivant, Diana Bullivant Holidays, Trebell Green, Lanivet, Bodmin PL30 5HR
T: (01208) 831336
F: (01208) 831336
E: diana@dbullivant.fsnet.co.uk
I: www.cornwall-online.co.uk/diana-bullivant

Pentire View ★★★★
Contact: Mrs Diana Bullivant, Diana Bullivant Holidays, Southwinds, Trebell Green, Lanivet, Bodmin PL30 5HR
T: (01208) 831336
F: (01208) 831336
E: diana@dbullivant.fsnet.co.uk
I: www.cornwall-online.co.uk/diana-bullivant

3 Pinewood Flats ★★★
Contact: Harbour Holidays - Rock, Trebetherick House, Polzeath, Wadebridge PL27 6SB
T: (01208) 863399
F: (01208) 862218

Seaview ★★★★
Contact: Mrs Diana Bullivant, South Winds, Trebell Green, Lanivet, Bodmin PL30 5HR
T: (01208) 831336
F: (01208) 831336
E: diana@d.bullivant.fsnet.co.uk
I: www.cornwall-online.co.uk/diana-bullivant

Stonechat ★★★
Contact: Mrs Teresa Smith, The Starlings, 2 Sunnybank, Shilla Mill Lane, Polzeath, Wadebridge PL27 6SS
T: (01208) 863172
E: tesspete@tiscali.co.uk
I: www.polzeathbeach.co.uk

Trecreege Barn ★★★
Contact: Harbour Holidays - Rock, Trebetherick House, Polzeath, Wadebridge PL27 6SB
T: (01208) 863399
F: (01208) 862218

10 Trenant Close ★★★
Contact: Mr & Mrs Goodright, Camel Coast Holidays, 5 Marshalls Way, Trelights, Port Isaac PL29 3TE
T: (01208) 880509
E: goodright@ndirect.co.uk

Trevarthian ★★★★
Contact: Mrs Diana Bullivant, Diana Bullivant Holidays, Trebell Green, Lanivet, Bodmin PL30 5HR
T: (01208) 831336
F: (01208) 831336
E: diana@dbullivant.fsnet.co.uk

Tywardale Cottage ★★★
Contact: Mr Swann, Tywardale Cottage, West Rae Road, Polzeath, Wadebridge PL27 6ST
T: (01208) 862721
F: (01208) 862721

Waders ★★★
Contact: Harbour Holidays - Rock, Trebetherick House, Polzeath, Wadebridge PL27 6SB
T: (01208) 863399
F: (01208) 862218

Westpoint ★★★
Contact: Harbour Holidays - Rock, Trebetherick House, Polzeath, Wadebridge PL27 6SB
T: (01208) 863399
F: (01208) 862218

5 Westward Apartments Rating Applied For
Contact: Mr Patrick Bradley, Sundial, Tredrizzick, St Minver, Wadebridge PL27 6PB
T: (01208) 862719

White Rose ★★★
Contact: Mrs Norma Arkell, Palladwr House, Bleke Street, Shaftesbury SP7 8AH
T: (01747) 852176

Windsong ★★
Contact: Harbour Holidays - Rock, Trebetherick House, Polzeath, Wadebridge PL27 6SB
T: (01208) 863399
F: (01208) 862218

PORKELLIS
Cornwall

Ivy's Cabin ★★★
Contact: Agent, Cornish Cottage Holidays, Godolphin Road, Helston TR13 8AA
T: (01326) 573808
F: (01326) 564992
E: enquiry@cornishcottageholidays.co.uk
I: www.cornishcottageholidays.co.uk

PORLOCK
Somerset

Church Farm Rating Applied For
Contact: Toad Hall Cottages, Elliot House, Church Street, Kingsbridge TQ7 1BY
T: (01548) 853089
F: (01548) 853086
E: thc@toadhallcottages.com
I: www.toadhallcottages.com

Coach House Apartments The Old Coach House & Stables ★★★
Contact: Mrs P A Lloyd, Coach House Apartments The Old Coach House & Stables, Doverhay Place, Porlock TA24 8HU
T: (01643) 862409
F: (01643) 862409
E: lloyd@oldcoachhouse.f9.co.uk
I: www.whatsonexmoor.co.uk/coachhouse

Green Chantry ★★★★
Contact: Mrs M Payton, Home Farm, Burrowbridge, Bridgwater TA7 0RF
T: (01823) 698330
F: (01823) 698169
E: maggie_payton@hotmail.com

Hartshanger Holidays ★★★★
Contact: Mrs Anna Edward, Hartshanger Holidays, Hartshanger, Toll Road, Porlock, Minehead TA24 8JH
T: (01643) 862700
F: (01643) 862700
E: hartshanger@lineone.net
I: www.hartshanger.com

Hunters Rest ★★★
Contact: Mr B West, Hunters Rest, Mill Lane, Hawkcombe, Porlock, Minehead TA24 8QW
T: (01643) 862349
F: (01643) 863295
E: west@huntersrest.info
I: www.huntersrest.info

The Watermill ★★★★
Contact: Mr & Mrs John & Diane Ames, 12 The Mead, New Ash Green, Longfield DA3 8EZ
T: (01474) 879810
F: (01474) 879810
E: james.ames1@btinternet.com

Woodside Cottage ★★★
Contact: Mr & Ms Lawrence & Daley, 41 Princes Road, Tivoli, Cheltenham GL50 2TX
T: (01242) 261435
E: woodside_cottage@hotmail.com

PORT GAVERNE
Cornwall

Carn-Awn ★★★
Contact: Mrs May, Port Gaverne, Port Isaac PL29 3SQ
T: (01208) 880716
F: (01208) 880716
E: jimmay@orcades.u-net.com
I: www.orcades.v-net.com

Green Door Cottages ★★★-★★★★★
Contact: Mrs M Ross, Green Door Cottages, Port Gaverne, Port Isaac PL29 3SQ
T: (01208) 880293
F: (01208) 880151
E: enquiries@greendoorcottages.co.uk
I: www.greendoorcottages.co.uk

PORT ISAAC
Cornwall

Atlanta ★★
Contact: Harbour Holidays - Rock, Trebetherick House, Trebetherick, Wadebridge PL27 6SB
T: (01208) 863399
F: (01208) 862218

Atlantic House ★★★
Contact: Mr Dennis Knight, Atlantic House, 41 Fore Street, Port Isaac PL29 3RE
T: (01208) 880498
F: (01208) 880934
E: info@cornishholidayhomes.co.uk

Locarno ★★★
Contact: Mrs R D Hicks, 7 New Road, Haven Park, Port Isaac PL29 3SD
T: (01208) 880268

9a Lundy Road ★★
Contact: Mrs E. E. Taylor, 9a Lundy Road, Port Isaac PL29 3RR
T: (01208) 880283
I: www.worthcornwall.co.uk

57a Springside ★★★
Contact: Mrs Catherine Armstrong, 66 Fore Street, Port Isaac PL29 3RE
T: (01208) 880780
E: cath.armstrong@tesco.net

Trevallion ★★★★
Contact: Mr F J Holpin, 1 Leaze Close, Berkeley GL13 9BZ
T: (01453) 810486

Trevathan Farm ★★★-★★★★★
Contact: Mrs J Symons, Trevathan Farm, St Endellion, Port Isaac PL29 3TT
T: (01208) 880248
F: (01208) 880248
E: symons@trevathanfarm.com
I: www.trevathanfarm.com

The White House ★★★
Contact: Dr Anthony Hambly, Bodrean Manor, St Clements, Bodrean, Truro TR4 9AG
T: (01872) 264400
F: (01872) 264400
E: anthonyhambly@hotmail.com
I: www.cornishholidays.uk.com

PORT PENDENNIS
Cornwall

Marinaside ★★★★
Contact: Mrs Margie Lumby, Special Places in Cornwall, Poachers Reach, Harcourt, Feock, Truro TR3 6SQ
T: (01872) 864400
E: office@specialplacescornwall.co.uk
I: www.specialplacescornwall.co.uk

PORTESHAM
Dorset

Rockfall Cottage ★★★
Contact: Mrs Philippa Roper, Rockfall Cottage, 5 Portesham Hill, Portesham, Weymouth DT3 4EU
T: (01305) 871879
I: www.rockfallcottage@portesham.com

Sleepers ★★★
Contact: Miss Parker, Gorselands Caravan Park, West Bexington, Dorchester DT2 9DJ
T: (01308) 897232
F: (01308) 897239

PORTHALLOW
Cornwall

Bank Cottage ★★★
Contact: Cornish Cottage Holidays, Godolphin Road, Helston TR13 8AA
T: (01326) 573808
F: (01326) 564992
E: enquiry@cornishcottageholidays.co.uk
I: www.cornishcottageholidays.co.uk

Cockle Island Cottage ★★★★
Contact: Mr Ian Hawthorne, Cornish Cottage Holidays, Porthallow, St Keverne, Helston TR12 6PN
T: (01326) 280370
E: hawthorne@valleyviewhouse-freeserve.co.uk

PORTHCOTHAN
Cornwall

Gull Cottage ★★★
Contact: Ms Nicky Stanley, Harbour Holidays - Padstow, 1 North Quay, Padstow PL28 8AF
T: (01841) 532555
F: (01841) 533115
E: sales@jackie-stanley.co.uk
I: www.harbourholidays.co.uk

Sunset ★★★
Contact: Ms Nicky Stanley, Harbour Holidays - Padstow, 1 North Quay, Padstow PL28 8AF
T: (01841) 532555
F: (01841) 533115
E: sales@jackie-stanley.co.uk
I: www.harbourholidays.co.uk

PORTHCURNO
Cornwall

Rospletha Farm ★★★★
Contact: Mrs P Thomas, Bosistow Farm, St Levan, Penzance TR19
T: (01736) 871254

Stargazey ★★★★
Contact: Ms Liz Trenary, Treeve Moor House, Sennen, Penzance TR19 7AE
T: (01736) 871284
E: info@firstandlastcottages.co.uk
I: www.firstandlastcottages.co.uk

PORTHLEVEN Cornwall

Above Beach Cottages ★★★-★★★★
Contact: Mrs Janice Benney, Chy-An-Gwel, Torleven Road, Porthleven, Helston TR13 9HR
T: (01032) 656 3198
E: motthouse@sandpebbles.com

An-Mordros ★★★★
Contact: Cornish Cottage Holidays, The Old Turnpike Dairy, Godolphin Road, Helston TR13 8GL
T: (01326) 573808
F: (01326) 564992
E: inquirey@cornishcottageholidays.co.uk
I: www.cornishcottageholidays.co.uk

Atlantic Cottage ★★★
Contact: Cornish Cottage Holidays, Godolphin Road, Helston TR13 8AA
T: (01326) 573808
F: (01326) 564992
E: enquiry@cornishcottageholidays.co.uk
I: www.cornishcottageholidays.co.uk

Crabpot Cottage ★★★
Contact: Cornish Cottage Holidays, The Old Turnpike Dairy, Godlophin Raod, Helston TR13 8GS
T: (01326) 573808
F: (01326) 564992
E: inquiry@cornishcottageholidays.co.uk
I: www.cornishcottageholidays.co.uk

The Haven ★★★★
Contact: Cornish Cottage Holidays, The Old Turnpike Dairy, Godolphin, Meneage Street, Helston TR13 8AA
T: (01326) 573808
F: (01326) 564992
E: enquiry@cornishcottageholidays.co.uk
I: www.cornishcottageholidays.co.uk

Kestrel House & Harbour View ★★★-★★★★
Contact: Cornish Cottage Holidays, The Old Turnpike Dairy, Godolphin Road, Helston TR13 8GS
T: (01326) 573808
E: inquiry@cornishcottageholidays.co.uk
I: www.cornishcottageholidays.co.uk

Mounts Bay Cottage & Morgolok ★★★
Contact: Mr & Mrs Hinton, Cornish Cottage Holidays, The Old Turnpike Dairy, Godolphin, Meneage Street, Helston TR13 8AA
T: (01326) 573808
I: www.cornishcottageholidays.co.uk

Mounts Bay Villa ★★
Contact: Mr Martin Raftery, Mullion Cottages, Churchtown, Mullion, Helston TR12 7HQ
T: (01326) 240315
F: (01326) 241090
E: martin@mullioncottages.com
I: www.mullioncottages.com

Pegs ★★★
Contact: Cornish Cottage Holidays, The Old Turnpike Dairy, Godolphin, Meneage Street, Helston TR13 8AA
T: (01326) 573808
F: (01326) 564992
E: enquiry@cornishcottageholidays.co.uk
I: www.cornishcottageholidays.co.uk

Peverell ★★★
Contact: The Old Turnpike Dairy, Godolphin, Meneage Street, Helston TR13 8AA
T: (01326) 573808
F: (01326) 564992
E: enquiry@cornishcottageholidays.co.uk
I: www.cornishcottageholidays.co.uk

Sea Cottage ★★★
Contact: Mrs Janice Benney, Chy-an-Gwel, Torleven Road, Porthleven, Helston TR13 9HR
T: (01326) 563198
E: seacottage@sandpebbles.com

Surf Cottage ★★★
Contact: Mr Martin Raftery, Churchtown, Mullion, Helston TR12 7HQ
T: (01326) 240315
F: (01326) 241090
E: martin@mullioncottages.com
I: www.mullioncottages.com

PORTLAND Dorset

The Bell & Lighthouse ★★★
Contact: Mr Zachary Stuart-Brown, Dream Cottages, 41 Maiden Street, Weymouth DT4 8AZ
T: (01305) 761347
E: admin@dream-cottages.co.uk
I: www.dream-cottages.co.uk

Blue Horizon ★★★
Contact: Dream Cottages, 41 Maiden Street, Weymouth DT4 8AZ
T: (01305) 761347
F: (01305) 789000

Chapel Cottage ★★★★
Contact: Ms Brenda Parker, Gorselands, West Bexington, Dorchester DT2 9DJ
T: (01308) 897232
F: (01308) 897239

Chesil Cottage ★★★★
Contact: Mrs Heather Parsons, Chesil Cottage, 31 Clements Lane, Portland DT5 1AS
T: (01305) 820940
E: heparsons@tiscali.co.uk

Endeavour ★★★★
Contact: Mr Zachary Stuart-Brown, Dream Cottages, 41 Maiden Street, Weymouth DT4 8AZ
T: (01305) 761347
E: admin@dream-cottages.co.uk
I: www.dream-cottages.co.uk

Fullerton House ★★★
Contact: Mr Zachary Stuart-Brown, Dream Cottages, 41 Maiden Street, Weymouth DT4 8AZ
T: (01305) 761347
E: admin@dream-cottages.co.uk
I: www.dream-cottages.co.uk

Greenhill Cottage ★★★
Contact: Mr Zachary Stuart-Brown, Dream Cottages, 41 Maiden Street, Weymouth DT4 8AZ
T: (01305) 761347
E: admin@dream-cottages.co.uk
I: www.dream-cottages.co.uk

Inglis Cottage ★★★★
Contact: Mr & Mrs Nigel & Judith Shaw, 145 Wakeham, Portland DT5 1HR
T: (01305) 821042
E: nigelshaw@seeshaws.freeserve.co.uk
I: www.seeshaws.freeserve.co.uk

Ivy Dene
Rating Applied For
Contact: Miss Jacqueline Treanor, Hillfield House, 592 Dorchester Road, Weymouth DT3 5LL
T: (01305) 814566

Kivel Cottage, Bilbo Cottage, Hobbiton★★★
Contact: Mrs Susan Boden, 17 South Street, Titchfield, Fareham PO14 4DL
T: (01329) 841104
E: sue_richardboden@hotmail.com

Lilac Cottage ★★★
Contact: Ms Shelagh Hepple, The Three Pips, Newstead Lane, Fitzwilliam, Pontefract WF9 5AX
T: (01977) 619453
E: hepple@lilaccott171.fs.co.uk
I: www.portlandholiday.co.uk

Mollys Cottage ★★
Contact: Mrs Mary Lenihan, 17 Wheeler Avenue, London RH8 9LF
T: (01883) 372020
E: mollyscottage@hotmail.com

Old Coastguard Cottage ★★★
Contact: Mr John Bunday, Brierley, Knellers Lane, Totton, Southampton SO40 7EB
T: (023) 8086 6421

Old Customs House ★★★★
Contact: Dream Cottages, 41 Maiden Street, Weymouth DT4 8AZ
T: (01305) 761347
F: (01305) 789000

The Old Higher Lighthouse ★★★★
Contact: Mrs Lockyer, The Old Higher Lighthouse, Portland Bill, Southwell, Portland DT5 2JT
T: (01305) 822300
F: (01305) 822300
E: f.lockyer@talk21.com

Polly's Cottage ★★★
Contact: D Leverton, Woodwater Causeway, Radipole Village, Weymouth DT4 9XX
T: (01305) 774360

Sunset Cottage ★★★★
Contact: Mr Zachary Stuart-Brown, Dream Cottages, 41 Maiden Street, Weymouth DT4 8AZ
T: (01305) 761347
E: admin@dream-cottages.co.uk
I: www.dream-cottages.co.uk

Tompot Cottage ★★★
Contact: Mr David Cooper, 91 Longfield Road, Tring HP23 4DF
T: (01442) 826344
E: dcooper@go-scuba.freeserve.co.uk

Twybill Cottage ★★★
Contact: Mr Zachary Stuart-Brown, Dream Cottages, 41 Maiden Street, Weymouth DT4 8AZ
T: (01305) 761347
E: admin@dream-cottages.co.uk
I: www.dream-cottages.co.uk

Wobblers ★★
Contact: Mr Zachary Stuart-Brown, Dream Cottages, 41 Maiden Street, Weymouth DT4 8AZ
T: (01305) 761347
E: admin@dream-cottages.co.uk
I: www.dream-cottages.co.uk

PORTREATH Cornwall

Cliff View ★★★
Contact: Powell's Cottage Holidays, High Street, Freystrop, Haverfordwest SA69 9EJ
T: (01834) 812791
F: (01834) 811731
E: info@powells.co.uk
I: www.powells.co.uk

Gull View ★★★
Contact: Holiday Homes & Cottages South West, 365A Torquay Road, Paignton TQ3 2BT
T: (01803) 663650

The Moorings ★★★
Contact: Powell's Cottage Holidays, High Street, Freystrop, Haverfordwest SA69 9EJ
T: (01834) 812791
F: (01834) 811731
E: info@powells.co.uk
I: www.powells.co.uk

Trengove Farm Cottages ★★★
Contact: Mrs Lindsey Richards, Trengove Farm, Cot Road, Illogan, Redruth TR16 4PU
T: (01209) 843008
F: (01209) 843682
E: richards@farming.co.uk

PORTSCATHO
Cornwall

Linhay Cottage
Rating Applied For
Contact: Holiday Homes & Cottages SW, 365A Torquay Road, Paignton TQ3 2BT
T: (01803) 663650
F: (01803) 664037
E: holcotts@aol.com

Pollaughan Farm Holidays
★★★★
Contact: Mrs V Penny, Pollaughan Farm Holidays, Pollaughan Farm, Portscatho, Truro TR2 5EH
T: (01872) 580150
F: (01872) 58010
E: pollaughan@yahoo.co.uk
I: www.pollaughan.co.uk

Puffins ★★★★
Contact: Mr Paul Riches, 19 Wyvern Road, Sutton Coldfield B74 2PS
T: (0121) 355 8785
E: RPaulflap@aol.com

Rosevine Holiday Cottages
★★★★
Contact: Rosevine Holiday Cottages, Portscatho, Truro TR2 5ET
T: (01872) 580480
F: (01872) 580480
E: enquires@roselandholidaycottages.co.uk

PORTWRINKLE
Cornwall

Westway ★★★
Contact: Ms Susan Irving, 33 Greyhound Lane, Streatham Common, London, London SW16 5NP
T: (0208) 769 7988
I: www.westwaycottage.co.uk

POTTERNE
Wiltshire

Abbotts Ball Farm ★★★
Contact: CH Ref: 12707, Holiday Cottages Group, Spring Mill, Earby, Barnoldswick BB94 0AA
E: sales@holidaycottagesgroup.com
I: www.country-holidays.co.uk

Stroud Hill Farm Holidays
★★★
Contact: Mrs Helen Straker, Stroud Hill Farm, Potterne Wick, Potterne, Devizes SN10 5QR
T: (01380) 720371
F: (01380) 739643
E: hstraker@amserve.net

POUGHILL
Cornwall

Atlantic Cottages ★★★
Contact: Mrs Rosemary Lauder, 2 Blackgate Cottages, Westleigh, Instow, Bideford EX39 4NS
T: (01271) 860232

1 Brightland Apartments
Rating Applied For
Contact: Mrs J Sames, 28 Creslow Way, Stone, Aylesbury HP17 8YW
T: (01296) 747425
E: jlpearce@tesco.net

Moor Farm ★★★
Contact: Farm & Cottage Holidays, Victoria House, 12 Fore Street, Northam, Bideford EX39 1AW
T: (01237) 479146
F: (01237) 421512
E: enquiries@farmcott.co.uk

Trevalgas Cottages
★★★-★★★★
Contact: Mrs Sarah Banning, Candytuft Green, Widmer End, High Wycombe HP15 6BX
T: (01494) 711540
E: info@trevalgascottages.co.uk
I: www.trevalgascottages.co.uk

POUNDISFORD
Somerset

Old Mapp's Garden ★★★
Contact: Mrs Carole Bartleet, Old Mapp's Garden, Corner House, Poundisford, Taunton TA3 7AE
T: (01823) 421737
F: (01823) 421197
E: stephenbartleet@lineone.net

POUNDSGATE
Devon

Bramblemoor Cottage ★★★★
Contact: Mrs Helen Hull, Bramblemoor Cottage, Leusdon, Poundsgate, Newton Abbot TQ13 7NU
T: (01364) 631410
E: helen.hull@eclipse.co.uk
I: www.bramblemoor.fsworld.co.uk

POUNDSTOCK
Cornwall

Pegsdown ★★★
Contact: Powell's Cottage Holidays, High Street, Saundersfoot SA69 9EJ
T: (01834) 812791
F: (01834) 811731
E: info@powells.co.uk
I: www.powells.co.uk

POXWELL
Dorset

Honeysuckle Cottage ★★★
Contact: Mr Zachary Stuart-Brown, Dream Cottages, 41 Maiden Street, Weymouth DT4 8AZ
T: (01305) 761347
E: admin@dream-cottages.co.uk
I: www.dream-cottages.co.uk

PRAA SANDS
Cornwall

Sea Meads Holiday Homes
★★★
Contact: Miss Nicky Hann, Best Leisure, North Hill, Shirwell, Barnstaple EX31 4LG
T: (01271) 850611
F: (01271) 850693
E: enquiries@bestleisure.co.uk

PRESTON
Dorset

Bayview ★★★
Contact: Mr Zachary Stuart-Brown, Dream Cottages, 41 Maiden Street, Weymouth DT4 8AZ
T: (01305) 761347
E: admin@dream-cottages.co.uk
I: www.dream-cottages.co.uk

Bella Rosa, Bella Vista & Villa de la Mer ★★★
Contact: Mr Zachary Stuart-Brown, Dream Cottages, 41 Maiden Street, Weymouth DT4 8AZ
T: (01305) 761347
E: admin@dream-cottages.co.uk
I: www.dream-cottages.co.uk

Deers Leap ★★★
Contact: Holiday Homes & Cottages South West, 365a Torquay Road, Paignton TQ3 2BT
T: (01803) 663650
F: (01803) 664037
E: holcotts@aol.com
I: www.swcottages.co.uk

Phoenix Holiday Flats ★★★★
Contact: Ms Janet Bennett, Phoenix Holiday Flats, 53 Coombe Valley Road, Preston, Weymouth DT3 6NL
T: (01305) 832134
F: (01305) 834955

Preston Heights ★★★
Contact: Mr Zachary Stuart-Brown, Dream Cottages, 41 Maiden Street, Weymouth DT4 8AZ
T: (01305) 761347
E: admin@dream-cottages.co.uk
I: www.dream-cottages.co.uk

Shingle Cottage ★★★
Contact: Dream Cottages, 41 Maiden Street, Weymouth DT4 8AZ
T: (01305) 761347
F: (01305) 789000

PUCKLECHURCH
South Gloucestershire

Fern Cottage ★★★★
Contact: Mrs Sue James, Fern Cottage Self Catering Accommodation, Fern Cottage, 188 Shortwood Hill, Pucklechurch, Bristol BS16 9PG
T: (0117) 937 4966

PUDDLETOWN
Dorset

Weatherbury Cottages
★★★★
Contact: Mr & Mrs Clive Howes, 7a High Street, Puddletown, Dorchester DT2 8RT
T: (01305) 848358
E: enquires@weatherburycottages.co.uk

PUNCKNOWLE
Dorset

Daisy Down Cottage & Puncknowle Manor Farmhouse
★★★★
Contact: Mrs L Hopkins, Hazel Lane Farmhouse, Puncknowle, Dorchester DT2 9BU
T: (01308) 898107
F: (01308) 898107
E: cottages@pknlest.com

Prosperous Cottage ★★★
Contact: Mr Zachary Stuart-Brown, Dream Cottages, 41 Maiden Street, Weymouth DT4 8AZ
T: (01305) 761347
E: admin@dream-cottages.co.uk
I: www.dream-cottages.co.uk

PUTSBOROUGH
Devon

11 Clifton Court ★★★★
Contact: Marsden's Cottage Holidays, 2 The Square, Braunton EX33 2JB
T: (01271) 813777
F: (01271) 813664
E: holidays@marsdens.co.uk
I: www.marsdens.co.uk

17 Clifton Court ★★★★
Contact: Marsden's Cottage Holidays, 2 The Square, Braunton EX33 2JB
T: (01271) 813777
F: (01271) 813664
E: holidays@marsdens.co.uk
I: www.marsdens.co.uk

25 Clifton Court ★★★★
Contact: Marsden's Cottage Holidays, 2 The Square, Braunton EX33 2JB
T: (01271) 813777
F: (01271) 813664
E: holidays@marsdens.co.uk
I: www.marsdens.co.uk

Flat 1 Clifton Court ★★★★
Contact: Marsden's Cottage Holidays, 2 The Square, Braunton EX33 2JB
T: (01271) 813777
F: (01271) 813664
E: holidays@marsdens.co.uk
I: www.marsdens.co.uk

Flat 22 Clifton Court ★★★★
Contact: Marsden's Cottage Holidays, 2 The Square, Braunton EX33 2JB
T: (01271) 813777
F: (01271) 813664
E: holidays@marsdens.co.uk
I: www.marsdens.co.uk

Flat 24 Clifton Court ★★★★
Contact: Marsden's Cottage Holidays, 2 The Square, Braunton EX33 2JB
T: (01271) 813777
F: (01271) 813664
E: holidays@marsdens.co.uk
I: www.marsdens.co.uk

Flat 32 Clifton Court ★★★★
Contact: Mr & Mrs Cornwell, Marsden's Cottage Holidays, 2 The Square, Braunton EX33 2JB
I: www.marsdens.co.uk

Flat 7 Clifton court ★★★★
Contact: Marsden's Cottage Holidays, 2 The Square, Braunton EX33 2JB
T: (01271) 813777
F: (01271) 813664
E: holidays@marsdens.co.uk
I: www.marsdens.co.uk

Vention ★★★★
Contact: Marsden's Cottage Holidays, 2 The Square, Braunton EX33 2JB
T: (01271) 813777
F: (01271) 813664
E: holidays@marsdens.co.uk
I: www.marsdens.co.uk

Vention Cottage ★★★
Contact: Mr & Mrs Peter & Janet Cornwell, Marsden's Cottage Holidays, 2 The Square, Braunton EX33 2JB
T: (01271) 813777
F: (01271) 813664
E: holidays@marsdens.co.uk
I: www.marsdens.co.uk

RAMPISHAM Dorset

Stable Cottage ★★★★
Contact: Mr & Mrs James & Diane Read, School House, Rampisham, Dorchester DT2 0PR
T: (01935) 83555

RATTERY Devon

Knowle Farm ★★★★
Contact: Mr & Mrs Richard & Lynn Micklewright, Knowle Farm, Rattery, South Brent TQ10 9JY
T: (01364) 73914
F: (01364) 73914
E: Holiday@knowle-farm.co.uk
I: www.knowle-farm.co.uk

REDRUTH Cornwall

Morthana Farm Holidays ★★-★★★
Contact: Mrs Sally Pearce, Morthana Farm Holidays, Morthana Farm, Wheal Rose, Scorrier, Redruth TR16 5DF
T: (01209) 890938
F: (01209) 890938

RESTRONGUET Cornwall

Regatta Cottage ★★★★
Contact: Mrs Margie Lumby, Poachers Reach, Harcourt, Feock, Truro TR3 6SQ
T: (01872) 864400
E: office@specialplacescornwall.co.uk
I: www.specialplacescornwall.co.uk

RIDDLECOMBE Devon

Manor Farm ★★★★
Contact: Mrs E Gay, Manor Farm, Riddlecombe, Chulmleigh EX18 7NX
T: (01769) 520335
F: (01769) 520335

RINGSTEAD Dorset

The Creek ★★
Contact: Mrs Fisher, The Creek, Ground Floor Flat, Ringstead, Dorchester DT2 8NG
T: (01305) 852251
E: michaelandfredafisher@btinternet.com

Upton Farm ★★★★★
Contact: Mr & Mrs Davis, Upton, Ringstead, Poxwell, Dorchester DT2 8NE
T: (01305) 853970
F: (01305) 853970
E: alan@uptonfarm.co.uk

ROADWATER Somerset

Tacker Street Cottage ★★
Contact: Mrs A J Thomas, Higher Rodhuish Farm, Rodhuish, Minehead TA24 6QL
T: (01984) 640253
F: (01984) 640253

ROBOROUGH Devon

Owlacombe Mill ★★★★
Contact: Mr James Thomas, Owlacombe Mill, Roborough, Winkleigh EX19 8AE
T: (01805) 603319
F: (01805) 603173
E: owlacombe@eclipse.co.uk
I: www.owlacombemill.com

ROCHE Cornwall

Owl's Reach ★★★★
Contact: Mrs Pride, Owl's Reach, Colbiggan Farm, Old Coach Road, Roche, St Austell PL26 8LJ
T: (01208) 831597
E: info@owlsreach.co.uk
I: www.owlsreach.co.uk

ROCK Cornwall

Cant Cove ★★★★★
Contact: Mr Sleeman, The Cottage, Cant Farm, St Minver, Wadebridge PL27 6RL
T: (01208) 862841
F: (01208) 862142
E: info@cantcove.co.uk
I: www.cantcove.co.uk

22 Croftlands ★★★★
Contact: Mr & Ms James & Dee Smith & McCormack, Tredrizzick, St Minver, Wadebridge PL27 6PB
T: (01208) 862278
E: jimmer2000000@aol.com

Flat 2 Trelawney Court ★★★
Contact: Harbour Holidays - Rock, Trebetherick House, Polzeath, Wadebridge PL27 6SB
T: (01208) 863399
F: (01208) 862218

Flat 8 Trelawney Court ★★★
Contact: Harbour Holidays - Rock, Trebetherick House, Polzeath, Wadebridge PL27 6SB
T: (01208) 863399
F: (01208) 862218

Gullway ★★★★★
Contact: Mrs Diana Bullivant, South Winds, Trebell Green, Lanivet, Bodmin PL30 5HR
T: (01208) 831336
F: (01208) 831336
E: diana@dbullivant.fsnet.co.uk
I: www.cornwall-online.co.uk/diana-bullivant

Half Way Tree ★★★
Contact: Mrs Diana Bullivant, Diana Bullivant Holidays, Trebell Green, Lanivet, Bodmin PL30 5HR
T: (01208) 831336
F: (01208) 831336
E: diana@dbullivant.fsnet.co.uk

Little Riggs ★★★
Contact: Mrs Diana Bullivant, Trebell Green, Lanivet, Bodmin PL30 5HR
T: (01208) 831336
F: (01208) 831336
E: diana@dbullivant.fsnet.co.uk
I: www.cornwall-online.co.uk/diana-bullivant

Maidenover ★★★★
Contact: Mrs Diana Bullivant, Diana Bullivant Holidays, Trebell Green, Lanivet, Bodmin PL30 5HR
T: (01208) 831336
F: (01208) 831336
E: diana@dbullivant.fsnet.co.uk
I: www.cornwall-online.co.uk/diana-bullivant

Mariners Rock ★★★-★★★★
Contact: Miss Grania Wills, 1 Ranelagh Avenue, London SW6 3PJ
T: (020) 7384 9105
I: www.marinersrock.com

Meadowside ★★★★★
Contact: Mrs Diana Bullivant, Diana Bullivant Holidays, Southwinds, Trebell Green, Lanivet, Bodmin PL30 5HR
T: (01208) 831336
F: (01208) 831336
E: diana@d.bullivant.fsnet.co.uk
I: www.cornwall-online.co.uk/diana-bullivant

Mullets ★★★★
Contact: Mrs Diana Bullivant, Southwinds, Trebell Green, Lanivet, Bodmin PL30 5HR
T: (01208) 831336
F: (01208) 831336
E: diana@d.bullivant.fsnet.co.uk
I: www.cornwall-online.co.uk/diana-bullivant

Musters ★★★
Contact: Mrs Diana Bullivant, Diana Bullivant Holidays, Trebell Green, Lanivet, Bodmin PL30 5HR
T: (01208) 831336
F: (01208) 831336
E: diana@dbullivant.fsnet.co.uk

No 3 Trelawney Court ★★★
Contact: Mrs Meg Godfrey, Highoaks, St Kew Highway, Wadebridge PL30 3ED
T: (01208) 841658

Seashells ★★★
Contact: Harbour Holidays - Rock, Trebetherick House, Polzeath, Wadebridge PL27 6SB
T: (01208) 863399
F: (01208) 862218

17 Slipway Cottages ★★★
Contact: Mrs Diana Bullivant, Southwinds, Trebell Green, Lanivet, Bodmin PL30 5HR
T: (01208) 831336
F: (01208) 831336
E: diana@dbullivant.fsnet.co.uk
I: www.cornwall-online.co.uk/diana-bullivant

The Studio ★★★
Contact: Mr & Mrs Gregan, The Studio, Porthilly, Wadebridge PL27 6JX
T: (01208) 862410

Trevethan ★★★
Contact: Harbour Holidays - Rock, Trebetherick House, Polzeath, Wadebridge PL27 6SB
T: (01208) 863399
F: (01208) 862218

Tristan House ★★★
Contact: Harbour Holidays - Rock, Trebetherick House, Polzeath, Wadebridge PL27 6SB
T: (01208) 863399
F: (01208) 862218

Wheel Cottage ★★★★
Contact: Mrs Diana Bullivant, Diana Bullivant Holidays, Trebell Green, Lanivet, Bodmin PL30 5HR
T: (01208) 831336
F: (01208) 831336
E: diana@d.bullivant.fsnet.co.uk

ROOKSBRIDGE Somerset

Garden Cottage & Dairy Cottage ★★★★
Contact: Mrs Mandi Counsell, Rooksbridge House, Rooksbridge, Axbridge BS26 2UL
T: (01934) 750630
E: rooksbridgehouse@btinternet.com

ROSE ASH Devon

Nethercott Manor Farm ★★★
Contact: Mrs Carol Woollacott, Nethercott Manor Farm, Rose Ash, South Molton EX36 4RE
T: (01769) 550483
F: (01769) 550483

ROSUDGEON Cornwall

Thatched Cottage ★★★★
Contact: Welcome Holidays, Embassy Mills, Embassy, Skipton BD23 6QR
T: (01756) 799999
F: (01756) 702235

ROUSDON Devon

The Lodge House ★★★★
Contact: Ms Kate Bartlett, Jean Bartlett Cottage Holidays The Old Dairy, Fore Street, Seaton EX12 3JB
T: (01297) 23221
F: (01297) 23303
E: holidays@jeanbartlett.com
I: www.netbreaks.com/jeamb

ROWDE Wiltshire

Lakeside Rendezvous ★★★★
Contact: Mrs Sarah Gleed, Lakeside Rendezvous, Devizes Road, Rowde, Devizes SN10 2LX
T: (01380) 725447
E: enquiries@lakesiderendezvous.co.uk
I: lakesiderendezvous.co.uk

RUAN HIGH LANES Cornwall

Chy Tyak ★★★★
Contact: Mrs P Carbis
T: (01872) 501339
F: (01872) 501339
E: pam@trenonafarmholidays.co.uk
I: www.trenonafarmholidays.co.uk

Lower Penhallow Farm ★★★★
Contact: Mr Johan Balslev, Lower Penhallow Farm, Ruan High Lanes, Truro TR2 5LS
T: (01872) 501105
F: (01872) 501105
E: enquiries@lowerpenhallowfarm.co.uk
I: www.lowerpenhallowfarm.co.uk

Trelagossick Farm ★★★
Contact: Mrs Rachel Carbis, Trelagossick Farm, Ruan High Lanes, Truro TR2 5JU
T: (01872) 501338

RUAN MINOR
Cornwall

Candle Cottage ★★★★
Contact: Mr Martin Raftery, Churchtown, Mullion, Helston TR12 7HQ
T: (01326) 240315
F: (01326) 241090
E: martin@mullioncottages.com
I: www.mullioncottages.com

Gwavas Vean ★★★
Contact: Mullion Cottages, Sea View Terrace, Churchtown, Mullion, Helston TR12 7HN
T: (01326) 240315
F: (01326) 241090

The Orchard ★★★
Contact: Mr Martin Raftery, Churchtown, Mullion, Helston TR12 7HQ
T: (01326) 240315
F: (01326) 241090
E: martin@mullioncottages.com
I: www.mullioncottages.com

Squires Cottage ★★★
Contact: Mr Martin Raftery, Churchtown, Mullion, Helston TR12 7HQ
T: (01326) 240315
F: (01326) 241090
E: martin@mullioncottages.com
I: www.mullioncottages.com

Tanuf ★★★
Contact: Mr Martin Raftery, Mullion Cottages, Churchtown, Mullion, Helston TR12 7HQ
T: (01326) 240315
F: (01326) 241090
E: martin@mullioncottages.com
I: www.mullioncottages.com

ST AGNES
Cornwall

Covean Cottage Little house ★★★
Contact: Mrs Heather Sewell, Covean Cottage Little house, St Agnes TR22 0PL
T: (01720) 422620
F: (01720) 422620

Croft Cottage ★★★★
Contact: Mrs Jane Sawle, Croft Cottage, Beacon Cottage Farm, Beacon Drive, St Agnes TR5 0NU
T: (01872) 553381
E: beaconcottagefarm@lineone.net

Gothic Cottages ★★
Contact: Mrs Gillian Willson, 6 Norfolk Lodge, Richmond Hill, Richmond TW10 6RJ
T: (0208) 948 0691
E: gillwillson@mac.com
I: www.users.waitrose.com/~gwillson

Lowertown Barn ★★★
Contact: Mrs Page, Shamley Green, Guildford GU5 0SU
T: (01483) 273805
F: (01483) 271606
E: robert@gcpage.freeserve.co.uk

Periglis Cottage ★★★
Contact: Mr Paget-Brown, Periglis Cottage, St Agnes TR22 0PL
T: (01720) 422366

ST AUSTELL
Cornwall

Bosinver Farm Cottages ★★-★★★★
Contact: Mrs Pat Smith
T: (01726) 72128
F: (01726) 72128
E: bosinver@holidays2000.freeserve.co.uk
I: www.bosinver.co.uk

The Engine House ★★★★★
Contact: Mrs Kitchen, Niche Retreats, Hunters Moon, Banns Road, Mount Hawke, Truro TR4 8BW
T: (01209) 890272

Lanjeth Farm Holiday Cottages Rating Applied For
Contact: Mrs Anita Webber, Lanjeth, High Street, St Austell PL26 7TN
T: (01726) 68438
E: anita@cornwall-holidays.uk.com

Nanjeath Farm ★★★★
Contact: Mrs Jill Sandercock, Nanjeath Farm, Lanjeth, High Street, St Austell PL26 7TN
T: (01726) 70666
E: peter@sandercocks.freeserve.co.uk
I: www.nanjeath.co.uk

Poltarrow Farm ★★★★
Contact: Mrs J D Nancarrow, Poltarrow Farm, St Mewan, St Austell PL26 7DR
T: (01726) 67111
F: (01726) 67111
E: enquire@poltarrow.co.uk
I: www.poltarrow.co.uk

Southfield ★★★
Contact: Mrs Pamela Treleaven, Trevissick Farm, Trenarren, St Austell PL26 6BQ
T: (01726) 75819
F: (01726) 68052

Tor View ★★★★
Contact: Ms Clare Hugo, Tor View, Corgee Farm, Luxulyan, Bodmin PL30 5DS
T: (01726) 850340
F: (01726) 850340
E: torview@btopenworld.com
I: www.torviewcentre.co.uk

Tregongeeves Farm Holiday Cottages ★★★★
Contact: Mr & Mrs John & Judith Clemo, Tregongeeves Farm Holiday Cottages, Polgooth, St Austell PL26 7DS
T: (01726) 68202
F: (01726) 68202
E: johnclemo@aol.com
I: www.cornwall-holidays.co.uk

ST BLAZEY
Cornwall

The Mill ★★★★
Contact: Mr & Mrs John & Caroline Tipper & Wey, Prideaux Road, St Blazey, Par PL24 2SR
T: (01726) 810171

ST BREOCK
Cornwall

Hustyns ★★★★★
Contact: Ms Katie Richards, Hustyns, St Breock, Wadebridge PL27 7LG
T: (01208) 893700
F: (01208) 893701
E: reception@hustyns.com
I: www.hustyns.com

ST BREWARD
Cornwall

Darrynane Cottages ★★★
Contact: Mrs Clark, Darrynane, St Breward, Bodmin PL30 4LZ
T: (01208) 850885
E: darrynane@eclipse.co.uk
I: www.darrynane.co.uk

Irish Farm ★★★★
Contact: Shenda Allgrove, Tywardreath, Par PL24
T: (01726) 812558

Meadowside Cottage ★★★★
Contact: Mr & Mrs Aileen & David Feasey, Meadowside Cottage, Mellon Farm, St Breward, Bodmin PL30 4PL
T: (01208) 851497
F: (01208) 851497
E: feaseymellon@aol.com
I: www.mellonfarm.co.uk

Morlanow ★★★★
Contact: Mrs Hillary B Bond, Morlanow, Limehead, St Breward, Bodmin PL30 4LU
T: (01208) 851169
F: (01208) 851169
E: morlanow@cornwall-county.com
I: www.morlanow.co.uk

ST BURYAN
Cornwall

Choone Farm Holiday Cottages ★★★
Contact: Mr Eric Care, Downs Barn Farm, St Buryan, Penzance TR19 6DG
T: (01736) 810658
F: (01736) 810658
E: bonnar.care@talk21.com
I: www.choonefarm.co.uk

Lands End Cottages Rating Applied For
Contact: Mrs Chris Wells, Ye Worlds End, Lower Treave, St Buryan, Penzance TR19 6HZ
T: (01736) 810072
E: kwells6166@aol.com

ST CLEMENT
Cornwall

Churchtown Farm ★★★
Contact: Mrs Margie Lumby, Poachers Reach, Harcourt, Feock, Truro TR3 6SQ
T: (01872) 864400
E: office@specialplacescornwall.co.uk
I: www.specialplacescornwall.co.uk

ST CLETHER
Cornwall

Forget-Me-Not Cottage ★★★★
Contact: Mr & Mrs Sheila Kempthorne, Forget-Me-Not Cottage, Trefranck, St Clether, Launceston PL15 8QN
T: (01566) 86284
E: holidays@trefranck.co.uk
I: www.forgetmenotfarmholidays.co.uk

Treven Farmhouse ★★★
Contact: Farm & Cottage Holidays, Victoria House, 12 Fore Street, Northam, Bideford EX39 1AW
T: (01237) 479146
F: (01237) 421512
E: enquiries@farmcott.co.uk

ST COLUMB
Cornwall

Tregatillian Cottages ★★★
Contact: Mr & Mrs Peter & Cathy Osborne, Cornish Horizons, Higher Trehemborne, St Merryn, Padstow PL28 8JU
T: (01841) 520889
F: (01841) 521523
E: cottages@cornishhorizons.co.uk
I: www.cornishhorizons.co.uk

ST COLUMB MAJOR
Cornwall

Trevellan ★★★★
Contact: Mr & Mrs Corinne & Bob Medhurst, Arcadia Mill, Reterth, St Columb Major, St Columb TR9 6DX
T: (01637) 889148

Walhalla Cottage ★★★
Contact: Ms Nicky Stanley, Harbour Holidays - Padstow, 1 North Quay, Padstow PL28 8AF
T: (01841) 532555
F: (01841) 533115
E: sales@jackie-stanley.co.uk
I: www.harbourholidays.co.uk

ST ENDELLION
Cornwall

Barton Cottage ★★★
Contact: Mrs Harris, Barton Cottage, Tolraggott Farm, St Endellion, Port Isaac PL29 3TP
T: (01208) 880927
F: (01208) 880927
I: www.rock-wadebridge.co.uk

Dinham Farm Courtyard Cottages ★★★
Contact: Mrs Harris, Dinham Farm Courtyard Cottages, Tolraggott Farm, St Endellion, Port Isaac PL29 3TP
T: (01208) 880927
I: www.rock-wadebridge.co.uk

ST ERTH
Cornwall

Trenedros Green ★★★
Contact: Cornish Cottage Holidays, The Old Turnpike Dairy, Godolphin Road, Helston TR13 8AA
T: (01326) 573808
F: (01326) 564992
E: enquiry@cornishcottageholidays.co.uk
I: www.cornishcottageholidays.co.uk

ST ERVAN
Cornwall

Treleigh Manor Farm ★★★
Contact: Mr & Mrs Michael Old, Treleigh Manor Farm, Rumford, Wadebridge PL27 7RT
T: (01841) 540075

ST EVAL
Cornwall

Trelorna ★★★
Contact: Ms Lorna Knott, Trevorgey Mowhay, St Eval, Wadebridge PL27 7UJ
T: (01841) 520992

ST GENNYS
Cornwall

Mineshop Holiday Cottages ★★★
Contact: Mr & Mrs Charlie & Jane Tippett, Mineshop Holiday Cottages, Mineshop, Crackington Haven, Bude EX23 0NR
T: (01840) 230338
F: (01840) 230103
E: tippett@mineshop.freeserve.co.uk
I: www.cornwall-online.co.uk/mineshop

Penrowan Farmhouse Rating Applied For
Contact: Farm & Cottage Holidays, Victoria House, 12 Fore Street, Northam, Bideford EX39 1AW
T: (01237) 479146
F: (01237) 421512
E: enquiries@farmcott.co.uk

Woodgate ★★★
Contact: Mr Francis Crocker, Woodgate, Barton Cottage, St Gennys, Bude EX23
T: (01840) 230492
I: www.wild-trevigue.co.uk

ST GERMANS
Cornwall

The White House ★★★
Contact: Mrs Daw, The White House, Old Quay Lane, St Germans, Saltash PL12 5LH
T: (01503) 230505
E: thewhitehouse_cornwall@hotmail.com

ST ISSEY
Cornwall

Blable Farm Barns ★★★★★
Contact: Mr & Mrs Mike & Alison Roberts, Blable Farm Barns, St Issey, Wadebridge PL27 7RF
T: (01208) 815813
F: (01208) 814834
E: blablefarm@btclick.com

Cannallidgey Villa ★★★
Contact: Mr D J Old, Cannallidgey Villa Farm, St Issey, Wadebridge PL27 7RB
T: (01208) 812276

Hawksland Mill ★★★★
Contact: Mr Richard Jenkins, Hawksland Mill, Hawkland, St Issey, Wadebridge PL27 7RG
T: (01208) 815404
F: (01208) 816831
E: hjc@hawkslandmill.idps.co.uk
I: www.4starcottages.co.uk

The Manor House ★
Contact: Mrs L Kirk, The Manor House, Churchtown, St Issey, Wadebridge PL27 7QB
T: (01841) 540346

Marshall Barn ★★★
Contact: Ms Nicky Stanley Harbour Holidays - Padstow, 1 North Quay, Padstow PL28 8AF
T: (01841) 532555
F: (01841) 533115
E: sales@jackie-stanley.co.uk
I: www.harbourholidays.co.uk

The Old Dairy ★★★
Contact: Ms Nicky Stanley, Harbour Holidays - Padstow, 1 North Quay, Padstow PL28 8AF
T: (01841) 532555
F: (01841) 533115
E: sales@jackie-stanley.co.uk
I: www.harbourholidays.co.uk

The Old Vicarage ★★★
Contact: Ms Nicky Stanley, Harbour Holidays - Padstow, 1 North Quay, Padstow PL28 8AF
T: (01841) 532555
F: (01841) 533115
E: sales@jackie-stanley.co.uk
I: www.harbourholidays.co.uk

Pentire View ★★★
Contact: Mrs Sarah Brewer, Pentire View & Trewint Farm Holiday Homes, St Issey, Wadebridge PL27 7RL
T: (01208) 816595

The Snug ★★★
Contact: Ms Nicky Stanley Harbour Holidays - Padstow, 1 North Quay, Padstow PL28 8AF
T: (01841) 532555
F: (01841) 533115
E: sales@jackie-stanley.co.uk
I: www.harbourholidays.co.uk

South House ★★★
Contact: Harbour Holidays - Padstow, 1 North Quay, Padstow PL28 8AF
T: (01841) 532555
E: contact@harbourholidays.co.uk

Valencia Cottage ★★★
Contact: Mr & Mrs Peter & Cathy Osborne, Cornish Horizons, Higher Trehemborne, St Merryn, Padstow PL28 8JU
T: (01841) 520889
F: (01841) 521523
E: cottages@cornishhorizons.co.uk
I: www.cornishhorizons.co.uk

ST IVES
Cornwall

Ayr Holiday Homes ★★★
Contact: Mrs Kerry Baragwanath, Ayr Holiday Homes, Ayr, St Ives TR26 1EJ
T: (01736) 795855
F: (01736) 798797
E: kerry@ayrholidays.co.uk

Carrack Widden ★★★★
Contact: Mrs C Perry, Tros-an-Mor, Treloyhan Manor Drive, St Ives TR26 2AS
T: (01736) 793370

Casa Bella ★★★★
Contact: Mrs C Perry, Tros-an-Mor, Treloyhan Manor Drive, St Ives TR26 2AS
T: (01736) 793370

Cheriton Self Catering Rating Applied For
Contact: Mr Alec Luke, Cheriton Self Catering, Cheriton House, Market Place, St Ives TR26 1RZ
T: (01736) 795083

Chy Mor and Premier Apartments ★★★
Contact: Mr M Gill, Beach House, The Wharf, St Ives TR26 1QA
T: (01736) 798798
F: (01736) 796831
E: mgill@stivesharbour.com
I: www.stivesharbour.com

Lamorna Apartment ★★★★
Contact: Ms Judy Dale, Lamorna Apartment, Treloyhan Park Road, St Ives TR26 2AH
T: (01736) 794384
F: (01736) 794384
E: gev@onet.co.uk

Nanjizal Cottage Rating Applied For
Contact: Mrs Judy Dale, Lamorna, Treloyhan Park Road, St Ives TR26 2AH
T: (01736) 794384
E: gev@onet.co.uk

The Studio ★★
Contact: Ms Carol Holland, Little Parc Owles, Pannier Lane, Carbis Bay, St Ives TR26 2RQ
T: (01736) 793015
F: (01736) 793258

Tregenna Castle Self-Catering, Tregenna Castle Hotel ★★-★★★★★
Contact: Mr Tony Smith, Tregenna Castle Self-Catering, Tregenna Castle Hot, Treloyan Avenue, St Ives TR26 2DE
T: (01736) 795254
F: (01736) 796066
E: hotel@tregenna-castle.co.uk
I: www.tregenna-castle.demon.co.uk

Trevalgan Holiday Farm ★★★★
Contact: Mrs Joan Osborne, Trevalgan Holiday Farm, Trevalgan Farm, Trevalgan, St Ives TR26 3BJ
T: (01736) 796433
F: (01736) 799798
E: holidays@trevalgan.co.uk
I: www.trevalgan.co.uk

ST JUST-IN-PENWITH
Cornwall

Nanquidno Vean ★★★
Contact: Mrs P M Gildea, 15 College Street, Stratford-upon-Avon CV37 6BN
T: (01789) 299338
F: (01789) 204554
E: pennyguildea@uku.co.uk

Swallows End ★★★★
Contact: Mr & Mrs Richens, Swallows End, Kelynack Moor Farmhouse, Bosworlas, St Just-in-Penwith TR19 7RQ
T: (01736) 787011
♿

ST JUST IN ROSELAND
Cornwall

Brambly Cottage ★★★★
Contact: Mrs Margie Lumby, Poachers Reach, Harcourt, Feock, Truro TR3 6SQ
T: (01872) 864400
E: office@specialplacescornwall.co.uk
I: www.specialplacescornwall.co.uk

Carrick View ★★★★
Contact: Mrs Margie Lumby, Poachers Reach, Harcourt, Feock, Truro TR3 6SQ
T: (01872) 864400
E: office@specialplacescornwall.co.uk
I: www.specialplacescornwall.co.uk

ST KEVERNE
Cornwall

East End Cottage ★★★★
Contact: Cornish Cottage Holidays, Godolphin Road, Helston TR13 8AA
T: (01326) 573808
F: (01326) 564992
E: enquiry@cornishcottageholidays.co.uk
I: www.cornishcottageholidays.co.uk

Eden House Wing ★★★
Contact: Cornish Cottage Holidays, Godolphin Road, Helston TR13 8AA
T: (01326) 573808
F: (01326) 564992
E: robertBOBhughes@aol.com
I: www.cornishcottageholidays.co.uk

Fatty Owls ★★★★
Contact: Ms Yvonne Cole, St Keverne, Helston TR12 6QQ
T: (01326) 280199
E: trenowethhouse@aol.com

Pedn-Tiere ★★★
Contact: Mr Martin Raftery, Mullion Cottages, Churchtown, Mullion, Helston TR12 7HQ
T: (01326) 240315
F: (01326) 241090
E: martin@mullioncottages.com
I: www.mullioncottages.com

Penrose Farm Cottage ★★★
Contact: Cornish Cottage Holidays, The Old Turnpike Dairy, Godolphin Road, Helston TR13 8GS
T: (01326) 573808
F: (01326) 564992
E: enquiry@cornishcottageholidays.co.uk
I: www.cornishcottageholidays.co.uk

Tarragon ★★★★
Contact: Cornish Cottage Holidays, The Old Turnpike Dairy, Godolphin, Meneage Street, Helston TR13 8AA
T: (01326) 573808
F: (01326) 564992
E: enquiry@cornishcottageholidays.co.uk
I: www.cornishcottageholidays.co.uk

Trenoweth Mill ★★★★
Contact: Cornish Cottage Holidays, The Old Turnpike Dairy, Godolphin Road, Helston TR13 8AA
T: (01326) 573808
F: (01326) 564992
E: enquiry@cornishcottageholidays.co.uk
I: www.cornishcottageholidays.co.uk

Trevallack House ★★★
Contact: Farm & Cottage Holidays, Victoria House, 12 Fore Street, Westward Ho!, Bideford EX39 1AW
T: (01237) 479146
F: (01237) 421512
E: bookings@farmcott.co.uk

ST KEW Cornwall

The Barn House ★★★★
Contact: Mrs Janet Chancellor, Ashley, Forty Green Road, Beaconsfield HP9 1XL
T: (01494) 670696
E: jeremy.chancellar@which.net
I: www.visitbarnhouse.co.uk

Lane End Farm Bungalow ★★★
Contact: Mrs Monk, Lake End Farm Bungalow, Pendoggett, St Kew, Bodmin PL30 3HH
T: (01208) 880013
F: (01208) 880013
E: nabmonk@tiscali.co.uk

Larna Vale ★★★★
Contact: Harbour Holidays - Rock, Trebetherick House, Trebetherick, Wadebridge PL27 6SB
T: (01208) 863399
F: (01208) 862218

Ogas Pol ★★★★
Contact: Mr B Greenhalgh, 43 Meadway, Southgate, London N14 6NJ
T: (020) 8882 1333
E: ogaspol_43@onetel.com

Paget & Every ★★★
Contact: Harbour Holidays - Rock, Trebetherick House, Trebetherick, Wadebridge PL27 6SB
T: (01208) 863399
F: (01208) 862218

Treharrock Farm Cottages ★★★★
Contact: Mrs Emerald Quinn, St Kew, Bodmin PL29 3TA
T: (01208) 880517
F: (01208) 880517
E: treharrockfarmcottages@btinternet.com

Trewethern Barn ★★★★
Contact: Harbour Holidays - Rock, Trebetherick House, Trebetherick, Wadebridge PL27 6SB
T: (01208) 863399
F: (01208) 862218

'Skisdon' ★★★-★★★★
Contact: Mr Tim Honeywill, 'Skisdon', Skisdon, St Kew, Bodmin PL30 3HB
T: (01208) 841372
E: Tim580208@aol.com
I: www.skisdon.com

ST LEVAN Cornwall

Bosistow Cottage ★★★★
Contact: Mrs PJ Thomas, Lower Bosistow, St Levan, Penzance TR19 6JH
T: (01736) 871254
F: (01736) 871551
E: bosistow.farm@virgin.net

The Land's End Vineries ★★
Contact: Mrs Clair Sutton, The Land's End Vineries, Polgigga, St Levan, Penzance TR19 6LT
T: (01736) 871437
E: vineries@clara.co.uk
I: www.cornwalltouristboard.co.uk

Longships & Tater-Du ★★★★
Contact: Cornish Cottage Holidays, The Old Turnpike Dairy, Godolphin, Meneage Street, Helston TR13 8AA
T: (01326) 573808

ST MARTIN Cornwall

Bodigga ★★★
Contact: Cornish Cottage Holidays, Godolphin Road, Helston TR13 8AA
T: (01326) 573808
F: (01326) 564992
E: enquiry@cornishcottageholidays.co.uk
I: www.cornishcottageholidays.co.uk

The Bull House ★★★★
Contact: Cornish Cottage Holidays, Godolphin Road, Helston TR13 8AA
T: (01326) 573808
F: (01326) 564992
E: enquiry@cornishcottageholidays.co.uk
I: www.cornishcottageholidays.co.uk

ST MARTIN'S Cornwall

Carron Farm ★★★
Contact: Mrs Julia Walder, Carron Farm, Higher Town, St Martin's TR25 0QL
T: (01720) 422893
I: www.carronfarm.co.uk

Churchtown Farm ★★★★
Contact: Mrs Julian, Churchtown Farm, Higher Town, St Martin's TR25 0QL
T: (01720) 422169
F: (01720) 422800
E: info@churchtownfarmholidays.co.uk
I: www.churchtownfarmholidays.co.uk

Connemara Farm ★★★
Contact: Mr T Perkins, 2 Coastguard Cottage, Higher Town, St Martin's TR25 0QL
T: (01720) 422814
F: (01720) 422814
E: taperkins@btinternet.com

Grans Cottage & The Stable ★★★★
Contact: Mrs D Williams, Grans Cottage & The Stable, Middle Town, St Martin's, Porkellis, Helston TR25 0QN
T: (01720) 422810
F: (01720) 422810
E: middletownfarm@tesco.net

The Stables ★★★
Contact: Mr John Boyle, Sunset, Salt Cellar Hill, Porthleven, Helston TR13 9DP
T: (01326) 563811
F: (01326) 563811
E: john@sharkbayfilms.demon.co.uk

ST MARY'S Isles of Scilly

The Aft Cabin ★★★
Contact: Mr & Mrs Terry & Elizabeth Parsons, The Cabin, 2 The Bank, St Mary's, Helston TR21 0HY
T: (01720) 422393
F: (01720) 422393

Ajax ★★★
Contact: Island Properties Holiday Lettings & Management, Porthmellon, St Mary's TR21 0JY
T: (01720) 422082
F: (01720) 422211
E: enquiries@isleofscillyholidays.com
I: www.isleofscillyholidays.com

Albany Flats & Thurleigh ★★-★★★
Contact: Mrs Isabel Trenear, Albany Flats, Church Street, Thurleigh, St Mary's TR21 0JT
T: (01720) 422601

Allwinds ★★★
Contact: Mrs Lewis, Henhurst Farm, Foots Lane, Burwash Weald, Etchingham TN19 7LE
T: (01435) 883239
E: henhurst@hotmail.com.co.uk

Amaryllis ★★★★
Contact: Mr Tony Dingley, Island Properties, Church Street, St Mary's TR21 0PT
T: (01720) 422082

Anchor Cottage ★★★
Contact: Island Properties Holiday Lettings & Management, Porthmellon, St Mary's TR21 0JY
T: (01720) 422082
F: (01720) 422211
E: enquiries@isleofscillyholidays.com
I: www.isleofscillyholidays.com

1 & 2 Quay House ★★★
Contact: Island Properties Holidays Lettings & Management, Porthmellon, St Mary's TR21 0JY
T: (01720) 422082
F: (01720) 422211
E: enquiries@isleofscillyholidays.com
I: www.isleofscillyholidays.com

Anglesea House ★★★★
Contact: Island Properties Holiday Lettings & Management, Porhtmellon, St Mary's TR21 0JY
T: (01720) 422082
F: (01720) 422211
E: enquiries@isleofscillyholidays.com
I: www.isleofscillyholidays.com

Ardwyn ★★★★
Contact: Mrs Gill Osborne, The Withies, Trench Lane, Old Town, Old Town, St Mary's TR21 0PA
T: (01720) 422986

Armorel Cottage ★★★
Contact: Island Properties Holiday Lettings & Management, Porthmellon, St Mary's TR21 0JY
T: (01720) 422082
F: (01720) 422211
E: enquiries@isleofscillyholidays.com
I: www.isleofscillyholidays.com

Avoca Holiday Homes ★★★★
Contact: Mr & Mrs Colin & Elizabeth Ridsdale, Avoca, Hospital Lane, Church Road, St Mary's, Helston TR21 0LQ
T: (01720) 422656

Bar Escapade ★★★
Contact: Island Properties, Church Street, St Mary's
T: (01720) 422082
F: (01720) 422111
E: enquiries@isleofscillyholidays.com
I: www.isleofscillyholidays.com

The Barn ★★★
Contact: Island Properties Holiday Lettings & Management, Porthmellon, St Mary's TR21 0JY
T: (01720) 422082
F: (01720) 422211
E: enquiries@isleofscillyholidays.com
I: www.isleofscillyholidays.com

1 Bay View ★★★
Contact: Mr Tony Dingley, Island Properties, Church Street, St Mary's TR21 0PT
T: (01720) 422082
F: (01720) 422211

3 Bay View ★★
Contact: Island Properties Holiday Lettings & Management, Porthmellon, St Mary's TR21 0JY
T: (01720) 422082
F: (01720) 422211
E: enquiries@isleofscillyholidays.com
I: www.isleofscillyholidays.com

Beach House Flat ★★★
Contact: Island Properties Holiday Lettings & Management, Porthmellon, St Mary's TR21 0JY
T: (01720) 422082
F: (01720) 422211
E: enquiries@isleofscillyholidays.com
I: www.isleofscillyholidays.com

Beach Mooring Flat 1, Smugglers Ride★★★★
Contact: Mrs Susan Eccles, Orchard Meadow, Well Lane, Gerrans, Portscatho, Truro TR2 5EG
T: (01872) 580997
E: norman_eccles@barclays.net

Beachside Maisonette Above Co-op★★
Contact: Island Properties Holiday Lettings & Management, Porthmellon, St Mary's TR21 0JY
T: (01720) 422082
F: (01720) 422211
E: enquiries@isleofscillyholidays.com
I: www.isleofscillyholidays.com

Beggars Roost ★★
Contact: Mr Kenneth Peay, 19 Langley Avenue, Surbiton KT6 6QN
T: (020) 8399 8364

Bodilly Cottage ★★★
Contact: Island Properties, Church Street, St Mary's TR21 0JY
T: (01720) 422082
F: (01720) 422211
E: enquiries@islesofscillyholidays.com

Bounty Ledge ★★★
Contact: Mr R T Jackman, Scillonian Estate Agency, 8 Lower Strand, St Mary's TR21 0PS
T: (01720) 422124

Buzza Ledge
Rating Applied For
Contact: Mr Jeremy Phillips, Rose Cottage, Strand, St Mary's TR21 0PT
T: (01720) 422028
F: (01720) 423588
E: jeremyphillips@rosecottagescilly.freeserve.co.uk

Bylet Holiday Homes ★★★
Contact: Mr D Williams, Bylet Holiday Homes, The Bylet, Church Road, St Mary's TR21 0NA
T: (01720) 422479
F: (01720) 422479
E: thebylet@bushinternet.com
I: www.geocities.com/bylet_holidays/

The Captains Cabin ★★★
Contact: Mrs Peggy Rowe, The Captains Cabin, Marine House, Church Street, St Mary's TR21 0JT
T: (01720) 422966
E: peggy@rowe55.freeserve.co.uk

Carnwethers Country House ★★★★
Contact: Mr Roy Graham, Carnwethers Country House, Pelistry Bay, St Mary's TR21 0NX
T: (01720) 422415
F: (01720) 422415

Christmas House ★★★
Contact: Mrs Jane Chiverton, Sally Port, St Mary's TR21 0JE
T: (01720) 422002

Church Hall Cottage ★★★★
Contact: Mr David Townend, Church Street, Thurleigh, St Mary's TR21 0JT
T: (01720) 422377
F: (01720) 422377
E: dtownend@netcomuk.co.uk

Chy Kensa ★★★★
Contact: Mr T Dingley, Island Properties, Church Street, St Mary's TR21 0JT
T: (01720) 422082

Clemys Cottage ★★
Contact: Mrs Cherry Cattran, Zennor, St Ives TR26 3BP
T: (01736) 796977
F: (01736) 794970
E: petche@cwcom.net

The Corner House Flat ★★★
Contact: Island Properties Holiday Lettings & Management, Porthmellon, St Mary's TR21 0JY
T: (01720) 422082
F: (01720) 422211
E: enquiries@islesofscillyholidays.com
I: www.isleofscillyholidays.com

Cornerways ★★★★★
Contact: Mr & Mrs Pritchard, Jacksons Hill, St Mary's TR21 0JZ
T: (01720) 422757
F: (01720) 422797

The Crow's Nest ★★★
Contact: Mrs Stella Carter, The Old Bakehouse, Winterborne Road, Abingdon OX14 1AJ
T: (01235) 520317
F: (01235) 527495
E: stella@bakehouse.supanet.com

Dolphins ★★★
Contact: Island Properties Holiday Lettings & Management, Porthmellon, St Mary's TR21 0JY
T: (01720) 422082
F: (01720) 422211
E: enquiries@isleofscillyholidays.com
I: www.isleofscillyholidays.com

Dunmallard, Lower Flat ★★★
Contact: Mr & Mrs Elliot, 2 Greenhill Mead, Pesters Lane, Somerton TA11 7AB
T: (01458) 272971

Ebor Cottage ★★★
Contact: Island Properties Holiday Lettings & Management, Porthmellon, St Mary's TR21 0JY
T: (01720) 422082
F: (01720) 422211
E: enquiries@isleofscillyholidays.com
I: www.isleofscillyholidays.com

Escallonia ★★★★
Contact: Mrs Susan Quinton, 31 Forest Ridge, Orpington BR2 6EG
T: (01689) 850216

Fishermans Arms ★★★
Contact: Mrs A L Walker, Bute Lodge, 182 Petersham Road, Petersham, Richmond TW10 7AD
T: (020) 8940 9808

The Flat ★★★★
Contact: Mrs Jill May, The Flat, The Sandpiper Shop, Hugh Town, St Mary's TR21 0HY
T: (01720) 422122
F: (01720) 422122

Flat 2 Madura ★★★
Contact: Mrs Winifred A Davis, 40 Hawkwell Chase, Hockley SS5 4NH
T: (01702) 203515
E: fredadavis@v21.me.uk

Flat 3 Rosevean ★★★
Contact: Mrs Talbot, 35 Barracks Lane, Macclesfield SK10 1QJ
T: (01625) 427059

Flat 4 Kenwyn ★★★
Contact: Mrs Patricia Vian, Southmead, Telegraph, St Mary's TR21 0NR
T: (01720) 423100
E: vian@btinternet.com

Flat 5, Spanish Ledge ★★
Contact: Island Properties, Porthmellon, St Mary's TR21 0JY
T: (01720) 422082
F: (01720) 422211
E: enquiries@isleofscillyholidays.com

Flat 6 Spanish Ledge Holiday Flats★★★
Contact: Mrs B Phillips, Guthers Church Road, St Mary's TR21 0NA
T: (01720) 422345

Flats 3 & 4 ★★★
Contact: Island Properties Holiday Lettings & Management, Porthmellon, St Mary's TR21 0JY
T: (01720) 422082
F: (01720) 422211
E: enquiries@isleofscillyholidays.com
I: www.isleofscillyholidays.com

Garrison Holidays ★★★
Contact: Mr & Mrs Ted & Barbara Moulson, Tower Cottage, Garrison, St Mary's TR21 0LS
T: (01720) 422670
F: (01720) 422625
E: tedmoulson@aol.com
I: www.isles-of-scilly.co.uk

Glandore Apartments ★★★★
Contact: Mr Stephen Morris, Glandore Apartments, St Mary's TR21 0NE
T: (01720) 422535
E: apartments@glandore.co.uk

2 Godolphin Flats ★★★★
Contact: Mr T Dingley, Island Properties, Church Street, St Mary's TR21 0JY
T: (01720) 422082
F: (01720) 422211
E: enquiries@isleofscillyholidays.com

6 Godolphin House & 8 Buzza Street ★★★
Contact: Mrs A S Hogg, 92 Brinklow Road, Coventry CV3 2HY
T: (024) 7645 0455

1 Golden Bay Mansions ★★★
Contact: Mrs M H Barnes, Three Gables, MacFarlands Down, St Mary's TR21 0NS
T: (01720) 423141

Greystones ★★★
Contact: Mr Tony Dingley, Island Properties, Church Street, St Mary's TR21 0PT
T: (01720) 422082
F: (01720) 422211

Gunner Rock ★★★
Contact: Mr & Mrs Heslin, Gunner Rock, Jackson's Hill, St Mary's TR21 0JZ
T: (01720) 422595

Harbour Lights with Smugglers Ride ★★★
Contact: Mr T C Clifford, 22 Trevallion Park, Feock, Truro TR3 6RS
T: (01872) 863537
F: (01872) 863537
E: tcclif@globalnet.co.uk
I: www.users.globalnet.co.uk/~tcclif/

5 Harbour View Mansions ★★★★
Contact: Mrs Sheila Thomas, 7 Porthcressa Road, St Mary's, Helston TR21 0JL
T: (01720) 422637
E: aurigascilly@aol.com

Harbour Walls ★★★
Contact: Island Properties Holiday Lettings & Management, Porthmellon, St Mary's TR21 0JY
T: (01720) 422082
F: (01720) 422211
E: enquiries@isleofscillyholidays.com
I: www.isleofscillyholidays.com

Haycocks ★★★
Contact: Island Properties Holiday Lettings & Management, Porthmellon, St Mary's TR21 0JY
T: (01720) 422082
F: (01720) 422211
E: enquiries@isleofscillyholidays.com
I: www.isleofscillyholidays.com

Inglenook ★★★
Contact: Mr J White, 36 Cotland Acres, Redhill RH1 6JZ
T: (01737) 248890
F: (01737) 242770
E: jon@holidayinglenook.co.uk
I: www.holidayinglenook.co.uk

Katrine ★★★★
Contact: Mrs Hayden, 2 Buzza Street, St Mary's TR21 0HX
T: (01720) 422178

Kingston House ★★★
Contact: Island Properties Holiday Lettings & Management, Porthmellon, St Mary's TR21 0JY
T: (01720) 422082
F: (01720) 422211
E: enquiries@isleofscillyholidays.com
I: www.isleofscillyholidays.com

Kirklees Holiday Flat ★★★
Contact: Mr P & Mrs G Coldwell, Kirklees, Porthcressa, St Mary's TR21 0JL
T: (01720) 422623

Kistvaen ★★
Contact: Mrs Chiverton, Kistvaen, Sally Port, St Mary's TR21 0JE
T: (01720) 422002
F: (01720) 422002
E: chivy002@aol.com

Lea View ★★★
Contact: Island Properties Holiday Lettings & Management, Porthmellon, St Mary's TR21 0JY
T: (01720) 422082
F: (01720) 422211
E: enquiries@isleofscillyholidays.com
I: www.isleofscillyholidays.com

The Lighthouse ★★★
Contact: Island Properties Holiday Lettings & Management, Porthmellon, St Mary's TR21 0JY
T: (01720) 422082
F: (01720) 422211
E: enquiries@isleofscillyholidays.com
I: www.isleofscillyholidays.com

Lower Ganilly Flat ★★★
Contact: Island Properties, Church Street, St Mary's TR21 0JY
T: (01720) 422082
F: (01720) 422211
E: enquiries@isleofscillyholidays.com
I: www.isleofscillyholidays.com

6 Lower Strand ★★★★
Contact: Mrs S Richards, Holy Vale, St Mary's TR21 0NT
T: (01720) 422904
F: (01720) 422904

Lunnon Cottage, The Quillet, Medlar ★★★
Contact: Mrs Rogers, Lunnon Cottage, The Quillet, Medlar, Lunnon, St Mary's TR21 0NZ
T: (01720) 422422
F: (01720) 422422

Madura I ★★★
Contact: Island Properties Holiday Lettings & Management, Porthmellon, St Mary's TR21 0JY
T: (01720) 422082
F: (01720) 422211
E: enquiries@isleofscillyholidays.com
I: www.isleofscillyholidays.com

Manilla Flats ★★★
Contact: Mrs Frances Grottick, Burgundy House, Rams Valley, St Mary's, Helston TR21 0JX
T: (01720) 422424
F: (01720) 422424

Maypole Farm ★★
Contact: Island Properties Holiday Lettings & Management, Porthmellon, St Mary's TR21 0JY
T: (01720) 422082
F: (01720) 422211
E: enquiries@isleofscillyholidays.com
I: www.isleofscillyholidays.com

Mellyns Holiday Home ★★★★
Contact: Jill & Bill Wilson, The Laundry House, Church Way, Ecton, Northampton NN6 0QE
T: (01604) 414906
F: (01604) 414906

Minalto Holiday Flats ★★★
Contact: Mr Richard Vaughan, Minalto Holiday Flats, Church Street, St Mary's TR21 0JT
T: (01720) 423159

Minmow Holiday Flats ★★★
Contact: Mr D K Simpson, Stoneraise, Old Town, St Mary's TR21 0NH
T: (01720) 422561

The Moos ★★★
Contact: Mrs Susan Williams, Polmenor, Pelistry, St Mary's TR21 0NX
T: (01720) 422605

Morgelyn ★★★
Contact: Mrs J Lishman, Morgelyn, McFarlands Down, St Mary's TR21 0NS
T: (01720) 422897
E: info@morgelyn.co.uk
I: www.morgelyn.co.uk

The Mount ★★★★
Contact: Mr Peter Loxton, Jerusalem Terrace, St Mary's TR21 0JH
T: (01720) 422484

Mount Todden Farm ★★★
Contact: Miss Anna Ebert, Mount Todden Farm, St Mary's TR21 0NY
T: (01720) 422311
E: annaebert@mounttodden.sol.co.uk

4 Myrtle Cottages ★★★
Contact: Island Properties Holiday Lettings & Management, Porthmellon, St Mary's TR21 0JY
T: (01720) 422082
F: (01720) 422211
E: enquiries@isleofscillyholidays.com
I: www.isleofscillyholidays.com

5 Myrtle Cottages ★★★
Contact: Island Properties Holiday Letings & Management, Porthmellont, St Mary's TR21 0JY
T: (01720) 422082
F: (01720) 422211
E: enquiries@isleofscillyholidays.com
I: www.isleofscillyholidays.com

Newfort House ★★★★
Contact: Island Properties Holiday Lettings & Management, Porthmellon, St Mary's TR21 0JY
T: (01720) 422082
F: (01720) 422211
E: enquiries@isleofscillyholidays.com
I: www.isleofscillyholidays.com

No. 3 Godolphin House ★★★
Contact: Island Properties Holiday Lettings & Management, Porthmellon, St Mary's TR21 0JY
T: (01720) 422082
F: (01720) 422211
E: enquiries@isleofscillyholidays.com
I: www.isleofscillyholidays.com

No 3 Bungalow ★★
Contact: Mrs M Sherris, Content Farm, St Mary's TR21 0NS
T: (01720) 422496

The Old Cottage ★★
Contact: Mrs Lethbridge, The Old Cottage, The Bank, St Mary's TR21 0HY
T: (01720) 422630

The Palms ★★
Contact: Mrs J Lethbridge, The Palms, Maypole, St Mary's TR21 0NU
T: (01720) 422404

Peacehaven ★★
Contact: Mr P A Bennett, Borough Farm, St Mary's TR21
T: (01720) 422326

Pelistry Cottage ★★★
Contact: Mr & Mrs John & Brenda Ashford, Hugh Street, St Mary's TR21 0LL
T: (01720) 422059

Pengarriss ★★★
Contact: Mrs Walker, 4 Copse View Cottages, Redenham, Andover SP11 9AT
T: (01264) 772758

Penlee Boathouse Rating Applied For
Contact: Mr Rod Tugwell, Penlee Boathouse, Porthcressa Road, St Mary's TR21 0JL
T: (01720) 423605
E: penleeboathouse_scilly@hotmail.com

Pennlyon ★★★
Contact: Mrs Majorie Feast, Bryer Cottage, Whitemoor Lane, Sambourne B96 6NT
T: (01527) 893619

1 Pentland ★★
Contact: Mr Dingley, Island Properties, Church Street, St Mary's
T: (01720) 422082
F: (01720) 422211
E: enquiries@isleofscillyholidays.com

Perran ★★★
Contact: Island Properties Holiday Lettings & Management, Church Street, St Mary's TR21 0JY
T: (01720) 422082
F: (01720) 422211
E: enquiries@isleofscillyholidays.com
I: www.isleofscillyholidays.com

Pharmacy Flat ★★★
Contact: Ms Helen Pearce, Pharmacy Flat, St Mary's Pharmacy, St Mary's TR21 0LG

Pilots Gig Flat ★★★★
Contact: Mrs Jay Holliday, Daventry Road, Staverton, Daventry NN11 6JH
T: (01327) 871053

Plumb Cottage ★★★★
Contact: Island Properties Holiday Lettings & Management, Porthmellon, St Mary's TR21 0JY
T: (01720) 422082
F: (01720) 422211
E: enquiries@isleofscillyholidays.com
I: www.isleofscillyholidays.com

2 Porthcressa View ★★★★
Contact: Mrs Diana Peat, Pelorus, Church Road, St Mary's, Helston TR21 0NA
T: (01720) 422376
E: cpeat@aol.com

Porthlow Farm ★-★★★
Contact: Mrs Mawer, Porthlow Farm, St Mary's TR21 0NF
T: (01720) 422636

Porthmellon House ★★★
Contact: Mrs Rosemary Clifton, Porthmellon House, Porthmellon, St Mary's TR21 0JY
T: (01720) 422748

Prospect House Flats ★★★★
Contact: Mr & Mrs Peter & Nicola Thompson, Prospect Lodge, Well Lane, St Mary's TR21 0HZ
T: (01720) 422948

The Retreat ★★★
Contact: Island Properties Holiday Lettings & Management, Porthmellon, St Mary's TR21 0JY
T: (01720) 422082
F: (01720) 422211
E: enquiries@isleofscillyholidays.com
I: www.isleofscillyholidays.com

Rocky Hill Chalets ★★
Contact: Mrs DK Edwards, Rocky Hill Chalets, Rocky Hill, St Mary's TR21 0NE
T: (01720) 422955

1 Rosevean ★★★
Contact: Raymond, 1 Cart Lane, Kents Bank Road, Grange-over-Sands LA11 7EF
T: (015395) 34780
F: (015395) 34780
E: gwyn.raymond@btopenworld.com

4 Rosevean House ★★★
Contact: Mr Mark Littleford, McFarlands Down, St Mary's TR21 0NS
T: (01720) 423102

The Round House ★★★
Contact: Island Properties Holiday Lettings & Management, Porthmellon, St Mary's TR21 0JY
T: (01720) 422082
F: (01720) 422211
E: enquiries@isleofscillyholidays.com
I: www.isleofscillyholidays.com

Sailcheck ★★★★
Contact: Miss Hodges, London Road, Hemel Hempstead HP1 2RE

Sallakee Farm ★★
Contact: Mrs P A Mumford, Sallakee Farm, St Mary's TR21 0NZ
T: (01720) 422391

22 Sally Port ★★
Contact: Mr J A Hyde, 30A St Peters Hill, Newlyn, Penzance TR18 5EH
T: (01736) 366199

Shamrock ★★
Contact: Ms Tracey Guy, Shamrock Self Catering, St Mary's TR21 0NW
T: (01720) 423269

Shipwrights Cottage Maisonettes ★★★★
Contact: Mrs Margaret Lorenz, Four Winds, Telegraph, St Mary's TR21 0NR
T: (01720) 422522

14 Silver Street ★★★
Contact: Island Properties Holiday Lettings & Management, Porthmellon, St Mary's TR21 0JY
T: (01720) 422082
F: (01720) 422211
E: enquiries@isleofscillyholidays.com
I: www.isleofscillyholidays.com

12 Silver Street and 1 Porthcressa★★★
Contact: Mrs L J Mills, 6 Highclere Drive, Longdean Park, Hemel Hempstead HP3 8BT
T: (01923) 270533
F: (01923) 268080

Smuggler's Den (flat 2) ★★★
Contact: Mrs Stella Carter, The Old Bakehouse, Winterborne Road, Abingdon OX14 1AJ
T: (01235) 520317
E: stella@bakehouse.supanet.com

2 Spanish Ledge ★★
Contact: Island Properties, Porthmellon, St Mary's TR21 0JY
T: (01720) 422082
F: (01720) 422211

3 Spanish Ledge ★★
Contact: Island Properties, Porthmellon, St Mary's TR21 0JY
T: (01720) 422082
F: (01720) 422211
E: enquiries@isleofscillyholidays.com

4 Spanish Ledge ★★
Contact: Island Properties, Porthmellon, St Mary's TR21 0JY
T: (01720) 422082
F: (01720) 422211
E: enquiries@isleofscillyholidays.com

Spanish Ledge Holiday Flats ★★★
Contact: Mr Tony Dingley, Island Properties, Church Street, St Mary's TR21 0PT
T: (01720) 422338
F: (01720) 422211

1 Springfield Court ★★★
Contact: Island Properties, Porthmellon, St Mary's TR21 0JY
T: (01720) 422082
F: (01720) 422211
E: enquiries@isleofscillyholidays.com
I: www.isleofscillyholidays.com

7 Springfield Court ★★★★
Contact: Island Properties Holiday Lettings & Management, Porthmellon, St Mary's TR21 0JY
T: (01720) 422082
F: (01720) 422211
E: enquiries@isleofscillyholidays.com
I: www.isleofscillyholidays.com

9 Springfield Court ★★★
Contact: Island Properties Holiday Lettings & Management, Porthmellon, St Mary's TR21 0JY
T: (01720) 422082
F: (01720) 422211
E: enquiries@isleofscillyholidays.com
I: www.isleofscillyholidays.com

Spy Hole ★★★
Contact: Island Properties Holiday Lettings & Management, Porthmellon, St Mary's TR21 0JY
T: (01720) 422082
F: (01720) 422211
E: enquiries@isleofscillyholidays.com
I: www.isleofscillyholidays.com

10 The Strand ★★★★
Contact: Mrs Pamela Murray, The Barn, Tremaine, Launceston PL15 8SA
T: (01566) 781270
E: cottage@madnmap.com
I: www.madnmap.com

Sunny Creek ★★★
Contact: Island Properties Holiday Lettings & Management, Porthmellon, St Mary's TR21 0JY
T: (01720) 422082
F: (01720) 422211
E: enquiries@isleofscillyholidays.com
I: www.isleofscillyholidays.com

Sunnyside Flats ★★-★★★
Contact: Mr Mike Brown, Sunnyside Flats, Rosemary Cottage, St Mary's TR21 0NW
T: (01720) 422903
E: mike@sunnysideflats.com

The Tardis ★★★
Contact: Mrs Margaret Helen Williams, The Tardis, c/o Briar Lea, Pelistry, St Mary's TR21 0NX
T: (01720) 422209

Teeki ★★★
Contact: Island Properties, Church Street, St Mary's
T: (01720) 422211

2 Telegraph Bungalows ★★★
Contact: Mrs S Mumford, Newford Farm, St Mary's TR21 0NS
T: (01720) 422650

Top Flat ★★★
Contact: Mrs Christine Hosken, Top Flat, Trenoweth Farm, St Mary's TR21 0NS
T: (01720) 422666

Treglesyn ★★★
Contact: Mr Thomas Holden, 11 Hurst Lane, Cumnor, Oxford OX2 9PR
T: (01865) 864022

Tremelethen Farm ★★★
Contact: Mrs Sarah Hale, Tremelethen Farm, St Mary's TR21 0NZ
T: (01720) 422436
F: (01720) 423226

Trevessa ★★★★
Contact: Mrs P A Browning, Wingletang Guest House, The Parade, St Mary's TR21 0LP
T: (01720) 422381

Upper & Lower Jacksons ★★★★
Contact: Mr Tony Dingley, Island Properties, Church Street, St Mary's TR21 0PT
T: (01720) 422082
F: (01720) 422211

Upper Flat, Dunmallard ★★★
Contact: Mr & Mrs D J Poynter, 17 Braybrooke Road, Wargrave, Reading RG10 8DU
T: (0118) 940 3539

Verona ★★★
Contact: Island Properties Holiday Lettings & Management, Porthmellon, St Mary's TR21 0JY
T: (01720) 422082
F: (01720) 422211
E: enquiries@isleofscillyholidays.com
I: www.isleofscillyholidays.com

Warleggan Holiday Flats ★★★
Contact: Mrs Hiron, Warleggan Holiday Flats, Church Street, St Mary's TR21 0JT
T: (01720) 422563
F: (01720) 422563
E: terry.hiron@virgin.net

The White Cottage ★★★
Contact: Mr Tony Dingley, Island Properties, Church Street, St Mary's TR21 0PT
T: (01720) 422082
F: (01720) 422211

Wisteria & Jasmine Cottages ★★★★
Contact: Claire Oyler, 2 Hamewith, The Parade, St Mary's TR21 0LP
T: (01720) 422111

1 Wras ★★★
Contact: Island Properties Holiday Lettings & Management, Porthmellon, St Mary's TR21 0JY
T: (01720) 422082
F: (01720) 422211
E: enquiries@isleofscillyholidays.com
I: www.isleofscillyholidays.com

3 Wras ★★★
Contact: Mr Tony Dingley, Island Properties, Church Street, St Mary's TR21 0PT
T: (01720) 422082
F: (01720) 422211

ST MARYCHURCH Devon

Little Grange ★★★
Contact: Mr & Mrs Edward & Jenifer Webber, Grange Cottage, Babbacombe Downs Road, St Marychurch, Torquay TQ1 3LP
T: (01803) 313809
E: littlegrange@bushinternet.com

Ludwell House Rating Applied For
Contact: Ms Sue Clark, Ludwell House, Cary Park, Babbacombe, St Marychurch, Torquay TQ1 3NH
T: (01803) 326032
F: (01803) 326032
E: sue.clark@ukonline.co.uk

ST MAWES Cornwall

Chy Ryn ★★★
Contact: Mrs Margie Lumby, Poachers Reach, Harcourt, Feock, Truro TR3 6SQ
T: (01872) 864400
E: office@specialplacescornwall.co.uk
I: www.specialplacescornwall.co.uk

Coppers ★★★★
Contact: Mrs Margie Lumby, Poachers Reach, Harcourt, Feock, Truro TR3 6SQ
T: (01872) 864400
E: office@specialplacescornwall.co.uk
I: www.specialplacescornwall.co.uk

Dolphins ★★★
Contact: Mrs Margie Lumby, Poachers Reach, Harcourt, Feock, Truro TR3 6SQ
T: (01872) 864400
E: office@specialplacescornwall.co.uk
I: www.specialplacescornwall.co.uk

The Gingerbread House ★★★★
Contact: Mrs Margie Lumby, Poachers Reach, Harcourt, Feock, Truro TR3 6SQ
T: (01872) 864400
E: office@specialplacescornwall.co.uk
I: www.specialplacescornwall.co.uk

Mariners ★★★★
Contact: Ms Margie Lumby, Poachers Reach, Harcourt, Feock, Truro TR3 6SQ
T: (01872) 864400
E: office@specialplacescornwall.co.uk
I: www.specialplacescornwall.co.uk

Oyster Haven & Prydes ★★★★-★★★★★
Contact: Mrs Margie Lumby, Poachers Reach, Harcourt, Feock, Truro TR3 6SQ
T: (01872) 864400
E: office@specialplacescornwall.co.uk
I: www.specialplacescornwall.co.uk

Penlee ★★★★
Contact: Mrs Margie Lumby, Poachers Reach, Harcourt, Feock, Truro TR3 6SQ
T: (01872) 864400
E: office@specialplacescornwall.co.uk
I: www.specialplacescornwall.co.uk

Pier Cottage Rating Applied For
Contact: Holiday Homes & Cottages SW, 365A Torquay Road, Paignton TQ3 2BT
T: (01803) 663650
F: (01803) 664037
E: holcotts@aol.com

Rocklee House ★★★★
Contact: Mrs Margie Lumby, Poachers Reach, Harcourt, Feock, Truro TR3 6SQ
T: (01872) 864400
F: (01872) 864400
E: office@specialplacescornwall.co.uk
I: www.specialplacescornwall.co.uk

Seaward ★★★★
Contact: Mrs Margie Lumby, Poachers Reach, Harcourt, Feock, Truro TR3 6SQ
T: (01872) 864400
E: office@specialplacescornwall.co.uk
I: www.specialplacescornwall.co.uk

Starboard ★★★
Contact: Mrs Margie Lumby, Poachers Reach, Harcourt, Feock, Truro TR3 6SQ
T: (01872) 864400
E: office@specialplacescornwall.co.uk

Sunnybanks ★★★★
Contact: Mrs Margie Lumby, Poachers Reach, Harcourt, Feock, Truro TR3 6SQ
T: (01872) 864400
E: office@specialplacescornwall.co.uk
I: www.specialplacescornwall.co.uk

Topdeck ★★★★
Contact: Mrs Margie Lumby, Poachers Reach, Harcourt, Feock, Truro TR3 6SQ
T: (01872) 864400
E: office@specialplacescornwall.co.uk
I: www.specialplacescornwall.co.uk

The Workshop ★★★★
Contact: Mrs Margie Lumby, Poachers Reach, Harcourt, Feock, Truro TR3 6SQ
T: (01872) 864400
E: office@specialplacescornwall.co.uk
I: www.specialplacescornwall.co.uk

ST MAWGAN
Cornwall

Polgreen Manor ★★
Contact: Mrs J A Wake, NDD, Polgreen Manor, St Mawgan, Newquay TR8 4AG
T: (01637) 860700
F: (01637) 875165

ST MERRYN
Cornwall

Chalet 83 ★★
Contact: Miss Elizabeth Kerry, Church Cottage, Church Street, Chiseldon, Swindon SN4 0NJ
T: (01793) 740284

Chyloweth
Rating Applied For
Contact: Mr & Mrs Roger & Sally Vivian, Chyloweth, Constantine Bay, Padstow PL28 8JQ
T: (01841) 521012
E: roger.vivian@ukgateway.net

Little Lancarrow ★★★
Contact: Mr & Mrs Peter & Cathy Osborne, Cornish Horizons Holiday Cottages, Higher Trehemborne, St Merryn, Padstow PL28 8JU
T: (01841) 520889
F: (01841) 521523
E: cottages@cornishhorizons.co.uk
I: www.cornishhorizons.co.uk

Lower Trevorgus ★★★
Contact: Mr & Mrs Peter & Cathy Osborne, Cornish Horizons, Higher Trehemborne, St Merryn, Padstow PL28 8JU
T: (01841) 520889
F: (01841) 521523
E: cottages@cornishhorizons.co.uk
I: www.cornishhorizons.co.uk

12 Peguarra Court ★★★
Contact: Mr & Mrs Peter & Cathy Osborne, Cornish Horizons, Higher Trehemborne, St Merryn, Padstow PL28 8JU
T: (01841) 520889
F: (01841) 521523
E: cottages@cornishhorizons.co.uk
I: www.cornishhorizons.co.uk

St Hilary ★★★
Contact: Mr & Mrs Peter & Cathy Osborne, Cornish Horizons, Higher Trehemborne, St Merryn, Padstow PL28 8JU
T: (01841) 520889
F: (01841) 521523
E: cottages@cornishhorizons.co.uk
I: www.cornishhorizons.co.uk

Spindrift ★★
Contact: Mr & Mrs Peter & Cathy Osborne, Cornish Horizons, Higher Trehemborne, St Merryn, Padstow PL28 8JU
T: (01841) 521333
F: (01841) 521523
E: cottages@cornishhorizons.co.uk
I: www.cornishhorizons.co.uk

Sunshine Cottage ★★
Contact: Mr & Mrs Peter & Cathy Osborne, Cornish Horizons, Higher Trehemborne, St Merryn, Padstow PL28 8JU
T: (01841) 520889
F: (01841) 521523
E: cottages@cornishhorizons.co.uk
I: www.cornishhorizons.co.uk

Trearth ★★★★
Contact: Mr & Mrs Peter & Cathy Osborne, Cornish Horizons, Higher Trehemborne, St Merryn, Padstow PL28 8JU
T: (01841) 520889
F: (01841) 521523
E: cottages@cornishhorizons.co.uk
I: www.cornishhorizons.co.uk

Tregerrick
Rating Applied For
Contact: Mr Andy Stefanczyk, 80 Westbrook End, Newton Longville, Milton Keynes MK17 0DF
T: (01908) 374451

Twizzletwig ★★★
Contact: Mr & Mrs Peter & Cathy Osborne, Cornish Horizons, Higher Trehemborne, St Merryn, Padstow PL28 8JU
T: (01841) 520889
F: (01841) 521523
E: cottages@cornishhorizons.co.uk
I: www.cornishhorizons.co.uk

Yellow Sands Cottages ★★★-★★★★
Contact: Mrs Sharron Keast, Yellow Sands Cottages, Harlyn Bay, St Merryn, Padstow PL28 8SE
T: (01637) 881548
E: yellowsands@btinternet.com

ST MINVER
Cornwall

April Cottage ★★★★★
Contact: Harbour Holidays - Rock, Trebetherick House, Trebetherick, Wadebridge PL27 6SB
T: (01208) 863399
F: (01208) 862218

The Bothy ★★★★
Contact: Harbour Holidays - Rock, Trebetherick House, Trebetherick, Wadebridge PL27 6SB
T: (01208) 863399
F: (01208) 862218

Brae Cottage ★★★★
Contact: Harbour Holidays - Rock, Trebetherick House, Trebetherick, Wadebridge PL27 6SB
T: (01208) 863399
F: (01208) 862218

Bunkers Cottage ★★★★
Contact: Harbour Holidays - Rock, Trebetherick House, Trebetherick, Wadebridge PL27 6SB
T: (01208) 863399
F: (01208) 862218

Caldarvan ★★★★
Contact: Harbour Holidays - Rock, Trebetherick House, Trebetherick, Wadebridge PL27 6SB
T: (01208) 863399
F: (01208) 862218

Casa Piedra Cottage ★★★★
Contact: Harbour Holidays - Rock, Trebetherick House, Trebetherick, Wadebridge PL27 6SB
T: (01208) 863399
F: (01208) 862218

Chy Petroc ★★★★
Contact: Harbour Holidays - Rock, Trebetherick House, Trebetherick, Wadebridge PL27 6SB
T: (01208) 863399
F: (01208) 862218

Cobwebs ★★★★
Contact: Harbour Holidays - Rock, Trebetherick House, Trebetherick, Wadebridge PL27 6SB
T: (01208) 863399
F: (01208) 862218

Cowrie ★★★★
Contact: Harbour Holidays - Rock, Trebetherick House, Trebetherick, Wadebridge PL27 6SB
T: (01208) 863399
F: (01208) 862218

The Farmhouse Roserrow ★★★★
Contact: Harbour Holidays - Rock, Trebetherick House, Polzeath, Wadebridge PL27 6SB
T: (01208) 863399
F: (01208) 862218

Gearys ★★★★
Contact: Harbour Holidays - Rock, Trebetherick House, Trebetherick, Wadebridge PL27 6SB
T: (01208) 863399
F: (01208) 862218

Gore's Cottage ★★★★★
Contact: Harbour Holidays - Rock, Trebetherick House, Trebetherick, Wadebridge PL27 6SB
T: (01208) 863399
F: (01208) 862218

Gwella ★★★★
Contact: Harbour Holidays - Rock, Trebetherick House, Trebetherick, Wadebridge PL27 6SB
T: (01208) 863399
F: (01208) 862218

The Haven ★★★★★
Contact: Harbour Holidays - Rock, Trebetherick House, Trebetherick, Wadebridge PL27 6SB
T: (01208) 863399
F: (01208) 862218

The Hawthorns ★★★★
Contact: Harbour Holidays - Rock, Trebetherick House, Trebetherick, Wadebridge PL27 6SB
T: (01208) 863399
F: (01208) 862218

Idle Rocks ★★★★
Contact: Harbour Holidays - Rock, Trebetherick House, Trebetherick, Wadebridge PL27 6SB
T: (01208) 863399
F: (01208) 862218

Janners Retreat ★★★★
Contact: Harbour Holidays - Rock, Trebetherick House, Trebetherick, Wadebridge PL27 6SB
T: (01208) 863399
F: (01208) 862218

Keepers ★★★★
Contact: Harbour Holidays - Rock, Trebetherick House, Trebetherick, Wadebridge PL27 6SB
T: (01208) 863399
F: (01208) 862218

Lundy Cottage ★★★★
Contact: Harbour Holidays - Rock, Trebetherick House, Trebetherick, Wadebridge PL27 6SB
T: (01208) 863399
F: (01208) 862218

Mayfield ★★★★
Contact: Harbour Holidays - Rock, Trebetherick House, Trebetherick, Wadebridge PL27 6SB
T: (01208) 863399
F: (01208) 862218

The Millhouse ★★★★
Contact: Harbour Holidays - Rock, Trebetherick House, Trebetherick, Wadebridge PL27 6SB
T: (01208) 863399
F: (01208) 862218

The Millhouse Barn ★★★★
Contact: Harbour Holidays - Rock, Trebetherick House, Polzeath, Wadebridge PL27 6SB
T: (01208) 863399
F: (01208) 862218

Mosseyoak ★★★★
Contact: Harbour Holidays - Rock, Trebetherick House, Trebetherick, Wadebridge PL27 6SB
T: (01208) 863399
F: (01208) 862218

The Nineteenth ★★★★
Contact: Harbour Holidays - Rock, Trebetherick House, Trebetherick, Wadebridge PL27 6SB
T: (01208) 863399
F: (01208) 862218

Numbers 3 & 4 Trevanger Cottages ★-★★★
Contact: Mrs Liisa Beagley, The Street, Pettistree Grange, Ufford, Woodbridge IP13 0HP
T: (01728) 746334
E: liisabeagley@hotmail.com

Oak Tree House ★★★★
Contact: Harbour Holidays - Rock, Trebetherick House, Trebetherick, Wadebridge PL27 6SB
T: (01208) 863399
F: (01208) 862218

2 The Old Dairy ★★★★
Contact: Harbour Holidays - Rock, Trebetherick House, Trebetherick, Wadebridge PL27 6SB
T: (01208) 863399
F: (01208) 862218

Pearl Springs ★★★
Contact: The Agent, Blakes Country Cottages, Springmill, Earby, Freystrop, Haverfordwest BB94 0AA
T: 08700 708090
F: (01282) 841539

Penahayle ★★★★
Contact: Harbour Holidays - Rock, Trebetherick House, Trebetherick, Wadebridge PL27 6SB
T: (01208) 863399
F: (01208) 862218

Pendragon Cottage ★★★
Contact: Mrs T J Smith, 2 Sunnybank, Shilla Mill Lane, Polzeath, Wadebridge PL27 6SS
T: (01208) 863172
E: tesspete@tiscali.co.uk

Penhayle ★★★★
Contact: Harbour Holidays - Rock, Trebetherick House, Trebetherick, Wadebridge PL27 6SB
T: (01208) 863399
F: (01208) 862218

Penkivel House ★★★★
Contact: Harbour Holidays - Rock, Trebetherick House, Trebetherick, Wadebridge PL27 6SB
T: (01208) 863399
F: (01208) 862218

Penteli ★★★★
Contact: Harbour Holidays - Rock, Trebetherick House, Trebetherick, Wadebridge PL27 6SB
T: (01208) 863399
F: (01208) 862218

Puffin House ★★★★
Contact: Harbour Holidays - Rock, Trebetherick House, Trebetherick, Wadebridge PL27 6SB
T: (01208) 863399
F: (01208) 862218

Ridgewood ★★★★
Contact: Harbour Holidays - Rock, Trebetherick House, Trebetherick, Wadebridge PL27 6SB
T: (01208) 863399
F: (01208) 862218

Rosewin Barn ★★★★
Contact: Harbour Holidays - Rock, Trebetherick House, Polzeath, Wadebridge PL27 6SB
T: (01208) 863399
F: (01208) 862218

Rosewin Farmhouse ★★★★
Contact: Harbour Holidays - Rock, Trebetherick House, Polzeath, Wadebridge PL27 6SB
T: (01208) 863399
F: (01208) 862218
I: www.rockholidays.com

The Roundhouse ★★★★
Contact: Harbour Holidays - Rock, Trebetherick House, Trebetherick, Wadebridge PL27 6SB
T: (01208) 863399
F: (01208) 862218

Sandy Cottage ★★★★
Contact: Harbour Holidays - Rock, Trebetherick House, Trebetherick, Wadebridge PL27 6SB
T: (01208) 863399
F: (01208) 862218

September ★★★★
Contact: Harbour Holidays - Rock, Trebetherick House, Trebetherick, Wadebridge PL27 6SB
T: (01208) 863399
F: (01208) 862218

Streth Tu ★★★★★
Contact: Harbour Holidays - Rock, Trebetherick House, Trebetherick, Wadebridge PL27 6SB
T: (01208) 863399
F: (01208) 862218

Talamore ★★★★
Contact: Harbour Holidays - Rock, Trebetherick House, Trebetherick, Wadebridge PL27 6SB
T: (01208) 863399
F: (01208) 862218

Tamarisk ★★★★
Contact: Harbour Holidays - Rock, Trebetherick House, Trebetherick, Wadebridge PL27 6SB
T: (01208) 863399
F: (01208) 862218

Taphouse ★★★★★
Contact: Harbour Holidays - Rock, Trebetherick House, Trebetherick, Wadebridge PL27 6SB
T: (01208) 863399
F: (01208) 862218

Tremaine ★★★★★
Contact: Harbour Holidays - Rock, Trebetherick House, Trebetherick, Wadebridge PL27 6SB
T: (01208) 863399
F: (01208) 862218

Trevelver Farm Cottage ★★★
Contact: Mrs Avice Wills, Trevelver Farm Cottage, St Minver, Wadebridge PL27 6RJ
T: (01208) 863290

Trewint Farm ★★
Contact: Mrs Sarah Brewer, Pentire View & Trewint Farm Holiday Homes, St Issey, Wadebridge PL27 7RL
T: (01208) 816595

Webbs Retreat ★★★★
Contact: Harbour Holidays - Rock, Trebetherick House, Trebetherick, Wadebridge PL27 6SB
T: (01208) 863399
F: (01208) 862218

Wedge Cottage ★★★★
Contact: Harbour Holidays - Rock, Trebetherick House, Trebetherick, Wadebridge PL27 6SB
T: (01208) 863399
F: (01208) 862218

ST STEPHEN
Cornwall

Court Farm Cottages ★★★★
Contact: Mr Bill Truscott, Court Farm Cottages, St Stephen, St Austell PL26 7LE
T: (01726) 822727
F: (01726) 822685
E: truscott@ctfarm.freeserve.co.uk
I: www.chycon.co.uk/cottages/court-farm/index.htm

ST TEATH
Cornwall

Barn Farm ★★★-★★★★
Contact: CH Ref:1042,10262, 8775,14636, Holiday Cottages Group, Spring Mill, Earby, Barnoldswick BB94 0AA
T: 08700 781200
E: sales@holidaycottagesgroup.com
I: www.country-holidays.co.uk

Cocks Cottage ★★★
Contact: Mrs Misson, Spring Farm, Warwick Road, Stratford-upon-Avon
T: (01789) 731966

Tregreenwell Farm ★★★★
Contact: Farm & Cottage Holidays, Victoria House, 12 Fore Street, Northam, Bideford EX39 1AW
T: (01237) 479146
F: (01237) 421512
E: enquiries@farmcott.co.uk

ST TUDY
Cornwall

The Linhay ★★★★★
Contact: Mrs C. Mavis Kingdon, The Linhay, The Oaks Barn, Redvale Road, St Tudy, Bodmin PL30 3PU
T: (01208) 851422

Potters ★★★★
Contact: Susan Susan Enderby, 48 Little Heath, London SE7 8BH
T: (020) 8855 8532
F: (020) 8855 8532
E: susanenderby@aol.com
I: www.westcountrynow.com

SALCOMBE
Devon

Coxswain's Watch ★★★
Contact: Mr Andrew Oulsnam, Robert Oulsnam & Co, 79 Hewell Road, Barnt Green, Birmingham B45 8NL
T: (0121) 445 3311
F: (0121) 445 6026
E: barntgreen@oulsnam-online.com
I: www.oulsnam-online.com

Longridge ★★★★
Contact: Mr B Curry, Meriden Cottage, Longburton, Sherborne DT9 5PH
T: (01963) 210622
F: (01963) 210622
E: curryb@btinternet.com

SALISBURY
Wiltshire

Charter Court ★★★★
Contact: Mr Nicholas Pash, Chapel House, Luke Street, Berwick St John, Shaftesbury SP7 0HQ
T: (01747) 828170
F: (01747) 829090
E: enq@hideaways.co.uk
I: www.hideaways.co.uk

12 Charter Court ★★★★
Contact: Mrs Moore, 28 Riverside Close, Laverstock, Salisbury SP1 1QW
T: (01722) 320188
E: charterho@hotmail.com

Fowlers Road ★★★
Contact: Mr Nicholas Pash, Chapel House, Luke Street, Berwick St John, Shaftesbury SP7 0HQ
T: (01747) 828170
F: (01747) 829090
E: enq@hideaways.co.uk
I: www.hideaways.co.uk

Hen View (The Fishing Lodge) ★★★★
Contact: Mrs Victoria Dakin, Church Farmhouse, Melbury Abbas, Shaftesbury SP7 0EA
T: (01747) 855976
E: vdakin@skymarket.org

Love Lane ★★★
Contact: Mr Nicholas Pash, Chapel House, Luke Street, Berwick St John, Shaftesbury SP7 0HQ
T: (01747) 828170
F: (01747) 829090
E: enq@hideaways.co.uk
I: www.hideaways.co.uk

Manor Farm Cottages ★★★★
Contact: Ms Gillie Strang, Strang Cottages, Manor Farm, Sutton Mandeville, Salisbury SP3 5NL
T: (01722) 714226
F: (01722) 714507
E: strangf@aol.com
I: www.strangcottages.com

The Old Stables ★★★★
Contact: Mr Gould, The Old Stables, Bridge Farm, Lower Road, Britford, Salisbury SP5 4DY
T: (01722) 349002
F: (01722) 349003
E: mail@old-stables.co.uk
I: www.old-stables.co.uk

Rojoy ★★★
Contact: Mr Nicholas Pash, Chapel House, Luke Street, Berwick St John, Shaftesbury SP7 0HQ
T: (01747) 828170
F: (01747) 829090
E: enq@hideaways.co.uk
I: www.hideaways.co.uk

Saint Ann Street ★★★
Contact: Mr Nicholas Pash, Chapel House, Luke Street, Berwick St John, Shaftesbury SP7 0HQ
T: (01747) 828170
F: (01747) 829090
E: enq@hideaways.co.uk
I: www.hideaways.co.uk

Winterbourne Cottage
★★★★
Contact: Mr Nicholas Pash, Chapel House, Luke Street, Berwick St John, Shaftesbury SP7 0HQ
T: (01747) 828170
F: (01747) 829090
E: enq@hideaways.co.uk
I: www.hideaways.co.uk

Wyndham ★★★★
Contact: Mr Nicholas Pash, Chapel House, Luke Street, Berwick St John, Shaftesbury SP7 0HQ
T: (01747) 828170
F: (01747) 829090
E: enq@hideaways.co.uk
I: www.hideaways.co.uk

SALWAY ASH
Dorset

Brinsham Farm Cottages
★★★★
Contact: Mrs Viv Harding, Brinsham Farm Cottages, Brinsham Farm, Pineapple Lane, Salway Ash, Bridport DT6 5HY
T: (01308) 488196
F: (01308) 488196
E: Brinsham@aol.com

SAMPFORD ARUNDEL
Somerset

Gorlegg Cottage ★★★
Contact: Farm & Cottage Holidays, Victoria House, 12 Fore Street, Westward Ho!, Bideford EX39 1AW
T: (01237) 479146
F: (01237) 421512
E: enquiries@farmcott.co.uk

SAMPFORD BRETT
Somerset

The Granary ★★★
Contact: CH Ref:68042, Country Holidays, Spring Mill, Earby, Barnoldswick BB94 0AA
T: 08700 781200
E: sales@holidaycottagesgroup.com
I: www.country-holidays.co.uk

SAMPFORD SPINEY
Devon

Withill Cottage ★★★
Contact: Farm & Cottage Holidays, Victoria House, 12 Fore Street, Westward Ho!, Bideford EX39 1AW
T: (01237) 479146
F: (01237) 421512
E: enquiries@farmcott.co.uk

SANDYWAY
Devon

Barkham Cottages ★★★★
Contact: Mr & Mrs J Adie, Barkham, Sandyway, South Molton EX36 3LU
T: (01643) 831370
I: www.exmoor-visitus.co.uk

SAUNTON
Devon

Lower Lease ★★★★
Contact: Marsden's Cottage Holidays, 2 The Square, Braunton EX33 2JB
T: (01271) 813777
F: (01271) 813664
E: holidays@marsdens.co.uk
I: www.marsdens.co.uk

Rhu & Little Rhu
★★★-★★★★
Contact: Marsden's Cottage Holidays, 2 The Square, Braunton EX33 2JB
T: (01271) 813777
F: (01271) 813664
E: holidays@marsdens.co.uk
I: www.marsdens.co.uk

Saunton Heath ★★★
Contact: Marsden's Cottage Holidays, 2 The Square, Braunton EX33 2JB
T: (01271) 813777
F: (01271) 813664
E: holidays@marsdens.co.uk
I: www.marsdens.co.uk

Surf ★★★
Contact: Marsden's Cottage Holidays, 2 The Square, Braunton EX33 2JB
T: (01271) 813777
F: (01271) 813664
E: holidays@marsdens.co.uk
I: www.marsdens.co.uk

Thorn Close Cottage ★★★★
Contact: Marsdens Cottage Holidays, 2 The Square, Braunton EX33 2JB
T: (01271) 813777
F: (01271) 813664
E: holidays@marsdens.co.uk

SEATON
Devon

Badgers Holt ★★★
Contact: Milkbere Holidays, 3 Fore Street, Seaton EX12 2LE
T: (01297) 20729
F: (01297) 22925
E: info@milkberehols.com
I: www.milkbere.com

Caruso ★★★
Contact: Milkbere Holidays, 3 Fore Street, Seaton EX12 2LE
T: (01297) 20729
F: (01297) 22925
E: info@milkberehols.com
I: www.milkbere.com

Conswalk ★★★
Contact: Ms Louise Hayman, Milkbere Cottage Holidays, 3 Fore Street, Seaton EX12 2LE
T: (01297) 20729
F: (01297) 22925

Drakes Nest ★★★
Contact: Milkbere Holidays, 3 Fore Street, Seaton EX12 2LE
T: (01297) 20729
F: (01297) 22925
E: info@milkberehols.com
I: www.milkbere.com

Farthings ★★★★
Contact: Ms Louise Hayman, Milkbere Cottage Holidays, 3 Fore Street, Seaton EX12 2LE
T: (01297) 20729
F: (01297) 22925
E: info@milkberehols.com

Flat 2, 8 Westcliffe Terrace
★★★
Contact: Ms Louise Hayman, Milkbere Holidays, 3 Fore Street, Seaton EX12 2LE
T: (01297) 20729

Glynsall Cabin ★★
Contact: Milkbere Holidays, 3 Fore Street, Seaton EX12 2LE
T: (01297) 20729
F: (01297) 22925
E: info@milkberehols.com
I: www.milkbere.com

Harrys ★★★
Contact: Ms Louise Hayman, Milkbere Cottage Holidays Ltd, 3 Fore Street, Seaton EX12 2LE
T: (01297) 20729
F: (01297) 24831
E: info@milkberehols.com
I: www.milkbere.com

Hawks Hideaway ★★★
Contact: Milkbere Holidays, 3 Fore Street, Seaton EX12 2LE
T: (01297) 20729
F: (01297) 22925
E: info@milkberehols.com
I: www.milkbere.com

Highclyffe Court ★★★★
Contact: Ms Louise Hayman, Milkbere Cottage Holidays, 3 Fore Street, Seaton EX12 2LE
T: (01297) 20729
F: (01297) 22925
E: info@milkberehols.com

Homestead Flats ★★★
Contact: Jean Bartlett Cottage Holidays, Fore Street, Beer, Seaton EX12 3JB
T: (01297) 23221

1 Inkerman Court ★★★★
Contact: Ms Louise Hayman, Milkbere Cottage Holidays Ltd, 3 Fore Street, Seaton EX12 2LE
T: (01297) 20729
F: (01297) 24831
E: info@milkberehols.com
I: www.milkbere.com

Last Penny Cottage ★★★★
Contact: Milkbere Holidays, 3 Fore Street, Seaton EX12 2LE
T: (01297) 20729
F: (01297) 22925
E: info@milkbere.com
I: www.milkbere.com

Little Cot ★★★
Contact: Jean Bartlett Cottage Holidays, Fore Street, Beer, Seaton EX12 3JB
T: (01297) 23221
F: (01297) 23303
E: holidays@jeanbartlett.com
I: www.netbreaks.com/jeanb

Little Oaks ★★★★
Contact: Milkbere Holidays, 3 Fore Street, Seaton EX12 2LE
T: (01297) 20729
F: (01297) 22925
E: info@milkberehols.com
I: www.milkbere.com

The Loft ★★★★
Contact: Ms Louise Hayman, Milkbere Cottage Holidays, 3 Fore Street, Seaton EX12 2LE
T: (01297) 20729
F: (01297) 22925
E: info@milkberehols.com

3 Lyme Mews ★★★
Contact: Jean Bartlett Cottage Holidays, Fore Street, Seaton EX12 3JB
T: (01297) 23221
F: (01297) 23303
E: holidays@jeanbartlett.com
I: www.netbreaks.com/jeanb

Manor Farm Cottages
★★★-★★★★
Contact: Mrs Parr, Manor Farm, Harepath Hill, Seaton EX12 2TF
T: (01297) 625349

The Nook ★★★★
Contact: Milkbere Holidays, 3 Fore Street, Seaton EX12 2LE
T: (01297) 20729
F: (01297) 22925
E: info@milkberehols.com
I: www.milkbere.com

Owls Retreat ★★★
Contact: Milkbere Holidays, 3 Fore Street, Seaton EX12 2LE
T: (01297) 20729
F: (01297) 22925
E: info@milkberehols.com
I: www.milkbere.com

Primrose ★★★
Contact: Milkbere Holidays, 3 Fore Street, Seaton EX12 2LE
T: (01297) 20729
F: (01297) 22925
E: info@milkberehols.com
I: www.milkbere.com

Rosemead ★★★
Contact: Milkbere Holidays, 3 Fore Street, Seaton EX12 2LE
T: (01297) 20729
F: (01297) 22925
E: info@milkberehols.com
I: www.milkbere.com

Sarnia ★★★
Contact: Ms Louise Hayman, Milkbere Cottage Holidays Ltd, 3 Fore Street, Seaton EX12 2LE
T: (01297) 20729
F: (01297) 24831
E: info@milkberehols.com
I: www.milkbere.com

Seafield Lawn
Rating Applied For
Contact: Ms Louise Hayman, Milkbere Cottage Holidays, 3 Fore Street, Seaton EX12 2LE
T: (01297) 20729
F: (01297) 22925
E: info@milkberehols.com

10 Seafield Road ★★★★
Contact: Milkbere Holidays, 3 Fore Street, Seaton EX12 2LE
T: (01297) 20729
F: (01297) 22925
E: info@milkberehols.com
I: www.milkbere.com

1 Seafield Road Flat 2 ★★★
Contact: Milkbere Holidays, 3 Fore Street, Seaton EX12 2LE
T: (01297) 20729
F: (01297) 22925
E: info@milkbere.com
I: www.milkbere.com

Seaside Flat 3★★★
Contact: Jean Bartlett Cottage Holidays, Fore Street, Beer, Seaton EX12 3JB
T: (01297) 23221
F: (01297) 23303
E: holidays@jeanbartlett.com
I: www.netbreaks.com/jeanb

Shalom ★★★
Contact: Milkbere Holidays, 3 Fore Street, Seaton EX12 2LE
T: (01297) 20729
F: (01297) 22925
E: info@milkbere.com
I: www.milkbere.com

Soo Soo San ★★★
Contact: Milkbere Holidays, 3 Fore Street, Seaton EX12 2LE
T: (01297) 20729
F: (01297) 22925
E: info@milkberehols.com
I: www.milkbere.com

Spindrift ★★★
Contact: Milkbere Holidays, 3 Fore Street, Seaton EX12 2LE
T: (01297) 20729
E: info@milkberehols.com

Swans Nest & Treasure Chest
Rating Applied For
Contact: Ms Louise Hayman, Milkbere Cottage Holidays, 3 Fore Street, Seaton EX12 2LE
T: (01297) 20729
F: (01297) 22925
E: info@milkberehols.com

27 West Acres ★★★
Contact: Milkbere Holidays, 3 Fore Street, Seaton EX12 2LE
T: (01297) 20729
F: (01297) 22925
E: info@milkberehols.com
I: www.milkbere.com

West Ridge Bungalow ★★★
Contact: Mrs H Fox, West Ridge Bungalow, Harepath Hill, Seaton EX12 2TA
T: (01297) 22398
F: (01297) 22398
E: foxfamily@westridge.fsbusiness.co.uk
I: www.cottageguide.co.uk/westridge

Westacres ★★★
Contact: Ms Kate Bartlett, Jean Bartlett Cottage Holidays, The Old Dairy, Fore Street, Seaton EX12 3JB
T: (01297) 23221
F: (01297) 23303
E: holidays@jeanbartlett.com
I: www.netbreaks.com/jeamb

Windrush ★★★
Contact: Ms Kate Bartlett, Jean Bartlett Cottage Holidays, Fore Street, Seaton EX12 3JB
T: (01297) 23221
F: (01297) 23303
E: holidays@jeanbartlett.com
I: www.netbreaks.com/jeanb

Yarty Cottage ★★★★
Contact: Milkbere Holidays, 3 Fore Street, Seaton EX12 2LE
T: (01297) 20729
E: info@milkberehols.com

SEATOWN
Dorset

Guard House Cottage
★★★★★
Contact: Mrs Joyce Whittaker, Seatown House, Seatown, Chideock, Bridport DT6 6JU
T: (01297) 489417
F: (01297) 489151
E: info@guardhouse.co.uk
I: www.guardhouse.co.uk

SECTOR
Devon

Brook Cottage ★★★★
Contact: Ms Kate Bartlett, Jean Bartlett Cottage Holidays, The Old Dairy, Fore Street, Seaton EX12 3JB
T: (01297) 23221
F: (01297) 23303
E: holidays@jeanbartlett.com
I: www.netbreaks.com/jeamb

Primrose Cottage ★★★★
Contact: Jean Bartlett Cottage Holidays, Fore Street, Seaton EX12 3JB
T: (01297) 23221
F: (01297) 23303
E: holidays@jeanbartlett.com
I: www.netbreaks.com/jeanb

SENNEN
Cornwall

3 & 4 Wesley Cottages ★★★
Contact: Mrs Jane Davey, Rosteague, Raginnis Farm, Mousehole, Penzance TR19 6NJ
T: (01736) 731933
F: (01736) 732344
E: wesley@raginnis.demon.co.uk
I: www.wesleyatnanquidno.co.uk

SENNEN COVE
Cornwall

Huer's Rock ★★★★
Contact: Mr Richard Puddiphatt, Albaston, Gunnislake PL18 9AL
T: (01822) 832985
E: huersrock@hotmail.com
I: www.sennen-cove.com

Jubilee Cottage ★★★
Contact: Mr J Nicholas, Harbour View, Sennen Cove, Penzance TR19 7DE
T: (01736) 871206
F: (01736) 871206
E: susannecook@supanet.com
I: www.pop3susannecook@supanet.com

Lynwood House ★★★
Contact: Mr J Nicholas, Harbour View, Sennen Cove, Penzance TR19 7DE
T: (01736) 871206
F: (01736) 871206
E: susannecook@supanet.com

The Old Success Inn
★★-★★★
Contact: Mr Martin Brookes, Sennen Cove, Sennen, Penzance TR19 7DG
T: (01736) 871232
F: (01736) 871457
E: oldsuccess@sennencove.fsbusiness.co.uk

SHALDON
Devon

Barton Cottage ★★★
Contact: Ms Susan Witt, Honeysuckle Cottage, Deane Road, Stokeinteignhead, Newton Abbot TQ12 4QF
T: (01626) 872441
E: bartoncottage@stokeinteignhead.freeserve.co.uk

Coombe Close Holidays ★★★
Contact: Mr M & Mrs P Huff, Coombe Close Holidays, Coombe Close, Brim Hill, Maidencombe, Torquay TQ1 4TR
T: (01803) 327215
F: (01803) 327215
E: peterhuff@onetel.net.uk
I: www.shines.net/maidencombe

Longmeadow Farm ★★-★★★
Contact: Mrs A Mann, Longmeadow Farm, Coombe Road, Ringmore, Shaldon, Teignmouth TQ14 0EX

SHEEPSTOR
Devon

Burrator House
★★★-★★★★★
Contact: Ms Sarah Bridger, Biznot Ltd, Burrator House, Sheepstor, Yelverton, Yelverton PL20 6PF
T: (01822) 855669
E: sarah.bridger@btopenworld.com
I: www.burratorhouse.com

SHEEPWASH
Devon

Swardicott Farm ★★★
Contact: Mrs M Purser, Swardicott Farm, Sheepwash, Beaworthy EX21 5PB
T: (01409) 231633
F: (01409) 231361
E: mpurser@btinternet.com
I: www.holidaycottages-devon.co.uk

SHEPTON MALLET
Somerset

Knowle Farm Cottages Ltd
★★★
Contact: Ms Helen Trotman, Knowle Farm Cottages, West Compton, Shepton Mallet BA4 4PD
T: (01749) 890482
F: (01749) 890405
E: helen@knowle-farm-cottages.co.uk
I: www.knowle-farm-cottages.co.uk

Leigh Holt ★★★★
Contact: Mrs Pamela Hoddinott, Burnt House Farm, Waterlip, West Cranmore, Shepton Mallet BA4 4RN
T: (01749) 880280
F: (01749) 880004

SHERBORNE
Dorset

1 & 2 Trill Cottages ★★★
Contact: Mrs Warr, 1 & 2 Trill Cottages, Trill House, Thornford, Yetminster, Sherborne DT9 6HF
T: (01935) 872305
E: trill.cottages@ic24.net

Blackberry Cottage ★★★
Contact: Mr John Michael Farr, 17 Marsh Lane, Yeovil BA21 3BX
T: (01935) 423148

Grange Farm ★★★★
Contact: Mrs K Flannery, Grange Farm, Oborne, Sherborne DT9 4LA
T: (01935) 812793
F: (01935) 432765
I: www.hideaways.co.uk

Millers Loft ★★★
Contact: Mrs Bridget Buckland, Millers Loft, The Mill, Goathill, Sherborne DT9 5JD
T: (01963) 250380
E: bandebuckland@aol.com

Old Orchard Cottage ★★★★
Contact: Mrs Alexa Buckland, Old Orchard Cottage, Goathill Farm, Goathill, Sherborne DT9 5JD
T: (01963) 251365
F: (01963) 251365

Stable Cottage ★★★
Contact: Mrs R E Dimond, Stable Cottage, Bridleways, Oborne Road, Sherborne DT9 3RX
T: (01935) 814716
F: (01935) 814716
E: bridleways@tiscali.co.uk

SHERFORD
Devon

Keynedon Barton ★★★★
Contact: Mrs Angela Heath, Keynedon Barton, Sherford, Kingsbridge TQ7 2AS
T: (01548) 531273
I: www.keynedon.fsnet.co.uk

Valley Springs Cottages
★★★★★
Contact: Ms Lynne Bentley, Valley Springs Cottages, The Spinney, Sherford, Kingsbridge TQ7 2DR
T: (01548) 856005
F: (01548) 856005
E: valleyspringscottages@btopenworld.com
I: www.valley-springs.com

SHERRINGTON
Wiltshire

Gingerbread Cottage ★★★★
Contact: Mrs Gabrielle Lewis, Gingerbread Cottage, Sheepfold Cottage, Sherrington, Warminster BA12 0SN
T: (01985) 850453
F: (01985) 850453
E: patlewis@lineone.net
I: www.gingerbreadcottage.co.uk

SHERSTON
Wiltshire

May Cottage ★★★★
Contact: Mrs S M Bristow, Mill Cottage, Thompsons Hill, Sherston, Malmesbury SN16 0PZ
T: (01666) 840655

SHIPTON GORGE
Dorset

Dolphins ★★★★
Contact: Mrs Jan Sorrell, 6 Rosamond Avenue, Shipton Gorge, Bridport DT6 4LN
T: (01308) 897277

Masons Cottage
Rating Applied For
Contact: Dream Cottages, 41 Maiden Street, Weymouth DT4 8AZ
T: (01305) 761347
E: admin@dream-cottages.co.uk

SHREWTON
Wiltshire

The Cottage ★★★★
Contact: Mrs Joan Robathan, Maddington House, Maddington Street, Shrewton, Salisbury SP3 4JD
T: (01980) 620406
F: (01980) 620406
E: rsrobathan@freenet.co.uk

Drovers' Barn ★★★★
Contact: Chapel House, Luke Street, Berwick St John, Shaftesbury SP7 0HQ
T: (01747) 828170
F: (01747) 829090
E: enq@hideaways.co.uk

SHUTE
Devon

Higher Watchcombe Farmhouse & Country Cottages★★★★
Contact: Mr & Mrs Paul & Jane Galloway, Higher Watchcombe Farmhouse & Country Cottages, Shute, Axminster EX13 7QN
T: (01297) 552424
F: (01297) 552424
E: galloways@ukgateway.net
I: www.higherwatchcombe.com

SIDFORD
Devon

6 Axe Vale ★★★
Contact: Jean Bartlett Cottage Holidays, Fore Street, Beer, Seaton EX12 3JB
T: (01297) 23221

Porch Cottage ★★★
Contact: Jean Bartlett Cottage Holidays, Fore Street, Beer, Seaton EX12 3JB
T: (01297) 23221

SIDMOUTH
Devon

Bayview ★★★
Contact: Mrs Rosemary Sidwell, Little Mead, Beatlands Road, Sidmouth EX10 8JH
T: (01395) 515668

Boswell Farm Cottages ★★★★
Contact: Mr & Mrs B P Dillon, Boswell Farm Holiday Cottages, Boswell Farm, Sidford, Sidmouth EX10 0PP
T: (01395) 514162
F: (01395) 514162
E: dillon@boswell-farm.co.uk
I: www.boswell-farm.co.uk

Cherry Tree Cottage ★★★
Contact: Mrs Rosemary Sidwell, Little Mead, Beatlands Road, Sidmouth EX10 8JH
T: (01395) 515668

Cliffe Cottage ★★★★
Contact: Jean Bartlett Cottage Holidays, Fore Street, Beer, Seaton EX12 3JB
T: (01297) 23221
F: (01297) 23303
E: holidays@jeanbartlett.com
I: www.netbreaks.com/jeanb

Clovelly ★★★
Contact: Jean Bartlett Cottage Holidays, Fore Street, Beer, Seaton EX12 3JB
T: (01297) 23221
F: (01297) 23303
E: holidays@jeanbartlett.com
I: www.netbreaks.com/jeanb

Farthings ★★
Contact: Ms Kate Bartlett, Jean Bartlett Cottage Holidays, The Old Dairy, Fore Street, Beer, Seaton EX12 3JB
T: (01297) 23221
F: (01297) 23303
E: holidays@jeanbartlett.com
I: www.netbreaks.com/jeamb

Flat 1, Fortfield Chambers ★★★
Contact: Mrs Parry, Sheko, Southway, Sidmouth EX10 8JL
T: (01395) 516150
F: (01395) 512775
E: parry@sheko.freeserve.co.uk

Flat 3, Fortfield Chambers ★★★★
Contact: Mrs Sylvia Brownlee, Flat 3, 5 Alexandria Road, Sidmouth EX10 9HD
T: (01395) 577993
F: (01395) 577993
E: brownlee@clara.co.uk
I: www.fortfieldchambers.com

Higher Thorn Barn ★★★★
Contact: Mrs Margaret Evans, Higher Thorn Cottage, Trow, Sidmouth EX10 0PA
T: (01395) 513813

Leigh Farm ★★★★
Contact: Mr & Mrs Geoff & Gill Davis, Leigh Farm, Weston, Sidmouth EX10 0PH
T: (01395) 516065
F: (01395) 579582
E: leigh.farm@virgin.net
I: www.streets-ahead.com/leighfarm

Riverside Cottage ★★★
Contact: Jean Bartlett Cottage Holidays, Fore Street, Beer, Seaton EX12 3JB
T: (01297) 23221
F: (01297) 23303
E: holidays@jeanbartlett.com
I: www.netbreaks.com/jeanb

SIMONSBATH
Somerset

Wintershead Farm ★★★★
Contact: Mrs J Styles, Wintershead Farm, Simonsbath, Minehead TA24 7LF
T: (01643) 831222
I: www.wintershead.co.uk

SITHNEY
Cornwall

Tregathenan Country Cottages ★★★-★★★★
Contact: Liz Fairweather & Ian Paterson, Tregathenan Country Cottages, Old Farmhouse, Tregathenen, Sithney, Helston TR13 0RZ
T: (01326) 569840
F: (01326) 572852
E: tregathenan@heatline.demon.co.uk

SLAPTON
Devon

Dittiscombe Holiday Cottages ★★★-★★★★
Contact: Mrs Ruth Saunders, Dittiscombe, Slapton, Kingsbridge TQ7 2QF
T: (01548) 521272
F: (01548) 521425
E: dittiscombe@lineone.net
I: www.dittiscombe.co.uk

Meadow Court Barn ★★★★
Contact: Toad Hall Cottages, Elliot House, Church Street, Kingsbridge TQ7 1BY
T: (01548) 853089
F: (01548) 853086
E: thc@toadhallcottages.com

SLAUGHTERFORD
Wiltshire

Carters Cottage ★★★
Contact: Mrs Janet Jones, Carters Cottage, Slaughterford, Chippenham SN14 8RE
T: (01249) 782243
F: (01249) 782243
E: hanfreeth@hotmail.com

SOMERTON
Somerset

Sleepy Hollow ★★★★
Contact: Mr & Mrs P Raine, Sleepy Hollow, Double Gates Drove, Mill Road, Barton St David, Somerton TA11 6DF
T: (01458) 850584
F: (01458) 850584
E: paul&rhian@sleepyhollowcottages.com
I: www.sleepyhollowcottages.com

SOUTH BRENT
Devon

Hillview
Rating Applied For
Contact: Brook Cottage,Old Warleigh Lane, Tamerton Foliot, Plymouth PL5 4ND
T: (01752) 774900

SOUTH BREWHAM
Somerset

Magpie Cottage & Jackdaw Cottage ★★★★
Contact: Mr David Dabinett, Haven Farm, South Brewham, Bruton BA10 0JZ
T: (01749) 850441
E: david@havenfarm.co.uk

SOUTH MILTON
Devon

Nancy's Cottage ★★★
Contact: Mrs R J Jones, 139 Franche Road, Kidderminster DY11 5AP
T: (01562) 66930

Savernake ★★★★
Contact: Mrs Nicola Godfrey, Torr View, Woodleigh, East Allington, Totnes TQ7 4DG
T: (01548) 559192

SOUTH MOLTON
Devon

Drewstone Farm ★★★★
Contact: Mrs Ruth Ley, Drewstone Farm, Twitchen, South Molton EX36 3EF
T: (01769) 572337
F: (01769) 572337
E: Ruth_ley@drewstonefarm.fsnet.co.uk
I: www.devonself-catering.co.uk

Great Whitstone Farm ★★★
Contact: Mrs Sally Meikle, Great Whitstone Farm, Meshaw, South Molton EX36 4NH
T: (01884) 860914

North Lee Farm Holiday Cottages ★★★★
Contact: Miss Rebecca Evans, North Lee Farm Holiday Cottages, Hacche Lane, Twitchen, South Molton EX36 3EH
T: (01598) 740248
F: (01598) 740248
E: beck@northlee.com
I: www.northleeholidaycottages.co.uk

The Willows ★★★
Contact: Marsden's Cottage Holidays, 2 The Square, Braunton EX33 2JB
T: (01271) 813777
F: (01271) 813664
E: holidays@marsdens.co.uk
I: www.marsdens.co.uk

SOUTH PETHERTON
Somerset

Tanwyn ★★★★
Contact: Mr & Mrs Rodney & Ann Tanswell, St Brides Major, Bossington, Minehead CF32 0SB
T: (01656) 880524
F: (01656) 880524
E: rodney.tanswell@btinternet.com

SPRYTOWN
Devon

Herb Cottage ★★★
Contact: Mrs J Earle, Bottom Cottage, Portgate, Lewdown, Sprytown, Lifton EX20 4PY
T: (01566) 783386

STAPLEGROVE
Somerset

The Barn ★★★★
Contact: Mrs Anita & Tom Harris, Higher Yarde Farmhouse, Staplegrove, Taunton TA2 6SW
T: (01823) 451553
E: anitaharris24@hotmail.com

STARCROSS
Devon

Aster House ★★★★
Contact: Holiday Homes & Cottages South West, 365A Torquay Road, Paignton TQ3 2BT
T: (01803) 663650
F: (01803) 664037
E: holcotts@aol.com
I: www.swcottages.co.uk

Autumn Cottage ★★★
Contact: Mr Ian Butterworth, Holiday Homes & Cottages South West, 365A Torquay Road, Paignton TQ3 2BT
T: (01803) 663650
F: (01803) 664037
E: holcotts@aol.com
I: www.swcottages.co.uk

Marina ★★★★
Contact: Holiday Homes & Cottages South West, 365A Torquay Road, Paignton TQ3 2BT
T: (01803) 663650
F: (01803) 664037
E: holcotts@aol.com
I: www.swcottages.co.uk

STATHE
Somerset

Walkers Farm Cottages
★★★★
Contact: Mr & Mrs William & Dianne Tiley, Walkers Farm Cottages, Walkers Farm, Stathe, Bridgwater TA7 0JL
T: (01823) 698229
F: (01823) 698063
E: booking@walkersfarmcottages.co.uk

STAVERTON
Devon

The Kingston Estate ★★★★
Contact: Mr Mark Stevens, Kingston House, Staverton, Totnes TQ9 6AR
T: (01803) 762235
F: (01803) 762444
E: info@kingston-estate.net
I: www.kingston-estate.net

STEEPLE ASHTON
Wiltshire

Elwyns Cottage ★★★★
Contact: Ref: E2484, Hoseasons Country Cottages, Raglan Road, Lowestoft NR32 2LW
T: 0870 5 342342
F: 0870 9 022090
I: www.hoseasons.co.uk/images/2002/ukcottages/cottages/aa99.html

Jasmine Cottage ★★★★
Contact: Mr Sharples, 4 St Margarets, Sutton Coldfield B74 4HU
T: (0121) 353 5258
E: stay@jasminecottage.info
I: www.jasminecottage.co.uk

STIBB
Cornwall

Claires Cottage ★★★
Contact: Mr & Mrs Roger & Brenda Dunstan, Claires Cottage, Strands, Stibb, Bude EX23 9HW
T: (01288) 353514

STITHIANS
Cornwall

Charis Cottage ★★★★
Contact: Mr A Drees & Ms T Schneider, Treweege, Trewithen Moor, Stithians, Truro TR3 7DU
T: (01209) 861003
E: astondrees@hotmail.com
I: www.chariscottage.co.uk

The Dhorlin ★★★★
Contact: Mrs Margaret Richards, Davaar, Vellandrucia, Stithians, Truro TR3 7AA
T: (01209) 860640
E: enquiries@thedhorlin.co.uk
I: www.thedhorlin.co.uk

Higher Trewithen ★★★
Contact: Mr Neil Pardoe, Higher Trewithen, Stithians, Truro TR3 7DR
T: (01209) 860863
F: (01209) 860785
E: trewithen@talk21.com
I: www.trewithen.com

STOGUMBER
Somerset

Periwinkle Cottage ★★★★
Contact: Miss Sheila Hubbard, Puzzle Tree, Wootton Courtenay, Minehead TA24 8RD
T: (01643) 841413
F: (01643) 841413

STOKE ABBOTT
Dorset

Canterburys Cottage ★★★
Contact: Mr Zachary Stuart-Brown, Dream Cottages, 41 Maiden Street, Weymouth DT4 8AZ
T: (01305) 761347
E: admin@dream-cottages.co.uk
I: www.dream-cottages.co.uk

Fossil Cottage ★★★
Contact: Mr J L Roberts, Chartknolle, Stoke Abbott, Beaminster DT8 3JN
T: (01306) 862220
F: (01306) 863989
E: john@jlro.demon.co.uk

Rectory Cottage ★★★
Contact: Mr Thomas Harmsworth, The Old Rectory, Stoke Abbott, Beaminster DT8 3JT
T: (01308) 868118

STOKE CANON
Devon

Bussells Farm Cottages
★★★★
Contact: Mr Andrew Hines, Bussells Farm, Huxham, Exeter EX5 4EN
T: (01392) 841238
F: (01392) 841345
E: hinesandrew@netscape.net
I: www.bussellsfarm.co.uk

STOKE GABRIEL
Devon

The Boathouse ★★★★★
Contact: Mr W Christopher, c/o 69 Seymouth Road, Newton Abbot TQ12 2PX
T: (01626) 366592
F: (01626) 334490
E: info@ula.com
I: www.ula.com

Jesters ★★★★
Contact: Holiday Homes & Cottages South West, 365A Torquay Road, Paignton TQ3 2BT
T: (01803) 663650
F: (01803) 664037
E: holcotts@aol.com
I: www.swcottages.co.uk

Thatch Cottage ★★★★★
Contact: Ms Anita Chisolm, Belsford Farmhouse, Harberton, Totnes TQ9 7SP
T: (01803) 863341
F: (01803) 840208
E: anita@smoothtransition.freeserve.co.uk

STOKE ST GREGORY
Somerset

Baileys Gallery ★★★
Contact: Mr Chedzoy, Fairholme, Stoke St Gregory, Taunton TA3 6JQ
T: (01823) 490644

Holly Farm ★★★★
Contact: Mr R & Mrs E Hembrow & Smith, Holly Cottage, Stoke St Gregory, Taunton TA3 6HS
T: (01823) 490828
F: (01823) 490590
E: robhembrow@btinternet.com
I: www.somerset-farm-holiday.co.uk

Lovells Farm ★★★
Contact: Mr & Ms Oppenlander/Bolton, Lovells Cottage, Dark Lane, Stoke St Gregory, Taunton TA3 6EU
T: (01823) 491437
F: (01823) 491433
E: sabine@somersetholidays.com
I: www.somersetholidays.com

STOKE ST MARY
Somerset

Centra ★★★★
Contact: Mrs Karen Freir, Centra, Stoke St Mary, Taunton TA3 5BS
T: (01823) 442443
E: info@centra-uk.com

Stoke Hill Studio ★★-★★★★
Contact: Mr Alan Coles, Stoke St Mary, Henlade, Taunton TA3 5BT
T: (01823) 443759
F: (01823) 443759
E: ajcoles@supanet.com

STOKE ST MICHAEL
Bath and North East Somerset

Pitcot Farm Barn Cottages
★★★★
Contact: Mrs Mary Coles, Pitcot Farm Barn Cottages, Pitcot Lane, Stratton-on-the-Fosse, Radstock BA3 4SX
T: (01761) 233108
F: (01761) 417710

STOKE SUB HAMDON
Somerset

Blackspur Cottage
Rating Applied For
Contact: Mr & Mrs John Fisher, Brook House, Little Street, Norton sub Hamdon, Stoke sub Hamdon TA14 6SR
T: (01935) 881789
F: (01935) 881789

East Stoke House ★★★★★
Contact: Mrs M A Shuldham, East Stoke House, Stoke sub Hamdon TA14 6UF
T: (01935) 823558
F: (01935) 824596

Fairhaven ★★★★
Contact: Mrs Magaret Wilson, Fairhaven, Montacute Road, East Stoke, Montacute TA14 6UQ
T: (01935) 823534
E: frank@fairhaven70.freeserve.co.uk

One Fair Place ★★★★
Contact: Mrs A A Wright, Holly Lodge, 39 The Avenue, Crowthorne RG45 6PB
T: (01344) 772461
F: (01344) 778389
E: aawright@btopenworld.com
I: www.somersetcottageholidays.co.uk

Top o Hill ★★★
Contact: Mrs Mary Gane, Top o Hill, Percombe, Stoke sub Hamdon TA14 6RD
T: (01935) 822089

STOKEINTEIGNHEAD
Devon

Church Barn Cottage ★★★★
Contact: Mr & Mrs Rees, Congdon Farm Cottages, Stokeinteignhead, Newton Abbot TQ12 4QA
T: (01626) 872433

Dean Cottage ★★★★
Contact: Holiday Homes & Cottages South West, 365a Torquay Road, Paignton TQ3 2BT
T: (01803) 663650
F: (01803) 664037
E: holcotts@aol.com
I: www.swcottages.co.uk

The Granary ★★★
Contact: Holiday Homes & Cottages South West, 365A Torquay Road, Paignton TQ3 2BT
T: (01803) 663650

STONEY STRATTON
Somerset

Red Tiles ★★★★
Contact: Mr Richard Neill, The Vicarage, Winkfield Street, Winkfield, Windsor SL4 4SW
T: (01344) 882322
E: neill.hall@care4free.net

Springfield Cottages
★★★-★★★★
Contact: Mrs Pat Allen, Springfield Cottages, Hill Springfield House, Maesdown, Evercreech, Shepton Mallet BA4 6EG
T: (01749) 830748
E: ted.allen@btinternet.com

STRATFORD SUB CASTLE
Wiltshire

Manor Cottage H107 ★★★★
Contact: Hideaways, Chapel House, Luke Street, Berwick St John, Shaftesbury SP7 0HQ
T: (01747) 828170
F: (01747) 829090
E: enq@hideaways.co.uk

Millers Barn ★★★
Contact: Mr Nicholas Pash, Chapel House, Luke Street, Berwick St John, Shaftesbury SP7 0HQ
T: (01747) 828170
F: (01747) 829090
E: enq@hideaways.co.uk
I: www.hideaways.co.uk

STRATTON
Cornwall

3 Crawford Cottages ★★★
Contact: Mr S Munday, Oketon, 11 Flexbury Park Road, Bude EX23 8HR
T: (01288) 359358

The Granary ★★★
Contact: Mrs Deborah Chivers, Marsh Farm Cottage, Howard Lane, Stratton, Bude EX23 9TE
T: (01288) 355503
F: (01288) 355503
E: ncsigns@ncsigns.co.uk
I: www.cottagesdirect.com/coa197

Ivyleaf Combe ★★★★
Contact: Mr Cheeseman, Ivyleaf Combe, Ivyleaf Hill, Stratton, Bude EX23 9LD
T: (01288) 321323
F: (01288) 321323
E: tony@ivyleafcombe.com
I: www.ivyleafcombe.com

Kitts Cottage ★★★
Contact: Farm & Cottage Holidays, Victoria House, 12 Fore Street, Westward Ho!, Bideford EX39 1AW
T: (01237) 479146
F: (01237) 421512
E: enquiries@farmcott.co.uk

No. 2 Bideford Mews
Rating Applied For
Contact: Mr Neil Harrold, Greensleeves, Heathton, Claverley, Wolverhampton WV5 7EB
T: (01746) 710147

Old Sanctuary Cottages ★★★★
Contact: Mrs Jane Berry, Diddies Road, Stratton, Bude EX23 9DW
T: (01288) 353159
F: (01288) 353159
E: kj.berry@virgin.net
I: www.freespace.virgin.net/kj.berry

Ronjon ★★★
Contact: CH Ref: 11610,15102, Holiday Cottages Group Owner Services Dept, Spring Mill, Earby, Barnoldswick BB94 0AA
T: 08700 723723
F: (01282) 844288
E: sales@ttgihg.co.uk
I: www.country-holidays.co.uk

The Tithe Barn ★★★
Contact: Mrs J. M. Walker, Falcon Mews, Vicarage Road, Bude EX23 8LN
T: (01288) 355148
E: jan-walker@freeuk.com

Tree Hill House ★★★
Contact: Mrs Christine Heybourn, 9 Frances Road, Windsor SL4 3AE
T: (01753) 852512
F: (01753) 852512
E: robert@heybourn.freeserve.co.uk

STREET
Somerset

Blue Lias ★★★
Contact: Mr Mark Foot, 8 Kingston Drive, Nailsea, Bristol BS48 4RB
T: (01275) 853612
F: (01275) 544936

STRETE
Devon

Garden Cottage ★★★
Contact: Mr & Mrs Michael Toms, Cobbolds House, Strete, Dartmouth TQ6 0RH
T: (01803) 770132
E: michaeltoms@onetel.com

Sunsets ★★★★
Contact: Powells Cottage Holidays, Springmill, Earby, Freystrop, Haverfordwest BB94 0AA
T: 08705 143076
F: (01834) 811731
E: info@powells.co.uk
I: www.powells.co.uk

SUTTON POYNTZ
Dorset

Magnolia Cottage ★★★
Contact: Mr Zachary Stuart-Brown, Dream Cottages, 41 Maiden Street, Weymouth DT4 8AZ
T: (01305) 761347
E: admin@dream-cottages.co.uk
I: www.dream-cottages.co.uk

SWANPOOL
Cornwall

Mobri ★★★★★
Contact: Mrs Broughton, Mobri, 1B Madeira Walk, Newlyn, Penzance TR11 4EJ
T: (01326) 314348

SWIMBRIDGE
Devon

Lane End ★★★
Contact: Marsden's Cottage Holidays, 2 The Square, Braunton EX33 2JB
T: (01271) 813777
F: (01271) 813664
E: holidays@marsdens.co.uk
I: www.marsdens.co.uk

SWINDON
Wiltshire

The Cottage ★★★★
Contact: Mrs Judith Stares, The Cottage, 101 Bath Road, Swindon SN1 4AX
T: (01793) 485461
F: (01793) 485462
E: judith@stares.co.uk
I: www.stares.co.uk

Southleigh Farm ★★★
Contact: Mrs M Gash, Mirwil, 4 Old Farm Close, Hanherton, Malmesbury SN16 9LR
T: (01666) 575135

SYDLING ST NICHOLAS
Dorset

Grace Cottage ★★★
Contact: Mrs Nicky Willis, Dorchester Road, Sydling St Nicholas, Dorchester DT2 9NU
T: (01300) 341659
F: (01300) 341699
E: nickywillis@tesco.net

Swain Cottage ★★★
Contact: Mrs Bryant, 9 Dorchester Road, Dorchester DT2 9NU
T: (01300) 341382

SYMONDSBURY
Dorset

Bathsheba ★★★★
Contact: Mrs Shelagh Mullins, Bathsheba, 1 Shutes Farm Cottage, Symondsbury, Bridport DT6 6HF
T: (01308) 425261
F: (01308) 425261
E: shelaghmullins@aol.com
I: www.shelaghsbathsheba.co.uk

Crepe Farmhouse
Rating Applied For
Contact: Ms Catherine Chick, The Estate Office, Symondsbury, Bridport DT6 6EX
T: 07940 839868
E: philip@holcot.com

TALATON
Devon

Westcot House Farm ★★★
Contact: Miss Melanie Peters, Westcot House Farm, Talaton, Exeter EX5 2RN
T: (01404) 822320
F: (01404) 823847
E: m.peters@farming.co.uk

TAUNTON
Somerset

Masons Arms ★★
Contact: Mr Jeremy Leyton, Masons Arms, Magdalene Street, Taunton TA1 1SG
T: (01823) 288916
E: jjmax@jleyton.freeserve.co.uk
I: www.masonsarms.freeuk

Meadowsweet Cottages ★★★★
Contact: Mrs Sue Wilson, Meadowsweet Cottages, Meadowsweet Farm, Newton, Bicknoller, Taunton TA4 4EU
T: (01984) 656323
F: (01984) 656933
E: info@meadowsweet-cottages.co.uk
I: www.meadowsweet-cottages.co.uk

Meare Court Holiday Cottages ★★★-★★★★★
Contact: Mrs E J Bray, Meare Court Holiday Cottages, Meare Court, Wrantage, Taunton TA3 6DA
T: (01823) 480570
F: 0870 167 3067
E: mearecourt@farming.co.uk
I: www.mearecourt.co.uk

TAVISTOCK
Devon

Acorn Cottage Cedar Lodge ★★★
Contact: Mr & Mrs Ashe, Acorn Cottage, Heathfield, Tavistock PL19 0LQ
T: (01822) 810038
I: www.fsmail.net

Downhouse Farm ★★★★
Contact: Ms Sarah Heaps, Downhouse Farm, Mill Hill Lane, Tavistock PL19 8NH
T: (01822) 614521
F: (01822) 613675
E: downhousefarm@aol.com
I: www.downhousefarm.co.uk

Edgemoor Cottage ★★★★
Contact: Mrs Mary Susan Fox, Edgemoor, Middlemoor, Tavistock PL19 9DY
T: (01822) 612259
F: (01822) 617625
E: Foxes@dartmoorcottages.info

Higher Chaddlehanger Farm ★★★
Contact: Mrs R Cole, Higher Chaddlehanger Farm, Tavistock PL19 0LG
T: (01822) 810268
F: (01822) 810268

Old Sowtontown ★★★
Contact: Mr Christopher Boswell, Old Sowtontown, Peter Tavy, Tavistock PL19 9JR
T: (01822) 810687
F: (01822) 810687
E: chrisboswe@aol.com
I: www.dartmoorholidays.co.uk

Tavistock Trout Fishery ★★★★
Contact: Miss A Underhill, Tavistock Trout Fishery, Parkwood Road, Tavistock PL19 9JW
T: (01822) 615441
F: (01822) 615401
E: abigail@tavistocktroutfishery.co.uk
I: www.tavistocktroutfishery.co.uk

TEIGNGRACE
Devon

Twelve Oaks Holiday Cottages ★★★
Contact: Mrs M A Gale, Twelve Oaks Holiday Cottages, Twelve Oaks Farm, Teigngrace, Newton Abbot TQ12 6QT
T: (01626) 352769
F: (01626) 352769

TEIGNMOUTH
Devon

Grendons Holiday Apartments ★★★
Contact: Mr Charles Gray, Grendons Holiday Apartments, 58 Coombe Vale Road, Teignmouth TQ14 9EW
T: (01626) 773667
F: (01626) 773667
E: grendonsholidayapts@cix.co.uk

Higher Venn Cottage ★★★
Contact: The Proprietor, Higher Venn Cottage, Venn Farm Lane, Teignmouth TQ14
T: (01626) 779679

The Old Post office
Rating Applied For
Contact: Holiday Homes & Cottages SW, 365a Torquay Road, Paignton TQ3 2BT
T: (01803) 663650
F: (01803) 664037
E: holcotts@aol.com

TELLISFORD
Somerset

Farleigh Wood ★★★★
Contact: Ms Bella Gingell, Farleigh Wood, Wood Cottage, Tellisford, Bath BA2 7RN
T: (01373) 831495
F: (01373) 830289
E: bellagingell@farleighwood.fsnet.co.uk

THE LIZARD
Cornwall

Dene House ★★★
Contact: Mr Martin Raftery, Churchtown, Mullion, Helston TR12 7HQ
T: (01326) 240315
F: (01326) 241090
E: martin@mullioncottages.com
I: www.mullioncottages.com

The Haven ★★★
Contact: Mr Martin Raftery, Churchtown, Mullion, Helston TR12 7HQ
T: (01326) 240315
F: (01326) 241090
E: martin@mullioncottages.com
I: www.mullioncottages.com

The Roundhouse ★★★★
Contact: Mr Martin Raftery, Churchtown, Mullion, Helston TR12 7HQ
T: (01326) 240315
F: (01326) 241090
E: martin@mullioncottages.com
I: www.mullioncottages.com

Sunny Corner ★★
Contact: Mr Martin Raftery, Churchtown, Mullion, Helston TR12 7HQ
T: (01326) 240315
F: (01326) 241090
E: martin@mullioncottages.com
I: www.mullioncottages.com

THORNBURY
Devon

Dairy Cottage & Beech Barn ★★★★
Contact: Farm & Cottage Holidays, Victoria House, 12 Fore Street, Westward Ho!, Bideford EX39 1AW
T: (01237) 479146
F: (01237) 421512
E: enquiries@farmcott.co.uk

THORNCOMBE
Dorset

Thatch Cottage ★★★★★
Contact: Mr John Mercer, 53 Heatherside Road, West Ewell, Epsom KT19 9QS
T: (0208) 393 8165
E: eileenjmercer@hotmail.com

THORVERTON
Devon

Fursdon Estate ★★★★
Contact: Mrs Catriona Fursdon, Fursdon Estate, Fursdon House, Cadbury, Thorverton, Exeter EX5 5JS
T: (01392) 860860
F: (01392) 860126
E: enquiries@fursdon.co.uk
I: www.fursdon.co.uk

Heathfield Barn ★★★★
Contact: Mr & Mrs Reuy & Mary Jehu, Heathfield Barn, Thorverton, Exeter EX5 5JP
T: (01392) 841941
F: (01392) 841438
E: 506003@eclipse.co.uk
I: www.heathfieldfarm.net

Ratcliffe Farm ★★★
Contact: Mr M & Mrs T Ayre, Ratcliffe Farm, Thorverton, Exeter EX5 5PN
T: (01392) 860434
E: ayre.ratcliffe@virgin.net

THROWLEIGH
Devon

Sue's House & The Cottage ★★-★★★
Contact: Mrs Joan White, Sue's House & The Cottage, Aysh Farm, Throwleigh, Okehampton EX20 2HY
T: (01647) 231266

THURLESTONE
Devon

April Cottage ★★★★
Contact: Toad Hall Cottages, Elliot House, Church Street, Kingsbridge TQ7 1BY
T: (01548) 853089
F: (01548) 853086
E: thc@toadhallcottages.com

Stable Cottage ★★★★★
Contact: Elliot House, Church Street, Kingsbridge TQ7 1BY
T: (01548) 853089
F: (01548) 853086
E: thc@toadhallcottages.com

TINCLETON
Dorset

The Old Dairy Cottage & Clyffe Dairy Cottage★★★★
Contact: Mrs Rosemary Coleman, The Old Dairy Cottage & Clyffe Dairy Cottage, Clyffe Farm, Tincleton, Dorchester DT2 8QR
T: (01305) 848252
F: (01305) 848702
E: coleman.clyffe@virgin.net
I: www.heartofdorset.easynet.co.uk

TINTAGEL
Cornwall

Barras House ★★
Contact: Mr Sleep, Barras House, Castle View, Tintagel PL34 0DH
T: (01840) 770457

Clifden Farm Cottages ★★★
Contact: Mrs Margaret Nute, Clifden Farm Cottages, Halgabron, Tintagel PL34 0BD
T: (01840) 770437
E: mnute@clifdenfarm.fsnet.co.uk

Glen House ★★★★
Contact: Mrs L White, Hazeldene, Crackington Haven, Bude EX23 0JQ
T: (01840) 230024
F: (01840) 230078
E: paul.bcfc@btinternet.com
I: www.cornwall-online.co.uk/glenhouse

Halgabron Holiday Cottages ★★★
Contact: Mrs Christine Alexander, Halgabron Holiday Cottages, Halgabron, Tintagel PL34 0BD
T: (01840) 770667
F: (01840) 770900
E: holidays@halgabron.co.uk
I: www.cornwall-online.co.uk/halgabron

Penpethy Holiday Cottages ★★★
Contact: Mrs Steadman, Penpethy Holiday Cottages, Lower Penpethy Farm, Tintagel PL34 0HH
T: (01840) 213903

Rosemary ★★★
Contact: Mrs M Dyer, Rosemary, Bossiney Road, Tintagel PL34 0AH
T: (01840) 770472
F: (01840) 770472

Tregeath Cottage ★★★
Contact: Mrs E M Broad, Davina, Trevillett, Tintagel PL34 0HL
T: (01840) 770217
F: (01840) 770217

TIPTON ST JOHN
Devon

Summer Cottage ★★★★
Contact: Mrs Ashford, Rose Cottage, Frogmore Road, East Budleigh, Otterton, Budleigh Salterton EX9 7BB
T: (01395) 442442
E: enquiries@rent-a-cottage.net

TISBURY
Wiltshire

The Old Coach House ★★★
Contact: Mr Nicholas Pash, Chapel House, Luke Street, Berwick St John, Shaftesbury SP7 0HQ
T: (01747) 828170
F: (01747) 829090
E: enq@hideaways.co.uk
I: www.hideaways.co.uk

TIVERTON
Devon

Cider Cottage ★★★★
Contact: Mrs Sylvia Hann, Cider Cottage, Great Bradley Farm, Withleigh, Tiverton EX16 8JL
T: (01884) 256946
F: (01884) 256946
E: hann@agriplus.net
I: www.devonfarms.co.uk

Coombe Cottage ★★★★
Contact: Mrs Mary Reed, Oakford, Tiverton EX16 9HF
T: (01398) 351281
F: (01398) 351211
E: coombehse@aol.com
I: www.exmoor-holiday-cottage.co.uk

Lilac Cottage ★★★★
Contact: Mrs Venner, Lilac Cottage, Battens Farm, Sampford Peverell, Tiverton EX16 7EE
T: (01884) 820226
I: www.cottageguide.co.uk/battensfarm

Tiverton Castle ★★★★
Contact: Mrs Alison Gordon, Tiverton Castle, Park Hill, Tiverton EX16 6RP
T: (01884) 253200
F: (01884) 254200
E: tiverton.castle@ukf.net
I: www.tivertoncastle.com

TIVINGTON
Somerset

Tethinstone Cottage ★★★★
Contact: Mr N G Challis, Tethinstone Cottage, Tivington, Minehead TA24 8SX
T: (01643) 706757
F: (01643) 706757

TOLLER PORCORUM
Dorset

11 High Street ★★★
Contact: Mrs Dot Thornton, 2 The George Yard, Broad Street, Alresford SO24 9EF
T: (01962) 732700
E: dot.thornton@virgin.net

TOLPUDDLE
Dorset

Cob Cottage ★★★★★
Contact: Miss Hilary Cobban, The Old Mill, Tolpuddle, Dorchester DT2 7EX
T: (01305) 848552
F: (01305) 848552
E: hlcobban@lineone.net

TOPSHAM
Devon

The Galley Restaurant with Cabins
Rating Applied For
Contact: Mr Mark & Paul Wright & Da-Costa Greaves, The Galley Restaurant with Cabins, 41 Fore Street, Topsham, Exeter EX3 0HY
T: (01392) 876078
F: (01392) 876078
E: mark@galleyrestaurant.co.uk

TORQUAY
Devon

Abbey Mews ★★★★
Contact: Holiday Homes & Cottages South West, 365a Torquay Road, Paignton TQ3 2BT
T: (01803) 663650
F: (01803) 664037
E: holcotts@aol.com
I: www.swcottages.co.uk

Abbey View Holiday Flats ★★★
Contact: Mr C & Mrs C Foss & Blockley, Abbey View, Rathmore Road, Chelston, Torquay TQ2 6NZ
T: (01803) 293722
E: abbeyflats@tinyworld.co.uk

Alexandra Lodge ★★★
Contact: Mrs Heather Armes, Alexandra Lodge, Grafton Road, Torquay TQ1 1QJ
T: (01803) 213465
F: (01803) 390933
E: alexalodge@aol.com
I: www.alexandra-lodge.co.uk

Appletorre Flats ★★★
Contact: Mr Steve Nevitt, Appletorre Flats, 20 Vansittart Road, Torquay TQ2 5BW
T: (01803) 296430
E: appletorrehols@email.com
I: appletorreflats.co.uk

Aster House Apartments ★★-★★★
Contact: Mr Coleman, Aster House Apartments, Warren Road, Torquay TQ2 5TR
T: (01803) 292747
E: info@asterhouse.freeserve.co.uk
I: www.asterhouse.freeserve.co.uk

Atherton Holiday Flats ★★
Contact: Mrs B K Kaye, Atherton Holiday Flats, 41 Morgan Avenue, Torquay TQ2 5RR
T: (01803) 296884

Atlantis Holiday Apartments ★★★
Contact: Mrs Pauline Roberts, Atlantis Holiday Apartments, Solsbro Road, Chelston, Torquay TQ2 6PF
T: (01803) 607929
F: (01803) 391313
E: enquiry@atlantistorquay.co.uk
I: www.atlantistorquay.co.uk

Babbacombe Downs ★★★
Contact: Mr Ian Butterworth, Holiday Homes & Cottages South West, 365A Torquay Road, Paignton TQ3 2BT
T: (01803) 663650
F: (01803) 664037
E: holcotts@aol.com
I: www.swcottages.co.uk

Barewell ★★★
Contact: Mr Ian Butterworth, Holiday Homes & Cottages South West, 365A Torquay Road, Paignton TQ3 2BT
T: (01803) 663650
F: (01803) 664037
E: holcotts@aol.com
I: www.swcottages.co.uk

Barramore Holiday Flats ★★★
Contact: Mr Trevor Ward, Barramore Holiday Flats, Solsbro Road, Chelston, Torquay TQ2 6PF
T: (01803) 607105
E: holidays@barramore.co.uk
I: www.barramore.co.uk

Bay Fort Mansions ★★★★
Contact: Mr & Miss Paul & Maria Freeman & Young, Bay Fort Mansions, Warren Road, Torquay, Torquay TQ2 5TN
T: (01803) 213810
F: (01803) 209057
E: freeman@bayfortapartments.co.uk
I: www.bayfortapartments.co.uk

Bedford House ★★-★★★
Contact: Mrs E J MacDonald-Smith
T: (01803) 296995
F: (01803) 296995
E: bedfordhotorquay@btconnect.com
I: www.bedfordhousetorquay.co.uk

The Beulah Holiday Apartments ★★-★★★
Contact: Mr & Mrs David & Caroline Perry, The Beulah Holiday Apartments, Meadfoot Road, Torquay TQ1 2JP
T: (01803) 297471
E: enquiries@thebeulah.co.uk
I: www.thebeulah.co.uk

Bronshill Court Holiday Apartments ★★★
Contact: Mr & Mrs Tony & Glenys Burden, Bronshill Court Holiday Apartments, Bronshill Road, St Marychurch, Torquay TQ1 3HD
T: (01803) 324549
F: (01803) 324549
E: holidays@bronshillcourt.co.uk
I: www.bronshillcourt.co.uk

Brunel ★★★★
Contact: Holiday Homes & Cottages South West, 365A Torquay Road, Paignton TQ3 2BT
T: (01803) 663650
F: (01803) 664037
E: holcotts@aol.com
I: www.swcottages.co.uk

Burley Court Apartments ★★★
Contact: Mrs B Palmer, Burley Court Apartments, Wheatridge Lane, Livermead, Torquay TQ2 6RA
T: (01803) 607879
F: (01803) 605516
E: burley.court@virgin.net
I: www.burleycourt.co.uk

Chelston Dene ★★★
Contact: Mr Rod Payne, Chelston Dene, Chelston Road, Chelston, Torquay TQ2 6PU
T: (01803) 605180
F: (01803) 605180
E: info@chelstondene.com
I: www.chelstondene.com

Chestnut Lodge Holiday Apartments ★★★
Contact: Mr George Baxter, Chestnut Lodge, Rowdens Road, Torquay TQ2 5AZ
T: (01803) 297242
E: enquiries@chestnutlodgetorquay.co.uk
I: www.chestnutlodgetorquay.co.uk

Cliff Court Holiday Apartments ★★★
Contact: Mr & Mrs Gary & Denise Tudor, Cliff Court Holiday Apartments, Cliff Road, Livermead, Chelston, Torquay TQ2 6RE
T: (01803) 294687
E: gary@cliffcourt.co.uk
I: www.cliffcourt.co.uk

Clydesdale Holiday Flats ★★★
Contact: Mr Terry Watson, 32 Croft Road, Torquay TQ2 5UE
T: (01803) 292759
I: www.clydesdaleholidayflats.co.uk

The Coach House & Butlers Flat ★★★★
Contact: Mr Ian Butterworth, Holiday Homes & Cottages South West, 365A Torquay Road, Paignton TQ3 2BT
T: (01803) 663650
F: (01803) 664037
E: holcotts@aol.com
I: www.swcottages.co.uk

The Corbyn ★★★★★
Contact: Mrs Sallie Stamp, The Corbyn, Torbay Road, Chelston, Torquay TQ2 6RH
T: (01803) 215595
F: (01803) 200568
I: www.thecorbyn.co.uk

Corbyn Lodge ★★-★★★
Contact: Holiday Homes & Cottages South West, 365A Torquay Road, Paignton TQ3 2BT
T: (01803) 663650
F: (01803) 664037
E: holcotts@aol.com
I: www.swcottages.co.uk

Cornerstone ★★★
Contact: Mr Ian Butterworth, Holiday Homes & Cottages South West, 365A Torquay Road, Paignton TQ3 2BT
T: (01803) 663650

The Cottage ★★★★
Contact: Mr & Mrs Vaughton, The Preferred Apartment Company, 21 Bishops Close, Torquay TQ1 2PL
T: (01803) 211116
F: (01803) 214023
E: info@hollington-house.com

Cranmere Court ★★★
Contact: Mrs Sally Noad, Cranmere Court Holiday Flats & Flatlets, Kents Road, Torquay TQ1 2NL
T: (01803) 293173
F: (01803) 293173

Derwent Hill Holiday Apartments ★★★
Contact: Mr & Mrs Gill & Derek Bryant, Greenway Road, Chelston, Torquay TQ2 6JE
T: (01803) 606793
F: (01803) 605793
E: info@derwent-hill.co.uk
I: www.derwent-hill.co.uk

Evergreen Lodge ★★★★
Contact: Mrs Louise Clifford, Evergreen Lodge, Ruckamore Road, Chelston, Torquay TQ2 6HF
T: (01803) 605519
F: (01803) 605519
E: evergreenlodge@dial.pipex.com
I: evergreenlodge.co.uk

Fairlawns Hall ★★-★★★
Contact: Ms Emma Hanbury, Fairlawns Hall, 27 St Michaels Road, Torquay TQ1 4DD
T: (01803) 328904
E: E.Hanbury@fairlawns.fsnet.co.uk

Florence Holiday Apartments Rating Applied For
Contact: Mr Ian J King, 39 Morgan Avenue, Torquay TQ2 5RR
T: (01803) 297264
F: (01803) 297264

Gainsborough ★★★
Contact: Holiday Homes & Cottages South West, 365A Torquay Road, Paignton TQ3 2BT
T: (01803) 663650
F: (01803) 664037
E: holcotts@aol.com
I: www.swcottages.co.uk

Glebeland ★★★
Contact: Holiday Homes & Cottages South West, 365A Torquay Road, Paignton TQ3 2BT
T: (01803) 663650
F: (01803) 664037
E: holcotts@aol.com
I: www.swcottages.co.uk

5 Hesketh Mews ★★★★
Contact: Holiday Homes & Cottages South West, 365A Torquay Road, Paignton TQ3 2BT
T: (01803) 663650
F: (01803) 664037
E: holcotts@aol.com

Hollows Way ★★★
Contact: Holiday Homes & Cottages South West, 365A Torquay Road, Paignton TQ3 2BT
T: (01803) 663650
F: (01803) 664037
E: holcotts@aol.com
I: www.swcottages.co.uk

Hollywater ★★★
Contact: Holiday Homes & Cottages South West, 365A Torquay Road, Paignton TQ3 2BT
T: (01803) 663650
F: (01803) 664037
E: holcotts@aol.com
I: www.swcottages.co.uk

Kingswood Holiday Flats ★★
Contact: Mr Peter Skinns, 22 Morgan Avenue, Torquay TQ2 5RS
T: (01803) 293164

Linden House Holidays ★★★
Contact: Mrs Keran Reilly, Linden House Holidays, Ruckamore Road, Chelston, Torquay TQ2 6HF
T: (01803) 607333
F: (01803) 401234
E: info@lindenholidays.com

Lisburne Place ★★★★-★★★★★
Contact: Lisburne Place, Lisburne Square, Torquay TQ1 2PS
T: (01803) 855282
F: (01803) 851825
E: bluechip@eclipse.co.uk

Little Walderlea ★★★
Contact: Holiday Homes & Cottages South West, 365A Torquay Road, Paignton TQ3 2BT
T: (01803) 663650
F: (01803) 664037
E: holcotts@aol.com
I: www.swcottages.co.uk

The Lodge ★★★★
Contact: Holiday Homes & Cottages South West, 365A Torquay Road, Paignton TQ3 2BT
T: (01803) 663650
F: (01803) 664037
E: holcotts@aol.com
I: www.swcottages.co.uk

Longdon Holiday Flats & Flatlets ★★-★★★
Contact: Mrs Jean Erdpresser, Higher Erith Road, Torquay, Torquay TQ1 2NH
T: (01803) 297240
E: jean@longdonholidayflats.fsnet.co.uk

Lydwell Park ★★★
Contact: Holiday Homes & Cottages South West, 365A Torquay Road, Paignton TQ3 2BT
T: (01803) 663650
F: (01803) 664037
E: holcotts@aol.com
I: www.swcottages.co.uk

Marina View & Bay View ★★★
Contact: Holiday Homes & Cottages South West, 365A Torquay Road, Paignton TQ3 2BT
T: (01803) 663650
F: (01803) 664037
E: holcotts@aol.com
I: www.swcottages.co.uk

Maxton Lodge Holiday Apartments ★★★
Contact: Mr Richard Hassell, Maxton Lodge Holiday Apartments, Rousdown Road, Chelston, Torquay TQ2 6PB
T: (01803) 607811
F: (01803) 605357
E: stay@redhouse-hotel.co.uk
I: www.redhouse-hotel.co.uk

Meadcourt ★★★★
Contact: Holiday Homes & Cottages South West, 365A Torquay Road, Paignton TQ3 2BT
T: (01803) 663650
F: (01803) 664037
E: holcotts@aol.com
I: www.swcottages.co.uk

Meadowside Holiday Flats ★★★
Contact: Mr & Mrs Wilson, 22 Vansittart Road, Torquay TQ2 5BW
T: (01803) 295683
E: meadowside@torquay38.freeserve.co.uk

Mirage & Oasis Apartments ★★★★-★★★★★
Contact: Mrs Sue Vaughton, The Preferred Apartment Company, 21 Bishops Close, Torquay TQ1 2PL
T: (01803) 211116
F: (01803) 214023
E: info@hollington-house.com
I: www.torbayapartments.com

Moongate Cottages ★★★
Contact: Holiday Homes & Cottages South West, 365A Torquay Road, Paignton TQ3 2BT
T: (01803) 663650
F: (01803) 664037
E: holcotts@aol.com
I: www.swcottages.co.uk

Moorcot Self Contained Holiday Apartments★★★
Contact: Mrs M C Neilson, Moorcot Self Contained Holiday Apartments, Kents Road, Wellswood, Torquay TQ1 2NN
T: (01803) 293710
E: holidayflats@moorcot.com
I: www.moorcot.com

Moorhaven Holiday Flats ★★★
Contact: Mr & Mrs Terry & Jackie Chandler, Moorhaven Holiday Flats, 43 Barton Road, Torquay TQ1 4DT
T: (01803) 328567
E: info@moorhaven.co.uk
I: www.moorhaven.co.uk

Moorings ★★★
Contact: Holiday Homes & Cottages South West, 365A Torquay Road, Paignton TQ3 2BT
T: (01803) 663650
F: (01803) 664037
E: holcotts@aol.com
I: www.swcottages.co.uk

Muntham Luxury Holiday Apartments ★★★★
Contact: Mr & Mrs Peter & Trudie Cross, Muntham Holiday Apartments, Barrington Road, Wellswood, Torquay TQ1 1SG
T: (01803) 292958
F: (01803) 291715
E: muntham@btinternet.com
I: www.torbay.gov.uk

Newhaven ★★★
Contact: Mr Brian Wiltshire, 49 Morgan Avenue, Torquay TQ2 5RR
T: (01803) 612836

The Preferred Apartment Company Rating Applied For
Contact: Mrs Sue Vaughton, The Preferred Apartment Company, 21 Bishops Close, Torquay TQ1 2PL
T: (01803) 211116
F: (01803) 214023
E: info@torbayapartments.com

Reddenhill ★★
Contact: Holiday Homes & Cottages South West, 365A Torquay Road, Paignton TQ3 2BT
T: (01803) 663650
F: (01803) 664037
E: holcotts@aol.com
I: www.swcottages.co.uk

Richmond Court ★★★
Contact: Ms Leslie J Creber, Richmond Court, 1 Rowdens Road, Torquay TQ2 5AZ
T: (01803) 293824

South Sands Apartments ★★★
Contact: Mr P W Moorhouse, South Sands Apartments, Torbay Road, Torquay TQ2 6RG
T: (01803) 293521
F: (01803) 293502
E: southsands.torquay@virgin.net
I: www.southsands.co.uk

Southern Comfort ★★★
Contact: Holiday Homes & Cottages South West, 365A Torquay Road, Paignton TQ3 2BT
T: (01803) 663650
F: (01803) 664037
E: holcotts@aol.com
I: www.swcottages.co.uk

Spa Cottage ★★★
Contact: Holiday Homes & Cottages South West, 365A Torquay Road, Paignton TQ3 2BT
T: (01803) 663650
F: (01803) 664037
E: holcotts@aol.com

Summerdyne Apartments ★★★
Contact: Mr & Mrs Dale & Mandy Tanner, Summerdyne Apartments, Greenway Road, Chelston, Torquay TQ2 6JE
T: (01803) 605439
F: (01803) 607441
E: stay@summerdyne.co.uk
I: www.summerdyne.co.uk

Suncourt ★★★
Contact: Holiday Homes & Cottages South West, 365A Torquay Road, Paignton TQ3 2BT
T: (01803) 663650
F: (01803) 664037
E: holcotts@aol.com
I: www.swcottages.com

Sunningdale Apartments ★★★
Contact: Mr Allan Carr, Sunningdale Apartments, 11 Babbacombe Downe Road, Torquay TQ1 3LF
T: (01803) 325786
F: (01803) 329611
E: allancarr@yahoo.com
I: www.sunningdaleapartments.co.uk

Vane Tower ★★★★
Contact: Holiday Homes & Cottages South West, 365A Torquay Road, Paignton TQ3 2BT
T: (01803) 663650
F: (01803) 664037
E: holcotts@aol.com
I: www.swcottages.co.uk

Villa Capri ★★★★
Contact: Mr Arthur Turner, Villa Capri, Daddyhole Road, Meadfoot, Torquay TQ1 2ED
T: (01803) 297959
F: (01803) 297959
E: villcapr@btinternet.com
I: www.torbay.gov.uk./tourism/t-self-c/villcapr.htm

Vomero Holiday Apartments ★★★
Contact: Mr Anthony Brown, Vomero Holiday Apartments, Stitchill Road, Torquay TQ1 1PZ
T: (01803) 293470
F: (01803) 293470
E: holidays@vomero.co.uk
I: www.vomero.co.uk

Waldon Court ★★★★
Contact: Mr Ian Butterworth, Holiday Homes & Cottages South West, 365A Torquay Road, Paignton TQ3 2BT
T: (01803) 663650
F: (01803) 664037
E: holcotts@aol.com
I: www.swcottages.co.uk

42 Warberry Road West ★★★★
Contact: Holiday Homes & Cottages South West, 365A Torquay Road, Paignton TQ3 2BT
T: (01803) 663650

Woodfield Holiday Apartments ★★★
Contact: Mr & Mrs T W Gaylard, Woodfield Holiday Apartments, Lower Woodfield Road, Torquay TQ1 2JY
T: (01803) 295974

Wrenwood ★★★★
Contact: Holiday Homes & Cottages South West, 365A Torquay Road, Paignton TQ3 2BT
T: (01803) 663650
F: (01803) 664037
E: holcotts@aol.com
I: www.swcottages.co.uk

TORRINGTON
Devon

Glebe Farm Cottage ★★★
Contact: Mr & Mrs Mike & Marilyn Cooper, Glebe Farm Cottage, Little Torrington, Torrington EX38 8PS
T: (01805) 622156
E: marilyn_mike@cornflowerblue.com
I: www.cornflowerblue.com

Hill Farm Cottages ★★★★
Contact: Mrs Mary Vickery, Hill Farm Cottages, Hill Farm, Weare Trees Hill, Torrington EX38 7EZ
T: (01805) 622432
F: (01805) 622432
E: info@hillfarmcottages.co.uk
I: www.hillfarmcottages.co.uk

2 Little Silver ★★★★
Contact: Mrs A Taylor, Torwood Lane, Kenley CR3 0HD
T: (020) 8763 0796
F: (020) 8763 0796
E: admin@devonshire-cottages.co.uk

Stowford Lodge & South Hill Cottages★★★
Contact: Mrs S Milsom, Stowford Lodge, Langtree, Torrington EX38 8NU
T: (01805) 601540
F: (01805) 601487
E: stowford@dial.pipex.com
I: www.stowford.dial.pipex.com

Week Farm Flat ★★★
Contact: Mrs Della Bealey, Week Farm Flat, Week Farm, Torrington EX38 7HU
T: (01805) 623029
F: (01805) 623029
E: weekfarm.flat@btinternet.com

TOTNES
Devon

The Annexe, The Talus ★★★
Contact: Mr & Mrs Pedley, The Annexe, The Talus, 12 Quarry Close, Follaton, Totnes TQ9 5FA
T: (01803) 865647
E: theannexe@talk21.com

Castle Foot ★★★★
Contact: Mr D G R Hales, 18 South Street, Totnes TQ9 5DZ
T: (01803) 865282
E: davidg.r.hales@sagainternet.co.uk

Hood Barton Barns ★★★★
Contact: Mrs P Baxendale, The Hayloft, Hood Barton Barns, Dartington, Totnes TQ9 6AB
T: (01803) 762756
F: (01803) 762697
E: info@hoodbartonbarns.co.uk
I: www.hoodbartonbarns.co.uk

The Little Elbow Room ★★★
Contact: Mrs Savin, North Street, Totnes TQ9 5NZ
T: (01803) 863480
F: (01803) 863480
E: elbowroomtotnes@aol.com

Rose Cottage ★★★
Contact: The Proprietor, Rose Cottage, Totnes TQ9
I: www.swcottages.co.uk

Wedge Cottage ★★★★
Contact: Mrs Shirley Seymour, 17 Bridgetown, Totnes TQ9 5BA
T: (01803) 862893

TREBETHERICK
Cornwall

Bars House ★★
Contact: Dr Anthony Hambly, Bodrean Manor, St Clements, Bodrean, Truro TR4 9AG
T: (01872) 264400
F: (01872) 264400
E: anthonyhambly@hotmail.com
I: www.cornishholidays.uk.com

Boskenna ★★★★
Contact: Mrs Diana Bullivant, Diana Bullivant Holidays, Southwinds, Trebell Green, Lanivet, Bodmin PL30 5HR
T: (01208) 831336
F: (01208) 831336
E: diana@d.bullivant.fsnet.co.uk
I: www.cornwall-online.co.uk/diana-bullivant

Church Lane House ★★★★
Contact: Mrs K Painter, 10 Chapel Street, Camelford PL32 9PJ
T: 07814 684822

Evergreen Lodge ★★-★★★
Contact: Mr Wright, Nyetimber, Chiltern Road, Amersham HP6 5PH
T: (01494) 726453
F: (01494) 726453
E: davidwright17@compuserve.com

Hillcroft Bungalow
Rating Applied For
Contact: Mr & Mrs P Beach, Longwood, West Street, Odiham, Hook RG29 1NX
T: (01256) 702650

2 The Martins ★★★
Contact: A P Duffield, 2 The Martins, Dunder Hill, Polzeath, Wadebridge PL27 6SX
T: (01208) 863638
F: (01208) 862940
E: information@seascapehotel.co.uk

Saint Moritz Villas ★★★★
Contact: Mr Stephen Rushworth, Saint Moritz Villas, Trebetherick, Wadebridge PL27 6SD
T: (01208) 862242
F: (01208) 862262
E: info@stmoritzhotel.co.uk
I: www.stmoritzhotel.co.uk

TREDETHY Cornwall

Brinkywell Holiday Cottages ★★★
Contact: Mr & Mrs Tocknell, Treetops, Ashmead Green, Dursley GL11 5EW
T: (01453) 545184
E: brian.tocknell@treetopscam.freeserve.co.uk
I: www.brinkywell.co.uk

TREDRIZZICK Cornwall

Ryth Hogh ★★★
Contact: Harbour Holidays - Rock, Trebetherick House, Polzeath, Wadebridge PL27 6SB
T: (01208) 863399
F: (01208) 862218

TREGADA Cornwall

Burdown Cottage ★★★★
Contact: Ms Janet Oxenbury, Burdown Cottage, Little Comfort, Tregada, Launceston PL15 9NA
T: (01566) 772960
I: burdowncottage.users.btopenworld.com

TREGONY Cornwall

The Bolt Hole
Rating Applied For
Contact: Miss Rebecca Nash, 43 Huntingtower Road, Banner Cross, Sheffield S11 7GT
T: (0114) 238 3966
E: rebnash@yahoo.com

TREGURRIAN Cornwall

Mandalay ★★★
Contact: Ms Nicky Stanley, Harbour Holidays - Padstow, 1 North Quay, Padstow PL28 8AF
T: (01841) 532555
F: (01841) 533115
E: sales@jackie-stanley.co.uk
I: www.harbourholidays.co.uk

TREKNOW Cornwall

Kittiwake Cottage ★★★
Contact: Mrs Jan Harwood, Kittiwake Cottage, Gull Rock, Treknow, Tintagel PL34 0EP
T: (01840) 770438
F: (01840) 770406
E: jan.harwood@btinternet.com

Parwin ★★★
Contact: Mr & Mrs Peter & Cathy Osborne, Cornish Horizons, Higher Trehemborne, St Merryn, Padstow PL28 8JU
T: (01841) 520889
F: (01841) 521523
E: cottages@cornishhorizons.co.uk
I: www.cornishhorizons.co.uk

Sunnyside ★★★
Contact: Mr & Mrs Hansen, West Green Common, Hartley Wintney, Hook RG27 8JD
T: (01252) 843986
E: hansen_harry@hotmail.com

TRELIGGA Cornwall

Caradoc Barn ★★★★
Contact: Harbour Holidays - Rock, Trebetherick House, Trebetherick, Wadebridge PL27 6SB
T: (01208) 863399
F: (01208) 862218

TRELIGHTS Cornwall

Hillside ★★
Contact: Harbour Holidays - Rock, Trebetherick House, Trebetherick, Wadebridge PL27 6SB
T: (01208) 863399
F: (01208) 862218

TRELILL Cornwall

The White House ★★★
Contact: Mr & Mrs Farmer, The White House, Trelill, St Tudy, Bodmin PL30 3HX
T: (01208) 850883
F: (01208) 851914
E: richard@farmer46.freeserve.co.uk

TREMAINE Cornwall

Tremaine Barn ★★★★★
Contact: Mr & Mrs Alan & Jillie Lamb, Tremaine Barn, Tremaine, Launceston PL15 8SA
T: (01566) 781636
F: (01566) 781309
E: welcome@stay-in-cornwall.co.uk
I: www.stay-in-cornwall.co.uk

TRENANCE DOWNS Cornwall

Little Robins & Woodpecker Lodge ★★★-★★★★
Contact: Farm & Cottage Holidays, Victoria House, 12 Fore Street, Westward Ho!, Bideford EX39 1AW
T: (01237) 479146
F: (01237) 421512
E: enquiries@farmcott.co.uk

TRENARREN Cornwall

East Wing Apartment ★★★
Contact: Mrs Treleaven, Trevissick Farm, Trenarren, St Austell PL26 6BQ
T: (01726) 72954
F: (01726) 72954
E: d.treleaven@farmline.com

TRENEGLOS Cornwall

Tregerry Farm ★★★★
Contact: Farm & Cottage Holidays, Victoria House, 12 Fore Street, Westward Ho!, Bideford EX39 1AW
T: (01237) 479146
F: (01237) 421512
E: enquiries@farmcott.co.uk

TRENTISHOE Devon

The Old Farmhouse ★★★
Contact: Mr & Mrs Ian & Ann Wright, The Old Farmhouse, Trentishoe, Barnstaple EX31 4QD
T: (01598) 763495
E: ian@oldfarmhouse.co.uk
I: www.oldfarmhouse.co.uk

TRESCO Cornwall

Boro Chalets ★★★
Contact: Mrs Margaret Christopher, Boro Chalets, Boro Farm, Tresco TR24 0PX
T: (01720) 422843

Borough Farm Chalets ★★★
Contact: Mrs Ann Oyler, The Bungalow, Borough, Tresco TR24 0PX
T: (01720) 422840

TRESPARRETT Cornwall

Underlanes ★★
Contact: Mrs S Prout, Penventon, St Juliot, Boscastle PL35 0DA
T: (01840) 250289

TREVIA Cornwall

The Garden Flat ★★★
Contact: Ms Irene Hislop, The Garden Flat, Green Valley, Trevia, Camelford PL32 9UX
T: (01840) 213415

TREVONE Cornwall

5 Atlanta ★★★
Contact: Ms Nicky Stanley Harbour Holidays - Padstow, 1 North Quay, Padstow PL28 8AF
T: (01841) 532555
F: (01841) 533115
E: sales@jackie-stanley.co.uk
I: www.harbourholidays.co.uk

1 Atlantic ★★★
Contact: Ms Nicky Stanley, Harbour Holidays - Padstow, 1 North Quay, Padstow PL28 8AF
T: (01841) 532555
F: (01841) 533115
E: sales@jackie-stanley.co.uk
I: www.harbourholidays.co.uk

The Bothy ★★★
Contact: Ms Nicky Stanley, Harbour Holidays - Padstow, 1 North Quay, Padstow PL28 8AF
T: (01841) 532555
F: (01841) 533115
E: sales@jackie-stanley.co.uk
I: www.harbourholidays.co.uk

The Bower ★★★
Contact: Ms Nicky Stanley, Harbour Holidays - Padstow, 1 North Quay, Padstow PL28 8AF
T: (01841) 532555
F: (01841) 533115
E: sales@jackie-stanley.co.uk
I: www.harbourholidays.co.uk

Chy an Porth ★★
Contact: Mr & Mrs Peter & Cathy Osborne, Cornish Horizons, Higher Trehemborne, St Merryn, Padstow PL28 8JU
T: (01841) 520889
F: (01841) 521523
E: cottages@cornishhorizons.co.uk
I: www.cornishhorizons.co.uk

Chy Vean ★★
Contact: Mr & Mrs Peter & Cathy Osborne, Cornish Horizons, Higher Trehemborne, St Merryn, Padstow PL28 8JU
T: (01841) 520889
F: (01841) 521523
E: cottages@cornishhorizons.co.uk
I: www.cornishhorizons.co.uk

Furlongs ★★★
Contact: Mrs Gill Vivian, 4 St Saviours Lane, Padstow PL28 8BD
T: (01841) 533791
F: (01841) 533843
E: neil.vivian@btopenworld.com
I: www.holiday-padstow.co.uk

Hill Rise
Rating Applied For
Contact: Mr Peter Alvey, The Drive, Henleaze, Westbury-on-Trym, Bristol BS9 4LD
T: (0117) 962 5862
E: hillrise1@aol.com

Jacaranda ★★★
Contact: Ms Nicky Stanley, Harbour Holidays - Padstow, 1 North Quay, Padstow PL28 8AF
T: (01841) 532555
F: (01841) 533115
E: sales@jackie-stanley.co.uk
I: www.harbourholidays.co.uk

Lamorna Cottage ★★★
Contact: Ms Nicky Stanley, Harbour Holidays - Padstow, 1 North Quay, Padstow PL28 8AF
T: (01841) 532555
F: (01841) 533115
E: sales@jackie-stanley.co.uk
I: www.harbourholidays.co.uk

Lesial ★★★★
Contact: Harbour Holidays - Padstow, 1 North Quay, Padstow PL28 8AF
T: (01841) 532555

Pentonwarra ★★★
Contact: Ms Nicky Stanley, Harbour Holidays - Padstow, 1 North Quay, Padstow PL28 8AF
T: (01841) 532555
F: (01841) 533115
E: sales@jackie-stanley.co.uk
I: www.harbourholidays.co.uk

Riviera ★★
Contact: Harbour Holidays - Padstow, 1 North Quay, Padstow PL28 8AF
T: (01841) 532555
F: (01841) 533115
E: sales@jackie-stanley.co.uk

Rosben ★★★
Contact: Ms Nicky Stanley, Harbour Holidays - Padstow, 1 North Quay, Padstow PL28 8AF
T: (01841) 532555
F: (01841) 533115
E: sales@jackie-stanley.co.uk
I: www.harbourholidays.co.uk

Sintra ★★★
Contact: Mrs Julie Fuller, Little Portion, Trevone Bay, Padstow PL28 8QJ
T: (01841) 521693
F: (01841) 520615
E: julie.collins@ukonline.co.uk

Trelyn ★★★
Contact: Mr & Mrs Peter & Cathy Osborne, Cornish Horizons, Higher Trehemborne, St Merryn, Padstow PL28 8JU
T: (01841) 520889
F: (01841) 521523
E: cottages@cornishhorizons.co.uk
I: www.cornishhorizons.co.uk

Warnecliffe Flat ★★★
Contact: Mr & Mrs Peter & Cathy Osborne, Cornish Horizons, Higher Trehemborne, St Merryn, Padstow PL28 8JU
T: (01841) 520889
F: (01841) 521523
E: cottages@cornishhorizons.co.uk
I: www.cornishhorizons.co.uk

Windmill Cottage ★★
Contact: Mr Christopher Hawkes, Loose Chippings, Lower Rads End, Eversholt, Milton Keynes MK17 9EE
T: (01525) 280385
F: (01525) 280385
E: hawkes@dial.pipex.com

TREVONE BAY
Cornwall

Atlanta Holiday Apartments ★★★-★★★★
Contact: Mr Michael Alken, Askrigg, Dobbin Road, Trevone Bay, Padstow PL28 8QW
T: (01841) 520442
E: mikealken@mail.com
I: www.cornwall-seaside-holidays.com

TREVOSE
Cornwall

Coastguard Cottage West ★★★★
Contact: Mr & Mrs Peter & Cathy Osborne, Cornish Horizons, Higher Trehemborne, St Merryn, Padstow PL28 8JU
T: (01841) 520889
F: (01841) 521523
E: cottages@cornishhorizons.co.uk
I: www.cornishhorizons.co.uk

TREYARNON BAY
Cornwall

Saint Cadocs ★★★
Contact: Mr & Mrs Peter & Cathy Osborne, Cornish Horizons, Higher Trehemborne, St Merryn, Padstow PL28 8JU
T: (01841) 520889
F: (01841) 521523
E: cottages@cornishhorizons.co.uk
I: www.cornishhorizons.co.uk

TROWBRIDGE
Wiltshire

Hinton Lodge ★★★★
Contact: Mrs C Gompels, Hinton House, Great Hinton, Trowbridge BA14 6BS
T: (01380) 871067
F: 0870 870 7026
E: sam@gompels.co.uk
I: www.hintonlodge.co.uk

TRULL
Somerset

Amberd Farmhouse - Old Barn ★★★★
Contact: Mr Tim Isaac, Amberd Lane, Trull, Taunton TA3 7AA
T: (01823) 331744
F: (01823) 331744
E: amberd@btopenworld.com
I: www.amberd.users.btopenworld.com

TRURO
Cornwall

Ancarva Cottage ★★★
Contact: Mrs Margie Lumby, Poachers Reach, Harcourt, Feock, Truro TR3 6SQ
T: (01872) 864400
E: office@specialplacescornwall.co.uk
I: www.specialplacescornwall.co.uk

The Coach House ★★★
Contact: Dr Hambly, Bodrean Manor, St Clements, Bodrean, Truro TR4 9AG
T: (01872) 264400
F: (01872) 264400
E: anthonyhambly@hotmail.com
I: www.cornishholidays.uk.com

Hill View ★★★
Contact: CH Ref: 1122, Holiday Cottages Group Owner Services Dept, Spring Mill, Earby, Barnoldswick BB94 0AA
T: 08700 723723
F: (01282) 844288
E: sales@ttghig.co.uk
I: www.country-holidays.co.uk

Trenerry Lodge ★★
Contact: Mrs Angela Parsons, Trenerry Farm, Mingoose, Truro TR4 8BX
T: (01872) 553755
F: (01872) 553755
E: babatrenerry@btopenworld.com

Westward & Mellangoose (Niche Retreats) ★★★-★★★★
Contact: Mrs J A Kitchen, Niche Retreats, Banns Road, Mount Hawke, Truro TR4 8BW
T: (01209) 890272
F: (01209) 891695
E: info@nicheretreats.co.uk

UFFCULME
Devon

Old Bridwell Holiday Cottages ★★★★
Contact: Ms Jackie Kind, Old Bridwell Holiday Cottages, Uffculme, Cullompton EX15 3BU
T: (01884) 841464
E: bridwellholidays@aol.com
I: www.oldbridwell.co.uk

UGBOROUGH
Devon

Coombe House and Cottages Rating Applied For
Contact: Mr & Mrs John & Faith Scharenguivel, Coombe House and Cottages, North Huish, South Brent TQ10 9NJ
T: (01548) 821277
F: (01548) 821277
E: coombehouse@hotmail.com

Donkey Cottage ★★★★
Contact: Mrs Gill Barker, 5 Meade King Grove, Woodmancote, Cheltenham GL52 9UD
T: (01242) 678568
E: gill@donkeycottage.co.uk
I: www.donkeycottage.co.uk

UMBERLEIGH
Devon

Little Wick ★★★★
Contact: Marsdens Cottage Holidays, 2 The Square, Braunton EX33 2JB
T: (01271) 813777
F: (01271) 813664
E: holidays@marsdens.co.uk

Millbrook ★★★★
Contact: Mr & Mrs Cornwell, Marsden's Cottage Holidays, 2 The Square, Braunton EX33 2JB
T: (01271) 813777

UPLODERS
Dorset

Butterwells ★★★
Contact: Mr Zachary Stuart-Brown, Dream Cottages, 41 Maiden Street, Weymouth DT4 8AZ
T: (01305) 761347
E: admin@dream-cottages.co.uk
I: www.dream-cottages.co.uk

Clematis Cottage Rating Applied For
Contact: Dream Cottages, 41, Maiden Street, Weymouth DT4 8AZ
T: (01305) 761347
E: admin@dream-cottages.co.uk

Moens Dairyhouse ★★★★
Contact: Mrs L Marston, Moens Farmhouse, Uploders, Bridport DT6 4PH
T: (01308) 420631

UPLOWMAN
Devon

West Pitt Farm ★★★-★★★★
Contact: Ms Susanne Westgate, West Pitt Farm Holidays, Whitnage, Uplowman, Tiverton EX16 7DU
T: (01884) 820296
F: (01884) 820818
E: susannewestgate@yahoo.com

UPLYME
Devon

The Bower ★★★★
Contact: Mrs Paula Wyon-Brown, The Bower, Hill Barn, Gore Lane, Uplyme, Lyme Regis DT7 3RJ
T: (01297) 445185
F: (01297) 445185
E: jwb@lymeregis-accommodation.com
I: www.lymeregis-accommodation.com

Higher Holcombe Farm Cottage ★★★
Contact: Mrs Duffin, Higher Holcombe Farm Cottage, Holcombe Lane, Uplyme, Lyme Regis DT7 3SN
T: (01297) 444078
E: ro3duffin@hotmail.com

Holmer Villas Rating Applied For
Contact: Mrs Pamela Boyland, Holmer Villas, 3 Ozone Terrace, Uplyme, Lyme Regis DT7 3JY
T: (01404) 861297
E: pab@barnparkfarm.fsnet.co.uk

Old Orchard ★★★-★★★★
Contact: Mr G L Smith, Cannington Farm, Cannington Lane, Uplyme, Lyme Regis DT7 3SW
T: (01297) 443172
F: (01297) 445005
E: tvecs@aol.com

Sherwood Apartments ★★★
Contact: Mrs W Blinman, Sherwood Apartments, Sherwood, Uplyme, Lyme Regis DT7 3LS
T: (01297) 445753
F: (01297) 443863
E: information@sherwoodapts.freeserve.co.uk
I: www.lymeregis.com/sherwood-apartments/htm

UPOTTERY
Devon

Courtmoor Farm ★★★★
Contact: Ms Rosalind Buxton, Upottery, Honiton EX14 9QA
T: (01404) 861565
E: courtmoor.farm@btinternet.com

The Haybarton ★★★★★
Contact: Mrs P A Wells, Bidwell Farm, Upottery, Honiton EX14 9PP
T: (01404) 861122
F: 08700 55496
E: pat@bidwellfarm.co.uk
I: www.bidwellfarm.co.uk

Hoemoor Bungalow ★★★
Contact: Mrs Phillips, Hoemoor Bungalow, Upottery, Honiton EX14 9PB
T: (01823) 601265
E: holidays@hoemoor.freeserve.co.uk

UPTON
Somerset

West Withy Farm Holiday Cottages ★★★★
Contact: Mr & Mrs Gareth & Mary Hughes, West Withy Farm Holiday Cottages, West Withy Farm, Upton, Taunton TA4 2JH
T: (01398) 371258
F: (01398) 371123
E: g.hughes@irisi.u-net.com
I: www.exmoor-cottages.com

UPWEY
Dorset

Appleloft & Brook Springs ★★-★★★
Contact: Mr Zachary Stuart-Brown, Dream Cottages, 41 Maiden Street, Weymouth DT4 8AZ
T: (01305) 761347
E: admin@dream-cottages.co.uk
I: www.dream-cottages.co.uk

Chapel Cottage & Old School Cottage ★★★
Contact: Mr Zachary Stuart-Brown, Dream Cottages, 41 Maiden Street, Weymouth DT4 8AZ
T: (01305) 761347
E: admin@dream-cottages.co.uk
I: www.dream-cottages.co.uk

The Retreat ★★★★
Contact: Mr Zachary Stuart-Brown, Dream Cottages, 41 Maiden Street, Weymouth DT4 8AZ
T: (01305) 761347
E: admin@dream-cottages.co.uk
I: www.dream-cottages.co.uk

Rock Rose Cottage ★★★
Contact: Mr Zachary Stuart-Brown, Dream Cottages, 41 Maiden Street, Weymouth DT4 8AZ
T: (01305) 761347
E: admin@dream-cottages.co.uk
I: www.dream-cottages.co.uk

Sixpenny Cottage ★★★★
Contact: Dream Cottages, 41 Maiden Street, Weymouth DT4 8AZ
T: (01305) 761347
F: (01305) 789000

Strawberry Cottage ★★★
Contact: Mr Zachary Stuart-Brown, Dream Cottages, 41 Maiden Street, Weymouth DT4 8AZ
T: (01305) 761347
E: admin@dream-cottages.co.uk
I: www.dream-cottages.co.uk

Wey Valley House ★★★★
Contact: Dream Cottages, 41 Maiden Street, Weymouth DT4 8AZ
T: (01305) 761347
F: (01305) 789000

URCHFONT
Wiltshire

Breach Cottage & The Pottery ★★
Contact: Mr & Mrs Philip & Clare Milanes, Breach House, Cuckoo Corner, Urchfont, Lydeway, Devizes SN10 4RA
T: (01380) 840402
F: (01380) 840150
E: breachhouse@btopenworld.com

WADEBRIDGE
Cornwall

The Barn ★★★
Contact: Mr & Mrs Peter & Cathy Osborne, Cornish Horizons, Higher Trehemborne, St Merryn, Padstow PL28 8JU
T: (01841) 520889
F: (01841) 521523
E: cottages@cornishhorizons.co.uk
I: www.cornishhorizons.co.uk

Colesent Cottages ★★★★
Contact: Mrs S Zamaria
T: (01208) 850112
F: (01208) 850112
E: holiday@colesent.co.uk
I: www.colesent.co.uk

Lowenna Holiday Flat ★★★
Contact: Mrs Katy Holmes, Lowenna House, 35 Egloshayle Road, Wadebridge PL27 6AE
T: (01208) 815725
E: pablo.holmes@talk21.com

15 & 16 Michaelstow Manor Holiday Park★★
Contact: Mr & Mrs John & Pam Hartill, 17 St Leonards, Bodmin PL31 1LA
T: (01208) 73676
F: (01208) 73676
E: pamhartill@ukonline.co.uk

Rock Barn ★★★★
Contact: Cornish Cottage Holidays, The Old Turnpike Dairy, Godolphin, Meneage Street, Helston TR13 8AA
T: (01326) 573808
F: (01326) 564992
E: enquiry@cornishcottageholidays.co.uk
I: www.cornishcottageholidays.co.uk

117 Talmena Avenue ★★★★
Contact: Mr Knapp, 9 Treforest Road, Wadebridge PL27 7HE
T: (01208) 813448

Tregolls Farm Cottages ★★★★
Contact: Mrs Marilyn Hawkey, Tregolls Farm, St Wenn, Withiel, Bodmin PL30 5PG
T: (01208) 812154
F: (01208) 812154
E: tregollsfarm@btclick.com
I: www.tregollsfarm.co.uk

Trenoweth ★★★★
Contact: Mr & Mrs Curtis-Clarke, 87 Talmena Avenue, Wadebridge PL27 7RP
T: (01208) 812483
E: anncurtis_clarke@hotmail.com
I: myweb.tiscali.co.uk/trenoweth

West Park Farm Holiday Cottages ★★★
Contact: Miss Helen Fishenden, No Mans Land, St Issey, Wadebridge PL27 7RF
T: (01208) 813882
E: helen@daymer.freeserve.co.uk

WARBSTOW
Cornwall

Cartmell Bungalow ★★★
Contact: Mrs Dawe, Cartmell Bungalow, Trelash, Warbstow, Launceston PL15 8RL
T: (01840) 261353

Fentrigan Manor Farm Cottage ★★★★
Contact: Farm & Cottage Holidays, Victoria House, 12 Fore Street, Northam, Bideford EX39 1AW
T: (01237) 479146
F: (01237) 421512
E: enquiries@farmcott.co.uk

WARLEGGAN
Cornwall

Treveddoe & Barley Crush ★★★-★★★★★
Contact: Lady Hill-Norton, The Barns, Newton Valence, Alton GU34 3RB
T: (01420) 588302
F: (01420) 587387
E: jennic@hill-norton.freeserve.co.uk
I: www.cornwall-online.co.uk/treveddoe

WARMINSTER
Wiltshire

The Annex ★★
Contact: Mrs Allery, The Annex, 'Wayside', 64 Weymouth Street, Warminster BA12 9NT
T: (01985) 218158

The Coach House ★★★★
Contact: Mrs Lynn Corp, Sturford Mead Farm, Corsley, Warminster BA12 7QU
T: (01373) 832213
F: (01373) 832213
E: lynn_sturford.cottage@virgin.net
I: lynn_sturford.cottage@virgin.net

Downside House H112 ★★★★
Contact: Chapel House, Luke Street, Berwick St John, Shaftesbury SP7 0HQ
T: (01747) 828170
F: (01747) 829090
E: enq@hideaways.co.uk

Whey Cottage ★★★★
Contact: Mr Zachary Stuart-Brown, Dream Cottages, 41 Maiden Street, Weymouth DT4 8AZ
T: (01305) 761347
E: admin@dream-cottages.co.uk
I: www.dream-cottages.co.uk

WARMWELL
Dorset

Apple Orchard ★★
Contact: Mr Geoffrey Stuart Murgatroyd, Apple Orchard, Skippet Heath, Warmwell Road, Warmwell, Dorchester DT2 8JD
T: (01305) 853702
F: (01305) 853702

Beech Farm ★★★
Contact: Mrs Ruth Goldsack, Beech Farm, Warmwell, West Knighton, Dorchester DT2 8LZ
T: (01305) 852414
F: (01305) 853138
E: rugold@lineone.net

Misery Farm ★★★
Contact: Mr Zachary Stuart-Brown, Dream Cottages, 41 Maiden Street, Weymouth DT4 8AZ
T: (01305) 761347
E: admin@dream-cottages.co.uk
I: www.dream-cottages.co.uk

WASHAWAY
Cornwall

Ferkins Barn ★★★
Contact: Mr & Mrs Peter & Cathy Osborne, Cornish Horizons, Higher Trehemborne, St Merryn, Padstow PL28 8JU
T: (01841) 520889
F: (01841) 521523
E: cottages@cornishhorizons.co.uk

WASHFORD
Somerset

Cedar House Cottages Rating Applied For
Contact: Mr & Mrs David & Christine Holmes, Cedar House Cottages, Cedar House, Old Cleeve, Washford, Watchet TA24 6HH
T: (01984) 640437
F: (01984) 640437

Monksway ★★★★★
Contact: Mr & Mrs Woolford, Parkside, Hailey, Ipsden, Wallingford OX10 6AD
T: (01491) 681229
E: barry.woolford@ntlworld.com
I: www.countrycottagesonline.com

WATCHET
Somerset

The Croft Holiday Cottages ★★★★
Contact: Mr & Mrs A M Musgrave, The Croft Holiday Cottages, The Croft, Anchor Street, Watchet TA23 0BY
T: (01984) 631121
F: (01984) 631134
E: croftcottages@talk21.com
I: www.cottageguide.co.uk/croft-cottages

The Square ★★★
Contact: Mrs C Court, 31 North Croft, Williton, Taunton TA4 4RP
T: (01984) 639089
E: clarecourt@supanet.com
I: www.somerset-cottage.com

WATERMOUTH
Devon

The Nut House ★★★
Contact: Marsden's Cottage Holidays, 2 The Square, Braunton EX33 2JB
T: (01271) 813777
F: (01271) 813664
E: holidays@marsdens.co.uk
I: www.marsdens.co.uk

WATERROW
Somerset

Halsdown Farm Holiday Cottages ★★★
Contact: Mrs James, Waterrow, Wiveliscombe, Taunton TA4 2QU
T: (01984) 623493
F: (01984) 623493
E: jamesathalsdown@tinyworld.co.uk

Handley Farm ★★★★
Contact: Farm & Cottage Holidays, Victoria House, 12 Fore Street, Westward Ho!, Bideford EX39 1AW
T: (01237) 479146
F: (01237) 421512
E: enquiries@farmcott.co.uk

WAYFORD
Somerset

Manor Farm ★★★
Contact: Mr Austin Emery, Manor Farm, Wayford, Crewkerne TA18 8QL
T: (01460) 78865
F: (01460) 78865
I: www.manorfarm.com

WEARE GIFFARD
Devon

Honeycomb ★★★★
Contact: Farm & Cottage Holidays, Victoria House, 12 Fore Street, Westward Ho!, Bideford EX39 1AW
T: (01237) 479146
F: (01237) 421512
E: enquiries@farmcott.co.uk

WEDMORE
Somerset

The Coach House ★★★★
Contact: Mr Mike Rippon, The Coach House, Holdenhurst, Cheddar Road, Wedmore BS28 4EQ
T: (01934) 713125
F: (01934) 710050
E: coach.house@holdenhurst.co.uk

WEEK ST MARY
Cornwall

5 Church Mews ★★★
Contact: Mrs Kabler, Clifton House, Week St Mary, Holsworthy EX22 6UH
T: (01288) 341499

Stewart House Holiday Cottages ★★★
Contact: Mrs G Cox, Stewart House Holiday Cottages, Stewart House, Week St Mary, Holsworthy EX22 6XA
T: (01288) 341556
E: simon.gaynor2@tinyworld.co.uk

WELCOMBE
Devon

Mead Barn Cottages ★★★-★★★★
Contact: Mrs Valerie Price, Mead Barn Cottages, Welcombe, Bideford EX39 6HQ
T: (01288) 331721
E: meadbarns@aol.com
I: www.meadbarns.com

Olde Smithy Bungalows ★★★
Contact: Mrs Sandra Millbourne, Olde Smithy Bungalows Self Catering, 18 Bude Street, Appledore, Northam, Bideford EX39 1PS
T: (01237) 421811
E: user@fearonsfsbusiness.co.uk

Saint Heligans ★★★★
Contact: CH Ref: 14788, Holiday Cottages Group Owner Services Department, Spring Mill, Earby, Barnoldswick BB94 0AA
T: 08700 723723
F: (01282) 844288
E: sales@ttgihg.co.uk
I: www.country-holidays.co.uk

WELLINGTON
Somerset

Tone Dale House ★★★★★
Contact: Mrs Beverley Netley, Tone Dale House, Milverton Road, Tonedale, Wellington TA21 0EZ
T: (01823) 662673
F: (01823) 662177
E: party@thebighouseco.com
I: www.thebighouseco.com

White Barn ★★★★
Contact: Mrs AM Reeve, White Barn, Ford St Hill, Wellington TA21 9PD
T: (01823) 663874

WELLOW
Bath and North East Somerset

Holly Cottage ★★★★
Contact: Mr & Mrs Alick & Mari Bartholowmew, Holly Cottage, The Hollies, Mill Hill, Wellow, Bath BA2 8QJ
T: (01225) 840889
F: (01225) 833150
E: enquiries@bath-holidays.co.uk
I: www.bath-holidays.co.uk

WELLS
Somerset

Garslade Cottage ★★★
Contact: Mrs Bridget Gooden, Garslade Farm Wing, Garslade Farm, Godney, Wells BA5 1RX
T: (01458) 833801

Hart Cottage ★★★
Contact: Mr A Williams, 21 St John Street, Wells BA5 1SW
T: (01749) 674897
E: nandi@clara.co.uk

Model Farm Cottages ★★★
Contact: Mrs Gill Creed, Model Farm Cottages, Model Farm, Milton, Wells BA5 3AE
T: (01749) 673363
F: (01749) 671566
E: gill_creed@talk21.com

The Old Farm House ★★★
Contact: Mrs Jayne Wood, The Old Farm House, 62 Bath Road, Wells BA5 3LQ
T: (01749) 673087
F: (01749) 674689
E: frankjwood@aol.com

The Potting Shed Holidays ★★★★
Contact: Mr & Mrs J Van Bergen-Henegouwen, Potting Shed Holidays, Harters Hill Cottage, Pillmoor Lane, Coxley, Wells BA5 1RF
T: (01749) 672857
F: (01749) 679925
E: cjvbhhol@aol.com
I: www.pottingshedholidays.co.uk

Shalom ★★
Contact: Mrs Rees, 60 Eastgrove Avenue, Sharples, Bolton BL1 7HA
T: (01204) 418576
F: (01204) 301345

Spiders End ★★★★
Contact: Mr & Mrs J Van Bergen-Henegouwen, Potting Shed Holidays, Harters Hill Cottage, Pillmoor Lane, Coxley, Wells BA5 1RF
T: (01749) 672857
F: (01749) 679925
E: cjvbhhol@aol.com
I: www.pottingshedholidays.co.uk

Spindlewood Lodges ★★★★
Contact: Mr & Mrs Peter/Linda Norris, Spindlewood Lodges, Lower Westholme, Pilton, Shepton Mallet BA4 4EL
T: (01749) 890367
F: (01749) 890367
E: info@spindlewoodlodges.co.uk
I: www.spindlewoodlodges.co.uk

15a Tucker Street ★★
Contact: Mr J Mullins, 15a Tucker Street, Wells BA5 2DZ
T: 07968 367803

Vicars' Close Holiday House ★★★
Contact: Mrs Debbie Jones, Cathedral Office, Chain Gate, Cathedral Green, Wells BA5 2UE
T: (01749) 674483
F: (01749) 832210
E: visits@wellscathedral.uk.net

WEMBDON
Somerset

Grange Farm Cottage ★★★★
Contact: English Country Cottages, Stoney Bank, Earby, Barnoldswick BB94 0AA
T: 0870 585 1155
F: 0870 585 1150
I: www.english-country-cottages.co.uk

WEMBURY
Devon

Traine Farm ★★★-★★★★
Contact: Mrs S Rowland, Traine Farm, Wembury, Plymouth PL9 0EW
T: (01752) 862264
F: (01752) 862264
E: rowland.trainefarm@eclipse.co.uk
I: www.traine-holiday-cottages.co.uk

WEMBWORTHY
Devon

Taw Mill ★★★★★
Contact: Mr Roger Bowley, Taw Mill, Wembworthy, Chulmleigh EX18 7SW
T: (01837) 83931
E: sheila@tawmill.com
I: www.tawmill.com

WEST ALVINGTON
Devon

Sunshine Cottage ★★★★
Contact: Mr Nicholas Pash, Hideaways, Chapel House, Luke Street, Berwick St John, Shaftesbury SP7 0HQ
T: (01747) 828170
F: (01747) 829090
E: enq@hideaways.co.uk
I: www.hideaways.co.uk

WEST ANSTEY
Devon

Brimblecombe ★★★★
Contact: Mrs C Hutsby
T: (01789) 840261
F: (01789) 842270
E: charhutsby@talk21.com
I: www.brimblecombe-exmoor.co.uk

Deer's Leap Country Cottages ★★★★
Contact: Mr & Mrs Michael & Frances Heggadon, Deer's Leap Country Cottages, West Anstey, South Molton EX36 3NZ
T: (01398) 341407
F: (01398) 341407
E: deersleapcottages@lineone.net
I: www.deersleap.com

Dunsley Farm ★★★
Contact: Mrs I M Robins, Dunsley Farm, West Anstey, South Molton EX36 3PF
T: (01398) 341246
F: (01398) 341246

Dunsley Mill ★★★★
Contact: Mr & Mrs John & Helen Sparrow, Dunsley Mill, West Anstey, South Molton EX36 3PF
T: (01398) 341374
F: (01398) 341374
E: helen@dunsleymill.co.uk
I: www.dunsleymill.co.uk

WEST BAY
Dorset

The Bay House ★★★
Contact: Mr D A Kimber, 5 Flaxfield Court, Basingstoke RG21 8FX
T: (01256) 470927

15 Bramble Drive ★★★
Contact: Mr & Mrs Gerald & Janet Paget, 3 Boundary Close, Tanners Brook, Southampton SO15 4PE
T: (02380) 345836
F: (01962) 877946
E: gerry.paget@hants.gov.uk

28 Chesil House ★★★
Contact: Mrs Frances Hunt, Spices, Stoney Lane, Curry Rivel, Langport TA10 0HY
T: (01458) 251203
F: (01458) 251203
E: frances.hunt@curryrivel.freeserve.co.uk
I: www.somersetcook.freeserve.co.uk

Harbour Lights ★★★
Contact: Mr Zachary Stuart-Brown, Dream Cottages, 41 Maiden Street, Weymouth DT4 8AZ
T: (01305) 761347
E: admin@dream-cottages.co.uk
I: www.dream-cottages.co.uk

18 Heron Court ★★★
Contact: Mrs Mary Fitzpatrick, Merlins Cottage, Looke Lane, Puncknowle, Dorchester DT2
F: (01308) 898261
E: merlinscottage@aol.com

Seafront Chalet ★★
Contact: Mrs Teresa Visram, 224 Perth Road, Gants Hill, Ilford IG2 6DZ
T: (020) 8554 1543
F: (020) 8554 1543
E: teresa.visram@btinternet.com

Westpoint Apartments ★★★-★★★★★
Contact: Mr D & Mrs B Slade, Westpoint Apartments, The Esplanade, West Bay, Bridport DT6 4HE
T: (01308) 423636
F: (01308) 458871
E: bed@westpoint-apartments.co.uk
I: www.westpointapartments.co.uk

Winnie Bustles ★★
Contact: Ms Anne Francis, Mole Cottage, 31 Loders, Merriott DT6 3SA
T: (01308) 427741
E: mole@theboops.fsnet.co.uk

2 Wreckers Cottage ★★
Contact: Mr D & Mrs B Slade, Westpoint Apartments, The Esplanade, West Bay, Bridport DT6 4HG
T: (01308) 423636
F: (01308) 458871
E: bea@westpoint-apartments.co.uk
I: www.westpoint-apartments.co.uk

WEST BEXINGTON
Dorset

Gorselands ★★-★★★
Contact: Mrs Pallister, Gorselands, West Bexington, Dorchester DT2 9DJ
T: (01308) 897232
F: (01308) 897239

Tamarisk Farm Cottages ★★★-★★★★★
Contact: Mrs Josephine Pearse, Tamarisk Farm Cottages, West Bexington, Dorchester DT2 9DF
T: (01308) 897784
F: (01308) 897784
E: tamarisk@eurolink.ltd.net
I: www.tamariskfarm.co.uk
♿

WEST CHINNOCK
Somerset

Weavers Cottage ★★★★
Contact: Lt Col Gordon Piper, Weavers Cottage, West Chinnock, Crewkerne TA18 7QA
T: (01935) 881370
E: thepipers@hotmail.com

Yeoman Cottage ★★★★
Contact: Mrs Marie Wheatley, Yeoman Cottage, Yeoman Wake, Higher Street, West Chinnock, Crewkerne TA18 7QA
T: (01935) 881421
F: (01935) 881421
E: jonwheat@aol.com

WEST DOWN
Devon

Fairview Farm Cottages ★★★
Contact: Mr Kevin Walker, Fairview Farm Cottages, West Down, Ilfracombe EX34 8NE
T: (01271) 862249
E: info@fairviewfarm.co.uk
I: www.fairviewfarm.co.uk

Kings Close ★★★★
Contact: Mrs Toni Buchan, Kings Close, Kings Down, West Down, Braunton EX34 8NF
T: (01271) 865222
F: 0870 130133

Rock Cottage ★★★
Contact: Mrs Virginia Sprason, Hagley Mews, Hagley Hall, Hall Drive, Hagley, Stourbridge DY9 9LQ
T: (01562) 883038
F: (01562) 886592
E: rock.cott@virgin.net
I: www.devoncottage.fsnet.co.uk

Tawny Cottage & Swallow Cottage ★★★★
Contact: Marsden's Cottage Holidays, 2 The Square, Braunton EX33 2JB
T: (01271) 813777
F: (01271) 813664
E: holidays@marsdens.co.uk
I: www.marsdens.co.uk

WEST MILTON
Dorset

Gore Cottage ★★★
Contact: Hon Mrs E G Maude, Sparrow Court, Chalk Hill Road, Kingsdown, Deal CT14 8DP
T: (01304) 389253
F: (01304) 389016
I: www.heartofdorset.easynet.co.uk

Leopard Cottage ★★★★
Contact: Mr & Mrs B Bushell, Leopard Cottage, Ruscombe Lane, West Milton, Bridport DT6 3SL
T: (01308) 485014
I: www.milkbere.com

WEST PENNARD
Somerset

Victoria Farm ★★
Contact: Mr & Mrs Rands, Victoria Farm, West Pennard, Glastonbury BA6 8LW
T: (01458) 850509

WEST STAFFORD
Dorset

Barton House Loft ★★★
Contact: Mrs J M Robertson, Barton House Loft, Barton Close, West Stafford, Dorchester DT2 8AD
T: (01305) 250472
F: (01305) 250472

WESTBURY
Wiltshire

Iron Box Cottage ★★★★
Contact: Mrs Hansford, 1 Carpenters Lane, Bratton, Westbury BA13 4SS
T: (01380) 830169
E: sue.hansford@tesco.net
I: www.ironboxcottage.co.uk

WESTBURY-SUB-MENDIP
Somerset

The Dairy ★★★
Contact: Mrs C Hancock, The Dairy, Cottage Farm, The Hollow, Westbury-sub-Mendip, Wells BA5 1HH
T: (01749) 870351
I: www.westbury-sub-mendip.org

Old Apple Loft ★★★
Contact: Mrs Anne Flintham, Old Apple Loft, Westbury Cross House, Crow Lane, Westbury-sub-Mendip, Wells BA5 1HB
T: (01749) 870557
F: (01749) 870997
E: enquiries@swan-networks.co.uk

WESTHAY
Somerset

The Courtyard New House Farm ★★★★
Contact: Mr Bell, The Courtyard New House Farm, Shapwick Road, Westhay, Glastonbury BA6 9TT
T: (01458) 860238
F: (01458) 860568
E: newhousefarm@farmersweekly.net

Riverside Farmhouse ★★★★
Contact: Mr & Mrs Graham Noel, Riverside Farmhouse, Main Road, Westhay, Glastonbury BA6 9TN
T: (01458) 860408
E: gn@venividi.co.uk
I: www.go-see.co.uk/riversidefarmhouse

WESTLEIGH
Devon

Farleigh Cottage ★★★★
Contact: Farm & Cottage Holidays, Victoria House, 12 Fore Street, Northam, Bideford EX39 1AW
T: (01237) 479146
F: (01237) 421512
E: enquiries@farmcott.co.uk

WESTON
Devon

5 Axe Vale ★★
Contact: Ms Kate Bartlett, Jean Bartlett Cottage Holidays, Fore Street, Seaton EX12 3JB
T: (01297) 23221
F: (01297) 23303
E: holidays@jeanbartlett.com
I: www.netbreaks.com/jeanb

9 Axe Vale ★★
Contact: Ms Kate Bartlett, Jean Bartlett Cottage Holidays, Fore Street, Seaton EX12 3JB
T: (01297) 23221
F: (01297) 23303
E: holidays@jeanbartlett.com
I: www.netbreaks.com/jeanb

E6 ★★★
Contact: Ms Kate Bartlett, Jean Bartlett Cottage Holidays, Fore Street, Seaton EX12 3JB
T: (01297) 23221
F: (01297) 23303
E: holidays@jeanbartlett.com
I: www.netbreaks.com/jeanb

8 Sidvale ★★★
Contact: Ms Kate Bartlett, Jean Bartlett Cottage Holidays, Fore Street, Seaton EX12 3JB
T: (01297) 23221
F: (01297) 23303
E: holidays@jeanbartlett.com
I: www.netbreaks.com/jeanb

2 Stoneleigh ★★★
Contact: Ms Kate Bartlett, Jean Bartlett Cottage Holidays, Fore Street, Seaton EX12 3JB
T: (01297) 23221
F: (01297) 23303
E: holidays@jeanbartlett.com
I: www.netbreaks.com/jeanb

Stoneleigh Bungalow ★★★
Contact: Ms Kate Bartlett, Jean Bartlett Cottage Holidays The Old Dairy, Fore Street, Seaton EX12 3JB
T: (01297) 23221
F: (01297) 23303
E: holidays@jeanbartlett.com
I: www.netbreaks.com/jeamb

WESTON-SUPER-MARE
Somerset

Batch Farm Cottage ★★
Contact: Mrs I D Wall, Batch Farm, Lympsham, Weston-super-Mare BS24 0EX
T: (01934) 750287
F: (01934) 750287

Clarence View ★★★★
Contact: Ms A Cantle, Champagne Holiday Lets, Broomrigg House, Broomrigg Road, Fleet, Aldershot GU51 4LR
T: (01252) 622789
F: (01252) 812948
E: alison@champagnelettings.fsnet.co.uk
I: www.holiday-rentals.com

Doubleton Farm Cottages ★★★
Contact: Mr & Mrs John & Victoria Southwood, Doubleton Farm Cottages, Hewish, Weston-super-Mare BS24 6RB
T: (01934) 520225
F: (01934) 520225
E: info@doubleton.com
I: www.doubleton.com

Hope Farm Cottages ★★★★
Contact: Mrs Liz Stirk, Hope Farm Cottages, Brean Road, Lympsham, Weston-super-Mare BS24 0HA
T: (01934) 750506
F: (01934) 750506
E: stirkhopefarm@aol.com
I: www.hopefarmcottages.co.uk

Manor House Cottages ★★★-★★★★★
Contact: Mrs V Hart, Manor House, Bleadon Road, Bleadon, Weston-super-Mare BS24 0PY
T: (01934) 812689
F: (01934) 812689
E: valerie@manor-house-cottages.com
I: www.manor-house-cottages.com

Royal Sands ★★★★
Contact: Ms A Cantle, Champagne Holiday Lets, Broomrigg House, Broomrigg Road, Fleet, Aldershot GU51 4LR
T: (01252) 622789
F: (01252) 812948
E: alison@champagnelettings.fsnet.co.uk
I: www.champagnelettings.co.uk

Sandhurst ★★★★
Contact: Ms Alison Cantle, Broomrigg House, Broomrigg Road, Seale, Farnham GU51 4LR
T: (01252) 622789
F: (01252) 812948
E: alison@champagnelettings.fsnet.co.uk
I: www.champagnelettings.co.uk

Westward Ho! Holiday Flats ★★-★★★
Contact: Mr & Mrs Ken & Janet Everard, Westward Ho! Holiday Flats, 39 Severn Road, Weston-super-Mare BS23 1DP
T: (01934) 629294
F: (01934) 624168
E: kenandjanet@westwardhohols.fsnet.co.uk
I: www.westonholidayflats.co.uk

WESTPORT
Somerset

Riverside ★★★★
Contact: Mrs Caroline King, Hemyock, Clayhidon, Cullompton EX15 3PT
T: (01823) 680447
F: (01823) 681008
E: cking@dunnsgreen.fsnet.co.uk
I: www.dunnsgreen.fsnet.co.uk

Wind in the Willows Cottage ★★★
Contact: Mr Baker, Cooks Lane, Axminster EX13 5SQ
T: (01297) 32051
F: (01297) 32051
E: cjbaker@eggconnect.net

WESTWATER
Devon

Woodhouse Cottage ★★★★
Contact: Ms Playford, Woodhouse Cottage, Woodhouse Farm, Westwater, Axminster EX13 7JD
T: (01297) 33666

WEYMOUTH
Dorset

Acropolis Hotel & Apartments ★★
Contact: Mr & Mrs Afedakis, Plantours Ltd, Dorchester Road, Weymouth DT4 7JT
T: (01305) 784282
F: (01305) 767172
E: acropolishotel@plantours.fsnet.co.uk

Amailia Holiday Flat ★★
Contact: Mrs H Webster, 15 Carlton Road South, Weymouth DT4 7PL
T: (01305) 768978

Amhurst Lodge Cottages and Apartments Rating Applied For
Contact: Ms Lesley Gyte, Amhurst Lodge Cottages and Apartments, 4 Spring Gardens, Fortuneswell, Portland DT5 1JG
T: (01305) 860960
F: (01305) 860960

Anchor Cottage ★★
Contact: Mr Zachary Stuart-Brown, Dream Cottages, 41 Maiden Street, Weymouth DT4 8AZ
T: (01305) 761347
E: admin@dream-cottages.co.uk
I: www.dream-cottages.co.uk

Anvil House ★★★
Contact: Mr Zachary Stuart-Brown, Dream Cottages, 41 Maiden Street, Weymouth DT4 8AZ
T: (01305) 761347
E: admin@dream-cottages.co.uk
I: www.dream-cottages.co.uk

April Grange Cottage ★★★
Contact: Mr Zachary Stuart-Brown, Dream Cottages, 41 Maiden Street, Weymouth DT4 8AZ
T: (01305) 761347
E: admin@dream-cottages.co.uk
I: www.dream-cottages.co.uk

Ashleigh Holiday Flats ★-★★
Contact: Mr Roger Littler, Ashleigh Holiday Flats, 53 Abbotsbury Road, Weymouth DT4 0AQ
T: (01305) 773715
E: ashleighhols@talk21.com

Ashwood ★★★★
Contact: Dream Cottages, 41 Maiden Street, Weymouth DT4 8AZ
T: (01305) 761347
F: (01305) 789000

The Barbican ★★★
Contact: Mr Zachary Stuart-Brown, Dream Cottages, 41 Maiden Street, Weymouth DT4 8AZ
T: (01305) 761347
E: admin@dream-cottages.co.uk
I: www.dream-cottages.co.uk

Bay Lodge Self-Catering Accommodation★★★★★
Contact: Mr & Mrs G Dubben, Bay Lodge, 27 Greenhill, Weymouth DT4 7SW
T: (01305) 782419
F: (01305) 782828
E: barbara@baylodge.co.uk
I: www.baylodge.co.uk

Baywatch ★★★
Contact: Mr T L Broadhead, Eastney Hotel, 15 Longfield Hotel, Weymouth DT4 8RQ
T: (01305) 761347
I: www.eastneyhotel.co.uk

The Beach House ★★★★
Contact: Ms Jo Skinner, Weymouth DT3
T: (01305) 770650

Beach View Apartment ★★
Contact: Mr Zachary Stuart-Brown, Dream Cottages, 41 Maiden Street, Weymouth DT4 8AZ
T: (01305) 761347
E: admin@dream-cottages.co.uk
I: www.dream-cottages.co.uk

Beachside - Weymouth ★★★
Contact: Mr Tarrant, Beachside - Weymouth, 45 Southwell, Portland DT5 2DP
T: (01305) 824108
F: (01305) 823182
E: eats@tesco.net
I: www.beachsideweymouth.co.uk

Blissco ★★
Contact: Mr Zachary Stuart-Brown, Dream Cottages, 41 Maiden Street, Weymouth DT4 8AZ
T: (01305) 761347
E: admin@dream-cottages.co.uk
I: www.dream-cottages.co.uk

Brewers House ★★★★
Contact: Ms Sue Thornton, Eastwood House, Stroudley Crescent, Preston, Weymouth DT3 6NT
T: (01305) 837474
F: (01305) 777515
E: sue@eastwoodquay.freeserve.co.uk

Bridges ★★★
Contact: Ms Lindsey Diment, 11 Love Lane, Weymouth DT4 8JZ
T: (01305) 759565
E: lyndseyd@madasafish.com

Cassis Cottage ★★
Contact: Mr Zachary Stuart-Brown, Dream Cottages, 41 Maiden Street, Weymouth DT4 8AZ
T: (01305) 761347
E: admin@dream-cottages.co.uk
I: www.dream-cottages.co.uk

Central Seafront Apartments ★★★
Contact: Mr & Mrs Wright, 21 Greenhill, Weymouth DT4 7SW
T: (01305) 766744

Cherry Tree Cottage ★★★
Contact: Mr Martin Rolls, 12 Great Western Terrace, Lodmoor, Weymouth DT4 7LU
T: (01305) 772952
F: (01305) 772952
E: cottage@rollsco.com
I: www.rollsco.com/cottage

Christopher Robin Holiday Flats ★★
Contact: Mrs Davies, Christopher Robin Holiday Flats, 70 The Esplanade, Weymouth DT4 7AA
T: (01305) 774870

Coates Way ★★★
Contact: Mr Zachary Stuart-Brown, Dream Cottages, 41 Maiden Street, Weymouth DT4 8AZ
T: (01305) 761347
E: admin@dream-cottages.co.uk
I: www.dream-cottages.co.uk

Cockleshells ★★
Contact: Mr Zachary Stuart-Brown, Dream Cottages, 41 Maiden Street, Weymouth DT4 8AZ
T: (01305) 761347
E: admin@dream-cottages.co.uk
I: www.dream-cottages.co.uk

Cove Walk Cottage ★★★★
Contact: Ms Rosemarie Latta, 7 Coniston Crescent, Weymouth DT3 5HA
T: (01305) 779144
E: dstone2880@aol.com

Crescent Cottage ★★★★
Contact: Mrs Tracy Buckwell, 38 Cleveland Avenue, Weymouth DT3 5AG
T: (01305) 771881
F: (01305) 768491
E: buckwell@btinternet.com

Crescent Cottage Rating Applied For
Contact: Dream Cottages, 41 Maiden Street, Weymouth DT4 8AZ
T: (01305) 761347
F: (01305) 789000

Crows Nest ★★★
Contact: Mr Zachary Stuart-Brown, Dream Cottages, 41 Maiden Street, Weymouth DT4 8AZ
T: (01305) 761347
E: admin@dream-cottages.co.uk
I: www.dream-cottages.co.uk

Daintree ★★
Contact: Mrs Sheila Snook, Daintree, 46 Chelmsford Street, Weymouth DT4 7HR
T: (01305) 782689

Dornare Holiday Flats ★-★★
Contact: Mrs Dorenne Fowler, Dornare Holiday Flats, Newberry Road, Weymouth DT4 8LP
T: (01305) 786359
F: (01305) 786359
E: dornare@fowler77.freeserve.co.uk

Dream Beach ★★★
Contact: Mr P Smith, 2 Littlemead, Weymouth DT3 5DL
T: (01305) 813455

Driftwood Cottage ★★★
Contact: Dream Cottages Ltd, 41 Maiden Street, Weymouth DT4 8AZ
T: (01305) 761347
E: admin@dream-cottages.co.uk
I: www.dream-cottages.co.uk

Dunvegan Holiday Cottages ★★★
Contact: Mr Ian Boudier, 1 Old Castle Road, Weymouth DT4 8QB
T: (01305) 783188
F: (01305) 783181
E: trelawney@freeuk.com

Eastleigh House ★★
Contact: Mr Zachary Stuart-Brown, Dream Cottages, 41 Maiden Street, Weymouth DT4 8AZ
T: (01305) 761347
E: admin@dream-cottages.co.uk
I: www.dream-cottages.co.uk

Ebb Tide ★★★
Contact: Mr Zachary Stuart-Brown, Dream Cottages, 41 Maiden Street, Weymouth DT4 8AZ
T: (01305) 761347
E: admin@dream-cottages.co.uk
I: www.dream-cottages.co.uk

Fairhaven Holiday Flats & Cottage ★★
Contact: Mr Peter Stark, 12 The Esplanade, Weymouth DT4 8EB
T: (01305) 760100
F: (01305) 760300
I: www.kingshotels.co.uk

Ferndale House ★★★
Contact: Mr Zachary Stuart-Brown, Dream Cottages, 41 Maiden Street, Weymouth DT4 8AZ
T: (01305) 761347
E: admin@dream-cottages.co.uk
I: www.dream-cottages.co.uk

Ferryboat Cottage ★★
Contact: Mr Zachary Stuart-Brown, Dream Cottages, 41 Maiden Street, Weymouth DT4 8AZ
T: (01305) 761347
E: admin@dream-cottages.co.uk
I: www.dream-cottages.co.uk

The Firs
Rating Applied For
Contact: Dream Cottages, 41, Maiden Street, Weymouth DT4 8AZ
T: (01305) 761347
E: admin@dream-cottages.co.uk

Fishermans Cottage ★★★
Contact: Mr Zachary Stuart-Brown, Dream Cottages, 41 Maiden Street, Weymouth DT4 8AZ
T: (01305) 761347
E: admin@dream-cottages.co.uk
I: www.dream-cottages.co.uk

Fleurs Apartment ★★★
Contact: Mr Zachary Stuart-Brown, Dream Cottages, 41 Maiden Street, Weymouth DT4 8AZ
T: (01305) 761347
E: admin@dream-cottages.co.uk
I: www.dream-cottages.co.uk

Footprints ★★★★
Contact: Mr Zachary Stuart-Brown, Dream Cottages, 41 Maiden Street, Weymouth DT4 8AZ
T: (01305) 761347
E: admin@dream-cottages.co.uk
I: www.dream-cottages.co.uk

Fuchsia's Edge ★★★
Contact: Dream Cottages, 41 Maiden Street, Weymouth DT4 8AZ
T: (01305) 761347
F: (01305) 789000

The Gables ★★★★
Contact: Mr Zachary Stuart-Brown, Dream Cottages, 41 Maiden Street, Weymouth DT4 8AZ
T: (01305) 761347
E: admin@dream-cottages.co.uk
I: www.dream-cottages.co.uk

The Gatehouse & Malthouse ★★★★
Contact: Mr Zachary Stuart-Brown, Dream Cottages, 41 Maiden Street, Weymouth DT4 8AZ
T: (01305) 761347
E: admin@dream-cottages.co.uk
I: www.dream-cottages.co.uk

Georges House ★★★★
Contact: Mr Zachary Stuart-Brown, Dream Cottages, 41 Maiden Street, Weymouth DT4 8AZ
T: (01305) 761347
E: admin@dream-cottages.co.uk
I: www.dream-cottages.co.uk

Glenthorne ★★★
Contact: Mrs Olivia Nurrish, Glenthorne, 15 Old Castle Road, Weymouth DT4 8QB
T: (01305) 777281
E: info@glenthorne-holidays.co.uk
I: www.glenthorne-holidays.co.uk

Grandview ★★★
Contact: Mr RF Downham, Grandview, 22 Greenhill, Weymouth DT4 7SG
T: (01305) 783796

Greenhill Lodge ★★★
Contact: Ms Marylou Delaplanque, Greenhill Lodge, 18 Greenhill, Weymouth DT4 7SG
T: (01305) 786351

Harbour Edge ★★★
Contact: Mr Zachary Stuart-Brown, Dream Cottages, 41 Maiden Street, Weymouth DT4 8AZ
T: (01305) 761347
E: admin@dream-cottages.co.uk
I: www.dream-cottages.co.uk

Harbour Retreat ★★★
Contact: Mr Zachary Stuart-Brown, Dream Cottages, 41 Maiden Street, Weymouth DT4 8AZ
T: (01305) 761347
E: admin@dream-cottages.co.uk
I: www.dream-cottages.co.uk

Harbour View Apartments ★★★
Contact: Mr Zachary Stuart-Brown, Dream Cottages, 41 Maiden Street, Weymouth DT4 8AZ
T: (01305) 761347
E: admin@dream-cottages.co.uk
I: www.dream-cottages.co.uk

Harbourside Apartments 1 & 2 ★-★★
Contact: Mr Zachary Stuart-Brown, Dream Cottages, 41 Maiden Street, Weymouth DT4 8AZ
T: (01305) 761347
E: admin@dream-cottages.co.uk
I: www.dream-cottages.co.uk

Holiday House ★★
Contact: Mr Saunders, 8 Sutcliffe Avenue, Weymouth DT4 9SA
T: (01305) 773307

Hops House ★★★★
Contact: Mr Zachary Stuart-Brown, Dream Cottages, 41 Maiden Street, Weymouth DT4 8AZ
T: (01305) 761347
E: admin@dream-cottages.co.uk
I: www.dream-cottages.co.uk

Howard Cottage ★★★
Contact: Mrs Barbara Willy, 5 Helston Close, Portesham, Weymouth DT3 4EY
T: (01305) 871799

Jacaranda ★★★
Contact: Mr Zachary Stuart-Brown, Dream Cottages, 41 Maiden Street, Weymouth DT4 8AZ
T: (01305) 761347
E: admin@dream-cottages.co.uk
I: www.dream-cottages.co.uk

Kenmuire Holiday Flats ★-★★★
Contact: Mr G Cotterill, Kenmuire Holiday Flats, 28 Alexandra Road, Lodmoor, Weymouth DT4 7QQ
T: (01305) 785659

Kingsview ★★
Contact: Ms Anne Breen, The Old Rectory, Lorton Lane, Weymouth DT3 5DJ
T: (01305) 814741

Lavender Cottage ★★★★
Contact: Dream Cottages, 41 Maiden Street, Weymouth DT4 8AZ
T: (01305) 761347
F: (01305) 789000

The Little Coachouse ★★★
Contact: Mr Zachary Stuart-Brown, Dream Cottages, 41 Maiden Street, Weymouth DT4 8AZ
T: (01305) 761347
E: admin@dream-cottages.co.uk
I: www.dream-cottages.co.uk

Littlecoombe Flat 1 Coombe House ★★★
Contact: The Agent, Dream Cottages, 41 Maiden Street, Weymouth DT4 8AZ
T: (01305) 761347

Lobster Pot ★★★
Contact: Mrs J Creed, Propect House, The Street, Yatton Keynell, Chippenham SN14 7BQ
T: (01249) 782713

Marina View Apartment ★★★★
Contact: Mr Zachary Stuart-Brown, Dream Cottages, 41 Maiden Street, Weymouth DT4 8AZ
T: (01305) 761347
E: admin@dream-cottages.co.uk
I: www.dream-cottages.co.uk

Mariners Way ★★★
Contact: Mr Zachary Stuart-Brown, Dream Cottages, 41 Maiden Street, Weymouth DT4 8AZ
T: (01305) 761347
E: admin@dream-cottages.co.uk
I: www.dream-cottages.co.uk

Melbury Holiday Flats ★★
Contact: Mr & Mrs Alison Lawrence, 18 Melbury Road, Weymouth DT4 0AP
T: (01305) 780052

Newlands Holiday Flats ★★-★★★
Contact: Mr & Mrs Hazel Brownsey, Newlands Holiday Flats, 10 Glendinning Avenue, Weymouth DT4 7QF
T: (01305) 784949

The Oast House ★★★★
Contact: Mr Zachary Stuart-Brown, Dream Cottages, 41 Maiden Street, Weymouth DT4 8AZ
T: (01305) 761347
E: admin@dream-cottages.co.uk
I: www.dream-cottages.co.uk

Ocean Wave ★★★★
Contact: Mr Zachary Stuart-Brown, Dream Cottages, 41 Maiden Street, Weymouth DT4 8AZ
T: (01305) 761347
E: admin@dream-cottages.co.uk
I: www.dream-cottages.co.uk

The Old Boathouse (Phoenix Holiday Flats)
Rating Applied For
Contact: Mrs Janet Bennett, Phoenix Holiday Flats, 53 Coombe Valley Road, Preston, Weymouth DT3 6NL
T: (01305) 832136
F: (01305) 834955

90 Old Castle Road
Rating Applied For
Contact: Mrs Angela Mary Blake, Weymouth Bay Holiday Apartments, 56 Greenhill, Weymouth DT4 7SL
T: (01305) 785003

Old Harbour Holiday Flats ★★
Contact: Mrs Ida Goddard, 451 Chickerell Road, Weymouth, Weymouth DT3 4DG
T: (01305) 776674

Oyster Cottage ★★★★
Contact: Mrs Burt, 46 Greenhill, Weymouth DT4 7SL
T: (01305) 761271
E: family@tburt.fsnet.co.uk

Panda Holiday Flats ★★★
Contact: Mrs Rose, Panda Holiday Flats, 12 Grosvenor Road, Weymouth DT4 7QL
T: (01305) 773817

Pear Tree Cottage ★★★
Contact: Mr Ian Boudier, 1 Old Castle Road, Weymouth DT4 8QB
T: (01305) 783188
F: (01305) 783181
E: trelawney@freeuk.com
I: www.trelawneyhotel.com

Pebble Cottage ★★★
Contact: Mr Zachary Stuart-Brown, Dream Cottages, 41 Maiden Street, Weymouth DT4 8AZ
T: (01305) 761347
E: admin@dream-cottages.co.uk
I: www.dream-cottages.co.uk

Petunia Apartment ★★★
Contact: Mr Zachary Stuart-Brown, Dream Cottages, 41 Maiden Street, Weymouth DT4 8AZ
T: (01305) 761347
E: admin@dream-cottages.co.uk
I: www.dream-cottages.co.uk

Poppies Cottage ★★★★
Contact: Mr Zachary Stuart-Brown, Dream Cottages, 41 Maiden Street, Weymouth DT4 8AZ
T: (01305) 761347
E: admin@dream-cottages.co.uk
I: www.dream-cottages.co.uk

Promenade Way
Rating Applied For
Contact: Dream Cottages, 41, Maiden Street, Weymouth DT4 8AZ
T: (01305) 761347
E: admin@dream-cottages.co.uk

Quayside ★★★
Contact: Mr A M Heath, Heath Developments Ltd, 2 St James Walk, Iver SL0 9EW
T: (01753) 654676
F: (01753) 653856
E: amhuk@aol.com

Quayside Apartment ★★★★
Contact: Mr Zachary Stuart-Brown, Dream Cottages, 41 Maiden Street, Weymouth DT4 8AZ
T: (01305) 761347
E: admin@dream-cottages.co.uk
I: www.dream-cottages.co.uk

Queensway Holiday Flats
Rating Applied For
Contact: Mr Martin Kelly, 46 Park Street, Weymouth DT4 7DF
T: (01305) 760747

Queensway Holiday Flats ★-★★★
Contact: Mr Martin Kelly, 46 Park Street, Weymouth DT4 7DF
T: (01305) 760747
I: www.precision.clara.net/queensway

Randall's Net Loft (Phoenix Holiday Flats)
Rating Applied For
Contact: Mrs Janet Bennett, Phoenix Holiday Flats, 53 Coombe Valley Road, Preston, Weymouth DT3 6NL
T: (01305) 832136
F: (01305) 834955

Rose Cottage ★★★
Contact: Mr Zachary Stuart-Brown, Dream Cottages, 41 Maiden Street, Weymouth DT4 8AZ
T: (01305) 761347
E: admin@dream-cottages.co.uk
I: www.dream-cottages.co.uk

Savoy Holiday Flats ★★★
Contact: Mr Mark Taylor, Savoy Holiday Flats, 112 The Esplanade, Weymouth DT4 7EA
T: (01305) 783254

Sea Horse Apartment ★★★★
Contact: Mr Zachary Stuart-Brown, Dream Cottages, 41 Maiden Street, Weymouth DT4 8AZ
T: (01305) 761347
E: admin@dream-cottages.co.uk
I: www.dream-cottages.co.uk

Sea Shells Holiday Flat ★★★
Contact: Mr & Mrs Duncan and Ramona Rosser, Sea Shells Holiday Flat, 26 High Street, Wyke Regis, Weymouth DT4 9NZ
T: (01305) 778540

Seabreeze ★★★
Contact: Mr Zachary Stuart-Brown, Dream Cottages, 41 Maiden Street, Weymouth DT4 8AZ
T: (01305) 761347
E: admin@dream-cottages.co.uk
I: www.dream-cottages.co.uk

Seafields ★★★
Contact: Mr Zachary Stuart-Brown, Dream Cottages, 41 Maiden Street, Weymouth DT4 8AZ
T: (01305) 761347
E: admin@dream-cottages.co.uk
I: www.dream-cottages.co.uk

Seafront Holiday Flats ★★★
Contact: Mr Stephen Taylor, 225 Dorchester Road, Weymouth DT3 5EQ
T: (01305) 780104
F: (01305) 780104

Seagull Cottage ★★★
Contact: Mr Zachary Stuart-Brown, Dream Cottages, 41 Maiden Street, Weymouth DT4 8AZ
T: (01305) 761347
E: admin@dream-cottages.co.uk
I: www.dream-cottages.co.uk

Seaside House ★★★
Contact: Mr Zachary Stuart-Brown, Dream Cottages, 41 Maiden Street, Weymouth DT4 8AZ
T: (01305) 761347
E: admin@dream-cottages.co.uk
I: www.dream-cottages.co.uk

Seaspray ★★★
Contact: Mr Zachary Stuart-Brown, Dream Cottages, 41 Maiden Street, Weymouth DT4 8AZ
T: (01305) 761347
E: admin@dream-cottages.co.uk
I: www.dream-cottages.co.uk

Seaview Cottage & Captains Cabin ★★
Contact: Mrs Wendy Evans, 811 Wyke Road, Weymouth DT4 9QN
T: (01305) 785037
E: wenjon@onetel.net.uk

The Shanty ★★★
Contact: Mr Zachary Stuart-Brown, Dream Cottages, 41 Maiden Street, Weymouth DT4 8AZ
T: (01305) 761347
E: admin@dream-cottages.co.uk
I: www.dream-cottages.co.uk

Shire Horse Mews ★★★
Contact: Mr Zachary Stuart-Brown, Dream Cottages, 41 Maiden Street, Weymouth DT4 8AZ
T: (01305) 761347
E: admin@dream-cottages.co.uk
I: www.dream-cottages.co.uk

Spinnaker House ★★★
Contact: Mr Zachary Stuart-Brown, Dream Cottages, 41 Maiden Street, Weymouth DT4 8AZ
T: (01305) 761347
E: admin@dream-cottages.co.uk
I: www.dream-cottages.co.uk

Stavordale House Holiday Flats ★★★
Contact: Mr Wallace, 49 Roman Road, Weymouth DT3 5JH
T: (01305) 789004

Stonebank Cottage ★★★★
Contact: Mrs Pru Westcott, Stonebank, 14 West Street, Chickerell, Fleet, Weymouth DT3 4DY
T: (01305) 760120
F: (01305) 760871
E: annexe@stonebank-chickerell.com
I: www.stonebank-chickerell.co.uk

Sunnywey Apartments ★★★★
Contact: Mr & Mrs Bond, Sunnywey Apartments, 27 Kirtleton Avenue, Weymouth DT4 7PS
T: (01305) 781767
E: bond@sunnywey.co.uk
I: www.sunnywey.co.uk

4 Sutcliffe Avenue ★★★
Contact: Mr MT Saunders, 8 Sutcliffe Avenue, Southill, Weymouth DT4 95A
T: (01305) 773307

Tamarisk Apartment ★★★
Contact: Mr Zachary Stuart-Brown, Dream Cottages, 41 Maiden Street, Weymouth DT4 8AZ
T: (01305) 761347
E: admin@dream-cottages.co.uk
I: www.dream-cottages.co.uk

Timbers ★★★
Contact: Mr Zachary Stuart-Brown, Dream Cottages, 41 Maiden Street, Weymouth DT4 8AZ
T: (01305) 761347
E: admin@dream-cottages.co.uk
I: www.dream-cottages.co.uk

Treetops ★★★★
Contact: Mr Zachary Stuart-Brown, Dream Cottages, 41 Maiden Street, Weymouth DT4 8AZ
T: (01305) 761347
E: admin@dream-cottages.co.uk
I: www.dream-cottages.co.uk

Trezise Holiday Home ★★★
Contact: Mr Barrie & Valerie Trezise, Riverside Cottage, 1 High Street, Wick, Bristol BS30 5QJ
T: (0117) 937 2304
E: b.trezise@btopenworld.com

Waters Edge ★★★
Contact: Mr Zachary Stuart-Brown, Dream Cottages, 41 Maiden Street, Weymouth DT4 8AZ
T: (01305) 761347
E: admin@dream-cottages.co.uk
I: www.dream-cottages.co.uk

Weyfarer Cottage ★★★
Contact: Mr Zachary Stuart-Brown, Dream Cottages, 41 Maiden Street, Weymouth DT4 8AZ
T: (01305) 761347
E: admin@dream-cottages.co.uk
I: www.dream-cottages.co.uk

Weymouth Bay Holiday Apartments ★★★
Contact: Mrs Angela Mary Blake, Weymouth Bay Holiday Apartments, 56 Greenhill, Weymouth DT4 7SL
T: (01305) 785003

Wheelwright House ★★★
Contact: Mr Zachary Stuart-Brown, Dream Cottages, 41 Maiden Street, Weymouth DT4 8AZ
T: (01305) 761347
E: admin@dream-cottages.co.uk
I: www.dream-cottages.co.uk

White Horse House ★★★
Contact: Mr Zachary Stuart-Brown, Dream Cottages, 41 Maiden Street, Weymouth DT4 8AZ
T: (01305) 761347
E: admin@dream-cottages.co.uk
I: www.dream-cottages.co.uk

Whitesands Seafront Apartments ★-★★★
Contact: Mr Harvey Bailey, Whitesands Holiday Apartments, 23 The Esplanade, Weymouth, Weymouth DT4 8DN
T: (01305) 782202

Winkle Cottage ★★★
Contact: Mr Zachary Stuart-Brown, Dream Cottages, 41 Maiden Street, Weymouth DT4 8AZ
T: (01305) 761347
E: admin@dream-cottages.co.uk
I: www.dream-cottages.co.uk

WHEDDON CROSS
Somerset

Cutthorne ★★★★
Contact: Mrs Ann Durbin, Cutthorne Farm, Wheddon Cross, Minehead TA24 7EW
T: (01643) 831255
F: (01643) 831255
E: durbin@cutthorne.co.uk
I: www.cutthorne.co.uk

Mill Cottage ★★★★
Contact: Mrs Ratcliff, Mill Cottage, Ford Farm, Draypers Way, Wheddon Cross, Minehead TA24 7EE
T: (01643) 841251
F: (01643) 841251
E: ratcliff@ford-farm.freeserve.co.uk

Pembroke ★★★
Contact: Mrs Escott, Wheddon Cross, Minehead TA24 7EX
T: (01643) 841550

Triscombe Farm ★★★★
Contact: Ruth Corby, Wheddon Cross, Minehead TA24 7HA
T: (01643) 851227
F: (01643) 851227
E: ruthattriscombe@aol.com

WHIMPLE
Devon

LSF Holiday Cottages ★★★
Contact: Mrs S Lang
T: (01404) 822989
F: (01404) 822989
E: lowersouthbrookfarm@btinternet.com

WHITCHURCH CANONICORUM
Dorset

Bereheyes Farm Cottages ★★★★
Contact: Mr & Mrs Winterbourne, Berehayes Farm Cottages, Whitchurch Canonicorum, Charmouth, Bridport DT6 6RQ
T: (01297) 489093
F: (01297) 489093
E: berehayes@tesco.net
I: www.berehayes.co.uk

Hinkhams Farm Willow View ★★
Contact: Mrs Marion Ray, Hinkhams Farm Willow View, Whitchurch Canonicorum, Ryall, Bridport DT6 6RJ
T: (01297) 489311

Taphouse Farmhouse, Courthouse Farmhouse & Courthouse Dairy★★
Contact: Mrs Sue Johnson, Cardsmill Farm, Whitchurch Canonicorum DT6 6RP
T: (01297) 489375
F: (01297) 489375
E: cardsmill@aol.com
I: www.farmhousedorset.com

WHITECROSS
Cornwall

Endsleigh ★★★
Contact: Mr & Mrs George & Sue Beresford, Endsleigh, Whitecross, Wadebridge PL27 7JD
T: (01208) 814477
E: george@gberesford.fsnet.co.uk
I: www.gberesford.fsnet.co.uk

WIDCOMBE

Highclere Rating Applied For
Contact: Mrs Elizabeth Daniel, Meadowland, 16 Cleveland Walk, Bath BA2 6JU
T: (01225) 465465
F: (01225) 465465
E: lizdaniel@tinyworld.co.uk

WIDEMOUTH BAY
Cornwall

Freestyle at Widemouth Bay Holiday Village★★
Contact: Mr Barker, 14 Brook Road, Montpelier, Bristol BS6 5LN
E: freestyle4me@yahoo.com
I: www.members.tripod.co.uk/freestyle/

Quinceborough Farm Cottages ★★★
Contact: Farm & Cottage Holidays, Victoria House, 12 Fore Street, Northam, Bideford EX39 1AW
T: (01237) 479146
F: (01237) 421512
E: enquiries@farmcott.co.uk

St Trinians ★★★
Contact: Mr D J Bluett, Derriton Mill, Pyworthy, Holsworthy EX22 6JU
T: (01409) 253064

WIDWORTHY
Devon

Sutton Barton ★★★★★
Contact: Jean Bartlett Cottage Holidays, Fore Street, Beer, Seaton EX12 3JB
T: (01297) 23221
F: (01297) 23303
E: holidays@jeanbartlett.com
I: www.netbreaks.com/jeanb

WILLITON
Somerset

Daisy Cottage ★★★★
Contact: Mrs Ann Bishop, 6 North Street, Williton, Taunton TA4 4SL
T: (01984) 632657
F: (01984) 632657

WILLSBRIDGE
South Gloucestershire

Clack Mill Farm ★★★
Contact: Mrs Gaile Gay, Clack Mill Farm, Keynsham Road, Willsbridge, Bristol BS30 6EH
T: (0117) 932 2399

WILTON
Wiltshire

Sycamore Cottage Rating Applied For
Contact: Mr & Mrs Richard & Cilla Pickett, Melrose Cottage, Lower Road, Quidhampton, Wilton, Salisbury SP2 9AS
T: (01722) 743160
E: cilla@sycamorecottage.biz

WINFORD
Somerset

Regilbury Farm ★★-★★★
Contact: Mrs J Keedwell, Regilbury Farm, Regil, Winford, Bristol BS40 8BB
T: (01275) 472265
E: janekeedwell@yahoo.co.uk

WINGFIELD
Wiltshire

Romsey Oak Cottages ★★
Contact: Mr Alan Briars, Romsey Oak Cottages, Romsey Oak Farmhouse, Bradford Road, Wingfield, Trowbridge BA14 9LS
T: (01225) 753950
F: (01225) 753950
E: enquiries@romseyoakcottages.co.uk
I: www.romseyoakcottages.co.uk

WINKLEIGH
Devon

Hen House & Donkeys Cottage ★★★
Contact: Farm & Cottage Holidays, Victoria House, 12 Fore Street, Westward Ho!, Bideford EX39 1AW
T: (01237) 479146
F: (01237) 421512
E: enquiries@farmcott.co.uk

WINSCOMBE
North Somerset

Mulberry and Medlar ★★★★
Contact: Mrs Symons, Winscombe Court, Winscombe Hill, Winscombe BS25 1DE
T: (01934) 842171
F: (01934) 842171
E: jsymons@winscombecourt.fsnet.co.uk
I: www.winscombecourt.co.uk

WINSFORD
Somerset

East Galliford ★★★
Contact: Mr Alexander, 28 Friars Stile Road, Richmond TW10 6NE
T: (020) 8940 8078
F: (020) 8940 6871
E: malcolm.alexander@interregna.com

Little Folly ★★★
Contact: Mrs Pat Hewlett, Little Folly, Folly, Winsford, Dulverton TA24 7JL
T: (01643) 851391
F: (01643) 851391
E: adrianh@softhome.net

WINTERBOURNE ABBAS
Dorset

Garden and Pine Studios ★★★
Contact: Mrs Anne Slattery, 14 Diggory Crescent, Dorchester DT1 2SP
T: (01305) 259127
E: slattery@slattery.fsnet.co.uk

WINTERBOURNE STOKE
Wiltshire

Scotland Lodge ★★
Contact: Mrs Jane Singleton, Scotland Lodge, Winterbourne Stoke, Salisbury SP3 4TF
T: (01980) 620943
F: (01980) 621403
E: scotland.lodge@virgin.net.co.uk
I: www.scotland-lodge.co.uk

WITHERIDGE
Devon

Maggies Cottage Rating Applied For
Contact: Little Quarme, Wheddon Cross, Minehead TA24 7EA
T: (01643) 841249
F: (01643) 841244
E: info@littlequarme.co.uk

WITHIEL
Cornwall

Southview Cottage ★★★
Contact: Harbour Holidays - Rock, Trebetherick House, Polzeath, Wadebridge PL27 6SB
T: (01208) 863399
F: (01208) 862218

WITHYPOOL
Somerset

Hillway Lodge ★★★
Contact: Ms Gillian Lamble, Hillway Farm, Withypool, Minehead TA24 7SA
T: (01643) 831182
E: gillian@hillwayfarm.com

Landacre Bungalow ★★★
Contact: Mrs P G Hudson, Landacre Cottage, Landacre Farm, Withypool, Minehead TA24 7SD
T: (01643) 831223

Leys Farm ★★★★★
Contact: Mr & Mrs Zurick, Leys Farm, Foxtwitchen, Withypool, Minehead TA24 7RU
T: (01643) 831427

River View ★★★
Contact: Mrs E Duthie, Walnut Tree Cottage, Llandevaud, Newport NP18 2AF
T: (01633) 400403
F: (01633) 400403

Westerclose House Cottages ★★★-★★★★★
Contact: Mrs Valerie Warner, Westerclose House Cottages, Westerclose House, Withypool, Minehead TA24 7QR
T: (01643) 831302
F: (01643) 831302
E: val@westerclose.f9.co.uk
I: www.westerclose.f9.co.uk

Westwater Cottage Rating Applied For
Contact: Mrs Sue Branfield, Westwater Cottage, Withypool, Minehead TA24 7RQ
T: (01643) 831360

WIVELISCOMBE
Somerset

The Granary ★★★★
Contact: Mr & Mrs David & Rachael Willcox, The Granary, Upcott Farm, Raddington, Chipstable, Taunton TA4 2QQ
T: (01398) 361256

Pinkhouse Farm Cottages ★★★★
Contact: Mrs D Davey, Higher Pinkhouse Farm, Waterrow, Wiveliscombe, Taunton TA4 2QX
T: (01398) 361428
F: (01398) 361428

WOODBURY
Devon

The Coach House ★★★★
Contact: Mr Paul Slade, The Coach House, Furze Close, Sanctuary Lane, Woodbury, Exeter EX5 1EX
T: (01395) 233704

Squirrel ★★★★★
Contact: Mrs Barlow, 56 Fore Street, Otterton, Budleigh Salterton EX9 7HB
T: (01395) 567676
F: (01395) 567440
E: info@thethatchedcottagecompany.com

WOODFORD
Cornwall

Woodlands Farm ★★★★
Contact: Mrs S M Webb, Woodford, Bude EX23 9HU
T: (01288) 331689
F: (01288) 331689
E: woodlandssandra@aol.com

WOOKEY
Somerset

Honeysuckle Cottage ★★★★
Contact: Mrs Luana Law, Honeysuckle Cottage, Worth, Wookey, Wells BA5 1LW
T: (01749) 678971

WOOLACOMBE
Devon

The Apartment ★★★★
Contact: Marsden's Cottage Holidays, 2 The Square, Braunton EX33 2JB
T: (01271) 813777
F: (01271) 813664
E: holidays@marsdens.co.uk
I: www.marsdens.co.uk

Baggy Leap ★★★★★
Contact: Marsdens Cottage Holidays, 2 The Square, Braunton EX33 2JB
T: (01271) 813777
F: (01271) 813664
E: holidays@marsdens.co.uk

Barricane Sands ★★★
Contact: Marsden's Cottage Holidays, 2 The Square, Braunton EX33 2JB
T: (01271) 813777
F: (01271) 813664
E: holidays@marsdens.co.uk
I: www.marsdens.co.uk

Bayview ★★★★
Contact: Mr & Mrs P & J Cornwell, Marsden's Cottage Holidays, 2 The Square, Braunton EX33 2JB
I: www.marsdens.co.uk

Beachcroft Holiday Apartments ★★★
Contact: Mrs Gill Barr, Beachcroft Holiday Apartments, Beach Road, Woolacombe EX34 7BT
T: (01271) 870655
F: (01271) 870655
E: robert@rbarr.freeserve.co.uk

Butchers Cottage ★★★
Contact: Marsden's Cottage Holidays, 2 The Square, Braunton EX33 2JB
T: (01271) 813777
F: (01271) 813664
E: holidays@marsdens.co.uk
I: www.marsdens.co.uk

40 Chichester Park ★★★
Contact: Mr & Mrs Cornwell, Marsden's Cottage Holidays, 2 The Square, Braunton EX33 2JB
I: www.marsdens.co.uk

Cove Cottage ★★
Contact: Ms Vivien Lawrence, Cove Cottage, Sharp Rock, Mortehoe, Woolacombe EX34 7EH
T: (01271) 870403

5 Devon Beach ★★★★
Contact: Mr & Mrs Peter & Janet Cornwell, Marsden's Cottage Holidays, 2 The Square, Braunton EX33 2JB
T: (01271) 813777
F: (01271) 813664
E: holidays@marsdens.co.uk
I: www.marsdens.co.uk

Dolphin Court ★★★★
Contact: Marsden's Cottage Holidays, 2 The Square, Braunton EX33 2JB
T: (01271) 813777
F: (01271) 813664
E: holidays@marsdens.co.uk
I: www.marsdens.co.uk

2 Dolphin Court ★★★★★
Contact: Marsden's Cottage Holidays, 2 The Square, Braunton EX33 2JB
T: (01271) 813777
F: (01271) 813664
E: holidays@marsdens.co.uk
I: www.marsdens.co.uk

1 Europa Park ★★
Contact: Mrs Rosemary Ann Facey, Sticklepath Lodge, Old Sticklepath Hil, Sticklepath, Barnstaple EX31 2BG
T: (01271) 343426
E: rosemary.facey@talk21.com
I: http//.www.rosemaryandderek.co.uk

Kirton ★★★
Contact: Marsdens Cottage Holidays, 2 The Square, Braunton EX33 2JB
T: (01271) 813777
E: holidays@marsdens.co.uk
I: www.marsdens.co.uk

Lundy Set ★★★★
Contact: Mr & Mrs P Cornwell, Marsden's Cottage Holidays, 2 The Square, Braunton EX33 2JB
T: (01271) 813777
F: (01271) 813664
E: holidays@marsdens.co.uk
I: www.marsdens.co.uk

Ocean View ★★★★
Contact: Marsden's Cottage Holidays, 2 The Square, Braunton EX33 2JB
T: (01271) 813777
F: (01271) 813664
E: holidays@marsdens.co.uk
I: www.marsdens.co.uk

Oysters ★★★★
Contact: Marsden's Cottage Holidays, 2 The Square, Braunton EX33 2JB
T: (01271) 813777
F: (01271) 813664
E: holidays@marsdens.co.uk
I: www.marsdens.co.uk

The Palms ★★★
Contact: Marsden's Cottage Holidays, 2 The Square, Braunton EX33 2JB
T: (01271) 813777
F: (01271) 813664
E: holidays@marsdens.co.uk
I: www.marsdens.co.uk

4 Pandora Court ★★★★
Contact: Marsden's Cottage Holidays, 2 The Square, Braunton EX33 2JB
T: (01271) 813777
F: (01271) 813664
E: holidays@marsdens.co.uk
I: www.marsdens.co.uk

5 Pandora Court ★★★★
Contact: Marsden's Cottage Holidays, 2 The Square, Braunton EX33 2JB
T: (01271) 813777
F: (01271) 813664

Potters View ★★★★
Contact: Marsdens Cottage Holidays, 2 The Square, Braunton EX33 2JB
T: (01271) 813777
F: (01271) 813664
E: holiday@marsdens.co.uk

Potters View ★★★★
Contact: Mr & Mrs Cornwell, Marsden's Cottage Holidays, 2 The Square, Braunton EX33 2JB
T: (01271) 813777

Seawatch ★★★
Contact: Marsden's Cottage Holidays, 2 The Square, Braunton EX33 2JB
T: (01271) 813777
F: (01271) 813664
I: www.marsdens.co.uk

Southover Apartments ★★★
Contact: Mr & Mrs Peter & Janet Cornwell, Marsden's Cottage Holidays, 2 The Square, Braunton EX33 2JB
T: (01271) 813777
F: (01271) 813664
E: holidays@marsdens.co.uk
I: www.marsdens.co.uk

Swallows Nest ★★★
Contact: Marsden's Cottage Holidays, 2 The Square, Braunton EX33 2JB
T: (01271) 813777
F: (01271) 813664
E: holidays@marsdens.co.uk
I: www.marsdens.co.uk

Swiss Cottage ★★★★
Contact: Marsden's Cottage Holidays, 2 The Square, Braunton EX33 2JB
T: (01271) 813777
F: (01271) 813664
E: holidays@marsdens.co.uk
I: www.marsdens.co.uk

Tamarin ★★★★
Contact: Marsden Cottage Holidays, 2 The Square, Braunton EX33 2JB
T: (01271) 813777
F: (01271) 813664
E: holidays@marsdens.co.uk

Tysoe ★★★★
Contact: Marsden's Cottage Holidays, 2 The Square, Braunton EX33 2JB
T: (01271) 813777
F: (01271) 813664
E: holidays@marsdens.co.uk
I: www.marsdens.co.uk

WOOTTON COURTENAY
Somerset

Bridge Cottage ★★
Contact: Mrs M Hawksford, Bridge Cottage, Crockford House, Wootton Courtenay, Minehead TA24 8RE
T: (01643) 841286

Exmoor View ★★★★
Contact: Mrs Carole Turner, Exmoor View, Green Close, Wootton Courtenay, Minehead TA24 8RA
T: (01643) 841482
E: info@exmoorview.co.uk
I: www.exmoorview.co.uk

Old Parlour Cottage ★★★★
Contact: Mr Bishop, Old Parlour Cottage, Hanny Cottage, Wootton Courtenay, Minehead TA24 8RE
T: (01643) 841440
E: bishop.dunn@virgin.net

Rose Cottage ★★★
Contact: Mr Bryan Fawcett, Pilgrims Way, Chew Stoke, Bristol BS40 8TZ
T: (01275) 331123
E: bryanfawcett@lineone.net

WOOTTON FITZPAINE
Dorset

Champernhayes Cottages ★★★★★
Contact: Mrs Tina Le-Clercq, Champernhayes Cottages, Wootton Fitzpaine, Bridport DT6 6DF
T: (01297) 560853
E: champernhayes@aol.com
I: www.champernhayes.com

Higher Wyld Farmhouse Annexe
Rating Applied For
Contact: Mrs Jo Day, Higher Wyld Farm, Monkton Wyld, Wootton Fitzpaine, Bridport DT6 6DE
T: (01297) 560479

WRANTAGE
Somerset

Ludwells Barn ★★★
Contact: Mr Dodd, Ludwells Barn, Wrantage, Taunton TA3 6DQ
T: (01823) 480316

WYKE REGIS
Dorset

Anchor House ★★★★
Contact: Ms Sue Thornton, Eastwood House, Stroudley Crescent, Preston, Weymouth DT3 6NT
T: (01305) 837474
F: (01305) 777515
E: sue@eastwoodquay.freeserve.co.uk

Church View ★★★
Contact: Mr Zachary Stuart-Brown, Dream Cottages, 41 Maiden Street, Weymouth DT4 8AZ
T: (01305) 761347
E: admin@dream-cottages.co.uk
I: www.dream-cottages.co.uk

Rippling Waters
Rating Applied For
Contact: Dream Cottages, 41, Maiden Street, Weymouth DT4 8AZ
T: (01305) 761347
E: admin@dream-cottages.co.uk

Serendipity ★★★★
Contact: Mr Zachary Stuart-Brown, Dream Cottages, 41 Maiden Street, Weymouth DT4 8AZ
T: (01305) 761347
E: admin@dream-cottages.co.uk
I: www.dream-cottages.co.uk

Still Waters ★★★
Contact: Mr Zachary Stuart-Brown, Dream Cottages, 41 Maiden Street, Weymouth DT4 8AZ
T: (01305) 761347
E: admin@dream-cottages.co.uk
I: www.dream-cottages.co.uk

YARCOMBE
Devon

Heaven's Mouth ★★★
Contact: Mrs Ruth Everitt, Heaven's Mouth, Beacon, Yarcombe, Honiton EX14 9LU
T: (01404) 861517
E: ruth-everitt@supanet.com

YELVERTON
Devon

Meadow Cottage ★★★★
Contact: Mrs Bridget Cole, Meadow Cottage, Greenwell Farm, Yelverton PL20 6PU
T: (01822) 853563
F: (01822) 853563
E: greenwellfarm@btconnect.com

ZELAH
Cornwall

Little Callestock Farm ★★★-★★★★★
Contact: Mrs Liz Down, Little Callestock Farm, Zelah, Truro TR4 9HB
T: (01872) 540445
F: (01872) 540445
E: liznick@littlecallestockfarm.co.uk
I: www.littlecallestockfarm.co.uk

SOUTH EAST

ABINGDON
Oxfordshire

Flat 1
Rating Applied For
Contact: Mrs Stella Carter, The Old Bakehouse, Winterborne Road, Abingdon OX14 1AJ
T: (01235) 520317
E: stella@bakehouse.supanet.com

Kingfisher Barn Holiday Cottages ★★★-★★★★
Contact: Ms Liz Beaumont, Kingfisher Barn Holiday Cottages, Culham, Abingdon OX14 3NN
T: (01235) 527590
F: (01235) 537538
E: info@kingfisherbarn.com
I: www.kingfisherbarn.com

The Old School ★★★
Contact: Mrs C A Radburn, The Old School, 16 High Street, Drayton, Abingdon OX14 4JL
T: (01235) 531557
E: gordon@theoldeschool.freeserve.co.uk

ACRISE
Kent

Ladwood Farm Cottages ★★★
Contact: Mr & Mrs Steve & Shirley Craigie, Ladwood Farm, Acrise, Folkestone CT18 8LL
T: 01303 891328
I: www.ladwood.com

ADDERBURY
Oxfordshire

Hannah's Cottage at Fletcher's ★★★★
Contact: Mrs Charlotte Holmes, Fletchers, High Street, Adderbury, Banbury OX17 3LS
T: (01295) 810308
E: charlotteaholmes@hotmail.com
I: www.holiday-rentals.com

ALBURY
Surrey

The Lodge at Overbrook
Rating Applied For
Contact: Ms Rebecca Greayer, Overbrook, Farley Green, Albury, Guildford GU5 9DN
T: (01483) 209579
F: (01483) 209579

ALCISTON
East Sussex

Rose Cottage Flat ★★★
Contact: Mrs Brenda Beck, Freedom Holiday Homes, 15 High Street, Cranbrook TN17 3EB
T: (01580) 720770
F: (01580) 720771
E: mail@freedomholidayhomes.co.uk
I: www.freedomholidayhomes.co.uk

Southdown Barn ★★★
Contact: Mr Richard Harris, Best of Brighton & Sussex Cottages Ltd, Windmill Lodge, Vicarage Lane, Rottingdean, Brighton BN2 7HD
T: (01273) 308779
F: (01273) 300266
E: brightoncottages@pavilion.co.uk
I: www.bestofbrighton.co.uk

The Studio ★★★
Contact: Mrs Brenda Beck, Freedom Holiday Homes, 15 High Street, Cranbrook TN17 3EB
T: (01580) 720770
F: (01580) 720771
E: mail@freedomholidayhomes.co.uk
I: www.freedomholidayhomes.co.uk

ALFRISTON
East Sussex

Cross House Cottage ★★★★★
Contact: Ms Jan Smith, 20 Peak Dean Lane, East Dean, Eastbourne BN20 0JD
T: (01323) 423540
F: (01323) 423540
E: jan@nightowldesign.co.uk
I: www.crosshousecottage.com

Danny Cottage ★★★★★
Contact: Mr Michael Ann, Alfriston, Polegate BN26 5XW
T: (01323) 870406
F: (01323) 870406
E: contact@dannycottage.co.uk
I: www.dannycottage.co.uk

Flint Cottage ★★★★
Contact: Mrs Shirley Moore, Renby Stables, Eridge Green, Royal Tunbridge Wells TN3 9LG
T: (01892) 864811
F: (01322) 666476
E: flintcott@aol.com
I: www.flintcottagesussex.co.uk

The Pony House ★★★★
Contact: Mrs Sandy Hernu, The Old Forge, Sloe Lane, Alfriston, Polegate BN26 5UP
T: (01323) 870303
F: (01323) 871664
E: hernu@supanet.com

Winton Barn ★★★
Contact: Mrs Fay Smith, Winton Barn, Winton Street, Alfriston, Polegate BN26 5UJ
T: (01323) 870407
F: (01323) 870407

ALTON
Hampshire

Butts House Studio ★★★
Contact: Mrs Sue Webborn, Butts House, The Butts, Alton GU34 1RD
T: (01420) 87507
F: (01420) 87624
E: chris@webborn.fsbusiness.co.uk

Woodside Farm Annexe ★
Contact: Miss V A Crisp & Mrs M Crisp, Woodside Farm, Gosport Road, Privett, Alton GU34 3NJ
T: (01730) 828359
F: (01730) 828006

ALVERSTOKE
Hampshire

28 The Avenue ★★
Contact: Mr Martin Lawson, 18 Upper Paddock Road, Watford WD19 4DZ
T: (01923) 244042
F: (01923) 244042

ALVERSTONE
Isle of Wight

Combe View ★★★
Contact: Mrs G D Oliver, Kern Farm, Alverstone, Sandown PO36 0EY
T: (01983) 403721

The Dairy, The Forge & The Grange ★★★★
Contact: Mrs J Clark, 27 Worsley Road, Gurnard, Cowes PO31 8JW
T: (01983) 294900

West Wing Kern Farmhouse ★★★★
Contact: Mrs G D Oliver, Kern Farm, Alverstone, Sandown PO36 0EY
T: (01983) 403721

ALVERSTONE GARDEN VILLAGE
Isle of Wight

Garstone ★★★★
Contact: Mrs J Clark, 27 Worsley Road, Gurnard, Cowes PO31 8JW
T: (01983) 294900

AMBERLEY
West Sussex

Culver Cottage ★★
Contact: Mrs Beryl Cruttenden
T: (01903) 746610
F: (01903) 743332

AMERSHAM
Buckinghamshire

Chiltern Cottages
Rating Applied For
Contact: Mr Stephen Hinds, Flexmore House, Hill Farm Lane, Chalfont St Giles HP8 4NT
T: (01494) 874826

AMPFIELD
Hampshire

The Den ★★★★
Contact: Mrs Beryl Knight, Birch House, Knapp Lane, Ampfield, Romsey SO51 9BT
T: (01794) 367291
F: (01794) 367291
E: beryl@knightworld.com

ANDOVER
Hampshire

Westmead ★★★
Contact: Mrs Dianna Leighton, Westmead, Amesbury Road, Weyhill, Andover SP11 8DU
T: (01264) 772513
E: westmeadweyhill@aol.com

APPLEDORE
Kent

Ashby Farms Ltd ★★-★★★
Contact: Mr Ashby, Ashby Farms Ltd, Place Farm, Woodchurch, Ashford TN26 2LZ
T: (01233) 733332
F: (01233) 733326
I: www.stay.at/ashby.farms/

ARDINGLY
West Sussex

Townhouse Bothy ★★★
Contact: Mrs Ann Campbell, Fairhaven Holiday Cottages, Derby House, 123 Watling Street, Gillingham ME7 2YY
T: (01634) 300089
F: (01634) 570157
E: enquiries@fairhaven-holidays.co.uk
I: www.fairhaven-holidays.co.uk

ARUNDEL
West Sussex

The Coachman's Flat and the Cottage ★★★
Contact: Mrs J Fuente, Mill Lane House, Slindon, Arundel BN18 0RP
T: (01243) 814440
F: (01243) 814436
E: jan.fuente@btopenworld.com
I: mill-lane-house.co.uk

Village Holidays ★★★-★★★★★
Contact: Mrs Pilkington & Miss C Booker, The William Booker Yard, The Street, Barnham, Bognor Regis BN18 0PF
T: (01243) 551073
F: (01243) 551073
E: tb@villageholidays.com
I: www.villageholidays.com

ASCOTT-UNDER-WYCHWOOD
Oxfordshire

Hedera Cottage ★★★★
Contact: Mrs Angela Richards, Manor Cottages & Cotswold Retreats, 33a Priory Lane, Burford, Oxford OX18 4SG
T: (01993) 824252
F: (01993) 824443
E: mancott@netcomuk.co.uk

ASH
Kent

Hawthorn Farm ★★★-★★★★★
Contact: Mr John Baker, Hawthorn Farm, Corner Drove, Ware, Ash, Canterbury CT3 2LU
T: (01304) 813560
F: (01304) 812482
E: info@hawthornfarm.co.uk
I: www.hawthornfarm.co.uk

ASHBURNHAM
East Sussex

Sliverick's Farm Folly ★★★
Contact: Mrs Brenda Beck, Freedom Holiday Homes, 15 High Street, Cranbrook TN17 3EB
T: (01580) 720770
F: (01580) 720771
E: mail@freedomholidayhomes.co.uk
I: www.freedomholidayhomes.co.uk

Thornden Holiday Cottages ★★★
Contact: Mr C Norman, Thornden Farm, Ashburnham, Battle TN33 9PE
T: (01435) 830207
F: (01435) 830000
I: www.country-cottages.net

ASHEY
Isle of Wight

The Springs ★★★★
Contact: Mrs Honor Vass, Island Cottage Holidays, Godshill Park Farm House, Godshill, Wroxall, Ventnor PO38 3JF
T: (01929) 480080
F: (01929) 481070
E: enq@islandcottagesholidays.com
I: www.cottageholidays.dmon.co.uk.

Tithe Barn & The Old Byre ★★★★★
Contact: Mrs Alison Jane Johnson, Little Upton Farmhouse, Little Upton Farm, Gatehouse Road, Ashey, Ryde PO33 4BS
T: (01983) 563236
F: (01983) 563236
E: alison@littleuptonfarm.co.uk
I: www.littleuptonfarm.co.uk

ASHFORD
Kent

Dean Farm ★★★★
Contact: Mrs Brenda Beck, Freedom Holiday Homes, 15 High Street, Cranbrook TN17 3EB
T: (01580) 720770
F: (01580) 720771
E: mail@freedomholidayhomes.co.uk
I: www.freedomholidayhomes.co.uk

Eversleigh Woodland Lodges ★★★
Contact: Mrs C J Drury, Eversleigh Woodland Lodges, Eversleigh House, Hornash Lane, Shadoxhurst, Ashford TN26 1HX
T: (01233) 733248
F: (01233) 733248
E: cjdrury@freeuk.com
I: www.eversleighlodges.co.uk

The Old Dairy ★★★
Contact: Mrs June Browning, Whatsole Street Farm, Elmsted, Ashford TN25 5JW
T: (01233) 750238
F: (01233) 750238

ASHINGTON
Dorset

Fripps Cottage ★★★★
Contact: Mrs Helen Edbrooke, 2 Rowlands Hill, Walford, Wimborne Minster BH21 1AN
T: (01202) 848312
F: (01202) 848349
E: john@stoneleighhouse.com

ASHLEY GREEN
Buckinghamshire

The Old Farm ★★★
Contact: Mrs Gillian Potter, The Old Farm, Hog Lane, Ashley Green, Chesham HP5 3PY
T: (01442) 866430
F: (01442) 866430
E: tc.eng@virgin.net

AYLESBURY
Buckinghamshire

Appletrees ★★★★
Contact: Hoseasons Country Cottages, Appletrees E2144, Lowestoft NR32 2LW
T: 0870 534 2342
F: 0870 902 2090
I: www.hoseasons.co.uk

AYLESFORD
Kent

Stable Cottage at Wickham Lodge ★★★★★
Contact: Mr & Mrs Bourne, The Quay, High Street, Aylesford ME20 7AY
T: (01622) 717267
F: (01622) 792855
E: wickhamlodge@aol.com

BAMPTON
Oxfordshire

Haytor Cottage ★★★
Contact: Mrs Phillips, Haytor, Lavender Square, Bampton OX18 2LR
T: (01993) 850321
E: smph@supanet.com

Tom's Barn ★★
Contact: Mr Thomas Freeman, Radcot Bridge House, Radcot, Bampton OX18 2SX
T: (01367) 810410
E: tmfreeman@btinternet.com

BANBURY
Oxfordshire

Little Good Lodge ★★★★
Contact: Ms Lynne Aries, Little Good Farm, Little Bourton, Banbury OX17 1QZ
T: (01295) 750069
F: (01295) 750069
E: littlegoodfarm@btopenworld.com
I: http://littlegoodfarm.users.btopenworld.com

Mill Wheel Cottage ★★★★
Contact: Mrs Sheila Nichols, Mill House Farm, King's Sutton, Banbury OX17 3QP
T: (01295) 811637
F: (01295) 811637
I: www.holiday-rentals.com

BARNHAM
West Sussex

Welldiggers ★★★★★
Contact: Mrs Penelope Crawford, Church Farm Barns, Hill Lane, Barnham, Bognor Regis PO22 0BN
T: (01243) 555119
F: (01243) 552779
E: welldiggers@hotmail.com
I: www.welldiggers.co.uk

BARTON ON SEA
Hampshire

Rose Cottage ★★★★
Contact: Mr Patrick Higgins, Rafters, Dilly Lane, Barton on Sea, New Milton BH25 7DQ
T: (01425) 613406
F: (01425) 613406

Solent Heights ★★★★★
Contact: Mrs Dee Philpott, Solent Heights, 53 Marine Drive East, Barton on Sea, New Milton BH25 7DX
T: (01425) 616066
F: (01425) 616066

Westbury Apartment ★★★
Contact: Mr Les Williams, 12 Greenacre, Barton on Sea, New Milton BH25 7BS
T: (01425) 620935
E: les@westbury-apartment.co.uk

BATTLE
East Sussex

Henley Bridge Stud ★★★
Contact: Mr & Mrs Martin White
T: (01424) 892076
F: (01424) 893990
E: martan@hbstud.fsnet.co.uk

Highfields ★★★
Contact: Mr & Mrs Martin Holgate, Highfields, Telham Lane, Battle TN33 0SN
T: (01424) 774865

Lonicera Lodge ★★★
Contact: Mrs Annette Hedges, Lonicera, 114 Hastings Road, Battle TN33 0TQ
T: (01424) 772835

Netherfield Hall Cottages ★★★
Contact: Mrs Jean Hawes, Netherfield Hall Cottages, Netherfield Hall, Netherfield, Battle TN33 9PQ
T: (01424) 774450
F: (01424) 774450

Stiles Garage (Battle) Ltd ★★-★★★
Contact: Mr John Stiles, Stiles Garage (Battle) Ltd, 2-3 Upper Lake, Battle TN33 0AN
T: (01424) 773155
F: (01424) 773155
E: stilesgarage@hotmail.com

BEACONSFIELD
Buckinghamshire

Roselands ★★★
Contact: Mrs June Koderisch, Roselands, 3 Beechwood Road, Beaconsfield HP9 1HP
T: (01494) 676864
F: (01494) 676864
E: dkoderisch@iname.com

BEARSTED
Kent

The Haven ★★★★
Contact: Mrs Valerie Jensen, Parsons Cottage, The Green, Bearsted, Maidstone ME14 4DL
T: (01622) 737479
E: johnvaljensen@aol.com
I: www.thehavenbearsted.co.uk

Laurel Cottage ★★★
Contact: Mr Kevin Street, 43 The Landway, Bearstead, Bearsted, Maidstone ME14 4BG
T: (01622) 739713
F: (01622) 631249

The Water Tower ★★★★
Contact: Country Holidays Ref: 13684, Country Holidays, Spring Mill, Earby, Barnoldswick BB94 0AA
T: 08700 723723
F: (01282) 844288
E: sales@holidaycottagesgroup.com
I: www.country-holidays.co.uk

BEAULIEU
Hampshire

Hill Top House Cottage ★★★★
Contact: Mr & Mrs Brett Johnson, Hill Top House, Palace Lane, Beaulieu, Brockenhurst SO42 7YG
T: (01590) 612731
F: (01590) 612743
E: bretros@interalpha.co.uk

Ivy Cottage ★★★
Contact: Mr & Mrs B R Gibb, 28 Church Street, Littlehampton BN17 5PX
T: (01903) 715595
F: (01903) 719176
E: gibb28@breathemail.net

Mares Tails Cottage ★★★★
Contact: Mrs Alice Barber, Mares Tails, Furzey Lane, Beaulieu, Brockenhurst SO42 7WB
T: (01590) 612160
E: marestails@ukonline.co.uk

Old Stables Cottage ★★★★
Contact: Mr & Mrs Peter & Jo Whapham, East Boldre, Beaulieu, Brockenhurst SO42 7WU
T: (01590) 626707
E: oldstablescott@aol.com

BECKLEY
East Sussex

Bixley ★★★
Contact: Ms Philippa Bushe, 93 Balfour Road, London N5 2HE
T: (0207) 226 9035
E: tim@busheassoc.com

The Herdsman & The Blacksmith's Cottage ★★★-★★★★
Contact: Mr Stuart Winter, Garden of England Cottages Ltd, The Mews Office, 189a High Street, Tonbridge TN9 1BX
T: (01732) 369168
F: (01732) 358817
E: holidays@gardenofenglandcottages.co.uk
I: www.gardenofenglandcottages.co.uk

BEECH
Hampshire

4B Wellhouse Road ★★★★
Contact: Mr Norman Adams, 4A Wellhouse Road, Beech, Alton GU34 4AH
T: (01420) 542011

BEMBRIDGE
Isle of Wight

Allandale ★★
Contact: Mrs Ellis, Bembridge Holiday Homes, 13 High Street, Bembridge PO35 5SD
T: (01983) 872335

1 Bay Cottages
Rating Applied For
Contact: Mrs J Ellis, Bembridge Holiday Homes, 13 High Street, Bembridge PO35 5SD
T: (01983) 872335

Bella Vista
Rating Applied For
Contact: Mrs Ellis, Bembridge Holiday Homes, 13 High Street, Bembridge PO35 5SD
T: (01983) 872335

Cara Cottage ★★★
Contact: Mrs J Ellis, Bembridge Holiday Homes, 13 High Street, Bembridge PO35 5SD
T: (01983) 872335

Casa Blanca
Rating Applied For
Contact: Mrs Ellis, Bembridge Holiday Homes, 13 High Street, Bembridge PO35 5SD
T: (01983) 872335

The Chalet
Rating Applied For
Contact: Mrs Ellis, Bembridge Holiday Homes, 13 High Street, Bembridge PO35 5SD
T: (01983) 872335

Cliff Cottage ★★
Contact: Mrs J Clark, 27 Worsley Road, Gurnard, Cowes PO31 8JW
T: (01983) 294900

Crab Cottage ★★★
Contact: Mrs J Ellis, Bembridge Holiday Homes, 13 High Street, Bembridge PO35 5SD
T: (01983) 872335

Crossways ★★★
Contact: Mrs J Ellis, Bembridge Holiday Homes, 13 High Street, Bembridge PO35 5SD
T: (01983) 872335

Dolphin Cottage ★★★
Contact: Ms Lisa Baskill, Home from Home Holidays, 31 Pier Street, Ventnor PO38 1SX
T: (01983) 854340
F: (01983) 855524

8 Downsview Road ★★
Contact: Mrs J Ellis, Bembridge Holiday Homes, 13 High Street, Bembridge PO35 5SD
T: (01983) 872335

3 Fairhaven Close ★★
Contact: Mrs J Ellis, Bembridge Holiday Homes, 13 High Street, Bembridge PO35 5SD
T: (01983) 872335

The Finches ★★★
Contact: Mrs J Ellis, Bembridge Holiday Homes, 13 High Street, Bembridge PO35 5SD
T: (01983) 872335

Flat 3 Pump Mews ★★★
Contact: Residential & Holiday Letting Agents, 177 High Street, Ryde PO33 2HW
T: (01983) 616644
F: (01983) 568822
E: rental_office@hose-Rhodes-Dickson.co.uk
I: www.island-holiday-homes.net

Folly Hill Cottage ★★
Contact: Ms Lisa Baskill, Home from Home Holidays, 31 Pier Street, Ventnor PO38 1SX
T: (01983) 854340
F: (01983) 855524

Forelands Cottage ★★
Contact: Mrs J Ellis, Bembridge Holiday Homes, 13 High Street, Bembridge PO35 5SD
T: (01983) 872335

Green Oaks ★★★
Contact: Mrs J Ellis, Bembridge Holiday Homes, 13 High Street, Bembridge PO35 5SD
T: (01983) 872335

Harbour Farm Cottage and Harbour Farm Lodge ★★★
Contact: Mr Kenneth Hicks, Embankment Road, St Helens, Ryde PO35 5NS
T: (01983) 872610
F: (01983) 874080
I: www.harbourfarm.co.uk

3 Harbour Strand ★★★
Contact: Mrs J Clark, 27 Worsley Road, Gurnard, Cowes PO31 8JW
T: (01983) 294900

4 Highbury Court ★★★
Contact: Mrs C Page, 32 Mays Avenue, Carlton, Nottingham NG4 1AU
T: (0115) 987 4420

Hilvana ★★
Contact: Mrs J Ellis, Bembridge Holiday Homes, 13 High Street, Bembridge PO35 5SD
T: (01983) 872335

Honeysuckle Haven ★★
Contact: Mrs J Ellis, Bembridge Holiday Homes, 13 High Street, Bembridge PO35 5SD
T: (01983) 872335

51 Howgate Road
Rating Applied For
Contact: Mrs Ellis, Bembridge Holiday Homes, 13 High Street, Bembridge PO35 5SD
T: (01983) 872335

Kestrel
Rating Applied For
Contact: Mrs Ellis, Bembridge Holiday Homes, 13 High Street, Bembridge PO35 5SD
T: (01983) 872335

Kings Close
Rating Applied For
Contact: Mrs J Ellis, Bembridge Holiday Homes, 13 High Street, Bembridge PO35 5SD
T: (01983) 872335

Kingsmere ★★
Contact: Mrs M Kersley, Kingsmere, Lane End, Bembridge PO35 5TB
T: (01983) 872778

Little Forelands ★★★★
Contact: Mrs J Ellis, Bembridge Holiday Homes, 13 High Street, Bembridge PO35 5SD
T: (01983) 872335

Meadow Dairy ★★★
Contact: Ms Lisa Baskill, Home from Home Holidays, 31 Pier Street, Ventnor PO38 1SX
T: (01983) 854340
F: (01983) 855524

Mimosa Cottage ★★★
Contact: Ms Lisa Baskill, Home from Home Holidays, 31 Pier Street, Ventnor PO38 1SX
T: (01983) 854340
F: (01983) 855524

Nine ★★★
Contact: Mrs B C Cripps, High Point, Brook Green, Cuckfield, Haywards Heath RH17 5JJ
T: (01444) 454474

Pitt Corner ★★★
Contact: Ms Lisa Baskill, Home from Home Holidays, 31 Pier Street, Ventnor PO38 1SX
T: (01983) 854340
F: (01983) 855524

11 Port St Helens ★★
Contact: Mrs J Ellis, Bembridge Holiday Homes, 13 High Street, Bembridge PO35 5SD
T: (01983) 872335

Portland House ★★★★
Contact: Mrs J Ellis, Bembridge Holiday Homes, 13 High Street, Bembridge PO35 5SD
T: (01983) 872335

Princessa Cottage & Coastwatch Cottage ★★★
Contact: Mrs Hargreaves, 1 Norcott Drive, Bembridge PO35 5TX
T: (01983) 874403
F: (01983) 874403
E: ssnharg@aol.com

Rosemullion
Rating Applied For
Contact: Mr Matthew White, Island Holiday Homes, 138 High Street, Newport PO30 1TY
T: (01983) 521114

Rothsay Cottage
Rating Applied For
Contact: Mrs Ellis, Bembridge Holiday Homes, 13 High Street, Bembridge PO35 5SD
T: (01983) 872335

Seahorses ★★★
Contact: Mrs Ellis, Bembridge Holiday Homes, 13 High Street, Bembridge PO35 5SD
T: (01983) 872335

September Cottage ★★
Contact: Mrs J Ellis, Bembridge Holiday Homes, 13 High Street, Bembridge PO35 5SD
T: (01983) 872335

Ship-n-Shore ★★★★
Contact: Mr Chris Durham, Dunmow Road, North End, Barnston, Great Dunmow CM6 3PJ
T: (01245) 237481
E: thebutchersarms@tesco.net

12a Solent Landings ★★★
Contact: Mr Matthew White, Island Holiday Homes, 138 High Street, Newport PO30 1TY
T: (01983) 521114

4 Swains Villas ★★★
Contact: Mrs J Ellis, Bembridge Holiday Homes, 13 High Street, Bembridge PO35 5SD
T: (01983) 872335

Will-o-Cott ★★
Contact: Mrs Betty Cripps, High Point, Brook Green, Cuckfield, Haywards Heath RH17 5JJ
T: (01444) 454474

Windmill Inn, Hotel & Restaurant ★★★-★★★★
Contact: Mrs Elizabeth Miles, Windmill Hotels Ltd, 1 Steyne Road, Bembridge PO35 5UH
T: (01983) 872875
F: (01983) 874760
E: enquiries@windmill-inn.com
I: www.windmill-inn.com

BENENDEN
Kent

Beacon Hall Farm Cottages/ Bluebell Cottage★★★
Contact: Mrs Brenda Beck, Freedom Holiday Homes, 15 High Street, Cranbrook TN17 3EB
T: (01580) 720770
F: (01580) 720771
E: mail@freedomholidayhomes.co.uk
I: www.freedomholidayhomes.co.uk

Coopers Cottage ★★★★
Contact: Mr Stuart Winter, Garden of England Cottages Ltd, The Mews Office, 189a High Street, Tonbridge TN9 1BX
T: (01732) 369168
F: (01732) 358817
E: holidays@gardenofenglandcottages.co.uk
I: www.gardenofenglandcottages.co.uk

Standen Barn ★★★★
Contact: Mr Stuart Winter, Garden of England Cottages Ltd, The Mews Office, 189a High Street, Tonbridge TN9 1BX
T: (01732) 369168
F: (01732) 358817
E: holidays@gardenofenglandcottages.co.uk
I: www.gardenofenglandcottages.co.uk

BEPTON
West Sussex

The Coach House ★★★
Contact: Dr Jennifer Randall, The Coach House, Bepton, Midhurst GU29 0HZ
T: (01730) 812351

BERE REGIS
Dorset

Brockhill Loft ★★★
Contact: Mrs Peg Browning, Cecily Cottage, Brockhill, Bere Regis, Wareham BH20 7NH
T: (01929) 471552
F: (01929) 471886
E: pegbrowning@aol.com

Troy, Bathsheba & Oak Cottages ★★★★
Contact: Mr Ian Ventham, Shitterton Farmhouse, Bere Regis, Wareham BH20 7HU
T: (01929) 471480
E: info@shitterton.com
I: www.shitterton.com

Victoria Cottage ★★★★
Contact: Mrs Patricia Sage, Regency Cottage, Church Lane, Wool, Wareham BH20 6DD
T: (01929) 462229
F: (01929) 462229
E: agbrend@fricsfciarb.demon.co.uk

BETHERSDEN
Kent

The Mill House ★★★★
Contact: Mrs Brenda Beck, Freedom Holiday Homes, 15 High Street, Cranbrook TN17 3EB
T: (01580) 720770
F: (01580) 720771
E: mail@freedomholidayhomes.co.uk
I: www.freedomholidayhomes.co.uk

Oast Mews ★★★
Contact: Mr Tim Bourne, Kent Holiday Cottages, Shepherd's View, Brissenden Court, Bethersden, Ashford TN26 3BE
T: (01233) 820746
F: (01233) 820746

BEXHILL
East Sussex

Beachcomber Flat ★★★
Contact: Mrs V Mathews, Miraleisure Ltd, 51 Marina, Bexhill TN40 1BQ
T: (01424) 730298
F: (01424) 212500
E: infomira@waitrose.com

Boulevard Flat ★★★
Contact: Mrs V Mathews, Miraleisure Ltd, 51 Marina, Bexhill TN40 1BQ
T: (01424) 730298
F: (01424) 212500
E: infomira@waitrose.com

Carlton Flat ★★★
Contact: Mrs V Mathews, Miraleisure Ltd, 51 Marina, Bexhill TN40 1BQ
T: (01424) 730298
F: (01424) 212500
E: infomira@waitrose.com

Devonshire Flat ★★★
Contact: Mrs V Mathews, Miraleisure Ltd, 51 Marina, Bexhill TN40 1BQ
T: (01424) 730298
F: (01424) 212500
E: infomira@waitrose.com

Eversley Flat ★★
Contact: Mrs V Mathews, Miraleisure Ltd, 51 Marina, Bexhill TN40 1BQ
T: (01424) 730298
F: (01424) 212500
E: informira@waitrose.com

Flat 1 Trent House ★★★
Contact: Mrs Brenda Beck, Freedom Holiday Homes, 15 High Street, Cranbrook TN17 3EB
T: (01580) 720770
F: (01580) 720771
E: mail@freedomholidayhomes.co.uk
I: www.freedomholidayhomes.co.uk

Haven Flat ★★★
Contact: Mrs V Mathews, Miraleisure Ltd, 51 Marina, Bexhill TN40 1BQ
T: (01424) 730298
F: (01424) 212500
E: infomira@waitrose.com

27 Linden Road ★★★
Contact: Mrs Mathews, Miraleisure Ltd, 51 Marina, Bexhill TN40 1BQ
T: (01424) 730298
F: (01424) 212500
E: infomira@waitrose.com

Mansion Flat ★★★★
Contact: Mrs V Mathews, Miraleisure Ltd, 51 Marina, Bexhill TN40 1BQ
T: (01424) 730298
F: (01424) 212500
E: infomira@waitrose.com

Marina Flat ★★★
Contact: Mrs V Mathews, Miraleisure Ltd, 51 Marina, Bexhill TN40 1BQ
T: (01424) 730298
F: (01424) 212500
E: infomira@waitrose.com

Mariners Flat ★★★
Contact: Mrs V Mathews, Miraleisure Ltd, 51 Marina, Bexhill TN40 1BQ
T: (01424) 730298
F: (01424) 212500
E: infomira@waitrose.com

Miramar Holiday Flats ★★★
Contact: Mrs Carolyn Simmonds, Miramar Holiday Flats, De La Warr Parade, Bexhill TN40 1NR
T: (01424) 220360

Mulberry ★★★
Contact: Mrs Valerie Passfield, Mulberry, 31 Warwick Road, Bexhill TN39 4HG
T: (01424) 219204

Pavilion Flat ★★★
Contact: Mrs V Mathews, Miraleisure Ltd, 51 Marina, Bexhill TN40 1BQ
T: (01424) 730298
F: (01424) 212500
E: infomira@waitrose.com

Promenade Flat ★★★
Contact: Mrs V Mathews, Miraleisure Ltd, 51 Marina, Bexhill TN40 1BQ
T: (01424) 730298
F: (01424) 212500
E: infomira@waitrose.com

Riviera Flat ★★★
Contact: Mrs V Mathews, Miraleisure Ltd, 51 Marina, Bexhill TN40 1BQ
T: (01424) 730298
F: (01424) 212500
E: infomira@waitrose.com

Sackville Hotel ★★★★
Contact: Ms Amanda Fiora, Sackville Hotel, De La Warr Parade, Bexhill-on-Sea, Bexhill TN40 1LS
T: (01424) 224694
F: (01424) 734132

Sea Whispers ★★★
Contact: Mrs V Mathews, Miraleisure Ltd, 51 Marina, Bexhill TN40 1BQ
T: (01424) 730298
F: (01424) 212500
E: infomira@waitrose.com

Seaside Flat ★★★
Contact: Mrs Mathews, Miraleisure Ltd, 51 Marina, Bexhill TN40 1BQ
T: (01424) 730298
F: (01424) 212500
E: infomira@waitrose.com

Sovereign Flat ★★★
Contact: Mrs V Mathews, Miraleisure Ltd, 51 Marina, Bexhill TN40 1BQ
T: (01424) 730298
F: (01424) 212500
E: infomira@waitrose.com

Sylvian ★★★
Contact: Adrian or Nicola Hazell, 40 Fairfield Chase, Bexhill TN39 3YD
T: (01424) 733955
F: (01424) 733955
E: nicola@ajcleaning.fsbusiness.co.uk

Wilton Flat ★★★
Contact: Mrs V Mathews, Miraleisure Ltd, 51 Marina, Bexhill TN40 1BQ
T: (01424) 730298
F: (01424) 212500
E: infomira@waitrose.com

BICESTER
Oxfordshire

Pimlico Farm Country Cottages ★★★★
Contact: Mr & Mrs John & Monica Harper, Pimlico Farm Country Cottages, Pimlico Farm, Tusmore, Bicester OX27 7SL
T: (01869) 810306
F: (01869) 810309
E: enquiries@pimlicofarm.co.uk
I: www.pimlicofarm.co.uk

BIDDENDEN
Kent

Garden Cottage
Rating Applied For
Contact: Mrs Brenda Beck, Freedom Holiday Homes, 15 High Street, Cranbrook TN17 3EB
T: (01580) 720770
F: (01580) 720771
E: mail@freedomholidayhomes.co.uk
I: www.freedomholidayhomes.co.uk

Tanyard Barn ★★★★
Contact: Mr Stuart Winter, Garden of England Cottages Ltd, The Mews Office, 189a High Street, Tonbridge TN9 1BX
T: (01732) 369168
F: (01732) 358817
E: holidays@gardenofenglandcottages.co.uk
I: www.gardenofenglandcottages.co.uk

BILSINGTON
Kent

Stonecross Farm Barn ★★★★
Contact: Mr & Mrs John & Jane Hickman, Stonecross Farm Barn, Stonecross Farm, Stonecross, Bilsington, Ashford TN25 7JJ
T: (01233) 720397
E: stonecrossbarn@tiscali.co.uk

BINFIELD
Berkshire

5 Bitterne Place
Rating Applied For
Contact: Mr Matthew White, Island Holiday Homes, 138 High Street, Newport PO30 1TY
T: (01983) 521114

BIRDHAM
West Sussex

The Old Dairy ★★★★
Contact: Mrs Diana Strange, Carthagena Farm, Bell Lane, Earnley, Chichester PO20 7HY
T: (01243) 513885

BISHOPSTONE
East Sussex

144 Norton Cottage ★★★
Contact: Mrs Carol Collinson, Inces Barn, Norton Farm, Bishopstone, Seaford BN25 2UW
T: (01323) 897544
F: (01323) 897544
E: norton.farm@farmline.com

BLANDFORD FORUM
Dorset

The Lodge, the Stable & Plumtree Cottage★★★
Contact: Mrs Penny Cooper, Dairy House Farm, Woolland, Blandford Forum DT11 0EY
T: (01258) 817501
F: (01258) 818060
E: penny.cooper@farming.me.uk
I: www.self-cateringholidays4u.co.uk

Old Rectory Cottage
Rating Applied For
Contact: Mrs Margaret Waldie, Old Rectory Cottage, Lower Blandford St Mary, Blandford Forum DT11 9ND
T: (01258) 453220

Shepherds Cottage ★★★
Contact: CH ref; 8002, 8003, 8322, Country Holidays, Spring Mill, Earby, Barnoldswick BB94 0AA
T: 08700 723723
F: (01282) 844288
E: sales@holidaycottagesgroup.com
I: www.country-holidays.co.uk

BLEAN
Kent

50 School Lane ★★★★
Contact: Mrs Brenda Beck, Freedom Holiday Homes, 15 High Street, Cranbrook TN17 3EB
T: (01580) 720770
F: (01580) 720771
E: mail@freedomholidayhomes.co.uk
I: www.freedomholidayhomes.co.uk

BOLDRE
Hampshire

Close Cottage ★★★
Contact: Mr & Mrs C J White, Close Cottage, Brockenhurst Road, Battramsley, Boldre, Lymington SO41 8PT
T: (01590) 675343

Orchard House ★★★
Contact: Mrs Valerie Barnes, Orchard House, Battramsley, Boldre, Lymington SO41 8ND
T: (01590) 676686

Springfield Wing, Boldre ★★★
Contact: Mr & Mrs David or Rosemary Scott, Springfield Wing, Boldre, Shirley Holms, Boldre, Pennington, Lymington SO41 8NG
T: (01590) 672491
E: david.scott@nfdc.gov.uk
I: www.vnewforest.co.uk

BONCHURCH
Isle of Wight

Ashcliff Holiday Apartments
Rating Applied For
Contact: Mrs Judith Lines, Ashcliff Holiday Apartments, The Pitts, Bonchurch, Ventnor PO38 1NT
T: (01983) 853919
F: (01983) 853919
E: ashcliff.iow@virgin.net

Fernwood Cottage ★★★★
Contact: Mrs J Clark, 27 Worsley Road, Gurnard, Cowes PO31 8JW
T: (01983) 294900

Hadfield Cottage ★★★
Contact: Mrs Honor Vass, Island Cottage Holidays, The Old Vicarage, Kingston, Wareham BH20 5LH
T: (01929) 480080
F: (01929) 481070
E: enq@islandcottageholidays.com
I: www.islandcottageholidays.com

Regent Court Holiday Bungalows ★★★
Contact: Mrs Smith, Windycroft, Park Road, Wootton Bridge, Ryde PO33 4RL
T: (01983) 883782
E: smith.windycroft@tinyworld.co.uk
I: www.cottageguide.co.uk/regentcourt

2 Regents Court Holiday Bungalows ★★★
Contact: Mrs Lyn Daly, 65 High Street, Carisbrooke, Newport PO30 1NT
T: (01983) 530825
E: ld@teas.fsbusiness.co.uk

Uppermount ★★★★
Contact: Mrs Honor Vass, The Old Vicarage, Kingston, Wareham BH20 5LH
T: (01929) 480080
F: (01929) 481070
E: enq@islandcottageholidays.com
I: www.islandcottageholidays.com

Wyndcliffe Holiday Apartments ★★★★
Contact: Mrs Rosalind Young, Wyndcliffe Holiday Apartments, 16 Spring Gardens, Ventnor PO38 1QX
T: (01983) 853458
F: (01983) 853272

BONNINGTON
Kent

Bonnington Court ★★
Contact: Mrs Monika Mann, Bonnington Court, Bonnington, Ashford TN25 7BA
T: (01233) 720521
F: (01233) 720521
E: m-mann@beeb.net
I: www.bonningtoncourt.com

BOOKHAM
Surrey

Woodlands ★★★
Contact: Mr Victor Edwards, Woodlands, 31 Woodlands Road, Bookham, Leatherhead KT23 4HG
T: (01372) 453281
F: (01372) 453281
E: vicedwards@btopenworld.com

BORDON
Hampshire

Tunford Cottage Lodge ★★
Contact: Mrs Anne Symon, Tunford Cottage Lodge, Tunford Cottage, Oakhanger, Selborne, Alton GU35 9JE
T: (01420) 473159
E: symon@tunford.freeserve.co.uk

BORTHWOOD
Isle of Wight

Borthwood Cottages ★★★
Contact: Ms Anne Finch, Borthwood Cottages, c/o Sandlin Boarding Kennels, Borthwood, Sandown PO36 0HH
T: (01983) 402011

BOSCOMBE
Dorset

Flat 2 St George's Mansions ★★
Contact: Mr Palmer, Greenmount, Cleeve Hill, Cheltenham GL52 3PR
T: (07711) 802788

BOSHAM
West Sussex

The Warren ★★★
Contact: Mrs Gillian Odell, The Warren, Main Road, Bosham, Hambrook, Chichester PO18 8PL
T: (01243) 573927
F: (01243) 573927

BOUGHTON MONCHELSEA
Kent

Dovecote ★★★★
Contact: Mrs Gill Beveridge, Dovecote, Wierton Oast, Wierton Hill, Boughton Monchelsea, Maidstone ME17 4JT
T: (01622) 741935
F: (01622) 741935
E: gill.beveridge@lineone.net

BOURNEMOUTH
Dorset

Sea Road Holiday Apartments ★★★
Contact: Mr S A Lees, 581 Christchurch Road, Boscombe, Bournemouth BH1 4BU
T: (01202) 721666
F: (01202) 303490

Shalbourne House Holiday Flats ★★★
Contact: Mr Tony Parker, Shalbourne House Holiday Flats, 17 Grand Avenue, Southbourne, Bournemouth BH6 3SY
T: (01202) 432735
I: www.bhfa.co.uk/shalbourne-house-holiday-flats

Woodview Holiday Apartments ★★★★
Contact: Mr Shane Busby, Woodview Holiday Apartments, 6 St Anthony's Road, Meyrick Park, Bournemouth BH2 6PD
T: (01202) 290027
F: (01202) 295959
E: woodview.holidays@virgin.net
I: www.SmoothHound.co.uk/hotels/woodview.html

BOWLHEAD GREEN
Surrey

The Barn Flat ★★
Contact: Mrs Grace Ranson, Bowlhead Green Farm, Bowlhead Green, Thursley, Godalming GU8 6NW
T: (01428) 682687

BOXLEY
Kent

Styles Cottage ★★
Contact: Mrs Sue Mayo, Styles Cottage, Styles Lane, Boxley, Maidstone ME14 3DZ
T: (01622) 757567
E: sue.mayo@virgin.net
I: www.freespace.virginnet.co.uk/styles.cottage/

BRACKLESHAM BAY
West Sussex

Broadwater ★★★★
Contact: Mr & Mrs Michael & Susan Wright, Broadwater, West Bracklesham Drive, Bracklesham Bay, East Wittering, Chichester PO20 8PH
T: (01243) 670059
F: (01243) 670059

39 Marineside ★★★
Contact: Mrs Kirsten Spanswick, 33 Cartier Close, Old Hall, Warrington WA5 5TD
T: (01925) 652334
F: (01925) 499552
E: chris.spanswick@ntlworld.com
I: homepage.ntlworld.com/chris.spanswick/

Searide ★★★
Contact: Mrs Karen Brooker, Baileys, 17 Shore Road, East Wittering, West Wittering, Chichester PO20 8DY
T: (01243) 672217
F: (01243) 670100
E: info@baileys.uk.com
I: www.baileys.uk.com

BRADING Isle of Wight

Albion House ★★★
Contact: Mr Gorton, Albion House, High Street, Brading, Sandown PO36 0DQ
T: (01983) 407749

Anemoen ★★★
Contact: Mrs J Clark, 27 Worsley Road, Gurnard, Cowes PO31 8JW
T: (01983) 294900

Moles Leap ★★
Contact: Mrs J Clark, 27 Worsley Road, Gurnard, Cowes PO31 8JW
T: (01983) 294900

The Old Bakery ★★★
Contact: Ms Lisa Baskill, Home from Home Holidays, 31 Pier Street, Ventnor PO38 1SX
T: (01983) 854340
F: (01983) 855524

The Stables ★★★
Contact: Mrs Diane Morris, New Farm, Coach Lane, Brading, Sandown PO36 0JQ
T: (01635) 200316

Thistlewaite ★★★★
Contact: Mrs Jan Hegarty, Rock Cottage, Melville Street, Sandown PO36 9JW
T: (01983) 409707
E: jananddon-rock2@yahoo.com

BRAISHFIELD Hampshire

Meadow Cottage & Rosie's Cottage ★★★
Contact: Mrs Wendy Graham, Farley Farm Cottage Holidays, Farley Farm, Braishfield, Romsey SO51 0QP
T: (01794) 368265
F: (01794) 367847

BRAMLEY Surrey

Converted Stable at Juniper Cottage ★★
Contact: Mr Bob Heyes, Juniper Cottage, 22 Eastwood Road, Bramley, Guildford GU5 0DS
T: (01483) 893706
F: (01483) 894001
E: heyes@tiscali.co.uk
I: www.users.totalise.co.uk/~bobheyes

Old Timbers ★★★
Contact: Mrs P Taylor, Old Timbers, Snowdenham Links Road, Old Timbers, Bramley, Guildford GU5 0BX
T: (01483) 893258
E: jpold_timbers@hotmail.com

BRANKSOME Dorset

Danehurst Holiday Flat ★★★
Contact: Mr John Richings, Danehurst Holiday Flat, 15 Brunstead Road, Branksome, Poole BH12 1EJ
T: (01202) 768632

BRASTED Kent

Courtside Cottage ★★★★
Contact: Mrs J R Couch, Courtside Lodge, Station Road, Brasted, Westerham TN16 1NT
T: (01959) 561494
E: jeannecouch@hotmail.com

BREDE East Sussex

Eastwood Cottage Rating Applied For
Contact: Mrs Gill Winter, Garden of England Cottages, The Mews Office, 189A High Street, Tonbridge TN9 1BX
T: (01732) 369168
F: (01732) 358817
E: holidays@gardenofenglandcottages.co.uk

BRIGHSTONE Isle of Wight

The Brew House ★★★★
Contact: Mrs Honor Vass, The Old Vicarage, Kingston, Wareham BH20 5LH
T: (01929) 480080
F: (01929) 481070
E: enq@islandcottageholidays.com
I: www.islandcottageholidays.com

Casses - Brighstone - Isle of Wight ★★★★
Contact: Mr & Mrs Nesbitt, Peartree Court, Old Orchards, Lymington SO41 3TF
T: (01590) 679601
E: jkn@casses.fsbusiness.co.uk

Chilton Farm Cottages ★★★
Contact: Mrs Susan Fisk, Chilton Farm Cottages, Chilton Farm, Chilton Lane, Brighstone PO30 4DS
T: (01983) 740338
F: (01983) 741370
E: info@chiltonfarm.co.uk
I: www.chiltonfarm.co.uk

2 The Granary ★★★★
Contact: Mr & Mrs David & Vanessa Lovett, 27 Dixons Hill Close, North Mymms, Hatfield AL9 7EF
T: (01707) 267976

Grange Farm - Brighstone Bay ★★★
Contact: Mr D J Dunjay, Grange Farm, Military Road, Brighstone Bay, Isle of Wight PO30 4DA
T: (01983) 740296
F: (01983) 741233
E: grangefarm@brighstonebay.fsnet.co.uk
I: www.brighstonebay.fsnet.co.uk

Ivy Cottage ★★★
Contact: Mr Matthew White, Island Holiday Homes, 138 High Street, Newport PO30 1TY
T: (01983) 521114

Pool Cottage ★★★★★
Contact: Mr John Russell, Thorncross Farm, Brighstone, Newport PO30 4PN
T: (01983) 740291
F: (01983) 741408

Rose Cottage ★★★★★
Contact: Mr John Russell, Thorncross Farm, Brighstone, Newport PO30 4PN
T: (01983) 740291

Stable Cottage ★★★★
Contact: Mrs Honor Vass, Island Cottage Holidays, The Old Vicarage, Kingston, Wareham BH20 5LH
T: (01929) 480080
F: (01929) 481070
E: enq@islandcottageholidays.com
I: www.islandcottageholidays.com

BRIGHTLING East Sussex

Great Worge Farm Barn ★★★★
Contact: Mrs Brenda Beck, Freedom Holiday Homes, 15 High Street, Cranbrook TN17 3EB
T: (01580) 720770
F: (01580) 720771
E: mail@freedomholidayhomes.co.uk
I: www.freedomholidayhomes.co.uk

BRIGHTON & HOVE East Sussex

The Abbey Self-Catering Flatlets ★-★★
Contact: Mr R A Smith, The Abbey Self-Catering Flatlets, 14-19 Norfolk Terrace, Brighton BN1 3AD
T: (01273) 778771
F: (01273) 729147
E: theabbey@brighton.co.uk
I: www.brighton.co.uk/hotels/theabbey

22 Astra House ★★
Contact: Mrs Janet Colman, Hightrees, 28 Highview Avenue North, Patcham, Brighton BN1 8WR
T: (01273) 505774

Brighton Lanes ★★-★★★
Contact: Miss Carol Coates, Brighton Lanes, Gordon House, 14A Ship Street, Hove, Brighton BN1 1AD
T: (01273) 325315
F: (01273) 323882
E: brightonlanes@easynet.co.uk
I: www.brighton.co.uk/hotels/brightonlanes

Brighton Marina Apartments ★★
Contact: Mr & Mrs Richard & Lorna Gartside, 16 Orchard Gardens, Hove, Brighton BN3 7BJ
T: (01273) 737006
E: bton-marina-apts@mistral.co.uk

Brighton Marina Holiday Apartments★★★★
Contact: Mrs A M Wills
T: (020) 8940 6945
F: (020) 8940 8907
E: info@brightonmarinaholidayapartments.co.uk
I: www.brightonmarinaholidayapartments.co.uk

18 Bristol Road ★★★
Contact: Mr Richard Harris, Best of Brighton & Sussex Cottages Ltd, Windmill Lodge, Vicarage Lane, Rottingdean, Brighton BN2 7HD
T: (01273) 308779
F: (01273) 300266
E: brightoncottages@pavilion.co.uk
I: www.bestofbrighton.co.uk

67 Britannia Court ★★★
Contact: Mr Richard Harris, Best of Brighton & Sussex Cottages Ltd, Windmill Lodge, Vicarage Lane, Rottingdean, Brighton BN2 7HD
T: (01273) 308779
F: (01273) 300266
E: brightoncottages@pavilion.co.uk
I: www.bestofbrighton.co.uk

9 Brunswick Mews ★★★
Contact: Mr Richard Harris, Best of Brighton & Sussex Cottages Ltd, Windmill Lodge, Vicarage Lane, Rottingdean, Brighton BN2 7HD
T: (01273) 308779
F: (01273) 300266
E: brightoncottages@pavilion.co.uk
I: www.bestofbrighton.co.uk

50 Brunswick Square Flat 4 ★★★
Contact: Mr Richard Harris, Best of Brighton & Sussex Cottages Ltd, Windmill Lodge, Vicarage Lane, Rottingdean, Brighton BN2 7HD
T: (01273) 308779
F: (01273) 300266
E: brightoncottages@pavilion.co.uk
I: www.bestofbrighton.co.uk

The Cabin ★★
Contact: Mr Richard Harris, Best of Brighton & Sussex Cottages Ltd, Windmill Lodge, Vicarage Lane, Rottingdean, Brighton BN2 7HD
T: (01273) 308779
F: (01273) 300266
E: brightoncottages@pavilion.co.uk
I: www.bestofbrighton.co.uk

Cobblers Cottage ★★★
Contact: Mr Richard Harris, Best of Brighton & Sussex Cottages Ltd, Windmill Lodge, Vicarage Lane, Rottingdean, Brighton BN2 7HD
T: (01273) 308779
F: (01273) 300266
E: brightoncottages@pavilion.co.uk
I: www.bestofbrighton.co.uk

Dale Court Family Holiday Flats ★★★
Contact: Ms Bettina Goodman, Dale Court Family Holiday Flats, 9 Florence Road, Brighton BN1 6DL
T: (01273) 326963

36 Dorset Court ★★★
Contact: Mr Richard Harris, Best of Brighton & Sussex Cottages Ltd, Windmill Lodge, Vicarage Lane, Rottingdean, Brighton BN2 7HD
T: (01273) 308779
F: (01273) 300266
E: brightoncottages@pavilion.co.uk
I: www.bestofbrighton.co.uk

44 Eastern Concourse ★★★
Contact: Mrs Pat Lowe, Palms Property Sales & Letting, 16 Village Square, Brighton Marina, Brighton BN2 5WA
T: (01273) 626000
F: (01273) 624449
E: enquiries@palmsagency.co.uk
I: www.palmsagency.co.uk

Flat 1 22 Brunswick Square ★★★
Contact: Mr Richard Harris, Best of Brighton & Sussex Cottages Ltd, Windmill Lodge, Vicarage Lane, Rottingdean, Brighton BN2 7HD
T: (01273) 308779
F: (01273) 300266
E: brightoncottages@pavilion.co.uk
I: www.bestofbrighton.co.uk

Flat 1 68 Marine Parade ★★★
Contact: Mr Richard Harris, Best of Brighton & Sussex Cottages Ltd, Windmill Lodge, Vicarage Lane, Rottingdean, Brighton BN2 7HD
T: (01273) 308779
F: (01273) 300266
E: brightoncottages@pavilion.co.uk
I: www.bestofbrighton.co.uk

Flat 10 4 Adelaide Mansions ★★★★
Contact: Mr Richard Harris, Best of Brighton & Sussex Cottages Ltd, Windmill Lodge, Vicarage Lane, Rottingdean, Brighton BN2 7HD
T: (01273) 308779
F: (01273) 300266
E: brightoncottages@pavilion.co.uk
I: www.bestofbrighton.co.uk

Flat 11 4 Adelaide Mansions ★★★★
Contact: Mr Richard Harris, Best of Brighton & Sussex Cottages Ltd, Windmill Lodge, Vicarage Lane, Rottingdean, Brighton BN2 7HD
T: (01273) 308779
F: (01273) 300266
E: brightoncottages@pavilion.co.uk
I: www.bestofbrighton.co.uk

Flat 14, 37-38 Adelaide Crescent★★★★
Contact: Mr Richard Harris, Best of Brighton & Sussex Cottages Ltd, Windmill Lodge, Vicarage Lane, Rottingdean, Brighton BN2 7HD
T: (01273) 308779
F: (01273) 300266
E: brightoncottages@pavilion.co.uk
I: www.bestofbrighton.co.uk

Flat 2 34 Bedford Square★★★
Contact: Mr Richard Harris, Best of Brighton & Sussex Cottages Ltd, Windmill Lodge, Vicarage Lane, Rottingdean, Brighton BN2 7HD
T: (01273) 308779
F: (01273) 300266
E: brightoncottages@pavilion.co.uk
I: www.bestofbrighton.co.uk

Flat 2, 7 Eastern Terrace ★★★★
Contact: Mr Richard Harris, Best of Brighton & Sussex Cottages Ltd, Windmill Lodge, Vicarage Lane, Rottingdean, Brighton BN2 7HD
T: (01273) 308779
F: (01273) 300266
E: enquiries@bestofbrighton.co.ukk
I: www.bestofbrighton.co.uk

Flat 2 Glenside Court ★★★
Contact: Mr Richard Harris, Best of Brighton & Sussex Cottages Ltd, Windmill Lodge, Vicarage Lane, Rottingdean, Brighton BN2 7HD
T: (01273) 308779
F: (01273) 300266
E: enquiries@bestofbrighton.co.ukk
I: www.bestofbrighton.co.uk

Flat 3, 4 Chichester Terrace ★★★★★
Contact: Mr Richard Harris, Best of Brighton & Sussex Cottages Ltd, Windmill Lodge, Vicarage Lane, Rottingdean, Brighton BN2 7HD
T: (01273) 308779
F: (01273) 300266
E: brightoncottages@pavilion.co.uk
I: www.bestofbrighton.co.uk

Flat 3, 9 Belgrave Place ★★★
Contact: Mr Richard Harris, Best of Brighton & Sussex Cottages Ltd, Windmill Lodge, Vicarage Lane, Rottingdean, Brighton BN2 7HD
T: (01273) 308779
F: (01273) 300266
E: enquiries@bestofbrighton.co.ukk
I: www.bestofbrighton.co.uk

Flat 3 1 Third Avenue ★★★
Contact: Mr Richard Harris, Best of Brighton & Sussex Cottages Ltd, Windmill Lodge, Vicarage Lane, Rottingdean, Brighton BN2 7HD
T: (01273) 308779
F: (01273) 300266
E: brightoncottages@pavilion.co.uk
I: www.bestofbrighton.co.uk

Flat 3 34 Brunswick Terrace ★★★★
Contact: Mr Richard Harris, Best of Brighton & Sussex Cottages Ltd, Windmill Lodge, Vicarage Lane, Rottingdean, Brighton BN2 7HD
T: (01273) 308779
F: (01273) 300266
E: brightoncottages@pavilion.co.uk
I: www.bestofbrighton.co.uk

Flat 3 35 First Avenue ★★
Contact: Mr Richard Harris, Best of Brighton & Sussex Cottages Ltd, Windmill Lodge, Vicarage Lane, Rottingdean, Brighton BN2 7HD
T: (01273) 308779
F: (01273) 300266
E: brightoncottages@pavilion.co.uk
I: www.bestofbrighton.co.uk

Flat 3 68 Marine Parade ★★★
Contact: Mr Richard Harris, Best of Brighton & Sussex Cottages Ltd, Windmill Lodge, Vicarage Lane, Rottingdean, Brighton BN2 7HD
T: (01273) 308779
F: (01273) 300266
E: brightoncottages@pavilion.co.uk
I: www.bestofbrighton.co.uk

Flat 5, 143 Western Road ★★★
Contact: Mr Richard Harris, Best of Brighton & Sussex Cottages Ltd, Windmill Lodge, Vicarage Lane, Rottingdean, Brighton BN2 7HD
T: (01273) 308779
F: (01273) 300266
E: enquiries@bestofbrighton.co.ukk
I: www.bestofbrighton.co.uk

Flat 5, 52 The Drive ★★★
Contact: Mr Richard Harris, Best of Brighton & Sussex Cottages Ltd, Windmill Lodge, Vicarage Lane, Rottingdean, Brighton BN2 7HD
T: (01273) 308779
F: (01273) 300266
E: enquiries@bestofbrighton.co.ukk
I: www.bestofbrighton.co.uk

Flat 5 35 First Avenue ★★
Contact: Mr Richard Harris, Best of Brighton & Sussex Cottages Ltd, Windmill Lodge, Vicarage Lane, Rottingdean, Brighton BN2 7HD
T: (01273) 308779
F: (01273) 300266
E: brightoncottages@pavilion.co.uk
I: www.bestofbrighton.co.uk

Flat 5 37 Brunswick Terrace ★★★
Contact: Mr Richard Harris, Best of Brighton & Sussex Cottages Ltd, Windmill Lodge, Vicarage Lane, Rottingdean, Brighton BN2 7HD
T: (01273) 308779
F: (01273) 300266
E: brightoncottages@pavilion.co.uk
I: www.bestofbrighton.co.uk

Flat 5 4 Medina Terrace ★★★
Contact: Mr Richard Harris, Best of Brighton & Sussex Cottages Ltd, Windmill Lodge, Vicarage Lane, Rottingdean, Brighton BN2 7HD
T: (01273) 308779
F: (01273) 300266
E: brightoncottages@pavilion.co.uk
I: www.bestofbrighton.co.uk

Flat 5 Lansdowne Court ★★★★
Contact: Mr Richard Harris, Best of Brighton & Sussex Cottages Ltd, Alnham, Whittingham, Alnwick NE66 4TJ
T: (01273) 308779
F: (01273) 300266
I: www.bestofbrighton.co.uk

Flat 6, 63 Regency Square ★★★
Contact: Mr Richard Harris, Best of Brighton & Sussex Cottages Ltd, Windmill Lodge, Vicarage Lane, Rottingdean, Brighton BN2 7HD
T: (01273) 308779
F: (01273) 300266
E: brightoncottages@pavilion.co.uk
I: www.bestofbrighton.co.uk

Flat 6 8 Regency Square ★★★
Contact: Mr Richard Harris, Best of Brighton & Sussex Cottages Ltd, Windmill Lodge, Vicarage Lane, Rottingdean, Brighton BN2 7HD
T: (01273) 308779
F: (01273) 300266
E: brightoncottages@pavilion.co.uk
I: www.bestofbrighton.co.uk

Flat 6 Glenside Court ★★★
Contact: Mr Richard Harris, Best of Brighton & Sussex Cottages Ltd, Windmill Lodge, Vicarage Lane, Rottingdean, Brighton BN2 7HD
T: (01273) 308779
F: (01273) 300266
E: brightoncottages@pavilion.co.uk
I: www.bestofbrighton.co.uk

Flat 6 Lansdowne Court ★★★★
Contact: Mr R T Harris, Best of Brighton & Sussex Cottages, Windmill Lodge, Vicarage Lane, Rottingdean, Brighton BN2 7HD
T: (01273) 308779
F: (01273) 300266
E: brightoncottages@pavilion.co.uk
I: www.bestofbrighton.co.uk

Flat 8 The Georgian House ★★★
Contact: Mr Richard Harris, Best of Brighton & Sussex Cottages Ltd, Windmill Lodge, Vicarage Lane, Rottingdean, Brighton BN2 7HD
T: (01273) 308779
F: (01273) 300266
E: brightoncottages@pavilion.co.uk
I: www.bestofbrighton.co.uk

Flat 9 28 Brunswick Terrace ★★★
Contact: Mr Richard Harris, Best of Brighton & Sussex Cottages Ltd, Windmill Lodge, Vicarage Lane, Rottingdean, Brighton BN2 7HD
T: (01273) 308779
F: (01273) 300266
E: brightoncottages@pavilion.co.uk
I: www.bestofbrighton.co.uk

Florence House ★★
Contact: Mr Geoff Hart, 18 Florence Road, Brighton BN1 6DJ
T: (01273) 506624
F: (01273) 506624
E: geoffhart@eggconnect.net

The Garden Flat ★★★
Contact: Mr Richard Harris, Best of Brighton & Sussex Cottages Ltd, Windmill Lodge, Vicarage Lane, Rottingdean, Brighton BN2 7HD
T: (01273) 308779
F: (01273) 300266
E: brightoncottages@pavilion.co.uk
I: www.bestofbrighton.co.uk

Garden Flat ★★★★
Contact: Mr Richard Harris, Best of Brighton & Sussex Cottages Ltd, Windmill Lodge, Vicarage Lane, Rottingdean, Brighton BN2 7HD
T: (01273) 308779
F: (01273) 300266
E: brightoncottages@pavilion.co.uk
I: www.bestofbrighton.co.uk

Hanover Cottage ★★★
Contact: Mrs Maureen Jackson, 51 Pinn Way, Ruislip HA4 7QG
T: (01895) 630107
F: (01895) 613540
E: mjackson@sunnyspells.biz

Holiday Flat 16 Lancaster Court ★★★
Contact: Mr Peter Anthony, Merrydown, 1A Fairfields, St Ives, Huntingdon PE27 5QQ
T: (01480) 495914
F: (01480) 495914
E: pastives@aol.com

2 Ivy Mews ★★★
Contact: Mr Richard Harris, Best of Brighton & Sussex Cottages Ltd, Windmill Lodge, Vicarage Lane, Rottingdean, Brighton BN2 7HD
T: (01273) 308779
F: (01273) 300266
E: brightoncottages@pavilion.co.uk
I: www.bestofbrighton.co.uk

3 Kemp Town Mews ★★★
Contact: Mr Richard Harris, Best of Brighton & Sussex Cottages Ltd, Windmill Lodge, Vicarage Lane, Rottingdean, Brighton BN2 7HD
T: (01273) 308779
F: (01273) 300266
E: brightoncottages@pavilion.co.uk
I: www.bestofbrighton.co.uk

13c Kemp Town Place ★★★★
Contact: Mr Richard Harris, Best of Brighton & Sussex Cottages Ltd, Windmill Lodge, Vicarage Lane, Rottingdean, Brighton BN2 7HD
T: (01273) 308779
F: (01273) 300266
E: brightoncottages@pavilion.co.uk
I: www.bestofbrighton.co.uk

Kilcolgan Bungalow ★★★★★
Contact: Mr J St George, 22 Baches Street, London N1 6DL
T: (020) 7250 3678
F: (020) 7250 1955

Lower Ground Floor Flat ★★★★
Contact: Mr Richard Harris, Windmill Lodge, Vicarage Lane, Rottingdean, Brighton BN2 7HD
T: (01273) 308779
F: (01273) 300266
E: brightoncottages@pavilion.co.uk

Lower Ground Floor Flat ★★★
Contact: Mr Richard Harris, Best of Brighton & Sussex Cottages Ltd, Windmill Lodge, Vicarage Lane, Rottingdean, Brighton BN2 7HD
T: (01273) 308779
F: (01273) 300266
E: brightoncottages@pavilion.co.uk
I: www.bestofbrighton.co.uk

82 Lowther Road ★★★
Contact: Mr Richard Harris, Best of Brighton & Sussex Cottages Ltd, Windmill Lodge, Vicarage Lane, Rottingdean, Brighton BN2 7HD
T: (01273) 308779
F: (01273) 300266
E: brightoncottages@pavilion.co.uk
I: www.bestofbrighton.co.uk

Lutyens Apartment ★★★
Contact: Mr Richard Harris, Windmill Lodge, Vicarage Lane, Rottingdean, Brighton BN2 7HD
T: (01273) 308779
F: (01273) 300266
E: enquiries@bestofbrighton.co.uk

63 Marine Parade ★★★
Contact: Mr Richard Harris, Best of Brighton & Sussex Cottages Ltd, Windmill Lodge, Vicarage Lane, Rottingdean, Brighton BN2 7HD
T: (01273) 308779
F: (01273) 300266
E: enquiries@bestofbrighton.co.ukk
I: www.bestofbrighton.co.uk

19A Metropole Court ★★★★★
Contact: Mr Richard Harris, Best of Brighton & Sussex Cottages Ltd, Windmill Lodge, Vicarage Lane, Rottingdean, Brighton BN2 7HD
T: (01273) 308779
F: (01273) 390211
E: enquiries@bestofbrighton.co.uk
I: www.bestofbrighton.co.uk

3A Metropole Court ★★★
Contact: Mr & Mrs Nigel & Viv Earwicker, Nivian Apartments, Acorn Cottage, Tudor Close, Pulborough RH20 2EF
T: (01798) 875513
E: nivianinc@aol.com

Metropole Court Apartments ★★★-★★★★★
Contact: Ms Katherine Draco, 5 Woodthorpe Road, Putney, London SW15 6UQ
T: (020) 8789 3520
I: www.brighton-apartments.com

19 North Gardens ★★★★
Contact: Mr Richard Harris, Best of Brighton & Sussex Cottages Ltd, Windmill Lodge, Vicarage Lane, Rottingdean, Brighton BN2 7HD
T: (01273) 308779
F: (01273) 300266
E: brightoncottages@pavilion.co.uk
I: www.bestofbrighton.co.uk

10 Oxford Mews ★★★★
Contact: Mr Richard Harris, Best of Brighton & Sussex Cottages Ltd, Windmill Lodge, Vicarage Lane, Rottingdean, Brighton BN2 7HD
T: (01273) 308779
F: (01273) 300266
E: enquiries@bestofbrighton.co.ukk
I: www.bestofbrighton.co.uk

Patio Flat 10 Brunswick Terrace★★★★
Contact: Mr Rupert Riley, Riley Properties, 10 Brunswick Terrace, Hove, Brighton BN3 1HL
T: (01273) 203758
F: (01273) 205608

20 Portside ★★★★
Contact: Mr Richard Harris, Best of Brighton & Sussex Cottages Ltd, Windmill Lodge, Vicarage Lane, Rottingdean, Brighton BN2 7HD
T: (01273) 308779
F: (01273) 300266
E: brightoncottages@pavilion.co.uk
I: www.bestofbrighton.co.uk

Regency Seafront Holiday Flats ★★
Contact: Mrs Edwards, 6 Highcroft Villas, Brighton BN1 5PS
T: (01273) 556227

28 Royal Crescent Mansions ★★★★
Contact: Mr Richard Harris, Best of Brighton & Sussex Cottages Ltd, Windmill Lodge, Vicarage Lane, Rottingdean, Brighton BN2 7HD
T: (01273) 308779
F: (01273) 300266
E: brightoncottages@pavilion.co.uk
I: www.bestofbrighton.co.uk

Seapoint ★★★★
Contact: Mr Richard Harris, Best of Brighton & Sussex Cottages Ltd, Windmill Lodge, Vicarage Lane, Rottingdean, Brighton BN2 7HD
T: (01273) 308779
F: (01273) 300266
E: enquiries@bestofbrighton.co.uk

South Lodge ★★★
Contact: Mr Richard Harris, Best of Brighton & Sussex Cottages Ltd, Windmill Lodge, Vicarage Lane, Rottingdean, Brighton BN2 7HD
T: (01273) 308779
F: (01273) 300266
E: brightoncottages@pavilion.co.uk
I: www.bestofbrighton.co.uk

18 St Vincents Court ★★★★
Contact: Mr Richard Harris, Best of Brighton & Sussex Cottages Ltd, Windmill Lodge, Vicarage Lane, Rottingdean, Brighton BN2 7HD
T: (01273) 308779
F: (01273) 300266
E: brightoncottages@pavilion.co.uk
I: www.bestofbrighton.co.uk

9 Starboard ★★★
Contact: Mrs Pat Lowe, Palms Property Sales & Letting, 16 Village Square, Brighton Marina, Brighton BN2 5WA
T: (01273) 626000
F: (01273) 624449
E: enquiries@palmsagency.co.uk
I: www.palmsagency.co.uk

6 Starboard Court ★★★
Contact: Mr Richard Harris, Best of Brighton & Sussex Cottages Ltd, Windmill Lodge, Vicarage Lane, Rottingdean, Brighton BN2 7HD
T: (01273) 308779
F: (01273) 300266
E: brightoncottages@pavilion.co.uk
I: www.bestofbrighton.co.uk

Upper Market Street ★★
Contact: Ms Marcia Stanton, 4 King Charles Road, Surbiton KT5 8PY
T: (020) 8979 1792
F: (020) 8399 6639

12 Western Concourse ★★★
Contact: Mrs M Bowen, 2 Lincoln Avenue, Peacehaven BN10 7HL
T: (01273) 584347

BROAD OAK
East Sussex

Austens Wood Farm ★★★★
Contact: Mrs Brenda Beck, Freedom Holiday Homes, 15 High Street, Cranbrook TN17 3EB
T: (01580) 720770
F: (01580) 720771
E: mail@freedomholidayhomes.co.uk
I: www.freedomholidayhomes.co.uk

BROADSTAIRS
Kent

Albert Cottage ★★★★
Contact: Mrs Brenda Beck, 15 High Street, Cranbrook TN17 3EB
T: (01580) 720770
F: (01580) 720771
E: mail@freedomholidayhomes.co.uk

Beacon Light Cottage ★★★
Contact: Mr Patrick Vandervorst, Duinhelmlaan 11, B-8420 Wenduine, Belgium
T: 0032 504 23207
F: 0032 504 23207
E: beaconlight.cottage@worldonline.be
I: www.beaconlightcottage.com

Bray Holiday Homes ★★★
Contact: Mr Bray, 34 Smithamdowns Road, Purley CR8 4ND
T: (020) 8660 1925

Broadstairs Holiday House ★★★
Contact: Mrs Bull, Millstone Cottage, 16 Beulah Road, Epping CM16 6RH
T: (01992) 576044
E: lynn.bull@btinternet.com

2 Church Square ★★★
Contact: Mr Philip Dennis, Sunnyside, St Peters Footpath, Margate CT10 2RA
T: (01843) 601996
E: phil.dennis@btconnect.com

Coachman's Flat ★★★
Contact: Mrs Ellen Barrett, Manningham, 15 Western Esplanade, Broadstairs CT10 1TD
T: (01843) 867925
F: (01843) 867925
E: ellen@stonar.com
I: www.stonas.com

1 Darren Gardens ★★★★
Contact: Mrs Jean Lawrence, J N Lawrence, 24 Winterstoke Crescent, Ramsgate CT11 8AH
T: (01843) 591422
F: (01843) 591422
E: jnancylawrence@aol.com

Fisherman's Cottage ★★★★
Contact: Mr John Linwood, 5 Union Square, Broadstairs CT10 1EX
T: (020) 8672 4150
E: linda.spillane@virgin.net
I: www.forge.co.uk/broadstairs

Flat 1
Rating Applied For
Contact: Mrs Linda Sear, Charity Farm, Eggington, Leighton Buzzard LU7 9PB
T: (01525) 210550

Flat 3
Rating Applied For
Contact: Mrs Linda Sear, Charity Farm, Eggington, Leighton Buzzard LU7 9PB
T: (01525) 210550

Homehaven House ★★★
Contact: Mrs Barbara Vandervord, 13 Granville Avenue, Ramsgate CT12 6DX
T: (01843) 585798
E: bvandervord@hotmail.com
I: www.members.eunet.at/j.krautgartner

Martin Holiday Homes ★★★★
Contact: Mrs Penny Martin, 21 Avebury Avenue, Ramsgate CT11 8BB
T: (01843) 592945
F: (01843) 599063
E: penny@martinholidays.co.uk

Martin Holiday Homes ★★★★
Contact: Mrs Penny Martin, 21 Avebury Avenue, Ramsgate CT11 8BB
T: (01843) 592945
F: (01843) 599063
E: penny@martinholidays.co.uk

2 Paragon Lodge ★★★
Contact: Mrs Ruth Kelsey, Stanhill Farm, Birchwood Road, Wilmington, Dartford DA2 7HD
T: (01322) 669711
F: (01322) 619037
E: r.kelsey@farming.me.uk

Sacketts Hill Farm
Rating Applied For
Contact: Mr Phil Dennis, Sacketts Hill Farm, Sacketts Hill, Broadstairs CT10 2QS
T: (01843) 601996
F: (01843) 601996

Secret Cottage ★★★
Contact: Mr John Ferris, 15 St Peters Park Road, Broadstairs CT10 2BG
T: (01843) 602656
F: (01843) 602656
E: info@bluesky-apart.com
I: www.bluesky-apart.com

Spero Court Apartments Flat 13 ★★★
Contact: Miss Carol Bowerman, 28 Heather Drive, Wilmington, Dartford DA1 3LE
T: (01322) 224869

BROCKENHURST
Hampshire

Avenue Lodge ★★★
Contact: Mr Paul Gillings, Avenue House, East Bank Road, Brockenhurst SO42 7RW
T: (01590) 624006
F: (01590) 623867
E: paul@cricketnet.net

Brookley Dairy
Rating Applied For
Contact: Mrs Tracey Boulton, Mayfield, 77 Burley Road, Bockhampton, Christchurch BH23 7AJ
T: (01425) 672013
F: (01425) 672013

Gorse Cottage ★★★★★
Contact: Mr Julian Gilbert, Suite E, Chiltern House, 180 High Street North, Dunstable LU6 1AT
T: 0870 321 0020
F: 0870 233 0151
E: info@gorsecottage.co.uk
I: www.bareford.com

Jacmar Cottage
Rating Applied For
Contact: Mrs Melanie Ayres, Jacmar Cottage, Mill Lane, Brockenhurst SO42 7UA
T: (01590) 622019
E: jacmarcottage@aol.com

Latchmoor Corner ★★★
Contact: Ms Jacquie Taylor, Three Corners, Centre Lane, Pennington, Lymington SO41 0JD
T: (01590) 645217
E: tommy.tiddles@virgin.net

Setley Brake East ★★★
Contact: Mr John Gorton, Setley Brake East, Tile Barn Lane, Brockenhurst SO42 7UE
T: (01590) 622160

BROOK
Isle of Wight

Brook Farm Cottages ★★★
Contact: Mrs Sonia Fry, Brook Farmhouse, Mottistone, Newport PO30 4ES
T: (01983) 740387

Holiday Homes Owners Services Ref: B5★★★★
Contact: Mr Colin Nolson, Holiday Homes Owners Services (West Wight), 18 Solent Hill, Freshwater PO40 9TG
T: (01983) 753423
F: (01983) 753423
E: holidayhomesiow@ic24.net

Holiday Homes Owners Services Ref: B7★★★★
Contact: Mr Colin Nolson, Holiday Homes Owners Services (West Wight), 18 Solent Hill, Freshwater PO40 9TG
T: (01983) 753423
F: (01983) 753423
E: holidayhomesiow@ic24.net

Holiday Homes Owners Services Ref: B6★★★
Contact: Mr Colin Nolson, Holiday Homes Owners Services (West Wight), 18 Solent Hill, Freshwater PO40 9TG
T: (01983) 753423
F: (01983) 753423
E: holidayhomesiow@ic24.net

Holiday Homes Owners Services Ref: B3★★★★
Contact: Mr Colin Nolson, Holiday Homes Owners Services (West Wight), 18 Solent Hill, Freshwater, PO40 9TG
T: (01983) 753423
F: (01983) 753423
E: holidayhomesiow@ic24.net

Holiday Homes Owners Services Ref: B1★★★
Contact: Mr Colin Nolson, Holiday Homes Owners Services (West Wight), 18 Solent Hill, Freshwater, PO40 9TG
T: (01983) 753423
F: (01983) 753423
E: holidayhomesiow@ic24.net

Holiday Homes Owners Services Ref: B4★★★
Contact: Mr Colin Nolson, Holiday Homes Owners Services (West Wight), 18 Solent Hill, Freshwater PO40 9TG
T: (01983) 753423
F: (01983) 753423
E: holidayhomesiow@ic24.net

Holiday Homes Owners Services Ref: B2★★
Contact: Mr Colin Nolson, Holiday Homes Owners Services (West Wight), 18 Solent Hill, Freshwater, PO40 9TG
T: (01983) 753423
F: (01983) 753423
E: holidayhomesiow@ic24.net

Sudmoor Cottage ★★★★
Contact: Mrs Honor Vass, The Old Vicarage, Kingston, Wareham BH20 5LH
T: (01929) 480080
F: (01929) 481070
E: enq@islandcottageholidays.com
I: www.islandcottageholidays.com

Wittensford Lodge ★★★
Contact: Ms Carol Smith, 14 Hunts Mead, Billericay CM12 9JA
T: (01277) 623997
F: (01277) 634976
E: mbmcarol@dircon.co.uk
I: www.wittensfordlodge.freeservers.com

BROOKLAND
Kent

Puddock Farm Pine Lodges ★★★★
Contact: Mrs Amanda Skinner, Puddock Farm Pine Lodges, Puddock Farm, Fairfield, Brookland, Romney Marsh TN29 9SA
T: (01797) 344440
F: (01797) 344440
E: amanda_skinner@talk21.com
I: www.cottageguide.co.uk/puddockfarmpinelodges.

BUCKINGHAM
Buckinghamshire

Huntsmill Holidays ★★★★
Contact: Mrs Fiona Hilsdon, Huntsmill Holidays, Huntsmill Farm, Shalstone, Buckingham MK18 5ND
T: (01280) 704852
F: (01280) 704852
E: fiona@huntsmill.com
I: www.huntsmill.com

BURFORD
Oxfordshire

Bruern Holiday Cottages ★★★★★
Contact: Ms Frances Curtin, Red Brick House, Bruern, Oxford OX7 6PY
T: (01993) 830415
F: (01993) 831750
E: enquiries@bruern.co.uk
I: www.bruern.co.uk

Candlemas ★★★★
Contact: Manor Cottages & Cotswolds Retreats, Priory Mews, 33A Priory Lane, Burford, Oxford OX18 4SG
T: (01993) 824252
F: (01993) 824443
E: mancott@netcomuk.co.uk

Park House Lodge ★★★
Contact: Mrs Therese Kennard, Park House Lodge, Park House, Witney Street, Burford, Oxford OX18 4SN
T: (01993) 823460
F: (01993) 823460
E: dken768542@aol.com

Pilgrims ★★
Contact: Cottage in the Country, Forest Gate, Frog Lane, Milton-under-Wychwood, Oxford OX7
T: (01635) 200316

BURGATE
Hampshire

Burgate Farmhouse ★★★
Contact: Mrs Christine Bennett, Burgate Farmhouse, Burgate, Fordingbridge SP6 1LX
T: (01425) 655909
E: christine@burgatefarm.freeserve.co.uk
I: www.burgate.fslife.co.uk

BURGESS HILL
West Sussex

Farnaby ★★★
Contact: Mr Richard Harris, Best of Brighton & Sussex Cottages Ltd, Windmill Lodge, Vicarage Lane, Rottingdean, Brighton BN2 7HD
T: (01273) 308779
F: (01273) 300266
E: brightoncottages@pavilion.co.uk
I: www.bestofbrighton.co.uk

BURITON
Hampshire

18 High Street ★★
Contact: Mr Michael Ayling, 14 High Street, Buriton, Petersfield GU31 5RX
T: (01730) 260366

Rose Cottage ★★★★
Contact: Mr Michael Ayling, 14 High Street, Buriton, Petersfield GU31 5RX
T: (01730) 260366
E: rosecottage18@hotmail.com
I: www.rosecot18.fsnet.co.uk

BURLEY
Hampshire

Brackenwood ★★★★★
Contact: Mrs Carole Stewart, Great Wells House, Beechwood Lane, Burley, Ringwood BH24 4AS
T: (01425) 402302
F: (01425) 402302
E: greatwells@cs.com
I: www.smoothhound.co.uk/hotels/greatwel

Cherry Tree Cottage ★★★
Contact: Mr & Mrs J Pannell, West Cliff Sands Hotel, 9 Priory Road, West Cliff, Bournemouth BH2 5DF
T: (01202) 557013

The Dairy ★★★★
Contact: Mrs Carole Stewart, Great Wells House, Beechwood Lane, Burley, Ringwood BH24 4AS
T: (01425) 402302
F: (01425) 402302
E: carolestewart@pobox.com

Honeysuckle Cottage ★★★
Contact: Mrs Wanda Williams, Oakapple Cottage, 5 Garden Road, Burley, Ringwood BH24 4EA
T: (01425) 402489
F: (01425) 402489
E: wanda@oakapplecottage.fsnet.co.uk
I: www.oakapplecottage.fsnet.co.uk

BURSLEDON
Hampshire

62 Goodlands Vale ★★★
Contact: Mr & Mrs Mike & Sue Batley, Town or Country Serviced Apartments & Houses, 60 Oxford Street, Southampton SO14 3DL
T: (023) 8088 1000
F: (023) 8088 1010
E: town@interalpha.co.uk
I: www.intent.co.uk/southampton/hotels/townorc/index.htm

BURWASH
East Sussex

Battenhurst Barn ★★★
Contact: Mr Stuart Winter, Garden of England Cottages Ltd, The Mews Office, 189a High Street, Tonbridge TN9 1BX
T: (01732) 369168
F: (01732) 358817
E: holidays@gardenofenglandholidays.co.uk
I: www.gardenofenglandcottages.co.uk

1 Rose Hill Cottages ★★★
Contact: Country Holidays Ref: 2805, Country Holidays Sales, Spring Mill, Earby, Barnoldswick BB94 0AA
T: 08700 723723
F: (01282) 844288
E: sales@holidaycottagesgroup.com
I: www.country-holidays.co.uk

BURWASH WEALD
East Sussex

Little Haycorns
Rating Applied For
Contact: Mrs Gill Winter, Garden of England Cottages, The Mews Office, 189A High Street, Tonbridge TN9 1BX
T: (01732) 369168
F: (01732) 358817
E: holidays@gardenofenglandcottages.co.uk

CALBOURNE
Isle of Wight

Holiday Homes Owners Services Ref: C1★★★★
Contact: Mr Colin Nolson, Holiday Homes Owners Services (West Wight), 18 Solent Hill, Freshwater PO40 9TG
T: (01983) 753423
F: (01983) 753423
E: holidayhomesiow@ic24.net

CAMBER
East Sussex

Bridle Cottage & Horseshoe Cottage & Poundfield Bungalow★★★★
Contact: Mr Stuart Winter, Garden of England Cottages Ltd, The Mews Office, 189a High Street, Tonbridge TN9 1BX
T: (01732) 369168
F: (01732) 358817
E: holidays@gardenofenglandcottages.co.uk
I: www.gardenofenglandcottages.co.uk

Brookside ★★★★
Contact: Mrs Anne Arnold, East Dene, Udimore, Rye TN31 6BA
T: (01424) 883020

The Bungalow ★★★
Contact: Mrs Jane Wood, The Bungalow, Poundfield House, Farm Lane, Camber, Rye TN31 7QY
T: (01797) 227391

Camber Farmhouse Barn ★★★★
Contact: Ms Georgina Holt, Camber Farmhouse Barn, Farm Lane, Camber, Rye TN31 7QY
T: (01797) 225202

CAMBERLEY
Surrey

Inglenook Apartment ★★★★
Contact: Mr D J Fuller, Inglenook Apartment, 11(b) Kings Ride, Camberley GU15 4HU
T: (01276) 24660
F: (01932) 562638
E: fullspur.cam@btinternet.com
I: www.geocities.com/apartment_camberley

CANTERBURY
Kent

Canterbury Holiday Lets ★★★★
Contact: Mrs Kathryn Nevell, 4 Harbledown Park, Harbledown, Canterbury CT2 8NR
T: (01227) 763308
F: (01227) 763308
E: rnevell@aol.com

The Canterbury Hotel & Apartments ★★★★
Contact: Mrs J Wigginton, The Canterbury Hotel & Apartments, 71 New Dover Road, Canterbury CT1 3DZ
T: (01227) 450551
F: (01227) 780145
E: canterbury.hotel@btinternet.com
I: www.canterbury-hotel-apartments.co.uk

11 Dunstan Court
Rating Applied For
Contact: Mrs Maria Cain, 39 London Road, Canterbury CT2 8LF
T: (01227) 769955

Ebury Hotel Cottages ★★★★
Contact: Mr Henry Mason, Ebury Hotel, 65-67 New Dover Road, Canterbury CT1 3DX
T: (01227) 768433
F: (01227) 459187
E: info@ebury-hotel.co.uk
I: www.ebury-hotel.co.uk

Henry's of Ash ★★★
Contact: Mr P H Robinson, Henry's of Ash, Darrington, Durlock Road, Ash, Canterbury CT3 2HU
T: (01304) 812563

Knowlton Court ★★★-★★★★
Contact: Miss Amy Froggatt, Knowlton Court, The Estate Office, Knowlton Court, Knowlton, Canterbury CT3 1PT
T: (01304) 842402
F: (01304) 842403
E: knowlton.cottages@farmline.com
I: www.knowltoncourt.co.uk

Luxury Holiday Apartment ★★★★
Contact: Mrs H A Homerstone, Courtfields, Lees Road, Brabourne Lees, Ashford TN25 6RN
T: (01303) 814020
F: (01303) 812333

Oriel Lodge ★★★★
Contact: Mr Keith Rishworth, Oriel Lodge, 3 Queens Avenue, Canterbury CT2 8AY
T: (01227) 462845
F: (01227) 462845
E: info@oriel-lodge.co.uk
I: www.oriel-lodge.co.uk

Queensview Cottage ★★★★
Contact: Mrs Woodifield, Queens Avenue, Canterbury CT2 8AY
T: (01227) 471914
F: (01227) 785348
I: www.cottageguide.co.uk/queensview/

St Mary's ★★★★
Contact: Mr R Allcorn, 115 Whitstable Road, Canterbury CT2 8EF
T: (01227) 450265
F: (01227) 478626
E: r.allcorn@discovercanterbury.com

Wagoners & Shepherds Cottages ★★★
Contact: Ms H Long, Wagoners & Shepherds Cottages, Denstroude Farm, Blean, Canterbury CT2 9JZ
T: (01227) 471513

CARISBROOKE
Isle of Wight

Alvington Manor Farm ★★
Contact: Mrs Margaret Marsh, Alvington Manor Farm, Carisbrooke, Newport PO30 5SP
T: (01983) 523463
F: (01983) 523463

Dairy Cottage ★★★★
Contact: Mrs E R Yapp, Luckington Farm, Bowcombe Road, Carisbrooke, Newport PO30 3HT
T: (01983) 822951

Froglands Farm ★★★-★★★★
Contact: Mrs L J Dungey, Froglands Farm, Carisbrooke, Newport PO30 3DU
T: (01983) 821027
E: s.dungey@btinternet.com
I: www.thecowshed.co.uk

New Close Farm ★★★★
Contact: Mrs V M Fisher-McAllum, Technifind, New Close Farm, Nunnery Lane, Carisbrooke, Newport PO30 1YR
T: (01983) 523996
F: (01983) 537378
E: newclosefarm@42net.co.uk

Toll Cottage
Rating Applied For
Contact: Mrs Siobhan Aubin, 8 Shide Road, Newport PO30 1YQ
T: (01983) 523685

CASTLETHORPE
Buckinghamshire

Balney Grounds
★★★-★★★★
Contact: Mrs Mary Stacey, Balney Grounds, Home Farm, Hanslope Road, Castlethorpe, Milton Keynes MK19 7HD
T: (01908) 510208
F: (01908) 516119
E: mary.stacy@tesco.net
I: www.lets-stay-mk.co.uk

CATERHAM
Surrey

The White Cottage ★★★
Contact: Mrs Josephine Crux, Birchwood House, Woldingham Road, Woldingham, Caterham CR3 7LR
T: (01883) 343287
F: (01883) 348066
E: alan.crux@virgin.net
I: www.oas.co.uk/ukcottages

CATHERINGTON
Hampshire

Lone Barn ★★★★
Contact: Mrs Melanie Flint, Lone Barn, Catherington, Waterlooville PO8 0SF
T: (023) 9263 2911
F: (023) 9263 2288
I: www.lonebarn.net

CAVERSFIELD
Oxfordshire

Grooms Cottage ★★★
Contact: Mr Albert Phipps, Grooms Cottage, Banbury Road, Caversfield, Bicester OX27 8TG
T: (01869) 249307
F: (01869) 249307

CHALE
Isle of Wight

Atherfield Green Farm Holiday Cottages★★★★
Contact: A Jupe, The Laurels, High Street, Newchurch, Sandown PO36 0NJ
T: (01983) 867613
F: (01983) 868214
E: alistair.jupe@btinternet.com

Chapel Cottage ★★★
Contact: Mrs J Clark, 27 Worsley Road, Gurnard, Cowes PO31 8JW
T: (01983) 294900

The Old Rectory ★★★★
Contact: Mrs Mary Coward, The Old Rectory, Chale Street, Chale, Ventnor PO38 2HE
T: (01635) 200316

CHALE GREEN
Isle of Wight

Greenedge ★★★
Contact: Mrs Jacqueline Miles, Greenedge, Chale Green, Whitwell, Ventnor PO38 2JR
T: (01983) 551419

North Appleford Cottages
★★★
Contact: Mrs Jan Clarke, Cridmore Farm, Binstead, Ryde PO33 3HH
T: (01983) 721206

CHALFONT ST GILES
Buckinghamshire

Hilborough ★★
Contact: Mr & Mrs Peter Bentall, Hilborough, Mill Lane, Chalfont St Giles HP8 4NX
T: (01494) 872536
F: (01494) 872536

Studio Flat at Applewood
★★★★
Contact: Mr & Mrs J E Newcombe, Applewood, Mill Lane, Chalfont St Giles HP8 4NX
T: (01494) 873343
E: JnA@stgiles.fsnet.co.uk

CHARLBURY
Oxfordshire

Banbury Hill Farm Cottages
★★★
Contact: Mrs Angela Widdows, Banbury Hill Farm, Charlbury, Oxford OX7 3JH
T: (01608) 810314
F: (01608) 811891
E: angelawiddows@gfwiddowsf9.co.uk
I: www.charlburyoxfordaccom.co.uk

CHARLTON
West Sussex

Orchard Cottage ★★★
Contact: Mrs Eve Jeffries, 34 Foxhall Lane, Chichester PO18 0HU
T: (01243) 811338

CHARLTON MARSHALL
Dorset

Bluebell Cottage ★★★
Contact: Mr Stuart-Brown, Dream Cottages, 41 Maiden Street, Weymouth DT4 8AZ
T: (01305) 761347

CHART SUTTON
Kent

Brick Kiln Cottage ★★★★
Contact: Mrs Susan Spain, White House Farm, Green Lane, Chart Sutton, Maidstone ME17 3ES
T: (01622) 842490
F: (01622) 842490
E: sue.spain@totalise.co.uk

Park House Farm ★★★
Contact: Mrs Brenda Beck, Freedom Holiday Homes, 15 High Street, Cranbrook TN17 3EB
T: (01580) 720770
F: (01580) 720771
E: mail@freedomholidayhomes.co.uk
I: www.freedomholidayhomes.co.uk

CHAWTON
Hampshire

Darcy House ★★★
Contact: Mrs Terri Burman, Winchester Road, Chawton, Alton GU34 1SA
T: (01420) 83357
F: (01420) 83357

CHECKENDON
Oxfordshire

Livery Cottage ★★★★
Contact: Ms Linda Tarrant, Livery Cottage, c/o Checkendon Equestrian Centre, Lovegrove's Lane, Checkendon, Reading RG8 0NE
T: (01491) 680225
F: (01491) 682801
E: linda@checkendon.f9.co.uk
I: www.checkendon.f9.co.uk

CHICHESTER
West Sussex

24 & 26 Oaklands Court ★★★
Contact: Mr Ryan & Mr M Stait, Southern Counties Lettings, 7 Loretto Gardens, Harrow HA3 9LY
T: (020) 8204 1188
F: (020) 8906 1940
E: info@southerncountieslettings.com
I: www.southerncountieslettings.com

Apple Tree Cottage ★★★★
Contact: Mrs Daphne Vickers, 34 King George Gardens, Broyle Road, Chichester PO19 4LB
T: (01243) 839770
F: (01243) 839771
E: vickersdaphne@aol.com

1a Blackfriars House ★★★
Contact: Mr & Mrs Laurie & Pat Burrell, 48 Stewart Avenue, Shepperton TW17 0EH
T: (01932) 564556
F: (01932) 564556
E: laurie.burrell@surreycc.gov.uk

5 Caledonian Road ★★★★
Contact: Miss Victoria Chubb, 33 Hillier Road, London SW11 6AX
T: (020) 7924 5446
E: victoriachubb@hotmail.com
I: www.visitsussex.org

Cornerstones ★★★★
Contact: Mrs V J Higgins, Greenacre, Goodwood Gardens, Runcton, Chichester PO20 1SP
T: (01243) 839096
F: (01243) 779658
E: vjrmhiggins@hotmail.com
I: www.visitbritain.com

Cygnet Cottage ★★★★
Contact: Mrs V J Higgins, Greenacre, Goodwood Gardens, Runcton, Chichester PO20 1SP
T: (01243) 839096
F: (01243) 779658
E: vjrmhiggins@hotmail.com
I: www.visitbritain.com

Flat 2, 4 Guildhall Street
★★★
Contact: Mr Ryan & Mr M Stait, Southern Counties Lettings, 7 Loretto Gardens, Harrow HA3 9LY
T: (020) 8204 1188
F: (020) 8906 1940
E: info@southerncountieslettings.com
I: www.southerncountieslettings.com

Flats 1 & 5 West Broyle House
Rating Applied For
Contact: Mrs Penelope Gurland, Flat 6, 21 De Vere Gardens, London W8 5AN
T: (020) 7937 6337
F: (020) 7938 2199

Honeysuckle Cottage ★★★★
Contact: Mr & Mrs Noel & Jenny Bettridge, Footpath Nursery, Post Office Lane, North Mondham, Runcton, Chichester PO20 1JY
T: (01243) 779823
F: (01243) 779823
E: noeljenny@onetel.net.uk

Hunston Mill ★★★-★★★★
Contact: Mr & Mrs R Beeny, Hunston Mill, Selsey Road, Hunston, Chichester PO20 1AU
T: (01243) 783375
F: (01243) 785179
E: rbeeny@freenetname.co.uk
I: www.hunstonmill.co.uk

Lavender Cottage ★★★★
Contact: Mr & Mrs Ron & Pam Foden, 4 York Road, Chichester PO19 7TJ
T: (01243) 771314
F: (01243) 839171
E: rdfoden@talk21.com

33 Melbourne Road ★★★
Contact: Mrs Jane Donnely, Clevelands, Fordwater Road, Chichester PO19 6PS
T: (01243) 537737

Muttons Farm House
★★★★★
Contact: Mr & Mrs Rist, Muttons Farm House, Keynor Lane, Sidlesham, Chichester PO20 7NG
T: (01243) 641675
F: (01243) 641675
E: rist@muttonsfh.fsnet.co.uk
I: www.smoothhound.co.uk/hotels/muttons.html

Oak Apple Barn ★★★★
Contact: Mrs Siobain Davies, Oak Apple Barn, The Lane, Summersdale, Chichester PO19 5PY
T: (01243) 771669
I: www.siobaindavies@virgin.net

201 Oving Road ★★★★
Contact: Ms Deborah Clark, Durley, Selsey Road, Sidlesham, Chichester PO20 7LS
T: (01243) 641858
F: (01243) 641231

Quay Quarters ★★★★★
Contact: Mrs Lorraine Sawday, Apuldram Manor Farm, Appledram Lane, Chichester PO20 7EF
T: (01243) 839900
F: (01243) 782052
E: info@quayquarters.co.uk

2 Rumbolds Close ★★★
Contact: Dr Ian White, 35 Baldwin Avenue, Eastbourne BN21 1UL
T: (01323) 648291
E: irwhite@nildram.co.uk

CHIDDINGFOLD Surrey

Combe Court Farm ★★★
Contact: Mrs Thelma Lane, The Dovecote, Chiddingfold, Godalming GU8 4XW
T: (01428) 683375
F: (01428) 683375

Prestwick Byre ★★★★
Contact: Mrs Valerie Mills, Prestwick Farm, Prestwick Lane, Chiddingfold, Godalming GU8 4XP
T: (01428) 654695
F: (01428) 654695
E: paul.prestwick@virgin.net

CHIDDINGLY East Sussex

Dove Cottage ★★★★
Contact: Mr Stuart Winter, Garden of England Cottages Ltd, The Mews Office, 189a High Street, Tonbridge TN9 1BX
T: (01732) 369168
F: (01732) 358817
E: holiday@gardenofenglandcottages.co.uk
I: www.gardenofenglandcottages.co.uk

Pekes ★★★-★★★★★
Contact: Ms Eva Morris, 124 Elm Park Mansions, Park Walk, London SW10 0AR
T: (020) 7352 8088
F: (020) 7352 8125
E: pekes.afa@virgin.net
I: www.pekesmanor.com

CHIDHAM West Sussex

Canute Cottages ★★★★
Contact: Ms Diana Beale, Cobnor House, Chidham, Chichester PO18 8TE
T: (01243) 572123
E: taylorbeales@yahoo.co.uk
I: www.canutecottages.co.uk

CHILD OKEFORD Dorset

Hillcrest ★★★
Contact: Mrs S Salisbury, Orchard Cottage, Duck Street, Child Okeford, Blandford Forum DT11 8ET
T: (01258) 861476
E: mikesal66@yahoo.co.uk
I: www.heartofdorset.easynet.co.uk

CHILHAM Kent

Monckton Cottages ★★★
Contact: Mrs Helen Kirwan, Monckton Cottages, Heron Manor, Mountain Street, Chilham, Canterbury CT4 8DG
T: (01227) 730256
F: (01227) 732423
E: monckton@rw-kirwan.demon.co.uk

CHILLERTON Isle of Wight

Roslin Farm Annexe ★★
Contact: Mrs Evelyn Murdoch, Roslin Farm Annexe, Chillerton, Newport PO30 3HG
T: (01983) 721662
E: bill.murdoch.2@btopenworld.com

Sunnybank Cottage ★★★
Contact: Mrs Honor Vass, The Old Vicarage, Kingston, Wareham BH20 5LH
T: (01929) 480080
F: (01929) 481070
E: enq@islandcottagesholidays.com
I: www.cottageholidays.dmon.co.uk

The Willows ★★★
Contact: Mrs Muriel Burns, Dove Cottage, Brook Lane, Chillerton, Newport PO30 3EW
T: (01983) 721630

CHILWORTH Hampshire

Lavender Cottage ★★★★
Contact: Mrs Susan Barnes, Holbrook House, Long Lawford, Rugby CV23 9BD
T: (01788) 543932

CHIPPING NORTON Oxfordshire

Grace Cottage ★★★
Contact: Mr Gordon Brown, Briery Cottage, Alexandra Square, Chipping Norton OX7 5HL
T: (01608) 641833
F: (01608) 641833
E: g-brown@netcomuk.co.uk

Heath Farm Holiday Cottages ★★★★-★★★★★
Contact: Mr & Mrs David & Nena Barbour, Heath Farm Holiday Cottages, Heath Farm, Swerford, Oxford OX7 4BN
T: (01608) 683270
F: (01608) 683222
I: www.heathfarm.com

14A New Street ★★★
Contact: Ms Kate Bluck, 20 New Street, Over Norton, Chipping Norton OX7 5LJ
T: (01608) 644084

CHRISTCHURCH Dorset

Avon Reach ★★★★
Contact: Mrs Wynne, Hollyoaks, 10 Ramley Road, Pennington, Lymington SO41 8GQ
T: (01590) 670220

The Black House ★★★
Contact: Andrew, The Black House, 51 Carbery Avenue, Southbourne, Bournemouth BH6 3LN
T: (07855) 280191
F: (01202) 483555
E: theblackhouse@hotmail.com
I: www.theblackhouse.co.uk

Burridge Lettings ★★-★★★
Contact: Mr Mark Pope, Burridge Lettings, 3 Mudeford, Mudeford, Christchurch BH23 3NQ
T: (01202) 481810
F: (01202) 476677
E: enquiries@burridge-property.co.uk
I: www.burridge-property.co.uk

Burton Farm House Annexe ★★★
Contact: Mrs Marylyn Etheridge, Burton Farm House, 159 Salisbury Road, Burton, Christchurch BH23 7JS
T: (01202) 484475

The Causeway ★-★★
Contact: Mrs Tomkinson, The Causeway, 32-34 Stanpit, Mudeford, Christchurch BH23 3LZ
T: (01202) 470149
F: (01202) 477558
E: thecauseway@nascr.net

The Holiday Cottage ★★
Contact: Mr & Mrs John Brewer, 61 Southwick Road, Southbourne, Bournemouth BH6 5PR
T: (01202) 420673

Mallard Cottage ★★★
Contact: Mr & Mrs David Pearce, Swan Lodge, 17 Willow Way, Christchurch BH23 1JJ
T: (01202) 480805
F: (01202) 480805

Riverbank Holidays ★★★
Contact: Mr & Mrs Gibson, 8 Willow Way, Christchurch BH23 1JJ
T: (01202) 477813

Riverbank House ★★★★
Contact: Ms S Burrows, Oakdene Orchard, Ringwood Road, Three Legged Cross, Wimborne Minster BH21 6RB
T: (01202) 828487
F: (01202) 828487
E: handbleisure@amserve.net
I: riverbankholidays.co.uk

Riverside Park ★★★
Contact: Mrs Lisa Booth, Riverside Park, Paddlegrade Limited, 28 Willow Way, Christchurch BH23 1JJ
T: (01202) 471090
E: holidays@riversidepark.biz
I: www.riversidepark.biz

CHURCH KNOWLE Dorset

Denorah ★★★
Contact: Mr & Mrs Ronald & Mary Wrixon, The Old Post Office, 16 Church Knowle, Church Knowle, Wareham BH20 5NG
T: (01929) 480234

CHURCHILL Oxfordshire

The Little Cottage ★★★★
Contact: Mr David Sheppard, Gables Cottage, Hackers Lane, Churchill, Oxford OX7 6XL
T: (01608) 658674
E: enquiries@littlecottage.co.uk
I: www.littlecottage.co.uk

CLANFIELD Oxfordshire

Grafton Manor Wing ★★★
Contact: Ms Sandra Eddolls, Manor Farm, Grafton, Clanfield, Bampton OX18 2RY
T: (01367) 810237

CLIFTONVILLE Kent

19 Majestic Court ★★★
Contact: Mrs Yvonne Forbes, 70/72 Harold Road, Cliftonville, Margate CT9 2HS
T: (01843) 298635
F: (01843) 298635
E: enquiries@elonville-hotel.demon.co.uk

CLIMPING West Sussex

The Dairy Cottage ★★★
Contact: Mrs Sue Beckhurst, The Dairy, Brookpit Lane, Climping, Littlehampton BN17 5QU
T: (01903) 724187
F: (01903) 724187
E: thedairy@tiscali.co.uk

COLWELL BAY Isle of Wight

The Acorns ★★★
Contact: Ms Lisa Baskill, Home from Home Holidays, 31 Pier Street, Ventnor PO38 1SX
T: (01983) 854340
F: (01983) 855524

Brambles Farm Bungalows ★★★
Contact: Mr & Mrs Trevor Bonner-Williams, Almond Lodge, Church Hill, Totland Bay PO39 0ET
T: (01983) 759773
F: (01983) 759773

Chalet 14 Island View Chalet Park ★
Contact: Ms Dorothea Lutticke, Unterer Hasselbach 14, 34359 Reinhardshagen, Germany
T: 0049 5544 7328
F: 0049 5544 7328
E: dorothealutticke@hotmail.com

Solent Heights ★★★
Contact: Mrs Honor Vass, The Old Vicarage, Kingston, Wareham BH20 5LH
T: (01929) 480080
F: (01929) 481070
E: enq@islandcottageholidays.com
I: www.islandcottageholidays.com

COMPTON West Sussex

3 The Old School House ★★★★
Contact: Mr & Mrs Brian & Val Parkinson, 47-48 Castle Garden, Petersfield GU32 3AG
T: (01730) 233747
E: val@comptoncottage.co.uk
I: www.comptoncottage.co.uk

Yew Tree House Annexe ★★★
Contact: Mr & Mrs James Buchanan, Yew Tree House Annexe, Yew Tree House, Compton, Chichester PO18 9HD
T: (023) 9263 1248
E: d.buchanan@btinternet.com

COMPTON ABBAS Dorset

The Smithy ★★★
Contact: Mrs Lucy Kerridge, The Old Forge, Fanners Yard, Compton Abbas, Shaftesbury SP7 0NQ
T: (01747) 811881
F: (01747) 811881
E: theoldforge@hotmail.com
I: www.smoothhound.co.uk

CORFE CASTLE
Dorset

Kingston Country Courtyard ★★★
Contact: Mrs Ann Fry, Kingston Country Courtyard, Greystone Court, Kingston, Corfe Castle, Wareham BH20 5LR
T: (01929) 481066
F: (01929) 481256
E: annfry@kingstoncountrycourtyard.co.uk
I: www.kingstoncountrycourtyard.co.uk

Knaveswell Farm ★★
Contact: Mrs Valerie Murray, Knaveswell Farm, Knitson Lane, Corfe Castle, Wareham BH20 5JB
T: (01929) 424184
F: (01929) 424184

Scoles Manor ★★★★
Contact: Mr & Mrs Peter Bell, Scoles Manor, Kingston, Corfe Castle BH20 5LG
T: (01929) 480312
F: (01929) 481237
E: peter@scoles.co.uk
I: www.scoles.co.uk

Tavern Way ★★★
Contact: Mrs Stuart-Brown, Dream Cottages Ltd, 41 Maiden Street, Weymouth DT4 8AZ
T: (01305) 761347
F: (01305) 789000
E: admin@dream-cottages.co.uk

COWES
Isle of Wight

Apartment Marivent ★★★
Contact: Mrs Segui, Apartment Marivent, 75 High Street, Gurnard, Cowes PO31 7AJ
T: (01983) 292148
F: (01983) 280174
E: julia@marivent.co.uk
I: www.marivent.co.uk

Cutters & Marina Glimpse ★★★★
Contact: Mrs Valerie Caws, 4/5 Shooters Hill, Gurnard, Cowes PO31 7BE
T: (01983) 295697
F: (01983) 281203
E: caws@lineoe.net

Debourne Lodge ★★★
Contact: Mrs J Clark, 27 Worsley Road, Gurnard, Cowes PO31 8JW
T: (01983) 294900

Dolphin House ★★★
Contact: Mrs Kimiko Ure, c/o 58 Place Road, East Cowes PO31 7UB
F: (01983) 294788
E: dolphin_house_iow@yahoo.co.uk
I: www.dolphinhousecowes.co.uk

Dormers Cottage ★★★
Contact: Mrs Honor Vass, Island Cottage Holidays, Godshill Park Farm House, Godshill, Wroxall, Ventnor PO38 3JF
T: (01929) 480080
F: (01929) 481070
E: enq@islandcottagesholidays.com
I: www.cottageholidays.dmon.co.uk.

Farthings ★★
Contact: Mr Michael Rabjohns, Firestone Cottage, Kite Hill, Wootton Bridge, Ryde PO33 4LE
T: (01983) 884122

Greenside ★★★★
Contact: Mrs Honor Vass, The Old Vicarage, Kingston, Wareham BH20 5LH
T: (01929) 480080
F: (01929) 481070
E: enq@islandcottageholidays.com
I: www.islandcottageholidays.com

Mariners ★★★★
Contact: Mrs Suzanne Thomas, 69 Airedale Avenue, Chiswick, London W4 2NN
T: (020) 8994 0856
F: (020) 8994 0856

87 Medina View ★★★
Contact: Ms Catherine Hopper, Island Holiday Homes, 177 High Street, Ryde PO33 2HW
T: (01983) 616644
F: (01983) 616640
E: enquiries@island-holiday-homes.net
I: www.island-holiday-homes.net

1 Middleton Terrace ★★-★★★
Contact: Mrs Sarah Cotton, 49 Linden Road, Newport PO30 1RJ
T: (01983) 523648
I: www.rjccowes

78 Park Road ★★★
Contact: Mrs Patricia Rooke, 202 Park Road, Cowes PO31 7NE
T: (01983) 298976
E: trish.rooke@virgin.net
I: www.zenalt.com/cowesholidayhomes

Point Cottages ★★★★
Contact: Mrs Fran Durrell, Point Cottages, 46 Medina Road, East Cowes PO31 7BX
T: (01983) 294974
F: (01983) 290255
E: pointcottages@medtec.co.uk
I: www.pointcottages.co.uk

24 Seaview Road ★★★
Contact: Ms Lisa Baskill, Home from Home Holidays, 31 Pier Street, Ventnor PO38 1SX
T: (01983) 854340
F: (01983) 855524

47 Victoria Road ★★★
Contact: Mr & Mrs Barker, 75 Lowndes Avenue, Chesham HP5 2HJ
T: (01494) 785948

64 York Street ★★★
Contact: Mrs Patricia Rooke, 202 Park Road, Gurnard, Cowes PO31 7NE
T: (01983) 298976
E: trishrooke@wight365.net
I: www.zenalt.com/cowesholidayhomes

CRANBROOK
Kent

Bakersbarn ★★★
Contact: Dr & Mrs Hooper, Bakersbarn, Golford Road, Cranbrook TN17 3NW
T: (01580) 713344

Little Dodges ★★★★
Contact: Mrs Brenda Beck, Freedom Holiday Homes, 15 High Street, Cranbrook TN17 3EB
T: (01580) 720770
F: (01580) 720771
E: mail@freedomholidayhomes.co.uk
I: www.freedomholidayhomes.co.uk

Mill Cottage ★★★★
Contact: Mr Stuart Winter, Garden of England Cottages Ltd, The Mews Office, 189a High Street, Tonbridge TN9 1BX
T: (01732) 369168
F: (01732) 358817
E: holidays@gardenofenglandcottages.co.uk
I: www.gardenofenglandcottages.co.uk

Oak Cottage ★★★
Contact: Mrs Brenda Beck, Freedom Holiday Homes, 15 High Street, Cranbrook TN17 3EB
T: (01580) 720770
F: (01580) 720771
E: mail@freedomholidayhomes.co.uk
I: www.freedomholidayhomes.co.uk

The Old Barn ★★★
Contact: Mrs Brenda Beck, Freedom Holiday Homes, 15 High Street, Cranbrook TN17 3EB
T: (01580) 720770
F: (01580) 720771
E: mail@freedomholidayhomes.co.uk
I: www.freedomholidayhomes.co.uk

CREECH
Dorset

The Cottage ★★★★
Contact: Mr & Mrs E Evans, The Cottage, Creech Bottom, Creech, Wareham BH20 5DQ
T: (01929) 556241

CROWBOROUGH
East Sussex

Cleeve Lodge ★★★★
Contact: Mr & Mrs Edward & Nina Sibley, The Old House, Harlequin Lane, Crowborough TN6 1HS
T: (01892) 654331
E: nina@the-old-house.co.uk
I: www.the-old-house.co.uk

Hodges ★★★★
Contact: Mrs Hazel Colliver, Hodges, Eridge Road, Hodges, Crowborough TN6 2SS
T: (01892) 652386
F: (01892) 667775

CROWHURST
East Sussex

Old Shop Cottage ★★★★
Contact: Miss Denise P Webster, Old Shop Cottage, Sampsons Lane, Crowhurst, Battle TN33 9AU
T: (01424) 830541
E: frank.73.sandgate@virgin.net

CRUNDALE
Kent

Farnley Little Barn ★★★★
Contact: Mrs Sylvia Hope, Farnley Little Barn, Denwood Street, Crundale, Canterbury CT4 7EF
T: (01227) 730510
F: (01227) 730510
E: farnleylittlebarn@supaworld.com

Ripple Farm ★★★
Contact: Ms Maggie Baur, Ripple Farm, Crundale, Godmersham, Canterbury CT4 7EB
T: (01227) 730748
F: (01227) 730748
E: ripplefarmhols@aol.com

CUDHAM
Kent

Fairmead Cottage ★★★★
Contact: Mrs Gillingham, Fairmead Farm, Cudham Lane South, Cudham, Sevenoaks TN14 7NZ
T: (01959) 532662
F: (01959) 534274

DEAL
Kent

The Chequers ★★★
Contact: Mr David Sworder, The Chequers, Golf Road, Deal CT14 6RG
T: (01304) 362288

Shirley House ★★★★
Contact: Mrs Brenda Beck, Freedom Holiday Homes, 15 High Street, Cranbrook TN17 3EB
T: (01580) 720770
F: (01580) 720771
E: mail@freedomholidayhomes.co.uk
I: www.freedomholidayhomes.co.uk

DENMEAD
Hampshire

Flint Cottage ★★★
Contact: Mr & Mrs John & Sheila Knight, High Trees, Ashling Close, Denmead, Waterlooville PO7 6NQ
T: (023) 9226 6345
E: sheila@flintcottagehants.fsnet.co.uk

DINTON
Buckinghamshire

Wallace Farm Cottages ★★
Contact: Mrs J M Cook, Wallace Farm, Dinton, Aylesbury HP17 8UF
T: (01296) 748660
F: (01296) 748851
E: jackiecook@wallacefarm.freeserve.co.uk
I: www.country-accom.co.uk

DITCHLING
East Sussex

Tovey Cottage ★★★★
Contact: Mr Richard Harris, Best of Brighton & Sussex Cottages Ltd, Windmill Lodge, Vicarage Lane, Rottingdean, Brighton BN2 7HD
T: (01273) 308779
F: (01273) 300266
E: brightoncottages@pavilion.co.uk
I: www.bestofbrighton.co.uk

Tovey Flat ★★★★
Contact: Mr Richard Harris, Best of Brighton & Sussex Cottages Ltd, Windmill Lodge, Vicarage Lane, Rottingdean, Brighton BN2 7HD
T: (01273) 308779
F: (01273) 300266
E: brightoncottages@pavilion.co.uk
I: www.bestofbrighton.co.uk

DODDINGTON
Kent

The Old School House ★★★★
Contact: Mr Stuart Winter, Garden of England Cottages Ltd, The Mews Office, 189a High Street, Tonbridge TN9 1BX
T: (01732) 369168
F: (01732) 358817
E: holidays@gardenofenglandcottages.co.uk
I: www.gardenofenglandcottages.co.uk

DORCHESTER ON THAMES
Oxfordshire

Vine Cottage ★★★★
Contact: Mr & Mrs Robert & Jenny Booth, Wellplace Barns, Wellplace, Ipsden, Wallingford OX10 6QY
T: (01491) 681158
F: (01491) 681158
E: wellplacebarns@aol.com

DORKING
Surrey

Bulmer Farm ★★★
Contact: Mrs Gill Hill, Bulmer Farm, Holmbury St Mary, Dorking RH5 6LG
T: (01306) 730210

DOVER
Kent

Meggett Farm Cottage ★★★★
Contact: Mr & Mrs Simon Price, Meggett Farm, Meggett Lane, Alkham, Dover CT15 7BS
T: (01303) 252764
F: (01303) 252764
E: simon-price.dover@virgin.net

DOWNEND
Isle of Wight

The Old Barn ★★-★★★
Contact: Mrs Anne Kennerley, The Old Barn, Duxmore Farm, Downend, Newport PO30 2NZ
T: (01983) 883993

DRAYTON
Oxfordshire

Brook Farm ★★★
Contact: Mrs Pam Humphrey, Brook Farm, Milton Road, Steventon, Abingdon OX14 4EZ
T: (01235) 820717
F: (01235) 820262

DYMCHURCH
Kent

Dymchurch House ★★★★
Contact: 53 Crescent Road, Sidcup DA15 7HW
T: (020) 8300 2100
E: dymchurchhouse@btopenworld.com

Seabreeze Holiday Homes ★★-★★★
Contact: Mr Peter Checksfield, Seabreeze Holiday Homes, 1 Sea Wall, Dymchurch, Romney Marsh TN29 0TG
T: (01635) 200316

EARNLEY
West Sussex

Poplars Farm House Rating Applied For
Contact: Mr & Mrs T Kinross, Poplars Farm House, Batchmere Road, Almodington, Earnley, Chichester PO20 7LD
T: (01243) 514969
F: (01243) 512081
E: poplarsfarmhouse@tiscali.co.uk

EAST BOLDRE
Hampshire

Greycott ★
Contact: Ms Catherine Gray, The Bungalow, Main Road, East Boldre, Brockenhurst SO42 7WL
T: (01590) 612162
F: (01590) 612162

EAST CHALDON
Dorset

Kay's Cottage ★★★
Contact: Mrs Noel Hosford, Heart of Dorset, Mill Cottage, Bramblecombe, Melcombe Bingham, Dorchester DT2 7QA
T: (01258) 880248
F: (01258) 880248
I: www.heartofdorset.easynet.co.uk/

EAST COWES
Hampshire

Buttercup Cottage ★★★★
Contact: Mr G Newnham, Alberts Dairy, Heathfield Farm, Whippingham, Isle of Wight PO32 6NQ
T: (01983) 884553
E: post@newnhams.freeserve.co.uk

Harbour View ★★★★
Contact: Ms Lisa Baskill, Home from Home Holidays, 31 Pier Street, Ventnor PO38 1SX
T: (01983) 854340
F: (01983) 855524

School House ★★★
Contact: Mr Matthew White, Island Holiday Homes, 138 High Street, Newport PO30 1TY
T: (01983) 521114

1 Seymour Court ★★★
Contact: Mrs Julia Maciw, 5 Orchard Close, Tilehurst, Reading RG31 6YS
T: (0118) 941 9866
E: holiday@seymourcourt.co.uk

EAST GRINSTEAD
West Sussex

Boyles Farmhouse Self-Catering Holidays★★★★
Contact: Mrs Emma Amos, Boyles Farmhouse, Harwoods Lane, East Grinstead RH19 4NQ
T: (01342) 315570
E: emmacamos@hotmail.com

EAST HAGBOURNE
Oxfordshire

The Oast House ★★★★
Contact: Mr Harries, Manor Farm, East Hagbourne, Didcot OX11 9ND
T: (01235) 815005

EAST HOATHLY
East Sussex

Fern Cottage ★★★★
Contact: Mr Robert Wallace/Tracie Greenland, The Kings Head, 1 High Street, East Hoathly, Lewes BN8 6DR
T: (01825) 840238
F: (01825) 880044
E: kingshead1648@hotmail.com
I: www.ferncottageholidays.co.uk

EAST KNIGHTON
Dorset

Dairy House Cottage ★★★
Contact: Mr Stuart-Brown, Dream Cottages, 41 Maiden Street, Weymouth DT4 8AZ
T: (01305) 761347

Lovers Knot ★★
Contact: Mr Stuart-Brown, Dream Cottages, 41 Maiden Street, Weymouth DT4 8AZ
T: (01305) 761347

Oaktree Cottage ★★★
Contact: Mr Stuart-Brown, Dream Cottages, 41 Maiden Street, Weymouth DT4 8AZ
T: (01305) 761347

EAST PECKHAM
Kent

Middle Cottage, Pippins Barn & Oak Weir★★★★
Contact: Mr Stuart Winter, Garden of England Cottages Ltd, The Mews Office, 189a High Street, Tonbridge TN9 1BX
T: (01732) 369168
F: (01732) 358817
E: holidays@gardenofengland.co.uk
I: www.gardenofenglandcottages.co.uk

EAST STOUR
Dorset

Crown Inn ★★★★
Contact: Mr Samuel Holmes, The Crown Inn, East Stour, Gillingham SP8 5JS
T: (01747) 838866
E: crown.inn@o2.co.uk

EAST WITTERING
West Sussex

Fairhaven ★★★
Contact: Mrs Karen Brooker, Baileys, 17 Shore Road, East Wittering, Chichester PO20 8DY
T: (01243) 672217
F: (01243) 670100
E: info@baileys.uk.com
I: www.baileys.uk.com

Little Thatch ★
Contact: Mrs J A Schofield, Canna, West Drive, Bracklesham Bay, Chichester PO20 8PF
T: (01243) 671209
E: info@baileys.uk.com
I: www.baileys.uk.com

1 Seagate Court ★★★★
Contact: Ms Karen Brooker, Baileys Estate Agents, 17 Shore Road, East Wittering, Chichester PO20 8DY
T: (01243) 672217
F: (01243) 670100
E: info@baileys.uk.com
I: www.baileys.uk.com

20 Seagate Court ★★★
Contact: Mr Ryan & Mr M Stait, 7 Loretto Gardens, Harrow HA3 9LY
T: (020) 8204 1188
F: (020) 8906 1940
E: southerncountieslets@hmeth.fsnet.co.uk
I: www.southerncountieslettings.com

Sunnyside ★★★
Contact: Mrs Karen Booker, Baileys, 17 Shore Road, West Wittering, Chichester PO20 8DY
T: (01243) 672217
E: info@baileys.uk.com
I: www.baileys.uk.com

EASTBOURNE
East Sussex

Black Robin Farm ★★★★
Contact: Mrs Jane Higgs, Black Robin Farm, Beachy Head, Eastbourne BN20 7XX
T: (01323) 643357
F: (01323) 643357
E: jane_higgsbrb@yahoo.co.uk

4 Boship Cottages ★★★
Contact: Country Hols Ref: 11983, Spring Mill, Earby, Barnoldswick BB94 0AA
T: 08700 723723
F: (01282) 844288
E: sales@holidaycottagesgroup.com
I: www.country-holidays.co.uk

4 Clovelly ★★★
Contact: Mr Richard Harris, Best of Brighton & Sussex Cottages Ltd, Windmill Lodge, Vicarage Lane, Rottingdean, Brighton BN2 7HD
T: (01273) 308779
F: (01273) 300266
E: enquiries@bestofbrighton.co.uk
I: www.bestofbrighton.co.uk

Courtney House Holiday Flats ★★★★
Contact: Dr E Toner, Courtney House Holiday Flats, 53 Royal Parade, Eastbourne BN22 7AQ
T: (01323) 410202
E: holidays@courtneyhouse.org.uk
I: www.eastbourne-web.co.uk/sites/courteneyhouse/index.html

Oysters ★★★★★
Contact: Mr Richard Harris, Best of Brighton & Sussex Cottages Ltd, Windmill Lodge, Vicarage Lane, Rottingdean, Brighton BN2 7HD
T: (01273) 308779
F: (01273) 300266
E: brightoncottages@pavilion.co.uk
I: www.bestofbrighton.co.uk

Quayside ★★★★★
Contact: Mr Richard Harris, Best of Brighton & Sussex Cottages Ltd, Windmill Lodge, Vicarage Lane, Rottingdean, Brighton BN2 7HD
T: (01273) 308779
F: (01273) 300266
E: brightoncottages@pavilion.co.uk
I: www.bestofbrighton.co.uk

Tom Thumb Cottages ★★
Contact: Mr & Mrs Roger Clark, 52 Royal Parade, Eastbourne BN22 7AQ
T: (01323) 723248
F: (01323) 723248
E: info@eastbourne-holidayflats.co.uk
I: www.eastbourne-holidayflats.co.uk

EASTCHURCH
Kent

Connetts Farm Holiday Cottages ★★★-★★★★
Contact: Mrs Maria Phipps, Connetts Farm Holiday Cottages, Plough Road, Eastchurch, Sheerness ME12 4JL
T: (01795) 880358
F: (01795) 880358
E: connetts@btconnect.com
I: www.connettsfarm.co.uk

EASTERGATE
West Sussex

Eastmere ★★★
Contact: Mrs Sarah Wilkins, Eastergate Lane, Eastergate, Chichester PO20 3SJ
T: (01243) 574389
E: wilkins45@hotmail.com
I: www.eastmere.com

EGERTON
Kent

Box Farm Barn ★★★★
Contact: Mr Stuart Winter, Garden of England Cottages Ltd, The Mews Office, 189a High Street, Tonbridge TN9 1BX
T: (01732) 369168
F: (01732) 358817
E: holidays@gardenofenglandcottages.co.uk
I: www.gardenofenglandcottages.co.uk

Coldharbour Farm Oast & Pond Cottage★★★★
Contact: Mrs Lisa Fraser, Coldharbour Farm Oast & Pond Cottage, Barhams Mill Road, Egerton, Ashford TN27 9DD
T: (01233) 756548
F: (01233) 756770

The Dering Suite & The Old Bakery ★★★
Contact: Mrs Brenda Beck, Freedom Holiday Homes, 15 High Street, Cranbrook TN17 3EB
T: (01580) 720770
F: (01580) 720771
E: mail@freedomholidayhomes.co.uk
I: www.freedomholidayhomes.co.uk

ELHAM
Kent

Lower Court Cottage ★★★★
Contact: Mr & Mrs J G Caunce, Lower Court, Shuttlesfield Lane, Ottinge, Canterbury CT4 6XJ
T: (01303) 862124
F: (01303) 864231
E: caunce@ottinge.fsnet.co.uk

ELMSTED
Kent

The Dairy ★★★
Contact: Mrs Brenda Beck, Freedom Holiday Homes, 15 High Street, Cranbrook TN17 3EB
T: (01580) 720770
F: (01580) 720771
E: mail@freedomholidayhomes.co.uk
I: www.freedomholidayhomes.co.uk

Great Holt Farm ★★★
Contact: Mr Stuart Winter, Garden of England Cottages Ltd, The Mews Office, 189a High Street, Tonbridge TN9 1BX
T: (01732) 369168
F: (01732) 358817
E: holidays@gardenofenglandcottages.co.uk
I: www.gardenofenglandcottages.co.uk

EMSWORTH
Hampshire

3 Avocet Quay ★★★
Contact: Mrs Jane Eastell, West Lychett, 111 East Lane, East Horsley, Leatherhead KT24 6LJ
T: (01483) 281819
E: janeeastell@aol.com

Hermitage Cottage ★★★
Contact: Mrs Sarah Evans, School Lane, Nutbourne, Chichester PO18 8RZ
T: (01243) 372554
E: hermitagecottage@btinternet.com
I: www.btinternet.com/~seeksystems

2 Heron Quay ★★★
Contact: Mrs Linda Sprules, Tandriway, 15 Godstone Road, Old Oxted, Oxted RH8 9JS
T: (01883) 732144
F: (01883) 722510

Westview Holiday Flat ★★★
Contact: Mrs Julia Oakley, 61 Bath Road, Emsworth PO10 7ES
T: (01243) 373002
E: j.oakley@bigfoot.com

EPSOM
Surrey

7 Great Tattenhams ★★★
Contact: Mrs Mary Willis, 7 Great Tattenhams, Epsom KT18 5RF
T: (01737) 354112

EPWELL
Oxfordshire

The Retreat of Church Farm ★★★★
Contact: Mrs Dawn Castle, Church Farm, Epwell, Banbury OX15 6LD
T: (01295) 788473

ETCHINGHAM
East Sussex

Moon Cottage ★★★★
Contact: Mrs Jan Harrison, The White Cottage, Union Street, Flimwell, Wadhurst TN5 7NT
T: (01580) 879328
F: (01580) 879729
E: enquiries@harrison-holidays.co.uk
I: www.harrison-holidays.co.uk

EVERTON
Hampshire

Gothic Cottage ★★★
Contact: Mrs Mary Brockett, The Old Boathouse, 13 Newlands Manor, Milford-on-Sea, Lymington SO41 0JH
T: (01590) 645941
E: gothic.everton@btopenworld.com

10 Newlands Manor ★★★
Contact: Mrs J A Rhoden, 10 Newlands Manor, Everton, Milford-on-Sea, Lymington SO41 0JH
T: (01590) 642830
F: (01590) 642830
E: newlandsmanor@eurolink.ltd.net

October Cottage ★★★
Contact: Mrs Val Williams, 12 Greenacre, Barton on Sea, New Milton BH25 7BS
T: (01425) 620935
E: val@westbury-house.co.uk
I: www.octobercottagenewforest.co.uk

2 Uplay Cottages ★★★★
Contact: Ms Jacquie Taylor, Three Corners, Centre Lane, Everton, Lymington SO41 0JP
T: (01590) 645217
F: (01590) 673633
E: tommy.tiddles@virgin.net
I: www.halcyonholidays.com

Wheatley Cottage ★★★
Contact: Mrs Jacquie Taylor, Centre Lane, Everton, Milford-on-Sea, Lymington SO41 0JP
T: (01590) 645217
E: tommy.tiddles@virgin.net

EXTON
Hampshire

Beacon Hill Farm Cottages ★★★★
Contact: Mrs J Smith, The Farm Office Manor Farm, Beacon Hill Lane, Warnford Road, Exton, Southampton SO32 3NW
T: (01730) 829724
F: (01730) 829833
E: chris@martin4031.freeserve.co.uk
I: www.beaconhillcottages.co.uk

FAIRLIGHT
East Sussex

Little Oaks ★★★★
Contact: Mrs Janet Adams, Warren Road, (Via Coastguard Lane), Fairlight, Hastings TN35 4AG
T: (01424) 812545
F: (01424) 812545
E: fairlightcottage@supanet.com

FAREHAM
Hampshire

Manor Croft ★★★★
Contact: Mr Thomson, Manor Croft Clinic Ltd, Manor Croft, Church Path, Fareham PO16 7DT
T: (01329) 280750
F: (01329) 280750
E: accom@btconnect.com
I: www.manor-croft-health.co.uk/visitor_accom_1.htm

FARNHAM
Surrey

High Wray ★★
Contact: Mrs Alexine Crawford, High Wray, 73 Lodge Hill Road, Farnham GU10 3RB
T: (01252) 715589
F: (01252) 715746
E: crawford@highwray73.co.uk

Tilford Woods ★★★★
Contact: The Booking Manager, Tilford Woods, Tilford Road, Tilford, Farnham GU10 2DD
T: (01252) 792199
F: (01252) 781027
E: admin@tilfordwoods.co.uk
I: www.tilfordwoods.co.uk

Kilnside Farm ★★
Contact: Mrs Ros Milton, Kilnside Farm, Moor Park Lane, Farnham GU10 1NS
T: (01252) 710325

FAVERSHAM
Kent

The Country Retreat ★★★
Contact: Mrs Maureen French, Country Retreat, Yew Tree Cottage, Syndale Park, Faversham ME13 0RH
T: (01795) 531257
F: (01795) 531257
E: countryretreat1@aol.com

Monks Cottage ★★★★
Contact: Mr & Mrs Graham Darby, Monks Cottage, Leaveland, Faversham ME13 0NP
T: (01233) 740419
F: (01233) 740419

Old Dairy ★★★
Contact: Mrs Gillian Falcon, Shepherds Hill, Selling, Faversham ME13 9RS
T: (01227) 752212
F: (01227) 752212
E: ag@agfalcon.f9.co.uk

Uplees Farm ★★★★
Contact: Mr & Mrs Chris & Heather Flood, Uplees Farm, Uplees Road, Luddenham, Faversham ME13 0QR
T: (01795) 532133

FELPHAM
West Sussex

Felpham Bungalow ★★★
Contact: Mrs Janet Yabsley, 4 Nicholas Road, Beddington, Croydon CR0 4QS
T: (0208) 680 4761

FERRING
West Sussex

5 Lamorna Gardens ★★★
Contact: Mrs Elsden & Mary Fitzgerald
T: (01903) 238582
F: (01903) 230266

FINCHDEAN
Hampshire

Wagtails ★★★★
Contact: Mrs Guess, Swallows Roost, Finchdean Farm, Finchdean, Waterlooville PO8 0AU
T: (023) 9241 3838
F: (023) 9241 3569
E: roger.guess@btinternet.com

FINSTOCK
Oxfordshire

Wychwood ★★
Contact: Mrs Bodil Grain, 40 School Road, Finstock, Oxford OX7 3DJ
T: (01993) 868249
E: bgrain@wychwoodcottage.co.uk
I: www.wychwoodcottage.co.uk

FISHBOURNE
West Sussex

The Tidings ★★★
Contact: Mrs Davies, The Tidings, Appledram Lane North, Fishbourne, Chichester PO19 3RW
T: (01243) 773958

The Willows ★★
Contact: Mrs Linda Proctor, The Willows, Main Road, Fishbourne, Chichester PO18 8AX
T: (01243) 576645
E: linda@proctor50.freeserve.co.uk

FIVE OAK GREEN
Kent

Stable Cottage ★★★★
Contact: Mrs Brenda Beck, Freedom Holiday Homes, 15 High Street, Cranbrook TN17 3EB
T: (01580) 720770
F: (01580) 720771
E: mail@freedomholidayhomes.co.uk
I: www.freedomholidayhomes.co.uk

FOLKESTONE
Kent

Bybrook Cottage ★★★
Contact: Mrs Gwendoline Baker, Bybrook House, The Undercliffe, Folkestone CT20 3AT
T: (01303) 248255

Flat 4 Leas House ★★★
Contact: Mr James Kitson, Flat 3 Leas House, 3 Castle Hill Avenue, Folkestone CT20 2TD
T: (01303) 248905

The Grand ★★-★★★
Contact: Mr Michael Stainer
T: (01303) 220440
F: (01303) 220220
E: enquiries@grand-uk.com
I: www.grand-uk.com

Llamados Apartments ★★★★
Contact: Ms Claire Stafford, 13 Harbour Point, The Stade, Folkestone CT19 6RB
T: (01303) 255895
F: (01303) 255895

Merriwinds ★★★★
Contact: Country Holidays, Merriwinds, 147 The Old Dover Road, Capel-le-Ferne, Folkestone CT18 7HX
T: 08700 726726
F: (01282) 841539
E: ownerservices@holidaycottagesgroup.com
I: www.varne-ridge.co.uk

Meyrick Court Studio Apartments ★★
Contact: Mr Julio Santos Hilario, Meyrick Court Studio Apartments, 8-10 Trinity Crescent, Folkestone CT20 2ET
T: (01303) 275388
F: (01303) 275325

Parkview Apartments ★★★
Contact: Miss Paula McGlynn, Parkview Apartments, 1 Grimston Gardens, Folkestone CT20 2PT
T: (01303) 251482
E: paulamcglynn6@hotmail.com

FOLKINGTON
East Sussex

Wood Barn at The Old Rectory ★★★
Contact: Mrs Janet Macdonald, Wood Barn, The Old Rectory, Folkington, Polegate BN26 5SD
T: (01323) 483367
F: (01323) 488156
E: geradin@pobox.com

FORDINGBRIDGE
Hampshire

Alderholt Mill ★★★
Contact: Mr & Mrs Richard & Sandra Harte, Alderholt Mill, Sandleheath Road, Alderholt, Fordingbridge SP6 1PU
T: (01425) 653130
F: (01425) 652868
E: alderholt-mill@zetnet.co.uk
I: www.alderholtmill.co.uk

Burgate Manor Farm Holidays ★★★★
Contact: Mrs Bridget Stallard, Burgate Manor Farm Holidays, Burgate Manor Farm, Fordingbridge SP6 1LX
T: (01425) 653908
F: (01425) 653908
E: info@newforestcottages.com
I: www.newforestcottages.com

Fir Tree Farm Cottage ★★★★
Contact: Mr & Mrs Colin & Sarah Proctor, Fir Tree Farm, Frogham Hill, Stuckton, Fordingbridge SP6 2HH
T: (01425) 654001
E: cjproctor@onetel.net.uk
I: www.firtreefarmcottage.co.uk

Garden Cottage ★★★
Contact: Mrs Adele Holmes, The Dial House, Rockbourne, Fordingbridge SP6 3NA
T: (01725) 518083
F: (01725) 518083
E: rockbourneprop@freeuk.com
I: www.rockbourne.4dw.com

Glencairn ★★★
Contact: Mrs C Tiller, 2 Fernlea, Sandleheath, Fordingbridge SP6 1PN
T: (01425) 652506

Hucklesbrook Farm ★★★★
Contact: Mr Sampson, Ringwood Road, South Gorley, Fordingbridge SP6 2PN
T: (01425) 653180
E: dh.sampson@btinternet.com

FRESHWATER
Isle of Wight

Afton Thatch ★★★★
Contact: Mrs Mylene Curtis, Afton Thatch, The Causeway, Freshwater PO40 9TN
T: (0208) 995 9288
F: (0208) 580 3911
E: mylene@blueyonder.co.uk

Applebarns House & Cottage ★★★-★★★★
Contact: Mr David Poole, 42 Frewin Road, London SW18 3LP
T: (01635) 200316

40 Brambles Chine ★★
Contact: The Lettings Administrator, Linstone Chine Holiday Services Ltd, Brambles Office, Monks Lane, Colwell Bay PO40 9NQ
T: (01983) 755933
F: (01983) 752015

60 Brambles Chine ★★
Contact: The Lettings Administrator, Linstone Chine Holiday Services Ltd, Heath Meadow, Colwell Bay PO40 9NQ
T: (01983) 755933
F: (01983) 752015

67 Brambles Chine ★★
Contact: The Lettings Administrator, Linstone Chine Holiday Services Ltd, Brambles Office, Monks Lane, Colwell Bay PO40 9NQ
T: (01983) 755933
F: (01983) 752015

87 Brambles Chine ★★
Contact: The Lettings Administrator, Linstone Chine Holiday Services Ltd, Brambles Office, Monks Lane, Colwell Bay PO40 9NQ
T: (01983) 755933
F: (01983) 752015

92 Brambles Chine ★★
Contact: Mrs April Mansbridge, Glen Gariff, Victoria Road, Yarmouth PO41 0QW
T: (01983) 761167
F: (01983) 752015

103 Brambles Chine ★★
Contact: Mrs April Mansbridge, Glen Gariff, Victoria Road, Yarmouth PO41 0QW
T: (01983) 761167
F: (01983) 752015

107 Brambles Chine ★★★
Contact: The Lettings Administrator, Linstone Chine Holiday Services Ltd, Brambles Office, Monks Lane, Colwell Bay PO40 9NQ
T: (01983) 755933
F: (01983) 752015

110 Brambles Chine ★★
Contact: The Lettings Administrator, Linstone Chine Holiday Services Ltd, Brambles Office, Monks Lane, Colwell Bay PO40 9NQ
T: (01983) 755933
F: (01983) 752015

111 Brambles Chine ★★
Contact: Mrs April Mansbridge, Glen Gariff, Victoria Road, Yarmouth PO41 0QW
T: (01983) 761167
F: (01983) 752015

131 Brambles Chine ★★★
Contact: The Lettings Administrator, Linstone Chine Holiday Services Ltd, Brambles Office, Monks Lane, Colwell Bay PO40 9NQ
T: (01983) 755933
F: (01983) 752015

160 Brambles Chine ★★
Contact: The Lettings Administrator, Linstone Chine Holiday Services Ltd, Brambles Office, Monks Lane, Colwell Bay PO40 9NQ
T: (01983) 755933
F: (01983) 752015

170 Brambles Chine ★★★
Contact: The Lettings Administrator, Linstone Chine Holiday Services Ltd, Brambles Office, Monks Lane, Colwell Bay PO40 9NQ
T: (01983) 755933
F: (01983) 752015

171 Brambles Chine ★★★
Contact: The Lettings Administrator, Linstone Chine Holiday Services Ltd, Brambles Office, Monks Lane, Colwell Bay PO40 9NQ
T: (01983) 755933
F: (01983) 752015

176 Brambles Chine ★★
Contact: Mr Neil Andrew Cain, 18 Osborn Gardens, Mill Hill East, London NW7 1DY
T: (020) 8346 6308

196 Brambles Chine ★★★
Contact: The Lettings Administrator, Linstone Chine Holiday Services Ltd, Brambles Office, Monks Lane, Colwell Bay PO40 9NQ
T: (01983) 755933
F: (01983) 752015

209 Brambles Chine ★★
Contact: The Lettings Administrator, Linstone Chine Holiday Services Ltd, Brambles Office, Monks Lane, Colwell Bay PO40 9NQ
T: (01983) 755933
F: (01983) 752015

210 Brambles Chine ★★★
Contact: The Lettings Administrator, Linstone Chine Holiday Services Ltd, Brambles Office, Monks Lane, Colwell Bay PO40 9NQ
T: (01983) 755933
F: (01983) 752015

222 Brambles Chine ★★
Contact: The Lettings Administrator, Linstone Chine Holiday Services Ltd, Brambles Office, Monks Lane, Colwell Bay PO40 9NQ
T: (01983) 755933
F: (01983) 752015

226 Brambles Chine ★★
Contact: The Lettings Administrator, Linstone Chine Holiday Services Ltd, Brambles Office, Monks Lane, Colwell Bay PO40 9NQ
T: (01983) 755933
F: (01983) 752015

12A Cliff End ★★
Contact: Mrs April Mansbridge, Glen Gariff, Victoria Road, Yarmouth PO41 0QW
T: (01983) 761167
F: (01983) 752015

36 Cliff End ★★
Contact: The Lettings Administrator, Linstone Chine Holiday Services Ltd, Brambles Office, Monks Lane, Colwell Bay PO40 9NQ
T: (01983) 755933
F: (01983) 752015

52 Cliff End ★
Contact: The Lettings Administrator, Linstone Chine Holiday Services Ltd, Brambles Office, Monks Lane, Colwell Bay PO40 9NQ
T: (01983) 755933
F: (01983) 752015

70 Cliff End ★★★
Contact: Mr R Armour, Glebelands, Afton Road, Freshwater PO40 9TP
T: (01983) 754453

Farringford Hotel ★★★
Contact: Miss L Hollyhead, Farringford Hotel, Bedbury Lane, Freshwater PO40 9PE
T: (01983) 752500
F: (01983) 756515
E: enquiries@farringford.co.uk
I: www.farringford.co.uk

Freshfields ★★★
Contact: Mr & Mrs Barry, 26 Calbourne Road, Carisbrooke, Newport PO30 5AP
T: (01983) 529901
E: jo@isle-of-wight.fsbusiness.co.uk

Holiday Homes Owners Services Ref: F1★★★
Contact: Mr Colin Nolson, Holiday Homes Owners Services (West Wight), 18 Solent Hill, Freshwater PO40 9TG
T: (01983) 753423
F: (01983) 753423
E: holidayhomesiow@ic24.net

Holiday Homes Owners Services Ref: F7★★★
Contact: Mr Colin Nolson, Holiday Homes Owners Services (West Wight), 18 Solent Hill, Freshwater PO40 9TG
T: (01983) 753423
F: (01983) 753423
E: holidayhomesiow@ic24.net

Holiday Homes Owners Services Ref: F8★★★
Contact: Mr Colin Nolson, Holiday Homes Owners Services (West Wight), 18 Solent Hill, Freshwater PO40 9TG
T: (01983) 753423
F: (01983) 753423
E: holidayhomesiow@ic24.net

Holiday Homes Owners Services Ref: F10★★★★
Contact: Mr Colin Nolson, Holiday Homes Owners Services (West Wight), 18 Solent Hill, Freshwater PO40 9TG
T: (01983) 753423
F: (01983) 753423
E: holidayhomesiow@ic24.net

Holiday Homes Owners Services Ref: F2/51★★★
Contact: Mr Colin Nolson, Holiday Homes Owners Services (West Wight), 18 Solent Hill, Freshwater PO40 9TG
T: (01983) 753423
F: (01983) 753423
E: holidayhomesiow@ic24.net

Holiday Homes Owners Services Ref: F2/168★★
Contact: Mr Colin Nolson, Holiday Homes Owners Services (West Wight), 18 Solent Hill, Freshwater PO40 9TG
T: (01983) 753423
F: (01983) 753423
E: holidayhomesiow@ic24.net

Holiday Homes Owners Services Ref: F2/203★★★
Contact: Mr Colin Nolson, Holiday Homes Owners Services (West Wight), 18 Solent Hill, Freshwater PO40 9TG
T: (01983) 753423
F: (01983) 753423
E: holidayhomesiow@ic24.net

Holiday Homes Owners Services Ref: F2/48★★
Contact: Mr Colin Nolson, Holiday Homes Owners Services (West Wight), 18 Solent Hill, Freshwater PO40 9TG
T: (01983) 753423
F: (01983) 753423
E: holidayhomesiow@ic24.net

Holiday Homes Owners Services Ref: F2/32★★
Contact: Mr Colin Nolson, Holiday Homes Owners Services (West Wight), 18 Solent Hill, Freshwater PO40 9TG
T: (01983) 753423
F: (01983) 753423
E: holidayhomesiow@ic24.net

Holiday Homes Owners Services Ref: F2/30★★
Contact: Mr Colin Nolson, Holiday Homes Owners Services (West Wight), 18 Solent Hill, Freshwater PO40 9TG
T: (01983) 753423
F: (01983) 753423
E: holidayhomesiow@ic24.net

Holiday Homes Owners Services Ref: F4★★★
Contact: Mr Colin Nolson, Holiday Homes Owners Services (West Wight), 18 Solent Hill, Freshwater PO40 9TG
T: (01983) 753423
F: (01983) 753423
E: holidayhomesiow@ic24.net

Little Rabbits ★★★
Contact: Mrs Helen Long, Windrush, Wellow, Yarmouth PO41 0TA
T: (01983) 761506
E: hugh7@bushinternet.com

Rose Cottage ★★★
Contact: Mrs Jo Gardner, 12 New Barn Lane, Alton GU34 2RU
T: (01420) 543385
F: (01420) 84587
E: jlightfoot.knowkedgeexchange@btinternet.com

St Martins Holiday Flats ★★
Contact: Mr & Mrs John Finch, St Martins Holiday Flats, Afton Down, Freshwater Bay PO40 9TY
T: (01983) 752389
E: stmartins.holidayflats@virgin.net

Soake Farm House Rating Applied For
Contact: Ms Annette Edmundson, Soake Farm House, Queens Road, Freshwater Bay PO40 9ES
T: (01983) 752383

Sunnyside ★★
Contact: Mrs Sara Yarwood, Waratah, Church Lane, Sway, Lymington SO41 6AD
T: (01590) 682863

Sunsets ★★
Contact: Mrs April Mansbridge, Glen Gariff, Victoria Road, Yarmouth PO41 0QW
T: (01983) 761167
F: (01983) 752015

Tree Tops ★★★
Contact: Ms Lisa Baskill, Home from Home Holidays, 31 Pier Street, Ventnor PO38 1SX
T: (01983) 854340
F: (01983) 855524

Wagtails 4 & Wagtails 5 ★★★
Contact: Mrs Fay McKay, Wagtails, 4 Gaggerhill Lane, Brighstone, Newport PO30 4DX
T: (01983) 740816

FRESHWATER BAY
Isle of Wight

Holiday Homes Owners Services Ref: F9★★★★
Contact: Mr Colin Nolson, Holiday Homes Owners Services (West Wight), 18 Solent Hill, Freshwater PO40 9TG
T: (01983) 753423
F: (01983) 753423
E: holidayhomesiow@ic24.net

Holiday Homes Owners Services Ref: F3★★★
Contact: Mr Colin Nolson, Holiday Homes Owners Services (West Wight), 18 Solent Hill, Freshwater PO40 9TG
T: (01983) 753423
F: (01983) 753423
E: holidayhomesiow@ic24.net

2 Tennyson View ★★★★★
Contact: Ms Catherine Hopper, Manager, Housing Letting Hose Rhodes Dickson, Island Holiday Homes, 177 High Street, Ryde PO33 2HW
T: (01983) 616644
F: (01983) 616640
E: enquiries@island-holiday-homes.net
I: www.island-holiday-homes.net

5 Tennyson View ★★★★
Contact: Mr Matthew White, Island Holiday Homes, 138 High Street, Newport PO30 1TY
T: (01983) 521114

10 Tennyson View ★★★★
Contact: Ms Catherine Hopper, Manager, Housing Letting Hose Rhodes Dickson, Island Holiday Homes, 177 High Street, Ryde PO33 2HW
T: (01983) 616644
F: (01983) 616640
E: enquiries@island-holiday-homes.net
I: www.island-holiday-homes.net

FRITTENDEN
Kent

Weaversden Oast House ★★★★
Contact: Mr Stuart Winter, Garden of England Cottages Ltd, The Mews Office, 189a High Street, Tonbridge TN9 1BX
T: (01732) 369168
F: (01732) 358817
E: holidays@gardenofenglandcottages.co.uk
I: www.gardenofenglandcottages.co.uk

FULBROOK
Oxfordshire

Footstool Cottage ★★★★
Contact: Mr Roger Bevan, The Ridge, Lower Basildon, Reading RG8 9NX
T: (0118) 984 4985
F: (0118) 984 5664
E: roger@bevanwoodlands.fsnet.co.uk
I: www.geocities.com/bevanwoodlands

FUNTINGTON
West Sussex

The Courtyard ★★★★
Contact: Mrs Claire Hoare, 3 The Cottages, Adsdean Farm, Funtington, Chichester PO18 9DN
T: (01243) 575464
F: (01243) 575586
E: tim.hoare@farming.co.uk

Dellfield ★★★★
Contact: Mr Hall Hall, Dellfield, Downs Road, West Ashling, Chichester PO18 9LS
T: (01243) 575244
F: (01243) 578916
E: holidays@dellfield.com
I: www.dellfield.com

FURZEHILL
Dorset

Grange Holiday Cottages ★★★★
Contact: English Country Cottages, Earby, Barnoldswick BB94 0AA
T: 0870 4 441101
F: (0128) 284 1539

FYFIELD
Hampshire

2 Rose Lane ★★★
Contact: Mr & Mrs Jan & Paul Martin, 2 Rose Lane, Fyfield, Andover SP11 8ER
T: (01264) 771556

GATCOMBE
Isle of Wight

Newbarn Country Cottages ★★★★
Contact: Mrs Diane Harvey, Gatcombe, Newport PO30 3EQ
T: (01983) 721202
I: www.wightfarmholidays.co.uk/stable

GILLINGHAM
Dorset

Meads Farm ★★★★
Contact: Mrs June Wallis, Meads Farm, Stour Provost, Gillingham SP8 5RX
T: (01747) 838265
F: (01258) 821123

Top Stall ★★★
Contact: Mrs Kathleen Jeanes, Top Stall, Factory Farm, Fifehead Magdalen, Gillingham SP8 5RS
T: (01258) 820022
F: (01258) 820022
E: factoryfarm@agriplus.net

Woolfields Barn ★★★★
Contact: Mr & Mrs B Thomas, Woolfields Barn, Woolfields Farm, Milton on Stour, Gillingham SP8 5PX
T: (01747) 824729
F: (01747) 824986
E: OThomas453@aol.com

GLYNDE
East Sussex

Caburn Cottages ★★★★
Contact: Mr & Mrs Philip Norris, Caburn Cottages, Ranscombe Farm, Glynde, Lewes BN8 6AA
T: (01273) 858062

GODALMING
Surrey

Magpie Cottage ★★★
Contact: Mrs Gabrielle Mabley, Tigbourne Wood, Wormley, Godalming GU8 5SU
T: (01428) 682702
E: Gabrielle.Mabley1@btinternet.com

GODSHILL
Isle of Wight

1, 2 & 3 Barwick Cottages ★★★-★★★★
Contact: Mrs P J Wickham, Barwick Cottage, Rookley Farm Lane, Niton Road, Rookley, Ventnor PO38 3PA
T: (01983) 840787
F: (01983) 840787
E: pam@barwickcottages.co.uk
I: www.barwickcottages.co.uk

Bagwich Cottage ★★★★
Contact: Mrs Honor Vass, The Old Vicarage, Kingston, Wareham BH20 5LH
T: (01929) 480080
F: (01929) 480080
I: www.islandcottageholidays.com

The Coach House Studio ★★★
Contact: Mrs Honor Vass, The Old Vicarage, Kingston, Wareham BH20 5LH
T: (01929) 480080
F: (01929) 481070
E: enq@islandcottageholidays.com
I: www.islandcottageholidays.com

Demelza ★★★★
Contact: Mrs Honor Vass, Island Cottage Holidays, The Old Vicarage, Kingston, Sturminster Newton BH20 5LH
T: (01929) 480080
F: (01929) 481070
E: enq@islandcottageholidays.com
I: www.islandcottageholidays.com

Glebelands Holiday Apartments ★★★★
Contact: Mrs Iris Beardsall, Glebelands Holiday Apartments, Church Hollow, Godshill, Wroxall, Ventnor PO38 3DR
T: (01983) 840371
F: (01983) 867482

Godshill Park House ★★★★
Contact: Mrs Nora Down, Godshill Park House, Shanklin Road, Godshill, Wroxall, Ventnor PO38 3JF
T: (01983) 840271
F: (01983) 840960
E: noradown@godshillpark.fsnet.co.uk

Graylands Cottage ★★
Contact: Professor Ian Bruce, 54 Mall Road, Hammersmith, London W6 9DG
T: (020) 8748 0611
F: (020) 8741 5621
E: tinab@cocoon.co.uk

Keepers Cottage ★★★★
Contact: Mrs Honor Vass, The Old Vicarage, Kingston, Wareham BH20 5LH
T: (01929) 480080
F: (01929) 481070
E: enq@islandcottageholidays.com
I: www.islandcottageholidays.com

Lambourn View Holiday Annexe ★★
Contact: Mrs Maureen Plumbley, Lambourn View Holiday Annexe, Beacon Alley, Godshill, Ventnor PO38 3JX
T: (01635) 200316

Loves Cottage ★★★
Contact: Mrs Honor Vass, The Old Vicarage, Kingston, Wareham BH20 5LH
T: (01929) 480080
F: (01929) 481070
E: enq@islandcottageholidays.com
I: www.islandcottageholidays.com

Milk Pan Farm ★★★
Contact: Mr & Mrs Tony & Leila Morrish, Milk Pan Farm, Bagwich Lane, Ventnor PO38 3JY
T: (01983) 840570
E: tony@milkpanfarm.fsnet.co.uk

Pheasant Cottage ★★★★
Contact: Mrs Kathy Domaille, Pheasant Cottage, Godshill Park Farm, Shanklin Road, Wroxall, Ventnor PO38 3JF
T: (01983) 840781
E: info@godshillparkfarm

Pilgrims Lodge ★★★
Contact: Mrs Honor Vass, The Old Vicarage, Kingston, Wareham BH20 5LH
T: (01929) 480080
F: (01929) 481070
E: enq@islandcottageholidays.com
I: www.islandcottageholidays.com

Rosemary Cottage ★★★★
Contact: Mrs Honor Vass, The Old Vicarage, Kingston, Wareham BH20 5LH
T: (01929) 480080
F: (01929) 481070
E: enq@islandcottageholidays.com
I: www.islandcottageholidays.com

Seymour Cottages ★★★
Contact: Mr & Mrs Arthur & Pat Lazenby, Seymour Cottages, Lower Yard Farm, Ventnor PO38 3LY
T: (01983) 840536

Stag Cottage ★★★★
Contact: Mrs Honor Vass, The Old Vicarage, Kingston, Wareham BH20 5LH
T: (01929) 480080
F: (01929) 481070
E: enq@islandcottageholidays.com
I: www.islandcottageholidays.com

GODSHILL WOOD
Hampshire

The Lodge (Ref: H212) ★★★★
Contact: Mr Nick Pash, Chapel House, Luke Street, Berwick St John, Shaftesbury SP7 0HQ
T: (01747) 828170
F: (01747) 829090
E: enq@hideaways.co.uk
I: www.hideaways.co.uk/property2.cfm?ref=H212

GOODWOOD
West Sussex

Bay Cottage ★★★
Contact: Mrs Rosemary Wilks, 58 North Acre, Banstead SM7 2EG
T: (01737) 358863

GORING-BY-SEA
West Sussex

Sea Place ★★
Contact: Mr Robert Brew, Promenade Holiday Homes, 165 Dominion Road, Worthing BN14 8LD
T: (01903) 201426
F: (01903) 201426
E: robert@promhols.fsbusiness.co.uk

GOSPORT
Hampshire

Avenue Corner ★★★★
Contact: Mr Kevin Macaulay, 21 Vernon Close, Alverstoke, Gosport PO12 3NU
T: (02392) 502222
F: (02392) 528338
E: enquiries@avenuecorner.co.uk
I: www.avenuecorner.co.uk

Captains Folly ★★★
Contact: Mr J M White, 8 Cambridge Road, Lee on the Solent PO13 9DH
T: (023) 9255 0883
I: www.brook.white1.btinternet.co.uk/index.html

Dolphins ★★★
Contact: Mrs Donnelly, 28 Crescent Road, Alverstoke, Gosport PO12 2DJ
T: (023) 9258 8179

Keefons ★★
Contact: Mr & Mrs Keith & Yvonne Hoskins, 6 Village Road, Alverstoke, Gosport PO12 2LF
T: (023) 9252 0982

The Laurels ★★★★
Contact: Manager, 1 Madden Close, Gosport PO12 2PT
T: (023) 9258 3637
E: enquiries@onewestlodge.co.uk
I: www.onewestlodge.co.uk

19 The Quarterdeck ★★★★★
Contact: Mr Dave Danns, 197 Portsmouth Road, Lee on the Solent, Gosport PO13 9AA
T: (023) 9255 2550
F: (023) 9255 4657
E: dave@thequarterdeck.co.uk
I: www.thequarterdeck.co.uk

GOUDHURST
Kent

Blackthorn Barn ★★★★
Contact: Mrs Brenda Beck, Freedom Holiday Homes, 15 High Street, Cranbrook TN17 3EB
T: (01580) 720770
F: (01580) 720771
E: mail@freedomholidayhomes.co.uk
I: www.freedomholidayhomes.co.uk

The Coach House ★★★
Contact: Mrs Brenda Beck, Freedom Holiday Homes, 15 High Street, Cranbrook TN17 3EB
T: (01580) 720770
F: (01580) 720771
E: mail@freedomholidayhomes.co.uk
I: www.freedomholidayhomes.co.uk

The Stables ★★★★
Contact: Mrs Brenda Beck, Freedom Holiday Homes, 15 High Street, Cranbrook TN17 3EB
T: (01580) 720770
F: (01580) 720771
E: mail@freedomholidayhomes.co.uk
I: www.freedomholidayhomes.co.uk

Three Chimneys Farm ★★★★
Contact: Mrs Marion Fuller, Three Chimneys Farm, Bedgebury Road, Goudhurst, Cranbrook TN17 2RA
T: (01580) 212175
F: (01580) 212175
E: marionfuller@threechimneysfarm.co.uk
I: www.threechimneysfarm.co.uk

3 Whitestocks Cottages
★★★★
Contact: Mrs Brenda Beck, Freedom Holiday Homes, 15 High Street, Cranbrook TN17 3EB
T: (01580) 720770
F: (01580) 720771
E: mail@freedomholidayhomes.co.uk
I: www.freedomholidayhomes.co.uk

GRAFTY GREEN
Kent

2 Fermor Cottages ★★★
Contact: Garden of England Cottages, The Mews Office, 189A High Street, Tonbridge TN9 1BX
T: (01732) 369168
F: (01732) 358817
E: holidays@gardenofenglandcottages.co.uk

The Old Chapel & Weirton Villas
Rating Applied For
Contact: Mrs Gill Winter, Garden of England Cottages, The Mews Office, 189A High Street, Tonbridge TN9 1BX
T: (01732) 369168
F: (01732) 358817
E: holidays@gardenofenglandcottages.co.uk

GRAVESEND
Kent

Russell Quay ★★★★
Contact: Mr Trevor Dickety, 1 Brimstone Hill, Meopham, Gravesend DA13 0BN
T: (01474) 573045
F: (01474) 573049
E: mikedickety@beeb.net
I: www.halcyon-gifts.co.uk/holidaylet.html

GREAT MILTON
Oxfordshire

Views Farm Barns ★★★★
Contact: Mr & Mrs C O Peers, Views Farm Barns, Views Farm, Great Milton, Oxford OX44 7NW
T: (01844) 279352
F: (01844) 279362
E: info@viewsfarmbarns.co.uk
I: www.viewsfarmbarns.co.uk

GREAT ROLLRIGHT
Oxfordshire

Blackbird Cottage ★★★★
Contact: Mrs Carol Dingle, Tyte End Cottage, Great Rollright, Chipping Norton OX7 5RU
T: (01608) 737676
F: (01608) 737330

Butlers Hill Farm ★★★
Contact: Mrs Campbell, Butlers Hill Farm, Great Rollright, Chipping Norton OX7 5SJ
T: (01608) 684430

GROOMBRIDGE
East Sussex

Sherlocks Cottage ★★★★
Contact: Mrs Brenda Beck, Freedom Holiday Homes, 15 High Street, Cranbrook TN17 3EB
T: (01580) 720770
F: (01580) 720771
E: mail@freedomholidayhomes.co.uk
I: www.freedomholidayhomes.co.uk

GUILDFORD
Surrey

Cathedral View Self-Catering Flat ★★★
Contact: Mrs Caroline Salmon, Cathedral View Self-Catering Flat, 7 Harvey Road, Guildford GU1 3SG
T: (01483) 504915
E: cathedralview@supanet.com

4 Grove End ★★★
Contact: Mr Colin Stoneley, 12 Pit Farm Road, Guildford, Guildford GU1 2JH
T: (01483) 560831
E: wtieurope@btclick.com

Lavender ★★★
Contact: Mr & Mrs E Liew, Mandarin, Pewley Point, Pewley Hill, Guildford GU1 4LF
T: (01483) 506819
F: (01483) 506819
E: shirleyliew9@hotmail.com

University of Surrey ★★
Contact: University of Surrey, Guildford GU2 7XH
T: (01483) 689157
F: (01483) 579266
E: k.stacey@surrey.ac.uk
I: www.surrey.ac.uk/conferences

GURNARD
Isle of Wight

3 & 160 Gurnard Pines ★★
Contact: Mrs Vanetta Westell, 69 Scarf Road, Canford Heath, Poole BH17 8QJ
T: (01202) 679777

136 Gurnard Pines ★★★
Contact: Mr Nigel Haward, 23 Highfield Road, East Cowes PO31 7UF
T: (01983) 297294

166 Gurnard Pines Holiday Village ★★
Contact: Mrs Maureen Orchard, 35 Cross Street, Cowes PO31 7TD
T: (01983) 200872
F: (01983) 292666

The Stable ★★★★
Contact: Mrs J Clark, 27 Worsley Road, Gurnard, Cowes PO31 8JW
T: (01983) 294900

GUSTON
Kent

Owl Cottage ★★★★
Contact: Mr & Mrs Michael & Gloria Morgan, 10 Cranleigh Drive, Whitfield, Dover CT16 3NL
T: (01304) 825732
F: (01304) 825732
E: owlcottage@lineone.net

HAILSHAM
East Sussex

Little Marshfoot Farmhouse
★★★★
Contact: Ms Kathryn Webster, Little Marshfoot Farmhouse, Mill Road, Hailsham BN27 2SJ
T: (01323) 844690
E: kew@waitrose.com

The Old Orchard Bungalow
★★★
Contact: Mr Brian Bennett, The Old Orchard House, The Platt, Bottom of Caburn Way, Hailsham BN27 3LX
T: (01323) 440977
F: (01323) 440977
E: bbrian985@AOL.com

HALLAND
East Sussex

Little Tamberry ★★★★
Contact: Mrs Brenda Beck, Freedom Holiday Homes, 15 High Street, Cranbrook TN17 3EB
T: (01580) 720770
F: (01580) 720771
E: mail@freedomholidayhomes.co.uk
I: www.freedomholidayhomes.co.uk

HARTGROVE
Dorset

Hartgrove Farm
★★★-★★★★
Contact: Mrs Susan Smart, Hartgrove Farm, Hartgrove, Shaftesbury SP7 0JY
T: (01747) 811830
F: (01747) 811066
E: cottages@hartgrovefarm.co.uk
I: www.hartgrovefarm.co.uk

HARTLEY MAUDITT
Hampshire

The Dairy Cottages ★★★★
Contact: Mr & Mrs Peter & Nicola Minns, Wick Hill Farm, Hartley Mauditt, Alton GU34 3BP
T: (01420) 511021
F: (01420) 511368
E: nicolashearer@aol.com

HARTLEY WINTNEY
Hampshire

Wintney Stable ★★★
Contact: Mr & Mrs Bernard Kilroy, 10 Hunts Common, Hartley Wintney, Hook RG27 8NT
T: (01252) 843133
F: (01252) 843133
E: bernardkilroy@uk2.net

HASLEMERE
Surrey

The Creamery ★★★★
Contact: Mr Nick Pash, Hideaways, Luke Street, Berwick St John, Shaftesbury SP7 0HQ
T: (01747) 828170
F: (01747) 829090
E: enq@hideaways.co.uk

Guard Hill ★★
Contact: Mr M J Wimbush, Guard Hill, 13 Hill Road, Haslemere GU27 2JP
T: (01428) 642166

HASTINGLEIGH
Kent

Staple Farm ★★★★
Contact: Mr & Mrs C H Martindale, Staple Farm, Hastingleigh, Ashford TN25 5HF
T: (01233) 750248
F: (01233) 750249

HASTINGS
East Sussex

Brooklands Coach House
★★★
Contact: Mrs Caroline McNally, Brooklands Coach House, 61 Old London Road, Hastings TN35 5NB
T: (01424) 421957
F: (01424) 437003
E: brooklandscoachhouse@btinternet.com

Bryn-Y-Mor ★★★-★★★★
Contact: Mrs Doreen Karen-Alun, Bryn-Y-Mor, 12 Godwin Road, Hastings TN35 5JR
T: (01424) 722744
F: (01424) 445933
E: karen-alun@brynymor.ndirect.co.uk

The Chestnuts ★★★
Contact: Country Holidays Ref: 8021, Country Holidays, Spring Mill, Earby, Barnoldswick BB94 0AA
T: 08700 723723
F: (01282) 844288
E: sales@holidaycottagesgroup.com
I: www.country-holidays.co.uk

12 The Coastguards ★★★
Contact: Mrs Janine Vallor-Doyle, Merton House, 11 Barrack Street, Bridport DT6 3LX
T: (01308) 423180

10A Courthouse Street ★★★
Contact: Mr Billson, 14 All Saints Street, Hastings TN34 3BJ
T: (01424) 425734

Lionsdown House ★★★★
Contact: Mrs Sharon Bigg, 116 High Street, Old Town, Hastings TN34 3ET
T: (01424) 420802
F: (01424) 420802
E: info@lionsdownhouse.co.uk
I: www.lionsdowhouse.co.uk

Number Six ★
Contact: Mr & Mrs Chris & Pat Hart, Number Six, 6 Stanley Road, Hastings TN34 1UE
T: (01424) 431984
F: (01424) 432690
E: famhart@supanet.com

14 Old Humphrey Avenue
★★★
Contact: Mrs Chris Nixey, 4 Southfield Cottages, Chalkshire Road, Princes Risborough, Aylesbury HP17 0TS
T: (01296) 625780
F: (01296) 625780

Rocklands Holiday Park ★★★
Contact: Mr & Mrs Joan & Len Guilliard, Rocklands Holiday Park, Rocklands Lane, East Hill, Hastings TN35 5DY
T: (01424) 423097
E: rocklandspark@aol.com

Rose House ★★★
Contact: Mrs Susan Hill, 1 Beauport Gardens, St Leonards-on-Sea, St Leonards, Hastings TN37 7PQ
T: (01424) 754812
F: (01424) 754812
E: hillbusybee@aol.com

St Marys Holiday Flats ★-★★
Contact: Mrs Edwards, 6 Highcroft Villas, Brighton BN1 5PS
T: (01273) 556227

Tillys Cottage ★★★
Contact: Mrs Celia Conway, Solent Breezes, Hook Lane, Warsash, Stevenage SO31 9HG
T: (01438) 565493
I: www.hastings-holidays.com

Wellington Holiday Apartments ★★-★★★
Contact: Mrs Joan Stevens, Ashen Grove Road, East Hill, Knatts Valley, Sevenoaks TN15 6YE
T: (01959) 524260

Westcliff Lodge ★★★
Contact: Mrs Celia Conway, The Captain's Cabin, Solent Breezes Hook Lane, Warsash, Southampton SO31 9HG
T: (01438) 216787
I: www.hastings-holidays.com

HAWKHURST Kent

Kent Bridge Croft ★★★
Contact: Mrs Brenda Beck, Freedom Holiday Homes, 15 High Street, Cranbrook TN17 3EB
T: (01580) 720770
F: (01580) 720771
E: mail@freedomholidayhomes.co.uk
I: www.freedomholidayhomes.co.uk

The Stables ★★★★
Contact: Mr Stuart Winter, Garden of England Cottages Ltd, The Mews Office, 189a High Street, Tonbridge TN9 1BX
T: (01732) 369168
F: (01732) 358817
E: holidays@gardenofenglandcottages.co.uk
I: www.gardenofenglandcottages.co.uk

HAWKINGE Kent

1 North Downs Cottage ★★★★
Contact: Mrs Brenda Beck, Freedom Holiday Homes, 15 High Street, Cranbrook TN17 3EB
T: (01580) 720770
F: (01580) 720771
E: mail@freedomholidayhomes.co.uk
I: www.freedomholidayhomes.co.uk

HAYLING ISLAND Hampshire

15 Anchor Court ★★★
Contact: Mr Roy Pine, 19 Mengham Road, Hayling Island PO11 9BG
T: (023) 9246 5951
F: (023) 9246 1321
E: millers@haylingproperty.co.uk
I: www.haylingproperty.co.uk

Bay Cottage ★★★★
Contact: Miss Kate Cross, Cockle Warren Hotel, 36 Sea Front, Hayling Island PO11 9HL
T: (023) 9246 4961
F: (023) 9246 4838

8 Chandlers Close ★★★
Contact: Mr Roy Pine, Millers, 19 Mengham Road, Hayling Island PO11 9BG
T: (023) 9246 5951
F: (023) 9246 1321
E: millers@haylingproperty.co.uk
I: www.haylingproperty.co.uk

69 Creek Road ★★★
Contact: Mr Roy Pine, Millers, 19 Mengham Road, Hayling Island PO11 9BG
T: (023) 9246 5951
F: (023) 9246 1321
E: millers@haylingproperty.co.uk
I: www.haylingproperty.co.uk

15 Fairlight Chalets ★
Contact: Mr Roy Pine, 19 Mengham Road, Hayling Island PO11 9BG
T: (023) 9246 5951
F: (023) 9246 1321
E: millers@haylingproperty.co.uk
I: www.haylingproperty.co.uk

30 Fairlight Chalets ★
Contact: Mr Roy Pine, 19 Mengham Road, Hayling Island PO11 9BG
T: (023) 9246 5951
F: (023) 9246 1321
E: millers@haylingproperty.co.uk

63 North Shore Road ★★★★
Contact: Mr Roy Pine, 19 Mengham Road, Hayling Island PO11 9BG
T: (023) 9246 5951
F: (023) 9246 1321
E: millers@haylingproperty.co.uk

1 Ramsey Road ★★
Contact: Mr Roy Pine, 19 Mengham Road, Hayling Island PO11 9BG
T: (023) 9246 5951
F: (023) 9246 1321
E: millers@haylingproperty.co.uk
I: www.haylingproperty.co.uk

7 Sandybeach Estate ★★
Contact: Mr Roy Pine, Millers, 19 Mengham Road, Hayling Island PO11 9BG
T: (023) 9246 5951
F: (023) 9246 1321
E: millers@haylingproperty.co.uk
I: www.haylingproperty.co.uk

78 Sandypoint Road ★★
Contact: Mr Roy Pine, 19 Mengham Road, Hayling Island PO11 9BG
T: (023) 9246 5951
F: (023) 9246 1321
E: millers@haylingproperty.co.uk
I: www.haylingproperty.co.uk

88 Southwood Road ★★
Contact: Mr Roy Pine, 19 Mengham Road, Hayling Island PO11 9BG
T: (023) 9246 5951
F: (023) 9246 1321
E: millers@haylingproperty.co.uk
I: www.haylingproperty.co.uk

88c Southwood Road ★★
Contact: Mr Roy Pine, 19 Mengham Road, Hayling Island PO11 9BG
T: (023) 9246 5951
F: (023) 9246 1321

5 Webb Close ★★★
Contact: Mr Roy Pine, 19 Mengham Road, Hayling Island PO11 9BG
T: (023) 9246 5951
F: (023) 9246 1321
E: millers@haylingproperty.co.uk
I: www.haylingproperty.co.uk

26 Wittering Road ★★★★
Contact: Mr Roy Pine, 19 Mengham Road, Hayling Island PO11 9BG
T: (023) 9246 5951
F: (023) 9246 1321
E: millers@haylingproperty.co.uk
I: www.haylingproperty.co.uk

HAYWARDS HEATH West Sussex

Stevens Barn ★★★
Contact: Mr Richard Harris, Best of Brighton & Sussex Cottages Ltd, Windmill Lodge, Vicarage Lane, Rottingdean, Brighton BN2 7HD
T: (01273) 308779
F: (01273) 300266
E: brightoncottages@pavilion.co.uk
I: www.bestofbrighton.co.uk

HEADINGTON Oxfordshire

Mulberry Self-Catering ★★★
Contact: Mr & Mrs Gojko & Nada Miljkovic, 265 London Road, Headington, Oxford OX3 9EH
T: (01865) 767114
F: (01865) 767114
E: mulberryguesthouse@hotmail.com
I: www.oxfordcity.co.uk/accom/mulberrysc

HEATHFIELD East Sussex

Boring House Farm The Cottage ★★★
Contact: Mrs Anne Reed, Boring House Farm The Cottage, Nettlesworth Lane, Vines Cross, Heathfield TN21 9AS
T: (01435) 812285
E: info@boringhousefarm.co.uk
I: www.boringhousefarm.co.uk

HEDGE END Hampshire

Twin Oaks ★★★★
Contact: Mrs Yvonne Main, Twin Oaks, 43 Upper Northam Road, Hedge End, Southampton SO30 4EA
T: (01489) 690054

HENFIELD West Sussex

New Hall Cottage & New Hall Holiday Flat★★★
Contact: Mrs M W Carreck, New Hall, Small Dole, Henfield BN5 9YJ
T: (01273) 492546

HENLEY-ON-THAMES Oxfordshire

2 Badgemore Lane ★★★
Contact: Ms Annabelle Arber, 6 Clarence Road, Henley-on-Thames RG9 2DP
T: (01491) 577550

The Clock Tower & Beechwood Cottage ★★★★
Contact: Mrs Liz Martin, The Clock Tower & Beechwood Cottage, Lovegroves Barn, Gallowstree Common, Wyfold, Reading RG4 9HS
T: (0118) 972 2365

141 Greys Road ★★★★
Contact: Mrs King, Jersey Farmhouse, Greys Road, Henley-on-Thames RG9 1TE
T: (01491) 628486
F: (01491) 628015
E: mjking@btinternet.com
I: www.holiday.btinternet.co.uk

Jersey Farmhouse ★★★
Contact: Mrs King, Jersey Farmhouse, Colmore Lane, Kingwood, Rotherfield Peppard, Henley-on-Thames RG9 5LX
T: (01491) 628486
F: (01491) 628015
E: mjking@btinternet.com
I: www.holiday.btinternet.co.uk

Rotherleigh House Annexe ★★★
Contact: Mrs Jane Butler, Rotherleigh House, Harpsden Way, Henley-on-Thames RG9 1NS
T: (01491) 572776
E: jvbutler57@hotmail.com

HERNE BAY Kent

Arlington Lodge ★★★★
Contact: Mr Adrian Webb, 45A Warren Road, Reigate RH2 0BN
T: (01737) 244385

Golf Lodge Cottage ★★★
Contact: Mrs Mariam Smallridge, 166 Mickleburgh Hill, Herne Bay CT6 6JZ
T: (01635) 200316

Iluka ★★★
Contact: Ms Maggie Hyde, Yamba, Spa Esplanade, Herne Bay CT6 8EP
T: (01227) 372282
E: maggie@coa.org.uk

Umballa ★★★
Contact: Ms Maggie Hyde, Yamba, Spa Esplanade, Herne Bay CT6 8EP
T: (01227) 372282
E: maggie@coa.org.uk

Westcliff ★★★
Contact: Ms Maggie Hyde, Yamba, Spa Esplanade, Herne Bay CT6 8EP
T: (01227) 372282
E: maggie@coa.org.uk
I: iluka@coa.org.uk

HERONS GHYLL
East Sussex

The Stables ★★★★
Contact: Mrs Brenda Beck, Freedom Holiday Homes, 15 High Street, Cranbrook TN17 3EB
T: (01580) 720770
F: (01580) 720771
E: mail@freedomholidayhomes.co.uk
I: www.freedomholidayhomes.co.uk

HIGH HALDEN
Kent

The Annexe ★★★
Contact: Mrs Brenda Beck, Freedom Holiday Homes, 15 High Street, Cranbrook TN17 3EB
T: (01580) 720770
F: (01580) 720771
E: mail@freedomholidayhomes.co.uk
I: www.freedomholidayhomes.co.uk

Crampton Lodge ★★★★
Contact: Mrs Brenda Beck, Freedom Holiday Homes, 15 High Street, Cranbrook TN17 3EB
T: (01580) 720770
F: (01580) 720771
E: mail@freedomholidayhomes.co.uk
I: www.freedomholidayhomes.co.uk

The Granary & The Stables ★★★★
Contact: Mrs Brenda Beck, Freedom Holiday Homes, 15 High Street, Cranbrook TN17 3EB
T: (01580) 720770
F: (01580) 720771
E: mail@freedomholidayhomes.co.uk
I: www.freedomholidayhomes.co.uk

Heron Cottage ★★★
Contact: Mr Stuart Winter, Garden of England Cottages Ltd, The Mews Office, 189a High Street, Tonbridge TN9 1BX
T: (01732) 369168
F: (01732) 358817
E: holidays@gardenofenglandcottages.co.uk
I: www.gardenofenglandcottages.co.uk

Mallard Cottage ★★★
Contact: Mr Stuart Winter, Garden of England Cottages Ltd, The Mews Office, 189a High Street, Tonbridge TN9 1BX
T: (01732) 369168
F: (01732) 358817
E: holidays@gardenofenglandcottages.co.uk
I: www.gardenofenglandcottages.co.uk

HIGHCLERE
Hampshire

Glencross Annexe ★★★
Contact: Mr Martyn Alexander, Glencross, Mount Road, Highclere, Newbury RG20 9QZ
T: (01635) 253244
F: (01635) 253244
E: martyn@owenalex.freeserve.co.uk

HIGHCLIFFE
Dorset

Cumberland Lodge ★★-★★★
Contact: Mr Paul Williamson, Flat 1, Cumberland Lodge, 424 Lymington Road, Highcliffe BH23 5HF
T: (01425) 280275
E: enquiries@cumberland-lodge.co.uk
I: www.cumberland-lodge.co.uk/info

The Flat Briarwood ★★★
Contact: Mrs Stella Ward, Briarwood, 1 Dunbar Crescent, Walkford, Christchurch BH23 5RY
T: (01425) 275523

Pedralves ★★★
Contact: Mrs Kenney, Pedralves, 48 Nea Road, Highcliffe BH23 4NB
T: (01425) 273858

Saffron ★★★
Contact: Mrs Rosemary Broadey, 14 Mallow Close, Christchurch BH23 4UL
T: (01425) 277507
E: rosemary@broadey.net

Wingfield Holiday Bungalow ★★★
Contact: Mrs Josephine Stevens, 15 Wingfield Avenue, Christchurch BH23 4NR
T: (01425) 278583
E: josephinemstevens@hotmail.com
I: www.wingfieldholidays.co.uk

HIGHMOOR
Oxfordshire

Bay Tree Cottage ★★★★
Contact: Ms Carolyn Wyndham, Witheridge Hill Farm, Witheridge Hill, Highmoor, Henley-on-Thames RG9 5PE
T: (01491) 641229
F: (01491) 642260
E: baytree@hotmail.com

HILDENBOROUGH
Kent

The Cottage ★★★
Contact: Mr Dudley Hurrell, Court Lodge, Coldharbour Lane, Hildenborough, Tonbridge TN11 9LE
T: (01732) 832081
F: (01732) 832081

HILTON
Dorset

Crown Farm ★★
Contact: Mrs Pamela Crocker, Crown Farm, Duck Street, Hilton, Blandford Forum DT11 0DQ
T: (01258) 880259

HOLBURY
Hampshire

Tree Tops ★★★
Contact: Mrs P I Ardern Smith, Tree Tops, 78 Rollestone Road, Holbury, Southampton SO45 2GZ
T: (023) 8089 3109

HOO
Kent

Whitehall Farmhouse ★★★★
Contact: Mr Dennis Reavell, Fairhaven Holiday Rentals, Whitehall Farm, Stoke Road, Hoo, Rochester ME3 9NP
T: (01634) 250251
F: (01634) 251112
E: reavell@waystarltd.freeserve.co.uk
I: www.selfkater.com

HORSHAM
West Sussex

Walnut Barn & Walnut Cottage ★★★★-★★★★★
Contact: Mrs Sally Cole, Hard's Farm Cottage, Kerves Lane, Horsham RH13 6RJ
T: (01403) 249159
E: jpcole@lineone.net
I: www.sussexholidaycottages.com

HORSMONDEN
Kent

Field Cottage ★★★
Contact: Mrs Brenda Beck, Freedom Holiday Homes, 15 High Street, Cranbrook TN17 3EB
T: (01580) 720770
F: (01580) 720771
E: mail@freedomholidayhomes.co.uk
I: www.freedomholidayhomes.co.uk

HUNSTON
West Sussex

Well Cottage ★★★★
Contact: Mrs Paula Fountain, Church Farm House, Church Lane, Hunston, Chichester PO20 1AJ
T: (01243) 530889
F: (01243) 537689
E: tomandpaula@lineone.net

HUNTON
Kent

Woolhouse Barn ★★★★
Contact: Mr Stuart Winter, Garden of England Cottages Ltd, The Mews Office, 189a High Street, Tonbridge TN9 1BX
T: (01732) 369168
F: (01732) 358817
E: holidays@gardenofenglandcottages.co.uk
I: www.gardenofenglandcottages.co.uk

HURN
Dorset

The Old Farmhouse ★★★
Contact: Mrs Jennifer Burford, The Old Farmhouse, Pitt House Farm, Hurn, Christchurch BH23 6AU
T: (01202) 479483

HYDE
Dorset

Forest Lodge
Rating Applied For
Contact: Mr Stuart-Brown, Dream Cottages, 41 Maiden Street, Weymouth DT4 8AZ
T: (01305) 761347

Holly Lea ★★★
Contact: Mr & Mrs Havelock, Fordingbridge SP6
T: (01425) 652456
F: (01425) 652456

HYTHE
Kent

Hydene Cottage ★★★★
Contact: Mrs Brenda Beck, Freedom Holiday Homes, 15 High Street, Cranbrook TN17 3EB
T: (01580) 720770
F: (01580) 720771
E: mail@freedomholidayhomes.co.uk
I: www.freedomholidayhomes.co.uk

Hythe Period Cottage ★★★
Contact: Mrs Clarissa Moncrieff, 70 Victoria Way, Stafford ST17 0NY
T: (01785) 662042
E: ctf.moncrieff@supanet.com

Keepers Cottage ★★★
Contact: Mrs Brenda Beck, Freedom Holiday Homes, 15 High Street, Cranbrook TN17 3EB
T: (01580) 720770
F: (01580) 720771
E: mail@freedomholidayhomes.co.uk
I: www.freedomholidayhomes.co.uk

Uppermill ★★★
Contact: Mrs Nicola Hooshangpour, 1 Stephendale Road, London SW6 2LU
T: (020) 7736 7133
F: (020) 7731 8412
E: ellie@marstonproperties.co.uk
I: www.marstonproperties.co.uk

Waterfront House ★★★★★
Contact: Mr & Mrs Cunningham, Shalimar, Lime Walk, Hythe, Southampton SO45 5RA
T: (023) 8084 2460
E: alexcunningham@waitrose.com
I: www.cunningham100.fsnet.co.uk

IBBERTON
Dorset

May Cottage ★★★
Contact: Mr Stuart-Brown, Dream Cottages, 41 Maiden Street, Weymouth DT4 8AZ
T: (01305) 761347

IBSLEY
Hampshire

Chocolate Box Cottage ★★★★
Contact: Mrs Frances Higham, 39 Helena Road, Rayleigh SS6 8LN
T: (01268) 741036
F: (01268) 741990
E: enquiries@chocolateboxcottage.co.uk
I: www.chocolateboxcottage.co.uk

Crofton ★★★★★
Contact: Mrs Julie Hordle, Air View, Mockbeggar Lane, Ibsley, Ringwood BH24 3PR
T: (01425) 471829
F: (01425) 461350
E: airview@tiscali.co.uk

ICKLESHAM
East Sussex

Broadstreet House ★★★
Contact: Mr Stuart Winter, Garden of England Cottages Ltd, The Mews Office, 189a High Street, Tonbridge TN9 1BX
T: (01732) 369168
F: (01732) 358817
E: holiday@gardenofenglandcottages.co.uk
I: www.gardenofenglandcottages.co.uk

Garden Cottage ★★★
Contact: Mr Stuart Winter, Garden of England Cottages Ltd, The Mews Office, 189a High Street, Tonbridge TN9 1BX
T: (01732) 369168
F: (01732) 358817
E: holidays@gardenofenglandcottages.co.uk
I: www.gardenofenglandcottages.co.uk

The Oast Cottage ★★★★
Contact: Mrs Brenda Beck, Freedom Holiday Homes, 15 High Street, Cranbrook TN17 3EB
T: (01580) 720770
F: (01580) 720771
E: mail@freedomholidayhomes.co.uk
I: www.freedomholidayhomes.co.uk

The Stable ★★★
Contact: Mr Stuart Winter, Garden of England Cottages, The Mews Office, 189a High Street, Tonbridge TN9 1BX
T: (01732) 369168
F: (01732) 358817
E: holidays@gardenofenglandcottages.co.uk
I: www.gardenofenglandcottages.co.uk

IFFLEY
Oxfordshire

13B Abberbury Road ★★★★
Contact: Mr Christopher Griffiths, 13B Abberbury Road, Iffley, Oxford OX4 4ET
T: (01865) 776904

IPING
West Sussex

River Meadow Flat ★★★
Contact: Mr & Mrs Tim & Rowena Hill, River Meadow Flat, Iping, Midhurst GU29 0PE
T: (01730) 814713

The Studio ★★★
Contact: Claudia Callingham, Kinrose House, Titty Hill, Iping, Midhurst GU29 0PL
T: (01428) 741561
F: (01428) 741561

IPSDEN
Oxfordshire

The Old Stables at Wellplace Barns ★★★★
Contact: Mr & Mrs Robert & Jenny Booth, Wellplace Barns, Wellplace, Ipsden, Wallingford OX10 6QY
T: (01491) 681158
F: (01491) 681158
E: wellplacebarns@aol.com

IVINGHOE
Buckinghamshire

Town Farm Holiday Cottages ★★★
Contact: Mrs A Leach, Town Farm Holiday Cottages, Town Farm, Ivinghoe, Leighton Buzzard LU7 9EL
T: (01296) 660279
F: (01296) 668455
E: angie@unlimitedlets.com
I: www.unlimitedlets.com

KEMSING
Kent

6 Dippers Close ★★
Contact: Mr & Mrs Ronald Rose, 6 Dippers Close, Kemsing, Sevenoaks TN15 6QD
T: (01732) 761937

KIDLINGTON
Oxfordshire

Ambassador's Oxford ★★★★★
Contact: Mr Karim Easterbrook, 2 Broad Field Road, Kidlington OX5 1UL
T: (01865) 849530
F: (01865) 849533
E: info@ambassadorsoxford.co.uk
I: www.ambassadorsoxford.co.uk

KILMESTON
Hampshire

College Down Farm Self Catering Holidays★★★★
Contact: Mr Eric Ruff, College Down Farm Self Catering Holidays, College Down Farm, Kilmeston, Alresford SO24 0NS
T: (01962) 771345

KING'S SOMBORNE
Hampshire

By the Way Annexe ★★★
Contact: Dr Penny Morgan, Romsey Road, Kings Somborne, King's Somborne, Stockbridge SO20 6PR
T: (01794) 388469
E: penny@bytheway4.freeserve.co.uk

KINGSDOWN
Kent

Chalet 115 Kingsdown Holiday Park ★★★
Contact: Mr Martin Jones, 40 Springfield Gardens, Bromley BR1 2LZ
T: (020) 8402 8614
F: (020) 8402 8614
E: martin.icon@ntlworld.com

Chalet 80, Kingsdown Park Holiday Village★★★
Contact: Mrs Trena Stokes, Dernford, Downs Road, East Studdal, Dover CT15 5DB
T: (01304) 365880

KINGSTON
East Sussex

Nightingales ★★★★
Contact: Mrs Jean Hudson, Nightingales, The Avenue, Kingston, Lewes BN7 3LL
T: (01273) 475673
F: (01273) 475673
E: Nightingales@totalise.co.uk
I: www.user.totalise.co.uk/nightingales/

Roman Way ★★★★
Contact: Mrs Pippa Campbell, Roman Way, Kingston Ridge, Kingston, Lewes BN7 3JX
T: (01273) 476583
F: (01273) 476583
E: camp1942@aol.com

KINTBURY
Berkshire

Limetree House ★★★
Contact: Mr & Mrs Felix Chapman, Limetree House, Inglewood, Kintbury, Hungerford RG17 9SL
T: (01488) 683297
E: fjc@supanet.com

LAKE
Isle of Wight

The Dolphins ★★★
Contact: Ms Lisa Baskill, Home from Home Holidays, 31 Pier Street, Ventnor PO38 1SX
T: (01983) 854340
F: (01983) 855524

LAMBERHURST
Kent

Goldings Barn ★★★
Contact: Mrs Brenda Beck, Freedom Holiday Homes, 15 High Street, Cranbrook TN17 3EB
T: (01580) 720770
F: (01580) 720771
E: mail@freedomholidayhomes.co.uk
I: www.freedomholidayhomes.co.uk

The Hideaway ★★★
Contact: Mrs Brenda Beck, Freedom Holiday Homes, 15 High Street, Cranbrook TN17 3EB
T: (01580) 720770
F: (01580) 720771
E: mail@freedomholidayhomes.co.uk
I: www.freedomholidayhomes.co.uk

Oast Cottage, Orchard Cottage & The Oast House - Barnfield Oast Self★★★-★★★★
Contact: Mrs Brenda Beck, Freedom Holiday Homes, 15 High Street, Cranbrook TN17 3EB
T: (01580) 720770
F: (01580) 720771
E: mail@freedomholidayhomes.co.uk
I: www.freedomholidayhomes.co.uk

Owls Castle Oast ★★★★
Contact: Mrs Sally Bingham, Owls Castle Oast, Hoghole Lane, Lamberhurst, Royal Tunbridge Wells TN3 8BN
T: (01892) 890758
F: (01892) 890215
E: sally.bingham1@btopenworld.com

LANGTON MATRAVERS
Dorset

Flat 5 Garfield House ★★★
Contact: Miss Susan Inge, Flat A, 147 Holland Road, London W14 8AS
T: (020) 7602 4945
E: sueinge@hotmail.com
I: www.langton-matravers.co.uk

Hyde View Cottage ★★★
Contact: Ms Leanne Hemingway, 11 Tyneham Close, Sandford, Wareham BH20 7BE
T: (01929) 553443
F: (01929) 552714
E: enquiries@dhcottages.co.uk
I: www.dhcottages.co.uk/hyde%20view%20cottage.htm

Island View ★★★
Contact: Mr Z Stuart-Brown, Dream Cottages, 41 Maiden Street, Weymouth DT4 8AZ
T: (01305) 761347
F: (01305) 789000
E: admin@dream-cottages.co.uk
I: www.dream-cottages.co.uk

5 North Street Rating Applied For
Contact: Mrs Ann Garratt, 5 Brasted Place, High Street, Brasted, Westerham TN16 1JE
T: (01959) 565145

Roxeth Cottage ★★★
Contact: Ms Leanne Hemingway, 11 Tyneham Close, Sandford, Wareham BH20 7BE
T: (01929) 553443
F: (01929) 552714
E: enquiries@dhcottages.co.uk

LAUGHTON
East Sussex

Holly Cottage ★★★
Contact: Mr & Mrs David & Pat Fuller, Holly Cottage, Lewes Road, Laughton, Lewes BN8 6BL
T: (01323) 811309
F: (01323) 811106
E: hollycottage@tinyworld.co.uk

LAVANT
West Sussex

South Cottage ★★★★
Contact: Mr Graham Davies, Raughmere Drive, Lavant, Chichester PO18 0AB
T: (01243) 527120
E: gmd@cix.co.uk

LAVENDON
Buckinghamshire

The Annexe ★★★★
Contact: Mrs Marion Rutherford, 37 Northampton Road, Lavendon, Olney MK46 4EY
T: (01234) 712755
E: mruther21@aol.com

Bell Cottage ★★★
Contact: Mrs Sally Wetherall, Bell House, 35 High Street, Lavendon, Olney MK46 4HA
T: (01234) 712614
F: (01234) 712614

Cobblers Barn ★★★★
Contact: Mr & Mrs A Ledson, 33 Northampton Road, Lavendon, Olney MK46 4EY
T: (01234) 713337
F: (01234) 246150

LEAFIELD
Oxfordshire

King John's Barn ★★★★
Contact: Mrs Vicky Greves, Langley Lodge, Leafield, Langley, Oxford OX29 9QD
T: (01993) 878075

LEATHERHEAD
Surrey

6 Lavender Court ★★★★
Contact: Mrs Liz Willis, 1 Old Dene Cottages, Ranmore Common Road, Westhumble, Dorking RH5 6AZ
T: (01306) 884408
F: (01306) 884404
E: liz.willis@btinternet.com

LEDWELL
Oxfordshire

Chapel Cottage ★★★
Contact: Country Holidays Ref: 12510, Country Holidays, Spring Mill, Earby, Barnoldswick BB94 0AA
T: 0870 4 446603
F: (01282) 844288
E: ownerservices@holidaycottagesgroup.com
I: www.country-holidays.co.uk

LEE COMMON
Buckinghamshire

The Cottage ★★★
Contact: Mrs Bette Brumpton, High Beeches, Ballinger Road, Lee Common, Great Missenden HP16 9NE
T: (01494) 837246

LEE ON THE SOLENT
Hampshire

Bay Tree Lodge ★★★
Contact: Mr Dave Danns, 197 Portsmouth Road, Lee on the Solent, Gosport PO13 9AA
T: (023) 9255 2550
F: (023) 9255 4657
E: dave@baytreelodge.co.uk
I: www.baytreelodge.co.uk

The Chart House ★★★
Contact: Ms Marion Kinnear-White, 6 Cambridge Road, Lee on the Solent PO13 9DH
T: (023) 9255 4145
E: marion_kinnear-white@talk21.com
I: www.brook.white1.btinternet.co.uk

Kinderton House ★★★
Contact: Mrs Jean Miller, Kinderton House, 31 Marine Parade West, Lee on the Solent PO13 9LW
T: (023) 9255 2056

One West Lodge ★★★★
Contact: Mrs Carole Rudin, 1 Madden Close, Gosport PO12 2PT
T: (023) 9258 3637
E: enquiries@onewestlodge.co.uk
I: www.onewestlodge.co.uk

LEEDS
Kent

1 & 2 Orchard View ★★★
Contact: Mr Stuart Winter, Garden of England Cottages Ltd, The Mews Office, 189a High Street, Tonbridge TN9 1BX
T: (01732) 369168
F: (01732) 358817
E: holidays@gardenofenglandcottages.co.uk
I: www.gardenofenglandcottages.co.uk

LENHAM
Kent

Apple Pye Cottage ★★★★
Contact: Mrs Patricia Diane Leat, Apple Pye Cottage, Bramley Knowle Farm, Eastwood Road, Ulcombe, Maidstone ME17 1ET
T: (01622) 858878
F: (01622) 851121
E: diane@bramleyknowlefarm.co.uk
I: www.bramleyknowlefarm.co.uk

7 Church Square ★★
Contact: Mrs Brenda Beck, Freedom Holiday Homes, 15 High Street, Cranbrook TN17 3EB
T: (01580) 720770
F: (01580) 720771
E: mail@freedomholidayhomes.co.uk
I: www.freedomholidayhomes.co.uk

Holiday Cottage Rating Applied For
Contact: Mrs Brenda Beck, Freedom Holiday Homes, 15 High Street, Cranbrook TN17 3EB
T: (01580) 720770
F: (01580) 720771
E: mail@freedomholidayhomes.co.uk
I: www.freedomholidayhomes.co.uk

5 Lime Tree Cottages ★★★
Contact: Mr Peter Hasler, 4 Lime Tree Cottages, Pilgrims Way, Lenham, Maidstone ME17 2EY
T: (01622) 851310
F: (01622) 853586
E: pvhasler@hotmail.com

The Olde Shoppe ★★★
Contact: Mrs Brenda Beck, Freedom Holiday Homes, 15 High Street, Cranbrook TN17 3EB
T: (01580) 720770
F: (01580) 720771
E: mail@freedomholidayhomes.co.uk
I: www.freedomholidayhomes.co.uk

LEWES
East Sussex

5 Buckhurst Close ★★★
Contact: Mrs S Foulds, 66 Houndean Rise, Lewes BN7 1EJ
T: (01273) 474755
F: (01273) 474755

Corset Cottage Rating Applied For
Contact: Mr & Mrs A Tammar, 134 High Street, Lewes BN7 1XS
T: (01273) 475631

24 St Johns Terrace ★★★
Contact: Mr Richard Harris, Best of Brighton & Sussex Cottages Ltd, Windmill Lodge, Vicarage Lane, Rottingdean, Brighton BN2 7HD
T: (01273) 308779
F: (01273) 300266
E: brightoncottages@pavilion.co.uk
I: www.bestofbrighton.co.uk

Sussex Countryside Accommodation ★★★★
Contact: Mrs Hazel Gaydon, Sussex Countryside Accommodation, Crink House, Barcombe Mills, Lewes BN8 5BJ
T: (01273) 400625
F: (01273) 401893
E: crinkhouse@hgaydon.fsnet.co.uk

LILLINGSTONE LOVELL
Buckinghamshire

Little Thatch ★★★★
Contact: Mrs Jane Scott, 9 Brookside, Lillingstone Lovell, Buckingham MK18 5BD
T: (01280) 860014
F: (01280) 860014
E: janegscott@lineone.net

LINTON
Kent

Loddington Oast ★★★★
Contact: Mr & Mrs Richard & Valerie Martin, Loddington Oast, Loddington Lane, Linton, Maidstone ME17 4AG
T: (01622) 747777
F: (01622) 746991
E: rm_trsystems@btinternet.com

LITTLEHAMPTON
West Sussex

Dormer Cottage Rating Applied For
Contact: Mrs S Ogrodnik, Victoria Holidays, 86 South Terrace, Littlehampton BN17 5LJ
T: (01903) 722644

Racing Greens ★★★
Contact: Mrs Eileen Thomas, Racing Greens, 70 South Terrace, Wick, Littlehampton BN17 5LQ
T: (01903) 732972
F: (01903) 732932

Victoria Holidays ★★★
Contact: Mrs Ogrodnik, Victoria Holidays, 86 South Terrace, Wick, Littlehampton BN17 5LJ
T: (01903) 722644

LOCKINGE
Oxfordshire

The Coach House ★★★★
Contact: Mrs Janine Beaumont, The Coach House, Andersey Farm, Grove Park Drive, Lockinge, Wantage OX12 8SG
T: (01235) 771866
F: (01235) 771866

LOCKS HEATH
Hampshire

Stepping Stones ★★★★
Contact: Mrs B A Habens, 126 Locksheath Park Road, Locks Heath, Southampton SO31 6LZ
T: (01489) 572604
E: jimhabens@aol.com
I: http://members.lycos.co.uk/selfcateringannexe/

LOOSE
Kent

Bockingford Steps Barn ★★★
Contact: Mrs Jennifer Buckley, Bockingford Steps, Bockingford Lane, Maidstone ME15 6DP
T: (01622) 756030

LOUDWATER
Buckinghamshire

Daisy's Cottage ★★★
Contact: Mrs Julia Newman, Derehams Farm, Derehams Lane, Loudwater, High Wycombe HP10 9RR
T: (01494) 520964
F: (01494) 520964
E: newmanwill@aol.com

LOWER BEEDING
West Sussex

Black Cottage, The Little Barn & the Old Dairy★★★-★★★★
Contact: Mrs V Storey, Newells Farm, Newells Farmhouse, Newells Lane, Lower Beeding, Horsham RH13 6LN
T: (01403) 891326
F: (01403) 891530
E: vicky.storey@btinternet.com

LYDD
Kent

1 & 2 Riddlers Cottages ★★★
Contact: Mr Glyn Swift, 1 & 2 Riddlers Cottages, Romney Farm, Romney Road, New Romney TN29 9LS
T: (01797) 361499

LYDD ON SEA
Kent

69 Coast Drive ★★★
Contact: Mrs Brenda Beck, Freedom Holiday Homes, 15 High Street, Cranbrook TN17 3EB
T: (01580) 720770
F: (01580) 720771
E: mail@freedomholidayhomes.co.uk
I: www.freedomholidayhomes.co.uk

LYMINGTON
Hampshire

8 Admirals Court ★★★★
Contact: Mrs Mayes, 4 Quay Hill, Lymington SO41 3AR
T: (01590) 679655
F: (01590) 670989
E: holidays@newforestcottages.co.uk
I: www.newforestcottages.co.uk

Badgers Holt ★★★★
Contact: Mrs Mary Brockett, Badgers Holt, Newlands Manor, Everton, Milford-on-Sea, Lymington SO41 0JH
T: (01590) 645941
E: gothic_cottage@hotmail.com

4 Belmore Lane ★★
Contact: Mrs Jacquie Taylor, Three Corners, Centre Lane, Everton, Milford-on-Sea, Lymington SO41 0JP
T: (01590) 645217
E: tommy.tiddles@virgin.net

Bourne House ★★★★
Contact: Mr & Mrs P J Mare, Maybury Wood Cottage, The Ridge, Woking GU22 7EG
T: (01483) 772086
F: (01483) 772086
E: jppmare@aol.com

The Chantry ★★★★
Contact: Country Holidays Ref: 9805, Holiday Cottages Group Owner Services Dept, Spring Mill, Earby, Barnoldswick BB94 0AA
T: 08700 723723
F: (01282) 844288
E: sales@ttholidaycottagesgroup.com
I: www.country-holidays.co.uk

Corner Cottages ★★★★
Contact: Mrs Ginny Neath, Main Road, East Boldre, Brockenhurst SO42 7WD
T: (01590) 612080
F: (01590) 612080
E: rg.neath@virgin.net
I: www.neath.bizland.com

3 Court Close ★★★
Contact: Mr Darren Roberts, Centre Lane, Everton, Milford-on-Sea, Lymington SO41 0JP
T: (01590) 645217
F: (01590) 673633
E: tommy.tiddles@virgin.net

1 Daniell's Close ★★★★
Contact: Ms Taylor, Three Corners Centre Lane, Everton, Milford-on-Sea, Lymington SO41 0JP
T: (01590) 645217
F: (01590) 673633
E: tommy.tiddles@virgin.net

De La Warr House ★★★-★★★★★
Contact: Mrs Joanne Broadway, All Saints Road, Lymington SO41 8FB
T: (01590) 672785
F: (01590) 672785
E: delawarrhouse@aol.com
I: www.delawarrhouse.co.uk

Elmers Court Country Club Rating Applied For
Contact: Jenny Young, Elmers Court Country Club, South Baddesley Road, Lymington SO41
T: (01590) 688548
F: (01590) 679780
I: www.barratt-resorts.com

7a Fairlea Road ★★★
Contact: Mrs Megan Hall, 1 Medley Close, Eaton Bray, Dunstable LU6 2DX
T: (01525) 220652

Fir Tree Cottage ★★★
Contact: Mrs B Saword, 1 Merlewood Court, Lyon Avenue, New Milton BH25 6AP
T: (01425) 617219

94 Queen Katherine Road ★★★
Contact: Mrs Jan Anstey Hayes, 2 Bonham Road, London SW2 5HF
T: (020) 7771 2384
E: j.anstey-hayes@talk21.com

Rainbow Cottage ★★★
Contact: Mr & Mrs Mare, Maybury Wood Cottage, The Ridge, Woking GU22 7EG
T: (01483) 772086
F: (01483) 772086
E: jppmare@aol.com

Saltmarsh ★★★★
Contact: Mr James Cecil-Wright, Garden Cottage, Kitwalls Lane, Milford-on-Sea, Lymington SO41 0RJ
T: (01590) 642965
E: gardctg@aol.com

Silkhouse Rating Applied For
Contact: Mrs Anne Paterson, Silkhouse, 77 Lower Buckland Road, Lymington SO41 9DR
T: (01590) 688797
F: (01590) 688797
E: annevp@ntlworld.com

17 Southampton Road ★★★★
Contact: Julie Stevens & Andrew Baxendine, Elm Cottage, Pilley Bailey, Pilley, Lymington SO41 5QT
T: (01590) 676445
E: juleestevens@aol.com

55 Waterford Lane Rating Applied For
Contact: Ms Sally Sargeaunt, 33 Barton Court Avenue, Barton on Sea, New Milton BH25 7EP
T: (01425) 628970
F: (01425) 620399

LYNDHURST
Hampshire

Acorn Cottage ★★★★
Contact: Mrs April Robinson, Boltons House, Princes Crescent, Lyndhurst SO43 7BS
T: (023) 8028 3000
E: visit@lyndhurstcottages.co.uk
I: www.lyndhurstcottages.co.uk

Alice Cottage, Dormouse Corner, Duchess Place & The Mad Hatter★★★★
Contact: Mr Mike Saqui, The Penny Farthing Hotel, Romsey Road, Lyndhurst SO43 7AA
T: (023) 8028 4422
F: (023) 8028 4488
E: cottages@pennyfarthinghotel.co.uk
I: www.pennyfarthinghotel.co.uk

Clematis Cottage Rating Applied For
Contact: Mr & Mrs David & Madalaine Cintra, Osborne, Pikes Hill, Lyndhurst SO43 7AY
T: (023) 8028 2200
F: (023) 8028 2200

The Cottage ★★★
Contact: Mrs Sheila Robinson, The Cottage, The Old Stables, Pikes Hill, Lyndhurst SO43 7AY
T: (023) 8028 3697

95B High Street ★★★
Contact: Mr & Mrs John Langston, Monkton Cottage, 93 High Street, Lyndhurst SO43 7BH
T: (023) 8028 2206
F: (023) 8028 2206

Holly Cottage ★★★★
Contact: Mr & Mrs F S Turner, Greensward, The Crescent, Woodlands Road, Ashurst, Southampton SO40 7AQ
T: (023) 8029 2374
F: (023) 8029 2374
E: sam@turner402.fsnet.co.uk
I: http://mysite.freeserve.com/hollycottnewforest

Link Place ★★★★
Contact: Mrs April Robinson, Boltons House, Princes Crescent, Lyndhurst SO43 7BS
T: (023) 8028 3000
E: enquiries@lyndhurstcottages.co.uk
I: www.lyndhurstcottages.supanet.com

Stable Cottage ★★
Contact: Mr Stephen Morris, Huntley Farm, Patch Elm Lane, Rangeworthy, Bristol BS37 7LU
T: (01454) 227322
F: (01454) 227323
E: newforest.cottage@btinternet.com
I: www.newforestcottages.net

Yorke Cottage ★★★★
Contact: Mr John Drew, Burwood Lodge, 27 Romsey Road, Lyndhurst SO43 7AA
T: (023) 8028 2445
F: (023) 8028 4104
E: burwood.1@ukonline.co.uk
I: www.burwoodlodge.co.uk

MAIDENHEAD
Berkshire

11 Cadwell Drive ★★★
Contact: Mrs Vivien Williams, 32 York Road, Maidenhead SL6 1SF
T: (01628) 627370
F: (01628) 627370
E: rvwilliams@btopenworld.com

Release Apartments Rating Applied For
Contact: Ms Margaret Appleton, Release Ltd, P O Box 2380, Maidenhead SL6 8WL
T: (01628) 674029
F: (01628) 674029
E: info@release-apartments.co.uk

Sheephouse Manor ★★-★★★
Contact: Mrs Caroline Street, Sheephouse Manor, Sheephouse Road, Maidenhead SL6 8HJ
T: (01628) 776902
F: (01628) 625138
E: info@sheephousemanor.co.uk
I: www.sheephousemanor.co.uk

MAIDSTONE
Kent

Brook House Barn ★★★★★
Contact: Mrs Linda Doust, Brook House, Old Loose Hill, Maidstone ME15 0BL
T: (01622) 743703
F: (01622) 747828

5 Kentish Court ★★★★
Contact: Mr Stuart Winter, Garden of England Cottages Ltd, The Mews Office, 189a High Street, Tonbridge TN9 1BX
T: (01732) 369168
F: (01732) 358817
E: holidays@gardenofenglandcottages.co.uk
I: www.gardenofenglandcottages.co.uk

20 Kings Walk ★★★★
Contact: Mr Stuart Winter, Garden of England Cottages Ltd, The Mews Office, 189a High Street, Tonbridge TN9 1BX
T: (01732) 369168
F: (01732) 358817
E: holidays@gardenofenglandcottages.co.uk
I: www.gardenofenglandcottages.co.uk

Lavender Cottage ★★
Contact: Mr & Mrs L R Hulm, Lavender Cottage, Headcorn Road, Grafty Green, Maidstone ME17 2AN
T: (01622) 850287
F: (01622) 850287
E: lavender@nascr.net
I: www.oas.co.uk/ukcottages/lavender

Orchard Flat ★★
Contact: Mrs Pamela Clark, Orchard Flat, Ferlaga, Vicarage Lane, East Farleigh, Maidstone ME15 0LX
T: (01622) 726919
E: pamclark@ferlaga.freeserve.co.uk

MAPLEDURHAM
Oxfordshire

Mapledurham Holiday Cottages ★★-★★★★
Contact: Mrs Lola Andrews, The Estate Office, Mapledurham House, Mapledurham, Reading RG4 7TR
T: (0118) 972 4292
F: (0118) 972 4016
E: mtrust1997@aol.com
I: www.mapledurham.co.uk

MARDEN
Kent

Redstock ★★★★
Contact: Mr Stuart Winter, Garden of England Cottages Ltd, The Mews Office, 189a High Street, Tonbridge TN9 1BX
T: (01732) 369168
F: (01732) 358817
E: holidays@gardenofenglandcottages.co.uk
I: www.gardenofenglandcottages.co.uk

MARGATE
Kent

House Palm Bay ★★★
Contact: Mrs Bowles, 57 Rectory Lane North, Leybourne, West Malling ME19 5HD
T: (01732) 843396
F: (01732) 843396
E: richardbowles@blueyonder.co.uk

Lombard House ★★★★
Contact: Ms Janet Williams, 71 Sea Road, Westgate on Sea, Margate CT8 8QG
T: 07879 630257

Salmestone Grange ★★★
Contact: Mr William Whelan, Salmestone Grange, Nash Road, Margate CT9 4BX
T: (01843) 231161
F: (01843) 231161
E: salmestonegrange@aol.com
I: www.salmestonegrange.co.uk

MARNHULL
Dorset

Trooper Farm ★★
Contact: Mr Cyril Bastable, Trooper Farm, Love Lane, Marnhull, Sturminster Newton DT10 1PT
T: (01258) 820753

MARSH GREEN
Kent

Littleworth Cottage ★★★★
Contact: Mr Stuart Winter, Garden of England Cottages Ltd, The Mews Office, 189a High Street, Tonbridge TN9 1BX
T: (01732) 369168
F: (01732) 358817
E: holidays@gardenofenglandcottages.co.uk
I: www.gardenofenglandcottages.co.uk

MEREWORTH
Kent

The Dairy ★★★★
Contact: Bl Hols Ref:KC89,90,91, etc, Blakes Holidays in Britain Sales, Stoney Bank Road, Earby, Barnoldswick BB94 0AA
T: 08700 723723
F: (01282) 844288
E: sales@holidaycottagesgroup.com
I: www.country-holidays.co.uk

MERSHAM
Kent

Gill Farm ★★★★
Contact: Mrs Jan Bowman, Gill Farm, Gill Lane, Mersham, Ashford TN25 7HZ
T: (01303) 261247
F: (01233) 721622
E: gillfarm@studio2uk.com
I: www.studio2uk.com/gillfarm

MERSTONE
Isle of Wight

Chapel Cottage ★★★★
Contact: Mrs Honor Vass, Island Cottage Holidays, The Old Vicarage, Kingston, Wareham BH20 5LH
T: (01929) 480080
F: (01929) 481070
E: enq@islandcottagesholidays.com
I: www.cottageholidays.dmon.co.uk.

MICHELDEVER
Hampshire

Hope Cottage ★★★★
Contact: Mrs Elaine Walker, Hope Cottage, Winchester Road, Micheldever, Winchester SO21 3DG
T: (01962) 774221
F: (01962) 774818
E: hopeis@btinternet.com

MIDHURST
West Sussex

Cowdray Park Holiday Cottages ★★★★
Contact: Mrs Sam Collins, Cowdray Park Holiday Cottages, Cowdray Estate Office, Cowdray Park, Midhurst GU29 0AQ
T: (01730) 812423
F: (01730) 815608
E: enquiries@cowdray.co.uk
I: www.cowdray.co.uk

MILBORNE ST ANDREW
Dorset

Garden Cottage ★★★
Contact: Mr John Blackwood, 9 St Michaels Way, Little Heath, Potters Bar EN6 1SN
T: (01707) 643485
F: (01707) 665504
E: blackwoodjohn@hotmail.com

Orchard Cottage ★★★
Contact: Mrs C Martin, 2 Deverel Cottages, Deverel Farm, Milborne St Andrew, Blandford Forum DT11 0HX
T: (01258) 837195
E: deverel@dialstart78.fsnet.co.uk
I: www.oas.co.uk/ukcottages/orchardcottage/

The Retreat ★★★
Contact: Mrs June Jenkins, 27 Fourgates Road, Dorchester DT1 2NL
T: (01305) 269194

MILFORD-ON-SEA
Hampshire

Bethany ★★★★
Contact: Mrs Jacqueline Green, The Vicarage, Station Road, Sway, Lymington SO41 6BA
T: (01590) 683389
F: (01590) 683389
E: jackiegreen@onetel.net.uk
I: www.bethany-milford.com

Curlew Cottage ★★★
Contact: Mrs Sally Edgar, Flexford Rise, Flexford Lane, Sway, Lymington SO41 6DN
T: (01590) 683744

Forest Farm ★★★
Contact: Ms Pippa Jarman, Forest Farm, Barnes Lane, Milford on Sea, Milford-on-Sea, Lymington SO41 0RR
T: (01590) 644365
F: (01590) 644365
E: driving@ffarm.fsnet.co.uk
I: www.forestfarmdriving.com

3 Kingfisher Court Rating Applied For
Contact: Mrs Olga Budden, 111 Milford Road, Lymington SO41 8DN
T: (01590) 671492
F: (01590) 672012
E: budden1@onetel.net.uk

The Old Bakery ★★★
Contact: Mrs A Braithwaite, Bay Tree Cottage, Bashley Common Road, New Milton BH25 5SQ
T: (01425) 620733

Old Walls ★★★
Contact: Mrs Kate Danby, Old Walls, Church Hill, Milford-on-Sea, Lymington SO41 0QJ
T: (01590) 642138
F: (01590) 642138
E: mrskatedanby@aol.com

Penny Pot ★★★★
Contact: Mrs Plummer, Penny Pot, Ha'penny House, 16 Whitby Road, Milford-on-Sea, Lymington SO41 0ND
T: (01590) 641210
E: pennypot@hapennyhouse.co.uk

Pine View Cottage ★★★★
Contact: Mrs Sheri Gadd, Cherry Trees, Lymington Road, Milford-on-Sea, Lymington SO41 0QL
T: (01590) 643746
E: cherrytrees@beeb.net
I: www.theaa.co.uk/region12/98653.htmlwww.newforest.demon.co.uk/cherrytrees.htm

Windmill Cottage ★★★
Contact: Mrs S M Perham, Danescourt, 14 Kivernell Road, Milford-on-Sea, Lymington SO41 0PQ
T: (01590) 643516
F: (01590) 641255

MILTON ABBAS
Dorset

Little Hewish Barn ★★★★★
Contact: Mr Terry Dunn, 2 Little Hewish Cottages, Milton Abbas, Blandford Forum DT11 0DP
T: (01258) 881235
F: (01258) 881393
E: terry@littlehewish.co.uk
I: www.littlehewish.co.uk

Luccombe Farm ★★★★
Contact: Mr & Mrs Murray & Amanda Kayll, Luccombe Farm, Milton Abbas, Blandford Forum DT11 0BE
T: (01635) 200316

Park Farm ★★-★★★★
Contact: Mrs Audrey Burch
T: (01258) 880828
E: burch@parkfarmcottages.co.uk
I: www.parkfarmcottages.co.uk

Primrose Cottage ★★★★
Contact: Mrs G D Garvey, Brook Cottage, 1 Long Street, Cerne Abbas, Dorchester DT2 7JF
T: (01300) 341352
F: (01300) 341352
E: tgarvey@ragtime99.freeserve.co.uk
I: www.miltonabbas-primrosecottage.co.uk

Three the Maltings ★★★
Contact: Mr Stuart-Brown, Dream Cottages, 41 Maiden Street, Weymouth DT4 8AZ
T: (01305) 761347

MILTON KEYNES
Buckinghamshire

33 and 35 Brookside Close ★★★
Contact: Mrs A Hepher, The Old Bakery, 5 Main Street, Cosgrove, Milton Keynes MK19 7JL
T: (01908) 562253
F: (01908) 562228
E: mksh@hepher.demon.co.uk
I: www.mksh.co.uk

MILTON-UNDER-WYCHWOOD
Oxfordshire

Washpool Cottage ★★★★
Contact: Mrs Angela Richards, Priory Mews, 33A Priory Lane, Burford, Oxford OX18 4SG
T: (01993) 824252
F: (01993) 824443

MINSTEAD
Hampshire

Minstead House ★★★★
Contact: Mrs Isabel Morton, Minstead House, School Lane, Minstead, Stoney Cross, Lyndhurst SO43 7GL
T: (02380) 813824
E: ismorton@aol.com

MINSTER-IN-THANET
Kent

Durlock Lodge ★★★
Contact: Mr David Sworder, Durlock Lodge, Durlock, Minster-in-Thanet, Ramsgate CT12 4HD
T: (01843) 821219
E: david@durlocklodge.co.uk
I: www.durlocklodge.co.uk

MINSTER LOVELL
Oxfordshire

Hill Grove Cottage ★★★★
Contact: Mrs Katharine Brown, Hill Grove Farm, Crawley Road, Minster Lovell, Oxford OX29 0NA
T: (01993) 703120
F: (01993) 700528
E: kbrown@eggconnect.net
I: www.country-accom.co.uk/hill-grove-farm/

MOLLINGTON
Oxfordshire

The Stables, The Shippon, The Byre - Anitas Holiday Cottages ★★★-★★★★
Contact: Mr & Mrs Darrel & Anita Gail Jeffries, Anitas Holiday Cottages, The Yews, Church Farm, Mollington, Banbury OX17 1AZ
T: (01295) 750731
F: (01295) 750731
E: anitagail@btopenworld.com

MONXTON
Hampshire

The Den at Millcroft ★★★★
Contact: Mrs Pat Hayward, Millcroft, Chalkpit Lane, Monxton, Andover SP11 8AR
T: (01264) 710618
F: (01264) 710615
E: millcroft@aol.com

MORETON
Dorset

The Courtyard ★★★
Contact: Mrs J P Lofts, The Courtyard, Moreford Hall, Moreton, Dorchester DT2 8BA
T: (01305) 853499
E: famlofts@aol.com

Glebe Cottage ★★
Contact: Mrs Gibbens, Glebe Cottage, Moreton, Dorchester DT2 8RQ
T: (01929) 462468

Meadowbrook Farm Holiday Cottages
Rating Applied For
Contact: Mrs Diana Wynn, Meadowbrook Farm, Watlington, Oxford OX9 2HY
T: (01844) 212116
F: (01844) 217503
E: rdwynn@ukonline.co.uk

MOTCOMBE
Dorset

The Dairy House ★★★★★
Contact: Mr Gilbert Archdale, The Dairy House, Church Farm, Motcombe, Shaftesbury SP7 9NT
T: (01747) 550968
E: enquiries@thedairyhouse.com
I: www.thedairyhouse.com

MUDEFORD
Dorset

Cherry Tree ★★★
Contact: Mrs Jean Bassil, 6 Woodland Way, Highcliffe, Christchurch BH23 4LQ
T: (01425) 271761

Flat 1 Digby Court ★★
Contact: Mrs Spreadbury, Merbury House, Vaggs Lane, Sway, Lymington SO41 0FP
T: (01425) 615605

Victoria Cottage ★★★★
Contact: Mr Stuart-Brown, Dream Cottages, 41 Maiden Street, Weymouth DT4 8AZ
T: (01305) 761347

MURSLEY
Buckinghamshire

The Barn ★★★★
Contact: Mrs Jenny Dobbs, Fourpenny Cottage, 23 Main Street, Mursley, Milton Keynes MK17 0RT
T: (01296) 720544
F: (01296) 720906
E: fourpennycottage@tinyworld.co.uk
I: www.fourpennycottage.co.uk

NEW MILTON
Hampshire

Dahlia Cottage ★★★★
Contact: Mr Ken Claxton, 19 Elmcroft Drive, Chessington KT9 1DZ
T: (020) 8397 8825
E: freqabev@hotmail.com

The Granary ★★
Contact: Mr & Mrs Daniel & Jane Fish, Woodcutters, St Johns Road, Bashley, Tiptoe, Lymington BH25 5SD
T: (01425) 610332
F: (01425) 610332
E: danfishsurface@onetel.net.uk

NEWBRIDGE
Isle of Wight

Laurel Cottage ★★★
Contact: Mrs Honor Vass, Island Cottage Holidays, The Old Vicarage, Kingston, Wareham BH20 5LH
T: (01929) 480080
F: (01929) 481070
E: enq@islandcottageholidays.com
I: www.islandcottageholidays.com

Lavender Cottage ★★★★
Contact: Ms Lisa Baskill, Home from Home Holidays, 31 Pier Street, Ventnor PO38 1SX
T: (01983) 854340
F: (01983) 855524

NEWBURY
Berkshire

Barn House ★★★★
Contact: Mrs Edwards, Enborne Street, Newbury RG20 0JP
T: (01635) 253443
F: (01635) 253443

Peregrine Cottage ★★★★★
Contact: Mrs Elizabeth Knight, Peregrine House, Enborne Street, Enborne, Newbury RG14 6RP
T: (01635) 42585
F: (01635) 528775
E: lizknight@amserve.net

Yaffles ★★★-★★★★
Contact: Mr & Mrs Tony & Jean Bradford, Yaffles, Red Shute Hill, Hermitage, Thatcham RG18 9QH
T: (01635) 201100
F: (01635) 201100
E: yaffles@ukonline.co.uk
I: www.cottagesdirect.com/yaffles

NEWCHURCH
Isle of Wight

Barn Cottage ★★★
Contact: Mrs Anne Corbin, Knighton Barn, Knighton Shute, Newchurch, Sandown PO36 0NT
T: (01983) 865349
F: (01983) 865349
E: bryan-annecorbin@newchurch.fsbusiness.co.uk
I: www.wightfarmholidays.co.uk

Clematis ★★★
Contact: Mr & Mrs A & B Jupe, The Laurels, High Street, Newchurch, Sandown PO36 0NJ
T: (01983) 867613
F: (01983) 868214
E: alistair.jupe@btinternet.com
I: www.btinternet.com/~alistair.jupe/

Knighton Gorges ★★★
Contact: Mrs Honor Vass, Island Cottage Holidays, The Old Vicarage, Kingston, Wareham BH20 5LH
T: (01929) 480080
F: (01929) 481 0700
E: enq@islandcottageholidays.com
I: www.islandcottageholidays.com

Mersley Farm ★★★
Contact: Mrs Jennifer Boswell, Mersley Farm, Mersley Lane, Newchurch, Sandown PO36 0NR
T: (01983) 865213
F: (01983) 862294
E: jenny@mersleyfarm.co.uk
I: www.mersleyfarm.co.uk

Paper Barn & Squire Thatchers Barn ★★★★
Contact: Mrs Honor Vass, The Old Vicarage, Kingston, Wareham BH20 5LH
T: (01929) 481555

NEWENDEN
Kent

The Bothy & The Barn ★★★-★★★★★
Contact: Mrs Brenda Beck, Freedom Holiday Homes, 15 High Street, Cranbrook TN17 3EB
T: (01580) 720770
F: (01580) 720771
E: mail@freedomholidayhomes.co.uk
I: www.freedomholidayhomes.co.uk

NEWHAVEN
East Sussex

The Old Farmhouse & Barn Owls Apartments ★★★-★★★★★
Contact: Mr & Mrs Frank & Gill Canham, 34 The Glade, Ewell, Epsom KT17 2HB
T: (0208) 786 5868

NEWICK
East Sussex

Manor House Cottage ★★★★
Contact: Mrs Jane Roberts, The Manor House, Church Road, Newick, Lewes BN8 4JZ
T: (01825) 722868
E: jane.roberts@tinyworld.co.uk
I: www.manorhousecottage.co.uk

NEWPORT
Isle of Wight

Bethel Cottage ★★★
Contact: Mrs Bridget Lewis, Blackbridge Brook House, Main Road, Ryde PO33 4DR
T: (01983) 884742
E: bridget.lewis@btinternet.com

The Cottage, Stone Farm ★★★★
Contact: Mrs Honor Vass, The Old Vicarage, Kingston, Wareham BH20 5LH
T: (01929) 480080
F: (01929) 481070
E: enq@islandcottageholidays.com
I: www.islandcottageholidays.com

Marvel Cottage ★★★★
Contact: Mr & Mrs Steven & Prudence Sweetman, Marvel Cottage, Marvel Farm, Marvel Lane, Carisbrooke, Newport PO30 3DT
T: (01983) 822691
F: (01983) 822692
E: s@mys.uk.com

Nobbys Cottage ★★★★★
Contact: Mrs Honor Vass, The Old Vicarage, Kingston, Wareham BH20 5LH
T: (01929) 480080
F: (01929) 481070
E: enq@islandcottageholidays.com
I: www.islandcottageholidays.com

2 Sydney Lodge ★★★★
Contact: Mrs Carol Henley, 2 Sydney Lodge, 44 Shide Road, Newport PO30 1YE
T: (01983) 537445

Therles Cottage
Rating Applied For
Contact: Mrs Jane R Phillips, Compton Farm, Military Road, Brook, Newport PO30 4HF
T: (01983) 740215

Waterside Cottage ★★★★
Contact: Mr & Mrs Janet & Alan Pollitt, 2 Highway Road, Maidenhead SL6 5AA
T: (01628) 670346
E: ihiow@ukonline.co.uk

West Standen Farm
Rating Applied For
Contact: Mr & Mrs Edwin & Sally Burt, West Standen Farm, Blackwater Road, Newport PO30 3BD
T: (01983) 522099
I: www.weststandenfarm.co.uk

NINGWOOD
Isle of Wight

The Granary ★★★★
Contact: Mrs Honor Vass, The Old Vicarage, Kingston, Wareham BH20 5LH
T: (01929) 480080
F: (01929) 481070
E: enq@islandcottageholidays.com
I: www.islandcottageholidays.com

NITON
Isle of Wight

Bridge Cottage ★★★
Contact: Ms Lisa Baskill, Home from Home Holidays, 31 Pier Street, Ventnor PO38 1SX
T: (01983) 854340
F: (01983) 855524

Enfield Cottage ★★
Contact: Ms Lisa Baskill, Home from Home Holidays, 31 Pier Street, Ventnor PO38 1SX
T: (01983) 854340
F: (01983) 855524

Gate Lodge ★★★
Contact: Mrs J Clark, 27 Worsley Road, Gurnard, Cowes PO31 8JW
T: (01983) 294900

Hoyes Farmhouse ★★
Contact: Mr & Mrs Willis, Ladyacre Farm, Pan Lane, Niton, Ventnor PO38 2BU
T: (01983) 730015

Jobsons Farm Cottage ★★
Contact: Ms Lisa Baskill, Home from Home Holidays, 31 Pier Street, Ventnor PO38 1SX
T: (01983) 854340
F: (01983) 855524

Pictou ★★★
Contact: Mrs J Clark, 27 Worsley Road, Gurnard, Cowes PO31 8JW
T: (01983) 294900

2 Puckaster Lodge ★★★
Contact: Ms Lisa Baskill, Home from Home Holidays, 31 Pier Street, Ventnor PO38 1SX
T: (01983) 854340
F: (01983) 855524

NITON UNDERCLIFF
Isle of Wight

Puckaster Cottage, Puckaster House & Puckaster Wing ★★★-★★★★★
Contact: Mrs Honor Vass, The Old Vicarage, Kingston, Wareham BH20 5LH
T: (01929) 480080
F: (01929) 481070
E: enq@islandcottageholidays.com
I: www.islandcottageholidays.com

NOKE
Oxfordshire

Manor Barn ★★★★
Contact: Ms Emma Righton, Oxford Shortlets, Lower Farm Offices, Noke, Oxford OX3 9TX
T: (01865) 373766
F: (01865) 371911
E: er@oxfordshortlets.co.uk
I: isisnokelets.co.uk

NORLEYWOOD
Hampshire

The Bee Garden ★★★★
Contact: Mr Mayes, 4 Quay Hill, Lymington SO41 3AR
T: (01590) 679655
F: (01590) 670989
E: holidays@newforestcottages.co.uk
I: www.newforestcottages.co.uk

NORTH LEIGH
Oxfordshire

Wylcot Cottage ★★★★
Contact: Mrs Joy Crew, Hollywell Cottage, New Yatt, North Leigh, Witney OX29 6TF
T: (01993) 868614

NORTH NEWINGTON
Oxfordshire

Herrieff's Cottage ★★★★
Contact: Mrs Mary T Bentley, Herrieff's Farmhouse, The Green, North Newington, Banbury OX15 6AF
T: (01295) 738835
F: (01295) 738835
E: mary@herrieffsfarm.freeserve.co.uk

NORTHBOURNE
Kent

New Mill ★★★
Contact: Mrs Brenda Beck, Freedom Holiday Homes, 15 High Street, Cranbrook TN17 3EB
T: (01580) 720770
F: (01580) 720771
E: mail@freedomholidayhomes.co.uk
I: www.freedomholidayhomes.co.uk

NORTHMOOR
Oxfordshire

Rectory Farm Cottages ★★★★
Contact: Mrs Mary Anne Florey, Rectory Farm, Northmoor, Oxford OX8 1SX
T: (01865) 300207
F: (01865) 300559
E: pj.florey@farmline.com

NUTLEY
East Sussex

Whitehouse Farm Holiday Cottages ★★-★★★
Contact: Mr Keith Wilson, Whitehouse Farm Holiday Cottages, Whitehouse Farm, Horney Common, Nutley, Uckfield TN22 3EE
T: (01825) 712377
F: (01825) 712377
E: keith.g.r.wilson@btinternet.com
I: www.streets-ahead.com/whitehousefarm

OLD CHALFORD
Oxfordshire

Beech House ★★★★★
Contact: Mrs Dorothy Canty, Oak House, Chalford Park, Old Chalford, Chipping Norton OX7 5QR
T: (01608) 641435
F: (01608) 641435

OLNEY
Buckinghamshire

Hyde Farm Cottages ★★★★
Contact: Mrs Penny Reynolds, Hyde Farm Cottages, Hyde Farm, Warrington Road, Olney MK46 4DU
T: (01234) 711223
F: (01234) 714305
E: accomm@thehyde.fsbusiness.co.uk

The Old Stone Barn ★★★-★★★★
Contact: Mr & Mrs G J Pibworth, Warrington, Olney MK46 4HN
T: (01234) 711655
F: (01234) 711855
E: accommodation@oldstonebarn.co.uk
I: www.oldstonebarn.co.uk

OTFORD
Kent

64 Pilgrims Way East ★★★
Contact: Mr Steley, 64 Pilgrims Way East, Sevenoaks TN14 5QW
T: (01959) 522254

OTTERDEN
Kent

Frith Farm House ★★★★
Contact: Mrs Susan Chesterfield, Frith Farm House, Otterden, Faversham ME13 0DD
T: (01795) 890701
F: (01795) 890009
E: markham@frith.force9.co.uk

OWSLEBURY
Hampshire

The Fo'c'sle
Rating Applied For
Contact: Mrs Barbara Crabbe, Hensting Lane, Owslebury, Winchester SO21 1LE
T: (01962) 777887
F: (01962) 777781
E: crabbesleg@aol.com

Hensting Valley Chalet ★★★
Contact: Mrs Diana Carter, Dell Croft, Hensting Lane, Owslebury, Winchester SO21 1LE
T: (01962) 777297

Little Glebe ★★★
Contact: Mrs Caroline Shipley, Glebe House, Owslebury, Winchester SO21 1LU
T: (01962) 777387
E: leashipley@orange.net
I: www.visit-winchester.org.uk

Lower Farm House Annexe ★★★★
Contact: Mrs Penelope Bowes, Lower Farm House Annexe, Lower Farm House, Whaddon Lane, Owslebury, Winchester SO21 1JL
T: (01962) 777676
F: (01962) 777675
E: pbowes@cwcom.net

OXFORD
Oxfordshire

Apartments in Oxford ★★★★★
Contact: Lindsay Edmunds, St Thomas' Mews Apartments in Oxford Limited, 58 St Thomas Street, Oxford OX1 1JP
T: (01865) 254000
F: (01865) 254001
E: based@oxstay.co.uk
I: www.oxstay.co.uk

7 Bannister Close ★★★
Contact: Mrs Irene Priestly, 7 Bannister Close, Iffley Road, Oxford OX4 1SH
T: (01865) 251095
F: (01865) 251095

17 Kingston Road ★★★
Contact: Mrs Pru Dickson, 17 Kingston Road, Oxford OX2 6QR
T: (01865) 516913
F: (01865) 516913
E: pru.dickson@tesco.net
I: www.oxfordcity.co.uk/accom/studioflat/

Manor House Cottages ★★★★
Contact: Mr & Mrs Edward Hess, Manor House Cottages, The Manor House, Wheatley OX33 1XX
T: (01865) 875022
F: (01865) 875023
E: chess@harcourtchambers.law.co.uk

Otmoor Holidays ★★★★
Contact: Mrs Emma Righton, Otmoor Holidays, Lower Farm, Noke, Oxford OX3 9TX
T: (01865) 373766
F: (01865) 371911
E: info@oxfordholidays.co.uk
I: www.oxfordholidays.co.uk

48 St Bernards Road ★★★
Contact: Ms Sian Lewis-Rippington, The Old Workshop, Bruncombe Lane, Bayworth, Abingdon OX13 6QU
T: (01865) 321100
E: greenhavenoxford@btconnect.com
I: www.holidayhomeoxford.co.uk

Tallet Cottage ★★★★
Contact: Mr & Mrs T C Hubbard, Tallet Cottage, Manor Farm Close, Kingham, Moreton-in-Marsh OX7 6YX
T: (01608) 658140
E: info@talletcottage.co.uk

45 Thackley End ★★★
Contact: Mr Kelvin Fowler, Gordon House, 276 Banbury Road, Oxford OX2 7ED
T: (01865) 557555
F: (01865) 557555
E: info@weeklymansion.co.uk

PANGBOURNE
Berkshire

Brambly Thatch ★★★
Contact: Mr & Mrs J N Hatt, Merricroft Farming, Goring Heath, Reading RG8 7TA
T: (0118) 984 3121
F: (0118) 984 4662
I: www.easisites.co.uk/bramblycottages

The Old Rectory Cottage ★★★
Contact: Mrs J H Short, The Old Rectory Cottage, Lower Basildon, Pangbourne, Reading RG8 9NH
T: (01635) 200316

Pennycroft ★★★★
Contact: Mrs Viveka Collingwood, 34 Ambleside Avenue, London SW16 1QP
T: (020) 8769 2742
F: (020) 8677 3023
E: info@pennycroft.com
I: www.pennycroft.com

Soldalen Annexe ★★
Contact: Mr & Mrs John & Bente Kirk, Soldalen, Riverview Road, Pangbourne, Tidmarsh, Reading RG8 7AU
T: (0118) 984 2924
F: (0118) 984 2924

PEACEHAVEN
East Sussex

Highseas ★★★
Contact: Mr Richard Harris, Best of Brighton & Sussex Cottages Ltd, Windmill Lodge, Vicarage Lane, Rottingdean, Brighton BN2 7HD
T: (01273) 308779
F: (01273) 300266
E: brightoncottages@pavilion.co.uk
I: www.bestofbrighton.co.uk

PEASMARSH
East Sussex

Pond Cottage ★★★★
Contact: Mr & Mrs Reeve, Pond Cottage, Clayton Farm, Church Lane, Rye Foreign, Rye TN31 6XS
T: (01797) 230394
I: rye.tourism.co.uk/pondcottage

Sharvels Oast House ★★★★
Contact: Mrs Brenda Beck, Freedom Holiday Homes, 15 High Street, Cranbrook TN17 3EB
T: (01580) 720770
F: (01580) 720771
E: mail@freedomholidayhomes.co.uk
I: www.freedomholidayhomes.co.uk

PETHAM
Kent

Lime Tree Farmhouse
Rating Applied For
Contact: Mrs Brenda Beck, Freedom Holiday Homes, 15 High Street, Cranbrook TN17 3EB
T: (01580) 720770
F: (01580) 720771
E: mail@freedomholidayhomes.co.uk
I: www.freedomholidayhomes.co.uk

PETT LEVEL
East Sussex

Laughing Water ★★★
Contact: Mrs L Robinson, Laughing Water, 80 Hayes Chase, West Wickham, Bromley BR4 0JA
T: (020) 8777 7517

PETWORTH
West Sussex

The Old Dairy ★★★★
Contact: Mrs Rosaleen Waugh, Coultershaw Farm House, Shrewsbury GU28 0JE
T: (01798) 342900
E: bookings@theolddairy.com

Polo Cottage
Rating Applied For
Contact: Mr & Mrs Peter & Deirdre Cope, Polo Cottage, Rotherbridge Lane, Petworth GU28 0LL
T: (01798) 344286
F: (01798) 344286
E: demalpas@aol.com

PLAXTOL
Kent

Golding Hop Farm Cottage ★★★
Contact: Mrs J Vincent, Golding Hop Farm, Bewley Lane, Plaxtol, Sevenoaks TN15 0PS
T: (01732) 885432
F: (01732) 885432
E: adrian@mvvincent.freeserve.co.uk
I: www.mvvincent.freeserve.co.uk

POLEGATE
East Sussex

Barn Cottage ★★★★★
Contact: Mr Richard Harris, Best of Brighton & Sussex Cottages Ltd, Windmill Lodge, Vicarage Lane, Rottingdean, Brighton BN2 7HD
T: (01273) 308779
F: (01273) 300266
E: brightoncottages@pavilion.co.uk
I: www.bestofbrighton.co.uk

POOLE
Dorset

The Boat House ★★★
Contact: Mr Martin Fuller, Holtwood, Holt, Gaunts Common, Wimborne Minster BH21 7DR
T: (01258) 840377
F: 0870 167 2994
E: baiter.holidays@btinternet.com
I: www.baiter.holidays.btinternet.co.uk

Dolphin Cottage, Seahorse & Starfish Apartments★★★
Contact: Mrs Middler, The Grovefield Manor Hotel, 18 Pinewood Road, Branksome Park, Poole BH13 6JS
T: (01202) 766798

Egret ★★★
Contact: Mr & Mrs Cocklin, 46 Perry Gardens, Poole BH15 1RA
T: (01202) 670046

Flat 8 Sandacres ★★
Contact: Miss Barker-Smith, Flat 7, Keythorpe, 27 Manor Road, Bournemouth BH1 3ER
T: (01202) 316230

Flats 5 & 6 Sandacres ★★-★★★
Contact: Mrs Rosemary Bond
T: (01202) 631631
F: (01202) 625749
I: www.beaconhilltouringpark.co.uk

17 Green Gardens ★★★
Contact: Ms Christina Harris, 46 Bournemouth Road, Parkstone, Poole BH14 0EY
T: (01202) 462485
E: christina.harris@breathemail.net

91 Labrador Drive ★★★★
Contact: Mrs Diane Lee, Forest Edge, Holtwood, Wimborne Minster BH21 7DX
T: (01258) 840952
E: diane@leedpm.fsnet.co.uk

Lakeside ★★★
Contact: Mrs Suzanne Fuller, Hollymoors, Holtwood, Holt, Gaunts Common, Wimborne Minster BH21 7DR
T: (01258) 840377
F: 08701 672994
E: baiter.holidays@btinternet.com

Quay Side ★★★★
Contact: Mr Martin Fuller, 12 Catalina Drive, Poole BH15 1UZ
T: (01258) 840377
F: 08701 672994
E: baiter.holidays@btinternet.com
I: www.baiter.holidays.btinternet.co.uk

Quayside ★★★
Contact: Mrs Mary Ball, 59 Oakwood Avenue, Beckenham BR3 6PT
T: (020) 8663 6426
F: (020) 8663 0038
E: quayside@oakwood59.freeserve.co.uk
I: www.oas.co.uk/ukcottages/quayside

Quayside Close Holiday Apartments ★★★
Contact: Mr & Mrs David & Susan Ellison, Bromlea, 23 Leicester Road, Canford Cliffs, Poole BH13 6DA
T: (01202) 764107
F: (01202) 764107
E: quaysideclose@aol.co.uk
I: www.quayside.co.uk

22 St Aubyn's Court ★★★
Contact: Mrs Rosalind Randle, 3B Nuns Road, Chester CH1 2LZ
T: (01244) 401591
F: (01244) 401591
E: rosrandle@cs.com
I: www.oas.co.uk/ukcottages/staubyns

43 Vallis Close ★★★
Contact: Miss Patricia Thomas, 65 Parr Street, Poole BH14 0JX
T: (01202) 743768

Wychcott & Quay Cottage ★★
Contact: Mrs Beryl Saunders, Wychcott, Spinnaker Reach & Quay Cottage, 1 Harbour Shallows, 15 Whitecliff Road, Poole BH14 8DU
T: (01202) 741637

PORCHFIELD
Isle of Wight

Squirrels ★★★★
Contact: Mrs Bridget Lewis, Blackbridge Brook House, Main Road, Ryde PO33 4DR
T: (01983) 884742
E: bridget.lewis@btinternet.com

PORTMORE
Hampshire

Rosemary Cottage ★★★★
Contact: Mrs Jacquie Taylor, Centre Lane, Everton, Milford-on-Sea, Lymington SO41 0JP
T: (01590) 645217
E: tommy.tiddles@virgin.net

PORTSMOUTH & SOUTHSEA
Hampshire

Alamar ★
Contact: Mr Alan Hyde, 1 Eastlake Heights, Horse Sands Close, Southsea PO4 9UE
T: (023) 9282 6352

Atlantic Apartments ★★★
Contact: Mr F Hamdani, Atlantic Apartments, 61A Festing Road, Southsea PO4 0NQ
T: (023) 9282 3606
F: (023) 9229 7046
E: atlantic@portsmouth-apartments.co.uk
I: www.portsmouthapartments.co.uk

Geminair Holiday & Business Flats ★★★
Contact: Mrs Pamela Holman, Geminair Holiday & Business Flats, 1 Helena Road, Southsea PO4 9RH
T: (023) 9282 1602
E: gemflat@aol.com
I: www.gemflat.co.uk

Greenhays Business/Holiday Accommodation★★★★
Contact: Mrs Christine Martin, Greenhays Business/Holiday Accommodation, 10 Helena Road, Southsea PO4 9RH
T: (02392) 737590
F: (02392) 737590

Helena Court Apartments ★★★
Contact: Mrs Wendy Haley, Helena Court Apartments, 3 Helena Road, Southsea PO4 9RH
T: (023) 9273 2116
F: (023) 9282 5793
E: tikitouch@mail.com

Kenilworth Court Holiday Flats ★★★★
Contact: Mrs Sparrowhawk, 1 Kenilworth Road, Southsea PO5 2PG
T: (023) 9273 4205
F: (023) 9273 4205
E: kenilworthcourt@onetel.net.uk

Lakeside Holiday & Business Apartments★★★
Contact: Mrs V Hamza, Lakeside Holiday & Business Apartments, 5 Helena Road, Southsea, Portsmouth PO4 9RH
T: 07810 436981
I: www.lakesidesouthsea.com

Ocean Apartments ★★★
Contact: Mr F Hamdani, Ocean Hotel & Apartments, 8-10 St Helens Parade, Southsea PO4 0RW
T: (023) 9273 4233
F: (023) 9229 7046
I: www.portsmouth-apartments.co.uk

Salisbury Apartments ★★★
Contact: Mr F Hamdani, Atlantic Apartments, 61A Festing Road, Southsea PO4 0NQ
T: (023) 9282 3606
F: (023) 9229 7046
E: salisbury@portsmouth-apartments.co.uk
I: www.portsmouth-apartments.co.uk

South Parade Apartments ★★★
Contact: Mrs Dawn Sait, South Parade Apartments, 29b South Parade, Southsea PO4 0SH
T: (023) 9273 4342
E: southparade@portsmouth-apartments.co.uk
I: www.oceanhotel.freeserve.co.uk

Sovereign Holiday Flatlets ★★
Contact: Mr & Mrs Michael Cummings, Sovereign Holiday Flatlets, 18 Victoria Grove, Southsea, Portsmouth PO5 1NE
T: (023) 9281 1398

University of Portsmouth ★★
Contact: Mr David Goodwin, University of Portsmouth, Langstone Centre, Furze Lane, Southsea PO4 8LW
T: (01635) 200316

Wallington Court ★-★★★
Contact: Mr Paul Stretton, Wallington Court, 64 Craneswater Avenue, Southsea PO4 0PD
T: (01635) 200316

PRINCES RISBOROUGH
Buckinghamshire

Old Callow Down Farm ★★★
Contact: Mrs C Gee, Old Callow Down Farm, Wigans Lane, Bledlow Ridge, High Wycombe HP14 4BH
T: (01844) 344416
F: (01844) 344703
E: oldcallow@aol.com
I: www.chilternscottage.co.uk

Windmill Farm ★★
Contact: Mrs Rosemarie Smith, Windmill Farm, Pink Road, Lacey Green, Princes Risborough, Aylesbury HP27 0PG
T: (01844) 343901
E: windmill_farm@hotmail.com

PRINSTED West Sussex

4 The Square ★★
Contact: Mrs Anne Brooks
T: (01243) 377489
E: brooksems@btclick.com
I: www.fourthesquare.co.uk

PUNNETTS TOWN East Sussex

The Bothy ★★★
Contact: Mrs Brenda Beck, Freedom Holiday Homes, 15 High Street, Cranbrook TN17 3EB
T: (01580) 720770
F: (01580) 720771
E: mail@freedomholidayhomes.co.uk
I: www.freedomholidayhomes.co.uk

RAMSGATE Kent

Hamilton House Holiday Flats ★-★★
Contact: Mrs Ann Burridge, Hamilton House Holiday Flats, 5 Nelson Crescent, Ramsgate CT11 9JF
T: (01843) 582592

23 The Lawns ★★★★
Contact: Mrs Jean Lawrence, J N Lawrence, 24 Winterstoke Crescent, Ramsgate CT11 8AH
T: (01843) 591422
F: (01843) 591422
E: jnancylawrence@aol.com

Ramsgate Holiday House ★★★
Contact: Mrs W E Martin, 20 Swinburne Avenue, Broadstairs CT10 2DP
T: (01843) 863014
E: wendy@martin3371.fsnet.co.uk

2 Westcliff Mansions Rating Applied For
Contact: Mr Chris Bowra, G E Bowra Group Ltd, Haine Industrial Park, 18 Leigh Road, Ramsgate CT12 5EU
T: 07717 511890
F: (01843) 580790

RINGWOOD Hampshire

Beech Cottage ★★★
Contact: Peter Grisdale, Flat 2 Canford Heights, 7 Western Road, Canford Cliffs, Poole BH13 7BE
T: (01202) 707885

Glenavon ★★★
Contact: Mrs Wareham, Glenavon, 12 Boundary Lane, West Moors, Wimborne Minster BH24 2SE
T: (01202) 873868
E: enquiries@glenavonhol.co.uk
I: www.glenavonhol.co.uk

Heather Cottage ★★★
Contact: Mr & Mrs Peter Harper, 93 Southampton Road, Ringwood BH24 1HR
T: (01425) 474567
F: (01425) 474567
E: pjh.hols@btinternet.com

Karelia Holidays ★★★
Contact: Mr R Gleed, Karelia Holidays, c/o The Studio, Ashley, Ringwood BH24 2EE
T: (01425) 478920
F: (01425) 480479
E: kareliahol@aol.com
I: http://members.aol.com/kareliahol

ROBERTSBRIDGE East Sussex

Butters Cottage ★★★★
Contact: Mrs Brenda Beck, Freedom Holiday Homes, 15 High Street, Cranbrook TN17 3EB
T: (01580) 720770
F: (01580) 720771
E: mail@freedomholidayhomes.co.uk
I: www.freedomholidayhomes.co.uk

Garden Cottage ★★★
Contact: Mrs Brenda Beck, Freedom Holiday Homes, 15 High Street, Cranbrook TN17 3EB
T: (01580) 720770
F: (01580) 720771
E: mail@freedomholidayhomes.co.uk
I: www.freedomholidayhomes.co.uk

Holly Cottage ★★★
Contact: Mrs Ann Campbell, Fairhaven Holiday Cottages, Derby House, 123 Watling Street, Gillingham ME7 2YY
T: (01634) 300089
F: (01634) 570157
E: enquiries@fairhaven-holidays.co.uk
I: www.fairhaven-holidays.co.uk

Tudor Cottage ★★★★
Contact: Mr Stuart Winter, Garden of England Cottages Ltd, The Mews Office, 189a High Street, Tonbridge TN9 1BX
T: (01732) 369168
F: (01732) 358817
E: holidays@gardenofenglandcottages.co.uk
I: www.gardenofenglandcottages.co.uk

○ ROCHESTER Kent

Merton Villa ★★
Contact: Mrs Nicola Radford, Merton Villa, 38 Maidstone Road, Rochester ME1 1RJ
T: (01634) 817190

Stable Cottages ★★★★
Contact: Mr & Mrs Jason Symonds, Stable Cottages, Fenn Croft, Newlands Farm Road, St Mary's Hoo, Rochester ME3 8QS
T: (01634) 272439
F: (01634) 272205
E: stablecottages@btinternet.com
I: www.stable-cottages.com

ROMSEY Hampshire

The Old Smithy Cottage ★★★
Contact: Mr Paul Reeves, The Old Smithy Cottage, Awbridge Hill, Romsey SO51 0HF
T: (01794) 511778
E: paul@smithycottage.co.uk
I: www.smithycottage.co.uk

ROOKLEY Isle of Wight

Dairy Cottage ★★★★
Contact: Mrs Jean Linaker, Dairy Cottage, Little Pidford Farm, Blackwater Hollow, Rookley, Ventnor PO38 3NL
T: (01983) 721841

ROPLEY Hampshire

Dairy Cottage ★★★★
Contact: Mr M Neal, Cowgrove Farm, Petersfield Road, Ropley, Alresford SO24 0EJ
T: (01962) 773348
E: theneals@virgin.net

ROTTINGDEAN East Sussex

38 Highcliff Court ★★
Contact: Mr Richard Harris, Best of Brighton & Sussex Cottages Ltd, Windmill Lodge, Vicarage Lane, Rottingdean, Brighton BN2 7HD
T: (01273) 308779
F: (01273) 300266
E: brightoncottages@pavilion.co.uk
I: www.bestofbrighton.co.uk

11 Highcliffe Court ★★
Contact: Mr Richard Harris, Best of Brighton & Sussex Cottages Ltd, Windmill Lodge, Vicarage Lane, Rottingdean, Brighton BN2 7HD
T: (01273) 308779
F: (01273) 300266
E: brightoncottages@pavilion.co.uk
I: www.bestofbrighton.co.uk

Horseshoe Cottage ★★★
Contact: Mr Richard Harris, Best of Brighton & Sussex Cottages Ltd, Windmill Lodge, Vicarage Lane, Rottingdean, Brighton BN2 7HD
T: (01273) 308779
F: (01273) 300266
E: enquiries@bestofbrighton.co.uk
I: www.bestofbrighton.co.uk

White Cliffs ★★★★
Contact: Mr Richard Harris, Best of Brighton & Sussex Cottages Ltd, Windmill Lodge, Vicarage Lane, Rottingdean, Brighton BN2 7HD
T: (01273) 308779
F: (01273) 300266
E: brightoncottages@pavilion.co.uk
I: www.bestofbrighton.co.uk

ROWLAND'S CASTLE Hampshire

Golf View Cottage ★★★★
Contact: Mrs M S Marshall, Golf View Cottage, 91 Castle Road, Rowland's Castle, Portsmouth PO9 6AR
T: (023) 9241 3404

ROYAL TUNBRIDGE WELLS Kent

Broad Oak House ★★★
Contact: Ms Tina Seymour, Broad Oak House, 9 Linden Park Road, Royal Tunbridge Wells TN2 5QL
T: (01892) 619065
F: (01892) 619066
E: tina@thctraining.co.uk

Flat 4 76 London Road ★★★
Contact: Mrs Brenda Beck, Freedom Holiday Homes, 15 High Street, Cranbrook TN17 3EB
T: (01580) 720770
F: (01580) 720771
E: mail@freedomholidayhomes.co.uk
I: www.freedomholidayhomes.co.uk

Ford Cottage ★★★
Contact: Mrs Wendy Cusdin
T: (01892) 531419
E: FordCottage@tinyworld.co.uk
I: www.fordcottage.co.uk

Hollambys ★★★
Contact: Mr Andrew Joad, Hollambys, Eridge Road, Groombridge, Royal Tunbridge Wells TN3 9NJ
T: (01892) 864203
E: ajoad@hollambys.co.uk
I: www.hollambys.force9.co.uk

Itaris Properties Limited ★★★★
Contact: Mrs Edward May, Itaris Properties Ltd, 12 Mount Ephraim, Royal Tunbridge Wells TN4 8AS
T: (01892) 511065
F: (01892) 540171
E: itaris_properties@yahoo.co.uk
I: www.itaris.co.uk

Kennett ★★★★
Contact: Mrs Lesley Clements, Kennett, London Road, Southborough, Royal Tunbridge Wells TN4 0UJ
T: (01892) 533363
E: gravels@onetel.net.uk

1 Stable Mews ★★★
Contact: Mrs Brenda Beck, Freedom Holiday Homes, 15 High Street, Cranbrook TN17 3EB
T: (01580) 720770
F: (01580) 720771
E: mail@freedomholidayhomes.co.uk
I: www.freedomholidayhomes.co.uk

Victoria House ★★★★
Contact: Mr Stuart Winter, Garden of England Cottages Ltd, The Mews Office, 189a High Street, Tonbridge TN9 1BX
T: (01732) 369168
F: (01732) 358817
E: holidays@gardenofenglandcottages.co.uk
I: www.gardenofenglandcottages.co.uk

RUCKINGE
Kent

The Old Granary ★★★★
Contact: Mrs Brenda Beck, Freedom Holiday Homes, 15 High Street, Cranbrook TN17 3EB
T: (01580) 720770
F: (01580) 720771
E: mail@freedomholidayhomes.co.uk
I: www.freedomholidayhomes.co.uk

The Old Post Office ★★
Contact: Mr Chris Cook
T: (020) 8655 4466
F: (020) 8656 7755
E: c.cook@btinternet.com
I: www.ruckinge.info

Willow Court ★★★
Contact: Mrs Brenda Beck, Freedom Holiday Homes, 15 High Street, Cranbrook TN17 3EB
T: (01580) 720770
F: (01580) 720771
E: mail@freedomholidayhomes.co.uk
I: www.freedomholidayhomes.co.uk

RUSHLAKE GREEN
East Sussex

The Coach House ★★★★
Contact: Mrs J B Desch, Beech Hill Farm, Cowbeech Road, Rushlake Green, Heathfield TN21 9QB
T: (01435) 830203
F: (01435) 830203
E: desch@lineone.net
I: www.sussexcountryretreat.co.uk

Stone House Coach House ★★★★
Contact: Mr Peter Dunn, Stone House, Rushlake Green, Heathfield TN21 9QJ
T: (01435) 830553
F: (01435) 830726

RUSTINGTON
West Sussex

The Bungalow ★★★★
Contact: Mr D R Baggs, Teigncombe, Park View Road, Woldingham, Caterham CR3 7DL
T: (01883) 653289

Chalet Bungalow ★★★★
Contact: Mr D R Baggs, Teigncombe, Park View Road, Woldingham, Caterham CR3 7DL
T: (01883) 653289

79 Mallon Dene ★★★
Contact: Mr Robert Brew, Promenade Holiday Homes, 165 Dominion Road, Worthing BN14 8LD
T: (01903) 201426
F: (01903) 201426
I: www.promenadeholidayhomes.co.uk

8 Mariners Walk ★★
Contact: Mr Robert Brew, Promenade Holiday Homes, 165 Dominion Road, Worthing BN14 8LD
T: (01903) 201426
F: (01903) 201426
E: robert@promhols.fsbusiness.co.uk

Papyrus ★★★
Contact: Mrs Joyce Smith, 16 Meadow Way, Rustington, Littlehampton BN17 6BW
T: (01903) 725345
E: joyce@16meadow89.freeserve.co.uk

Seaway ★★★
Contact: Mrs Millidge, Four Seasons, 27 Mill Lane, Rustington, Littlehampton BN16 3JR
T: (01903) 772548

RYDE
Isle of Wight

Beachcomber ★★
Contact: Ms Tina Clift, Beachcomber, 18 The Esplanade, Ryde PO33 2DZ
T: (01983) 566333

Benham Lodge & Forelands ★★★
Contact: Mrs Kathleen Yaxley, Bellair, East Hill Road, Ryde PO33 1LB
T: (01983) 616841
E: kathy@appleyfarmcottages.co.uk
I: www.appleyfarmcottages.co.uk

Bramble Cottage ★★★★
Contact: Ms Lyn Cooper-Hall, Island Holiday Homes, Hose Rhodes Dickson, 177 High Street, Ryde PO33 2HW
T: (01983) 616655
F: (01983) 568822
I: www.island-holiday-homes.net

Claverton House ★★★
Contact: Dr H Metz, Claverton, 12 The Strand, Ryde PO33 1JE
T: (01983) 613015
F: (01983) 613015
E: clavertonhouse@aol.com

Coast View Cottage ★★★
Contact: Mr & Mrs Richard & Lynn Pester, Cynara, Winford Road, Newchurch, Sandown PO36 0NE
T: (01983) 865373
F: (01983) 865373

Dungen ★★★
Contact: Mrs Bernadette Sessions, Hilltop Dairy Farm, Long Lane, Newport PO30 3NW
T: (01983) 564370
F: (01983) 528880

Fairfields Farm ★★★
Contact: Mr Simon Read, Fairfields Farm, Stroudwood Road, Haylands, Ryde PO33 4BY
T: (01983) 616292

Holmwood ★★★★
Contact: Mrs Nicola Newton, Channers Ltd, 7 Argyll Street, Ryde PO33 3BZ
T: (01983) 614852
E: nicola@holmwood-holidays.co.uk

Island Retreat ★★★
Contact: Ms Lisa Baskill, Home from Home Holidays, 31 Pier Street, Ventnor PO38 1SX
T: (01983) 854340
F: (01983) 855524

Jubilee Cottage ★★★★
Contact: Ms Catherine Hopper, Manager, Housing Letting Hose Rhodes Dickson, Island Holiday Homes, 177 High Street, Ryde PO33 2HW
T: (01983) 616644
F: (01983) 616640
E: enquiries@island-holiday-homes.net
I: www.island-holiday-homes.net

Kemphill Barn ★★★★★
Contact: Mr Ron Holland, Kemphill Barns, Stroud Wood Road, Upton, Ashey, Ryde PO33 4BZ
T: (01983) 563880
F: (01983) 563880
E: ron.holland@farming.me.uk
I: www.kemphill.com

Lionstone House ★-★★★
Contact: Mrs Hermiston-Hooper, Lionstone House, 13 The Strand, Ryde PO33 1JE
T: (01983) 563496
F: (01983) 563496

OakLawn Cottages ★★★★
Contact: Mrs Lynette Haywood, Oak Lawn, Woodside, Wootton Bridge, Ryde PO33 4JR
T: (01983) 884080

The Oaks ★-★★★
Contact: Mrs Christine Rossall, 56 West Hill Road, Ryde PO33 1LW
T: (01983) 565769

Owls Cottage ★★★
Contact: Mrs Diana Price, 79 Rounton Road, Waltham Abbey EN9 3AP
T: (01992) 769500

Percy House ★★★
Contact: Ms Catherine Hopper, Manager, Housing Letting Hose Rhodes Dickson, Island Holiday Homes, 177 High Street, Ryde PO33 2HW
T: (01983) 616644
F: (01983) 616640
E: enquiries@island-holiday-homes.net
I: www.island-holiday-homes.net

Silver Birches
Rating Applied For
Contact: Mrs Kathy Domaille, Godshill Park Farm House, Shanklin Road, Godshill, Wroxall, Ventnor PO38 3JF
T: (01983) 840781
E: truelovek@btconnect.com

Strand House ★★★
Contact: Ms Jan Johnston, Strand House, 17 The Strand, Ryde PO33 1JE
T: 07973 683722

Upwood Holiday Flats ★★-★★★
Contact: Mrs Angela Harris, Upwood Holiday Flats, East Hill Road, Ryde PO33 1LS
T: (01983) 568965
E: angie.harris@virgin.net

10 Vernon Square
Rating Applied For
Contact: Mr Matthew White, Island Holiday Homes, 138 High Street, Newport PO30 1TY
T: (01983) 521114

The Victorian Lodge ★★★
Contact: Mrs Herbert, The Victorian Lodge, 8 Easthill Road, Ryde PO33 1LS
T: (01983) 563366

22 Westfield Park
Rating Applied For
Contact: Mr Patrick Mann, 16 Westfield Park, Ryde PO33 3AB
T: (01983) 614758

RYE
East Sussex

Apothecary House ★★★★
Contact: Mr Trevor Esdaile, Perrinhurst Ltd, 4 Highgrove, Battle TN33 0EL
T: (01424) 774254

Boat House ★★★
Contact: Mr Melville-Brown, The Manor House, Durrington, Salisbury BN13 2PX
T: 07803 189031
E: chris@ryeholidays.co.uk
I: www.ryeholidays.co.uk

10 The Boathouse
Rating Applied For
Contact: Mr Robert Lever, Seascape, Coastguard Lane, Fairlight, Hastings TN35 4AB
T: (01424) 813566
F: (01424) 813566
E: rslever@tn35ab.freeserve.co.uk
I: www.tn354ab.freeserve.co.uk

15 The Boathouse ★★★
Contact: Mr Mike Hickmott, Glynton Hurst, Penshurst Road, Speldhurst, Royal Tunbridge Wells TN3 0PH
T: (01892) 863037
E: mike@rye4ukbreaks.co.uk
I: www.rye4ukbreaks.co.uk

Brandy's Cottage ★★★★
Contact: Mrs Jane Apperly, Brandy's Cottage, Cadborough Farm, Udimore Road, Rye TN31 6AA
T: (01797) 225426
F: (01797) 224097
E: info@cadborough.co.uk
I: www.cadborough.co.uk

Caer Glow ★★★
Contact: Mr Stuart Winter, Garden of England Cottages Ltd, The Mews Office, 189a High Street, Tonbridge TN9 1BX
T: (01732) 369168
F: (01732) 358817
E: holidays@gardenofenglandcottages.co.uk
I: www.gardenofenglandcottages.co.uk

Chapel Cottage ★★★
Contact: Mr Stuart Winter, Garden of England Cottages Ltd, The Mews Office, 189a High Street, Tonbridge TN9 1BX
T: (01732) 369168
F: (01732) 358817
E: holidays@gardenofenglandcottages.co.uk
I: www.gardenofenglandcottages.co.uk

Chesterfield Cottage ★★★
Contact: Ms Sally Bayly, 44 1/2 The Mint, Rye TN31 7EN
T: (01797) 222498
F: (01797) 223826

Christmas Cottage ★★★★
Contact: Dr & Mrs D P North-Coombes, Farthings, Brox Lane, Ottershaw, Chertsey KT16 0LL
T: (01932) 872220
E: sue@north-coombes.co.uk
I: mail@north-coombes.co.uk

Crispin/Arend Apartments ★★★
Contact: Mr & Mrs David & Sarah Nixon, 75 The Mint, Rye TN31 7EW
T: (01797) 226837
F: (01797) 226837
E: crispins@talk21.com

Driftwood ★★★
Contact: Mrs Brenda Beck, 15 High Street, Cranbrook TN17 3EB
T: (01580) 720770
F: (01580) 720771
E: mail@freedomholidayhomes.co.uk

Ellis Bros (Ironmongers) Ltd ★★
Contact: Miss H K Gill, Ellis Bros (Ironmongers) Ltd, 1 High Street, Rye TN31 7JE
T: (01797) 222110

Homelands ★★★
Contact: Mrs Margaret Royle, South Chailey, Lewes BN8 4RS
T: (01825) 723294
F: (01825) 723294

2 Hucksteps Row ★★★
Contact: Mrs Brenda Beck, Freedom Holiday Homes, 15 High Street, Cranbrook TN17 3EB
T: (01580) 720770
F: (01580) 720771
E: mail@freedomholidayhomes.co.uk
I: www.freedomholidayhomes.co.uk

Lapwings
Rating Applied For
Contact: Mrs Sandra Fenn, Northlands, Chitcombe Road, Broad Oak Brede, Rye TN31 6EU
T: (01424) 882607
F: (01424) 883417
E: sandra@northlands.co.uk

Larkin House ★★★
Contact: Stella Larkin, 31 London Road, Shenley, Radlett WD7 9EP
T: (01923) 857095
E: stella.larkin@freenet.co.uk
I: www.interiorstylist.com

Mermaid Cottage ★★★★
Contact: Mrs Suzie Warren, Tanners, Freight Lane, Cranbrook TN17 3PF
T: (01580) 712046
E: mermaidcottage@supanet.com
I: www.mermaidcottage.supanet.com

22 Mermaid Street ★★★
Contact: Mr Grimes, 36 Poets Road, Highbury, London N5 2SH
T: (0207) 704 8470
E: frankwoof@yahoo.com

41 Military Road ★★★
Contact: Mrs Valerie John, c/o Smugglers Steps, 13 Love Lane, Rye TN31 7NE
T: (01797) 223785

Ockman Cottage ★★★
Contact: Mrs Brenda Beck, Freedom Holiday Homes, 15 High Street, Cranbrook TN17 3EB
T: (01580) 720770
F: (01580) 720771
E: mail@freedomholidayhomes.co.uk
I: www.freedomholidayhomes.co.uk

Riverview Cottage ★★★
Contact: Mr & Mrs Henderson, 18 Chipstead Park, Riverhead, Sevenoaks TN13 2SN
T: (01732) 457837

Seaview Terrace ★★★
Contact: Mrs Pamela Pettigrew, The Folly, Folly Road, Upper Lambourn, Hungerford RG17 8QE
T: (01488) 71569
F: (01488) 71569

Thacker House ★★★
Contact: Ms Bridget Green, Thacker House, Old Brickyard, Rye TN31 7EE
T: (01797) 226850
E: abb25@supanet.com

RYE FOREIGN
East Sussex

Oak Cottages & Rose Cottage ★★★
Contact: Mr Reeve, Clayton Farm, Church Lane, Rye Foreign, Rye TN31 6XS
T: (01797) 230394
E: jackiereeve@peasmarsh68.fsnet.co.uk
I: www.country-holidays.co.uk

RYE HARBOUR
East Sussex

1a Coastguard Square ★★★
Contact: Mrs Brenda Beck, Freedom Holiday Homes, 15 High Street, Cranbrook TN17 3EB
T: (01580) 720770
F: (01580) 720771
E: mail@freedomholidayhomes.co.uk
I: www.freedomholidayhomes.co.uk

Harbour Lights ★★★
Contact: Mrs Penelope Webster, 24 Moorcroft Close, Sheffield S10 4GU
T: (0114) 230 6859
E: holidays@harbourlights.info

Harbour Point South ★★★
Contact: Mrs Brenda Beck, Freedom Holiday Homes, 15 High Street, Cranbrook TN17 3EB
T: (01580) 720770
F: (01580) 720771
E: mail@freedomholidayhomes.co.uk
I: www.freedomholidayhomes.co.uk

ST HELENS
Isle of Wight

1 & 2 Glade House ★★★★
Contact: Mrs Peggy Stephens, Mill Road, St Helens, Ryde PO33 1UE
T: (01983) 872507
E: oldmill@fsb.dial.co.uk
I: www.oldmill.co.uk

Carpenters Farm ★★
Contact: Mrs Mary Lovegrove, Carpenters Farm, Carpenters Road, St Helens, Ryde PO33 1YL
T: (01983) 872450

Island Lights ★★
Contact: Ms Lisa Baskill, Home from Home Holidays, 31 Pier Street, Ventnor PO38 1SX
T: (01983) 854340
F: (01983) 855524

Isola ★★★★
Contact: Mr & Mrs Tim & Anne Baker, 79 Staunton Road, Headington, Oxford OX3 7TL
T: (01865) 761558
E: timbaker@isola-iow.freeserve.co.uk

The Little Shell House ★★★
Contact: Mrs Christina Hind, 11 Byng Road, High Barnet, Barnet EN5 4NW
T: (0208) 449 8867
F: (0208) 449 8867
E: thehinds@ntlworld.com

The Poplars ★★★
Contact: Mrs Honor Vass, The Old Vicarage, Kingston, Wareham BH20 5LH
T: (01929) 480080
F: (01929) 481070
E: enq@islandcottageholidays.com
I: www.islandcottageholidays.com

9 Port St Helens ★★★
Contact: Mrs Peggy Stephens, Mill Road, St Helens, Ryde PO33 1UA
T: (01983) 872507
E: old_mill@netguides.co.uk

Seagull Cottage ★★★
Contact: Dr & Mrs Simon Baker, High Tree Cottage, Wood Lane, Willingale, Ongar CM5 0QU
T: (01277) 896364
F: (01920) 877513
E: kcf88@dial.pipex.co

ST LAWRENCE
Isle of Wight

Beech Cottage ★★★★
Contact: Mr & Mrs Davies, Mole End, 27 Foxhills, Whitwell, Ventnor PO38 1LX
T: (01983) 857608
E: s&r@daviesmoleend.worldonline.co.uk

Charles Wood House ★★★★
Contact: Ms Lisa Baskill, Home from Home Holidays, 31 Pier Street, Ventnor PO38 1SX
T: (01983) 854340
F: (01983) 855524

Copse Hill ★★
Contact: Ms Lisa Baskill, Home from Home Holidays, 31 Pier Street, Ventnor PO38 1SX
T: (01983) 854340
F: (01983) 855524

Heshcot ★★★
Contact: Mrs J Clark, 27 Worsley Road, Gurnard, Cowes PO31 8JW
T: (01983) 294900

Manor Retreat ★★★
Contact: Mrs Jeanie Brown, Manor Retreat, Salem Manor, Salem Close, St Lawrence, Ventnor PO38 1XN
T: (01983) 854485

The Spinnaker ★★★
Contact: Mr & Mrs Derek Morris, The Spinnaker, Undercliff Glen, The Undercliffe Drive, St Lawrence, Ventnor PO38 1XY
T: (01983) 730261

1 St Rhadagunds Cottages ★★★★
Contact: Mrs Julie Banks-Thompson, The Garden House, Green Lane, Chobham, Woking GU24 8PH
T: (01276) 858168
F: (01276) 485821
E: JB-T@talk21.com

ST LEONARDS
East Sussex

Flat 4 42 Marina ★★★★
Contact: Mrs Brenda Beck, Freedom Holiday Homes, 15 High Street, Cranbrook TN17 3EB
T: (01580) 720770
F: (01580) 720771
E: mail@freedomholidayhomes.co.uk
I: www.freedomholidayhomes.co.uk

Flats 5 & 6 ★★★
Contact: Mrs Brenda Beck, Freedom Holiday Homes, 15 High Street, Cranbrook TN17 3EB
T: (01580) 720770
F: (01580) 720771
E: mail@freedomholidayhomes.co.uk
I: www.freedomholidayhomes.co.uk

Glastonbury Self-Catering ★★
Contact: Mr W L Campbell, Glastonbury Self-Catering, 45 Eversfield Place, St Leonards, Hastings TN37 6DB
T: (01424) 436186
E: glastonburyselfcatering@btinternet.com
I: www.hastings.gov.uk

Ground Floor Flat
Rating Applied For
Contact: Mr Richard Harris, Windmill Lodge, Vicarage Lane, Rottingdean, Brighton BN2 7HD
T: (01273) 308779
F: (01273) 300266
E: brightoncottages@pavilion.co.uk

St Leonards Flat ★★★
Contact: Mrs V Mathews, Miraleisure Ltd, 51 Marina, Bexhill TN40 1BQ
T: (01424) 730298
F: (01424) 212500
E: infomira@waitrose.com

60 Warrior Square ★★★★
Contact: Mrs Brenda Beck, Freedom Holiday Homes, 15 High Street, Cranbrook TN17 3EB
T: (01580) 720770
F: (01580) 720771
E: mail@freedomholidayhomes.co.uk
I: www.freedomholidayhomes.co.uk

ST MARGARET'S BAY
Kent

Reach Court Farm Cottages ★★★★
Contact: Mrs Jacqui Mitchell, Reach Court Farm Cottages, Reach Court Farm, St-Margarets-at-Cliffe, Dover CT15 6AQ
T: (01304) 852159
F: (01304) 853902

ST MARY BOURNE
Hampshire

Trestan Cottage ★★★
Contact: Mrs Carolann Sutton, Trestan Cottage, Church Street, St Mary Bourne, Andover SP11 6BL
T: (01264) 738380
E: gardenlodge@ukworld.net

ST MARY'S BAY
Kent

Edenhurst ★★★
Contact: Country Holidays Ref : 4691, Country Holidays, Spring Mill, Earby, Barnoldswick BB94 0AA
T: 08700 723723
F: (01282) 844288
E: sales@holidaycottagesgroup.com
I: www.country-holidays.co.uk

ST MICHAELS
Kent

6 The Terrace ★★★
Contact: Mrs Brenda Beck, Freedom Holiday Homes, 15 High Street, Cranbrook TN17 3EB
T: (01580) 720770
F: (01580) 720771
E: mail@freedomholidayhomes.co.uk
I: www.freedomholidayhomes.co.uk

SALFORD
Oxfordshire

Mill Cottage ★★★★
Contact: Mr & Mrs Charles & Liz Teall, Salford Mill, Worcester Road, Salford, Chipping Norton OX7 5YQ
T: (01608) 641304
F: (01608) 644442
E: teall@compuserve.com

Stable Cottage & The Granary ★★★★
Contact: Mrs Barbara Lewis, Stable Cottage & The Granary, Larches Farmhouse, Salford, Chipping Norton OX7 5YY
T: (01608) 643398
E: babbylew@supanet.com

SALTDEAN
East Sussex

11b Nutley Avenue ★★★★★
Contact: Mr Richard Harris, Best of Brighton & Sussex Cottages Ltd, Windmill Lodge, Vicarage Lane, Rottingdean, Brighton BN2 7HD
T: (01273) 308779
F: (01273) 300266
E: brightoncottages@pavilion.co.uk
I: www.bestofbrighton.co.uk

Westpoint ★★★
Contact: Mr Richard Harris, Best of Brighton & Sussex Cottages Ltd, Windmill Lodge, Vicarage Lane, Rottingdean, Brighton BN2 7HD
T: (01273) 308779
F: (01273) 300266
E: brightoncottages@pavilion.co.uk
I: www.bestofbrighton.co.uk

SANDFORD
Isle of Wight

The Cottage ★★★
Contact: Ms Sue Dyer, S D Residential, 6 Velsheda Close, Totland Bay PO39 0AJ
T: (01983) 759861
F: (01983) 759861
E: sue.dyer2@virgin.net
I: www.iowcottage.com

SANDHURST
Kent

Little Brook
Rating Applied For
Contact: Mr Nick Pash, Hideaways, Chapel House, Luke Street, Berwick St John, Shaftesbury SP7 0HQ
T: (01747) 828170
F: (01747) 829090
E: enq@hideaways.co.uk

SANDLING
Kent

Dingley Cottage & Dell Cottage ★★★★
Contact: Mr Robert Lawty, Cobtree Manor House, Forstal Road, Sandling, Maidstone ME14 3AX
T: (01622) 671160
F: (01622) 750378
E: mail@cobtree.com
I: www.cobtree.com

SANDOWN
Isle of Wight

Barcelona Holiday Flats ★★★
Contact: Mr Nick Clemens, Barcelona Holiday Flats, 6 Leed Street, Sandown PO36 8JQ
T: (01983) 402481
I: barcelonahouse.co.uk

Beaulieu Cottage ★★★
Contact: Mrs Honor Vass, Island Cottage Holidays, Godshill Park Farm House, Godshill, Wroxall, Ventnor PO38 3JF
T: (01929) 480080
F: (01929) 481070
E: enq@islandcottagesholidays.com
I: www.islandcottageholidays.com

Brackla Apartments ★★★★
Contact: Mrs Lindsay Heinrich, Brackla Apartments, 7 Leed Street, Sandown PO36 9DA
T: (01983) 403648
F: (01983) 402887
E: enquire@brackla-apartments.co.uk
I: www.brackla-apartments.co.uk

19 Copse End ★★★
Contact: Ms Lisa Baskill, Home from Home Holidays, 31 Pier Street, Ventnor PO38 1SX
T: (01983) 854340
F: (01983) 855524

Hope Cottage ★★★
Contact: Ms Gail Whiting, Hillrise House, 11 Vaughan Way, Shanklin PO37 6SD
T: (01983) 864103

Kintore Court Holiday Apartments ★★★
Contact: Mr Bass, Kintore Court Holiday Apartments, 15 Broadway, Sandown PO36 9BY
T: (01983) 402507

Little Parklands Holiday Apartments ★★★
Contact: Mrs Karen Hudson, Little Parklands Holiday Apartments, 7 Winchester Park Road, Sandown PO36 8HJ
T: (01983) 402883
E: info@sandownholidays.com

Mayfair ★★★★
Contact: Mrs J Clark, 27 Worsley Road, Gurnard, Cowes PO31 8JW
T: (01983) 294900

P & J Holiday Chalets 173 & 174 Sandown Bay Holiday Centre★★
Contact: Mr & Mrs Paul Horobin, 22 St Boniface Cliff Road, Lake, Sandown PO37 6ET
T: (01983) 868184
F: (01983) 868409

Parklands Apartments
Rating Applied For
Contact: Mr Hugh McGee, Parklands Apartments, 9 Winchester Park Road, Sandown PO36 8HJ
T: (01983) 409602
F: (01983) 407644

Parterre Holiday Flats ★★★
Contact: Mr Roger Hollis, Parterre Holiday Flats, 34 Broadway, Sandown PO36 9BY
T: (01983) 403555
E: roger@parterre.freeserve.co.uk

Royal Cliff Apartments ★★★
Contact: Mr Peter Smith, Royal Cliff Apartments, Beachfield Road, Sandown PO36 8NA
T: (01983) 402138
F: (01983) 402368

Royal Court & Garden Apartments ★★★★
Contact: Mr & Mrs Blake, The Town House, Beachfield Road, Sandown PO36 8ND
T: (01983) 405032

35 Sandown Bay Holiday Centre ★★
Contact: Mr & Mrs Sitton, 24 Jeals Lane, Sandown PO36 9NS
T: 07974 971595
E: grahamsitton@hotmail.com

Victoria Lodge ★★★
Contact: Mr Gibbens & Mrs P Jackson, Victoria Lodge, 4-6 Victoria Road, Sandown PO36 8AP
T: (01983) 403209

SANDWICH
Kent

The Old Dairy ★★★★
Contact: Mrs J R Montgomery, Little Brooksend Farm, Birchington CT7 0JW
T: (01843) 841656
F: (01843) 841656

Quay Location ★★★
Contact: Mrs Janet Cross, 1 Kings Avenue, Deal CT13 9PH
T: (01304) 612880
E: janet@quaylocation.com
I: www.quaylocation.com

The Way Out Inn ★★★
Contact: Ms Hazel Cruttwell, The Way Out Inn, Westmarsh, Canterbury CT3 2LP
T: (01304) 812899
F: (01304) 813181
E: Mail@TheWayOutInn.com
I: www.TheWayOutInn.com

2 Worth Farm Cottages ★★★
Contact: Mrs Patricia Mallett, Vine Farm, Marshborough, Sandwich CT13 0PG
T: (01304) 812276
F: (01304) 812694
E: worthcotts@vinefarm.plus.com

SEAFORD
East Sussex

Cuilfail ★★★
Contact: Mrs Lois Fuller, Cuilfail, Firle Road, Seaford BN25 2JD
T: (01323) 898622

Dymock Farm ★★★
Contact: Mrs White, Dymock Farm, Chyngton Lane North, Seaford BN25 4AA
T: (01323) 892982

Hardy's Coffee House
Rating Applied For
Contact: Mr & Mrs Hardy, Fletching Cottage, Richmond Road, Seaford BN25 1DN
T: (01323) 894877

2 Kingsway Court ★★★★
Contact: Mrs Pauline Gower, 6 Sunningdale Close, Southdown Road, Seaford BN25 4PF
T: (01323) 895233
E: sific@bgower.f9.co.uk

21 Marine Parade ★★★
Contact: Mr Richard Harris, Best of Brighton & Sussex Cottages Ltd, Windmill Lodge, Vicarage Lane, Rottingdean, Brighton BN2 7HD
T: (01273) 308779
F: (01273) 300266
E: brightoncottages@pavilion.co.uk
I: www.bestofbrighton.co.uk

SEAVIEW
Isle of Wight

The Bolt Hole at Linden ★★★★
Contact: Mrs Barbara Hughes, Linden, Seaview Lane, Seaview, Seaview PO34 5DJ
T: (01983) 810324
F: (01983) 810324
E: barbara_hughes@btinternet.com
I: www.theboltholeiow.co.uk

Glynn Cottage ★★★
Contact: Mrs J Clark, 27 Worsley Road, Gurnard, Cowes PO31 8JW
T: (01983) 294900

44 Horestone Drive ★★★★
Contact: Mrs Honor Vass, Island Cottage Holidays, The Old Vicarage, Kingston, Wareham BH20 5LH
T: (01929) 480080
F: (01929) 481070
E: enq@islandcottagesholidays.com
I: www.cottageholidays.dmon.co.uk.

Pepita ★★
Contact: Mrs J Clark, 27 Worsley Road, Gurnard, Cowes PO31 8JW
T: (01983) 294900

1 Pond Lane ★★★
Contact: Mrs S M Capon, 11 Circular Road, Ryde PO33 1AL
T: (01983) 564267
F: (01983) 564267
E: smcapon@aol.com

SEDLESCOMBE
East Sussex

Acorn Chalet ★★★★
Contact: Mr Stuart Winter, Garden of England Cottages Ltd, The Mews Office, 189a High Street, Tonbridge TN9 1BX
T: (01732) 369168
F: (01732) 358817
E: holidays@gardenofenglandcottages.co.uk
I: www.gardenofenglandcottages.co.uk

SELHAM
West Sussex

The Annex ★★★
Contact: Mrs Belinda Hurst, Great Ham Mead, Selham, Petworth GU28 0PJ
T: (01798) 861450

SELSEY
West Sussex

Stable Annexe ★★
Contact: Mr & Mrs Kenneth Child, Post Cottage, Rectory Lane, Selsey, Chichester PO20 9DU
T: (01243) 604264

40 Toledo ★★
Contact: Mr & Mrs Robert Jones, 47 Colne Avenue, West Drayton UB7 7AL
T: (01895) 446352

SEVENOAKS
Kent

Harveys ★★★
Contact: Mrs Pat Harvey, Harveys, 143 West End, Kemsing, Sevenoaks TN15 6QJ
T: (01732) 761862

Linden Beeches Cottages ★★★
Contact: Mr Peter & Lynda Gilbert, Linden Beeches Cottages, 81 Bradbourne Park Road, Sevenoaks TN13 3LQ
T: (01732) 461008
E: lindenbeeches@rmplc.co.uk
I: www.smoothhound.co.uk/hotels/linde.html

SHAFTESBURY
Dorset

Dairy Cottage ★★
Contact: Mrs Pope, Broadlea Farm, Sutton Waldron, Blandford Forum DT11 8NS
T: (01747) 811330
F: (01747) 811330
E: maryp2@tinyworld.co.uk

South View ★★★
Contact: Mr Keith Westcott, Stonebank, 14 West Street, Fleet, Weymouth DT3 4DY
T: (01305) 760120
F: (01305) 760871
E: elmvale@stonebank-chickerell.co.uk
I: www.stonebank-chickerell.com

25 St James's Street ★★★
Contact: Mrs Jane Pyrgos, Port Regis, Motcombe Park, Motcombe, Shaftesbury SP7 9QA
T: (01747) 856343
E: pjp@portregis.com

Stable Cottage, Shire Cottage & Granary Cottage ★★★-★★★★
Contact: Mrs Trevor, Middle Farm, Fifehead Magdalen, Gillingham SP8 5RR
T: (01258) 820220
F: (01258) 820220

Thatch Cottage
Rating Applied For
Contact: Mrs Lynne Sekree, Four Seasons, Beech Road, Chandler's Ford, Chandlers Ford, Eastleigh SO53 1LR
T: (023) 8026 5945
F: (023) 8048 6259
E: thatchcottage@ntlworld.com

Vale Farm Holiday Cottages ★★★★
Contact: Mrs Sarah Drake, Vale Farm, Sutton Waldron, Blandford Forum DT11 8PG
T: (01747) 811286
F: (01747) 811286
E: jandsdrake@ukonline.co.uk
I: www.valeholidays.co.uk

SHALFORD
Surrey

The Flat, Shalford Mill ★★
Contact: Mr & Mrs Brian Bagnall, The Flat, Shalford Mill, The Street, Shalford, Guildford GU4 8BS
T: (01483) 561617
F: (01483) 561617

SHANKLIN
Isle of Wight

1 Apse Castle Cottages ★★
Contact: Ms Lisa Baskill, Home from Home Holidays, 31 Pier Street, Ventnor PO38 1SX
T: (01983) 854340
F: (01983) 855524

Braeholme ★★★
Contact: Mr Roger Charlo, Braeholme, 8 Arthurs Hill, Shanklin PO37 6EF
T: (01635) 200316

Byre Cottage ★★★
Contact: Mrs J Clark, 27 Worsley Road, Gurnard, Cowes PO31 8JW
T: (01983) 294900

Chestnut Mews ★★★★★
Contact: Mrs Carol Bowkis, Squirrels, 17 Vaughan Way, Old Village, Shanklin PO37 6SD
T: (01983) 861143
F: (01983) 861143
E: chestnut@bowkis.fsnet.co.uk

Dairymaid Cottage ★★★
Contact: Mrs J Clark, 27 Worsley Road, Gurnard, Cowes PO31 8JW
T: (01983) 294900

Fair Winds ★★★
Contact: Ms Lisa Baskill, Home from Home Holidays, 31 Pier Street, Ventnor PO38 1SX
T: (01983) 854340
F: (01983) 855524

Fernhurst Holiday Apartments ★★★
Contact: Mrs Sandra Petcher, Fernhurst Holiday Apartments, 42 Western Road, Shanklin PO37 7NF
T: (01983) 862126
E: bpetcher@talk21.com
I: www.isleofwight.uk.com/fernhurst

Glendower ★★★
Contact: Mr William Eglinton, Glendower, 14 Furze Hill Road, Shanklin PO37 7PA
T: (01983) 865925
E: williameglinton@yahoo.com
I: www.members.lycos/glendowershanklin/

Green Gable ★★★
Contact: Mrs J Clark, 27 Worsley Road, Gurnard, Cowes PO31 8JW
T: (01983) 294900

Heatherdene ★★★★
Contact: Mrs J Clark, 27 Worsley Road, Gurnard, Cowes PO31 8JW
T: (01983) 294900

Laramie ★★★
Contact: Mrs Sally Ranson, Laramie, Howard Road, Lake, Sandown PO37 6HD
T: (01983) 862905
E: sally@ranson2.worldonline.co.uk

Laurel Court Holiday Apartments ★★
Contact: Mr & Mrs Brash, Downdale Lodge, Priory Road, Shanklin PO37 6SA
T: (01983) 868025

Lavender Cottage & Magnolia Cottage ★★★★
Contact: Mrs Honor Vass, The Old Vicarage, Kingston, Wareham BH20 5LH
T: (01929) 480080
F: (01929) 481070
E: enq@islandcottageholidays.com
I: www.islandcottageholidays.com

Lovecombe Cottage ★★★
Contact: Mrs Anne Kennerley, Duxmore Farm, Downend, Newport PO30 2NZ
T: (01983) 883993

Luccombe Villa ★★★
Contact: Mrs Christine Williams, Luccombe Villa, 9 Popham Road, Shanklin PO37 6RF
T: (01983) 862825
F: (01983) 862362

Ninham House ★★★★
Contact: Mrs Veronica Harvey, Ninham House, Ninham, Shanklin PO37 7PL
T: (01983) 864243
F: (01983) 868881

The Old Grange Apartments ★★★★
Contact: Mr Willoughby Douglas, The Old Grange Apartments, 9 Eastcliff Road, Shanklin PO37 6AA
T: (01983) 862385
F: (01983) 868385

Percy Cottage ★★★
Contact: Mr David Hirst, 47 George Street, Hoyland, Barnsley S74 9AE
T: (01226) 744754

2 Rubstone Court ★★★★
Contact: Mrs Elaine Hedley, 19 Palmerston Road, Shanklin PO37 6AU
T: (01983) 867695
E: rubstone2@aol.com

Shanklin Manor Mews ★★★★
Contact: Mr Thomas McLinden, Shanklin Manor House Hotel, Manor Road, Old Village, Shanklin PO37 6QX
T: (01983) 862777
F: (01983) 863464
I: www.hotels.iow.co.uk

The Stables ★★★★
Contact: Mr N Rigby, The Stables, 29 Sandy Lane, Shanklin PO37
T: (01983) 866702

Summerhill Apartments ★★★
Contact: Pat, Summerhill Apartments, 4 Culver Road, Shanklin PO37 6ER
T: (01983) 865545
F: (01983) 865545
I: www.summerhill.f9.co.uk

Upper Chine Holiday Cottages & Apartments ★★★★
Contact: Mr Henry Butcher, Upper Chine Holiday Cottages & Apartments, 22a Church Road, Old Village, Shanklin PO37 6QU
T: (01983) 867900
F: (01983) 867900
I: www.upperchinecottages.co.uk

Upper Hatch ★★★
Contact: Ms Lisa Baskill, Home from Home Holidays, 31 Pier Street, Ventnor PO38 1SX
T: (01983) 854340
F: (01983) 855524

Winchester House ★★★
Contact: Mrs Caryl Morrison, Winchester House, Sandown Road, Lake, Sandown PO37 6HU
T: (01983) 862441
F: (01983) 863513
E: winchesterhouse@lineone.net

SHAWFORD
Hampshire

Kingsmere Cottage ★★★★
Contact: Mrs Caroline Daniels, Kingsmere Cottage, Kingsmere Acres, Bridge Lane, Shawford, Winchester SO21 2BL
T: (01962) 714876
F: (01962) 717398

SHELDWICH
Kent

Littles Manor Farmhouse ★★★★
Contact: Mr Tim Bourne, Kent Holiday Cottages, Shepherd's View, Brissenden Court, Bethersden, Ashford TN26 3BE
T: (01233) 820425
F: (01233) 820746

SHERE
Surrey

Five Pines ★★
Contact: Ms Gill Gellatly, Lockhurst Hatch Farm, Lockhurst Hatch Lane, Shere, Guildford GU5 9JN
T: (01483) 202689

SHILLINGSTONE
Dorset

Orchard House Cottage ★★★★
Contact: Ms Fiona Chapman, Orchard House, Everetts Lane, Shillingstone, Blandford Forum DT11 0SJ
T: (01258) 860257
F: (01258) 863784
E: fiona@chapman1807.fsnet.com

SHILTON
Oxfordshire

The Chestnuts ★★★★
Contact: Miss Christine Burton, The Chestnuts, Shilton, Oxford OX18 4AB
T: (01993) 844905
F: (01993) 841508

SHIPBOURNE
Kent

The Old Stables ★★★★
Contact: Mrs Cohen, Great Oaks House, Puttenden Road, Shipbourne, Tonbridge TN11 9RX
T: (01732) 810739
F: (01732) 810738
E: kent.lets@virgin.net
I: www.heartofengland.org.uk

SHIPTON-UNDER-WYCHWOOD
Oxfordshire

Plum Cottage ★★★★
Contact: Mrs Angela Richards, Priory Mews, 33A Priory Lane, Burford, Oxford OX18 4SG
T: (01993) 824252
F: (01993) 824443
E: mancott@netcomuk.co.uk

Turkey Cottage ★★★★
Contact: Cottage in the Country, Forest Gate, Frog Lane, Milton-under-Wychwood, Chipping Norton OXY 6JZ
T: (01993) 831495
F: (01993) 831095
E: cottage@cottageinthecountry.co.uk
I: www.cottageinthecountry.co.uk

6 Westgate ★★★
Contact: Mrs Helen Harrison, Northgate, Shipton Court, Shipton-under-Wychwood, Oxford OX7 6DG
T: (01993) 830202
F: (01993) 830202

SHOREHAM-BY-SEA
West Sussex

140 Old Fort Road ★★★★
Contact: Mr Richard Harris, Windmill Lodge, Vicarage Lane, Rottingdean, Brighton BN2 7HD
T: (01273) 308779
F: (01273) 390211
E: brightoncottages@pavilion.co.uk

SHORTGATE
East Sussex

White Lion Farm Cottages ★★★
Contact: Mrs Diana Green, White Lion Farm, Shortgate, Halland, Lewes BN8 6PJ
T: (01825) 840288
F: (01825) 840288

SHORWELL
Isle of Wight

Cheverton Farm Cottage & Brummell Barn
Rating Applied For
Contact: Mrs Sheila Hodgson, Cheverton Farm, Cheverton Shute, Shorwell, Newport PO30 3JE
T: (01983) 741017
F: (01983) 741017

Marylands ★★★
Contact: Mrs Honor Vass, The Old Vicarage, Kingston, Wareham BH20 5LH
T: (01929) 480080
F: (01929) 481070
E: enq@islandcottageholidays.com
I: www.islandcottageholidays.com

Sandfoot ★★★★
Contact: Mrs Honor Vass, The Old Vicarage, Kingston, Wareham BH20 5LH
T: (01929) 480080
F: (01929) 481070
E: enq@islandcottageholidays.com
I: www.islandcottageholidays.com

Stone Place Cottage ★★★
Contact: Ms Lisa Baskill, 31 Pier Street, Ventnor PO38 1SX
T: (01983) 854340
F: (01983) 855524

SIDLESHAM
West Sussex

Cloverlands Cottage ★★★
Contact: Mrs Diana Pound, Cloverlands Cottage, Chalder Lane, Sidlesham, Chichester PO20 7RJ
T: (01243) 641243
F: (01243) 641243

Lackers ★★★★
Contact: Mrs Alison Bickmore, 307 Upland Road, East Dulwich, London SE22 0DL
T: (020) 8693 7385
E: alibick@aol.com

Little Durley ★★★★
Contact: Ms Deborah Clark, Durley, Selsey Road, Sidlesham, Chichester PO20 7LS
T: (01243) 641858
F: (01243) 641231

Tombrec ★★
Contact: Mrs Christine Morris, The Old Bakery, Mill Lane, Sidlesham, Chichester PO20 7LZ
T: (01243) 641379
F: (01243) 641129
E: chris_morris@onetel.net.uk
I: www.tombrec.com

SIDLESHAM COMMON
West Sussex

Lockgate Dairy Cottages ★★★★
Contact: Mrs Jean Buchanan, Lockgate Road, Sidlesham Common, Chichester PO20 7QH
T: (01243) 641452
F: (01243) 641452
E: buchanan.j@virgin.net

SIXPENNY HANDLEY
Dorset

Summer Cottage ★★★
Contact: Miss Suzanne Harding, Stockfield House, 41 High Street, Sixpenny Handley, Salisbury SP5 5ND
T: (01725) 553161
F: (01725) 553161
E: roomreview@hotmail.com

SMARDEN
Kent

Bakehouse ★★★
Contact: Mrs Brenda Beck, Freedom Holiday Homes, 15 High Street, Cranbrook TN17 3EB
T: (01580) 720770
F: (01580) 720771
E: mail@freedomholidayhomes.co.uk
I: www.freedomholidayhomes.co.uk

The Cobbles
Rating Applied For
Contact: Mrs Brenda Beck, Freedom Holiday Homes, 15 High Street, Cranbrook TN17 3EB
T: (01580) 720770
F: (01580) 720771
E: mail@freedomholidayhomes.co.uk
I: www.freedomholidayhomes.co.uk

Dering Barn ★★★★
Contact: Mrs Brenda Beck, 15 High Street, Cranbrook TN17 3EB
T: (01580) 720770
F: (01580) 720771
E: mail@freedomholidayhomes.co.uk
I: www.freedomholidayhomes.co.uk

SOUTH CHAILEY
East Sussex

Fantasy Cottage ★★★
Contact: Mr Stuart Winter, Garden of England Cottages Ltd, The Mews Office, 189a High Street, Tonbridge TN9 1BX
T: (01732) 369168
F: (01732) 358817
E: dave@Fantasy2000.Freeserve.co.uk
I: www.gardenofenglandcottages.co.uk

SOUTH WONSTON
Hampshire

'Burwood' ★★★★
Contact: Mrs Alice Lowery, 'Burwood', 128 Downs Road, South Wonston, Winchester SO21 3EH
T: (01962) 881690
E: lowery@euphony.net

SOUTHAMPTON
Hampshire

Bridge Terrace Apartments ★★
Contact: Mr & Mrs Mike & Sue Batley, Town or Country Serviced Apartments & Houses, 60 Oxford Street, Southampton SO14 3DL
T: (023) 8088 1000
F: (023) 8088 1010
E: town@interalpha.co.uk
I: www.intent.co.uk/southampton/hotels/townorc/index.htm

Bridge Terrace Studio Apartments ★★
Contact: Mr & Mrs Mike & Sue Batley, Town or Country Serviced Apartments & Houses, 60 Oxford Street, Southampton SO14 3DL
T: (023) 8088 1000
F: (023) 8088 1010
E: town@interalpha.co.uk
I: www.intent.co.uk/southampton/hotels/townorc/index.htm

4 Canada Place ★★★
Contact: Mr & Mrs Mike & Sue Batley, Town or Country Serviced Apartments & Houses, 60 Oxford Street, Southampton SO14 3DL
T: (023) 8088 1000
F: (023) 8088 1010
E: town@interalpha.co.uk
I: www.intent.co.uk/southampton/hotels/townorc/index.htm

7 Canada Place ★★★
Contact: Mr & Mrs Mike & Sue Batley, Town or Country Serviced Apartments & Houses, 60 Oxford Street, Southampton SO14 3DL
T: (023) 8088 1000
F: (023) 8088 1010
E: town@interalpha.co.uk
I: www.intent.co.uk/southampton/hotels/townorc/index.htm

27 The Grenwich ★★★★
Contact: Mr & Mrs Mike & Sue Batley, Town or Country Serviced Apartments & Houses, 60 Oxford Street, Southampton SO14 3DL
T: (023) 8088 1000
F: (023) 8088 1010
E: town@interalpha.co.uk
I: www.intent.co.uk/southampton/hotels/townorc/index.htm

45 The Grenwich ★★★★
Contact: Mr & Mrs Mike & Sue Batley, Town or Country Serviced Apartments & Houses, 60 Oxford Street, Southampton SO14 3DL
T: (023) 8088 1000
F: (023) 8088 1010
E: town@interalpha.co.uk
I: www.intent.co.uk/southampton/hotels/townorc/index.htm

307 Imperial Apartments ★★★★
Contact: Mr & Mrs Mike & Sue Batley, Town or Country Serviced Apartments & Houses, 60 Oxford Street, Southampton SO14 3DL
T: (023) 8088 1000
F: (023) 8088 1010
E: town@interalpha.co.uk
I: www.intent.co.uk/southampton/hotels/townorc/index.htm

315 Imperial Apartments ★★★★
Contact: Mr & Mrs Mike & Sue Batley, Town or Country Serviced Apartments & Houses, 60 Oxford Street, Southampton SO14 3DL
T: (023) 8088 1000
F: (023) 8088 1010
E: town@interalpha.co.uk
I: www.intent.co.uk/southampton/hotels/townorc/index.htm

Pinewood Lodge Apartments ★★★
Contact: Dr or Mrs S W Bradberry, Pinewood Lodge Apartments, Pinewood Lodge, Kanes Hill, Southampton SO19 6AJ
T: (023) 8040 2925
E: stan.bradberry@tesco.net

STANDLAKE
Oxfordshire

Gaunt Mill Cottage & Fishermans Loft ★★★
Contact: Mrs Moira Glynn, Gaunt Mill Cottage & Fishermans Loft, Standlake, Witney OX8 7QA
T: (01865) 300227
F: (01865) 300117
E: moiraglynn@aol.com

Wheelwrights Cottage ★★★★
Contact: Mrs Nora Hunt
T: (01865) 300536
E: bobnora@huntb1.fsnet.co.uk
I: www.oxtowns.co.uk/wheelwrights

STANFORD IN THE VALE
Oxfordshire

The Paddock ★★★★
Contact: Cottage in the Country, Forest Gate, Frog Lane, Shipton-under-Wychwood, Oxford OX7 6JZ
T: (01993) 831495
F: (01993) 831095
E: cottage@cottageinthecountry.co.uk
I: www.cottageinthecountry.co.uk

STAPLE
Kent

Piglet Place ★★★★
Contact: Mr & Mrs Richard & Bronwen Barber, Greengage Cottage, Lower Road, Barnsole, Staple, Canterbury CT3 1LG
T: (01304) 813321
F: (01304) 812312

STAPLEHURST
Kent

Gardeners Cottage ★★★★
Contact: Mr Stuart Winter, Garden of England Cottages Ltd, The Mews Office, 189a High Street, Tonbridge TN9 1BX
T: (01732) 369168
F: (01732) 358817
E: holidays@gardenofenglandcottages.co.uk
I: www.gardenofenglandcottages.co.uk

6 Headcorn Road ★★
Contact: Mrs I B Maxted, 6 Headcorn Road, Staplehurst, Tonbridge TN12 0BT
T: (01580) 891219

Rose Cottage Oast ★★★
Contact: Mrs Brenda Beck, Freedom Holiday Homes, 15 High Street, Cranbrook TN17 3EB
T: (01580) 720770
F: (01580) 720771
E: mail@freedomholidayhomes.co.uk
I: www.freedomholidayhomes.co.uk

Tudor Hurst Cottage ★★★★
Contact: Mrs Brenda Beck, Freedom Holiday Homes, 15 High Street, Cranbrook TN17 3EB
T: (01580) 720770
F: (01580) 720771
E: mail@freedomholidayhomes.co.uk
I: www.freedomholidayhomes.co.uk

STEEPLE ASTON
Oxfordshire

Westfield Farm Motel ★★★
Contact: Mrs Julie Hillier, Westfield Farm Motel, Fenway, Steeple Aston, Oxford OX25 4SS
T: (01869) 340591
F: (01869) 347594
E: info@westfieldmotel.u-net.com

STOCKBRIDGE
Hampshire

7 Prospect Place ★★★
Contact: Mrs Caroline Sellick, Parfitts Farm, Chequers Lane, Eversley Cross, Hook RG27 0NT
T: (01189) 732155

STOCKBURY
Kent

The Old Dairy ★★
Contact: Mrs Anthony, Wheatsheaf Farm, Hazel Street, Stockbury, Sittingbourne ME9 7SA
T: (01622) 884222

STOKENCHURCH
Buckinghamshire

5 Gardens Close ★★★
Contact: Mrs Mary Langston, Box Tree Cottage, Postcombe, Oxford OX9 7DY
T: (01844) 281501
F: (01844) 281501

STONE-IN-OXNEY
Kent

Old Forge Cottage ★★★
Contact: Mrs Brenda Beck, Freedom Holiday Homes, 15 High Street, Cranbrook TN17 3EB
T: (01580) 720770
F: (01580) 720771
E: mail@freedomholidayhomes.co.uk
I: www.freedomholidayhomes.co.uk

STONEGATE
East Sussex

Coopers Cottage ★★★★★
Contact: Ms Jane Howard, Coopers Farm, Stonegate, Wadhurst TN5 7EH
T: (01580) 200386
E: jane@coopersfarmstonegate.co.uk
I: www.coopersfarmstonegate.co.uk

STONOR
Oxfordshire

White Pond Farm ★★★★
Contact: Mrs Lindy Stracey, White Pond Farm, Stonor, Henley-on-Thames RG9 6HG
T: (01491) 638224
F: (01491) 638428

STORRINGTON
West Sussex

Byre Cottages ★★★
Contact: Mrs Gail Kittle, Byre Cottages, Sullington Manor Farm, Sullington Lane, Storrington, Pulborough RH20 4AE
T: (01903) 745754
F: (01903) 745754
E: kittles@waitrose.com

STOWTING
Kent

Cavalry Farm ★★★
Contact: Mrs Marion Britton, Cavalry Farm, Stowting Common, Stowting, Ashford TN25 6BG
T: (01233) 750319
F: (01233) 750225

STREAT
West Sussex

The Gote Lodge ★★★
Contact: Mrs Caroline Tower, Streat, Hassocks BN6 8RN
T: (01273) 890976
F: (01273) 891656
E: thegote@amserve.com

STUDLAND
Dorset

Corner Cottage ★★
Contact: Mrs Antonia Ives, Faun's Cottage, Swanage Road, Studland, Swanage BH19 3AE
T: (01929) 450309
E: antnives@aol.com
I: www.members.aol.com/antnives

STURMINSTER NEWTON
Dorset

The Homestead ★★★
Contact: Mrs Carol Townsend, The Homestead, Hole House Lane, off Glue Hill, Sturminster Newton DT10 2AA
T: (01258) 471390
F: (01258) 471090
E: townsend@dircon.co.uk
I: www.townsend.dircon.co.uk

SWANAGE
Dorset

Alrose Villa ★★★
Contact: Mrs Jacqueline Wilson, Alrose Villa, 2 Highcliffe Road, Swanage BH19 1LW
T: (01929) 426318
E: enquiry@alrosevilla.co.uk
I: www.alrosevilla.co.uk

Ballard Lee & Ballard Ridge ★★★
Contact: Mr & Mrs Ian Lever, Old Stables, Grange Road, Stoborough, Wareham BH20 5AL
T: (01929) 551320

6 Cluny Crescent ★★★★
Contact: Ms Catherine Suttle, Miles & Son, Railway House, 2 Rempstone Road, Swanage BH19 1DW
T: (01929) 423333
F: (01929) 427533
E: info@milesandson.co.uk
I: www.milesandson.co.uk

Coastguards Return ★★★★
Contact: Mrs Anna Morrison, 6 Sunnydale Villas, Durlston Road, Swanage BH19 2HY
T: (01929) 424630
F: (01929) 424630
E: jamesrmorrison@aol.com

5 Durlston Mews ★★★★
Contact: Ms Leanne Hemingway, 11 Tyneham Close, Sandford, Wareham BH20 7BE
T: (01929) 553443
F: (01929) 552714
E: enquiries@dhcottages.co.uk
I: www.dhcottages.co.uk/durlston_mews.htm

Flat 3 Sunnybank Court ★★★
Contact: Mrs Pamela Oliver, 27 Prospect Crescent, Swanage BH19 1BD
T: (01929) 425984
E: rob@oliverr80.fsnet.co.uk

Flat 32 ★★★★
Contact: Mrs Chris Hobson, 17 Moorside Road, Corfe Mullen, Broadstone BH21 3NB
T: (01202) 696222
F: 0871 433 4879
E: mel.hobson@lds.co.uk
I: www.lds.co.uk/holidayhome

Flat 8 Sandringham Court ★★★★
Contact: Mrs Nicola Russ, 137a High Street, Swanage BH19 2NB
T: (01929) 422776
F: (01929) 422002

Forge Cottage ★★★
Contact: Ms Leanne Hemingway, 11 Tyneham Close, Sandford, Wareham BH20 7BE
T: (01929) 553443
F: (01929) 552714
E: enquiries@dhcottages.co.uk
I: www.dhcottages.co.uk

10 The Haven ★★★★
Contact: Mrs Russ, Wyke Holiday Properties, 137a High Street, Swanage BH19 2NB
T: (01929) 422776
F: (01929) 422002
E: bookings@wykeholiday.co.uk
I: www.wykeholiday.co.uk

13 The Haven ★★★★
Contact: Ms Nicky Russ, Wyke Holiday Properties, 137a High Street, Swanage BH19 2NB
T: (01929) 422776
F: (01929) 422002
E: bookings@wykeholiday.co.uk
I: www.wykeholiday.co.uk

Holiday Bungalow ★★★
Contact: Mrs Mary Brennan, 10 Hillsea Road, Swanage BH19 2QN
T: (01929) 425715
F: (01929) 425715

Island View ★★★
Contact: Mr & Mrs Jones, Island View, 19A Priests Road, Swanage BH19 2RG
T: (01929) 426614
E: ray.jones@btinternat.com

The Isles Apartments ★★-★★★
Contact: Ms P McGrath, The Pyghtle, Fleet Hill, Finchampstead, Wokingham RG40 4LJ
T: (0118) 973 3116
F: (0118) 973 3116

27 Manwell Road Rating Applied For
Contact: Mrs Jill Henstridge, 10 Moor Road, Swanage BH19 1RG
T: (01929) 427276

No 3 Exeter Road ★★★★
Contact: Mrs Anna Morrison, 6 Sunnydale Villas, Durlston Road, Swanage BH19 2HY
T: (01929) 424630
F: (01929) 424630
E: jamesrmorrison@aol.com

5 Peveril Heights ★★★
Contact: Miles & Son Chartered Surveyors, Estate Agents, Railway House, 2 Rempstone Road, Swanage BH19 1DW
T: (01929) 423333
F: (01929) 427533
E: property@milesandson.co.uk
I: www.milesandson.co.uk

Pips Cottage ★★
Contact: Mr Michael Padfield, Grubwood Lane, Cookham, Cookham Dean, Cookham, Maidenhead SL6 9UB
T: (01628) 472113
E: mike@thepadfields.com

Purbeck Cliffs ★★★★
Contact: Mrs Sue McWilliams, 3 Boundary Close, Swanage BH19 2JY
T: (01929) 424352

1B Purbeck Terrace Road ★★★
Contact: Ms Nicky Russ, Wyke Holiday Properties, 137a High Street, Swanage BH19 2NB
T: (01929) 422776
F: (01929) 422002
E: bookings@wykeholiday.co.uk
I: www.wykeholiday.co.uk

The Quarterdeck ★★★
Contact: Ms Leanne Hemingway, 11 Tyneham Close, Sandford, Wareham BH20 7BE
T: (01929) 553443
F: (01929) 552714
E: reservations@dhcottages.co.uk
I: www.purbeckholidays.co.uk

2 Quayside Court ★★
Contact: Mr Michael Padfield, Greenways, Grubwood Lane, Cookham Dean, Cookham, Maidenhead SL6 9UB
T: (01628) 472113
E: mike@thepadfields.com

St Mark's Cottage Rating Applied For
Contact: Mr David Evans, 38 Blackborough Road, Reigate RH2 7BX
T: (01737) 224441
F: (01737) 240952
E: david@asdellevans.co.uk

Sea Wall ★★★
Contact: Ms Leanne Hemingway, 11 Tyneham Close, Sandford, Wareham BH20 7BE
T: (01929) 553443
F: (01929) 552714
E: enquiries@dhcottages.co.uk
I: www.dhcottages.co.uk/sea%20wall.htm

Seaviews ★★★
Contact: Mr Robert Moon, Bryanstone Road, Talbot Woods, Bournemouth BH3 7JF
T: (01202) 513671
E: moon-enterprises@cwctv.net

Swanwic House ★★
Contact: Mrs Carole Figg, Swanwic House, 41A Kings Road, Swanwic House, Swanage BH19 1HF
T: (01929) 423517

Tanglewood ★★★★
Contact: Probert, 9 Longfield Drive, Amersham HP6 5HD
T: (01494) 721849
F: (01494) 721849
E: audrey.probert@btopenworld.com

2 Wilksworth Cottage ★★
Contact: Mr Stuart-Brown, Dream Cottages, 41 Maiden Street, Weymouth DT4 8AZ
T: (01305) 761347

SWAY
Hampshire

Dormie ★★★★★
Contact: Mr Chris Cutting, 9 Munnery Way, Orpington BR6 8QD
T: (01689) 862709
F: (01689) 862533

Hackney Park ★★★
Contact: Mrs Helen Beale, Hackney Park, Mount Pleasant Lane, Sway, Lymington SO41 8LS
T: (01590) 682049

High Bank ★★
Contact: Mr Stuart Bailey, Homefield, Silver Street, Sway, Lymington SO41 6DG
T: (01590) 682025
F: (01590) 683782
E: cottages@stuartbailey.net

4 Laurel Close ★★★★
Contact: Mrs Jacquie Taylor, Three Corners, Centre Lane, Everton, Milford-on-Sea, Lymington SO41 0JP
T: (01590) 645217
E: tommy.tiddles@virgin.net

Little Corner Cottage ★★★★
Contact: Mrs Maureen Jones, 315 Vale Road, Ash Vale, Aldershot GU12 5LN
T: (01252) 664428
E: maureengaryl@hotmail.com

The Old Exchange Rating Applied For
Contact: Mrs Sarah Alborino, Gabetti Cottage, Priestlands Lane, Pennington, Lymington SO41 8HZ
T: (01590) 679228
E: arcobaleno_1@hotmail.com

TARRANT GUNVILLE
Dorset

Underwood ★★★
Contact: Mrs Belbin, Home Farm, Tarrant Gunville, Blandford Forum DT11 8JW
T: (01258) 830208

TENTERDEN
Kent

Cromwell Cottage ★★★
Contact: Mrs Valerie Ernst, Aventine, Ingleden Park Road, Tenterden TN30 6NS
T: (01580) 762958
F: (01580) 762958
E: val@cromwellcottage.fsnet.co.uk

Meadow Cottage & Tamworth Cottage ★★★★
Contact: Mrs Cooke, Meadow Cottage & Tamworth Cottage, Great Prawls Farm, Stone in Oxney, Tenterden TN30 7HB
T: (01797) 270539
E: p.cooke.prawls@tinyworld.co.uk
I: www.prawls.co.uk

Quince Cottage ★★★★
Contact: Mrs H E Crease, Laurelhurst, 38 Ashford Road, Tenterden TN30 6LL
T: (01580) 765636
F: (01580) 765922
E: quincott@zetnet.co.uk
I: quincecottage.co.uk

44 Rogersmead ★★★★
Contact: Mrs Brenda Beck, Freedom Holiday Homes, 15 High Street, Cranbrook TN17 3EB
T: (01580) 720770
F: (01580) 720771
E: mail@freedomholidayhomes.co.uk
I: www.freedomholidayhomes.co.uk

THAME
Oxfordshire

Goldsworthy Cottage ★★★
Contact: Mrs Janet Eaton, Cuttle Cottage, 17 Southern Road, Thame OX9 2EE
T: (01844) 213035
E: janet-eaton@virgin.net
I: www.enquiries@cottageinthecountry.co.uk

The Hollies ★★★★
Contact: Ms Julia Tanner, Little Acre, 4 High Street, Tetsworth, Thame OX9 7AT
T: (01844) 281423
E: info@theholliesthame.co.uk
I: www.theholliesthame.co.uk

Honeysuckle Cottage ★★★
Contact: Mr & Mrs A Lester, Honeysuckle Cottage, Frogmore Lane, Long Crendon, Aylesbury HP18 9DZ
T: (01635) 200316

THORLEY
Isle of Wight

Holiday Homes Owners Services Ref: Y20★★★
Contact: Mr Colin Nolson, Holiday Homes Owners Services (West Wight), 18 Solent Hill, Freshwater PO40 9TG
T: (01983) 761193
F: (01983) 753423
E: holidayhomesiow@ic24.net
I: www.newclose.co.uk

Southlee ★★★★
Contact: Mr & Mrs Steve & Jill Cowley, Coast and Country, Lee Farm, Wellow, Yarmouth PO41 0SY
T: (01983) 760327
F: (01983) 760327

THREE LEGGED CROSS
Dorset

The Gables ★★★
Contact: Mr & Mrs David Priest, The Gables, Verwood Road, Three Legged Cross, Wimborne Minster BH21 6RW
T: (01202) 821322
F: (01202) 821322

TINGEWICK
Buckinghamshire

Lily Cottage ★★★
Contact: Mrs Rosemary Shahani, Carolyn Cottage, 22 Main Street, Tingewick, Buckingham MK18 4NN
T: (01280) 848047
F: (01280) 848047
E: rosemaryshahani@yahoo.co.uk

TIPTOE
Hampshire

Brockhill Farm ★★★-★★★★
Contact: Mr David Turner, Brockhill Farm, Sway Road, Tiptoe, Lymington SO41 6FQ
T: (01425) 627 457

TONBRIDGE
Kent

88 Avebury Avenue ★★★★★
Contact: Mr Ragnhild Baker, 88 Avebury Avenue, Groombridge, Royal Tunbridge Wells TN9 1TQ
T: (01732) 353298
E: charles@cgbaker.eclipse.co.uk
I: www.gardenofenglandcottages.co.uk

Goldhill Mill Cottages ★★★★★
Contact: Mr & Mrs V Cole, Goldhill Mill Cottages, Goldhill Mill, Golden Green, Tonbridge TN11 0BA
T: (01732) 851626
F: (01732) 851881
E: vernon.cole@virgin.net
I: www.goldhillmillcottages.com

High Barn Farm Cottage ★★★★
Contact: Mrs Sue Brooks, High Barn, High Barn Farm, Tonbridge Road, Tonbridge TN11 9JR
T: (01732) 832490
F: (01732) 832490

Oast Barn ★★★★
Contact: Mr Ragnhild Baker, Oast Barn, Groombridge, Royal Tunbridge Wells TN9 1TQ
T: (01732) 353298
E: charles@cgbaker.eclipse.co.uk
I: www.gardenofenglandcottages.co.uk

Postern Heath Oast ★★★
Contact: Mrs Brenda Beck, Freedom Holiday Homes, 15 High Street, Cranbrook TN17 3EB
T: (01580) 720770
F: (01580) 720771
E: mail@freedomholidayhomes.co.uk
I: www.freedomholidayhomes.co.uk

Waters Edge ★★★★
Contact: Mr Stuart Winter, Garden of England Cottages Ltd, The Mews Office, 189a High Street, Tonbridge TN9 1BX
T: (01732) 369168
F: (01732) 358817
E: holidays@gardenofenglandcottages.co.uk
I: www.gardenofenglandcottages.co.uk

TOTLAND BAY
Isle of Wight

Alum Bay House ★★
Contact: Mr Geoffrey Hurrion, Alum Bay House, Alum Bay Old Road, Totland Bay PO39 0JA
T: (01983) 754546
I: www.cottageguide.co.uk/heritageholidays

The Coach House ★★★
Contact: Mr C E Boatfield, Frenchman's Cove, Alum Bay Old Road, Alum Bay, Totland Bay PO39 0HZ
T: (01983) 752227
F: (01983) 755125
E: boatfield@frenchmanscove.co.uk

Holiday Homes Owners Services Ref: T7★★★★
Contact: Mr Colin Nolson, Holiday Homes Owners Services (West Wight), 18 Solent Hill, Freshwater PO40 9TG
T: (01983) 753423
F: (01983) 753423
E: holidayhomesiow@ic24.net

Holiday Homes Owners Services Ref: T1★★★
Contact: Mr Colin Nolson, Holiday Homes Owners Services (West Wight), 18 Solent Hill, Freshwater PO40 9TG
T: (01983) 753423
F: (01983) 753423
E: holidayhomesiow@ic24.net

Holiday Homes Owners Services Ref: T6★★★
Contact: Mr Colin Nolson, Holiday Homes Owners Services (West Wight), 18 Solent Hill, Freshwater PO40 9TG
T: (01983) 753423
F: (01983) 753423
E: holidayhomesiow@ic24.net

5 Manor Villas ★★
Contact: Ms Lisa Baskill, Home from Home Holidays, 31 Pier Street, Ventnor PO38 1SX
T: (01983) 854340
F: (01983) 855524

Nodewell House ★★★
Contact: Mrs Angela Morgan, Westways, The Mall, Colwell Bay PO39 0DS
T: (01983) 753157

Seawinds Self-Catering Bungalows
Rating Applied For
Contact: Mrs Jacquie Simmonds, Norton Lodge, Granville Road, Totland Bay PO39 0AZ
T: (01983) 752772

Stabula ★★★
Contact: Country Holidays Ref; 7311, Country Holidays, Spring Mill, Earby, Barnoldswick BB94 0AA
T: 08700 723723
F: (01282) 844288
E: sales@holidaycottagesgroup.com
I: www.country-holidays.co.uk

Stonewind Farm ★★★
Contact: Mrs Pat Hayles, Barn Cottage, Middleton, Freshwater PO40 9RW
T: (01983) 752912
F: (01983) 752912

Summers Lodge ★★★★
Contact: Mrs Honor Vass, Island Cottage Holidays, The Old Vicarage, Kingston, Wareham BH20 5LH
T: (01929) 480080
F: (01929) 481070
E: enq@islandcottagesholidays.com
I: www.cottageholidays.dmon.co.uk.

TUDELEY
Kent

Latters Farm Barn ★★★★
Contact: Mr Stuart Winter, Garden of England Cottages, The Mews Office, 189a High Street, Tonbridge TN9 1BX
T: (01732) 369168
F: (01732) 358817
E: holidays@gardenofenglandcottages.co.uk
I: www.gardenofenglandcottages.co.uk

Latters Oast ★★★★
Contact: Mr Stuart Winter, Garden of England Cottages Ltd, The Mews Office, 189a High Street, Tonbridge TN9 1BX
T: (01732) 369168
F: (01732) 358817
E: holidays@gardenofenglandcottages.co.uk
I: www.gardenofenglandcottages.co.uk

TURNWORTH
Dorset

The Old Post Office ★★★
Contact: Ms Adele Martin, Okeden House, Turnworth, Blandford Forum DT11 0EE
T: (01258) 454331
F: (01258) 454331

TWYFORD
Dorset

Buddens Farm Holidays ★★★-★★★★★
Contact: Mrs Sarah Gulliford, Buddens Farm Holidays, Buddens Farm, Twyford, Shaftesbury SP7 0JE
T: (01747) 811433
F: (01747) 811433
E: buddensfarm@eurolink.ltd.net
I: www.buddensfarm.co.uk

Embessy Cottage ★★★
Contact: Mrs Caroline Rees, Old Rectory Lane, Twyford, Winchester SO21 1NS
T: (01962) 712921
F: (01962) 712921
E: reescj@hotmail.com

UCKFIELD
East Sussex

Keen's Lodge
Rating Applied For
Contact: Mr & Mrs Bill & Sue Keen, Keen's Lodge, Little Horsted, Uckfield TN22 5TT
T: (01825) 750616

UDIMORE
East Sussex

Billingham Byre ★★★★
Contact: Mrs Nanette Hacking, Billingham Farm, Udimore, Rye TN31 6BD
T: (01424) 882348
E: hackingnan@aol.com

Devonia House ★★★★
Contact: Mr Stuart Winter, Garden of England Cottages Ltd, The Mews Office, 189a High Street, Tonbridge TN9 1BX
T: (01732) 369168
F: (01732) 358817
E: holidays@gardenofenglandcottages.co.uk
I: www.gardenofenglandcottages.co.uk

Finlay Cottage & Tibbs Bungalow ★★★★
Contact: Mr Stuart Winter, Garden of England Cottages Ltd, The Mews Office, 189a High Street, Tonbridge TN9 1BX
T: (01732) 369168
F: (01732) 358817
E: holidays@gardenofenglandcottages.co.uk
I: www.gardenofenglandcottages.co.uk

The Jays ★★★★
Contact: Mrs Brenda Beck, Freedom Holiday Homes, 15 High Street, Cranbrook TN17 3EB
T: (01580) 720770
F: (01580) 720771
E: mail@freedomholidayhomes.co.uk
I: www.freedomholidayhomes.co.uk

ULCOMBE
Kent

Kingsnorth Manor Farm ★★★★
Contact: Mrs Brenda Beck, Freedom Holiday Homes, 15 High Street, Cranbrook TN17 3EB
T: (01580) 720770
F: (01580) 720771
E: mail@freedomholidayhomes.co.uk
I: www.freedomholidayhomes.co.uk

UPCHURCH
Kent

The Old Stable ★★★
Contact: Mr Stuart Winter, Garden of England Cottages Ltd, The Mews Office, 189a High Street, Tonbridge TN9 1BX
T: (01732) 369168
F: (01732) 358817
E: holidays@gardenofenglandcottages.co.uk

UPTON
Dorset

Sandon House ★
Contact: Mrs Whittingham, Sandon House, 641-643 Blandford Road, Upton, Poole BH16 5ED
T: (01202) 622442

VENTNOR
Isle of Wight

Bay Lodge ★★★
Contact: Ms Lisa Baskill, Home from Home Holidays, 31 Pier Street, Ventnor PO38 1SX
T: (01983) 854340
F: (01983) 855524

Bush Cottage ★★★
Contact: Mrs J Clark, 27 Worsley Road, Gurnard, Cowes PO31 8JW
T: (01983) 294900

Clarence House ★★★★
Contact: Mrs Sue Lawson, Clarence House, Park Avenue, Ventnor PO38 1LE
T: (01983) 852875
F: (01983) 855006
E: c.a.c@btinternet.com
I: www.iowholidayapartments.co.uk

1 Cleeve Court ★★★
Contact: Ms Catherine Hopper, Island Holiday Homes, 177 High Street, Whitwell, Ventnor PO33 2HW
T: (01983) 616644
F: (01983) 616640
E: enquiries@island-holiday-homes.net
I: www.island-holiday-homes.net

Cliff Cottage ★★★
Contact: Ms Lisa Baskill, Home from Home Holidays, 31 Pier Street, Ventnor PO38 1SX
T: (01983) 854340
F: (01983) 855524

Cove Cottage ★★★
Contact: Ms Lisa Baskill, Home from Home Holidays, 31 Pier Street, Ventnor PO38 1SX
T: (01983) 854340
F: (01983) 855524

Daisy Cottage ★★★
Contact: Mrs Valerie Anderson, Mari Laetare, Esplanade, Ventnor PO38 1JX
T: (01983) 855189
F: (01983) 855189
E: samval@marilaetare.freeserve.co.uk

Dudley House ★★★
Contact: Mrs J Clark, 27 Worsley Road, Gurnard, Cowes PO31 8JW
T: (01983) 294900

Garfield Holiday Flats ★★★
Contact: Mrs Susan Stead, Garfield Holiday Flats, 13 Spring Gardens, Ventnor PO38 1QX
T: (01983) 854084

Gatcliff ★★★★
Contact: Ms Lisa Baskill, Home from Home Holidays, 31 Pier Street, Ventnor PO38 1SX
T: (01983) 854340
F: (01983) 855524

Glenlyn ★★★
Contact: Mr Louis Stritton, c/o Eversley Hotel, Park Avenue, Ventnor PO38 1LB
T: (01983) 852244
F: (01983) 856534
E: eversleyhotel@fsbdial.co.uk
I: www.eversleyhotel.com

Halcyon ★★★
Contact: Ms Lisa Baskill, Home from Home Holidays, 31 Pier Street, Ventnor PO38 1SX
T: (01983) 854340
F: (01983) 855524

Holiday Homes Owners Services Ref: V1 ★★★
Contact: Mr Colin Nolson, Holiday Homes Owners Services (West Wight), 18 Solent Hill, Freshwater PO40 9TG
T: (01983) 753423
F: (01983) 753423
E: holidayhomesiow@ic24.net

Ivy Cottage ★★★
Contact: Ms Lisa Baskill, Home from Home Holidays, 31 Pier Street, Ventnor PO38 1SX
T: (01983) 854340
F: (01983) 855524

Jules Cottage ★★★★
Contact: Mrs J Clark, 27 Worsley Road, Gurnard, Cowes PO31 8JW
T: (01983) 294900

Marina Apartments ★★★★
Contact: Mr Redding, Marina Apartments, Marine Parade, Ventnor PO38 1JN
T: (01983) 852802
E: information@marinaapartments.co.uk
I: www.marinaapartments.co.uk

Marula ★★★
Contact: Mrs J Clark, 27 Worsley Road, Gurnard, Cowes PO31 8JW
T: (01983) 294900

Old Park Hotel ★★★★
Contact: Mrs Sharp, Old Park Hotel, Old Park Road, St Lawrence, Ventnor PO38 1XS
T: (01983) 852583

2 Palmerston House ★★★
Contact: Mrs J Clark, 27 Worsley Road, Gurnard, Cowes PO31 8JW
T: (01983) 294900

Petit Tor ★★★
Contact: Ms Lisa Baskill, Home from Home Holidays, 31 Pier Street, Ventnor PO38 1SX
T: (01983) 854340
F: (01983) 855524

Russet Spinney ★★★
Contact: Ms Lisa Baskill, Home from Home Holidays, 31 Pier Street, Ventnor PO38 1SX
T: (01983) 854340
F: (01983) 855524

Sea Haze ★★★
Contact: Mrs J Clark, 27 Worsley Road, Gurnard, Cowes PO31 8JW
T: (01983) 294900

Seagate Lodge ★★★
Contact: Ms Julia Warr, 8 Dartmouth Park Road, London NW5 1SY
T: (0207) 485 4809

3 Seaview ★★★
Contact: Mr & Mrs Smithers, Dykebeck Farm, Wymondham NR18 9PL
T: (01953) 602477
F: (01953) 602157
E: peter@isleofwightholidays.com
I: www.isleofwightholidays.com

1 St Catherines View ★★
Contact: Ms Lisa Baskill, Home from Home Holidays, 31 Pier Street, Ventnor PO38 1SX
T: (01983) 854340
F: (01983) 855524

Stoneplace Cottage ★★★
Contact: Mrs J Clark, 27 Worsley Road, Gurnard, Cowes PO31 8JW
T: (01983) 294900

Trelawney ★★
Contact: Mrs J Clark, 27 Worsley Road, Gurnard, Cowes PO31 8JW
T: (01983) 294900

Valerian ★★★
Contact: Mrs J Clark, 27 Worsley Road, Gurnard, Cowes PO31 8JW
T: (01983) 294900

Ventnor Holiday Villas ★-★★
Contact: Mr Stephen King, Ventnor Holiday Villas, Old Fort Place (Reception), Wheelers Bay Road, Ventnor PO38 1HR
T: (01983) 852973
F: (01983) 855401
E: steve@ventnor-holidayvillas.co.uk
I: ventnor-holidayvillas.co.uk

Verbena ★★★
Contact: Mrs J Clark, 27 Worsley Road, Gurnard, Cowes PO31 8JW
T: (01983) 294900

Western Lines ★★★
Contact: Ms Lisa Baskill, Home from Home Holidays, 31 Pier Street, Ventnor PO38 1SX
T: (01983) 854340
F: (01983) 855524

Westfield Lodges ★★★
Contact: Mrs MacLean, Westfield Lodges, Shore Road, Bonchurch, Ventnor PO38 1RH
T: (01983) 852268
F: (01983) 853992
E: info@westfieldlodges.co.uk
I: www.westfieldlodges.co.uk

Woodcliffe Holiday Apartments ★★★
Contact: Mr Bryce Wilson, Woodcliffe Holiday Apartments, The Undercliffe Drive, St Lawrence, Ventnor PO38 1XJ
T: (01983) 852397
F: (01983) 852397
E: bryce.wilson@virgin.net
I: www.business.virgin.net/bryce.wilson

VERWOOD
Dorset

West Farm Lodges & West Farm Cottage ★★★
Contact: Mr & Mrs Roger & Penny Froud, West Farm, Romford, Verwood, Wimborne Minster BH31 7LE
T: (01202) 822263
F: (01202) 821040
E: west.farm@virgin.net

VINES CROSS
East Sussex

Cannon Barn ★★★★
Contact: Mrs Anne Reed, Cannon Barn, Boring House Farm, Nettlesworth Lane, Vines Cross, Heathfield TN21 9AS
T: (01435) 812285
E: info@boringhousefarm.co.uk
I: www.boringhousefarm.co.uk

WADHURST
East Sussex

Bewl Water Cottages ★★★★
Contact: Mr & Mrs Bentsen, Bewl Water Cottages, Newbarn, Wards Lane, Wadhurst TN5 6HP
T: (01892) 782042
E: bentsen@bewlwatercottages.com
I: www.bewlwatercottages.com

Old Stables ★★★
Contact: Mrs Le May, Old Stables, Ladymeads Farm, Lower Cousley Wood, Wadhurst TN5 6HH
T: (01892) 783240
F: (01892) 783240
E: camrosa.equestrian@virgin.net

WALLINGFORD
Oxfordshire

Oak Cottage ★★★★
Contact: Mr & Mrs Philip & Wendy Burton, Oak House, New Road, Wallingford OX10 0AU
T: (01491) 836200
E: pburton@dircon.co.uk

WALMER
Kent

The Coach House ★★
Contact: Mr Martin O'Neill, Rashleigh, 9a Liverpool Road, Walmer, Deal CT14 7HW
T: (01304) 239201

Cottage In Deal ★★
Contact: Mr Alan Hay, Leipziger Str 13D, 91058 Erlangen, Germany
T: 00499 131 65921
F: 00499 131 65733
E: alan.hay@t-online.de

Fisherman's Cottage ★★
Contact: Dr & Mrs Morris, 39 Dorset Road, Merton Park, London SW19 3EZ
T: (020) 8542 5086
F: (020) 8540 9443

The Gulls & Sea Watch ★★★★
Contact: Mr & Mrs Sandra & Kenneth Upton, 51 The Strand, Deal CT14 7DP
T: (01304) 371449
F: (01304) 371449
E: palmers3@freenetname.co.uk

Holm Oaks ★★★
Contact: Mrs Annie Spencer-Smith, Holm Oaks, 72 The Strand, Deal CT14 7DL
T: (01304) 367365
E: holm_oaks@hotmail.com

32 York Road ★★
Contact: Mrs Janice Twaits, 44 Mayfield Road, Chingford, London E4 7JA
T: (0208) 524 3320

WALTHAM
Kent

Springfield Cottage and Springfield Barn★★★
Contact: Mr Stuart Winter, Garden of England Cottages Ltd, The Mews Office, 189a High Street, Tonbridge TN9 1BX
T: (01732) 369168
F: (01732) 358817
E: holidays@gardenofenglandcottages.co.uk
I: www.gardenofenglandcottages.co.uk

WALTON-ON-THAMES
Surrey

Guest Wing ★★★★
Contact: Mr A R Dominy, 30 Mayfield Gardens, Walton-on-Thames KT12 5PP
T: (01932) 241223

WARBLETON
East Sussex

Well Cottage ★★★★
Contact: Mr Stuart Winter, Garden of England Cottages, The Mews Office, 189a High Street, Tonbridge TN9 1BX
T: (01732) 369168
F: (01732) 358817
E: holidays@gardenofenglandcottages.co.uk
I: www.gardenofenglandcottages.co.uk
holiday@gardenofengland cottages.co.uk

WAREHAM
Dorset

Bronte Cottage ★★★★
Contact: Mr Stuart-Brown, Dream Cottages, 41 Maiden Street, Weymouth DT4 8AZ
T: (01305) 761347

East Creech Farm House ★★★
Contact: Mrs Best, East Creech Farm House, East Creech Farm, East Creech, Wareham BH20 5AP
T: (01929) 480519
F: (01929) 481312
E: debbie.best@euphony.net
I: www.pages.euphony.net/debbie.best/holiday

WATCHFIELD
Oxfordshire

The Coach House ★★★★★
Contact: Cottage in the Country Cottage Holidays, Forest Gate, Frog Lane, Shipton-under-Wychwood, Oxford OX7 6JZ
T: (01993) 831495
F: (01993) 831095
E: info@cottageinthecountry.co.uk

WELLOW
Isle of Wight

Blakes Barn & Dairy Cottages ★★★★
Contact: Mr & Mrs Alan Milbank, Mattingley Farm, Main Road, Wellow, Yarmouth PO41 0SZ
T: (01983) 760503
F: (01983) 760503
E: i.milbank@btinternet.com

Brook Cottage & Mrs Tiggywinkles Cottage★★★★
Contact: Mrs Anne Longford, The Warren, 1 Elenors Grove, Wootton Bridge, Ryde PO33 4HE
T: (01983) 883364
F: (01983) 884980
E: anne.longford@btinternet.com
I: www.warrenholidays.com

Jubilee Villa ★★★★
Contact: Mr & Mrs Steve & Jill Cowley, Lee Farm, Wellow, Yarmouth PO41 0SY
T: (01983) 760327
F: (01983) 760327

WEST ASHLING
West Sussex

Hills Cottage ★★★★
Contact: Mrs Virginia Jack, The Thatched House, Down Street, West Ashling, Chichester PO18 8DP
T: (01243) 574382
F: 07092 217358
E: hills.cottage@btinternet.com
I: www.hillscottage.com

WEST HORSLEY
Surrey

West View ★★★
Contact: Mrs Janet Steer, West View, Shere Road, West Horsley, Leatherhead KT24 6EW
T: (01483) 284686
E: cliveandjan@aol.com

WEST LULWORTH
Dorset

Advantage Point ★★
Contact: Mr Stuart-Brown, Dream Cottages, 41 Maiden Street, Weymouth DT4 8AZ
T: (01305) 761347

Butterfly Cottage ★★
Contact: Mrs Claire Bellenis, 68 Haverstock Hill, London NW3 2BE
T: (020) 7485 6997
E: fotinibell@aol.com

Flat 2 Chestnut Court ★★★
Contact: Mrs Patricia Coulson, Laleham, The Glade, Tadworth KT20 6JE
T: (01737) 832282
E: pat.coulson@talk21.com

Villa Buena Vista ★★★
Contact: Mr Stuart-Brown, Dream Cottages, 41 Maiden Street, Weymouth DT4 8AZ
T: (01305) 761347

WEST MALLING
Kent

The Shire ★★★★
Contact: Mr & Mrs S Garrard, Manor Farm, West Malling ME19 6RE
T: (01732) 842091
F: (01732) 873784
E: barbaralambert@lineone.net

WEST MARDEN
West Sussex

Barley Cottage ★★★★
Contact: Mr & Mrs Martin Edney, West Marden Farmhouse, West Marden, Chichester PO18 9ES
T: (023) 9263 1382
E: carole.edney@btopenworld.com
I: www.barleycottage.co.uk

Laundry Cottage ★★★★
Contact: Mrs Julia Baker, Watergate House, West Marden, Chichester PO18 9EQ
T: (023) 9263 1470
F: (023) 9263 1767

The Old Stables ★★★★★
Contact: Mr & Mrs Martin Edney, West Marden Farmhouse, West Marden, Chichester PO18 9ES
T: (023) 9263 1382
E: carole.edney@btopenworld.com

WEST MELBURY
Dorset

Allans Farm Cottage ★★★★
Contact: Ms Sally Nutbeem, Allans Farm, Pitts Lane, West Melbury, Shaftesbury SP7 0BX
T: (01747) 852153
F: (01747) 852153
E: sally@eurolink.ltd.net

Lakeside Cottage ★★★
Contact: Mrs Jane Cecil, Lakeside Cottage, Incombe Farm, Compton Abbas, Shaftesbury SP7 0LZ
T: (01747) 811081
F: (01747) 812029
E: info@cecil.com

WEST MEON
Hampshire

Alma
Rating Applied For
Contact: Dr John Kelly, Alma, West Meon, Petersfield GU32 1LU
T: (01730) 829237

WEST PARLEY
Dorset

Church Farm ★★
Contact: Mr Andrew Ross, Church Farm, Church Lane, West Parley, Bournemouth BH22 8TR
T: (01202) 579515
F: (01202) 591763
E: andyross@eurolink.ltd.net
I: www.churchfarmcottages.co.uk

WEST PECKHAM
Kent

Beech Farmhouse ★★★★
Contact: Mr & Mrs H Wooldridge, Beech Farmhouse, Stan Lane, West Peckham, Maidstone ME18 5JT
T: (01622) 812360
F: (01622) 814659

WEST TYTHERLEY
Hampshire

Brightside Cottage Annexe ★★★
Contact: Mrs Barbara Wilks, Church Lane, West Tytherley, Salisbury SP5 1JY
T: (01794) 341391
F: (01794) 341775
E: bwilks@talk21.com

WEST WITTERING
West Sussex

The Breeze ★★★★
Contact: Baileys Estate Agents, 17 Short Road, West Wittering, Chichester PO20 8DY
T: (01243) 672217
F: (01243) 670100
E: info@baileys.uk.com

Brendon ★★★
Contact: Mr Michael Palmer, Greensleeves, 120 Hillside, Banstead SM7 1HA
T: (01737) 355401
E: info@wittering.info/
I: www.wittering.info/

WESTBROOK
Kent

The Cottage ★★★
Contact: Mr & Mrs R T Smith, The Cottage, 190 Canterbury Road, Westbrook, Margate CT9 5JW
T: (01843) 834545
F: (01843) 834545

WESTCOTT
Surrey

The Garden Flat ★★★★
Contact: Ms Louise Scillitoe Brown, The Garden Flat, Chartfield, Guildford Road, Westcott, Dorking RH4 3LG
T: (01306) 883838
F: (01306) 883838

WESTERHAM
Kent

The Barn at Bombers ★★★★★
Contact: Mr & Mrs Roy or Brigitte Callow, The Barn at Bombers, Bombers Farm, Westerham Hill, Cudham, Sevenoaks TN16 2JA
T: (01959) 573471
F: (01959) 540035
E: roy@bombers-farm.co.uk
I: www.bombers-farm.co.uk

WESTFIELD
East Sussex

Mashe Foldes Stable ★★★
Contact: Mr Stuart Winter, Garden of England Cottages, The Mews Office, 189a High Street, Tonbridge TN9 1BX
T: (01732) 369168
F: (01732) 358817
E: holidays@gardenofenglandcottages.co.uk
I: www.gardenofenglandcottages.co.uk

WHIPPINGHAM
Isle of Wight

Daisy Cottage ★★★★
Contact: Ms Lyn Cooper-Hall, Island Holiday Homes, Hose Rhodes Dickson, 177 High Street, Ryde PO33 2HW
T: (01983) 616644
F: (01983) 568822

WHITSTABLE
Kent

Fairway View ★★★★
Contact: Mrs Maria Hudson, 35 Cedar Road, Romford RM7 7JS
T: (01708) 766599
E: brian_hudson@novar.com

Flat 31 Grand Pavilion ★★★★
Contact: Mr Robert Gough, 1 Joy Lane, Whitstable CT5 4LS
T: (01227) 779066
F: (01227) 779066
E: bobgough57@aol.com

3 Harbour Mews ★★★★
Contact: Mr & Mrs John Kaye, 46 Marine Parade, Whitstable CT5 2BE
T: (01227) 280391
E: jkaye46@hotmail.com

38 Marine Parade
Rating Applied For
Contact: Mrs Janet Adams, 98 Northwood Road, Whitstable CT5 2HA
T: (01227) 282095
E: janetwadams@btinternet.com

4 Saxon Shore ★★★★
Contact: Mrs Bryant, 29 Summerfield Avenue, Whitstable CT5 1NR
T: (01227) 263958

Trappers End ★★★
Contact: Mrs J M Reed, 11 Woodlands Avenue, New Malden KT3 3UL
T: (020) 8942 0342
F: (020) 8942 0344
E: janette.reed07@btopenworld.com
I: www.kenttourism.co.uk/trappers

WHITWELL
Isle of Wight

Ashdale ★★★
Contact: Mr A V Woodford, Lane End Nursery Cottage, Macketts Lane, Arreton, Newport PO30 3AS
T: (01983) 865727

43 Bannock Road ★★★
Contact: Mrs Sally Morris, 1 Upper Ash Drive, Whitwell, Ventnor PO38 2PD
T: (01983) 730153

Castleview Flat
Rating Applied For
Contact: Mr Matthew White, Island Holiday Homes, 138 High Street, Ryde PO33 1TY
T: (01983) 521114

2 Farm Cottages ★★★
Contact: Mrs J Clark, 27 Worsley Road, Gurnard, Cowes PO31 8JW
T: (01983) 294900

Fossil Cottage ★★★
Contact: Mrs Honor Vass, The Old Vicarage, Kingston, Wareham BH20 5LH
T: (01929) 480080
F: (01929) 481070
E: enq@islandcottageholidays.com
I: www.islandcottageholidays.com

Greystone Cottage ★★
Contact: Mrs Steele, Mardon, 79 New Road, Sandown PO36 0AG
T: (01983) 407221

Nettlecombe Farm ★★★
Contact: Mrs Jose Morris, Nettlecombe Farm, Nettlecombe Lane, Whitwell, Ventnor PO38 2AF
T: (01983) 730783
F: (01983) 730783

The Old Dairy ★★★
Contact: Mrs Denham, Lower Dolcoppice Farm, Dolcoppice Lane, Whitwell, Ventnor PO38 2PB
T: (01983) 551445
F: (01983) 551445

Pyrmont Cottage ★★★
Contact: Hose Rhodes Dickson, Residential and Holiday Letting Agents, 177 High Street, Ryde PO33 2HW
T: (01983) 616644
F: (01983) 568822
E: rental_office@hose-rhodes-dickson.co.uk
I: island-holiday-homes.net

Sunglaze ★★★★
Contact: Mrs A M Evans, Kingsmede, Kemming Road, Whitwell, Ventnor PO38 2QX
T: (01983) 730867

Westwood ★★★★
Contact: Mr Douglas Shrubsole, The Willows, 2 Waddon Way, Croydon CR0 4HU
T: (020) 8686 1120
F: (020) 8686 1120

Whitwell Station ★★★
Contact: Mrs Julia Carter, Old Station House, Nettlecombe Lane, Whitwell, Ventnor PO38 2QA
T: (01983) 730667
F: (01983) 730667
E: enqs@whitwellstation.co.uk
I: www.whitwellstation.co.uk

Willow Bank ★★★
Contact: Mrs Eldridge, 28 Mulgrave Road, Ealing, London W5 1LE
T: (020) 8997 7903

The Wing, Dean Farm ★★★★
Contact: Mrs Honor Vass, The Old Vicarage, Kingston, Wareham BH20 5LH
T: (01983) 730236
F: (01983) 730202
E: enq@islandcottageholidays.com
I: www.islandcottageholidays.com

WICKHAM
Hampshire

Meonwood Annexe ★★★
Contact: Mrs Susan Wells, Meonwood, Heath Road, Wickham, Fareham PO17 6JZ
T: (01329) 834130
F: (01329) 834380

WILMINGTON
East Sussex

Old Inn House ★★★★
Contact: Mrs Annette Whamond, Old Inn House, The Street, Wilmington, Polegate BN26 5SN
T: (01323) 871331
F: (01323) 871331
E: awhamond@netscape.net
I: www.tourismsoutheast.com/member/webpages/M0302.htm

WIMBORNE MINSTER
Dorset

Hillberry ★
Contact: Mr & Mrs P L Cheyne, Hillberry, Blandford Road, Corfe Mullen, Wimborne Minster BH21 3HF
T: (01202) 658906

Millstream ★★★★
Contact: Mrs Mary Ball, 59 Oakwood Avenue, Beckenham BR3 6PT
T: (020) 8663 6426
E: millstream@oakwood59.freeserve.co.uk

Owls Lodge ★★★
Contact: Miss Mary King, Hope Farm, Holtwood, Gaunts Common, Wimborne Minster BH21 7DU
T: (01258) 840239
E: kinger@owls-lodge.freeservenet.co.uk

WINCHELSEA
East Sussex

Greyfriars
Rating Applied For
Contact: Mrs N Haynes, Greyfriars, Friars Road, Winchelsea TN36 4ED
T: (01797) 226745
F: (01797) 226749

WINCHELSEA BEACH
East Sussex

Tamarix ★★★
Contact: Mr & Mrs Miller, Sanderlings, Plovers Barrows, Buxted, Uckfield TN22 4JP
T: (01825) 732034

WINCHESTER
Hampshire

147 Alresford Road ★★★
Contact: Mrs Madeline Lawless, 26 Minden Way, Winchester SO22 4DT
T: (01962) 853650

87 Christchurch Road
Rating Applied For
Contact: Mrs Elisabeth Peacocke, 87 Christchurch Road, St Cross, Winchester SO23 9QY
T: (01962) 854902
F: (01962) 843458
E: peacockes@hotmail.com

Flat 7 Kingsway Court ★★
Contact: Mr Peter Bulmer, Flat 14 Kingsway Court, Kingsway Gardens, Chandlers Ford, Eastleigh SO53 1FG
T: (023) 8025 3159

Gyleen ★★★★★
Contact: Mr & Mrs Paul Tipple, 9 Mount View Road, Olivers Battery, Winchester SO22 4JJ
T: (01962) 861918
F: 08700 542801
E: pauliz@tipple.demon.co.uk
I: www.cottageguide.co.uk/gyleen

Little Acres ★★★
Contact: Mrs Joy Welch, Kennel Lane, Littleton, Winchester SO22 6PT
T: (01962) 882295
F: (01892) 882295

Mallard Cottage ★★★
Contact: Mrs Tricia Simpkin, Mallard Cottage, 64 Chesil Street, Winchester SO23 0HX
T: (01962) 853002
F: (01962) 853002
E: mallardsimpkin@aol.com
I: www.geocities.com/mallardcottageuk

Milnthorpe ★★★★★
Contact: Mrs Alison Dudgeon, Milnthorpe, Sleepers Hill, St Cross, Winchester SO22 4NF
T: (01962) 850440
F: (01962) 890114
E: alison@milnthorpehouse.deamon.co.uk
I: alison@milnthorpehouse.demon.co.uk

18 Swanmore Close ★★
Contact: Mrs Carole Wilkins, 18 Swanmore Close, Harestock, Winchester SO22 6LX
T: (01962) 883341

WINDSOR
Berkshire

Castle Mews Apartment ★★★
Contact: Miss Mary George, Woodbank, The Knotts, Watermillock, Penrith CA11 0JP
T: 07811 175706
F: (01768) 486355
E: info@lakedistrict-cottages.com

9 The Courtyard ★★★
Contact: Mrs Hitchcock, 1 Agar's Place, Datchet, Slough SL3 9AH
T: (01753) 545005
F: (01753) 545005
E: jhhitchcock@btinternet.com

Flat 6 The Courtyard ★★★
Contact: Mr Gavin Gordon, 5 Temple Mill Island, Marlow SL7 1SG
T: (01628) 824267
F: (01628) 828949
E: gavingordon@totalise.co.uk

House in the Courtyard
Rating Applied For
Contact: Mrs Eva Brooks, Belmont House, 64 Bolton Road, Windsor SL4 3JL
T: (01753) 860860
F: (01753) 830330

Manor View Apartment ★★★
Contact: Mrs Clare Smith, 32 Matthews Chase, Binfield, Bracknell RG42 4UR
T: (01344) 485658
E: manorview@care4free.net
I: www.manorview.care4free.net

Oak Cottage ★★★★
Contact: Miss Mary George, Woodbank, The Knotts, Watermillock, Penrith, Penrith CA11 0JP
T: 07811 175706
F: (01768) 486355
E: info@lakedistrict-cottages.com

Riverviewaccommodation ★★★★
Contact: Mrs Janet Noakes, Riverviewaccommodation, 7 Stovell Road, Windsor SL4 5JB
T: (01753) 863628

Wisteria & Gardeners Bothy
Rating Applied For
Contact: Mr Peter Smith & Sarah Everitt, Wisteria & Gardeners Bothy, The Old Place, Lock Path, Dorney, Windsor SL4 6QQ
T: (01753) 827037
F: (01753) 855022
E: sarah@pjsmith.co.uk
I: www.pjsmith.co.uk

WINGHAM
Kent

Charolais Cottages ★★★★
Contact: Mr & Mrs Pagdin, Staple Road, Wingham, Canterbury CT3 1LU
T: (01227) 720082
F: (01227) 720082
E: info@pagoast.co.uk
I: www.pagoust.co.uk

WINTERBORNE WHITECHURCH
Dorset

3 Rose Cottages ★★★
Contact: Mrs Anne Macfarlane, Barn Court, West Street, Winterborne Kingston, Blandford Forum DT11 9AX
T: (01929) 471612
F: (01929) 472293
E: rosecottages5137@aol.com
I: www.cottageguide.co.uk/rose.cottage

WITCHAMPTON
Dorset

The Old Exchange ★★★★
Contact: Mr & Mrs Martin & Carol Smith, The Old Exchange, c/o High Lea Cottage, Witchampton Lane, Witchampton, Wimborne Minster BH21 5AF
T: (01258) 840809
E: msmithhighlea@aol.com
I: www.heartofdorset.easynet.co.uk

WITNEY
Oxfordshire

Gleann Cottages ★★★
Contact: Mr S Murtagh, Gleann Cottages, Northfield Farm, Woodstock Road, Witney OX8 6UH
T: (01993) 778007
F: (01993) 775957
I: www.cottageguide.co.uk/gleanncottages

Little Barn ★★★★
Contact: Mrs Harrison, Little Barn, c/o Stable Barn, New Yatt Road, Witney OX29 6TA
T: (01993) 706632
F: (01993) 706689
I: info@stablebarn.co.uk

Melrose Villa & Mews ★★★
Contact: Mrs Susan Petty, 74 Corn Street, Witney OX28 6BS
T: (01993) 703035
F: (01993) 771014
E: petty@witneyserve.net

Sighs Cottage ★★
Contact: Mr Peter Crowther, 11 Bridge Street, Witney OX28 1BY
T: (01993) 709596
F: (01993) 709596
E: pjccrowth@hotmail.com

Swallows Nest ★★★★
Contact: Mrs Janet Strainge, Springhill Farm Bed & Breakfast, High Cogges, Witney OX29 6UL
T: (01993) 704919
E: jan@strainge.fenet.co.uk

WOOBURN TOWN
Buckinghamshire

Magnolia House ★★★
Contact: Mr Alan Ford, Magnolia House, Grange Drive, Wooburn Green, Wooburn Town, High Wycombe HP10 0QD
T: (01628) 525818
F: (01628) 810367
E: sales@lanford.co.uk

WOODCHURCH
Kent

The Stable ★★★★
Contact: Mrs Carol Vant, The Stable, Coldblow Lodge, Woodchurch, Ashford TN26 3PH
T: (01233) 860388
F: (01233) 860388
E: carol.vant@btinternet.com
I: www.thestablecottage.co.uk

Tuckers Farm
Rating Applied For
Contact: Mrs Bernadette Restorick, Warehorne, Woodchurch, Ashford TN26 2ER
T: (01233) 733433
F: (01233) 733700
E: prestorick@aol.com

WOODLANDS
Dorset

Meadow Cottage
Rating Applied For
Contact: Mrs Pamela Brickwood, Meadow Cottage, Horton Road, Woodlands, Wimborne Minster BH21 8NB
T: (01202) 825002

Purlins ★★★
Contact: Mrs Kay Lindsell, Purlins, 159 Woodlands Road, Woodlands, Southampton SO40 7GL
T: (023) 8029 3833
F: (023) 8029 3855
E: Kay@purlins.net
I: www.purlins.net

WOODMANCOTE
West Sussex

Woodhouse Cottages ★★★
Contact: Mrs Jane Cragg, Old School House, Church Lane, Pyecombe, Brighton BN45 7FE
T: (01273) 846011
F: (01273) 846011
E: jane.cragg@virgin.net

WOODNESBOROUGH
Kent

Sonnet Cottage ★★
Contact: Mrs Brenda Beck, Freedom Holiday Homes, 15 High Street, Cranbrook TN17 3EB
T: (01580) 720770
F: (01580) 720771
E: mail@freedomholidayhomes.co.uk
I: www.freedomholidayhomes.co.uk

WOOLSTONE
Oxfordshire

Cartwheel Cottage
Rating Applied For
Contact: Mrs A K Walker, Cartwheel Cottage, Oxleaze Farm, Woolstone, Faringdon SN7 7QS
T: (01367) 820116
F: (01367) 820116
E: ridgewayholidays@amserve.net

WOOTTON
Kent

Captains & Colonels ★★★
Contact: Mrs Brenda Beck, Freedom Holiday Homes, 15 High Street, Cranbrook TN17 3EB
T: (01580) 720770
F: (01580) 720771
E: mail@freedomholidayhomes.co.uk
I: www.freedomholidayhomes.co.uk

WOOTTON BRIDGE
Isle of Wight

Alpine Cottage ★★★
Contact: Mrs Honor Vass, Island Cottage Holidays, The Old Vicarage, Kingston, Wareham BH20 5LH
T: (01929) 480080
F: (01929) 481070
E: enq@islandcottagesholidays.com
I: www.islandcottageholidays.com

The Barn ★★★★
Contact: Ms Lisa Baskill, Home from Home Holidays, 31 Pier Street, Ventnor PO38 1SX
T: (01983) 854340
F: (01983) 855524

Grange Farm ★★★
Contact: Mrs Rosemarie Horne, Grange Farm, Staplers Road, Wootton, Wootton Bridge, Ryde PO33 4RW
T: (01983) 882147

The Hayloft ★★★★
Contact: Ms Lisa Baskill, Home from Home Holidays, 31 Pier Street, Ventnor PO38 1SX
T: (01983) 854340
F: (01983) 855524

The Hayloft & New Barn Cottage ★★★★
Contact: Mrs Honor Vass, Island Cottage Holidays, Godshill Park Farm House, Godshill, Wroxall, Ventnor PO38 3JF
T: (01929) 480080
F: (01929) 481070
E: enq@islandcottagesholidays.com
I: www.cottageholidays.dmon.co.uk.

The Orangery ★★★
Contact: Mrs Honor Vass, The Old Vicarage, Kingston, Wareham BH20 5LH
T: (01929) 480080
F: (01929) 481070
E: enq@islandcottagesholidays.com
I: www.islandcottageholidays.com

West Wing Westwood House ★★★
Contact: Mrs Honor Vass, The Old Vicarage, Kingston, Wareham BH20 5LH
T: (01929) 480080
F: (01929) 481070
E: enq@islandcottageholidays.com
I: www.islandcottageholidays.com

Wootton Keepers Cottage ★★★
Contact: Mrs Honor Vass, Island Cottage Holidays, The Old Vicarage, Kingston, Wareham BH20 5LH
T: (01929) 480080
F: (01929) 481070
E: enq@islandcottageholidays.com
I: www.islandcottageholidays.com

WORTH MATRAVERS
Dorset

Drovers Cottage ★★★★
Contact: Mrs Ann Cockerell, Weston Farm Cottage, Worth Matravers, Swanage BH19 3LJ
T: (01929) 439254
F: (01929) 439254
E: drovers@worthmatravers.freeserve.com
I: www.drovers-cottage.co.uk

One London Row ★★★
Contact: Mr & Mrs Philip & Monica Sanders, 54 Hillway, Highgate, London N6 6EP
T: (020) 8348 9815
F: (020) 8347 7124
E: info@philamonic.com
I: www.philamonic.com

WORTHING
West Sussex

Aldine House ★★★
Contact: Mr & Mrs Hills, 311 South Farm Road, Worthing BN14 7TL
T: (01903) 266980
E: hills.aldine@supanet.com

12 Byron Road ★★
Contact: Mr Robert Brew, Promenade Holiday Homes, 165 Dominion Road, Worthing BN14 8LD
T: (01903) 201426
F: (01903) 201426

Exmoor House ★
Contact: Mr & Mrs Harrison, Exmoor House, 32 Chesswood Road, Worthing BN11 2AD
T: (01903) 208856

Flat 16 Heene Court Mansions ★★
Contact: Mr Robert Brew, Promenade Holiday Homes, 165 Dominion Road, Worthing BN14 8LD
T: (01903) 201426
F: (01903) 201426
E: robert@promhols.fsbusiness.co.uk

Flat 1A Heene Court Mansions ★★
Contact: Mr Robert Brew, Promenade Holiday Homes, 165 Dominion Road, Worthing BN14 8LD
T: (01903) 201426
F: (01903) 201426
E: robert@promhols.fsbusiness.co.uk
I: www.promenadeholidayhomes.co.uk

Flat 3 ★★
Contact: Mr Robert Brew, Promenade Holiday Homes, 165 Dominion Road, Worthing BN14 8LD
T: (01903) 201426
F: (01903) 201426

Flat 4 6 Heene Terrace ★★★★
Contact: Mr Robert Brew, Promenade Holiday Homes, 165 Dominion Road, Worthing BN14 8LD
T: (01903) 201426
F: (01903) 201426
I: www.promenadeholidayhomes.co.uk

Flat wA ★★
Contact: Mr Robert Brew, Promenade Holiday Homes, 165 Dominion Road, Worthing BN14 8LD
T: (01903) 201426
F: (01903) 201426
E: robert@promhols.fsbusiness.co.uk
I: www.promenadeholidayhomes.co.uk

Garden Flat ★★
Contact: Mr Robert Brew, Promenade Holiday Homes, 165 Dominion Road, Worthing BN14 8LD
T: (01903) 201426
F: (01903) 201426
E: robert@promhols.fsbusiness.co.uk
I: www.promenadeholidayhomes.co.uk

2 Harley Court ★★★
Contact: Mr Robert Brew, Promenade Holiday Homes, 165 Dominion Road, Worthing BN14 8LD
T: (01903) 201426
F: (01903) 201426
I: www.promenadeholidayhomes.co.uk

6 Heene Terrace ★★
Contact: Mr Robert Brew, Promenade Holiday Homes, 165 Dominion Road, Worthing BN14 8LD
T: (01903) 201426
F: (01903) 201426
E: robert@promhols.fsbusiness.co.uk
I: www.promenadeholidayhomes.co.uk

Holiday Bungalow ★★★
Contact: Mr & Mrs Graham Haynes, Bahnstrasse 59, 3008 Bern, Switzerland
T: 004131 381 1876
F: 004131 381 1876
E: grahamhaynes@tiscalinet.ch

2 Knightsbridge House ★★★
Contact: Ms Greta Paull, 35 Cheyne Avenue, South Woodford, London E18 2DP
T: (020) 8530 2336
F: (020) 8530 2336

Navarino Flat ★★★
Contact: Mrs Cynthia Hanton, Navarino Flat, 46 Navarino Road, Worthing BN11 2NF
T: (01903) 205984
F: (01903) 520620
E: chantan@cwctv.net

Park Cottage ★★★
Contact: Ms Tina Williams, 27 Madeira Avenue, Worthing BN11 2AX
T: (01903) 521091

17 Pendine Avenue ★★★
Contact: Mrs Sue Harding, 17 Pendine Avenue, Worthing BN11 2NA
T: (01903) 202833
E: sue.harding@catlover.com

Torrington Holiday Flats ★★
Contact: Mrs Elsden & Mary Fitzgerald
T: (01903) 238582
F: (01903) 230266

WROXALL
Isle of Wight

Appuldurcombe Holiday Cottages ★★★-★★★★
Contact: Mrs Jane Owen, Appuldurcombe Holiday Cottages, Appuldurcombe Road, Wroxall, Ventnor PO38 3EW
T: (01983) 840188
F: (01983) 840188
I: www.appuldurcombe.co.uk

The Brewhouse & Stable Cottage ★★★
Contact: Mrs Felcity Corry, Little Span Farm, Rew Lane, Wroxall, Ventnor PO38 3AU
T: (01983) 852419
F: (01983) 852419
E: info@spanfarm.co.uk
I: www.spanfarm.co.uk

Clevelands House Rating Applied For
Contact: Mrs Nicolette Roberts, Clevelands House, Clevelands Road, Wroxall, Ventnor PO38 3DZ
T: (01983) 853021
F: (01983) 852340

Malmesbury Cottage ★★★★
Contact: Mrs J Clark, 27 Worsley Road, Gurnard, Cowes PO31 8JW
T: (01983) 294900

Poppies ★★★
Contact: Mrs J Clark, 27 Worsley Road, Gurnard, Cowes PO31 8JW
T: (01983) 294900

Sundown ★★★
Contact: Mrs J Clark, 27 Worsley Road, Gurnard, Cowes PO31 8JW
T: (01983) 294900

Sunflower Holiday Chalets ★
Contact: Ms Patricia Quennell, Sundance Lodge Sunflower Holiday Lodges, Clevelands Road, Wroxall, Ventnor PO38 3DZ
T: (01983) 853194

Wroxall Manor Farmhouse ★★★
Contact: Mrs Virginia Grace, Wroxall Manor Farmhouse, Manor Road, Wroxall, Ventnor PO38 3DH
T: (01983) 854033

YAPTON
West Sussex

West Cottage ★★★
Contact: Mrs Karen Blackman, Barnham Court Farm, Church Lane, Barnham, Bognor Regis PO22 0BP
T: (01243) 553223
F: (01243) 553223
E: farmoffice@btinternet.com

YARMOUTH
Isle of Wight

Alma Cottage ★★★★
Contact: Mr Matthew White, Island Holiday Homes, 138 High Street, Newport PO30 1TY
T: (01983) 521114

Holiday Homes Owners Services Ref: Y21★★★
Contact: Mr Colin Nolson, Holiday Homes Owners Services (West Wight), 18 Solent Hill, Freshwater PO40 9TG
T: (01983) 753423
F: (01983) 753423
E: holidayhomesiow@ic24.net

Holiday Homes Owners Services Ref: Y11★★★★
Contact: Mr Colin Nolson, Holiday Homes Owners Services (West Wight), 18 Solent Hill, Freshwater PO40 9TG
T: (01983) 753423
F: (01983) 753423
E: holidayhomesiow@ic24.net

Holiday Homes Owners Services Ref: Y18★★★
Contact: Mr Colin Nolson, Holiday Homes Owners Services (West Wight), 18 Solent Hill, Freshwater PO40 9TG
T: (01983) 753423
F: (01983) 753423
E: holidayhomesiow@ic24.net

Holiday Homes Owners Services Ref: Y15★★★
Contact: Mr Colin Nolson, Holiday Homes Owners Services (West Wight), 18 Solent Hill, Freshwater PO40 9TG
T: (01983) 753423
F: (01983) 753423
E: holidayhomesiow@ic24.net

Holiday Homes Owners Services Ref: Y17★★★
Contact: Mr Colin Nolson, Holiday Homes Owners Services (West Wight), 18 Solent Hill, Freshwater PO40 9TG
T: (01983) 753423
F: (01983) 753423
E: holidayhomesiow@ic24.net

Holiday Homes Owners Services Ref: Y3★★★
Contact: Mr Colin Nolson, Holiday Homes Owners Services (West Wight), 18 Solent Hill, Freshwater PO40 9TG
T: (01983) 753423
F: (01983) 753423
E: holidayhomesiow@ic24.net

Holiday Homes Owners Services Ref: Y6★★★★
Contact: Mr Colin Nolson, Holiday Homes Owners Services (West Wight), 18 Solent Hill, Freshwater PO40 9TG
T: (01983) 753423
F: (01983) 753423
E: holidayhomesiow@ic24.net

Holiday Homes Owners Services Ref: Y12★★★
Contact: Mr Colin Nolson, Holiday Homes Owners Services (West Wight), 18 Solent Hill, Freshwater PO40 9TG
T: (01983) 753423
F: (01983) 753423
E: holidayhomesiow@ic24.net

Holiday Homes Owners Services Ref: Y9★★★
Contact: Mr Colin Nolson, Holiday Homes Owners Services (West Wight), 18 Solent Hill, Freshwater PO40 9TG
T: (01983) 753423
F: (01983) 753423
E: holidayhomesiow@ic24.net

Holiday Homes Owners Services Ref: Y13★★★
Contact: Mr Colin Nolson, Holiday Homes Owners Services (West Wight), 18 Solent Hill, Freshwater PO40 9TG
T: (01983) 753423
F: (01983) 753423
E: holidayhomesiow@ic24.net

Holiday Homes Owners Services Ref: Y5★★★
Contact: Mr Colin Nolson, Holiday Homes Owners Services (West Wight), 18 Solent Hill, Freshwater PO40 9TG
T: (01983) 753423
F: (01983) 753423
E: holidayhomesiow@ic24.net

Holiday Homes Owners Services Ref: Y8★★★
Contact: Mr Colin Nolson, Holiday Homes Owners Services (West Wight), 18 Solent Hill, Freshwater PO40 9TG
T: (01983) 753423
F: (01983) 753423
E: holidayhomesiow@ic24.net

Portside, Sail Loft Annexe, Sail Loft and Starboard★★★
Contact: Mr John Brady, Manor House, Church Hill, Totland Bay PO39 0EU
T: (01983) 754718

Prosper Cottage ★★★
Contact: Mrs Susan Robinson, The Loft, High Street, Yarmouth PO41 0PL
T: (01983) 760987
F: (01983) 760245

River Cottage ★★★★
Contact: Mr Nigel Howell, River Cottage, Station Road, Yarmouth PO41 0QX
T: (01983) 760553
F: (01983) 760553
E: nigel@isle-wight.co.uk
I: www.isle-wight.co.uk

The Excellence in England awards 2004

The Excellence in England Awards are all about blowing English tourism's trumpet and telling the world what a fantastic place England is to visit, whether it's for a day trip, a weekend break or a fortnight's holiday.

The Awards, now in their 15th year, are run by VisitBritain in association with England's regional tourist boards. This year there are 12 categories including B&B of the Year, Hotel of the Year and Visitor Attraction of the Year and an award for the best tourism website.

Winners of the 2004 awards will receive their trophies at an event to be held on Thursday 22nd April 2004 followed by a media event to be held on St George's Day (23 April) in London. The day will celebrate excellence in tourism in England.

The winners of the 2003 Excellence in England Self-Catering Holiday of the Year Award are:

Gold winner over 50 bedrooms:
Park Hall Country Cottages, St Osyth, Nr Clacton-on-Sea, Essex
Silver winners:
Barnacre Cottages, Barnacre, Garstang, Preston, Lancashire
Bruern Stable Cottages, Chipping Norton, Oxfordshire

For more information about the Excellence in England Awards visit
www.visitengland.com

Safeway
EXCELLENCE IN ENGLAND

Marketing **English** Tourism
VISIT BRITAIN™

www.visitengland.com

What makes the perfect break? Big city buzz or peaceful country panoramas? Take a fresh look at England and you may be surprised that everything is here on your very own doorstep. Where will you go? Make up your own mind and enjoy England in all its diversity.

Experience....*remember paddling on sandy beaches, playing Poohsticks in the forest, picnics at open-air concerts, tea-rooms offering home-made cakes........*

Discover....*make your own journey of discovery through England's cultural delights: surprising contrasts between old and new, traditional and trend-setting, time-honoured and contemporary........*

Explore....*while you're reading this someone is drinking in lungfuls of fresh air on a hill-side with heart-stopping views or wandering through the maze that can be the garden of a stately home or tugging on the sails of a boat skimming across a lake....*

Relax....*no rush to do anything or be anywhere, time to immerse yourself in your favourite book by a roaring log fire or glide from a soothing massage to a refreshing facial, ease away the tension......*

To enjoy England, visitengland.com

Information

Contents

The National Quality Assurance Scheme

★ ★ ★
SELF-CATERING

RATINGS YOU CAN TRUST

Wherever you see a national rating sign, you can be sure that one of our trained impartial assessors has been there before you, checking the place on your behalf - and will be there again, because every place with a national rating is assessed annually.

The Star ratings reflect the quality that you're looking for when booking accommodation. All properties have to meet an extensive list of minimum requirements to take part in the scheme. From there, increased levels of quality apply. For instance, you'll find acceptable quality at One Star, good to very good quality at Three Star and exceptional quality at Five Star establishments.

Quite simply, the more Stars, the higher the overall level of quality you can expect to find. Establishments at higher rating levels also have to meet some additional requirements for facilities.

Minimum entry requirements include the following:

- High standards of cleanliness throughout
- Pricing and conditions of booking made clear
- Local information to help you make the best of your stay
- Comfortable accommodation with a range of furniture to meet your needs
- Colour television (where signal available) at no extra charge
- Kitchen equipped to meet all essential requirements

The brief explanation of the Star ratings outlined below show what is included at each rating level.

• ONE STAR

An acceptable overall level of quality with adequate provision of furniture, furnishings and fittings.

• TWO STAR
(in addition to what is provided at ONE STAR):

A good overall level of quality. All units self-contained.

• THREE STAR
(in addition to what is provided at ONE and TWO STAR):

A good to very good overall level of quality with good standard of maintenance and decoration. Ample space, good quality furniture. All double beds have access from both sides. Microwave.

• FOUR STAR
(in addition to what is provided at ONE, TWO and THREE STAR):

An excellent overall level of quality with very good care and attention to detail throughout. Access to a washing machine and drier if not provided in the unit, or a 24-hour laundry service.

• FIVE STAR
(in addition to what is provided at ONE, TWO, THREE and FOUR STAR):

An exceptional overall level of quality with high levels of decor, fixtures and fittings with personal touches. Excellent standards of management, efficiency and guest services.

The rating awarded to an establishment is a reflection of the overall standard, taking everything into account. It is a balanced view of what is provided and, as such, cannot acknowledge individual areas of excellence. Quality ratings are not intended to indicate value for money. A high quality product can be over-priced; a product of modest quality, if offered at a low price, can represent good value. The information provided by the quality rating will enable you to determine for yourself what represents good value for money.

ALL ASSESSED

All holiday homes listed in this guide have been assessed or are awaiting assessment under VisitBritain's national quality assurance standard. The ratings in the accommodation entries were correct at the time of going to press but are subject to change.

An information leaflet giving full details of VisitBritain's national quality assurance standard - which also covers hotels, motels, guesthouses, inns, B&Bs, farmhouses, motorway lodges and caravans, chalets and camping parks - is available from any Tourist Information Centre.

AWAITING CONFIRMATION OF RATING

At the time of going to press some establishments featured in this guide had not yet been assessed for their rating for the year 2004 and so their new rating could not be included. These are indicated as 'Rating Applied For'.

For your information, the most up-to-date information regarding these establishments' ratings is in the listings pages at the back of this guide.

General **Advice** and **Information**

MAKING A BOOKING

When enquiring about accommodation, make sure you check prices and other important details. You will also need to state your requirements, clearly and precisely - for example:

- **Arrival and departure dates,** with acceptable alternatives if appropriate.
- **The accommodation you need.**
- **Number of people in your party,** and the ages of any children.
- **Special requirements,** such as ground-floor bathroom, garden, cot.

Booking by letter

Misunderstandings can easily happen over the telephone, so we strongly advise you to confirm your booking in writing if there is time.

Please note that VisitBritain does not make reservations - you should write direct to the accommodation.

PRICES

The prices shown in Where to Stay 2004 are only a general guide; they were supplied to us by proprietors in summer 2003. Remember, changes may occur after the guide goes to press, so we strongly advise you to check prices when you book your accommodation.

Prices are shown in pounds sterling and include VAT where applicable. The prices shown are per unit per week.

Also remember that prices may be higher in summer and during school holidays, and lower in the autumn, winter and spring.

DEPOSITS

When you book your self-catering holiday, the proprietor will normally ask you to pay a deposit immediately, and then to pay the full balance before your holiday date.

The reason for asking you to pay in advance is to safeguard the proprietor in case you decide to cancel at a late stage, or simply do not turn up. He or she may have turned down other bookings on the strength of yours, and may find it hard to re-let if you cancel.

CANCELLATIONS

Legal contract

When you accept accommodation that is offered to you, by telephone or in writing, you enter a legally binding contract with the proprietor.

This means that if you cancel your booking, fail to take up the accommodation or leave early, you will probably forfeit your deposit, and may expect to be charged the balance at the end of the period booked if the place cannot be re-let.

You should be advised at the time of the booking of what charges would be made in the event of cancelling the accommodation or leaving early. If this does not happen you should ask, to avoid any further disputes. Where you have already paid the full amount before cancelling, the proprietor is likely to retain the money. If the accommodation is re-let, the proprietor will make a refund, normally less the amount of the deposit.

And remember, if you book by telephone and are asked for your credit card number, you should check whether the proprietor intends charging your credit card account should you later cancel your reservation. A proprietor should not be able to charge your credit card account with a cancellation unless he or she has made this clear at the time of your booking and you have agreed.

However, to avoid later disputes, we suggest you check with the proprietor whether he or she intends to charge your credit card account if you cancel.

Insurance

There are so many reasons why you might have to cancel your holiday, which is why we strongly advise people to take out a cancellation insurance policy. In fact, many self-catering agencies now insist their customers take out a policy when they book their holiday.

Code of Conduct

The operator/manager is required to observe the following Code of Conduct:

- To maintain standards of guest care, cleanliness, and service appropriate to the type of establishment;
- To describe accurately in any advertisement, brochure, or other printed or electronic media, the facilities and services provided;
- To make clear to visitors exactly what is included in all prices quoted for accommodation, including taxes, and any other surcharges. Details of Charges for additional services/facilities should also be made clear;
- To give a clear statement of the policy on cancellations to guests at the time of booking i.e. by telephone, fax, email as well as information given in a printed format;
- To adhere to, and not to exceed prices quoted at the time of booking for accommodation and other services;
- To advise visitors at the time of booking, and subsequently of any change, if the accommodation offered is in an unconnected annexe or similar, and to indicate the location of such accommodation and any difference in comfort and/or amenities from accommodation in the establishment;
- To give each visitor, on request, details of payments due and a receipt, if required;
- To deal promptly and courteously with all enquiries, requests, bookings and correspondence from visitors;
- Ensure complaint handling procedures are in place and that complaints received are investigated promptly and courteously and that the outcome is communicated to the visitor;
- To give due consideration to the requirements of visitors with special needs, and to make suitable provision where applicable;
- To provide public liability insurance or comparable arrangement and to comply with applicable planning, safety and other statutory requirements;
- To allow a VisitBritain representative reasonable access to the establishment, on request, to confirm the Code of Conduct is being observed.

COMMENTS AND COMPLAINTS

Information

The proprietors themselves supply the descriptions of their establishments and other information for the entries (except VisitBritain Ratings and Awards). They have all signed a declaration that their information conforms to the Trade Description Acts 1968 and 1972.

VisitBritain cannot guarantee the accuracy of information in this guide, and accepts no responsibility for any error or misrepresentation.

All liability for loss, disappointment, negligence or other damage caused by reliance on the information contained in this guide, or in the event of bankruptcy or liquidation or cessation of trade of any company, individual or firm mentioned, is hereby excluded.

We strongly recommend that you carefully check prices and other details when you book your accommodation.

Problems

Of course, we hope you will not have cause for complaint, but problems do occur from time to time.

If you are dissatisfied with anything, make your complaint to the management immediately. Then the management can take action at once to investigate the matter and put things right. The longer you leave a complaint, the harder it is to deal with it effectively.

In certain circumstances, VisitBritain may look into complaints. However, VisitBritain has no statutory control over establishments or their methods of operating. VisitBritain cannot become involved in legal or contractual matters or in seeking financial compensation.

If you do have problems that have not been resolved by the proprietor and which you would like to bring to our attention, please write to: Quality Standards Department, VisitBritain, Thames Tower, Black's Road, Hammersmith, London W6 9EL.

About the **Guide Entries**

ENTRIES

All the acommodation featured in this guide has been assessed or has applied for assessment under VisitBritain's quality assurance standard. Assessment automatically entitles establishments to a listing in this guide. Additionally proprietors may pay to have their establishment featured in either a Standard Entry (includes description, facilities and prices) or Enhanced Entry (photographs and extended details).

LOCATIONS

Places to stay are listed under the town, city or village where they are located. If a place is out in the countryside, you may find it listed under a nearby village or town.

Town names are listed alphabetically within each regional section of the guide, along with the name of the county or unitary authority they are in (see note on page 678), and their map reference.

MAP REFERENCES

These refer to the colour location maps at the front of the guide. The first figure shown is the map number, the following letter and figure indicate the grid reference on the map.

Only place names under which Standard or Enhanced entries (see above) are included appear on the maps.

Some entries were included just before the guide went to press, so they do not appear on the maps.

ADDRESSES

County names, which appear in the town headings, are not repeated in the entries. When you are writing, you should of course make sure you use the full address and postcode.

PRICES

The prices shown are only a general guide; they were supplied to us by proprietors in summer 2003. A number of establishments have included in their enhanced entry information about any special offers, short breaks, etc. that are available. Please see page 663 for further details about prices.

OPENING PERIOD

If an entry does not state 'Open All Year' please check opening period with the establishment.

SYMBOLS

The at-a-glance symbols included at the end of each entry show many of the facilities and equipment available at each place. You will find the key to these symbols on the back-cover flap. Open out the flap and you can check the meanings of the symbols as you go.

SMOKING

Some places prefer not to accommodate smokers, and in such cases the accommodation entry makes this clear.

PETS

Many places accept guests with dogs, but we do advise that you check this when you book, and ask if there are any extra charges or rules about exactly where your pet is allowed. The acceptance of dogs is not always extended to cats, and it is strongly advised that cat owners contact the establishment well in advance. Some establishments do not accept pets at all. Pets are welcome where you see this symbol .

The quarantine laws have changed in England, and a Pet Travel Scheme (PETS) is currently in operation. Under this scheme pet dogs and cats are able to come into Britain from over 50 countries via certain sea, air and rail routes into England.

Dogs and cats that have been resident in these countries for more than six months may enter the UK under the Scheme, providing they are accompanied by the appropriate documentation. Pet dogs and cats from other countries will still have to undergo six months' quarantine.

For dogs and cats to be able to enter the UK without quarantine under the PETS Scheme they will have to meet certain conditions and travel with the following documents: the official PETS certificate, a certificate of treatment against tapeworm and ticks and a declaration of residence.

A European Regulation on the movement of pet animals will apply from 3 July 2004. Broadly, the rules of PETS will continue to apply to dogs and cats entering the UK but certain other pet animals will also be included.

For details of participating countries, routes, operators and further information about the PETS scheme and the new EU Regulations please contact the PETS Helpline, DEFRA (Department for Environment, Food and Rural Affairs), 1a Page Street, London SW1P 4PQ
Tel: +44 (0) 870 241 1710
Fax: +44 (0) 20 7904 6834
Email: pets.helpline@defra.gsi.gov.uk, or visit their website at www.defra.gov.uk/animalh/quarantine.

CREDIT AND CHARGE CARDS

The credit and charge cards accepted by an establishment are listed in the entry following the letters CC.

If you do plan to pay by card, check that the establishment will take your card before you book.

Some proprietors will charge you a higher rate if you pay by credit card rather than cash or cheque. The difference is to cover the percentage paid by the proprietor to the credit card company.

If you are planning to pay by credit card, you may want to ask whether it would, in fact, be cheaper to pay by cheque or cash. When you book by telephone, you may be asked for your credit card number as 'confirmation'. But remember, the proprietor may then charge your credit card account if you cancel your booking. See under Cancellations on page 664.

Welcome *to* Excellence

Look out for the Welcome to Excellence sign – a commitment to achieve excellence in customer care

Displaying this logo signifies that the business aims to exceed visitor needs and expectations, and provides an environment where courtesy, helpfulness and a warm welcome are standard.

Their house is **your home**

Owners and agencies offering holiday homes in this guide want you to enjoy your holiday so please make yourself at home – but do also remember that it is someone else's property.

Here are a few tips to ensure a smooth-running, problem-free holiday:

Allow plenty of time for your journey but please do not arrive at the property before the stated time – and please leave by the stated time. This enables the owner to make sure everything is ready for you and for whoever follows you.

If you've booked for, say, six people please don't turn up with more.

Do respect the owner's rules on pets – if, for example, one small pet is allowed please don't take a Great Dane.

Do report any damages or breakages immediately (and offer the cost of repair), so that the owner can ensure everything is in order for the next letting.

Do leave the place clean and tidy – no dirty dishes in the sink, please – and all the furniture back where it was when you arrived.

Despite the best endeavours of the owners and agents, problems can occur from time to time. If you are dissatisfied in any way with your holiday home, please give the owner or agent a chance to put matters right by letting them know immediately.

Distance Chart

The distances between towns on the chart below are given to the nearest mile, and are measured along routes based on the quickest travelling time, making maximum use of motorways or dual-carriageway roads. The chart is based upon information supplied by the Automobile Association.

To calculate the distance in kilomet[res] multiply the mileage by 1.6

For example: Brighton to Dover 82 miles x 1.6 =131.2 kilometres

	Aberdeen	Aberystwyth	Barnstaple	Birmingham	Brighton	Bristol	Cambridge	Cardiff	Carlisle	Carmarthen	Dorchester	Dover	Edinburgh	Exeter	Fort William	Glasgow	Gloucester	Guildford	Hereford	Holyhead	Hull	Inverness	Kendal	Leeds	Lincoln	Liverpool	Maidstone	Manchester	Middlesbrough	Newcastle	Northampton	Norwich	Nottingham	Oxford	Penzance	Perth	Peterborough	Plymouth	Portsmouth	Preston	Salisbury	Sheffield	Shrewsbury	Southampton	Stoke-on-Trent	Stranraer	Taunton	Wick	York
Aberystwyth	472
Barnstaple	608	214
Birmingham	436	124	180
Brighton	613	288	210	171
Bristol	518	130	100	90	169
Cambridge	463	215	267	97	120	170
Cardiff	537	111	128	109	202	44	203
Carlisle	236	236	371	199	376	281	256	300
Carmarthen	520	48	190	172	264	107	266	68	284
Dorchester	600	206	94	172	119	62	184	120	364	182
Dover	587	326	272	208	82	205	124	239	381	301	200
Edinburgh	126	336	471	299	476	381	333	400	100	386	463	458
Exeter	593	198	44	165	178	84	259	113	356	175	57	248	455
Fort William	156	435	570	398	576	480	456	499	199	485	562	580	137	554
Glasgow	150	332	467	295	472	377	353	396	96	382	459	477	47	451	102
Gloucester	484	113	126	56	155	36	150	63	248	125	118	192	346	110	445	343
Guildford	571	224	175	128	44	106	96	139	335	201	97	97	433	150	532	430	99
Hereford	487	79	144	59	189	54	153	59	250	85	136	225	349	129	448	346	34	133
Holyhead	464	102	339	167	345	249	259	202	228	150	331	369	326	323	425	323	215	302	156
Hull	376	227	320	139	258	230	138	250	170	311	312	262	247	304	367	266	196	239	198	218
Inverness	106	496	631	459	637	541	517	561	260	546	623	641	157	616	66	176	507	595	510	488	430
Kendal	283	189	324	153	330	234	251	254	47	240	316	354	145	309	245	143	200	288	203	181	164	307
Leeds	329	173	301	120	262	211	146	230	123	224	293	271	200	285	321	219	177	220	179	165	59	383	110
Lincoln	388	199	275	98	216	185	95	205	182	267	246	220	258	260	379	277	151	173	154	204	44	441	176	74
Liverpool	362	110	272	101	278	182	193	202	126	158	264	302	224	257	324	222	148	236	151	102	128	386	79	74	139
Maidstone	545	284	234	166	50	167	82	200	339	262	161	41	416	209	537	435	153	58	186	327	220	599	313	231	178	261
Manchester	357	134	261	89	266	171	160	190	120	184	253	290	219	245	318	216	136	224	139	125	97	380	74	44	85	34	248
Middlesbrough	276	244	357	176	318	267	197	286	95	294	349	322	146	341	283	190	232	276	235	235	89	308	84	64	122	145	280	114
Newcastle	235	275	388	207	349	298	229	317	60	325	380	353	106	372	242	153	264	307	266	266	142	267	102	95	154	176	311	145	39
Northampton	486	174	212	56	133	115	56	162	249	224	159	155	348	196	447	345	79	90	111	217	152	509	203	136	94	151	113	139	189	220
Norwich	488	278	329	160	168	233	63	266	282	328	241	172	359	313	480	378	212	160	215	321	147	542	276	174	103	240	130	185	223	254	118
Nottingham	395	162	232	51	193	142	86	161	189	223	224	210	266	216	387	285	107	151	110	178	93	449	164	77	39	112	168	71	130	161	64	119
Oxford	510	160	170	68	109	73	82	107	274	169	115	146	373	154	472	370	48	67	81	242	190	534	228	174	132	176	107	164	227	258	44	146	102
Penzance	702	308	108	274	287	193	368	222	466	284	167	357	564	109	663	562	220	259	238	434	415	726	419	403	370	367	318	356	451	482	326	433	326	265
Perth	86	388	523	351	529	433	378	453	152	438	515	503	42	507	102	64	399	486	401	379	291	114	199	245	303	278	461	275	192	150	400	404	310	426	617
Peterborough	435	204	263	86	158	173	37	193	229	255	204	162	306	248	427	325	139	115	142	225	110	489	223	121	51	159	120	132	170	201	45	78	58	86	357	351
Plymouth	633	239	62	205	218	124	299	153	397	215	98	288	495	44	594	493	151	190	169	365	346	657	350	334	301	298	249	287	382	413	257	364	257	196	78	544	288
Portsmouth	596	244	162	154	53	125	137	158	360	220	73	141	458	132	558	456	118	45	152	328	276	620	314	260	215	262	102	250	313	344	130	204	188	85	241	508	157	172
Preston	326	146	281	110	287	191	209	211	89	197	273	311	188	266	287	185	157	245	160	138	122	349	43	69	134	36	269	35	103	139	159	235	121	184	375	237	180	306	270
Salisbury	549	184	118	121	90	52	145	98	313	160	39	160	411	93	511	409	72	62	105	281	261	573	267	244	202	215	121	203	298	329	115	212	173	70	203	461	165	134	44	223
Sheffield	397	166	272	91	233	182	122	201	161	263	264	247	236	256	359	257	148	191	150	157	66	421	115	38	47	79	205	39	100	131	104	148	45	142	366	309	93	297	228	73	212
Shrewsbury	417	75	220	48	226	130	140	111	181	110	212	250	279	205	379	277	96	184	52	105	162	441	135	119	124	65	208	71	190	221	98	203	87	123	314	329	129	245	209	92	161	88
Southampton	578	225	142	135	66	106	136	140	342	201	53	152	440	111	539	437	100	49	133	309	258	601	295	241	199	243	113	232	294	325	111	204	169	67	221	489	157	152	20	252	23	209	191
Stoke-on-Trent	392	112	220	48	226	130	140	150	156	211	212	250	254	205	353	251	96	184	99	123	129	415	109	93	91	57	208	46	164	195	98	172	54	123	314	303	99	245	209	66	161	50	38	191
Stranraer	235	342	477	305	482	387	363	406	106	392	469	487	132	461	181	86	352	440	355	333	276	261	153	229	288	232	445	229	201	163	354	388	295	380	571	149	333	502	466	195	418	267	287	447	261
Taunton	560	165	50	132	160	51	226	80	323	142	45	224	422	34	521	419	77	126	96	291	272	583	277	261	228	225	185	213	309	340	183	291	184	123	144	471	215	75	114	234	70	224	172	94	172	429
Wick	207	597	732	560	738	642	618	662	361	647	724	742	258	716	166	277	608	695	610	588	531	104	408	484	543	487	700	484	409	367	609	644	550	635	826	215	589	757	721	451	673	523	542	702	516	362	684
York	323	201	314	133	275	224	154	243	116	251	306	279	193	298	314	212	189	233	192	192	38	376	91	24	79	102	237	71	51	89	146	180	87	184	408	239	125	339	269	96	254	57	146	251	120	223	265	477
LON[DON]	550	239	216	121	54	120	59	153	314	215	125	78	413	200	512	410	102	31	136	282	186	574	268	201	143	216	39	204	254	285	68	118	129	56	310	462	86	241	75	225	85	169	163	77	161	420	167	675	211

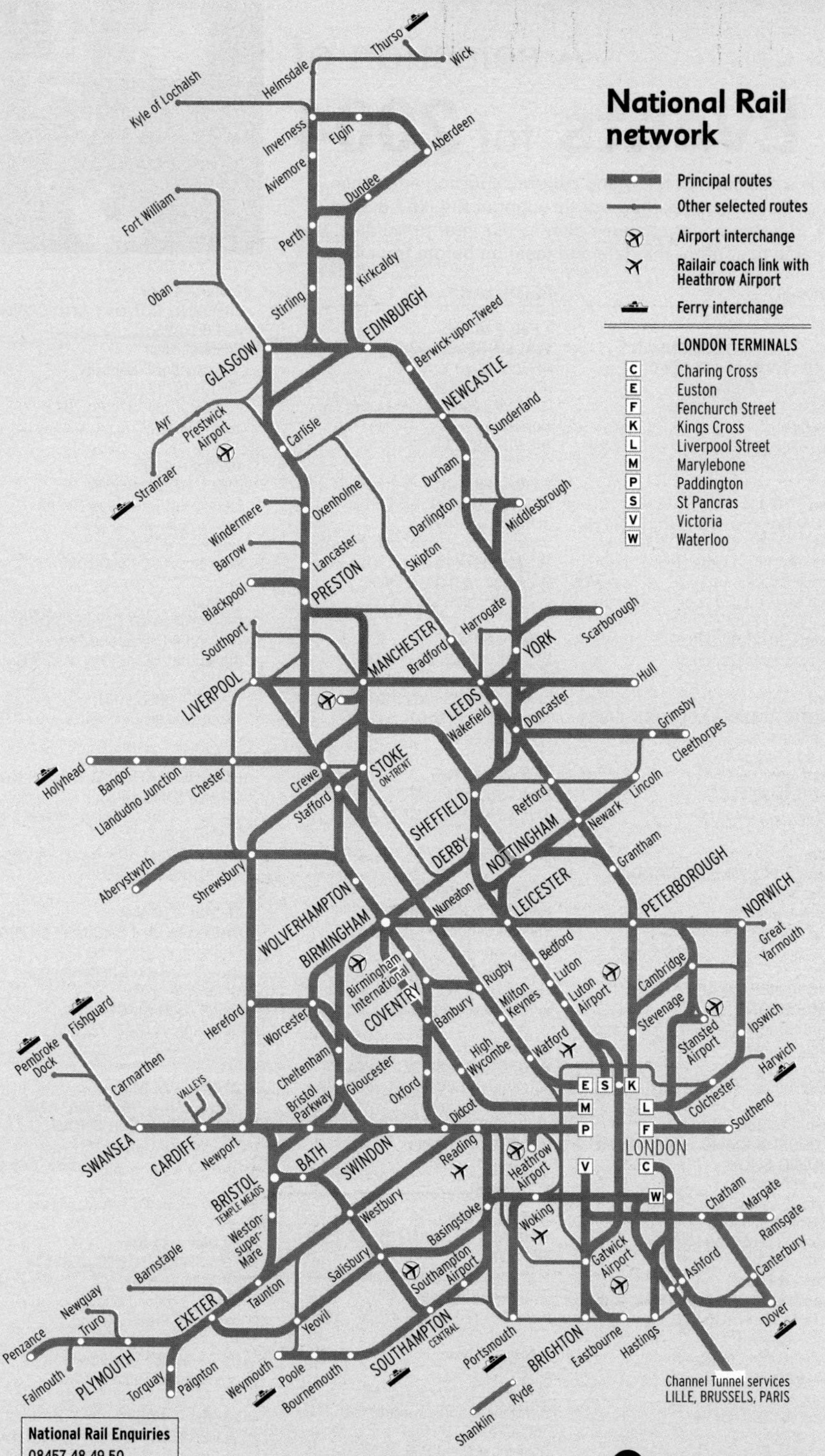

National Rail Enquiries
08457 48 49 50
www.nationalrail.co.uk

© ATOC 2000. All rights reserved. MCD/BAJS-2S 11/00

National Rail

03/NRE/1216

A selection of Events for 2004

This is a selection of the many cultural, sporting and other events that will be taking place throughout England during 2004. Please note, as changes often occur after press date, it is advisable to confirm the date and location before travelling.

JANUARY

11 Jan
LANCASTER OLD CALENDAR WALKS - NEW YEAR'S EVE
John O'Gaunt Gateway
Lancaster Castle, Lancaster, Lancashire
Tel: (01524) 32878
www.lancaster.gov.uk

17 Jan – 18 Jan
PIGEON RACING: BRITISH HOMING WORLD SHOW OF THE YEAR
Winter Gardens, Opera House and Empress Ballroom
Church Street, Blackpool, Lancashire
Tel: (01452) 713529
Bookings: (01253) 292029
www.pigeonracing.com

18 Jan
ANTIQUE AND COLLECTORS' FAIR
Alexandra Palace and Park
Alexandra Palace Way, Wood Green, London
Tel: (020) 8883 7061
www.allypally-uk.com

25 Jan
CHARLES I COMMEMORATION
Banqueting House
Whitehall, London
Tel: (01430) 430695

25 Jan
CHINESE NEW YEAR CELEBRATIONS
Gerrard Street, Leicester Square and Trafalgar Square
London
www.chinatownchinese.com

25 Jan – 26 Jan
THE CHESHIRE AND LANCASHIRE WEDDING SHOW
Tatton Park (NT)
Knutsford, Cheshire
Tel: (01625) 534400
Bookings: (01625) 534400

29 Jan – 8 Feb
WAKEFIELD RHUBARB TRAIL AND FESTIVAL OF RHUBARB
Various venues
Wakefield, West Yorkshire
Tel: (01924) 305911
Bookings: (01924) 305911
www.wakefield.gov.uk

FEBRUARY

1 Feb – 28 Feb
WALSINGHAM ABBEY SNOWDROP WALKS
Walsingham Abbey Grounds
Little Walsingham, Walsingham, Norfolk
Tel: (01328) 820259

1 Feb – 29 Feb*
JORVIK VIKING FESTIVAL – JOLABLOT 2004
Various venues throughout York
Tel: (01904) 643211
Bookings: (01904) 543402
www.vikingjorvik.com

6 Feb – 8 Feb
BIC WEDDING EXHIBITION
Bournemouth International Centre
Exeter Road, Bournemouth, Dorset
Tel: (01202) 456501
www.bic.co.uk

14 Feb – 28 Feb
KING'S LYNN MART TUESDAY MARKET PLACE
King's Lynn, Norfolk
Tel: (01508) 471772

20 Feb – 21 Feb
RALLYE SUNSEEKER
Various Venues
Bournemouth
Tel: (020) 8773 3404
Bookings: (020) 8773 3404
www.rallyesunseeker.co.uk

28 Feb – 6 Mar
BEDFORDSHIRE FESTIVAL OF MUSIC, SPEECH AND DRAMA
Corn Exchange
St Paul's Square, Bedford
Tel: (01234) 354211

MARCH

2 Mar – 7 Mar
FINE ART AND ANTIQUES FAIR
Olympia
Hammersmith Road, London
Tel: 0870 736 3105
Bookings: 0870 739 31054

4 Mar – 7 Mar
CRUFTS 2004
National Exhibition Centre
Birmingham, West Midlands
Tel: (020) 7518 1069
Bookings: 0870 909 4133
www.crufts.org.uk

7 Mar – 4 Apr
LAMBING SUNDAY AND SPRING BULB DAYS
Kentwell Hall
Long Melford, Sudbury
Tel: (01787) 310207
Bookings: (01787) 310207
www.kentwell.co.uk

10 Mar – 4 Apr
IDEAL HOME SHOW
Earls Court Exhibition Centre
Warwick Road, London
Tel: 0870 606 6080
Bookings: 0870 606 6080

14 Mar
ANTIQUE AND COLLECTORS' FAIR
Alexandra Palace and Park
Alexandra Palace Way, Wood Green, London
Tel: (020) 8883 7061
www.allypally-uk.com

14 Mar
BESSON NATIONAL BRASS BAND CHAMPIONSHIPS
Winter Gardens, Opera House and Empress Ballroom
Church Street, Blackpool, Lancashire
Tel: (0161) 707 3638

16 Mar – 18 Mar
CHELTENHAM RACING FESTIVAL
Cheltenham Racecourse
Prestbury Park, Cheltenham, Gloucestershire
Tel: (01242) 513014
Bookings: (01242) 226226
www.cheltenham.co.uk

20 Mar – 21 Mar
AMBLESIDE DAFFODIL AND SPRING FLOWER SHOW
The Kelsick Centre
St Mary's Lane, Ambleside, Cumbria
Tel: (015394) 32252
www.ambleside-show.org.uk

20 Mar – 21 Mar
THE SHIRE HORSE SOCIETY SPRING SHOW
East of England Showground
Alwalton, Peterborough,
Tel: (01733) 234451
Bookings: (01733) 234451
www.eastofengland.co.uk

26 Mar – 4 Apr*
ULVERSTON WALKING FESTIVAL
Various Venues, Ulverston, Cumbria
Tel: (01229) 580640
www.ulverston-festivals.fsnet.co.uk/walking.htm

27 Mar – 28 Mar
THRIPLOW DAFFODIL WEEKEND
Various Venues
Thriplow, Royston, Hertfordshire
Tel: (01763) 208538
www.thriplow.org.uk

28 Mar
OXFORD AND CAMBRIDGE BOAT RACE
River Thames
London
Tel: (020) 7611 3500
www.theboatrace.org

APRIL

9 Apr
MIDDLEHAM STABLES OPEN EVENT
Middleham Key Centre, Park Lane, Middleham, Leyburn, North Yorkshire
Tel: (01969) 624500
Bookings: (01969) 624502
www.middlehamstablesopenevent.co.u

9 Apr – 12 Apr
BLICKLING CRAFT SHOW
National Trust: Blickling Hall
Blickling, Norwich
Tel: (01263) 734711
www.paston.co.uk/easternevents

9 Apr – 12 Apr
GREAT EASTER EGG HUNT QUIZ AND RE-CREATION OF TUDOR LIFE
Kentwell Hall
Long Melford, Sudbury
Tel: (01787) 310207
Bookings: (01787) 310207
www.kentwell.co.uk

10 Apr – 11 Apr*
GATESHEAD SPRING FLOWER SHOW
Gateshead Central Nurseries
Whickham Highway, Lobley Hill, Gateshead, Tyne and Wear
Tel: (0191) 433 3838
Bookings: (0191) 433 3838

12 Apr
LONDON HARNESS HORSE PARADE
Battersea Park
London
Tel: (01737) 646132

12 Apr
MORRIS DANCING ON EASTER MONDAY
Various Venues
Norfolk
Tel: (01553) 768930
www.thekingsmorris.co.uk

15 Apr – 18 Apr
BRITISH OPEN SHOW JUMPING CHAMPIONSHIPS
Hallam FM Arena
Broughton Lane, Sheffield
Tel: (0114) 256 5656
Bookings: (0114) 256 5656
www.hallamfmarena.co.uk

18 Apr
FLORA LONDON MARATHON
Greenwich Park to The Mall
London
Tel: (020) 7902 0199
www.london-marathon.co.uk

22 Apr – 25 Apr
HARROGATE SPRING FLOWER SHOW
Great Yorkshire Showground
Harrogate, North Yorkshire
Tel: (01423) 561049
Bookings: (01423) 561049
www.flowershow.org.uk

29 Apr – 3 May*
CHELTENHAM INTERNATIONAL JAZZ FESTIVAL
Various venues throughout Cheltenham, Gloucestershire
Tel: (01242) 775888
Bookings: (01242) 227979
www.cheltenhamfestivals.co.uk

MAY

1 May – 3 May*
SWEEPS FESTIVAL
Various Venues
Rochester, Kent
Tel: (01634) 843666
www.medway.gov.uk/tourism

1 May – 23 May
BRIGHTON FESTIVAL
Various Venues
Brighton
Tel: (01273) 700747
Bookings: (01273) 709709
www.brighton-festival.org.uk

8 May
HELSTON FLORA DAY
Around Streets of Helston
Helston, Cornwall
Tel: (01326) 572082

9 May
ANTIQUE AND COLLECTORS' FAIR
Alexandra Palace and Park
Alexandra Palace Way, Wood Green, London
Tel: (020) 8883 7061
www.allypally-uk.com

16 May 2004
NORTHUMBRIAN WATER UNIVERSITY BOAT RACE
River Tyne
Quayside, Newcastle upon Tyne
Tel: (0191) 433 3820
www.gateshead.gov.uk

16 May – 17 May
INTERNATIONAL KITE FESTIVAL
Lower Promenade
Kingsway, Cleethorpes, North East Lincolnshire
Tel: (01472) 323352
www.nelincsevents.co.uk

20 May – 22 May
DEVON COUNTY SHOW
Westpoint Exhibition Centre
Devon County Showground, Clyst St Mary, Exeter, Devon
Tel: (01392) 446000
Bookings: (01392) 446000

25 May – 28 May
CHELSEA FLOWER SHOW
Royal Hospital Chelsea
Royal Hospital Road, Chelsea, London
Tel: (020) 7834 4333
Bookings: 0870 9063781
www.rhs.org.uk

27 May – 6 Jun*
BRITISH INTERNATIONAL MOTOR SHOW LIVE
National Exhibition Centre
Birmingham, West Midlands
Tel: (020) 7235 7000
www.motorshowlive.com

28 May – 13 Jun
BATH FRINGE FESTIVAL
Various Venues
Bath
Tel: (01225) 480079
www.bathfringe.co.uk

29 May – 31 May
CHATHAM NAVY DAYS
The Historic Dockyard Chatham
Chatham, Kent
Tel: (01634) 823800
Bookings: (01634) 403868
www.chdt.org.uk

31 May*
NORTHUMBERLAND COUNTY SHOW
Tynedale Park
Corbridge, Northumberland
Tel: (01697) 747848
Bookings: (01749) 813899
www.northcountyshow.co.uk

JUNE

Jun*
RACING AT ASCOT: THE ROYAL MEETING
Ascot Racecourse
Ascot, Berkshire
Tel: (01344) 876876
Bookings: (01344) 876876
www.ascot.co.uk

Jun*
THE MERSEY RIVER FESTIVAL
The Albert Dock
Suite 22, Edward Pavilion, Albert Dock, Liverpool, Merseyside
Tel: (0151) 233 3007

Jun*
TROOPING THE COLOUR – THE QUEEN'S BIRTHDAY PARADE
Horse Guards Parade
London
Tel: (020) 7414 2479
Bookings: (020) 7414 2479

* provisional/date not confirmed at time of going to press

2 Jun – 5 Jun
THE ROYAL BATH AND WEST SHOW
The Royal Bath and West Showground
Shepton Mallet, Somerset
Tel: (01749) 822200
Bookings: (01749) 822200
www.bathandwest.co.uk

4 Jun*
OAKS AND CORONATION CUP HORSE RACE MEETING
Epsom Downs Racecourse
Epsom Downs, Epsom, Surrey
Tel: (01372) 470047
Bookings: (01372) 470047
www.epsomderby.co.uk

4 Jun – 6 Jun
HOLKER GARDEN FESTIVAL
Holker Hall and Gardens
Cark in Cartmel, Grange-over-Sands, Cumbria
Tel: (015395) 58328
Bookings: (015395) 58328
www.holker-hall.co.uk

5 Jun*
D-DAY COMMEMORATIVE CHANNEL CROSSING
Portsmouth Harbour
Tel: (023) 9282 7261
www.portsmouthmuseums.co.uk

5 Jun*
DERBY HORSE RACE MEETING
Epsom Downs Racecourse
Epsom Downs, Epsom, Surrey
Tel: (01372) 470047
Bookings: (01372) 470047
www.epsomderby.co.uk

9 Jun – 10 Jun
CORPUS CHRISTI CARPET OF FLOWERS AND FLORAL FESTIVAL
Cathedral of Our Lady and St Philip Howard
London Road, Arundel, West Sussex
Tel: (01903) 882297
www.arundelcathedral.org

10 Jun – 12 Jun
ROYAL CORNWALL SHOW
Royal Cornwall Showground
Wadebridge, Cornwall
Tel: (01208) 812183
Bookings: (01208) 812183
www.royalcornwall.co.uk

10 Jun – 12 Jun
SOUTH OF ENGLAND AGRICULTURAL SHOW
South of England Showground
South of England Centre, Ardingly, Haywards Heath, West Sussex
Tel: (01444) 892700
Bookings: (01444) 892700
www.seas.org.uk

13 Jun
ROYAL AIR FORCE COSFORD 2004 AIR SHOW
Royal Air Force Museum, Cosford
Cosford, Shifnal, Shropshire
Tel: (01902) 376200
Bookings: (01902) 373520
www.cosfordairshow.co.uk

17 Jun – 20 Jun*
BLENHEIM PALACE FLOWER SHOW BLENHEIM PALACE
Woodstock, Oxfordshire
Tel: (01737) 379911
Bookings: (0115) 912 9188
www.bpfs2003.co.uk

17 Jun – 27 Jun
GOLOWAN FESTIVAL INCORPORATING MAZEY DAY
Various Venues
Theatre, Marquee, Street
Penzance, Cornwall
Tel: (01736) 332211
Bookings: (01736) 365520
www.golowan.com

18 Jun – 20 Jun
THE EAST OF ENGLAND COUNTRYSHOW 2004
East of England Showground
Alwalton, Peterborough,
Tel: (01733) 234451
Bookings: (01733) 234451

18 Jun – 26 Jun*
NEWCASTLE HOPPINGS
Town Moor
Grandstand Road,
Newcastle upon Tyne
Tel: (0191) 232 8520

19 Jun – 27 Jun
BROADSTAIRS DICKENS FESTIVAL
Various Venues
Broadstairs, Kent
Tel: (01843) 861827
Bookings: (01843) 861827
www.broadstairs.gov.uk/dickensfestival.html

21 Jun – 4 Jul
TENNIS: WIMBLEDON LAWN TENNIS CHAMPIONSHIPS
All England Lawn Tennis & Croquet Club
Church Road, London
Bookings: (020) 8946 2244

25 Jun – 27 Jun*
GLASTONBURY FESTIVAL
Worthy Farm
Pilton, Shepton Mallet, Somerset
Tel: (01458) 834596
Bookings: (01749) 890470
www.glastonburyfestivals.co.uk

27 Jun – 3 Jul
ALNWICK FAIR
Market Square
Alnwick, Northumberland
Tel: (01665) 711397
www.fair01.freeserve.co.uk/index.html

JULY

30 Jun – 1 Jul
ROYAL NORFOLK SHOW 2004
The Showground
New Costessey, Norwich
Tel: (01603) 748931
Bookings: (01603) 748931
www.royalnorfolkshow.co.uk

30 Jun – 4 Jul*
HENLEY ROYAL REGATTA
Henley Reach
Regatta Headquarters,
Henley-on-Thames, Oxfordshire
Tel: (01491) 572153
Bookings: (01491) 572153
www.hrr.co.uk

30 Jun – 11 Jul
WARWICK FESTIVAL
Various Venues throughout Warwick
Northgate, Warwick, Warwickshire
Tel: (01926) 410747
Bookings: (01926) 410747
www.warwickarts.org.uk

Jul*
AIRSHOW: FARNBOROUGH INTERNATIONAL 2004
Farnborough Airfield
PO Box 122, Farnborough, Hampshire
Tel: (020) 7227 1043
Bookings: (020) 7227 1043
www.farnborough.com

Jul*
FORMULA 1 BRITISH GRAND PRIX
Silverstone, Towcester, Northamptonshire
Bookings: (01327) 850260

Jul*
GOODWOOD FESTIVAL OF SPEED
Goodwood Park
Goodwood, Chichester, West Sussex
Tel: (01243) 755055
Bookings: (01243) 755055
www.goodwood.co.uk

Jul*
NETLEY MARSH STEAM AND CRAFT SHOW
Meadow Farm
Ringwood Road, Netley Marsh, Southampton
Tel: (023) 8086 7882

2 Jul – 11 Jul
YORK EARLY MUSIC FESTIVAL
Various venues, York
Tel: (01904) 645738
Bookings: (01904) 658338
www.ncem.co.uk

2 Jul – 25 Jul
GREENWICH AND DOCKLANDS INTERNATIONAL FESTIVAL
Various venues in Greenwich
Greenwich, London
Tel: (020) 8305 1818
Bookings: (020) 8305 1818
www.festival.org

3 Jul – 4 Jul
BEDFORD RIVER FESTIVAL
River Great Ouse
Ely, Cambridgeshire
Tel: (01234) 343992

3 Jul – 4 Jul
GRAND FIREWORKS CONCERT
Warwick Castle
Warwick, Warwickshire
Tel: 0870 4422000
Bookings: 0870 4422395
www.warwick-castle.co.uk

3 Jul – 4 Jul
HARTLEPOOL MARITIME FESTIVAL
Hartlepool Historic Quay
Maritime Avenue, Hartlepool, Cleveland
Tel: (01429) 523407
www.destinationhartlepool.com

3 Jul – 4 Jul*
SUNDERLAND INTERNATIONAL KITE FESTIVAL
Northern Area Playing Fields
Stephenson, Washington,
Tyne and Wear
Tel: (0191) 514 1235
www.sunderland.gov.uk/kitefestival

3 Jul – 18 Jul
ROTHERHAM WALKING FESTIVAL
Various Venues throughout the Borough of Rotherham
Rotherham, South Yorkshire
Tel: (01709) 835904
www.rotherham.gov.uk

4 Jul – 7 Jul
ROYAL SHOW
National Agricultural Centre
Stoneleigh Park, Warwickshire
Tel: (024) 7685 8276
Bookings: 0870 3666544
www.royalshow.org.uk

6 Jul – 11 Jul
HAMPTON COURT PALACE FLOWER SHOW
Hampton Court Palace
Hampton Court, East Molesey, Surrey
Tel: (020) 7649 1885
Bookings: 0870 906 3791
www.rhs.org.uk

11 Jul
GRASMERE RUSHBEARING
Grasmere Parish Church
Grasmere, Ambleside, Cumbria
Tel: (015394) 35537

13 Jul – 15 Jul
GREAT YORKSHIRE SHOW
Great Yorkshire Showground
Harrogate, North Yorkshire
Tel: (01423) 541000
Bookings: (01423) 541000
www.yas.co.uk

16 Jul – 11 Sep
THE PROMS
Royal Albert Hall
Kensington Gore, London
Tel: (020) 7765 5575
Bookings: (020) 7589 8212
www.bbc.co.uk/proms

17 Jul – 6 Aug*
THE KESWICK CONVENTION
The Convention Centre
Skiddaw Street, Keswick, Cumbria
Tel: (01435) 866034
www.keswickconvention.org

23 Jul – 25 Jul
WEYMOUTH NATIONAL BEACH VOLLEYBALL
The Beach
Weymouth, Dorset
Tel: (01305) 785747
www.weymouth.gov.uk

24 Jul
CLEVELAND SHOW
Stewart Park
The Grove, Marton, Middlesbrough, Cleveland
Tel: (01642) 312231
Bookings: (01642) 312231

24 Jul – 25 Jul*
CUMBRIA STEAM GATHERING CARK AIRFIELD
Flookburgh, Grange-over-Sands, Cumbria
Tel: (015242) 71584
Bookings: (015242) 71584

24 Jul – 26 Jul*
POTFEST IN THE PARK
Hutton-in-the-Forest
Penrith, Cumbria
Tel: (017684) 83820
www.potfest.co.uk

27 Jul – 29 Jul
NEW FOREST AND HAMPSHIRE COUNTY SHOW
The Showground, New Park,
Brockenhurst, Hampshire
Tel: (01590) 622400
Bookings: (023) 8071 1818
www.newforestshow.co.uk

30 Jul – 6 Aug
SIDMOUTH INTERNATIONAL FESTIVAL
Various venues
Sidmouth, Devon
Tel: (01296) 433669
Bookings: (01296) 433669
www.mrscasey.co.uk/sidmouth

31 Jul – 1 Aug*
GATESHEAD SUMMER FLOWER SHOW
Gateshead Central Nurseries
Whickham Highway, Lobley Hill,
Gateshead, Tyne and Wear
Tel: (0191) 433 3838
Bookings: (0191) 433 3838

AUGUST

Aug*
INTERNATIONAL BEATLES FESTIVAL
Various venues
Liverpool
Tel: (0151) 236 9091
Bookings: (0151) 236 9091
www.cavern-liverpool.co.uk

Aug*
SKANDIA LIFE COWES WEEK 2004
The Solent
Cowes, Isle of Wight
Tel: (01983) 293303

6 Aug – 8 Aug*
LOWTHER HORSE DRIVING TRIALS AND COUNTRY FAIR
Lowther Castle
Lowther Estate, Lowther, Penrith, Cumbria
Tel: (01931) 712378
Bookings: (01931) 712378
www.lowther.co.uk

6 Aug – 8 Aug*
POTFEST IN THE PENS
Skirsgill Auction Market
Skirsgill, Penrith, Cumbria
Tel: (017684) 83820
www.potfest.co.uk

7 Aug
GARSTANG SHOW
Show Field
Wyre Lane, Garstang, Preston
Tel: (01995) 603180
Bookings: (01995) 603180
www.abarnett.co.uk

* provisional/date not confirmed at time of going to press

7 Aug – 14 Aug*
BILLINGHAM INTERNATIONAL FOLKLORE FESTIVAL
Forum Theatre
Town Centre, Billingham, Cleveland
Tel: (01642) 651060
Bookings: (01642) 552663
www.billinghamfestival.co.uk

12 Aug – 15 Aug
AIRBOURNE: EASTBOURNE'S INTERNATIONAL AIR SHOW
Seafront and Western Lawns
King Edwards Parade, Eastbourne, East Sussex
Tel: (01323) 411400
www.eastbourneairshow.com

21 Aug – 27 Aug
WHITBY FOLK WEEK
Various venues
Whitby, North Yorkshire
Tel: (01757) 708424
Bookings: (01757) 708424
www.folkwhitby.freeserve.co.uk

22 Aug*
GRASMERE LAKELAND SPORTS AND SHOW SPORTS FIELD
Stock Lane, Grasmere, Ambleside, Cumbria
Tel: (015394) 32127
Bookings: (015394) 32127

28 Aug – 30 Oct
MATLOCK BATH ILLUMINATIONS AND VENETIAN NIGHTS
Derwent Gardens
Matlock Bath, Matlock, Derbyshire
Tel: (01629) 761224

29 Aug – 30 Aug
NOTTING HILL CARNIVAL
Streets around Ladbroke Grove
London
Tel: (020) 8964 0544

30 Aug
LANCASTER GEORGIAN FESTIVAL FAIR & NATIONAL SEDAN CHAIR CARRYING
Lancaster Castle Green & Priory Churchyard
Lancaster, Lancashire
Tel: (01524) 32878
www.lancaster.gov.uk

SEPTEMBER

1 Sep – 5 Sep
THE GREAT DORSET STEAM FAIR
South Down
Tarrant Hinton, Blandford Forum, Dorset
Tel: (01258) 860361
Bookings: (01258) 488928
www.steam-fair.co.uk

Sep*
GOODWOOD REVIVAL MEETING
Goodwood Motor Circuit
Goodwood, Chichester, West Sussex
Tel: (01243) 755055
Bookings: (01243) 755055
www.goodwood.co.uk

Sep*
THE ROYAL COUNTY OF BERKSHIRE SHOW
Newbury Showground
Priors Court, Hermitage, Thatcham, Berkshire
Tel: (01635) 247111
Bookings: (01635) 247111
www.newburyshowground.co.uk

3 Sep – 7 Nov
BLACKPOOL ILLUMINATIONS
Blackpool Promenade
Blackpool
Tel: (01253) 478222
www.blackpooltourism.com

4 Sep – 6 Sep
WOLSINGHAM AND WEAR VALLEY AGRICULTURAL SHOW
Scotch Isle Park
Wolsingham, Bishop Auckland, County Durham
Tel: (01388) 527862
Bookings: (01388) 527862

6 Sep – 11 Sep
SCARBOROUGH OPEN GOLF WEEK
Various venues
Scarborough, North Yorkshire
Tel: (01723) 367579
Bookings: (01723) 367579

9 Sep*
WESTMORLAND COUNTY SHOW
Westmorland County Showfield
Lane Farm, Crooklands, Milnthorpe, Cumbria
Tel: (015395) 67804
www.westmorland-county-show.co.uk

10 Sep*
35TH ANNUAL KENDAL TORCHLIGHT CARNIVAL
Kendal, Cumbria
Tel: (015395) 63018
Bookings: (015395) 63018
www.lakesnet.co.uk/kendaltorchlight

11 Sep – 12 Sep
CARAVAN EXTRAVAGANZA
The Lawns
University of Hull, Harland Way, Cottingham, East Riding of Yorkshire
Tel: (01276) 686654
www.hercma.co.uk

11 Sep – 12 Sep
MAYOR'S THAMES FESTIVAL
River Thames
London
Tel: (020) 7928 0960
Bookings:
www.ThamesFestival.org

11 Sep – 12 Sep*
THE GREAT LEEDS CASTLE BALLOON AND VINTAGE CAR WEEKEND
Leeds Castle and Gardens
Maidstone, Kent
Tel: (01622) 765400
www.leeds-castle.com

18 Sep*
RNAS YEOVILTON: INTERNATIONAL AIR DAY
RNAS Yeovilton, Ilchester, Yeovil, Somerset
Tel: 0870 800 4030
Bookings: 0870 800 4030
www.yeoviltonairday.co.uk

18 Sep – 19 Sep
MIDLAND GAME & COUNTRY SPORTS FAIR
Weston Park
Weston-under-Lizard, Shifnal, Shropshire
Tel: (01952) 852100
www.weston-park.com

24 Sep – 26 Sep
NANTWICH LOCAL FOOD AND DRINK FESTIVAL 2004
Various Venues
Nantwich, Cheshire
Tel: (01270) 610983

26 Sep
ANTIQUE AND COLLECTORS' FAIR
Alexandra Palace and Park
Alexandra Palace Way, Wood Green, London
Tel: (020) 8883 7061
www.allypally-uk.com

OCTOBER

24 Oct
TRAFALGAR DAY PARADE
Trafalgar Square
London
Tel: (020) 7928 8978

NOVEMBER

3 Nov
PORTSMOUTH BONFIRE AND FIREWORK DISPLAY
King George V Playing Field
Northern Road, Cosham, Portsmouth
Tel: (023) 9282 6722
www.portsmouthcc.gov.uk/visitor

5 Nov
BRIDGWATER GUY FAWKES CARNIVAL TOWN CENTRE
Bridgwater, Somerset
Tel: (01278) 421795
www.bridgwatercarnival.org.uk

5 Nov
TAR BARRELS
Town Centre
Ottery St Mary, Devon
Tel: (01404) 813964
www.cosmic.org.uk

5 Nov
THE CITY OF LIVERPOOL FIREWORKS DISPLAY
Sefton Park, Liverpool
Tel: (0151) 233 3007

7 Nov
VETERAN CAR RUN
Madeira Drive
Brighton, East Sussex
Tel: (01753) 765100
www.msauk.org

13 Nov
LORD MAYOR'S SHOW
City of London
Tel: (020) 7606 3030

21 Nov
ANTIQUE AND COLLECTORS' FAIR
Alexandra Palace and Park
Alexandra Palace Way, Wood Green, London
Tel: (020) 8883 7061
www.allypally-uk.com

27 Nov – 28 Nov
THE BIRMINGHAM TATTOO
National Indoor Arena
King Edwards Road, Birmingham, West Midlands
Tel: (0118) 930 3239
Bookings: 0870 909 4144
www.telinco.co.uk/maestromusic

DECEMBER

16 Dec – 20 Dec 2004
OLYMPIA INTERNATIONAL SHOWJUMPING CHAMPIONSHIPS
Olympia
Hammersmith Road, London
Tel: (020) 7370 8206
Bookings: (020) 7370 8206
www.olympia-show-jumping.co.uk

* provisional/date not confirmed at time of going to press

VisitBritain's Where to Stay Self-Catering Holiday Homes 2004

Published by: VisitBritain, Thames Tower, Black's Road, Hammersmith, London W6 9EL

Publishing Manager: Michael Dewing

Production Manager: Iris Buckley

Compilation, Design & Production: Jackson Lowe Marketing, www.jacksonlowe.com

Typesetting: Tradespools Ltd, Somerset and Jackson Lowe Marketing, Lewes

Maps: © Maps in Minutes™ (1999)

Printing and Binding: Mozzon Giutina S.p.A, Florence and Officine Grafiche De Agostini S.p.A, Novara

Advertisement Sales: Jackson Lowe Marketing, 173 High Street, Lewes, East Sussex BN7 1YE.
(01273) 4874487

©**VisitBritain** (except where stated)

ISBN 0 7095 7755 9

IMPORTANT:
The information contained in this guide has been published in good faith on the basis of information submitted to VisitBritain by the proprietors of the premises listed, who have paid for their entries to appear. VisitBritain cannot guarantee the accuracy of the information in this guide and accepts no responsibility for any error or misrepresentation. All liability for loss, disappointment, negligence or other damage caused by reliance on the information contained in this guide, or in the event of bankruptcy, or liquidation, or cessation of trade of any company, individual or firm mentioned, is hereby excluded. Please check carefully all prices and other details before confirming a reservation.

PICTURE CREDITS:

Front Cover: Orion Holidays, South Cerney, Heart of England **Back Cover: (Top)** Mill House, Somerton, South West **(Bottom)** Culver Cottage, Amberley, South East

Cumbria: Cumbria Tourist Board

Northumbria: Northumbria Tourist Board, Graeme Peacock, Mike Kippling, Colin Cuthbert and Michael Busselle

North West: North West Tourist Board, Chessire County Council, Lancashire County Council, Marketing Mancheste

Yorkshire: Yorkshire Tourist Board

Heart of England: Heart of England Tourist Board

East of England: East of England Tourist Board

South West: South West Tourism

South East England: Tourism South East, Peter Titmuss, Chris Cove-Smith, Chris Parker and Iris Buckley

National Accessible Scheme **Self-Catering Index**

Establishments taking part in the National Accessible Scheme are listed below. Listings in blue have a detailed entry in the regional sections. Use the Town Index at the back of the guide to find the page numbers of their full entries.

MOBILITY Level 1

Abberley, Worcestershire - Old Yates Cottages
Alnwick, Northumberland - Village Farm
Ambleside, Cumbria - The Larches
Ashburton, Devon - Wooder Manor Holiday Homes
Atherstone, Warwickshire - Hipsley Farm Cottages
Bailey, Cumbria - Bailey Mill
Bakewell, Derbyshire
- Haddon Grove Farm Cottages
Bath, Bath and North East Somerset
- Greyfield Farm Cottages
Beaminster, Dorset - Stable Cottage
Bettiscombe, Dorset - Conway Bungalow
Beverley, East Riding of Yorkshire
- Rudstone Walk Country Accommodation
Bicester, Oxfordshire
- Pimlico Farm Country Cottages
Bolton, Cumbria - Glebe Hayloft and Glebe Stable
Bosley, Cheshire - The Old Byre
Bradworthy, Devon - Lympscott Farm Holidays
Bridgwater, Somerset
- Ash-Wembdon Farm Cottages
Buckland in the Moor, Devon - Pine Lodge
Caldbeck, Cumbria - Monkhouse Hill
Castle Acre, Norfolk - Cherry Tree Cottage
Chapel Amble, Cornwall - The Olde House
Chichester, West Sussex - Cornerstones
Clitheroe, Lancashire - Higher Gills Farm
Colyford, Devon - Whitwell Farm Cottages
Craven Arms, Shropshire - Upper Onibury Cottages
Cressbrook, Derbyshire - Cressbrook Hall Cottages
Crosthwaite, Cumbria - Greenbank
Darley Dale, Derbyshire
- Nether End c/o Nether Hall
Dilham, Norfolk - Dairy Farm Cottages
Dorking, Surrey - Bulmer Farm
Dulverton, Somerset - Northmoor House & Lodge
Farnham, Surrey - High Wray
Foxley, Norfolk - Moor Farm Stable Cottages
Framlingham, Suffolk - Boundary Farm
Gainford, Durham - East Greystone Farm Cottages
Grassington, North Yorkshire - The Barn
Harrogate, North Yorkshire
- Brimham Rocks Cottages
Hartgrove, Dorset - Hartgrove Farm
Hereford, Herefordshire - Anvil Cottage
Horning, Norfolk
- Horning Lodges 1,2,3, Kates & Lady Lodge & Eagle Cottage
Horsington, Lincolnshire - Wayside Cottage
Kilmersdon, Somerset - The Creamery
Lavenham, Suffolk - The Rector's Retreat
Ledbury, Herefordshire - The Old Kennels Farm
Little Dewchurch, Herefordshire - The Granary
Little Tarrington, Herefordshire - Stock's Cottage
Looe, Cornwall - Bocaddon Holiday Cottages
Maltby le Marsh, Lincolnshire
- Yew Tree Cottage and The Granary
Middleton-in-Teesdale, Durham
- Hyland View and The Hideaway
Middlewich, Cheshire - Forge Mill Farm Cottages
Moretonhampstead, Devon - Budleigh Farm
Ogwell, Devon - Rydon Ball
Old Brampton, Derbyshire
- Chestnut Cottage and Willow Cottage
Oundle, Northamptonshire - Oundle Cottage Breaks
Pateley Bridge, North Yorkshire
- Helme Pasture, Old Spring Wood
Pickering, North Yorkshire
- Beech Farm Cottages
- Easthill Farm House and Gardens
- Keld Head Farm Cottages
Plymouth, Devon - Haddington House Apartments
Portreath, Cornwall - Trengove Farm Cottages
Potterne, Wiltshire - Abbotts Ball Farm
Reepham, Norfolk - Rookery Farm
Sandwich, Kent - The Old Dairy
Sawley, North Yorkshire - Lacon Hall Cottages
Shanklin, Isle of Wight - Laramie
Sibton, Suffolk - Bluebell, Bonny, Buttercup & Bertie
Sleights, North Yorkshire - Groves Dyke
Smardale, Cumbria - Leases
Stanford Bridge, Worcestershire - The Riseling
Staveley, Cumbria - Avondale
Stoke-on-Trent, Staffordshire - Jay's Barn
Stoven, Suffolk
- Stringers Woodlands, Wood Farm Stables & Dairy
Telford, Shropshire - Church Farm Cottages
Thorpe Bassett, North Yorkshire
- The Old Post Office
Truro, Cornwall - Trenerry Lodge
Whitbourne, Herefordshire
- Crumplebury Farmhouse
Wildboarclough, Cheshire - Lower House Cottage
Windermere, Cumbria - Beaumont
Wisbech, Cambridgeshire - Common Right Barns
Woodhall Spa, Lincolnshire - Mill Lane Cottage
Yapham, East Riding of Yorkshire
- Wolds View Holiday Cottages
York, North Yorkshire - York Lakeside Lodges Ltd

MOBILITY Level 2

Abbotsbury, Dorset - Gorwell Farm Cottages
Ashbourne, Derbyshire - Dove Farm
Ashburton, Devon - Wooder Manor Holiday Homes

Ashover, Derbyshire - Holestone Moor Barns
Barnstaple, Devon - Country Ways
Bath, Bath and North East Somerset
- Church Farm Country Cottages
Beaminster, Dorset - Lewesdon Farm Holidays
Beckley, East Sussex
- The Herdsman & The Blacksmith's Cottage
Beeston, Norfolk - Holmdene Farm
Bicester, Oxfordshire
- Pimlico Farm Country Cottages
Bispham, Blackpool - Burbage Holiday Lodge
Buckden, North Yorkshire
- Dalegarth and The Ghyll Cottages
Bridgnorth, Shropshire - Bulls Head Cottages
Bolton Abbey, North Yorkshire
- The Beamsley Project
Butterton, Staffordshire - Swainsley Farm
Cawood, North Yorkshire - Cawood Holiday Park
Chew Magna, Bath and North East Somerset
- Woodbarn Farm Cottages
Church Stretton, Shropshire - Botvyle Farm
Commondale, North Yorkshire - Fowl Green Farm
Coniston, Cumbria - Red Dell Cottage
Cotton, Suffolk - Coda Cottages
Craster, Northumberland - Craster Pine Lodges
Craven Arms, Shropshire
- Swallows Nest and Robin's Nest
Diss, Norfolk - Norfolk Cottages Malthouse Farm
Exeter, Devon - Coach House Farm
Farnham, Surrey - High Wray
Froghall, Staffordshire - Foxtwood Cottages
Gainford, Durham - East Greystone Farm Cottages
Gillingham, Dorset - Top Stall
Hadleigh, Suffolk - Stable Cottages
Hallow, Worcestershire - The New Cottage
Halwill, Devon - Anglers Paradise
Harrogate, North Yorkshire
- Brimham Rocks Cottages
Hartgrove, Dorset - Hartgrove Farm
Hartington, Derbyshire
- Dairy Cottage,Piggery Pl,Shire's Rs
Horham, Suffolk - Alpha Cottages
Horning, Norfolk
- Hall Farm Cottages
- Horning Lodges 1,2,3, Kates & Lady Lodge & Eagle Cottage
Ilam, Staffordshire
- Beechenhill Cottage and The Cottage by the Pond
Kessingland, Suffolk - Four Winds Retreat
Kirkby Lonsdale, Cumbria - Barkinbeck Cottage
Kirkoswald, Cumbria - Howscales
Knightcote, Warwickshire
- Knightcote Farm Cottages
Langport, Somerset - Hay Loft & Stables
Ledbury, Herefordshire - The Old Kennels Farm
Leek, Staffordshire - Larks Rise
Lenham, Kent - Apple Pye Cottage
Looe, Cornwall
- Bocaddon Holiday Cottages
- Bucklawren Farm
Lostwithiel, Cornwall - Hartswheal Barn
Malvern, Worcestershire - Hidelow House Cottages
Market Rasen, Lincolnshire - Pelham Arms Farm
Okehampton, Devon - Beer Farm
Oldcroft, Gloucestershire - Cider Press Cottage
Pickering, North Yorkshire - Rawcliffe House Farm
Salisbury, Wiltshire - The Old Stables
Sandwich, Kent - The Old Dairy
Sandy, Bedfordshire - Acorn Cottage
Selby, North Yorkshire - Lund Farm Cottages
Shrewsbury, Shropshire
- Newton Meadows Holiday Cottages
Silverdale, Lancashire - The Stables
Skegness, Lincolnshire - Ingoldale Park
Sledmere, North Humberside - Life Hill Farm
South Kilvington, North Yorkshire
- Mowbray Stable Cottages
Stoke St Gregory, Somerset - Holly Farm
Stroud, Gloucestershire
- Whitminster House Cottages
Wembury, Devon - Traine Farm
Whitby, North Yorkshire - Captain Cook's Haven
Wisbech, Cambridgeshire - Common Right Barns
Witney, Oxfordshire - Swallows Nest
Yapham, East Riding of Yorkshire
- Wolds View Holiday Cottages

MOBILITY Level 3

Bishops Down, Dorset - Monks Barn
Broadclyst, Devon - Hue's Piece
Bude, Cornwall - Forda Lodges
Charmouth, Dorset - The Poplars
Cockfield, Durham - Stonecroft and Swallows Nest
Colyton, Devon - Smallicombe Farm
Commondale, North Yorkshire - Fowl Green Farm
Godney, Somerset - Swallow Barn
Harrogate, North Yorkshire
- Brimham Rocks Cottages
Hartgrove, Dorset - Hartgrove Farm
Kielder Water, Northumberland
- Calvert Trust Kielder
Knightcote, Warwickshire
- Knightcote Farm Cottages
Malvern, Worcestershire - Hidelow House Cottages
Skegness, Lincolnshire - Ingoldale Park
St Just-in-Penwith, Cornwall - Swallows End
West Bexington, Dorset - Tamarisk Farm Cottages

MOBILITY Level 4

East Harling, Norfolk - Berwick Cottage
Norwich, Norfolk - Spixworth Hall Cottages
Skegness, Lincolnshire - Ingoldale Park

HEARING IMPAIRMENT Level 1

Commondale, North Yorkshire - Fowl Green Farm
Kielder Water, Northumberland
- Calvert Trust Kielder
Pickering, North Yorkshire
- Easthill Farm House and Gardens
Sledmere, North Humberside - Life Hill Farm
Yapham, East Riding of Yorkshire
- Wolds View Holiday Cottages

HEARING IMPAIRMENT Level 2

East Harling, Norfolk - Berwick Cottage

VISUAL IMPAIRMENT Level 1

Commondale, North Yorkshire - Fowl Green Farm
Pickering, North Yorkshire
- Easthill Farm House and Gardens

VISUAL IMPAIRMENT Level 2

East Harling, Norfolk - Berwick Cottage
Kielder Water, Northumberland
- Calvert Trust Kielder
Sledmere, North Humberside - Life Hill Farm

In which **region** is the county I wish to visit?

COUNTY/UNITARY AUTHORITY	REGION
Bath & North East Somerset	South West
Bedfordshire	East of England
Berkshire	South East England
Bristol	South West
Buckinghamshire	South East England
Cambridgeshire	East of England
Cheshire	North West
Cornwall	South West
Cumbria	Cumbria
Derbyshire	Heart of England
Devon	South West
Dorset (Eastern)	South East England
Dorset (Western)	South West
Durham	Northumbria
East Riding of Yorkshire	Yorkshire
East Sussex	South East England
Essex	East of England
Gloucestershire	South West
Greater London	London
Greater Manchester	North West
Hampshire	South East England
Herefordshire	Heart of England
Hertfordshire	East of England
Isle of Wight	South East England
Isles of Scilly	South West
Kent	South East England
Lancashire	North West
Leicestershire	Heart of England
Lincolnshire	Heart of England
Merseyside	North West
Norfolk	East of England
North East Lincolnshire	Yorkshire
North Lincolnshire	Yorkshire
North Somerset	South West
North Yorkshire	Yorkshire
Northamptonshire	Heart of England
Northumberland	Northumbria
Nottinghamshire	Heart of England
Oxfordshire	South East England
Rutland	Heart of England
Shropshire	Heart of England
Somerset	South West
South Gloucestershire	South West
South Yorkshire	Yorkshire
Staffordshire	Heart of England
Suffolk	East of England
Surrey	South East England
Tees Valley	Northumbria
Tyne & Wear	Northumbria
Warwickshire	Heart of England
West Midlands	Heart of England
West Sussex	South East England
West Yorkshire	Yorkshire
Wiltshire	South West
Worcestershire	Heart of England
York	Yorkshire

UNITARY AUTHORITIES

Please note that many new unitary authorities have been formed - for example Brighton & Hove and Bristol - and are officially separate from the county in which they were previously located. To aid the reader we have only included the major unitary authorities in the list above and on the colour maps.

Finding
accommodation
is as easy as 1 2 3

Where to Stay makes it quick and easy to find a place to stay. There are several ways to use this guide.

1 TOWN INDEX

The town index at the back, lists all the places with accommodation featured in the regional sections. The index gives a page number where you can find full accommodation and contact details.

2 COLOUR MAPS

All the place names in black on the colour maps at the front have an entry in the regional sections. Refer to the town index for the page number where you will find one or more establishments offering accommodation in your chosen town or village.

3 ACCOMMODATION LISTING

Contact details for **all** VisitBritain assessed accommodation throughout England, together with their national Star rating are given in the listing section of this guide. Establishments with a full entry in the regional sections are shown in blue. Look in the town index for the page number on which their full entry appears.

TOWN INDEX

The following cities, towns and villages all have accommodation listed in the full colour regional pages of this guide. If the place where you wish to stay is no shown, the location maps (starting on page 18) will help you to find somewhere to stay in the area.

Y PAGE

USE YOUR *i*s

There are more than 550 Tourist Information Centres throughout England offering friendly help with accommodation and holiday ideas as well as suggestions of places to visit and things to do. There may well be a centre in your home town which can help you before you set out. You'll find addresses in the local Phone Book.